# THE UNIVERSAL SELF-INSTRUCTOR

## AND MANUAL OF GENERAL REFERENCE

*A facsimile of the 1883 edition with an introduction by*

ANNETTE K. BAXTER

*Winter House Ltd*
*New York*
1970

Library of Congress Catalog Card Number 74-127421
ISBN: 0-87806-007-3

Manufactured in the United States of America

# INTRODUCTION

At the conclusion of Professor George H. Curtis' presentation of "The Art of Music," one of sixty-four unhurried articles that make up the informational cornucopia that is *The Universal Self-Instructor,* a characteristically cautionary note is sounded. Having detailed for us the uses of music from the Hebrews, who "cultivated it as a consolation in time of peace, and as a powerful incentive in war," through the Apostles, among whom it became "a joy in their conversions, and was accompanied by miraculous results in dungeons and imprisonments," on to the Troubadours, Palestrina and Liszt, and having classified and examined music as both a science and an art, the author now invokes its essential neutrality, its power for good or evil depending on "the extent of its union with elevating or debasing scenes." The modern reader of *The Universal* will, by the time he has reached this passage, quickly recognize its unabashedly moralistic vein —an effort to wed utility to ethics in an amalgam of salubrious Americanism. Indeed, *The Universal* is a continuous celebration of the belief that such an amalgam was not just possible, it was ordained.

It is no accident that this resplendent volume, half handbook and half homily, appeared in 1883, the year that simultaneously saw the publication of William Graham Sumner's *What Social Classes Owe To Each Other* and Lester Frank Ward's *Dynamic Sociology*. In their radically divergent philosophies these two most influential American Darwinians forecast the conflicting directions in which their society was moving, directions which *The Universal* indiscriminately cheers along. Ward, and his voluble adherents, proclaimed that human inequities and indignities could ultimately be eradicated by man's own effort to reshape his environment, and *The Universal* plunges us forward in this brave assumption. Sumner, on the contrary, supposed that inequality was a law of nature and therefore of society, and *The Universal,* in its unvarnished allegiance to both nature and society, frequently concurs.

Thus *The Universal,* probably without its authors' having realized it, marshalled both hope and disillusionment, and in succeeding decades its readers would see themselves as occupants of one or the other philosophical camp. The military metaphor is not presumptuous, for in 1883 ideological battle lines were beginning to be drawn. Yet as one reads *The Universal* there is scarcely a hint of this, for America's credal faith in the ethical imperatives of freedom and equality was still comfortably co-existing with native utilitarianism. When on page 293 Professor Curtis exhorts families, school teachers and "collegians" to intensify their study of music, he clearly supposes that Americans, goaded onward, will not simply make music a power for good, but a power for Some Greater Good.

Basic to *The Universal's* purpose is this concept of a steadily expanding community upon which the high hopes and practical benefits of American civilization must rapidly be conferred. A readership presumably susceptible, on the one hand, to the numbing commercial transactions of the firm of Rodgers and Wolcott (pp. 96–109) and, on the other, to thirty-six pages feverishly listing the achievements of those ensconced in a "Biographical Dictionary of Distinguished Persons" must have collaborated in a fundamental editorial assumption: that "the wants of everyday life," as the Preface puts it, range from instruction to inspiration, and that they are equal partners in *The Universal's* encyclopedic agglomerate. Actually, the tedium of "Book-Keeping" is punctured by the exploits of a capital young fellow, Stephen Steady, who borrows $25 from his father "with which to seek his fortune in the city"—thereby giving us an idea of what has happened to the purchasing power of $25. And by an occasional buried joke like the $2400 ten-day loan to Mark Twain (p. 85 ff.). The author of these felicities was Charles Ezra Sprague, who, as everyone remembers, had been wounded at Gettysburg and was the first American advocate of Volapük, a predecessor of Esperanto. Bookkeeping of course is given considerably greater space than the section devoted to the enlightened choice of a spouse (pp. 354-358), and evidently the priorities of the 1883 moral order required no apology: if homework in bookkeeping will fatten the youthful businessman's bank account, will his family life not thereby be enhanced? In *The Universal* the ethical and the utilitarian are everywhere in harmony—as the blessings of the modern era radiate from its pages to the remotest hamlets.

Here was a treasury of moral and practical benefactions, and the treasurer-editor was convinced that its contents were attractively illustrated and properly authenticated ("the information contained in their articles is entirely trustworthy") and that they were generously available to all stations in American life ("there is no home in the land where . . . the *Universal Self-Instructor* will not be welcomed . . ."). The immigrant, the black man and the poor white might have little need for counsel in the niceties of the cotillion or for caution against employing "fine language, long words, or high-sounding phrases," but such inconsistencies troubled neither the editor nor his "efficient corps of specialists." Today, our consciences laced with the guilts and anxieties of a post-industrial society, we shrink perceptibly before *The Universal's* claim to universality, but to the authors it must have seemed axiomatic that those on the periphery of the ever-enlarging middle class would soon be included in it.

It was, after all, 1883, and if ever it was possible to believe that *The Universal's* relentless mission of elevating the masses was attainable it was then. Three years would elapse before industrial unrest triggered the hysteria over well-meaning anarchists in the Chicago Haymarket bombing. The farmer, mainstay of the nation's economy, was enjoying a prosperity that would not begin to totter until the second half of the decade. And the nation's railroads, after a shadowy period of fiscal license, had almost formed a continental network, promising far-flung exchanges of goods, immigrants and ideas. The fifteen years, on and off, of political scandal, launched by exposés of the Tweed Ring, the Credit Mobilier and the Erie Railroad, had given way, by accident of assassination, to the Presidency of Chester Alan Arthur. That former collector of the port of New York, veteran of the rough and tumble of machine politics, was unpredictably abetting civil service reform, heedless of anguished cries from his erstwhile cronies. Six years earlier, Reconstruction in the South, strewn with the debris of mixed motives, had ground to a halt when President Hayes recalled Union troops to the North.

As the nation collectively determined to erase its memories of civil conflict (and there is noticeably little reference to it in *The Universal*), it permitted the former slaves to remain variously victimized. The famous 1883 Supreme Court vetoes of acts intended to check discrimination against blacks were affirming America's version of *laissez-faire;* and it could all be rationalized in the name of progress. When Charles Darwin had died a year earlier, his burial in Westminster Abbey marked the victory of evolution's irresistible measuring out of the human, as well as of the vegetable, mineral and other-animal, condition: progress obeyed its own laws. And if Americans left well enough alone, its march would somehow whisk the oppressed into a joyful rear guard. So perhaps it is not surprising that *The Universal's* only substantive attention to slavery appears in a historical vignette under "Commerce and Transportation" and makes no mention of American slavery.

Such evasiveness hardly marks its references to other persons of distinctly modest stations. The article on "Letter Writing," for example, informs us that "there is no condition of life, humble or elevated, in which the 'art of letter writing' will not at times be found of much importance. It is a comfort and blessing to the poor; with the middle and upper classes an indispensable acquirement—a boundless means of pleasure and gratification." And a trifle embarrassing to us. What the well-to-do are entitled to experience as good clean fun is permitted to the poor only in the guise of spiritual blandishment. Evidently some post-Emersonian law of compensation was supplanting Darwinism here; today's reader translates it as Victorian condescension.

But if *The Universal* patronized the poor in extending the range of its authors' pedagogical powers, it also warned the comfortable middle class about affluent idleness. In "Domestic Duties," the mistress of the household is charged with "daily inspection of the ice-box, meat-safe, pantries and cellar" so that her servants may be reassured of their own value by the honor she accords the dull routines of home management. In fact, the mistress is crassly more at fault than her servants if she has not guided her "inferiors to a conscientious discharge of the duties of the position they have assumed." This echoes the then prevailing politics of domesticity, whose vigorous spinster spokesman, Catharine Beecher, had died five years earlier. With her celebrated sister Harriet, Miss Beecher had elaborated the principles of domestic science in *The American Woman's Home*. A bible for countless young women of the period, it approached the question of class with a combined faith in puritanical attention to duty and democratic practice, along with a healthy infusion of *noblesse oblige*. Respect for human equality would foster acceptance of differences rooted in social role and, while distinctions based on "accidents of birth, fortune or occupation"—to quote the Beechers—were deplored, it was essential that "children be subordinate to parents, pupils to teachers, the employed to their employers, and subjects to magistrates."

In *The Universal* too, this snappy adjustment in one's image is repeatedly prescribed. As "Letter Writing" releases its piquant thoughts on "comparative social position" and "difference in station," promptly atoning with threats that everybody "whether of high or low degree" deserves a "Mr.," "Master," "Mrs.," or "Miss" before his name, real uneasiness sets in with "Esquire." Use it for "gentlemen of high social standing," as well as members of the legal profession; but wait, in the next sentence, "Esquire" is dismissed as "a distinction more strictly English," and "should seldom be used unless really appropriate." *The Universal's* policy on social distinctions is perhaps more, or possibly less, precise in the luminous section on "The Etiquette of Conversation," where "women, clergymen, and men of learning or years should always be addressed with respect and attention"—regardless, presumably, of their intrinsic claims to our good will or even of their economic circumstances. But money, and what money means, speaks out redundantly from the pages of *The Universal*, and its authors here again betray their discomfort at the tentativeness of class differences in a country undergoing vast economic metamorphoses. How could they ignore this, when the dramatic acquisition, and equally dramatic turnover, of the fortunes from which these differences issued were witnessed daily?

Wedded to their egalitarian principles, the authors of *The Universal* nonetheless knew that their readers were wholly enamored of the professional success-mongers, whose advocacy of a place on top of the pile strongly implied that equality was hardly a desirable state of being, unless interpreted as equality with a Carnegie or a Vanderbilt. It was the heyday of the Sunday morning sermon that couched its approval of plunder in high places in the language of the "secular calling," when ministers competed with fly-by-night journalists and tycoons-turned-educator in rendering unto Caesar. Business expansion obviously partook of the Divine Order.

During the weeks when *The Universal* was being assembled in Broome Street, John D. Rockefeller was consolidating the Standard Oil trust and Phineas T. Barnum was publishing *The Art of Money-Getting*. How was the editor of a volume marked with encyclopedic detachment and moral refinement to address himself to American lust for success and acquisition? If he felt any uncertainty, he shielded his readers from it. In the article on "Business Habits" (with the predictable subtitle, "Qualifications Essential to Success"), its author recites the orthodoxies of diligence and perseverance, and then recommends honesty primarily as a strategem—"to be a rogue is to be a fool." Nowhere does he suggest that moral scruple might occasionally stop a zealous businessman in his tracks or, at the least, give him a sleepless night or two. Instead, his concerns center around such matters as good health ("firmness of purpose and ability to perform great deeds are rarely found in a puny and effeminate body"), the cultivation of a pragmatic outlook ("it is not so much what a man knows, as the use he is able to make of his knowledge for practical purposes") and the value of decisiveness ("a vacillating man, no matter what his abilities, is invariably pushed aside by the man of determined will"). Then, just before a torrent of advice and maxims, the author slips into his identity as a Man of the New Age. The standard virtues need invigorating with technical and commercial creativity; old methods are attacked and new ones encouraged. Enlightened enterprise, an openness to the advanced and the experimental, are loosening the puritanical constrictions of earlier generations. A fresh idiom of adventure vies with the tired vocabulary of responsibility.

"Business Habits" is not the only arena in which *The Universal* tangles with the status quo. "Farming as a Fine Art" was written by Frank H. Norton, who several years earlier had edited Frank Leslie's *Historical Register of the Philadelphia Centennial* and had been struck with the fair's array of inventions and improvements, among them American farm implements far ahead of the European. His introduction to the *Historical Register* is an ecstatic celebration of Progress: "The Centennial Exhibition was, in itself, the culminating effort of a century of grand achievements. Presenting a panorama of intellectual and industrial results of a hundred years of toil, it stands before humanity as a vast and complete exemplification of the progress of the past—to be utilized as a picture of experience for the benefit of the future." Norton's *Universal* article is almost poignant in its eagerness for new ideas out on the farm, in its conviction that rural torpor could be exterminated by the "progress of civilization." He strikes out against those who resist the knowledge spouting from farmers' clubs, county fairs, and farming journals, and those whose attitude toward model farming was less sanguine than his own. Furthermore, in hailing the union of ethics with utility that inspired so many of *The Universal's* authors, he asserts that agriculture "in its moral and social relations" would be vastly benefited by the application of scientific farming and adds with magisterial impatience that "where conservatism breeds only stagnation, the most advanced radicalism is preferable to it."

This essay deserves special attention for its reference to women on the farm. Norton, unlike some of *The Universal's* masculine contributors, concedes the existence of the weaker sex. (William Blaikie's article on "Physical Culture" is eloquent on the theme of sound bodies for boys and girls—*Harper's* published his manual of that title a year later—but the exercises he advocates are clearly intended for boys and men, not their sisters and wives.) Commiserating with the farmers' wives and daughters who are deprived not simply of recreation but of "mental improvement" and "intellectual pursuits" as well, Norton concludes that the quality of farm life stifles even the desire for these satisfactions. While his observations are hardly as forceful as those of contemporary feminists, he obviously sees farm women as cruelly oppressed.

Few male voices joined Norton's. One addressed itself to "The Rights of Married Women" under "Mercantile Law and Legal Forms" and briefly took notice of the agitation to grant women the right to vote for school committees under "Petitions," and another perfunctorily mentioned the "Woman's Rights Party" under "Political Parties." The voice closest to being provocative belonged to *The Universal's* literary expert, Edward M. Kingsbury, then 28 years old. Turning away from the law, for which he was trained at Harvard, he had begun a long and consequential career in journalism—for 62 years he wrote editorials, first for the *New York Sun* and later for the *New York Times*—and was doubtless as sensitive to issues of the day as any of *The Universal's* contributors. Tucked into his list of 707 subjects for "Compositions and Debates" are 27 relating to women. The titles of some of them hint at a swelling controversy over women's activities in circles outside the domestic: "The rights of married women"; "The desirability of retaining married women as teachers in the public schools"; "How far the extension of the right of suffrage to women is desired by woman"; "The co-education of the sexes," and so on. These speculative forays halt abruptly before any raw confrontation with the "woman problem."

They stand in revealing contrast to parts of *The Universal* written exclusively by and intended primarily for women. The gentle feminine acquiescence with which women were enjoined to undertake their domestic duties first appears in the smothering amenities of "The Domestic Circle." Thumbnail sketches of the ideal husband and wife predictably honor biblical submissiveness in the wife and masterfulness in the husband: "Fortunate, indeed, is the woman who possesses as husband a man who knows more of the world and of all things than she can know." Each sketch is preceded by a series of ruthless psychological portraits of marital anti-heroes and -heroines, such as "The Reckless Husband" and "The Nagging Wife." Always more recognizable than their syrupy counterparts, they provide some of the most entertaining reading in *The Universal.* (The idea of a general reference manual offering guidance in the choice of a mate finds a ready parallel in the computerized mate-matching of the present. Both are manifestly American examples of "How-to-ism," each employing a genre enmeshed in its own time.) Mary Kyle Dallas, author of "The Domestic Circle," had previously published the saga of a Miss Charity Grinder, "wherein are detailed her numerous hairbreadth escapes and wonderful adventures while on a visit to New York from the country." While the tedious proprieties she champions in *The Universal* suggest that an element of wish-fulfillment enlivened her heroine's adventures, her position on the role of woman shares its outlines with those of the three remaining female authors in their articles on "Home Occupations," "Domestic Duties," and "Social Etiquette."

The oversimplifications of these ladies were not to be matched until the resurgence of domestic orthodoxy in the 1950's, when the proliferation of household gadgets was again regarded as the woman's passport to a harmless degree of self-realization. The author of "Domestic Duties" breezily assures her readers that these new conveniences would allow them time for "art studies, scientific research, or some money-yielding branch of industry," but her assurances are somewhat dampened by the exhausting catalogue of basic household tasks prescribed in her essay. In a harbinger of split-level domesticity, the wife is promised that, if she complies with *The Universal's* canons and creates a pleasant atmosphere in the home, her husband "will invite people to dine with him on the slightest provocation." Piling insult on injury, the author reveals that a husband's "vanity is gratified by his wife's superior housekeeping, because he attributes it to his own personal influence." Since readers are told that "the desire to please and the love of admiration" are "especially characteristic of their sex," chances are slim that wives will escape the delights of male autonomy.

Little in *The Universal* better measures the gulf between it and us than the "Household Receipts," for which read "recipes." Such a listing was no recent arrival to publishing: the *hortus sanitatis,* or household book of recipes and remedies, dates back at least to the fifteenth century, when recipes must have been more plausible than in 1883. Any bride today, venturing to feed her husband the beefsteak, or a chop or two, for the breakfast recommended on page 407, will think seriously of returning to mother during the rice farther down that page and will surely have become unhinged before completing the Mock Turtle Soup on page 409. *The Universal's* disclaimers to the contrary, veteran cooks were obviously determined to humiliate neophytes: it was not until the twentieth century that cook books appeared that would consistently register ingredients, spoonfuls and oven temperatures.

"Practical Housekeeping" was thus clearly the operative center of a woman's life, despite the ritual nod to Women's Rights at the start of that section, almost unavoidable for writers on the subject by the last quarter of the century, and the concession to the "polished training her mental faculties have attained, through co-education perhaps," at its conclusion. Departure from the pattern was hardly possible, or even, as yet, apparently desirable. *The Universal's* mood underscores the fact that in 1883 the women's movement had come to a temporary standstill, with the two major Woman Suffrage Associations—the National and the American—not to unite until 1890, when women would begin making perceptible strides in the world beyond the home. Exactly a decade after *The Universal* another now-forgotten handbook was published. As expansive in its mood if somewhat less bulky in content than the present volume, it was entitled *What Can A Woman Do; or, Her Position in the Business and Literary World.* Like the editor of *The Universal,* who claims that it "may be said to occupy a field peculiarly its own," its editor modestly calls it "the only book of its kind that has been published." Unlike *The Universal,* however, its editor was a woman.

If housekeeping still held the practical center of woman's existence, children occupied its spiritual center. Today's perpetrators of child-rearing manuals may note that the succinct passage on "Confidence Between Parents and Children" (p. 359) anticipates many of their advanced findings. It repudiates physical punishment and recommends close, easy relations: "The grim old-fashioned stateliness that keeps them at arms' length will never do with this independent generation." Timorous restrictions on child behavior are out: "You cannot expect your future explorer, who will one day make his way to the North Pole or the interior of Africa, to abstain from excursions into the city or the woods, even if he loses himself." And parents are alerted to the baleful influence of peer groups: "When you see a girl anxious to tell your daughter something she must not repeat to mother, check the intimacy at once." Couched in good-humored mockery, there is even a warning to mothers against Oedipal possessiveness of sons developing an interest in the opposite sex: "What can he want of Betty Martin, when he has you?" Note also among "Essays" in that "List of Subjects for Compositions and Debates": number 333, "The younger generation always seems degenerate to the generation before it," and number 407, "How far the affection of parents for their children is returned by the latter."

*The Universal's* readiness to Face These Issues, its burgeoning liberalism, accurately reflects the pronounced shift in thinking, heralded by the appearance in 1847 of Horace Bushnell's *Christian Nurture,* away from the old rigidities of training children. As the nineteenth century rolled on, Calvinist suspicions of the child's inherent sinfulness were steadily losing ground. Jacob Abbott's *Gentle Measures in the Management and Training of the Young,* published in 1871, was another milestone in the "nature versus nurture" controversy; it took a hopeful view of the child's potential, relying on reasonable disciplinary measures and the beneficence of the environment. Following the appearance of G. Stanley Hall's *The Study of Children* in the same year as *The Universal,* and the ideas of contemporary proponents of the kindergarten, children's educational and psychological welfare called out for increasing expertise. The church had already relinquished the child to the home and now, with the ever-accelerating growth of public schools and of normal schools for the training of teachers, home was beginning to sense that it was losing ground to school. The persistence with which home values are defended in *The Universal* divulges this anxiety.

The waning of the church's influence on child-rearing could be surmised from its fugitive image throughout *The Universal.* Doctrinal pieties are sounded, but hardly in the accents of secure commitment. Could it be that three of those "Subjects for Forensic Discussions"—"Is there a smaller attendance at churches now than formerly?," "Should the Bible be read in the public schools?" and "Is the influence of the clergy less than formerly?"—are as symptomatic as they are forensic? The section on "Religions of the World" is a model of detachment, and the discussion of Christianity not only betrays no temptation to proselytize, it is almost self-effacingly spare.

While the persuasiveness of Protestant theology was dwindling in the minds of Americans in the last decades of the century, Protestant morality remained largely unchallenged. It asserts itself valiantly in the pages of *The Universal,* as in the section on "The Care of Health," for example, where the reader is assured that "to be always well is an attainable blessing—the uniform result of self-denial, temperance, and an industrious life," but there are occasional signs of erosion. "The Domestic Circle," under the sub-heading of "The Girls' Beaux," cites some unsettling changes in what a later generation would call "dating habits." These range from "the utter want of supervision and decorum, which has obtained a footing in our rural districts" to city daughters' accepting gentlemen's invitations without asking permission and then coming home, thanks to their own latch-keys, long after their parents have turned in. In the face of all this deterioration, a modest gregariousness is sanctioned in "Social Intercourse"—and qualified with lofty resignation: "A gay scene, a crowd now and then is good for every one. It cures young people of embarrassment, and brightens up old ones, but it is not society in the best sense."

This tension between the profane and the sacred was echoed in a diary written at the same time and, like *The Universal,* brought to light and published decades later. It was kept by Isabella Maud Rittenhouse, a Cairo, Illinois, grain merchant's eighteen-year-old daughter, who certainly belonged in the group of late adolescents to whom *The Universal's* social strictures were addressed. On January 20, 1883, she quoted the local minister's concession that Christianity might see recreation and amusement as beneficial "but not in such excess that it ruined the health" or diverted the mind "when it should at times be devoted to graver meditations." Like *The Universal's* wayward daughters, Maud did not fully acquiesce in these inhibitions. While alert to the dangers of over-indulgence, she set down her own convictions: "I love parties and dancing—they rest me in many ways, they animate me—I can do more work and more energetic cheerful work in anticipation of a jolly evening than otherwise." So the youth of the land, or at least conscientious youth, were trying to resolve the work-play dilemma that still plagues America. *The Universal* too was doing its best, stretching the Standard Protestant Precepts to fit the protean shapes of the future. The struggle occasionally required a strategic capitulation: "The old Puritanic rules, 'Eat what is set before you, and leave nothing upon the plate to be wasted,' is a physical impossibility to a 19th century mortal" (p. 403). Christian morals were coming to rest at a half-way house between Calvinist restrictiveness and a later *ad libitum* eclecticism.

If Puritanism was waning, other components of the American personality were just as surely in flux. The jugglings in the social order resulting from the phenomenal increase in population and the growth of cities in the years after the Civil War, plus the shifting from farm to industry, and the fertilization of American culture by immigrant groups—all were turning America away from her vaunted provincialism and were compelling a keener awareness of the world outside her borders. *The Universal* quivers with internationalism. Notice the non-American topics listed as "Subjects for Compositions and Debates," the attention given to the physical and political features and natural resources of other countries, the sections on "Heads of Principal Nations" and "Journalism of the World," and the three closely-packed pages of "Foreign Terms and Phrases."

Equally non- or perhaps new-American is *The Universal's* gusto for well-deserved leisure. The words of Benjamin Hardwick, in his introduction to "Out-Door Sports and Pastimes," resound more than once: "As wealth increases, a larger number of persons are set free from the obligations of daily toil." Free enough to spur the "headlong progress of arts and sciences in this teeming age of wonders," as the article on "Journalism" puts it, and, by reaching out toward Europe, to make the first diffident gestures toward a heightened aestheticism. Some months earlier Oscar Wilde, lily in hand, was enlightening his American lecture audiences and finding them not utterly uncomprehending. "We care so much more than our grandparents did about surrounding ourselves with beauty," asserts the author of "Home Occupations," adding a bit later, "Never was there a time when so many people took an interest in, and understood something about art." And pages other than hers in *The Universal* bolster her claim, "Architecture," for example, properly acknowledging its debt to Europe in the popularity of Gothic and Queen Anne dwellings. This penchant for the "picturesque" appeared earlier in the landscape paintings of the Hudson Valley. Now, in architecture, it provoked *The Universal's* dogged practicality: "While picturesqueness is very effective in country houses, care must be taken not to sacrifice comfort or room to this end." Innovation was encouraged with the assurance that "the best Architects . . . do not allow themselves to be fettered by any style, as a house should be what it aims to be, —a *home,* and not simply a reproduction in brick, stone, or wood of certain set rules." The precedence given to interior planning—"It is well to settle on the plans and interior arrangements first, as these make up the comforts, and then try to make as good an exterior to them as possible"—had been circulating for several decades and would soon be reiterated by Louis Gibson, whose *Convenient Houses, with Fifty Plans for the Housekeeper* asserted that "the exterior will be formed in a natural way by the requirements of the interior." *The Universal* thus endorses the blending of European and vernacular traditions that was at this moment inspiring the prodigious architectural confections of H. H. Richardson and McKim, Mead and White.

If the arts felt the pull of native experimentalism and pragmatism against the push of European extravagance, the sciences matched this with their own uncertainties. *The Universal's* attention to medicine occupies precisely one page, 298, and it consists of an aloof presentation of the four "schools of medicine," two of which are all but forgotten today, the other two having merged. But how could a *Universal Self-Instructor* have failed to list at least a few, or a few dozen, of the hundreds of household remedies that every grandmother and most doctors were administering night and day? Why does *The Universal* totally ignore therapeutics when it offers every other conceivable sort of advice? Were the authors so perceptive as to leave bad enough alone? Was medicine too forbidding, or too indecisive, to warrant more than a single page? There may well have been an editorial battle about this, but unless some missing memoirs or correspondence surfaces, it will remain one of *The Universal's* mysteries. (Another is why Australia keeps popping up: somebody down on Broome Street had an *idée fixe* on Australia.)

Contrast this diffidence toward scientific controversy with *The Universal's* bland, authoritative voice on "The Care of Health." That muffled ring of Puritanism is heard again in the injunction that diet "should be plain and wholesome," just as exercise should be taken "in moderation to keep the blood pure." Furthermore, "the three great elementary principles of every healthy community, as well as of individuals, are pure air, perfect cleanliness, and well-cooked food." Was it moderation—plainness and wholesomeness—that guided *The Universal*?—or was it perfection —pure air and perfect cleanliness? (Perfect cleanliness seems compromised a few paragraphs above by the recommendation of "a warm soap and water bath . . . taken at bed-time once a week, or once a fortnight . . . ."). Evidently 1883 could not be confident of a distinction between moderation and perfection.

Usually moderation wins the day; a prime example is "Phrenology." Its author was the noted phrenologist, Nelson Sizer, and it must therefore have been his editor's qualms that qualified so encompassing an interpretation of human behavior thus lamely: "widely disseminated and much discussed." But however tentatively presented, or even scientifically suspect, phrenology emphatically serves *The Universal's* cause in assuring its readers that the proper adjustment and co-ordination of "temperaments" can "give harmony of character and excellent health."

This frequent intoning of the personal ideal of "harmony" or of "moderation" is in some sense an unconscious evasion, tidily assisting the self-instructed to reconcile the old moralisms with the new freedoms of perception and inquiry. Like the parallel effort to accommodate ethics to utility in the culture itself, this would surely, if faced squarely, lead to conflict. The problem was not really acknowledged, which is to say that *The Universal* successfully dodged conflict by ignoring it. And it deftly restricted itself to whichever half of the equation suited its subject: in the articles particularly directed at women, it stresses the past; in those directed at men, the future. It is simultaneously loyal to the home and to technology, to formalism and to innovation, to sentiment and to logic.

One of the best examples of *The Universal's* virtuosity is found in "In-Door Amusements," written by Margaret Elizabeth Sangster, who had recently joined the staff of *Harper's Young People* and was to become editor in 1889 of *Harper's Bazaar.* The prolific author of such captivating works as "Home and Heaven," "Little Knights and Ladies," and "Home Fairies and Heart Flowers," Mrs. Sangster surely rejoiced in "the hurrying life of the present century" even while deploring its failure "to study the art of recreation." Her career bespeaks nothing so much as dedication to the home, yet she regrets that "in plain sober fact, many homes are dreadfully dull and tedious places to live in. They have no flavor, no spice; nothing ever goes on to make them interesting."

To provide the missing spice and flavor, she recommends fortune-telling, along with an assortment of less jaded amusements. She is not content to recommend it without a high-minded defense of superstition: "Our superstitions are akin to that vein of poetry which lies under the surface of the finest civilization, and is found at the root of what is best and simplest among the peoples who are still primitive and rude." Lest the reader be so transported by exposure to this world of fate and intrigue that he turn his back upon the familiar moral codes, the concluding paragraphs on fortune-telling remind him that "our fortunes, good or ill, are very much in our own control," and testify to the enduring truth of salvation by works, salvation being given the late nineteenth century reading of financial success: "As a general rule riches and honor come to the diligent and faithful, while poverty and reproach are inherited by the idle and reckless." Immediately following Mrs. Sangster's words on "Fortune-Telling" are her instructions on "Toy-Making" where, in an admirable twist of reasoning, the poor inherit the kingdom of pleasure: "Plenty of toys may be bought by those who have Fortunatus's purse to go to for funds, but it is doubtful whether those who can buy whatever they wish, have half the fun which belongs to those who with a knife, a few tacks, screws, and strings, a little paper, and some other simple materials, construct ingenious toys of their own, for the diversion of their friends."

Mrs. Sangster's skill extends beyond the tactics of conflict-avoidance. Undeterred by so mundane a title as "Home Occupations," she delivers a generous array of *The Universal's* more intimate messages to its readers: a lecture on the evils of time-wasting ("your sixteen-year old daughter might certainly indulge in more profitable occupations than gossiping, reading novels, and flirting at her window with the young gentleman over the way"), a defense of practical skills as an essential adjunct of book learning ("every boy, however deeply he may plunge into the classics, should know how to use tools, to drive a nail, to wield a hammer, to mend a hinge, or to make some pretty article for his mother and sisters"), and a promise that utilitarianism is entirely compatible with individuality ("in the ideal home there is liberty to indulge the individual, so that each person may be developed symmetrically, and the happiness of all be insured").

Leisure was welcomed outdoors as vehemently as in. "Out-Door Sports and Pastimes" sees the sudden access of free time as a blessing. From the healthful consequences upon the puny bodies of the city-bred to the opportunities it affords the socially ambitious ("the knowledge of games is a part of polite breeding. . . . it is also useful to us in society"), the enthusiasm for physical activity is unquestionably one of the distinguishing marks of the period. In the swelling dust of cyclists, the League of American Wheelmen was founded in 1881, the same year that the Intercollegiate Football Association approved the rules that punted Rugby into modern football. Croquet and lawn tennis were in full, ladies-included, swing, and while golf, in *The Universal,* is allocated one entire paragraph, some 43 rules of cricket are deployed over two pages. Baseball is still underhand, and in Polo "yelling, excitement, or severity to the pony are very bad form." And how we revere the memory of Hare and Hounds, a "favorite sport . . . almost too well known to require a description . . . the runs are from eight to fifteen miles [*on foot*], and generally wind up with a good dinner." This galloping interest in outdoor sports, documented by the comprehensive treatment the subject receives in *The Universal,* conveys in a curiously flavorful way the expansiveness of the nation's mood.

*The Universal* is fun to read. Such fun to discover the language of flowers, to appraise the haunting Egyptian cowcatchers, to spot mistakes —Scylla and Charybdis were not two rocks; Calvert Vaux was not two people, Calver and Vaux— and fun to be told the exact cost of the "War of the Revolution" ($135,193,703) and that you should learn to fence ambidextrously, in case you lose an arm. Fun to see the picture of the brand new Brooklyn Bridge and find that in 1880 North America had more railroad mileage than Europe —101,240 to 100,920—compared with Japan's 67 and China's, apparently, none. How many of us knew that in 1790 North Carolina was the third most populous state and New York the fifth? Or that in 1883 the President's salary was a whopping $50,000, while the Vice President earned $8,000, less than the U.S. Minister to Chili (sic)? Look for favorites in the "Celebrated Characters in Fiction, Poetry, and the Drama," heavily weighted with Dickens, Scott and Shakespeare. There is inside-drollery to be tracked down, like the specimen of "The Art of Flourishing" in "Penmanship" which has *The Universal's* very own sports editor declining a young lady's invitation to lawn tennis because of "journalistic duties." Read the model letters in "Letter Writing," pulsing with an eloquence now totally lost in correspondence, and savor the precisions of distinction among "English Synonyms," most of them still quite useful today.

Other than those tables of compound interest, which are probably accurate, there is little in *The Universal* that is not enjoyable reading. But what can it tell us, as we thumb through it, nearly a hundred years after it wrapped it all up? Where we find fun we know that in 1883 there was perplexity, but that it was perplexity informed with a lively consciousness of what was human, unfettered by European cynicism or later American misgivings. Nowhere else, it might be suggested, in all the catalogues of Western endeavor, could so much hopeful yearning for knowledge, for style, for evidence of unfolding potentials, be found enunciating a tradition firmly posited on two thousand years of motion forward. That was a moment when hindsight and foresight were equally focussed and clear: only from America could the world's past and future be viewed with such stunning certainty.

And how did Americans view *themselves* in 1883? This is one of the few questions *The Universal* did not consciously pose, but to us the volume's usefulness in answering it unquestionably is its greatest value. People were comprehensible, their behavior the result of decisions reached through the processes of rationality. Thus all the admonitions, the precepts, the aphorisms which the authors somehow believed their readers would heed. In its assumption that exhaustiveness was possible, that all essential knowledge could be contained within its pages, *The Universal* revealed an America never more confident of knowing its own place in a world that was structured and predictable. Because that world operated according to laws that could be explained and understood in these 672 pages, there was little doubt that it could also be controlled.

America's urge for self-assertion, just beginning to be felt in international politics, was at this point still complemented by an equally powerful urge for domestic harmony. This is evident as much by what *The Universal* ignores as by the optimistic data it characteristically chooses to proclaim. The stinging realities of slums, infant mortality, fouling factories, prostitution, the dreariness of the small town, the brutalizing asylums for the insane, the tyrannizing of helpless minorities, and the rapid disappearance of a frontier to which the American dream was fatefully joined, nowhere ruffle *The Universal's* poise and are, in fact, barely discernible. The texture of American life is portrayed as uniformly cheerful. Cheerful as it is, *The Universal* is essentially humorless, almost devoid of self-criticism or irony, although a tiny exception slipped in, Henry James' observation (p. 646) that American civilization was "rotten before it is ripe."

With *The Universal* as his sole guide to enlightenment about America in 1883, one would never guess that the nation was embarking upon what we would now label a prolonged identity crisis. Naively trusting in the alchemy of the melting pot, America welcomed hundreds of thousands of immigrants, while the editor seems to have drawn an almost total blank on the subject of immigration. Judging from the relaxed tone of its formulations on other potentially troubling themes, it is fair to conclude that *The Universal* may have acknowledged the immigrants only by indirection. As it invested each wave of the newly-rising middle class with a sense of belonging to venerable bourgeois traditions by dint of those observances obligingly laid bare in its "Epitome of Forms," it may have assumed that it was doing the same for the nation's immigrants. Certainly *The Universal* was offering a sense of continuity to the lives of people who were rarely able to trace their ancestry beyond their grandfathers. It sought to solve for them not the problems of survival, or even of existence, but of life style. As that foremost student of American institutions, Lord Bryce, observed a few years later, the absence of artificial rank oddly made social acceptance more difficult to achieve. How then was the alien to find his way in the lonely landscape of America? For those who perused it with care, *The Universal* provided assistance far beyond its generous encyclopedic core of tables and glossaries—everything from the arcana of proofreading to the consolations of poetry for the weary (see "Rock Me To Sleep," p. 666). But also it taught the technique of changing one's awkward name and the tactics of gracious male response to feminine overtures.

*The Universal* deserves our respect along with our amused condescension. It negotiated the rapids between major epochs of American history without flinching. And its eagerness to establish the guidelines for conformity may, paradoxically, have furthered American uniqueness. More than a half-century later another European visitor, Jean-Paul Sartre, was to note that "every American is educated by other Americans and educates others in turn. . . . all the advice with which his path is marked is so perfectly motivated, so penetrating, that he feels lulled by an immense solicitude that never leaves him helpless or abandoned." He might have been writing about *The Universal.*

*Annette K. Baxter*
*August 1970*

KNOWLEDGE IS POWER
HISTORY

# THE UNIVERSAL SELF-INSTRUCTOR

AND

## MANUAL OF GENERAL REFERENCE,

INCLUDING

MANY VALUABLE VOCABULARIES AND CAREFULLY COMPILED TABLES.

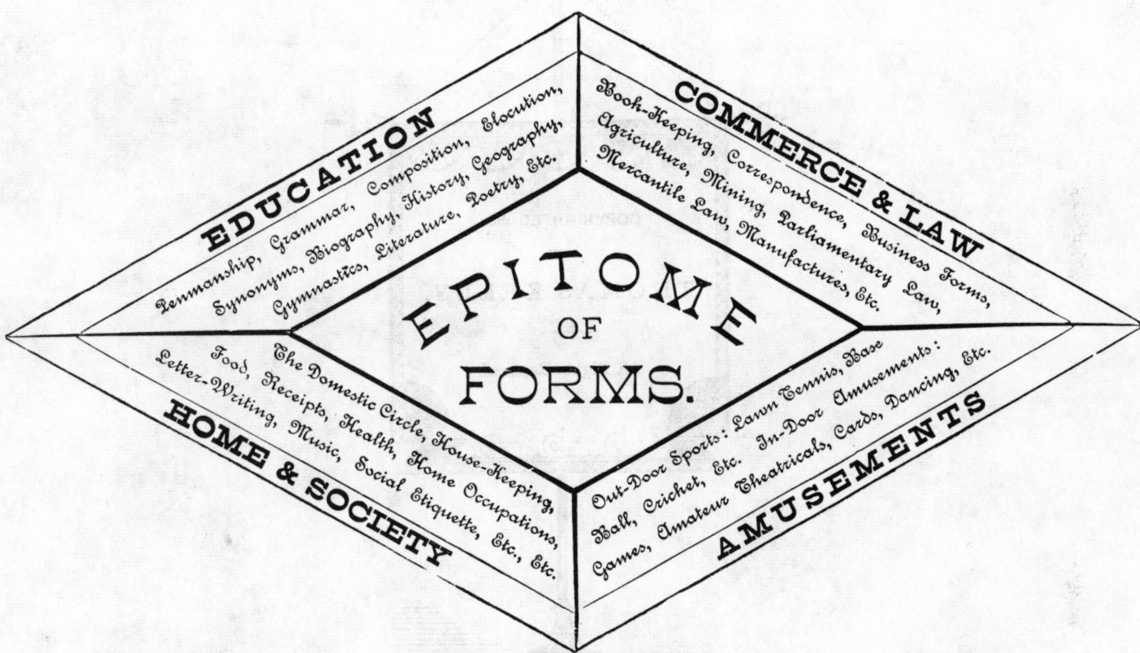


HANDSOMELY ILLUSTRATED WITH ORIGINAL DRAWINGS.


EDITED BY

ALBERT ELLERY BERG,

Assisted by an Efficient Corps of Specialists.



THOMAS KELLY, Publisher,

358 AND 360 BROOME ST., NEW YORK.

171 S. CLARK ST., CHICAGO; 216 S. EIGHTH ST., PHILADELPHIA; 208 SUPERIOR ST., CLEVELAND; WILDER'S ARCADE, ROCHESTER; 18 HALL BUILDING, TROY; 36 SIXTH ST., PITTSBURG.

JAMES A. HOYE & CO., 178 Devonshire St., Boston. A. L. BANCROFT & CO., 721 Market St., San Francisco. RICE & FARRINGTON, 203½ S. 5th St., St. Louis. L. H. BARKDULL, 69 W. 7th St., Cincinnati. BARNEY & KOHLER Detroit.

1883.

A WITTY Frenchman said that marriage is a tedious volume with a very fine preface, and he might have added, if he had lived in this country, that the title page of many modern publications is chiefly remarkable as an announcement of what the book does *not* contain. It can be honestly claimed, however, that the UNIVERSAL SELF-INSTRUCTOR is nothing less than it pretends to be,—an Epitome of Forms, especially adapted for purposes of self-instruction and general reference in the various departments of Education, Commerce, Law, Home, Society, and Amusements. Every young man and young woman; every business man, farmer, and mechanic; every housewife and lady of society;—in fact every intelligent member of the community should have it within reach for consultation on those numerous minor matters that a well-educated person is supposed to know.

The Reading Public has been amply supplied for years with reference books of every description, but the present volume may be said to occupy a field peculiarly its own, as the people have never before been furnished with a publication embracing in a single volume such a quantity of practical information, and treating the *wants of every-day life* in a lucid, instructive and agreeable manner.

Such articles as Elocution, Penmanship, Book-keeping, Letter-writing, Mercantile Law, Music, Stenography, Phrenology, Agriculture, Social Etiquette, Out-door Sports, In-door Amusements, Physical Culture, The Domestic Circle, Household Receipts, Parliamentary Law, etc., have been prepared by writers of reputation and large experience in the special subjects given them for treatment. The information contained in their articles is entirely trustworthy, and the Editor desires to express his obligation to these contributors for the interesting and conscientious manner in which they have handled their respective topics.

It has been the aim of the Publishers to produce a work that will become a standard authority on the matters it contains, and no labor or expense has been spared to make it the most attractive and useful book of its kind ever published. The illustrations are artistic, appropriate and original; while the literary features have been made entertaining as well as instructive. The Publishers feel confident, therefore, that the book will meet with the great success it deserves, and that there is no home in the land where the introduction of the UNIVERSAL SELF-INSTRUCTOR will not be welcomed as a cause of immediate gratification and a source of lasting pleasure.

A. E. B.

NEW YORK, *November, 1882.*

# LIST OF CONTRIBUTORS.

**EDWARD M. KINGSBURY.**
The English Language.
Elocution, Oratory and Declamation.
Distinguished Persons.

**Prof. GEO. H. THOMPSON.**
Penmanship.
Telegraphy.

**ROBERT D. TOWNSEND.**
Mercantile Law.
Resolutions, Petitions, Etc.
Outlines of History.

**FRANK H. NORTON.**
Agriculture.
Commerce and Transportation.
Manufactures and Mining.

**FRANKLIN J. OTTARSON.**
Parliamentary Law.
Government of the United States.
The Calendar.

**WILLIAM BLAIKIE.**
Physical Culture.

**CHARLES E. SPRAGUE.**
Book-Keeping.
Commercial Transactions.
Banking.

**Prof. GEORGE H. CURTIS.**
The Art of Music.

**ASHLEY W. COLE.**
Stenography.

**BENJAMIN HARDWICK.**
Out-Door Sports and Pastimes.

**Prof. N. SIZER.**
Phrenology.

**EDWARD W. CURTIS.**
Letter Writing.

**MARY KYLE DALLAS.**
The Domestic Circle.

**MARGARET E. SANGSTER**
In-Door Amusements.
Home Occupations.

**HELEN MORSE BERG.**
Domestic Duties.
Household Receipts.

**MARY A. BARR.**
Social Etiquette.

## ARTISTS

**HENRY A. OGDEN.**
**JOHN DE JONGH.**
**DANIEL T. AMES.**
**W. P. SNYDER.**

# TABLE OF CONTENTS.

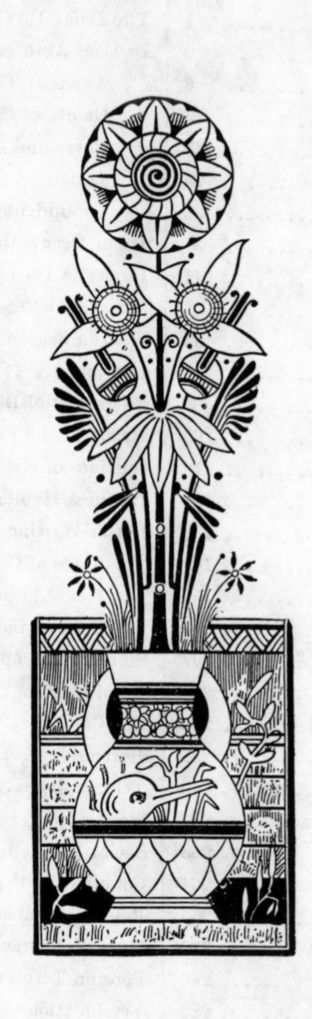

## D



## E

## F



## G

## Q



## R

## T



## U

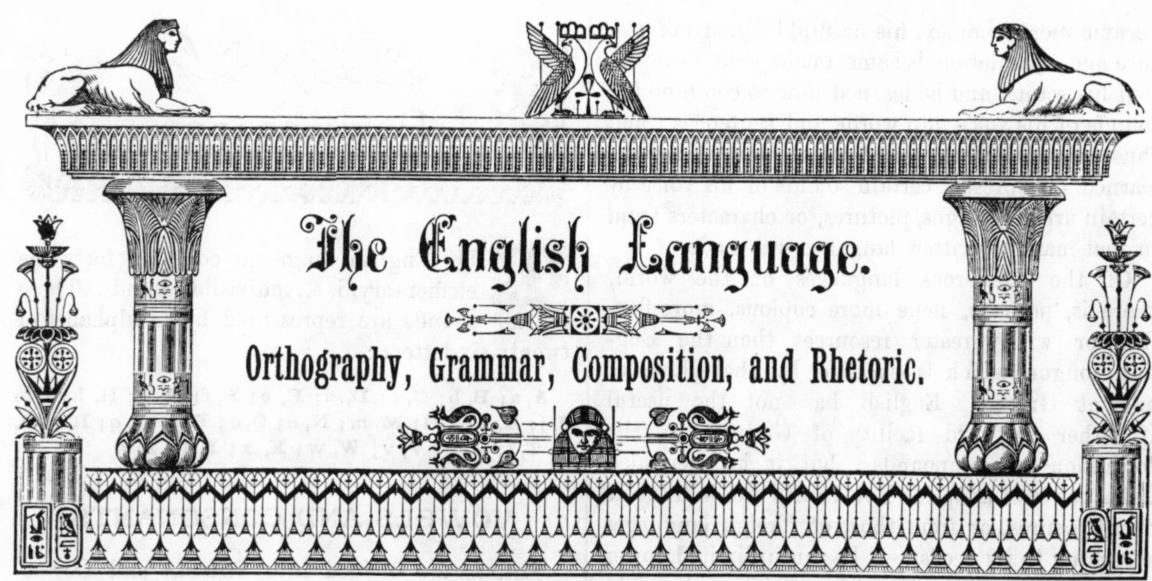


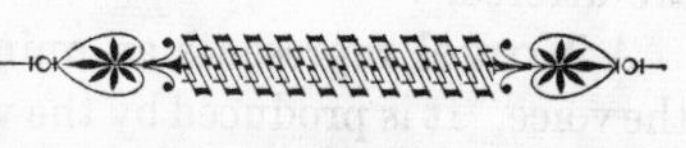

"LANGUAGE," said Talleyrand, "was given to conceal men's thoughts." It was a true saying, no doubt, so far as the witty French diplomat was concerned; and society, in our own day, frequently resorts to this subterfuge.

The possibilities of an existence without a language do not offer much that is enticing; for even the deaf-and-dumb, and all those who converse by means of signs, employ a language—the *word* meaning, as we use it, a medium for communicating one with another, whether this be by speaking, writing, or signs.

In connection with the study of this subject, Philology offers us the hieroglyphics of Egypt, the cuneiform inscriptions of Babylon, the picture-writing of the Aztecs, and other ancient American races; besides the numerous written languages which have come down to us. These extend back to the Sanskrit; and in our ENGLISH language we have representatives of almost all of the great language families, it being one of the peculiar characteristics of the history of languages, that to a certain extent they are always assimilating, cohering, coalescing—one with another.

Languages also take up many of the characteristics of those to whom they belong; and are, in fact, the creatures, to a great extent, of their environment. Thus in the rugged Norse tongue we can discern the elements which made sea-kings out of the Danes and Norwegians: just as in the liquid vowel preponderance of the south of Europe we recognize the soft languor of the Italian, Spanish and Portuguese people.

The early language of man must have consisted very largely of exclamations, of abrupt cries, and an extremely limited vocabulary of sounds. Many savage races of the present time have no other means of communication than an imperfect series of primitive sounds and various movements of the face, trunk, and limbs.

The writer has seen Indian scouts accompanying a United States army expedition use no other language for weeks in conversing with its commander than signs, and the well-known deaf and dumb alphabet is only a civilized extension of a leading principle of natural language. Any person who will take the trouble to study the language of the common domestic animals, and the utterances of very young children, will acquire a good deal of information upon the subject of natural language.

As the condition of man improved, and his wants

became more complex, his natural language of gesture and ejaculation became inadequate to represent his wants, and he learned how to combine the sounds of his voice into words and sentences ; and thus spoken language had its origin. Later, he learned to represent certain sounds of his voice by certain arbitrary signs, pictures, or characters ; and in that manner written language was made.

Of the numerous languages of the world, there is, perhaps, none more copious, more flexible, or with greater resources than the English tongue, which is excelled by that alone of ancient Greece. English has not the useful if rather awkward facility of German in the formation of compounds ; but it is unequaled in its power of adopting new coined words from its own treasures, or from those of foreign languages according to its needs. It has an unlimited power of extension and growth, and considering the rapid increase of population in America and Australia, seems destined at no distant day to be spoken by more people than any other modern language.

Before proceeding to the consideration of the spoken and written English language it may be well to mention briefly the group of languages to which it belongs.

## THE INDO-EUROPEAN LANGUAGES.

English is a member of the so-called Indo-European family of languages, of which four belong to Europe, and two to Asia. The parent language of this family was spoken in Asia, on the high table-lands of Iran. The family comprises :

1. The **Indian** branch, including Sanscrit, and dialects descended from it.

2. The **Medo-Persian** branch, of which the Zend, or Old Persian was the principal language.

3. The **Graeco-Latin** branch, including Greek, Latin, and languages derived from the Latin, *i.e.*, Spanish, Italian, Portuguese, French, Wallachian, Provençal, etc.

4. The **Slavonic** branch, including Russian, Polish, Lithuanian, etc.

5. The **Teutonic** branch, including Gothic, Anglo-Saxon, Friesic, Dutch, German, Flemish, Icelandic, Danish, Swedish, Norwegian, and English.

6. The **Celtic** branch, including Welsh, Gaelic, Irish, Cornish, Armorican, and Manx, a dialect spoken in the Isle of Man.

THE English language contains forty-one elementary, i. e., indivisible sounds. These sounds are represented by an alphabet of twenty-six letters :

**A, a; B, b; C, c; D, d; E, e; F, f; G, g; H, h; I, i; J, j; K, k; L, l; M, m; N, n; O, o; P, p; Q, q; R, r; S, s; T, t; U, u; V, v; W, w; X, x; Y, y; Z, z.**

## VOWELS AND CONSONANTS.

Letters are divided into Vowels and Consonants, according to the manner in which they are uttered.

A **Vowel** represents an uninterrupted sound of the voice. It is produced by the voice, varied but uninterrupted by the positions of the tongue and lips. The English vowels are *a, e, i, o, u, w* at the end of a syllable, and *y* not at the beginning of a syllable. The difference in sound of the vowels is regulated by the relation between the inside of the mouth and the opening of the lips—a relation varied by the different positions of the tongue.

A *Diphthong* is the union of two vowels uttered with one impulse of the voice. Diphthongs are either *proper* or *improper*. In a proper diphthong both vowels are sounded, as *oi*, in rejoice, or *oy* in toy. In an improper diphthong but one vowel is sounded, as *ei* in either, *ay* in play.

A *Triphthong* is a union of three vowels uttered with one impulse of the voice, as *ieu* in adieu.

A **Consonant** is a letter that cannot be perfectly uttered without the aid of a vowel. In passing through the organs of speech its sound is modified and interrupted. They are nineteen in number, exclusive of *y* and *w*, which are consonants only when followed by a vowel sounded in the same syllable ; in other cases *y* and *w* are vowels.

The consonants are divided into *mutes* and *semi-vowels*.

The Mutes *b, d, c* and *g* hard, *k, p,* and *t,* cannot be uttered unaided by a vowel sound.

The SEMI-VOWELS are *f, l, m, n, r, s, v, x, y, c* soft, and *g* soft. They can be uttered of themselves, with only small interruption from closing the organs of speech.

The Semi-Vowels *l, m, n,* and *r* are further distinguished as *liquids,* from their smooth, flowing sound, and the ease with which they combine with other consonants.

*K, q, c* hard, and *g* hard, are known as *gutturals,* being mostly pronounced by the throat.

The *labials* are *b, f, m, p,* and *v,* and are so called from being sounded by the lips.

The *dentals, d, g* soft, *j, s, t,* and *z,* are chiefly sounded by the teeth.

The *nasals, m, n,* and the combined sound or digraph *ng,* are chiefly pronounced through the nose.

The *palatals, d, g, j, k, l, n, q,* are sounded by the aid of the palate.

A DIGRAPH is a combination of two vowels or consonants in a single sound, as *Ph* in Philadelphia.

A SILENT LETTER is one not pronounced, as *w* in wretch.

## SYLLABLES.

A SYLLABLE is a letter, or a combination of letters, pronounced with one impulse of the voice, as *a, ba.*

A *Monosyllable* is a word of one syllable, as *cat.*

A *Dissyllable* is a word of two syllables, as *dif-fer.*

A *Trissyllable* is a word of three syllables, as *in-ter-pret.*

A *Polysyllable* is a word of more than three syllables, as *in-ter-pre-ta-tion.*

In dividing a word into syllables it should be remembered that so far as possible those letters which are closely connected in pronunciation should be kept together. The following general rules may be of service:

1. Every syllable contains a vowel.
2. Every pronounced consonant goes with a vowel or a diphthong.
3. The number of syllables in a word equals the number of words or diphthongs pronounced in that word.
4. A single consonant (other than x) between two vowels goes with the latter. *Re-search,* but *ex-ample.* This rule does not apply to compound words. *Un-easy, in-active.*
5. Two consonants capable of beginning a word are not to be divided, *ta-ble;* but two consonants between two vowels, and incapable of beginning a word, are divided, as *blun-der, ter-ror.*
6. Three consonants in the middle of a word, if capable of beginning a word, are to be divided, and one of them goes to the preceding syllable if the vowel of that syllable is short, *dis-tress, dis-trust.*
7. Of three or more consonants (incapable of beginning a word) between two vowels, one goes to the first syllable, *in-scription.*
8. Two vowels not diphthongs are divided, *tri-al, She-ol.*
9. Compound words must be resolved into their components, *over-come.*
10. Grammatical endings are divided, *reach-es, reach-est, reach-ing.*
11. A word broken at the end of a line is separated by syllables, but the syllable itself is not to be broken.

These rules are subject to some exceptions.

## SPELLING.

Spelling, or Orthography, is the art of forming words by arranging their letters correctly and in order. The spelling of English words is extremely irregular and arbitrary, and correct spelling is a matter of no small difficulty of attainment. The following rules will be found useful:

1. When *ing* is added to verbs ending in a single final *e,* the *e* is dropped, except in *dye, dyeing, hoe, hoeing, shoe, shoeing, singe, singeing, swinge, swingeing,* and *tinge, tingeing.* Examples of the rule are, *raise, raising, sneeze, sneezing.*
2. Monosyllabic verbs, with a single final consonant following a single vowel, on the addition of another syllable double such final consonant, *sham, shammed, hem, hemming.*
3. Verbs of two syllables, with a single final consonant following a single vowel and accented on the last syllable, double the final consonant on the addition of another syllable, *forget, forgetting, wed, wedded.*
4. When *ing* is added to verbs ending in *ie,* the *ie* becomes *y, die, dying.*
5. When *ing* is added to verbs with a final *y* preceded by a consonant, the *y* remains unchanged, *fry, frying.*
6. When *ed* is added to verbs with a final *y* preceded by a consonant, the *y* becomes *i, fry, fried.* If *s* is added to such verbs *y* becomes *ie, try, tries.*
7. When *ed, ing,* or *s* is added to verbs with a final *y* following another vowel, *y* is unchanged, *bay, baying, bays.*

N. B.—*Say, said, stay, staid* (or *stayed*), *lay, laid,* and *pay, paid,* are exceptions to this rule.

8. Words with final *e* drop that ending before the adjective ending *able,* as *love, lovable.* But words ending in *ce* or *ge* keep the *e* before *able, change, changeable.*
9. Adverbs in *ly* derived from words ending with *e* retain the *e,* as *wise, wisely.*
10. Nouns ending in *ment,* derived from words ending in *e,* keep the original *e, enslave, enslavement.*

11. Words of more than one syllable ending in an unaccented *l*, do not double the final *l*, *reproachful*. But otherwise, if the final syllable be accented, as *rebel*, *rebellious*.

12. Compounds consisting of a syllable or word before a single syllable ending in *all*, generally, but not always, keep the *ll*, as *downfall;* but *withal*, *therewithal*, *wherewithal*.

13. Compounds from words with final *y*, change *y* to *i*, *duty*, *dutiful*.

14. Nouns with final *o* following another vowel add *s* to their plural, *olio*, *olios*.

15. Nouns with final *o* following a consonant generally add *es* to form their plural, *embargo*, embargoes. But *canto*, *cento*, *duodecimo*, *grotto*, *portico*, *solo*, and a few others, add *s* only.

16. Nouns with final *ey* add *s* to form the plural, *valley*, *valleys*.

17. Nouns ending in *y* following a consonant, drop *y* in the plural and add *ies*, *county*, *counties*.

## SPELLING REFORM.

It is always advisable to refer to a good dictionary when there is any doubt as to the proper spelling of a word. The imperfection of the English alphabet, which attempts to represent forty-one elementary sounds with only twenty-six letters, has long engaged the attention of scholars. Several alphabets have been devised in which each letter represents but one and a uniform sound. Societies have been formed, both in England and America, with the object of improving the present system of English spelling. It cannot, however, be said that many of the changes proposed have met, or are likely to meet, with any extensive success, so far as a general introduction of them is concerned. The elaborate and sweeping changes which have been proposed by some of the more enthusiastic reformers can have little hope of going into immediate effect. At the same time, some of the proposed changes are entirely desirable and feasible. Such are the omission of one of two double consonants, and the omission of letters not heard in pronunciation. The omission of such letters would save much both in time and money.

More than a cursory treatment of the subject does not belong to this place; but for the benefit of those interested in the subject we subjoin the five rules adopted by the SPELLING REFORM ASSOCIATION. These rules are simple, and are followed by quite a number of newspapers, printers, and educators.

1. Use *e* for *ea*, equal to short *e*.
2. Drop silent *e* (not following *g* or *o*) after a diphthong or short vowel.
3. Use *f* for *ph*.
4. Omit one letter of a double consonant, unless both are pronounced.
5. Use *t* instead of *ed* when it represents the sound.

## ACCENT.

ACCENT is the vocal stress laid upon some particular syllable of a word. The mark placed above a syllable to indicate what modulation of the voice is to be given it, is also called an accent.

The *acute* accent (´) over a letter or syllable shows it is to be uttered with a rising inflection.

The *grave* accent (`) indicates a falling inflection.

The *circumflex* accent (ˆ) is a combination of the grave and acute accents. It indicates a vibratory movement of the voice.

The *breve* (˘) shows that the letter beneath it has a short sound, as *ĕlĕgant*.

The *macron* (¯) shows that the letter beneath has a long sound, as *fāme*.

The *cedilla* (¸) shows that the letter *c* written above it is pronounced soft like *s*, *leçon*. Its most frequent use is in French words, or derivatives.

A *diæresis* (¨) over the latter of two successive vowels, shows that they are to be separately pronounced.

All English words containing more than one syllable have at least one accented syllable, and most words of more than three syllables have, in addition to their principal or primary accent, another inferior accent called secondary; thus *det′ri-ment′al*, *leg′is-la′ture*, in which the accent on the first syllable is secondary.

The last syllable but one of a word is called a *penult*.

The last syllable but two is called the *antepenult*.

## ADVICE ABOUT PRONUNCIATION.

Many words have a different pronunciation according as they are used as nouns or as adjectives, or as nouns or verbs. Pronunciation is subject to frequent changes, and often appears to be largely a matter of fashion. The safe rule on this point has been often stated,—not to be the first to adopt a new pronunciation of a word, or the last to retain the old pronunciation. The real authority on pronunciation is the usage of the greatest number of cultivated persons. Observe carefully how words in regard to the pronunciation of which you feel doubtful are pronounced by educated persons upon whose knowledge you can rely. Always keep a good pronouncing dictionary, and consult it whenever you are not absolutely certain of the spelling and pronunciation of a word. A useful adjunct to a large dictionary is one of the little dictionaries, or list of words frequently mispronounced.

The habit of reading aloud is also of great service in enlarging one's knowledge of pronunciation.

After you have thoroughly familiarized yourself with the standard pronunciation of the day, it will be found interesting to note the licenses taken by poets in the accentuation. You can also learn from poetry many interesting details of the ever-changing fashions of speech. Thus you will find in Byron and Rogers *balcóny;* in Pope, *bohea* and *tea* pronounced *bohay'* and *tay;* and in Shakespeare *reven'ue, persev'er, sepul'chre,* and many other pronunciations no longer permissible. In this way, after a good practical knowledge of modern pronunciation has been obtained, some historical knowledge of it may be gained conjointly with the study of the best English literature.

## WORDS AND THEIR ORIGIN.

The number of words in the English language is not accurately known, and is variously stated. The most common estimate is in the vicinity of 100,000 words. But when it is considered that new terms relating to the arts and sciences are being introduced every day, and that many words found in literature of even recent date are either obsolete or are fast becoming so, it will be seen that any estimate of the number of words in the English language at a given time must be based to a great extent on mere guesswork. Only a small part of these words constitutes a large vocabulary for most persons. Probably the average man does not use more than 3,000 words. An extremely well-read person may use 6,000, while Shakespeare himself only used four times the latter number.

Of these words, exclusive of the immense number of scientific and technical terms taken from Greek and Latin, between one-half and five-eighths are of Anglo-Saxon origin.

A Primitive word is one that cannot be farther resolved: as, *ox, go, hunt.*

A Derivative word is derived from a primitive word by joining letters or syllables to the latter. Such an addition placed before the primitive word is called a *prefix,* as *pre* in the word *prefix;* placed after such word, it is called a *suffix,* as *ing* in *going.*

### PREFIXES.

The chief **prefixes** are *a*=at, in, etc.; *be*=for, upon; *for*=against; *fore*=before; *mis*=wrong; *out*=beyond, in excess of, over; *un*=not; and *under.* Thus, *afield, bespeak, forbid, forestall, misconception, outswear, overestimate, unequalled, undervalued.*

The most important **Greek** prefixes are *a*=without; *amphi*=about, around; *anti*=against; *apo*=from; *cata*=down; *dia*=through; *hyper*=above, in excess of; *hypo*=under; *peri*=about, around; *pro*=before; *syl, sym, syn*=with. Thus, *a*catalectic, *amphi*bology, *anti*-slavery, *apo*stle, *cata*leptic, *dia*meter, *hyper*bole, *hypo*chondria, *pro*leptic, *sym*metrical.

The chief **Latin** prefixes are *a, ab* or *abs*=from; *ac, ad, af, ag, al, ap, ar*=to; *ante*=before; *circum*=around; *co, com, con,* etc.=with; *de*=down; *dis*=apart, or not; *e, ex*=out of; *in* (before an adjective)=not; *in* (before a verb)=in; *ob*=in the way of; *per*=through; *pre*=before; *retro*=backward; *se*=apart; *sub, sus,* etc.=under; *super*=above; *trans*=beyond:—*a*verse, *ab*hor, *abs*tract, *ac*cept, *ad*vise, *af*firm, *ag*ree, *al*lude, *ap*ply, *ar*rest, *ante*date, *circum*navigate, *co*ëval, *com*municate, *con*nect, *de*base, *dis*similar, *dis*place, *e*lude, *ex*pel, *in*nocuous, *in*spire, *ob*trude, *pre*pare, *retro*grade, *se*clude, *sub*stratum, *sus*pect, *super*pose, *trans*late.

### SUFFIXES.

The chief **Anglo-Saxon suffixes** are *er*=he who; *ful*=full of; *hood*=condition, character; *less*=without, deprived of; *ly* (after a noun)=like, after an adjective indicates the manner of; *ness*=with the quality of; and *ship*=state of:—mak*er*, thought*ful*, child*hood*, thought*less*, god*ly*, right*ly*, thoughtless*ness*, steward*ship*.

The chief **Latin** suffixes are *able, ble, ible*=capable of; *ant, ent* (after a noun)=the person who, (after adjective)=the participial ending *ing; ity, tude*=the state of; *ous*=with the quality of; *fy*=to make; as, litig*ant*, depend*ent*, familiar*ity*, desue*tude*, furi*ous*, beauti*fy*.

From the **Greek** come the suffixes *ic* and *ical*=relating to; *graphy*=describing, treating of; *logy*=descriptive of, the science of; *ize*=to make:—misanthrop*ic*, misanthrop*ical*, tele*graphy*, geo*logy*, empha*size*.

It should be said that in many cases the suffixes and the affixes take a different meaning from the above, according to the word with which they were compounded.

GRAMMAR is the art of speaking and writing correctly according to established usage. The English language is termed our *mother tongue* because it is our native language, which we were taught to speak when we first began to talk.

The study that teaches the correct use of the English language in speaking and in writing is called ENGLISH GRAMMAR, and is divided into Etymology and Syntax.

ETYMOLOGY treats of the origin and derivation of words.

SYNTAX treats of the construction of sentences.

## ETYMOLOGY.

The English language has ten PARTS OF SPEECH, including the participle :

| | |
|---|---|
| 1. The ARTICLE, | 6. The ADVERB, |
| 2. The NOUN, | 7. The PREPOSITION, |
| 3. The PRONOUN, | 8. The CONJUNCTION, |
| 4. The ADJECTIVE, | 9. The INTERJECTION, |
| 5. The VERB, | 10. The PARTICIPLE. |

The **Article** is placed before a noun to define or restrict its meaning.

The **indefinite** article, *a*, or *an*, points out indefinitely a single thing or person of the kind; as, *a* man, *an* ox.

The form *an* is used before a vowel, elsewhere *a*. But *an* is to be used before a silent *h* followed by a vowel; as, *an* heirloom; and also before words beginning with *h* not silent, and accented on the second syllable; *an* historic stone. *A* is used before words whose initial vowel has a consonant sound like *y* or *w;* as, *a union*, *a one*-man power.

The **definite** article, *the*, is placed before nouns both in the singular and the plural numbers. It points the particular object referred to; as, "Find *the* place." *The* is also used to form the comparative and superlative degree of adjectives and adverbs.

A **Noun**, or **Substantive**, is the name of an object; as, a *man*. Nouns are either *common* or *proper*.

A **common** noun is a name common to a whole class of objects; as, *bird, boy.*

A proper noun is the name of an individual person or thing; as, *Cicero, America, John.*

Nouns have *Gender, Number*, and *Case.*

### GENDER.

GENDER is the distinction which marks the difference of sex in the classification of objects.

Names of females, and of objects conceived as female, are of the *feminine* gender.

Names of males, and of objects conceived as males, are of the *masculine* gender.

Names of things are of the *neuter* gender.

There are in English four ways of indicating gender.

1. By the use of two forms for the two genders of the word; as, goose, gander; duck, drake.

2. By a special ending for the feminine; as, baron, baron*ess;* count, count*ess*.

3. By prefixing a pronoun; as, *he*-goat, *she*-goat.

4. By prefixing a noun; as, *man*-servant, *maid*-servant.

### NUMBER.

Nouns have two NUMBERS, the *singular* and the *plural* number, according as they signify one object or more than one object.

The PLURAL is formed in most cases by the addition of *s* to the singular; as, road, road*s;* owl, owl*s*.

When nouns end in sounds that do not easily combine with *s*, the plural is formed by adding *es* to the singular; as, church, church*es;* loss, loss*es;* galosh, galosh*es;* box, box*es*.

Some nouns ending in *f* or *fe* make their plural by changing *f* or *fe* into *ves;* half, hal*ves;* knife, kni*ves*.

Nouns ending in *y* following a consonant add *es* to form the plural, and change *y* to *i;* lady, lad*ies*.

Nouns ending in *y* following a vowel form their plural in the regular way by the addition of *s* to the singular; volley, volley*s*.

A number of words of Greek or Latin origin form their plurals either according to the language from which they are derived, or according to the English language. Thus memorandum, memorandum*s*, or memorand*a*. As a rule the English form is to be preferred, unless the word be one lately introduced, or not yet common in English.

### CASE.

CASE distinguishes the relation between nouns and pronouns, and the words to which they are joined.

There are in English four cases, the *nominative*, the *possessive*, the *objective*, and the *vocative.*

The NOMINATIVE case simply points out the person or thing without showing the construction of the sentence.

The POSSESSIVE case denotes possession; as, *John's book.*

The possessive case, singular, is formed by writing *apostrophe s* (*'s*) after the singular noun; as, mother, *mother's*.

The possessive case, plural, is formed by writing the apostrophe after the *s* of plural nouns; as, mothers, *mothers'*. But when the plural does not end in *s* the *'s* is added; as, children, *children's*.

The OBJECTIVE case depends upon a verb or a preposition, being the case in which the *object* of the verb is placed, when denoting what is produced or affected by the act expressed by the verb. "Strike for your *altars* and your *fires*."

The VOCATIVE is the case by which a person is directly addressed; as, "Bay not me, *Brutus*."

A **Pronoun** is a word used to take the place of a noun, with the object of preventing inelegant repetition of the word for which it stands.

Pronouns are either *personal, possessive, interrogative*, or *adjective*. The latter are more commonly called *pronominal adjectives*.

The **personal pronouns** take the place of nouns indicating persons. They are *I, thou, he, she, it*, and their plural, *we, you* [or *ye*], *they*.

*I* and *we* are pronouns of the first person, and denote the speaker.

*Thou* and *you* are of the second person, and denote the person spoken to.

*They, she*, and *it* are of the third person, and denote the person spoken of.

The **relative pronouns** refer to some preceding word or expression called the antecedent. They are *who, which, what, that*.

*Who* relates only to persons.

*Which* relates only to things.

*That* relates to both persons and things.

The **interrogative pronouns** are used to ask questions. They are *who, which*, and *what*.

The **adjective pronouns**, or **pronominal adjectives**, are so called because they have the character of both adjectives and pronouns. They are divided into *demonstrative, distributive, indefinite*, and *possessive*.

The POSSESSIVE pronouns are *my, mine, thy, thine, his, her, our, your, their*.

The DEMONSTRATIVE pronouns point out a person or thing. They are *this, these, that, those*.

The DISTRIBUTIVE pronouns denote one of several persons or things taken individually. They are *each, every, either, neither*.

The INDEFINITE pronouns denote indefinitely the object to which they refer. They are *all, any, one, other, some*, and *such*.

An **Adjective** is a word joined to a noun to show the quality or restrict the meaning of the latter.

The **comparison** of an adjective is its formation to show different degrees of the quality expressed.

The POSITIVE is the original form of the adjective; as, *bold*.

The COMPARATIVE indicates a higher degree of the quality as compared with the quality of some other object or person; "*bolder* than a lion."

The SUPERLATIVE degree denotes the highest degree of the quality expressed; as, "The *boldest* might tremble."

The comparative degree is formed in words of one syllable by the addition of *r* or *er* to the positive; bold, bold*er*; pale, pale*r*. In adjectives of more than one syllable it is formed by placing *more* before the positive; anxious, *more* anxious.

The superlative degree of adjectives of one syllable is formed by the addition of *st* or *est* to the positive; bold, bold*est*; pale, pale*st*. In adjectives of more than one syllable it is formed by placing most before the positive; anxious, *most* anxious.

N. B.—The following adjectives are irregular in their comparison:

| POSITIVE. | COMPARATIVE. | SUPERLATIVE. |
|---|---|---|
| Good, | Better, | Best. |
| Bad, | Worse, | Worst. |
| Little, | Less, | Least. |
| Many, } Much, } | More, | Most. |
| Near, | Nearer, | Nearest, } Next. } |
| Late, | Later, } Latter, } | Last. |
| Old, | Older, } Elder, } | Oldest, } Eldest. } |

A **Verb** expresses action, existence, or affirms something about some person or object. The person or object in regard to which the affirmation is made, is styled the subject.

Verbs are either *transitive* or *intransitive*.

A **transitive** verb expresses an action by some person or object upon some person or object. Its sense is incomplete unless it is followed by an object. Such object (noun or pronoun) is put in the objective case. "God *created* man."

An **intransitive** verb expresses existence, or state of existence. The sense of an intransitive verb is complete without an object; as, the rain *falls*.

Besides *person* and *number*, verbs have *mood* and *tense*.

## MOOD.

MOOD, OR MODE, is the form of the verb which shows the manner of the action or condition expressed. The English verb has five moods: *indicative, potential, subjunctive, infinitive*, and *imperative*.

The INDICATIVE mood expresses an absolute affirmation.

The POTENTIAL mood expresses possibility, inclination, ability, duty. Its signs are the auxiliary verbs, *may, can, must, will, might, could, would, should*.

The SUBJUNCTIVE expresses a condition. Its ordinary sign is *if*.

The INFINITIVE mood expresses action or condition without restriction of number or person. A verb in the infinitive mood has no subject, and consequently can make no affirmation.

The IMPERATIVE mood expresses a command.

### TENSE.

Tense is the form of the verb which indicates the time of the action or condition.

The English verb has six tenses, the *present, imperfect, perfect, pluperfect, first future,* and *second future.*

The PRESENT tense expresses a present action or condition; "It rains."

The IMPERFECT tense expresses what took place, or was taking place in time past; "It rained."

The PERFECT tense expresses an action or condition indefinitely passed; "It has rained."

The PLUPERFECT tense expresses what had occurred before some past time; "It had rained before my departure."

The FUTURE tense expresses what will happen in future time; "It will rain."

The SECOND FUTURE tense expresses what will have happened after some future time specified or implied; "It will have rained by the time we arrive."

The **conjugation** of a verb is the regular arrangement according to person, number, mood, and tense.

A **passive** verb is made by joining the perfect participle of a transitive verb to some tense of the verb *to be*; "I was lost."

**Voice** is that form of the verb which shows whether it is active or passive.

An **auxiliary** verb is one used in the conjugation of a verb. The auxiliary verbs are *be, can, do, have, must, shall, will,* in all their forms.

The **Participle** is sometimes classed as a mere form of the verb, and not a separate part of speech. It has the character both of a verb and of an adjective or noun. Like the verb, it denotes action, being, suffering, but it does not affirm anything.

The forms of the participle are three.

The **present participle** denotes present action, being, or suffering. It is formed by the addition of *ing* to the stem of the verb; lov*ing*, fear*ing*.

The **perfect or past participle** denotes past action, being, or suffering. It is formed in the case of regular verbs by the addition of *ed* to the stem of the verb, as, lov*ed*, fear*ed*.

The **compound perfect participle** is formed by the combination of the perfect participle with the present participle of an auxiliary verb; as, having loved, having feared.

The participle is made a noun by placing the definite article *the* before it; the *suffering*

An **Adverb** is a word joined with a verb, an adjective, or another adverb, to qualify the meaning of the latter; as, an *exceedingly good* book, *very* well done, he does *well.*

Many adverbs are derived from adjectives by the addition of *ly*; as, bold, bold*ly*; warm, warm*ly*. Others change final *e* to *y*; as, able, abl*y*; terrible, terribl*y*.

A **Conjunction** is a participle used to connect words and sentences; as, "He *and* I went;" "Fate ordains it, *and* we bow to its decrees."

The two chief classes of conjunctions are **copulative**, which add a word or sentence, such as, *and;* and **disjunctive**, which join the words, but not the sense, as, *but.*

A **Preposition** is a particle governing a noun or pronoun in the objective case, and showing the relation in which such noun or pronoun stands to some other word in the sentence.

Prepositions are usually placed before the word which they govern; as, he was running *to* the house.

Prepositions are *inseparable* when they can only be used in compounding words; as, *mis*-calculate; or *separable*, when they may be separately used, as *in.*

An **Interjection** expresses some mental affection or emotion; as, *alas!*

## SYNTAX.

A SENTENCE is a collection of words grammatically connected and making a complete sense.

Every sentence must have a *subject*, of which something is said, and a *predicate*, which is said of the subject; as, *I run.*

The SUBJECT of a sentence is a noun or pronoun in the nominative case.

The PREDICATE is a verb agreeing with its subject and in number and person.

The Infinitive may be the subject of a sentence; as, *To die* is gain."

The Object of a transitive verb is put in the objective case; as, "Why have they slain *him?*"

The less immediate relations of an object to the verb of the sentence are denoted by prepositions governing the objective case. "*To* what base *uses* we may return, Horatio."

A Noun may be qualified by a noun or by an adjective.

A qualifying noun is said to be in *apposition*, or to be an *appositive* substantive, when its relation to its noun is assumed *as already existing* in the sentence, not as created by the sentence; as, "Cicero, the consummate *orator*, was proscribed."

In the same case the qualifying adjective is said to be *attributive;* as, "The *eloquent* Cicero was proscribed."

When the qualifying substantive comes into relation with the qualified *by means of the sentence* it is called a *predicate noun*, or *predicate;* as, "Ye call me *chief.*"

In the same case the qualifying adjective is called a *predicate adjective;* as, "He was called *generous.*"

The qualified noun is called the *subject* of the appositive, or predicate, and the subject noun must be in the same case.

It will be noticed that the appositive, as a rule, is merely descriptive of its subject, while the attributive is intimately connected with it.

A Verb must agree with its subject in number and person.

A Pronoun must agree with its antecedent in number.

Two or more subjects joined by the conjunction *and* take a plural verb. "Fire and sword *have* done their work."

The Subject of a verb is in the nominative case.

The Object addressed is in the vocative case.

The Possessive case is often more elegantly replaced by *of* with the objective.

**Sentences** are either *simple* or *compound.*

A SIMPLE SENTENCE is one in which the subject and predicate are found but once.

A COMPOUND SENTENCE is composed of a principal or independent sentence, and a subordinate sentence dependent upon the principal sentence.

The ADVERB usually precedes the adjective or adverb modified by it.

It should always be placed as near as possible to the word which it modifies.

The adverb usually follows the verb; as, "He spoke *frequently,*" but in connection with the compound forms of the verb it comes between the auxiliary and the verb; as, "He had been *frequently* spoken of."

## CONVERSATIONAL ERRORS.

The following are a few of the errors most frequent in conversation:—

1. The use of two negatives instead of one; as, "I didn't hear *no* bell."

2. *Don't* for *doesn't* in the third person singular of the indicative; as, "It *don't* matter." This is a mistake of frequent occurrence even among cultivated men.

3. Use of the nominative for the objective of the pronoun; as, "*Who* are you looking for?" instead of *whom.* This is an error which can always be avoided by putting the preposition at the beginning of the sentence, not at the end; as, "For *whom* are you looking?"

4. Use of the objective in place of the nominative; as, "Him and me went."

5. Use of *like* instead of *as;* "He looked *like* he did a year ago."

6. Use of *them* for *those;* as, "See *them* people."

7. Improper conjugation of the verb; "He done it," for "He did it," "He *drinked* it," for "He *drank* it;" "He *knowed it,*" for "He *knew* it."

8. Confusion of one word with another. "I will *lay* down on the sofa," for "I will *lie* down." "He is too weak to *set* up," for "*sit up.*" "Learn me to sing," for *teach*, etc.

9. Singular instead of plural form of the verb with plural subject, or more than one subject. "The horse and carriage *is* at the door;" "The theatres *is* crowded."

10. Use of a plural verb with a singular noun. This often happens when a plural noun or two connected singular nouns immediately precede the subject; as, "The recital of all these transactions and proceedings *make* a long story," instead of *makes.*

11. Confusion of *each other* and *one another.* The former should only be used in reference to two objects; "Let us all then promise *each other,*" for one another.

12. Use of *oughter* for *ought to* (or *should*). "You *oughter,*" instead of "You *ought to.*" "He *oughter do it,*" for "He *should* do it."

In writing, few of the above errors are likely to pass unnoticed, as their absurdity is evident to the eye. In conversation, however, they are often heard. A little practice and carefulness will lead one to avoid them. To speak the English language grammatically is really a very simple matter, if one will take a little pains, for the number of possible errors is not very large. To learn to pronounce every word properly, is a much more difficult matter. But any person who will keep his ears open and thumb his dictionary assiduously, will easily conquer the difficulty.

## SLANG.

Care must be taken not to use slang, or vulgar expressions. A certain amount of slang does indeed find its way into conversation; but the habit of using slang expressions should be guarded against by every person who cares to have any reputation for correct and cultivated speech. It is simply an indication of poverty of ideas.

## VULGARISMS.

Avoid a certain class of words which bear the stamp of vulgarity, and are only heard among the ignorant, though often used by persons of considerable pretensions.

The most frequent mistakes are the use of *gent* for *gentleman*; *pants* for *trousers*; *genteel* for *elegant*; *distinguished*, *first-class* for *excellent*; *party* for *person*; *mad* for *angry*.

Avoid all provincial expressions, such as *guess*; *expect* for *think*, *suppose*, *imagine*.

Avoid the excessive and unnecessary use of *get*, *got*. This verb properly means to *possess*, *obtain*. To combine it with the auxiliary *have* is mere waste of words. "He *has* it," means just the same as "he *has got* it," and has the merit of being short and correct. "He *has got* to go" is incorrect. Say "he must go," or "he is obliged to go." Perhaps there is no word in the English language made to serve such a variety of incorrect uses as the word *get*.

Care must be taken not to confound the two auxiliaries of the future tense *shall* and *will*. A little reflection will easily show which is to be used in a particular case. The general rule for their use is as follows:

*Shall*, in the first person, simply marks a future event, as, "I *shall* go;" in the second and third persons, it marks a command, threat, or promise, as, "you *shall* go," "he *shall* die."

*Will*, in the first person, marks a promise or a threat, as, "I *will* go to-morrow," "I *will* be heard;" in the second and third persons, it simply marks a future event, as, "he *will* speak," "thou *wilt* listen."

## ADVICE ABOUT WRITING.

To write good English is an accomplishment not easily attained. The colloquial expressions, the occasional inelegancies, and the abrupt changes permissible in conversation are to be carefully avoided in writing. The important thing is to have something to say, and to express it in as simple, clear, and intelligible a manner as possible.

Avoid roundabout expressions, and rhetorical phrases. Anybody who writes grammatically, who uses as few words as will clearly express his meaning, and who escapes slang, writes good English; but to write English of the most finished elegance it requires a painstaking study of the best models, and a degree of patient and conscientious labor for which most persons have neither the time nor the inclination.

It will be found to be of service to take some English prose-writer with a style of acknowledged excellence, and read his works thoroughly and attentively. In this way one may obtain an insight into the secret of good writing, and may to a certain extent form his style after that of the author whom he has chosen as his model. Addison and Cardinal Newman are good models of all that is clear, simple, and at the same time elegant in style.

There is no better way of cultivating one's sense of style than to study the works of the great masters. Nobody can read with any degree of care Goldsmith's "Vicar of Wakefield," and not get a deeper understanding of the character and value of simple and natural writing. Persons whose reading is confined to newspapers are liable to fall into a hasty and incorrect method of expression. The best safeguard against this danger is the study of good English prose.

## FIGURES.

A FIGURE OF RHETORIC OR RHETORICAL FIGURE is a method of speech in which words are used in other than their literal sense. These figures are of frequent occurrence in poetry and imaginative literature, and when properly and discriminatingly used do much to strengthen and adorn a composition. The rhetorical figures are as follows:

An **Allegory** is a figure in which the words used have another signification beside their literal and usual one. Bunyan's "Pilgrim's Progress" is perhaps the most famous English instance of an allegory.

**Allusion** is an indirect reference to or mention of something similar and well-known. "He was lost in a *labyrinth* of doubts, from which escape seemed hopeless."

**Alliteration** is the use of the same initial in two or more successive words. "Apt alliteration's artful aid."

**Antithesis** is the opposition or contrast of contraries. "From grave to gay, from lively to severe."

**Climax** is a gradual rising from an inferior thought or expression up to a higher thought or expression. "It is an outrage to bind a Roman citizen; to scourge him is an outrageous crime; to put him to death is almost parricide; but to *crucify* him—what shall I call it?"

**Apostrophe** is a sudden change in the discourse, to address a person or thing immediately. "Oh, ever-loving, lovely, and beloved! Dear to a heart where naught is left so dear!"

**Exclamation** expresses any passion or emotion.

"Oh, Sleep, it is a gentle thing,
Beloved from pole to pole!"

**Hyperbole** is the use of an exaggerated or extravagant expression, signifying more than the literal truth, and not supposed to be understood in a literal sense.

"By Heaven, methinks it were an easy leap
To pluck bright Honor from the pale-faced moon!"

**Interrogation** is the expression of an opinion or a sentiment by means and in the form of a question. "What can ennoble sots, or slaves, or cowards ?"

**Irony** is the expression of something other than is meant. "It requires great courage to make war on helpless women and children." "Brutus is an *honorable* man."--*Shakespeare.*

**Euphemism** is the substitution of a more agreeable expression for one which would be harsh or offensive if directly related. "He was out in the forty-five," (*i. e.*, he took part in the Jacobite rising in Scotland in 1745.)

**Metaphor** is a figure which expresses the resemblance of one object to another by an implied comparison. "I'll be your *foil*, Laertes."

**Metonymy** is a figure by which the cause is put for the effect, the effect for the cause, the sign for the object signified. "The crown (*i.e.*, royalty) itself was not safe from attack."

**Paralipsis** is a figure which pretends to omit what is really expressed. "We must not call this proceeding a swindle, for that would be impolite."

**Personification** represents an inanimate object as a person.

"And Freedom shall awhile repair
To dwell a weeping hermit there."

**Onomatopoeia** is the use of a word whose sound answers to the sense.

"Sea-nymphs hourly ring his knell,
Hark, I hear them—ding-dong, bell!"

**Repetition** is the frequent use of a word or phrase in the same sentence.

"Alone, alone, all all alone,
Alone on a wide, wide sea."

**Simile** is a direct and express comparison. "As a woodcock to mine own springe, Osric, I am justly killed with mine own treachery."

**Synecdoche** puts the whole for the part, or the part for the whole. "A squadron of forty sail" (*i.e.*, ships).

A FIGURE OF SYNTAX is a deviation from the rules of syntax. Among the figures of syntax, the following deserve mention :

**Aposiopesis** is a sudden break in the sentence, leaving something to be supplied. "Him I may yet—but truce to idle vaunts."

**Enallage** is the substitution of one part of speech or form of a word for another. It is unnecessary, and frequently incorrect. "Marry come up, *says* I."

**Ellipsis** is the omission of some part necessary to the construction but not to the meaning. "The beginning and (*the*) end." "Would he were fatter,"="*I* would *that*," etc.

**Hyperbation** or Inversion is a transposition of words from their simple, natural grammatical order. "Eftsoons his hand dropt he"; "Out of the sea rose he."

**Pleonasm** is the use of words not necessary to the sense. "*Verily, verily*, I say unto you, all ye *inhabitants* of the world, *and dwellers on the earth*."

**Zeugma** is the reference of a word to two or more words, when, strictly construed, it can agree with but one of them. "Nor e'er had changed, nor wished to change his *place*."

An **Archaism** is an antiquated expression. "Right little peace one hath of it, God *wot*."

A FIGURE OF ORTHOGRAPHY is a deviation from the regular spelling or pronunciation :

**Apocope** is the cutting off of a final letter or syllable. "What cannot you and I perform upon *th'* unguarded Duncan?"

**Aphaeresis** is the cutting off of an initial letter or syllable. "And since *'tis* hard to combat, learn to fly."

**Diaeresis** is the pronunciation of an unaccented *e*. It is sometimes indicated by the accent ′. It is frequent in poetry in the termination *ed*.

**Prosthesis** is the prefixing of a word or a syllable; *be*smeared.

**Syncope** is the cutting off of a letter or syllable in the middle of a word. "Nor *e'er* (ever) had changed."

**Paragoge** is the addition of a syllable to a word; *deary* for *dear*.

**Tmesis** is the separation of the parts of a compound word. "In what way *soever*," *i.e.*, "in what soever way."

## PUNCTUATION.

Punctuation is the art of separating written discourse into sentences, or parts of sentences, by the use of points. The points used in punctuation are :

| | |
|---|---|
| Comma | , |
| Semicolon | ; |
| Colon | : |
| Period | . |
| Interrogation Point | ? |
| Exclamation Point | ! |
| Dash | — |
| Parenthesis | ( ) |
| Apostrophe | ' |
| Hyphen | - |
| Quotation Marks | " " or ' ' |
| Ellipsis | . . . . . |
| Brackets | [ ] |
| Caret | ^ |

The **Comma** (,) indicates the shortest pause, and is used—

I. To separate (1) adjectival, (2) absolute, (3) adverbial, and (4) participial expressions from the context.

1. Bitter as was the *strife*, *it* ended at last.
2. To tell the *truth*, *this was* the proper course.
3. The *proposition*, greatly to my *surprise*, *was* refused.
4. Resuming the *subject*, *it* may be said that action is the soul of oratory.

Conjunctions and adverbs connecting one sentence with another or modifying a sentence are often to be separated from the context by a comma.

*Finally*, I will say. *There*, *nevertheless*, *is* to be found the true solution of the problem.

*Too*, *however*, *indeed*, *then*, *now*, when used as conjunctions, are separated from the context by commas ; used as adverbs they are not so separated.

*However* great our obligation to others, it must not be forgotten, *however*, that our chief obligation is to him alone.

II The comma separates two words or phrases in apposition ; but not if they are used as one phrase or as a compound word, thus : *Emmet, the* hero of Ireland. But *Lord Herbert.*

The dash, or both the dash and comma, may be used to separate expressions in apposition.

The two controlling influences of his character,—*Patriotism* and *Humanity.*

III. Relative clauses explaining or adding something to the antecedent are divided from the context by commas.

*Addison, who* afterwards made an unhappy *marriage, was* at this time single.

In our *generation, when* the power of wealth is so much *greater, the* importance of integrity is also greater.

Relative clauses which simply restrict the meaning of the antecedent are not to be divided from the context.

The *few who survive* remember the bitter sufferings of that memorable year.

IV. A comma is used between two closely connected independent clauses connected by a conjunction, in a short sentence.

He destroyed his country's *liberties, and* his country forgave him.

V. The comma may be used to set off parenthetic expressions.

His *reward, though* undoubtedly *large, was* less than he had anticipated.

Marks of parenthesis ( ), brackets [ ], and dashes, with or without other stops, are also used to set off parenthetic expression. Commas should not be used for this purpose in a sentence in which several commas are already found.

The **Semicolon** (;) is used between two independent clauses connected by a conjunction, if the sentence is long, and the clauses are not closely connected.

" This exploit, as unexpected as it was heroic, rekindled the flagging public *interest ; and* the name of the young general soon became famous."

The semicolon is inserted between dependent expressions in a series ; such expressions depend upon words either at the beginning or at the end of a sentence.

We must remember that the country is still suffering from the effects of those *decrees ; that* a long period of commercial depression may still lie before *us ; and* that no hasty remedy can cure an inveterate evil.

The semicolon (1) or colon (2) may connect short sentences between which no close connection exists.

1. The streets are *wide ; most* of them are well *paved ; some* of them are beautifully shaded with elms.

2. But in this he was not different from his *contemporaries : Clay*, Benton, Calhoun, Cass, were exposed to a similar reproach.

The semicolon is inserted between clauses divided up by commas.

He was bold, not rash, in *battle ; generous*, not ostentatious, in *peace ; and* cautious, but not timid or hesitating, in his political career.

The **Colon** (:) separates two parts of a sentence, one or both of which consist of clauses divided by semicolons.

Peace on such terms is impossible ; war for such a cause is *welcome : peace* would bring nothing but dishonor ; war can bring no more than ruin.

The colon is used to introduce formal statements.

Once *more : the* presumption has no basis either in law or fact.

The colon (1), the dash and colon (2), the comma (3), or the dash and comma (4), may introduce quotations denoted by quotation marks.

1. In this correspondence occurs the following *passage :* " *You* will use your good offices in favor of Peru."

2. If I remember, it is thus that the quotation *runs :*—
" *Perhaps* it was right to dissemble your love,
But why did you kick me down stairs ? "

3. It cried in a loud *voice,* " *Beware !* "

4. In the grand words of *Byron,*—
" *Death* rides upon the sulphury Siroc."

The **Caret** (∧) indicates that an omitted letter, word, or expression will be found above the line.

```
           a of
" She wore a wreth roses."
              ∧ ∧
```

The **Hyphen** (-) connects the parts of compound and derivative words, and divides words at the end of a line, or is used to show pronounciation.

Sister-in-law. Self-made. Re-elect.

The **Exclamation point** (!) follows an exclamation, or any expression indicating emotion.

" Oh, all ye host of Heaven ! Oh, Earth ! "

The **Interrogation** (?) follows every sentence asking a question.

Has the gentleman done ? Has he completely done ?

The **Period** (.) follows every complete affirmative or negative sentence, abbreviations, headings, and sub-headings.

" And thereby hangs a tale."
Lieut. Jones, U.S.A.

**Quotation marks** (" ") (1) denote expressions quoted from anotner. A quotation in a quotation (2) is enclosed by single marks. Names of books, magazines, newspapers, and vessels are generally enclosed in quotation marks, or italicized (3).

1. "There was a ship," quoth he.

2. " It shows no remarkable degree of poetical power," says Hazlitt, " to call snuff ' the pungent grains of titillating dust.' "

3. A characteristic article in the *Times.*

The **Dash** (—) denotes a sudden suspension or change of the construction or meaning of a sentence (1), emphasis (2), the omission of words, letters, or figures (3).

1. Greece, lovely Greece, " the land of scholars and the nurse of *arms* " —*where* and what is she ?

2. What shall be done for *them—for* our dearest boast ?

3. N—w—Y—k, 18—

The **Apostrophe** (') denotes the ommission of letters or figures (1), the possessive case (2), and the formation of a few plurals (3).

1. { The spirit of '76.
A change came *o'er* the spirit of my dream. }

2. *Shakespeare's* Sonnets.

3. Mind your *P's* and *Q's.*

**Parentheses** ( ) enclose a parenthetical, explanatory, or intermediate sentence,

Gladstone (who had up to this time been a Tory) now went over to the Whigs.

The place of marks of parenthesis is now often supplied by dashes or commas.

**Brackets** [ ] are used to inclose a reference, explanation, or note, or a part to be excluded from a sentence, to indicate an interpolation, to rectify a mistake, or to supply an omission.

The President [Mr. Davis] in the chair.

The **Ellipsis** ( . . . . ) denotes the omission of letters, syllables, or words.

## CAPITAL LETTERS.

The majority of words begin with small letters, but capitals must be used in the following cases.

Every sentence beginning a paragraph or preceded by a period or other full stop, and every line of poetry must begin with a capital.

Every proper name and every word used as a proper name must begin with a capital.

Thus: *d*emocratic institutions, but the *D*emocratic party; *w*ar and *r*ebellion, but the *W*ar of the *R*ebellion.

It should be noted that the words *gentleman* and *sir*, not at the beginning or end of a composition, though used as proper names, are not begun with capitals. This is believed to be the only exception to the general rule.

Every direct quotation must begin with a capital.

Every noun, and as a rule, every pronoun referring to or indicating the Deity, must begin with a capital.

Titles of persons and of books must begin with capitals.

Titles of chapters and other parts of books must begin with capitals.

Clauses numbered separately, as, 1st, 2d, etc., must begin with a capital.

The days of the week, the name of the month, of religious denominations, of political parties, of educational, religious, and charitable institutions, begin with a capital.

The pronoun *I* and the interjection *O* must be written as capitals; but "oh" is not written as a capital unless it begins a sentence.

The word immediately following the address of a letter must be given with a capital.

*Sir, Father, Mother, Friend*, etc., in the address should begin with a capital.

The formal phrase beginning or ending a letter must begin with a capital. Thus: Yours sincerely, J. A. T.; and, My dear Sir.

All these words in the body of a composition or letter are to be begun with a small letter.

Finally any word upon which it is desired to lay particular stress may begin with a capital. But capital letters should not be used too freely for this purpose.

COMPOSITION is the arrangement of the different parts of a discourse, and is divided into PROSE and POETRY.

**Prose** is that form of discourse in which the expression and arrangement are independent of metre or poetic measure.

**Poetry** is a metrical composition. The principal divisions of poetry, according to the manner of representation employed, are *epic, lyric*, and *dramatic.*

EPIC poetry is narrative in form, and treats in an elevated style the exploits of heroes, etc., as Milton's *Paradise Lost.*

LYRIC poetry relates to the feelings and thoughts of the person who composes it; in a restricted sense, it is such poetry as is composed for musical recitation.

DRAMATIC poetry does not relate an action, but represents it. [In regard to the metres used in poetry, see the article on Versification.]

The principal subdivisions of prose are argumentative discourses, essays, descriptions, letters, and narratives.

STYLE is the distinctive manner of composition peculiar to a writer or a body of writers.

## DESCRIPTIONS AND NARRATIONS.

Description is a composition giving an account of the characteristics of some thing or person; as, a description of Niagara Falls, a description of the assassination of President Garfield.

In description it is important to grasp the salient peculiarities of the object described, and to bring them out clearly before the reader's mind. Fullness of detail is often necessary, but care must be taken not to present a dead mass of uninteresting detail. The important thing is to dwell with special emphasis on the parts likely to be most interesting to the reader. Whether a man attempts to write a sublime description of a storm at sea, or a humorous description of a street fight, he must not be tedious. While his description should be true, he is not obliged to tell everything, or to follow an exact order of description. He should exercise judgment in the choice of his details, and skill in their arrangement. If one undertake to describe something which he has not actually seen, he should first fill his mind so far as possible with ideas and images suitable to the subject. The best descriptive writing, with the exception of a few works of a high order of imagination, is the result and record of actual eye and ear experience.

A common fault into which persons attempting description are liable to fall is fine writing, so called. This is particularly the case with descriptions of natural scenery. Yet a simple, natural, and unaffected style is, above all others, appropriate to this class of objects. A description consisting of a collection of sounding phrases will perhaps convey to the reader's mind little or no idea of the object described; while a few simple touches, accurately and graphically expressed, will instantly call up a picture superior in vividness and effect to pages of windy rhetoric.

The first rule for good descriptive writing is to study carefully what you wish to describe, till you are able to give an accurate account of it, and then to write an account in simple language, such as every reader can understand.

Narration is an account of real or imaginary incidents. Its great divisions are Biography, Fiction, History, and Travels. The consideration of the proper style of writing for each of these classes of narration does not belong to the plan of this work. It is sufficient to say that in narration, as in every other kind of composition, clearness is the first requisite. Without clearness the meaning of the author is not understood, or is only understood with difficulty, and consequently the object of the writer is entirely or partially sacrificed.

## STYLE.

The errors of undue conciseness and of undue prolixity can be avoided by repeating and varying the expression of the same idea. This can be done by the use of synonomous words, by arranging the arguments in a different order.

In the choice of words, other things being equal, a short, universally intelligible word should be preferred to a longer word more liable to be misunderstood. Within the same limits a word of Anglo-Saxon origin should be preferred to a word of Latin or French origin.

In the construction of sentences, such as are extremely long should be avoided. On the other hand, a series of extremely short sentences should be avoided, as harsh and unmusical. Where it is necessary to use a very long sentence, care should be taken to construct it so that each part of it shall be intelligible, and shall have a distinct meaning, though the sense in each part is not completed; in this way a long sentence can be constructed, every part of which is intelligible to the reader as he proceeds. The use of involved or parenthetical sentences should be avoided as far as possible. Every new thought or argument should constitute a new sentence. The subject should not be too far separated from its predicate, nor the pronoun from its antecedent. The preposition should be kept with the noun which it governs. Modifying words should stand near the words which they modify.

Avoid the excessive use of quotations, and be very sparing of foreign words. Whatever one has to say should be said in English. Avoid sprinkling your composition with French phrases. You do not write to show your knowledge of the French language, but to make other people understand your ideas. If you have no ideas to communicate, don't write. If you have ideas to communicate, use words that everybody can understand. Avoid, as far as possible, the use of technical words, and of newly coined words.

## ENERGY OF EXPRESSION.

Next to clearness, the most important quality of style is energy or vivacity, which is the general name for whatever tends to give strength, spirit, vividness, or animation to the expression. As a rule, the briefer an expression is made, the greater is its energy. But some kinds of writing do not admit of the energy of conciseness to the same extent as others. Campbell mentions as "less susceptible of this ornament, the Descriptive, the Pathetic, and the Declamatory."

Great care should be taken to avoid the use of too many words,—a fault, perhaps, the most injurious of all to energy. It will be found useful to go over a composition carefully after it is finished, and see what words can be omitted without loss to the sense, and with a gain to the energy of the expression. Search carefully for sentences which can be worked over and abridged, so that, perhaps, out of two or three sentences a single sentence may be made expressing fully the idea of the sentences whose place it has taken, but expressing it with more energy and force. In regard to the selection of terms for the energy which they express, it should be said that *specific* are always to be preferred to general and abstract terms. The latter should never be employed except as a sort of euphemism to mitigate an offensive expression.

An **Epithet**, in Rhetoric, is an adjective which does not enlarge the meaning of the noun which it qualifies, but simply denotes something already signified by the noun. Epithets should be but sparingly used in prose. According to Whately, no epithet should be used "which does not fulfill one of these two purposes: 1st, to explain a metaphor; 2d, when the epithet expresses something which, though implied in the subject, would not have been likely to occur at once spontaneously to the hearer's mind, and yet is important to be noticed with a view to the purpose in hand."

## RHETORICAL FIGURES.

The appropriate and judicious use of rhetorical figures adds much to the energy of an expression. This is especially the case with the METAPHOR and the SIMILE. Of these two figures, the metaphor or implied comparison is, as a rule, more energetic than the simile, or direct comparison. The strongest metaphors are those which are personified, so that a personal activity and animation are attributed to inanimate objects; as, the *wild* waves, the *howling* wilderness. But the employment of well-known and hacknied metaphors and comparisons is to be avoided. Care must be taken also to avoid a mixture of metaphors.

On the whole, the proper guide in using or rejecting the use of a metaphor or simile is to determine whether the expression in which it is to occur is more significant with them than without them. If the passage will be as significant without them, they are not to be retained.

## DISCOURSES.

An ARGUMENTATIVE DISCOURSE is an attempt by a writer or speaker to persuade his readers or hearers of the truth of the proposition which he maintains. An argumentative discourse treating of a religious or theological topic is called a SERMON; an argumentative discourse upon some other than a religious or theological topic is called an ORATION.

In classical antiquity it was the custom of rhetoricians and public speakers to arrange an oration according to the following formal divisions:

1. The EXORDIUM, containing the introductory matter by which the speaker sought to ingratiate himself into the good graces of his audience.

2. The DIVISION, in which the orator sketched the method which he intended to follow in his discussion of the proposition.

3. The STATEMENT, which stated the proposition and the necessary facts in relation to it.

4. The REASONING, which supported the proposition, and disproved the argument of the orator's opponent.

5. The APPEAL to the feelings and passions of the audience.

6. The PERORATION, which recapitulated the argument, and often the appeal, and contained, briefly expressed, the author's conclusion.

An arrangement of the discourse after the method given above is still frequently used by preachers, orators, and writers at the present day.

Some regular division and plan of argument should be mapped out by every speaker and writer who is to use argumentative discourse. The proposition to be proved must be clearly formulated in the author's mind, so as to admit of clear and unmistakable statement.

An **Argument** is a reason offered to prove some proposition advanced.

**Rhetoric,** in its more restricted and immediate sense, is the art of inventing and arranging arguments.

An argument *a priori* is an argument from Cause to Effect.

An argument *a posteriori* is an argument from Effect to Cause.

## PUBLIC DISCUSSIONS.

In beginning the discussion of a question, it is important to determine upon which side the burden of proof lies, *i.e.*, which side of the question has the least antecedent probability in its favor. The side which has the most antecedent probability in its favor is said to have a presumption in its favor. The presumption is generally in favor of existing systems, customs, and institutions, and against novelties in opinion and doctrine. In regard to the arrangement of arguments no general rule can be given, except that the most obvious should be placed first. An argument is often made much clearer by the use of an illustration and example. An illustration or analogous example is also often the best method of exposing the weakness and fallacy of an opponent's position. What is a proper argumentative style will always depend upon the character of the class of readers or hearers whom it is attempted to persuade. In making a political speech, or any other oration before a popular audience, a florid and highly ornamented style may be used with advantage. In any composition to be read before a cultivated audience, however, the expression should be pruned of all luxuriances and redundancies. It will be a good plan to go carefully over a composition after it is completed, and strike out all unnecessary expressions. As a rule, a young writer will find it advisable to strike out whatever portion of his composition seems to him most striking and beautiful. Such a revision will generally add to the strength of his argument, as the portions struck out will be mostly sounding and meaningless tautology.

Where a speaker is discussing any other than a sentimental question, and desires to persuade the intelligence rather than to play upon the passions of his hearers, it will be the best rule to make a clear statement of the question, and then to support his side of it by logical, connected, and rational argument.

In discussing a question of finance or of political economy, the advantages of a rational and logical method are evident. Heated statements and passionate vituperation are eminently out of place in a discussion of this kind. It is, indeed, more difficult to carry along the attention of an audience on an abstruse question of this nature than it is to inflame their passions by an appeal to their feelings; but by making every proposition in the plainest language, and illustrating it by well-chosen and apposite examples, it is entirely possible to win their judgments.

In writing of almost every description, where there is no need of using sophistry, or of obscuring one's meaning in order to mislead the reader, the simplest language is usually the most effective. Simplicity of style is a mark of the highest art. It is a mistake to suppose that a verbose, florid style is elegant. Simplicity is the surest mark of polish, and can be attained only by constant labor and revision. Simplicity is especially requisite in argumentative discourse, where it is difficult to hold the attention of the reader or hearer. If the attention is distracted by a multitude of words, the hearer or reader is bewildered, and fails to follow the argument. If he once loses the thread of the argument, he cannot find it again if the discourse is oral; and if the discourse is written, he will have to reread the sentence in which it occurs, a trouble which he is not likely to take.

## ESSAYS AND DISSERTATIONS.

An Essay is a short composition upon some subject.

A composition upon a subject which demands argument is usually called a Dissertation.

The remarks already made as to the use of style and language and the arrangement of arguments, apply also to these species of compositions.

In beginning an essay upon a given subject, it is the best plan to define the subject. If it has an ordinarily accepted and popular sense, and at the same time a limited and more restricted sense, the reader or hearer should never be left in doubt of the precise meaning which you attach to it. Then make clear just how far your treatment of the subject is to extend, and what you intend to prove, describe, narrate, or illustrate. If it is a subject which admits of historical treatment, give a historical exposition of it; show how it originated, to what changes, if any, it was subjected, what it was formerly, and what you conceive it to be now. In giving such a summary, care should be taken not to make it a mere barren chronological table. Seize and group together the salient and most important points only. Follow the connection of events which have the relation of cause and effect, but do not slavishly follow their exact sequence in point of time. It is a matter of no small difficulty to write a summary which is not merely narrative but also shows philosophically the interdependence of the events recounted.

Historical illustration is an effective way of making clear a proposition or supporting an argument. It is well not to refer too frequently to historical characters of antiquity, who are known only in a vague way to the majority of readers or hearers. Be very sparing of allusions to Solon, Lycurgus, Darius, Themistocles, etc. Indeed, an illustration drawn from the history of one's own country is, other things being equal, to be preferred to a classical illustration. Young writers are very free with the use of illustrations from the Greeks and Romans, mainly, perhaps, from a certain desire to manifest their acquaintance with classical literature.

Many writers overload their compositions with quotations, and it is said that the essays of young women are especially subject to this fault. Say what you have to say in your own words, and introduce but a few quotations. Poetical quotations often forcibly illustrate a point, but as a rule they do not add to the strength of a composition. Sparing and appropriately used they are not inelegant, and they are often useful in ending a composition gracefully.

## CHOICE OF SUBJECTS.

Much of the difficulty experienced by beginners in writing an essay or dissertation arises from the unfortunate choice of subject. It is too general a habit among schoolmasters to give abstract subjects for compositions. A boy or girl cannot be expected to know anything in particular about "Vice," or "The Folly of Inconsistent Expectations," or "The Vanity of Human Wishes." The primary object of exercises in composition is not to make boys and girls great authors, or profound reasoners, or philosophical disputants, but to teach them to write, spell, and speak the English language correctly. It cannot be expected that their ideas upon many subjects should be of value or interest, but it is certain that they will write with greater ease and even enthusiasm upon subjects in which they take an interest, and which do not rise above the habitual scope of objects and ideas with which they are familiar. Let the first exercises be descriptive of some object before their eyes, such as the house in which they live. Let them write letters describing what they have done during the day, what they expect to do the next day, their sports, their work, any concrete subjects, not above their reach. Allow them to use their own language, simply correcting mistakes. It will be found that a good idea of composition can be gained in this way, not only because it is the simplest way, but because it interests as well as instructs the dullest learner. If, on the contrary, the learner is compelled to write upon abstruse or abstract subjects beyond his comprehension, he will take no interest in the composition, will really have no ideas of his own on the subject, and will simply set down a number of stereotyped phrases derived from others. A list of subjects for compositions and essays is appended. It contains some subjects too abstract and vague to fully coincide with some of the foregoing remarks, but it has designedly been made general to accommodate persons belonging to literary and debating societies, competent to deal with the more difficult topics. A separate list of subjects for the forensic disputations appears below. But debating societies can turn many of the subjects given for compositions, into subjects for forensic disputations, by a little change. Thus the composition subject, "How far should punishment for crime be vindictive," by being put in an affirmative form, becomes a subject for forensic disputation, viz.: *Resolved,* "That punishment for crime should be vindictive."

In connection with the subjects for composition, etc., young writers are recommended to give particular attention to the discussion of questions of common interest at the present time, in politics, art, science, literature, religion and morals. Every person is more familiar with questions of the present day, which he reads about in the newspapers and hears discussed constantly, than with abstract or historical questions. About questions of present importance he feels a higher degree of enthusiasm than he does about more abstract questions or questions of the past. His mind being full of actual information upon such subjects, his arguments are more likely to be interesting, and his conclusions will certainly prove more valuable.

## PRACTICAL SUGGESTIONS.

In places where there is no means of access to a good library, it may perhaps be difficult to study sufficiently some of the historical and other questions of which we have furnished a list. But it is always easy to find subjects for discussion. When you have finished reading a book draw up a summary of its contents. Then write an essay upon the author's style, or his opinions. Afterwards write a dissertation upon books of that kind, comparing the author's style and opinions with those of other authors in the same field. Lend the book to your friends to read in order to have them form an opinion. Then you can talk with them about it (colloquy), or can discuss it from a literary, philosophical, or historical point of view. There is no better method than this to fix the contents of a book in one's mind, and by treating it in this way you will probably derive a good deal of information from discussion of the book and kindred matters with persons whose views are different from yours. Take Thackeray's *Henry Esmond* for example. Read it carefully till you are thoroughly familiar with the plot. Then write an account in your own words of the action. Study the style thoroughly and write an essay on it. If you have read some other of Thackeray's novels, compare the style, plots, characters and general merits of the two books. Write an essay on some of the principal characters, as "Henry Esmond, or Thackeray's Ideal of a Gentleman and a Soldier," or "Beatrice, or a Woman of Fashion in Queen Anne's Time," etc., etc. If you have read other novels of Thackeray, you can write on "Thackeray's Idea of Women," "Rachel in *Henry Esmond* compared with Helen in *Pendennis*," etc. Then you can compare Thackeray with Dickens, or with any other novelist with whose works you are familiar.

It is evident that every standard book properly and thoroughly understood will furnish a great store of interesting subjects, and suggest many more that are nearly or remotely connected with it. To study *Henry Esmond* in the manner indicated, requires only a few books. The principal works of Dickens, Thackeray, Scott, and George Eliot will be found in the smallest village; and with these and some good historical work relating to the period, Lord Mahon's "History of the Reign of Queen Anne," for instance, all the subjects mentioned above, and many other cognate subjects that will readily suggest themselves, may be treated in an interesting manner, and with a certain degree of knowledge.

A few evenings every month devoted to study and discussion of this kind will not only result in the attainment of a good deal of information, but with proper criticism and direction will be valuable in forming style and in teaching how to conduct an argumentative discussion. This plan puts the means of choosing fresh subjects of debate, and of having tolerably competent information in regard to them within the reach of all.

## CRITICISM.

Wherever persons associate themselves together for improvement in discussion, it ought to be a rule of their society that every essay or dissertation read before it shall be criticized by the other members. Criticism should be to the point, and not be prompted by any captious spirit. But every improper use of language, every fault of style, every feebleness of argument ought to be noted for correction. A little temporary resentment is sometimes caused by the freedom of criticism proper to such occasions; but this custom of general and searching criticism by the whole society, of the individual performances of each member is in the highest degree serviceable, and only demands a spirit of mutual forbearance and courtesy.

## HOW TO CONSULT A LIBRARY.

In preparing for a discussion of any kind it is often desirable to consult authorities in order to fortify your position with statistics. If you have access to a large public library, such as is to be found in most cities of consequence, this is a very simple matter. It is only necessary to consult the catalogue, which is usually divided into two parts, one containing a list of books arranged alphabetically according to their subjects, the other containing a list of books arranged alphabetically according to the names of the authors. If, for instance, you wish to write a dissertation on American literature, and desire to get a connected view of the subject, you will find in the catalogue, under the head "Literature, American," all the works which the library contains upon that subject. If you want to find some particular work by an author whose name you are familiar with, as, for instance, Tyler's *History of American Literature*, look up the name TYLER, M. C., in the list of authors.

A list of books comprising what is most important in fiction, history, philosophy, science, etc., will be found in another part of this work. It will be useful to consult this list when studying any particular subject with a view to writing about it. It represents all classes of opinions, and is indispensable to the writer or debater seeking authorities in support of his side of the question.

## DIARIES.

Persons who are so situated as not to be able to belong to a debating club or a literary society, will find it useful to keep a diary in which they may record the daily events of their life. In keeping a diary one should especially guard against being self-conscious. Write simply and naturally as if nobody but yourself would ever see your diary. Note down in it what you are reading, your opinions of books, and of contemporary events. In this way a diary may be made a regular literary exercise, and may supply the place of more formal means of improvement in composition.

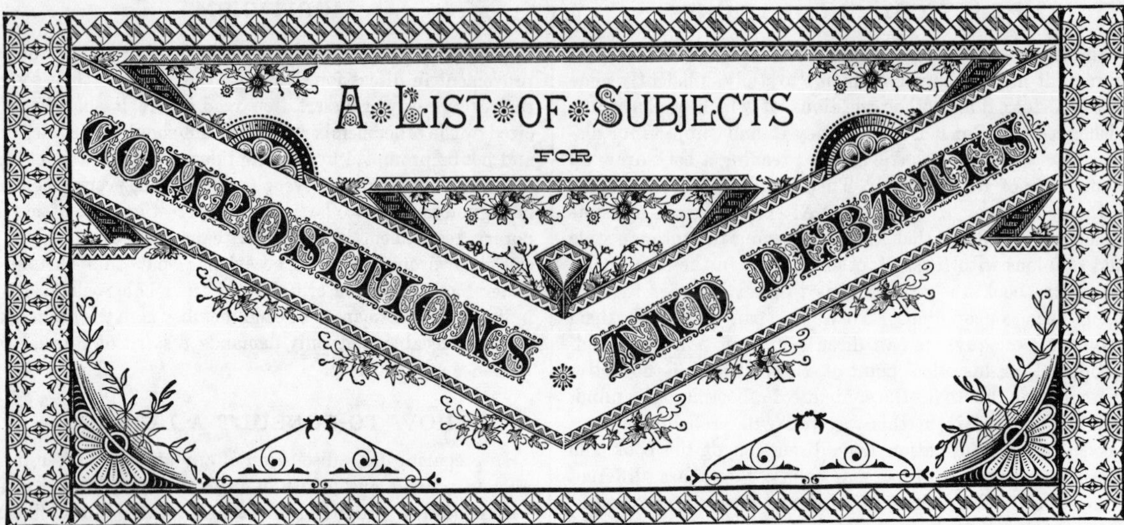


# SUBJECTS FOR ESSAYS.

THE benefits derived from novel reading.
2. Injudicious novel reading.
3. The influence of the press.
4. The influence of democracy upon public opinion.
5. The growth of toleration in religion.
6. The evils of an elective judiciary.
7. The evils of an appointed judiciary.
8. The growth of Australia.
9. The rights of married women.
10. The need of reform in divorce laws.
11. The English and American physique.
12. Education in Australia.
13. Indifference in religion.
14. Indifference in politics.
15. The abuse of the caucus.
16. The introduction of the caucus into England.
17. The workings of the Land Act in Ireland.
18. The influence of the Land League agitation upon the tenure of land in England.
19. The growth of democracy in England.
20. The gold product of Australia.
21. Municipal government in America.
22. The modern relation of England to her colonies.
23. The effect of the physical upon the mental condition.
24. The novels of George Eliot.
25. The writings of Oliver Goldsmith.
26. The poetry of Ireland.
27. The ballad poetry of Scotland.
28. The object of punishment.
29. Describe the life of a parish priest.
30. Describe the qualities requisite for a successful lawyer.
31. The importance of learning a trade.
32. The overcrowding of the learned professions.
33. Stock farming.
34. The effect of the modern improvements in machinery upon the working classes.
35. Benefits of the old system of apprenticeship.
36. The usefulness of village improvement societies.
37. Weather prophecies.
38. Effect of the weather upon the feelings.
39. Give an account of your favorite studies.
40. Give an account of the most remarkable event in your life.
41. Tell your political opinions and the grounds upon which they are based
42. Who is your favorite author, and why.
43. The politeness of the heart.
44. The increase of wealth in America.
45. The temptations of mercantile life.
46. The qualities requisite for success in a mercantile career.
47. The demand for skilled artisans.
48. The life and the opportunities of a mechanic.
49. Modern standing armies.
50. The cultivation of the taste by reading.
51. American wit and humor.
52. Irish wit and humor.
53. English wit and humor.
54. Scotch wit and humor.
55. The distinction between wit and humor.
56. The effect of physical exercise upon the mind.
57. The writings of Thomas Carlyle.
58. Carlyle as a historian.
59. The character of Thomas Carlyle.
60. The cause of the American Civil War.
61. The economical evils of slavery.
62. The introduction of slavery into America.
63. The improvement in the condition of the colored race in America.
64. The persecution of the Jews in the Middle Ages.
65. The modern persecution of the Jews in Russia.
66. Vanity in men ; vanity in women.
67. The pleasures of Hope.
68. The pleasures of the Imagination.
69. The advantages of a liberal education.
70. Self-made men.
71. The discomforts of celibacy.
72. The theory of religious persecution.
73. The advantages of routine in making a proper use of one's time.
74. What books I have read.
75. The progress of Australia.

76. The influence upon civilization of the modern improvements in transportation.
77. The desirableness of an international system of penny postage.
78. The proper basis for suffrage.
79. The best method of study.
80. "How small, of all that human hearts endure,
The part that laws or kings can cause or cure."
81. Physiognomy as an indication of character.
82. How far the study of phrenology is based upon scientific data.
83. Why an untarnished reputation is of more importance to a woman than to a man.
84. The arguments (humane) against vivisection.
85. The arguments (scientific) against vivisection.
86. The legal responsibility of insane criminals.
87. The workings of usury laws.
88. The evils of excessive commercial speculations.
89. The position of woman in modern society.
90. The position of woman among the ancient Greeks.
91. Describe the best actor you have seen, and analyze his style of acting.
92. The effect of modern scientific speculations upon the religious beliefs of the present generation.
93. Give a brief account of the Government and institutions of the country in which you live.
94. The study of history.
95. The true objects of Government.
96. How far the extension of the right of suffrage to women is desired by woman.
97. The growth of radicalism in England.
98. "The voice of the people is the voice of God."
99. The pleasures of Memory.
100. What constitutes the true ideal of physical beauty.
101. The comparative morality of the city and of the country.
102. The chief causes of insanity.
103. Emigration as an outlet for excess of population.
104. A farmer's life.
105. "Fancy" farming.
106. A walk in the woods.
107. The first of May in the country.
108. The first of May in the city.
109. Flowers which bloom in June (describe those you are familiar with).
110. Flowers which bloom in July (describe those you are familiar with).
111. Give an account of the first birds to appear in the Spring where you live.
112. Describe the growth of a tree.
113. Describe the growth of a plant.
114. Describe the principal varieties of roses familiar to you.
115. A walk through a country pasture.
116. Describe the most beautiful natural scenery you ever saw.
117. Describe the most sublime natural scenery you ever saw.
118. The pleasures of the chase.
119. Give an account of the principal kinds of game in your vicinity.
120. What constitutes a good English education.
121. The characteristics of Longfellow's poetry.
122. The political opinions of Thomas Jefferson.
123. In what cases it is desirable for a nation to declare war with another nation.
124. Literary women.
125. Protection against fire.
126. The benefits of life insurance.
127. A journey on the water.
128. The increase in the average duration of human life.
129. The study of astronomy.
130. The progress of Arctic discovery.
131. The navies of the world.
132. The pleasures of horseback riding.
133. "Fears of the brave, and follies of the wise."
134. Dancing.
135. "A great memory is usually accompanied by a poor judgment."
136. "Ill fares the land, to hastening ills a prey,
Where wealth accumulates, and men decay."
137. The pleasures of angling.
138. Describe the principal varieties of fish with which you are familiar.
139. The diminution of forests as a cause of a diminished rainfall.
140. The hardships inflicted by game laws.
141. Harvesting.
142. "One swallow does not make a summer."
143. The capacity of the Red Indian for civilization.
144. Intemperance.
145. The pleasures of childhood.
146. The consolation of old age.
147. The sorrows of old age.
148. The study of the English language.
149. Common errors in the use of the English language.
150. The pleasure of doing nothing. (*Dolce far niente.*)
151. The pleasure of doing good.
152. "Eternal vigilance is the price of liberty."
153. The first settlement of Australia.
154. The discovery of the Mississippi River.
155. The cultivation of the memory.
156. The importance of learning to read aloud according to the rules of elocution.
157. The importance of acquiring a good knowledge of the English language.
158. Difficulties in the way of learning how to spell the English language correctly.
159. Importance of learning to spell correctly.
160. Skating.
161. Swimming.
162. Taste in dress.
163. How to furnish a room in good taste.
164. The simplest pleasures are the most enjoyed.
165. The characteristics of woman.
166. The characteristics of genius and of talent compared.
167. The value of time.
168. The dignity of labor.
169. The effect of commerce upon civilization.
170. The effect of the Crusades upon commerce and civilization.
171. Nihilism and the Nihilists.
172. Humanity.
173. Philanthropy.
174. "Necessity is the mother of invention."
175. The prose of Matthew Arnold.
176. The poetry of Matthew Arnold.
177. The writings of Cardinal Newman.
178. The character and career of Cardinal Newman.
179. The Catholic Church in America.
180. The Catholic Church in Australia.
181. The advantages and pleasures of a life of contemplation.
182. The advantages and pleasures of a life of action.
183. "A thing of beauty is a joy forever."
184. "The moral uses of dark things."
185. The domestic affections.
186. Occupation as a means of health.
187. The proper sphere of Government.
188. Description of a constitutional monarchy.
189. What reforms, if any, are desirable in the present system of criminal law?
190. The reform of criminals.
191. What is the best education for women?
192. Give an account of the principal colleges in Australia.
193. "There is no royal road to learning."
194. "We are such stuff as dreams are made on,
And our little life is rounded with a sleep."
195. What are the wages received by day laborers in your vicinity, and are they, in your opinion, sufficient for their support?
196. Give an account of the principal manufacturers in your vicinity.

197. "Great wits to madness nearly are allied,
And thin partitions do their walls divide."

198. Give an account of the principal agricultural productions in your vicinity.

199. Give an account of the principal mineral productions in your vicinity.

200. Peculiarities of national character.

201. Characteristics of an Irishman.

202. Characteristics of an Englishman.

203. Characteristics of an American.

204. The French national character.

205. National character as affected by climate.

206. Give a sketch of the career of the present Pope.

207. Give an account of the present Government of France.

208. "'Tis better to have loved and lost,
Than never to have loved at all."

209. Has Democratic Government been a success in cities?

210. The career of Mr. Gladstone.

211. The character of a statesman.

212. The distinction (if any) between a statesman and a politician.

213. The evils of indiscriminate charity.

214. The evils of poverty.

215. The blessings of poverty.

216. The responsibility of wealth.

217. The opportunities of wealth.

218. How to make a duty a pleasure.

219. Athletic sports.

220. The qualities desirable in a husband.

221. The qualities desirable in a wife.

222. Is the anticipation of a pleasure more delightful than the actual enjoyment of it?

223. The beauty of the human voice as heard in song compared with the beauty of the sounds of musical instruments.

224. The treatment of pauperism.

225. The treatment of "tramps."

226. The town meeting.

227. The village school.

228. "Knowledge is power."

229. The principal religions of the world.

230. The proper basis of faith.

231. The necessity of religion to society.

232. The effect of education upon the manners.

233. Good manners.

234. What is good society?

235. The origin of architecture.

236. Modern church architecture.

237. The comparative value as a means of mental discipline of the study of the classics and the study of mathematics.

238. The prose writings of John Milton.

239. The political opinions of John Milton.

240. The characteristics of Milton's poetry.

241. The character of Lord Byron.

242. Was Hamlet insane?

243. "The critics are the men who have failed in literature and art."

244. "He never loved who loved not at first sight."

245. Characteristics of good conversation.

246. International copyright.

247. How far will arbitration succeed war as a method for the settlement of international disputes?

248. "Money makes the mare go."

249. Description of an autumn sunset.

250. Description of a summer sunrise.

251. Description of a sunset on the mountains.

252. Description of a river.

253. What is a good sermon?

254. What is a good poem?

255. What is a good political speech?

256. Is Civil Service Reform desirable in the United States?

257. Is the proverb true that "Home is home, be it ever so homely"?

258. Does the habitual reading of poetry on the whole weaken or strengthen the mind?

259. "There are more things in heaven and earth, Horatio,
Than are dreamt of in your philosophy.

260. Comparison between Paganism and Christianity.

261. Has physical beauty any relation to, or connection with, moral beauty?

262. Remedies for a hasty temper.

263. The evils of covetousness.

264. The evils of prodigality.

265. Write an Allegory.

266. Write a Fable.

267. "The truth is not to be spoken at all times."

268. The characteristics of Lord Byron's poetry.

269. The poetry of Keith.

270. The poetry of Aubrey de Vere.

271. The moral importance of cultivating the faculty of veneration.

272. The importance of industry in literary labor.

273. "The fault, dear Brutus, is not in our stars, but in ourselves that we are underlings."

274. The best method of teaching history.

275. The importance of knowing the history of one's own country.

276. The position of women among savage nations.

277. How far, if at all, drunkenness ought to be a palliation for crime committed under its influence.

278. Habitual drunkenness as a disease.

279. The moral aspect of drunkenness.

280. The treatment of drunkenness by the State.

281. Melancholy.

282. The value and the dangers of high animal spirits.

283. The love of country.

284. The love of home.

285. Protestantism in the nineteenth century.

286. The character of Andrew Jackson.

287. The character of Queen Elizabeth.

288. "Uneasy lies the head that wears a crown."

289. The assassination of rulers.

290. The effects of disease upon the temper.

291. The use of slang.

292. The use of profane language.

293. Vulgarity in thought, feeling, language, and action.

294. A perfect gentleman.

295. A perfect lady.

296. "A government of the people, by the people, and for the people."

297. "Man wants but little here below,
Nor wants that little long."

298. The knowledge of style to be derived from a constant perusal of the best authors.

299. The beneficial effects of the use of tobacco.

300. The injurious effects of the use of tobacco.

301. Description of a walk in the country.

302. Description of a country churchyard.

303. The proposed interoceanic ship canal across the Isthmus of Tehuantepec. (Geographical division of Mexico.)

304. The proposed canal across the Isthmus of Darien.

305. The pleasures and the inconveniences of solitude.

306. The differing standards of morality enforced by different civilizations.

307. Morality and immorality in fiction.

308. The clouds.

309. The distinction between vanity and pride.

310. The distinction between true and false pride.

311. Women as rulers.

312. The impetus to civilization given by the invention of the printing press.

313. How far are canals superseded by railroads.

314. "Throw physic to the dogs."

315. The best tragedy of Shakespeare, and the reasons why.

316. The best comedy of Shakespeare, and the reasons why.

317. Dyspepsia as a cause of ill temper.

318. Old and new systems of postal service.
319. The trotting horse.
320. Description of a railway journey.
321. Description of a steamboat journey.
322. The pleasures and inconveniences of a strong imagination.
323. "Hope springs eternal in the human breast."
324. "Sovereign Law, the world's collective will."
325. The distinction between the Fancy and the Imagination.
326. Superstition.
327. The importance of a general system of primary education.
328. Art in America.
329. "Worth makes the man, the want of it the fellow."
330. The domestic life of literary people.
331. The formation of habits, and their effect upon character and mode of life.
332. The antithetical style in the works of Alexander Pope.
333. The younger generation always seems degenerate to the generation before it.
334. Health is the indispensable condition to human happiness.
335. Tell a ghost story.
336. "Gratitude is a lively sense of favors expected."
337. The influence of natural scenery upon the character.
338. Modesty and prudery.
339. The art of making one's self agreeable.
340. True hospitality.
341. Generosity and prodigality.
342. Happiness is independent of outward things.
343. "Thrice is he armed who hath his quarrel just."
344. Virtue often makes itself as offensive as vice.
345. Virtue, however ostentatiously manifested, is always more agreeable than vice.
346. In cultivating the greater virtues, many men forget the smaller ones.
347. The decline of the English aristocracy.
348. What is an aristocracy ?
349. "Blessings brighten as they take their flight."
350. Describe the kind of life that seems to you most desirable.
351. "Shakespeare's works are a library in themselves."
352. The most agreeable things are not always the most useful.
353. Honesty is the best policy.
354. "Our birth is but a sleep and a forgetting."
355. To what extent are lawyers useful to the community ?
356. The dangers of overwork.
357. To what extent is the remark true, that a great mathematician is also a great poet ?
358. "An undevout astronomer is mad."
359. The advantages of labor strikes.
360. The evils of labor strikes.
361. The benefits of co-operation.
362. The benefits of trades-unions.
363. The relation between intelligence and morality.
364. The character and public services of Abraham Lincoln.
365. Describe some striking incident within your own knowledge.
366. Describe some humorous incident within your own knowledge.
367. Describe some pathetic incident within your own knowledge.
368. "Discretion is the better part of valor."
369. Enthusiasm as a factor in the character.
370. The conduct of most men is guided by their passions, not by their judgment.
371. The best means of conquering susceptibility to physical fear.
372. The conditions of material success in a new country.
373. Public opinion.
374. Influence of personal character in political life.
375. The importance to a lawyer of a knowledge of the methods of conducting mercantile business.
376. The character of Mary, Queen of Scots.
377. Women in politics.
378. Office-seeking.
379. The poetry of Robert Burns.
380. The study of elocution.
381. Importance in a free Government of a free discussion of political questions.
382. Suffrage, as based upon property.
383. Suffrage, as based upon intelligence.
384. Universal suffrage.
385. Show the fallacy of the common saying that "The exception proves the rule."
386. Julius Cæsar as he appears in Shakespeare's play of that name.
387. "For forms of government let fools contest,
Whate'er is best administered is best."
388. Toleration a necessary quality to enjoyment of literature.
389. The Puritans.
390. The influence of Puritanism upon literature and art.
391. Prejudice, how formed and how overcome.
392. Brevity is the soul of wit.
393. "Does death end all ?"
394. "Is life worth living ?"
395. The English Constitution.
396. The American Constitution.
397. Liberty and license.
398. Should personal property be taxed by the State ?
399. The benefits conferred upon civilization by Christian missions.
400. Life of a missionary among the heathen.
401. Horticulture.
402. A flower garden.
403. A snow-storm.
404. The advisability of the enactment of sumptuary laws.
405. Changes in the art of naval warfare.
406. The character of Lord Nelson.
407. How far the affection of parents for their children is returned by the latter.
408. The precarious livelihood to be derived from unskilled labor.
409. The inferiority of knowledge acquired from books to that acquired by experience.
410. How far punishment for crime should be vindictive.
411. The evils of crowded tenement-houses.
412. Political parties in Australia.
413. Political parties in the Canadian Dominion.
414. Political parties in the United States ; their history and opinions.
415. The manufactured and the agricultural products of the United States.
416. The manufactured and the agricultural products of the Canadian Dominion.
417. The manufacturing and agricultural interests of Australia.
418. The colonial systems of the ancient Greeks.
419. Dancing, ancient and modern, religious and secular.
420. Free libraries in the United States; their circulation and how they are conducted.
421. The early explorers of America from Scandinavia.
422. The Thirty Years' War ; its causes and consequences.
423. The influence of the fine arts upon civilization.
424. The importance of education at the present time.
425. The great statesmen of ancient and modern times.
426. Geographical progress and discovery.
427. Astronomical phenomena and progress.
428. The Eastern question.
429. Ireland and the Irish question.
430. The Army of the United States.
431. International exhibitions.
432. Hero worship.
433. The great cathedrals of Europe.
434. Indoor and outdoor sports.
435. Political assassinations of recent times.
436. The standard of technical and scientific knowledge in the medical profession.
437. Public opinion in the United States.
438. The desirability of England changing her policy of free-trade for a more or less protective policy.
439. The countries of the world; describing climate, mountains, lakes, rivers, great cities, products, industry, and commerce.

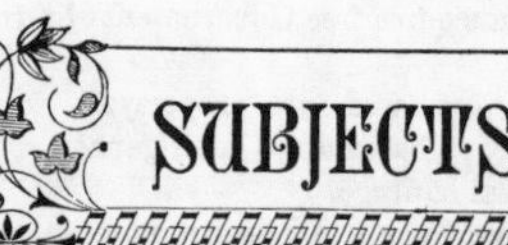

# SUBJECTS FOR DISSERTATIONS.

PHOTOGRAPHY in astronomy.
2. The connection of the physical sciences.
3. The revolution of 1688 compared with that of 1789.
4. The causes of the decline of poetry in England during the eighteenth century.
5. The endowment of scientific research.
6. Summary of the scientific doctrines of Leibnitz.
7. The influence of the French trouvères upon the poetry of Chaucer.
8. The establishment of the new German empire.
9. The Homeric question as affected by recent discoveries at Troy.
10. A parallel between the Greek drama and the modern opera.
11. American literature since 1776.
12. The advantages and disadvantages of gold as a standard of value.
13. Insanity among the early Roman Emperors.
14. The proposed introduction of the clôture in the British Parliament.
15. Celtic literature.
16. The advantages and disadvantages of home rule in Ireland.
17. The influence of English models on American literature.
18. A critical estimate of the philosophy of Ralph Waldo Emerson.
19. The defects of Macaulay as a historian.
20. The importance of making changes in the tariff laws of the United States.
21. A comparison of the works of Dickens and of Thackeray.
22. The arguments for and against bi-metalism.
23. The phenomena of hypnotism.
24. Modern church music.
25. The growth of cities as compared with the growth of country towns.
26. Literary criticism in America.
27. Contemporary English criticism.
28. Modern tendencies towards centralization.
29. The contributions of America to Arctic exploration.
30. A critical estimate of the philosophy of Herbert Spencer.
31. The amendments to the Constitution of the United States.
32. The effects of competition among railroads.
33. The evils of class legislation.
34. The commercial relations of Australia and the United States.
35. Social life among the ancient Greeks.
36. The military talents of George Washington.
37. The value of competitive examinations as a means of testing the fitness of applicants for government offices.
38. The "spoils system" in American politics.
39. The constitutional and political theories of John C. Calhoun.
40. Art Museums in America.
41. The assessment of office-holders for political purposes.
42. Materialism and Agnosticism.
43. The public debts of the great nations of the world.
44. The present relations of Italy and the Vatican.
45. The foreign policy of the Earl of Beaconsfield.
46. Clay, Calhoun, and Webster.
47. English as a universal language.
48. Fiction in public libraries.
49. American novelists.
50. American playwrights.
51. The genius and character of Edgar A. Poe.
52. Curran as an advocate at the bar.
53. The philosophical writings of Edmund Burke.
54. Pitt and Fox.
55. The cause of the Franco-Prussian war of 1870–71.
56. The growth of Socialism.
57. Socialism and Communism.
58. The æsthetic revival in England.
59. English opinions about America.
60. The standing armies of the great continental powers.
61. The coal supply of the United States.
62. The future of Australia.
63. Agriculture in Australia.
64. The mineral deposits of Australia.
65. The doubtful plays of Shakespeare.
66. The political opinions of Alexander Hamilton.
67. The causes of the American war with England in 1812.
68. The growth of Ritualism in the Church of England.
69. Military genius of the Duke of Marlborough.
70. The life and writings of Daniel Defoe.
71. Recent experiments in the use of the electric light.
72. The phenomena of reflex action.
73. The novels of Henry James, Jr.
74. The growth of the United States in the decade 1870–1880.
75. The effect of the study of the physical sciences upon religious belief.
76. Changes in the political geography of Europe during the twenty years 1860–1880.
77. The reforms instituted by Mr. Gladstone during his first ministry.
78. The co-education of the sexes.
79. The character and career of Gambetta.
80. Government land grants to railroads.
81. The Pan-Slavic movement.
82. The military talents of General von Moltke.
83. The character and career of Bismarck.
84. The writings of John Stuart Mill.
85. The comparative merits of Bancroft's and of Hildreth's History of the United States.
86. The treatment of criminals.
87. The writings of Nathaniel Hawthorne.
88. The decline in influence of the British House of Lords.
89. Means of protection against railroad accidents.
90. The relation of the State to the education of its inhabitants.
91. The Hartford Convention.
92. The decline of dogmatic theology in the Protestant Church.
93. The relations of Canada with the British Empire.
94. American inventors and inventions.
95. The college and the university.
96. The poetry of Edmund Spenser.
97. The connection of Sir Walter Raleigh with the settlement of the United States.
98. Lord Bacon as a lawyer and a judge.
99. The characteristics of the Elizabethan age.
100. Longfellow, Lowell, and Whittier.
101. The prose writings of Longfellow.
102. Railroads and the State.
103. The study of English literature.
104. The causes of suicide.
105. The military talents of General Grant and General Lee.
106. The use of money at elections.
107. The rights and responsibilities of neutrals in time of war.
108. The religious belief of John Milton.
109. The comparative study of religions.
110. Fairy tales and ancient myths.
111. National homogeneity as a condition of lasting national greatness.

EDMUND BURKE as an orator and as a Parliamentary leader.

2. The comparative merits of the dictionaries of Webster and Worcester.
3. The relative rank of Sir Walter Scott as a novelist and a poet.
4. The practical value of an education obtained at a business college.
5. The wages of women as compared with those of men for the same work.
6. The desirability of retaining married women as teachers in the public schools.
7. The means of preventing inundations by the Mississippi River.
8. The system of granting subsidies to ocean steamers for carying the mails.
9. The protection afforded by the United States Government to its citizens.
10. The influence of the new Platonic speculations upon Christian dogma.
11. The workings of a prohibitory compared with those of a license liquor law.
12. The merits and demerits of a civil service holding office during good behavior.
13. The arguments in favor of the right of a State to secede.
14. Constitutional amendments setting a limit to municipal indebtedness.
15. The arguments for total abstinence and for moderate drinking.
16. The arguments for and against the contract system of convict labor.
17. The proper limits of newspaper criticism of public men.
18. The position of Coleridge as a critic, a philosopher, and a poet.
19. The increased cost of living as a preventive of marriage.
20. The introduction of German methods into American universities.
21. The natural oratorical gifts of the Celtic race.
22. Victor Hugo as a poet, a novelist, and a politician.
23. The comparative merits of recent English translations of Virgil.
24. Canada and the United States as a desirable field for immigration.
25. Australia and Canada as desirable fields for immigration.
26. Daniel Webster as a diplomatist and writer of letters.
27. Daniel Webster as an orator compared with Edmund Burke.
28. The society of New York City as a field for the novelist and playwright.
29. The limits of, and distinctions between, comedy, farce, and burlesque.
30. The disasters and the successes of Arctic exploring expeditions.
31. The physical health of women of to-day compared with that of women of the past generation.
32. A comparison between Grote's and Thirlwall's histories of Greece.
33. The comparative knowledge and impartiality of Hume and Lingard as historians.
34. The influence exerted by the clergy on other than religious subjects.
35. The persecution of the Christians by the Pagans, and of the Pagans by the Christians.
36. Business methods and business morality of the present day.
37. The beneficial results of the study of comparative mythology.
38. The arguments against the present system of trial by jury.
39. The comparative strength of the religious sentiment in men and in women.
40. The great famines of history, and their supposed causes.
41. The extent to which health and personal beauty are hereditary.
42. The extent to which talent and genius are hereditary.
43. The duty of the State to encourage art, science, and literature.
44. The difference between the Christian and the Pagan systems of morality.
45. Debating and writing as a means of improving one's style and language.
46. The comparative value of history and philosophy as mental instructors.
47. The reproach and disgrace, deserved or undeserved, attached to suicide.
48. The Metaphor and the Simile in poetry and in prose.
49. The poetry of Robert Browning and of his wife.
50. The position of the day-laborer in England and in the United States.
51. The effect of the improvements in agricultural labor upon the condition of the agricultural laborer.
52. Daniel O'Connell and John Wilkes as political agitators.
53. Bribery and intimidation at elections in England and in the United States.
54. The imitation of English models by the fashionable society of America.
55. Dr. Johnson as a man of letters, a novelist, and a politician.
56. The practical value of a college education as compared with its cost.
57. Witchcraft, sorcery, and magic in Pagan and in Christian times.
58. The comparative labor and income of the journalist and the lawyer.
59. Luxury among the ancient Romans and modern Americans.
60. Gladstone and Disraeli as orators, statesmen, and parliamentary leaders.
61. The reign of Victoria and the reign of Queen Anne.
62. The literature of the reign of Victoria, and that of the reign of Anne.
63. The study of poetry compared with that of prose as a means of attaining a knowledge of style.
64. The resources of Carthage and those of Rome at the outbreak of the First Punic War.
65. The military talents of Napoleon and of the Duke of Wellington.
66. The Anglo-Saxon and the Celtic contributions to the English language.
67. The relations of England to Ireland compared with those to Scotland.
68. The American Revolutionary War compared with the War of 1812.
69. Alexander Hamilton, James Madison, the Constitution, and the *Federalist*.
70. The commercial relations of the United States with Mexico.
71. Richard Brinsley Sheridan as an orater, a politician, a wit, and a man of fashion.
72. George Washington as a writer and speaker upon political subjects.
73. Novels and novelists in England and in the United States.
74. Benjamin Franklin as a political philosopher and a man of science.
75. English reviews and reviewers of American books.
76. Samuel Adams and the beginnings of the American Revolution.

# SUBJECTS FOR FORENSIC DISCUSSIONS.

HOULD the protective system be maintained in the United States ?

2. Is the assassination of rulers ever capable of justification ?

3. Would reciprocity between the United States and Canada be advantageous to the former, or to the latter more than the former ?

4. Ought personal property to be exempt from taxation ?

5. Was the war of Great Britain against the Boers necessary ?

6. Are the conditions of modern life favorable to the production of great works of literature ?

7. Is it desirable to put restrictions upon the emigration of the Chinese to the United States or to Australia ?

8. Ought the Capitol of the United States to be at Washington ?

9. Ought the largest city of a State to be the capital of that State ?

10. Shall the editor of a newspaper be responsible for the personal opinions of his contributors ?

11. Has the abolition of slavery improved the condition of the blacks?

12. Have many of the good results hoped for from the abolition of serfdom in Russia been obtained ?

13. Was Thomas Jefferson or Alexander Hamilton the greater man ?

14. Was Edmund Kean or David Garrick the greater actor ?

15. Will the coal supply of the United States hold out ?

16. Is universal suffrage to be pronounced a success ?

17. Is the growth of sects injurious to the welfare of Protestantism ?

18. Is there a smaller attendance at churches now than formerly ?

19. Was the Tichborne claimant clearly shown to be an impostor ?

20. Was General Lee a greater general than General Grant ?

21. Is it true that the drama is immoral and needs to be reformed ?

22. Is a tax upon incomes a judicious method of raising revenue ?

23. Ought the United States National Bank system to be abolished ?

24. Does the diminution of forests cause a diminished rainfall ?

25. Was it for the interest of mankind that Rome should conquer Carthage ?

26. Was Abraham Lincoln a Christian in the proper sense of that word ?

27. Is it possible to maintain both a gold and a silver standard of coinage ?

28. Is the extension of the right of suffrage to women advisable ?

29. Was the war of the United States with Mexico justifiable ?

30. Is cremation a desirable substitute for burial ?

31. Should the State assume control of the railroads and telegraphs ?

32. Is corruption as prevalent in political life now as formerly ?

33. Ought the President of the United States to be directly elected by the popular vote ?

34. Was the electoral commission of 1876-1877 constitutional ?

35. Is Great Britain tending towards a republican form of government ?

36. Will Chicago ever have a greater population than New York ?

37. Will Australia always be a colony of Great Britain ?

38. Ought property in land to be abolished ?

39. Ought restrictions to be put upon the amount of property inheritable ?

40. Has the aristocracy of Great Britain done more harm than good ?

41. Is it probable that international arbitration will definitively succeed war ?

42. Is it probable that English will ever become a universal language ?

43. Has the State a constitutional right to enact a prohibitory liquor law ?

44. Is imprisonment for life as a punishment for murder likely to be more effectual as a prevention of crime and a terror to criminals than capital punishment ?

45. Would the substitution of the garrote or the guillotine for the gallows make capital punishment more effective ?

46. Was Guiteau, the assassin of President Garfield, insane ?

47. Should drunkenness be a palliation for a crime committed without evidence of previous intent ?

48. Is the "total abstinence" movement injurious to the real interests of temperance ?

49. Are the weather reports of the signal service trustworthy ?

50. Is the system of trial by jury a failure in large cities ?

51. Was the execution of Mrs. Surratt for complicity in the murder of President Lincoln justified by the evidence ?

52. Should public museums and parks be opened on Sunday ?

53. Should drawing be taught in the public schools ?

54. Should the Bible be read in the public schools ?

55. Should the right to vote in large cities be made dependent upon a property qualification?

56. Should religious and educational institutions be taxed ?

57. Ought railroads and transportation companies to be allowed to give more favorable terms to one shipper of freight or merchandise than to others ?

58. Is it constitutional for the Congress of the United States to disfranchise the Mormons of Utah ?

59. Has the general Government of the United States any constitutional right to provide for education in the several States ?

60. Should corporal punishment be abolished in schools ?

61. Are there any reasonable grounds for the common prejudice against Jews, either individually or as a class ?

62. Should the hours of labor be restricted by law to eight hours ?

63. Is a Republican form of government desirable for Great Britain ?

64. Is a Republican form of government likely to be permanent in France ?

65. Is a knowledge of Greek and Latin of any practical value ?

66. Is a course of training in the sciences preferable to a classical or solely literary education ?

67. Are early marriages desirable in an economic sense?

68. Do the wages of working-men bear a proper relation to the cost of living ?

69. Is an aristocracy in process of formation in the United States ?

70. Was Bacon the author of the plays attributed to Shakespeare ?

71. Was the annexation of Schleswig-Holstein by Prussia justifiable either historically or politically ?

72. Should French and German be taught in the public schools ?

73. Ought the House of Lords to be abolished ?

74. With all the modern business improvements and advantages, is life more desirable than it was among the Greeks ?

75. Is it desirable that Ireland should be separated from Great Britain ?

76. Is the influence of the clergy less than formerly ?

77. Should the internal revenue system of the United States be abolished ?

78. Will the colored race ever be amalgamated with the white ?

79. Is journalism prejudicial to the cultivation of literature pure and simple ?

80. Is the present English system of land tenure likely to last ?

81. Was the play of *Henry the Eighth* written by Shakespeare ?

N. B.—The proper form for debating societies to discuss questions of this kind is as follows : *Resolved*, That the play of *Henry the Eighth* was written by Shakespeare, etc., etc.

THE PLATFORM
THE PULPIT
THE STAGE
AT THE BAR
THE LEGISLATURE
H.A. Ogden

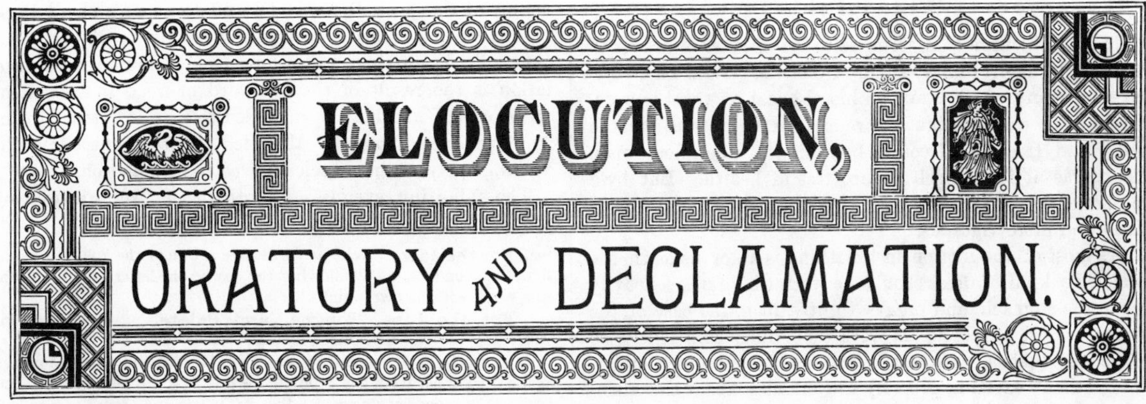


ELOCUTION is the art which treats of the management of the voice in speaking and reading.

The study of elocution is of great importance to all persons who are liable to be called upon to do any considerable share of public speaking. Under any form of government which permits or encourages the free discussion of questions of public interest, the ability to speak easily and gracefully is highly desirable. No man, however polished his language, or however strong and original his thought, can exercise the sway to which he aspires over his audience, or do full justice to his mental powers without some training in elocution. Half the effect of his words is lost if his delivery of them be indistinct, or feeble, or even monotonous. There have, indeed, been instances of persons with extraordinary vocal gifts, who have received from Nature what the rest of mankind can only learn by patient application to the art of speaking. But probably a majority of the persons who strive to attain distinction in public speaking, not only have no extraordinary vocal endowment, but in many cases have, at least in the beginning of their efforts, positive defects.

Owing to the unscientific manner in which, till quite recently, elocution was taught, where it was taught at all, many persons have been brought up without any proper idea of the cultivation of the qualities of the voice. The very class of persons who are habitual speakers in public, have most neglected their manner of delivery. It is not too much to say that the clergy of all denominations might greatly add to the force of their discourses, and to the impressiveness of their reading of the Scriptures and other services of the church, if they paid more attention to this matter of elocution.

It is sometimes said that elocution cannot be taught; but this error is only the result of pursuing wrong methods of instruction. The voice can be strengthened and improved, and a defective articulation can be remedied by exercise and drill in elocution, just as muscular strength can be gained, and a thin chest filled out by gymnastic exercise. The difficulty is that students of elocution too commonly insist on beginning at the wrong end. They waste their time by attempting to declaim elaborate and difficult passages before they have learned to breathe properly and to pronounce the elementary sounds correctly in order to remedy a defective articulation. By beginning at the beginning, by cultivating a proper carriage, by taking exercise calculated to expand the chest and lungs, and by studying the position of the vocal organs necessary to produce each sound or combination of sounds, the voice may be greatly improved and strengthened, and a fair degree of elocutionary skill be obtained. The mere declamation of pieces learned by rote will not be sufficient, although that is the extent of the instruction in elocution given in most schools. Persistent physical and vocal training is indispensable to every person who wishes to be a good speaker or reader.

## BREATHING.

It is of the utmost importance to the speaker or reader to form right habits of BREATHING. Otherwise he will be unable to endure any severe strain on his physical or vocal powers, and will be easily fatigued through his inability to breathe fully and freely. Of course breathing is dependent upon health, as it is in itself a sure test of health. But by a proper course of training the action of the lungs can be made freer and more vigorous.

As most of the motion in breathing is at or beneath the waist, no kind of dress should be worn which rests heavily upon the stomach and presses tightly upon the base of the lungs. Most people do not work their lungs sufficiently, so to speak; that is, they breathe too weakly and superficially, and without exerting properly the muscles about the abdomen and waist.

The following physical exercises will be of advantage in strengthening the breathing and developing the lungs :

1. **Abrupt Breathing.** Draw in a full breath quickly, and give it out in a short whispered sound like Hoo !

2. **Effusive Breathing.** Inhale a full breath slowly, and then give it out very slowly and gradually through the mouth open, making a kind of long drawn *h* sound.

3. **Deep Breathing.** Put the hands on the hips, with the elbows turned outward. Without changing the position of the shoulders draw in through the nostrils a deep, full, slow breath; then, keeping the chest well out, emit the breath gently through the nostrils.

4. **Expulsive Breathing.** Draw in the breath through the nostrils, and send it out full and strong through the mouth, with a sort of prolonged, whispered *h* sound.

5. **Unequal Breathing.** Standing erect, put the left palm to the side, near the arm-pit as possible, then bend the right arm over the head and breathe deeply.

6. **Prolonged Breathing.** Inhale the breath easily and slowly, with lips drawn together, and emit in the same manner.

It is of great importance to learn to use freely, in breathing, the muscles around the back, abdomen, and waist. The following are among the exercises designed by teachers of elocution for this purpose :

1. **For the Muscles of the Back.** Put the hands on the waist, with the thumbs well forward, and the fingers resting on the small of the back. Inhale the breath, and in doing so draw outward the muscles pressed by the fingers, and then emit the breath, throwing the same muscles outward.

2. **For the Muscles of the Abdomen.** Put the hands on the hips, with the elbows turned outward. Draw in and emit the breath through the nostrils.

3. **For the Muscles of the Ribs and Waist.** Put the palms on the lower ribs and draw in the breath through the nostrils, throwing out the waist sidewise ; then, pressing the palms against the lower ribs and drawing in the waist sidewise, give out the breath.

## ARTICULATION.

ARTICULATION is the distinct and correct utterance of all the elementary sounds of a word. It is produced by the action of the jaws, lips, palate, and tongue ; and all these organs must act easily, surely, and readily, or the articulation will be indistinct. An imperfect or mumbling articulation is the result of the awkward or weak movement of these organs, and may be remedied to a great extent by constant practice of sounds calculated to bring out a free and vigorous play of the muscles moved in articulation.

The following exercises in articulation were devised by the late Professor L. B. Monroe, of Boston:

1. **For the Jaws.** Whisper, with free action of the jaw, in alternation, the sounds *ē*, *ah*, "allowing the jaw in the latter sound to drop, as it were, with its own weight."

2. **For the Lips, Tongue, and Palate.** (*a*) Pronounce *ip*, "bringing the lips in contact, and separating them with a smart, percussive recoil." (*b*) Pronounce *it*. "The tip of the tongue touches against the upper teeth and promptly recoils." (*c*) Pronounce *ik*. "The back of the tongue shuts against the soft palate and promptly recoils." Then go over the same exercises, leaving out the vowel. Practice in the same way the consonants *b*, *d*, and *g*.

3. **For the Lips and Jaws.** (*a*) Pronounce *e* with the lips stretched out sidewise, and showing the tips of the teeth. (*b*) Pronounce *ah*, dropping the jaw and opening the mouth to its widest extent. (*c*) Pronounce *oo* (as in cool), contracting the lips. Then pronounce all these sounds successively, rapidly, and without pause ; as, *E-ah-oo ; e-oo-ah ; ah-e-oo ; ah-oo-e ; oo-ah-e ; oo-e-ah.*

4. **For the Lips and Tongue.** Practice the same exercises as in No. 3, but without moving the jaw. Set the teeth at a fixed distance apart —say the width of two fingers—then form the above-named vowels exclusively by the action of the tongue and lips.

## QUALITY OF VOICE.

The qualities of voice most frequently used are the PURE TONE, the ASPIRATED, the GUTTURAL, and the OROTUND.

The **Pure Tone** is a smooth, clear, flowing sound, used in tranquil discourse, to express gentle, moderate, and pleasant emotions, and to denote sadness in which there is no element of solemnity.

The **Aspirated** is a strong whispered or breathed tone, expressing secrecy, remorse, fear, terror, etc.

The **Guttural** is a modification of the Aspirated, deeply uttered, and expressing contempt, hatred, dislike, etc.

The **Orotund** is a deep, full tone, expressing sublimity, pathos, grandeur, vastness, etc.

## HOW TO PRODUCE TONE.

Assume an erect position, keep the chest well out, fill the lungs with air, paying special attention to the muscles around the abdomen and waist. Follow these directions, no matter what the tone to be produced.

In order to make the tone **full** and **free**, let the jaw fall easily, keep the corners of the mouth drawn in, and the lips a little drawn out.

For exercises in **Pure** Tone, take all the vowel sounds, long, intermediate, short, etc., *ā* as in May ; *â* as in fall ; *ă* as in cat ; *ä* as in bar ; *ē* as in be ; *ĕ* as in pet ; *ī* as in my ; *ĭ* as in wit ; *ō* as in cold ; *ô* as in booze, etc., etc. Practice each sound till a satisfactory quality of voice is obtained.

To produce an **Aspirated** Tone, draw in a full breath through the nostrils, and emit it through the mouth opened, uttering a sort of whispered *h*.

The **Orotund** Tone is an enlargement of the Pure Tone. The lungs are filled out to their full capacity, all the muscles used in breathing are vigorously moved, and the vocal passage is opened as widely as possible.

**Modulation** is the art of inflecting the voice musically and agreeably. It comprises the subjects of Pitch or Key, Force, Rate or Movement, Variation, and Stress.

## PITCH.

PITCH OR KEY is the tone in which a particular passage is to be spoken or read. There are three principal pitches or keys, which are to be used according to the nature of the passage.

A **middle pitch** is used in general and practical discourse in which no emotion is meant to be expressed. This is the tone in which ordinary conversation is pitched. A sermon dealing argumentatively with questions of dogmatic theology; a speech or oration upon a practical subject, in which the question discussed is treated directly on its merits without any attempt to influence the passions of the audience; essays, papers, or articles upon literary, philosophical, and scientific topics; plain historical narration, narrative portions of fiction without emotional intent; as well as the greater part of descriptive, narrative, and didactic poetry, etc., should be delivered in the middle key.

A **high pitch** is used to express lively, gay, joyous, and light emotions, and in passages expressing the extremes of grief, fear, and pain. The height of these emotions finds utterances in sharp, shrill, high-pitched cries.

A **low pitch** is used in serious and solemn discourse, where awe, wonder, melancholy, profound grief, etc., are expressed.

The **monotone** is a full, slow, prolonged tone, produced in one uniform key without going up or down on the scale. It is used to express the supernatural; as, for instance, the lines of the ghost of Hamlet's father, which are delivered by the actors playing that part in a monotone. The monotone is useful in practicing the voice, as it produces a full and slow sound, rendering distinct every passage uttered in that tone. A proper and discriminating use of modulation is essential to good reading and speaking.

Anybody who has ever heard boys and girls reading aloud must have noticed their tendency to deliver every passage, irrespective of the meaning, in the same dull, monotonous drone. A kind of shrill, high-pitched sing-song seems to be the favorite style of delivery at schools. Many public speakers spoil their delivery by their failure to modulate their voices according to the sentiment of the various passages in their discourse. No fault, with the exception of an indistinct and feeble articulation, is more offensive to an audience, or throws such a damper upon their enthusiasm. If they hear a speaker uttering the humorous, the pathetic, and the practical in the same wearisome key, without distinction of manner or matter, they lose interest in his remarks, and soon cease to give him their undivided attention. No rules can be given which would be of any use in correcting this common but unpardonable fault. He who wishes to modulate his voice correctly must possess a correct ear for music, a correct taste, and an understanding of the exact shade of feeling expressed by each passage which he utters. If he does not possess these requisites, he must seek adequate instruction. He should be thoroughly drilled in the utterance of vowels, syllables, words, and sentences in each pitch. When he is able to produce these tones fully and at will, he will be able to modulate his voice according to the varying feeling or thought of each passage, and will use the proper keys instinctively.

## FORCE.

FORCE is the volume of voice to be used in reading a passage in any given key. The force requisite to render faithfully a given passage is regulated by several considerations, such as the character of the thought or emotion expressed by the passage, the size of the audience who are to hear it, and the size of the space which the reader's or speaker's voice must fill. The degree of force used must be sufficient to render the speaker's voice distinctly audible to the hearer at the greatest distance from him. On the other hand, if too great a degree of force is used, the volume of voice will be so loud as to be unpleasant to the auditors nearest the speaker; and a continuously loud voice not only exhausts the speaker and wearies the audience, but makes it impossible to give the requisite degree of force to passages which express a thought or emotion upon which an increased volume of voice should be spent. The practice of repeating vowels, syllables, words and passages in a loud tone is of great value in strengthening the voice, but care must be taken not to fall into a habit of using an unnaturally loud, shouting tone.

## RATE.

RATE OR MOVEMENT indicates the time in which a given passage should be uttered. It is of extreme importance in reading and speaking. It depends upon the thought or emotion to be expressed. Solemnity, seriousness, and dignity require a slow rate. Gayety, playfulness, animation, joyousness, and all agreeable emotions require a quick rate. Sudden emotions, wild and vehement passions, require an irregular movement. Care should be taken not to adopt a movement so quick as to cause indistinctness, or so slow as to allow the hearers time to forestall the next sentence before it is uttered. An undue rapidity is, perhaps, more common than the opposite fault. A slow movement, if successfully maintained, is very impressive and dignified. The main body of a discourse should be uttered with a moderate rate, which may be increased or diminished as may be requisite. Both a very slow and a very rapid rate should be at the command of every speaker and reader. It is a good drill in rate to take a paragraph and read it with varying rates of rapidity and slowness. In attempting a rapid rate be careful to pronounce each syllable distinctly.

## VARIATION.

A Variation is the movement of the voice in changing from a given key in uttering a passage. The Variations comprehend the Bend, the Close, the Slide, and the Sweep.

The **Bend** is a gentle upward inflection of the voice at a place in the sentence where a slight pause is made without completing the sense. In beginning a reading or a speech the use of the Bend is to be recommended, as it is of much advantage in conciliating the attention and winning the sympathies of an audience. Its use, wherever proper and practicable, adds vivacity and spirit to the discourse. While the Sweeps are perhaps more important variations, the skillful use of the Bend is indispensable to form an accomplished reader or speaker.

The **Close** is a downward inflection of the voice at end of a sentence or of a part of a sentence. The Partial Close (ˊ) is merely antecedent to the Perfect Close (ˋ). It is a downward inflection of the voice, generally to the pitch, or a tone near to the pitch, at the close of one part of the sentence. The Partial Close prepares the way for the Perfect Close, which comes at the close of the whole sentence, and drops the voice to a tone below the pitch. Sometimes the Perfect Close only drops to a point near to the pitch.

The **Slides** or **Inflections** are the upward and downward movements of the voice on the sounds of the vowels. When a question is asked directly, the voice is at first low, and gradually slides up to a high tone. This is the Upward Slide. In the answer to a direct question the slides go correspondingly downward. This is the Downward Slide. Thus, "Did he live' ?" is an Upward Slide, while "No', he died'!" is a Downward Slide. The so-called Waving Slide is identical with the Emphatic Sweep. The Double Slide is a combination of the Upward and Downward Slides. It is used in disjunctive interrogative sentences, connected by the conjunction, as, "Is' he' living', or is' he' dead` ?" It will be noticed that the conjunction is the dividing line between the two Slides, the voice sliding upward to *or*, and thence downward to the end of the sentence. The Waving Slide is sometimes called the Circumflex Slide (ˆ). It is of frequent occurrence in ironical passages where a double meaning is intended to be produced. The Waving or Circumflex Slide rises or falls according as the voice has an upward or downward movement at the end of the sentence. The monotone, which, strictly speaking, is an inflection, has already been mentioned. The student should practice the various slides, first with the vowels, and then with words and sentences. The nature of the expression will almost always show with what slide it should be delivered, so that no rules need be given here.

The **Sweeps** denote a movement of the voice upward above the key, or downward below the key, and then back. They are the Emphatic Sweeps and the Accentual Sweeps. The Upper Emphatic Sweep raises the voice above the pitch up to the word to be emphasized. The Lower Emphatic Sweep brings the voice from the emphasized word to a point below the pitch, and thence carries it back to the pitch. The force of Accentual Sweeps is spent, as a rule, upon a single word, or a single syllable of a word. They carry the voice upward or downward, like the Emphatic Sweeps, but with a greatly reduced movement.

## STRESS.

Stress denotes the way in which a tone receives its force. According to the portion of the sound to which force is applied, Stress is divided into Radical, Median, and Terminal. These three kinds of Stress denote that the force is applied to the beginning, middle, and end of the sound respectively.

The **Radical Stress** is generally violent and explosive. It is used in passages expressive of sudden or surprising emotions, or of deliberate and settled conviction. It is sometimes used, however, in unimpassioned discourse, for the purpose of animating the delivery by a clear and incisive utterance.

The **Median Stress** is a smooth, flowing, harmonious movement, appropriate to peaceful and thoughtful emotions. It is of great use in poetry.

The **Terminal Stress** begins gently, but ends abruptly and explosively. It is appropriate to passages expressing scorn, defiance, determination, querulousness, revenge, etc.

Another division of Stress is into Thorough, Compound, and Intermittent. The latter is sometimes called the Tremor.

The **Thorough Stress** denotes a strong, full tone, lasting as long as the sound is prolonged. It is used where a continuously full, loud voice is necessary, because some distant person is addressed. This is the Stress habitually employed by street venders, and to a greater or less extent by speakers in the open air. It is not a natural tone, and its cultivation is not to be recommended. Nothing is more wearisome than a sustained loud tone of this kind. For some unknown reason, it seems to be the favorite Stress of pupils in the schools, and readings by a class in concert are too frequently carried on in this high-pitched, fatiguing shout. In conversation the use of this Stress is a pretty sure test of a person's want of cultivation.

The **Compound Stress** is a combination of the Radical

Stress and the Terminal Stress upon one sound. It denotes, therefore, the application of force at the beginning and the end of the sound. The words upon which this Stress falls will generally be found to require the Circumflex or Waving Slide also. The Compound Stress denotes a mixture of emotions at the same time, as, hatred, anger, and surprise.

The **Intermittent Stress** or **Tremor** denotes that the voice trembles. This Stress is appropriate to sorrow, old age, etc. It should be used in moderation.

## STYLE.

The manner in which a piece should be read or spoken depends entirely upon the STYLE. The volume of voice to be used, the gesture, the whole general delivery are regulated by the style. Distinguish the different styles which may occur in the same discourse. Read over carefully the piece to be delivered, and determine the general style in which it is written. This will determine the manner in which it should be delivered — whether argumentative, descriptive, serious, conversational, didactic, or emotional.

## HOW SENTENCES ARE DELIVERED.

Sentences are either DECLARATIVE, INTERROGATIVE, or EXCLAMATORY. Declarative sentences affirm or deny something about some person or thing. Exclamatory sentences express emotion. Interrogative sentences ask a question.

**Declarative** sentences take the Partial Close at pauses not completing the sentence, where particular emphasis is necessary, or sadness or grief is to be expressed.

**Exclamatory** sentences may be either Interrogatory or Declarative. They require the same delivery as the sentences after which they are modeled, besides the utterance and expression appropriate to the emotions and passions which they represent.

**Interrogative** sentences are divided into *Definite*, *Indefinite*, and *Indirect*.

DEFINITE or DIRECT Interrogative sentences ask a direct question, which may be answered categorically, *Yes* or *No*. This class of Interrogative sentences begins with a verb. INDEFINITE interrogative sentences ask a question which cannot be answered by a direct *Yes* or *No*. They begin with Interrogative pronouns, or adverbs of place, time, manner, etc. DEFINITE Interrogative sentences require to be delivered with the Rising Slide. Indefinite Interrogative sentences take the Upper Emphatic Sweep till the emphatic word is reached; from that point till the end of the sentence they take the Downward Slide. Indirect interrogative sentences, or such as put a question in the form of a declaration, take the Circumflex or Waving Slide; they are delivered with the Upper Sweep till the emphatic word is reached, and with the Lower Sweep from that point to the end of the sentence.

## GESTURE.

GESTURE is the action accompanying a word, and enforcing or expressing more vividly some thought or emotion. It should never be used except where it comes in naturally, and makes more forcible the meaning of the expression which it accompanies. Between excessive and too scanty gesture, it is better to err in the direction of the latter. If gestures are appropriately and gracefully made, they enhance the strength of the expression, and impress the hearer much more than if they are awkwardly introduced at every turn. Even if gracefully made, they pall upon the audience if used to excess. It should be remembered that repose is as essential in a person's style of delivery as it is in his style of writing. To accent every sentence with a gesture is as much a waste of energy and as much of a demand upon the patience of an audience as to use one's utmost volume of voice in all or most parts. An economy of gesture will produce a greater effect than a prodigality of gesture. In the same way that the orator is more effective who spares his voice and husbands his resources for those passages, and those only, in his discourse which require a loud and forcible and passionate utterance, so the orator who keeps his gestures for those parts of his speech which are most forcible and impressive will produce a greater effect upon the audience than if he had already accustomed them to his action, and had exposed to them his whole store of gesture, so that no surprises are left for them. There are, of course, some gestures, such as the use of the index finger to point out an object, to which these remarks do not apply. They do apply to argumentative discourse, but gesture is not of much importance in other branches of composition, where it is little used except in referring to an object.

Care must be taken to avoid awkward and unbecoming gestures. Some speakers, who use gestures very little or not at all to their knowledge, have an unconscious habit of moving the body to and fro, standing on tiptoe from time to time, putting one hand behind the back or in a pocket, etc. A gesture ought, indeed, to be natural; but it ought, at the same time, to be graceful. Gracefulness of gesture, if not a natural gift, must and can be acquired to a considerable extent by constant practice, in the same way that a graceful carriage of the body can be acquired by dancing or by athletic exercise. The trouble with even the most graceful gestures, artificially learned, is that their artificiality is liable to be detected by the audience; and an audience is easily disgusted with anything that seems to be studied or artificial. This is an additional reason for being sparing of gesture, so that your delivery, while studied in the extreme, may not seem so to your hearers. Most speakers who have certain mannerisms of voice, have, in addition, certain mannerisms of gesture. Many speakers seem to have only one gesture, which they repeat constantly in all sorts of connections, and perhaps to enforce the most opposite meanings.

It is better to have no gesture at all than to be confined to only one.

It is generally the direction of books on elocution to complete the gesture at the moment of uttering the syllable or word which it accompanies. Archbishop Whately contends, and with some show of reason, that the gesture ought to precede somewhat the utterance of the words. He maintains that such "is always the natural order of action. An emotion, struggling for utterance, produces a tendency to a bodily gesture, to express that emotion more *quickly* than *words* can be framed; the words follow, as quickly as they can be spoken. And this being always the case with a real, earnest, unstudied speaker, this mode of placing the action foremost gives (if it be otherwise appropriate) the appearance of earnest emotion actually present in the mind." It will be found, perhaps, that Whately's views are not really inconsistent with the ordinary rule. The bodily gesture is begun first, but the word is produced so quickly by the voice that usually the gesture is not completed till the utterance of the word is completed. The matter cannot well be tested in speaking the words of others; but in delivering one's own words, if one feels called upon naturally and unpremeditatedly to use a certain gesture at a certain point, that gesture will probably be made at the proper time, whether it be made *before* or *during* the utterance of the word which it accompanies. In any case, a gesture should not be made or linger after its word.

## ORDINARY GESTURES.

In gesture the right hand should be used more than the left. Double gestures, *i. e.*, with both hands, should not be used too frequently. The hand in gesture should be open, with the fingers a little curved, and the thumb slightly above the fingers, and in the same direction. In debate and argumentative discourse, the most common gesture is the so-called "ARGUMENTATIVE" gesture. In making this, the index finger is held straight, while the remaining fingers are curved. Next in importance to the argumentative gesture is a gesture used to present some argument or state some position to the audience. This gesture keeps the hand open, the index finger straight, the other fingers a little curved. In the expression of very forcible arguments or powerful emotions, the fist may be brought down. This gesture should not be used too frequently. Some speakers use it with absurd frequency, hammering the desk or pulpit almost constantly. Never use it except in very strong, vehement passages.

## THE PASSIONS.

The speaker must always feel what he attempts to express. He must have his mind filled with the passion or emotion which his words represent, so as to insure a correct and striking delivery. He must seem to his audience to be under the control of the feeling with which he is seeking to impress them. Having wrought himself up to a proper pitch, he must then suppress every mental process except the object which he wishes to accomplish by his oratory, and the feeling which he wishes to express. The highest art of oratory, like the highest art of acting, is not to be attained simply by a painstaking and conscientious study, resulting in a careful, polished, but cold delivery. To fully represent any strong and thrilling passion, the orator and the actor must throw themselves into that passion with a momentary excitement, with a complete mental abandonment, for the time, of themselves and of every other passion or thought to the dominant passion to be expressed. To do this is often a severe strain upon the nerves; it requires an expenditure of mental energy, of nervous force, and sometimes of muscular activity, such as few persons are capable of enduring. The professed actor or elocutionist has to submit to the severest strain in this regard. The orator who is using his own language to express thoughts and feelings by which he is himself deeply moved, and of whose truth and force he is firmly convinced, has less difficulty in affecting and persuading his hearers, because he is himself already affected and persuaded. But the orator and elocutionist who is, perhaps, obliged to represent in quick succession powerful emotions of the most opposite character, finds his energies severely taxed, and is often forced to repay by hours of weakness for the applause which he has earned by his successful representation. In the midst of all his excitement, however, it should be remembered that he does not lose entire control of himself, although he may seem to do so. He seems to be mastered by the passion, but in reality the passion is mastered by him, "In the very torrent, tempest, and whirlwind of his passion," he retains his self-possession, and so "acquires a temperance that may give it smoothness." Inexperienced or incompetent actors and speakers, on the other hand, confuse strength with violence, and mistake a noisy and vehement declamation for a powerful and passionate delivery.

Every passion has its own sign, and expresses itself by a number of indications, such as a change in pitch, in force, in inflection, in articulation, in the position of the body, and in the expression of the face. To give any general rules for the expression of the various passions is very difficult, though it has been many times attempted. An anonymous writer, quoted with approval by Walker in his Treatise on Elocution, has, perhaps, been more successful than others in catching the exterior marks of the principal passions and states of feeling. A few of his directions are given in a condensed form below. This writer's detailed description of the passion of love as represented on the stage is not inserted here, as it may be supposed that every reader will have sufficiently clear and practical ideas of his own on that subject, and will not require any directions as to the proper mode of expressing that passion.

## HOW TO EXPRESS THE PASSIONS.

**Tranquillity.**—The body and face are kept in a state of repose, without muscular movement. The countenance is open and natural, the forehead smooth and unwrinkled, the mouth is just not entirely closed, the eyebrows are slightly arched, and the eyes are passing easily from one object to another without dwelling long upon one.

**Cheerfulness.**—The same as tranquility with the addition of a smile; the mouth, too, is open a little wider.

**Raillery.**—(Without ill feeling.) The same as cheerfulness. The countenance is smiling, the voice gay and sprightly.

**Joy.**—The face wears a moderate smile ; or in the extremes of joy the hands are clasped together suddenly, the eyes are lifted upward, the body springs gayly and elastically. (Delight is the same as extreme joy.) See Illustration.

**Shame.**—The face is turned away, the eyes seek the ground, the eyebrows are drawn down, the body looks weak.

**Pity.**—The voice is soft and sympathetic, the eyebrows are drawn together, the hands are raised, and then dropped, and the mouth is somewhat open.

**Hope.**—The face looks bright and happy, the arms are spread out, the hands are open, the breath is drawn a little more strongly than usual, the voice is plaintive and a little eager. See Illustration.

**Hatred.**—The body is drawn backward, the hands are thrown out as if to keep back the hated object, the face is turned away as if to avert it from what it loathes, the eyes sparkle angrily and are turned obliquely in the same direction as the hands, the eyebrows are drawn together, the teeth are set, the voice has a rough and harsh sound.

**Anger.**—The voice is high (but not always ; in suppressed anger, for instance, it is low), the nostrils are expanded more than usual, the fist is clinched, the brow is wrinkled, the foot stamps upon the ground.

**Fear.**—The eyes are wide open, the mouth is also open, the breath is short and quick, the body shakes, one foot is drawn back of the other, the elbows are held parallel with the sides, the hands are open, with the fingers spread out to the height of the breast. See Illustration.

PEEVISHNESS.

**Sorrow.**—The eyes look down upon the ground, the hands are open, the fingers are spread out, the voice is soft, plaintive, slightly tremulous. If the sorrow to be expressed is excessive, the hands are wrung, the body shrunk, the eyes are covered with the hands, etc.

**Remorse.**—The head hangs down, the eyes are lifted up for a moment, and then cast down, the body writhes, the voice has a harsh and low sound.

**Despair.**—The eyebrows are bent down, the eyes are rolled, the mouth is opened, the nostrils expand and enlarge, the fist is clinched, the teeth gnash, the body is moved violently to and fro.

**Surprise.**—(Wonder, admiration, etc.) The eyes are opened wide, the mouth is open, the hands are held up.

**Pride.**—The eyes are open full and wide, the eyebrows are drawn down, the lips are drawn together tightly, the words are uttered slowly and deliberately, the step is slow and stately, the body is held erect and unbending, the legs are apart.

**Courage.**—The head is held high and straight, the breast is thrown out, the eyes are clear, the voice is firm.

**Boasting.**—The arms are held akimbo, the foot stamps upon the ground, the strides are long, the voice is loud. See Illustration.

**Anxiety.**—(Perplexity, etc.) The eyebrows are contracted, the head hangs down, the eyes are cast upon the ground, the lips are drawn together tightly, the movements of the body are irregular and agitated, the tone of the voice is uneven, and frequently varied.

**Peevishness.**—The forehead is somewhat wrinkled, the upper lip is drawn up, the eyes take an oblique direction. See Illustration.

**Malice.**—The jaws are set resolutely, the fist is clinched, the elbows are bent in till they touch the body. See Illustration.

**Command.**—The hand is held out with the palm upward. Sometimes a nod is given to the person commanded.

**Scorn.**—The eyebrows are turned up, the body is straight, the open hand is thrown out, with the palm downward, the face is slightly turned away.

## TRANSITION.

In reading or speaking it is of the highest importance to avoid the too continuous use of the same tone. The ear soon wearies unless it is appeased with a little variety. Unless a composition be unpardonably dull, it is susceptible of a variety of intonations, and it will lose much of its effect if it is delivered monotonously, without bringing out its contrasts by fitting vocal contrasts. To do this the speaker or reader must clearly understand the thought and feeling, and must be able to give its proper representation by his voice. To attain such a control over the voice as to be able to make a rapid transition from one tone to another requires a long course of training, unless a person is exceptionally gifted by nature. Yet he who aspires to be a good reader must be able to take advantage of every opportunity to give significance to his reading by changing, as contrast demands, the volume, pitch, rate, and quality of his voice. Constant practice must be had in passing from pure tone to orotund, from orotund tone to aspirated, from aspirated tone to pure, from loud to soft, from middle pitch to low, from slow time to quick, from loud to moderate, etc., etc.

## POSITION AND CARRIAGE.

Support the weight of the body upon one foot. Rest the weight of the body at first upon the left foot, resting the right foot, with the knee slightly bent, about three inches in advance of the left. When you grow tired of this position, reverse it by resting the weight of the body on the right foot, with the left advanced. Expand the chest easily. Let the arms, when not employed in gesture, hang down at the sides. Keep the shoulders at the same height, the body erect, the chin a very little drawn in, the eyes looking straight. In coming on the platform or stage, bow to the chairman or president, if there is one. Bow the body and not the head simply. Walk easily and gracefully to the front of the stage, bow slightly to the audience and begin. In coming on the stage, or walking across in the course of your speech (if you have occasion) hold the head up straight, keep the body erect, the chest expanded, the eyes straight ahead. The feet should incline outwards about thirty degrees. Swing the arms easily and naturally. Take steps of the same length, and with a uniform time.

## SITTING POSITION.

In reading from a sitting position, adopt the following rules in that regard : Keep the feet on the floor at an angle of from fifty to sixty degrees with one another. Bend the knees to an angle of about eighty-five degrees. Keep the shoulders square, the body erect, the head straight, the chest well out, the chin a little in. Hold the book or manuscript in the left hand, with three fingers under it. Put the thumb and little finger above the leaf to hold it down. Raise the fore-arm from thirty-five to forty-five degrees, throwing the elbow a little forward. The book is in a proper position when the reader can see to read, and at the same time is not obliged to bend his neck or body.

IN an ancient Assyrian document, which was written during the reign of Sardanapalus V., it is said that the god Nebo revealed to the ancestors of the King the cuneiform characters of their language. This account of the sacred origin of their writings was universally believed by the people. To many persons, trained in the customs and modes of thought peculiar to our age, it seems quite incredible that this idea was ever seriously entertained; but, according to statements of reliable historians, such a belief was universal.

Nearly every nation of antiquity has, at some period of its history, attributed the origin of letters to the beneficence of the god in which it trusted. This appears not only from statements of the writers, but from the nature and signification of their words. In the Egyptian language, the term *writing* signified, according to Lenormant, "Writing heavenly words." This meaning is not only beautiful but essentially true, for whatever may be the origin of letters, no gift or invention has been as useful, nor contributed so much to the civilization of mankind, as the ART OF WRITING.

That a people like the Assyrians, for the most part uneducated, having but little intercourse with other nations, should believe that none but the gods could see meaning in the wedge-like forms of their language is not strange; but it seems extraordinary that such an enlightened people as the Egyptians should have attributed anything supernatural to their hieroglyphics.

The true origin of the art of writing could not well be understood by a person confining his observations to any one language or time. To the student of philology, however, it is not a surprising fact that writing was not invented by a single man, but gradually worked out by the contributions of numerous generations. The invention of written characters is due to the genius of man working through ages, and proving, indeed, that "art is long."

Under these circumstances, it is natural that the accounts of the origin of writing should be somewhat varied, but there is a very general agreement that the first developments of written language are to be found among the Egyptians. It might have been expected that the three great classes of kindred languages, the Aryan, the Semitic, and the Turanian, would give us the source of our written characters; but the connection between thought and the symbols of thought has not proved strong

PLATE 1.

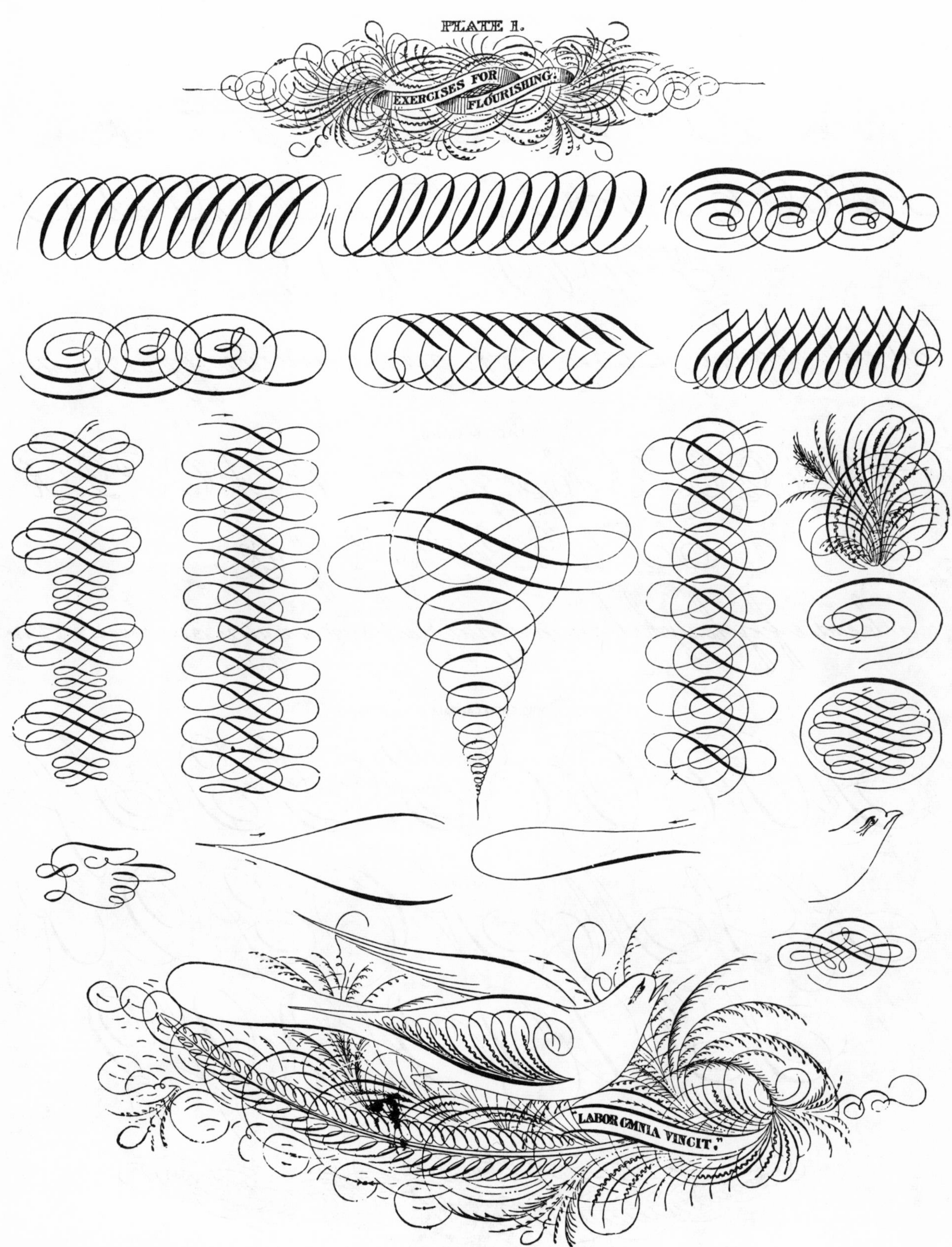

## PLATE II.

### STANDARD LETTERS.

enough to decipher the ancient characters without a key or alphabet. Owing, therefore, to our limited knowledge, we can only trace three principal sources from which the various nations have derived their letters—the Chinese, the Assyrian and the Egyptian. It is claimed, moreover, that the Assyrian ought not to be classed as a source at all, as that language is manifestly the product of long experience with more simple forms.

All writing has been divided into two classes—*Ideographic* and *Phonetic.*

IDEOGRAPHIC writing is the art of expressing ideas by means of images or pictures, and is the natural language of children and primitive men everywhere. The most perfect examples of this writing have been found in Egypt, and have been known as the hieroglyphs. The Egyptians developed four languages, which, by their resemblances and variations, enable us to trace, with considerable certainty, the course of linguistic evolution. The oldest of these languages is the HIEROGLYPHIC, in which the pictorial element prevails to the largest extent. This language was in use more than three thousand years before the Christian era, but it was confined to the priests; it was chiefly employed in religious services, and in the rituals for the dead. The second of these languages of Egypt, and that which was by far the most useful to the world, was the HIERATIC. This language was in use twenty centuries before the close of the old era, and was the medium of the best thought of Egyptian literature. To this also we must look for the source from which the nations of Europe have principally derived their letters. This language, though ideographic, was rather symbolical than pictorial; it had so far departed from the original forms that it may be considered a cursive writing; and it is probably the first example known among men. The other two languages found among the Egyptians were the DEMOTIC and COPTIC, but their influence was far less than the hieratic.

The characters of the HIERATIC language, which the Phœnicians had adopted, were soon taken from the service of ideographic writing, and became the basis of another system called the PHONETIC, in which the characters represent sounds. Of the phonetic languages there are two classes: the *syllabic,* in which each character represents a combination of sounds, and the *alphabetical,* in which each character is the symbol of a single sound. It required a long experience to bring into use the system of phonetic writing now employed by the most enlightened nations of the world. Time and experience, however, developed our present art of writing, for which no price was too great to pay.

The difficulties which men have encountered in the development of this art can scarcely be understood unless we study the materials which men have employed in the attempt to express their ideas in written forms. The laborious chiseling upon stone, the slow tracing of the iron style upon the palm leaf, the papyrus and the wooden blocks, and the separate process of filling or rubbing into the lines the chosen pigment, involved difficulties which the writers of our day would not willingly undertake. If persons of to-day were compelled to use those modes for a short time, they would return to our present methods with the consciousness of exalted privilege and blessing.

The study of the writings of the different nations shows us that there were generally two motives that guided their course of progress. The more important was the desire to save work; the other motive was the love of beauty. It is hard to believe that men have always been moved by these causes, when we see some of the ugly characters which they have used; yet there are very few systems in which we do not find (even from our own peculiar standpoint) many illustrations of the æsthetic and economic qualities of men. As an example of the latter, we note the cuneiform inscriptions of the Assyrians. These are supposed to have been developed from the linear style of cutting in stone. Experience showed that the wedge could be cut much more quickly than the angle formed by two narrow lines.

The desire for beauty was especially predominant among the peoples of northern and western Europe from the close of the twelfth to the sixteenth century. During this time the Gothic script prevailed, and it still has a representation in the characters of the German language. These were the characters used in the famous "Black Letter Books," as the first books published in Germany imitated the heavy lines of the Gothic script in use with the people at that time. But the Gothic characters do not seem to have been very satisfactory. The French modified them, and gave to their forms the name "*lettres de somme.*" The Italians rejected them altogether, and produced the forms now known as the ROMAN. These appeared in an edition of Pliny's Natural History, published in Venice in the year 1469. It is a circumstance worthy of note that the ornamental Gothic letters, which were rejected by most of the European nations so many years ago, are now beginning to lose favor even among the Germans themselves, and there are very many who long to see them exchanged for the simpler form of the Roman.

It is impossible to foresee the changes which are in store for the written languages of to-day; but it is certain they are not fixed. Some changes will undoubtedly take place. There is work enough of an excellent kind for those who will undertake it. Many persons look upon writing as something which *anybody* may accomplish, and think it does not matter very much how it is done. They like to see individuality in writing. But we must remember that writing is an art; that while there is a certain scope for the individuality of each one who writes, there are also inexorable laws. Whatever improvement we have made in the expression of thought by means of script, we have made by discovering and obeying the laws of this Art. So long as writing consisted only in imitating a copy without regard to principles of letter construction, and without care for the position of the body, or for the movements of the arm and hand, it depended for interest solely upon its utility in conveying intelligence and preserving to men the important events of history. But when men began to study the subject more carefully, they found there were more things in this Art of Writing than were dreamed of in the old philosophies. Observation taught them that mere imitation could never give the best results. The process of writing involved a series of movements of the arm and hand, the laws of which could not be ignored without serious loss in time and in the skill of execution. A few persons may be skillful artists without formulated rules, but only those who are gifted with superior powers of imagination and elegance of taste can ever attain great skill by any other means than practical familiarity with rules. But the study of this Art has done more than to reveal the fact of a loss in time and skill; it has demonstrated another fact of the utmost importance to writers, book-keepers and copyists, that the use of the pen, even for long periods of time, is not unhealthful nor greatly exhausting, when the method is natural and physiological. While, on the other hand, there is no occupation more tedious, and none that makes a more severe draft upon the energies of man, than the use of the pen by improper methods. Diseases of the hand and ruin of the whole nervous system are often the result. Many men and women, whose health has broken under the task of writing, have failed and suffered, not so much from the difficulty of their work as from the attempt to do it in an unnatural way. It is of no use to fight against Nature, and whoever attempts it must suffer. It is inexcusable to shut your eyes to the light of science, and employ a method which is condemned by the plainest laws of your own body. Penmanship may now be justly termed a science. The knowledge pertaining to it has been classified, and the rules of a natural method have been made so complete, that any one who will follow them carefully for a few months will be rewarded by a power of easy and rapid execution which could never be attained under the old method of learning to write. In the development of every art there is a tendency to adornment. Indeed, there are few things which man attempts in which you will not find evidence of his æsthetic nature, consciously or unconsciously expressed. Even in so practical an art as writing this has appeared, and has brought discredit to some extent upon the schools. But this has been simply from a misunderstanding of the uses of the ornamental style. Apart from its peculiar use in decoration, it is of the highest service in training the muscles of the arm and hand, and in allaying, when properly employed, all unnatural excitement of the nerves. Viewed in this light, the development of the ornamental style is to be regarded as an important part of the advances in the art of writing. Whoever has used the method of training, in which the ornamental style has been employed as a means of giving the best control over the muscles, will need no other evidence to convince him of its great utility. But if any examples were needed, it may justly be said that those institutions, which have employed it most carefully, have been most successful in sending forth pupils expert in the use of the pen, and possessed of a ready and legible handwriting.

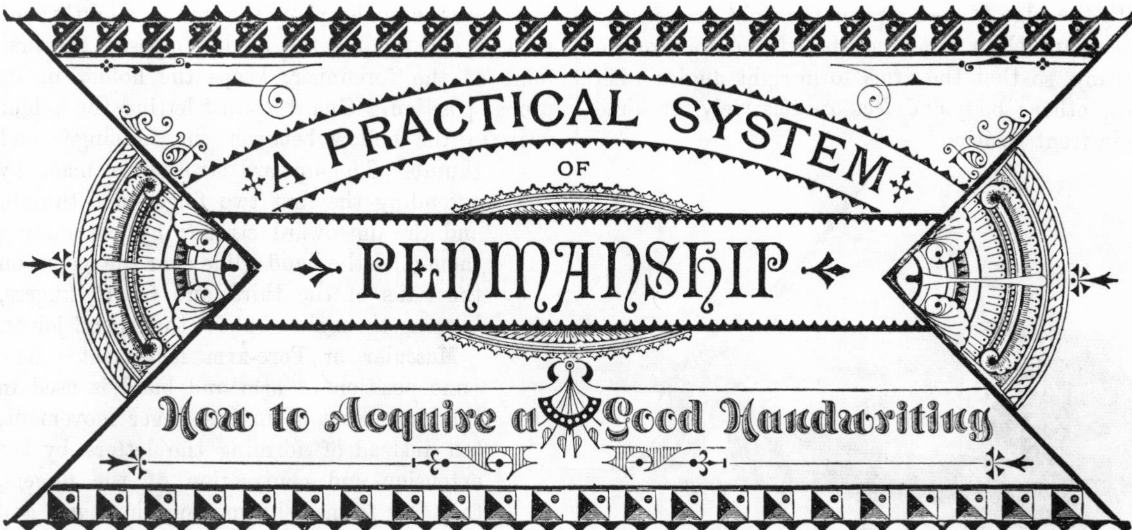


PERSONS who desire to acquire a good handwriting cannot pay too much attention to the assumption of a CORRECT POSITION, of which there are three, the FRONT, the RIGHT side, and the LEFT side. The **Front Position** is most commonly used, and we always recommend it, especially to students learning to write. In this position sit square with the desk, but not in contact with it; keep the body erect, the feet level on the floor; place the paper in front of the body, in an oblique position, and square with the right arm; rest the left arm on the desk, with the hand on the paper to the left, above the right hand, and forming a right angle with it.

**Right Side Position.** Sit with the right side to the desk without touching it; let the paper lie square

FRONT POSITION.

with the edge of desk; place the right arm on the desk parallel to edge, and the left hand above the writing, so that the arms form right angles with each other; body and feet are relatively the same as in front position.

POSITION OF THE HAND (REAR VIEW).

**Left Side Position.** Sit with the left side to the desk; body erect; left arm parallel to edge of desk with the hand on the paper above the writing; paper square with desk; and right arm at a right angle with the left. This position is recommended especially in the counting-house where large books are used, that have to be placed at right angles to the edge of the desk. The right arm should always be parallel to the sides of the paper or book.

## MOVEMENTS.

IN writing, three MOVEMENTS are necessary, viz: FINGER movement, MUSCULAR or FORE-ARM movement, and OFF HAND or WHOLE ARM movement.

**Finger Movement.** Let the arm touch the table on the muscles only, about three inches from elbow; hold the wrist clear from the table and square, so that a pencil laid on the back of wrist would be in a horizontal position; hold the pen between the thumb and first and second fingers; keep the second finger nearly straight and about three quarters of an inch from point of pen, resting the holder halfway between the end of finger and first joint; the forefinger, which is also nearly straight, rests over the holder; and the thumb, slightly bent with its end against the holder opposite the first joint of the forefinger, keeps the holder in its proper position. Guard against letting the holder drop in the hollow between the forefinger and thumb. The upward strokes are made by extending the first two fingers and thumb, and the downward strokes by contracting them; let the hand glide over the paper on the nails of the third and fourth fingers, keeping them closed above the second joints.

**Muscular or Fore-arm Movement.** The same position of arm and hand is used in this movement as in the finger movement, but instead of forming the letters by the extension and contraction of the fingers, they are formed by moving the hand and wrist with the pen, letting the arm roll on the muscle near the elbow, and sliding the hand over the paper on the nails of the third and fourth fingers. This is the proper movement for business writing, and beginners will acquire a good business hand much sooner by constantly practicing it.

**Off Hand or Whole Arm Movement.** In this movement raise the elbow from the desk, and move the whole arm from the shoulder with the pen, letting the hand slide on the nails of the third and fourth fingers. This movement is only used in making large Capitals.

**Formation** is the manner in which letters are made. All letters are formed with straight lines and curves called principles. The straight lines are all parallel and of the same slant. Curves are of three kinds, *convex*, *concave*, and *compound*.

POSITION OF THE HAND (FRONT VIEW).

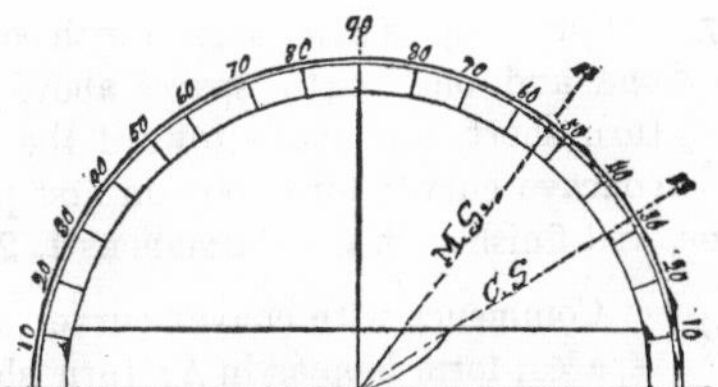


**Slant.** All straight lines in the formation of letters should be at an angle of fifty-three degrees (53°), and all curved lines in small letters connecting straight lines should be at an angle of thirty-two degrees (32°); when the space between letters is diminished this angle is increased, but in all cases the main slant should remain the same. The above engraving shows the MAIN SLANT (53°) and the CONNECTING SLANT (32°).

**Space.** The line on which the writing rests is called the BASE line, that at the head of the small letters the HEAD line; and the line to which the Capitals extend, the TOP line. A space in small letters is the width of the letter *u* and height of *i*, excepting the loop letters that have the height of capitals; d, p and t, that are two spaces above the base line; and f, g, j, p, q, y and z, that are two spaces below the base line.

**Shading.** It is better that students in learning to write should make all small letters without shading except the letters d, p, and t; and in shading Capitals there should be but one shade in a single letter. After one has learned the formation of small letters, shading may be practiced, making two or three in a word of eight or nine letters.

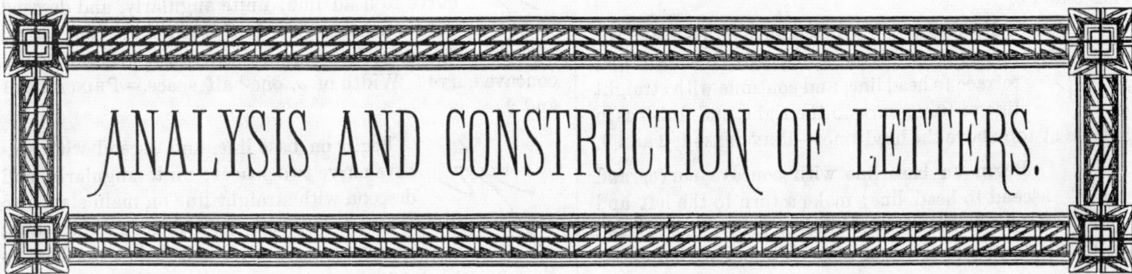


NOTHING is of greater importance in learning to write than that the student should acquire a thorough knowledge of the analysis and construction of all the letters of the alphabet. Many persons fail to acquire a good handwriting, because they have never taken the trouble to inform themselves in this respect, and merely imitate the general characteristics of a letter without the slightest knowledge of its regular construction. Some individuals even boast of their ignorance, and pride themselves on the legibility or individuality of their style of writing. Educated people, however, consider a knowledge of the formation of letters essential to those who wish to acquire a graceful or genteel handwriting. After this has been accomplished, individuality will develop itself, and by constant practice you will gradually work out a peculiar style of your own; but without a knowledge of the fundamental laws of penmanship you can no more learn to write properly, than you could draw a fine picture unless you had first mastered certain rules relating to the art of drawing.

### HOW SMALL LETTERS ARE FORMED.

The three PRINCIPLES given below are those employed in the formation of all letters. They should be thoroughly understood before attempting to construct either small letters or capitals, as one, two, or all three of these principles are used in every case.

*Prin. 1. Convex curve.* Head line / Base line

I. The **first principle** of small letters is a convex curve, commencing at base line, and ascending to head line at an angle of thirty-two degrees (32°).

*Prin. 2. Concave curve.*

II. The **second principle** is a concave curve, commencing at base line, and ascending to head line at an angle of thirty two degrees (32°).

*Prin. 3, Oblique St. line.* 53°

III. The **third principle** is a straight line, commencing at head line and descending to base at an angle of fifty-three degrees (53°).

*a* Begin on base line, and ascend with convex curve to head line; retrace one-half space, and finish the movement with convex curve to base line; turn to the right and ascend with concave curve to head line, forming a pointed oval; descend with a straight line on main slant to base; turn to right, and finish with concave curve.—PRINCIPLES 1, 2 and 3.

Begin on base line, and ascend with convex curve to top line; turn to the left, and descend with straight line to base, crossing upward movement at head line; turn to the right on base line, and ascend with concave curve to head line; finish with a horizontal concave curve to the right, one-half space in length.—PRINCIPLES 2 and 3.

Begin on base line, and ascend with concave curve, leaving space enough between its highest point and the head line for the passage of another curve; unite angularly, and descend with straight line on main slant one-fourth space; make a short turn to the right, and ascend with concave curve; turn to the left over the upward curve, touching the head line; descend to base with straight line on main slant, and finish as in *a*.—PRINCIPLES 2 and 3.

Form the pointed oval as in *a*; continue the second principle one space above the head line; retrace to head line, and continue with straight line to base; turn to the right, and finish as in *a*; shade at top above the head line.—PRINCIPLES 1, 2 and 3.

Begin on base line with concave curve, and ascend to head line; make a turn to the left and descend with a straight line on main slant to base; turn to the right, and finish as in *a*.—PRINCIPLES 2 and 3.

Begin as in *h* with the upward and downward movement, crossing at head line; continue the straight line two spaces below the base; turn to the right, and ascend with concave curve, touching straight line at base; unite angularly, and finish with the concave curve to the right.—PRINCIPLES 2 and 3.

First, second and third movement same as in *a*; uniting angularly with a straight line on main slant, and finishing as in *j*.—PRINCIPLES 1, 2 and 3.

Begin on base line, and ascend with concave curve three spaces; turn to the left, and descend with straight line to base, crossing curve at head line; unite angularly, and ascend with convex curve to head line; turn to the right, and descend with a straight line on main slant to base; finish as in *a*.—PRINCIPLES 1, 2 and 3.

Begin at base line; ascend with concave curve to head line; unite angularly, and descend with straight line on main slant to base; finish same as in *a*; dot one space above third principle, on same slant.—PRINCIPLES 2 and 3.

Begin as in *i*; continue straight line on main slant two spaces below the base line, and finish as in *g*.—PRINCIPLES 1, 2 and 3.

Form loop as in *h*; ascend with convex curve one and one-fourth spaces above base line; turn short, and move toward the left with a concave curve; form loop on first principle at the head line, and finish as in *i*.—PRINCIPLES 1, 2 and 3.

Commence with convex curve; ascend two spaces; form loop as in *h*; turn short to the right, and finish as in *i*.—PRINCIPLES 2 and 3.

Begin with convex curve on base line; ascend to head line; turn, and descend with straight line on main slant to base; unite angularly; ascend to head line, repeating the above, and finish as in *i*. Width of *m*, two spaces.—PRINCIPLES 1, 2 and 3.

Commence and finish same as *m*. Width, one space.—PRINCIPLES 1, 2 and 3.

Begin on base line, and ascend with concave curve to head line; unite angularly, and descend with convex curve to base; turn short, and ascend with concave curve, forming an oval; finish with horizontal concave curve. Width of *o*, one-half space.—PRINCIPLES 1 and 2.

Begin on base line, and ascend with concave curve two spaces; unite angularly, and descend with straight line on main slant two spaces below base line; retrace to base line; complete as in *n*; shade below the base.—PRINCIPLES 1, 2 and 3.

Form pointed oval as in *a*; unite angularly, and descend with straight line on main slant two spaces below base line; turn short to the right, and ascend with convex curve to head line.—PRINCIPLES 1, 2 and 3.

Begin on base line, and ascend with concave curve one and one-fourth spaces; descend with a vertical curve to head line; turn short, and descend with straight line to base; turn short to the right, and finish same as *i*. Width, one-half space.—PRINCIPLES 2 and 3.

First movement as in *r*; descend with concave curve on main slant to base line; turn to the left, terminating with a dot on first curve, one-third space from base; retrace to base line, and finish with concave curve. Width, one-half space.—PRINCIPLE 2.

Begin on base line, and ascend with concave curve two spaces; descend with straight line to base; turn to the right, and end as in *i*. Shade above head line; cross with a straight line horizontally one-half space from top.—PRINCIPLES 2 and 3.

Commence with concave curve, ascending to head line; unite angularly with straight line on main slant, and descend to base; turn, repeat the same thing, and finish as in *i*. Width, one space.—PRINCIPLES 2 and 3.

PLATE V.

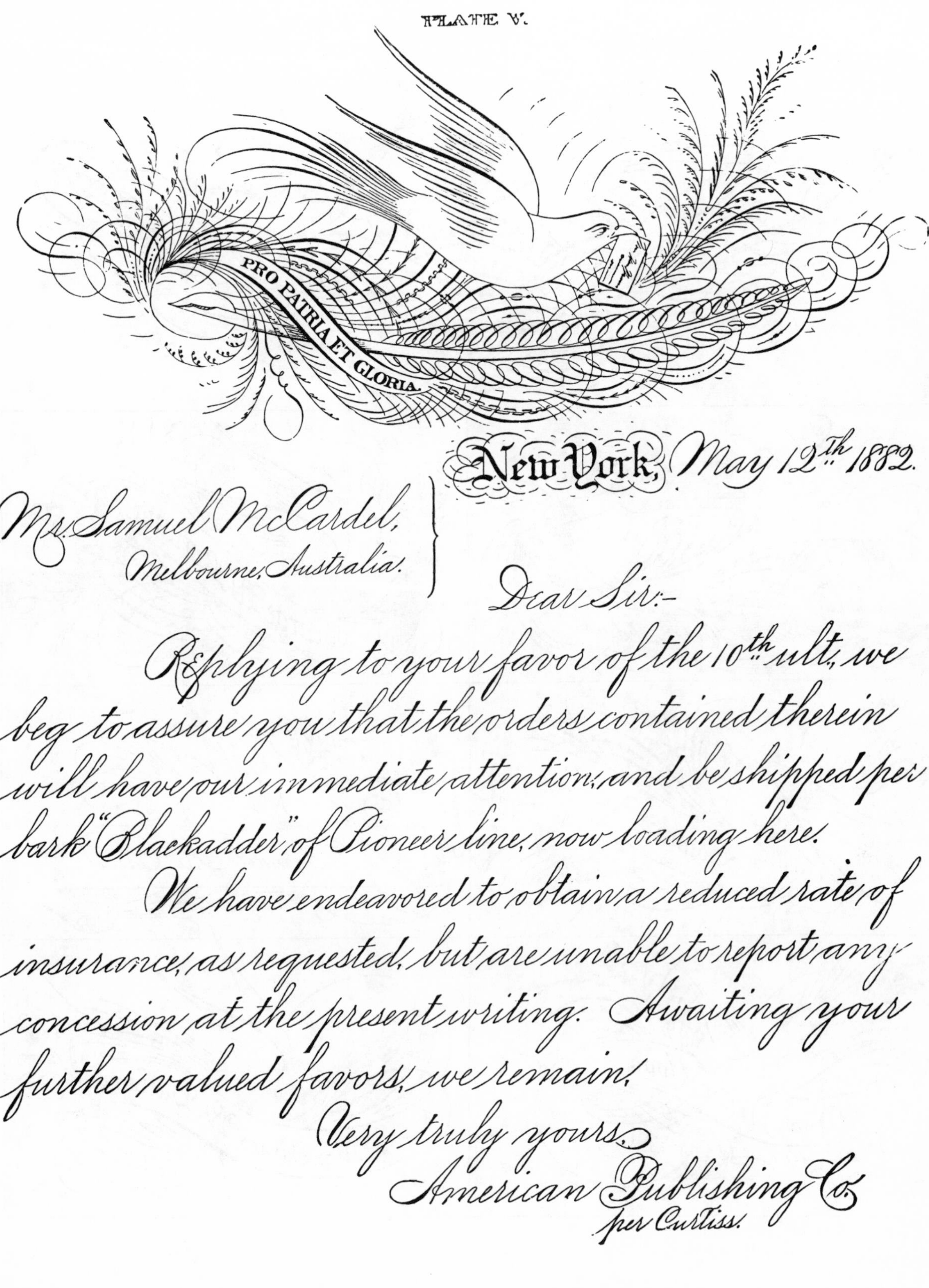


New York, May 12th 1882.

Mr. Samuel McCardel,
Melbourne, Australia.

Dear Sir:-

Replying to your favor of the 10th ult., we beg to assure you that the orders contained therein will have our immediate attention, and be shipped per bark "Blackadder," of Pioneer line, now loading here.

We have endeavored to obtain a reduced rate of insurance, as requested, but are unable to report any concession at the present writing. Awaiting your further valued favors, we remain,

Very truly yours,
American Publishing Co.
per Curtiss.

PLATE VI.

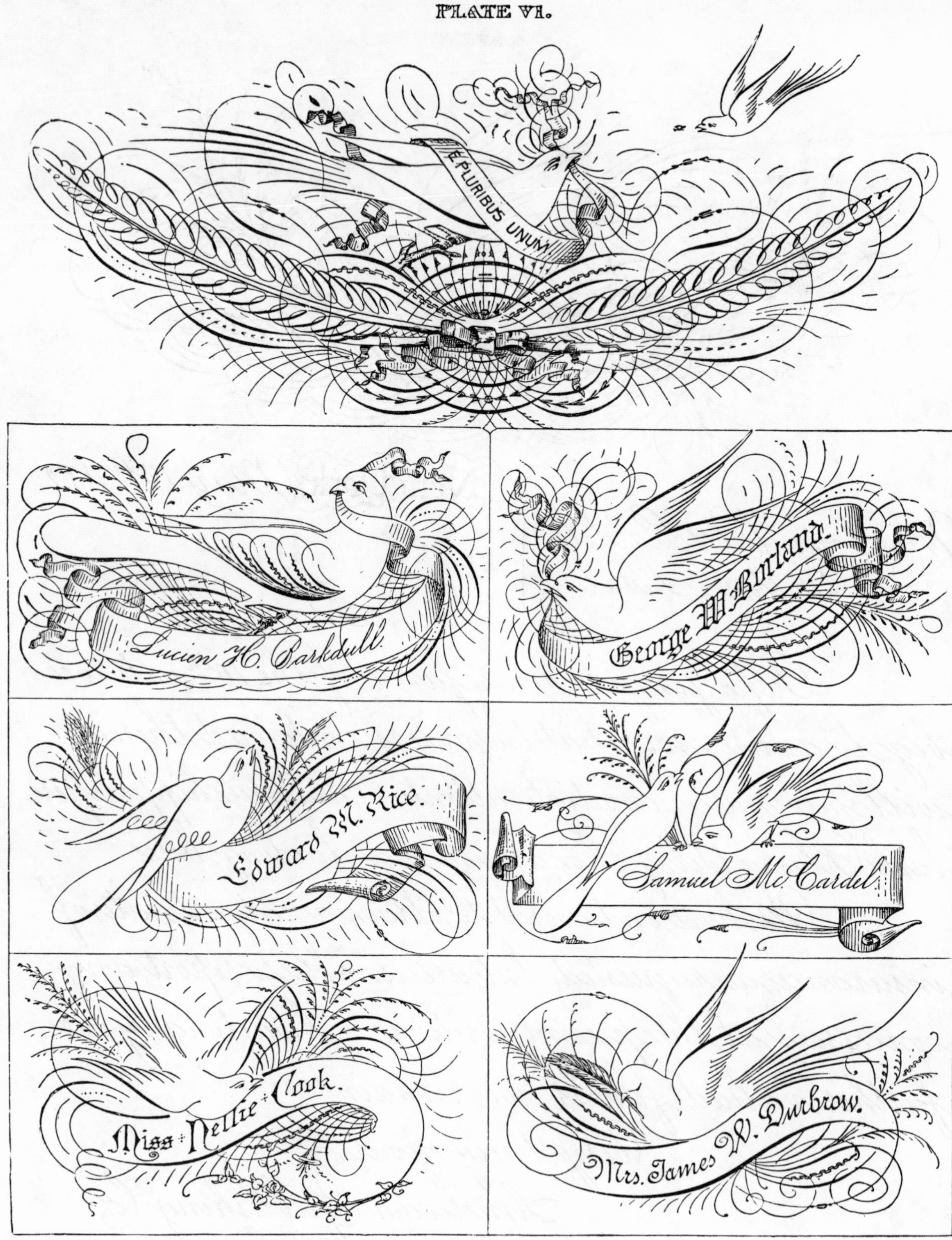
E PLURIBUS UNUM
Lucien H. Parkdull
George W. Borland
Edward M. Rice
Samuel Mc Cardel
Miss Nellie Cook.
Mrs. James W. Durbrow.

Begin at base line, and ascend with convex curve to head line; turn to the right, and descend with straight line on main slant to base; turn to the right, and ascend with concave curve to head line one-half space from top of second movement, and finish with a horizontal curve to the right. Width of letter, one-half space.—PRINCIPLES 1, 2 and 3.

The first two movements are the same as in *n;* turn to the right, and ascend with concave curve to head line; unite angularly, with a straight line on main slant, and finish with the last movement of *v*. Width, one and one-half spaces.—PRINCIPLES 1, 2 and 3.

First two movements same as in *n;* the third movement begins at the head line, and, descending, traces the second movement one-third of its length; continue to the base line; turn to the right, and finish with the concave curve.—PRINCIPLES 1, 2 and 3.

Begin on base line, and ascend with convex curve to head line; turn, and descend with a straight line on main slant to base; turn to the right, and ascend with concave curve to head line; unite angularly with a straight line on main slant, and finish as in *j*.—PRINCIPLES 1, 2 and 3.

Three first movements as in *r;* unite angularly with a convex curve; ascend slightly, then turn to the right, and descend with a concave curve two spaces below base line; turn to the left, and finish as in *j*.—PRINCIPLES 1, 2 and 3.

## CONSTRUCTION OF CAPITALS.

We first present the three principles of the capitals, which a student should practice before writing the letters. They are formed by the convex and concave curve, which are the first and second principles of writing.

**Capital Stem.** — Formed with principles 1 and 2. Height, three spaces; finished with an oval one-half its height.

The **Oval.**—Formed with principles 1 and 2. Height, three spaces. Width, one-half its height.

The **Inverted Oval.**—Formed with principles 1 and 2. Begin one and one-half spaces from base line, ascend to top line, making an oval two-thirds its height. With this principle the letters *Q, U, V, W, X, Y* and *Z* are made.

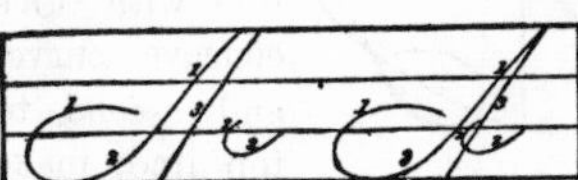

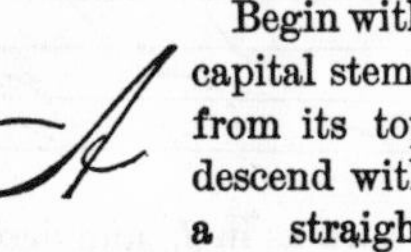

Begin with capital stem; from its top descend with a straight line on main slant to base line; begin a slight curve to the left on the straight line, one and one-fourth spaces from base line, and descend one-half space; cross straight line, and ascend with a concave curve to head line. Commence shade on the stem, one-fourth space above head line, and finish on base line. PRINCIPLES 1, 2 and 3.

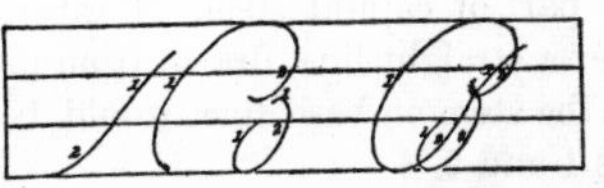

Begin two and one-half spaces from base line, and descend with capital stem on main slant; make an oval turn to the left, and ascend to top line; make an oval turn to the right, and descend to one and one-half spaces from base line; cross the capital stem, and form a loop pointing upward; then descend with a right curve to base line; turn, and ascend one space. PRINCIPLES 1 and 2.

Begin on base line and ascend to top line with concave curve; turn to left, and descend to base line, forming loop as in *l;* finish with oval one-half the full height. PRINCIPLES 1, 2 and 3.

Begin two and one-fourth spaces from base line, and descend with compound curve to base line; form a horizontal loop, and touch the base at the right of crossing; ascend with convex curve to head line, crossing compound curve two spaces from base line; finish with oval extending downward two and one-half spaces from head line. PRINCIPLES 1 and 2.

Begin near the top line; after forming a small oval, descend one space from top line; form a small loop pointing downward, and finish with an oval two spaces touching the base. PRINCIPLES 1 and 2.

Begin *F* with convex curve (same as small letter *n*) one-half space from top line; ascend to top line; turn to the right, and descend with a straight line one-third of a space; form a horizontal compound curve to the right, one space; form loop pointing upward at top line, and descend with capital stem same as in the capital letter *A;* cross capital stem one and one-half spaces from base line. The capital *T* is formed in the same manner as *F*, without the crossing on the stem. PRINCIPLES 1 and 2.

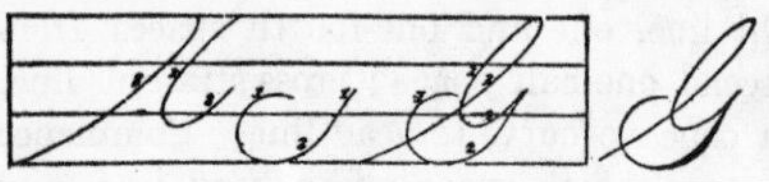

Begin as in small letter *l;* after forming loop, make an oval turn, which should be three-fourths of a space from base line; ascend to a point one and one-half spaces from base line; unite angularly, and finish with lower part of capital stem. Position of loop should be such that a straight line, drawn from its top to the centre of oval of the stem on base line, would be on main slant. PRINCIPLES 1 and 2.

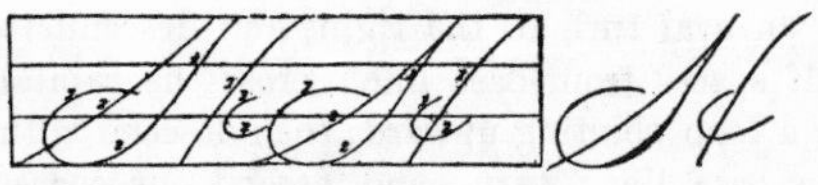

Begin on base line, and ascend with concave curve three spaces; unite angularly, and complete with capital stem; begin second part at top line, one space to the right of stem; descend to base line with a slight convex curve; finish as in *A.* PRINCIPLES 1 and 2.

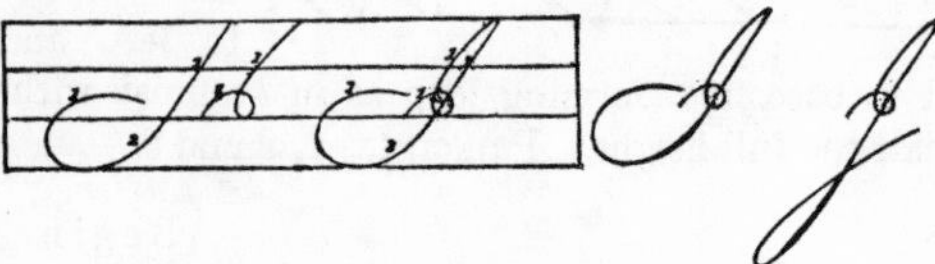

Begin *I* one space from base line, and ascend one-half space with convex curve; carry it well toward the right, and form a broad loop pointing downward one space from base line; ascend with convex curve to top line on main slant; make a short turn, and finish with capital stem, passing downward through the centre of loop. PRINCIPLES 1 and 2. *Capital J.*—Begin as in *I;* after passing through the loop, descend with a straight line on main slant two spaces below the base line; make a left turn, and ascend with a convex curve, crossing downward movement at base line and ending one space above. PRINCIPLES 1, 2 and 3.

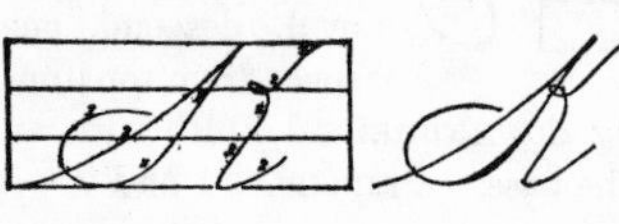

Form the first part as in *H;* begin second section at a point on top line one space to the right of stem, and descend with a compound curve one space from top line; form a loop across capital stem, pointing upward; descend with a straight line on main slant to base line, turning to the right; finish with concave curve. PRINCIPLES 1, 2 and 3.

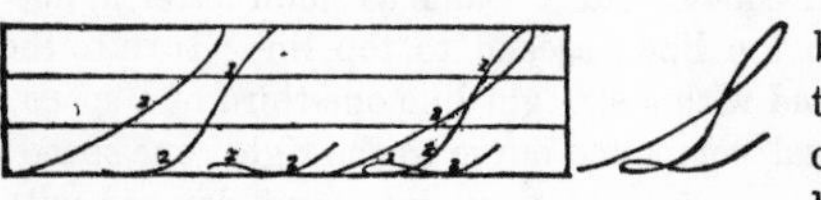

Ascend from base line with the concave curve to top line; turn short to the left, and descend with capital stem to base line, crossing the concave curve: one and one half spaces from base line; form horizontal loop touching base line to the right of crossing; finish with concave curve. PRINCIPLES 1 and 2.

Begin as in *A* with capital stem; begin second downward movement at top line connecting with top of capital stem; descend to base in a straight line, touching one space from the point on base line touched by oval of capital stem; from base line ascend with concave curve to top line to a point one space to the right of capital stem; unite angularly, and descend with concave curve to base line; finish with an oval one and one half spaces from base line. PRINCIPLES 1, 2 and 3.

Begin with the capital stem; unite at top with a downward straight line as in *A;* finish with a short turn, and concave curve, one and one half spaces from base line. PRINCIPLES 1, 2 and 3.

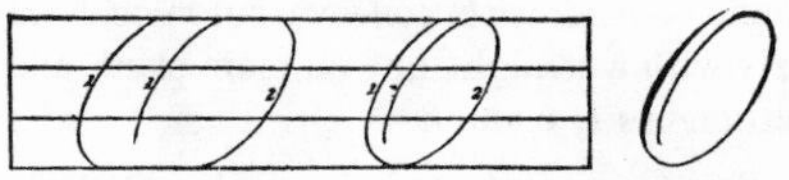

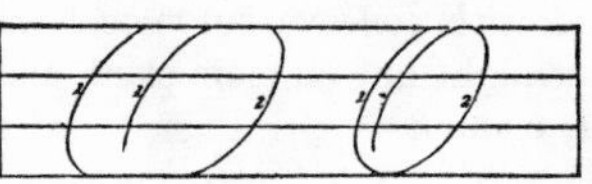

Same as oval or second principle of capital letters. Width: one half its height. Last downward movement should be parallel to the first, and finish at one half space above base line. PRINCIPLES 1 and 2.

Begin with capital stem, and finish in the same manner as *B,* as far as the crossing loop. PRINCIPLES 1 and 2.

Begin with inverted oval, or third principle of capital letters; the oval should be two spaces from top line; form a horizontal loop on base line, touching the base at the right of crossing; finish with concave curve. PRINCIPLES 1 and 2.

Form R with capital stem the same as *B,* as far as crossing loop; descend to base with a straight line, touching one space from that point touched by the turn in stem; make a turn to the right, and finish with concave curve. PRINCIPLES 1, 2 and 3.

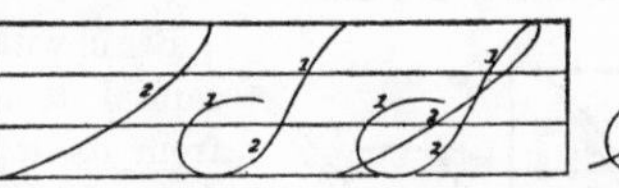

Begin at base line with the concave curve, and ascend to top line; make a turn as in *L,* and descend with convex curve: one and one half spaces from top line; cross upward curve, and finish with lower part of capital stem. PRINCIPLES 1 and 2.

[*The letter T will be found in diagram with letter F.*]

Begin with inverted oval (the third capital principle); oval should be two spaces from top line; make a turn on base line, and ascend with concave curve two and one half spaces; unite angularly, and descend with straight line to base; make a turn to the right, and finish with the concave curve. Width of *U* in centre one space. PRINCIPLES 1, 2 and 3.

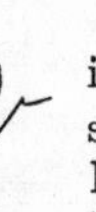

Form *V* with inverted oval: same as *U* to base line; make a turn to the right, ascend with a concave curve two spaces, and finish with a short horizontal concave curve to the right. PRINCIPLES 1 and 2.

Commence with inverted oval, and continue to base line; unite angularly, and ascend with concave curve nearly three spaces; unite angularly, and descend with straight line to base, one space from first section; unite angularly, and ascend with convex curve one and one half spaces. PRINCIPLES 1, 2 and 3.

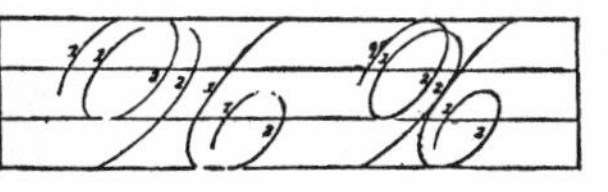

Commence with inverted oval, and continue to base line same as in *W;* begin second section at the top line, and with the convex curve descend, touching first section at the centre, or one and one half spaces above base line; make a broad turn to the right on base line, and finish with oval, which should be one and one half spaces in height. PRINCIPLES 1 and 2.

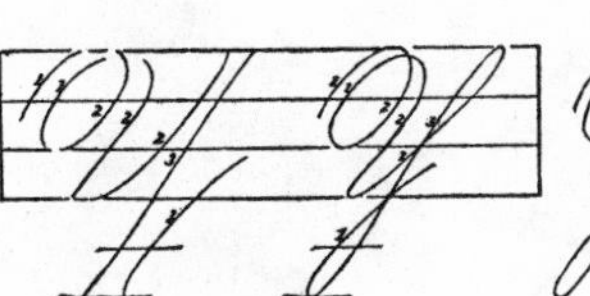

Commence, as in *U*, with the inverted oval; make a turn at base line, and ascend with the concave curve to top line; turn to the left as in *l*, and descend with a straight line two spaces below the base line; turn to the left, and with the convex curve ascend, crossing downward movement at base line; and finish same as in *J*. PRINCIPLES 1, 2 and 3.

Commence with inverted oval, and continue to base line, same as first section of *X;* form a loop pointing downward, and after crossing the downward movement, descend with concave curve two spaces below base line; and finish as in *Y*. PRINCIPLES 1 and 2.

# The Art of Flourishing.

FLOURISHING is the art of delineating figures by means of a rapid, whole-arm movement of the pen. This species of the penman's art has been practiced from time immemorial; not only as a distinctive feature of penmanship in the production of designs representing birds, animals, fishes, and fanciful designs, but also for the embellishment of writing and lettering. In former times, *flourishing* was of greater practical value and more highly esteemed than it is to-day.

Before the discovery of printing, when the books of the world were written and illuminated by the pen, and during the centuries immediately following the discovery of printing, the art of flourishing was extensively practiced. It was greatly prized, and considered a valuable accomplishment for professional teachers of artistic pen-work.

The exercise of the hand in flourishing tends to give ease and dexterity in the execution of practical writing. The plates connected with this subject present a series of exercises adapted for the practice of learners in this fascinating department of the penman's art.

*Plate I.* presents the Elementary Principles of Flourishing. These principles should be practiced until they are thoroughly mastered, and the hand begins to reproduce by the mere force of habit. When this is accomplished, the mastery of the more complicated designs presented upon other plates will be a comparatively easy task.

*Plate II.* contains the alphabet of flourished capitals and the standard practical alphabets of capitals and small letters.

*Plate III.* represents blackboard writing and flourishing.

*Plate IV.* consists of an elegant specimen of ladies' epistolary writing and an artistic design of flourishing; also a specimen of a gentleman's handwriting suitable for social correspondence.

*Plate V.* has a letter written in a practical hand, suitable for the practice of gentlemen engaged either in business or correspondence.

*Plate VI.* presents at the top of the page a highly artistic design, adapted to the use of penmen in the execution of specimen work, while beneath are six original and unique designs, suitable for cards or pages for albums.

[All of the above plates have been prepared expressly for this work by Mr. Daniel T. Ames, an experienced and well-known pen artist, and editor of the *Penman's Art Journal*, New York.]

POSITION IN FLOURISHING.

## POSITIONS IN FLOURISHING.

The first cut on this page represents the correct attitude of the body, as well as the position of the hand and pen, while in the act of flourishing.

It will be observed that the hand and pen are reversed, so as to impart the shade to the upward or outward stroke of the pen, instead of the downward or inward stroke, as in the direct or ordinary position, while writing.

Sit square at the desk, as close as is practicable without touching it, the left hand resting upon and holding the paper in the proper position, which must be always in harmony with the position of the hand and pen. The penholder is held between the thumb and first and forefingers, the thumb pressing upon the holder about two inches from the point of the pen. The first finger is bent at the centre joint, forming nearly a right angle, and is held considerably back of the second finger, which rests upon the under side of the holder, about midway between the thumb and the point of the pen. The third finger rests upon the fourth; the nail of the latter rests lightly upon the paper about one and a half inches from the pen, in a straight line from its point, parallel with the arm.

**Another position of the hands,** which is used and advocated by some penmen and authors, is: rest the arm upon the ball of the hand instead of the finger nail. [See the illustration.] The latter method is preferable in the execution of work requiring large sweeps of the pen, as in the former the fingers are liable to strike into the ink lines and mar the work. In the ornamentation of lettering and the execution of small designs—in short, most kinds of off-hand pen-work—the position described in the previous paragraph is the best.

The **movement** employed in all flourishing is that of the whole arm, which is obtained by raising the entire arm free from the table, resting the hand lightly upon the nail of the fourth finger, all motion of the arm being from the shoulder, which gives the greatest freedom and scope to the movements of the pen. This same movement is used in striking whole-arm capitals. What dancing is for imparting grace and ease of movement to the body, flourishing is to one's handwriting. Its practice is thus of double importance, as a discipline to the hand, and as a separate accomplishment.

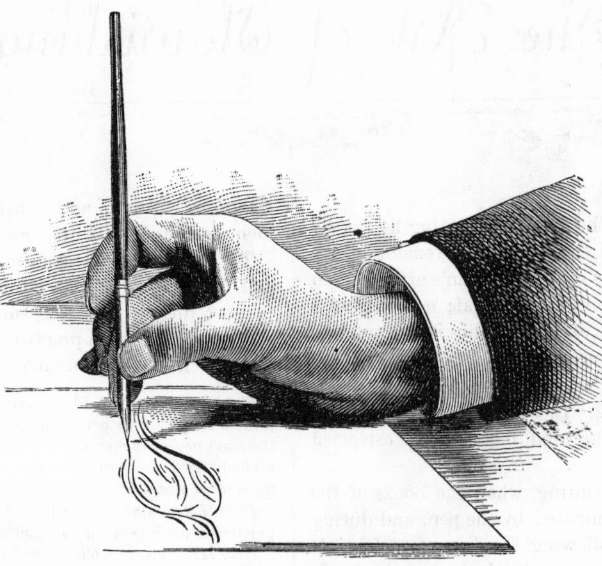

ANOTHER POSITION OF THE HAND.

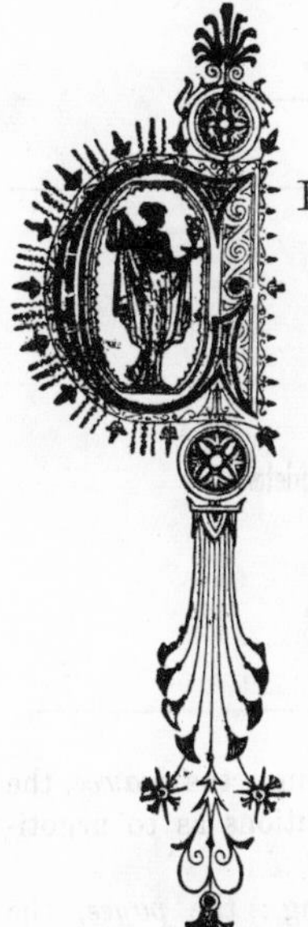

GENERAL BUSINESS FORMS are Commercial Documents, used for the everyday transactions of business, which custom has established, and which experience has pointed out as the best. Every person, though not actively engaged in business, needs to understand the meaning and force of such papers and should never affix his signature unless he fully comprehends them.

The majority of the forms in common use are often *printed in blank;* that is to say, those words which are supposed to be applicable to all the cases of a certain class, are *printed,* while spaces or *blanks* are left for the words and figures which should be inserted in order to make the document serve for a particular case. This practice of printing blank forms has of late years become very much extended. It not only saves time, but it promotes accuracy, legibility, uniformity, and readiness of reference to any portion of the matter.

Blank forms are often bound up into books or fastened together in pads. Then, as soon as one of them is filled up, it is torn out or detached. In books of blanks there is frequently a margin left on which to record the filling-in or particulars, opposite the torn-out document. This margin is called the "STUB."

Although printed forms are very convenient, our collection of models will enable any one to write out a document in proper form when no printed blanks are at hand, and also to furnish a suitable copy for the printer if he desires to have them printed.

We print in ordinary Roman type those parts of the forms which are applicable generally; the words which would be inserted by a person who was having a printed blank made for his own use are in SMALL CAPS, and the filling up, or words inserted in writing, are in *italics.*

## LETTER-HEADS.

It is a very convenient and useful practice to have a printed heading for business correspondence, giving the name of the writer of the letter, his business, if desired, the location from which he writes, and a space for the date. We mention this here because this same heading may be inserted with propriety in almost any of the forms whichwe shall give.

It is advisable to keep a copy of all business communications and documents which are sent off, and the best means of doing this is by a copying press which gives a fac-simile. If the heading or other printed matter be done in an aniline ink, it will copy together with the writing, making reference easier.

The following are specimens of business letter-headings, taken from actual examples:

Law Offices of Arnoux, Ritch & Woodford,

THOMAS G. RITCH,
STEWART L. WOODFORD,

HALEY FISKE,

22 PARK PLACE

*Please direct all letters by mail to*
P. O. Box 400.

New York, .................. 18......

---

LACKAWANNA IRON AND COAL CO.,

MANUFACTURERS OF STEEL AND IRON RAILS,

*NEW YORK OFFICE,*
52 Wall Street.

Scranton, Pa., .................. 18......

---

St. James Hotel,

COR. FIFTH AND WALNUT ST.,

AMERICAN AND EUROPEAN PLANS.

THOS. P. MILLER, Proprietor.

Opposite the New Southern Hotel.

St. Louis, Mo., .................. 18......

---

## MONETARY DOCUMENTS.

This division of our subject may be arranged in three heads:

1. The **Receipt,** an acknowledgment that money has been paid.

2. The **Order,** an authorization or command that money be paid.

3. The **Note,** a promise that money shall be paid.

Using the language of grammar, we might say that the RECEIPT is in the perfect indicative; the order is in the imperative mood; and the note is in the future indicative.

Each document of these three classes contains the following elements: the *date;* the *amount;* the *signature;* besides others peculiar to its class.

The receipt also contains these elements: "*from whom,*" and *consideration,* or "*for what.*"

The ORDER also contains the following: the *drawee,* the *payee,* and words expressing the conditions as to negotiability.

The NOTE also contains the following: the *payee,* the *words defining negotiability,* the *time of payment,* and the *place of payment.*

The DATE is usually at the beginning. It contains the place and the time, thus:

"Boston, Mass., Dec. 16, 1883."

It is proper always to write the name of the State or province, as well as of the town or city.

The AMOUNT should usually be written in the body of the document in words or letters, thus: — "Twenty-nine $\frac{65}{100}$ dollars," and repeated in figures at the top or bottom, thus: $29.65.

If the words do not fill all the space allotted to the amount, the blank remaining should be filled up with a dash or waving line to avoid alteration. Thus, if the amount be written without this precaution, for example:

"Seven dollars,"
there is nothing to prevent its being altered into
"Seven*teen* dollars,"
"Seven *hundred and ninety* dollars," or,
"Seven*teen thousand* dollars."

The proper way would have been:
"Seven ——————— dollars."

The SIGNATURE is usually at the bottom. It should be uniformly written. If you adopt "Geo. W. Smith" as your form of signature, do not capriciously change to "George W. Smith," "Geo. Washington Smith," "G. W. Smith," or "G. Washington Smith." Banks often reject commercial paper, refusing to pay it by reason of such discrepancies either in signature (on the face) or in indorsements (on the back).

It is almost superfluous to say that a signature ought to be legible, but many persons appear to think that the more confused and illegible is their style of writing their names, the more business-like it is. We do not agree with this opinion.

Provided the signature is genuine, it makes no difference by whom the filling in of the body of the document is done.

## THE RECEIPT.

We now take up the first class of business documents.

### 1. A BLANK RECEIPT.

New York, N. Y., ________________, 18____

Received of ________________________________

________________________________ Dollars,

________________________________________

$________ ________________

The first line contains the *date;* the second, "*from whom;*" the third, the *amount* in words; the fourth, the *consideration;* and the fifth the *signature*, and the amount in figures. We give the same form filled in as a

### 2. RECEIPT IN FULL OF ALL DEMANDS.

*No. 13.*

New York, N. Y., Feb. 16 1883.

Received of Lawrence Finn

Three hundred and seventy-five $\frac{25}{100}$ Dollars,

in full of all demands to date.

$375.25 Samuel Knapp.

Documents of this kind are often *numbered* in order, as in the above example.

We now give other examples of receipts. The same elements are present, but are not always placed in the same order.

### 3. RECEIPT ON ACCOUNT.

$300.$\frac{00}{00}$

CHICAGO, ILL., *Jan.* 14, 1883.

Received from *Henry G. Ely & Co. Three hundred* —— DOLLARS *on account.*

No. 229. FRANCIS W. HUNT.

### 4. RENT RECEIPT.

Received,

NEWBURGH, N. Y., *Feb.* 1, 1884,

from *Alexander McLean*——————————
*one hundred and five* ———Dollars, being *one* month's rent in advance for No. 122 *Main st.*, property of *James Nevins.*

$105.00 *Wm. Robinson*, Agent.

### 5. RECEIPT FOR INTEREST.

No. 223.

NEW YORK, *March* 27, 1883.

Received, from *Peter A. Welch, One hundred and fifty* Dollars, for Interest to *March* 1, on his Bond and Mortgage; receipt to be acknowledged also on the bond.

Principal, $5,000. *Alfred P. Burbank,*
Rate, 6 %. Time, 6 Months, — Days. Executor.
$150.00.

### 6. RECEIPT ON ACCOUNT OF A MORTGAGE.

No. 261.

NEW YORK, *Feb.* 28, 1884.

Received from *Nathaniel Johnson, One thousand*—— Dollars, on account of Principal of his Bond, and $32.$\frac{25}{100}$ interest on said payment, leaving $6,000 Principal unpaid; receipt to be acknowledged on said bond.

$1,032.$\frac{25}{100}$. *Albert Parmele.*

### 7. RECEIPT FOR INTEREST ON NOTE.

LITCHFIELD, CONN., *April* 19, 1883.

I have this day received from Jasper C. Goodman, Thirteen $\frac{50}{100}$ Dollars, in full of interest to date on his promissory note for Four hundred and fifty Dollars made in my favor on the 19th of October, 1880.

CHRISTOPHER SPERLING.

The forms of Receipts given thus far are entirely for money or cash, and they are in each case signed by the person who receives the payment. We will now explain other forms which vary in some respects from this and which will now be better understood.

1. Instead of money, the thing acknowledged as received may be some other valuable thing, as MERCHANDISE, DOCUMENTS, OR SERVICES.

2. The CASH paid on the one hand and the VALUABLE exchanged for it on the other may both be expressed in the receipt. In fact, this is the case in nearly all the receipts we have given. There is an exchange of values. Cash on the one side, and some other form of value on the other. But in all the cases given, it has been the party *receiving* the cash who signed the receipt. This may be reversed, and the document (then called a *statement*) bear the signature of the one who *pays* the money and *receives* the equivalent.

3. The receipt may appear on the face of a bill or statement of goods, usually at the bottom, making it a *receipted bill.*

### 8. RECEIPT FOR MERCHANDISE.

NEW YORK, March 19, 1883.

Received of *Fayette S. Giles, one Gold Watch, No.* 130,561 (*value* $475), on approval, to be returned or paid for in one week.

*Cornelius O'Reilly.*

### 9. RECEIPT FOR NOTE.

Received from Wilkins Micawber his note at Ninety days for $100, in settlement of bill of July 16, 1880.

PARK AND TILFORD.

New York, Feb. 17, 1881.

### 10.

NEW HAVEN, April 24, 1883.

Received from Peter Henderson Bill of Exchange on London for Fifteen Pounds, proceeds to be credited his account when collected.

JONES AND SMILEY.

### 11. STATEMENT OF PAYMENT.

PHILADELPHIA, June 16, 1884.

Messrs. Harper Brothers,
New York, N. Y.,

Gentlemen:
I herewith deliver to you Ten Dollars in New York Draft, for which you will please forward by mail ten copies of, etc.

PETER BROWNSTONE.

### 12. STATEMENT OF RENT PAID.
(Corresponding to Form 4.)

SIR:

NEWBURGH, N. Y., Feb. 1, 1883.

I enclose herewith my check for One hundred and five Dollars for one month's rent in advance of No. 122 Main st.

ALEXANDER MCLEAN.

To Wm. Robinson, Agent.

## 13. INVOICE.

New York, August 22, 1883

Mr. Andrew B. Rogers

**Bought of** ROGERS & PYATT,
Brokers and Commission Merchants,
23 LIBERTY STREET.

| | | | | | |
|---|---|---|---|---|---|
| 1 | No. 5 Coach Duster | $6 | 00 | | |
| | Less 40 % | 2 | 40 | | |
| | | 3 | 60 | | |
| | 10 % | | 36 | | |
| | | 3 | 24 | | |
| | 5 % | | 16 | $3 | 08 |

In the above model of a bill of goods, several points are worthy of attention. Instead of "Bought of Rogers and Pyatt," many employ the form (which, however, we do not consider an improvement) "To Rogers and Pyatt, Dr." Observe the successive discounts, 40 %, 10 %, and 5 %, which equal the single discount 48 6-10 %. As it stands, the bill is a statement from R. & P. of the delivery of the goods; when receipted, as below, it becomes also an acknowledgment of the payment therefor.

## 14. A RECEIPTED BILL OF GOODS.

NEW YORK, *August* 22, 1883.

*Mr. Andrew B. Rogers.*

Bought of ROGERS & PYATT,
BROKERS AND COMMISSION MERCHANTS,
23 LIBERTY STREET.

| | | | | | | |
|---|---|---|---|---|---|---|
| | 1 | *No.* 5 *Coach Duster* | $6 | 00 | | |
| | | *Less* 40 % | 2 | 40 | | |
| | | | 3 | 60 | | |
| | | *Less* 10 % | | 36 | | |
| | | | 3 | 24 | | |
| | | *Less* 5 % | | 16 | $3 | 08 |

Received Payment, Aug. 23, 1881.

ROGERS & PYATT.

Bills presented against a city government or against a large corporation, are usually made out on a form provided by the proper disbursing officers, and known as a VOUCHER. This is in a more complete form than the ordinary bill, and contains appropriate space for all the signatures which may be requisite in order to enforce proper control and responsibility. An example of such a voucher will be interesting and useful, as showing the methods of business when conducted on a great scale and with perfect system.

*No.*........ ..................................*Account*

**New York, Lake Erie & Western R. R. Co.,**

*To*.......................................*Dr.*

*Memo. No*........ *(Address,)* ..............................

| 188 | *For the following, as per Bill rendered, filed in Auditor's Office at New York, and certified by*...........*viz.:* | *Dolls.* | *Cts.* |
|---|---|---|---|
| | | | |
| | | | |
| | | | |
| | | | |
| | | | |
| | | | |
| | | | |
| | | | |
| | | | |
| | | | |
| | | | |
| | | | |
| | | | |
| | | | |
| | | | |

*I certify that the above account is correct; that the items therein specified were duly authorized and contracted for, and were received for the use and benefit of the New York, Lake Erie & Western Railroad Co.*

..............................*Gen'l Sup't.*

*I certify that the above account has been examined by me and found correct, and is hereby approved for payment.*

..............................*Auditor.*

*Countersigned,*..............................*Auditor of Disbursements.*

*Received,*............188 , *of the* TREASURER *of the* NEW YORK, LAKE ERIE & WESTERN R. R. Co...............................*Dollars, in full of the above account.* 100

$.............. ..............................

# The Order.

Under this general term we have included all documents in which a first party (the drawer) directs a second party (the drawee) to deliver value to a third (the payee). All modern business of importance is carried on by the aid of papers of this class, the advantage of which is that the risk and expenses of the transportation of valuables are saved. The principal documents classed under this head are CHECKS, DRAFTS, BILLS OF EXCHANGE, besides simple ORDERS payable in merchandise.

A **Check** is an order on a bank or banker.

A **Draft** is an order on a private individual, firm or corporation, or by one bank on another bank in another city of the same country. In the latter sense it is also called a "Domestic Bill of Exchange," or an "Inland Bill of Exchange," or a "Bank Draft."

A **Bill of Exchange**, or, as it is sometimes called, a Foreign Bill, is an order on a bank or person in another country.

As to **time of payment**, checks, drafts and bills of exchange may be "*on demand*," "*at sight*," "*at so many days' sight*," or "*at so many days from date.*"

"**On demand**" means literally on presentation.

In the other forms spoken of, the laws of the States usually allow three days' "grace;" that is, if a certain number of days or months is specified, three days more are to be allowed before the paper matures. This is, properly speaking, no grace or indulgence for the drawer, as interest is charged for the three days. Thus, "*one day's sight*" really means "*four days after date*," and "*sixty days after date*" means "*sixty-three days.*" It is perfectly proper, however, to insert the words "*without grace*," in which case the three days are not to be computed. Checks are usually "*on demand.*"

As to the **payee** of a check, draft or bill of exchange, his name may be inserted in various ways, which affect the negotiability of the paper.

1. Simply "To Bearer." In this case the drawee may pay to any one who presents the paper, and will be discharged by so doing.

2. "To JOHN DOE or Bearer." This is practically the same as the preceding, but indicates to whom the drawer intended that it should be paid.

3. "To JOHN DOE." This would, strictly speaking, be non-negotiable; that is, it should be paid to John Doe himself. This form is seldom used.

4. "To the order of JOHN DOE," or "To JOHN DOE or order." These two forms are practically the same. The amount will not be paid until JOHN DOE has written his name on the back, either as an acknowledgment that he himself receives it, or as authority for some one else to receive it. The various ways in which this may be done will be fully explained under the heading "ENDORSEMENTS."

Of the preceding forms, Nos. 1, 2 and 4 are called "*negotiable;*" that is, they may be transferred from one person to another by delivery alone (Nos. 1 and 2), or by delivery and endorsement (Nos. 2 and 4). The person into whose hands it has rightfully come is called the holder. The holder and endorsers of negotiable paper have certain rights, privileges and duties under the law merchant which will be hereafter explained.

**16. A CHECK.**

No. 14562 New York, Jan. 15, 1883

The Chemical National Bank,

Pay to the order of Jay Gould

Five hundred thousand Dollars.

Wm. H. Vanderbilt.

$500,000.00

For other information respecting checks see the article "BANKING."

## 17. A DRAFT.

(At sight, on private party.)

Indianapolis, Ind., Feb. 19, 1883

At sight, pay to the order of

John Kidd, Esq.,

Three hundred seventeen 53/100 Dollars.

and charge account of

Smith and Robinson.

To Solomon Rosenbaum,
119 Pearl St.,
Albany, N. Y.

The above method is often used for the collection of debts.

## 18. A BANK DRAFT.

$617.50. No.——

STATE TRUST COMPANY,
RUTLAND, Vt., *June* 29, 1883.

Pay to the order of..*David W. Rogers*,...............
*Six hundred and seventeen*.................... $\frac{50}{100}$ Dollars.
*Charles Clement*, President.
*John N. Woodfin*, Treasurer.

To the Continental National Bank,
New York, N. Y.

Bank drafts are usually paid on demand, like a check. They are often drawn in sets of two, the "original" and the "duplicate."

## 19. A BILL OF EXCHANGE.

BILLS OF EXCHANGE are generally drawn in sets of three, so that if the original is lost in transmission, one of the others may be paid. They are drawn in the money of the country where payable.

OFFICE OF BROWN BROTHERS & Co.,
59 WALL ST., NEW YORK, *March* 18, 1883.

£100. 0. 0.

Sixty days after sight of this, our First of Exchange (second and third of the same tenor and date unpaid), pay to the order of *Walter Lawrence, One hundred pounds*, for value received, and charge account of

BROWN BROTHERS & Co.

To Messrs. BROWN & SHIPLEY,
Founders' Court, Lothbury, London.

OFFICE OF BROWN BROTHERS & Co.,
59 WALL ST., NEW YORK, *March* 18, 1883.

£100 0. 0.

Sixty days after sight of this our Second of Exchange (first and third of the same tenor and date unpaid), pay tc the order of *Walter Lawrence, One hundred pounds*, for value received, and charge account of

BROWN BROTHERS & Co.

To Messrs. BROWN & SHIPLEY,
Founders' Court, Lothbury, London.

OFFICE OF BROWN BROTHERS & Co.,
59 WALL ST., NEW YORK, *March* 18, 1883.

£100 0. 0.

Sixty days after sight of this our Third of Exchange (first and second of the same tenor and date unpaid), pay to the order of *Walter Lawrence, One hundred pounds*, for value received, and charge account of

BROWN BROTHERS & Co.

To Messrs. BROWN & SHIPLEY,
Founders' Court, Lothbury. London

If Mr. Lawrence, of New York, desired to pay some one in London a sum of one hundred pounds, he would purchase a bill of exchange in three parts like the above form. He might send the "first" immediately, (making it over to his correspondent by endorsement) and send the "second" by the next steamer for safety, keeping the "third" till he heard from the first.

If he bought it on the date of the bill, he probably paid about $486 as the quotations were "$4.86 for 60 day bills and $4.89½ for demand." In such quotations the price of a pound sterling is given in dollars. In quotations of exchange on France or other countries where the franc is the money unit, this is reversed and the price of a dollar in francs is given. Thus on the day mentioned, the price of exchange in francs was "5.20⅝ for 60 day bills." That is, $1 would buy five francs twenty centimes and five-eighths, or in that proportion.

## ACCEPTANCE.

In the foregoing examples, we have used the expression "so many days after sight." These days begin to run from the date when the bill is *accepted*. The "acceptance" of a draft or bill of exchange is denoted by writing or stamping across the face the word "accepted" (with the date in case of time paper) and affixing the signature of the drawee. The acceptance is a promise to pay the amount named.

We give the forms of acceptance corresponding to the forms Nos. 17 and 19:

### 20. ACCEPTANCE OF DRAFT (No. 17.)

*Accepted payable*
*at the*
*Albany County Bank.*
*March 21, 1882.*
*Solomon Rosenbaum.*

### 21. ACCEPTANCE OF BILL OF EXCHANGE (No. 19.)

*Accepted,*
*March 30, 1882.*
*Brown & Shipley.*

The acceptance of a check or bank draft is termed *certification*. It will be more fully explained under "Banking."

## ENDORSEMENTS.

To *endorse*, or *indorse*, a check, draft, bill of exchange or promissory note, is to write one's name on the back in such a way as to transfer the title to another.

As has already been stated, a check or other order, if payable to bearer or to a certain person *or* bearer, does not require endorsement to be negotiable. Nevertheless the endorsement is frequently made. As it passes from hand to hand, a person receiving it, especially if unacquainted with the maker, will desire to have the endorsement of the person from whom he has received it, in order to have recourse to him in case the check should not be good.

But if payable "*to the order*" of a certain person or if to that person "*or order*," his endorsement is necessary. For instance, in form No. 16, the bank would not pay the check without the endorsement of Mr. GOULD. If in that endorsement he specified another person to whose order it should be paid, then this person's signature must also appear on the back, and so on.

The following are the principal varieties of endorsement:

### 1. SPECIAL ENDORSEMENT.

*Pay to the order of Russell Sage.*
*Jay Gould.*

Or

*Pay Russell Sage, or order.*
*Jay Gould.*

Mr. Sage's endorsement will now be required. If the words "to the order of" are on the face, they need not be repeated on the back, and the endorsement may read simply:

*Pay Russell Sage.*
***Jay Gould.***

Mr. Gould might send the check to Mr. Sage by mail in its present state without risk, because it would not be good to any one until Mr. Sage had written his name on the back. A check which is to be sent away should always be endorsed *specially* to the person entitled to the money, to avoid the risk of loss which there would be if the style that follows were adopted.

2. The check may be endorsed thus:

*Pay to bearer.*
***Jay Gould.***

This should be done only where it is desired to send by messenger to the bank and draw the money.

3. Instead of inserting the words "to bearer," it may be preferable to leave the name of the payee in blank, so that it may be afterwards inserted. Thus:

*Pay to ............................ or order.*
***Jay Gould.***

As far as Mr. Gould is concerned, it makes no difference whether he endorses in the above manner or to bearer; but the next holder may prefer to insert his own name in the blank, thus making the check valueless to any other person, and rendering it safe to keep it.

4. Practically the above form is seldom used as given, but the endorser merely writes his name:

*Jay Gould.*

Any holder may fill in any order for payment above a name thus written. This is called an ENDORSEMENT IN BLANK, and is more frequently used than any other. Simply writing the name on the back passes the title.

5. An endorsement may specify the consideration for which the paper passes. This form of endorsement serves as proof of payment in the absence of a receipt. Thus if the payee of a bank draft (form 18) desired to make a payment with it for certain securities purchased, he may endors it in this manner:

"*Pay to the order of*
*Fisk & Hatch, for*
$500 *N. Y. gold* 6s *of* 1901.
*David W. Rogers.*"

6. By inserting the words "without recourse" above his signature the endorser avoids liability for the payment of the paper.

Other directions as to endorsing will be given under "BANKING."

Endorsements should always be made *across* the back. The endorser should observe which side is to be the top when endorsing. To ascertain this, hold a check or similar paper before you with both hands, as if to read the face. What is now the left hand end of the check will be the top when turned over for endorsing.

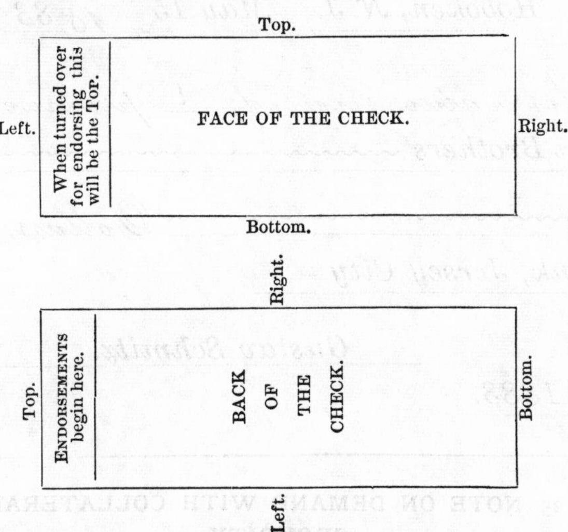


Each holder of a check, draft, or bill of exchange is responsible to all his successors for the amount if the paper is not paid on presentation. The last endorser looks to all the previous endorsers, to the maker and to the acceptor. In case of paper payable at a future time, certain formal notice is required in order to hold the endorsers, and this notice must be given without delay; but the acceptor and maker do not require such notice. This will be more fully explained under "Promissory Notes."

# Promissory Notes.

Instead of accepting a draft signed by a creditor, a person may issue his note, *promising* to pay such creditor. The person who signs, corresponding to the acceptor of the draft, is called the maker of the note.

It is usual to insert in promissory notes the words "*for value received,*" although this is not essential. The defense of want of consideration is good between the original parties only; if a third party, an innocent holder, has given value for a bill or note, he must be paid, even though the paper may have been originally given without consideration received, or obtained by fraud, or compulsion, or theft, either of which reasons would make it invalid as between the original parties.

A note frequently contains, besides the particulars already given, a statement of the *place where* payable. This is necessary, because it will have to be presented for payment. It is usual for business men to make their notes payable at the bank where their account is kept; then, on the day of maturity, that bank pays it from the funds on deposit just the same as a check. "*At a bank*" means on the face of a note "*through the agency of that bank,*" and gives authority to the bank to pay out so much of the maker's deposit. Sometimes a note which has matured is certified like a check instead of being paid.

All the three forms, the receipt, the order, and the note, are so similar in their nature that they are convertible one into the other.

A receipt for money entrusted to another to deliver in exchange therefor, is in effect an order.

A draft when accepted is equivalent to a note.

A check dated ahead is equivalent to a note payable at the bank.

The endorsements of checks, notes, and bills are in effect receipts for the money.

A note payable at a bank becomes, when due, a check.

Notes are sometimes drawn "*with interest.*" If no rate is specified, the legal rate in the State or country where payable is understood. But if the words "*with interest*" are not inserted, only the principal can be collected at maturity.

If a note (or time-draft) is presented for payment on the day of maturity and payment is refused, each endorser must be promptly notified, otherwise he is not liable. It is advisable in any important case to have this done by a notary public, who will, if necessary, protest. The protest is a formal declaration to all concerned, signed and sealed by the notary, stating the fact of non-payment and calling upon the parties liable to make it good. In paper drawn in another State or a foreign country, the protest should never be omitted. The fees of the notary for making the protest become part of the principal of the note and are payable with it.

## 22. A BLANK NOTE.

*No.* ________ ________, ________, *18* ____

________ *after date, for value received,* ____ *promise to pay to the order of* ________

________ *Dollars,*

*at* ________

*$* ________ *Due,* ________

The above form of note will serve for almost all cases. It is advisable to draw all notes to order, not to bearer.

## 23. 60 DAY NOTE PAYABLE AT BANK.

*No.* *622.* *Hoboken, N. J.*, *May 15*, *1883*

*Sixty days* *after date, for value received,* *I* *promise to pay to the order of* *Baumann Brothers*

*One hundred and twenty-five* *Dollars,*

*at* *the Hudson County National Bank, Jersey City*

*Gustav Schmitz.*

*$ 125—.* *Due,* *June 14-17, 1883.*

## 24. PAYABLE AT PLACE OF BUSINESS.

No. 96. PHILADELPHIA, *Jan.* 17, 1881.

*Three months* after date, for value received *I* promise to pay to the order of ________William Penn________

*Seven hundred* ________ dollars,

at *No.* 1,243 *Market St.*

BENJ. FRANKLIN.

$700 $\frac{00}{100}$. Due *Apl.* 17/20, 81.

## 25. NOTE ON DEMAND WITH COLLATERAL SECURITY.

Loans which are made between brokers and bankers are usually *on demand* and are secured by the deposit of valuable property or evidences of property. The usual name of such obligations is "call-loans."

Frequently, the only documentary evidence of the loan is a memorandum on the envelope containing the securities, but corporations generally require a note to be given.

*Loan No.* 2,066, *Folio* 324.

$100,000$\frac{00}{100}$ New York, *November* 5, 1884.

On demand, we promise to pay to the Union Dime Savings Institution of the City of New York, or order, *One hundred thousand* dollars, for value received, with interest at 3½ per cent. per annum, having deposited or pledged with said institution, as collateral security for the payment of this note, $100,000 *U. S.* 4 % *Consols of* 1907, coupon, and we hereby give to said institution, or its treasurer, full power to sell said collateral security, or any other collaterals that may have been substituted therefor, at the Board of Brokers in the City of New York, or at public or private sale, on the non-performance of the above promise, or at any time thereafter, without notice or demand, and without advertising the same or giving any notice of sale, applying the proceds of any such sale to payment of this note, accounting to us for the surplus, if any ; and in case of any deficiency, we promise to pay said institution the amount thereof, forthwith after such sale.

Vermilye & Co.

## 26. FIRM NOTE.

No.—— Boston, Mass, *Apl.* 13, 1885.

*One month* after date, *without grace, we* promise to pay to the order of *ourselves*——————
*One hundred and fifty*——————dollars, at *any Bank in Boston.*

Smith & Co.,

$150. Due *May* 13/85. 113 Temple Place.

## 27. DATE OF PAYMENT SPECIFICALLY NAMED.

This form has not been much used, but expresses the maturity clearly.

Amsterdam, N. Y., *Aug.* 17, 1855.

On the 17th of October, 1855 (without grace), I promise to pay to the order of Harlan P. Kline, for value received, *Five hundred*————dollars, at the Farmers' Bank.

Xenophon Haywood.

## 28. NOTE BY A MARRIED WOMAN.

One year after date, for value received, I promise to pay to the order of *Gerrit Smith*, at the People's Bank, *One thousand Dollars*, and I hereby declare that the debt secured hereby was created for the benefit of my separate estate which I hereby charge with the payment thereof.

$1,000 —. Elizabeth Cady Stanton.

Dated, New York, Feb. 29, 1864.

## 29. JOINT AND SEVERAL NOTE.

Chicago, Ill., *March* 18, 1873.

Ninety days after date we promise jointly and severally to pay to the order of Joseph Wright (6) Six hundred and fifty-three $^{25}/_{100}$ Dollars, (value received) at the First National Bank.

$653.$^{25}$ W. H. Nichols.
Saml. N. Rexford.

## 30. NOTE WITH SURETY.

$1500. St. Louis, Mo., *Aug.* 29, 1873.

Three months after date, for value received, I promise to pay to the order of H. B. Claflin & Co., of New York,—*Fifteen hundred*————Dollars at the Planter's National Bank.

Everett Leavenworth.

I hereby guarantee the payment of the above note.

J. Hopkins Witherspoon.

The same effect would have been attained by drawing the note to the order of Mr. Witherspoon and having him endorse it to Messrs. Claflin & Co.

## 31. JUDGMENT NOTE.

Poughkeepsie, N. Y., *Apl.* 16, 1885.

$833 $\frac{33}{100}$

On demand, for value received, I promise to pay to the order of Felix McIntyre,————Eight hundred and thirty-three $^{33}/_{100}$————Dollars. And I hereby confess judgment for said sum with interests and costs, a release of all errors, and a waiver of all rights of appeal and to the benefit of all laws exempting property from levy and sale.

Allan McDonald.

## 32. DUE BILL.

Schenectady, N. Y.,
*March* 19, 1884.

Due Garret Veeder, Fifty dollars, payable in goods at our store.

Clute and Barhydt.

The above and the following are merely acknowledgments of debt, not strictly speaking promissory notes.

## 33. AN "I O U."

Newark, N. J., *May* 31, 1876.

Roswell Van Buskirk, Esq.;
I O U $50.
Bartholomew Flanagan.

# Interest.

Interest is the value of the use of money or its equivalent.

How much must I pay to some one for lending me "One hundred Dollars" for one year ? If the reply is "Six Dollars," then the *use* of the hundred dollars is worth, or costs, six dollars ; six dollars is the *interest;* one hundred dollars is the *principal;* one year is the *time.*

What is in this case the rate ? It is, in the words of the statute, "Six dollars for the use or forbearance of one hundred dollars for one year, and in like proportion for a greater or less sum for a greater or less time." But in ordinary language is called briefly SIX PER CENT., and is written in any of the following ways :

Six per centum per annum ; Six per centum ; Six percent. ; Six one-hundredths ; 6%; 6 ℔ c.; .06 ; 6|100 ; 6 : 100 ; all of which expressions mean the same. The decimal .06 is the one to be used in arithmetical operations.

**Compound Interest** is interest on interest. That is, at certain periods, the interest is added to the principal and a new or increased principal is formed on which the next interest is computed. In simple interest, the principal remains the same ; in compound interest it constantly increases.

In books on arithmetic, the sum of the principal and interest is called the *amount;* but this term is not so used among business men.

## COMPUTATION OF INTEREST.

For a person who seldom has occasion to compute interest, the best method is the one which is simplest, most easily understood and remembered, and the least arbitrary. "Short cuts" and "lightning methods" are practicable only for those who are constantly working interest, and even they can do better work by means of a book of interest tables.

In order to solve any problem in interest, answer the following questions:

1. At the given rate and on the given principal, what is the interest for one year ?
2. If there are years in the required time, what is the interest for that number of years ?
3. If there are months in the time, what is the interest for *one* month, or $\frac{1}{12}$ of a year's interest ?
4. What is the interest for the given number of months ?
5. If there are days as well as months, what is one day's interest, or $\frac{1}{30}$ of a month's interest ?
6. If the time is expressed in days, regardless of months, what is the interest for *one* day, or $\frac{1}{365}$ of a year's interest ?
7. What is the interest for the given number of days ?

Now add together the interest for years, for months, and for days, and you have the entire interest.

To find the interest for one year : Multiply the number of dollars by the rate ; the result is cents.

What is the interest on $26,280 at 7 per cent. for one year ?

| | |
|---|---|
| | $26,280 |
| | .07 |
| Answer : | $1,839.60 |

What is it for 3 years ?

| | |
|---|---|
| | $1,839.60 |
| | 3 |
| Answer : | $5,518.80 |

What is it for one month ? $\frac{1}{12}$ of $1,839.60, or $153.30.
What is it for 5 months ? 5 times $153.30, or $766.50.
What is it for one day ? $\frac{1}{30}$ of $153.30, or $5.11.
What is it for 14 days ? 14 times $5.11, or $71.54.
What is it for 3 years, 5 months, 14 days ?

| | |
|---|---|
| 3 years, | $5,518.80 |
| 5 months, | 766.50 |
| 14 days, | 71.54 |
| Answer : | $6,356.84 |

If instead of "5 months and 14 days," the time were expressed in days only, then we must take so many 365ths of a year's interest. From January 1 to June 15 would be 5 months and 14 days, but reckoning by days only it would be 165 days.

Let us then change the form of our question, and ask, "What is the interest of $26,280 for 3 years and 165 days ?"

If we disregard months, a day's interest is $\frac{1}{365}$th as much as a year's interest. We, therefore, divide $1,839.60 by 365 and get exactly $5.04 for a day's interest, instead of $5.11 as before. The answer would then be:

| | |
|---|---|
| 3 years, | $5,518.80 |
| 165 days, | 831.60 |
| Answer : | $6,350.40 |

In this case the borrower would profit $6.44 by computing interest on days only, instead of months and days. At some periods of the year he would lose by so doing.

We will explain one of the brief methods already allude to, which is frequently useful, especially at 6 per cent.

As the interest of $1 for one year is six cents, the interest for two months, or $\frac{1}{6}$ of a year, is one cent. On this principle, we obtain two months' interest at 6 per cent. by drawing a line between the tens and the hundreds of dollars.

What is two months' interest on $600 ? 6|00, or $6.
On $7,300 ? 73|00, or $73.
On $69 ? |69, or 69c.
On $6,375 ? 63|75, or $63.75.

Now, having the interest for two months (or, as we may say for convenience, 60 days), it may be found for any other number of days by dividing, multiplying and adding. Practice will give skill in this.

What is the interest on $720 for 1 month, 13 days, at 6 per cent. ?

| | | |
|---|---|---|
| We first cut off two places for two months. | 7\|20 | 2 mo. |
| $\frac{1}{2}$ as much | 3\|60 | 1 mo. |
| $\frac{1}{3}$ of that | 1\|20 | 10 days. |
| $\frac{1}{5}$ of that | \|24 | 2 days. |
| $\frac{1}{2}$ of that | \|12 | 1 day. |
| Answer : | $5.16 | |

At 4 per cent. the figures cut off would be for 3 months, or 90 days (at 30 days to the month).

What is the interest on $720 for 1 month, 13 days, at 4 per cent. ?

| | | |
|---|---|---|
| Operation : | 7\|20 | 3 mos. |
| | 2\|40 | 1 mo. |
| $\frac{1}{10}$ of 7.20 | \|72 | 9 days. |
| $\frac{1}{3}$ of .72 | \|24 | 3 days. |
| $\frac{1}{3}$ of .24 | \|08 | 1 day. |
| Answer : | 3.44 | |

At 5 per cent. the time obtained by cutting off is 72 days ; at 7 per ent. (approximately), 52 days ; at 8 per cent., 45 days ; at 9 per cent., 40 days ; at 3 per cent., 120 days (4 months); at 2½ per cent., 144 days ; at 4½ per cent., 80 days.

THE business of banking consists in dealing in money and credit.

The following are some of the branches of this business: DEPOSITS, CIRCULATION, REMITTANCE, COLLECTION, DISCOUNTS, LOANS, EXCHANGE, INVESTMENT, AGENCY.

Banks are frequently classified as belonging to or practising one of these branches of the business, and are termed accordingly Banks of Deposit, Banks of Discount, Savings Banks, etc. Most banks unite two or more of these branches, being Banks of Circulation and Discount, Banks of Deposit and of Remittance, etc.

## DEPOSITS.

The receiving of DEPOSITS is the most universal and important of the functions of a bank. The person entrusting money to the care of a bank is called the Depositor. He has the advantage of the safekeeping of his cash and generally the further convenience of being able to make payments from it whenever he desires and in whatever sums he desires, transferring his title to any portion of it by means of a *check*. As other persons who keep accounts at the same or other banks will make their payments to him in similar checks, he can also deposit these the same as so much money and the bank will collect them for him. Thus vast amounts of payments are effected daily without any handling of money.

This system of payment by checks which are again deposited as cash, is more widespread in the United States and Canada than in any other part of the world. On the continent of Europe it is very little practised. The holder of a check there presents it to the bank and receives the money. In America he deposits it in his own bank and receives credit for it. In this way alone can the greatest saving of time and risk be effected.

A regular depositor, or dealer, as he is frequently called, is regarded as entitled to accommodation and preference in the various other branches of the business, such as discounts, loans, exchange and agency.

The safe keeping and convenience of his check-account, with the other favors he receives, are generally sufficient compensation for the use of the depositor's money. But in exceptional cases, where a large balance is kept, a moderate rate of interest is allowed by the bank—less of course than what it can obtain in turn.

When a person not a regular dealer wishes to make a single deposit—to be withdrawn in the same amount, he receives a *certificate of deposit*. This is issued by the bank itself and is payable either on demand or at a certain time, and may bear interest. See example page 56.

## CIRCULATION.

CIRCULATION is the issue by a bank of its promises to pay to bearer on demand. These ordinarily circulate from hand to hand as a substitute for money, and are commonly called bank notes or bank bills. In the United States, only the National Banks issue circulation, as there is a tax of ten per cent. on any other kind of circulating notes.

Its redemption is guaranteed by the national government, which holds, as security, bonds to a larger amount, belonging to the banks, and also holds a five per cent. fund for immediate redemption.

The national treasury itself performs the office of a bank of circulation in issuing its notes, commonly called "greenbacks." Opinions vary as to the expediency of the government's exercising this function; some contending that the government alone should have the power of issuing paper currency, and others holding that it ought not to engage in any kind of banking-business at all; still others believe that for every paper dollar in circulation, the government should hold a dollar of coin in the treasury.

## REMITTANCE.

For the purpose of enabling persons to send money to distant points, the bank keeps money on deposit at the principal centres. It charges the person who desires to remit, a small amount for its services and sells him its *draft* (Business

## A CERTIFICATE OF DEPOSIT.

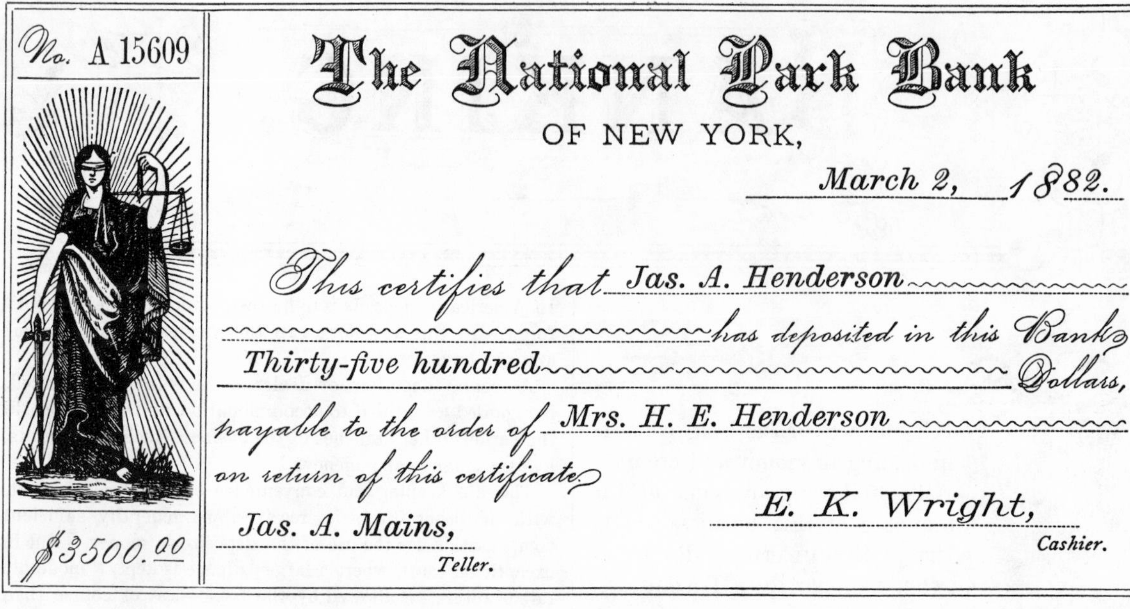

No. A 15609

The National Park Bank
OF NEW YORK,

March 2, 1882.

This certifies that Jas. A. Henderson has deposited in this Bank Thirty-five hundred Dollars, payable to the order of Mrs. H. E. Henderson on return of this certificate

$3500.00

Jas. A. Mains, Teller.

E. K. Wright, Cashier.

Forms, No. 18) on that place. Much expense and risk in the transportation of funds is thus saved. The Money Order Department of the Post Office serves as a Bank of Remittance.

**Collection** is the reverse of remittance. The bank receives drafts or checks payable at distant points, and through its correspondents these are finally presented at the places of payment. Notes, time-drafts and bills of exchange, whether locally payable or elsewhere, are also left with the bank for collection previous to maturity. The bank takes care of them and sees that they are duly presented, and, if necessary, protested, unless paid. When paid, it passes over the amount to the dealer, usually by giving him credit on his deposit account.

**Discount** is paying to a person the proceeds of a note or other paper not yet due, deducting therefrom the interest till maturity. As the sum received is not the full amount of the paper, the borrower really pays more than the nominal rate of interest.

For example, if a note for $1000 due 3 months hence is discounted at 6 per cent., the operation is as follows:

| | |
|---|---|
| From the face.................... | $1,000 00 |
| subtract the discount, being interest for 3 months at 6 per cent.................. | 15 00 |
| and the remainder is the proceeds or amount received by borrower.......... | 985 00 |

At the end of three months he has to repay $1,000, or $985 and $15 interest. But $15 for three months on $985 is at the rate of about $6\frac{1}{11}$ (six and one-eleventh) per cent. per annum.

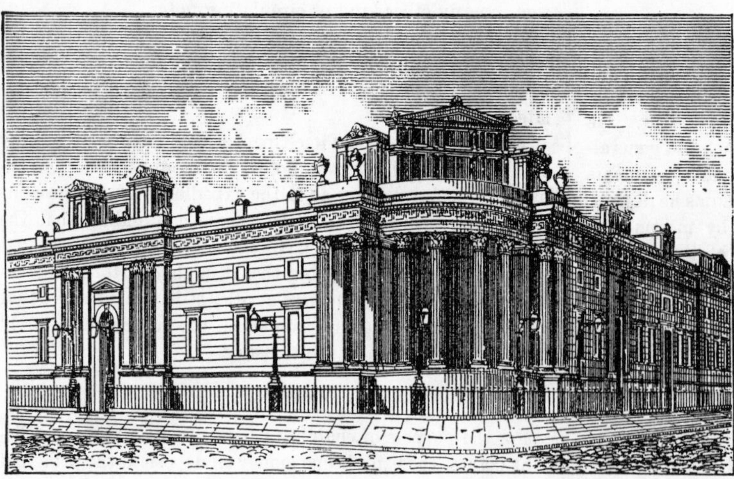

BANK OF ENGLAND.

The security for a discounted bill lies in the solvency of the parties to it. Discounts are made by some banks to their dealers only; by all they are granted most readily to dealers, although it is often required that there be one or more good endorsers.

**Loans.** The principal distinction between a discount and a LOAN is that in the former the bank becomes the owner of a note or bill, while in a loan valuable property of some kind, or the evidence of such property, is pledged to the bank. A form of note for demand loans is given in the article "Commercial Transactions," Form 25.

**Exchange.** DOMESTIC or INLAND EXCHANGE is the operation described under "Remittances." Foreign Exchange involves also the reduction of the money of one country to that of another.

**Investments.** Money not otherwise employed is used in the purchase of various securities, both for the income to be derived from them and for the profit to be realized in their sale. Savings banks have for their chief object the collective investment of small sums.

**Agency.** Many banks act as the financial agents of their customers in various ways other than those stated above, such as purchasing or selling securities, for their account.

**Capital.** A bank has (with the exception of savings banks) a CAPITAL, which it is usually required to keep invested in some stable form of security, as a guarantee to those who have dealings with it. That is, the values which the bank handles belong partly to its stockholders (the capital) and partly to others (depositors, note-holders, certificate-holders.)

## BANK OFFICERS AND EMPLOYEES.

The stockholders of an incorporated bank elect a BOARD OF DIRECTORS, who manage its affairs. These elect a President, one or more Vice-Presidents, and a Cashier. The Cashier is the Executive officer of the bank and controls its interior management. He is assisted by a number of employees. The principal ones are the PAYING TELLER and the RECEIVING TELLER, who are at the head of the DEBIT and CREDIT DEPARTMENTS; the NOTE TELLER; the DISCOUNT CLERKS; the COLLECTION CLERKS; the BOOK-KEEPERS, each in charge of certain ledgers; ASSISTANT TELLERS; ASSISTANT BOOK-KEEPERS; CHECK-CLERKS; MESSENGERS or "RUNNERS." Of course the number of these employees and the division of their duties, vary according to the size of the bank. In England "Cashier" means what we term "Teller," while "Teller" is applied to the Messengers, and "Chief Cashier," or "Manager," to the Cashier.

## HOW TO DRAW AND ENDORSE A CHECK.

We give an engraved specimen of a check, filled, certified, and endorsed, to show the proper way of doing it. The following observations should be carefully noted:

1. The first endorsement should correspond exactly with the face. If the face reads "J. F. Wilkins" and your usual signature is "Joseph F. P. Wilkins," then endorse both ways, thus

{ J. F. Wilkins.
{ Joseph F. P. Wilkins.

2. Do not endorse the check wrong side up. Notice the example and also the rules in "Commercial Transactions."
3. Write across the paper, not lengthwise.
4. Begin near the top so that those coming after you may have room.
5. Do not send away a check endorsed in blank, but make it payable to the person to whom you send it. Then, if lost, it cannot be paid to any one else.
6. When you deposit a check it is well to write or stamp above your endorsement, "For Deposit" or "For Deposit only," or "For Deposit in the —— Bank." In the example the Tradesmen's National Bank has stamped its clearing-house number "10," as an acknowledgment that the check passed through its hands.

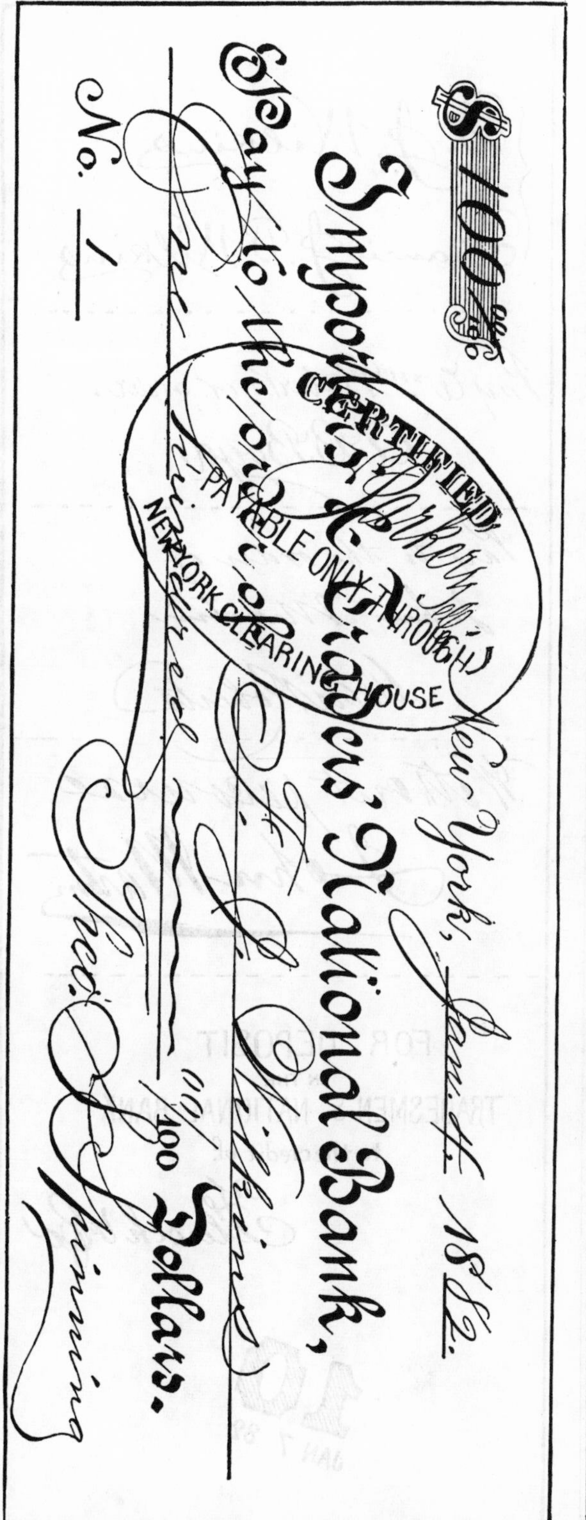

$100 00/100 New York, Jan. 4, 1882.

Importers' & Traders' National Bank,

Pay to the order of J. F. Wilkins

One hundred 00/100 Dollars.

No. 1 Theo. L. Spinning

CERTIFIED
Parker, Jr.
PAYABLE ONLY THROUGH
NEW YORK CLEARING HOUSE

F. J. Wilkins

Francis J. P. Wilkins

Pay Wm Roberts or order.

A. B. Boyd,

Pay to the order of

John Martin

Wm Roberts

Without recourse

John Martin

FOR DEPOSIT
IN THE
TRADESMEN'S NATIONAL BANK
to the credit of

Fleisch & Co

## CERTIFICATION.

A bank is said to "certify" a check, when it writes on the face of it an acknowledgment that the check is good and binds itself to pay it. This is usually done by the paying teller. When a check is certified, it is immediately charged against the dealer's account as paid, for the bank has assumed its payment. Certified checks will often be accepted where an uncertified one would not. This practice of certification is comparatively recent. Where it is unknown, as in Boston, the use of check accounts is less extended, and bank notes and certificates of deposit are more employed. [The engraved example of a check shows the certification.]

## CROSSED CHECKS.

In England when it is desired to make a check payable only through a certain bank or banker, this is done by writ-

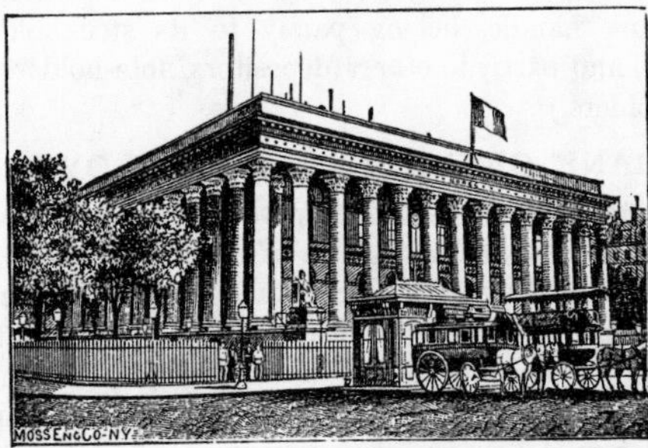


PARIS BOURSE.

ing the name of the latter *across* the face, between two parallel lines. For example, suppose John Smith has his account at the London and Westminster Bank, and James Jones has his with Messrs. Brown and Shipley. Smith wishes to send a check to Jones, and to prevent the check, if lost, from being cashed by the finder; he *crosses* it, that is writes across the face "Brown & Shipley," knowing them to be Mr. Jones's bankers. Thus :

London and | BROWN & SHIPLEY. | Westminster Bank. London, March 16, 1881.
Pay to James | | Jones or order, the sum of
One hundred | | and Fifty Pounds.
£150. 0. 0. | | John Smith.

Now the check being "crossed" would not be cashed by the London and Westminster Bank unless presented by Brown and Shipley. But if Smith, instead of inserting a name, merely draws the two lines and writes "—— & Co.," it may be paid through any banker, but not over the counter.

[The certified check shown on page 57 is equivalent to a crossed check, as the bank has marked it "payable through the New York Clearing-house only."]

## HOW TO OPEN AN ACCOUNT

In order to open an account with a bank, it is necessary to be introduced to its officers as a proper person to deal with. The Cashier or Assistant Cashier will request you to write your name in the Signature book. Be careful to do this in the style which you propose to adopt permanently, and do not vary your signature. You will then be given a PASS BOOK, a CHECK-BOOK, and a number of blank DEPOSIT SLIPS. Of course you will have brought a deposit with you, and will proceed to make use of your blanks. The deposit slips will read as follows:

### DEPOSITED BY

in the Importers' and Traders' National Bank,

New York, ——————, 18—.

| | | | |
|---|---|---|---|
| Gold. | | | |
| Bills. | | | |
| Checks. | | | |

Write your name and the date in the proper blanks at the head. Then enter in the MONEY COLUMNS the AMOUNTS you propose to deposit, and add them up. Do not omit to *endorse* the checks if you have any. The bank will not take them otherwise, even if payable to bearer.

Having made out your deposit slip, place it upon the bills and checks in the pass-book, and present this at the receiving teller's desk, If others are there, await your turn in line. The teller, having compared your deposit slip with the cash, will enter the total on the left hand page of the pass-book. Your account is now fairly opened. The book-keeper will in due course write your name at the head of the ledger-page where your account will be kept. Thus there will be *three* copies of your account kept: one in the BANK LEDGER for their information, one in your CHECK-BOOK for your own purposes; and one in the PASS-BOOK as a kind of arbiter between you.

Every DEPOSIT you make must be entered also in your check-book. The left hand page (when the book is open) of the stub or margin is intended for that purpose. The right hand page is for the description of the checks drawn. Both sides should be kept footed; then the excess of the left hand total over the right always gives the balance in bank. We give an example of the way the stubs should look after the checks of a page have been detached.

### STUB OF CHECK-BOOK.

| | | | |
|---|---|---|---|
| 1882.<br>Jan. 3, Deposit.<br>Coin ........$ 50 00<br>Bills ........ 100 00<br>Check.<br>Smith....... 30 00<br>Jones....... 18 75<br>Brown...... 833 33 | $1,032 08 | No. 1.<br>Jan. 4, 1882.<br>Amount............<br>Order of<br>F. J. Wilkins. | $ 100 00 |
| Jan. 6. Deposit.<br>Bills. | 500 00 | No. 2.<br>Jan. 5, 1882.<br>Amount............<br>Order of<br>L. P. Morton. | 62 50 |
| Jan. 7. Deposit.<br>Check, R. Dix. | 75 99 | | |
| $ 1,608 07<br>491 65<br>1,116 42 | | No. 3.<br>Jan. 8, 1882.<br>Amount...... .....<br>Order of<br>Alex. T. Stewart & Co | 329 15 |
| | $1,608 07 | | $ 491 65 |

The totals should be carried forward to the top of the next pages, thus:

| | | | | | |
|---|---|---|---|---|---|
| Forward, etc. | 1,608 | 07 | Forward, etc. | 491 | 65 |

This is preferable to subtracting each check, or the total of each page, from the previous balance, as some do, which makes the tracing of an error very difficult.

In drawing a check, insert all the particulars in the stub before doing it in the body of the check. It is a good plan to enter also on the stub the *purpose* for which the check is drawn.

At suitable intervals, the bank will ask you to leave your pass-book to be balanced. The left hand page has been gradually filling up with your deposits, but the other page, which is to contain the amounts of your checks, is blank. When the pass-book is handed in to be balanced or written up, the book-keeper takes the checks which have been paid and cancelled since the last balance, and writes their amounts only on the right hand page. He returns you the book with the balance to your credit brought down, and gives you at the same time the checks which you have drawn, and which have been presented, paid, and cancelled by cutting.

You must now balance your own account on the stub of your check book, and see if there is any difference. If the balances agree, and your checks are all returned, your book is correct. But if there is a difference, you must find what causes it. First, compare your left hand total with the total of the left hand page of the pass-book. These should agree at all events. If not, either some deposit, or some addition, must be incorrect. By comparing and examining, you will discover the error. Next, compare the checks with your stubs, and make a note of any which are not returned. There must be an allowance made for those checks which have been drawn, but have not yet been presented for payment, known as the "outs," or "outstanding checks." This allowance should be made on both sides of the check-book as a guide for the next balance, when some of these checks will probably have come in. Suppose your actual balance as shown by your stub is $492.47, but on the books of the bank you appear to have $739.82, because there are three checks outstanding amounting to $247.35. Then this amount of $247.35 should be added to both sides of your stub, thus:

| | | | | |
|---|---|---|---|---|
| Balance brought down; | | $492.47 | | |
| Checks outstanding: | | | | |
| No. 7, | 100.00 | | | |
| " 12, | 59.80 | | | |
| " 14, | 87.55 | 247.35 | Checks outstanding as opposite | 247.35 |
| Balance per pass-book, | | 739.82 | | |

Then, as you recommence with the same balance in the check-book as in the pass-book, your footing will also agree with that of the pass-book on the next occasion of balancing.

You should examine the checks as soon after they are returned from the bank as possible, that any errors may be promptly rectified.

Be careful in filling out your checks not to make it easy, by leaving blanks, for dishonest persons to increase the amount, which is called "raising." Do not give your checks to strangers, who may wish to use them for purposes of fraud.

Make your deposits as early in the day as possible, in order to save the time of the clerks.

Treat the officials of the bank with consideration and courtesy and you will meet with similar treatment.

## BANKING CONCERNS.

According to their mode of organization, banking concerns are classified as PRIVATE BANKS, INCORPORATED BANKS, (State and National), TRUST COMPANIES and SAVINGS INSTITUTIONS.

A BANKER, INDIVIDUAL BANKER, OR PRIVATE BANKER, is one who engages with his private capital in the banking business or some branch of it. Frequently it is a firm of bankers who carry on the business. In England the word "banker" is applied in many phrases to incorporated banks. In America you are asked, "Have you a bank account?"—in England the question is, "Do you keep a banker?" The Englishman says "at my banker's," where the American would say "at the bank where I deal."

**Incorporated Banks** are associations formed under the laws of a country for the purpose of carrying on this business. In England they are called JOINT-STOCK BANKS. The CAPITAL OR STOCK of these banks is always fixed at a certain sum and divided into a certain number of shares. The owner of a share has the right to sell it if he likes. Thus the list of proprietors varies from time to time.

For a long time the only banks in the United States were chartered by the several States, and the requirements varied in different States. These banks were permitted to issue circulation, and consequently a great many different kinds of bank bills were in use as paper money. The tax of ten per cent., already spoken of, drove these bills out of circulation, so that now only three kinds of paper money are in general circulation. 1. NATIONAL BANK NOTES; 2. LEGAL TENDERS OR GREENBACKS, issued and redeemed by the U. S. Treasury; 3. SILVER CERTIFICATES, representing silver coin actually in the Treasury.

**National Banks** are chartered by the United States, under laws first passed in 1864. Not less than five persons may organize a new bank. They must subscribe and pay in cash not less than $50,000 capital. In places of more than 6,000 inhabitants it is $100,000. Stockholders are responsible for twice the amount of their shares. Thus, suppose a bank through misfortune or fraud meets with losses which are great enough to use up all the surplus or accumulated earnings; then the stockholders may lose all the money they have put into the stock, for the depositors must first be paid; finally, if this is not enough, the stockholder who had one share of one hundred dollars must pay in one hundred dollars more.

STATE and NATIONAL BANKS are also known as BUSINESS BANKS, COMMERCIAL BANKS, or BANKS proper. They transact what is called a general banking business, which includes the branches of Deposits, Remittance, Collection, Exchange, Discounts, and Loans. Private Bankers engage in more or less of the same branches. They also act as agents for the purchase and sale of securities on commission. This, however, is more properly the function of a broker, especially where the greater part of the purchase money is advanced by him.

**Trust Companies** act as BANKS OF DEPOSIT, and as financial agents, besides their proper office of executing trusts.

**Saving Institutions** or **Savings Banks** differ widely from Commercial Banks. Under the United States laws, however, they are classed as banks. A SAVINGS BANK is properly a Bank of Investment only. Its function is to receive small amounts, keep them in safety, invest so much as is prudent, and be ready to repay them on proper notice with a just share of the profits. Small sums, which could not be invested separately, thus become a mighty force when aggregated. Some Savings Banks are organized without capital—that is, they have no money except that paid them by depositors and the accumulated earnings of the same. In some States they may be organized also with a capital stock. In this case, the stockholders being responsible for losses, receive a higher rate of income in the way of dividends, than that paid as interest to depositors. In the Eastern States and New York there are no savings banks except the former or "mutual" class. In other States both kinds are permitted to exist, and the Stock Savings Banks are even permitted to transact a "general banking business," being Savings Banks in little more than name.

The **"Cheque-Bank"** is an institution in London which carries on its business in a somewhat peculiar manner. Its method is to receive deposits and to issue its blank cheques to the depositor, each guaranteed as good *up to* a certain amount, which amounts are held by the banks. Thus, a person may deposit £100 and receive a book of 5 cheques, each marked "good for £20 or under," or 20 cheques of £5 each, or 50 cheques of £2 each. Suppose the latter case. The limit, £2, is perforated in each cheque, and the bank guarantees the payment of £2 or under, according as each is filled out. If you fill one up for £1 15s., sign it and pay it away, then at your next settlement the bank will allow you 5s. for the remainder. These "Cheque-bank cheques" are readily received where the check of a private person would be refused, because it is known that the money must have been deposited. Thus they take the place of a certificate of deposit, and also of a certified check. They are equivalent to saying: "This certifies that —— —— has deposited in this bank —— pounds, *the whole or any part of which is* payable to his order on the return of this certificate.

### HISTORICAL, STATISTICAL AND GENERAL.

The Bank of Venice was founded in 1171.
The Bank of Amsterdam was founded in 1609.
The Bank of Hamburg was founded in 1619.
The Bank of England in 1693.
The first Bank of the United States in 1791.
The Bank of France in 1803.
The National Banking system of the United States in 1863.
The London Clearing-house in 1775.
The New York Clearing-house in 1853.
Number of incorporated Banks in the United States, over 3,000.
Number of Clearing-houses in the world 32, of which 26 are in the United States.

Total clearings in one year in the world, ninety-seven thousand millions of dollars, $97,000,000,000; of which $49,000,000,000 were in the New York Clearing-house.

Greatest amount cleared in one day (at the London Clearing-house), $309,000,000.

The first bankers in England were goldsmiths.

The first bankers in Italy were money-changers, who had benches in the market-place. *Bank* is derived from the Italian word *banco*, a bench.

## THE CLEARING-HOUSE.

This is an association of banks in one town, which hold regular meetings for the purpose of exchanging the checks held by each bank, and payable by the others.

If checks were paid "over the counter" in money only, no such arrangement would be needed. But this kind of banking results in comparatively little saving of labor, and is unsuited to large transactions. The business man in America who receives a check seldom thinks of sending it to the bank on which it is drawn in order to receive the money. If he is doubtful of its goodness, he merely has it "certified." But he deposits it in his own bank as cash. Consequently, every bank has, at the close of the day, many checks on other banks. Instead of sending to these banks separately, the bank assorts the checks, and places them in envelopes marked with the names of the banks, and with the total amount. A list of the total contents of the envelopes is made up. A clerk and a messenger take all the envelopes and the list to the clearing-house.

Each clerk, after reporting the amount brought, takes his seat at a desk; the messengers stand outside of the desks. Each messenger passes in succession to the clerk of each other bank, and gives him the proper envelope, getting his receipt on the list. The clerks enter the same amounts on another list.

Thus, let us suppose there are four banks, which we will call A, B, C, and D. The following are the lists of envelopes which they bring with them.

| A. | | B. | | C. | | D. | |
|---|---|---|---|---|---|---|---|
| On B, | $569.18 | on A, | $262.75 | on A, | $479.42 | on A, | $279.48 |
| On C, | 322.13 | on C, | 629.43 | on B, | 818.00 | on B, | 979.16 |
| On D, | 272.75 | on D, | 937.82 | on D, | 678.99 | on C, | 1,542.72 |
| | 1,164.06 | | 1,830.00 | | 1,976.41 | | 2,801.36 |

The clearing-house therefore receives in all:

| | |
|---|---|
| From A, | $1,164.06 |
| From B, | 1,830.00 |
| From C, | 1,976.41 |
| From D, | 2,801.36 |
| | $7,771.83 |

Now, the same envelopes will be carried away which have been brought in. Therefore, when the envelopes have been re-distributed so that each bank has the checks against itself instead of those against others, though each bank has a different amount, the aggregate will be the same. Thus, if we arrange the above amounts, according to banks drawn on, we have the following lists of checks to be taken out:

| Against A. | | Against B. | | Against C. | | Against D. | |
|---|---|---|---|---|---|---|---|
| From B. | $262.75 | From A. | $569.18 | From A. | $322.13 | From A. | $272.75 |
| " C. | 479.42 | " C. | 818.00 | " B. | 629.43 | " B. | 937.82 |
| " D. | 279.48 | " D. | 979.16 | " D. | 1,542.72 | " C. | 678.99 |
| | $1,021.65 | | $2,366.34 | | $2,494.28 | | $1,889.56 |

TOTALS.

| | |
|---|---|
| Against A. | $ 1,021.65 |
| " B. | 2,366.34 |
| " C. | 2,494.28 |
| " D. | 1,889.56 |
| | $ 7,771.83 |

As the same result, $7,771.83 is obtained in both cases, the "proof is made." Then comes the question of settlement. For this purpose a balance sheet is made up thus:

THE NEW YORK CLEARING-HOUSE.

| Dr. Balance. | Dr. Balance. | Name of Bank. | Cr. Total. | Cr. Balance. |
|---|---|---|---|---|
| | $1,021 65 | A. | $1,164 06 | $142 41 |
| 536 34 | 2,366 34 | B. | 1,830 00 | |
| 517 87 | 2,494 28 | C. | 1,976 41 | |
| | 1,889 56 | D. | 2,801 36 | 911 80 |
| $1,054 21 | $7,771 83 | | $7,771 83 | $1,054 21 |

Then B. and C. pay into the clearing-house by a certain hour the balances against them, which settles their account.

| | |
|---|---|
| B. pays | $536.34 |
| C. " | 517.87 |
| | $1,054.21 |

The $1,054.21 received from these "debtor banks" is just sufficient to pay the "creditor banks," viz.:

| | |
|---|---|
| A. receives | $ 142.41 |
| D. " | 911.80 |
| | $1,054.21 |

In this manner, exchanges of many millions of dollars are daily effected at our large clearing-houses by the transfer of a few thousands.

# THE BANKS OF THE UNITED STATES.

The Revised Statutes of the United States require the Comptroller of the Currency to present annually to Congress a statement of the condition of the banks and savings banks organized under State laws. Returns of capital and deposits are made by these institutions and by private bankers, semi-annually, to the Commissioner of Internal Revenue for purposes of taxation.

We condense from the last annual report of the Comptroller of the Currency the following table, exhibiting in concise form, by geographical divisions, the total average capital and deposits of all the State and savings banks and private bankers of the country, for the six months ending May 31, 1880:

| Geographical Divisions. | State Banks and Trust Companies. | | | Private Bankers. | | | Savings Banks with Capital. | | | Savings Banks Without Capital. | |
|---|---|---|---|---|---|---|---|---|---|---|---|
| | No. | Capital. | Deposits | No. | Capital. | Deposits | No. | Capital | Deposits. | No. | Deposits. |
| | | *Millions.* | *Millions.* | | *Mill'ns.* | *Millions.* | | *Milln's.* | *Milln's.* | | *Milln's.* |
| New England States | 40 | 6.86 | 16.47 | 74 | 5.16 | 3.74 | .. | .... | .... | 422 | 368.76 |
| Middle States | 234 | 38.98 | 154.89 | 885 | 40.01 | 71.54 | 6 | 0.53 | 3.19 | 175 | 386.00 |
| Southern States | 241 | 26.69 | 38.51 | 252 | 4.81 | 13.54 | 3 | 0.34 | 0.57 | 2 | 0.88 |
| Western States and Territories | 481 | 41.44 | 108.91 | 1,591 | 26.14 | 93.85 | 20 | 3.17 | 30.85 | 30 | 27.39 |
| United States | 996 | 113.97 | 318.78 | 2,802 | 76.12 | 182.67 | 29 | 4.04 | 34.61 | 629 | 783.03 |

The table below exhibits the aggregate average capital and deposits for the six months ending May 31, 1880, of all classes of banks other than national, and the capital and deposit of the national banks on June 11 following:

| Geographical Divisions. | State Banks, Savings Banks, Private Bankers, &c. | | | National Banks. | | | Total. | | |
|---|---|---|---|---|---|---|---|---|---|
| | No. | Capital. | Deposits. | No. | Capital. | Net Deposits | No. | Capital. | Deposits. |
| | | *Millions.* | *Millions.* | | *Millions.* | *Millions.* | | *Millions.* | *Millions.* |
| New England States | 536 | 12.02 | 388.97 | 548 | 165.60 | 161.96 | 1,084 | 177.62 | 550.93 |
| Middle States | 1,300 | 79.51 | 615.62 | 654 | 170.44 | 480.06 | 1,954 | 249.95 | 1095.68 |
| Southern States | 498 | 31.85 | 53.50 | 177 | 30.79 | 45.90 | 675 | 62.64 | 99.40 |
| Western States and Territories | 2,122 | 70.76 | 261.00 | 697 | 89.08 | 212.87 | 2,819 | 159.84 | 473.87 |
| United States | 4,456 | 194.14 | 1319.09 | 2,076 | 455.91 | 900.79 | 6,532 | 650.05 | 2,219.88 |

From this table it will be seen that the total number of banks and bankers in the country at the dates named was 6,532, with a total banking capital of $650,049,390, and total deposits of $2,219,883,290.

The following table exhibits for corresponding dates in each of the last five years, the aggregate amounts of the capital and deposits of each of the classes of banks given in the foregoing table:

| Years. | National Banks. | | | State Banks, Private Bankers, &c. | | | Savings Banks with Capital. | | | Savings Banks Without Capital. | | Total. | | |
|---|---|---|---|---|---|---|---|---|---|---|---|---|---|---|
| | No. | Capital. | Deposits. | No. | Capital. | Deposits. | No. | Capital. | Deposits. | No. | Deposits. | No. | Capital. | Deposits |
| | | *Mill'ns.* | *Mill'ns.* | | *Mill'ns.* | *Mill'ns.* | | *Mill's* | *Mill's.* | | *Mill'ns.* | | *Mill'ns.* | *Mill'ns.* |
| 1876 | 2,091 | 500.4 | 713.5 | 3,803 | 214.0 | 480.0 | 26 | 5.0 | 37.2 | 691 | 844.6 | 6,611 | 719.4 | 2,075.3 |
| 1877 | 2,078 | 481.0 | 768.2 | 3,799 | 218.6 | 470.5 | 26 | 4.9 | 38.2 | 676 | 843.2 | 6,579 | 704.5 | 2,120.1 |
| 1878 | 2,056 | 470.4 | 677.2 | 3,709 | 202.2 | 413.3 | 23 | 3.2 | 26.2 | 668 | 803.3 | 6,456 | 675.8 | 1,920.0 |
| 1879 | 2,048 | 455.3 | 713.4 | 3,639 | 197.0 | 397.0 | 29 | 4.2 | 36.1 | 644 | 747.1 | 6,360 | 656.5 | 1,893.9 |
| 1880 | 2,076 | 455.9 | 900.8 | 3,798 | 190.1 | 501.5 | 29 | 4.0 | 36.6 | 629 | 783.0 | 6,532 | 650.0 | 2,219.9 |

## VALUE OF FOREIGN COINS IN UNITED STATES MONEY.

| Country. | Monetary Unit. | Standard. | Value in U. S. Money. | Standard Coin. |
|---|---|---|---|---|
| Austria | Florin | Silver | $ .40,6 | |
| Belgium | Franc | Gold and silver | .19,3 | 5, 10, and 20 francs. |
| Bolivia | Boliviano | Silver | .82,3 | Boliviano. |
| Brazil | Milreis of 1000 reis | Gold | .54,6 | |
| British Possessions in North America | Dollar | Gold | 1.00 | |
| Chili | Peso | Gold and silver | .91,2 | Condor, doubloon, and escudo. |
| Colombia (United States of) | Peso | Silver | .82,3 | Peso. |
| Cuba | Peso | Gold and silver | .93,2 | $\frac{1}{16}$, $\frac{1}{8}$, $\frac{1}{4}$, $\frac{1}{2}$, and 1 doubloon. |
| Denmark | Crown | Gold | .26,8 | 10 and 20 crowns. |
| Ecuador | Peso | Silver | .82,3 | Peso. |
| Egypt | Piaster | Gold | .04,9 | 5, 10, 25, 50, and 100 piasters. |
| France | Franc | Gold and silver | .19,3 | 5, 10, and 20 francs. |
| Great Britain | Pound Sterling | Gold | 4.86,6½ | ½ sovereign and sovereign. |
| Greece | Drachma | Gold and silver | .19,3 | 5, 10, 20, 50, and 100 drachmas. |
| German Empire | Mark | Gold | .23,8 | 5, 10, and 20 marks. |
| Hawaiian Islands | Dollar | Gold | 1.00 | |
| Hayti | Gourde | Gold and silver | .96,5 | 1, 2, 5, and 10 gourdes. |
| India | Rupee of 16 annas | Silver | .39 | |
| Italy | Lira | Gold and silver | .19,3 | 5, 10, 20, 50, and 100 lire. |
| Japan | Yen | Silver | .88,7 | 1, 2, 5, 10, and 20 yen, gold and silver yen. |
| Liberia | Dollar | Gold | 1.00 | |
| Mexico | Dollar | Silver | .89,4 | Peso or dollar, 5, 10, 25 and 60 centavo. |
| Netherlands | Florin | Gold and silver | .40,2 | |
| Norway | Crown | Gold | .26,8 | 10 and 20 crowns. |
| Peru | Sol | Silver | .82,3 | Sol. |
| Portugal | Milreis of 1000 reis | Gold | 1.08 | 2, 5, and 10 milreis. |
| Russia | Rouble of 100 copecks | Silver | .65,8 | ¼, ½, and 1 rouble. |
| Spain | Peseta of 100 centimes | Gold and silver | .19,3 | 5, 10, 20, 50, and 100 pesetas. |
| Sweden | Crown | Gold | .26,8 | 10 and 20 crowns. |
| Switzerland | Franc | Gold and silver | .19,3 | 5, 10, and 20 francs. |
| Tripoli | Mahbub of 20 Piasters | Silver | .74,3 | |
| Turkey | Piaster | Gold | .04.4 | 25, 50, 100, 250, and 500 piasters. |
| Venezuela | Bolivar | Gold and silver | .19,3 | 5, 10, 20, 50, and 100 bolivar. |

## THE WORLD'S PRODUCTION OF GOLD AND SILVER.

The following statement will exhibit the amount of the precious metals estimated to have been obtained from the surface and mines of the earth from the earliest times to the close of 1879.

[Estimate based, in part, upon a work on "Gold and Silver," by the Russian Councillor Otreschkoff, published in 1856.]

| Period. | Gold. | Silver. | Total. |
|---|---|---|---|
| A. C. | $1,415,000,000 | $2,913,000,000 | $4,328,000,000 |
| A.D. to 1492 | 3,842,374,000 | 521,000,000 | 4,363,374,000 |
| 1493 to 1842 | 2,726,000,000 | 5,800,000,000 | 8,526,000,000 |
| 1843 to 1852 | 907,000,000 | 450,000,000 | 1,357,000,000 |
| 1853 to 1862 | 2,220,000,000 | 560,000,000 | 2,780,000,000 |
| 1863 to 1879 | 2,958,000,000 | 1,071,000,000 | 4,029,000,000 |
| Grand Total | $14,068,374,000 | $11,315,000,000 | $25,383,374,000 |

**Note—Regarding this and all other estimates of the aggregate amount of the precious metals existing in the world at any period, it is only candid to state that they cannot rise above the domain of conjecture. Statistical science, even now in its infancy, was not born before the present century; and where no census even of the numbers of mankind existed, nothing could possibly be known regarding the amount of the precious metals.—A. R. Spofford.**

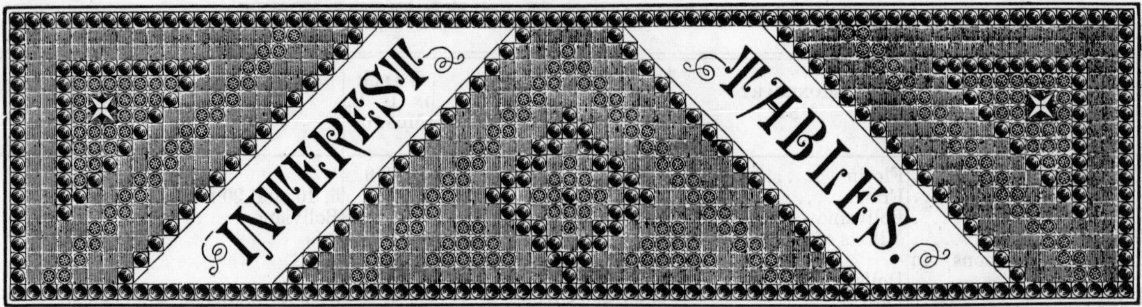


## FIVE PER CENT.

| Time. | $1 | $2 | $3 | $4 | $5 | $6 | $7 | $8 | $9 | $10 | $25 | $50 | 100 | 1,000 |
|---|---|---|---|---|---|---|---|---|---|---|---|---|---|---|
| 1 day | 0 | 0 | 0 | 0 | 0 | 0 | 0 | 0 | 0 | 0 | 0 | 0 | 1 | 13 |
| 2 days | 0 | 0 | 0 | 0 | 0 | 0 | 0 | 0 | 0 | 0 | 0 | 1 | 2 | 21 |
| 3 " | 0 | 0 | 0 | 0 | 0 | 0 | 0 | 0 | 0 | 0 | 1 | 2 | 4 | 47 |
| 4 " | 0 | 0 | 0 | 0 | 0 | 0 | 0 | 0 | 0 | 0 | 1 | 2 | 5 | 54 |
| 5 " | 0 | 0 | 0 | 0 | 0 | 0 | 0 | 0 | 0 | 0 | 1 | 3 | 7 | 68 |
| 6 " | 0 | 0 | 0 | 0 | 0 | 0 | 0 | 0 | 0 | 0 | 2 | 3 | 9 | 82 |
| 7 " | 0 | 0 | 0 | 0 | 0 | 0 | 0 | 0 | 0 | 1 | 2 | 4 | 10 | 95 |
| 8 " | 0 | 0 | 0 | 0 | 0 | 0 | 0 | 0 | 1 | 1 | 2 | 5 | 11 | $1.10 |
| 9 " | 0 | 0 | 0 | 0 | 0 | 0 | 0 | 1 | 1 | 1 | 3 | 6 | 12 | 1.23 |
| 10 " | 0 | 0 | 0 | 0 | 0 | 0 | 1 | 1 | 1 | 1 | 3 | 6 | 13 | 1.37 |
| 12 " | 0 | 0 | 0 | 0 | 0 | 1 | 1 | 1 | 1 | 1 | 4 | 8 | 17 | 1.64 |
| 14 " | 0 | 0 | 0 | 0 | 1 | 1 | 1 | 1 | 1 | 2 | 4 | 9 | 18 | 1.92 |
| 15 " | 0 | 0 | 0 | 0 | 1 | 1 | 1 | 1 | 2 | 2 | 5 | 10 | 20 | 2.05 |
| 16 " | 0 | 0 | 0 | 1 | 1 | 1 | 1 | 1 | 2 | 2 | 5 | 10 | 21 | 2.19 |
| 18 " | 0 | 0 | 0 | 1 | 1 | 1 | 1 | 2 | 2 | 2 | 6 | 12 | 23 | 2.46 |
| 20 " | 0 | 0 | 0 | 1 | 1 | 1 | 2 | 2 | 2 | 3 | 6 | 13 | 25 | 2.64 |
| 22 " | 0 | 0 | 0 | 1 | 1 | 1 | 2 | 2 | 2 | 3 | 7 | 14 | 27 | 2.86 |
| 24 " | 0 | 0 | 0 | 1 | 1 | 2 | 2 | 2 | 3 | 3 | 8 | 15 | 29 | 3.11 |
| 25 " | 0 | 0 | 0 | 1 | 1 | 2 | 2 | 2 | 3 | 3 | 8 | 15 | 31 | 3.24 |
| 26 " | 0 | 0 | 0 | 1 | 1 | 2 | 2 | 3 | 3 | 3 | 8 | 16 | 33 | 3 37 |
| 28 " | 0 | 0 | 0 | 1 | 2 | 2 | 2 | 3 | 3 | 4 | 9 | 18 | 37 | 3.63 |
| 1 mo. | 0 | 0 | 1 | 2 | 2 | 2 | 3 | 3 | 4 | 4 | 10 | 21 | 42 | 4.16 |
| 2 mos. | 1 | 1 | 2 | 3 | 4 | 5 | 6 | 6 | 7 | 8 | 21 | 42 | 83 | 8.38 |
| 3 " | 1 | 2 | 4 | 5 | 6 | 7 | 9 | 10 | 11 | 12 | 31 | 63 | 1.25 | 12.50 |
| 4 " | 2 | 3 | 5 | 7 | 8 | 10 | 12 | 13 | 15 | 16 | 42 | 83 | 1.66 | 16.66 |
| 5 " | 2 | 4 | 6 | 8 | 10 | 12 | 15 | 17 | 19 | 21 | 52 | 1.04 | 2.08 | 20.83 |
| 6 " | 3 | 5 | 7 | 9 | 12 | 15 | 18 | 20 | 23 | 25 | 63 | 1.25 | 2.50 | 25.00 |
| 1 year | 5 | 10 | 15 | 20 | 25 | 30 | 35 | 40 | 45 | 50 | 1.25 | 2.50 | 5.00 | 50.00 |

## SIX PER CENT

| Time. | $1 | $2 | $3 | $4 | $5 | $6 | $7 | $8 | $9 | $10 | $25 | $50 | 100 | 1,000 |
|---|---|---|---|---|---|---|---|---|---|---|---|---|---|---|
| 1 day | 0 | 0 | 0 | 0 | 0 | 0 | 0 | 0 | 0 | 0 | 0 | 0 | 1 | 16 |
| 2 days | 0 | 0 | 0 | 0 | 0 | 0 | 0 | 0 | 0 | 0 | 0 | 1 | 3 | 33 |
| 3 " | 0 | 0 | 0 | 0 | 0 | 0 | 0 | 0 | 0 | 0 | 1 | 2 | 5 | 50 |
| 4 " | 0 | 0 | 0 | 0 | 0 | 0 | 0 | 0 | 0 | 0 | 1 | 3 | 6 | 67 |
| 5 " | 0 | 0 | 0 | 0 | 0 | 0 | 0 | 0 | 0 | 0 | 2 | 4 | 8 | 83 |
| 6 " | 0 | 0 | 0 | 0 | 0 | 0 | 0 | 0 | 1 | 1 | 2 | 5 | 10 | $1.00 |
| 7 " | 0 | 0 | 0 | 0 | 0 | 0 | 0 | 1 | 1 | 1 | 3 | 6 | 12 | 1.20 |
| 8 " | 0 | 0 | 0 | 0 | 0 | 0 | 1 | 1 | 1 | 1 | 3 | 6 | 13 | 1.33 |
| 9 " | 0 | 0 | 0 | 0 | 0 | 0 | 1 | 1 | 1 | 1 | 3 | 7 | 15 | 1.50 |
| 10 " | 0 | 0 | 0 | 0 | 0 | 1 | 1 | 1 | 1 | 1 | 4 | 8 | 16 | 1.67 |
| 12 " | 0 | 0 | 0 | 0 | 1 | 1 | 1 | 1 | 1 | 2 | 4 | 9 | 18 | 2.00 |
| 14 " | 0 | 0 | 0 | 0 | 1 | 1 | 1 | 2 | 2 | 2 | 5 | 11 | 23 | 2.33 |
| 15 " | 0 | 0 | 0 | 1 | 1 | 1 | 1 | 2 | 2 | 2 | 6 | 12 | 25 | 2.50 |
| 16 " | 0 | 0 | 0 | 1 | 1 | 1 | 1 | 2 | 2 | 2 | 6 | 13 | 26 | 2.67 |
| 18 " | 0 | 0 | 0 | 1 | 1 | 1 | 2 | 2 | 2 | 3 | 7 | 14 | 30 | 3.00 |
| 20 " | 0 | 0 | 0 | 1 | 1 | 2 | 2 | 2 | 2 | 3 | 8 | 16 | 33 | 3.33 |
| 22 " | 0 | 0 | 0 | 1 | 1 | 2 | 2 | 3 | 3 | 3 | 9 | 18 | 36 | 3.66 |
| 24 " | 0 | 0 | 0 | 1 | 1 | 2 | 2 | 3 | 3 | 4 | 10 | 20 | 40 | 4.00 |
| 25 " | 0 | 0 | 0 | 1 | 2 | 2 | 3 | 3 | 3 | 4 | 10 | 21 | 41 | 4.17 |
| 26 " | 0 | 0 | 0 | 1 | 2 | 2 | 3 | 3 | 3 | 4 | 11 | 22 | 43 | 4.33 |
| 28 " | 0 | 0 | 1 | 2 | 2 | 3 | 3 | 4 | 4 | 5 | 12 | 24 | 48 | 4.67 |
| 1 mo. | 0 | 1 | 1 | 2 | 2 | 3 | 3 | 4 | 4 | 5 | 12 | 25 | 50 | 5.00 |
| 2 mos. | 1 | 2 | 3 | 4 | 5 | 6 | 7 | 8 | 9 | 10 | 25 | 50 | 1.00 | 10.00 |
| 3 " | 1 | 3 | 4 | 6 | 6 | 9 | 10 | 12 | 13 | 15 | 37 | 75 | 1.50 | 15.00 |
| 4 " | 2 | 4 | 6 | 8 | 10 | 12 | 14 | 16 | 18 | 20 | 50 | 1.00 | 2.00 | 20.00 |
| 5 " | 2 | 5 | 7 | 10 | 12 | 15 | 17 | 20 | 22 | 25 | 62 | 1.25 | 2.50 | 25.00 |
| 6 " | 3 | 6 | 9 | 12 | 15 | 18 | 21 | 24 | 27 | 30 | 75 | 1.50 | 3.00 | 30.00 |
| 1 year | 6 | 12 | 18 | 24 | 30 | 36 | 42 | 48 | 54 | 60 | 1.50 | 3.00 | 6.00 | 60.00 |

## SEVEN PER CENT.

| Time. | $1 | $2 | $3 | $4 | $5 | $6 | $7 | $8 | $9 | $10 | $25 | $50 | 100 | 1,000 |
|---|---|---|---|---|---|---|---|---|---|---|---|---|---|---|
| 1 day | 0 | 0 | 0 | 0 | 0 | 0 | 0 | 0 | 0 | 0 | 0 | 1 | 2 | 19 |
| 2 days | 0 | 0 | 0 | 0 | 0 | 0 | 0 | 0 | 0 | 0 | 1 | 2 | 4 | 38 |
| 3 " | 0 | 0 | 0 | 0 | 0 | 0 | 0 | 0 | 0 | 0 | 1 | 3 | 5 | 57 |
| 4 " | 0 | 0 | 0 | 0 | 0 | 0 | 0 | 0 | 0 | 0 | 2 | 4 | 8 | 77 |
| 5 " | 0 | 0 | 0 | 0 | 0 | 0 | 0 | 0 | 0 | 1 | 2 | 4 | 9 | 96 |
| 6 " | 0 | 0 | 0 | 0 | 0 | 0 | 0 | 1 | 1 | 1 | 2 | 5 | 11 | $1.16 |
| 7 " | 0 | 0 | 0 | 0 | 0 | 0 | 1 | 1 | 1 | 1 | 3 | 6 | 13 | 1.35 |
| 8 " | 0 | 0 | 0 | 0 | 0 | C | 1 | 1 | 1 | 1 | 3 | 7 | 15 | 1.55 |
| 9 " | 0 | 0 | 0 | 0 | 0 | 1 | 1 | 1 | 1 | 1 | 4 | 8 | 17 | 1.72 |
| 10 " | 0 | 0 | 0 | 0 | 0 | 1 | 1 | 1 | 1 | 1 | 4 | 9 | 19 | 1.92 |
| 15 " | 0 | 0 | 0 | 1 | 1 | 1 | 1 | 2 | 2 | 2 | 7 | 14 | 29 | 2.91 |
| 20 " | 0 | 0 | 1 | 1 | 1 | 2 | 2 | 3 | 3 | 3 | 9 | 19 | 38 | 3.84 |
| 25 " | 0 | 0 | 1 | 1 | 2 | 3 | 3 | 3 | 4 | 4 | 12 | 24 | 48 | 4.81 |
| 1 mo. | 0 | 1 | 2 | 2 | 3 | 3 | 4 | 4 | 5 | 6 | 14 | 29 | 58 | 5.83 |
| 2 mos. | 1 | 2 | 3 | 5 | 6 | 7 | 8 | 9 | 10 | 12 | 29 | 58 | 1.17 | 11.67 |
| 3 " | 2 | 3 | 5 | 7 | 9 | 10 | 12 | 14 | 16 | 18 | 44 | 88 | 1.75 | 17.50 |
| 4 " | 2 | 4 | 7 | 9 | 12 | 14 | 16 | 18 | 21 | 23 | 58 | 1.17 | 2.33 | 23.33 |
| 5 " | 3 | 6 | 9 | 12 | 15 | 17 | 20 | 23 | 26 | 29 | 73 | 1.46 | 2.91 | 29.17 |
| 6 " | 4 | 7 | 11 | 14 | 18 | 21 | 25 | 28 | 32 | 35 | 88 | 1.75 | 3.50 | 35.00 |
| 1 year | 7 | 14 | 21 | 28 | 35 | 42 | 49 | 56 | 63 | 70 | 1.75 | 3.50 | 7.00 | 70.00 |

## EIGHT PER CENT.

| Time. | $1 | $2 | $3 | $4 | $5 | $6 | $7 | $8 | $9 | $10 | $25 | $50 | 100 | 1,000 |
|---|---|---|---|---|---|---|---|---|---|---|---|---|---|---|
| 4 days | 0 | 0 | 0 | 0 | 0 | 0 | 0 | 0 | 0 | 1 | 2 | 4 | 9 | 88 |
| 8 " | 0 | 0 | 0 | 0 | 1 | 1 | 1 | 1 | 1 | 1 | 4 | 9 | 17 | $1.76 |
| 12 " | 0 | 0 | 0 | 1 | 1 | 1 | 2 | 2 | 2 | 2 | 6 | 13 | 26 | 2.63 |
| 16 " | 0 | 0 | 1 | 1 | 2 | 2 | 2 | 3 | 3 | 3 | 9 | 17 | 35 | 3.52 |
| 20 " | 0 | 0 | 1 | 2 | 2 | 2 | 3 | 3 | 4 | 4 | 11 | 22 | 44 | 4.40 |
| 24 " | 0 | 0 | 1 | 2 | 2 | 3 | 4 | 4 | 5 | 5 | 13 | 26 | 53 | 5.28 |
| 28 " | 0 | 1 | 2 | 2 | 3 | 4 | 4 | 5 | 5 | 6 | 16 | 31 | 61 | 6.16 |
| 1 mo. | 0 | 1 | 2 | 3 | 3 | 4 | 5 | 5 | 6 | 7 | 17 | 33 | 67 | 6.67 |
| 2 mos. | 1 | 2 | 4 | 5 | 6 | 8 | 9 | 10 | 12 | 13 | 33 | 67 | 1.33 | 13.33 |
| 3 " | 2 | 4 | 6 | 8 | 10 | 12 | 14 | 16 | 18 | 20 | 50 | 1.00 | 2.00 | 20.00 |
| 4 " | 3 | 5 | 8 | 11 | 13 | 16 | 18 | 21 | 24 | 26 | 67 | 1.33 | 2.67 | 26.67 |
| 5 " | 3 | 7 | 10 | 13 | 17 | 20 | 23 | 27 | 30 | 33 | 83 | 1.67 | 3.33 | 33.33 |
| 6 " | 4 | 8 | 12 | 16 | 20 | 24 | 28 | 32 | 36 | 40 | 1.00 | 2.00 | 4.00 | 40.00 |
| 1 year | 8 | 16 | 24 | 32 | 40 | 48 | 56 | 64 | 72 | 80 | 2.00 | 4.00 | 8.00 | 80.00 |

## TEN PER CENT

| Time. | $1 | $2 | $3 | $4 | $5 | $6 | $7 | $8 | $9 | $10 | $25 | $50 | 100 | 1,000 |
|---|---|---|---|---|---|---|---|---|---|---|---|---|---|---|
| 4 days | 0 | 0 | 0 | 0 | 0 | 0 | 0 | 1 | 1 | 1 | 2 | 5 | 11 | $1.10 |
| 8 " | 0 | 0 | 0 | 0 | 1 | 1 | 1 | 2 | 2 | 2 | 5 | 11 | 22 | 2.19 |
| 12 " | 0 | 0 | 1 | 1 | 1 | 2 | 2 | 2 | 3 | 3 | 8 | 16 | 33 | 3.28 |
| 16 " | 0 | 0 | 1 | 2 | 2 | 3 | 3 | 3 | 4 | 4 | 11 | 22 | 44 | 4.38 |
| 20 " | 0 | 1 | 2 | 2 | 3 | 3 | 4 | 4 | 5 | 5 | 14 | 27 | 55 | 5.48 |
| 24 " | 0 | 1 | 2 | 2 | 3 | 4 | 4 | 5 | 6 | 6 | 17 | 33 | 66 | 6.57 |
| 28 " | 0 | 1 | 2 | 3 | 4 | 5 | 5 | 6 | 7 | 7 | 19 | 38 | 77 | 7.67 |
| 1 mo. | 1 | 1 | 3 | 3 | 4 | 5 | 6 | 6 | 7 | 8 | 21 | 42 | 83 | 8.33 |
| 2 mos. | 2 | 3 | 5 | 6 | 8 | 10 | 12 | 13 | 15 | 17 | 42 | 83 | 1.67 | 16.67 |
| 3 " | 2 | 5 | 7 | 10 | 13 | 15 | 17 | 20 | 23 | 25 | 62 | 1.25 | 2.50 | 25.00 |
| 4 " | 3 | 6 | 10 | 12 | 17 | 20 | 23 | 27 | 30 | 33 | 83 | 1.67 | 3.33 | 33.33 |
| 5 " | 4 | 7 | 13 | 15 | 21 | 25 | 29 | 33 | 37 | 42 | 1.04 | 2.08 | 4.17 | 41.67 |
| 6 " | 5 | 10 | 15 | 20 | 25 | 30 | 35 | 40 | 45 | 50 | 1.25 | 2.50 | 5.00 | 50.00 |
| 1 year | 10 | 20 | 30 | 40 | 50 | 60 | 70 | 80 | 90 | 1.00 | 2.50 | 5.00 | 10.00 | 100.00 |

## COMPOUND INTEREST TABLE.

SHOWING the amount of $1, from 1 Year to 15 Years, with Compound Interest added semi-annually at different rates.

| PER CENT. | 3 | 4 | 5 | 6 | 7 | 8 | 9 | 10 |
|---|---|---|---|---|---|---|---|---|
| ½ Year | $1.01 | $1.02 | $1.02 | $1.03 | $1.03 | $1.04 | $1.04 | $1.05 |
| 1 " | 1.03 | 1.04 | 1.05 | 1.06 | 1.07 | 1.08 | 1.09 | 1.10 |
| 1½ " | 1.04 | 1.06 | 1.07 | 1.09 | 1.10 | 1.12 | 1.14 | 1.15 |
| 2 " | 1.06 | 1.08 | 1.10 | 1.12 | 1.14 | 1.16 | 1.19 | 1.21 |
| 2½ " | 1.07 | 1.10 | 1.13 | 1.15 | 1.18 | 1.21 | 1.24 | 1.27 |
| 3 " | 1.09 | 1.12 | 1.15 | 1.16 | 1.22 | 1.26 | 1.30 | 1.34 |
| 3½ " | 1.10 | 1.14 | 1.18 | 1.22 | 1.27 | 1.31 | 1.36 | 1.40 |
| 4 " | 1.12 | 1.17 | 1.21 | 1.26 | 1.31 | 1.36 | 1.42 | 1.47 |
| 4½ " | 1.14 | 1.19 | 1.24 | 1.30 | 1.36 | 1.42 | 1.48 | 1.55 |
| 5 " | 1.16 | 1.21 | 1.28 | 1.34 | 1.41 | 1.48 | 1.55 | 1.62 |
| 5½ " | 1.17 | 1.24 | 1.31 | 1.38 | 1.45 | 1.53 | 1.62 | 1.71 |
| 6 " | 1.19 | 1.26 | 1.34 | 1.42 | 1.51 | 1.60 | 1.69 | 1.79 |
| 6½ " | 1.21 | 1.29 | 1.37 | 1.46 | 1.56 | 1.66 | 1.77 | 1.88 |
| 7 " | 1.23 | 1.31 | 1.41 | 1.51 | 1.61 | 1.73 | 1.85 | 1.97 |
| 7½ " | 1.24 | 1.34 | 1.44 | 1.55 | 1.67 | 1.80 | 1.93 | 2.07 |
| 8 " | 1.26 | 1.37 | 1.48 | 1.60 | 1.73 | 1.87 | 2.02 | 2.18 |
| 8½ " | 1.28 | 1.39 | 1.52 | 1.65 | 1.79 | 1.94 | 2.11 | 2.29 |
| 9 " | 1.30 | 1.42 | 1.55 | 1.70 | 1.85 | 2.02 | 2.20 | 2.40 |
| 9½ " | 1.32 | 1.45 | 1.59 | 1.75 | 1.92 | 2.10 | 2.30 | 2.52 |
| 10 " | 1.34 | 1.48 | 1.63 | 1.80 | 1.98 | 2.19 | 2.41 | 2.65 |
| 11 " | 1.38 | 1.54 | 1.72 | 1.91 | 2.13 | 2.36 | 2.63 | 2.92 |
| 12 " | 1.42 | 1.60 | 1.80 | 2.03 | 2.28 | 2.56 | 2.87 | 3.22 |
| 13 " | 1.47 | 1.67 | 1.90 | 2.15 | 2.44 | 2.77 | 3.14 | 3.55 |
| 14 " | 1.51 | 1.73 | 1.99 | 2.28 | 2.62 | 2.99 | 3.42 | 3.62 |
| 15 " | 1.56 | 1.80 | 2.09 | 2.42 | 2.80 | 3.24 | 3.74 | 4.32 |

## NUMBER OF DAYS FROM ANY DAY IN ONE MONTH TO THE SAME DAY IN ANOTHER MONTH.

| | Jan. | Feb. | March. | April. | May. | June. | July. | Aug. | Sept. | Oct. | Nov. | Dec. |
|---|---|---|---|---|---|---|---|---|---|---|---|---|
| January | 365 | 31 | 59 | 90 | 120 | 151 | 181 | 212 | 243 | 273 | 304 | 334 |
| February | 334 | 365 | 28 | 59 | 89 | 120 | 150 | 181 | 212 | 242 | 273 | 303 |
| March | 306 | 337 | 365 | 31 | 61 | 92 | 122 | 153 | 184 | 214 | 245 | 275 |
| April | 275 | 306 | 334 | 365 | 30 | 61 | 91 | 122 | 153 | 183 | 214 | 244 |
| May | 245 | 276 | 304 | 335 | 365 | 31 | 61 | 92 | 123 | 153 | 184 | 214 |
| June | 214 | 245 | 273 | 304 | 334 | 365 | 30 | 61 | 92 | 122 | 153 | 183 |
| July | 184 | 215 | 243 | 274 | 304 | 335 | 365 | 31 | 62 | 92 | 123 | 152 |
| August | 153 | 184 | 212 | 243 | 273 | 304 | 334 | 365 | 31 | 61 | 92 | 122 |
| September | 122 | 153 | 181 | 212 | 242 | 273 | 303 | 334 | 365 | 30 | 61 | 91 |
| October | 92 | 123 | 151 | 182 | 212 | 243 | 273 | 304 | 235 | 365 | 31 | 61 |
| November | 61 | 92 | 120 | 151 | 181 | 212 | 242 | 273 | 304 | 334 | 365 | 30 |
| December | 31 | 62 | 90 | 121 | 151 | 182 | 212 | 243 | 274 | 304 | 335 | 365 |

EXAMPLE.—To find the number of days from the 10th of May to the 10th of October following: Find May in the first column, and then in a line with that under October, is 153 days. If from the 10th of May to the 25th of October, it would be 15 days more, or 168 days; but if from the 10th of May to the 1st of October, it would be 10 days less, or 143 days. In leap-year, when the last day of February is included between the two dates, there will be one day more than by the table.

## A TABLE OF DAILY SAVINGS AT COMPOUND INTEREST.

| Cents per day. | Per Year. | In Ten Years. | Fifty Years. |
|---|---|---|---|
| 2¾ | $ 10 | $ 130 | $ 2,900 |
| 5½ | 20 | 260 | 5,800 |
| 11 | 40 | 520 | 11,600 |
| 27½ | 100 | 1,300 | 29,000 |
| 55 | 200 | 2,600 | 58,000 |
| 1 10 | 400 | 5,200 | 116,000 |
| 1 37 | 500 | 6,500 | 145,000 |

By the above table it appears that if you save 2¾ cents per day from the time you are 21 till you are 70, the total with interest will amount to $2,900, and a daily saving of 27½ cents reaches the important sum of $29,000.

# CONDENSED INTEREST TABLES.

Showing at different rates the Interest on $1 from 1 Month to 1 Year, and on $100 from 1 Day to 1 Year.

| | Time. | 4 Per Cent. | | | 5 Per Cent. | | | 6 Per Cent. | | | 7 Per Cent. | | | 8 Per Cent. | | |
|---|---|---|---|---|---|---|---|---|---|---|---|---|---|---|---|---|
| | | Dolls. | Cents. | Mills. | Dolls. | Cents. | Mills. | Dolls. | Cents. | Mills. | Dolls. | Cents. | Mills. | Dolls. | Cents. | Mills. |
| One Dollar. | 1 month | 0 | 0 | 3 | 0 | 0 | 4 | 0 | 0 | 5 | 0 | 0 | 5 | 0 | 0 | 6 |
| | 2 months | 0 | 0 | 7 | 0 | 0 | 8 | 0 | 1 | 0 | 0 | 1 | 1 | 0 | 1 | 3 |
| | 3 " | 0 | 1 | 2 | 0 | 1 | 6 | 0 | 1 | 5 | 0 | 1 | 7 | 0 | 2 | 0 |
| | 6 " | 0 | 2 | 0 | 0 | 2 | 5 | 0 | 3 | 0 | 0 | 3 | 5 | 0 | 4 | 0 |
| | 12 " | 0 | 4 | 0 | 0 | 5 | 0 | 0 | 6 | 0 | 0 | 7 | 0 | 0 | 8 | 0 |
| One Hundred Dollars. | 1 day | 0 | 1 | 1 | 0 | 1 | 3 | 0 | 1 | 6 | 0 | 1 | 9 | 0 | 2 | 2 |
| | 2 days | 0 | 2 | 2 | 0 | 2 | 7 | 0 | 3 | 2 | 0 | 3 | 8 | 0 | 4 | 2 |
| | 3 " | 0 | 3 | 4 | 0 | 4 | 1 | 0 | 5 | 0 | 0 | 5 | 8 | 0 | 6 | 7 |
| | 4 " | 0 | 4 | 5 | 0 | 5 | 3 | 0 | 6 | 6 | 0 | 7 | 7 | 0 | 8 | 9 |
| | 5 " | 0 | 5 | 6 | 0 | 6 | 9 | 0 | 8 | 2 | 0 | 9 | 7 | 0 | 11 | 1 |
| | 6 " | 0 | 6 | 7 | 0 | 8 | 3 | 0 | 10 | 0 | 0 | 11 | 6 | 0 | 13 | 3 |
| | 1 month | 0 | 33 | 4 | 0 | 41 | 6 | 0 | 50 | 0 | 0 | 58 | 3 | 0 | 66 | 7 |
| | 2 months | 0 | 66 | 7 | 0 | 83 | 2 | 1 | 0 | 0 | 1 | 16 | 6 | 1 | 33 | 3 |
| | 3 " | 1 | 0 | 0 | 1 | 25 | 0 | 1 | 50 | 0 | 1 | 75 | 0 | 2 | 0 | 0 |
| | 6 " | 2 | 0 | 0 | 2 | 50 | 0 | 3 | 0 | 0 | 3 | 50 | 0 | 4 | 0 | 0 |
| | 12 " | 4 | 0 | 0 | 5 | 0 | 0 | 6 | 0 | 0 | 7 | 0 | 0 | 8 | 0 | 0 |

## Table Showing the Time in which a Sum will Double Itself at the following Rates of Interest.

| Rate. | Simple Interest. | Compound Interest. | |
|---|---|---|---|
| 2 per cent | 50 years | 35 years | 1 day. |
| 3 " | 33 years 4 months | 23 years | 164 days. |
| 4 " | 25 years | 17 years | 246 days. |
| 5 " | 20 years | 14 years | 75 days. |
| 6 " | 16 years 8 months | 11 years | 327 days. |
| 8 " | 12½ years | 9 years | 2 days. |
| 10 " | 10 years | 7 years | 100 days |

## One Dollar Loaned 100 Years at Compound Interest would Amount to the Following Sums.

| Rate | Amount | Rate | Amount |
|---|---|---|---|
| 1 per cent | $2.75 | 12 per cent | $84,675.00 |
| 3 " | 19.25 | 15 " | 1,174,405.00 |
| 6 " | 340.00 | 18 " | 15,145,207.00 |
| 10 " | 13,809.00 | 24 " | 2,551,799,404.00 |

## INTEREST RULES.

Four Per Cent.—Multiply the principal by the number of days to run ; separate the right hand figure from product, and divide by 9.

Five Per Cent.—Multiply by number of days, and divide by 72.

Six Per Cent.—Multiply by number of days ; separate right hand figure, and divide by 6.

Seven and Three-Tenths Per Cent. — Multiply by number of days, and double the amount so obtained. On $100 the interest is just two cents per day.

Eight Per Cent.—Multiply by number of days, and divide by 45.

Nine Per Cent.—Multiply by number of days ; separate right hand figure, and divide by 4.

Ten Per Cent.—Multiply by number of days, and divide by 36.

Twelve Per Cent.—Multiply by number of days; separate right hand figure, and divide by 3.

Fifteen Per Cent.—Multiply by number of days and divide by 24.

Eighteen Per Cent.—Multiply by number of days; separate right hand figure, and divide by 2.

Twenty Per Cent.—Multiply by number of days and divide by 18.

# Interest Laws of the United States and Canada.

Compiled from the latest State and Territorial Statutes.

*Laws of each State and Territory regarding Rates of Interest and Penalties for Usury, with the Law or Custom as to Day of Grace on Notes and Drafts.*

| States and Territories. | Legal Rate of Interest. | Rate Allowed by Contract. | Penalties for Usury. | Grace or No Grace. |
|---|---|---|---|---|
| | per cent. | per cent. | | |
| Alabama | 8 | 8 | Forfeiture of entire interest. | Grace. |
| Arizona | 10 | Any rate. | None. | Grace. |
| Arkansas | 6 | 10 | Forfeiture of principal and interest. | No statute. |
| California | 7 | Any rate. | None. | No grace. |
| Colorado | 10 | Any rate. | None, except of excess. | Grace. |
| Connecticut | 6 | 6 | Forfeiture of excess. | Grace. |
| Dakota | 7 | 12 | Forfeiture of interest. | Grace. |
| Delaware | 6 | 6 | Forfeiture of principal. | Grace. |
| District of Columbia | 6 | 10 | Forfeiture of entire interest. | Grace. |
| Florida | 8 | Any rate. | None. | No statute. |
| Georgia | 7 | Any rate. | None. | Grace. |
| Idaho | 10 | 18 | Fine of $100 or imprisonment. | No grace. |
| Illinois | 6 | 8 | Forfeiture of entire interest. | Grace. |
| Indiana | 6 | 8 | Forfeiture of excess of interest. | Grace. |
| Iowa | 6 | 10 | Forfeiture of 10 per cent. on amount. | Grace. |
| Kansas | 7 | 12 | Forfeiture of excess of interest. | Grace. |
| Kentucky | 6 | 8 | Forfeiture of entire interest. | Grace. |
| Louisiana | 5 | 8 | Forfeiture of entire interest. | Grace. |
| Maine | 6 | Any rate. | None. | Grace. |
| Maryland | 6 | 6 | Forfeiture of excess of interest. | Grace. |
| Massachusetts | 6 | Any rate. | None. | Grace. |
| Michigan | 7 | 10 | None. | Grace. |
| Minnesota | 7 | 12 | Forfeiture of excess over 12 per cent. | Grace. |
| Mississippi | 6 | 10 | Forfeiture of excess of interest. | Grace. |
| Missouri | 6 | 10 | Forfeiture of entire interest. | Grace. |
| Montana | 10 | Any rate. | None. | No grace. |
| Nebraska | 7 | 10 | Forfeiture of interest and cost. | Grace. |
| Nevada | 10 | Any rate. | None. | Grace. |
| New Hampshire | 6 | 6 | Forfeiture of thrice the excess. | Grace. |
| New Jersey | 6 | 6 | Forfeiture of entire interest. | Grace. |
| New Mexico | 6 | 12 | Forfeiture of entire interest. | No statute. |
| New York | 6 | 6 | Forfeiture of principal and interest. | Grace. |
| North Carolina | 6 | 8 | Forfeiture of entire interest. | Grace. |
| Ohio | 6 | 8 | Forfeiture of excess above 6 per cent. | Grace. |
| Oregon | 8 | 0 | Forfeiture of principal and interest. | Grace. |
| Pennsylvania | 6 | 6 | Forfeiture of excess of interest | Grace. |
| Rhode Island | 6 | Any rate. | None. | Grace. |
| South Carolina | 7 | Any rate. | None. | Grace. |
| Tennessee | 6 | 6 | Forfeiture of excess of interest and $100 fine. | Grace. |
| Texas | 8 | 12 | None. | Grace. |
| Utah | 10 | Any rate. | None. | Grace. |
| Vermont | 6 | 6 | Forfeiture of excess of interest. | Grace. |
| Virginia | 6 | 8 | Forfeiture of excess over 6 per cent. | Grace. |
| Washington Territory | 10 | Any rate. | None. | ...... |
| West Virginia | 6 | 6 | Forfeiture of excess of interest. | Grace. |
| Wisconsin | 7 | 10 | Forfeiture of entire interest. | Grace. |
| Wyoming | 12 | Any rate. | No | Grace. |
| Canada | 6 | Any rate. | | Grace. |
| New Brunswick | 6 | Any rate. | | Grace. |
| Nova Scotia | 6 | Any rate. | | Grace. |

No agreement to pay a higher than the legal rate can be enforced unless such agreement is expressly authorized by statute, the established presumption of the law, in the absence of such legislation, being that such a rate is usurious.

# The Statutes of Limitations of the United States and Canada.

| State. | Open Accounts. | Notes and Contracts in writing. | Sealed Instruments. | Judgments of a Court of Record. | (The Figures Indicate Years.) |
|---|---|---|---|---|---|
| * Alabama | 3 | 6 | 10 | 20 | |
| Arkansas | 3 | 5 | 5 | 10 | Judgments of Justice's court, 5 years. Judgment liens expire in 3 years. |
| * Arizona | 2 | 4 | 4 | 5 | |
| California | 2 | 4 | 4 | 5 | An action upon a judgment rendered or contract made out of the State is barred in 2 years. |
| Colorado | 6 | 6 | 6 | 3 | When the cause of action accrues without the State, the periods of limitation are 2 years for notes and accounts; 3 years for sealed instruments and judgments. |
| Connecticut | 6 | 6 | 17 | 17 | Promissory notes not negotiable are barred in 17 years. Demand notes, when indorsed, must be protested 4 months from date, without grace, to hold the indorser. |
| Dakota | 6 | 6 | 20 | 20 | |
| Delaware | 3 | 6 | 20 | 20 | |
| District of Columbia | 3 | 3 | 12 | 12 | |
| Florida | 4 | 5 | 20 | 20 | |
| Georgia | 4 | 6 | 20 | | Judgments become dormant in 7 years from date of last return on execution issued, but may be revived. Foreign judgments barred in 5 years. |
| Idaho | 2 | 4 | 4 | 5 | Sealed instruments, judgments, notes, in 3 years if defendant resided out of Territory when the cause of action accrued. |
| * Illinois | 5 | 10 | 10 | 20 | |
| * Indiana | 5 | 20 | 20 | 20 | |
| * Iowa | 5 | 10 | 10 | 20 | |
| * Kansas | 3 | 5 | 5 | .. | Judgments become dormant in 5 years. |
| * Kentucky | 5 | 15 | 15 | 15 | "Store account" for goods sold and delivered 2 years from 1st January next succeeding date of last item. Merchandise accounts between merchants, 7 years. |
| * Louisiana | 3 | 5 | 10 | 10 | |
| Maine | 6 | 6 | 20 | 20 | Witnessed notes, 20 years. |
| Maryland | 3 | 3 | 12 | 12 | |
| * Massachusetts | 6 | 6 | 20 | 20 | Witnessed notes, 20 years. |
| Michigan | 6 | 6 | 10 | 10 | |
| * Minnesota | 6 | 6 | 10 | 10 | |
| Mississippi | 3 | 6 | 7 | 7 | Years from date of last execution. Foreign judgments barred in three years. Accounts stated, 3 years. |
| Missouri | 5 | 10 | 10 | 20 | |
| * Montana | 5 | 10 | 10 | 10 | |
| * Nebraska | 4 | 5 | 5 | 5 | |
| * Nevada | 2 | 6 | 4 | 5 | Liabilities incurred out of State, 3 years. |
| New Hampshire | 6 | 6 | 20 | 20 | |
| New Jersey | 6 | 6 | 16 | 20 | |
| New Mexico | 4 | 6 | 6 | 15 | |
| New York | 6 | 6 | 20 | 20 | |
| North Carolina | 3 | 3 | 10 | 10 | |
| * Ohio | 6 | 15 | 15 | 15 | For foreign judgments. Domestic judgments become dormant in 5 years, but may be revived in 21 years after it becomes dormant. |
| * Oregon | 6 | 6 | 10 | 10 | |
| * Pennsylvania | 6 | 6 | 20 | 20 | Mercantile accounts are not affected by the statute as long as they remain open. |
| Rhode Island | 6 | 6 | 20 | 20 | |
| South Carolina | 6 | 6 | 20 | 20 | |
| * Tennessee | 6 | 6 | 10 | 10 | |
| * Texas | 2 | 4 | 4 | 10 | |
| * Utah | 2 | 4 | 4 | 5 | Action "for specific recovery of personal property," or "for relief on the ground of fraud," 3 years. |
| * Vermont | 6 | 6 | 8 | 8 | Witnessed notes, 14 years. |
| Virginia | 5 | 5 | 20 | 20 | Judgments of other States, period of limitation under the law of that State, not exceeding 10 years. "Store account," 2 years. |
| * Washington | 5 | 6 | 6 | 6 | |
| West Virginia | 5 | 10 | 10 | 10 | Judgments of another State, same as in Virginia. "Store account," 3 years. |
| * Wisconsin | 6 | 6 | 20 | 20 | Judgments of other States and sealed instruments, where the liability accrued out of the State, 10 years. |
| * Wyoming | 4 | 5 | 5 | .... | Judgments become dormant in 5 years. Foreign debts and judgments, 1 year. |
| **Canada.** | | | | | |
| Province of Ontario | 6 | 6 | 10 | 10 | |
| Province of Quebec | 5 | 5 | 30 | 30 | |

Notes.—A statute of limitation begins to run from the time at which a creditor is authorized first to commence suit. Upon mutual, concurrent and open accounts, the statute, in general, begins to run with the date of the last item. A debt, otherwise barred, may be revived by a new promise made within the period of limitation. The new promise may be either express, or implied from a part payment, or any unqualified acknowledgment from which a promise may be inferred.

* In the States thus marked, it is provided by statute, that a cause of action shall be barred, which first accrued in another State and is barred by the statute of limitations of that State. This is contrary to the general rule, by which a debtor must have resided in the State during the statute period, before he can take advantage of it.

BOOK-KEEPING is the art of recording mercantile transactions in a regular and systematic manner, so that a man may know the true state of his business and property by an inspection of his books. *Book-keeping by single entry,* is the method of keeping books by carrying the record of each transaction to the debit *or* credit of a single account. *Book-keeping by double entry* is the art of keeping accounts by making a separate record of every transaction in a debit *and* a credit account; it is sometimes called, from the place of its origin, the *Italian method.*

1. The method of KEEPING ACCOUNTS is especially practical; nevertheless it depends strictly on scientific principles. There is, or should be, nothing arbitrary about it; there is a reason for every word and figure in properly kept accounts. These reasons and principles must be learned, if the book-keeper would be anything more than a mechanical copyist. It is a mistake to suppose that book-keeping can best be acquired by experience in a counting-room without previous study; on the other hand, after the principles are not only learned, but thoroughly worked into the mind by well-directed exercises, then experience is necessary to make the finished accountant. The object of this article is to thoroughly explain the laws governing the process of recording the history of property, which constitutes the branch of mathematics known as book-keeping. If you acquire a knowledge of these laws, you can learn to understand and use intelligently any set of books whatever. In every system which you are called upon to examine or to work in, you will find something new in form, but you will never find any new principles involved.

2. This treatise, however, is not theoretical. Forms in actual use will be constantly exhibited: for the most part the modern, live forms which the active business spirit of the nineteenth century, has developed. If we give specimens of the old cumbersome routine which survives mainly in the pages of books of instruction, it is that the reader may understand such forms when he meets with them.

3. We expect our reader to study with pen or pencil in hand; to perform every process which we explain, and besides working the practical exercises given, to make others for himself. The qualifications for beginning the study are very simple; to write plainly and uniformly, to understand the

chief rules of arithmetic, to be especially accurate in adding, and to be able to draw straight lines with a ruler. Beyond this, book-keeping is merely the application of common sense to money records.

4. Even though you never expect to keep books as a profession, a knowledge of accounts will be found a great protection in any walk of life.

## CHAPTER I.

What are Accounts ?—Increase and Decrease—Cash Account—Form—Example 1—Stephen Steady's Diary—He makes up a Cash Account—Balancing—Rule—Short Method—Exercises—Review of Cash Account—*More* and *Less*—Property Accounts—Personal Accounts—Debtors and Creditors—Owing and Trusting—Profit and Loss—The Struggle for Wealth—Balance Sheets—Resources, Liabilities, and Capital—Exercises.

5. An account is a statement of Increase and Decrease, for the purpose of showing a Result. The account always contains two columns, one for increase and one for decrease. It usually contains also a space for explanations, and a column for dates.

6 The first thing to be learned in book-keeping is to put any statement of financial increase and decrease into the form of a regular account.

7. An account may be the record of increase and decrease of *money* or only of *money's worth.* In either case, the amount of increase and decrease is measured in money. Therefore the columns of amount must correspond with the money of the country. In the United States and Canada they are ruled for dollars and cents ; in Great Britain or wherever sterling money is used, for pounds, shillings, and pence.

8. An account of money is called a *cash* account, because *cash* originally meant a box, or money-chest.

9. Money received is *increase ;* money paid is *decrease.* The *result* is what remains on hand.

10. The following diagram of a cash account illustrates the usual form of account :

CASH.

| Receipts. [Date.] | [For what received.] | [$ | cts.] | Payments. [Date.] | [For what paid.] | [$ | cts.] |
|---|---|---|---|---|---|---|---|
| | | | | | | | |

11. Make a copy of the ruling of the above lines from memory.

12. We will now give a list of receipts and payments of money to be placed in the above form of account.

### EXAMPLE 1.

(*a*) Stephen Steady borrows $25 from his father, William Steady, with which to seek his fortune in the city, Jan. 1, 1882. His diary is as follows :

(*b*) Jan. 2 ; Paid for railroad fare, $4.65 ; (*c*) for lunch, 30c. ; (*d*) for hotel bill, $1.00.

(*e*) Jan. 3 ; Engaged board with Mrs. Malone at $4.50 per week. Paid one week's board in advance. (*f*) Deposited $10 in the City Savings Bank.

Jan. 4 ; Obtained employment with Messrs. Cheeryble Brothers at $12.00 per week.

(*g*) Jan. 11 ; Received from Cheeryble Brothers one week's wages, $12.00.

(*h*) Jan. 12 ; Sent my father $5.00 to apply on loan.

(*i*) Jan. 13 ; Lent Fred Watson $4.00.

(*j*) Jan. 17 ; One week's board ending to-day, $4.50.

(*k*) Jan. 18 ; One week's wages, $12.00. (*l*) sent my father $6 ; (*m*) deposited $3.

(*n*) Jan. 20 ; Fred Watson repaid me $3. (*o*) drew from the bank $4.

(*p*) Jan. 23 ; purchased an overcoat, $8.50. (*q*) A pair of shoes, $3.

13. Although all of Stephen's transactions had been in ready money, he decided that they were not kept with sufficient system in his diary. It required considerable calculation to ascertain at any time the *result* of his receipts and expenditures, that is the amount on hand. We therefore proceed to show how the same transactions would appear when made into the form of a cash account.

14. The transactions marked *a, g, k, n* and *o*, are all receipts of money or *increase* of the cash-balance ; those marked *b, c, d, e, f, h, i, j, l, m,* and *p*, are payments or *decrease.* The receipts are entered in the left hand side of the account, and the payments in the right hand side. The date is entered opposite each transaction, and a brief explanation of it next.

## CASH ACCOUNT

RECEIPTS. of STEPHEN STEADY. PAYMENTS.

| | | | | | | | | | |
|---|---|---|---|---|---|---|---|---|---|
| 1882. | | | | | 1882. | | | | |
| Jan. | 1 | *a.* Borrowed of William Steady........ | $25 | 00 | Jan. | 2 | *b.* Railroad fares.................. | $4 | 65 |
| | 11 | *g.* One week's wages................ | 12 | 00 | | " | *c.* Lunch ...... ........... | | 30 |
| | 18 | *k.* do. do. ............... | 12 | 00 | | " | *d.* Hotel bill................... | 1 | 00 |
| | 20 | *n.* Repaid by Fred Watson............ | 3 | 00 | | 3 | *e.* One week's board to Jan. 10........ | 4 | 50 |
| | " | *o.* Drew from City Savings Bank...... | 4 | 00 | | " | *f.* Deposited in City Savings Bank.... | 10 | 00 |
| | | | | | | 12 | *h.* Repaid Wm. Steady............... | 5 | 00 |
| | | | | | | 13 | *i.* Lent Fred Watson................ | 4 | 00 |
| | | | | | | 17 | *j.* One week's board to date.......... | 4 | 50 |
| | | | | | | 18 | *l.* Repaid Wm. Steady............... | 6 | 00 |
| | | | | | | " | *m.* Deposited in City Savings Bank.... | 3 | 00 |
| | | | | | | 23 | *p.* Overcoat.. ..................... | 8 | 50 |
| | | | | | | " | *q.* Shoes........................... | 3 | 00 |

15. Without referring to the above solution, make up an account from the narrative in Example I.

### BALANCING.

16. By adding up each side of the cash account, we learn that the total receipts are $56.00; and the total payments $54.45. What then is the *result* or amount now on hand?

| | | |
|---|---|---|
| Total receipts.... | $56 00 | Minuend |
| Total payments.. | 54 45 | Subtrahend |
| On hand......... | 1 55 | Difference. |

17. This is correct, but is not the book-keeper's way of writing it down. He never subtracts the smaller side of an account from the greater: he always *adds* to the less enough to make it equal to the greater. Thus:

| | | | |
|---|---|---|---|
| Receipts... | $56 00 | Payments....... | $54 45 |
| | | *Balance on hand.* | *1 55* |
| | $56 00 | | $56 00 |

18. This operation is called "balancing" or closing, and is one of the most important in book-keeping.

**Rule for Balancing.**—Enter the difference or result in red ink on the smaller side; rule across each column at the first clear line; add each side; draw double lines to denote equality or "closed."

To recommence: Bring down the difference or "balance" in black ink to the *opposite* side as the first entry of the new account.

19. The use of red ink is not essential, but it adds to the appearance of the books to draw all lines and write all results in that manner. When we use *italic words and figures,* red ink is to be used.

20. We now give Stephen Steady's cash account as it would appear when balanced:

## CASH ACCOUNT

RECEIPTS. of STEPHEN STEADY. PAYMENTS.

| | | | | | | | | | |
|---|---|---|---|---|---|---|---|---|---|
| 1882. | | | | | 1882. | | | | |
| Jan. | 1 | Borrowed of William Steady........ | $25 | 00 | Jan. | 2 | Railroad fares....... ............. | $4 | 65 |
| " | 11 | One week's wages.................. | 12 | 00 | | " | Lunch.............................. | | 30 |
| " | 18 | do. do. | 12 | 00 | | " | Hotel bill.......................... | 1 | 00 |
| " | 20 | Repaid by Fred Watson............ | 3 | 00 | | 3 | One week's board to Jan. 10......... | 4 | 50 |
| " | " | Drew from City Savings Bank...... | 4 | 00 | | " | Deposited in City Savings Bank...... | 10 | 00 |
| | | | | | | 12 | Repaid William Steady ............. | 5 | 00 |
| | | | | | | 13 | Lent Fred Watson................... | 4 | 00 |
| | | | | | | 17 | One week's board to date............ | 4 | 50 |
| | | | | | | 18 | Repaid William Steady............... | 6 | 00 |
| | | | | | | " | Deposited in City Savings Bank...... | 9 | 00 |
| | | | | | | 23 | Overcoat ........................... | 8 | 50 |
| | | | | | | " | Shoes .............................. | 3 | 00 |
| | | | | | | " | *Balance* ........................... | *1* | *55* |
| | | | $56 | 00 | | | | $56 | 00 |
| Jan | 24 | Balance.......................... | $1 | 55 | | | | | |

21. The operation of balancing may be facilitated by performing the addition and the subtraction of the smaller side at the same time. Write down the $56.00 under the greater side: write the same opposite, under the smaller side. Now add downward, and when you come to the bottom, *supply* the necessary figure to bring out the total, carrying as in addition. Thus if you are required to balance these figures:

| | |
|---|---|
| 63 | 25 |
| 26 | 19 |
| 32 | |

First add the greater side:

| | |
|---|---|
| 63 | 25 |
| 26 | 19 |
| 32 | |
| 121 | |

Then set down the same amount under the other side:

| | |
|---|---|
| 63 | 25 |
| 26 | 19 |
| 32 | ..? |
| 121 | 121 |

Now add the last column downward, inserting figures where the dots are, thus: "Five,—fourteen, and—how many? SEVEN are twenty-one: put down one; carry two; two,—four,—five and—how many? seven are twelve." Answer, 77.

| | |
|---|---|
| 63 | 25 |
| 26 | 19 |
| 32 | 77 |
| 121 | 121 |
| | 77 |

22. **Exercise 1.**—Balance the following accounts:

| | | | | | |
|---|---|---|---|---|---|
| 254 | 618 | 317 | 254 | 4.37 | 2.45 |
| 376 | 213 | 219 | 726 | 5.25 | 3.00 |
| 793 | 19 | 614 | | 10.19 | 6.17 |
| 121 | | 110 | | 5.17 | 10.00 |

23. **Exercise 2.**—Continue Stephen Steady's account, beginning with the balance brought down ($1.55), and entering the following occurrences:

(*a*) Jan. 24. Received from Fred Watson the balance due, $1.00.

(*b*) Jan. 25. One week's wages, $12 00. (*c*) Paid one week's board to the 24th, $4.50.

(*d*) Jan. 26. Bought paper and postage stamps, 75 cents.

(*e*) Jan. 27. Sent William Steady on account, $5.

(*f*) Jan. 28. Paid for cutting hair, 25c.

(*g*) Jan. 29. Earned by extra work, $6.

(*h*) Jan. 31. Paid one week's board, $4.50.

Balance the account and bring down the balance.

24. **Exercise 3.**—Place the following cash transactions of Joseph R. Skinner in the form of a cash account. Balance the account and bring down the balance.

Feb. 14, 1881. Received from the executors of my father's will, my inheritance, $5,000.

Feb 16. Purchased a truck, $100; a pair of horses, $300.

Feb. 17. Purchased Ohio bonds, par value, $4,000; cost @ 110, $4,400. —Received for labor with team, $8.—Paid for shoeing horses, $4.

Feb 18. Received for labor with team, $7.

Feb. 20.—Sold truck for $90. Sold horses for $350. Paid for keep of horses, $10.

25. Let us now review what has been learned about a cash account.

26. It has, like all accounts, two sides, denoting increase and decrease, or more and less.

27. On the left is entered every transaction whereby I *have more.*

28. On the right is entered every transaction whereby I *have less;* also the *result* (balance or difference), making the two equal.

## PROPERTY ACCOUNTS.

29. The cash account is only one of many accounts which record increase and decrease of property of various kinds. In such property-accounts, the arrangement of the sides always is

| LEFT HAND COLUMN. | | RIGHT HAND COLUMN. |
|---|---|---|
| *Have more* | = | *Have less + result.* |

30. For example, turn again to the cash account of Stephen Steady. He parted on Jan. 3 with some of his money to the City Savings Bank; instead of money he has a share in that institution and its property. Again on the 18th he made a deposit; he thereupon *had more* in the savings bank and *had less* in his pocket. On the 20th, requiring the use of some of his savings, he reversed the operation; he then *had more* in cash and *had less* in the bank. Now if he desired to keep an account of how much he has in the bank, and how it grows more or less, he must do so on precisely the same plan as that of the cash account.

*When you* ***have more,*** *enter the amount on the left side.*
*When you* ***have less,*** *enter the amount on the right side.*
*Enter the* ***result*** *on the right side, which will make the two sides equal.*

31. We select from the transactions in paragraph 12, those which express increase or decrease of the savings bank account, viz., transactions *f*, *m*, and *o*.

(*f*) Jan. 3; deposited $10 in the City Savings Bank.
(*m*) Jan. 18; deposited $3.
(*o*) Jan. 20; drew from the bank $4

These, placed in the form of an account, will appear thus:

### CITY SAVINGS BANK

| DEPOSITS. | | | | | IN ACCOUNT WITH STEPHEN STEADY. | | | | DRAFTS. |
|---|---|---|---|---|---|---|---|---|---|
| 1882. | | | | | 1882. | | | | |
| Jan. | 3 | Deposit | 10 | 00 | Jan. | 20 | Draft | 4 | 00 |
| | 18 | " | 3 | 00 | | 23 | *Balance* | *9* | *00* |
| | | | 13 | 00 | | | | 13 | 00 |
| Jan. | 24 | Balance | 9 | 00 | | | | | |

## PERSONAL ACCOUNTS,
### Or Debtors and Creditors.

32. Turning again to Steady's transactions, we find several in which the principle of trusting or credit is involved. Steady trusts Watson with $4, which the latter repays gradually. In order to ascertain how much Watson owes at any time, it is necessary to select these transactions from the others and place them together in an account. This will be an account of Watson's indebtedness.

33. As Watson's indebtedness is a kind of property, or valuable, because Steady believes, or trusts, that it will be paid, so the same rule is followed as with cash and other

kinds of property ; *more* indebtedness is on the left and *less* on the right, or

*What you* **trust more**, *is on the left ;*
*What you* **trust less**, *is on the right, and the result, or what is now owing, is also on the right, making the two sides equal.*

34. The person whom you trust is called your *debtor ;* and you are called his *creditor.* You are said to *debit* him or *charge* him with the amounts you enter in the left-hand side of the account as trusted. On the other hand, when he diminishes his debt to you, he is said to be *credited,* although he is not yet your creditor. Dr. stands for " Debtor" and Cr. for " Creditor" or "credit."

Watson's account made up and balanced, would read as follows :

### FRED WATSON

IN ACCOUNT WITH STEPHEN STEADY.

| DR. | | | | | | CR. | | |
|---|---|---|---|---|---|---|---|---|
| 1882. | | | | | 1882. | | | |
| Jan. | 13 | Loaned him........ | 4 | 00 | Jan. 20 | Received on account... | 3 | 00 |
| | | | | | 23 | *Balance.............* | *1* | *00* |
| | | | 4 | 00 | | | 4 | 00 |
| Jan. | 24 | Balance............... | 1 | 00 | | | | |

35. When Watson gets into debt an entry is made on the left hand, or debit side ; when he gets out of debt, the entry is on the credit side.

In any mercantile business, there are a large number of accounts like the above—accounts of *personal debtors*, or customers. They buy goods *on credit*, or as far as we are concerned, on *debit*. The left hand side of the account fills up with charges for merchandise, and when they settle in whole or in part, they are credited just as Watson is.

36. Before going any farther, let us look back at those entries which have been taken up a second time. They are *f, i, m, n,* and *o.* Each of these appears both in the cash account and in one of the other accounts, *but on opposite sides.* When we *have more* (left hand) in the savings bank, we *have less* (right hand) in cash. When we *trust less* by Watson's payment, we *have more* in cash.

37. It begins to be evident that we cannot have a complete set of accounts until we have entered every occurrence in some other account, as well as in the cash account, making in each case a double entry.

38. Let us look through the whole list of Steady's transactions, and see if any other account can be opened which will give useful information. The very first (*a*) is a borrowing transaction like that with Watson, except that Stephen is now the debtor, or borrower. The increase and decrease to be recorded are when he *owes more,* and *owes less.*

39. But here comes in an important distinction. The increase in an account like this is entered on the *right* hand side, not on the left, because it is just the opposite kind of increase to that in Watson's account. On the left side is entered the decrease of Stephen's indebtedness to his father. But considered as debits and credits, the respective sides are the same as in Watson's account.

In any person's account the left side contains debits against that person. The right side contains credits in favor of that person.

### WILLIAM STEADY

IN ACCOUNT WITH STEPHEN STEADY

| DR. | | | | | | | CR. | |
|---|---|---|---|---|---|---|---|---|
| 1882. | | | | | 1882. | | | |
| Jan. | 12 | Repaid on account (*h*)... | 5 | 00 | Jan. 1 | Borrowed of him (*a*).... | 25 | 00 |
| " | 18 | " " (*l*). | 6 | 00 | | | | |
| " | *23* | *Balance.........* | *14* | *00* | | | | |
| | | | 25 | 00 | | | 25 | 00 |
| | | | | | Jan. 24 | Balance............ | 14 | 00 |

40. The result is, Stephen now owes William fourteen dollars. If William Steady keeps accounts, he will have one with Stephen exactly the reverse of this.

41. If we compare these entries with the cash account, we again see that what is on the left of that account is on the right of this, and *vice versa*, carrying out the idea of " double entry."

## PROFIT AND LOSS.

42. Now we still have the following transactions unclassified :

(*b*) Jan. 2. Paid for railroad fare, $4.65.
(*c*) For lunch, 30c.
(*d*) For hotel bill. $1.00.

(*e*) Jan. 3. Paid one week's board in advance. $4.50.
(*g*) Jan. 11. Rec'd from Cheeryble Bros. one week's wages, $12.00.
(*j*) Jan. 17. One week's board, $4.50.
(*k*) Jan. 18. One week's wages. $12 00.
(*p*) Jan. 23. Purchased an overcoat, $8.50.
(*q*) A pair of shoes, $3.00.

43. These occurrences represent the history of Stephen's struggle with the world. When he earns money by his labor he is *worth more ;* when he has to pay out some of his earnings for food and clothes, etc., he is *worth less.* Such payments and receipts as these are very different from those we have heretofore considered.

44. The question now is, has Stephen gained or lost? is he better off than when he started with nothing, or worse? (for a person may be worth "less than nothing;") is he ascending or descending the hill of prosperity? on the 23d of January, is he *worth more* or *worth less* than on New Year's day? how much? and why? To answer these questions is the duty of the DOUBLE ENTRY BOOK-KEEPER. Whether he keeps the accounts of poor Stephen Steady or of the great firm which employs him, it is all the same. The history of the progress towards wealth or poverty must be carefully recorded and carefully scrutinized.

45. The account which contains this history is called the PROFIT AND LOSS ACCOUNT. Increase of wealth, or *worth more*, is entered on the right hand side; decrease, or *worth less*, on the left hand side. We select this arrangement because it will preserve the rule already noticed: that a transaction on the left side of cash account appears on the right side of another account, and *vice versa.*

## PROFIT AND LOSS ACCOUNT

EXPENSES. OF STEPHEN STEADY. EARNINGS.

| | | | | | | | | | |
|---|---|---|---|---|---|---|---|---|---|
| 1882. | | | | | 1882. | | | | |
| Jan. | 2 | Railroad fare (*b*)....... | 4 | 65 | Jan. | 11 | One week's wages (*g*)... | 12 | 00 |
| " | 2 | Lunch (*c*)............ | | 30 | " | 18 | " " (*k*)... | 12 | 00 |
| " | 2 | Hotel bill (*d*).......... | 1 | 00 | | | | | |
| " | 3 | One week's board (*e*).... | 4 | 50 | | | | | |
| " | 17 | " " (*j*)... | 4 | 50 | | | | | |
| " | 23 | Overcoat (*p*).......... | 8 | 50 | | | | | |
| " | 23 | Shoes (*q*)............ | 3 | 00 | | | | | |

46. The left hand column foots up..........................$26 45
And the right hand.............................................24 00

It would seem therefore that Stephen has gone behind, or lived beyond his income..........................$2 45

47. This however is not quite true. Stephen has chosen to balance up his accounts at a time when several days have elapsed since pay-day. He has earned wages for four work days, at $2 per day, or $8, though he has not yet received them. Messrs. Cheeryble Brothers are indebted to him $8. Therefore, he must, in order to give a correct statement of his affairs, open an account with the firm, and debit them with the amount.

## CHEERYBLE BROTHERS

DR. IN ACCOUNT WITH STEPHEN STEADY CR.

| | | | | | | | | | |
|---|---|---|---|---|---|---|---|---|---|
| 1882. | | Balance of wages to last | | | | | | | |
| Jan. | 24 | night............... | 8 | 00 | | | | | |

48. Now, the same amount is entered in the Profit and Loss Account on the right hand side; Stephen is *worth more* than was shown by the Cash transactions.

49. On the other hand, while Stephen's wages have been running on, his board-bill has also been accumulating. Out of the eight dollars which he has counted on as earned, Mrs. Malone will claim six days' board at $4.50 per week. What is $^6/_7$ of $4.50? $3.86. Mrs. Malone must have an account, and the same amount must be added to the expense side of the Profit and Loss Account.

50. With these two amendments made, the Profit and Loss Account may be balanced, and the result brought down, showing that the subject of the history has earned abov ehis expenses $1.69.

## MARY MALONE

DR. IN ACCOUNT WITH STEPHEN STEADY. CR.

| | | | | | | | | | |
|---|---|---|---|---|---|---|---|---|---|
| | | | | | | | Balance due to last | | |
| | | | | | 1882. | | night, 5 days at $4.50 | | |
| | | | | | Jan. | 24 | per week............ | 3 | 86 |

## PROFIT AND LOSS ACCOUNT

EXPENSES. OF STEPHEN STEADY. EARNINGS.

| | | | | | | | | | |
|---|---|---|---|---|---|---|---|---|---|
| 1882. | | | | | 1882. | | | | |
| Jan. | 2 | Railroad fares.......(b) | 4 | 65 | Jan. | 11 | One week's wages....(g) | 12 | 00 |
| " | " | Lunch ..........(c) | | 30 | " | 18 | " " ....(k) | 12 | 00 |
| " | " | Hotel bill.........(d) | 1 | 00 | " | 23 | 4 days' " (accrued).. | 8 | 00 |
| " | 3 | One week's board ...(e) | 4 | 50 | | | | | |
| " | 17 | " " ....(j) | 4 | 50 | | | | | |
| " | 23 | Overcoat..........(p) | 8 | 50 | | | | | |
| " | " | Shoes..............(q) | 3 | 00 | | | | | |
| " | " | 6 days' board (accrued). | 3 | 86 | | | | | |
| " | " | *Balance*............. | *1* | *69* | | | | | |
| | | | 32 | 00 | | | | 32 | 00 |
| | | | | | Jan. | 24 | Ba ance of earnings.... | 1 | 69 |

51. We have now gone through the entire list of transactions in paragraph 12, and have recorded, or, as book-keepers say, "posted" each entry twice: once in the Cash Account, once in some other account, always on opposite sides. Each account has been balanced, and the results brought down, always to the side denoting *more*, which is sometimes the right and sometimes the left. Combining these results we have a general statement of Steady's affairs, which is called a "Balance Sheet." It is an account—not an account of transactions, but of results.

52. If all our work has been correctly done, this account will add up the same on both sides. If it does not, there has been an error somewhere.

53. We give this account in a little different form from the one hitherto used.

### BALANCE SHEET.

STEPHEN STEADY.

Jan. 24, 1882.

| | | |
|---|---|---|
| | RESOURCES: | |
| 1 55 | Cash. | |
| 1 00 | Fred. Watson. | |
| 9 00 | City Savings Bank. | |
| 8 00 | Cheeryble Brothers. | |
| | LIABILITIES: | |
| | Wm. Steady .......... | 14 00 |
| | Mrs. Malone .......... | 3 86 |
| | CAPITAL: | |
| | [or Profit and Loss].... | 1 69 |
| 19 55 | | 19 55 |

54. The examination of this balance sheet will explain, better than any definition, the meaning of "Resources" and "Liabilities." "Capital" is the difference of these two, or the *worth* of the person or of the business enterprise, whose history is the subject of record.

My Resources = what I *have* + what I *trust* to have.
My Liabilities = what I *owe*.
My Capital = my resources minus my liabilities = what I am *worth*.

What I have + what I trust = what I owe + what I am worth.

Steady's resources amount to.................................. $19.55
His liabilities amount to..................................... 17.86
His capital to................................................ 1.69

19.55 = 17.86 + 1.69.

## RESOURCES = LIABILITIES + CAPITAL.

This last is the formula of all balance sheets. In accordance with it, construct balance sheets from the following facts:

55. **Exercise 4.**—James Jones has the following resources and liabilities: Cash, $3,506.75; Merchandise, $22,166.73; due from various Personal Debtors, $15,972.18; Real Estate, $10,000; Mortgage (to be paid by Jones), $4,000; due to various Personal Creditors, $18,718.62; Capital to be ascertained from the above.

56. **Exercise 5.**—Armstrong & Baylis are a firm of lawyers. They have: Cash, $542.63; in Pacific Bank, $1,574.00; Notes of other parties [these are called in book-keeping, Bills Receivable], $7,000; Library, value $3,000; due from Clients, $6,922.50; due James Gordon Bennett (for Rent), $433.33. (*a*) Make a balance sheet showing their joint capital. (*b*) Make a second balance sheet showing under Capital the share of each partner; let Armstrong's be $9,452.90: how much is Baylis's?

57. **Exercise 6.**—Joseph Anderson has the following resources and liabilities, which we give in confused sequence; arrange them in proper order, putting the most available resources first: Due to William Simpson, $50; Due from Peter Brown, $100; Merchandise, $562; due on a note held by another party [this is called in book-keeping, Bills Payable], $300; due from Samuel Cohen, $30; Cash, $279; due to Albert Barnes, $76; Horses, $250; Wagon, $125; due from Samuel Wilkins, $43; due from Arthur Knight, $29; due from James Jackson, $5; 26 shares of Bank Stock, $2,600; United States Bonds, worth $595.

## CHAPTER II.

Posting and Balancing explained—Books of Original Entry—The Journal—Debits and Credits—Journalizing—A Table—Example of the Journal—Practical Exercises, Introducing Various Accounts.—Merchandise—Bills Receivable—Bills Payable—Capital—Opening Entries—"Sundries"—Profit and Loss Accounts.

58. By the few transactions which we have taken as examples, we have illustrated in a general manner the processes of all book-keeping. They may be all explained as *posting* and *balancing*.

*Posting* is distributing a transaction to its proper accounts.

*Balancing* is reducing an account to its result.

59. In posting, we find what accounts are increased or decreased by the transaction; we record the increase or decrease on the proper sides of those accounts.

60. In balancing, we find what amount added to the *less* side will make both sides equal; this amount (the result, difference or balance) we enter on the less side; add and rule off: the result we enter on the opposite side of the ac-

count or to some other account to which we desire to transfer it.

61. In current business, we first enter the transactions in the order of their occurrence in a book or books, called the books "of original entry." These ought to be so arranged that they point out to which accounts and to which sides the amounts are to be posted.

62. The names of the principal Books of Original Entry in common use are the JOURNAL, the CASH BOOK, the SALES BOOK, the INVOICE BOOK, the BILL BOOK, the CHECK BOOK, the DAY BOOK or BLOTTER.

63. While the original book-entry is made in one of these books, there is frequently a previous entry on a document or business paper of some kind. The use of such memorandums as a basis of record has become very extended; in fact, it may be said that modern business on a large scale is done in writing, not by word of mouth.

64. The Journal is the most *general* of the books of entry. It is adapted to receive entries of any transaction whatever; while the other books are adapted to some special kind of transactions, as receipts and payments of money, purchases and sales of merchandise, etc.

We will show how a transaction is put into the form of a "journal entry." It is necessary to know what accounts are affected and on which side.

65. The reader has noticed that in personal accounts the left hand side is marked "Debtor," and the right hand side "Creditor." These names are for convenience extended to all accounts, even where there is no owing nor trusting.

66. The left hand side of any account is called for convenience the **DEBIT SIDE**; the right hand the **CREDIT.**

67. All accounts represent what we *have*, what we *trust*, what we *owe* or what we are *worth*. In two of these classes, the left hand or *debit* side is devoted to increase; the right hand or *credit* to decrease. In the other two classes, this is exactly reversed, because the tendency of the accounts is the reverse. We will now furnish a table for ascertaining the debits and credits of any transaction, which is called "journalizing."

## 68. JOURNALIZING TABLE.

| DEBITS. | CREDITS. |
|---|---|
| 1. Have more. | 1. Have less. |
| 2. Trust more. | 2. Trust less. |
| 3. Owe less. | 3. Owe more. |
| 4. *Am worth less.* | 4. *Am worth more.* |

69. As an example of the manner of using this table, take the first entry (*a*) in paragraph 12, Chapter I., and try to find what debits and what credits are involved in it. If you do this correctly, the following will be the result:

70. **Transaction.** Borrowed $25 from William Steady.

Looking down the list of debits in the table, I see that *have more* is the only one which applies.

I *have more* cash.

Therefore, a debit entry must be made in Cash account, or briefly,

"Cash Dr. $25."

Looking down the list of credits, I see that *have less* is not true, for I have as much property as before; neither do I *trust less* through this transaction; but I *owe more*.

Therefore, a credit entry must be made in the account of the person whom I owe, or

"William Steady, Cr. $25."

71. Instead of "Cash Dr."
we may write "By Cash."
Instead of "Wm. Steady, Cr."
we may write "To Wm. Steady."

Note carefully these different expressions.

72. In combining the debit and the credit into a single "journal entry," the form "Cash Dr. to Wm. Steady," is the one oftenest used, meaning that Cash account is to be debited and Wm. Steady's account credited the given amount.

73. As written out in full, the journal entry will be as follows:

| | | Dr. | | Cr. | |
|---|---|---|---|---|---|
| | Jan. 1, 1882. | | | | |
| **Cash** Dr. | | $25 | 00 | | |
| | To **William Steady**. | | | $25 | 00 |
| | For amount borrowed from him. | | | | |

74. We will now give the journalization of all the transactions in paragraph 12, and opposite each one we give the reasoning in each case.

75. "D. 1" in the explanation refers to No. 1 of the debits in the journalizing table. "C. 3" to the third credit, &c.

## 76.

| JOURNAL. Jan. 1, 1882. | Dr. | | Cr. | | EXPLANATION. |
|---|---|---|---|---|---|
| **Cash** Dr. | $25 | 00 | | | |
| To **Wm. Steady**. | | | $25 | 00 | (*a*) Cash is debited because I *have more* of it (D. 1). Steady is credited because I *owe* him *more* (C. 3). |
| *For amount borrowed from him.* | | | | | |
| —2— | | | | | The day of the month is in the middle of the line. |
| **Profit** *and* **Loss** Dr. | 4 | 65 | | | |
| To **Cash**. | | | 4 | 65 | (*b*) Profit and Loss is debited because I am *worth less* than before (D. 4). Cash is credited because I *have less* of it (C. 1). |
| *For amount of railroad fare.* | | | | | |
| " | | | | | |
| **Profit** *and* **Loss** Dr. | | 30 | | | (*c*) Similar to *b*. |
| To **Cash**. | | | | 30 | |
| *For amount paid for lunch* | | | | | |
| " | | | | | |
| **Profit** *and* **Loss** Dr. | 1 | 00 | | | (*d*) Similar to *b*. |
| To **Cash**. | | | 1 | 00 | |
| *For hotel bill paid.* | | | | | |
| —3— | | | | | |
| **Profit** *and* **Loss** Dr. | 4 | 50 | | | (*e* Similar to *b*. |
| To **Cash**. | | | 4 | 50 | |
| *For one week's board in advance, paid Mrs. Malone.* | | | | | |
| " | | | | | |
| **City Savings Bank** Dr. | 10 | 00 | | | (*f*) I *have more* property as far as the bank account is concerned (C. 1), and *less* in money (D. 1). |
| To **Cash**. | | | 10 | 00 | |
| *For amount deposited.* | | | | | |
| " | | | | | |
| **Cash** Dr. | 12 | 00 | | | (*g*) I *have more* cash (C. 1), and having given no other property for it I am *worth more* (D. 4). |
| To **Profit** *and* **Loss**. | | | 12 | 00 | |
| *For one week's wages received.* | | | | | |
| —12— | | | | | |
| **Wm. Steady** Dr. | 5 | 00 | | | (*h*) I *owe* him *less* (C. 4), and *have less* (C. 1). |
| To **Cash**. | | | 5 | 00 | |
| *For amount paid him.* | | | | | |
| —13— | | | | | |
| **Fred. Watson** Dr. | 4 | 00 | | | (*i*) I *trust* him the amount, and *have* so much *less* money. |
| To **Cash**. | | | 4 | 00 | |
| *For amount loaned him.* | | | | | |
| —17— | | | | | |
| **Profit** *and* **Loss** Dr. | 4 | 50 | | | (*j*) Similar to *b*. |
| To **Cash**. | | | 4 | 50 | |
| *For one week's board to date.* | | | | | |
| —18— | | | | | |
| **Cash** Dr | 12 | 00 | | | (*k*) Similar to *g*. |
| To **Profit** *and* **Loss**. | | | 12 | 00 | |
| *For one week's wages.* | | | | | |
| " | | | | | |
| **Wm. Steady** Dr. | 6 | 00 | | | (*l*) Similar to *h*. |
| To **Cash**. | | | 6 | 00 | |
| *For amount paid him.* | | | | | |
| " | | | | | |
| **City Savings Bank** Dr. | 3 | 00 | | | (*m*) Similar to *f*. |
| To **Cash**. | | | 3 | 00 | |
| *For amount deposited.* | | | | | |
| —20— | | | | | |
| **Cash** Dr. | 3 | 00 | | | (*n*) I now *have more* and *trust less*. |
| To **Fred. Watson**. | | | 3 | 00 | |
| *For amount received from him.* | | | | | |
| " | | | | | |
| **Cash** Dr | 4 | 00 | | | (*o*) I *have more* in money and *less* in the bank. |
| To **City Savings Bank** | | | 4 | 00 | |
| *For amount withdrawn.* | | | | | |
| *Carried forward* | $96 | 95 | $96 | 95 | |

| JOURNAL. | | | | | EXPLANATION. |
|---|---|---|---|---|---|
| Jan. 23, 1882. | Dr. | | Cr. | | |
| *Brought forward........* | $96 | 95 | $96 | 95 | |
| **Profit** *and* **Loss** Dr..... | 8 | 50 | | | (*p*) Similar to *b*. |
| To **Cash**.................. | | | 8 | 50 | |
| *For amount expended for overcoat.* | | | | | |
| **Profit** *and* **Loss** Dr..... | 3 | 00 | | | (*q*) Similar to *b*. |
| To **Cash**.................. | | | 3 | 00 | |
| *For amount expended for shoes.* | | | | | |
| —24— | | | | | |
| **Cheeryble Bros.** Dr..... | 8 | 00 | | | This and the following entry are not of cash transactions, but of the facts stated in paragraphs 47 to 50. |
| To **Profit** *and* **Loss**. | | | 8 | 00 | Cheeryble Brothers owe me, or I *trust* them this amount, as if I had lent them so much money. I am *worth more*, as much as if I had received the money for my labor. |
| *For wages to date unpaid.* | | | | | |
| " | | | | | |
| **Profit** *and* **Loss** Dr..... | 3 | 86 | | | I am *worth less* because I have incurred this expense, and I *owe more*, namely, to Mrs. Malone. |
| To **Mary Malone**... | | | 3 | 86 | |
| *For board to date unpaid.* | | | | | |
| | $122 | 31 | $122 | 31 | The equality shows that the total amount of the debits and of the credits is the same. |

77. **Exercise 7.**—In mercantile business, the account of goods bought and sold is called the **Merchandise** Account. Put the following transactions into the journal form.

April 3, 1882. Bought for Cash, merchandise amounting to $500.

April 4. Sold for Cash, merchandise, $100.

April 5. Sold James Jones merchandise, $50, and trusted him for the same.

A sale of this kind is called "on account," or "on credit," or "on time."

April 6. Bought of Abram Smith, on credit, merchandise, $400.

April 7. Received from Abram Smith, in part payment, merchandise, $200.

78. **Exercise 8.**—The department of negotiable paper is an important one in business. It includes Notes, also Bills of Exchange, and Drafts, if payable at a future time. The forms of such documents are given in this book under "Commercial Forms."

Notes, etc., payable *to* us are recorded in an account entitled "Bills Receivable;" notes payable *by* us, in an account called "Bills Payable." The former constitutes a Resource, the latter a Liability.

May 1, 1882. Loaned Peter Skinner $500 cash, for which he gave me *his* note at 30 days [Bills Rec.].

May 2. Sold Jeremiah Black merchandise, and took in payment *his* note for 30 days at $400.

May 3. Bo't [abbreviation for *bought*] of Abram Smith mdse. [abbreviation for "merchandise"], and gave him *my* note at 30 days for $556.75. [Bills Pay.]

June 3. Peter Skinner paid his note in cash, $500.

June 4. Jeremiah Black paid his note in cash, $400.

June 5. Redeemed my note to Abram Smith, $556.75, in cash.

79. **Exercise 9.**—Place in the form of Journal entries the transactions in paragraph 24.

80. The *Profit and Loss* account is used to record the current losses and gains of the business, but the account which shows the total amount of investment is the *Capital* account. Frequently the net result of the Profit and Loss account is transferred every year or half year to the Capital. This is almost always the case with a single proprietor. The Profit and Loss is then a temporary account, and really is a part of Capital account. Where there are several partners, each of them usually has a Capital account, and at the end of the year (or half year) the result of Profit and Loss is divided according to their contract, and the share of each partner is carried to his Capital account. In a corporation, bank, or joint-stock company, the Capital account represents the shares into which the proprietorship of the concern is divided, and remains a fixed quantity. The earnings are in part paid in cash, so much per share, and in part carried to such an account as "Surplus," "Undivided Profits," or "Reserve." *Capital* Account is sometimes called "Stock Account."

81. **Example** of a JOURNAL ENTRY representing INVESTMENT.

*Transaction.*—Jan. 1, 1882. Invested in the grocery business cash, $3,000; with which I open my books.

*Journal Entry.*

**Cash** Dr....................................$3,000.00
To **Capital**......... ........... $3,000.00
for amount invested in the grocery business.

82. **Example** of a Journal entry representing investment of several different kinds of property. "Sundries" in journal means "the following accounts;" but the words in brackets may be omitted and the second form used.

*Transaction*—July 1, 1882. Invested in business the following resources: Cash, $1,000; Goods, $2,344.50; Notes of various parties, $500; store and land, $6,000.

*Journal Entry.* 1. Ancient Form.

[Sundries] Dr. to **Capital**............ $9,844.50
for amount invested in business this day.

**Cash** on hand and in bank ................$1,000.00
**Mdse.**, as per Inventory.................. 2,344.50
**Bills Receivable,** as per Bill Book....... 500.00
**Real Estate,** appraised value........... 6,000.00

2. Simple Form.

| | | |
|---|---|---|
| **Cash** on hand and in banks...........Dr. | $1,000 00 | |
| **Mdse**., as per Inventory ........ " | 2,344 50 | |
| **Bills Receivable,** as per Bill Book.. " | 500.00 | |
| **Real Estate**, appraised value....... " | 6,000 00 | |
| To **Capital**.................. | | $9,844.50 |
| for total amount of my investment in business. | | |

83. **Example** of ENTRY showing INVESTMENT of TWO PARTNERS.

*Transaction.*—Messrs. Smith and Jones enter into a copartnership in the dry goods business. William Smith invests Cash, $1,000; Goods, $8,966.25. Thomas Jones invests Cash, $4,000; Building to be used for store, $9,000. Required a journal entry showing the investments and each partner's interest.

*Journal Entry.*

[Sundries Dr. to Sundries]

| | | |
|---|---|---|
| To open the books of the firm of Smith & Jones. | | |
| **Cash**...........Dr., as per Cash Book.. | $5,000.00 | |
| **Mdse**.......... " as per Inventory... | 8,966.25 | |
| **Real Estate** ... " as valued ......... | 9,000.00 | |
| To **William Smith** (Capital)..... | | $ 9,966.25 |
| " **Thomas Jones** (Capital)...... | | 13,000.00 |
| for amounts of their respective proprietary interests. | | |
| | $22,966.25 | $22,966.25 |

84. **Example** of an ENTRY for INVESTMENTS, where there are LIABILITIES OUTSTANDING.

*Conditions.*—Stephen Steady on the 24th of January, 1882, desires to open books of account for his private affairs. He has the following Resources (see paragraph 53): Cash, $1.55; Due from Fred Watson, $1.00; City Savings Bank, $9.00; Cheeryble Brothers, $8.00. Liabilities—due William Steady, $14.00; Mrs. Malone, $3.86.

*Journal Entry.*

[Sundries Dr. to Sundries.]

| | | |
|---|---|---|
| To record the condition of my affairs this day. | | |
| **Cash,** amount on hand.......................... | $1.55 | |
| **Fred Watson,** amount due from him.......... | 1.00 | |
| **City Savings Bank,** amount on deposit...... | 9.00 | |
| **Cheeryble Brothers**, wages to date........... | 8.00 | |
| To **Wm. Steady,** amount due him...... | | $14.00 |
| **Mrs. Malone,** board to date........ | | 3.86 |
| **Capital,** what I am now worth...... | | 1.69 |
| | $19.55 | $19.55 |

85. Besides the General Profit and Loss account, there are usually kept several special Profit and Loss accounts. For example, the **Expense** account records the cost of carrying on the business, salaries, rent, insurance, etc. Sometimes even this is subdivided into **Salaries** account, **Rent** account, **Insurance** account, **Postage** account, etc. The **Interest** account records the loss or the gain, the cost or proceeds, as the case may be, of borrowing money or of lending it on interest. The following are also specimens of Profit and Loss accounts; their purpose will be learned from their titles: Commission, Discount, Exchange, Brokerage, Bad Debts, Taxes.

86. The debit side of a Profit and Loss account, of course, always contains the expenses and losses, which make us *worth less;* the credit side the earnings and profits, which make us or our enterprise *worth more.*

87. In such subordinate accounts, the balance is seldom carried down, but is transferred to the more general account. Thus the result of the Expense, Interest, Commission and other like accounts would be carried at the close of the year to the Profit and Loss account. The result of the Profit and Loss account would be carried to the Capital account or to the Partners' accounts.

## CHAPTER III.

Posting—The Ledger—"Single Entry"—Example—Stephen Steady again—Practical Exercises.

88. We have now illustrated the Journal, and our readers should be able to find the debits and credits of any ordinary transaction.

89. The Journal, however, is merely a mechanism preparatory to posting in the LEDGER. The *Ledger* is the book of accounts. A complete ledger contains an account with every department of the resources, liabilities and capital. An incomplete or "Single Entry" ledger contains personal accounts and sometimes property accounts.

90. The complete ledger always contains the same amount of debits as of credits. This furnishes a valuable test of correctness, called the *Trial Balance*, which will be hereafter explained.

91. POSTING from the journal is a very simple process. Take the first entry of the journal in paragraph 76, which reads:

January 1, 1882.

| | | | |
|---|---|---|---|
| 1 | "**Cash, Dr.,** | $25.00, | |
| 2 | To **William Steady,** | | $25.00, |
| | for amount borrowed from him." | | |

92. Turn to the page of the ledge rcontaining the Cash account, and write on the first line of the debit side:

First, the date;
Second, the opposite account credited;
[Third, the explanation;]
Fourth, the page of the journal from which you post;
Fifth, the amount, thus:

PAGE 1.

CASH.

| Dr. | | | | | | | | | | | | | Cr. |
|---|---|---|---|---|---|---|---|---|---|---|---|---|---|
| 1882. Jan. | 1 | To Wm. Steady, for amount borrowed.... | 1 | 25 | 00 | | | | | | | | |

Then, returning to the journal, insert in the left hand column the number of the page of the Ledger where you have just posted, viz.: 1.

93. Turn to the account of William Steady, credit side, and make the same posting, except that the account debited is inserted, thus:

PAGE 2.

WILLIAM STEADY.

| | | | | | | | | | | | |
|---|---|---|---|---|---|---|---|---|---|---|---|
| | | | | | | 1882. Jan. | 1 | By Cash, for amount loaned by him....... | 1 | 25 | 00 |

Returning to the Journal, we insert the page number, 2.

94. We may remark several variations in the wording. We have given the full form:

"By Cash, for amount loaned by him." (1)

This is not so frequently used as the less explicit form:

"By Cash." (2)

The words "By" and "To" are not of the slightest use. Hence many book-keepers omit them altogether, and write

"Cash." (3.)

Others again omit all reference to the opposite or "per contra" account, and insert only the specification, thus:

"Amount of loan, 25.00." (4.)

Form 2 is the most frequently used; but in the writer' opinion it is not the best.

95. We now give the whole of Stephen Steady's Ledger, as posted (Form 2) and balanced. We have opened a capital account, to which we have carried Steady's earnings. Transfer or balancing entries are not entered in the Journal (although we shall show how this may be done), but the amount is entered in red ink [italics] in the account *from* which, and in black ink in the account *to* which it is transferred.

96. **LEDGER.**

STEPHEN STEADY.

1. CASH.

| Dr. | | | | | | | | | | | Cr. |
|---|---|---|---|---|---|---|---|---|---|---|---|
| 1882. Jan. | 1 | To William Steady | 1 | 25 | 00 | 1882. Jan. | 2 | By Profit and Loss..... | 1 | 4 | 65 |
| | 11 | " Profit and Loss...... | 1 | 12 | 00 | " | " | " " ...... | 1 | | 30 |
| | 18 | " " " ...... | 2 | 12 | 00 | " | " | " " ...... | 1 | 1 | 00 |
| | 20 | " Fred. Watson..... | 3 | 3 | 00 | | 3 | " " | 1 | 4 | 50 |
| | " | " City Savings Bank.... | 2 | 4 | 00 | " | " | " City Savings Bank | 1 | 10 | 00 |
| | | | | | | | 12 | " William Steady..... | 1 | 5 | 00 |
| | | | | | | | 13 | " Fred. Watson | 1 | 4 | 00 |
| | | | | | | | 17 | " Profit and Loss. | 1 | 4 | 50 |
| | | | | | | | 18 | " William Steady.... | 2 | 6 | 00 |
| | | | | | | | " | " City Savings Bank.... | 2 | 3 | 00 |
| | | | | | | | 23 | " Profit and Loss..... | 2 | 8 | 50 |
| | | | | | | | " | " " ...... | 2 | 3 | 00 |
| | | | | | | | " | *By Balance*.......... | | *1* | *55* |
| | | | | 56 | 00 | | | | | 56 | 00 |
| Jan. | 24 | To Balance.......... | | 1 | 55 | | | | | | |

### 2. WILLIAM STEADY.

| DR. | | | | | | CR. | | | | |
|---|---|---|---|---|---|---|---|---|---|---|
| 1882. | | | | | | 1882. | | | | |
| Jan. | 12 | To Cash | 1 | 5 | 00 | Jan. | 1 | By Cash | 1 | 25 | 00 |
| | 18 | " " | 2 | 6 | 00 | | | | | | |
| | *23* | *To Balance* | | *14* | *00* | | | | | | |
| | | | | 25 | 00 | | | | | 25 | 00 |
| | | | | | | Jan. | 24 | By Balance | | 14 | 00 |

### 3. FRED. WATSON.

| DR. | | | | | | CR. | | | | | |
|---|---|---|---|---|---|---|---|---|---|---|---|
| 1882. | | | | | | 1882. | | | | | |
| Jan. | 13 | To Cash | 1 | 4 | 00 | Jan. | 20 | By Cash | 2 | 3 | 00 |
| | | | | | | | *23* | *By Balance* | | *1* | *00* |
| | | | | 4 | 00 | | | | | 4 | 00 |
| | 24 | To Balance | | 1 | 00 | | | | | | |

### 4. CITY SAVINGS BANK.

| DR. | | | | | | CR. | | | | | |
|---|---|---|---|---|---|---|---|---|---|---|---|
| 1882. | | | | | | 1882. | | | | | |
| Jan. | 3 | To Cash | 1 | 10 | 00 | Jan. | 20 | By Cash | 2 | 4 | 00 |
| | 18 | " " | 2 | 3 | 00 | | *23* | *By Balance* | | *9* | *00* |
| | | | | 13 | 00 | | | | | 13 | 00 |
| Jan. | 24 | To Balance | | 9 | 00 | | | | | | |

### 5. PROFIT AND LOSS.

| DR. | | | | | | CR. | | | | | |
|---|---|---|---|---|---|---|---|---|---|---|---|
| 1882. | | | | | | 1882. | | | | | |
| Jan. | 2 | To Cash | 1 | 4 | 65 | Jan. | 11 | By Cash | 1 | 12 | 00 |
| | 2 | " " | 1 | | 30 | | 18 | " " | 2 | 12 | 00 |
| | 2 | " " | 1 | 1 | 00 | | 23 | " Cheeryble Bros. | 2 | 8 | 00 |
| | 3 | " " | 1 | 4 | 50 | | | | | | |
| | 17 | " " | 1 | 4 | 50 | | | | | | |
| | 23 | " " | 2 | 8 | 50 | | | | | | |
| | 23 | " " | 2 | 3 | 00 | | | | | | |
| | 23 | " Mary Malone | 2 | 3 | 86 | | | | | | |
| | *23* | *To Capital* | *L.8* | *1* | *69* | | | | | | |
| | | | | 32 | 00 | | | | | 32 | 00 |

### 6. CHEERYBLE BROTHERS.

| DR. | | | | | | CR. | | | | | |
|---|---|---|---|---|---|---|---|---|---|---|---|
| 1882. | | | | | | *1882.* | | | | | |
| Jan. | 23 | To Profit and Loss | 2 | 8 | 00 | *Jan.* | *23* | *By Balance* | | *8* | *00* |
| | 24 | To Balance | | 8 | 00 | | | | | | |

## 7. MARY MALONE.

| | | | | | | | | | | | Cr. |
|---|---|---|---|---|---|---|---|---|---|---|---|
| *1882.* *Jan.* | *23* | *To Balance............* | | *3* | *86* | 1882. Jan. | 23 | By Profit and Loss...... | 2 | 3 | 86 |
| | | | | | | | 24 | By Balance............ | | | 86 |

## 8. CAPITAL.

| Dr. | | | | | | | | | | | Cr. |
|---|---|---|---|---|---|---|---|---|---|---|---|
| *1882.* *Jan.* | *23* | *To Balance............* | | *1* | *69* | 1882. Jan. | 23 | By Profit and Loss...... | L. 5 | 1 | 69 |
| | | | | | | Jan. | 24 | By Balance............ | | 1 | 69 |

97. **Exercise 10.**—Continue Stephen Steady's accounts, making up a Journal and posting it to the Ledger from the occurrences stated in paragraph 23, Exercise 2. Carry the result of Profit and Loss account into Capital; balance all accounts and make a balance sheet.

98. **Exercise 11.**—Journalize the statement in paragraph 57, Exercise 6, as if to open a set of books.

99. **Exercise 12.**—Journalize the following transactions:

Bo't mdse. costing $500; paid cash $300, and my note $200.

Sold mdse. for $560; received cash $200, *my* note for $200, and Philip Nolan's note for $160.

Remember the use of "Sundries;" refer to paragraph 82.

100. Repeat the journalizing table, paragraph 68, from memory.

# CHAPTER IV.

Transferring—Property Accounts—Gain or Loss on Property—Merchandise Account—The Inventory—Closing the Ledger—The Trial Balance—Forms—Example—Exercise in Journalizing, Posting, and Closing.

101. We transferred, in the last chapter, the result of Profit and Loss account to Capital. We wrote the result with red ink on the less side, and then carried it in black ink to the opposite side of Capital account.

102. As the result of Profit and Loss is carried to Capital, so the results of Expense, Interest, etc., are carried to Profit and Loss. Capital is like the sea into which great rivers flow, which are fed by little brooks.

103. But sometimes Property accounts also give results which are carried to Profit and Loss, instead of being brought down as balances. This is the case when there is a *change of value.*

104. We buy a pair of horses for $300. We may open a property account entitled Horses, and make the journal entry thus: "Horses Dr. to Cash $300.

The value of the horses may stand thus until for some reason it is desired to revalue them. Perhaps we may be offered $350, so that $300, although correct as to cost, may no longer be a true representation of their value. We have no more horses than before, but they represent more dollars; we *have more* value invested in horses, and are consequently, as we have parted with no other value nor run into debt, *worth more.* It is then proper to debit Horses account, and credit Profit and Loss with the increase $50.

## HORSES.

| | | | | | | | | | | |
|---|---|---|---|---|---|---|---|---|---|---|
| | | To Cash (cost)......... | 300 | | | | | | | |
| | | " Profit and Loss..... | 50 | | | | | | | |
| | | | 350 | | | | | | | |

105. In like manner we have bought a truck for $100. "Truck Dr. to Cash $100."

When we come to sell it, however, we find we can get only $90 for it. "Cash Dr. to Truck $90."

Truck account then stands:

TRUCK.

| | To Cash............. | 100 | 00 | | By Cash............. | 90 | 00 |
|---|---|---|---|---|---|---|---|

106. If we should now balance the account and bring down the result, it would appear as if we had ten dollars worth of truck still on hand. Instead of balancing the account, we should transfer the loss to Profit and Loss account. Then the two accounts would stand thus:

TRUCK.

| | To Cash............. | 100 | 00 | | By Cash............. | 90 | 00 |
|---|---|---|---|---|---|---|---|
| | | | | | *By Profit and Loss.....* | *10* | |
| | | | | | | 100 | |

PROFIT AND LOSS.

| | To Truck............ | 10 | 00 | | | | |
|---|---|---|---|---|---|---|---|

107. **Merchandise Account** is one where this process is regularly necessary. We always buy merchandise at one price for the express purpose of selling it at a higher price. Thus the debit side of merchandise account in a retailer's business is filled with entries of merchandise *bought* at wholesale prices, and the credit side with entries of *sales* at retail prices. It is evident that if all the merchandise were sold the account would not balance, but there would be a resulting profit to carry to the Profit and Loss account. But usually there is a stock of merchandise remaining on hand. In most kinds of business this stock is gone over once or twice a year, and a list made up, with prices, called an "Inventory." This is called "taking stock" or "taking account of stock." As most merchants do not keep their books in such a way as to know what is the profit on the several sales, they cannot tell until stock-taking what their total profit has been. The time of stock-taking is also the date at which the books are balanced so as to make up the Statement of Results, or Balance Sheet.

108. In closing the Merchandise account, then, there will be a double result: the amount remaining on hand (which must be taken at present wholesale rates), and the profit or margin on sales. The latter result must be obtained from the former.

109. **Example.**—My merchandise has cost during the year $4,000. My sales have been $3,000. My stock remaining on hand is $1,600. What is my profit?

| | |
|---|---|
| Actual proceeds of sales at retail price...... ....... | $3,000 |
| Inventory, or anticipated proceeds at wholesale price. | 1,600 |
| | $4,600 |
| Cost........................................ | 4,000 |
| Profit (being 15 %)................ ............... | $600 |

110. We treat the balance on hand as if it were a sale. It might be said that 1881, to close up its business, *sells* the contents of the inventory to 1882 at wholesale rates.

111. The above transactions would give the following Merchandise Account:

MERCHANDISE.

| | To Sundries [purchases] ....... | 4,000 | 00 | | By Sundries [Sales]....... .... | 3,000 | 00 |
|---|---|---|---|---|---|---|---|
| | *To Profit and Loss* ........... | *600* | *00* | | *By Balance [Inventory]*....... | *1,600* | *00* |
| | | 4,600 | 00 | | | 4,600 | 00 |
| | To Balance.................. | 1,600 | 00 | | | | |

112. **Rule for Balancing Merchandise Account.**—(1) Credit it by the amount on hand as per inventory. (2) Find the difference of the two sides as they now stand. (3) Carry this result to Profit and Loss account. (4) Bring down the balance. Or, arithmetically: To the sales add the inventory; subtract the cost; this difference is the profit.

113. **Exercise 13.**—Purchases, $5,000; Sales, $3,000; Inventory, $2,500. Profit? What per cent.? Make an account of this. **Exercise 14.**—Purchases, $6,000; Sales, $3,000; Inventory, $2,500. Profit or loss? How much?

114. There is nothing particularly abstruse or difficult about the yearly or half-yearly "closing of the ledger," although it may be made to appear mysterious. It merely consists in obtaining the accurate *results* of all accounts, and placing them in a balance sheet.

115. To transfer an account, enter the result on the less side, and rule off as if to balance the account; but instead of carrying down the balance, place it on the opposite side of the account to which it is to be transferred.

116. The process of closing a ledger is as follows:

1. The first step is to transfer into Profit and Loss account all accounts which are subdivisions of that account, like Expenses, Interest, Commission, etc. 2. Take up those property accounts like Merchandise in which there is a fluctuating value, which has to be ascertained by inventory and appraisal. Find the gain or loss, and close the account doubly, as explained in paragraphs 107 to 112, transferring one result to Profit and Loss, and bringing down the other, the balance. 3. Transfer the result of Profit and Loss to Capital account or accounts. 4. Bring down the balances of this and all the remaining accounts. 5. Copy these balances into a balance sheet, the two sides of which should foot up an equal amount.

117. The TRIAL BALANCE is a test of the correctness of the ledger, which may be applied at any time when the posting is complete to date. It consists in adding up both sides of every account in pencil, then copying these totals into a list like a balance-sheet. Add up the two sides of the trial balance; if they are not alike, there is *surely* an error somewhere; if they are alike, the work is *probably* correct.

118. If a second trial balance is taken, it is only necessary to go back as far as to include the figures of the last trial balance in each account. Many book-keepers take a trial balance at the end of every month.

119. **Example of a Trial Balance.**—The accounts in the Ledger are Cash, Merchandise, Bills Receivable, Bills Payable, Expense, Interest, Profit and Loss, and Capital. Then the trial balance is prepared in one of the following ways:

TRIAL BALANCE.—Form 1.

| Dr. Totals. | ACCOUNTS. | P. | Cr. Totals. |
|---|---|---|---|
| | Cash .................... | | |
| | Mdse ..................... | | |
| | Bills Receivable .......... | | |
| | Bills Payable ............ | | |
| | Expense ................. | | |
| | Interest ................. | | |
| | Profit and Loss........... | | |
| | Capital .................. | | |

TRIAL BALANCE.—Form 2.

| ACCOUNTS. | P. | Dr. | Cr. |
|---|---|---|---|
| Cash.................. | 1 | | |
| Mdse.................. | 2 | | |
| Bills Receivable....... | 3 | | |
| Bills Payable.......... | 4 | | |
| Expense .............. | 5 | | |
| Interest .............. | 6 | | |
| Profit and Loss........ | 7 | | |
| Capital .............. | 8 | | |

TRIAL BALANCE.—Form 3.

| ACCOUNT. | P. | January. | | February. | | March. | | April. | | May. | | June. | |
|---|---|---|---|---|---|---|---|---|---|---|---|---|---|
| | | Dr. | Cr. | Dr. | Cr. | Dr. | Cr. | Dr. | Cr. | Dr. | Cr. | Dr. | Cr. |
| Cash............. | | | | | | | | | | | | | |
| Mdse............. | | | | | | | | | | | | | |
| Bills Receivable..... | | | | | | | | | | | | | |
| Bills Payable ........ | | | | | | | | | | | | | |
| Expense ............ | | | | | | | | | | | | | |
| Interest ............ | | | | | | | | | | | | | |
| Profit and Loss....... | | | | | | | | | | | | | |
| Capital ............. | | | | | | | | | | | | | |

Form 3 is used by those who take monthly trial balances. A very convenient form is in a book where, by using the two open pages, the titles of the accounts need only be written once a year.

119. Pursuing the routine, with Form 1, we take first the Cash account; add up the debit side and the credit side, and place the totals, $12,860 and $9,638, in the money columns. In Merchandise the totals are $10,000 and $9,360, which we set down likewise. In Bills Receivable there are no credits. When we have thus copied all the totals we have the following result:

TRIAL BALANCE.

Jan'y 12, 1882.

| Dr. | Accounts. | Cr. |
|---|---|---|
| 12,860 | Cash. | 9,638 |
| 10,000 | Merchandise. | 9,360 |
| 3,900 | Bills Receivable. | ......... |
| 3,000 | Bills Payable. | 6,000 |
| 225 | Expense. | ......... |
| 3 | Interest. | ......... |
| ......... | Profit and Loss. | ......... |
| ......... | Capital. | 5,000 |
| 29,988 | | 29,998 |

120. From the fact that there is a difference of $10 in the totals, we know that there is somewhere an error or errors of at least that amount. It would be well to look at the footing of the journal up to this point so as to know whether the error is in the debits or the credits. We find that the debit column of the trial balance agrees perfectly with the debit column of the journal, but that the credit side does not agree. Hence we look in the credit figures for the mistake. We go over the additions of that side carefully again, and we compare every amount with its original in the journal until we detect and correct the mistake.

121. We now give, as an exercise, a few transactions to be made into a journal and posted to the ledger. The accounts required are: Cash (14 lines needed), Merchandise (8 lines), Bills Receivable (5 lines), Bills Payable (3 lines), Expense (9 lines), Interest (4 lines), Profit and Loss (3 lines), Capital (3 lines).

122. **Exercise 15.**—— —— [Name of student] begins business to-day, Jan. 1, 1882, with a cash capital of $5,000. Jan. 3—Bo't merchandise costing $7,000; paid cash $4,000 and my note for the remainder (to bear interest at 6 per cent. till paid). Jan. 4. Sold merchandise for $3,000; received $1,500 cash and $1,500 in note of Job Williams at 60 days. Jan. 5. Paid for stationery, $50. Jan. 6. Paid for signs, $100. Jan 7. Paid clerk hire, $75; Bo't merchandise on my note for $3,000, payable in $30 days; sold for cash merchandise $2,360. Jan. 9. Paid off my note given on the third, principal $3,000, interest $3. Jan. 10. Sold for cash merchandise, $4,000. Jan. 11. Lent Mark Twain $2,400 on his note, payable on demand with interest at 6 per cent. [When the posting is done to this point, take a trial-balance. If it does not prove, find out on which side the error is and trace it out.] Jan. 14. Paid clerk hire, $75. Jan. 16. Bo't merchandise for cash, $3,000. Jan. 18. Sold merchandise for cash, $2,000. Jan. 21. Sold merchandise $2,000 for note at 30 days; paid clerk hire, $75; paid for various expenses, $30; received payment in cash of Mark Twain's note, principal $2,400, interest $4. Jan. 23. Bought merchandise for cash, $1,800. Jan. 28. Paid clerk hire, $75. Jan. 30. Sold merchandise for cash, $400. Jan. 31. Paid clerk hire to date, $37.50; paid rent for the month of January, $400; drew out of the business for personal use, cash, $1,000. [Debit capital.]

Now close your ledger. Your inventory shows that you have $3,000 worth of merchandise on hand. Find the result of each account and bring it down or transfer it to Profit and Loss, as may be proper. Transfer the result of Profit and Loss to Capital. Balance this and bring it down. The balance will be $5,043.50. Make a balance sheet.

## CHAPTER V.

Use of the Ledger—Books of Original Entry—The Day Book not Used—The Historical Journal Obsolete—The Cash Book, Sales Book and Invoice Book—Forms of the Cash Book—Journalizing and Direct Posting—The Bank Account Introduced into the Cash Book—Special Columns in the Cash Book—Cash Book Used for all Entries—Model.

123. The Ledger is the book of results. It is the source to which we look for information as to our dealings with any party, or our transactions in any branch of our business. Its office is to classify. The other books are all arranged so as to facilitate this classification, varying in method with the nature of the business.

124. The Journal, as we have given it, is not a practical book for any business even of moderate extent. The transactions in any actual business run in certain lines. In a mercantile business, the great mass of transactions consist of purchases, sales, receipts, payments; not one entry in hundreds but will be included in one or the other of these four. To enter these transactions in a journal indiscriminately and post both the debit and the credit of each transaction separately would be a crude and unscientific plan, and is not used in modern business.

125. Books of instruction on book-keeping usually speak of the Day Book as a book preparatory to the journal, in which a narrative of all the events of the business is written in ordinary language without regard to the accounts they will affect. The writer knows of no business house where such a book is kept. It is just as easy and is the universal practice to make the first record in proper form. The practical way is to have different books for different kinds of entries; in mercantile business all sales are entered in the sales book, all purchases in the invoice book, all receipts and payments in the cash book.

127. These specialized books are prepared with a view to the sole purpose which each is destined for. As the sales book is to contain nothing but a long series of records of sales, it must be so arranged that every particular relating to a sale may find a convenient place and be stated with the least possible labor.

128. But there are two ways of carrying the contents of these books to the ledger—Direct Posting and Journalizing. Book-keepers are divided in opinion as to which of these methods is preferable, and we will express no further judgment on the matter than this: In our experience, we have known of a number of book-keepers who had dropped the journal and adopted the Direct Posting system, but we have never met with a case where the journal was introduced and the direct method dropped.

129. Whether the posting is done direct or through the medium of the journal, it is most usual to group the like transactions of an entire month together. For example, the salesbook is kept in such a way as to show the total sales for the month; the invoice book in such a way as to show the total purchases for the month. Sometimes, but not so frequently, the period is made weekly or daily.

130. We will first explain the cash book, for it is almost invariably kept in every kind of business.

131. *Receiving* and *paying* are two distinct classes of operations, but they are almost always kept in the same book on opposite pages. In accordance with the rules of the cash account as explained in Chapter I., the left hand side is devoted to receipts and the right side to payments.

132. The balance of cash on hand should be counted every day at the close of business and should be compared with the difference of the two sides of the cash book.

## CASH

| Month | Day | Particulars | Folio | Dollars | Cents |
|---|---|---|---|---|---|
| 1882. Jan. | 1 | To **Capital**, amount invested |  | 5,000 |  |
|  | 3 | " **Mdse.**, sold Job Williams (Sales 1), 3,000 |  |  |  |
|  |  | Note, 1,500 |  | 1,500 |  |
|  | 7 | " **Mdse.**, sold Andrew J. Provost (Sales 2) |  | 2,360 |  |
|  |  |  |  | 8,860 |  |
| Jan. | 8 | To **Balance** brought down |  | 4,635 |  |
|  | 10 | " **Mdse.**, sold R. K. Munkittrick (Sales 3) |  | 4,000 |  |
|  |  |  |  | 8,635 |  |
| Jan. | 15 | To **Balance** brought down |  | 3,157 |  |
|  | 18 | " **Mdse.**, sold A. R. Haven (Sales 3) |  | 2,000 |  |
|  | 21 | " **Bills Receivable**, collected M. Twain's note |  | 2,400 |  |
|  |  | " **Interest on above note to date @ 6%** |  | 4 |  |
|  |  |  |  | 7,561 |  |
| Jan. | 22 | To **Balance** brought down |  | 4,456 |  |
|  | 30 | " **Mdse.**, sold P. T. Barnum (Sales 4) |  | 400 |  |
|  |  |  |  | 4,856 |  |
| Feb. | 1 | To **Balance** brought forward from January |  | 2,543 | 50 |

## BOOK.

| | | | | | |
|---|---|---|---|---|---|
| 1882. Jan. | 3 | By **Mdse.** Bo't of Alex. T. Stewart & Co., Inv. 1, $7,000 ; note, $3,000. ........ | | 4,000 | |
| | 5 | " **Expense,** paid Corlies Macy & Co. for books and stationery..... | | 50 | |
| | 6 | " " paid G. H. Macarthy for painting signs........... | | 100 | |
| | 7 | " " paid Salaries........... | | 75 | |
| | *7* | " *Balance, amount on hand*........... | | *4,635* | |
| | | | | 8,860 | |
| Jan. | 9 | By **Bills Payable,** paid note to Alex. T. Stewart & Co........... | | 3,000 | |
| | 9 | " **Interest** on above note, 6 d. @ 6½........... | | 3 | |
| | 11 | " **Bills Receivable,** loaned Mark Twain on note on demand with interest........... | | 2,400 | |
| | 14 | " **Expense,** paid Salaries........... | | 75 | |
| | *14* | " *Balance, amount on hand*........... | | *3,157* | |
| | | | | 8,635 | |
| Jan. | 16 | By **Mdse.,** bo't of Alex. T. Stewart & Co., Inv. 2........... | | 3,000 | |
| | 21 | " **Expense,** sundries as per petty C. B........... | | 30 | |
| | 21 | " " paid Salaries........... | | 75 | |
| | *21* | " *Balance, amount on hand*........... | | *4,456* | |
| | | | | 7,561 | |
| Jan. | 23 | By **Mdse.,** bo't of Arnold Constable & Co., Inv. 3........... | | 1,800 | |
| | 28 | " **Expense,** paid Salaries........... | | 75 | 50 |
| | 31 | " " " " to date........... | | 37 | *50* |
| | 31 | " " " rent for one month........... | | 400 | |
| | *31* | " *Balance, amount on hand*........... | | *2,543* | |
| | | | | 4,856 | |

133. There are many devices for improving the Cash book, and fitting it to special requirements. We shall give ample instructions on this subject hereafter, but, confining ourselves for the present to the simple form of cash book given above, will show how its contents are to be transferred to the ledger, by the two methods of Journalizing and Direct Posting.

134. The following is an example of the journal entries which are made from the cash book transactions of the preceding pages.

## JOURNAL.—JANUARY, 1882.

| | | | |
|---|---|---|---|
| **Cash**. Dr. to Sundries.... Total receipts for month. | 17,664 00 | | |
| To **Capital** for amount invested. | | 5,000 00 | |
| " **Mdse**., for cash sales, viz., Jan. 3....1,500; " 7....2,360; " 10....4,000; " 18....2,000; " 30....400 | | 10,260 00 | |
| To **Bills Receivable**, collected Mark Twain's note.... | | 2,400 00 | |
| " **Interest**, 10 days at 6%.... | | 4 00 | |
| Sundries Dr. to **Cash**.... Total payments for month. | | 15,120 50 | |
| **Mdse**., for cash purchases, viz., Jan. 3....4,000; " 16....3,000; " 23....1,800 | 8,800 00 | | |
| **Expense**, viz., Jan. 5....50; " 6....100; " 7....75; " 14....75; " 21....105; " 31....512 50 | 917 50 | | |
| **Bills Payable**, redeemed note to A. T. Stewart & Co.... | 3,000 00 | | |
| **Bills Receivable**, loaned on demand to Mark Twain.... | 2,400 00 | | |
| **Interest** on demand-note to A. T. Stewart & Co.... | 3 00 | | |

135. The posting of these entries requires no explanation. Our readers are familiar with the operation.

136. The method of direct posting dispenses with the journalizing of the cash book altogether. The left hand or "received" page may be considered as a continuous entry. "Cash Dr. to Sundries." Every account to which Cash is Dr., we know, without journalizing, should be credited, "By Cash." Similarly all entries on the credit side of the Cash book are posted to the debit of other accounts. We may state the rule.

137. **Rule for posting from the Cash Book.**—Post from the left of the cash book to the right of the ledger; and from the right to the left.

138. In fact, the cash book is nothing more nor less than the Cash Account in full, removed from the ledger, placed in a book by itself, and used for original entry of all transactions involving cash. It is therefore superfluous to keep a cash account as well as the cash book. When you take a trial balance or make up a balance sheet, include among the resources the balance of cash as shown by the cash book. The page of the account to which the posting is made is inserted in the column next to the money column.

139. As we have already said there are very many modifications in the mode of keeping the cash book. The skill of the experienced accountant is often called into action to devise a cash book for the special requirements of some particular branch, or some individual business concern. It will be interesting and useful to consider some of these peculiarities.

140. (1.) The scope of "Cash" is considerably widened beyond that of mere money. Bank deposits and bank checks, whether drawn by ourselves or by other people, are now very usually included as cash; that is to say, we consider the money in the bank and that in hand as both together making up our cash. This is the simplest way of treating the bank account, and saves the necessity of keeping a regular ledger account for it. Deposits are not noted at all, neither are checks for which we draw the money, and checks are entered simply as cash payments. For the particulars of the bank account the stub of the check book is referred to.

As an illustration of this use of the cash book, and also of another arrangement of the columns that facilitates posting by bringing the amounts close to the title of the account, we re-write the entries in the cash-book from January 15th to 21st. It will be seen that the only division of the bank balance from the money in hand is at the time of striking the balance, and that the two amounts may be consolidated as they are brought down.

## CASH.

| 1882. | | Receipts. | | Cr. | Account. | Dr. | Payments. | | Specification. |
|---|---|---|---|---|---|---|---|---|---|
| Jan. | 15 | 2,457 | 00 | | .................. | | | | Balance in Bank. |
| | 15 | 700 | 00 | | .................. | | | | " in Drawer. |
| | 16 | | | | Mdse. | | 3,000 | 00 | Invoice 2, Alex. T. Stewart & Co. |
| | 18 | 2,000 | 00 | | Mdse. | | | | Sales 3, A. R. Haven. |
| | 21 | | | | Expense. | | 30 | 00 | As per Petty Cash book. |
| | " | 2,400 | 00 | | Bills Receivable. | | | | Note, Mark Twain. |
| | " | 4 | 00 | | Interest. | | | | On above note, 10 days @ 6%. |
| | " | | | | Expense. | | 75 | 00 | Salaries; ck., $25, money, $50. |
| | | | | | .................. | | *4,361* | *00* | *Balance in Bank.* |
| | | | | | .................. | | *95* | *00* | " *in Drawer.* |
| | | 7,561 | 00 | | | | 7,561 | 00 | |
| Jan. | 22 | 4,456 | 00 | | | | | | Balance brought down. |

141. The method of keeping the stub of the check book is fully explained in that part of this work entitled "Banking." We now give, however, an illustration of the stub corresponding to this extract from the cash book. It is assumed that the merchant drew $75 from the bank on Friday for the purpose of paying the salaries due next day, but that one of his employees (Mr. A. Clerk) preferred to receive the amount due him in a check.

| | | | | | |
|---|---|---|---|---|---|
| 1882. | | | | | |
| January 15, Balance............... | 2,457 | 00 | No. 5. Date, January 16, 1882. Amount................ Order of Alex. T. Stewart & Co., for Mdse. | 3,000 | 00 |
| " 18, Deposited A. R. Haven's Check........$2,000 Money......... 600 | 2,600 | 00 | | | |
| " 21, Deposited Mark Twain's Check............. | 2,404 | 00 | | | |
| | | | No. 6. Date, January 20, 1882. Amount................ Order of Bearer, for Money. | 75 | 00 |
| | | | No. 7. Date, January 21, 1882. Amount................ Order of A. Clerk, for Salary. | 25 | 00 |
| | | | Balance.............. | 4,361 | 00 |
| | 7,461 | 00 | | 7,461 | 00 |

142. There are other ways of treating the bank deposit in connection with the cash book. Two columns may be kept on each side, one for the bank account, one for the cash on hand.

RECEIVED. **CASH.** PAID.

| | | | BANK. | | DRAWER. | | | | | BANK. | | DRAWER. | |
|---|---|---|---|---|---|---|---|---|---|---|---|---|---|
| Jan. | 15 | Balances.................. | 2,457 | 00 | 700 | 00 | Jan. | 16 | **Mdse.**, Inv. 2, Ck. 5....... | 3,000 | 00 | | |
| " | 18 | **Mdse.**, 3, A. Haven.....} | 2,000 | 00 | | | " | 18 | Money for deposit.. | | | 600 | 00 |
| " | 18 | Dep. money.....} | 600 | 00 | | | " | 20 | Cashed Ck. No. 6... | 75 | 00 | | |
| " | 20 | Ck. cashed........ | | | 75 | 00 | " | 21 | **Expense**, as per P. C. B... | | | 30 | 00 |
| " | 21 | **Bill Rec.**, M. Twain.....} | 2,400 | 00 | | | " | 21 | **Expense**, Salaries......... | 25 | 00 | 50 | 00 |
| " | 21 | **Interest**, " .....} | 4 | 00 | | | " | 21 | *Balances*................. | *4,361* | *00* | *95* | *00* |
| | | | 7,461 | 00 | 775 | 00 | | | | 7,461 | 00 | 775 | 00 |
| " | 22 | Balances................ | 4,361 | 00 | 95 | 00 | | | | | | | |

143. Others again keep the cash book purely for the cash and checks on hand, making an entry on the credit side when a deposit is made, but making no entry when a check is drawn except it be drawn in money. The other checks are posted from the stub (which is considered as a regular book of account) to the debit of the proper accounts. Thus checks No. 5 and No. 7 in the example would be posted to the debit of Mdse. and Expense, while the manner of making up the cash book will be found in the following example, in which is introduced still another arrangement of the columns of the cash book.

**CASH.**

| | | | | Dr. | | Cr. |
|---|---|---|---|---|---|---|
| Jan. | 15 | Balance | √ | 700 | | |
| | 18 | **Mdse.**, A. R. Haven | 2 | 2,000 | | |
| | | **Bank**, deposited | | | √ | 2,600 |
| | 20 | **Bank**, drew | √ | 75 | | |
| | 21 | **Expense**, P. C. B. | | | 5 | 30 |
| | 21 | do. Salaries | | | 5 | 50 |
| | 21 | **Bills Rec.**, Mark Twain | 3 | 2,400 | | |
| | 21 | **Interest**, do. | 6 | 4 | | |
| | 21 | **Bank**, deposited | | | √ | 2,404 |
| | *21* | *Balance* | | | √ | *95* |
| | | | | 5,179 | | 5,179 |
| | 22 | Balance | √ | 95 | | |

The check-marks (√) in the columns used for the ledger page, indicate that the entry has been compared with the stub.

144. (2.) Another extension of the cash book is in introducing special columns in order to group together the entries which go to certain accounts. It will be noticed in our model cash book that many of the entries on the debit side are to be credited to Merchandise Account, and many on the

## CASH

RECEIPTS AND CREDITS.

| Date, 1882. | | Consideration. | Voucher No. | Account Credited. | Page. | Merchandise. | General. |
|---|---|---|---|---|---|---|---|
| Jan. | 1 | Amount invested this day | | Capital | | | 5,000 |
| | 3 | Sold Job Williams on cash and note (see opposite) | 1 | Merchandise | | 3,000 | |
| | 3 | Gave note to A. T. Stewart in payment of bill | 2 | Bills Payable | | | 3,000 |
| | 7 | Sold Andrew J. Provost | 6 | Merchandise | | 2,360 | |
| | 7 | Gave note to Abm. Watkins in payment for mdse. (see opp.) | 7 | Bills Payable | | | 3,000 |
| | 10 | Sold R. K. Munkittrick | 9 | Merchandise | | 4,000 | |

Proof of Cash.

| | | | |
|---|---|---|---|
| 9,360 | 10,000 | | |
| 11,000 | 300 | | |
| | 6,903 | Bank | 2,457 |
| 20,360 | | | |
| 17,203 | 17,203 | Drawer | 700 |
| 3,157 | | | 3,157 |

| Date, 1882. | | Consideration. | Voucher No. | Account Credited. | Page. | Merchandise. | General. |
|---|---|---|---|---|---|---|---|
| | | | | | | *9,360* | *11,000* |
| | 18 | Sold A. R. Haven | 13 | Merchandise | | 2,000 | |
| | 21 | Sold Philip Muller on note | 14 | Merchandise | | 2,000 | |
| | 21 | Collected Mark Twain's note, principal and interest | 21 | Bills Receivable | | | 2,400 |
| | | | | Interest | | | 4 |
| | 30 | Sold P. T. Barnum | 24 | Merchandise | | 400 | |
| | | Total for month | | **Merchandise** | | 13,760 | 13,760 |
| | | Total receipts | | **Cash, Dr.** | | | 27,164 |
| Feb. | 1 | Balance forward | | | | | 2,543 50 |

credit side are to be charged to Expense Account. If the journal is used, these are naturally grouped together and posted in one sum; but in direct posting, it would be necessary to make many entries in those accounts. But these accounts are of the very kind in which a total is more valuable than separate items. We therefore split the columns into two or more and only post the aggregate at the end of the month. We retain one column for "general" or miscellaneous items; into this we carry all the special columns at the end of the month. If it is desired to "prove the cash" this requires a little more calculation than in the single-column methods.

145. (3.) The cash book may be made to contain *all* entries, even those in which there is really no delivery of money, by treating these last as *both* receipts and payments. For example, take the following transaction:

Bought merchandise for $3,000, giving my note for that amount.

The Merchandise Account is evidently to be debited, and the Bills Payable account to be credited. The journal entry would be

| | | | |
|---|---|---|---|
| Mdse., | Dr., | $3,000, | |
| | To Bills Payable, | | $3,000. |

But, by a sort of fiction, it may be supposed that the money for the goods was handed out to the seller, and immediately handed back by him in exchange for the note. We did not literally give him money for the goods, but we gave him the value of them in the note. He did not actually pay us the money for the note, but he paid us the same value in merchandise. And the receipt and payment are only postponed. The money is embodied in the merchandise, from which it will be forthcoming when wanted to pay the note.

## BOOK.

PAYMENTS AND CHARGES.

| Date, 1882. | | Consideration. | Voucher No. | Account Debited. | Page | Merchandise. | Expense. | | General. | |
|---|---|---|---|---|---|---|---|---|---|---|
| Jan. | 3 | Bo't of Alex. T. Stewart & Co. cash and note (see opp) | 2 | Merchandise..... | | 7,000 | | | | |
| | " | Took Job Williams' note in payment of bill......... | 1 | Bills Receivable.. | | | | | 1,500 | |
| | 5 | Corlies & Macy Co., books and stationery......... | 3 | Expense......... | | | 50 | | | |
| | 6 | Geo. H. Macarthy, painting sign......... | 4 | Expense......... | | | 100 | | | |
| | 7 | Salaries, as per pay roll...... | 5 | Expense......... | | | 75 | | | |
| | " | B'ot of Abm. Watkins on note......... | 7 | Merchandise...... | | 3,000 | | | | |
| | 9 | Paid note to Alex. T. Stewart & Co., principal and interest......... | 8 | { Bills Payable.. <br> { Interest......... | | | | | 3,000 <br> 3 | |
| | 11 | Loaned Mark Twain note on demand, with interest.... | 10 | Bills Receivable.. | | | | | 2,400 | |
| | 14 | Salaries as per pay roll..... | 11 | Expense......... | | | 75 | | | |
| | | | | | | *10,000* | *300* | | *6,903* | |
| | 16 | Bo't of A. T. Stewart & Co. | 12 | Merchandise...... | | 3,000 | | | | |
| | 21 | Took P. Muller's note in payment.............. | 14 | Bills Receivable.. | | | | | 2,000 | |
| | " | Salaries as per pay roll.... | 15 | Expense......... | | | 75 | | | |
| | " | Sundry bills per C. B...... | 16 to 20 | Expense......... | | | 30 | | | |
| | 23 | Bought of Arnold, Constable & Co.......... | 22 | Merchandise...... | | 1,800 | | | | |
| | 28 | Salaries as per pay roll.... | 23 | Expense......... | | | 75 | | | |
| | 31 | Rent for January......... | 25 | Expense......... | | | 400 | | | |
| | " | Salaries to date, to close the month.......... | 26 | | | | 37 | 50 | | |
| | | Total for month....... | | **Expense**......... | | | 917 | 50 | 917 | 50 |
| | | Total for month....... | | **Merchandise**.... | | 14,800 | | | 14,800 | |
| | | Total payments...... | | **Cash. Cr.** | | | | | 24,620 | 50 |
| | | *Balance in bank*...... | | *2,401* | | | | | | |
| | | *" on hand*...... | | *142 50* | | | | | *2,543* | *50* |
| | | | | | | | | | 27,164 | 00 |

| RECEIVED. | | PAID. | |
|---|---|---|---|
| From **Bills Payable,** the equivalent of cash, (viz. goods.) | $3,000 | For **Merchandise,** the equivalent of cash, (viz., note.) | $3,000 |

| DR. | CASH. | | CR. |
|---|---|---|---|
| To **Bills Payable,** (deferred payment.) | $3,000 | By **Merchandise,** (deferred receipt.) | $3,000 |

This last way of looking at it is on the principle that to avoid a payment is equivalent to receiving, and to excuse a receipt is the same in its effect on the cash as making a payment.

146. In whatever way it is explained, the following is the method of journalizing through the cash book:

The account to be credited is entered on the debit side of the cash; the account to be debited is entered on the credit side of the cash; the cash, being equally swelled both ways, is not affected in the result.

147. The following example of a cash book illustrates the method by columns and also the journalizing through the cash book. It furthermore illustrates the registration of vouchers

NOTE. The preservation and registration of written vouchers for all payments cannot be too strenuously insisted upon. Correct models are given in this work under "Commercial Transactions." The tendency in recent times is not only to insist upon vouchers for all payments, but upon corresponding statements accompanying *receipts* of cash, in order that the intent of the parties may be determined and the amount and consideration placed beyond dispute.

148. Our reason for dwelling so long on the cash book is that it is the one book which is universally required. If a person in private or professional life has not the time or the inclination to keep a full set of accounts, a well arranged cash book may supply all his needs. If it be divided into columns, these will take the place of ledger accounts. If there be any credit transactions with persons, these will probably be very simple, and can be readily traced by running back through the cash book. Again, if a special trust (such as an executorship or the treasurership of an association) be assumed, the trustee will require as his principal book, and possibly as his only one, a well arranged cash book.

## CHAPTER VI.

Other Auxiliary Books—The Merchandise Books—Invoice Book—Sales Book—Description—Models—Rules for Posting—Cash Sales—Journalizing the Merchandise Books—Improved Methods—Copying Press and Posting—Summary Invoice and Sales Books—Models.

149. The **Sales Book** and **Invoice Book** are in the department of merchandise what the cash book is in the department of settlements. They are hardly ever dispensed with in any branch of trade where buying and selling are the means of profit.

150. The INVOICE BOOK is a detailed statement of goods purchased. The SALES BOOK is a detailed statement of goods sold. The former is the same as an entry "Mdse. Dr. to Sundries;" the latter is in effect an entry "Sundries Dr. to Mdse." They might be contained in one book—the invoice on the left-hand page and the sales to the right, corresponding to the cash book:

| More Cash. | Less Cash. |
|---|---|
| More Merchandise. | Less Merchandise. |

But they are generally kept in separate books, for two reasons: because the sales are more numerous, and there would be waste room on the invoice side, and because we do not prove the balance of the merchandise as we do that of the cash.

151. In general arrangement the sales book and invoice book are the same. Each of them contains the following spaces:

| Ledger Page. | [Date] | Page of Account. | Prices. | Totals. |
|---|---|---|---|---|
| | [Entry] ........................................ | | | |
| | ........................................ | | | |

152. The date occupies a line, as in the Journal. The buyer or seller's name comes next; then the quantity and rate of each item. The "extension" or price of the given quantity is in the first money column; the total value of the sale or purchase in the second column. The terms of the sale are either at the beginning or the end of the entry.

153. We give an example of a very simple sales book and invoice book, each in a single page. In practice they are carried forward, page after page, till the end of the month.

## INVOICE BOOK.

| | | | | | |
|---|---|---|---|---|---|
| | Jan. 3, 1882. | | | | |
| | J. J. Cauchois, New York. | | | | |
| | 4 months. | | | | |
| | 5 bags Rio Coffee ................ 680 lbs. | | | | |
| | Tare ........................ 80 " | | | | |
| | 600 " @ .35 | 210 | | | |
| | 3 bags Java Coffee ........................ 370 lbs. | | | | |
| | Tare ........................ 48 " | | | | |
| 17 | 322 " @ .31 | 99 | 82 | 309 | 82 |
| | 4 | | | | |
| | J. Fisher & Co., New York. | | | | |
| | 10 bbls. Canso Herrings ........................ @ 3.50 | 35 | | | |
| | 5 " Round " ........................ @ 3.00 | 15 | | | |
| | 4 " Whitefish ........................ @ 5.00 | 20 | | 70 | |
| C. 1 | Cash | | | | |
| | 5 | | | | |
| | L. Pomeroy, Boston. | | | | |
| | 50 bush. Winter Apples ........................ @ 1.50 | 75 | | | |
| | 40 bush. Potatoes ........................ @ .75 | 30 | | 105 | |
| 23 | Note @ 30 d. | | | | |
| | 10 | | | | |
| | Moller & Co., New York. | | | | |
| | 20 bbls. Mackerel ........................ @ 5 | | | 100 | |
| 14 | 30 d. | | | | |
| | 20 | | | | |
| | Havemeyers & Elder, Brooklyn. | | | | |
| | 20 bbls. No. 2 Sugar ................ 4,390 lbs. | | | | |
| | 300 " tare. | | | | |
| | 4,090 " net @ .10¼ | | | 419 | 22 |
| 28 | 60 d. | | | | |
| | 25 | | | | |
| | J. J. Cauchois, New York. | | | | |
| | 6 bags Rio Coffee ........................ 720 lbs. | | | | |
| | Tare ........................ 90 " | | | | |
| | 630 " @ .34 | | | 214 | 20 |
| 17 | 4 months. | | | | |
| | 31 | | | | |
| | Park & Tilford, New York. | | | | |
| 34 | 10 doz. cans Tomatoes ........................ @ 1.05 | | | 10 | 50 |
| 6 | Total Purchases, Mdse. Dr. ........................ | | | 1,228 | 74 |

## SALES BOOK.

| | | | | | |
|---|---|---|---|---|---|
| | Jan. 3, 1882. | | | | |
| | M. Conkling. | | | | |
| | 3 lbs. Rio Coffee ........ @ .42 | 1 | 26 | | |
| 139 | 2 " Java " ........ @ .40 | | 80 | 2 | 06 |
| | 5 | | | | |
| | P. Wilson. | | | | |
| | 1 bbl. Herring ........ | 4 | 00 | | |
| 182 | 1 bag Coffee, 125 lbs ........ @ .36 | 45 | 00 | 49 | 00 |
| | " | | | | |
| C. 2 | Cash Sales as per tickets ........ | | | 18 | 75 |
| | 6 | | | | |
| | Alexander Hamlin. | | | | |
| | 10 lbs. Java ........ @ .40 | 4 | 00 | | |
| 116 | 2 boxes Raisins ........ @ 3.50 | 7 | 00 | 11 | 00 |
| | " | | | | |
| C. 2 | Cash Sales as per tickets ........ | | | 23 | 25 |
| | 10 | | | | |
| | M. Conkling. | | | | |
| 139 | 1 bbl. Mackerel ........ | | | 6 | 50 |
| | " | | | | |
| | P. Wilson. | | | | |
| | 3 bush. Apples ........ @ 1.75 | 5 | 25 | | |
| 182 | 1 bush. Potatoes ........ | 1 | 00 | 6 | 25 |
| | " | | | | |
| C. 2 | Cash Sales as per tickets ........ | | | 82 | 17 |
| | 15 | | | | |
| | Mrs. Robertson. | | | | |
| | 5 lbs. Tea ........ @ .80 | 4 | 00 | | |
| | 8 " Coffee (mixed) ........ @ .41 | 3 | 28 | | |
| 175 | 1 bbl. Herring ........ | 4 | 00 | 11 | 28 |
| | " | | | | |
| C. 2 | Cash Sales as per tickets ........ | | | 62 | 50 |
| | 31 | | | | |
| | Alexander Hamlin. | | | | |
| | 3 bush. Apples ........ @ 1.75 | 5 | 25 | | |
| 116 | 3 cans Tomatoes ........ @ .15 | | 45 | 5 | 70 |
| 6 | Total Sales, Mdse. Cr. ........ | | | 278 | 46 |

154. Of course we have only given a few transactions, and those on a few days. In actual business, the sales book and invoice book often fill many pages in a month.

155. These books, like the cash book, may be either journalized or posted direct.

RULES.

*Post from the sales book to the debit of the ledger*, and
*Post from the invoice book to the credit of the ledger*.

In cash sales and purchases, the cash book takes the place of the ledger, therefore

*Cash sales appear in the debit of the Cash and in the sales book, and require only the pages to be inserted.*

*Cash purchases appear in the credit of the Cash and in the invoice book, and require only the pages to be inserted:*

156. Thus, if a cash sale appears on page 16 of the cash book, and on page 25 of the sales book, no further posting is necessary. We write in the page columns as follows:

In the Cash book, "S. 25."
In the Sales book, "C. 16."

A cash purchase is marked thus:

In the Cash book, "I. 19."
In the Invoice book, "C. 18."

157. The monthly total of the sales book is posted to the credit of Merchandise.

158. The monthly total of the invoice book is posted to the debit of Merchandise.

159. A sale or purchase is often said to be for "cash," when in reality there is an interval of a few days between the purchase and the receipt. In some kinds of business seven days are regularly allowed on cash bills. In such a case the posting may be deferred, if the purchaser has no account on the books. Some prefer to post all purchases to a personal account, even if immediately settled for.

160. For those who prefer to "journalize" everything, the sales book and invoice book are very simple, and we give the form. We omit the specification under each entry, because many book-keepers, who retain the journal, do so. We also use for this purpose a form of the journal which is not much in vogue, and which certainly is inferior to the one where each ledger-title stands opposite the amount to be posted. This, too, we give because our readers may meet with such a journal, and desire to understand it.

## JOURNAL.

| | | | | | |
|---|---|---|---|---|---|
| | Jan. 31, 1882. | | | | |
| | Mdse. Dr. to Sundries. | | | | |
| | To J. J. Cauchois, 3d. | 309 | 82 | | |
| | 25th | 214 | 20 | | |
| | | | | 524 | 02 |
| | To Bills Payable, 5th. | | | 105 | 00 |
| | " Moller & Co., 10th | | | 100 | 00 |
| | " Havemeyers & Elder, 20th. | | | 419 | 22 |
| | " Park & Tilford, 31st. | | | 10 | 50 |
| | | | | 1,158 | 74 |
| | " | | | | |
| | Sundries Dr. to Mdse. | | | | |
| | M. Conkling. 3d | 2 | 06 | | |
| | 10th | 6 | 50 | 8 | 56 |
| | P. Wilson, 5th | 49 | 00 | | |
| | 10th. | 6 | 25 | 55 | 25 |
| | Alex. Hamlin, 6th | 11 | 00 | | |
| | 31st | 5 | 70 | 16 | 70 |
| | Mrs. Robertson, 15th. | | | 11 | 28 |
| | | | | 91 | 79 |

161. It will be noticed that in the journal the cash sales and purchases are not entered with the others. They must be omitted either from the entry "Mdse. Dr. to Sundries," or from "Sundries Dr. to Cash;" and either from "Cash Dr. to Sundries," or from "Sundries Dr. to Mdse.," to avoid journalizing the same transactions twice.

162. This is a disadvantage of the journalizing method, that the sales and purchases appear in two parts, thus:

## MERCHANDISE.

| DR. | | | | | | | | | CR. |
|---|---|---|---|---|---|---|---|---|---|
| Jan. | 31 | To Cash | 70 | .. | Jan. | 31 | By Cash | 186 | 67 |
| | | " Sundries | 1,158 | 74 | | | " Sundries | 91 | 79 |
| | | *Instead of—* | | | | | *Instead of—* | | |
| Jan. | 1-31 | Total Purchases | 1,228 | 74 | Jan. | 1-31 | Total Sales | 278 | 46 |

163. Instead of copying out the bills into the sales book and the invoice book, an easier way is to use the original bill or a press copy of it. The seller makes out the bill or invoice; he puts it between the dampened leaves of a copying book, and takes a copy with the press. Then the sales book need only contain the name, date, terms, and amount. When the buyer receives the invoice, he pastes it into a book made like a scrap-book, and his invoice book may also be condensed into a single line for each purchase. Sometimes the invoices are folded and kept in bundles, instead of being pasted in a book. So that the modern plan is to make one writing answer for three: copy in the press invoices outward, preserve invoices inward.

164. The sales book and invoice book are still required, but only in a summary or skeleton form:

## INVOICE BOOK.

| DATE. | | INV. | FROM | TERMS. | PAGE. | AMOUNT | |
|---|---|---|---|---|---|---|---|
| 1882. | | | | | | | |
| Jan. | 3 | 1 | J. J. Cauchois, N. Y....... | 4 m. | 17 | 309 | 82 |
| | 4 | 2 | J. Fisher & Co., " ....... | C. | C. 1 | 70 | 00 |
| | 5 | 3 | L. Pomeroy, Boston ....... | B. | 23 | 105 | 00 |
| | 10 | 4 | Moller & Co., N. Y. ....... | 30 d. | 14 | 100 | 00 |
| | 20 | 5 | Havemeyers & Elder, B'klyn | 60 d. | 28 | 419 | 22 |
| | 25 | 6 | J. J. Cauchois, N. Y....... | 4 m. | 17 | 214 | 20 |
| | 31 | 7 | Park & Tilford, " ...... | | 34 | 10 | 50 |
| | | | Mdse. Dr.......... | | 6 | 1,228 | 74 |

## SALES BOOK.

| DATE. | | INV. | BUYER. | PAGE | AMOUNT | |
|---|---|---|---|---|---|---|
| 1882 | | | | | | |
| Jan. | 3 | 1 | M. Conkling........................ | 139 | 2 | 06 |
| | 5 | 2 | P. Wilson........................ | 182 | 49 | 00 |
| | 5 | | Cash Tickets........................ | C. 2 | 18 | 75 |
| | 6 | 3 | A. Hamlin........................ | 116 | 11 | 00 |
| | 6 | | Cash Tickets........................ | C. 2 | 23 | 25 |
| | 10 | 4 | M. Conkling........................ | 139 | 6 | 50 |
| | 11 | 5 | P. Wilson........................ | 182 | 6 | 25 |
| | 11 | | Cash Tickets........................ | C. 2 | 82 | 17 |
| | 15 | 6 | Mrs. Robertson........................ | 175 | 11 | 28 |
| | 15 | | Cash Tickets........................ | C. 2 | 62 | 50 |
| | 31 | 7 | Alex. Hamlin........................ | 116 | 5 | 70 |
| | | | Mdse. Cr........................ | 6 | 278 | 46 |

# CHAPTER VII.

**Model Set of Mercantile Books for practice—Transactions of the firm of Rodgers and Wolcott—Cash Book—Sales Book—Invoice Book—Journal—Ledger—Trial Balances—Balance Sheet.**

165. We have now explained the principles on which book-keeping is based, and propose to give an example of a set of books in mercantile business in which those principles will be exemplified.

166. We have said very little about SINGLE ENTRY BOOK-KEEPING, for we consider it merely as a fragment of Book-keeping proper. It may serve all the purposes of some kinds of business. If the student should strike out all except the personal accounts in the following ledger, he would duce it to a single-entry basis.

167. We recommend that the transactions now given be worked into a set of books by the student. He will be able to correct his work by the models given.

168. The methods employed are severely practical, and are in use in the best houses. We may state the general plan as follows: Cash-book, Sales-book and Invoice book posted direct to the ledger. Cash sales and cash purchases offset each other. The journal used only for entries not appropriate to either of the other books. No cash account in the ledger. Cash on hand and in bank consolidated. Sales book, a summary of the original bills, taken from the copying book. Invoice book, a summary of the original bills which are pasted in a blank book. Trial balance taken monthly, by totals. Transfers from one account to another made through the journal; but the bringing down of a balance in the same account not journalized. Accounts doubtful of collection not closed into profit and loss, but a corresponding amount is reserved from the profit and loss account to cover loss.

# Transactions of the Firm of Rodgers and Wolcott.

Jan. 1. Our Resources and Liabilities are as follows : RESOURCES—Cash, $2,314.97 (of which $1,869.17 is in the People's Bank), Merchandise as per Inventory, $7,819.23 ; Real Estate (building used for trade), $4,000 ; Bills Receivable, $1,250 ; (being one of J. B. Woodward, due Jan. 10, for $1,000, and one of L. P. Bain, due March 19, for $250.) LIABILITIES : on our Notes, $1,500 ($1,000 to H. B. Claflin, due Feb. 10 ; $500 to the same, due Jan. 20). Our capital is shared equally between the two partners.

Our book-keeper is instructed to keep the following books : a Ledger, a Cash book, a Sales book (giving totals of bills only, a press copy of the originals being retained), an Invoice book (giving totals only, the invoices being preserved) ; a Journal, for entries not coming under either of the above books of entry. The Cash book is to contain all entries, whether by check or in money. No cash account to be kept in the Ledger.

Jan. 10. Purchased goods on account, from Arnold & Constable, $3,300 ; from Lord & Taylor, $1,892.17. Sold, on account : to L. Plummer, $362 50 ; to F. P. Simmons, $29.30 ; Mrs. A. J. Provost, $516.92 ; P. L. Jackson, $272.13 ; A. J. Redding, $493.18 ; Cash Sales, $1,563.17. Collected, J. B. Woodward's note, $1,000. Mr. Rodgers drew for private use $100. Paid Expense, $15. Discounted for Patrick Gleason his note due Feb. 10, for $1,000 ; paid him the proceeds in cash, $995.

Jan. 20. Sales : Mrs. A. J. Provost, $213.92 ; P. L. Jackson, $433.19; L. Plummer, $52.00; R. Smith, $718.53 ; R. Wolcott (for private use), $33.69 ; Cash Sales, $1,719.34. Paid Expense, $32.50. Paid our note to H. B. Claflin & Co., due to-day. Mr. Rodgers drew for private use $25. Bought merchandise of L. Cohen & Co., giving our note at 30 days, $575. Paid Arnold, Constable & Co. for bill of Jan. 10th, $3,300. Received on account from L. Plummer, $362.50 ; from Mrs. A. J. Provost, $500.

Jan. 31. Sales : F. P. Simmons, $37.89 ; P. L. Jackson, $526.82 ; A. J. Redding, $829.17 ; R. Smith, $100 ; M. B. Vandervoort, $427.18. Bought of Lord & Taylor, $497.18.

Cash Sales, $1,825.35. Received on account from F. P. Simmons, $67.19 ; from A. J. Redding, $200. Paid Salaries, $800 ; other Expenses, $29.25. Paid Lord & Taylor on account, $1,500.

Balance the Cash book daily. Foot the Sales book and Invoice book at the end of the month and post the totals to Merchandise. Take a trial balance.

Feb. 10. Purchases : Lord & Taylor, $2,600 ; Arnold, Constable & Co., $417.25. Sales : L. Plummer, $215.92 ; F. P. Simmons, $317.44 ; M. B. Vandervoort, $180 ; R. Smith, $29.75 ; A. J. Redding, $334.96 ; P. L. Jackson, $679.18. Cash Sales, $1,560,19. Received on account, from P. L. Jackson, $1,232.14 ; from Mrs. Andrew J. Provost, $100 ; from R. Smith, $100. Collected P. Gleason's note $1,000. Paid Expense, $37.65. Mr. Wolcott drew for private use $300. Paid our note to H. B. Claflin, $1,000.

Feb 20. Sales : Mrs. A. J. Provost, $220.57 ; P. L. Jackson, $318.20 ; M. B. Vandervoort, $622.14 ; F. P. Simmons, $55.17 ; R. Smith, $219.26. Bought of H. B. Claflin, $1,719,26 ; of Bates, Reed & Cooley, $2,316.95. Cash Sales, $1,792.13. Paid Expense, $45.50. Paid our note to L. Cohen & Co., due to-day, $575. Received of A. J. Redding his note in settlement, $1,457.31. Paid Lord & Taylor on account, $3,000. Mr. Rodgers drew for private use $100. Bought of Duncan A. Grant, for cash, mdse., $217.92. Received cash on account from Mrs. A. J. Provost, $100 ; from M. B. Vandervoort, $350.

Feb 28. Sales : P. L. Jackson, $472 18. M. B. Vandervoort, $119.73 ; R. Smith, $230.19 ; L. Baker, $10.25 ; Mrs. A. J. Provost, $318.75 ; A. J. Redding, $293.17. Cash Sales, $2,039.45. Paid Salaries, $800 ; other expenses, $32.75. Gave H. B. Claflin & Co our note for $1,719.26 in settlement of bill of 20th inst. Bought of Lord & Taylor bill amounting to $1,317.92 ; of Arnold, Constable & Co. $2,518.39. Made cash payments to Arnold, Constable & Co $417,25 ; to Bates, Reed & Cooley, $2,000. Sold L. Plummer, $320 ; F. P. Simmons, $213.25. Paid Lord & Taylor $1,000. Received from Mrs. A. J. Provost, on account, $200 ; from R. Smith, $500.

Take another trial balance and compare it with the one in the model.

March 10. Sales : L. Baker, $314.52 ; R. Smith, $213.97 ; L. Plummer, $150 ; P. L. Jackson, $217.95 ; Mrs. A. J. Provost, $142.14 ; F. P. Simmons, $679.18 ; A. Redding, $413.92. Cash Sales, $1,927.18. Collected L. P. Bain's note, $250. Received on account from P. L. Jackson, $1,469.65 ; from L. Plummer, $587.92 ; from Mrs. A. J. Provost, $200. Bought for $1,000 cash, plot adjoining our building, to be used as an extension. Mr. Rodgers took for private use in goods $216.92. Received on account from F. P. Simmons, $585.86 ; from R. Smith, $400 ; from M. B. Vandervoort, $500. Bought of Arnold, Constable & Co. merchandise, $2,132.17. Paid them on account, $2,518,39. Paid expense, $17.25.

March 20. Mr. Rodgers drew for private account $200 ; Mr. Wolcott drew $200. Sales to-day : P. L. Jackson, $220.33 ; L. Plummer, $172.13. Mrs. A. J. Provost, $534.16 ; A. J. Redding, $118.79 ; F. P. Simmons, $239.14 ; R. Smith, $110.92. Cash Sales, $2,019,74. Purchases, Arnold, Constable & Co., $1,319.20 ; Lord & Taylor, 617.93 ; Duncan A. Grant, for cash, $179.18. Paid Expense, $16.50. Paid Lord & Taylor on account, $500 ; Arnold, Constable & Co., $2,132.17. Collections, L. Baker, $314.52 ; L. Plummer, $150.

March 31. Sales : Mrs A. J. Provost, $218 ; A. J. Redding, $115.22 ; R. Smith, $379.24. Cash Sales, $1,579.16. Bought of Lord & Taylor, $1,600. Paid Salaries, $800 ; other expenses, $25.33. Paid Bates, Reed & Cooley, in full, $316.95. Paid Lord & Taylor on account, $1,000. Collections : Mrs. A. J. Provost, $400 ; R. Smith, $450. Received A. J. Redding's note in payment, $941.10.

It is desired to balance the accounts and divide the profits equally between the partners, reserving $400 to meet contingent losses, bad debts, etc.

First, take a trial balance to see whether the work is right to this point.

The Inventory shows a total of merchandise on hand valued at $5,279. From this find what is the profit on the sales of the last six months. What per cent. is it ?

Transfer this profit, also the results of the Expense and interest accounts to Profit and Loss, by journal entries.

Find the result of Profit and Loss account ; transfer it, less $400, in equal parts to the capital accounts of the partners. Transfer the private accounts of the partners to their respective capital accounts.

Bring down the balances of all the accounts now open (without journal entries).

Make up from these balances a balance sheet or statement of the business.

# Cash Book.

RECEIPTS.

| Date | | | Account | Folio | Dollars | Cents |
|---|---|---|---|---|---|---|
| 1882. | | | | | | |
| Jan. | 1 | | **Balance,** from old books, Bank, 1,869.17 | | | |
| | | | Drawer, 445.80 | J. 1 | 2,314 | 97 |
| | 10 | | **Mdse.,** cash sales | S. 1 | 1,563 | 17 |
| | 10 | | **Bills Receivable,** J. B. Woodward's note | 3 | 1,000 | 00 |
| | 10 | | **Interest,** discount on P. Gleason's note as opposite | 9 | 5 | 00 |
| | | | | | 4,883 | 14 |
| Jan. | 11 | | **Balance,** brought forward | | 3,768 | 14 |
| | 20 | | **Mdse.,** cash sales | S. 1 | 1,719 | 34 |
| | 20 | | **L. Plummer,** on account | 17 | 362 | 50 |
| | 20 | | **Mrs. A. J. Provost,** on account | 18 | 500 | 00 |
| | | | | | 6,349 | 98 |
| Jan. | 21 | | **Balance,** brought forward | | 2,492 | 48 |
| | 31 | | **F. P. Simmons,** on account | 21 | 67 | 19 |
| | 31 | | **A. J. Redding,** do. | 19 | 200 | 00 |
| | 31 | | **Mdse.,** cash sales | S. 1 | 1,825 | 35 |
| | | | | | 4,585 | 02 |
| Feb. | 1 | | **Balance,** brought forward, Bank, 1916.82 | | | |
| | | | Drawer, 338.95 | | 2,255 | 77 |
| | 10 | | **P. L. Jackson,** on account | 16 | 1,232 | 14 |
| | 10 | | **Mrs. A. J. Provost,** on account | 18 | 100 | 00 |
| | 10 | | **R. Smith,** do. | 20 | 100 | 00 |
| | 10 | | **Bills Receivable,** collected P. Gleason's note | 3 | 1,000 | 00 |
| | 10 | | **Mdse.,** cash sales | S. 2 | 1,560 | 19 |
| | | | | | 6,248 | 10 |
| Feb. | 11 | | **Balance,** brought forward | | 4,910 | 45 |
| | 20 | | **Mrs. A. J. Provost,** on account | 18 | 100 | 00 |
| | 20 | | **M. B. Vandervoort,** do. | 22 | 350 | 00 |
| | 20 | | **Mdse.,** cash sales | S. 2 | 1,792 | 13 |
| | | | | | 7,152 | 58 |

# Cash Book.

PAYMENTS.

| Date | Day | Particulars | Folio | $ | cts |
|---|---|---|---|---|---|
| 1882. Jan. | 10 | **W. Rodgers,** (private) paid him | 6 | 100 | 00 |
| | 10 | **Expense,** as per petty cash | 8 | 15 | 00 |
| | 10 | **Bills Receivable,** discounted P. Gleason's note: | | | |
| | | Disct. 30 d. @ 6 % 5.00 | | | |
| | | Proceeds 995.00 | 3 | 1,000 | 00 |
| | *10* | *Balance, carried forward* | | *3,768* | *14* |
| | | | | 4,883 | 14 |
| Jan. | 20 | **Bills Payable,** pd. note due to-day | 4 | 500 | 00 |
| | 20 | **W. Rodgers,** (private) paid him | 6 | 25 | 00 |
| | 20 | **Expense,** as per petty cash | 8 | 32 | 50 |
| | 20 | **Arnold, Constable & Co.,** pd. on account | 11 | 3,300 | 00 |
| | *20* | *Balance, carried forward* | | *2,492* | *48* |
| | | | | 6,349 | 98 |
| Jan. | 31 | **Expense,** paid Salaries, as per pay roll | 8 | 800 | 00 |
| | 31 | **Lord & Taylor,** paid on account | 12 | 1,500 | 00 |
| | 31 | **Expense,** as per petty cash book | 8 | 29 | 25 |
| | *31* | *Balance, carried forward* | | *2,255* | *77* |
| | | | | 4,585 | 02 |
| Feb. | 10 | **Expense,** as per petty cash book | 8 | 37 | 65 |
| | 10 | **R. Wolcott,** (private) paid him | 10 | 300 | 00 |
| | 10 | **Bills Payable,** pd. note due to-day | 4 | 1,000 | 00 |
| | *10* | *Balance, carried forward* | | *4,910* | *45* |
| | | | | 6,248 | 10 |
| Feb. | 20 | **Expense,** as per petty cash book | 8 | 45 | 50 |
| | 20 | **Lord & Taylor,** paid on account | 12 | 3,000 | 00 |
| | 20 | **W. Rodgers,** (private) paid him | 6 | 100 | 00 |
| | 20 | **Mdse.** bought of Duncan A. Grant | I. 1 | 217 | 92 |
| | 20 | **Bills Payable,** pd. note due to-day | 4 | 575 | 00 |
| | *20* | *Balance, carried forward, page 3* | | *3,214* | *16* |
| | | | | 7,152 | 58 |

# Cash Book.

RECEIPTS.

| | | | | | |
|---|---|---|---|---|---|
| 1882. Feb. | 21 | **Balance,** from page 2 | | 3,214 | 16 |
| | 28 | **Mdse.,** cash sales | S 2 | 2,039 | 45 |
| | 28 | **Mrs. A. J. Provost,** on account | 18 | 200 | 00 |
| | 28 | **R. Smith,** do. | 20 | 500 | 00 |
| | | | | 5,953 | 61 |
| March. | 1 | **Balance,** brought forward, Bank, 1,501.19<br>Drawer, 202.42 | | 1,703 | 61 |
| | 10 | **Mdse.,** cash sales | S. 3 | 1,927 | 18 |
| | 10 | **Bills Receivable,** L. P. Bain, collected | 3 | 250 | 00 |
| | 10 | **P. L. Jackson,** on account | 16 | 1,469 | 65 |
| | 10 | **L. Plummer,** do. | 17 | 587 | 92 |
| | 10 | **Mrs. A. J. Provost,** on account | 18 | 200 | |
| | 10 | **F. P. Simmons,** do. | 21 | 585 | 86 |
| | 10 | **R. Smith,** do. | 20 | 400 | |
| | | **M. B. Vandervoort,** do. | 22 | 500 | |
| | | | | 7,624 | 22 |
| March. | 20 | **Balance,** brought forward | | 4,088 | 58 |
| | 20 | **Mdse.,** cash sales | S. 3 | 2,019 | 74 |
| | 20 | **L. Baker,** on account | 15 | 314 | 52 |
| | 20 | **L. Plummer,** on account | 17 | 150 | 00 |
| | | | | 6,572 | 84 |
| March. | 21 | **Balance,** brought forward | | 3,344 | 99 |
| | 31 | **Mdse.,** cash sales | S. 3 | 1,579 | 16 |
| | 31 | **Mrs. A. J. Provost,** on account | 18 | 400 | 00 |
| | | **R. Smith,** do. | 20 | 450 | 00 |
| | | | | 5,774 | 15 |
| Apl. | 1 | Balance brought forward | | 3,631 | 87 |

# Cash Book.

PAYMENTS.

| | | | | | |
|---|---|---|---|---|---|
| 1882. Feb. | 28 | **Expense,** paid salaries as per pay roll | 8 | 800 | 00 |
| | 28 | do. as per petty cash book | 8 | 32 | 75 |
| | 28 | **Arnold, Constable & Co.,** on account | 11 | 417 | 25 |
| | 28 | **Bates, Reed & Cooley,** do. | 13 | 2,000 | 00 |
| | 28 | **Lord & Taylor,** do. | 12 | 1,000 | 00 |
| | *28* | *Balance, carried forward* | | *1,703* | *61* |
| | | | | 5,953 | 61 |
| March. | 10 | **Real Estate,** bought adjoining plot to warehouse | 2 | 1,000 | 00 |
| | 10 | **Arnold, Constable & Co.,** on account | 11 | 2,518 | 39 |
| | 10 | **Expense,** as per petty cash book | 8 | 17 | 25 |
| | | *Balance, carried forward* | | *4,088* | *58* |
| | | | | 7,624 | 22 |
| March. | 20 | **W. Rodgers,** (private) paid him | 6 | 200 | 00 |
| | 20 | **R. Wolcott,** (private) do. | 10 | 200 | 00 |
| | 20 | **Mdse.** bo't of Duncan A. Grant | I. 1 | 179 | 18 |
| | 20 | **Expense,** as per petty cash | 8 | 16 | 50 |
| | 20 | **Lord & Taylor,** on account | 12 | 500 | 00 |
| | 20 | **Arnold, Constable & Co.,** on account | 11 | 2,132 | 17 |
| | | *Balance, carried forward* | | *3,344* | *99* |
| | | | | 6,572 | 84 |
| March. | 31 | **Expense,** as per petty cash book | 8 | 25 | 33 |
| | 31 | do. salaries as per pay roll | 8 | 800 | 00 |
| | 31 | **Bates, Reed & Cooley,** in full | 13 | 316 | 95 |
| | 31 | **Lord & Taylor,** on account | 12 | 1,000 | 00 |
| | *31* | *Balance, viz., in Bank, 3,284.25* | | | |
| | | *in Drawer, 347.62* | | *3,631* | *87* |
| | | | | 5,774 | 15 |

## SALES BOOK.

| 1882. | | | Page Copybook. | Page Ledger. | $ | cts. |
|---|---|---|---|---|---|---|
| Jan. | 10 | L. Plummer.......... | 1 | 17 | 362 | 50 |
| | | F. P. Simmons......... | 1 | 21 | 29 | 30 |
| | | Mrs. A. J. Provost.... | 2 | 18 | 516 | 92 |
| | | P. L. Jackson........ | 3 | 16 | 272 | 13 |
| | | A. J. Redding........ | 4 | 19 | 493 | 18 |
| | | Cash Sales............ | — | C1 | 1,563 | 17 |
| | 20 | Mrs. A. J. Provost.... | 5 | 18 | 213 | 92 |
| | | P. L. Jackson......... | 6 | 16 | 433 | 19 |
| | | L. Plummer.......... | 6 | 17 | 52 | 00 |
| | | R. Smith............ | 7 | 20 | 718 | 53 |
| | | R. Wolcott, priv'te acc't | 8 | 10 | 33 | 69 |
| | | Cash Sales............ | — | C1 | 1,719 | 34 |
| | 31 | F. P. Simmons........ | 8 | 21 | 37 | 89 |
| | | P. L. Jackson......... | 9 | 16 | 526 | 82 |
| | | A. J. Redding........ | 10 | 19 | 829 | 17 |
| | | R. Smith............. | 10 | 20 | 100 | — |
| | | M. B. Vandervoort.... | 11 | 22 | 427 | 18 |
| | | Cash Sales............ | — | C1 | 1,825 | 35 |
| | | Total to credit of Mdse. | | 1 | 10,154 | 28 |
| | | 2. | | | | |
| Feb. | 10 | L. Plummer.......... | 12 | 17 | 215 | 92 |
| | | F. P. Simmons........ | 13 | 21 | 317 | 44 |
| | | M. B. Vandervoort.... | 14 | 22 | 180 | 00 |
| | | R. Smith............ | 14 | 20 | 29 | 75 |
| | | A. J. Redding........ | 15 | 19 | 334 | 96 |
| | | P. L. Jackson........ | 16 | 16 | 679 | 18 |
| | | Cash Sales............ | — | C1 | 1,560 | 19 |
| | 20 | Mrs. A. J. Provost ... | 17 | 18 | 220 | 57 |
| | | P. L. Jackson........ | 18 | 16 | 318 | 29 |
| | | M. B. Vandervoort.... | 19 | 22 | 622 | 14 |
| | | F. P. Simmons........ | 20 | 21 | 55 | 17 |
| | | R. Smith............ | 20 | 20 | 219 | 26 |
| | | Cash Sales............ | — | C1 | 1,792 | 13 |
| | 28 | P. L. Jackson, | 21 | 16 | 472 | 18 |
| | | M. B. Vandervoort... | 22 | 22 | 119 | 73 |
| | | R. Smith............ | 22 | 20 | 230 | 19 |
| | | Forward .. ...... | | | 7,367 | 10 |
| | | Forward ......... | | | 7,367 | 10 |
| | | L. Baker.......... | 22 | 15 | 10 | 25 |
| | | Mrs. A. J. Provost.... | 23 | 18 | 318 | 75 |
| | | A. J. Redding........ | 23 | 19 | 293 | 17 |
| | | Cash Sales............ | — | C1 | 2,039 | 45 |
| | | L. Plummer.......... | 24 | 17 | 320 | — |
| | | F. P. Simmons....... | 24 | 21 | 213 | 25 |
| 1882. | | Total to credit of Mdse. | | 1 | 10,228 | 97 |
| March | 10 | 3. | | | | |
| | | L. Baker........... | 25 | 15 | 314 | 52 |
| | | R. Smith............ | 26 | 20 | 213 | 97 |
| | | L. Plummer.......... | 27 | 17 | 150 | — |
| | | P. L. Jackson......... | 27 | 16 | 217 | 95 |
| | | Mrs. A. J. Provost.... | 28 | 18 | 142 | 14 |
| | | F. P. Simmons | 29 | 21 | 679 | 18 |
| | 20 | A. J. Redding........ | 30 | 19 | 413 | 92 |
| | | Cash Sales.......... | — | C3 | 1,927 | 18 |
| | | Rodgers (private)...... | 31 | 6 | 216 | 92 |
| | | P. L. Jackson......... | 31 | 16 | 220 | 33 |
| | | L. Plummer.......... | 32 | 17 | 172 | 13 |
| | | Mrs. A. J. Provost.... | 33 | 18 | 534 | 16 |
| | | A. J. Redding........ | 34 | 19 | 118 | 79 |
| | 31 | F. P. Simmons........ | 35 | 21 | 239 | 14 |
| | | R. Smith............. | 35 | 20 | 110 | 92 |
| | | Cash Sales............ | — | C3 | 2,019 | 74 |
| | | Mrs. A. J. Provost.... | 36 | 18 | 218 | — |
| | | A. J. Redding........ | 36 | 19 | 115 | 22 |
| | | R. Smith............. | 37 | 20 | 379 | 24 |
| | | Cash Sales............ | — | C3 | 1,579 | 16 |
| | | Total to credit of Mdse. | | 1 | 9,982 | 61 |

## INVOICE BOOK.

| 1882. | | | No. Invoice. | Ledger Page. | $ | cts. |
|---|---|---|---|---|---|---|
| Jan. | 10 | Arnold, Constable & Co. | 1 | 11 | 3,300 | 00 |
| | | Lord & Taylor........ | 2 | 12 | 1,892 | 17 |
| | 20 | Bills Payable (L. Cohen & Co).......... | 3 | 4 | 575 | 00 |
| | 31 | Lord & Taylor........ | 4 | 12 | 497 | 18 |
| | | Total to debit of Mdse. | | 1 | 6,264 | 35 |
| Feb. | 10 | Lord & Taylor......... | 5 | 12 | 2,600 | 00 |
| | | Arnold, Constable & Co. | 6 | 11 | 417 | 25 |
| | 20 | H. B. Claflin & Co.... | 7 | 14 | 1,719 | 26 |
| | | Bates, Reed & Cooley.. | 8 | 13 | 2,316 | 95 |
| | | Cash (Duncan A. Grant) | 9 | C2 | 217 | 92 |
| | 28 | Lord & Taylor....... | 10 | 12 | 1,317 | 92 |
| | | Arnold, Constable & Co. | 11 | 11 | 2,518 | 39 |
| | | Total to debit of Mdse. | | 1 | 11,107 | 69 |
| 1882. | | | | | | |
| March | 10 | Arnold, Constable & Co. | | 11 | 2,132 | 17 |
| | 20 | Arnold, Constable & Co. | | 11 | 1,319 | 20 |
| | | Lord & Taylor......... | | 12 | 617 | 93 |
| | | Cash (Duncan A. Grant) | | C4 | 179 | 18 |
| | 31 | Lord & Taylor......... | | 12 | 1,600 | 00 |
| | | Total to debit of Mdse. | | 1 | 5,848 | 48 |

# JOURNAL.

| | | | | | |
|---|---|---|---|---|---|
| | Jan. 1, 1882. | | | | |
| | Sundries Dr. to Sundries. | | | | |
| | To open the books of Rodgers & Wolcott, with the following Resources, Liabilities and Capital: | | | | |
| C. 1 | **Cash**, amount on hand and in bank.................... .... | 2,314 | 97 | | |
| 1 | **Merchandise**, as per Inventory............................ | 7,819 | 23 | | |
| 2 | **Real Estate**, building corner Main and State Streets......... | 4,000 | 00 | | |
| 3 | **Bills Receivable**, J. B. Woodward, Jan. 10..................... | 1,000 | 00 | | |
| 3 | " " L. P. Bain, March 10.................... | 250 | | | |
| 4 | To **Bills Payable**, H. B. Claflin, Feb. 10.............................. | | | 1,000 | 00 |
| 4 | " " " Jan. 20............................ | | | 500 | 00 |
| 5 | **W. Rodgers**, Capital account.................................. | | | 6,942 | 10 |
| 7 | **R. Wolcott**, Capital account.................................. | | | 6,942 | 10 |
| | | 15,384 | 20 | 15,384 | 20 |
| | Feb. 20 | | | | |
| 3/19 | **Bills Receivable**, Dr............................ ........... | 1,457 | 31 | | |
| | To **A. J. Redding**.................................... ......... | | | 1,457 | 31 |
| | Took his note in payment to Feb. 10. | | | | |
| | 28 | | | | |
| 14/4 | **H. B. Claflin & Co.**, Dr............................................ | 1,719 | 26 | | |
| | To **Bills Payable**.................................................... | | | 1,719 | 26 |
| | Gave note for bill of 20th. | | | | |
| | | 3,176 | 57 | 3,176 | 57 |
| | March 31 | | | | |
| 3/19 | **Bills Receivable**, Dr................................................ | 941 | 10 | | |
| | To **A. J. Redding**................................................ | | | 941 | 10 |
| | Took his note in settlement to date. | | | | |
| | " | | | | |
| 1/23 | **Mdse.**, Dr ..................................................... | 4,938 | 11 | | |
| | To **Profit and Loss.** | | | 4,938 | 11 |
| | For amount of profit on sales for the past three months. | | | | |
| | Total Sales (Trial Balance) .................................30,698.86 | | | | |
| | Total cost (including stock on hand) Jan. 1..31,039.75 | | | | |
| | Of which there is still on hand as per Inv....5,279.— | | | | |
| | Leaving cost of goods sold.............................25,760.75 | | | | |
| | Margin of profit thereon (16 per cent.)............. 4,938.11 | | | | |
| | " | | | | |
| 9/23 | **Interest**, Dr................................................ .... | 5 | 00 | | |
| | To **Profit and Loss**.......................................... | | | 5 | 00 |
| | To transfer result for the three months. | | | | |
| | " | | | | |
| 23/8 | **Profit and Loss**, Dr.............................................. | 2,651 | 73 | | |
| | To **Expense**.................................................... | | | 2,651 | 73 |
| | To transfer result for the three months. | | | | |
| | " | | | | |
| 23 | **Profit and Loss** Dr. to Sundries.................................. | 1,891 | 38 | | |
| | To transfer the net profit to accounts of partners, reserving $400 to meet contingent losses: | | | | |
| 5 | To **W. Rodgers**, Capital, his half. ....................... | | | 945 | 69 |
| 7 | " **R. Wolcott**, Capital, his half.............................. | | | 945 | 69 |
| | " | | | | |
| 5/6 | **W. Rodgers**, Capital, Dr.......................................... | 641 | 92 | | |
| | To **W. Rodgers**, Private.......................................... | | | 641 | 92 |
| 7/10 | **R. Wolcott**, Capital ................................................ | 533 | 69 | | |
| | To **R. Wolcott**, Private.......................................... | | | 533 | 69 |
| | To transfer balances of private accounts. | | | | |
| | | 11,602 | 93 | 11,602 | 93 |

# LEDGER.

## 1. MERCHANDISE.

| Date | | | Fo. | Amount | | Date | | | Fo. | Amount | |
|---|---|---|---|---|---|---|---|---|---|---|---|
| 1882 | | | | | | 1882. | | | | | |
| Jan. | 1 | Sundries.........J | 1 | 7,819 | 23 | Jan. | 31 | Sales............... | 1 | 10,154 | 28 |
| | 31 | Purchases.........I | 1 | 6,264 | 35 | Feb. | 28 | " ............... | 2 | 10,561 | 97 |
| Feb. | 28 | " ......... | 1 | 11,107 | 69 | Mar. | 31 | " ............... | 3 | 9,982 | 61 |
| Mar. | 31 | " ......... | 1 | 5,848 | 48 | | " | *Balance*............... | | *5,279* | *00* |
| | " | Profit and Loss...J | 1 | 4,938 | 11 | | | | | | |
| | | | | 35,977 | 86 | | | | | 35,977 | 86 |
| April. | 1 | Balance........... | | 5,279 | 00 | | | | | | |

## 2. REAL ESTATE.

| Date | | | Fo. | Amount | | Date | | | Fo. | Amount | |
|---|---|---|---|---|---|---|---|---|---|---|---|
| 1882 | | | | | | *1882.* | | | | | |
| Jan. | 1 | Sundries.........J | 1 | 4,000 | 00 | *Mar.* | *31* | *Balance*.......... | | *5,000* | |
| Mar. | 31 | Cash ............C | 4 | 1,000 | | | | | | | |
| | | | | 5,000 | | | | | | 5,000 | |
| April. | 1 | Balance ........... | | 5,000 | | | | | | | |

## 3. BILLS RECEIVABLE.

| Date | | | Fo. | Amount | | Date | | | Fo. | Amount | |
|---|---|---|---|---|---|---|---|---|---|---|---|
| 1882. | | | | | | 1882. | | | | | |
| Jan. | 1 | Sundries (J. B. Woodward)....J | 1 | 1,000 | 00 | Jan. | 10 | Cash (J. B. W.) C | 1 | 1,000 | |
| | " | Sund. (L. P. Bain) " | 1 | 250 | 00 | Feb. | 10 | " P. G......... | 1 | 1,000 | |
| | 10 | Cash (P. Gleason) C | 2 | 1,000 | | Mar. | 10 | " L. P. B........ | 3 | 250 | |
| Feb. | 20 | A. J. Redding....J | 1 | 1,457 | 31 | | *31* | *Balance*.......... | | *2,398* | *41* |
| Mar. | 31 | do. " | 1 | 941 | 10 | | | | | | |
| | | | | 4,648 | 41 | | | | | 4,648 | 41 |
| Apl. | 1 | Balance........... | | 2,398 | 41 | | | | | | |

## 4. BILLS PAYABLE.

| Date | | | Fo. | Amount | | Date | | | Fo. | Amount | |
|---|---|---|---|---|---|---|---|---|---|---|---|
| 1882 | | | | | | 1882. | | | | | |
| Jan. | 10 | Cash............. | 2 | 500 | | Jan. | 1 | Sundries (H.B. Claflin & Co).......J | 1 | 1,000 | |
| Feb. | 10 | " ............. | 2 | 1,000 | | | " | Sundries (H.B. Claflin & Co).......J | " | 500 | |
| Feb. | 20 | " ............. | 2 | 575 | | | 20 | Mdse (L. Cohen)..S | 2 | 575 | |
| *Mar.* | *31* | *Balance*.......... | | *1,719* | *26* | Feb. | 28 | H. B. Claflin & Co. J | 1 | 1,719 | 26 |
| | | | | 3,794 | 26 | | | | | 3,794 | 26 |
| | | | | | | Apl. | 1 | Balance........... | | 1,719 | 26 |

## 5. W. RODGERS, CAPITAL.

| Date | | | Fo. | Amount | | Date | | | Fo. | Amount | |
|---|---|---|---|---|---|---|---|---|---|---|---|
| 1882. | | | | | | 1882. | | | | | |
| Mar. | 31 | Private account..J | 1 | 641 | 92 | Jan. | 1 | Sundries.........J | 1 | 6,942 | 10 |
| " | " | *Balance*........... | | *7,245* | *87* | Mar. | 31 | Profit & Loss.....J | 1 | 945 | 69 |
| | | | | 7,887 | 79 | | | | | 7,887 | 79 |
| | | | | | | Apl. | 1 | Balance........... | | 7,245 | 87 |

## 6. W. RODGERS, PRIVATE.

| Date | | | Fo. | Amount | | Date | | | Fo. | Amount | |
|---|---|---|---|---|---|---|---|---|---|---|---|
| 1882. | | | | | | 1882. | | | | | |
| Jan. | 10 | Cash.............. | 2 | 100 | 00 | Mar. | 31 | Capital account...J | 1 | 641 | 92 |
| | 20 | " .............. | 2 | 25 | 00 | | | | | | |
| Feb. | 10 | " .............. | 2 | 100 | | | | | | | |
| Mar. | 10 | Mdse.............S | 3 | 216 | 92 | | | | | | |
| | 20 | Cash.............C | 4 | 200 | | | | | | | |
| | | | | 641 | 92 | | | | | 641 | 92 |

## 7. R. WOLCOTT, CAPITAL.

| | | | | | | | | | | | |
|---|---|---|---|---|---|---|---|---|---|---|---|
| 1882. | | | | | | 1882. | | | | | |
| Mar. | 31 | Private account...J | 1 | 533 | 69 | Jan. | 1 | Sundries.........J | 1 | 6,942 | 10 |
| " | " | *Balance*........... | | *7,354* | *10* | Mar. | 31 | Profit and Loss...J | 1 | 945 | 69 |
| | | | | 7,887 | 79 | | | | | 7,887 | 79 |
| | | | | | | Apl. | 1 | Balance........... | | 7,354 | 10 |

## 8. EXPENSE.

| | | | | | | | | | | | |
|---|---|---|---|---|---|---|---|---|---|---|---|
| 1882. | | | | | | 1882. | | | | | |
| Jan. | 10 | Cash.............. | 2 | 15 | 00 | Mar. | 31 | Profit and Loss...J | 1 | 2,651 | 73 |
| | 20 | " .............. | 2 | 32 | 50 | | | | | | |
| | 31 | " .............. | 2 | 800 | 00 | | | | | | |
| | " | " .............. | 2 | 29 | 25 | | | | | | |
| Feb. | 10 | " .............. | 2 | 37 | 65 | | | | | | |
| | 20 | " .............. | 2 | 45 | 50 | | | | | | |
| | 28 | " .............. | 4 | 800 | | | | | | | |
| | " | " .............. | 4 | 32 | 75 | | | | | | |
| Mar. | 10 | " .............. | 4 | 17 | 25 | | | | | | |
| | 20 | " .............. | 4 | 16 | 50 | | | | | | |
| | 31 | " .............. | 4 | 25 | 33 | | | | | | |
| | " | " .............. | 4 | 800 | | | | | | | |
| | | | | 2,651 | 73 | | | | | 2,651 | 73 |

## 9. INTEREST.

| | | | | | | | | | | | |
|---|---|---|---|---|---|---|---|---|---|---|---|
| 1882. | | | | | | 1882. | | | | | |
| Mar. | 31 | Profit and Loss ..J | 1 | 5 | 00 | Jan. | 10 | Cash.............. | 1 | 5 | 00 |

## 10. R. WOLCOTT, PRIVATE.

| | | | | | | | | | | | |
|---|---|---|---|---|---|---|---|---|---|---|---|
| 1882. | | | | | | 1882. | | | | | |
| Jan. | 30 | Mdse............S | 1 | 33 | 69 | Mar. | 31 | Capital account..J | 1 | 533 | 69 |
| Feb. | 10 | Cash............C | 2 | 300 | | | | | | | |
| Mar. | 20 | " .............. | 4 | 200 | | | | | | | |
| | | | | 533 | 69 | | | | | | |

## 11. ARNOLD, CONSTABLE & CO.

| | | | | | | | | | | | |
|---|---|---|---|---|---|---|---|---|---|---|---|
| 1882. | | | | | | 1882. | | | | | |
| Jan. | 20 | Cash.............. | 2 | 3,300 | | Jan. | 10 | Mdse.............. | 1 | 3,300 | |
| Feb. | 28 | " .............. | 4 | 417 | 25 | Feb. | 10 | " .............. | 1 | 417 | 25 |
| Mar. | 10 | " .............. | 4 | 2,518 | 39 | | 28 | " .............. | 1 | 2,518 | 39 |
| | 20 | " .............. | 4 | 2,332 | 17 | Mar. | 10 | " .............. | 1 | 2,132 | 17 |
| | *31* | *Balance*........... | | *1,319* | *20* | | 20 | " .............. | 1 | 1,319 | 20 |
| | | | | 9,687 | 01 | | | | | 9,687 | 01 |
| | | | | | | Apl. | 1 | Balance........... | | 1,3 9 | 20 |

## 12. LORD & TAYLOR.

| | | | | | | | | | | | |
|---|---|---|---|---|---|---|---|---|---|---|---|
| 1882. | | | | | | 1882. | | | | | |
| Jan. | 31 | Cash.............. | 2 | 1,500 | | Jan. | 10 | Mdse.............. | 1 | 1,892 | 17 |
| Feb. | 20 | " .............. | 2 | 3,000 | | | 31 | " .............. | 1 | 497 | 18 |
| | 28 | " .............. | 4 | 1,000 | | Feb. | 10 | " .............. | 1 | 2,600 | 00 |
| Mar. | 20 | " .............. | 4 | 500 | | | 28 | " .............. | 1 | 1,317 | 92 |
| | 31 | " .............. | 4 | 1,000 | | Mar. | 20 | " .............. | 1 | 617 | 93 |
| | " | *Balance*........... | | *1,525* | *20* | | 31 | " .............. | 1 | 1,600 | |
| | | | | 8,525 | 20 | | | | | 8,525 | 20 |
| | | | | | | Apl. | 1 | Balance........... | | 1,525 | 20 |

### 13. BATES, REED & COOLEY.

| 1882. | | | | | | 1882. | | | | | |
|---|---|---|---|---|---|---|---|---|---|---|---|
| Feb. | 28 | Cash | 4 | 2,000 | 00 | Feb. | 20 | Mdse. | 1 | 2,316 | 95 |
| Mar. | 31 | " | 4 | 316 | 95 | | | | | | |
| | | | | 2,316 | 95 | | | | | 2,316 | 95 |

### 14. H. B. CLAFLIN & CO.

| 1882. | | | | | | 1882. | | | | | |
|---|---|---|---|---|---|---|---|---|---|---|---|
| Feb. | 28 | Bills Payable.....J | 1 | 1,719 | 26 | Feb. | 20 | Mdse. | 1 | 1,719 | 26 |

### 15. L. BAKER.

| 1882. | | | | | | 1882. | | | | | |
|---|---|---|---|---|---|---|---|---|---|---|---|
| Feb. | 28 | Mdse. | 2 | 10 | 25 | Mar. | 20 | Cash | 3 | 314 | 52 |
| Mar. | 10 | " | 3 | 314 | 52 | " | *31* | *Balance* | | *10* | *25* |
| | | | | 324 | 77 | | | | | 324 | 77 |
| Apl. | 1 | Balance | | 10 | 25 | | | | | | |

### 16. P. L. JACKSON.

| 1882. | | | | | | 1882. | | | | | |
|---|---|---|---|---|---|---|---|---|---|---|---|
| Jan. | 10 | Mdse. | 1 | 272 | 13 | Feb. | 10 | Cash | 1 | 1,232 | 14 |
| | 20 | " | 1 | 433 | 19 | Mar. | 10 | " | 3 | 1,469 | 65 |
| | 31 | " | 1 | 526 | 82 | | *31* | *Balance* | | *438* | *28* |
| Feb. | 10 | " | 2 | 679 | 18 | | | | | | |
| | 20 | " | 2 | 318 | 29 | | | | | | |
| | 28 | " | 2 | 472 | 18 | | | | | | |
| Mar. | 10 | " | 3 | 217 | 95 | | | | | | |
| | 20 | " | 3 | 220 | 33 | | | | | | |
| | | | | 3,140 | 07 | | | | | 3,140 | 07 |
| Apl. | 1 | Balance | | 438 | 28 | | | | | | |

### 17. L. PLUMMER.

| 1882. | | | | | | 1882. | | | | | |
|---|---|---|---|---|---|---|---|---|---|---|---|
| Jan. | 10 | Mdse. | 1 | 362 | 50 | Jan. | 20 | Cash | 1 | 362 | 50 |
| | 20 | " | 1 | 52 | 00 | Mar. | 10 | " | 3 | 587 | 92 |
| Feb. | 10 | " | 2 | 215 | 92 | | 20 | " | 3 | 150 | 00 |
| | 28 | " | 2 | 320 | 00 | | *31* | *Balance* | | *172* | *13* |
| Mar. | 10 | " | 3 | 150 | | | | | | | |
| | 20 | " | 3 | 172 | 13 | | | | | | |
| | | | | 1,272 | 55 | | | | | 1,272 | 55 |
| Apl. | 1 | Balance | | 172 | 13 | | | | | | |

### 18. MRS. A. J. PROVOST.

| 1882. | | | | | | 1882. | | | | | |
|---|---|---|---|---|---|---|---|---|---|---|---|
| Jan. | 10 | Mdse. | 1 | 516 | 92 | Jan. | 20 | Cash | 1 | 500 | 00 |
| | 20 | " | 1 | 213 | 92 | Feb. | 10 | " | 1 | 100 | 00 |
| Feb. | 20 | " | 2 | 220 | 57 | | 20 | " | 1 | 100 | 00 |
| | 28 | " | 2 | 318 | 75 | | 28 | " | 3 | 200 | 00 |
| Mar. | 10 | " | 3 | 142 | 14 | Mar. | 20 | " | 3 | 200 | |
| | 20 | " | 3 | 534 | 16 | | 31 | " | 3 | 400 | |
| | 31 | " | 3 | 218 | 00 | | " | *Balance* | | *664* | *46* |
| | | | | 2,164 | 46 | | | | | 2,164 | 46 |
| Apl. | 1 | Balance | | 664 | 46 | | | | | | |

## 19. A. J. REDDING.

| | | | | | | | | | | | |
|---|---|---|---|---|---|---|---|---|---|---|---|
| 1882. | | | | | | 1882. | | | | | |
| Jan. | 10 | Mdse............ | 1 | 493 | 18 | Jan. | 31 | Cash............ | 1 | 200 | |
| | 31 | " ............ | 1 | 829 | 17 | Feb. | 20 | Bills Receivable..J | 1 | 1,457 | 31 |
| Feb. | 10 | " ............ | 2 | 334 | 96 | Mar. | 31 | " " J | 1 | 941 | 10 |
| | 28 | " ............ | 2 | 293 | 17 | | | | | | |
| Mar. | 10 | " ............ | 3 | 413 | 92 | | | | | | |
| | 20 | " ............ | 3 | 118 | 79 | | | | | | |
| | 31 | " ............ | 3 | 115 | 22 | | | | | | |
| | | | | 2,598 | 41 | | | | | 2,598 | 41 |

## 20. R. SMITH.

| | | | | | | | | | | | |
|---|---|---|---|---|---|---|---|---|---|---|---|
| 1882. | | | | | | 1882. | | | | | |
| Jan. | 20 | Mdse............ | 1 | 718 | 53 | Feb. | 10 | Cash............ | 1 | 100 | |
| | 31 | " ............ | 1 | 100 | | | 28 | " ............ | 3 | 500 | |
| Feb. | 10 | " ............ | 2 | 29 | 75 | Mar. | 10 | " ............ | 3 | 400 | |
| | 20 | " ............ | 2 | 219 | 26 | | 31 | " ............ | 2 | 450 | |
| | 28 | " ............ | 2 | 230 | 19 | | " | *Balance*.......... | | *551* | *86* |
| Mar. | 10 | " ............ | 3 | 213 | 97 | | | | | | |
| | 20 | " ............ | 3 | 110 | 92 | | | | | | |
| | 31 | " ............ | 3 | 379 | 24 | | | | | | |
| | | | | 2,001 | 86 | | | | | 2,001 | 86 |
| Apr. | 1 | Balance.......... | | 551 | 86 | | | | | | |

## 21. F. P. SIMMONS.

| | | | | | | | | | | | |
|---|---|---|---|---|---|---|---|---|---|---|---|
| 1882. | | | | | | 1882. | | | | | |
| Jan. | 10 | Mdse............ | 1 | 29 | 30 | Jan. | 31 | Cash............ | 1 | 67 | 19 |
| | 31 | " ............ | 1 | 37 | 89 | Mar. | 10 | " ............ | 3 | 585 | 86 |
| Feb. | 10 | " ............ | 2 | 317 | 44 | | *31* | *Balance*.......... | | *918* | *32* |
| | 20 | " ............ | 2 | 55 | 17 | | | | | | |
| | 28 | " ............ | 2 | 213 | 25 | | | | | | |
| Mar. | 20 | " ............ | 3 | 679 | 18 | | | | | | |
| | 20 | " ............ | 3 | 239 | 14 | | | | | | |
| | | | | 1,571 | 37 | | | | | 1,571 | 37 |
| Apl. | 1 | Balance.......... | | 918 | 32 | | | | | | |

## 22. M. B. VANDERVOORT

| | | | | | | | | | | | |
|---|---|---|---|---|---|---|---|---|---|---|---|
| 1882. | | | | | | 1882. | | | | | |
| Jan. | 31 | Mdse............ | 1 | 427 | 18 | Feb. | 20 | Cash............ | 1 | 350 | 00 |
| Feb. | 10 | " ............ | 2 | 180 | 00 | Mar. | 20 | " ............ | 3 | 500 | |
| | 20 | " ............ | 2 | 622 | 14 | | *31* | *Balance*.......... | | *499* | *05* |
| | 28 | " ............ | 2 | 119 | 73 | | | | | | |
| | | | | 1,349 | 05 | | | | | 1,349 | 05 |
| Apl. | 1 | Balance.......... | | 499 | 05 | | | | | | |

## 23. PROFIT AND LOSS.

| | | | | | | | | | | | |
|---|---|---|---|---|---|---|---|---|---|---|---|
| 1882. | | | | | | 1882. | | | | | |
| Mar. | 31 | Expense.......... | | 2,651 | 23 | Mar. | 31 | Mdse..... ......J | 1 | 4,938 | 11 |
| | " | Sundries.......... | | 1,891 | 38 | | " | Interest.........J | 1 | 5 | |
| | " | *Balance*.......... | | *400* | | | | | | | |
| | | | | 4,943 | 11 | | | | | 4,943 | 11 |
| | | | | | | Apr. | 1 | Balance.......... | | 400 | |

## 6. TRIAL BALANCES.

| PAGE | ACCOUNT. | JANUARY. | | FEBRUARY. | | MARCH. | | APRIL. | | MAY. | | JUNE. | |
|---|---|---|---|---|---|---|---|---|---|---|---|---|---|
| 1 | Merchandise | 14,083 58 | 10,154 28 | 25,191 27 | 20,716 25 | 31,039 75 | 30,698 86 | | | | | | |
| 2 | Real Estate | 4,000 00 | | 4,000 00 | | 5,000 00 | | | | | | | |
| 3 | Bills Receivable | 2,250 00 | 1,000 00 | 3,707 31 | 2,000 00 | 4,648 41 | 2,250 00 | | | | | | |
| 4 | Bills Payable | 500 00 | 2,075 00 | 2,075 00 | 3,794 26 | 2,075 00 | 3,794 26 | | | | | | |
| 5 | W. Rodgers (Capital) | | 6,942 10 | | 6,942 10 | | 6,942 10 | | | | | | |
| 6 | " (Private) | 125 00 | | 225 00 | | 641 92 | | | | | | | |
| 7 | R. Wolcott (Capital) | | 6,942 10 | | 6,942 10 | | 6,942 10 | | | | | | |
| 8 | Expense | 876 75 | | 1,792 65 | | 2,651 73 | | | | | | | |
| 9 | Interest | | 5 00 | | 5 00 | | 5 00 | | | | | | |
| 10 | R. Wolcott (Private) | 33 69 | | 333 69 | | 533 69 | | | | | | | |
| 11 | Arnold, Constable & Co. | 3,300 00 | 3,300 00 | 3,717 25 | 6,235 64 | 8,367 81 | 9,687 01 | | | | | | |
| 12 | Lord & Taylor | 1,500 00 | 2,389 35 | 5,500 00 | 6,307 27 | 7,000 00 | 8,525 20 | | | | | | |
| 13 | Bates, Reed & Cooley | | | 2,000 00 | 2,316 95 | 2,316 95 | 2,316 95 | | | | | | |
| 14 | H. B. Claflin & Co. | | | 1,719 26 | 1,719 26 | 1,719 26 | 1,719 26 | | | | | | |
| 15 | L. Baker | | | 10 25 | | 324 77 | 314 52 | | | | | | |
| 16 | P. L. Jackson | 1,232 14 | | 2,701 79 | 1,232 14 | 3,140 07 | 2,701 79 | | | | | | |
| 17 | L. Plummer | 414 50 | 362 50 | 950 42 | 362 50 | 1,272 55 | 1,100 42 | | | | | | |
| 18 | Mrs. A. J. Provost | 730 84 | 500 00 | 1,270 16 | 900 00 | 2,164 46 | 1,500 00 | | | | | | |
| 19 | A. J. Redding | 1,322 35 | 200 00 | 1,950 48 | 1,657 31 | 2,598 41 | 2,598 41 | | | | | | |
| 20 | R. Smith | 818 53 | | 1,297 73 | 600 00 | 2,001 86 | 1,450 00 | | | | | | |
| 21 | F. P. Simmons | 67 19 | 67 19 | 653 05 | 67 19 | 1,571 37 | 653 05 | | | | | | |
| 22 | M. B. Vandervoort | 427 18 | | 1,349 05 | 350 00 | 1,349 05 | 850 00 | | | | | | |
| | Cash Balance | 2,255 77 | | 1,703 61 | | 3,631 87 | | | | | | | |
| | | 33,937 52 | 33,937 52 | 62,147 97 | 62,147 97 | 84,048 93 | 84,048 93 | | | | | | |

## 7. BALANCE SHEET OF THE FIRM OF RODGERS & WOLCOTT.

April 1, 1882.

| | | | | | |
|---|---|---|---|---|---|
| **RESOURCES.** | | | | | |
| **Cash,** as per Cash-book, p. 4. | | | | | |
| On hand | $347.62 | | | | |
| In bank | 3,284.25 | 3,631 | 87 | | |
| **Merchandise,** as per Inventory, p. 9 | | 5,279 | 00 | | |
| **Real Estate,** as per Ledger, p. 2 | | 5,000 | 00 | | |
| **Bills Receivable,** as per Ledger, p. 3: | | | | | |
| A. J. Redding | 1,457.31 | | | | |
| Do. | 941.10 | 2,398 | 41 | | |
| **Customers,** as per Ledger: | | | | | |
| L. Baker p. 15 | 10.25 | | | | |
| P. L. Jackson 16 | 438.28 | | | | |
| L. Plummer 17 | 172.13 | | | | |
| Mrs. A. J. Provost. 18 | 664.46 | | | | |
| R. Smith 20 | 551.86 | | | | |
| F. P. Simmons 21 | 918.32 | | | | |
| M. B. Vandervoort. 22 | 499.05 | 3,254 | 35 | | |
| **LIABILITIES.** | | | | | |
| **Dealers,** for purchases as per Ledger: | | | | | |
| Arnold Constable & Co., p. 11 | 1,319.20 | | | | |
| Lord & Taylor, 12 | 1,525.20 | | | 2,844 | 40 |
| **Bills Payable** (H. B. Claflin & Co.) | | | | 1,719 | 26 |
| **Reserve** to meet loses in collection | | | | 400 | 00 |
| **CAPITAL.** | | | | | |
| **W. Rodgers'** investment | 7,245.87 | | | | |
| **R. Wolcott's** " | 7,354.10 | | | | |
| Total value of business | | | | 14,599 | 97 |
| | | 19,563 | 63 | 19,563 | 63 |
| **RESULTS.** | | | | | |
| Total sales, 3 months | | | | 30,698 | 86 |
| Cost of same goods | | | | 25,760 | 75 |
| Profit on sales | | | | 4,938 | 11 |
| Interest | | | | 5 | 00 |
| | | | | 4,943 | 11 |
| Deduct: Expense | | 2,651 | 73 | | |
| Estimated loss in collection | | 400 | 00 | 3,051 | 73 |
| Net profits | | | | 1,891 | 38 |
| Each half or | | | | 945 | 69 |

# AVERAGING ACCOUNTS;

## OR, EQUATION OF PAYMENTS.

It very often happens that the items composing an account fall due at various times, and in order to make a settlement with justice to both parties, it becomes necessary to calculate the *average* time when the entire amount may fairly be paid.

Although a number of different methods are used for this purpose they all depend upon one principle which may be thus stated. To keep three dollars for two days is worth just as much as to keep six dollars for one day or one dollar for six days, no matter what is the rate of interest. Multiply the number of time units by the number of money-units and you have what we shall call the *value product*, or simply the product. The value product of a certain number of dollars for a certain number of days tells us how many dollars may be kept *one* day, or how many days *one* dollar may be kept to make an equivalent amount of use.

**Example.** What is the value product of $60 for 9 days? Answer, 540. That is, 540 is the number of dollars that may be kept for one day, or the number of days that one dollar may be may be kept to equal, in either case, the use of $60 for 9 days.

What is the value product of $50 for 16 days?

Of $49 for 10 days? Of $23 for 15 days?

What is the value product of £20 for 9 months? 180.

But this product is in pounds and months, instead of dollars and days, and represents 180 pounds for one month or one pound for 180 months.

As we obtain the value product by multiplying the number of money-units by the number of time units, we may reverse the process when the value product is given, and find, by division, the time for a certain amount of money.

**Example**. For the use of $60 for 9 days, how many days may $108 be kept? The value product is 540. Divide 540 by 108 and we have 5, the number of days that $108 can be kept.

When various sums for various times are to be averaged, we find the value product of each, and then add these products together, giving the total value.

What is the total value of the following amounts for the various periods of time! $30 for 2 days; $30 for 4 days; $40 for 5 days; $8 for 20 days.

First find the products:

30 × 2 = 60
30 × 4 = 120
40 × 5 = 200
8 × 20 = 160

The addition of which gives 540, the total value.

The total amount due is $108. If we are required to find the average time when this total amount may be paid, we divide the total value by the total amount.

108)540(5.

That is, instead of paying $30 after 2 days, $30 at 4 days, $40 at 5 days and $8 at 20 days' time, it would be perfectly just to pay the whole $108 in 5 days. The first two payments are delayed and the last payment is advanced, and the advance counterbalances the delay.

The first 30 dollars are delayed 3 days; value product 90
The other 30 dollars are delayed 1 day; value product 30

Total value of delay.................... 120

The 8 dollar payment is anticipated 15 days; product 120. Therefore, the advance payment compensates for the delay.

We may now frame a set of rules for averaging an account like this, where all the items are payable *one way*.

1. Multiply each payment by its time.
2. Add all these products together.
3. Divide this total by the sum of all the payments.

Average the following:

| (1.) | (2.) |
|---|---|
| $100 for 8 days. | $400 for 3 days. |
| $150 for 9 days. | $600 for 5 days. |
| $200 for 17 days. | $100 for 23 days. |
| $125 for 20 days. | $ 50 for 30 days. |
| **(3.)** | **(4.)** |
| $300 for 2 months, 17 days. | $ 50 for 1 month, 15 days. |
| $500 for 3 months, 12 days. | $ 60 for 2 months, 1 day. |
| $200 for 4 months, 9 days. | $100 for 3 months, 27 days. |

When there are both months and days, as in examples 3 and 4, it is usual to consider the days as thirtieths of a month. Thus, to find the product of $300 for 2 months, 17 days, take $2\frac{17}{30}$ times $300, which is 770.

In the foregoing examples, the number of months or days has always been given, but in most real cases, only a *date* is given for each item. For example,

Jan. 10, $100.
Feb. 12, $200.
March 3, $500.

How are the products to be obtained? We cannot multiply by a date. We must take some fixed date as a starting point, and calculate the length of time between that starting point and the date of each item.

This fixed date is called the **Focal Date**, because it is like a *focus* to which all the other lines of measurement converge. The question is, in any problem, **What shall I take for the focal date?** and the answer is, **Any date whatever**. It makes no difference whatever, as to getting the correct answer, whether you take the date of the earliest item, or that of some other item, or a date in the past or one in the future. It is merely a matter of convenience. But your answer must always be measured from the same focal date.

We will take an example illustrating the use of the following different focal dates: (1). The date of the earliest item; (2) the last day of the previous month; (3) the last day of the previous year; (4) the date of the latest item.

### EXAMPLE.

| *Dates.* 1883. | *Amounts.* |
|---|---|
| March 10, | $252 50 |
| March 20, | 300 00 |
| June 4, | 93 75 |
| July 20, | 165 00 |
| Total due, | $811 25 |

Required the average date.

### SOLUTIONS.

**1. Focal Date.** March 10, 1883.

| | |
|---|---|
| 252 50 × 0 = | 0 |
| 300 00 × 0 m. 10 d. = | 100 00 |
| 93 75 × 2 m. 24 d. = | 262 50 |
| 165 00 × 4 m. 10 d. = | 715 00 |
| 811 25 | ) 1077 50 |

Ans. 1 m. 10 d. from March 10, 1883, or **Apr. 20, 1883.**

**2. Focal Date.** Feb. 28, 1883.

| | |
|---|---|
| 252 50 × 0 m. 10 d. = | 84 17 |
| 300 00 × 0 m. 20 d. = | 200 00 |
| 93 75 × 3 m. 4 d. = | 293 75 |
| 165 00 × 4 m. 20 d. = | 770 00 |
| 811 25 | ) 1347 92 |

Ans. 1 m. 20 d. from Feb. 28, 1883, or **Apr. 20, 1883.**

**3. Focal Date.** Dec. 31, 1882.

| | |
|---|---|
| 252 50 × 2 m. 10 d. = | 589 17 |
| 300 00 × 2 m. 20 d. = | 800 00 |
| 93 75 × 5 m. 4 d. = | 481 25 |
| 165 00 × 6 m. 20 d. = | 1100 00 |
| 811 25 | ) 2970 42 |

Ans. 3 m. 20 d. from Dec. 31, 1882, or **Apr. 20, 1883.**

**4. Focal Date.** July 20, 1883.

| | |
|---|---|
| 252 50 × 4 m. 10 d. = | 1094 17 |
| 300 00 × 4 m. = | 1200 00 |
| 93 75 × 1 m. 16 d. = | 143 75 |
| 165 50 × 0 = | 0 |
| 811 25 | ) 2437 92 |

Ans. 3 mos. before July 20, 1883, or **Apr. 20, 1883.**

Thus the same result is obtained, whatever be the focal date assumed. If all the dates are in the same month, or in two consecutive months, the second method is usually the best; if the dates are scattered through the year, the third method.

Where the account to be averaged is one which contains both debits and credits, proceed as follows: Take an *early* focal date (not later than that of the earliest item); find the products of the debit side and of the credit side separately; subtract the less sum of products from the greater; divide the difference by the balance of the account; the result is the time which, measured from the focal date forward, gives the average date. But if the greater side of the account gives the smaller total product, then the time is to be measured backward.

COMMERCE, though the term is sometimes used as a definition for transactions across water—since so much of it occurs in ships—yet really means only the interchange of products or articles of manufacture, by whatsoever means may be found most convenient and competent.

Almost from the very beginning trade and transportation were allied. As early as beasts were set to bear burdens the processes of barter were effected by their mediation, and the very beginning of transportation in its relation to commerce was undoubtedly to be found in the caravans that transported their burdens across the deserts of Africa, Palestine, Persia, and so on to India and Tartary. The first commerce of which we have any detailed account was that which occurred among the Arabs, and was carried on by caravans. They were in fact traders by profession, conducting the business between different countries having different products and different manufactures, and their periodical movements were very extended and involved materials and articles of great value. They brought ivory and gold from the interior of Africa to the sea coast, and in time transported large numbers

COMMERCE.

of slaves from the same region ; these articles being exchanged for the products and manufactures of countries in which they were desirable.

Navigation in ships appears to have been originated by the ancient Egyptians. Boat travel antedated that, and extended back to a period beyond the reach of human knowledge. The Egyptians are thought to have extended their voyages to the western coast of India, and also to have navigated the Mediterranean. But the first who made sea transportation of goods a business were the Phœnicians, possibly the most remarkable people whose history is preserved to us. In fact the known history of the Phœnicians extends back only to a period fourteen centuries before Christ, while it is well known that even at that early date the country was a flourishing one, whose people covered the shores around the Ægean and Mediterranean seas with their colonies, their factories, and their strongholds. Phœnicia was the Great Britain of remote antiquity. Manufacturing for all existing races, and conducting the commerce of all of them in its own ships and by its own caravans, while founding colonies in different parts of the then known world, each of which in time became an empire—the people of this little territory, 200 miles long by 12 miles wide, present the most striking picture of remote antiquity. Energetic, cunning, and industrious, the Phœnicians made all the world pay tribute to their acuteness and business capacity. They were the "middle-men" between all nations. Meanwhile in the arts they were as great as in commerce and in manufactures, while to them we owe our first knowledge of letters, of astronomy, and of arithmetic. From the Phœnicians Europe received her first lessons in civilization, and imbibed a taste for the elegancies of life. The Phœnicians continued to flourish until 332 B. C., when occurred the capture of Tyre by Alexander, after which period the very name Phœnicia disappears from history, lost in the rising glory of Athens, Corinth, Argo, Carthage, and Alexandria, the great seaport founded by the conqueror.

CARAVAN AT A HALT.

Principal among these colonies was Carthage, whose fleets, passing the Pillars of Hercules with no better guide than the stars, are believed to have sailed northward to the British Isles, and southward for some distance along the west coast of Africa. Rome wrested from Carthage its vast trade, which it placed in the hands of the Italian sailors. The vessels employed up to this period and later were galleys, which changed from time to time in size, but probably not in any other particular. Regular fleets were maintained, both in the Mediterranean and on the coast of Gaul, for the protection of commerce. With the fall of the Roman empire the art of navigation became almost extinct in the Mediterranean, but the islanders of Venice, the Genoese and Pisans soon became the carriers of that great inland sea. Their merchants traded to the farthest Indies, and their markets became the exchanges for the produce of the world. Vast fleets of merchant galleys from these flourishing republics braved the storm, while their constant rivalries gave occasion for the growth of nautical tactics. Naturally their commerce became so rich and extensive that it tempted to piracy, and the Moorish Corsairs penetrated everywhere on both sides of the Straits of Gibraltar in quest of prey.

PIRATES OF THE EIGHTEENTH CENTURY.

Venice, founded in the fifth century by a colony from Padua, was the queen of mediæval commerce. In the fifteenth century her annual exports were valued at 10,000,000 ducats, of which amount 8,000,000 ducats were clear profit. She possessed 300 seagoing and 3,000 smaller vessels, besides a fleet of 47 galleys; and 36,000 men were employed by her on the sea alone. At this time her argosies traversed the ocean in all directions. Intimate intercourse was kept up with every European country, as well as with Syria, Egypt, and even India, and among the imported articles of Venetian merchandise were the iron of Staffordshire, the tin of Cornwall and Devon, and the wool of Sussex. But the fifteenth century, which witnessed the height of her grandeur, was the beginning of her fall. A vast commercial activity was now springing up among the western nations of Europe, due mainly to the discovery of America, and the great commercial city sank rapidly into a decline, which was completed in the latter part of the eighteenth century when Napoleon destroyed its government and ceded its provinces to Austria.

## PIRATES AND PIRACY.

Another element which entered largely into the prosecution of commerce in those days, but which for the last hundred years has been practically extinguished, was the institution of piracy. Traffic by sea from the earliest ages was subject not only to the dangers of the sea—the sudden storm, the sunken rock, the lee shore, and the generally prevailing ignorance with regard to navigation—but was also constantly brought into the presence of a danger more horrible, if possible, than these, threatening not only loss of property and of life, but the dreaded condition of slavery to foreign masters. The Grecian Archipelago was in ancient times particularly infested by sea robbers, and the pirates on the coast of Africa were so daring and audacious that they did not hesitate to attack cities in Italy, until they were defeated by the Romans and their fleets destroyed. Later on, the Gauls took possession of the Bosphorus and its coast, of the Black Sea and the Adriatic, and huge yellow-haired barbarians periodically pillaged the surrounding countries. The Vikings or Sea Kings of the North had no hesitation in pillaging the shores of Norway, Sweden, Denmark, Germany, France, and

England, but these Norsemen found their parallel in the pirates of the China Seas and indeed the whole coast of Asia. The Arabs infested the west coast of India, and gained rich booty from the magnificent commerce between its ports and those of Europe. As late as the close of the eighteenth century there was formed on the coast of Malabar a dangerous combination of pirates including Mussulmans, Hindoos, and Mahrattas, who, for half a century, were the terror of the Malabar coast. In the East Indies there have always been thousands of pirates who, following during a portion of the year the honest calling of fishermen or cultivators of the soil, devoted the greater portion of their time to predatory excursions against the heavily laden merchantmen that traversed those seas. Twelve thousand islands of all sizes and shapes, in the most genial and productive climate in the world, were so infested with these marauders—Malays, Papuans, and others—that they are stated to have numbered as many as 100,000, and the costly spices of the Moluccas, the ebony, pearls, and ostrich feathers of New Guinea ; the rice, pepper, and coffee of Java and Sumatra ; the diamonds, camphor, and gold of Borneo, formed rich and attractive booty for those whose only inclinations were to pillage and depredation, and whose myriads of war prahus darted in and out of the innumerable hidden channels, on the constant lookout for traders. The Arabs gained for themselves possessions in Borneo, and pressed forward the system of piracy which was chiefly organized by them. The wealth which they obtained through its means they invested in the same pursuits, buying gunpowder, arms, and provisions to supply the natives in their excursions, and receiving their pay with unlimited interest in slaves and rich commodities. The Sulus, who were natives of Borneo and adjacent islands, and whose fleets were so large that even the Dutch and Spaniards—most hostile to piracy—never dared to cope with them, formerly sent out fleets of two or three hundred prahus every spring. These Sulus were so brave and daring that they would not only attack junks and prahus, but even European square-rigged ships, Spanish, English, Dutch, and others, murdering the crews, and pillaging and burning their ships. Not to extend this portion of the subject further, it is sufficient to mention the Algerine and Barbary pirates and those that infested the West Indies even so late as the beginning of this century, and our readers will appreciate something of the difficulties in the face of which trade and commerce have been conducted from the beginning of time.

## SLAVES AND SLAVERY.

All kinds of traffic and most of the manufactures and arts were in the flush times of Roman history in the hands of slaves. We meet with slavery in the very earliest history, although in Egypt in the most ancient times the system was unknown. The institution of the slave-trade is believed to have been originated by the Phœnicians, who in many instances sold as slaves those whom they captured in their raids on different countries. In the time of Sylla, Italy contained about 13,000,000 slaves ; Corinth had 450,000 slaves, and Ægina 470,000. Among the eastern Asiatic nations slavery was not frequent, but in Africa, as is well known, it has been customary from time immemorial, derived, doubtless, from the Carthaginians. In time it became a trade of vast importance and value, and has continued down to our own days. Slaves abounded even in England in early times, and Domes Day Book gives a list of 25,000 of them. As late as the twelfth century the Anglo-Saxon slave-dealer sent his human stock to Ireland for sale. In Rome, in its palmy days, there were over 300 different kinds of slaves ; a fact which has a decided bearing on the general subject we are considering, from its significance of the number and variety of articles necessarily occurring in trade to produce so many different vocations for servants. Inasmuch, also, as the entire menial labor of navigation in ancient times was performed by slaves—galley-slaves as they were called—it may be readily perceived how important a part they played in the history of commerce.

### BAZARS.

Owing to the fact that the first ideas of general traffic would necessarily carry with them the notion of a shop or place for the disposition of wares, so that they could be readily observed and inspected by customers, originated the bazars of the Oriental countries, which became in time the markets and market-places of the rest of the world. Goods which were brought by caravans from distant countries were displayed in the open market-place of the town, city, or settlement where the largest number of buy-

ers could be brought to congregate, and after purchase were carried to the bazars and displayed by each individual purchaser in his special section or department. The word bazar is from the Persian, and means market. In Turkey, Egypt, Persia and India, as has been the case from time immemorial, portions of towns are exclusively appropriated to the bazars. These comprise a connected series of streets and lanes, sometimes vaulted, with high brick roofs, domes, or cupolas. The porches of these vast markets are commonly lined with small shops in which goods of little value are exposed for sale. The shops of the bazars are nothing more than small closets six feet square and eight or ten feet high, entirely open in front. The owner usually sits cross-legged on the floor or counter with his goods about him arranged for his convenience. It is said that the Persian, Armenian, and Jewish shopkeepers in the bazars are more obliging than the Turks, and more anxious to obtain customers, but the latter are alleged to be more honest in their business methods. Various portions of the bazar are assigned to different classes of goods. Nearly all of them are supplied with khans or coffee houses to which merchants resort after a successful trade. Women, except of the lower class, are rarely seen in the bazars, while men resort to them for conversation and to pass away the time, as well as for business. Trade begins there at present, as formerly, at daybreak and ends at sundown. The bazars are well watched, but larcenies are almost unknown, and shopkeepers do not hesitate to leave their places unguarded during brief absences.

TURKISH BAZAR.

## FAIRS, ANCIENT AND MODERN.

From the bazar and market place of general traffic to the fair was an easy transition, and it occurred very early in the history of trade. The idea of competition entered into trade practices almost at the beginning of commerce, and it soon became obvious that this would be greatly facilitated by competitive exhibitions held periodically. The word fair is derived possibly from the Latin *forum*, a market place, or from *feriæ*, holidays. Originating partly in the difficulties surrounding transportation, they occurred at considerable intervals, and were a subject of long and careful preparation. The Romans undoubtedly derived the institution from the East, and the custom of making a holiday of this special market season was quite likely to originate the name given to it. Even down to a comparatively recent period European fairs were held on some saint's day or the occasion of a religious festival. The idea of fairs spread all over Europe, and they were held in England in very early times, facilitated by a grant from the crown with the provision that no two fairs should interfere with or impede each other. Among early instances of this character cattle fairs were common, being held once a year in different places in England—at Exeter, Norwich, Norfolk and Carlisle. The great Saint Bartholomew fair became one of great importance and among the most interesting features of London life. In the time of William the Conqueror a fair was established at St. Giles's Hall, near Winchester, England, and in the reign of Henry III. this fair lasted sixteen days, and its jurisdiction covered a space of seven miles. On the continent of Europe the most important fair was that of Beaucaire, in France. In Germany the fairs (*messe*) of Frankfort-on-the-Maine, Frankfort-on-the-Oder, and Leipsic were the most celebrated, the latter adding more particularly a book fair, occurring at Easter, and lasting sometimes three weeks. A great fair and very ancient is still conducted at Sinigaglia, in Italy, and which lasts from the 20th of July until the 10th of August each year. In Hungary a similar fair is that of Pesth, which is the center of Hungarian commerce. But the most remarkable fair known to us is that of Nijni-Novgorod, the foremost commercial and manufacturing town in Russia, 715 miles from St. Petersburg. Fairs were introduced in France as early as the fifth century. The great fair of St. Denis was instituted in 629 ; those of Aix la Chapelle and Troyes about 800. At the fair of St. Denis slaves were sold, and French children were taken away to foreign countries in exchange. Fairs for the sale of slaves were quite common in Germany and in the north of Europe generally, in the eleventh century, and were even encouraged in England by William the Conqueror. The fair of St. Denis was continued until 1777, and in the year 1789 most of the great fairs in France were abolished, and their place taken by permanent markets, but the fair of Beaucaire still continues, its sales amounting to £1,000,000 or $5,000,000 annually. This fair is held from July 1st to July 28th, and merchants come to it even from so far as Persia and Armenia, there being as many as 100,000 people sometimes in attendance. Here the chief articles of commerce are silks, wines, oil, almonds, fruit, wool, and cotton. In Holland there are annual fairs of importance at Amsterdam, Rotterdam, and other cities. They are less frequent in Italy, Spain, and Portugal than in other parts of Europe. The fairs of Leipzig date from the twelfth century, and are the most frequented of any in Germany. The principal articles of trade are silk, cloth, cotton, china, glass, earthenware, drugs, hides, leather, bread-stuffs, dye-stuffs, colors, oils, alcohol, coal, and paper.

RUSSIAN FAIR AT NOVGOROD.

On the American continent fairs date from an early period. In ancient Mexico, where there were no shops, they very frequently attracted large crowds, a particular quarter of the city being allotted to each trade. Fairs were regularly held at Azcapazalco, near the capital, where slaves were sold, and at Tlascala, where were held great pottery fairs. The most important fair, however, was that held at the city of Mexico, the number of visitors being estimated at 40,000 to 50,000. In Peru, the Incas instituted fairs for facilitating agricultural exchange. They took place three times a month in some of the most populous places, the trade being altogether by barter. At Puerto Bello, on the northern shore of the isthmus, four miles north of the town of Panama, was formerly held a great fair under the Spanish rule.

In the United States agricultural fairs were the first held, and have since become the most important of any. These started in the New England States shortly after the Revolution, the first on record being a display of sheep, and out of which have sprung the entire catalogue of state and county agricultural and cattle fairs throughout the country. These fairs have been of vast importance in encouraging invention and discovery in their application to agriculture, and in awakening an interest in the advancement of breeds of cattle, horses, sheep, hogs, and poultry, which has resulted in placing the United States in the forefront of all nations as regards these important elements of agriculture. But besides agricultural fairs there have also been organized those which comprehended especially the display of the improvements in manufactures and mechanical ingenuity. Associations have been formed in the principal cities, like the American Institute in New York, by which

THE FAIR AT LEIPZIG.

fairs have been annually organized, at which prizes and other premiums have been bestowed, awakening an energetic and honorable competition among manufacturers and producers. The same system has been applied to the dairy, and state dairy associations, with their annual fairs, have resulted, as a part of their work, in the formation of the International Dairy Fair Association of New York city, by which organization an annual fair for the competitive exhibition of dairy products has been for several years conducted with marked success. The general tendency of fairs in this country has been shown to be in the direction of the improvement of products and manufactures.

LONDON EXHIBITION, 1851.

## NATIONAL AND INTERNATIONAL EXHIBITIONS.

The Industrial Exhibition originated naturally in the great fair. It was an expansion of the original idea with the element of competition made more prominent than had previously been the case, and that of compensation by prizes and premiums more generally introduced as an additional inducement to contribution. Fairs were originally held for profit only, and are still so held in some parts of the world. When the element of sale ceased to enter into their composition they became exhibitions. It was quite at a recent date that this idea assumed somewhat of the form it holds at present. The first Industrial Exhibition was held in Paris in 1798, and comprised principally specimens of arts and manufactures loaned by their owners. It was in fact the origin of the "Loan Exhibition" of the present day. This display was sufficiently successful to be continued, and under the Consulate of Napoleon such exhibitions were frequent. In England local exhibitions were held in Manchester, Leeds, Birmingham, and other cities, in 1828, 1837, 1839, and 1849. In Ireland the Royal Society of Dublin began a series of triennial exhibitions of Irish manufactures in 1829. Similar exhibitions were held in Ghent in 1839, in Berlin in 1832, and Vienna in 1835. But the International Exhibition originated in London, and under the paternal care of the "London Society of Arts." This Society was organized in 1753, and by a judicious system of prizes did much service to English arts and manufactures, and even promoted the improvement of the fishery trade and commerce in the British colonies. In 1845 Prince Albert became President of the Society, and four years later an annual exhibition of articles of utility, invented, registered, or patented dur-

VIENNA EXHIBITION, 1873.

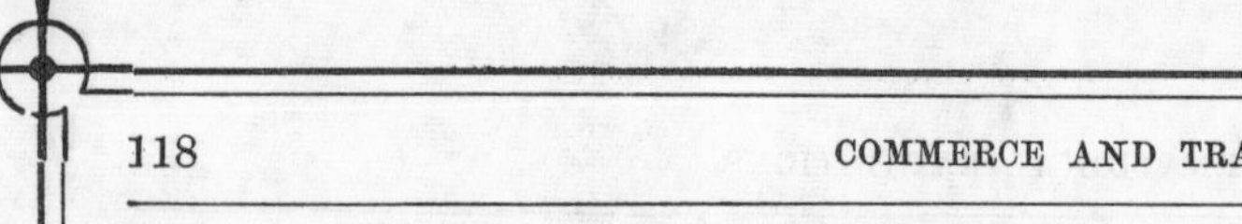

ing the preceding twelve months was organized. In that same year Prince Albert recommended the establishment of an International Exhibition, which was held in 1851 in the Crystal Palace in Hyde Park, the first of its kind which ever took place in the world. It was opened in May by Queen Victoria, and was closed in October of the same year, having been visited by over six million persons. This Exhibition was followed by a similar one in Dublin in 1853, which was visited by 1,150,000 people. In the same year occurred in New York an Industrial Exhibition, which was held in a building covering 170,000 square feet, with an additional one of 33,000 square feet. This building was called the Crystal Palace, and the Exhibition, which contained exhibits from many foreign countries, was moderately successful. In 1854 an Industrial Exhibition was held in Munich, Bavaria, and in 1855 occurred the great Paris Exposition, in a building 800 feet long by 350 feet wide, and which cost $5,000,000. This Exhibition was kept open on Sundays, and the entire number of visitors was 4,533,464. The number of exhibitors was more than 21,000, representing nearly 53 countries and 22 colonies. In 1862 another International Exhibition occurred in London in a building erected for the purpose at South Kensington, and which afterwards became the Alexandra Palace, destroyed by fire in 1873. There were at this Exhibition 17,861 foreign exhibitors. It was open 171 days, and the number of visitors was 6,211,-103.

The Paris International Exposition of 1867 was the largest up to that date, there being 50,226 exhibitors and 10,200,000 visitors. The Exhibition building cost about 21,000,000 francs, of which the government paid 13,-000,000 francs. The receipts for admission, etc., were $2,000,-000, and there resulted, as was claimed, a profit of $600,000. Annual Exhibitions occurred in London in 1871, '72, and '73. In 1872 a great Russian Exhibition was organized in Moscow under the patronage of the Imperial Government. The Vienna International Exhibition of 1873 was conducted in a building of brick and glass, 2,985 feet long and 82 feet wide, and other buildings, the whole covering about 60 acres. The entire number of exhibitors, exclusive of Oriental countries, was 42,584, and the total number of visitors was 7,254,867.

The Centennial Exposition of 1876 originated in an act of Congress passed March 3d, 1871. The area covered by this Exposition was 75 acres, the number of buildings being about 200. The main building was 1880 feet long by 464 feet wide; the art gallery or "Memorial Hall" 365 feet long by 210 wide and 59 high; the Machinery Hall 1402 x 360,

OPENING OF THE PARIS EXHIBITION, 1878.

with an annex 208 x 210; Horticultural Hall, 383 x 193 and 72 feet high; the Agricultural Building, 465 x 630, covering a space of 7½ acres; the United States Government building, 260 x 300. The ground inclosed for the site of all the Exposition buildings, including, besides those already named, numerous annexes, state buildings, and special buildings, was 236 acres. There were 7 miles of avenues and walks, and 7½ miles of railway within the grounds. This Exhibition was open from May 10th to November 10th—159 days, and received 9,892,625 visitors. The largest attendance on any one day was on "Pennsylvania Day," September 28th, 274,919. The total cash receipts amounted to $3,819,497. The total receipts, including concessions and royalties, amounted to $4,314,507.75. After paying all its expenses and returning the $1,500,000 loaned by the United States Government, the Centennial Commissioners were able to divide among the purchasers of its stock a small percentage of their investment. The Paris Exposition of 1878 took place in buildings erected on the Champ de Mars and including the palace of the Trocadero on the hill of that name and the Main Building on the opposite side of the Seine. The gross receipts from entrance fees of this Exhibition amounted to about 13,000,000 francs. The number of strangers who stayed in Paris during the progress of the Exhibition was 571,792. Of these nearly 15,000 were Americans, and about 64,000 English. Thirty-six royal personages visited the Exposition, including the Shah of Persia. In August, 1879, the Agricultural Society of New South Wales held an Exhibition at Sydney, continuing for four months, and which attracted universal attention, and was very successful. The main building, situated on what is known as the "Domain," covered 7½ acres of space, affording 11,000,000 cubic feet of available room, and cost £100,000. Numbers of American manufacturers contributed to this Exhibition. A second Australian Exhibition, which took place at Melbourne, Victoria, South Australia, commenced on October 1st, 1880. The opening ceremonies were attended by more than 22,000 persons, and during the first half month 119,659 admissions were recorded. The total number of admissions during the seven months of the Exhibition amounted to 1,309,496. In the division of awards at this antipodal exhibition the United Kingdom received the largest number, 559; after which came Victoria, S. A., 373; France, 338; Germany, 259; Italy, 138; and the United States, 115; the remaining countries exhibiting, of which there were 15 in all, receiving much less than the smallest number of awards just given. The largest number of admissions on any one day was on the 22d of March, when the awards were declared, and amounted to 25,189.

In 1881 a large Cotton Exposition was held in the United States at Atlanta, Georgia. The number of exhibits was 1,113, divided among 37 States, of which the New England and Middle furnished 374; the Western, 261; and the Southern, 478. The Exposition was open 76 days; the number of admissions being 289,774: and the cash receipts for admisions $95,802.25.

## THE EAST INDIA AND OTHER COMPANIES.

From the time of the Phœnicians and Carthaginians the trade with India has always been an object of desire among the commercial nations of the earth. Endowed with almost fabulous wealth, the seat of manufactures unrivaled elsewhere among the empires of the earth, with a facility of production unsurpassed, there is little wonder that India should have always been an attraction to the commercial eyes of the West. Combining the central and south-eastern peninsulas of Asia, India comprises an area of 1,576,746 miles, and a population of nearly 240,000,000. The first trade with this extensive, rich, and populous country, was carried on by the ancient cities of Tyre and Carthage, from which it descended to Genoa and Venice, when those cities gained their commercial supremacy; from them again to the Portuguese, Dutch, and English, at periods ranging between the middle ages and the eighteenth century. The commerce with India prior to the Turkish conquest of Constantinople and Egypt, was conducted chiefly by the Italian republics; in later days by means of the overland route, via Suez. Late in the fifteenth century Vasco da Gama made a voyage from Lisbon around the Cape of Good Hope, across the Indian Ocean and to Calicut, now Calcutta. The result of his expedition was that Portugal organized a commerce with India, which it monopolized for nearly a century, holding sections of country with which they traded by means of viceroys appointed by the Portuguese king. In 1587 the government chartered an East Indian Company, which, however, was abolished in 1640. In the mean time Holland grasped at the same rich

INDIGO FACTORY AT ALLAHABAD, INDIA.

prize, and in 1595 a Dutch East India Company was formed, which soon returned large dividends, and captured or purchased immense properties in valuable colonies. The charter of this company was renewed for the last time in 1776, and in 1795 it terminated its existence, its affairs passing into the hands of the government. A French East India Company was founded in 1664, and was broken up in 1770. A Danish East India Company, founded in 1618, was dissolved in 1634, reconstructed in 1670, again dissolved in 1729, and reformed in 1732. It continued prosperous during the eighteenth century, after which time it declined. All of these companies, however, in the extent of their wealth, their commerce, and their political significance were totally eclipsed by the great British East India Company, which was chartered at London in 1600, and was abolished by act of Parliament August 2d, 1858, when the East Indian possessions, trade, and power reverted to the crown. It may be said of this corporation that it reached a height of power, wealth, and aggrandizement never equaled by any other similar association. It owned vast and thickly populated provinces, held native rulers tributaries, and their governments as appendages, and drew from the wealth of Indian provinces sums amounting to millions of pounds annually. For more than two centuries the East India Company wielded this tremendous power, and was only finally overturned by the corruptions engendered within itself, although the immediate cause of its destruction was the bloody Indian revolt of 1857–8. The foreign trade of India has been for centuries famous for its value and importance. In 1871–2 there were engaged in it 1,230 square-rigged vessels, 948 steamers, and 50,000 native craft. In Bengal and Mysore there are extensive manufactures of silk, while Delhi is celebrated for its manufactures of this article. Benares and Ahmenabad are noted for gold brocade; the Punjaub for silks, woolens, and white and colored cottons, amounting to £5,000,000, or $25,000,000 annually; while the cotton manufactures of Oude, the Central Provinces, and Mysore are likewise of great importance, and in the latter section cutlery works and manufactures of gold and silver lace are extensive and flourishing. The products of India are rice, maize, and wheat; opium, coffee, tea—the yield of which in 1872 was more than 6,000,000 pounds—Peruvian bark, cotton, jute, India-rubber, and indigo, of which Bengal produces annually about 9,000,000 pounds. From all of this we may see to what a tremendous extent the growth of the Indian trade was fostered and forwarded by the East India Company. In 1869 the Suez Canal, built by Ferdinand de Lesseps, was opened in the presence of the Viceroy and a vast native assemblage, besides the Empress Eugenie, who traveled from Paris for the purpose. During the first five years of its existence the number of vessels passing through the Suez Canal increased from 491 to 1,264; the tonnage from 635,000 to 2,500,000; the receipts increasing during the same period from 5,000,000 francs to five times that amount. The Suez Canal is managed by a company, 2,500 shares of the stock being divided between the Viceroy and French holders, nearly 200,000 belonging to England, and 222,358 in the hands of French capitalists.

The extension of commerce through the agency of companies such as the British East India Company is still further susceptible of demonstration by investigation into the colonizing of America by means of similar methods. Plymouth Colony, and Providence Plantations, as they were termed, originating in their settlement in religious movements, were none the less influenced by commercial necessities or encouraged and developed by commercial means. The more southern colony of James River was directly founded and pushed to a successful establishment by means of a colonizing company of London. Companies were employed, in the first instance, to open up new fields for settlement and for trade, and in the second place to encourage and facilitate the prosecution of such settlement and trade. Thus, the Peninsular and Oriental Company, the vast enterprises of the Cunards and other trans-oceanic steamship lines, have quite circumnavigated the globe in their active and energetic movements in this direction.

DEPARTURE OF AN OCEAN STEAMER.

## STEAM IN ITS RELATION TO TRANSPORTATION AND TRADE.

THE introduction of steam as a motive force and its adaptation to general use was important in its relation to commerce not only as concerned its application to transportation —thereby lessening the time while increasing the accommodation for the transportation of goods—but, in a fair degree, by increasing the possibilities of manufacture and the production of articles to be used in trading. Whether in the first half of the sixteenth century steam as a motive power was applied or not is of little importance. It was not until the eighteenth century that its powerful influence began to be seriously felt in connection with the establishment and development of trade. The application of steam to manufactures and the introduction of the factory system, at first in England and soon afterwards throughout manufacturing countries, gave a tremendous impetus to the quantity of production. It was quite half a century later that its uses for transportation became evident and practicable.

EXPRESS BUSINESS—LOADING AT MAIN OFFICE.

The date of the invention of tramways would appear to have been very early in the seventeenth century. They were first used in the coal districts of England and in the south of Scotland ; but it was not until the beginning of the following century that the original idea was developed into something presenting more practicable methods. The first application of steam to locomotion on land was made by George Stephenson in 1814, but the Stockton and Darlington Railway, under an Act of Parliament of 1821, may be considered to have been the first railroad in England built on this plan. The first railroad in the United States was at Quincy, in Massachusetts. The first American engine was the "Tom Thumb," constructed by Peter Cooper, and placed on the Baltimore and Ohio road in 1830. The Baltimore and Ohio Railroad was commenced in 1828, and three years later transported nearly 100,000 passengers, and 6,000 tons of freight. From this time to the present there has occurred the constant construction of railroads, and in later years their consolidation into complete systems, tapping vast territories and contrived to convey the largest possible quantities of freight from the interior to the seaboard and for exportation. At the beginning of the year 1880 there were in the United States 85,580 miles of railroad, employing 16,455 locomotive engines, 11,683 passenger cars, and 423,013 freight cars. As an illustration of the vast capacity of the railroad systems of the United States it is to be observed that in the year 1879 thirteen lines moved 67,092,549 tons of freight, the receipts therefor being $116,311,452. It is to be further noted, in regard to this question of capacity, that a freight car load is estimated at 26,000 pounds. Thus an ordinary railroad freight car will hold of corn, 450 bushels ; barley, 400 bushels ; oats, 800 bushels ; rye, 400 bushels ; wheat, 425 bushels ; bran, 1,000 bushels ; apples, 360 bushels; potatoes, 480 bushels; whiskey, 60 barrels; salt, 70 barrels; lime, 70 barrels ; flour, 90 barrels; flour,200 sacks; cattle, 18 head ; hogs, 50 head; sheep, 80 head; hardwood, 6 cords; solid board, 6,000 feet; shingles, 40,000 feet, hard lumber, 20,000 feet; green lumber, 15,000 feet; joist, scantling, and large lumber, 4,000 feet.

EXPRESS BUSINESS—AT A RAILWAY STATION.

## THE EXPRESS BUSINESS.

ONE special development in connection with railroad traffic has been the express business, which, from the smallest possible beginning, has, in less than half a century, become an established institution for carriage of the greatest possible value and importance to large and widely separated populations. The express business commenced in 1839, with the advertisement of William F. Harnden, of Boston, of his design to make regular trips as a messenger and package-carrier between Boston and New York by way of the Providence Railroad and steamboat therefrom. In accordance with this announcement Harnden made his first trip March 4th, 1839, with a few packages, some orders, and small amounts of money to exchange and deliver. From this beginning originated

the entire business of carrying, which increased and grew more lucrative from the first. Mr. Harnden made contracts with railroad and steamboat companies, increased the frequency of his trips, and gained the favor of the press by bringing them matter in advance of the regular mails.

The advantages of this system were speedily recognized by the mercantile interests of the two cities originally involved, and shortly afterwards a similar express was commenced by Alvin Adams, which was designed to connect Boston and New York by another route. At the beginning of this undertaking a carpet-bag was found sufficient for the accommodation of the entire business, and from this has grown the vast express transportation business with its immense capital, its trains of cars, armies and relays of assistants, and its widely extended connections. In 1841 the express was extended to Philadelphia and Albany ; a year or two later to Washington, and thence to Buffalo and other cities of the West by other companies which were rapidly formed. In 1854 four of the railroad companies were consolidated in Adams's Express Company with a capital of $1,200,000. At present the entire capital invested is supposed to be in the neighborhood of $30,000,000. Express companies now transport nearly all the specie and bullion, as well as a considerable portion of the bank notes, bills of exchange, drafts, bonds, and other securities, and the prices of exchange between cities depend in some measure upon the express charges for conveyance. Merchandise of nearly every description is now forwarded from place to place, however distant apart, by this method. The development of commerce has still further been extended by inland water navigation through the means of rivers, lakes, and canals, these means being ordinarily used for slow freight and non-perishable articles in contradistinction to the employment and use of railroads for more rapid transit.

After transportation, of course the means of communication with as much rapidity as is practicable becomes a most important factor in the prosecution of commerce. For this purpose two systems have been organized—the MAIL CARRIAGE and the TELEGRAPH SYSTEM, followed by a third in more recent times—the system of communication by TELEPHONE. The establishment of the POSTAL SERVICE, by which letters and packages may be regularly conveyed from place to place has proved to be one of the most efficient instruments of civilization, as well as one of the most important adjuncts of commerce by diffusing intelligence and information and facilitating business between persons placed at a distance from each other.

## MONEY AND EXCHANGES.

O facilitate the conduct and extension of commerce throughout the world other agencies have been found necessary besides those already mentioned. Such are, for instance, the use of an available circulating medium ; the institution of banking; and the organization of exchanges in the different departments of trade. Next to the management of trade by means of actual barter or exchange of articles, to which we have already alluded, came in the establishment and organization, as far as was practicable, of the use of money so-called ; meaning, briefly, a circulating medium or means for accommodating the wants of buyer and seller without the necessity of resorting to the cumbrous and often expensive method of direct exchange.

In 1435 the amount of coined money in existence was estimated at $150,000,000. At the end of the seventeenth century it amounted to $1,900,000,000. In 1847 the entire amount of gold coin and bullion in the world was stated at $3,000,000,000. The yield of the mines of California in the next ten years added about $500,000,000 to this amount, and those of Australia from 1851 to 1859 yielded about $500,000,000 more. The entire yield of the American mines, both gold and silver, from 1848 to 1876 was $1,500,000,000. The total amount of gold existing in the world in 1881 is estimated by the highest authorities to have been $7,763,223,772, and that of silver to have been $6,757,843,025—making an aggregate of gold and silver to the value of $14,521,066,797.

In order to facilitate trade, what are called EXCHANGES have been organized in all the principal financial and trade centers. The term "exchange" is applied to buildings or places of resort for merchants. The name *bourse* (literally, purse) is applied in France and Belgium to a resort of this kind, and in Berlin, Hamburg, and other German cities there is the equivalent *börse*. Usually the word has been made to comprehend an open quadrangle surrounded by an arcade, but in some cases large reading-rooms constitute resorts of this kind, and as such are open only to subscribers, and the visitors these introduce to them. Exchanges originated in the commercial cities of Italy, Germany, and the Netherlands, and from the last-named country were copied by England in the latter part of the sixteenth century. The first Exchange of London was almost entirely destroyed by the great fire of 1666. Two others afterwards erected met a similar fate. The foundation-stone of the third was laid by Prince Albert on January the 17th, 1842, and was opened on the 1st January, 1845, by Her Majesty Queen Victoria. There are also PRODUCE EXCHANGES, COTTON EXCHANGES, MINING EXCHANGES, etc., according to the character of the trade existing in the localities where they are organized. Other institutions of a similar character are termed BOARDS OF TRADE or CHAMBERS OF COMMERCE. All of these are voluntary associations of merchants and traders formed to discuss matters appertaining to commerce, to buy and sell stocks, bonds, or produce, and to promote commercial interests generally. The idea of the Chamber of Commerce is originally attributed to Oliver Cromwell, who, in 1655, appointed his son Richard, with many distinguished persons, and about twenty noted merchants of London and other cities of England "to meet and consider by what means the trade and navigation of the country might be best promoted." As to such institutions as we have named, their members are generally termed brokers, excepting members of Boards of Trade and Chambers of Commerce.

## STOCK AND STOCK BROKERS.

The term **Stock** is used under several significations. Among others, it expresses the capital or money invested in business by individuals or firms, and also that of banking or other money establishments. The word "stocks," however, is the general name by which the public debt or debt of the Government, and the securities of railroads, gas companies, and other corporations, are generally known. These stocks always have a market value, sometimes above and sometimes below their nominal value. They form the subject of speculation, being bought or sold in the expectation of profit. Business is conducted under the rules and terms of organization of the Stock Exchange and for a fixed commission from which brokers are not permitted to deviate. The New York Stock Exchange was first regularly organized in 1789. A similar organization had previously existed in Philadelphia. The stocks at first dealt in were United States stocks, and State, bank, and insurance stock. Railroad stocks first came into the market in 1830. In 1823 the initiation fee of the New York Stock Exchange was $25; in 1827, $100; in 1833, $150. At present a seat in the Board is worth $26,000. The number of members is 1,060. From 300,000 to 500,000 shares of stock change hands on the New York Stock Exchange daily, and the operations frequently cover more than $2,000,000 value of securities handled.

The record of transactions is abbreviated in its expressions in the printed reports and on the "tape" of the telegraphic stock indicator; as, for instance, "L. S. 400 : 125 s. 60," which means 400 shares of the Lake Shore and Michigan Southern Railroad stock at $125, to be delivered at the seller's option any time within 60 days. If recorded "b. 60," the option is with the buyer. The letters "ex." mean "less dividend." Applied to bonds "c." means "coupon," and "r." "registered;" "o. b." stands for "delivered at the opening of the books of transfer." Stock is bought either for its full value in cash or on a margin. In the latter instance the client deposits with his broker 10 per cent. of the par value of the stock, thus securing the latter against loss, since he may sell if the stock falls to the point which the margin covers, or can call for more margin, and sell if the client declines further risk.

Those who contract to deliver stock at a certain price at a future day are said to "sell short" and are technically called "bears," because they desire to squeeze or depress the market. "Bulls," on the contrary, buy stock for a rise, and are called "long of the stock" or "bulls," because their interest is to raise the market price. The broker's commission for buying or selling is one-eighth of 1 per cent. except to members of the Board, who pay $2 per one hundred shares. The business in "stock privileges," as they are called, is a peculiar one, involving the technical terms "puts" and "calls." A broker who sells a "put" agrees to buy a specified stock, in a certain number of shares, within a stated time at a specified price, provided the seller be willing to deliver the stock at the time and price named. If the broker sells a "call," he agrees to deliver a certain number of shares of a given stock on call, within a stated time at a specified price. The cost of these privileges is arranged between the parties in accordance with the condition of the market, the time involved, etc.

STOCK EXCHANGE, NEW YORK.

## COMMERCIAL TERMS AND AGENTS.

A **broker** is an agent or intermediate person who transacts special business on account of another. The province of a broker is to find buyers and sellers and bring them together to make their bargains, or to transact for them himself the business of such buying and selling. The class is generally limited to cities and large towns, since in small places where the amount of trade done is very limited, buyers and sellers are generally familiar with each other and do not require to go to the expense of employing a third party or intermediary. Brokers are divided into different classes, according to the nature of the property in which they deal.

A **bill broker** is one who buys and sells notes and bills of exchange. An **exchange broker** buys and sells uncurrent money, and deals in exchanges relating to money in different countries. An **insurance broker** effects insurance on lives or property. A **stock broker** negotiates transactions in the public funds and deals in stocks of mining corporations, railroads, and other securities. The **real estate broker** buys and sells houses and lands and obtains loans of money upon mortgage. The **merchandise broker** buys and sells goods. The **shipping broker** deals with the purchase and sale of vessels, procures freights, etc. The **pawnbroker** advances money on various kinds of goods taken on pledge, conditionally on being allowed to sell them if the sum or sums advanced be not repaid within a certain time. Other brokers appraise or sell household furniture, etc. All these different classes of intermediary agents obtain their profits chiefly by commission on their transactions, though many of them indulge in speculations in their own behalf.

Among the mediums in use for the payment of indebtedness and for other use of the circulating medium, the **bill of exchange** or draft may properly be considered here. This is a written order or request from one person to another desiring him to pay a sum of money therein named to a third person mentioned, on his account. Like a note of hand it must be made payable to order or bearer, in order to be negotiable or transferable. This was a method devised by merchants in different countries for the more ready remittance of money from one to another. By this means, at the present day, a man in any part of the civilized world may receive money from any trading country, instead of being obliged to carry from home all over the earth the money he requires. Transactions of this kind are usually conducted by persons known as exchange brokers, who are acquainted with different merchants in various places at home and abroad.

Another important element which enters into commercial transactions and the value of goods is that which is known as **Insurance.** MARINE INSURANCE is that by which vessels of every kind, with or without their cargoes, are secured against the dangers of the sea, and is a special branch of the business. The underwriters who attend to this kind of insurance ascertain, as far as possible, what the risks are on every voyage by any particular vessels, and charge commission for insurance accordingly.

A **drawback** in commerce is an allowance made to merchants on the re-exportation of certain goods, which in some cases consists of the whole and in others of a part of the duties which had been paid upon the merchandise. A **debenture** is a certificate delivered at the Custom House when the exporter of any goods or merchandise has complied with the regulations, in consequence of which he is entitled to a bounty on the exportation. This certificate is signed by the officer of customs when the goods are regularly entered and shipped, and the vessel cleared for her intended voyage. A **certificate of clearance** gives her permission to sail. A "**bill of credit**" among merchants is a letter sent by an agent or other person to a merchant desiring him to give credit to the bearer for goods or money. A **bill of entry** is a written account of goods entered at the Custom House, whether imported or intended for exportation. A **bill of lading** is a written account of goods shipped by any person on board of a vessel, signed by the master of the vessel, who acknowledges the receipt of the goods, and promises to deliver them safely at the place directed, dangers of the sea excepted. It is usual for the master to sign two or three copies of the bills, one of which he keeps in his possession, while one is kept by the shipper, and another is sent to the consignee or person who is to receive the goods at the end of the voyage. A **bill of store** is a license granted at the Custom House to merchants to carry such stores and provisions as are necessary for the voyage free of duty. An **invoice** is an account of goods shipped by merchants for their purchasers or agents abroad, in which the peculiar marks of the goods, the value, prices and other particulars are given. The duties and charges upon them of every kind are recorded, and a book is kept in which they are duly entered. A **foreign agent** or **factor** is a person in some foreign country employed by a merchant to transact business for him, for which he receives a commission of so much per cent. on all the sales he effects. He may buy and sell in his own name and is entrusted with the possession and control of the goods. In these respects he differs from a broker. Factors are also employed for domestic business, as, for instance, the cotton factors in the Southern States, who make advances upon crops, and who store, sell, and ship the cotton when baled, all of which business they do upon commission. An **embargo** is an order from the Government prohibiting the departure of ships or merchandise from all or some of the ports within its dominions. Such detentions generally occur in actual war or when one nation is in a hostile attitude towards another. **Quarantine** is the time during which a vessel suspected of having malignant sickness on board, or of having come from a port where such malignant sickness is known to prevail, is forbidden to have any intercourse with the shore at which she arrives. The word is derived from the Italian *quaranta*, meaning forty, because forty days' detention was commonly prescribed for all vessels delayed under such circumstances.

# Commerce of Various Countries.

WHEN it is remembered that the national wealth of the United States is over fifty thousand million dollars, and that it increases at the rate of five hundred millions per annum, some idea of the vastness, the frequency, and the comprehensive nature of its transactions will be obtained. Meanwhile an important element, which has gone to the increase of the wealth of the country, should not be ignored in this connection. This element is immigration, which for the last five years has amounted to from 150,000 to 500,000 per annum.

The commerce of the United States, like that of most other countries, is both internal and external. It is a fact but little known, that the value of the commodities transported on the railroads of the United States many times exceeds the total value of the foreign commerce of the United States, including imports and exports. To illustrate this fact, it may be remarked that the value of the commodities composing the freight traffic of the Pennsylvania Railroad between Philadelphia and Pittsburg (including branch lines) amounted during the year 1876 to $560,903,462, this being exclusive of express freights, the value of which is very much greater in proportion to the weight carried than is the value of the ordinary commodities transported in freight cars. The growth of the internal commerce has been more rapid during the last ten years than has been the case during any preceding decade in the history of the country. The growth of the great east and west commercial movement between the Atlantic seaboard States and the Western and Northwestern States serves to illustrate this statement. The tonnage movement over the New York State Canals, the New York Central and Hudson River Railroad, the New York, Lake Erie and Western Railroad, and the Pennsylvania Railroad, during the last ten years, increased as follows:

| | Year. | Tons. |
|---|---|---|
| New York State Canals | 1871 | 6,467,888 |
| " " " | 1880 | 6,462,290 |
| N. Y. C. & H. R. R.R | 1871 | 4,532,056 |
| " " " | 1880 | 10,576,754 |
| N. Y., L. E. & W. R.R | 1871 | 4,844,208 |
| " " " | 1880 | 9,445,392 |
| Pennsylvania R.R | 1871 | 7,100,294 |
| " " | 1880 | 16,341,568 |

It will be seen from the foregoing statement that the tonnage moved on the New York State Canals was not so great in the year 1880 as in the year 1871, but that the tonnage moved on the three railroads mentioned increased from 16,476,558 tons in 1871 to 36,363,714 tons in 1880, an increase of 120.7 per cent. It is also a fact that the aggregate tonnage on thirteen of the principal railroads of the United States increased from 1873 to 1880 by the amount of 71.5 per cent. Of the total number of freight cars employed in the United States in 1880, 6 per cent. belong to railroads in the New England States, 47 per cent. to railroads in the Middle States, 5 per cent. to railroads in the Southern States, 40 per cent. to railroads in the Western, Northwestern and Southwestern States, and 2 per cent. to the railroads of the Pacific States and Territories. The rapid growth of the internal commerce of the country during the last twenty years has given rise to a demand for largely increased means of transportation. The tonnage employed in the domestic trade of the United States, on the lakes, on rivers, and in the coastwise trade amounted in 1880 to 2,637,685 tons, the tonnage unit being 100 cubic feet of space; but the capacity of railroad cars of all descriptions employed on the railroads in the United States in 1880, according to the latest information, amounted to about 7,900,000 similar tons of 100 cubic feet of space. Meanwhile the cost of railroad transportation has greatly decreased. The average rate per ton charged on the thirteen principal railroads of the United States fell from 1.77 cent per ton per mile in 1873 to 1.07 cent per ton per mile in 1880, a decrease of 39.5 per cent. While this decrease in the cost of railroad traffic was occurring that on the New York State Canals decreased also, but to the amount of 7 per cent. less in the same period. The reductions in the charges of transportation on railroads have conferred immense benefits upon the interests of agriculture, mining, and commerce. Thus the increase in the value of the domestic exports of the United States to foreign countries from $442,820,178 in 1871 to $902,319,473 in 1881 has been largely due to such reductions, as is evident from the fact that such exports are chiefly the products of the Western and Northwestern States, a large proportion of which is transported to the seaboard on railroads. "The freight charges for the movement from Chicago to Boston, a distance of 1,000 miles, of one year's subsistence of grain and meat for an adult working-man amounts to but $1.25, which sum is only one day's wages of a common laborer, or half the daily wages of a good carpenter or mason."—*Edward Atkinson.*

LOADING COTTON AT SAVANNAH.

### FOREIGN COMMERCE.

The vast increase of the foreign commerce of the United States is quickest seen in the following comparison. In 1840, in the beginning of successful ocean steam navigation, the entire receipts of foreign merchandise of the United States amounted to $86,250,335. In 1880 the total imports of merchandise amounted to $667,954,746. The exports in 1840 were $111,660,561; in 1880, $823,946,353. The principal countries to which the agricultural and other products of the United States are sent stood in the order of value of exports in 1879 as follows:

ON THE LEVEE AT NEW ORLEANS.

|  |  |
|---|---|
| Great Britain and Ireland | $346,485,881 |
| France | 88,194,041 |
| Germany | 56,164,394 |
| British America | 28,281,569 |
| Belgium | 27,470,003 |
| Russia | 15,959,701 |
| Netherlands | 13,802,840 |
| Spain | 12,438,903 |
| Cuba | 12,201,691 |
| Italy | 8,657,203 |
| Brazil | 8,106,928 |
| Australia | 7,042,875 |
| British West Indies | 6,779,153 |
| China | 5,930,594 |
| Mexico | 5,400,380 |
| Colombia | 5,199,648 |
| Portugal | 4,897,290 |
| Turkey | 3,989,230 |
| Hayti | 3,148,757 |
| Japan | 2,674,601 |
| Austria | 2,640,648 |
| Hawaian Islands | 2,288,178 |
| Denmark | 2,284,784 |
| British Africa | 2,168,076 |
| Sweden and Norway | 2,138,461 |
| Argentine Republic | 2,033,401 |
| Venezuela | 1,926,923 |
| Porto Rico | 1,771,483 |
| British Guinea | 1,719,827 |
| French West Indies | 1,535,768 |
| Dutch East Indies | 1,447,510 |
| Gibraltar | 1,297,820 |
| Peru | 1,293,991 |
| Chili | 1,253,555 |
| British East Indies | 1,142,196 |
| Central America | 1,110,603 |
| All other countries | 8,538,276 |
| Total | $699,538,742 |

BLOOMER CUTTING ON THE PACIFIC RAILROAD.

The difference of values and other conditions brought about in the United States during the past decade may be best seen in the following figures: In 1870 the commerce of the country amounted to $860,000,000; in 1880, to $1,505,000,000. In 1870 the manufactures were valued at $3,410,000,000; in 1880, at $4,400,000,000; mining, which produced $190,000,000 in 1870, reached $360,000,000 in 1880; agriculture was $2,075,000,000 in 1870, and $2,625,000,000 ten years later; the carrying trade increased from $575,000,000 to $705,000,000 in the same ten years; and the banking, which was $200,000,000 in 1870, had risen to $260,000,000 in 1880. In no country, in fact, that we are about to consider, has there not been an increase in the value of the factors that go to make countries rich through commerce; yet, as will be seen by the following table of such increase during the ten years from 1870 to 1880, the public debt and taxation have held their own with the rest of the advanced influences:

| | | | |
|---|---|---|---|
| Population increased.. | 9.76 per ct. | Carrying trade....... | 53.22 per ct. |
| Agriculture.......... | 8.58 " " | Earnings of nations.. | 19.84 " " |
| Manufactures........ | 18.60 " " | Public wealth........ | 10.57 " " |
| Commerce.......... | 38.20 " " | *Taxes*.............. | 22.34 " " |
| Mining............ | 47.06 " " | *Public Debt*.......... | 43.39 " " |

## AUSTRO-HUNGARY.

In the empire of Austro-Hungary the production of milk is estimated at 1,672,000,000 gallons per annum; that of cheese at 200,000,000 pounds; of wool there is produced 60,000,000 pounds annually, and of spun silk to the value of $3,500,000; the annual amount from the bee culture is 50,000,000 pounds of honey and 3,000,000 pounds of wax. Game of all descriptions makes up an important product in many districts of the empire, as does also the catch of sea-fish along the shores of Dalmatia and Istria. About one-third of the population are engaged in agriculture and forestry. Austrian industry is extensively carried on in manufactures, for the export trade, of paper, stationery and paper fancy goods, leather and articles of leather, India rubber, articles of bone, wood, glass and stone, earthenware, hardware, carriages, boats and vessels, machinery, tools and implements, piece goods and small ware, drugs and chemical products. The principal industrial pursuits of the empire are carried on in Bohemia, Moravia, Silesia, and Lower Austria. About 8,000,000 persons in the empire may be considered to earn their livelihood by industrial occupations. The official value of imports into Austro-Hungary increased from the year 1863 to the year 1877 from $125,000,000 to $260,000,000, or more than double. Exports during the same period increased from $135,000,000 to $265,000,000. In order to animate progress in industry, patents are granted for new discoveries, and exclusive patents for articles to be introduced from foreign states. Producers and manufacturers are also allowed to make use of symbols and characters, or other devices, as trade-marks. In all divisions of the empire there are chambers of commerce and trade, numbering twenty-nine in Austrian and thirteen in the Hungarian dependencies. The length of railway line in use in Austria in 1878 was 12,000 miles. The weight of the goods forwarded amounted to more than 45,000,000 tons. The postal service includes 4,115 offices in Austria and 1,959 in Hungary. The number of telegraph stations was, in 1876, 2,329 in Austria and 911 in Hungary. The Austro-Hungarian commercial navy at the end of 1877 comprised about 95 steamers and 7,010 sailing vessels. The merchant service in 1878 numbered 7,608 sailing vessels and 100 steamers.

## BELGIUM.

The kingdom of Belgium is rich in minerals and certain metals. Slate is very common, and bricks for building are made everywhere throughout the kingdom. The configuration of the country is such that it has been readily covered, at small expense, with roads, canals and railways. The railway system in 1877 amounted to 2,500 miles. The imports of the kingdom amount to about $450,000,000, and the exports to $400,000,000 annually. An important product is derived from the mines of lead, zinc, and iron, the production of iron ore in 1877 being 234,000 tons. Steel is manufactured to some extent, and there are copper and zinc works. Important industries are the manufacture of glass and mirrors. In 1877 the glass industry employed nearly 12,000 workmen in seventy-six factories, and produced goods worth $7,000,000. Terra cotta, stoneware, and porcelain are also manufactured extensively and exported. The manufacture of chemical products is an important industry, and Belgian cutlery enjoys a universal reputation. The kingdom exports steamers, engines, machinery, and iron work to the value of $10,000,000 per annum. The candles of Belgian manufacture are of high repute. The country possesses two of the most important stearine factories in the world. Belgium is also famous for linen and for lace-making. Ever since the eighteenth century lace has been one of the principal articles of exportation, including Valenciennes lace, Brussels point, guipure, etc. Several descriptions of embroidery are made in Belgium, which are in high favor for religious vestments, banners, trimmings, etc. The manufacture of wool is one of the oldest industries in the country; in 1877 the exportation was 158,000 pieces. The manufactories make scarcely any use of native wool, but purchase from Russia, Germany, Austria, etc. The importations of wool amount annually to 100,000 000 pounds. Another important industry in Belgium comprises the imitation Smyrna, and the Brussels and Aubusson carpets. A valuable production is that of malt. Belgium, having 60 malt houses, produces from 500,000 to 600,000 sacks a year. Distillation occupies also an important place in the national industries. A large trade is carried on in chocolate, also in sweet liquors. Wood-carving and the manufacture of fancy goods and art bronzes, and that of small arms, are also important industries. In 1876 nearly 700,000 guns and pistols of all descriptions, besides 350,000 revolvers, were made at Liege. The exportation of Belgian paper amounts to 35,000,000 pounds per annum.

## CHINA.

The Chinese have always been noted as a manufacturing nation. Porcelain originated with them, as did also the art of spinning silk, so far as its introduction into the West is concerned. In the manufacture

of lacquered ware, and in the arts of carving and inlaying, the Chinese have no superiors, while their ivory and mother-of-pearl industries are widely known and appreciated. An enormous population and extended and comprehensive devotion to agriculture, and a generally mild and beneficent climate, combine to bring labor to its lowest possible cost, and it therefore enables the production of enormous quantities of manufactured articles at a cost quite below the possibilities of any other people to compete with. It is only within a comparatively recent date that Chinese manufactures have been introduced into Europe, America, and Australia. The occurrence of international expositions, in which China participated to a great extent, has occasioned the introduction. The total imports into China in 1878 were valued at about $100,000,000, and the exports to nearly the same. In the period from 1869 to 1878, the exports increased seven per cent. over the imports. More than two-thirds in value of the total exports of China consist of one article, tea. In 1878 the amount of this to Great Britain and Ireland alone was 154,000,000 pounds, valued at $45,000,000. Raw silk is also exported to a considerable extent, and latterly enormous quantities of porcelain, bronzes, lacquered ware, and arms of various kinds. Some of the bronze vases exhibited at the Centennial were valued at from $2,000 to $3,000. One carved bedstead was priced at $4,000. Other exportations for the ornamenting of foreign drawing-rooms comprised bamboo work, silk, panel screens, porcelain tablets, and carved work of all sorts. The lacquered ware comes chiefly from Loo-choo and Canton, and includes chairs, sofas, dressing-tables, screens, chess-tables, etc. Articles in silver, toys, fans, lanterns, pongees, grass cloth, and matting are all important manufactures.

SORTING TEA IN CHINA.

## FRANCE.

The industries of France are generally too well known to need enumeration, incuding porcelain, glass, sugar, textile manufactures, silks, carpets, jewelry, and small articles. Cheese and butter, refined sugar, wools and manufactured leather form an important part of the export trade of France. The special commerce of 1879 reached the following amounts: Imports, $900,000,000; exports, $600,000,000; total, $1,500,000,000. The merchant navy in 1880 numbered 14,939 sailing vessels and 588 steamers. The value of the French ceramic industry, including porcelain and the commoner wares, amounts to $12,000,000 annually; that of glass to $22,000,000; paper and pasteboard to $21,000,000; stearine lights, $11,000,000; soaps, $21,000,000. The product of native sugar is averaged at $110,000,000. The State controls a number of the principal manufacturing establishments, including the Gobelins tapestry, Sévres porcelain, the carpet factories of Beauvais, the great machine shops and gun factories, and lastly the tobacco factories, tobacco being a government monopoly. The total value of the general commerce of France for 1878 amounted to $1,800,000,000. The average yearly product of wine is about 1,000,000,000 gallons.

VINTAGE IN FRANCE.

## GERMANY.

Nearly fifty per cent. of the entire soil of Germany is devoted to agriculture, the most important crops being wheat, rye, barley, oats, potatoes, and tobacco. Of these the exportation amounts to but very little, except in the article of potatoes, of which 410,000 tons were exported in 1878 In the matter of trade in live stock, the importation is largely greater than the export, except in the case of sheep, in which, in 1878, the latter nearly doubled the former in amount. The extent of railroad service in Germany in 1877 was 13,500 miles. The number of sea-going vessels in 1879 amounted to 4,453 sailing ships and 351 steamships. The number of post offices in 1878 was 8,890. The length of telegraph lines in the same year was 40,000 miles. By the industrial census of Germany of 1875, there were in the German Empire nearly 3,000,000 different business enterprises carried on, occupying in them 6,470,630 persons, of whom one-sixth were females. These different lines included mining, metal working, the manufacture of machines, chemical industry, paper and leather, wood and carving, food products, building, commercial business, lodging and refreshments. Of these the largest number of persons in any one was 1,053,142 engaged in clothing and cleaning. Nearly as many were employed in the textile industry, the next largest being commercial industry. The production of salt, metals, and other products of mines engages an enormous number of men and quantity of machinery.

The oldest and most important of the German industrial arts are the manufacture of linen and woolen goods, toys, wooden clocks, and wood carving. Saxony and Prussia are noted for their china and earthen wares. The commerce of Germany, which amounted to $1,300,000,000 in 1869, was nearly $2,000,000,000 in 1880; and the carrying trade, in the same period, had risen from $190,000,000 to $320,000,000. The imports in 1869 were $700,000,000; in 1880, $900,000,000. The exports $645,000,000 in 1869, and $945,000,000 in 1880.

## GREAT BRITAIN.

The commerce of Great Britain amounts to nearly £1,000,000,000 annually, of which that with the United

States amounted, in 1881, to £141,819,-820, the imports from the United States being more than double the exports thitherward. Great Britain imports heavily of breadstuffs, timber, metals, cotton, meat, and butter. Her exports are machinery, textile fabrics, hardware, coal, iron, salt, rails, etc. The railways of the United Kingdom cover 17,333 miles, and their annual traffic amounts to 245,000,000 tons. The number of vessels carrying the British flag is greater than that of any other nation in ancient or modern times, her tonnage amounting to 6,399,000 tons, and that of her colonies to 1,735,000 tons. Textile Industries are of enormous extent, employing nearly one million hands. The metal manufactures come next, employing 650,000 hands.

HAULING TIMBER IN AUSTRALIA.

**AUSTRALIA.**

With the wonderful antipodal colonial possession of Great Britain, Australia, we shall conclude this brief glance at a few of the leading countries of the world in regard to their commerce and transportation.

The British flag was first planted on the shores of New Holland, near the site of the present city of Sydney, in 1788. Twelve years later there were not 6,000 inhabitants in the colony. But by the end of the next half century the population amounted to nearly half a million, and since the discovery of gold, in 1851, it has increased five-fold. Gold and sheep-farming have been the great resources of Australia, the value of the gold exported in 1877 being £7,400,000, and that of wool £19,000,000. But the

SYDNEY, AUSTRALIA.

gold production from 1852 to 1878 averaged £9,000,000 per annum. The wool trade, which in 1830 was only 2,000,000 pounds, had reached in 1877 the enormous quantity of 354,000,000 pounds. The wealth at present represented by the farming stock in the country amounts to £70,000,000. Meanwhile the exportation of grain averages 15,000,000 bushels, and the vintage averages 1,800,000 gallons of wine. The annual value of the farming products may be set down at £53,000,000. The extent of the railway service of Australia, including all the colonies, is 3,977 miles, and there are 25,400 miles of telegraph. In 1874 the colonies owned 2,000 vessels, aggregating 223,000 tons.

TRANSPORTATION IN SOUTH AFRICA.

The capacity of Australia for the cultivation of the vine is quite beyond what is generally supposed. The United States Consul at Melbourne writes to the State Department in 1881 that "it may confidently be asserted that every variety of vine grown on the continent of Europe is capable of being produced in the southern half of the continent of Australia." The number of acres under cultivation in this culture in 1879 were 14,128, divided as follows: Victoria, 4,284; New South Wales, 4,266; Queensland, 743; South Australia, 4,117; Western Australia, 718. The average product of wine per acre varies between 111 gallons in South Australia and 172 in New South Wales, the average of Victoria being 134 gallons.

Some idea of the extent and importance of the colonies of Australia may be derived from the following facts concerning one of them: The colony of Victoria has an area of 88,198 square miles, being only a thousand square miles smaller than Great Britain. It possesses 43 per cent. of the population of the entire continent, amounting to 900,000, in round numbers, in 1881. The splendid city of Melbourne alone contains a quarter of a million of inhabitants, and in all that goes to the creation of a beautiful and impressive city, ranks with those of Europe and the United States. The character of the division of the inhabitants of this colony, as regards industrial vocations, was, in 1880—mechanical, 51,000; mining, 39,600; agricultural, 110,000; land and sea transportation, 18,000; food products, 17,000; domestic servants, 28,000; laborers, 34,000. The foreign trade of Victoria amounted in 1879, imports and exports, to £25,000,000, The post-office system of the colony comprises 1,069 offices. All the railways in the colony are the property of the State.

## AFRICA.

Many of the productions of other countries have been introduced both in the tropical and temperate parts of Africa. Gold is found abundantly in the sands of the great rivers that flow out of the central region, on the coast of Guinea, and also in the south-east of Africa. The Sierra Leone coast has valuable iron ore; and copper, salt, saltpeter, sulphur, and emery are found in various portions of the continent. Of the interior commerce or barter of the natives among themselves, our knowledge is scanty. The chieftains in the desert are the principal traders; and Timbuctoo, on the southern edge of Sahara, is the chief commercial depot and central station for the caravans which arrive from Tafilet, Tripoli, and other places in North Africa. Algeria exports large quantities of "Esparto grass" for making paper, and the principal export of the Cape Colony is wool

The commerce of Egypt is very large, but consists to a great extent of goods carried in transit. In 1880, the total value of the imports amounted to £6,752,500, and of the exports to £13,390,000. To the entire trade Great Britain contributed 63 per cent., and the rest was divided between France, Austria, Italy, Russia, and the United States. Cotton, corn, and flour are the largest articles of export.

## The Conduct of Trade.

To a man entering upon business life, there is no doubt that much advice could be given with propriety by those better experienced or informed in the laws of trade than himself. Thus it may be suggested that it is wise to buy in the cheapest and sell in the dearest market; that one should not buy at all, if he can avoid it, on a falling market; that "economy is wealth," and "the nimble sixpence is better than the slow shilling." All these are aphorisms which come with experience, and will eventually be learned by any thoughtful business man. Ideas that are not so generally understood, and are frequently never learned by the very ones to whom they would be the most beneficial, are, for instance, that advertising, to be successful, and permanently so, should be rather *discriminating* than universal; and that it is better to sell a large number of any article at a small profit than a smaller number at a heavy profit. Even supposing the net results to be the same, in the one case the dealer adds largely to his patronage by the extension of his acquaintance, while in the other he confines it to the limited circle of those who can afford to pay his high prices. In the matter of advertising, there is still much to be learned. Paying a thousand dollars for a page in a newspaper in a metropolitan city has no longer the effect that it had when the extravagance was a novelty. The running advertisements in "patent outsides" in a thousand and one country journals of a few hundred circulation is not now as popular as it once was; and the concealed advertisement in the apparently harmless bosom of an anecdote or an exciting legend, with sensation head-lines, has ceased to deceive. Indeed, it is found that the constant iteration of this class of advertising tends to annoy readers, and finally to awaken in their minds a determination to avoid the articles thus advertised. It is beginning to be learned that the true plan of advertising is to bring the matter to be introduced to the attention of exactly the persons likely to be interested in it, by personal appeal through pamphlets and circulars possessing some attractive features. In the constant and increasing competition existing in every line of trade, it is certainly essential that a dealer should make himself well known and *hold his patronage*. The latter duty is the most important one of all in the accomplishment of success in trade. And this is easily performed by assiduity, promptitude, and an obliging habit. A customer always goes where he is well treated, and where "to take trouble" is considered an important function in business. Equally, he soon leaves a tradesman by whom he is treated with rudeness, who fails in punctuality, who is forgetful, who tries to impose upon him, or who will not take a little extra trouble to retain his custom.

COFFEE WAREHOUSE IN BRAZIL.

## Classes of Trade.

The different lines of trade are sharply defined in the large commercial cities, but gradually drift into less exact methods as the centres of population are left behind. Thus the manufacturers sell to the jobbers, who sell to the retail dealers, who, in their turn, sell to the consumers. This subdivision of trade enhances the price, while accommodating both manufacturer and consumer. The business of "picking up trade" is an art in itself, and one which the manufacturer cannot afford to undertake. Just as the study of the taste of the consumer, and the extensive advertising must be done by the retailer, who is brought into immediate contact with him. As a matter of fact, the introduction of intermediary steps in trade falls upon the consumer—so far as its cost is concerned. But, again, he has the advantage of being placed in the presence, by means of the retail dealer, of goods which he would never see if he had to depend upon their exhibition to him by the manufacturer. And so the retail dealer finds the jobber a great convenience, willing to act between the manufacturer and himself, to take the risk of giving him credit, to accept from him orders so small that the manufacturer never would bother with them, and, in fact, to enable him to successfully conduct a business to any extent in accordance with his custom.

## The Commercial Traveler.

The system of the employment of "Drummers," as they are called in this country, is quite an old one, having been long in vogue in England and France, in which latter country they are known as *commis voyageurs*. This institution has assumed an importance in our internal commerce, which is not likely to be diminished, though in certain lines of business their use has been curtailed or even abandoned. This system serves the purpose of bringing business establishments into personal acquaintance with each other; saves provincial and country buyers the necessity of making long and expensive journeys—by carrying samples of goods to their own counters; acquaints manufacturers and importers with the changing tastes of different localities; enables the latter to gain a knowledge of the standing and business success and prospects of their customers by personal investigation without the interposition of mercantile agencies; and, in fine, effects in commercial relations what neither telegraph nor post-office could ever do half so well—an acquaintance with the business situation all over the country, through personal intercommunication. This system also reacts, by educating a class of judicious, experienced and sensible business men, whose knowledge of the ins and outs, tactics, and ways and means of business, is of the greatest possible service to their employers in the mean time, and will become of equal aid to themselves, when they, in turn, employ others.

The number of commercial travelers in actual employment in Great Britain and Australia is over forty thousand, and in the United States as many as seventy-five thousand. In 1881 they formed a National Association at Atlanta, Ga., for the purpose of influencing legislation in their behalf, and to effect arrangements for transportation that will render the performance of their duties as economical as possible.

Any one who has traveled much throughout the United States will have had frequent opportunities of observing the shrewd, alert commercial traveler, with his acute "man-of-the-world" look, his affability and his "eye to the main chance." Hardly a hotel, in the season, is without one or more rooms furnished with conveniences for displaying "a line" of samples; and, indeed, the hotel-keepers and railroad companies would be the first to suffer if the system were abolished.

GRAIN-ELEVATORS.

## The "Bazar" System.

In the early part of this paper we described the *bazars* of the countries of the East. Within the past ten years this plan of selling goods has been largely adopted in our principal cities. It is, in fact, merely going back to first principles, and is not even novel with us, since every "country store" or cross-roads headquarters has conducted business on the same system during our history. The Bazar, as applied to modern city shopping, consists in adapting an enormous structure, or series of buildings, perhaps covering a whole square, to the sale of every imaginable article for which a customer can be found. Dry goods, shoes, fancy goods, perfumery, china ware, domestic hardware, books and stationery—all these, and many other lines of business are carried on under one roof, and in one name. But it must not be imagined that the business is therefore in the hands of one firm. This is by no means always the case. Not infrequently the space is rented to distinct concerns, and the establishment is practically only a number of different shops running in agreement in the same building, or in a number of contiguous buildings. These concerns are, in a measure, coöperative (with each other), buying from the manufacturer direct at prices so reduced as to be able to undersell competitors.

The first result of their introduction into a town or city, on this principle, is to break down all the small tradespeople in the neighborhood, whom they afterwards usually absorb, as clerks and salesmen. It is a commercial fact that the more different business establishments there are supported in a given place, the greater is the commercial prosperity of that place. On this point observe the words of the last annual Report on the Internal Commerce of the United States: "A family whose necessities compel all or most of its members to engage in remunerative occupations, is much more ready to adopt as a permanent home a city where each can secure such employment as is desired, than one where only such of their members as are inclined to, or are capable of engaging in, a certain specific occupation can hope to obtain a satisfactory means of subsistence. The highest degree of human happiness, and the most permanent conditions of prosperity, are doubtless attained in communities where the largest number of the population necessarily engaged in labor can secure such employment as is suited to their abilities and tastes." This passage refers more particularly to manufacturing, but is none the less appropriate in connection with the "Bazar" system, since this latter dispenses with the existence of a great number of small establishments, each of which would support a number of individuals and families. It is the principle of "Centralization" applied to trade, which when carried to excess becomes disastrous.

## Co-operative Stores.

Co-operative stores, proper, have been long employed in Great Britain in local commerce, but have not succeeded when attempted in the United States. The "Civil Service Stores" in England were started about 1866 by some clerks in the London Post Office buying a chest of tea and distributing it among themselves, thereby saving a considerable sum from the retail price, and obtaining the best quality. The plan worked so well that a small room was hired and a trustworthy man employed to take charge, and there were stored articles for daily domestic consumption, which were purchased at wholesale and distributed among the subscribing clerks, who also divided the small expense involved. The idea soon spread, assumed a more comprehensive shape, and there are at this writing a number of immense organizations in London, and others in other parts of Great Britain, all conducted on the same general principle. This principle is, of course, directly opposed to that of jobbers, retail-dealers, and middlemen in general, and has for its purpose the distribution of the profits of these agents among the co-operating subscribers, in the form of reduced charges for commodities. The sales of one such company in London amount to more than $1,000,000 per month, and are increasing, and the increase of the income of its subscribers through this species of economy is said to equal twenty-five per cent. of the same. The plan has been tried in New York and elsewhere in the United States in a number of instances, but has never worked well. It is at present in course of being conducted in New York in the case of the "Co-operative Dress Association: Limited," which has not yet been in existence sufficiently long to have its success or failure decided.

## Trade Policy.

The questions that must come before the manufacturer and the dealer in commodities are not unlike in their nature and general bearing. The question of overproduction is paralleled by that of overstocking; if the manufacturer adulterates his goods, or the dealer gives short weight or short measurement, each eventually meets with the same failure of public confidence; both manufacturer and dealer must study the economies of trade in order to successfully prosecute it. Yet there is no sound judgment in lack of enterprise, or fear to make experiments. A. T. Stewart probably took more chances in the conduct of his business than would be ventured upon by most merchants, yet his success is recognized. We have in our mind an instance of a business conducted in the city of New York in the midst of a tremendous competition, which started three years ago with five men and a little shop, which now employs seventy-five men, and has a pay-roll of $800 per week. It has been fostered by assiduity and enterprise; by invariably supplying the best article in the market at a fair price; by catering to the best custom, and being first to offer novelties; and by judicious advertising (not newspaper). The richest and most successful newsdealer in the United States started life as a newsboy, peddling papers about the streets of New York.

But while *enterprise* is a most valuable and necessary factor in commerce, we are far from recommending that species of enterprise which is known as "speculation." The latter trusts to chance for success, while the former conquers it by energy and wisdom. A steady trade, built upon the sure foundation of integrity, and conducted with a sense of duty to the buyer who confides in him, is the only safe reliance of the young man who enters into commercial life for himself. And with regard to one who labors in the employment of another, it should be remembered that while he is being paid for his time and his labor, he is also receiving, as a part of his wages, the knowledge of business which is, in time, to fit him in turn to be an employer of others. This fact is but little appreciated by those who enter business as clerks or other subordinates. Such, in fact, if they are watchful, are placed in a position to profit by all the knowledge and experience which has been acquired by their employers. A business house, under these circumstances, becomes a higher school, from which the pupil graduates into the great commercial world fully equipped—if he has taken advantage of his opportunities—to enter into the battle for subsistence and wealth on an equality with the best of his competitors. This is a point with regard to a business life which should not be lost sight of. The acquisition of the methods and rules of business are of far more value to the learner than any pay he may receive for his services.

From the first simple traffic by barter, one may follow the wonderful movement of commerce--and its hand-maid, transportation—through all its numerous ramifications, among different races, increased constantly through discovery and invention by new accessions of commodities, forwarded constantly by all the arts and all the sciences, until it reaches its present gigantic state, when thousands of millions of articles change hands daily by means of the proper representatives of value. It has been estimated that there are about twelve hundred millions of human beings at all times engaged in buying and selling, wearing and eating, wasting and destroying. It would, therefore, take many books the size of this one to tell half of the story—but sufficient has been told here to induce the *thinking man* to enter upon and conduct his business life with a just recognition of its responsibilities, its difficulties and its magnitude, when taken in the mass.

Returning From Pasture.

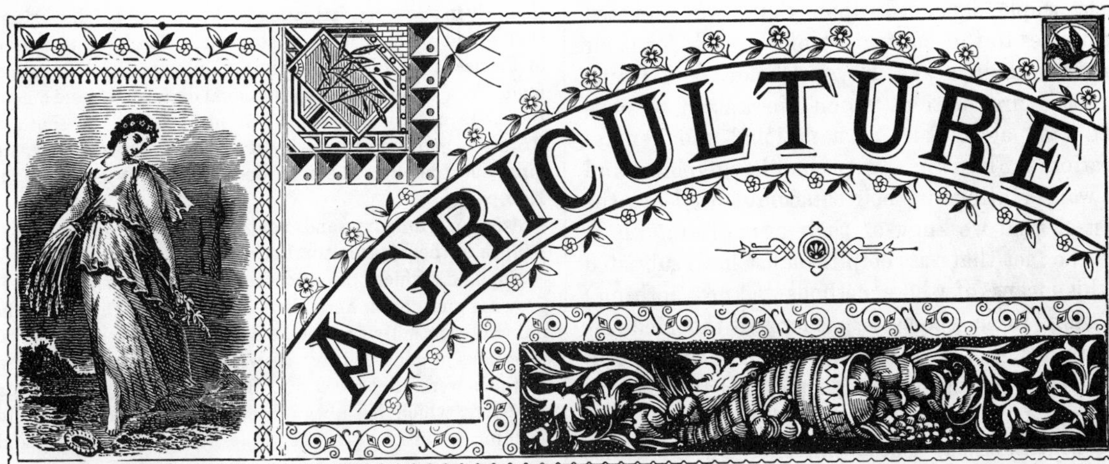


WE derive our word *Agriculture* from the Romans, the Latin word *ager* being field, and *cultura* cultivation; and beyond what the Latin writers have told us, we know very little concerning the agriculture of the ancients. But ordinary reasoning would inform us that primeval man must first have depended for subsistence upon the chase, and not upon the culture of the soil. It was a far advanced step in civilization when man first discovered and applied the reproductive capacity of the seeds of food-plants: as it was an evidence of mature reflection, and a confidence in the continuance of existence, when he began to make provision for the fruitfulness of future seasons. In fact the discoveries of flint implements, the first employed by man, show that he pursued animals to kill them for food, there being arrows and spear-heads and knives, but no tools apparently designed for excavating, or for cultivating the soil. And even later, when the use of iron had been discovered, and weapons for the chase of land animals had been supplemented by fish-hooks and fish-spears, indicating that the sea had also been forced to yield fish as food for man, there were still disclosed no evidences of agriculture. Human beings, at that far distant period, dwelt in caves, where their bones have been found, accompanied by the flint and bronze implements they used. Later, they built themselves houses, now known as "lake-dwellings," which were reared on piles in the midst of lakes—not only in Europe, but in Asia, and in the East India Islands. In the discoveries which have been made of the remains of these lake-dwellings, as in the tombs of the ancient Egyptians, have been found the first indications of earth-culture, in the actual grain and corn which was grown, and which differ but little from existing varieties.

It was doubtless the accumulation of large numbers of human beings in settlements—communities thus occurring on account of the necessity for self-protection—that, by necessity, awakened the knowledge of the possibilities of agriculture in the mind of man. The recurring season of fruitfulness must have been the suggestion, and the demand of hunger the occasion which gave rise to the custom of planting seed and reaping the result. Thus, also, it was with regard to domesticating animals of certain species for food, and for the skins which could be employed for protective covering in inclement seasons. Like causes producing like effects, and the human intelligence being the same, or nearly the same, everywhere, in the beginning, agriculture, like every other custom, will have been spontaneous in different parts of the world, whenever the local circumstances demanded it. But some of the ancient nations grew into commerce, as a vocation, others into manufactures: the Phœnicians are an instance of this character.

Such people depended upon those who devoted themselves to the cultivation of the soil, for their grain and their meat. Egypt, Chaldea and China were the first nations which are known to have conducted agriculture as a national and general vocation. From the Egyptian hieroglyphics, and the wall-paintings in their catacombs, we learn the most of what we know of their agriculture. It is also the fact that vast empires must have subsisted by this means, of whose methods we know nothing: Babylon, India, the eastern shores of the Mediterranean Sea, the great plains bordering on the Euphrates River—myriads of people—led the life of a constant farmer, not to speak of those of eastern and central Asia, whose existence was at times nomadic, and at times settled and agricultural, and who always reared large herds of cattle and sheep.

## ANCIENT CONDITIONS.

**Climatic Changes.**—The conditions of ancient times were much the same as those of the present, with the difference that there has evidently been a constant change of relation between localities and the recurrence of the seasons, bringing about similar changes in the products of countries. Indications are that in both hemispheres, or parts of them, the tendency of product-belts—so to speak—is northward: thus the wheat belt, the vine region, and the cotton region have sensibly displayed a northward movement; and the finest agricultural regions of Italy have changed, from ancient times, from the southern part of the peninsula to the plains about Lombardy, which are now a veritable garden spot.

The same has been the case with regard to Spain, which, under the Moorish dominion, was, in its southern regions, raised to the highest pitch of cultivation, including rich crops of wheat and maize; while now their principal yield is the olive, oranges, and the fruit of the vine. The great European wheat belt, which extends south from the Baltic to the regions about the Black Sea, is the parallel of that of America, running northward and westward from the Ohio River; just as the vine regions of Spain, Portugal, Italy, and France, are paralleled by those of California.

## AGRICULTURE IN EUROPE.

The extent to which artificial irrigation is used in Europe and the Eastern countries, and the results obtained by this mode of cultivation, are astonishing, and should give rise to thoughtful consideration in America. In the great plain of northern Italy watered by the river Po, as much as 1,600,000 acres are under irrigation, and, by the system of rotation of crops, are made the most productive lands in all Europe. On the farms of Lombardy large numbers of cattle are kept, the land being often a complete network of canals, with their accompanying minor channels. In the south of France, particularly in Provençe, irrigation has reclaimed much territory that would without it be waste land. The farming system of France is peculiar in its division into small allotments of land, French law requiring the equal division of land among the heirs on the death of a parent. While the south of France is given up to the cultivation of the mulberry, the vine, and the olive, the northwest is the most fertile land in Europe.

Austria, Hungary, and Southern Russia are much like France in their agricultural conditions.

England, which, prior to the 16th century, was a wool-growing and not an agricultural country, became such later on, and eventually grew to be an exporter of wheat, and an enormous grazing country as well. Excellent agricultural methods were introduced into England in early times from Flanders, which has always been a careful and successful farming country. In the western counties of England, stock-raising and dairy-farming predominate.

## AGRICULTURE IN ASIA.

Throughout eastern and southern Asia rice is the most important food-crop, irrigation is generally practiced, and, particularly in China, agriculture is conducted on the most economical principles, with the free use of fertilizers and with the most liberal results. What we know of the interior tribes of Central Africa, and those of the Polynesian Islands, gives evidence that food-crops have been raised among them from time immemorial. The methods which were in use in the remote past among these semi-civilized races, and which were of the simplest character, obtain at present. Such has also been the case with the aborigines of America, North and South. Generally of a nomadic nature, the native tribes have wandered over the vast territories in their possession, and depending mainly upon the chase for food, have otherwise lived upon esculent roots, cultivating maize, at intervals, as a standard article of food. It is a fact that as many as twenty-five different roots, and sixty varieties of berries, fruits, nuts, and wild plants, unknown as food to the whites, have always been among the articles of diet of North American Indians.

Perhaps there has been no country that has offered such interesting material for the history of agriculture as the Empire of Japan. Dating from a remote antiquity, this vocation has been conducted in the Japanese Islands with unfailing regard for ancient forms, and yet these have been found to include a thorough and comprehensive knowledge of the best methods extant. There the whole water system of the empire is utilized in irrigation; fertilizers are employed with rigid adherence to their known properties, and the most thorough tillage is conducted with the end scrupulously in view of gaining from the land its utmost possibilities of return for cultivation. Labor being exceedingly cheap, and the land exceptionally fertile, the effect has been to occasion the most remarkable results in production in every part of the empire, about one-half of which is under the closest cultivation, while four-fifths of the adult male population are agriculturists. The principal products are rice, wheat, barley, cotton, tobacco, sugar, hemp, flax, and fruits. The whole area of the settled portion of the Japanese Islands is not much larger than the New England States, while here is concentrated a population four-fifths as great as that of the United States. By not allowing an ounce of fertilizing material of any kind to go to waste, though without live-stock to any extent, unaided by mechanical appliances, without the system of rotation of crops, the Japanese farmer produces annually from one acre of land the crops which require four seasons in the United States; and this with the crudest and simplest aids in the way of implements.

## AGRICULTURE IN AUSTRALIA.

Australia is divided into seven colonies, viz.: New South Wales, Victoria, South Australia, Queensland, Western Australia, Tasmania and New Zealand. Of these, Victoria and South Australia are the most interested in agriculture.

### VICTORIA.

In 1880 the number of acres in this colony under cultivation was 1,687,400, the number of occupiers being 49,025. The five principal crops included wheat, 707,738 acres; oats, 167,721; barley, 43,208; potatoes, 41,600; hay, 210,169. Green forage, and permanent artificial grasses covered 307,475 acres; vines, 4,284; gardens and orchards, 20,305 acres. The other crops were maize (Indian corn), rye, peas and beans, mangel wurzel, turnips, beets, carrots, parsnips, onions, chicory, hops, and tobacco. The produce of wheat was 9,407,503 bushels, or 13.3 bushels to the acre; that of oats, 4,024,962 bushels, or 24 to the acre; barley, 1,065,759 bushels, or 25 to the acre; potatoes, 167,986, or 4 tons to the acre; and hay, 291,781 tons, or $1\frac{1}{2}$ tons to the acre. The area under tillage has doubled, and that under wheat much more than doubled during the last ten years.

### NEW SOUTH WALES.

This colony is devoted principally to sheep-farming, being the greatest wool-producing country in the world. It is also beginning to assume importance for its production of meat, shipping it in a frozen condition to the London market. The area of land under cultivation is continually increasing, and maize, in particular, is becoming a highly successful crop. The yield of vegetable products and fruits covers the semi-tropical as well as those of colder climates. The production of sugar is considerable, as is also that of tobacco; and dairy-farming is assuming prominence in the southern districts, while the culture of the vine has resulted in a production which has attracted attention in Europe.

The following figures give the crop production for 1878–9:

|  |  |
|---|---|
| Wheat | 3,439,326 bushels. |
| Oats | 447,912 " |
| Barley | 132,072 " |
| Maize | 4,420,580 " |
| Other Cereals | 27,621 " |
| Potatoes | 53,590 tons. |
| Hay | 172,407 " |
| Wine | 684,733 gallons. |

## QUEENSLAND.

This colony contains an area of 669,520 square miles, nearly all of which is leased, or otherwise occupied, and nearly all of which is productive land. In the northern part there are well-marked tropical wet and dry seasons, but in the rest of the colony moisture is uncertain. There are as yet only 130,000 acres under cultivation in the whole of Queensland, the colony being only thinly populated. The pastoral country is large and very rich, the great detriment being scarcity of surface water. The coast country of Southern Queensland grows an enormous variety of vegetables and fruit, and all the cereals, sugar-cane, tobacco, tea, and coffee. The northern coast lands contain large tracts of fine sugar country. The coffee bush thrives well along the whole coast. This colony had, in 1878, 2,469,555 head of cattle; and in 1879 the number of its sheep, 5,796,742.

The following is a table of the principal productions of Queensland:

| | | |
|---|---|---|
| Wheat | 130,452 | bushels. |
| Oats | 1,274 | " |
| Barley | 16,904 | " |
| Maize | 1,539,510 | " |
| Other Cereals | ——— | " |
| Potatoes | 9,063 | tons. |
| Hay | 18,553 | " |
| Wine | 64,407 | gallons. |

## SOUTH AUSTRALIA.

The area of cultivated land in this colony is about 2,250,000 acres, and about 177,000 square miles are leased for pastoral purposes. In that year there were in South Australia 130,000 horses, 266,000 horned cattle, over 6,000,000 sheep, 90,500 pigs, and 11,200 goats. The favorite breed of sheep in the interior is the merino, but on the coast longwools are sometimes preferred. The value of the export of wool during 1878 amounted to over £1,750,000 for 56,500,000 pounds.

Nearly two-thirds of the area under cultivation is given up to wheat, 1,500,000 acres being reaped in the harvest of 1880, an aggregate over 14,000,000 bushels. This wheat brings the highest price in the London market, and has received the highest award at international exhibitions. During the season of 1879-'80, there were grown 202,000 bushels of barley, 61,000 of oats. 58,000 of peas, 296,000 tons of hay, and 27,000 tons of potatoes. Hops are grown with success in the southern districts. Flax, tobacco, the castor oil plant, opium, and many plants used for distilling perfumes are grown in this colony. The mulberry and silkworm thrive well, but there is no important silk culture. The annual vintage is about half a million gallons, the most of the wine being consumed in the colony. Fruits of all the European varieties are produced easily.

## WESTERN AUSTRALIA.

This is the largest of all the Australian Colonies, but is the least devoted to agriculture, the population being under 30,000. There were 45,933 acres of land under cultivation in 1877, and the live stock comprised 33,502 horses, 54,050 cattle, and 899,494 sheep.

## TASMANIA.

The soil and climate of Tasmania are peculiarly adapted for the production of cereals and fruit. The total area of land cleared or in cultivation is 366,911 acres, the chief products being wheat, oats, barley, potatoes, peas, and English grasses.

The number of acres in wheat in 1880 was over 45,000, with 37,000 in oats. Hops are extensively and profitably cultivated, their export in 1879 amounting to over £26,000, and all the fruits of temperate climates grow here luxuriantly.

The number of sheep in the colony is nearly 2,000,000; cattle, about 130,000; horses, 25,000; and pigs, 38,000.

## NEW ZEALAND.

All the grains, grasses, fruits, and vegetables grown in England are cultivated in New Zealand with perfect success, being excellent in quality and heavy in yield; while, besides these, the vine is cultivated in the open air, and maize, the taro, and the sweet potato are cultivated to some extent in the sunny valleys of the north island. The principal crops are wheat, oats, barley, potatoes, and sown grass. The climate of New Zealand is one of the finest in the world; and owing to the prevalence of light and easily-worked soils, all agricultural processes are performed with unusual ease.

## AMERICAN COLONIAL AGRICULTURE.

The early history of the British colonists in America displays a constant succession of dangers and hardships, in the midst of which agriculture could hardly thrive. Down to as late a period as the middle of the 18th century, the James River colonists cultivated one field until it was exhausted, when they deserted it for another which they cleared for the purpose. Cattle had been introduced as early as 1609, and were much thought of; but when it is remembered that the practice of cultivating grasses and roots for fodder was not even introduced into England until 1633, the manner in which they were cared for may be imagined. They were permitted to roam at will, picking up such subsistence as they might, and faring badly in consequence. Under this treatment the cattle of the colonists continued to deteriorate until after the Revolution. Farming was conducted under many disadvantages in those days, one of the most serious being the want of proper implements. For twelve years after the landing of the Puritans the farmers had no plows, and later on it was customary for one owning a plow to travel about and do the plowing for the farmers over a considerable extent of territory. The massive old plow required a strong team, a stout man to bear on, another to hold, and a third to drive. The work it did was slow and laborious. The other tools in use were a heavy spade, a clumsy wooden fork, and later, a harrow. The plows used by the French settlers of Illinois from 1682, were made of wood, with a small point of iron fastened upon the wood by strips of rawhide. They used carts that had not a particle of iron about them ; the thrashing was done with a flail, the winnowing by the wind. In fact, previous to the beginning of the present century, a strong man could have carried on his shoulders all the implements used on an American farm, except the old wooden cart and the harrow. The Plymouth colonists found corn in cultivation by the Indians, and soon learned to grow it after the Indian fashion. This was to dig with a clam-shell small holes in the ground about four feet apart, drop in a fish or two (alewives), plant in them four or six kernels of corn, and cover them up. For the clam-shell the colonists soon employed the heavy mattock, or grub-hoe. Indian corn, pumpkins, squashes, potatoes, and tobacco were at this time new to the Europeans. Wheat, rye, oats, and barley were grown by the Puritan settlers, but wheat was never a successful crop in New England. It will have been seen that the Indians understood the value of fertilizers, and an early chronicler of the history of Plymouth colony wrote of this as follows : "According to the manner of the Indians, we manured our ground with herrings, or rather shads (alewives), which we have in great abundance, and take with great ease at our doors." But the condition of agriculture could hardly be worse than it was at this time. With poor and inefficient tools in scant quantity, illy-kept and profitless cattle, meager crops, and ignorant farming, the early settlers could with difficulty raise sufficient food to keep themselves from starvation. During the Revolution there was general stagnation in farming, and this condition continued until some years later. It was not until the last decade of the eighteenth century that the establishment of agricultural societies in a few of the States gave a positive impetus to agriculture. This impetus was perhaps first given in the agricultural convention held in Georgetown, D. C., in 1809 ; and which was followed, May 10, 1810, by the first agricultural exhibition ever held in the country, which took place in Georgetown. In October of the same year, the exhibition of three merino sheep at Pittsfield, Mass., became the germ of the Berkshire County Agricultural Society, whose regular exhibitions began in 1811, the first county exhibition ever held in this country.

## AGRICULTURAL IMPLEMENTS.

All of this progress naturally brought about improvements in the form and capacity of agricultural implements. Charles Newbold, of Burlington, N. J., had received a patent in 1797 for his cast-iron plow. Peacock improved on this in 1807, while Thomas Jefferson had written a treatise on the requisite form of the mold-board, based on scientific principles. These early efforts were the beginning of that wonderful march of invention in its application to agricultural implements, which has resulted in revolutionizing farming to that extent that the number of two-horse reapers in use in the country, in 1861, performed an amount of work equal to that of a million of men. Horse hay-rakes, mowers and reapers, thrashing-machines, and many smaller improved implements have, on every well regulated farm, usurped the place of the old clumsy and cumbersome tools, their very possession stimulating to the increased activity and energy which have placed us foremost among the agricultural peoples of the earth.

What has been said with regard to the antiquity of certain tools of the farmer, merely shows the simplicity with which farm work was for ages performed. As men advanced in powers of invention, this faculty became devoted to making agriculture more certain and more scientific by devising new implements. The number of these is incalculable, and every well-informed farmer should acquaint himself with the nature and uses of all those likely to be needed in the kind of farming he prosecutes. Especially in handling the soil by the subsoil plow, harrow, and cultivator, do the latest implements come in play. Everything is gained by being properly equipped in this direction, and the farmer who possesses the best article of mower and reaper, or horse-rake, is just so far better able to handle his crops than is his neighbor who is not thus supplied. There is nothing to which labor-saving is so generally and so ingeniously applied as to farm implements, and there is no economy in doing without them. Any farmer can obtain gratuitously an illustrated catalogue of new implements by applying to the manufacturers, who always advertise in the agricultural journals and magazines, which is one good reason why every farmer should supply himself with agricultural literature in that form.

### MODERN IMPLEMENTS.

The gang-plow, for instance, has placed the weak and infirm, so far as plowing is concerned, on a par with the strong and active. This machine consists of a gang of two plows, whose beams are attached to an axle resting upon two wheels. One of these wheels is so arranged that by means of a lever the driver can so adjust the height of the wheel that it shall correspond to the wheel running in the furrow, and thus keep the plow-soles on a level in the bottom of the furrow. Another lever on the opposite side, with a catch working into notches on an arc serves the double purpose of either regulating the depth of the plow, or of entirely throwing the plows out of the ground at the end of a furrow for the purpose of turning around. Upon the machine is provided a comfortable seat for the driver, where he may sit and plow, and even smoke his pipe in perfect freedom of action. Upon examining the work done by this implement at sundown, we find that one man with four horses has thoroughly turned over and broken up the soil of about five acres, to a uniform depth of about eight inches, leaving no balks and hollows, but all smooth and level, indicating the thoroughness of the work. The improved sulky harrow both harrows and seeds, and will accomplish from ten to fifteen acres a day with one man and a pair of horses. The driver from his comfortable seat superintending the various operations of harrowing the soil, sowing the fertilizer, grain, and grass seed, all at one operation. The reaper, horse-rake, mower, corn-planter, cultivator, etc., one and all, exhibit the value of inventive genius as applied to agriculture.

### COMPARATIVE GRAIN STATISTICS.

In default of having statistics of the production of corn and wheat in the United States, prior to 1840, we can only give certain figures of their exportation, which will, however, serve, by comparison, as some indication of the vast increase in the product of these grains. In 1748, South Carolina exported 39,308 bushels of corn, and in 1754, 16,428 bushels. In 1753 North Carolina exported 61,580 bushels ; in 1770

Savannah exported 13,598 bushels; and the total quantity exported from all the colonies in the latter year was 578,349 bushels. Even as late as 1800 the entire exportation was only 2,032,425 bushels. The export of wheat was in 1791, 1,018,339 bushels, and 619,681 barrels of flour; in 1800 it had fallen to 26,853 bushels of wheat, with 653,052 barrels of flour; in 1810 it was 325,024 bushels of wheat and 798,431 barrels of flour. In comparison with these figures, consider the 150,575,577 bushels of wheat, and the 7,945,786 barrels of flour exported from the United States in 1881.

## TOBACCO.

The culture of tobacco began with the first settlement of the James River colony, and it is recorded that in 1615 the gardens, fields, and streets of Jamestown were planted with tobacco. It became the great staple crop, and also the currency of the colony. In 1622 the product amounted to 60.000 pounds, and it doubled during the next twenty years. At a period nearer to that of the Revolution, when the soil had become exhausted and manure was not procurable, the tobacco crop fell off, but from 1744 to 1766 the exports of it amounted to 40,000,000 a year.

## COTTON.

The cotton crop in America is the growth of the last century. Prior to the invention of the cotton-gin by Eli Whitney, 1793, comparatively little of it had been raised in the Southern States. The difficulty of freeing the cotton from the seed had previously been so great that a hand could clean but a pound a day. Whitney's invention enabled a hand to clear 360 pounds per day, and of course stimulated the planting of cotton. The application of power to machinery in carding, spinning, and weaving cotton, which was made in England about this time, created a demand for all the cotton that could be grown. In the factories the power of a hand in the manufacture of cotton cloth had been increased twenty-two hundred times, as in the field it had been multiplied by three hundred and sixty. Cotton-growing now became of immense importance in the colonies, and it soon constituted a third part of the entire export of the country. Each decade showed an increase of about 100 per cent. in production, and in 1840 it amounted to six times that of 1820, being, in quantity, 2,177,835 bales, which is, again, about one-third of the quantity which this product has since reached, as will be seen on reference to our tables of productions. The hay crop has also grown up in the United States mainly during the past century, having been increased by reason of the labor-saving machinery in this direction which has been invented, making possible the sufficiently rapid and economical cutting of our grasses. The improved methods in gathering, curing, and preserving these grasses for fodder have of course resulted in great advantage in the breeding and care of cattle.

## COTTON-SEED FOR SHEEP.

While it is not designed in this place to propound theories of agriculture, or even to enumerate or describe accepted methods—matters which strictly find their place in the text-books and treatises on practical farming—there are many recent discoveries and applications, both scientific and practical, to which it seems proper to allude. And, for instance, in the matter of sheep-farming, it has been very clearly shown by recent experiment, that this industry can be greatly economized in the cotton States, by using cotton-seed as winter feed. Mr. Edward Atkinson's plan of four-field rotation in Southern farming involves this. For he advises dividing a farm into four fields—one to be put in grass, one in peas, one in corn, one in cotton; the peas to be fed off by sheep on the ground, and then the cotton-seed to be fed to the sheep in the field where the peas grew. This course would so enrich the field by means of the sheep manure that a good cotton crop could be raised on it without the use of commercial fertilizers. About 100 pounds of seed will be sufficient for each sheep during a hard winter, and half that quantity in a mild winter.

## THE SILO AND ENSILAGE.

In considering the subject of raising stock, we may properly refer to the important subject of *ensilage*. Ensilage is fodder cut green and deposited in pits termed *silos*, and taken out as it is needed for feed for cattle. The idea of preserving green fodder was known to the ancients, and such pits have been found in Egypt. The modern silo originated with Auguste Goffart, a Frenchman, who began his experiments in 1850. In America the plan has been carried to great success by Dr. Bailey, of Billerica, Mass.; C. W. Mills, of New Jersey; Samuel Remington, of Ilion, N. Y.; Theodore A. Havemeyer, New York, on his model farm at Pompton, N. J.; and others. By this plan it is found that corn or grasses can be preserved with all their nutritious qualities, and to such advantage, that one hundred and twenty head of horned cattle and twelve horses have been kept during two winters (1880-82) on the product of thirteen acres of land, at a cost of five hundred dollars for the fodder, the two silos in which it was kept having cost seven hundred dollars. Fed on hay for the same time the stock would have cost for their keeping seventy-five hundred dollars. This extraordinary statement has been frequently verified, and the conclusion of all those who have faithfully fed stock on ensilage has been entirely favorable to its use. One system of silos is thus described: They occupy the north wing of the barn of the owner, 99 feet long by 40 wide; upon a massive stone foundation, concrete walls 2½ feet thick were constructed, forming four large silos, two 59 feet long and 14 feet wide; and two 35 feet long and twelve feet wide, the depth of each of them being 25 feet. They may, however, and to advantage, be made much smaller than these, requiring less time and fewer hands to fill them. and avoiding the danger of fermentation by being filled and closed rapidly. The corn (for instance) is harvested in the latitude of New Jersey, in the latter part of September, when the stalks are fully matured, but while still green in color. It is cut with an ensilage-cutter into half-inch or inch lengths. and is then filled into the silo as rapidly as possible. When all the fodder is in, the surface is leveled, and is then covered with boards, on which heavy weights are placed to accomplish a uniform pressure. These weights may be barrels of stones or cement, loose stones, bags of sand, or anything else to answer the purpose. When the fodder is to be used for cattle, a portion of the cover is taken off, and it is then cut down perpendicularly as required. It has been found that cattle will leave all other feed for this, that they will thrive better upon it than upon any other, and that their milk is richer and will produce a better quality of butter under its use. It has been clearly shown, moreover, that cattle can be fed on this system at a cost of $12 (£2.10) per head per annum, when the usual expense of feeding by the ordinary process is $80 (about £16.6) per head. The silo which was closed up at the Atlanta Cotton Exposition in October 1881, was opened in May 1882, and the fodder was found pure and wholesome, and fit for immediate use.

## FERTILIZERS.

The importance of chemical science to agriculture was, perhaps, first made known to the civilized world through the experiments of Sir Humphry Davy, about the first part of the present century. But it was not until 1840, when Liebig announced his important scientific proposition regarding fertilizers, that intelligent farmers were awakened to the tremendous character of their possible powers in sustaining or renewing the fertility of the soil. Said Liebig: "To manure an acre of land with forty pounds of bone-dust, is sufficient to supply three crops of wheat, clover, potatoes, turnips, &c., with phosphates; but the form in which they are restored to the soil does not appear to be a matter of indifference; for the more finely the bones are reduced to powder, and the more intimately they are mixed with the soil, the more easily they are assimilated. The most easy and practical mode of effecting their division is to pour over the bones, in the state of fine powder, half of their weight of sulphuric acid, diluted with three or four parts of water." These simple words opened the way to the whole system of concentrated fertilizers, which has extended so far in modern times and grown to such gigantic proportions as to affect the commerce of the whole civilized world. It was not, in fact, until 1840 that guano was first used in England, twenty casks being landed there in that year. Five years later the importation had grown to 200,000 tons, employing 679 vessels. By 1856 the quantity taken from the Chincha Islands alone amounted to 2,000,000 tons, and the sales from 1840 to that time to $100,000,000 (£20,000). In 1848 fertilizers to the quantity of 1,000 tons were imported into the United States; in 1849, over 21,000 tons, and in the next twenty years, to 1,230,372 tons. But these figures are small compared to those of the commercial fertilizers manufactured in the United States.

The exhaustion of the soil by the constant growth of cotton on the same land in the South has rendered the use of fertilizers in enormous quantities, indispensable.

## AGRICULTURE IN THE UNITED STATES.

There is, perhaps, no other country on the face of the earth so admirably adapted for agricultural purposes as the United States. The area of the country is 1,936,384,000 acres, exclusive of Alaska, which in itself comprises 370,000,000 acres. The mountain ranges —the Appalachian chain towards the east, the Rocky Mountains in the centre, and the Sierra Nevada in the west, divide the United States into four great regions: The Atlantic slope, the basin of the Mississippi and the Missouri, the country between the Rocky Mountains and the Sierra Nevada, and the Pacific slope. Of the total area of the United States, 35,584,000 acres are water, leaving 1,900,800,000 acres in land. The climate of such an extent of territory, running through 24 degrees of latitude and nearly 60 of longitude, of course varies considerably, giving a great variety of products. Thus apples, pears and plums flourish in the North, melons and grapes in the Middle States, pine-apples, pomegranates, figs, almonds and oranges in the South. Maize is grown from Maine to Louisiana, and wheat throughout the Union; though, within the last generation, the corn centre has been transferred from the South to the West, and the wheat centre from the Middle States to the extreme West and Northwest. In 1842, 59 per cent. of the corn was grown in the Southern States, in 1880 not more than thirty-three per cent. was raised in that section. Very little cotton is grown north of 37 degrees, though it does grow as far north as 39. Sugar cane grows as far north as 33 degrees, though it does not thoroughly succeed beyond 31. Vines and the mulberry grow in various parts of the Union, oats, rye and barley throughout the North and the mountainous parts of the South, and hemp, flax and hops in the Western and Middle States. The cash value of the farms in the United States, by the ninth census, (the figures of the tenth as to this not being yet accessible) was $9,262,803,861; of farm implements and machinery, $336,878,429; of live stock, $1,525,276,457; total estimated value of all farm productions, $2.447,538,658; the value of orchard products, $47.335.189; products of market-gardening. $26,719,229. There were in 1879 in the various States of the United States, live stock valued at $1,576,917,556, divided according to the following table:

Statistics of the United States.

| STATES. | Horses. | | | Milch Cows. | | | Oxen and Other Cattle. | | | Sheep. | | | Hogs. | | |
|---|---|---|---|---|---|---|---|---|---|---|---|---|---|---|---|
| | Number. | Average Price. | Value. | Number. | Average Price. | Value. | Number. | Average Price. | Value. | Number. | Average Price. | Value. | Number. | Average Price. | Value. |
| Maine | 81.700 | $60 15 | $ 4,914,255 | 160,600 | $24 10 | $3,870,460 | 203,700 | $24 00 | $4,888,800 | 596,300 | $3 23 | $1,926,049 | 60,000 | $7 93 | $ 475,800 |
| New Hampshire | 57,100 | 61 40 | 3.505,940 | 98,100 | 28 00 | 2,746.800 | 122,500 | 29 36 | 3,596,600 | 242,100 | 2 83 | 685,143 | 45,000 | 11 75 | 528,750 |
| Vermont | 77,400 | 63 55 | 4,918,770 | 207,100 | 25 05 | 5,187,855 | 126,500 | 21 03 | 2,666,295 | 498,600 | 3 48 | 1,735,138 | 49,400 | 7 61 | 375,934 |
| Massachusetts | 136,200 | 95 52 | 13,009,824 | 167,100 | 35 00 | 5,848,500 | 114,900 | 34 14 | 3 922,686 | 63,300 | 3 58 | 226,614 | 84,900 | 12 46 | 1,057.854 |
| Rhode Island | 16,200 | 94 50 | 1,530,900 | 22,000 | 30 00 | 660,000 | 15,700 | 30 05 | 471,785 | 28,200 | 3 70 | 104.340 | 13,800 | 8 70 | 120,060 |
| Connecticut | 54,000 | 59 20 | 3,196,800 | 118,800 | 29 37 | 3,489,156 | 125.600 | 28 95 | 3,636,120 | 97,100 | 3 40 | 330,140 | 60,600 | 8 84 | 535,704 |
| New York | 898.900 | 76 41 | 68,684,949 | 1,431,700 | 29 06 | 41,605,202 | 668,600 | 26 22 | 17,530,692 | 2,205,800 | 3 57 | 7,874,706 | 936.000 | 7 16 | 6,701,760 |
| New Jersey | 114,500 | 79 76 | 9,132,520 | 153,700 | 35 10 | 5,394,870 | 84,500 | 29 77 | 2,515,565 | 127,400 | 4 01 | 510,874 | 152,900 | 7 40 | 1,131.460 |
| Pennsylvania | 602,200 | 67 22 | 40,479,884 | 836,700 | 26 66 | 22,306,422 | 659,500 | 21 69 | 14,304,555 | 1,649,300 | 3 01 | 4,964,303 | 909.200 | 6 88 | 6,255,296 |
| Delaware | 20,300 | 74 25 | 1,507,275 | 24.800 | 32 50 | 806,000 | 32,000 | 30 67 | 981,440 | 38,800 | 3 83 | 148,604 | 47,600 | 5 63 | 267,988 |
| Maryland | 108,600 | 62 30 | 6,765,780 | 99,500 | 27 20 | 2,706,400 | 120.400 | 19 74 | 2,376,696 | 152,700 | 3 13 | 477,951 | 264,800 | 4 99 | 1,321,352 |
| Virginia | 214,900 | 56 72 | 12,075,688 | 240,600 | 18 86 | 4,537,766 | 431,100 | 15 51 | 6,686,361 | 426,100 | 3 23 | 950,203 | 692,100 | 3 50 | 2,422,350 |
| North Carolina | 146,700 | 59 22 | 8,687,574 | 230,000 | 12 60 | 2.898,000 | 415,800 | 8 31 | 3,455,298 | 425,000 | 1 45 | 616,250 | 1,262,600 | 3 15 | 3,977,190 |
| South Carolina | 62,000 | 79 69 | 4,940,780 | 132,600 | 15 25 | 2.022,150 | 191,800 | 10 52 | 2,017,736 | 176.500 | 1 76 | 310,640 | 546,000 | 2 81 | 1,528,640 |
| Georgia | 119,200 | 67 60 | 8,057,920 | 273.100 | 13 26 | 3,621,306 | 400,800 | 7 93 | 3,178,344 | 374,400 | 1 44 | 539.136 | 1,684,800 | 3 14 | 5,290,272 |
| Florida | 22,400 | 59 00 | 1,321,600 | 72,800 | 9 27 | 674,856 | 518,900 | 6 08 | 3,154,912 | 59,900 | 1 75 | 104,825 | 217.300 | 2 33 | 506 309 |
| Alabama | 113,900 | 56 63 | 6,450,157 | 217,300 | 13 50 | 2,933.550 | 267,800 | 7 75 | 2,075,450 | 214,200 | 1 55 | 332,010 | 1,117,000 | 2 78 | 3,105.260 |
| Mississippi | 99,100 | 57 73 | 5,721,043 | 190,700 | 13 06 | 2,490,542 | 247.500 | 7 69 | 1,903,275 | 200,300 | 1 52 | 304,456 | 1,636,300 | 2 70 | 4,418.010 |
| Louisiana | 82,500 | 38 15 | 3,147,375 | 115,200 | 18 00 | 2,073,600 | 119,900 | 9 60 | 1,151,040 | 135,100 | 1 67 | 225,617 | 378,500 | 4 02 | 1,521,570 |
| Texas | 963,900 | 22 13 | 21,331,107 | 566,300 | 13 85 | 7,843,255 | 4,464,000 | 8 88 | 39,640,320 | 5,148,400 | 1 89 | 9,730.476 | 1,817,800 | 2 55 | 4,635,390 |
| Arkansas | 191,100 | 45 28 | 8,653,008 | 199,000 | 13 66 | 2,718,340 | 371,300 | 10 48 | 3,891,224 | 293,500 | 1 56 | 457,860 | 1,146,000 | 2 97 | 3,403,620 |
| Tennessee | 326,900 | 49 75 | 16,263,275 | 248,100 | 17 09 | 4,240,029 | 397,400 | 10 94 | 4,347,556 | 858.500 | 1 60 | 1,373,600 | 1,710,000 | 3 43 | 5,865,300 |
| West Virginia | 124,600 | 47 86 | 5,963,356 | 131.800 | 20 97 | 2,763,846 | 232,700 | 18 76 | 4,365,452 | 600,500 | 2 14 | 1,285,070 | 287,100 | 3 60 | 1,033,560 |
| Kentucky | 402,400 | 45 04 | 18,121,096 | 270,000 | 22 62 | 6,107,400 | 460,700 | 19 05 | 8,776,335 | 1,009,800 | 2 53 | 2,554,794 | 1,812,000 | 3 26 | 5,907,120 |
| Ohio | 811,300 | 57 53 | 46,674,089 | 700,000 | 26 44 | 18,508,000 | 792,000 | 22 37 | 17,717,040 | 4,080,400 | 2 83 | 11,547,532 | 2,045,200 | 5 01 | 10,246,452 |
| Michigan | 350,500 | 75 68 | 26,525,840 | 416,900 | 26 68 | 11,122,892 | 432 600 | 22 51 | 9,737,826 | 1,856,400 | 2 53 | 4,696.692 | 538,800 | 4 92 | 2.650.896 |
| Indiana | 688,800 | 54 60 | 37,608,480 | 434,800 | 25 09 | 10,909,132 | 756,600 | 18 65 | 14,110,590 | 1,019,000 | 2 29 | 2,333,510 | 2,186,000 | 4 70 | 10,274,200 |
| Illinois | 1,078,000 | 51 66 | 55,689,480 | 695,400 | 26 63 | 18,518,502 | 1,235,300 | 21 09 | 26,052,077 | 1,110,800 | 2 60 | 2,888,080 | 3,202,600 | 5 61 | 17,966.586 |
| Wisconsin | 392,100 | 60 24 | 23,620,104 | 458,200 | 21 79 | 9,984,178 | 522,700 | 17 83 | 9,319,741 | 1,316,100 | 2 39 | 3,145,479 | 571,800 | 5 07 | 2,899,026 |
| Minnesota | 274,500 | 64 58 | 17,727,210 | 304,000 | 20 16 | 6,128,640 | 322,400 | 17 46 | 5,629,104 | 307,500 | 2 13 | 654,975 | 194,200 | 5 28 | 1,025,376 |
| Iowa | 778,400 | 55 19 | 42,959,896 | 724,500 | 24 20 | 17.532,900 | 1,370,400 | 19 44 | 26,640,576 | 454,400 | 2 54 | 1,154,176 | 2,778 400 | 5 36 | 14,892,224 |
| Missouri | 639.800 | 40 37 | 25,828,726 | 526,500 | 19 21 | 10,114,065 | 1,648,300 | 17 47 | 28,795,801 | 1,523,300 | 1 83 | 2,787,639 | 2,620,400 | 3 44 | 9,014,176 |
| Kansas | 299,700 | 48 62 | 14,571,414 | 351,400 | 23 68 | 8,321,152 | 647,700 | 20 32 | 13,161,264 | 371,900 | 2 23 | 829,337 | 1,208.700 | 5 28 | 6,381.936 |
| Nebraska | 176,100 | 64 34 | 11,330,274 | 142,900 | 26 00 | 3,715,460 | 428,000 | 21 52 | 9,210,560 | 172,800 | 2 73 | 471,744 | 698,700 | 5 21 | 3,640,227 |
| California | 273,000 | 46 18 | 12,607,140 | 473,400 | 28 65 | 13.562,910 | 999,900 | 18 47 | 18,468,153 | 7,646,800 | 1 62 | 12,387,816 | 661,000 | 3 97 | 2,624,170 |
| Oregon | 117,400 | 51 93 | 6,096,582 | 121,400 | 17 71 | 2,149,994 | 201,500 | 11 39 | 2,295,085 | 1,265,100 | 1 46 | 1,847,046 | 228,500 | 2 60 | 594,100 |
| Nevada, Colorado and Territories | 287,500 | 47 56 | 13,673,500 | 470,000 | 20 82 | 9,785,400 | 1,080,000 | 17 68 | 19.694,400 | 4,019.600 | 1 92 | 7,717,632 | 170,100 | 6 97 | 1,185,597 |
| Total | 11,201,800 | ........ | $613,296,611 | 12,027,000 | ........ | $279,899,420 | 21,231,000 | ........ | $341,761,154 | 40,765,900 | ........ | $90,230,537 | 34,034,300 | ........ | $145,781,515 |
| Grand average of prices | .......... | $54 75 | .......... | .......... | $23 27 | .......... | .......... | $16 10 | .......... | .......... | $2 21 | .......... | .......... | $4 28 | .......... |

# DAIRY FARMING.

DAIRY farming is among the most profitable lines of business in which the practical farmer can engage. As a matter of course, this business has to be carried on in the vicinity of centers of population. To meet with that success, however, of which it is justly capable, it is especially necessary that it should be conducted with the most absolute care and consideration for the animals, and the most complete cleanliness as to every element that goes to its making up. While it is necessary that the dairy industry should be settled near the centers of population, it is quite astonishing to what a distance milk can be profitably shipped. Thus, the city of New York receives milk daily from the city of Rutland, Vt., distant 241 miles, and from Pittsfield, Mass., distant 167 miles, on another route. Not many years ago St. Louis, then having a population of 310,000, obtained all its supply from the suburbs; now, an estimated proportion of one-eighth of its supply is received by rail from distances up to 95 miles. We have not the statistics of the milk supply of great cities in recent years, but some such figures of a period a decade back will not be without interest. Thus, in 1871, the trade in fresh country milk for the single market of New York represented a yearly gross income to producers of $4,170,000, while the entire expenditure for city consumption exceeded $15,000,000. Judging from the increase of population up to 1880, this latter figure has doubtless increased by this time to $20,000,000. Comparatively little milk is received in Chicago from points distant more than 50 miles from the city. In Boston the extreme distance is about 60 miles. That from Philadelphia about 50. In the vicinity of Cincinnati there are probably 300 dairies, averaging each 30 cows, and 40 gallons of milk per day. Many wealthy families of that city and the immediate suburbs keep their own cows. Probably one-half of the dairymen use "dry feed," including brewer's grain, corn meal, bran, shorts and sheaf oats; the other half use still-slop, refuse from starch factories, with oil cake, etc. The city of Washington obtains its milk by the Baltimore and Ohio and other roads, and from distances up to 80 miles. From these facts and figures it will probably be inferred that with the increase of population increases the necessary radius of supply. Dairy farmers finding their markets in small towns require to be nearer to them than is the case in regard to larger cities.

The manner of shipping milk has been brought to a nicety by the arrangements which have been perfected by the chief railroad lines of the country. Special milk cars are afforded, having the right of way; the shippers owning their own cans, which are returned to them. One of the great obstacles to success in regard to the shipment of milk is the difficulty of impressing the producer with the importance of absolute cleanliness in his milking, and the care of milk vessels, and in establishing him in accurate methods of cooling. The loose management which may suffice for milk not subjected to transportation will not answer for milk which is to be carried long distances and made liable to considerable delay before consumption. When the producer has once established a reputation as a prompt, skillful and cleanly dairyman, his account with the dealer generally suffers little deduction for sour milk. The most reliable dairymen now use tin milking vessels. Wooden pails are not considered safe in respect to perfect cleanliness. Milk cans are stoppered with bungs of maple or other close-grained wood, these being preferable to tin stoppers on account of the jamming to which the neck of the can is liable in handling of collectors, etc. The return cans are very foul, often mouldy. These should be thoroughly scrubbed by hand inside, using warm water, then scalded and rinsed, and placed bottom up out of doors to dry. The wooden stoppers are scrubbed and boiled when they are offensive to the smell. Lye is used in the process. At milking time the milk is strained into the can, which is set into a vat of cold water, the milk stirred from time to time and brought to the proper temperature for shipment. The evening's milk is left over night in the water, and taken up with the morning's milk for the train. It is required that the can before forwarding be filled, and the bungs driven down firmly on the milk. This point of complete filling is strongly insisted on by the dealers in order to prevent injurious agitation of the milk during transportation. The proper temperature of milk for shipment is 58°.

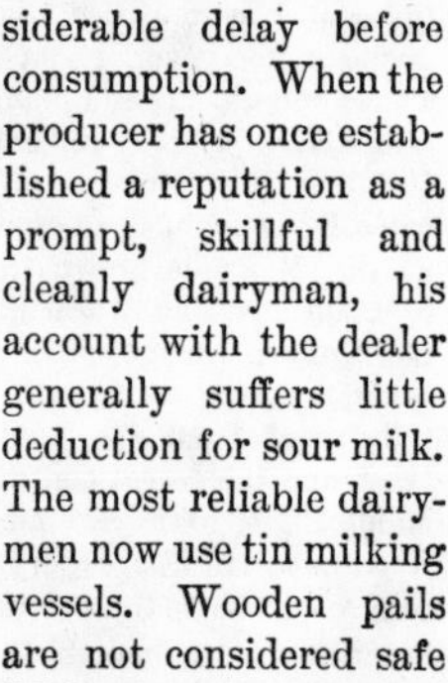

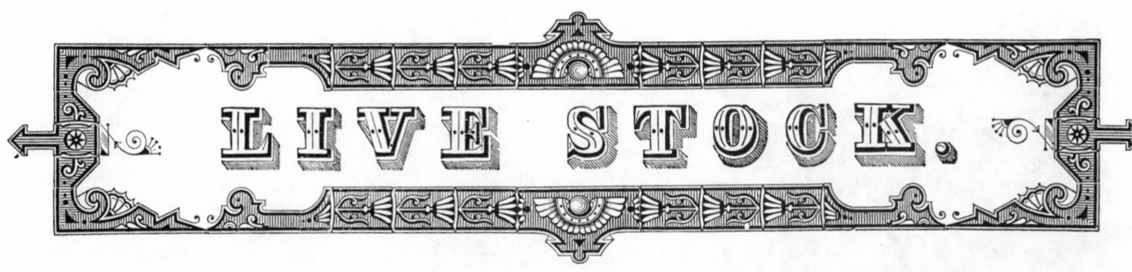

The relation of live stock to the business of the farmer is of the most intimate nature, precisely as with regard to the agriculture of the country it resolves itself into a factor of surpassing importance. As has been already shown in this article, the rearing of cattle in the early history of the American colonies, and even down to a period within the latter part of the last century, was not conducted with any special degree of care, or even judgment. Cattle and sheep were permitted, as a rule, to roam at will, picking up a precarious livelihood wherever they might chance to find it, and of such a character as the sparse vegetation of the New England lands afforded. It has been shown that cattle and sheep and hogs of good breeds were at length imported from Europe, crossed in the instance of the latter with fine Asiatic breeds, and that these became the parents of a long line of progeny. Of recent years, not only has the cattle business grown enormously with the great increase of population and its spread over the vast plains west and south-west, but the devotion of numbers of farms specifically to cattle raising, chiefly for dairy purposes, has become a marked feature in American agriculture. While an enormous business is constantly being done in the transportation of cattle to market from the vast ranches of Texas, Indian Territory and Kansas, in more settled localities splendid arrangements have been effected for the best care of the best cattle for dairy uses, combined with the wisest choice, no matter at what expense, of breeds calculated to improve and sustain those most

JERSEY COW.

HEAD OF DEVON BULL.

favored in the United States. Of such breeds may be named as to cattle the Herefords, Short-horns, Devonshires, Hol-

HEAD OF SHORT-HORN BULL.

steins, Jerseys, Guernseys, etc. The organization and successful conduct of great cattle fairs in the United States have done much towards the improvement of breeds and the awakening of a proper interest in this important industry. Enormous prices have been paid for imported stock, and whole herds are not unfrequently sold at figures for each animal which would stun our ancestors, could they be present and witness such sales.

While each farmer may have a predilection for a certain breed of cattle, the best dairymen in various countries are now growing to regard the Jersey as the most economical and reliable for milk and butter. "No breed of animal is receiving more attention from practical and theoretical breeders, and none have ever proved more responsive or more profitable." Though reckoned an English breed, they

HEAD OF HEREFORD COW.

undoubtedly originated on the coast of France, a close resemblance between the cattle of Jersey and Brittany being observable today. The cows of this breed weigh about 800 pounds. Their eyes are large and mild; the head small and lean; the face dished; the horns small, uncurved, and yellow; the ears small, thin, and yellow inside ; the neck and throat straight, thin, and clean ; back level and broad at loins ; the barrel well ribbed, and deep at flanks ; legs short and small ; tail fine and long ; hide thin and mellow, and yellow ; hair soft ; disposition kind and quiet. Records exist of Jersey cows producing 700 and 800 pounds of butter in twelve running months, besides developing a calf during the period, without showing any falling off in vigor of constitution either in herself or in her offspring. The Jersey gives richer milk than other breed, and the cream rises quicker. Cream cheese from the milk of this breed is highly esteemed, and Jersey veal brings a high price in the market. Of the Holstein cattle it may be said that the cows are large milkers, and the bulls gentle and docile, and excellent workers in the yoke. They are easily fattened, and males often attain a weight of 2,000 to 3,000 pounds, females ranging from 1,200 to 2,000 pounds. The Ayrshire cattle, although not a beef breed, are said to unite the properties of yielding a great deal of milk and beef. They will feed kindly and profitably, and their meat will be good. They will fatten on farms and in districts where others could not be made to thrive at all, unless partially or principally supported by artificial food. The Ayrshire excels in yielding a large quantity of milk in proportion to the food consumed. The Oneida Community's herd of 37 Ayrshire cows averaged for one year 2,557 quarts. She is preëminently the farmer's cow ; responds to good treatment, and under less favorable circumstances does surprisingly well. There is no dairy breed that, with an equal amount of roughing, under bad treatment or poor food, can surpass her yield or condition.

HEAD OF SHORT-HORN COW.

The system of co-operative dairies or factories has increased until it numbers as many as 5,000, including many thousands of dairymen. In 1874, New York had 1,139 of these co-operative factories, with over 300,000 cows. At present, it is estimated that in New York at least 30,000 farmers and 30,000 farms are now identified with this interest. The great dairy fairs have done much to establish this industry. So, also, have the Dairy Boards of Trade, the one at Little Falls, N.Y., effecting annually an exchange of more than 25,000,000 pounds of cheese. England imports annually of butter and cheese to the amount of £15,000,000. The entire cheese exports from the United States for 1878, amounted to 134,000,000 pounds. The entire annual butter product is estimated at from 1,000,000,000 to 1,400,000,000 pounds, nearly all of which is consumed at home. The system of ensilage for preserving green fodder, to which allusion has been already made, the new milking machine, and inventions for extracting cream from the milk immediately after being drawn from the cow, all promise the means of cheapening the production of butter and cheese very considerably. All of which shows the opportunity which exists in the business of dairy-farming.

HEAD OF LONG-HORN BULL.

# HORSES.

HORSES are almost universally employed for draught, although for some purposes oxen supply their place, and in some localities—as in the Southern States—mules are actually preferred for farm work. In mountain travel, as in the Cordilleras, mules take the place of horses, as being more sure-footed. Horses whatever may be their breed, should be selected for their good size, shape and soundness, as the best animals of any stock can be fed and kept at the same expense as those which are inferior. They also perform their work more satisfactorily; and, when it is desirable to sell them, they bring a better price. Oats and hay are the staple articles of food for horses which are expected to do hard work. A few beans or peas can also be given; half a bushel, with a bushel of oats and hay being a fair allowance for farm-horses. Cut fodder is usually given in the winter months, which the animal can sooner masticate, and thus have more time for rest. A weekly bran-mash may also be given, containing in winter an ounce of pounded niter. Horses should be allowed free access to water, except when overheated or fatigued. It is now acknowledged by the most experienced in horse-keeping that the animal knows better than his master when he wants water, and how much of it he requires. Even in summer, when the horse is taking green food, hard worked horses may properly receive a fair proportion of oats. The new system of feeding with ensilage is found to agree well with horses. Horses should be cared for with the greatest assiduity in regard to cleanliness of their surroundings. They should have roomy, well-lighted, and well-ventilated stables, and should be thoroughly groomed. Nothing is ever lost in good work by the cleanly as well as healthy condition of farm horses. Soiled or wet litter should be promptly removed, and, if necessary, it is well to scatter about the stalls a little disinfecting powder. Treated in this manner, horses seldom need dosing, but if this is to be done it should always be under the advice of some experienced person, whether a veterinary surgeon or otherwise.

# Sheep.

SHEEP-farming, as a business, to be made very profitable, has to be conducted on a large scale, except in instances where they are kept for breeding purposes, as is the case in Vermont, for instance. And here, as in cattle, personal prejudice or predilection comes in with regard to breed, and according as the farmer rears chiefly for mutton or for wool. Thus, the Leicesters produce a fleece weighing seven to eight pounds, valuable as fine combing wool. This breed is popular in the South, and in Kentucky, where it is preferred as a fit companion to the short-horn bullock on the blue grass pastures. The mutton of Leicesters is too fat to suit the American taste. The value of the South-Down is too well known to need notice. The Shropshire is of a larger size than the South-Down, which they also excel in yield both of mutton and wool, the meat being next to the latter in quality. Hampshires, Oxford-Downs, Cotswolds, Black Faces, and Merinos are also popular in the United States, the latter having been especially cultivated and improved since its first importation from Spain in 1802. It is said by the best judges of sheep who have visited the flocks of Merinos in foreign countries, that nowhere else has the improvement in these sheep for practically profitable wool bearing purposes reached so great perfection, and that the best specimens in America are without rivals. While the sheep imported from Spain sheared only seven per cent. of unwashed wool to live weight of carcass, whole flocks of the American Merino will shear from twenty to thirty per cent. Of these sheep there are about 350 registered flocks in Vermont, 100 or more in Ohio, about the same number in Michigan, about 60 in New York, 50 more in Wisconsin, and smaller numbers in other States. No other county in England has finer sheep than Lincolnshire, and the Negretti sheep are considered an excellent breed. The Cheviot sheep is now very widely diffused over a considerable part of England, and almost all parts of Scotland. The rich grasses of Australia support many millions of sheep, and it is now the chief wool-growing country in the world.

LINCOLN AND NEGRETTI SHEEP.

HOGS.

# Hogs.

THE business of swine breeding in the United States has until reecent years been conducted in an unmethodical and unscientific manner. Associated effort, conventions, and organized societies at length brought about an improvement in this matter, and now some care and thought are devoted to the breeding and rearing of hogs, as well as of cattle and sheep. Breeds of importance are the Chester Whites, a good sized, easily fattened and good bacon hog; Victorias, a medium sized white hog, which matures early, and is covered with a good coat of hair to protect it from the cold in winter and the heat in summer. The flesh is fine grained and firm, with small bone, and thick side pork. The pigs easily keep in condition, and can be made ready for slaughter at any age. Cheshires are also pure white, with very thin skin of a pink color, and with very little hair. The flesh of these hogs is fine grained, and they are commended on account of their extra amount of mess pork in proportion to the amount of offal. What is called the "Farmer's Hog" is a cross between a Siamese boar and a native English Berkshire. It is a hardy, prolific stock, furnishing meat of an excellent quality, the fat and lean well mixed. The Essex is remarkable for easy fattening, and is a great lard producer. The Yorkshire is claimed to be the most thorough bred hog known. It is of a size, shape, and flesh desirable for the family or packer's use ; has a hardy, vigorous constitution, feeds well, and fattens quickly. The Middlesex breed has been considerably imported into the United States.

# POULTRY.

In order to make the keeping of poultry as profitable as any other adjunct of general farming, it should be conducted with care and attention. It in fact involves much less trouble and labor than most other kinds of farm employment. In the milder seasons of the year domestic fowls, if left to themselves, are almost invariably healthy. They secure exercise, pure air, pure water, variety of food, and access to fine dry soil themselves. As health is the first condition of success in poultry keeping, this fact presents the key to the whole matter of profitable management of poultry on farms and in large numbers as a specialty. If 50 hens kept in health can be made to produce a clear annual profit of $50, a thousand in like condition may be made to yield a proportionate profit. The proportion of range necessary, of shelter, space, food, water, care, etc., must be extended mathematically in proportion to the number of fowls kept, and then, other things being equal, the profit is as certain with many hens as with few. Poultry require room for exercise, and a place for rest, laying, and brooding. The best soil in which to keep poultry is a sandy one, resting upon gravel, as it absorbs the least moisture, and stagnant moisture is a fruitful source of disease. Any soil upon which an enclosure for fowls is erected should be well drained. The place should have a southern or southeastern slope, be sheltered from the north and east, and obtain the warmth of the sun, and security from cold winds. The hen house should afford proper shelter and warmth. Perches and nests should be kept clean, and the air pure without any perceptible draft. The floor should be hard and perfectly dry, concrete or solidly packed earth being the best material. For 25 hens a room eight to ten feet square is large enough for a roosting and laying house. If the walls are plastered, the pro-

WHITE SHANGHAE FOWLS.

tection against vermin and cold will be greater than when otherwise. The sunny side, except for the nest room, should be composed of glass, commencing one foot above the ground or floor. The perches should be low, especially for the heavier breeds, unless there is convenient access to them by means of steps. The ground beneath should be strewn with sand or ashes removed often enough to prevent taint. Boxes for nests for setting should be movable for convenience of cleaning, and should be placed low. Many put them upon the ground. Chopped straw is a good material with which to fill nest boxes, and should be clean. An enclosed yard should adjoin the hen house to which they may have access. An eighth of an acre in grass is the proper proportion for 25 hens, but a smaller yard will answer if kept perfectly clean, and if a sufficient amount of vegetable food is supplied. Feed and water troughs or boxes of sufficient capacity should be provided.

As a general series of rules, it may be said : 1. That the cheapest and most accessible land for poultry keeping is the most desirable, always provided that a near and sure market is at command ; 2. That the utmost economy consistent with the safety, comfort, and health of the poultry should be exercised in the erection of the buildings and fences ; 3. That an abundance of pure water should be accessible or attainable ; 4. That fowls over three years old are not profitable, and a stock should be thoroughly renewed every two years ; 5. That only the largest, hardiest, and best fowls should be used as breeders. It is asserted by the best poultry keepers that under the general circumstances here indicated a thousand pounds of poultry can be produced cheaper than the same weight of mutton, beef, or pork. As great profit comes from turkeys as from hens, and greater with more attention. The large bronze turkeys, Poland geese, which lay earliest, and light Brahma hens are good breeds. The Brahmas mature early for spring chickens, are handsome, hardy, good layers, look well when dressed, and are large size. Black Spanish and white Leghorn are better for eggs, but are undesirable for the table. Feed may be corn, wheat, chopped turnips, refuse cabbage, with sour milk and burnt bones, lime, etc., for shell making. Especially must fowls have space and cleanliness.

A few instances of successful poultry keeping may be given here as indications of what may be easily done. During the month of January 56 hens laid 868 eggs ; February, 891 ; March, 984 ; with 14 of the hens setting from about the middle of the month. The eggs were sold for $66.98. The expense of keeping was $26.13. The profit on eggs for the three months was $40.85. 12 common yellow hens and one cock for two months cost $3.25, receipts 472 eggs, which sold for $15.02—profit, $11.77. These hens had a clean, warm house, with plenty of outdoor range, and were well supplied with food, pounded oyster shells, ashes, etc. For one year, ending March 4th, starting with 90 hens and 11 cocks, the following was the record: 115 fowls of the increase were sold and used. At the close of the year, 127 hens and 23 young chickens remained. The eggs produced numbered 8001. The total credit was $390.70 ; expenses, $182.21 ; leaving a profit of $208.49. From these figures it will be seen that poultry keeping, even simply as an adjunct to ordinary small farming, may be made exceedingly profitable with comparatively little trouble. While, if conducted in the neighborhood of a good market, it may, being sufficiently extended, be made a highly valuable business of itself.

## Fruit Culture.

THE movement of the cultivation of wheat and corn westward has served to open up lands for other farming purposes, grain crops proving unprofitable. The wise farmer, under such circumstances, seeks about him for knowledge of the next best crop to raise in place of the one forbidden by reason of changes such as we have indicated. Always having a view to the proximity and nature of the nearest accessible market, the selection must of course be governed also by conditions of soil, etc. In Ulster County, N.Y., the change was made by farmers to fruit orchards, and as many as five million peach trees have been planted during the last five or six years. The result has been to open up a new source for this valuable crop to take the place of Delaware and New Jersey, where it has fallen off materially. Fruit is always a profitable crop to handle if care be taken in watching the growth of the trees, pruning, grafting, and so on. Much attention has been paid of late years to the cultivation of small fruits, and with remarkable success in many instances. In the vicinity of large cities small fruits and vegetables can be handled with the result of making a most profitable business. All the necessary directions concerning their cultivation can be obtained from any of the large seedsmen, and like dairy-farming and poultry-keeping these industries, as the population grows more dense, become more necessary and more profitable.

## Silk Culture.

HE earliest effort at silk culture in America was made on the settlement of Virginia, being proposed by James I., who sent supplies of silkworms' eggs to the colony from his private stores. Soon after all the colonies became interested in this business, and more or less silk was raised in all of them from Massachusetts to Georgia. It is only in comparatively recent years, however, that it has been conducted on a large scale. In California and in some of the Eastern and Middle States it has been made a great and growing business.

Mulberry trees can be planted from the first of October until the first of May, according to the climate ; standard trees, 30 feet apart in avenues ; medium trunks, 14 feet apart ; dwarf trees, 4 feet in a hedge ; the rows 12 to 15 feet apart. Trees and cuttings can be obtained at the lowest market price by applying to the Women's Silk Culture Association, Philadelphia, where can also be purchased eggs at $1 per thousand ; $3 per half ounce ; $5 per ounce. Books of instruction can also be obtained at the same address. The *Morus Japonica* or Japanese Mulberry, and the *Morus Alba* or White Mulberry are the best for food. Silk culture has two limits. One is the climate ; it being possible to get either too far south or too far north. Another limit is that of economy, which occurs when this culture meets with another of the same importance at the same time. As an instance when this is not the case may be mentioned silk culture in Mississippi, where in early spring, while the men are plowing for cotton, the lady of the house with her children, for three weeks, has little trouble to feed the young silk worms. The last week, when work needs hurrying, there are plenty of colored boys to pick the leaves while the lady and children of the house are attending the larvæ. All this will be done in April. Then will come the cash money from the silk factory in exchange for the cocoons, and this will help a good deal to enlarge the cotton and other crops. Silk culture being considered only as an important addition to general farming, the same general principles which obtain in Mississippi in reference to cotton planting will be found to exist elsewhere within the range of possible silk culture in regard to other kinds of farming.

Eggs should be procured in February and March, and should be of a pale slate or clay color. They should be kept in a cold dry place, but where water will not freeze, until the leaf buds of the mulberry begin to swell. If the eggs are soiled, the paper or cloth to which they adhere should be dipped in water once or twice to wash off the coat with which they are covered, which will otherwise hinder the hatching of the worms. They should then be dried quickly in a draught of air, and put in shallow boxes lined with paper, in a small room, with a temperature of 64°. This temperature should be kept up for two days, by means of an open fire, or of a stove, charcoal being good for fuel. The third day the heat should be increased to 66°; the fourth to 68°; the fifth to 71°; the sixth to 73°; the seventh to 75°; the eighth to 77°; the ninth to 80°; the tenth, eleventh, and twelfth to 82°. After the worms are hatched they go through five ages or moults, during which time they are fed with the tender leaves of the mulberry. The first moulting takes place between the fifth and seventh days; and each of the moultings takes place after about the same length of time, the temperature being kept between 68° and 73° during the moultings. About the tenth day of the fifth age the worms attain perfection, when bundles of twigs of chestnut, hickory, oak, or birch are arranged over them so that they can climb up to work their cocoons. These bundles of twigs are arranged on the feeding trays, and the worms soon rise into them and begin to spin. At this period it is essential that they should be kept in total stillness. About the eighth or ninth day after the rising, the cocoons are taken off in baskets, being afterwards laid in trays, certain of them being kept apart for the production of eggs. Cocoons kept at a temperature of 66° begin to be hatched after fifteen days, when the moths come forth in great numbers, males and females immediately uniting.

To conduct this culture on a fairly large scale, there are required two cheap buildings of rough boards, with fixtures, built with a view to thorough ventilation, each 100 x 24 feet. Of course attention has to be paid to the locality as regards the method for keeping the temperature at the proper point. The following statement of expenses applies to the production of 3000 pounds of cocoons from about seven acres of mulberry trees:

| | |
|---|---|
| First moult at 75c. per day, 6 days, 1 lady | $4 50 |
| 60c. from first to second moult, 4 days, 4 girls | 4 80 |
| 60c. from second to third moult, 4 days, 4 girls | 9 60 |
| 60c. from third to fourth moult, 6 days, 6 girls | 21 60 |
| 60c. from fourth moult to spinning cocoons, 8 days, 8 girls | 38 40 |
| Picking cocoons at 1c. per pound | 30 00 |
| Picking leaves at 30c. per hundred pounds, 30,000 pounds | 90 00 |
| Rent of two stables 15 days for use of cocoonery | 30 00 |
| Rent of capital used for shelves, trees, and land, $400, at 10 per cent | 40 00 |
| Overseer and other little expenses | 100 00 |
| Total expenses | $368 90 |

# FARMING AS A FINE ART.

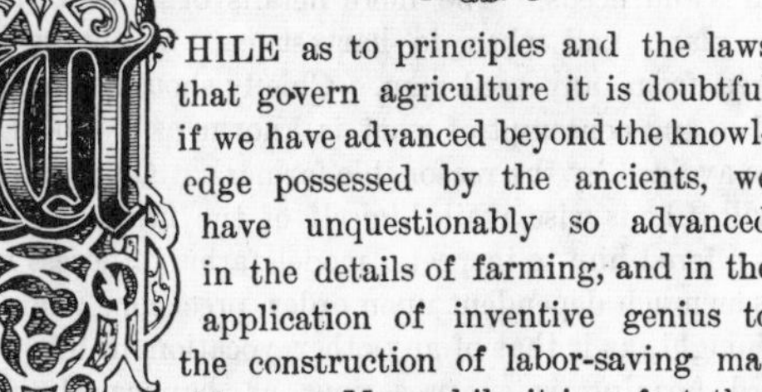

WHILE as to principles and the laws that govern agriculture it is doubtful if we have advanced beyond the knowledge possessed by the ancients, we have unquestionably so advanced in the details of farming, and in the application of inventive genius to the construction of labor-saving machinery. Meanwhile it is a fact that the moral atmosphere of farm life has deteriorated, though the progress of civilization has been constant. It is credibly alleged that the proportion of insanity among the farming population is larger than in any other class of labor. It is a well recognized fact, that as a rule the farming population of most countries are, comparatively speaking, ignorant. It is a constant subject of complaint among farmers in the United States at their conventions, State fairs, and meetings of State and county agricultural associations, that the best of their young men cannot be induced to follow a farming life, but resort in crowds to the cities, where for the few who are successful in making permanent business engagements, there are multitudes who fall by the wayside and are carried down hill by the tide of idleness and iniquity. Especially is it recognized in America that the customary nature of a farm life presses with extraordinary severity upon the wives of farmers. The toil which would seem to be inseparable from this vocation, so far as women are concerned, results, in its influence upon them, in producing a most unsatisfactory and uncomfortable condition. The wives and daughters of the average working farmer have little or no opportunity for recreation, and little inclination for it. Neither have they time or desire for mental improvement or intellectual pursuits. The instances where such is not the case serve only to establish as exceptions the general wide-spread character of the rule.

It becomes us to learn wisdom from the lessons of the past. It becomes us to discern if possible the source of such obnoxious and unhealthy elements as may exist in our own system of agriculture in its moral and social relations. And as to these points it is beginning to be recognized that the more science is applied to the conduct of the farm, the more intelligence stands at its head, and the amenities of life are associated with it, the higher will be the type of farming, the more profitable its results, and the more graceful its associations. There is nothing about farming of itself that should be crude, ungraceful, or undignified. There is nothing in the constant association with nature that should do other than sweeten home association and mollify the disturbing influences that necessarily occur in every kind of life. Where conservatism breeds only stagnation, the most advanced radicalism is preferable to it. It is better to err in seeking to advance than to be correct in the well-worn ruts of an absurd slavery to precedent. No farmer is going to be any worse off for joining a "farmer's club;" for traveling some miles to attend a State or county fair; for uniting himself with an agricultural association; or subscribing to an agricultural periodical. No farmer is going to be any worse off because his leisure hours in the long winter nights are passed in reading and in thought, instead of the ordinary farm gossip of the period; and as the home is refined and made intelligent, and the spirit of grace and brightness is diffused about it, the children of the home circle will lose their anxiety to fly out into the unknown world, and by association with the pleasanter side of agriculture will grow to possess a fondness for it.

A WESTERN FARM.

A few years ago a man from one of the Atlantic ship yards who had accumulated a little money, invested it in land in one of the Middle States, and commenced farming. It was a business that was entirely new and strange to him, and in the beginning he made many mistakes, but before he had been thirty months engaged in it, he was observed to be in advance of his neighbors in nearly everything which he undertook. We have related this anecdote, which is true, for the purpose of making an important point in connection with the general argument of this article. The man from the ship yard was successful for two reasons. First, because he was not tied up by any conservative tendencies or inherited manners or customs; second, because his previous life and association among men where activity was the rule, and the atmosphere was always filled with floating intelligence, this life had trained him to investigate, to inquire, and to accept new ideas. By the application of his habits of mind to his new duties he succeeded. To the man who begins farming as a new business, say in middle life, there are to be made a few practical suggestions which will be found of general application. Some such have already been offered. No man should buy poor land if he can possibly avoid it. Good land, though dearer in the beginning, is cheaper in the end. Having bought his land, he should acquaint himself with its characteristics. Some kinds of soil are excellent for producing one crop; others, useless for that, are successful with something else, and so on. At any experiment station the farmer may obtain an analysis of his soil, and the constituents of the various plants are no more difficult to find, the books being accessible from any agricultural publisher. A knowledge of the nature of the soil enables one to know with what fertilizing material to treat it. Some soils require potash; others lime; others ammonia, while crops vary equally in their demands in this direction. Scientific farming is by no means so difficult to learn as is imagined. Any agricultural editor or superintendent of an experiment farm will gladly put the inquisitive farmer in the way of obtaining the knowledge he desires and needs. The mere details of when to plow, when to plant, and when to harvest can be obtained with the seed from any seedsman. Chiefly should obnoxious criticism and contempt of what is known as "model farming" be avoided by the reasonable farmer. On the contrary, he will if he is wise avail himself of the first opportunity that is offered him to inspect a model farm. Success in farming is as much dependent upon order, precision, cleanliness, and thought, as is that of any other vocation in life. Haphazard farming is as precarious as haphazard navigation. Death awaits in the one instance, failure in the other. Both are conclusions to be avoided.

## LEGAL WEIGHT OF A BUSHEL IN POUNDS, IN DIFFERENT STATES AND TERRITORIES.*

| States and Territories. | Wheat. | Rye. | Oats. | Barley. | Buckwheat. | Shelled Corn. | Corn on Cob. | Corn Meal. | Potatoes. | Sweet Potatoes. | Onions. | Turnips. | Beans. | Peas. | Dried Apples. | Dried Peaches. | Flaxseed. | Timothy Seed. | Blue-grass Seed. | Clover Seed. | Coal, Anthracite. |
|---|---|---|---|---|---|---|---|---|---|---|---|---|---|---|---|---|---|---|---|---|---|
| Arkansas | 60 | 56 | 32 | 48 | 52 | .. | 70 | 50 | 60 | 50 | 57 | .. | 60 | 46 | 24 | 33 | 56 | 45 | 14 | 60 | 80 |
| Arizona | 60 | 56 | 32 | 45 | .. | 54 | .. | .. | .. | .. | .. | .. | 60 | .. | .. | .. | .. | .. | .. | .. | .. |
| California | 60 | 54 | 32 | 50 | 40 | 52 | .. | .. | .. | .. | .. | .. | .. | .. | .. | .. | .. | .. | .. | .. | .. |
| Colorado | 60 | 56 | 32 | 48 | 52 | 56 | 70 | 50 | 60 | .. | 57 | .. | 60 | .. | .. | .. | .. | 45 | 14 | 60 | .. |
| Connecticut | 60 | 56 | 32 | 48 | 48 | 56 | .. | 50 | 60 | .. | 50 | 50 | 60 | 60 | .. | .. | .. | .. | .. | .. | .. |
| Dakota | 60 | 56 | 32 | 48 | 42 | 56 | 70 | .. | 60 | 46 | 52 | 60 | 60 | 60 | .. | .. | 56 | 42 | .. | 60 | 80 |
| Delaware | 60 | .. | .. | .. | .. | 56 | .. | 48 | .. | .. | .. | .. | .. | .. | .. | .. | .. | .. | .. | .. | .. |
| District Columbia | 60 | 56 | 32 | .. | .. | 56 | .. | 48 | 60 | .. | .. | .. | .. | .. | .. | .. | .. | .. | .. | .. | .. |
| Georgia | 60 | 56 | 32 | 47 | 52 | 56 | 70 | 48 | 60 | 55 | 57 | 55 | 60 | 60 | 24 | 33 | 56 | 45 | 14 | 60 | 80 |
| Illinois | 60 | 56 | 32 | 48 | 52 | 56 | 70 | 48 | 60 | 55 | 57 | 55 | 60 | .. | 24 | 33 | 56 | 45 | 14 | 60 | 80 |
| Indiana | 60 | 56 | .. | 48 | 50 | 56 | 68 | 50 | 60 | .. | 48 | .. | 60 | .. | 25 | 33 | .. | 45 | 14 | 60 | .. |
| Iowa | 60 | 56 | 32 | 48 | 52 | 56 | 70 | .. | 60 | 46 | 57 | .. | 60 | .. | 24 | 33 | 56 | 45 | 14 | 60 | 80 |
| Kansas | 60 | 56 | 32 | 48 | 50 | 56 | 70 | 50 | 60 | 50 | 57 | 55 | 60 | .. | 24 | 33 | 54 | 45 | 14 | 60 | 80 |
| Kentucky | 60 | 56 | 32 | 47 | 55 | 55 | 70 | 50 | 60 | 55 | 57 | 60 | 60 | 60 | 24 | 39 | 56 | 45 | 14 | 60 | 76 |
| Louisiana | 60 | 32 | 32 | 32 | .. | 50 | .. | .. | .. | .. | .. | .. | .. | .. | .. | .. | .. | .. | .. | .. | .. |
| Maine | 60 | 50 | 30 | 48 | 48 | 56 | .. | 50 | 60 | .. | 52 | 50 | 64 | 60 | .. | .. | .. | .. | .. | .. | .. |
| Maryland | 60 | 56 | 32 | 47 | 48 | 56 | 70 | 48 | .. | 56 | 56 | .. | 60 | .. | .. | .. | .. | 45 | 14 | 64 | .. |
| Massachusetts | 60 | 56 | 32 | 48 | 48 | 56 | .. | 50 | 60 | 56 | 52 | .. | .. | .. | .. | .. | .. | .. | .. | .. | .. |
| Michigan | 60 | 56 | 32 | 48 | 48 | 56 | 70 | 50 | 60 | 56 | 54 | 58 | 60 | 60 | 22 | 28 | 56 | 45 | 14 | 60 | .. |
| Minnesota | 60 | 56 | 32 | 48 | 42 | 56 | .. | .. | 60 | .. | .. | .. | .. | .. | 28 | 28 | .. | .. | .. | 60 | .. |
| Missouri | 60 | 56 | 32 | 48 | 52 | 56 | .. | .. | 60 | .. | 57 | .. | 60 | .. | 24 | 33 | 56 | 45 | 14 | 60 | .. |
| Montana | 60 | 56 | 35 | 48 | 52 | 56 | .. | 50 | 60 | .. | 57 | 50 | 60 | .. | .. | .. | .. | 45 | 14 | 60 | .. |
| Nebraska | 60 | 56 | 34 | 48 | 52 | 56 | 70 | 50 | 60 | 50 | 57 | 55 | 60 | 60 | 24 | 33 | 56 | 45 | 14 | 60 | 80 |
| Nevada | 60 | 56 | 32 | 50 | 40 | 52 | 70 | .. | 60 | .. | .. | .. | .. | 60 | .. | .. | .. | .. | .. | .. | .. |
| New Hampshire | 60 | 56 | 32 | .. | .. | 56 | .. | 50 | 60 | .. | .. | .. | 60 | 60 | .. | .. | .. | .. | .. | .. | .. |
| New Jersey | 60 | 56 | 30 | 48 | 50 | 56 | .. | .. | 60 | 54 | 57 | .. | 60 | 60 | 25 | 33 | 55 | .. | .. | 64 | .. |
| New York | 60 | 56 | 32 | 48 | 48 | 56 | .. | .. | 60 | .. | .. | .. | 62 | 60 | .. | .. | 55 | 44 | .. | 60 | .. |
| North Carolina | 60 | 56 | 30 | 48 | 50 | 54 | .. | 46 | .. | .. | .. | .. | .. | 50 | .. | .. | .. | .. | .. | 64 | .. |
| Ohio | 60 | 56 | 32 | 48 | 50 | 56 | 70 | .. | 60 | 50 | 50 | .. | 60 | 60 | 22 | 33 | 56 | 45 | .. | 60 | .. |
| Oregon | 60 | 56 | 36 | 46 | 42 | 56 | .. | .. | 60 | .. | .. | .. | .. | .. | 28 | 28 | .. | .. | .. | 60 | .. |
| Pennsylvania | 60 | 56 | 30 | 47 | 48 | 56 | .. | .. | 56 | .. | .. | .. | .. | .. | .. | .. | .. | .. | .. | 62 | .. |
| Rhode Island | .. | 56 | 32 | 48 | .. | 56 | .. | 50 | 60 | .. | 50 | .. | .. | .. | .. | .. | .. | .. | .. | .. | .. |
| South Carolina | 60 | 56 | 33 | 48 | 56 | 56 | 70 | 50 | 60 | 50 | 57 | .. | 60 | 60 | 26 | 33 | 44 | .. | 14 | 60 | .. |
| Tennessee | .. | 56 | 32 | 48 | 50 | 56 | 72 | 50 | 60 | 50 | 56 | .. | 60 | 60 | 26 | .. | 56 | 45 | 14 | .. | .. |
| Vermont | 60 | 56 | 32 | 48 | 46 | 56 | .. | .. | 60 | .. | 52 | 60 | 60 | 60 | .. | .. | .. | 45 | .. | 60 | .. |
| Virginia | 60 | 56 | 32 | 48 | 52 | 56 | 70 | 50 | 60 | 56 | 57 | 55 | 60 | 60 | 28 | 32 | 56 | 45 | 14 | 60 | 80 |
| Washington T. | 60 | 56 | 36 | 45 | 42 | 56 | .. | .. | 50 | .. | 50 | 50 | 60 | 60 | 28 | 28 | .. | 40 | .. | 60 | .. |
| West Virginia | 60 | 56 | 32 | 48 | 52 | 56 | .. | .. | 60 | .. | .. | .. | 60 | .. | 25 | 33 | 56 | 45 | .. | 60 | .. |
| Wisconsin | 60 | 56 | 32 | 48 | 50 | 56 | 70 | .. | 60 | .. | 50 | 42 | 60 | .. | 28 | 28 | 56 | 45 | .. | 60 | .. |

* Some States, not here mentioned, only legalize and recognize the Standard United States bushel, without reference to weight.

### *Table—Showing the Price per cwt. of Hay, at given Prices per Ton.*

| Price per ton. | ½ hundred. | 1 hundred. | 2 hundred. | 3 hundred. | 4 hundred. | 5 hundred. | 6 hundred. | 7 hundred. | 8 hundred. | 9 hundred. | 10 hundred. | 11 hundred. |
|---|---|---|---|---|---|---|---|---|---|---|---|---|
| $ | cts. | cts. | $ cts. | $ cts. | $ cts. | $ cts. | $ cts. | $ cts. | $ cts. | $ cts. | $ cts. | $ cts. |
| 4 | 10 | 20 | 40 | 60 | 80 | 1.00 | 1.20 | 1.40 | 1.60 | 1.80 | 2.00 | 2.20 |
| 5 | 12 | 25 | 50 | 75 | 1.00 | 1.25 | 1.50 | 1.75 | 2.00 | 2.25 | 2.50 | 2.75 |
| 6 | 15 | 30 | 60 | 90 | 1.20 | 1.50 | 1.80 | 2.10 | 2.40 | 2.70 | 3.00 | 3.30 |
| 7 | 17 | 35 | 70 | 1.05 | 1.40 | 1.75 | 2.10 | 2.45 | 2.80 | 3.15 | 3.50 | 3.85 |
| 8 | 20 | 40 | 80 | 1.20 | 1.60 | 2.00 | 2.40 | 2.80 | 3.20 | 3.60 | 4.00 | 4.40 |
| 9 | 22 | 45 | 90 | 1.35 | 1.80 | 2.25 | 2.70 | 3.15 | 3.60 | 4.05 | 4.50 | 4.95 |
| 10 | 25 | 50 | 1.00 | 1.50 | 2.00 | 2.50 | 3.00 | 3.50 | 4.00 | 4.50 | 5.00 | 5.50 |
| 11 | 27 | 55 | 1.10 | 1.65 | 2.20 | 2.75 | 3.30 | 3.85 | 4.40 | 4.95 | 5.50 | 6.00 |
| 12 | 30 | 60 | 1.20 | 1.80 | 2.40 | 3.00 | 3.60 | 4.20 | 4,80 | 5.40 | 6.00 | 6.60 |
| 13 | 32 | 65 | 1.30 | 1.95 | 2.60 | 3.25 | 3.90 | 4.55 | 5.20 | 5.85 | 6.50 | 7.15 |
| 14 | 35 | 70 | 1.40 | 2.10 | 2.80 | 3.50 | 4.20 | 4.90 | 5.60 | 6.30 | 7.00 | 7.70 |
| 15 | 37 | 75 | 1.50 | 2.25 | 3.00 | 3.75 | 4.50 | 5.25 | 6.00 | 6.75 | 7.50 | 8.25 |

## FOOD SUPPLY OF ALL NATIONS.

| | Grain—Million Bushels. | | | | Meat—Thousand Tons. | | | | Production of | | |
|---|---|---|---|---|---|---|---|---|---|---|---|
| | Production. | Consumption. | Surplus. | Deficit | Production. | Consumption. | Surplus. | Deficit | Wine. Million Gals. | Beer. Million Gals. | Spirits Million Gals. |
| Great Britain | 410 | 690 | .. | 280 | 1,205 | 1,808 | .. | 603 | 0 | 1,110 | 31 |
| France | 740 | 910 | .. | 170 | 1,002 | 1,228 | .. | 226 | 660 | 192 | 33 |
| Germany | 950 | 1,065 | .. | 115 | 1,340 | 1,700 | .. | 360 | 90 | 880 | 61 |
| Russia | 1,620 | 1,440 | 180 | .. | 2,116 | 1,925 | 191 | .. | 20 | 50 | 105 |
| Austria | 560 | 530 | 30 | .. | 960 | 975 | .. | 15 | 290 | 245 | 24 |
| Italy | 270 | 275 | .. | 5 | 224 | 215 | 9 | .. | 660 | 20 | 8 |
| Spain | 305 | 300 | 5 | .. | 196 | 188 | 8 | .. | 260 | 0 | 4 |
| Belgium | 95 | 120 | .. | 25 | 92 | 140 | .. | 48 | 0 | 170 | 15 |
| Holland | 50 | 65 | .. | 15 | 144 | 87 | 57 | .. | 0 | 35 | 1 |
| Denmark | 74 | 62 | 12 | .. | 112 | 52 | 60 | .. | 0 | 25 | 86 |
| Sweden and Norway | 78 | 80 | .. | 2 | 213 | 146 | 67 | .. | 0 | 35 | 27 |
| Portugal | 30 | 35 | .. | 5 | 54 | 47 | 7 | .. | 88 | 0 | 1 |
| Turkey, Greece, etc. | 90 | 80 | 10 | .. | 250 | 250 | .. | .. | 24 | 0 | 1 |
| Europe | 5,272 | 5,652 | .. | 380 | 7,908 | 8,761 | .. | 853 | 2,092 | 2,762 | 334 |
| United States | 2,390 | 2,020 | 370 | .. | 3,816 | 2,740 | 1,076 | .. | 20 | 360 | 76 |
| Australia | 58 | 41 | 17 | .. | 990 | 152 | 838 | .. | 2 | 0 | 4 |
| Canada | 170 | 160 | 10 | .. | 287 | 270 | 17 | .. | 0 | 0 | 1 |
| River Plate | 6 | 6 | .. | .. | 1,310 | 272 | 1,038 | .. | 1 | 1 | 1 |
| Algeria | 20 | 15 | 5 | .. | 110 | 82 | 28 | .. | 9 | 0 | 0 |
| * Total | 7,916 | 7,894 | 22 | .. | 14,421 | 12,277 | 2,144 | .. | 2,124 | 3,123 | 416 |

* There are, moreover, 200 million bushels of wheat grown in India, of which one-tenth is exported; and besides the wine crop here given the Cape produces 4½ million gallons, and Madeira, Canaries, etc., 5 millions.

## AGRICULTURAL AND PASTORAL INDUSTRIES.

| | Grain Cultivation. | | | Pastoral Farming. | | | |
|---|---|---|---|---|---|---|---|
| | Acres under grain. | Do. per Adult male.* | Bushels per acre. | Cows. | Sheep. | Cows per 100 inhabitants. | Sheep per 100 inhabitants. |
| Great Britain | 11,260,000 | 1·63 | 36·40 | 9,912,000 | 32,174,000 | 29 | 93 |
| France | 40,300,000 | 5·45 | 18·50 | 11,315,000 | 23,674,000 | 30 | 64 |
| Germany | 43,200,000 | 4·75 | 22·05 | 15,800,000 | 25,200,000 | 35 | 55 |
| Russsia | 158,000,000 | 9·95 | 10·25 | 28,000,000 | 64,000,000 | 35 | 80 |
| Austria | 37,300,000 | 4·78 | 15·04 | 13,133,000 | 21,418,000 | 33 | 55 |
| Italy | 19,560,000 | 3·43 | 13·80 | 3,490,000 | 7,150,000 | 12 | 25 |
| Spain | 25,000,000 | 7·50 | 12·20 | 1,550,000 | 14,000,000 | 9 | 84 |
| Belgium | 2,910,000 | 2 65 | 32·72 | 1,242,000 | 586,000 | 22 | 10 |
| Holland | 1,730,000 | 2·16 | 28·80 | 1,466,000 | 941,000 | 37 | 24 |
| Denmark | 2,670,000 | 6·70 | 27·72 | 1,348,000 | 1,720,000 | 68 | 88 |
| Sweden and Norway | 4,380,000 | 3·37 | 17·80 | 3,205,000 | 3,276,000 | 49 | 50 |
| Portugal | 2,570,000 | 2·84 | 11·64 | 523,000 | 2,417,000 | 12 | 55 |
| Greece | 610,000 | 2·90 | 15·20 | 58,000 | 2,100,000 | 3 | 130 |
| Europe | 349,490,000 | 5·82 | 15·06 | 91,042,000 | 198,656,000 | 30 | 66 |
| United States | 102,500,000 | 10·25 | 23·30 | 33,500,000 | 38,000,000 | 67 | 76 |
| Australia | 3,400,000 | 6·10 | 17·10 | 7,879,000 | 65,914,000 | 287 | 2,402 |
| Canada | 8,500,000 | 9·90 | 20·00 | 2,702,000 | 3,331,000 | 63 | 77 |
| River Plate | 330,000 | 0 60 | 19·00 | 18,850,000 | 76,000,000 | 630 | 2,580 |
| South Africa. | 600,000 | 2·40 | 9·90 | 1,730,000 | 11,700,000 | 130 | 890 |
| WORLD | 464,820,000 | 6·44 | 17·02 | 155,703,000 | 393,601,000 | 43 | 109 |

* Counting one-fifth of the population as adult males.

## MEASUREMENT OF CORN.

**In Cob.**—Two heaping bushels of corn on the cob will make one struck bushel of shelled corn. Some claim that one and one-half bushels of ear will make one bushel of shelled corn. Much will depend upon the kind of corn, shape of the ear, size of the cob, etc.

**In Crib.**—To measure corn in a crib, multiply the length of the crib in inches by the width in inches, and that by the height of the corn in the crib in inches, and divide the product by 2,748, and the quotient will be the number of heaped bushels of ears. If the crib flares at the sides, measure the width at the top and also at the bottom, add the two sums together, and divide by two, which will give the mean width.

## CISTERNS AND CASKS.

**To Measure the Contents of Cisterns.**—To ascertain the contents of circular cisterns, multiply the square of the diameter in feet by the depth in feet, and that product by $\frac{373}{4000}$ for the contents in hogsheads, or by $\frac{373}{2000}$ for barrels, for $\frac{47}{8}$ for the contents in gallons.

**Square Cisterns.**—Multiply the width in feet by the length in feet, and that by the depth in feet, and that again by $\frac{19}{160}$ for hogsheads, or $\frac{19}{80}$ for barrels, or $7\frac{48}{100}$ for gallons.

Another and simpler method is to multiply together the length, width, and depth, in inches, and divide by 231, which will give the contents in gallons.

**Cask Gauging.**—To measure the contents of cylindrical vessels multiply the square of the diameter in inches by 34, and that by the height in inches, and point off four figures. The result will be the contents or capacity, in wine gallons and decimals of a gallon. For beer gallons multiply by 28 instead of 34. If the cask be only partially filled, multiply by the height of the liquid instead of the height of the cask, to ascertain actual contents. In ascertaining the diameter, measure the diameter at the bung and at the head, add together, and divide by 2 for the mean diameter.

## MEASUREMENT OF HAY.

The only exact method of measuring hay is to weigh it, but the rules given below will be found sufficient for ordinary practical purposes.

**To Find the Number of Tons of Meadow Hay in Windrows.**—Multiply together the length, breadth, and height, in yards, and divide the product by 25. The quotient will be the number of tons in the windrow.

**To Find the Number of Tons of Hay in a Mow.**—Multiply together the length, height, and width, in yards, and divide by 15 if the hay be well packed. If the mow be shallow, and the hay recently placed therein, divide by 18, and by any number from 15 to 18, according as the hay is well packed.

**To Find the Number of Tons of Hay in Square or Long Stacks.**—Multiply the length of the base in yards by the width in yards, and that by half the height in yards, and divide by 15.

**To Find the Number of Tons of Hay, in a Load.**—Multiply together the length, width, and height, in yards and divide the product by 20.

To ascertain the value of a given number of lbs. of hay, straw, or other commodity sold by the ton, at a given price per ton, multiply the number of lbs. by one-half the price per ton, and point off three figures from the right. The result will be the price of the article.

## MEASUREMENT OF WOOD AND LUMBER.

**A Cord of Wood** contains 128 cubic feet. To ascertain how many cords there are in a pile of wood, multiply the length by the height, and that by the width, and divide the product by 128.

To ascertain the circumference of a tree required to hew a stick or timber of any given number of inches square, divide the given side of the square by .225. and the quotient is the circumference required.

Round timber, when squared, loses one-fifth.

To measure round timber take the girth in inches at both the large and small ends, add them, divide by two, which gives the mean girth; then multiply the length in feet by the square of one-fourth of the mean girth, and the quotient will be the contents in cubic feet. This rule is commonly adopted, and gives four-fifths of the true contents, one-fifth being allowed to the purchaser for waste in sawing.

**To Measure Inch Boards.**—Multiply the length in feet by the width in inches, and divide the product by 12. The quotient will be the contents in feet. For lumber 1¼ inches thick, add ¼ to the quotient. If 1½ inches thick add ½. If 1¾ inches thick, add ¾. If 2 inches thick, divide by 6, instead of by 12. If 2¼ inches thick, add ¼ to the quotient, and so on. If 3 inches thick, divide by 4. If 4 inches thick, divide by 3. If 6 inches thick, divide by 2. To ascertain the contents (broad measure) of timber, multiply the width in inches by the thickness in inches, and that by the length in feet, and divide the product by 12. The result will be the number of feet.

To ascertain how many feet of lumber can be sawed from a log, from the diameter of the log in inches subtract 4; one-fourth the remainder squared and multiplied by the length of the log in feet, will give the correct amount of lumber that can be sawed from the log.

## MEASUREMENT OF LAND.

If the field be a square or parallelogram, multiply the length in rods by the width in rods, and divide by 160, the number of square rods in an acre. If the field is triangular, multiply the length of the longest side in rods by the greatest width in rods, and divide half the product by 160. If the field be of irregular shape, divide it into triangles, and find the acreage of each triangle as above. All straight-sided fields can be thus measured. Where the sides are crooked and irregular, take the length in rods in a number of places at equal distances apart, add them, and divide by the number of measurements, which will give the mean length; proceed similarly with the width, multiply the mean length by the mean width, and divide by 160. Where the field is in a circle, find the diameter in rods, multiply the square of the diameter by 7.854, and divide by 160.

**To Lay Out an Acre in Rectangular Form.**—An acre of land contains 160 square rods, or 43,560 square feet. Hence, to lay out an acre at right angles (square corners), when one side is known, divide the units in the square contents by the units of the same kind in the length of the known side. Thus: if the known side be 4 rods, divide 160 by 4, and the quotient, 40, will be the depth of the acre-plot. If the length of the known side be 90 feet, divide 43,560 by 90, and the quotient, 48, will be the depth of an acre-plot.

## MEASURES OF AN ACRE PLOT.

Either of the following measures include an acre plot:

| | | |
|---|---|---|
| 3 by 53 1-8 rods. | 7 by 22 6-7 ods. | 10 by 16 rods. |
| 4 by 40 " | 8 by 20 " | 11 by 14 6-11 " |
| 5 by 32 " | 9 by 17 7-8 " | 12 by 13 1-3 " |
| 6 by 26 2-3 " | | |

12 rods 10 feet and 8½ inches square make an acre.

### Square Feet and Feet Square in Fractions of an Acre.

| Fraction of an acre. | Square feet. | Feet square. | Frac'n of an acre. | Square feet. | Feet square. |
|---|---|---|---|---|---|
| 1-16 | 2722½ | 52¼ | ½ | 21780 | 147½ |
| 1-8 | 5445 | 73¾ | 1 | 43560 | 208¾ |
| 1-4 | 10890 | 104½ | 2 | 87120 | 295¼ |
| 1-3 | 14520 | 120½ | | | |

### Rails, Riders, and Stakes Required for Every Ten Rods of Crooked Fence.

| Length of rail—feet. | Deflection from right line—feet. | Length of panel. | Number of panels. | No. rails for each 10 rods. | | | Number of stakes. | Number of riders, single. |
|---|---|---|---|---|---|---|---|---|
| | | | | 5 rails high. | 6 rails high. | 7 rails high. | | |
| 12 | 6 | 8 | 20 5–8 | 103 | 123 | 144 | 42 | 21 |
| 14 | 7 | 10 | 16½ | 83 | 99 | 116 | 34 | 17 |
| 16½ | 8 | 12 | 13¾ | 69 | 84 | 95 | 28 | 14 |

## Relative Number of Plants or Hills in an Acre.

Giving the number in an acre when the direct and cross rows are of equal or unequal width :

| In | 10 in. | 12 in. | 15 in. | 18 in. | 20 in. | 2 ft. | 2½ ft. | 3 ft. | 3½ft. | 4 ft. | 4½ ft | 5 ft. |
|---|---|---|---|---|---|---|---|---|---|---|---|---|
| 10 | 62726 | | | | | | | | | | | |
| 12 | 52272 | 43560 | | | | | | | | | | |
| 15 | 41817 | 34848 | 27878 | | | | | | | | | |
| 18 | 34848 | 29040 | 23232 | 19360 | | | | | | | | |
| 20 | 31362 | 26136 | 20908 | 17424 | 15681 | | | | | | | |
| 24 | 26132 | 21780 | 17424 | 14520 | 13068 | 10890 | | | | | | |
| 30 | 20908 | 17424 | 13939 | 11616 | 10454 | 8712 | 6969 | | | | | |
| 36 | 17424 | 14520 | 11616 | 9680 | 8712 | 7260 | 5808 | 4840 | | | | |
| 42 | 14935 | 12446 | 9953 | 8297 | 7467 | 6223 | 4976 | 4148 | 3565 | | | |
| 48 | 13068 | 10890 | 8712 | 7260 | 6534 | 5445 | 4356 | 3630 | 3111 | 2722 | | |
| 54 | 11616 | 9680 | 7744 | 6453 | 5308 | 4840 | 3872 | 3226 | 2767 | 2420 | 2151 | |
| 60 | 10454 | 8712 | 6969 | 5808 | 5227 | 4356 | 3484 | 2004 | 2489 | 2178 | 1936 | 1742 |

## TABLE SHOWING THE NUMBER OF DRAINS REQUIRED FOR AN ACRE OF LAND.

| DISTANCE APART. | 12-inch Tiles. | 13-inch Tiles. | 14-inch Tiles. | 15-inch Tiles. |
|---|---|---|---|---|
| Drains 12 feet apart require.. | 3,630 | 3,351 | 3,111 | 2,934 |
| " 15 " " ... | 2,904 | 2,681 | 2,489 | 2,323 |
| " 18 " " ... | 2,420 | 2.234 | 2.074 | 1,936 |
| " 21 " " ... | 2,074 | 1,914 | 1,777 | 1,659 |
| " 24 " " ... | 1,815 | 1,675 | 1,556 | 1,452 |
| " 27 " " ... | 1,613 | 1,480 | 1,383 | 1,291 |
| " 30 " " ... | 1,452 | 1,340 | 1,245 | 1.162 |
| " 33 " " ... | 1,320 | 1,218 | 1,131 | 1,056 |
| " 36 " " ... | 1,210 | 1,117 | 1,037 | 968 |

## FACTS ABOUT WEEDS.

Dr. Lindley estimates as a low average the following number of seeds from each of these four plants :

One plant of Groundsel produces ........ 2,080 }
One plant of Dandelion " ........ 2,740 }
One plant of Sow Thistle " ........ 11,040 } 16,400 plants,
One plant of Spurge " ........ 540 }

Or enough seed from these four plants to cover three acres and a half, at three feet apart. To hoe this land will cost 6s. (sterling) per acre, and hence a man throws away 5s. 3d. a time, as often as he neglects to bend his back to pull up a young weed before it begins to fulfill the first law of nature. He recommends every farmer, whose vertebral column will not bend, to count the number of dandelions, sow thistles, etc., on the first square rod he can measure off.

This operation may be repeated by applying all the above estimates to pig weed, burdock, fox-tail, chick-weed, and purslane.

**Dry Measure.**—36 bushels make 1 chaldron. The standard bushel is the Winchester, containing 2,150.42 cubic inches, or 77.627 pounds, avoirdupois, of distilled water at its *maximum* density. Its diameter inside is 18½ inches ; its depth is eight inches. Vegetables, fruit, meal, bran, and corn on the ear, are usually sold by the heaping bushel measure 32 British or Imperial bushels are equal to 38 of our bushels.

**Weighing Liquids.**—One gallon of pure water weighs nearly 8⅓ lbs. avoirdupois. The gallon, containing 231 cubic inches, is the standard unit of wine measure. The British gallon, called the Imperial gallon, contains 277.274 cubic inches.

**To Measure Grain in Bins.**—Multiply the length of the bin in inches by the width in inches, and that by the height in inches, and divide by 2,150 for struck bushels, and by 2,748 for heaped bushels. The quotient will be the number of bushels contained in the bin.

## TO ESTIMATE THE WEIGHT OF CATTLE.

Multiply the girth in inches, immediately back of the shoulders, by the length in inches from the square of the buttock to the point of the shoulder blade, and divide the product by 144, which will give the number of superficial feet. If the animal has a girth of from 3 to 5 feet, multiply the number of superficial feet by 16, which will give the weight of the animal. If the girth is from 5 to 7 feet. multiply by 23, and if from 7 to 9 feet, multiply by 31. If less than 3 feet girth, as in the case of small calves, hogs, sheep, etc., multiply by 11. Of course many circumstances, such as the build of the animal, mode of fattening, condition, breed, etc., will influence the weight, but the above will be found approximately correct.

## Time required for Digesting Food.

| Food. | How Cooked. | H.M. |
|---|---|---|
| Apples, sour, mellow | Raw | 2.00 |
| Apples, sour, hard | Raw | 2.50 |
| Apples, sweet, mellow | Raw | 1.30 |
| Bass, striped | Broiled | 3.00 |
| Beans, pod | Boiled | 2.30 |
| Beans and green corn | Boiled | 3.45 |
| Beef | Fried | 4.00 |
| Beefsteak | Broiled | 3.00 |
| Beef, fresh, lean, dry | Roasted | 3.30 |
| Beef, fresh, lean, rare | Roasted | 3.00 |
| Beets | Boiled | 3.45 |
| Brains, animal | Boiled | 3.45 |
| Bread, corn | Baked | 3.15 |
| Bread, wheat, fresh | Baked | 1.30 |
| Cabbage | Raw | 2.30 |
| Cabbage, with vinegar | Raw | 2.00 |
| Cabbage | Boiled | 4.30 |
| Carrot, orange | Boiled | 3.13 |
| Catfish | Fried | 3.30 |
| Cheese, old, strong | Raw | 3.30 |
| Chicken, full grown | Fricasseed | 2.45 |
| Codfish, cured dry | Boiled | 2.00 |
| Custard | Baked | 2.45 |
| Duck, tame | Roasted | 4.00 |
| Duck, wild | Roasted | 4.30 |
| Eggs, fresh | Raw | 2.00 |
| Eggs, fresh | Whipped | 1.30 |
| Eggs, fresh | Roasted | 2.15 |
| Eggs, fresh | Soft boiled. | 3.00 |
| Eggs, fresh | Hard | 3.30 |
| Eggs, fresh | Fried | 3.30 |
| Fowls, domestic | Roasted | 4.00 |
| Fowls, domestic | Boiled | 4.00 |
| Gelatine | Boiled | 2.30 |
| Goose, wild | Roasted | 2.30 |
| Hashed meat & vegetables | Warmed | 2.30 |
| Heart, animal | Fried | 4.00 |
| Lamb, fresh | Broiled | 2.30 |
| Liver, beeve's, fresh | Broiled | 2.00 |
| Milk | Boiled | 2.00 |
| Milk | Raw | 2.15 |
| Mutton, fresh | Broiled | 3.00 |
| Mutton, fresh | Boiled | 3.00 |
| Mutton, fresh | Roasted | 3.15 |
| Oysters, fresh | Raw | 2.55 |
| Oysters, fresh | Roasted | 3.15 |
| Oysters, fresh | Stewed | 3.30 |
| Parsnips | Boiled | 2.30 |
| Pig, sucking | Roasted | 2.30 |
| Pig's feet, soused | Boiled | 1.00 |
| Pork steak | Broiled | 3.15 |
| Pork, fat and lean | Roasted | 5.15 |
| Pork, recently salted | Stewed | 3.00 |
| Pork, recently salted | Broiled | 3.15 |
| Pork, recently salted | Fried | 4.15 |
| Pork, recently salted | Boiled | 4.30 |
| Potatoes, Irish | Roasted | 2.30 |
| Potatoes, Irish | Baked | 2.30 |
| Potatoes, Irish | Boiled | 3.30 |
| Salmon, salted | Boiled | 4.00 |
| Sausages, fresh | Broiled | 3.20 |
| Soup, barley | Boiled | 1.30 |
| Soup, bean | Boiled | 3.00 |
| Soup, chicken | Boiled | 3.00 |
| Soup, mutton | Boiled | 3.30 |
| Soup, oyster | Boiled | 3.00 |
| Soup, beef, vegetables | Boiled | 4.00 |
| Soup, marrow bones | Boiled | 4.15 |
| Tripe, soused | Boiled | 1.00 |
| Trout, salmon, fresh | Boiled | 1.30 |
| Trout, salmon, fresh | Fried | 1.30 |
| Turkey, wild | Roasted | 2.18 |
| Turkey, domesticated | Roasted | 2.30 |
| Turkey, domesticated | Boiled | 2.25 |
| Turnips | Boiled | 3.30 |
| Veal, fresh | Boiled | 4.00 |
| Veal, fresh | Fried | 4.30 |
| Venison steak | Broiled | 1.35 |

## Relative Nutritive Qualities of Food.

| | Warmth producing | Flesh producing. |
|---|---|---|
| Barley | 57 | 10 |
| Beef | 17 | 10 |
| Buckwheat | 130 | 10 |
| Milk, cow's | 30 | 10 |
| Milk, human | 40 | 10 |
| Mutton, fat | 27 | 10 |
| Oatmeal | 50 | 10 |

## Yield per acre.

| Articles. | lbs. pr acre. |
|---|---|
| Hops | 442 |
| Wheat | 1,260 |
| Barley | 1,600 |
| Oats | 1,840 |
| Peas | 1,920 |
| Beans | 2,000 |
| Plums | 2,000 |
| Cherries | 2,000 |
| Onions | 2,800 |
| Hay | 4,000 |
| Pears | 5,000 |
| Grass | 7,000 |
| Carrots | 6,800 |
| Potatoes | 7,500 |
| Apples | 8,000 |
| Turnips | 8,420 |
| Cinque-foil grass | 9,600 |
| Vetches, green | 9,800 |
| Cabbage | 10,900 |
| Parsnips | 11,200 |
| Mangel Wurtzel | 22,000 |

## Effects of Heat.

| | Deg. F. |
|---|---|
| Fine Gold melts | 2,590 |
| " Silver " | 1,250 |
| Copper melts | 2,548 |
| Wrought Iron melts | 3,980 |
| Cast " " | 3,479 |
| Glass melts | 2,377 |
| Common fire | 790 |
| Brass melts | 1,900 |
| Antimony melts | 951 |
| Bismuth melts | 476 |
| Cadmium | 600 |
| Steel | 2,500 |
| Lead | 504 |
| Tin | 424 |
| Heat, cherry red | 1,500 |
| Heat, bright red | 1,860 |
| " red visible by day | 1,077 |
| " white | 2,900 |
| Mercury boils | 622 |
| " volatilizes. | 806 |
| Platinum melts | 3,080 |
| Zinc melts | 740 |
| Highest natural temperature (Egypt) | 177 |
| Greatest natural cold (below zero) | 56 |
| Greatest artfic'l cold | 106 |
| Heat of human blood | 98 |
| Snow and salt, equal parts | 0 |
| Ice melts | 32 |
| Water in *vacuo* boils. | 98 |
| Furnace under steam boiler | 1,100 |

## Life Period of Birds.

| | Years. |
|---|---|
| Blackbird | 10 to 12 |
| Blackcap | 15 |
| Canary | 24 |
| Chaffinch | 20 to 24 |
| Crane | 24 |
| Crow | 100 |
| Eagle | 100 |
| Partridge | 15 |
| Pigeon | 20 |
| Raven | 100 |
| Robin | 10 to 12 |
| Skylark | 10 to 30 |
| Sparrow Hawk | 40 |
| Starling | 10 to 12 |
| Swan | 100 |
| Thrush | 8 to 10 |
| Titlark | 5 to 6 |
| Wheatear | 2 |
| Wren | 2 to 3 |

## Number of Eggs for a Setting.

| | |
|---|---|
| Eagle | 2 to 3 |
| Falcon | 2 to 4 |
| Fowl, domestic | 6 to 20 |
| Hawk | 2 to 4 |
| Partridge | 14 to 20 |

## HOW TO TELL THE AGE OF CATTLE.

**Age of Cattle.**—A cow's horn is generally supposed to furnish a correct indication of the age of the animal. This is not always true. However, for ordinary purposes, the following will be found to be approximately correct. At two years of age a circle of thick matter begins to form on the animal's horns, which becomes clearly defined at 3 years of age, when another circle or ring begins to form, and so on year after year. Its age, then, can be determined by counting the number of rings, and adding two to their number. The rings on the bull's horns do not show themselves until he is 5 years old, so to the number of rings we must add 5 to arrive at his age. Unless the rings are clear and distinct this rule will not apply. Besides, dealers sometimes file off some of the rings of old cattle to make them appear younger.

**Age of Sheep and Goats.**—At 1 year old they have eight front teeth of uniform size. At two years of age the two middle ones are supplanted by two large ones. At 3 a small tooth appears on each side. At 4 there are 6 large teeth. At 5 all the front teeth are large, and at 6 the whole begin to get large.

## CLASSIFICATION OF SOILS ACCORDING TO THE AMOUNT OF SAND THEY CONTAIN.

1. *Pure Clay*, from which no sand can be removed by washing.
2. *Strong Clay*, when the soil contains from 5 to 29 per cent. of sand.
3. *Clay Loam*, when it contains from 20 to 40 per cent. of sand.
4. *Loam*, from 40 to 70 per cent. of sand.
5. *Sandy Loam*, from 70 to 90 per cent of sand.
6. *Light Sand*, less than 90 per cent. of sand.
7. *Calcareous* (or Marly) soils are those which contain a large amount of calcium carbonate.
8. *Peaty Soils*, (vegetable mold) are those showing a large percentage of organic matter.
9. *Heavy*, the presence of a large quantity of clay makes a soil sticky when wet, and causes it to hold moisture a long time, hence such soils are said to be heavy; a large quantity of sand gives the opposite property, that is, of not retaining moisture, and hence these are said to be light.

The *soil* proper is the surface layer down to where a change in the character of the material takes place, generally from six to ten inches, and beneath this is the sub-soil.

### Quantity of Seed or Plants Required per Acre.

| | | |
|---|---|---|
| Asparagus in 12-inch drills | 16 | quarts. |
| " plants 4 by 1½ feet | 8,000 | " |
| Barley | 2½ | bushels. |
| Beans, bush, in drills 2½ feet | 1½ | " |
| " pole, Lima, 4 by 4 feet | 20 | quarts. |
| " Carolina, prolific, etc., 4 by 3 | 10 | " |
| Beets and mangolds, drills, 2½ feet | 9 | pounds. |
| Broom corn in drills | 12 | " |
| Cabbage, outside, for transplanting | 12 | ounces. |
| Cabbage sown in frames | 4 | " |
| Carrot in drills 2½ feet | 4 | pounds. |
| Celery, seed | 8 | ounces. |
| " plants 4 by ½ feet | 25,800 | " |
| Clover, white Dutch | 12 | pounds. |
| " Lucerne | 10 | " |
| " Alsike | 6 | " |
| " large red with timothy | 12 | " |
| " " " without | 16 | " |
| Corn, sugar | 10 | quarts. |
| Corn, field | 8 | " |
| Corn salad, drill 10 inches | 25 | pounds. |
| Cucumber, in hills | 3 | quarts. |
| " in drills | 4 | " |
| Egg plants, plants 3 by 2 feet | 4 | ounces. |
| Endive in drills 2½ feet | 3 | pounds. |
| Flax, broadcast | 20 | quarts. |
| Grass, timothy with clover | 6 | " |
| " " without " | 10 | " |
| " orchard | 25 | " |
| " red tops, or herds | 20 | " |
| Grass, blue | 28 | quarts. |
| " rye | 20 | " |
| " millet | 32 | " |
| Hemp, broadcast | ½ | bushels. |
| Kale, German greens | 3 | pounds. |
| Lettuce, in rows, 2½ feet | 3 | " |
| Leek | 4 | " |
| Lawn grass | 35 | " |
| Melons, water, in hills, 8 by 8 feet | 3 | " |
| " citron " 4 by 4 " | 2 | " |
| Oats | 2 | bushels. |
| Okra, in drills, 2½ by ½ feet | 20 | pounds. |
| Onion, in beds for sets | 50 | " |
| " in rows for large bulbs | 7 | " |
| Parsnips, in drills, 2½ feet | 5 | " |
| Pepper, plants, 2½ by 1 | 17,500 | " |
| Pumpkins, in hills, 8 by 8 feet | 2 | quarts. |
| Parsley, in drills 2 feet | 4 | pounds. |
| Peas, in drills, short varieties | 2 | bushels. |
| " " " " | 1 to 1½ | " |
| " broadcast | 3 | " |
| Potatoes | 8 | " |
| Radish, in drills 2 feet | 10 | pounds. |
| Rye, broadcast | 1½ | bushels. |
| " drilled | 1½ | " |
| Salsify, in drills 2½ feet | 10 | pounds. |
| Spinach, broadcast | 20 | " |
| Squash, bush, in hills, 4 by 4 feet | 3 | " |
| " running, 8 by 8 feet | 2 | " |
| Sorghum | 4 | quarts. |
| Turnips, in drills, 2 feet | 3 | pounds. |
| " broadcast | 2 | " |
| Tomatoes, in frame | 3 | ounces. |
| " seed in hills, 3 by 3 feet | 8 | " |
| " plants | 3,800 | " |
| Wheat, in drills | 1½ | bushels. |
| " broadcast | 2 | " |

## THE NUMBER OF LOADS OF MANURE AND NUMBER OF HEAPS TO EACH LOAD REQUIRED TO EACH ACRE, THE HEAPS AT GIVEN DISTANCES APART.

| Distance of heaps apart in yards. | NUMBER OF HEAPS IN A LOAD. | | | | | | | | | |
|---|---|---|---|---|---|---|---|---|---|---|
| | 1 | 2 | 3 | 4 | 5 | 6 | 7 | 8 | 9 | 10 |
| 3 | 538 | 269 | 179 | 134 | 108 | 89½ | 77 | 67 | 60 | 54 |
| 3½ | 395 | 168 | 132 | 99 | 79 | 66 | 56½ | 49½ | 44 | 39½ |
| 4 | 203 | 151 | 101 | 75½ | 60½ | 50½ | 43¼ | 37¼ | 33½ | 30¼ |
| 4½ | 239 | 120 | 79½ | 60 | 47¾ | 39¾ | 34¼ | 30 | 26½ | 24 |
| 5 | 194 | 97 | 64½ | 48½ | 38¾ | 32¼ | 27¾ | 24¼ | 21½ | 19¼ |
| 5½ | 160 | 80 | 53½ | 40 | 32 | 26¾ | 22¾ | 20 | 17¼ | 16 |
| 6 | 131 | 67 | 44¾ | 33½ | 27 | 22½ | 19¼ | 16¼ | 15 | 13½ |
| 6½ | 115 | 57½ | 38¼ | 28⅓ | 23 | 19 | 16¼ | 14¼ | 12¼ | 11½ |
| 7 | 99 | 49½ | 33 | 24⅔ | 19¾ | 16½ | 14 | 12¼ | 11 | 10 |
| 7½ | 86 | 43 | 28¾ | 21½ | 17¼ | 14¼ | 12¼ | 10¼ | 9½ | 8½ |
| 8 | 75½ | 37½ | 25¼ | 19 | 15¾ | 12½ | 10¼ | 9½ | 8½ | 7½ |
| 8½ | 67 | 33½ | 22¼ | 16½ | 13½ | 11¼ | 9½ | 8½ | 7½ | 6¼ |
| 9 | 60 | 30 | 20 | 15 | 12 | 10 | 8½ | 7¼ | 6⅔ | 6 |
| 9½ | 53½ | 26¾ | 18 | 13½ | 10¾ | 9 | 7¼ | 6¼ | 6 | 5¼ |
| 10 | 48½ | 24¼ | 16¼ | 12 | 9¾ | 8 | 7 | 6 | 5½ | 4¼ |

## SUGGESTED ROTATION OF CROPS.

| 3 years. | 4 years. | 6 years. | Tobacco. | Cotton. |
|---|---|---|---|---|
| Corn.<br>Wheat.<br>Clover. | Turnips.<br>Other roots.<br>Barley.<br>Clover.<br>Wheat. | Clover.<br>Wheat.<br>Wheat.<br>Clover.<br>Corn.<br>Wheat. | Clover.<br>Clover.<br>Tobacco.<br>Wheat. | Clover or peas.<br>Cotton.<br>Wheat. |

## COMPARATIVE VALUE OF GOOD HAY AND OTHER FOOD FOR STOCK.

| 100 lbs. hay are equal to | 100 lbs. hay are equal to |
|---|---|
| 504 lbs. turnips. | 50 lbs. oats. |
| 300 " carrots. | 46 " wheat. |
| 201 " uncooked potatoes. | 54 " rye. |
| 175 " boiled potatoes. | 64 " buckwheat. |
| 339 " mangel wurzel. | 57 " Indian corn. |
| 442 " rye straw. | 45 " peas and beans. |
| 360 " wheat straw. | 105 " wheat bran. |
| 180 " barley straw. | 109 " rye bran. |
| 150 " pea straw. | 167 " wheat, pea, and oat chaff. |
| 200 " buckwheat straw. | 179 " rye and barley mixed. |
| 275 " green Indian corn. | 68 " acorns. |

## TABLE SHOWING AMOUNT OF HAY OR ITS EQUIVALENT REQUIRED EACH DAY FOR EVERY 100 LBS. OF LIVE STOCK.

| | |
|---|---|
| Working Horses | 3.08 lbs. |
| " Oxen | 2.40 " |
| Fatting Oxen | 5.00 " |
| " " when fat | 4.00 " |
| Milch Cows | from 2.25 to 2.40 " |
| Dry " | 2.42 " |
| Young growing cattle | 3.08 " |
| Steers | 2.84 " |
| Pigs | 3.00 " |
| Sheep | 3.00 " |

## CAPACITY OF CORN-CRIBS 10 FEET HIGH.

| Breadth in Ft. / Lgth. | 10 | 11 | 12 | 13 | 14 | 15 | 16 | 18 | 20 | 22 | 24 | 26 | 28 | 30 |
|---|---|---|---|---|---|---|---|---|---|---|---|---|---|---|
| 3 | 135 | 149 | 162 | 175 | 189 | 202 | 216 | 243 | 270 | 297 | 324 | 351 | 378 | 405 |
| 3½ | 158 | 173 | 189 | 205 | 221 | 236 | 258 | 284 | 315 | 347 | 378 | 410 | 451 | 473 |
| 4 | 180 | 198 | 216 | 234 | 252 | 270 | 288 | 324 | 360 | 396 | 432 | 468 | 504 | 540 |
| 4½ | 203 | 223 | 243 | 263 | 283 | 304 | 324 | 365 | 405 | 446 | 448 | 527 | 567 | 608 |
| 5 | 225 | 248 | 270 | 292 | 315 | 337 | 360 | 405 | 450 | 495 | 540 | 585 | 630 | 675 |
| 5½ | 248 | 272 | 297 | 322 | 347 | 371 | 396 | 446 | 495 | 545 | 594 | 644 | 693 | 743 |
| 6 | 270 | 297 | 324 | 351 | 378 | 405 | 432 | 486 | 540 | 594 | 648 | 702 | 756 | 810 |
| 6½ | 293 | 322 | 351 | 380 | 410 | 439 | 468 | 527 | 585 | 644 | 702 | 761 | 819 | 878 |
| 7 | 315 | 347 | 378 | 409 | 441 | 472 | 504 | 567 | 630 | 693 | 756 | 819 | 882 | 945 |
| 7½ | 338 | 371 | 405 | 439 | 473 | 506 | 540 | 608 | 675 | 743 | 810 | 878 | 945 | 1013 |
| 8 | 360 | 396 | 432 | 468 | 504 | 540 | 576 | 648 | 720 | 792 | 864 | 936 | 1008 | 1080 |
| 8½ | 383 | 421 | 459 | 497 | 536 | 574 | 612 | 689 | 765 | 842 | 918 | 995 | 1071 | 1148 |
| 9 | 405 | 446 | 486 | 526 | 567 | 607 | 648 | 729 | 810 | 891 | 972 | 1053 | 1134 | 1215 |
| 10 | 450 | 495 | 540 | 585 | 539 | 675 | 720 | 810 | 900 | 990 | 1080 | 1170 | 1260 | 1350 |
| 11 | 495 | 545 | 594 | 643 | 693 | 742 | 792 | 891 | 990 | 1089 | 1188 | 1287 | 1386 | 1485 |
| 12 | 540 | 594 | 648 | 702 | 756 | 810 | 864 | 972 | 1080 | 1188 | 1296 | 1404 | 1512 | 1620 |

## CAPACITY OF GRAIN BINS 10 FEET HIGH.

| Width in Ft. | Bin 6 ft. Lg. | Bin 7 ft. Lg. | Bin 8 ft. Lg. | Bin 9 ft. Lg. | Bin 10 ft Lg. | Bin 11 ft Lg. | Bin 12 ft Lg | Bin 13 ft Lg. | Bin 14 ft Lg. | Bin 15 ft. Lg. | Bin 16 ft Lg. | Bin 20 ft. Lg. | Bin 22 ft. Lg. |
|---|---|---|---|---|---|---|---|---|---|---|---|---|---|
| | Bu. | Bu. | Bu. | Bu. | Bu. | Bu. | Bu. | Bu. | Bu. | Bu. | Bu. | Bu. | Bu. |
| 3 | 145 | 169 | 192 | 217 | 241 | 265 | 289 | 313 | 338 | 362 | 386 | 482 | 530 |
| 4 | 193 | 225 | 257 | 289 | 321 | 354 | 386 | 418 | 450 | 482 | 514 | 643 | 708 |
| 5 | 241 | 282 | 321 | 362 | 402 | 442 | 482 | 522 | 563 | 603 | 643 | 804 | 884 |
| 6 | 290 | 338 | 386 | 434 | 482 | 530 | 579 | 627 | 675 | 723 | 771 | 964 | 1060 |
| 7 | 338 | 394 | 450 | 500 | 563 | 619 | 675 | 731 | 788 | 844 | 900 | 1125 | 1238 |
| 8 | 386 | 450 | 514 | 579 | 643 | 707 | 771 | 836 | 900 | 964 | 1029 | 1286 | 1414 |
| 9 | 434 | 507 | 579 | 651 | 723 | 796 | 868 | 940 | 1013 | 1085 | 1157 | 1446 | 1592 |
| 10 | 482 | 563 | 643 | 723 | 804 | 884 | 964 | 1045 | 1125 | 1205 | 1286 | 1607 | 1768 |
| 11 | 531 | 619 | 707 | 796 | 884 | 972 | 1061 | 1149 | 1238 | 1326 | 1414 | 1768 | 1944 |
| 12 | 579 | 675 | 771 | 868 | 964 | 1061 | 1157 | 1254 | 1350 | 1446 | 1543 | 1929 | 2122 |

## AMOUNT OF BUTTER AND CHEESE CONTAINED IN MILK.

| | | |
|---|---|---|
| 100 lbs. milk contain about | 3 | lbs. pure butter. |
| 100 " " " " | 7.8 | " cheese. |
| 100 " " average " | 3.5 | " common butter. |
| 100 " " " " | 11.7 | " common cheese. |
| 100 " skim milk yield " | 13.5 | " skim milk cheese. |

Time required for cream to rise to the surface of new milk at different temperatures:

10 to 12 hours if the temperature of the air is 77° Fahr.
18 to 20 " " " " 68° "
24 " " " " 55° "
36 " " " " 50° "

## DISTANCE TRAVELED BY A HORSE IN PLOWING AN ACRE OF LAND, WITH THE QUANTITY OF LAND WORKED, AT THE RATE OF 16 AND 18 MILES PER DAY OF 9 HOURS.

| Width of furrow in inches. | Miles trav'd in plowing an acre. | Acres plowed per day. 18 miles. | 16 miles. | Width of furrow in inches. | Miles trav'd in plowing an acre. | Acres plowed per day. 18 miles | 16 miles. |
|---|---|---|---|---|---|---|---|
| 7 | 14 1-8 | 1 1-4 | 1 1-8 | 22 | 4 1-2 | 4 | 3 1-2 |
| 8 | 12 1-4 | 1 1-2 | 1 1-4 | 23 | 4 1-4 | 4 1-5 | 3 7-10 |
| 9 | 11 | 1 3-5 | 1 1-2 | 24 | 4 | 4 1-3 | 3 9-10 |
| 10 | 9 9-10 | 1 4-5 | 1 3-5 | 25 | 4 | 4 1-2 | 4 |
| 11 | 9 | 2 | 1 3-4 | 26 | 3 4-5 | 4 3-4 | 4 1-5 |
| 12 | 8 1-4 | 2 1-5 | 1 9-10 | 27 | 3 3-5 | 4 9-10 | 4 1-2 |
| 13 | 7 1-2 | 2 1-3 | 2 1-10 | 28 | 3 1-2 | 5 3-8 | 4 1-2 |
| 14 | 7 | 2 1-2 | 2 1-4 | 29 | 3 1-2 | 5 1-4 | 4 3-5 |
| 15 | 6 1-2 | 2 3-4 | 2 2-5 | 30 | 3 1-2 | 5 3-4 | 4 4-5 |
| 16 | 6 1-6 | 2 9-10 | 2 3-5 | 31 | 3 1-5 | 5 | 5 |
| 17 | 5 3-4 | 3 1-10 | 2 3-4 | 32 | 3 1-10 | 5 4-5 | 5 1-4 |
| 18 | 5 1-2 | 3 1-4 | 2 9-10 | 33 | 3 | 6 | 5 1-3 |
| 19 | 5 1-4 | 3 1-2 | 3 1-10 | 34 | 2 9-10 | 6 1-5 | 5 1-2 |
| 20 | 4 9-10 | 3 3-5 | 3 1-4 | 35 | 2 4-5 | 6 1-3 | 5 3-5 |
| 21 | 4 7-10 | 3 4-5 | 3 1-3 | 36 | 2 3-4 | 6 1-2 | 5 4-5 |

## HOW TO FORETELL THE WEATHER THROUGH THE LUNATIONS OF THE MOON.

(Compiled from the Works of Dr. Herschell and Adam Clarke.)

| If the New Moon, the First Quarter, the Full Moon or the Last Quarter, enters— | In Summer. | In Winter. |
|---|---|---|
| Between midnight and 2 A. M. | Fair. | Hard frost, unless wind is S. or E. |
| Bet. 2 and 4 A. M. | Cold, fr't showers. | Snowy and stormy. |
| " 4 and 6 A. M. | Rain. | Rain. |
| " 6 and 8 A. M. | Wind and Rain. | Stormy. |
| " 8 and 10 A. M. | Changeable. | Cold rain if wind is W., snow if E. |
| " 10 and 12 A. M. | Frequent showers. | Cold and high wind. |
| At 12 M. and 2 P. M. | Very rainy. | Snow and rain. |
| Bet. 2 and 4 P. M. | Changeable. | Fair and mild. |
| " 4 and 6 P. M. | Fair. | Fair. |
| " 6 and 8 P. M. | Fair if wind N. W., rainy if S. or S. E. | Fair and frosty if wind is N. or W., rain or snow if S. or S. E. |
| " 8 and 10 P. M. | Do. | Do. |
| " 10 and midnight | Fair. | Fair and frosty. |

Notes.—1. The nearer the time of the moon's change, first quarter, full, and last quarter, is to *midnight*, the fairer the weather during 7 following days. Range for this is from 10 at night till 2 next morning. 2. The nearer to *mid-day* the phases of the moon happen, the more foul or wet weather during the 7 days following. 3. The moon's change entering from 4 to 10 of the afternoon, may expect fair weather.

## WHAT POULTRY WEIGHS.

| | Lbs. | oz. |
|---|---|---|
| Black Polish cock, 3 years old | 5 | 3 |
| Black Polish hen, 3 years old | 3 | 4 |
| Golden Polish cock | 5 | 0 |
| Golden Polish hen | 3 | 8 |
| White-crested Golden Poland pullet | 2 | 3 |
| Golden Hamburgh hen, molting | 2 | 3 |
| Silver Hamburgh hen | 3 | 1 |
| Speckled Surrey hen, 2 years old | 5 | 12 |
| Spanish hen | 5 | 0 |
| Dorking cock | 7 | 0 |
| Dorking hen | 6 | 8 |
| Pheasant Malay cock, 2 years old | 7 | 0 |
| Pheasant Malay hen | 5 | 1 |
| Cochin-China cock, 16 months old | 6 | 5 |
| Cochin-China hen, 16 months old | 4 | 6 |
| Game cock | 4 | 10 |
| Game hen | 3 | 0 |
| Turkey cock, 16 months old | 16 | 0 |
| Turkey hen, 3-4 years old | 8 | 6 |
| White China gander, 6 years old | 12 | 3 |
| White China goose | 11 | 3 |
| Black Spanish cockerel | 2 | 11 |
| Black Spanish pullet | 2 | 11 |

MERCANTILE LAW is that branch of the law which governs mercantile transactions of any kind. The law of all English-speaking countries is based upon the common law of England. *Common law* is that body of law which originates in principles of justice and the needs of society, becomes well established custom, and is finally sanctioned, limited and defined by the decisions of the higher courts. Its principles must therefore be sought in treatises on its various branches and in the numerous reports of decisions by the courts of last resort. *Statute law,* on the other hand, consists of special legislative enactments, such as acts of parliament, of Congress, and of state or colonial legislatures. Statutes are definite and formal in their nature. Common law gives way to a statute, and an old statute to a new one on the same subject. When a statute which repeals another is itself repealed, the old statute becomes again in force.

In the United States the supreme law is the Federal Constitution. This, with treaties and acts of Congress, is the highest law in all States and territories and cannot be interfered with by local legislation. The general government is sovereign in those matters entrusted to it by the Constitution; the States are sovereign in all other matters within their own domain. In any particular State we have, therefore, to regard—1. The Constitution and laws of the United States. 2. The Constitution of the State. 3. The public and private statutes of the State, and—4. The common law, which is that of England at the time of the revolution, modified and developed by the decisions of the State courts of appeal. To this there is one exception, Louisiana, which was formerly a French possession, and hence derives its unwritten law from the *Civil* or *Roman Law.*

It will thus be seen that there may be great diversity in the exact provisions of the law on a given subject in different states and countries. Yet the general principles are everywhere founded on the same considerations, and are identical. Especially is this true of the branch of law known as commercial or mercantile law. The very nature of commerce and trade compelled business men of different lands to adopt similar customs and modes of doing business. The usages and customs to which they voluntarily conformed in their mutual intercourse became almost identically the same in all parts of the civilized world; they were soon recognized as binding law by the courts, and in many cases are confirmed and defined by special statutes. It is thus not impractical to give to business men a collection of useful rules and principles of legal forms, the application of which shall not be confined to any locality. Such a collection will be found in the following pages; and to it we shall add, when practicable and desirable, the substance of special statutory enactments and requirements. To draw forms to suit every imaginary set of circumstances is of course impossible, but in most cases the necessary alterations in the form given will at once suggest themselves. The utility of a law compendium of this kind, we need not dwell upon at length. We do not claim that it will literally make "every man his own lawyer;" but it will often save time, temper and money. We shall endeavor to present in a clear, condensed and handy form (free, as far as possible, from technical language) a mass of useful, varied and reliable information on topics of importance to business men.

## Accord and Satisfaction.

IN legal phrase, ACCORD and SATISFACTION means an agreement between two parties by which one, the *injurer*, undertakes to give, and the other, the *injured*, to receive some valuable consideration as a satisfaction for a wrong done, followed by the actual giving and receiving of such consideration. This is a bar to all actions on account of such injury. Accord and satisfaction by a co-partner is a bar to an action by or against his fellow partners. But payment of part of a whole debt is not good satisfaction, even though accepted as such, unless the acceptor receives additional advantage in some shape The new promise must be founded on a new consideration. An agreement to cancel and annul mutual claims or to discontinue mutual suits is good accord and satisfaction, and will bar further proceedings. If a third party make accord and satisfaction with a creditor for the debtor, the test as to whether it will hold good or not, is whether the actual debtor can be shown to have treated it as sufficient.

An accord and satisfaction made before a breach of contract is not a bar to an action for a subsequent breach.

If a promise be executed formally and literally, but is of no value to the creditor, because by some act or omission of the debtor it is really inoperative, this will have no effect as an accord and satisfaction. If a new promise is in its nature executory, that is, one to be fulfilled at some future time, and in point of fact is not so fulfilled, there is no satisfaction. Even though the promise is for performance at a fixed future day, the creditor may bring his original action before the new promise becomes due.

## AFFIDAVITS.

WRITTEN statements of facts under oath or affirmation are called AFFIDAVITS. The word in itself means "he has sworn." Affidavits may be made in law suits, or independently of legal proceedings to verify certain facts. They must be made in the presence of an officer qualified to administer an oath, as a justice of the peace; and must be made within the personal jurisdiction of such officer or court. Voluntary affidavits, not to be used in legal proceedings and not made under a statute, cannot be the cause of a prosecution for perjury, even though totally false. A *deposition* differs from an affidavit in that in the former the opposing party has the right to be represented when the deposition is taken and to make a cross examination on the subject matter. The seal of the officer taking the affidavit should be affixed, if he has one. Amendment to the affidavit may be made by order of the court, and the document must then be resworn to. When deponent cannot write, the affidavit must be read to him and that fact stated in the oath. He must then make his mark.

A COUNTER-AFFIDAVIT is one made in opposition to an affidavit already made. The *jurat* is that part of the affidavit in which the proper officer certifies that the same was sworn to before him. The instrument should show on its face that it was made before some officer competent to take affidavits. *Venue* is the place where the affidavit is taken. Omission of the venue from an affidavit is a fatal defect. The affidavit will not be vitiated by *surplusage,* the statement of immaterial matter, provided it is not inconsistent with the principal and necessary averments. Statements as to descriptions, amounts and parties should be clear, particular and positive.

## GENERAL FORM OF AFFIDAVIT.

STATE OF ——, —— COUNTY, TOWN OF ——, *ss.:*

A. B. (of ——), being duly sworn, deposes and says (*or, alleges and says*):

That :—(*Here set out in full and accurate language the matters to be alleged*).

[SEAL.] (*Signature of Affiant.*)

*Sworn (or affirmed) before me, this —— day of* ——, A. D. 18—.

(*Signature of Justice or other officer.*)

(If the affiant is unable to read, the subscription should be as follows):

Subscribed and sworn to before me, this —— day of ——, A. D. 18—, the same having been by me (*or, in my presence*) read to this affiant, he being illiterate (*or blind*), and understanding the same.

(*Officer's signature and title.*)

## AFFIDAVIT TO ACCOUNTS.

STATE OF ——, —— COUNTY, *ss.:*

Before me, the undersigned, one of the justices of the peace in and for said county, personally came F. G., of ——, and being duly sworn according to law, deposes and says: That the above account, as stated, is just and true.

That the above sum of —— dollars is now justly due and owing to this deponent by the above-named L. P.

That he, the said F. G., has never received the same or any part thereof, either directly or indirectly, nor any person for him, by his direction or order, knowledge, or consent.

F. G.

*Sworn and subscribed before me, this —— day of* ——, A. D. 18—.

M. N.,
*Justice of the Peace.*

## AFFIDAVIT TO PETITION.

STATE OF ——, —— COUNTY, *ss.:*

A. B., being duly sworn, says: That the facts set forth in the foregoing petition are true to the best of his knowledge and belief.

A. B.

*Sworn, etc. (as in other forms above).*

## AFFIDAVIT TO PUBLICATION.

STATE OF ——, —— COUNTY, *ss.:*

A. B., being duly sworn, says that he is the printer of (*or, is in the employ of C. D., the printer of*) the —— ——, a newspaper published in and of general circulation in said county; and that the notice, of which the annexed is a true copy, was published for —— consecutive days (*or weeks, as the case may be*) in said newspaper, beginning on the —— day of ——, A. D. 18—.

A. B.

*Subscribed and sworn to before me this —— day of* ——, A. D. 18—.

F. G., *Justice of the Peace.*

## AFFIDAVIT OF ASSETS.

STATE OF ——, —— COUNTY, *ss.:*

A. B., being duly sworn, says and declares, that he is the owner in fee simple of the following described real estate, free from all liens and incumbrances, to wit: (*here give description by metes and bounds*), all of the aggregate value of (*amount*); that he is also the absolute owner of the following described personal property, to wit: (*give description*) all of the aggregate value of (*amount*); that he is worth at least —— dollars over and above all his debts, exemptions and liabilities.

(*Signed*) A. B.

*Subscribed and sworn to, etc. (as above).*

## SURETIES' OATH.

STATE OF ——, —— COUNTY, *ss.:*

We, the undersigned, sureties on the within undertaking, do solemnly swear that we are residents of said county and State, and that we are each of us worth —— dollars beyond the amount of our debts, exemptions and liabilities, and have property therein subject to execution equal to said sum. So help us God.

(*Signed*) A. B.
C. D

*Subscribed and sworn, etc.*

## AFFIDAVIT TO SIGNATURE OF ABSENT OR DECEASED WITNESS.

STATE OF ——, —— COUNTY, *ss.:*

**Be it remembered,** that on the —— day of ——, A. D. 18—, before me the undersigned, F. P., one of the justices of the peace in said county, personally appeared N. H., who, being duly sworn, deposes and says: That C. S., one of the subscribing witnesses to the within (*will or deed*) is (*dead, or absent from the state, as the case may be*).

That he has frequently seen said C. S. write, and that he is well acquainted with the handwriting of said C. S.

That to the best of his knowledge and belief (*or he verily believes*) the name of C. S., signed to the same as one of the subscribing witnesses, is the proper and individual handwriting of said C. S.

(*Signed*) N. H.

*Subscribed and sworn to before me, this —— day of* ——, A. D. 18—.

F P.,
*Justice of the Peace.*

# Agents and Attorneys.

AGENTS are those employed to transact business or to act for others. A *general agent* is one who is employed to do all the business of his principal, or all the business of a certain kind or at a particular place. A *special agent* is one who is appointed for a particular purpose and under a limited power. Authority may be given to an agent orally, in writing under seal, or in writing without a seal. When it is in writing the authority is called a power of attorney. It is a general rule of law that, when the thing to be done requires the execution of an instrument under seal, the power must itself be under seal. Even when no express authority has been given either in writing or by word of mouth, the law will often consider the relation of agent and principal to exist; that is, it is presumed or implied from the circumstances. Thus a wife who is accustomed to do certain business for her husband (for instance, paying or collecting rents) will be considered his agent in such acts; so with a child, a domestic servant, or a clerk. A person, even, who is not qualified to make a contract on his own account (as a minor, married woman, or alien) may legally act as agent for another.

The acts of general agents bind their principals so long as they are within the general scope of the authority given, even though they are contrary to his private instructions, or even after the actual revocation of the authority, if the agency were known and the revocation unknown to parties dealing in good faith with the agent. It is, therefore, a common and proper practice for the principal to advertise publicly the revocation of a power. Notice to the agent is notice to the principal.

The agent is bound to use reasonable care in transacting the business of his agency, such as a prudent and careful man would use in his own affairs. If he goes beyond the scope of his authority he is liable both to his principal and to third parties. If given power to sell, the agent cannot himself become the purchaser (or, if to buy, the *seller*) without special authority to that effect. He should keep separate accounts. The agent is often paid by commission, for which he has a lien. An authority to sell does not imply an authority to sell on credit, unless such is the general custom of the trade. As a rule, an agent cannot substitute another in place of himself without special power. This is usually given in written instructions or powers of attorney by inserting the clause "with full power to substitute."

The proper manner for an agent to sign is thus, "B., by A.," not "A. for B." A. in each case representing the agent and B. the principal.

Agency is terminated by the full execution and completion of the business entrusted; by the written revocation of the power by the principal; by the legal incapacity of either agent or principal, as when caused by insanity or the marriage of a woman; or by the death of principal or agent. There is only one class of *powers* which are not destroyed by the death of the principal. These are "powers coupled with an interest," an example of which will be found among the forms below. A power given by A. to B. to sell certain shares of stock belonging to A., and with the proceeds to reimburse himself for certain debts due to him (B.) from A., would be a power coupled with an interest.

RATIFICATION is the acceptance by the principal of the unauthorized act of an agent as his own. It may either be express and open, as a declaration in a letter, or implied, as where the principal takes advantage of the act and says nothing.

Agents are of very many classes, such as clerks, salesmen, and others governed by the ordinary rules which control the relations of master and servant, factors and brokers, auctioneers, "ships' husbands," ship masters, and attorneys.

A BROKER is one employed by others to make and conclude bargains for them, and is usually the agent of both parties. He is bound entirely by his instructions, is liable for any negligence, fraud, or breach of orders, and has a lien on goods or money in his possession for his fee or commission. A power to sell does not include the power to pledge. There are several classes, such as real estate, note, insurance, ship, and stock brokers. The usual commission of a stock broker in the United States is one-eighth of one per cent. on the par value of all sales or purchases.

A FACTOR differs from a broker in that he usually has actual possession of goods entrusted to him, and may buy and sell in his own name. He is often called a commission merchant or consignee. He may pledge the goods for advances to his principal or for his own charges and commission. The factor may even use his own name in suits at law concerning the goods of which he is consignee. A foreign factor is one who acts for a principal living in a different country ; as regards third parties he is almost always regarded as himself a principal and personally liable.

A SHIP'S HUSBAND is usually, but not of necessity, a part owner, and is the agent of the owners to equip and repair the ship, furnish her with proper papers, make contracts for freight or passage, and collect dues. His authority may be written or oral. He cannot borrow money on the ship, nor insure, nor appoint a substitute without special authority. The master of a ship, on the other hand, has special powers arising from the nature of his position. He may, if driven by circumstances, borrow money on ship or cargo, or pledge the same, or even, in extreme necessity, sell the ship, without special authority so to do.

ATTORNEYS may be *attorneys-in-fact* or *attorneys-at-law*. An attorney-in-fact is one appointed by a special act (power of attorney) to do some specific thing. An attorney-at-law is a sworn officer of a court, employed by others (clients) to conduct legal proceedings for them. He has authority in all matters necessary to the prosecution and termination of the cause, but he cannot settle the points in dispute or give a release for damages or costs without the consent of his client. He is bound to use due diligence, to professional secrecy, and to a full accounting with his client. On all papers of his client in his hands and on judgments and costs which he may obtain he has a lien for his fees, which must be reasonable.

In England the attorney does not plead causes in court, but prepares briefs and submits them to the *barrister*, who conducts all court proceedings. In the United States the functions of the barrister and attorney are united in one and the same person. When a power of attorney is for use in a foreign country or another state, it should be acknowledged before a notary public. His signature should be attested, in the first case, by the consul of the foreign government in which the power is to be used ; in the second case, by the clerk of the superior court, or according to the statutory provisions of the State where it is executed.

## POWERS OF ATTORNEY.

### SHORT GENERAL FORM.

**Know all Men by these Presents** : That I, the undersigned, of (*place*), do hereby make, constitute and appoint John Doe, of (*place*), my true and lawful attorney, for me, and in my name and stead to (*here insert the subject matter of power*), to do and perform all the necessary acts in the execution and prosecution of the aforesaid business, and in as full and ample a manner as I might do if I were personally present.

**In witness whereof,** I have hereunto set my hand and seal this 10th day of May, A. D. 1881.

JAMES SMITH. [L. S]

*Signed, Sealed and Delivered in the Presence of*

### FULLER GENERAL FORM.

**Know all Men by these Presents**: That I. James Smith, of (*place of residence*), have by these presents ordained, made and constituted, and in my name and place, put John Doe, of (*residence of attorney*), to be my lawful and sufficient attorney, for me and in my name, place and stead, to (*here insert the purpose or purposes for which the power is given*).

That I hereby grant unto my said attorney full authority and power, in and about said premises : and to use all due course, means and process of law for the complete, effectual and full execution of the business above described ; and for said premises to appear and me represent before any governors, judges, justices, and ministers of law whomsoever, in any court or courts of judicature, and there on my behalf defend and prosecute all actions, causes and matters whatsoever, relating to the premises : and in all said premises make and execute all due acquittances, discharges, and releases.

That said attorney shall have full power and authority to do, act, determine, accomplish and transact all matters and things relating to the premises, as amply as I, his said constituent and principal, if present, might or ought, although said matters and things should require more special authority than is herein comprised and included.

That I hereby allow, ratify and hold firm and valid all matters and things whatsoever my said attorney or his substitutes shall lawfully do or cause to be done in and about said premises, by virtue of these presents.

**In witness whereof,** etc. (*as in previous form*).

## POWER TO CARRY ON MERCANTILE BUSINESS.

(*Draw the form as above, and with the same acknowledgment; where it is indicated that the subject matter should be stated, insert this clause:*) to carry on, conduct and manage the entire business concerns included in and pertaining to (*here state name and description of business*) at (*name of place*) in (*State and county*).

For me, and in my name to use and employ all such means, rights, remedies and uses, as are best calculated for the safe and successful prosecution of said business, and to insure accessions, increase and preservation of all property; the diligent collection and settlement of indebtedness, the most judicious purchases and largest sales therein, and for all and every other matter or thing, belonging or pertaining to said business.

## POWER TO PURCHASE, SELL, AND LEASE REAL ESTATE.

PURCHASE—(*Insert this clause:*)—to purchase any real estate on my account, in fee simple or otherwise, at any prices or any exchanges whatsoever; and for these purposes to receive, confirm, make and execute any deeds, conveyances, contracts, or other instruments whatsoever.

SALE—(*Insert this clause:*)—to sell, barter, or exchange any real estate on my account to any person or persons whatsoever, for any price or any manner; and for these purposes to execute and acknowledge all deeds, conveyances, and assurances, with general covenants of warranty against all persons or incumbrances, or any other covenants whatsoever.

LEASE. (*Insert this clause:*)—to receive all rents, issues, and profits of all my lands or tenements, or other real estate to which I am or may be entitled, and from time to time to renew the leases thereof, not extending the same, however, beyond the —— day of ——, A. D. 18—.

(Where these powers of lease, purchase or sale are to be confined to certain specific property, that should be fully described.)

## FULL POWER TO DEMAND, SUE FOR, AND RECOVER DEBTS.

**Know all Men by these Presents:** That I, Edward Wilson, have constituted, ordained and made, and in my place and stead put, and by these presents do constitute, ordain and make, and in my stead and place put, Thomas Grant, to be my true, sufficient and lawful attorney for me and in my name and stead and to my use, to ask, demand, levy, require, recover and receive of and from all and every person or persons whomsoever the same shall or may concern, all and singular sums of money, debts, goods, wares, merchandise, effects, and things whatsoever and wheresoever they shall and may be found, due, owing, payable, belonging and coming to me the constituent, by any ways or means whatsoever.

**Giving and hereby granting** unto my said attorney full and whole strength, power and authority in and about the premises; and to take and use all due means, course and process in the law for the recovery and obtaining the same, and of recoveries and receipts thereof; and in my name to make, seal and execute due acquittance and discharge; and for the premises to appear, and the person of me the constituent to represent, before any governors, justices, officers and ministers of the law whatsoever, in any court or courts of judicature; and there on my behalf to answer, defend and reply unto all actions, causes, matters and things whatsoever, relating to the premises. Also to submit any matter in dispute to arbitration, with full power to make and substitute one or more attorneys as my said attorney, and the same again at pleasure to revoke. And generally to say, do, act, transact, determine, accomplish and finish all matters and things whatsoever relating to the premises, as fully, amply and effectually, to all intents and purposes, as I, the said constituent, if present, ought or might personally, although the matter should require more special authority than is herein comprised, I, the said constituent, ratifying and allowing and holding firm and valid, all, and whatsoever my said attorney or his substitutes shall lawfully do, or cause to be done in and about the premises, by virtue of these presents.

**In witness whereof,** I have hereunto set my hand and seal this fourth day of January, in the year of our Lord one thousand eight hundred and eighty.

(*Signed*) EDWARD WILSON. [L. S.]

*Signed, Sealed and Delivered in Presence of us,*

ANTHONY TOWLE,
RICHARD BRINTON.

## POWER TO RECEIVE DIVIDENDS ON STOCK.

**Know all Men by these Presents:** That I, Willis Sayre, of New York city, do authorize, constitute, and appoint Edward Livingstone of the same place to receive from the Morris and Essex Railroad Company the dividend now due to me on all stock standing on the books of said company, and receipt for the same; hereby ratifying and confirming all that may lawfully be done in the premises by virtue hereof.

**Witness** my hand and seal, this —— day of ——, 18—.

(*Signature.*) [L. S.]

*Signed, Sealed and Delivered in the Presence of*

GEORGE WRIGHT.

## PROXY TO VOTE ON STOCK.

*With Revocation of Previous Proxies and Affidavit as to Ownership.*

**Know all Men by these Presents:** That I, the undersigned, stockholder in the (*name of company*), do hereby constitute and appoint John Doe my true and lawful attorney, with power of substitution, for me, and in my name to vote at the meeting of the stockholders in said company, to be held at (*name of place*) or at any adjournment thereof, with all the powers I should possess if personally present. And I do hereby revoke all previous proxies granted by me for such purpose.

(*Signed*) GEORGE STERN.

**Witness:** EDWARD DOE. This 5th day of July, A. D. 1881.

I do swear (*or affirm*) that the shares on which my representative and attorney in the above proxy is entitled to vote, do not belong and are not hypothecated to the said company, and that they are not hypothecated or pledged to any other corporation or person whatever; that such shares have not been transferred to me for the purpose of enabling me to vote thereon at the ensuing election, and that I have not contracted to sell or transfer them upon any condition, agreement or understanding in relation to my manner of voting at the said election.

*Sworn to this* —— *day of* ——, 18—, *before me,* ——, J. P.

(*Signature.*)

## A POWER COUPLED WITH AN INTEREST.

For value received from John Stokes, I have sold to him 200 shares of the capital stock of the Midland Railway Company, now standing in my name upon its books; and I hereby constitute and appoint the said John Stokes my attorney irrevocable to transfer the said stock upon the books of said company to himself or any other person; and I also authorize him to substitute any other person as attorney for me and in my name to make such transfer.

(*Signed*) SAMUEL FRENCH.

**Witness** my seal, this 4th day of June, A. D. 1870. [L. S.]

## REVOCATION OF POWER.

**Whereas,** I, James Smith, of (*residence*), on July 5, A. D. 1881, did by my letter of attorney under my hand and seal, appoint John Green my true and lawful attorney to sell and convey lands (*or for whatever purpose the power was given*) for me, now

**Know all Men by these Presents,** that I have revoked and annulled such letter and authority, and I do hereby revoke and annul it, and declare the said John Green no longer my attorney for such purpose.

JAMES SMITH. [L. S.]

**Witness** my hand and seal, this 12th of November, A. D. 1881.

MINORS bound to service for a term of years to learn some trade, art, or profession, are termed APPRENTICES. In return for such service they receive instruction in their master's trade or art. An infant may be thus bound by his own free will and act, with the consent of father, mother, or guardian (or by public officers where there is no guardian or the infant is a pauper), until the age of 21 in the case of males and of 18 in the case of females.

The master cannot transfer his rights over the apprentice without his consent and that of parent or guardian. If the master neglects his part of the contract, the parent's right revives and the discharge of the apprentice may be compelled. Neither sickness nor inaptness in the trade will release the master from his obligations. If the apprentice runs away and enters the employment of another, the master is not bound to take him back, but is entitled to whatever he may earn, provided that he can show that the new employer was aware of the existence of the apprenticeship. The death of the master discharges the apprentice. The relation may also be terminated by a deed of mutual release or by a decree of a court, as where ill treatment, neglect, and abuse are shown.

### AN INDENTURE OF APPRENTICESHIP.

**This Indenture of Apprenticeship** between ——, minor, of the age of —— years, by and with the consent of his father (*or mother, or guardian, as the case may be*) — and —— master, **Witnesseth**: That the said ——is hereby bound as an apprentice to the said —— for the full term of —— years from the date hereof, to learn the art and trade of a ——; and the said ——, minor, acting with the consent of his (*parent or guardian*), hereby covenants faithfully to serve the said —— for the full term of years, to watch carefully his master's interest, to abstain from all vice, negligence and wastefulness, and to obey the commands of said —— in all lawful and proper matters.

And the said ——, master, on his part, doth promise and covenant that he will to the best of his power teach the said —— his trade or art, that he will give and provide for said —— good and sufficient meat, drink, clothing, washing and lodging, such as are suitable for an apprentice, that he will give him —— months' schooling during the year and at the expiration of the term of apprenticeship will furnish him with a suit of substantial wearing apparel, and —— in money. And for the true performance of all and singular the covenants and agreements aforesaid, the said parties bind themselves, each unto the other, firmly by these presents.

**In Witness Whereof,** the parties hereto have set their hands and seals this —— day of ——, in the year of our Lord, 18—.

*Executed and delivered before*

(*Witnesses.*) (*Signatures.*) (*Seals.*)

*To this should be annexed the written consent of parent or guardian, as follows:* I do hereby consent to and approve of the binding of my son (*or ward*) as in the above indenture is set forth.

*Dated this —— day of ——,* A. D. 18—.

(*Signature.*) [L. S.]

### INDENTURE BY PUBLIC OFFICERS.

**This Indenture Witnesseth:** That —— of ——, minor, with the consent of —— and ——, justices of the peace (*or overseers of the poor, or selectmen, or Judge of the —— Court*) of the town of ——, hereon endorsed, doth hereby bind himself as apprentice, *etc.* (*as above*).

### RELEASE OF APPRENTICESHIP.

**Know all Men by these Presents:** That ——, son of ——, of ——, did by his indenture, bearing date the — day of ——, A.D. 18—, bind himself as an apprentice unto, —— of ——, for a term of — years (*or, until he should be of legal age*) from the date thereof, as by said indenture more fully appears.

That (*here state fully the reasons for the release*).

By reason whereof, the said —— doth hereby release, and forever discharge said —— and his father —— (*or, mother or guardian*) of and from said indenture and all service and all other agreements, covenants, matters and things contained therein, on their, or either of their parts, to be observed and performed whatsoever, unto the date of this release.

**In Witness Whereof** I have hereby set my hand, this —— day of ——, A. D. 18—, (*Signature.*)

PARTIES who have mutual claims may submit the matter in dispute to a third party or to two or more third parties. The agreement of the injured and injuring parties, followed by the decision of the arbitrators and the compliance of both parties therewith is an ARBITRATION. The agreement is called the *submission,* and the decision the *award.*

The SUBMISSION may be by word of mouth, by written agreement, or by order of the court. The more formal method is for the parties to enter into bonds to one another, the conditions of which are the compliance with the award, the payment of sums of money as directed, and the mutual discharge of all claims and causes of action. A bond, however, is not at all necessary. Either party may revoke his submission at any time before the award is made, by giving notice to the other party. This is not true, however, when the arbitration is by order of a court.

The AWARD must not go beyond the subject matter submitted; it must be clear, certain, possible, reasonable, final and conclusive.

Arbitration is favored by the law as an inexpensive and peaceable way of settling disputes; an award will not, therefore, be set aside by the courts, except upon very strong grounds, such as impropriety or irregularity in the conduct of the arbitrators, or when "procured by corruption or undue means." A mere mistake in the facts by arbitrators, unless very important and very patent, will not be considered by the court. The award when completed should be sealed, addressed to all the parties, and opened in their presence, or if made under order of court, returned to the clerk.

The death of either party, or one of the arbitrators, will revoke the submission, if not made by order of the court.

It is a common practice to submit the matter in dispute to two parties, one selected by each disputant, and to give to them power to select a third and disinterested arbitrator, in case they are not able to agree upon a decision.

### FORM OF SUBMISSION.

**Memorandum of an Agreement** made May 8, 1879, between Max Kohn on the one part, and Egbert Wilson of the other part, to submit a matter in controversy between them to arbitration.

The said Max Kohn, on his part, makes a claim against the said Egbert Wilson for labor and services (*or whatever the claim may be, giving full particulars*). And the said Egbert Wilson disputes the claim as being excessive (*or as the case may be*), and in his turn claims (*give full particulars of counter claim, if any*).

They now mutually agree to leave the said claims to the arbitrament and award of James Stiles and Jonas Allen as arbitrators by them selected, who are to hear the proofs and allegations of the parties, and determine whether any, and if any what, moneys or damages are due and should be properly paid from either party to the other by reason thereof, and to make an award thereon. And if they cannot agree upon an award they are to select a third person, who shall be indifferent and disinterested between the parties hereto, and the award of one of such arbitrators, together with that of such third person, made in writing and delivered to the party in whose favor it may be (with notice to the other party) within twenty days hereof, shall be final.

And the parties hereto, each to the other, doth bind himself to pay to the other such sum as may by such award become payable, without fraud or delay.

**Witness** our hands and seals:— { MAX KOHN. [L.S.]<br>EGBERT WILSON. [L.S.]

*On this may be endorsed the oath of the arbitrators, as follows:*

STATE OF ——, —— COUNTY, TOWN OF ——, *ss.:*

James Stiles, Jonas Allen and Henry Bell, being duly sworn, each for himself, severally saith, that he will faithfully and fairly hear and examine the matter in controversy submitted to these deponents by the within submission, and will make a just and fair award thereon according to the best of his understanding.

*Signed and sworn to before me,* John Gray, J. P., *this 12th of May, A.D.* 1879. (*Signatures.*)

### GENERAL FORM OF AWARD.

**Know all Men by these Presents**: That we the undersigned, arbitrators of all the matters in difference, of every name, kind, and nature, between Max Kohn and Egbert Wilson, by virtue of their agreement of submission of May 9. 1879, do award, order, judge and determine of and concerning the same, as follows: That (*then state the award in full*).

**In Witness Whereof,** we have, in each other's presence, hereunto set our hands, this 25th day of May, 1879. (*Signatures.*)

### FORM OF AWARD WHEN BONDS ARE GIVEN.

**To all to whom these Presents shall come**: We (*here insert names of the arbitrators*), to whom was submitted as arbitrators the matter in controversy between —— and ——, as by the condition of their respective bonds of submission, executed by the said parties respectively, each unto the other, and dated —— of ——, 18—, and which —— more fully appears.

**Now therefore, know ye,** That we, the arbitrators named in the above bonds, having been first duly sworn according to law, and having heard the proofs and allegations of the parties, and examined the matter in controversy by them submitted, do make this award in writing; that is to say, the said (*here follows the award, specifying fully what is to be done or paid by either party, declaring the bonds to henceforth cease and determine, together with all causes of action existing before the submission was entered into, and requiring the parties to execute mutual releases of all mutual accounts, debts, damages, demands or causes of action*).

**In Witness Whereof,** We have hereunto subscribed these presents, this —— day of, —— 18——.

*In Presence of* (*Signatures.*)

### REVOCATION OF SUBMISSION.

**Whereas,** the subscriber, Max Kohn, with Egbert Wilson, did on the 9th day of May, 1879, submit to James Stiles and Jonas Allen, arbitrators, with power to select a third, the arbitrament and award of certain claims existing between me, the said Max Kohn and the said Egbert Wilson, and now for certain reasons I desire to revoke the submission; **Now Therefore,** I do hereby revoke the said submission, and declare the same null and void.

Given under my hand and seal this 15th day of May, A.D. 1879.

(*Signed*) MAX KOHN.

To James Stiles and Jonas Allen.

### REVOCATION NOTICE.

To Egbert Wilson: Dear Sir—I have this day revoked the powers of James Stiles and Jonas Allen as arbitrators under the agreement of submission entered into between us on the 9th day of May, 1879, by an instrument of which the annexed is a copy.

(*Signed*) MAX KOHN.

Dated this 15th day of May, 1879.

RECEIPTS signed by the master of a ship for cargo to be carried as freight, are called BILLS OF LADING. They specify the goods, ship, price, names of consignor and consignee, and such other things as may be requisite. They are usually signed in triplicate, one copy being kept by the consignor and the others sent to the consignee by different channels. *Average* is the charge on such small expenses of the ship as harbor dues, pilotage and towage. *Primage* is a small percentage on the freight, which goes to the master as a perquisite.

Bills of lading are transferable and assignable, and the assignee may sue for the recovery of the goods. If the goods perish without fault of the master the freight must be paid, but if proper precautionary measures have not been adopted, the master or ship owners are liable for the damage.

### BILL OF LADING.

**Shipped** in good order, and well conditioned, by James Grant, on board the ship called the *Water Witch*, whereof John Old is master, now lying in the port of Liverpool and bound for New Orleans, **to wit**: One hundred and fifty bales merchandise, marked and numbered as in the margin, which are to be delivered in like good order and condition at the aforesaid port of New Orleans (the acts of God, the public enemies and the perils of the sea only excepted), unto Edward Kirsch or his assigns, he or they paying freight for the said boxes, with primage and average accustomed.

**In Witness Whereof** the master (*or purser*) of the said vessel hath affirmed to three bills of lading, all of this tenor and date, one of which being accomplished, the others to stand void.

Dated in Liverpool, the 8th day of April, 1878.

JOHN OLD, *Master.*

Nos. 1—150.
Edw. Kirsch,
New Orleans.

### ASSIGNMENT OF BILL OF LADING.

**Know all Men by these Presents:** That I, the within named, Edward Kirsch, in consideration of the sum of nine thousand dollars ($9,000), the receipt of which is hereby acknowledged, do by these presents grant, assign and transfer unto Joseph Gale the within written bill of lading, and the full right, title and ownership to all the property therein described. To have and to hold the same unto himself, his heirs and assigns forever. And I do covenant, promise and agree that said bales of merchandise therein described are and shall be free and clear of all debts and encumbrances whatsoever, by or through my means, consent or procurement, except only the proper charges for freight, average and primage.

Given under my hand and seal at New Orleans, this 25th day of May, 1878.

(*Signed*) EDWARD KIRSCH.

A BILL OF SALE is a written instrument by which the ownership of personal property is transferred. It is not necessary that there should be a seal. The validity of the sale does not depend on the actual possession of the goods passing from the seller to the buyer. If the seller retains possession, however, the buyer runs the risk of having the goods attached by third parties having claims against the seller, and will then have to prove *affirmatively* that the sale was in good faith and not to defraud creditors.

A warranty of the seller's title is usual in bills of sale, and such warranty is implied by law, though not stated. On the other hand, warranty of quality or condition must be expressed. The general rule of law is that the buyer must look out for his own interests. But the seller will not be protected where actual fraud has been practiced. Where goods are sold by sample, there is an implied warranty that the goods correspond with the sample.

### GENERAL FORM.

**Know all Men by these Presents:** That I, (*name of seller*), of (*place*), for and in consideration of the sum of (*amount*), to me in hand well and truly paid by (*buyer's name*), the receipt of which is hereby acknowledged, do by these presents grant, bargain, sell and convey unto the said (*buyer's name*), his heirs, executors, administrators and assigns, the following goods and chattels. (*Here describe property.*)

**To Have and to Hold** all the said bargained and granted goods and chattels for the own proper use and behoof of the said (*buyer*), his heirs, executors, administrators and assigns forever. And the said (*seller*) doth hereby vouch himself to be the only lawful owner of said goods and chattels, and doth covenant with said (*buyer*) that he has good right and lawful authority to dispose of said goods and chattels; that they are free from all incumbrances, and that he will warrant and defend the same against the lawful claims and demands of all persons whomsoever.

**In Witness Whereof** the said (*seller*) has hereunto set his hand and seal this — day of ——, A. D. 18—.

*Witness:—*

(*Signature.*) [L. S.]

## BILL OF SALE OF A SHIP.

**To all to whom these Presents shall come, Greeting:**

**Know ye,** that we, John Smith and James Jones, in consideration of the sum of sixty thousand dollars ($60,000), to us in hand paid by Edward Grant, have bargained and sold and transferred to him all the hull and body of the good ship, the Osprey, now lying in the port of New London, together with her masts, spars, rigging, tackle, boats and furniture, and all her other appurtenances, the certificate of whose register is as follows. (*Here give certificate in full.*)

**To Have and to Hold** the same to the said Edward Grant; and we avouch the said John Smith and James Jones to be the owners of said ship with her appurtenances above mentioned, and hereby agree to warrant and defend the said Edward Grant in the peaceable possession of the same against all persons lawfully claiming, or to claim, the same or any part thereof.

**Witness** our hands and seals, this 5th day of May, A.D. 1874.

JOHN SMITH. [L. S.]
JAMES JONES. [L. S.]

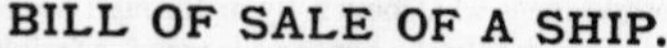

BONDS are written instruments by which one party binds himself to pay another a certain sum of money. If this is all, the bond is called a "simple bond;" but the word bond is more generally applied to bonds with a condition attached, upon fulfillment of which the promise of payment is to be of no effect. The party executing the bond is the *obligor*, the other party the *obligee*, and the amount specified the *penal sum*.

The bond must be sealed, except in States where the use of private seals has been abolished by statute. Under the common law, the use of a seal makes it unnecessary to prove a consideration; it also extends the right of action (under most statutes of limitation) to twenty years.

Should the condition of the bond be not fulfilled, the *obligee* cannot recover the full amount of the penal sum, as might be supposed, but will obtain only principal, interest and expenses, if the condition was the payment of money, or actual damages and costs if the condition was for the doing or not doing of certain things. The penal sum in a bond is usually made double the amount involved in the transaction.

## BOND TO PAY MONEY.

**Know all Men by these Presents:** That I, John Doe, of New York City, am held and firmly bound unto Richard Roe, of the same place, in the sum of ten thousand dollars ($10,000), to be paid to the said Richard Roe, or his certain attorney, executors, administrators or assigns; to which payment well and truly to be made I also bind my heirs, executors, and administrators by these presents. Sealed with my seal, this 4th day of June, A. D. 1881.

**The condition of this obligation** is such that if I, the said John Doe, shall pay to said Richard Roe the sum of five thousand dollars ($5,000) and legal interest, on or before the 4th day of December 1881, then the obligation shall be of no effect and void, but otherwise to remain in full power, force and virtue.

*Sealed and Delivered in the Presence of*
(*Name of witness.*)

(*Signed*) JOHN DOE. [L. S.]

## BOND TO GIVE A DEED.

**Know all Men by these Presents:** That I, ——— ———, of ———, am held and firmly bound unto ————, of ———, in the penal sum of ——— dollars, to be paid to the said ————, his executors, administrators, or assigns; to which payment I hereby bind myself, my heirs, executors, and administrators.

**The condition of this obligation** is such that if the above bounden ————, shall within ——— months from this date make, execute and deliver to the said ———— a good and sufficient deed to convey to the said ———— the (*here describe in full the property to be conveyed*), to hold the same in fee simple absolute with a covenant of warranty of the title, then this obligation shall be void, otherwise of force.

(*Signature.*) [L. S.]

*Signed, Sealed, and Delivered in the Presence of*

## CONDITION OF BOND FOR PERFORMANCE OF CONTRACT.

### TO BE INDORSED ON AN AGREEMENT OR CONTRACT.

(*Make the bond proper as in first form, and add this clause*):

**The condition of this obligation** is such that if the above bounden John Doe, his executors, administrators or assigns, shall in all things well and truly keep, stand to, abide by, and perform all and singular the conditions, covenants and agreements contained in the within instrument, on his or their part to be kept and performed, at the time and in the manner and form therein specified, then the above obligation shall be void, otherwise to be of full virtue and effect.

(*Signed and Sealed as above.*)

PERSONAL as well as real property may be mortgaged. A CHATTEL MORTGAGE is a mortgage of personal property. It is in effect a bill of sale of the goods together with a clause providing for the making the sale void and of no effect upon the payment of the debt for which the mortgage is made. The mortgagor retains possession of the property, and the instrument provides that the mortgagee may enter into possession if the condition of the mortgage is not fulfilled. A man cannot mortgage property which he does not own; hence a chattel mortgage made by a merchant upon all goods which he may hereafter purchase is of no effect. No seal is necessary in a chattel mortgage. If the mortgagor retains possession, the instrument is of no avail as against third parties unless *recorded* in accordance with the law of the place where it is made.

Care must be taken to follow the statutes in regard to NOTICE, FORECLOSURE, RECORDING and EQUITY of REDEMPTION, which is usually sixty days. We give below an abstract of the principal provisions as to chattel mortgages in the States and Territories.

If it can be shown that a mortgage was given to defraud creditors, it will be void.

## FORM OF CHATTEL MORTGAGE.

**Know all Men by these Presents:** That I, Charles Lewis, in consideration of the sum of one hundred dollars ($100), to me in hand paid by Susan Gay, have sold and transferred, and hereby sell and transfer, to her and her assigns, the goods and chattels mentioned in the schedule hereto annexed, marked Schedule A, and subscribed by me.

**This Instrument** is a mortgage given by me to secure to the said Susan Gay and her assigns the payment of the said sum of one hundred dollars with the interest thereon (as promised in a promissory note made by me, bearing date the first day of June, A.D. 1875, payable to the said Susan Gay) six months after date; and it is a condition hereof that if I or my legal representatives or assigns, pay the said Susan Gay, her legal representatives or assigns, such sum of money with the interest thereon, without fraud or delay, this instrument shall be void; and until default therein I am to retain the possession of the same goods and chattels.

But if there shall be any default in the payment of said sum of money, or the interest thereon, or any part thereof, the said Susan Gay, or her legal representatives or assigns, may, with the aid and assistance of any person or persons, enter my dwelling house, store or other premises, or other place where the said goods and chattels are or may be placed, and take and carry them away, and sell and dispose of them for the best price they can obtain, and out of the money arising therefrom retain and pay the said sum above mentioned, with interest and all charges touching the same, rendering the overplus (if any) unto me, my legal representatives or assigns.

**Witness** my hand and seal, June 1, 1875.

(*Signed*) CHARLES LEWIS. [L. S.]

*Executed and delivered in presence of* WILLIAM EDDY. [L. S.]

STATE OF ——, —— COUNTY, *ss.*

This mortgage was acknowledged before me by Charles Lewis, this 1st day of June, 1875. MAX LANT, *J. P.*

## FORM WITH POWER OF SALE.

(*Draw the mortgage as before, and insert this clause before the signature:*)

**Provided, also,** that until default by said mortgagor, or his executors or administrators, in performing the condition aforesaid, it shall be lawful for him to keep possession of and to use and enjoy said granted property; but in case of such default, or in case such goods and chattels are attached by other creditors of said mortgagor at any time before payment, or if said mortgagor, or any person or persons whatsoever, shall attempt to sell, conceal, carry away, or in any way dispose of said property without notice to the said mortgagee, his executors, administrators or assigns, and without his or their written consent, then it shall be lawful for said mortgagee, his executors, administrators or assigns, to take immediate possession of all said granted property to his or their own use, and to sell and dispose of the same at public auction or at private sale, or any part thereof, giving due notice of the time and place of such sale, if public, to the said mortgagor or his legal representatives; and after satisfying the amount of the debt due said mortgagee as above set forth, with interest and all expenses, the surplus, if any there may be, shall be paid over to said mortgagor or his legal representatives.

## LAWS OF THE STATES AND TERRITORIES ON CHATTEL MORTGAGES.

In most of the States mortgages on personal property must be recorded in the place where the grantor lives, and are null and void unless so recorded, as regards creditors and purchasers. This may be assumed to be the case *unless the contrary is expressly stated.* Where the words "recorded *also* in the county where the goods may be" are used, it is to be understood that the mortgage must be recorded in both that county and that which is the residence of the mortgagor, if they are not the same. When mortgagor is non-resident, the record must always be in county where property is situated. If there is delivery of the property, recording is unnecessary.

**Alabama.**—Chattel mortgages must be recorded *also* in the county where the property is, and if removed to a different county from where the grantor resides, must be there recorded within six months.

**Arkansas.**—They must be acknowledged before some person authorized to take acknowledgments by law. After condition broken and suit, judgment is rendered for sale on three months' credit, the purchaser to give bond.

**Arizona.**—Certain classes of property are specified on which mortgage can be placed. If mortgagee has possession of property, recording is not necessary.

**California.**—Only the following may be mortgaged: Railroad rolling stock and locomotives; steamboat, mining and other machinery; printing presses and materials; professional libraries; surgeons', physicians' and dentists' instruments; vessels of more than five tons' burden; growing crops; and upholstery and furniture of hotels and boarding-houses for their purchase money. To hold against creditors, the mortgage must not only be recorded in county where grantor lives, and where property is situated, but must also be accompanied by an affidavit of all parties that it is made in good faith.

**Colorado.**—Not valid as to third parties unless there is actual delivery or acknowledgment before a justice of the peace in the justice's district where grantor lives. No provision as to foreclosure, except when in the form of trust deeds, when the trustee may sell at public auction.

**Connecticut.**—Recorded like deeds of real estate; foreclosed by suit in equity, and property sold by order of court.

**Columbia, District of.**—Recorded within twenty days after execution. If property is exempt from execution the mortgage must be signed by wife of grantor.

**Dakota.**—Original or authenticated copy must be deposited with register of deeds in county where property is situated. Must be renewed every three years. Two witnesses; no other acknowledgment necessary.

**Delaware.**—Recorded within ten days; must be renewed every three years. Foreclosure by order of court; no equity of redemption.

**Florida.**—Recorded like deeds of real estate, unless there is actual transfer of possession. Also executed like deeds. Foreclosure by petition to Circuit Court of county where property lies. When mortgagor retains possession, mortgagee may, upon making affidavit of debt, have an attachment issued before foreclosure is granted.

**Georgia.**—Executed in presence of and attested by a notary public, judge or clerk of court. Should be recorded within three months; but record at any time is due notice. Foreclosure by affidavit before justice, notary or (if non-resident) commissioner for the State, as to debt, filed with clerk of Superior Court of county where *mortgagor* resides. The clerk issues execution. Sale after eight weeks and advertising weekly by sheriff.

**Idaho.**—Recorded *also* in county where goods may be. Affidavit must be made as to good faith and no intention to defraud creditors.

**Illinois.**—Acknowledged before justice of peace in district where

mortgagor lives. Power of sale to sheriff is usually inserted, and he may sell after thirty days' notice; mortgagee may be a purchaser.

**Indiana.**—Acknowledged like deeds of real property. No foreclosure law. The mortgagee may take possession on judgment after an action to recover.

**Iowa.**—Must be acknowledged like deeds. Chattel mortgages for the payment of money may be foreclosed and sold after notice to mortgagor, served and published as in case of sale of real property on execution.

**Kansas.**—Need not be acknowledged. Mortgage or copy is deposited with register of deeds in county where mortgagor lives; the mortgagee must file an affidavit each year that his interest is a continuing one, Property may be seized and sold after notice by handbills posted in four different places in township where sale is to take place, ten days before the sale.

**Kentucky.**—Foreclosure by suit in equity. The mortgagor may redeem property within five years; and five years' possession by mortgagor acts as bar to mortgagee.

**Louisiana.**—Chattel mortgages are unknown to the law in this State.

**Maine.**—If for less than $30, good without delivery or recording; otherwise not. Foreclosed after notice left with mortgagor, or published once a week for three weeks in a paper of the town where mortgage is recorded. The notice, with affidavit of service or copy of publication, must also be recorded. The mortgagor has right of redemption for sixty days after notice is recorded.

**Maryland.**—Acknowledged and recorded within twenty days of date. A seal must be used. Foreclosure by sale, after twenty days' notice by advertisement, or in accordance with terms of the instrument. Mortgagee must give bond to execute any decree made by a court of equity in the premises. Sale must be confirmed by court.

**Massachusetts.**—Recorded within fifteen days in town where mortgagor resides, and also the town or city where he transacts business. Notice to mortgagor personally in writing, or by advertisement once a week for three weeks. In other respects foreclosure as in Maine.

**Michigan.**—No statute provision as to foreclosure. Recorded with town or city clerk. Affidavit as to continuing interest must be filed by mortgagee every year.

**Minnesota.**—Recorded *also* in the city or town where the property is. Foreclosure as in Maine, unless special terms are stipulated in the instrument.

**Mississippi.**—Must be acknowledged. Recorded in office of clerk of Court of Chancery of county where property is. Foreclosed according to terms of instrument.

**Missouri.**—Foreclosed, if for less than $100 (exclusive of interest), by the mortgagee after sixty days' notice, and thirty days' notice of time and place; if for larger amount, by petition to Circuit Court and judgment.

**Montana.**—Valid for one year only after date of record. If mortgagor sells chattel while the lien still exists, the purchaser may demand twice the value thereof, and the mortgagor is also liable criminally for misdemeanor.

**Nebraska.**—Mortgagee must yearly record his continuing interest. Foreclosure by sale at public auction after twenty days' notice.

**New Hampshire.**—Recorded with town clerk with affidavits of both parties as to good faith and actual debt. Sale at auction after thirty days from time condition is broken, and after four days' notice to mortgagor and public. Right of redemption until the sale.

**New Jersey.**—Recorded with register of deeds or county clerk. Copy of mortgage and affidavit of interest must be filed yearly by mortgagee. Foreclosure by suit in equity; no right of redemption.

**New Mexico.**—Mortgagee must file affidavit yearly as to his continuing interest and the extent thereof and the amount remaining due, if payments have been made. Growing crops are not subject to chattel mortgage.

**New York.**—Recording and affidavit as in New Jersey, *etc.* No seal. Foreclosure by seizure and sale after three days' notice, or according to terms of instrument. No right of redemption after sale.

**North Carolina.**—Foreclosure by seizure and sale after twenty days' notice in three public places.

**Ohio.**—Recorded with clerk of township. Mortgagee must file copy and affidavit of his interest and account yearly. Foreclosure as with real estate mortgages.

**Oregon.**—Recorded as in Ohio, *etc.* Mortgagee gains possession by attachment and suit on affidavit of facts.

**Pennsylvania.**—The personal property must be delivered, except the following articles, and the exception is even then not good unless the value is over $500; petroleum or coal oil in bulk; iron tanks and tank cars; iron ore already mined, pig-iron, blooms, rolled and hammered iron in bars or sheets; manufactured slates; saw logs, pickets, laths, spars, lumber (sawed), hewn timber; canal boats; and leases of collieries, factories and other premises. Mortgagee must file statement once a year. Sale by public auction after thirty days' notice to mortgagor, or publication once a week for four weeks. No redemption after sale.

**Rhode Island.**—Foreclosure by seizure and sale. Redemption right for sixty days after breach of condition.

**South Carolina.**—Recorded with register of mesne conveyances within sixty days of date. Seizure and sale. Right of redemption in mortgagor for two years after breach of condition.

**Tennessee.**—Foreclosure by bill in equity.

**Texas.**—Foreclosure by suit based on affidavit. Sale by sheriff after sixty days' notice. No right of redemption after sale.

**Utah.**—No statutory provisions in regard to chattel mortgages.

**Vermont.**—Delivery must be made, except in case of fixed machinery, when mortgage must be executed, acknowledged and recorded like deeds of real estate. Foreclosure by bill in equity. Sale by order of court, which will allow not more than one year for redemption to mortgagor.

**Virginia.**—Recorded, acknowledged and executed like deeds of real property. To avoid necessity of foreclosure by suit in equity, it is common to make the chattel mortgage a trust deed, when the trustee can, of course, sell on breach of condition.

**West Virginia.**—Same law as Virginia.

**Washington.**—Acknowledged and recorded like deeds of real estate, and accompanied by affidavits of both parties as to good faith, *etc.* When the goods pledged are exempt from execution, the wife must join in the mortgage.

**Wisconsin.**—Recorded with town or city clerk. Mortgagee files statement of interest yearly. No foreclosure law; seizure and sale.

**Wyoming.**—Acknowledged and executed like deeds of real estate. Valid as to third parties, when recorded, for two months after time mentioned in the instrument; between the mortgagor and mortgagee, until the period set by the statute of limitations expires. It is a statute felony to sell the goods without the consent of mortgagee.

HE who undertakes as a regular business to convey goods or passengers for a compensation, is a COMMON CARRIER. His liability is greater than that of one who makes a special contract to carry for an individual in a particular instance. The common carrier is considered as an insurer for the safe delivery of goods intrusted to him, and responsible for all loss, except that occasioned by the "act of God" or of the public enemy; even though there has been no negligence on his part. He has a lien upon goods and baggage of passengers for his compensation.

Examples of common carriers are railroads, expressmen, steam and sailing vessels (having an established line and general business) truckmen and stage coaches. A common carrier may also be a warehouseman, wharfinger or forwarding merchant. When he is acting in such a capacity he is liable only for injury caused by his own negligence. The distinction made is this: that when he stores the goods as the agent of the owner or at his express orders, he is a depositary and not a carrier; but when he stores them for his own convenience, and as a matter subordinate to the carriage, he is a carrier and fully liable.

From the public nature of his business, the carrier is not at liberty to refuse to receive goods or passengers, unless the former are dangerous, or the latter are drunk, disorderly or insane. He may, however, demand his compensation in advance, or may refuse upon the ground that his means of conveyance are insufficient. Yet it has been held in the case of railroad companies that the latter is not a valid excuse, and that the company is bound to furnish means of transportation after having sold tickets or received freight.

The carrier is bound to carry his passengers over the whole route agreed upon, or, if accident prevents, to furnish other means of transportation; to provide suitable accommodations for all, and to treat all alike, and is liable for all damage to life, limb or property caused by his negligence in any particular and in the least degree. It has even been held that where a passenger has been put in a position of danger and has incurred injury by attempting to escape, it is not a good defence for the carrier to show that he would have been unharmed if he had not made such attempt.

Goods must be delivered in time, way, and place as agreed with the sender, and only to the consignee or his accredited agent. If the consignee will not or cannot take the goods, the carrier must keep them subject to the owner's order, and is then only liable as a warehouseman. Such directions as, "This side up," "Glass, with care," or "To be kept dry," must be complied with, unless unreasonable from the nature of the case.

What constitutes *good delivery* of the property? This depends greatly on the nature of the goods. Thus a box or parcel may, and should, be delivered at the house or office of the consignee. This is usually done by what are known in this country as express companies, but not by railroad or steamboat companies. Goods in bulk, as coal or lumber, must be left at the wharf or freight depot nearest the consignee, to which the carrier has access. Notice should be given by the carrier, upon the arrival of the goods at such place, to the consignee. It has been held that this is obligatory with carriers by water, but not with railroad companies.

Stoppage in transitu is the right which the seller of goods upon credit has to recall them while in the hands of the common carrier or warehouseman, upon learning of the insolvency of the purchaser. The carrier may hold the goods until he can determine whether the right really exists. If he delivers them to the wrong party he is liable to the full value of the property. If the goods are claimed by a third party (not the consignor or consigneee) he also acts at his own risk in either delivering or not delivering them; but he may ask for evidence of the claimant's title, and if not satisfied, may demand security.

The common carrier has a right to retain goods until he receives his compensation, and, this being refused, he may, after a reasonable delay, sell them at auction, after notice and public advertisement. The balance, after paying his dues, if any, must be paid over to the owner.

We have said that the carrier is not liable for the "act of God" or the public enemy, or (in shipping) for the perils of the sea. But *fire*, unless caused by lightning, does not come under these exceptions. Robbery or theft will not relieve him from liability, however ample his precautions and care. In all cases the act of an agent is the act of the carrier himself. When the carrier undertakes to forward the goods beyond the end of his own route by another common carrier, his liability ceases when they are fairly in the possession of the second. But it is a common thing with railway companies to unite or "pool" in the business and profits over a long route of which each controls part. They are then all liable for a loss on any part of the combined line.

It is clear that the general principles as to liability above stated may be done away with by special agreement between the carrier and the owner. It is, therefore, usual for all general carrying companies to give notice to owners of what obligations they are unwilling to accept and what regulations they require to be followed, by means of printed receipts or bills of lading. We give below the form of receipt used by one of our large express companies. In order to make such a notice a binding contract, it must be shown that the stipulations were brought to the knowledge of the consignor. Thus it was held, in a case where a passenger was a German and the printed ticket was in English, that the railroad company must prove that he had actual knowledge of the stipulations. But showing common usage will often suffice.

Free passes on railroads often contain a stipulation that the company are not liable for injury to the holder. In the absence of such agreement, the holder has all the rights of other passengers. Even when it is made, the company will be liable for *gross* negligence.

When an employee or agent of the company is injured through the fault of a fellow servant, he cannot claim damages from the company, unless it has also been negligent in the matter, as in providing unsafe machinery.

## FREIGHT RECEIPT.

[DUPLICATE.]

UNION EXPRESS COMPANY,
FAST FREIGHT LINE,
*April* 4, 1882.

Received from John Doe, the following packages, in apparent good order, contents and value unknown:

Advanced charges, $4.25.

RATES.

Double 1st class — cents per 100 lbs.
1st class....... — cents per 100 lbs.
2d class....... — cents per 100 lbs.
3d class....... — cents per 100 lbs.
4th class....... — cents per 100 lbs.
As per classification on back.

Marked and numbered as in the margin, to be forwarded by railroad and delivered at Easton, upon payment of freight therefor, as noted in the margin, subject to the conditions and rules on the back hereof, and those of the several railroads over which the property is transported, which constitute a part of this contract.

(*Signed*) WM. SMITH, *Agent*.

## EXPRESS COMPANY'S RECEIPT.

[*No.* —. *Not Negotiable.*] ADAMS EXPRESS COMPANY.

**Received** of John Doe, at New York, N. Y., May 12, 1881 (*description of goods.*) Value $—. For which this company charges $—.
**Marked**: Richard Roe, Chicago, Ill.

Which it is mutually agreed is to be forwarded to our agency nearest or most convenient to destination only, and there delivered to other parties to complete the transportation.

It is part of the consideration of this contract, and it is agreed, that the said express company are *forwarders only*, and are not to be held liable or responsible for any loss or damage to said property while being conveyed by the *carriers* to whom the same may be by said express company intrusted, or arising from the dangers of railroad, ocean or river navigation, steam, fire in stores, depots or in transit, leakage, breakage, or from any cause whatever; unless in every case, the same be proved to have occurred from the fraud or gross negligence of said express company or their servants; nor, in any event, shall the holder hereof demand beyond the sum of $50, at which the article forwarded is hereby valued, unless otherwise herein expressed, or unless specially insured by them and so specified in this receipt, which insurance shall constitute the limit of the liability of The ADAMS EXPRESS COMPANY. And if the same is entrusted or delivered to any other express company or agent (which said Adams Express Company are hereby authorized to do) such company or person so selected shall be regarded exclusively as the agent of the shipper or owner, and as such alone liable, and the Adams Express Company shall not be, in any event, responsible for the negligence or non-performance of such company or person; and the shipper and owner hereby severally agree that all the stipulations and agreements in this receipt contained shall extend to and inure to the benefit of each and every company or person to whom the Adams Company may entrust or deliver the above described property for transportation, and shall define and limit the liability therefor of such other company or person. In no event shall the Adams Express Company be liable for any loss or damage unless the claim therefor shall be presented to them, in writing, at this office, within thirty days after date, in a statement to which this receipt shall be annexed. All articles of glass, or contained in glass, or of a fragile nature, will be taken at the shipper's risk only, and the shipper agrees that the company shall not be held responsible for any injury by breakage or otherwise, nor for damage to goods not properly packed and secured for transportation. It is further agreed that said company shall not, in any event, be liable for any loss, damage or detention caused by the acts of God, civil or military authority, or by rebellion, piracy, insurrection or riot, or the dangers incident to a time of war, or by any riotous or armed assemblage. If any sum of money, besides the charges for transportation, is to be collected from the consignee on delivery of the above described property, and the same is not paid within thirty days from the date hereof, the shipper agrees that this company may return said property to him at the expiration of said time, subject to the conditions of this receipt, and that he will pay the charges for transportation both ways, and that the liability of this company for such property while in its possession for the purpose of making such collection, shall be that of warehousemen only.

(*Signed*) *For the Company*,
JOHN SMITH.

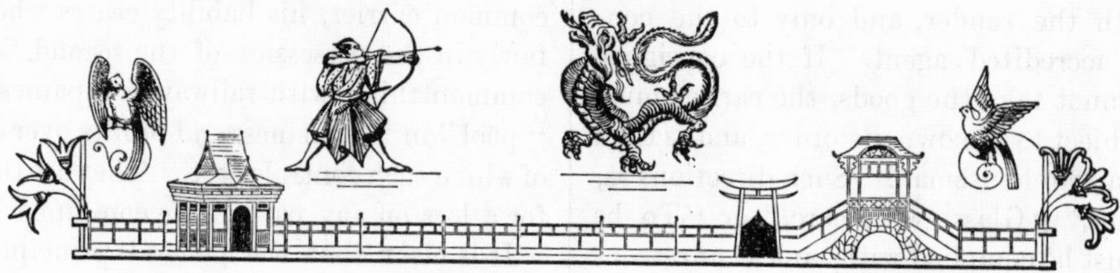

WHEN two or more persons agree, upon sufficient consideration, to do or not to do a certain thing, the result is a CONTRACT.

Contracts may be in express terms or implied by acts of the parties; they may be made by word of mouth or in writing, but by the "Statute of Frauds," in force both in England and United States, it is required that a contract shall be in writing and signed by the party charged thereby or his authorized representative: 1. When it is not to be performed within one year from the making thereof. 2. When it is to charge any person to answer for the debt or default of another, or to charge an executor or administrator to answer damages out of his own estate. 3. When made in consideration of marriage, except mutual promises to marry. 4. When the contract is for the sale of lands or some interest in real property, except leases for not more than three years. 5. In case of the sale of personal property beyond a certain value (in England, £10; in most of the United States, $50) unless there was delivery in part of the goods or payment in whole or part. In all these cases by common law the consideration must be stated in the writing, unless it is under seal. But the consideration may be merely nominal.

The essence of the contract is the actual agreement or coming together of the minds of the two parties; that is, there must be proposal on the one side and acceptance on the other, and the promises implied form the mutual considerations and make the contract. The proposal may be revoked any time before acceptance, but not after. Thus if a proposal is made to me for a sale of certain goods at a certain price, and I write and post a letter accepting the proposal, the contract is complete and can be enforced by law. In a very recent English case it was held that this is true, even though the letter posted never reaches its destination.

Who can make a contract? Persons of either sex under twenty-one years of age cannot for most purposes bind themselves by promises. An exception is the case of necessaries of life, when not furnished by those whose duty it is to do so. But a minor may after coming of age confirm a promise previously made. One wholly bereft of reason cannot contract. A person so drunk as to be incapable of knowing what he is doing cannot bind himself to one who knows his condition. By common law a married woman is incapable of making a contract. But this rule has in many places been modified or done away with by statute. (See RIGHTS OF MARRIED WOMEN.)

Contracts are said to be *voidable* when they may be legally annulled or avoided, but until then have force and effect. Thus a contract by an infant with an adult may be either affirmed or made void by the former when he comes of age. *Void* contracts are such as the law altogether refuses to recognize. Such are agreements made for an illegal consideration or in opposition to public morality; agreements in restraint of trade, except for a limited time; agreements in restraint of marriage (as opposed to public policy), and agreements for the suppression of criminal prosecutions. Fraud of any kind or concealment of such facts as a party is legally bound to disclose will void a contract. But the general rule of law is "let the buyer beware," and unless the concealment was of facts of importance, which it was impossible, in the nature of the case, for him to discover, it will not void the contract. Neither is a merely "hard bargain" ground for relief at law. A contract made under *duress* or force is void. A *naked* contract is one made without consideration, and therefore void.

Misspelling or bad punctuation will not void a contract, if the meaning of the parties is clear. A contract written with pencil is not void for that reason, but ink should always be used. Contracts made on Sunday are void, but if written on that day and delivered on another, they will hold good.

In drawing a contract technical language is not necessary, and had better be avoided. The instrument should be made and executed in duplicate, and a copy kept by each of the contracting parties. It should contain :—1. The true date. 2. The full names and titles of the parties, who may be conveniently distinguished and referred to as "the party of the first part," "the party of the second part," *etc.* 3. The subject matter of the contract, with full details and specifications, and time and place of performance. 4. The covenants, warranties, forfeitures or penalties to be performed or incurred. 5. The signatures of the parties or their authorized agents, and of the witnesses. An agent should sign thus: A. B., by his agent (or attorney) C. D.

## CONTRACT—SHORT GENERAL FORM.

**This Agreement Witnesseth**: That A. B., of (*place of residence and profession or business*), and C. D., of (*as before*), have agreed together at (*place*), this —— day of ——, A. D. 18—, and do hereby mutually agree and promise to each other, as follows: The said A. B., in consideration of the promises hereinafter made by the said C. D., and in consideration of (*here state any other consideration A. B. may have, as money received*), doth promise, covenant, and agree with said C. D. that (*here set out in detail what A. B. undertakes to perform*).

And said C. D., in consideration of the promises hereinbefore made by A. B., *etc.*, (*as before*), doth on his part covenant and agree with said A. B. that (*here state what C. D. undertakes to do*).

**Witness** our hands and seals to two copies of this agreement interchangeably.

*Signed, Sealed, and Interchanged in Presence of* E. F. G. H. (*Signed*) A. B. [L. S.] C. D. [L. S.]

## FORM WITH LIQUIDATED DAMAGES.

(LIQUIDATED DAMAGES are sums of money agreed and fixed upon by the parties as a forfeit or penalty for non-compliance. The sum mentioned will be considered by a court to be liquidated or fixed when from the nature of the case it appears that the parties have in advance agreed upon the sum after fair calculation and adjustment, or when it is impossible to fix the amount of actual damage by any rule. Otherwise the sum mentioned will not necessarily be awarded, but the measure of damages will be the actual loss incurred.)

*Insert this clause*:—And for the true and faithful performance of each and all the promises and agreements above made and described, the said parties bind themselves, each to the other, in the sum of —— dollars, as liquidated damages, to be paid by the failing party.

## FOR SALE OF REAL ESTATE.

**Articles of Agreement**, made this —— day of ——, in the year of our Lord one thousand eight hundred and ——, between A. B., party of the first part, and C. D., party of the second part, **Witnesseth**: That said A. B., in consideration of the sum of —— dollars, to be paid as hereinafter mentioned, shall on or before the —— day of —— next ensuing, well and sufficiently grant, sell and release unto the party of the second part, his heirs and assigns, all that tract or parcel of land situated in ——, and described as follows, **to wit**: (*give description of lot or parcel by boundaries*), by a good and sufficient warranty deed. That said conveyance shall be at the costs of said party of the second part (excepting only counsel fees), and shall contain the usual covenants, that said premises are free from all demands and incumbrances whatsoever at the time of such conveyance, and all other reasonable and usual conveyances. That said party of the second part, in consideration thereof, shall well and truly pay unto said party of the first part the sum of —— dollars, in manner and form following, **to wit**: the sum of —— dollars, cash in hand, the receipt of which is hereby acknowledged, and the balance (*state terms of part payments, if any*), the entire sum to be paid in full at or before the time herein fixed for the execution of said conveyance. And in case of the failure of said party of the second part to make such payment as above specified, this agreement shall be forfeited and of no effect, if so determined by the party of the first part; and all payments already made shall be forfeited to said party of the first part, and by him retained in full liquidation of all damages by him sustained, and he, the said party of the first part, shall have the legal right to re-enter and take full possession of the premises above described. (*Executed as in first form.*)

## CONTRACT FOR SERVICES.

**Memorandum of an Agreement** made this —— day of —— A. D. 18—, between A. B. and C. D.

The said A. B. agrees to serve C. D. as foreman in his business of machinist in the City of Cleveland, Ohio, for one year from this date, at a salary of eighteen hundred dollars per annum, payable in equal monthly payments on the last day of each month by said C. D. And the said A. B. agrees to devote all his attention and skill to that business and superintend the same under the directions of the said C. D., as they may from time to time be given him; and at all times to furnish said C. D. with any desired information concerning the business. (*Executed as in first form.*)

## FORM OF BUILDING CONTRACT.

**Articles of Agreement**, made this —— day of ——, A. D. 18—, between A. B. of the first part, and C. D. of the second part. The party of the second part doth **Agree, Promise,** and **Covenant**, to and with the party of the first part, that he, said party of the second part, will erect, build and complete, or cause to be erected, built and completed, on the land of the party of the first part situated as follows, to wit: (*describe lot by number and bounds*), a good and substantial dwelling house of the dimensions, description and materials mentioned and specified in the paper hereto annexed and bearing even date herewith, marked "Specifications of Dwelling House, Work and Materials" and signed by said parties, and according to a plan made by E. F., architect, with reference to which said specifications are drawn; and said party of the second part agrees to furnish and provide at his own expense all materials, tools, workmen and foremen, necessary for the erecting and completing of said dwelling house according to said specifications, and to deliver said building to said party of the first part, completely finished and ready for occupancy, on the —— day of ——, A. D. 18—, unless such delivery be prevented by accidental fire, not occurring from neglect of any kind upon his part.

The party of the first part, in consideration of the agreements and covenants aforesaid, to be performed by said party of the second part, doth on his side promise, agree, and covenant to and with said party of the second part, that upon said party of the second part performing said covenants and agreements, he will pay or cause to be paid unto said party of the second part, for completing and erecting said building in the manner aforesaid, and providing the materials therefor, the sum of —— thousand dollars in the following manner, to wit: (*Here describe terms of payment, as: "one third at the execution of this agreement, the receipt of which is hereby acknowledged by said party of the second part; one third, when the walls are built, the roof completed and the floors laid; and one third when the house is fully completed and delivered to said party of the first part on said —— day of ——, A. D.* 18—).

**And it is hereby further agreed:** That the party of the first part may make, or require to be made, alterations in the plans of construction and specifications, without annulling this agreement; and that in case of such alterations, the increase or diminution of expense occasioned thereby shall be estimated, as far as possible, in accordance with the price fixed by these presents for the whole work and materials, and allowances shall be made on one side or the other as the case may be. And in case the parties fail to agree as to the allowances to be made for such changes, or in case the parties fail to agree in regard to any conditions or covenants herein contained or to the performance of the same, then such disagreement shall be referred to three disinterested persons, one to be chosen by each party and they to choose another, as arbitrators, and the decision in writing of any two of them to be final.

**And it is further agreed,** that if there shall be any delay on the part of the party of the second part in erecting or completing said building, that in the opinion of the superintendent will prevent its being completed on the day herein specified, then the party of the first part may, at his option, either employ persons other than the party of the second part to do the whole or any part of said work and furnish the whole or any part of said materials, and deduct the cost of the same from the sum hereinbefore mentioned to be paid by the party of the first part; or he may leave the completion of said building unto the party of the second part and enforce his claim for damages, should said building not be completed on the day specified.

**And it is further agreed,** that if said building shall not be completed by said —— day of ——, A. D. 18—, the party of the second part shall forfeit the sum of —— dollars for each and every day from and after that date during which the said building shall remain unfinished and not completed, to be deducted from the sum to be paid by said party of the first part.

And for the true performance of the aforesaid **Agreements, Promises,** and **Covenants,** and on their parts respectively, the said parties bind themselves, each to the other, in the penal sum of —— dollars. (*Executed as before.*)

(*To this annex plans and specifications, which cannot be too exact and minute.*)

# DAMAGES.

REPARATION in money for injury to property or person is known in law as DAMAGES.

NOMINAL DAMAGES will be awarded when, though there has been a breach of contract, no actual loss has been sustained by the injured party. The actual loss sustained is usually the measure of damages to be awarded. Thus, where a price is set in the contract, and performance of the bargain has been made in part only, the measure of damages will be the contract price, or, if not practicable, the actual value of the goods furnished or services rendered. Any expenditure or outlay which has been actually made under the contract will be considered, but *anticipated* profits or benefits cannot be included in the damages. When the contract is to deliver goods on demand, their value at the time demand is made will be the measure; when time and place for delivery are fixed, the value of the goods at such time and place will be the measure.

With common carriers the rule is, that upon total failure to deliver, the carrier is liable for the value of goods at the place of destination, together with interest thereon, and deducting the freight. If he fails to take the goods for transportation, then he must pay the difference in value at the place of destination and of shipment, less freight. When there is delay in the delivery, the changes in market value will be considered.

Where the contract is for services for a certain time and at a fixed rate of compensation, if the employer discharges the employee before the time agreed upon has elapsed, and without good cause, the employee may claim full compensation for the whole time upon showing that he was ready and willing at all times to perform his part of the contract. If he engages in other work, and receives compensation therefor, deduction may be made from his claims.

VINDICTIVE OR EXEMPLARY DAMAGES are awarded in cases where the injury inflicted is of a nature that cannot be compensated in money by any fixed rule or calculation, or when the wrong-doing of the injuring party requires the infliction of a punishment for public policy or the sake of public morals. Thus, where one is injured in a railway accident, and the company are clearly to blame, not only the actual loss from medical services, attendance, loss of employment, etc., will be considered, but also the physical suffering, mental anguish, general loss of health, and the degree of culpability on the part of the company will be taken into account. This is sometimes called "smart money."

As a rule, *interest* is not to be recovered upon claims for damages which are unliquidated (*i.e.*, not fixed or certain), nor in actions founded upon *torts* (*i.e.*, wrongs or injuries inflicted).

*Contributory negligence* exists when the plaintiff has himself been in some degree in fault. He cannot then recover damages.

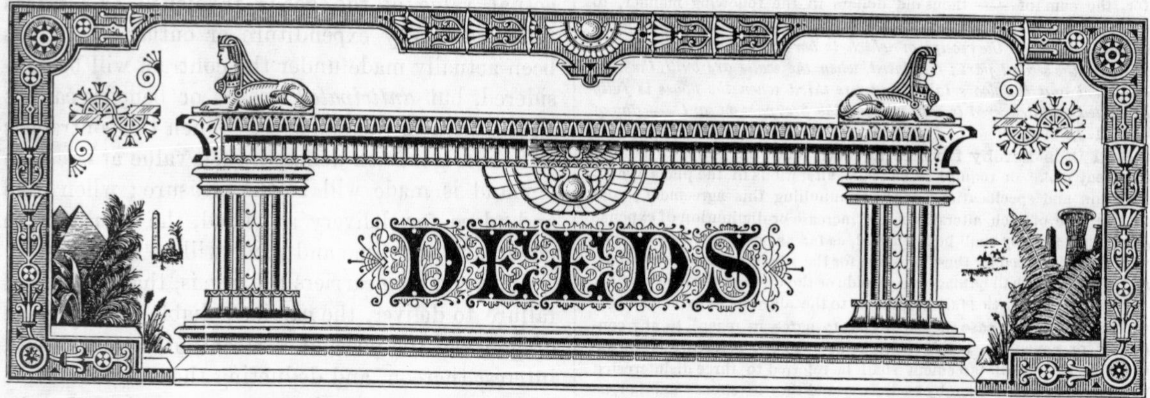


A DEED is an instrument in writing and under seal, whereby real property or some interest therein is conveyed.

A *deed poll* is one executed by a single party, as distinguished from an *indenture*, which purports to be executed by several parties. The difference is one of form rather than of meaning; the deed poll purports to be a direct *grant* from the grantor, while the indenture is in form of an *agreement* between the grantor and grantee.

A QUIT-CLAIM DEED conveys all the right, title and interest in and to the land possessed by the grantor, and *only* that. In other words, there is no warranty that the grantor has any title to convey. Such a deed should never be accepted when a warranty deed can be obtained. To make the deed clearly a quit-claim, the words "release and quit-claim" should be used, instead of the usual words of conveyance, "give, grant, sell and convey," as it is thought by some authorities that the latter words *imply* a certain assertion of title.

The DEED must be made by a party legally capable of making contracts, and to a party able to be contracted with (*see* CONTRACTS). It must be signed with ink distinctly, or if the grantor cannot write, his mark must be attested. If signed by an agent or attorney, the seal should be that of the principal, and the authority of the agent to use the seal should itself be under seal. The statute requirements as to signing, sealing and acknowledgment must be minutely observed, as a formal error is fatal. We give below the requirements of the different States and Territories, which are far from uniform. Any interlineation or erasure must be explained in writing on the face of the instrument, and the explanation duly attested.

The CONSIDERATION on which the deed is based may be either *good* (as for love and affection), or *valuable* (as for money or other property). It is customary, though not necessary, to mention some nominal sum, as one dollar, or one pound, even when no money price is paid. The seller is not so far bound by his acknowledgment of the receipt of the price paid as to prevent him from suing to recover it, and proving that it has not in fact been paid.

The PROPERTY to be conveyed should be described by boundaries as minutely as possible. It is customary to refer to previous deeds of the same property, which by this reference become themselves a part of the deed last made.

The estate passes upon the actual delivery of the deed. If it is retained until the grantor's death, it becomes void and of no effect. But where it is delivered to a third person to transfer to the grantee upon the happening of some event, as the death of the grantor, the estate will pass upon that final delivery. Such a deed is called an ESCROW.

It is always best that the execution of the deed should be witnessed, even though not required by statute. A witness should have no interest in the deed. Therefore a wife is not a proper witness of a deed to her husband. If witnesses are dead, proof of their handwriting will be admitted; if this cannot be obtained, proof of the grantor's handwriting is sufficient. As between parties, acknowledgment is not necessary to make the deed valid, but it cannot be recorded without such acknowledgment before an officer appointed by law to receive it, as a justice of the peace, or, if the land is situated in a different State from the one where the deed is executed, a commissioner for the State where the land is. If the deed is executed in a foreign country, it should be acknowledged before a consular agent of the country where the land is situated.

The object of the public recording of a deed is not to give validity as between the grantor and grantee, but to protect the grantee against subsequent *bona fide* purchasers or mortgagees, and against the grantor's creditors. Copies from the records have the same force as the records themselves. An acknowledged deed is considered as recorded from the minute it reaches the hands of the legal recording officer, and not from the time when he actually writes the copy. A deed not recorded is perfectly valid as against a deed subsequently obtained, even though recorded, *provided* that the second grantees had knowledge of the first conveyance; and this even though they have paid a full price.

The COVENANTS usually made in a deed are: 1. That the grantor is lawfully seized (or possessed) of the land; 2. That he has good right to convey; 3. That the land is free from incumbrances; 4. That the grantee shall quietly enjoy; 5. That the grantor will warrant and defend. The covenants of warranty and quiet enjoyment are said to "run with the land," because they may be taken advantage of by the heirs and assigns of the original grantee.

Deeds are construed according to the intent of the parties, so far as it can be ascertained from the instrument itself. When the terms are doubtful they are construed in favor of the grantee and against the grantor.

TAX DEEDS are made by a public officer after sale of the land for non-payment of taxes. They differ from common deeds in that they do not *in themselves* transfer title. That is to say, any irregularity or illegality in the sale or other proceedings on which the deed is based will invalidate the deed itself. In many States the grantee of such a deed holds the property subject to the right of the owner to redeem it within a specified time, by paying taxes, costs and interest on the purchase money, at a fixed rate, greater than the usual rate of interest.

## FORMS OF DEEDS.

(It is of course impracticable to give here the various forms of deeds used in the different States. Printed blanks of such forms may be readily obtained in the several localities. The forms here given will illustrate the general method of drawing deeds.)

### QUIT-CLAIM DEED.

**(With Covenant against Acts of Grantor.)**

**This Conveyance,** made the — day of —, between A. B., of (*residence*), of the first part, and C. D., of (*residence*), of the second part, **Witnesseth.**

That the said party of the first part, for and in consideration of the sum of (*amount*) lawful money, to him in hand paid by the party of the second part, at or before the sealing and delivery of these presents, the receipt whereof is hereby acknowledged, hath remised, released and quit-claimed, and by these presence doth remise, release and quit-claim unto the party of the second part, and to his heirs and assigns forever, all (*describe accurately the land or premises granted*): together with all and singular the tenements, hereditaments and appurtenances thereunto belonging, or in any wise appertaining; and the reversion and reversions, remainder and remainders, rents, issues and profits thereof. And also all the estate, right, title and interest (*insert "dower and right of dower," if necessary*), property, possession, claim and demand whatsoever, as well in law as in equity, of the said party of the first part, of, in or to the above described premises, and every part and parcel thereof, with the appurtenances:—**To Have and to Hold** all and singular the above mentioned and described premises, together with the appurtenances, unto the said party of the second part, his heirs and assigns forever.

And the said party of the first part, for himself and his heirs, executors and administrators, doth covenant, promise and agree to and with the said party of the second part, his heirs, executors, administrators and assigns, that he hath not made, done or committed, executed or suffered any act or acts, thing or things whatsoever, whereby or by means whereof the above mentioned and described premises, or any part or parcel thereof, now are, or at any time hereafter, shall or may be impeached, charged or incumbered in any way or manner whatever.

**In Witness Whereof,** the said party of the first part has hereunto set his hand and seal the day and year before written.

A. B. [L. S.]

*Sealed and Delivered in Presence of*

STATE OF ——, COUNTY OF ——, ss.

On this —— day of ——, in the year ——, before me personally came A. B., who is known by me to be the person described in, and who executed, the foregoing instrument, and acknowledged that he executed the same.

(*Signature.*) [L. S.]

### SHORT WARRANTY DEED.

(*Used in New York.*)

**To all People to whom these Presents shall come, Greeting:—Know ye** that I, A. B., of ——, —— county, State of ——, of the first part, for the consideration of (*amount*), the receipt of which is hereby acknowledged, of C. D., of ——, in —— county, State of ——, of the second part, do grant, bargain, sell and confirm unto the said C. D., his heirs and assigns, all (*here give minute description of property by boundaries*):—**To Have and to Hold** the above granted and bargained premises, with the appurtenances thereof, unto the said C. D., his heirs and assigns to his and their proper use and behoof forever. And I do, for myself, and my heirs, executors and administrators, covenant with the said C. D., his heirs and assigns, that at and until the ensealing of

these presents, I am well seized of the premises as a good and indefeasible estate in fee simple, and have good right to bargain and sell the same, in manner and form aforesaid; and that the same is free from all incumbrance whatever. And further, I do by these presents bind myself, and my heirs, to warrant and forever defend the above granted and bargained premises unto the said C. D., his heirs and assigns, against all claims and demands whatsoever.

**In Witness Whereof** I have hereunto set my hand and seal the year and day above written.

A. B. [L. S.]

## COVENANTS.

*(To be inserted as may be necessary.)*

THAT THE GRANTOR IS LAWFULLY SEIZED.—And the said A. B., for himself and his heirs, executors and administrators, doth covenant, grant and agree to and with the said party of the second part, his heirs and assigns, that the said party of the first part, at the time of the sealing and delivery of these presents, is lawfully seized in his own right, of a good, absolute and indefeasible estate of inheritance in fee simple, of and in all and singular the above granted and described premises, with the appurtenances, and hath good right, full power, and lawful authority to grant, bargain, sell and convey the same, in manner aforesaid.

FOR "QUIET ENJOYMENT."—And that the said party of the second part, his heirs and assigns, shall at all times hereafter, peaceably and quietly have, use, hold, occupy, possess and enjoy the above granted premises, and every part and parcel thereof, with the appurtenances, without any let, suit, trouble, molestation, eviction or disturbance of the said party of the first part, his heirs or assigns, or of any other person or persons lawfully claiming or to claim the same.

THAT THERE ARE NO INCUMBRANCES.—And that the same now are free, clear, discharged and unincumbered of and from all former and other grants, titles, charges, estates, judgments, taxes, assessments and incumbrances, of whatever nature or kind soever.

TO EXECUTE FURTHER CONVEYANCES IF NECESSARY.—And also that the said party of the first part and his heirs, and all and every person or persons, whomsoever, lawfully or equitably deriving any estate right, title, or interest of, in or to the herein granted premises, by, from, under or in trust for him or them, shall and will, at all time or times hereafter, upon the reasonable request, and the proper costs and charges in the law, of the said party of the second part, his heirs and assigns, make, do and execute, or cause to be made, done and executed, all and every such further and other lawful and reasonable acts, conveyances and assurances in the law, for the better and more effectually resting and confirming the premises herein granted, or so intended to be, in and to the said party of the second part, his heirs and assigns, forever, as by the said party of the second part, his heirs or assigns, or his or their counsel, learned in the law, shall be reasonably advised, desired or required.

CLAUSE FOR A TRUST DEED.—**To Have and to Hold** the same, together with all and singular the tenements, hereditaments and appurtenances thereunto belonging, or in anywise appertaining, forever, in fee: **In Trust,** nevertheless, and to and for the uses, interests and purposes hereinafter limited, described and declared; that is to say, in trust, to *(here state the purposes and nature of the trust)*.

TO WAIVE HOMESTEAD AND DOWER.—And the said party of the first part, A. B., and M. B., his wife, hereby expressly waive, release and relinquish unto the said party of the second part, the said grantee, his heirs, executors and administrators and assigns, all right, title, claim, interest and benefit whatever in and to the above described premises and each and every part thereof, which is given by or results from all laws of this State pertaining to the exemption of homesteads: PROVIDED that the said grantor and his heirs and assigns may hold and enjoy said premises, and the rents, issues and profits thereof, until default shall be made as aforesaid, and that when the said note and all expenses accruing hereby shall be fully paid, the said grantee or his legal representatives, shall reconvey all the estate acquired hereby in said premises, or any part thereof, then remaining unsold to (and at the cost of) the said grantor or his heirs, assigns or representatives. *(This form is to be used in a trust deed to secure a note; the first part or waiver may be used in any deed.)*

## ABSTRACT OF THE LAWS OF THE STATES AND TERRITORIES OF THE UNITED STATES RELATING TO DEEDS.

IN THE FOLLOWING STATES NO SEAL OR SCROLL NEED BE USED: Alabama, Arkansas, California, Indiana, Iowa, Kansas, Kentucky, Louisiana, Nebraska, Tennessee, Arizona, Dakota and Montana. In the other States and Territories a seal of some kind is requisite. In most States a scroll or scrawl is sufficient. The exceptions are: Massachusetts, New Hampshire, New York, Rhode Island and Vermont.

**Alabama.**—One witness is required; acknowledgment before judges of a court of record or their clerks, justices of the peace or notary public. The husband must join in a conveyance of a wife's separate property. The wife may relinquish her right of dower by joining the husband in a conveyance and acknowledging the relinquishment. **Arkansas.**—Two witnesses required, either for the execution or acknowledgment; the latter before the same officers as in Alabama. **Arizona** and **Dakota.**—Acknowledgment may be made at any place in the Territory before a justice or clerk of the Supreme Court, or of any court of record, a justice of the peace, a mayor of a city, or a register of deeds. The officer taking the acknowledgment must affix thereto his official seal. All rights of *dower* and *curtesy* are abolished. In Arizona the wife must be examined apart from her husband to ascertain if she acts by her own free will, and without undue influence on his part. In Dakota the wife need not join in conveying property of the husband, except in case of homesteads. **California.**—Deeds are known as grants. Two witnesses are required. Acknowledgment may be made before the recorder of the county where the land is situated, or the other usual officers. Husband or wife can convey *separate* property without the other joining, but both must join when the property is owned in common. **Colorado.**—No witnesses required expressly. Acknowledgment should be in the county where the land lies. The whole estate conveyed passes unless there is an express limitation. **Columbia, District of.**—Acknowledgment is before any judge, justice of the peace, notary public, or commissioner of the Circuit Court of the district in the place where the person making the deed lives. The officer must annex to the deed a certificate under his hand and seal. **Connecticut.**—Two witnesses. Acknowledgment before a judge of a court of record, justice of the peace, notary public, town clerk, commissioner of the Superior Court, or commissioner of the school fund. Recording to be done by town clerk of the town where lands are situated. Wife must join with husband in conveyance of her separate real estate, but not in that of his own. **Delaware.**—One witness is sufficient. Deeds must be recorded in the county where the land lies, within one year. Wife must relinquish her right of dower, and is to be examined separately, and the examination certified. **Florida.**—At least two witnesses are necessary. Deeds are acknowledged before any judge, justice of the peace, or notary public, or before the clerk of a Circuit Court. They must be recorded within six months after delivery, or are void as against creditors, subsequent purchasers, or mortgagees for value. The right of dower must be relinquished by the wife's joining in conveyance with the husband. **Georgia.**—At least two witnesses are necessary. If not recorded within one year, the deed loses priority over a subsequent deed recorded within the year. The right of dower need not be relinquished, except in conveying lands to which the husband gained title through the wife, prior to the statute of 1866. **Idaho.**—No witnesses are required. Acknowledgment as in Dakota. No rights of dower or curtesy exist. The husband must join in conveying the real estate of the wife, who must be examined separately as to free will, etc. **Illinois.**—No witnesses required. Acknowledgment in county where land lies and before any of the usual officers. Husband and wife must join in conveying property of either, and dower is released by the wife's thus joining. No deed will release or waive homestead right, unless it is so expressly stated both in the deed and certificate of acknowledgment. **Indiana.**—No witnesses required. It is not necessary to use the words "heirs and assigns." The recording must be in the recorder's office of the county where the land lies, and within ninety days of the execution. There is no right of dower or curtesy. Husband and wife must join in conveying

the separate estate of the wife. **Iowa.**—No witnesses are necessary. Acknowledgment and recording under the usual rules. The wife should join husband in conveying, whether the property is her separate estate or not. **Kansas.**—No witness necessary. Corporations only use a private seal. Must be recorded in office of register of deeds for the county where the land lies. Married women must join in the conveyance, unless non-resident. Separate examination of the wife is not required. **Kentucky.**—No witnesses are required. Acknowledgment may be before the clerk of a county court. The deed must be recorded within sixty days from the date; but four months is allowed to non-residents, and, if living out of the United States, twelve months. The record dates from the time when the clerk's fee is paid. Separate examination of married women is not necessary. **Louisiana.**—Acknowledgment before a notary public or recorder, besides whom there should be two witnesses. Recording in the *parish* where the land lies. Husband and wife must join in conveying the separate estate of either. There must be separate examination of the wife as to her free will and knowledge of the nature of the act. **Maine.**—One witness is required; two customary. Acknowledgment before a justice of the peace. Wife must join in order to release her right of dower. No separate examination is required. **Maryland.**—At least one witness is necessary. Deeds must be recorded within six months from the date of execution; when property lies in more than one county, or in the City of Baltimore and a county adjoining, the deed must be recorded in each of them. The wife must join in deeds for fee simple to release her dower. No separate examination is required. **Massachusetts.**—Witnesses are not necessary. To bar dower, the wife must join husband in a conveyance. A separate examination is not required. **Michigan.**—At least two witnesses are needed. The deed must be recorded in the county where the land lies. When a wife joins in the deed, her acknowledgment must be taken separately. She may convey her separate estate without her husband's joining. **Minnesota.**—Two witnesses are necessary. The deed must be acknowledged and recorded in the county where the property is situated. Dower is released by the wife's joining in a conveyance with her husband. Separate acknowledgment is not required. **Mississippi.**—At least two witnesses are necessary, if the deed is not acknowledged; otherwise one will do. Recording is in the office of the chancery clerk of the county where the land lies. Married women must be examined privately, and release dower by joining in a conveyance. **Missouri.**—Witnesses are not necessary. Corporations must attach the corporate seal. Acknowledgment may be before a justice of the peace, notary public, judge or clerk of a court having a seal, or before a mayor of a town. Married women must be examined separately. **Montana.**—Acknowledgment and recording as in Dakota and Arizona. A wife must be separately examined. Dower is practically abolished. **Nebraska.**—At least one witness is required. The acknowledgment must be indorsed on the instrument. Dower and courtesy are barred by wife or husband joining in the conveyance. Separate examination is not customary. Recording must be with the clerk of the county where the land lies; if it is in an unorganized district, then in the county to which that district is attached for judicial purposes. **Nevada.**—No witnesses are required, but are customary. If the grantor repudiates the deed, his signature may be proved by witnesses, or, if there are none, by other competent parties. The wife must join in the conveyance, and should be separately examined. **New Hampshire.**—At least two witnesses are called for. The seal (not a scroll) must be attached, and the deed recorded in the county where the land lies. Dower is barred and homestead privilege released by the wife's joining in the conveyance, but she need not be examined apart, or make a separate acknowledgment. **New Jersey.**—One witness is required, and two are customary. The word "heirs" must be used to convey an estate in fee simple. Recording must be within fifteen days after delivery. Seals must be on wax or wafers. Dower is barred by the wife joining in the deed. Husband and wife must join in conveying the property of either. **New Mexico.**—Witnesses are not required. Acknowledgment and recording as in Montana. The husband must join in conveying the wife's separate property, and she must be examined privately and make separate acknowledgment. The wife need not join in conveyance when she has no right to the property independent of the husband. **New York.**—One witness is required, if the deed is not acknowledged before delivery. Seals must be of wax, wafers, or a piece of paper capable of taking an impression, gummed or wafered to the deed. Acknowledgment is before commissioners of deeds, notaries public, or judicial officers generally. Married women must be separately examined. If non-resident, the wife may join with her husband and convey as if she were unmarried. **North Carolina.**—One or more witnesses are necessary. Recording must be within two years after delivery, in the county where the land lies. Dower is relinquished by the wife joining. She must first acknowledge her signature, and afterwards be examined apart. She cannot convey her separate property unless the husband joins in the conveyance or gives his written consent. **Ohio.**—Deeds must be acknowledged before two attesting witnesses, before any officer legally empowered to take depositions. Recording must be within six months of the execution. Wife and husband must join in conveying the property of either. Dower is barred by the wife's joining. Separate examination of the wife is required. **Oregon.**—Two witnesses are demanded. Acknowledgment before the proper judicial officer, and recording in the county where the land is, within five days after the execution of the deed. Married women must be examined separately. **Pennsylvania.**—Witnesses are not required by statute, but are customary. Acknowledgment may be before the usual judicial officers, notary public, recorder of deeds, or mayors, recorders and aldermen of Philadelphia, Pittsburg, Alleghany or Carbondale. Recording must be within six months after execution, in the office of the recorder of deeds for the county where the land lies. Dower is barred when the wife joins in the conveyance. She must be examined separately. **Rhode Island.**—No witnesses are called for. Seals must be of wax, wafers or adhesive paper. Acknowledgment before the usual judicial officers, notary public, town clerk or senator. With corporations the deed should be signed by the president or treasurer and the corporate seal attached. Dower is barred by the wife joining. Husband and wife must join in conveying the property of either. Married women in this State must be examined apart from their husbands. **South Carolina.**—Two witnesses necessary. Acknowledgment before a trial justice or notary public. Recording in the office of the registrar of mesne conveyances for the county where the land lies within thirty-three days after execution. Dower released by a separate instrument, but barred when the wife joins in the deed. Separate examination of the wife prevails. **Tennessee.**—The deed must be acknowledged before two attesting witnesses and registered in the county where the land lies. The wife need not join to bar dower when the conveyance is in fee simple, but must in trust deeds. Husband and wife join in conveying joint property. **Texas.**—Two witnesses are required to grantor's signature, when the deed is not acknowledged before delivery. No technical words are necessary to convey a fee simple. Married women are examined separately. **Utah.**—One witness is necessary; two, customary. Dower is abolished. Married women convey in the same way as single women. Recording in the recorder's office of the county where the land lies. **Vermont.**—Two witnesses are necessary. Acknowledgment before a master in chancery, justice of the peace or notary. Recording in the office of the city or town clerk where the land is located. Married women are not examined separately. Seals must be of wax, wafers or adhesive paper. **Virginia.**—Acknowledgment may be proved by two witnesses. The deed must be recorded in the county where the land lies within sixty days after execution. Dower is barred by the wife joining. The acknowledgment of a married woman must be attested by an officer having a seal or two justices of the peace. Separate examination is required. **Washington.**—Two witnesses are necessary. Acknowledgment as in Dakota. Dower and curtesy are abolished. A married woman must be joined by her husband and separately examined. **West Virginia.**—Two witnesses will prove grantor's signature, if deed has not been acknowledged before delivery. Dower is barred by the wife joining, and she must be examined separately. **Wisconsin.**—Two attesting witnesses are required. Recording with the register of deeds in proper county. Dower is barred by the wife joining. Married women convey as though they were single, and no separate examination is necessary. **Wyoming.**—Two witnesses should attest signature. Acknowledgment as in Dakota. The deed must be recorded with register of deeds within three months after the delivery. Dower and curtesy are abolished. Married women join in conveying common property, otherwise they convey like single women. No separate examination is required.

EXEMPTION LAWS exist in all the States, providing that certain specified articles of personal property shall be exempt, or free from execution and attachment. The usual articles specified are food and fuel to a certain amount; bed, bedding and necessary furniture; clothing; Bibles and school books; tools of a trade or professional library; arms and uniforms of men or officers in the State militia, and a limited amount of stock and fodder. Sometimes after mentioning a number of specific articles the statute provides that other necessary personal property to a certain fixed value is also exempt. In the abstract of exemption and homestead laws of the States and Territories given below, space cannot be afforded to give in minute detail the personal property exempt. For this reference must be had to the general statutes. Only the more important articles are mentioned, and it may be assumed that articles of the kind above described are also exempt.

HOMESTEAD LAWS do not exist in all the States, but in most of them the home and its appurtenances are free from all attachments and executions, to a certain value; except, in some cases, for taxes and labor wages to a fixed sum.

## ABSTRACT OF HOMESTEAD AND EXEMPTION LAWS IN THE STATES AND TERRITORIES.

**Alabama.**—A homestead is exempt, if not in a city, town or village, and not exceeding 160 acres, or, if in a city, town or village, not exceeding $2,000 in value. Personal property to the value of $1,000 may be selected by the debtor. Also lots in cemeteries, pews in a church, wages of laborers not over $25 per month, *etc.*

**Arkansas.**—The homestead of a married man or head of a family, not in village, town or city, and not exceeding 160 acres, or, if in town, city or village, not worth above $5,000. Personal property to the value of $2,000 may be selected by the debtor.

**California.**—The homestead on which debtor resides, to the value of $5,000, if he is the head of a family; if not, to the value of $1,000. The personal property exempt is specified very minutely, and includes the earnings of a judgment debtor for personal services rendered within thirty days next preceding, when necessary for family support; the cabin of a miner, not over $500 in value, with all tools and gear necessary for his work; seed, grain and vegetables for sowing not above $200 in value; two oxen, or two horses, or two mules and harness; one cart or wagon; sewing machine and piano in actual use or belonging to a woman, and many other lesser articles.

**Colorado.**—Homestead of farm or city lots to the value of $2,000 to the head of a family. The fact of homestead being claimed must be recorded with title. The head of a family may select personal property to the value of $1,000; others to the value of $300. Also are exempt, working animals to the value of $200; provisions and fuel for six months; family furniture not over $100 in worth, and beds, cooking utensils, *etc.*; one cow and calf, ten sheep, with fodder; one wagon, plow, harrow, *etc.*, *etc.*

**Connecticut.**—No homestead exemption. Among the articles of personal property exempt are, libraries not above $500 in value; a cow not above $150 in value; ten sheep, not over $50 in value; two hogs and two hundred lbs. of pork; two tons of coal and twenty-five bushels of charcoal; two cords of wood; two tons of hay; 200 pounds each of wheat flour, beef and fish; oyster or shad boat and equipment; sewing machine, and other lesser articles.

**Dakota.**—Homestead of not more than 160 acres, with buildings and appurtenances, and personal property of specified kinds to the value of $1,500. A non-householder may hold exempt 80 acres, or a half acre in a city or town, with personal property.

**Delaware.**—No homestead law. Personal property not above $100 in value. The articles exempt are specified, but if the debtor does not possess articles of the description specified to the value, others may be substituted.

**District of Columbia.**—No homestead exemption. Personal property (not, however, exempt from execution and sale for laborers' wages), provisions and fuel for three months; household furniture to the value of $300; farmers' utensils to the value of $100; library and family pictures not above $400 in value; mechanics' tools worth $200; library of a professional man not over $300 in value.

**Florida.**—Homestead of 160 acres, or, in city or town, one-half acre. Personal property to the value of $1,000, to be selected by the debtor; also all improvements of real estate. The exemption does not extend to tax liens, nor to debts for purchase money or improvements.

**Georgia.**—Homestead of 50 acres of land, including house and improvements not above $200 in value, with 5 acres in addition for each child under sixteen years; but in a city or town, real estate to the value of $500. Personal property—one horse or mule, cow and calf, ten swine, and provisions to the value of $50, and $5 additional for every child; library of professional man not to exceed $300 in value; and other necessaries specified in the statutes.

**Idaho.**—Homestead to head of a family not exceeding in value $2,000. Personal property may be selected by the debtor to the value of $300 from various articles enumerated in the statute. But the exemption does not extend to purchase money, nor to mortgages on the property.

**Illinois.**—Homestead to the value of $1,000 to a householder having a family. Personal property may be selected by the debtor, if a householder, to the value of $300; if not, wearing apparel, Bibles, school books, family pictures and $100 worth of other property is exempt. After the death of a householder his family are entitled to the exemption. The exemption does not extend to debt for purchase money or improvement.

**Indiana.**—No homestead exemption. The debtor may select personal property to the amount of $600, as exempt from execution or debts founded on contract; if the debt was formed before May 31, 1879, only $300 worth of property is exempt.

**Iowa.**—Homestead of 40 acres, or, if in town or city, one-half acre, not exceeding in value $500; if less than $500 in value the number of acres may be increased till the value reaches that amount. Among articles of personal property exempt are, household furniture to the value of $200; printing press and types in newspaper office not above $1,200 in value; provisions and fuel for six months; the personal earnings of the debtor for ninety days preceding the execution; two cows, one horse, fifty sheep, five swine, *etc.*, *etc.* With non-residents, single men not heads of families, and those who are leaving the State, only wearing apparel and trunks, to the value of $75, are exempt. Purchase money is not protected by exemption laws.

**Kansas.**—Homestead of 160 acres with improvements, occupied as residence of the debtor, is exempt. No limit as to value. Personal property—household furniture and implements of industry not exceeding $500 in value; two cows, ten hogs, one yoke of oxen, one horse or mule, or in place of the oxen and mule, a span of horses or mules; provisions and fuel for one year; miners' and mechanics' tools not above $400 in value, *etc., etc.*

**Kentucky.**—Homestead to the value of $1,000, with buildings. Personal property exempt to a householder, two work beasts, or one and a yoke of oxen; two cows and calves; one wagon or cart; household furniture not to exceed $100; provisions and provender for one year; on liabilities created since May 1, 1870, the tools of a mechanic to the extent of $100, and professional libraries not over $500 in value.

**Louisiana.**—Homestead of 160 acres, occupied by debtor as a residence, together with personal property, all not exceeding in value $2,000; and, also, bedding, furniture, tools, and a few minor articles. There is no homestead exemption in cities and towns; nor, if the wife in her own right owns property to the amount of $1,000.

**Maine.**—Homestead of a householder to the value of $500, or any lot purchased from the State as a homestead. After death of the debtor his family is entitled to the exemption. Personal property, bed and bedding; household furniture not to exceed $50 in value; library not worth more than $150, one or two horses, not worth more than $300, or one pair of working cattle or span of mules; five tons of anthracite and fifty bushels of bituminous coal; twelve cords of wood; $10 worth of lumber; a cow and heifer, ten sheep with lambs; a boat of two tons; plow and cart, and minor articles.

**Maryland.**—No homestead exemption. Personal property, all wearing apparel, books and tools used for earning a living, and other property not exceeding $100 in value.

**Massachusetts.**—Homestead not exceeding $800 in value, to a householder having a family. The homestead claim must be set forth in the deed of conveyance of the property. Personal property, tools and implements of trade, not worth over $100; materials and stock in trade to the amount of $100; library not worth more than $50; provisions to the amount of $50; boats, nets and tackle actually used by fishermen; fuel, wearing apparel, bedding, *etc., etc.*

**Michigan.**—Homestead of 40 acres, with buildings and appurtenances, not in town plat, city or village. If situated in town or city, one lot and dwelling house, not above $1,500 in value. No exemption from execution for purchase money. Personal property, library not above $150 in value; provisions and provender for six months; two cows, five swine, ten sheep and fleeces, or the yarn or wool from the same; tools, stock, materials, apparatus, horses or harness vehicles or teams, not exceeding $250 in value; spinning wheel, loom for weaving, one sewing machine, *etc., etc.*

**Minnesota.**—Homestead of 80 acres, or if in incorporated city, town or village, one lot and dwelling house. No limit as to value. Personal property, the usual articles of household furniture and apparel and articles not enumerated, to the value of $500; farming tools and utensils not above $300 in value; three cows, ten swine, twenty sheep, one yoke of oxen and a horse (or one span of horses or mules); provisions and provender for one year. Also (not to exceed $50) wages due for personal services of debtor or his family, rendered within ninety days before process is issued.

**Mississippi.**—Homestead of 80 acres, to a householder, head of a family, for debts on contract since September 1, 1870; in an incorporated town, lot and dwelling house to the value of $2,000. Personal property, tools, implements, and books of students and teachers; agricultural implements for two laborers; professional libraries to the value of $250; two cows and calves, five swine, five sheep, one horse or mule, or one yoke of oxen, with food for the same; cart or wagon, worth not more than $100: household furniture not exceeding $100.

**Missouri.**—Homestead not exceeding 160 acres in extent or $1,500 in value; in cities of more than 40,000 inhabitants, not to exceed 18 square rods, or $3,000 in value; in cities of less than 40,000 inhabitants, not to exceed 30 square rods, or $1,500 in value. Personal property, household furniture not over $100; provisions, not more than $100 worth; working animals and cattle not to exceed $300, or, in place thereof, any kind of property selected. Those not heads of families can claim only necessary tools and implements and wearing apparel, Wages for a month preceding issue of process are exempt.

**Montana.**—Homestead of 80 acres, or, if in city or town, lot and dwelling not to exceed one-quarter acre, and in either case not to exceed in value $2,500. But exemption will not hold against a mortgage or the lien of mechanics or laborers. Personal property to the value of $1,400 is also exempt.

**Nebraska.**—Homestead of 160 acres, or if in a city, town or village, a lot of twenty acres, or two contiguous lots on a recorded plot. Personal property, provisions, fuel and provender for six months; one yoke of oxen or span of horses; one wagon, cart or dray; two plows and other farming instruments not above $50 in value; household furniture not exceeding $100; bedding, clothes, books, *etc.*, as usual. A head of a family having no homestead may hold $500 worth of personal property exempt.

**Nevada.**—Homestead held by the head of a family not to exceed $5,000 in value. Personal property, provisions and fodder for a month; seeds for planting within six months; two oxen, or horses and mules, with harnesses; cabin of a miner, not worth over $500, and mining tools; sewing machine below $150 in value; household furniture, books to the value of $100, *etc., etc*

**New Hampshire.**—Household for the head of a family not to exceed $500 in value; clothes, bedding, furniture to the value of $100; one cow, one hog and pig, six sheep and their fleeces; one horse or a yoke of oxen; four tons of hay; one sewing machine; library to the value of $200.

**New Jersey.**—Homestead and buildings to the value of $1,500. Personal property, wearing apparel, and $200 worth of any property, on appraisment. The same exemption may be claimed by the widow of a householder.

**New York.**—Homestead to the value of $1,000 occupied by a householder having a family. Personal property, household furniture and library to the value of $250; ten sheep, one cow, two hogs; a team and provender for ninety days; tools of a mechanic not above $25 in value, professional implements; cooking utensils, *etc.*, as specified. Homestead is not good as against an execution upon a judgment founded on fraud.

**New Mexico.**—Homestead to the value of $1,000 in farm land. Personal property, provisions to the amount of $25; furniture for kitchen not to exceed $10; mechanical and agricultural tools to the value of $20; wearing apparel, bed and bedding, school books, *etc.*

**North Carolina.**—Homestead to the value of $1,000, when occupied by the head of a family, whether in country or town. Personal property to the value of $500, to be selected by the debtor.

**Ohio.**—Homestead to the value of $1,000. If it exceed that amount the homestead may be partitioned. If the head of a family have no homestead, he may select personal property to the value of $500 in addition to the articles specified by the statutes as exempt. Personal property, provisions to the value of $50; household furniture not to exceed $50; tools and implements worth not more than $100; one cow, two hogs, six sheep, and provender for sixty days, or in lieu of these animals, $35, $15 and $15 in household furniture, respectively; one sewing machine, beds, bedding, *etc.*, as usual; scientific collections, if not exhibited for money; one horse, or yoke of oxen, one wagon, cart or dray. For an unmarried woman are exempt, wearing apparel to the value of $100, sewing or knitting machine, and books to the value of $25. Widows may claim the exemption, and wives may do so, if the husband will not.

**Oregon.**—No homestead exemption. Personal property, tools, implements, apparatus, team and food therefor for sixty days, or professional library to the value of $400; wearing apparel to the value of $50 for each member of the family, or to the value of $100, if debtor is not a householder; two cows, ten sheep, five hogs; furniture and utensils to the value of $300; provisions for three months and provender for six months. Exemption does not hold good against an action brought to recover the price of an article.

**Pennsylvania.**—No special homestead exemption. But property to the value of $300 is exempt, whether real or personal, as is also wearing apparel for the debtor and his family, all Bibles and school books, and nothing else. It is a common thing to waive the exemption in notes of hand.

**Rhode Island.**—No homestead exemption. Personal property, household furniture not above $300 in value; tools and implements of occupation to value of $200; library to value of $300; one cow, one hog, one pig, one and a half tons of hay; mariner's wages till the end of voyage on which they were earned; wages to the amount of $10, when the suit is not for necessaries furnished; debts secured by bills of exchange or negotiable promissory notes.

**South Carolina.**—Homestead to value of $1,000 to head of family, or after his death to the widow and orphans. Personal property, as specified in the statute, but not beyond the value of $500. Exemption of the homestead will not hold good as against execution for purchase money, improvements or taxes. One-third of the yearly gains of members of the family other than its head, is exempt.

**Tennessee.**—Homestead to the head of a family, not exceeding $1,000 in value, including improvements. None but heads of families are entitled to any exemption. Personal property, beds, bedding and household furniture (very minutely specified in statute); two horses or mules, or one and a yoke of oxen; two cows and calves, or if family has six or more persons, three cows and calves; one wagon or cart, not above $75 in value; mechanic's tools; a limited amount of various kinds of grain and provisions; $50 worth of lumber and material to each mechanic, and minor articles.

**Texas.**—Homestead to the value of $5,000, not to exceed 200 acres, if in the country, or a lot or lots in a city, town or village. The limit of value applies to either. Personal property; all household furniture; tools or implements of a trade or profession; library; two yoke of oxen, two horses and one wagon; twenty hogs, twenty sheep; all provisions and provender for home use, *etc.*, *etc.* A person not the head of a family is entitled to exemption on clothing, tools, books, a horse, bridle and saddle.

**Utah.**—Homestead to the value of $1,000, to be selected by the debtor, if the head of a family. Personal property may be selected, to the value of $700, from articles specified by the statute. In addition to the homestead, each member of the family is entitled to $250. Exemption does not apply in case of mortgages, mechanics' liens or purchase money.

**Vermont.**—Homestead of the head of a family to the value of $500, with products and improvements. Personal property; all growing crops; bedding, furniture, sewing machine and provisions to a limited amount, specified in the statute; one cow, one hog, or the pork; one yoke of oxen or two work horses, and forage for the winter, and such personal property as the debtor may select to the value of $200 in lieu of oxen; physicians' books and instruments; other professional libraries to the value of $200.

**Virginia.**—Homestead to the value of $2,000, to be selected by the head of a family from either real or personal property. Personal property, to be selected from articles specified by the statute, to a value ranging from $50 to $500, according to the size of the family and occupation of the head thereof.

**Washington.**—Homestead to the value of $1,000, when actually occupied by family. Personal property, household furniture, *etc.*, to the value of $1,500; two cows, five swine, one span of horses and harness, or two yoke of oxen; twenty-five fowls; provision and fuel for six months; professional libraries not exceeding $500 in value; small boats, and, to persons engaged in lightering, two lighters and a small boat, not to exceed $250 in value.

**West Virginia.**—Homestead to the value of $1,000. The fact of homestead being claimed must be recorded in the land records of county where the property lies. Children of deceased parents may claim the homestead right. Personal property to the value of $300 is exempt to the father of a family.

**Wisconsin.**—Homestead not exceeding forty acres of farm land, or a lot in city, town or village, not to exceed one-fourth of an acre. Personal property, household furniture to the value of $200; one gun or rifle not above $50 in value; one horse or mule and one yoke of oxen, or in place thereof, a span of horses or mules, two cows, ten swine, ten sheep and the fleeces, with provender for a year; one cart, wagon or dray, one sleigh, one plow, one drag; provisions and fuel for a year; tools or stock in trade of mechanic or miner; or professional library, not to exceed $200 in value; printing press and material to the value of $1,500; inventions; earnings of head of family for sixty days before process is issued, if necessary for support of family. Insurance money on exempt property destroyed, is itself exempt.

**Wyoming.**—Homestead not exceeding 160 acres, or a lot in city, town or village, the value in either case not to be above $1,500, to a *bona fide* resident and householder. Personal property, articles specified by the statute to be selected by the debtor to the value of $500; tools, stock in trade of miner or mechanic, or professional library, not over $300 in value.

## JURISDICTION OF COURTS.

**Alabama.**—Justices of the peace have jurisdiction under $100 in cases of contract; $50 in cases of torts. **Arizona.**—Justices have jurisdiction for amounts less than $300; district courts over $100. **Arkansas.**—Justices have exclusive jurisdiction under $100; concurrent jurisdiction with circuit courts under $300. **California.**—The limit of the jurisdiction of a justice is $300. Appeal lies directly to the superior court. **Colorado.**—Justices are limited in jurisdiction to the value of $300; county courts to $2,000, concurrently with district courts. **Connecticut.**—Justices may decide in cases under $100; common pleas jurisdiction under $500, or, concurrently with superior court, $1000. **Dakota.**—Justices' jurisdiction is under $100; district courts any amount above. **Delaware.**—Amounts under $100 may be brought before a justice; no district or county court. **Florida.**—Amounts under $100 may be sued for before a justice; appeal to county or circuit court. **Georgia.**—Appeal lies from justice (jurisdiction $100) in cases above $50; county courts decide up to $300; appeal to superior court. **Idaho.**—Amounts over $100 must be carried to district court, which has original and appellate jurisdiction. **Illinois.**—Justices have jurisdiction to the amount of $200; county and circuit courts have concurrent jurisdiction. **Indiana.**—Suits for $200 may be brought before a justice, who may also give judgment for $300 *on confession*; circuit courts are concurrent with the superior court. **Iowa.**—By consent of parties the jurisdiction of a justice may be extended from $100 to $300; circuit courts have no criminal jurisdiction, and are concurrent with district courts in civil cases. **Kansas.**—The limit of justices' decision is $300; no county courts; appeal from district to supreme court. **Kentucky.**—Justices may not give judgment of over $50; quarterly courts $200. **Louisiana.**—Justice courts, $100; court of appeals, $1,000. **Maine.**—Justices, $20; appeal to superior court. **Maryland.**—Justices, $100, concurrent jurisdiction with circuit court above $50. **Massachusetts.**—Trial justices, $300; municipal court of Boston, $100. **Michigan.**—Justices, $100; concurrent with circuit court under $300. **Minnesota.**—Justices, $100; appeal from district to supreme court. **Mississippi.**—Justices, $150; county courts abolished. **Missouri.**—Justices, original jurisdiction, $150; in cities over 50,000 inhabitants, $250. **Montana.**—Justices, $50; probate courts, $500. **Nebraska.**—Justices, $200; county courts, $1,000. **Nevada.**—Justices, $300; district courts, $300. **New Hampshire.**—Justices, in civil cases, $13.33; police courts, $100. **New Jersey.**—Justices, $200; in cities, $100; circuit courts concurrent with supreme court. **New Mexico.**—Justices, $100; district courts, unlimited. **New York.**—Justices, $200, in case of confession, $500. Appeal lies from supreme court to court of appeals. **North Carolina.**—Justices, $200; no circuit or county courts. **Ohio.**—Justices, $100; concurrent with common pleas, $300. **Oregon.**—Justices, $150; county courts, $500. **Pennsylvania.**—Justices, $300; appeal to common pleas court. **Rhode Island.**—Justices, $100; beyond, common pleas or probate court. **South Carolina.**—Justices, $100; appeal to common pleas or probate. **Tennessee.**—Justices, $500; chancery and circuit courts concurrent. **Texas.**—Justices, $200; county court, $500; district court beyond. **Utah.**—Justices, $300, except land cases; beyond, district courts. **Vermont.**—Justices, $200; county court, beyond that amount. **Virginia.**—Appeal from county courts to circuit courts; from corporation courts to supreme court. **Washington.**—Justices, $100, except in land cases; beyond that, district courts. **West Virginia.**—Justices, $300; appeal to circuit courts; county courts have no civil jurisdiction. **Wisconsin.**—Justices, $200; appeal to circuit courts. **Wyoming.**—Justices, $100; appeal to district court.

CONTRACTS by which one party, the *insurer*, agrees to indemnify another party, the *insured*, against loss or damage to certain property or interests are termed in law INSURANCE. The consideration on which the contract rests is called the *premium*. The instrument by which the contract is made is called the *policy*.

Insurance may be of three kinds, *fire*, *marine*, and *life* insurance. Many general principles, however, are applicable to all of the three varieties. Insurance is now almost universally made by incorporated companies, but sometimes by individuals.

In all kinds of insurance, the holder of the policy must have a personal interest in the property or life insured. What will constitute an insurable interest will be discussed below. As a rule, all persons capable of making contracts of any kind may enter into a contract of insurance. (See CONTRACTS.)

It has been held that insurance contracts may be made by word of mouth; but they should always be in writing. All stipulations and conditions contained in the policy are binding upon both parties, though signed by but one, the insurer. This is because of the acceptance of the policy by the insured and his intent to profit by its benefits in case of loss.

A policy in which the property upon which the risk is taken, is not fully described, but is referred to in general terms, as "all the property of the insured on board the ship 'Ella,'" is called an *open* policy. Such contracts are not common.

In addition to stock and mutual insurance companies, there is a class of mixed companies in which members, who may or may not be insured, hold certificates for capital contributed, and are entitled to interest or to a definite share of receipts after payment of losses and expenses.

## Fire Insurance.

FIRE INSURANCE includes all contracts by which the insurer agrees to indemnify the insured against losses by fire, whether upon buildings, ships, or the goods and stock contained therein, or live stock. The insurance only holds good while the property is left in the same general condition as when the contract was made. If goods are removed from one place to another, notice must be given to the company, and the policy altered in accordance with the new state of facts. It is common with fire insurance companies to classify various kinds of property as to the probable danger, as *ordinary*, *hazardous*, *extra-hazardous*. Any misrepresentation at the time when the policy is obtained, as to the material, construction, or position of a building, or as to the use to which it is to be put, will relieve the insurers from responsibility. But changes after the policy is issued, for which the insured is not responsible, will not affect the contract. All warranties are to be strictly construed.

It is held that actual *ignition* or burning must take place to make the company responsible; otherwise steam explosions or damage by lightning will not come under the policy. But damage caused by water used in extinguishing the fire, or by blowing up property, under the orders of proper authorities, to hinder the spreading of the fire, will be included.

In case of a loss occurring, the company must be notified, and proof furnished strictly in accordance with the provisions of the policy.

Mutual insurance companies differ from the common stock companies in that every one who is insured becomes by that fact a member, and entitled to a share of the profits of the concern. The expense of insuring in such a company is usually less than in a joint-stock concern; but, on the other hand, the latter will generally insure closer to the value of the property.

Insurable Interest. The law holds that a policy issued to a person who has no interest in the subject of insurance is void, as being a *gaming* policy. An insurable interest is possessed by a trustee, factor, or commission merchant, and he may insure the goods either for his own benefit or that of his principal; by a lessee of a building under his lease; by a mortgagee in possession, or by a mortgagor to the whole value of the property; by one holding a mechanics' or builders' lien on the building; by an administrator of an insolvent estate; by a purchaser holding an executory contract for future conveyance, but having as yet no title; by a sheriff holding goods under process; by a partner in a building bought with partnership funds, though standing on ground belonging solely to the other partner; and, in general, any interest which would be recognized as such by a court of law or equity, is an "insurable interest;" but not a mere expectation or *probable* interest, however well-grounded it may be.

It is not a good defence for an insurance company to assert that the fire was caused by the negligence of the insured or his servants, unless, indeed, the negligence is so great as to be criminal or to indicate fraud. If an insured party alienates the property, the insurance does not pass with it, as the contract is held to be a personal one, and policies usually have a provision specifying that transfer of the property or policy shall void the contract. But the death of the insured is not an alienation, such as to void the contract.

The sum paid to the insured must be such as to indemnify him for actual loss. Goods are estimated at their actual value at the time of the fire. Mutual insurance companies are usually forbidden by their charters to insure for more than two-thirds of the full value of the property. It is usually required by a company that if any other company has an insurance upon the property offered, it shall be stated and indorsed upon the policy. This, of course, is to prevent the insured from obtaining more than full value in case of loss. It is also required that when different insurers have granted policies on the same property, in case of loss the insurance should be treated as *one* insurance and paid by the different companies in proportion. When two policies cover the same insurable interest against the same risks and in the name of the same person, it is called a *double* insurance. In marine insurance the company pays only that proportion of the sum for which insurance is taken which is equal to the proportion which the actual loss bears to the entire value. Thus, if a ship is valued at $15,000 and insured for $9,000 and the loss is one-third, the company will pay only $3,000. But in fire insurance the whole amount of the loss is paid, if it does not exceed the amount for which insurance is taken.

## Life Insurance.

In Life Insurance, the insurer agrees to pay a fixed sum of money, upon the death of the person whose life is insured, to his family or legal representatives, or to the person (other than he whose life is insured) who has taken out the policy, and who has an insurable interest in the life proposed for insurance. If there is no *insurable interest*, the contract is void, as being a gaming policy. The consent of the person whose life is insured must be obtained to a policy issued in favor of a third party. If the insurable interest exists when the policy is issued and ceases before the death, the contract still holds good.

An insurable interest is possessed by a creditor in the life of his debtor; by a father in the life of his minor child; by a wife in the life of her husband; by a sister in the life of her brother; by a clerk in one who has agreed to employ him for a fixed time; and, in general, whenever by the death of the insured there would naturally follow actual and pecuniary loss or disadvantage to him to whom the policy is issued. If a wife is treated as a single woman by the laws of the place in which she lives, as regards her property rights, she may insure her husband's life for her own benefit, and the policy will be beyond his control to cancel or transfer, will not be made void by his misrepresentations at the time of insurance, and will inure to the benefit of her children, if she dies first.

Any material misrepresentations made by the insured at the time the policy is issued will render it void. Thus a false statement as to health, such as a denial that the applicant had heart disease, would void the contract. But in view of the great number of questions put by the insurers, and the difficulty of having certain knowledge as to one's health, the courts are inclined to construe such warranties liberally in favor of the applicant, unless it appears that there has been deliberate suppression or misstatement. Examination by a physician in the employ of the company is usually required. Questions usually put are, as to the applicant's use of intoxicating liquors, whether he is subject to fits, as to consumption and other hereditary diseases, as to his manner of life, etc. *Restrictions* are usually imposed by the company, such as to travel only within certain limits, or not to engage in hazardous employments. In this case, if the insured desires to overstep the restrictions, permission must be obtained for the purpose. Death by suicide will void the policy.

Life insurance policies are *assignable.* The policy itself usually specifies the way in which the transfer must be made. Notice to the insurance company is usually called for. The policy itself must be transferred with the assignment and notice indorsed upon it. But actual transfer is unnecessary, if assignment is made by a separate deed duly executed and delivered. The following form may be used for an indorsed assignment:

I, the undersigned *A. B.*, insured by the within policy issued by the (*name of company*), in consideration of one dollar to me in hand paid by *C. D.*, and for other good and sufficient consideration, do hereby assign and transfer to the said *C. D.* the said within policy, together with all the right, title, interest and claim which I now have or hereafter may have, in, to, or under the same.

**Witn ss** my hand and seal this —— day of ——, A. D. 18—.

(*Signed*) *A. B.* [L. S.]

*Executed in the Presence of E. F.*

The payment of the premium on the day specified must be made in order to keep the policy in force. But it is sometimes provided by statute that the insured shall not lose all pecuniary interest in his policy by failing to pay the premium. It is the rule in most places that seven years' absence of the insured with silence on his part will afford a presumption of death.

The amount of the premium to be paid is based in great measure upon the age of the individual to be insured. The "expectation of life," as it is called, is founded on statistics accumulating for many years. We give a table in common use. It will be seen that the first column contains the age, and the second the number of years which a person of that age may, on the average, be expected to live.

TABLE OF LIFE EXPECTATION.

| Age. | Expectation in years. | Age. | Expectation in years. | Age. | Expectation in years. | Age. | Expectation in years. | Age. | Expectation in years. |
|---|---|---|---|---|---|---|---|---|---|
| 0 | 28.15 | 20 | 34.22 | 40 | 26.04 | 60 | 15.45 | 80 | 5.85 |
| 1 | 36.78 | 21 | 33 84 | 41 | 25.61 | 61 | 14.86 | 81 | 5.50 |
| 2 | 38.74 | 22 | 33.46 | 42 | 25.19 | 62 | 14.26 | 82 | 5.16 |
| 3 | 40.01 | 23 | 33.08 | 43 | 24.77 | 63 | 13.66 | 83 | 4.87 |
| 4 | 40.73 | 24 | 32.70 | 44 | 24.35 | 64 | 13.05 | 84 | 4.66 |
| 5 | 40.88 | 25 | 32.33 | 45 | 23.92 | 65 | 12.43 | 85 | 4.57 |
| 6 | 40 69 | 26 | 31.93 | 46 | 23 37 | 66 | 11.96 | 86 | 4.21 |
| 7 | 40.47 | 27 | 31.50 | 47 | 22.83 | 67 | 11.48 | 87 | 3.90 |
| 8 | 40.14 | 28 | 31.08 | 48 | 22.27 | 68 | 11.01 | 88 | 3 67 |
| 9 | 39.72 | 29 | 30.66 | 49 | 21.72 | 69 | 10.50 | 89 | 3.56 |
| 10 | 39.23 | 30 | 30.25 | 50 | 21.17 | 70 | 10.06 | 90 | 3.43 |
| 11 | 38 64 | 31 | 29 83 | 51 | 20.61 | 71 | 9 60 | 91 | 3.32 |
| 12 | 38 02 | 32 | 29.43 | 52 | 20.05 | 72 | 9.14 | 92 | 3 12 |
| 13 | 37.41 | 33 | 29.02 | 53 | 19.49 | 73 | 8 69 | 93 | 2.40 |
| 14 | 36.79 | 34 | 28.62 | 54 | 18.92 | 74 | 8.25 | 94 | 1.98 |
| 15 | 36 17 | 35 | 28.22 | 55 | 18.35 | 75 | 7.83 | 95 | 1.62 |
| 16 | 35.76 | 36 | 27.78 | 56 | 17.78 | 76 | 7.40 | | |
| 17 | 35.37 | 37 | 27.34 | 57 | 17.20 | 77 | 6.99 | | |
| 18 | 34.98 | 38 | 26.91 | 58 | 16.63 | 78 | 6.59 | | |
| 19 | 34 59 | 39 | 26.47 | 59 | 16.04 | 79 | 6.21 | | |

## Marine Insurance.

In Marine Insurance, the insurer agrees to indemnify the insured against any injury which may occur to his ship or goods contained therein, or in their profits and earnings. A *time* policy is one framed to cover possible loss within a specified time. Other policies are made to cover the risk in a certain specified voyage. As in the other forms of insurance, there must be an insurable interest; and what that is will be determined by the rules before spoken of.

The form of the policy used in marine insurance is very ancient and peculiar. It is usually partly written and partly printed, and the written parts will prevail over the printed. Any alteration in the contract should be indorsed on the policy. The policy often requires that a change of owners or a change in the master of the vessel shall be notified to the insurer under penalty of voiding the policy. Goods may be moved from one ship to another, if necessary, without voiding the policy.

The premium is very commonly paid by a promissory note, called the premium note, and part of its value will be, under certain contingencies, returnable; as when the risk insured against is not actually incurred in its full extent.

Marine insurance, from the nature of the subject, is less certain and definite in the description of the property to be insured than fire insurance. Thus the insured may obtain a policy upon a cargo to be sent him from a certain port, without designating its charactér, quality or exact value, and even without knowing in what vessel it is to be shipped; but whatever is known should be clearly stated in the policy. It is held that a general policy does not include cargo carried on deck unless there is special provision therefor, as this method of transport is considered extra-hazardous.

Marine insurance will be void when the purpose of the voyage is illegal; or if made to cover the property of a public enemy; or to violate the revenue laws of the country where insurance is made. Goods contraband of war may be insured. The risks insured against, as commonly enumerated, are, the perils of the sea, fire, barratry, theft, robbery, piracy, capture, arrests and detentions. Insurers are not liable for ordinary wear and tear or breakage. By *barratry* is meant an illegal act done by the master, officers or crew as against the owner.

When the insurance is for a certain voyage, the place of sailing and that which is to be the termination of the voyage must be specified, and the voyage must be by the ordinary course from the one port to the other unless deviation is allowed by the terms of the policy. Policies usually contain a provision that the insurance shall continue until twenty-four hours after the ship has arrived and been safely moored, and upon the goods until they have been safely landed.

Any breach of warranty or misrepresentation by the insured party will void the policy. Warranties may be expressed or implied. The express warranties are, in general, as to the ownership of the vessel, its neutrality, the time of sailing, and the present position of the ship. Of the implied warranties, the most important is that of *sea-worthiness*. If the ship becomes unseaworthy after the policy is issued, it is the duty of the owner or master to restore her to a proper condition as soon as possible, and if she leave a port in unseaworthy condition when that condition might there have been remedied, the insurers will not be liable for damage that may ensue.

The loss may be *total* or *partial*. Total loss may be *actual* or *constructive*—the latter when, though the entire property has not been actually destroyed, yet the insured parties are by law allowed to abandon their title upon what remains to the insurers, and to claim from them payment in full as for a total loss. The general rule is that such abandonment may be made when the loss exceeds *one half* of the value of the property insured. But if a ship is brought into the port of termination of the voyage, she cannot be so abandoned, though necessary repairs might cost more than half the value. The rule "one third off, new for old" applies to a partial loss, and means that when the insurers repair a vessel to indemnify the insured for damages, and in so doing replace old material by new, the insured is not permitted to retain the entire advantage of the replacement, which would be obviously unfair, but is obliged to assume that the old material had at the time of the damage already lost one third of its value. The proportion of one third is taken arbitrarily, but is considered a fair average.

Uncarned freight is a proper subject for insurance, whether on the goods of others carried in the ship, or in the nature of the benefit which a shipowner will receive by carrying his own goods in his own ship.

## INTEREST AND USURY.

MONEY paid for the use of money is INTEREST. The sum on which interest is paid is called the *principal*; the ratio of the annual interest to the principal, the *rate per cent.*, and the sum of principal and interest, the *amount*. *Usury* is a higher rate of interest than is allowed by law. *Simple* interest is paid as it falls due; *compound* interest is interest on principal and interest, the interest being successively added to the principal at the dates on which it falls due.

Interest may be on a debt actually due, as borrowed money, or upon a judgment of a court, or for the price of goods, when it is understood that no credit is to be given. When damages claimed are unliquidated, *i. e.,* not fixed or certain, interest will not be allowed. Neither will it be allowed in actions founded on *tort,* or wrong. The interest will begin to run as soon as the debt is payable, and not before. Thus, with a note without interest payable at ninety days, interest will begin when the ninety days have elapsed; but with a note payable on demand, interest will begin to accrue at the date on which the note is given.

Laws fixing a rate of interest and forbidding usury may, as a penalty, declare that if usury is taken the whole sum due shall be forfeited, or they may declare forfeit only the usurious interest. The tendency of the age is toward leaving the right of contract as free as possible, and hence many States allow the parties to agree upon any rate they may choose, but establish a legal rate to be observed when no special bargain is made. To make a contract for interest usurious, there must be a *usurious intent.* Thus, if by a mistake in reckoning a greater amount than legal interest is received, the mistake may be rectified and the penalty not imposed. On the other hand, if the contract appears on the face to be not usurious, but the intent of the parties to avoid the law can be made evident, the court will set aside the contract as usurious.

The "law of place" (*lex loci*) applies to interest and usury. That is to say, a rate of interest which is lawful in the State where it is made may be enforced in another State where it would otherwise be usurious; and, *vice versa,* if a contract is for a rate which is usurious in the State where the contract is made, it cannot be enforced in the second State, though the rate may be lawful in that State. We give below an abstract of the rates of interest and laws as to usury in the United States. It should be borne in mind that changes are frequently made from year to year.

## INTEREST AND USURY LAWS.

**Alabama.**—The legal rate is eight per cent. Usurious interest cannot be recovered.

**Arizona.**—Legal rate, ten per cent. Any rate by written contract.

**Arkansas.**—Parties may contract for any rate; if no contract is made, six per cent. must be paid.

**California.**—Legal rate, seven per cent.; but ten per cent. can be claimed on money overdue on any written instrument.

**Colorado.**—Legal rate, ten per cent. Any rate by written contract.

**Connecticut.**—Any rate may be agreed upon. In the absence of any contract, six per cent. is the legal rate, Tables for computing interest which reckon three hundred and sixty days to the year may be used.

**Dakota.**—Legal rate, seven per cent. Contract may be made for twelve.

**District of Columbia.**—Legal rate, six per cent. But contracts may be made as high as ten per cent. The whole interest is forfeited if usury is taken.

**Delaware.**—Legal rate, six per cent. If usury is taken half the debt is forfeited; one half the amount forfeited goes to the prosecuting party, the other half to the State.

**Florida.**—Legal rate, eight per cent. There is no penalty existing for taking usury.

**Georgia.**—Legal rate, seven per cent.; but a contract in writing may be made for any rate not to exceed eight per cent.

**Idaho.**—Legal rate, ten per cent. Contract may be made for one and a half per cent. per month.

**Illinois.**—Legal rate, six per cent. Special contract (which need not be in writing) may be made for as high as eight per cent. The penalty for usury is the forfeiture of all interest.

**Indiana.**—Legal rate, six per cent. Contracts may be made in writing for as high as eight per cent. Any excess of interest is forfeited.

**Iowa.**—Legal rate, six per cent. Ten per cent. may be agreed upon in writing. In case of usury the principal only can be recovered, and ten per cent. of the amount is forfeited to the State.

**Kansas.**—Legal rate, seven per cent. Agreement may be made for any rate not above twelve per cent. Usury forfeits all interest, and any payment of usurious interest to the creditor is held as part payment of the principal.

**Kentucky.**—Legal rate, six per cent. Contract may be made for eight per cent. All interest above the legal rate is forfeited.

**Louisiana.**—Legal rate, five per cent. Contract may be made for not more than eight per cent. The penalty is the forfeiture of all interest. If usurious interest has been paid it may be recovered by suing within a year.

**Maine.**—Legal rate, six per cent. Exception is made in case of certain contracts, such as bottomry bonds, and marine insurance, contracts between farmers for farming purposes, and the course of exchange in practice among merchants. Suit for recovery of excessive interest paid must be brought within twelve months.

**Maryland.**—Legal rate, six per cent. The penalty is the forfeiture of excessive interest.

**Massachusetts.**—Legal rate, six per cent. Agreement may be made in writing for any rate.

**Michigan.**—Legal rate, seven per cent. Contract can be made for any rate not over ten per cent.

**Minnesota.**—Legal rate, seven per cent. Contract may be made for any rate not above ten per cent. Interest on judgments is six per cent.

**Mississippi.**—Legal rate, six per cent. A written contract may be made for not more than ten per cent.

**Missouri.**—Legal rate, six per cent. Any rate not above ten per cent. may be agreed upon. Interest cannot be compounded oftener than once a year. If usurious interest is taken the principal only can be recovered, and ten per cent. is forfeit to the State.

**Nebraska.**—Legal rate, seven per cent. Contract may be made for not more than ten per cent.

**Nevada.**—Legal rate, ten per cent. Any rate may be taken, if a written agreement is made.

**New Hampshire.**—Legal rate, six per cent. Some exceptions are made (*see Maine*). The penalty of usury is the forfeiture of three times the excessive interest by the party receiving it.

**New Jersey.**—Legal rate, six per cent. If usury is agreed upon, all interest is forfeit.

**New Mexico.**—Legal rate, six per cent. Contracts for any rate may be made.

**New York.**—Legal rate, six per cent. A contract for more than legal interest is wholly void.

**North Carolina.**—Legal rate, six per cent. Written contract may be made for not more than eight per cent.

**Ohio.**—Legal rate, six per cent. Contract in writing may be made for not over eight. An exception is made in case of railroad companies, which may borrow at seven per cent.

**Oregon.**—Legal rate, ten per cent. Agreement may be made for as high as twelve per cent.

**Pennsylvania.**—Legal rate, six per cent. If excessive interest is paid, it may be recovered on suit brought within six months.

**Rhode Island.**—Legal rate, six per cent. Agreement may be made for any rate whatever.

**South Carolina.**—Legal rate, seven per cent. Any rate may be agreed upon.

**Tennessee.**—Legal rate, six per cent. Any excess is usury and is forfeited.

**Texas.**—Legal rate, eight per cent. Written contract may be made for twelve per cent.

**Utah.**—Legal rate, ten per cent. Any rate by contract.

**Vermont.**—Legal rate, six per cent. Exception is made in contracts for letting of cattle by farmers, *etc.* (*as in Maine*).

**Virginia.**—Legal rate, six per cent. All contracts for a greater rate are void.

**Washington Territory.**—Legal rate, ten per cent. Any rate by contract.

**West Virginia.**—Legal rate, six per cent. Excess cannot be recovered.

**Wisconsin.**—Legal rate, seven per cent. Contract may be made for any rate not above ten per cent. Penalty for usurious interest is the forfeiture of three times the amount paid in excess, by the creditor who has received it.

**Wyoming.**—Legal rate, twelve per cent. Any rate by written contract.

# LEASES.

LEASES are contracts by which one party, called the *lessor*, or landlord, gives to a second, called the *lessee*, or tenant, possession of land or other real estate, for a fixed period of time, receiving in return for the use, possession and profits thereof a fixed compensation called the *rent*. The lease of real property carries with it all appurtenances necessary for the proper enjoyment of the same.

Leases may be for life, at will, by sufferance, or for a term of years. A lease for life will be terminated by the death of the lessee or of some other person specified, upon whose life the lease is made to depend. A lease by sufferance of the lessor is presumed to exist when a lease for years or life has expired and the tenant is nevertheless allowed to remain in possession. Such possession may be terminated without notice. A lease at will is one which exists only during the will of the grantor. It may be terminated at the will of either party, by any act of the lessor in assertion of his right of possession, by any act of abandonment of possession by the tenant, or by the death of either party. An estate for years is one which begins and ends at certain and specified dates. The lessee possesses greater privileges than in the other varieties mentioned. Thus he may enter upon the land and remove crops after his term has ended, when the termination falls between planting and harvest.

It is usual for a landlord to agree to make all necessary repairs, but, unless the lease expressly requires it, he is not bound to do so. The tenant usually covenants to leave the premises in good condition, "ordinary wear and usage excepted." The tenant is not bound to make general repairs nor to pay taxes, unless he specially covenants so to do. He may always underlet the premises unless forbidden to do so by the lease. It is not uncommon to insert a clause in the lease forbidding the tenant to use the premises for other than certain specified things. In case of a tenant at will, or one who holds over after the term is complete, a notice to quit is necessary to compel him to give up his possession. This notice must, as a rule, be given at a date before some "rent day," and distant from it by the usual period at which rent is payable. Thus, if it is payable monthly, there should be a month's notice ending on the day when rent is payable. If the rent is in arrears, only a brief notice is required. In most of the States this is fixed at two weeks, fourteen days. Such notice need not be made to end upon the day when rent is payable.

Many States require leases to be recorded. Leases for more than one year must be recorded in the following States:—Connecticut, Mississippi, Oregon, Rhode Island, South Carolina, Tennessee, and Vermont. In Connecticut and Mississippi leases must be executed in all respects like deeds. Leases for more than seven years must be recorded in Maine, Maryland, Massachusetts, and New Hampshire. Leases for more than three years must be recorded in Ohio. In North Carolina and Texas all leases must be recorded. In Delaware and Pennsylvania all leases for more than twenty-one years must be recorded.

## SHORT LEASE (used in New York).

### Agreement of Landlord.

**This is to certify,** that I have let unto A. B. my dwelling house known as No. —, ——— street, New York city, for the term of one year from the first day of May, A.D. 18—, at the annual rent of ——— dollars, payable quarterly on the first days of August, November, and February, and the last day of April.

The premises are not to be used or occupied for any business deemed extra-hazardous on account of fire; nor shall the same, or any part thereof, be let or underlet, except with my consent in writing, under the penalty of forfeiture and damages. I or my agent shall have the right to enter said premises at reasonable hours in the daytime, to examine the same or to make such repairs and alterations therein as shall be necessary for the safety and preservation thereof, and to exhibit the premises after the first day of February to persons desirous of renting, and to put upon the walls or doors thereof the usual notice—"To Let."

Given under my hand and seal this —— day of ——— A.D. 18—

(*Signed*) C. D. [L.S.]

### Tenant's Agreement.

**This is to certify,** that I have hired and taken from C. D. his dwelling house known as No. —, ——— street, New York city, for the term of one year from the first day of May, A.D. 18—, at the annual rent of ——— dollars, payable quarterly, to wit, on the first days of August, November, and February, and the last day of April; and to pay the water tax for said premises. And I hereby promise to make punctual payment of the rent in manner aforesaid, and quit and surrender the premises, at the expiration of said term, in as good state and reasonable condition as usual and reasonable use and wear thereof will permit (damages by the elements excepted) and engage not to let or underlet the whole or any part of said premises, nor occupy the same for any business regarded as extra-hazardous on account of fire, without the written consent of the landlord, under the penalty of forfeiture and damages. The landlord or his agent shall have the right to enter said premises at reasonable hours in the daytime to examine the same, or to make such repairs and alterations therein as shall be necessary for the safety and preservation thereof, and to exhibit the said premises, after the first day of February, to persons desirous of renting, and to put on the walls or doors thereof the usual notice—"To Let."

Given under my hand and seal, this —— day of ———, A.D. 18—.

(*Signed*) A. B. [L. S.]

## LEASE OF A FARM.

**This Indenture,** made this —— day of ———, A.D. 18—, between A. B., of the first part, and C. D., of the second part, **Witnesseth**: that said A. B. has leased and to farm let, and doth hereby lease and to farm let to the said C. D., his legal representatives and assigns, his farm in the township of ———, consisting of —— acres, bounded as follows, to wit: (*give boundaries if necessary to identify land*) called and generally known as the ——— farm, for the term of —— years, to commence on the —— day of ——, A.D. 18—, and to end on the last day of ——, A.D. 18—, at the rent of —— dollars yearly, to be paid at the end of each year and at the close of the term.

The lessee covenants to and with the lessor, to pay all the taxes that may be charged, imposed or assessed thereon, during the term, of every description whatever, to maintain the buildings and fences in as good repair as they are now (ordinary wear and tear, and natural decay, and accidents beyond human control, and fire not occasioned by his negligence, excepted); to work the farm only in a husbandman-like manner, and not to commit, nor permit waste to be committed upon it. He is to have the right to cut wood for fuel for the place, and for timber for the repairing of buildings and fences upon it, and for tools to be used upon it, and generally for the use of the farm, but not to remove or sell any.

The lessor on his part covenants with the lessee, his legal representatives and assigns, that while he or they faithfully keep and perform the acts to be by him and them kept and performed, he and they shall quietly and peaceably have and enjoy the said premises without hindrance or disturbance by any one having any right to hinder or disturb him or them in the possession and use thereof.

On a failure for thirty days to pay rent, as herein provided, the lessor, or his heirs or assigns, may put an end to the term hereby created, may regard all persons holding possession as tenants at will wrongfully holding over their term without permission, and re-enter and dispossess them in any manner provided by law for that purpose.

**In witness whereof,** the parties have hereunto set their hands and seal, the day first above written.

(*Signed*) A. B. [L. S.]
C. D. [L. S.]

*Executed in Presence of* }

## SURRENDER OF LEASE.

**This Indenture,** made the —— day of ——, 18—, between A. B., of the first part, and C. D., of the second part, **Witnesseth**: that inasmuch as the said party of the second part did, by a certain lease bearing date the —— day of ——, A. D. 18—, demise unto the said party of the first part a farm situated and described as follows (*give township, county, and bounds*), for the term of — years from and after the —— day of ——, A. D. 18—; **Now Therefore,** in consideration of the sum of —— dollars paid by the party of the second part to the party of the first part, and to the intent that the said term in said land may be extinguished, the party of the first part hath surrendered and doth hereby surrender unto the said party of the second part, his heirs and assigns, the premises in the said lease described, and all estate, claim and demand whatsoever of the said party of the first part of, in or to the same, or any part or parcel thereof. And the said party of the first part doth hereby covenant and agree to and with the said party of the second part, that the said party of the first part hath not at any time heretofore, done, committed or suffered any act or thing whatsoever, by reason or means whereof the said premises surrendered, or any part or parcel thereof, are, or is, or may be, in any wise impeached or encumbered.

**In witness whereof,** *etc.* (*Signed and sealed as above.*)

# RIGHTS OF MARRIED WOMEN.

UNDER the common law MARRIED WOMEN were most unjustly deprived of nearly all rights pertaining to the use and disposal of their own property, and had no power whatever to enter into contracts on their own account. By statutory enactments of the different States, these disabilities have been done away with, in some cases in part, in others altogether. But as the common law principles will still apply, unless specifically revoked, we must know what that common law theory was in order to understand the force of the statutes, an abstract of which is given below. Briefly stated, it was this: The wife's *personal* property, at time of marriage, became absolutely the husband's property. He could use it, sell it, or dispose of it by will, except only her *paraphernalia*, by which was meant dress, jewelry, *etc.*, suited to her condition in life. In her real estate the husband was possessed during her life, and if a child were born, to the end of his own life, in case he survived her. This latter right for life was called *curtesy*. Property not actually in the wife's possession, but to which she had a right *in action* (as debts due her), might be reduced to possession by the husband, and was then his. All separate earnings of the wife might be seized by the husband. To reserve property to the separate use of the wife, it was necessary to make a contract before marriage, or marriage settlement, by which it was put into the hands of trustees for her benefit. Upon death of her husband without a will, the wife was entitled to one third of the real estate, or *dower*, and if a will was made and a legacy left her she could choose between taking it or claiming her dower right.

In only one respect did the common law bear rather hardly on the husband. He was liable for all debts contracted by his wife *before* marriage. He was also bound to supply her with necessaries according to her station in life; and, if he neglected to do so, she could contract for them in his name, and bind him thereby. The wife's right to support and protection can be forfeited only if she abandons him without good cause or is divorced by law.

## ABSTRACT OF STATE LAWS AS TO THE RIGHTS OF MARRIED WOMEN.

**Alabama.**—All property acquired before marriage and all afterwards acquired by gift, grant, devise or inheritance is separate estate, not liable for the husband's debts, and may be devised or bequeathed as by a single woman. This separate estate is liable for debts contracted by the woman before marriage, and for contracts after marriage for articles of comfort and support of the family. Wife is entitled to dower of one-half of husband's real estate if he leave no lineal descendants; one-third if there are any; *provided* she has no separate estate. If her separate estate is less than the dower interest would be, she is entitled to as much as will make it equal.

**Arizona.**—Separate property as in Alabama. She may control and dispose of it in all respects like a single woman. It is liable for her own, but not for her husband's debts. Married women may carry on business and sue and be sued in their own names.

**Arkansas.**—Wife's separate property should be scheduled, under the act of 1875, and is then hers to dispose of by gift, grant, devise or inheritance, and not subject to her husband's debts. If not scheduled, the burden of proof is on the wife to show that the property in question is separate estate. To render the separate property liable for debts contracted by the wife, the contract must be made with reference to such liability.

**California.**—No rights of dower or curtesy exist. Separate property of wife as in Alabama. All property acquired by husband or wife after marriage, except such as is acquired by gift, bequest, devise or descent, is common property, and under the absolute management of the husband. Upon his death the wife is entitled to one half after paying debts, expenses, *etc.* In case of divorce, not on account of adultery or extreme cruelty, the wife is also entitled to one half the property.

**Colorado.**—Married women are treated in all respects as to their property rights as if they were single. A wife may transact business, sue and be sued, transfer real estate, and in all ways bind her separate estate without the husband's joining. Her separate property is not bound for her husband's debts.

**Connecticut.**—By the act of 1877 the rights of married women are materially enlarged. Any woman married after April 20, 1877, may make contracts, convey real estate and sue or be sued in regard to any property owned by her at the time of marriage or afterwards acquired. The estate is liable for her debts, and, jointly with her husband, for debts contracted for joint benefit of both or household expenses. After the death of the husband or wife, the survivor is entitled to one half of all property; absolutely, if there is no will, for life in any case. But if there are children, the half is reduced to one third. In case of women married before 1877, the property of the wife vests in the husband in trust for the wife, and at his death vests in the wife as a *femme sole*. The separate earnings of a wife are her sole property.

**Dakota.**—Neither husband nor wife has any interest in the separate property of the other. A married woman may do business in all respects like a *femme sole*. Her earnings and accumulations are her separate property and not liable for the husband's debts, nor even for household debts contracted by her as her husband's agent.

**Delaware.**—By the acts of 1873 and 1879, all property, real or personal, now held or hereafter in any way acquired from any person but the husband, is separate estate and not subject to his disposal, or liable for his debts. The wife may receive wages, sue and be sued in respect to her own property, and give bonds in all respects like a *femme sole*.

**District of Columbia.**—Real or personal property belonging to the wife at the time of the marriage, or afterwards acquired, is separate estate. In regard to it she may contract, sue and be sued, convey and devise as a single woman. But the earnings of a married woman are still her husband's property.

**Florida.**—Separate property is not liable for husband's debts, nor for debts contracted for family expenses. By the law of 1879, a married woman may gain entire control of her property, sue and be sued, and become a "free dealer" by making a petition to the Circuit Court judge sitting in chancery, and upon a license issued by that court, and published four weeks in a newspaper of the circuit or posted at the county court house.

**Georgia.**—A married woman may contract, sue and be sued as to her separate estate in her own name, unless she have a trustee. She may become a free trader with consent of her husband advertised for four weeks. The wife and children, after the husband's death, are entitled to one year's support from his property, and all other claims yield to this.

**Idaho.**—Separate estate of wife or husband as in Alabama. The property acquired after marriage except by gift, devise, bequest or descent, is common. Separate property of the wife should be inventoried with the county recorder. The husband has control of it during marriage, but cannot sell or encumber unless joined by the wife, who must be examined separately, as to her free will, *etc*. A trustee may be appointed by the District Court to manage separate property, if the husband commits waste. Upon the death of husband or wife, half the common property goes to the survivor, or, if there are no direct descendants, all.

**Illinois.**—Married women may own in their own right real or personal property, obtained by gift, descent or purchase; may convey the same, sue or be sued, or make a will, in all respects like single women. The wife's separate earnings are her own. The property of both is liable for family expenses and education of children. A surviving wife or husband takes one third of all the real estate of the deceased.

**Indiana.**—A married woman holds her real and personal property, and all profits therefrom, absolutely as her separate property, not liable for her husband's debts; but she cannot convey or encumber her real estate unless the husband joins. Personal property she may sell. A married woman's note is not binding unless it can be shown that it was made with special reference to her separate property. A widow takes one third of her husband's personal estate, and, of the realty one third, free from creditors, if valued under $10,000; one fourth, if the estate is more than $10,000 and under $20,000, and one fifth, if above $20,000. In any case she takes $500 without accounting.

**Iowa.**—A married woman may own, sell, convey or devise by will her separate property in the same manner as her husband can his. Neither is liable for the debts of the other before marriage, nor for separate debts incurred afterwards; but either or both are liable for family expenses and education of children. The wife's earnings are her own. Her note is good against her own estate.

**Kansas.**—A married woman may bargain, sell, convey and control her separate estate in all respects, as the husband may his. She may make contracts or carry on any trade or business, and her earnings or profits are her own.

**Kentucky.**—A wife can act as a *femme sole* only if the husband abandons her, leaves her without maintenance, or is in the penitentiary for more than one year. She cannot make contracts, buy goods or give notes unless authorized so to do by a decree of a court. By petition to a court in chancery, in which the husband must join, she may acquire the right to transact business in her own name. She takes a dower of one third of the real estate, and one half of the personal estate if there are no descendants; otherwise one third.

**Louisiana.**—If the wife have separate property at the time of marriage (as by marriage settlement) the husband cannot sell it. All property acquired after marriage by husband or wife is common property. At the dissolution of the marriage by death or divorce the property is equally divided. There is no right of dower to the wife. A wife has a mortgage upon her husband's real estate to secure repayment of all sums received by him on her account since marriage. To have effect against third parties it must be recorded. The wife may carry on a separate business, but her husband will be bound by her contracts so long as the community of property exists. If separation of property has been obtained, the wife must duly contribute from her separate estate for family expenses, *etc*.

**Maine.**—Married women have now the same property rights, power to sue and be sued and make contracts that men have. A married woman's property is liable only for her own contracts. If the husband abandon her and leave the State, she may obtain authority from a court to receive and use his personal property.

**Maryland.**—Separate property is protected from a husband's debts, unless it has been transferred to the wife after marriage by the husband to avoid his creditors. Married women who by skill, industry or personal labor may acquire property (real or personal) to above the value of $1,000, may manage, sell or dispose of such property like single women. Other property must be conveyed by joint deed with the husband, but may be devised by will. The husband is not liable for wife's debts contracted before marriage. The wife has dower in the real estate.

**Massachusetts.**—Separate property is that which comes to a married woman by descent, devise, bequest, gift or grant, before or after marriage, or is acquired by her trade, business or personal services, or received for releasing dower. All such property she may sell, lease, convey, manage and control like a single woman. She may make any contracts except to or with her husband. Personal ornaments, clothing, etc., to the value of $2,000, are her separate property. A married woman's note is good as against her alone. A married woman doing business on her own account must file a certificate in the town or city clerk's office, stating the facts. Such certificate may be filed by the husband. If not filed at all the husband will be liable for the debts of the wife.

**Michigan.**—Separate property is owned and controlled by married women in the same manner as by single women. A wife may carry on business in her own name and may contract with all persons, including her husband. All common law restrictions have been removed, except that in becoming surety for her husband or a third party, she does not bind her separate estate. When execution issues against husband and wife jointly for a wrong committed by the wife, her separate property only can be seized.

**Minnesota.**—Married women have full property rights as to their separate estate, power of contracts and proceeds of their personal skill or labor. But in case of selling or conveying real estate or any interest therein, except mortgages for purchase money and leases for not more than three years, the husband must join in the conveyance. Contracts or powers of attorney between husband and wife are void, if they relate to real estate.

**Mississippi.**—Married women may acquire and hold any kind of property free from any control or liability of the husband. Income therefrom and earnings for services to others than the husband are the wife's. Deeds from husband to wife are void as to creditors at the time of execution. A wife may carry on any business on her own account like a single woman. If a husband converts his wife's income to his own use, he is liable, but action must be brought within one year.

**Missouri.**—Before the act of 1875 the intervention of a trustee was necessary to relieve a married woman's separate property from liability for the husband's debt. She may now sell or dispose of real or personal estate, make contracts, sue or be sued, trade and give notes. To make property acquired by her, her husband's, a written transfer is now necessary.

**Montana.**—Property claimed to be a married woman's separate estate must be recorded as such with the register of deeds in the county where she resides, to exempt it from liabilities or debts of the husband. If she desires to become a sole trader she must also record her intention, and, if the capital invested is over $10,000, must make oath that the surplus did not come from funds belonging to her husband. A surviving wife or husband takes one half of the property of the deceased if there are no children, one third if there are.

**Nebraska.**—All property owned by the wife at marriage and all acquired by her in any way, except only by gift of the husband, is separate and may be disposed of or sold freely. The wife may carry on business on her own account and her earnings are her own. Her note is good only as against her own estate. A will of a married woman conveying real property is not valid unless the written consent of the husband thereto is annexed.

**Nevada.**—Separate property is that owned at the time of marriage. Any acquired afterwards, except by gift, devise or descent, is common property. Of the common property, the husband has absolute control and may dispose of it as of his own. Curtesy and dower are abolished. At the death of the husband, or after divorce for other cause than adultery or extreme cruelty, the wife takes half the common property after paying all expenses.

**New Hampshire.**—Married women may hold, convey, sell, devise and bequeath real or personal property as freely as single women. They may make contracts, engage in business, buy goods, give notes, etc., for their sole benefit and without the husband's intervention. The wife may even contract with her husband and may sue him as her agent. The husband cannot convey real estate to his wife.

**New Jersey.**—A wife's separate property is not liable for her husband's debts. Since Jan. 1, 1875, a married woman has had the right to bind herself by contract as if she were single, but she cannot become an accommodation indorser, guarantor or surety, nor liable on any promise to answer for the debt, default or liability of another party. She cannot convey or encumber real estate unless the husband joins, unless she be separated from him by decree of court.

**New Mexico.**—Married women have a separate estate in whatever they own, inherit or acquire. But the husband has the management of the wife's property, and the profits thereon become joint property. The husband must join in the wife's conveyance of real estate. There is no dower. On the husband's death the wife's private property is first deducted, then debts and expenses are paid, and the residue is equally divided between the wife and the husband's estate.

**New York.**—A married woman has the same rights and is subject to the same liability as a single woman. She may carry on any trade or business in her own name, and dispose of the profits as she chooses. She may make negotiable paper, but only to bind her separate estate, and may charge the same by indorsing as security. The right of dower exists. Real property may be devised by females of the age of twenty-one, personal property by females of the age of sixteen. Life insurance policies in favor of a wife on her husband's life may be assigned by the wife with the written consent of the husband.

**North Carolina.**—The separate property of the wife is secured from liability for the husband by constitutional provision. The wife may devise or bequeath, and, with the written consent of the husband, convey. She cannot make contracts even to pay her debts before marriage without the husband's written consent. But she may become a "free trader" by filing her intention so to become, and her husband's full consent thereto, in the register's office of the place where she is to carry on business. The common law rule as to dower prevails.

**Ohio.**—All separate property is free from liability on the husband's account, except personal property which has been reduced to his possession with her assent. The husband must unite in all conveyances of real estate or interest therein, except leases for less than three years. If the husband abandon his family the wife may apply for an order of court giving her the property rights of a single woman. A widow is entitled to dower. A married woman's note of hand binds only her separate estate.

**Oregon.**—The property of a married woman possessed by her at the time of her marriage, or afterwards acquired by gift, devise or inheritance, is not subject to the husband's debts or control. Conveyances and transfers between man and wife are valid, and other contracts may be made by the wife and business transacted by her as if she were a *femme sole.* The wages of a wife's labor are her own. Husband and wife are liable for the separate debts of each other, but not if incurred before marriage.

**Pennsylvania.**—Separate property is not liable for the husband's debts. The wife cannot make a valid contract (except for necessaries); her note is not binding; she cannot convey real estate unless the husband joins. But if the husband has been adjudged a lunatic, the wife may act as a single woman. The wife's earnings belong to the husband, but may be secured by a petition to the Court of Common Pleas. Married women may devise by will, subject to the right of curtesy; they may also transfer railroad and other stocks as if unmarried, and keep bank accounts in their own names, and draw thereon without the husband's consent.

**Rhode Island.**—The wife's separate property cannot be attached for the husband's liabilities, and upon his death reverts to her sole use. The wife may sell or transfer personal property, except household furniture, pla e, jewels, stock or shares, money on deposit and debt secured by mortgage; but she cannot transact business as a trader nor bind herself by a promissory note. Rights of dower and curtesy are fully preserved.

**South Carolina.**—By provisions in the constitution of 1868 all property held by a woman at time of marriage, or afterwards acquired by gift, grant, inheritance, devise or otherwise, is not subject to levy for the husband's debts, but is separate, and may be bequeathed, devised or alienated by her as if she were unmarried. But no gift from husband to wife is valid if detrimental to the claims of his creditors. In every respect the wife deals like a single woman. Dower exists.

**Tennessee.**—Married women can dispose of separate property by deed or will, unless the power of disposition is expressly withheld by the instrument under which she holds. Real estate not separate is conveyed by joint deed of husband and wife, and separate examination is required. After death of the husband the wife has dower in all real estate to the extent of one-third, without abatement on account of mortgages and creditors' claims, and of the personal estate, after paying debts, *etc.*, she takes all, if there are no children; if there are children, the wife and children share equally. If the husband dies intestate and without heirs, the wife inherits all his real estate.

**Texas.**—All property owned by husband or wife at marriage, or afterwards acquired by gift, devise or descent, and the increase of such property, is separate estate. All acquired after marriage, otherwise than by gift, devise or descent, is in common. The husband has the control and management of the wife's separate property. The common property is liable for the debts of either, and may be disposed of by the husband without the wife's consent. On the death of either one-half of the community property goes to the survivor and half to the children. A married woman cannot become a free trader or partner in business. She may, however, act as security for her husband by creating a lien on her separate property.

**Utah.**—The separate property of a married woman may be held, managed, transferred, controlled and disposed of without limitation or restriction by reason of marriage. The wife may carry on business on her own account, sue and be sued, give a valid promissory note, or make any form of contract.

**Vermont.**—Separate property is not liable for the husband's debts; nor can real estate not separate be attached for such debt, except for family necessaries, labor, material and improvements upon the real estate. At law a married woman can make no contracts, but if a woman is doing business in her own name a court of *equity* will enforce judgments against her separate property. The wife may devise by will, but the husband must join in conveying real property. The wife's earnings cannot be attached by trustee or garnishee process for the husband's debts.

**Virginia.**—Important changes were made by the acts of 1874, 1877, and 1878. As the law now stands, the separate property of a married woman is not subject to the husband's debts or disposal, but she cannot contract in relation thereto, or sue and be sued, unless her husband joins her, except only in case of property acquired by her as a sole trader. She may devise or bequeath as a single woman (subject to the

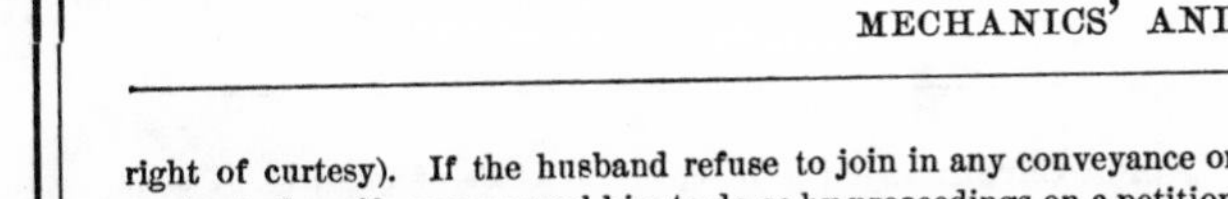

right of curtesy). If the husband refuse to join in any conveyance or contract, the wife may compel him to do so by proceedings on a petition in equity, showing the court that her interests require the transaction.

**West Virginia.**—Separate property is secured to the wife's own use, but the husband must join in the conveyance or disposal of real estate, unless the wife is living apart from him. Dower exists, and the wife must therefore join in the conveyance of real estate in order to release dower. A married woman may make a will, keep a separate bank account, and in most respects has the same rights as a single woman.

**Wisconsin.**—Property held by a married woman at the time of marriage, or afterwards acquired in any way, is under her full control. She may convey real estate without the husband joining. In suing for charges against the separate estate of a wife, the husband must be joined as a defendant, but the wife may bring suit alone. Dower exists. After the wife's death the husband holds her realty.

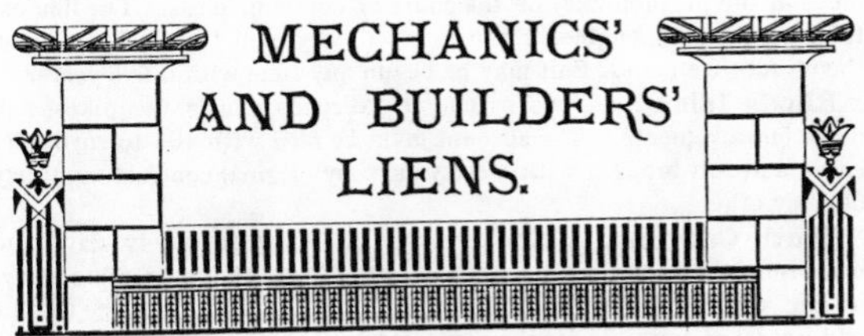

VALID claims against property (or, as the word itself signifies, a *hold* upon it), are termed LIENS. One who holds a lien may, within a time specified by law and by duly prescribed methods, enforce his claim by having the property sold to satisfy the amount due him.

Special liens are given by the statutes of the different States to mechanics, material-men—that is, those who supply material—and to builders. Before beginning action to enforce such a lien, notice must be given in writing by the holder of the lien to the owner of the property and in order to guard against fraud to third parties, the certificate of the claim must be filed with the county clerk or other officer as provided by the statute. The following form may be used:

### NOTICE OF LIEN.

**Take Notice**, that I, A. B., of (*residence*), hereby claim a lien against C. D. of (*residence*), amounting to the sum of (*amount*), due to me; and that the claim is made for and on account of (*here state in full the nature of the work done or materials furnished, with bill of particulars*), work done and performed (*or materials furnished*), by me in building the premises (*describe building in full*), owned by the said C. D.

And I claim a lien upon said house or building and the appurtenances thereof, and the lot on which the same stands, pursuant to the provisions of an act of the Legislature of the State of ——, to secure the payment of mechanics, laborers, and persons furnishing materials towards the erection, altering, or repairing of buildings.

Dated this —— day of ——, A. D. 18—. (*Signed*) A. B.

## MECHANICS' LIENS. ABSTRACT OF STATE LAWS.

**Alabama.**—Liens are extended to railroad laborers, as well as to the usual classes, mechanics, contractors, *etc.* Proceedings must commence within six months after the work is finished. The process is by attachment.

**Arizona.**—Besides liens of the usual description, any mechanic or artisan who makes, alters, or repairs any article of personal property, has a lien thereon to secure his just charges, and may retain possession until he is paid.

**Arkansas.**—Account of the claim must be filed with the clerk of the circuit court of the county where the land lies within ninety days after the work is done. Suit must begin within nine months.

**California.**—Liens have precedence over subsequent or previous unrecorded incumbrances. An original contractor may file his claim within sixty days; others must do so in thirty days. Suit must be brought within ninety days from the date of filing the claim.

**Colorado.**—There is a lien for work and materials over $25 in value. Claim must be filed within forty days and suit brought within six months.

**Connecticut.**—Liens exist for amounts over $25. Claims must be verified by oath and filed within sixty days from the time when claimant *began* to furnish materials or work.

**Dakota.**—The lien lies upon land as well as buildings. Machinery is included in materials furnished. The taking of collateral security will destroy the lien.

**Delaware.**—Liens are allowed for amounts above $25. Original contractors must file claims not sooner than sixty or later than ninety days after the building is finished; others, within sixty days.

**District of Columbia.**—Claims must be filed with the clerk of the supreme court of the District within sixty days after the work is completed. The amount claimed must be above $20.

**Florida.**—Contracts under which the lien is claimed must be in writing, the amount liquidated or certain, and a net balance struck. Such contracts must be recorded within thirty days. Claims must be filed within six months after the work is done or materials furnished, and suit brought within a year.

**Georgia.**—Claims must be recorded within thirty days with the clerk of the superior court of the county where the property lies. Suit must be brought within a year. Mechanics and laborers have also a lien on personal property given them to repair or alter, but lose it on giving up possession of the goods.

**Idaho.**—Claims must be not less than $25. The improvement and development of mines, claims, flumes, ditches, and bridges come under the law of mechanics' liens. Accounts must be filed with the county recorder within sixty days by an original contractor; within thirty, by others. Suit must be brought within six months. Mechanics have a lien on articles left with them to repair or alter, and may sell them, if the charges are not paid within two months, after advertising the sale for three weeks.

**Illinois.**—Suit must be brought within six months. Liens for labor and materials take precedence to the extent to which they have increased the value of the property. If the time for completion of the work is fixed by contract at more than three years from the beginning, or the time of payment at more than one year from the time stipulated for the completion of the work, there is no lien.

**Indiana.**—Notice must be filed within sixty days after the completion of the work. Suit must be brought within a year. Tradesmen and mechanics have a lien for work done on personal property and may sell the same if not paid for within six months.

**Iowa.**—Claims must be filed within ninety days after the work is done or materials furnished. Suit must be brought within two years. Liens hold against railroads. Taking collateral security will destroy the lien.

**Kansas.**—Claims may be filed by sub-contractors within sixty days; by others, within four months. Suit must be begun within the year. Tradesmen and mechanics may hold articles ordered to be repaired or constructed, if their charges are not paid, and after three months may sell the same.

**Kentucky.**—Claims must be filed within sixty days. Suit must begin within six months after filing the account.

**Louisiana.**—Liens are known as "privileges." Privileges are given to architects, contractors, and material men on the buildings and lot of land not to exceed one acre. The privilege must be recorded with the register of privileges in the parish where the property lies.

**Maine.**—Statements of accounts must be filed within thirty days after ceasing to labor, in the office of the clerk of town or city where the building is. Attachments may issue against buildings ninety days after the work is finished or materials furnished; against vessels four days after they are launched.

**Maryland.**—Liens lie on buildings, machines, wharfs, and bridges erected or repaired to the extent of one fourth the value. Notice must be given to the owner within sixty days and the claim recorded within six months. Kent, Charles, Calvert, and St. Mary's counties are not included in the list of those in which the lien laws apply.

**Massachusetts.**—Claims must be filed with town or city clerk thirty days after the service is rendered. Suit must be commenced within ninety days after the work has ceased. In case of materials furnished written notice must be given to the owner (in case he is not the purchaser), that it is intended to claim a lien.

**Michigan.**—Liens lie for constructing, repairing, or furnishing materials for buildings, wharves, machinery or appurtenances. A contractor must file a copy of his contract with the register of deeds, notify the owner of his claim, and begin suit within six months after the work has ceased.

**Minnesota.**—Liens lie on buildings, appurtenances, boats, vessels, and land on which the buildings stand, not to exceed forty acres, or, if in the city, one acre. The account must be filed within a year and action brought within a year after the date of filing. There is a lien on personal property for work done thereon, and it may be sold after three months, if proper charges are not paid.

**Mississippi.**—Liens lie on buildings, bridges, fixed machinery or gearing, boats and vessels. Claims must be filed in the office of the chancery clerk of the county where the land lies. Suit must be brought within six months after the money claimed is due.

**Missouri.**—Claims must be filed within six months by original contractors, thirty days by journeymen and day laborers, and four months by other persons. Actions must begin within ninety days after filing claims. Liens lie on buildings, land, fixtures, engines, and boilers.

**Montana.**—Original contractors must file accounts within ninety days from the time work ceases; sub-contractors within thirty days. All liens filed within thirty days of the time the first lien is filed are entitled to share alike. Suit must be begun within ninety days by sub-contractors; within a year by original contractors.

**Nebraska.**—Accounts should be filed within four months of the time the work is done, or materials furnished, with the clerk of the county where the property lies. Suit must be brought within two years. The account filed must be sworn to.

**Nevada.**—Liens lie in case of railroads, canals, mines, tunnels, and ditches, as well as buildings. The amount due must be as much as $25. Claims must be recorded by original contractors within sixty days, by other persons within thirty days, after the work has ceased. Suit must be brought within six months after filing the claim.

**New Hampshire.**—Liens lie for amounts of $15, or more. Suit must be brought within ninety days. Railroad contractors and lumberers have a like lien for sixty days only.

**New Jersey.**—Liens lie on buildings, materials, fixtures, and machinery. Original contractors, by filing a copy of their contract before any work has been done or material furnished, may confine the liability for liens to themselves alone. Claims must be filed and suit brought within a year.

**New Mexico.**—Liens lie on land as well as buildings. Claims must be filed within sixty days after the work is done, and must be sworn to. Suit must be brought within a year. Tradesmen and mechanics have a lien upon articles given them for repair. Landlords and innkeepers have a lien on property and baggage of tenants and guests.

**New York.**—Claims, with specifications and a copy of the contract, if any exist, must be filed from two to three months after the work ceases. Suit must be brought within a year. The law differs in some respects in the different counties.

**North Carolina.**—Liens lie upon any kinds of property. Claims under $200 may be filed with a justice of the peace. Over that amount they must be filed with the clerk of the superior court for the county where the work was done. Notice must be filed within thirty days. Personal property held for charges by mechanics and tradesmen may be sold after thirty days if not above $50 in value, after ninety days if worth more than that.

**Ohio.**—Liens lie on buildings, bridges, or vessels. Claims, with copy of the original contract, if in writing, must be filed within four months. Suit must begin within the year.

**Oregon.**—Liens lie for any amount over $20. Claims must be filed within three months. Suit must be brought within a year. Personal property held for charges by artisans or mechanics may be sold after three months.

**Pennsylvania.**—Claims must be recorded within six months in the office of the prothonotary of the court of common pleas. The lien extends to wharves, engines, fixtures, machinery, and the land on which the structure stands. Suit may be begun any time within five years.

**Rhode Island.**—Liens extend to railroads, canals, turnpikes, and other improvements. The account must be filed with the town or city clerk, and suit brought within sixty days by original contractors, thirty days by others.

**South Carolina.**—Claims must be filed within ninety days and suit brought within the year. If the owner is not the contracting party, he may prevent the lien from attaching by giving written notice that he will not be responsible for the contractor's debts.

**Tennessee.**—Nôtice must be given of intention to claim a lien when the work is begun or materials furnished by sub-contractors and workmen. Suit must be brought within a year. In case of vessels and steamboats, suit must be brought within three months after the money is due.

**Texas.**—Claims must be recorded within thirty days. The owner, when served with notice by sub-contractors or workmen, may retain enough to pay them out of the sum due the original contractor.

**Utah.**—Liens extend to mining property as well as to buildings and improvements. Claims must be filed in the recorder's office within three months. Suit must be brought within a year of the completion of the work, unless the amount is not due within that time, when suit may be brought at any time within three months after it is due.

**Vermont.**—In case of work and materials for building, suit must be brought within three months. When the lien is on a vessel or steamboat, suit must be brought within eight months after the completion of the same. Claims must be filed with the town or city clerk of the place where the building is.

**Virginia.**—General contractors must file claims within thirty days after the completion of the work; sub-contractors and workmen must give notice to the owner within ten days of the amount due.

**Washington.**—Liens for wages extend to lumber and timber. Such claims must be recorded with the county auditor within sixty days from the time the work ceased. Suit must begin within four months. Wages of servants, mechanics, laborers and others are preferred claims to the extent of $100 each, in cases of insolvency. Also all sums earned for sixty days previous thereto.

**West Virginia.**—Claims must be filed with the county clerk within thirty days. The owner, upon notice by sub-contractors or workmen of sums due them, may reserve their pay from the amount due the general contractor. Suit must be brought within six months.

**Wisconsin.**—Liens extend to land on which buildings stand, but not to exceed forty acres or a city lot. Sub-contractors and workmen must give notice to the owner within thirty days after completing their services. Suit must be brought within a year. Personal property held for charges may be sold after six months.

**Wyoming.**—Claims must be filed within sixty days. Suit must be brought within a year. Artisans and mechanics may hold personal property for charges due them.

DEEDS conveying real property for the securing of a debt, the evidence of which may be a bond or obligation, or a promissory note, are known in law as MORTGAGES. The conveyance of the property is subject to the right of the debtor to redeem his estate by paying his debt, with interest, as agreed upon, and at the specified time. He who makes the conveyance is called the *mortgagor;* he who receives it the *mortgagee.*

The bond or note is drawn precisely like any other instrument of the kind. In the case of notes, it is customary to state therein that they are secured by a mortgage of even date.

Strictly speaking, the *mortgagee* has the right to take possession of the property at once, and hold it until the condition is fulfilled, but it is now almost universal for the deed to provide that the mortgagor may retain possession.

EQUITY OF REDEMPTION.—By the theory of the transaction the mortgagee has the right to take immediate possession, when the debt for which the mortgage is security falls due and is not paid. But courts of equity, deeming this an undue hardship, long ago gave the mortgagor further time within which to redeem his title. This is called the *equity of redemption.* The rule has been adopted by courts of law and by statutory enactment. The time very generally allowed for redemption is three years. The right is such a positive one that it may be itself sold, and is of such a character that the law refuses to allow it to be foregone, even by the express agreement of the mortgagor himself. Thus a distinct contract in the deed itself that the mortgagee shall have full title as soon as the debt is due and unpaid, is void and of no effect, and the three years' equity still remains.

POWER OF SALE.—It is now permitted, however, to insert an agreement to the effect that upon the debt becoming due, the mortgagee may, after a fixed time, enter upon the land, sell it, pay himself debt, interest and costs, and return the balance left, if any there be, to the mortgagor. This is called a *power of sale.* The equity of redemption, or three years' grace, begins to run at the date when the mortgagee takes the property into his own possession with the avowed intention of *foreclosing.* That is, the note or bond may call for payment of the debt in, say six years, but the debt may run on unpaid for ten, and the right of redemption be not exhausted and not even begun, because the mortgagee has taken no steps to foreclose.

INSURANCE CLAUSES are often inserted, providing that insurance shall be maintained on the property at the expense of the mortgagor. Where this is not done, the mortgagee must insure at his own cost, or run the risk of losing his security by fire. Where the right of dower still exists, the wife should join in the deed to release or extinguish her dower right. The execution and acknowledgment of mortgages must be performed exactly as in the case of deeds absolute.

A RELEASE of a mortgage must be in writing, and duly signed, sealed, acknowledged and recorded. It must distinctly declare that the debt which the deed was designed to secure has been fully paid and discharged. It may take the form of a quit-claim deed from the mortgagee to the mortgagor. A more common and convenient practice is for the register or recorder of deeds to draw a form of release and discharge on the margin of the record of the deed, and to obtain thereto the signature of the mortgagee.

Unless stipulation is made to the contrary, the mortgagee, upon foreclosing absolutely, that is, not under a power of sale, is entitled to all fixtures and buildings which have been added to the property by the mortgagor. On the other hand, if the mortgagee has made such additions after taking possession with intention to foreclose, they fall to the mortgagor, if he redeems in time. The latter is also entitled to rents and profits received by the mortgagee while in possession.

Mortgages may be assigned, and the written assignment should be indorsed on the back of the deed or attached thereto.

## FORM OF MORTGAGE WITH POWER OF SALE.

**This Indenture,** made the —— day of ——, A. D. 18—, between A. B. of (*mortgagor's residence*), the party of the first part, and C. D., of (*mortgagee's residence*), the party of the second part: **Whereas,** the said A. B. of the first part is justly indebted to the said C. D. of the second part, in the sum of (*amount*), lawful money, secured to be paid by a certain bond or obligation (*or promissory note, as the case may be*) bearing even date with these presents, in the penal sum of (*amount of penalty, if on a bond, and describe the bond or note*) as by the said bond or obligation (*or promissory note*) and the condition thereof, reference being thereunto had, may more fully appear.

**This Indenture Witnesseth,** That the said party of the second part, for the more fully securing the payment of the said sum of money mentioned in said bond (*or note*) with interest thereon, according to the true intent and meaning thereof, and also for and in consideration of the sum of one dollar to him in hand paid by the said party of the second part, at or before the ensealing and delivery of these presents, the receipt whereof is hereby acknowledged, has granted, bargained, sold, aliened, released, conveyed and confirmed, and by these presents doth grant, bargain, sell, alien, release, convey and confirm unto the party of the second part, and to his heirs and assigns forever, all those premises known (*here describe land by bounds and metes with great particularity*). **Together** with all and singular the tenements, hereditaments and appurtenances thereunto belonging or in any way pertaining, and the reversion and reversions, remainder and remainders, rents, issues and profits thereof; and also all the estate, right, title, interest, property, possession, claim and demand whatsoever, as well in law as in equity, of the said party of the first part, of, in and to the same, and every part and parcel thereof, with the appurtenances: **To have and to hold,** the above granted, bargained and described premises, with the appurtenances, unto the said party of the second part, and his heirs and assigns, to his and their own proper use, benefit and behoof forever.

**Provided Always,** and these presents are upon this express condition, that if the said party of the first part, his heirs, executors or administrators, shall well and truly pay unto the party of the second part, his executors, administrators or assigns, the said sum of money mentioned in the condition of the above mentioned bond (*or in the note*) according to the true intent and meaning thereof, and the interest thereon at the time and manner mentioned in the said condition, that then these presents and the estate hereby granted shall cease, determine and be void. And the said A. B., for himself and his heirs, executors and administrators, does covenant and agree to pay unto the said party of the second part, C. D., or his executors, administrators or assigns, the said sum of money and interest as mentioned above, and expressed in the condition of the said bond. And if default shall be made in the payment of the said sum of money, or the interest or any part thereof, that then and from thenceforth, it shall be lawful for said party of the second part, his executors, administrators or assigns, to enter into and upon all and singular the premises hereby granted, or intended so to be, and to sell and dispose of the same and all benefit and equity of redemption of the said party of the first part, or his heirs, executors, administrators or assigns therein, at public auction. And out of the money arising from such sale, to retain the principal and interest, which shall then be due on the said bond or obligation (*or note*), together with the costs and charges of advertisement and sale of the same premises, rendering the overplus of the purchase money (if any there shall be) unto the said A. B., his heirs, executors, administrators or assigns; which sale, so to be made, shall forever be a perpetual bar, both in law and in equity, against the said party of the first part, and his heirs and assigns and all other parties claiming, or to claim, the premises, or any part thereof, by, from or under him or them, or any of them.

**In Witness Whereof,** *etc.* (*Executed and acknowledged like other deeds. See* Deeds.)

### Clause to Release Dower.

*Insert when dower right is to be extinguished*:—And for the consideration aforesaid, I, L. B., the wife of the said A. B., of the first part, do hereby release unto the said C. D., of the second part, his heirs, executors, administrators and assigns, all my right of dower and homestead in the above described, bargained and granted premises.

### Insurance Clause.

And it is expressly agreed, by and between the parties to these presents, that the said party of the first part shall and will keep the buildings erected and to be erected upon the lands above conveyed, insured against loss and damage by fire, by insurers approved by the said party of the second part, and in an amount approved by said party of the second part; and assign the policy and certificates thereof to the said party of the second part, and in default thereof, it shall be lawful for the said party of the second part to effect such insurance, and the premium or premiums paid for effecting the same shall be a lien on said mortgaged premises, added to the amount of the said bond or obligation (*or note*), and secured by these presents, and payable on demand with interest at the rate of — per cent. per annum.

## RELEASE OF MORTGAGE.

**This Debt,** secured by the deed of mortgage dated the — day of ——, A. D. 18—, and recorded with the recorder of deeds for the city of ——, (*or* county —), *lib.* ——, *fol.* ——, has been paid to me by A. B., of ——, the mortgagor therein, and in consideration thereof I do discharge the mortgage and release the mortgaged premises to said A. B., his heirs, executors, administrators and assigns.

**Witness** my hand and seal, this — day of ——, A. D. 18—.

(*Signed*) A. B. [L. S.]

*Executed and Delivered in Presence of*

## ASSIGNMENT OF MORTGAGE.

**Know all Men by these Presents:** That I, C. D., of (*residence*) the mortgagee named in a certain mortgage given by A. B., of (*residence*) to said C. D., to secure the payment of (*amount*) and interest, dated the —— day of ——, A. D. 18—, recorded in volume ——, on page——, of the registry of deeds for the county of ——, in consideration of the sum of —— dollars to me paid by E. F., of (*residence*), the receipt of which is hereby acknowledged, do hereby sell, transfer, set over, and convey unto said E. F., his heirs and assigns, said mortgage and the real estate thereby conveyed, together with the promissory note, debt, and claim thereby secured and the covenants therein contained (*and to redemption according to law*).

**In Witness Whereof,** I have hereunto set my hand and seal, this —— day of ——, A. D. 18—.

(*Signature*) [L. S.]

*Signed, sealed, and delivered in Presence of* }

## MORTGAGE BOND.

**Know all Men by these Presents:** That I, A. B., of (*residence*) am held and firmly bound unto C. D., of (*residence*) in the penal sum of (*insert twice the amount of the actual debt*) to be paid to the said C. D., his heirs, executors, administrators, or assigns, and to this payment I hereby bind myself, my heirs, executors and administrators firmly by these presents.

*Sealed with my seal this —— day of ——*, A. D. 18—.

**The Condition** of the above obligation is: That if I, the said A. B., or my heirs, executors, or administrators, shall pay or cause to be paid unto the said C. D. the sum of (*amount of debt*) on the —— day of ——, with interest at the rate of —— per cent. per annum, payable —— months from the date hereof and every —— months thereafter, until the said sum is paid, then the obligation shall be void and of no effect; but otherwise it shall remain in full force.

And I further agree and covenant that if any payment of interest be withheld or delayed for —— days after such payment shall fall due, the said principal sum and all arrearage of interest thereon, shall be and become due immediately on the expiration of —— days, at the option of said C. D., his executors, administrators, or assigns.

A. B. [*Seal.*]

*Executed and delivered in presence of* }

# Partnership.

NO especial form of contract is necessary to constitute a partnership. When two or more persons agree to unite together their money, property, labor or skill, or all of these, for the purpose of carrying on business for their common profit and at their common risk, the compact is a PARTNERSHIP. The persons may be any able to contract, and the business any lawful one. Written articles of partnership should always be drawn, though the partnership may be proved by a parole contract or even by the acts of the parties. The rights of third parties against those who hold themselves out as partners are very carefully guarded by the law, and as regards these rights persons may be held to be partners, though as between themselves only, they would not be so considered.

THE FIRM is the name, style or title under which the partners do business, or may mean the partners themselves, taken collectively. The firm-name should be set forth in the articles of partnership. The signing of the firm name by any one of the partners will bind all, and each and every partner is liable to the full extent of the firm's indebtedness, except in case of limited partnership.

An *ostensible* partner is one who is known as such to the world at large. A *silent* partner is one who has an interest, but whose name is not published as a partner. A *nominal* partner is one who is held out to the world as such, but has no actual interest. He is fully liable for the firm's debts, as credit may have been given them on the strength of his name.

In all matters properly pertaining to partnership business, the act of one partner is the act of all. But if one attempts to bind the rest by using the firm's signature in matters outside the regular course of business, the contract will not hold. Conveyance of real estate should be joined in by all the partners, but if made by one and subsequently ratified by any act of the others, it will hold good. *Releases* may be made by a single partner. Upon the death of one partner his personal representatives become tenants in common with the others.

PROFITS.—When no other stipulation appears in the articles of partnership, the partners will share the profits equally. And the fact that one partner furnished most or all of the capital, the other giving only time and services, or special skill, will not contradict this presumption.

LIMITED PARTNERSHIPS were wholly unknown to the common law, and must be formed and carried on in strict conformity with the statutory regulations which allow of their existence. The object is to allow a *special* partner, whose name does not appear in that of the firm, to invest a fixed sum of money in the business, and to receive profits and share losses only in proportion to the amount thus invested. The statutes generally require such a partnership to be defined in a certificate, acknowledged like a deed, which must set forth the firm name, nature of business, names of general and special partners, distinguished as such, and the amount which each special partner contributes.

DISSOLUTION.—A partnership may be dissolved: 1. By the death of one of the partners. The dissolution takes effect from the time of death. Insanity or absolute incapacity of one partner also effects a dissolution. But articles may provide for the continuance of the partnership after the death or incapacity of a member, by stipulating that his heirs, legal representatives or other persons designated, may take his place. 2. By act of the parties. If the partnership is for a fixed period, the mutual consent is necessary. If not, any partner may dissolve the compact at his pleasure by giving notice to the others. 3. By act of law, as in bankruptcy or insolvency, or by the decree of a court of equity founded on fraud, misconduct or gross incapacity of one partner. 4. By assignment for benefit of creditors or by one partner of his interest to a stranger or another partner. 5. By expiration of the period of partnership; by extinction of the subject matter of business; by the absconding of one partner, or by the breaking out of war between states in which the trade is carried on. After dissolution the partners are, in respect to the property, tenants-in-common. Their power as co-partners extends to winding up the business of the firm, and completing unfulfilled engagements, but no further.

## ARTICLES OF PARTNERSHIP.

**Articles of Agreement**, made this —— day of ——, A.D. 18—, between A. B., C. D., and E. F.

This agreement witnesseth, that the above named A. B., C. D., and E. F. have this day, and do by these presents, associate themselves together as copartners in the trade or business of ——, and in buying and selling at wholesale and retail, all sorts of goods and merchandise belonging to said trade or business, under the name and firm title of A. B., C, D. & Co. That said partnership shall continue from the date of this agreement for and during the term of —— years, next ensuing. That to this end and purpose A. B. has contributed the sum of (*amount*), and the said C. D. the sum of (*amount*), and the said E. F. the sum of (*amount*), as stock, to be used, invested and employed in common between them in the management of the said business for their utmost general advantage and benefit. That said parties shall not at any time hereafter use, follow or exercise said business or occupation, or another, during said term, to their private benefit or advantage, but shall at all times during said term, and with their utmost skill and ability, conduct and act only for their mutual advantage with said stock and its increase. That the said copartners shall and will discharge and pay all rents, salaries, and other expenses of carrying on the business, equally between them. That all increase, gain, and profit which may accrue or arise in the course of, and resulting from said trade or business, shall be from time to time equally divided between them, the aforesaid copartners, share and share alike. And also that all losses and decrease that may be incurred in said joint trade or business, by reason of bad debts, falling off in value, ill commodities, or in any way, except by the fraud or gross misconduct of one of the partners, shall be borne and paid equally between them, share and share alike. That there shall be kept during said term and joint business, just and true books of account, wherein each of the said copartners shall duly enter and set down, as well all money by him received and expended, as also the goods, wares, and merchandise by him bought and sold on account of said partnership and all other things relating thereto, and to the conduct thereof, so that either of the partners may at any time have free and full access thereto. That said partners shall once every three months, or oftener if so required by any one of them, make and render, each to the other, or to the legal representatives of the other, a true and perfect account of all profits and gains by them made, and of all losses sustained; and also of all receipts, disbursements and other things whatsoever concerning said partnership; and thereupon shall cancel, adjust, pay and deliver unto each other their equal shares of all profits, if any there shall be. That at the end of the said term of —— years, heretofore agreed upon, or other sooner determination of the copartnership, by death, process of law or otherwise, the said partners, or their survivors, shall and will make and render to each other, or to the legal representatives of each other, a final and true account of all things as aforesaid, and in all things well and truly adjust the same, and fully, fairly and completely divide equally among themselves, or between themselves and the legal representatives of a partner deceased, all and every the accrued profits, stock in hand, accounts payable, and all the joint property of the copartnership in whatsoever form, share and share alike.

(*Signatures.*)

**In Witness Whereof**, etc.

## ARTICLES OF LIMITED PARTNERSHIP.

**Articles of Partnership** agreed upon this first day of June, 1882, between Edward Grant and John Heald. The parties hereto agree to form a limited partnership, under the laws providing for limited partnerships, under the style of Edward Grant, as wholesale dealers in flour and grain, to be conducted in the city of Boston, to commence this day and continue five years.

Edward Grant is to be the general partner, and contribute to the capital $4,000. He is to have charge and management of the business and devote his time and attention to it, and use his best exertions to make it profitable. He is to keep correct and proper books of account, in a proper manner, to show all the partnership transactions, which are to be open for examination to said Heald at all times, and shall communicate to said Heald, from time to time, all information that he may desire as regards the business.

John Heald is to be the special partner, and, at the time of executing these articles, has contributed to the capital eight thousand dollars in cash to the common stock.

From the profits, if any, each partner is to receive the interest upon his contribution to the capital, and the residue of the profit is to be divided between them. An accounting is to be had once in six months, the profits and losses ascertained, and the losses, if any, are to be borne by the partners in proportion to their respective contributions to the capital.

EDWARD GRANT.
JOHN HEALD.

## CERTIFICATE OF LIMITED PARTNERSHIP.

**This is to Certify,** That the undersigned have, pursuant to the provisions of the statutes of the State of Massachusetts, formed a limited partnership under the firm name of Edward Grant, that the general nature of the business to be transacted is that of wholesale dealers in flour and grain; that it is to be conducted in the city of Boston; that Edward Grant is the general partner and John Heald the special partner; that the said John Heald has contributed the sum of eight thousand dollars as capital toward the common stock; and that said partnership is to begin on the first day of June, 1882, and is to terminate on the first day of June, 1887.

*Dated this first day of June*, 1882.

EDWARD GRANT.
JOHN HEALD.

CITY OF BOSTON, SUFFOLK COUNTY, ss.

On the first day of June, 1882, before me came Edward Grant and John Heald, to me known to be the individuals described in and who executed the above certificate, and they severally acknowledged that they executed the same.

JAMES SMITH,
*Judge Superior Court.*

## CLAUSES TO BE INSERTED, IF DESIRED.

TO BUY OR SELL.—That either party may, upon the dissolution of said partnership, make a written offer to the other parties, to buy their or sell his own entire interest in the partnership effects, at a certain price, which shall be specified in said written offer. And that thereupon and within —— days thereafter, the other parties or partners shall in writing signify to the party proposing, their acceptance or rejection of his offer; and failing so to do, the said party proposing may within —— days buy or sell at his own option and according to the terms of his proposal.

PROPORTION OF PROFITS.—That all profits and losses shall be apportioned according to the capital furnished by each partner, and in no other manner.

CONTINUATION OF PARTNERSHIP.—It is hereby agreed that the partnership evidenced by the within articles of agreement shall be continued upon the same terms and under the same provisions and restrictions as are therein contained. for the further term of —— years from the —— day of —— next ensuing.

CLERK TO BE CASHIER.—That the chief clerk for the time being shall act as cashier and be the general receiver of all the money belonging to the said partnership, and shall pay out therefrom all demands as ordered by said partners, and from time to time shall pay all surplus cash to such parties as said partners shall designate.

NOT TO INDORSE OR BIND FIRM WITHOUT CONSENT.—That neither of said parties shall, during the existence of said partnership, without the consent of the others being first obtained thereto, make any note, accept any bill, or indorse any or either of the same for himself or any other person whatsoever, nor enter into any bond, conveyance, covenant or other obligation without the consent of the others first obtained.

(Other common stipulations are, as to division of duties; drawing for personal expenses by partners; admission of new partners; retiring partners not to establish similar business in the same place; providing for arbitration in case of dispute; denying the right of partners to assign their interests; binding each not to trust any whom the copartners shall forbid, *etc., etc.*

## NOTICE OF DISSOLUTION,

Notice is hereby given that the partnership hitherto existing between the undersigned under the firm title of "B. and D.," in the town of ——, is this day dissolved by mutual consent. By agreement between the undersigned all liabilities of the firm are hereby assumed by C. D., who will henceforth carry on the business under his own name. All debts to the firm may be paid to the said C. D., and promptness is requested in such settlement.

(*Signed*) A. B.
C. D.

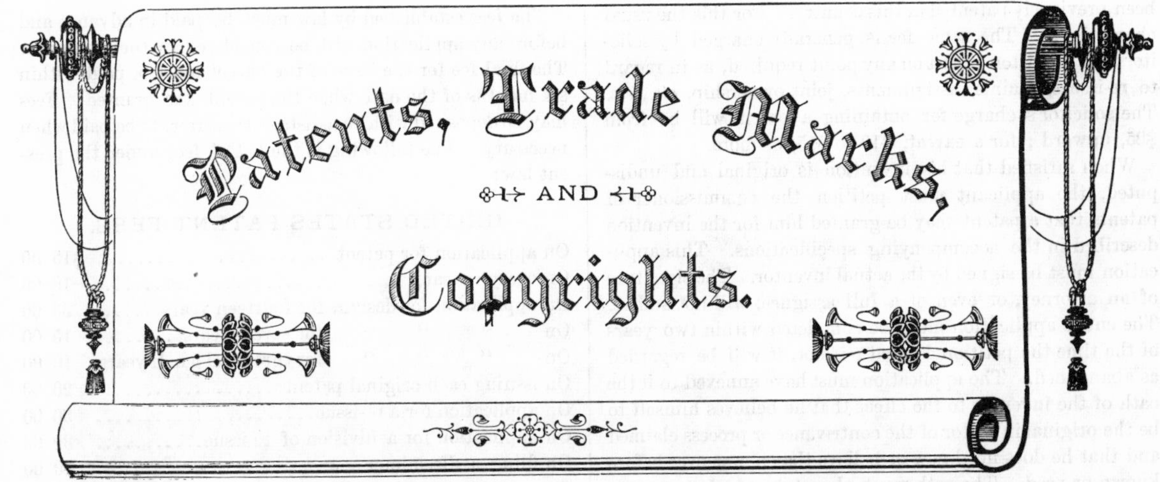


ORIGINAL contrivances and literary property belong to the inventor or author alone, so long as they are kept within his exclusive possession. When circulated abroad with the consent of the inventor or author they become public property, and the right of the originator is lost. The object of PATENT and COPYRIGHT laws is to secure to the originator the benefits of his inventive or literary skill and at the same time to allow the public to enjoy the fruits of his invention or composition. The consideration received by the inventor or author is protection in the sale and use of his production; the compensation gained by the public is the privilege of benefiting by his skill for adequate remuneration, and the encouragement of invention and talent.

**A Patent** is an exclusive right given to an inventor by a government, for a fixed time to use, manufacture and sell an invention or improvement, made by him and not before known.

**What is Patentable.**—Patents may be obtained under the Acts of Congress governing the subject for "any new and useful art, machine, manufacture or composition of matter, or any new and useful improvement thereof, not before known or used by others in this country, and not at the time patented or described in any printed publication in this or any foreign country; or for any new and original design for a manufacture, bust, statue, alto-relievo or bas-relief; or for any new and original ornament, impression, pattern, print or picture to be placed on or worked into any article of manufacture; or any new and original shape or configuration of any such article, the same not having been known or used by others before the application for a patent."

**Who May Obtain Patents.**—Aliens as well as citizens may obtain patents. When the inventor dies before application has been made, his executor or administrator may apply for and obtain a patent.

**Duration.**—The exclusive right to use, sell and manufacture is granted for the term of seventeen years. No extension can be granted upon any patent issued since March 2, 1861, and as more than seventeen years have now elapsed since that date, no patents capable of extension are now in existence. Patents for designs may be granted for fourteen years, seven years, or three years and six months, as the applicant may elect and petition for in his application. No patents issued for designs after March 2, 1861, can be extended.

**Re-issue.**—When the original patent is invalid, because of an inefficient or defective specification arising from mistake or accident, the original patent may be surrendered and a re-issue for the same period granted. All parties having any interest in the patent must concur in the surrender, which must be verified by oath that the original patent is not valid and available, that the error has arisen from inadvertence, mistake or accident, and without fraudulent or deceptive intention. The re-issue may be granted to the original patentee or his heirs, or to the collective assignees.

**How to Get a Patent.**—In obtaining a patent it is by far the best plan to employ a patent solicitor, who will fully understand the steps to be taken and who has experience in all pertaining to patent law. The first thing to be done is to have a special examination made at the Patent Office in Washington to discover whether the alleged invention has been previously patented in this country. For this the usual charge is $5. The same fee is generally charged by solicitors for a written report on any point required, as in regard to re-issues, claims, assignments, joint ownership, *etc., etc.* The solicitor's charge for obtaining a patent will be from $25, upward ; for a caveat, $10 to $15, or more.

When satisfied that his invention is original and undisputed, the applicant must petition the commissioner of patents that a patent may be granted him for the invention described in the accompanying specifications. This application must be signed by the actual inventor. The signature of an attorney, or even of a full assignee, will not suffice. The entire application must be completed within two years of the time the petition is filed ; if not, it will be regarded as abandoned. The application must have annexed to it the oath of the inventor to the effect that he believes himself to be the original inventor of the contrivance or process claimed and that he does not know or believe that it was ever before known or used. The oath must also state of what country the applicant is a citizen. The *specifications* must also be signed by the inventor and by two witnesses. In the specification the exact thing for which a patent is claimed must be described fully and in precise detail. When the claim is for an improvement on an old machine, art or manufacture, the specification must clearly show what is new and what old in the completed product. Whenever possible, distinct inventions should be made the subject of separate applications, but when there is mutual dependence and connection between two or more inventions, one patent may be asked for to cover the whole. The specifications must be accompanied by *drawings,* when the nature of the invention makes it possible. These must be referred to by sections, letters or figures in the specification itself. Drawings must be in duplicate, one copy on stiff paper, 20 inches by 15, to fold in the middle. This must be signed and attested by two witnesses.

**Models** must be sent where possible. They should be of durable material, and have the name of the inventor inscribed upon them. If practicable, working models should be sent. In case of works of design, photographs or drawings will be accepted. The negative of a photograph should be sent. In the case of a composition of matter, specimens of the composition and of each ingredient must be forwarded, with statement of proportion. For improvements, in most cases a model of the part to be patented will suffice.

**Caveats.**—A caveat is a petition to the commissioner from an inventor, who has not as yet fully perfected his invention, setting forth that he intends to apply for a patent, and asking that this notice or caveat be filed. Its effect is to prevent, for one year, the issue of a patent for the same purpose to another, except after due notice to the applicant. After such notice is given him he must complete his own application within three months. Caveats may be renewed for a second year by renewing the fee. They cannot be filed by aliens. The description in a caveat need not be as precise as in ordinary specifications, but the commissioner must be enabled to judge whether interference would exist with a subsequent applicant.

The fees established by law must be paid in advance and before any application will be considered by the examiner. The final fee for the issue of the patent must be paid within six months of the date when the patent was granted. Fees may be deposited with an assistant treasurer, to be paid when necessary. The following is the list of fees under the present law:

## UNITED STATES PATENT FEES.

| | |
|---|---|
| On application for patent........................ | $15 00 |
| On every caveat................................ | 10 00 |
| On application for design, for fourteen years....... | 30 00 |
| On " " " for seven years......... | 15 00 |
| On " " " for three and a half years. | 10 00 |
| On issuing each original patent.................. | 20 00 |
| On application for a re-issue..................... | 30 00 |
| On application for a division of re-issue........... | 30 00 |
| On filing a disclaimer........................... | 10 00 |
| On appeal to examiners-in-chief.................. | 10 00 |
| On appeal from examiners-in-chief to commissioner. | 20 00 |
| On every copy of patent or other instrument, per 100 words.................................... | 10 |
| On copy of drawing............*the cost of having it made.* | |
| For recording assignment, under 300 words........ | 1 00 |
| " " " over 300 and under 1,000 words...................................... | 2 00 |
| For recording assignment, over 1,000 words........ | 3 00 |

When the formalities already described have been fully complied with, the alleged inventions will be thoroughly examined by the examiners in the order of the dates of application. Applications for re-issue, inventions for which a foreign patent has issued and inventions which are supposed to be of importance to the public service may be taken up out of turn. If the application is rejected, the inventor may demand a second examination. If he fails in this he has the right of appeal to the examiner-in-chief, and from his adverse decision he may again appeal to the Commissioner of Patents. Failing here, the only remaining right of appeal is to the Supreme Court of the District of Columbia. The applicant has the right to amend after the first or second rejection.

**Interference** is said to exist when two parties claim to be the original inventor of the same " art, machine, manufacture or composition of matter." When a patent has been granted to one person, and the commissioner has reason to believe that another was the true inventor, he may grant a patent to the second also, and thus place them on an equal footing. And if, after interference has been declared, a third claimant appears, he will be allowed to come into the case. As a rule the burden of proof will lie on those who oppose the party first making oath to the invention. Appeal lies in regard to decisions in interference cases in the same manner as when an application is rejected.

**Assignments.**—Patents may be assigned in whole or in part. The assignment must be in writing, but need not be sealed or attested. When the assignment is made before the patent issues, it should be recorded in the patent office five days before the issue, if the patent is to be made out in the name of the assignee. The assignment of exclusive territorial right should also be recorded. If not recorded within three months, the assignment will be void as against a subsequent purchaser or mortgagee for value. A five-cent stamp is required for every sheet on which the assignment is written.

**Sale of Patent Rights.**—If the entire right is not sold, one of three methods is employed in selling patent rights, by *territorial* privilege, by *shop* right, and on a *royalty.* The territorial right may or may not include the right to manufacture; it gives the purchaser exclusive right to sell the article within certain territory, as a State. By shop right is meant the privilege of manufacturing the article in a certain shop or factory and not elsewhere, without limit as to the number of articles sold. Royalty is a fixed sum paid to the patentee by some other person on each article made or sold. It is usual to stipulate that the royalty shall be paid on at least an agreed number of articles, whether sold or not.

## PETITION FOR PATENT.

**To the Commissioner of Patents:**

Your petitioner, A. B., of Hartford, Connecticut, prays that a patent may be granted to him for the invention set forth in the annexed drawings and specifications.

(*Signed*) A. B.

## FORM OF OATH.

State of Connecticut,
City of Hartford, Hartford County. } ss.

Personally appeared before me, the subscriber, a justice of the peace, in and for said city and county, on this 12th day of May, 1882, the within named A. B., and made solemn oath that he verily believes himself to be the original and first inventor of the machine and mechanical contrivance (*or process, or composition, or art, as the case may be*) herein described; and that he does not know or believe the same was ever before known or used; and that he is a citizen of the United States.

C. D., *Justice of the Peace.*

## APPLICATION FOR DESIGN.

**To the Commissioner of Patents**:—The petition of A. B., of the City of Hartford, Hartford County, State of Connecticut, respectfully represents:

That your petitioner aforesaid has invented or produced a new and original design for (*describe nature and use of design*), which he verily believes has not been known prior to the production thereof by your petitioner. He therefore prays that letters patent of the United States may be granted him therefor, for the term of (*state whether* 14, 7, or 3½ *years are desired*), vesting in him and his legal representatives the exclusive right to the same upon the terms and conditions expressed in the Act of Congress in that case made and provided, he having paid —— dollars into the Treasury, and complied with the other provisions of the act.

(*Signed*) A. B.

## FORM OF CAVEAT.

(*Begin as in previous form*). That he has made certain improvements and discoveries in regard to (*describe what is the subject of the invention and in general terms what has been accomplished and is intended*), and is now engaged in perfecting the same, preparatory to his applying for letters patent therefor. He therefore prays that the subjoined description of his invention may be filed as a caveat in the confidential archives of the Patent Office, agreeably to the provisions of the Act of Congress in that case made and provided; he having paid ten dollars into the treasury of the United States, and otherwise complied with the conditions of the said act. (*Signed, dated and with oath annexed*).

## TERRITORIAL GRANT.

**Whereas** the undersigned, A. B., of —— (*residence*), did obtain letters patent of the United States for (*describe invention briefly*), which letters patent bear date the —— day of ——, A. D. 18—, and whereas C. D., of (*residence*), desires an interest therein; **This Indenture Witnesseth,** that for and in consideration of the sum of (*amount*) to me in hand paid, and the receipt of which is hereby acknowledged, I do hereby grant, sell and transfer unto the said C. D., all right, title and interest which I have in said invention and letters patent, for, to and in the States of Georgia and Arkansas, and in no other place or State, the same to include the rights of manufacture as well as of sale, to be held and enjoyed by the said C. D., for his own use and behoof and that of his executors, administrators, or assigns, to the full end of the term for which said letters patent are granted, as fully and entirely as the same would have been held and enjoyed by me, had this grant and sale not been made.

**In Witness Whereof,** *etc.* (*Signed, sealed and delivered*).

# Copyright.

**What it Is.**—Copyright is defined by the act of 1874 as the sole liberty of printing, reprinting, publishing, compiling, copying, executing and vending any original book, map, chart, dramatic or musical composition, engraving, print, photograph or negative thereof, or of a painting, drawing, chromo, statue or statuary, and of models or designs intended to be perfected as works of art.

**How to get it.**—To obtain this right a printed copy of the title of the book or other article must be sent by mail, prepaid, to the Librarian of Congress, at Washington. For recording the title there is a fee of fifty cents; also fifty cents for a certificate of such record. After publication, two complete copies of the best edition of the work must be sent to the Librarian of Congress, charges prepaid. Notice must also be given by inserting on the title page of the book or inscribing on some part of the article the words: "Entered according to act of Congress in the year ——, by ——, in the office of the Librarian of Congress, at Washington;" or, "Copyright, 18—, by ——." To reserve the right of translation or of dramatization the words: "All rights reserved," or "Right of Translation reserved," should be added.

**Duration.**—The right lasts for twenty-eight years. A renewal for fourteen years may be obtained by the author or designer, or his widow or children, by application made six months before the expiration of the twenty-eight years. In such application a distinct claim of ownership on the part of those applying must be made.

**Assignment.**—The copyright is assignable, and the written assignment must be recorded with the Librarian of Congress within sixty days after its execution. The fee is one dollar, and a certificate of record will be furnished for the same sum.

**Penalties and Remedies.**—Any person falsely printing a claim of copyright on any book, work of art, *etc.*, is liable to a fine of $100; half to go to the prosecutor, and half to the United States. In cases of infringements, injunctions may be obtained from Circuit Courts and District Courts having the jurisdiction of Circuit Courts, upon a bill in equity. Action must be brought within two years of the date when the cause of action arose. A petition should set out : 1. That the petitioner is a citizen or resident. 2. That he is the author, designer or proprietor of the work in question. 3. That he has complied with all regulations and obtained his copyright in due form, giving dates of each act. 4. He must describe the time and manner of infringement, and declare that the printing, publishing, *etc.*, was done without his written consent and in violation of his copyright. Upon such a presentation of facts he may demand : 1. That an injunction may issue restraining the defendant from further printing and publishing, *etc.* 2. That defendant shall forfeit all copies already printed to him, the petitioner. 3. That defendant shall render an account of all printing, *etc.*, already done. 4. That he shall pay damages to be fixed by the Court. 5. That petitioner's costs shall be paid by defendant. From the Circuit or District Court there is a right of appeal to the United States Supreme Court.

**Originality.**—The true test of originality has been defined as, "whether the claimant's book contains any substantive product of his own labor." (*Curtis.*) Quotations may, of course, be used; but if they are used to such an extent as to show that their purpose was not for comparison or review, piracy will be inferred. It is not necessary that a book should be original in the sense that the facts related should be of the author's own observing, or even that the reflections should be novel and now first brought before the world. Such a test would be too severe. The great store-house of accumulated knowledge is open to all to use, but not to abuse. In fact it may be said that the laws of copyright apply more strictly to form than to thought. The plan, arrangement, selection of material, the point of view from which the subject is regarded may render a compilation of old and well-known facts, an original work, as regards the copyright law. A test often used to decide whether one work is copied from another, is to learn by examination whether the inaccuracies and errors of the earlier work are to be found in the later. The fact that an infringer did not know of the copyright, or supposed it had expired, is no defence. A new copyright may be obtained on a new edition of an old work, if enough new matter has been added to make it practically a new book. An abridgment of a work may be an infringement.

## CERTIFICATE OF COPY OF TITLE.

[L. S.] LIBRARY OF CONGRESS, COPYRIGHT OFFICE,
*No.—C.* WASHINGTON, D. C.

**To wit :—Be it Remembered :**

That on the — day of —, A. D. 18—, A. B., of —, hath deposited in this office the title of a book (*or map, chart, or other article, as the case may be*), the title or description of which is in the following words, to wit : (*here follows title or description*), the right of which he claims as author (*originator or proprietor, as the case may be*) in conformity with the laws of the United States respecting copyrights.

(*Signed*) ——, *Librarian of Congress.*

## ASSIGNMENT OF COPYRIGHT.

**Know all Men by these Presents,** That for and in consideration of the sum of —— dollars, to me in hand paid, the receipt of which is hereby acknowledged, I, the undersigned A. B., do hereby assign, transfer and set over to C. D. all my right, title and interest in and under a certain copyright and the certificate thereof of the date and number as follows ; to wit : (*give date, number and description of certificate*), the rights whereof I claim as author, (*proprietor or originator, as the case may be*) **To have and to hold** the same unto the said C. D., his heirs, executors, administrators and assigns forever.

**In Witness Whereof,** *etc.*

(*Signed*) A. B.

## SHORT CONTRACT BETWEEN AUTHOR AND PUBLISHER.

**This agreement,** made this — day of —, A. D. 18—, between A. B., author, of the first part, and C. D., publisher, of the second part. **Witnesseth:**—That the said party of the first part, having now in preparation a book to be called by the title or description (*here give title in full*), to be in — octavo volumes, of — pages each, he the said party of the first part hereby agrees and promises to said C. D. of the second part to complete said book for the press within a reasonable time and in as rapid a manner as the nature of the work will permit, and to sell to the said party of the second part for the sum of —— dollars, to be paid to him in manner and form as hereinafter mentioned, the sole and exclusive right of printing, publishing and selling the first edition thereof, to consist of —— copies. The copyright of said work to be secured and retained by said A. B., as author and proprietor.

And the said C. D., publisher, hereby agrees and promises to publish said edition of —— copies, and to pay to said A. B., the aforesaid sum of —— dollars, by his negotiable promissory notes, payable at three and six months after the day of publication of said edition, and also to give to the said A. B. —— copies of said work as presentation copies.

(*Signatures.*)

(*This agreement should be executed in duplicate.*)

# Trade Marks.

**A Trade Mark** is a mark, emblem or symbol, which a tradesman or manufacturer attaches or puts upon his goods. It may be in the form of letters, words or ornamental designs. To such a trade mark there is an exclusive right arising from first use, but to enforce such right it is necessary for the manufacturer to first comply with the requirements of the law as to registration, etc.

**Registration.**—By the statutes of the United States on the subject, as revised in 1874 and amended in 1876, protection in the use of trade marks may be obtained by citizens or corporations of the United States or by residents of foreign countries which grant similar privileges to citizens of the United States, by complying with the following requirements : 1. The names, residences and places of business of the applicants for protection must be recorded in the patent office. 2. Also must be recorded a description of the class of goods and of the special quality of goods to which the trade mark is to be applied. 3. Also a description and *fac-simile* of the mark itself and a description of the manner in which it is intended to apply it. 4. A statement of the time in which the mark has already been in use, if it is not a new one. 5. A fee of twenty-five dollars must be paid in the same manner as in the case of patents. 6. Any special regulations prescribed by the commissioner of patents must be complied with. 7. The applicant must file a declaration under oath that the *fac-similes* and descriptions of the marks are correct and true copies, that he has a right to use the same arising from first use,. and that no other person or firm has a right to such use, either in the identical form presented, or in such close resemblance as might be calculated to deceive. The claim as to essential features should be clearly set forth.

**Duration.**—After registration, the right to protection at once begins and continues for thirty years, when, by payment of a second fee, it may be renewed for the same time.

From the decision of the trade mark examiner an appeal may be taken to the commissioner of patents. No trade mark will be registered which so nearly resembles one already existing as to be calculated to deceive the public. When dispute as to prior right occurs and an interference is declared, the proceedings are very similar to those in an interference in a patent case. The name alone of a manufacturer, firm or corporation, cannot become a lawful trade mark, if there is nothing (in the way of ornamentation or otherwise) to distinguish it from the same name when used without fraud by other persons. Assignments of trade marks must be recorded in the patent office within sixty days after execution. The fees are the same as in case of patents. If this is not done, the assignment will be void as against subsequent purchasers or mortgagees for valuable consideration.

The reproduction, copying or imitating any trade mark and affixing such imitation or counterfeit to goods of the same class and nature, renders the offending party liable in an action for damages and costs in any court of original jurisdiction.

# WILLS.

A WILL, or Last Will and Testament, is an instrument by which property is disposed of, either absolutely or conditionally, to take effect from the time of the death of the maker thereof.

The maker, if a man, is spoken of as the *testator;* if a woman, as the *testatrix.* An *executor* is one appointed by the will to carry out its provisions and settle the estate. The feminine form of the word is *executrix. Administrators* are persons appointed by the proper court to settle the estate when there is no will, or when the executors refuse to serve, which they may do. In appointing an administrator the court will regard the decree of relationship to the accused, but is not bound strictly by that consideration.

It is not necessary that a will should be drawn in any particular form, and where the provisions are few or simple in their nature, any clear-headed man can draw his own will as well as a lawyer, *provided* that he takes due care in regard to the provisions of the State where he lives, as regards attestation and execution. The proper attestation of a will may, indeed, be said to be its most important part. But when any of the gifts are to be made under conditions, or where trusts are to be established, or remainders and life estates to be created, then the best legal advice should be sought and followed.

Any person may make a will who is of "sound and disposing" mind, and has arrived at the age of discretion. This is usually fixed by statute at twenty-one years. But personal property may be bequeathed by minors. In regard to mental incapacity, absolute idiocy or lunacy, will, of course, debar the victim as incapable. If he has lucid intervals, he may, during one of them, execute a will, but it would be necessary to show that his restoration, though temporary, was, for the time being, complete. *Monomania* may or may not prove incapacity, according to its extent and connection. So with *senile dementia.* The best test is to ask the question, "Did the testator, at the time of executing the will, understand fully the nature of what he was doing, the extent of the property, the number and claims of those to whom he was related or connected, and clearly perceive the effect on these of the disposition he was about to make?" Undue influence may be proved. Unwritten or *nuncupative* wills are not unknown, but they are rare, and admitted only when made in solemn form and under peculiar circumstances, as of a soldier on the battle-field.

**Revocation.**—A will may be revoked by the actual destruction thereof, as by burning, tearing, or obliterating, or by the making of a new will of later date. If the second will is itself destroyed and the first remains in existence, that is considered *prima facie* evidence of the intention of the testator to have it prevail. The statement should always be made in the instrument that this is the testator's *last* will, and if others have been previously drawn, it is well to use the phrase, "Hereby revoking all previous wills."

**Interpretation.**—In construing the meaning of a will the chief rule regarded by the court will be to ascertain, as closely as may be, the real intention of the testator. Technical terms are, therefore, unnecessary, and when used will be understood in the sense usually given them by the law, unless it clearly appears that the testator used them in a different sense, in which case that will be adopted. Words which have no meaning or are evidently contrary to the testator's intent will be rejected, and where it is clear that words have been omitted by mistake the court will supply the omitted words.

**Codicil.**—A codicil is a supplement or addition to a will. It must be executed and witnessed with all the formalities required for the will itself. The codicil is construed as being part of the will itself. The codicil may in part confirm and part revoke the provisions of the main body of the will. It is common to use such a form of words, as: "I hereby expressly confirm my former will, dated ——, excepting so far as the disposition of my property is changed by this codicil."

**Witnesses.**—Great care should be taken in regard to the attesting witnesses. The number is fixed by statute at two in some States and three in others. No person who is a legatee can serve as a witness. In no case can it do any harm to make use of three witnesses. The testator, in signing his name, should be clearly seen by each of the witnesses. It is not necessary that they should see the body of the will. The attestation must state that the witnesses have subscribed their names in the presence of the testator and at his request, and in the presence of each other. A good form of attestation clause will be found at the close of the form or example of a will given below.

**Probate.**—The will must be *probated* or proved by the executor in the court having jurisdiction and in the manner prescribed by statute. (See the abstract below.) The attesting witnesses must all, if possible, be produced. If any are dead, or have left the State, proof of their handwriting may be required. Wills, however, which are over thirty years old, which come from proper custody and appear to be regular, are said to prove themselves. Wills which have been lost or destroyed accidentally may be admitted on sufficient proof of their execution, contents and loss.

LEGACY is the word more commonly applied to the gift by will of money or personal property. The word *bequeath* applies to the gift of personal and *devise* to that of real property. A *lapsed* legacy is one which has never vested because of the death of the legatee before that of the testator. A *residuary* legacy is a bequest of all the testator's personal property not otherwise disposed of by the will.

RELEASE OR SATISFACTION OF DEBT.—It is sometimes doubtful, when a legatee was indebted to the testator, whether the legacy is, or is not, intended to release the debt. The presumption is that it is not, but the testator's intentions may be shown.

A will was revoked by common law, when the testator, after executing it, married and had a child. In this country this is regulated by statutes, and as a rule the claims of children born subsequently to the execution of a will, are guarded. A bequest may be left to a wife *in lieu* of dower, where dower still exists, and the wife may then elect whether she will accept the legacy or retain her dower right.

## SHORT AND SIMPLE WILL.

**Know all Men by these Presents,** That I, James Grant, merchant, of Springfield, Hampden County, Massachusetts, being in good health of body and sound and disposing state of mind and memory, and being desirous of settling my worldly affairs, while I have strength and capacity, do make and publish this, my last will and testament; hereby revoking and making void all former wills by me at any time heretofore made.

*First*:—I direct my executors, hereinafter named, to pay all my just debts and funeral expenses from my personal property not hereinafter disposed of.

*Second*:—I give to my wife, Mary, all the household furniture which may be contained in my homestead at the time of my death, also my library, carriage, carriage-horses and harness appertaining thereto, of which I may die possessed.

*Third*:—I give to my wife, Mary, an annuity of $1,500 annually, which annuity I direct shall be a charge upon my estate.

*Fourth*: I devise to her for her natural life my homestead in Springfield, Hampden County, Massachusetts, known as No. 432 Main street, and all the land thereto pertaining, to be received and held by her without impeachment for waste, on condition, however, that she receive the same in lieu of her dower, and that on the request of my executors after this will is proved, that she release her dower in the residue of my real estate.

*Fifth*:—I give to my friend, William Edson, my gold watch and chain and the seals of the same.

*Sixth*:—I give to my cousin, Ellen White, three thousand dollars to be paid out of my personal estate not otherwise disposed of.

*Seventh*:—I bequeath and devise to my three children, all the residue of my estate, whether real or personal, to be divided into equal shares by my executors, one share or third of the personal and one share or third of the real property to be allotted to each, so that each child who shall survive me shall take one such share, and the children or issue of any child who may die before my death shall take one share, and hold the share of the personal property absolutely, and the share of the real to his, her, or their heirs and assigns forever; the issue of any child taking the share of such child *per stirpes* and not *per capita*.

*Lastly*:—I appoint Charles Grant and Edward Fox my executors.

**In Witness Whereof,** I have hereto set my hand and seal, and published and declared this instrument to be my last will and testament, the first day of May, 1882, in presence of the persons whose names are subscribed as attesting witnesses.

(*Signed*) JAMES GRANT. [L. S.]

On the first day of May, 1882, the above named James Grant, in our presence signed the foregoing instrument, and declared to us that the same was his last will and testament, and requested us to subscribe our names hereto as witnesses; and we in his presence and in the presence of each other, have, in compliance with such request, hereto subscribed our names.

(*Here follow the signatures of witnesses; the residences of each should be added.*)

## CODICIL TO ABOVE.

Codicil to the last will and testament of James Grant.

I, James Grant, having made my last will and testament, and published the same on the first day of May, 1882, do hereby make, declare and publish this codicil to the same.

*First*:—Instead of giving to my cousin, Ellen White, the sum of three thousand dollars, I hereby give her an annuity of two hundred dollars, commencing at my death and to be a charge upon my estate.

*Second*:—In addition to the provision already made for my wife, Mary

Grant, I now further give to her, to be hers absolutely, the sum of five thousand dollars, to be paid to her from my personal property before any division is made thereof.

**In Witness Whereof,** (*Signed, sealed, acknowledged and attested in every respect like the will itself.*)

## ABSTRACT OF STATE LAWS REGARDING WILLS.

**Alabama.**—Two witnesses. Recorded in office of Judge of Probate Court. No nuncupative will can dispose of more than $500 worth of property. Wills are to be executed out of the State in the same way as if within the State. All persons over twenty-one years of age can dispose of real estate; all over eighteen, of personal property.

**Arizona.**—Two or more witnesses. Nuncupative wills cannot dispose of more than $300 worth of property. Soldiers and sailors in active service may dispose of personal property by unwritten wills. The statute provides in great detail the manner in which wills shall be executed.

**Arkansas.**—All over twenty-one years may devise realty and personalty; all over eighteen, personalty. Two witnesses. Nuncupative wills not to exceed $500. A will, the body of which was written by the testator as well as the signature, may be established by three disinterested witnesses as to handwriting, when there are no attesting witnesses.

**California.**—All persons over eighteen years of age may dispose by will of either real or personal property. Two or more witnesses required. Nuncupative wills, not to exceed $2,000, are valid, but must be reduced to writing within thirty days.

**Colorado.**—Real estate may be devised by all over twenty-one; personal estate by all over seventeen. Two or more witnesses. A married man may not leave more than half of his property away from his wife, nor can a wife leave more than half away from her husband without his written consent thereto.

**Connecticut.**—Three witnesses required. All persons over eighteen years of age can dispose of real or personal property. Subsequent marriage revokes a will, and so also the birth of a child, unless provision is made in the will for the contingency. Wills must be offered for probate within ten years.

**Dakota.**—Both real and personal property may be disposed of by all persons above eighteen years of age. Wills of which the body is in the testator's handwriting and which are signed and dated by him, need not be attested. Two or more witnesses are necessary for other wills. Wills made out of the Territory are proved in the same way as those made within it. A will made by an unmarried woman is revoked by her marriage. Married women may dispose by will of all their property as though single.

**Delaware.**—Two or more witnesses. Any person of sound mind, and above the age of twenty-one years, may dispose of real or personal property. A married woman must obtain the written consent of her husband, signed, sealed and attested by two witnesses, to enable her to dispose by will of her property.

**District of Columbia.**—Males of twenty-one and females of eighteen years of age may dispose of real estate or interest therein. Three or more witnesses are required. The person making the will must be of sound mind and capable of making a deed or contract.

**Florida.**—Persons above twenty-one years of age may dispose of real or personal property. Three or more witnesses are required. Nuncupative wills must be proved by the oath of at least three witnesses who were present when it was made. Such a will must be reduced to writing and sworn to within six days. Foreign wills must be executed according to the law of the State.

**Georgia.**—Three or more witnesses are necessary. Persons of fourteen years of age may make a will. Wills are recorded in the Ordinary's Court. Married women may dispose by will of their separate estate.

**Idaho.**—Persons over twenty-one years of age may dispose of real or personal estate; persons over eighteen, of personal estate. Married women may dispose by will of all separate estate, real or personal. Two witnesses are required. Copies of the will must be recorded in every county where there is any real estate conveyed by the will.

**Illinois.**—All males above twenty-one, and all females above eighteen years of age may dispose of real or personal property. Two or more witnesses are required. Wills made out of the State must be probated within the State.

**Indiana.**—All persons twenty-one years of age or more may will real or personal property. Married women may dispose by will of their separate property. Nuncupative wills must not exceed $100. Two witnesses. Record must be made in the office of the County Clerk where probated.

**Iowa.**—Testator must be twenty-one years of age. Nuncupative wills cannot exceed $300 worth of property, and must be sworn to by at least two disinterested witnesses. Wills valid where made, are valid in the State. All foreign wills must be probated in the State.

**Kansas.**—Two or more witnesses. Persons must be of age to make a valid will. Wills made in other States must be probated in the county where the property lies, and are then valid. Wills are recorded in the Probate Office.

**Kentucky.**—Persons must be twenty-one years of age and of sound mind to make a valid will. Married women may dispose by will of their separate property. Two witnesses are required. Wills must be proved in the County Court of the county where testator resided. Personal property owned by persons living outside the State may be disposed of by a will made in accordance with the requirements of the place where made. In case of devise of real estate, the will must be proved where made, and an authenticated copy of the certificate of probate offered for probate in this State.

**Louisiana.**—Four kinds of wills are recognized: nuncupative by public act; nuncupative by private act; mystic or sealed wills, and olographic wills. The first must be dictated by testator to a notary public and read in the presence of three resident or five non-resident witnesses, and must be signed by the testator and witnesses. The second must be written in the presence of five resident or seven non-resident witnesses, read to them and signed by the testator and the witnesses, or at least two of them. In the country three resident or five non-resident witnesses will suffice, if more cannot be obtained. The third form, or *mystic* will, is first signed by the testator, then enclosed in an envelope and sealed up. The testator then declares in the presence of a notary and seven witnesses that that paper contains his will, signed by himself, the notary endorses the act of superscription on the will or envelope, and that act is signed by the notary, the testator and the witnesses. Olographic testaments are written entirely by the testator himself, and dated and signed by him. No attestation or other form is required. The following cannot act as witnesses: women of any age; males under sixteen; the deaf, dumb, blind or insane; those debarred by the criminal law from exercising civil functions; those who stand as heirs or legatees under the will, except in case of *mystic* testaments.

**Maine.**—Three witnesses not interested as heirs or legatees. Real estate acquired afterwards may pass. A posthumous child or other child not provided for by will takes the same share as if the deceased had died intestate, unless it is shown that the omission of mention in the will was intentional. Nuncupative wills made in the last sickness and at the testator's residence, or made by sailors and soldiers, are valid, but must be reduced to writing within six days, and, if they dispose of more than $100 worth of property, must be sworn to by at least three witnesses.

**Maryland.**—Wills of personal property are valid without witnesses; wills of real estate must be attested by three or four witnesses. Real estate may be disposed of by males above twenty-one and females above eighteen years of age, of sound mind and capable of making a deed or contract. Wills are probated before the "Orphan's Court," and recorded with the Registrar of Wills. A married woman can will her property to her husband or to others only with his written consent subscribed to the will. She must also be examined apart from her husband, as in case of deeds; and such will must be made sixty days before the death of the testatrix.

**Massachusetts.**—Persons of legal age may dispose by will of real or personal property. Three or more witnesses are required, but they need not sign in the presence of each other. A bequest to a subscribing witness is void. A married woman may devise as though single, but she cannot leave more than half of her personal property away from her husband, nor deprive him of his *curtesy* in her real estate without his written consent. Wills must be offered for probate within thirty days after the executor knows of the death of the testator.

**Michigan.**—Two or more competent witnesses are required. Nuncupative wills must not dispose of more than $300 worth of property. Devisees and legatees are incompetent witnesses. Wills must be recorded in the Probate Court, and a copy of the probate thereof registered with the Registrar of every county in which there may be land conveyed by the will.

**Minnesota.**—Two or more witnesses. Nuncupative wills can be made only by soldiers in active service or sailors at sea. All persons of legal age and sound mind may devise. Married women may make wills as if they were single. Legatees and devisees are not competent witnesses. Probate as in Michigan.

**Mississippi.**—Any person of legal age may devise real or personal property. Two witnesses are required in case of all wills made after November 1, 1880. Nuncupative wills can be made by soldiers or sailors in actual service, or by others only in the last sickness and at the residence of the testator. If for more than $100 such a will must be sworn to by at least two witnesses.

**Missouri.**—Real estate may be disposed of by males above the age of twenty-one and females above that of eighteen years. Personal property may be devised by all above eighteen years of age. Two witnesses are necessary. Married women may make wills as though single. Wills should be recorded with the recorder of deeds for the county where probate is made, and a copy registered in every county where there is land disposed of in the will.

**Montana.**—All persons more than eighteen years of age may dispose by will of either real or personal property. Two witnesses are required. Married women may dispose of their separate estate. Nuncupative wills must not exceed $1,000 in amount, must be made by soldiers or sailors in actual service, and must be sworn to by two competent witnesses. The law of descent for real and personal property is provided for by the Probate Practice Act.

**Nebraska.**—Wills must be attested by two or more witnesses. Nuncupative wills are allowed under stringent statutory limitations. Married women may dispose of their property as if single. All foreign wills which have been probated in accordance with the law of the State or country where made, will be admitted to probate in this State.

**Nevada.**—All persons over eighteen may make wills as to realty or personalty. Two witnesses required. A child unprovided for shall take the share he would have had if testator had died intestate, unless the omission is shown to be intentional. Married women may dispose of separate estate and, with the husband's consent, of their interest in common property.

**New Hampshire.**—The testator must be twenty-one years of age. Three or more witnesses are called for. Married women may dispose of separate estate. Nuncupative wills must be attested by three witnesses, reduced to writing within six days and offered for probate within six months.

**New Jersey.**—Testator must be twenty-one years old. A married woman may dispose of personal or real estate, but cannot defeat the husband's right of curtesy in the realty. Two witnesses are required. A legacy or devise to a witness is void.

**New Mexico.**—Males over fourteen and females over twelve may make wills. Wills may be written or verbal. Verbal wills must be attested by five witnesses, two of whom must swear that the testator was of sound mind; written wills must be attested by three witnesses. The probate judge may disapprove a will after hearing the witnesses, and return it to the party applying. It may be then brought before the district court, and finally approved or disapproved.

**New York.**—Personal property may be disposed of by males of eighteen and females of sixteen. Two witnesses. Wills properly proved in the State or country where made will be admitted to probate in this State.

**North Carolina.**—Two witnesses are required. Wills, written, dated and signed in testator's handwriting throughout will be admitted on proof of handwriting by at least three witnesses. Nuncupative wills are strictly limited. Wills made out of this State and conveying real estate within this State must be executed according to the laws of this State; *i.e.*, the *lex rei sitæ* prevails.

**Ohio.**—Two witnesses. Verbal wills may be made in the last sickness as regards personal estate. They must be reduced to writing and subscribed by two disinterested witnesses within ten days. A devisee or legatee cannot be a witness. Bequests for religious, benevolent, educational or charitable purposes are void as against children unless the will is executed at least one year before the decease of the testator. Wills executed and allowed in other States will be admitted to probate in this State.

**Oregon.**—All persons over twenty-one may dispose of real or personal estate by will. Personal estate may be bequeathed by all above eighteen. Married women may make wills as if single, but cannot destroy the right of curtesy in real estate. Two or more witnesses. Children not provided for in a will may take as if the parent had died intestate. Real estate owned in this State may be disposed of by will made in another State and admitted to probate in this State,

**Pennsylvania.**—All persons of legal age may make wills. Unless the testator is on his deathbed, the will must be in writing. Two witnesses must be present, but they need not subscribe the instrument; no acknowledgment before witnesses by the testator is necessary, except in case of a married woman, or of a bequest for religious or charitable purposes.

**Rhode Island.**—Two witnesses are required. Both must be produced when the will is probated, if alive and within the State. Real estate may be disposed of by will by all persons above twenty-one years of age. Personal property by all above eighteen years of age. Married women may dispose of separate estate, but cannot impair the right of curtesy in real estate.

**South Carolina.**—Three or more witnesses are called for. Wills are recorded in the probate court of the county where testator had his domicile. Common law principles generally prevail.

**Tennessee.**—Two witnesses A will written throughout and signed and dated in the testator's handwriting, and found among his papers, or lodged by him with another for safe keeping, will be admitted, though unattested, on the evidence of at least three witnesses as to the handwriting. Nuncupative wills must not exceed $250, and are further limited in various ways by the statutes. No subscribing witnesses are necessary to wills of personal property, except in case of married women.

**Texas.**—Testator must be of full age. Unless the will is olographic, there must be at least two competent witnesses. A will properly executed and probated in another State will be admitted to probate here upon application. Nuncupative wills exceeding $30 must be sworn to by three credible persons, made in the last sickness, and offered for probate within six months.

**Utah.**—Real and personal property may be disposed of by will by all persons of sound mind and of the age of eighteen years. Married women may make wills as if single. Two witnesses are necessary.

**Vermont.**—Three witnesses are required. Wills made and executed legally in another State or country may be proved, allowed, and recorded in this State. Wills must be recorded in the probate office and also in the town clerk's office in every town where real estate disposed of may lie.

**Virginia.**—All persons over twenty-one may dispose of real property; all over eighteen of personal property. Two witnesses. Married women may dispose of separate property, but cannot impair the husband's right of curtesy. The circuit, county and corporation courts have probate jurisdiction.

**Washington.**—Males above twenty-one and females above eighteen years of age may dispose by will of realty or personal property. Two or more subscribing witnesses. Nuncupative wills for above $200 must be sworn to by two witnesses, except in case of sailors or soldiers in actual service.

**West Virginia.**—Testator must be of legal age. Two subscribing witnesses, except in case of an olographic will. A will executed outside of the State, must still be executed according to the laws of the State, in order to convey real estate therein.

**Wisconsin.**—Two subscribing witnesses are necessary. Probate is had in the county court. Wills duly executed, proved and allowed in other States will be admitted to probate here.

**Wyoming.**—There are no statutes in regard to the execution of proof of wills. The common law principles must be followed. Probate must be had in the county probate court.

# Laws of the Dominion of Canada.

## PROVINCE OF QUEBEC.

[NOTE.—The civil laws of this Province are founded on the French "customary" or common law. A code exists; the laws having been first codified in 1866. As it now exists, the code is in many respects similar to the *Code Napoleon*, but contains many of the distinctive features of the English and United States statute law. The criminal code in this and all the Provinces is founded on English law, and is identical throughout the Dominion.]

**ATTACHMENTS.**—The plaintiff may attach, in case of movables, fifteen days after judgment or sooner, and even before judgment, by making affidavit that the debt is above five dollars, that the debtor has absconded or is about to do so, or is secreting his property; or that defendant is a general trader, is notoriously insolvent, and has refused to make any arrangement with his creditors. The affidavit must aver also that the affiant believes that without the attachment the debt will be lost.

**Chattel Mortgages.**—There is no such thing as a chattel mortgage, except in case of vessels in the course of construction, to which a special act applies. Money can be raised on movables only by actually placing them in the hands of the lender.

**Deeds.**—When parties residing in the United States execute deeds to property in the Province, the laws of the place where the deed is made are followed. The witnesses, or one of them, must make affidavit as to the signatures before the mayor or chief magistrate of the place, who must give a certificate to that effect which should be attested by the nearest British consul. Such and all other deeds must be registered in the county where the land lies, in conformity with the requirements of the code. If the authenticity of a deed made out of the Province is questioned, it must be established where made before a commissioner appointed by the court.

**Exemptions**—The following articles of personal property are exempt from execution: bed and bedding, wearing apparel, furniture, cooking utensils, hunting and agricultural implements, minutely specified in the statute; fuel and food for thirty days, not above $20 in value; one cow, two hogs, four sheep, fifteen hives of bees; tools of a trade not over $30 in value; ten books. But when the suit and execution is for the price, there is no exemption. Also are exempt, sums of money given as *aliment*, or when the donor specifies in the gift that the money shall be exempt, and wages and salary not yet due.

**Interest.**—Any rate may be agreed upon. The legal rate is six per cent. Six per cent. is charged on judgments.

**Married Women.**—Three estates of property exist after marriage. The husband and wife each retains control of all the immovable property belonging to him and her at the time of marriage. The third, or *community* estate, over which the husband has full control, consists of all movables owned by either at time of marriage and all property of any kind acquired by either afterwards. The wife's separate estate is also administered by the husband, and she cannot part with it without his consent. The wife may will separate property as she chooses; the husband cannot bequeath more than his half interest in the common property. If a married woman becomes a public trader she binds her husband, unless she is separated and has her deed of separation recorded. Full divorce cannot be obtained without a special act of the Dominion Legislature, sanctioned by the Crown.

**Mechanics' Liens.**—Builders, workmen, and architects have a lien on the additional value resulting from their work. An official statement of the state of the premises must be made previously by an expert appointed by the court, and within six months the work must be accepted by another expert.

**Mortgages.**—HYPOTHECS or mortgages are classed as legal, judicial, or conventional; the first resulting from the law, the second from judgments of courts, and the third from agreements. Mortgages cannot be acquired upon the immovables of persons notoriously insolvent to the prejudice of their creditors.

**Wills.**—All persons above twenty-one and of sound intellect can will property. There are three kinds of wills: 1. The *authentic* or French will, executed before two notaries, or one notary and two witnesses, not females. 2. The English will, for which at least two attesting witnesses, male or female, are necessary. 3. The olograph will, written throughout in testator's handwriting and signed by him, for which no witnesses are required. The English and the olograph wills must be probated.

## PROVINCE OF ONTARIO.

**Aliens.**—The disabilities formerly imposed on aliens have been removed. Aliens can buy, sell, and hold real and personal property in the same way as citizens. A non-resident who brings an action in the Province is bound, if asked, to give security for costs.

**Attachments.**—A judge's order may be obtained for attachment of property, upon the affidavit of the creditor that the debtor has absconded to defraud the plaintiff or to avoid arrest and service. Other creditors may come in by issuing attachments within six months of the date of the first writ.

**Chattel Mortgages.**—All sales and pledges of personal property are void as against creditors and subsequent purchasers or mortgagees in good faith, unless there is immediate delivery, or unless the chattel mortgage is registered with the clerk of the county court where the mortgagor or seller lives within five days, together with affidavit as to execution by a subscribing witness, and the affidavit of the buyer or mortgagee as to good faith. To keep up the debt, a statement must be filed within thirty days of the expiration of the year, showing the amount due and payments made, with affidavit of the mortgagee as to truth and good faith.

**Deeds.**—A seal must be used; a scroll will not suffice. Two witnesses attest the signatures. The deed is proved by affidavit of a subscribing witness, on a memorial left for permanent record with the registrar of the county where the property lies. The word "heirs" must be used to make an estate in fee. Affidavit to prove deeds or mortgages may be taken within the Province before a commissioner, the registrar of deeds, or the judge of a court of record; in Great Britain, before the judge of a superior or county court, the mayor or chief magistrate of a town, borough, or city, under the common seal of such town, city, or borough, or a commissioner of deeds; in foreign countries, before the mayor of any city, town, or borough corporate, certified under the common seal, before any British consul or vice-consul there resident, or before a notary public or court of record.

**Exemptions**.—Free grants and homesteads to actual settlers in the districts of Algoma and Nipissing, and of certain lands between the Ottawa River and the Georgian Bay, are exempt from execution. Personal property: beds, bedding, furniture (a few articles), tools of a trade to the value of $60, fifteen hives of bees, provisions to the value of $40, one cow, four sheep, two hogs, and fodder for thirty days are exempt.

**Insolvency.**—The act of the Parliament of the Dominion of 1880 repealed all insolvency acts, except as to cases where the estate had vested in an assignee before the passing of the act.

**Interest.**—Legal rate, six per cent. Contract may be made for any rate. Banks cannot recover more than seven per cent.

**Married Women.**—If the marriage took place since May 4, 1859, the wife holds all her property, real or personal, free from the control or debts of the husband, except that given to her by him after marriage. If the marriage was prior to that date, the wife has control of all real estate not already reduced to possession by the husband. The separate property of the wife is liable for her debts before marriage. The wife may carry on a business, trade, or profession as though she were a single woman, and her wages and earnings are free from the husband's control. She may sue and be sued, hold stocks, make deposits, and execute deeds and wills in all respects as though she were a single woman. She may insure her husband's life for her own benefit, and the insurance will be free from his creditors. The right of dower still exists. A husband becomes tenant by curtesy of all lands of which his wife died seized.

**Mechanics' Liens.**—Builders, mechanics, miners, contractors, or machinists have a lien to the extent of the owner's interest on both land and buildings. The lien must be registered within one month of the completion of the work, in the county register's office.

**Mortgages.**—The execution is in all respects like that of other Deeds (*which see*). The certificate of registration is also drawn in the same manner. A mortgage is foreclosed by suit in equity before the high court. A special Dominion act regulates the recovery of interest on mortgage debts. There is no equity of redemption after the decree and sale.

**Wills.**—All persons over twenty-one, and of sound mind, can make a will. Two attesting witnesses are necessary. No special form of attestation is required. A devise or legacy to a witness, or the husband or wife of a witness, is void. An executor is competent as a witness.

## NEW BRUNSWICK.

**Attachments.**—By an act of the General Assembly of 1880, all previous laws in regard to attachment were repealed.

**Chattel Mortgages.**—Mortgages on personal property are recognized. They must be recorded with the registrar of the county where the vendor, or mortgagor, lives ; the registry need not be renewed from year to year. Bills of sale must be recorded.

**Deeds.**—Deeds must be in writing, signed and sealed. A wafer or adhesive paper may be used for a seal ; a scroll will not suffice. At least one witness must attest the signature. A deed is acknowledged in or out of the Province in the same manner as in Ontario (*which see*). When a married woman joins her husband in conveying, she must be examined apart from him, and the magistrate must certify that she acknowledged that she joined in conveying of her own free will.

**Exemptions.**—The Homestead Act gives the owner of a homestead exemption to the value of $600. Personal property: household effects to the value of $60 ; wearing apparel, bedding, kitchen utensils, and tools of a trade or calling, to the value of $100, are exempt.

**Interest.**—Any rate may be agreed upon. If none is contracted for, and upon all judgments, the legal rate is six per cent.

**Jurisdiction.**—Magistrates have jurisdiction when the amount involved is not greater than $20 ; if from $20 to $200, the county court has jurisdiction ; supreme court from $200 upward.

**Married Women.**—The real or personal property belonging to a woman before or accruing after her marriage, excepting only gifts from the husband after marriage, is her separate property, and free from her husband's control or debts. The wife's separate property is liable for her ante-nuptial debts. In case of separation or abandonment or desertion by the husband, the wife may carry on business, sue and be sued, and control her property as if a single woman. A widow is entitled to dower.

**Mortgages.**—A mortgage must be executed in all respects like a deed. A scroll will not answer for a seal. The execution is proved by a memorial, and if out of the Province, before a proper officer. See the rules laid down for deeds in Ontario. Foreclosure is by bill in equity. There is no equity of redemption after decree and sale. "Tacking" is not allowed. When the mortgagee has entered into possession, suit to redeem must be brought within twenty years.

**Wills.**—Any person of age and of sound mind may make a will. Married women, however, must obtain the consent of the husband, endorsed upon the will. Two or more witnesses are required. No special form of attestation is prescribed. A devisee or legatee is a competent witness, but the will is void so far as regards the legacy or devise to him.

## NOVA SCOTIA.

**Aliens.**—By act of the Dominion Parliament the disabilities formerly existing have been removed ; aliens may buy, sell, and hold real or personal property in the same manner as citizens.

**Attachments.**—When the suit is for twenty dollars or more and the debtor has absconded, an order of attachment will issue upon an affidavit of the facts by the creditor. Subsequent attachments are allowed by other creditors.

**Chattel Mortgages.**—The law does not recognize mortgages of personal property. To make the pledge there must be actual transfer of possession. Bills of sales must be recorded with the registrar of deeds of the county where the maker resides.

**Deeds.**—A deed must be in writing, signed and sealed (a scroll will not suffice), and attested by at least two witnesses. The rules as to registry and proof by means of memorial or attached certificate are about the same as in Ontario. By an act of 1879, all deeds executed out of the Province are admitted in evidence upon such proof of their due execution as is required to entitle such deeds to registry in the Province.

**Exemption.**—By an act of 1877 the law in regard to Free Grants and Homesteads was repealed, but no rights acquired by any party located on land under the provisions of that act are affected. Personal property: necessary wearing apparel and bedding, tools of a trade, a stove, and one cow, are exempt from execution.

**Interest.**—Legal rate, six per cent. Contract may be made in writing for any rate not above seven per cent., when the security is real estate or chattels real, or for ten per cent. where the security is personal property or personal responsibility. Excess of interest forfeits the excess only.

**Jurisdiction.**—Magistrates have jurisdiction up to $20 ; county courts from $20 to $200 ; supreme court from $200 upward.

**Married Women.**—The husband's property is liable for debts contracted by the wife before marriage. The husband has full control over wife's property acquired after marriage. In general, the common law principles prevail. When the wife has been deserted or a separation has taken place, an order of protection will be issued, and she may then manage her estate as though she were a single woman.

**Mechanics' Liens.**—The act of 1879 establishes liens in favor of mechanics, machinists, contractors, and sub-contractors. The extent of the lien is limited by the interest of the person upon whom the claim is made. A statement of claim and the written contract must be registered. Disputed claims of sub-contractors may be settled by arbitration. The registry must be made within thirty days of the time when the work was done or materials furnished. If suit is not brought within ninety days after the claim is registered, the lien expires.

**Mortgages.**—The execution, attestation, and proof of mortgages is in every respect like those of other deeds. Foreclosure is by petition and decree in a court of equity. A mortgage is deemed to be satisfied in twenty years if there has been no payment of interest or written acknowledgment.

**Wills.**—No person under twenty-one years of age can make a will. Married women must have the written consent of the husband before making a will. At least two witnesses must attest the will. No special form of attestation is required. Nuncupative wills may be made by sailors or soldiers in actual service. Marriage revokes a will. Executors, devisees, and legatees are competent witnesses. But a legacy or devise to an attesting witness will be void.

# LEGAL MAXIMS.

LEGAL maxims are principles of law universally admitted as just and consonant with reason. They have been compared by Blackstone to axioms in geometry. When once established, they form part of the common law of the land, and are good authority. Bouvier's Law Dictionary gives over a thousand of these maxims, from among which we have selected the following as the most important and best known. Most of the maxims are usually quoted in the Latin form, which we therefore give first for convenience of reference. A few are in "Law French."

*A l'impossible nul n'est tenu.* No one is bound to do what is impossible.

*Abundans cautela non nocet.* Abundant caution does no harm.

*Accusare nemo debet se nisi coram Deo.* No one ought to accuse himself except before God.

*Aqua currit et debet currere.* Water runs and ought to run.

*Æquitas sequitur legem.* Equity follows the law.

*Æquum et bonum, est lex legum.* What is good and equal is the law of laws.

*Aliud est celare, aliud tacere.* To conceal is one thing, to be silent another.

*Argumentum à simili valet in lege.* Argument by analogy avails in law.

*Causa proxima, non remota spectatur.* Immediate, not remote cause is to be regarded.

*Caveat emptor.* Let the buyer beware.

*Commodum ex injuria sua non habere debet.* No one ought to derive benefit from his own wrong.

*Communis error facit jus.* Common error makes law, *i. e.*, what is at first illegal, by repetition may gain the force of common usage and become law.

*Communis error non facit jus.* Common error does not make law.

*Consensus facit legem.* Consent makes law (in contracts).

*Consuetudo debet esse certum.* Custom ought to be certain.

*Consuetudo est altera lex.* Custom is another law.

*Conventio vincit legem.* Agreement prevails against the law.

*Cujus est solum, ejus est usque ad cœlum.* Who owns the soil owns up to the sky.

*Culpæ pœna par esto.* Let punishment be proportioned to the offense.

*Currit tempus contra desides et sui juris contempores.* Time runs against the slothful and those who neglect their rights.

*De minimis non curat lex.* The law does not concern itself for trifles

*De similibus idem est judicium.* With similar things the judgment is the same.

*Debet esse finis litium.* There ought to be an end of law suits

*Delegatus non potest delegare.* An agent cannot delegate his power.

*Derivta potestas non potest esse major primitiva.* The power which is derived cannot be greater than that from which it is derived.

*Domus sua cuique est tutissimum refugium.* Every man's house is his castle.

*Dormiuntur aliquando leges, nunquam moriuntur.* The laws sometimes sleep, but never die.

Equality is equity.

Equity suffers not a right without a remedy.

Equity looks upon that as done which ought to be done.

*Ex dolo malo non oritur actio.* Out of fraud no action arises.

*Facta sunt potentiora verbis.* Facts are more powerful than words.

*Falsus in uno, falsus in omnibus.* False in one thing, false in all.

*Fiat justitia, ruat cœlum.* Let justice be done though the heavens fall.

*Fraus est celare fraudem.* It is a fraud to conceal a fraud.

*Fraus latet in generalibus.* Fraud lies hid in general expressions.

*Generale dictum generale est interpretandum.* A general expression is to be generally construed.

*Hæredem Deus facit, non homo.* God, not man makes the heir.

He who has committed iniquity shall not have equity.

*Id certum est quod certum vidi potest.* That is certain which may be rendered certain.

*Idem est scire aut scire potuisse.* To be able to know is the same as to know.

*Idem non esse et non apparere.* It is the same thing not to exist and not to appear.

*Id possumus quod de jure possumus.* We may do anything allowed by law.

*Ignorantia facti excusat, ignorantia legis non excusat.* Ignorance of facts excuses, ignorance of the law does not.

*Ignorantia legis neminem excusat.* Ignorance of the law excuses no one.

*Impotentia legem excusat.* Impossibility excuses the law.

*In dubio pars melior est sequenda.* In a doubtful case the gentler course is to be pursued.

*In dubio sequendum quod tutius est.* In doubt follow the safest course.

*In propria causa nemo judex.* No one may be judge in his own cause.

*Incerta pro nullo habenda sunt.* Things uncertain are held for nothing.

*Intentio cœca mala.* A hidden intention is a bad one.

*Interest republicæ est sit finis litium.* It is for the public interest that lawsuits come to an end.

*Judex est lex loquens.* The judge is the law speaking.

*Judicia posteriora sunt in lege fortiora.* The later decisions are stronger in law.

*Jus publicum privatorum pactis mutari non potest.* A public right cannot be changed by private agreement.

*Jus respicit æquitatem.* Law regards equity.

*Lata culpa dolo æquiparatur.* Gross negligence is equivalent to fraud.

*Le contrat fait le loi.* The contract makes the law.

*Leges posteriores priores contrarias abrogant.* Subsequent laws repeal previous ones to the contrary.

*Legis interpretatio legis vim obtinet.* Construction of law obtains the force of law.

*Lex de futuro, judex de præterito.* Law provides for the future, the judge for the past.

*Lex favet doti.* The law favors dower.

*Lex nemini faciat injuriam.* The law wrongs no one.

*Lex prospicit non respicit.* Laws look forward, not backward.

*Lex reprobat moram.* Law dislikes delay. (Clients sometimes doubt this maxim.)

*Magna culpa dolus est.* Great neglect is fraud.

*Major continet in se minus.* The greater contains the less.

*Malum non presumitur.* Evil is not presumed.

*Mens testatoris in testamento spectanda est.* In wills the intention of the testator is to be considered.

*Misera est servitus, ubi jus est vagum aut incertum.* When law is vague or uncertain, there is miserable slavery.

*Mors omnia solvit.* Death dissolves all things.

*Natura non facit saltum, ita nec lex.* Nature makes no leap, nor does the law.

*Necessitas est lex temporis et loci.* Necessity is the law of time and place.

*Necessitas facit licitum quod alias non est licitum.* Necessity makes that lawful which is otherwise unlawful.

*Necessitas non habet legem.* Necessity has no law.

*Negatio duplex est affirmatio.* A double negative is an affirmative.

*Neminem oportet esse sapientiorem legibus.* No one should be wiser than the law.

*Nemo bis punitur pro eodem delicto.* No one can be punished twice for the same crime.

*Nemo contra factum suum venire potest.* No one may contradict his own deed.

*Nemo dat qui non habet.* A man cannot give what he does not own.

*Nemo est hæres viventis.* No one is heir to a living man.

*Nemo tenetur se ipsum accusare.* No one is bound to accuse himself.

*Non consentit qui errat.* He who errs does not consent.

*Non debet cui plus licet, quod minus est, non licere.* He who is permitted to do the greater may, with greater reason, do the less.

*Non est certandum de regulis juris.* About rules of law there is no disputing.

*Non decipitur, qui scit se decipi.* He is not deceived who knows himself to be deceived.

*Non omne quod licet honestum.* Not everything legal is honorable.

*Non refert verbis aut factis fit revocatio.* It matters not whether a revocation be by word or deed.

*Novatio non presumitur.* A novation is not presumed.

*Nul prendra advantage de son toit demesne.* No one may take advantage of his own wrong.

*Nulle regle sans faute.* No rule without exceptions.

*Omne testamentum morte consummatum est.* Every will is consummated by death.

*Omne sacramentum debet esse de certa scientia.* Every oath should be founded on positive knowledge.

Once a fraud always a fraud.

Once a mortgage, always a mortgage.

Once a recompense, always a recompense.

*Optimus judex qui minimum sibi.* He is the best judge who relies least on himself.

*Partus sequitur ventrem.* Offspring follow the mother (in condition). This applies to slaves and animals only.

Possession is a good title, where no better appears.

*Præsumptio violenta valet in lege.* Strong presumption avails in law.

*Prior tempore, potior jure.* First in time, first in right.

*Quæ in curia acta sunt rite agi præsumuntur.* What is done in court is presumed to have been rightly done.

*Quæ non valeant singula, juncta uvant.* Things which do not avail singly, may when united.

*Quando aliquid prohibitur ex directo, prohibitur et per obliquum.* What is prohibited directly is prohibited indirectly.

*Quando lex aliquid alicui concedit, omnia incidentia tacite conceduntur.* When the law gives anything, it gives tacitly what is incident to it.

*Qui confirmat nihil dat.* Confirming is not giving.

*Qui facit per alium, facit per se.* He who acts through another, acts for himself.

*Qui hæret in litera hæret in cortice.* He who adheres to the letter, adheres to the bark.

*Qui jure suo utitur nemini facit injuriam.* He who uses his legal rights, harms no one.

*Qui non improbat, approbat.* He approves who does not disapprove.

*Qui potest et debet vitare, jubet.* Neglect to forbid is equivalent to a command.

*Qui vult decipi, decipiatur.* Let him who wishes to be deceived be deceived.

*Qui tardius solvit, minus solvit.* Who pays too late, pays too little.

*Quicquid plantatur solo, solo cedit.* Whatever is affixed to the soil (or realty) belongs to it.

*Quod ab initio non valet in tractu temporis non convalescere.* What is not good at the beginning cannot be rendered good by time.

*Quod in uno similium valet, valebit in altero.* What avails in one of two similar things will avail in the other.

*Quod vanum et inutile est lex non requirit.* The law does not demand that which is vain and useless.

*Ratio legis est anima legis.* The reason of the law is the soul of the law.

Remedies ought to be reciprocal.

*Reproba apecunia liberat solventem.* Money refused (*i. e.* tender) liberates the debtor.

*Res judicata pro veritate accipitur.* A thing adjudged must be taken for truth.

*Respondeat superior.* Let the superior answer.

Rights never die.

*Salus populi est suprema lex.* The safety of the people is the supreme law.

*Scribere est agere.* To write is to act.

*Semper necessitas probandi incumbit qui agit.* The burden of proof lies on the claimant.

*Si quis custos fraudem pupillo fecerit a tutela removendus est.* A guardian, guilty of fraud toward his ward, shall be removed.

*Sic utere tuo ut alienum non lædas.* So use your own as not to injure another's property.

*Silent leges inter arma.* Laws are silent amidst arms.

*Solo cedit quod solo implantatur.* What is planted in the soil belongs to the soil.

*Summum jus summa injuria.* The height (extreme rigor) of the law is the height of wrong.

Superfluities do no injury.

Surplusage does no harm.

*Tacite quædam habentur pro expressis.* Things silent are sometimes considered as expressed.

*Tantum bona valent, quantum vendi possunt.* Things are worth what they will sell for.

*Terra transit cum onere.* Land passes with the incumbrances.

*Testibus deponentibus in pari numero dignioribus credendum.* When the number of witnesses is equal on both sides, the more worthy are to be believed.

*Testis oculatus unus plus valet quam auriti decem.* One eye witness is worth ten ear witnesses.

Trusts survive.

*Tout ce que le loi ne defend pas, est permis.* The law permits everything it does not forbid.

*Tutius erratur ex parte mitiore.* It is safer to err on the side of mercy.

*Ubi eadem ratio, ibi idem lex.* Where there is the same reason there is the same law.

*Ubi jus, ibi remedium.* Where there is a right, there is a remedy.

Usury is odious in law.

*Utile per inutile non vitiatur.* What is useful is not vitiated by the useless.

*Valeat quantum valere potest.* It shall avail as far as it can have effect.

*Verba fortius accipiuntur contra proferentem.* Words are to be taken most strongly against him using them.

*Verba generalia generaliter sunt intelligenda.* General words are to be understood generally.

*Verba nihil operandi melius est quam absurde.* It is better that words should have no interpretation than an absurd one.

*Veritas nihil veretur, nisi abscondi.* Truth fears nothing but concealment.

*Vir et uxor consentur in lege una persona.* Man and wife in law are considered one person.

*Volunti non fit injuria.* He who consents cannot receive an injury.

When the foundation fails all fails.

When two rights concur, the most ancient shall be preferred.

Where there is equal equity, the law must prevail.

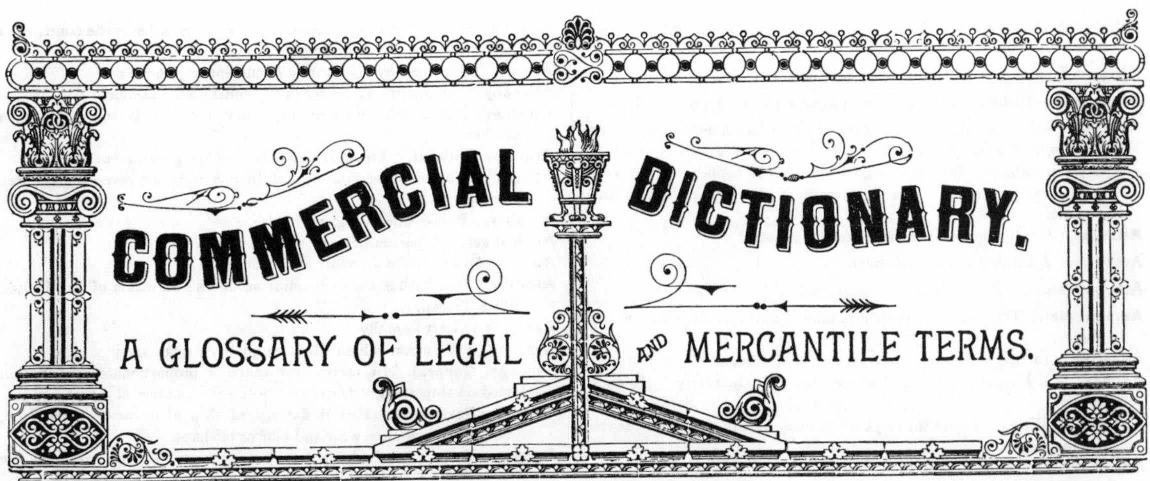


**A.** Capital A endorsed on the face of an account or document may mean *Audited, Accepted*, or *Approved*. Small *a*, written @, means *at*, as, 10 yds. @ 14 cts.

**A. 1.** Of first quality. Used technically in shipping, but applied to other matters. The mark originated with the English Lloyds, who rate vessels A1, A2, and so down. In the American system the registry descends from A by fractions, A1, A1¼, A1½, A1¾, A2.

**Abandonment.** In marine insurance, the abandonment of property insured to the insurers.

**Abatement.** Amount deducted from a bill for any cause; a discount; removal of a nuisance.

**Abator.** One who removes a nuisance.

**Abeyance.** Held in suspense, as an unsettled estate.

**Abstract.** Abridgment or epitome of a deed or other document.

**Acceptance.** Agreement by the *drawee* of negotiable paper to pay the same. Agreement to terms offered.

**Acceptance supra Protest.** Agreement to pay a note or bill after it has been protested, for the honor of the maker or an indorser.

**Acceptor.** He who by his signature makes acceptance.

**Accession.** Acquiring property attached as an incident.

**Accessory.** One who instigates, encourages or aids in the offence of another.

**Accommodation Paper.** Notes or bills not representing an actual sale or trade transaction, but merely drawn to be discounted for the benefit of drawer, acceptor or indorsers, or all combined.

**Accord and Satisfaction.** Offer and acceptance of one thing in place of another due.

**Account.** A statement of sums and amounts due from one person to another and their offsets, arising from mutual transactions. Summary of *debits* and *credits*.

**Accountant.** An expert in examining books.

**Account Current.** A running account for a certain period, showing what is due at the present time.

**Account Sales.** The account of a broker or commission agent, showing amount and rate of sales, expenses of freight, commission, etc., and *net* amount due the principal.

**Accretion.** Gradual increase of land through natural causes.

**Accroach.** To attempt to use power without authority.

**Accrue.** To increase, to be due as profits.

**Acknowledgment.** A receipt. In law, admission of facts.

**Acquittance.** A written receipt in full, or discharge from all claims.

**Actionaire** (*French*). The holder of shares in a stock company.

**Act.** A formal writing expressing what has been done, as, an act of Congress, an act of bankruptcy.

**Actuary.** Officer of a life insurance company; expert in vital statistics and annuities.

**Act of God.** A cause of injury not to be prevented by human means.

**Adjustment.** Settlement of claims in marine or fire insurance. Determining amount of loss and of liability. In accounts, the settling of a disputed account.

**Admiralty Court.** A court having jurisdiction in maritime matters.

**Ad Valorem** (*Latin*). According to the value.

**Ad Valorem Duties.** Duties levied on goods according to value; not by quantity, weight or measure. Opposed to *Specific Duties*.

**Administer.** To settle an estate as adminstrator or executor.

**Administrator.** One who has charge of the estate of a man dying without a will, or appointed in place of an executor.

**Advance.** Increase in value.

**Advances.** Money paid before goods are delivered to buyer, or sold by broker.

**Adventure.** Shipment of goods on shipper's own account. Merchants keep a debit and credit account with each enterprise, as, Adventure to Rio Janeiro.

**Adventure, Bill of.** Writing signed by master of ship which carries goods at the owner's risk.

**Adventure in Co.** Shipment of goods at joint risk of shipper and consignee.

**Adverse Posession.** Posession of real property avowedly contrary to the claim of another person.

**Advice.** Mercantile information sent by letter, called *Letter of Advice*.

**Affiant.** One who makes an affidavit.

**Affidavit.** Declaration under oath.

**Affiliation.** Establishment of paternity.

**Affinity.** Connection resulting from marriage.

**Affreightment.** The act of hiring a ship for transportation of goods.

**Agent.** One who acts for another.

**Aggravation.** In law, something enhancing crime or increasing damages.

**Agio** (*Italian*). Difference in value between bank notes and gold, or between one kind of paper money and another.

**Agiotage.** Speculation on fluctuation of public securities.

**Agrarian.** Relating to land.

**Agreement.** A contract. Literally, the meeting of minds.

**Alias** (*Latin*). A second or assumed name.

**Alien.** One of foreign birth and allegiance.

**Alimony.** In divorce law, provision for support of a wife.

**Allegation.** Rule for obtaining the proportion of ingredients in making mixtures, and the value of such mixtures.

**Alliquot Part.** A number contained within a larger number an exact number of times.

**Allonge** (*French*). A paper pasted on a note or bill of exchange to allow more indorsements than the bill has room for.

**Allegiance.** Obedience and support due to the government.

**Allotment Ticket.** Order for payment of wages to seaman's family at stated intervals during the voyage.

**Allow.** To yield to another's profit; to concede; to discount.

**Allowance.** Deduction from gross weight or amount. Sailor's rations.

**Alloy** (*French*, *á la loi*). Baser metal introduced in coinage; the union of different metals. Neither of the precious metals is used in absolute purity in coinage. Gold is alloyed with silver or copper; silver, with nickel, brass, or copper. The proportion of alloy differs in different countries.

**Alluvion.** Gradual increase of the shore of a stream.

**Amotion.** A turning away or removal.

**Amount Gross.** The total sum or aggregate.

**Amount Net.** Total sum less proper deduction for expenses, discount, or charges.

**Ancestor.** In law, embraces collaterals as well as lineals.

**Anchorage.** A spot near shore where ships are in safety. Holding ground.

**Ancient Writings.** Deeds thirty years old may be admitted to evidence without proof.

**Anker.** A foreign measure of about ten gallons.

**Annex.** To take permanently, as to annex territory; fixtures are annexed to the freehold.

**Annuity.** A sum paid yearly or at stated intervals.

**Answer.** To be responsible for; to reply.

**Antedate.** To date beforehand.

**Application.** In insurance, the first step in obtaining a policy.

**Appellate Jurisdiction.** Courts having power to review decisions of lower courts.

**Apply.** To dispose of in a particular manner, as, to apply funds in payment of a note.

**Appraisement.** Ascertaining the value of goods or property.

**Appraiser.** He who appraises. In particular, an officer of government who ascertains the value of dutiable goods.

**Appreciate.** To rise in value.

**Apprentice.** A minor bound out to learn a trade.

**Apprize.** Another form of *appraise.*

**Appropriation.** Setting apart for a specific purpose. Government grant of money.

**Appurtenance.** Something incidental to another.

**Arbitration.** Settlement of disputed claims or accounts by arbitrators.

**Arbitrators.** Disinterested parties called in to settle disputes.

**Arbitration of Exchanges.** Comparison of currency of intermediate places, to discover whether it is more profitable to forward money directly or indirectly.

**Archives.** State papers, records, charters, and other important documents.

**Article.** A single piece of goods; a division of a document or contract.

**Arson.** The malicious burning of another's house.

**Articles of Partnership.** The contract between the parties.

**Articles of War.** Rules for the government of army and navy.

**Assay.** To test the purity of precious metals.

**Assess.** To levy a tax or share of expenses.

**Assets.** Funds of an individual, firm, or corporation; resources; opposed to liabilities.

**Assignats.** Paper money of France after the revolution, never redeemed.

**Assignee.** A person to whom an assignment is made; trustee for the creditors of a bankrupt estate.

**Assignment.** Conditional transfer of property for safe keeping, or adjustment.

**Assignor.** One who transfers his property to assignees for the benefit of creditors or for other reasons.

**Assizes.** A criminal court for jury trials held from place to place. (*English*).

**Association.** A body of men; a stock company; a society.

**Assortment.** A quantity of goods varying in form, color, style, size, or price.

**Assumpsit.** An action to recover damages for breach of contract.

**Assurance.** Nearly synonymous with insurance; an agreement to pay on a contingency *sure to occur.*

**Attachment.** A seizure of property or person by order of the court, to be held until the cause is decided.

**Attest.** To witness by signature a document or judicial act

**Attorney.** An agent; an officer of the court; a counsellor.

**Attorney, Power of.** Written authority for one person to act for another.

**Attorney General.** The chief law officer of the government.

**Attorn.** To agree to become tenant to one to whom reversion has been granted.

**Auction.** Public sale to highest bidder.

**Auctioneer.** A person licensed to sell by auction.

**Audit.** To scrutinize accounts and vouchers.

**Auditor.** One authorized to examine accounts; an officer of the United States Treasury.

**Aver.** To assert formally.

**Average.** The mean value; Medium quality; a fair sample.

**Average, General.** In marine insurance, a proportionate contribution levied on ship and goods to cover necessary sacrifice of a part.

**Average, Particular.** Partial damage of ship alone, or of cargo alone, arising from ordinary wear and tear or mishaps.

**Average, Petty.** Small charges, such as pilotage, port charges, and the like, borne in part by ship and part by cargo.

**Average of Payments.** Method of finding the time when payment may be made of several sums due at different dates without loss to either party.

**Avoid.** In law, to nullify.

**Avulsion.** Lands torn by the current from one estate and added to another.

**Bail.** A surety for appearance; the amount pledged.

**Bailments.** In law of contracts, delivery of goods for some purpose.

**Balance.** Difference necessary to make *debit* and *credit* sides of an account equal; weighing scales.

**Balance Account.** An account made up of balances of different accounts; a brief summary of the state of a business.

**Balance Sheet.** A paper giving a summary and balance of accounts.

**Balance of Trade.** Difference in value between total exports and imports of a country.

**Ballast.** Weight used to steady a ship; *in balance*, loaded with ballast instead of cargo.

**Bale.** A package of goods or produce.

**Banco.** Difference between bank value and current value of money.

**Bank.** An institution for deposit, discount, and circulation.

**Bankable.** Capable of passing at par at a bank.

**Bankbook.** Passbook of a bank, showing state of depositor's account.

**Bank Hours.** Usually from 9 or 10 A. M. to 3 P. M.

**Banker.** A dealer in money; one entrusted with funds by others.

**Bankrupt.** One unable to meet his business liabilities; the word literally means *broken up.*

**Bank Stock.** Shares in a banking company; paid up capital of a bank divided into shares.

**Bar.** A final defence; profession of law.

**Bargain.** An agreement of sale; an advantageous commercial transaction.

**Barque or Bark.** A three-masted vessel, rigged square as to fore and main masts, and "fore and aft" as to mizzen mast.

**Barratry.** In shipping, any wilful breach of duty or trust by master or crew, as against owners or insurers; in common law, malicious stirring up of litigation.

**Barrel.** A measure of capacity, containing 31½ gallons, wine measure; 36 gallons, beer measure; 32 gallons, ale measure.

**Barrel Bulk.** In freight measurement, 5 cubic feet.

**Barrister.** English name for a lawyer who practices in the courts.

**Barter.** To exchange one kind of goods for another.

**Base Court.** An inferior court, not one of record.

**Bazaar** (*Turkish*). Place of trade; specially applied to shops for sale of fancy articles.

**Beacon.** General word for light-house or light-ship.

**Bear.** In Stock Exchange slang, one who strives to depress the price of stocks.

**Bearer.** He who holds and presents for payment a note, bill, check, or draft.

**Bearer, Payable to.** Negotiable paper so drawn need not be indorsed.
**Bench Warrant.** One issued by a superior court judge.
**Bill.** A statement of accounts due ; general term for all negotiable paper.
**Bill Book.** In bookkeeping, the account kept of all notes, drafts and bills of exchange.
**Billhead.** A printed form for bills, with business address at the top.
**Bill of Discovery.** Application to equity court to compel disclosure of facts.
**Bill of Entry.** A bill of goods entered at the custom-house.
**Bill of Exceptions.** A written list of exceptions to a court's decisions.
**Bill of Exchange.** A written order from one person to another, ordering or requesting him to pay a certain sum of money to a third person at a given date.
**Bill, Domestic or Inland.** A bill of exchange payable in the country where drawn.
**Bill, Foreign.** A bill of exchange payable in a foreign country ; usually drawn in duplicate or triplicate.
**Bill of Lading.** A receipt given by a ship's master for goods received for carriage, promising to deliver the same at a certain time and place, dangers of the sea excepted : four copies are usually made, one for master, one for shipper, one to be sent in ship to consignee, the fourth sent by some other ship.
**Bill of Parcels.** Sometimes used for invoice.
**Bill of Particulars.** Specification of demands for which an action is brought.
**Bill of Sale.** A contract under seal for the sale of goods.
**Bill of Sight.** A form of Custom-House entry, allowing consignee to see goods before paying duty.
**Bills Payable.** Notes and bills issued in favor of other parties by a merchant.
**Bills Receivable.** Notes and bills made by others and payable to ourselves.
**Blank Credit.** Permission to draw money on account, no sum being specified.
**Bona Fide** (*Latin*). In good faith.
**Blackmail.** Extortion of money by threats.
**Blockading.** Obstructing an enemy's ports.
**Board of Trade.** About equivalent to *Chamber of Commerce* or *Merchant's Exchange* ; an association of business men to regulate matters of trade and further their interests, and for the settlement of differences between its members.
**Bond.** A legal document by which a person binds himself to pay money or do something under penalty of paying a sum fixed.
**Bond Creditor.** A creditor whose debt is secured by a bond.
**Bond Debt.** A debt contracted under obligation of a bond.
**Bonded Goods.** Goods on which bonds instead of cash have been given for import duties.
**Bonded Warehouse.** Buildings owned by persons approved of by the Secretary of the Treasury, and who have given bonds or guarantee for the strict observance of the revenue laws ; used for storing imported merchandise until the duties are paid or the goods re-shipped without entry.
**Bondsman.** One who gives security for the payment of money, performance of an act, or integrity of another.
**Bonus.** Additional money paid beyond interest ; extra profits.
**Book Debts.** Accounts charged on the books.
**Bookkeeper.** One who keeps mercantile accounts.
**Bookkeeping, Single Entry.** That system of bookkeeping which requires only one entry for a single transaction.
**Bookkeeping, Double Entry.** The system of bookkeeping which requires for every transaction two entries, one on the debit and one on the credit side.
**Borough.** An incorporated town or village.
**Bottomry Bond.** The mortgage of a vessel for sums advanced for the use of the ship.
**Bought and Sold Notes.** Notes given by a broker to the seller and buyer respectively.
**Bounty.** A bonus or premium given to encourage trade.
**Brand.** Literally a mark of designation made by a hot iron ; any trade-mark, device, or name ; the particular quality of a class of goods.
**Breach of Trust.** Violation of his duty by a trustee.
**Breadstuffs.** Any kind of grain, corn, or meal.
**Breakage.** Allowance made by a shipper for loss by the destruction of fragile wares.
**Breaking in.** Such violence as is necessary to constitute burglary.
**Breaking Bulk.** Opening packages of goods in transit.
**Brief.** A concise summary or statement of a case.
**Broker.** An agent or factor ; a middleman paid by commission ; the most common are *Bill*, *Exchange*, *Insurance*, *Produce*, *Ship*, and *Stock Brokers*.
**Bull.** Stock Exchange slang for a broker or dealer who believes that the value of stocks will rise and speculates for a rise, "goes long" on a stock.
**Bullion.** Uncoined gold or silver.
**Burden of Proof.** Obligation of a party asserting a fact to prove it.
**Burglary.** At common law, breaking into a house in the night time with felonious intent.
**Bushel.** A cylindrical measure, 18½ inches in diameter and 8 inches deep inside ; its capacity is 2,150 42-100 cubic inches.
**By-Law.** Local or restricted municipal regulations.

**Cabinet.** Advisory council of a sovereign or president.
**Calculate.** To determine by reckoning ; to adjust by comparison.
**Call.** Demand for payment of instalments due on stock.
**Call.** In Stock Exchange slang, a privilege given to another to "call" for delivery of stock at a time and price fixed.
**Cancel.** To annul or erase ; often done by stamp or punch.
**Canon.** A precept of ecclesiastical law.
**Capias.** Writ commanding sheriff to take defendant or a witness into custody.
**Capital.** Money invested in business ; amount of assets.
**Capitalist.** One having money to invest ; a wealthy man.
**Capital Offence.** One punishable by death.
**Capital Stock.** The aggregate amount invested in a stock company ; total value of stock at par.
**Capitation.** Tax levied by polls.
**Carat.** A measure of weight for gold and precious stones.
**Cargo.** Merchandise laden on a ship for transportation.
**Carrier.** One who carries goods for another.
**Cartage.** The amouut due for carting goods.
**Carte Blanche** (*French*). Literally white paper · free or full powers.
**Case.** A box for holding goods or merchandise ; at law, an action or suit.
**Case, Action on the.** A common law form of action.
**Cash.** Ready money ; gold, silver, bank-notes ; checks and drafts are usually included.
**Cash-Book.** A book of entry for money paid in and out.
**Cashier.** One who has charge of money ; a bank officer.
**Cassation** (*French*). Act of annulling ; reversal.
**Cash Sales.** Sales for cash.
**Caveat.** Formal notice not to interfere with one's rights.
**Certificate.** A written voucher, as, a certificate of deposit, a stock-certificate.
**Certified Check.** One accepted by the bank on which it is drawn as good.
**Chamber of Commerce.** An association of merchants for the encouragement of trade.
**Charter.** A grant by a State empowering a corporated association to do business.
**Charter-Party.** A written contract for the hire of a vessel for a given voyage.
**Check.** An order on a bank for payment of money on demand to bearer or the order of some person.
**Check-Book.** A printed book of blank checks.
**Check-Clerk.** One who examines accounts of other clerks ; a bank clerk who enters up checks.
**Choses in Action** Personal property for which the right of action exists but which has not been reduced to possession.
**Circular.** A printed letter of advertisement.
**Circular Note.** A note or bill issued by bankers for the accommodation of travelers, calling upon correspondents at different places to pay money on demand.
**Clearance.** A Custom House certificate that a ship is free to leave.

**Clearing.** 1. Entering a ship at the Custom House and obtaining clearance. 2. In banking, exchange of checks and settling balances at the Clearing House.
**Clearing House.** A banking exchange for daily settlements.
**C. O. D.** Collect on delivery; method of payment for goods sent by express.
**Collateral.** In law of descent, that which is not lineal; a grandson is of lineal, a nephew of collateral descent.
**Collateral Security.** A secondary security to be available if the chief security fail.
**Collector.** One authorized to receive money for another; chief officer of a Custom House.
**Commerce.** Extended trade or traffic.
**Commission.** An agent's percentage for transacting business.
**Commission Broker.** One who buys or sells on commission.
**Commissioner of Deeds.** An attorney or notary authorized to take acknowledgment of deeds in a foreign State.
**Common Carrier.** A public conveyer of goods or passengers.
**Common Law.** Unwritten law, as distinguished from written or statute law.
**Company.** An association in business; a joint stock concern.
**Compound Interest.** Interest on both principal and interest.
**Composition.** A payment by a debtor of a percentage of his debts as settlement in full.
**Consideration.** Value received; a bonus.
**Consignee.** One to whom goods are sent.
**Consignment.** Goods sent to an agent to be sold.
**Consols.** Government securities of England, paying three per cent.
**Consul.** A representative of one country in a port of another to protect trade interests and the rights of seamen and other citizens.
**Consulage.** Duty paid by merchants for protection of commerce abroad.
**Contraband.** Prohibited goods or merchandise; smuggled goods.
**Contraband of War.** Goods which neutral ships are forbidden to carry to belligerents; as munitions of arms.
**Contract.** An agreement; a bargain.
**Contractor.** One who engages to do certain work or furnish goods at fixed rates; a public supply agent.
**Conveyance.** A written instrument by which property is transferred; a deed.
**Cooperage.** Charge for putting hoops on casks or barrels.
**Copying-Press.** An instrument for taking impressions from damp paper.
**Corner.** In stock and grain broker's slang, the buying up of a large quantity of stock or grain to raise the price.
**Corporation.** A body of business men authorized by law to transact certain business.
**Counter-Entry.** An entry in a contrary sense.
**Counting Room.** A merchant's business office.
**Coupon** (*French*). A certificate of interest attached to bonds or stock, to be cut off when due.
**Court of Equity.** One having a chancery or equity jurisdiction; not limited by the common law.
**Cr.** Abbreviation for *Credit;* the *Cr.* side of an account is on the right hand.
**Credit.** In bookkeeping, value received or transferred from the party; opposite of *debit;* financial standing; power to obtain loans.
**Creditor.** One to whom money or value is due.
**Credit Mobilier.** An association intending to buy up and conduct railroads or other companies on limited liability principles; in this country the most noted was the Credit Mobilier Company of the Pacific Railroad.
**Curbstone Broker.** Brokers not members of the regular Stock-Exchange.
**Currency.** The circulating medium of a country.
**Current.** Passing freely; now running, as, *current accounts.*
**Customs.** Taxes on goods exported or imported.
**Custom House.** A place appointed to receive customs.
**Custom House Entry.** A statement made and fees paid in clearing a ship.
**Customary Law.** Practices which have become law through the long usage of the mercantile world.
**Damages.** Compensation for injury received.
**Date.** Day of the month and year.
**Day-Book.** A book for recording daily transactions.
**Days of Grace.** Three days allowed for payment of notes or bills after the time specified has elapsed. In some other countries more than three are allowed.
**Debase.** To lessen in value; as, a debased coinage.
**Debenture.** A Custom House certificate entitling an exporter to a drawback on duties paid.
**Debit.** To make debtor; opposite of credit; a charge entered.
**Debtor.** One who owes; opposite of creditor.
**Decimal.** A tenth part; by tenths.
**Declined.** Decreased in value.
**Deed.** A sealed legal instrument, transferring property, usually land.
**Default.** Failure to pay.
**Defendant.** In law, the one against whom a claim or charge is made.
**Deficit.** A lack of funds to balance accounts.
**Del Credere** (*Italian*). Extra commission given an agent in consideration of his warranting the solvency of the purchaser.
**Demand.** Claim for payment.
**Demurrage.** Forfeit money for detention of vessels beyond the time allowed by a charter-party.
**Deposit.** Money left with a bank subject to order; payment on account.
**Depot.** A place of storage or warehouse; improperly used of a railway station.
**Derelict.** Ship or cargo abandoned at sea.
**Deterioration.** Lessening in value.
**Deviation.** The departure of a ship from her regular course to stop at other ports.
**Directors.** The managers of a stock company.
**Discharge.** To pay a debt; to unload a ship.
**Discount.** A sum thrown off the amount of a note or bill; a deduction; *to discount* is to lend money on bills after deducting the interest.
**Discount Broker.** One who lends money on notes or bills.
**Dissolution.** Breaking up of a partnership.
**Dividend.** Payment of the profits of a joint stock concern, *pro rata;* proportional payment to creditors out of a bankrupt estate.
**Dockage or Dock Dues.** Charges for the use of a dock.
**Docket.** A ticket or mark on goods showing measurement or destination; a list of cases before a court.
**Donee.** One to whom something is given.
**Draft.** An order to pay money; a rough copy of a writing; a deduction from gross weight of goods; number of feet which a ship sinks in the water.
**Draw.** To make a draft; to call for funds.
**Drawback.** An allowance or return of duties paid at the Custom House.
**Drawer.** The maker of a draft or bill of exchange.
**Drawee.** The one on whom a draft or bill is drawn.
**Drayage.** Charges on goods hauled by a dray; cartage.
**Drummer.** One who solicits custom for a merchant by showing samples.
**Dry Goods.** Commercial name for textile fabrics.
**Due.** Owing; that which is owed.
**Due Bill.** A written acknowledgment of debt, not negotiable.
**Dun.** To demand payment.
**Dunnage.** Loose articles of a cargo; loose material laid on the bottom of the ship's hold to raise goods and prevent injury by water.
**Duplicate.** A copy; a second article of the same kind.
**Duress.** Confinement; restraint; compulsion.
**Duties.** Taxes levied by a government on exports or imports.
**Eagle.** A gold coin of the United States, value ten dollars.
**E. E.** Abbreviation for *errors excepted.*
**Effects.** Property; goods on hand; the possessions of a firm.
**Ejectment.** Dispossession of houses or land; forcing out.
**Ell.** A measure of length, 1 yard, 9 inches.
**Embargo.** Order of a government forbidding ships to leave its ports.
**Embark.** To enter a ship for a voyage; to engage in any enterprise.
**Emporium.** A commercial city; a place of trade.
**Endorse.** To transfer notes, bills, or checks by writing one's name on the back; to guarantee payment.
**Endorsee.** He in whose favor endorsement is made.
**Endorser.** One who endorses.

**Engrosser.** One who takes the whole of a line of goods; a forestaller; one who "corners the market" on commodities; an ornamental penman.
**Engrossing Clerk.** A copyist; a copying clerk.
**Entrepot.** A place where goods are deposited without paying duty, to await transportation elsewhere; a free port.
**Entry.** In bookkeeping, any record made; depositing a ship's papers with the Custom House.
**Equity** A branch of jurisprudence distinct from the common law.
**Equity of Redemption.** Privilege allowed to a mortgagor to redeem property within a given time.
**Estoppal.** Preclusion of a person from asserting a fact or doing an act inconsistent with previous acts or declarations.
**Examiner.** A Custom House officer who compares goods with invoices.
**Exchange.** Place where merchants meet to transact business; percentage on sale of bills; difference of value between different currencies.
**Exchange Broker.** One who negotiates foreign bills of exchange.
**Exchequer.** A treasury; summary of finances.
**Excise.** Internal revenue tax.
**Executed.** Finished; accomplished in legal form.
**Executor.** One appointed to carry out the provisions of a will.
**Executory.** To be performed in the future.
**Executrix.** Feminine form of *executor*.
**Exhibit.** Voucher or document presented in court; transcript of ledger balances.
**Export.** To send goods to a foreign country.
**Export Duty.** Tax imposed on exports.
**Exporter.** One who exports.
**Exports.** The goods or merchandise exported.
**Express.** To transmit with celerity.
**Express Company.** A corporation engaged in the business of transporting goods and money from one place to another more quickly than can be done by sending as ordinary freight.
**Extension.** Allowance of time for payment to a debtor; carrying out items of a bill or account.
**E. & O. E.** "Errors and Omissions Excepted.

**Face.** The amount for which a note is drawn.
**Fac Simile** (*Latin*). An exact copy; a counterpart.
**Factor.** An agent appointed to sell goods on commission; a consignee.
**Factorage.** Commissions allowed to factors.
**Facture.** An invoice or bill of goods.
**Failure.** Becoming bankrupt; suspension of payment.
**Fair.** Of average quality; above middling.
**Fall.** Decrease in price or value.
**False Pretences.** Misstatements made with intent to defraud.
**Fancy Goods.** Light fabrics, ribbons, laces, etc.
**Fare.** Charge for passage.
**Farthing.** An English copper coin worth half a cent; an insignificant value.
**Fee.** Payment; charge of a professional man; a gratuity.
**Fee-Simple.** In real estate, an absolute title; one with no conditions attached.
**Finance.** Funds; public money; revenue.
**Financier.** One skilled in money matters.
**Fire Insurance.** Indemnity against loss by fire.
**Fire Policy.** The writing by which insurers agree to pay fire insurance.
**Firm.** Name, style or title of a business concern; the partners taken collectively.
**Five-Forties.** United States Bonds, issued during the war, redeemable any time after five years, payable at not more than forty years after date, bearing 6 per cent. interest.
**Five-Twenties.** United States Bonds, redeemable any time after five years, payable twenty years from date, bearing 6 per cent. interest.
**Fixtures.** Anything of an accessory nature annexed to real estate; that which forms a part of the reality.
**Flat.** Inactive; depressed; dull; *flat value* of stock and bonds is the value without interest.
**Flotsam.** Goods thrown into the sea which swim.
**F. O. B.** "Free on board;" transportation and shipping expenses included.
**Footing.** Amount of a column of figures.
**Forced Sales.** Sale of commodity under compulsion or foreclosure.
**Foreclose.** To seize property under the conditions of a mortgage.
**Foreign Bill.** A bill of exchange drawn in one country upon a citizen of another.
**Forestall.** To buy up goods before the regular time of sale; to bring about an increase in the price of provisions.
**Forwarder.** A merchant or agent who transmits or forwards goods.
**Fractional Currency.** United States paper money for sums less than a dollar.
**Franc.** French unit of coinage; 100 *centimes*; value, 18 3-5 cents.
**Franking.** Privilege of sending letters free of charge.
**Fraud.** In law, any wrongful artifice, device or concealment by which pecuniary damage is done to another.
**Free Goods.** Goods admitted without an import tax.
**Free Port.** A port where ships may load and unload free from duties.
**Free Trade.** Trade not restricted by tariff duties for "protection."
**Freight.** Sums paid for transportation of merchandise or hire of a ship; less properly, the goods carried.
**Funded.** Made into a permanent loan on which interest is paid.
**Funds.** Ready money; shares in a national debt; public securities.

**Garbles.** Dust, filth or soil removed from spices, drugs, etc; *to garble* is to separate this refuse.
**Garnishment.** Legal notice attaching goods or money of one person in the hands of another.
**Garnishee.** The person on whom is served a writ of garnishment or "trustee process," ordering him to appear in court and give information in regard to the goods of another, the original debtor, in his hands.
**Gauge.** To measure the contents of a cask; measure or standard.
**General Order Store.** A bonded warehouse to which merchandise not claimed within a certain time is sent under a "General Order."
**Goods.** Merchandise; movable property.
**Good Will.** The interest of an established business in the way of trade and custom.
**Grain.** Collective name for all cereals.
**Great Gross.** Twelve gross; i. e., 1,728 articles.
**Gross.** Twelve dozen; total amount; opposed to ***net***.
**Gross Ton.** Twenty-two hundred and forty pounds.
**Guarantee.** The one to whom security is given or guaranty made.
**Guarantor.** One making a guaranty.
**Guaranty.** Security; an undertaking that one person will pay money to another or fulfil a contract.
**Gunny-Bags.** Sacks of coarse material used for coffee.

**Hand.** Measure of animals' height; about four inches.
**Hand-Money.** Money paid to bind a bargain.
**Harbor.** A place of security for vessels.
**Harbor-Dues.** Charges made for use of a harbor.
**Harbor-Master.** An officer having charge of a harbor.
**Hogshead.** A measure of capacity; 2 barrels, or 63 gallons; a large cask.
**Holder.** He in whose possession a note or bill may be.
**Hollow-Ware.** Trade name for cast or wrought iron vessels, kettles, etc.
**Honor.** To accept and pay a note, draft or bill.
**Husbandage.** Compensation paid to a "ship's husband," (***which see***).
**Hypothecate.** To pledge as security; to mortgage chattels.

**Immovables.** Land, houses, and fixtures; real estate.
**Importer.** A merchant who imports goods.
**Imports.** Goods brought from a foreign country.
**Impost.** Government tax on imported goods.
**Income.** Total amount of receipts from all sources; yearly gains.
**Income Tax.** A government tax of a percentage on the income of individuals or corporations.
**Indemnification.** Making good a loss; securing one against damages.
**Indemnity.** Guarantee against loss; freedom; compensation for damages suffered.
**Index.** Names of titles or accounts arranged alphabetically.
**Indorse.** See *Endorse*, etc.
**Indulgence.** Extension of time for payment.

**Inland Bill.** A bill of exchange or draft drawn upon a person in the same State or Country.
**Insolvent.** Unable to pay outstanding liabilities; bankrupt.
**Instalment.** A part payment or part delivery of goods.
**Instant.** Of the present month, as, the 12th inst.
**Insurable Interest.** Such an interest as will entitle a person to obtain insurance on the life or property of another.
**Insurance.** A contract in which one party, the *insurer*, agrees in consideration of the *premium*, to pay a certain sum on the death of the *insured* or to indemnify him for loss to property by fire or marine risks.
**Insurance Broker.** One who negotiates insurance contracts.
**Interest.** Money paid for use of money; share in a business or venture.
**Interest Account.** In bookkeeping, a separate account of sums paid and received as interest.
**Internal Revenue.** Government revenue derived from domestic sources.
**Intestate.** Not disposed of by a valid will; one who dies without a will.
**In Transitu** (*Latin*). On the road; not brought to an end.
**Inventory.** A list of goods and merchandise on hand; any enumeration of articles; a schedule.
**Investment.** Placing of money in business or securities.
**Invoice.** Account of merchandise shipped, with prices and charges annexed.
**Invoice Book.** A book for entering copies of invoices.
**Involved.** Confused; embarrassed by liabilities.

**Jettison.** Throwing goods overboard or cutting away masts and sails to save a vessel.
**Jetsam.** Goods thrown into the sea which have sunk.
**Jobber.** One who buys from importers or manufacturers and sells to retailers; a middleman.
**Job Lot.** Goods left over; an odd assortment.
**Joint Stock.** That held in company; stock formed by the union of several companies.
**Joint Stock Company.** A business association, the capital of which is represented by shares of stock.
**Joint Tenants.** Those who have not only unity of possession, but also of title and interest, and the survivor takes the whole.
**Journal.** An account book intermediate between Day-Book and Ledger.
**Judgment.** A judicial decree; decision of a court.
**Judgment Note.** One containing a power of attorney from maker to payee to confess judgment for the maker to the extent of face and interest.
**Jurisdiction.** Extent of a court's authority as to place, sum, or subject matter.

**Lame Duck.** Stock-brokers' slang for one unable to meet his liabilities.
**Land.** To discharge cargo; to disembark.
**Law, Merchant.** Body of law relating to mercantile customs.
**Law Days.** Days allowed in a charter-party for unloading a ship.
**Lay Down.** Cost of merchandise, including charges and freight to place of shipment.
**Lazzaretto** (*Italian*). A place in Quarantine where goods are fumigated.
**Leakage.** An allowance made for waste by leaking of casks.
**Lease.** An agreement for letting lands or tenements for life, a term of years or months, or at will.
**Legal Tender.** Currency or coin which a government has declared shall be received in payment of debts; a formal proffer of money to pay a debt; if refused, the creditor cannot recover.
**Lessee.** One to whom a lease is given.
**Lessor.** One who makes a lease.
**Letter Book.** That in which copies of letters sent and received are made.
**Letter of Advice.** One giving notice of a shipment made, bill drawn, or other business transaction.
**Letter of Credit.** One authorizing credit to a certain amount to be given to the bearer.
**Letter of License.** One by which creditors of an insolvent debtor postpone their claims and allow him to continue trade.
**Letter of Marque.** Commission from a government to a private ship to seize and destroy ships and property of a hostile country.
**Letters of Administration.** Authority given to administer an intestate estate, or one in regard to which the executor has refused to act.
**Letters Patent.** A writing executed and sealed, granting power and authority to do some act, or enjoy some right.
**Letters Testamentary.** Authority to an Executor to act as such, after probate of will has been made.
**Liability.** That for which one is responsible; debts; obligations.
**Lien.** A hold or claim on property to secure a debt.
**License.** Permission to trade or act, as *liquor license*, *pedlar's license.*
**Lighterage.** Payment for unloading ships by lighters or boats.
**Liquidation.** Settlement or adjustment of liabilities.
**Lloyds'.** An old association of English marine underwriters (insurers) which formally met at Lloyd's coffee house, London. The company possesses complete records of everything pertaining to marine matters and has a vast correspondence. To rate on Lloyd's books as A1 is accepted as conclusive evidence of excellence.
**Lloyds' Register.** A yearly register of tonnage, age, build, character, and condition of ships, issued by the Lloyds.
**Loan.** Money or property furnished for temporary use; a public debt.
**Loan Office.** An office where loans are negotiated.
**Log-Book.** A book in which is recorded the daily progress of a vessel, weather notes, and all incidents.
**Long Price.** Price after duties are paid.
**Longshoremen.** Laborers who load and unload vessels.

**Manifest.** A list or invoice of a ship's cargo and passengers to be exhibited at Custom Houses.
**Manifold Writer.** A contrivance by which several copies may be obtained at once; it consists of several sheets covered with a preparation of plumbago.
**Manufactures.** Articles which have undergone some process; not crude or raw.
**Marine Insurance.** Insurance on vessels and cargo.
**Mark.** A letter, figure, or device, by which goods and prices are distinguished; private marks are usually made by selecting a word of ten letters and letting each letter stand for a digit.
**Market.** A public place of sale for provisions or other wares.
**Mart.** A market; a place of traffic.
**Maturity.** Time fixed for payment; becoming due.
**Maximum.** The highest price or sum.
**Measurement Goods.** Goods on which freight is charged by measurement.
**Mercantile Agency.** A concern which procures and furnishes information as to the financial standing and credit of business firms.
**Mercantile Paper.** Notes or bills issued by merchants for goods bought or consigned.
**Merchantable.** Fit for market; in sound condition.
**Merchant.** One who buys and sells goods, generally applied to wholesalers or large dealers.
**Merchant Service.** Trading ships taken collectively; the management of merchant vessels.
**Merger.** Absorption of a lesser by a greater debt or obligation.
**Metallic Currency.** Silver, gold, and copper coinage.
**Metric System.** A decimal system of weights and measures, first established in France; now in general use in Europe and growing into use in English-speaking countries.
**Minimum.** Lowest price; least quantity possible.
**Mint.** A place for coining money.
**Misfeasance.** The doing of a lawfu act in an unlawful manner.
**Mitigation.** Reduction of a penalty or fine; that which in part excuses.
**Mixed Fabrics.** Those composed of more than one kind of fibre, as wool and cotton.
**Money.** The measure of value and medium of exchange; strictly speaking, money must have intrinsic value to the amount it represents, as gold or silver; but bank notes and sometimes checks are included.
**Money-Broker.** One who deals in money.
**Money Market.** The general system of cash loans; the exchange of different kinds of currency.
**Money Order.** An order requesting one person to pay money to another; not negotiable; most commonly used of post-office orders.
**Monopoly.** Sole power of dealing in certain class of goods.
**Mortgage.** A conditonal conveyance of property, to become void upon fulfillment of the condition, as, the payment of a note.

**Mortgage Deed.** A deed of the nature of a mortgage.
**Mortgagee.** The person to whom property is mortgaged.
**Mortgagor.** One who gives a mortgage.
**Movables.** Personal property ; property not fixed.
**Muster.** A collection of samples.

**National Banks.** Banks organized under the conditions of an Act of Congress ; they can issue bank notes only to the amount of United States Bonds they have deposited in the U. S. Treasury.
**Negotiable Paper.** Notes, bills, and drafts which may be transferred with all their rights by indorsement or assignment.
**Negotiation.** Agreeing upon a mercantile transaction ; making a bargain ; fixing a price.
**Net.** The clear amount ; what remains after deducting charges and expenses.
**Net Profits.** Clear profit, after deducting losses.
**Net Weight.** Weight of merchandise without bag, box, or covering.
**Nominal.** In name only ; very small, as, a nominal price.
**Non-feasance.** The not doing of what ought to be done.
**Notary Public.** A public officer who attests or certifies to acknowledgment of deeds and other papers, protests notes and bills, etc.
**Notarial Seal.** Seal of a notary public.
**Note of Hand.** A written undertaking to pay money at a certain time.
**Note Book.** A book in which notes of hand are recorded.

**Obligation.** A duty ; a binding engagement ; bond with condition annexed.
**On Sale.** Goods left with another person to sell on account.
**Open Account.** A running or unsettled account.
**Opening.** The display of a new stock of goods for sale.
**Open Policy.** In marine insurance, a policy which covers undefined risks.
**Option.** Permission to choose ; in stock-broking, privilege of taking or delivering stock at a given day and price.
**Order.** A commission to purchase ; directions to pay money or deliver goods.
**Order Book.** That in which orders received are entered.
**Ordinary.** A ship in harbor is said to be in ordinary ; of medium quality.
**Outstanding Accounts.** Book debts not yet collected.
**Overdraw.** To call for more money than is on deposit.
**Overdue.** Applied to a note or draft the specified time for payment of which has passed.
**Overt.** Apparent ; manifest ; open.

**Package.** A bundle : a parcel ; a bale.
**Panic.** A monetary pressure ; financial crisis.
**Paper.** Negotiable evidence of indebtedness.
**Paper Money.** Bills of banks or the government passing current as money.
**Parole** (*French*). Not written, as, parole evidence.
**Par Value.** The face or nominal value.
**Par of Exchange.** The value of a unit of one country's coinage expressed in that of another's.
**Partner.** An associate in business ; member of a partnership.
**Partnership.** Contract of two or more persons to join money, stock, or skill in trade for mutual benefit.
**Part Owner.** One of several owners of a ship ; the relation differs materially from partnership.
**Pass Book.** A book kept by a customer in which entries of purchases are made ; a bank book.
**Passport.** A permission from a government to travel, with identification and certificate of nationality.
**Pawnbroker.** One who lends money at interest on security of goods deposited.
**Payable.** Justly due ; capable of payment.
**Payee.** The person to whose order a note, bill, or draft is to be paid.
**Per Cent** (*Latin*). By the hundred ; rates of interest, discount, etc.
**Per Centage** (*Latin*). An allowance reckoned by hundredth parts ; commission.
**Per Contra** (*Latin*). To the opposite side of an account.
**Permit.** Written authority to remove dutiable goods.
**Petty Cash Book.** Account of small receipts and expenses.
**Policy.** The instrument by which the contract of insurance is made.
**Port.** A harbor for vessels ; a commercial city.
**Port of Entry.** A port where a Custom House is established for the entry of imports.
**Post-Date.** To date after the real time.
**Posting.** To transfer from day-book or journal to the ledger.
**Post Orbit.** A promise to pay loans after the death of some person.
**Power of Attorney.** Written authority from one person to another to act for him.
**Preferred Creditor.** One whose claims a bankrupt debtor elects to settle first.
**Premium.** A sum beyond par value : the amount paid annually in insurance contracts.
**Price Current.** A statement showing prevailing price of merchandise, stock, or securities.
**Price List.** A list of articles with prices attached.
**Prime.** Of high quality ; superior.
**Principal.** The sum on which interest is paid.
**Proceeds.** The sum realized by a sale.
**Procuration.** A general letter or power of attorney.
**Produce.** Farm products of all kinds.
**Profit and Loss.** An account in which gains and losses are balanced.
**Promissory Note.** (*See Note*).
**Pro Rata** (*Latin*). A proportional distribution.
**Protective Tariff.** Duty imposed on imports to encourage manufactures.
**Protest.** Notice to the sureties of a note that it was not paid at maturity or to the drawer of a draft that acceptance was refused.
**Purveyor.** One who supplies provisions.

**Quarantine.** Restraint of intercourse to which a ship is subjected on suspicion of infection ; the place of such restraint.
**Quitrent.** Rent paid by tenant of a freehold, discharging him from other rent.
**Quotation.** Current Prices of stocks or commodities.

**Real Estate.** Land, houses and fixtures ; all immovable property.
**Rebate.** Deduction ; abatement ; discount ; giving back part of sum already paid.
**Receipt.** A written acknowledgment of payment.
**Receipt Book.** A book in which receipts are filed.
**Receiver.** An officer appointed by a court to hold in trust property in litigation, or to wind up the affairs of a bankrupt concern.
**Recoup.** To counterbalance losses by gains.
**Rectification.** Second distillation of alcoholic liquors.
**Register.** A ship's paper, issued by the Custom House, stating description, name, tonnage, nationality, and ownership.
**Re-insurance.** Transfer of part of the contract of insurance from one insurer to another.
**Remittance.** Transfer of funds from one party to another.
**Renewal.** Giving a new note for an old one ; extension of time.
**Rent.** Compensation for the use of real estate.
**Rente.** A French term equivalent to government annuity.
**Repository.** A warehouse or storehouse.
**Reprisal.** The seizure of ships or property to indemnify for unlawful seizure or detention.
**Respondentia Bond.** A bond for a loan secured by the cargo of a ship.
**Retail.** To sell in small quantities.
**Returns.** Profit on an investment.
**Revenue.** Income of a State ; taxes received.
**Revenue Cutter.** A small government vessel used in collecting taxes and preventing smuggling.
**Reversion.** Right to possess property after the happening of some event, as the death of a person.

**Sale.** Transfer of property for a consideration.
**Salvage.** Compensation given those who rescue ship or cargo from loss
**Salvor.** One who voluntarily engages in saving a ship or cargo from peril.
**Sample.** A small portion of merchandise taken as a specimen of quality.
**Sans Recours** (*French*). Without recourse ; sometimes added to an indorsement of a note or bill to protect indorser from liability.
**Scrip.** Certificate of stock given before registration.
**Seaworthy.** Fit for a voyage and properly equipped.

**Securities.** Documents securing a right to property.
**Sell.** To make a sale; to transfer for consideration.
**Sett-Off.** A counter claim or cross debt arising from a different matter from the one in question.
**Share.** Interest owned by one of a number; unit of the division of stock.
**Ship.** Technically, a three-masted square-rigged vessel; commonly used for any large vessel.
**Shipment.** Quantity of goods dispatched.
**Shipper.** One who dispatches goods by vessel or other conveyance.
**Shipping.** Collective term for a number of vessels.
**Shipping Articles.** Articles of agreement between captain and seamen.
**Shipping Clerk.** One who oversees the forwarding of merchandise.
**Ship's Husband.** One who attends to the requisite repairs of a ship while in port, and does all the other necessary acts preparatory to a voyage.
**Ship's Papers.** Papers which a vessel must carry; register, sea-letter, logbook, bill of health, shipping articles, etc.
**Ship's Stores.** Provisions, fuel, cables, extra spars, etc.
**Short.** To "sell short" is to sell for future delivery what one has not got in hopes that prices will fall.
**Short Exchange.** Bills of exchange payable at sight or in a few days.
**Shrinkage.** Reduction in bulk or measurement.
**Sight.** The time when a bill is presented to the drawee.
**Sight Draft.** One payable *at sight*, i. e., when presented.
**Signature.** The name of a person written by himself.
**Silent Partner.** One who furnishes capital but takes no active part in a business.
**Simple Interest.** Interest on principal alone; not compound.
**Sinking Fund.** A fund set apart from revenue to pay a public or corporation debt.
**Smuggling.** Introducing goods into a country without paying duties.
**Solvent.** Able to meet all liabilities.
**Specialty.** A written, sealed, and delivered contract.
**Specie.** Any kind of coined money.
**Specification.** A written description and enumeration of particulars.
**Speculation.** A business investment out of the ordinary run of trade.
**Stamp Duty.** Law requiring stamps to be affixed to checks and proprietary articles.
**Staple.** Principal commodity of a country or district.
**Statute Law.** Body of laws established by legislative enactment; written as opposed to unwritten or common law.
**Sterling.** Lawful or standard money of Great Britain.
**Stock.** Shares in the capital of corporations; goods on hand.
**Stock Broker.** One who buys and sells stock on commission.
**Stock Exchange.** Place where shares of stock are bought and sold.
**Stock-Holder.** One who holds shares of stock.
**Stock Jobber.** One who speculates in stocks.
**Stoppage in Transitu** (*Latin*). Right of a seller to stop goods "on their passage" if purchaser has become insolvent.
**Storage.** Sums paid for storing goods.
**Storekeeper.** Officer in charge of a bonded warehouse.
**Stowage.** Careful arrangement of cargo in a ship.
**Subpœna.** A writ commanding a witness to appear in court.
**Subpœna duces tecum.** A subpœna requiring witness to bring papers with him.
**Subrogation.** Putting one thing in place of another; substituting one creditor for another.
**Sundries.** Unclassified articles.
**Supercargo.** An agent who accompanies cargo to care for and sell it.
**Surety.** One who binds himself to pay money in case another person fails to pay, to fill a contract, or to serve with integrity.
**Surveyor.** Agent of an insurance company to examine and report on applications for marine or fire insurance.
**Suspend.** To fail; to stop payment.
**Suspense Account.** An account made of doubtful balances to ascertain probable profit or loss.
**Sutler.** One authorized to sell goods to an army.
**Suttle Weight.** Weight after *tare* is deducted.
**Tale Quale** (*Latin*). "Such as;" used to denote that cargo is presumed to correspond with sample, and that buyer takes the risk of deterioration.
**Tally.** Keeping account by checking off.
**Tally-Man.** One who receives payment for goods in weekly instalments.
**Tare.** Allowance in weight or quantity on account of cask, bag, or covering. *Actual tare:* when each cask, *etc.* is weighed. *Average tare:* when one is weighed as a sample. *Estimated tare:* when a fixed percentage is allowed.
**Tariff.** Rate or list of duties; price list.
**Teller.** Officer of a bank who receives or pays out money.
**Tenants.** Those who lease or rent real estate.
**Tenants in Common.** Persons holding the same property in common, i. e., by distinct titles and not as joint tenants.
**Tender.** Offer to supply money or articles. (*See Legal Tender.*)
**Ten Forties.** United States Government Bonds, which could be redeemed by the government in ten years or allowed to run for forty.
**Tenor.** Intent, nature, character; sometimes an exact copy.
**Textile Fabrics.** All woven or piece goods.
**Testator.** One who has made a will; feminine form, *testatrix.*
**Time Bargain.** A contract for the future sale of stock.
**Tonnage.** The weight a ship will carry in tons; capacity of a vessel.
**Tort.** A private or civil injury for which damages will lie.
**Trade.** Buying and selling; commerce; traffic.
**Trade Discount.** An allowance made to dealers in the same line.
**Trade Mark.** Letters, figures, or devices used on goods and labels which a manufacturer has the sole right to use.
**Trade Price.** That allowed by wholesalers to retailers.
**Trade Sale.** An auction by and for the trade; especially of booksellers.
**Trades Union.** A combination of workingmen to protect their own interests.
**Traffic.** Business done; especially that of a railroad.
**Transhipment.** Removing goods from one ship or conveyance to another.
**Transportation.** Conveying goods from one place to another.
**Transit Duty.** Tax imposed on goods for passing through a country.
**Traveler.** A commercial agent; a drummer.
**Treasury Notes.** Those issued by government and passing current as money.
**Treaty.** An agreement or compact between two or more nations.
**Tret.** Allowance for waste of 4 lbs. in 104 lbs., after tare has been deducted.
**Triplicate.** To make three copies of a paper; the third copy.
**Trustee Process.** Same as *Garnishment*, which see
**Ullage.** What a cask lacks of being full.
**Unclaimed Goods.** Goods in government storehouses unclaimed after three years from importation, or on which duties have not been paid, may be sold at auction.
**Undersell.** To sell below the trade price.
**Underwriter.** A marine insurer; an individual, not a company.
**Unseaworthy.** Unfit for a voyage in condition or equipment.
**Unsound.** In bad condition; of doubtful solvency.
**Usance.** The time allowed by usage for the payment of a bill of exchange; it differs greatly in different countries; any business custom.
**Usury.** Interest beyond the lawful rate.
**Valid.** Of force; binding; good in law.
**Value.** To estimate; worth.
**Value Received.** Phrase used in notes and bills to express a consideration indefinitely.
**Vendee.** One to whom something is sold.
**Vendor.** A seller.
**Vendue.** An auction sale.
**Venture.** A mercantile speculation or investment.
**Void.** That which is of no legal effect.
**Voidable.** That which may become of no legal effect if proper steps are taken.
**Voucher.** A book, receipt, entry, or other document which establishes the truth of accounts.
**Warehouseman.** One who stores goods for pay.
**Waiver.** Relinquishment of a legal right or privilege.
**Warranty.** An undertaking that goods or title are as represented.
**Wastage.** Loss in handling; shrinkage.
**Waste.** Refuse material.
**Way Bill.** List of goods given to a carrier.
**Wharfage.** Fees paid for use of a wharf.
**Wreckage.** Merchandise saved from a wreck.

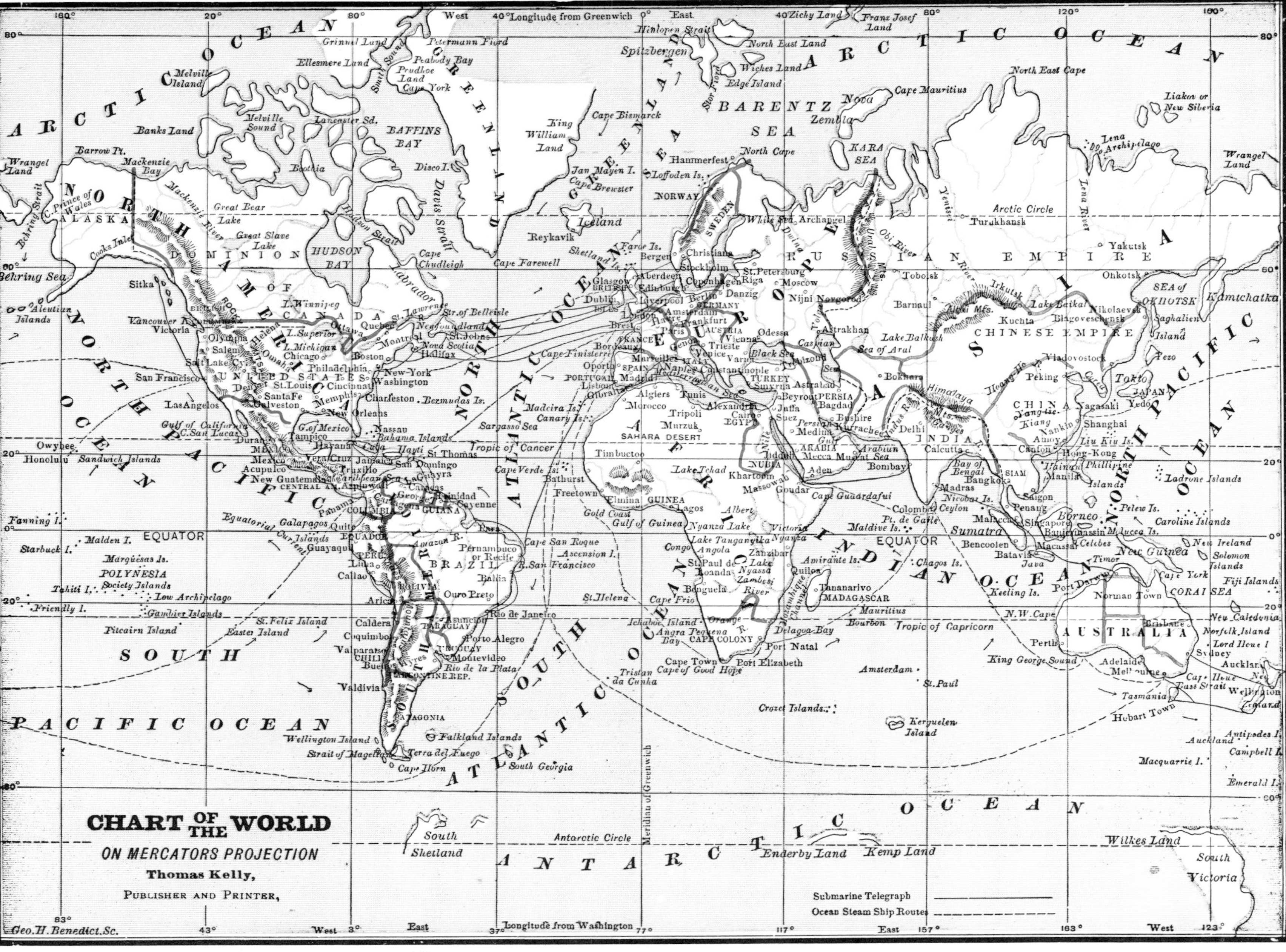
CHART OF THE WORLD
ON MERCATORS PROJECTION
Thomas Kelly,
PUBLISHER AND PRINTER,
Submarine Telegraph
Ocean Steam Ship Routes
Longitude from Greenwich
Longitude from Washington
Geo. H. Benedict. Sc.

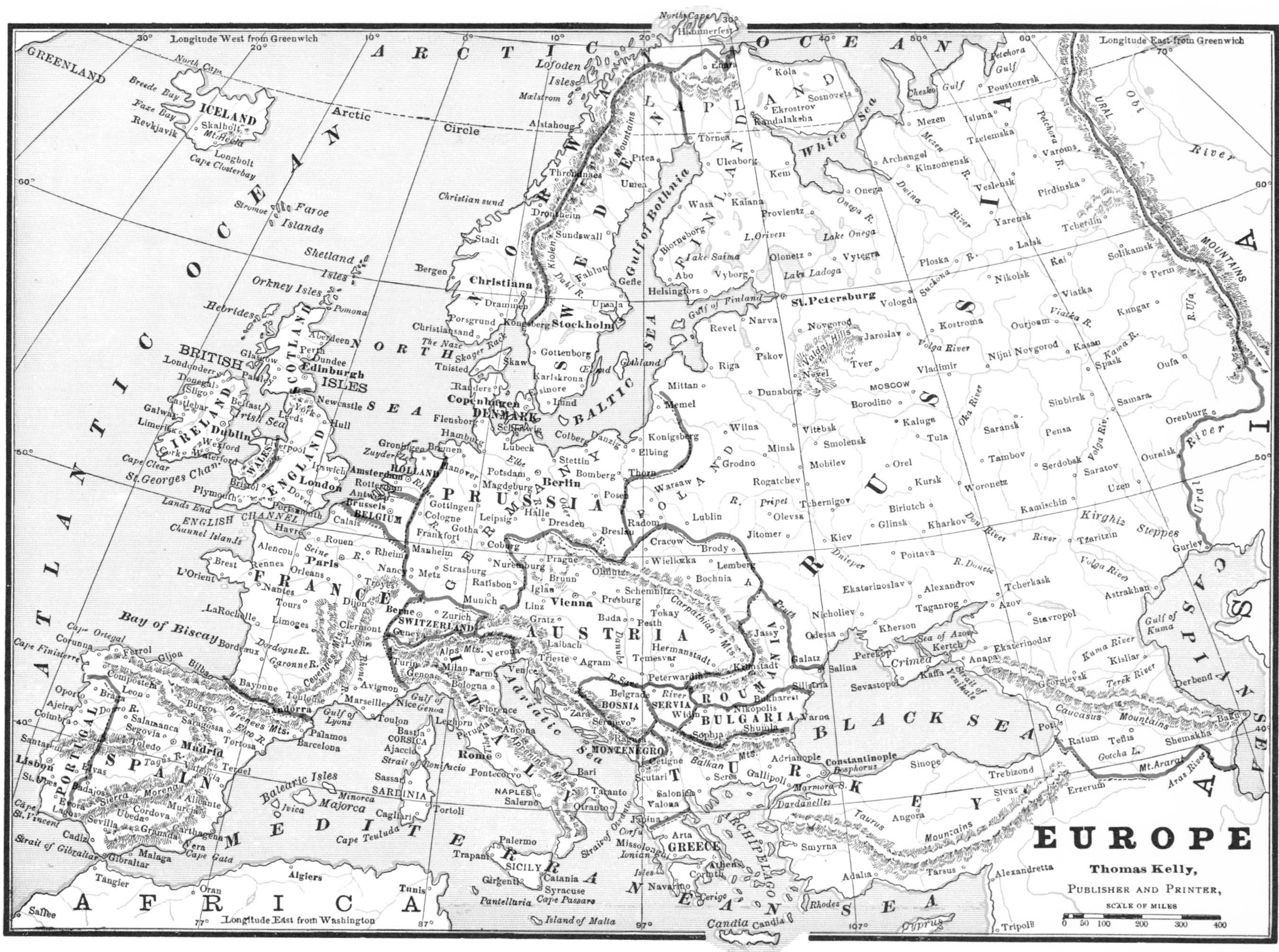
EUROPE
Thomas Kelly,
PUBLISHER AND PRINTER,
SCALE OF MILES
0 50 100 200 300 400
Longitude West from Greenwich
Longitude East from Greenwich
Longitude East from Washington
ARCTIC OCEAN
ATLANTIC OCEAN
MEDITERRANEAN SEA
BLACK SEA
CASPIAN SEA
NORTH SEA
BALTIC SEA
AFRICA
ASIA
ICELAND
GREENLAND
BRITISH ISLES
SCOTLAND
ENGLAND
IRELAND
WALES
FRANCE
SPAIN
PORTUGAL
HOLLAND
BELGIUM
DENMARK
SWITZERLAND
PRUSSIA
GERMANY
AUSTRIA
ITALY
SARDINIA
CORSICA
SICILY
NAPLES
GREECE
TURKEY
BOSNIA
SERVIA
MONTENEGRO
ROUMANIA
BULGARIA
NORWAY
SWEDEN
LAPLAND
FINLAND
POLAND
RUSSIA
London
Paris
Berlin
Vienna
Rome
Madrid
Lisbon
Stockholm
Christiania
Copenhagen
St. Petersburg
MOSCOW
Constantinople
Edinburgh
Dublin
Brussels
Amsterdam
Berne
Athens
Arctic Circle
Bay of Biscay
Gulf of Bothnia
White Sea
Adriatic Sea
Sea of Azov
Strait of Gibraltar
ENGLISH CHANNEL
Balearic Isles
Faroe Islands
Shetland Isles
Orkney Isles
Hebrides
Lofoden Isles
Caucasus Mountains
Taurus Mountains
Balkan Mts.
Pyrenees Mts.
Alps Mts.
Carpathian Mts.
Apennine Mts.
Ural Mountains
Kirghiz Steppes
Volga River
Dnieper
Danube
Don River
Ural River
Obi River
ARCHIPELAGO
Crimea
Cyprus
Candia
Rhodes
Island of Malta

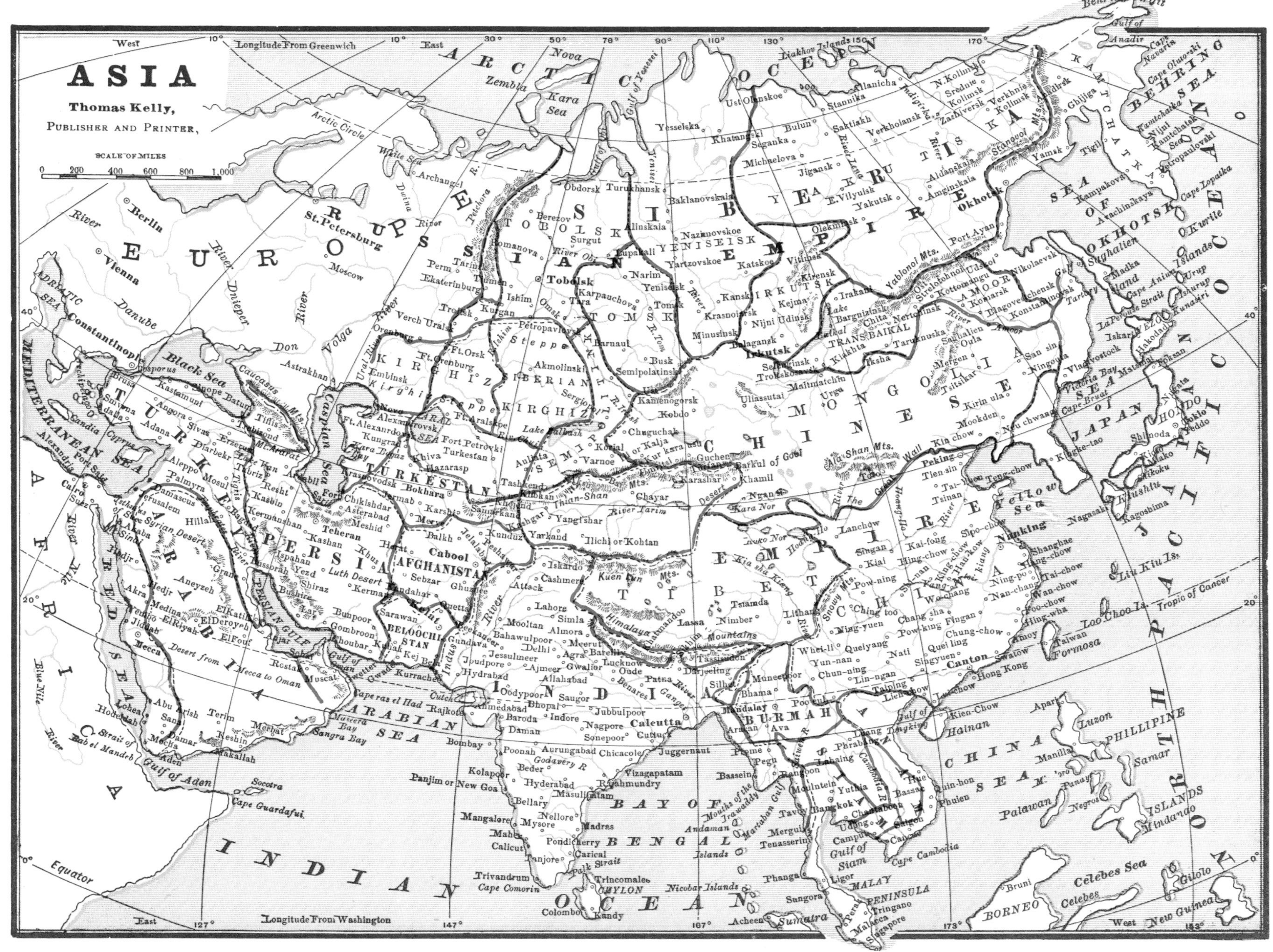

ASIA
Thomas Kelly,
PUBLISHER AND PRINTER,
SCALE OF MILES
0 200 400 600 800 1,000
West
Longitude From Greenwich
East
Longitude From Washington
Arctic Circle
Tropic of Cancer
Equator
ARCTIC OCEAN
Nova Zembla
Kara Sea
Gulf of Yenisei
White Sea
Archangel
St. Petersburg
Moscow
Berlin
Vienna
Constantinople
EUROPE
RUSSIAN EMPIRE
SIBERIA
TOBOLSK
TOMSK
YENISEISK
IRKUTSK
YAKUTSK
TRANS BAIKAL
AMOOR
KAMTCHATKA
BEHRING SEA
Behring Strait
Gulf of Anadir
SEA OF OKHOTSK
Okhotsk
Yablonoi Mts.
Tobolsk
Irkutsk
Danube
Dnieper
Don
Volga
Caucasus Mts.
Black Sea
Caspian Sea
ARAL SEA
Lake Balkash
KIRGHIZ
Steppe
TURKESTAN
Bokhara
Khiva
TURKEY
Tiflis
Mt. Ararat
Tigris
Euphrates
Damascus
Jerusalem
Syrian Desert
ARABIA
Mecca
Medina
Desert from Mecca to Oman
RED SEA
Strait of Bab el Mandeb
Gulf of Aden
Aden
Cape Guardafui
Socotra
PERSIA
Teheran
Ispahan
Shiraz
Luth Desert
PERSIAN GULF
AFGHANISTAN
Cabool
Herat
BELOOCHISTAN
Kelat
ARABIAN SEA
Bombay
INDIA
Indus
Ganges
Delhi
Calcutta
Madras
Himalaya Mountains
BAY OF BENGAL
CEYLON
Colombo
Cape Comorin
INDIAN OCEAN
TIBET
Lassa
Kuen Lun Mts.
CHINESE EMPIRE
MONGOLIA
CHINA
Peking
The Great Wall
Hoang-Ho
Nanking
Canton
Hong Kong
Yellow Sea
Formosa
Loo Choo Is.
Liu Kiu Is.
SEA OF JAPAN
JAPAN
HONDO
Yeddo
YEZO
Saghalien
Kurile Islands
PACIFIC OCEAN
BURMAH
SIAM
ANAM
Bangkok
Saigon
Gulf of Siam
Cape Cambodia
MALAY PENINSULA
Singapore
Sumatra
Hainan
CHINA SEA
PHILLIPINE ISLANDS
Luzon
Manilla
Samar
Mindanao
Palawan
BORNEO
Celebes
Celebes Sea
Gilolo
New Guinea
AFRICA
Suez
Cairo
Alexandria
Port Said
River Nile
Blue Nile
MEDITERRANEAN SEA
ADRIATIC SEA
Cyprus
Candia
Archipelago

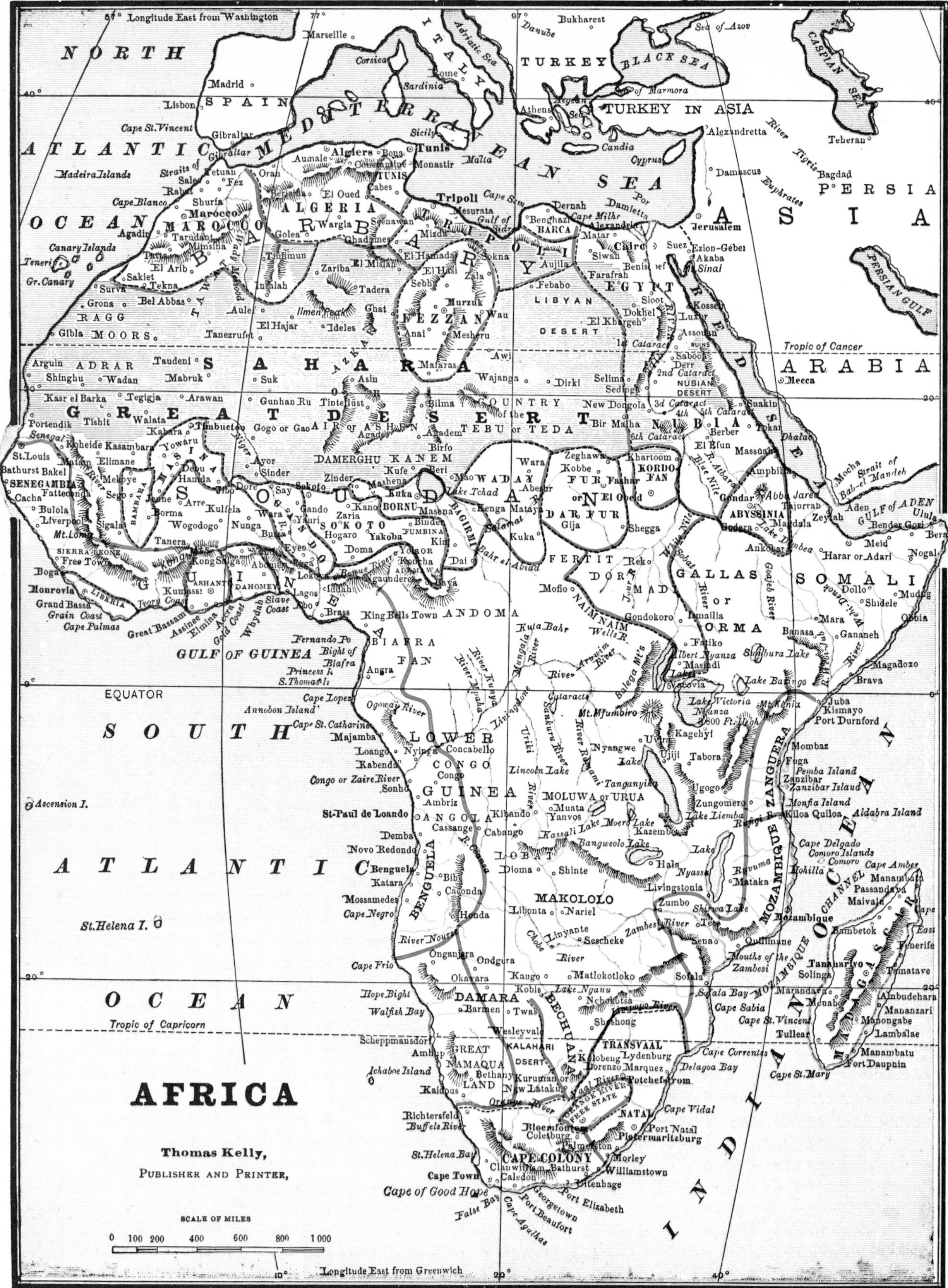

AFRICA
Thomas Kelly,
PUBLISHER AND PRINTER,
SCALE OF MILES
0 100 200 400 600 800 1 000
Longitude East from Washington
Longitude East from Greenwich
NORTH
ATLANTIC
OCEAN
SOUTH
ATLANTIC
OCEAN
EQUATOR
Tropic of Cancer
Tropic of Capricorn
MEDITERRANEAN SEA
BLACK SEA
CASPIAN SEA
PERSIAN GULF
RED SEA
INDIAN OCEAN
GULF OF GUINEA
GULF OF ADEN
MOZAMBIQUE CHANNEL
SPAIN
ITALY
TURKEY
TURKEY IN ASIA
PERSIA
ASIA
ARABIA
MAROCCO
ALGERIA
TUNIS
TRIPOLI
BARCA
EGYPT
NUBIA
ABYSSINIA
BARBARY
SAHARA
GREAT DESERT
LIBYAN DESERT
FEZZAN
SOUDAN
SENEGAMBIA
GUINEA
DAHOMEY
ASHANTI
LIBERIA
SIERRA LEONE
BORNU
SOKOTO
WADAY
DAR FUR
KORDOFAN
GALLAS or ORMA
SOMALI
ZANGUEBAR
MOZAMBIQUE
LOWER GUINEA
CONGO
ANGOLA
BENGUELA
MAKOLOLO
DAMARA
GREAT NAMAQUA LAND
KALAHARI DESERT
BECHUANA
TRANSVAAL
ORANGE RIVER FREE STATE
NATAL
CAPE COLONY
MADAGASCAR
Madrid
Lisbon
Gibraltar
Algiers
Tunis
Tripoli
Cairo
Alexandria
Jerusalem
Mecca
Khartoom
Timbuctoo
Monrovia
Cape Town
Cape of Good Hope
Port Elizabeth
Zanzibar
Mombaz
Lake Victoria Nyanza
Albert Nyanza
Tanganyika Lake
Lake Nyassa
Bangweolo Lake
Lake Tchad
Canary Islands
Madeira Islands
Ascension I.
St. Helena I.
Annobon Island
Fernando Po
Princess I.
S. Thomas I.

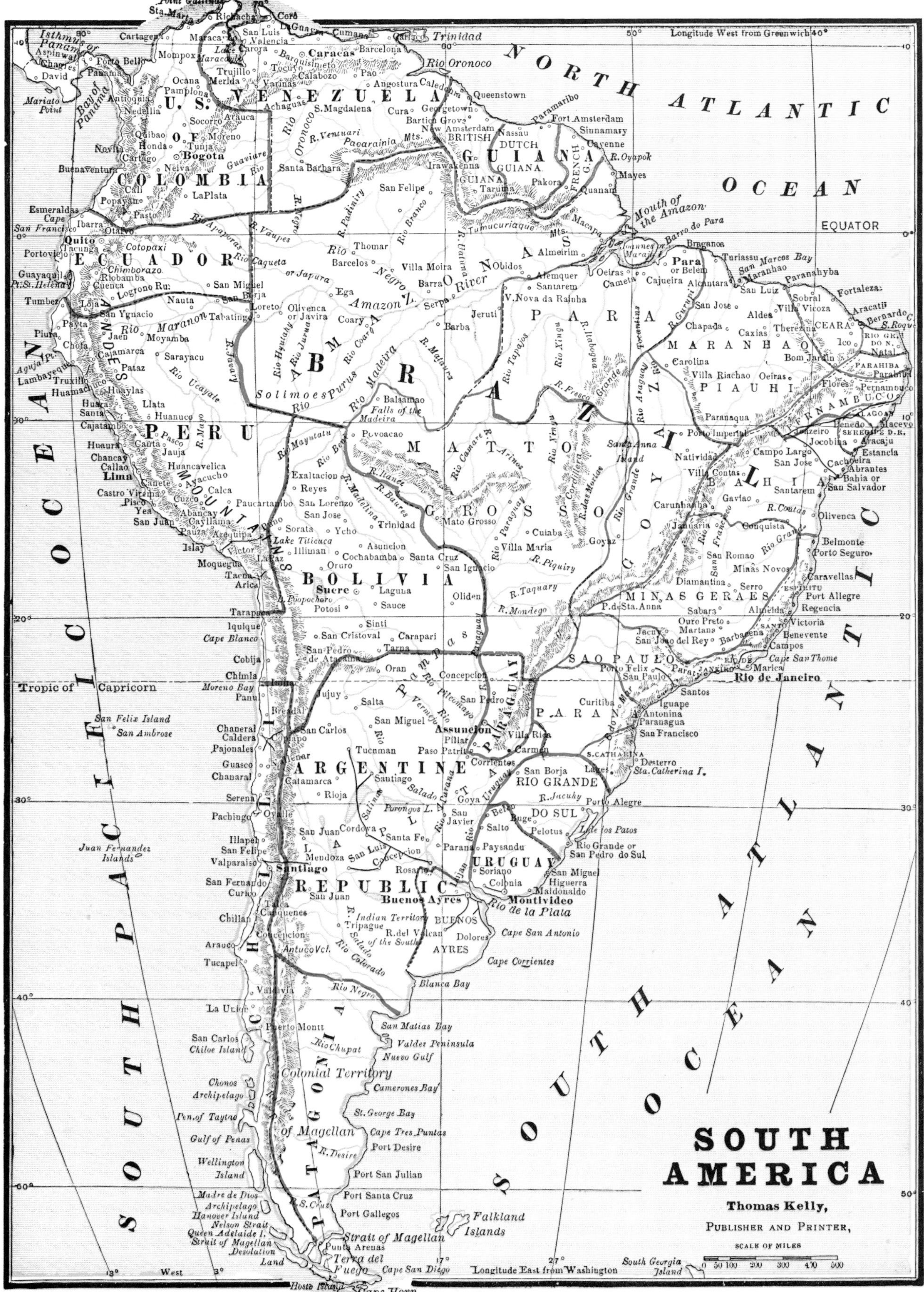
SOUTH AMERICA
Thomas Kelly,
PUBLISHER AND PRINTER,
SCALE OF MILES
0 50 100 200 300 400 500
Longitude West from Greenwich
Longitude East from Washington
Tropic of Capricorn
EQUATOR
NORTH ATLANTIC OCEAN
SOUTH ATLANTIC OCEAN
SOUTH PACIFIC OCEAN
U. S. OF COLOMBIA
VENEZUELA
GUIANA
BRITISH GUIANA
DUTCH GUIANA
FRENCH G.
ECUADOR
PERU
ANDES MOUNTAINS
BRAZIL
AMAZON
PARA
MARANHAO
PIAUHI
CEARA
PERNAMBUCO
BAHIA
GOYAZ
MATTO GROSSO
MINAS GERAES
SAO PAULO
PARANA
S. CATHARINA
RIO GRANDE DO SUL
BOLIVIA
PARAGUAY
URUGUAY
ARGENTINE REPUBLIC
LA PLATA
BUENOS AYRES
CHILI
PATAGONIA
Colonial Territory of Magellan
Indian Territory of the South
Point Gallinas
Sta. Marta
Isthmus of Panama
Bay of Panama
Porto Bello
Panama
Aspinwall
Chagres
David
Mariato Point
Cartagena
Mompox
Maracaibo
Lake Maracaibo
Coro
La Guaira
Caracas
Cumana
Trinidad
Barcelona
Rio Oronoco
Valencia
San Luis
Carora
Barquisimeto
Tocuyo
Calabozo
Pao
Trujillo
Merida
Ocana
Pamplona
Angostura
Caledonia
Queenstown
Achaguas
Yarinas
S. Magdalena
Cura
Georgetown
Bartica Grove
New Amsterdam
Nassau
Paramaribo
Fort Amsterdam
Sinnamary
Cayenne
R. Oyapok
Mayes
Pakora
Tarumia
Quanani
Irawakenna
Pacaraima Mts.
R. Ventuari
Arauca
Socorro
Moreno
Quibao
Honda
Tunja
Bogota
Nedellin
Antioquia
Novita
Cartago
Neiva
Guaviare
Buenaventura
Cali
Popayan
LaPlata
Pasto
Santa Barbara
San Felipe
Esmeraldas
Cape San Francisco
Ibarra
Otalvo
Quito
Tacunga
Cotopaxi
Chimborazo
Riobamba
Cuenca
Portoviejo
Guayaquil
Pt. St. Helena
Loja
Tumbez
Logrono Ru.
San Miguel
San Borja
Nauta
Loreto
Tabatinga
San Ygnacio
Payta
Piura
Chota
Jaen
Moyamba
Sarayacu
Cajamarca
Pataz
Lambayeque
Aguja Pt.
Truxillo
Huamachuco
Huaylas
Huaras
Santa
Llata
Huanuco
Cajatambo
Huaura
Pasco
Canta
Jauja
Chancay
Callao
Lima
Huancavelica
Ayacucho
Canete
Castro Virreina
Pisco
Yea
Calca
Cuzco
Abancay
Paucartambo
San Juan
Cayllama
Arequipa
Islay
Moquegua
Tacna
Arica
Puno
Lake Titicaca
Sorata
Illiman
La Paz
Victor
Ycho
Trinidad
Asuncion
Cochabamba
Oruro
Santa Cruz
San Ignacio
Sucre
Laguna
Potosi
Sauce
Oliden
L. Poopochoro
Tarapaca
Iquique
Cape Blanco
Cobija
Chimla
Moreno Bay
Panul
San Felix Island
San Ambrose
Chaneral
Caldera
Pajonales
Guasco
Chanaral
Serena
Pachingo
Ovalle
Illapel
San Felipe
Valparaiso
Santiago
San Fernando
Curico
Talca
Cauquenes
Chillan
Concepcion
Arauco
Tucapel
Antuco Vol.
Valdivia
La Union
Puerto Montt
San Carlos
Chiloe Island
Chonos Archipelago
Pen. of Taytao
Gulf of Penas
Wellington Island
Madre de Dios Archipelago
Hanover Island
Nelson Strait
Queen Adelaide I.
Strait of Magellan
Desolation Land
Punta Arenas
Terra del Fuego
Cape San Diego
Hoste Island
Cape Horn
Juan Fernandez Islands
Sinti
San Cristoval
Carapari
San Pedro de Atacama
Tarija
Oran
Concepcion
Jujuy
Salta
San Pedro
San Miguel
Rio Pilcomayo
Rio Vermejo
Assuncion
Pillar
Villa Rica
Carmen
Paso Patria
Corrientes
San Carlos
Tucuman
Catamarca
Santiago
Rioja
Saladc
Porongos L.
San Javier
Santa Fe
Cordova
San Juan
Mendoza
San Luis
Concepcion
Parana
Rosario
Buenos Ayres
San Juan
Tripague
R. del Valcan
Dolores
Rio Colorado
Rio Negro
Blanca Bay
Cape San Antonio
Cape Corrientes
Rio de la Plata
Montevideo
Colonia
Soriano
Maldonaldo
Higuerra
San Miguel
Paysandu
Salto
Pelotus
Lake los Patos
Rio Grande or San Pedro do Sul
Porto Alegre
R. Jacuhy
San Borja
Lages
Desterro
Sta. Catherina I.
San Francisco
Curitiba
Antonina
Paranagua
Iguape
Santos
San Paulo
Porto Felix
Rio de Janeiro
Cape San Thome
Marica
Campos
Barbacena
San Joao del Rey
Jacuhy
Ouro Preto
Martana
Sabara
Victoria
Benevente
Regencia
Port Allegre
Almeida
Caravellas
Serro
Minas Novos
San Romao
Diamantina
Porto Seguro
Belmonte
Olivenca
Conquista
Januaria
Carunhanha
Gaviao
R. Contas
Santarem
San Salvador
Bahia or
Abrantes
Cachoeira
Estancia
Aracaju
Jocobina
Joazeiro
Campo Largo
San Jose
Villa Contas
Natividad
Porto Imperial
Paranagua
Santa Anna Island
Goyaz
Cuiaba
Villa Maria
Mato Grosso
R. Piquiry
R. Taquary
R. Mondego
P. de Sta. Anna
Barra
Jeruti
V. Nova da Rainha
Santarem
Alemquer
Obidos
Almeirim
Macapa
Mouth of the Amazon
Barro do Para
Braganca
Para or Belem
Cameta
Oeiras
Cajueira
Alcantara
San Luiz
Turiassu
San Marcos Bay
Maranhao
Paranahyba
Fortaleza
Sobral
Villa Vicoza
Aracati
Bernardo
S. Roque
Ico
Natal
Parahiba
Pernambuco
Flores
Bom Jardin
Oeiras
Villa Riachao
Carolina
Chapada
Caxias
Therezina
Aldea
San Jose
Tumucuriaque Mts.
Thomar
Barcelos
Villa Moira
Ega
Olivenca or Javira
Coary
Serpa
Barba
Balsamao
Falls of the Madeira
Povoacao
Exaltacion
Reyes
San Lorenzo
San Jose
Rio Negro
River
Solimoes
Rio Purus
Rio Madeira
Rio Mayutatu
Rio Beni
R. Itanez
R. Baures
Cordillera
R. Fresco
R. Xingu
R. Tapajos
Rio Araguay
Rio Tocantins
Rio Grande
Rio Parana
Rio Uruguay
R. Desire
Cape Tres Puntas
Port Desire
Port San Julian
Port Santa Cruz
Port Gallegos
R. S. Cruz
Falkland Islands
South Georgia Island
San Matias Bay
Valdez Peninsula
Nuevo Gulf
Rio Chupat
Camerones Bay
St. George Bay
West
60°
50°
40°
30°
20°
10°
0°

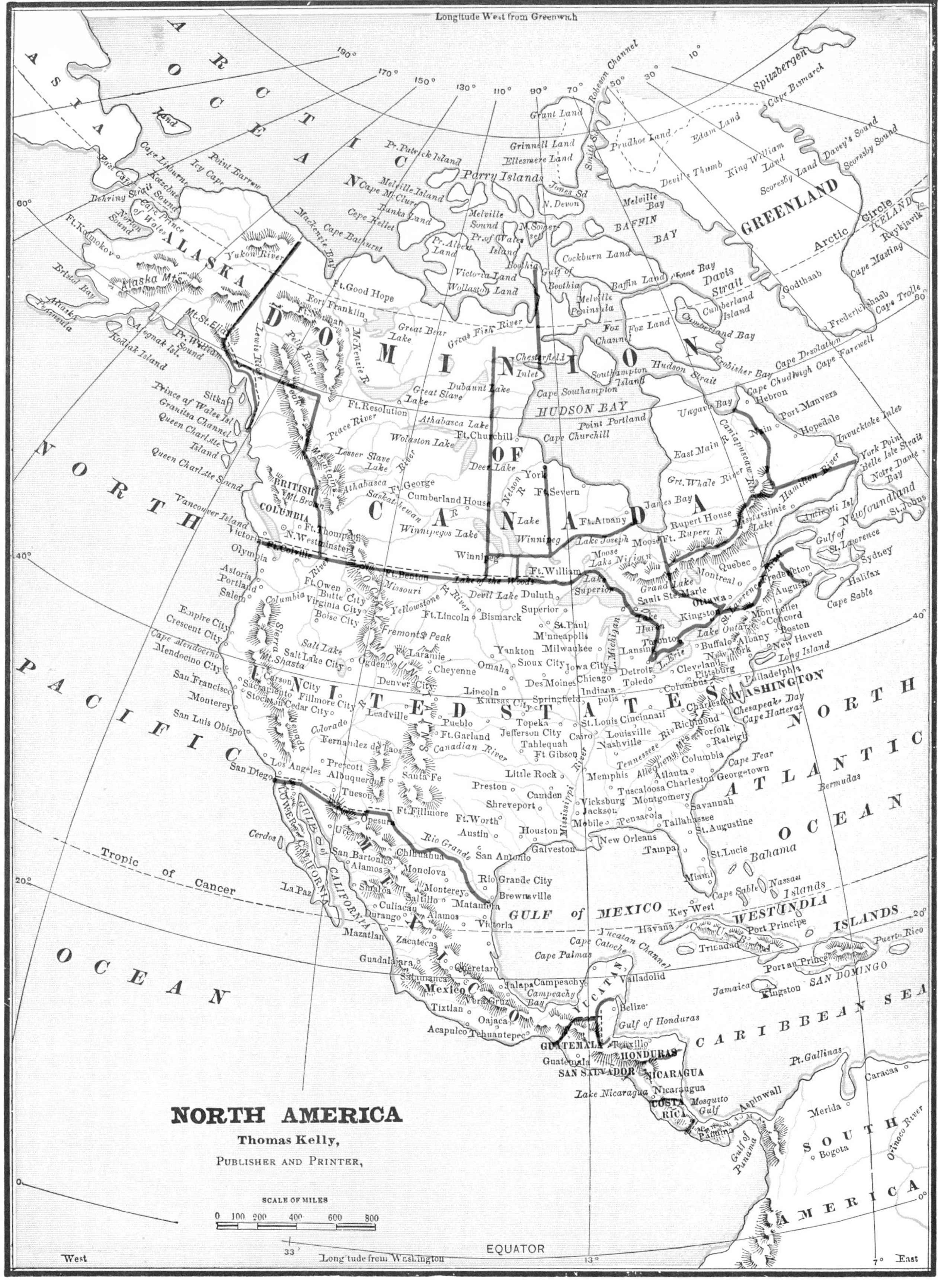

Longitude West from Greenwich
ARCTIC OCEAN
ASIA
Spitzbergen
Cape Bismarck
Grant Land
Robeson Channel
Smith Sd
Grinnell Land
Ellesmere Land
Prudhoe Land
Edam Land
Devil's Thumb
King William Land
Scoresby Land
Davey's Sound
Scoresby Sound
GREENLAND
Arctic Circle
ICELAND
Reykjavik
Cape Masting
Godthaab
Frederickshaab
Cape Trolle
Cape Farewell
Cape Desolation
Pr. Patrick Island
Parry Islands
Jones Sd
N. Devon
Melville Bay
BAFFIN BAY
Melville Island
Cape McClure
Banks Land
Cape Kellet
Melville Sound
M. Somerset
Pr. of Wales Island
Pr. Albert Land
Victoria Land
Wollaston Land
Boothia
Gulf of Boothia
Melville Peninsula
Cockburn Land
Baffin Land
Home Bay
Davis Strait
Cumberland Island
Cumberland Bay
Fox Channel
Fox Land
Frobisher Bay
Southampton Island
Hudson Strait
Cape Chudleigh
Hebron
Ungava Bay
Port Manvers
Hopedale
Invucktoke Inlet
York Point
Belle Isle Strait
Notre Dame Bay
Newfoundland
St. Johns
Point Barrow
Icy Cape
Cape Lisburne
Kotzebue Sound
East Cape
Behring Strait
Cape Prince of Wales
Norton Sound
Ft. Kolmokov
ALASKA
Yukon River
Alaska Mts.
Bristol Bay
Aliaska Peninsula
Afognak Isl.
Kodiak Island
Mt. St. Elias
Pr. William Sound
Sitka
Prince of Wales Isl.
Granitsa Channel
Queen Charlotte Island
Queen Charlotte Sound
Vancouver Island
Victoria
Mackenzie Bay
Cape Bathurst
Ft. Good Hope
Fort Franklin
Ft. Norman
Great Bear Lake
Great Fish River
DOMINION OF CANADA
Lewis R.
McKenzie R.
Great Slave Lake
Dubaunt Lake
Chesterfield Inlet
Cape Southampton
HUDSON BAY
Point Portland
Cape Churchill
Ft. Resolution
Peace River
Athabasca Lake
Wollaston Lake
Ft. Churchill
East Main R.
Lesser Slave Lake
Deer Lake
York
Ft. Severn
Grt. Whale River
Hamilton River
BRITISH COLUMBIA
Mt. Brown
Athabasca
Ft. George
Saskatchewan
Cumberland House
Nelson R.
James Bay
Rupert House
Ft. Rupert R.
Anticosti Isl.
Gulf of St. Lawrence
Sydney
Halifax
Cape Sable
Ft. Thompson
N. Westminster
Winnipegos Lake
Lake Winnipeg
Ft. Albany
Winnipeg
Lake Joseph
Moose
Quebec
Fredericton
Augusta
Montreal
Ft. Colville
Ft. Benton
Lake of the Woods
Ft. William
Lake Superior
Lake Nipigon
Grand Lake
Sault Ste. Marie
Ottawa
Kingston
Olympia
Astoria
Portland
Salem
Columbia
Ft. Owen
Butte City
Virginia City
Boise City
Missouri
Yellowstone
Devil Lake
Duluth
Superior
Ft. Lincoln
Bismarck
St. Paul
Minneapolis
Lake Huron
Lake Michigan
Toronto
Lake Ontario
Montpelier
Concord
Boston
New Haven
Long Island
Albany
New York
Buffalo
Lansing
Milwaukee
Fremonts Peak
Empire City
Crescent City
Cape Mendocino
Mendocino City
Sierra Nevada
Mt. Shasta
Salt Lake
Salt Lake City
Ogden
Ft. Laramie
Cheyenne
Yankton
Sioux City
Omaha
Iowa City
Detroit
L. Erie
Cleveland
Pittsburg
Philadelphia
WASHINGTON
Carson City
Sacramento
San Francisco
Stockton
Fillmore City
Cedar City
Monterey
Denver City
Lincoln
Kansas City
Des Moines
Chicago
Indianapolis
Toledo
Columbus
Springfield
UNITED STATES
Charleston
Richmond
Chesapeake Bay
Cape Hatteras
NORTH ATLANTIC OCEAN
San Luis Obispo
Colorado
Leadville
Pueblo
Topeka
St. Louis
Cincinnati
Jefferson City
Louisville
Norfolk
Raleigh
Ft. Garland
Fernandez de Taos
Canadian River
Tahlequah
Cairo
Nashville
Tennessee
Ft. Gibson
Alleghany Mts.
Columbia
PACIFIC OCEAN
San Diego
Los Angeles
Prescott
Albuquerque
Santa Fe
Little Rock
Memphis
Atlanta
Cape Fear
Georgetown
Tucson
Preston
Camden
Tuscaloosa
Charleston
Bermudas
Shreveport
Vicksburg
Montgomery
Savannah
Jackson
Ft. Fillmore
Ft. Worth
Mississippi River
Mobile
Pensacola
Tallahassee
St. Augustine
Austin
Houston
New Orleans
Opesura
Ures
Gulf of California
LOWER CALIFORNIA
Cerdos
Rio Grande
San Antonio
Galveston
Tampa
St. Lucie
Bahama Islands
Chihuahua
San Bartonico
Alamos
Monclova
Rio Grande City
Brownsville
Miami
Cape Sable
Nassau
Tropic of Cancer
La Paz
Sinaloa
Saltillo
Monterey
Matamoros
Culiacan
Durango
Alamos
Victoria
GULF OF MEXICO
Key West
Havana
WEST INDIA ISLANDS
Port Principe
Puerto Rico
Mazatlan
Zacatecas
MEXICO
Cape Catoche
Yucatan Channel
Cape Palmas
Trinidad
Port au Prince
SAN DOMINGO
Guadalajara
Queretaro
Valladolid
Salamanca
Mexico
Jalapa
Campeachy
Campeachy Bay
Vera Cruz
Jamaica
Kingston
CARIBBEAN SEA
Tixtlan
Oajaca
YUCATAN
Belize
Acapulco
Tehuantepec
Gulf of Honduras
GUATEMALA
Truxillo
HONDURAS
Guatemala
SAN SALVADOR
NICARAGUA
Pt. Gallinas
Caracas
Lake Nicaragua
Nicaragua
COSTA RICA
Mosquito Gulf
Aspinwall
Merida
Panama
Gulf of Panama
Orinoco River
SOUTH AMERICA
Bogota
NORTH AMERICA
Thomas Kelly,
PUBLISHER AND PRINTER,
SCALE OF MILES
0 100 200 400 600 800
EQUATOR
West
Longitude from Washington
East

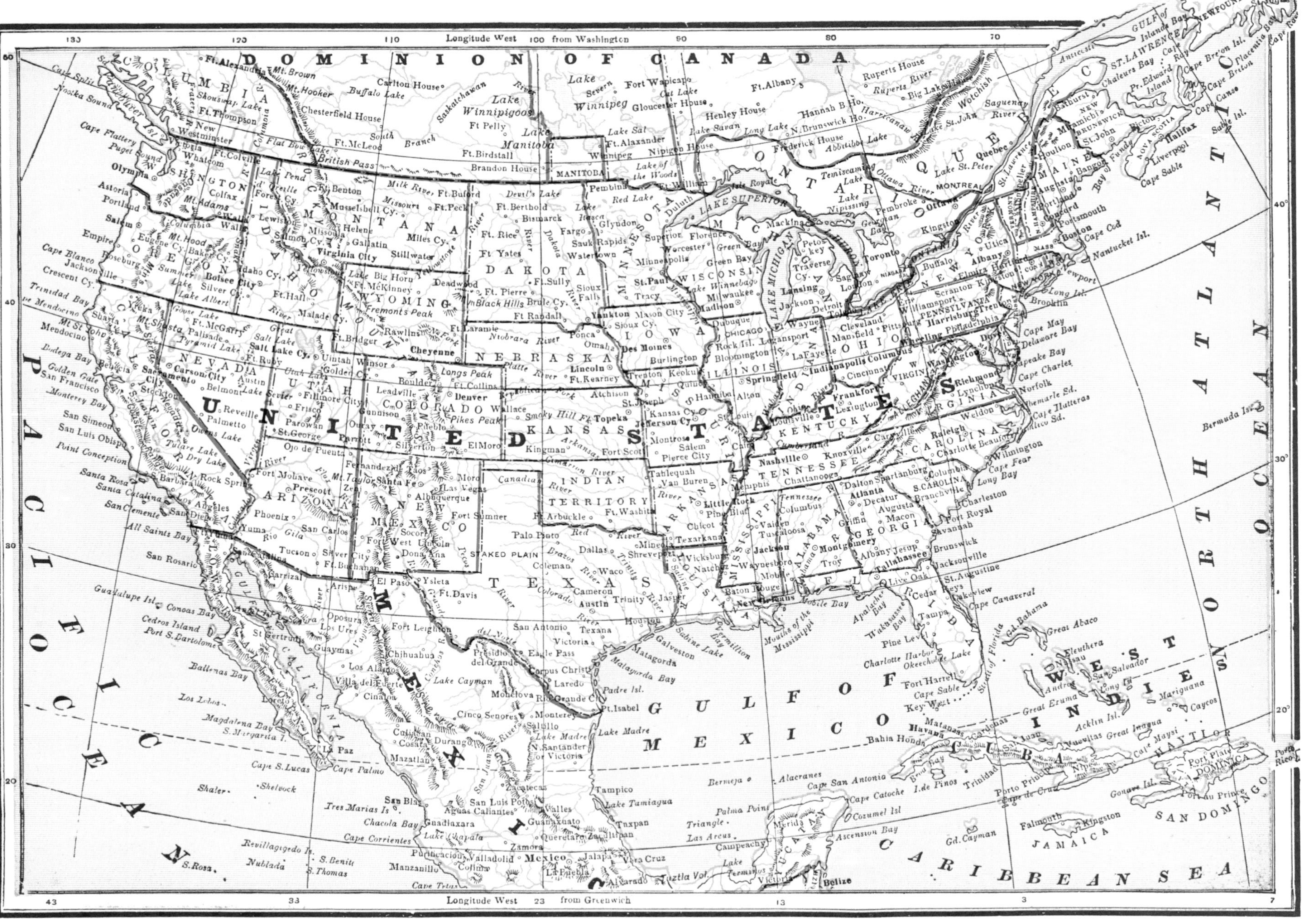

Longitude West from Washington
DOMINION OF CANADA
UNITED STATES
MEXICO
WEST INDIES
GULF OF MEXICO
PACIFIC OCEAN
NORTH ATLANTIC OCEAN
CARIBBEAN SEA
MANITOBA
ONTARIO
QUEBEC
NEW BRUNSWICK
NOVA SCOTIA
NEWFOUNDLAND
GULF of ST. LAWRENCE
WASHINGTON
OREGON
IDAHO
MONTANA
WYOMING
DAKOTA
NEVADA
UTAH
COLORADO
NEBRASKA
KANSAS
INDIAN TERRITORY
ARIZONA
NEW MEXICO
TEXAS
MINNESOTA
IOWA
MISSOURI
ARKANSAS
WISCONSIN
ILLINOIS
INDIANA
MICHIGAN
OHIO
KENTUCKY
TENNESSEE
MISSISSIPPI
ALABAMA
GEORGIA
FLORIDA
LOUISIANA
PENNSYLVANIA
NEW YORK
VIRGINIA
N. CAROLINA
S. CAROLINA
MAINE
CALIFORNIA
CUBA
HAYTI
SAN DOMINGO
JAMAICA
YUCATAN
LAKE SUPERIOR
LAKE MICHIGAN
Lake Winnipeg
Lake Winnipigoos
Lake Manitoba
STAKED PLAIN
Bermuda Isl.
Longitude West from Greenwich

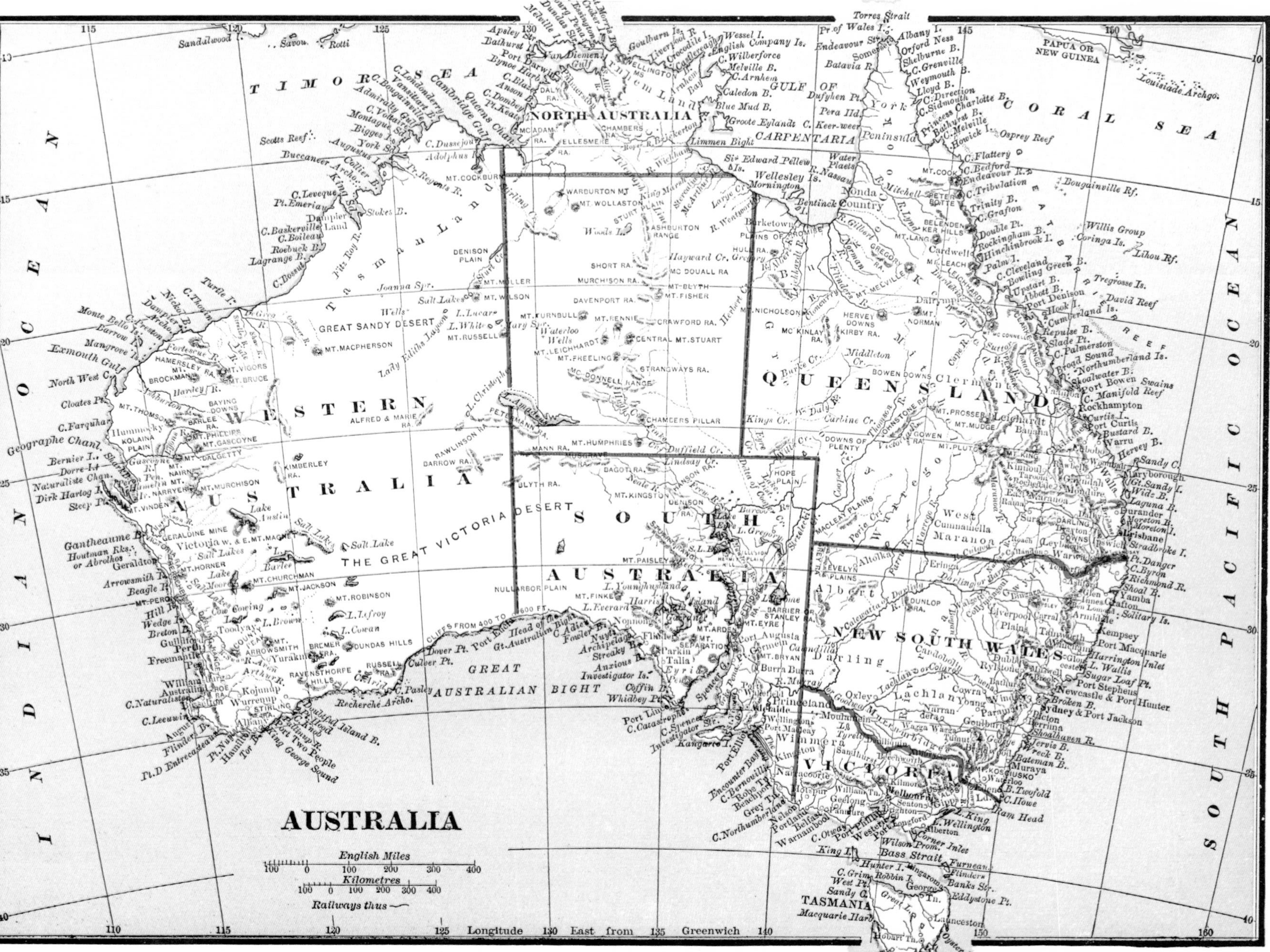

AUSTRALIA
English Miles
Kilometres
Railways thus
Longitude East from Greenwich
INDIAN OCEAN
SOUTH PACIFIC OCEAN
TIMOR SEA
CORAL SEA
GULF OF CARPENTARIA
GREAT AUSTRALIAN BIGHT
PAPUA OR NEW GUINEA
NORTH AUSTRALIA
WESTERN AUSTRALIA
SOUTH AUSTRALIA
QUEENSLAND
NEW SOUTH WALES
VICTORIA
TASMANIA
GREAT SANDY DESERT
THE GREAT VICTORIA DESERT
NULLARBOR PLAIN
Torres Strait
Bass Strait
Cambridge Gulf
Exmouth Gulf
Geographe Chan.
Spencer G.
Kangaroo I.
Melville I.
Groote Eylandt
Wellesley Is.
Rockhampton
Brisbane
Sydney & Port Jackson
Newcastle & Port Hunter
Port Macquarie
Launceston
Hobart Tn.
Macquarie Harb.
Port Darwin
Port Augusta
Geraldton
Fremantle
King George Sound

FLAGS OF VARIOUS NATIONS.

# ARMS OF VARIOUS NATIONS.

UNITED STATES
BELGIUM
CHINA
EGYPT
GREECE
HONDURAS

ARGENTINE REPUBLIC
BRAZIL
CUBA
FRANCE
GUATEMALA
IONIAN ISLANDS

AUSTRALIA
CANADA
DENMARK
GERMANY
HAWAIIAN ISLANDS
IRELAND

AUSTRIA
CHILI
ECUADOR
GREAT BRITAIN
HAYTI
ITALY

# ARMS OF VARIOUS NATIONS.

JAPAN
MEXICO
PARAGUAY
RUSSIA
SPAIN
TURKEY

COLOMBIA
NETHERLANDS
PERSIA
SAN SALVADOR
SWEDEN
TUSCANY

LIBERIA
NORWAY
PERU
SCOTLAND
SWITZERLAND
URUGUAY

LUXEMBURG
ORANGE FREE STATES
PORTUGAL
SIAM
TUNIS
VENEZUELA

# Arms of the States and Territories of the American Union.

| | | | | | |
|---|---|---|---|---|---|
| MAINE | RHODE ISLAND | PENNSYLVANIA | WEST VIRGINIA | GEORGIA | LOUISIANA |
| NEW HAMPSHIRE | CONNECTICUT | DELAWARE | DISTRICT OF COLUMBIA | FLORIDA | TENNESSEE |
| VERMONT | NEW YORK | MARYLAND | NORTH CAROLINA | ALABAMA | ARKANSAS |
| MASSACHUSETTS | NEW JERSEY | VIRGINIA | SOUTH CAROLINA | MISSISSIPPI | TEXAS |

# Arms of the States and Territories of the American Union.

| | | | | | |
|---|---|---|---|---|---|
| OHIO | MICHIGAN | MISSOURI | OREGON | IDAHO TER. | UTAH TER. |
| INDIANA | WISCONSIN | KANSAS | NEVADA | MONTANA TER. | ARIZONA TER. |
| ILLINOIS | MINNESOTA | NEBRASKA | COLORADO | NEW MEXICO TER. | DAKOTA TER. |
| KENTUCKY | IOWA | CALIFORNIA | WASHINGTON TER. | WYOMING TER. | INDIAN TER. |

INTERNATIONAL CODE

INTERNATIONAL CODE

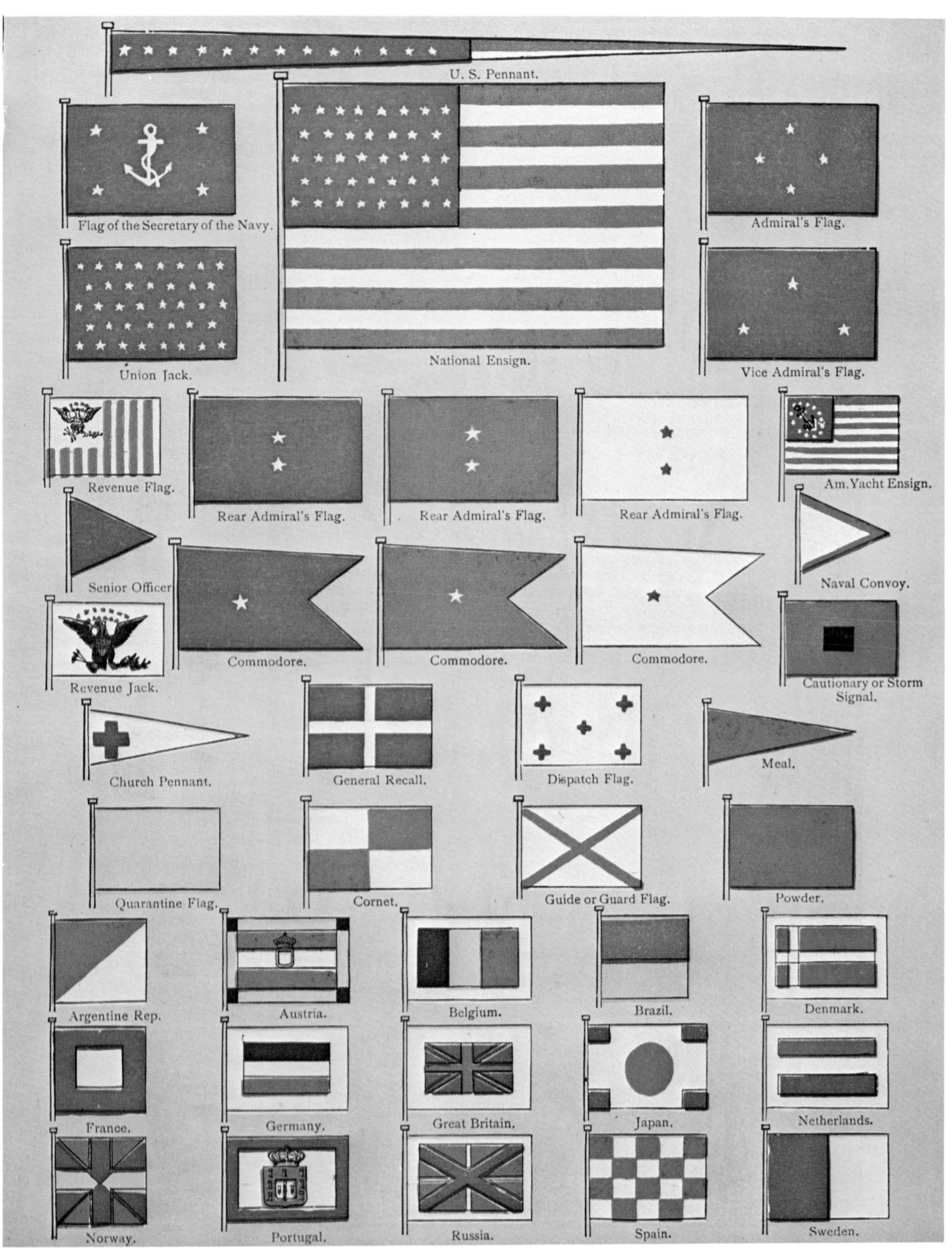


U. S. NAVAL FLAGS, ETC. PILOT SIGNALS OF VARIOUS NATIONS.

# Shoulder Straps for Officers of the United States Army.

General of Army.

Lieutenant General.

Major General.

Brigadier General.

Colonel.

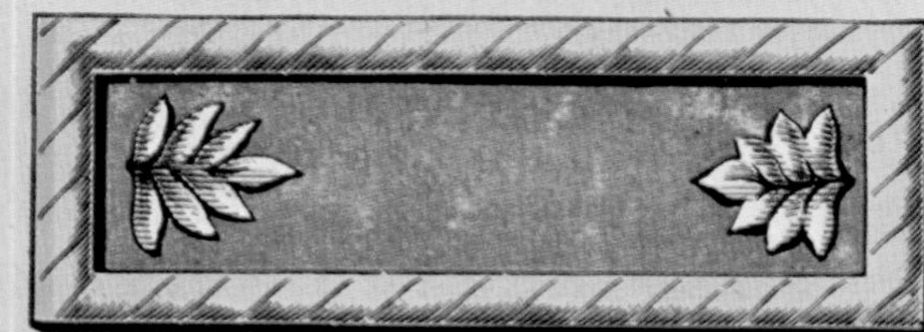

Lieutenant Colonel (Silver Leaves).

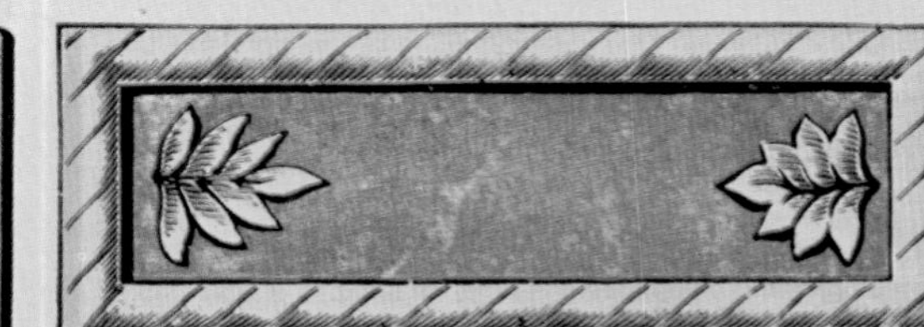

Major (Gold Leaves).

Captain.

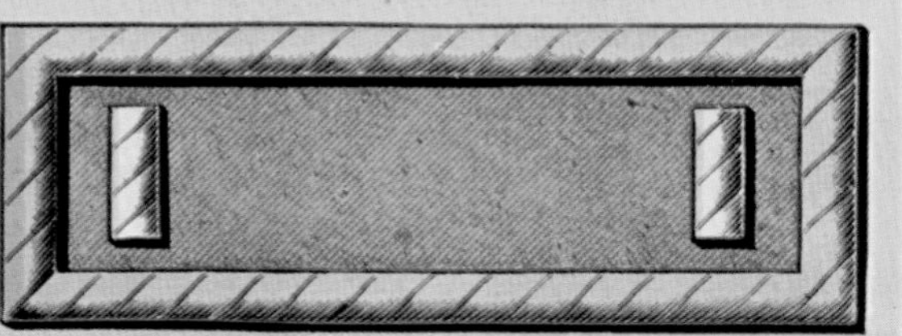

First Lieutenant.

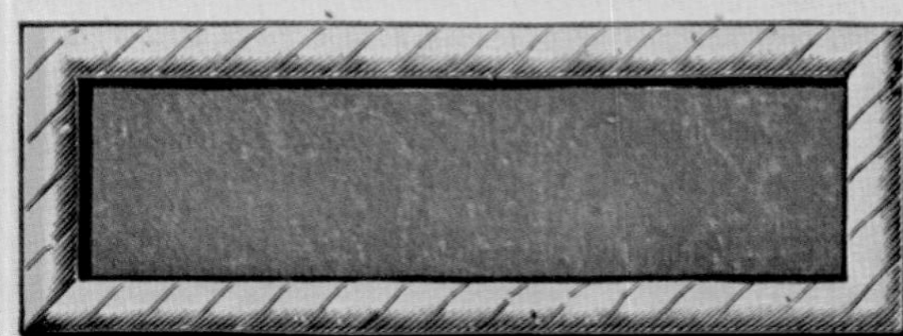

Second Lieutenant.

For Generals and Staff Officers on Dark Blue Cloth.
" Officers of Artillery on Red Cloth.

For Officers of Cavalry on Yellow Cloth.
" " " Infantry on Light Blue Cloth.

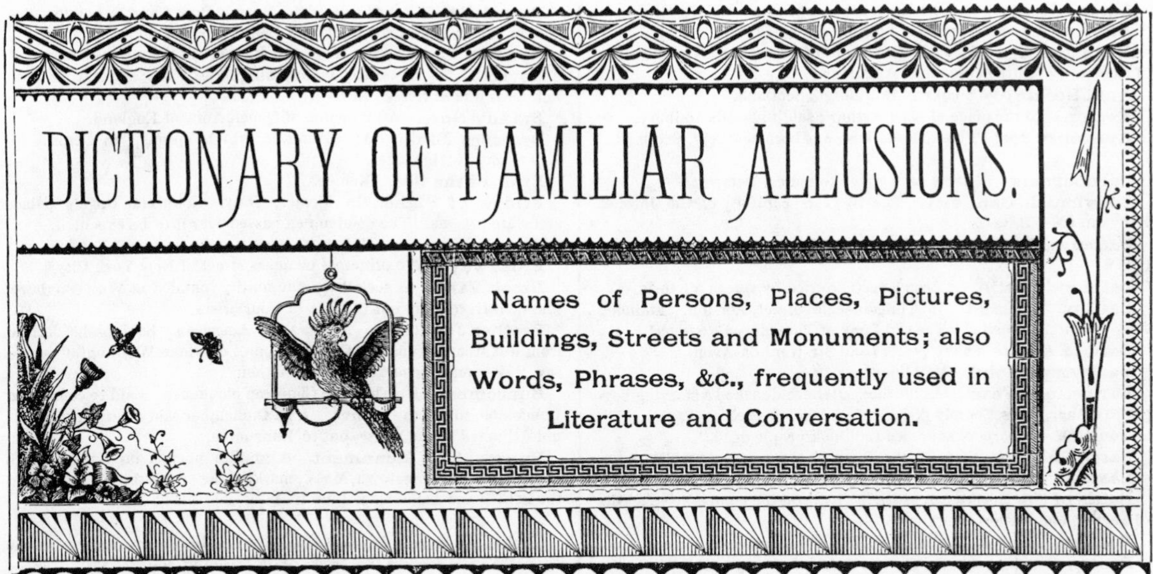


**Abderite.** A scoffer; from Abdera, where Demócritus lived.

**Abraham's Bosom.** The rest of the blessed dead. Luke xiv. 22.

**Abyla.** One of the "Pillars of Hercules;" Calpë, being the other.

**Academics.** The disciples of Plato, so called from the academy.

**Academy** (Academia). A gymnasium in the suburbs of Athens, where Plato founded his school, 368 B. C. The Academy (as a philosophic school) was divided into the OLD (by Plato and his disciples); the MIDDLE (by Arcesiláos), and the NEW (by Carneades).

**Academy, The French.** (*Académie Française.*) One of the five academies constituting the French Institute; founded by Richelieu; deals with the French language, and consists of 40 members.

**Acadia.** The former name of Nova Scotia.

**Adams and Liberty.** Patriotic American song, by R. T. Paine, Jr.

**Adam's Apple** Caused by a piece of forbidden fruit sticking there.

**Admirable Crichton, The.** James Crichton; Scotch prodigy of the 16th century. Hence a person of great accomplishments.

**Admiral.** English admirals were of three kinds according to the color of their flag. ADMIRAL OF THE BLUE, kept the rear in a fight; ADMIRAL OF THE RED, the center; ADMIRAL OF THE WHITE, the van.

**Æneid.** Virgil's epic poem, of which Ænéas is the hero.

**Ages.** According to Hesiod there were five ages of the world. The GOLDEN, the SILVER, the BRAZEN, the HEROIC, and the IRON.

**Agnus Dei.** The Lamb of God. A cake stamped with the figure of a lamb, given out by the Pope on the Sunday after Easter.

**Alabama.** A Confederate privateer built in England, and commanded by Capt. Semmes. After great depredations on American commerce, she was sunk by the "*Kearsarge*," June 19, 1864.

**Aladdin's Window (To finish).** To try to finish something left unfinished by a great man. One window in Aladdin's palace was left for the Sultan to finish, but his treasure gave out.

**Albany Regency.** Nickname of a set of able Democratic politicians, 60 years ago, at Albany, N. Y.

**Albino.** Person with unusually white skin and hair, and red eyes.

**Albion.** England. Said to mean the chalk cliffs. (*Albus*, white.)

**Aldine Press.** Founded by Aldus Manutine, at Venice, 1496. Hence came the famous *Aldine* editions.

**Alexandrian Library.** Founded by Ptolemy Soter, at Alexandria, Egypt. Contained 100,000 volumes. Burned 47 B. C.

**Alexandrine Age.** 323-640, when Alexandria was the seat of the highest culture.

**Alhambra.** Palace and fortress of the Moors at Granáda, Spain.

**All Souls' Day.** Nov. 2. Day of prayer for souls in Purgatory.

**Allah.** ("The Adorable.") Arabic name of God.

**Almack's.** Once a famous London assembly-room where balls were given of the most exclusive, aristocratic character.

**Almighty Dollar.** A phrase from Irving's *Creole Village.*

**Alsatia.** The Whitefriars (London) refuge for criminals.

**Alto-Relievo.** (High relief.) Figures in marble, etc., cut so as to project one-half or more from the tablet.

**Ambrosia.** The food of the gods.

**Amuck, To run amuck.** Run foul of. Malays, drunk with opium, run about, armed with daggers, shouting "**Amuck**" (kill).

**Anacreontics.** Verses in praise of love or wine, after Anacreon.

**Ancient Regime.** The French Government before the Revolution.

**Andersonville Prison.** In Georgia. Union soldiers were confined there during the Civil War of the United States.

**Angelic Doctor, The.** Thomas Aquínas.

**Angelus, The.** A prayer to the Virgin, recited thrice a day.

**Angling, The Father of.** Izaak Walton.

**Annunciation, Day of.** Festival, celebrated March 25th, the day the angel announced to the Virgin that she would bear Our Lord.

**Annus Mirabilis.** (Wonderful Year.) 1666. Plague, fire of London, and English victory over the Dutch.

**Anthony, Saint.** ST. ANTHONY'S FIRE. Erysipelas.

**Antoninus, The Wall of.** Turf entrenchment across Scotland from the Clyde to the Frith of Forth, built by the Romans 140.

**Apollo Belvedere.** A marble statue of Apollo in the Belvedere Gallery of the Vatican at Rome.

**Appian Way.** Oldest of the Roman roads, from Rome to Cápua.

**Apples of Sodom.** Lovely fruit, but within full of ashes.

**Arabesque.** Moorish (Arabic) patterns in decoration.

**Arcadian.** A shepherd; belonging to shepherds. So called from the Greek country Arcadia, a pastoral region.

**Arch of Triumph.** At the west end of the Champs Elysées, Paris, 116 ft. high, 145 wide. Begun by Napoleon.

**Arctic, The.** A Collins steamer, sunk, with great loss of life, in 1854.

**Argo.** The ship in which Jason went after the golden fleece.

**Argonauts.** The heroes who sailed in the Argo.

**Argus-eyed.** Extremely watchful. Juno, jealous of Io, had her watched by the hundred-eyed Argus.

**Arians.** Disciples of Arius; maintained that the Father and Son are distinct beings.

**Armada, The Spanish.** Fleet collected by Philip of Spain, in 1588, to conquer England.

**Artesian Well.** From Artois in France, where they were first dug.

**Aryans.** The parents of the Indo-European peoples.

**Astor Library.** In New York city, founded by J. J. Astor.

**Athens, The Modern.** 1. Edinburgh. 2. Boston.

**Augustan Age.** The palmiest period of a literature ; the best days of Roman literature being under Augustus.

**Auld Reekie** (Old Smoky). Edinburgh, Scotland.

**Avalon.** Burial place of King Arthur ; said to be Glastonbury.

**Ayreshire Poet, The.** Burns, who was born near Ayr, Scotland.

**Barnburners.** A name once given to radical Democrats.

**Babylonish Captivity.** The 70 years' captivity of the Jews at Babylon, 608–538 B. C.

**Baconian Philosophy.** The inductive philosophy of Lord Bacon.

**Balmoral Castle.** A Scotch castle owned by Queen Victoria.

**Bank of England.** In Threadneedle Street, London. Founded 1694. Sometimes called "The Old Lady of Threadneedle Street."

**Bard of Avon.** Shakespeare, from Stratford-on-Avon.

**Barleycorn, John.** Malt liquor.

**Barmecide's Feast.** An illusion. Barmecide asked a starving beggar to dinner, and set empty dishes before him. (*Arabian Nights.*)

**Basilisk.** A serpent supposed to "look people dead."

**Basso-Relievo.** Figures cut on marble, etc., projecting a little.

**Bastile.** French prison and fortress, destroyed by the mob, 1789.

**Battle of the Books.** A satire by Swift on the comparative merits of ancient and modern literature.

**Battery, The.** A park in New York city adjoining the river.

**Beacon Street.** The aristocratic residence street of Boston.

**Beauty and the Beast.** A fairy tale. Beauty lives with the Beast to save her father's life. Beast, disenchanted by love, is made a handsome prince.

**Bedlam** (Bethlehem). A lunatic asylum.

**Bee, The Attic.** Plato, from his sweet style.

**Beelzebub.** God of flies ; a Philistine deity.

**Begging the question.** Assuming as true what you are to prove.

**Belle France, La** (Fair France.) A general name of France.

**Belgravia.** Fashionable quarter of London.

**Bell the Cat.** A wise mouse proposed that a bell should be hung upon the cat's neck to apprise the mice of her coming ; a young mouse inquired, "Who will put the bell on ?"

**Bell, The Passing.** Rung formerly when persons were dying.

**Beloved Disciple.** St. John.

**Benicia Boy.** John C. Heenan, the American pugilist, born at Benicia, Cal.

**Bess, Good Queen.** Queen Elizabeth.

**Bibliothèque Nationale.** (National Library.) At Paris, contains over 1,000,000 books, 150,000 MSS., etc.

**Billingsgate.** Coarse language, such as is used by the fishwomen of Billingsgate, the London fish market.

**Black Death.** A contagious, putrid typhus, which desolated Europe, Asia and Africa in the 14th century.

**Black Friday.** Sept. 26, 1869 ; financial panic in Wall street, N. Y.

**Black Hole.** Dark cell in Calcutta prison where Surajah Dowlah shut up 146 British soldiers; 23 lived till morning.

**Black Prince.** Edward, Prince of Wales, son of Edward III.

**Black Republicans.** The Republican party in the U. S., from their opposition to the extension of slavery.

**Blarney Stone.** In Blarney Castle, near Cork, Ireland. Supposed to impart a flowing tongue to whoever kisses it.

**Bluebeard.** A wife-killing tyrant ; a sort of Henry VIII.

**Blue Laws.** A nickname of early severe New England statutes.

**Blue Stocking.** A female pedant; so called from a literary society at Venice in 1400, whose members wore blue stockings.

**Bohemian.** An artist or literary man living loosely by his wits.

**Bois de Bologne.** A Paris promenade.

**Border, The.** The frontiers of England and Scotland.

**Border Minstrel, The.** Sir Walter Scott.

**Border States.** Maryland, Delaware, Virginia, Kentucky, Missouri.

**Bourgeoisie.** French tradesmen and manufacturers as a class.

**Boulevard.** In Paris, a wide street or promenade.

**Bourse.** The Parisian Stock Exchange.

**Bloody Mary.** Queen Mary of England ; so called on account of her bloodthirsty persecution of English Protestants.

**Bow Bells.** A set of bells in St. Mary-le-Bow Church, London. A person "born within sound of Bow Bells" is a Cockney.

**Bowery, The.** A New York thoroughfare of the lower classes.

**Boycott.** To refuse to have anything to do with. Boycott, an Irish landlord, was so treated in 1881.

**Brandy Nose.** A nickname of Queen Anne of England.

**Breeches Bible.** An edition in which aprons, in Genesis iii. 7, is rendered "breeches."

**Bride of the Sea.** Venice.

**Bridge of Sighs.** In Venice, Italy. Connects Doge's palace and state prisons. The condemned passed over it to be executed.

**British Museum.** A famous library and museum of London.

**Broadway.** The principal business street of New York City.

**Brook Farm.** A socialistic community founded at West Roxbury, Mass., 1841, to carry out the idea of Fourierism.

**Brother Jonathan.** America, an American. Said to be derived from Jonathan Trumbull, Gov. of Conn., of whom Washington would say, "We must consult Brother Jonathan."

**Buncombe or Bunkum.** Clap-trap eloquence. Said to come from Buncombe, in North Carolina. A N. C. member said a fiery speech was not delivered to the house, but to Buncombe.

**Bunker Hill Monument.** A granite obelisk on Bunker (once Breed's) Hill, Charlestown, Mass., marking the site of the battle between the British and Americans, June 17, 1775.

**Cachet, Lettres de.** (Sealed letters). Blank warrants with the French King's seal, to free from, or imprison in the Bastile.

**Caledonia.** A poetical name for Scotland.

**Campagna.** (The country). The plain around the city of Rome.

**Carbonari.** Italian secret political society, organized in 1820.

**Carmagnole.** Song and dance in the French Revolution.

**Cartesian Philosophy.** (Descartes.) "I think, therefore I exist."

**Castle Garden.** The landing-place of emigrants, New York city.

**Catacombs.** The subterranean burial-places in Alexandria, Egypt ; also in Rome, used by the early Christians.

**Cavalier Servente.** The escort of a married woman.

**Cecilia, Saint.** A Roman Christian martyr ; patroness of music.

**Celestial Empire.** China, whose first emperors were all divinities.

**Central Park.** The great park of N. Y. City, contains 863 acres.

**Champs de Mars.** A field in Paris for military manœuvres.

**Champs Elysées.** A promenade in Paris, 1¼ miles long.

**Charter Oak.** A tree in Hartford, Conn., in which the Colonial Charter was secreted in 1688. Blown down in 1856.

**Chauvinism.** Narrow-minded braggart patriotism; from Chauvin, a character of Scribe's.

**Cheapside.** A great and crowded London thoroughfare.

**Chestnut Street.** The fashionable street of Philadelphia, Penn.

**Chiltern Hundreds, To accept the.** To resign one's seat in Parliament. An English M. P. resigns his seat by taking office. Stewardship of the Chiltern Hundreds is a sinecure for this purpose.

**Christ Church.** The largest college in the University of Oxford.

**Cid, The.** Don Roderigo Laynez, Count of Bivar ; Spanish hero.

**Cincinnati, The.** Society of American Revolutionary officers.

**Citizen King, The.** Louis Philippe of France.

**Cockaine, Land of.** An imaginary land of pleasure and laziness.

**Colossus of Rhodes.** A brass statue at Rhodes, 126 feet high.

**Columbia.** Poetical name of the United States, from Columbus.

**Column of Vendome.** **(Colonne Vendome.)** Stone pillar in Paris, erected by Napoleon ; razed by the Commune in 1871.

**Confederate States.** The 11 States which seceded in 1861, viz., Alabama, Arkansas, Florida, Georgia, Louisiana, Mississippi, North Carolina, South Carolina, Tennessee, Texas, Virginia.

**Congressional Library.** At Washington, largest in United States.

**Consols.** English public securities at 3 per cent.

**Copperheads.** Northern sympathizers with the South in the American Civil War.

**Corncrackers, The.** Kentuckians.

**Corn Law Rhymer, The.** Ebenezer Elliott.

**Corso.** (The Course.) The chief thoroughfare of Rome.

**Crapaud** (a toad) **Johnny.** A Frenchman. The ancient device of French royalty was three toads (subsequently the *fleur de lys*).

**Credit Mobilier.** A company authorized to do a stock-jobbing business. The American C. M. in connection with the Pacific railroads was famous in 1873.

**Crocodile Tears.** Hypocritical grief. The crocodile was fabled to weep as it ate its victim.

**Cumberland.** A United States vessel sunk by the Confederate ram *Merrimac* in Hampton Roads, March 8, 1862. Went down with colors flying, firing a broadside as she sunk.

**Curfew Bell.** A bell rung at sunset in the time of William I. and II. in England, to order fires and candles to be put out.

**Dámocles' Sword.** Presentiment of evil. Dionysius the Elder, tyrant of Syracuse, invited his flatterer Damocles to a splendid feast, but hung over his head a sword dangling by a single hair.

**Darby and Joan.** An affectionate married couple. From a ballad.

**Dartmoor Prison,** in Devonshire, England. A prison of war.

**Darwinian Theory.** A theory proposed by Charles Darwin in his *Origin of Species*; the different species came from one or a few original forms, present differences being the result of development and natural selection.

**De Profundis** (Out of the depths). The first two words of the Latin version of the 130th Psalm. Sung at burials.

**Debatable Ground.** Land on the western border of Scotland, disputed between Scotland and England.

**Defender of the Faith.** Title given by Pope Leo X. to Henry VIII. of England.

**Dies Iræ.** (Day of wrath.) First two words of a celebrated mediæval hymn by Thomas of Celáno.

**Directory, The French.** By the constitution of 1795 the Executive power was vested in 5 directors. It lasted 4 years only.

**Dixie. The Land of Dixie.** The Southern States.

**Dizzy.** A nickname of Benjamin Disraeli, Earl of Beaconsfield.

**Doctors' Commons.** Where the Ecclesiastical Court sat in London.

**Doctrinaire.** An impracticable politician. First applied to the French Constitutional Monarchists, of whom Guizot was one.

**Doe, John.** Fictitious plaintiff in ejectment; Doe versus Roe.

**Doomsday Book.** A book containing the value of all English estates in the reign of William the Conqueror.

**Donnybrook Fair.** A once celebrated annual fair near Dublin.

**Douay Bible, The.** The English Bible authorized by the Roman Catholic Church. First published at Douay, France.

**Downing Street,** in London. The official residence of the Prime Ministers is situated there since the time of Sir Robert Walpole.

**Drachenfels** (Dragon Rock). A castle on a mountain of the same name, high above the Rhine, not far from Bonn.

**Drury Lane Theater.** A London playhouse, opened in 1668.

**Dunciad.** A satire on Dunces by Pope. Colley Cibber is the hero.

**Dying Gladiator.** An ancient statue in the Capitol at Rome.

**Eastern States, The.** Maine, Vermont, New Hampshire, Massachusetts, Rhode Island, and Connecticut.

**Ecce Homo.** (Behold the man.) A famous painting by Corregio representing the Savior crowned with thorns.

**École Polytechnique.** (Polytechnic School). A Parisian school whose graduates are given places in the public service.

**El Dorado.** (The Golden.) General name for wealthy country.

**Elephant, Seeing the.** Seeing the world; "life."

**Elgin Marbles.** A collection of Greek sculptures (mainly from the Athenian Parthenon), made by Lord Elgin; now in British Museum.

**Escorial, The.** Granite palace and mausoleum near Madrid.

**Eternal City, The.** Rome.

**Eulenspiegel, Tyl.** Hero of a German story; a vagrant Brunswicker who cuts up all sorts of pranks.

**Euréka.** (I have found it.) A saying attributed to the Archimedes when he discovered the way to test the purity of Hiero's crown.

**Evangelists, Symbols of the.** MATTHEW has a scroll before him and holds a pen. MARK sits writing, with a winged lion by his side. LUKE has a pen and scroll; near him is an ox. JOHN is a young man behind whom is an eagle.

**Exclusion, Bill of.** A bill which passed the English Commons in 1679, proposing to exclude the Duke of York (afterwards James II.) from the throne, because he was a Roman Catholic.

**Expounder of the Constitution, The.** Daniel Webster.

**Fabian Policy.** A policy of delay, such as was pursued by Q. Fabius Maximus, called Cunctátor, "The Delayer."

**Fabius, The American.** George Washington.

**Fairmount Park,** in Philadelphia, contains nearly 3,000 acres. It was the site of the Centennial Exhibition of 1876.

**Faery Queen.** A rhymed romance of Edmund Spenser.

**Fainéants, Les Rois.** (Do-nothing Kings). Nicknames of the last kings of the Merovingian dynasty in France.

**Falérnian.** A celebrated ancient Italian wine grown at Falernum.

**Faneuil Hall,** in Boston, Mass., first built in 1742. Revolutionary orators frequently addressed public meetings in it.

**Farmer George.** George III. of England; so called from his bluff manners, thriftiness, and love of agriculture.

**Fata Morgána.** A mirage observed in the Straits of Messina.

**Father of his Country.** George Washington.

**Fathers of the Latin Church.** Ambrose, of Milan; Augustine, St. Bernard, Hilary, Jerome, Lactantius.

**Faubourg, St. Antoine.** The part of Paris in which the workingmen live. Once the scene of many insurrections and riots.

**Faubourg St. Germain.** The aristocratic residence quarter of Paris, where are the houses of the old nobility.

**Fenians.** A society of Irishmen organized in the United States in 1865 to make Ireland a Republic.

**Field of the Cloth of Gold.** Plain in France where Francis I. met Henry VIII.; so called from the magnificent display made.

**Fifth Avenue.** A celebrated residence street in New York City.

**Fighting Joe.** The American general Joseph Hooker.

**First Gentleman in Europe.** George IV. of England.

**Five Points.** A locality in New York once famous as the abode of poverty and crime; now greatly changed.

**Flagellants.** Religious fanatics of the 13th century, who went about naked and scourging themselves.

**Fleet, The.** A famous London prison, taken down in 1845.

**Flowery Kingdom, The.** China, where flowers are abundant.

**Flying Dutchman.** A spectre ship seen, in bad weather, about the Cape of Good Hope; supposed to presage bad luck.

**Fort Sumter.** In the harbor of Charleston, S. C. Here was done the first fighting in the late Civil War of the United States.

**Fourierism.** A system of communism proposed by Charles Fourier. The world was to be divided into "phalansteries" of 400 families, who were to live and work in common.

**Freshman.** A student in his first year at college.

**Funk, Peter.** A mock auction; a person employed at auction sales in making bids in collusion with the owner of the property to be sold.

**Gadshill,** near Rochester, in Kent, England; famous for Falstaff's highway robbery. Charles Dickens lived there.

**Genre Painting.** One representing domestic rural ordinary scenes.

**George, St., and the Dragon.** St. George, the patron saint of England, is said to have slain in Libya a huge dragon, to which every day a virgin was offered up.

**Gerrymander.** To so apportion, geographically, legislative, congressional, or other electoral districts, as to give an unfair preponderance to some one political party. Started in Massachusetts, and named after Elbridge Gerry, then Governor of the State.

**Ghetto.** The quarter in Rome to which the Jews were formerly restricted. Also in many other European cities.

**Ghibelline.** In the Middle Ages an adherent of the Holy Roman Empire against the Papacy.

**Girondists; The Gironde.** In the French Revolution the party of moderate "constitutional" Republicans.

**Glencoe.** A pass in Argyleshire, Scotland. Here, Feb. 13, 1691, occurred the famous massacre of Glencoe, in which 38 of the McDonalds were murdered by 120 soldiers under Capt. Campbell.

**Gobelins.** A tapestry and carpet manufactory at Paris, founded about 1515 by J. Gobelin, a dyer.

**Godiva, Lady.** Wife of Leofric, Earl of Mercia, who offered to remit certain exactions to his tenants if she would ride naked through the streets of Coventry. She did so, everybody keeping indoors except one "Peeping Tom," who was struck blind for peeping at her.

**Golcónda.** A locality in India containing some rich diamond mines.
**Golden Age.** An age of innocence and prosperity. The palmy time of a nation or a literature.
**Golden Gate.** The entrance to the harbor of San Francisco, Cal.
**Golden Horn.** The estuary of the Bosphorus, upon whose banks Constantinople is built.
**Golden House.** Palace of gold built by Nero in Rome.
**Gordian Knot.** A vexed question, an obstacle. Gordius, a Phrygian peasant, when chosen king, consecrated his wagon to Jupiter, tying the yoke and beam together so that it could not be untied, till Alexander, hearing that the untier of the knot should rule over all the East, cut the knot with his sword.
**Gordon Riots, The.** In 1780, at London, under Lord George Gordon, a weak-minded nobleman, to force the repeal of the bill passed by the House of Commons to relieve the Roman Catholics.
**Gotham.** A name sometimes applied to New York City.
**Gotham, The Wise Men of,** were noted for their folly. Gotham was an English village.
**Great Commoner, The.** William Pitt.
**Great Duke, The.** The Duke of Wellington.
**Great Eastern.** A great steamship, the largest vessel ever launched. She was made to carry 1,000 passengers and 5,000 tons of cargo. Since 1864 only used in laying cables.
**Great Pyramid, The.** At Gheezeh, Egypt, was built about 3100 B. C. It is 484 feet high, and contains 577,600 square feet.
**Greenbacks.** U. S. Treasury notes ; so called from their color.
**Green Isle, The.** Ireland, from the greenness of its vegetation; also called the Emerald Isle.
**Greenwood.** A cemetery in Brooklyn, N. Y. ; largest in America.
**Gregórian Year.** The year as reformed by Gregory XIII., in 1582. He took away 10 days.
**Gretna Green.** A Scotch village, once a famous place for runaway matches. A declaration before witnesses of an intention to marry was formerly sufficient to make a valid marriage in Scotland.
**Grub Street.** A London street, once noted for literary hacks.
**Guelphs.** In mediæval Europe the adherents of the Papacy as against the Holy Roman Empire.
**Guildhall.** The London Town Hall ; the hall of the guilds.
**Gunner's Daughter, Kissing the.** To be flogged. Boys in the English navy, before being flogged, are tied to a gun breech.
**Gunpowder Plot, The.** A plot to blow up the English Parliament in its House, Nov. 5, 1605, with gunpowder. Catesby conceived the scheme, which was to have been carried out by Guy Fawkes.
**Gyges' Ring.** A ring which made the wearer invisible. Gyges, a Lydian, found in a brazen horse, in a cavern, a man's corpse, from the finger of which he took a brazen ring which made him invisible. With this ring he went into the chamber of the King of Lydia, whom he murdered and succeeded.

**Habeas Corpus Act, The.** Passed in the time of Charles II., provides that the body of an accused person must be brought (if he insist) before a judge, and the reason of his confinement stated. The judge will then determine whether or not to admit the accused to bail. The guilt of an accused person is to be finally decided by a jury.
**Halcyon Days.** A period of happiness. The halcyon (kingfisher) was thought by the ancients to lay its eggs, and brood for 14 days preceding the winter solstice, on the surface of the ocean, which was always calm during this time.
**Handicap.** In horse-racing, assigning different weights to horses of different speed, age, etc., so they may run with an equal chance. So called from an ancient game of cards.
**Hansard.** The debates of the British Parliament, which are printed by a firm named Hansard.
**Hanse Towns.** The North German seaboard cities which once constituted the Hanseatic League.
**Hanseatic League.** A union of a number of maritime towns in Northern Germany for purpose of trade and mutual safety. Founded in the 13th century. Their triennial legislature was called *hansa*.
**Hare, Mad as a March.** The hare is excessively wild in March.
**Harpies.** Creatures with a woman's head and breasts, and the rest of the body like vultures, hungry and emitting a terrible stench.
**Hari-Kari** (happy dispatch). Japanese official suicide. Civil officials ordered by the government to dispatch themselves, rip out their bowels with two cross-gashes.
**Harvest Moon.** The full moon at or nearest to the fall equinox ; rises for a number of days about sunset.
**Heathen Chinee.** A nickname of the Chinese in America.
**Heidelberg Castle.** A ruined palace-fortress near Heidelberg, Germany.
**Heel-tap.** "No heel-taps ;" *i. e.*, drain the glass to the bottom. A heel-tap is a shoe-peg stuck in the heel, but taken out when the shoe is done.
**Hegíra.** The date of Mahomet's flight from Mecca, July 16, 622. The Mahommedan epoch begins with it.
**High Church.** That section of the English clergy which maintains the apostolic descent of the clergy, and absolution by priests.
**High Seas, The.** The sea beyond three miles from the coast.
**History, The Father of.** The Greek historian. Herodotus.
**Hob-and-Nob.** To touch glasses together in drinking ; to talk confidentially to. A hob, at the corner of the hearth, was to heat the water or spirit. A nob is a small table.
**Hobson's Choice.** What is offered, or nothing. It is said that Tobias Hobson, an English stable-keeper, whenever a customer came to hire a horse, made him take the horse nearest the stable door.
**Holborn.** A London street by which criminals used to be carried out to execution at Tyburn.
**Holy Alliance,** formed in 1816 by Austria, Prussia, and Russia.
**Holy Family, The.** The name of many mediæval pictures representing the infant Jesus, Joseph, the Virgin, John the Baptist, Anna, and Elizabeth. Perhaps the most celebrated are by Michael Angelo, at Florence ; by Rubens, at Florence ; by Raphael, in London ; and by Leonardo da Vinci, in the Louvre.
**Holy Land, The.** Palestine, as the birthplace of Christ.
**Holy League, The.** The alliance of Pope Julius II., France, Germany, Spain, and some of the Italian Republics in 1508, against Venice.
**Honi soit qui mal y pense.** (Shame to him who evil thinks.) Motto of the Order of the Garter. At a ball given by Edward III. of England, the Countess of Salisbury's blue garter came off accidentally. The King picked it up, made the remark quoted above, and fixed it round his own knee. This led to his instituting the Order of the Garter.
**Honors of War.** Allowing a surrendered enemy to keep his arms.
**Hotel de Rambouillet.** A Paris palace, the resort of wits, literary ladies, etc., in the 17th century. Ridiculed by Molière.
**Hotel de Ville.** The City Hall of French and Belgian cities.
**Houris,** in the Koran, black-eyed, beautiful virgins of Paradise ; 72 are alloted to each believer.
**Humble Pie, To eat.** To make submission. From *umbles*, the entrails and other inferior portions of the deer.
**Hundred Days, The,** from March 20, 1815, when Napoleon escaped from Elba, to June 22, 1815, when he abdicated.

**Iconoclast** (Image-breaker). A radical reformer ; so called from the 8th century reformers who objected to (and threw down) statues, pictures, etc., in churches.
**Iliad.** The story of the siege of Troy by the Greeks, a Greek epic poem, by Homer.
**Immaculate Conception.** The dogma of the Catholic Church that the Virgin Mary was conceived without original sin.
**Independence, Declaration of,** issued July 4, 1776, asserting the independence of the American Colonies of Great Britain.
**Independence Hall,** in Philadelphia, Penn. ; the meeting-place of the Continental Congress, where the Declaration of Independence was adopted.
**Index Expurgatorius.** A list of printed works, the reading of which is prohibited by the Church of Rome ; published annually.
**Inns of Court.** The four London law societies which have the sole right of admitting candidates to the bar. They are GRAY'S INN, LINCOLN'S INN, the INNER TEMPLE, and the MIDDLE TEMPLE.
**Inquisition** (An inquiry into.) A tribunal to inquire into transgressions against the Roman Catholic Church.
**Irish Agitator, The.** Daniel O'Connell.
**Iron City, The.** Pittsburgh, Pa., celebrated for its iron industries.
**Iron Duke, The.** The Duke of Wellington.

**Iron Mask, The Man in the.** A mysterious French state prisoner.

**Jack Ketch.** The hangman ; the name of an English hangman.

**Jack Robinson.** Before you can say Jack Robinson, meaning *at once*. Halliwell notes the derivation "Jack, Robes on " from an old play. According to Grose, one Jack Robinson was noted for the short ness of his visits ; the servants had hardly time to repeat Jack Robinson, before he would leave. (Very doubtful.)

**Jack the Giant-Killer.** A nursery hero, who has an invincible sword, a cap of wisdom, shoes of swiftness, and an invisible coat.

**Jack, the American, or Union.** The blue ground of the American flag with the stars, but without the stripes.

**Jacobins.** A famous political club in the French Revolution. It met at a convent of the Jacobins (Dominicans).

**Jacobites.** Adherents of James II. of England, and the Stuarts, his descendants ; from Jacobus (James).

**Jardin des Plantes.** Botanical and zoölogical garden in Paris.

**Jardin Mabille.** A once famous garden in Paris ; the home of the *can-can*. Pleasure resort of the *demi-monde*. Shut up in 1882.

**Jericho, Gone to.** Disappeared, ruined. Henry VIII. had a manor called Jericho. When he went there to visit some of his mistresses it used to be said of him, "He has gone to Jericho." (Very doubtful.)

**Jerusalem Delivered.** An Italian epic poem by Torquato Tasso.

**Jingo ; Jingoism.** Expressions which arose during the ministry of Lord Beaconsfield, 1874–1880. Applied to those who wished England to take an aggressive foreign policy. It originated in a music-hall song.

**Joan, Pope.** A pretended female Pope who was said to have succeeded Leo IV. The falsity of the legend has been shown.

**John Bull.** Nickname for an Englishman ; England. A choleric, plethoric, bull-headed, well-meaning fellow.

**John Chinaman.** Nickname for the Chinese in America.

**Johnny Reb.** Nickname of Southerners in American Civil War.

**Jubilee, Year of.** Among the Jews came every 50th year; all debts were considered to be paid, and land reverted to its original owners. In the Catholic Church it comes once in every 25 years.

**Juggernaut.** A Hindoo god who has a famous temple in India.

**Julian Era, The,** begins 46 B.C., when Cæsar reformed the calendar.

**Junius, Letters of.** A celebrated series of political letters signed "Junius," written in the reign of George III., of doubtful authorship.

**Kansas, Bleeding.** So called on account of the fierce struggles between its anti-slavery and pro-slavery settlers.

**Kensington Gardens.** A great London pleasure ground adjoining Kensington Palace (where Queen Victoria was born).

**Kilkenny Cats, The,** fought in a saw-pit till only their tails remained.

**King can do no wrong, The.** Meaning *he* is not responsible, but his *ministers* are, for mistakes in administration.

**King of Yvetot.** A "good, little king." A pretentious person. The holders of the little seigneurie of Yvetot, had the title of king.

**King Cole.** A legendary British king, who "loved his pipe and bowl."

**King Cotton.** Cotton, the great product of the Southern States, was so called before the Civil War.

**King's Evil.** The scrofula. It was an ancient notion that the touch of a sovereign could heal scrofula. Doctor Johnson was the last Englishman "touched" for scrofula.

**King Log.** An ineffectual, do-nothing ruler. Jupiter, in answer to the prayer of the frogs for a king, gave them a log.

**King-Maker, The.** Richard Neville, the great Earl of Warwick, who set up and deposed English kings in the 15th century.

**King Stork.** A tyrant. The frogs, dissatisfied with the let-alone policy of King Log, prayed for a new king, whereupon Jupiter sent them the Stork, who devoured them miscellaneously.

**Kit Kat Club, The.** A famous London Club, founded in 1688, at the shop of one Christopher Katt, pastry-cook. Among the members were Addison, Congreve, Halifax, the Duke of Marlborough, Steele, and Vanbrugh.

**Knickerbocker.** A member of an "old" New York family ; especially persons descended from the original Dutch settlers.

**Knights of Malta.** Also called Hospitallers of St. John of Jerusalem. A once powerful association. The original knights had charge of a church and hospital at Jerusalem consecrated to St. John. Thence they moved to Rhodes, and in 1523 to Malta.

**Know Nothings.** Political party in the United States insisting that nobody but "native Americans should hold office." Sprang up suddenly about 1853, and (after carrying a few State elections) disappeared.

**Kohinoor** (Mountain of Light.) A diamond from the mines of Golconda, India. When found (1550) it weighed 793 carets; the present weight is 106 1-16. It came into the possession of Queen Victoria in 1850. Estimated value, 625,000 dollars, or 125,000 pounds.

**Koran or Alkoran.** (The Reading.) The Mahommedan Bible.

**Kremlin.** A quarter in Moscow, Russia, in which are several palaces, cathedrals, towers, etc.

**Labyrinth, The.** A celebrated structure of ancient Egypt. A maze of difficulties, so called from an inextricable series of winding passages, constructed by Minos, King of Crete.

**Laconic.** Brief, from Laconia, another name for Sparta ; the Spartans cultivated curtness of speech.

**Lacrymæ Christi.** Italian wine grown about Mount Vesuvius.

**Lake School, The.** The poetry of Coleridge, Wordsworth, and Southey, who lived in the Lake district of England.

**Land of Bondage.** Egypt, so called by the Jews.

**Land of Cakes.** Scotland, famous for its oatmeal cakes.

**Land of Nod.** Popular phrase for sleep.

**Land of Promise, or Promised Land.** Among the Jews, Canaan, which God promised to Abraham.

**Lang Syne,** is Scotch for long since. The famous song *Auld Lang Syne* is generally credited to Robert Burns, who said he took this song down from an old man's singing.

**Langue d'Oc.** (Language of Yes.) Provençal, formerly the language of southern France.

**Langue d'Oïl.** (Language of Yes). French, in distinction from Provençal.

**Laocoön.** A statue in the Belvedere of the Vatican representing the death of Laocoön, strangled to death (with his sons) by serpents.

**Laodicean.** "Luke-warm" in religious matters. See Rev. iii. 14-18.

**Lares and Penates.** The household gods of the Romans.

**Last Judgment.** The subject of many mediæval paintings. The most famous is the fresco by Michael Angelo, in the Sistine Chapel in the Vatican. There is a fresco of it in the Campo Santo, at Pisa, supposed to be the work of Orcagna ; and a picture on this subject by Luca Signorelli, in Orvieto Cathedral, is considered his master-piece.

**Last Supper, The,** is the subject of many mediæval paintings, of which the most famous is Leonardo da Vinci's, at Milan. Next is Andrea del Sarto's in the Salvi convent, near Florence.

**Lateran Palace, The,** at Rome, was the residence of the Popes till late in the 14th century.

**Laughing Philosopher, The.** Democritus of Abdéra.

**Leaning Tower, The,** at Pisa, Italy ; leans about 13 feet from the perpendicular ; 178 ft. high ; 50 ft. in diameter.

**Learned Blacksmith, The.** Elihu Burritt, an American writer and linguist, originally a blacksmith.

**Leonine Verses.** Verses in which end and middle words rhyme.

**Libby Prison.** A famous Confederate prison of war at Richmond, Va., during the Civil War of the United States.

**Lilliput.** A region inhabited by pigmies, in *Gulliver's Travels*.

**Lingua Franca.** A corrupt Italian-French spoken along the Mediterranean.

**Lion and Unicorn,** on the British royal arms. The lion is English ; the unicorn, Scotch. Added in 1603.

**Lion of the North.** Gustavus Adolphus of Sweden.

**Lion's Share.** All or most. The lion, in Æsop, hunts with some other beasts. In dividing the spoils he claims four quarters.

**Little Corporal.** Napoleon I., from his shortness of stature.

**Little Giant.** Stephen A. Douglas, who was of small stature.

**Lloyds.** Rooms in London, resorted to by bankers and brokers.

**Lombard Street.** The great financial street of London.

**Lone Star State, The.** Texas, whose flag bears a single star.

**Long Parliament, The.** Sat from Nov. 3, 1640, till April 20, 1653.

**Lorelei.** A water spirit who enticed sailors till they were dashed to pieces by the rapids around the high rocks called Lorelei, on the Rhine.

**Lotus Eaters, The.** A people in Homer's Odyssey who ate the lotus tree, which made them forget home, and only wish "to live at ease."

**Louvre.** A palace in Paris filled with works of art.

**Low Church.** That section of the English Church which lays little or no stress on ceremonies and is extremely "evangelical."

**Lusiad.** A Portuguese epic by Camoens, recounts the adventures of the Lusians (Portuguese) under Vasco de Gama, the first to sail to India.

**Lynch Law.** Hanging by a mob; its judgments are pronounced by "Judge Lynch." Said to be derived from a Virginian named Lynch, who acted as a judge in the 17th century, by appointment of his neighbors. According to others, derived from an Irish James Lynch, Warden of Galway, who sentenced his own son to death for murder.

**Mab, Queen.** "The fairies' midwife," *i. e.*, employed by the fairies as midwife of dreams (to deliver man's brain of dreams).

**Macadamize.** To pave a street with broken stones; so called from Sir John Macadam, who invented that system of paving.

**Macaronic Verse.** Ludicrous verses consisting of words from different languages mixed.

**Machiavellism.** Political or diplomatic trickery; so called from Nicholas Macchiavelli, author of a political treatise called *The Prince*.

**Madame Tussaud's Exhibition.** An exhibition in London of waxwork figures, many being modelled from life.

**Mad Poet, The.** Nathaniel Lee, the insane English dramatist.

**Madman of Macedonia, The.** Alexander the Great.

**Madman of the North.** Charles XII. of Sweden.

**Madonna.** (My Lady.) The Virgin Mary. Of the immense number of pictures on this subject, we mention the Sistine Madonna, by Raphael, and the Madonna di San Georgio, by Correggio, at Dresden; and the Madonna della Seggiola, by Raphael, in the Pitti Palace, Florence.

**Maecénas.** A friend and patron of literary men. Caius Cilnius Mæcenas, a Roman general and statesman, friend of Augustus, was a liberal patron of literary men, especially Horace and Virgil.

**Magna Charta.** (Great charter.) The charter securing the liberty (or at least fair trial) of English subjects; granted by King John.

**Mahomet's Coffin,** was said to be hung in mid-air at Medina.

**Maid of Orleans, The.** Joan of Arc (Jeanne Darc.)

**Maid of Saragossa.** Augustina Zaragoza, famous for her valor during the siege of Saragossa, in Spain, by the French (1808-1809).

**Maiden Queen, The.** Queen Elizabeth of England.

**Maine Law.** A prohibitory liquor law first adopted in Maine.

**Malthusian Doctrine, The.** So called from the English economist Malthus, who claimed that population increases faster than the means of living; so that, unless population is checked, either a part of it must starve to death, or the whole of it be insufficiently fed.

**Mammoth Cave,** near Green River, Ky., is the largest in the world.

**Man in the Moon, The,** is the man who picked up sticks on the Sabbath. *Numbers*, xv. 32-36; another legend says he is Cain.

**Man of Destiny, The.** Napoleon Bonaparte.

**Man of Iron. The.** Bismarck.

**Man of Straw.** An irresponsible person. Professional false witnesses or givers of "straw bail" in the English courts are said to have worn a straw in their shoes as a professional sign.

**Mare's Nest, To find a.** To find something which seems of importance, but doesn't amount to anything. The nightmare was thought to be a vampire which guarded treasures in its secret nest.

**Marriage à la Mode.** ("Fashionable Marriage.") A series of six satirical pictures by William Hogarth.

**Marseillaise.** A famous French Revolutionary song, now the French national air. Composed by Rouget de Lisle.

**Martinet.** A rigid disciplinarian, so called from M. de Martinet, a French infantry tactician in the 17th century.

**Mason and Dixon's Line.** So called because run by two English surveyors, Charles Mason and Jeremiah Dixon, 1763-1767. It was 39° 43′ 26″ north latitude, being the northern boundary of the then Slave States, dividing Pennsylvania from Maryland and Virginia.

**Mausoleum.** The marble monument built by Artemisia, queen of Caria, to her husband. Mausolus; one of the seven wonders of the world.

**Mayfair.** An aristocratic region in London.

**Mayflower, The.** The vessel in which the founders of the Plymouth Colony, in Mass., sailed from Southampton, England, in 1620.

**Medicine, The Father of.** Hippocrates of Cos.

**Merlin.** A celebrated enchanter in the Arthurian legends.

**Mermaid.** A sea nymph with a fish's tail.

**Merry Andrew.** A buffoon; so called from Andrew Borde, the eccentric physician of Henry VIII.

**Merry England.** A common designation of England; in the old sense of the word *merry*, meaning *pleasant, agreeable*.

**Merry Monarch, The.** Charles II. of England.

**Mesmerism,** is named after the German physician, Mesmer.

**Mezzo-Relievo.** (Middle Relief.) Figures cut in stone, etc., which project from the tablet more than figures in Basso-Relievo, and less than figures in Alto-Relievo.

**Middle Ages, The.** The period between the destruction of the Roman Empire and the revival of learning in Italy, from 476-1500.

**Middle States, The.** New York, Pennsylvania, New Jersey, and Delaware.

**Minnesingers.** (Love-singers.) The German lyric poets of the 12th and 13th centuries.

**Miserere** (Pity.) The 51st psalm; a penitential psalm.

**Mississippi Bubble, The.** See South Sea Scheme.

**Missouri Compromise, The,** prohibited slavery north of 36° 30′ north.

**Mistress of the Seas.** England.

**Molly Maguires.** A secret society in the United States; many crimes were attributed to it, especially in Pennsylvania, in the coal regions of which State it is still active.

**Monarque, Le Grand.** (The Great Monarch.) Louis XIV. of France.

**Monroe Doctrine.** The United States is not to meddle in European affairs, nor to allow European governments to meddle in the affairs of the American continent. European forms of government not to be permitted in North America. This doctrine really belongs, not to President Monroe, but to Adams, his Secretary of State.

**Mont de Pieté** ("Mountain of Piety"). A pawnbroker's shop; in particular the famous Paris pawnbroking establishment.

**Montmartre.** A Parisian cemetery.

**Monumental City, The.** Baltimore, Md., so called from the number of its public monuments.

**Morey Letter, The.** A forged letter (1880) attributing anti-Chinese sentiments to Gen. Garfield.

**Morganatic Marriage.** The marriage of a person of high rank to a woman of inferior rank, who does not take her husband's title.

**Mother of Presidents.** Virginia; six Virginians have been President of the United States.

**Mother Carey's Chickens.** Stormy petrels. Mother Carey is said to be *Mater Cara* ("Dear Mother"), *i. e.*, The Virgin Mary.

**Mother Goose,** nursery rhymer, lived in Boston; sang her rhymes to her grandson, Thomas Fleet, who printed them in 1719.

**Mount Vernon.** The home of Washington in Virginia.

**Muscular Christianity.** Healthy religion, "a sound mind in a sound body." The phrase originated with Charles Kingsley.

**Music of the Spheres.** According to Plato each planet has a siren who sings a song harmonizing with the motion of her own planet, and also with the other planets.

**Namby-Pamby.** Wishy-washy, childish. A name given by Pope to certain verses written by Ambrose Philips for the children of Lord Carteret; a babyish way of pronouncing Ambry (Ambrose) and Philips.

**Nantes, Edict of.** Issued at Nantes, France, in 1598, by Henry IV., granting toleration to the Protestant religion; repealed by Louis XIV. in 1685.

**Nation of Shopkeepers.** The English; so called by Napoleon I.

**Natural Bridge, The.** A natural arch 200 feet high spanning Cedar Creek, near James River, Virginia.

**Newgate.** The oldest of the London prisons.

**New World.** The Americas.

**Nibelungen-Lied.** A German epic poem of the 13th century.

**Nightmare of Europe, The.** Napoleon Bonaparte.

**Nine Worthies, The.** David, Joshua, Judas Maccabæus, Alexander, Hector, Julius Cæsar, Arthur, Charlemagne, and Godfrey of Bouillon.

**Noctes Ambrosianae.** (Ambrosian nights.) The title of a

celebrated work by Prof. Wilson ("Christopher North"). Lockhart and Wilson used to frequent Ambrose's, an Edinburgh tavern.

**Noel**. Christmas-day. From *nouvelles* (news).

**Nonconformists**. Dissenters from the Church of England. Originally applied to the 2,000 clergymen who left that Church in 1662, because they would not conform with the Act of Uniformity.

**Northern Giant, The**. Russia.

**Nôtre Dame**. The cathedral of Paris.

**Odyssey**. Homer's narrative poem dealing with the adventures of Odysseus (Ulysses) on his voyage from Troy to Ithaca.

**Ogres**. Giants who devour human flesh. Said to come from the Ogurs, a fierce Asiatic tribe.

**Oi Polloi**. (Hoi Polloi.) The many. The mob.

**Old Abe**. Abraham Lincoln.

**Old Bailey**. A famous London criminal court.

**Old Dominion, The**. Virginia.

**Old Guard, The**. Favorite regiment of Napoleon I. The supporters of Gen. Grant for the Presidency at the Chicago Convention of 1880.

**Old Hickory**. A nickname of Andrew Jackson.

**Old Probabilities**. A nickname for the U S. signal service.

**Old Public Functionary**. President James Buchanan.

**Old South, The**. A famous church in Boston, Mass., connected with many events in the Revolution.

**Orangeman**. A Protestant Irishman; from the Protestants espousing the cause of William of Orange (William III. of England).

**Orange Peel**. Sir Robert Peel, from his anti-Catholic policy.

**Ordinance of 1787**. Passed in 1787; fixes the government of the Northwest Territory of the U. S.

**Orlando Furioso**. An Italian epic poem by Ariosto.

**Ossian**. Son of Fingal, a Scotch bard. James McPherson, published in 1760 *Ossian's Poems*, which he pretended to have translated from Erse manuscripts. The work, however, is McPherson's own, the pretended MSS. never having existed.

**Ostend Manifesto**. Issued during Pierce's administration by Buchanan, Mason, and Soulé, U. S. Ministers to England, France, and Spain respectively, declaring that Cuba must belong to the United States.

**Ostracism**, comes from the Greek *ostrakon*, an oyster shell. The Athenians expelled every dangerous public man against whom a sufficient number of votes (inscribed on oyster shells) could be cast.

**Palimpsest**. A parchment in which the original writing has been rubbed out, and a new writing substituted.

**Pall Mall**. (Pell Mell.) A street in London famous for its clubs.

**Palladium**. An object that insures protection. The Palladium of Troy was a statue of Pallas, believed to have fallen from Heaven.

**Pantheon**. A circular building in Rome built in the time of Augustus; now a church called the Rotonda.

**Paradise Lost**. Milton's great epic, treating of the fall of man.

**Paradise Regained**, by Milton, treats of the temptation and triumph of Jesus.

**Paris of America**. Cincinnati.

**Parthenon**. A celebrated temple of Athena (Minerva) on the Acropolis, Athens; the noblest specimen of Doric architecture.

**Partington, Mrs**. Famed for her misuse of words. The invention of the American, B. P. Shillaber.

**Pasquinade**. A sarcastic political squib; so called from Pasquino, a sarcastic tailor. An antique statue opposite Pasquino's house in Rome is called Pasquino, and political squibs are affixed to it.

**Peeler**. A policeman. So called from Sir Robert Peel, the founder of the Irish constabulary.

**Peninsular War**. The war of the English against France in Spain and Portugal, 1808–1812.

**People's William**. A nickname of William E. Gladstone.

**Père-la-Chaise**. A famous cemetery near Paris.

**Philippic**. A severe invective; so called from the orations of Demosthenes against Philip of Macedon.

**Philistine**. Narrow-minded person; in common use in the German Universities to designate tradesmen, etc.

**Philosopher's Stone, The**. A substance for which the alchemists were always searching; it was to turn the other metals into gold.

**Pleiad, The French**. Seven 16th-century poets, viz: Ronsard, Joachim du Bellay, Remi-Belleau, Jodelle, Baïf, Pontus de Thiard, Dorat.

**Plon Plon**. A nickname of Prince Napoleon J. C. Bonaparte.

**Plumed Knight, The**. Nickname of J. G. Blaine, American statesman.

**Plymouth Rock**. A rock at Plymouth, Mass., where the Pilgrims are thought to have landed in 1620.

**Poet's Corner**. A corner in Westminster Abbey where Chaucer, Spenser, and other poets are buried. Poetical column of newspapers.

**Pons Asinorum**. (The bridge of asses.) The 5th proposition of the 1st Book of Euclid's Geometry; difficult to dunces.

**Poor Richard**. Benjamin Franklin.

**Porkopolis**. The nickname of Cincinnati.

**Prater, The**. The fashionable promenade of Vienna, Austria.

**Phœnix**. A fabulous bird, said to live 500 years, when it burns itself on a nest of spices, and renews its life 500 years more.

**Pied Piper of Hamelin, The**. He was offered a reward to drive out the rats and mice from Hamelin in Westphalia; which he did by drawing them into the river by the sound of his pipe. The authorities refusing to pay him the reward, he piped the children of the town into Koppelberg Hill, where 130 of them died.

**Pigeon English**. English, Chinese, and Portuguese mixed; used in business affairs in China.

**Pre-Raphaelites**. A name given to the English school of artists, comprising Hunt, Millais, etc.

**Protestant Duke, The**. The Duke of Monmouth, natural son of Charles II. of England.

**Puke**. Nickname of a Missourian.

**Pyramids**. A number of remarkable ancient buildings in Egypt. The most famous are at Gheezeh.

**Quaker City, The**. Philadelphia, Pa.

**Quaker Poet, The**. John G. Whittier.

**Quartier Latin** (The Latin Quarter.) A region in Paris south of the Seine, whose population consists largely of students.

**Queen of the Antilles**. The island of Cuba.

**Railway King, The**. George Hudson, an Englishman, who made an immense fortune out of railway speculations.

**Red Letter Day**. A fortunate day. In old calendars the saints days were marked by a red letter.

**Ranz des Vaches**. The tunes played by the Swiss mountaineers on their horns while driving their cattle to pasture.

**Rebellion, The Great**. The war between Charles I. of England and Parliament.

**Rebellion, War of the**. The civil war of the United States between the Southern and Northern States, 1861-1865.

**Red Tape**. Official routine. Law papers are tied with red tape.

**Reign of Terror**. The time in the French Revolution from the overthrow of the Girondists, May 31, 1793, to the overthrow of Robespierre, July 27, 1794.

**Reynard, the Fox**. A beast epic of the 14th century.

**Rialto, The**. A bridge over the Grand Canal, Venice.

**Rights, Declaration of**. An instrument drawn up after the English Revolution of 1689, and accepted by William and Mary. It summarizes the leading points of the English Constitution. Annual parliaments, trial by jury, free elections, and the right of petition are secured. The crown is not to keep a standing army or to levy taxes.

**Roast, To rule the**. To be at the head. Roast means *council*. (German *rath*.)

**Robert the Devil** (*le Diable*). First Duke of Normandy; called the Devil on account of his crimes.

**Robin Goodfellow**. A mischievous domestic spirit.

**Roland, (A) for an Oliver**. Tit for tat. Roland and Oliver, two of Charlemagne's peers, fought five days without gaining the slightest advantage over each other.

**Romantic School**. A term applied to a number of German poets and painters in the beginning of this century. They aimed at a truly national German literature, independent of French influence.

**Romantic School**, in France, the poets and dramatists, of whom Victor Hugo is now (1882) the last survivor. They aimed at the natural in distinction from the classical. *i. e.*, conventional.

**Roscius, The British**. David Garrick.

**Rough and Ready**. General Zachary Taylor.

**Round Robin.** Petition with signatures in a circular form.

**Round Table**, in the Arthurian legends, was made by Merlin; Arthur's 150 knights of the Round Table had seats at it.

**Roundheads.** The Puritans, who wore short hair.

**Royal Martyr, The.** Charles I. of England.

**Royal Society, The.** A society for the advancement of natural science, founded at London in 1645.

**Rozinante.** The horse of Don Quixote; hence a miserable nag.

**Rubicon, To pass the.** To take an irretrievable step. The Rubicon separated Italy from Cisalpine Gaul, Cæsar's province. When he crossed he became an enemy of the Republic.

**Rule Britannia.** An English song, the words of which are by Thomson, author of *The Seasons*, and the music is by Dr. Arne.

**Rump Parliament.** What was left of Parliament in 1648, after Cromwell had imprisoned and driven out the others for refusing to condemn Charles I.

**Rye House Plot.** A conspiracy in 1683 to assassinate Charles II. and the Duke of York. The conspirators met at Rye House Farm.

**Sabbath Day's Journey.** About one mile. See *Exodus* xvi. 29.

**Sack. To get the sack**; to be discharged. When the Sultan wants to get rid of one of his harem, he puts her in a sack, which is thrown into the Bosphorus.

**Sadducees.** Jewish sect disbelieving the resurrection of the dead.

**Sagas.** Scandinavian books containing the Northern mythology.

**Sailor King, The.** William IV., of England, entered the navy 1779.

**Saint Bartholomew, Massacre of.** Massacre of the French Huguenots, in the reign of Charles IX., on St. Bartholomew's Day, Aug. 24–25, 1572.

**Saint Cloud.** Once a famous French palace near the Seine; destroyed in the Franco-Prussian war.

**Saint James, The Court of.** The English Court; so called from the palace of St. James, formerly a royal residence in London.

**St. Mark's.** The famous cathedral of Venice, Italy.

**Saint Paul's.** The cathedral of London; designed by Wren.

**Saint Peter's.** The metropolitan church of Rome; the most splendid in the world. Area, 240,000 square feet.

**Saint Sophia.** A mosque in Constantinople, Turkey; the finest of Mohammedan temples.

**Saint Stephen's.** A famous Gothic cathedral at Vienna, Austria.

**Salt River.** Oblivion, ruin. *Gone up Salt River*; forgotten.

**Sambo.** A general nickname for a colored man; the colored race.

**Sanctum.** (Holy.) One's private room or office, as an editor's *sanctum*. The *Sanctum Sanctorum* (holy of holies) in the Jewish Temple was inaccessible to any one but the high priest.

**Sandwich.** A piece of meat between two pieces of bread. The English Earl of Sandwich used to take that form of refreshment.

**Sang Bleu.** (Blue blood.) High, aristocratic descent.

**Sanhedrim.** The Jewish court of seventy elders.

**Sans Culottes.** (Without trousers.) A nickname given by the Royalists to the French Revolutionists.

**Sans Souci.** Palace of Frederick the Great, at Potsdam, near Berlin.

**Santa Croce.** (Holy Cross.) A church in Florence, Italy; the burial-place of Michael Angelo, Galileo, Machiavelli, etc.

**Satanic School.** A name sometimes applied to some modern writers, supposed to entertain irreligious ideas, such as Byron, Shelley, Victor Hugo, Swinburne, Rousseau, George Sand.

**Saturnalia.** A period of disorder and debauch. The Romans kept the Saturnalia, or feast of Saturn, Dec. 17, 18, and 19.

**Schoolmen.** The mediæval theologians, whose lectures were delivered in the cathedral *schools*.

**Scotland Yard.** The headquarters of the London police.

**Scourge of God, The.** Atilla, king of the Huns.

**Scratch, Old.** The Devil; from Scrat, a Northern familiar demon.

**Scylla.** *Avoiding Scylla, he fell into Charybdis.* In trying to avoid one danger he fell into another. Scylla and Charybdis were two opposite rocks in the Straits of Messina, Italy.

**Sea-girt Isle. The.** England, which is surrounded by the ocean.

**Secessia.** Nickname of the *seceding* Southern States, 1861–1865.

**Secular Games.** The games held by the Romans once in a century

**Seltzer Water.** Water from the Lower Selters, Germany.

**Semiramis of the North.** Catherine II., Empress of Russia.

**September Massacres.** The massacre of the French Royalist prisoners in Paris, Sept. 2, 3, and 4, 1792. About 8,000 were killed.

**Septuagint.** A Greek version of the Old Testament; so called because there were 70 (*septuaginta*) revisers. (There were really 72.)

**Seven-hilled City, The.** Rome, which was built on seven hills.

**Seven Wonders of the World.** The Pyramids of Egypt; the Temple of Diana at Ephesus; the Hanging Gardens of Babylon; the Colossus at Rhodes; the Mausoleum at Halicarnassus; the statue of Zeus, by Phidias, at Olympia; and the Pharos (lighthouse) of Alexandria in Egypt.

**Seven Years' War.** The war of Frederick the Great against Austria, France, and Russia, 1756–1763.

**Shamrock.** The national emblem of Ireland, because St. Patrick proved with it the doctrine of the Trinity.

**Shibboleth.** The password of a secret society; a countersign. When the Ephraimites, who had been routed by Jephthah, tried to pass the Jordan, they were made to pronounce the word *Shibboleth*; they pronounced it *Sibboleth*, and were thus detected.

**Sick Man, The.** The Ottoman Empire; so called by the Czar Nicholas of Russia.

**Sinews of War, The.** Money, which hires men to fight.

**Single-Speech Hamilton.** W. G. Hamilton, an English statesman of the 18th century, never made but one speech; the one he did make was surprisingly eloquent.

**Six Hundred, Charge of the.** A charge on the Russians by the British light cavalry, 670 strong, at the battle of Balaclava, Oct. 25, 1854. Result of a mistake as to orders. See Tennyson's poem.

**Sleeping Beauty, The,** was shut by enchantment in a castle; after a sleep of 100 years, she is rescued by and marries a young prince.

**Smell of the Lamp.** A too labored literary work. Pytheas first applied the phrase to the orations of Demosthenes, who studied constantly in a cave lighted by a lamp.

**Song of Roland.** An old French epic recounting the deaths of Oliver and Roland at Roncesvalles.

**Sorbonne, The.** A Parisian university founded in the 13th century by Robert de Sorbonne. Once famous for theological discussions.

**Sortes Biblicae.** Telling one's fortune by consulting the Bible. The first passage touched at random by the finger is the decisive passage.

**South Kensington Museum.** A collection of works of art, manufactures, etc., in London.

**South Sea Bubble, The.** About 1710 a company was formed in England to pay the national debt, taking in return the sole privilege of trading in the South Seas. The scheme collapsed (about 1720), ruining thousands of persons.

**Spanish Main.** The northern coast of South America.

**Sphinx.** A monument near Cairo, Egypt; half woman, half lion; an emblem of silence and mystery.

**Stabat Mater.** A famous Latin hymn on the crucifixion.

**Stalwart.** A follower of the Republican party in the United States, who firmly adheres to the principles, methods and rules of his party. In contradistinction to the "Half-Breeds," applied to Republicans unwilling to be dictated to by the so-called "Machine," meaning the political organization controlled by party leaders.

**Star Chamber.** A former English civil and criminal court with jurisdiction over offences whose punishment was not provided for by law.

**"Stonewall" Jackson.** Gen. Thomas J. Jackson, a famous Confederate general in the late civil war of the United States.

**Strasburg Cathedral.** At Strasburg; one of the noblest works of Gothic architecture; 468 ft. high; containing a wonderful clock.

**Swedish Nightingale.** Jenny Lind (Mme. Goldschmidt).

**Tabooed.** Prohibited; from a Polynesian word meaning consecrated, devoted. Applied to anything out of date or in bad taste.

**Tammany Hall.** A section of the Democratic party in New York City; Tammany Hall is the building where they meet.

**Tammany Ring** (also called the Tweed Ring, and, generally, the Ring). A corrupt set of New York City officials who stole large sums from the city. They were exposed in 1871.

**Tammany, St.** The patron saint of the Democratic party in New York. He was an Indian chief; how made a saint, does not appear. The principal officer of the Tammany Society is called Grand Sachem.

**Tapis, On the.** On the carpet; proposed, in discussion. So called from the tapis or cloth on the council table, or speaker's table, on which motions, bills, etc., are laid.

**Temple Bar,** in London, was a stone house above which the heads of traitors were formerly exposed. It was removed in 1878.

**Termagant.** A shrew; originally the name of a Saracen god. The word was formerly applied to both sexes.

**Terra Firma.** Dry land as distinguished from water.

**Tertium Quid.** A third person or party that shall be nameless.

**Théâtre Français.** A theatre in Paris devoted to the production of the classic and the best modern French drama. Celebrated for the excellence of its company of actors.

**Thelème, Abbey of.** The abbey founded by Gargantua in Rabelais' *Gargantua.* Its motto was "Do as you please."

**Thirty Years' War, The,** was between the Catholics and Protestants, in Germany, 1618–1648.

**Thistle.** The national emblem of Scotland. According to tradition, the Danes were attempting to surprise an encampment of the Scotch one night, and had come very near it without being observed. A Dane trod on a thistle, cried out with pain, and the Scotch were aroused, and defeated their assailants, whereupon the thistle was made the insignia of Scotland.

**Thor,** in Scandinavian mythology, is the god of war, son of Odin.

**Threadneedle Street, The Old Lady of.** The Bank of England in Threadneedle Street, London.

**Three Estates of the Realm.** The nobility, the clergy, and the commonalty, represented in the two Houses of Parliament.

**Thunderer, The.** A nickname given to the London *Times.*

**Tick, On.** On credit; for *on ticket.* Ticket was formerly used for a promissory note.

**Tit for Tat.** An equivalent. Said to be the Dutch *dit vor dat,* this for that.

**Tom Thumb.** The famous American dwarf, Stratton.

**Tory.** The name of the great English party whose place is to a certain extent taken by the Conservatives. Said to come from *toruigh,* a robber. Whig and Tory were originally terms of reproach.

**Tour, The Grand.** From England through France, Switzerland, Italy, to Germany and home. All aristocratic families used to send their sons on the grand tour.

**Tower, The.** The citadel of London, on the Thames.

**Transfiguration, The.** The most famous of Raphael's pictures, now in the Vatican. Represents the miraculous change of Christ on the mount.

**Trimmer.** A person who takes a moderate course in politics. First applied as a term of reproach to the great Halifax, who was not violently attached to any political party.

**Trinity Church.** A famous Episcopal church on Broadway, at the head of Wall Street, New York City. The richest church in America.

**Triple Alliance, The.** The alliance of Great Britain, Holland, and Sweden, in 1668, against Louis XIV. of France.

**Troubadours.** Provençal poets, from the 11th to the 14th century.

**Trouvères.** Northern French poets, 1100–1400.

**Trumpet. To sound one's own trumpet,** *i. e.,* to boast. The coming of the knights into the list used to be announced by the heralds with a flourish of trumpets.

**Tuft-hunter.** A toady. At Oxford University a nobleman is called a *tuft,* because of the gold tuft on his college cap.

**Tuileries.** A French royal palace, burned by the Commune in 1871.

**Tulip Mania.** A 17th-century European craze for buying tulip bulbs. Holland was the great seat of it.

**Tune that the old cow died of.** Words instead of alms. In the old song, a man who has nothing on which to feed his cow plays her this tune, "Consider, good cow, consider, This isn't the time for grass to grow." Also applied to inharmonious tunes.

**Tyburn.** Once a London place of execution. The site is now occupied by Grosvenor Square and Portman Square, and called Tyburnia, a wealthy and fashionable quarter.

**Uffizi.** A building in Florence containing a celebrated art collection.

**Ultramontanes.** The extreme "high" Roman Catholics. The word, which means "beyond the mountains," was first used in France of those Catholics who ascribe everything to the Pope "beyond the Alps," in contradistinction to the Gallicans who insist upon a self-governing national church.

**Underground Railroad.** A phrase which expressed all the means used to further the escape of runaway slaves in America.

**Under the Rose.** (Sub rosa.) Confidentially. The rose was considered by the ancients an emblem of secrecy.

**Unknown, The Great.** First applied to Sir Walter Scott; so called on account of the anonymous publication of the Waverley novels.

**Unlicked Cub.** An awkward, ill-bred boy. The bear cub was said to be out of shape till its dam licked it into shape.

**Unter den Linden.** (Under the Linden.) A famous street in Berlin, Prussia; it has four rows of lime trees.

**Unwashed, The Great.** The mob; first used by Edmund Burke.

**Upas Tree.** An object that exerts a hurtful influence. There was a tradition that a noisome river rose in a upas tree in Java, the vapor of which was a deadly poison.

**Upper Ten Thousand.** The aristocracy; fashionable society. A phrase first used by N. P. Willis.

**Utilitarians.** Those who believe that utility, *i. e.* the fitness of a thing to promote human happiness, is the proper standard of morality.

**Utopia.** (No place.) The imaginary island which Sir Thomas More makes the scene of his romance of *Utopia;* an ideal commonwealth. Hence the adjective *Utopian, i. e.* visionary, impracticable.

**Valhalla.** In Scandinavian mythology, the palace where dwell the heroes slain in battle.

**Vampire.** An extortioner. The vampire is a dead man who returns to life in the night, and sucks the blood of persons asleep.

**Vatican.** The palace of the Popes, on the bank of the Tiber, Rome.

**Vatican, Council of the.** The Œcumenical Council which met in 1869, and promulgated the doctrine of Papal Infallibility.

**Vedas.** The four sacred books of the Hindu religion.

**Veni, Vidi, Vici.** ("I came, I saw, I conquered.") The phrase with which Julius Cæsar announced his victory at Zela.

**Venus de' Medici.** A celebrated Greek statue at Florence; attributed to Cleomenes, a sculptor of the 2d century B.C.

**Venus of Milo.** Considered the most beautiful of Greek statues; found in the Island of Melos in 1820. It is now in the Louvre.

**Verbum Sap.** A word to the wise; for *verbum sapienti.*

**Veronica.** A relic at St. Peter's, Rome, said to be the handkerchief on which Jesus wiped his brow on his way to Calvary. It is said to contain the true likeness (Vera icon) of our Saviour.

**Versailles.** A splendid palace at Versailles, 10 miles from Paris.

**Vespers, The Sicilian.** The massacre of the French in Sicily by the Sicilians, March 30, 1282. The sounding of the vesper bell was the signal for the massacre.

**Via Dolorosa.** (The way of pain.) The way by which the Lord went from the Mount of Olives to Golgotha.

**Vinegar Bible, The,** printed at Oxford, 1767, has vinegar for vineyard in the headline of Luke xxii.

**Virgin Queen, The.** Queen Elizabeth of England.

**Vitus, St.** St. Vitus' dance is so called because St. Vitus was thought to have control of hysterical complaints.

**Wabash Avenue.** A street in Chicago, noted for fine buildings.

**Wall of China, The.** A wall 1,200 miles long and 20 feet high, built by the Chinese in the 3d century B.C. as a protection against the Tartar invasions.

**Wall Street.** The great financial street of New York. Most of the bankers and brokers are on this street or in its vicinity.

**Wallack's.** A famous New York theatre, conducted by J. Lester Wallack.

**Walton. An Izaak Walton.** An angler. Izaak Walton published his *Complete Angler* in 1655.

**Wandering Jew, The.** A famous personage in mediæval legend. Our Saviour, wearied with carrying his cross, is said to have stopped before the house of one Ahasuerus, a cobbler, who pushed him off, saying, "Away with you." Jesus answered, "I go away, but thou shalt tarry till I come." Ahasuerus wandered over the world, seeking death, but condemned to live till the coming of our Lord. The Wandering Jew was seen from time to time in Europe. His last recorded appear ance was late in the 18th century, in Belgium. According to another legend, the Wandering Jew's name was Kartophilus, the doorkeeper of the Hall of Judgment. He struck our Saviour, telling him to go faster.

**War of 1812.** Between Great Britain and the United States, 1812–15.

**War of the Roses.** The English civil wars, between the houses of York and Lancaster, in the 14th and 15th centuries. The red rose was the symbol of Lancaster, the white rose of York. See Shakespeare's I. Henry VI. II. 4.

**Ward, Artemas.** Pseudonym of the American humorist, C. F. Browne.

**Washington Street.** The principal business street of Boston, Mass.

**Wassail.** An old Saxon salutation, "What, hail!" The wassail bowl is the bowl of spiced ale used on New Year's Day.

**Wat.** A hare, from his wattles, *i. e.* long ears.

**Waters, The Father of.** The Mississippi River (said to be a translation of the Indian name).

**Watling Street.** A road across Southern Britain from Dover to Cardigan; a corruption of *Vitellina Strata*, "the street of Vitellin." The Milky Way was called Watling Street by the English peasantry.

**Ways and Means, Committee of the.** A most important Committee of the American House of Representatives, charged with devising the methods by which money for the current expenses of the Government is to be supplied.

**Wedding.** The first anniversary of a wedding is called a PAPER wedding, the gifts being paper articles; the fifth, WOODEN; the tenth, TIN; the fifteenth, CRYSTAL; twenty-fifth, SILVER; fiftieth, GOLDEN; seventy-fifth, DIAMOND.

**Well of St. Keyne.** A well in Cornwall whose virtue is such that whoever of a married couple first tastes its waters will "wear the breeches" in the household.

**Westminster Abbey.** The celebrated abbey-church of London, where many of the illustrious dead of England are buried.

**Wetherell, Elizabeth.** Pseudonym of the American novelist, Miss Susan Warner, author of *The Wide, Wide World*.

**Whig.** Once the name of great political parties in England and the United States. The term is said to come from Whiggamore, a Scotch (Celtic) word for a thief, a freebooter. The Marquis of Argyle collected a troop of these thieves to oppose some measures of James I., and finally the epithet *Whig* was applied to all opponents of the Government. The Whigs at the English Revolution opposed the government of James II. The Whig party in America favored a protective tariff, and a U. S. bank. Gen. Scott was their last candidate for President (1852).

**Whistle.** TO PAY TOO DEARLY FOR THE WHISTLE. Dr. Franklin tells a story of buying a whistle, when a boy, for four times its value. Hence, something which does not equal our expectations, though costly.

**White Elephant.** Something you don't know what to do with. The king of Siam sends a white elephant to a courtier whose fortune he wishes to destroy.

**White Feather, To show the.** To display cowardice. A white feather in a bird marks a cross breed, and is not found on a game-cock.

**White House.** The residence of the President of the United States at Washington; so called from its color.

**White Stone.** A DAY TO BE MARKED WITH A WHITE STONE is a day to be pleasantly remembered. The ancient Romans marked a lucky day on the calendar with a white stone; an unlucky day with charcoal.

**Whiteboys.** A secret organization who engaged in "agrarian outrages" in Ireland in 1789; so called from wearing white shirts.

**Whitehall.** A region in Westminster, London, where the royal palace formerly stood.

**Wild Huntsman, The.** In German legend a spectral huntsman in the Black Forest. The English name is "Herne the Hunter."

**Windmills, To fight with.** To oppose imaginary objects; to fight with crotchets. The phrase comes from Don Quixote's adventure in assailing windmills, which he mistook for giants.

**Windsor Castle.** Famous royal castle and residence near London.

**Wise Men of the East, The.** The three Magi who were guided by the star of Bethlehem to our Saviour's birthplace.

**Witch of Endor, The.** A soothsayer who, at the request of Saul, invoked the ghost of Samuel, who foretold the death of Saul.

**Witch-Hazel.** A forked hazel twig used for finding witches; still in use to find a suitable place for digging a well.

**Witches' Sabbath.** The nightly meeting of witches and demons.

**Wooden Horse, The.** After the death of Hector, the Greeks besieging Troy built a gigantic wooden horse, pretending that it was an offering to the gods to insure a safe return to Greece. The horse was filled with Greek warriors; the Trojans dragged it into the city, and at night the Greeks came out of the horse, opened the city gates to their companions, and sacked the town.

**Woolsack, To sit on the.** To be Lord Chancellor of England. His seat in the House of Lords is called the *woolsack*, an armless, backless bag of wool.

**Wyoming Massacre.** A band of British and Indians ravaged the valley of Wyoming in 1778.

**Xanthos.** The horse of Achilles in the Trojan war; like Balaam's ass, prophetic.

**Xantippe.** A shrew. She was the wife of Socrates, and an intolerable scold.

**Yahoo.** A rowdy; a brutal, ill-bred man. The Yahoos in Swift's *Gulliver's Travels* are brutes with the shape of men.

**Yankee.** An American. The word is used in America itself as a nickname of persons born in the New England States. The usual account of the introduction of the word is this: Jonathan Hastings, a Cambridge, Mass., farmer, in the 18th century, used it as an epithet denoting excellence, as "Yankee cider," *i. e.* good, home-made cider. The word was taken up by the students of Harvard College, and gradually spread through the country. This is doubtful. The word is probably a corrupted Indian form of English.

**Yankee Doodle.** An American national air.

**Yarmouth Bloater.** A red herring. Yarmouth, England, is noted for them.

**Yellow Jack.** A cant term for the yellow fever. The Yellow Jack is the flag over vessels in quarantine, marine hospitals, etc.

**Yggdrasil.** In Scandinavian mythology, an ash-tree, whose roots run to heaven, to the under-world, and to the Frost Giants. The serpent Nithöggr gnaws its roots.

**Young America.** American boys and girls; the younger generation, supposed to be very irreverent.

**Young Chevalier.** Charles Edward Stuart, the second or young Pretender to the throne of Great Britain (1720–88).

**Young Germany.** The literary school of Heinrich Heine, and his followers.

**Yosemite Valley,** in California, famous for its natural scenery; also a well-known picture by the American artist, Bierstadt.

**Yule.** Christmas. The "turn" of the sun at the winter solstice.

**Yule-log.** An immense log of wood put across the fire on the hearth at Christmas.

**Zend Avesta.** The old Persian scriptures. It is written in the Zend language. Avesta means "the living word."

**Zodiac.** An imaginary belt in the heavens, divided into 12 equal parts of 30 degrees each, with a sign for each part. The six signs north of the equator are: *Aries*, "the ram;" *Taurus*, "the bull;" *Gemini*, "the twins;" *Cancer*, "the crab;" *Leo*, "the lion;" *Virgo*, "the virgin." The six signs south of the equator are: *Libra*, "the balance;" *Scorpio*, "the scorpion;" *Sagittarius*, "the archer;" *Capricornus*, "the goat;" *Aquarius*, "the water-carrier," and *Pisces*, "the fishes." The first six are summer signs, the next three autumn signs, the last three winter signs.

**Zollverein.** A commercial association between the German States to maintain the same tariff rates.

WHEN LITTLE BIRDS HAVE WINGS, 'TIS BEST
THEY SOON SHOULD LEARN TO FLY;
THE PARENTS PERCHED ABOVE THE NEST
ARE COAXING THEM TO TRY.

BUT WHEN AT NIGHT THEIR WINGS ARE FURLED,
AND BIRDIES CEASE TO ROAM,
THE SWEETEST SPOT IN ALL THE WORLD
IS EVER "HOME! SWEET HOME!"

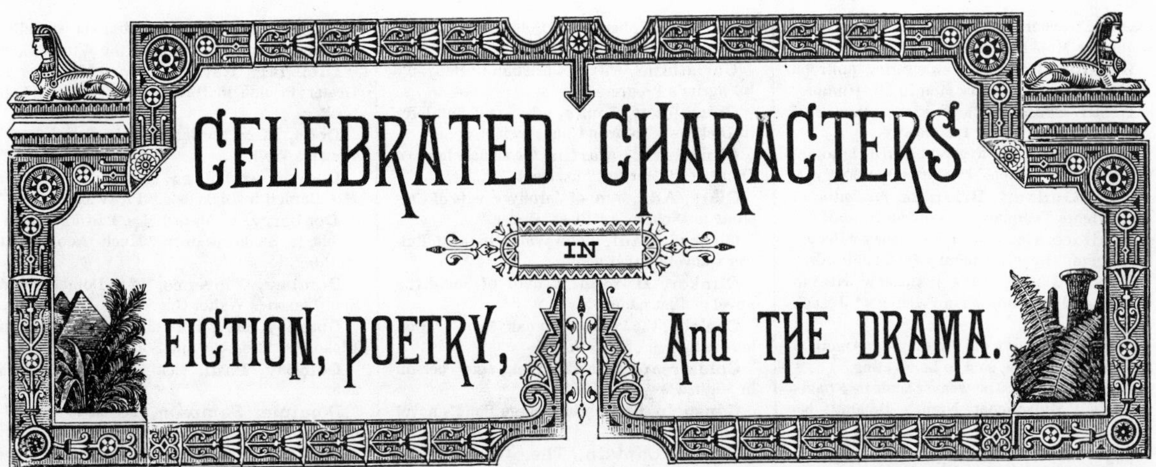


**Abdiel,** the angel who opposed Satan, and remained faithful when he revolted.

**Abigail,** a common name for a waiting-maid. See I. Sam. xxv. 3.

**Ablewhite, Godfrey,** a sneak in Wilkie Collins's "The Moonstone."

**Abon Hassan,** a character in the "Arabian Nights," who is duped for a short time into believing himself Caliph.

**Absalom,** in Dryden's "Absalom and Achitophel;" the Duke of Monmouth, natural son of Charles II.

**Absolute, Captain,** a gallant, high-spirited character in Sheridan's "The Rivals."

**Absolute, Sir Anthony,** father of the above, an irascible but generous character in "The Rivals."

**Achitophel,** the Earl of Shaftesbury in Dryden's "Absalom and Achitophel."

**Acres, Bob,** whose "courage oozes out at his fingers' ends," a character in "The Rivals."

**Acrasia,** in Spenser's "Faëry Queen," a witch, the personification of Intemperance.

**Adam Bell,** a famous archer, celebrated in many old ballads.

**Adams, Parson,** a learned, good, eccentric, simple divine in Fielding's "Joseph Andrews."

**Adriana,** the wife of Antipholus, in "Comedy of Errors."

**Ague-cheek, Sir Andrew,** a foolish knight in Shakespeare's "Twelfth Night."

**Aladdin,** the hero of the "Arabian Nights" tales, possessed of a wonderful ring and lamp.

**Allworthy, Squire,** a benevolent character in Fielding's "Tom Jones."

**Alp,** the hero of Byron's "Siege of Corinth"

**Amadis de Gaul,** the hero of a widespread romance of Portuguese origin.

**Amelia,** the heroine of Fielding's novel of that name. Drawn from Fielding's wife.

**Amine,** a wicked woman in the "Arabian Nights," who leads her three sisters as hounds in a leash.

**Amlet, Richard,** a gambler in Vanbrugh's "Confederacy."

**Amri,** in Dryden's "Absalom and Achitophel," Sir H. Finch.

**Andrews, Joseph,** the hero of Fielding's novel of that name; brave and pure.

**Anerley, Mary,** the heroine of Blackmore's novel of that name.

**Apemantus,** a cynic in Shakespeare's "Timon of Athens."

**Arden, Enoch,** the hero of Tennyson's poem of that name.

**Argante,** a giantess in Spenser's "Faëry Queen."

**Ariel,** a spirit in Shakespeare's "Tempest."

**Artful Dodger,** a bright young thief in Dickens's "Oliver Twist."

**Arthur, King,** a legendary British king, famous in romance, celebrated by Tennyson.

**Ashton, Lucy,** the heroine of Scott's "Bride of Lammermoor."

**Atalanta,** one of Diana's maids, skilled as an archer, the heroine of Swinburne's "Atalanta in Calydon."

**Athelstane, The Unready,** a Saxon thane in Scott's "Ivanhoe."

**Autolycus,** "a snapper up of unconsidered trifles," in Shakespeare's "The Winter's Tale."

**Baba, Ali,** a character in the "Arabian Nights," who, having overheard "sesame," the password of the Forty Thieves, opens their cave.

**Baba, Cassim,** brother of the above, forgets the password.

**Backbite, Sir Benjamin,** a slanderous character in Sheridan's "School for Scandal."

**Bagstock, Joe,** a pompous, boastful character in Dickens's "Dombey and Son." He always speaks of himself in the third person, as "Joey B.," "J. B.," "Old Joey," "Josh," etc.

**Bailey, Young,** a precocious youth, servant, etc., in Dickens's "Martin Chuzzlewit."

**Balderstone, Caleb,** the Master of Ravenswood's butler, in Scott's "Bride of Lammermoor."

**Balthazar,** a merchant in Shakespeare's "Comedy of Errors."

**Balthazar,** a servant in Shakespeare's "Much Ado About Nothing."

**Banquo,** a chieftain in Shakespeare's "Macbeth," murdered by Macbeth.

**Bardell, Mrs.,** a widow who sues Mr. Pickwick for breach of promise in Dickens's "Pickwick Papers."

**Bardolph,** a red-nosed follower of Falstaff in Shakespeare's "Henry IV."

**Barkis,** an eccentric character in Dickens's "David Copperfield;" his form of proposal was, "Barkis is willin'."

**Bath, Major,** a pompous person in Fielding's "Amelia."

**Bayes,** the hero of the Duke of Buckingham's play of "The Rehearsal," a satire upon the poet Dryden.

**Baynes, Charlotte,** Philip's sweetheart in Thackeray's "Philip."

**Bede, Adam,** the hero of George Eliot's novel of that name.

**Belch, Sir Toby,** the bibulous uncle of Olivia in Shakespeare's "Twelfth Night."

**Belford,** the friend of Lovelace in Richardson's "Clarissa Harlowe."

**Belinda,** the heroine of Pope's "Rape of the Lock."

**Bell, Laura,** finally marries Arthur in Thackeray's "Pendennis."

**Bell, Peter,** the hero of Wordsworth's poem of that name.

**Bellaston, Lady,** a woman of gallantry in Fielding's "Tom Jones."

**Bellenden, Lady,** a Tory gentlewoman in Scott's "Old Mortality."

**Belphoebe,** in Spenser's "Faëry Queen," a portrait of Queen Elizabeth.

**Belvidera,** the heroine of Otway's "Venice Preserved."

**Benedict,** a humorous gentleman in Shakespeare's "Love's Labor Lost," finally married to Beatrice.

**Bennet, Mrs.,** a woman of gallantry in Fielding's "Amelia."

**Benvolio,** in Shakespeare's "Romeo and Juliet," the friend of Romeo, and nephew of old Montague.

**Bertram,** the hero of Shakespeare's "All's Well that Ends Well." He marries Helena.

**Bianca,** Cassio's mistress in Shakespeare's "Othello."

**Birch, Harvey,** the hero of Cooper's "Spy."

**Blifil,** a sneak in Fielding's "Tom Jones," nephew of Mr. Allworthy.

**Blimber, Miss Cornelia,** a prim and grim

classical teacher in "Dombey and Son," subsequently Mrs. Feeder, B.A.

**Bobadil, Captain**, a swaggering poltroon in Ben Jonson's "Every Man In His Humor."

**Boeuf. Front de**, a ferocious follower of King John in Scott's "Ivanhoe."

**Boffin, Noddy**, a good-natured, ignorant ex-servant in Dickens's "Our Mutual Friend."

**Bois, Guilbert, Brian de**, preceptor of the Knights Templars in Scott's "Ivanhoe."

**Boniface**, a landlord in Farquhar's "Beaux' Stratagem," hence, generally for a landlord.

**Booby, Lady**, plays Potiphar's wife to Joseph Andrews' Joseph in Fielding's "Joseph Andrews."

**Booth**, the hero of Fielding's "Amelia," husband of Amelia, said to be Fielding.

**Bottom, Nick**, the weaver-actor in Shakespeare's "Midsummer Night's Dream," beloved of Titania.

**Bounderby, Josiah**. a wealthy manufacturer and matter-of-fact man in Dickens's "Hard Times."

**Bowles, Tom**, blacksmith and manufacturer in Bulwer's "Kenelm Chillingly."

**Bowline, Tom**, a very nautical person in Smollett's "Roderick Random."

**Box and Cox**, the heroes of Morton's farce of that name.

**Bradwardine, Baron**, in Scott's "Waverley," father of Rose B.

**Bramble, Matthew**, a very dyspeptic person in Smollett's "Humphry Clinker."

**Brangtons**, vulgarians in Miss Burney's "Evelina."

**Brass, Sally** and **Sampson**, sister and brother, shysters in Dickens's "Old Curiosity Shop."

**Brick, Jefferson**, an American patriot in Dickens's "Martin Chuzzlewit."

**Bridgenorth, Major Ralph**, prominent in Scott's "Peveril of the Peak."

**Bridget, Mrs.**, a remarkable lady in Sterne's "Tristram Shandy."

**Brown, Tom**, the hero of Thomas Hughes's "Tom Brown at Oxford," etc.

**Bucket, Inspector**, the detective in Dickens's "Bleak House."

**Bumble**, the conceited beadle in Dickens's "Oliver Twist."

**Caius, Doctor**, Welsh suitor of Anne Page's in the "Merry Wives of Windsor."

**Caliban**, a monstrosity in Shakespeare's "Tempest."

**Candor, Mrs.**, a slanderer in Sheridan's "The Rivals."

**Carker**, a plausible scoundrel, managing clerk of Mr. Dombey in "Dombey and Son."

**Cassio**, Othello's lieutenant in Shakespeare's "Othello."

**Caudle, Mrs.**, scold and heroine of Douglas Jerrold's "Curtain Lectures."

**Caustic, Colonel**, satirical character in Mackenzie's "Lounger."

**Celia**, cousin of Rosaline and daughter of Frederick in Shakespeare's "As You Like It."

**Chadband**, an oily, hypocritical preacher in Dickens's "Bleak House."

**Chamont**, leading male character in Otway's "The Orphan's."

**Chillingly, Kenelm**, hero of Bulwer's novel of that name.

**Christabel**, heroine of Coleridge's poem of that name.

**Christiana**, wife of Christian in Bunyan's "Pilgrim's Progress."

**Chuzzlewit, Jonas**, miser and murderer in Dickens's "Martin Chuzzlewit."

**Chuzzlewit, Martin**, the selfish hero of Dickens's "Martin Chuzzlewit."

**Clare, Ada**, ward of Jarndyce, wife of Carstone in Dickens's "Bleak House."

**Clifford, Paul**, highwayman hero of Bulwer's novel of that name.

**Clinker, Humphry**, hero of Smollett's novel of that name.

**Coelebs**, the hero of Hannah More's "Cœlebs in Search of a Wife."

**Coldstream, Sir Charles**, *blasé* person in Mathew's "Used Up."

**Consuelo**, heroine of George Sand's novel of that name.

**Copper Captain, The**, the nickname of Perez, braggart and coward in Beaumont and Fletcher's "Rule a Wife and Have a Wife."

**Copperfield, David**, the hero of Dickens's "David Copperfield."

**Cordelia**, the youngest and faithful daughter of Lear in Shakespeare's "King Lear."

**Corinne**, heroine of Mme. de Staël's romance of that name.

**Costigan, Captain**, a bibulous and disreputable person in Thackeray's "Pendennis."

**Coverly, Sir Roger De**, country gentleman in Addison's "Spectator."

**Crane, Ichabod**, the schoolmaster in Irving's Legend of "Sleepy Hollow."

**Crawley, Rawdon**, the husband of Becky Sharpe in Thackeray's "Vanity Fair."

**Cressida**, heroine of Shakespeare's "Troilus and Cressida."

**Crummles, Vincent**, theatrical manager in Dickens's "Nicholas Nickleby."

**Crusoe, Robinson**, hero of De Foe's "Robinson Crusoe."

**Cuttle, Captain**, simple nautical person in Dickens's "Dombey and Son."

**Cymbeline**, a British King, whose name is preserved in Shakespeare's "Cymbeline."

**Dalgarno, Lord**, a profligate young Scotch nobleman in Scott's "The Fortunes of Nigel."

**Davy**, Shallow's servant in Shakespeare's "Second Part of Henry IV."

**Deans, Dovce Davie**, pious Presbyterian in Scott's "The Heart of Mid-Lothian;" father of Effie and Jeanie.

**Deans, Effie**, a betrayed woman in the same.

**Deans, Jeanie**, the heroine of the same.

**Dedlock, Lady**, proud, beautiful, and unfortunate character in Dickens's "Bleak House."

**Dedlock, Sir Leicester**, husband of the above, narrow-minded but noble.

**Delamaine, Geoffrey**, a muscular man in Wilkie Collins's "Man and Wife."

**Delphine**, heroine of Mme. de Staël's novel of that name.

**Deronda, Daniel**, the hero of George Eliot's novel of that name.

**Desdemona**, heroine of Shakespeare's "Othello," wife of Othello.

**Diddler, Jeremy**, impecunious swindler in Kinny's farce of "Raising the Wind."

**Dimsdale, Rev. Arthur**, the seducer of Hester Prynne in Hawthorne's "Scarlet Letter."

**Dods, Meg**, the landlady in Scott's "St. Ronan's Well."

**Dodson and Fogg**, shyster attornies for Mrs. Bardell in Dickens's "Pickwick Papers."

**Dogberry**, an absurd Mrs. Partington constable in Shakespeare's "Much Ado About Nothing."

**Dombey, Florence**, in "Dombey and Son," marries Walter Gay.

**Dombey, Mr.**, a proud, stern merchant in Dickens's "Dombey and Son."

**Dombey, Paul**, sickly little son of the above.

**Dominie, Sampson**, eccentric schoolmaster in Scott's "Guy Mannering."

**Don Quixote**, the hero of Cervante's romance of that name; made insane by excessive reading of the romances of chivalry.

**Dora**, David Copperfield's first and child wife in Dickens's "David Copperfield."

**Dorimant**, the fashionable hero of Etherege's "The Man of Mode."

**Dorothea**, the heroine of George Eliot's "Middlemarch."

**Dorrit, Edward**, "the father of the Marshalsea" in Dickens's "Little Dorrit."

**Drawcansir**, the bully in the Duke of Buckingham's "Rehearsal."

**Dulcinea del Toboso**, a country maid, beloved of Don Quixote.

**Dundreary, Lord**, an original in Taylor's "Our American Cousin."

**Edgar**, legitimate son of Gloucester in Shakespeare's "King Lear."

**Edmund**, natural son of Gloucester.

**Emilia**, wife of Iago in Shakespeare's "Othello."

**Escalus**, associated with Angelo in the government in Shakespeare's "Measure for Measure."

**Esmond, Beatrix**, the beautiful heroine of Thackeray's "Henry Esmond."

**Esmond, Henry**, the high-spirited and witty hero of that novel.

**Eugenia**, the beautiful but unfortunate heroine of Hardy's "Return of the Native."

**Evangeline**, heroine of Longfellow's poem of that name.

**Evans, Sir Hugh**, a Welsh parson in Shakespeare's "Merry Wives of Windsor."

**Evelina**, the heroine of Miss Burney's novel of that name.

**Eyre, Jane**, the heroine of Charlotte Brontë's novel of that name.

**Fag**, a lying servant in Sheridan's "The Rivals."

**Fagin**, Jew thief, and receiver in Dickens's "Oliver Twist."

**Faithful, Jacob**, the hero of Marryatt's novel of that name.

**Falkland**, a jealous character in Sheridan's "The Rivals."

**Falstaff, Sir John**, the greatest of Shakespeare's comic creations, in "Merry Wives of Windsor" and "Henry IV."

**Fanny**, a pretty schoolmistress, heroine of Hardy's "Under the Greenwood Tree."

**Fat Boy, The,** given to mincepies and sleep, in Dickens's "Pickwick Papers."

**Faust,** the hero of Goethe's poem of that name; sells his soul to the devil.

**Feeble,** one of Falstaff's "most forcible" recruits in Shakespeare's Henry IV.

**Felton, Septimius,** the hero of Hawthorne's romance of that name.

**Ferdinand,** son of the King, marries Miranda in Shakespeare's "Tempest."

**Ferrers, Endymion,** the hero of Disraeli's "Endymion."

**Figaro,** the sharp-witted hero of Beaumarchais' "Le Mariage de Figaro."

**Firmin, Philip,** the hero of Thackeray's "The Adventures of Philip."

**Florizel,** the Prince of Bohemia in Shakespeare's "Winter's Tale."

**Fluellen,** a pedantic Welsh captain in Shakespeare's "Henry V."

**Foker, Harry,** a good-natured, simple friend of Arthur's in Thackeray's "Pendennis."

**Fondlewife,** a vexatious old fellow in Congreve's "Old Bachelor."

**Foppington, Lord,** a weak-brained fop in Vanbrugh's "The Relapse."

**Fosco, Count,** a subtle, all-accomplished villain, in Collins's "Woman in White."

**Frankenstein,** a monstrous creation which gives its name to a romance by Mrs. Shelley.

**Friar Tuck,** the jolly and inseparable companion of Robin Hood.

**Friday,** Crusoe's servant and man in De Foe's "Robinson Crusoe."

**Gamp, Sarah,** a nurse, talkative and bibulous in Dickens's "Martin Chuzzlewit," the friend of Betsey Prig.

**Gargantua,** the hero of Rabelais' work of that name.

**Gaunt, Griffith,** husband of Kate, the nominal hero of Reade's "Griffith Gaunt."

**Gay, Walter,** nephew of Sol Gills, husband of Florence Dombey in Dickens's "Dombey and Son."

**Gibbie, Goose,** a half-witted boy in Scott's "Old Mortality."

**Gil Blas,** the hero of a celebrated novel of Spanish manners by Le Sage.

**Gills, Sol,** nautical-instrument seller in Dickens's "Dombey and Son."

**Gilpin, John,** a "London Citizen," whose ride is celebrated by Cowper.

**Ginevra,** the heroine of a poem by Samuel Rogers.

**Gobbo, Launcelot,** a merry servant in Shakespeare's "Merchant of Venice."

**Goneril,** Lear's eldest daughter in Shakespeare's "King Lear."

**Gonzalo,** an honest old counselor in Shakespeare's "Tempest."

**Gosling, Giles,** the landlord in Scott's "Kenilworth."

**Gradgrind, Jeremiah,** a lover of "facts" in Dickens's "Hard Times."

**Gradgrind, Louisa,** daughter of the above, and wife of Josiah Bounderby.

**Grandison, Sir Charles,** the elaborate hero of Richardson's novel of that name.

**Gray, Vivian,** the hero of Disraeli's novel of that name.

**Greaves, Sir Launcelot,** the hero of a novel by Smollett.

**Grundy, Mrs.,** a character in Morton's "Speed the Plough."

**Gulliver, Lemuel,** the hero of Swift's "Gulliver's Travels."

**Hamlet,** the hero of Shakespeare's tragedy of that name.

**Harley,** the hero of Mackenzie's "Man of Feeling."

**Harlowe, Clarissa,** the unfortunate heroine of Richardson's novel of that name.

**Harris, Mrs.,** a non-existent person who is constantly referred to, and whose identity is stoutly asserted by Mrs. Gamp in Dickens's "Martin Chuzzlewit."

**Headstone, Bradley,** a passionate schoolmaster in Dickens's "Our Mutual Friend."

**Heep, Uriah,** a hypocritical sneak in Dickens's "David Copperfield."

**Helena,** the heroine of Shakespeare's "All's Well that Ends Well."

**Hero,** daughter of Leonato in Shakespeare's "Much Ado About Nothing."

**Hexam, Lizzie,** in love with Wrayburn in Dickens's "Our Mutual Friend."

**Holofernes,** a pedantic schoolmaster in Shakespeare's "As You Like It."

**Holt, Felix,** the hero of George Eliot's novel of that name.

**Honeyman, Charles,** a fashionable preacher in Thackeray's "Newcomes."

**Honor, Mrs.,** Sophia Western's waiting-woman in Fielding's "Tom Jones."

**Hopeful,** a pilgrim in Bunyan's "Pilgrim's Progress."

**Horatio,** the "scholar" friend of Hamlet in Shakespeare's "Hamlet."

**Howe, Miss,** the friend of the heroine in Richardson's "Clarissa Harlowe."

**Hudibras,** the hero of Butler's poem of that name; a model Presbyterian.

**Hunter, Mr.** and **Mrs. Leo,** "lion" hunters in Dickens's "Pickwick Papers."

**Iago,** the villain in Shakespeare's "Othello."

**Imogen,** the heroine of Shakespeare's "Cymbeline."

**Isabella,** the heroine of Shakespeare's "Measure for Measure."

**Ivanhoe,** the hero of Scott's novel of that name.

**Jack, Colonel,** the hero of De Foe's novel of that name.

**Jaffier,** the hero of Otway's "Venice Preserved."

**Jaques,** a melancholy philosopher in Shakespeare's "As You Like It."

**Jarndyce, John,** a benevolent gentleman in "Bleak House."

**Javert,** a detective in Victor Hugo's "Les Miserables."

**Jessica,** daughter of Shylock in Shakespeare's "Merchant of Venice."

**Jingle, Alfred,** an adventurer in Dickens's "Pickwick Papers."

**Katherine,** a lady in attendance upon the French princess in Shakespeare's "Love's Labor Lost."

**Kilmansegg, Miss,** the heroine (with one golden leg) of Hood's "The Golden Legend."

**Kitely,** merchant and jealous husband in Ben Jonson's "Every Man in His Humor."

**Lady Bountiful,** a gentlewoman in Farquhar's "The Beaux' Stratagem."

**Laertes,** the son of Polonius in Shakespeare's "Hamlet," "killed by his own poisoned foil."

**Lafeu,** a witty old lord, attendant of the French princess, in Shakespeare's "Love's Labor Lost."

**Lalla Rookh,** the heroine of Moore's poem of that name.

**Languish, Lydia,** the romantic heroine of Sheridan's "The Rivals."

**Lear,** the hero of Shakespeare's tragedy of King Lear, father of Regan, Goneril, and Cordelia.

**Leatherstocking, Natty,** otherwise Natty Bumpo, hunter, the most famous of Cooper's characters; he appears in "The Pioneer," "The Last of the Mohicans," "The Pathfinder," "The Deerslayer," and "The Prairie."

**Legree,** a brutal slave-master in Mrs. Stowe's "Uncle Tom's Cabin."

**Leigh, Aurora,** the heroine of Mrs. Browning's poem-novel of that name.

**Leila,** the heroine of Byron's romantic poem, "The Giaour."

**Leontes,** the King of Sicily in Shakespeare's "Winter's Tale."

**Lightwood, Mortimer,** barrister, and friend of Eugene Wrayburn in Dickens's "Our Mutual Friend."

**Lismahago, Captain,** a retired Scotch officer, suitor of Tabitha Bramble in Smollett's "Humphry Clinker."

**Little, Henry,** the hero of Reade's "Put Yourself in His Place."

**Little Nell,** a precocious and good child in Dickens's "Old Curiosity Shop."

**Locksley,** an archer in Scott's "Ivanhoe," the name of Robin Hood.

**Long Tom Coffin,** in Cooper's "The Pilot," the most famous of his sea characters.

**Lorenzo,** the lover of Jessica in Shakespeare's "Merchant of Venice."

**Lothair, Marquis of,** the hero of Disraeli's "Lothair;" the Marquis of Bute.

**Lothario,** a rake in Rowe's tragedy of "The Fair Penitent."

**Lovelace,** a man of fashion and gallantry, the hero of Richardson's "Clarissa Harlowe."

**Lucio,** a witty gossip and liar in Shakespeare's "Measure for Measure."

**Lumpkin, Tony,** an oafish country squire in Goldsmith's "She Stoops to Conquer."

**Macbeth,** thane of Cawdor, hero of Shakespeare's tragedy of that name.

**Macduff,** a Scottish chief, the slayer of Macbeth in Shakespeare's "Macbeth."

**Mac Ivor, Flora,** the heroine of Scott's "Rob Roy."

**Mackenzie, Mrs,** a termagant widow, mother-in-law of Clive, in Thackeray's "Newcomes."

**Malagrowther, Sir Mungo,** an old, ill-natured courtier in Scott's "Fortunes of Nigel."

**Malaprop, Mrs.,** famed for verbal blunders, a character in Sheridan's "The Rivals."

**Mavolio,** Olivia's conceited steward in Shakespeare's "Twelfth Night."

**Manfred**, the gloomy, solitary hero of Byron's tragedy of that name.

**Manson, Æneas**, the villain in Hardy's "Desperate Remedies"

**Mantalini**, the dandy husband of a milliner in Dickens's "Nicholas Nickleby."

**Marchioness, The**, the little, ill-used maid-servant of the Brasses, in Dickens's "Old Curiosity Shop."

**Margaret**, the heroine of Goethe's "Faust," seduced by Faust.

**Mariana**, the deserted wife of Angelo in Shakespeare's "Measure for Measure."

**Mariana**, the daughter of Pericles, in Shakespeare's "Pericles, Prince of Tyre."

**Marlow, Young**, the hero of Goldsmith's "She Stoops to Conquer."

**Medora**, the heroine of Byron's "The Corsair."

**Merdle, Mr.**, a speculator and financier in Dickens's "Little Dorrit."

**Meister, Wilhelm**, the hero of Goethe's novel of that name.

**Mephistopheles**, the devil in Goethe's "Faust."

**Mercutio**, a highly-accomplished friend of Romeo in Shakespeare's "Romeo and Juliet."

**Micawber, Wilkins**, always "waiting for something to turn up," in Dickens's "David Copperfield."

**Miggs, Miss**, elderly servant of Mrs. Varden, enamored of Tappertit in Dickens's "Barnaby Rudge."

**Miller, Daisy**, the very American heroine of Henry James, Jr.'s, novelette of that name.

**Minna**, joint heroine with Brenda, of Scott's "The Pirate."

**Miranda**, daughter of Prospero, loved by Ferdinand in Shakespeare's "The Tempest"

**Monimia**, the heroine of Otway's "The Orphan."

**Moth**, Armado's page in Shakespeare's "Love's Labor Lost."

**Mouldy**, one of Falstaff's recruits in Shakespeare's "2d Part of King Henry IV."

**Mucklewrath, Habbakuk**, a fanatical preacher in Scott's "Old Mortality."

**Nathaniel, Sir**, a remarkable curate in Shakespeare's "Love's Labor Lost."

**Nerissa**, Portia's waiting-woman in Shakespeare's "Merchant of Venice."

**Neuchatel, Adriana**, a very rich young lady in Disraeli's "Endymion."

**Newcome, Clive**, the hero of Thackeray's "The Newcomes," son of the Colonel.

**Newcome, Colonel**, a simple, noble gentleman in Thackeray's "The Newcomes."

**Newcome, Ethel**, the beautiful cousin, and finally the wife, of Clive Newcome.

**Nickleby, Mrs.**, an irrelevant and credulous person in Dickens's "Nicholas Nickleby."

**Nickleby, Nicholas**, the hero of Dickens's novel of that name.

**Norna**, a sort of insane Sibyl in Scott's "The Pirate."

**Nydia**, a blind flower-girl in Bulwer's "The Last Days of Pompeii."

**Nym**, a rascally follower of Falstaff's in Shakespeare's "Merry Wives of Windsor."

**Obadiah**, a servant in Sterne's "Tristram Shandy."

**Oberon**, King of the Fairies in Shakespeare's "Midsummer Night's Dream."

**Ochiltree, Edie**, a beggar who plays a prominent part in Scott's "The Antiquary."

**Oldbuck, Jonathan**, connoisseur and collector, gives his name to Scott's "The Antiquary."

**Old Mortality**, gravestone cleaner, gives his name to Scott's "Old Mortality."

**Olifaunt, Nigel**, the hero of Scott's "The Fortunes of Nigel."

**Oliver**, elder brother of Orlando in Shakespeare's "As You Like It."

**Ophelia**, daughter of Polonius, in love with Hamlet, in Shakespeare's "Hamlet."

**Orlando**, the nephew of Charlemagne, hero of Ariosto's "Orlando Furioso."

**Orlando**, the son of Sir Rowland, and lover of Rosalind in Shakespeare's "As You Like It."

**Orsino**, the Duke of Illyria, in Shakespeare's "Twelfth Night."

**Orville, Lord**, the lover of Evelina in Miss Burney's novel of that name.

**Osric**, an affected courtier in Shakespeare's "Hamlet."

**Othello**, husband of Desdemona, and hero of Shakespeare's "Othello."

**O'Trigger, Sir Lucius**, an Irish adventurer in Sheridan's "The Rivals."

**Overreach, Sir Giles**, a usurer in Massinger's "A New Way to Pay Old Debts."

**Page, Mrs.**, beloved of Falstaff.

**Page, Anne**, beloved of Felton and Dr. Caius in Shakespeare's "Merry Wives of Windsor."

**Pamela**, the ever-virtuous heroine of Richardson's novel of that name.

**Pangloss**, a pedant in Colman's "The Heir at Law."

**Pantagruel**, the learned and mighty-stomached hero of Rabelais' satire of that name.

**Panurge**, the licentious and cowardly follower of Pantagruel.

**Parisina**, in love with her stepson, the heroine of Byron's "Parisina."

**Parolles**, the lying and cowardly attendant of Bertram in Shakespeare's "All's Well that Ends Well."

**Partridge**, barber and schoolmaster, the trusty follower of Fielding's "Tom Jones."

**Pecksniff, Miss Charity**, beloved of Moddle in Dickens's "Martin Chuzzlewit."

**Pecksniff, Mercy**, wife of Jonas Chuzzlewit.

**Pecksniff, Mr.**, architect and hypocrite, father of the above.

**Peebles, Peter**, drunkard and liar in Scott's "Redgauntlet."

**Pendennis, Arthur**, the clever and conceited hero of Thackeray's "Pendennis."

**Pendennis, Helen**, a noble woman, mother of Arthur.

**Pendennis, Major**, an elderly man of fashion, uncle of Arthur.

**Perdita**, the sweetheart of Florizel in Shakespeare's "Winter's Tale."

**Petruchio**, the madcap husband of Katherine in Shakespeare's "Taming of the Shrew."

**Pickle, Peregrine**, the dissolute hero of Smollett's "The Adventures of Peregrine Pickle."

**Pickwick, Samuel**, the hero of Dickens's "Pickwick Papers," founder of the "Pickwick Club."

**Pierre**, one of the conspirators in Otway's "Venice Preserved."

**Pinch, Miss**, Tom's pretty sister, John Westlock's sweetheart, in Dickens's "Martin Chuzzlewit."

**Pinch, Tom**, a simple, noble character in Mr. Pecksniff's family.

**Pipes, Tom**, a retired boatswain's mate in Smollett's "Peregrine Pickle."

**Pistol, Ancient**, a swaggering, loud-mouthed, rascally follower of Falstaff in Shakespeare's "Merry Wives of Windsor" and "Henry the IV."

**Pleydell, Paulus**, a lawyer in Scott's "Guy Mannering."

**Poins, Ned**, a gay companion of the young Prince in Shakespeare's "Henry IV."

**Polonius**, the lord chamberlain of the King of Denmark in Shakespeare's "Hamlet."

**Portia**, the heroine of Shakespeare's "Merchant of Venice."

**Posthumus**, the husband of Imogen in Shakespeare's "Cymbeline."

**Poundtext, Peter**, a preacher in Scott's "Old Mortality."

**Primrose, Doctor**, the noble-minded vicar in Goldsmith's "Vicar of Wakefield."

**Primrose, Moses**, his simple, credulous son.

**Proteus**, one of Shakespeare's "Two Gentlemen of Verona."

**Proudfute**, a bonnet-maker in Scott's "Fair Maid of Perth."

**Prynne, Hester**, the heroine of Hawthorne's "Scarlet Letter."

**Pumblechook, Uncle**, bully and sycophant in Dickens's "Great Expectations."

**Pynchon, Phoebe**, the heroine of Hawthorne's "House of the Seven Gables."

**Quasimodo**, a deformed monster in Victor Hugo's "Our Lady."

**Quickly, Mrs.**, hostess of the Eastcheap tavern in Shakespeare's "Henry IV."

**Quilp**, a vicious, ill-tempered dwarf in Dickens's "Old Curiosity Shop."

**Quince, Peter**, carpenter-actor in Shakespeare's "Midsummer Night's Dream."

**Random, Roderick**, the sensual, unfeeling hero of Smollett's novel of that name.

**Rashleigh**, the villain in Scott's "Rob Roy."

**Rasselas**, prince of Abyssinia, the hero of Dr. Johnson's romance of that name.

**Rattler, Jack**, a nautical character in Smollett's "Roderick Random."

**Ravenswood**, the haughty hero of Scott's "Bride of Lammermoor."

**Rebecca**, a gentle, lovable Jewess, the real heroine of Scott's "Ivanhoe."

**Redgauntlet**, the violent hero of Scott's novel of that name.

**Regan**, the second daughter of Lear in Shakespeare's "King Lear."

**Rob Roy**, a Scottish chief whose name is given to one of Scott's novels.

**Roderigo**, a dupe of Iago in Shakespeare's "Othello."

**Romeo**, a Montagne, beloved of Juliet in Shakespeare's "Romeo and Juliet."

**Romola,** the heroine of George Eliot's novel of that name.

**Rosalind,** daughter of the deposed Duke in Shakespeare's "As You Like It."

**Rosaline,** an attendant of the French princess in Shakespeare's "Love's Labor Lost."

**Rosencrantz,** a courtier in Shakespeare's "Harold."

**Rowena,** a Saxon princess, the ostensible heroine of Scott's "Ivanhoe."

**Roxana,** one of Nathaniel Lee's "Rival Queens."

**Rudge, Barnaby,** a half-witted youth, the hero of Dickens's "Barnaby Rudge."

**Rugby,** a servant of Dr. Caius in Shakespeare's "Merry Wives of Windsor."

**Ruggiero,** a Saracen knight in Ariosto's "Orlando Furioso." He has a winged horse, the hippogriff.

**Sabrina,** a river-nymph in Milton's "Comus."

**Sacripant,** King of Circassia, in love with Angelica in Ariosto's "Orlando Furioso."

**Saddletree, Bartoline,** a learned peddler in Scott's "Heart of Mid-Lothian."

**Salanio,** a friend of Antonio in Shakespeare's "Merchant of Venice."

**Sampson,** servant to Capulet in Shakespeare's "Romeo and Juliet."

**Sandford, Harry,** one of the heroes of Day's "History of Sandford and Merton."

**Sangrado, Doctor,** a physician in Le Sage's "Gil Blas;" he is always bleeding his patients; a satire on Helvetius.

**Scheherezade, Queen,** the Sultaness who tells the tales in "The Arabian Nights."

**Schlemihl, Peter,** hero of Chamisso's work of that name; sells his shadow to the devil.

**Scrub,** a facetious valet in Farquhar's "The Beaux' Stratagem."

**Sedley, Amelia,** an amiable woman in Thackeray's "Vanity Fair." She has many lovable qualities, but no talent or force of character.

**Sedley, Joseph,** a rich, fat, selfish, bashful East Indian in Thackeray's "Vanity Fair."

**Selim,** the hero of Byron's poem, "The Bride of Abydos."

**Shafton, Sir Piercie,** a pedantic courtier in Scott's "The Monastery."

**Shallow,** a silly gentleman in Shakespeare's "Merry Wives of Windsor."

**Shandy, Mrs.,** a woman of no force of character in Sterne's "Tristram Shandy."

**Shandy, Tristram,** her son, nominally the hero of that novel.

**Shandy, Walter,** Tristram's eccentric father, a man of strange opinions.

**Sharp, Rebecca,** the clever, selfish heroine of Thackeray's "Vanity Fair."

**Shylock,** a vindictive Jew in Shakespeare's "Merchant of Venice."

**Silence,** a simple gentleman in Shakespeare's "Second Part of Henry IV."

**Silvia,** the sweetheart of Valentine in Shakespeare's "Two Gentlemen of Verona."

**Simple,** the servant of Slender in Shakespeare's "Merry Wives of Windsor."

**Skimpole, Harold,** a gay, child-like, impecunious "beat" in Dickens's "Bleak House."

**Slender,** a silly suitor of Anne Page's in Shakespeare's "Merry Wives of Windsor."

**Slipslop, Mrs.,** a waiting-woman of more than doubtful character in Fielding's "Joseph Andrews."

**Slop, Doctor,** an irascible physician in Sterne's "Tristram Shandy."

**Sly, Christopher,** a drunken tinker in the "Induction" to "The Taming of the Shrew."

**Slyme, Chevy,** impecunious "gent" in Dickens's "Martin Chuzzlewit."

**Smike,** a poor, half-witted pupil of Squeers in Dickens's "Nicholas Nickleby."

**Sneerwell, Lady,** a gossip and backbiter in Sheridan's "School for Scandal."

**Snodgrass, Augustus,** a poetical companion of Mr. Pickwick in Dickens's "Pickwick Papers."

**Snout,** a tinker and amateur actor in Shakespeare's "Midsummer Night's Dream."

**Snow, Lucy,** the heroine of Charlotte Brontë's "Villette."

**Snug,** a joiner and amateur actor in Shakespeare's "Midsummer Night's Dream."

**Sparkler, Edmund,** ass and man of fashion in Dickens's "Little Dorritt."

**Speed,** the punning servant of Valentine in the "Two Gentlemen of Verona."

**Square,** pedant, philosopher, and moralist in Fielding's "Tom Jones."

**Squeers, Wackford,** the brutal master of the Dotheboys Hall in Dickens's "Nicholas Nickleby."

**Squeers, Master Wackford,** in the same, a spoiled child, and chip of the old block.

**St. Leon,** the hero of William Godwin's novel of that name; he has the secret of perpetual youth, and of the transmutation of the metals.

**Starveling,** tailor and amateur actor in Shakespeare's "Midsummer Night's Dream."

**Steerforth, James,** talented but profligate character in Dickens's "David Copperfield."

**Steggs, Miss Carolina Wilhelmina Amelia,** in Goldsmith's "Vicar of Wakefield," a vulgar pretender to gentility.

**Stephano,** a bibulous butler in Shakespeare's "Tempest."

**Stiggins, Elder,** in Dickens's "Pickwick Papers," fond of pineapple rum and Mrs. Weller.

**Strap, Hugh,** a faithful follower of Roderick Random in Smollett's "Roderick Random."

**Surface, Sir Charles,** a brilliant, generous rake in Sheridan's "School for Scandal."

**Surface, Joseph,** a hypocrite in the same play.

**Swiveller, Dick,** a gay, rattle-pated fellow in Dickens's "Old Curiosity Shop."

**Tamora,** the Gothic queen in Shakespeare's "Titus Andronicus."

**Tapley, Mark,** the "jolly-under-difficulties" servant in Dickens's "Martin Chuzzlewit."

**Tappertit, Simon,** a small but ferocious apprentice in Dickens's "Barnaby Rudge."

**Tartuffe,** the hypocritical hero of Molière's play of that name.

**Teazle, Lady,** the heroine of Sheridan's "School for Scandal."

**Teazle, Sir Peter,** her old husband.

**Thalaba,** "The Destroyer," hero of a poem by Southey.

**Thersites,** a foul-mouthed Greek in Homer's "Iliad," and Shakespeare's "Troilus and Cressida."

**Thwackum,** philosopher and pedagogue in Fielding's "Tom Jones."

**Tilburina,** a very much crossed-in-love maiden, in Sheridan's "The Critic."

**Timon,** a misanthropic Athenian, hero of Shakespeare's "Timon of Athens."

**Tinto, Dick,** an artist in Scott's "Bride of Lammermoor," and "St. Ronan's Well."

**Titania,** queen of the fairies in Shakespeare's "Midsummer Night's Dream."

**Titmouse, Tittlebat,** the vulgar hero of Warren's "Ten Thousand a Year," the type of the "gent."

**Tito,** the handsome, but weak hero of George Eliot's "Romola."

**Todgers, Mrs.,** keeper of a commercial boarding-house in Dickens's "Martin Chuzzlewit."

**Toots,** a simple, eccentric fellow in Dickens's "Dombey and Son."

**Topsy,** an ignorant young slave-girl in Mrs. Stowe's "Uncle Tom's Cabin."

**Touchstone,** a clown in Shakespeare's "As You Like It."

**Touchwood, Peregrine,** an irascible East Indian in Scott's "St. Ronan's Well."

**Tox, Miss,** a simple and eccentric spinster in Dickens's "Dombey and Son."

**Traddles, Tom,** barrister, and friend of Copperfield in Dickens's "David Copperfield."

**Tranio,** Lucentio's servant in Shakespeare's "Taming of the Shrew."

**Trapbois,** a usurer in Scott's "The Fortunes of Nigel."

**Trim, Corporal,** the trusty follower of Uncle Toby in Sterne's "Tristram Shandy."

**Trinculo,** a jester in Shakespeare's "Tempest."

**Troil, Magnus,** a wealthy Zetlander in Scott's "The Pirate."

**Trotwood, Betsy,** Copperfield's kind, eccentric aunt in Dickens's "David Copperfield."

**Trulliber, Parson,** an ignorant clergyman in Fielding's "Joseph Andrews."

**Trunnion, Commodore Hawser,** an eccentric nautical character in Smollett's "Peregrine Pickle."

**Tulkinghorn, Mr.,** a crafty solicitor in Dickens's "Bleak House."

**Tulliver, Maggie,** the heroine of George Eliot's "Mill on the Floss."

**Tulliver, Tom,** her selfish, conceited brother.

**Tupman, Tracy,** a fat lover of the fair sex in Dickens's "Pickwick Papers."

**Turveydrop,** dancing master and "model of deportment" in Dickens's "Bleak House."

**Tusher, Thomas,** a sycophantic clergyman in Thackeray's "Henry Esmond."

**Twemlow, Mr.,** diner-out and friend of Veneering in Dickens's "Our Mutual Friend."

**Twist, Oliver,** a charity boy, hero of Dickens's "Oliver Twist."

**Twysden, Talbot,** public officer and flunkey in Thackeray's "Philip."

**Tybalt,** nephew of Lady Capulet, slain by Romeo in Shakespeare's "Romeo and Juliet."

**Ulrica**, an old witch in Scott's "Ivanhoe."

**Una**, the personification of Truth in Spenser's "Faery Queen."

**Uncas**, a Mohican chief in Cooper's "The Last of the Mohicans."

**Uncle Toby**, a noble old soldier, the hero of Sterne's "Tristram Shandy."

**Uncle Tom**, a pious slave, the hero of Mrs. Stowe's "Uncle Tom's Cabin."

**Valentine**, one of Shakespeare's "Two Gentlemen of Verona."

**Varden, Dolly**, the heroine of Dickens's "Barnaby Rudge."

**Vathek**, the hero of Beckford's Eastern romance, of great gifts, but of violent passions and inordinate ambition.

**Verges**, a silly, self-important watchman in Shakespeare's "Much Ado about Nothing."

**Vernon, Die**, the heroine of Scott's "Rob Roy."

**Vholes**, a cold-blooded, crafty solicitor in Dickens's "Bleak House."

**Vincentio**, Duke of Vienna, in Shakespeare's "Measure for Measure."

**Viola**, in love with Orsino in Shakespeare's 'Twelfth Night."

**Virgilia**, wife of Coriolanus in Shakespeare's "Coriolanus."

**Virginia**, the heroine of St. Pierre's "Paul and Virginia."

**Vivian**, mistress of Merlin in Tennyson's "Idyls of the King."

**Volumnia**, mother of Coriolanus in Shakespeare's "Coriolanus."

**Wadman, Widow**, in Sterne's "Tristram Shandy," tries to marry Uncle Toby.

**Wamba**, a clown in Scott's "Ivanhoe."

**Wardle, Mr.**, a jolly country gentleman in Dickens's "Pickwick Papers."

**Warrington, George** and **Harry**, grandsons of "Henry Esmond," and heroes of Thackeray's "The Virginians."

**Warrington, George**, the cynical, but kind-hearted friend of Arthur in Thackeray's "Pendennis."

**Wegg, Silas**, a one-legged, crafty schemer in Dickens's "Our Mutual Friend."

**Weller, Tony**, a jovial and rubicund coachman in Dickens's "Pickwick Papers."

**Weller, Sam**, son of Tony, Mr. Pickwick's humorous servant.

**Werther**, the sentimental hero of Goethe's "Sorrows of Werther."

**Western, Sophia**, the heroine of Fielding's "Tom Jones."

**Western, Squire**, her father, a pig-headed, foul-mouthed country squire.

**Westlock, John**, friend and finally brother-in-law of Tom Pinch in Dickens's "Martin Chuzzlewit."

**Whiskerandos, Don Ferolo**, lover of Tilburina, in Sheridan's "The Critic."

**Wickfield, Agnes**, the lovable heroine of Dickens's "David Copperfield," and David's second wife.

**Wild, Jonathan**, highwayman, the hero of Fielding's "History of Jonathan Wild." He is drawn from a famous highwayman of that name, who was executed in 1725.

**Wildair, Sir Harry**, man of fashion and gallantry, the hero of Farquhar's "Constant Couple" and "Sir Harry Wildair."

**Wildfire, Madge**, a woman crazed by seduction, and by the murder of her infant, in Scott's "Heart of Mid-Lothian."

**Wilfer, Bella**, the beautiful, wilful heroine of Dickens's "Our Mutual Friend."

**Wilfer, Lavinia**, her irrepressible sister, beloved of George Sampson.

**Wilfer, Reginald**, their father, a commercial cherub.

**Wilfrid**, son of Oswald Wycliffe, in Scott's "Rokeby," in love with Matilda, heiress of Rokeby, at whose feet he dies.

**Willet, John**, an obstinate innkeeper in Dickens's "Barnaby Rudge."

**Willet, Joe**, his son, in love with Dolly Varden.

**Williams, Caleb**, the hero of William Godwin's novel of that name.

**Wilmot, Arabella**, George Primrose's sweetheart in Goldsmith's "Vicar of Wakefield."

**Wilton, Ralph de**, finally marries Lady Clare, daughter of the Earl of Gloucester, in Scott's "Marmion."

**Wimble, Will**, a good-natured, simple, and officious character in "The Spectator," said to be a portrait of Thomas Morecroft, who died at Dublin in 1741.

**Winkle, Nathaniel**, a would-be sporting character in Dickens's "Pickwick Papers."

**Winkle, Rip Van**, good-natured, bibulous, blessed with a scolding wife; he and his long sleep are commemorated in Irving's "Sketch Book."

**Wishfort, Lady**, a witty, vain character in Congreve's "The Way of the World."

**Wititterly, Mr.**, a snob and tuft-hunter in Dickens's "Nicholas Nickleby."

**Wititterly, Mrs. Julia**, in the same, his wife, a languid lady, whose "soul was too large for her body." She "dearly loved a lord."

**Witwould, Sir Willful**, a pig-headed gentleman in Congreve's "Way of the World."

**Worldly Wiseman, Mr.**, in Bunyan's "Pilgrim's Progress," tries to persuade Christian from his journey,

**Wray, Enoch**, an aged and noble character in Crabbe's "Village."

**Wrayburn, Eugene**, a calm and briefless barrister in Dickens's "Our Mutual Friend."

**Wren, Jenny**, doll's-dressmaker in Dickens's "Our Mutual Friend."

**Wronghead, Sir Francis**, a country gentleman, the hero of Vanburgh's "The Provoked Husband."

**Xury**, a servant of Crusoe in De Foe's "Robinson Crusoe."

**Yellowley, Mistress Baby** (Barbara), sister and housekeeper of Triptolemus, in Scott's "The Pirate."

**Yellowley, Triptolemus**, a Scotch-Yorkshireman, of agricultural tendencies, in Scott's "The Pirate."

**Yorick**, a witty, heedless parson in Sterne's "Tristram Shandy," represented as a descendant of Shakespeare's jester of that name, in "Hamlet."

**Yseult** or **Isolde**, beloved of Tristram, celebrated in many mediæval romances, and in the "Tristram and Yseult" of Matthew Arnold, and of A. C. Swinburne. She was the wife of King Mark, of Cornwall, and mistress of his nephew, Tristram, with whom she fell in love from drinking a love-philter. She was called Isolde the Fair.

**Zadoc**, in Dryden's "Absalom and Achitophel," is Sancroft, Archbishop of Canterbury.

**Zanoni**, alchemist, etc., the hero of Bulwer's "Zanoni." He is a member of an occult fraternity who deal familiarly with the world of spirits, can make precious stones and metals, and can live as long as they please.

**Zeluco**, a prodigal nobleman, hero of Dr. J. Moore's "Zeluco."

**Zenobia**, a beautiful woman in Hawthorne's "Blithedale Romance."

**Zerbino**, a Scotch warrior in Ariosto's "Orlando Furioso."

**Zimri**, the Duke of Buckingham in Dryden's "Absalom and Architophel."

**Zobeide**, the favorite wife of Haroun-Al-Raschid in "The Arabian Nights." Her story is told in the tale of the "Three Calendars."

**Zodig**, a rich Babylonian, hero of Voltaire's novel of that name.

**Zophiel**, in Milton's "Paradise Lost," the swiftest of the cherubim.

**Zuleika**, the heroine of Byron's "Bride of Abydos."

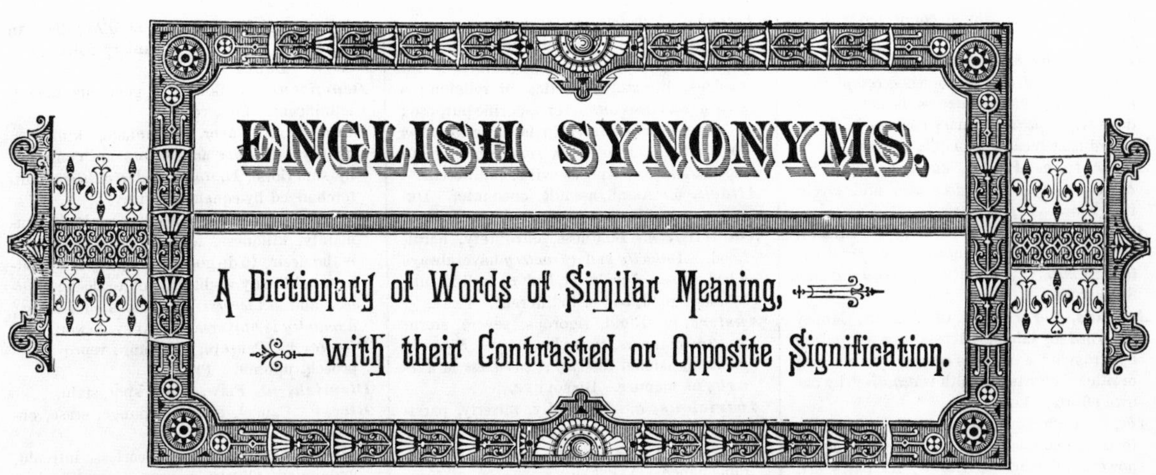


SYNONYMS are words which have the same or a similar meaning. A dictionary of synonyms is intended to enable the person who consults it to repeat an expression in a new form, and avoid the awkwardness of style produced by the too frequent occurrence of the same word.

In preparing the following short list of synonyms, the works of Crabb, Graham, Whately, Soule, and Roget, and the dictionaries of Webster and Worcester have been carefully consulted. It was impossible within the space here available to adopt the scientific classification made by Roget in his "Thesaurus." A complete list of synonyms after the manner of the ordinary dictionary of synonyms was equally impracticable. A short explanation, however, of the more important synonyms (the plan adopted by Crabb), has been attempted in the following list. For convenience, a few synonyms are given without explanation:

A word in capitals standing alone at the end of a paragraph indicates an opposite or contrasted word, to which reference may be made. This opposite or contrasted word is sometimes not to be found separately in the list. In such cases the word under which it occurs is also indicated. Thus under ***Temporary*** the contrasting word PERMANENT is at the end of the paragraph followed by the words (See DURABLE); by turning to ***Durable*** the synonym permanent will be found.

N. B. *a.* stands for adjective; *adv.* for adverb; *n.* for noun; *v.* for verb; *conj.* for conjunction; *prep.* for preposition.

## A.

***Abandon,*** *v.* Desert, forsake, relinquish. A sinking vessel is *abandoned;* a soldier *deserts* his post; a creditor *relinquishes* his claims; a man in trouble is *forsaken* by his friends. KEEP.

***Abash,*** *v.* Confuse, confound. Pride is sometimes *abashed;* ignorance or wickedness *confounded;* diffidence and modesty *confused.* ENCOURAGE.

***Abate,*** *v.* Diminish, lessen, decrease. INCREASE.

***Abhor,*** *v.* Abominate, detest, loathe. We *abhor* mean, base actions; *abominate* impiety; *detest* a hypocrite; *loathe* an offensive object. ESTEEM.

***Ability,*** *n.* Capacity, faculty, talent, dexterity address. *Ability* denotes a human power which may be acquired; *faculty* a natural gift. *Capacity* is a particular species of *ability;* a *talent* is a particular gift given in a remarkable degree; *dexterity* and *address* are degrees of *ability; dexterity* is a peculiar facility of execution; *address* a peculiar mode of setting one's self to work. INABILITY.

***Abolish,*** *v.* Abrogate, repeal, annul, cancel, revoke. An institution is *abolished;* a contract *annulled;* an edict *revoked;* a law *repealed* or *abrogated.* PRESERVE.

***Abridge,*** *v.* Curtail, shorten. EXTEND.

***Abridgment,*** *n.* A compendium, digest, epitome, summary, abstract. An *abridgment* is a shorter form of a literary work; a *compendium,* a short, general view of a subject; a *digest,* an orderly arrangement of details; an *epitome,* a concise account of the whole of a subject; a *summary* recapitulates the subject; an *abstract* is a short general account of a particular thing. An *abridgment* of Gibbon's Roman Empire; a *compendium* of geology; a *digest* of the law of evidence; an *epitome* of American history; a *summary* of an argument; an *abstract* of a deed.

***Abstemious,*** *a.* Abstinent, sober, temperate. A *sober* man does not use strong drink to excess; a *temperate* man is moderate in his use of liquor; an *abstemious* man habitually refrains from the use; an *abstinent* man refrains temporarily. INTEMPERATE.

***Abundance,*** *n.* Plenty, copiousness, plentifulness. SCARCITY.

***Accident,*** *n.* Chance, contingency, casualty. An *accident* is a thing that has been; a *chance* is yet to be; a *casualty* is unavoidable and independent of ourselves; a *contingency* denotes a circumstance connected with an event.

***Accomplish,*** *v.* Achieve, effect, execute. A purpose is *effected;* an object *accomplished;* a *design executed;* success is *achieved;* a duty *performed.* Ordinary means *effect;* extraordinary means *accomplish.* FAIL.

***Accurate,*** *a.* Precise, exact, correct. *Exact* is stronger than *accurate;* and *precise* than *exact.* INACCURATE.

***Acquaintance,*** *n.* Familiarity, intimacy. *Intimacy* expresses more than *familiarity; familiarity* more than *acquaintance.* STRANGER.

***Acquire,*** *v.* Earn, gain, obtain, win. Money is *earned* by labor; success *won* or *gained* by struggle; a result is *obtained* by our own or others' efforts; wealth is *acquired* by our own efforts. LOSE.

***Act,*** *v.* Do, make, work, operate. To *act* is to exert a simple power; to *work* a complex power. A machine *works;* its parts *act. Operate* is intransitive; *Do* is always transitive; *Act* usually transitive. *Make* is to *do* for a special purpose or in a special way.

***Active,*** *a.* Busy, brisk, agile, nimble, diligent, industrious. A *busy* person is always employed; an *active* person constantly willing to be employed; an *industrious* person is constantly seriously employed; a *diligent* person is active for some particular purpose. *Briskness* relates to sport; *nimbleness* to quickness of movements; *agility* to ease of carriage. INACTIVE.

***Add,*** *v.* Join, coalesce, unite.

***Admit,*** *v.* Allow, permit, suffer, tolerate. *Permit* is more positive than *allow. Suffer* and *tolerate* refer to important matters. We *grant* what is agreed to be true. DENY.

***Advantageous,*** *a.* Beneficial. HURTFUL.

***Affection,*** *n.* Love. *Affection* is a lasting, tender feeling; *love* is a warmer feeling, subsisting (more frequently) between persons of different sex. AVERSION.

***Affectionate,*** *a.* Fond, kind.

***Agreeable,*** *a.* Pleasant, pleasing, charming. A *pleasant* day; a *pleasing* landscape; a *charming* girl. DISAGREEABLE.

***Alternating,*** *a.* Intermittent. CONTINUAL.

***Ambassador,*** *n.* Envoy, plenipotentiary, minister. A *plenipotentiary* is intrusted with some special mission; a *minister resident* and *ambassador* are permanent officials; an *envoy* is more commonly employed for a special purpose.

***Amend,*** *v.* Improve, correct, better, mend. IMPAIR.

***Anger,*** *n.* Ire, wrath, indignation, resentment. *Wrath* and *ire* are hasty; *anger* sometimes lasting; *resentment* is caused by a feeling of personal injury. GOOD NATURE.

***Appropriate,*** *v.* Assume, ascribe, arrogate, usurp. We *usurp* by taking to ourselves violently and wrongfully; *appropriate* by taking to ourselves, rightfully or wrongfully. We *arrogate* a title; *assume* a right; *ascribe* to ourselves a merit.

***Argue,*** *v.* Debate, dispute, reason upon.

***Arise,*** *v.* Flow, emanate, spring, proceed, rise, issue.

***Artful,*** *a.* Disingenuous, sly, tricky, insincere. CANDID.

***Artifice,*** *n.* Trick, stratagem, finesse.

***Association,*** *n.* Combination, company, partnership, society. An *association* is for business, literature, politics, or religion; a *society* is an *association* for a specific purpose; a *company* or *partnership* is an *association* for trading purposes; a *combination* is an *association* for purposes evil or indifferent.

***Attack,*** *v.* Assail, assault, encounter. DEFEND.

***Audacity,*** *n.* Boldness, effrontery, hardihood. *Audacity* and *effrontery* have always a bad sense; *hardihood,* bad or indifferent; *boldness,* good, bad or indifferent. FEAR.

***Austere,*** *a.* Rigid, rigorous, severe, stern. *Austere* manners, *severe* language. *Rigor* is great occasional *severity; sternness* is a *severity* of manner. DISSOLUTE.

***Avaricious,*** *a.* Niggardly, miserly, parsimonious. EXTRAVAGANT.

***Aversion,*** *n.* Antipathy, dislike, hatred, repugnance. AFFECTION.

***Awe,*** *n.* Dread, reverence. Sublime and sacred things excite *awe;* terrific things, *dread;* noble things, *reverence.*

***Awkward,*** *a.* Clumsy. *Awkward* denotes carriage; *clumsy,* natural shape. GRACEFUL.

***Axiom,*** *n.* Adage, aphorism, apothegm, by-word, maxim, proverb, saying, saw. An *axiom* is a self-evident proposition; an *apothegm, saw* or *saying,* a pithy sentiment; an *aphorism,* a pointed truth; a *proverb,* or an *adage,* an old and common saying; a *by-word* had some local origin; a *maxim* is a practical moral truth.

B.

***Babble,*** *v.* Chatter, prattle, prate.

***Bad,*** *a.* Wicked, evil. Things disagreeable to the taste and sentiments are *bad;* to the principles, *wicked;* what is highly *bad* or *wicked* is *evil.* GOOD.

***Baffle,*** *v.* Confound, defeat, disconcert.

***Base,*** *a.* Vile, mean. We abhor *baseness;* are disgusted with *vileness;* despise *meanness.* NOBLE.

***Battle,*** *n.* Action, combat, engagement.

***Bear,*** *v.* Carry, convey, transport. To *bear* is to support the weight of a thing; to *carry,* to take it from the place where it was; *convey* and *transport* are modes of carrying.

***Bear,*** *v.* Endure, suffer, support. We *endure* great evils; *bear* small or great; *support* our own or others; *suffer* is entirely involuntary.

***Beat,*** *v.* Defeat, overpower, overthrow, rout.

***Beautiful,*** *a.* Fine, handsome, pretty. *Beautiful* is the strongest. *Pretty* is simple and small; *fine* implies (generally) a good-sized figure. A man is *handsome;* a woman *beautiful, pretty,* or *fine.* HOMELY.

***Becoming,*** *a.* Decent, fit, seemly, suitable. UNBECOMING.

***Beg,*** *v.* Beseech, crave, entreat, implore, solicit, supplicate. We *beg* in want; *crave* from physical want; *beseech, entreat,* and *solicit* from pressing necessity; *implore* and *supplicate* from extreme distress. GIVE.

***Behavior,*** *n.* Carriage, conduct, deportment, demeanor.

***Belief,*** *n.* Credit, faith, trust. *Belief* is the general word; it is *trust* in facts or opinions; *trust* in religious opinions is *faith; trust* in a person's veracity or pecuniary solvency is *credit.* DOUBT.

***Beneficent,*** *n.* Bountiful, generous, liberal, munificent. COVETOUS.

***Benefit,*** *n.* Favor, advantage, kindness, civility. *Benefits* and *favors* are conferred by superiors; *kindness* and *civilities* are interchanged by equals. INJURY.

***Benevolence,*** *n.* Beneficence, benignity, humanity, kindness, tenderness. *Benevolence* is the desire to do good; *benignity* is a goodness habitually visible in look or deed; *kindness* and *tenderness* are modes of feeling; *humanity* is universal. MALEVOLENCE.

***Blame,*** *v.* Censure, condemn, reprove, reproach, upbraid. PRAISE.

***Blemish,*** *n.* Flaw, speck, spot, stain.

***Blot,*** *v.* Cancel, efface, expunge, erase, obliterate.

***Bold,*** *a.* Brave, daring, fearless, intrepid, undaunted. TIMID.

***Border,*** *n.* Brim, brink, edge, margin, rim, verge.

***Border,*** *n.* Boundary, confine, frontier. *Boundary* denotes the limit of place; *frontier* is (mostly) a military term; *confines* is used in reference to two places.

***Bound,*** *v.* Circumscribe, confine, limit, restrict.

***Brave,*** *v.* Dare, defy.

***Bravery,*** *n.* Courage, valor. *Bravery* is unreasoning; *courage,* the result of reflection; *valor* combines *bravery* and *courage.* COWARDICE.

***Break,*** *v.* Bruise, crush, pound, squeeze.

***Breeze,*** *n.* Blast, gale, gust, hurricane, storm, tempest. A gentle *breeze;* a brisk *gale;* a sudden *gust;* a violent *blast.* A *storm* is a disturbance of the whole atmosphere; a *tempest* is a storm with thunder and lightning; a *hurricane* is the most violent of storms.

***Bright,*** *a.* Clear, radiant, shining. DULL.

***Business,*** *n.* Avocation, employment, engagement, occupation. *Business* takes our thoughts, time, and strength; *occupation* and *employment,* time and strength only. An *engagement* employs partially; an *avocation* prevents from doing something else.

***Business,*** *n.* Art, profession, trade. Buying and selling merchandise is *trade;* learning is requisite for a *profession;* employment of knowledge and experience for profit is *business;* exercise of art an *art.*

C.

***Calamity,*** *n.* Disaster, misfortune, mischance, mishap.

***Calm,*** *a.* Collected, composed. *Calm* relates to the state of the feelings; *collected,* of the thoughts; *composed,* of thoughts and feelings both. STORMY.

***Calm,*** *a.* Placid, serene. *Calm* is a transient mental state: placidity and serenity; permanent mental habits.

***Capable,*** *a.* Able, competent. INCOMPETENT.

***Captious,*** *a.* Fretful, cross, peevish, petulant.

***Care,*** *n.* Anxiety, concern, solicitude. HEEDLESSNESS. (See NEGLIGENT.)

*mous* and *huge* relate to size; *immense* and *vast* to extent, quantity, and number. *Enormous* is larger than *huge; immense* than *vast*.

***Enroll,*** *v.* Enlist, list, register, record.

***Enthusiast,*** *n.* Fanatic, visionary. The *enthusiast* feels a peculiar mental fervor; the *fanatic* believes himself inspired; the *visionary* sees supernatural visions.

***Equal,*** *a.* Equable, even, like, alike, uniform. An *equable* temper; an *even* surface; *like* or *alike* in face and color. UNEQUAL.

***Eradicate,*** *v.* Root out, extirpate, exterminate.

***Erroneous,*** *a.* Incorrect, inaccurate, inexact. EXACT.

***Error,*** *n.* Blunder, mistake. *Error* is the general term; a *blunder* is *error* in action; a *mistake* an error of choice.

***Especially,*** *adv.* Chiefly, particularly, principally. GENERALLY.

***Essay,*** *n.* Dissertation, tract, treatise.

***Establish,*** *v.* Confirm. Things permanent and important are *established;* things partial or temporary, *confirmed.* OVERTHROW.

***Esteem,*** *n.* Regard, respect. *Esteem* and *respect* come from the understanding; *regard*, from the heart. *Regard* is felt among friends; *respect* for superiority. *Esteem* is for worth.

***Estimate,*** *v.* Appraise, appreciate, esteem.

***Estimate,*** *v.* Compute, rate. We *estimate* expenses; *compute* interest; *rate* a man's commercial standing.

***Estrangement,*** *n.* Abstraction, alienation.

***Eternal,*** *a.* Endless, everlasting. The *eternal* has no beginning or end; the *endless* a beginning but no end; the *everlasting* is without cessation or interruption.

***Evade,*** *v.* Equivocate, prevaricate. We *evade* by changing the subject; *equivocate* by using equivocal expressions; *prevaricate* by using loose, unsatisfactory expressions.

***Even,*** *a.* Level, plain, smooth. The *even* is free from great roughness; the *smooth* from any roughness; the *level* from rise and fall; the plain from obstruction. UNEVEN. (See ROUGH.)

***Event,*** *n.* Accident, adventure, incident, occurrence. An *event* is anything which is going on in the world; an *accident* is an accidental *event;* an *adventure* an extraordinary *event;* an *incident* a personal *event;* an ordinary *event.*

***Evil,*** *n.* Ill, harm, mischief, misfortune. GOOD.

***Exact,*** *a.* Nice, particular, punctual. *Particular* and *punctual* are applied to persons only; *exact* and *nice* either to persons or things. *Exact* and the two former are always used in a good sense; the two latter may be carried to excess. INEXACT. (See ERRONEOUS.)

***Exalt,*** *v,* Ennoble, dignify, raise. HUMBLE.

***Examination,*** *n.* Investigation, inquiry, research, search, scrutiny. *Examination* is a general term; an *inquiry* is made by putting questions; an *investigation* is a minute *inquiry;* a *search*, a painstaking *examination;* a *research*, a thorough *search;* a *scrutiny*, a rigid examination.

***Exceed,*** *v.* Excel, outdo, surpass, transcend. FALL SHORT. (See FAIL.)

***Exceptional,*** *a.* Uncommon, rare, extraordinary. *Uncommon.*

***Excite,*** *v.* Awaken, provoke, rouse, stir up. LULL.

***Excursion,*** *n.* Jaunt, ramble, tour, trip.

***Execute,*** *v.* Fulfill, perform. *Execute* is stronger than *fulfill* or *perform.* We *fulfill* a moral duty; *perform* an ordinary task. *Execute* (bring about to an end) something extraordinary.

***Exempt,*** *a.* Free, cleared. SUBJECT.

***Exercise,*** *v.* Practice. An art is *exercised;* a profession *practiced.*

***Exhaustive,*** *a.* Thorough, complete. CURSORY

***Exigency,*** *n.* Emergency. The former is more frequent; the latter more pressing.

***Experiment,*** *n.* Proof, trial, test. *Trial* finds the quality of a thing; *experiment* develops some truth; *proof* is the result of experiment; *test* is the most convincing proof.

***Explain,*** *v.* Expound, interpret, illustrate, elucidate. Single words are *explained;* a work is *expounded;* a prophecy or the sense of a work *interpreted;* a commentary *elucidates;* an example *illustrates.*

***Express,*** *v.* Declare, signify, utter, tell.

***Extend,*** *v.* Reach, stretch. ABRIDGE.

***Extravagant,*** *a.* Lavish, profuse, prodigal. *Extravagant* is the general term. The *extravagant* spend their money unreasonably; the *prodigal* in excesses. The *lavish* man spends wastefully without considering the value of what he spends; *profuseness* spends liberally from a full store. PARSIMONIOUS. (See AVARICIOUS.)

## F

***Fable,*** *n.* Apologue, novel, romance, tale. A *fable* or *apologue* is a short tale enforcing a moral. A *novel* deals with a variety of characters and incidents; a *romance* presents extraordinary incidents; a *tale* is a simple kind of fiction.

***Face,*** *n.* Visage, countenance.

***Facetious,*** *a.* Pleasant, jocular, jocose. *Facetious* is used of either writing or conversation; the others only of conversation. SERIOUS.

***Factor,*** *n.* Agent. A *factor* merely buys and sells for others; an *agent* transacts all kinds of business.

***Fail,*** *v.* To fall short, be deficient. ACCOMPLISH.

***Faint,*** *a.* Languid. *Faint* is slighter than *languid;* a *faintness* spread through the whole frame is *languor.*

***Fair,*** *a.* Clear. What is *fair* has brightness; what is *clear* is spotless. *Fair* weather is somewhat sunny; *clear* weather, cloudless. STORMY.

***Fair,*** *a.* Equitable, honest, reasonable. UNFAIR. (See UNJUST.)

***Faith,*** *n.* Creed. A *creed* is an established form of faith.

***Faithful,*** *a.* True, loyal, constant. FAITHLESS.

***Faithless,*** *a.* Perfidious, treacherous. *Perfidy* is in the will; *treachery* in the action; *faithlessness* is a violation of faith for one's own interest without attempting to deceive. FAITHFUL.

***Fall,*** *v.* Drop, droop, sink, tumble. RISE.

***Fame,*** *n.* Renown, reputation. *Fame* may be good or bad; *renown* is used only of brilliant and great deeds and men; *reputation* is gained only by actual distinction in something, as the *reputation* of a lawyer, of a surgeon.

***Famous,*** *a.* Celebrated, renowned, illustrious, OBSCURE.

***Fanciful,*** *a.* Capricious, fantastical, whimsical.

***Fancy,*** *n.* Imagination. *Fancy* relates to light objects; *imagination* to things grand, extraordinary, remote.

***Fast,*** *a.* Rapid, quick, fleet, expeditious. SLOW.

***Fatigue,*** *n.* Weariness, lassitude. *Fatigue* is a physical or mental exhaustion; *Weariness* an exhaustion of strength or spirits; *lassitude* a weakness of the whole frame produced by *fatigue* or illness.

***Fear,*** *n.* Timidity, timorousness. BRAVERY.

***Feeling,*** *n.* Sensation, sense. *Feeling* is transitory and changeable; *sense* permanent. A *feeling* of pity; a *sense* of justice. A *sensation* is an act of *feeling.*

***Feeling,*** *n.* Sensibility, susceptibility. INSENSIBILITY.

***Ferocious,*** *a.* Fierce, savage, wild, barbarous. MILD.

***Fertile,*** *a.* Fruitful, prolific, plenteous, productive. STERILE.

***Fiction,*** *n.* Falsehood, fabrication. *Fiction* tells what may be, but is not; *fabrication* and *falsehood* tell what is not as what is.

***Figure,*** *n.* Allegory, emblem, metaphor, symbol, type.

***Find,*** *v.* Find out, descry, discover, espy. We may *find* by accident; we may *find out* by exertion; *discover* what is remote or hidden. A thing is *descried* at a distance; we *espy* something remote. LOSE.

***Fine,*** *a.* Delicate, nice. *Fine* applies to large or small objects: *delicate* to small objects only. In a moral sense *delicacy* rests upon the taste; *nicety* upon a minute, searching scientific examination; *delicate* is pleasant to sense and taste; what is *nice* refers to the appetite. COARSE.

***Fine,*** *n.* Forfeit, forfeiture, mulct, penalty.

***Fire,*** *n.* Glow, heat, warmth. *Warmth* is a gentle *heat;* *glow* a partial *heat* or *warmth;* *fire* in action emits *heat;* *heat* is less active than *fire*, more active than *warmth.*

***Firm,*** *a.* Constant, solid, steadfast, fixed, stable. WEAK.

***First,*** *a.* Foremost, earliest. LAST.

***Fit,*** *v.* Accommodate, adapt, adjust, suit.

***Fix,*** *v.* Determine, establish, settle, limit.

***Flame,*** *n.* Blaze, flare, flash, glare. *Flash* is a sudden *flare*, an unsteady *flame;* *blaze* is a broad, bright *flame;* *glare* a strong, glowing *flame.*

***Flat,*** *a.* Level. *Flat* is the opposite of *round;* *level* of *uneven.*

***Flexible,*** *a.* Pliant, pliable, ductile, supple. *Pliant* is used only in a moral sense; *flexible* and *pliable* mean easily bent; *suppleness* is an extreme *pliability;* *ductile* means easily drawn. INFLEXIBILITY.

***Flourish,*** *v.* Prosper, thrive. *Thrive* denotes the process of becoming prosperous or full-grown; *flourish* the state; *prosper* is used only in a moral sense.

***Flow,*** *v.* Gush, emanate, issue, stream, glide, proceed.

***Follow,*** *v.* Ensue, succeed. *Follow* is to go in order; *succeed* marks an immediate succession; *ensue* a following by necessary connection.

***Follower,*** *n.* Adherent, partisan. *Follower* is general; an *adherent follows* a person's cause; a *partisan* his party.

***Fondness,*** *n.* Affection, likeness. DISLIKE.

***Foolhardy,*** *a.* Adventurous, rash. The *adventurous* man ventures from love of danger; the *rash* from thoughtlessness; the *foolhardy* from foolish scorn of consequences. CAUTIOUS. (See WARY.)

***Forbid,*** *v.* Interdict, prohibit. *Forbid* is the common word; *prohibit* the judicial; *interdict* the moral. PERMIT.

***Forerunner,*** *n.* Harbinger, messenger, precursor.

***Foresight,*** *n.* Forecast, forethought and premeditation. Business requires *foresight;* statesmanship *forecast; premeditation* denotes knowledge obtained by meditation; *forethought* is seeing something before it happens.

***Foretell,*** *v.* Predict, prognosticate, prophesy. An eclipse is *foretold;* a calamity *predicted* or *prophesied;* the result of a disease *prognosticated* from the symptoms.

***Forgive,*** *v.* Absolve, pardon, remit. We *forgive* an injury; *pardon* a crime; *remit* a penalty; *absolve* from a sin.

***Form,*** *v.* Compose, constitute, make.

***Form,*** *n.* Ceremony, observances, rite. *Form* is general; *ceremony* is the *form* of outward behavior; *rites* and *observances* are religious.

***Formal,*** *a.* Ceremonious, ceremonial. *Formal* in a bad sense is the opposite of easy; *ceremonious* to cordial; *ceremonial* relates to established ceremonies; *formal and ceremonious* may be used in an indifferent sense.

***Formidable,*** *a.* Dreadful, terrible, shocking, terrific.

***Forswear,*** *v.* Perjure, suborn. *Perjury* is a false oath before a court; *forswear* is applied to oaths of all kinds; *suborn* is to make to *perjure* or *forswear.*

***Fortunate,*** *a.* Lucky, prosperous, successful. *Fortunate* and *lucky* relate to things happening beyond the control of man; *prosperous* and *successful* denote the escape of evil as well as the acquisition of good; *fortunate* applies to single circumstances; *prosperous* to a series of circumstances. UNFORTUNATE. (See UNHAPPY.)

***Foster,*** *v.* Cherish, harbor, indulge, nourish, nurse.

***Foundation,*** *n.* Base, basis, ground. The *foundation* is underground; *basis* or *base* above ground; the *foundation* for a report, the *grounds* of a suspicion.

***Fragile,*** *a.* Brittle, frail. *Frail* is only used figuratively. A *fragile* thing is liable to be broken; a *brittle* one will break under the slightest violence. STRONG.

***Frame,*** *n.* Constitution, temper, temperament. *Frame* denotes the body or the mental powers in a universal sense; *temper* the general or particular state or feeling of the individual; *temperament* and *constitution* his general state; the latter has a physical sense only.

***Frank,*** *a.* Candid, free, ingenuous, open, plain. DISINGENUOUS. (See ARTFUL.)

***Freedom,*** *n.* Liberty. *Freedom* is private; *liberty* public; a *freedom* may be innocent and agreeable; a *liberty* disagreeable and insulting. SLAVERY.

***Friend,*** *n.* Well-wisher. FOE.

***Frolic,*** *n.* Gambol, prank. A *gambol* is a trick of movement; a *prank,* a humorous, eccentric freak; a merry, laughing, noisy performance is a *frolic.*

***Fulfill,*** *v.* Accomplish, complete, keep, realize.

***Full,*** *a.* Replete, filled, abounding. EMPTY.

G.

***Gain,*** *n.* Emolument, profit, lucre. *Gain* is the general term; *profit* is what comes from each article or venture; *emolument* is the *gain* from one's office or position; *lucre* is only used in an abstract (and bad) sense. LOSS.

***Gait,*** *n.* Walk, carriage. *Gait* is the manner of carrying the body and limbs when in motion; *walk* the manner of carrying them when walking; *carriage* applies either to motion or repose.

***Gape,*** *v.* Gaze, stare. *Gape* and *stare* have a bad sense; the former is the result of ignorance; the latter of impertinence; *gaze* has a good sense; to *gaze* at a picture.

***Gather,*** *v.* Collect. We *gather* from necessity or convenience; we *collect* from choice or design; we *gather* fruit; *collect* pictures. SCATTER. (See SPREAD.)

***Generation,*** *n.* Age. The latter denotes the period; the former the persons living in that period.

***Genius,*** *n.* Talent. *Genius* is a most extraordinary and original mental endowment; *talent* is acquisitive and imitative rather than original.

***Gentiles,*** *n.* Heathen, Pagans. *Gentiles* were all nations except the Jews; *Heathen* and *Pagans* are all nations practicing idolatry or false worship; *Heathen* is more frequently applied to cultivated *Pagan* nations like the Greek and Romans.

***Gentle,*** *a.* Tame. *Gentleness* is natural; *tameness* the result of art or breeding; *gentle* is the opposite of fierce or rude; *tame* of wild or spirited; in a moral sense *gentle* has a good, *tame* a bad signification. ROUGH.

***Get,*** *v.* Gain, obtain, procure, acquire, earn. LOSE.

***Give,*** *v.* Bestow, grant. We *give* what is asked or unasked for; *grant* what is asked for; *bestow* what is expressly wished; *bestow* indicates the need of the receiver. TAKE.

***Give up,*** *v.* Cede, concede, deliver, surrender, yield.

***Glad,*** *a.* Cheerful, joyful, pleased. *Glad* is stronger than *cheerful* and weaker than *joyful; glad* denotes a lively and transient, *pleased* a less vivid but more lasting sentiment; *cheerfulness* is an even frame of mind. SAD. (See MOURNFUL.)

***Gloomy,*** *a.* Morose, sullen. *Gloomy* is in the frame of mind; *morose* and *sullen* in the temper; *sullenness* is shown by reserve; *moroseness* by roughness of voice and language. CHEERFUL.

***Glory,*** *n.* Honor. *Glory* is attained by splendid exploits; *honor* by a conscientious discharge of one's duty.

***Good,*** *a.* Virtuous, worthy. BAD.

***Good,*** *n.* Advantage, benefit. *Good* as a universal term includes *benefit* and *advantage;* a *benefit* is a positive *good;* an *advantage* an indirect *good;* an *advantage* is not a *benefit* unless good use is made of it. EVIL.

***Good Nature,*** *n.* Good humor. The former is a permanent habit; the latter a temporary state of the spirits.

***Goods,*** *n.* Chattels, effects, furniture, movables.

***Govern,*** *v.* Regulate, rule. *Govern* has always a good sense; *rule* may have a bad one; *regulate* is governing with judgment.

***Grace,*** *n.* Favor. *Grace* is the result of kindness; *favor* is voluntary, without obligation or hope of reward; *favor* is a positive good; *grace* a kindness to offenders deserving punishment.

***Grace,*** *n.* Charm. *Grace* is merely physical; *charm* either physical or mental; *grace* depends on bodily movement; *charm* is an innate quality.

***Graceful,*** *a.* Comely, elegant. AWKWARD.

***Grandeur,*** *n* Magnificence. The latter is the highest degree of *grandeur.*

***Gratify,*** *v.* Humor, indulge. *Humor* is generally used in a bad sense.

***Grave,*** *a.* Serious, solemn. *Grave* means more than *serious;* less than *solemn; gravity* is a characteristic of persons; *seriousness* of persons and things; *gravity* of demeanor; a *serious* charge; a *solemn* invocation. FACETIOUS.

***Great,*** *a.* Big, large. *Great* refers to all dimensions; *large* to extent, quantity, space; *big* to capacity or expansion. SMALL. (See LITTLE.)

***Greediness,*** *n.* Avidity, eagerness. *Avidity* refers to mental desires; *greediness* to physical; *eagerness* is a passing feeling; *greediness* a fixed habit.

***Grief,*** *n.* Affliction, sorrow. JOY.

***Grieve,*** *v.* Lament, mourn. *Grief* is inward feeling; *mourning* and *lamentation* the outward sign of grief; *lament* expresses a passing and partial feeling; *mourning* a permanent one. REJOICE.

***Gross,*** *n.* Total. *Gross* is the whole from which nothing has been taken; *total* the whole to which nothing need be added; deductions may be made from the *gross,* but not from the *total.*

***Guarantee,*** *v.* To be responsible for, be security for, warrant. *Guarantee* refers to either private or public matters; *be security* to private only; one is *security* by contract; *responsible* by his office or situation; *warrant* is a commercial term.

***Guard,*** *v.* Defend, watch, shield, keep, protect.

***Guard,*** *n.* Sentinel. A *sentinel* is a military guard.

***Guess,*** *v.* Conjecture, divine. We *guess*

what is; *conjecture* what may be; *divine* things mysterious or supernatural.

***Guile,*** *n.* Deceit, fraud. *Guile* denotes extreme deceitfulness; *deceit* is the general word; *fraud* is a mode of deceit.

***Guiltless,*** *a.* Harmless, innocent. The *innocent* do not directly harm; the *guiltless* do not mean harm; the *harmless* want the power or will to inflict physical injury. GUILTY.

***Guilty,*** *a.* Criminal. *Guilty* marks the fact of the offence; *criminal* its character; *guilt* is a matter of evidence. GUILTLESS.

H.

***Habit,*** *n.* Custom. *Custom* is the frequent repetition of an act; *habit* the involuntary movement resulting from that repetition.

***Hail,*** *v.* Accost, address, greet, salute, welcome.

***Happiness,*** *n,* Beatitude, blessedness, bliss, felicity. *Felicity* is more than happiness; *bliss* than both. *Beatitude* is heavenly *happiness*; *blessedness* the *happiness* of those favored by Heaven. UNHAPPINESS. (See UNHAPPY.)

***Harbor,*** *n.* Haven, port. A *haven* is a natural *harbor;* a *port* an artificial *harbor.*

***Hard,*** *a.* Firm, solid. Bodies are *hard* by the adhesion of their component parts; the adherence of different bodies to each other is firmness. *Hard* denotes a closer adherence of the parts of a body than *solid*. *Hard* is opposed to *soft; solid* to *fluid.* SOFT.

***Hard,*** *a.* Arduous, difficult. *Hard* is positive; *difficult* negative; *arduous* means more than either. A *difficult* task requires exertion; a *hard* task, great exertion; an *arduous* task, extraordinary exertion. EASY.

***Harsh,*** *a.* Rough, rigorous, severe, gruff, morose. GENTLE.

***Hasten,*** *v.* Accelerate, despatch, expedite, speed. *Hasten* denotes a quick movement towards a point; *accelerate*, a bringing something to a point; *speed*, a quick, forward movement; *despatch*, bringing to an end; *expedite*, bringing to an end important affairs. DELAY.

***Hateful,*** *a.* Odious. *Hateful* applies to whatever transgresses the rules of morality; *odious* to things relating to the interests of others.

***Hatred,*** *v.* Enmity, ill-will, rancor. *Hatred* is stronger than *enmity; enmity* than *ill-will. Rancor* is a bitter, inveterate *enmity. Ill-will* is in the mind only. FRIENDSHIP.

***Haughtiness,*** *n.* Arrogance, pride. *Haughtiness* and *arrogance* are founded on a lofty idea of one's own merits; *disdain* on a low opinion of others. MODESTY. (See MODEST.)

***Haughty,*** *a.* Arrogant, disdainful, supercilious, proud.

***Hazard,*** *v.* Risk, venture. *Hazard* denotes an absence of design; *risk*, a choice, the result of necessity. *Venture* implies a calculation of the chances.

***Healthy,*** *a.* Salubrious, salutary, wholesome. *Healthy* is the general word; *wholesome* is what does not injure the health; *salubrious*, what improves it; *salutary*, what cures a disorder. UNHEALTHY. (See SICKLY.)

***Heap,*** *v.* Accumulate, amass, pile. We *heap* without order; *pile* in order; *accumulate* by adding *heap* to *heap*; *amass* by forming into a mass.

***Hearty,*** *a.* Cordial, sincere, warm. *Sincere* expresses a weaker feeling than *warmth* or *cordialty.* A *warm* heart; *sincere* professions; a *cordial* greeting; a *hearty* welcome. (See ARTFUL.) INSINCERE.

***Heavy,*** *a.* Burdensome, ponderous, weighty. *Weighty* is more than *heavy*; *ponderous* more than *weighty.* LIGHT.

***Heed,*** *n.* Care, attention. *Heed* applies to important things; *care* to less important. *Attention* is the generic term.

***Heighten,*** *v.* Enhance, exalt, elevate, raise.

***Heinous,*** *a.* Atrocious, flagitious, flagrant A *heinous* crime is a serious violation of law; a *flagrant* offence is in direct disregard of established opinions; a *flagitious* offence is a gross violation of morality; an *atrocious* crime is accompanied with revolting and horrible circumstances. VENIAL.

***Help,*** *v.* Aid, assist, relieve, succor. *Help* and *assist* are personal services; the former physical, the latter physical or mental. *Assistance* is given; *aid* sent. *Succor* is *assistance* given immediately; *relief* is the removal of pain. HINDER.

***Heretic,*** *n.* Sectary, sectarian, schismatic, dissenter, nonconformist. *Heretic* applies to matters of faith; *schismatic* to matters of discipline. A *sectary* or *sectarian* is a member of a sect; a *dissenter* dissents from an established church; a *nonconformist* does not conform to a national religion.

***Hesitate,*** *v.* Falter, stammer, stutter. *Stammer* and *stutter* relate to physical defects; *hesitation* is the result of an interruption in the thoughts; *faltering* of disturbed feeling.

***Hideous,*** *a.* Grim, ghastly, grisly. *Grim* refers to the face only; *grisly* to the whole form; *hideous* to natural objects; *ghastly* to things supernatural or death-like. BEAUTIFUL.

***High.*** *a.* Lofty, tall, elevated; the opposite of *deep.*

***Hinder,*** *v.* Impede, obstruct, prevent. We are *hindered* temporarily; *prevented* altogether *Impede* and *obstruct* relate to more important things than hinder; and cause longer delay. HELP.

***Hint,*** *v.* Allude, refer, suggest, intimate, insinuate.

***Hold,*** *v.* Detain, keep, retain, *Hold* is merely physical; *keep* is to have by at one's disposal. *Detain* and *retain* are methods of *keeping.* What is *detained* is *kept* without the consent of the owner; what is *retained* is *kept*, but under altered circumstances.

***Holiness,*** *n.* Sanctity, piety, sacredness.

***Holy,*** *a.* Devout, pious, religious. *Holiness* is both Divine and human; *devoutness, religion, piety*, merely human. *Piety* is a feeling of love and obedience to a Supreme Being; *devotion* the outward mark of piety. *Religion* is a matter of conduct and principle.

***Homely,*** *a.* Plain, ugly, coarse. BEAUTIFUL.

***Honesty,*** *n.* Integrity, probity, uprightness. *Honesty* is the general term; it implies only a negative virtue. *Probity* is a tried, solid virtue; *uprightness* implies also a *resistance* to temptation; *integrity* is soundness of principle either (like uprightness) with reference to particular trusts, or without reference to any outward circumstances. DISHONESTY.

***Honor,*** *v.* Respect, reverence. *Honor* expresses an outward act; *reverence* is either mental or exterior; *respect* is generally mental, though it may be expressed by acts. DISHONOR. (See DISCREDIT.)

***Hope,*** *n.* Confidence, expectation, trust. We *hope* for things desirable; *expect* what may be desirable or undesirable. *Confide* and *trust* express a dependence on some person or thing to effect something which we desire.

***Hopeless,*** *a.* Desperate. *Hopeless* applies only to things; *desperate* to persons or things. *Desperate* is stronger than *hopeless.*

***Hot,*** *a.* Ardent, burning, fiery. *Ardent* is only used figuratively. *Hot* expresses the presence of heat; *fiery* of fire and heat; *burning* of fire now in progress. (See COOL.) COLD.

***However,*** *conj.* Nevertheless, notwithstanding, yet. *Yet* marks a simple contrast; *nevertheless* and *notwithstanding* consequences the opposite of what was to be expected. *However* marks a deduction drawn from the whole.

***Humble,*** *a.* Modest, submissive. *Modesty* relates to ourselves only; *humility* to ourselves and others; *submissiveness* to others. *Humility* is a frame of mind; *submissiveness* a form of action. HAUGHTY.

***Humble,*** *v.* Degrade, humiliate; mortify, abase. EXALT.

***Humor,*** *n.* Mood, temper. *Humor* and *mood* are partial and temporary; the former is chiefly produced by physical, the latter by mental or moral causes. *Temper* is the general permanent state.

***Hunt,*** *n.* Chase. The *hunt* begins as soon as we begin to look for game; the *chase* when the game is found.

***Hurtful,*** *a.* Noxious, pernicious. What is *hurtful* simply *hurts;* what is *pernicious* tends to destroy; what is *noxious* inflicts only physical *hurt.* BENEFICIAL. (See ADVANTAGEOUS.)

***Husbandry,*** *n.* Cultivation, tillage. *Cultivation* includes everything relating to the production of the fruits of the earth; *tillage* is the preparation of the ground for seed; *husbandry* is *cultivation* for domestic purposes.

***Hypocrite,*** *n.* Dissembler. The *hypocrite* pretends to be what he is not; the *dissembler* conceals what he is. The *hypocrite* must be a *dissembler*; but the *dissembler* is not necessarily a *hypocrite.*

I.

***Idea,*** *n.* Thought, imagination. The *idea* represents the object; *thought* reflects it. *Imagination* combines *ideas* already in the mind.

***Ideal,*** *a.* Imaginary. The *ideal* is what belongs to the idea, independent of the reality; the *imaginary* is created by the mind itself. The *ideal* is abstracted from the real; the *imaginary* directly opposed to it.

***Idle,*** *a.* Indolent, lazy. *Idle* expresses less than *lazy*; *lazy* less than *indolent.* An *idle* man does nothing useful; an *indolent* man does not care to do anything; a *lazy* man does nothing which he can help doing. *Idle* in a derived sense is synonymous with *vain;* an *idle* pursuit is a useless one by one who might have turned his time to better use; a *vain* pursuit is one which is not attended by the hoped-for consequences. (See ACTIVE.) INDUSTRIOUS.

***Ignorant,*** *a.* Illiterate, unlearned, unlettered. *Ignorant* is the general term; it implies simply a want of knowledge; *illiterate* implies total want of education and is used in an unfavorable sense; *unlettered* and *unlearned* imply want of education, but have no unfavorable sense. LEARNED.

***Illegal,*** *a.* Unlawful, illicit. LAWFUL.

***Illusion,*** *n.* Delusion. The latter refers especially to the mind; the former to the senses and imagination.

***Imitate,*** *v.* Ape, mimic. *Imitate* is the general word. *Ape* implies an absurd imitation; *mimic* a ludicrous one.

***Imitate,*** *v.* Follow. We *imitate* what is external only; we *follow* what is external or internal.

***Immaterial,*** *a.* Insignificant, trifling. SIGNIFICANT.

***Imminent,*** *a.* Impending, threatening. *Threatening* evils are discoverable; *impending* and imminent ones are not. An *impending* danger has been for some time gradually coming on; *imminent* conveys no idea of duration. REMOTE.

***Impair,*** *v.* Injure, deteriorate, lessen. IMPROVE.

***Impatient,*** *a.* Vehement, fretful. PATIENT.

***Imperfection,*** *n.* Defect, fault. *Imperfection* is want of perfection; *defect* shows that something is wanting; fault is a positive *imperfection.*

***Imperious,*** *a.* Lordly, domineering, overbearing, haughty.

***Impertinent,*** *a.* Impudent, insolent, rude, saucy. *Impertinence* assumes to itself what belongs to others; *rudeness* implies an extreme breach of decorum; *sauciness* is a pert *impertinence; impudence* a shameless *impertinence; insolence* an outrageous *impertinence.*

***Impervious,*** *a.* Impassable, impermeable, inaccessible.

***Implacable,*** *a.* Inexorable, unrelenting, relentless. GENTLE.

***Implant,*** *v.* Inculcate, infuse, instil, ingraft.

***Implicate,*** *v.* Involve, intangle, infold.

***Importance,*** *n.* Consequence, moment, weight. *Importance* is in things themselves. A thing is of *consequence* on account of its *consequences. Weight* is a very great degree of *importance; moment* is the *importance* belonging to a thing from its power to affect our interests; it applies only to things relating to our happiness or prosperity.

***Impossible,*** *a.* Impracticable. POSSIBLE.

***Imprint,*** *v.* Engrave, stamp, indent, impress, print upon.

***Impugn,*** *v.* Attack, assail, gainsay, oppose, contradict.

***Inability,*** *n.* Disability. *Inability* is a general absence of ability; *disability* an *inability* in particular cases. ABILITY.

***Inaccurate,*** *a.* Inexact. ACCURATE.

***Inactive,*** *a.* Inert, lazy, sluggish, slow, slothful. ACTIVE.

***Incapable,*** *a.* Incompetent, inadequate, insufficient. CAPABLE.

***Inclination,*** *a.* Propensity, proneness. *Inclination* marks the first movement of the will towards an object; *tendency,* a continued *inclination; propensity,* a still stronger inclination; *proneness* an habitual *inclination.*

***Inconsistent,*** *a.* Incongruous, incoherent. *Inconsistency* belongs to human feelings or actions; *incongruity* to the qualities of things; *incoherency* to thought or speech. CONSISTENT.

***Incorruptible,*** *a.* Honest, upright. VENAL.

***Increase,*** *n.* Accession, addition, augmentation. *Increase* is the general word. *Addition* is an intentional, *accession* an accidental increase. *Augmentation* increases value of a thing as well as quantity or number. DECREASE. (See ABATE.)

***Indecent,*** *a.* Immodest, indelicate. *Indecency* is weaker than *immodesty;* stronger than *indelicacy.* The latter comes from deficient education; *indecency* from unrestrained desire. *Immodest* conduct; *indelicate* language; *indecent* dress. (See BECOMING.) DECENT.

***Indifference,*** *n.* Insensibility, apathy. *Indifference* is generally a partial, temporary state; *apathy* a permanent one. *Insensibility* is either temporary or permanent; it is incapacity for feeling. (See FEELING.) SENSIBILITY.

***Indolent,*** *a.* Careless, listless. *Indolence* is indisposition to exertion; *listlessness* a sort of temporary torpor; the *careless* man from want of thought takes little or no concern about things. INDUSTRIOUS.

***Indubitable,*** *a.* Indisputable, incontrovertible, undeniable, unquestionable. DOUBTFUL.

***Ineffectual,*** *a.* Unavailing, powerless. EFFECTUAL.

***Infamous,*** *a.* Scandalous. *Infamous* applies to persons and things; *scandalous* to things only. *Infamous* implies a worse offense against morality. An *infamous* crime; a *scandalous* fraud.

***Inflexible,*** *a.* Unyielding, immovable. FLEXIBLE.

***Influence,*** *n.* Authority, ascendency, sway. *Influence* implies a power unconnected with a right; *authority* implies a power by right, superiority, etc. *Ascendency* and *sway* imply an extreme *influence.*

***Inform,*** *v.* Acquaint, apprise, instruct, notify, advise, tell.

***Information,*** *n.* Intelligence, instruction, advice.

***Infringe,*** *v.* Violate, transgress. Civil and moral laws are *infringed;* treaties and compacts *violated;* moral laws *transgressed.*

***Inherent,*** *a.* Inborn, inbred, innate.

***Injury,*** *n.* Damage, harm, hurt, mischief. *Injury* is the general word; damage is an *injury* accompanied by loss; *harm* the smallest kind of injury; *hurt* an *injury* impairing the soundness of a thing; *mischief* an *injury* disturbing the order of things. BENEFIT.

***Inside,*** *n.* *Interior.* The latter applies more properly to objects of considerable size; the former to things either great or small. OUTSIDE.

***Insist,*** *v.* Persist. We *insist* upon a right; we *persist* in doing a thing simply because we wish to do it.

***Insnare,*** *v.* Allure, entrap, entangle, inveigle.

***Insolvency,*** *n.* Failure, bankruptcy. *Insolvency* is an inability to pay one's debts; *failure,* a stopping of business from the same cause; *bankruptcy,* a voluntary or involuntary assignment of assets to creditors.

***Institute,*** *v.* Erect, establish, found. *Institute* is to form according to a definite plan; *erect* to build; *establish* to fix in position a thing already formed; *found* to lay the foundation of. *Found* a college; *erect* a college building.

***Insurrection,*** *n.* Rebellion, revolt, sedition. *Insurrection* may have either a good or a bad sense; *sedition* and *rebellion* have always a bad. *Revolt* is the throwing off of foreign rule; *sedition* and *rebellion* are directed against one's own government. *Sedition* may be open or secret.

***Intercede,*** *v.* Interfere, intermeddle, interpose, mediate.

***Intemperate,*** *a.* Immoderate, excessive, self-indulgent. ABSTEMIOUS.

***Intercourse,*** *n.* Communication, connection, commerce.

***Interest,*** *n.* Concern. *Interest* is on account of profit or amusement; *concern* is involuntary and disagreeable.

***Intermediate,*** *a.* Intervening. The latter relates to time or circumstances; the former to time and space.

***Interval,*** *n.* Respite. The latter denotes ceasing from action for a time.

***Intoxication,*** *n.* Drunkenness. *Intoxication* may be produced by various things; *drunkenness* is produced by the use of *intoxicating* liquors. SOBRIETY.

***Intrinsic,*** *a.* Genuine, native, real, true, inherent, inward.

***Invasion,*** *n.* Incursion, inroad, irruption. *Invasion* is the act of a regular, organized force; *irruption* and *inroad* of irregular forces. *Incursion* is the frequent raid from one State to another bordering upon it.

***Invent,*** *v* Fabricate, feign, forge, frame. *Invent* is the general word. *Feign* marks the creation of unreal objects; *frame* marks an invention which combines and arranges objects. *Fabricate* and *forge* mark *inventions* entirely false. *Invent* a story; *frame* an apology; *feign* repentance; *fabricate* a letter; *forge* a signature.

***Invincible,*** *a.* Insuperable, unconquerable, insurmountable.

***Irrational,*** *a.* Absurd, foolish, preposterous. *Foolish* is stronger than *irrational;* less than *absurd* and *preposterous. Irrational* commonly applies to things; *foolish* to persons or things. RATIONAL.

***Irregular,*** *a.* Disorderly, inordinate, intemperate, immethodical. *Irregular* is stronger than *immethodical;* weaker than *disorderly. Irregular* is not in order; *disorderly* positively out of order. *Inordinate* is out of order morally. *Intemperate*, contrary to a proper temper. *Intemperate* language, *inordinate* jealousy; *disorderly* conduct; *immethodical* habits; *irregular* proceedings.

***Jealous,*** *a.* Suspicious in love, envious. Persons are *jealous* of what is their own; *envious* of what is another's; *suspicious* of the designs or character of others.

***Jeopard,*** *v. a.* Hazard, peril, endanger.

***Jest,*** *v.* Joke, sport, divert, make game of. A person *jests* to make others laugh; he *jokes* or *diverts* for his own amusement or the amusement of others. Only persons can be *made game of;* both persons and things can be *made sport of.*

***Journey,*** *n.* Travel, tour, passage. A *journey* is on land; a *voyage* on the water; *travel* generally a long *voyage* or *journey*, or both. A *tour* is made for amusement and instruction. *Passage* now more frequently refers to travel on the water.

***Joy,*** *n.* Gladness, mirth, delight. *Joy* is a strong, lively sensation, evident in the face; *gladness* a more quiet, internal feeling; *mirth* a loud, noisy, externally expressed feeling. GRIEF.

***Judge,*** *n.* A person who decides; a justice. A *judge* may determine any matter; an *arbiter, referee*, or *umpire* only special matters submitted to them.

***Joyful,*** *a.* Glad, rejoicing, exultant. MOURNFUL.

***Judgment,*** *n.* Discernment, discrimination, understanding. *Judgment* is the generic name for the power of discriminating right and wrong; *discretion* and *prudence* apply to particular cases. *Judgment* combines experience and knowledge; *discretion* implies reflection in regard to the present; *prudence*, calculation of the future.

***Justice,*** *n.* Equity, right. *Justice* is right as established by law; *equity* according to the circumstances of each particular case. INJUSTICE. (See WRONG.)

***Justness,*** *n.* Accuracy, correctness, precision. *Justness* is an agreement with certain fixed principles; *correctness*, conformity to a certain standard. A statement is *correct;* the thought expressed in it is *just.*

## K.

***Keep,*** *v.* Preserve, save. Things are *kept* under all circumstances; *preserved* from dangers and difficulties; *saved* from threatened destruction. ABANDON.

***Kill,*** *v.* Assassinate, murder, slay. *Kill* is the general word. *Murder* is *killing* unlawfully with malice; *assassination, killing* by surprise; *slaying, killing* in battle.

***Kindred,*** *n.* Affinity, consanguinity, relationship. *Kindred* is the general word. *Relationship* applies to particular families; *affinity* is a close relationship; *consanguinity* is between persons descended directly from the same relations.

***Knowledge,*** *n.* Erudition, learning, science. *Knowledge* is the general word; *science*, a systematic species of *knowledge; learning*, the *knowledge* received by instruction; *erudition*, a profound *knowledge* acquired by long, laborious study. IGNORANCE. (See IGNORANT.)

## L.

***Language,*** *n.* Dialect, idiom, speech, tongue. *Language* is the general word. *Idiom* marks the peculiar construction of *language;* a *dialect* is a peculiar form of language. *Speech* is an abstract term, denoting either the power of uttering articulate sounds, or the words uttered. *Tongue* generally refers to the spoken language only.

***Last,*** *a.* Final, latest, ultimate. *Last* is opposed to first; *latest* to earliest; *final* to the introductory; *ultimate* to the immediately preceding. FIRST.

***Laudable,*** *a.* Commendable, praiseworthy. Things are *laudable* in themselves; *commendable* or *praiseworthy* in particular persons. A *praiseworthy* action is entitled to general respect; a *commendable* one to temporary approbation. BLAMABLE.

***Laughable,*** *a.* Comical, droll, ludicrous, ridiculous. The *laughable* is composed of things in general; the *ludicrous* and *ridiculous* have usually a personal reference; the former less so than the latter. The *comical* and *droll* apply to whatever is the cause of *laughter.* SERIOUS.

***Lawful,*** *a.* Legal, legitimate, licit. *Lawful* relates to law in general; *legal* to the established law of the land; *legitimate* to scientific standards as well as law; *licit* to moral laws only. A *legal* remedy; a *lawful* wife; a *legitimate* conclusion; an *illicit* intrigue. ILLEGAL.

***Lead,*** *v.* Conduct, guide. The two latter are modes of the former. FOLLOW.

***Lean,*** *a.* Meagre. *Lean* denotes want of fat; *meagre* of flesh. FAT.

***Learned,*** *a.* Erudite, scholarly. IGNORANT.

***Leave,*** *v.* Quit, relinquish. We *leave* what we may possibly return to; we *quit* a thing finally; *relinquish* it unwillingly.

***Leave,*** *n.* Liberty, permission, license. *Leave* and *liberty* may be taken; *license* and *permission* must be granted. *Leave* refers to familiar things; *liberty* to more important ones.

***Life,*** *n.* Existence, animation, spirit, vivacity. DEATH.

***Lifeless,*** *a.* Dead, inanimate. *Dead* and *lifeless* mark the absence of life where it once existed; *inanimate* where it never existed. The *inanimate* world; a *dead* body; a *lifeless* corpse.

***Lift,*** *v.* Erect, elevate, exalt, raise. LOWER.

***Light,*** *a.* Clear, bright. DARK.

***Lightness,*** *n.* Flightiness, giddiness, levity, volatility. SERIOUSNESS. (See SERIOUS.)

***Likeness,*** *n.* Resemblance, similarity. *Likeness* is the general word; *resemblance* relates to external properties only; *similarity* to circumstances or properties. *Likeness* is actual *resemblance* apparent. UNLIKENESS. (See DISSIMILARITY.)

***Linger,*** *v.* Lag, loiter, tarry, saunter. *Linger* is to stop or move slowly; *tarry* to stop; *loiter* to move slowly; *lag* has a bad sense; *saunter* is the lazy movement of an idler. HASTEN.

***Little,*** *a.* Diminutive, small. *Little* is the opposite of great; *small* of large. *Diminutive* is smaller than it ought to be. GREAT.

***Livelihood,*** *n.* Living, maintenance, subsistence, support.

***Lively,*** *a.* Jocund, merry, sportive, sprightly, vivacious. *Lively* is the general word; *sprightly*, full of spirits; *vivacious*, same as lively; *merry and jocund* are social forms of liveliness.

***Long,*** *a.* Extended, extensive. SHORT.

***Look,*** *v.* Appear. The former marks the impression which a thing makes upon the senses; the latter the act of coming into sight. A woman *looks* handsome; *appears* suddenly.

***Lose,*** *v.* Miss. What is *lost* is gone entirely; what is *missed* is temporarily out of sight or reach. GAIN.

***Loss,*** *n.* Detriment, damage, deprivation. GAIN.

***Loud,*** *n.* Clamorous, high-sounding, noisy. *Loud* is the general word; *clamorous* is disagreeably loud; *high-sounding* implies the use of big words; *noisy* is offensively loud. LOW.

***Love,*** *n.* Affection. HATRED.

***Low,*** *a.* Abject, mean. *Low* is stronger than *mean; abject* than both *mean* and *low.* NOBLE.

***Lunacy,*** *n.* Derangement, insanity, lunacy, mania, madness. *Derangement* denotes the beginning of mental unsoundness; *insanity* is a positive disease; *lunacy* a violent *insanity; madness* and *mania* denote a confirmed and furious stage of *insanity* or *lunacy.* SANITY.

***Lustre,*** *n.* Brightness, brilliancy, splendor. *Brightness* and *lustre* apply generally to natural, *brilliancy* and *splendor* to artificial or extraordinary lights. Figuratively *brightness* applies to ordinary, *lustre* to remarkable cases of virtue, heroism, etc. *Splendor* is the effect of size and richness of light, *brilliancy* of variety and brightness of light.

***Luxuriant,*** *a.* Exuberant. The former denotes the perfection, the latter the superabundance of vegetation. SPARSE.

## M.

***Madness,*** *n.* Fury, rage, frenzy. *Frenzy* and *madness* are either physical or moral; *fury* and *rage* moral only. *Madness* is a permanent, *frenzy* a temporary derangement; *rage* is a highly inflamed passion; *fury* the bursting out of rage.

***Magisterial,*** *a.* August, dignified, majestic, pompous, stately. The *majestic* is real, the *magisterial* assumed; *stately* relates to rank and splendor, *pompous* to personal importance; *dignified* is a characteristic of manner or action; *august* marks an essential characteristic of an object.

***Make,*** *v.* Form, create, produce. *Make* is the general word; *form* is to *make* after a certain form; *produce* to bring into existence; *create* to bring into existence by an absolute power and intelligence. *Make* implies a conscious agent; *form* does not. DESTROY.

***Malediction,*** *n.* Anathema, curse, imprecation, execration. *Malediction* is a general declaration of evil; *curse*, a solemn utterance and wish of evil; anathema, an ecclesiastical *malediction; execration* and *imprecation* denounce some great evil.

***Malevolent,*** *a.* Malicious, malignant. *Ma-*

*levolence* is a permanent temper of the mind; *maliciousness* may be only temporary; *malignity* is a characteristic of things rather than persons. BENEVOLENCE.

***Malice,*** *n.* Grudge, pique, rancor, spite. *Malice* is rooted in the heart; *rancor* is a permanent hatred; *spite*, a petty *malice; grudge* and *pique* are spiteful feelings caused by personal resentment; a *grudge* exists longer than a *pique*.

***Maritime,*** *a.* Marine, naval, nautical. Countries on the sea are *maritime; marine* is belonging to the sea as opposed to the land; *naval* is opposed to military; *nautical* is a scientific term denoting the science of navigation.

***Mark,*** *n.* Impression, print, stamp. Anything which changes the exterior appearance of an object is a *mark; an impression* is a *mark* stamped upon or into an object; a *print* is a specific *mark* upon an object; a *stamp* a *mark* stamped in or upon an object.

***Mark,*** *n.* Indication, note, sign, symptom, token. A *sign* is a representation of some object; a *note* is a *sign* composed of *marks; a symptom* a *mark* which shows the cause of complaints; a *token* a permanent *mark* (in a moral sense); an *indication* a *sign* given by persons, and denoting the act of persons.

***Mark,*** *n.* Footstep, track, trace, step. A *mark* is a fresh, recent line; a *trace* an old, broken one; a *vestige* a *mark* or *trace* left by the works of men; a *footstep* is the *step* of a person; a *track* is made by the steps of many.

***Mark,*** *n.* Badge, stigma. a *badge* is a *mark* of distinction; a *stigma* a *mark* of disgrace.

***Matter,*** *n.* Materials, subject. *Matter* is opposed to spirit; *materials* are a part of *matter;* the *subject* of a work is the question which it discusses; the *matter* is the thoughts, opinions, and words in it.

***Mean,*** *a.* Pitiful, sordid. *Mean* is what is low, degraded, beneath us; *pitiful* is bad as well as low; *sordid* applies particularly to the love of money-getting. NOBLE.

***Mean,*** *n.* Medium. *Mean* is used in speculative, *medium* in practical things.

***Meeting,*** *n.* Interview. *Meeting* is ordinary, *interview* extraordinary.

***Memoirs,*** *n.* Annals, chronicles. *Memoirs* are a personal narrative of an individual in regard to things public or private; *annals* and *chronicles* relate to public events only; *chronicles* record events in the order of their occurrence; *annals* arrange events by the year.

***Memory,*** *n.* Recollection, remembrance, reminiscence. *Memory* is the power of recalling mental images; the other three are methods of exerting that power; *remembrance* is a voluntary exercise of memory; *recollection* is the recalling of a thing forgotten; *reminiscence* is an abstract, intellectual exercise of the memory.

***Mental,*** *a.* Intellectual. *Mental* is opposed to corporeal, *intellectual* to physical or sensual. Objects are *mental; subjects intellectual*. PHYSICAL.

***Mere,*** *a.* Bare. *Bare* has a positive sense; *mere* a negative.

***Mien,*** *n.* Air, look. *Mien* marks any state of external circumstances; *air* an habitual, *look* a particular state.

***Mindful,*** *a.* Observant, regardful. *Mindful* relates to what is wanted of others; *regardful* to what demands serious consideration, generally from its importance to others; *observant* is applicable to either. HEEDLESS. (See NEGLIGENT.)

***Mirth,*** *n.* Merriment, hilarity, joviality, jollity. *Mirth* denotes the feeling of joy shown in outward conduct; the other words denote the cause or outward expression; *merriment* is what will cause *mirth; hilarity, jollity*, and *joviality* refer to social *mirth*, the pleasures of the table, etc. GRIEF.

***Misconstrue,*** *v.* Misinterpret. The former is usually the result of ignorance; the latter of prejudice.

***Mix,*** *v.* Blend, confound, mingle. Things *mixed* lose their individuality; things *mingled* may still be distinguished; *blending* is a partial mixture; *confounding* an erroneous mixture; *blend* and *confound* usually refer to mental operations.

***Mixture,*** *n.* Medley, miscellany. Whatever can be *mixed* may form a *mixture;* a *medley* is a *mixture* of incongruous objects; *miscellany* applies only to intellectual objects.

***Modest,*** *a.* Bashful, diffident. *Modesty* is a becoming self-distrust; *bashfulness* a feeling shown in the face and demeanor; *diffidence*, an undue self-distrust. IMMODEST.

***Moisture,*** *n.* Dampness, humidity. *Dampness* is the portion of *moisture* remaining in bodies capable of retaining *moisture; moistness* is the general term to express the presence of liquid in a body; *humidity* the scientific equivalent of *moistness*.

***Mournful,*** *a.* Sad, sorrowful, grievous. JOYFUL.

***Moving,*** *a.* Affecting, pathetic. Only the tender feelings are *affected;* either good or bad feelings may be *moved*. The *affecting* appeals to the sense and understanding; the *pathetic* to the heart alone. An *affecting* scene; a *pathetic* appeal.

***Mutilate,*** *v.* Maim, mangle. *Mutilate* is the most general; *mangle* denotes irregular wounds anywhere on the body; *maim* denotes wounds in the limbs, especially the hands.

***Mutual,*** *a.* Reciprocal. *Mutual* denotes an equality of condition; *reciprocal* a succession of favors. Friends render one another *mutual*, master and servants *reciprocal*, services.

## N.

***Naked,*** *a.* Bare. *Bare* is without any particular covering; *naked* without any covering at all. CLOTHED.

***Name,*** *v.* Call. *Name* is to address one by name; *Call* to address loudly. We *call* to proclaim; *name* to distinguish.

***Name,*** *n.* Appellation, title. *Name* is the general word; an *appellation* is a *name* given for some specific purpose; a *title* is an *appellation* given for purposes of honor or distinction.

***Name,*** *v.* Designate, denominate, entitle, style. *Name* is to give a *name* to or call by *name; entitle* is to call by a specific *title; denominate* to distinguish by a specific *name; style* to address by a specific *name*.

***Name,*** *n.* Credit, repute, reputation. *Name* and *repute* have either a good or a bad sense; *credit* always, and *reputation* generally a good one; *name* and *reputation* are known to the public; *repute* and *credit* to a smaller number.

***Necessary,*** *a.* Essential, requisite. *Necessary* is a general term; *essential* and *requisite* are modes of *necessity*. The *requisite* may be *requisite* only in part; without the *essential* a thing cannot exist. UNNECESSARY. (See SUPERFLUOUS.)

***Necessary,*** *a.* Needful. The *necessary* may refer to any object; *needful* relates only to partial and temporary wants.

***Negative,*** *a.* Positive denying. POSITIVE.

***Neglect,*** *v.* Omit. We *neglect* what ought to be done; *omit* what is inconvenient for us to do.

***Negligent,*** *a.* Careless, remiss, heedless, inattentive, thoughtless. *Negligence* and *remissness* fail to do what they ought; *carelessness* is want of care in doing things; *heedlessness*, want of thought; *inattentiveness*, want of attention. CAREFUL.

***Neighborhood,*** *n.* Vicinity. The former denotes the nearness of persons to each other or to objects in general; the latter the nearness of one object to another. We live in a quiet neighborhood in the *vicinity* of New York.

***New,*** *a.* Fresh, modern, novel, recent. *New* is what has not long existed; *novel*, something strange; *fresh*, something showing yet no marks of use; *modern*, something of the present time; *recent*, something just done or made. OLD.

***News,*** *n.* Tidings. *News* is unexpected; *tidings* expected.

***Noble,*** *a.* Grand. *Noble* denotes the quality by which a thing is more excellent than others; *grand* the existence of one of those qualities by which a thing is *noble*. BASE.

***Noise,*** *n.* Clamor, cry, outcry. A *noise* is a loud sound; *clamor, cry*, and *outcry* are kinds of *noise*. A *cry* is produced only by animate objects; a *noise* either by animate or inanimate. *Outcry* and *clamor* are irregular sounds; the latter the joint work of many; *outcry* may be made by one or many. SILENCE.

***Noted,*** *a.* Notorious. *Noted* is used both in a good and a bad sense; *notorious* only in a bad sense. OBSCURE.

***Nourish,*** *v.* Cherish, nurture. Things *nourish:* persons *nurture* and *cherish. Nourish* is physical; *cherish*, physical and mental. A mother *nourishes* her child with her breast; *nurtures* it while it is dependent on her; *cherishes* it in her bosom.

***Numb,*** *a.* Benumbed, torpid. *Numb* denotes the quality, *benumbed* the state; what is permanently *benumbed* is *torpid*. LIVELY.

## O.

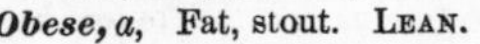

***Obduracy,*** *n.* Impenitence.

***Obedient,*** *a.* Obsequious, submissive. We are *obedient* to command, *submissive* to power or will, *obsequious* to persons. UNRULY.

***Obese,*** *a,* Fat, stout. LEAN.

***Object,*** *v.* Oppose. *Opposition* is longer, more premeditated, than *objection.*

***Obnoxious,*** *a.* Offensive. *Obnoxious* is applicable to persons only; *offensive,* to both persons and things.

***Obscure,*** *a.* Undistinguished, unknown. DISTINGUISHED.

***Obstinate,*** *a.* Contumacious, headstrong, stubborn. *Obstinacy* is a mental habit; *contumacy* a mode of action or particular state of feeling or mode of action. The *stubborn* man is *obstinate* from a perverted will; the *headstrong,* from perverted understanding. YIELDING.

***Occasion,*** *n.* Opportunity. The former decides our action; the latter invites to action.

***Offense,*** *n.* Affront, misdeed, misdemeanor, transgression, trespass. *Offense* is the general word; it may be either private or public. A *misdemeanor* is an *offense* against public law; *misdeed* is private; *affront,* personal; *trespass,* in regard to land and property; *transgression,* moral.

***Offensive,*** *a.* Insolent, abusive, obnoxious. INOFFENSIVE.

***Office,*** *n.* Charge, function, place.

***Offspring,*** *n.* Issue, progeny. *Progeny* denotes a number; *issue* has no reference to number; *offspring* applies to one or many.

***Old,*** *a.* Ancient, antique, antiquated, obsolete, old-fashioned. The *old* has long existed and still exists; *ancient* once existed, but perhaps does not now; *antique* has long been *ancient; antiquated, obsolete,* and *old-fashioned* have long been out of use. YOUNG.

***Omen,*** *n.* Presage, prognostic. *Omens* and *prognostics* are drawn from external objects; *presages* from one's own feelings.

***One,*** *a.* Single. *One* is opposed to none; *single* to double or two.

***Opaque,*** *a.* Dark. *Opaqueness* is the *darkness* of solid bodies which do not admit light. BRIGHT.

***Opinionated,*** *a.* Conceited, egoistical. A *conceited* man has a high *conceit* of himself; an *opinionated* man is free with, and fond of, his opinions; an *egoistical* man admires and constantly talks of himself.

***Opinion,*** *n.* Notion, sentiment. *Opinions* relate to speculation, *notions* to sensible objects, *sentiments* to matters of practice.

***Oppose,*** *v.* Resist, withstand, thwart.

***Option,*** *n.* Choice. *Option* is given, *choice* made.

***Order,*** *n.* Method, rule. *Order* is a proper accord of time, object, and place; *method,* the right choice of means; *rule,* what will keep us right.

***Outlive,*** *v.* Survive. The former denotes a comparison between two lives; the latter, existence beyond any given term.

***Outward,*** *a.* External, outside, exterior. INSIDE.

***Over,*** *prep.* Above. UNDER.

***Overbalance,*** *v.* Outweigh, preponderate.

***Overbear,*** *v.* Bear down, overwhelm, overpower, subdue. *Overpower* and *overwhelm* denote a partial, *subdue* a permanent, superiority; *bear down* implies greater force and violence than *overbear.*

***Overflow,*** *v.* Inundation, deluge. *Overflow* denotes abundance; *inundation,* abundance and impetuosity; the *deluge* sweeps everything before it.

***Overrule,*** *v.* Supersede. The former applies only to the acts of persons; the latter, to things as agents also.

***Overspread,*** *v.* Overrun, ravage.

***Overturn,*** *v.* Invert, overthrow, reverse, subvert. *Overturn* turns over; *overthrow* throws over with violence. Small matters are *overturned;* great ones *subverted.* A decision is *reversed;* the order of things *inverted.*

***Overwhelm,*** *v.* Crush. *Overwhelm* makes a thing sink by putting a heavy body over it; *crush* destroys its consistency by violent pressure.

## P.

***Pain,*** *n.* Pang, agony, anguish. *Pang* is a particular feeling; *anguish* always, and *agony* generally, denotes a state. *Pain* is the general word. PLEASURE.

***Pallid,*** *a.* Pale, wan. The mere absence of color is *paleness; pallidness* is excessive *paleness; wan* denotes extreme *pallor.*

***Part,*** *n.* Division, portion, share. *Part* is indefinite, opposed to the whole; *division* is done by design; *portion* relates to individuals without distinction; *share,* to individuals specially referred to.

***Particular,*** *a.* Eccentric, odd, singular, strange. What is *particular* belongs to some small point; what is *singular* is the only one of its kind; *odd* without an equal; *eccentric* deviates from ordinary rules; *strange* is different from what we are accustomed to.

***Patient,*** *a.* Passive, submissive. *Patience* is a virtue; *passiveness,* an involuntary nonresistance. *Submissive* means conforming to another's will.

***Peace,*** *n.* Calm, quiet, tranquillity. *Peace* is a general term; *quiet,* freedom from noise, or interruption; *calm,* an absence of violent motion and noise; *tranquillity,* an entire freedom from every discomposing element.

***Peaceable,*** *a.* Pacific, peaceful. Persons and things are *peaceable;* things *peaceful. Pacific* means either making, or disposed to make, peace.

***Penetrate,*** *v.* Bore, pierce, perforate. *Penetrate* makes an entrance into a thing; *pierce* goes deeper; *perforate* and *bore* generally indicate mechanical means.

***Penetration,*** *n.* Acuteness, sagacity.

***People,*** *n.* Nation. A *nation* is a *people* connected by birth.

***People,*** *n.* Persons, folks. *People* is general; *persons* specific; *folks* familiar or disrespectful.

***Perceive,*** *v.* Discern, distinguish. We *perceive* what is obvious; *discern* what is remote; *distinguish* things.

***Perception,*** *n.* Conception, notion, idea. Our impression of a present object is a *perception;* its revival in the absence of the object, an *idea;* a combination of *ideas* to present an image to the mind, a *conception;* the *association* of *ideas* to form a decision, a *notion.*

***Permit,*** *v.* Allow. FORBID.

***Persuade,*** *v.* Allure, entice, prevail upon.

***Physical,*** *a.* Corporeal, bodily, material. MENTAL.

***Picture,*** *n.* Engraving, print. *Picture* is by the hand of the artist; *print* is a *printed* copy of the painting; *engraving* the work of an engraver.

***Piteous,*** *a.* Doleful, woful, rueful. *Piteous* marks the external expression of mental or physical pain; *doleful* sounds implying pain; *rueful* the looks; *woful* applies to human situations.

***Pity,*** *n.* Compassion. *Pity* is excited by weakness; *compassion* by misfortune.

***Place,*** *n.* Position, post, situation, station.

***Place,*** *v.* Order, dispose. *Place* is to assign a place to a thing; *dispose* is to place according to a certain rule; *order,* to place in a certain order.

***Place,*** *n.* Spot, site. *Spot* is a small *place; site* the place on which anything stands.

***Plain,*** *a.* Open, manifest, evident. SECRET.

***Play,*** *n.* Game, sport. *Play* is irregular; *game* a systematic exercise; *sport* any action or motion for pleasure. WORK.

***Please,*** *v.* Gratify, pacify. DISPLEASE.

***Pleasure,*** Charm, delight, joy. *Delight* and *joy* are modes of pleasure; joy *fleeting, delight* less so; *charm* implies a high degree of *pleasure.* PAIN.

***Plentiful.*** Abundant, ample, copious, plenteous.

***Poise,*** *v.* Balance. A thing is *poised* as respects itself; *balanced* as respects other things.

***Positive,*** *a.* Absolute, peremptory. The two former refer to persons or things; peremptory, only to personal objects. NEGATIVE.

***Possessor,*** *n.* Owner, master, proprietor.

***Possible,*** *a.* Practical, practicable. IMPOSSIBLE.

***Poverty,*** *n.* Penury, indigence, need, want. *Want* is a low state of *poverty; penury* an extreme degree of *want. Need* is an immediate, present *want; indigence,* the want of things to which one has been accustomed. RICHES.

***Power.*** Authority, force, strength, dominion.

***Powerful,*** *a.* Mighty, potent. WEAK.

***Praise,*** *v.* Commend, extol, laud. BLAME.

***Prayer,*** *n.* Entreaty, petition, request, suit.

***Pretense,*** *n.* Pretext.

***Prevailing,*** *a.* Predominant, prevalent.

***Prevent,*** *v.* Obviate, preclude. *Prevent* applies to circumstances; *obviate* and *preclude,* to mental objects.

***Previous,*** *a.* Introductory, preparatory, preliminary. *Previous* applies to matters in general; *preliminary,* to matters of contract; *preparatory,* to matters of arrangement; *introductory,* to matters of science and discussion. SUBSEQUENT.

***Pride,*** *n.* Vanity, conceit. We are *proud* of what we have; *conceited* of what we think we have; *vain* in regard to small things from frivolity or weakness. HUMILITY. (See HUMBLE.)

***Primary,*** *a.* Original, primitive, pristine. Primary is general, denoting merely the order of succession; *original* is or belongs to the birth of a thing; other things are formed after the *primitive;* the *pristine* comes after the *primitive,* and becomes customary.

***Prince,*** *n.* Monarch, potentate, sovereign.

***Priority,*** *n.* Precedence, pre-eminence, preference.

***Privacy,*** *n.* Retirement, seclusion. *Privacy* is opposed to publicity; *retirement* to freedom of access. *Seclusion* is excess of *retirement.* PUBLICITY.

***Privilege,*** *n.* Exemption, immunity, prerogative. *Privilege* applies to all desirable things. *Prerogative* is the exercise of some special power; *exemption* exempts from some burden or payment; *immunity* from some service.

***Proceeding,*** *n.* Transaction. The latter includes only things deliberately brought to a conclusion.

***Profess,*** *v.* Declare. We *profess* by words or action; *declare* only by words.

***Profligate,*** *a.* Abandoned, reprobate. VIRTUOUS.

***Promiscuous,*** *a.* Indiscriminate. *Promiscuous* refers to the mingling of any number of different objects; *indiscriminate* to an action which does not criminate different objects. SELECT.

***Promise,*** *n.* Engagement, word. We *promise* in set form of words; *engage* generally. *Word* includes both.

***Proof,*** *n.* Evidence, testimony. *Proof* proves; *evidence* makes evident; *testimony* is *evidence* by witnesses.

***Proportionate,*** *a.* Commensurate. UNPROPORTIONATE. (See UNEQUAL.)

***Prorogue,*** *v.* Adjourn. *Prorogue* is to *adjourn* for an indefinite time; *adjourn* implies generally a shorter time.

***Prove,*** *v.* Demonstrate, evince, manifest. *Prove* is to make good by proofs; *demonstrate proves* clearly; *evince* shows by convincing proof something of ourselves.

***Provide,*** *v.* Furnish, procure, supply. *Provide* against contingencies; *furnish* comforts; *procure* necessaries; *supply* wants.

***Publish,*** *v.* Disclose, divulge, publish, promulgate, reveal. *Publish* is the general word; things of general interest are *promulgated;* things concealed *divulge, disclosed,* and *revealed.*

***Purpose,*** *v.* Propose. We *purpose* things to be done at once; *propose* things more distant.

***Put,*** *v.* Lay, place, set. *Put* is the general word. *Place* is to *put* in a specific manner. *Lay* applies only to things that will *lie; set* to things that will stand.

Q.

***Quality,*** *n.* Property, attribute. *Quality* is inherent in the thing; *property* belongs to it for the time being; *attribute* is the *quality* which can be assigned to an object.

***Quarrel,*** *n.* Broil, feud.

***Question,*** *n.* Query. *Question* may be reasonable or not; *query* is generally reasonable.

***Quickness,*** *n.* Celerity, fleetness, rapidity, swiftness, velocity. SLOWNESS. (See SLOW.)

R.

***Rapacious,*** *a.* Ravenous, voracious.

***Rashness,*** *n.* Hastiness, precipitancy, temerity. *Rashness* refers to physical, *temerity* to moral action. *Hastiness* and *precipitancy* are modes of *rashness.*

***Ravage,*** *n.* Desolation, ravage.

***Ready,*** *a.* Apt, prompt.

***Recede,*** *v.* Retreat, retire, withdraw, secede. ADVANCE.

***Recover,*** *v.* Repair, retrieve. *Recover* is the general word. We *recover* and *repair* by our own efforts only. LOSE.

***Recovery,*** *n.* Restoration. *Recovery* is the regaining of something; *restoration* bringing it back to its former state.

***Redeem,*** *v.* Ransom. Persons and things are *redeemed;* only persons *ransomed.*

***Redress,*** *n.* Relief.

***Refer,*** *v.* Regard, relate, respect.

***Refresh,*** *v.* Revive, restore, invigorate. WEARY.

***Refuse,*** *v.* Decline, rebuff, reject, repel. *Refusal* is unqualified; *decline* means a gentle *refusal; reject* is direct and implies disapprobation. *Repel* is to reject with violence; *rebuff* to refuse with scorn. ALLOW. (See ADMIT.)

***Rejoice,*** *v.* Exult, triumph. GRIEVE.

***Relate,*** *v.* Describe, recount.

***Relation,*** *n.* Narration, narrative, recital.

***Relative,*** *n.* Kinsman, kindred. *Relation* denotes the person to whom one is related; *kinsman* a particular *relation; kindred* is a collective term for all one's relations.

***Remote,*** *a.* Far, distant.

***Repeat,*** *v.* Recite, rehearse.

***Repentance,*** *n.* Contrition, compunction, remorse, penitence. *Contrition* is a lasting, *compunction* an occasional, *remorse* an acute sorrow for offenses. *Penitence* applies only to offenses against God; *repentance* is more general. IMPENITENCE. (See OBSTINACY.)

***Repetition,*** *n.* Tautology.

***Reproach,*** *n.* Contumely, obloquy.

***Reprobate,*** *v.* Condemn. *Reprobate* is to *condemn* severely.

***Reserved,*** *a.* Unsocial, uncommunicative. SOCIAL.

***Rest,*** *n.* Remainder, remnant, residue. *Rest* is the general word, applying both to persons and things; *remnant* a small *remainder; remainder* applies to things only. *Residue* is a *remainder* after a distribution of some kind.

***Restitution,*** *n.* Amends, reparation.

***Retaliation,*** *n.* Reprisal. The latter usually refers to a state of war.

***Retard,*** *v.* Hinder. We *retard* a thing; *hinder* a person. HASTEN.

***Retort,*** *n.* Repartee. *Retort* is censure for censure; *repartee* wit for wit.

***Retrospect,*** *n.* Review, survey. PROSPECT. (See VIEW.)

***Revive,*** *v.* Refresh, renew, renovate.

***Riches,*** *n.* Affluence, opulence, wealth. POVERTY.

***Right,*** *a.* Fit, just, proper. *Right* applies to everything; *just* mostly to important, *fit* and *proper* to less essential things. WRONG.

***Rise,*** *v.* Emerge, issue. A thing may *rise* in or out of a body; it *emerges* or *issues* out of a body. FALL.

***Rot,*** *v.* Corrupt, putrefy. *Corrupt* denotes the beginning, *putrefy* the continuance, *rot* the last stage of the internal dissolution of bodies.

***Rough,*** *a.* Uneven, coarse, rude. SMOOTH, EVEN, GENTLE.

***Royal,*** *a.* Regal, kingly. *Royal* is belonging, *regal* appertaining, *kingly,* becoming, to a king.

***Rupture,*** *n.* Fracture. Soft substances are *ruptured;* hard ones *fractured.*

***Rural,*** *a.* Rustic, countrified. *Rural* applies to all country objects except man, *rustic* only to persons. *Countrified* means uncultivated, having manners or appearance of the country. URBAN.

S.

***Safe,*** *a.* Secure. *Safe* is exemption from harm; *secure,* exemption from danger. UNSAFE.

***Satisfy,*** *v.* Cloy, satiate, glut. *Satisfaction* is enough; *satiety* satisfaction of the appetite; *glutting* the satisfaction of an inordinate appetite.

***Save,*** *v.* Preserve, protect, spare. We are *saved* and *spared* from small, *preserved* and *protected* from great evils. LOSE.

***Scarcity,*** *n.* Dearth. *Dearth* is an extreme *scarcity.* ABUNDANCE.

***Scoff,*** *v.* Gibe, jeer, sneer. *Scoff* is the general word. *Gibe, jeer, sneer* imply ill-natured words.

***Search,*** *v.* Examine, explore. We *search* for things hidden, *examine* things near, *explore* unknown things and countries.

***Second,*** *v.* Support. *Support* is stronger than *second.*

***Second,*** *a.* Inferior, secondary. *Second* refers only to order; *secondary* to merit; *inferior* to condition or quality. FIRST.

***Secret,*** *a.* Hidden, latent, occult, mysterious. The *secret* is known to somebody; the *hidden* may be known to nobody; the *latent* ought to be known; the *occult* is hidden from most people; the *mysterious* is strange or supernatural. MANIFEST. (See PLAIN.)

***Sedulous,*** *a.* Assiduous, diligent, industrious, laborious. NEGLIGENT.

***See,*** *v.* Perceive, observe, behold, look at.

***Seem,*** *v.* Appear. *Appear* is stronger than *seem.*

***Select,*** *a.* Choice, chosen, excellent. PROMISCUOUS.

***Senior,*** *a.* Elder, older. JUNIOR.

***Sentence,*** *n.* Period, phrase, proposition.

***Sentence,*** *v.* Condemn, doom.

***Sentiment,*** *n.* Perception, sensation. *Sentiment* belongs to the heart, *perception* to the understanding, *sensation* to the senses.

***Separate,*** *v.* Divide, part, disjoin, detach, disunite, sever, sunder. JOIN. (See ADD.)

***Serious,*** *a.* Sober, solemn, earnest. FACETIOUS.

***Servitude,*** *n.* Bondage, slavery. FREEDOM.

***Shake,*** *v.* Quake, quiver, shudder, totter, tremble. We *shake* with cold, *totter* from weakness, *quake, quiver,* or *tremble* with fear, *shudder* (*i. e.,* tremble violently) at something horrible.

***Sharp,*** *a.* Acute, keen. *Acute* is not only *sharp,* but *sharp*-pointed; *keen,* extremely *sharp.* DULL.

***Shine,*** *v.* Glare, glitter, radiate, sparkle. *Shine* simply expresses the steady emission of light, *glitter* its unsteady emission, *sparkle* the emission in small portions, *radiate* in long lines, *glare* in a high degree.

***Short,*** *a.* Brief, concise, succinct, summary. LONG.

***Show,*** *v.* Indicate, mark, point out, exhibit, display.

***Show,*** *n.* Exhibition, representation, sight, spectacle.

***Sick,*** *a.* Diseased, sickly, unhealthy, morbid. *Sickly* is inclined to be *sick,* or permanently unwell; *diseased* is an extreme disorder; *morbid* applies to the character and feelings. HEALTHY.

***Sickness,*** *n.* Illness, indisposition. *Illness* is a particular, *indisposition* a slight *sickness.* HEALTH. (See HEALTHY.)

***Significant,*** *a.* Expressive. The former has an indifferent, the latter a good sense. INSIGNIFICANT. (See IMMATERIAL.)

***Signification,*** *n.* Import, meaning, sense.

***Silence,*** *n.* Speechlessness, dumbness. NOISE.

***Silent,*** *n.* Dumb, mute, speechless. *Silence* is the general word; *dumb* denotes physical incapacity; *mute,* temporary inability to speak; *speechless,* physical inability from some incidental cause. TALKATIVE.

***Simile,*** *n.* Comparison, similitude. *Simile* compares things so far as they are alike; *comparison,* generally. *Similitude* is a prolonged *simile.*

***Simple,*** *a.* Single, uncompounded, artless, plain. COMPLEX. COMPOUND.

***Simulate,*** *v.* Dissimulate. We *simulate* what we are not, *dissimulate* what we are.

***Sincere,*** *a.* Candid, hearty, honest, pure, genuine, real. INSINCERE. (See ARTFUL.)

***Situation,*** *n.* Condition, plight, predicament, state. *Situation* marks the relative, *condition* the accidental *state,* the habitual circumstances of a person or thing. *Predicament* is a temporary embarassed *situation; plight,* an unpleasant *condition.*

***Size,*** *n.* Bulk, greatness, magnitude.

***Slavery,*** *n.* Servitude, enthrallment, thralldom. FREEDOM.

***Sleep,*** *n.* Doze, drowse, nap, slumber. *Sleep* is the general word; *nap* is a short *sleep; slumber,* a soft, light *sleep; doze* and *drowse,* an inclination to sleep.

***Sleepy,*** *a.* Somnolent. WAKEFUL.

***Slow,*** *a.* Dilatory, tardy. *Slow* is a general word; *dilatory* and *tardy* apply to the operations of persons only. FAST.

***Smell,*** *n.* Fragrance, odor, perfume, scent. *Smell* and *scent* apply to what gives or receives *smell;* the other words only to what gives it out. *Fragrance* and *perfume* are always pleasant; *odor* and *smell* pleasant or unpleasant.

***Smooth,*** *a.* Even, level, mild. ROUGH.

***Soak,*** *v.* Drench, imbrue, steep.

***Social,*** *a.* Sociable. The former denotes an active, the latter a passive quality. UNSOCIAL.

***Soft,*** *a.* Gentle, meek, mild. *Soft* applies to objects that act pleasantly on the ear or eye; *mild* and *gentle* to objects that act not unpleasantly on the senses; *meek* denotes non-resistance to force. HARD.

***Solicitation,*** *n.* Importunity. *Importunity* is a troublesome *solicitation.*

***Solitary,*** *a.* Sole, only, single. *Solitary* and *sole* denote one object left by itself; *only* conveys an idea of deficiency; *single* denotes merely one or more detached from others.

***Sorry,*** *a.* Grieved. *Grieved* is stronger than *sorry.* GLAD.

***Soul,*** *n.* Mind, spirit. As a rule, the *soul* acts, the *mind* receives. *Soul* is opposed to body, *mind* to matter.

***Sound,*** *a.* Healthy, sane. *Sane* refers to mental *soundness; sound* to things essential for life; *healthy* to every part. UNHEALTHY. (See SICK.)

***Sound,*** *n.* Tone. *Tone* is a kind of *sound* made by particular bodies. SILENCE.

***Space,*** *n.* Room. *Space* is limited or unlimited; *room* limited.

***Sparse,*** *a.* Scanty, thin. LUXURIANT.

***Speak,*** *v.* Converse, talk, converse, say, tell.

***Special,*** *a.* Particular, specific. The *special* is part of the general, the *particular* of the special. *Specific* relates to inherent properties. GENERAL.

***Spend,*** *v.* Expend, exhaust, consume, waste, squander, dissipate. SAVE.

***Spread,*** *v.* Disperse, diffuse, expand, disseminate, scatter. *Spread* is the general word; *scatter* applies to divisible bodies only. *Dispersion* spreads in many directions; *diffusion* pours out in different ways; *disseminate* is to sow in different parts; *expand* is to spread by unfolding the parts.

***Spring,*** *n.* Fountain, source.

***Staff,*** *n.* Prop, support, stay.

***Stagger,*** *v.* Reel, totter. *Staggering* and *reeling* are caused by drunkenness or sickness; *tottering,* by weakness.

***Stain,*** *v.* Soil, discolor, spot, sully, tarnish.

***State,*** *n.* Commonwealth, realm. The United *States;* a peer of the *realm;* the *commonwealth* of New York.

***Sterile,*** *a.* Barren, unfruitful. FERTILE.

***Stifle,*** *v.* Choke, suffocate, smother.

***Stormy,*** *a.* Rough, boisterous, tempestuous. CALM.

***Straight,*** *a.* Direct, right. *Straight* applies to material objects; *right* and *direct* to material or moral. CROOKED.

***Stranger,*** *n.* Alien, foreigner. FRIEND.

***Strengthen,*** *v.* Fortify, invigorate. WEAKEN.

***Strong,*** *a.* Robust, sturdy. *Strong* is the general word; *robustness,* a high degree of strength; *sturdiness,* a strong build. WEAK.

***Stupid,*** *a.* Dull, foolish, obtuse, witless. CLEVER.

***Subject,*** *a.* Exposed to, liable, obnoxious. EXEMPT.

***Subject,*** *a.* Inferior, subordinate.

***Subsequent,*** *a.* Succeeding, following. PREVIOUS.

***Substantial,*** *a.* Solid. Things which admit of handling are *substantial;* things so hard as to have to be cut, *solid.* UNSUBSTANTIAL.

***Suit,*** *v.* Accord, agree. DISAGREE.

***Superficial,*** *a.* Flimsy, shallow. SOLID. (See FIRM.)

***Superfluous,*** *a.* Unnecessary, excessive. NECESSARY.

***Surround,*** *v.* Encircle, encompass, environ.

***Sustain,*** *v.* Maintain, support. *Maintain* is always active; *sustain* and *support* may be passive. *Sustain* implies the bearing of a great weight; *support,* of any weight, great or small.

***Symmetry,*** *n.* Proportion.

***Sympathy,*** *n.* Commiseration, compassion, condolence. *Sympathy* may apply either to pleasure or pain; the other words can be used only in reference to things painful.

***System,*** *n.* Method. The former is a stronger word than the latter. *System* is the arrangement of things according to a fixed plan; *method,* either the manner or principle of such arrangement.

## T.

***Take,*** *v.* Accept, receive. *Take* is the general word; we *take* anything; *accept* and *receive* what is offered or sent. GIVE.

***Talkative,*** *a.* Garrulous, loquacious. SILENT.

***Taste,*** *n.* Flavor, relish, savor. *Taste* is the general word; *flavor,* the peculiar *taste; relish,* a particular, artificial *taste; savor* applies to what smells as well as *tastes.* TASTELESSNESS.

***Tax,*** *n.* Custom, duty, impost, excise, toll. *Tax* is the general word; *customs, duties* and *imposts* are *taxes* on imports; *excise* is a tax on articles of home consumption; *toll,* a local *tax; tribute,* 'a payment to a foreign state.

***Tax,*** *n.* Assessment, rate. A *tax* is laid directly, a *rate* indirectly; an *assessment* is the *tax* at a *given rate* laid upon an individual.

***Tease,*** *v.* Taunt, tantalize, torment, vex. *Tease* is trifling; *torment,* more serious; *taunt,* in contemptuous words; we are *vexed* by the misconduct of others.

***Temporary,*** *a.* Fleeting, transient, transitory. *Temporary* lasts only for a time; *transient,* for a moment. *Fleeting* is still stronger than *transient; transitory* means apt to pass away. PERMANENT. (See DURABLE.)

***Tenacious,*** *a.* Pertinacious, retentive.

***Tendency,*** *n.* Aim, drift, scope. *Tendency* applies only to things; the other words also to thoughts.

***Tenet,*** *n.* Position. The former denotes our own individual mental opinion; the latter an opinion about which we argue for the conviction of others.

***Term,*** *n.* Boundary, limit. *Term* is the point that terminates; *limit,* a point or line that marks where to stop; *boundary,* a line which includes a space; a *term* of office, the *limits* of the Russian Empire; the *boundary* of France.

***Territory,*** *n.* Dominion. The latter denotes rather the power exerted; the former the limits within which that power is exercised.

***Thankfulness,*** *n.* Gratitude. The former

is the outward expression of the latter. THANKLESSNESS.

***Thanklessness,*** *n.* Ingratitude. THANKFULNESS.

***Theory,*** *n.* Hypothesis, speculation. *Theory* rests on inferences from established principles; an *hypothesis* is a supposition to explain certain phenomena; a *speculation* belongs to the imagination mostly, and is more or less fanciful. FACT.

***Therefore,*** *adv.* Accordingly, consequently. *Therefore* marks a deduction; *accordingly*, an agreement; *consequently*, a consequence.

***Thick,*** *a.* Dense, close. THIN.

***Thin,*** *a.* Slender, slight, slim. *Thin* is the general word; *slender* is at once small and long. *Slightness* and *slimness* are defects; *slimness* is extreme *slightness*. THICK.

***Think,*** *v.* Deliberate, meditate, ponder, reflect. *Think* is the general word; *reflection*, *thinking* by recalling ideas; *ponder* and *meditate* relate to serious matters; *deliberation* is *thinking* as a preparation for some action.

***Think,*** *v.* Deem, believe, imagine, suppose. We *think* or *believe* a statement to be true; *imagine* it may be so; *suppose* a thing may have happened. *Deem* is to conclude.

***Thoughtful,*** *a.* Considerate, deliberate. The *thoughtful* man remembers his duty; the *considerate* considers it, the *deliberate* considers it deliberately. *Deliberate* may have a bad sense, as *deliberate* murder. THOUGHTLESS.

***Thoughtless,*** *a.* Inconsiderate, heedless. THOUGHTFUL.

***Threat,*** *n.* Menace. A *menace threatens* great evils.

***Time,*** *n.* Age, date, epoch, era, period, season. *Time* is the general word; *season*, a given portion of *time; period*, a space of *time* between two points of *time; date*, a point of *time; epoch* and *era*, periods distinguished in some way; *age*, the *period* included in one life, or the lives of many living about the same time.

***Torment,*** *n.* Torture.

***Trade,*** *n.* Commerce, traffic, dealing. *Trade* is the general word; *commerce* is a *trade* by exchange of commodities; *dealing*, a *trade* by bargains. *Commerce* is always wholesale, and between different countries; *trade* is wholesale or retail.

***Transfigure,*** *v.* Transform, metamorphose.

***Treacherous,*** *a.* Traitorous, treasonable. *Treacherous* relates to private relations; *traitorous*, to betrayal of one's country. An act is *treasonable* that is aimed against the government of a country. FAITHFUL.

***Trembling,*** *n.* Tremor, trepidation. *Tremor* is a slight, *trepidation* a violent *trembling*.

***Trifling,*** *a.* Frivolous, petty, trivial. *Trivial* is stronger than *trifling*. A *petty* consideration; a *frivolous* amusement; a *trifling* dispute; a *trivial* remark. SERIOUS.

***Trouble,*** *v.* Disturb, molest, derange. *Trouble* is the general word; *molestation* and *disturbance* are *temporary troubles*.

***Truth,*** *n.* Verity, reality, fact. UNTRUTH.

***Tumultuous,*** *a.* Mutinous, turbulent, seditious. *Mutinous* denotes resistance to military or naval authority; *seditious*, resistance to government; *tumultuous*, an inclination to noise; *turbulent*, resistance to authority. CALM.

***Turgid,*** *a.* Bombastic, tumid. SIMPLE.

***Turn,*** *v.* Bend, distort, twist, wrest, wrench, wring. A thing is *turned* by being moved from point to point; *bent*, by changing its direction; *distorted*, by being *bent* from its right course; *twisted*, by being often *bent; wrested* or *wrenched*, by *twists; wrung*, by violent *twists*.

***Turn,*** *v.* Wind, whirl, writhe. *Turn* is the general word; *whirl* is to *turn* about violently; *twirl*, to *turn* aimlessly; *writhe*, to *turn* with pain and agony.

***Turn,*** *n.* Bent. The former denotes a slight or beginning inclination; the latter a decided and positive one.

## U.

***Unbecoming,*** *a.* Indecent, indecorous, unsuitable. BECOMING.

***Unbelief,*** *n.* Infidelity. incredulity. *Incredulity* is unbelief in ordinary matters; *infidelity* in Divine revelation. *Infidelity* and *incredulity* denote an active rejection of belief. BELIEF.

***Unchangeable,*** *a.* Immutable, unalterable. CHANGEABLE.

***Uncover,*** *v.* Disclose, discover. *Uncover* is generally to take off the artificial covering; *discover*, to take off the natural or moral covering. *Disclosure* opens what has been closed. A country is *discovered*, hidden treasure *disclosed*. CONCEAL.

***Under,*** *prep.* Below, beneath. *Beneath* is stronger than *below* or *under*. *Under* denotes retirement or concealment; *below*, inferiority or lowness; *beneath*, a great degree of the same. ABOVE. (See OVER.)

***Undermine,*** *v.* Sap. *Undermine* is to form a mine under the ground or anything on the ground; *sap*, to dig down to the root of.

***Understanding,*** *n.* Intelligence, intellect. *Understanding* is the more common, familiar word. *Intellect* denotes the operation of the mind on higher objects. *Intelligence* is acquired by observation, from books, etc.; *understanding* and *intellect* are natural gifts.

***Undertaking,*** *n.* Attempt, enterprise. An *undertaking* is more complicated than an *attempt*, less hazardous than an *enterprise*.

***Undetermined,*** *a.* Unsettled, unsteady, wavering *Undetermined* implies a want of determination; *wavering* and *unsteady* denote habitual mental states. *Wavering* is generally used in a bad sense. DETERMINED.

***Unequal,*** *a.* Disproportionate, unlike. EQUAL.

***Unfold,*** *v.* Develop, unravel. *Unfold* reveals what has been kept secret; *unravel* what has been confused and mixed up; *develop*, what has been studiously kept out of sight.

***Unhappy,*** *a.* Miserable, wretched, unfortunate. *Unhappy* is simply not happy; *miserable*, what deserves pity; *wretched*, what is peculiarly *miserable*. HAPPY.

***Unimportant,*** *a.* Immaterial, inconsiderable, insignificant. *Unimportant* relates to the consequences of our actions; *inconsiderable* marks the low value of things; *insignificant* has a contemptuous sense; *immaterial* is *unimportant* in regard to ordinary matters. IMPORTANT.

***Unjust,*** *a.* Unfair, partial, inequitable. FAIR.

***Unless,*** *adv.* Except. The former refers only to a particular case; the latter denotes an exception to a general rule.

***Unoffending,*** *a.* Harmless, inoffensive. *Unoffending* marks a temporary state; *inoffensive* and *harmless* the habitual disposition. OFFENSIVE.

***Unruly,*** *a.* Refractory, ungovernable. *Unruly* marks a temporary, *ungovernable* a permanent, fault of temper. A *refractory* child is extremely *unruly*. OBEDIENT.

***Unsafe,*** *a.* Insecure, perilous, dangerous. SAFE.

***Unspeakable,*** *a.* Irrepressible, ineffable, unutterable. *Unspeakable* and *ineffable* denote what is beyond the power of man to express. The *unutterable* and *inexpressible* cannot be communicated even by signs.

***Unsubstantial,*** *a.* Unreal, flimsy. SUBSTANTIAL.

***Untruth,*** *n.* Falsehood, falsity, lie. TRUTH.

***Unwillinglg,*** *adv.* Reluctantly. WILLINGLY.

***Unworthy,*** *a.* Worthless. *Unworthy* conveys less reproach than *worthless*, which implies entire absence of worth. WORTHY.

***Urban,*** *a.* Belonging to a city. RUSTIC.

***Usage,*** *n.* Custom, prescription. *Usage* is what we have been used to do; *custom*, what we generally do; *prescription*, what *usage* prescribes to be done.

***Utter,*** *v.* Articulate, pronounce, speak. *Utter* is the general word; *speech* is a method of utterance; *articulate* and *pronounce* denote methods of speaking.

## V.

***Vacancy,*** *n.* Inanity, vacuity. *Vacancy* and *vacuity* are used in an indifferent, *inanity* in a bad sense. FULLNESS.

***Vain,*** *a.* Conceited, puffed up, inflated. MODEST.

***Vain,*** *a.* Fruitless, ineffectual, destitute of force. *Vain* is the general word; *ineffectual* marks the inadequacy of the means to the end; *fruitlessness*, the waste of labor to obtain a particular object. SUCCESSFUL. (See FORTUNATE.)

***Valuable,*** *a.* Costly, precious. The latter means highly valuable. WORTHLESS.

***Value,*** *n* Worth, rate, price. *Value* is the general word; *worth*, the acknowledged *value; rate* is the general, while *price* is the particular measure of the *value* or *worth* of things.

***Value,*** *v.* Esteem, prize. The former applies both to physical and mental objects; the latter two only to mental objects. *Prize* refers to either sensible or moral things; *esteem*, to moral objects only.

***Variation,*** *n.* Variety. The latter denotes either the thing changed, or the change itself.

***Venal,*** *a.* Mercenary. *Venal* is much stronger than *mercenary*. The *mercenary* seek their own interest irrespective of principle; the *venal* sell themselves without principle. INCORRUPTIBLE.

***Verbal,*** *a.* Oral, vocal. *Verbal* and *oral*

distinguish what is spoken from what is written; *vocal*, the sound of the human voice from other sounds.

***Vexation***, *n.* Chagrin, mortification. *Mortification* is an extreme *vexation; chagrin*, a mixture of the other two. PLEASURE.

***View***, *n.* Prospect, survey. *View* and *survey* mark the act of the person; *prospect*, what is seen.

***Violent***, *a.* Boisterous, furious, impetuous, vehement. *Violent* is the general word; *furious* implies a higher degree of *violence; boisterous* refers to *violent* noise; *impetuous*, to bodies moving with great *violence; vehement*, to affections or passions. GENTLE.

***Virtuous***, *a.* Upright, honest, moral. PROFLIGATE.

***Vision***, *n.* Apparition, ghost, phantom, spectre. A *vision* is a supernatural effort of the vision; *apparition*, a supernatural object seen; *phantom*, a false *apparition; spectre* and *ghost, apparitions* of immaterial things.

***Voluptuary***, *n.* Epicure, sensualist. The *sensualist* devotes himself to the indulgence of his senses, the *voluptuary* to his pleasures; the *epicure* is a refined *voluptuary*.

***Vote***, *n.* Suffrage, voice. A *vote* is a wish in favor of a thing; it may be expressed (*i. e.*, cast) or not; a *voice* or *suffrage* is expressed.

***Vouch***, *v.* Affirm, asseverate, assure, aver. *Affirm* declares a fact on our own credit; *asseverate*, confidently; *aver*, unequivocally; *assent* marks the conviction of the speaker; we *vouch* for the truth of another's declaration on our own responsibility.

## W.

***Wait***, *v.* Await, expect, look for, wait for. *Wait* and *wait for* refer to remote, uncertain matters; *await, look for* and *expect* to what is liable to happen.

***Wakeful***, *a.* Vigilant, watchful. *Wakefulness* depends upon the body, *watchfulness* upon the will; *vigilance* is an extreme *watchfulness*. SLEEPY.

***Wander***, *v.* Range, ramble, roam, rove, stroll. We *wander* by irregular paths; *stroll* by *wandering* out of our path; *range* within regular limits; *ramble* by wandering at random; *roam* and *rove*, without plan or object.

***Want***, *v.* Lack, need. We *want* comforts, *need* necessaries. *Lack* is simple deficiency. ABUNDANCE.

***Wary***, *a.* Circumspect, cautious. FOOLHARDY.

***Waterman***, *n.* Ferryman, boatman.

***Wave***, *n.* Breaker, billow, surge. *Wave* is the general word; a *wave* with an unusual swell is a *billow;* a very high *wave* a *surge;* a *wave* clashing strongly on the shore a *breaker*.

***Way***, *n.* Course, manner, means, method. *Way* is general; *manner* and *method* are *ways* chosen by design. *Course* and *means* are moral *ways; mode*, an habitual *way*.

***Weak***, *a.* Feeble, infirm. *Weak* is general; *infirmity*, a particular kind of weakness; *feebleness*, a qualified *weakness*. STRONG.

***Weaken***, *v.* Debilitate, enfeeble, enervate, invalidate. *Weaken* is the general word; it may apply to either a temporary or permanent result. *Enfeeble* denotes a permanent result, either mental or physical. Weaken refers to persons or things; *invalidate* only to things. *Enervation* is a relaxation of the nervous system; *debilitation*, a weakening of a particular power. STRENGTHEN.

***Wearisome***, *a.* Tedious, tiresome. *Wearisome* is the general word; *tedious* and *tiresome* are kinds of wearisomness.

***Weary***, *v.* Harass, jade, tire, fatigue. REFRESH.

***Weight***, *n.* Gravity, heaviness. *Weight* is indefinite; *heaviness* belongs to bodies of great *weight*; *gravity* is a scientific term. LIGHTNESS.

***Weight***, *n.* Burden, load. *Weight* may refer either to persons or things; *burden* usually relates to persons only; *load* may refer to either. A *weight* may be accidental; a *burden* may be self-imposed or imposed by others; a *load* is always put upon one. Morally, a *load* is an extreme *weight; a burden* depends upon the feeling of the person bearing it.

***Well-being***, *n.* Happiness, prosperity, welfare. *Well-being* more frequently applies to the condition of a body of persons; *welfare* to the individual. *Prosperity* and *happiness* include everything that can add to human enjoyment.

***Whole***, *a.* Entire, complete, total, integral. Nothing has been subtracted from the *whole;* the *entire* has not been divided; nothing is wanted to the *complete*. *Total* is more limited than *whole; integral* relates to unbroken parts or numbers. PART.

***Wicked***, *a.* Iniquitous, nefarious. *Iniquitous* is stronger than *wicked; nefarious* than *iniquitous*. VIRTUOUS.

***Will***, *n.* Wish. *Will* is an effectual impulse of the soul towards action; *wish* is a feeble impulse which may be directed to things which we cannot obtain.

***Willingly***, *adv.* Spontaneously, voluntarily. We do a thing *willingly*, with a good will; *voluntarily*, of our own accord; *spontaneously* applies more frequently to inanimate objects. UNWILLINGLY.

***Wisdom***, *n.* Prudence. The latter is a branch of the former; a foresight in regard to things future, the result of an experience of things past. *Wisdom* applies equally to the past and the future.

***Wit***, *n.* Humor. *Wit* is more pointed and brilliant than *humor*. *Humor* is more genial than *wit*, and applies to words and actions.

***Wonder***, *v.* Admire, amaze, astonish, surprise. *Wonder* is the general word; *admiration* is *wonder* and esteem; *astonishment* and *surprise* are caused by the unexpected; *amazement* is *surprise* and perturbation.

***Wonder***, *n.* Marvel, miracle, prodigy.

***Word***, *n.* Expression, term. *Word* is general; *term*, a *word* with a specified meaning; *expression*, a *word* with a forcible meaning. *Words* are determined by usage; the meaning of *terms* is settled by science; *expression* gives a voice to feelings and opinions. A forcible style employs suitable *expressions;* a pure style is the result of a proper selection of *words;* an exact style is produced by an apt selection of *terms*.

***Work***, *n.* Labor, task, toil. *Work* is the general word; *labor* is hard *work; toil*, still harder; *task* is a work imposed by others. PLAY.

***Worthless***, *a.* Valueless. VALUABLE.

***Writer***, *n.* Author, penman. *Writer* includes both the latter terms. The *author* invents; the *writer* may be a penman.

***Wrong***, *n.* Injustice, injury. JUSTICE.

## Y.

***Yet***, *adv.* and *conj.* But, however, still, nevertheless, hitherto, besides.

***Yield***, *v.* Concede, give, resign, surrender.

***Yielding***, *a.* Compliant, mild. OBSTINATE.

***Youth***, *n.* Boy, lad.

***Youthful***, *a.* Juvenile, puerile. *Youthful* and *juvenile* have an indifferent, *puerile* a contemptuous sense. OLD.

## Z.

***Zeal***, *n.* Earnestness. INDIFFERENCE.

***Zealot***, *n.* Bigot. enthusiast, fanatic.

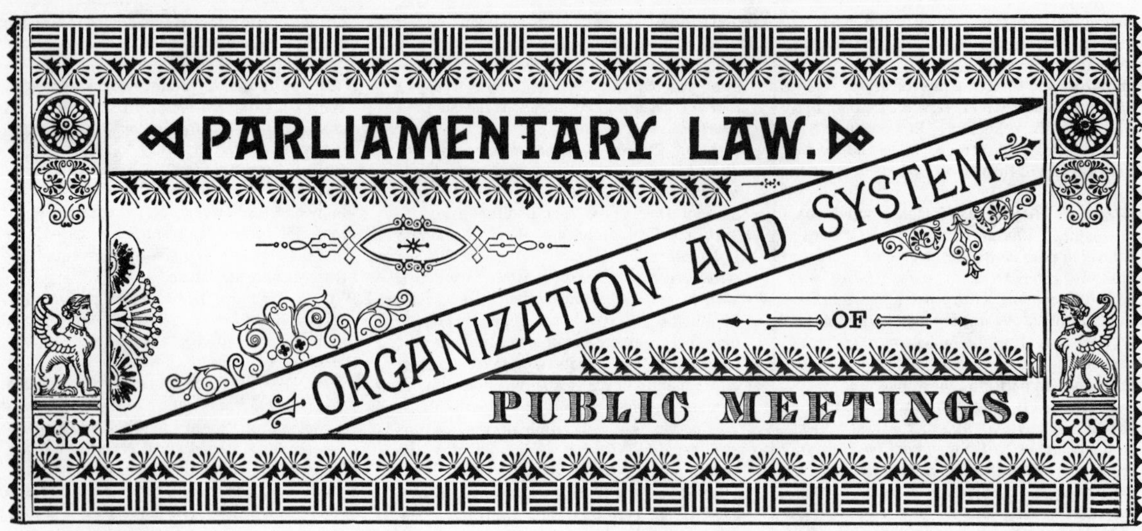


ONE of the highest rights of citizens is that of holding meetings for the consideration of matters affecting the general welfare, or the interests of a particular class, profession, or trade. The first amendment to the Constitution made this right secure, and in no country is it more frequently or fully exercised. Hence it is useful and necessary to know how to proceed in the organization and conduct of such meetings.

### ORGANIZING A PUBLIC MEETING.

Preparations for a meeting should be made by one or more prominent citizens, and a call issued through the newspapers, or by written or printed notices, in which the object of the meeting should be expressed. When a sufficient number of people have convened, one of the leaders will call the assembly to order by saying, "Gentlemen (or ladies and gentlemen), you will please come to order." Silence having been secured, the same person, or any one in sympathy with the object for which the people have met, will say:

"I nominate Mr. A. for chairman of this meeting."

Any one may nominate another person, and the question must be taken first on the latest nominee until one is chosen.

Suppose Mr. A. to be chosen ; the person who called the meeting to order will then say :

"Mr. A., having been duly elected to preside over this meeting, will please take the chair."

Mr. A. assumes the place of chairman, returns thanks for the honor conferred upon him, and closes by asking, "Who will you have for secretary ?"

Some one is nominated, perhaps two or more, but usually no opposition is offered. The secretary being chosen, the meeting is now fully organized for business.

In large meetings it is common to name a great number of prominent citizens for vice-presidents and secretaries, but this is for effect, as perhaps not one in ten may be present.

The meeting being duly organized, it is in order for the chairman, or some one familiar with the object in view, to state concisely for what purpose the people were called together. Suppose it to be to build a town hall. The speaker explains, and moves that a committee be appointed to present resolutions expressing the desire of the originators of the movement. The motion is seconded and carried. The chairman asks, How many members of the committee shall there be ? Some one suggests a certain number—say five; and if no other suggestion is made the number is considered adopted as much as if it had been carried by a vote. Then the chairman asks, "How shall the committee be appointed ?"

Some one suggests "by the chair;" another "by ballot." Questions being seconded are taken in order, and it is voted that the chair appoint. The committee is appointed, and retire; and while they are preparing their resolutions or report it is usual for the assembly to take a recess, and indulge in general conversation. Upon the appearance of the committee the presiding officer calls to order, and the chairman of the committee offers their report. It is now before the meeting, and generally a motion is made that "the report of the committee be received." This opens discussion, and some one moves that the report be adopted. Suppose this motion to fail, then the whole movement is substantially a failure; but other cognate propositions may be made and lead to further action. If the report is adopted, the next business is to take steps to carry the resolutions into effect by such means as raising subscriptions, or whatever other method may seem feasible. And, now, the business for which the meeting met being finished, at the suggestion of the chairman, or on motion of some one present, the meeting will adjourn to some future day, or indefinitely.

## RECORD OF PROCEEDINGS.

It is the duty of a secretary to make a brief but exact record of the proceedings, whether they are to be published or not. For such a meeting as we have indicated the secretary's minutes would read about as follows:

In accordance with public notice, a meeting of citizens of Slatstown was held at the Phœnix Hotel on the evening of the 8th October, 1895. The object of the meeting was to secure the building of a Town Hall. Mr. A. was chosen chairman, and Mr. B. secretary. The following gentlemen were appointed a committee on resolutions: G. B., J. D., and E. F. While the committee were out, Mr. J. N. spoke of the importance of the purpose for which the people had assembled.

The committee on resolutions made the following report. [Here insert the full report.]

After discussion, in which Mr. G. supported and Mr. H. opposed the committee's report, a vote was taken, and the report and resolutions were adopted. The meeting then adjourned to the 11th of November next [or *sine die*, if such be the fact].

A DEBATING SOCIETY.

## DUTIES OF A PRESIDENT.

HE President or Chairman of a public meeting should be familiar with the purpose in view, and a person acquainted with the usages of deliberative bodies ; of firmness, and of ready decision. He should set forth the purposes for which the meeting is called, or call upon some person competent to do so with precision and clearness. It is the Chairman's duty to keep strict order and enforce all rules ; decide points of order; appoint committees whose selection is not specially provided for; see that a quorum is present (if there is a quorum necessary under the rule); sign the proceedings or necessary documents ; keep members to the business on hand as far as possible, and at all times preserve strict impartiality in his official conduct.

**A Vice-President** is merely a substitute for the chief officer, and when acting for him possesses all his powers and assumes all his duties.

## THE SECRETARY.

In regular bodies holding frequent meetings, the Secretary has much to do with the direction of business, as he is best informed of what has been done and what is unfinished. He reads all papers when so desired; furnishes copies for publication or personal information of interested parties; keeps a full and faithful record of the actual proceedings; records in full all papers when so directed by the President or the meeting; is careful to note the substance if not the exact words of all motions, with name of mover and of seconder, and the result of the vote thereon. He is to record, file, and preserve all papers of importance, and have them ready for inspection by those who are so entitled. He notifies committees of their appointment and duties, and his signature attests all official documents or proceedings.

## THE TREASURER.

In many cases the Secretary acts as Treasurer also, but where there is a Treasurer his duties are very simple—to give bonds (in some cases), to receive and disburse all funds of the association or society as directed by rules or by special votes. He usually reports at stated periods the condition of his accounts.

## A QUORUM FOR BUSINESS.

An important point to determine, if not set down in the rules, is how many shall constitute a quorum. This is an unsettled matter. In a regular legislative body at least a majority must be present for any action, except that a less number may adjourn from time to time. In the New York Legislature there must be three-fifths of all members of each house present to make the adoption of an act legal. Where there is a fixed number to constitute a quorum, the presiding officer must see that the required number are present. The moment the quorum is broken it is his duty to announce the fact, and declare the session "adjourned for want of a quorum." Such an adjournment is a matter of course, and needs no vote. But as soon as enough come in to form a quorum, business may be resumed.

## SPECIAL COMMITTEES.

The only, or at least the best, method of starting business in a meeting or association, is by forming committees who have charge of special subjects. Therefore all regular bodies have a large number of Standing Committees. In Congress the most important of such committees are on Finance, Commerce, Appropriations, Foreign Relations, Judiciary, Banking and Currency, etc. In temporary bodies committees are appointed as required by the business contemplated. Standing committees are appointed by prescribed rules; temporary committees by the chair or the meeting. Members of a committee may choose their own chairman, although it is usual to accept as chairman the person first named on the committee.

## COMMITTEE OF THE WHOLE.

This means all the members of a deliberative body in session for general or particular discussion. In Congress much of the minor work is done in Committee of the Whole, where voting by calling the roll is dispensed with, and where the previous question is not in order. A Committee of the Whole chooses its own Chairman, perhaps a different person at every session. After sufficient debate the Committee rises, the regular body resumes its former session, and the Chairman of the Committee of the Whole makes a report, which is discussed and voted upon by the main body. Usually the recommendations of the Committee of the Whole are adopted.

## COMMITTEE WORK.

Much of the real work of meetings of citizens as well as of regular bodies is done by committees. In Congress the Ways and Means Committee practically shapes all financial legislation. In a meeting of citizens the business is best put in shape by deputizing a committee to present resolutions or some plan for action, and such committee should consist of the best informed persons present. The person first named is usually the chairman, but the committee may choose some other member. In the absence of specific direction the committee uses its own judgment, but commonly takes its cue from the call or object of the meeting, and drafts resolutions or motions, and perhaps an address to carry out such objects. It is in order to refer any appropriate matter or paper to this committee, and report must be made on all such matters. Having finished their work, the committee report to the meeting in writing for or against propositions referred to them. Some one moves that the report be received. The adoption of this motion does not adopt the report; only puts it before the meeting for action. Motions may then prevail to adopt, to reject, to re-commit to the committee, and so on. An action on the report (except to re-commit) discharges the committee. A report agreed to by a majority is the report of the committee, but any member of a committee may make a minority report.

Committee sessions, if not fixed at stated times, are called by the chairman at his discretion. Unless so ordered, or the business demand it, committees will not hold sessions during the sitting of the main body.

In the matter of reports there is no special formality. When the committee or a majority thereof are agreed upon the matter referred to them, a report to that effect is made to the main body. A minority of any number is equally entitled to make a report adverse or different from that of the majority.

## ACTION ON A REPORT FROM A COMMITTEE.

In case of a special committee, if the report be exhaustive, the usual course is to move that the report be received and the committee discharged. If that prevails, the committee no longer exists, and the matter referred to them is before the meeting. Here may come in a great variety of motions —to adopt, amend, reject, etc. There is no precise form of

## PRECEDENCE OF MOTIONS.

But the order in Congress is about as follows: 1. To adjourn. 2. To lay on the table. 3. Previous question (in the House only). 4. Postponement to a certain time. 5. Indefinite postponement. A question to adjourn is always first in order. Next, a question of privilege. Next, the order of the day. Next, a point of order on the subject in hand. Next, the reading of papers concerning such subject. A motion to suspend the rules takes precedence of the proposed action from which such motion arose. A motion to lay on the table comes before all other subsidiary questions; that for the previous question goes before one to postpone, commit, or amend, if made first; a motion to postpone to a definite time supersedes the previous question, commitment and amendment; a motion to commit comes before amendment, postponement, and previous question, but only if it be made first. A motion to amend is to be voted on before the vote on the subject to be amended, and, if made first, comes before indefinite postponement, or the previous question. A motion to adjourn to a particular date takes precedence of a motion to adjourn without day.

## WHAT CAN BE DONE WITH MOTIONS.

The following careful synopsis gives the leading facts about motions and their course in legislative bodies, societies and public meetings:

**First.**—***Motions that can neither be amended nor debated:*** 1. To adjourn. [But a motion to adjourn may be in effect amended by specifying a future date, and then, on the time or date only, discussion may ensue.] 2. An appeal from the chair. 3. A call to order. 4. To allow a member to continue speaking. 5. To lay on the table. 6. An objection to considering a question at the time. 7. A call for the order of the day. 8. The previous question. 9. Reading of papers appropriate to the subject under consideration. 10. That the committee do rise (generally meaning the committee of the whole). 11. To suspend the rules. 12. To take a matter from the table. 13. To take a question out of its proper order. 14. To withdraw a motion.

**Second.**—***Motions that need not be seconded:*** 1. Call to order. 2. Objecting to consideration. 3. The order of the day. 4. Whether discussion shall continue.

**Third.**—***Motions that cannot be reconsidered:*** 1. To adjourn. 2. To reconsider. 3. That the committee rise. 4. To suspend the rule. 5. To lay on the table (if carried). 6. To take from the table (if carried).

**Fourth.**—***Motions requiring a two-thirds vote to adopt:*** 1. To suspend or amend the rules. 2. To close debate. 3. To limit debate. 4. Objecting to consideration. 5. For the previous question. 6. Whether the matter shall now be discussed. 7. Making the subject a special order. 8. To take a subject up out of its regular order.

**Fifth.**—***Motions in order although a member has the floor:*** 1. Appeal from the decision of the chair. 2. A call to order. 3. Objecting to consideration of the question. 4. The order of the day. 5. Whether the subject shall be discussed.

## COURSE OF BUSINESS IN PUBLIC MEETINGS.

The work of a meeting begins by the presentation of a motion, the object of which the mover explains. If seconded, debate ensues. If not seconded it has no effect. But commonly an initial resolution goes to action by general consent; that is, no one objects to its consideration. The right to the floor, or to speak, goes by majority. If two or more rise at the same moment, the chair decides which has the floor. If that decision is questioned, the matter is decided by vote or by the voluntary yielding of competitors. All motions and amendments ought to be in writing, except such as to lay on the table or to postpone. A motion being made and seconded, the chair states it, and then it is open for debate. It is then in possession of the body, and cannot be withdrawn without unanimous consent. It must be read as often as any member shall call for its reading. Thereafter its course is determined by the usual rules of order. If it is determined to crowd it through, the mover or some other supporter moves the previous question. This stops all discussion, and a vote on the resolution must be taken at once. [In the United States Senate this previous question, or, as some call it, the "gag rule," is not permitted.] If the previous question is sustained, the resolution is dead, and cannot be renewed unless at a future time in some modified form. If the previous question is not sustained, motion may be made to adopt, to postpone indefinitely, to postpone to another time, to lay on the table, to refer to a committee, to amend, to substitute a different motion, all of which must be considered in their place under the rules of order.

## RIGHTS OF MINORITIES.

Certain minority rights are everywhere recognized. So small a number as one-quarter may demand a vote by yeas and nays; but in some cases it takes two-thirds. Sometimes a plurality only may elect or take action, but usually a majority is required. Not long ago in several of our States a majority was required to elect a Governor by the people. If there were a tie or more than two candidates, and no one had a majority, the Legislature was charged with the election. But this majority principle has gone by, and in nearly all cases of vote by the people the candidate having the greatest number of votes is chosen. If there were a thousand candidates for Governor of New York, and nine hundred and ninety-nine had each nine hundred and ninety-nine votes, and one had one thousand votes, that one would be legally chosen Governor by a large minority but a legal plurality.

## COURTESY IN DEBATE.

Courtesy and a careful regard for the opinions and rights of others should be the aim of every speaker, even in meetings of the least importance. A person wishing to speak should rise and say, "Mr. President," or "Mr. Chairman," and wait for recognition. If recognized he has the floor and may hold it, in the absence of special rules, as long as he desires to speak. If a point of order is raised, he should be seated and silent until the point is decided. He should not be interrupted unless clearly out of order, or in a case where a member has information very pertinent and important to the subject of the speech. In that case the member asks the speaker to yield for a moment and give him an opportunity to make a statement. If the speaker refuses, he cannot insist. To indulge in calls to order, or call question, or rise to explain, or in any way annoy a member who has the floor is excessively ill-mannered. When making an address the speaker must stand up, unless in case of infirmity. (Senator Morton was for years unable to stand, and of course was permitted to speak from his seat.) It is irregular in formal debate to mention other members by name; the form is, *the gentleman from Ohio*, or *the Senator from Maine*, or *my honored colleague;* and in ordinary meetings, *the gentleman who has just spoken*, or *the mover of the amendment*, or *my worthy friend on the right*—any form except *Mr. Jones* and *Mr. Smith*. A speaker should not be prolix in any case, nor spin out words without meaning. All statements should be terse, compact, and clear; the plainer and simpler the language of an argument the greater is its effect. He should avoid all matters not pertinent to his subject, be careful to use no disrespectful language, give no reason for offense to any one. If a point of order should be raised, no matter how irrelevant, he should gracefully yield the floor until permitted to go on. In regular bodies there are rules defining the number of times or the length of time a man may speak. In ordinary meetings no person should speak more than once if any one else desires to speak, or unless he has general consent. It is proper, however, to give the mover of a resolution the last words upon his motion. As to language we need only say that it should be dignified, courteous, and good-tempered, and that nothing whatever of a coarse or vulgar character should be used.

## DISCUSSION AND VOTING.

A subject should be discussed until the body can fully understand it, and opposition should be fair and courteous. Sometimes an attempt is made to "talk the matter to death," and the patience of an assembly is worn out in irrelevant debate. This may be stopped by a call for the previous question, or if that is not admissible, by the general opposition of the assembly in calling "question," as in the English House of Commons, until the offending speaker is silenced.

Debate being over, and suppose there to be a single question, the chairman says: "Are you ready for the question?" Silence gives consent, and he says: "All who are in favor of the adoption of the resolution will say aye." Response is made. "All who are opposed will say nay." If it seems to be clear, he says: "The resolution is adopted," or, "The chair is in doubt; all who are in favor of the resolution will rise." They rise. "Gentlemen will please be seated. All who are opposed will rise." If he is still in doubt they rise again and stand until counted, when the chairman decides that the ayes or nays have it, as the case may be. In Congress and most legislative bodies (except in committee of the whole) votes on important matters are taken by calling the roll, each member answering yea or nay as he hears his name. In the matter of ordinary voting by yea and nay, any member may question the decision of the chair, and call for a division or a rising vote. After a motion has been formally adopted it is still in order to move reconsideration, and if such a motion prevails the subject is opened back to the original motion. But this hardly ever happens; yet to prevent the revival of the subject it is not unusual for one who voted with the majority to "clinch it," as the saying is, by moving that the vote just taken (adopting the resolution) be reconsidered, and that the said motion to reconsider do lie upon the table. This being carried, the subject is finished, for the session at least.

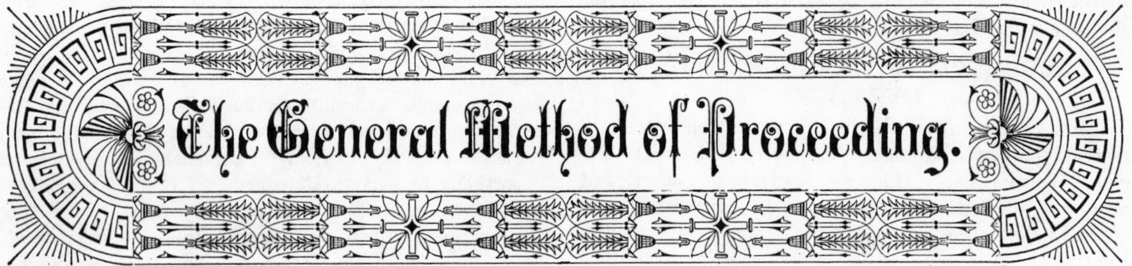

# The General Method of Proceeding.

WHEN there has been a previous meeting the first business in order is reading the minutes of such meeting. If no one objects the minutes are approved. Reports of standing and special committees follow in order, and are variously disposed of. Then comes unfinished business, next new business, which generally comes in the form of a motion or resolution. This should be written out, and read by the President, and passed to the Secretary. If seconded it may be debated, amended, referred, postponed, or voted upon. Whenever the members are asked to vote the chairman should state precisely what they are to vote for or against. In regular societies votes are frequently taken by calling the roll, each member answering "aye" or "nay" as he hears his name. Any person in doubt can ask to have the question stated again, which the chairman must do. Only one subject or question can be considered at a time. Where a matter is important and fully understood, the sooner it is disposed of the better. The great evil in legislative bodies, from Congress down, is unnecessary delay.

## FORWARDING A QUESTION.

The mover of a question ought to be reasonably sure of a respectable number of supporters and well informed of the views of the society or meeting on the subject. He should bring in his resolution in time for full discussion and at a full meeting, and also at a time when it will not interfere with other business. The member making the motion is the only proper person to open its advocacy, which he should do as clearly as possible and with the least waste of words or time. In case the matter is referred to a committee, he should personally enlighten them in the matter. Ordinarily if there be any opposition it will come in the form of motions to lay on the table, to postpone, to amend in such manner as to destroy the original proposition—as a motion to strike out the enacting clause, if carried, would kill a legislative act. If the friends of a question feel sure of victory they may shut off opposition by moving the

## PREVIOUS QUESTION.

This is differently understood in various bodies. In the Senate of the United States it is not permitted. In some bodies when the previous question is moved it is the rule to vote consecutively upon the latest motions back to the original question; as, for instance, first on the motion to lay on the table, next on the motion to amend, and lastly on the main question. But the more general and preferable method is that when the previous question is moved all additional motions are disregarded, and the vote is taken at once and without debate on the main question. If the opponents have a majority the whole business is killed, and cannot come up again unless in some very different form.

## OPPOSITION TACTICS.

The resources of the opposition in deliberative and legislative bodies are very great. Usually their first action is to procure delay by moving adjournment; to lay on the table for a time on plea of want of information on the subject; to lay on the table without time, which would permit the taking up of the question at the next moment or the next meeting; to postpone without day, which if carried absolutely kills the subject; to postpone to a future time, when by proper effort the opponents may appear in a majority, when they may take the question and kill it, or they may try the previous question suddenly when members not informed of the object of the motion will be sure not to vote for it. These are some of the strangling motions, but when the opposition is not strong enough to defeat they resort to interference and delay by proposing damaging amendments and dilatory motions in great variety. One course is confusion of amendments. An opponent moves to amend, another to amend the amendment, another to amend the amendment to the amendment—all to produce confusion. This is as far as heaping up amendments can go; and, after perhaps almost interminable debate, question is to be taken, beginning with the latest amendment and going back to the original motion. Further complication can be made before these questions are taken by a motion to postpone, which must be put before that on the amendment to the amendment, or by a motion to refer, which comes before that to postpone. The very last resource of the opposition is to leave the body without a quorum, but that is seldom effective, except to procure delay.

## QUESTIONS OF PRIVILEGE.

When a question has been regularly proposed, seconded, and put by the presiding officer in due form, it must be voted upon as the first business in order. But motion to adjourn may be made, which is always first in order, and must be voted upon without discussion. Yet if any other question has been actually put and voting thereon commenced, the motion to adjourn cannot be entertained until such voting is finished. Another privileged question is the order of the day. If a matter has been postponed to a given hour, when that time arrives it must be taken up, regardless of other business, unless a motion to suspend the order of the day be carried. The previous question is privileged, and always in order.

### MISCELLANEOUS PROVISIONS.

When a subject has been postponed to a given time, every member may insist upon its being taken up at that time.

Where the sense will admit, a resolution or subject may be divided into two or more parts, to be voted upon separately. But such division should not be proposed unless the parts naturally form different questions.

In filling blanks, the remotest dates and the largest sums are voted upon first.

Points of order are decided by the presiding officer, but any member may appeal from such decision, when the presiding officer must put the question whether the members sustain the appeal. If they do, the question is "Shall the decision of the Chair stand?" In most cases of appeal the Chairman's decision is sustained.

A motion for the reading of papers pertinent to a matter under consideration, must be put before the main question. But usually there is no objection to the reading of such papers.

To expedite business, it is permissible to allow unimportant motions such as approving minutes, reading papers, etc., to go by consent, the presiding officer saying, in case of the minutes: "You have heard the minutes of the last meeting read. If there is no objection they will be approved." (After waiting a moment and hearing no voices.) "They are approved."

In some bodies the presiding officer has a vote only when there is an equal division, or a tie, as in the Senate of the United States. In some bodies, a Speaker of the Assembly, for instance, is recorded alphabetically, as "Mr. Speaker," who votes on all questions, or he may delay until the roll is finished and then vote. A presiding officer cannot properly take part in debate, unless some other member takes his chair. His arena for discussion is in committee of the whole. A presiding officer may vote or not, as he pleases, though in certain cases other members may be compelled to vote. If a body be divided sixteen to fifteen, the Chair may make a tie and defeat the motion, or keep silent and permit it to pass.

No one has a right to read or speak in a public body, unless by consent or after vote of permission.

When a speaker finds that little attention is paid by members to his remarks, he ought to know that it is time to conclude.

By common usage, the person making a proposition is entitled to speak upon it before any other person.

Whoever moves (and carries) an adjournment, is entitled to the floor when the meeting again convenes.

When an advocate and an opponent of a motion rise at the same time, it is usual to give the opponent the floor, and the advocate almost always has the last word.

No member ought to speak more than once to a question if any other member desires the floor; but in case of an amendment, though essentially the same matter, he may speak to that.

Suspending the rules has often been arbitrarily done in deliberative bodies, but should be as little resorted to as possible. In some bodies it requires the consent of two-thirds or three-fourths of the members present to effect such suspension.

Methods of voting are different in casual and permanent bodies. In a public meeting it is usually by "Yea" or "Nay" in general voice; if there is a doubt, there may be a count. In some bodies it is by raising the hand; in others by calling the roll; in others by secret ballot.

It is becoming common for women to attend public meetings, and proper accommodations should be made for them. In assemblies where women are officers, such as boards of education or school trustees, they may be addressed as "Mrs." or "Miss Chairman" (not Chairwoman), or "Mrs. President" (not Presidentess). With the exception of the sexual prefix, the titles for female officers are the same as those for males, and should be so used, however awkward it may seem.

# FORMS OF CONSTITUTIONS.

CONSIDERABLE social enjoyment is attained in the country and small villages by the organization of clubs, unions, societies, or associations for mutual improvement. Such societies may be formed in almost any section, even of sparsely settled country, as there need be but a handful of members, so to speak. When it is thought proper to form such an association, the projectors should agree upon its general purpose and outline of formation, by consultation at a private or public gathering. If it is to be a small society of neighbors and friends, no publicity need be given, and all the work may be done at the homes of the parties most interested. But if it be thought desirable to include persons farther off, or out of the immediate circle, or if the object be of public and general interest, a public notice or call would be in order. This may be given by advertising in a newspaper, or by handbills posted in the district, or by written or printed notices sent through the mails. When a sufficient number have come together, some one, on behalf of the object, moves another friend for chairman, and either the chairman or the mover, or some one previously agreed upon, will explain the purpose for which the people are called together, and give an outline of the club, society, or association which it is proposed to organize. His proper course, in finishing his remarks, is to move the appointment of a committee to prepare a constitution and by-laws. If that work has already been done, as it might well be, the meeting may take a recess for half an hour, at the close of which time the committee may report. If no such preparation has been made, it will be necessary, after an interchange of opinion, to adjourn to a future time. In the interval, friends of the object will enlighten the committee in the matter. On reconvening, the officers of the former meeting will preside without further notice; the committee report the desired laws, and they should be at once fully and carefully discussed, article by article, and section by section, and so voted upon. If adopted, the club or association is formed, and the members at once proceed to elect the officers required by the rules just adopted. The temporary officers give their places to those newly elected, and the organization is complete.

In forming an association of any kind, the first step to be taken is the adoption of a CONSTITUTION. By this is meant a formal agreement, defining the purpose and intention of the association, the course of action which the members of the society propose to pursue, and the rules and regulations by which they will be governed in their proceedings. Lesser regulations in regard to the conduct of members and order of proceeding, and, especially, rules which are added after the adoption of the Constitution, and are not of such importance as to be made Amendments, may be framed into a set of BY-LAWS.

The language of the Constitution should be precise, clear, and free from verbiage or unnecessary statements. If desired, the document may begin with a PREAMBLE, setting out in general terms the reasons which have led to the forming of the association. This, however, is by no means essential, and, we think, is now regarded as an old-fashioned custom. For convenience of reference, the Constitution must be divided and subdivided into ARTICLES and SECTIONS. The Articles should be numbered by Roman, and the Sections by Arabic numerals. The substance of each Article should be placed either as a heading or at the left side. Examples of the two methods are given below.

When the Constitution has been framed by a committee appointed for that purpose, it is to be brought before the society and considered, either as a whole, or section by section. After its adoption, it should be neatly engrossed in a suitable book, which may be the minute book of the society. To signify the acceptance of it as the fundamental law, all members must sign it. Plenty of blank space must be left for the signatures of new members, and also for the adding of such amendments as may afterwards be adopted. When an amendment is added, reference should be made to it in the main body of the Constitution either by foot or side notes.

## A LYCEUM OR INSTITUTE.

### PREAMBLE.

KILL in debate and oratory, fluency in public speaking, and ease in rhetorical exercises, being obtainable only by constant practice in public; and freedom of thought and discussion in regard to questions of public importance, whether political, social or religious, being one of the most desirable means both of culture and enlightenment, we, whose names are undersigned, do hereby agree to form an association to further these ends; and for its government do hereby establish and adopt the following

## Constitution.

### TITLE.

**ARTICLE I.** The title and name of this association shall be THE EASTON INSTITUTE.

### OBJECTS.

**ARTICLE II.** The objects of this society shall be mutual improvement in debate and composition, the diffusion of knowledge among its members, and the cultivation of the social qualities.

### OFFICERS.

**ARTICLE III.** The officers of this society shall consist of a President, Vice-President, a Recording Secretary, a Corresponding Secretary, a Treasurer, and a Librarian.

### ELECTION OF OFFICERS.

**ARTICLE IV.** Officers shall be elected at the first regular meetings of the society in the months of January, May and September, and shall hold office for the four months following.

*Sec.* 2. An absolute majority of all votes cast shall not be necessary to elect an officer. A plurality shall suffice.

### DUTIES OF OFFICERS.

**ARTICLE V.** The President shall preside at all meetings of the society. In his absence the Vice-President shall take the chair.

*Sec.* 2. The Recording Secretary shall keep a clear and accurate record of the proceedings at each meeting and be prepared to read the same at the next succeeding meeting.

*Sec.* 3. The Corresponding Secretary shall conduct all correspondence of the society, and inform honorary members of their election in appropriate form.

*Sec.* 4. The Treasurer shall receive all dues and fines, shall pay out money as directed by the vote of the society, and shall make a report of the society accounts at the first regular meetings of the society in January, May and September.

*Sec.* 5. The Librarian shall have charge of all books, records and manuscripts belonging to the society, shall loan books to the members in accordance with the by-laws relating to the subject, and shall keep an account of the whereabouts of such books.

### COMMITTEES.

**ARTICLE VI.** Standing Committes shall be appointed by the President immediately after his election, as follows: Executive Committee, committees on finance, library, lectures and printing; special committees shall be appointed upon other subjects by a vote of the society. Standing committees shall consist of three members each.

### MEMBERSHIP.

**ARTICLE VII.** Any person residing within the town of Easton, whether lady or gentleman, may become a member of this association, by a majority vote of the members present at the regular meeting next following that at which his or her name has been proposed. After such election the membership shall begin only when the member elect has signed this constitution and paid to the Treasurer three dollars ($3), as an initiation fee.

*Sec.* 2. Honorary memberships may be conferred by vote of the association upon any persons eminent in literature, science, art or statesmanship. Honorary members shall not be called upon to pay the initiation fees or dues.

### RULES OF ORDER.

**ARTICLE VIII.** The proceedings and deliberations of this society shall be governed by the rules of order laid down in "Cushing's Manual of Parliamentary Law," unless said manual should in any respect conflict with this Constitution, its Amendments, or the By-laws.

### EXPULSION OF MEMBERS.

**ARTICLE IX.** Any member guilty of disgraceful, corrupt or immoral conduct, or who shall persist in neglecting the duties imposed upon him by the society, or without good cause absent himself persistently from its meetings, may be expelled by a two-thirds vote of the members present at any meeting; *Provided*, that no member shall be expelled before his case has first been presented to the Executive Committee, who shall inform him of the charges made against him, give him an opportunity to be heard on his own behalf, and report the result of the inquiry to the society at large to take action upon.

### TIME OF MEETINGS.

**ARTICLE X.** The regular meetings of this society shall be held at eight o'clock on the Tuesday of each week, at Wilcox's Hall.

*Sec.* 2. Special meetings may be called by the President on the written request of five members.

### AMENDMENTS.

**ARTICLE XI.** This Constitution may be altered or amended, at any regular meeting, by a vote of two-thirds of the members present; *Provided*, that written notice of the nature of said amendment or alteration shall have been given at a previous meeting.

## By-Laws.

### LIBRARY.

**ARTICLE I.** No member shall be allowed to have more than two books from the library at one time in his possession. A fine of two cents per day shall be imposed upon members keeping books more than two weeks. The library shall be open before and after the regular meetings of the society.

### QUORUM.

**ARTICLE II.** Twelve members of good and regular standing shall constitute a quorum of this society.

### MONTHLY DUES.

**ARTICLE III.** Each member shall pay a monthly due of fifty cents to the Treasurer.

*Sec.* 2. The Treasurer shall post upon the bulletin board every month the names of those who have not paid dues for the three months preceding. If, at the next meeting, any are still delinquent, he shall refer the matter to the Executive Committee.

### APPOINTMENTS.

**ARTICLE III.** Members shall be appointed to take part in the exercises in turn by the President. The orator shall be entitled to two weeks' notice of his appointment: debaters to one week's notice; the critic shall be appointed at the opening of each meeting.

*Sec.* 2. Failure to fill an appointment shall subject the delinquent to a fine of fifty cents for each offense. The fine may be remitted by a vote of the society.

### ORDER OF EXERCISES.

**ARTICLE IV.** The following shall be the regular order of exercise at each regular meeting, after the meeting has been called to order:

1. Calling the roll.
2. Reading minutes of last meeting.
3. Reports of committees and officers.
4. Debate.
5. Reading (*selected*).
6. Oration.
7. Criticism of literary exercises.
8. Election of members.
9. Election of officers (in Jan., May and Sept.)
10. New business.
11. Adjournment.

## A Farmer's Club.

### ARTICLE I.

Name and Object.

This association shall be known as the Midfield County Agricultural Society. Its objects shall be the promotion of the knowledge of practical and scientific farming among its members and the community at large, and social enjoyment among its members and their families.

### ARTICLE II.

Membership.

Any person residing within this State, and more than twenty-one years of age, may become a member of this club by receiving a majority vote of the members present at any meeting, and by paying the fee of three dollars ($3.00) to the Treasurer, and the same sum annually thereafter.

### ARTICLE III.

Officers.

The officers of this Club shall be a President, a Secretary (who shall also be the Treasurer), and three members who, with the President and Secretary, shall constitute the Executive Committee. These officers shall be elected annually by ballot at the regular meeting in May of each year.

### ARTICLE IV.

Duties of Officers.

The President and Secretary shall have like powers and perform like duties with like officers in similar organizations. The Executive Committee shall have general charge of the interests of the Club and the carrying out of its objects. It shall fill vacancies among its own members, make rules, regulate expenditures, manage fairs or exhibitions, invite speakers or lecturers, and shall report at the annual meeting of the Club, and whenever else it may have matter to communicate. Three members of the Executive Committee shall constitute a quorum.

### ARTICLE V.

Sections.

The Club shall be divided into the following sections, namely: 1. Soils, their culture and management; 2. Cereals and grasses; 3. Vegetables; 4. Fruit and flowers; 5. Farm buildings; 6. Implements of agriculture; 7. Stock, its food and care; 8. Miscellaneous affairs. To one or more of the sections each member shall attach himself as soon as convenient after joining the club. Papers and questions relating to the several departments shall be referred to the appropriate sections, and reports thereon made to the Club from time to time.

### ARTICLE VI.

Meetings.

The meetings of this Club shall take place monthly on the first Tuesday of each month, and at such other times as the President, at the request of at least five members, shall name. The regular meeting on the first Tuesday of May shall be known as the "Annual Meeting."

### ARTICLE VII.

Annual Fair.

An annual county fair shall take place in the last week of September under the auspices of this Club. The Executive Committee shall have the general charge of such fair, and other special committees may be appointed by the Executive Committee. Such articles shall be exhibited in competition and otherwise, and such premiums shall be paid to exhibitors as the committees, by and with the consent of the Club, shall determine.

### ARTICLE VIII.

Amendments.

This Constitution may be altered or amended by a vote of two-thirds of the members present at any regular meeting of the Club; but a written notice of the proposed alteration or amendmen must be given at a previous regular meeting.

[NOTE. It will be observed that the rules in the last Constitution are less minute and stringent than in the case of the Lyceum. In a debating club every opportunity should be given for parliamentary practice, and strict method should be followed. In a farmers' club less formality and fewer arbitary rules of order are required. In fact, the more informal and conversational the proceedings of such a club, the more likely is it to be a success.]

## An Insurance Club.

In all great societies, such as the Freemasons or Odd Fellows, it is now the practice to agree upon a mutual guaranty of help in cases of sickness and decease. The Society, or some section thereof, forms itself practically into a mutual Insurance Company confined in membership. The main advantage lies in the fact that no large salaries have to be paid to officers and agents. There is no reason why such an arrangement may not be applied to any organization, if the number of members is moderately large. The introduction of the following Articles into the Constitution will effect the purpose:

**Article I.** On the death of any member of this association in good and regular standing, each member shall, upon being notified thereof by the Treasurer, pay to him the sum of one dollar and ten cents ($1.10), of which amount the Treasurer shall pay one dollar to the widow or nearest relative of the deceased member, and shall retain the remaining ten cents to cover expenses of notification and collection, rendering a report to the Society of the expense in each case and paying the surplus, if any, into the General Benefit fund, or otherwise, if directed by the Society.

**Article II.** If any member fails to respond to the notice of the Treasurer for the payments as specified in Article I., the amount shall be charged against him as *dues;* and no member who shall be in arrears for his dues for six months shall be entitled to the benefit given by Article I.

**Article III.** Every member must at all times keep his residence registered in the books of the Society. Failure to do so shall forfeit his rights as to insurance.

**Article IV.** If any member shall fail to pay the one dollar and ten cents, as above specified, within sixty days after proper notice has been given to him by the treasurer, his name shall be dropped from the Insurance Club roll, he shall cease to have any rights under its provisions, and shall forfeit any assessments already paid.

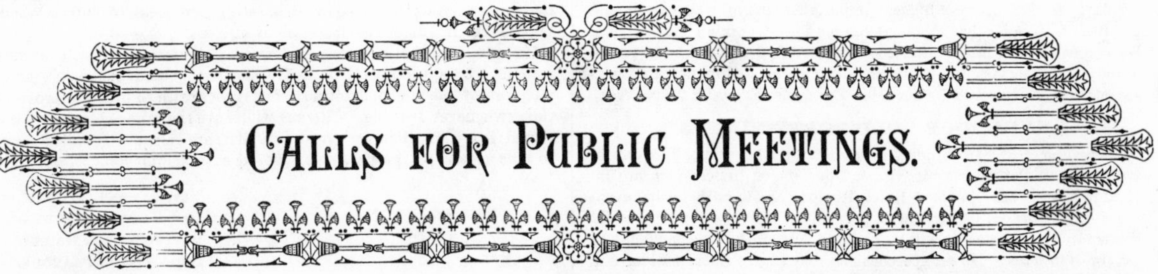

# CALLS FOR PUBLIC MEETINGS.

IN no small measure does the success of a public meeting depend upon the amount of publicity given by its originators to the time and place when and where it is to be held. With proper energy and a good cause, a very few persons can arouse and attract the attention of the multitude in such a way as to insure a spirited and well attended meeting. In issuing the call the object should be set forth not only clearly and distinctly, but *strikingly* and, if possible, in an original form. Display type is here very properly used, and a moderate degree of "sensationalism" not out of place.

The principal points to be mentioned, besides the place and hour of assembly, are usually the names of speakers who may be present, the object of gathering together, the presence of a glee club, music or other attractions, and the general merits of the cause to be discussed. The following forms will suggest many variations to suit special cases.

### REPUBLICAN RALLY!

AT MUSIC HALL, Thursday, Oct. 5, at 8 P. M., *sharp*. The first GRAND RALLY of the Campaign. REPUBLICANS, stand by the cause! WORKINGMEN, remember your interests! CITIZENS, the country's prosperity is at stake! The meeting will be addressed by the HON. JOHN SHERMAN, ROBERT G. INGERSOLL, and others. The Young Voters' Union Glee Club will render stirring campaign songs. *Ladies cordially invited.* COME ONE! COME ALL!

### ATTENTION! BALSTON ZOUAVES!

Members of Company A, Balston Zouaves, are hereby notified to meet at the armory at eight o'clock on the evening of Thursday, the 10th inst., for drill and company meeting. The question as to visiting Syracuse and joining in the Decoration Day parade will be considered. A full attendance is specially desired. By order of the captain.

JAMES PIKE, *Orderly.*

### VETERAN FIREMAN.

All persons who were formerly members of the old Volunteer Fire Companies of this city are earnestly requested to meet at Tompkins Hall on Wednesday night next at eight o'clock. It is desired to form an association of old Veterans for purposes of mutual enjoyment, and possibly to parade at some future time. Come and talk over the old times.

### SHALL WE HAVE A GOOD SCHOOL?

Many citizens who are greatly dissatisfied with the present management of the district schools of this town, propose to meet at the house of Mr. William Edgarton, Wednesday night, at half-past seven, to discuss the practicability of establishing a good select school where our children may receive proper instruction. An opportunity is now offered to engage a capable and experienced teacher, if a reasonable number of pupils can be obtained. All interested in the cause of education are earnestly urged to be present.

### INDEPENDENCE DAY.

All patriotic citizens of Greenville who wish to see the anniversary of the Nation's independence celebrated in a fitting manner to do honor to our town and our public spirit, will please meet at the Town Hall on Wednesday next, at three o'clock in the afternoon, to take appropriate measures. Let every one come out. A committee, consisting of Messrs. J. L. Hunt, William Robinson, and Selah Strong, will be on hand to receive subscriptions, or will call on you at your homes. Let us have a glorious old-fashioned FOURTH OF JULY.

## PRISON REFORM.

A meeting of all interested in reforming the well-known abuses existing in the prisons, jails, reform schools and almshouses of this State, will be held at Allyn Hall, Hartford, on Friday, June 29th, at two o'clock in the afternoon. Papers of great interest will be read on Prison Management, Almshouse Abuses, and Convict Labor. Rev. THOMAS W. WYANS, who has devoted much time to the investigation of this subject, will address the meeting and give the result of his studies, describing the atrocities which have existed in other States and the defects of our own system. Hon. FRANCIS WAYLAND, of New Haven, will give an account of the pauper systems of England and Europe, and deal with the subject of "Our Tramps."

## LABOR MEETING.

CAR-DRIVERS, TAKE NOTICE! *Shall we strike?* A meeting of all car-drivers employed on the Third Avenue horse railroad will be held Sunday evening at eight o'clock at Steinway Hall to determine whether a "strike" shall be instituted for a raise of wages of twenty-five cents per day. It is of the very highest importance that all who can should be present, in order that a general expression of opinion may be had. Good speakers and music will be on hand. We desire to let the public know the real facts as to our treatment by the bloated monopolists who are enriching themselves by our toil. *Per Order Executive Committee.*

## REUNION OF "OLD FORTY-NINERS."

All residents of San Francisco or vicinity, who originally came to California in the "Forty-nine Rush," of 1849, or thereabouts, are invited to meet at the Crawford Hotel, Rooms 8 and 9, on Saturday evening, for the purpose of forming a permanent organization of a social character. Refreshments will be on hand, and stories and incidents of old times in order. No set speeches are asked for. Come and have a good time.

## SUPPRESSION OF VICE.

The undersigned, at the request of many citizens, have determined to call a meeting to consider the advisability of forming a permanent organization to be known as the "Society for the Suppression of Vice in the City of Chicago." The meeting will be held in the lecture-room of the First Presbyterian Church, on Main Street, at two o'clock in the afternoon of Monday, the 12th inst.

The reasons which have led to this call are:

1. The fact that several gambling dens of the lowest description are now in full operation in this city, enticing our young men to destruction; that, though their attention has been called to this fact, the city authorities have seemed to be unwilling or unable to cope with the evil.

2. The fact that daily observation shows that drunkenness is on the increase, and a long train of crime follows in its wake; that, though laws have been made to restrain the sale of liquor, forbidding the opening of saloons on Sunday, selling liquor to minors and keeping open after midnight, yet these laws are constantly and defiantly violated, and the proper authorities declare themselves powerless to enforce them without the intelligent co-operation of citizens.

It is proposed that a society be formed to investigate this deplorable state of affairs, to appoint detective agents to obtain evidence against violators of the law, and to raise funds wherewith to institute prosecutions whenever feasible. Citizens who have the true interests of the city at heart, of whatever creed or belief, are vehemently called upon to take a stand on the right side. Let us save the fair fame of our city.

*Signed,*
REV. JAMES L. BELL.
REV. THOMAS WALKER.
REV. JOSIAH Y. GRIGGS.
HON. WILSON PEABODY.
DANIEL MCCARTHY.

# Petitions.

PETITIONS are formal requests or memorials addressed by one or more citizens to officers or bodies having power to grant the thing sought for. When the petition is negative in its character, requesting that something shall not be done, it is called a *remonstrance*. Among the persons to whom petitions may properly be made in this country are, the President or Congress of the United States, the Governor or Legislature of the various States, courts of law, and the Mayor and Common Council of a city. Affidavits should be attached to all legal petitions addressed to a court.

The petition should be formal in its direction and close. The address to the President should be, "To Chester A. Arthur, President of the United States;" to a Governor, "To Hobart B. Bigelow, Governor of the State of Connecticut." In neither of these cases should the title of "Excellency" be prefixed. After the address the object of the petition is introduced in this manner:

"The petition of the undersigned, citizens of New York, respectfully represents: That ——" The object of the petition must then be set out in a brief and lucid shape.

It is customary to close petitions to courts and legislative bodies with the phrase: "And your petitioners will ever pray," etc.

## PETITIONS TO CITY OFFICERS.

### 1. FOR EXTENSION OF WATER FACILITIES.

TO THE MAYOR AND COMMON COUNCIL OF THE CITY OF WESTBROOK:

*Gentlemen:*—Your petitioners, citizens and taxpayers residing on Sylvan Avenue and Myrtle Street in the city of Westbrook, respectfully petition and solicit your honorable body to extend the system of the city waterworks by laying pipes through the streets above mentioned. We would respectfully represent to your honorable body that within the past year many new houses have been erected on those streets and the immediate vicinity, and that the residents are totally without the water facilities to which as taxpayers they are justly entitled.

WESTBROOK, NEW YORK, June 12, 1881.

(*Signed by all residents on Sylvan Avenue and Myrtle Street.*)

### 2. FOR ABATEMENT OF A NUISANCE.

TO THE MAYOR AND ALDERMEN OF THE CITY OF HOBOKEN, IN COMMON COUNCIL ASSEMBLED:

*Gentlemen:*—The undersigned, citizens, residents of the Fourth Ward, respectfully represent that the building, 406 South Street, owned by a corporation known as the "New Process Soap Company," is now, and for some months has been, used by the said company for the purpose of manufacturing soap, and for other purposes to your petitioners unknown; that the process of manufacture is so carried on as to produce a most unendurable stench, to the great annoyance and serious discomfort of your petitioners, their families, and all persons resident in or passing through the neighborhood; that your petitioners are informed by medical authority, and verily believe, that the gases thus generated and diffused are injurious to health, as well as unpleasant to the senses. Your petitioners further represent that the carrying on of this business is in all respects a nuisance, and request your honorable body to have it abated as such.

HOBOKEN, NEW JERSEY, July 5th, 1882.

(*Signed by fifty persons living in the neighborhood.*)

### 3. REMONSTRANCE AGAINST SALOON LICENSES.

TO THE MAYOR AND COMMON COUNCIL OF YONKERS, NEW YORK:

Your petitioners, residents and taxpayers, respectfully represent that the increase in crime in this city within the last year, as shown by the records of the City Court, and especially the fearful prevalence of intoxication, a fact which may daily be observed on our streets, are, in the opinion of your petitioners, in great measure due to the increased number of licenses granted by the city authorities to carry on the business of liquor selling; that the number of saloons in our city is already far too large in proportion to the size of the place, and that it is also larger than in other cities of the same size. We, therefore, respectfully solicit and urge your honorable body to permit no more such licenses to be granted in the future, and to take prompt action against such licensed vendors of spirituous liquors as have violated the laws and conditions under which they were granted.

(*Signed by ten clergymen and many citizens.*)

## PETITIONS TO STATE LEGISLATURES.

### 1. REMONSTRANCE AGAINST DIVISION OF TOWNS.

TO THE HONORABLE THE SENATE AND HOUSE OF REPRESENTATIVES OF THE STATE OF MAINE IN LEGISLATURE ASSEMBLED:

The petition of the undersigned, citizens of the village of Pawckassett, now a portion of the borough of Podunk, respectfully represents that they have learned that a bill is now before the two Houses of Assembly, for the purpose of erecting the village aforesaid into a separate corporate borough; that they, your petitioners, fully believe that such action would be opposed to the best interests of both village and borough, and earnestly remonstrate against such action, both as unnecessary and injurious, and as opposed, as they are informed and verily believe, to the will of the majority of the people of said village and borough. And your petitioners, as in duty bound, will ever pray, etc., etc.

### 2. WOMEN ON SCHOOL COMMITTEES.

TO THE GENERAL ASSEMBLY OF THE STATE OF WISCONSIN:

The undersigned, citizens and voters of the State of Wisconsin, respectfully present to your honorable body the following reasons in favor of the bill now before the State Legislature providing that all women above the age of twenty-one, who are owners or part-owners of property on which taxes are assessed, should be permitted to cast their ballots at the election of school committees in the several towns and boroughs, and to serve as members of such school committees, if elected thereto:

1. That, as taxpayers, they are entitled to have a voice in the disposition of the funds raised in part by assessment of their property, on the principle declared by our forefathers, "no taxation without representation."

2. That the care and education of children is a subject in which women are peculiarly and specially interested, and that therefore their tastes and training make them fully competent to assist in the selection of school committees and to serve with credit thereon.

3. That it is, as we believe, the general opinion of the voters of this State that a step should be taken toward the enfranchisement of woman; that to many it seems expedient that full electoral rights should not be conferred at once; and that the grant proposed in the bill referred to will furnish an excellent test of the capacity of the women of this State to properly use the full right of suffrage in case it may hereafter seem advisable to bestow it upon them.

For these reasons and others which will be set before your honorable body by those members having charge of said bill, the undersigned respectfully but earnestly petition your honorable body to consider the subject at an early date, feeling assured that its immediate passage will meet with the warm approbation of a large majority of citizens. And your petitioners, as in duty bound, will ever pray, etc.

### 3. FOR CHANGE OF NAME.

TO THE HONORABLE SENATE AND HOUSE OF REPRESENTATIVES OF THE STATE OF GEORGIA:

Your petitioner, the undersigned, respectfully represents to your honorable body that he is a citizen of Dahlonega, Lumpkin County; that through the unintentional misjudgment of his parents, he at present bears the unmelodious name of Nebuchadnezzar Nubbins; that said name is disagreeable in sound and ridiculous in writing; that it is a cause of great annoyance to him as furnishing a source of mirth to ill-disposed persons, and that he verily believes it is the cause of pecuniary loss to him in business matters. He therefore prays your honorable body to allow him to exchange it for the more euphonious name of Algernon Sydney Gordon, by passing the following bill, which will be presented to you by the member from Lumpkin County.

Private Bill No.—Be it enacted that the name of Nebuchadnezzar Nubbins, of Lumpkin County, be and hereby is changed to Algernon Sydney Gordon.

And your petitioner will ever pray, etc.

### PETITION TO GOVERNOR.

TO ALONZO B. CORNELL, ESQ., GOVERNOR OF THE STATE OF NEW YORK:

The petition of the undersigned, citizens of New York, respectfully represents:

That on the twelfth day of January, 1876, William Wallace, of the City of New York, was convicted before the Court of Oyer and Terminer in said city of the crime of burglary, and sentenced therefor to the State prison at Sing Sing for the term of eight years; that he has already served five years of said sentence, and that three remain to be served; that his conduct while in prison has been uniformly excellent and his character has greatly improved, as will be seen from the enclosed letters written by the Warden and Chaplain: that the evidence upon which he was convicted is not altogether conclusive as to the breaking-in necessary to constitute burglary; that said Wallace has a wife and child greatly in need of his support and care; that, in the opinion of all acquainted with the case, the said Wallace will faithfully adhere to his resolve to live henceforth an industrious and honest life. Your petitioners, therefore, believing that the best interests of society will be served thereby, and that the demands of justice have been already sufficiently answered, respectively implore the executive clemency in his behalf, and petition that the unexpired portion of his sentence be remitted.

And your petitioners will ever pray, etc.

By means of written Resolutions assemblies or bodies of people put upon record their opinions, sentiments, or intentions regarding any matter before them for consideration. Resolutions may be of a purely business character, as resolutions of instruction to members of a legislature, or of stockholders in favor of a certain route, or they may be resolutions of condolence or congratulation. In framing the first class, care should be taken to use brief, clear, and business-like language, and to express what is desired in the fewest, plainest, and most forcible words possible. When condolence or congratulation is to be extended, the task of drawing satisfactory resolutions is more difficult. On the one hand is the danger of appearing unfeeling by being too curt and business-like; on the other, the danger of falling into too sentimental and "high-flown" language, making bathos of what is meant for pathos. The only guide that can be followed is that suggested by honest feeling and a refined literary taste.

It is usual to preface resolutions with a preamble, beginning with the word "Whereas," and setting out the reasons or occasion for the following resolutions. When the preamble naturally divides itself into two or more parts, each should form a separate clause beginning with the word "Whereas." The resolutions should each begin with the words "Be it Resolved," or simply "Resolved." The preamble may in many cases be omitted altogether. While it is well to use considerable formality in framing a set of resolutions, precision and brevity must not be sacrificed.

The following forms of Resolutions may, with alterations which will readily suggest themselves, serve for many occasions.

## RESOLUTIONS OF CONDOLENCE.

### 1.—ON THE DEATH OF A PUBLIC OFFICER.

Whereas, It has pleased Almighty God in His infinite wisdom to remove from our midst our honored and worthy fellow-member, Edwin Stone; and

Whereas, The pleasant and intimate relations which for twenty years he held with this Board as a fellow Director make it eminently fitting that we should place upon record our feelings of appreciation of his services and regret for his loss; therefore

*Resolved*, That this Board of Directors will ever hold in grateful remembrance the sterling business qualities, the patience, integrity, and clear-sightedness displayed for many years by our late fellow-member, Edwin Stone, in the work of this Board.

*Resolved*, That the sudden removal by death of our esteemed fellow-citizen from the position which he held as a public officer creates a vacancy not easily filled, and that his fellow-members fully realize and deeply deplore the loss occasioned to themselves and to the public at large.

*Resolved*, That we hereby extend our deepest sympathy to the bereaved relatives and friends of the deceased, hoping that even in the sadness of their affliction they may yet find some consolation in knowing that the worth of his private qualities and the value of his public services are properly appreciated.

*Resolved*, That a copy of these Resolutions be properly engrossed and sent to the family of our deceased fellow-member, and that the Resolutions be also published in each of the daily papers of this city.

### 2.—DEATH OF A SOCIETY MEMBER.

At a special meeting of the Greenville Literary Institute and Lyceum, held at Union Hall on the evening of Wednesday, the 12th inst., the following preamble and resolutions were unanimously adopted:

Whereas, It has seemed good to the Ruler of the Universe to remove from among us our talented and beloved friend and fellow-member, James Austin Gregory, therefore, in view of the loss we have sustained, and the still heavier loss occasioned to his respected relatives, be it

*Resolved*, That the members of this society hereby desire to express their sense of bereavement and grief at the loss of one of their earliest, most faithful, and most gifted members, and to record the enjoyment and profit which they have long had in the genial social qualities and the brilliant intellectual acquirements of the deceased.

*Resolved*, That we sincerely sympathize with the relatives and near friends of our late beloved associate, and that we respectfully commend them for consolation to that Divine Power which, though sometimes inscrutable in its dispensations, yet 'doeth all things well,' feeling sure that to them, as to us, there is comfort in the knowledge that the deceased was not only honorable and manly in all respects, but was also a devoted and consistent Christian;

*Resolved*, That in token of our sorrow at the death of our friend, the members of this association wear a badge of crape upon the left arm for thirty days.

*Resolved*, That the secretary of this meeting is instructed to send a copy of these resolutions to the parents of the deceased, as a testimonial of our grief and sympathy.

## CONGRATULATION AND COMPLIMENT.

### 1. PROMOTION OF AN OFFICER.

At a meeting of the members and officers of the Fire Department of the city of Providence, held in Turners' Hall, on the evening of Wednesday, the following resolutions were unanimously adopted:

WHEREAS, At the last meeting of the Board of Fire Commissioners for the city of Providence, Edgar C. Jenkins, foreman of Engine Company No. 2, was unanimously appointed Chief of the Fire Department of this city; now, therefore be it—

*Resolved*, That we, the officers and members of the different companies, desire to declare, in the warmest manner, our approbation of this appointment as a wise and suitable one, and to express our opinion that it will result in greatly increasing the efficiency of the Department in every respect.

*Resolved*, That we also desire to congratulate our comrade and associate, Edgar C. Jenkins, on his well-deserved promotion, to express our confidence in his ability to fill the important post with credit and honor, and to assure him of our hearty coöperation in his efforts to make our Fire Department the best in the State.

*Resolved*, That these resolutions be handsomely engrossed at the expense of this meeting and presented to the new Chief, Edgar C. Jenkins, and that copies be sent to the daily papers and to the Board of Fire Commissioners.

### 2. RETIREMENT OF PUBLIC OFFICER.

At a meeting of the Aldermen and Councilmen of the city of Weston, in Common Council assembled, the following resolutions were adopted without a dissenting vote:

WHEREAS, Our esteemed fellow-citizen, Lucius A. Judson, has handed to us his written resignation of the office of Town Treasurer, assigning as reasons therefor his increasing age and bodily infirmity, and—

WHEREAS, The said Lucius A. Judson has filled the office from which he now retires for thirty-five years, to the great satisfaction of all citizens, of whatever political parties; and during this time our taxes have been lighter than those of other neighboring towns, and at the same time our public improvements have been more extensive; and—

WHEREAS, During all this time the said Lucius A. Judson has absolutely refused to accept any pay whatever for his services, therefore, be it

*Resolved*, That in unwillingly accepting the resignation of Treasurer Judson, the Mayor and Common Council of this town desire to express to him in the heartiest and most sincere manner the thanks both of themselves and of the public, for his prolonged, valuable and unrequited labor in behalf of the public interest, and to hope that in his retirement from office he will enjoy the happiness of a peaceful and serene old age, with the confidence and regard of his fellow-citizens.

*Resolved*, That, in the opinion of this meeting, the prosperity and growth of Weston is due, more than to any other one cause, to the disinterested exertions of our late Town Treasurer in its behalf.

*Resolved*, That a copy of these resolutions be handsomely engrossed, at an expense of not more than fifty ($50) dollars, and presented to the retiring Treasurer as a mark of our esteem.

*Resolved*, That a committee of three be appointed by the Mayor to engage some skillful artist to paint a portrait of the Hon. Lucius A. Judson, at an expense of not more than three hundred ($300) dollars, to be borne by the town, and that such portrait, when completed, shall be hung in a prominent position in the new Town Hall.

(*Signed by the Mayor, Aldermen and Councilmen.*)

### 3. COMMENDING OFFICERS OF A SHIP.

WHEREAS, On the night of June 4, the steamship *Ocean Wave*, Capt. Watson, from Liverpool to New York, came into collision with the steamship *Alice*, under circumstances which, in the judgment of the undersigned, passengers in the *Ocean Wave*, fully exonerate the captain and officers of that vessel from all blame in the premises, and

WHEREAS, The conduct of the captain, officers and crew in the trying emergency is deserving of the highest praise and gratitude; therefore

*Resolved*, That we, the passengers of the *Ocean Wave*, do hereby extend our earnest thanks to the captain, officers, and crew for the cool, determined, and efficient manner in which they took instant and efficacious measures for the safety of the passengers under their charge and the preservation of the ship, and that we congratulate the owners of the line on the possession of officers so manly, courageous, and gentlemanly, and of a crew so well disciplined and obedient.

*Resolved*, That especial praise is due to Captain Watson, whose quick appreciation of the situation and thorough seamanship preserved, as we believe, the lives of the passengers and crew, and assured the safety of the *Ocean Wave;* also to Second Mate Lowry and the boat-crew under his command, who, at the imminent risk of their own lives, saved the crew of the *Alice*, by putting out to her in a very heavy sea.

*Resolved*, That a copy of these resolutions be sent to the owners, to Captain Watson, and to Mate Lowry.

(*Signed by all the passengers.*)

### 4. THANKS TO OFFICERS OF A CONVENTION.

*Resolved*, That the thanks of this convention are due, and are hereby given, to the President, for the able, impartial, and dignified manner in which he has presided over its deliberations, and to the other officers, for the satisfactory manner in which they have fulfilled the duties assigned them.

(*A resolution of this kind should be put to the vote by the member offering it, the subject being personal to the chair.*)

## BUSINESS RESOLUTIONS.

### 1. INSTRUCTIONS TO MEMBERS OF LEGISLATURE.

At a meeting of citizens of Palmer, the following Preamble and Resolutions were adopted by a large majority:

WHEREAS, The various Horse Railroad Companies of this city see fit to charge the fare of six cents for a single ride on each road, and will grant no transfer tickets; and

WHEREAS, This charge was first adopted in "war times," when the purchasing value of money was less, and the population of the city much smaller.

*Resolved*, That in our opinion the present charge is excessive and vexatious, and that in view of the public privileges conceded to them, and the large profits accruing, the companies should be compelled to reduce the fare.

*Resolved*, That the members of the Legislature for this district be, and hereby are, instructed to prepare a bill reducing the fare from six to five cents and providing for the issue of transfer tickets by the Main Street road from their main line to their depot branch, at the price of six cents for the full trip, to present such bill to the Legislature, and to do all in their power to procure its immediate passage.

### 2. PROTEST AGAINST STREET PAVING.

At a meeting of the residents on Pine Street, held last evening, the following Resolutions were adopted:

WHEREAS, The Board of Public Works of this city have passed an Order for the paving of Pine Street, from Walnut to Penn, with Belgian blocks:

*Resolved*, That it is the unanimous opinion of the residents and property owners on that part of the street that such street-paving is unnecessary and injudicious:

1. Because the road is already macadamized and in excellent condition.

2. Because the street is occupied almost entirely by private houses and villas, is distant from the center of the city, and is not subject to heavy or business travel.

3. That the assessments will be a heavy and uncalled-for burden on the residents, whose taxes are already very high.

*Resolved*, That a committee of three be named by the chairman of this meeting, to draw up a petition setting forth our opinion, to circulate the same for signatures, and to present it to the proper authorities, praying for relief.

### 3. OBJECTING TO RAILROAD ROUTE.

At a town meeting of the town of Bolton, regularly called by the proper officers, and held at the Town Hall, on Tuesday, the 12th inst., the following Resolutions were passed by a vote of 146 to 37:

WHEREAS, The Hampton and Midland Railroad Company have obtained a charter from the Legislature of this State allowing them to lay a track through this town ; and

WHEREAS, The surveyors and construction company have chosen for the position of such track a line beginning forty-three feet northeast of the south corner of the large barn belonging to Jared Hall, and proceeding thence due west, along what is commonly known as the Bolton Flats :

*Resolved*, That the citizens of Bolton, in town meeting assembled, protest against such line being adopted ; because such line passes directly in the rear of our finest residences, and would prove an intolerable nuisance ; because it runs parallel to the highway, crossing it at two points, and would therefore prove a source of danger to life and limb, and, finally, because another route beginning five hundred feet south from the point mentioned, and proceeding in a westerly direction, would be free from the objections mentioned, and could be adopted without a serious increase of expense.

*Resolved*, That Abram Wilcox and Jared Hall be appointed a committee to lay our objections before the company, and to induce them, if possible, to change the route as suggested ; and that the committee, in case the company refuse, are instructed to take legal advice and opinion in the name of the town, and to report on the subject at a special town meeting which they are hereby given authority to call.

Attest : JOHN ADDISON, *Clerk.*

# Public Celebrations.

UNDER the denomination of public celebrations may be included the general observance of certain legal holidays, anniversaries of important historical events, and extensive society reunions. Compared with other countries, our national holidays are few, and their observance slight. At the present time only Independence Day and Decoration (or Memorial) Day are honored by the holding of public exercises, and the observance of even the Fourth of July seems constantly diminishing. This greatly to be regretted fact is due, perhaps, to the over-formal and sometimes bombastic fashion in which it was formerly customary to celebrate that most important day. In arranging the exercises for this or any other public celebration, it should be borne in mind that the public like to be amused and not preached to. "Shorten the high-flown oratory and have plenty of brass bands" is a good motto for the committee to follow. The taste for turgid rhetoric and delight in the soaring of the American eagle which Dickens ascribed to us, if it ever existed at all, is surely long since extinct.

Let us see what is to be done to carry out a Fourth of July celebration in a suitable manner. The first thing is to arouse public attention to the importance of the matter. Steps should be taken at least two weeks before the arrival of the day. In every town there are men of the proper character to start such a movement. It is a valuable opportunity for young professional men and politicians to place themselves in the glare of publicity, which, if they possess shrewdness, is just what they want. No matter how indifferent the public mind at the outset, two or three energetic and popular men can surely make a success by careful attention to details. After talking the matter over thoroughly, let them issue and widely distribute printed notices of a public meeting to consider the subject of celebrating the Fourth in a manner to do credit to the town. A suitable form will be found under "Calls for Public Meetings." If the town boasts of a newspaper, advertise the meeting and interest the editor in the subject. He will gladly assist, both out of patriotism and with the view of obtaining interesting matter for his columns.

Before the meeting, let the projectors use all spare time in talking the matter up. Do not leave the meeting to "run itself." In such a matter the crowd will readily follow the lead of those who have thought the subject over and have definite plans to propose. Let one of the projectors nominate officers, who should previously be informed of their proposed honors and given time to prepare their "extemporaneous" speeches. Select for officers "solid" men of wealth and reputation. Their assistance is indispensable, and men will do a great deal more through public spirit and self-glorification combined than through patriotism alone. After the meeting is organized, let the best speakers among the projectors present the subject. His speech should be earnest, clear, not too eloquent, and, if possible, witty. The ball thus started, other speeches will readily follow, and the sense of the meeting soon be determined. Do not attempt to go into details of business. Keep the assembly in good humor and bring them to the resolve of having a "good time" and a "glorious Fourth."

If a celebration is decided upon, the most important business for the meeting to transact is the appointment of an executive committee or committee of arrangements, as it may be called. Upon the men selected depends the entire success of the celebration. They must be popular, shrewd, and energetic. A single incompetent member will greatly endanger the whole scheme. Let the list be carefully prepared beforehand and the president instructed on the subject. The committee of arrangements should contain ten or twelve members. The projectors will naturally be included.

At the close of the public meeting let the executive committee meet at once and divide into sub-committees. Let the sub-committees, of three, two, or even one, be in constant consultation, and have general meetings of the whole committee of arrangements as often as possible. The following list of sub-committees may, of course, be varied to meet the circumstances:

1. On finance. To collect funds, pay bills, and audit expenses.
2. On printing. To advertise thoroughly the celebration, and "see" the newspapers.
3. On invitations. To invite societies, military companies, and eminent men.
4. On procession. To organize the line, assign places to different bodies, select the line of route, and appoint marshals of the day.
5. On decoration. To urge citizens to decorate their houses and to see to the decorating of the hall where the exercises are to take place.
6. On orators. To select speakers for the occasion.
7. On salutes. To see to firing of cannon and ringing of bells.
8. On public fireworks.
9. On music. To engage brass bands and glee clubs.
10. On "Antiques and Horribles." A burlesque feature in a procession adds greatly to the general amusement.

PUBLIC DINNERS may be (1) in honor of some distinguished guest, (2) anniversary, as the Alumni dinner of a college, or (3) society dinners. In the first case a formal invitation should be drawn and signed by leading citizens or by the body proposing to give the dinner. A day may be named, or the guest may be requested to name one which will suit his convenience. Other guests may receive cards of invitation, or tickets may be sold. It is not uncommon to invite guests at a distance who, it is well-known, cannot be present. In such case their letters of regret are read at the table and should be framed with that end in view.

At a public dinner the president of the occasion takes the head, and the vice-president the foot of the table. The guest of the evening occupies a position at the right of the president. The etiquette during the continuance of the dinner is the same as at a private dinner table. The custom of one diner asking another to take a glass of wine with him is now almost obsolete.

## TOASTS.

The observance of the custom of drinking healths, with some complimentary or sympathetic allusion, is so natural a social act that it is doubtless as ancient as wine-drinking itself. It became general in England, however, in the seventeenth century, when the habits of society there were more convivial than ever before, and when the reigning beauty of a county or district became, so to speak, the "toast" at all dinner-parties and other social gatherings. The name is supposed to have originated from the custom of floating pieces of toast in a bowl of punch, which was common in England after that beverage was introduced from India, in the Sixteenth century. The Earl of Rochester, advising as to the construction of a drinking-cup, says:—

Make it so large, that filled with sack
Up to the swelling brim,
Vast toasts, on the delicious lake,
Like ships at sea may swim.

The term of health-giving "I'll pledge you," originated in the frequency of assassinations while drinking, the person so speaking pledging himself for the safety of the drinker. From England, the custom of drinking Toasts spread to France, and so over the Continent, and at present every civilized community follows this custom "in its cups."

After the dessert has been served the toasts of the evening are in order. At civic banquets, corporation feasts, and all public dinners, it is usual to set down beforehand a line of toasts to be followed in regular order, and with the persons named who are appointed to respond to them. The first to be proposed should be "The Day We Celebrate," if the occasion be an anniversary. On other public occasions the custom is to begin with "The President of the United States." or, if in Great Britain or its dependencies "Her gracious Majesty the Queen;" this first toast is drunk standing, and if the royal family or the President be in mourning, in silence. Next should follow a toast to the guest of the occasion, whose speech should be the principal one of the dinner. After this come the "Army and Navy," "the Bench and Bar," "the Press," and then the names of distinguished guests, coupled with some complimentary allusion. The persons who are to respond to special toasts should be selected with regard for their profession, office, and attainments. They should be informed as soon as possible of the toast to which they are to be called upon to respond. The last formal or regular toast should be "The Ladies." Afterwards the president may call for extemporaneous toasts, speeches and songs at his own judgment. To make a good after-dinner speech is an attainment which few possess. Such a speech should be colloquial, humorous, spontaneous, and appropriate.

At private dinners the first toast is "Our worthy host," who after acknowledging the compliment usually calls up some special guest, who in return proposes "the Ladies," and so the cup goes round. Sometimes humorous toasts are given, as:—

"One loaf between four of us :
Thank the Lord there are no more of us!"

Or as in this old-fashioned sentiment :—"Here's to you and your folks and us and our folks, hoping that when us and our folks go to visit you and your folks, you and your folks will treat us and our folks, as us and our folks treated you and your folks, when you and your folks came to visit us and our folks!"—in which the eccentricity of the grammar may be forgiven in consideration of the forethought of the sentiment. Another toast somewhat of the same character is the following :—

"Here's a health to all those that I love,
And a health to all those that love me,
Here's a health to all those that love them that I love,
And all those that love them that love me."

The French, in drinking healths, say "A vous," or, if to a lady, "A vos beaux yeux;" the English "Your good health," or "Here's to you;" the Germans "Auf Wiedersehen;" thieves slang "I looks t'vards yer," "I likewise bows," "Ere's hall the air hoff yer ead," etc. Of late years it has become customary to place upon the walls—embroidered, painted, printed or otherwise set forth—mottoes which are in the nature of sentiments or toasts, and are most commonly to be found in the family dining-room. Besides many selections from the Scriptures, and religious apostrophizing, such as "God bless Our Home!" "Give us this Day Our Daily Bread," etc., there are found the following, "Eat, Drink and be Merry," "Eat and be Filled," "Let Good Digestion Wait on Appetite, and Health on Both," all of which may be considered to be of the nature of sentiments, fitly concluding with

"What is a table richly spread,
Without a Woman at its Head?"

At wedding breakfasts the custom is to toast the "Happy pair" or the "Bride and groom," and send them on their way rejoicing, with the conventional old shoe cast after them for luck. After their departure the guests settle down to the good things on the board, and toasts are drunk to the fancy of those present. "Absent Friends" is a favorite toast at all private tables, not infrequently followed even in these days, by singing "Auld Lang Syne," all rising and taking hands. On shipboard, "The Ship," "The Voyage," "The Company," "The Captain," "The Doctor," are the favorite toasts. Of course, on all public occasions where it is desirable to get some special wit, or humorist, or otherwise notable personage "upon his legs," the plan adopted is to drink his health with some reference to his noteworthy qualifications. Another plan, if he be a stranger, is to drink to his native land, or its emblems, as, in the case of a Scotchman "The Land O'Cakes," or "the Land of Burns;" if an American "the Stars and Stripes," "Columbia," or "Uncle Sam;" Italy, "Garibaldi" or "Victor Emmanuel," as the case may be; Great Britain, either "The Queen, God bless her!" "the Flag that braved a thousand years," etc, "the land of Shakespeare;" Australia, "The Governor," "the Prosperity of the Colony," etc., and Ireland, "The Green Isle of Erin," "Tom Moore," etc. The custom of toast-giving has been often the source of song, as in "Drink to me only with thine eyes," "Here's a health to thee, Tom Moore," Byron's "Farewell to Tom Moore," and finally, that gloomy chant of the plague-stricken soldiers in India :—

"Then stand to your glasses, steady,
We drink to our comrades' eyes;
One cup to the dead already—
Hurrah for the next that dies."

In offering wine to another—and when a toast is proposed all glasses should be filled—it is customary to pour a little first into your own glass, in order that if there be any cork or other foreign matter in the bottle it may fall to your share, an act of consideration which forms one of the finer shades of social observance at table. Any one may propose a toast, after catching the eye of the host, or master of the feast, and rising; but at public banquets and on important occasions, it is customary to appoint a "toast-master," to whom all toasts are given, and whose duty it is to read them off at the proper moment.

# List of Toasts for Public and Private Occasions.

**New Year's Day.**—Many happy returns of the Day.

Compliments of the Season.

A New Year and new luck.

Our good resolutions: May they never be broken.

The Old Year: He was not so bad after all.

The Mile-posts of Life: May they never seem farther apart.

The New Year: Like wine, may it improve with age.

New Year's Day: To the Ladies it is the fountain of everlasting youth: every year they grow a year younger.

**Christmas Day**—The World's Festival: England furnishes the plum pudding and America the mince-pie; everybody is Hungary, and we swim in Greece, and devour Turkey.

St. Nicholas: A noble character: the only Saint in the Calendar who is *for-giving.*

"Father Christmas:"—Well dressed from top to toe. [Snow-crown and Mistle-toe]

A Christmas Dinner: The printer's misery—since everything ends in *Pi.*

The Plum-Pudding: A Dream before—a Nightmare after.

Our Stockings: The only time in the year when we leave them empty and find them full.

The Holly Green Festival: May we never be so *wholly green* as to give it up.

Christmas Hospitality, and the ladies who make it delightful by their *mincing* ways.

**Washington's Birthday.**—"First in Peace, first in War, and first in the hearts of his Countrymen."

George Washington: The Father of his Country. May his offspring never dishonor his memory.

Our First President: He created an Empire and refused a Crown.

**Independence Day.**—The day we celebrate.

The "Fourth of July:" The birth-day of a brood of Giants,—"Columbia," "Uncle Sam," "Brother Jonathan," and "The Star-Spangled Banner."

The "Flag of Our Union:" By the Light of its Stars we are shown the Stripes and Sufferings of our Forefathers.

The "Stars and Stripes:" Each of them represents a State—a Diamond in a necklace of Gems.

**Thanksgiving Day.**—The first American invention.

The Pilgrim Fathers: The "foothold" for which they gave thanks has become the homestead of a mighty people.

The "Great Reunion Day," on which we welcome the seceders who have come back to join the Old Family Group; and show our aversion to gluttony by punishing the *gobblers.*

**Birthdays.**—The only day in the year that nobody could dispense with.

The more we have the more we want.

Signs of Progress that baffle the Census-taker.

**Weddings.**—The happy pair: Two are company, three are not.

May they be well broken to double harness.

The bride: Although she *reigns* over this *bridal* party, *sadd'll* be her lot unless she learns to submit to the *curb.*

**Wooden Weddings.**—The Bride and Bridegroom: And may the hearts they trust never prove *hollow-ware.*

The Wooden Wedding of our Friends: And may all the children be *chips of the old block.*

The Happy Pair: Their first wedding was a neat bit of *joiner work;* the second has furnished employment to the *coopers.*

**Tin Weddings.**—Ten years of wedded happiness: A *decade* that leaves affection *undecayed.*

The Golden Rule of Matrimony: Marry the first time for love—the second for the *Tin.*

The Fair Bride: She blushed at her first marriage, but she exhibits more *metal* to-day.

**Crystal Weddings.**—The Fifteenth Year of Wedlock: A matrimonial *stage* chiefly remarkable for its *Tumblers.*

The New Married Couple: They will not find the friendship of their guests as brittle as their gifts.

Crystal Weddings: The medium through which the bliss of enduring affection is *magnified, reflected,* and made *transparent* to everybody.

**Silver Weddings.**—The Bridal Pair: Their admirable performances in double harness well entitle them to the *plate.*

A quarter of a century of Happy Matrimony: The best five-twenty bond in the world.

Silver threads among the Gold: May they never *part* in the future with what they have won *bi-metal* in the past.

**Golden Weddings.**—May they long continue to bask in the golden sunshine of old age.

Matrimony's Pleasant Autumn: May it always bear a golden Harvest.

The Fiftieth Year of Wedlock: Affection's age of Gold.

## NATIONAL PARTIES.

THE first distinctive array of parties after the War of Independence, grew out of the successive attempts to form the Constitution. When the Constitution came before the people for adoption, its friends were called **Federalists**, and its opponents **Anti-Federalists.** Washington was the head of the former, and Jefferson of the latter.

A little later the Anti-Federals took the name of **Republicans**, accusing their opponents of secret hostility to popular institutions. The other side then called themselves **Federal-Republicans**, and stigmatized the Anti-Federalists as **Democrats**, meaning it to be a name of reproach. The only Federalists in the presidential chair were Washington and John Adams. From Jefferson onward to Monroe the Republicans, or Democratic-Republicans as they called themselves, had undisturbed possession of power. In 1824 there were four candidates for president, each one claiming to be a Democratic-Republican. There was no choice by the people, and the House of Representatives elected John Quincy Adams, who was after that called a **National-Republican.** The Democrats came into complete power, in 1828, by selecting Jackson, and their rule was perpetual under Van Buren. Meantime, Clay ran against Jackson (in 1832), as a National-Republican. In this canvass the **Anti-Masons** appeared, nominating William Wirt for president, but it was a party of no consequence except in the State of New York, and never carried any State except Vermont. Henceforward the National-Republicans became **Whigs**, with Clay as their leader; and in 1840 triumphed in the election of Harrison. His death and the course of Tyler turned the balance the other way, and the Democrats elected Polk in 1844. The **Liberty** party or Abolitionists appear feebly in 1842, but in 1844 they cast votes enough to give New York and Michigan to the Democrats, and so defeat Clay and elect Polk. The Whigs then took advantage of his fame in the Mexican war (in 1848), and easily elected General Taylor. Four years later they were defeated, and Pierce (Democrat) elected. Now came up the **Free-Soil** party, composed mainly of Democrats opposed to slavery extension. They ran Van Buren in 1848, and Hale in 1852, but did not carry a State. In 1856 the **American** party appeared with Fillmore as their candidate, carrying only Maryland. In 1860 the **Republicans** (successors of the Whig party) came upon the field to elect Lincoln against three others, Douglas, Independent Democrat; Breckinridge, Democrat; and Bell, Constitutional Union. The Republicans re-elected Lincoln in 1864; Grant in 1868, 1872; Hayes in 1876, and Garfield in 1880.

## MINOR PARTIES.

**Anti-Renters**, in New York, about 1841, who resisted the collection of back rents on Van Rensselaer manor near Albany. They had strength enough to defeat Wright, the regular Democratic candidate for Governor, and elected an Independent Democrat.

**Barn-burners**, New York, 1846, seceders from the Democratic party. They were opposed to slavery extension.

**Buck-Tails**, New York, about 1815, supported Madison and opposed Clinton.

**Conservatives**, New York and some other States, 1837; a paper-money faction of the Democrats, opposed to the establishment of the sub-treasury.

**Constitutionalists**, opposed to Friends of the People, Pennsylvania, 1805; rival factions of the Republican party.

**Doughfaces**, 1820, northern members of Congress who voted in favor of allowing slavery in Missouri. John Randolph gave them the name.

**Hunkers**, New York, a faction of the Democrats favoring the South, Barnburners being the other factor.

**Know-Nothings**, New York, 1854, opposed to naturalization of foreigners unless they had been twenty-one years in the country.

**Loco-Focos**, New York, 1835; a branch of the Democratic party.

**Liberal Republicans**, 1872; name of such Republicans as joined with the Democrats in support of Greeley for president.

**Native American**, New York, at various periods; same as Know-Nothings.

**State Rights**, 1787 and other dates; opposed to the encroachment upon the rights of the States by the Federal Government.

**Temperance**, or Prohibition, 1830 down, in many States; in favor of preventing or restricting the sale of liquors.

**Tories**, during the revolution; those who were in favor of Great Britain.

**Whigs**, in the revolution; those who were in favor of the freedom of the colonies.

**Woman's Rights**, 1860 down, in many States; in favor of granting to women the same right to vote that men now enjoy.

UNDER a Republican government the sovereign power is exercised by representatives elected by the people. The United States Government is a simple republic, its head and its law-making power being chosen by the people in popular elections. By the Constitution the government is intrusted to three separate authorities—the EXECUTIVE, the LEGISLATIVE, and the JUDICIAL. The head of the executive branch is the President, who is chosen once in four years. He must be a native-born citizen, at least thirty-five years of age. He (as well as the Vice-President) is chosen by electors, who are elected by vote of the people. Each State has as many electors as it has senators and congressmen. The electors meet on a given day at the capitals of their States, vote, and send the record to Washington. On a specified day these votes are opened before both Houses of Congress, when the result is declared. If no one has a majority of the electoral votes for President, the choice is made by the House of Representatives from the three persons having the largest vote of the electors. In such a choice by the House, each State has but one vote, and a majority of all the States (now thirty-eight) is necessary to elect a President. In case of no choice for Vice-President by the electors, the Senate makes the choice.

In case of the removal, death, resignation, or inability of both the President and Vice-President of the United States, the President of the Senate, or, if there is none, then the Speaker of the House of Representatives for the time being, acts as President until the disability is removed or a President elected. Whenever the offices of President and Vice-President both become vacant, the Secretary of State shall forthwith cause a notification to be made to the executive of every State, and shall also cause the same to be published in at least one of the newspapers printed in each State. The notification shall specify that electors of a President and Vice-President of the United States shall be appointed or chosen in the several States as follows: *First*—If there shall be the space of two months yet to ensue between the date of such notification and the first Wednesday in December next ensuing, such notification shall specify that the electors shall be appointed or chosen within thirty-four days preceding such first Wednesday in December. If there shall not be the space of two months between the date of such notification and such first Wednesday in December, and if the term for which the President and Vice-President last in office were elected will not expire on the 3d of

March next ensuing, the notification shall specify that the electors shall be appointed or chosen within thirty-four days preceding the first Wednesday in December in the year next ensuing; but if there shall not be the space of two months between the date of such notification and the first Wednesday in December then next ensuing, and if the term for which the President and Vice-President last in office were elected will not expire on the 3d day of March next ensuing, the notification shall not specify that the electors are to be appointed or chosen.

# The President and Vice-President.

THE President is commander-in-chief of the army and the navy, and the militia in time of war. He may grant reprieves and pardons for offences against the nation, except in impeachment cases. With the Senate, he makes treaties, appoints representatives to foreign countries, and names all United States officers whose appointment is not otherwise provided for in the Constitution or by law of Congress. He fills vacancies during the recess of the Senate. He is to inform Congress of matters affecting the country, and suggest legislation. He can at will call together either or both Houses of Congress. In case of a disagreement of the two houses as to the time of adjournment of a session, he may adjourn (prorogue) them to such time as he pleases. He receives ambassadors and other foreign representatives, and is to

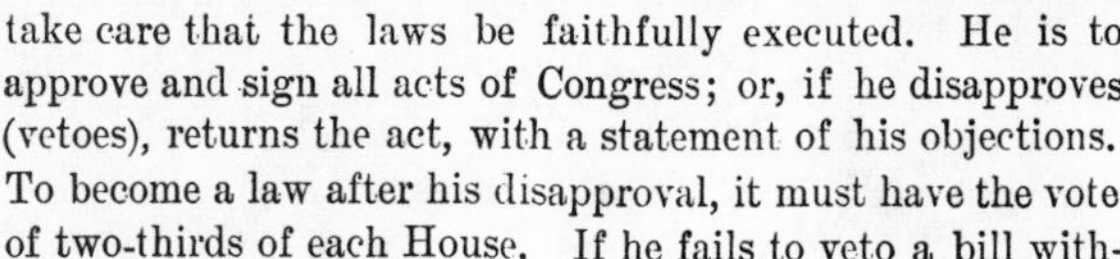

take care that the laws be faithfully executed. He is to approve and sign all acts of Congress; or, if he disapproves (vetoes), returns the act, with a statement of his objections. To become a law after his disapproval, it must have the vote of two-thirds of each House. If he fails to veto a bill within ten days after Congress adjourns, it becomes a law without his signature. His salary is $50,000 a year, and his establishment (the White House) is furnished at the charge of the nation. The President may be removed on impeachment and conviction of treason, bribery, or other high crime.

THE CABINET ROOM IN THE WHITE HOUSE.

## THE VICE-PRESIDENT.

This officer presides over the Senate, but has no vote except upon an equal division. He has very little power in the government, and is less noticed than any other officer of high position. At the commencement of the government, the electors of President and Vice-President voted two names, without specifying the office. The one having the highest vote became President, and the next highest Vice-President. This rule was changed in 1801, when there was a tie between Jefferson and Burr, and thereafter it was ordered that the electors should name the office with their votes.

## THE CABINET.

The President nominates, and with consent of the Senate appoints, heads of departments, or secretaries. They are his advisers, and he may require from any of them, at any time, advice or opinions on matters concerning administration. The first Cabinet consisted of Jefferson (who was then in France), Secretary of State; Alexander Hamilton, Secretary of the Treasury; Gen. Henry Knox, Secretary of War and Navy; and Edmund Randolph, Attorney-General. In 1797, the War and Navy were made two departments. In 1829, a Postmaster-General was added. Now, in 1882, the Cabinet consists of the Secretaries of State, Treasury, War, Navy, Interior, Postmaster-General and Attorney-General. The heads of departments have a salary of $8,000 a year. Public offices in the departments are open for business eight hours a day in winter and ten hours in summer. Women may be, and are, appointed to certain clerkships on the same terms as men. Each department makes at least one report every year, giving all information as to the operations of that branch of public service. All departments file in the office of the Secretary of the Interior complete lists of clerks and employes.

# STATE DEPARTMENT.

## DUTIES OF THE SECRETARY AND HIS CHIEF SUBORDINATES.

IN the United States the Secretary of State is charged, under the President, with correspondence with diplomatic officers of the nation, with representatives of foreign powers accredited here, and with various negotiations relating to foreign affairs. He is the medium of official correspondence between the President and the Executives of the several States. He is the official keeper of the great seal of the United States, and affixes it to commissions, proclamations, warrants, pardons, and extradition papers. He is the custodian of the originals of laws passed by Congress, and of treaties with foreign powers. He officially publishes the laws, and amendments to the constitution. From his office passports and exequators are issued. He proclaims the admission of new states. He reports annually on the affairs of his department, and furnishes commercial information collected by our representatives abroad.

**The Assistant Secretary of State** acts for the head of the department, in the latter's disability or absence. There are two assistants, who care for correspondence with our agents in other countries.

**The Examiner of Claims** (who is subordinate to the Attorney-General) looks after questions of law regarding claims before the State Department. The various nations are divided among their bureaus, and there are three divisions in the Consular Bureau. The other prominent officers are the Chief of the Bureau of Accounts, or disbursing clerk, and the custodian of archives and the library. The office of Secretary of State requires the services of persons well versed in the principal languages.

## DIPLOMATIC SERVICE OF THE UNITED STATES.

Our representatives in foreign countries consist of Envoys Extraordinary and Ministers Plenipotentiary, Ministers Resident, Chargés d'Affaires, Consuls-General, Consuls, and Commercial Agents. The highest class of Ministers are those sent to France, Germany, Great Britain, and Russia; they are paid $17,500 per year. The second class ($12,000 a year) are sent to Austria, Hungary, Brazil, China, Italy, Japan, Mexico, and Spain. The third class ($10,000 a year) go to Chili, Peru, and the Central American States. Ministers Resident receive $7,500 (with the exception of the one in Bolivia, $5,000, and the one in Liberia, $4,000), and are in the Argentine Republic, Belgium, Colombia, Hawaian Islands, Hayti, Netherlands, Sweden and Norway, Turkey, and Venezuela. Chargés d'Affaires have $5,000 a year, and are in Denmark, Portugal, Switzerland, Uraguay, and Paraguay. There are five Consuls-General in British dominions—at Calcutta, Melbourne, London, Halifax, and Montreal; two in Germany—at Berlin and Frankfort; two in Turkey, at Cairo and Constantinople; and one each in Paris, Vienna, Rome, St. Petersburg, Bucharest, Bangkok, Shanghai, Kanagawa, Havana, and Mexico. Their salaries range from $2,000 to $6,000. There are the following ranks of consulates: Five at $6,000 a year; two at $5,000; one at $4,500; six at $4,000; eight at $3,500; twenty-one at $3,000; sixteen at $2,500; thirty-seven at $2,000; forty-seven at $1,500, and twenty at $1,000. All consuls receiving a fixed salary pay into the treasury all fees received by virtue of their office. But there are many consuls and agents whose only compensation comes from fees. Such officers are usually allowed to go into business.

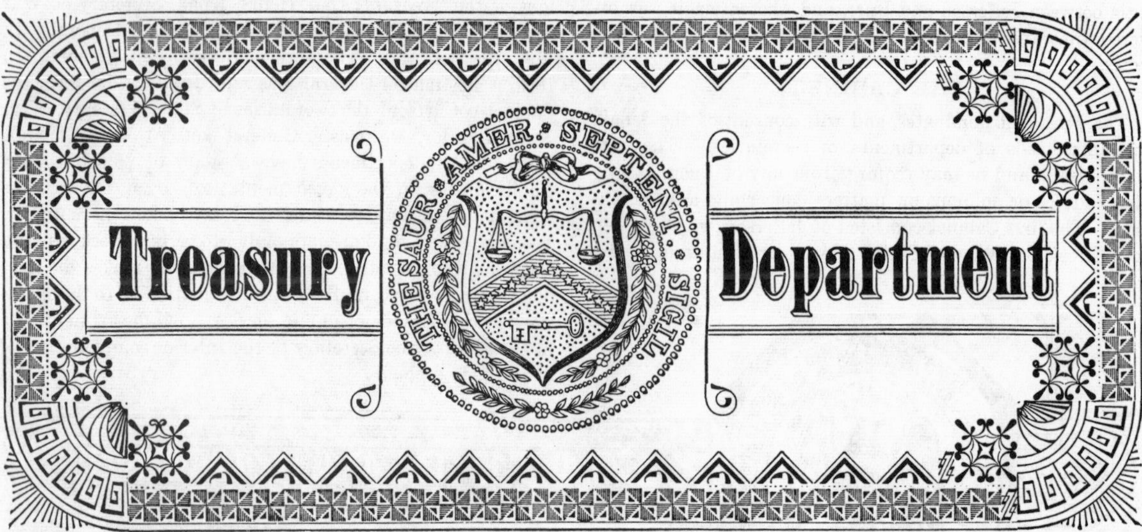


## FINANCIAL BRANCH OF THE GOVERNMENT —DUTIES OF CHIEF OFFICERS.

ONE of the most important cabinet officers is the Secretary of the Treasury, who has charge of the finances, and, with Congress, of the public credit of the country. He must not be concerned in trade, or commerce, or shipping, or public lands, or property, or deal in public securities. All his subordinates are in this manner restricted. The secretary prepares plans for revenue, prescribes forms for keeping accounts, grants warrants for payments from the treasury, gives information to Congress or the President, when required, on matters concerning his department; controls coinage, the printing of currency, the erection of public buildings, the collection of commercial statistics, the marine hospital, the revenue service, the life-saving service, and is chief of the light-house board. He makes provision, as directed by Congress, for the payment of the public debt; publishes monthly statements of the condition of the debt, and prepares annual estimates of receipts and expenditures to guide Congress in making appropriations.

There are nine divisions in the Treasury Department.

### DIVISION OF APPOINTMENTS.

Has supervision of all matters relating to appointment, suspension, and removal of officers under the department; examines complaints; prepares reports; inspects accounts; verifies pay-rolls; prepares estimates, and publishes the *United States Treasury Register*.

### DIVISION OF WARRANTS, ESTIMATES AND APPOINTMENTS.

Has charge of accounts, and particularly of the issue of warrants; publishes estimates, and the condition of appropriations for the information of Congress; prepares a statement every day showing the condition of treasury balances; prepares the monthly statements of the public debt, and prepares tables for the Secretary's annual report. This division is supposed at any time to know exactly how any account stands, whether involving millions of dollars or a few cents only.

### DIVISION OF PUBLIC MONEYS.

Has supervision of the independent treasury offices, of national banks and other depositories of public money; looks after their securities; keeps a general account of receipts into the treasury; directs all public officers except postmasters as to their deposits of public money; supervises outstanding liabilities, transportation of money and securities, and directs transportation of all public funds; has also care of and disposition of fines, penalties and forfeitures under internal revenue laws.

### DIVISION OF CUSTOMS.

Examines all tariff questions on appeals from collections as to rates, amounts, errors, refunding and abatement of duties, drawbacks, and all questions arising under customs laws and regulations; supervises appraisers to secure uniform valuation at all ports; supervises the seal fishery and other interests in Alaska.

### DIVISION OF INTERNAL REVENUE AND NAVIGATION.

Looks after petitions for remission of fines and penalties under custom, internal revenues, navigation, and steamboat inspection laws, and applications for compromise, except in customs cases; examines all questions concerning entry and clearances of vessels, tonnage taxes, and transportation of merchandise.

### DIVISION OF LOANS AND CURRENCY.

Has supervision of all matters relating to loans and other redemption; negotiation of securities; printing of bonds and their issue, care, redemption and cancellation; of the redemption and destruction of currency and stamps; and charge of the paper on which bonds and notes are printed.

### DIVISION OF REVENUE MARINE.

Has supervision of the revenue marine service, the building and repair of vessels, and over their officers and crews, payments, etc.; examines all matters concerning light-houses and the coast survey; has charge of standard weights and measures, supervises the life-saving service, and prepares statistics and annual reports on these matters.

### DIVISION OF STATIONERY, PRINTING, AND BLANKS.

Supplies stationery, blanks, books for keeping accounts; superintends the department of printing, except bonds, currency, and stamps; superintends the Treasury Department advertising and newspaper subscriptions; distributes postage-stamps for the departments, and cigar-stamps to customs officers, and accounts for them.

## DIVISION OF SPECIAL AGENTS.

Assigns and details all special agents; looks after their accounts, and examines their reports; supervises regulations to prevent smuggling and other frauds in the revenue; supervises the operations of customs affairs; looks after the transportation of merchandise in bond; approves the bonds of warehousemen; enforces the laws regulating trade with Canada and Mexico, so far as relates to the establishment of bounded routes and modes of transportation.

**Assistant Secretaries.**—There are two; one has supervision of the work assigned to the division of appointments, public money, revenue marine, stationery, printing, and blanks, loans and currency, engraving and printing, and of the director of the mint; the signature of letters and papers as assistant secretary, or "by order of the secretary," that do not by law require the signature of the head of the department; and performs such other duties as may be prescribed by law.

The other assistant secretary has supervision of the work of the divisions of customs, special agents, internal revenue, and navigation; has supervision of the accounts of the chief architect, the surgeon-general, of marine hospitals, the bureau of statistics, of inspection of steamboats; signs papers as assistant secretary, or "by order of the secretary;" signs certain warrants, and does whatever is required by law.

**The First Comptroller** countersigns a certain class of warrants; looks after the accounts, and reports, and payment of foreign ministers and consuls; also examines requisitions drawn by United States marshals, collectors of internal revenue, secretaries of territories, and some other disbursing affairs. He is charged also with responsible duties appertaining to claims against the United States.

**The Second Comptroller** has charge of the accounts of the army; of the Indians; of homes of soldiers; of annual pensions; of marine corps and navy-yard expenses; of the accounts of disbursing agents abroad, and of the financial agent in London.

**The Commissioner of Customs** revises and certifies all revenue accounts relating to duties, tonnage, marine hospitals, and fines, penalties and forfeitures under navigation laws; he also approves the securities of customs officers.

THE NEW BUILDING OF THE DEPARTMENTS OF STATE, ARMY, AND NAVY.

## THE SIX AUDITORS.

**The First Auditor** has under his charge five divisions of accounts: 1. Customs; 2. Judiciary; 3. Public debt; 4. Warehouse and bonded goods; 5. Miscellaneous.

**The Second Auditor** has the following six divisions: 1. Army paymaster; 2. Miscellaneous claims; 3. Indian affairs; 4. Bounties; 5. Investigating frauds; 6. Book-keeping.

**The Third Auditor** has six divisions: 1. Book-keeper; 2. Quartermaster; 3. Subsistence and engineering; 4. State war claims; 5. Miscellaneous; 6. Collection division.

**The Fourth Auditor** has three divisions: 1. Prize money; 2. Navy agents; 3. Paymasters.

**The Fifth Auditor** has two divisions: 1. Diplomatic and consular division; 2. Internal revenue division.

**The Sixth Auditor** has eight divisions, all of which deal with post-office accounts. The auditor superintends the collection of debts due the postal department, directs suits, etc.

**The United States Treasurer.**—The Treasurer of the United States is charged with official custody of public money in all parts of the country, in banks, sub-treasuries, or in the care of officers. He pays warrants; issues and redeems treasury notes; is agent for the redemption of national bank notes; agent for paying interest on the public debt, and custodian of Indian trust funds.

**The Register of the Treasury** has charge of the account books of the Government; he signs and issues bonds, treasury notes, and other securities; registers warrants; issues registers and licenses to vessels; makes return annually of vessels built, lost or destroyed; prepares statements of tonnage and imports.

**The Comptroller of the Currency** has, under the Secretary of the Treasury, supervision and control over the national banks.

**The Solicitor of the Treasury** takes cognizance of revenue-frauds, and has general supervision of legal measures for their prevention and detection. He has general charge of the legal business of the

department, and charge of secret service operations. He is required, when requested by his superior officer, to give his opinion on any law matter. He is also an officer in the department of justice.

**The Commissioner of Internal Revenue** makes all assessments and apportionments for collecting taxes. He has a Deputy Commissioner, and in his bureau are the following divisions: 1. Appointments; 2. Laws; 3. Accounts; 4. Tobacco; 5. Distilled Spirits; 6. Stamps; 7. Assessments. There are also under him special agents to look after proceeds in the manufacture and handling of whisky.

**The Superintendent of the Coast Survey** has charge of all surveys of ocean and coast, the making of maps and charts, etc.

**The Bureau of Statistics.**—This is a useful branch of the Treasury Department, charged with collecting and publishing, from the best sources, information in regard to trade and commerce, shipping, emigration, imports and exports, and other kindred matters. These statistics are published quarterly, in compact form, and may be had on application to the bureau.

**The Bureau of the Mint.**—The Government has mints in Philadelphia, San Francisco, New Orleans, Carson, and Denver; each has a superintendent, assayer, teller, refiner, coiner, and assistants; and at Philadelphia, an engraver. The director of the mint at Philadelphia makes report annually of all operations of all the mints in the country.

**The Life-Saving Service.**—The Secretary of the Treasury has power to establish and sustain life-saving stations on the Atlantic and the lake coasts. There are three lake and seven sea districts. The stations are supplied with boats, ropes, mortars for throwing lines to ships, cradles for bringing off passengers, and whatever may serve to save life from shipwreck. There is a superintendent for each district, with the rank and authority of an inspector of customs. Each station is in charge of a keeper, and some have assistants.

E who fills the office of Secretary of War performs such duties as the President, who is the commander-in-chief, may devolve upon him concerning the military service. He prepares for Congress estimates of appropriations needed for the army, fortifications, arms, etc. He prescribes the kind and amount of supplies to be purchased; regulates transportation, storage, and keeping of supplies, arms, etc.; and the transportation of troops; provides for the working of the weather bureau to give notice of storms; has oversight of all details of the service; makes an annual report for Congress; reports the progress of river and harbor surveys; and gives yearly a return of the number of militia in the several States. There are ten branches or divisions in the War Department.

**The Adjutant-General** promulgates orders, conducts correspondence, issues commissions, superintends recruiting, has charge of papers relating to drafting, or enlisting of volunteers; has general charge of matters of discipline, papers of the departments, etc.

**The Inspector-General** and his assistant have charge of *personnel* and material at posts, stations and depots; and inspect the accounts of all disbursing officers.

**The Quartermaster-General** and assistants provide quarters, transportation, clothing, equipage, horses, wagons, fuel, light, hospital stores, medicines, etc.; pay funeral expenses of officers and men, and have charge of the national cemeteries.

**The Commissary-General** has control of the subsistence department, including provisions, rations, and all articles that may be sold to officers or men.

**The Surgeon-General** has charge of the medical department, selects medical officers and directs their duties; directs the purchase of medical supplies; has charge of the Army Medical Museum, and control over the publications of the Surgeon-General's office.

**The Paymaster-General** is the principal disbursing officer; pays officers and men, and makes return of his accounts to the Treasury Department.

**The Chief of Engineers** commands the engineer corps, and superintends the construction and repair of fortifications and other works of defense or attack; he has charge of the torpedo service, of military bridges, and surveys for such purposes, and for movements in the field. He also has charge of harbor and river improvements, and of military and geographical explorations and surveys.

**The Chief of Ordnance** provides arms and ammunition for the field and for fortifications in peace or in war, and if necessary for the militia. He may direct the forms of cannon and small arms, and provides for their distribution and presentation.

**The Judge Advocate-General** and his assistant revise and record the proceedings of courts martial, courts of inquiry and military commissions, and make reports to the Secretary. There are eight judge-advocates of the army, who are under the general direction of this branch of the War Department.

**The Chief Signal Officer** superintends the instruction of officers and men in signal service; supervises the preparation of maps and charts, and has charge of the weather bureau, from which is sent the daily reports of the temperature, wind pressure, and prospects of weather from all parts of the United States and Canada.

**The Military Academy** at West Point is under the immediate control of the War Department (as well as the military prison, at Rock Island, Ill.). The chief officers at West Point are the superintendent, the commander of cadets, and a dozen or more of professors and instructors. They are appointed by the President. Cadets are nominated usually by members of Congress.

**The Military Code.**—The statutes contain a code of laws for the government of the army, commonly called the Articles of War, to which every one, from the highest to the lowest, is bound to yield implicit obedience under danger of penalty. These articles reach all ranks and conditions in the army, the formation of courts, and all the machinery of justice. The army is limited to 30,000 enlisted men.

# DEPARTMENT OF THE INTERIOR.

## BUREAUS AND DUTIES OF OFFICERS—HOW TO SECURE A HOMESTEAD.

NO greater responsibilities are connected with any cabinet office than those resting upon the Secretary of the Interior, who has supervision of patents, pensions, public lands, bounty lands, mines on public lands, Indian affairs, public education, the decennial census, the distribution of public documents, and certain duties connected with the government of the territories of the United States. He makes a detailed report at the opening of each stated session of Congress.

There is an assistant Secretary, who, in the absence of the chief, acts as the head of the department.

**The Commissioner of the General Land Office** performs all duties in regard to the survey and sale of the public domain, or that in any way concerns public lands, private claims, patents for grants of homesteads, etc. Land patents are countersigned by him, and recorded in his office. The business of the Land Office is divided into the following bureaus: Public lands; Private land claims; Surveying and Drafting; Pensions; Railroad lands; Bounty lands; Swamp lands; Pre-emption claims, and Accounts.

**The Commissioner of Patents** is charged with the administration of the patent laws, and the issuing of letters patent. In his office are kept all records, models, drawings, specifications, etc., relating to inventions and improvements. Among his assistants are an assistant commissioner; three examiners-in-chief; a chief clerk; an examiner of interferences; an examiner of trade marks; twenty-four principal examiners; twenty-four first, twenty-four second, and twenty-four third assistant examiners (two of whom are women); a librarian; a machinist; draughtsmen, copyists, and employees of lower grade. No person can be employed in the office who is in any way interested in any patent issued therefrom. The Commissioner of Patents makes an annual report to Congress.

**The Commissioner of Indian Affairs** oversees and directs all matters concerning the Indian outside of the Indian Territory; directs the distribution of supplies, and has charge of various agents, superintendents, inspectors, teachers, traders, etc There are four bureaus in his office, viz.: 1. Finance; 2. Land accounts; 3. Civilization; 4. Education and Records.

**The Commissioner of Pensions** attends to all matters concerning pensions, and laws affecting them; to their payment, and the detection and prosecution of attempts at fraud, and performs such other duties as may be required of him by the President or Secretary of the Interior.

Pension agents are appointed by the President for four years, and give bonds and security for the faithful performance of their duties.

**The Commissioner of Education** collects facts concerning the condition and progress of education in the various states and territories, and distributes such information among the people. He is assisted by a chief clerk, a statistician, and a translator.

**United States Surveyors.**—These officers are appointed by the President, but the Secretary of the Interior looks after the progress of their work, and their records are kept in his office.

**The Census.**—This important work, executed every tenth year, is under the general charge of the Department of the Interior, but the special charge of the Superintendent of the Census.

**Public Documents.**—In the office of Returns, under the Secretary of the Interior, are filed all contracts made by the war, navy, and interior departments, carefully indexed, and accessible to the public.

**The Secretary of the Interior** has supervision of the Government Hospital for the Insane, and the Columbian Institution for the Deaf and Dumb, both in the District of Columbia.

**The Public Lands—Homestead Privileges.**—There are public lands open to settlement in nineteen states and eight territories, and there are land offices in most sections where such lands lie, where the records of all surveyed lands are kept, and all applications concerning lands in each district are filed, and inquiries answered. The public lands are divided into two great classes. The one class have a dollar and a quarter an acre designated as the minimum price, and the other two dollars and a half an acre. Titles to these lands may be acquired by private entry or location under the homestead preëmption and timber-culture laws; or, as to some classes, by purchase for cash, in the case of lands which may be purchased at private sale, or such as have not been reserved under any law. Such tracts are sold on application to the Land Register, who issues a certificate of purchase, the Receiver giving a receipt for the money paid, subject to the issue of a patent, or complete title, if the proceedings are found regular, by the Commissioner of the General Land Office at Washington.

Entries under the preëmption law are restricted to heads of families or citizens over twenty-one, who may settle upon any quarter-section (or 160 acres), and have the right of prior claim to purchase on complying with certain regulations.

The homestead laws give the right to one hundred and sixty acres of a dollar and a quarter lands, or to eighty acres of two dollar and a half lands, to any citizen or applicant for citizenship over twenty-one who will actually settle upon and cultivate the land. This privilege extends only to the surveyed lands, and the title is perfected by the issue of a patent after five years of actual settlement. The only charges in the case of homestead entries are fees and commissions, varying from a minimum of $7 to a maximum of $22 for the whole tract entered, according to the size, value, or place of record.

Another large class of free entries of public lands is that provided for under the timber-culture acts of 1873-78. The purpose of these laws is to promote the growth of forest trees on the public lands. They give the right to any settler who has cultivated for two years as much as five acres in trees, to an eighty-acre homestead, or if ten acres, to a homestead of one hundred and sixty acres; and a free patent for his land is given him at the end of three years instead of five. The limitation of the homestead laws to one hundred and sixty acres for each settler is extended in the case of timber culture so as to grant as many quarter sections of one hundred and sixty acres each as have been improved by the culture for ten years of forty acres of timber thereon, but the quarter sections must not be immediately contiguous.

## DEPARTMENT OF AGRICULTURE.

It is the purpose of this Department or rather Bureau to acquire and distribute among the people of the country, especially among farmers and fruit-growers, useful information on all matters affecting agriculture, and to procure, propagate, and distribute new and valuable seeds and plants. The commissioner of agriculture is the head of the bureau, and has for his assistants, a chief and other clerks; a chemist and assistant; a botanist; a microscopist; an entomologist; a superintendent of gardens and nurseries; librarian; engineer; carpenter; attendants of the museum, etc. In the propagation garden at Washington are many rare and valuable exotic plants. In the library are reports and papers from all the prominent agricultural and pomological societies of the world. The monthly reports on the state of the crops and cognate subjects are of great value.

## MACHINERY OF THE MAILS—CHIEF OFFICERS AND THEIR DUTIES.

AMONG the most important branches of the General Government is the Postal Department, which is directed by the Postmaster-General, with three chief assistants and an army of lower officers all over the country. The principal duties of the Postmaster-General are briefly as follows: To appoint postmasters, whose annual pay does not exceed one thousand dollars; to establish or discontinue post-offices; prescribe forms of official papers and keeping of accounts; direct the expenses of his department; negotiate (with the President and Senate) all postal treaties with other Governments; to make an annual report of the operations of his department, with an estimate of appropriation necessary for its support, and perform all other duties properly pertaining to his office.

**The First Assistant Postmaster-General** has immediate charge of appointments, bonds, salaries and allowances, free delivery in cities, and blanks for the use of the Department.

**The Second Assistant Postmaster-General** has charge of contracts for carrying mails; the registration of the arrival and departure of mails; the supervision of route agents, and the furnishing of pouches, locks and keys, etc.

**The Third Assistant Postmaster-General** looks after the financial affairs of the department; receives and pays drafts, and keeps accounts. He issues stamps, stamped envelopes, and postal cards; provides for the registration of letters; has charge of dead letters, of the foreign mail service, and the money-order system.

**General Postal Information.**—In the large cities, at the post office, business is divided into branches, such as delivery, receiving and distributing, registration, box, and money-order departments.

Special agents superintend railway service, and watch the doings of employes.

Stamps, stamped envelopes, and postal cards are to be had at all post-offices in considerable towns or villages.

Uncalled-for or dead-letters finally go to Washington, where they are opened. If they are of any considerable value, efforts are made to return them to the writers. If of little or no value, they are destroyed.

Letters not called for are advertised at the end of a week, and the lists are posted in the offices for general information.

Letter-boxes are put up at the discretion of the Postmaster-General. Letter-carriers give security for the performance of their duties. It is a felony for any unauthorized person to wear the uniform of a letter-carrier. Carriers are not allowed to take fees or gratuities of any kind.

## INSTRUCTIONS TO THE PUBLIC.

Direct your mail matter plainly, and if to a city add the street and number of the person's residence or the number of his post-office box. Matter not addressed to a post-office cannot be forwarded. Give the county in which the post-office is, and be sure to spell the name of the State in full.

If you have your own address written or printed on the upper left-hand corner of a letter or package it will insure the speedy return to you of the package, in case it should be wrongly directed or insufficiently paid. If such letters are all right and should not be called for by the persons to whom they are addressed they may be returned free to the writer without going through the dead letter office; but if you use an envelope with another person's address printed thereon cross out such address with ink.

It is well to register valuable letters and packages. The registry fee is ten cents, besides the regular postage. Registered letters must have the name and address of the sender on the outside.

Mail all letters, etc., as early as practicable, especially when sent in large numbers, as is frequently the case with circulars. Be sure to write the name of the country, as a letter addressed simply "London," meaning England, might go to London in Canada. Many letters intended for Burlington, Nova Scotia, have gone to Burlington, New York, because of the similarity of the abbreviations "N. S." and "N. Y." Write State and county in full; use tolerably stout envelopes; very thin ones are apt to split open. Never send money, indorsed checks, or other valuable articles except by money order or registered letter. If you desire a letter to be returned write outside "Return if not delivered within —— days" with your address.

Postage stamps should always be placed on the upper right-hand corner of a letter or package. Postmasters are not obliged to take more than 25 cents at one time of nickel or copper coin, nor are they obliged to make change though it is usual to do so. They are not to affix stamps themselves, and must not give credit for postage. Write nothing on the address side of a postal card except the address of your correspondent and your own. No letter will be forwarded unless it has upon it a stamp.

No money order can be issued upon credit; the buyer must pay money down in current legal tender. Manuscripts for books, magazines, newspapers, etc., pay full letter postage, unless they are accompanied by proof sheets corrected or for correction, in which case the postage will be one cent for each two ounces.

*Rates of Postage.*—On letters to any part of the United States or Canada, three cents for each half ounce or fraction thereof. Postal cards are already stamped and cost one cent each, which pays for their transmission free in the mails.

Second class matter concerns only publishers and news agents.

Third class is printed matter in unsealed wrappers only, and goes at one cent for each two ounces or fraction thereof. This class includes newspapers, books, circulars, handbills, chromos, engravings, lithographs, magazines, music, pamphlets, photographs, proof sheets, and manuscript accompanying them, reproductions by the electric pen, hektograph, metalograph, papyrograph, and in fact, any reproduction upon paper by any process, except handwriting and the copying press, not in the nature of a personal correspondence. The limit of weight for one package is four pounds, except if a book it may weigh more.

Fourth class matter takes all not included in the first three classes which is so prepared for mailing as to be easily withdrawn from the wrapper and examined. It goes for one cent an ounce or part of an ounce; limit of weight, four pounds.

These rates apply to all British North America, except Newfoundland, except that merchandise is excluded in Canada, but samples not over eight ounces may be sent subject to ten cents postage. For rates to foreign countries, ask your postmaster, or procure a copy of the "U. S. Postal Guide," published monthly.

Obscene books, letters, papers, pictures, and postal cards; lottery circulars and letters; liquids of any kind; gunpowder and other explosives; live animals (except queen bees); poisons, and articles liable to injure the mails or those who handle them are rigidly excluded.

*Money Orders*—The following are the rates of fees for the issue of domestic and international money orders.

*Domestic* or anywhere in the United States: For a sum not exceeding $15, ten cents; over $15 and not over $30, fifteen cents; $30 to $40, twenty cents; $40 to $50, twenty-five cents.

*Foreign.*—On England, Scotland, Ireland, and adjacent islands: Not over $10, twenty-five cents; $10 to $20, fifty cents; $20 to $30, seventy cents; $30 to 40, eighty-five cents; $40 to $50, one dollar. For Switzerland, the German Empire, Italy, France, Algeria, New South Wales, Victoria, New Zealand, Jamaica, Dominion of Canada, and Newfoundland: For $10 or less, fifteen cents; $10 to $20, thirty cents; $20 to $30, forty-five cents; $30 to 40, sixty cents; $40 to $50, seventy-five cents.

The following table shows the whole number of postoffices in the United States on the 24th of June, 1882:—

| States and Terr. | Whole No. | States and Terr. | Whole No. |
|---|---|---|---|
| Alabama | 1255 | Mississippi | 782 |
| Alaska | 4 | Missouri | 1866 |
| Arizona | 114 | Montana | 185 |
| Arkansas | 975 | Nebraska | 837 |
| California | 947 | Nevada | 132 |
| Colorado | 431 | New Hampshire | 479 |
| Connecticut | 459 | New Jersey | 712 |
| Dakota | 529 | New Mexico | 172 |
| Delaware | 117 | New York | 3041 |
| Dist. Columbia | 5 | North Carolina | 1584 |
| Florida | 392 | Ohio | 2543 |
| Georgia | 1226 | Oregon | 394 |
| Idaho | 130 | Pennsylvania | 3589 |
| Illinois | 2074 | Rhode Island | 120 |
| Indiana | 1728 | South Carolina | 734 |
| Indian Territory | 112 | Tennessee | 1622 |
| Iowa | 1554 | Texas | 1438 |
| Kansas | 1558 | Utah | 208 |
| Kentucky | 1507 | Vermont | 498 |
| Louisiana | 523 | Virginia | 1841 |
| Maine | 953 | Washington | 282 |
| Maryland | 750 | West Virginia | 996 |
| Massachusetts | 769 | Wisconsin | 1395 |
| Michigan | 1479 | Wyoming | 82 |
| Minnesota | 1026 | | |
| | | | 46,159 |

There are 1,950 offices of which the President has the appointment of postmasters, and 5,436 money order offices.

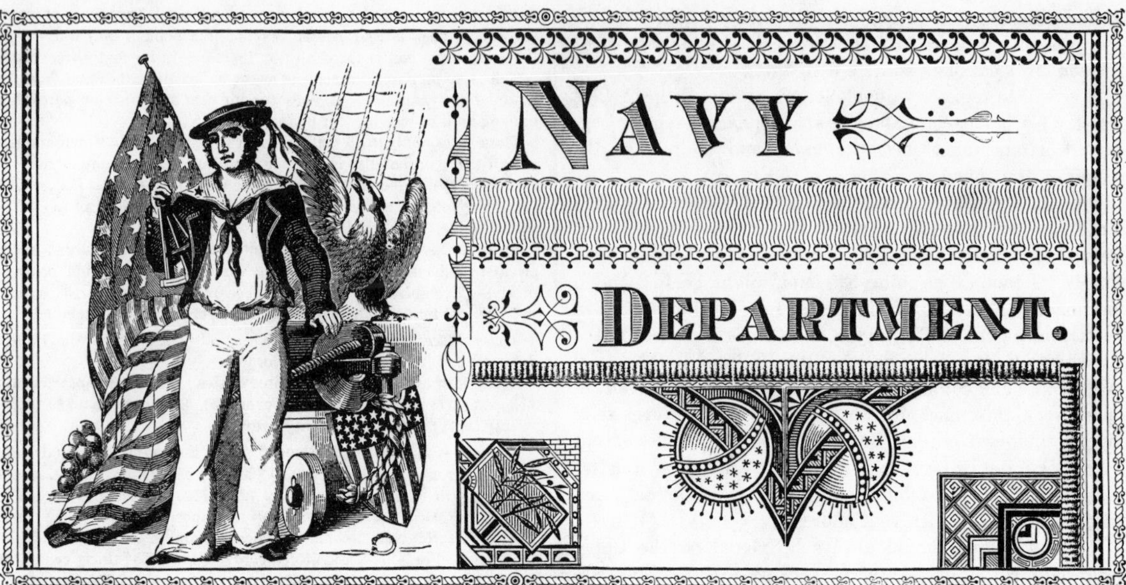


WE have in this country a Cabinet officer called the Secretary of the Navy, who performs such duties as the President, who is Commander-in-chief, may assign to him. He has the general superintendence of the construction, manning, government, equipment, and employment of vessels of war. His chief clerk has general charge of the records and correspondence of the department.

The office of Secretary of the Navy was not established until 1798, before which date the Secretary of War had charge of naval affairs. At the latest report (1881) there were in the naval service sixty-five steam vessels, all except six being screw propellers; twenty-three wooden sailing vessels; twenty-four iron-clad vessels, two torpedo boats, and twenty-five tugs. Only about one-half of these one hundred and thirty-nine vessels were fit for duty. The number of guns was one thousand and thirty-three. The active list of the Navy is composed of one admiral, one vice-admiral, twelve rear-admirals, twenty-five commodores, fifty captains, ninety commanders, eighty lieutenant-commanders, two hundred and eighty lieutenants, one hundred masters, one hundred ensigns, eighty-two midshipmen, one hundred and thirty cadet-midshipmen, and one hundred and forty-two cadet-midshipmen on probation at the Naval Academy, all of whom are officers of the line. Medical officers, paymasters, engineers, professors, chaplains, naval constructors, &c., make up on the active list one thousand one hundred and three officers of the line, six hundred and ninety-three officers of the staff, and two hundred and forty-two warrant officers, making a total of two thousand and thirty-eight officers of all grades. At the same time (July, 1881,) there were in the service seven thousand five hundred enlisted men and boys, besides the marine corps of seventy-seven officers and one thousand five hundred men. On the retired list there were forty-two rear-admirals, twenty commodores, twelve captains, ten commanders, fifteen lieutenant commanders, eight lieutenants, eleven masters, and two midshipmen, besides one hundred and seventeen staff officers, thirty-eight warrant officers, and six professors of mathematics. The number of students in the Naval Academy in 1881 was: Cadet-midshipmen, one hundred and sixty-one; cadet-engineers, one hundred. Total two hundred and sixty-one. There are eight bureaus in the Navy Department, viz.:—

**Chief of the Bureau of Yards and Docks** has charge of navy yards and naval stations, their construction and repair, and the purchase of timber and other materials for coustructing and repairing vessels.

**Chief of the Bureau of Navigation** supplies vessels of war with maps, charts, chronometers, barometers, flags, signal lights, glasses, and stationery: has charge of the publication of charts, the Nautical Almanac, and surveys; and the Naval Observatory and Hydrographic Office in Washington are under his charge.

**Chief of the Bureau of Ordnance** supervises the manufacture of naval ordnance and ammunition, small arms, the armament of vessels, arsenals and magazines, and the torpedo service.

**Chief of the Bureau of Provisions and Clothing** is charged with the duty of supplying, for all branches of the service, food, clothing, and small stores.

**Chief of the Bureau of Medicine and Surgery** superintends and directs the purchase and distribution of medical stores, hospital supplies, surgical instruments, etc.

**Chief of the Bureau of Construction and Repairs** has charge of dry docks, and repairs of vessels; the building and fitting out of vessels, and the arming of iron-clads.

**Chief of the Bureau of Equipment and Recruiting** is charged with the business of recruiting and enlisting men for naval service, and furnishing rigging, anchors, and fuel for ships.

**The Engineer-in-Chief** directs the repairing, fitting out, and running of steam marine engines and their accompaniments, and supervises the shops where they are repaired.

**The Naval Academy** is at Annapolis, Md. Cadets are appointed annually, ten from the nation at large, one for each member of Congress, and one for the District of Columbia.

COMPRISED in the judicial organization of the Government are the Supreme Court, District and Circuit Courts. Nearly all the States comprise a single Circuit. New York has three Circuits, a few States have two, and some of the less densely populated States combine in a single district. For each district there is a judge, a district attorney, and a marshal. The Chief Justice and the associate justices of the Supreme Court are alloted among the Circuits by order of the Court, while for each Circuit there is appointed a Circuit Judge having the same power and jurisdiction therein as the justice of the Supreme Court. Circuit Courts are held by the Circuit Justice, or the judge of the Circuit, or by the Judge of the District, or by any two of the said judges sitting together.

## THE SUPREME COURT.

The Supreme Court, the highest legal tribunal in the nation, consists of a chief justice and eight associate justices, who appoint a clerk, a marshal, and a reporter. This court holds one term at Washington annually, and such adjourned or special terms as may be necessary. The original jurisdiction of the United States is divided among the other classes of courts named. Original jurisdiction in a majority of cases is vested in the District Courts.

The Supreme Court has exclusive jurisdiction in all civil controversies where a State is a party, except between a State and its citizens, or between a State and citizens of other States, or aliens, in which latter case it has original but not exclusive jurisdiction. It has also exclusively all such jurisdiction of suits or proceedings against ambassadors and public ministers and their servants as is consistent with their privileges under the law of nations; also original but not exclusive jurisdiction of suits brought by ambassadors or public ministers, or in which a foreign consul is a party. The trial of all issues of faction, all actions at law against citizens of the United States, must be by jury.

The Supreme Court also has power to issue writs of prohibition to the District Courts when proceeding as courts of admiralty and maritime jurisdiction, and writs of mandamus to all inferior courts and officers of the United States, where a State, or an ambassador, or a public minister, or a consul is a party.

## THE CIRCUIT COURTS.

The Circuit Courts have original jurisdiction in all suits of a civil nature at common law or in equity when the matter in dispute exceeds $500 and an alien is a party, or where the suit is between citizens of different States; of all suits in equity where the amount in dispute exceeds $500, and the United States are petitioners; of all suits at common law where the United States, or any officer thereof, ruling under authority of an act of Congress, are plaintiffs; of all suits and proceedings arising under certain acts of Congress relating to tonnage dues, the slave trade, patents and copyrights, banking associations, etc.; of suits to recover possession of office, and of all proceedings by writ of *quo warranto*, and of all suits authorized to be brought under the Acts of Congress for enforcing the amendments to the Constitution.

The Circuit Courts have exclusive jurisdiction of all crimes and offenses recognizable under the authority of the United States, except as otherwise provided by law, and concurrent jurisdiction with the District Courts of crimes and offenses cognizable therein.

The Circuit Courts hear and determine appeals from the decrees of the District Courts in cases of equity or of admiralty and maritime jurisdiction when the matter in dispute exceeds $50. All final judgments of District Courts in civil actions, when the matter in dispute exceeds $50, may be re-examined upon a writ of error by the Circuit Court held in the same district. Jurisdiction of cases, civil or criminal, may also be transferred from a District Court into the Circuit Court by reason of the disability from sickness, interest, or other cause, of the district judge.

Suits commenced in State courts wherein the matter in dispute exceeds $500 may, in cases provided, be removed into the Circuit Court on petition, for the purpose of protecting the rights and interests of aliens or citizens of States other than those in which such suits are instituted, and also where parties claim land under titles from different States. Suits against revenue and registration officers of the United States, and against corporations organized under acts of Congress, may also be removed on petition to the Circuit Courts of the United States.

## COURT OF CLAIMS.

In 1855, the United States Court of Claims was instituted and directed to hear and determine claims against the nation, and report the cases and facts to Congress, with the opinions of the court thereon. In 1863, this court was authorized to render final judgment, with right of appeal to the Supreme Court. The Court of Claims has five judges.

## DUTIES OF THE ATTORNEY-GENERAL AND HIS ASSISTANTS.

**The Attorney-General** represents the Government where questions of land or rents are concerned; gives advice and opinions when required by the President or heads of departments; determines the validity of titles to real estate before purchased by the Government; has superintendence over District Attorney and marshals; furnishes counsel for the Government when necessary in any department, and makes an annual report to Congress. Either House of Congress may call upon the Attorney-General for information on any matter within the scope of his office, and it is his duty to communicate such information. It has been always understood that the opinion of the Attorney-General is not conclusive upon the President or the Secretaries, but it has been the practice for the different departments to govern the administration of their affairs according to his advice.

It is a settled rule that he has no right to give an opinion in any other cases than those in which the statutes make it his duty to give it. Therefore, he will not give an opinion to any subordinate officer of any of the departments, nor will he give an opinion to individuals in respect to their claims against the Government, nor will he advise upon speculative or hypothetical cases, nor upon any point of law, unless it has actually arisen in a case presented for the action of a department.

He may direct the Solicitor-General to argue causes in the Court of Claims in which the United States is interested, and appeals from that court to the Supreme Court in such cases as are committed to him and the Solicitor-General.

**The Solicitor-General** assists the Attorney-General, and, in the absence of the latter, performs his official duties.

**Assistant Attorneys-General.**—There are two of these; one assists in the argument of cases before the Supreme Court, and in preparing legal opinions; and the other represents the Government before the Court of Claims. All the law officers of the various departments exercise their functions under the supervision and control of the Attorney-General. These officers are: Assistant Attorney-General for the Department of the Interior; Assistant Attorney-General for the Post-Office Department; Solicitor of the Treasury, and Solicitor of Internal Revenue in the Treasury Department; Naval Solicitor in the Navy Department, and the Examiner of Claims in the State Department.

THE LIBRARY OF CONGRESS.

## THE LIBRARY OF CONGRESS.

The Library of Congress was founded on the establishment of the seat of government in Washington in 1800. In 1814 the Capitol was burned by the British, and the library, which contained about 3,000 volumes, was entirely destroyed. An annual appropriation being made for the purchase of books, the library continued to grow slowly, and in 1851 numbered 55,000 volumes. In the same year, a second conflagration destroyed all but 20,000 volumes, which fortunately formed the more valuable portion, but from that period the library increased more rapidly than ever, especially as 40,000 volumes of the Smithsonian Institute were transferred to the library of Congress. It now contains 300,000 volumes and about 60,000 pamphlets.

The act of Congress, passed Aug. 10, 1846, made it incumbent on the author or publisher of every book, map, print, etc., for which a copyright was secured, to forward, within three months after publication, one copy each to the librarians of the Smithsonian Institute and congressional library. The average number of deposits under this act amount to 25,000 articles per annum. Information concerning the method of obtaining a copyright is given under "Mercantile Law."

# The Legislative Department.

## THE UNITED STATES CONGRESS, THE SENATE AND THE HOUSE OF REPRESENTATIVES, POWERS AND DUTIES.

THE House of Representatives is chosen directly every second year by the electors, it is the popular branch of the Government. The qualifications and duties of members of the House are fully set forth in Section 2 of Article I. of the Constitution of the United States. The growth of the House in numbers has been rapid. After each decennial census a new apportionment is made; the sitting congress agrees upon the whole number of members, and they are apportioned among the States according to the population. The increase of the House has been as follows: in 1789, it had sixty-five members; in 1793, one hundred and five; in 1803, one hundred and forty-nine; in 1813, one hundred and eighty-nine; in 1823, two hundred and thirteen; in 1833, two hundred and forty; in 1843, two hundred and twenty-three; in 1853, two hundred and thirty-seven; in 1863, two hundred and forty-three; in 1873, two hundred and ninety-three; in 1883, it will be three hundred and twenty-five. When a new State is admitted a member (from that State) is added. The Speaker of the House may in a certain contingency act as President of the United States.

THE NATIONAL CAPITOL.

The Senate is the only permanent body in the Government, members being divided into classes so that two-thirds are always in office. The qualifications and duties of senators are clearly set forth in the constitution.

All the State governments are modeled on the plan of federal government. Each State has a governor or a lieutenant-governor (and some of them other State officers) elected by the people; a legislature also chosen by the people, consisting of a Senate, or upper house, and an Assembly, or lower house. Governors are chosen for one, two, three or four years, State senators for one, two, and four, and assemblymen for one and two years. Nearly all State legislatures meet bi-annually, only eight of the thirty-eight now holding annual sessions.

The following table shows the great variation among the different States in the ratio of representation. New York, for instance, has but 128 members of the lower house to a population of 5,082,871, or one member to very nearly 40,000 inhabitants; New Hampshire has 379 members in the lower house or one member to 917 inhabitants:

| | Sen. | Rep. | | Sen. | Rep. |
|---|---|---|---|---|---|
| Alabama | 33 | 100 | Mississippi | 33 | 107 |
| Arkansas | 31 | 93 | Missouri | 34 | 143 |
| California | 40 | 80 | Nebraska | 30 | 84 |
| Colorado | 26 | 49 | Nevada | 26 | 50 |
| Connecticut | 21 | 246 | New Hampshire | 12 | 379 |
| Delaware | 9 | 21 | New Jersey | 21 | 60 |
| Florida | 24 | 53 | New York | 32 | 128 |
| Georgia | 44 | 168 | North Carolina | 50 | 120 |
| Illinois | 51 | 153 | Ohio | 37 | 111 |
| Indiana | 50 | 100 | Oregon | 30 | 60 |
| Iowa | 50 | 100 | Pennsylvania | 50 | 201 |
| Kansas | 40 | 125 | Rhode Island | 36 | 72 |
| Kentucky | 38 | 100 | South Carolina | 33 | 124 |
| Louisiana | 36 | 125 | Tennessee | 25 | 75 |
| Maine | 34 | 151 | Texas | 31 | 93 |
| Maryland | 26 | 84 | Vermont | 30 | 242 |
| Massachusetts | 40 | 240 | Virginia | 44 | 132 |
| Michigan | 32 | 100 | West Virginia | 25 | 65 |
| Minnesota | 22 | 47 | Wisconsin | 33 | 100 |

## NAMES AND NICKNAMES OF STATES.

**Alabama** is named from its principal river, which in the Indian tongue means *quiet*, or "here we rest."

**Arkansas,** an Indian name, supposed to mean the Bow Indians, experts in bow-shooting. Its nickname is "Bear State."

**California,** from a Spanish romance, in which is described "the great island of California where an abundance of gold and precious stones are found." Nickname, "The Golden State."

**Colorado,** ruddy or blood-red, from the color of the water of Colorado river. But the river is not in the State.

**Connecticut,** "The land on a long tidal river," called in Indian "Quin-neh-tu-kgut." Nicknames, "Nutmeg State," and "Land of Steady Habits."

**Delaware,** after Lord De-la-war. Nicknames, "The Diamond State" (from its shape), and "The Blue Hen's Chicken."

**Florida,** "The Land of Flowers," so-named by Ponce de Leon, the discoverer, who landed there on "Pascha Florida," or "Flowery Easter," in 1512. Nickname, "Land of Flowers."

**Georgia,** after George II., King of England. Nickname, "Empire State of the South."

**Illinois,** the original name of a confederation of Indian tribes, meaning "real" or "superior men." Nickname, "Prairie" or "Sucker State."

**Indiana,** either from the American Indians, or from an old land company having possessions. Nickname, "Hoosier State."

**Iowa,** an Indian name, and the name of its chief river, meaning "the sleepy ones." Nickname, "Hawkeye State."

**Kansas,** an Indian name, from its principal river, meaning "the smoky water."

**Kentucky,** from its principal river. Nickname, "The Dark and Bloody Ground."

**Louisiana,** after Louis XIV. of France. Nickname, "Creole State."

**Maine,** "the mainland," meaning that portion of New England granted by Charles I. to Sir Fernando Gorges. Nickname, "Pine Tree State."

**Maryland,** after Henrietta Maria, queen of Charles I. No nickname, but might be "The Oyster State."

**Massachusetts,** from an Indian tribe. Nickname, "Bay State."

THE SENATE CHAMBER.

THE HOUSE OF REPRESENTATIVES.

**Michigan,** from an Indian term signifying "the lake country." Nickname, "Wolverine State."

**Minnesota,** from the Indian "Mini-sotah" or turbid water, applied to St. Peter's river.

**Mississippi,** from an Indian term meaning "the great river." Nickname, "Bayou State.

**Missouri,** after its river, meaning "muddy water," and a tribe of Indians of the same name.

**Nebraska,** from its river, in Indian meaning "shallow water."

**Nevada,** from the Spanish, meaning "snowy." The Sierra Nevada are "the snowy mountains." Nickname, "Silver State."

**New Hampshire,** after Hampshire county, in England. Nickname, "Granite State."

**New Jersey,** so named in honor of the defense of the Isle of Jersey by its first proprietor, Sir George Cartaret.

**New York,** after Charles II., when he was Duke of York. Originally New Amsterdam, after Amsterdam, in Holland. Nickname, "Empire State."

**North Carolina,** and **South Carolina,** whether after Charles I., of England, or Charles IX., of France, is not decided, but probably from the British king. Nicknames—North Carolina is "Old North" or "Tar State;" South Carolina is "Palmetto State."

**Ohio,** from a Wyandot term meaning the "beautiful" or "great river." Its nickname is "Buckeye State."

**Oregon,** from its river, in Indian meaning "River of the West."

**Pennsylvania,** from William Penn, the first proprietor. Nickname, "Keystone State."

**Rhode Island,** probably from the Dutch "Roode" or "red" island, from the appearance of the soil. Nickname, "Little Rhody."

**Tennessee,** perhaps from an important Cherokee settlement called Tanasse. Nickname, "Big Bend State."

**Texas,** of doubtful derivation. Some say from an Indian tribe of the name; some say from the Spanish "tejas," or covered houses. Nickname, "Lone Star State."

**Vermont,** from the French *verd mont*, or green mountain. Nickname, "Green Mountain State."

**Virginia,** from Elizabeth, "the virgin queen." Nicknames, "Old Dominion," or "Mother of States."

**West Virginia** is merely a geographical designation. The northern part is sometimes called, from its shape, "The Panhandle State."

**Wisconsin,** from its chief river, in French *Ouisconsin*, from *ouest*, or flowing westward. Nickname, "Badger State."

ARCHITECTURE is the art or science of building; especially the art of constructing buildings for the purpose of civil life.

The oldest erections of any kind known to mankind, were not dwellings, but buildings, enclosures, or stone groves, devoted to the worship of deities, or else consecrated to the dead. The most notable examples among these are the mounds, or large circular raised graves, of the mound builders, which are found in different parts of the world. The oldest buildings extant are in Egypt, and are chiefly notable for their solidity, and for the huge stones used in their construction, which were put together without mortar. Many of these buildings are many thousand years old. In India, however, there still exist temples which are hewn out of one solid rock each, and are supposed to date from remote antiquity.

The influence of race and epoch have made such marked changes in the manner of building, that each variation from former models is known as a different "style." The principal architectural styles are the EGYPTIAN, ASSYRIAN or BABYLONIAN, PERSIAN, INDIAN, CHINESE, GRECIAN, ROMAN, MOORISH or SARACENIC, BYZANTINE, EARLY CHRISTIAN, ROMANESQUE, GOTHIC and RENAISSANCE. Many of these styles have numerous subdivisions. In GOTHIC, there are the *Norman, Early English, Pointed, Perpendicular, Flamboyant, Elizabethan* or *Tudor*. In RENAISSANCE, there are many subdivisions, such as *Italian Renaissance, French Renaissance, French Château, Rococo, German Renaissance, Queen Anne,* etc.

## ARCHITECTURAL STYLES.

The chief characteristic of each style and the materials generally used are briefly given below; while illustrations of the most important styles will be found on Plate I. But as the main object of this article is to impart information concerning the best means of establishing a comfortable home, it will be principally devoted to practical points of building, and valuable hints regarding the selection of an architect, mason, or carpenter. We must, therefore, refer persons desiring further information about architectural styles, etc., to Fergusson's History of Architecture.

**Egyptian.**—In Egyptian, huge blocks of stone were used, tombs were cut into the solid rock, including whole chambers, with colonnades, etc. Obelisks, pyramids and sphinxes are well known objects of Egyptian Architecture, also huge temples, with approaches of miles of colonnades of stone work. The slanting outlines of walls, great solidity of construction, bell-shaped capitals and the frequent use of hieroglyphics and the lotus flower in their decorations are marked characteristics of this style. See plate I., No. 3.

**Assyrian, Babylonian and Persian** were built chiefly in sun-dried bricks and wood; the buildings were mostly palaces, very fanciful in design, and had many terraced approaches, with grand flights of steps; also many roof gardens, etc. See Plate I., No. 4.

**Indian** architecture was very ornamental, and chiefly in stone. Many of the temples and tombs are cut out of solid rock, and are very elaborate. The outside of the temple was first formed by cutting away the rock for hundreds of feet around, and then the interior was carved out, leaving columns (often highly ornamented and carved) to support the solid rock roof.

**Chinese** architecture is mostly in wood, and very ornamental. It is chiefly known by the turned-up eaves of its roofs, and the many roofs, tapering in size, built one above the other. See Plate I., No. 1.

**Grecian.**—The Greeks are thought by many to have brought Architecture to its highest perfection. Their buildings were mainly supported on columns, and were mostly temples of similar shape to the illustration given. The Greeks developed very carefully the proportions of each part to the whole, and had many ways of overcoming optical illusions, which so often spoil grand buildings. They never used the arch, believing that "the arch never sleeps," on account of its constant tendency to spread. They used three kinds of capitals to their columns, known as three of the five Orders of Architecture, viz.: the *Doric* (very plain), the *Ionic* (with the volute), and the *Corinthian* (very elaborate and imitating the Alanthus plant growing round a stone or basket). See Plate I., No. 8 and No. 10.

**Roman.**—There is no distinctively Roman style. Roman architecture was mainly based on the Grecian, with the addition of the constant use of the arch, which was borrowed from the Etruscans. The Romans added the two last to the five Orders of Architecture, viz.: the *Tuscan* (resembling the Doric, but more elaborate), and the *Composite*, as its name implies, composed of the Ionic and Corinthian. See Plate I., No. 10.

When the Roman Empire was divided, its Architecture also divided, the Eastern Empire developing the *Byzantine*, and the Western the *Early Christian* and *Romanesque*.

**The Byzantine** has a leaning to the Eastern and Moorish architecture, but has much color and decoration, and frequently striped exteriors of different colored stones, and onion-shaped roofs. See Plate I., No. 6.

**The Early Christian** is extremely simple, and, like the Romanesque, has principally round arched openings. See Plate I., No. 7.

**The Romanesque** has the barrel-shaped vaulted ceilings as a peculiar feature, and many quaint bits of detail here and there.

**The Moorish or Saracenic** is very brilliant in color and elaborate in detail, and has the peculiar shaped horse-shoe arch as a characteristic. See Plate I., No. 2.

**Gothic.**—The Gothic style is almost too well known to require description. Its divisions are known by the different shaped arches of the openings, and the difference in the manner and amount of ornamentation. In Gothic, the chief aim has been to build high, airy and light vaulted buildings on very slender supports, many feats of construction often being necessary. The ornamentation is chiefly done in carvings of imitations of animals and nature. Some of the most beautiful and elaborate buildings ever built have been in Gothic. See Plate I., No. 5.

**Renaissance,** literally the new birth, is a revival of Grecian Architecture, adapted to modern wants, and in many respects has been a failure. Gothic Architecture was gradually verging on the extreme, often ludicrously so, and a reaction toward simplicity and toward classicism set in. Renaissance is chiefly a use of the "Five Orders of Architecture" in modern buildings. See Plate I., No. 9.

**The Five Orders of Architecture** are represented by specimens of Doric, Ionic, Corinthian, Tuscan, and Composite capitals on Plate I., No. 10.

## HOW TO CHOOSE AN ARCHITECT.

It is the general custom among architects to insist upon being engaged for all the services usually rendered by them, and to charge for their services whether their clients are satisfied or not. It is, therefore, very important to know what kind of an architect you engage. Legally the architect can recover the usual charge for his services, if once engaged by the client, whether the client afterwards discharge him or not. A good architect should not only be a good artist, but a practical man as well, and be thoroughly familiar with all the details of building a house. Most architects are either too artistic or too practical ; the one will put up an extremely original, quaint and pretty house, but it may be poorly built, lack many comforts and conveniences, and be badly planned. On the other hand, the other may put up a convenient, comfortable and well planned house, but very ugly or common-place in design. The latter generally proves to be more satisfactory for people building homes, though either extreme should be avoided. Select, if you can, an architect who will not copy his design, one who has the reputation of building well, of being a practical man and attending to the superintendence or supervision of his work personally and thoroughly, and above all make sure that your architect is not one who is noted for extravagance and the habit of making a house cost two or three times what he originally promised.

## DUTIES AND CHARGES OF ARCHITECTS.

The duties of the architect consist in making all the necessary general drawings, specifications, details, and contracts for the house and in superintending the construction of it.

The architect draws up the contract, and is the impartial judge between his client and contractor in all questions of dispute. He decides what should or should not be done by the contractor. As superintendent, however, he is the direct representative of his client, and sees that his client's interests at the building are protected, and that his client gets the kind and amount of work he pays for.

The usual charges of architects for their services are five per cent. on the total outlay, for full professional services; charging only three and a half per cent. on the outlay, if they are not engaged to superintend.

During the progress of the building the architect makes the necessary detail drawings. These are drawings of every part of the building—every window, door, molding, for instance—and are made to scales four or more times as large as the general drawings; the moldings, carvings, and other important points being drawn full size.

In cases where it is impossible to obtain an architect, it is well for the party intending to build to get books, or to look at all the houses he can, in order to make up his mind thoroughly as to what he wants, and then to get some capable carpenter or mechanic to draw him the plans, etc. It is well in this case not to contract for the work unless one is perfectly sure that the contractor is thoroughly honest. If work is not executed by contract it is done by "day's work;" that is, some carpenter or mason undertakes the work and charges for the material and men just what it costs him; he furnishes all necessary scaffolding, machinery, utensils, etc., and for these and his own time he charges a commission on his outlay, varying from five per cent. to fifteen per cent., usually about ten per cent.

## PLANS AND SPECIFICATIONS.

The general drawings consist of a plan or horizontal section of each floor and a flat elevation or vertical plan of each side of the house, also drawings of sections of the house. These drawings are made to a scale, usually so that each foot in reality is represented either by one-eighth or one-quarter inch on the drawing. The general drawings are carefully made, showing arrangements of floors, rooms, windows, doors, closets, stairs and halls, flues, fire-places, heating, plumbing, drainage, ventilation, etc. They should be so thoroughly studied out and figured that no mistakes can arise afterward. Before making the general drawings it is usual to make pencil sketches to a small scale, and perhaps one or two rough perspective drawings, which are submitted to the client, and then altered to suit his particular wants.

Accompanying the general drawings are the specifications, which are long written descriptions of every part of the building, specifying the quality, amount, and what kind of material to use; also how to put things together. If the

PLATE I.

PAVILION OF THE GREAT TEMPLE AT CANTON
No 1
No 2
IN THE ALHAMBRA SPAIN
GREAT TEMPLE AT THE ISLAND OF PHILÆ
No 3
No 4
KHORSABAD-ASSYRIAN TEMPLE RESTORED
No 5
WEST FRONT OF THE COLOGNE CATHEDRAL
No 6
INTERIOR OF ST. SOPHIA - CONSTANTINOPLE
No 7
CATHEDRAL OF ANGOULÊME
No 8
TEMPLE OF NEPTUNE AT PÆSTUM
No 9
FRONT OF ST. PETER'S AT ROME
No 10.
DORIC
IONIC
CORINTHIAN
TUSCAN
COMPOSITE
H.D. BERG - INV.
H.A. Ogden del

specifications are full and carefully drawn, there should be no chance for extras afterward. Before making contracts a client should carefully study these plans and specifications, be certain that they include everything, and that he is well satisfied with everything, as alterations after the contracts are drawn generally involve many extras and much expense.

In England and Australia it is customary for architects to furnish a "bill of quantities," besides the specifications, giving the exact number of feet of masonry, timber, etc.; but this is not customary in America, where each contractor has to take out his own quantities.

## ESTIMATES AND CONTRACTORS.

After general drawings and specifications have been approved by the client they are submitted to the different tradesmen to obtain estimates on them. The man usually chosen to execute the work is he who furnishes the lowest estimates. This is not obligatory, however, except in public works, where the law compels it. It is often necessary to have the different tradesmen furnish bonds that they will finish the work and execute it properly, as to change tradesmen in the middle of the erection of a structure involves much expense and trouble.

It is generally advisable to let the architect have the selection of persons to execute the work, as it is as much to his interest as to the client's to have the work faithfully and honestly executed. With dishonest or ignorant contractors or tradesmen the best architect could not guarantee a satisfactory job, and if he is obliged to constantly reject materials the building is apt to be delayed beyond all measure. It is customary to let the contracts to but one or two parties, and they sub-let other parts of the building to other tradesmen. This is done that the client may not be forced to deal with too many principals. The mason usually contracts for all the excavating, masonry, fire-proofing, lathing, plastering, stone-work, iron-work, heating, drainage, and grading. The carpenter usually contracts for the timbering, joinery, cabinet-work, glass-work, plumbing, painting, etc. Sometimes but *one* man contracts for everything. The men who are chosen to do the work should be, above all, honest; men who will carry out the architect's plans and specifications faithfully. They should be competent mechanics, who understand their respective trades thoroughly. A contractor should also have plenty of money to stand a possibly serious loss on his contract without failing or stopping his work.

## WHERE TO BUILD A HOUSE.

In the city, town, or village other considerations than those of the architect usually settle the site—such as business, cost of land, etc. In the country, however, this is not the case. The most important consideration there is to get the house so located that the principal rooms are well exposed to the sunshine. The dining-room should have the morning sun, while the principal chamber and the sitting-room should be located on a corner, and so as to receive both morning and afternoon sun. The other chambers, parlors, etc., should get either morning or afternoon sun, while the less important rooms, like the kitchen, bath-room, store-rooms, halls, etc., can be put in the parts not exposed to direct sunshine.

The house should be set on high ground, if practicable, so as to avoid damp cellars, and be on well-drained ground. It should not be near any swampy ground, stagnant pools, or ponds, which breed malaria and other malignant fevers. A broad lawn of well-kept grass is very desirable, and should slope away from the house gently for good effect.

A very important consideration are the views. If the possible views from different parts of the house are kept in mind when locating and planning the same, it will often add greatly to the interior appearance.

## WHAT KIND OF A HOUSE TO BUILD.

A frame house is, of course, the cheapest, but unless built in a very solid and expensive manner, it is neither durable nor as good as a brick or stone house, besides needing frequent painting and many repairs; it is also subject to much cracking, owing to the unavoidable shrinkage of all timbering. A brick or stone house is not only more desirable but more durable; it is warmer, strogner, and if properly built, drier and healthier than a frame house. Between brick and stone there is no real practical difference. Brick will make the stronger house and withstand fire longer, but in a country house this advantage is not so apparent as in a large city building. Stone is perhaps more adapted to country houses, its treatment being more rustic in character.

## DESCRIPTION OF PLATE II.

The house is intended to be built of stone with either stone or brick trimmings. It might be built of brick and stone trimmings, if desired. The roof should be either slated or tiled. On entering the first story hall, the dining room is to the right and the parlor to the left, with a library or small sitting room in the rear of the parlor. The parlor has a large bay-window, while both parlor and dining room, and three of the chambers on the second floor have large open fire-places for wood fires, with tiled hearths. In the rear of the hall is a large pantry and store room, with plenty of lockers, shelves, closets and place to wash dishes. The kitchen adjoins this, and is intended to have stationary range and hot water boiler.

From the kitchen the back stairs lead up to the second story, having doors both at the head and foot,to keep the smells from the kitchen out of the house. In passing from the kitchen to either the hall or dining room it is also necessary to pass through two doors for the same reason. If the hall were wainscotted and the windows filled with stained glass, it would be very effective on entering the house.

In the second story there are four large chambers, each with ample closet room, and connecting with each other, without necessarily passing through the hall, except the chamber over the kitchen; the latter would be used as spare chamber, while the connecting rooms are for the family. There is a sewing or day sitting room in front, and bath room in the rear, which might be used as bed room if there is no plumbing in the house. The linen closet is conveniently located in the hall. The hall gets direct ventilation and light from the back hallway, and also through sewing room; besides this there would be a skylight overhead. If the attic were finished it would give from three to four rooms and storage room besides.

From the pantry on first floor stairs lead down to cellar, where the milk room, storage rooms, coal and wood cellars would be located, with a small laundry directly under the kitchen.

The style of this house is modern, with an English "feeling" in the detail. The approximate cost of building it would amount to $5,000–$10,000, according to the price of labor, convenience of transportation, style of interior finish, etc.

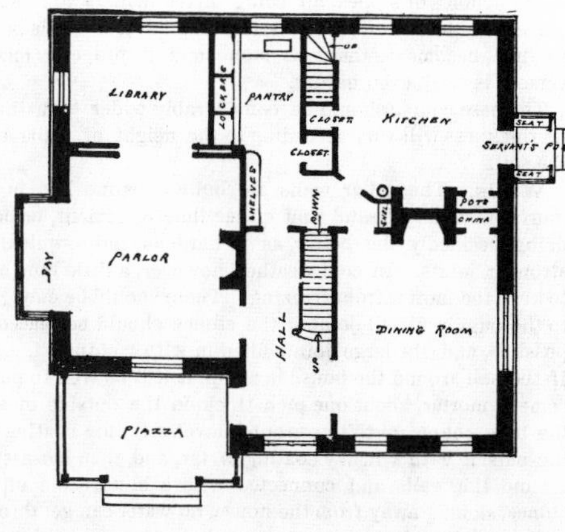


FIRST STORY PLAN

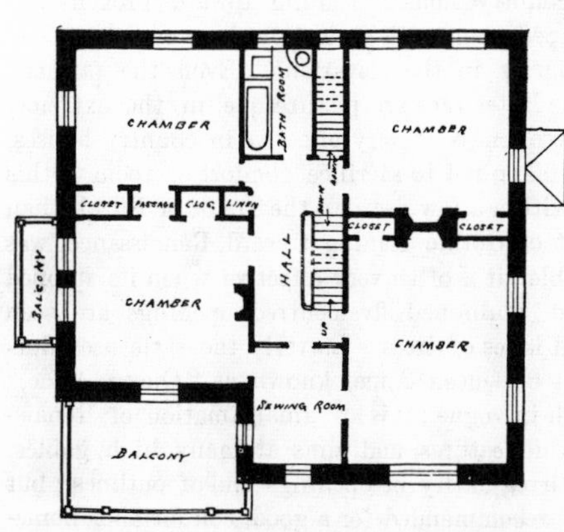


SECOND STORY PLAN

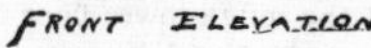

FRONT ELEVATION

SIDE ELEVATION.

LOUIS DECOPPET BERG,

ARCHITECT.

## WHAT STYLE TO BUILD IN.

The French, German and Italians incline to great regularity and symmetry in their country houses ; the English-speaking people, on the other hand, have always built more picturesque country houses, leaning toward broken outlines, odd shaped plans with projections here and there, and much irregularity in the elevations. Even the farmers' cottages of the latter race are picturesque in the extreme. While picturesqueness is very effective in country houses, care must be taken not to sacrifice comfort or room to this end. Up to within a few decades, the Tudor or Elizabethan Gothic, a sort of Gothic leaning toward Renaissance, was very fashionable ; it is often very effective when its stepped up gables and mullioned five-centred openings are seen through broad lanes of trees. Latterly the style used during the reign of Queen Anne, known as "Queen Anne," has been much in vogue ; it is an amalgamation of Renaissance and Gothic features, and aims at many high gables, broken roofs, irregularity of openings and of outlines ; but it cannot be recommended for a good, comfortable homelike house. It is expensive, its roofs are apt to be leaky, and the chimneys smoky, while the rooms are very much cut up. In America a style known as "Colonial," is now coming into fashion. It is the Renaissance, as interpreted by skillful local Dutch and English Architects during the Colonial times, and many interesting designs are being reproduced and preserved.

The best Architects, however, do not allow themselves to be fettered by any style, as a house should be what it aims to be,— a *home*, and not simply a reproduction in brick, stone, or wood of certain set rules. It is well to settle on the plans and interior arrrangements first, as these make up the comforts, and then try to make as good an exterior to them as possible. Avoid particularly too much height in a country house, it being always better to spread the house out, as ground costs but little in the country, and a low house looks more as if it were native to the place, and not like a high heap placed there.

## GENERAL ADVICE.

It has not been attempted to give more than one design, as each case requires different treatment, the same as one coat will only fit one man. We would advise every one to get an architect and try to give him the fullest particulars of what is wanted, leaving him to carry out your ideas in his own way. Those persons, however, who wish to make a selection from a variety of designs embodying the latest ideas should subscribe to some architectural publication, such as the London *Building News*, the London *Architect*, or the American *Architect*, published in Boston. These papers have weekly editions, are moderate in cost, and give numerous illustrations every week of all kinds of buildings, from a lodge to a cathedral.

Before closing this article we propose giving a few hints of some practical points and details, not generally known or employed in country houses. They will greatly improve the strength, durability and healthfulness of the same, without adding very seriously to the expense.

**Cellar.**—After staking out the house, excavate for the cellar, which should be under the whole house, so as to make the first story dry and warm. After the excavating is done, the base courses are laid under all the walls. Timbers are used sometimes, but these are bad, as they are apt to rot. Large flat stones make good base courses, but better yet is a mixture known as concrete, which is made of cement, sand, and sharp pebbles or stones, all being mixed with water and rammed into place and then allowed to "set," *i. e.* harden. This base course will, in time, become as hard as stone, and if properly mixed, and good cement is used, even harder.

The base course should be considerably wider than the cellar walls, its thickness will vary according to the height of walls and nature of the soil.

**Walls.**—The cellar walls are built of stone laid in mortar. The mortar is made of sand and either lime or cement, or both, the latter being decidedly the better, as it hardens more quickly and makes stronger joints. In cold weather, however, a little lime has to be used to keep the mortar from freezing. There should be enough mortar used to thoroughly fill all joints ; the stones should be placed as closely as possible, and the large joints filled in with "chips," i. e. small stones. If the soil around the house is damp, it will be well to put a coating of cement mortar, about one inch thick on the outside of all walls, from the base course up to the ground level. If this coating is covered on the outside with a heavy coating of tar, and then loose stones filled in around the walls and connected with a blind drain of similar loose stones, sloping away from the house, no water can get through the cellar walls. If there is danger of water being drawn up into the walls by capillary attraction, a coating or course of tarred felt, or else a course of slate should be built into all the cellar walls, just at the cellar bottom, and should extend entirely through the wall. The cellar bottom should be covered with concrete, similar to that for the base courses, but not as thick, say three to four inches. On top of this, if very good work is desired, a coating one inch thick of cement and sand should be put. All sand used should be coarse and very clean and pure, and free from earth or salt. Water should not be spared in mixing concrete and mortar, nor in laying bricks. The walls above the cellar should be laid similarly to those in cellar, though it is not so necessary to use cement in the mortar here ; lime will answer, though not making as good a job. The finish of the stone work, where seen on the outside, is a matter of taste and design. It can be left rough, or parts or all of it may be dressed by hand or rubbed smooth by machinery.

**In building projections, window sills, etc.,** care must be taken to provide a "drip moulding" underneath, so that rain water will drip off ; otherwise it will take up the dust gathered on top of the projections, sills, etc., and will run down the walls, leaving long muddy streaks in its tracks. Strong arches of brick work should be built behind the stone facings over all openings. The different parts of the stonework and walls are tied and bound together by strong pieces of wrought iron of different shapes, known as anchors, dowels, clamps, etc. The walls are covered usually with flat stones, nicely dressed, known as coping stones ; or else the cornices are made of wood, tin or galvanized sheet iron. In building the beams into walls their ends should be cut to a bevel, so that in case of fire they will fall out if burned through, without pulling the wall over with them. In bringing the beams up to the same level, it should be done by putting small pieces of slate under the ends, not wood and chips, which shrink and are apt to split and crush down.

**Floors.**—The floors of a house are laid with boards which have a tongue one side and a groove the other, fitting into each other. The narrower the boards, the better the floor will be, as when shrinkage takes place the cracks will be correspondingly smaller. Sometimes floors of rough boards are first laid and the nicer floors laid across these ; in this case the joints of the upper floor should run at right angles to those of the rough lower floor to keep the rough boards from curling. Floors are deafened in several ways, sometimes heavy felt paper, made for this purpose, is laid on the beams under the floor ; and sometimes rough boards are laid between the beams, about half way of their height, on small cleats which are nailed to the sides of the beams. On these boards a coating of mortar is laid about one inch thick. This is a good method for deafening and also helps to retard a fire very much. The inside walls or partitions are built of wood, a strip is laid on the floor and under ceilings and upright pieces or studs are secured between.

**Shrinkage.**—A great point to be remembered in building a house is, that wood will shrink *across* the grain, but not *lengthwise* of the piece. The shrinkage amounts even in ordinarily well seasoned stuff, to from a quarter inch to a half inch in a foot thickness. In building up partitions, etc., all timber must therefore be put on end as much as possible, and the bottom and head pieces should be as narrow as possible. Where beams rest on girders there will always be considerable shrinkage; the only method to avoid this is to rest beams against girders, but this involves expensive framing, which would be impracticable in most country houses. Some shrinkage is unavoidable, but if all unnecessary thickness *across* the grain is avoided it can be reduced to a minimum. Shrinkage and jarring of beams and partitions are apt to crack the plastering. To avoid this it is advisable to "cross furr" ceilings and partitions; that is securely nail parallel small strips of wood to them, close together, to distribute the shrinkage, etc., over a greater area.

**Dampness.**—Water and dampness will work its way through the best brick or stone walls. To prevent the plastering and inside of house from getting damp, the walls are either built hollow, allowing the water to drip down in the inside of hollow, or else blocks of wood are built in every now and then and the walls are furred off, same as described for the partitions, leaving a hollow space behind the plastering.

**To avoid rats or fire spreading** through a house, it is advisable to put one course of bricks laid in mortar, at each floor level, in all the furrings and partitions.

**Plastering.**—In plastering the best work is to put on three coats or three thicknesses; the first coat is well scratched so as to hold the second, the last coat is generally finished white and smooth with plaster of Paris. The first two coats are made of lime and sand, and there should be plenty of long and strong hair in them to hold the plastering together. Goats' hair is best. Narrow strips of wood, called laths, are nailed to the furrings of walls and ceilings, and the plastering is worked in and between and behind these, so that when it hardens it is thoroughly "clinched" to them.

**Painting.**—In painting, three coats should be put on for good work. White lead or zinc is mixed with the oil to give the paint body; there should be plenty of oil, however, in the first coat, as it soaks in rapidly, while the last should have more body. In choosing colors remember that they will all fade or bleach out more or less, and this should be allowed for. All knots in the wood must be covered with shellac or sizing, or else they will absorb all the oil and show right through the paint. Nail holes are puttied up. Sometimes the interior wood-work of houses is oiled and shellaced and not painted; this makes a cheap and effective finish if well done. Sometimes the pores of the wood are filled with preparations made for the purpose and the wood is then oiled, varnished and polished; but this makes very expensive work. If the wood is finished this way, remember that a dull or dead polish is considered in much better taste than a high, shiny polish.

**The Roofs** are made of many different materials, shingles, tin, zinc, slate, tiles, etc. If shingles are used it is bad to paint them in case the rain water is run into a cistern; though paint helps to preserve the wood, it is apt to poison the water. All metal roofs must be painted with metallic paints, prepared for this purpose, or they will rust out. The best and handsomest roofs are undoubtedly slate and tile, particularly the latter, though they make rather heavy roof framing necessary, on account of their great weight.

**Plumbing.**—Be sure that there is a trap under every fixture, and that from the top of every trap there is a ventilation pipe out to the open air. Also be sure that there is a large trap at the foot of the soil pipe just outside of the house, and that fresh air is let into the foot of the soil pipe, just inside of this trap; the other end of the soil pipe itself should be carried up to the roof and there capped with a ventilator. The best and simplest trap to use is a lead pipe cast to resemble the letter S on its side, thus : ∽.

**Hot Water.**—In houses where there is no plumbing, a good way to provide hot water baths, is to put the bath room next to the kitchen. Put the range right against the bath room partition, and put a large tin boiler on the back of the range. From the back of the tin boiler, carry a faucet right through the partition to open over a bath tub on the other side of the partition. This does away with carrying hot water to and fro. If it is desired to discharge the water from bath, run a small pipe to a distance fifteen to twenty feet from the house, and let it end there in a large hole filled in with loose stones and covered over with earth. The water will then soak away in the ground and do no harm, as it is not polluted.

**Cisterns.**—If the rain water is gathered in a cistern, it should be built circular of stone or brick, and made water-tight by coating it inside with cement. It is domed over on top, and a manhole left for cleaning out, which is covered with a flat stone. There should be small openings in top of the cistern to ventilate the same and prevent the water from getting foul. It is a good idea to build two cisterns in connection, with shut off cock between, and arrangement to turn the water into either, so that either can be cleaned out at pleasure. All water before entering the cistern should be allowed to run through a filter. This is a small brick, cement-coated box or smaller cistern (sometimes a part of the main cistern itself), which is filled with layers of sand, pebbles and charcoal, which purify the water as it bubbles through them. Filters should be cleaned out at least twice a year, and new charcoal put in.

**Cesspools** have generally been built with walls laid up with loose stones, without mortar, in order to allow the matter collecting in cesspools to soak away into the earth. This, however, is a very bad practice, as the ground for many, often hundreds of feet around becomes foul, and breeds malaria and all kinds of fevers; and if there is a spring or well anywhere near, its waters are sure to be polluted and poisoned. It is better to build the cesspool tight, same as the cistern, and clean it out when full. In this latter case it is absolutely necessary to provide ventilation to the same, and a pipe should be carried up eight or ten feet, from the top of the cesspool; if a tree is handy to the cesspool, run the pipe up still higher along the trunk of the tree. The pipe should be of good size, in proportion to the size of the cesspool.

**Stables.**—In building a stable there are one or two points worth knowing. The floor of the loft should be strong and well supported. The floors and partitions of the stalls should be very thick and strong. There should be no windows in the stalls except directly in front of the horses, or else they will keep twisting their heads and eyes toward the light and get blind in one or both eyes. The harness and carriage rooms should be as far as possible from the stalls; there should be at least two doors and a passage, stairs, or other ventilated space between them, as the fumes of the stalls destroy the varnish, and rust the metal parts of both harnesses and carriages.

**Ice-houses.**—In building ice-houses, there should be hollow spaces in walls and roofs, which are filled in with sawdust. Drainage must be provided at the bottom to lead off the water as fast as melted. There must also be ventilation on top to prevent warm air gathering under the roof. The door leading into the interior should be doubled and packed with sawdust in the same manner as the walls. It is well also to have both interior and exterior doors.

LOUIS DECOPPET BERG.

JOURNALISM has had a wonderful growth in modern times. Our grandfathers were glad to get hold of a seven by-nine country newspaper once a week. To-day we grasp half a dozen sheets of a morning, each almost large enough for a cradle quilt. The man who does not read newspapers will soon be a curiosity indeed. In the cities, and all over the land, they fall every morning as the autumn leaves fall when a sudden storm shakes the forest.

Printing with movable types began in 1452. In 1457 a newspaper was published. In England the *London Gazette* was the pioneer, starting in November, 1665, ten months before the great fire. The first American newspaper was "Publick Occurrences, both Foreign and Domestick," issued at Boston, September 25, 1690. It lived through one issue only—the authorities found it too free of speech, and squelched it. But in 1704 (April 24) the *Boston News-Letter* was started, and managed to live until the Revolution. Philadelphia's first paper started December 22, 1719, and New York's first October 16, 1725.

The circulation of newspapers was very small until the application of steam power to printing; and even then their circulation was within narrow limits until the invention of stereotyping came in. By this means any number of forms may be made and any number of presses run, so that now the circulation of newspapers is practically unlimited. The press on which Franklin laboriously "pulled off" two or three hundred sheets in an hour, printed on one side only, the sheet no larger than a card table, has given place to a seemingly living creature, that takes in its teeth the end of a roll of paper a mile long, and grinds it out at the rate of 20,000 to 30,000 per hour of completed newspapers of eight pages each, pasted at the back, cut at the edges, and folded ready for the mails.

Journalism has abandoned the pony-express and the steamboats, and harnessed in their stead the lightning. Its hand reaches under oceans and over continents, to the uttermost ends of the earth, to satisfy its insatiable craving for news. Its agents are ubiquitous, under the equator; at the poles; on the battle-field; in the drawing-room; step by step with exploration, step by step with science; even the secrets of State are kept with difficulty from the untiring search of journalism. It is no longer a means of making a poor living; journalism is a high and responsible profession. Where so many newspapers are read, there is little room for books—the newspaper, therefore, becomes the teacher, and although the reader may not suspect it, his opinions are more or less influenced by his favorite journal.

The tables given herewith present an interesting study. In the United States there are more than 11,000 newspapers and magazines. It is not easy to get at the amount of printed matter, for some are of four pages, others eight, twelve, sixteen, and on to thirty-two. Some vary from day to day—one day twelve pages, the next twenty-eight. The pages are of all sizes, and so are the types One illustration may give an idea of the vast amount of reading (we include advertisements) in the modern newspaper. In April, 1882, a New York paper issued as its regular sheet 28 pages of six columns each, or 168 columns of type. Rated as all nonpareil, the "ems" in printer's parlance in this sheet were eleven hundred thousand (1,108,800.) The New

Testament, revised edition, contains only 443,000 ems ; so this single copy of a newspaper might have printed two full copies and half of another of the entire New Testament. The newspaper on this occasion issued 120,000 copies, the whole edition being equal to 300,000 copies of the New Testament.

In the entire world there are published 34,274 newspapers, journals and magazines. Europe stands at the head in numbers, circulation, and influence, having 19,557 publications, or 57.07 per cent. of all in existence. North America comes next, with 12,400 publications, with which, in consideration of her youth, she may well be satisfied. Europe and North America have 31,957 newspapers, leaving but 2,317 to the remainder of the world. These are distributed as follows: In Asia, 775, or 2.27 per cent. of all in the world ; South America, 699, or 2.05 per cent ; Australia, 661, or 1.91 per cent.; Africa, 182, or 0.54 per cent. Europe and North America, with an area of less than 25 per cent. of the habitable globe, contain 93.23 per cent. of all the publications in existence. Europe and North America combined have a population of 377,390,145 ; the remainder of the world has an aggregate population of 1,245,788,016. Rating the average family at six persons it appears that in Europe and North America there is one publication for every two thousand families. In the other division there is one publication for about 90,000 families.

In the matter of language, English stands far ahead, having 16,500 publications. Next comes German with 7,350 ; French with 3,850 ; Spanish, 1,600.

The gathering of news for the press outside of merely local affairs, is a matter of vast importance and expense, and is conducted mainly by two great associations, Reuter's Telegram Company, of London, for Europe, Asia, and Africa; and the Associated Press, of New York, for America. The scope of Reuter's Company is boundless. Its agents and correspondents are found all over the world. It was originated by Jules Reuter, a Prussian, who was for many years employed as a courier between European courts. In 1858, he proposed to send brief dispatches of continental news to a London paper, and from that small beginning came the immense business now going on. No paper can afford to be beaten in news; that would be its funeral dirge. But in the early days of the telegraph the expense of special dispatches was hard to bear. So the leading journals in New York city organized the Associated Press, sharing the expenses and the news in common. Like Reuter's its agents and correspondents are everywhere, apparently waiting for news to happen. The offices in New York, London, San Francisco and other large cities are never closed, for, like the British flag, the sun never sets upon its work. To this Associated Press intelligence comes from all quarters, from over the land, from under the seas ; from countries that are in darkness when the midday sun shines over the New York office. The telegraph is at work at all hours bringing messages to headquarters, The click, click goes on incessantly over the wires, wires which converge from all quarters of the globe except northeastern Asia ; the messages are written out on manifold paper, a copy for each newspaper belonging to the Association is clapped into a little cylinder, the cylinder into a pneumatic tube, and in five seconds the cylinder drops upon the night editor's desk in the office to which it is destined. Time is so precious just before going to press by a morning paper, that even the messenger boy who had to run but a few hundred yards is dispensed with. Then in most editorial offices of the leading papers there is a wire over which notice is given of what is about coming or to be expected. It may notify the breaking out of a fire a few blocks away, a vote in Congress or in Parliament, a wreck off the Southern coast, or the death of a man of note. When the correspondent of a London paper was captured by the Boers in South Africa he showed his newspaper credentials, was at once released and treated with distinguished courtesy ; and further, the victorious savages requested him to bear a flag of truce to his army so that care would be taken of their wounded. He reached the British camp the night after the battle and prepared a dispatch to his paper. This dispatch was sent by the army telegraph to the coast, thence over the East India lines to the Gulf of Aden, then through the sea that swallowed Pharaoh and his hosts, across the Isthmus of Suez, under the blue Mediterranean, over Italy, over the snows of the Alps, across France, under the troubled Channel to the Reuter's London office, on, on without rest, to Valentia Bay, under two thousand miles of ocean to Newfoundland, to Halifax, to New York, away, away without rest, until far ahead of the lagging sun it reaches its ultimate western limit in the San Francisco office of the Associated Press. What would old Ben Franklin say to that !

Another instrument for gathering news of a local character is in its infancy—the telephone. Taking up a little tube and speaking in it in an ordinary tone of voice, you are distinctly heard as much as five miles away, the only means of communication between the speaker and the listener being a simple insulated or covered wire. This instrument is rapidly displacing the old speaking trumpet. It is the means in many cases of bringing local news up to the moment of going to press. When we remember that the telegraph is still young, that the railroad is but half a century old ; when we look back but a little distance, as it were, and see the old stage-coach as our beau-ideal of speed, we cannot but be amazed at the headlong progress of arts and sciences in this teeming age of wonders.

### THE PRESS OF THE WORLD.

*Number of Daily, Weekly, and Monthly Publications in Various Countries ; Number of Copies Issued Annually ; Number of Copies per year to Each Inhabitant.*

| *Country.* | *No. of Publication.* | *Annual Issue.* | *No. to each inhabitant.* |
|---|---|---|---|
| United States........... | 11,202 | 2,262,633,569 | 51.06 |
| Great Britain............ | 4,082 | 2,262,459,131 | 64.01 |
| France................... | 3,265 | 1,557,211,229 | 39.86 |
| Germany.................. | 5,529 | 1,748,086,209 | 38.67 |
| Italy.................... | 1,174 | 269,426,360 | 9.70 |
| Austria-Hungary.......... | 1,803 | 371,101,575 | 9.83 |
| Belgium.................. | 591 | 324,222,455 | 59.20 |
| Netherlands.............. | 435 | 122,560,660 | 31.76 |
| Sweden and Norway..... | 484 | 77,314,100 | 12.12 |

| *Country.* | *No. of Publication.* | *Annual Issue.* | *No. to each inhabitant.* |
|---|---|---|---|
| Denmark | 61 | 41,798,225 | 21.01 |
| Switzerland | 512 | 100,122,870 | 35.18 |
| Russia | 454 | 123,824,408 | 1 45 |
| Spain | 750 | 46,463,155 | 14.81 |
| Portugal | 179 | 54,520,145 | 12.82 |
| Turkey | 121 | 23,533,760 | 1.17 |
| Greece | 89 | 10,045,100 | 5.98 |
| British India | 373 | 25,573,286 | 5.29 |
| China | 22 | 7,693,174 | 0.001 |
| Japan | 251 | 143,730,000 | 4.18 |
| Algeria | 54 | 5,048,460 | 1.70 |
| Mexico | 283 | 46,779,858 | 4.67 |
| Central America | 71 | 10,145,840 | 3.82 |
| West Indies | 213 | 33,552.900 | 7.45 |
| Cuba | 81 | 25,505,000 | 16.91 |
| Argentine Republic | 39 | 11,317,700 | 4.52 |
| Bolivia | 27 | 1,188,820 | 0.06 |
| Brazil | 279 | 41,214,200 | 4.42 |
| Chili | 95 | 21,663,170 | 8.66 |
| Peru | 26 | 5,834,800 | 2.16 |
| Ecuador | 8 | 1,938,000 | 1.43 |
| Uruguay | 57 | 12,431,200 | 27.62 |
| Colombia | 40 | 4,920,500 | 1.64 |
| Venezuela | 117 | 12,670,550 | 6.73 |
| Australia | 451 | 66,067,400 | 24.08 |
| Melbourne | 40 | 14,266,000 | 56.66 |
| Tasmania | 19 | 3,042,112 | 26.31 |
| New Zealand | 170 | 42,345,150 | 86.59 |

SUMMARY.

| | | | |
|---|---|---|---|
| North America | 12,400 | 2,787,842,262 | 36.66 |
| Europe | 19,557 | 7,344,956,805 | 24.38 |
| Asia | 775 | 195.010.924 | 0.01 |
| Africa | 182 | 31,751,795 | 0.01 |
| Australia | 661 | 112,417,322 | 30.63 |
| South America | 699 | 117,520,340 | 3.92 |
| Totals | 34.274 | 10,589,499,448 | 6.52 |

*Cities.*

| | | | |
|---|---|---|---|
| New York | 587 | 516,322,752 | 291.21 |
| Boston | 161 | 147,977.838 | 408.17 |
| Philadelphia | 199 | 179,225,607 | 211.60 |
| Washington | 43 | 21,543,224 | 146.24 |
| Baltimore | 65 | 51,121.251 | 153.98 |
| New Orleans | 27 | 18,504,160 | 85.66 |
| Cincinnati | 91 | 79,916,784 | 813.09 |
| Chicago | 211 | 149,548,750 | 297.13 |
| St. Louis | 106 | 72,186,700 | 206.24 |
| San Francisco | 100 | 76,633,068 | 327.49 |
| London | 1,962 | 1,013.884,463 | 266.67 |
| Paris | 1,553 | 1,084,225,700 | 545.45 |
| Rome | 213 | 46,689,920 | 203.88 |
| Madrid | 253 | 126,407,000 | 343.97 |
| St Petersburg | 183 | 61,524,080 | 312.54 |
| Constantinople | 66 | 19,598,660 | 27.99 |
| Calcutta | 43 | 4,721,900 | 5.29 |
| Pekin | 1 | 3,130,000 | 1.56 |
| Tokio | 99 | 56,078,000 | 7.19 |
| Algiers | 21 | 2,112,700 | 40.08 |
| Mexico | 94 | 29,748,600 | 111.30 |
| Havana | 35 | 15,124,600 | 50.41 |
| Rio Janeiro | 30 | 28,666,200 | 104.32 |

[*Note.*—Of course the last column does not represent readers, as the cities are the great warehouses frcm which the various countries are supplied with printed matter.]

## THE PRESS OF THE UNITED STATES.

*Number of Daily, Weekly, and Other Serial Newspapers and Periodicals Issued in Each State, with Aggregate Number of Each Regular Issue.*

| *State.* | *No of Publication.* | *Total of One Issue.* |
|---|---|---|
| Alabama | 122 | 102,697 |
| Arkansas | 115 | 101,956 |
| California | 334 | 776,297 |
| Colorado | 93 | 132,060 |
| Connecticut | 145 | 221,701 |
| Delaware | 27 | 36,032 |
| District of Columbia | 43 | 211,737 |
| Florida | 42 | 21.641 |
| Georgia | 194 | 240,388 |
| Illinois | 971 | 2,192,051 |
| Indiana | 492 | 646,577 |
| Iowa | 573 | 560,016 |
| Kansas | 365 | 250,939 |
| Kentucky | 182 | 396,849 |
| Louisiana | 109 | 185,362 |
| Maine | 115 | 178,061 |
| Maryland | 156 | 405,589 |
| Massachusetts | 449 | 2,008,643 |
| Michigan | 475 | 585,217 |
| Minnesota | 236 | 239,053 |
| Mississippi | 109 | 77,089 |
| Missouri | 456 | 1,015,796 |
| Nebraska | 225 | 112,356 |
| Nevada | 31 | 19,895 |
| New Hampshire | 90 | 140.341 |
| New Jersey | 214 | 249,289 |
| New York | 1,385 | 7,489,926 |
| North Carolina | 124 | 101,907 |
| Ohio | 740 | 2,150,779 |
| Oregon | 75 | 75,404 |
| Pennsylvania | 927 | 2.984.698 |
| Rhode Island | 39 | 90,329 |
| South Carolina | 76 | 65,823 |
| Tennessee | 187 | 559,486 |
| Texas | 288 | 349,744 |
| Vermont | 68 | 135,129 |
| Virginia | 173 | 168,828 |
| West Virginia | 98 | 87,925 |
| Wisconsin | 351 | 468,724 |
| Territories | 223 | 148,611 |
| Totals | 11,207 | 25,988,945 |
| British America | 624 | 1,335,579 |

Hubbard rates the annual circulation in the United States at 2,562,633,569 papers. Assuming that these sheets, as we hold them open to read, measure three feet across, and laying them down in a line, we have the above number of yards, which makes 14,560,417 miles of paper. If we allow two feet for the other measure, or six square feet for each sheet, the year's issue would carpet about 550 square miles of ground, or 352,000 acres.

There are in the United States 936 daily newspapers (of which 449 are evening papers), 244 exclusively Sunday, 55 tri-weeklies, 112 semi-weeklies, 8,256 weeklies, and 1,604 semi-monthly and monthly issues. *Political Division*—Republican, 2,793; Democratic, 2,244; Independent, 1,315; Greenback, 164; neutral, 158 *Religious Division*—Methodist, 65; Baptist, 66; Presbyterian, 45; Universalist, 9; Episcopalian, 29; Evangelical, 124; Spiritualist, 7; Unitarian, 2; Liberal, 1; Congregational, 10; Swedenborgian, 3; Roman Catholic, 60; Second Advent, 9; Lutheran, 24; Reformed Church, 13; Moravian, 2; Quaker, 6; Mennonite, 4.

Devoted to agriculture, 107; literature, 184; education, 162; temperance, 56; commerce and trade, 172. There are also publications specially adapted to horticulture, stock-raising, amusements; papers for children, organs of freemasonry, odd-fellowship, and other societies; mechanics, law, real estate, sporting, fashions, women's rights, etc. Papers are issued in English, German, French, Spanish, Portuguese. Italian, Danish, Swedish, Norwegian, Welsh, Polish, Dutch, Bohemian, Cherokee, Chinese, Hebrew; in sign language (for the deaf and dumb), and in phonography, or short-hand writing.

IN all civilized Christian countries the claims of music upon the attention of persons of influence are now fully recognized. Its picturesque written sign language is probably more generally known and accepted among the races of Christendom than that of any other written language. The Russian musician from St. Petersburgh, the German from Berlin, the Italian from Naples, the Frenchman from Paris, the Englishman from London, the inhabitant of the United States of America or of Australia, in fact, all nationalities agree in rendering similarly the written signs of a language common to them all, a language founded upon scales and laws of harmony which are permanent and unchangeable. It is important, therefore, in developing systems of education designed to improve the religious, moral, and social condition of a people, that well-known and intelligent views of music as a science and as an art should be properly cultivated.

Music, which has been defined as "poetry sung," may be considered in its historic, scientific, technic, and æsthetic relations. It deserves a treatment in consonance with its ever growing influence, and with its extraordinary power over the emotions of civilized man. While the antediluvian Jubal is mentioned as the "father of all such as handle the harp and organ," it is clear that among the descendants of Abraham no names stand out more

MOZART.

prominently than those of Moses and his sister Miriam, whose knowledge of the divine art was unquestionably obtained in Egypt. By them it was engrafted upon the religious rites of the Hebrews, who also cultivated it as a consolation in time of peace, and as a powerful incentive in war. A magnificent array of patriarchs, prophets, judges, warriors and kings in Jewish history claim profound regard from the musical student as he looks back upon the past, and attempts to analyze the sources of music's subtle influence upon these chosen servants of God. It was one grand Te Deum, from Moses at the Red Sea to Solomon in his wonderful temple at Jerusalem. And this passionate love and devotion to music still animates the breasts of God's ancient people wherever they may be found. Not less marked was its influence upon the apostles and immediate followers of Christ. It was a joy in their conversions, and was accompanied by miraculous results in dungeons and imprisonments. Even before the coming of Christ, the Greek mind had already measured and appropriated its power in issuing laws, in upholding reforms, in instructing the young, and in pacifying the miserable. Fortified by its celestial harmony Apollo dwelt among the gods, Minerva spread light and wisdom among her worshipers, and Arion with his lovely voice charmed the very fishes of the sea. Homer himself attuned his lyre to its rhythmic flow, and Pythagoras, enlightened by his early Egyptian training, originated ideas of harmony which lie at the foundation of the whole modern system of concords and discords.

BEETHOVEN.

After the Greek and Roman civilizations had reached their height, the Christian bishop sang his love of the Messiah in Latin lines surmounted by Greek letters, to denote the rising and the falling inflections of the voice. St. Ambrose, A.D. 386, retained the four Greek modes founded upon the Greek tetrachords, which were used in the church for two hundred years, and St. Gregory, A.D. 590, added four more, thus completing what have since been known as the eight Gregorian tones, which are still in extensive use in the church.

The organ was introduced into the church during St. Gregory's pontificate, and the church has ever since retained it as the most effective accompaniment of human voices in worship. Harmony and counterpoint, or the system of concords and discords in music, arose with the use of the organ.

The most successful teacher of music during the Middle Ages was Guido Aretino, a Benedictine monk, A.D. 1000, who was the inventor of the vocal gamut, Ut, Re, Mi, Fa, Sol, La, Si. Little is known of music in the following two centuries until the appearance of the Troubadours, who were the immediate progenitors of the succeeding poetry and melody of Italy and France. Soon afterward the madrigal, a composition in parts for companies of four, eight, or sixteen voices, presented its claims for recognition, and for two centuries charmed the ears of the cultivated. More tender, sweet, and delightful concerted music for human voices has never been composed than the madrigals of the sixteenth and seventeenth centuries.

It is an interesting fact to notice, that at this period of time, A.D. 1537, the *Conservatorio Santa Maria di Loretto* was founded in Naples by Giovanni di Tappia, a Spanish clergyman, which is truly named as the pattern of all subsequent conservatories of music. Many were afterward established in Italy, some of which remain to this day. The conservatory of music in Paris, the most brilliant and thoroughly furnished of modern times, was founded A.D. 1793. All others have been founded during the present century.

Two very remarkable men lived in the sixteenth century, the influence of whose musical life and example upon later generations can hardly be overestimated. Palestrina, the father of strict church music forms, and Martin Luther, who established music in the parish schools of his day and clime, and gave the choral to the people. In the following century the Oratorio grew out of the church musical exhibitions entitled mysteries, and contemporaneously the Opera, or secular musical drama, originally of Greek origin, was presented to admiring audiences. Of later musicians, Domenico Scarlatti and John Sebastian Bach deserve to rank as the most distinguished predecessors of that grand galaxy of names consisting of Handel, Haydn, Mozart, Beethoven, and Mendelssohn.

BACH.

## THE SCIENCE OF MUSIC.

Modern Music, as known among Christian nations, is founded upon laws of harmony, which, since their origin, have never changed, because they rest upon mathematical data which render change impossible. The reason why concords in music, as distinguished from discords, are agreeable to the ear, is because the former resemble each other in the number and regularity of their vibrations, while the latter are void of such agreement. Melody may and does change with each succeeding generation; but harmony, or the relation of concords to discords, and *vice versa*, remains the same from age to age. These laws of harmony govern all changes in vocal and instrumental effect. The human voice may be trained to a more extensive compass; its dynamic power may be increased to a point not previously known; and all instrumental music, either for one or many, may be elaborated to a degree positively bewildering: yet all these results are achieved without one radical change in the harmony which lies at the bottom of them all. It may be stated as an axiom, without fear of rejection, that in musical composition, concords must be the rule and discords the exception, if the aim be to win the hearts of all classes of hearers.

## TECHNIC.

The *technical* in music precedes the *artistic*, if it do not in a great measure embrace it. To make the ear quick in distinguishing the difference between one sound and another, in pitch, power and quality of tone; to train the eye promptly to recognize the characters constituting the musical sign language; to require the voice and hand by perpetual drilling to obey the behests of a resolute will and a truthful conception,—these are the constant and never ending necessities of the true musical artist, which are not to be dispensed with, however facile his power of imitation, or however largely endowed he may be with the intuitions of genius. It is with the artistic renderings of musical compositions of unending variety, that the intelligent critic has chiefly to deal, and by which he judges of the character of the technic resources of either singer or player. Tke original outline and construction are the result of the composer's invention, and are to be properly estimated by their scientific relations; but the execution reveals the artistic proclivities of the performer through his mastery of technic. This subject of technic in music assumes a very comprehensive phase in view of the infinite variety of effects produced by different kinds of human voices, such as Base, Baritone, Tenor, Contralto, Mezzo-Soprano, and Soprano, and through the grand and numerous changes wrought by the stringed and wind instruments of an orchestra. With the increased compass, power, and flexibility of the human voice must be named the improvements in all kinds of instruments, with the single exception of the violin, which, it would seem, arrived at the height of its excellence in beauty of tone fully two centuries ago. From the rehearsals of the first Italian conservatories of music nearly three centuries and a half ago to the present time, the combined effects of voices and instruments have steadily increased, until now in the sacred oratorio and in the grand opera, as well as in other forms of united vocal and instrumental effort, the result is a splendid advance beyond all former conception.

## MUSIC AS A FINE ART.

Music cannot present in graphic outline the animate and inanimate forms of nature with the facility and success which attend the devotees of drawing, painting and sculpture in their charming work. And all of these fine arts, including music, cannot present to the intellect and imagination those delicate analyses of the sources of beauty, which Poesy, in the hands of its great masters, makes plain to the æsthetic sensibilities of man. Yet Music, it must be fairly acknowledged, by its more direct and stirring effect upon the emotions, does sway the soul in a manner hardly attainable by any other fine art. Its effect is also more general than that of any other fine art upon all classes of persons, young and old. Even a military band, which does not rely for its effect so much upon its delicate and tasteful appeals to the ear as it does upon its full, resonant and martial strains, will cause man, woman and child to stop and listen with rapt attention to its measured beat.

LISZT.

## COMPOSITION AND COMPOSERS.

For the sake of convenience in classification, and as tending to a higher æsthetic culture, three styles of musical composition may be mentioned, the CLASSIC, the ROMANTIC, and the SENTIMENTAL. These three styles may each embrace the *sacred* and *secular*, the distinctions in the styles arising from the musical, and not from the religious, moral, or poetic form of the composition; the character of the composer affording the real key to these points of difference. Thus it may be stated that Palestrina, Pergolesi, Scarlatti, Bach, Marpurg, Handel, Haydn, Mozart, Beethoven, Cherubini, Spohr, Mendelssohn, Schuman, and Rubenstein are composers chiefly of that which is classic.

In a degree less classic, and embracing much of the romantic, may be named Clementi, Cremer, Field, Dussek, Hummel, Czerny, Kalkbrenner, Moscheles, Chopin, Herz, Thalberg, Liszt, and Wagner. To the romantic school belong the operatic and descriptive song composers, such as Paisiello, Glück, Pacini, Rossini, Meyerbeer, Boildieu, Auber, Von Weber, Schubert, Bellini, Hiller, Kücken, Donizetti, Verdi, and many others.

"The mob of gentlemen who write (music) with ease" are the prolific sentimental song writers and composers of waltzes, fantasias, polkas, etc., a vast army of whom rise yearly to compete with each other in a very superficial school indeed. Most of this music is soon forgotten, and the shelves that knew it once, will know it no more forever.

A certain class of virtuosi, such as organists, pianists, violinists, violoncellists, cornetists, etc., achieve a world-wide reputation as soloists, and amass respectable fortunes. The most highly accomplished and celebrated of these, in modern days, are the violinists: Paganini, De Beriot, Ole Bull, Vieuxtemps, Ernst, Sivori, Joachim and Wieniawski. The great reputation they have achieved reveals this interesting fact, that next to the human voice the violin makes the most searching appeals to the human ear and heart. It is the King of the orchestra, and probably will long remain so.

## THE CULTIVATION OF MUSIC.

The systematic cultivation of music in the common schools now fostered by many States, together with the attention given to it as a science by Harvard and other seats of advanced learning, will, in due time, bear legitimate and abundant fruit. Conservatories, which are now the outcome of individual enterprise, will be chartered by the State and be placed upon a permanent foundation. Some, even now, are doing a flourishing business under State charters. These movements toward a higher and more intelligent appreciation of music among all classes of people must necessarily rescue it from many degrading associations with which it is now unfortunately united. Music, like language, has unlimited power for good or for evil, in exact proportion to the extent of its union with elevating or debasing scenes. What cheerful influence in the family can so cordially bind together its members as the faithful study and practice of the highest and best forms of concerted music? What charming relief from the tedium and confined air of class rooms in schools does the music drill afford! The young and lively collegian would also make his future life in society infinitely more pleasant to himself and to others, if, instead of singing the miserable doggerel lines with which he makes night hideous during his student days, he gave a limited portion of his time to the systematic cultivation of his voice and to the development of a strong and flexible finger in practicing classic music. Indeed, there are hardly any gatherings, large or small, in human society, where good music, appropriate to the occasion, would not be acceptable and confer increased happiness upon the hearer. At marriage, on the birthday, at the funeral, at home, in church, in school, on the graduation day, with the party of pleasure, the summer sail, the military review, at early dawn, by moonlight walk, in war, in peace, in all scenes, at all times, and in all places "the concord of sweet sounds" completely fills those intervals between the more prosaic acts of life which otherwise might be a succession of aching voids.

# Chronological List of Eminent Musical Personages.

| NAME. | CALLING. | BIRTHPLACE. | BIRTH. | DEATH. |
|---|---|---|---|---|
| | | | A. D. | A. D. |
| Abelard, Peter | Theologian and Composer | Paris | 1079 | 1142 |
| Abt, Franz | Composer | Ellenburg | 1819 | .... |
| Abbot, Asahel | Composer | New Hampshire | 1804 | .... |
| Albani, Emma | Soprano | Canada | 1850 | .... |
| Albrechtsberger, J. E. | Composer | Klosternenberg. | 1736 | 1803 |
| Allegri, Gregorio | Composer | Rome | 1600 | 1652 |
| Amati Brothers | Violin makers | Cremona | 1600 | 1650 |
| Ambrose, Saint | Bishop and Composer | Milan | 340 | 397 |
| Aretino, Guido | Monk and Instructor | Arezzo | 990 | 1050 |
| Arion | Poet and Musician | Lesbos | B. C. 600 | .... |
| Attwood, Thomas | Composer | London | A. D. 1767 | A. D. 1838 |
| Auber, D. F. E | Composer | Caen | 1784 | 1871 |
| Bach, J. S | Composer | Eisenach | 1685 | 1750 |
| Balfe, Michael | Composer | Dublin | 1808 | 1870 |
| Bargiel, W | Composer | Berlin | 1828 | .... |
| Beethoven, L. V | Composer | Bonn | 1770 | 1827 |
| Bellini, V | Composer | Catania | 1802 | 1835 |
| Benedict, Sir Jules | Composer and Director | Stuttgart | 1804 | .... |
| Berg, Albert W | Organist and Composer | Frankfort | 1825 | .... |
| Berlioz, Hector | Composer | Cote St. André. | 1803 | 1869 |
| Bishop, Sir H. R | Composer | London | 1782 | 18— |
| Boildieu, F. A | Composer | Rouen | 1770 | 1834 |
| Boyce, Dr. Wm | Organist and Composer | London | 1710 | 1799 |
| Bradbury, Wm | Composer | Maine | 1817 | 1861 |
| Braham, John | Tenor | London | 1774 | 1856 |
| Brahms, Jno | Composer | Hamburg | 1833 | .... |
| Bristow, G. F | Composer | New York | 1825 | .... |
| Buck, Dudley | Organist and Composer | Hartford | 1842 | .... |
| Bulow, Hans von | Pianist and Composer | Dresden | 1830 | .... |
| Burney, Dr. Ch | Historian and Composer | Shrewsbury | 1726 | 1814 |
| Calcott, Dr | Author and Composer | Kensington | 1766 | 1821 |
| Carey, Anna Louise | Contralto | Maine | .... | .... |
| Catalani, Angelica | Soprano | Sinigaglia | 1783 | 1842 |
| Catel, Ch. S | Professor of Harmony | Aigle | 1773 | 1830 |
| Cherubini, L | Author and Composer | Florence | 1760 | 1842 |
| Chladni, Dr. E. F | Writer on Acoustics | Wittenburg | 1756 | 1827 |
| Chopin, Fred | Pianist and Composer | Zelagona-Wola. | 1810 | 1849 |
| Choron, Alex. E | Author and Composer | Caen | 1772 | 1834 |
| Cimarosa, D | Composer | Naples | 1754 | 1801 |
| Clementi, Muzio | Pianist and Composer | Rome | 1752 | 1832 |
| Corelli, Arcangelo | Violinist and Composer | Fusignano | 1653 | 1713 |
| Costa, Sir Michael | Composer and Director | Naples | 1810 | .... |
| Cramer, J. B | Pianist and Composer | Germany | 1771 | 1858 |
| Croft, Dr. Wm | Organist and Composer | Nether Eatington | 1677 | 1727 |
| Crotch, Dr. Wm | | Norwich | 1755 | 1847 |
| Curtis, G. H | Author and Composer | Troy, N. Y | 1819 | .... |
| Czerny, Carl | Pianist and Composer | Vienna | 1791 | 1857 |
| Damoreau, Mad. Cinti. | | Paris | 1801 | 1863 |
| David | King and Psalmist | Bethlehem | B. C. 1050 | .... |
| David, Felicien | Composer | Codenet | A. D. 1810 | A. D. 1876 |
| De Begnis, G | Baritone | Lugo | 1795 | 1849 |

| NAME. | CALLING. | BIRTHPLACE. | BIRTH. | DEATH. |
|---|---|---|---|---|
| | | | A. D. | A. D. |
| Deborah | Prophetess and Singer | B. C. | 1295 | .... |
| Donizetti, G. | Composer | Bergamo | 1797 | 1848 |
| Duprez, Gilbert | Tenor | Paris | 1806 | .... |
| Durante, Fran | Composer and Instructor | Grumo | 1693 | 1755 |
| Dussek, J. L. | Pianist and Composer | Czaslan | 1761 | 1810 |
| Elizabeth | Queen and Virginal Player | England | 1533 | 1603 |
| Erard, P | | Paris | 1796 | 1855 |
| Farinelli, C. B. D | Singer | Naples | 1705 | 1782 |
| Farrant, Richard | Organist and Composer | London | .... | 1580 |
| Ferrari, G. G | Composer and Instructor | Roveredo | 1759 | 1842 |
| Fétis, F. J | Author and Composer | Mons | 1784 | 1871 |
| Feux, J. J | Author and Composer | Styria | 1660 | 1741 |
| Field, John | Pianist and Composer | Dublin | 1782 | 1837 |
| Fioravanti, V | Composer | Rome | 1770 | 1837 |
| Franc, G | Composer | Strasburg | 1535 | .... |
| Franz, Robert | Composer | Halle | 1815 | .... |
| Garcia, M | Tenor | Seville | 1775 | 1832 |
| Gilmore, P. S | Comp. & Director | Dublin | 1829 | .... |
| Giardini, Felice | Violinist and Composer | Turin | 1716 | 1796 |
| Gibbons, Orlando | Organist and Composer | Cambridge | 1583 | 1628 |
| Glück, C | Composer | Weidenwangen. | 1714 | 1787 |
| Goss, Sir John | Organist and Composer | Fareham | 1800 | ... |
| Gottschalk, L | Pianist and Composer | New Orleans | 1820 | 1865 |
| Goudimel, C | Composer | Franche Compté | 1510 | 1572 |
| Gounod, C. F | Composer | Paris | 1818 | .... |
| Gregory, Saint | Roman Pontiff and Composer | Rome | 550 | 604 |
| Grisi, Giulia | Soprano | Milan | 1812 | 1869 |
| Guglielmi, P | Composer | Massa di Carrau | 1729 | 1804 |
| Gungl, J | Composer and Director | Zambek | 1810 | .... |
| Halévy, J. F | Composer | Paris | 1799 | 1862 |
| Handel, G. F | Composer | Magdeburg | 1684 | 1759 |
| Hasse, G. A | Composer | Bergedorf | 1699 | 1783 |
| Hasse, Faustina | Soprano | Venice | 1700 | 1783 |
| Hastings, Thomas | Author and Composer | New York | 1790 | 1875 |
| Hauptmann, M | Harmonist and Composer | Dresden | 1792 | 1868 |
| Hawkins, Sir John | Historian of Music | London | 1719 | 1789 |
| Haydn, F. J | Composer | Rohran | 1732 | 1810 |
| Heller, Stephen | Pianist and Composer | Pesth | 1815 | .... |
| Henselt, Adolph | Pianist and Composer | Swabach | 1814 | .... |
| Herold, L. J. F | Composer | Paris | 1791 | 1833 |
| Herz, Henri | Pianist and Composer | Coblentz | 1806 | .... |
| Hesse, A. F | Organist and Composer | Breslau | 1809 | 1863 |
| Hiller, Ferd | Pianist and Composer | Frankfort-on-Main | 1811 | .... |
| Hoffman, R | Pianist and Composer | England | 1828 | .... |
| Horn, C. E | Tenor and Composer | London | 1822 | 1849 |
| Horsley, Ch. Ed | Composer and Director | London | 1786 | 1876 |
| Horsley, Wm | Organist and Composer | London | 1774* | 1858 |
| Hullah, Dr. John | Instructor and Author | Worcester | 1812 | .... |
| Hummel, J. P | Pianist and Composer | Presburg | 1778 | 1837 |
| Hünten, F | Pianist and Composer | Coblentz | 1793 | 1878 |
| Jackson, Wm | Author and Composer | Exeter | 1730 | 1803 |
| Jackson, Wm | Organist and Composer | Masham | 1816 | 1866 |
| Jackson, Sam'l | Organist and Composer | New York | 1816 | .... |
| Jaell, Alfred | Pianist and Composer | Trieste | 1832 | .... |
| Jomelli, N | Composer | Naples | 1714 | 1774 |
| Joseffy, R | Pianist and Composer | Prussia | ... | .... |
| Kalkbrenner, F | Pianist and Composer | Cassel | 1788 | 1849 |
| Kalliwoda, J. W | Composer | Prague | 1800 | 1866 |
| Kellogg, Clara L | Soprano | Sumpterville, S. C. | 1842 | .... |
| Kelly, Michael | Tenor and Composer | Dublin | 1764 | 1826 |
| King, M. P | Composer | London | 1773 | 1823 |
| King, Wm. A | Pianist and Organist | London | 1810 | 1867 |
| Kirnberger, J. P | Harmonist and Author | Berlin | 1721 | 1783 |
| Kollman, A. F. C | Organist and Author | Engelbostel | 1756 | 1829 |
| Kreutzer, R | Violinist and Composer | Versailles | 1766 | 1831 |
| Kullak, Theo | Pianist and Composer | Krotoschin | 1818 | 1882 |
| Labitzky, J | Composer | Schönfeld | 1802 | .... |
| Lablache, Louis | Basso | Naples | 1794 | 1858 |
| Lamperti, F | Author and Instructor | | 1813 | .... |
| Lang, B. J | Organist | Boston | .... | .... |
| Lasso, Orlando Di | Composer | Mons | 1520 | 1593 |
| Leslie, Henry D | Composer | London | 1822 | .... |
| Lind, Jenny | Soprano | Stockholm | 1820 | .... |
| Lindpainter, P. J | Composer | Coblentz | 1791 | 1855 |
| Liszt, Franz | Pianist and Composer | Raeding | 1811 | .... |
| Litolff, H. C | Pianist and Composer | London | 1818 | .... |
| Lock, Matthew | Composer | Exeter | 1635 | 1677 |
| Loewe, J. C. G | Composer | Loebejuen | 1796 | 1869 |
| Lucca, Pauline | Soprano | Vienna | 1846 | .... |
| Lulli, J. B | Violinist and Composer | Florence | 1634 | 1687 |
| Luther, Dr. Martin | Theologian and Composer | Isleben | 1483 | 1547 |
| MacFarren, Dr. Geo. A. | Composer | London | 1813 | .... |
| Mainzer, Dr. Joseph | Author and Director | Treves | 1801 | 1851 |
| Malibran, Madame | Soprano | Paris | 1808 | 1836 |
| Marcello, B | | | | |
| Mara, Madame | Soprano | Cassel | 1749 | 1833 |
| Marenzio, Luca | Composer | Coccaglia | 1550 | 1599 |
| Mario, Conte di Candia | Tenor | Genoa | 1812 | .... |
| Marpurg, F. W | Author and Composer | Mospergshof | 1718 | 1795 |
| Marschner, H | Composer | Zittau | 1796 | 1861 |
| Martini, G. B | Composer and Author | Bologna | 1706 | 1784 |
| Martini, G. P. E | Composer | Friegstall | 1741 | 1811 |
| Marx, Dr. A. B | Author and Composer | Halle | 1799 | 1866 |
| Mason, Dr. Lowell | Author and Composer | Medfield, Mass | 1792 | 1872 |
| Mason, William | Pianist and Composer | Boston | 1828 | .... |
| Mayseder, Jos | Violinist and Composer | Vienna | 1789 | 1863 |
| Mazzinghi, Jos | Organist and Composer | London | 1765 | 1844 |
| Mehul, E. H | Composer | Givet | 1763 | 1817 |
| Mendel, H | Author and Historian | Halle | 1834 | 1876 |
| Mendelssohn, Dr. F. B. | Composer | Hamburg | 1809 | 1847 |
| Mercadante, S | Composer | Altamura | 1797 | 1870 |
| Metastasio, P. H. D. P. | Author and Composer | Rome | 1698 | 1782 |
| Meyerbeer, G | Composer | Berlin | 1794 | 1863 |
| Mills, S. B | Pianist and Composer | Manch'ter, Eng. | 1835 | .... |
| Mollenhauer Brothers | Violinists | Erfurt | '18, '28, '30 | .... |
| Monk, Dr. E. G | Organist and Composer | Frome | 1819 | .... |
| Monk, Wm. H | Organist and Composer | London | 1823 | .... |

| Name. | Calling. | Birthplace. | Birth. | Death. |
|---|---|---|---|---|
| | | | A. D. | A. D. |
| Monteverde, Claudio P. | Violinist and Composer | Cremona | 1568 | 1643 |
| Moore, Thomas | Poet and Composer | Dublin | 1779 | 1852 |
| Morley, T. | Organist | England...circa | 1550 | 1604 |
| Morgan, George W. | Organist | Gloucester | 1823 | |
| Mornington, Earl of | Composer | Dangan | 1735 | 1781 |
| Moscheles, Ignaz | Pianist and Composer | Prague | 1794 | 1870 |
| Mozart, W. A. | Composer | Salzburg | 1756 | 1791 |
| Nantier-Didiée, C. B. R. | Soprano | St. Denis | 1831 | 1867 |
| Nares, Dr. James | Organist and Composer | Stanwell | 1715 | 1783 |
| Nava, Gaetano | Instructor | Milan | 1802 | 1875 |
| Neukomm, Sigismund | Composer | Salzburg | 1778 | 1858 |
| North, Roger | Author of "Memoirs of Music." | Rougham | 1650 | 1733 |
| Nourrit, L. | Tenor | Montpelier | 1780 | 1839 |
| Novello, Vincent | Organist and Composer | London | 1781 | 1861 |
| O'Carolan, Turlogh | Harpist and Composer | Newtown | 1670 | 1738 |
| Offenbach, J. | Composer | Cologne | 1819 | .... |
| Ole Bull | Violinist and Composer | Bergen | 1810 | 1881 |
| Onslow, George | Composer | Clermont Ferrand | 1784 | 1853 |
| Osborne, Geo. H. | Pianist and Composer | Limerick | 1806 | .... |
| Ouseley, Rev. Sir F. A. | Organist and Composer | London | 1825 | .... |
| Pacini, G. | Composer | Catania | 1796 | 1867 |
| Paer, F | Composer | Parma | 1771 | 1839 |
| Paèsiello, G. | Composer | Taranto | 1741 | 1815 |
| Paganini, N. | Violinist | Genoa | 1784 | 1840 |
| Paine, J. K. | Organist and Composer | Portland | 1839 | .... |
| Palestrina, G. P. D. | Composer | Rome | 1529 | 1594 |
| Panseron, A. | Composer and Instructor | Paris | 1796 | 1859 |
| Parepa-Rosa, Madame | Soprano | Edinburgh | 1836 | 1874 |
| Parish, Alvars | Harpist and Pianist | Teignmouth | 1816 | 1849 |
| Parsons, Sir Wm. | Mus. Doc | London | 1746 | 1817 |
| Pasta, Giuditta | Mezzo-Soprano | Milan | 1798 | 1865 |
| Paton, Mary Anne | Soprano | Edinburgh | 1802 | 1854 |
| Patti, Adelina | Soprano | Madrid | 1843 | .... |
| Patti, Carlotta | Soprano | Florence | 1840 | .... |
| Pepusch, Dr. J. E. | Author and Composer | Berlin | 1667 | 1752 |
| Pergolesi, G. B. | Composer | Jesi | 1710 | 1736 |
| Phillidor, F. A. D. | Composer | Dreux | 1726 | 1795 |
| Phillips, Harry | Baritone | Bristol | 1801 | 1876 |
| Piccolomini, Maria | Soprano | Siena | 1834 | .... |
| Pierson, H. H. | Composer | Oxford | 1815 | 1873 |
| Pinsuti, Ciro | Composer | Sinalunga | 1829 | .... |
| Pixis, J. P. | Pianist and Composer | Munich | 1788 | 1874 |
| Pleyel, Camille | Composer | Strasburg | 1792 | 1855 |
| Pleyel, Ignaz | Composer | Vienna | 1757 | 1831 |
| Pleyel, Marie F. | Pianiste | Paris | 1811 | 1875 |
| Porpora, Nicolo | Composer | Naples | 1686 | 1767 |
| Potter, Cipriani | Composer and Instructor | London | 1792 | 1871 |
| Purcell, H. | Composer | London | 1658 | 1695 |
| Pythagoras | Philosopher and Inventor | Samos | B. C. 580 | B. C. 500 |
| Raff, Joachim | Composer | Lachen | 1822 | 1882 |
| Rameau, J. P. | Organist and Author | Dijon | 1683 | 1764 |
| Reeves, J. Sims | Tenor | Woolwich | 1821 | .... |
| Reicha, Anton | Author and Composer | Prague | 1770 | 1836 |
| Ries, F. | Pianist and Composer | Bonn | 1784 | 1838 |
| Righini, V. | Composer | Bologna | 1756 | 1812 |
| Rinck, C. H. | Organist and Composer | Erfurt | .... | 1846 |
| Romberg, Dr. Andreas | Violinist and Composer | Gotha | 1767 | 1821 |
| Root, George F. | Author and Composer | Reading, Mass. | 1820 | .... |
| Rosa, Salvator | Painter and Composer | Renessa | 1615 | 1673 |
| Rossini, G. | Composer | Pesaro | 1792 | 1868 |
| Rousseau, J. J. | Author and Composer | Geneva | 1712 | 1778 |
| Rubinstein, Anton | Composer | Bessarabia | 1830 | .... |
| Rubini, G. B. | Tenor | Romano | 1795 | 1854 |
| Rush, Dr. Benj | Writer on Voice | Bristol, Pa | 1745 | 1813 |
| Salieri, A. | Composer | Leguano | 1750 | 1825 |
| Sarti, G. | Composer | Faenza | 1730 | 1802 |
| Scarlatti, A. | Composer | Trapani | 1659 | 1725 |
| Scarlatti, D. | Composer | Naples | 1685 | 1757 |
| Schmitt, Aloys | Pianist and Composer | Erlenbach | 1789 | .... |
| Schneider, J. C. F. | Organist and Composer | Gersdorf | 1785 | 1853 |
| Schubert, Franz | Composer | Himmelspfort-grand | 1797 | 1828 |
| Seguin, E. | Basso | London | 1810 | 1852 |
| Shield, Wm. | Composer | England | 1754 | 1829 |
| Sivori, C. | Violinist | Genoa | 1817 | .... |
| Smart, Sir G. T. | Composer | London | 1776 | 1867 |
| Sontag, Henrietta | Soprano | Coblentz | 1805 | 1855 |
| Spohr, L. | Violinist and Composer | Brunswick | 1784 | 1859 |
| Storace, S. | Composer | London | 1763 | 1796 |
| Stradella, Alessandro | Violinist and Composer | Naples | 1645 | 1679 |
| Strakosch, Maurice | Pianist and Composer | Lemburg | 1825 | .... |
| Strauss, John | Composer | Vienna | 1804 | 1849 |
| Tacchinardi, N. | Violinist and Composer | Florence | 1776 | 18— |
| Tallis, Thomas | Organist and Composer | England | 1529 | 1585 |
| Tappia, G. | Priest and Direc. | Spain | 1528 | .... |
| Taubert, W. | Pianist and Composer | Berlin | 1811 | .... |
| Thalberg, S. | Pianist and Composer | Geneva | 1812 | 1870 |
| Thayer, Eugene | Organist | Boston | 184– | .... |
| Thomas, Theodore | Violinist and Director | Germany | 1835 | .... |
| Thursby, Emma C. | Soprano | Brooklyn | 1844 | .... |
| Toulon, J. L. | Flutist and Composer | Paris | 1786 | 1843 |
| Turini, F. | Organist and Composer | Prague | 1590 | 1656 |
| Tyrteus | Composer of Martial Music | Athens | B. C. 685 | B. C. .... |
| | | | A. D. | |
| Urso, Camilla | Violinist | Italy | .... | .... |
| Vaccaj, N. | Composer | Tolentino | 1791 | .... |
| Vaccari, F. | Violinist | Modena | 1793 | .... |
| Vanhall, J. | Composer | Bohemia | 1739 | 1813 |
| Verdi, G. | Composer | Busseto | 1816 | .... |
| Vestris, Madame | Soprano | London | 1797 | 1856 |
| Vieuxtemps, H. | Violinist and Composer | Verriers | 1820 | 1881 |
| Vinci, L. D. | Composer | Naples | 1690 | 1732 |
| Viotti, G. B. | Violinist and Composer | Piedmont | 1753 | 1824 |
| Vogler, Abbé G. J. | Author and Composer | Wurzburg | 1749 | 1814 |
| Wagner, R. | Composer | Leipsic | 1813 | 1883 |
| Webb, Geo. J. | Composer | England | 1805 | .... |
| Webbe, S. | Composer | England | 1740 | .... |
| Webbe, S., Jr. | Composer | England | 1770 | .... |
| Weber, C. M. V. | Composer | Eutin | 1786 | 1826 |
| Wesley, C. | Organist and Composer | Bristol | 1757 | 1815 |
| Wesley, S. | Organist and Composer | Bristol | 1766 | 1837 |
| Wieck, Clara | Pianiste and Composer | Leipsic | 1818 | .... |
| Willmers, F. J. R. | Pianist and Composer | Copenhagen | 1820 | .... |
| Woelfl, J. | Pianist and Composer | Salzburg | 1772 | 1811 |
| Xavier, A. M. | Pianist and Composer. | Paris | 1769 | . . |
| Zanetti, A. | Violinist | Venice | 1650 | .... |
| Zelter, C. F. | Author and Composer | Berlin | 1758 | 1832 |
| Zerrahn, Carl | | Germany | 1752 | 1837 |
| Zingarelli, N. | Composer | Naples | 1752 | 1837 |

# Sign Language of Music.

THE different signs used in writing or reading music may be appropriately embraced under three general divisions: namely, Tune, Time, and Expression.

I. TUNE includes (1.) the *Staff* consisting of five horizontal lines and four intermediate spaces, to support the notes, rests, etc. (2.) *The Clefs*, to determine the pitch of the different Voices, Soprano, Alto, Tenor, and Bass, and the pitch of instruments; the Bass, or F clef, being on the 4th line from the bottom of the Staff; the Baritone, or F clef, on the 3d line; the Tenor, or C clef, on the 4th line; the Alto, or C clef, on the 3d line; the Mezzo-Soprano, or C clef, on the 2d line; the Soprano, or C clef, on the 1st line; and the Violin, or G clef, on the 2d line. Of these seven clefs the F and the G are those chiefly in use. (3). *The Letters*, A, B, C, D, E, F, G, ascending, or G, F, E, D, C, B, A, descending, are applied to the lines and spaces of the Staff by means of the clefs. The Letters also are used to denote the absolute and unchangeable pitch of the Key-notes, or starting points of the scale. (4.) *The Numerals*, 1, 2, 3, 4, 5, 6, 7, 8, ascending, or 8, 7, 6, 5, 4, 3, 2, 1, descending, are used to locate the sounds of the scale in their proper order, of which *One*, the beginning, is the most important, and therefore called the Key-note. (5) *The Syllables*, Do, Re, Mi, Fa, Sol, La, Si, Do, ascending, or Do, Si, La, Sol, Fa, Mi, Re, Do, descending, are used to impress the sounds of the scale upon the ear and memory. The following diagram shows the order of tones and half-tones (steps and half-steps) in the *Major Scale*:

(6.)

| 1 | | 2 | | 3 | | 4 | | 5 | | 6 | | 7 | | 8 |
|---|---|---|---|---|---|---|---|---|---|---|---|---|---|---|
| Do | Tone. | Re | Tone. | Mi | ½ Tone. | Fa | Tone. | Sol | Tone. | La | Tone. | Si | ½ Tone. | Do. |

This scale is called Major or Greater, because its first third, 1 to 3, contains two tones, or four half-tones, *i. e.* one half-tone more than the minor third, which contains but three half-tones. *The Minor Scale*, so called because its first third contains but a tone and a half, or three half tones, has two forms, as follows:

(7.) *First Form, or Melodic—Ascending.*

| La | Tone. | Si | ½ Tone. | Do | Tone. | Re | Tone. | Mi | Tone. | Fi | Tone. | Si | ½ Tone. | La. |
|---|---|---|---|---|---|---|---|---|---|---|---|---|---|---|

*Descending*

| La | Tone. | Sol | Tone. | Fa | ½ Tone. | Mi | Tone. | Re | Tone. | Do | ½ Tone. | Si | Tone. | La. |
|---|---|---|---|---|---|---|---|---|---|---|---|---|---|---|

(8.) *Second Form, or Harmonic.*

| La | Tone. | Si | ½ Tone. | Do | Tone. | Re | Tone. | Mi | ½ Tone. | Fa | Tone and ½ Tone. | Si | ½ Tone. | La. |
|---|---|---|---|---|---|---|---|---|---|---|---|---|---|---|

ascending and descending alike. (9.) *The Chromatic Scale, or Scale of Half-tones:*

| 1 | | 2 | | 3 | | 4 | | 5 | | 6 | | 7 | | 8 | | 9 | | 10 | | 11 | | 12 | | 13 |
|---|---|---|---|---|---|---|---|---|---|---|---|---|---|---|---|---|---|---|---|---|---|---|---|---|
| Do | ½ Tone | Di | ½ | Re | ½ | Ri | ½ | Mi | ½ | Fa | ½ | Fi | ½ | Sol | ½ | Si | ½ | La | ½ | Li | ½ | Si | ½ | Do. |

In a strictly musical and technical sense, all melodies and harmonies are founded upon the Major, the Minor, and the Chromatic Scales. (10.) *The Chromatic Signs* are the sharp (♯), raising a half-tone; the flat (♭), lowering a half-tone; the natural (♮), taking away the sharp by lowering a half-tone; the natural (♮), taking away the flat by raising a half-tone; the double sharp (×), raising a half-tone after a single sharp; the natural and sharp (♮♯), taking away the double sharp; the double flat (♭♭), lowering a half-tone after a single flat; the natural and flat (♮♭), taking away the double flat. Twelve Keys Major, six in the order of sharps and six in the order of flats, together with the twelve Minor Keys, constitute the entire circle of harmony:

*Major.*

C : G : D : A : E : B : F♯ ‖ C : F : B♭ : E♭ : A♭ : D♭ : G♭

The two Cs, commencing on the same sound, count for one scale. F♯ and G♭ also count for one scale.

*Minor.*

A : E : B : F♯ : C♯ : G♯ : D♯ ‖ A : D : G : C : F : B♭ : E♭

The two As, commencing on the same sound, count for one scale. D♯ and E♭ minor also count for one scale.

II. TIME includes (1.) the rhythmic name and value of the *Notes*, fractionally considered.

| OLD NAMES. | *Large.* | *Long.* | *Breve.* | *Semibreve.* | *Minim.* | *Crotchet.* |
|---|---|---|---|---|---|---|
| NEW NAMES. | *Large.* | *Long.* | *Double Whole Note.* | *Whole Note.* | *Half.* | *Quarter.* |

| *Quaver.* | *Semiquaver.* | *Demisemiquaver.* | *Hemidemisemiquaver.* |
|---|---|---|---|
| *Eighth.* | *Sixteenth,* | *Thirty second.* | *Sixty-fourth.* |

(2.) The rhythmic name and value of the *Rests*, fractionally considered:

*Eight Wholes.* *Four.* *Two.* *Whole Rest.* *Half.*

*Quarter.* *Eighth.* *Sixteenth.* *Thirty-second.* *Sixty-fourth.*

Each note or rest is equal to two of the next in regular fractional order; as, a whole is equal to two halves, etc. (3.) Any note or rest may be lengthened in its time-value one-half as long again by a *Dot* placed after it; as, 𝅝 · = 𝅝 𝅗𝅥; it may be lengthened three-quarters by two dots; as, 𝅝 · · = 𝅝 𝅗𝅥 𝅘𝅥; and it may be lengthened seven-eighths by three dots; as, 𝅝 · · · = 𝅝 𝅗𝅥 𝅘𝅥 𝅘𝅥𝅮, etc. (4.) Abbreviations in time appear as, three, to be played or

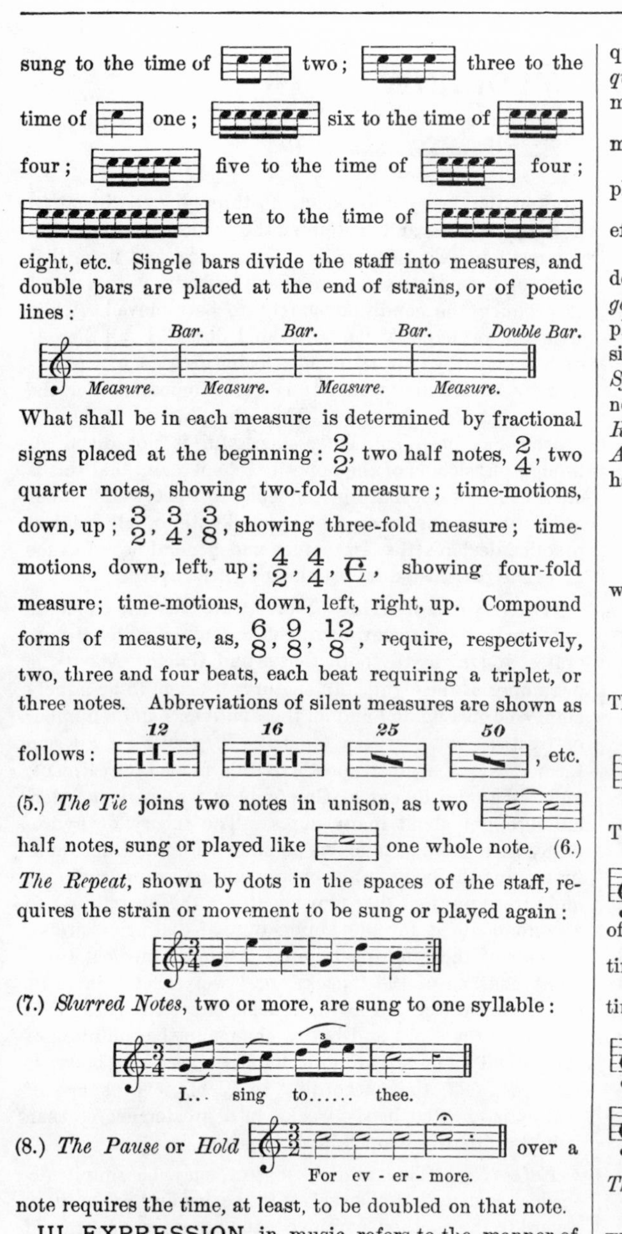

sung to the time of two; three to the time of one; six to the time of four; five to the time of four; ten to the time of eight, etc. Single bars divide the staff into measures, and double bars are placed at the end of strains, or of poetic lines:



What shall be in each measure is determined by fractional signs placed at the beginning: $\frac{2}{2}$, two half notes, $\frac{2}{4}$, two quarter notes, showing two-fold measure; time-motions, down, up; $\frac{3}{2}$, $\frac{3}{4}$, $\frac{3}{8}$, showing three-fold measure; time-motions, down, left, up; $\frac{4}{2}$, $\frac{4}{4}$, C, showing four-fold measure; time-motions, down, left, right, up. Compound forms of measure, as, $\frac{6}{8}$, $\frac{9}{8}$, $\frac{12}{8}$, require, respectively, two, three and four beats, each beat requiring a triplet, or three notes. Abbreviations of silent measures are shown as follows: 12, 16, 25, 50, etc.

(5.) *The Tie* joins two notes in unison, as two half notes, sung or played like one whole note. (6.) *The Repeat*, shown by dots in the spaces of the staff, requires the strain or movement to be sung or played again:

(7.) *Slurred Notes*, two or more, are sung to one syllable:



(8.) *The Pause* or *Hold* over a note requires the time, at least, to be doubled on that note.



III. **EXPRESSION** in music refers to the manner of taking, or attacking the note or musical phrase, to degrees of loudness or softness, to a proper conception of the composer's meaning, a natural and effective emission of tone, a distinct articulation and pronunciation; in a word, to style, which, though the singer or player may have attained to a perfect *technique*, is only to be acquired through a will and inspiration of his own. Helps, in the shape of signs and names, are here in order. *Forte*, or *f*, for loudness. *Piano*, or *p*, for softness. *Mezzo-forte*, or *mf*, for moderately loud. *Mezzo-piano*, or *mp*, for moderately soft. *Fortissimo*, or *ff*, for very loudly. *Pianissimo, or pp*, for very softly. *Allegro, Vivace*, and *Presto*, for cheerfulness, vivacity, and quickness of movement. *Moderato, Andantino, Allegretto quasi Andantino*, and *Andante*, for a moderate degree of movement. *Grave, Adagio*, and *Largo* for slowness of movement. The *demi-staccato* or dots placed above or below notes, express a partially detached effect. *Staccato*, or sharp points, denote the shortest possible effect. *Legato*, smoothly; *Legatissimo*, very smoothly, like the curved line ⌒ over phrases of any length. *Crescendo* and *Diminuendo*, or the sign <>, equivalent to the words swell and diminish. *Sforzando*, or >, a sudden but diminishing force upon one note; ∧ or ∨, an attack of still greater force. *Rallentando, Ritardando*, a gradual slackening of the movement. The *Appoggiatura*, or fore-note, without a cross, usually takes half the value of the succeeding note:

*Written.* *Performed.*

with the cross, it is sung or played quickly into the next note:

*Written.* *Performed.*

The *Accaciacatura*, two introductory grace notes:

*Written.* *Performed.*

The *Groupetto*, or turn, direct and inverted. Sign of the direct turn ~; of the inverted ≀; with accidentals, sometimes above, sometimes below. The *Trillo*, trill, or shake, sometimes on the half-tone, sometimes on the tone:

*The Arpeggio*, or broken chord:

This sign ▭, indicates a sustained and firm tone. The *Brace*, { connects two or more staves. This sign, 𝆖, is the *direct* to the same note on the succeeding staff. *V. S., Volti Subito*, turn the leaf quickly. *Metronome*, or time-keeping and movement marks: (♩ = 50, *slow*); (♩ = 100, *moderate*); (♩ = 150, *fast*); (♩ = 200, *very quick*). Transient shake . *Ped.* for pedal; ⊕, without pedal. *D. C., Da Capo al fine*, return to the beginning, and stop at *fine*, or end.

# SCHOOLS OF MEDICINE.

MEDICINE was first employed as an art in Rome about 200 B. C., and Rome produced two great authorities, Celsus and Galen. Next, the Arabian school sprung up, introducing many valuable drugs—rhubarb, cassia, senna, camphor—and a knowledge of the principles of distillation and medical chemistry. The first public dissection occurred early in the fourteenth century, and the next two centuries developed a knowledge of anatomy, which was of the greatest value to the art of healing. In the eighteenth century, a similar acquaintance with physiology was spread throughout Europe, and the existing knowledge of practice and of drugs began to be concentrated and systematized. The present century has been mainly devoted to experimental research and clinical practice, and a broad investigation into the resources of chemistry in providing new material for practical use in medical treatment. The number of sects or schools into which medical practice is divided may be properly reduced to four, viz.: Allopathic, Homœopathic, Hydropathic, and Eclectic.

***Allopathy.***—This term was invented by Hahnemann, the father of Homœopathy, to designate the mode of treatment employed by the "Old School" of practitioners. It is derived from two Greek words, and means simply the employment of remedies which produce a change from a condition of the system caused by disease. This school employs all known drugs in doses which are the result of experience, but are modified in accordance with the constitution, habits, and recognized condition of the patient. Its practitioners deny the certain efficacy of specifics, and will not be limited by generalizations such as are accepted by the opposite school. They utterly scout and ridicule the theory of the value of infinitesimal doses, and, while not absolutely denying the existence of the homœopathic law of *similia similibus curantur*, look upon its application as merely incidental, and without force other than as that of a metaphysical abstraction. This school may be said to represent the accumulated medical wisdom of all nations, from Hippocrates down, and, while admitting that medical practice is not an exact science, it gives almost equal value to the recorded teachings of experience.

***Homœopathy.***—The Homœopathic School was founded by Hahnemann at the close of the last century, and practices on the theory that medicines have the power of curing morbid conditions (disease) which they have the power to excite in a healthy person, the doctrine being signified by the expression—*similia similibus curantur*, "like things are cured by like." This doctrine was not entirely new, even Hippocrates having suggested something of the kind, as, for instance, to cure mania, "Give the patient a draught from the root of mandrake, *in a smaller dose than sufficient to induce mania.*" Hahnemann worked the theory into a doctrine through experiment on healthy patients, and laid down the proposition that only one medicine should ever be given at once, and none that had not been "proved" on a healthy body, with a result to produce the condition sought to be removed. This, with the principle of "infinitesimal doses," is all there is of homœopathy, the latter idea being carried to a reduction by trituration, which it is quite impossible for the human mind to conceive. That the practice of homœopathy has been eminently successful is not disputed, though physicians of the opposite school claim that this is on account of the natural tendency to "get well" under ordinary circumstances, while the skeptic of all medical practice declares the less potent and general use of drugs gives the patient the fairest chance for recovery.

***Hydropathy.***—The "Water Cure," as it is called, is very ancient treatment, having been employed by Hippocrates, and favored by both Celsus and Galen. About the beginning of the eighteenth century, it began to be largely employed in England and on the Continent, and a number of treatises were written upon it. Priessnitz, a Silesian farmer, was the great apostle of this mode of treatment, and his establishment at Graefenberg was very popular, and brought about many cures. The theory of hydropathy is, to cure as much as possible without drugs, and, by placing the body in a proper condition as to cleanliness and freedom for the movement of the secretions, to accommodate it for the application of dieting, exercise, the uses of the atmosphere, etc. Absolute medical treatment consists of the "pack," or "wet sheet;" in acute cases, the shower, sitz bath, douche, etc. The point held in view is the rapid and entire change in the condition of the patient by an alteration in the particles of the body, so rapid, in fact, that, according to Liebig, "a change of matter is effected in six weeks, in a greater degree than would ordinarily happen in three years."

***Eclectics.***—This school, or sect, may be simply described as devoting themselves to the healing art without regard to the method employed, the nature or quantity of the drugs used, or anything else, but the single object in view. To this end, they employ all kinds of treatment, recognized or rejected by the schools, including electricity, herbs. movement cure, rubbing, etc.

Medical practice is to-day divided into many specialties, physicians being surgeons, oculists, aurists, or devoting themselves to pulmonary complaints, obstetrics, mental diseases, etc., as the case may be. Hospitals afford much general practice for students, who must be graduated from some medical school, or college, in good standing, with a diploma, before being permitted to practice their profession.

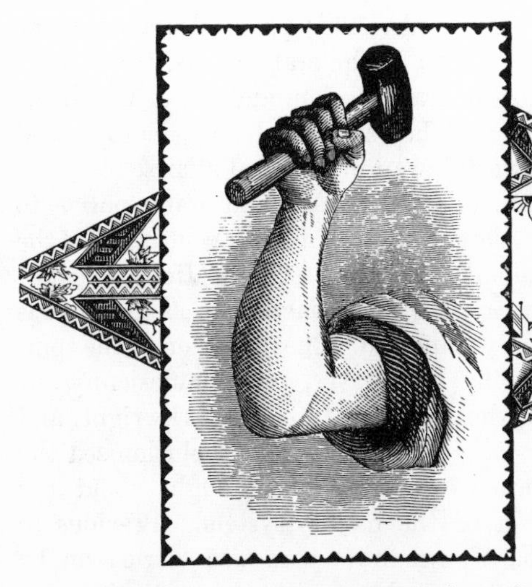

OUR word manufacture comes from two Latin words, meaning to make by hand, but since the introduction of power, it has grown to be the definition, rather, of work done by machinery. The first hand-work consisted in the making of implements for the chase of flint, and afterwards of iron or bronze. Very early, also, in the history of man was the making of pottery, and this after nearly the same design in all countries, the forms being of course the simplest possible. Wicker-work was also practiced at a very early period in human history, these simple arts developing naturally from human ingenuity, which readily devised methods of employing various materials to manufacture articles for convenience or necessity.

From the records left by the ancient Egyptians, in their hieroglyphics and wall-paintings, we know that they practiced many of the arts in use in our own day. They had mills with which they ground their corn; they understood the art of glass-blowing 3,500 years ago, and made beads, bottles, vases, and other utensils; they manufactured linen, and all of their mummies are wrapped in it. They used rude hand-looms, similar to those still employed in India and other Eastern countries; they made nets with needles made of wood, or sometimes of bronze; they embroidered in gold thread. Cotton and wool were also manufactured by the Egyptians into clothing, and they made rope and twine from various fibrous plants. Besides, potters, carpenters and cabinetmakers flourished in Egypt, and they constructed boats of water-plants, and even of planks. The Egyptians possessed many tools, including the axe, adze, hand-saw, chisels, drill, planes, rule, plummet, square, nails, and even glue. Their furniture was made with much skill and taste. The Phœnicians, by their great system of colonization, carried the arts to many

ANCIENT BLACKSMITHS.

distant points. The Assyrians, Hindoos, and Persians were skilled, at an early period, in the manufacture of many articles of utility and beauty ; and the Grecians, Romans, and Carthaginians derived their knowledge on such matters from these nations. And by these means the arts and manufactures spread throughout Europe with the progress of civilization, increasing in variety and improving in kind.

In the palmy days of Rome the artisans were all slaves. These were metal-workers, carpenters, tile-burners, builders, spinners, weavers, shoemakers, cobblers, coopers, cartwrights, armorers, etc. They were wonderfully artistic and expert, and the articles of their make which are found in the European collections are most interesting illustrative specimens. After the fall of Rome, the arts languished during the dark ages, but sprang into new life from the tenth century.

The middle ages were remarkable for their contribution in the direction of the handicrafts, and men became so expert in the manipulation of materials that specimens of the work of that period are now eagerly sought after by public and private collectors. In wood carving, and generally in the construction of furniture, and in architectural embellishment, that period has never been equaled. The same is true of the treatment of metals, and brass, bronze, and iron were formed into domestic utensils and common objects with a skill and beauty now entirely lost.

It was, moreover, peculiar to the handicrafts of that period, that they were conducted with entire and scrupulous *honesty*. The linen and wool fabrics of Holland and Flanders were woven faithfully, and the heavy and rich satins, damasks, and velvets were honest stuffs, whose lasting as well as their artistic qualities could not be gainsaid. The furniture of the time was solid, and firmly put together, lasting in good condition even to the present day, besides being decorated and ornamented with taste and refined sentiment.

In the reign of King John of England, they used iron chandeliers and candelabra, each of which was finished and shaped with the hammer, and with the truest art-taste. In those days, too, the blacksmith, the cordwainer (shoemaker), and the goldsmith were proud of their crafts and of their handiwork, and were esteemed for the quality of what they produced. This pride of craft was one cause of the origin of the craft-guilds, which were a higher sort of trades union, and out of which the latter sprung. They existed all over Europe, and became powerful even in political affairs.

The application of steam and water-power to machinery, late in the eighteenth century, was the cause of an entire change in the relations of labor, and of the origin of manufacturing, as the term is now generally employed. The invention of the spinning-jenny by Hargraves, the mule-jenny by Crompton, the spinning-frame by Arkwright, and the power-loom by Cartwright, revolutionized the manufacture of fabrics, and brought about the introduction of the factory system. Previous to this period this manufacture was carried on by individuals, by hand, occasionally in the employ of a master. But now, with the advent of machinery and the introduction of capital, immense factories were established in England, and the system soon spread to other countries, and was applied to other branches of manufacture.

## COTTON MANUFACTURE.

#### FROM THE FIELD TO THE LOOM.

A POUND of cotton is equivalent to four yards of cloth, and one man laboring in a cotton field can furnish the raw staple for 16,000 yards of cloth. The manufacture of cotton begins at the plantation and the gin-house. After the lint or wool is picked it is put through a machine called the cotton-gin, of which there are two varieties—one termed the saw and the other the roller-gin. The process which the cotton undergoes at this stage is that of separating the wooly fiber from the seeds, and this is accomplished in the implements named, by carrying the mass as it comes from the field over the saws or between the rollers in the gin, when the fiber runs through, the seed being left behind. Twelve hundred pounds as it comes from the field will be separated by the gin into 300 pounds of lint and 900 pounds of seed. The former is packed in bales of about 500 pounds, hooped with iron and sent to the factory. In the factory the cotton first enters the mixing-room, where it is assorted, the various qualities being laid out in layers and pressed close together. It is now carried to the cleaner, where it is freed from bits of leaves, stems, sand or other impurities; thence it goes to the picker, where it is prepared for carding, coming out in a continuous band or lap, as it is called. From the picker the lap goes to a card which delivers the fiber thoroughly cleaned and straightened in small bands called slivers, to several machines, which gradually reduce it in size until it reaches the ordinary thread of commerce. The sliver is first drawn out gradually until it is not thicker than a quill, when it is called a roving. It is then run through rollers which continually lessen its size until the finished roving is thirty-two times longer than the sliver; from the last roller it is wound on spools or reels, and thence transferred to the spinning-frames; here it is drawn through rollers again, at each process getting thinner and thinner until it reaches the desired size; it is then carried to a spindle which revolves with great rapidity, and which, by means of a simple arrangement, is made both to twist the thread and wind it on the spindle ready for the weaver.

**Weaving** consists of passing one set of threads transversely through another set, divided into two series, working alternately up and down, so as to receive the transverse threads in passing and interlock them, forming thereby a united surface which is cloth: the power-loom accomplishes this in every factory, the process being too complicated to be popularly described. The two kinds of cotton, long and short, staple or upland, are respectively used in the manufacture of finer and coarser fabrics; from the former are made cambrics, calicoes, shirtings, sheetings, etc., and from the latter fustians, osnaburgs, etc. Cotton is also used in combination with wool, silk, or linen, in making some fabrics.

**Statistics.**—The cotton manufacture of the United States includes about 1,000 mills, having 10,500,000 spindles, and manufacturing about 1,500,000 bales, or about one-quarter of the entire American cotton product. Great Britain has 480,000 operatives, and 40,000,000 spindles. The whole world employs 1,330,000, and the actual number of spindles is 70,000,000.

BLAST FURNACES.

FEEDING A BLAST FURNACE.

THE FURNACE MOUTH.

## IRON MANUFACTURE.

REDUCTION OF THE ORE—PUDDLING AND SQUEEZING.

THE first process in the manufacture of iron is that of the reduction of the ore as it comes from the mine, usually by means of the blast furnace. Some of the ores, before being smelted, are broken into small pieces, and mixed with charcoal or coke, after which the whole mass is roasted. This operation is sometimes performed in close kilns, and sometimes in open heaps. The process dissipates the sulphur, carbonic acid, and other volatile matter. The blast furnace is a massive tower of stone or brick, shaped narrower at the bottom than at the top. The roasted ore is fed into this—the blast from the bottom being produced by a blowing engine, and the materials raised to a very high heat, and gradually fused into a softened mass.

**Cast Iron.**—The combination for a ton of pig iron is as follows: two tons of roasted ore, two and a half tons of coal, of which about one-quarter is required for the blowing engine, and from twelve to sixteen hundred weight of broken limestone. The molten metal in the furnace sinks to the bottom, where it lies in a thick liquid mass; thence it is run into sand molds which form it into pig or cast iron.

**Malleable, or Wrought Iron.** — To make malleable iron, the pigs are placed on the floor of a puddling furnace, where the metal is freed from carbon and other extraneous matters by being stirred up as it melts, by means of a long bar of iron called a puddler—the mass being constantly watched and removed by the puddler, at the proper moment, in fiery balls or lumps, weighing about sixty pounds each. These lumps are carried to the hammer, where they are beaten into an oblong mass, or bloom, as it is called, or the red hot mass of iron is forced into a machine called by the hands a "coffee mill," which is a serrated wheel, revolving horizontally, and from which it emerges in a flat, oblong slab; or it passes through a squeezer termed the "crocodile," being shaped like the jaws of that reptile; the object of both these processes being to remove the slag or impurities from the iron, leaving the pure metal. The slab is now run through rollers or grooves, according as it is designed to make bar iron or round iron. From each of these rollers or grooves it comes out a little smaller, and by continuing the process may be drawn into fine wire. Girders, channel iron, T iron, etc., used in building bridges and large buildings, are all produced by being passed through rollers made in the form desired, and running from eight to twenty inches in width. Great girders can be sawn through by means of a steel disk, without teeth, which is run at as many as 1,800 revolutions per minute. Horseshoes are made in a patented machine, which produces the article from a bar, cut of a proper length. One such machine will make fifteen tons of complete horseshoes in a day. Screw-bolts are made by machinery, which cuts, threads, heads, and finishes them perfectly. One factory will make from 25,000 to 30,000 finished bolts in a day. In making nails the bar iron from the rolling mill is sheared into lengths of about a foot, and is then cut into nails of all sizes in small machines, the whole mechanism being driven by steam. Cast iron is used for the heavy portions of engineering work, such as bed plates for machines, cylinders, columns, cisterns, low-pressure boilers, water and gas pipes, rollers, girders, and the like. A large quantity is made into hollow ware, which includes pots, pans, and other cooking vessels. It is also used in the manufacture of ornamental objects, being readily cast into molds. Malleable iron is very ductile at a high temperature, and can be rolled into sheets as thin as paper, or drawn into the finest wire; it also possesses the property of welding by hammering two pieces together at a white heat. This iron is employed for the manufacture of general hardware, such as locks, keys, hinges, bolts, nails, screws, and tin plate, which is sheeted iron dipped into melted tin.

THE SOW AND LITTLE PIGS.

PUDDLING FURNACE.

**Steel.**—Steel differs from malleable iron in containing about one per cent. of carbon. It is made by first converting cast into malleable iron, by depriving the former of its carbon, and then adding carbon by heating the iron with charcoal. The Bessemer steel is made by blowing air through molten pig-iron, till the whole of the carbon and silicon is removed, and then introducing into the melted iron a given quantity of a peculiar kind of cast iron, containing a known percentage of carbon. Steel possesses valuable properties, which do not belong to cast or wrought iron. It is harder, denser, and whiter in color. It is also more elastic, takes a higher polish and rusts less easily. It is weldable and may be tempered to any degree of hardness. Steel is not only manufactured into edged tools, but is made into field guns, shafting, rails, boiler-plates and steamships.

## BOOTS AND SHOES.

Until within a very recent period the boot and shoe manufacture was carried on entirely by hand. The first machine applied to this art was the pegging machine. The next great invention was the stitching machine, invented by Elias Howe, patented in 1846. By this machine a single operator can do the work of about twenty by the old hand-process. The next important introduction was the McKay sewing-machine, stitching the uppers and bottoms together. Between 1861 and 1871 the introduction of new machinery completely revolutionized the business of shoemaking; besides the machines already mentioned, were applied the Goodyear welting machine, the cable screw, wire and wire tacking machine, etc.

**Ladies' Shoes.**—In making ladies' shoes the first process occurs in the sole-leather department. Here the hides are cut into strips, which are next passed through a machine, in which, by a system of knives, the soles are formed to the necessary width; these are then assorted according to quality, and after being wet are run through the splitter, which reduces them to a uniform thickness; thence they are passed between rollers, where they are made firm and solid. A machine now cuts each into the exact shape required; another channels the outer soles, leaving room for the stitches; another molds or presses the sole to the shape of the bottom of the last, when this part of the work is completed. Uppers are made from goat and calf-skin and cloth, and are cut by means of dies; the linings are made of drillings, strengthened around the top and edges of the upper with goat-skin and sheep-skin. The several parts of the upper are united properly by sewing-machines; they are then attached to the soles by the McKay sewing-machine, which will sole about 500 pairs a day. The heels are attached by machinery, which also works a semi-circular knife, shaving the heel in an instant. Another machine trims and burnishes the edges, and the bottoms are scoured and sanded by rollers revolved by power, and are smoothed by others covered with fine material; the shanks are then blacked and burnished, the inner soles lined, and the trimming put on, if there be any, when they are ready to be packed in cases. This description, with slight modifications, applies to all kinds of shoemaking by machinery.

## THE LINEN MANUFACTURE.

Linen is most extensively manufactured, and of the best quality, in France and the Netherlands, though formerly Ireland achieved a reputation in this direction. It is made wholly of flax, and very fine lawns are still manufactured in

Belfast, Armagh, and other Irish districts. Common sheeting and toweling are made in Scotland, and at Leeds and Barnsley, in England. The process of manufacturing linen is the same as that used for cotton cloths. The first mill or linen manufactory in the United States was set up at Fall River, Massachusetts, in 1834. The importation into the United States, in 1879, of flax and its manufactures, amounted to more than twenty-three millions of dollars. Jute is sometimes mixed with flax, in the manufacture, being cheaper, and is largely manufactured alone into gunny-bags and other heavy and coarse fabric. The factories of the world contain 3,500,000 spindles. Russia grows half the flax, and the factories of Great Britain consume one-third of the earth's production.

## PAPER MAKING.

### ANCIENT WRITING MATERIAL.

THE earliest writings were upon stone, or stamped upon bricks, or engraved upon metallic plates; bark and the leaves of trees and papyrus, which was the inner bark of an Egyptian water-plant, were the next employed. Parchment made from sheepskin was used generally during the middle ages; but paper itself has been known to the world since a very early period, and is supposed to have been introduced into Europe as early as the seventh or eighth century. Paper, made from linen, of the date 1178, is still in existence; and paper mills are said to have been in operation in Spain, in the eleventh century. For writing and printing paper, the materials used are fibers from cotton or linen rags. It is also made from wood fiber, and straw, rope, etc. The material is reduced by various processes to a watery pulp, which, being run out into thin sheets upon felt cloths, the water is drawn off, leaving the sheet of pulp, which is then pressed dry and subjected to other manipulations, according to the kind of paper to be made.

**The Paper Machine.**—The first machine for making paper was invented, in 1798, in France. The inventor sold his patent to the Messrs. Fourdrinier, a firm in England, who expended about £60,000 in experiments upon the machine, and then became bankrupt. But the machine itself, as perfected, is still employed in the paper manufacture. The process by this machine is to allow the prepared pulp to flow from the vat upon an endless web; during its passage it is partially drained, a process which is completed by passing it through rollers. It is then dried by being passed around drums heated with steam, and is delivered finished in a long sheet, which is afterwards cut into the required lengths. A paper machine at a cost of about $20,000, and being kept at work the twenty-four hours of a day, makes two and one-half tons of paper. This machine occupies a space of 1,200 square superficial feet. After the paper is made, it is calendered, which consists in rolling it between a smooth copper roller and one made of paper, this last material being the best substance known for giving a smooth surface; when finished and arranged in reams containing twenty quires of twenty-four sheets each, the paper is stamped with any device by means of dies. The manufacture of fine writing-paper in the United States amounts to some sixty-five tons a day. It has been computed that the total production of all the mills in Great Britain is not less than 6,000,000 yards, or 3,400 miles daily.

**Making Paper Pulp.**—The production of the pulp is accomplished by boiling the material, linen or cotton rags, wood fiber, or whatever else it may be, in a strong lye of caustic alkali. This effectually cleans it, and it is then placed in a washing-machine, out of which it comes pure vegetable fiber. The water being drawn away, the stuff goes into the bleaching vats where it is subjected to the action of a strong solution of chloride of lime, after which it is transferred to a hydraulic press, which presses out the liquid and the bleaching material. It is now passed into a beating engine, where the fibers are entirely separated and arranged much the same as with cotton in a carding machine. The pulp is now ready to be made into paper, and is either *wove* or *laid* as it is placed in a mold in which the wires are woven across each other, forming a very fine gauze; or in one made up of coarse bars and straight wires, the former about an inch apart, the latter about twenty to the inch. Paper when it is first made cannot be written upon, which is remedied by dipping it into a weak solution of hot size, sometimes tinged with color, after which it is pressed dry, folded, and made up into quires. Hot pressing and glazing are done by passing the sheets through hot and polished iron rollers. The successful manufacture of paper depends materially on the possession of pure water for washing and pulping. In making colored papers, if the color is introduced into the pulp, it runs through the body of the paper; if mixed with the size it is only applied to the surface. In England, the best paper is made in Kent, after which come Hertfordshire, Buckinghamshire, Oxfordshire, and Lancashire. In America, the best paper-mills are those of New York, Massachusetts, Pennsylvania, Ohio, and Connecticut.

## GLASS MAKING.

THERE are five different kinds of glass, varying a little in the materials used in making them, and more in the proportions used and the method of manufacture employed. These are bottle glass, window glass, plate glass, flint glass, and colored glass.

**Bottle Glass.**—The commonest kind is the first, which is that employed in the manufacture of black bottles for beer, etc. It is made of soap-maker's waste (which contains soda salts), fresh-water river sand, brick dust, calcined lime, and marl; to these there is added during the making a small quantity (proportionate) of the broken glass of the works, called *cullet*. In France, kelp and wood ashes furnish the alkaline portion of the mixture; sometimes a small proportion of oxide of manganese is added, and all establishments have their secret methods of coloring.

**Window Glass** is made of much more carefully selected materials, and, usually, of sand and alkali, a little lime without lead or any other metallic oxide, except a minute quantity of manganese and sometimes of cobalt, which are added to counteract the effect of any impurities in giving color to the glass; this kind of glass requires a higher degree of heat than the others. Window glass is blown in circular plates, but to obtain large plates for windows and looking-glasses the glass is blown in cylinders, which are cut through with shears (red hot), when they break at the cut, and, being placed on the floor of a furnace, spread themselves flat. These plates cannot be blown more than four feet in length, and when great plates are wanted for mirrors or shop windows, a different process has to be used, that of casting.

CUT GLASS.

**Plate Glass.**—When glass is to be cast, it is melted in great quantities in large pots or reservoirs, until it is in a state of perfect fusion, in which condition it is kept for a long time. It is then drawn out by means of iron cisterns of considerable size, which are lowered into the furnace, filled, and raised out by machinery. The glass is poured from the cisterns upon tables of polished copper, of a large size, having a rim elevated as high as the desired thickness of the plate. In order to spread it perfectly and to make the two surfaces parallel, a heavy roller of polished copper, weighing five hundred pounds or more, is rolled over the plate, resting upon the rim at the edges; the excess falls off at the extremity of the table. These plates are ground with wet sand or emery, the grinding substance being placed between two plates, the surfaces of which are both ground at once. Emery of fine grain is used for a second grinding, and the plate is polished with putty.

**Flint Glass.**—Flint glass differs from ordinary window glass in containing a large quantity of red oxide of lead. The proportions of the materials used are about three parts of fine sand, two of red lead, and one of pearl ash, with small quantities of nitre, arsenic, and manganese. This glass is very transparent, is soft, has a great refractive power, and is employed in making fine glass vessels, and also for lenses and other optical glasses.

**Molding and Annealing.**—Ornamented forms may be molded upon the surface of glass vessels when in a hot state by employing metallic molds. The mold is usually made of copper, and the glass is blown into it. The term "cut glass" is applied to that which is cut upon the surface in fine figures by using rapidly revolving wheels of stone, iron, or wood. Glass when first made is exceedingly brittle; so much so, that a grain of sand dropped in a glass tumbler in that condition will cause it to burst into a thousand fragments. To obviate this difficulty, the glass is annealed by passing it through a long gallery heated to different temperatures, until at the point of withdrawal it has become quite cool.

**Toughened and Colored Glass.**—What is known as the De Bastie process for toughening glass, consists in exposing the red-hot glass to a bath of melted paraffine or wax, which leaves it so toughened that it will bear a heavy blow or a fall without breaking. Colored glass is made by mixing with the melted glass various metallic oxides, which is either worked into the body of the fused metal, or is applied (more commonly) as a surface color.

**The Process of Fusing.**—In a general way and in simple form, glass metal—as it is termed—is obtained by fusing in a clay pot, under intense heat, various proportions of sea or river sand, carbonate of potash or pearl ash, litharge or red lead, and black oxide of manganese, with sometimes pounded or broken glass added. The pots are made of fine clay, and are carefully built up by hand, and require from four to six months to perfect and dry ready for use; they are then annealed and inserted in the furnace, where they will last from three to six months, when they have to be renewed. The glass is withdrawn from the pots, when melted, on the ends of iron blowing rods, and is thus carried to the artificers, who are to make bottles, decanters, gas shades, or chimneys, or to mold tumblers, or employ it for whatever purpose is in hand The men who are employed at the furnaces wear masks of wood covered with tin, having holes cut for the eyes, and present a most peculiar appearance: the safeguard is rendered necessary, however, by the fierce heat.

**Statistics.**—Glass, in some of the coarser forms, was manufactured in America during the Colonial period, but it was not until about the middle of the eighteenth century that the business was established in the United States, one of the earliest factories being at Brooklyn, L. I., in 1754. In 1870 the number of glass factories in the United States was 201, employing 15,822 operatives, a capital of $14,000,000, and making a product valued at $20,000,000. This product is believed to have increased one-half in 1880. The exports have increased; in 1880 they amounted to $749,866; in 1881, $756,022. In England the value of the exports of the chief kinds of glass in 1876 was £917,043.

## SEWING MACHINES.

ABOUT the year 1841 Elias Howe, a native of Massachusetts, invented the sewing-machine, although mechanism for the same purpose had been made and patented more than 100 years before. Howe's machine used a needle with the eye in the point, and a shuttle for the purpose of uniting two edges in a seam, making the stitch by interlocking two threads. From Howe's time down to 1871, nearly 1,000 different patents relating to sewing-machines were issued. At present these machines are made in four classes as follows:

1. The shuttle or lock-stitch machines intended for family use.
2. The same machine intended for manufacturing purposes.
3. Double chain-stitch.
4. The single thread, tambour, or chain-stitch machines.

Of the first and second class the Weed, Howe, Singer, Wheeler & Wilson, and others, are chief representatives; of the third class the old Grover & Baker was a specimen, and of the fourth class the Willcox & Gibbs. Of late years attention has been chiefly directed in this connection to mechanical devices which should render the machines, as far as possible, noiseless, and to improvement in the feeding and tension. In the single-thread machine the needle is pointed at each end, and is pushed through the fabric on one side and caught at the other by pincers; the thread being thus pulled through backwards and forwards. This machine is used in shoemaking. In chain-stitch the thread is looped upon itself, by means of a curved shuttle, after it has passed through the cloth.

## CLOCKS AND WATCHES.

CLOCKS were first made about the twelfth century, and though materially improved in the course of time, the principle of their manufacture has remained the same: that of a series of cog-wheels working into each other, finally revolving the hands on a dial containing the numerals representing the hours, the wheels being worked by the gradual descent of a heavy weight wound up by a cord on a drum. Watches or pocket-clocks were made first in the fifteenth century, and the earliest of them were run by weights. Later on, the steel spring was adopted to produce the power necessary for turning the wheels: the spring, being coiled up in a box by winding, acts, during its extension, to drive the general mechanism. Watches were first made by machinery near Boston in 1850; by this means the inner works made of brass and steel can be duplicated exactly in large quantities, thousands of wheels a day being cut by a single machine under the guidance of one man.

## PRINTING PRESSES.

THE first printing press comprised merely the action of the screw, or the lever, upon a movable plate which pressed the paper against the type and thus took the impression. The first steam press was built in 1814 for the London *Times*. It was on the principle now generally used, of a revolving cylinder, carrying the sheet to be printed over the form containing the types. The capacity of this press has increased since its invention from 1,100 to 20,000 impressions in an hour, newspapers being printed by it at present from continuous rolls of paper fed and cut by machinery. The principles involved in the cylinder press were first made known in 1790, and only their application has been improved since. In America, the greatest improvements have been made by Richard M. Hoe. By this manufacturer the idea was applied of placing the type in frames on a horizontal cylinder, against which the sheets were pressed by exterior and smaller cylinders; the frames containing the type are called "turtles," and form segments of a circle about the cylinder. The substitution of stereotype plates for type has still further simplified printing by this method. The improvements of Bullock and Walter have brought about the "web-perfecting" press, printing from a continuous roll of paper four miles or more in length. A machine for taking impressions of type in soft paper, to be afterward stereotyped, is an American invention of date 1867. Printing by improved hand-presses still continues in the case of a limited number of impressions, in small job-work where extra care and elegance of typography are required, and where steam-power is not obtainable. Visiting

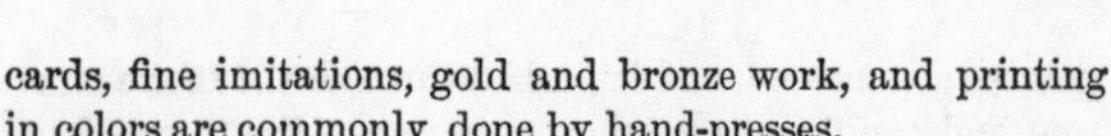

cards, fine imitations, gold and bronze work, and printing in colors are commonly done by hand-presses.

## SHIP BUILDING.

Ship-Building may be said to have started with Noah's Ark and to have culminated in the present steel or iron steamships, with water-tight compartments and screw propellers. Until the foundation of the American Government but little attention was paid to either speed or beauty in ship construction; since then the consideration of the proper lines to accomplish the greatest speed with the least resistance and friction has become general among commercial nations. The first process in ship-building is to make a model of alternate strips of pine and cedar, three or more feet in length, the exact representation of the vessel to be built. From this model three drawings are made, one giving the entire side of the ship, another a section of the length of the ship, the third a vertical section dividing the ship in halves. From enlarged patterns of these plans the workmen select and shape to the required dimension every timber for the ship. In the ship-yard the keel is laid on blocks close to the water's edge, next the stern and stern-posts are set, and then the ribs, or curved timbers called "futtocks," which make the frame of the ship and determine its shape. The planks and timbers which need curving are steamed and bent, the solid timbers are usually live-oak, the outside planking of oak planks, varying in thickness from four to ten inches, the decks of yellow pine; the rudder is made of oak and elm. The planking is calked by driving oakum into the seams, which are then covered with pitch, the bottom is covered with sheets of copper four feet long and fourteen inches broad, nailed on. Iron is now frequently used even in wooden ships for knees, deck-beams, and even for hollow masts. A vessel constructed wholly of iron is much lighter than a wooden vessel of the same size. For an iron ship each plate is prepared in the rolling-mill from exact drawings, holes for the rivets being punched by machinery; the keel is made of iron bars riveted together, and the plates are riveted, overlapping each other, to iron upright ribs, making each compartment a floating vessel in itself, greatly increasing the security of the ship.

IRON SHIP IN FRAME ON THE STOCKS.

## MUSICAL INSTRUMENTS.

All musical sounds are produced, instrumentally speaking, by vibration, either through percussion, as in the piano, or by the passage of a current of air through an aperture, upon the reed of the metal or other material, as in reed instruments, or by means of the human fingers, or by a bow, as in stringed instruments. The organ is one of the earliest instruments based upon what are known as "Pan's Pipes," hollow reeds of various lengths bound together and played upon by the mouth, each pipe being graded in size to some natural note of music. This being the principle, it is easy to see that the mechanism could be worked by water or a bellows, and in many other ways changed and improved according to taste. The cabinet or parlor organ is an American invention. About 32,000 of these were made and sold in America in 1870, and nearly as many of pianofortes; and the manufacture of these instruments has greatly increased during the last ten years. The principle of the pianoforte, that of percussion, simply involved the vibration of a series of wires by the tapping of hammers within the body of the instrument, controlled by keys on a key-board in front, operated by the performer. The first American piano was made in Philadelphia in 1775, and that city, by the latter part of the eighteenth century, had reached a considerable reputation in the manufacture of musical instruments. At that time, while American pianos were put together with screws, those made abroad were only glued. Pianos were not invented until 1714, and at first the hammer was raised from below by a button attached to an upright wire fixed on the back end of the key. This was afterwards gradually remedied until the present action was perfected. Formerly the strings of the pianoforte were all thin wire; now the bass strings are very thick and coated with a thin coil of copper wire, and the thickness, strength and tension of the strings, all diminish from the lower to the upper notes. In the upright piano, the strings run vertically from top to bottom, instead of horizontally as in grand and square pianos. The grand pianoforte has three strings to each of the upper and middle notes, and only two to the lower notes. Musical instruments, in general, are more largely manufactured in Germany, and more cheaply, than in any other country, these including reed instruments such as the clarionet, and brass instruments—trumpets, trombones, etc. The American piano is, perhaps, the best in the world, although those of certain makers in England and France have a high reputation. The best church organs are the German.

## BOOK-MAKING.

The manufacture of books has become so extensive, that in many instances it is conducted in large factories, wherein every process is completed. Great publishing houses not infrequently produce their own books, even so far as casting the type from which they are printed. Type-metal is composed of a large proportion of tin compounded with lead and antimony, The type is made in molds of copper, in which the form of the letter is impressed by a punch of hardened steel on which the letter is cut. In the manufacture of books, the type, which is kept in cases, divided alphabetically, is first set in a "composing stick," from which it is transferred to galleys, the latter being small wooden frames designed to receive the type in columns. From the galley it goes into pages, which are locked up in iron chases or frames, and placed in a printing-press for printing. From the composing-room to the press-room—if the book is to be electrotyped, to the foundry, and thence to the press-room—is the order of movement. The process of electrotyping is simply the transfer of the face of a page of type to a metal plate, by means of the galvanic battery, which takes a thin impression of the face of the type in copper. After electrotyping, the type is distributed and again ready for use. From the printing-press the printed sheets go to the drying-room, where they are dried under a temperature of 100 to 120 degrees. They are afterwards subjected to hydraulic pressure, then folded into pages by machinery, and hammered, pressed and sewed, when they are bound according to taste in pasteboard covered with muslin, morocco, or calf-skin.

## CIGARS AND TOBACCO.

The process of making cigars is simple. A sound piece of leaf shaped like one of the gores of a globe is placed on the work-bench. A bundle of fragments of leaves is then laid across the center of this gore, and rolled up in it, by passing the hand over it. The point of the cigar is shaped with a pair of scissors, and secured by means of gum and chicory. The cigar is next placed against a gauge, and a portion of the broad end cut off square. In European countries female labor is chiefly employed in cigar-making. The city of Bremen alone employs more than five thousand persons in this business, and exports over three hundred millions annually. In 1879 the total acreage of tobacco in the United States was 638,841; the amount of product, 472,661,159 pounds; the value being about $50,000,000. Up to 1877 tobacco had paid to the United States Government a revenue of more than four hundred and twenty-six millions of dollars in sixteen years. The number of cigars manufactured in New York in 1880 was about six hundred and fifty millions; of cigarettes, about three hundred and fifty millions. Manufactured tobacco for smoking and chewing comprises granulated, fine-cut, and long-cut; the Virginia tobaccos being the most popular for this purpose. Louisiana is noted for an especial brand called "Perique," which is not grown elsewhere. Kentucky tobaccos are usually of a darker grade, while those of North Carolina and Virginia are of the bright yellow, highly-flavored class. In the manufacture of cigars a coloring liquid is used, by which any desired tint may be obtained, without regard either to the quality of the leaf or mode of curing. The consumption averages one and a half pounds per inhabitant in England, and six pounds in the United States.

## CONFECTIONERY.

The cultivation of the sugar-cane and the manufacture of sugar and rock-candy are of great antiquity, being brought into Europe from Asia about the eighth century. Immediately after the discovery of America this industry was established in San Domingo. There are in the United States several hundred concerns engaged in manufacturing confectionery; twenty-five or thirty in New York City alone. The materials used in this business comprise sugar, honey, molasses, cream, gum-arabic, alum, cocoanuts, peanuts, chocolate, liquorice, jujube, flax-seed, coriander-seed, caraways, cinnamon, cloves, and Iceland-moss. The flavors used are birch, boneset, cayenne pepper, cinnamon, ginger, horehound, lemon, musk, peppermint, raspberry, rose, sassafras, and wintergreen. Coloring materials are cochineal, indigo, and saffron. Candy is manufactured into rock, stick, plumbs drops, lozenges, and broken candy. The principal process is to boil a strong syrup of sugar, and then to crystalize it, color it, and shape it for drying into its various forms. Both machinery and hand-labor are used. Candy is largely adulterated with plaster-of-paris, glucose, lamp-black, glue, tonka-beans, tartaric acid, sulphuric acid, aniline, gamboge and chrome yellow, ultramarine, oil of turpentine, prussic acid, extract of rotten cheese, and fusel-oil.

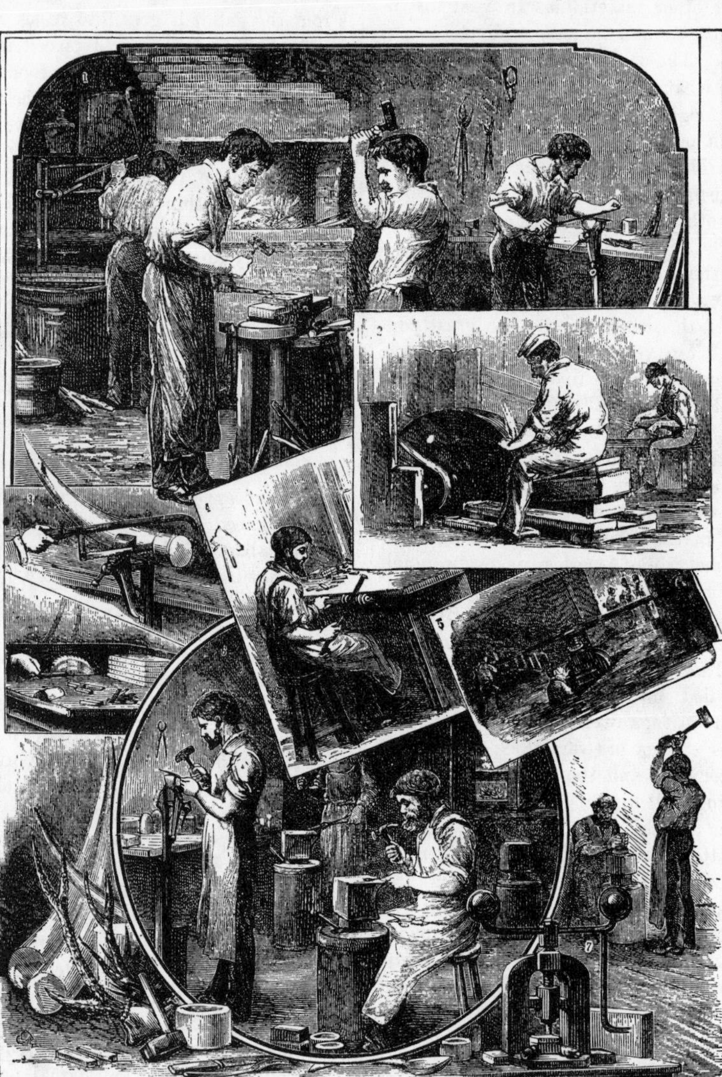

KNIFE, FORK, AND SPOON MAKERS.

1. Forging, filing, and tempering blades.
2. Grinding and polishing blades.
3. Cutting ivory.
4. Boring the handle for shaft of blade.
5. Stamping spoons.
6. Forging spoons and forks.
7. Press for cutting out spaces between prongs of forks.

## CUTLERY.

Until within a comparatively recent period the best cutlery had been manufactured in England, which supplied the civilized world. The manufacture was introduced into the United States early in the present century, and the introduction of the trip-hammer for forging blades—an American improvement—gave a great impetus to the business. The introduction of machinery for shaping the blades was the next improvement, and by these means the manufacture became greatly cheapened. The processes through which a knife has to pass before being finished number sixteen, and these are all done by machinery. As an illustration of the extent of this manufacture, it may be stated that in one establishment, the following raw materials were used in a single year: 2,000 tons of anthracite coal; 25,000 bushels of charcoal; 400,000 pounds of grindstones; 44,000 pounds of emery; 3,000 pounds of beeswax; for handles, 36,000 pounds of ivory; 112,000 pounds of ebony; 57,000 pounds of rosewood; 305,000 pounds of cocoawood; every day two tons of steel were used, and a large amount of silver was employed in plating blades and handles.

## SUGAR REFINING.

Sugar is first put into copper dissolving pans, about eight feet in diameter, with hot water. The solution is raised to the required heat by means of the steam-heated coils which encase the pans. From the pans the syrup passes through filters of thick twill cotton cloth, from which it runs free from the mass of its impurities, but still colored. To remove the color, it is passed through iron cylinders from five to ten feet in diameter, and fifty feet in height, filled with granulated charcoal or bone-black. From these cylinders it comes out perfectly colorless, and is evaporated and crystalized in a vacuum pan; thence it goes to a heating pan, where it is raised to a temperature of 180 degrees, when it is drawn off and poured into conical iron molds and left to drain. In the manufacture of crystal and crushed sugar, the crystals are separated by means of what is called a centrifugal machine. Sugar is also made from the sorghum, or Chinese sugar-cane, and from maple sap. Within recent years it has been extensively made in the United States from the French white sugar-beet, from which, in France, a very large quantity is annually manufactured.

## BRUSHES.

Brushes are made from hairs, hogs' bristles, strips of whalebone, vegetable filaments, etc., fastened together in a handle, or in holes drilled for the purpose in a stock of wood or bone. Bristles, however, are chiefly used in this manufacture, and are mostly obtained from Russia, those of the Ukraine being the most esteemed. Germany also supplies a large quantity of bristles. When taken from the animal they are assorted by hand into different colors and sizes, being first thoroughly washed. The white bristles are bleached with sulphur and by other chemical agents. The assorting is done by passing them through a species of combs, which catches and removes the coarser of the bristles, using at each process a finer comb. In making the brushes each operator devotes himself to a special variety. The packing, papering, and labeling, and other processes of shipments, are done by boys and girls. In tooth-brushes and some others, the bristles are fastened with wire. The delicate brushes for artists are made from the fur of badgers, squirrels, and sable; the hairs being thrust into a large end of a quill, which has been soaked beforehand, and in shrinking holds the brush. Small brushes of this kind are also often made by being mounted in metallic taps, with wooden handles.

## PETROLEUM OIL.

Before the discovery of petroleum oil wells, the illuminating mineral oil was made from a species of coal called "albertite," by distillation, the mineral being heated in a retort, and the product afterwards condensed into crude oil. So much of the process being found to be conducted subterraneously, the manufacture of kerosene oil takes it up at this point, the remaining work being simply the refining and removal of the volatile constituents of naphtha, benzine, keroseline, etc. From the residiuum, after the refining and hydraulic pressure, comes the paraffine used in the manufacture of candles. In refining, various acids and other ingredients are employed, the process being conducted in a machine called the "agitator." The principal oil grounds of the United States are located in Pennsylvania, Ohio, and West Virginia. The business of boring for oil began about 1845, near Pittsburgh, but was not conducted extensively until ten years later, when the great oil fever commenced. Of late years the petroleum trade is said to have employed, in America, as many hands as coal-mining and the working of iron.

## OUT-DOOR AND IN-DOOR GAMES.

The manufacture of material for out-door and in-door amusements has grown into an enormous value and extent during the last half century. The various kinds of cards, chess, and checker-men, dice, and other articles for in-door amusements are mostly made in Germany, France and England, though considerable manufactures in this line have sprung up in the United States during the past twenty years. The manufacture of billiard-tables and their appointments is largely conducted in America, and extensive concerns with large factories make out-door games, such as croquet, lawn-tennis, base-ball, cricket, etc., and this line of business is conducted exclusively by large firms in all the principal cities. Billiard-table manufacturers make as many as 1,000 billiard-tables each a year, valued at from $100 to $1,000 each, according to size and style. The bed of a billiard-table is made of solid slabs, four being required for each; the woodwork is rosewood, walnut, birch, mahogany, the California laurel, maple, oak, etc. The ivory balls are turned by machinery; the billiard-cloth is made in France and Belgium; the cues are turned and seasoned, as many as fifty dozen per day being made in a single manufactory.

## HATS.

The materials used for hat-making are the furs of the beaver, seal, rabbit, and other animals, and the wool of the sheep. The furs of most animals are mixed with the longer kind of thin hair, which is obliged to be first pulled out, after which the fur is cut off with the knife. The materials to be felted are intimately mixed together by the operation of bowing, which depends upon the vibrations of an elastic string, the rapid alternations of its motion being peculiarly well adapted to remove all irregular knots and adhesions among the fibres, and to dispose them in a very light uniform arrangement. This mass is dipped into a liquor containing a little sulphuric acid, and when intended to form a hat it is first molded into a large conical figure, and this is afterwards reduced in its dimensions by working it for several hours with the hands. It is then formed into a flat surface with several concentrated folds, which are still further compacted, in order to make the brim and the circular part of the crown, and forced on a block which serves as a mold for the cylindrical part. The nap or outer portion of the fur is raised with a fine wire brush, and the hat is subsequently dyed and stiffened on the inside with glue.

A silk hat consists of a light, stiff body, covered with a plush of silk, the manufacture of this plush being itself an important industry. The fabrication of silk hats has been carried to great perfection, not only in England, but in other European countries and the United States.

## INDIA-RUBBER.

**Caoutchouc.**—This substance, called also elastic gum and india-rubber, is obtained from different vegetables, but chiefly from the Iatropha Elastica. It exists in the form of juice, and is dried by applying it in successive coatings to clay molds of various shapes. After it is dry the clay is crushed and shaken out. This substance is wonderfully flexible and elastic, and restores itself instantly after being extended to many times its original dimensions. Slips of india-rubber may be made to cohere by boiling them in contact for a certain time in water, and in this way some articles are made. When heated to about 200 degrees Fahrenheit this substance may be spread by rollers upon cloth so as to form a permanent coating. Caoutchouc is of great use in the formation of many instruments which require to be elastic and impenetrable to water. Shoes are now made of it in great numbers, and found to exclude perfectly the wet. A solution of this gum spread upon leather and cloth renders them water-proof and even air-tight. An elegant elastic web is made from fibers of caoutchouc wound with silk and woven. The elasticity which is lost by stretching is restored by a hot smoothing-iron. Its adhesiveness and friction are the properties by which india-rubber erases black lead from paper.

## FURNITURE.

As in most other instances in manufacture, in furniture that which was formerly an art and a craft is now almost wholly performed by machinery. Vast factories now turn out every article for household decoration or use by the thousand, and even the construction of each of these is subdivided so that every part is made by its appropriate mechanism. Furniture is chiefly made of wood: rosewood, black walnut, chestnut, cherry, oak, ash, pine, mahogany, satinwood, maple, etc., each becoming in turn fashionable, but all being extensively used. In metals, brass, iron and bronze are used. Decorations are gilding, carving, turning, inlaying, painting, enameling, varnishing and staining. Furniture takes its name, as to style, from the period indicated, as "Louis Quinze," "Queen Anne," "Renaissance," etc. The manufacture of chairs from maple, beech, etc., with split-rattan seats, is carried on by steam-power in great establishments, and enormous quantities are exported to all parts of the world. Some of the larger factories for cabinetmaking work up from 4,000,000 to 8,000,000 feet of lumber every year, and employ from 500 to 1,000 men. A return has been made recently to mediæval designs. In England and Australia, fashions prevalent during the last century have been revived; in America the Louis XIV. style is very popular.

PITS IN A TANNERY YARD.

## LEATHER.

The preparation of animal skins for the purpose of changing them to leather, comprises simply their subjection to the action of tannic acid, which preserves them from decomposition. Among the skins which are subjected to this process are those of the ox, cow, calf, buffalo, horse, sheep, lamb, goat, kid, deer, dog, seal, and hog. The lighter forms of leather are called skins; the heavier, hides. Sheep and lamb skins are dressed for use in book-binding, deer-skins are made into the *shamoy* of trade, so called from the chamois of the Alps, of which it was formerly made; dog-skins furnish gloves—as do also kid and rats; seal-skins are made into "patent leather" by varnishing one side; hog and pig skins are used in making saddles. In tanning, the hides are soaked in water to wash and soften them; they are then heaped up for a time, and afterwards hung in a heated room until the softening loosens the hair, which is easily removed; they are now ready for the tan-bark, and are placed in pits in layers, with oak-bark or other tanning material between them, and are suffered to remain there for months, water being let into the pits. This is the proper, healthy mode of tanning, which is now, however, very generally superseded by new processes to hurry the work. In these new processes there are employed catechu, cutch, gambier, valonia (a species of acorn), sumac leaves, and other materials. After being tanned, the hides are submitted to pressure by being rubbed and rolled, by this means becoming compact and solid. Morocco leather is made from goat and sheep skins, and gains its peculiar appearance by being finished with engraved boxwood balls. Russia leather obtains its well-known aromatic odor from the oil of the birch-bark used in tanning it.

## FIRE-ARMS.

Fire-arms are divided into small-arms and artillery, or ordnance. The former include rifles, pistols, muskets, and fowling-pieces; the latter, heavy guns for fortifications and war-vessels, and light artillery for field-batteries. Small-arms are bored or drilled, heavy guns are cast. Rifling is done by reaming out the interior of a barrel spirally to give the projectile a certain twist which affords greater directness, speed, and penetrating force. The principles of rifling, breech-loading, and the revolving cylinder, are of ancient date, but failed to be perfected until modern times. In heavy ordnance the German Krupp manufacture excels all others. In rifled small-arms (breech-loading) it is doubtful if the American Peabody, Sharps, and Remington arms have been equaled anywhere. The American revolvers of Colt, and Smith & Wesson have a no less high reputation. Of English make, the Whitworth heavy guns and the Martini-Henry breech-loading rifle are celebrated ; so also are the German "needle-gun" and the French Minié rifle.

## CLOTHING.

FORMERLY clothing was "made to order," as a rule, by professional tailors, excepting in those instances when it was "home-made" of homespun, as was the case in the early history of the American Colonies. The clothing trade, as it now exists, grew out of the "slop-shops" of English and American seaport towns, where rough goods made up for sailors were sold at high prices, and from the business in second-hand clothing carried on by the Jews in all the principal European and American cities. The "ready-made clothing" business, springing from these sources, rapidly grew in extent and improved in character, until at present this is one of the most important manufactures, especially in the United States. With the aid of the sewing-machine, and by the employment of an army of workers, male and female, in their homes, enormous establishments in the principal cities carry on this business, in which many great fortunes have been made during the past twenty-five years.

## POTTERY AND CHINA, OR PORCELAIN.

POTTERY is made of baked clay, and may be glazed, but is always opaque ; the difference between it and porcelain being that the latter is finer in quality and translucent. Ordinary pottery has been made, from time immemorial, of common brick clay, mixed with water, shaped in molds, by the hand, or on a wheel, and baked. Porcelain is made from kaolin, a fine white clay. The process is nearly the same in both instances, differing only in the material, the care used in the manufacture, and the nature and quality of the decorations employed. The great Staffordshire works in England cover a district of forty-eight square miles, and employ more than 100,000 operatives. The porcelain works at Sèvres, near Paris, France, are noted for the manufacture of costly and beautiful vases and domestic ware. China and Japan have long held high rank in this art, and within recent years their chinaware and common pottery have been extensively imported into Europe and America. Holland was long noted for the production of *delft*, so called after the town of Delft, where it was first made.

## CARPETS.

WOVEN carpets were first used in Oriental countries, and until a comparatively modern date were imported thence, the manufacture not being elsewhere carried on. At present, carpets are made in most of the European countries, and in the United States. Though sometimes made by hand, they are usually woven by machinery, and either printed on a fabric by means of rollers, or formed of different colored yarns. The leading carpets in use are Turkey, Brussels, tapestry-Brussels, Wilton, Kidderminster, velvet, and ingrain.

## SALT.

THE manufacture of salt, either from the product of natural springs or by mining, is practically the same as in the case of rock-salt; it has to be dissolved in water to form the brine, which in springs flows naturally. Salt is mined in England, Germany, Poland, and in other parts of the world. The immense salt mines of Salzburg are noted. Salt springs are found in England, and in the United States the manufacture is one of the most important industries, rock-salt being found in Western Virginia, Louisiana, and elsewhere, and salt springs in nearly every State, New York, however, furnishing nearly one-half the entire domestic supply, chiefly from the celebrated springs of Onondaga County. The salt-water or brine is pumped from these springs to reservoirs, where the impurities sink to the bottom, being aided in the movement by the addition of a small percentage of alum. It is then run into tanks six inches deep, and 16x18 feet in dimensions, exposed to the air, where it is evaporated ; or it is boiled in kettles holding 100 gallons each, when the impurities are precipitated. New York produces about 10,000,000 bushels annually, and the total production in the United States, in 1880, was 29,800,298 bushels, Michigan being the heaviest producer, in quantity about 15,000,000 bushels. The annual production of salt in Great Britain is equal to £1,500,000.

**General Statistics.**—If we sum up all branches of manufacture in the United States and Great Britain, we find the following result :

| | *Operatives.* | *Manufactures.* | *Per Operative.* | *Total Horse-Power.* |
|---|---|---|---|---|
| United States | 2,704,600 | £888,000,000 | £312 | 3,153,000 |
| Great Britain | 2,930,000 | 758,000,000 | 224 | 3,828,000 |
| Australia | ........ | 13,000,000 | .... | ........ |

VARIOUS subterraneous excavations for the purpose of obtaining the deposits of metals and other minerals are termed Mines. Mining is the process of digging to, and otherwise approaching, these deposits which lie singly or in groups in certain geological strata. Minerals are the metalliferous ores and other products which have been deposited by the processes of Nature, but which have generally undergone considerable change in composition and relation, being sometimes found as a native metal, or more usually a component of different metals. What is known as "placer" mining is surface work performed on sand, supposed to contain metallic deposits, usually by the side of a river or in the bed of a mountain torrent. In the latter instance the treatment consists simply of washing the sand in a movable vehicle called the "cradle," the metallic product sinking to the bottom, by gravity, where it is found after the sand is washed out. Minerals usually lie in sections, or divisions, called veins, which are sheets of metalliferous matter, and either occur in vertical or horizontal fissures—as is the case in the Galena limestone, of the upper Mississippi, or in segregated veins interposed between strata which occur in metamorphic rocks, as is the case in the granitoid rock of the Alleghanies. Fissure veins, true veins or lodes, are formed in fissures, which have been produced by volcanic or earthquake action. The horizontal direction of a vein is called the "strike" or "cross;" the vertical angle which it makes with the horizontal is called the "dip." The ores contained in fissure veins are various, such as silver, copper, lead, tin, zinc, antimony, and other metals. Gold is less common in this form than in isolated veins. Silver, in the largest quantities, occurs in this class of vein. The Comstock Lode and various others in Nevada are examples. In mining, where the mineral occurs in veins or lodes, as copper and lead ore, shafts are sunk perpendicularly for raising the ore, and these are crossed by horizontal galleries, termed levels, which are driven upon the lode with small upright shafts called "winces." The levels are generally sixty feet apart, and are known by their depths in feet or fathoms. One consolidation of four lead mines in Cornwall, England, comprises sixty-three miles of underground workings. The ore is struck out from the solid body with picks, and is transported on small wagons, sometimes drawn by boys, sometimes by horse-power, and at others by endless chains worked by steam. By one or other of these methods, it is carried to the base of the shaft, where the wagons are run on to an elevator, hoisted to the top of the shaft, and dumped. Sometimes the hoisting is performed by simple hand or horse-power windlass, but usually in well-appointed mines this is done by steam. In such mines, also, Bessemer iron cages are used for hoisting the minerals. In some instances steam is made at the surface, and carried into the mine in pipes; in others, chambers are hewn out of the solid rock or mineral, underground, and in these powerful engines perform the work. The principal metals and other minerals which are employed in the arts and manufactures, and which are mined for use, are the following: gold, silver, mercury, copper, iron, lead, zinc, tin, nickel, antimony, manganese, bismuth, cobalt, platinum, coal, sulphur, gypsum, graphite, etc.

**Coal Mining.**—The usual mode of reaching coal is to sink a perpendicular shaft, though sometimes an inclined plane is adopted. When the shaft has been sunk to the necessary depth, a level is driven on each side, which serves to conduct the accumulation of water from the workings. From this point the coal is worked out as far as is practicable along the rise of the stratum. In some mines the coal is taken out in parallel spaces of fifteen feet wide, intersected by passages at right angles, between the two, masses of coal being left for the support of the roof of the seam. In getting out the coal, the miner undercuts the seam with a light pick for two or three feet inwards, and then, driving in wedges at the top of the seam, breaks away the overhanging portion. Blasting is sometimes, though not often, used. In a shaft there are usually four divisions, the two center ones being used for sending up and down the men and the coal; one of the others contains the pumps, and the other is used to withdraw foul air from the mine, a furnace being constructed at the bottom of it. The cages are suspended to a flat wire rope, and run up and down on guide rods. The ventilation in the mine is secured by doors in the passages, called traps, which open and shut at proper intervals. Coal is found chiefly in Great Britain and in the United States, of all the countries in the world. In 1876 the amount of coal mined in Great Britain was 148,989,385 tons; the production of the United States, in the same year, was 49,005,748 tons. Germany came next with 43,364,968 tons. The product of all the rest of the world amounted to 150,000,000 tons, the entire product for that year being 276,830,965 tons. Coal is classified as bituminous, or soft coal, and anthracite, or hard coal. The principal deposit of the latter, in the United States, is in an area of about 470 square miles, in Pennsylvania. In 1878 Australia produced coal to the amount of £710,000.

"HEWERS," "HOLERS," AND "PUTTERS."

**Copper Mining.**—Copper, in its native or metal state, or in combination with other metals and minerals, is generally distributed throughout the world. It is found in large quantities in Russia, Norway, Sweden, Great Britain, Prussia, Austria, France, Spain, Italy, Turkey, Algeria, Australia, East Indies, Japan, South America, Cuba, Jamaica, Mexico, and the United States. Copper was enumerated among the minerals of New England as early as 1632, and smelting-works were set up in Massachusetts in 1648. It was discovered in Maryland, Virginia, North Carolina, and South Carolina during the colonial period, and very rich mines were found in Tennessee. In 1709 the oldest mining charter in the country was granted to a company to work copper-mines in Connecticut. In 1766, 80 tons of copper ore valued at £100 sterling a ton, were exported from New York. The Lake Superior copper-mines were known to the French Jesuits before 1660. This region was surveyed about 1825, and in 1843 was ceded to the United States by the Chippeways. The following year the great copper-fever broke out, when speculators and miners went mad over Lake Superior copper. Innumerable companies were formed, and thousands of miners and adventurers settled in the region. It was not until 1850 that coppermining at Lake Superior was based on a firm basis. From that time the annual product from the mines was enormous; much of it was native metal, though silver was sometimes found in connection with it. Copper is classed as follows: 1. Mass-copper is cut out with cold-chisels in lumps of several hundred weight, and yields from 70 to 80 per cent. of pure metal. 2. Barrel-work, consisting of pieces too large to be stamped, and which are packed in barrels for transportation. 3. Stamp-work, which is the ore crushed in steam stamp-mills and packed in casks and barrels; before crushing, the ore is roasted, when care must be taken to prevent the copper from fusing and oxidizing. In extracting copper from its ores, the process that is followed out is tedious and complicated, arising from the difficulty of separating the iron and sulphur found in combination with the copper. In 1872 a single mine in the Lake Superior region yielded 8,000 tons of pure copper, nearly one-tenth of the production of the whole world. It is estimated that the total production of copper has more than doubled within a quarter of a century, the increase being largely due to the Lake Superior mines. Notwithstanding this, the United States still import ore from Cuba and Chili, pig and bar copper from other parts of South America, and sheathing-copper from Great Britain. In England the Cornwall and Devon mines are enormously rich. The value of copper is derived from its properties of tenacity, softness, and ductility. It is brought to market in sheets and plates, and is made into sheathing, stills, condensers, boilers, rods, and innumerable utensils. Copper, when combined with zinc, becomes brass; combined with tin, it makes bronze, gun-metal, and bell-metal. Formerly it was largely employed in coinage, but has been considerably superseded by a composition of nickel and copper, and in England by bronze. The name copper is derived from that of the island of Cyprus, where it was obtained first by the Greeks. In 1878 Australia produced copper and tin amounting to £1,771,000, the average yield of copper being 14,500 tons.

**Tin Mining.**—Tin is a soft metal, very malleable, and can be beaten out into thin leaves, in which form it is known as tin-foil. It was one of the earliest metals known, as it entered into the composition of bronze, of which the most ancient metallic weapons and tools were made. Tin was obtained from Cornwall, England, by the Phœnicians, and to this date England is the greatest tin-producing country, having raised in 1876 about 13,690 tons of dressed ore, or 8,500 tons of metal. Tin is found in Bohemia and Saxony, Spain, Portugal, and Malacca, and the neighboring islands. It has been found in large quantities in Tasmania, Van Diemen's Land, and in Queensland, Australia. In the latter district it was discovered in 1872, when 2,000 men obtained the metal to the value of £100,000 sterling, which was doubled in the next year. In 1876, Australia exported 8,392 tons. In 1878 prices fell, and the yield was much lessened. In reducing tin ore it is stamped to a very fine powder, after which it is washed to remove the impurities from the ore, and is next deprived of its sulphur and arsenic in a reverberatory furnace; from this furnace the reduced tin is run off into a cast-iron pan, from which it is ladled into molds to produce blocks or ingots of a convenient size; it still has to go through a refining process to remove the oxide of tin and other impure properties.

**Lead Mining.**—Pure lead is of very rare occurrence; it is usually obtained from the native sulphide of lead, known as *galena*, which, when tolerably pure, is smelted readily. The ore is roasted in a reverberatory furnace, in masses of twenty to forty cwts. at a time, being first washed in an apparatus for the purpose, to remove impurities. After the first roasting the ore is thoroughly mixed, the furnace temperature is suddenly raised, sulphureous acid is thrown off, and the lead is partially reduced. Lime is now thrown in, mixed with slag and unreduced ore, when the lead becomes entirely separated and runs off through a tap-hole. Lead reduced from galena contains from eight to ten ounces to the ton, of silver. It also contains antimony and tin as impurities, and these are separated by fusing the metal in shallow pans, when these metals come to the surface in the form of oxides and are skimmed off. Lead is desilverized by melting it and allowing it to cool slowly, the process being accompanied by brisk stirring, when a portion of the lead crystalizes in small grains, the remainder being rich in silver. The granulated portion is then taken away in a strainer, and this process is repeated until the silver and lead are completely separated and in different vessels.

The great lead district of the United States lies on either side of the Mississippi River in Northwestern Illinois, Southwestern Wisconsin, and Iowa, and in the State of Missouri. It is bounded by the Wisconsin River on the north, by the Apple River in Illinois on the south, and on the east by the eastern branch of the Pecatonika; on the west it extends to twelve miles west of the Mississippi. In 1846 the quantity of American lead sold in St. Louis and New Orleans was about 55,000,000 pounds. The lead-mines of Great Britain and Spain yield the largest quantity of this metal—about 75,000 tons each annually. The importation into the United States of lead in pigs, bars, and ore, declined between 1871 and 1881 from $3,711,785 to $325,076. Lead ore is found to some extent in New Hampshire, Massachusetts, New York, Pennsylvania, Virginia, Tennessee, North Carolina, and Kentucky. In Colorado, the silver-mining district shows a large proportion of lead, which is, however, neglected for the rich output of silver.

**Mercury.**—Mercury, popularly known as "quicksilver," is the only metal that remains fluid at ordinary temperatures, though it freezes at − 39° and boils at 662°, when it vaporizes. This metal is usually obtained from deposits of cinnabar, in which it occurs in the proportion of 86.2 to 13.8. Cinnabar is a rare mineral, and the most productive mines of it are those of Almaden, in Spain, which have been worked for nearly 2,500 years. Next to these in importance are the mines of Idria, in Austria, which were discovered in 1497, and which produce 330 tons of quicksilver annually; other mines exist in Germany, Hungary, Peru, California, China, Japan and, Mexico. In California, mercurial ore was discovered before gold, and in 1845 a company began to work the New Almaden mine, near San José. The annual yield of all the California mines is about 2,000,000 pounds, or about one-third of the total production of the world. In obtaining the metal from the ore the latter is burned in a furnace, when the mercury is collected in a condensing chamber, or it is distilled with iron filings or slaked lime, which combines with the sulphur and sets the mercury free. From certain chemical preparations of mercury we obtain calomel and corrosive sublimate, the latter a virulent poison, whose antidote is the white of eggs; we also get from it vermilion, and it is largely used as an amalgam for separating gold from the pulverized quartz, and in the manufacture of mirrors, being spread upon one surface of plate glass.

It is said that the Old Almaden mine in Spain controlled the Chinese market for quicksilver until a few years ago, when the New Almaden mine shipped 10,000 flasks (of 76½ lbs.) to Hong Kong, and sold them so much below the market price as to drive out the Spanish article. The export of quicksilver from the United States, which was 2,152,499 pounds, fell off after that year, the production being lessened, and in 1874 the export was only 501,389 pounds. It has, however, recovered, and in 1880 amounted to 3,574,412 pounds.

**Gold Mining.**—The first mines of gold were probably worked in Eastern Asia. Ethiopia, Nubia, and Egypt also contributed largely of this metal, down to a period as late as the fifteenth or sixteenth century. At about this period gold mining was prosecuted through Central and Northern Europe, and especially in Germany, though the average annual production of gold in the mines of Europe was not more than £100,000. About the year 1700 gold mines were discovered in Russia, and in the latter part of the eighteenth century, the product had doubled. Gold was first shipped from America in 1502, and for the next twenty years this country produced about $250,000 a year. Mexico and Peru added largely to the gold of the world, and by 1520 the supply from the Western Continent reached ten million dollars. From 1700 to 1810 the product of the American mines amounted to 4,000 million dollars. In 1848 gold was discovered in California, where at first "placer" mining prevailed, and for the following ten years California produced 500 million dollars. In 1851 gold was discovered in Australia, near Bathurst, and the total value of the gold mines in Australia, between 1851 and 1859, was 100,000,000 pounds.

Gold had been discovered in New South Wales as early as 1839, but it was not until February, 1851, that Edward Haman Hargraves, a California miner, verified this by "striking" it in paying quantities. The first "nugget" discovered weighed thirteen ounces, and at once crowds flocked to the new "El Dorado," as many as 1,800 men being counted in one day *en route* to Bathurst. At first a license of 30s. per head was charged by the Government for the privilege of searching for gold, but this was soon greatly reduced. In the same year (1851) of the discoveries in New South Wales, gold was discovered in Victoria, about seventy miles northwest of the city of Melbourne, again by a California miner, one James William Esmond. Discoveries at Mount Alexander and Ballarat followed, a Government license system was adopted, and speedily the usual scenes of a new gold-mining locality were re-enacted. At first alluvial deposits were worked (placer-mining), but this gave place to quartz-mining, and in 1878 only 35 per cent. of the gold obtained was alluvial, the remaining 65 per cent. being from quartz. Rich veins were found at a depth of 2,393 feet, 1,200 feet below the sea level, and at Sandhurst and Ballarat veins were worked at depths of 1,458 and 1,114 feet respectively. The average yield was found to be 11 dwts. and a fraction. In 1878 there were 1,036 steam-engines employed in mines, 750 of which were on quartz reefs. The number of miners employed in 1879 was 37,553, the number of Chinese being 9,110. The total value of the machinery in use was £1,899,788. The proximate area of the gold-fields was 1,234 square miles, and at least seventeen shafts were sunk more than 1,000 feet deep. From the first discovery of the Victoria gold-fields to 1880, the quantity of gold obtained amounted to 48,817,596 ounces, valued at £195,270,384, at £4 per ounce; the average yield was about 1,700,000 ounces per annum. Gold was also mined largely in Queensland, though not of so pure a quality as that found in Victoria. The Queensland yield amounted in 1873 to £717,540, and in 1877 had increased to £1,611,103. In 1860 gold was discovered in Nova Scotia, and since that time has been regularly mined in that province with a fair average yield. The value of the total amount of gold produced in the United States in 1881 was $36,500,000; the total amount produced since 1848, $1,557,141,532. The total amount of gold in existence in the world at the end of 1881 was $7,763,223,772. Quartz-mining is conducted by tunnelling the side of a hill where the gold is found, or excavating a shaft from the surface; galleries, cross-cuts, and winces being laid at intervals. As the quartz is got out it is taken to the stamp mill, where it is pulverized by a number of strong iron pestles, worked by steam or water-power: each stamp can pulverize from one to three tons of rock in twenty-four hours: as the rock becomes dust a stream of water carries it through a fine iron screen, whence it flows away in a shallow sluice, where the gold is extracted by mercury. Much of the ore passes away in tailings, and is treated by roasting or by chemical process. To extract the metal, new modes of reduction are constantly being invented, and greatly increase the gross product; the gold, when extracted, is assayed and molded into ingots for the market.

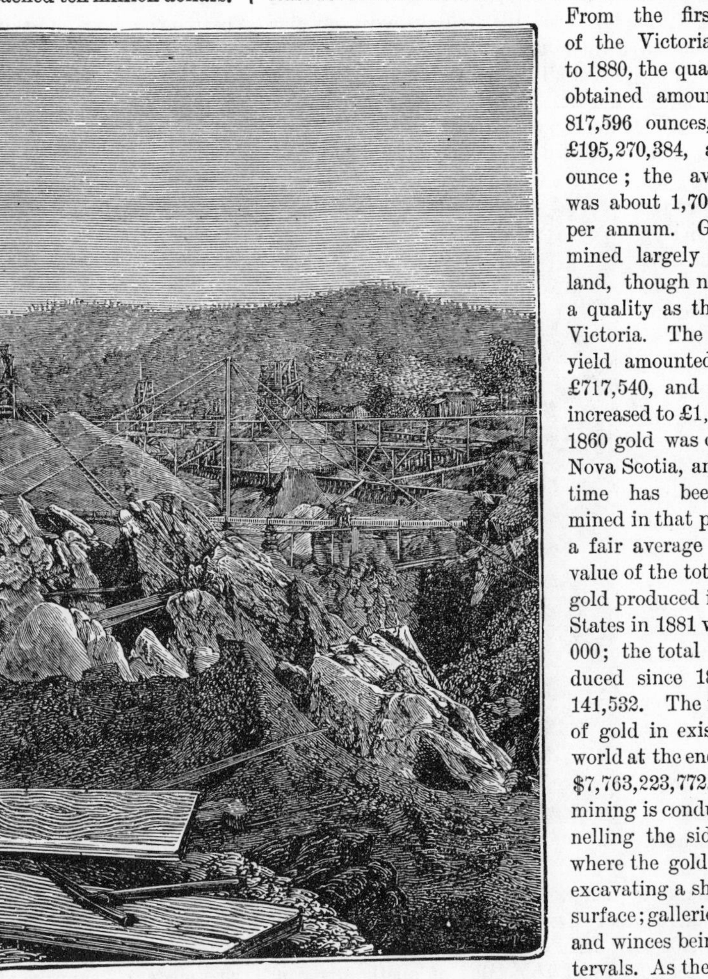

AUSTRALIAN GOLD MINE.

**Silver Mining.**—Silver is found in combination with

gold, mercury, lead, antimony, arsenic, sulphur, etc. It is also occasionally found in crystallized masses. The silver mines of Mexico were until quite recently the richest known to exist. Chili and Peru stood next for their silver production. Bolivia is also rich in silver, and of European countries Spain had the most product, but it has declined since 1858. The great silver-mining industry of the United States began in 1860, when it was discovered in Nevada, in the Comstock Lode. By 1865 the leading mines on this lode had yielded over thirty million dollars, and from 1859 to 1866 the total product of all the mines on this lode was about seventy million dollars. Silver was soon discovered in Colorado, Idaho, Montana, and Utah. Up to December, 1878, the value of silver yielded in Colorado was about sixteen million dollars, but the discovery of the Leadville mining district in 1877 added greatly to the quantity mined, the output of ore in those mines being valued at $15,286,936 in 1880. The general principles of silver-mining are the same as those employed in gold; the reduction of the ore is accomplished by ordinary smelting, the crushed ore being mixed with other constituents and heated in a furnace, when the silver and lead come down as an alloy. The silver is afterwards separated in a proper furnace, the lead being removed as litharge or oxide of lead, and a cake of silver left. The total product of silver in the United States in 1881 was $42,100,000; from 1848 to that date the total product was $501,072,260. The value of all the silver in existence in the world in 1881 was $6,757,843,025.

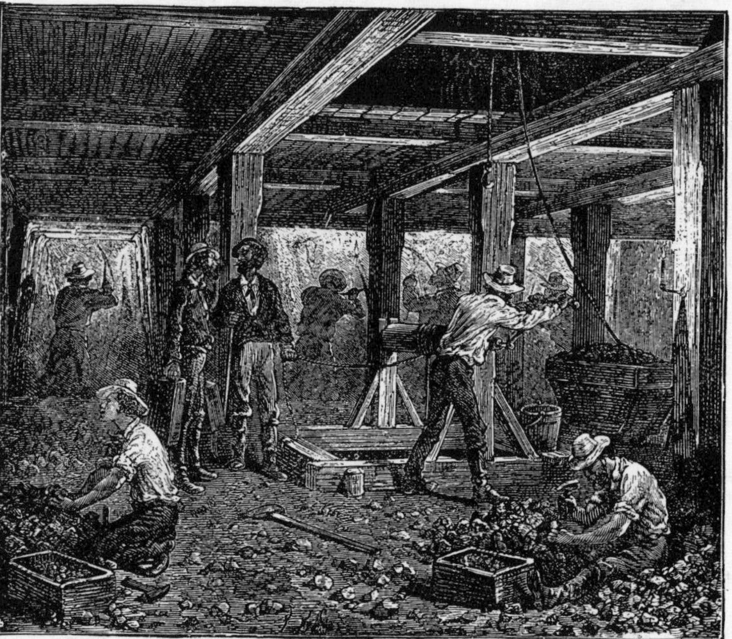

IN THE SILVER MINES OF NEVADA.

**Iron Mining.**—Iron is seldom met with in its native state, being usually alloyed with sulphur, arsenic, or phosphorus. This metal was known very early in the history of man, and it has been found all over the world. The chief kind are: 1. Magnetic iron ore. 2. Red hematite, specular, or red iron ore. 3. Brown hematite, or brown iron ore. 4. Carbonate of iron. The first of these is the richest in metal. Iron ore is reduced by smelting in a blast furnace, as has already been described in MANUFACTURES. This metal is found occupying extensive areas in the United States, Pennsylvania being specially rich in it, while the region about Lake Superior produces a valuable quality. The total product of iron ore in the United States for 1879 was 7,061,829 tons, the value being $20,470,756. The annual production of iron ore in Great Britain is sixteen and a half million tons, and the total production of the rest of the world is twenty-two million tons.

**Zinc Mining.**—Zinc is a hard, bluish-white metal, very brittle at ordinary temperatures, but which becomes ductile and malleable at 212°, when it can be drawn into wire, or beaten or rolled into thin plates. It is never found in the native state, but in the form of sulphuret or carbonate of zinc, usually associated with the ores of tin, lead, or copper. Sweden is rich in zinc, and it is found in Great Britain; red oxide of zinc occurs in New Jersey and in other parts of the United States. The metal is extracted from its ores by chemical processes too complicated for description here. It is used for coating wire and sheet-iron, making what is known as galvanized iron. It is also employed in the manufacture of paint, and certain preparations of it have important medical uses. Zinc ores have been found in Pennsylvania, Missouri, North Carolina, Arkansas, Wisconsin, Tennessee, etc. The first zinc made in the United States was in 1838, but in 1851 a block weighing 16,400 pounds was exhibited from the State of New Jersey in the London Exhibition. It was estimated several years since that of the entire product of the world Prussia yields 58 per cent., Belgium 27, Russia 7, and the United States 3. The sheet-zinc made in Pennsylvania is considered equal to the finest European manufacture.

**Nickel.**—This metal is only found in a native state in meteoric stones. It occurs in combination with arsenic, and is mined extensively in Saxony, Westphalia, Hungary, Sweden, and other European countries. It is much used in the manufacture of German-silver and other alloys, and for plating on other metals, being capable of receiving a high polish and of resisting atmospheric influences. In coinage, it is alloyed with zinc and copper, the proportions used in the United States cent of 1857 being 88 per cent. copper and 12 nickel.

**Diamond Mining.**—Diamonds are found not only in the form of perfect crystals, but also rolled grains; and they are obtained partly from alluvial soils and the sand of rivers, and partly from rocks, chiefly a quartzy sandstone or conglomerate, in which they are often associated with gold. A number of localities in India have been long celebrated as productive of diamonds, particularly Golconda; they are found also in Malacca, Borneo, and other parts of the East; nor were any diamonds procured in any other part of the world till the beginning of the eighteenth century, when they were discovered in remarkable abundance in the district of Serra do Frio, in the province of Minas Geraes, in Brazil. Previous to that time, diamonds found in Brazilian gold mines had been disregarded as mere pebbles; their nature became known in consequence of some of them accidentally finding their way to Europe. In 1829 they were discovered in the Ural Mountains. They have also been found in Rutherford Co., North Carolina; in Hale Co., Georgia; in the province of Constantine, Algeria; in Australia, and in South Africa. Diamond mines consist in general of mere diggings and washings of alluvial deposits. In Brazil the method pursued is to rake the alluvial matter backwards and forwards on inclined planes, over which a stream of water is made to run, till the lighter particles are carried away, when large stones are picked out by the hand, and what remains is carefully examined for diamonds. The work is carried on by slaves, and when a diamond of 17 carats is found, the slave who finds it is entitled to his liberty. Large diamonds are comparatively rare among those of Brazil, all the notable diamonds in the world being Indian. Brazil produces yearly from 25,000 to 30,000 carats of diamonds, of which, however, not more than 9,000 carats are capable of being cut, the rest being either very small or of inferior quality.

DIAMOND MINE AT KIMBERLEY, SOUTH AFRICA.

**Antimony.**—A brittle metal, bluish-white in color, which is found associated with silver, iron, and other metals, in Germany, and in the islands of Singapore and Borneo. The metal is obtained by heating the crude ore, covered with charcoal, on the bed of a furnace, when the sulphide of antimony fuses, and is drawn off in a liquid form into iron molds, where it solidifies in cakes or loaves. These are pulverized and placed on the bed of a reverberatory furnace, in which the sulphur is removed in the form of a gas, when, the roasted mass being mixed with powdered charcoal, and the whole wet with a solution of carbonate of soda, and raised to a bright red heat in crucibles, the metal falls to the bottom, leaving the impurities at the surface. Antimony is much used in alloys, as for britannia and type-metal and plate pewter, and is also employed in the casting of bells to improve their sound.

**Manganese.**—This metal is grayish-white in color, capable of a high degree of polish, and is so hard as to scratch glass and steel. But it oxidizes rapidly when exposed to the atmosphere, and should be preserved in naphtha. It is only found native in connection with iron in meteoric stones, and is usually obtained by reducing one of its oxide by carbon at an extreme heat From manganese are obtained purple and black colors used in staining glass.

**Bismuth.**—A brittle metal, white, tinged with red, found occurring in veins of fissures, in Cornwall (England), Germany, France, and Sweden. It is obtained by heating the ore in iron tubes in a furnace, when the metal volatilizes in a vapor, to be afterwards condensed and run into molds. It is used in the manufacture of porcelain for fixing the gilding. It is also employed in medical practice as a tonic and anti-spasmodic, and in the manufacture of cosmetics, in which use it becomes highly injurious, frequently causing paralysis.

**Graphite, Plumbago, or Black Lead.**—This mineral is one of the forms of carbon, and is found in Spain, Ceylon, Norway, Scotland, and various parts of the United States. An enormous mine of graphite was discovered in Siberia, near Irkutsk, in 1850. The principal use of the mineral is in the manufacture of black lead pencils, for which purpose the crude black lead is purified, dried, pulverized, made into a paste with water, and pressed into the desired shape, when it is cut into lengths and fitted between two grooved lengths of cedar or other wood, which are glued together, and being made in fours, are sawn apart to become pencils. Graphite is also used in combination with clay in the manufacture of crucibles, in the preparation of stove-polish, and to relieve friction in machinery.

**Cobalt.**—This metal is found in combination with arsenic and sulphur, and in a native state in meteoric stones. Preparations of it are employed in the manufacture of colors used in painting on porcelain. It is also manufactured into sympathetic inks in some of its compounds, the inks being pink, blue, green, or yellow, according to the combination employed.

**Platinum.**—This is designated as one of the "noble metals," and is found in the native state in small, steel-gray granules, though sometimes in lumps, varying in size from that of a pigeon's egg to twenty pounds. The metal is extracted from the ore by first removing the metals associated with it by the action of powerful acids, when the platinum is precipitated in the form of a salt, containing chlorine and ammonia, which are afterwards expelled by the action of heat, leaving the platinum in the form of a spongy mass. It is then powdered, pressed, heated to an intense heat in a blast furnace, and hammered into ingots. Platinum is the heaviest known form of matter; it is insoluble in any acid except aqua regia; does not undergo oxidation in the air, and is of great importance in experimental and manufacturing chemistry, when formed into crucibles, stills, spatulas, etc.

HYDRAULIC MINING.

**Sulphur.**—Sulphur is found, either in a free state, or combined with other elements, distributed over a large portion of the globe. When free it is usually found in regularly-formed crystals, and in this state it occurs extensively at Urbino in Italy, Girgenti in Sicily, and in Croatia. The same mineral, mixed with earthy matter, is found in Italy, Moravia, and Poland. Iceland is also rich in both varieties, but the mineral resources of that country have been but little developed. In the form of sulphide, sulphur occurs abundantly in connection with iron, copper, lead, zinc, etc.; and as sulphates in lime, magnesia, baryta, etc. The preparation of sulphur from the ore consists of removing the grosser impurities by fusion and distillation, usually carried on at the point of production. Refined sulphur is still further purified by distillation in a large cast-iron still, being afterward condensed in a cool receiver. Sulphur is extensively used in the manufacture of matches and gunpowder, and also of bleaching agents, but its chief employment is in the manufacture of sulphuric acid.

**Gypsum.**—This mineral is composed of sulphate of lime and water, and is found extensively deposited throughout the world. It often occurs in considerable masses, and in totally different geological positions. In form it varies from very perfect six-sided crystals to shapeless masses, and in color from white to yellow, red, brown, or black, according to the nature of the impurities combined with it. With the water driven from it by heat, and pulverized, it is known as *plaster of Paris*, and in this form is greatly in use for molding figures and ornamentation, making casts of heads, etc. But its most important use is as a fertilizer, for which purpose it is finely pulverized before using. A beautiful variety of uncrystalized gypsum is alabaster, used in the manufacture of many ornamental objects. *Satin spar* is also a fibrous variety of the same mineral, and is much used in making necklaces and for inlaid work.

**Amber.**—A peculiar resinous substance, similar in some particulars to ordinary tree-gums ; amber is, nevertheless, even now, a mystery as to its origin, though it is generally believed to be derived from an extinct tree, of the family of conifers. It appears in some parts of the world in masses or beds, like coal, while it is also found cast up by the sea, on the coast of the Baltic, and in considerable quantities. It is found in lumps of different sizes and shapes, is slightly brittle, has a pleasant, aromatic odor when burned, is made negatively electric by friction, and from this fact gave the name electricity, *elektron* being the Greek word for amber. Amber is found on the coasts of Sicily and the Adriatic, in different parts of Europe, Siberia, Greenland, etc. The Kingdom of Prussia derives an annual revenue of about £4,000 a year from the collection of amber between Königsberg and Memel. Here it is found thrown by the tide upon the shore after a storm, or is caught in nets where it is found floating, entangled with seaweed, and is also excavated from a local bed of bituminous wood. From amber is obtained, by distillation, a volatile oil, which is said to have therapeutic virtues as an anti-spasmodic. It is employed in the arts for the manufacture of a great many different ornamental articles—jewelry, mouth-pieces for pipes, etc. By many it is considered to be a specific against fever, and particularly hay fever, when worn as a necklace of beads. It is found of different characters, transparent, semi-transparent, translucent, and opaque. Sometimes insects of non-existent species are found enclosed in it, and specimens of this character are rare and greatly sought after by collectors. The largest piece of amber known is in the royal cabinet at Berlin, and weighs eighteen pounds.

**Albertite.**—A variety of cannel coal, highly bituminous, a considerable deposit of which formerly existed in New Brunswick, on the coast of the Bay of Fundy. This mineral is black, with a brilliant surface, and susceptible of being carved into ornaments, having the appearance of jet. From it is obtained, by distillation, an illuminating oil, and this was the ordinary means for obtaining coal-oil, prior to the discovery of the petroleum fields of Pennsylvania, West Virginia, and elsewhere. Limited beds of this coal have been found in Pennsylvania and in certain parts of Europe. The Boghead coal, found near Bathgate, Scotland, is of this variety, yielding a large proportion of paraffine oil and naphtha. It is still a mooted question whether this mineral is to be considered as a coal or a shale, and much discussion on the subject has occurred among scientific men.

QUEER as it may seem, there are a great many persons who would never take bodily exercise if it were not designated and prescribed as "Out-Door-Sport." *Mens sana in corpore sano* was the old Latin aphorism, for the body cannot be maintained in health if all the work is thrown on the brain. Man is so constituted that every organ, both of a mental and physical nature, requires to be severally exercised. Without this the machinery of the body gets out of order, and the mind suffers for it.

Providence in all these matters has implanted in us instincts which under due control are excellent guides. In all rapid actions involving the exercise of the muscles, when engaged in any skillful pastime, there is an instinctive pleasure. What it is we can hardly say. Why the keeping of a shuttle-cock in the air, or the return of a ball at tennis, or the skillful delivery of the ball in base-ball give pleasure, is much too metaphysical a question for us to debate here. Sufficient to say that where any difficulty has to be overcome or a feat of skill executed, the actor is delighted with his act. This is the same whether executed alone or in the presence of others; although no doubt the pleasure of exciting approbation has considerable influence on the result.

In these days of self-culture, the knowledge of games is a part of polite breeding, and is good for us in many other respects. It exercises the muscles, quickens the action of the heart, throws off humors and old tissue, and renders many a dose of medicine unnecessary. It is also useful to us in society. It gives people something to do, quickens companionships, and excites amusement and competition. It gives people something to talk about, promotes conversation, and enables young people to amuse each other without dullness or *ennui*.

The most important influence of Out-Door-Sports is on the growth of the figure in young persons, and this is especially the case with ladies. The type of figure among the female population of our large cities, is essentially weakened by the want of out-door sport in several generations. The shoulders slope, the back stoops, often one shoulder is higher than another. The chest is narrow, and the limbs are shrunken. Now, this is only the want of exercise. America and Australia have produced some of the most magnificent specimens of the human race. Our forefathers were not Lilliputians, but the tendency to excessive brain labor has dwarfed the present generation,

SKATING.
BASE-BALL
ARCHERY
ICE-YACHTING
TOBOGGANING
LAWN TENNIS
TUG-OF-WAR
H. A. Ogden

and given an undue predominance to mental over physical exercise, developing the brain at the expense of the body.

In the following pages we have been able to do no more than sketch the outline of the principal games, but we have done our best in each instance to give the latest and most authentic edition of the various rules. As wealth increases, a larger number of persons are set free from the obligations of daily toil. For them it is most important that healthful and legitimate recreation should be provided. It is so easy to be idle. Climate is often made the excuse. There is, however, a languor proceeding from a condition of the blood, which is often mistaken for fatigue, and which can best be thrown off by exercise.

LAWN tennis is played on a court laid out either on turf, asphalt, or hardened clay. It may also be played on a wooden floor. The court should be laid out as in the diagram on page 324, the lines being marked with whitewash or paint, or with cord piping fastened down with hair-pins. First mark the sides of a parallelogram, m l (twenty-seven feet) m k (seventy-eight feet), which, with the parallel lines k i and i l, form the boundaries of a single court for a two-handed game. M l and k i are called "base lines." Twenty-one feet from the net, draw the "service lines," d c and h g. Then draw the center line, and the court is complete for a single game. For double matches, extend the base lines to 36 feet, and add external side lines.

The choice of a racket is an important matter. It should be from 12½ ounces to 13½ ounces for a lady, and from 13½ ounces up to 15½ ounces for a gentleman. Some players prefer a still heavier weight.

For the instruction of persons who have no opportunity of seeing the game in operation, the elementary steps may be accurately indicated with the aid of the diagram. Where two persons play, one is called "striker-in," or "server," and the other, "striker-out." Suppose the server to be playing from m l (court, a), he places one foot on, or within, the base line, and the other foot without. In this position he strikes the ball with the racket so as to serve it over the net into the diagonally opposite court, f, where the striker-out awaits it, behind the service line. The striker-out lets the ball bound once, and before it reaches the ground a second time, he must strike it back over the net so it will fall anywhere within the court. Now, the server is required to send it back so it will fall anywhere within the opposite court, and to do this he may "volley" the ball (that is, strike it before it reaches the ground), or strike it after one bound. The ball is sent thus back and forth so long as it is in play, that is, until it twice touches the ground, or is struck out of court or into the net, or strikes the person of either player, in which case the ball is said to be "dead." When a service ball strikes the top of the net, yet passes over, it is called a "let," and does not count. A failure to keep the ball in play makes a score for the opponent. A ball is not in play until it has been served as above into the court of the striker-out. A failure to serve within the court of the striker-out is called a "fault." Two successive faults count a score against the server. The second ball is served from the left base line, into the left court e; and so on from right to left until the game is out. The modern game is counted like ancient tennis. Before either player has scored, the score is called "Love all." The first score, or ace, counts 15; the second, 15 more, or 30 all told; the third, 10 more, or 40; and the fifth scores game. When both sides are 40 at the same time, it is called "deuce;" then two successive scores, on either side, are necessary to win. The first score after deuce is called "advantage." If the next score is in favor of the opponent, then it is deuce again, and so on until one or the other makes two successive scores. In the second game, the striker-out becomes the server, or striker-in. The sides alternate as servers until one has won six games, thereby winning the "set." The outer lines indicate the boundaries of the court for four-handed games. Partners play right and left, each taking the service in his own court.

The partner who is not serving usually plays in near the service line, toward his own side, or the center, it being better for the server to defend the rear of the court. In three-

FIG. 1.—UNDERHAND SERVICE.

handed games, it is two against one, the partners playing as in four-handed games.

There are three ways of serving: the underhand, the overhand, and the high service. For the simple underhand service, grasp the racket in the middle of the handle, and stooping, drop the ball, striking it with the racket full faced. (Figure 1.)

To put "twist" on the ball, strike it with the racket nearly horizontal but slightly inclined forward. This will put a right-hand twist on the ball, so that when it bounds it will skew toward the striker-out in a very puzzling way. If he is prepared for a straight stroke, he must alter his position or play a back-hander.

The overhand service is made with the racket held nearly on a level with the shoulder. To produce a twist, turn the racket nearly face uppermost, and drop the ball on to the surface, cutting rather than striking the ball. This will give a strong left-hand twist, so that on striking the ground the ball will bound away from the opponent's right.

The same result, to a greater extent, may be produced by the high service. In making it, throw the ball up nearly in a line with the right shoulder, and in striking, hold the racket on a slant, so that it will strike the ball on the right side. If this stroke is cleverly made, it will cause the ball to swerve while in the air, so strong is the effect of the twist, and when it strikes the ground it will bound outward.

In returning a service ball, or a ball in play, the player should always endeavor to drive as near the top of the net as possible without cutting into the net. There is a right and a wrong moment for taking a ball. After bounding, it should be struck when its upper momentum is spent and it is about to fall. The reason of this is clear. If the ball is struck on the rise, it will leave the racket at an angle equal to that of its incidence. In other words, it will lob up. The same principle must be borne in mind in taking a "skyer." It will leave the racket at a descending angle equal to that at which it strikes the racket. In fast play, you must take the ball how and when you can. It is better to hold the racket long. But for ordinary forehand play, especially where the driving is not hard, the better plan is to hold the racket short, and let the stroke be given more from the shoulder than the elbow.

## THE EIGHT STROKES.

There are eight principal strokes at tennis, each of which should be thoroughly mastered. In order to do this, a person anxious to become a good player should practice each separately, having the ball pitched to him at a certain spot, and standing so as to play one particular stroke until it can be played with certainty. Some strokes only occur at rare intervals, and, consequently, unless practiced separately, are never really learned.

**Fore Overhand.**—The first and principal stroke is the fore overhand. For this stroke, hold the racket short, well up to the face, with a very slight backward incline. In order to play a ball in this manner, you should stand about eighteen inches to the left of its course, and strike it as it passes you. While it is of the utmost importance to be quick, more misses are made from being too quick than too slow. You should let your racket hover, as it were, a moment before striking. If you do this there will be no force in the stroke except that intended for the ball. When you have to run forward to a ball, recollect to deduct the force of your run from the force of the stroke, or you will strike out of court, and, if you run back, increase the force, as your run will deduct so much from the blow. Try to strike the ball well in the center of the racket. If you hit the wood it is almost sure to score against you. In making this stroke the left foot should be forward and the right back. (Figure 2.)

**Fore Underhand** is a stroke made with the racket held at the extreme end of the handle. It is most useful in taking half-volleys, quick services, and long drives. When the play is very fast and the ball is returned close over the net, the ball rises only a few inches after striking the ground. Consequently it must be taken underhand, or not at all. In good underhand play the ball should not be lobbed up in the

FIG. 2.—FORE OVERHAND STROKE.

air. Be sure to turn the elbow well in, and return as close to the top of the net as you can.

**The High Stroke.**—Where a ball passes over the player, but at a pace that will cause it to fall behind him and within the court, he should play it down just over the net. Such a ball, played either at the opponent's feet or in some undefended part of the court, is almost sure to score. Be careful not to cut into the net.

**Back Overhand.**—In case a ball twists suddenly, or is returned so quickly that you cannot get to the left of it so as to take it forehand, you must strike backhanded. The difficulty is to get behind the ball in time. The right foot should be well forward and the left back. Turn the body from the waist well to the left, so as to throw its whole weight into the stroke. The racket should be held long or half-handle. If it passes you before you strike, the ball will fly to the left and out of the court. By drawing the arm in as the blow is made, a very considerable twist may be imparted to the ball.

**Back Underhand** is a stroke given with the right foot forward and the left back. The racket must be held at the extreme end of the handle, and, as in the preceding stroke, turn the body well to the left. One great point in this stroke is to keep the elbow well up at the moment of striking; it should be as nearly as possible over the ball. The result of this is that the ball will not rise over the net more than a couple of feet at the most. This stroke has a tendency to drive the ball to the opponent's left corner, which is always his weakest point, and where he can only reply by a backhanded stroke. Next to the forehand this is, perhaps, the most important stroke in the game. In these two strokes the great science of the game consists. Without them the player is, as it were, half-handed, and can only play such balls as come on his right, whereas with them he covers the whole space which his arm can reach on either side.

**Forward Play Overhand and Underhand.**—These

FIG. 3.—FORWARD OVERHAND STROKE.

FIG. 4.—FORWARD UNDERHAND STROKE.

strokes are required chiefly for volleys and twisting balls. For the overhand, hold the racket short and firm. When the ball is driven very hard, little more than its own returned momentum is required to send it back over the net. A very telling play in single games, when you are near the net and your opponent is at or near the base line, is to loosen the racket in the hand when the stroke is given. This stops the ball without returning its force, and drops it just over the net, where it falls long before the opponent can get to it. (Fig. 3.)

**Forward Underhand Strokes** should be played as much as possible with the racket under the arm and the elbow upwards and outwards. The effect of this is to keep the ball from rising, and to return it just over the net. Nearly all that has been said with regard to the back underhand applies to this stroke. Except that being played in the front of the player, there is no room to swing the racket unless it is brought down with a semi-circular twist. The elbow, as in the previous stroke, should be well up and nearly over the ball. This stroke is generally used where balls twist so suddenly that the striker has no time either for a forehand or backhanded stroke, and consequently is used to swiftly played balls, requiring very little force to return them. (Figure 4.)

The **Back Stroke** is very seldom used It is a "show" play, and provokes great applause. When a ball twists so suddenly that you cannot get the racket behind it in time, pass the racket behind your back and play the back stroke.

**Placing.**—What is understood as *placing*, consists in returning the ball to that spot in the court where the opponent is not and cannot get. If he is forward, play over his head; if he is near the base line, drop the ball just over the net. Also drive the ball to his right or left, whichever way will make the return most perplexing. A good player will keep his opponent racing from side to side till he tires him out. Thus, if the ball be played so that while striking the ground in the right side of the opponent's court it twists outward, he must go out of his court to take it. If it be returned with a volley to the left side, it is almost impossible for him

to get there in time. When a ball cannot be played away from an opponent, the most embarrassing play is to place it at his feet. He must then step back to take it, and will very likely miss.

## RULES OF LAWN TENNIS.

The accepted rules of the game are :

1. The choice of sides and the right of serving during the first game shall be decided by toss; provided that if the winner of the toss choose the right to serve, the player shall have the choice of sides, and *vice versa*. The players shall stand on opposite sides of the net; the player who first delivers the ball shall be called the *Server*, the other the *Striker-out*. At the end of the first game, the striker-out shall become server, and the server shall become striker-out; and so on alternately in the subsequent games of the set.

2. The server shall stand with one foot outside the base line, and shall deliver the service from the right and left courts alternately, beginning from the right. The ball served must drop within the service line, half-court line, and side line of the court which is diagonally opposite to that from which it was served, or upon any such line.

3. It is a *fault* if the ball served drop in the net, or beyond the service line, or if it drop out of court, or in the wrong court. A fault may not be taken. After a fault, the server shall serve again from the same court from which he served that fault.

4. The service may not be *volleyed, i. e.,* taken before it touches the ground.

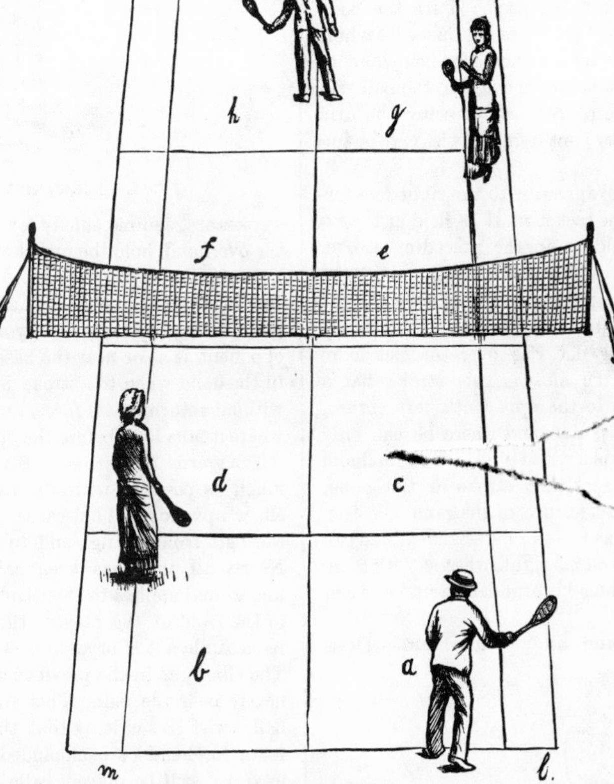

TENNIS COURT.

5. The server shall not serve until the striker-out is ready. If the latter attempt to return the service, he shall be deemed to be ready. A good service delivered when the striker-out is not ready annuls a previous fault.

6. A ball is *returned*, or *in play*, when it is played back, over the net, before it has touched the ground a second time.

7. It is a good return, although the ball touch the net.

8. The server wins a stroke if the striker-out volley the service; or if he fail to return the service or the ball in-play; or if he return the service or ball in-play so that it drop outside any of the lines which bound his opponent's court; or if he otherwise lose a stroke, as provided by Law 10.

9. The striker-out wins a stroke, if the server serve two consecutive faults; or if he fail to return the ball in-play; or if he return the ball in-play so that it drop outside any of the lines which bound his opponent's court; or if he otherwise lose a stroke, as provided by Law 10.

10. Either player loses a stroke if the ball in-play touch him or anything that he wears or carries, except his racket in the act of striking; or if he touch or strike the ball in-play with his racket more than once.

11. On either player winning his first stroke, the score is called fifteen for that player; on either player winning his second stroke, the score is called thirty for that player; on either player winning his third stroke, the score is called forty for that player; and the fourth stroke won by either player is scored game for that player; except in the following cases:

If both players have won three strokes, the score is called deuce; and the next stroke won by either player is scored advantage for that player. If the same player win the next stroke, he wins the game; if he lose the next stroke, the score is again called deuce; and so on until either player wins the two strokes immediately following the score of deuce, when the game is scored for that player.

12. The player who first wins six games wins a set. except as below.

If both players win five games, the score is called games-all; and the next game vantage game for that player. If the same player wins the next game, he wins the set; if he lose the next game, the score is again called games-all; and so on until either player wins the two games immediately following the score of games-all, when he wins the set.

*Note*—Players may agree not to play advantage-sets, but to decide the set by one game after arriving at the score of games-all.

13. The players shall change sides at the end of every set. When a series of sets is played, the player who was server in the last game of one set shall be striker-out in the first game of the next.

## THREE-HANDED AND FOUR-HANDED GAMES.

The above laws shall apply to three-handed and four-handed games, except as below:

In the three-handed game, the single player shall serve in every alternate game.

In the four-handed game, the pair who have the right to serve in the first game may decide which partner shall do so, and the opposing pair may decide similarly for the second game. The partner of the player who served in the first game shall serve in the third; and the partner of the player who served in the second game shall serve in the fourth; and so on in the same order in all the subsequent games of a set or series of sets.

The players shall take the service alternately throughout each game; no player shall receive or return a service delivered to his partner: and the order of service and of striking-out once arranged shall not be altered, nor shall the strikers-out change courts to receive the service, before the end of the set.

### THE IMPLEMENTS.

SOME cardinal points are to be considered in the selection of a bow. The best are of Italian or Spanish yew, but they are very costly. Bows made of snake-wood, or lance-wood, backed with hickory, are not expensive. Lance-wood, or lemon-wood, makes good bows, as also beef-wood, backed with lance-wood. The great points in a bow are elasticity, standing power and *sweetness* of draw. When unstrung, the bow must go back to its original form. Still the best bows will slightly follow the string. The bow must not require to be straightened by the hand. It must not weaken in shooting, and the draw must be easy and india-rubber like, not resisting and stubborn.

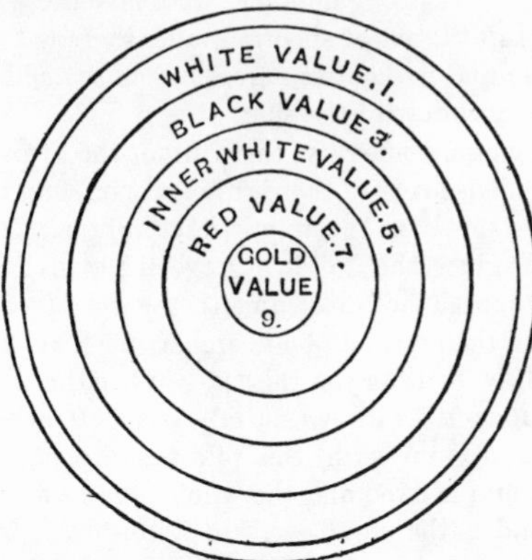


THE TARGET.

The arrows should be straight and smooth, with a slight taper from the feather to the nock. The grain should run as nearly as possible from end to end. They will be less liable to break. The weight should be about 4.6 to 4.9, or lighter, in proportion to the bow. These figures imply the weight of English shillings: 4.6 means four shillings and six pence in silver; 4.9 means four shillings, a six pence, and a three-penny bit. The left wrist should be protected by a leather guard, buckled on, but not so tight as to interfere with the circulation. The three fingers of the right hand must be protected by finger-tips or a glove. The importance of having these well made can only be appreciated by those who know the misery of shooting in tips too large, or too small. They should be a perfect fit, bending easily with the finger-joints, and distribute the pressure of the string well over the points of the fingers. When the fingers become very tender, small pieces of bone, horn, or quill, may be inserted as a further protection. Sore fingers are an inevitable part of the training of a beginner, and must be patiently borne with.

A quiver for the arrows should be worn on the left hip, well out of the way. The pull of the bow should be in proportion to the strength of the archer. For a lady, from 20 to 30 lbs.; and for a gentleman, from 35 to 50 lbs.

### POSITION.

In shooting, especially with beginners, great care should be taken to study a good form.

The feet should be flat on the ground, with the heels about six inches apart. By this position the weight is equally distributed on both feet. The left toe should not point directly to the target, but a little to the right. Turn the face well over the left shoulder. Hold the bow firm in the left hand, about the level of the waist, at an angle of forty-five degrees with the horizon. Now draw an arrow out of the quiver, and lay it over the bow and string, just above the plush. First shoot out the first finger of the left hand, and retain the arrow in its place; then nock the arrow with the

ARCHERY—STANDING POSITION.

ARCHERY—STRINGING THE BOW.

right hand, holding it with the finger and thumb; slip it into its place, having first turned it so as to bring the cock-feather uppermost, and run the first and second fingers round the string, taking a grip on the arrow, which should be well home in the groove on the string. Let go the left forefinger, so that the arrow rests on the left hand, retained only in its place by its own weight, and the grip of the right-hand fingers.

Now raise the bow to the full stretch of the left arm, all the muscles of which must be firmly knit. In doing this, draw the right arm back about two-thirds of the arrow's length. Take your aim with your right eye well over the point of the arrow, with the left arm sufficiently over towards the right, so that the loosed string shall not touch it, and as soon as the aim is certain, complete the draw and let go. It is of great importance to begin by studying a good position; and this can be better done by watching a good archer than from any amount of description. The attitude described is not at first easy to acquire, but experience shows that it is by far the best. It is important never to vary in the slightest degree. The weight, for instance, thrown on one foot instead of both, the toe an inch more to the right or left, will make all the difference in the position of the muscles. The beginner must be content to get one thing right at a time, and not try, as many do, to vanquish the difficulties of archery by adopting fancy positions.

## THE AIM.

The next point after the position is the aim. In point blanc ranges, the direction of the arrow only has to be considered, but at long ranges the elevation has also to be reckoned. In taking the direction with the right eye well over the point of the arrow, some slight allowance must be made for the width of the bow, which will send the arrow slightly to the left. The judgment soon gets accustomed to this, and provides for it. Where the range requires elevation, practice will give the sense of the amount required. For this purpose, it is most important that each draw should be precisely similar. An inch longer pull, a clumsy let go, will materially alter the freedom and force of the arrow's flight. If it wag in the air, the parabola of its course will be shorter, with the same force, than if it flies straight. In aiming, it is as well to fix the attention on the gold rather than the target, and watch each arrow to see in what it failed, whether in direction or in elevation. A great deal of art consists in loosing the arrow. Some recommend that the tips should be slipped off as part of the draw, others that the tips be thrown forward, so as to impart no twang to the string as it flies. As these rules are intended especially for beginners, we will not linger on this point, merely saying that a clean draw and a neat loose are absolute necessities to a good shot. The arrow should be drawn precisely the same length each time, that is, so far back that the point nearly rests on the left hand, and when once drawn, it should be discharged without being thrust forward again by the pressure of the string on the muscles of the right arm. We may remark here that it is better to pull a bow a pound or so below the archer's power, than one just up to it, for several reasons. In the first place, the force of the muscles is not the same every day, and a bow we can just manage one day, may be just a pound too strong another. To have the bow well under control in the act of shooting, and thereby to do everything easily and without too great an effort, adds undoubtedly to the accuracy of the shot.

In taking aim, some raise the point of the arrow above the point intended, lower to the right elevation, and then loose; others raise slowly to the required elevation. Mr. Maurice Thompson gives the following excellent advice: "First by careful experiment determine the height of your point of aim. Take the position of an archer, nock an arrow, raise the bow, drawing it as you raise it. When the arrow is little less than four-fifths drawn, steady your left arm and cover your point of aim with the pile (point) of your arrow. When the aim is fixed and the whole arrow has been placed directly under the right eye, finish the draw by a steady motion to just below the chin, and there loose quickly and smoothly.

## SCORING—MATCHES—THE YORK ROUND.

In large archery fields, it is usual to arrange a series of targets side by side, and not more than four persons shoot at each at the same time. Each target has another opposite,

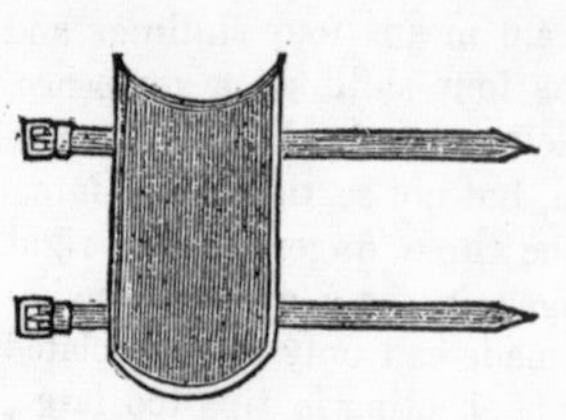

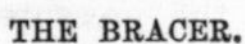

THE BRACER.

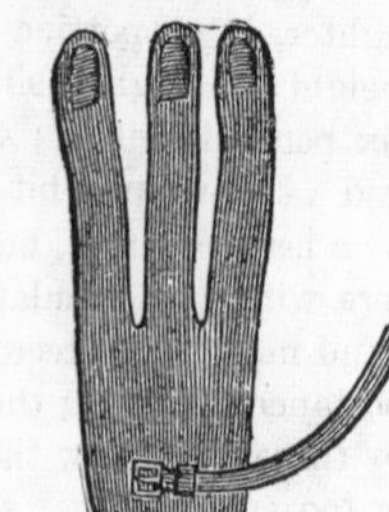

THE SHOOTING GLOVE.

and the archers walk to and fro between the two, shooting three arrows each time. This is better than a larger number. The exertion of drawing the bow when repeated three times, requires some little rest before the muscles regain their force, and the walk, picking up the arrows, and arranging for the next shots, just affords the required time.

The target contains four concentric rings.

The gold counts for nine.
The red " " seven.
The blue " " five.
The black " " three.
The white " " one.

Outside this, should the arrow strike the straw, it is called a horn spoon, and does not score anything.

The **York** round, which is generally adopted at matches, consists of 72 arrows at 100 yards, 48 at 80 yards, and 24 at 60 yards.

The **National** round, shot by all ladies in Great Britain and Australia, consists of 48 arrows at 60 yards, and 24 arrows at 50 yards.

The **Columbia** round, which is adopted for most ladies' contests in America, is 24 arrows at 30 yards, 24 arrows at 40 yards, and 24 at 50 yards.

LA CROSSE is of Indian origin. When the French first visited Canada they found it in vogue with the Iroquois tribe. It has since spread through the country, becoming in fact the national game of Canada.

It derives its name from the Crosse, with which it is played (like to a crosier), which is a hickory wood stick bent at the end and covered with a net work of string or catgut. The object, as in shinney or football, is to play the ball through the opponent's goal. The field should be large, say 200 yards at least, by 80 to a hundred wide. The goals are marked by flags.

Unlike other games, the players on both sides are posted all over the field (see cut) two and two. There is no rule as to off side. The object being to pass the ball from man to man till the goal is won.

The game is commenced by the players in the center, facing each other. They struggle for the ball, and the man who gets it, throws it up towards the enemy's goal to the nearest player on his own side. If it goes out of bounds, it must be thrown in straight, and faced for by the nearest players on each side. The ball can be thrown forwards, sideways, or backwards over his head. The great art consists in *esprit du corps*, and the way in which a side plays into one another's hands. Great speed is required, but the game involves little or no danger.

RUNNING.

THE CROSSE.

The rules are as follows:

### LAWS OF LACROSSE.

**Rule I.—The Crosse.**—Section 1. The Crosse may be of any length to suit the player; woven with cat-gut, which must not be bagged. ("Cat-gut" is intended to mean raw-hide, gut, or clock strings; not cord or soft leather.) The netting must be flat when the ball is not on it. In its widest part the crosse shall not exceed one foot. A string must be brought through a hole at the side of the tip of the turn, to prevent the point of the stick catching an opponent's crosse. A leading string resting on the top of the stick may be used, but must not be fastened, so as to form a pocket, lower down the stick than the end of the length strings. The length strings must be woven to within two inches of their termination, so that the ball cannot catch in the meshes.

Section 2. No kind of metal, either in wire or sheet, nor screws or nails, to stretch strings, shall be allowed upon the crosse. Splices must be made either with string or gut.

Section 3. Players may change their crosse during a match.

**Rule II.—The Ball.**—The ball must be india-rubber sponge, not less than eight, nor more than nine inches in circumference. In matches it must be furnished by the challenged party.

**Rule III.—The Goals.**—The goals must be at least 125 yards from each other, and in any position agreeable to the captains of both sides.

The top of the flag-poles must be six feet above the ground, including any top ornament, and six feet apart. In matches they must be furnished by the challenged party.

**Rule IV.—The Goal Crease.**—No attacking player must be within six feet of either of the flag-poles, unless the ball has passed cover-point's position on the field.

**Rule V.—Umpires.**—Section 1. There must be two umpires at each goal who shall be disinterested parties; they shall stand behind the flags when the ball is near or nearing the goal. In the event of "*game*" being called, they shall decide whether or not the ball has fairly passed through the goal; and if there be a difference of opinion between them, it shall be settled as provided for by Rule VI.

Section 2. When "*foul*" has been called, by either Captain, the Referee or any Umpire shall cry "*time*," after which the ball must not be touched by either party, nor must the players move from the position in which they happen to be at the moment until the Referee has called "*play*." If a player should be in possession of the ball when "*time*" is called, he must drop it on the ground. If the ball enters goal after "*time*" has been called, it will not count. The jurisdiction of Umpires shall not extend beyond the day of their appointment.

**Rule VI.—Referee.**—The Referee shall be selected by the Captains. No person shall be chosen to fill the position who is not thoroughly acquainted with the game, and in every way competent to act.

Section 2. Before the match begins, he shall draw the players up in lines, and see that the regulations respecting the ball, crosses, spiked soles, &c., are complied with. Disputed points, whereon the Umpires or Captains disagree, shall be left to his decision.

**Rule VII.—Captains.**—Captains to superintend the play shall be appointed by each side previous to the commencement of a match. They shall be members of the club by whom they are appointed, and no other. They may or may not be players in a match: if not, they shall not carry a crosse, nor shall they be dressed in Lacrosse uniform. They shall select Umpires and Referee, and toss for choice of goals, and they alone shall be entitled to call "foul" during a match. They shall report any infringement of the laws, during a match, to the Referee.

**Rule VIII.—Names of Players.**—The players on each side shall be designated as follows:—"Goal-keeper," who defends the goal; "Point," first man out from goal; "Cover-point," in front of point; "Centre," who faces; "Home," nearest opponent's goal; others shall be termed Fielders.

**Rule IX.—Miscellaneous.**—Section 1. Twelve players shall constitute a full field. They must be regular members in good standing of the club they represent, and of no other, for at least thirty days before becoming eligible to play in a match for their club.

Section 2. The game must be started by the Referee facing the ball in the centre of the field between a player of each side; the ball shall be laid upon the ground between the sticks of the players facing, and when both sides are ready the Referee shall call "*play!*" The players facing shall have their left side toward the goal they are attacking.

Section 3. A match shall be decided by the winning of three games out of five, unless otherwise agreed upon.

Section. 4. Captains shall arrange, previous to a match, whether it is to be played out in one day, postponed at a stated hour in the event of rain, darkness, etc., or to be considered a draw under certain circumstances; and, if postponed, if it is to be resumed where left off.

Section 5. Either side may claim at least five minutes' rest, and not more than ten, between each game.

Section 6. After each game players must change goals.

Section 7. No change of players must be made after a match has commenced, except for reasons of accident or injury during the game.

Section 8. Should any player be injured during a match, and compelled to leave the field, the opposite side shall drop a man to equalize the teams.

**Rule X.—Rough Play, &c.**—No player shall grasp an opponent's stick with his hands, hold with his arms, or between his legs, nor shall any player hold his opponent's crosse with his crosse in any way to keep him from the ball until another player reaches it. No player, with his crosse or otherwise, shall hold, deliberately strike, or trip another, nor push with the hand; nor must any player jump at to shoulder an opponent from behind, while running for or before reaching the ball; nor wrestle with the legs entwined, so as to throw an opponent.

# Curling.

URLING is played with large stones, each of which is fitted with a handle. The stones are of spherical form, flattened above and below. The under surface or sole, is polished so as to slide easily over the ice. Their weight is from thirty to fifty pounds. The rink is a smooth piece of ice, forty-two yards in length, but this length may be altered by mutual consent. At each end a tee is marked on the center line, and round it two concentric circles of different diameters. Through the two tees a line is drawn, extending two yards beyond each tee. On the left of this line (looking towards the other tee) a circle is drawn, which touches, but does not bisect the tee line. A line is drawn across the rink, one-sixth from each end called the hog score. The rink should be cleared at least ten feet wide, and ten or twelve feet beyond each tee. The number of players at each rink should be four, with two stones each, the player on each side alternate with a player on the other side. The object of the first player is to lay his stone as near the tee as he can, but a little short of it. The player who follows either tries to do the same or to dislodge the first stone. The object of the next player is to guard the stone played by his side, that is, so as to place his stone before the preceding one, that it cannot be struck out of its position, or if there is no stone near the tee to draw a shot i. e. to place his stone on or close to the tee. As the game proceeds the playing becomes more and more scientific. The object being when the center stones are so surrounded or guarded as to be unapproachable to play on to one and so strike the center stone, or to play on to another, and with that strike the center stones. This will be best understood by the following diagram. There is one art still to be mentioned, and that is to put a twist on the stone. This may be either the in-turn or the out-turn. By doing this a screw is imparted

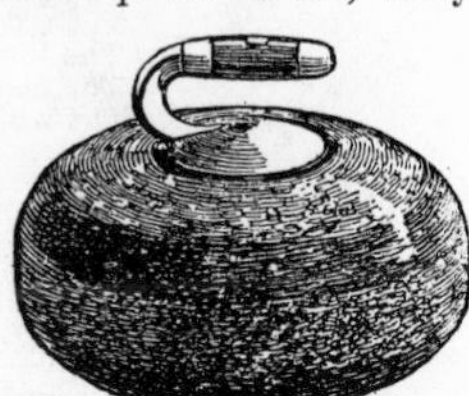

CURLING-STONE.

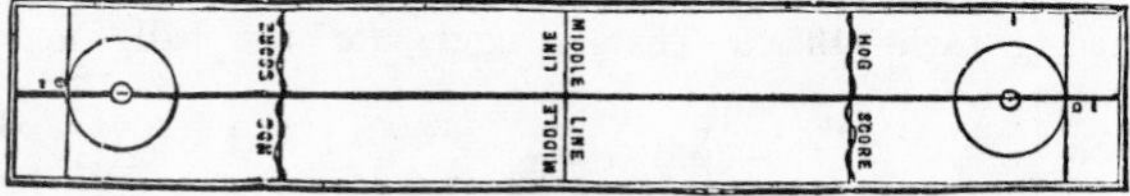


THE RINK.

to the stone, and the impetus given may be to the right or left of "a guard," as the "turn" will bring the stone back into the line.

FOR the game of croquet a level piece of turf or a surface of hardened earth slightly sanded is required. The best dimensions of the hoops or wickets are 4 to 4½ in. wide and 8 to 10 in. above ground. The stakes should be 72 feet apart, the first arch 7 feet from the starting stake, the second 7 feet from that, the third 14 feet to the right of and one foot in advance of the second, the fourth on a line with and 22 feet in advance of the second, the remaining five at the same relative distances, so as to have five in a line between the stakes and 4 wing arches. The mallets should be of boxwood, 7 to 7½ in. long by 2½ to 2⅝ in. diameter, and the handle about 15 in. long. The best balls are made of hard rubber; they should be 2⅝ inches in diameter.

### THE RULES OF CROQUET.

1.—There is no restriction as to the size of the mallet nor as to the place where the handle may be grasped; but the handle must not be used like a billiard cue; nor the side of the mallet head, except in cases where the striking is impeded.

[The latter part of this rule "bars" two strokes known as the cue stroke and the mace stroke.]

2.—The player who wins the toss has the choice of balls and of commencing the game. The game is begun as soon as a ball is struck from the starting-point; such ball being in play whether it passes the first hoop or not.

3.—No ball can be roqueted twice consecutively without a point having been made in the interval.

4.—If the striker's ball touch another at the beginning of a turn, a roquet is supposed to have been already made.

[Herein croquet differs from billiards, where touching balls prevent scoring.]

5.—If a ball pass through a hoop and roquet a ball lying beyond in the same stroke, both the point and the roquet are made; but if a ball pass through a hoop after a roquet the point is not made, as a ball is in hand after a roquet.

6.—A ball sent off the ground is brought out at right angles to the boundary line and three feet from the spot where it crossed the line.

7.—A ball lying within *less* than three feet of the boundary *must* be brought out three feet, unless it is that of the striker, who has the option of bringing it out, or playing it where it is.

8.—Croquet *must* be taken from a ball which has been roqueted either by simply "taking off" or by a splitting, rolling, or stop stroke. The striker is *not* allowed to place his foot on his ball.

9.—If in *taking croquet* the player causes either of the balls to cross the boundary, the turn *ceases*, and the balls remain as they are; that sent off the ground being replaced (according to Rule 6); this latter ball being said to be "killed."

[This rule is called the Dead Boundary Rule, and was first framed by the Fourshire Club, to whom a great debt is due for it. Its introduction quite revolutionized the tactics of the game, and made judgment of strength a *sine quâ non* for a good player.]

10.—A player makes *foul strokes* when he

- (*a*) Hits another ball besides his own;
- (*b*) Makes an inaudible stroke, *alias* "spoon;"
- (*c*) Hits his own ball twice, *i. e.*, by following on with his mallet;
- (*d*) Allows any ball, when *in play*, to touch any part of his person;
- (*e*) Lets a ball rebound from a wire or stick upon his mallet;
- (*f*) Moves a ball, which is resting against a wire or peg, by striking that wire or peg.

The penalty for a foul stroke is that the turn ceases, and the balls remain where they are.

11.—A turn *ceases*

- (i.) On the player failing to make a point or roquet a ball;
- (ii.) On his failing to shake the ball off which he is taking croquet;
- (iii.) On his "killing" a ball;
- (iv.) On his making a foul stroke.

12.—If a player play out of turn or with the wrong ball, the remainder of the turn is lost, and any point or roquet made after the mistake. The adversary has the option of letting the balls remain where they lie, or replacing them as they were before the last stroke, also playing with whichever of his own balls he chooses.

If, however, the adversary play without discovering the mistake, the turn holds good, and all points made after the mistake are scored.

13.—If a player, after making a wrong hoop, makes a second stroke, the remainder of the turn is lost, and any point or roquet made by that stroke; the previous rule applying to the position of the balls. But if the adversary does not discover the mistake before a third stroke, the turn holds good, and the player who made the wrong point proceeds as if he had made no mistake.

[The severe penalties enacted in Rule 12 are necessary in public matches to prevent careless play, and the confusion resulting from it. In private games it often obviates sore feeling if a player warns his antagonist, should he see him about to play with the wrong ball.]

14.—If a striker in roqueting any of his own balls, after it is a rover, drive it against the finishing peg, that ball is "dead," and the turn of the striker's ball ceases.

[*e. g.*, B and A are both rovers, and it is A's turn. A wishes to roquet B gently, and then after croqueting it against the peg "peg out" himself; but misjudging the required force, A roquets B against the peg; B is then dead, but A's turn ceases, so that the adversary has another shot at it before it can go out. The theory of this rule depends on Rule 8, as there is now no ball off which to take croquet, B being dead.]

15. No ball has the power of making an adversary's rovers dead unless it is itself a rover.

[The point of this rule is that it is often advantageous to make a hostile ball dead, if its partner is some way behind, as a player has then two turns to his adversary's one; but this privilege is only allowed to a player who has a rover with which to do it.]

16.—A ball lying in a hole may be moved away from the direction in which it is to be played, and may be also brought out more than three feet from the boundary, if the stroke cannot be freely taken.

# Bowls.

OWLS is probably the oldest of English pastimes. Although in but little use in America, the memory of it still lingers in the name of Bowling Green at the lower end of Broadway, New York. The first requisite for the game is a smooth and perfectly level piece of turf, which must be perfectly

BOWLS.

level. Nearly all Scotch towns have a bowling green. It should be from 90 to 150 feet long and about 30 wide. It is surrounded by a narrow trench about six or eight inches deep. The bowls were formerly of stone, but now they are universally of *lignum vitæ*. They are circular, with rounded edges, and are heavier on one side than the other. The result of this weight, or bias, as it is called, is to give the bowl a tendency to fall over in one direction as soon as its momentum begins to be exhausted. This makes its course end almost with a curl before it falls over. The game is commenced by sending the "Jack" along the green about 80 to 100 feet. The object of the player is to lay his bowl nearest to the jack. Each player is provided with two bowls. There may be as many as four or five players on a side, but not more. The nearest bowl to the jack only counts, but if two bowls of one player are nearer than his adversary, or if in the case of several players there are several bowls belonging to one side nearer than any of the other side, then they all count. The number of the game is arbitrary, as may be agreed upon. The skill is in the use of the bias. When several bowls are laid between the player and the jack, it would be impossible to get to it were it not for the bias. By sending the bowl at a curve it runs round (as it were) all the others, and sometimes the last bowl will cut out all its predecessors. There is considerable knack in bowling. A strong wrist is essential, but most especially that peculiar instinct of weight and distance which some writers have believed to be an extra sense. In addition to the implements above-mentioned, some others are also requisite. Pegs are required when it is uncertain which of the two bowls is nearest the jack. Pegs are a length of cord attached to a wooden or bone peg. This is stuck in the ground, touching the jack, and the comparative distance of any two bowls easily ascertained. If they are less than a yard from the jack the standard may be used, which is a light lattice. If either the jack or bowl strikes a stone, stick, or other impediment it is called a "rub." Casts or points are the name for each bowl that counts. For instance, supposing the game to be ten up, whichever side first reckons ten, wins. A dead bowl is the name given to one in the ditch or touching one in the ditch, or one improperly played, which last should be picked up at once. If the green is bounded by a fence, any bowl touching the fence is reckoned as dead. "To mark" means to bowl the jack at the commencement of the game. It must be bowled more than sixty-three feet, and must not be nearer to the end of the green than three feet. The footer is a small piece of carpet or matting used to stand on when delivering the bowl. It is usual to bowl from alternate ends of the green. A "void end" is when neither can score. "Turning the jack" is claiming the game before playing the last ball, which the last player only can do.

# Golf.

This game is much played in Scotland. It requires a series of circular holes, four inches in diameter, situated at various distances, ranging from eighty to five hundred yards from each other, which are generally cut on a patch of

smooth turf. The players are either two or four (two on a side) in number. The object of the game is to drive the ball from hole to hole round the course in the fewest number of strokes, the player succeeding in "holing" the ball in the fewest number, winning that hole. The greatest number of holes thus gained in one or more rounds ordinarily decides the match, though sometimes it is agreed to award victory to the smallest aggregate number of strokes taken to hole the course. Each player must be furnished with a set of clubs of different lengths and shapes, to be employed according to the position of the ball or distance to be driven.

CRICKET is making its way so steadily in America and Australia that we give a short description of the game, and manner of play. The implements of the game consist of a bat, ball, and stumps. The weight, height, and size of these are duly set forth in the rules. Two or more persons can play at the game. The object of the player is to make the greatest number of runs. The ball is bowled to the in-player, who with his bat drives it as far as he can, and while it is afield makes as many runs as he can till it is returned to the wicket. Every run counts one point. If the batman miss and his wicket is knocked down by the ball, or if he strike the ball up in the air and it is caught, or if while making runs the ball is returned and the wicket knocked down before he gets back to the crease, he is out. These are called respectively "bowled out," "caught out," or "run out." He may also be out "leg before wicket," that is, when he stands so that the ball which would have struck his wicket, hits his leg.

Cricket is played either single wicket, in which case the player-in must run to the bowling stump and back to get a run, or double wicket in which he runs only to the other wicket, crossing his partner on the way. Single wicket may be played by four persons ; double wicket requires at least eight on a side, and better still, the full number, eleven.

THE CUT.

THE BOWLER.

## THE RULES OF CRICKET.

1.—The Ball must weigh not less than five ounces and a half, nor more than five ounces and three-quarters. It must measure not less than nine inches, nor more than nine inches and one-quarter in circumference. At the beginning of each innings either party may call for a new ball.

2.—The Bat must not exceed four inches and one-quarter in the widest part ; it must not be more than thirty-eight inches in length.

3.—The Stumps must be three in number ; twenty-seven inches out of the ground ; the Bails eight inches in length ; the stumps of equal and of sufficient thickness to prevent the ball from passing through.

4.—The Bowling Crease must be in a line with the stumps ; six feet eight inches in length ; the stumps in the center ; with a return crease at each end towards the Bowler at right angles.

5.—The Popping Crease must be four feet from the wicket, and parallel to it ; unlimited in length, but not shorter than the bowling crease.

6.—The Wickets must be pitched opposite to each other by the Umpires, at the distance of twenty-two yards.

7.—It shall not be lawful for either party during a match, without the consent of the other, to alter the ground by rolling, watering, covering, mowing, or beating except at the commencement of each innings, when the ground shall be swept and rolled, unless the side next going in object to it.

8.—After rain the wickets may be changed with the consent of both parties.

9.—The Bowler shall deliver the ball with one foot on the ground behind the bowling crease, and within the return crease, and shall bowl *one over* before he change wickets, which he shall be permitted to do *twice* in the same innings, *and no bowler shall bowl more than two overs in succession.*

10.—The ball must be bowled. If thrown or jerked the Umpire shall call "No Ball."

11.—The Bowler may require the Striker at the wicket from which he is bowling to stand on that side of it which he may direct.

12.—If the Bowler shall toss the ball over the Striker's head, or bowl it so wide that in the opinion of the Umpire it shall not be fairly within the reach of the batsman, he shall adjudge one run to the party receiving the innings, either with or without an appeal, which shall be put down to the score of "Wide Balls"; such ball shall not be reckoned as one of the four balls; but if the Batsman shall by any means bring himself within reach of the ball, the run shall not be adjudged.

"THE DRIVE."

13.—If the bowler deliver a "No Ball" or a "Wide Ball," the Striker shall be allowed as many runs as he can get, and he shall not be put out except by running out. In the event of no run being obtained by any other means, then one run shall be added to the score of "No Balls" or "Wide Balls," as the case may be. All runs obtained for "Wide Balls" to be scored to "Wide Balls." The names of the Bowlers who bowl "Wide Balls" or "No Balls," in future to be placed on the score, to show the parties by whom either score is made. If the ball shall first touch any part of the Striker's dress or person (except his hands) the Umpire shall call "Leg Bye."

14.—At the beginning of each innings the Umpire shall call "Play;" from that time to the end of each innings no trial ball shall be allowed to any Bowler.

15.—**The Striker is out** if either of the bails be bowled off, or if a stump be bowled out of the ground;

16.—Or, if the ball, from the stroke of the bat, or hand, but not the wrist, be held before it touch the ground, although it be hugged to the body of the catcher;

17.—Or, if in striking, or at any other time while the ball shall be in play, both his feet shall be over the popping crease, and his wicket put down, except his bat be grounded within it;

18.—Or, if in striking at the ball he hit down his wicket;

19.—Or, if under pretense of running, or otherwise, either of the Strikers prevent a ball from being caught, the Striker of the ball is out;

20.—Or, if the ball be struck, and he willfully strike it again;

21.—Or, if in running the wicket be struck down by a throw, or by the hand or arm (with ball in hand), before his bat (in hand) or some part of his person be grounded over the popping crease. But if both the bails be off, a stump must be struck out of the ground;

22.—Or, if any part of the Striker's dress knock down the wicket;

23.—Or, if the Striker touch or take up the ball while in play, unless at the request of the opposite party;

24.—Or, if with any part of his person he stop the ball, which in the opinion of the Umpire at the Bowler's wicket, shall have been pitched in a straight line from it to the Striker's wicket, and would have hit it.

25.—If the players have crossed each other, he that runs for the wicket which is put down is out.

26.—A ball being caught, no run shall be reckoned.

27.—A Striker being run out, that run which he and his partner were attempting shall not be reckoned.

28.—If a lost ball be called, the Striker shall be allowed six runs; but if more than six shall have been run before lost ball shall have been called, then the Striker shall have all which have been run.

29.—After the ball shall have been finally settled in the Wicket-keeper's or Bowler's hand it shall be considered dead; but when the Bowler is about to deliver the ball, if the Striker at his wicket go outside the popping crease before such actual delivery, the said Bowler may put him out, unless (with reference to the 21st law) his bat in hand, or some part of his person be within the popping crease.

30.—The Striker shall not retire from his wicket, and return to it to complete his innings after another has been in, without the consent of the opposite party.

31.—No substitute shall in any case be allowed to stand out or run between wickets for another person without the consent of the opposite party; and in case any person shall be allowed to run for another, the Striker shall be out if either he or his substitute be off the ground in manner mentioned in laws 17 and 21, while the ball is in play.

32.—In all cases where a substitute shall be allowed, the consent of the opposite party shall also be obtained as to the person to act as substitute, and the place in the field which he shall take.

33.—If any Fieldsman stop the ball with his hat, the ball shall be considered dead, and the opposite party shall add five runs to their score; if any be run, they shall have five in all.

34.—The ball having been hit, the Striker may guard his wicket with his bat, or with any part of his body except his hands; that the 23d law may not be disobeyed.

35.—The Wicket-keeper shall not take the ball for the purpose of stumping until it has passed the wicket; he shall not move until the ball be out of the Bowler's hand; he shall not by any noise incommode the Striker; and if any part of his person be over or before the wicket, although the ball hit it, the Striker shall not be out.

36.—The Umpires are the sole judges of fair or unfair play, and all disputes shall be determined by them, each at his own wicket; but in case of a catch which the Umpire at the wicket bowled from cannot see sufficiently to decide upon, he may apply to the other Umpire, whose opinion shall be conclusive.

37.—The Umpires in all matches shall pitch fair wickets; and the parties shall toss up for choice of innings. The Umpires shall change wickets after each party has had one innings.

38.—They shall allow two minutes for each Striker to come in, and ten minutes between each innings. When the Umpire shall call "Play," the party refusing to play shall lose the match.

WICKET-KEEPER.

39.—They are not to order a Striker out unless appealed to by the adversaries;

40.—But if one of the Bowler's feet be not on the ground behind the bowling crease and within the return crease when he shall deliver the ball, the Umpire at his wicket, unasked, must call "No Ball."

41.—If either of the Strikers run a short run, the Umpire must call "One Short."

42.—After the delivery of four balls the Umpire must call "Over," but not until the ball shall be finally settled in the Wicket-keeper's or Bowler's hand; the ball shall then be considered dead; nevertheless, if an idea be entertained that either of the Strikers is out, a question may be put previously to, but not after, the delivery of the next ball.

43.—The Umpire must take especial care to call "No Ball" instantly upon delivery; "Wide Ball" as soon as it shall pass the Striker.

FOOTBALL is undoubtedly one of the oldest of English sports, and was apparently very popular as early as the fourteenth century. The old-fashioned game, played without any recognized rules, was a rather rough and brutal kind of sport, but it appears to have been improved in the course of time, and dignified with codes of rules.

The modern game is played in a field 200 yards long, and 100 yards wide. This space must be marked out as follows :

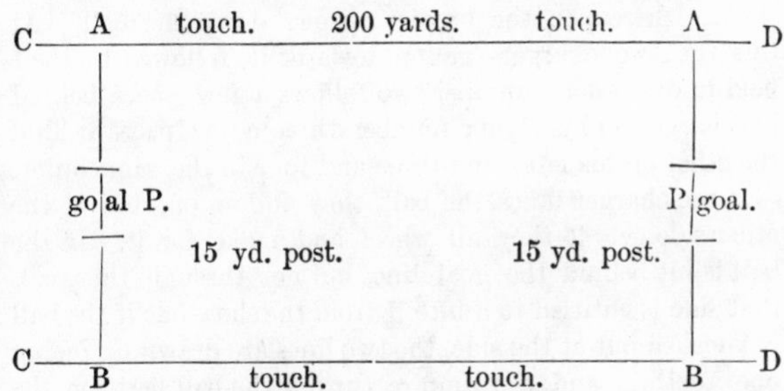


The players are divided into two parties who face one another in the field. The object of each side is to protect their own goal, and force the ball through their opponent's goal.

A football team consists of fifteen men. Of these ten are *forwards;* their duty is to follow the ball up wherever it is. Two are *half backs*, and remain just behind the forwards, waiting for a run or to prevent a run with the ball by the other side. A short distance behind the half backs comes

FOOTBALL—"DRIBBLING."

the *three-quarter back*. His post enables him to back up the half backs, or to tackle any opponent who gets past them with the ball. Behind him come the last two *backs*, who should be the steadiest players in the team. The captain should keep outside a scrimmage, and direct his men. The captain is generally a half back. The teams having met in the field, the captains toss for choice of goals, the loser taking the kick-off.

The rules of the association game are as follows:

### LAWS OF THE FOOTBALL ASSOCIATION.

1. The limits of the ground shall be : maximum length, 200 yards; minimum length, 100 yards; maximum breadth, 100 yards; minimum breadth, 50 yards. The length and breadth shall be marked off with flags; and the goals shall be upright posts, 8 yards apart, with a tape or bar across them, 8 feet from the ground.

2. The winners of the toss shall have the option of kick off or choice of goals. The game shall be commenced by a place-kick from the center of the ground; the other side shall not approach within ten yards of the ball until it is kicked off, nor shall any player on either side pass the centre of the ground in the direction of his opponent's goal until the ball is kicked off.

FOOTBALL—THE DROP KICK.

3. Ends shall only be changed at half-time. After a goal is won, the losing side shall kick off, but after the change of ends at half-time the ball shall be kicked off by the opposite side from that which originally did so; and always as provided in Law 2.

4. A goal shall be won when the ball passes between the goal-posts under the tape or bar, not being thrown, knocked on, nor carried. The ball hitting the goal, or boundary posts, or goal bar, or tape, and rebounding into play, is considered in play.

5. When the ball is in touch, a player of the opposite side to that which kicked it out shall throw it from the point on the boundary line where it left the ground, in any direction the thrower may choose. The

ball must be thrown in at least six yards, and shall be in play when thrown in, but the player throwing it in shall not play it until it has been played by another player.

6. When a player kicks the ball, or it is thrown out of touch, any one of the same side who at such moment of kicking or throwing is nearer to the opponent's goal line is out of play, and may not touch the ball himself, nor in any way whatever prevent any other player from doing so until the ball has been played, unless there are at least three of his opponents nearer their own goal line; but no player is out of play when the ball is kicked from the goal line.

7. When the ball is kicked behind the goal line by one of the opposite side, it shall be kicked off by any one of the players behind whose goal line it went, within six yards of the nearest goal post; but if kicked behind by any one of the side whose goal-line it is, a player of the opposite side shall kick it from within one yard of the nearest corner flag.post. In either case no other player shall be allowed within six yards of the ball until it is kicked off.

8. No player shall carry or knock on the ball, and handling the ball under any pretence whatever, shall be prohibited, except in the case of the goal-keeper, who shall be allowed to use his hands in defence of his goal, either by knocking or throwing, but shall not carry the ball. The goal-keeper may be changed during the game, but not more than one player shall act as goal-keeper at the same time, and no second player shall step in and act during any period in which the regular goal-keeper may have vacated his position.

9. Neither tripping nor hacking shall be allowed, and no player shall use his hands to hold or push his adversary nor charge him from behind. A player with his back towards his opponents' goal cannot claim the privilege of Rule 9 when charged behind.

10. No player shall wear any nails—except such as have their heads driven in flush with the leather—iron plates, or gutta-percha, on the soles or heels of his boots, or on his shin guards.

11. In the event of any infringement of Rules 6, 8, 9, or 14, a free kick shall be forfeited to the opposite side from the spot where the infringement took place.

12. In no case shall a goal be scored from any free kick, nor shall the ball be again played by the kicker until it has been played by another player. The kick off and corner-flag kick shall be free kicks within the meaning of this rule.

13. That in the event of any supposed infringement of Rules 6, 8, 9, 10, or 14, the ball be in play until the decision of the umpire, on his being appealed to, shall have been given.

14. No player shall charge an opponent by leaping on him.

15. By mutual agreement of the competing clubs in matches, a referee shall be appointed whose duties will be to decide in all cases of dispute between the umpires; he shall also keep a record of the game, and act as timekeeper, and in the event of ungentlemanly behavior on the part of any of the contestants, the offender or offenders shall, in the presence of the umpires, be cautioned, and in the case of violent conduct the referee shall have the power to rule the offending player out of play, and to order him off the ground, and transmit his name to the committee of the association under whose rules the game was played, and in whom shall be solely vested the right of accepting an apology.

### DEFINITION OF TERMS.

A *Place Kick* is a kick at the ball while it is on the ground, in any position in which the kicker may choose to place it.

*Hacking* is kicking an adversary intentionally.

*Tripping* is throwing an adversary by the use of the legs.

*Knocking on* is when a player strikes or propels the ball with his hands or arms.

*Holding* includes the obstruction of a player by the hand or any part of the arm extended from the body.

*Touch* is that part of the field, on either side of the ground, which is beyond the line of flags.

A *Free Kick* is a kick at the ball in any way the kicker pleases, when it is lying on the ground, none of the kicker's opponents being allowed within six yards of the ball, but in no case can a player be forced to stand behind his own goal-line.

*Handling* is understood to be playing the ball with the hand or arm.

*Dribbling* consists in working the ball along with the feet, pushing it on with a series of gentle kicks, in order to pilot it past opponents towards the desired goal.

## Polo.

POLO can be best described as shinny on horseback. It is played in a field 250 yards long and 150 wide. The space should be marked out by a post and rail fence, to protect spectators watching the game. The selection and purchase of the ponies is one of the most important points. The best come from Texas. The pony should be 14 to 14½ hands high, quick, with a good temper, and above all not ball-shy. A pony who fears the ball and swerves from it, rarely, if ever, gets over the trick; blinkers have been tried and given up. The clubs are about four feet long in the handle, with a strong head about three inches square and eight long. The number of players engaged is about five on a side. Of these one guards the home; another is told off as the charger, and the rest constitute the field; each side has its captain. At the commencement of the game the umpire, standing opposite the flag in the center of the field, calls, "Are you ready?" If the sides are ready they raise their sticks, whereupon the umpire throws down the ball. At this the two chargers gallop towards it, followed by their field in due order; number two follows a few paces behind his charger on his right; number three a few paces behind the other on his left; and three and four in the same order.

If the charger takes the ball, they follow on, but if the other side gets it they all wheel and make for it. If the ball is hit behind the goal line, but not through the goal, that side is entitled to a hit-off from the shot, but if the ball is knocked out at the side, the two lines are drawn up facing one another, and the umpire throws the ball between the two. In the play there are three strokes. The ordinary *fore-hand* stroke to the right of the pony. Formerly there was a restriction that the arm could not be lifted above the shoulder; this is now abolished, and the striker may swing his weapon as he pleases. The next stroke is called *over-hand*; it is made to the left of the pony; this may be made either backwards or forwards. The third is the *back-stroke* to the right of the pony, knocking the ball in the opposite direction. Hooking and checking are both permitted. Hooking is where a player lifts his stick to strike, and an opponent in his rear hooks his stick in so as to bar the strike. Checking is to insert your stick between the ball and the blow, and so turn it aside.

All that applies to good riding applies to polo. The seat should be firm and yet easy, with the grip from the knees. The rider should be able to lean well over, and, as it were, hang from the saddle on either side. He should not drag at the pony's mouth, and if he wears spurs they should be without rowels. The pony's forelegs should be swathed in bandages so as to save them from chance blows.

N. B.—Good temper is an essential qualification of a polo player, and no one should shout except the captain, whose duty it is to direct. Yelling, excitement, or severity to the pony are very bad form.

Skate Sailing
Polo
Rowing
Bowling
Cricket
Foot-Ball
Bicycling
H. A. Ogden

ASE-BALL is the national game of America. It is played in a field at least 500 feet long by 450 wide. The in-field is laid out in a diamond shape. The space between the positions of the pitcher and catcher should be laid in hard ground, as should also the paths from base to base. The field can be measured out as follows :—First, mark the home base. Then measure down the field 127 feet 4 inches, which will give the second base. Then take a cord 180 feet long, fasten one end at the home base, the other at the second base; mark the center of this cord, and carry it out right and left till it is fully stretched. This will give the position of the first and third bases. On a line from the home base to the second base, and distant 45 feet, is the pitcher's position. The space is six feet long and four wide. The foul-ball posts are on a line with the home and first, and home and third bases, and are at least 100 feet distant. Flags should be placed on the posts so as to make them conspicuous. The home base should be a block of stone sunk in the ground, with its sides parallel to the lines between the bases. The other bases may be marked by canvas bags attached to posts sunk in the ground. The batsman's position is marked by a space three feet by six, at the side of the home base.

### THE NINE PLAYERS.

The catcher and pitcher—these players are called the battery of the team. They are selected for their skill. These two should understand one another thoroughly, and, by a preconcerted code of signals, play into one another's hands. The catcher should be a good thrower. He should also be a good stopper and fielder. When the striker has made his first base, the catcher must come up close behind him so as to be ready to take the ball and throw it to the second base, in case the runner tries to steal a base on the pitcher. If no men are running, he can stand further back.

The pitcher, as his name implies, throws up the ball to the striker. He must be within his ground with both feet when he delivers the ball. He must not deliver the ball overhand or round hand, it must be underhand. His great art is to deliver the ball so that it misleads the striker, being in fact difficult to take. He must be a good catch and not afraid of a "hot" ball.

The three positions occupied by the first, second, and third basemen require different qualifications. The first baseman has to look out for swift balls thrown up. The second baseman has to touch players running to his base. The third baseman has to catch difficult foul balls with great twist in them.

The first baseman should be a good ball catcher. He ought to be able to catch and hold a ball that comes anywhere within six or eight feet of the base. He must remember that the ball must be held by him with some part of his person touching the base, before the striker reaches it, otherwise he is not out.

The second baseman should also be an active player. When a hard batter goes in and swift balls are delivered by the pitcher, he should fall back; but as his duty is to touch players, as soon as the batsman has made his first base, he should always have this duty in his mind.

The third baseman has most of the heavy fielding to do, and on his dexterity and quickness the score of the opponents will depend. All the players should be prepared at any moment to support each other.

The short-stop—his duty is to back up any other player, or take his place while on the run after a ball. He also fields for the pitcher any balls not stopped by him, if thrown up from the catcher.

The three out-fielders occupy respectively the left, center, and right fields ; they should be able to throw a ball at least eighty yards, good runners, and excellent judges of fly-balls.

## THE RULES OF BASEBALL.

**Section 1.** The ball must weigh not less than five nor more than five and one-quarter ounces avoirdupois. It must measure not less than nine nor more than nine and one-quarter inches in circumference. It must be composed of woolen yarn, and shall not contain more than one ounce of vulcanized rubber in mold form, and shall be covered with leather.

Sec. 2. In all match games the ball or balls played with shall be furnished by the home club, and shall become the property of the winning club.

Sec. 3. The bat must be round, and must not exceed two and one-half inches in diameter in the thickest part. It must be made wholly of wood, and shall not exceed forty-two inches in length.

Sec. 4. The bases must be four in number, and they must be placed and securely fastened upon each corner of a square, the sides of which are respectively thirty yards. The bases must be so constructed and placed as to be distinctly seen by the umpire. The first, second and third bases must cover a space equal to fifteen inches square, and the home base one square foot of surface. The first, second, and third

bases shall be canvas bags, painted white, and filled with some soft material. The home base shall be of white marble or stone, so fixed in the ground as to be even with the surface, and wholly within the diamond. One corner of said base shall face the pitcher's position, and two sides shall form part of the foul lines.

SEC. 5. The base from which the ball is struck shall be designated the home base, and must be directly opposite the second base. The first base must always be that upon the right hand, and the third base that upon the left hand side of the striker when occupying his position at the home base. In all match games, lines connecting the home and first bases, and the home and third bases, and also the lines of the striker's and pitcher's position, shall be marked by the use of chalk or other suitable material, so as to be distinctly seen by the umpire.

SEC. 6. The game shall consist of nine innings to each side, but should the score then be a tie, play shall be continued until a majority of runs for one side, upon an equal number of innings, shall be declared, when the game shall end. All innings shall be concluded when the third hand is put out.

SEC. 7. The pitcher's position shall be within a space of ground four feet wide by six feet long, the front or four feet line of which shall be distant fifty (50) feet from the center of the home base, and the center of the square shall be equidistant from the first and the third bases. Each corner of the square shall be marked by a flat iron plate, or stone, six inches square, fixed in the ground even with the surface.

THE STRIKER AND CATCHER.

SEC. 8. The player who delivers the ball to the bat must do so while wholly within the lines of the pitcher's position. He must remain within them until the ball has left his hand, and he shall not make any motion to deliver the ball to the bat while any part of his person is outside the lines of the pitcher's position. The ball must be delivered to the bat with the arm swinging nearly perpendicular at the side of the body, and the hand in swinging forward must pass below the waist. The pitcher, when taking his position to deliver the ball, must face the batsman.

SEC 9. Should the pitcher make any motion to deliver the ball to the bat, and fail so to deliver it—except the ball be accidentally dropped—or should he unnecessarily delay the game by not delivering the ball to the bat, or should he, when in the act of delivering the ball, have any part of his person outside the lines of his position, the umpire shall call a "balk," and players occupying the bases shall take one base each.

SEC. 10. Every ball fairly delivered and sent in to the bat over the home base and at the height called for by the batsman, shall be considered a good ball.

SEC. 11. All balls delivered to the bat which are not sent in over the home base and at the height called for by the batsman, shall be considered unfair balls, and every ball so delivered must be called. When "seven balls" have been called, the striker shall take first base and all players who are thereby forced to leave a base shall take one base. Neither a "ball" nor a "strike" shall be called until the ball has passed the home base.

SEC. 12. All balls delivered to the bat which shall touch the striker's bat without being struck at, or his (the batsman's) person while standing in his position, or which shall hit the person of the umpire—unless they be passed balls—shall be considered *dead* balls, and shall be so called by the umpire, and no players shall be put out, base be run, or run be scored on any such ball; but if a dead ball be also an unfair ball, it shall be counted as one of the seven unfair balls that entitle the striker to a base.

SEC. 13. The batsman's or striker's position shall be within a space of ground located on either side of the home base, six feet long by three feet wide, extending three feet in front of and three feet behind the line of the home base, and with its nearest line distant one foot from the home base.

SEC. 14. The batsmen must take their position in the order in which they are directed by the captain of their club, and after each player has had one time at bat, the striking order thus established shall not be changed during the game. After the first inning, the first striker in each inning shall be the batsman whose name follows that of the last man who has completed his turn (or time) at bat in the preceding inning.

SEC. 15. The batsman on taking his position, must call for either a "*high ball*," a "*low ball*," or a "*fair ball*," and the umpire shall notify the pitcher to deliver the ball as required; such call shall not be changed after the first ball delivered.

SEC. 16. A "*high ball*," shall be one sent in above the belt of the batsman, but not higher than his shoulder. A "*low ball*" shall be one sent in at the height of the belt, or between that height and the knee, but not higher than his belt. A "*fair ball*" shall be one between the range of shoulder high and the knee of the striker. All the above must be over the home base, and when fairly delivered shall be considered fair balls to the bat.

SEC. 17. Should the batsman fail to strike at the ball he calls for, or should he strike at and fail to hit the ball, the umpire shall call "*one strike*," and "*two strikes*," should he again fail. When two strikes have been called, should the batsman not strike at the next good ball the umpire shall warn him by calling "*good ball*," but should he strike at and fail to hit the ball, or should he fail to strike at or hit the next good ball, "*three strikes*" must be called, and the batsman must run toward the first base as in case of hitting a fair ball.

SEC. 18. The batsman, when in the act of striking at the ball, must stand wholly within the lines of his position.

SEC. 19. Should the batsman step outside the lines of his position and strike the ball, the umpire shall call "foul strike and out," and base runners shall return to the bases they occupied when the ball was hit.

SEC. 20. The foul lines shall be unlimited in length, and shall run from the right and left hand corners of the home base through the center of the first and third bases to the foul posts, which shall be located at the boundary of the field and within the range of home and first base, and home and third base. Said lines shall be marked, and on the inside, from base to base, with chalk or some other white substance, so as to be plainly seen by the umpire.

SEC. 21. If a ball from a fair stroke of the bat first touches the ground, the person of a player, or any other object, either in front of, or on the foul ball lines, or the first or third base, it shall be considered fair.

If the ball from a fair stroke of the bat first touches the person of the batter, or the ground, the person of a player, or any other object, behind the foul ball lines, it shall be declared foul, and the ball so hit shall be called foul by the umpire even before touching the ground, if it be seen falling foul.

SEC. 22. When the batsman has fairly struck a fair ball, or has had "three strikes," or "seven balls" called on him, he shall vacate his position, and he shall then be considered a base runner until he is put out or scores his run.

SEC. 23. The batsman shall be declared "out" by the umpire as follows: If a fair ball be caught before touching ground, or any object other than the player who catches it, except it be caught in such player's cap or dress. If a foul ball be caught before touching ground, or after touching ground but once, except it touch some object other than the player who catches it before touching ground or being caught, or be caught by the player in his cap or dress. If a fair ball be securely held

by a fielder while touching first base with any part of his person before the batsman touches first base. If after "three strikes" have been called, the ball be caught before touching the ground. If after "three strikes" have been called, he fails to touch first base before the ball is legally held there. If he plainly attempts to hinder the catcher from catching the ball, evidently without effort to make a fair strike, or if he makes a foul strike. If in running the last half of the distance from home base to first base he runs outside a line three feet distant from the foul line and parallel thereto.

Sec. 24. Players running bases must touch each base in regular order, viz.: first, second, third, and home bases: and when obliged to return to bases they have occupied, they must retouch them in reverse order, when running on fair or foul balls. In the latter case the base runner must return to the base where he belongs on the run and not at a walk. No base shall be considered as having been occupied or held until it has been touched.

Sec. 25. No player running the bases shall be forced to vacate the base he occupies unless the batsman becomes a base runner. Should the first base be occupied by a base runner when a fair ball is struck, the base runner shall cease to be entitled to hold said base until the player running to first base shall be put out. The same rule shall apply in the case of the occupancy of the other bases under similar circumstances. No base runner shall be forced to vacate the base he occupies if the base runner succeeding him is not thus obliged to vacate his base.

Sec. 26. One run shall be scored every time a base runner, after having regularly touched the first three bases, shall touch the home base before three hands are out. If the third hand is forced out, or is put out before reaching the first base, a run shall not be scored.

Sec. 27. If the player running the bases is prevented from making a base by the obstruction of an adversary, he shall be entitled to that base and shall not be put out.

Sec. 28. Any player running the bases shall be declared out if, at any time, while the ball is in play, he be touched by the ball in the hand of a fielder, without some part of his person is touching the base. The ball must be held by the fielder after touching the runner.

Sec. 29. Any base runner failing to touch the base he runs for shall be declared out if the ball be held by a fielder, while touching said base, before the base runner returns and touches it.

Sec. 30. Any base runner who shall in any way interfere with or obstruct a fielder while attempting to catch a fair fly ball, or a foul ball, shall be declared out. If he willfully obstructs a fielder from fielding a ball, he shall be declared out, and, if a batted fair ball strike him, he shall be declared out, and no base be run or run be scored.

Sec. 31. The umpire is master of the field from the commencement to the termination of the game, and must compel the players to observe the provisions of this and of all the Playing Rules, and he is invested with authority to order any player to do or omit to do any act necessary to give force and effect to any and all of such provisions.

# Rackets.

ONE of the noblest of pastimes is the game of Rackets, which is played in a court eighty feet long by forty feet wide. The front wall is thirty feet high, and the back twelve. It is lighted by skylights from the roof. The walls are of brick covered with plaster, hard and perfectly smooth. They are painted either red or black. The entrance is through the twelve foot wall, and the door is flush with it. One or two galleries for the spectators are placed over this wall, protected by a wire blind, about half way down, so as to receive any balls coming from above. The front wall to the height of twenty-six inches is covered with wood painted black. Above this, seven feet nine inches from the floor, is the cut line. The floor is divided by a line running from side to side about half, and by another running at right angles from the center of this to the back of the court, which is thus divided into two spaces, C and D. Where the cross line meets the wall two spaces six by eight are enclosed, called service spaces, A and B.

Front Wall.
A
B
C
D
Back Wall.

RACKET COURT.

The implements used in the game are rackets, not unlike a small tennis bat, with a longer handle, strung with catgut. The ball is about one-third the size of a tennis ball, and covered with white leather. Two persons can play the game at one time, or three or four, but not more. The first player-in stands on the right-hand service space, and serves on the front wall above the cut line, so that the ball rebounds into the other court. If he makes two faults, it puts him out. If the service is good, the other player must return the ball and need not strike above the cut line, but may return anywhere on to the end wall above the wood, which, if struck, gives a loud reverberating sound, telling that his opponent has won the ace. The player is not bound to strike the end wall first. He may angle off either of the side walls, and indeed in this consists the great skill of the game. The ball, if played on to the side wall at anything like an angle of forty-five degrees, will take the two other walls at the same angle and never return to the back of the court at all. If, therefore, the player is far back he will not reach it in time to save the ace. The ball may be volleyed as in lawn tennis. By this play it strikes the end wall at a descending angle, and takes the ground at once before it can be played by the adversary. Another very skillful play is to return into the corner, so that the ball in its return keeps close to the side wall, and thus renders the return very difficult. The striker-out must take the ball not later than on its second bound. Sometimes it strikes the back of the court before its first bound, and he then takes it in its rebound before the second bound. The skill in play consists to a great extent in the back strokes. Much of the play described under our chapter on lawn tennis applies equally to rackets. The only difference is that lawn tennis is played more gently. The racket player has nothing to fear from hard hitting, and consequently there is more activity and exercise in the game.

# BICYCLING.

MANY of our readers may not be within reach of a bicycling school, and for such we give the following advice :—

The learner should first be assisted by a tutor or friend, who will hold the machine while he mounts. The machine should be held close to the saddle, so as not to strain it. On a level road the non-rider should push it along, walking beside it, and keeping the equilibrium, so that the rider has nothing to do but to follow the pedals with his feet. He holds the handle with the knuckles uppermost. The handle-bars must be sufficiently high to clear the knee as the pedal reaches the uppermost point. If, in riding, the machine veers over, the rider can always recover himself by turning the handle-bars in that direction. This swerves the wheel in the line towards which the machine leans, and at once recovers the balance. In commencing to work the pedals let the pressure at first be very slight and even. A strong push will make the machine swerve with each stroke of the pedals, giving an unsteady and ungraceful gait. It is unnecessary to say that the rider should sit perfectly straight, and when riding slowly, the center of gravity should as nearly as possible run down the column of the spine; as the pace increases, the body may lean forward, until, at high speed, it rests against the pedals. The best riders, however, maintain the erect posture. Keen, at his greatest speed, sits perfectly erect, and it is to be noticed that the riders who adopt this position run the "cleanest line." Stanton adopts the leaning position, and his machine sways from side to side like a locomotive loosely coupled.

BICYCLING—MOUNTING.

**Dismounting.**—There are several ways of dismounting, first by the step. Take your feet off the pedals, and looking under the left arm, put the left foot on the step. Then rise on it, stretching out the arms, which will throw the body back, until you can drop to the ground with one leg on each side of the hind wheel. Having done this several times, try to remount without removing the left foot, touch the ground and spring back. Then hop twice on the right foot then three times and remount after each. You may then learn to mount, which is only the same motion, without the previous dismount. The next method of dismounting is by the backbone. Put the toe of the left foot round the backbone, raise the body, and drop off behind.

**Dismounting by the Pedals.**—As the right pedal approaches the lowest point, drop, throw the weight on the handles, and lift the seat from the saddle by pressure of the foot on the pedal, and spring off behind. Be careful that the machine does not kick and send you flying over its head.

**Dismounting over the Handles.**—Sit well back and throw either leg over the handles, catching the handle as the leg passes over; lean the machine the way you are going to dismount. It is a pretty and graceful feat.

**Dismounting by a Vault.**—Lift the body from the cross-bar and spring to the ground, bring the left foot over and round the backbone, and drop to the ground, still holding the handle. There are several positions more or less fanciful. For instance, on going down hill, throw both legs over the cross-bar and let the bicycle go of itself. Dismounting by a vault, when properly learned, is the best of all dismounts, as it is of service in any emergency.

**The Parts of a Bicycle.**—The bicycle consists of the framework and the wheels. The framework is composed of the head, handles, handle-bars, forks, break, backbone, springs, saddle, hind forks, and step. The large wheel consists of axles, cranks, hubs, pedals, spokes, bearings, and rims. At first these machines were made with wheels of the same size ; but no satisfactory speed was obtained until Parisian builders hit upon the device of a small hind wheel. There are two general styles : the "Racer," built very light for speed, and the "Roadster," heavier, for steady service.

LL nations, especially the more hardy ones, have from the very earliest days of their history, been fond of some kind of athletic sports, and our own country certainly forms no exception to the general rule.

A programme of sports generally includes the following contests: short distance race; long distance race; hurdle races; high jump and broad jump; putting the shot; throwing the hammer, and a walking race.

### SPRINTING

includes all races under 440 yards. To prepare for a short race, say 100 yards, the first thing is to walk steadily every day from five to seven miles at a good swinging pace, say four miles an hour. At the expiration of a week spurts of running two or three hundred yards should be added, but not too fast at first. As the muscles harden and the wind improves, 100 yards at full speed may be tried. Trainers recommend that the full strength should not be tried every day, but say every four days, to see if the powers are increasing. Every day for half an hour starting should be practiced. In starting, posture has a good deal to do with getting away well. Whichever foot is the strongest should be kept back; stretch out the arms with the hands clenched, and a cork or piece of paper in each, with the weight well on the back foot. This will enable the whole body to be instantaneously thrown forward. This should be well practiced, as a good start makes a great difference.

### QUARTER MILE RACE.

To train for this begin by walking as in the preceding case. Do not attempt to run the whole distance at once; not more than 250 yards, and that only as the muscles harden. Do not press your powers at first. Spins of 50 to 120 yards are enough, doing the whole distance not more than once in four days, and *not* for four days before the race. Stamina is wanted in this race, and so long as the muscles are lithe and the wind in good order, the last few days before the race should be a time of comparative rest.

The same remarks apply to one mile races, only the distances in training must be increased.

### HURDLE RACING.

These races are generally 120 yards with ten flights of hurdles 3 feet 6 inches high, and ten yards apart. This arrangement enables experienced runners to take each hurdle without stopping in the stride. Instead of jumping the hurdle fairly, they "buck" jumping off one foot and alighting on the other, generally off the right and on to the left. This requires less effort than a *bona fide* jump.

### THE HIGH JUMP.

Jumping has much increased in favor in late years. Four feet six used to be considered a marvelous feat. It is so no longer. The great art is to throw all the force into the upward-bound, and to do this the take off should be one-half the height of the jump—thus if the jump is five feet, take off at two and a half feet. Throw the body forward, tucking the legs well under it. Some jumpers still prefer the "buck;" approaching the bar sideways they spring, getting one leg over and throwing the other up so as to draw it after them. It is an ungraceful effort, but it saves several inches; in "bucking" the legs, the jumper, as it were, sits in the air describing two semi-circles with his legs.

### THE LONG JUMP.

The run should not be too long, twenty paces are enough. There is great art in so commencing the run that the last stride is not shortened or lengthened to suit the take off.

### POLE JUMPING.

Grasp the pole with both hands, the palms facing each other about three feet apart. The lower hand should grasp the pole at about the height of the object to be cleared. Take a short run, and in the high jump plant the pole six inches from the bar in front of the body, but a little to the left; as he body rises stiffen the arms and back, throwing the legs well out so as to fly over the bar, then let go the pole with a slight push, sufficient to let it fall back. In the long jump the body should be in front of the pole.

### PUTTING THE WEIGHT.

The shot used is 16 pounds. The putter takes it in his right hand, steadying with the left. He then raises and lets fall his hand, raising himself on his toes so as to get the swing. He then steps off with his right, takes two hops with the left leg; on landing off the second hop, he strides with his right and delivers the shot, but he must not cross the line, otherwise it is no put.

## HARE AND HOUNDS.

This favorite sport is almost too well known to require a description. The hares (there are generally two) are supplied with small sacks full of colored paper torn up very small. As they run they throw out handfuls, and so show the "scent." The hares get ten minutes to a quarter of an hour's law. They generally try to baffle the field by adopting a course of considerable difficulty, but they are "on honor" to fairly scatter the paper. At every gap, at every turn, and at every few yards in fact, out goes a handful. The hounds wait the required time, and then start off in full cry. There are huntsmen and whippers-in duly provided with horns. The runs are from eight to fifteen miles, and generally wind up with a good dinner. This pastime is a favorite during the winter and early spring. The party generally rendezvous at some hotel, from which they start, and to which they return to change clothes and dine.

HARE AND HOUNDS.

## WALKING.

Walking races are coming very much into vogue. It is as well to have some slight, light substance such as a cork or a piece of paper in the hands. One should wear walking slippers with no heels and spikes in the ball of the foot, a light jersey and knee pants not too tight. At the word *go*, the walker swings himself by working each arm and shoulder-blade with the corresponding step, so as to help the body by the action of these muscles. The foot must come down on the heel, the knee must be straight when the heel touches the ground and when it leaves it, but it may be bent in the middle of the pace. The great art is to twist the hips. By this means each stride is lengthened, and the leg carried more forward than in an ordinary pace.

## THROWING THE HAMMER.

The regulation hammer is 16 pounds, with a handle of three feet and six inches. Stand firm, the feet well apart; bring the hammer back, then swing forward, then back, not higher than the shoulder, then forward and let go.

## SKITTLES

May be termed nine pins on a large scale. The ground is laid out with planks of hard wood, and well fitted. The pins are set up as marked, and must be pushed down by the ball. There are several ways of scoring. One is to make thirty-one in the fewest throws, each pin scoring one. On the final throw, if more than the required number are knocked down it does not count, and the player throws again.

Another plan is for the players to throw alternately, getting as many as they can. The best game is where two players are allowed not more than three throws to clear the board. "A floorer," where the board is cleared in one throw, counts three; if in two throws, two; and in three, one. If a single pin remains after the third throw, it counts nothing.

## FIVES

Is probably the oldest game of ball. It is played with the palm of the hand against a wall. Along the base of the wall a wooden planking is nailed, about three feet up from the ground. The aim of each player is to strike the wall above the wooden planking, called the "baulk." The ground in front is marked out in counts by lines running from the wall and a line running parallel with it ten feet from the base. The striker-in plays the ball on to the wall, so that it bounds back beyond the ten-foot line. His opponent then returns it, and so on, till one lets it drop. If the striker-in drops it, it puts him out. If his adversary fails, he scores one point. The game is generally fifteen, but sometimes twenty-one.

## ICE YACHTING.

Ice yachting, of which we give a good illustration, requires an ice yacht which should be cutter rigged. The pace at which these yachts fly over smooth ice with a strong wind must be seen to be appreciated. The skill consists in handling the rudder and main-sheet. In approaching the wind the main-sheet must be hauled in. Before turning, ease her off the wind and then come up, not too quickly. There are a number of ice yachts on the Hudson, which affords one of the finest opportunities for the sport during frost in the world.

## LAWN BILLIARDS.

This is a pretty game for ladies. A revolving ring is set up. Each player has a ball and a cue, consisting of a long stick with a ring at the end.

The players start from a point, playing one after another at the ring, so as to pass through it. A player may either go at the ring or strike an opponent and then go through. The first counts one, "a carom" two. There is considerable skill in the game as it proceeds. A good player will so leave his opponent that the edge of the ring is towards him; in which case it is impossible to play through except by giving the ball a kind of twist which strikes the ring aside as it touches, and so enables the ball to pass through. The game is 31 up.

## QUOITS

Are iron rings (the cistus of the Romans), which are thrown so as to fall over a peg. The nearest only count, but if two or more of one side are nearer than the opponents, then each counts one.

## CANOEING

Is a sport of recent invention. Canoes are made of various builds. The navigator sits with his face to the prow and urges himself on with a paddle, worked alternately on each side. It is an excellent method of navigating shallow rivers, and affords an opportunity for very pleasant excursions.

## TOBOGANNING

Is a capital pastime in winter, much enjoyed in Canada. A course is cleared on the side of a hill, with a long reach of level ground at the base. The tobogan is a slip of birch bark, turned up at one end. The fun is to sit on it and go down hill at a tremendous pace. Serious accidents often occur, and a season rarely passes without some broken bones. Nevertheless, the excitement of the sport makes it very popular.

## TEN PINS

Are played in an alley, at the end of which is a triangular space on which the pins are set up, thus: . . . . Each player has three balls. If he clears the . . . board with one shot it counts 10. If not, as . . many pins as he knocks down are scored to . him.

## THE GAME OF SHINNY.

This game may be played either in a field or on the ice. If in the latter case every player must be a good skater, and the art of turning short, stopping, backing, etc., must be well known; a beginner on skates has no chance. Two goals are marked out either with poles or snow, and the ball has to be knocked through them. Sides being chosen, the players toss for first hit, which is made from the opposite goal. Sticks with a bend in the end are used. In England the game is called "Hockey."

## TUG-OF-WAR.

This is a good exercise. All that is required is a good rope. A knot is made in the middle, and on the ground a line is drawn. The sides then take hold, and those who first pull their adversaries over the line win. In pulling get your heel well into the ground. The more the body approaches the horizontal position the better tug can you give.

The great thing is for each side to pull with their leader well together, and by a series of jerks haul the adversaries over the line.

## BADMINTON.

This game is little more than lawn-tennis played with a battledore and shuttlecock instead of a ball. A net five feet high, at least, in the center of the court which is marked out in lines as in tennis. The player must serve so that the shuttlecock would fall into the further court. When one side fails to return, it scores one for the adversary. The game requires little skill.

DEVELOPMENT of the body through physical culture should undoubtedly be recognized as one of the most important branches of education.

The moral and mental education of the masses is fast attracting the attention of those most fit to guide in the national councils. In Germany, Austria, France, and in many of the United States, mental education is compulsory.

But the education of the body, who attends to that? Who spends time, money, rears buildings, trains teachers for that? Who points out to boy or girl what will bring vigor, size and shape to the body and limbs, however weak they may now be, bloom to the cheeks, buoyancy to the spirits, and health to the bones? Surely in any intelligent community this branch, of vital importance, cannot be overlooked.

Oh, but we do not want our children athletes! Well, is every hale, manly, well-knit man an athlete? Or every blooming, shapely, gracefully-stepping woman? No more than a fair conversationalist is an orator, or a house-painter an artist. An athlete first gets ready, and then contends in some sharp test of speed, strength or stay, or two or all of these. In doing so he goes on after heart and lungs are tired, and had better stop. Go with him only till he begins to tire, till the risk *begins*, and you avoid that risk, at the same time getting most of the benefit. Temporary fame and some trifling memento, or, if he is a professional, a portion—often but a small portion—of money, are the rewards of the athlete's efforts and for the risk he takes. Yours, if you have stopped in time, health, no risk, and, in the muscles and parts used, size and strength. But only in those used. Rowell, the great go-as-you-please traveler, has colossal legs, but his arms are not developed. The machinists, stone-masons and other swingers of heavy hammers have a strong hammering arm, another arm not so strong, and legs worth little on a race-course. And so down the whole range of men who use their muscles either for sport or for bread—or both.

Now if we learn how to get strength in one part from one class of men, in another from another, why may not the whole man, and the boy, and girl and woman be built well, not only here and there, but throughout? And so gain not only strength, but health; for, while not identical, who has not observed how intimately related are these two, and how apt to go together?

Every intelligent man must have often been struck with the fact that the well-built man or woman, boy or girl, to-day is, especially in cities and towns, the exception and not the rule, and this town population, both in England and America, is rapidly on the increase.

The country-bred boy gets years of pure air, ample out-door exercise for some of his principal muscles, though seldom for all, and is vigorous and hearty, though often slow of movement and lacking spring. But these years of out-door active life lay him up an annuity-fund of vigor and health, on which he may draw all his after life, if he spends that life in the city. But what annuity-fund does the city boy roll up? Will the top, kite, or marbles bring deep lungs and sturdy limbs? Can one city-boy in ten run three miles, or even one? Or avoid being left out of sight in a race with his country cousin with hoe or spade, with fork, sickle, or scythe? And, as soon as he is out of school, at thirteen, fourteen, or fifteen, do eight, ten, and, when business is driving, twelve hours a day of confinement in dusty factory, or behind counters, or over a set of books, bringing him home at night jaded and exhausted, tend to build up that fund, and make him reasonably certain to live out even half his days?

Growing faster at sixteen than in any other year, his body needing much of his strength to meet the unusual call, the Greeks and Romans spent hours daily at this period in building and toughening the youth, and fitting him for the exacting demands of after-life, sure to come to all. We, too often, bring him up to sixteen with nothing worth calling strength; and then put him, immature and half-built, where he stands excellent chance of never getting any more, and of losing what he has.

And again, would not a vigorous body aid him greatly in his life's work, though that work be of a sort calling for every hour of severe and often anxious brain tension he can possibly stand? If that brain is fed with blood, will it not work better fed with rich blood, than with a poor article—with—figuratively—cream than with skimmed milk. But, if the blood-making machinery gets sluggish, clogged, and run down, will it supply as good food to the brain as that important organ demands? If one member suffers, do not all the members suffer with it?

Is the course of him who brings his body up to manhood a poor, often spindling affair, when half developed in muscular or vital power, likely to make him win in the very struggle his every energy is bent on? Dash away he may at the start, and hold the lead for a while; but who in a five-mile race can rush the first mile up into one prolonged, mad spurt, and hope to be anywhere at the end of the fifth mile or even of the second, however trained and tough he may be? The steadier man beside him, a little less forward perhaps mentally, though not necessarily so, is the one he has to fear in that contest, where "all that makes a man" is sure to tell. The exercise and pastimes of the girl are usually not even as vigorous as the boy's, nor as likely to fit her to safely face the exacting demands, the anxieties, the privations, and bereavements of her later life. If the boy's body needs careful, sensible building, her body needs it even more.

And what is being done to meet this so general need? The athletes and those who take exercise more than they need are, in many communities, scarcely one per cent. of the population. A majority of the rest grope about in their physical education without definite aim, and not knowing what parts they are using, what they are ignoring. If their daily work uses the muscles, it uses only some and leaves the rest as idle as the unexercised muscles of the athlete.

If the education of the body were made a branch in every day-school and every class-room, if the teacher of the mind knew how to train the body also, and devoted even twenty minutes daily to the forty or more pupils under his or her charge, the effect would be beneficial and gratifying in the extreme. Without going, in the brief space allotted here, into definite and specific suggestions as to what course such teacher should follow, it may yet be well enough to point out what muscles and parts are called into play by the use of most of the well-known appliances for exercise, whether indoors or out, and so to indicate in what field or fields of development they had better labor.

The facilities and contrivances for directly enlarging and strengthening any muscles one wishes are many, easy to construct, and inexpensive. For those desiring great progress and proficiency in any athletic, gymnastic, or acrobatic line, books have been written, and may be readily obtained, guiding them in the work, and pointing out its peculiar advantages, and the chief performances thus far accomplished in it. The aim here will be rather to name just what sort of development one may look for in practicing assiduously any of the better known and popular exercises, and so enable him or her, or the teacher, to at once pick out work for any muscles which have been neglected, and, by daily practice, though only for a few minutes, soon bring them a good degree of size and strength.

LET us first look at those exercises which may be taken in-doors, most of them without cumbrous apparatus, indeed many of them in an ordinary sized room. One of the most graceful ones practiced widely to-day in some countries—notably in Germany, is fencing.

### FENCING.

This is capital work for the calves, the front of the thighs, the abdominal muscles, one shoulder, the extensor muscles of one arm, and the muscles of one wrist and hand, while it also keeps the lungs fully occupied. Of course it leaves the other shoulder, arm, and hand practically idle, and gives most of the muscles of the trunk only light work, nothing like as hard as it does those of the parts just named. It would be hard to find any exercise better fitted to bring grace, nerve, swiftness of eyes and of judgment, dash, and agility, or more useful in war times, especially for any one liable to fill any position where he will wear a sword. But it is a pity that every fencer was not required to fence as much with one hand as with the other; then he would have two good hands, two good arms, and two good shoulders, instead of only one of each, hence would come far nearer to becoming a well-built man. Should he ever lose his fencing-arm, he could also thus save himself the need of beginning all over again.

### BOXING.

Here is better work in many ways than fencing. You always have your tools with you. You use about every muscle you do in fencing, and while the wrists have less to do, you use two arms instead of one, and of course also two shoulders. It does little for the biceps or flexor muscles of the upper arms, but it is grand for the back-arms, which do so much of the pushing when you press with the hands against anything, indeed it is one of the best-known exercises for them from the marvelous rapidity and strength combined, which are essential in order to deserve the name of boxer It would be well if every boy or man were at least a fair boxer, and for all males whose occupation is sedentary, if they practiced this famous exercise a few minutes daily.

### SINGLE-STICK

is in many respects very similar to fencing in its effects on the muscles, slower, because the weapon is heavier, taking the biceps and the inner part of the back-arm more, because, instead of lunging out the point of the weapon, you bring it down with a sharp blow or swipe. It keeps the entire shoulder ceaselessly active, the wrist and fore-arm also, and the abdominal muscles, fronts of the thighs, and the calves always going. But, as in fencing, two hands should learn it—not one,—else, a one-sided man.

### WRESTLING

is now much practiced in-doors on a large soft mat, though of course the turf is always a good place for it. No other exercise has yet been discovered which so swiftly and surely brings power to the sides of the waist. No weak-waisted boy or man is much of a wrestler. It is one endless tugging at the side muscles, in a hundred directions almost, but at these muscles all the time. It also uses every part of the legs and hips vigorously, and gives both arms, both shoulders, and the entire trunk constant exercise, though the waist and legs get the giant's share. Strength in every muscle will aid the wrestler, but a sturdy waist and tough, well-knit legs are simply indispensable to his success at his chosen sport. Probably no other exercise comes nearer calling all the muscles into play, but to bring the arms, especially the extensor muscles of the arms, up to great size and power, harder work directly for them will be needed.

### DANCING.

This most popular of in-door exercises gives spring, elasticity, and as ordinarily practiced, considerable strength to the muscles of the foot, the ankles, calves, and front or upper muscles of the thighs, while the abdominal muscles and those of the sides of the waist are not idle. Professional dancers, those who for years practice this work for hours daily, come by-and-by to marvelous strength and grace in these muscles thus used. The arms, shoulders, and upper end of the trunk have practically nothing to do, save that the breast and lungs are rather more active in their duties than ordinarily.

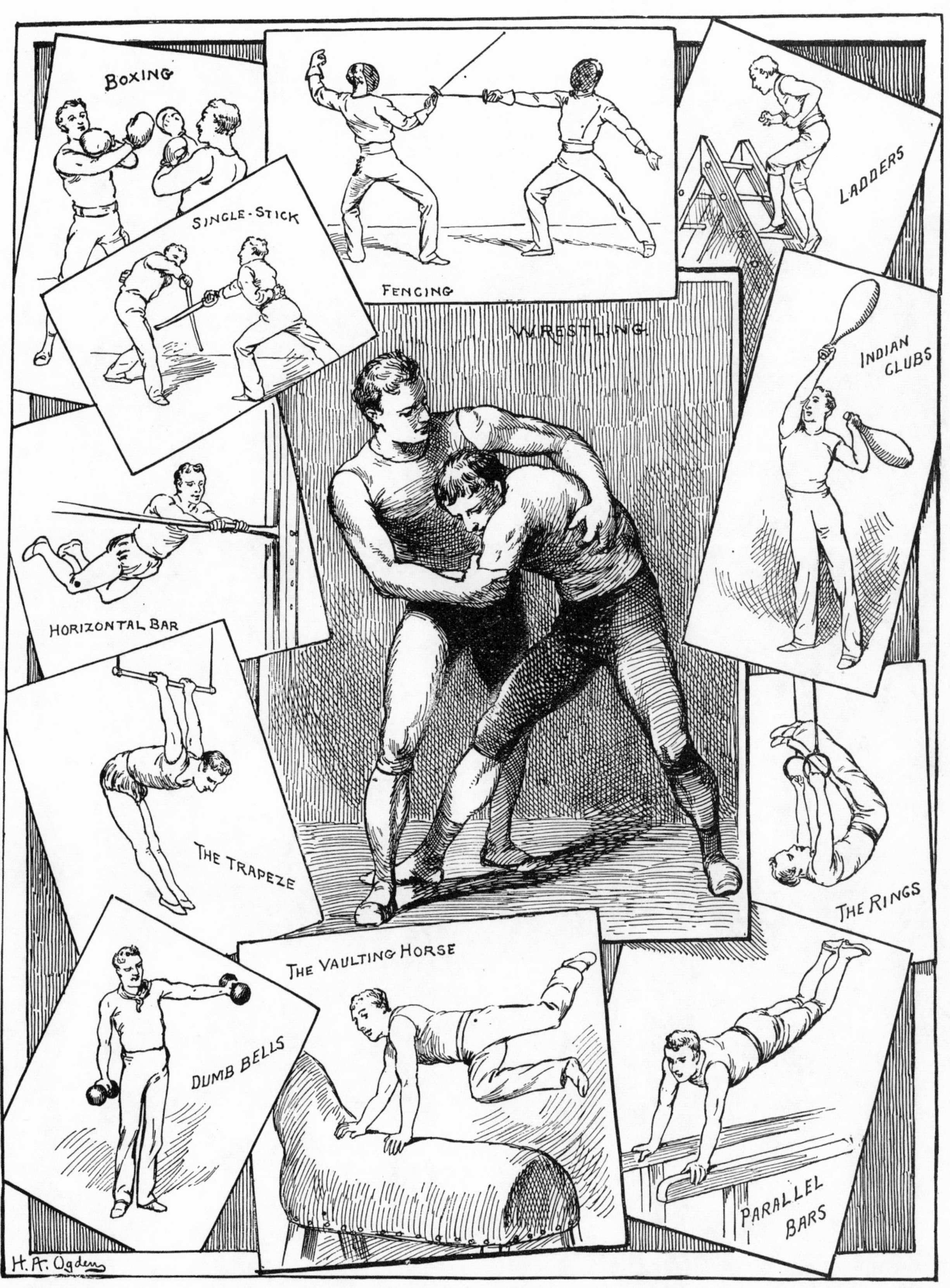
BOXING
SINGLE-STICK
FENCING
LADDERS
WRESTLING
INDIAN CLUBS
HORIZONTAL BAR
THE TRAPEZE
THE RINGS
THE VAULTING HORSE
DUMB BELLS
PARALLEL BARS
H. A. Ogden

## Exercises in the Gymnasium.

N the five preceding exercises the development of particular muscles was a secondary matter, often indeed not thought of, the chief purpose in all but one of them being to out-do one's antagonist. But the machinery of the gymnasium looks directly, among other things, to the education of the various parts of the body, and its tools are the body's school-books, by the judicious use of which it gradually comes to facility and fitness for its demands, as surely as the mind, by its training, does to those of our intellectual life. Let us consider first :—

### THE VAULTING HORSE.

This sturdy, headless monster is still seen in the gymnasium, though the room he takes is grudged far more than formerly, because you can get, on other apparatus, almost any exercise he can offer. Largely, work on this animal calls out the legs, especially the muscles of the calf and front thigh. The trunk is more of the time idle, though occasionally rushed into vigorous use, and the same is true of about all parts of the arms and shoulders. But so suddenly do these demands come that they are liable to strain and overdo the parts thus called on ; and it would be better, with persons not already fully developed above the waist, to first become so by exercises on other appliances before becoming intimate with this anchored steed.

### THE SPRING-BOARD

is a glorious friend of the legs, indeed would be a valuable adjunct to every home in any land, certainly every home whose people were confined most hours of the twenty-four in-doors. For bringing grace, size and power to the lower limbs, it stands almost unrivaled. As most exercises on it are practiced, that is, with the knees more or less bent, the upper thighs, the calves, the abdominal and sides, get the bulk of the work. But now keep the body erect, the legs rigidly stiff, and the knees sprung hard back all the time you are springing and alighting, and you suddenly find that a new set of muscles—those on the under side of the thighs —not large, but very important ones in bringing symmetry and graceful shape to the legs—are brought into vigorous action. The higher you jump on the spring-board, and especially the higher you raise your knees, the more vigorously you set the muscles across the abdomen at work, muscles which, if kept tough and in good condition by a little steady, daily exercise, are almost sure to prove great friends to good digestion and assimilation, and to sound health as well.

### LIFTING.

The standing astride of a heavy weight and lifting it, has become popular of late years, until the "health lift" is a well-known term, especially in American cities. The tendency of this exercise, is to give certain muscles violent work to do, their very utmost, and to partly or wholly ignore the others. Of course, one result is to make the muscles used strong, and to do nothing for the others. The pushing muscles of the arms for instance, those which take so prominent a part in the make-up of a well-shaped arm, are idle here. A natural tendency of trying to lift as many hundred pounds as you can every day—or nearly as many—is to stiffen the lifter, and make him slow and unwieldy, like a draft-horse, unless he takes special pains to counteract it by exercises calling for spring, agility, and pace. The late Dr. Winship, of Boston, who introduced this exercise in America, said also that it tended to depress the instep, and make a man flat-footed, and it would seem as if supporting from half a ton to a ton for a while every day, so that practically the whole weight came directly on the feet, could not fail to have this tendency.

These are the more prominent leg-exercises of the gymnasium, especially now when athletic clubs and field-sports invite both boy and man out-doors to take his foot work in pure air, and under the clear sky. Large and well made mattresses, many inches thick, laid on the floor, also invite the hand-springs, cart-wheels, and single and double, forward and back somersaults, the building of pyramids of men, the hard jumping, the alighting from a height, and in general the high and lofty tumbling of the acrobat, in which, of course, the two chief sets of the muscles of the legs already mentioned play a conspicuous part.

### THE PARALLEL BARS

are an excellent contrivance for developing principally the back-arms, the muscles on the front of the shoulders, and those across the chest. The whole weight rests, not on the feet but on the hands, and the more the elbows are bent in practicing on these bars, the harder the work, and especially on the muscles named. Any of the exercise practiced with the elbows much bent, and followed up daily, until one begins to feel tired, will soon tell noticeably and satisfactorily on the size and strength of the back-arms, and of the breast muscles. They also serve to expand the chest and throw the shoulders well back, which effect will be increased if the chin is held up high throughout each exercise. But, before using these bars, the muscles called into action ought, in most persons, to be prepared for this severe work by lighter exercises, as where part only of the weight rests on the hands, and the other part on the feet.

### HIGH PARALLEL BARS.

These two bars, about as high as one can comfortably reach, take hold of the arms in a way almost exactly the opposite of that just described. They do little or nothing for the back-arms, as the exercises do not call for pushing or lifting the body's weight by pushing against any substance, but by pulling. Hanging with one hand on each bar, and lifting yourself along by steps or springs, the fore-arms, the biceps muscles, and those of the upper back just behind the upper arm, get the bulk of the work, holding as they do pretty much the whole weight of the body, to

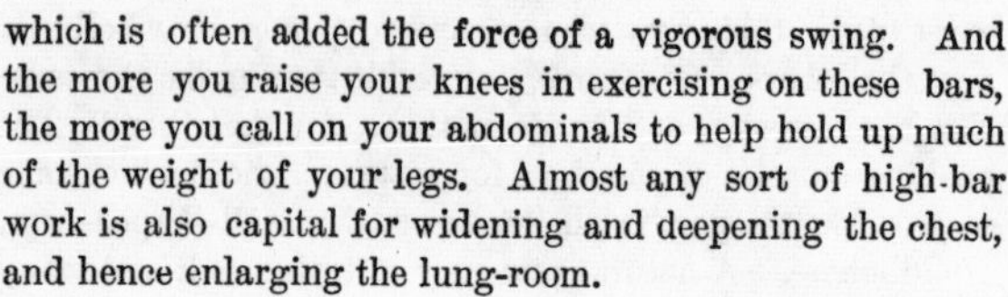

which is often added the force of a vigorous swing. And the more you raise your knees in exercising on these bars, the more you call on your abdominals to help hold up much of the weight of your legs. Almost any sort of high-bar work is also capital for widening and deepening the chest, and hence enlarging the lung-room.

## THE HORIZONTAL BAR.

A round bar of ash or other hard wood, about two inches thick, and seven to eight feet long, placed horizontally across between two upright posts, and capable of being raised or lowered at pleasure, is one of the tools of the acrobat, rather than of him who merely seeks moderate and harmonious muscular development. While it uniformly does little for the legs, there is scarcely a muscle of the arms or trunk which is not brought into vigorous play by some or other of the numerous exercises practiced on this simple bar, the abdominals especially, and the muscles used most in the high parallels getting the hardest of the work. Hanging by the knee, heel, or toes, of course also gives the leg so used something to do. If by the toes, a small muscle along the shin bone—one which in most exercises is idle—is hurried into active service.

## THE VAULTING BAR

is a little thicker and stiffer than the horizontal bar, and fitting into the same frame, may of course be raised or lowered at will. Standing with your side to it, and taking hold with the hand nearest it, you give a sharp spring jump over the bar, and land on the other side, never letting go your grip until your body is well over. After thus jumping and raising the bar steadily, until you can no longer clear it with one hand, you now face the bar, grasp it with both hands, and go on thus vaulting over it till you get it up as high as you can clear, or with the bar as high as your waist, grasping it with both hands, you spring and bring your feet over the bar, this time not outside of but between your hands, not letting go till your feet are past it. These, and the other exercises of the vaulting bar are grand for bringing spring and strength to the muscles of the foot, calf, and front-thigh, and to those of the abdomen, but the arms have no hard work here.

## THE TRAPEZE

is practically a swinging horizontal bar, or often two such bars, one hung a little above the other. You repeat on the trapeze the very exercises you first learn to do on the horizontal bar, and bring the same muscles into play. But it is harder for them, and the side and abdominal muscles are sharply at work much of the time, because of your effort to keep the bar still, and yourself from swaying. Often too the gymnast will purposely swing off from the trapeze, and spring to another trapeze or to the floor below, in the latter case, if the height is great, severely testing the strength of his feet and knees, and of the muscles of the fronts of his thighs, his calves, and of his feet. Where two persons work together on the trapeze, they generally merely give the muscles used a much harder task, but seldom use different muscles from those either person would were he up there alone. The trapeze is one of the best devices in the gymnasium for teaching one to keep cool in exciting and hazardous situations, and if the performer is well-made, and also skilled at his work, it offers a wide field for the exhibition of agility and grace.

## THE STRIKING BAG

Made of sheep or calf-skin, round, a foot in diameter, and full of sawdust, and hung by a single rope, the center of the bag being about as high as your chin, is a simple and valuable contrivance for setting nearly all the muscles of the arms, shoulders, body, and legs at work. Of course the exercise is substantially that of boxing, lacking, however, the advantage the latter has in keeping before you a shadowy, evasive, and often dangerous object, ever on the alert to bring that object's fist and some point of your head or body in close, and at times painful, contact. But the bag is inviting and handy, ready when, as is often the case, you cannot get any one to spar with, just when it is convenient to you, and would do much for many an indoor man's digestion and wind, if he would only punch it faithfully a hundred good times each day.

## THE RINGS.

Two iron rings, eight or ten inches in diameter, the iron being about an inch thick and covered tightly with leather, or better yet, with rubber, hung from the ceiling, or a frame overhead, by two ropes long enough to bring the bottom of the rings as high as you can comfortably reach, and about twenty inches apart; these are among the best tools in the gymnast's outfit for developing strength and daring. While the legs have little to do, the abdominal muscles are severely at work during all the forward swing, and through the latter half of the swing backward as well. In fact, the abdominal muscles are kept longer under tension, and given more to do, while one is swinging on the rings, than in almost any other exercise in the gymnasium. The chest also is stretched to its utmost capacity, the upper back, just behind the arms, is on fatigue duty, the bicep muscles likewise, and the grip of the hands must be simply perfect, or their owner's usefulness is liable to be temporarily impaired,—for all depends on that grip.

Sometimes, instead of only two rings, a row of six or eight, hung not twenty inches apart, but seven or more feet, are stretched along a room, so that, in swinging, you pass rapidly from one to the next, and so on to the end, the feet of course never touching the floor, and the weight being sustained, now wholly by one hand, then by the other. This is harder on the arms and shoulders—easier on the abdominals.

## EXERCISING-WEIGHTS

Are placed in spouts, or long narrow upright boxes, which are about as high as one's head. From each weight a rope runs up over a pulley at the top of the box, then out to a handle of which you take hold. Instead of the upright boxes, Dr. Sargent, of the Hemenway Gymnasium, at Harvard University, has introduced two upright rods of iron, just far enough apart to let a loaded weight-box travel up and down between the rods, thus avoiding the bumping and noise of the old plan, and allowing you to put what weight in the boxes you like. Standing, facing these weights, and pulling, the hands, wrists, fore-arms, biceps muscles, inner side of the upper-arms, and whole upper half of the back, are vigorously at work, and also the back of the neck, while, if you sit down to it, you also call on the lower half of the back as well, and, if you raise your feet at all, you give the fronts of your thighs, and your calves, active service. But while this pulling alone tends to enlarge the back, and rather flatten the chest, by turning with your back to the weights, and now pushing the handles out in front, you get the opposite effect, opening and expanding your chest, drawing the shoulders backward, and taking now the muscles on the front of the shoulders and chest, instead of those on the back of them. Hence an equal share of each sort of work will tend to bring equal development to both front and back.

## INDIAN CLUBS

Give the hands, fore-arms, and shoulders much to do, the upper arms not much, except the outer side of the back-arms, or that farthest from the body. They expand the chest and stretch the abdominal muscles, so counteracting the tendency of sedentary life to make one cramp both the chest and abdomen, and they take the large muscles just under and back of each arm. But there is a strong tendency in club-swinging to hold the shoulders so far back that it pitches the head forward, so both making one inerect, and expanding the lower part of the chest more than the upper. About all that can be done with clubs can also be done with dumb-bells, and a good deal more besides, while, from taking much less space, they often prove more profitable. The legs and lower-back, of course, do not get much hard work from clubs, scarcely, in fact, have anything to do.

## THE WRIST WEIGHT

Has a rope running from it up over a thick horizontal bar, hung about breast-high. By grasping this bar with both hands, on top instead of under it, and then turning your knuckles outward and away from you, or by turning them strongly towards you, your wrists soon get all the exercise they want, and the effect on their size and strength will ere long be noticeable. Exercise of this sort will greatly aid the fencer for the arduous wrist-work his favorite accomplishment demands.

## EXERCISING LADDERS,

Broad, strong, and unmovable, are set either horizontally a little higher than you can reach, or sloping upward to the ceiling. They keep the hands, forearms, biceps muscles, and the muscles of the back, just behind the upper-arms ceaselessly at work, while the moment you raise foot or knee the abdominals, which before were somewhat stretched by the weight of your legs hanging down, are now promptly contracted and given plenty to do. As it is practically impossible to put your hands up over your head without, for the time opening and expanding your chest, of course all kinds of ladder-work are excellent at affecting this desirable end.

## THE CLIMBING POLE.

A smooth, round ash pole, about two and a quarter inches thick, and hung from the ceiling—or a rope not quite so thick and hung in the same way—encourage a vice-like grip, as much as any known apparatus. For, as you mount either hand over hand, letting your legs hang straight downward, the entire weight of the body and limbs is held up, now by one hand, now by the other. No one can do much on this valuable, though simple apparatus, who has not good forearms, and its steady use soon brings up those very useful members of the body corporate. Besides using the same muscles which are called into action by work on the ladders, rings, and high bars, the pole or rope teach one to use his feet strongly in gripping with them, and with the inner and under muscles of the thighs, as these parts are often required to sustain much or all of one's weight.

## DUMB-BELLS.

There is scarcely any exercise of the countless ones which may be taken on the various gymnastic appliances already named that cannot be had, at least in part, if not wholly, without any of them, and by using dumb-bells only. If you want to push, pull, grip, or twist, if you want to use almost any muscle of your body, or of any limb, the dumb-bells are always at your service, patient friends, within the reach of all, so little do they cost, and never wearing out. Hold them out horizontally and twist them, now one way, now the other, and your hands, wrists, forearms, and shoulders are all busy—lift them from your knees to your shoulders, and the biceps muscles are at once the busy ones. Hold them up high behind you, and the backs of your shoulders and inner muscles of your upper-arms are doing the lion's share ; keep putting them up and down above your head, and your chest is stretched and opened ; and, if you then slowly lower them from as high as you can reach till your arms are out straight at your sides, as they would be on a cross, and at the same time hold your chin up high, and breathe a deep, full breath, your chest will be stretched to its utmost. Stoop down low, forty or fifty times, with dumb-bells in your hands, and the fronts of your thighs will be the busiest parts of you ; stand erect, with bells in hand, and now simply raise your heels as high as you can without taking your feet off the floor, then lower; then so raise and lower a hundred times, and, if you are not used to it, your calves will ache so that you can scarcely stand up.

We have thus taken a look at the chief and best-known appliances of the gymnasium, the indoor school for body-building, and at their simpler and principal uses. But there is a range of exercise almost more extensive, which combines far more of the element of play and sport, and has the commanding advantage of being practiced in perfectly pure air, and in the cheering sunlight. Let us glance at each, and at its part in muscle-making.

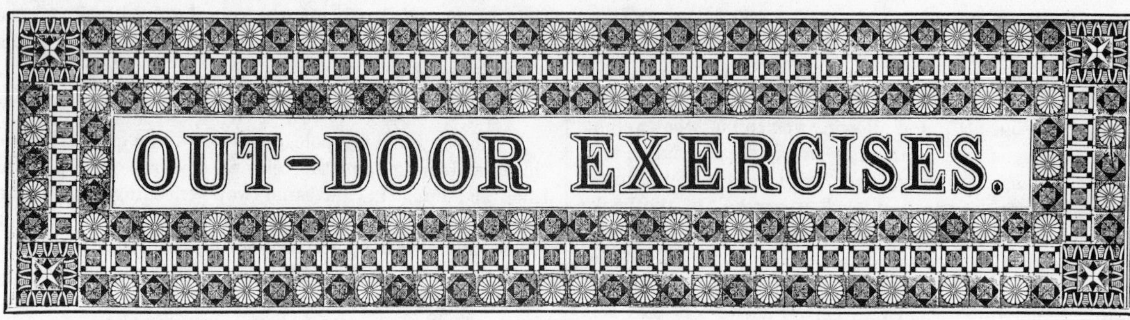

# OUT-DOOR EXERCISES.

## RIDING.

RIDING may be very easy exercise, or very severe, so much depends both on the gait of the horse, and on the skill of the man in avoiding effort. While the calves and fronts of the thighs are both always busy, unless the horse is standing or walking, it makes a great difference in the result on the muscles in these parts whether one places only the ball of each foot in the stirrup or pushes each so far in that the hollow of the foot rests on the stirrup. In the latter case the calves are almost idle, but in the former, they do an important—often the most important—share of the task of sustaining the whole body, and that not at rest, but ever rising and falling. One unused to riding, and to any other exercise calling much on his calves, will be sure, if he will only insert his feet but a little way in the stirrups, to have aching calves on the morning after a two or three hours' brisk ride, and probably stiff knees as well. And another kind of annoyance is liable to come, which may not leave so promptly as does the ordinary ache from suddenly giving unused muscles too much to do, and that is not only sore abdominal muscles, for these bands are ceaselessly active in helping to keep the body erect, but, in many cases, actual rupture. Indeed, it is a very common thing, at the breaking out of a war, to see cavalrymen, who have not been accustomed to riding and are suddenly required to do much of it, get ruptured and unfit for service. Strong abdominal muscles, kept in good order by even two minutes brisk daily exercise, would have saved them the discomfort and chagrin of having to go through much or all of the rest of their lives unsound men.

## WALKING

Slowly, or at a moderate pace, will not bring much size or strength to any muscles, unless long distances are systematically covered in this way. But quicken the pace till it averages four or more miles an hour, and the work gets vigorous enough to bring the fronts of the thighs plenty to do. If one does not raise his heels much, as is very frequently the fact, but walks almost flat-footed, he gives his toes, soles, insteps, and calves little to do, and his whole step lacks spring. But, if he will push hard with toes and soles, as they leave the ground, will step short, rather than overstep, and will spring his knees well back, at the same time holding his chin well up, he will find his calves full of work, going in fact all they know how, while not only the fronts of his thighs are as busy as ever, but the back or under muscles as well. Walking up hill takes his calves and the backs of his thighs in the same way, also his hips. A strong walker wants good lungs and loins, sides and abdominals, while light shoulders and arms give him less to carry, hence render his task easier.

## RUNNING

Is sharper leg work, and, followed up sensibly, is apt to bring strong and good-sized legs in much shorter time than walking will. You may walk so as to use neither calf, underthigh, nor hip to any appreciable extent; but it is hard work to run in any way so as not to develop all three, while the faster you run the more they have to do, for you then lift the heels much higher, and, in good running, go on the toes and soles only, never touching the heels to the ground. The breathing power, or "wind," gets good and enduring from steady practice, hence the lungs are enlarged and strengthened. Power of arm and shoulder a runner does not need, but strong abdominal muscles, especially at sharp, short-distance work, he must have. But the great shaft-horse muscles of the runner, especially over long distances —many miles—are those of the front thigh. Downright power he must have here, or he will not stay far at a fast pace. He may ease his abdominals, his under-thighs, and calves by flat-footed work, but upper-thigh he cannot do without, and scarcely a day passes but power here avails any man, even at his ordinary round of work or play, as it makes each step an easy one.

## JUMPING

Is the sharpest sort of work for front-thigh, calf, and abdominals, likewise about the quickest known work for bringing spring, size, and power to each of these parts. Put your hand on your calf as you spring, and you will feel it suddenly harden and knot up like whipcord. Five minutes of jumping daily, either flat or high, forward, backward, or sideways, upward or downward, will, in even one month, bring very gratifying results to him desiring good legs and a light, active step. The arms help a little, but nothing to speak of, the exercise being preëminently leg-work. Some physicians recommend this exercise as having an admirable effect on the nervous system, making one less sensitive to sudden noises, jars, and excitement, and tending to bring calm and quiet nerves.

### PUTTING THE SHOT

Is glorious work for the arm and shoulder which do the putting, good for both legs, and capital for one side of the waist. One puts into a supreme effort every atom of power he can muster, hoping, by throwing the heavy weight even one-eighth of an inch further than his adversaries, to win the prize. The whole pushing side of his body is stretched upward to its uttermost, while the opposite side of his waist is compacted and hardened, and given all it can stand. The lungs also are swollen to their fullest, and then all the air held in till the effort is over. Change the game to the best score from *both* one's hands, instead of from one only, and the small and unused back-arm and shoulder would catch up with its fellow, bringing even, instead of, as now, only partial development.

### THROWING THE HAMMER

Takes a firm grip in both hands, strong and reliable fore-arms, able biceps muscles, and great power of both shoulders. It lifts and expands the whole chest, stretches the abdominals instead of contracting them, needs a sturdy grip on the ground with the feet, and sides and waist, in general, which will not let the thrower sway at the moment he most wants to stand rigidly firm. It is as if a hardy axeman gathered all the strength of the ten thousand blows he strikes in a day into one mighty effort. Hence to prepare for this kind of work, one should build up the parts used, by lighter exercises, before doing much of it.

### SWIMMING,

One of the best-known exercises to bring capacious and powerful lungs, gives also to the whole calf, thigh, hip, loin, side, and abdominal muscles quick and active work, leaves the biceps idle, toughens the fore-arm, and calls steadily and even severely on the back-arm, the entire shoulder, and the muscles of the back just behind the shoulder. The breast muscles also have fair, though not very hard work to do.

### SKATING

Takes hold of the sides and abdominal muscles far more than walking, owing to the constant and often vigorous effort to keep from falling over. Needing good ankles, it is fine work for the lungs, calves, fronts of the thighs, and hips. Of course the arms have an easy time of it.

### ROWING,

Especially if you sit on a sliding-seat, and push your best with toes and soles against the stretcher, sets the calves and fronts of the thighs at very sharp work, takes hold of the loins almost more than anywhere else, and cannot be done at all rapidly, and for any length of time, without good development of the abdominal muscles. The upper-back does much and so do the fore-arms, the inner muscles of the upper arms next the body, and the backs of the shoulders, while the biceps and breast muscles and most of the back-arm have so little to do that rowing alone never brings them to much size or power. A good oar also needs a strong neck, and plenty of lung room, but foot-work, and exercises which will raise and expand his chest, are far more likely than rowing to give him the latter.

### BICYCLING

Incites a man to add to the size and power of the fronts of his thighs, his calves, his abdominal muscles, and the sides of his waist, and the firm grip on the handle brings strong hands, fore-arms, and inner muscles of his upper arms, while, if the hands are held nails upwards, the biceps muscles and fronts of the shoulders suddenly have a deal to do. The muscles of the back, just behind and above the elbows, are also not idle, while, if one will determinedly carry his head well back, he will also build up a good back-neck.

### THE TUG-OF-WAR

Is often extremely severe work, and he who attempts it, unless in at least fair muscular condition, and accustomed to considerable active exercise, stands a good chance of injuring his heart—possibly of stopping its action. The front of each thigh, the whole of each calf, back and forearm, the inner side of the upper-arm, and the back of the neck, as well as the lungs and heart, are worked as violently as their owner's will can drive them, the effort often being kept up till he can stand it no longer, and becomes absolutely exhausted. His breast-muscles, and those of all of the back-arm, save its inner side, are practically left unused, likewise those of the fronts and sides of his shoulders.

We have thus looked at the chief parts called into action by about all of the well-known out-door and in-door exercises which are indulged in for the purpose of recreation, health, or strength. Baseball, cricket, and numerous other games that have been described in the article "Out-door Sports and Pastimes," tend to promote a healthy action of the body, as well as develop certain muscles which are brought into play. The various trades and callings which bring a man bread by manual labor, of course, also each develop the muscles used, and leave the rest as they were, the aim being to get through the work, and the effect on the workman usually quite a secondary matter. Hence, men so occupied, if they care for symmetry of make and strength throughout, instead of only in parts, must single out and practice such exercises as will give the unused muscles also due attention, and, from the extensive field above, there should be no difficulty in readily selecting the sort of work needed, and then a little steady persevering effort at it each day will do the rest.

# The Care of Health.

N the care of health there are certain essentials which, in a work of this kind, it is only possible to glance at; we shall, however, give a few directions concerning those which are most important:—

1. **Diet.** This should be plain and wholesome, and of a mixed character. It should also be moderate as to quantity, and regular, allowing neither too long nor too short intervals between meals.

2. **Exercise.** Daily exercise is necessary to the enjoyment of good health, and if possible should be taken when the air is good and free from smoke and other impurities. The best forms of exercise are walking, riding, rowing, etc. When outdoor exercise is impracticable, the dumb-bells, single-stick, and billiards may be advantageously substituted. (See "Physical Culture" and "Out-Door Sports and Pastimes.")

3. **Pure Air.** The thorough ventilation of the house or rooms we live in is another essential to health, and must on no account be neglected. Nothing is so conducive to sickness as hot and stuffy rooms; and this remark is especially applicable to the bed-room, which should be of sufficient size, permitting a free current of pure air to pass through it during the hours when it is not occupied. And here it may not be out of place to observe that it is not sufficient to open doors leading into passages or staircases, which may contain all the bad air of the house; neither does it do to open windows looking into confined and impure spaces. Ventilation, to be of any service, must permit of the exit of the bad air in such a way that it cannot reenter, and of the admission of the pure air from the best source without.

4. **Clothing.** This should be comfortable only, too much wrapping up being quite as prejudicial to health as too little. It should be adapted to the season of the year, and should always in this country include thick under-clothing for the winter and light for the summer. The feet also should be well protected by warm stockings and strong boots. The custom of placing thick layers of flannel on the chest in the form of a chest-protector is very much to be deprecated, except in the case of really delicate people.

5. **The Bath.** This is a valuable adjunct to health, and should be taken cold during the summer months, and with the chill taken off for the remainder of the year. A warm soap and water bath should be taken at bed-time once a week, or once a fortnight, or the Turkish bath may be enjoyed by those who can indulge in the luxury, care being taken not to drive but to walk briskly home afterward, if the distance is not too great.

6. **A Calm Temperament.** Those who are so constituted, or who have sufficient command over themselves as to preserve this condition, have a most valuable adjunct to health, as there is perhaps nothing so prejudicial in this age of overwork both of brain and body as the worries and anxieties of every-day life. As a general rule the easy-going even-tempered man must digest his food better, and is less affected by the daily wear and tear of life, than the passionate, impetuous, and impatient man, and will live longer.

7. **Rest and Amusement.** These are essentials to health, hence the proverbs, "You cannot burn the candle at both ends," and "All work and no play make Jack a dull boy." The want of rest may endanger life; Jack's dullness will end in sickness.

## HEALTH MAXIMS.

Early to bed and early to rise make a man healthy and wealthy and wise.

When you are well, let yourself alone; you can never be better than well.

The almost universal cause of dyspepsia is eating too fast, too often, and too much.

Never take a cold bath while tired, nor less than two hours after a regular meal.

Sameness of food is a great drawback to health, for nature craves a variety of elements.

That man lives longest who wisely divides the occupations of life between brain and muscle.

Never eat when you are not hungry, nor drink when you are not thirsty; it imposes on nature.

Marriage is the natural condition of man, and without it no man or woman ever feels settled in life.

To be always well is an attainable blessing—the uniform result of self-denial, temperance, and an industrious life.

Either cold feet or constipated bowels attend a large majority of human ailments, the cure of which would be effected by their removal.

The three great elementary principles of every healthy community, as well as of individuals, are pure air, perfect cleanliness, and well-cooked food.

Go to bed at a regular hour, leave it as soon as you wake up, and do not sleep a moment in the daytime. This will give you all the sleep your system requires.

Eat regularly. Keep the feet warm. Get the utmost amount of sleep. Have one daily action of the bowels. Spend one or two hours in cheery out-door activities.

By using water in abundance to keep clean, taking exercise in moderation to keep the blood pure, and having a regular diet to sustain and strengthen, a man may maintain good health to the utmost limit of fourscore.

In recovering from any sickness: 1st, keep abundantly and comfortably warm; 2d, studiously avoid taking cold; 3d, watch against over-exercise; 4th, eat moderately and at regular intervals, of plain, nourishing food.

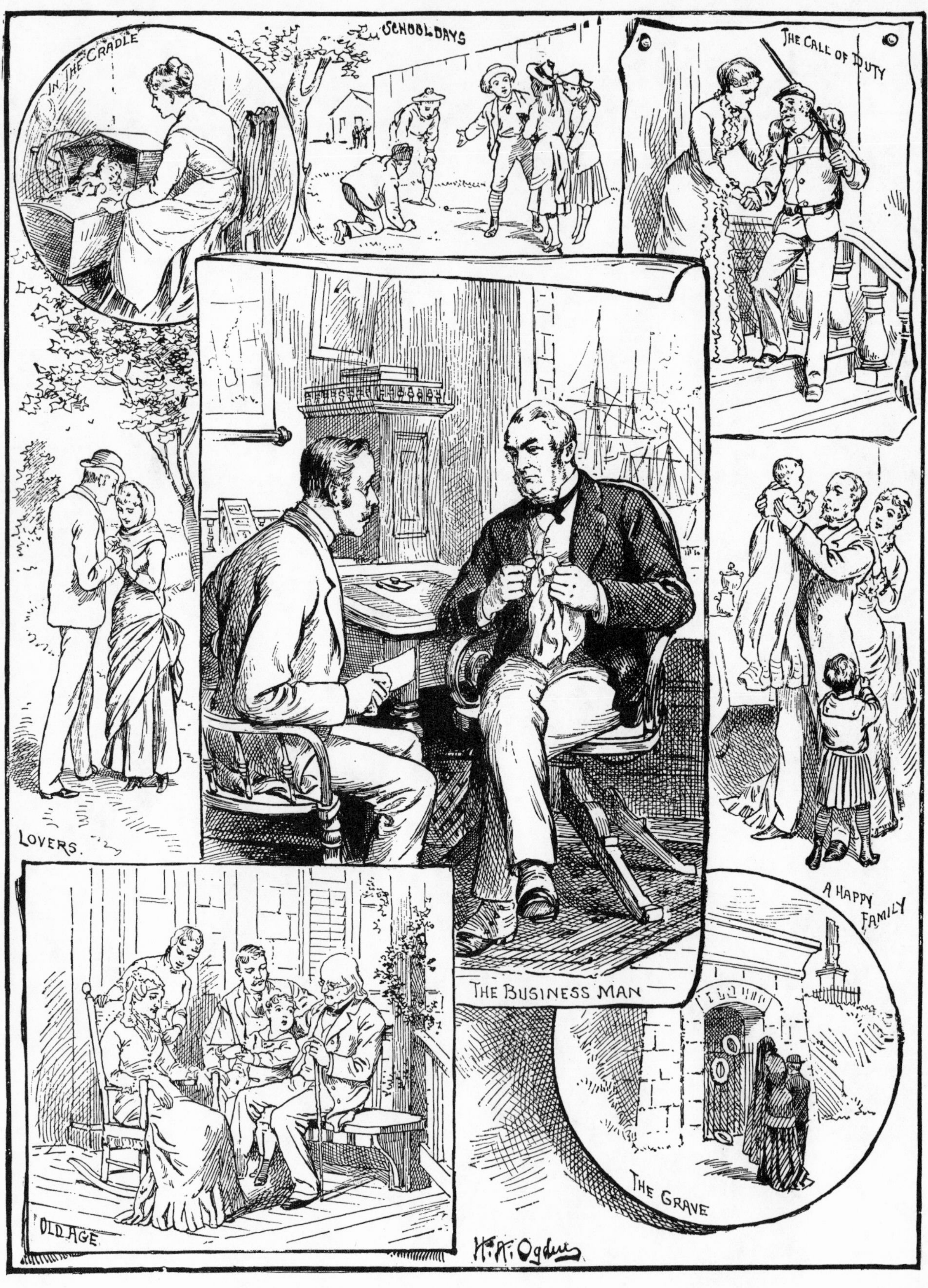
IN THE CRADLE
SCHOOL DAYS
THE CALL OF DUTY
LOVERS.
THE BUSINESS MAN
A HAPPY FAMILY
OLD AGE
THE GRAVE
H. A. Ogden

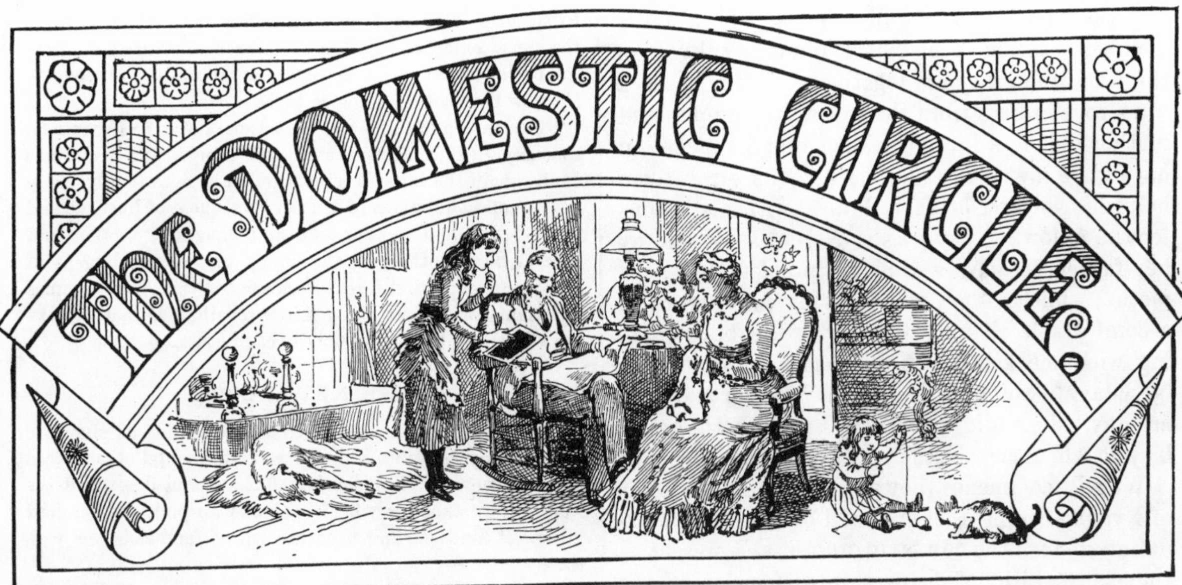

"HOME, Home! Sweet Home! There's no place like home!" sang John Howard Payne, in his lonely exile, many years ago, and who that has ever been blessed with a happy home would be willing to dispute the poet's assertion. "Be it ever so humble, there's no place like home!" It is the one spot on earth that we cherish in our hearts forever. We may travel in foreign lands, and enjoy all the luxuries that mortal man could desire. We may dine with kings and potentates, and have honors showered upon us, but there is nothing in this world that stirs the heart to its very depth, like the thought of home, and of the loved ones awaiting us on our return.

Mothers, who have conferred the great boon upon their families of creating a happy home, have accomplished more than if they had written a dozen learned books, while leaving their children uncared for. Children should grow up with the idea that they can have a better time at home than anywhere else. This can only be brought about by making it bright and cheerful, and providing them with better opportunities for amusement and recreation than is afforded them in other places. It is certainly not strange that Frank should prefer to go to Tom's home after school hours, if his own home is kept in a slovenly manner, and his parents have forbidden him to invite any playmates to the house. There is always some rollicking fun going on at Tom's house, and he has a big play-room to himself, in which he can make just as much noise as he pleases. Nor is it singular that Frank's sister, Nellie, is generally to be found visiting some intimate friend, whose mother is very kind to her and shows her how to sew and embroider, while at home no one ever offers to do anything for her.

Parents cannot take too great pains to make the domestic circle dear to their children. If boys and girls have a congenial home they are seldom anxious to part with it. Tom is not likely to wish to run away to sea, nor Nellie anxious to marry the first young man who makes her a proposal. Tom is proud of his family, and works to distinguish himself in the career he has chosen with his father's approval. Nellie becomes an accomplished young lady, and dreads the time when she will have to part with the pleasant associations of her childhood.

Indeed, too much cannot be said on the importance of cultivating the domestic circle. How great a contrast exists between the household that only assembles at meals, with glum faces and silent lips, and the family with smiling faces, where every member contributes his share towards enlivening the time when they are together. Father reads a humorous extract from the paper after supper, and mother tells of a funny incident that happened in her native town when she was a young girl. Tom helps his younger brother, Frank, with his lessons for the following day ; sister Nellie is assisted by her father to solve a difficult problem in arithmetic ; while mother, who is doing needlework in a comfortable chair, watches over the baby playing with the kitten. Nellie has a party on her birthday, to which all the cousins from far and near are invited ; while Tom and Frank both get a bicycle when their birthdays come around.

We will commence, however, with the wedding of a young couple, that may well be called the foundation stone of the DOMESTIC CIRCLE, and present to the reader a series of pictures drawn from every-day life, which, we trust, will afford entertainment as well as instruction.

## THE WEDDING.

A quiet, old-fashioned family wedding, in a brown old farm house, fifty years ago. The bride, a pretty girl in white muslin. The bridesmaid's friend, who has braided her hair for her, another pretty girl in more white muslin. Grandpa and grandma from over the hill. Cousins from everywhere within thirty miles. The bridegroom very red in the face. The groomsman in a jocular mood. The bridegroom's mother, a widow lady in black silk and a cap, is greatly disposed to tears. The bride's mother, ready to add her tears. The bride's father serious and silent. All the little sisters of the bride in muslin and blue ribbons, wondering when their turn will come. The bride's brother wondering why people make such a fuss about everything. Friends and neighbors. The bland, smooth-faced minister and his young wife. Then a hush falls and all rise : " Wilt thou, William, take this woman, to be thy wedded wife ?"

"I take, thee, Esther, to be my wedded wife, for better for worse, for richer for poorer, to love and to cherish, till death us do part ; and thereto I plight thee my troth."

" Wilt thou, Esther, take this man to be thy wedded husband?"

"I take thee, William, to be my wedded husband, for better for worse, for richer for poorer, in sickness and in health, to love, cherish, and obey, till death us do part ; and thereto I plight thee my troth !" Then follows all the rest of the beautiful old service.

They are man and wife, and the bride is kissed by everybody, while the bridegroom's hand is shaken until it aches. They all go out to supper; the bride cuts the cake, and the bridesmaid gets the ring that has been baked in it. She blushes very much, and later on the young couple go away to spend a week in New York before they settle down in their new home amongst the hills, where everything, from the parlor carpet to the saucepan, is bran new, and seems to the new housekeeper too nice to use.

Fifty years ago ! and why do we speak of it ? Because on that day, in that old homestead, were forged the first links of the chain that should bind together a new family circle in the holiest relations of human love, those of husband and wife—father and mother, son and daughter, brother and sister. Because that was the object of that wedding as of all others since that day. Because, for this, love becomes a passion, and draws young hearts together, so that forsaking all others, they cling only to each other.

## THE NEW HOME.

Last Christmastide I watched a pretty bride as she wove bright evergreens into a motto over the mantel of a certain home I know. When she had finished and descended the step-ladder, standing with her cheeks all pink and her hair all moist and curling over her white forehead, we read these words :—

**God Bless Our Home.**

Surely no motto more fitting for any fireside than this prayer. One to which all nations, all religions, all people who know the signification of that sweet word Home, must say " Amen," and if that prayer be answered all is well with us.

But God helps those who help themselves, and we must do our share to make the blessing fall. Yes, even in these first days of married life, when the two lovers have become husband and wife, and expect nothing but honey-moon bliss and rapture amidst the commonplace surroundings of ordinary life ; when for the first time they begin really to know each other, to discover failings never suspected, opinions that are averse to each other, habits and manners that never could display themselves in " courting times."

It is acknowledged that the first year of married life is frequently very uncomfortable, even for those couples who afterwards find themselves extremely happy. This, then, is the period at which to begin to consider not only the pleasures but the duties of married life, to begin those cares for others which are part of home life, to refrain from finding fault unnecessarily or from being touchy about little things. To those young couples who really and truly love, this will not be a hard task if both appreciate its importance.

## HUSBANDS.

IT is a certain and serious fact that no woman can ever tell what sort of husband she has chosen until she has actually married him. Now and then one who marries quite as confidently as all others finds that she has made a mistake. Miserable, indeed, is she who discovers too late that she has:—

## A HEARTLESS HUSBAND.

How bitter must be her recollections, when after that fleeting passion, that assumed the guise of love, is over, she discovers that she is not treasured in her husband's heart. Ah ! how all has changed since the days of his wooing, when flattering speeches, admiring glances, and gallant attentions were bestowed upon her. How cold his manner now, how carelessly he blames her, how heedless of her pain and shame when he flirts with other women, and snubs her before their very eyes; when he even makes love to those who are bad enough to enjoy a neglected wife's jealousy.

It is usually an honest, well-meaning woman with little power of self-assertion who is used in this way, and she often ends the little tragedy by dying early, anxious perhaps to gain as much appreciation of her virtues as shall be written on her tombstone in the words, "Miranda, beloved wife of Samuel Simpkins," since she knows it is all she will ever have in this world.

## THE BUSY HUSBAND.

There are other women whose husbands are perfectly true to them, who never dream of flirting, who provide them with plenty of housekeeping money or even blank checks ; but who have no time to give to them.

THE BUSY HUSBAND.

They gobble their breakfast behind a newspaper and seldom come home to dinner, which they take very often at the club or some restaurant. They never accept any of those invitations addressed on glossy cards to Mr. and Mrs.———, and it never occurs to them to bring home tickets for any place of amusement, or to ask their wives to take a walk.

This man s wife may have a Parisian hat if she likes, he will pay the bill without question, but he would not know it if he met her on the street. The children are in bed when he returns at night, and not up yet in the morning when he goes out. He is making money somewhere, that is all they know of him.

He is always civil to his wife, and says "oh, certainly" when she proposes anything, and he dutifully kisses the family when they go to the country in the summer and when they return. He considers himself an exceedingly good husband and father ; his wife declares that he is, but she is not happy. All her solitary life she longs for something, she hardly knows what. A "might have been " of some sort, and she loses her beauty very fast, and although her heart does not break, the moss grows over it as over an old ruin, while she frets about little things and seems to be needlessly discontented. The husband means well but "*he does not understand.*"

## THE FUSSY HUSBAND.

There is the fussy husband ; he is not delightful, nothing ever suits him. The coffee can never be clear or the tea strong enough. His mother always made better cake or better pudding than his wife ; he cannot tell why she can never have beefsteak broiled properly, or how it is that things never look neat about the house ; he re-arranges rugs, curtains and tidies, and has a knack of discovering cobwebs and dust; he putters about the kitchen so much that the cook is inclined to pin a dish cloth to his dressing-gown. Until he is convinced of his mistake by experience, he is sure that he can iron a collar better than any woman living.

When his wife is ill he nurses her himself, tears up the doctor's prescriptions, and buys all sorts of patent medicines. He cooks strange messes for her, flavors her gruel with peppermint by mistake, and makes her some jelly in the onion saucepan. It takes all the combined efforts of nurse and the two mothers-in-law to keep him from toning up the constitution of his first baby, a week after its arrival, with a shower bath and an electric battery.

When he sees a flame in the kitchen, he rushes bareheaded down the street to summon the firemen, who discover that cook has burned her ironing holder.

When he takes his wife anywhere, as he is fend of doing, he stands dancing in the hall. From the moment she begins to dress herself he keeps calling up the stairs, "My dear, I'm afraid we'll be late !" until she is ready to scream from nervousness.

On a journey he is always on the lookout for an accident.

But after all he is not a bad fellow, and she soon gets used to him.

## THE RECKLESS HUSBAND.

He is always good-humored, and seldom comes home without a present. He buys his wife more clothes than she can wear, and gets tickets for anything and everything, however great the cost. He entertains his friends with champagne. He has hot-house peaches, and boned turkey, and all sorts of costly things sent in from the restaurant, but fails to pay his baker's bill.

He surprises his wife on her birthday with a set of pearls, but leaves her to meet the landlord, who "would like to have his rent," which is very natural, and as he never receives it, the landlord finally turns the family out.

He spends four times his income, and when his wife softly remonstrates, chucks her under the chin, and calls her a "little goose." She is always afraid of duns, and spends her life flying about from place to place. She loves him dearly, and if he would only let her manage a little, they would be perfectly happy. But he does not, and the time comes when "the business" goes to pieces, and the household goods are seized, he is arrested, and in despair shoots himself, leaving her to support the children by taking in fine shirts.

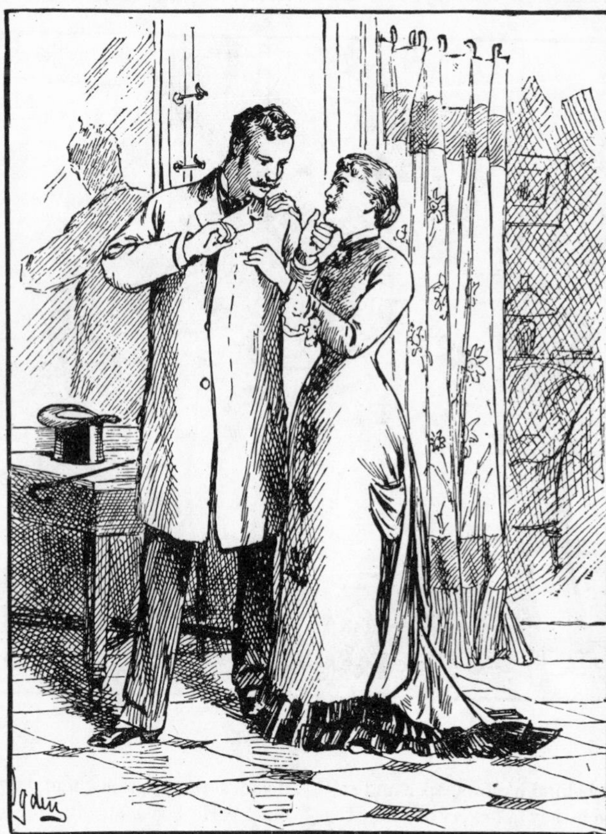

THE RECKLESS HUSBAND.

## THE STINGY HUSBAND.

The stingy husband is always poring over bills, inquiring into the price of butter, watching the servants to see that they do not give away bread, measuring the coal in the bins, and declaring that every one is cheating him.

He draws the price of every calico wrapper or pair of shoes, for which his wife asks him, from the depths of his pocket with a groan. He cannot see why a woman wants a new bonnet *every* year. He wears the same hat a long while, and if she were not foolish, she would do the same.

He asks her often if she really knows how much the children cost, and how they wear out their clothing. He has "Waste not, want not," and "A penny saved is a penny got," pasted up over the dining room mantel-piece. He turns off the gas and uses oil if he lives in the city, and if in the country, he uses tallow candles. He is always reading aloud to his family terrible stories of rich people, who, by recklessness and thriftlessness, have come to beggary, and wakes his wife up in the night to tell her that he shall probably die in the poor-house himself. But if she seems troubled he declares that it is not for himself he minds, but for her and the children.

When he has worried her to death, and perhaps starved himself into the grave, the children will probably find that he has left behind him a large fortune, which they frequently quarrel over, and generally waste.

## A GOOD HUSBAND.

Happy is the wife whose husband makes her his confidant, who helps her with her share of the burden, and is neither miserly nor a spendthrift, who always loves her, and who is wise enough to be her counselor in all things.

Fortunate, indeed, is the woman who possesses as husband a man who knows more of the world and of all things than she can know, and keeps a pure and tender heart through all vicissitudes; who is neither a bear nor a flirt in society; who enjoys her company, and is happiest at home; whose children think father perfection.

The good husband understands that, having sons and daughters, he is responsible for more than their food and clothing, and must take his share in their moral and intellectual education. He intends to have them grow up healthy men and women, if care and thought can make them so. His wife can truly say "I have a good husband," and from her heart she should thank heaven for being wed to him.

The woman who possesses a good husband is certainly to be envied, while the woman who is married to a man of an ill-natured disposition is greatly to be pitied, for, though she may, in time, grow hardened and even resigned to her fate, she never ceases to regret the happiness that might have fallen to her lot if she had not chosen so unwisely in the folly of her youth. If young people who contemplate matrimony would "look before they leap" they would seldom find that they had "married in haste, to repent at leisure."

## WIVES.

OF course wives are on the average better than husbands—we all know that, but now and then a poor young man discovers that he has:—

### A SLOVENLY WIFE.

She has never been used to keeping house, perhaps, and does not try to learn. The things lie about anywhere. Her curtains are pulled half down, and stay so. There is a rip in her carpet, which increases until some day it trips some one down. If she is living with her mother-in-law, she never hears the last of it, so that she pays dearly for that bit of negligence.

She always forgets to wind the clock, and sometimes to order the dinner. The handles are off the cups in no time, and the edges of the plates are all chipped. Spoons disappear; they get thrown out with the slops.

She neglects her husband's buttons; and goes about with a yard of braid dragging behind her skirt. In fact, the stitch in time that saves nine never occurs to her.

She used to be tidy and neat when he called to see her, and so she is now, when she has company or goes out; but at home, when he only sees her, she contents herself with crimping pins and old wrappers. Who can blame him if he does not feel flattered?

THE OVER-TIDY WIFE.

### THE OVER-TIDY WIFE.

There are wives who are over-tidy; who set the house before its dwellers, and forget that the "body is more than raiment." In the home over which the over-tidy wife presides, it is perpetually cleaning day. She resembles the old woman who was so neat that she scrubbed the floor through and fell into the cellar.

There is never a place where her husband can be at peace in all his house. He is not allowed to drink out of the polished goblets, or come into the newly swept house by the front door, nor lean his head against the wall, nor put his feet upon the sofa, nor smoke anywhere. She does not like a litter of newspapers about, nor to have the books taken down from the case. She hates to see the parlor blinds drawn up, and likes a religious gloom all over the house.

Above all things she detests whittling, and hammering, and chipping. She makes him put his shaving papers in a tin box, and fold his clothes away in a bureau drawer when he goes to bed.

As long as he is in the house, she follows him about with a broom and duster, feeling quite confident that he at least is made of dust, and to dust he will return.

It never surprises me to hear that the husband of this sort of woman is "out a great deal," for men will have freedom somewhere.

### THE NAGGING WIFE.

There is the nagging wife, who is always uttering her warnings and complaints, and is never contented. She is sure her husband is doing wrong, and when he makes a mistake she has always "told him so." She delivers "Caudle" lectures at night, and long homilies at breakfast. She cannot see why he doesn't make his fortune, or why they can never dress and live like other people.

She tells him of her old beaux, and how well off they have become, and sighs drearily. She is sure that he is getting the liver complaint, and that the children have symptoms of spine disease and consumption.

When he invites her to go out with him, she assures him she has nothing to wear, and declines for that reason. She is always telling him how her "Pa" succeeded, because *he* was a man of sense. Her father had always told his daughters never to marry a husband without a fortune.

If one hears at last that this man has "taken to drink," who can wonder? The tavern offered him jolly companionship and peace, if only he would drink enough. He wanted his pipe and easy chair, by his own fireside, a nice little woman to laugh at his jokes, and sympathize with his worries. He could not have it, and, therefore, took what he could get instead. In this case the woman is certainly to blame.

### THE WASTEFUL WIFE.

There is the woman who never considers how hard her husband works for the money she squanders. She orders home a new cloak, that costs a month's salary, and a set of parlor curtains, which necessitates his going without an overcoat in order to pay for them.

She spends the market money in lunching at restaurants and going to matinées, and then asks him for more with a babyish giggle. She may be pretty and caressing, but is too selfish to consider any one but herself. She thinks the world was made for her, and she means to enjoy it. She does not consider that a wife should be her husband's helpmeet in all things.

### A TOUCHY WIFE.

A husband has a hard time with a touchy wife. She is forever suspecting him of not considering her sufficiently, or of not loving her enough. A tone or look will send her into hysterics or weeping. She feels sure he "meant something dreadful," when he is quite unconscious of any meaning whatever. He is constantly obliged to apologize, and spends half his evenings in coaxing her into good humor, kissing away the tears she has been shedding all day over something he had no idea that he said that morning.

Visitors usually find her with red eyes and a swollen upper lip, and he is aware they suspect him of being a brute and of making her unhappy.

As a general thing, however, the wife of this sort, who is only too sensitive, grows more sensible with years, and ends by being a pleasant and contented woman. She only needs the proper management, for her heart is all right.

### A GOOD WIFE.

Ah ! long ago, happy husband of a good wife, did Solomon describe your treasure, and never since have better words been found, never will they be found in this world. "Her price is far above rubies. The heart of her husband doth safely trust in her, so that he shall have no need of spoil. She will do him good, and not evil, all the days of her life. She seeketh wool and flax, and worketh willingly with her hands. She is not afraid of the snow for her household : for all her household *are* clothed with scarlet. Her children arise up, and call her blessed; her husband *also*, and he praiseth her. Give her of the fruit of her hands ; and let her own works praise her in the gates."

After all the centuries that have come and gone, nothing better has been written of a good wife and mother. She is the greatest blessing that can possibly come to a man, and he should, therefore, in selecting a wife, care more for a noble character and amiable disposition than wealth and good looks.

## THE CHILDREN.

#### THE BABIES NEW AND OLD.

In France they have a saying that children govern the nation. Since they govern their mothers, who in turn govern the fathers, who are the rulers?

In all happy homes everywhere, much more is thought of the children than cross old bachelors, who have always boarded at hotels where they are only allowed at second table, and are turned out of the parlors, could possibly imagine.

There is the first baby, and what a commotion he causes ! The family doctor, nurse, grandmas, and aunts, all arrive for the great event. On the word of the doctor this is the largest, handsomest, and healthiest baby ever born in the county. Mamma is proud—papa prouder. All the female relatives rise in their own estimation, and grandpa positively takes all the credit to himself. Is it not to be named after him, and did he not get the scales and discover that it turned them at twelve pounds, while the new baby over the way only weighs eleven ?

Uncle Jack looks doubtful, hopes that it will turn out all right, and not remain so bald and wrinkly. He sends it up a velocipede that very night. Lady friends call, and go off into ecstacies over its beauty, with ohs! and ahs! like the children over skyrockets. The fact that its eyes are open, and the notice it takes of everything, is another source of infinite delight to them.

For weeks the existence of that house turns on the health and happiness of that child. The grandmas stay, and are constantly jumping up in the night, and bumping against each other in dark entries on the way to see why the baby cried. Advice is given by the yard, and consultations held as to its flannel jackets. When it is really certain that it has said "a-goo," bulletins are sent to absent relatives. When it cuts its teeth, they think of writing to the papers. Alas ! is it possible, King Baby the First, that you are ever to be deposed, that you can ever become the old baby ?

### POOR OLD BABY.

A word for you. You may be very young in years when the title is thrust upon you, and I think it is very hard on you to tell you so often that "your nose is out of joint." That soft, dreadful little bundle of white in mamma's arms gives you no pleasure. It squeaks like your toy lamb when you squeeze the bellows, and you hate it.

They call you cross, and no one has time to mend your horsey's leg, or pity you because your red balloon has collapsed. You have had a terrible downfall from the throne of babyhood to common life, when you are told you are "a little boy now," and must be "good." You are to go to school soon, and you find refuge at last in grandma's bed. You tell her you think you must be sick, and she had better give you a powder, or tie a rag round your finger. You do not understand your heart-ache, and find it worse than the measles.

Ah ! care-hardened "grown-ups," be very gentle to that ancient infant at this time. Be "to his faults a little kind, and to his failings very blind." Take time to cuddle him, and play with him a little; he is commencing a new life, he is no longer the principal object of interest in the family circle, and he feels it sorely.

### SORROWS OF CHILDHOOD.

As one new baby follows another, the children become factors in the domestic circle. There they stand, one a little taller than the other, like so many steps. There are little mouths to feed, little figures to clothe, little minds and hearts to develop, and oh, how sensitive they are! What deep impressions little things make upon them! They enjoy compliments, and are pained by neglect. They long for appreciation, and understand glances and hints better than you do. They see everything with their long-lashed eyes, and hear everything with their little pitcher ears.

If you remember your own childhood, you know that children are not the perfectly happy, untroubled little creatures that some people are apt to think them. Can you not remember when you were a little girl at school, how your heart used to beat and your face flush over the lessons you did not know? How miserable you were when Miss Birch called out to you, "Talking again, hey?—a *demerit!*" How could you contrive to be as silent as a mute when there was so much to say? Miss Birch talked as much as she wanted to herself, and there was that awful "demerit" to show the family. What anxiety you suffered, when you could not remember General Wolfe's dying words, or the year in which Columbus discovered America. Your heart was very sore when Cornelia received, with a triumphant look, the medal you so desired to win. At least she need not have let you see how pleased she was.

What a little sinner people sometimes thought you, when you really meant to do no harm, and how often they forgot their promises, when you had been calculating on their performance for days. In your little world you saw the shadow of the great one, when your sworn friend, Celestina, abandoned your society for that of Ann Hopkins, who was your foe and rival, because your pocket money was all gone while Ann was provided with a pound of French mixed candy and two big green pickles. How it grieved you when you heard Belle Brown declare to Fannie Flip that she thought you were "real mean." Then it was dreadful to have to wear that apron cut after an old-fashioned pattern you detested, because it kept your dress clean.

Don't you remember when you were *only a boy*, how frankly you "hated school." How you longed to play truant, and could not tell what good "knowing the English kings" would do you. How the band of street boys used to descend upon you, and steal your marbles. How old Jones at the corner raved and reported you at home, if you climbed his cherry trees, full of tempting fruit. How the boys despised you if you refused to fight your enemies, and your father threatened to flog you if you did. How all the resolutions in the world could not keep you from "snooping" preserves and cake, and how you were locked up all one Saturday holiday for it. How you followed the band all over the city, and went away with the organ man and monkey. How you drew caricatures of Deacon Hopkins on the barn door, and was reproached for it by your mother. How you made a ghost with two broomsticks and a sheet to frighten the old washerwoman. How you flew wildly up the road, with your shrieking little sister's doll in your wagon.

You did not really mean to be bad. You loved everybody, you only wanted fun. Perhaps these memories will make you more lenient to your Tom, who takes after you.

## CONFIDENCE BETWEEN PARENTS AND CHILDREN.

Of all things be sure that you establish confidence between your little ones and yourselves. Encourage them to tell you everything. The grim, old-fashioned stateliness that keeps them at arms' length will never do with this independent generation. Neither does the old adage of "spoiling the child by sparing the rod" prove itself useful at the present time. When it was the regular thing to trounce boys, it may have been less degrading, but now it is a pretty well spoiled boy who needs the rod, or who is not made worse by it. Above all things let no mother whip a boy. It is the most ridiculous and undignified spectacle possible. Make your boys love you, and mother's word will be weightier than a cowhide in a giant's hand.

Be intimate with your little ones, teach them their tasks, and play with them. Help them in their fancy work and mechanics, read their books with them, go into the woods with them, and take them to such entertainments as you approve of. It is not beneath mamma's dignity to turn the rope while her girls jump, and it elevates papa in his son's estimation, if his father proves the best skater on the pond and the best ball player in the field.

Having once become parents your first duty is to your children, their happiness should be your greatest care. But for you they would never have had this hard life to live, and the future beyond this world for which you are preparing them. Your precepts and practice cannot fail to have a great influence in forming their characters.

## BOYS.

The mother has a very extraordinary influence over her boys, and they have a peculiar love for her. It is a fact which must interest every woman—to know that there has scarcely ever been a great man who had not a wise and good mother. Over and over again in the zenith of their fame have such men said: "My mother made me all I have become. She taught me my duty, she encouraged me in every worthy effort. She believed in my success from the first."

The Hebrew women rejoiced when a "man-child" was born to them, and mothers are generally very proud to say "my son," as they look into the baby's cradle. Of course boys are troublesome. Even in their cradles they tear their frills, and scream, and kick the covers off as girls never do.

They come in from play with dirty hands and faces and torn clothes, when their sisters have learned to mince along at your side with due respect to their best flounces and sash ribbons. At night you empty their pockets of a terrible mixture of gingerbread, marbles, fish hooks, earth worms, and apple cores.

They tear their buttons off when their sisters have learned to sew them on. They wade in the gutters, ride away behind ice carts, dissect kittens, climb trees, and fight with other boys, but remember they are "mere children." You cannot expect your future explorer, who will one day make his way to the North Pole or the interior of Africa, to abstain from excursions into the city or the woods, even if he

loses himself. It is not presumable that the soldier in embryo will refrain from fighting the butcher's boy, at the risk of black eyes and bleeding forehead; or that the sailor, of twenty years to come, will not paddle in your wash-tub over the pond; that the naturalist born will not take an interest in snails and beetles; or the surgeon of the future feel it his duty to investigate the interior arrangements of the family kitten. Bear with them and look forward, for in the future lies the great happiness for the mother of boys.

## SENDING GIRLS TO BOARDING-SCHOOL.

Ah! those sweet little girls. How meekly they play at motherhood beside their dolls' cradles. How they set up their little households on closet shelves, cook nothing in shiny sauce-pans over toy stoves, hoard their little possessions of inch-long furniture, brush and dust, and wash and iron in imitation of their elders.

How can mothers send their little girls away from them, and yet this is frequently done by fashionable women, who are afraid of seeming old, or who have no time for the nursery, on account of what they call their social duties. It is only for motherless little girls that boarding-schools offer any advantages, and even then only the best and most wisely managed of such institutions. Sent from home, the little victims suffer terribly at first, for children crave the love and care that never yet were paid for; but finally they forget and grow hardened. They mature with miserable rapidity, and learn besides their lessons a thousand things they should not.

I suppose it is on the principle that you might crush plucked rosebuds together until they were withered and decayed, that little girls, who under home influence would grow up sweet and fresh and innocent, come from a boarding-school, where they have been crowded together, worldly, affected, with thoughts beyond their years, and knowledge they should only have gained with experience and age.

Madame sends her pupils home "finished"; they play, sing, dance, courtesy properly, introduce with grace, and bear themselves without awkwardness; but most parents would rather have for a *daughter* the simple young thing who is not "finished."

Fortunately, it is unnecessary to give advice on this subject to most mothers, for they would not send their little girls away on any condition, as their home would be desolate without them. But there are mothers, who send their daughters to boarding-schools to gratify their selfish vanity. We allude to the woman who is given over to fashion, who is ambitious that men shall admire her face and figure, and that women shall envy her gowns. She spends her days and evenings in enjoying herself, without a thought that she has duties towards her children. Her husband is simply the money spinner who draws the checks. She preserves sufficient reputation to insure her being "invited everywhere." To such women a poodle is dearer than a baby, and a growing daughter only a reminder that she is no longer a girl herself. But to the true wife and mother children are priceless jewels and the very sunshine of her existence.

THE MOTHER AND HER GIRLS.

## OCCUPATIONS FOR GIRLS.

A wise mother never allows her girls to be idle as they grow older. In households where servants are kept there is no need of ordinary household toil, and girls are very apt to fall into a habit of lounging about doing nothing, gaping out of the windows or napping on the sofas. Encourage exercise, long walks in the fresh air, proper gymnastics, riding and rowing where the opportunity exists, but give them also plenty of indoor work.

Among their occupations should be good reading, of course, elocution if they have a taste for it, and music if they have talent enough to become creditable performers. Let them learn to draw and paint, if possible. But even if they are not talented for accomplishments of that sort, there are many other things that any bright girl can do to pass the time and decorate the dwelling.

I like to see a home full of pretty things made by the ladies' own fingers. I like to see the girls sitting together busy at their pleasant tasks while some one reads aloud.

Here is a professor's home. The professor is not rich; and with a dowdy family, who did not know how to manage things, might look shabby; but what a home it is, with that wife of his and those girls!

Come into his study now and look at it carefully. Who do you suppose painted that floor? Why, the girls! You would think it rosewood, and it shines like a mirror. Look at that rug before the desk, and the other one before the grate. No, they are not Turkish; the girls made them of woolen rags hooked through a bit of burlaps. Then, that chair! Why it was the shabbiest old thing you ever saw, until they stuffed it with cotton and covered it with chintz. You see they have heightened the pattern of wild roses and butterflies with silk, so that it looks like rich embroidery. That stand was a little pine table; they stained the legs, covered it with plush, and put a fringe around it. The plush was from an old sack, and they wove the fringe themselves.

That looking-glass between the windows? Well, it was the most old-fashioned thing in the house, but Jack made a pine frame for it, and the girls painted it with grasses. You can see some of them run over on the mirror. Feast your eyes on the mantel lambrequin matching the chairs and two little ottomans, on which the girls love to sit. They are soap boxes with casters put on, stuffed and covered with black cloth from an old cloak, and embroidered in crewels. The brackets were carved by Jack, and that seeming China jar on one of them is only a big glass pickle jar. One of the girls pasted gay figures on the inside and then filled it with salt. Those two Japanese-looking things are ginger jars decorated.

The curtains are only cheese cloth and antique lace. That window, designed by mamma, is only blotting-paper of bright colors, cut into geometrical figures, divided by black lines. With the light shining through, it looks exactly like painted glass; it is varnished as you see. I cannot enumerate everything in the room, but it is beautiful, and so is all the house. The ladies are always busy and happy, not only with these things, but with more serious occupations, and have always plenty of good work for the poor on hand.

Making scrap-books is a pleasant occupation. If good selections are made, valuable volumes may be created. There are a great many fugitive pieces of poetry, essays, and tales in papers, that are not preserved to bind, that are well worth collecting.

Knitting is nice for odd moments, and beautiful sofa quilts may be made of strips of silk, cut and sewed as for carpet-rags, and knit on big wooden needles; nice quilts of the legs of worn stockings of all colors, cut round and round, knit in the same manner in breadths and crotcheted together. The prettiness of this work is only to be known by those who have seen it, and it saves material frequently thrown into a rag-bag, and actually costs nothing.

You can make funny little book-racks by threading empty spools on wire, painting and varnishing them; and we all know the hoop-skirt paper holders are useful when done, though hard to make.

If you are not rich let some good dressmaker give your girls lessons on making dresses, so that they can make their own. Bonnet-making comes naturally to most women. And let no girl grow up without knowing how to cook a good dinner, however rich she may be. Servants respect a mistress who knows how their work should be done.

## SOCIAL INTERCOURSE.

To entertain one's friends is a duty as well as a pleasure. Inhospitable people are very disagreeable, but there is no hospitality in simply making a display. There is no happiness in making the acquaintance of persons you only meet at large parties or grand dinners. A few warm friends, that you can welcome into the interior of your home, are worth far more than a list of five hundred chance acquaintances, who would forget you in a week if you were to die to-morrow.

Make sure that people suit you, so that you do not enter into great intimacies which you must break. Let your friendships be life-long. Do not give invitations that you do not mean, and say, "Come at any time," when response to the general welcome would be very inconvenient. Say, "I should like you to come to see me on such a day or evening, at such an hour," and ask only those you really hope will come.

A gay scene, a crowd now and then is good for every one. It cures young people of embarrassment, and brightens up old ones, but it is not society in the best sense. Above all watch your young people. Let their associates always be those who have been well brought up, and when you see a girl anxious to tell your daughter something she must not repeat to mother, check the intimacy at once. A girl should never have a secret from her mother, or even wish to have one.

Let the boys and girls enjoy themselves together as much as possible, but let the boys never forget to show respect to their sister's presence in language and conduct, or the girls fail in propriety of demeanor in their presence. There should never be too much freedom of manner, for it coarsens both sexes. When they meet in the parlor, let it be with neat dresses and pleasant manners. A boy should never be allowed to "snub" his sister, or a girl to "snap" at her brother, at any age.

## THE GIRLS' BEAUX.

As your girls grow up, young men will call on them. I think that American mothers manage this part of their lives very badly. English mothers do better. It is a pleasant thing that young people should meet freely, and I do not believe the French system of *espionage* necessary for American girls, but I consider the utter want of supervision and decorum, which has obtained a footing in our rural districts, utterly unpardonable.

The mother too often forgets her dignity as hostess and parent, and retires bashfully from the parlor not to appear again, when a young man calls on her daughter. She spends her evening in some remote room, and both father and mother retire early, leaving their daughter to sit up into the "wee sma'" hours with a young man they scarcely know, and who is, at all events, simply a *young man*. In the cities some "gentleman," who has been introduced to the young lady of the family, invites her to a concert, the opera, or the theater, and she accepts without asking permission of her parents. She has her latch-key, and the family go quietly to bed. Nobody knows just when the girl comes home. She tells them the next day that she has had a "lovely evening," and had champagne and oysters after the play. She has half a dozen beaux, perhaps, who offer her their attentions, and it should be said to her credit, that she generally retains her own self-respect and that of her cavalier, but not always.

One hears bad stories now and then, and there is much one never hears. Though custom may sanction it, young people are very apt in the present condition of things to brush the bloom from their love affairs too early. A little tender mystery should linger about a girl until she is "courted and married and all," if she wishes to be a happy wife; and no matter how much she may trust her daughter, a mother should not relinquish her guardianship until a husband claims it.

A good many women acknowledge this for a truth of late, and the sooner they all recognize this fact the better. Any sensible mother can draw the line between suspicious tyranny and the utter recklessness with which we now astonish well-bred foreigners.

## YOUTHS AND MAIDENS.

### HOW MOTHER GRIEVES WHEN THE FLOCK SCATTERS.

When the children are grown up, how often does the mother look back with regret to those years when they were her little boys and girls. Oh! to have them again sitting in their little pinafores about the table. Oh! to see the little flock climbing the stairs before her on their way to bed. Could she but once more put on their little night-gowns, hear them say their prayers, and then go down stairs to talk their perfections over to papa; telling him how Katy hemmed his handkerchief, Bessie beat the eggs for the cake, and Jany played the "White Cockade" all through correctly. How Charlie brought home the prize for arithmetic, and Ben dug all the garden-beds for you.

There were cares and troubles then, sleepless nights if they were ill, and many little stockings to darn; but she thinks she would be happier even to have them with the measles and mumps together, than to sit, as she does now, and fret about them.

Charlie is in town at present with his uncle, who has been very good about getting him into business, but she hears he is always going to see Miss Spruce, and she doesn't like to have him calling on a girl she does not know. What sort of a disposition may she not have, and she thinks he should ask her advice.

To be sure, Ben, who is to farm the place with his father, will not listen to her about Betty Martin. She knew things about Betty Martin's mother, and the girl looks like her. How can she endure it to have her brought home, with that way she has of throwing up her chin and pursing up her mouth?

And here is Dr. Black, always driving up to see Bessie. She can't endure the thought of that match. And Lizzie is almost certain to marry her cousin, Robin. Now, Robin is well enough, but what nonsense. She would like to kiss them all and put them to bed in their little night-gowns again, and tell them never, never to think about Sally Spruces, Betty Martins, Dr. Blacks, and Cousin Robins any more. But alas! they are beyond her reach, and all are taller than she is, even Jany. Can Jany be ready to follow her sister's footsteps, too? She is very unhappy. Ah! poor mother, the nest is about to be robbed, and you see the shadow of the thieves' wings with your sharp eyes. That abominable nest-robber, Cupid, is hovering about your home. You want to keep your girls and boys forever, but you cannot do it.

You feel sorest about Ben. He is your eldest boy. What can he want of Betty Martin, when he has you? And you have always mended his socks and made his shirts. When he has told you everything, you think it would be better if it were some other girl, but no loving mother ever yet had the right daughter-in-law.

You suffer from a form of jealousy people have no sympathy for, yet it is a very painful one. All the emotion does not die out of us with our own love affairs. It is so hard, so hard, while Ben is only angry with you, and Pa surprised; and they comfort you with platitudes, when there is no comfort for you. This is the last great trial of your maternal nature. Endure it bravely, conceal it if you can, be a Spartan for once, and let the fox gnaw your heart out without a word. Only thus will you save yourself from quarrels that may forever break the once happy family circle. Say nothing, lest the words you utter bring on you life-long resentment.

The girl who is about to be opposed to you, comes armed with the usual opinion of mothers-in-law. She knows she has stolen your son, and that you secretly hate her for it. She is ready for battle. Be prudent, and the danger will pass by. Time will heal your heart wound, and for the little ones you have lost others will come. You will be grandma one day, and will wonder why you were so sorry that Ben married, if only you can live through these months of courting and wedding, and billing and cooing that are before you now.

## COURTING.

I have always felt that it was very hard on Eve that Adam had no chance to court her. Perhaps if he had, she might not have been so fond of forbidden fruit, or taken counsel from the serpent. How she felt we are not told, but we know that Adam awoke and found a wife without having the least trouble about it.

It is a good thing for a man to have plenty of courting to do, to have hard work to get his wife, and to be in wholesome dread of the mitten for some time. It takes some of the vanity out of him, and is better for his wife, for no man cares much for what he can get too easily.

The girl who places herself in the position of trying to catch a beau, or a husband, does a very foolish thing. It is the man's place to do the "catching"—even savages recognize that.

Properly managed, courting days are the happiest a woman ever lives through. At this period she is a queen, and the less she grants the more sure she is of crown and scepter. To be sure, a real queen is not particularly happy on such occasions. Her Most Gracious Majesty, Queen Victoria, tells us in her autobiography that she was obliged to offer herself to Prince Albert, and informs us of her confusion in doing so. No subject dared offer himself to the Queen of England, and it was, therefore, no more unwomanly for her to help him than it would be for a girl, whose lover was blind, to put out her hand to lead him through a gate into her garden, even though she knew he was intending to propose when he got there. The Prince Consort had done all he could in the way of sighs and glances, we are led to understand, and Queen Victoria knew he loved her.

There are many stories told of women who have offered themselves in marriage, but I doubt if half of them are true. I knew an old lady who always said of her daughter-in-law: "She ran arter Peter and would hev him," but I consider this somewhat of a spiteful exaggeration. I do, however, believe in the story of the Yankee girl who had been courted for many days by a speechless lover. As he never did anything but stare at her, she at last gave a jump and a scream, and said: "Stop that, now!" "I ain't touchin' you," declared the youth. "Well, why don't you, then?" asked the lady. Whereupon he gained courage and grew bold.

Men no longer go upon their knees to pop the question, but they did so once. Cases have been known where stout and elderly lovers, getting upon their knees, were unable to rise, and cruel fair ones were sometimes so unkind as to leave them there for the servants to help up. To-day all sorts of off-hand speeches, and even no speeches at all, serve a man. All he has to do is to ask a girl to have him somehow. This reminds me of the case of the bashful lover who did not wish to run the risk of getting the mitten. He, therefore, resorted to the ruse of putting the question in the following ingenious manner: "Pussy," he said, seizing the young lady's favorite kitten, "Ask your mistress if she will have me for a husband?" "Say yes, Pussy," was the favorable reply of his blushing sweetheart.

The wise lover wins the affections of the parents first. He does not tread on the mother's corns as he flies past her to shake hands with his divinity. He never shows that he is not interested in the silver question or the comet, if papa is talking of either. He never alludes to them as the "old folks," or makes unpleasant remarks about mothers-in-law, in their hearing. He is modest in his manners, and pretends to have come to the home simply to be instructed by its master whom he reveres. Having won his way in this quarter, he does not lose his lady's esteem by being over bold. A girl of spirit is very apt to dislike a man who bounces at her and tries to kiss her before he has revealed his matrimonial intentions. Yet he is not too tardy, as though his mind was not made up.

"I was so glad when Harry offered himself," said a girl to me one day. "I have longed for a chance to refuse him; he always seemed so sure that I would have him whenever he chose to offer himself. That 'no' was the most delightful syllable I ever uttered." Yet she was not a spiteful creature, only an aggrieved young lady.

Be careful in your choice, and be sure that you are suited before you court at all. If you can say, "I have no mercenary motive, I feel pure affection, real esteem," you may look forward to a very happy comfortable life, I suppose; but between you and me, I do not really believe in anything but mutual love at first sight. There is such a thing. It comes like a flash of lightning, and people are safe to marry when it comes. That sort of love never changes, never grows humdrum, if it be the genuine article.

I am not sure that it is really best to marry unless you are what is called "madly in love," but I admit that in that case half the world would live single lives.

To these happy young folks you can give no advice about courting; they know all about it, and their wooing is something to remember as a little breath of Paradise. Oh, the happy lives such people lead! Oh, the beautiful homes they have; the brave children they leave behind them to love as they loved! Pray that this love may come to your sons and daughters, and if it does, have no fear, for such matches were made in Heaven.

## THE SINGLE DAUGHTER.

But there is one member of the home circle we have forgotten, and she deserves to be remembered. The single daughter. She is no disappointed "old maid," no matter what her years are. She has chosen to live single, and has not regretted it. She is her father's joy, and her mother's comfort. She takes up the work the old people have grown weary of, and is always busy. She has refused offers, and men have lost a good wife. In some cases she finds she has happily missed a bad husband.

She is the most useful of the whole family, and generally the most popular. The married people are wrapped up in their own interests, but Aunt Jany has time and sympathy for every one. She advises all the boys and helps all the girls. She is sent for when children are sick, and can always make them take their medicine.

The single daughter has a remedy for every ill, and a pattern for every garment known. She enjoys life greatly, and sometimes ends, after all, by marrying at fifty or sixty somebody who has waited for her all her life, understanding that she could not leave her parents. Nobody laughs, for she is sensible in everything, and does even this with dignity.

## THE OLD FOLKS AT HOME.

Oh, you young people who have married and gone away from home, and have your new family about you, don't forget the old folks. Down in the country they live a very quiet life, and think a great deal about you. Do not put off writing to them, for you do not know how drearily they turn away from the post-office without their letters, and ask each other if there "can be anything the matter." Go and see them as often as you can. Have them visit you often. Do you never think of all their sacrifices for you, of all their toil, of all their love? Do you never feel that you neglect them cruelly?

The time will come when you will be "old folks" yourselves, and fate gives us tit for tat very often. If you have forgotten, remember now. Spare the time, and run down. Ask them on a visit to town; remember no family circle is complete without grand-parents and a baby; and remember, too, that to honor your father and your mother is a divine command.

## A GOLDEN WEDDING.

I began with a wedding. I will end with one. A golden wedding. Grandpa and grandma have been married fifty years, and the young folks feel that the occasion should be celebrated. It is not given to all to live together as man and wife for fifty happy years. It is a long, long time as this short life goes, and worthy of celebration.

Jany, the single sister, has been at work a week, and there will be a supper which a French cook might envy and an epicure devour.

There they all are, Ben's family, and Charlie's family, Bessie's family, and Katie's also, and here is Bessie's eldest girl and her husband and baby, making the old people great grand-parents.

THE GOLDEN WEDDING.

There are some of the friends who came to the first wedding, and most of those who were the little sisters and brothers then. Here is the bland minister, who married them, nearly ninety now, but as bland as ever. His little wife is not here; she has slept in the grave-yard many a long year.

"To think of the children surprising us so, and what beautiful presents," says grandma. "The love is what makes them valuable to us, though. And have we been married fifty years, William; it is like a dream."

"It has been too real and good for that. We don't get such wives in dreams, Esther," says the old man, and kisses her blue-veined hand.

"And what good children we have," says grandma, "and how well they have married, exactly to suit us. What a happy life ours has been."

They are growing old, and do not mind making a little love to each other before folks now. She pats him on the arm, and he chucks her under the chin.

Jany says "supper is ready," and they all go to the long table together.

"Fifty years ago," says grandma again, "fifty years ago!"

"Fifty years ago," repeats the dear old man, fondling the golden locks of his little grandson, while gazing into his bright blue eye. And then Bessie's married daughter brings her little baby around to where grandpa and grandma stand, puts its little hands each in one of theirs, and so joins the last link of the yet unbroken family circle to the first; while Ben lifts his glass high and gives the toast, "God bless our dear old home."

TWIRL THE PLATTER.
COTTON FLIES
DANCING.
"FINE OR SUPERFINE?"
PARLOR CONJURING.
FORFEITS
PRIVATE THEATRICALS
SCHOOLMASTER.
H. A. Ogden
BLIND MAN'S BUFF

DEMANDS upon our time for business and other purposes are so numerous in the hurrying life of the present century, that we are very apt to neglect the duty of amusing ourselves. One of the best signs of the times is the present tendency to multiply holidays, and yet the average individual goes back to his counting-room with an air of relief when his holiday is over, and the farmer, on his part, feels very much easier in his working clothes.

We really need, as a people, to study the art of recreation, and learn how to take our pleasures with a light heart and a graceful manner. In our variable climate the greater part of our family and social life must be carried on in-doors. What to do, and how to do it within our homes, are questions of importance to all who wish to rise above the mere humdrum monotony of existence.

It is all very well to talk about "Home, Sweet Home," to sing its sweet familiar strains, and to chide the young if they look elsewhere for happiness. But, in plain sober fact, many homes are dreadfully dull and tedious places to live in. They have no flavor, no spice ; nothing ever goes on to make them interesting. Human nature craves a certain degree of excitement ; but what possible stimulus to the better part of a boy or girl is found in a gloomy, chill, quiet, simply well regulated home, if it be only that and nothing more.

The old require amusements of some sort to cheer them in the loneliness which creeps over their declining years. The middle-aged need something to win their thoughts away from anxiety and help them to forget care. As for the young, their blood flows with swift and vital force, and they cannot keep in stagnation. Somehow they must be occupied.

"Satan finds some mischief still
For idle hands to do."

No bright lad or merry lass should be expected to work or study forever. They must have play, and wholesome play at home is both their safeguard and their privilege.

So great a man as Sir Walter Scott used to find relaxation from his almost incessant brain-work by playing with a dear little girl named Marjorie Fleming. These two charming people, Sir Walter, with his honors clustering on his brow, and Pet Marjorie, with her dimpled cheeks and her merry eyes, would spend hours in amusing each other. Sometimes she recited to him ballads, poems, or passages of Shakespeare, which her wonderful memory had retained. Sometimes he gave her stirring border romances, or told her splendid fairy-tales from his inexhaustible resources ; and sometimes—listen, my grave reader in buckram, who may fear—to step from your pedestal to be merry with a child, Sir Walter would stand before her, as if to recite a task, and say : "Ziccotty, diccotty, dock, the mouse ran up the clock, the clock struck one, down the mouse ran, ziccotty, diccotty, dock."

This done repeatedly till she was pleased, she gave him his new lesson, gravely and slowly, timing it on her small fingers, he saying it after her:

"Wonery, twocry, tickery seven,
Alibi, crackaby, ten and eleven,
Pin pan, musky-dan;
Tweedle-um-twoddle-um Twenty-wan
Eerie, ourie, you--are--out."

Nonsense! Well, yes, but "a little nonsense now and then, is relished by the best of men," and very likely there would be less dyspepsia, less ill-temper, and fewer domestic jars, very likely fewer sudden deaths, if we would be more tolerant of harmless nonsense, and take more time to indulge in it.

All parlor games are not merely amusing. There are not a few which require memory and attention, and combine not a little instruction with their drollery.

The object of this article is to indicate and describe, in a plain, practical way, some of the many INDOOR AMUSEMENTS, which may be relied upon to furnish innocent fun and pastime in the group at the fireside, or in the social party.

Some of these mirthful games and laughable tricks are best adapted for rainy evenings at home, when only father, mother, aunt Mary, and the children are there. Others are intended for occasions when friends have gathered. Everybody knows how terrible to host and hostess is the solemn atmosphere that sometimes invests a company of people met for an evening's entertainment. They sit about like ghosts, or stand here and there like figures carved out of wood.

A frantic desire deepens in the mind of the hostess who has invited them and who wants their evening to be pleasant, to stir them up somehow, break up the stilted talk, and set the ball of fun rolling. By trying the following game the hostess would probably accomplish her purpose.

## CONSEQUENCES.

ONE of the oldest games is CONSEQUENCES, but it has never yet worn out. Seat the company at a table, and give every one a long piece of paper and a pencil. Each person at the top of the paper must write the *quality* of a gentleman, the fascinating, the awkward, or what not. Nobody may see what his neighbor writes. Fold down the top of the paper, and pass it to the person on the right who now writes the name of a gentleman. The papers are again folded and passed to the right. Now write in succession, always folding and passing, the quality of a lady, a lady's name, where they met, what he said to her, what she said to him, the consequence, and what the world said. Read the papers aloud. There will be no more stiffness in that party.

## PROVERBS.

IN PROVERBS, a familiar adage, like "A bird in the hand is worth two in the bush," is selected. A word is assigned from this in rotation to each player, and he is told to bring it into his answer to the question which will be asked him by the leader. The leader guesses the proverb from the evasive or peculiar words which he hears in his answers.

"I love my love with an A," because he is amiable, or, "I hate him with an A," because he is arrogant, is a good alphabetical exercise, going from A through all the letters except X, which is unmanageable.

## THUS SAYS THE GRAND MUFTI.

ONE of the company must sit in a chair, and may make what motion he pleases, winking, sneezing, coughing, etc. At each movement he says, "Thus says the Grand Mufti," and every body imitates him; but if he says, "So says the Grand Mufti," whoever imitates has a forfeit to pay.

## YES AND NO.

A quiet game. One of the players thinks of something, and the rest ask him questions about it, to which he replies only yes or no. From the knowledge thus gained, each guesses what it was that he thought about, and after a while they find out.

## RHYMES.

RHYMES is an easy game. The performer thinks of a word which rhymes with another which he mentions.

We will suppose the word in his mind to be "cat." The first person in the circle will ask him, "Is it an abode for a cultivated family?"

The answer will be :—

"No, it is not flat."

"Is it a covering for the head?"

"No, it is not hat."

"Is it a useful article in muddy weather?"

"No, it is not mat."

"Did it come over in the ship with Columbus and his men?"

"No, it is not rat."

"Is it part of a bedstead?"

"No, it is not slat."

"Is it a foe to rats and mice?"

"Yes, it is a cat."

The fortunate guesser now takes his turn in thinking of a word. The pleasant peculiarity of this game is that while grown people may enjoy it for half an evening, it does not exclude even little children, who enter into it with great spirit.

### HOW DO YOU LIKE IT.

How Do You Like It, When Do You Like It, And Where Do You Like It?" is a game of guessing. One goes out. The others think of a word, suppose it to be *money*. "How do you like it?" The answer might be "In abundance." "When do you like it?" "When I need it." It is as well to choose words which have two meanings, and can be spelled in two ways for this game, as cord, chord, key, quay, etc.

### SCHOOLMASTER.

This is a game which is very successful when played with animation. The one who is chosen to be master places himself in front of his class, who are all seated in a row. He examines the pupils in geography, history, or natural science. Deciding to begin with zoology, he asks the person at the head of the class to name a bird beginning with C. Should the pupil fail to name a bird beginning with this letter, while the master rapidly counts ten, it is passed to the next, the next, until some one calls out Cuckoo or Crow, and of course goes up to the head.

This game can be varied indefinitely if the schoolmaster is a capable leader. The questions must be asked without a pause, and the game must not lag. Authors, singers, heroes, and cities, states, rivers, etc., may be selected for topics of examination.

### SHADOW BUFF.

This is a pretty game for a family reunion on Christmas eve, or on a wedding anniversary. A large white sheet is first hung securely on one side of the room, and on a table some distance behind a very bright lamp must be placed. All other lights being extinguished, one of the party takes a seat on a low stool between the lamp and the sheet, but nearer the latter than the former. One after another the company pass behind him, their shadows of course falling upon the sheet as they pass. It is more difficult than most would imagine to distinguish the original from the shadow, especially as it is allowable in this game for the players to disguise themselves to some extent, by wearing false faces, wigs, whiskers, or mob-caps, and grotesque articles of dress, arranging their hair differently, etc. Any such liberty may be taken, in order to add to the general fun.

### SHOUTING PROVERBS.

This is a rather boisterous game, and one not to be played in a house where there are invalids.

A proverb is selected, such as "Too many cooks spoil the broth," or, "A bird in the hand is worth two in the bush." One word of this is given to each person in the company, and he is directed at the signal to shout this clearly and distinctly. One person has of course been left out. He is to guess the proverb from the shouting. Standing as near the rest as they will permit, this person says "Charge! Present! Fire!"

As soon as he utters the word "Fire!" the whole party shout their words vociferously, and from the confusion of sounds he is to guess the proverb. This is often a difficult task.

## Blind Man's Buff.

THERE are several methods of playing Blind Man's Buff. It is sometimes a very boisterous game, and if the players are careless or rough it is dangerous, but nobody ought ever to be so carried away by excess of spirits, that young ladies or little girls may get hurt. With this caution to the boys, and begging their pardon if it be superfluous, we will tell you all how to play Blind Man's Buff Seated.

The blind man may be chosen by lot, unless somebody volunteers to take the part. If the person be a gentleman, a handkerchief must be bound over his eyes by a lady, and if a lady, a gentleman must do the binding. Before this, the company may be seated close together on chairs in a circle. After the blindfolding they must change their places very quietly.

The blind man is forbidden to grope or to extend his hands, but he must approach the circle and seat himself in the lap of the first person he comes across, and without touching the person, but by simply listening to the smothered laughter around him, or to the rustling of clothes, must guess who it is, tell the name or describe the individual, so that he or she may be identified.

If the blind man guesses correctly, the person discovered takes his place, puts on the bandage, and performs the same part. If, on the contrary, he is mistaken, the company clap their hands to inform him of his error, and he tries again and again until he succeeds.

It is allowable for the company to resort to little stratagems to prevent the blind man from guessing correctly. Ladies may place shawls over their dresses, or gentlemen spread the skirts of a neighbor's dress over their laps.

In Blind Man's Buff by the Profile the player does not have his eyes bandaged, but the task is none the easier on that account. A piece of white and fine linen is stretched upon a frame like a screen, in the same way as when exhibiting a magic lantern. The blind man is seated on a stool, so low that his shadow is not represented on the linen, which is spread over the screen. Some distance behind him a single lighted taper is placed upon a stand, and all the other lights in the room are extinguished. The company now form a line of procession, and pass in single file before the blind man (who is expressly forbidden to turn his head) and the table on which the light is placed.

This produces the expected effect. The light of the candle, intercepted by each of the company in turn, as he passes before it, casts upon the piece of white linen a succession of shadows, quite accurately defined.

As these shadows move before him the blind man names aloud the person whom he supposes to be passing, and the errors he is sure to make cause shouts of laughter.

Each one passing before the light tries to disguise his height, makes up a funny face, or assumes a limp, in order that he may baffle the blind man.

Forfeits are not usually demanded in this game, but it

would add to its interest were they insisted upon from those who were too readily discovered.

Blind Man's Buff with the Wand is played in a very lively way. The company join hands, form a circle, and wheel round the blind man, whose eyes are securely bandaged, and in whose hands is a long wand. As they go round him at a quick pace, they sing some popular air; when the song is finished they stop, and the blind man, extending his wand, points it at some one in the company, who is obliged to take hold of it by the end presented. Then the blind man utters three cries, which the other imitates. He must try to disguise his voice. If he cannot do so, he will be readily found out. The person first discovered takes the blind man's place. The circle wheels round him singing, and the game proceeds.

Porco, or Italian Blind Man's Buff, is still another droll variation. Several persons of both sexes form a circle by joining hands. One person, who is blindfolded, is placed in the center, with a small stick in his or her hand. The players dance around the blind man, who tries to touch one with the wand. If he succeeds, they all stop. The player then grunts like a pig, brays like a donkey, neighs like a horse, or crows like a rooster, and the person touched endeavors to imitate the noise as closely as he can, without discovering himself. If the person touched is discovered the bandage is speedily transferred to him, the former blind man takes the vacant place in the ring, the dance begins again and the game goes merrily on.

A French Blind Man is not a blind man at all, but a pinioned man. One of the players has his hands tied tightly behind his back, and in this condition he is set to catching a companion if he can. Whoever is captured takes his place.

None of these are a bit more satisfactory, though each has its good points, than the common, old-fashioned blind man's buff, in which we have all engaged on Christmas Eve and at Thanksgiving, in which the blind man gropes here and there, reaches out his arms wildly, and tries to catch the eager throng who brush against him, elude his grasp, and stifle their laughter in a resolute determination not to betray themselves. Put all traps like footstools and little tables aside, see that no sharp-cornered furniture is in the way, and then ho! for the blind man, and give him a fair field and no favor.

## THE COTTON FLIES.

Form a circle close together. One player casts a flake of cotton into the air and puffs with his breath to keep it afloat. The person toward whom it floats must puff in the same way, to keep it from falling into his lap, as then he would have to pay a forfeit.

Nothing is more ludicrous than to see a dozen people puffing with all their might to keep this bit of cotton afloat, and send it from one to the other. Somebody is sure to laugh, and it is very hard work to laugh and puff at the same moment. Down falls the tuft into some widely opened mouth, and the unfortunate vainly trying to blow it away, is sentenced to pay a forfeit.

## THE RIBBONS.

Everybody takes a ribbon, and holds it by one end. The other ends are all held by one person, who is in the middle of the circle, and leads the game.

When he says *Pull*, they must let go. When he says *Let go*, they must pull their end of the ribbon. As many forget the rule, and do what they are told, instead of the exact opposite, a great number of forfeits are won.

## BRAVO FOR COPENHAGEN.

Who has not pleasant recollections of this frolicsome game on winter evenings of auld lang syne? What young person has not played it when he was younger than now? Do not count the children out of Copenhagen, friends.

First, you must be provided with a long piece of tape from mother's basket. It must be quite long enough to go all round the whole company, who must stand in a circle, holding in their hands each a part of the string; the last person holds both ends. One player remains in the center of the circle, and is called "The Dane." He must endeavor to slap the hands of one of those who are holding the string before they can be withdrawn. Whoever allows his hands to be slapped must take the place of the Dane.

## THE CAT AND THE MOUSE.

Join hands in a circle, letting one person stay inside to be the mouse, and leaving one outside to be the cat. The circle run around uplifting their arms. The cat springs in and the mouse slips out. Then down with everybody's arms, and keep the cat a prisoner. She goes around mewing, trying to get out. The circle keep dancing, and presently puss finds a weak place, and breaks through. The instant she is out she chases the mouse, who tries to get in, for which purpose the circle raise their arms. If the mouse gets in without being followed by the cat, the cat pays a forfeit, and then tries again. If the mouse is caught, she must pay a forfeit. They then name their successors, and the game, which is a splendid one, proceeds.

## THE HUNTSMAN.

One player is styled the Huntsman. The others are named after the accoutrements of a sportsman, thus: one is the coat, another the hat, another powder-flask, shot, shot-belt, dog, gun, etc. Arrange as many chairs as there are players in two rows, back to back, and bid all the players seat themselves. The Huntsman then walks around and calls out the names, for instance, "Gun!" when that player gets up, takes hold of the coat-skirts of the Huntsman, who continues his walk, calling for "Dog," "Coat," "Hat," and the others. As each is summoned, he jumps up and takes hold of the skirts of the player before him, and when all have been called, the huntsman begins to run, with the whole train after him, running as fast as they can. When he has run round the chairs three times, he suddenly shouts "bang!" and immediately sits down on one of the chairs, leaving his followers to scramble into places the best way they can.

Of course, one player is left standing, as no chair was set for the Huntsman. The player so left must pay a forfeit. The game is continued until all have paid three forfeits, when the penalties are declared. The huntsman is not changed throughout the game, unless he becomes tired and asks for relief.

## HUNT THE HARE.

This is something like the Cat and the Mouse. The players form a circle, joining hands. One is left out. This is the hare, who runs several times around the circle, and at last stops and taps a player on the shoulder. This person leaves the ring and chases the hare. The circle join hands, and the hare runs in and out in every direction, until caught by the pursuer, who in his turn becomes the hare. The circle must always be friendly to the hare, assisting his escape as well as they can.

## HUNT THE SLIPPER.

This is a great favorite. The company sit on the floor, a slipper is given them, and somebody standing in the center guesses who has it by its tap on the ground. The persons seated close together, pass it along, and prevent its being seen. When discovered, the one with whom it is found takes the hunter's place.

## THE GAME OF THE KEY.

In this case the players are seated on chairs in a ring, one standing in the middle. Each sitter with his left hand takes hold of the right *wrist* of the neighbor on his left. When all have joined hands, they begin moving them from left to right, making a circular motion, and touching each other's hands, as if for the purpose of taking something from them. The player in the center then presents a *key* to one of the sitters, and turns his back, so as to allow it to be passed on. It is quickly passed from hand to hand. Presently the player in the center turns, and tries to find out who has the key, and to seize it in its passage from one to another. The person in whose hand it is found must pay a forfeit, take his place in the center, and in his turn give and hunt the key. A player having paid three forfeits, is out.

## CATCH THE RING.

Place the chairs just so far apart that each sitter can easily reach the hand of another on either side of him. Let one person stand in the middle. A piece of string with a plain gold or brass ring upon it, is then tied, of a sufficient length to reach all around the circle, so that each may take hold of it. The players slide the ring along the string, passing it from one to another, and the person in the center must try to catch it. The one on whom he finds it is out, and must leave the circle.

## TWIRL THE TRENCHER.

For this game a wooden, earthen, or silver plate is needed, china being too fragile. The leader, who assumes either a name or a number himself, gives a name or a number to each of the company. The names may be those of flowers or of animals, but whatever they are, the players must be on the alert, and not forget their designations. A circle is formed, the leader gives the plate a twirl, and sets it spinning, calling out the name of the person who is to catch it, and running to his own place. If the person called fails to catch it before it stops spinning, he must pay a forfeit.

## THE FIELD OF THE CLOTH OF DAMASK.

Clear the table of everything upon it, and arrange yourselves around it, choosing partners. You need a small, round plate, or a circular piece of wood.

Select two of the liveliest and most genial of the party to be leaders. Call them Sir Loin, and General Kettle. They must alternately choose their soldiers, performing the ceremony of conferring titles, by giving each gentleman a tap with a stick across the shoulders, and each lady a kiss on the cheek, as the name is announced.

The officers and privates will be as follows :—

| | |
|---|---|
| SIR LOIN. | GENERAL KETTLE. |
| GENERAL GOOSE. | GENERAL TONGS. |
| LIEUTENANT-GENERAL DUCK. | LIEUTENANT-GENERAL CARVER. |
| MAJOR-GENERAL MUFFIN. | MAJOR-GENERAL FORK. |
| COLONEL CRUMPET. | COLONEL COFFEE POT. |
| COLONEL CARROT. | COLONEL CORKSCREW. |
| MAJOR O'MUTTON. | MAJOR CRACKER. |
| PRIVATE PARTRIDGE. | MAJOR SPIT. |
| " PINE. | CORPORAL STEEL. |
| " POTATO. | " TOASTRACK. |
| " PLUM. | PRIVATE PLATE. |
| " PEACH. | " PAIL. |
| " PIGEON. | " POTLID. |
| " PEAR. | " POKER. |

And as many more as may be convenient.

### THE GAME.

General Kettle begins: He takes the plate, which is called the Plum-Pudding, between his fingers and thumb, ready for spinning on the table, and tells a story which may be like this : "As I was sitting on the fire this morning, spluttering with rage at having no enemy to boil, who should come along in his bag and string but old Plum-Pudding. The moment he saw me, off he ran, and I after him, when turning a corner, I ran up against Major O'Mutton."

At this word General Kettle spins round the "Plum-Pudding," which Major O'Mutton has to keep up, the Major now going on with the story, until he has mentioned Plum-Pudding and introduced the name of some one on the other side, who, in his turn, continues the game.

The only troublesome thing about this, is to remember who you are. You are no longer yourself, but a Private Plate, or a Private Poker, a Carrot, a Corkscrew, or a Crumpet. If you do not succeed in keeping the Plum-Pudding spinning, or if you do not bring in the name of an opponent you will have to give a forfeit.

Forfeits in this game are expected for letting the Pudding fall, for alluding to yourself as a human being, since you must always speak in character, for hesitation in continuing the story, and for omitting the name Plum-Pudding, as well as for calling an enemy by a wrong title.

If the party is a large one, as many as a hundred forfeits may be won, but the fun is often fast and furious when the number is small.

At the end of the game, the army which has given the fewest forfeits is declared victorious. A Court Martial is then called, and the forfeits are redeemed. Perhaps there may be such penalties as these: If you belong to Sir Loin's Army, you may be *Basted*—which means, pursued with handkerchiefs around the room; *Seasoned*—which obliges you to kiss every lady in the room, and perhaps to receive a slap in return; *Trussed*, or skewered with two walking sticks into a corner, until some lady releases you with a kiss, or, *Roasted*, when you must walk up to every lady in the room, and entreat her for a salute. If she refuses it, you are said to be *done*.

As a member of General Kettle's army, you are liable to be *Scrubbed*; you must entreat each lady to kiss you. She will probably refuse and scrub your face with her handkerchief. *Sharpened*, when two gentlemen will obstruct your progress toward the lady of your choice. *Blackleaded*, you must go around the company, and inquire of each his or her opinion of you, which they will make, not in the least flattering. *Washed*, you ask the opinion of the company, and receive the most exaggerated praise.

These penalties are intended for gentlemen, but they may be varied for ladies. Indeed they may be dispensed with entirely, and other and quite different punishments given. The above forfeits apply also to other games.

## THE ELEMENTS.

The party sit in a circle. One throws a handkerchief at another and calls out AIR. The person hit must call the names of Dove, Eagle, Owl, Sparrow, and other creatures which belong to the air, in a loud voice, and as rapidly as possible, before the caller can count ten.

If a creature that does not belong to the air is named, or if a name is repeated, a forfeit must be paid.

Throw the handkerchief in the same way for the other elements. At FIRE keep perfect silence.

## WIGGLES.

A few pieces of writing-paper, or small sheets of cardboard, and a pencil for each player, are the only outfit required for the very amusing game of Wiggles.

A sort of humorous outline drawing-lesson, which leads to a good deal of merry laughter, is managed in the following way:—

Upon each paper, its possessor draws rather heavily either a straight or crooked line, and then passes it on to his neighbor on the right. He takes the line given him as his foundation, and proceeds to draw a picture of some kind. The results are often absurd, and often too they are very pretty.

Sometimes one person who is the artist of the evening, draws a picture which he does not show. Giving merely his first line or wiggle, he lets the rest of the group try how nearly they can approach his idea. When at last the pictures are compared with his, there is a perfect explosion of fun.

## THE SPANISH NOBLEMAN.

This, as its title implies, is a rather gallant and chivalrous game.

The company arrange themselves in a straight line at one end of the room, excepting one person who is to be the nobleman, and he must take his place at the other end of the room. Advancing to his friends, the nobleman must sing the following lines:—

"I am a nobleman from Spain,
Coming to court your daughter Jane.

The rest reply to this in concert,

"Our daughter Jane is yet too young,
She has not learned her mother-tongue."

The nobleman replies,

"Be she young, or be she old,
For her beauty she must be sold;
So, fare you well, my ladies gay,
I'll call again another day."

The company now advance, singing,

"Turn back, turn back, you noble knight,
And brush your boots and spurs so bright."

Whereupon the Spanish nobleman assumes an air of disdain, and sings,

"My boots and spurs gave you no thought,
For in this land they were not bought,
Neither for silver nor for gold,
So fare you well, my ladies gay,
I'll call again another day.

All then advance, saying,

"Turn back, turn back, you noble knight,
And choose the fairest in your sight."

The nobleman, fixing upon, we will suppose, Kitty, says,

"The fairest one that I can see
Is pretty Kitty—Come to me."

The couple go back hand in hand. The whole performance is now recommenced, only this time two noblemen advance instead of one. With graceful steps and gay dresses, this little bit of play may be quite effective in giving variety to a dull evening.

## THROWING LIGHT.

In this clever game, a word is chosen to be the subject of conversation, by two of the party, and it must be known only to themselves. It should be a word to which several meanings are attached, so that the remarks made in reference to it, may be puzzling to the rest of the company. The two persons who are in the secret, refer to the word in all its meanings, the others joining in the conversation as soon as they have guessed what the word is.

Suppose the word fixed upon to be Hare, which is also Hair, the colloquy could begin in this style :—

1st player.—"I saw one the other day, when I was out driving in the country."

2d player.—"I had one sent in a Christmas box."

1st player.—"My own is nearly black."

2d player.—"And mine is dark brown."

1st player.—"Do you prefer it hot or cold?"

2d player.—"Between the two, I think."

Here some one on whom light is dawning, may inquire : "Don't we read of some one in the Bible, who might have lived longer if he had not had so much of it?"

Thus the chat runs on, until the players, one by one, as they guess the word, are entitled to take part in the conversation. The penalty for making a mistake, and joining in the talk without discovering the right word, is to have a handkerchief thrown over the blundering person's head. This must be worn until the word is really found out.

Ball (bawl), dear (deer), key (quay), pen (Penn), boy (buoy), handel (handle), whale (wail), and similar words are legitimate.

## TOILET.

This beautiful old game was brought to England in the train of William the Conqueror. But in the rude days of the old Norman barons, it must have been played with more simplicity than in ours, when the articles of necessity and luxury which pertain to a lady's toilet are almost endless.

The idea is to fix upon some article indispensable to a lady's dress. Her fan, handkerchief, slipper, scent-bottle, hair-brush, dressing-glass, etc., are chosen, and one article is assigned to each player. The leader, who holds a wooden trencher, generally begins by announcing the fact, that my lady is invited to a ball, consequently her wants during the time of dressing will be numerous.

Perhaps the brush and comb will first be called for to dress the lady's hair, when the owner of these articles must respond to the call, by taking up the trencher, before it has ceased spinning; it being the rule that every one who makes a call, shall spin the trencher. Instead of articles of dress, flowers have frequently been called for, each young lady choosing her favorite, and boys may alter it to their principal tools and toys, as knife, saw, balls, skates, etc.

There would be little fun in playing this or any other round game, were it confined to boys only, or to girls only. It is a game for both sexes, and they enjoy it the more, if they play it together. Nor is it beneath the dignity of grown up men and women, to unbend, and at times play merrily like children.

Stage-Coach, Kitchen Furniture, and The Trades, all belong to the same class of games as Toilet.

## THE AVIARY.

The keeper of the Aviary must be fluent and glib of tongue, and able to make a speech, resembling those which we have all heard from the lips of itinerant showmen. The more bombastic it is, the better.

Before making his speech, the keeper sets down the names of the players, and also the name of the bird, which each player decides to represent. This latter fact he keeps to himself.

He steps to the front, makes a bow, waves his hand, and begins, with a flourish :—

"I have the honor of presenting to this assembly of the brave, the beautiful, and the distinguished, my world-renowned Aviary, with which I have made the tour of the globe, and which has been admired by all the crowned heads of Europe. My birds are unrivaled for their magnificent plumage, their splendid colors, their sweet voices, and their wonderful intelligence."

Then he repeats the names of his birds, and expresses a wish to know which of them are liked or hated by the company.

Turning to the nearest lady, he says :—

"To which of my birds will you give your heart?"
"To which will you reveal your secret?"
"From which would you pluck a feather?"

The lady may reply :—

"I will give my heart to the eagle."
"I will tell my secret to the nightingale."
"I will pluck a feather from the owl."

The keeper makes a note of these dispositions, and then turns to a gentleman, who may answer to the questions :—

"I will give my heart to the dove."
"I will tell my secret to the lark."
"I will pluck a feather from the bird of Paradise."

When any player says he will give his heart to a bird already chosen by another, he must pay a forfeit. He must pay a forfeit if he happens to mention a bird that is not in the aviary. He must make a new choice, and should he a second time blunder, he must again pay a forfeit.

When all have answered, the keeper announces the names of the persons represented by the birds, and commands each to salute the one to whom his heart was given, to whisper a secret in the ear of the one deemed worthy of confidence, and to receive a forfeit from the one whose feather was to be plucked.

## CANDY PULL.

None of the games under review will so enchant the children of the house as a genuine CANDY-PULL. For this the merry party must invade Bridget's domains, and deprive that functionary, for an interval, of the control of the range. But, she, good soul, is generally willing to bear a hand, and she presides like a benevolent genius over the giddy band, who watch the molasses bubbling in the pan, stirring it with many a quip and quere. Bridget herself advises that a little soda (bi-carbonate) be sifted into the boiling mass, in the proportion of a half-teaspoonful to a quart. This helps to whiten it. She tells the girls that their hands must be floured or buttered before they begin to pull the strands of candy, which grow pliant and toothsome, and under skillful treatment, may be braided, twisted or flattened. A candy-pull or a cooking party, is, in these days, very popular, and few rainy-day frolics are half so sensible.

# Forfeits and Penalties.

ENALTIES should be as mirth-provoking as possible. During the progress of games of forfeits, gloves, handkerchiefs, fans, bracelets, pocket knives, pencil cases, etc., may be given up as forfeits for mistakes. When the time comes to redeem them,,this is the common method:—

A lady who undertakes to cry the forfeits, sits on a chair, and another, whose office it is to decide what the punishment shall be to reclaim the article, kneels down before her.

She holds the article above his head, so that he cannot see it, and says:—

"Here's a pretty thing, and a very pretty thing,
And what shall the owner of this thing do?"

"Is it fine or superfine," asks the sentence-giver. Fine stands for a gentleman's property, and superfine for a lady's, and very different tasks must be set, according to the sex.

The doomster should be well up in his part beforehand, and the parties who have to redeem their forfeits, should do so with good nature, no matter how ridiculous they may be, or else the pleasure of all will be marred.

PRISON DIET is sometimes given. A glass of water and a teaspoon are brought into the room. The prisoner is blindfolded, and is then fed with water by the teaspoonful by every one in the room, unless he succeeds in guessing who is feeding him.

To hop on one foot three times around the room, to laugh, cry, cough, and sneeze in every corner; to count fifty backwards; to kiss your shadow; to play the judge sitting solemnly while funny stories are related to shake your gravity; to pay six compliments to six persons, leaving out the letter *l* or *s* in them, or mounted on a chair to be put in whatever absurd attitude any of the company may propose, you personating, meanwhile, a Grecian statue, are among ordinary forfeit penalties.

To BRUSH OFF A DIME is a trick which, well played, is very funny. A dime in a wet cloth is pressed against the victim's forehead, but he is forbidden to put his hands up. The cloth is removed, but the forehead feels as if the dime were there, and the poor fellow vainly tries to take it off by shaking his head, etc.

A favorite redemption is that of THE KNIGHT OF THE RUEFUL COUNTENANCE. He must take a lighted candle in his hand, select a friend to be his squire, and then the two must together make the circuit of the room. The squire must touch the hand of each lady very respectfully with his lips, after the fashion of a subject doing homage to a queen. After each kiss he must wipe the Knight's mouth with a handkerchief. The Knight must carry the candle throughout the ceremony, and on no account venture to smile.

HUSH-A-BYE-BABY. This obliges you to yawn till your sleepiness sets everybody in the room to yawning also.

THE MEDLEY. Sing without pause or rest, lines from a half dozen old and new songs, each as different as possible from the other

POETIC NUMBERS. The unfortunate being who is condemned to pay this penalty, must recite a verse of poetry in this way:—

Tell (one) me (two) not (three) in (four) mournful (five) numbers (six)
Life (seven) is (eight) but (nine) an (ten) empty (eleven) dream (twelve).

This must be repeated without hesitation, and is to some people a problem.

In cases where some ladies of the party have objections to promiscuous kissing, and decline to assist in games which may require forfeits of that character, it is best to choose penances in which the kiss is not imperative. There are plenty of jolly and absurd forfeits—penances which require no kisses. For instance, there is THE FLORIST'S CHOICE. Three flowers, Tulip, Rose, and Geranium, are selected. Two of the party may assist the forfeiter in choosing persons whom the flowers are to typify. Then he is asked, "What will you do with the Tulip?" "Dip it in water." "What with the Rose?" "Wear it next my heart." "What with the Geranium?" "Press it between old newspapers." The names with which the flowers are identified are now mentioned, and their fate excites laughter or commiseration.

THE FOOL'S LEAP is provocative of mirth, because the silly dupe, being ordered to set two chairs back to back, to take off his shoes and jump over them, is almost sure to jump, if he can, over the chairs, when the shoes only are meant for such gymnastics.

GOING TO SERVICE. The person who is bidden go to service, must demonstrate her ability to be a maid of all work, by going through the motions of various domestic processes, in answer to questions like

"How do you iron? How do you wash dishes? How do you sweep? How do you scrub?

To kneel to the wittiest, bow to the prettiest, and kiss the one you love best, is of time-honored celebrity, but a less enviable duty is his who, being asked to name his favorite musical instruments, is obliged to imitate them, or his who is at the mercy of the company, and compelled to fulfill whatever difficult task they may impose.

## TWENTY QUESTIONS.

The play of "TWENTY QUESTIONS" has been the cause of uproarious laughter in drawing-rooms where among the players have been learned professors, eminent legal authorities, and grave divines. It is a very intellectual game, yet has a mathematical precision which leads straight to the bottom facts of the topic under discussion.

"Is your subject animal, vegetable, or mineral?"
"What is its size?"
"To what age does it belong?"
"Is it historical or natural?"
"Is it ancient or modern?"
"Is it a manufactured article?" etc.

Many puzzling subjects may be found to baffle the most astute in playing Twenty Questions. The topmost stone in Milan Cathedral, the dew-drop in a Morning Glory, the Queen's slippers, and the wedding-ring of Princess Louise, have been guessed in companies where this sport has been indulged in.

### CRAMBO.

Two pieces of paper, unlike both in size and color, are given to each person. On one of them a noun must be written, and on the other a question. Two gentlemen's hats must now be called for, into one of which the nouns must be dropped, and into the other the questions, and all well shuffled. The hats must then be handed round, until each person is supplied with a question and a noun.

The thing now to be done is for each player to write an answer in rhyme to the question he finds written on the one paper, bringing in the noun he sees written on the other paper.

The questions and nouns are usually so very inappropriate that it is not easy to write decent poetry. The player need not be disturbed, for the less sensible the poetry, the greater the fun. The thing to be done is to write an answer to your question with the noun you have received. Perhaps your question is "Do you like ices?" and your noun is "Coquette."

A person might write a stanza like this:—

"Over ices we met
On a night of July,
If there was a coquette
It was she and not I,
But ices I like, for my Bessie and I
First broke ice together one eve of July."

### DUMB CRAMBO.

This is quite different from the other. After dividing the company into two equal parts, one half leave the room. In their absence, the remaining players fix upon a verb, to be guessed by those who have gone out on their return. As soon as the word is chosen, those outside the room are told with what word it rhymes. A consultation ensues when the absent ones come in, and silently act the word they think may be the right one. Suppose the word chosen to have rhymed with *sell*, the others might come in and begin felling imaginary trees with imaginary hatchets, but on no account uttering a single syllable. If *fell* were the verb the spectators, on recognizing the action, would clap their hands, as a signal that the word had been discovered. But if *tell*, or any other word has been thought of, the spectators would begin to hiss loudly, which the actors would understand as a notice that they were wrong, and must try again.

The rule in this game is absolute silence. If only an exclamation is uttered, a forfeit must be paid.

## Fortune Telling.

ORTUNE TELLING is an ancient amusement, in which no wise person believes, and to which only the superstitious pin their confidence. Without being in the least credulous, and only indulging that delight in mystery, which most of the human race feel, we may derive a great deal of entertainment, if we have a gifted friend among us, who will now and then use her talent for palmistry, by acting as a Sybil, or prophetess.

Which of us, however superior, does not own to a quick throb of pleasure on finding a four-leaved clover? Who has not counted the petals of the daisy, and been glad that the stray cat who persisted in adopting our domicile was black as Erebus? Where is the man who enjoys sitting down to a table where the guests number thirteen, or the woman who does not feel an involuntary shiver when her looking-glass falls from her hand? Most of us prefer to see the moon over the right shoulder, and do not prefer to begin an important piece of work, or to set out on a journey on Friday.

Our superstitions are akin to that vein of poetry which lies under the surface of the finest civilization, and is found at the root of what is best and simplest among the peoples who are still primitive and rude.

If you can coax your fortuneteller, provided she is to exercise her skill at a party, a church fair, or any assemblage of friends, to adopt the dress of a gypsey, to wear a striped shawl, muffle her voice, and sit in the shadow of an improvised tent, you will add to the mystery, and, of course, to the attractiveness of the occasion.

There are several ways of telling fortunes. Mademoiselle Le Normand, the shrewd and keen-eyed French woman, who discerned the star of Napoleon from afar, and predicted that the little Corsican would rise to fame, left a pack of thirty-six symbolic cards, which may be purchased anywhere at the book-stores. Among these, the ship is the symbol of commerce; the clover leaf foretells good news; the house means prosperity; trees stand for good health; the rod indicates quarrels in the family, and impending misfortunes; the scythe is the shadow of danger; a serpent betokens false friends and treachery, and a coffin is the herald of death.

All these cards are modified as to their signification by the manner in which they are held, and their relations to other cards. A pack of them will certainly do no harm in any house, and, if cleverly manipulated, they may be the source of much pleasurable occupation.

Ordinary playing-cards are of course used by the fortuneteller. The Queen of Hearts brings good luck; the King of Hearts increases it, and the Ace of Spades is to be deeply dreaded. Far, far away to the cloud-land of the earliest mythologies, where the three weird sisters, Atropos, Clotho, and Lachesis sit and spin the web of mortal destinies these mystic interpretations point.

The old Greeks and Romans went reverently to the oracles, before they entered on new adventures, or set forth to fierce wars, and the oracles, muttering in ambiguous phrases, sent them on their way rejoicing. The Pharaohs, at a younger, blither period of the earth's history, had their soothsayers, astrologers, and magicians, whose office it was to interpret the royal dreams, and pave the unseen future for the kingly feet with untold gifts and shining splendor.

PALMISTRY, or telling fortunes by the lines of the hand is easily learned. The lines running through the hand show delicacy or the reverse, will or vacillation; artistic deftness, or stupid clumsiness. Common sense and habit of observation will enable most people to tell fortunes by hands.

As for the prettiest way of all, the telling fortunes by

tea-leaves, that requires daintiness of wrist and eye, and a happy turn for hitting off the salient points in character.

The reader, however, will please take notice that it is only as a graceful indoor pastime, that fortune-telling is recommended. Do not suffer yourselves to think that the momentous issues of fate are ever decided by the fantasy of a floating tea-leaf, or the chance of a pretty picture on a card. Do not go to the vulgar and ignorant persons, who prey on the weakness of their neighbors, and earn their livings by telling fortunes for money.

Our fortunes, good or ill, are very much in our own control. The honest, the true, the brotherly, the persevering, usually arrive at final good fortune, even though they meet with sorrow and disappointment. The thriftless, the mean, the selfish, and the indolent most frequently reap the whirlwind, because they sow the wind. As a general rule riches and honor come to the diligent and faithful, while poverty and reproach are inherited by the idle and the reckless.

## TOY-MAKING.

The exercise of a little mechanical skill by young folks who have brains in their finger-tips, helps to swell the tide of home enjoyment.

Plenty of pretty toys may be bought by those who have Fortunatus's purse to go to for funds, but it is doubtful whether those who can buy whatever they wish, have half the fun which belongs to those who with a knife, a few tacks, screws, and strings, a little paper, and some other simple materials, construct ingenious toys of their own, for the diversion of their friends.

One can hear the shouts of laughter with which the assembled family greet Jack and Nellie, as by their combined efforts they produce, what is after all not a toy, but a trick.

## THE APPLE WOMAN.

For this nothing is wanted except a baby's or an old lady's cap, a pocket-handkerchief, and a live human hand.

Clench the fist, and then hold it with the knuckles upward, covering the top joint of the thumb with the top joints of the fingers. Draw on these portions of the fore-finger and thumb, forming the front of the clenched fist, a face, using a few bold dots and lines to represent the eyes, eyebrows, nose, etc. Make a cap to fit the hand, and drape a pocket-handkerchief over all, fastening it like a shawl in front. The old woman so made may be made to seem to speak, by slightly moving the knuckle of the thumb up and down, and to smoke by sticking a pipe between the fore-finger and the thumb, the space between which joints will represent the mouth.

## THE DANCING HIGHLANDER.

This is another curious hand performance. Get an old glove, and cut off the tops of the first fingers down to about the second joint; next will be required a very small pair of baby's socks, which are to be painted some plaid pattern, and fitted to the first and second fingers. Draw on the glove, then pull the socks on the first two fingers, padding out that for the first finger, so as to be equal in length to that for the second. The figure of a Highlander in his national costume, which should have been first prepared out of cardboard, and appropriately colored, is then to be pasted on to the back of the glove; the tops of the first two fingers of the gloves should do duty for shoes, and the uncovered portions of the performer's fingers will show as the bare knees of the kilted Scot, who may then be made to dance or perform any of those wild antics usually attributed to the Highlander when his foot is on his native heath.

## The Magic Fan.

FANS have a long and eventful history. They figure in the annals of courts, and are treasured by withered old ladies among the relics, scented and ribbon-bound, of their days of belle-hood and youthful bloom. Brought from the distant East, they are wielded with most grace by the lovely ladies of Spain, who can do what they please with the pretty weapon which they use with such aerial sprightliness.

To make a fan of paper tied with a bit of satin or lutestring is an easy accomplishment to most school girls. But whoever, in want of amusement, shall venture on the manufacture of THE MAGIC FAN, will find that much dexterity is required to insure success.

In its manufacture a piece of good stout paper will be required, in size twenty-four inches by nineteen, or proportionately larger or smaller. The paper is to be measured into six equal parts, the divisions being marked on the margin, as shown in Fig. 1. Double the paper in half, as shown in Fig. 2. Fold the uppermost half outwards, making the fold as shown in the same figure by the letters AA.

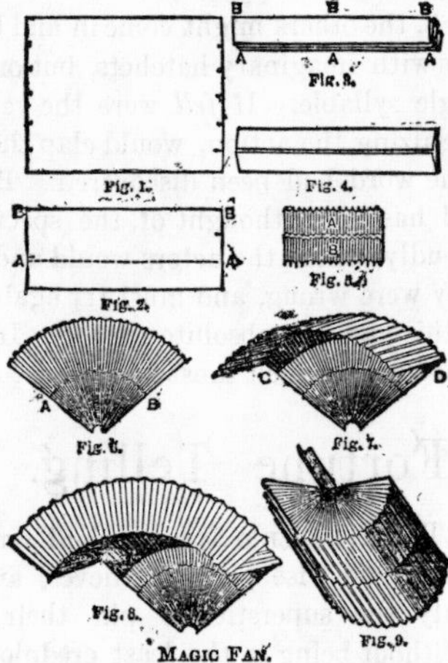

MAGIC FAN.

Turn the paper over and fold the other half in precisely the same way, thus making the paper as shown in Figure 3. Upon examining the edge A A A, two openings between the folds will be seen, whereas at the edge B B B, three openings will be found. The hand has next to be inserted into the middle of these latter openings, and the paper folded outward to the right and left, and turned over, when it will show as in Fig. 4. Then pinch the paper from end to end, in plaits like a ruff, three-eighths of an inch in depth, so that when it is all pinched it will be in small compass, as in Fig. 5.

The magic fan is now complete, and all that remains is to learn how to produce its variety of shapes. It is said that as many as from sixty to seventy varieties have been produced; a few only will, however, be here indicated, as by attention to the directions now given, it will be a comparatively easy matter to ring the changes on the kinds specified.

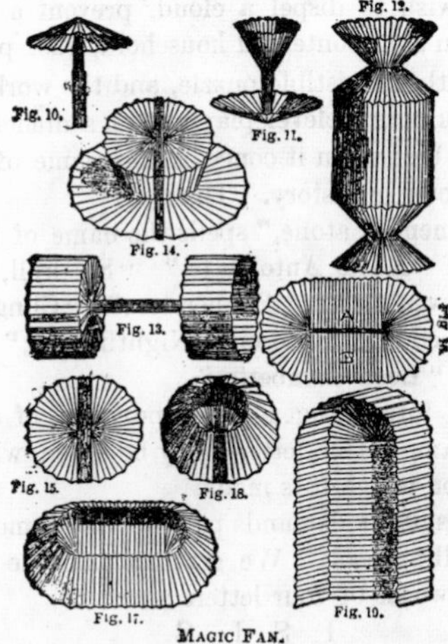

Magic Fan.

It must always be remembered that every time the form of the fan is changed, the paper must be again well pinched together, in order that the folds of the plaits may remain plainly and strongly marked. Unless the folds are kept in order, the fan cannot be properly worked.

To produce the first form, the common-shaped fan (Fig. 6), catch the folded paper (Fig. 5) at the bottom with both hands, pinch it in, and spread out the top. For Fig. 7 insert the fingers at A, and pass them round to B, raising the paper. To turn Fig. 7 into Fig. 8, insert the fingers at C, and pass them round to D.

For the next change catch the paper by the part now uppermost, pinch that part well together, and the paper takes the form of a scoop (Fig. 9), the upper part of the fan (Fig. 8) becoming the handle of the scoop.

Pinch the paper again into the form of Fig. 5, lift up the upper part A, bring the lower plaits B well together, and and with one hand arrange the upper part, so as to form the head of a mushroom (Fig. 10). A new form may be got by raising part of the double head of the mushroom. For Fig. 11 reverse the paper and spread out the lower part, so that it may represent the body of a wine-glass; that which in Fig. 10 was the head of the mushroom will soon appear as the foot of the glass.

To make the Chinese lantern (Fig. 12), open out all the paper and twist it around; catch it now by the central part, and by compressing the central folds well together, something like two of the enormous wheels of the steam stone-crusher will be produced (Fig. 13). The butter-cooler (Fig. 14) is obtained by opening the paper out again and catching it at the two ends.

The original form Fig. 5 must then be again reverted to, and a fresh start may be made by catching the paper at both ends, and folding it up so as to represent Fig. 15. By drawing it out the table mat, Fig. 16 will next be shown.

Raise up the paper at the letters A and B of Fig. 16, and there will appear a dish in the form of Fig. 17, and Fig. 18 is obtained by then pressing the paper inwards. The sentry-box, Fig. 19, comes by drawing the paper out, and letting it loose at the foot and so on. Many other shapes may be obtained.

Experiment as freely as you please on the Magic Fan. If spoiled, it costs only a little patience and a few minutes of time to remake, and a dexterous lad will produce chairs, sofas, flower-pots, staircases, windows and window-blinds, night-caps, boxes, etc.

Paper lends itself obligingly to many other queer devices, as boats, pusses, hats, and parachutes.

From pasteboard and paper united, Aunt Mary and Uncle Dick, putting their heads together, might evolve for the mystification and delight of a bevy of young visitors.

## THE PROPHET.

The Prophet, as his office is, predicts the future. To make his figure, procure a piece of cork, and cut out a stately man, dress him in flowing robes, give him a venerable beard, and in his hand put a small wand, pointing downwards.

Cut a piece of pasteboard in a circular shape, let it be a few inches in diameter, and ornament the edges with pieces of fancy paper. Then mark on the white surface of the pasteboard twenty equal divisions, by means of lines radiat-

ing from the center, and within each division place a number ranging in order from one to twenty.

Mount the card on a small wooden stand, through the center of which a steel wire is placed, and fix the figure of the Prophet in such a manner on the wire that it will revolve freely.

The next thing to be done is to draw up a table of prognostications, and, indeed, it is as well to have several of these and if they are somewhat indefinite all the better. The person who wishes his fortune told then signifies it, and the showman sets the Prophet spinning. As he comes to a standstill, his wand points to the number nearest to it, and that indicates the person's fortune.

### TELLING STORIES.

The gift of telling a story well is one that entitles its possessor to deserved popularity. There are days when every amusement wearies, and we pine for something new, and the new thing, being proposed, fails to please. Then how happy the fireside which has a story-teller of its own. Some dear grandparent or favorite cousin, or, it maybe, some charming girl or accomplished collegian, fills up the tedious hour and gives it wings of enchantment by relating the legends of the past, or evoking memories of stories read in the pages of great authors.

So, in the days of our ancestors, the troubadour and the palmer, wending their way from one castle to another, and from baron's hall to earl's abode, or else to the hospitable convent or monastery, which never refused shelter to the wandering and wayfaring, gained their welcome and seats above the salt. The teller of a good story is a benefactor, and should not be undervalued.

### PLAYING AND SINGING.

Music, too, is one of the home resources which, universal as the art is, is far too little prized. Everybody cannot sing like Gerster, or play like Joseffy. Home artists should not refuse to play for the home circle and for friends, because they are not ambitious and cannot produce dazzling effects on the piano or violin.

On the contrary, every performer should take pains to learn by heart, so as to be entirely independent of "notes" a half-dozen favorite arrangements, and, when asked, he or she should not wait to be coaxed and persuaded, before gratifying the company. She pleases twice who does her best when first invited. It is of all things most annoying to have a lady, known to be a good player, excuse herself from playing because her music is not at hand. Always to require music is like building a house and leaving the scaffolding visible.

Young people should learn to play in perfect time and touch, that is staccato or legato as may be needed, for dancing. No exercise is more graceful and beautiful than this, in which the body moves in rhythm to the sound of music, and a dance at home in the parlor, with the young folks flying light as birds to the inspiring tune, and the old folks looking on till their blood begins to glow, and father suddenly rising, whirls mother, laughing and protesting, into the center of the room, is a sight to behold and remember as a glimpse of Arcadia.

Learn to play for dancing, girls and boys, too. There is no reason why only girls should study music. It affords a very delightful indoor amusement for young gentlemen.

Song should be cultivated around the hearth, and where there are a number of voices, the different parts should be taken, and the evening should be turned at times into an amateur philharmonic rehearsal.

## Puzzles.

SOCIETY might be broadly divided into two parts. One part might consist of the people who cannot make out a puzzle to save their lives, and the other, of the people to whom a puzzle is a challenge to the most congenial of intellectual tournaments. The puzzle columns in the weekly papers are one of their most popular features, and in more houses than we can count, the nuts which the puzzle-editor provides for cracking, are sturdily tried by bright youngsters and shrewd adults, who never know when they are beaten, but if at first they don't succeed, try, try again. All America went wild over the little solitaire amusement, known as the fifteen-puzzle; and if you wish to dispel a cloud, prevent a quarrel, or make peace in a discontented household, just present them with a perfectly irresistible puzzle, and the work is done.

THE ANAGRAM is a clever play upon a sentence, or phrase, and is at its best when it conceals the name of some celebrated character in history. Thus:—

"Tear it, men; I atone," spells the name of the ill-fated and beautiful "Marie Antoinette." "So droll, pert man," transposed, reveals "Lord Palmerston." "Cling on, feeling heart," is, of course, "Florence Nightingale;" and "Able man to get," "Leon Gambetta."

J and I are interchangeable for purposes of convenience in the anagram, but no letters may be taken, which are not in the name on which it is made.

THE WORD SQUARE demands patience and some familiarity with the spelling-book. We give an example of a square composed of words of four letters:—

I S I S<br>
S I D E<br>
I D E A<br>
S E A T

The reader will observe that the letters across the top, and down the left side, spell the same word. The second column and the second row the same, and so on.

To set any one guessing this square, you would, having composed it, write as follows:—

1. A river in Oxfordshire.
2. A portion of our bodies.
3. A thought.
4. A chair.

The difficulty is very greatly increased when squares are formed of words containing five or six letters. Thus the square now given is harder than its predecessor:—

1. A poetical name of old England.
2. A Portuguese province in Africa.
3. A town in East Prussia.
4. Something aimed at or designed.
5. A town in Denmark.
6. A town in France.

A L B I O N<br>
L O A N D A<br>
B A R T E N<br>
I N T E N T<br>
O D E N S E<br>
N A N T E S

**ENIGMAS** are of various forms. We will suppose birds to be the subject of enigmas around the wintry fire :

1. What a severe attack of quinsy prevents your doing ? *Swallow.*
2. An architect well known to fame. *Wren.*
3. A portion of a whole, and a range of hills. *Part-ridge.*
4. What a coward does in the hour of danger. *Quail.*

Or fruits are cunningly hidden in the enigma, or it may be flowers. Then,

1. A vowel and a cooking apparatus are *Orange.*
2. To give way to anxiety and sorrow, is *Pine.*
3. The greatest crime in a school-boy's calendar, is *Peach.*
4. What a good conscience gives to its possessor, is *Heartsease.*
5. An Irish vehicle and a people who live under one king. *Car-nation.*
6. A noted Quaker, and a handy article of dress. *Fox-glove.*

**DIAMONDS** are made by selecting letters or words that may be set forth in the form of a diamond. For instance in the example, the central letters downward and horizontally spell the name of a great novelist.

1. A letter that is both vowel and consonant.
2. A Jewish tribe.
3. A woman who set two ancient peoples at war.
4. A character in Guy Mannnering.
5. A Grecian hero.
6. A novelist and poet.
7. A character in The Tempest.
8. A character in Love's Labor Lost.
9. Effervescence.
10. A letter of the Greek alphabet.
11. A consonant.

W<br>
D A N<br>
H E L E N<br>
B E R T R A M<br>
A G A M E M N O N<br>
W A L T E R S C O T T<br>
S E B A S T I A N<br>
M E R C A D E<br>
F R O T H<br>
E T A<br>
T.

## CHARADES.

Though weak to a proverb my first has been reckoned,
The game is so constantly made of my second.
Yet to hosts without number my whole bade defiance,
And the world stood amazed at the beauteous alliance.

This it is obvious is *Waterloo.*

I sent my second to my first, but many a whole passed before I saw him. *Sea-son.*

My first I hope you are, my second I see you are, and my whole I know you are, is *Wel-come.*

A verbal charade is sometimes composed by precocious seven and eight year olds, and twenty-seven or eight needs not blush at making a good numerical charade. In the latter, a word or proverb is selected, and the way to begin is to announce · "I am composed of so many letters. My 1, 5, 6, 7 is such a thing. My 8, 9, 10 such another, etc," spelling as many words as may be, by combining various letters. Finally a clue is given, not too distinctly, please, when it is admitted that, "My whole is a great discoverer or a marvelous invention."

The verbal charade, often called ENIGMA, is after this pattern :—

My first is in lamb, but not in sheep,
My second in shallow, but not in deep.
My third is in rat, but not in mouse,
My fourth is in villa, but not in house.
My fifth is in love, but not in hate,
My sixth is in door, but not in gate.
My seventh 's in plant, but not in a tree,
My whole is a Christian name you 'll see—*Matilda.*

ACROSTICS, LOGOGRAMS, CHRONOGRAMS, METAGRAMS, and PARAGRAMS, all invite the study of the curious. And, except that the young people are apt to survey them with suspicion, regarding the whole host of mathematical puzzles as veiled ambassadors, in league with schoolmasters and professors to cheat them into severer studies than play-time cares for, the various number puzzles are warranted to confuse the average head in the very pleasantest way.

For instance :—

"A room with eight corners, had a cat in each corner, seven cats before each cat, and a cat on every cat's tail. What was the total number of cats ?" Eight, and no more.

A countryman having a fox, a goose, and a peck of corn, came to a river, where he could carry over but one at a time. Now, as no two were to be left together that might destroy each other, he was at his wit's end, for, says he, "Though the corn can't eat the goose, nor the goose eat the fox, yet the fox can eat the goose, and the goose eat the corn." How shall he carry them over that they may not destroy each other.

*Answer.*—Let him first take over the goose, leaving the fox and corn ; then let him take over the fox, and bring the goose back ; then take over the corn, and lastly bring back the goose again.

Place three sixes together so as to make seven.

Will the little man who took the medal last week for his proficiency in fractions, think at once of the answer $6\frac{6}{6}$ ?

The three Graces, carrying each an equal number of oranges, were met by the nine Muses, who asked for some of them ; and each Grace having given to each Muse the same number, it was then found that they had all equal shares. How many had the Graces at first ?

*Answer.*—Any multiple of 12 will answer the conditions of this question.

Desire a person to think of a number, say 6. Let him multiply it by 3. Add 1. Multiply by 3. Add to this the number thought of. Let him inform you what is the number produced. It will always end with 3, Strike this off, and you have the original number, 63—6.

Desire a person to think of a number, say 6,

Let him multiply it by itself = 36.
Take one from the number thought of, 5.
Multiply this by itself = 25.
Tell you the difference between this and the former product, 11.
Add one to it, 12.
Halve this number, 6.

The result will invariably be the number thought of.

There are several methods in which this particular puzzle may be varied, but we pass on to something less abstruse and yet more curious.

# Sleight of Hand.

ERE you ever taken as a child to view some wonderful wizard, who wore a fantastic Oriental gown and a Persian-looking cap, all embroidered with queer signs and hieroglyphics? Mystery seemed shaking from his very robes, and his stage paraphernalia, innocent as it looked on the surface, concealed you knew not what of strange, bizarre, and incomprehensible things.

Since you have grown older, you have learned to your surprise that most of the tricks practiced by jugglers and necromaneers are quite simple, and within the range of any quick and deft person who will take the trouble to learn them. Ventriloquism adds to their effect, and something must be set down to the natural credulity, which makes most of us quite willing to be now and then imposed upon.

The only unsurpassed jugglers in the world, whose devices are performed with very little machinery, and who do the most amazing things, with a celerity that captivates the senses, and defies them to penetrate the magical secrets, are the jugglers of India.

Let us see what legerdemain performances we may safely try in a parlor exhibition at home.

## TO GUESS THE TWO ENDS OF A LINE OF DOMINOS.

Cause a set of dominos to be shuffled together as much as any of the company may desire. You propose to leave the room in which the audience are assembled, and you assert, that from your retreat, be it where it may, you can see and will be able to tell, the two numbers forming the extremes of a line composed of the entire set, according to the rules established for laying one domino after another in the draw game.

All the magic consists in taking up and carrying away, unknown to every one, one domino (not a double), taken at hazard; for the two numbers on it must be the same as those on the ends of the two outer dominos. You may renew the experiment as often as you choose, by taking each time a different domino, which changes the numbers to be guessed.

Another pretty little bit of mystery with dominos, is that of seeing and counting them through all obstacles. Lay a set of dominos on their faces, one beside the other, in one black line. Then tell the company that you will go into another room and submit to having your eyes bandaged, and they in the meantime may take from the line any number of dominos they please, *provided they be taken from the end now at your right hand*, and they may place them at the opposite end, and the line, except for the change of pieces, will remain in appearance precisely the same.

If you have mastered this feat of conjuring, you will be able to enter and, still with bandaged eyes, tell your friends the exact number transported from one end to the other. And you may assure them you have seen everything, notwithstanding that there was a wall to look through, and that you were blindfolded. You may even boast that you will do more. You may promise to take from the midst of these dominos, of which they have changed the position, one, which by the addition of its spots, will tell the very number they took from right to left.

The key to this trick is in the arrangement of the first thirteen dominos, *beginning at the left*, so that the spots on the first form the number *twelve*; of the second, *eleven*; of the third, *ten*; and so on up to a double blank for the thirteenth and last. You place the dominos afterwards in the order in which they happen to present themselves.

## THE MAGIC HANDKERCHIEF.

Take any handkerchief and put a quarter or a dime into it. You fold it up, laying the four corners over it, so that it is entirely hidden by the last one. You ask the audience to *touch and feel the coin inside*. You then unfold it, and the coin has disappeared.

The method is as follows: Take a dime and privately put a piece of wax on one side of it, place it in the middle of the handkerchief with the *waxed side up*; at the same time bring the corner of the handkerchief marked A (in Fig 1), and completely hide the coin; this must be carefully done.

Now press the coin very hard, so that by means of the

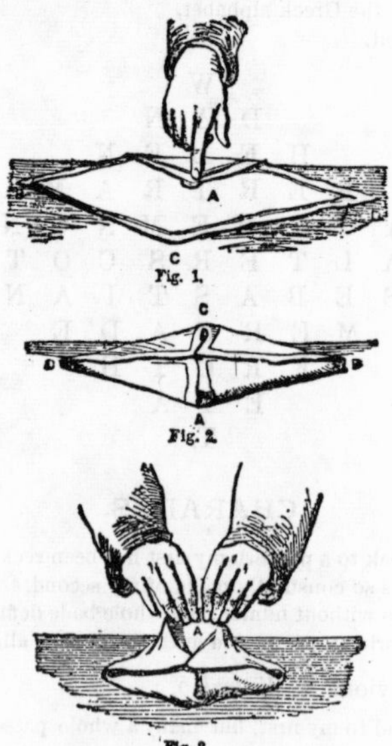


wax it will stick to the handkerchief; then fold the corners B, C, D, and it will resemble Fig. 2.

Then fold the corners B, C, and D, leaving A open (see Fig. 2). Having done this, take hold of the handkerchief with both hands, as represented in Fig. 3 at the opening A, and sliding along your fingers at the edge of the same, the handkerchief becomes unfolded, and the coin adheres to it, coming into your right hand. Detach it, shake the handkerchief out, and the coin will have disappeared.

To convince the spectators that the coin is in the handkerchief at first, drop it on the table and it will sound against the wood.

## THE MAGNETIZED CANE.

Take a piece of horsehair or black silk thread, about two feet long, and fasten to each end of it bent hooks of a black color. Fasten the hooks in the back part of your pantaloons, about two inches below the bend of the knees. Then place the cane, which should be a dark one, and not too heavy, within the inner part of the thread, and by a simple movement of the legs you may make it dance about, and perform a great many funny antics. At night the black thread is invisible, and you should tell the onlooker that you are magnetizing the cane, and by moving and making passes with your hands, you will hide the motion of the legs.

## THE ERRATIC EGG.

To transfer an egg from one wine-glass to another, and back again, without touching either egg or glasses, or letting any one else do so, is not impossible nor very difficult. Blow smartly on one side of the egg, and it will hop into the neighboring glass. Blow a second time, and it will obligingly hop back.

## THE MAGIC CANISTER.

Get a tinman to make a double canister, with an opening on each end, which must so slide within a tin tube that either end can be concealed within it alternately, as seen in the illustration, where the end of *A* is shown and *B* concealed.

In this position it resembles an ordinary canister. The interior is divided into two parts. Into *B* put a bit of cambric, to look like a handkerchief.

Borrow a handkerchief, and say: "Now, ladies and gentlemen, I shall burn this handkerchief to ashes, place them in this canister (so saying, you put it into *A*) and when I have uttered a spell it will be restored perfectly whole. Will the owner please mention what mark it has?"

This diverts the attention of the audience to the owner, and while they are looking at him or her you turn the canister over, and push it up till the shoulder of *B* is on a level with the the top of the tube. When the mark has been declared, you open *B*, take out the square of cambric, and pretend to examine the mark with anxious care. Having scrutinized it, put it into a candle flame, and when it has entirely burned up slip the ashes into *B*, and rapidly reverse it as you turn round to your audience with *A* now uppermost.

Say any nonsense you please, and take the handkerchief triumphantly out to be returned to its owner.

In tricks performed by sleight of hand it is important to preserve composure of manner. Nervousness is apt to betray the conjurer, and keep him from remembering details, and on the perfection of small details depends successful results.

The amateur magician should care more for the pleasure of his friends than for any glory or credit he may gain. In amusements, as in most other things, unselfishness wins the most laurels and gets the most solid returns. It is well to practice a new trick by yourself a number of times before venturing to display it to an audience. Failure is as mortifying in the parlor as on the battle-ground, and in most cases, thoroughness of preparation, united to a cool head and a steady hand, will make failure improbable.

## TIT-TAT-TO.

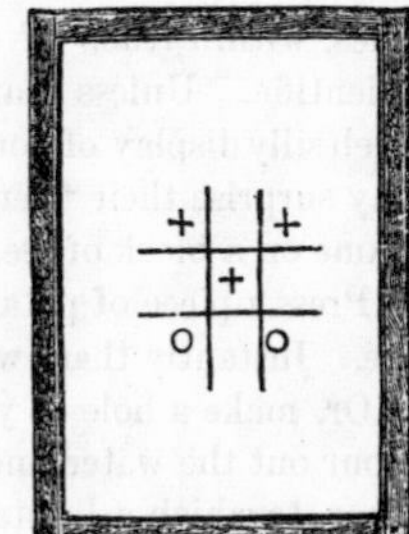

Draw a figure on the slate (*see cut*). The object is to draw three crosses in a row before your antagonist can draw three noughts in the same way. Each to mark but one at a time, and the two to mark by turns.

## LOTO.

There are twenty-four cards in this game, and they are to be found at all toy shops.

Each card is divided into three rows, and each row contains nine squares, five numbered and four blank. These numbers are arranged in columns down the card, the first column containing the units, the second the tens, the third the twenties, and so on up to ninety, which is the highest number. Each card contains fifteen numbers, and each number is four times contained in the set. There are also two bags, one containing numbers from one to ninety on little wooden discs, the other about two hundred counters of glass. The counters are used for covering the numbered squares. One of the players shuffles the loto cards, mixing them well, and then distributes them equally, reserving a share for himself. Any number of persons up to twelve may play loto. The dealer then puts his hand in the bag of numbers, calling them aloud, and the players cover their numbers on the cards with the glass counters as they hear their names. Prizes of nuts or candy may go with this game. The player who first covers five numbers in a row is entitled to the first share, etc.

That nobody should be left out is a cardinal rule in happy homes. We have felt pained in some houses at the loneliness of the old people. They have grown too feeble to mingle in gaieties which tax their strength, they cannot see to read, and even conversation tires them.

It is very hard for them, particularly if they have been of an active turn, and used to doing their share, to sit still with folded hands, passed over in the plans for amusement. It would not be a great sacrifice for some younger person to play loto, or bagatelle, or go-bang, or bring the never-failing backgammon board, and win the aged face to smiles, and the heart to forget its troubles. The rules for all these games are simple, and they are not so difficult but that a novice can learn to take part with very little effort. Do not leave grandpa and grandma out of your calculations when you are making your plans for household fun.

## CHEMICAL EXPERIMENTS.

In these days when every inquisitive person is poking his fingers into science, and trying to discover her secrets, there are not a few chemical experiments which are astonishing to the uninitiated.

Of these, the student will constantly find out new and marvelous combinations for himself, but some of the easier ones, within reach of every one, are safe even for the unscientific. Unless mamma declares that she will have no such silly display of contrasts, Eugene and Clifford may some day surprise their friends by showing them a blaze of vivid flame on a block of ice.

Press a piece of potassium with a penknife upon a cake of ice. Instantly there will be a burst of reddish-purple fire.

Or, make a hole in your cake of ice with a poker red-hot. Pour out the water and fill the cavity with spirits of camphor, to which a lighted match may be applied.

Fill a glass bottle with alkali in which you have dissolved copper filings. The liquid is blue, while uncorked. Cork it, and the color disappears. Uncork it, and it returns.

## THE MAN IN THE MOON.

This gentleman is supposed to be stationary in his lunar abode, but he can be brought to earth on occasion.

Suspend a large sheet across the folding doors of an old-fashioned parlor. In the front room place the company, in darkness. In the back room, on the floor, set a lighted lamp with a reflector of looking-glass or highly polished tin.

A person standing between the light and the sheet will be seen magnified to immense proportions, in the other room, and if he jumps over the light, it will appear as though he jumped to the ceiling. He may perform a variety of humorous feats, to the amusement of the spectators, and the graver countenance he can preserve while cutting up his capers, the louder will be the laughing to reward his good acting.

There is no danger of our growing too frivolous or too fond of play, from our learning how to indulge that part of our nature which protests against being fastened in a strait jacket. The best of books says that a merry heart hath a continual feast. Laughter is medicinal.

It is economy to lay in a stock of apples and nuts for long winter evenings, because to homes where there is an intelligent preparation for household pleasure, the doctor's visits are few. With the fire on the hearth, the cheerful parlor, the shining lamp on the center table, encourage the flow of good spirits. Invite the neighbors in, and with song or dance, gay conversation, and sprightly games, let the evening wear on till it is time to say good-night.

## JACK-STONES.

JACK-STONES are very amusing. Five smooth little pebbles are used. Little silk bags, filled with rice, are substituted for pebbles by some players.

The first player takes up a stone and tosses it in the air. While it is rising he takes up another and tosses it, catching the first as it descends. There are many pretty ways of playing jack-stones, and at the end the players say :—

" F for figs and J for jigs,
And N for knucklebones,
And J. S. for jack-stones.

BATTLEDORE and SHUTTLECOCK, the GRACES, CUP and BALL, SCHIMMEL, BANDILOR, and BAGATELLE are all among those games which develop physical gracefulness, and are good for the health, as well as for recreation. Full directions for playing all these accompany them, and their cost is very trifling.

## BILLIARDS.

There is a variety of games played on the billiard table but the most common at present is the carom game. It is played with three balls. The colored is spotted, *i. e.*, placed on the spot at the further end of the table. The players first string for first stroke, that is, they play up the table so that the ball returns to the lower cushion, and the one who rests nearest plays off. The two players' balls are white ; one marked with a small speck is termed "spot white," the other " plain." The non-striker spots his ball on the spot in baulk, and the striker plays up the table, endeavoring to bring his ball back so as to strike the other on the baulk line also. If he succeeds he scores one, and then continues until he misses striking both balls, when the other player comes in. This game is rarely played by more than two, although sometimes four play, in which case two are partners and strike alternately.

## POOL.

Another favorite game of billiards is POOL. This is played with pockets. The balls are of different colors, and the strikers follow one another in order. The object of each is to hole the ball he plays on, in which case he plays on the nearest. Each player has three lines marked on the board by little stars. As he loses each life he pays so much to the player who holed him. The player left in last wins the pool, which is generally three times the value of a life paid in by each player.

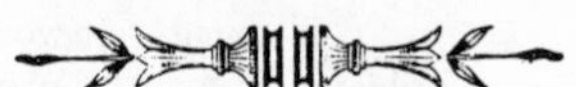

Childhood's Happy Hours.

(An Appreciative Audience.)

# Amateur Theatricals.

MONG indoor amusements, few offer more attractions than theatrical performances ; and in almost any considerable number of associates, or group of guests, there will be found several who have real dramatic talent, and enough others who can act passably, to make up a company. The first thing to do when this amusement has been decided upon is to select a stage manager, to whose decree all shall submit graciously, and who shall select the players and the pieces, cast the latter, and direct at rehearsals and at the performance. Of course, this selection does not prevent the offering suggestions and giving advice on the part of the general company, but much time will be saved and trouble spared if the directing power be finally placed in the charge of one person. For this position the one chosen should possess qualifications gained by experience, and should be competent to decide all disputed questions. In default of a manager thus qualified, the nearest to such an one should be preferred. And as almost every one knows something about "behind the scenes," it will not usually be a matter of much difficulty.

## THE PLAY.

In selecting a play for amateur performances the frequent mistake of choosing the most difficult in the whole range of the drama should be avoided. It should be remembered that it requires trained actors to play "School" or "Rosedale," as much as "Macbeth," or "East Lynne," or "Camille." Amateurs are usually venturesome, but they will do well to be advised in this and select pieces that are short, with few characters, and with the parts evenly distributed and not too long. When a different choice is made the amusement ceases to be such and becomes a task. Any theatrical publisher will supply collections of plays desirable for amateur performances, but among those which are suitable may be mentioned the following: "A Kiss in the Dark," "Jack of all Trades," "A Terrible Secret," "A Spanking Legacy," "Money Makes the Man," "High Life," "Marry in Haste and Repent at Leisure," "Love."

## THE STAGE AND AUDITORIUM.

It is very easy to arrange in any ordinary city or country house for the performance of a simple play requiring only "interior" stage-fitting and appointment. The front and back parlor, or double drawing-room, can be divided by curtains prettily draped, or even by an impromptu "proscenium," made of muslin, stretched on a fine framework and ornamented according to taste. If scenery be desired, and there be present any one qualified to paint it, arrangements can easily be made for its accommodation by running two poles the length of the room chosen for the stage, one on either side, from the folding or sliding-doors to the extreme rear. From these poles the side-scenes can be hung on hooks or rings, like maps, the "flat" or back scene being stretched from standards and stationary. It is desirable to have a raised platform for the floor of the stage, and the front should have the foot-lights (candles or lamps) carefully and strongly fitted, and securely protected by wire gauze. The "green curtain" may be made of baize, but should have a heavy roller secured at the bottom. Strong ropes should be firmly fastened at the top where there should be a pully-block at each end, and should be managed by a careful person attentive to his duty. If the room employed for the stage be very deep, the rear of it can be separated for dressing-rooms; otherwise arrangements must be made in accordance with the accommodations of the house.

## REHEARSALS.

The only pleasure to be derived from the performance of a play is furnished by the familiarity of the actor with his part, and the skill with which he delineates it. No one should undertake a part who is not willing to give the necessary time and study to commit it perfectly. It is a rudeness to players and audience to appear with a part half remembered, and therefore imperfectly played. Rehearsals are essential to accommodate the players to each other, and to familiarize them with the entrances and exits, cues, etc. Every person cast in a play should be made to attend rehearsals under penalty of having his or her part taken away if absent, imperfect, or negligent. Inattention at rehearsals is the secret of half the failures of amateur performances, and this evil is one easily remedied. Rehearsals should be frequent, and not too many of them, as this becomes wearisome.

## COSTUMES.

As a rule, for amateur performances, it is best to choose plays requiring only modern costumes—reliance being had on the wit of the dialogue or its pathos, or the interest of the situation for amusement or sentimental gratification. But it will be found very easy to manufacture out of the ordinary wardrobe, with a few ribbons and ornaments added, by the aid of taste and ingenuity, almost any ordinary style of dress. Such are, for instance, peasant dresses, sailor costumes, army and navy uniforms, and the dress of a gypsy, policeman, bandit, Neapolitan fisherman, miner, etc.

## THE PERFORMANCE.

It is the stage manager's business to see that everything to be used is in readiness on the night of performance. Each player should be responsible for his or her own costume; but the "properties," *i. e.,* the various articles to be used in the course of the play, should be in charge of the stage manager and be at hand when wanted. Careful rehearsal having familiarized the actors with their parts, and with the stage and movements of the play, there need be no hitches, and but very little "prompting." The *prompter* should have become perfectly familiar with the play, and should speak clearly and in a low voice, as little audible as possible "in front." He should be placed on one side or the other of the stage, concealed behind tne jamb, or by the proscenium, if one be built.

It will be found desirable to have an orchestra of a few instruments, or at least a piano, to play interludes between the acts, or chords as entrances, exits, or "situations." Musical pieces—operettas, burlettas, and extravaganzas—will be found very amusing and interesting, and not difficult to learn or to produce.

## CHARADES AND TABLEAUX VIVANTS.

CHARADES and TABLEAUX VIVANTS are delightful home amusements, but belong more properly to dramatic representation. Clever young people can generally manage them. Living statuary is always effective; there are no end of pretty groups in painting, scenes in literature, and striking situations in history, which may be represented in tableaux, and there is great fun in getting them up, in rifling old trunks and garrets for appropriate costumes, in begging and borrowing jewelry and ornaments from their chary owners, and in practicing over and over for the final triumph and splendor of the evening selected.

The following, among other words, are suitable for charade acting:—

Adulation, Andrew, Arrowroot, Artichoke, Articulate; Bayonet, Bellman, Bondmaid, Bonfire, Bookworm, Bracelet, Bridewell, Brimstone, Brushwood; Cabin, Carpet, Castaway, Catacomb, Champagne, Chaplain, Checkmate, Childhood, Cowslip, Cupboard, Cutlet; Daybreak, Dovetail, Downfall, Dustman; Earrings, Earshot, Exciseman; Farewell, Footman; Grandchild; Harebell, Handiwork, Handsome, Hardship, Helpless, Highgate, Highwayman, Homesick, Horn-book; Illwill, Indigent, Indulgent, Inmate, Insight, Intent, Intimate; Jewell, Jonquil, Joyful; Kindred, Knee-deep; Label, Lawful, Leap-year, Life-like, Loophole, Love-knot; Madcap, Matchless, Milkmaid, Mistake, Misunderstand, Mohair, Moment, Moon-struck; Namesake, Necklace, Nightmare, Nightshade, Ninepin, Nutmeg; Orphanage, Outside, Oxeye; Padlock, Painful, Parsonage, Penmanship, Pilgrim, Pilot, Pinchbeck, Purchase; Quarto, Quicklime, Quicksand, Quickest, Quicksilver; Ragamuffin, Ringleader, Roundhead, Ruthful; Scarlet, Season, Sentinel, Sightless, Skipjack, Sluggard, Sofa, Solo, Somebody, Sonnet, Spare-rib, Sparkling, Spectacle, Speculate, Speedwell, Spinster, Starling, Statement, Stucco, Supplicate, Sweetmeat, Sweetheart; Tactic, Tartar, Tenant, Tendon, Tenor, Threshold, Ticktack, Tiresome, Toadstool, Token, Torment, Tractable, Triplet, Tunnel; Upright, Uproar; Vampire, Vanguard; Waistcoat, Watchful, Watchman, Waterfall, Wayward, Wedding, Wedlock, Welcome, Welfare, Willful, Willow, Workmanship; Yokemate, Youthful.

## WHIST.

WHIST is played by four persons who sit round a table, the opposite players being partners. The cards are dealt out by the one who cuts the lowest card; beginning with the player on his left hand. He turns up the last card, and that suit is trumps for that round. Each player takes up and arranges his hand without his opponents or partner seeing what he holds. The player on the dealer's left then leads, the dealer's partner follows, then the next player, and lastly the dealer. Whoever takes the trick leads next, and so on through the game.

The ace is the highest card, then the king, queen, knave, ten, and so on. If a player has a card of the suit led he must play it, but if not, he may trump, that is, play one of the same suit turned up as the last card. As the fifty-two cards in the pack are divided between the four players, each commences with thirteen; there are consequently thirteen tricks. Every trick above six counts one.

The game is seven; whoever scores that number first wins. The best out of three games is called a rubber. It is impossible to do more than hint at the science and finesse of the game.

The partners try and help one another, and play up to each other's strong suits. These are indicated by the leads. If a player leads a suit it is noticed that he has strong cards in it. The second player as a rule plays a low card, the third plays his highest, and the fourth takes the trick if he can. If the third player takes the trick he generally leads the same suit back to his partner, on the supposition that the partner can take it.

Discarding is playing another suit than that led. It can only be done where the player has no cards of the suit led in his hand, and it enables him sometimes to trump the suit in a succeeding round. A player who trumps, having one of the suit played in his hand, revokes, and forfeits three tricks as a penalty.

The following general principles will be found valuable.

#### FIRST HAND.

1.—Lead from your strongest suit.

2.—Lead the highest of a head sequence.

3.—Lead the highest of a numerically weak suit.

4.—Try to avoid changing suits.

5.—In the second round of a suit return the lowest of a four suit, the highest of a three suit.

#### SECOND HAND.

6.—The second hand player in the first round of a suit should generally play the lowest card, and also win with the lowest of a sequence.

7.—If you do not head a trick you should throw away with your lowest card.

8.—Young players often make the mistake of imagining that it does not signify which card they play when they hold only small cards or cards in sequence.

9.—They have still to learn that a reason ought to exist for the playing of every card on the table, and that the winning of a single trick is not all that ought to be taken into consideration ; the information afforded to one's partner must also be thought of.

THIRD HAND.

10.—Play your highest card third hand. Presuming that your partner who may lead a small card, plays from his strong suit, meaning to get the winning cards of it out of his way, you therefore play your highest, remembering that you play the lowest of a sequence.

11.—When your partner leads a high card, however, the case is different. You must not put ace on your partner's king, thus parting with ace and king in one trick.

12.—If you think that your partner has led from a weak suit, you may then finesse king, knave, etc., or pass his card altogether, so as not to give up the entire command of the suit: but if you are not sure whether his card is intended to signify strength or weakness, do not finesse.

FOURTH HAND.

13.—Less skill is required by the fourth player than any of the others; all he has to do is to try to beat the three cards on the table before him, and thus win the trick, unless, of course, it has already been taken by his partner, who has either played the highest card or trumped. In that case the player should play a low one of the same suit, or if he cannot do that he should discard.

## LAWS OF WHIST.

1.—The rubber is the best of three games. If the first two games are won by the same players the third game is not played.

2.—A game consists of ten points (five in Short Whist). Each trick above six counts one point.

3.—Honors, *i. e.*, ace, king, queen, and knave of trumps, are thus reckoned :—

If a player and his partner, either separately or conjointly, hold—

1st. The four honors, they score four points.

2d. Three of the honors, they score two points.

3d. Two honors only, they do not score. (In Short Whist honors do not count.)

4.—Those players who at the commencement of a deal are at the score of nine cannot score honors.

5.—If an erroneous score be proved, such mistake can be corrected prior to the conclusion of the game in which it occurred, and such game is not concluded until the trump card of the following deal has been turned up.

6.—If an erroneous score, affecting the amount of the rubber, be proved, such mistake can be rectified any time during the rubber.

7.—In cutting, the ace is the lowest card.

8.—Three players cutting cards of equal value cut again.

9.—The pack must be shuffled above the table, but not so that the cards can be seen.

10.—The pack must not be shuffled during the play of the hand.

11.—The dealer's partner must collect the cards for the ensuing deal, and has the first right to shuffle that pack.

12.—Each player, after shuffling, must place the cards, properly collected and face downwards, to the left of the player about to deal.

13.—The dealer has always the right to shuffle last, but should a card or cards be seen during his shuffling, or any other time, he must reshuffle.

14.—Each player deals in his turn ; the right of dealing goes to the left.

15.—The player on the dealer's right cuts the pack, and, in dividing it, must not leave fewer than four cards in either packet ; if, in cutting, a single card be exposed, or if there be any confusion of the cards, there must be a fresh cut.

16.—After the pack is cut, should the dealer shuffle the cards he loses his deal.

17.—A misdeal loses the deal.

18.—The trump card must be left on the table until the first trick has been won.

19.—A revoker must give three tricks to his opponent.

20.—A revoke cannot be claimed after the cards have been cut for the next deal.

## CRIBBAGE.

This is a favorite game for two persons. A cribbage board has a double line of holes on each side, and two pegs to mark with for each player. The players cut for the deal, the lowest deals 5 or 6 cards to each. Each player then discards two cards which form the crib. Then the non-dealer cuts and the card is turned up. If it is a knave the dealer counts two for his heels. They then play, first the non-dealer, then the dealer. The object of each player is to score, which he may do in one of three ways, either by a sequence, or by pairs, or by fifteen or thirty-one. Thus: supposing the non-dealer plays a seven of any suit, the dealer if he plays eight makes up fifteen and scores two; supposing the non-dealer then plays nine, he makes a sequence of three—seven, eight, nine. A sequence may be reckoned either way, backwards, forwards, or by playing a middle card, as a seven between six and eight. When the other player cannot play so as to make up thirty-one or under, the other player scores one for a go. Court cards count as tens. The players then show their hands, counting two for as many fifteens as they can show in different combinations, sequences, pairs, or triplets. The dealer first reckons his own hand, and then takes up the crib. The players alternate the deal.

The hand is counted up thus:—

| | |
|---|---|
| For knave turned up (heels) | 2 points. |
| For sequence of three or four cards | 3 or 4 " |
| For a flush, that is, three cards of same suit | 3 " |
| For a full flush, when cards in hand and turn-up are of same suit | 4 " |
| For every fifteen, as 6 and 9; 10, 3, and 2; 7 and 8, court card and 5, etc | 2 " |
| For a pair (two of a sort, as 2 threes, 2 fours, &c.) | 2 " |
| For a pair royal (three of same sort) | 6 " |
| For a double pair royal, or four of same sort | 12 " |
| For knave of trumps in hand (nob) | 1 " |

## ÉCARTÉ.

Écarté is a French game. First throw out all the cards between ace and seven (not inclusive), leaving thirty-two cards in the pack.

The game consists of five points. The king is the highest card, the ace counting after the knave. The dealer shuffles and puts the pack on the table. His opponent cuts. Then three cards are dealt to each, then two, and the eleventh turned up. If the turn-up is a king the dealer scores one, and says "I mark king." If either player hold the king in his hand, he is bound to declare it before the first trick is played, otherwise he forfeits the point. If the non-dealer is not satisfied with his hand, he says, "I propose;" if dealer is also not satisfied, he accepts and says, "how many?" The non-dealer states how many he wishes. The dealer then deals these to his opponent, who throws out the same number first. Then the dealer throws out likewise and deals to himself; when both or either are satisfied they play. The non-dealer plays first. The dealer must follow suit. Whoever takes three tricks counts one, five tricks, two.

## CASSINO.

To play this game deal four cards to each player, and then four on the table, face upwards.

Each player (non-dealer first) alternately tries to take as many as he can. To do this he covers a card on the table with one of his own, thus, a six with a six, or two threes with a six, or he may "build," that is, place a card from his hand on one on the table, thus, put a three on a six and make nine, then, if his opponent does not take it, he takes the two with a nine. Cards so built up cannot be separated. Royal cards can only be taken by their own kind. When a player can do nothing, he throws down a card. If a player clears the board by taking all the cards down, he scores one. The taker of the last cards clears the board at the end of the game.

The game is generally 11 points, sometimes twenty-one.

The score is counted thus:—

Great cassino, 2 points.
Little cassino, 1 point.
Each ace, 1 point.
Majority of spades, 1 point.
" " cards, three points.
Clear board, 1 point.

The terms used in the game are as follows:—

*Great Cassino.*—The ten of diamonds reckons for two points.

*Little Cassino.*—The two of spades for one point.

*The Cards.*—When you have a greater number than your adversary, three points.

*The Spades.*—When you have the majority of the suit, one point.

*The Aces.*—Each of which reckons for one point.

*The Sweep.*—Matching all the cards on the board.

*Building up.*—Suppose the dealer's four cards in hand to be a seven, ten, and two aces; his adversary plays a six—the dealer puts an ace upon it, and says, "Seven," with a view of taking them with his seven; the non-dealer throws a two upon them, and says, "Nine," hoping to take them with a nine then in his hand; the dealer again puts upon the heap his other ace, and cries "Ten," when, if his adversary has ten, he plays some other card, and the dealer takes them all with his ten. It will be observed that a player in announcing the denomination of a build always employs the singular number. Thus—"Nine" or "Ten," not "Nines" or "Tens." This is called "Building up."

*Build from the Table.*—Employing cards on the table to continue a build.

*Call.*—Suppose a player to have in his hand two or more cards of the same denomination, and one or more cards of the same denomination remain upon the board, he may play one of them on the table, at the same time calling the denomination, and his opponent is thereby debarred from taking it with a card of any other denomination. In calling the denomination, the plural is always used. Thus—"Fours," not "Four." This is termed *calling*.

*Build.*—A card already built up.

*False Build.*—A build made without any card in hand to redeem it.

*Combine.*—To play a card which will take two or more cards of a different denomination whose aggregate number of pips or spots exactly equals those of the card played. Thus: a ten will take a seven, two, and ace, the combined spots on those cards being precisely ten.

*Last Cards.*—Those cards remaining on the board after the last trick is taken, all of which go to the winner of the last trick.

*Eldest Hand.*—The player sitting at the left hand of the dealer, so called because he is the first to play.

*Misdeal.*—An error in giving out the cards, the penalty for which is the forfeiture of the game and all depending upon it.

### LAWS OF CASSINO.

1. The pack must consist of fifty-two cards.
2. The dealer deals four cards, one after another, to each player, beginning at the elder hand, after which he deals four cards into the center of the table, face upwards. He then gives each player four more cards putting no more, however, into the center of the table.
3. In case of a misdeal, the dealer forfeits his deal.
4. Any number up to twelve may play, though four is the preferable number.

## DRAW POKER.

Any number of persons may play, but generally seven is the outside. Each player has counters or chips. The dealer puts up a stake called *ante*. Five cards are then dealt to each person. A player can either throw up his hand, or play, or exchange cards while any are left in the pack.

When the dealer's turn comes to make his choice, if he determine to play, he is bound to add an equal amount to what he had previously staked. This is called making good the *ante;* by so doing the dealer places himself on an equal footing with the other players.

Should he rather than raise his stake prefer to go out, the next player is requested to raise; but should he, like the dealer, also prefer to go out rather than raise, the next player is asked, and so on, until some player expresses himself willing to raise. This being the case, the next player has three alternatives: he must either *go better*, which means stake some larger amount; *see the raise*, which signifies staking an equal amount; or he must *go out*. The choice of these three alternatives is given to each player, until after full opportunity has been afforded to all of deciding, no one has *gone better*, but each of those remaining in has elected to see the raise, the stakes consequently remaining equal.

The person who is now requested to show his hand is the player seated next to him who last saw the raise, though if such player should not have a good hand to show, he may, if he likes, go out without showing his cards.

Perhaps to a greater extent in Poker than in any other card game, the great aim of a good player is to conceal his system of playing; therefore, although a player going out relinquishes all hold upon his stakes, he would rather do that than show an inferior hand.

Many of the technical terms used in Poker being peculiar to the game, a knowledge of them will be found necessary to the learner.

*Age.*—Same as eldest hand.

*Ante.*—The stake deposited in the pool by the dealer at the beginning of the game. At Straight Poker each player puts up an *ante*.

*Blind.*—This name is given to the bet made by the eldest hand before the cards are cut to be dealt.

The eldest hand alone has the privilege of starting the *blind*, though the player to the left of him may, if he likes, double it, and again, the next player, still to the left, may *straddle* it, which means double it again.

Any player refusing to *straddle* thus prevents any one else doing so afterwards.

*Bluffing Off.*—When a player with a weak hand bets so high that he makes his opponents believe he has a very strong hand, and they are deterred from *seeing* him or *going better*.

*Brag.*—To bet for the pool.

*Call.*—To call a show of hands is for the player whose *say* is last to deposit in the pool the same amount bet by any preceding player, and demand that the hands be shown.

*Chips.*—Another name for counters.

*Draw.*—To discard one or more cards, and receive a corresponding number from the dealer.

*Flush.*—Five cards of the same suit, not necessarily in order.

*Fours.*—Four cards of the same denomination, as four threes or four fives.

*Full.*—Three cards of the same denomination and a single pair.

*Going Better.*—When any player makes a bet, the next player to the left may raise him or run over his bet, which means that he may deposit more in the pool than his adversary has done.

*Pair.*—Two cards of the same denomination, as two queens.

*A Straight.*—Five cards in numerical sequence, though not of the same suit.

*Triplets.*—Three cards of the same denomination, as three aces.

Although the ace is the highest card in this game for sequence purposes, it may be counted as next to the two or next to the king, as may best suit the player. The player, however, is not on this account entitled to use the ace as a connecting link between the king and the two, so as to form a sequence between them.

## EUCHRE

Is played with a pack of thirty-two cards, that is, with all below seven thrown out, except the ace. The knave of trumps is the right-bower. The knave of the other suit of the same color is the left-bower. The cards rank as follows: Right-bower, left-bower, ace, king, queen, etc. The other suits rank from the ace downward.

### RULES FOR TWO PLAYERS.

The cards are dealt as follows :—First deal two to each, then three to each.

The eleventh card is then turned up, and to whatever suit it belongs that suit is trumps.

Five points constitute the game. If a player win three tricks, they count for one point; if he win four tricks, they also count for one point; but if he win all five tricks, they count two points.

The eleventh card being turned up, the first player begins the game by looking at his hand to ascertain if, in his own estimation, it is sufficiently strong to score—that is, to make three, four, or five tricks. Should he be able to do so, he will say, "I order it up;" that is, that the dealer is to take up the turn-up card in his hand, and put out any card he likes. If, on the contrary, he thinks he cannot score, he says, "I pass."

If the first player orders the turn-up card up, the game begins at once by his playing a card and the dealer following suit. Should the dealer not be able to follow suit, he must either throw away or trump, as in Whist.

The winner of the trick then leads, and so the game goes on until the ten cards are played.

If either the dealer or the other player order the card up and fail to get three or more tricks, he is *euchred*—that is, his adversary scores two.

Suppose the first player passes, not, in his own estimation, being strong enough to make three tricks, the dealer can, if he likes, take the card and put one of his own out, but if he fails to score he is *euchred.*

If they both pass, the first player may change the trump, and the dealer is compelled to play. If, however, the former does not score he is *euchred.*

If he passes for the second time the dealer can alter it, the same penalty being enforced should he not score.

If they both pass for the second time, the round is over, and the first player begins to deal.

If trumps are led, and you only have *left bower*, you must play it, as it is considered a trump.

### THREE-HANDED EUCHRE.

Fifteen cards are dealt in this game, but the rules are exactly the same as in two-handed euchre.

There are, however, a few differences in the tactics. If one player has scored four points, and the other two players two each, it is allowable for the two latter to help each other to prevent the player with the four tricks from winning.

### FOUR-HANDED EUCHRE.

In this game the players go two and two, being partners, the same as in Whist.

The game is won when the combined tricks taken by a player and his partner amount to five.

If all pass in the first round, the first player is allowed to alter trumps; if he does not care to do so, the second, then the third, and lastly the fourth.

If one should fail to score, having ordered up the card, he and his partner are *euchred*, and their opponents count two.

Should one player be exceedingly strong, he can say, "I play a lone hand," whereupon his partner throws up his hand, and the *lone hand* plays against the other two.

If the single player gets all five tricks he counts four, if three or four tricks, he counts only one, and if two, or less, he is *euchred*.

There is yet another variation to this game, and one that generally meets with approval.

A blank card is taken and on it is written "Joker." This card always counts highest in the pack whatever suit may happen to be trumps.

If "Joker" should be the turn-up card, the dealer has the privilege of naming any suit he likes for trumps.

## COMMERCE.

This game is well named, for it is carried on throughout simply by a series of exchanges and business transactions.

A full pack of cards is used, which are all dealt one by one to the players.

The ace counts as eleven, tens and court cards for ten each, and the rest of the cards according to the number of their pips.

Before dealing, a pool is formed, by each player contributing to it an equal stake. The eldest hand then begins by exchanging a card with his left hand neighbor, who again changes with his left-hand neighbor, and so on until some one, finding that he has a hand consisting entirely of one suit, cries out "My ship sails," and thereupon takes to himself the contents of the pool.

The object aimed at by all the players is one of three things: to make what is called a *tricon* (three cards alike), or a *sequence* (three cards following each other of the same suit), or a *point* (which is the smallest number of pips on three cards of the same suit).

The winner of the pool is the player who has the highest tricon; but should no tricon be displayed, the highest sequence has it; or in case of a failure also in sequence-making, then the player who has the best point takes the pool.

In case of ties, the banker or dealer is regarded as the eldest hand, but should he hold a lower tricon or sequence than either of the others, he loses the game, and forfeits a counter to each player higher than himself.

## BÉZIQUE.

Before describing the game of Bézique, it will perhaps be advisable to give a list of the technical terms employed in it.

*Single Bézique.*—The queen of spades and knave of diamonds, which count 40.

*Double Bézique.*—Two queens of spades and two knaves of diamonds, which count 500.

*Brisques.*—The aces and tens in the tricks taken count 10 each.

*Common Marriage.*—The king and queen of any suit but trumps, which count 20.

*Bézique Pack.*—The same as the Euchre, Piquet, or Ecarté pack, composed of thirty-two cards, all under the sevens, except the aces, being discarded.

*Quint Major.*—Same as sequence.

*Royal Marriage.*—The king and queen of trumps, which count 40.

*Sequence.*—Ace, king, queen, knave, and ten of trumps, which count 250.

*Stock.*—The number of packs of cards corresponding with the number of players, shuffled together, and ready to be dealt.

*Talon.*—The cards remaining after the dealer has distributed eight to each player.

*Declaration.*—Showing and scoring any combinations, such as those mentioned above.

Four aces count 100.
Four kings count 80.
Four queens count 60.
Four knaves count 40.
Seven of trumps, when turned or played, counts 10.
Exchanging or playing the seven of trumps counts 10.
The last trick counts 10.

This game is most commonly played by two persons with two packs of cards; but there must be a pack for every person playing, so that if four play four packs must be used, from which, as has been said, all cards under seven have been taken out, excepting aces. After shuffling and cutting, the dealer gives three cards to his adversary and three to himself, then he gives two, then three again, until both players are supplied with eight cards each. The remainder of the pack, which is called the talon, are left on the table, and the top card of it is turned up for the trump. Should the turn-up happen to be a seven, the dealer is thereby entitled to score ten to himself. After a trick has been made, the holder of a seven of trumps can, if so inclined, exchange it for the trump card, and for the exchange he scores ten.

The value of the cards in making the tricks is as follows:—

Ace (which takes all other cards), ten, king, queen, knave, nine, eight, and seven. Trumps are of no special value until the last eight tricks are in the hands of both players.

The player who wins the first trick takes the top card from the talon, thus completing his original number of eight. The person also who has lost the trick does the same; and so on, until all the cards in the talon are exhausted. As in other card games, the winner of a trick is entitled to the next lead.

When cards of the same value are played at the same round, the first that was turned up wins the trick, unless, of course, it should be trumped or beaten by a card higher in value.

When a player wishes to *declare*, he must do so immediately after taking a trick, and before supplying himself with a new card from the talon; and such cards as form a combination, after being declared, should be placed on the table, face upwards; being of the same value as if in the hand, they may be played away as they are needed. When the talon is exhausted, the combinations that have been made are taken into the owner's hand, and the last eight cards belonging to both players are disposed of the same way as in whist, the second player following suit, and heading the trick, if he can possibly do so, either by trumping or playing a higher card.

After bézique has been declared, the cards forming the combination cannot be employed to form any other. It is wise, therefore, to keep back the queen and knave to help to form other combinations before declaring bézique, especially when diamonds or spades happen to be trumps. In that case the queen may assist in making a royal marriage, a sequence, or one of four queens, while the knave may help to form a sequence or one of four knaves, both being also used afterwards in the declaration of bézique. All kings and queens are better kept in hand until they can be married; consequently, should the player be uncertain whether to throw away an ace or a king, if practicable, let it be the former. Although four aces count more than four kings, the declaration of four aces is not an easy matter to accomplish, while it is very probable that an opportunity may arise for marrying a king, when the pair may be thrown into the adversary's tricks. The aces and tens of trumps are better reserved for the last eight tricks, and a player should try to get the lead by taking the trick previous to exhausting the talon. The adversary will thus be obliged to part with his aces and tens by playing them on the cards that are led. The leader, if strong in trumps, may thus secure all the tricks, and may also earn the privilege of making the last declaration.

## BÉZIQUE WITHOUT A TRUMP.

This is very much like the ordinary game, the difference being that the trump card is decided, not by the last turned up after the deal, but by the first marriage that is declared. The seven of trumps also does not count ten points.

The béziques, four kings, four queens, etc., are counted the same as in bézique when the trump is turned, and can be declared before the trump is determined. It is the same with the other cards which constitute combinations; their value is the same as in the proper game of bézique.

## OLD MAID

Is a very simple game. One queen is thrown out. The cards are dealt round. The dealer then offers his cards to the next player who draws one; if he can match two cards he throws them out. He then offers his cards, face downwards, to the next player, and so on, until one player is left in with the queen, and is called old maid.

Sometimes instead of Whist Cards real Old Maids' Cards are used. Each card is made of white cardboard, with a pointed end on which a number is written. A couple of cards are marked 1, another couple 2, another couple 3, and so on until as many couples as are required have been figured. On the last single card the words *The Old Maid* are written, and the pack must then be well shuffled.

# CHESS AND CHEQUERS.

## CHESS.

CHESS is the most profound and intellectual amusement ever invented. It is a severe strain on the mental faculties, and requires a power of pursuing different moves through many combinations which only a very far-seeing mind can accomplish. It is played on a board with sixty-four squares alternately colored. The board is placed between the players so that each has a white square to his right hand. The men are placed on the board in two rows, the most important in the rear row and the pawns in front. The players move alternately. When a piece is on the line of attack of one of the opposite side it can be "taken," that is, removed from

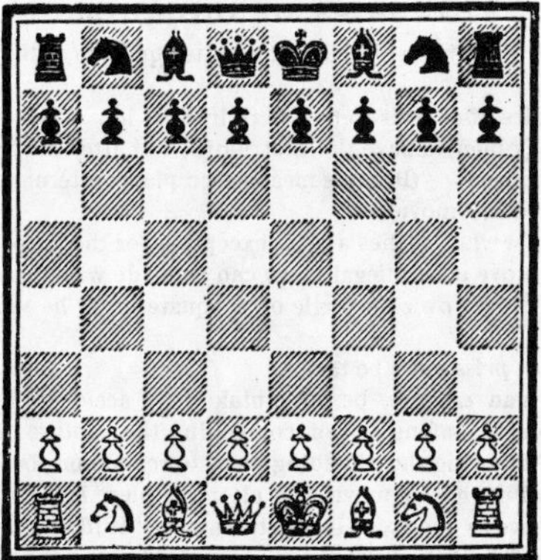


the board, the opponent's piece being placed on the square instead. The only piece that cannot be taken is the king, which can only be "checked," that is, threatened by an opponent's piece. In that case the king must be protected by covering it with another piece, or moved. The game is won by checkmate; that is, the king is so hemmed in by the adversary's attack that he is checked on the square where he is, cannot be covered, and cannot be moved. If he is so situated that he cannot move without going into check, and is not in check at the time, it is termed stale-mate, which counts as a drawn game.

### THE LAWS OF CHESS.

1. *Position of the Board.*—If during the progress of a game either party discover that the chess-board has been improperly placed, he may insist upon its being adjusted; the game to proceed from the point where the adjustment took place, as if no mistake had been made.

2. *Omission or Misplacement of Men.*—If at any time in course of a game it be found that the men were improperly placed, or that one or more of them were omitted, the game must be annulled. (N. B.—An annulled game is to be considered in all respects as if it had never been played.)

3. *First Move and Choice of Color.*—The right to the first move in the first game of a sitting is determined by lot. The choice of color must be determined in the same way, if either party require it. Unless another arrangement be made, each player has the first move alternately throughout any one sitting or match, whether the games be won or drawn. But in the case of an annulled game, the player who had the first move in that game shall also have the first move in the next.

4. *Commencing Out of Turn.*—If a player make the first move when it is not his turn to do so, the game must be annulled if the discovery be made before the completion of the fourth move. If the error be not discovered until afterwards, the game must proceed in due course. In a match an extra first move must be allotted to the player thus deprived of his move.

5. *Playing Two Moves.*—If a player in the course of a game make a move when it is not his turn to play he must retract the last move, and, if his adversary chooses, after he himself has moved, must play the man wrongly moved, if it can be played legally. But the adversary can enforce this penalty only before touching a man in reply. If the error be discovered later, it must be rectified simply by the *giuoco a monte*, *i. e.*, the moves must be retraced to the point where the error took place.

6. *Touch and Move.*—A player who touches with his hand one of his own men, when it is his turn to play, must move it, if it can be legally moved, unless before touching it he say *j'adoube* (I adjust), or words to that effect. And a player who touches one of his adversary's men (under the same conditions), must take it. If in either case the move cannot legally be made the offender must move his king, and in the event of the king having no legal move, he must play any other man legally movable that his adversary pleases. If a player, however, touches a man in consequence of a false cry of "check," or being checked and not apprised of it by his adversary, touches a man, he is not obliged to play it, or, having played it, may retract the move without penalty.

7. *Definition of a Move.*—A move is complete and irrevocable the moment the piece or pawn has quitted the player's hand; but as long as the hand remains on the man touched, it may be played to any square it commands. This stipulation does not, of course, apply to illegal moves.

8. *False Moves.*—If a player move a piece or pawn of his own to a square to which it cannot be legally moved, or capture an adverse man by a move which cannot legally be made, he must, at the choice of his adversary, either—

Firstly—Move his own or take the adverse man legally;

Secondly—Forfeit his turn to move; or

Thirdly—Play any other man legally movable which his adversary may select. Castling wrongfully is to be considered a false move.

9. *Touching more than one Man.*—If a player, when it is his turn to move, touch with his hand more than one of his own men (unless in castling), he must play any one of them legally movable that his opponent selects. If he touch more than one of his adversary's men, he must capture whichever of them his adversary chooses, provided it can be legally taken. If in such case it happens that none of the men so touched can be moved or captured, then the offender must move his king, or, if the king cannot legally be moved, he must play any other piece or pawn legally movable that his opponent may name.

10. *Enforcing Penalties.*—A penalty can only be enforced before the party who has not committed the error has touched a man in reply. If the illegality be discovered at a later period the moves must be retraced, the error rectified, and the game renewed from that point. But if the source of an illegality cannot be discovered, the game must be annulled. When the king is moved as a penalty, the party paying the penalty cannot castle on that move.

11. *Check.*—A player must audibly say "check," when he makes a move which puts the hostile king in check. A player is not compelled to give check because he utters it. But if it is uttered and not given, the move on which it is uttered must be retracted and another made, if the adversary require it. If a player move his king into check; if he remove a piece which covered his king, and thereby place him in check; if, while his king is in check, he touch or move a man which does not

cover the check—in each of these cases he subjects himself to the penalties laid down in Section 6.

12. *A King Remaining in Check.*—If the king of either player is placed in check, and the check has not been announced or discovered until one or more moves have been made, all moves subsequently made must be retracted, and the player who ought to have announced the check must make some other move. If the check has been duly announced, but still not provided against, the moves must only be retracted as far as that of the king, which must be placed out of check in any manner its player chooses. If the moves cannot be remembered, the game must be annulled.

13. *J'adoube.*—When a person touches a man for the purpose of adjusting it, and not with the intention of moving it, he must before touching it say *j'adoube*, or words to that effect. But it is of no avail to say *j'adoube* after the man has been touched. In that case the piece or pawn must be moved.

14. *Counting Fifty Moves.*—If at any period of a game one player should persist in repeating a particular check or series of checks, or the same line of play, his adversary can demand that the game shall be limited to fifty more moves on each side; and if within that limit neither party win, the game must terminate as a drawn one.

Secondly, when a player has only the king on the board, he may insist upon his adversary winning in fifty moves, or upon the game being drawn.

Thirdly, when one player has only a king and queen, king and rook, king and bishop, or king and knight, against an equal or superior force, he may insist equally upon the fifty-move limit.

Fourthly, whenever one player considers that the game ought to be drawn, or that one side can force a win, the umpire or bystanders shall decide whether the fifty-move limit ought to be applied; it being understood that the limit is not applicable in cases where several pieces remain on the board at the same time.

None of the foregoing clauses apply to games wherein one party undertakes to mate with a particular man or on a particular square.

15. *Upsetting the Board or Men.*—If the board or any of the men be upset or displaced, the pieces must be rearranged as they were when the accident took place, and the game proceed in due course. The opinion of the player who did not upset the board shall always prevail over that of the player who did. Willfully upsetting the board is equivalent to resigning the game.

16. *Dropped Man.*—If at any time it is discovered that a man has been dropped off the board, and moves have been made during its absence, such moves shall be retracted and the man restored. If the players cannot agree as to its restoration, the game must be annulled.

17. *Umpire.*—The umpire shall have authority to decide any question whatever that may arise in the course of a game, but must never interfere, except when appealed to by one of the players, unless a violation of the fundamental principles of the game has taken place. When a question is submitted to the umpire or to bystanders, their decision shall be final.

## CHEQUERS.

HEQUERS or draughts is played on the same board as chess. The pieces are of similar value, and are placed on the alternate white squares in the three rows nearest the side, placing the board so that the black square is to the right hand. The movement is diagonal, one square at a time. When two men of opposite color are so placed that one can leap over another to a square beyond in a diagonal line, he "takes" it, and the piece taken is removed from the board. When the pieces are moved so far forward as to have reached the opposite extremity of the board, they are crowned, that is a second piece is laid on top. A king can move backwards or forwards. The game is won by taking all the opponent's men.

BLACK.

WHITE.

### THE LAWS OF CHEQUERS.

1. The board is to be so placed that a white square is at the upper right-hand corner.
2. The choice of color is to be determined by lot.
3. The black men to have the first move, and after the first game the men to be changed. (By this means each player alternately takes the black men and first move.)
4. The player who touches a man, excepting for the purpose of adjusting it, must move it, if a legal move can be made with that man.
5. A man moved over the angle of a square must be moved to that square.
6. A man *en prise* must be taken.
7. If the man *en prise* be left untaken by accident, the adversary has the option of huffing; or of compelling the capture of the offered piece; or of allowing the offending piece to remain on its square.
8. The huff is not a move, and after the piece is huffed, the player makes his move as usual. (Hence the saying "Huff and move.")
9. *Five* minutes is the limit of time for considering a move. (In match games an umpire is appointed to call the time).
10. When a piece is *en prise*, and there is only one way of taking it, *one* minute is the maximum time allowed for the move.
11. The penalty for exceeding the time stated is the loss of the game. (In friendly contests time is not necessarily insisted on).
12. A player making a false move, must either replace the men and make a legal move, or resign the game, at the option of his adversary.
13. When, in the act of taking, the player removes one of his own men from the board, he cannot replace it without the consent of his opponent, who can either play or insist on the move standing, or of the piece being replaced.
14. When only two kings remain on either side, if neither player can force a win within twenty moves, the game is *drawn*.
15. When three or more kings are opposed to two, the player with the weaker force may claim a draw if his opponent fail to win within forty moves. (The forty moves are counted for each side.)
16. Notice must be formally given of the intention to count the moves.
17. When several pieces are taken by one move, no man must be lifted from the board till the move is completed; and if the player fail to take all the men he can, his opponent may huff him.
18. When a man arrives at the last row of squares on his opponent's side of the board, it must immediately be crowned; and such king cannot be moved until a move has been made by the other player.
19. All disputes to be decided by an umpire, or by the majority of the company present.
20. During the progress of a game neither player is allowed to leave the room without the consent of the other.
21. A breach of any of the above laws to be considered a loss of the game.

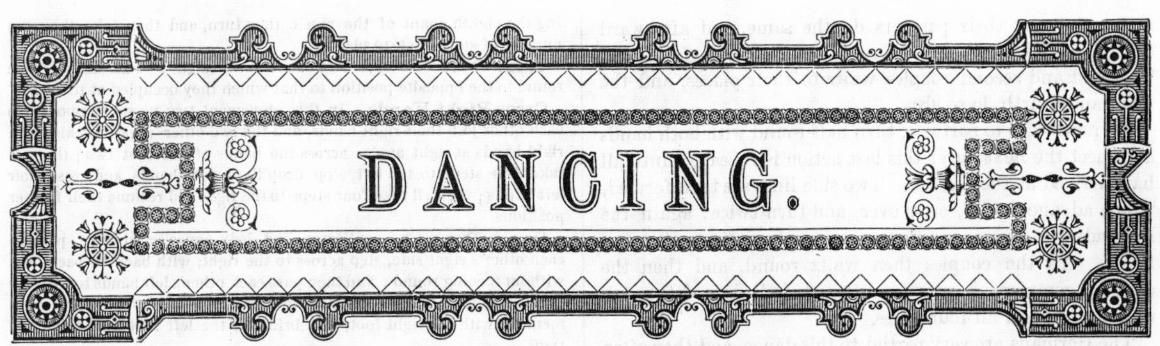

DANCING is one of the most popular forms of social amusement. It is also to be recommended as a healthful exercise, when the rooms for this purpose are not over-heated and ill-ventilated.

ROUND DANCES are performed by separate couples, who make circular movements round the room while performing them. They are preferred by many to those which are termed SQUARE DANCES (the Lancers, the Quadrille, etc.); the Round Dances, therefore, occupy most of the numbers set down in ball programmes.

The best known Round Dances are the Polka, Galop, and Waltz, which are danced in the following manner :—

### THE POLKA.

The step of the Polka is simple enough when once learned. It consists merely of three steps and one rest. The gentleman commences with a slight spring on his right foot, at the same time sliding the left forward. This is the first movement (the toe of the left foot being pointed outward, and the heel pointed toward the right foot). The right foot is then brought up to the left with a slight spring, the left foot being at the same time raised. This is the second movement. Then fall on the left foot, raising the right foot behind, which is the third movement. After a rest of one quaver, spring with the left foot, and slide the right foot forward, thus reversing the movement.

The lady dances the Polka the same as the gentleman, except the feet are reversed, she starting with the right foot instead of the left.

### THE GALOP.

This dance is simply a slide with one foot, and a chassez with the other, as long as the dancers continue in the same direction; then a half turn, repeating the same in the opposite direction, reversing the feet.

The gentleman slides the left foot sideways ; *count one.* Bring the right foot up behind the heel of the left ; *count two.* This is repeated until a change of direction is desired.

To *reverse* the direction, repeat the same movement, sliding with the right foot first in the opposite direction.

The lady executes the same steps as the gentleman, except the feet are reversed.

### THE WALTZ.

Assume the correct position, placing the right foot in front.

Glide the left foot directly backward about twelve inches ; *count one.* Pass the right foot two or three inches behind the left heel, at the same time turning on the ball of each foot ; *count two.*

Complete the turn by bringing the right foot front in the third position ; *count three.* Glide the right foot directly forward, about twelve inches ; *count four.* Advance the left foot about six inches in front of the right, at the same time turning on the ball of each foot ; *count five.* Complete the turn by bringing the right foot in front ; *count six.*

The lady follows the same order, with the exception that she begins with the reverse foot, each time.

#### THE REVERSE.

1. In reversing the gentleman glides the left foot directly forward and *counts one.* 2. Advance the right foot six inches in front of the left, at the same time turning on the ball of each foot toward the left hand ; *count two.* 3. Complete the turn to the left, by bringing the left foot in front; and you then *count three.* 4. Glide the right foot backward ; *count four.* 5. Pass the left behind the right, at the same time turning toward the left hand, on the ball of the feet ; *count five.* 6. Complete the turn to the left, by bringing the left foot in front ; *count six.*

### THE GERMAN, OR COTILLION.

Eight dancers take their places as for an ordinary quadrille. The first couple commence by waltzing once round, inside the group. Then the first and second ladies advance twice, and cross over; their partners do the same, and afterward the third and fourth couples repeat the same performance. The first and second couples waltz to their places, and the third and fourth do so also.

All now waltz to partners, turn half round with both hands and meet the next lady; this last action is repeated until all have arrived at their places. Two side lines are then formed, which advance twice, cross over, and turn twice; again the lines advance twice, and then cross to their places, turning twice. All the couples then waltz round, and then the dance is commenced again, and the whole is danced through as described—in all four times.

The Germans are very partial to this dance, and they often introduce variations. One form is this: Beforehand a basket of small bouquets and a cushion, whereon are a number of small rosettes, are prepared. When the dancers (the number is not limited) are arranged, the first lady takes her seat on a chair placed in the middle; the master of the ceremonies brings to her two gentlemen. If she wishes to dance with either of them, she takes a rosette from the cushion and pins it on the coat of the one she chooses. If she declines both, two other partners are brought. When she has made her choice she rises, pins on the rosette, and the couple then waltz round the room. The next lady then takes her place.

When all the ladies have observed this ceremony, the first gentleman takes a bouquet, goes to the lady with whom he wishes to dance, and offers it. If she refuses it, he tenders it to another; when he is accepted he waltzes once round with the lady. Then the next gentleman offers a bouquet, and so on. The dance is finished by all the couples waltzing at the same time.

## DICTIONARY OF DANCING TERMS.

**Allemand.**—Four steps are taken by each gentleman toward the lady of the right hand couple, who advances in order to meet him; after swinging her half way round, he advances four steps toward his partner (the latter advancing to meet him), and they swing (with left hands joined) to places.

**Balance to Corners.**—The gentleman, after turning toward the lady of the couple on his left, makes three glides to the right, and stops; then he makes three glides to the left, and stops; turns the lady with both hands, and all return to places.

**Balance in Place** consists in sliding the right foot to the right, bringing the left foot in front of the right; then sliding the left foot to the left, bringing the right foot in front of the left, after which the whole movement is repeated.

**Balance to Partners.**—The partners face each other, take three steps to the right, and stop; take three steps back to the left, and stop; then, joining hands, turn around once in their places.

**Chassez Across.**—The gentleman slides the right foot sideways to the right three times, bringing the left foot in front each time; then slides three times to the left with the left foot, bringing the right foot in front.

The lady at the same time takes similar steps to the left, passing across in front of her partner, and then takes three steps sideways back to place.

**Chassez All.**—Ladies take four steps sideways to the left, bringing the right foot close up to the left, and then take four similar steps back again; the gentlemen *chassez* four steps to the right, behind their partners, and return; partners then turn with both hands to places.

**Chassez in Promenade.**—The gentleman takes seven steps with his left foot, while the lady takes seven steps with her right foot. During the eighth count of the music they turn, and then take the same number of steps back to places.

**Cross Over.**—The partners dance in a straight line across, and face round in the opposite position to that which they occupied at the start.

**Cross Right Hands.**—In this movement two persons opposite to each other join their right hands, and the two other opposites also join right hands at right angles across the hands of the first two; then all take four steps to the left, stop, drop their right hands, and cross their left hands; then all take four steps to the right and resume their former positions.

**Dos à Dos.**—The gentleman and lady opposite advance, pass on each other's right side, step across to the right, with back to back, and without turning round; and then pass each other's left hands to places.

**Forward and Stop** consists in taking three steps forward, commencing with the right foot, and bringing the left foot up behind the right.

**Forward and Back** consists in taking three steps forward, beginning with the right foot, and bringing the left foot up behind the right; then three steps are taken backward, beginning with the left foot, bringing the right foot in front of the left.

**Forward and Ladies to the Center.**—The partners join their right hands, and advance four steps; then return four steps to their places. Advance again four steps toward the center. The gentleman then swings his partner half way round, so as to face him; the lady remains in the center, and he returns to his place.

**Gentlemen to the Right.**—See Ladies to the Right.

**Grand Chain.**—All eight chassez all the way round, giving alternately right and left hands to partners, beginning with the right. When the gentleman meets his partner half way round the quadrille, he salutes her. This movement is frequently called *Right and Left all Round.*

**Half Grand Chain** is the same as the above, except that the gentleman, instead of saluting his partner, joins right hands with her, and after both have swung half way round, so as to face in the opposite direction, they return left and right to places.

**Hands All Round.**—All the couples form a ring by joining hands, and then swing entirely round in a circle back to places. Another way is to swing eight steps to the left, then stop, and return with eight steps to places.

**Ladies to the Right.**—In this movement each lady takes four steps to the right, in front of her right hand couple, dances four steps in front of the gentleman on her right, turns him round by joining hands, and remains standing on his right side, taking the place of his former partner.

**Ladies' Chain.**—The ladies of the two opposite couples cross over and give the right hand to each other in passing; they return in the same manner, and are swung by partners with left hand to places.

**Ladies' Grand Chain.**—All four ladies cross right hands in the center, make a half turn, drop right hands, and join hands with opposite gentleman, being swung half round to his side. The movement is then repeated back to places.

**Promenade.**—The partners cross hands and cross over, passing on the right of the opposite advancing couple to the place directly opposite from which they started. They then return in the same manner to places.

**Promenade All.**—The partners cross hands, and all couples *chassez* to the right to opposite places. They then stop, and repeat the same movement to places.

**Right and Left.**—Two opposite couples cross over, the gentleman touching right hands with the opposite lady in passing; then the partners join left hands, and turn half way round in the places of the opposite couple. They return to their original places by repeating the same movement.

**Right Hand Across and Left Hand Back Again.**—The opposite couples cross over, the ladies on the inside and touching right hands with the opposite gentleman in passing. All four face round to return, each lady joining left hands with opposite gentleman, whose hand she retains; she then, after crossing her right hand over her left, joins right hands with her partner.

**Turn Partners** consists in the gentleman taking his partner with both hands, and turning her round once to the left.

**Vis à Vis** (*face to face*) is the French term for the partner (facing you) of the opposite couple.

## THE LANCERS.

### *FIRST FIGURE.

| | | |
|---|---|---|
| Head Couples : | Forward and Back | 4 bars. |
| | Forward and Turn Opposite Partners | 4 " |
| | Cross Over | 4 " |
| | Back to Places | 4 " |
| | Balance to Corners | 8 " |

### *SECOND FIGURE.

| | | |
|---|---|---|
| Head Couples : | Forward and Back | 4 bars. |
| | Forward and Ladies to the Center | 4 " |
| | Chassez to Right and Left | 4 " |
| | Turn Partners to Places | 4 " |
| Side Couples : | Divide, all Forward in two Lines | 4 " |
| | Forward again and Turn Partners to Places | 4 " |

### *THIRD FIGURE.

| | | |
|---|---|---|
| Head Couples : | Forward and Back | 4 bars. |
| | Forward and Salute | 4 " |
| Ladies All : | Cross Right Hands Half Round | 4 " |
| | Left Hands Back Again | 4 " |

Instead of cross Right Hands Half Round, the Ladies' Chain is sometimes substituted.

### *FOURTH FIGURE.

| | | |
|---|---|---|
| Head Couples : | To the Right, and Salute | 4 bars. |
| | To the Left, and Salute | 4 " |
| | Turn Partners to Places | 4 " |
| | Right and Left | 8 " |

### *FIFTH FIGURE.

| | | |
|---|---|---|
| All : | Right and Left All Round | 16 bars. |
| † First Couple : | Face Outward | 8 " |
| All : | Chassez Across | 8 " |
| First Couple : | Down the Center and Back | 8 " |
| Al : | Forward and Back | 4 " |
| | Forward again and Turn Partners to Places | 4 " |

† Each couple faces outward in turn, and the entire figure closes with Right and Left All Round.

## THE PLAIN QUADRILLE.

### *FIRST FIGURE.

| | |
|---|---|
| Right and Left | 8 bars. |
| Balance | 8 " |
| Ladies' Chain | 8 " |
| Half Promenade | 4 " |
| Half Right and Left, to Places | 4 " |

### *SECOND FIGURE.

Forward Two:

| | |
|---|---|
| Forward and Back | 4 bars. |
| Cross Over (Ladies inside) | 4 " |
| Chassez to Partners | 4 " |
| Cross Over to Places (Ladies inside) | 4 " |
| Balance | 8 " |

### *THIRD FIGURE.

| | |
|---|---|
| Right Hand Across, and Left Hand Back | 8 bars. |
| Balance (four in center) | 4 " |
| Half Promenade (cross to opposite side) | 4 " |
| Two Ladies Forward and Back | 4 " |
| Two Gentlemen Forward and Back | 4 " |
| Forward Four and Back | 4 " |
| Half Right and Left, to Places | 4 " |

### *FOURTH FIGURE.

| | |
|---|---|
| Forward Four and Back | 4 bars. |
| Forward again, and leave the first lady on the left of the opposite gentleman | 4 " |
| Forward Three—twice; the second time, both ladies cross over to opposite gentleman, and the first gentleman advances to receive them and retires with the two ladies | 8 " |
| Forward Three—twice; the second time stop in the center and turn the two ladies round | 8 " |
| Four Hands Half Round—The four join hands, turning to the left, and cross over to opposite places | 4 " |
| Half Right and Left, to Places | 4 " |

### *FIFTH FIGURE.

| | |
|---|---|
| All Promenade Round (or Ladies' Chain) | 8 bars. |
| Forward Two, } *Same as in second figure* | 16 " |
| Balance. } | 8 " |
| All Chassez, saluting partners with a bow and courtesy | 8 " |

## THE VIRGINIA REEL

OR

### SIR ROGER DE COVERLY.

| | |
|---|---|
| First gentleman and last lady, forward and back | 4 bars. |
| First lady and last gentleman, " " " | 4 " |
| First gentleman and last lady, swing right hands. | 4 " |
| First lady and last gentleman, " " " | 4 " |
| First gentleman and last lady, swing left hands | 4 " |
| First lady and last gentleman, " " " | 4 " |
| First gentleman and last lady, swing both hands | 4 " |
| First lady and last gentleman, " " " | 4 " |
| First gentleman and last lady, dos à dos | 4 " |
| First lady and last gentleman, " " " | 4 " |
| First couple turn right hands | 2 " |
| Separate and turn second couple, left hands | 2 " |
| Turn right hands | 2 " |
| Separate and turn third couple, left hands | 2 " |

Continue in the same manner to bottom.

All join hands and back to places at top.

Gentlemen to left, ladies to right, march down outside, and up the middle.

Head couple : Down the middle to bottom.

---

*This figure is danced four times: twice in succession by the head couples, and afterwards twice in succession by the side couples.

F OR what purpose do young ladies look at the moon?

To see the man in it.

Why ought Shakespeare's dramatic works to be considered unpopular?

Because they contain *Much Ado About Nothing*.

Why are suicides invariably successful people in the world?

Because they always manage to accomplish their own ends.

Why was Pharaoh's daughter like a broker?

Because she got a little prophet (profit) from the rushes on the bank?

Why are potatoes and corn like certain sinners of old?

Because, having eyes, they see not, and having ears they hear not!

If a woman were to change her sex, what religion would she be of?

She would be a he'then (heathen).

What is the difference between a donkey and a postage stamp?

One you lick with a stick, the other you stick with a lick!

What sort of tune do we all enjoy most?

For-tune, made up of bank notes!

Why are birds melancholy in the morning?

Because their little bills are all over dew!

Why is a pretty young lady like a wagon wheel?

Because she is surrounded by felloes (fellows).

Why is a newspaper like an army?

Because it has leaders, columns, and reviews.

What is the difference between killed soldiers and repaired garments?

The former are dead men, and the latter are men-ded (dead).

Why was the whale that swallowed Jonah like a milkman who has retired on an independence?

Because he took a great profit (prophet) out of the water.

Why is a short man struggling to kiss a tall woman like an Irishman going up to Vesuvius?

Because, sure, he's trying to get at the mouth of the crater!

When is a schoolboy like a postage-stamp?

When he is licked and put in the corner, to make him stick to his letters!

Why is opening a letter like taking a very queer method of getting into a room?

Because it is breaking through the sealing (ceiling).

When is a newspaper like a delicate child?

When it appears weekly.

What is the difference between a tight boot and an oak tree?

One makes acorns, the other—makes corns ache.

Why are sugar-plums like race-horses?

Because the more you lick them the faster they go!

How many young ladies does it take to reach from New York to Philadelphia?

About one hundred, because a Miss is as good as a mile.

Why is a spendthrift, with regard to his fortune, like the water in the filter?

Because he soon runs through it, and leaves many matters behind to settle!

What animals are admitted at the opera?

Puppies and white kids.

What is Majesty deprived of its externals?

A jest (M-ajest-y)!

Why are your nose and chin constantly at variance?

Because words are continually passing between them!

Where did Noah strike the first nail in the ark?

On the head!

What fur did Adam and Eve wear?

Bear (bare) skin.

Why are fixed stars like wicked old men?

Because they sin till late (scintillate).

Why are laundresses good navigators?

Because they are always crossing the line, and going from pole to pole!

What sort of sympathy would you rather be without?

You don't want to be pitted by the small-pox!

Why is a kiss like a rumor?

Because it goes from mouth to mouth!

Why are bald-headed men in danger of dying?

Because death loves a shining mark!

Why should a man troubled with the gout make his will?

Because he will then have his leg at ease (legatees).

Why is a dog's tail a great novelty?

Because no one ever saw it before.

Why was Herodias's daughter the *fastest* girl mentioned in the New Testament?

Because she got *a-head* of John the Baptist on a *charger*.

How do young ladies show their dislike to mustaches?

By setting their faces against them!

Why would Sampson have made an excellent actor?

Because he could so easily bring down the house!

When is a young lady not a young lady?

When she's a sweet tart (sweetheart).

Why is a ship like a woman?

Because she is often tender to a man-of-war; often running after a smack; often attached to a great buoy; and frequently making up to a pier!

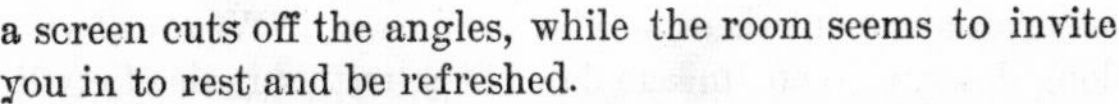



a screen cuts off the angles, while the room seems to invite you in to rest and be refreshed.

Every lady who gives her mind to it, whether greatly skilled or not, can improve a dull and dingy room by a few judicious alterations, and every young girl may, if she choose, learn to embroider at odd moments, and little by little may transform her abode from ugliness to beauty.

Crewels are used for working on linen, serge and flannel. Tapestry wool is much thicker than crewel and is useful on coarse fabrics. Embroidery silk is preferred for silk, satin, or fine materials. In working with crewels, cut your threads into short lengths. It is difficult to use too long a thread without puckering up the work.

Plush, which is the most elegant and effective material for banners, draperies, and covers, is very costly. A good quality is worth $4.50 a yard. Woolen plush is a little less than silk, but is also expensive. Canton flannel which comes in double width, and finished alike on both sides, in all the rich and desirable colors, can be bought for ninety cents a yard.

Felting, which is thick and stubborn, though useful for some purposes, costs $1.50 a yard, and is two yards wide. Velveteen can be had from $1.00 a yard and upward. Velvets and satins cost anywhere from $3.00 to $6.00, and satin brocatelle is $10.00 a yard.

Stitches. Stem-stitch is very simple. It is just a single long stitch forward, and a short one backward, and then another long stitch a little in advance of the first. In working outlines, great care must be taken to keep precisely the line of the pattern, and to keep the thread to the left of the needle. Some knowledge of drawing is necessary to a good embroiderer. Leaves and flowers or conventional designs, should be nicely drawn or stamped before beginning to work, though sometimes a lady is so deft with her needle that she can compose her pattern as she goes on. The stem-stitch may be longer or shorter according to fancy, but it must be even.

Split-stitch is a variety of stem-stitch, but in bringing the needle up through the material, it is passed through the embroidery silk or crewel.

Satin-stitch is the same on both sides. The needle must be taken back each time to the point from which it started. Rope-stitch is a twisted chain-stitch; blanket-stitch is the ordinary buttonhole stitch less closely worked, and feather-stitch is a broken stitch, worked in a light airy way, to suit the convenience of the seamstress.

Drawn-Work consists in drawing out the threads of linen, and working designs, or filling in the sort of lace foundation thus made with whatever stitch the lady pleases. This is very lovely for tidies, and for the bordering of pillow-shams, spreads, and curtains.

The embroiderer needs a smooth thimble, as a sharp one catches in her silk, a very sharp and pointed pair of scissors, and a set of needles of different sizes.

The best crewels will not be injured by a careful laundress. Covers of linen or sheeting, should be dipped in water in which bran has been boiled. Never use soda, soap, or washing-powders for your pretty things. Do not wring them, but rinse with care, hang up to dry, and when almost dry stretch carefully on a flat surface and fasten with pins; you may thus safely clean all cheap embroidered work. Very costly articles, when soiled, which need not be the case in years of use, should be taken to a cleaner.

Appliqué Work is simply transferred work. Cut out pretty figures from damask or cretonne, or the best parts of old and worn embroideries, and fasten them securely on a foundation of lace, linen, or silk.

## PRETTY THINGS WHICH MAY BE EMBROIDERED.

To leave curtains, lambrequins, screens, and panels, which are larger undertakings than some busy women have time for, cushions and chair-backs may be made in great variety. Sofa cushions are always desirable as gifts. A long narrow cushion for the back of an invalid's chair, or a neck-rest for a rocker, covers of cool gray linen to be slipped over a chair that has lost its freshness, covers of all kinds, little round mats for the table, scarf-shaped pieces to brighten the center of a dinner-table, portfolios and letter-cases, slippers, neck ribbons, and dainty sewing and knitting-aprons, with pockets to hold a bit of work and a thimble, and the needles in their sheath, are among the articles clever girls can have on hand.

## TATTING.

This cannot be learned from printed directions, but is easily acquired in a lesson or two from one who does it well. It is graceful looking work, and forms a very neat and strong trimming for underclothing. Collars and edging, closely resembling the finest lace, are made of tatting.

## TAPE WORK.

At present old-fashioned, it may at any time come into favor. It is made of tape in different widths, as a trimming for children's aprons, and it almost never wears out.

## TISSUE PAPER.

Lulu and Jennie must not think we have forgotten them. It rains and Jennie has a cold. Mamma forbids going out doors. "What shall we do?" is the perplexing question. Dolls are tiresome and games have been tried. Well, little girls, get your scissors and ask mamma for several sheets of bright-tinted tissue paper. Tell her you will make her a beautiful lamp mat. And this is the way to do it.

Cut a piece of paper the size you wish your mat to be, including the fringe. The mat is prettiest made of two contrasting colors, and you need two whole sheets cut into eight square pieces.

Take the sixteen pieces and fold each one over about three-quarters of an inch wide. After all are folded, braid or weave them together, half one way and half another, to form a square.

Sew the outside pieces as far as the center of your mat, then cut the fringe as deep as you wish it, and dampen it by pressing on it a wet cloth. Shake it very gently till it is dry. The fringe will curl up and be very pretty.

Tissue paper flowers are made by cutting the petals as much like real flowers as possible, and fastening them by stems of flexible wire. This is nice work for little fingers.

### CHENILLE WORK.

A glove or handkerchief box of plush or satin, worked in chenille, would be a beautiful birthday present. Line the box with quilted silk.

### CROCHET.

The little crochet hook is very old. Its charm is that with so small a tool so many beautiful things may be produced. From a counterpane to a collar, almost anything may be made with the crochet needle. Babies' afghans and sofa quilts for convalescents are often crocheted. There are few occupations more fascinating than this.

### KNITTING.

The delight of knitting is its sociability. One must give her close attention to her embroidery, but the lady who knits may talk at the same time, and be witty or wise as she pleases. What pictures rise in our mind's eye of dear old ladies knitting by the fire, their silvery needles flashing and their thoughts busy with the past. Shawls for breakfast or evening wear are both knitted and crocheted. Among our most dearly-prized treasures is a sofa-quilt, knitted in broad stripes, each like a gay Roman ribbon, and crotcheted together in black and gold, with deep fringe knotted in the edge, the work of a lady who has counted her seventy-six years, and reached life's evening leisure.

### PATCH WORK.

Let no one despise this homely art. It is an accomplishment worth boasting of to make a really elegant patch-work quilt. If you have pretty patterns or can procure them, save them carefully, for sooner or later you will meet some elderly woman who keeps a quilt on hand, and fills up her "betweenities" by combining tints and matching pieces with poetic harmony.

### DECALCOMANIE.

Beautiful jars, vases, umbrella holders, and boxes may be made in this favorite work, for which scrap pictures are necessary. It requires taste to arrange these tastefully, and when well-gummed, they should be varnished to preserve them, and to impart a finish. POTICHOMANIE requires glass for its foundation. Choose boxes, vases, or bowls of clear, flawless glass. Cut and gum your picture very carefully on the vase, which must then be varnished. Imitate Chinese, Assyrian, or Etruscan vases, if you wish, but do not undertake this work in a hurry. Pass a coating of gum over the inside of the vase, then, if the outside is quite dry, paint it in oil, in any color you please. Tall vases to fill with cattails, grasses, and clematis, or to stand with a pot-pourri inside, shedding, whenever stirred, its faint, spicy odor over the drawing room, are very important decorations. They have an air about them as who should say, "We are of very long descent. Our lineage dates back to the cradle of civilization. Egypt knew us in her palmy days, and so did Greece and Rome."

## Wax Flowers.

THOUGH three-fourths of the wax-flowers made are but clumsy imitations of the lovely blossoms which adorn the garden, or smile at us from their hiding-places in woods and wayside fields, we need not sneer at the artist in wax, nor laugh at her handiwork. For there are artists in wax flowers and fruits who are so successful as almost to cheat the bees and the birds.

In order to make a violet, a pond lily, or a pansy, well, or to combine a dish of plums and grapes with the sun-kissed peach, and the yellow pear, you must study your original and work from it. Take a real flower, or a real plum or peach as your model, and imitate it as closely as you can. If at first you don't succeed, try, try again, and keep on trying till you see as the result of your efforts, not a clumsy wooden affair, but something that is worth having and worth giving away.

You do not need a great many tools, but those you have should be of the best, and should be kept clean and neat, and by themselves. Nobody should think it too much trouble to take good care of her brushes, paints, and wax.

Wax should be kept in a box, closely covered from dust, and in a cool place. You require a brush for every color you use, strictly kept for that one tint. It is well to have a separate brush for every shade. Your sable pencils may be cleansed after using for one color, and employed in another.

Always use a pair of scissors to cut out your petals, and take as your pattern the flower you wish to copy.

In purchasing it is economy to go to the most trustworthy dealers and buy the very best wax. You will need white, cream-tinted, very pale green, smilax, tea-rose leaf, pale spring, and deep spring-green tints for wax, but you need not buy these all at once. It is necessary to purchase at first only a very few materials. In paints, both in powder and cake, the wax-worker should have carmine, chrome-yellow, burnt sienna, burnt umber, Prussian blue, indigo, crimson-lake, violet, carmine, rose-madder, French ultramarine, magenta, flake-white, and Indian yellow; fifteen tinting-brushes, and four sable pencils; some modeling pins, No. 1 and No. 3, wires covered with silk for fine, and with cotton for coarse stems; a palette and a palette knife; some best Bermuda arrow-root; green and white down for leaves; two sizes of wooden molds for the lily of the valley, and a cutter for heliotrope, and a bar of India ink. That is a much larger outfit than the novice requires. If you succeed with your work, you will probably obtain it gradually.

To take the pattern of a petal, place it on white paper, and brush it over with a tinting-brush. The form of the petal will be left white on the paper, and may be cut out. If you like, however, you may lay your petal on a piece of paper, and cut its pattern in that way. Always cut the petals with the grain of the wax. The fingers are excellent modeling tools. A few drops of glycerine used on the hands an hour or two before working makes them soft and pliant. Do not work with brittle wax. To remove its brittleness, set it awhile in a warm room, if it has been in the cold.

To take a mold for flower or fruit, mix some very fine plaster of Paris in a bowl with water, to the thickness of cream. Pour it lightly over leaf, or fruit, or bud, which it is well to place for the purpose on a glass slab. In about ten minutes the plaster will have hardened sufficiently to lift it from the slab. Pare away with a penknife any plaster that may have run over. Let the mold stay in the sun, having removed the leaf or bud, until it has hardened. In twenty-four hours it will be ready for a coat of varnish, which must be very thin indeed.

"To take the mold of such a flower as a fuchsia or an unopened bud; oil it, pour your thick plaster into a paper form, and allow the bud to sink on its side in the plaster. Let it sink only to the center line, leaving one-half exposed." This direction is given by a teacher of experience. "Lift the mold out of the plaster before it is set too hard, scrape the rim smooth, and with the point of a pen-knife make two little cavities, one at the stem end, the other at the point where the four sepals of the calyx fold, and carefully brush away any little particles of plaster; place this half of the mold back in the paper form, and paint the rim, the hollow, and the little cavities with sweet oil; place the bud again in the cast, and pour enough plaster over the exposed part to fill the paper form."

In order to take a wax mold from this, dip it into cold water, and pour melted wax into one half; fit the other half to it, turn it upside down, slowly, and hold it in your hand till it has hardened. On removing the mold you will have the perfect bud. If you were able before the plaster became too firm, to bore a little hole in the mold at the stem end, you can slip the wire stem through before the wax hardens.

Proceed in the same manner to make molds for fruit, using your judgment, according to shape and size.

A panel covered with black velvet, on which is fastened a dainty tea-rose and bud with a cluster of leaves, and this set upon a silvered or gilted easel is an ornament on any table. A cross of white pine, covered with wax roughly coated to resemble coral, the whole wreathed with a passion vine and flower, is a beautiful symbol at Easter; or a cross of dark wood garlanded with autumn leaves is very lovely. Exquisite bouquets of apple-blossoms, lilacs, and crocuses may be set in slender vases. Pond lilies look best mounted on dark green velvet, and covered with a glass case.

Wax-flowers and fruit are very salable at fairs and bazaars, and the lady who knows how to make them well, is always sure of presenting her favorite table with something which will make a fine display, and bring in a good profit when disposed of.

## PHANTOM LEAVES.

Phantom or skeleton leaves are the ghosts of the leaves that wave on the trees in summer. They are troublesome to prepare, but are very pretty when finished. Gather the leaves when they are perfect, and lay them in a large jar, filled with water. Leave them there until they decay, and the fleshly part of the leaves is easily detached from the frame-work, or what we may call the bones. The etherial, thread-like form of this delicate veined work is very beautiful. Having loosened the green part, bleach the remainder by infusion in a strong solution of soda. When quite white, make bouquets or wreaths of different leaves in combination, and arrange them on a dark back-ground, or set under glass.

## A FEW WORDS ABOUT GATHERING FERNS.

Many a happy hour is passed by the dear folks at home in gathering and pressing ferns and autumn leaves, with which to brighten the house when winter winds are wild.

Never have too many of these in one apartment, for ornament should always be subordinate, and never ought to appear overloaded or too profuse. A parlor ought not to be smothered with either growing vines or plants, nor should ferns and branches be so multiplied as to give a spotty effect to walls.

All the young people may help in decorating the home with leaves, the girls pressing and preparing them, dipping the brilliant maple and the somber oak foliage into thinnest wax, or varnishing it, or perhaps merely pressing it with a half-warm flat-iron, and the boys climbing the step-ladder, and placing the bright bunches and vivid festoons where their sisters direct.

The fern-gatherer should go the woods with a long basket, the sides and bottom of which are lined with fresh leaves. Lay the ferns in this, and as they wilt very quickly, cover them with leaves.

Press them immediately on arriving at home, between old newspapers, or, if you have it handy, large sheets of blotting-paper. Large old books will answer if you have such. Place a layer of ferns, face down; cover with several thicknesses of paper, on which lay a thin, smooth piece of board. Cover this with a weight evenly. Three or four weeks will press them perfectly.

Ferns and autumn leaves make a pretty picture framed against a black ground. They are a substitute for a bouquet in winter, when no plants are in bloom.

## BASKETS AND WALL-POCKETS.

Loosely plaited straw baskets, lined with satin, silk, soft worsted, or even silesia, tied with an immense bow, and ornamented with artificial flowers, or pressed ferns, a bunch of wheat, oats, grass, or corn ears, make charming wall pockets. These pockets are not only pretty in relieving the monotony of a wall, but they are very useful, enabling the neat housekeeper to put aside the baker's dozen of odds and ends that accumulate in spite of her, and assisting her to live up to that golden maxim, "A place for everything, and everything in its place."

## LACE.

Macrame lace is made of cord and is too intricate to be learned withont personal instruction. It is by no means difficult when one has the knack of it, and is utilized for the making of pretty bags for shopping, and of drapery, to finish off brackets, or lambrequines, and add variety to table-covers. Finer laces, made of thread, and a pretty lace-like trimming of which feather-edge braid is the foundation, are strong, lasting almost forever, and are very useful where one has many garments to adorn, but they are, one and all, exceedingly trying to the eyesight.

### WHITE EMBROIDERY.

Except for the marking of initials on handkerchiefs or table linen, no lady ought to practice white embroidery in these days of cheap Hamburg edging. Machinery executes such work, with a precision and elegance to which few hands can attain, and life is too short to be spent in the slow setting of white wreaths and eyelets and button-holes and hem-stitching, when daintily perfect work of the same kind can be bought for a song.

### TRIFLES.

Among pretty articles to give one's brother or young gentleman friend, a shaving case may be mentioned. Take a small Japanese paper fan, cover it with silk or silesia, cut a piece of pasteboard the size of the fan, and cover with silk or satin. Trim the edge with plaited ribbon, paint a spray of flowers on it, or paste a graceful picture. Fasten paper leaves nicely pinked to the fan part, and then join the two sides together finishing with a bow, and a loop to hang it by.

An embroidered hat band, or band to hold a dinner napkin are pretty gifts for a gentleman.

A foot-rest, worked on canvas in the old fashioned cross-stitch, filled in, and made up by an upholsterer over a box to contain blacking brushes and shoe polish is sure to be acceptable to papa.

Pretty little work-baskets may be made of the paper boxes in which one carries home ice-cream from the confectioners. Scrap-pictures are easily procured to ornament them. They may be cozily lined, and finished with a bow.

Exquisite little hair-receivers are made of Japanese umbrellas, bought for three cents, inverted and hung by a loop of ribbon.

These and many other little things are the merest trifles, but mother and the girls have good times together while they are tossing them off: the foam of merry hours, when good-natured talk, gossip without a spice of malice, and lively jests make home the blithest place in the world.

## Drawing and Painting.

ARTISTS of great reputation are few. The masters of their art, whose work in the world's great markets is paid in a golden shower, may be counted on a short muster roll. But never was there a time when so many people took an interest in, and understood something about art, when so many could paint in a manner to give pleasure to their friends and themselves, and when homes were so adorned by simple and uncostly works of beauty.

We were very much touched the other day on being shown, in the parlor of a friend, some lovely panels painted by her husband, who had for some time been ill. Accustomed to an active business life, the enforced routine of the household wearied him, yet he was not strong enough to go out, except when the weather was neither very hot nor very cold, the rare days, when "heaven tries the earth if it be in tune, and softly above it her warm ear lays." So the good wife, bethinking herself what new thing to suggest to make the tedium less, advised that he should learn to paint in water-colors.

Boys as well as girls may practice drawing and painting.

Every young person should learn to sketch from nature. An artist-friend who spends days out of doors with pencil and note-book, says it is wonderful how much more one sees, who draws what he sees, than others do. Then, too, the curious groups of spectators one gathers about him, afford food for speculation. Barefooted children, philosophic tramps, and curious cows sometimes look at my friend's pictures as they grow. A faithful dog is found to be a quite pleasant companion on long expeditions.

Seriously, it is well worth while to acquire so accurate a knowledge of drawing that one may jot down with a few facile strokes, enough of a situation or a landscape, to fill out the picture in after hours. Drawing is at the bottom. Unless you draw well, you will not succeed in any style of painting, either in oils, water-colors, or mineral painting.

It is well to learn drawing from the object as well as from copies. A professor of the art whose pupils take high rank, makes beginners draw the furniture of the room, and after a while tells them to draw their idea of "Tired!" "Happy!" "Sorrowful!" etc. But a great deal of pleasure may be had, by those who paint only from copies. They can preserve for themselves some beautiful pictures which they could not possess otherwise, and they may ornament with lovely devices, fans, ribbons, scent-bottles, and mouchoir-cases.

Very exquisite dresses for parties have been painted by clever girls, at a trifling expense, except of time and taste. At a commencement this summer, one graduate wore a dress of corded silk painted in the most delicately perfect way, and another had on a dress thick sown with embroidery of pearls, fit only for a royal princess, or a little Republican belle.

M. Taine, the great French painter and critic, says that success depends on learning to endure drudgery, and not getting angry at failure. Do not fret dear young friends, if your first attempts are not received with rapture, and please only the partial eyes of mother. You will improve in time, and not only panels, but lovely hand-painted covers for books, Easter and Christmas cards, invitations, and dinner-menus, will prove your skill.

### CHINA PAINTING.

This is very captivating. Procure your colors in tubes, and you will acquire a greater variety than you would for either oil or water-color painting. Though it is permitted to use water-color brushes, it is advisable to have a different set, and, if you try both, keep your tools separate. The colors most in use are black, white, gray, five shades of red, two of brown, three of green, four of yellow, and two of purple. These may be obtained at any art-store. The tube colors are diluted with turpentine. You will require a porcelain palette, a glass slab eight inches square, several camel's hair brushes of different sizes, several blenders, a quart bottle of spirits of turpentine, a quart bottle of 98 per cent. alcohol, a small bottle of oil of turpentine, one of oil of lavender, and one of balsam of copaiva. A steel palette knife, and one of horn or ivory; a rest for the hand while painting, made of a strip of wood about an inch long and twelve inches wide, supported at each end by a foot, an inch and a half in height; a small glass muller; and a fine needle set in a handle for removing tiny particles of dust.

Such an outfit will cost from ten to twelve dollars (about £2 to £2 10s.).

A plate, a flat plaque, or a tile is best to begin with. Let your first design be very simple. You will learn by degrees how to use the colors which will best stand the firing, which is the crucial test. There are places in the cities to which cups and saucers, vases, plates, and all china articles may be sent to be fired, few people having the facilities for doing this in their homes.

Painting can be applied to china, to velvet, to satin, to cloth, and to almost every fabric and material in use among civilized peoples.

By study, careful watching of processes, attention to details, and obedience to the directions of the best manuals, one may learn to paint creditably without a master. But all arts are rendered less difficult by a painstaking teacher, and therefore it is well, if one can, to join a class.

A circle of young people at home, and a few friends with them, might club together and engage the services of a good teacher, who would come to them twice a week. They would find that their rapid progress would well repay them for time given and money spent.

## THE CARE OF PETS.

A very engrossing home occupation is found in the care of pets. Sometimes, indeed, the pets take more of the family attention than outside friends approve. Over-indulged pets behave a good deal like spoiled children. When the parrot has his napkin on the dinner table, and poising there, utterly refuses to eat anything except a dainty morsel on a guest's plate, when Puss occupies the easiest chair and Ponto the sofa, the pets are too daintily lodged and too much considered.

But every boy should have some dear dumb animals to love and care for. Pigeons, rabbits, a feathered owl with his wise phiz, a frolicksome monkey, a darling chipmunk, a chattering parrot, a faithful dog, a pony, a gentle Alderney cow—how long is the list of our four-footed and two-footed friends in fur or in feathers, who serve us, amuse us, bear with us, love us, mind us, and no doubt wonder at our queer vagaries and odd dispositions.

Pets should be regularly tended, kept clean and comfortable, given pleasant and roomy houses of their own, fed plentifully, and, by gentle means, trained to obey their masters and mistresses. Well-cared for, they will reward by the pleasure they give, and sometimes they will manifest a kind and degree of intelligence, which might shame some stupid bipeds who belong to our human race.

## PHOTOGRAPHY.

To have one's picture taken used to be talked of as a family event, in the early days before we had found out what a swift and obliging miniature painter was our friend, the Sun. In these days photography is put to medical and scientific uses, and helps nearly all the other arts.

An amateur photographer's outfit is not very expensive, and a young man possessed of any skill in carpentering, can easily build himself a little cabin outdoors, where he can keep his apparatus and chemicals, and obtain great popularity among the girls by taking their charming faces on tin-types, if not on paper.

## COLLECTIONS.

A geological or mineralogical cabinet, or a fine collection of moths and butterflies, is a never-ending source of pleasure and profit to the young student of natural history. No matron, however neat, should object if her sons, bent on botany and geology, bring weeds and stones into the house for classification. A boy must have elbow-room. He will be the better man, the larger every way, and very likely the more affectionate son, brother, and, after a time, husband, if he is allowed to feel that his tastes are of some account, and that he may have sufficient space in the house to indulge them.

A hobby sometimes grows tiresome to others, if ridden too constantly. But if Emily has her painting, Louise her music, Ailee her books, Nanette her pretty dresses, and Lucille her housekeeping, why shall not Ned go poking among the rocks with his bag and little mallet, always making wonderful discoveries, and Rex prepare lures for the moths, and sally out with box and net for beetles and butterflies, and Tom take photographs, and Hugh collect stamps and postmarks. In the ideal home there is liberty to indulge the individual, so that each person may be developed symmetrically, and the happiness of all be insured.

## CHISEL AND PLANE.

Change of work is often the best way of resting. A young man, occupied in the store or the counting-room, and using one set of faculties exclusively, has a great advantage over his companion who doesn't know what to do with himself out of business hours, if he has a turn for carpentering.

Such a youth can do wonders, if the ladies help him, with old furniture. There is a discarded sofa in the attic; it began life in the drawing-room, in great pride and honor; went from there to the dining-room, in the course of time was taken to the privacy of a bedroom, and at last, being scorned as a miracle of ugliness, was packed off to the obscurity of old lumber. But Arthur and Susie, with new springs and stuffing, gay covering, varnish, and brass-headed nails, renew the despised article, and it is restored to its former glory, and becomes the family boast.

Bookcases, only tolerable where people use and love their books, may be made by the handy young man, who thinks nothing of undertaking a set of portable shelves, their edges finished with a band of bright morocco, deep enough to shield the precious volumes from dust.

Every pleasant thing that boys and girls can do together should be welcomed in home life. So, if Mary wants a mirror in her room, and the only one she can have is set in a mahogany frame with half the veneering off, and a crack down the northwest corner of the glass, is she to give up in despair? Not at all.

Fred looks at the glass with a professional eye, and straight away makes a new frame of white wood, which his sister paints in a lovely running wreath of eglantine and blackberry vines. As if by accident, a long spray drops over the unlucky corner, and the very defect is turned into an ornament.

It takes a great deal of tinkering to keep house, grounds, fences, and gates in that state of perfect repair which indicates the highest thrift. If Charlie has tools and knows how to use them, then, when a shutter is awry, or a sash-cord breaks, or a door creaks, or a gate hangs badly, he attends to it at once, and the neighbors admire the manner in which the folks at Charlie's keep things up.

## Fret-Sawing—Wood-Carving.

WOOD-CARVING and fret-sawing is often left as a home occupation for the boys, but it is not exclusively theirs. Panels, easels, brackets, boxes, frames, and the various pretty carved articles for the table in which ladies delight, may be made by both brothers and sisters.

The more accurate and perfect work is done by the machine, a Rogers or Holly saw turning out the loveliest things you can think of; but wood-carving by hand is the more artistic, and leaves room for the finest play of individual taste.

The amateur wood-carver must be provided with a strong deal table, which should stand in a good light. He must have three chisels of different sizes, one an eighth of an inch wide, the others a quarter and a half inch wide. These should be ground rather slantingly. An oil-stone to set the edges, a number of gouges, which are chisels of a different pattern, and a supply of wood—a bit of smooth pine or an old cigar-box will do—are all that are indispensable at first.

Try some simple leaf, with very few indentations at first. Draw it on paper, the back of which is rubbed with red chalk; pin this on the board, and press over it a bodkin or crotchet-needle, and when lifted the outline will be found on the wood. Next stab out your outline, either with a chisel or with a little wheel, a notched instrument which is very easy to manage.

In cutting away the wood, the chisel should be held in the right hand, the wrist of the left hand being held firmly on the panel, and the tool guided by the forefinger of the left hand. Begin to cut out the wood at some distance from the outline, shaving gradually to it.

Do everything very neatly, and without haste. Leave no litter about when you are done. Be sure to cut thoroughly, not digging or tearing away the wood.

The fret-saw consists of a frame with a cross-bar and two side pieces. There are hand saws, and there are foot-power saws worked by treadles. The pattern must always be outlined first, and the operator must not hurry. The cost of a good fret-saw is from $1 to $5, according to size. Full directions accompany the machines.

A lad who is ambitious may make a good deal of pocket-money by selling the pretty articles he turns out from his fret-saw. Wood-carving is much used in house-building, and railings, shelves, and cornices may be made for the new home, if the family are to have one, by the cunning hands of the sons and daughters.

### AMATEUR PRINTING.

There is still another fascinating pastime for young gentlemen, and one which effectually keeps them removed from outside temptation, and that is the printing-press. Many a little fellow's highest ambition is gratified when he is able to print visiting cards for his friends among the ladies, and circulars for his business acquaintances. The number of amateur newspapers edited, composed, set up, and passed through the press by boys on their small presses is very much larger than the uninitiated suppose.

"Art is long and time is fleeting." Change and vicissitude come to us all. The fledglings find their wings and fly from the home nest. While they are still there, it is good economy to make the nest so cozy, and to so fill the air with song and sweetness, that every memory of the dear place in all coming days shall vibrate to the air of "Home, Sweet home."

OUNG GIRLS seldom realize the fact that a knowledge of housekeeping is of greater practical value after marriage than the preservation of bright eyes and rosy cheeks, if they wish to retain the affection and admiration of their husbands. It was once said by an observing member of the gentler sex that "the only way to reach a man's heart is through his stomach," but this malicious piece of cynicism was probably offered by her as a witty retaliation for the many cruel things that have been said by man, from time immemorial, about her own sex. There is no doubt, however, that a good dinner does put the lord of creation in an amiable frame of mind, and married ladies who have observed this potent charm by practical experience, frequently resort to this method of obtaining the promise of a stylish bonnet or new dress.

No matter how slovenly a man may be himself, he generally desires to see his house kept in good order. He seldom invites his friends to visit him, if he is not sure that the parlor will be in proper condition to receive them. On the other hand, where he has good cause to be proud of the general air of comfort and refinement that his wife has managed to give his home, he will invite people to dine with him on the slightest provocation. His vanity is gratified by his wife's superior housekeeping, because he attributes it to his own personal influence. To a certain extent a husband is the motive power that prompts women to take pride in their domestic duties, for the desire to please and the love of admiration is only human nature, and especially characteristic of the female sex. Man is a creature of habit, and after he is married and settled in life, there is nothing that so attaches him to his loving helpmate as a pleasant, comfortable, and refined home.

In former centuries housekeeping was considered the whole of "Woman's Sphere," but in those days there were no "Women's Rights;" each wife and mother held undisputed sway in her own realm, and generally ruled with order and economy. Her maids of honor were daughters of the household, while her cabinet and aides-de-camp were her husband and sons.

The many discoveries and inventions, the added conveniences to the house, make the drudgery of the past century unnecessary, so that the "daughters of Eve" can always combine supervision of their households with the pursuit of art studies, scientific research, or some money-yielding branch of industry. Homes must be built and furnished, and how to commence is the knotty question for the young housekeeper—a question that each one must practically decide alone. Although no fixed rules can be laid down upon paper, germ-like suggestions can be given; but the development of them must depend greatly upon circumstances.

## HOW TO SECURE A HOME.

Primarily it would be well for no young couple to start out in life till the means for building the nest were assured.

Every one can form some estimate as to the probable yearly income that may be set apart for household and personal expenses. In the country, the proportion for rent is less than in a city, where, generally, one-third of the annual income is taken by the landlord. But this is too much ; one-fourth or one-fifth is as much as ought to be taken for this purpose. This paying of rent is a great bugbear, both to the very poor and to the well-to-do. Owning one's house or farm is the only wise starting point. Even if a mortgage remain, it is better than a hired home. The interest and taxes will not equal the annual rent ; the repairs will be an item, but they are for the benefit of the property, and can be made at convenience, not at the caprice of the landlord. Many a dollar that would be wasted in luxuries or pleasure seeking will be laid aside to pay off the debt on the homestead. Were it not for the modern boarding-house, to which impecunious couples can flee, there would be a greater incentive for young men and maidens to save up toward buying a piece of ground, at least, upon which a modest structure might be erected till the means warranted a better one.

## THE KITCHEN.

"We are getting nicely settled in our new home ; the parlor carpet is down, and all the ornaments and pretty things are set about, making it look so cozy like," said a young woman to an elderly matron. That bride of a few weeks has never, in a score of years, forgotten the expression in the face of the more experienced friend, as she simply remarked, "You have thought of the parlor before the kitchen."

Begin, therefore, with the workshop of home, for out of this, when well ordered, proceed peace and joy unspeakable. Let the kitchen contain every thing needful, but no superfluous utensils. The modern architect provides for comfort in the improved range, the never-failing supply of hot water, the ash-slide and laundry conveniences. The pantries and cupboards are numerous and roomy, but do not allow that to be a temptation to extravagance in order to see them well filled.

Start the kitchen machinery with the least possible complications ; with no labor-saving inventions such as apple-corers, patent egg-beaters, chocolate foamers, pie crimpers, etc., etc. These cost much money, need careful handling, and, after all, accomplish nothing that cannot be done with knife, fork, and spoon. Though economy is recommended, let there be vessels in number to equal the different viands to be prepared ; fruit should never be cooked in a saucepan that has served for meat or vegetables, and the milk pot should be dedicated solely to milk. Copper, tin, and iron ought not to be used, now that the porcelain and agate wares are brought to such perfection. They are more easily cleaned and safer for the health.

The ordinary pottery pipkins are very inexpensive, though not very durable, but, with careful usage till they are well *tempered*, they will do good service. Before bringing them to the fire they must be well greased upon the under side, then allowed to stand some twenty-four hours, after which fill with cold water and set them upon the back of the range, to be slowly heated to the boiling point ; they must never be placed upon the *open* fire, as the intense heat melts the glazing, giving a bad flavor to the contents. Used in the way described, they will last a number of years.

All kitchen utensils must be kept very clean, and a simple method, after the meal is served, is to fill the pots and saucepans with water and leave them on the fire ; when they are very greasy, a small bit of soda should be added. By the time the meal is cleared away, any food adhering to the cooking vessels will be well softened, and they can then be washed without the terrible din of "scraping pots and pans" so offensive to sensitive ears. The iron dish cloth is a capital thing for this purpose. It is a bit of *chain* cloth, and costs from ten to twenty-five cents.

If every cook were a chemist, it would not be so imperative to give this fixed rule : never to use iron spoons or steel knives in the preparation of acid vegetables or fruit. Wooden spoons and a silver-plated knife will give a delicate flavor to food that otherwise would be spoiled. An earthen colander is also often very desirable for draining currants or other fruit intended for jelly or syrup. Cranberry sauce is much nicer if the skins are removed by pressing the cooked fruit through a colander, then add the sugar and return to the fire just long enough to bring to a boil.

The ideal kitchen is very roomy, with a scullery attached. It is in a pleasant country place ; shady trees, creeping vines, and green fields delight the eye and soften the breeze on hot summer days. The fresh fruits and vegetables grow at the very door. Life in such a kitchen is a poem read only in the rich man's domain, or in a New England farmhouse. But the actual kitchen is only a cookshop that must be attached to a house. It is a small, wee corner of a flat, or a dark, damp, half under-ground room. The burden of daily toil presses heavily upon those who serve in such a workshop. The only rules for mitigating the discomfort inevitable are : to systematize the work in every way possible, and to keep perfect order, not on one day in the week, when there has been a "setting to rights," but there must be a place for everything, and these places must be occupied by their rightful owners. Some persons will cook a meal or perform other labors, and as the work is finished there will be no disorder, nothing to clear away, while others in preparing a simple meal will have the kitchen table heaped full of dirty dishes, the sink choked up and unapproachable.

A tidy plan is to set the dish-pan, filled with cold water (warm if accessible), upon the dresser, and gather up the cups, spoons, plates, or whatever one uses ; it takes but a moment to rinse them out, dry, and put them away. If there is time it is best to wash the pots and pans while the family are at table ; this leaves room for the dishes, as they are brought from the dining-room. The quicker the dishes are washed, before the dirt has hardened, the easier it is and then it keeps away the horde of flies that delight in an untidy kitchen.

## MEALS.

Nothing helps so essentially in the maintenance of order as early rising and an early breakfast, for neither mistress nor maid can work well fasting. The foreign custom of a light breakfast has much in its favor, as the cup of tea or coffee and roll without butter is quickly served, and then each one is ready for work; children clatter off to school, in summer at seven, in winter at eight, and a long morning is spread out before the busy housewife.

This light breakfast involves an early dinner, which does not suit American business hours in large cities. But those who can adopt it will find the weariness and lassitude of the early morning disappearing with the warm draught of tea, coffee, or milk, and they bring a far lighter heart to the daily tasks. After the long rest of the night, the stomach is unable to receive heavy food, but needs to be toned up gradually. Midway between coffee and dinner many take a light luncheon of fruit and bread.

If, however, an *American* breakfast must be served, let the cook be up betimes, make a bright fire, brush around the range, sweep out the area, the yard, and the sidewalk, if that be her duty also, though it is the work for the up-stairs girl if there are two servants. In filling the tea-kettle be sure to rinse it thoroughly, and never fill with the first running of the water near the faucet, which has been standing all night, and is likely to have absorbed lead from the pipe. With a good smart fire, a breakfast of hominy, rolls, toast, eggs boiled, meat, etc., can be prepared in an hour's time, and it will relish so much better if eaten immediately. Morecver, food that stands simmering and stewing, keeping warm for a laggard, is far from wholesome.

## SERVING MEALS.

While the cooking is going on get every thing ready for dishing up. The platters, plates, and vegetable dishes must be wiped with a dry cloth to free them from dust, and placed where they will get warm, not hot—a mistake often made. It ruins chinaware to continually over-heat it, and it is very disagreeable to have the platter so hot that the meat simmers upon it, and the plates in such a white heat that a napkin is essential to hold them as passed around the table. Unless there is a closet under or near the range expressly for this purpose, let them be dipped into boiling water and dried —they will be the right temperature then.

The food should be dished as quickly as possible, and taken to the table at once. If there are several courses, each course should be dished in the order of serving. Some incline to a great variety upon the table at once, others prefer one or two dishes at a time, which is the better way. It prolongs the meal, thereby aiding digestion. Salads, asparagus, cauliflower, and many of these delicate vegetables relish far better eaten alone than served with meat.

## FOOD.

The quantity and variety of food must be regulated by the taste and needs of each family; indeed, of each individual. It is not always daintiness that gives to one a craving for something better than what another finds good enough. Habits of life, constitutional weakness, and the kind of daily occupation regulate these apparent whims. The old Puritanic rules, "Eat what is set before you, and leave nothing upon the plate to be wasted," is a physical impossibility to a nineteenth-century mortal.

The wiser and cheaper way is to study the tastes of those one caters for. It pays in the long run; for in the usual variety of the markets, taking things in their proper season, one article is as cheap as another. Then why not eat that for which there is a preference?

There are many valuable receipts for the disposition of cold meats, etc., but the most sensible of all economies is to cook about what is needed for each meal. Of course roast and boiled meat cannot be measured so accurately, and a larger piece makes a better roast; but vegetables and puddings are best fresh cooked, and a little observation and management will soon enable one to gauge the appetites of the consumers, so that nothing need be wasted, and yet all have enough.

It is very unwise to advance upon the natural order of the seasons. The facilities for transportation are so perfected that one needs a calendar to know winter from summer in passing through the city markets. Every clime and every season is represented. But of what use to eat strawberries at $8 per quart, with the snow a foot deep without? Those strawberries grew where there was warmth and sunshine, the proper condition for enjoying acid fruit. As the warm weather approaches in the northern regions, the earth bears there also the fruits that the system craves. Grown near at hand and in abundance, they are cheap. Moreover, only fresh ripe fruits and vegetables are wholesome. There is no extravagance so utterly foolish as the buying of unseasonable importations.

## THE STORE-ROOM.

The old-fashioned one, with its barrels of sugar and flour, chests of tea, bags of coffee to be roasted at home, nuts, raisins, spices, etc., in profusion, is almost an impossibility in the modern "flats" and small houses—and perhaps by no means desirable. There is economy in buying by wholesale, but there are many disadvantages also.

Instead of the morning hour in the store-room, weighing and measuring the daily supplies, the modern housekeeper dons a market hat and delegates the task to the retail grocer. Ordering in small quantities is a check upon waste, and relieves the mistress from much care in guarding the supplies. Of course the retailer's profit must be reckoned, but time, nowadays, is such a priceless commodity that in a city home there is more gain than loss through this method.

In very large establishments, in country places, on farms, and wherever there are ample store-rooms suitably constructed for the protection of stores against heat, cold, and the ravages of vermin, by at all means buy at wholesale. But rich or poor, in a large or small households, the mistress should never omit the daily inspection of the ice-box, meat-safe, pantries, and cellar. There are few servants unwilling to submit to this supervision, provided they see the mistress thoroughly intent upon making the work of housekeeping an honor, and not a task.

## SERVANTS.

It is said that a finished education is essential to the right teaching of the rudiments in any branch; and certain it is that a lady, gifted and cultured, will conduct the ordinary details of housework with method and dispatch impossible to a servant trained to drudgery. Therefore a well-intentioned servant soon appreciates the oversight of the intelligent mistress, teaching many deft ways that had never entered into her philosophy.

In many families the domestics are retained for years; in others there is a "long procession passing to and fro." We need stricter laws in this respect; laws to govern those who hire and those who serve alike.

The tyrannical mistress has too much latitude, and the servant too much independence. But unless there is really criminal conduct on the servant's part, a big share of the blame justly belongs to the master or mistress. They look for virtues in a servant that they themselves, with the advantages of superior education, do not possess. In making an engagement, both parties ought to clearly state their wishes, and then the lady or gentleman must never forget that they, being the superiors, are bound to guide their inferiors to a conscientious discharge of the duties of the position they have assumed.

It is a pity when the mistress of a house, although able to keep many servants, does not choose to abridge the number and perform light tasks herself, instead of devising plans to occupy her whole time with fancy work, light reading, amusements, etc. Any one who will devote one or two hours a day to the house, will soon be able to dispense with much extra work, perhaps with one servant altogether. Then there is a certain individuality about the house that hirelings can never give.

## WEEKLY WASHING.

The horrors of "blue Monday" might be lessened if part of the clothes were washed on Saturday; if not hung out, they can be left in the suds and are soon ready for the line, and will dry while another lot is being washed on Monday. It takes but an hour or two to wash out all the bedding and pieces from the Saturday's changing. Still, domestics have a strong objection to this plan, although dividing the work, and giving Sunday for rest between, is greatly to their own advantage. If one cannot convince, however, the best way is to give up and get the wash started as early as possible on Monday.

There are now so many preparations for lightening the labors of the laundry, that the ordinary wash ought to be all out of the way shortly after noon.

There was formerly a tacit agreement to accept a poor dinner upon wash-day; the custom is now rightfully obsolete. There is no reason why an exception should be made for wash-day more than sweeping-day, and men returning from business need food one day just as much as another.

It is well to order a dinner that requires but little preparation; instead of a roast, a nice steak with some of the cold meat left over from Sunday, some freshly cooked vegetables, and fruit for dessert, can be just as easily prepared as the programme of hash-ups and stews, thought good enough for wash-day.

## THE DINING-ROOM.

Sometimes the dining and breakfast rooms are separate apartments, the one large and suggestive of hospitality unbounded, the other a cheerful room looking to the east, that the morning sun may brighten and gladden all who enter. But usually the breakfast, dining, and sitting room are combined, and it ought to be the most home-like one of all in the house.

The carpet can cover the entire floor, or if the boards are stained and polished, it suffices to put a square under the table, and rugs elsewhere. There should be some soft carpet to moderate the noise, especially when there are children. In no room is harmony of color more desirable, and quiet tone is in good taste.

A large extension table, with round corners and substantial center pedestal is the handsomest and most useful. Economy must not rule in the choice of this one piece of furniture. A strong, well-made table will last for a lifetime, and a cheap one is soon rickety and unserviceable. If finely polished, luncheon and tea can be served without a cloth, and in this way quite an item is saved in the way of linen. Happy those who can have mahogany, but an endless variety of woods are used for dining-rooms now, which should be stained, oiled, or polished, in preference to varnish.

It is best to have straight-back chairs for the table, but a comfortable sofa and two arm-chairs suggest that an after-dinner nap winds up the bill of fare. Landscapes and portraits have no place here—fruit and game pieces belong upon these walls—but many prefer only flowers and fruit, leaving the game out entirely. It is not relishing to eat a delicate fish and look at a dead one hung upon the opposite panel; or, while enjoying a tit-bit of some rare bird, to see a whole string of them upon the walls.

Decorations are minor points compared with the table appointments. Here artistic taste can have full sway, and it were better to pause in furnishing till this room and the adjoining pantries are fully arranged.

The true housewife can show her skill in serving, to make a simple repast appear like a banquet—nice table linen, pretty dishes, plenty of knives and forks, flowers and fruit—who has not felt a thrill of delight upon entering such a feast chamber?

There is another style of dining-room, which, if not elegant, is thoroughly cheerful and inspiring—the farmer's kitchen. In winter the cooking stove is in there, but in summer it is usually carried out to a shed, or some structure adjoining, to avoid the discomfort of the heat. In no banquet hall is there the same enjoyment of food as in these places, where, at five o'clock of a summer morning, the farmer's wife has a table loaded with pies, doughnuts, fried pork, potatoes, and good steaming coffee. After a hearty breakfast, the men go forth to the toilsome work upon the farm, and the women to the household cares, the principal one being to cook fresh supplies of food for the noon-day meal and for the supper.

There must be plenty of food in such a dining-room, and there is never fault-finding—the appetites of the heavy toilers are too keenly whetted for that.

## THE PARLOR OR DRAWING-ROOM.

This is generally the room set apart for receiving visitors. It is often kept more exclusively than any other for ornament rather than for use. But a drawing-room possesses its greatest charm when it impresses those who enter it with a sense of being constantly occupied by a lady. Unless the room be in daily use, the atmosphere of home and enjoyment will be wanting. The parlor may be said to be the most difficult room to furnish so that elegance and comfort should appear together. Stiffness and uniformity should be banished from it, and refined comfort should reign supreme.

There is a certain house upon which thousands have been expended, and yet there is neither a parlor nor a drawing-room in it. The visitor is ushered from a curtained vestibule into a room which seems to cry out a welcome from every nook and corner. In a large bay window, filled with flowers and plants, stands a writing table, note paper and pen lying ready for use. Chairs and tables are placed as if some one had just occupied them. Papers and periodicals are at hand; low book-cases are stocked with books that have not been misused, but certainly have been well read. A map or two of some portion of the globe, to which, for the moment, all thoughts are directed, suggest an interest in current events.

There are many choice oil paintings, a few rare engravings, and lovely children's portraits. On a table near the sofa are some finely-illustrated works, near-by a low chair and a pretty basket, with some half-finished work. There is bric-à-brac also, but not too much, and very curious of its kind. There is an enchanting home-look about the whole place. The parlor leads into the piano-room, thence into the dining-room.

This is the reception floor in a very rich man's house, the idea of which could be carried into a poorer home, where often the largest and pleasantest room is extravagantly furnished and kept for the use of company. Guests in such parlors feel ill at ease, for the family seem constrained, and there is an unused look to everything, that belies words of cordial welcome.

## BEDROOMS.

Let them be as light and airy as possible. The foreign fashion of no carpets is becoming very popular, and deservedly so. The bare floor can be washed or wiped with a damp cloth, the movable rugs carried to the yard or roof and thoroughly beaten, and that terrible dust and lint arising from bedroom floors is avoided. The gain to health for the strong can hardly be estimated, and what must it be for the sick?

Wire springs are now universally adopted, some are covered with ticking, but the open spring is the best; it is nice and clean and capitally ventilated.

One would think the airing of the sleeping apartments would be an axiom comprehended by the feeblest intellect, and yet there is hardly one servant in a hundred who will attend to this properly. Indeed, the care of this ought not to be left to the domestics. Any lady or gentleman, worthy of bearing the name, ought to have learned in youth to throw back the bedding immediately upon rising, and to open the windows before quitting the room. Closets must not only be well aired every day, but at least once a month they need a complete routing out, the dust to be wiped up with a damp cloth, the garments shaken and refolded, the boxes and budgets set to rights. This insures against the ravages of insects.

## CLEANLINESS.

Insects of all kinds delight in dust and dirt; deprive them of this and they will generally seek a home elsewhere. Better than all moth powders is a good airing and brushing of garments, washing such as are soiled, or sponging the spots at least. If a housewife complains of the moths in her woolens and furs, or of creatures nameless to polite ears, be sure there is carelessness in the storing of the former and a criminal negligence in the inspection of the servants' quarters. Two things should be strenuously enforced: absolute purity in the attic, and the same in the cellar. And this work must be intelligently overlooked. The former insures comfort for the entire household, the latter may serve to ward off a pestilence.

If the thousands who suffer from malaria would descend to the caverns under their mansions, they would often find germs of disease that might well have inoculated ten times ten thousand. Cobwebs and dust of ages every-where, old rubbish piled about, harboring vermin, and very likely the whole place is reeking with dampness from badly constructed or neglected drains.

## MODERN HOUSEKEEPING.

Keeping house is a science and an art. It must be conducted on business principles, too, and the mistress of a good home has earned a right to be ranked with the successful merchant or broker, or a great general, even. In fact, none of these could have done what one woman may have accomplished in a single day. We hear of the "new profession," a favorite theme with one of our great orators. May the time be not far distant when we shall hear of the "new sphere" for woman's energies, viz.: to regulate her home in accordance with the polished training her mental faculties have attained, through co-education perhaps, and not to feel her life is being wasted, or her education for naught. Then we shall have reached the harmonious blending of old and new ideas; the old idea of responsibilities and duties beyond purely selfish interests, and the graceful discharge of those duties as the result of "higher culture."

RECEIPTS of any kind, but especially household receipts, are not easily given in a lucid manner. It is, therefore, somewhat difficult for novices to cook or do housework, following the usual printed directions.

Those who attempt to give information generally so thoroughly understand the matter that they forget to be instructors, and omit the minor details that must be known to insure success. What to an experienced matron, from long practice, has become a second nature, is a profound mystery to a young creature, making vain essays to show off her skill in a branch that has been wholly overlooked in her studies at the college where she graduated with high honors. Mamma, too, was so proud of her daughter's proficiency that she never thought of allowing her to waste time "pothering about the house."

If there is a cook, make her observe carefully how everything is done, that she can do it, by herself, another time. Train servants to be self-reliant—do not perform their tasks for them. Give careful instructions, and insist upon having them followed. But, by all means, in the first weeks of housekeeping superintend everything. See to the serving of each meal. The experience will be invaluable for future guidance, and in those emergencies, which come at times, there will be a delightful feeling of independence worth all the trouble taken to acquire it. For it must be remembered that, whether a woman's future life obliges her to do these things or not, and even if her position in the world allows her to keep as many servants as she chooses, she will always command more respect if she knows how to do all the work she requires of them. We know of a home where, though living in affluence, the mother requires the daughters, each in her turn, to put on a woolen wrapper, to guard against fire, and go into the kitchen to oversee the dishing of the meals.

Not every young woman is so unsophisticated as to make the comical mistakes of the heroine in "Mrs. Jerningham's Journal," who orders a "leg of lamb" one day, and a "leg of beef, for variety," the next. Terrible blunders, however, will be made, and often sad mishaps occur, till, after a while each housekeeper settles down to a code of her own, despite cook-books and theories. Before studying the Cooking and other Household Receipts, given in the following pages, it will be of benefit to the reader to carefully peruse a quotation from Ruskin on the subject of the culinary art. "What does cookery mean? It means the knowledge of all fruits and herbs and balms and spices, and of all that is healing and sweet in fields and groves, and savory in meats. It means carefulness, and inventiveness, and watchfulness, and willingness, and readiness of appliance. It means the economy of your great grandmother, and the science of modern chemists. It means much tasting and no wasting; it means English thoroughness and French art and Arabian hospitality; and it means, in fine, that you are to be perfectly and always ladies—*loaf-givers*; and as you are to see imperatively that everybody has something pretty to put on, so you are to see even yet more imperatively that everybody has something nice to eat."

## BREAKFAST.

Hurry down stairs before the master of the house is up, or if he is also an early riser, be sure the newspaper is at hand to occupy him while you give the breakfast room a glance, and then help with the breakfast.

The beefsteak, or a chop or two, will be all the meat needed, a few of the cold potatoes fried brown, some hot rolls, and boiled eggs, with tea or coffee, give a very nice breakfast.

## A DINNER FOR TWO PERSONS.

WHEN the wedding journey is over the husband reports at his office, and the wife is, for the first time, alone, with the weight of her new dignity and the burden of ordering dinner.

Get a nice steak—porterhouse is the most economical for a tête-à-tête; sirloin where five or six dine. Have it cut an inch thick, and be sure it is not fresh killed. Do not try to *look* experienced till you really are. Throw trades-folk upon their honor and they will seldom impose upon you—if they do so once, return the article; if the second time, go elsewhere for supplies. Altercations with trades-people are not profitable. Order a few apples, some potatoes, and one seasonable vegetable; a nice dish of fruit, with a cup of coffee, and cigar afterwards, will be a dinner fit for a prince, in the opinion of the young Benedict.

## GOING INTO THE KITCHEN.

Throw off the dusty traveling dress, slip on a wrapper, and give a look to affairs in the kitchen. Have the potatoes peeled, cut lengthwise into four parts, so that the pieces are shaped like the quarters of an orange; then throw them into cold water.

### RICE.

Cull and wash the rice, and then pour boiling water over it, in proportion; three pints of water to one cup of rice, but half a cup will suffice for a dinner, if there be but a small party to dine. Salt to taste. By putting on the full quantity of water at once, the ebullition of boiling keeps the rice from sticking to the saucepan. Stir it *at first*, and be sure that not one kernel adheres; but after the rice has swelled so as to absorb most of the water, do not stir at all, if the kernels are to remain whole, but drain off the rest of the water and set the saucepan away from the hot fire, cover closely and let it finish cooking in its own steam. It ought to boil *rapidly* for ten minutes, and then steam for three-quarters of an hour. Just before serving, drop a little piece of butter into the saucepan, but do not stir at all; dish it as lightly as possible. Every kernel ought to be dry, yet perfectly soft. Sometimes while the rice is steaming a little milk can be added; but be very careful then not to let it burn; the milk is easily scorched. If water enough is put on at first, and the rice carefully stirred, not one particle will adhere to the saucepan. Cooked in this way rice is an excellent vegetable, and no dinner ought to be served without it, even if there are potatoes, which many use instead.

### APPLE SAUCE.

While the rice is steaming the apples can be pared, cored, and stewed, to eat *hot* with the beefsteak. This is an old-fashioned New England relish, and delicious, too.

Put just enough water on the apples to keep them from burning—not a drop more. Too much water makes them flat and insipid. Never *stir* apple sauce. Stirring lets the steam escape, and then the sauce is lumpy, and must be sifted through a colander. Let the apples cook briskly. Shake the saucepan once or twice, keep them on the boil till done; never let them simmer or cook over a very slow fire, it makes the sauce dark. Add the sugar, less to eat with meat than for tarts, or to eat with bread and butter. Cook the sugar one minute, watch it all the time, lest it burn; then to bring out the flavor put in a pinch of salt. Do not forget this. Never peel apples with a steel knife; stir with a clean wooden spoon. Keep one spoon for apple sauce. Of course it has been cooked in a porcelain or agate saucepan; but, as soon as done, take it up at once, so it will be light-colored and transparent. If the apples are peeled long before cooking, they will turn dark unless laid in cold water, but they certainly lose some of their flavor by being in the cold water any length of time.

The quicker food is prepared and the sooner served, the better it is. The apple sauce can stand on one side in the sauce dish, as it need not be piping hot.

### POTATOES.

The potatoes will be better for lying a while in cold water; if old they should lie an hour at least. Throw the pieces into some water that is boiling sharp—enough to cover them. Salt it well. Keep them boiling till soft to the touch, but not broken. Strain off every drop of water, put them in a vegetable dish that will bear heat, and place in the oven; then quickly put into the hot spider that is ready upon the range or stove, a piece of butter, and, as on the first day there are no drippings, take a small bit of the fat from the beefsteak, and cut it into little pieces to simmer with the butter, throw into the hot butter and fat a handful of fine breadcrumbs; or, if there is time, cut the bread into small dice; brown, but do not burn, and turn them over the potatoes. The hot fat can be seasoned with about a quarter of a small onion, chopped very, very fine, but it is not best to venture that always, for every one does not like onion, though it is a great aid to digestion. One secret of French cooking being healthful is that onion and garlic are largely used, but disguised. Chopped onion, gently browned, imparts a delicate flavor to sauces and ragouts that nothing else gives.

### BEEFSTEAK.

Get the gridiron ready, lay the steak in good shape upon it, put it over the brisk coals, but not too near; it is a great mistake to scorch meat in broiling. In less than a minute one side will be slightly browned, turn and sprinkle evenly with salt and perhaps a little pepper; turn again, sprinkle the second browned side with salt. Keep turning every minute, till done, to prevent juice escaping upon the fire. If the fat blazes up, hold the steak away a moment so that it does not catch the smoke.

Five minutes is long enough to cook the steak; put it upon a hot platter with a small bit of butter—not too much, it spoils the flavor of the meat to have it swimming in butter.

## DRESSING FOR DINNER.

Now that everything is ready, there will be time enough to run up stairs, cool the flushed face with a dash of *rice* powder—never use water to the face when over-heated—smooth the hair, and change the wrapper for that pretty dress lying ready upon the bed; the ruffles are basted at neck and wrist, so it takes but a minute to slip in on. There is a ring at the door. Be ready to receive your sole guest, for the first home dinner.

## NEVER WASTE COLD VICTUALS.

There was quite a large piece of steak left over. It was put aside in the meat safe with the other remnants from dinner —never waste one morsel of food; there are too many suffering for the want of it. There is no need of throwing away any thing.

### USING UP THE COLD STEAK.

The cold steak should be cut into very thin, long strips. Take the cold gravy, pour a table-spoonful of boiling water over the platter, in order to get it all, rub a spoonful of butter and flour together, add to the gravy a very little more water, not too much—you do not wish to deluge the meat—sprinkle a little pepper into the pipkin, and let the gravy just come to a boil; as it boils, put in the meat and turn it out at once into a dish in which you have laid a half slice of buttered toast. If you do not *cook* the meat, just warming it in the gravy, it will be tender and juicy as the day before. Any cold roast or boiled meat can be warmed up in this way. But most cooks insist upon *cooking* the meat, which makes it tough as shoe-leather. The gravy can be seasoned with onion, parsley, Worcestershire sauce, or whatever one fancies.

### SEASON LIGHTLY.

It is best when young to avoid the excessive use of spices and condiments of all kinds. A little spice and seasoning is not injurious; indeed, it not only makes food more palatable, but aids the digestion. But the use of too highly seasoned food leads to the development of very serious organic diseases, and, as the appetite grows by what it feeds upon, the taste of those who habitually use these things becomes cloyed, and finally relishes nothing. Study so to cook that the natural flavor of every dish shall be preserved.

### FRESH EGGS.

It is a mistake to eat an egg before it is one day old—it requires ten hours for the white to set properly, and not before that do they acquire their delicate flavor.

In using eggs be sure to break each one separately into a cup, for sometimes a dish full of fresh eggs will be spoiled by a careless cook breaking a suspicious one into the mass, just at the last. Try each egg by itself, even if the product of your own poultry-yard; an unworthy one may chance amongst them.

### BOILING EGGS SOFT.

Of the many receipts for boiling eggs there is really but one sure. Some put them in cold water and let it come to a boil, but they are apt to let the water boil a while, and then the eggs are too hard. Others take boiling water at first, and stand, watch in hand, counting three minutes. Still another counts just one hundred, and yet the eggs come to grief.

There is an egg-boiler made of block-tin, double sides, to retain the heat; the eggs are put into a rack, the tin is filled with boiling water, closed, and set upon the table at once.

Eggs cooked in this manner cannot get too hard, and the white is like a jelly, never tough and leathery. One needs to eat the white as well as the yolk of an egg to get the full amount of nourishment contained in it.

If you have no egg-boiler take a small tin pail—a pint pail is big enough for two eggs—put in the eggs, fill with boiling water; but as the sides are not double, to prevent the heat radiating too quickly, before the eggs are done, wrap the pail in a thick napkin as it is placed upon the table.

### HARD BOILED EGGS.

Let the eggs boil *six* minutes, dip them for a moment in cold water, which contracts the inner membrane so that the shell can be easily removed without breaking the egg. Cut each egg in halves, lengthwise, put a bit of butter and a little salt upon each half. They must be eaten while very hot.

Eggs done in this manner are delicate and digestible, and if nicely prepared it is a very pretty dish. The bright yellow yolk in the clear white frame has a very appetizing look.

Never boil eggs for salads, sauces, or any other purpose, more than ten minutes. Place them for *five* minutes to cool before removing their shells. Nothing is more indigestible than an egg too hard boiled.

### MAKING COFFEE.

It is simple enough to make, but few can do it. In hotels and restaurants the tea and coffee are made by steam, and to those who come first it is good, but as the coffee must remain some hours before all are served, the last running is sure to have a dead insipid taste. There are various coffee machines adapted to private use, and many by experience are known to be good, but they are expensive and complicated, needing intelligent handling; and coffee is never better than when made as it was in New England a century ago.

Then it was fresh roasted, under a careful supervision, that not one kernel should burn; it was ground while the kettle was boiling. The coffee-grounds were just wet with cold water and a little white of egg, or a bit of the shell, or even a piece of fish skin the size of a shilling, the boiling water added; it cooked briskly for five minutes, then a table-spoonful of cold water was put into the pot, a little of the coffee poured into a cup, then poured back into the pot—this was to clear the nose from the grounds that gathered in boiling—then the coffee-pot was put to the back of the hearth or stove to settle, while the breakfast was dished. Good rich cream was served with that coffee, which had as delicious aroma as any cup made from the most expensive coffee machine. The whole secret lies in the boiling hot water, the freshly ground coffee, the quick boiling and quick serving before all the true flavor has steamed away. Boiled coffee is said to be more nutritious and less exciting to the nerves than French or leached coffee. Here the grandmother's quaint invention served every purpose. A flannel bag, to hold the coffee, hung inside of a fine muslin one, allowed the coffee to slowly distill into the closed pitcher below. But this mode never became popular in old New England. It took more coffee, and they thought the liquid had a *raw* taste compared with the old method. The grounds can be boiled and the water used to wet the fresh coffee, but it detracts somewhat from its fine flavor, so the old grounds are best used as an extra beverage for persons working hard and needing some stimulant more than plain water.

### TEA.

The Russians boil the water for tea one hour. Certainly no tea tastes like theirs. The best Russian tea is brought in caravans over-land and has not suffered from seasickness. They drink it from glasses, held in silver frames, like our soda-water glasses. No milk is used, and generally a little arrack brings out the true flavor. It is certain the water must not only boil, but it must boil thoroughly to make good tea, and that is all the boiling to be done. The tea must never boil. Rinse the tea-pot with hot water; while it is still steaming, put in the tea; add a few spoonsful of water, take off the lid of the tea-kettle, set the tea-pot in the place of it. After about two minutes fill up the tea-pot and take it away from the fire. It is sure to get to simmering if left standing near the stove.

The English have a tea-cosy, a thick hood, more or less ornamental, to put over the tea-pot while it is brewing; but if you have no cosy take a square of flannel and wrap it close around the teapot, and let it brew for five or six minutes. If the tea is made upon the table by a spirit lamp, do not draw off all the good tea and then fill up the teapot, but keep adding a little water after every two or three cups. In this way the tea is good to the last. But the water must boil. The New England rule was to put the sugar and cream into each cup before pouring in the tea. It was thought that it changed the flavor to add them afterwards. Then again they say milk should never be used with tea (cream perhaps), as the tannin, in the tea, forms with the milk a very indigestible curd.

### ICED TEA

Is now offered at supper and at lunch. If you wish to have it perfect, and without the least trace of bitterness, put the tea in cold water hours before it is to be used; the delicate flavor of the tea and abundant strength will be extracted, and there will not be a trace—if one's taste is the judge—of the tannic acid which renders tea so often disagreeable and undrinkable. You need not use more than the usual quantity of tea. If it is to be served at a 1 o'clock meal, put it in water soon after breakfast, and ice a few minutes before serving. The best way is to have ice broken in a pitcher and put one lump in each glass.

### CHOCOLATE AND COCOA.

Chocolate is rather a heavy article for breakfast. It is more a dainty for lunch or to offer a visitor out of meal hours. There are various preparations of cocoa that are excellent, and each package is marked with directions that must be followed accurately. Many boil the chocolate and milk together, which is a mistake. The chocolate should be cooked in water and allowed to boil thoroughly, which is impossible when there is milk mixed with it. It is very indigestible cooked with milk.

The boiled milk or cream should be served separately. Sometimes the white of egg is added to chocolate, and the whole brought to a light foam with a wheel for that purpose like an egg-beater. It is very delicate this way.

## SOUPS.

SOUP is the standard for the first course at dinner. Eminent physicians have written against diluting the gastric juice with fluids before commencing a hearty meal, but the latest authority states that a few spoonfuls of light bouillon is quickly absorbed by the digestive organs, and serves to tone up the system for the harder work upon the solids of the meal.

Therefore, a soup to precede a dinner should be a clear soup with little body, but for lunch a vegetable, or some of the great variety of heavier soups, for which the French and Germans are so famous, could be taken with advantage.

These soups are made with or without meat stock for the foundation. There are always a great many scraps of meat bones of roast meat, trimmings of chops, the bones of fowls, etc., that ought to be put into the stock-pot, boiled for several hours, skimmed and strained. This serves for the basis of gravies, ragouts, and, with the addition of vegetables and thickening, makes an excellent soup.

Be sure to crack all the bones, as they contain a great deal of gelatine.

**Mock Turtle Soup.**—Ingredients: Half a calf's head with the skin on, 2 lbs. lean veal, 2 lbs. beef, ½ lb. mild, lean bacon, three onions, three carrots, a head of celery, a small bunch of mixed sweet herbs, a little parsley, some seasoning, a pinch of curry powder, a table-spoonful of anchovy sauce, 4 ozs. butter, some roux, a little soy, a little allspice, a blade of mace, a handful of basil, four lemons, a pinch of sugar, and half a pint of sherry.

How to use them: Well wash and trim the half head, place it in a stew-pan, cover with water, and boil until tender (time, about two hours or less); when cooked take it out of the liquor and let it get cold; add to the liquor the veal and beef, some seasoning, the sweet herbs (including the handful of herb basil), some allspice, a blade of mace, and the celery; let boil, take off the scum, and let simmer three hours; peel, scrape, and wash the carrots and onions, cut them in thin slices, and fry them in 4 ozs. butter a light brown; add the curry powder, bacon cut up finely, let fry together a few minutes; then stir in two table-spoonfuls of flour, mix well together, fry one minute; then stir in with the meat, boil up quickly; skim it, add a little roux, some soy, a pinch of sugar, and the anchovy sauce; strain through a fine hair sieve, add the sherry and the juice of two lemons, simmer, and take off the scum as it rises; cut the meat off the head into square pieces (about an inch in size), add it to the soup. Let boil, and serve immediately. Cut lemons and cayenne pepper to be served with the soup.

**Consommé.**—This is a rich nourishing broth, made with lean beef and chicken. Old fowl make stronger broth than young ones. A hen gives a more delicate flavor, and the meat is tender and good for fricassée or salad, if not boiled too long. Sometimes the chicken is partly roasted, and then thrown into the pot with the beef. Boil the chicken two, the beef four, hours. For two quarts of good consommé two or three chickens and four lbs. of beef is not too much.

Season lightly with pepper and salt, and with vegetables and herbs also, unless one object to their flavor in the meat. In that case the broth can be strained, cooled, and set aside, the vegetables cooked separately and added as required.

For an invalid this broth is often more palatable without vegetables or seasoning of any kind but salt.

Highly seasoned, a small cup of it is placed by each guest at supper parties, or is offered at afternoon teas to gentlemen, and those persons who object to spoiling their six o'clock dinner with the sweets served at receptions. It acts in these cases as a tonic and appetizer.

**Mutton Broth** with barley, or **Veal Broth** with rice, are very palatable, and less heating to the system, particularly in the spring of the year.

**Tomato Soup.**—Two quarts ripe tomatoes, remove the skins, stew half an hour, put in an even tea-spoonful of soda. 1 pint sweet milk, 1 pint water, 1 table-spoonful flour, mixed with the milk, 1 table-spoonful butter; pepper and salt to taste; cook one-half hour longer.

**Spring Soup.**—When the young vegetables begin to appear in market, a spring soup relishes, when everything else fails.

Take a delicate soup stock—chicken or veal broth is better than beef stock. Take a handful of each kind of vegetable in the market, a few green peas, a bunch of young carrots, a few beans, one small turnip, a few button onions, a sprig of parsley, a leaf or two of young celery, and a head of lettuce. Cook the peas, carrots, onions, turnips, and beans till soft, add to the soup, just before dishing or putting into the tureen, the parsley and celery cut fine, and the inner leaves of the lettuce; do not put in the thick part of the lettuce leaves which are bitter, tear out the center rib of the larger leaves. This is delightfully refreshing on a hot spring day, when nothing tastes good. It must be made with great care, not to cook it too long to wither the fresh young greens, and to be sure that the flavor of one vegetable does not predominate over another.

**Beef Tea.**—Broil beef slightly, cut into small pieces, and press out the juice with a lemon squeezer. This gives the pure juice of the meat alone, and if there be great exhaustion is quickly made.

Another way: Cut the meat into small pieces, put them in a bottle, cork, and let it boil for one or two hours in a pot of water.

The late Dr. Peaslee maintained that the Liebig receipt was preferable, as it extracted all the substance by the double action of heat and water. Take fresh, lean meat, cut into small dice, or chop fine, just cover the meat with cold water, let it stand where it is warm, but not hot enough to bring it to a boil, for one hour. When on the *point* of boiling remove at once from the fire.

## FRUIT.

THE table ought never to be without it—fresh or cooked—oranges, melons, apples, pears, berries, grapes, or whatever is in season, set off the breakfast table, and the best time to eat them is before commencing the meal.

For dessert, for luncheon and dinner, fruit ought to supplement pies and puddings to a great extent.

Many persons cannot digest the raw fruits, who are able to eat them cooked.

Fruit should be cooked quickly; add just water enough to keep it from burning—some fruits require none at all—use very little sugar, which must be added just as it is done, and allowed to cook in but a moment. If the sugar and fruit simmer together it destroys the natural flavor, giving sweetmeats instead of sauce. Stewed fruit must be eaten when quite fresh, as there being so little sugar it soon spoils if kept more than a day or two.

Sweetmeats are made by specialists, and sold almost cheaper than one can make them, but it seems nicer to have a few things of one's own preparing.

### CURRANT JELLY

Is a relish for roast mutton and game that nothing else supplies. Heat the currants in an earthen jar or porcelain kettle. Throw the heated mass on a hair sieve to drain, part at a time, to let it cool so as to be able to handle it in the bag, through which the remainder of the juice must be pressed. Extract all the juice and as much of the pulp as possible, as this makes the jelly stiffer. If properly made there is no necessity of using gelatine to stiffen the jelly. Our grandmothers did without it, and we can, too. After the mass has been squeezed perfectly dry, measure the juice; for each pint weigh out a pound of granulated sugar, or order it weighed by the grocer to be very accurate. Put the juice on the fire to boil, the sugar into a large pan, and set it into the oven to become perfectly hot. Do not melt or scorch the sugar. Keep the juice boiling constantly for about twenty minutes, skimming it, or till the watery part is evaporated; then add the sugar, which, being perfectly hot, does not cool the syrup, which ought to continue to boil, but for not more than ten minutes, when it will be ready to put into the glasses. Set where the light and sun will strike them for twenty-four hours, then cut a piece of paper the size of the jelly glass, dip in brandy and lay it upon the tops, afterwards put on the covers of the jars, or, if there are no covers, tie paper tightly round each one, or paste the edges to the glass.

Follow these directions carefully, and the jelly will be a success. On or about the 20th of July is the best season for preserving. The currants are then fully ripe, and in a better state than later. Some object to the exceeding acid of the currant alone, and take one-third raspberry juice to two-thirds currant, but as a relish for meat it is better pure. With the raspberry it is nicer for tarts and cakes.

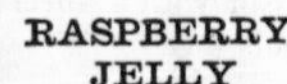

### RASPBERRY JELLY

Is made in the same manner, but it is not necessary to take quite as much sugar. The secret of getting the jelly is to thoroughly extract the water by boiling the juice before adding the sugar; for when the sugar and juice are cooked too long together, the syrup becomes of a ropy consistency, and will seldom make a stiff jelly, and this is why inexperienced persons think it necessary to add gelatine, which spoils the delicate color and taste, and renders the jelly much more likely to mold and spoil.

### RASPBERRY JAM.

Get nice fresh fruit, pick it carefully and break with a wooden spoon. Do not rub it into a pulp, breaking the seeds. Boil the fruit first about fifteen minutes, then put sugar and fruit together, a little less than pound for pound; six pounds of fruit and five of sugar. Cook, simmering gently but steadily, for twenty minutes. Never stew sweetmeats over a slow fire. They must be watched constantly. If visitors cause interruptions they are apt to be spoiled.

## THE MYSTERY OF MAKING BREAD.

A LADY who has kept house for many years is of the opinion that, "Loaf bread interferes with the salvation of more housekeepers than any other one thing in the world."

To make two quarts of bread or rolls, take four or five nice, large Irish potatoes, peel and cut them up, and put to boil in just water enough to cover them. When done mash smooth in the same water, and when cool (not cold), add a half tea-cupful of yeast, or if you use compressed yeast, the sixth part of a cake dissolved in tepid water; a dessert-spoonful of sugar, a little salt, a table-spoonful of lard, and a pint of flour. Mix together lightly. This batter should be very soft and quite sticky. Set it (covered) in a warm place to rise. In two or three hours it will be risen; it will be full of bubbles and look like yeast. Now work in the rest of the flour, and, if necessary, add a little cold water. The dough should be rather soft, and must not be kneaded more than half an hour. Set it to rest in a moderately warm place for about four hours. If wanted, it can now be baked at once; but, if not, take a spoon and push the dough down from the top and sides of the vessel containing it, and let it rise again. It can rise thus three times. Now knead until smooth, perhaps add a little more flour. Some of it can be taken, rolled out thin, and baked for rolls. Let the rolls rise a while after they are in the pan. The baking pan must be greased, and the rolls must not touch each other.

The bread must rise a few minutes after it is put in the baking tins.

It has long been known in Vienna, that if an oven be cleaned with a wisp of moist straw, the crust of the bread baked in it assumes a beautiful yellow tint. In Paris they have acted upon this idea, and constructed ovens in which a bunch of moist straw can be placed near the opening, so that the current of air drives in the moisture from the straw.

**PARKER HOUSE ROLLS (Boston Receipt).**—Two quarts flour, 1 tea-spoonful lard, 1 table-spoonful butter, 2 table-spoonfuls sugar, 1 tea-spoonful salt, 1 pint scalded milk (cooled), half cup of yeast. Make a hole in the center of the flour, pour in the milk and yeast, and stir in part of the flour The next morning knead in the rest of the flour, the sugar, lard, and butter. Roll out half an inch thick, cut in squares, spread each square with a little butter, fold the sides together, let them rise again until light, and bake in a very quick oven.

**SARATOGA ROLLS.**—Two quarts of flour, 1 tea-spoonful salt, large table-spoonful yeast, butter (size of an egg), 1 pint warm milk. Make over night.

**GERMAN PUFFS.**—Half pound butter, half pint milk, boil; beat in very smoothly a cup of sifted flour, cook; set to cool. When cold stir in six eggs, leaving out whites of two; sugar to taste, flavor also. Bake in well-buttered cups. Sauce: one cup white wine, two cups of sugar and one egg, and the extra white well-beaten; stir gradually into the boiling wine, and serve at once.

**SALLY LUNN.**—One quart flour, 3 spoonfuls Royal Baking Powder, 1 pint milk or cream, heaping table-spoonful butter, 2 spoonfuls white sugar; melt the butter; add the milk; salt slightly. Sift the flour, sugar, and baking powder together. Stir the flour quickly into the milk. The mixture should be just stiff enough to drop from a spoon into the baking pan. One spoonful for each bun. Do not drop too near together. Bake in very hot oven. Break them apart and lay upon a napkin to serve. Instead of baking powder use yeast, and set to rise over night.

**JOHNNY CAKE.**—One quart meal, 1 pint flour, 2 eggs, 2 spoonfuls baking powder; water or milk to make a stiff batter. If water is used a small piece of butter must be added. Some like a little sugar also.

**PANCAKES** (French style).—Make a thin paste with 1 pound of flour, 4 eggs, 2 table-spoonfuls of sweet-oil, 1 of French brandy, a little salt, the necessary quantity of lukewarm milk and water. Let it stand two or three hours, then put an ounce of butter, lard, or oil in the frying-pan, and set it over a brisk fire; when hot, put some of the batter in it with a ladle, spreading it so as to cover the bottom of the pan; brown and dust white sugar over both sides. Serve warm. Buckwheat and other pancakes can be made the same way.

**WAFFLES.**—Make a thin batter with 8 ounces of flour, 6 ounces of pulverized sugar, 2 eggs, a few drops of essence to flavor, half a liquor-glass of brandy or rum, and milk sufficient for batter. Warm the mold; butter both sides; put in some of the paste, close gently; turn to heat both sides equally; dust with sugar. Eat either warm or cold. With a good fire a minute suffices to bake them.

**MUHLENBERG GINGER BREAD.**—One pint of molasses, half pound brown sugar, 3 eggs, quarter of a pound of butter, quarter of a pound of lard, ½ pint of sour milk, 4 tea-spoonfuls baking soda, 1¾ pounds of flour; ginger, cloves, and cinnamon to taste. Bake in large loaf; or add raisins and currants, and bake in small, shallow tins.

**HOMINY or SPIDER BREAD.**—Mash cold boiled hominy (to free from lumps), into milk, 2 eggs to a quart, a little salt, white meal and flour to form a batter; beat thoroughly. Bake in quick oven. Spread the mixture about one-half inch thick over the pan. Use but little flour, the hominy must predominate.

**BREAD CAKES.**—Take bread crumbs, well dried, soak over night in just enough milk to soften them. In the morning add a little salt; beat the crumbs till smooth, add two eggs well beaten separately, and drop one spoonful at a time upon a hot griddle.

**MUFFINS.**—One quart of milk, 2 eggs, well beaten separately, a piece of butter the size of an egg, and flour enough to make a stiff batter. Stir in half a pint of yeast, and let stand till perfectly light. Bake in quick oven, in well-greased muffin rings.

**BUCKWHEAT CAKES.**—One quart of buckwheat flour, half a cupful of yeast, half a pint of corn meal, 2 eggs, a little salt, 1 table-spoonful of molasses. Mix with warm water into a thin batter, and let it rise over night. The eggs can well be omitted in winter when expensive and scarce.

The remains of the batter must be left in the dish in which it is mixed. A pitcher is the best for this purpose. This batter will serve to raise the cakes for the next morning without additional yeast, and the cakes will be better than the first.

## MEATS.

ROASTS require that, as far as possible, the nutritive juices should be well preserved, without which a joint is rendered comparatively worthless.

Let the meat be kept in the ice-box or a cool place till ready to cook. Scrape clean, rather than wash it. If washing be necessary let it be done quickly, allowing the water to run over the meat, not plunging it into the pan. Rub well with pepper and salt, and tie in a compact shape instead of using skewers, which are so difficult to remove when the meat is cooked.

The larger the piece the juicier and better the roast. Have a quick oven to start with, letting it be cooler after a while. But if meat is put into a slow oven it will be tough, the pores will not close quickly and much of the juice is wasted.

If impossible to attain heat enough, as is often the case with poor ovens, then take a small bit of butter and some clean drippings, or a piece of the fat from the meat itself; put it into the baking pan, set it over the fire, when hot place the meat in it, turning it upon all sides till browned crisp, but not burned. Then add a table-spoonful or two of water, and set in the oven; it must be kept basted, and it is well to dredge once or twice with flour.

Some cooks will declare that not one drop of water should go into the pan; there should never be enough to *steam* the meat, merely enough to keep the gravy from burning. It is properly baking meat to cook it in an oven; roasting meat requires an open fire, and the cold, fresh air, coming in contact with it while cooking imparts a peculiar flavor that cannot be attained in a close oven. Baked meat has a dead taste compared with roast. An English cook acknowledges no other method; but the American arrangements rarely allow the luxury of the big, clear fire and ample space required for the roasting jack. Some housekeepers, who insist upon it, manage to get their meat roasted by the usual small fire-grate of the range.

Meat requires about one-quarter of an hour for each pound, but every cook needs to exercise her judgment, in this, as well as in all other household matters; there is no rule without its exception.

Meat should be so well basted that it does not dry up, and, when cut, the juice ought to stream out in the track of the knife. There should be enough of this gravy for every one, and it is much more healthful than made gravy. However, some prefer the latter. This is made, after the meat is placed upon the platter, by draining off nearly all the fat from the dripping-pan, then set it upon the open fire; dredge in flour, stirring till it is brown; add a little water and strain into gravy boat. There is usually salt and pepper enough that has come from the meat; otherwise some can be added, or any other seasoning according to taste.

**Boiling** is one of the most ordinary modes of cooking meat, and yet it is very seldom done properly.

The water must boil when the meat is first placed in it, and be kept boiling for about two or three minutes till the pores of the meat are well closed, then the pot must be placed where it will not boil any more, but it must simmer constantly, and be kept well skimmed and tightly covered. Have as little water as possible.

Let the cooking be done mostly by the steam. If the water boil away add more, which must be at the boiling point.

Do not salt the meat till partly done. Salt toughens, and the long cooking destroys the flavor of the salt itself. When the meat is done there ought to be barely water enough to make the amount of gravy needed. Capers are used for mutton, oysters for boiled turkey.

Boiled meat should be served at least once a week. In France and Germany it is used every day. But this is the meat that has furnished the stock for the soup, and would scarcely contain nourishment enough for the exhausting effects of the American climate and greater activity in business habits.

**POT ROAST.**—Prepare meat as for roasting, lay in an iron or porcelain-lined pot a piece of butter, onion, herbs, bay leaf, or whatever seasoning one likes. Let the meat brown in the butter, turning upon all sides; then cover very closely, and steam for two or three hours, shaking and turning from time to time.

**YORKSHIRE PUDDING.**—Six table-spoonfuls of flour, six eggs, beaten, a little salt, and a gill of milk; mix well together with a wooden spoon, that there are no lumps, then add three gills more of milk. Set in a shallow pan under a piece of meat roasting before the fire, or if the fire is not large enough, bake in the oven, adding a few tea-spoonfuls of the gravy as it drips from the roast. It can be made with less eggs by using prepared flour, and is quite as good.

## TIME REQUIRED TO COOK MEATS.

MUTTON.—A leg of 8 lbs., will require two hours and a half. A chine or saddle of 10 or 11 lbs., two hours and a half. A shoulder of 7 lbs., one hour and a half. A loin of 7 lbs., one hour and three quarters; and about the same time (1¾ h.) is required for a neck and breast.

BEEF.—The sirloin of 15 lbs., from three hours and three quarters to four hours. Ribs of beef, from 15 to 20 lbs., take three hours to three hours and a half.

VEAL.—A fillet from 12 to 16 lbs., takes from four to five hours, with a good fire. A loin generally takes three hours. A shoulder from three hours to three hours and a half. A neck two hours. A breast from an hour and a half to two hours.

LAMB.—Hind quarter of 8 lbs., takes from an hour and three-quarters to two hours. Fore-quarter of 10 lbs., about two hours. Leg of 5 lbs., from an hour and a quarter to an hour and a half. Shoulder or breast, an hour, with a good fire.

PORK.—A leg of 8 lbs., requires about three hours. Griskin, an hour and a half. A spare-rib of 8 or 9 lbs. requires about two hours and a half to three hours to roast it thoroughly. A bald spare-rib of 8 lbs., an hour and a quarter. A loin of 5 lbs., from two hours to two hours and a half, when very fat. A sucking pig (3 weeks old), about an hour and a half.

POULTRY.—A large turkey requires about three hours. A turkey weighing 10 pounds, two hours, and a small one an hour and a half. A full-grown fowl, about an hour and a half; a pullet, from half an hour to forty minutes. A large goose, two hours. A green goose, forty minutes. A large duck, from an hour and a quarter to an hour and three quarters.

**DANIEL WEBSTER'S CHOWDER.**—Four table-spoonfuls of onion fried in salt pork, one quart of boiled potatoes well mashed, one and one half pounds of sea biscuit, one tea-spoonful of thyme and summer savory, half bottle of mushroom catsup, one bottle of claret or port wine, half nutmeg grated, some cloves, a little mace and allspice, six pounds of sea-bass or cod, cut in slices; 25 large oysters, a little black pepper, a few slices of lemons; the whole put in a pot and covered with an inch of water, let it boil one hour, stir it gently. Chowders are made in a dozen different ways, but the result is about the same. It is generally admitted that boatmen prepare it better than others.

**OYSTERS.**—Stew in their own liquor, butter, salt, and pepper, and many think them improved with the addition of milk or cream, mace, parsley, or nutmeg. Cracker is preferable to flour for thickening. Lay the grated cracker in the tureen and pour in the oysters.

A nice way for a sick person is to lay a few good sized oysters in a little pan with their liquor. Set in the oven or upon the fire for two or three minutes, or just long enough to scald, without cooking. They are as delicate as raw oysters, without the chilling effect to which many object.

**PUFF OMELET.**—Take half a table-spoonful of flour and make it into a smooth paste, with a little cream. Break five or six eggs, beat all together. Then add a cup of cream, and a little salt. Put a piece of butter the size of an egg into the omelet pan, when it bubbles, pour in the eggs, when it is half cooked over the fire, set it in a hot oven to finish cooking, and serve as soon as done, or it will fall and be soggy. Have it ready, but it is best cooked after the family have assembled.

**APPLE OR PEACH FRITTERS.**—Chop the apples or cut in thin slices, make a light batter of two eggs, a little milk and flour, one tea-spoonful baking powder, stir in fruit, drop from ladle into hot fat. They will assume fantastic shapes. Drain well, sprinkle with sugar. Must be eaten with wine, lemon juice, or cider. Pineapple can be used, or any kind of fruit.

**NEW ENGLAND SHORT CAKE.**—Take cream (if no cream is to be had, take milk), and melt a large piece of butter, one quart flour, three tea-spoonfuls baking powder, one pint milk, one quarter pound butter, half tea-spoonful salt. Sift flour, baking powder, and salt together; stir into milk and butter quickly as possible. Do not knead or work over at all. Keep it soft as can be shaped. Bake in thin cakes (size of pie-plate), prick the cakes with a fork, to prevent air bubbles puffing one part more than another. Split, butter evenly, and grate a little nutmeg upon the crust, fill with strawberries, raspberries, stewed apples, or any kind of fruit. These are far more wholesome than pies made of rich pastry.

**OLD FASHIONED COMPOSITION CAKE.**—One and three quarter pounds of sugar, one and three quarter pounds of flour, three quarters pound of butter, one nutmeg, four eggs, one pint of milk, one tea-spoonful saleratus, one glass of brandy. Raisins and other fruit can be added.

**WEDDING CAKE.**—Take 1 lb. of flour, 1 lb. of sugar, 1 lb. of butter, 10 eggs, half pint of brandy, one-half ounce each of mace, nutmeg, cinnamon, and cloves; half pint of rose water, 2 lbs. of almonds, 4 lbs. of currants, 2 lbs. of raisins, 1 lb. of citron, 1 wine-glass of lemon peel chips, 1 wine-glass of orange peel chips, the juice of the lemon and orange, and 1 tea-spoonful saleratus. This makes one loaf, bake in a six-quart pan, the sides and bottom lined with a paste made of flour and water without salt or butter, rolled out very thin. If it commences to burn, lay an oiled paper over the top. It is best baked in a brick oven, and needs two hours.

**COTTAGE PUDDING.**—One cup sugar, two eggs, butter size of one egg, one cup sweet milk, about three cups of flour, or enough to thicken, three tea-spoonfuls baking powder. Bake.

**SAUCE FOR COTTAGE PUDDING.**—Rub butter and sugar together, add a little cream and beat into it cut, ripe peaches.

**RICE PUDDING.**—Four table-spoonfuls of rice to one quart of milk, salt, sugar, and vanilla or other flavor. Wash the rice in cold water, add the milk, set in moderate oven, must bake very slowly, stirring it very often, add a little cold milk each time it is stirred, this gives it a creamy consistency.

**PLUM PUDDING.**—One pound of raisins, one pound of currants, one pound of suet, quarter of a pound of flour or *grated bread*, three ounces of sugar, one ounce and a half of grated lemon peel, one blade of mace, a little nutmeg and ginger grated, six eggs; work it well together, put in a cloth, tie firmly, allowing room to swell, and never let it stop boiling till done. Time to boil five or six hours.

## Miscellaneous Receipts.

**Airing.**—A sheet of finely perforated zinc, substituted for a pane of glass, in one of the upper squares of a chamber window, is the cheapest and best form of ventilation. No bedroom should be without it.

**Ants, To Destroy.**—1. Perfect cleanliness. 2. Pulverized borax sprinkled in places they frequent. 3. A few leaves of green wormwood, scattered among their haunts. 4. The use of camphor. 5. A sponge can be sprinkled with sugar and laid upon shelves where ants are numerous; the next morning plunge quickly into boiling water, and most of the intruders will be destroyed. 6. Carbolic acid wiped around the edges of the shelves and wherever they seem to come from. Little red ants cannot travel over wool or rag carpet. Set the meat-safe on coarse baize, cover the closet or pantry shelves with flannel, and the ants will disappear.

**Blankets, To Wash.**—The great secret of washing blankets properly is to give them plenty of water, and to change the water. The soap must be dissolved in the water; the water must not be too hot. Of course, blankets should not be boiled.

**Brass, To Polish.**—It is a mistake to clean brass with Bath brick, as is often done; the metal cleaned with it tarnishes quickly, besides having a pale yellow color, instead of the true golden hue. Rotten stone and oil are, thus far, the best things known for the purpose.

**Black Lace, To Clean.**—Dip a sponge into beer or cold tea, and damp the lace, taking care not to make it wet; place brown paper over it, and press with a warm iron. The lace will look glazed if the paper is not put between it and the iron. The lace must be brushed free from dust before it is made damp.

**Black Silk, To Clean.**—Ox-gall dissolved in hot water. Lay the silk out on a table—a marble one is the best; sponge both sides with the liquor; rinse in clean water. Or use beer and water, or gin and water. Again, an old black kid glove can be boiled in a quart of water till it is reduced to one pint; sponge the silk with this; it restores the color and stiffens the silk. A weak solution of gum arabic will stiffen silk, or a spoonful of honey placed in the last sponging water will give it the quality of new. Never iron with hot irons. Spread the silk over any smooth surface, or, better still, lay papers between the folds, and press under boards or two mattresses.

**Boards, To Take Ink Out of.**—Strong muriatic acid, or spirits of salts, applied with a piece of cloth, afterwards well washed with water.

**Bed-Bugs, To Exterminate.**—1. Perfect cleanliness. No bed-bugs or other vermin will infest a house, when the mistress is of orderly and cleanly habits and fine tastes. 2. Two ounces of red arsenic, one-fourth of a pound of white soap, one-half an ounce of camphor dissolved in a tea-spoonful of spirits, rectified, made into a paste of the consistency of cream. Place this mixture in the openings and cracks of the bedstead. 3. Where bed-bugs are present, the best, quickest, and handiest exterminator is kerosene or crude petroleum oil, drenching all parts of the article of furniture thoroughly and effectively. March and September are the best months for making an attack on bugs. Putting spirits of turpentine in the water for scrubbing floors destroys vermin.

**Burns.**—Should you ever burn your fingers while getting up a dinner, wet them with cold water, and hold as near the fire as you can without burning the other fingers. It will smart, but grin and bear it; the pain will leave as quick as it came, before you can count fifty. It will leave no blister, and you'll need no bandage; in fact, you will hardiy know which finger was burned. This receipt was given by a blacksmith, a poor, old, life-time convict, and it has never been found to fail.

**Clinkers.**—Oyster shells on top of a coal fire will cause the clinkers adhering to the sides of the grate, or to the fire-brick, to drop off.

**Candles.**—To make a candle burn all night, when, as in case of sickness, a dull light is wished, put finely powdered salt on the candle till it reaches the black part of the wick. In this way a mild and steady light may be kept through the night by a small piece of candle.

**Crickets.**—Cucumber rinds thrown around will destroy crickets.

**Cockroaches.**—Can also be destroyed by laying freshly cut cucumber rinds near their haunts.

**Complexions, Suitable Colors for.**—Complexions vary considerably, and, therefore, every one should not wear any particular color which may be in fashion. Blue and violet suit most complexions; orange and its companion tints of amber, yellow, primrose, etc., look well with a dark complexion, provided that it has some color, and is not sallow; scarlet and crimson are also becoming to brunettes; blondes can wear green, peach, brown, and pale blue; black also suits a fair complexion. Brown is the most becoming color to people who have reddish hair or freckled complexion. Drabs, grays, and neutral tints do not suit people who have pale or sallow complexions.

**Cold Cream** is best made of olive oil and white wax. It is often made of lard, but it is not so soothing and healing.

**Carpets, To Sweep.**—Sprinkle tea leaves, squeezed quite dry, over the carpet before sweeping. If tea leaves are scarce, tear up moist newspapers, or take small bits of cotton and linen rags, wet, and use like the leaves. The rags can be rinsed, dried, and used several times. Wheat bran moistened is good for almost any kind of carpets but Brussels. When carpets are well cleaned, sprinkle with salt, and fold; when laid, strew with slightly moistened bran before sweeping. This, with salt, will freshen them up wonderfully.

**Doors, To Prevent Creaking.**—Apply a little soap to the hinges, or take lard, soap, and blacklead, equal parts, mix and apply. Swing the door to and fro a few times to bring the entire hinge in contact with the mixture.

**Drink for Hot Weather.**—Two table-spoonfuls of Scotch oatmeal put into a large tumbler or small jug, and filled up with clear, cold water, well stirred up, and allowed to settle only until the large particles of meal fall to the bottom, forms a most refreshing drink in hot weather, and quenches thirst more than any other liquid.

**Deodorizers.**—One pound of green copperas, dissolved in one quart of boiling water, will destroy foul smells. Platt's chlorides, sprinkled over and under the bed, and diffused through the room with an atomizer, will instantly remove offensive odors. A few drops in water, used as a gargle, will sweeten a bad breath. A saucerful set in the kitchen, will counteract the fumes from frying or boiling. Chloride of lime, carbolic acid, and several other things are deservedly coming into general use. Many highly perfumed articles are often used for the purpose of deodorizing sick rooms; they are of no value whatever. They merely hide the offensive odor by adding something which for the time overpowers it without removing the cause, and actually do more harm than good.

**Flies, To Drive Away.**—Buy an ounce of oil of lavender, pour half of it in a pint bottle of cold water, and shake it up; the mixture is a mechanical one only; if dissolved in alcohol it is a perfect solution; but this becomes more expensive; scatter your water and oil of lavender on the table-cloth, and the flies will go away.

**Freckles.**—Take of corrosive sublimate 5 grains; muriatic acid, 30 drops; lump sugar, 1 ounce; alcohol, 2 ounces; rose water, 7 ounces. Agitate together till all is dissolved. Apply night and morning. Another remedy is to take of sal ammoniac, 2 drams; cologne water, 1 ounce; soft water, 1 pint. Mix.

**Glass Chimneys, To Prevent Cracking.**—If the chimney glass of a lamp be cut with a diamond on the convex side (outside), it will never crack, as the incision affords room for the expansion produced by the heat, and the glass, after it is cool, returns to its original shape, with only a scratch visible where the cut is made.

**Marble, To Clean.**—Mix together with water three parts of common soda, one part of finely-powdered chalk, and one part of pumice-stone; rub this well over the marble, and afterwards wash off with soap and water.

**Moths.**—These insects make very quick work when they attack woolens or furs—and great care must be taken to anticipate them. The moth millers begin to fly about with the first warm spring days, and then the housewife must look to her closets; remove everything from the shelves and hooks, brush the walls and ceiling carefully, lift the shelves and wipe out the corners with a damp cloth, wipe up the floor with a damp cloth or have it scrubbed, but do not sweep out the closet, as that disperses the eggs into the room to hatch and do more mischief. Sprinkle a little moth powder, pepper, or powdered camphor behind the shelves and along the surface. Hang all the woolens and furs, in the yard, or where they can get the sun and air. Choose a warm day, otherwise the moths will hide away from the cold in the seams and folds. Brush and beat the garments. Those that can be spared should be folded, wrapped in a newspaper—the ink is a good moth preventive. Pin them in linen cloths also, but be sure to close the bundles tight; moth powder, lumps of camphor, or carbolic paper, can be placed in each bundle, but careful airing and cleaning is the most effectual remedy against these destructive insects.

When the moths have once attacked a garment, do not, upon the first impulse, give it a good shaking, but take it to the yard at once, pick off the larvae, then lay the article in a tightly-covered wash-boiler, place this in hot water, and leave till the garment is heated through and through, and all life destroyed. Then it can be beaten and brushed, but ought never to be put away with other things lest there might be a stray moth left in spite of all these precautions.

Spirits of turpentine sprinkled in boxes and drawers will destroy and drive away moths. Almost any one of the essential oils is more or less efficacious.

**Mosquitoes and Fleas** can be driven out of a room by sprinkling oil of pennyroyal upon a cloth, and waiving it to and fro in every corner of the room will drive them towards the window or door. Hang up the cloth near the place where they are likely to enter. Insects dislike all strongly aromatic herbs. Cologne or camphor sprinkled upon the pillow will drive them away for a time.

**Picture Frames, To Prevent Flies from Injuring.**—Boil three or four onions in a pint of water; then with a gilding brush do over your glasses and frames, and the flies will not alight on the article so washed. This may be used without apprehension, as it will not do the least injury to the frames.

**Paste.**—To two large spoonfuls of fine flour put as much pounded resin as will lie on a shilling; mix with strong beer and boil half an hour. Let it cool before using. Rye flour and a little alum added while boiling, makes an adhesive paste as strong as glue.

**Rats, To Extirpate.**—The extirpation of rats may be accomplished either by means of trapping or poisoning. The rat-trap must be rendered attractive by some dainty morsel of food, and may also be sprinkled with rat scent. Rats are said to be very fond of powdered cantharides steeped in French brandy. Pastes and powders made from arsenic, tartar emetic, nux vomica, and other poisons, are very effective.

**Silver, To Clean.**—The best way to clean silver articles is to wash them first with warm water and soap, and afterwards polish them with pure London whiting and a piece of leather. As pure whiting, free of grits, cannot always be had, except in London, you may substitute hartshorn powder for it.

**Soot.**—If through careless handling of stove-pipes, or draughts from the chimney, soot fall upon the carpet, cover the spot thickly with salt, and the soot can be brushed up without injury to the carpet.

The fine soot that collects in the chimney and in the joints of the pipe is excellent for scouring tins, etc.

Use kerosene, or bath-brick, or powdered lime, to scour iron, tin, or copper; wash in hot suds, and polish with dry whiting.

**Stairs, To Wash.**—The sides of stairs and carpeted passages should be washed with a sponge, instead of linen or flannel, and then the edges will not be soiled.

**Tooth Powder.**—Pound together in a mortar, cream of tartar and chalk, of each half an ounce; myrrh, powdered, one drachm; orris root, powdered, half a drachm; and powdered bark, two drachms.

**To Remove Ink Stains from Linen.**—With a clear rag rub the spot with lemon juice in which is dissolved a small quantity of salt.

**To Remove Ink Stains from Dress Goods.**—Dissolve ten cents worth of oxalic acid in a pint of soft water; dip the stained spots in it quickly, and then into clear water, and rub well. If the goods remain in the acid the texture will be destroyed. If the color is affected, wet with a solution of ammonia and water; this will restore the original color.

**To Remove Nitrate of Silver Stains (Indelible Ink.)**—Cyanide of potassium is the most effective, but being highly poisonous, is extremely dangerous to use.

The cloth must be stretched over a bowl or cup of hot water, a little of the powder laid upon the stain or writing, then hot water dropped upon it—gently stirring the powder over the spot—then rinse. Be very careful not to inhale the steam arising from the cyanide.

Chloride of copper completely removes nitrate of silver stains from colored cotton cloth. It should be rinsed with hyposulphite of soda, and well washed afterward with clean water.

From white cloth they are best removed with a dilution of permanganate of potash and hydrochloric acid, washing with hyposulphite of soda and plain water.

If the writing is not very black it can be removed with salt, wet with lemon juice; lay the article in a very hot sun and rinse in boiling water. It will fade the ink at any rate, if it does not entirely remove it.

**Water** that has stood in an open dish over night should not be used for cooking or drinking, as it will have absorbed many foul gases. If obliged to occupy a freshly-painted room set pails and pans of water about; the water absorbs the unwholesome odors.

**Window Glass—To Prevent the Sun from Passing Through.**—Dissolve gum tragacanth in the white of eggs well beaten, twenty-four hours. Then paint the inner side of the glass.

**To Wash Colored Woolens.**—Buy quarter of a pound of soap-bark, at the druggists; boil in earthenware, for half an hour or more, in two quarts of water; strain, and unless the color is very delicate, use it quite warm, especially if the garment is much soiled. Let every part be thoroughly saturated with the bark-suds; shake it about, leave to soak awhile, rub and squeeze it out (do not wring); rinse in tepid water, hang to drain. fold in cloth, iron while very damp. There will be none of the disagreeable odor that woolens have when washed with soap. Woolen coats and pantaloons can be cleaned as follows: Brush and beat them well, spread them out upon a large table, scrub hard with a brush dipped in strong suds of soap-bark; as fast as one side is cleaned, rub it dry with a clean, coarse towel; get off every drop of the suds, so the clothes do not get wet through and shrink; clean conscientiously, and the result is surprising.

### JANUARY.

**Fish.**—Barbel, brill, carp, cod, crabs, crayfish, dace, eels, flounders, haddocks, herrings, lampreys, lobsters, mussels, oysters, perch, pike, porgy, prawns, shrimps, skate, smelts, soles, sprat, sturgeon, tench, thornback, turbot, whiting.

**Meat.**—Beef, house lamb, mutton, pork, veal, venison.

**Poultry.**—Capons, fowls, tame pigeons, pullets, turkeys.

**Game.**—Grouse, hares, partridges, pheasants, rabbits, snipes, wild-fowl, woodcock.

**Vegetables.**—Beetroot, broccoli, cabbages, carrots, celery, chervil, cresses, cucumbers, (forced), endive, lettuces, parsnips, potatoes, savoys, spinach, turnips,—various herbs.

**Fruit.**—Apples, grapes, medlars, nuts, oranges, pears, walnuts, almonds, raisins, plums, prunes, figs, dates.

### FEBRUARY.

**Fish.**—The same fish that are seasonable in January.

**Meat.**—Beef, house lamb, mutton, pork, veal.

**Poultry.**—Capons, chickens, ducklings, tame and wild pigeons, pullets with eggs, turkeys, wild fowl, though not now in full season.

**Game.**—Grouse, hares, partridges, pheasants, snipes, woodcock.

**Vegetables.**—Beetroot, broccoli (purple and white), Brussels sprouts, cabbages, carrots, celery, chervil, cresses, cucumbers (forced), endive, kidney-beans, lettuces, parsnips, potatoes, savoys, spinach, turnips,—various herbs.

**Fruit.**—Apples (golden and Dutch pippins), grapes, medlars, nuts, oranges, pears, walnuts, almonds, raisins, plums, prunes, figs, dates.

### MARCH.

**Fish.**—The same fish that are seasonable in January, with the exception of cod.

**Meat.**—Beef, house lamb, mutton, pork, veal.

**Poultry.**—Capons, chickens, ducklings, tame and wild pigeons, pullets with eggs, turkeys, wild-fowl, though not now in full season.

**Game.**—Grouse, hares, partridges, pheasants, snipes, woodcock.

**Vegetables.**—Beetroot, broccoli (purple and white), Brussels sprouts, cabbages, carrots, celery, chervil, cresses, cucumbers (forced), endive, kidney-beans, lettuces, parsnips, potatoes, savoys, sea-kale, spinach, turnips,—various herbs.

**Fruit.**—Apples, grapes, medlars, nuts, oranges, pears, walnuts, almonds, raisins, plums, prunes, figs, dates.

### APRIL.

**Fish.**—Brill, carp, cockles, crabs, dory, flounders, ling, lobsters, mullet, mussels, oysters, perch, prawns, salmon, shad, shrimps, skate, smelts, soles, tench, turbot, whiting.

**Meat.**—Beef, lamb, mutton, veal.

**Poultry.**—Chickens, ducklings, fowls, pigeons, pullets.

**Game.**—Hares, rabbits, leverets.

**Vegetables.**—Broccoli, celery, lettuces, young onions, parsnips, radishes, small salad, sea-kale, spinach, sprouts,—various herbs.

**Fruit.**—Apples, nuts, pears, forced cherries, etc., for tarts, rhubarb, dried fruits.

### MAY.

**Fish.**—Carp, clams, crabs, dory, eels, halibut, herrings, lobsters, mackerel, mullet, prawns, salmon, shad, smelt, soles, trout, turbot.

**Meat.**—Beef, lamb, mutton, veal.

**Poultry.**—Chickens, ducklings, fowls, green geese, pullets.

**Vegetables.**—Asparagus, beans, early cabbages, carrots, cauliflowers, cresses, cucumbers, lettuces, peas, early potatoes, salads, sea-kale, —various herbs.

**Fruit.**—Apples, green apricots, cherries, currants for tarts, gooseberries, melons, pears, rhubarb, strawberries.

### JUNE.

**Fish.**—Clams, crayfish, herrings, lobsters, mackerel, mullet, pike, prawns, salmon, soles, tench, trout, turbot.

**Meat.**—Beef, lamb, mutton, veal, buck venison.

**Poultry.**—Chickens, ducklings, fowls, green geese, plovers, pullets, turkey poults, wheatears.

**Vegetables.**—Artichokes, asparagus, beans, cabbages, carrots, cucumbers, lettuces, onions, parsnips, peas, potatoes, radishes, small salads, sea-kale, spinach,—various herbs.

**Fruit.**—Apricots, cherries, currants, gooseberries, melons, nectarines, peaches, pears, pineapples, raspberries, rhubarb, strawberries.

### JULY.

**Fish.**—Bluefish, blackfish, bass, catfish, clams, crabs, dory, flounders, haddocks, herrings, lobsters, mackerel, mullet, pike, plaice, prawns, salmon, shrimps, soles, sturgeon, tench, thornback.

**Meat.**—Beef, lamb, mutton, veal, buck venison.

**Poultry.**—Chickens, ducklings, fowls, green geese, plovers, pullets, turkey poults, wheatears, wild ducks (called flappers).

**Vegetables.**—Artichokes, asparagus, beans, cabbages, carrots, cauliflowers, celery, cresses, endive, lettuces, mushrooms, onions, peas, radishes, small salading, sea-kale, sprouts, turnips, vegetable marrow,—various herbs.

**Fruit.**—Apricots, cherries, currants, figs, gooseberries, melons, nectarines, pears, pineapples, plums, raspberries, strawberries, walnuts in high season, and pickled.

### AUGUST.

**Fish.**—Bluefish, blackfish, clams, crabs, dory, eels, flounders, grigs, herrings, lobsters, mullet, pike, porgy, salmon, shrimps, skate, soles, sturgeon, thornback, trout, turbot, weakfish.

**Meat.**—Beef, lamb, mutton, veal, buck venison.

**Poultry.**—Chickens, ducklings, fowls, green geese, pigeons, plovers, pullets, turkey poults, wheatears, wild ducks.

**Game.**—Blackcock, grouse, leverets, rabbits.

**Vegetables.**—Artichokes, asparagus, beans, carrots, cabbages, cauliflowers, celery, cresses, endive, lettuces, mushrooms, onions, peas, potatoes, radishes, sea-kale, small salading, sprouts, turnips, various kitchen herbs, vegetable marrows.

**Fruit.**—Currants, figs, filberts, gooseberries, grapes, melons, mulberries, nectarines, pears, peaches, pineapples, plums, raspberries.

### SEPTEMBER.

**Fish.**—Brill, carp, cod, eels, flounders, lobsters, mullet, oysters, plaice, prawns, skate, soles, turbot, whiting, whitebait.

**Meat.**—Beef, lamb, mutton, pork, veal.

**Poultry.**—Chickens, ducks, fowls, geese, larks, pigeons, pullets, teal, turkey.

**Game.**—Blackcock, buck venison, grouse, hares, partridges, pheasants, rabbits.

**Vegetables.**—Artichokes, asparagus, cabbage sprouts, beans, carrots, celery, lettuces, mushrooms, onions, peas, potatoes, salading, sea-kale, sprouts, tomatoes, turnips, vegetable marrows,—various herbs.

**Fruit.**—Bullaces, damsons, figs, filberts, grapes, melons, morella cherries, mulberries, nectarines, peaches, pears, plums, quinces, walnuts.

### OCTOBER.

**Fish.**—Barbel, brill, cod, crabs, eels, flounders, gudgeons, haddocks, lobsters, mullet, oysters, plaice, prawns, shrimps, smelts, skate, soles, tench, turbot, whiting.

**Meat.**—Beef, mutton, pork, veal, venison.

**Poultry.**—Chickens, fowls, geese, larks, pigeons, pullets, teal, turkeys, widgeons, wild duck.

**Game.**—Blackcock, grouse, hares, partridges, pheasants, rabbits, snipes, woodcock, doe venison.

**Vegetables.**—Artichokes, beets, cabbages, cauliflowers, carrots, celery, lettuces, mushrooms, onions, potatoes, sprouts, tomatoes, turnips, vegetable marrows,—various herbs.

**Fruit.**—Apples, black and white bullaces, damsons, figs, filberts, grapes, pears, quinces, walnuts.

### NOVEMBER.

**Fish.**—Brill, carp, cod, crabs, eels, gudgeons, haddocks, oysters, pike, soles, tench, turbot, whiting.

**Meat.**—Beef, mutton, veal, doe venison.

**Poultry.**—Chickens, fowls, geese, larks, pigeons, pullets, teal, turkeys, widgeons, wild duck.

**Game.**—Hares, partridges, pheasants, rabbits, snipes, woodcock.

**Vegetables.**—Beetroot, cabbages, carrots, celery, lettuces, late cucumbers, onions, potatoes, salading, spinach, sprouts,—various herbs.

**Fruit.**—Apples, bullaces, chestnuts, filberts, grapes, pears, walnuts.

### DECEMBER.

**Fish.**—Barbel, brill, carp, cod, crabs, eels, dace, gudgeons, haddocks, herrings, lobsters, oysters, perch, pike, shrimps, skate, sprats, soles, tench, thornback, turbot, whiting.

**Meat.**—Beef, house lamb, mutton, pork, venison.

**Poultry.**—Capons, chickens, fowls, geese, pigeons, pullets, teal, turkeys, widgeons, wild ducks.

**Game.**—Hares, partridges, pheasants, rabbits, snipes, woodcock.

**Vegetables.**—Broccoli, cabbages, carrots, celery, leeks, onions, potatoes, parsnips, Scotch kale, turnips, winter spinach.

**Fruit.**—Apples, chestnuts, filberts, grapes, medlars, oranges, pears, walnuts, dried fruits, such as almonds and raisins, figs, dates, etc.,—crystallized preserves.

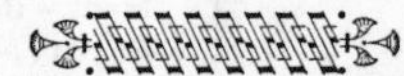

KILLFUL CARVING is one of the most useful accomplishments which the master or mistress of a household can possess. To carve well and elegantly requires considerable practice, but the importance of acquiring this art is not likely to be underrated by those who have experienced the discomfort and the delay which arise from an unskilled carver being seated at the head of the table.

The dish should be sufficiently near the carver to enable him to reach it without rising, while at the same time his seat should be high enough for him to have perfect command over the joint. As in work of this kind a great deal more depends upon knowledge and skill than upon physical strength, all exhibitions of violent exertion are out of place. They only give rise to suspicion, either that the carver is unaccustomed to his post, or that he is working with bad tools upon inferior materials. A good carver always performs his task quietly, and dispenses without partiality to each guest a portion of such parts of the joint as are considered the best.

The carving-knife should not be too heavy ; it should be of sufficient size ; but above all, it should have a sharp edge.

A carver should be careful never to cut across the grain of the meat. Beef, veal, ham, tongue, and breasts of poultry, should be cut very thin ; mutton, pork, and lamb a little thicker.

**Beef.**—The under part of a sirloin of beef should be cut first when hot, and the upper part should be cut straight from the backbone to the outside of the ribs. The ribs of beef should be carved in the same way. The round of beef and the aitchbone of beef should have a slice half an inch thick taken from the outside ; then thin slices taken off, and one of these with a little fat given together.

**Veal.**—A shoulder of veal should be commenced at the knuckle, and thin slices taken off in a slanting direction. Neck and loins should have the bones divided with a small saw before being sent to the table. The bone should then be cut quite through in a slanting direction by the carver. A loin of veal should be carved like the sirloin of beef, a little of the kidney and a little of the fat being apportioned to each person.

**Mutton.**—The usual plan of carving a saddle of mutton is to cut long slices the whole length of the bone. Instead of this, Alexis Soyer recommends that the knife should be put under the meat to cut it away from the bone, and that afterwards it should be divided into thin chops, fat and lean together. A leg of mutton should be carved into cutlets. A quarter of lamb should have the ribs sawed through before it is cooked. The shoulder should then be raised, the ribs divided, and a rib and a piece of the brisket served to each person.

**Fish** requires very little carving, but care must be taken not to break the flakes. Part of the roe, melt, or liver should be served to each person, and the heads of salmon and cod are also considered delicacies.

**Fowl.**—The fork should never be put through the back of a fowl, but the knife should run gently down each side of the breast, and the leg and the wing be taken off at the same time. A little practice is required for the smaller bones, and it is advisable to observe the manner in which it is done by an expert carver. The merry-thought is taken out by slipping the knife through at the point of the breast. After the neck bones have been drawn out, the trunk should be turned over, and the knife thrust through the backbone.

**Turkey.**—In carving a turkey, first cut slices each side of the breast down to the ribs ; the legs should then be removed, and the thighs divided from the *drum-sticks.* The pinions of the wing and the white part of the wing are preferred by many to the breast. The stuffing is usually placed in the breast, but frequently truffles, mushrooms, or oysters are put in the body, which compels the carver to make an opening by cutting through the apron.

**Goose.**—After the apron has been cut off in a circular direction, a glass of port wine mixed with a tea-spoonful of mustard is sometimes poured into the body. The neck of the goose should then be turned towards the carver, and the flesh of the breast sliced on either side of the bone. The wings are cut off next, and then the legs. The rest is carved in the same manner as fowl.

**Duck.**—Large ducks are carved like goose, and small ones like fowl.

**Ham.**—Carve in thin slices from the knuckle to the blade.

**Pork.**—The spare-rib of pork should be carved by separating the chops. After cutting as far as the joint, return the knife to the point of the bones. A loin of pork is carved in the same manner as a loin of mutton. A leg of pork is carved like ham, only in thicker slices.

**Tongue.**—Carve across in thin slices.

**Pheasant.**—The breast is carved in slices. The legs and wings in the same way as fowl.

**Partridges** are carved by cutting off the breast and afterwards dividing it.

**Woodcocks** are cut through the center, from head to tail.

**Pigeons** are carved like partridges or woodcocks.

BORN. DIED.

**Aaron.** First Jewish high priest; associate of Moses. B.C. 1574—1451

**Abbott, J. S. C.** American historian. *Life of Napoleon Bonaparte; History of Russia* ........ 1805—1877

**Abbott,** Charles (Lord Tenterden). Lord Chief Justice of England. *Treatisè on the Law of Merchant Ships and Shipping* ........ 1762—1832

**Abelard,** Peter. French schoolman, and lover of Heloise. *Letters to Heloise* ........ 1079—1142

**Abercrombie,** John. Scotch metaphysician. *The Intellectual Powers* ........ 1781—1844

**Abinger,** Lord James Scarlett. Great English jury advocate. 1769—1844

**About,** Edmond F. V. French author. *The Notary's Nose* ........ 1828 —

**Abraham.** The Jewish patriarch; led his people from Ur of the Chaldees. ........ B.C. 1996—1821

**Abraham-a-Sancta-Clara.** (His real name was Ulric Megerle). Eloquent German preacher; chaplain to the Imperial Court at Vienna ........ 1642—1709

**Abrantes,** Duchess d'. French authoress. *Memoirs in regard to Napoleon Bonaparte* ........ 1784—1838

**Accorso,** Francis. Italian jurist. *Great Glossary* ........ 1180—1260

**Achilles Tatius.** Bishop of Alexandria, and rhetorician, flourished in the 6th century. *The Sphere* ........

**Adalbert,** Saint. Archbishop of Prague, "Apostle of the Prussians," whom he converted to Christianity ........ 939— 997

**Adams,** Charles Francis. Statesman and diplomatist, son of J. Q.; Minister to England (1861-8), American negotiator of the Treaty of Geneva ........ 1807 —

**Adams,** John. American statesman and diplomatist, graduated at Harvard; school-teacher and lawyer; defended British soldiers implicated in Boston Massacre, 1770; delegate to Continental Congress, 1774; commissioner to France, 1778; minister to Holland, 1781; one of the negotiators of treaty of peace with Great Britain, 1782; minister to Great Britain, 1785-88; Vice-President, 1789-97. President, 1797-1801 ........ 1735—1826

**Adams,** John Quincy (son of John). American statesman and diplomatist, graduated at Harvard; minister to Holland, 1794; to Prussia, 1797; elected to U. S. Senate by Federalists, 1803; resigned, 1808; minister to Russia, 1809; one of the negotiators of the treaty of peace with Great Britain, 1814; minister to England, 1816-17; Secretary of State, 1817-1825; President, 1825-29; M. C., 1830 till his death ........ 1767—1848

**Adams,** Samuel. American Revolutionary patriot and statesman. Governor of Massachusetts, one of the foremost popular leaders of the Revolution ........ 1722—1803

BORN. DIED.

**Addington,** Henry, English statesman. Chancellor of the Exchequer. Afterwards created Lord Sidmouth ........ 1755—1844

**Addison,** Joseph. English man of letters, poet, humorist, moralist, dramatist. *The Spectator* and *Cato*. Under-Secretary of State, 1705; M. P. 1708. His first English composition was some complimentary verses to Dryden in 1704. His poem *The Campaign*, on the battle of Blenheim, had a great success. Much of the *Tatler* (edited by Steele) and three-fourths of the *Spectator* is his ........ 1672—1719

**Adelaide,** Queen. Wife of William IV. of England; daughter of the Duke of Saxe Meiningen ........ 1792—1849

**Adelung,** John C., German philologist. *Mithridates* ........ 1732—1806

**Ælian,** Claudius. Roman historian of the 3d century. *Various History*. Flourished about ........ 250

**Ælius Spartianus.** Historian of the Roman Emperors; flourished in the 4th century. *History in single Biographies of the Roman Emperors* ........ 4th Cent'y.

**Æmilius Paulus.** Roman general and statesman; Conqueror of Macedonia ........ B.C. 220— 160

**Æneas Sylvius,** scholar and patron of letters. Pope Pius II. Supposed to practice the black art ........ 1405—1464

**Æschines.** Athenian orator; rival of Demosthenes, and supporter of Philip of Macedon. *Orations* ........ B.C. 389— 314

**Æschylus.** Sublime Athenian tragic writer. *Agamemnon the Persian* ........ B.C. 525— 456

**Æsop.** Greek fabulist of the 6th century B.C. *Fables* ....

**Afranius,** Lucius. Roman comic writer. Only fragments of his works; flourished ........ 1st Cent'y.

**Agassiz,** Louis. Swiss naturalist and man of science, Professor at Harvard; founder of the Museum of Comparative Zoölogy at Cambridge, Mass. *Researches on Fossil Fishes* ........ 1807—1873

**Agricola,** Cnæus Julius. Roman general; built line of fortresses across Scotland; father-in-law of the historian Tacitus ........ 37— 93

**Agrippa,** Henry Cornelius. German scientist and author. *On the Vanity of the Sciences* ........ 1486—1535

**Agrippina.** Mother of the Emperor Nero, infamously cruel and sensual; put to death by Nero ........ 15— 60

**Aguilar,** Grace. English novelist. *Home Influence* ........ 1816—1847

**Aikin,** Lucy. English author. *Life of Joseph Addison* ........ 1747—1822

**Ainsworth,** William Harrison. British novelist. *Jack Sheppard; The Tower of London* ........ 1805—1882

**Akenside,** Mark. British poet. *The Pleasures of the Imagination* ........ 1721—1770

**Alain de Lille.** "The Universal Doctor." French scholar and theologian ........ 1114—1203

N. B. The names of the principal works of authors and artists are printed in *Italics*.

BORN. DIED.

**Alaric I.** King of the Visigoths, captured Rome ........ 350— 410

**Albert,** Archduke of Austria. Ruler of the Netherlands; captured Ostend (1609), after a memorable siege ........ 1559—1621

**Albert,** Prince Consort of England; husband of Queen Victoria; man of noble character. .................. 1819—1861

**Alberti,** Leon Baptiste. Italian painter, architect, and sculptor. Designed the Church of St. Francis, at Rome .... 1404—1472

**Albertus Magnus.** German scholar and theologian, one of the greatest of the schoolmen. He left many works on logic, metaphysics and theology .......... 1190—1280

**Alboin.** King of the Lombards. Conqueror of Northern Italy. ........................ —— 573

**Albornoz,** Gil A. C. Spanish ecclesiastic; Cardinal; legate of Innocent VI .................... 1300—1367

**Alcaeus.** Lesbian lyric poet. Fragments only of his works. Flourished ................ B.C. 620— 580

**Alcibiades.** Athenian statesman and commander. Led Athenian fleet; conquered at Cyzicus and Cynossema; annexed Chalcedon and Byzantium. Handsome, talented, fickle, vain. ........................ 450— 404

**Alcman.** Sardian lyric poet. Fragments only of his works. Flourished ........................ B.C. 600 ——

**Alcott,** Louisa M. American author. *Little Women; An Old Fashioned Girl; Hospital Sketches*.................. 1833 ——

**Alcuin.** Anglo-Saxon theologian; most learned man of his age; lived at court of Charlemagne; founded schools in France........................ 725— 804

**Aldrich,** Thomas Bailey. American novelist and poet. *Prudence Palfrey; The Story of a Bad Boy* ............ 1836 ——

**Alexander the Great,** King of Macedonia, conqueror. Aristotle was his tutor. He came to the throne in 336, razed Thebes, and was chosen by the Greeks commander of the forces against Persia; invaded Asia Minor (334), beat Darius at the Granicus, and cut the Gordian knot; defeated Darius at Issus (333); captured Tyre (332), invaded Egypt and founded Alexandria; routed Darius at Arbela (331); took Babylon, Persepolis, Susa, and invaded India till his army refused to proceed farther; died at Babylon..............B.C. 356— 323

**Alexander VI.** (Borgia). Pope 1492-1503. Infamous for his crimes .................. 1430—1503

**Alexander I.** Czar of Russia (1801-25); one of the chief opponents of Napoleon, reorganized Russian army.... 1777—1825

**Alexander II.** Czar of Russia, liberator of the serfs. Assassinated........................ 1818—1881

**Alexander of Hales.** English schoolman. *System of Theology* .......................... —— 1245

**Alfieri.** Vittore. Italian poet. *Virginia. Saul*....... 1749—1803

**Alfonso VII.** King of Spain; son of ex-Queen Isabella II........................ 1857 ——

**Alfred the Great.** King of Wessex. Came to throne 871; lived in concealment to escape Danes: routed Danes, 878; allowed them to settle in his kingdom; repelled invasion of the Northmen, 896; founded a navy; established schools and a police system; encouraged literature 849— 901

**Alfric,** Archbishop of Canterbury; Anglo-Saxon ecclesiastic. *Homilies.* Flourished in the 10th century..........

**Alison,** Sir Archibald, British historian. *History of Europe. from the commencement of the French Revolution to the Restoration of the Bourbons*.......................... 1792—1867

**Allegri,** Gregorio. Italian composer. *Miserere*.......... 1580—1652

**Allen,** Ethan. American Revolutionary soldier; captured Ticonderoga "in the name of the great Jehovah and the Continental Congress".................... 1737—1789

**Allston,** Washington. American painter and poet. *Elijah in the Desert. The Sylphs of the Seasons*.............. 1779—1843

**Alphonso X.,** King of Castile and Leon. "The Wise." Lawgiver and astronomer.................. 1203—1284

**Alva,** Ferdinand Alvarez, Duke of. Spanish general. Regent of the Netherlands; conspicuous in the war with the Netherlands; annexed Portugal to Spain.......... 1508—1582

BORN. DIED.

**Ambrose,** Saint. Italian ecclesiastic; Bishop of Milan. *The Ambrosian Chant*.............................. 340— 397

**Ames,** Fisher. American orator and statesman; Federalist member of Congress. *Speeches*.................. 1758—1808

**Amherst,** William Pitt, Earl. English statesman; ambassador to China; governor-general of India.......... 1773—1857

**Ammirato,** Scipio. Italian historian. *History of Florence*.............................. 1531—1601

**Ampère,** Jean Jacques Antoine. French author. *History of French Literature before the 12th Century*............ 1800—1864

**Amurath I.** Sultan of Turkey; first of the Sultans to make European conquests.................. 1319—1389

**Amyot,** Jacques. French scholar and translator of Plutarch's *Lives*.............................. 1513—1593

**Anacharsis.** Scythian philosopher. Contemporary of Solon. Only barbarian admitted to Athenian citizenship. Flourished....................B.C. 594

**Anaxagoras.** Greek philosopher; held eternity of matter; excluded chance; father of modern science..B.C. 500— 482

**Anaximander.** Greek philosopher; invented the sun dial; discovered obliquity of the ecliptic..........B.C. 610— 544

**Ancus Marcius,** 4th king of Rome. Organizer and lawgiver of the Plebeian class.................. B.C. —— 614

**Andersen,** Hans Christian. Danish author. *Fairy Tales for Children; The Improvisatore; The Poets' Bazaar*.. 1805—1875

**Anderson,** Sir Edmund. Lord Chief Justice of England. *Reports*.............................. 1531—1630

**André,** Major John. English soldier in the American Revolution, hanged as a spy.................. 1731—1780

**Andrea da Pisa,** Italian sculptor. *Bronze Gate of Baptistry of S. Giovanni at Florence*.................. 1270—1345

**Andrew,** John A. American lawyer and statesman; "War Governor" of Massachusetts.................. 1818—1867

**Andrews,** Lancelot, Bishop of Winchester. English theologian; one of the translators of the Pentateuch. *Tortura Torti*.............................. 1555—1626

**Andros,** Sir Edmund. Colonial governor of New York, and of New England; an arbitrary, tyrannical ruler; deposed by people.............................. 1637—1714

**Angoulême,** Charles de Valois, Duke of. Son of Charles IX. of France; General; opened siege of Rochelle..... 1573—1650

**Anna Comnena.** Byzantine chronicler. *Alexiad,* a history of the reign of her father Alexis.................. 1083—1148

**Anne,** of Austria. Queen of Louis XIII. of France; Regent during the minority of Louis XIV.............. 1602—1666

**Anne.** Daughter of James II. Queen of England. Literature flourished in her reign.................. 1664—1714

**Anselm.** Archbishop of Canterbury; reviver of metaphysics; defender of the church against English king, *Cur Deus Homo*.............................. 1033—1109

**Anson,** George. Lord. English admiral and navigator; defeated French fleet 1747.................. 1697—1762

**Anspach,** Elizabeth. Margravine of. English dramatist, artist and musician; immoral. *Memoirs*.............. 1750—1828

**Anthony,** Saint. Egyptian ascetic; founder of the Monastic system.............................. 201— 356

**Antiochus,** King of Syria. "The Great:" invaded Greece; defeated by the Romans..................B.C. 237— 187

**Antoinette,** Marie. Queen of Louis XVI. of France. guillotined.............................. 1755—1793

**Antonelli,** Giacomo. Cardinal. Italian ecclesiastic and statesman. Secretary of Foreign Affairs for Pius IX... 1806—1876

**Antoninus,** Marcus Aurelius. Emperor of Rome; philosopher. *Meditations*.............................. 121— 180

**Antoninus Pius.** Emperor of Rome; "Father of his Country." A most humane and just ruler.............. 86— 161

**Antonius,** Marcus. Roman orator and statesman; triumvir with Octavianus and Lepidus. Lover of Cleopatra; defeated at Actium..............................B.C. 83— 36

**Apelles.** Greek painter. *Venus Anadyomene.* Flourished in..............................B.C. 330

BORN. DIED.

**Apollinaris,** Sidonius. Roman poet. *Carmina. Epistolæ.* 431—484

**Appollonius Rhodius.** Greek poet. *Argonautica.* .B.C. 235

**Appollonius of Tyana.** Greek philosopher and thaumaturgist. Flourished in 1st cent....

**Appian.** Roman historian. *Roman History.* Flourished. 98—150

**Appius Claudius.** Roman patrician. Decemvir; attempted to dishonor Virginia, daughter of Virginius.......B.C. — 449

**Appuleius.** Roman philosopher and writer. *The Golden Ass.* Flourished. ... 150

**Aquinas,** Thomas, Saint. "The Angelic doctor." Italian theologian. *Summa Theologiæ.* Greatest of the schoolmen; born at Aquino, near Naples, of a noble family, his father being a nephew of Frederick Barbarossa. At the age of 16 he joined the order of St. Dominic; studied with Albertus Magnus; refusing any higher ecclesiastical preferment taught theology and preached at Paris and Rome; was one of the greatest thinkers of the middle ages ........ 1224—1274

**Arago,** François J. D. French astronomer; director of the Paris Observatory; popularized astronomy......... 1786—1853

**Aratus.** Greek poet. *Phænomena*........B.C. 271—213

**Archilochus.** Greek lyric poet; inventor of Iambic verse. Flourished.........B.C. 750

**Archimedes.** Syracusan mathematician and engineer; made many discoveries in hydrostatics and mechanics. *On the Sphere and Cylinder*.........B.C. 287—212

**Aretino,** Pietro. Italian poet. *Dialogues; Comedies*..... 1492—1557

**Argyle,** Archibald Campbell, 8th Earl of. Scotch Covenanter leader. Defeated by Montrose; executed for treason......... 1598—1661

**Argyll,** George Douglas Campbell, 7th Duke of. Scotch Liberal, statesman and author. Secretary of State for India. *The Reign of Law*......... 1823 —

**Ariosto Ludovico.** Italian poet. *Orlando Furioso.* In the service of the Cardinal Ippolito d' Este, and of his brother Alphonso, Duke of Ferrara; began (1505) to compose the *Orlando Furioso*, which he completed in 1516. He made sonnets, elegies, canzones, 7 satires, and 5 comedies in verse, of which *The Magician (Il Negromante)* is the best known......... 1474—1533

**Aristarchus.** Greek grammarian and critic. Severe commentator on Homer. Flourished.........B.C. 150

**Aristides.** "The Just." Athenian statesman. Rival of Themistocles; famous for integrity.........B.C. — 468

**Aristophanes.** Greatest Greek comedy writer. *The Knights. The Clouds. The Birds*.........B.C. 444—380

**Aristotle.** Greek philosopher. *Ethics.* Father of scientific natural history, and of logic. Tutor of Alexander the Great; taught at Athens in the Lyceum; left works on physics, metaphysics, ethics, dialectics, logic, mathematics, politics, economics.........B.C. 384—322

**Arius.** Founder of Arianism; denied that the Son is co-existent and co-eternal with the Father......... — 336

**Arkwright,** Sir Richard. English inventor. The Spinning Jenny......... 1732—1792

**Arlington,** Henry Bennet, 1st Earl of, English statesman; Secretary of State; member of the "Cabal" Ministry.. 1618—1683

**Arminius,** James. Dutch theologian; founder of Arminianism; denied Calvinistic doctrines of grace and predestination......... 1560—1609

**Arnauld,** Antoine. French theologian and Port Royalist. *On Frequent Communion*......... 1612—1694

**Arnim,** Louis A., von. German romantic writer. *Angelica the Genoese, and Cosmos the rope dancer*......... 1781—1831

**Arnobius.** Christian apologist. *Contra Gentes.* He flourished about......... 290

**Arnold,** Benedict. American traitor. Tried to surrender West Point to the British......... 1740—1801

**Arnold,** Edwin. English journalist and poet, editor of the London *Telegraph. The Light of Asia*......... 1832 —

**Arnold,** Matthew. English poet and critic. *God and the Bible; Poems; Essays in Criticism*......... 1822 —

**Arnold,** Thomas. English educator and historian. Master of Rugby School. *History of Rome*......... 1795—1842

**Arnold of Brescia.** Italian reformer; maintained clergy should have no temporal property or power. Executed for heresy......... — 1155

**Arnoldus de Villa Nova.** French theologian, alchemist, physicist and astrologist......... 1235—1314

**Arrian.** Greek historian. *Expedition of Alexander*...... 90—170

**Artaxerxes I.** ("Longimanus"). King of Persia. Subjected most of Egypt.........B.C. — 425

**Artaxerxes II.** ("Mnemon.") King of Persia. Defeated his brother Cyrus at Cunaxa.........B.C. 463—362

**Artaxerxes III.** ("Ochus.") King of Persia. Notorious for cruelty and sensuality. Poisoned.........B.C. — 339

**Artemisia.** Queen of Caria. Built Mausoleum..B.C. — 350

**Artevelde,** James von. Brewer and demagogue of Ghent; led revolt of Ghent; ally of Edward III. of England; slain by populace......... — 1345

**Artevelde,** Philip von. Son of the above. Popular leader; slain at Rosebec......... — 1382

**Arthur,** Chester A. American statesman; born in Vermont and educated at Union College; admitted to the bar; Quartermaster-General of New York during the Civil War; Collector of the Port of New York, 1871–78; Vice-President, 1881; succeeded to Presidency on death of President Garfield, Sept. 1881......... 1830 —

**Ascham,** Roger. Tutor of Queen Elizabeth. *The Schoolmaster; Toxophilus or the School of Shooting*......... 1515—1568

**Asser,** John. English (Saxon) writer. Reputed author of a biography of Alfred the Great......... — 909

**Astor,** John Jacob. American millionaire......... 1763—1848

**Athanasius,** Saint. Bishop of Alexandria. *Discourse on the Incarnation*......... 296—373

**Athenaeus.** Roman grammarian. *Banquet of the Learned.* Flourished......... 200

**Atterbury,** Francis. English Bishop of Rochester, Deprived of his see for correspondence with the Jacobites. His style is praised by Dr. Johnson......... 1662—1732

**Atticus,** Titus Pomponius. Roman Knight. Friend and correspondent of Cicero.........B.C. 109—32

**Attila.** "The Scourge of God." King of the Huns. Invaded the Roman Empire......... — 453

**Auber,** Daniel F. E. French composer. *Masaniello; Fra Diavolo*......... 1782—1871

**Audubon,** John James. American naturalist. *Birds of America*......... 1782—1831

**Auerbach,** Berthold. German novelist. *Country House on the Rhine*......... 1812—1882

**Auersperg,** Anton A., Count. ("Anastasius Grün.") Austrian poet. *The Last Knight*......... 1806—1876

**Augier,** Guillaume V. E. French dramatist. *La Ciguë*......... 1820 —

**Augustine,** Saint. Bishop of Hippo in Africa. Theologian. *De Civitate Dei* Professor of rhetoric and philosophy at Milan, 384; was for a time immoral, but was converted about 386. Ordained priest 391; made bishop of Hippo 396. He wrote against the Pelagians, the treatises *On the Grace of Christ*, and *On Original Sin*......... 354—430

**Augustus** (Octavianus). First Roman Emperor. Conqueror at Actium. Patron of literature.........B.C. 65—A.D. 14

**Aulus Gellius.** Roman grammarian. *Noctes Atticæ*..... 117—180

**Aurelian.** Roman Emperor. Conquered Zenobia and annexed her kingdom of Palmyra......... 212—275

**Aurungzebe.** Emperor of Hindostan; annexed Golconda; increased the imperial revenue $200,000,000.... 1618—1707

**Ausonius,** Decimus Magnus. Roman poet. *Idyllia Epigrammata*......... 310—389

**Austen,** Jane, English novelist. *Sense and Sensibility; Pride and Prejudice; Emma*......... 1775—1817

BORN. DIED.

**Averroes.** Arabian philosopher and expounder of Aristotle. *The Great Commentary* ........ 1149—1198
**Avicenna.** Arabian philosopher. *Rule* ........ 980—1037
**Ayrer,** Jacob. Early German dramatist. Author of sixty-six dramas ........ — 1605
**Aytoun,** William E. Scotch poet, and professor. *Lays of the Scottish Cavaliers; Bothwell a Poem* ........ 1813—1865

**Bach,** John Sebastian. German composer. *The Nativity.* He was court organist at Weimar, where he produced many of his first performances for the organ; was musical director of the St. Thomas school, Leipsic, from 1723 till his death; produced both secular and sacred music in great variety ........ 1685—1750
**Bacon,** Francis, Viscount St. Albans, Lord Verulam. English statesman and philosopher. *Novum Organum. Advancement of Learning.* Counsel to Queen Elizabeth at 28: M. P. 1585-1614; Knighted, 1603; Solicitor General, 1603; Attorney General, 1606; Keeper of the Great Seal; Lord High Chancellor, 1618; Viscount St. Albans, 1619; found guilty of corruption, 1621. Among his works are *Essays;* and *On the Wisdom of the Ancients.* His *Novum Organum* applies inductive method to study of science ........ 1561—1626
**Bacon,** Roger. English friar, philosopher, and scientist. *Opus Majus.* Anticipated discovery of gunpowder; wrote works on Greek, Hebrew, philosophy, metaphysics, theology, the sciences ........ 1214—1292
**Bailey,** Philip J. English poet. *Festus; The Mystic* ........ 1816 —
**Baillie,** Joanna, Miss. English dramatist. *De Montfort; Plays of the Passions* ........ 1762—1831
**Bajazet,** I. Sultan of Turkey. Conqueror of Asia Minor ........ 1347—1403
**Balboa,** Vasco Nuñez de. Spanish adventurer. Discoverer of the Pacific ........ 1475—1517
**Baldwin,** I. (IV. of Flanders). Emperor of the East. In the 4th Crusade. Brother of Godfrey; captured Acre and Sidon ........ 1171—1206
**Balfe,** Michael William. Irish composer and violinist. *The Bohemian Girl* ........ 1808—1870
**Baliol,** John. King of Scotland. Rival of Bruce ........ 1257—1314
**Baltimore,** George Calvert, 1st Lord. Founder of Maryland ........ 1580—1632
**Balzac,** Honoré de. French novelist. *Comèdie Humaine.* 1799—1850
**Bancroft,** George. American diplomatist and historian. Minister to England, and to Germany; secretary of the navy. *History of United States* ........ 1800 —
**Bandello,** Matteo. Italian monk; novelist and poet. *Novelle* ........ 1480—1561
**Barbauld,** Anna Lætitia, Mrs. English authoress. *Hymns in Prose* ........ 1743—1825
**Barclay,** Alexander. British poet. Translator of *Brandt's Ship of Fools* ........ — 1552
**Bareith,** Frederica, S. N. Margravine of. Sister of Frederick the Great. *Memoirs* ........ 1709—1758
**Barham,** Rev. Richard H. English poet and humorist. *Ingoldsby Legends* ........ 1788—1845
**Barlow,** Joel. American poet. *Columbiad* ........ 1755—1812
**Barnave,** Antoine R. J. French statesman. Best debater in National Assembly; Constitutionalist; guillotined 1761—1793
**Barneveldt,** Jan van Olden. Dutch statesman. Grand Pensionary of Holland: chief of the Republican party; beheaded ........ 1547—1619
**Barnum,** Phineas T. American showman ........ 1810 —
**Barrow,** Isaac. English theologian and mathematician. *Lectiones Opticæ; Sermons* ........ 1630—1677
**Basil,** Saint. Bishop of Cæsarea. Christian Father. *Homilies* ........ 329— 379
**Bassompierre,** François de. French general. *Memoirs.* 1579—1646
**Bastiat,** Frederic. French political economist. *Harmonies Economiques* ........ 1801—1850

BORN. DIED.

**Baur,** Ferdinand C. German theologian. *Doctrine of the Atonement* ........ 1750—1806
**Baxter,** Richard. English Dissenting minister, and writer. *The Saints' Rest* ........ 1615—1691
**Bayard,** Peter du Terrail, Chevalier de. French soldier. "Without fear and without reproach." ........ 1476—1524
**Bayle,** Peter. French philosopher and critic. *Dictionary* .. 1647—1706
**Beattie,** James. Scotch poet. *The Minstrel* ........ 1735—1803
**Beaufort,** Henry, Cardinal. English prelate. Bishop of Winchester; Lord Chancellor. Guardian of the infant Henry VI ........ 1370—1440
**Beauharnais,** Alexander, Vicomte de. First husband of the Empress Josephine ........ 1760—1794
**Beauharnais,** Eugene de. Son of the above. Viceroy of Italy; made masterly retreat from Moscow ........ 1781—1824
**Beauharnais,** Hortense Eugenie. Sister of Eugene, Queen of Holland ........ 1783—1837
**Beaumarchais,** Pierre A. C. de. French dramatist. *Le Mariage de Figaro* ........ 1732—1799
**Beaumont,** Francis. English dramatist. Associate of Fletcher. *The Two Noble Kinsmen.* Among their numerous works in collaboration are *The Maid's Tragedy; Philaster; The Coxcomb,* and *Cupid's Revenge.* He was a friend of Jonson and Shakespeare ........ 1586—1616
**Beccaria,** Cæsar B. Marquis of. Italian publicist. *Crimes and Punishments* ........ 1738—1793
**Becket,** Thomas á. Archbishop of Canterbury. Murdered; had controversy in defence of rights of the Church with Henry II. of England, whom he excommunicated ........ 1117—1170
**Beckford,** William. English author, and plutocrat. *Vathek* ........ 1760—1844
**Bede,** "The Venerable." Anglo-Saxon historian. *Ecclesiastical History of the English Nation* ........ 672— 735
**Bedford,** John, Duke of. Regent of France during the minority of Henry VI ........ 1389—1453
**Beecher,** Lyman. American Congregational preacher, and theologian. *Views on Theology* ........ 1775—1836
**Beecher,** Henry Ward. American preacher, lecturer, and orator, at Brooklyn, N. Y. *Star Papers* ........ 1813 —
**Beethoven,** Louis von. German composer. *Ninth Symphony.* For a time organist to the Elector of Cologne; settled in Vienna where he produced (1802) his *Sinfonia Eroica.* In 1805 appeared his opera of *Lenore.* He composed many symphonies, cantatas, and overtures ........ 1770—1827
**Belisarius.** Byzantine general under Justinian. Defeated Vandals, Ostrogoths, and Persians ........ 505— 565
**Bellamy,** George Anne, Mrs. English actress. *Apology* .. 1733—1786
**Bellarmine,** Robert. Italian Cardinal. Ablest defender of the Church. *Treatise on the Duty of Bishops. Controversies* ........ 1542—1621
**Bellini,** Giovanni. Venetian painter. *Coronation of the Virgin* ........ 1426—1512
**Bellini,** Vincente. Italian composer. *La Norma* ........ 1802—1835
**Bembo,** Pietro, Cardinal. Italian poet and historian. *History of Venice* ........ 1470—1547
**Benedict,** Saint. Italian ecclesiastic. Founder of the Benedictines ........ 480— 543
**Bennett,** James Gordon. American journalist. Proprietor of the *N. Y. Herald* ........ 1795—1872
**Bentham,** Jeremy. English utilitarian philosopher and economist. *Principles of Morals and Legislation* ........ 1748—1832
**Bentivoglio,** Guido. Italian Cardinal and historian. *Civil Wars of Flanders* ........ 1579—1644
**Bentley,** Richard. English classical scholar and critic. *The Epistles of Phalaris* ........ 1662—1742
**Benton,** Thomas H. American statesman. Senator from Missouri. *Thirty Years' View* ........ 1782—1858
**Béranger,** Jean P. de. French lyric and patriotic poet ... 1780—1857
**Bergerac,** Cyrano de. French dramatist and duelist. *Pedant Joue; Agrippina* ........ 1620—1655

BORN. DIED.

**Berkeley,** George, Bishop. English metaphysician. *The Principles of Human Knowledge* ........ 1684—1753

**Berlichingen,** Goetz von ("The Iron-Handed"). German hero. Immortalized by Goethe. Slain in war of peasants against nobles ........ 1480—1562

**Berlioz,** Louis Hector. French composer. *Romeo and Juliet* ........ 1803—1869

**Bernadotte.** French general. King of Sweden (Charles XIV.) ........ 1764—1846

**Bernard,** Saint. Abbot of Clairvaux. French ecclesiastic. Born at Dijon in Burgundy; when very young entered the Cistercian monastery at Clairvaux with five of his brothers, and, 1115, was chosen abbot. He refused to her ecclesiastical preferment, exerting in that position a great power over Europe. He induced the French and English to recognize Innocent II. as Pope, procured in 1140 the condemnation of Abelard's works, and was active in bringing about the crusade of 1146; canonized in 1174 ........ 1091—1153

**Berni,** Francis. Italian burlesque poet. *Rime* ........ 1490—1536

**Beroald de Verville,** François. French author. *Moyen de Parvenir* ........ 1558—1612

**Berryer,** Pierre Antoine. French statesman. Chief of the legitimists ........ 1790—1868

**Berthier,** Alexandre. Prince of Wagram. One of Napoleon's marshals, and his Chief of Staff ........ 1753—1815

**Berwick,** James Fitzjames, Duke of. Natural son of James II. French marshal. Defeated Spaniards at Almanza, and established Philip V. on the Spanish throne ........ 1670—1734

**Beza,** Theodore. French reformer. Translation of the Testament ........ 1519—1605

**Biddle,** Nicholas. American financier. President U. S. Bank ........ 1786—1844

**Bigelow,** George T. Chief Justice of Massachusetts ........ 1810—1878

**Bion.** Greek pastoral poet. *Idylls* ........ B.C. 4th cent.

**Bismarck,** Otto von. German statesman; 1847, member United Diet and leader of Conservatives; ambassador to Russia 1809; Prime Minister of Prussia 1862; Chancellor of the German Empire ........ 1813 —

**Black,** William. Scotch novelist; originally a journalist. *A Daughter of Heth; Strange Adventures of a Phaeton; A Princess of Thule; Madcap Violet* ........ 1841 —

**Black Hawk.** Indian chief. Hero of the Black Hawk War. 1768—1838

**Blackstone,** Sir William. English judge, and law writer. *Commentaries* ........ 1723—1780

**Blaine,** James Gillespie. American Republican politician. U. S. Senator from Maine; Speaker House of Representatives; Secretary of State ........ 1830 —

**Blake,** Robert. English Admiral. Defeated Von Tromp and De Witt in war with Holland, 1652 ........ 1599—1657

**Blake,** William. English artist. *The Book of Job* ........ 1757—1827

**Blanche of Castile.** Queen of Louis VIII. of France. Mother of St. Louis. Regent of France during his minority ........ 1197—1252

**Bloomfield,** Robert. English bucolic poet. *The Farmer's Boy* ........ 1766—1823

**Blücher,** Gebhard L. von. Prussian field marshal; decided the battle of Waterloo by coming up with his force in the evening ........ 1742—1819

**Boccaccio,** John. Italian poet. *The Decameron* ........ 1313—1375

**Boehm,** Jacob. German mystic. *Aurora* ........ 1575—1624

**Boerhaave,** Herman. Dutch botanist, physician, and philosopher. *Elements of Chemistry* ........ 1668—1732

**Boethius,** Ancius M. T. Severinus. Roman senator and author. *De Consolatione Philosophiae* ........ 475— 525

**Boiardo,** Matteo M. Italian poet. *Orlando Innamorato.* 1434—1494

**Boileau, Despréaux,** Nicholas. Bishop of Meaux. French poet and critic. *Art of Poetry* ........ 1636—1711

**Boleyn,** Anne. 2d Queen of Henry VIII. Beheaded ........ 1507—1536

**Bolingbroke,** Henry St. John, Viscount. English statesman and author. *Dissertation on Parties.* Principal negotiator of the Treaty of Utrecht. Entered into treasonable correspondence with the Pretender; fled to France ........ 1678—1751

BORN. DIED.

**Bolivar,** Simon. Freer of the Spanish South American colonies ........ 1783—1830

**"Bolognese"** (J. F. Grimaldi). Italian painter. His specialties were landscapes and architectural pieces ........ 1606—1680

**Bonaparte,** Caroline M. A. Sister of Napoleon I. Wife of Murat ........ 1782—1839

**Bonaparte,** Jerome, " Joseph, " Louis Napoleon, } brothers of Napoleon. Kings respectively of Westphalia, Spain, Holland .... } 1784—1860, 1766—1844, 1778—1846

**Bonaparte,** Maria Letitia. Mother of Napoleon I ........ 1750—1836

**Bonaparte,** Napoleon. Napoleon I. Emperor of France, Captain of artillery, 1792; crushed insurrection in Paris, 1795; married Josephine Beauharnais, and took command of the army of Italy, 1796; conquered Austria and the Pope, 1797; made an expedition to Egypt, 1798; made First Consul, 1799; conquered at Marengo, 1800; made peace with England, 1802, and about this time produced his *Civil Code.* Became Emperor, 1804; engaged in war with England, Russia, Sweden, Prussia; married Marie Louise, 1810; made a disastrous campaign in Russia, 1812; was beaten at Leipzig, 1813; retired to Elba, 1814; returned to France, and was conquered at Waterloo, and sent to St. Helena, 1815 ........ 1769—1821

**Bonaparte,** Napoleon E. L. J. J. French Prince Imperial; killed by the Zulus ........ 1856—1879

**Bonheur,** Rosalie (usually called "Rosa"). French animal painter. *The Horse Fair* ........ 1822 —

**Boniface,** Saint. "Apostle of Germany," which he converted to Christianity; Archbishop of Mentz ........ 680— 755

**Boniface VIII.** Pope; 1294-1303. Excommunicated Colonna family and destroyed Praeneste. Excommunicated Philip the Fair of France; the latter accused him of heresy, and imprisoned him; but he was soon rescued .. 1228—1303

**Bonnivard,** François de. "The Prisoner of Chillon." ... 1496—1570

**Boone,** Daniel. American explorer and hunter. Father of the present State of Kentucky ........ 1735—1820

**Booth,** Edwin. American actor. Among his best parts are *Richelieu, Iago, Hamlet,* and *Berbuccio* in the *Fool's Revenge* ........ 1833 —

**Booth,** John Wilkes. American actor. Assassin of President Lincoln ........ 1839—1865

**Booth,** Junius Brutus. English Tragedian. Great in Shakespearean parts, especially *Richard III.;* came to America. Father of Edwin and John Wilkes ........ 1796—1852

**Borgia,** Caesar. Natural son of Pope Alexander VI. Duc de Valentinois; attempted conquest of the cities in the Romagna ........ 1457—1507

**Borgia,** Lucretia. Duchess of Ferrara, sister of the above; married Giovanni Sforza; for her second husband Alfonso, natural son of the King of Naples; for her third, Alfonso of Este ........ — 1523

**Borromeo,** Charles, Saint. Cardinal, and Archbishop of Milan. Famous for benevolence and care of the sick. 1538—1584

**Bossuet,** Jacques, B. C. Bishop of Meaux. French ecclesiastic and author. *Discourse on Universal History.* 1627—1704

**Boswell,** James. Scotch biographer of Dr. Johnson. *Boswell's Life of Johnson* ........ 1740—1795

**Bothwell,** James Hepburn, Earl of. Husband of Mary Queen of Scots. Probable murderer of her husband Darnley ........ 1526—1576

**Botticelli,** Alessandro. Italian painter. *Frescoes in the Vatican* ........ 1437—1515

**Bouillon,** Godfrey de, Duke of Lorraine. Hero of the first Crusade: King of Jerusalem ........ 1058—1100

**Bourbon,** Charles, Duke of. Constable of France. Leader of Imperial forces at the battle of Pavia. Slain while storming Rome ........ 1489—1527

BORN. DIED.

**Bourdaloue,** Louis. Eloquent French Jesuit preacher..... 1632—1704

**Bouterwek,** Frederic. German scholar and author. *History of Spanish Literature*..... 1766—1828

**Bowditch,** Nathaniel. American mathematician. *Navigation*..... 1773—1838

**Bowdoin,** James. American statesman. Governor of Massachusetts. Founder of Bowdoin College..... 1727—1790

**Boyle,** Richard, Earl of Cork. British statesman. Prominent in suppressing Irish rebellion in 1641..... 1566—1643

**Boyle,** Robert. Irish chemist and physicist. Discovered law of the air's elasticity. *Disquisition on Final Causes* 1627—1691

**Bozzaris,** Marco. Greek patriotic leader in the Greek war of Independençe. Slain near Missolonghi..... 1789—1823

**Bracciolini,** Poggio. Italian scholar. Leader in the Renaissance; accomplished Latinist..... 1380—1459

**Braddock,** Edward. British general in America. Defeated by Indians..... 1715—1755

**Brahé,** Tycho. Danish astronomer. Erected an observatory, and made many discoveries..... 1546—1601

**Bramante d'Urbino.** (Donato Lazzari.) Italian architect of St. Peter's..... 1444—1514

**Brandon,** Charles, Duke of Suffolk. Favorite of Henry VIII. Married widow of Louis XII. of France..... — 1545

**Brandt,** Sebastian. German poet. *Ship of Fools*..... 1458—1520

**Brantôme, Pierre de Bordeilles.** French historian. *Vies des Dames Illustres*..... 1540—1614

**Breckenridge,** John C. American politician. Vice-President (1857-1861). Confederate general. A Democratic candidate for President, 1860..... 1821—1875

**Brentano,** Clemens. German novelist and poet of the romantic school. *Foundation of Prague*..... 1777—1842

**Brewster,** Sir David. English man of science. Made many discoveries in optics. Inventor of kaleidoscope.. 1781—1868

**Bright,** John. English Radical, statesman and orator. Opponent of Corn Laws; member of Gladstone's cabinet.. 1811 —

**Brillat-Savarin,** A. French author. *Physiology of the Taste*..... 1755—1826

**Brinvilliers,** Marguerite d'Aubrai, Marchioness. French poisoner..... — 1676

**Brissot,** Jean P. French Revolutionist. Head of the "Brissotins"..... 1754—1793

**Brodie,** Sir Benjamin C. English surgeon. *On Local Nervous Affections*..... 1783—1862

**Bronté,** Charlotte. "Currer Bell." English novelist. *Jane Eyre.* Daughter of the curate of Haworth, Yorkshire; teacher and governess; in 1846, with her sisters, published *Poems;* 1848, *Jane Eyre;* 1849, *Shirley;* 1852, *Villette;* 1854, married Rev. Arthur B. Nichols.... 1816—1855

**Brougham,** Henry Lord. English lawyer, statesman and author. Lord Chancellor..... 1778—1868

**Browne,** Charles F. "Artemus Ward." American humorous writer..... 1835—1867

**Browne,** Sir Thomas. English author, physician and philosopher; practiced medicine for many years at Norwich; published *Religio Medici*, 1642; *Enquiries into Vulgar and Common Errors* (*Pseudodoxia Epidemica*), 1646; was knighted by Charles II..... 1605—1682

**Browning,** Mrs. Elizabeth Barrett. English poetess. *Casa Guidi Windows;* daughter of a London merchant; finely educated; knew Greek and Latin; wrote verses at ten; in 1826, published *Essay on Mind;* 1838, *The Seraphim;* 1839, *The Romaunt of the Page;* 1840, *The Drama of Exile;* 1844, *Poems;* 1856, *Aurora Leigh;* married Robert Browning in 1846..... 1809—1861

**Browning,** Robert, English poet. *The Ring and the Book;* born at Camberwell, near London; educated at University of London; in 1835 appeared *Paracelsus;* 1837, *Strafford;* 1846, two volumes of shorter poems; 1855, *Men and Women.* Among his other works are *Pippa Passes; The Blood on the Scutcheon; The Red-Cotton Night-Cap Country,* and *Idylls*..... 1812 —

BORN. DIED.

**Bruce,** Robert. King of Scotland. Defeated Edward II. at Bannockburn, 1314..... 1274—1329

**Brummell,** George B. "Beau Brummell." English man of fashion..... 1778—1840

**Brunelleschi,** Philip. Florentine architect; designed Santa Maria del Fiore, at Florence..... 1377—1444

**Brunetto Latini.** Florentine grammarian and poet. Dante's master. *Il Tesoro.*..... 1230—1294

**Bruno,** Giordano. Italian pantheist. *Della Causa, Principio, e Uno.* Burned..... 1550—1600

**Bruno,** Saint. German ecclesiastic. Founder of the Carthusian order of Monks..... 1030—111

**Brutus,** Lucius Junius. Roman patriot; overthrew Tarquin and established Republican government at Rome. Flourished 6th century, B.C.

**Brutus,** Marcus Junius. One of Cæsar's assassins. Defeated at Philippi. Committed suicide.....B.C. 85— 42

**Bryant,** William Cullen. American poet. *Thanatopsis.* Born in Massachusetts; at 13 wrote *The Embargo* and *The Spanish Revolution;* entered Williams College; studied law; wrote *Thanatopsis* in 1816; published *The Ages,* 1821; became an editor of the New York *Evening Post* in 1826; more than forty years later appeared his translation of Homer..... 1794—1878

**Buchanan,** George. Scotch poet and historian. *History of Scotland*..... 1506—1582

**Buchanan,** James. American statesman; born Pa.; admitted to bar, 1812; M.C., 1821-31; minister to Russia, 1832-4; U. S. Senator, 1834-45; Sec'y of State, 1845-9; minister to England, 1853-6; signed Ostend Manifesto, 1854; President, 1857-61..... 1791—1868

**Buckle,** Henry Thomas. English historian. *History of Civilization*..... 1822—1862

**Buffon,** George L. L. Comte de. French naturalist; made intendant of the royal garden at Paris in 1739. His great works are *Natural History* and *Epochs of Nature;* he discovered the law of the geographical distribution of animals according to climate, and attempted to show the unity of the human species..... 1707—1788

**Bunsen,** Christian C. J., Baron. German philologist and diplomatist. Prussian Minister at Rome and London. *Egypt's Place in Universal History*..... 1791—1860

**Bunsen,** Robert W. E. German physicist; one of the founders of stellar chemistry..... 1824 —

**Bunyan,** John. English author. *Pilgrim's Progress, The Holy City, The Holy War.* Born at Elston, near Bedford; son of a tinker, and followed that occupation; for several years led a dissipated, wandering life; served in the Parliamentary army; joined Anabaptists in 1654; became Baptist minister, 1655; was sentenced to transportation for life for promoting seditious assemblies; in prison, 1660-'72; there wrote part of *Pilgrim's Progress* (1678); after his release, was minister at Bedford. 1628—1688

**Burgoyne,** John. British general. Surrendered at Saratoga..... 1730—1792

**Burke,** Edmund. English (Irish) orator, statesman and writer. Before entering public life, published his *Philosophical Inquiry into the Origin of our Ideas of the Sublime and Beautiful;* became M.P. in 1766, and sat for many years; was paymaster of the forces, 1782; made a noble speech for the prosecution at the impeachment of Warren Hastings in 1788. His last great work was *Reflections on the Revolution in France*..... 1730—1797

**Burlingame,** Anson. American diplomatist; Chinese Ambassador; negotiator of treaty with United States... 1822—1870

**Burnet,** Gilbert. English bishop and historian. *History of My Own Times*..... 1643—1715

**Burns,** Robert. Scotch lyric poet. *The Cotter's Saturday Night.* Born at Ayr; the son of a poor farmer; had little opportunity for education; worked hard on his father's farm, but heard "many tales and songs";

BORN. DIED.

studied mensuration and surveying, but was always falling in love; fell into dissipated habits; 1785, formed a *liaison* with Jean Armour, whom he married in 1788; conceived project of emigrating, but the great applause which his poems, first gathered in full in 1787, received determined him to remain in Scotland; afterwards an officer of the excise. *Tam O'Shanter*, *To the Unco Guid*, *Halloween*, *The Jolly Beggars*, *Holy Willie's Prayer*..... 1759—1796

**Burr**, Aaron. American lawyer and statesman; Vice-President. Tried for (and acquitted) of treason. Killed Alexander Hamilton in a duel.... 1756—1836

**Burton**, Robert. English author, philosopher and humorist. *Anatomy of Melancholy*.. 1576—1640

**Bussy**, Roger Rabutin, Count of. French writer. *Histoire Amoureuse des Galles*.... 1618—1693

**Butler**, Benjamin F. American lawyer, politician and general; member of Congress; military governor of New Orleans .... 1818 ——

**Butler**, Joseph. English theologian. Bishop of Bristol and of Durham. *Analogy of Natural and Revealed Religion to the Constitution and Course of Nature*...... 1692—1752

**Butler**, Samuel. English poet. *Hudibras*. Born in Strensham, Worcestershire; when young, clerk to one Jeffreys, a justice of the peace; afterwards in the service of Sir S. Luke, one of Cromwell's officers; after the Restoration, steward of Ludlow Castle; married Mrs. Herbert, whose fortune he lost by bad investments; died poor; published first part of *Hudibras*, 1663; second part, 1664; third part, 1678.... 1612—1680

**Byng**, John. English admiral. Shot for cowardice..... 1704—1757

**Byron**, George Gordon, Lord. English poet. *Childe Harold*, *Don Juan*; travelled 1809-11, and on his return produced first cantos of *Childe Harold*; 1813, *Giaour* and *Bride of Abydos*; 1814, *Corsair*; married Anne Isabel Millbanke, 1815; separated from her and left England 1816; lived in Italy; espoused cause of Greek independence, and died at Missolonghi. *Cain*; *Manfred*; *Marino Faliero*; *The Two Foscari*; *Beppo*; *The Vision of Judgment*; *The Prisoner of Chillon*; *The Siege of Corinth*; *Mazeppa*; *English Bards, and Scotch Reviewers*; *Parisina*; *The Deformed Transformed*.... 1788—1824

**Cabanis**, Pierre J. G. French physician and philosopher. *Relation between the Physical System and the Mental Faculties of Man*.... 1757—1808

**Cade**, John. Hero of "Jack Cade's Rebellion." Irish rebel. —— 1450

**Cadoudal**, George. French Bourbon general and conspirator. Executed for plotting dethronement of Napoleon I. 1769—1804

**Caedmon**. Anglo-Saxon poet. *The Creation*.... —— 680

**Cæsar**, Caius Julius. Roman general and statesman. Dictator. Quæstor, 58 B.C.; Aedile, 65; pontifex maximus 64; consul, 59 (alliance with Pompey and Crassus called first triumvirate); was granted both the Gauls for 5 years; conquered many tribes, and invaded England; crossed Rubicon and entered Rome; conquered Pompey at Pharsalia (48); subdued Spain and Africa; made imperator; assassinated by Brutus, Cassius, and others. B.C. 99— 44

**Cagliostro**, Alexander (Joseph Balsamo). Italian, adventurer and impostor. Physician, alchemist. Free Mason. 1743—1795

**Cajetan**, Theodore de Vios, Cardinal. Italian theologian. One of the first propounders of the doctrine of papal infallibility .... 1469—1534

**Calderon de la Barca**. Spanish dramatist and poet. Served as a soldier, but afterwards entered the church, after which he wrote only sacred dramas; he left some 500 plays, of which the most famous are *The Constant Prince*, *Life is a Dream*, and *The Physician of his own Honor*.... 1601—1681

**Calhoun**, John Caldwell. American statesman. Vice-President. Born S. C; elected to Congress, 1810; Secretary of War, 1817; Vice-President, 1829-32; resigned in latter year and entered Senate; Sec'y of State, 1844; re-entered Senate, 1845; "State's Rights" leader; left, among other writings, a *Treatise on the Nature of Government* 1783—1850

**Caligula**. Emperor of Rome (37-41). Insanely cruel, sensual, impious. Built temple to himself.... 12— 41

**Callimachus**. Alexandrian poet and grammarian. His only extant works are *Hymns* and *Epigrams*...... B.C. — 246

**Calonne**, Charles A. de. French statesman and financier. Controller-general of finance; proposed Assembly of Notables.... 1734—1802

**Calvin**, John. French theologian. Withdrew to Geneva, where his religion and political principles made him extremely unpopular; went to Germany, but was ultimately recalled to Geneva. His *Institutes of Christian Religion* was intended to vindicate the Reformed Church. The fundamental doctrines of his theology were unconditional reprobation and election. He published *Commentaries on the Harmony of the Gospel*.... 1509—1564

**Cambacères**, Jean J. R. de. French statesman. Second Consul; took a leading part in compiling the *Civil Code*. 1753—1824

**Cambyses**. King of Persia. Conqueror of Egypt. B.C. — 521

**Cameron**, Richard. Scotch Covenanter. Founder of the Cameronian sect.... —— 1680

**Cameron**, Simon. American politician; Secretary of War; Senator from Pennsylvania.... 1799 ——

**Camillus**, Marcus Furius. Roman general. Dictator; Conqueror of the Gauls.... B.C. — 365

**Camoens**, Louis de. Portuguese poet. *The Lusiad*. A soldier in Morocco, and in 1553 went to India; was exiled from Goa to Macao (1559) for his political satires, *Follies in India*. Returning to Lisbon, he lived in extreme poverty, and finally died in a hospital. His great poem *Os Lusiadas*, *The Lusiad*, celebrates the exploits of Vasco de Gama and the other Portuguese navigators. He also wrote many songs, odes, and sonnets.... 1524—1579

**Campbell**, Thomas. Scotch poet. *The Pleasures of Hope*. Son of a Glasgow merchant; educated at University of Glasgow; 1799, published *Pleasures of Hope*; 1800, visited Continent, and soon after his return published *Exile of Erin*, *Ye Mariners of England*, *Lochiel's Warning*; 1803, married his cousin, Miss Sinclair; 1806, was pensioned; 1809, published *Gertrude of Wyoming*; was author of biographies of Petrarch, Frederick the Great, and Mrs. Siddons.... 1777—1844

**Canning**, George. English statesman and orator. Prime Minister; entered Parliament 1793; with Frere and others, wrote *Anti-Jacobin*; 1807, Secretary for foreign affairs; fought duel with Castlereagh; again secretary of foreign affairs, 1822; premier, 1827.... 1770—1827

**Canova**, Antonio. Italian sculptor. *Venus Victorious*. His *Daedalus and Icarus* (1778), and *Theseus and the Minotaur* were the beginning of a new era in modern sculpture. Among his works are *Venus and Adonis*; *The Graces*; and a *statue of Washington*.... 1757—1822

**Cantu**, Cesare. Italian historian. *History of Italian Literature*.... 1805 ——

**Canute**. King of Denmark and England. Conqueror of England.... 990—1035

**Caracalla**. Emperor of Rome (211-217). Cruel and vicious. Assassinated.... 188— 217

**Caracci**, Annibal. Italian painter. One of the masters of the Bolognese school; his best pieces are in the Farnese Gallery .... 1560—1609

**Caracci**, Ludovico. Italian painter, founder of the Bolognese school. *The Preaching of St. John the Baptist* 1555—1619

**Caravaggio**, Michael Angelo. Italian painter. *Supper at Emmaus*.... 1569—1609

**Cardan**, Jerome. Italian physician and scientist. *On the Subtlety of Things*.... 1501—1576

**Carey**, Henry C. American political economist. *Political Economy*.... 1793—1879

BORN. DIED.

**Carlisle,** George W. F. Howard, 7th Earl of. English writer and statesman. Lord Lieutenant of Ireland..... 1802—1864

**Carlyle,** Thomas. Scotch historian and essayist; educated at University of Edinburgh; became thoroughly familiar with German literature; married Jane Welch (1825), and settled on a farm; published *Sartor Resartus*, 1834; *French Revolution*, 1837; *Chartism*, 1839; *Heroes and Hero Worship*, 1840; *Past and Present*, 1843; *Latter Day Pamphlets; Oliver Cromwell's Letters and Speeches*, 1845; *Life of John Sterling*, 1851; *Life of Frederick the Great*, 1858-64 .................................................. 1795—1881

**Carnarvon,** Henry H. M. Herbert, 3d Earl. English statesman, Secretary for the Colonies, 1874-78............ 1831 ——

**Carroll,** Charles (of Carrollton). American Revolutionary statesman. Signer of the Declaration of Independence. Very wealthy .......................................... 1737—1832

**Casas,** Bartholomew de las. Spanish missionary and historian. Friend and inculcator of humanity to the Indians. *History of the Indians*.... 1474—1566

**Casaubon,** Isaac. Swiss scholar and critic. *Athenæus*.. 1559—1614

**Cass,** Lewis. American statesman and diplomatist. U. S. Senator from Michigan. Democratic candidate for President, 1840; Secretary of State ......................... 1782—1866

**Cassiodorus,** Magnus Aurelius. Roman statesman and author. *History of the Goths* ........................ 470— 560

**Castelar y Rissollo,** Emilio. Spanish Republican orator and statesman; President of the Cortes, 1873. *Old Rome and New Italy* .................................. 1832 ——

**Castiglione,** Balthasar. Italian statesman and author. *The Courtier* ............................................. 1478—1529

**Castlereagh,** Robert Stewart, Viscount. Marquis of Londonderry. English statesman. Prominent in suppressing Irish Rebellion of 1798, in bringing about the Union with Ireland; in opposing Bonaparte. Committed suicide 1769—1822

**Catherine, Saint.** Italian Dominican nun at Siena. Mediator between the rival Popes in the great schism.. 1347—1380

**Catherine of Aragon.** Queen of Henry VIII. of England. Divorced............................................. 1486—1536

**Catherine de Medici.** Queen of Henry II. of France. Strenuous opponent of Protestantism and the Huguenots................................................... 1519—1589

**Catherine I.** Wife of Peter the Great. Empress of Russia; succeeded to government on his death........ 1682—1727

**Catherine II.** Empress of Russia. Married, 1745, the nephew of the Empress Elizabeth, who became Emperor as Peter III. in 1762. Catherine deposed him in July of that year. She took part in the partition of Poland (1772); beat the Turks, and annexed land along the Black Sea; and in 1793 got additional territory by the second partition of Poland. Notoriously immoral . 1729—1796

**Catiline,** Lucius Sergius. Roman conspirator; slain..B.C. 108— 62

**Cato,** Dionysius. Latin didactic poet. *Disticha de Moribus*. 3d cent.

**Cato,** Marcus Portius (The Elder). Roman statesman and author. Censor. *De Re Rustica* ............B.C. 235— 149

**Cato,** Marcus Portius (The Younger). "Uticensis." Opponent of Cæsar; famed for probity. Committed suicide...........................................B.C. 95— 46

**Catullus,** Caius Valerius. Roman lyric poet. *Carmina*.B.C. 87— 47

**Cavaignac,** Louis E. French general and statesman. Put down the insurrection of 1848; for a time Dictator........ 1802—1857

**Cavour,** Camillo B. Count. Italian statesman. First Prime Minister of the Kingdom of Italy, whose unity he did more than any other man to bring about........... 1810—1861

**Caxton,** William. English printer. Introducer of printing into England.......................................... 1412—1492

**Cecil,** William, Lord Burleigh. Lord Treasurer of England, under Elizabeth........................................ 1520—1598

**Cellini,** Benvenuto. Italian artist, sculptor, and engineer. *Life of B. Cellini. Statue of Perseus*................... 1500—1570

**Celsus.** Aurelius Cornelius. Latin medical writer. *De Medicina*................................................. 2d cent.

BORN. DIED.

**Cenci,** Beatrice. A Roman girl, called "the beautiful parricide." Executed for her crime ..................... 1583—1599

**Cervantes Saavedra,** Miguel. Spanish novelist. *Don Quixote*. Was wounded at the battle of Lepanto, 1571; imprisoned in Algiers, where he suffered cruelly; lived in poverty; produced dramas, pastorals, and other works. 1547—1616

**Chalmers,** Thomas. Scotch preacher and theologian. Founder of the "Free Church" in Scotland. *Astronomy in its Connection with Religion*........................ 1780—1847

**Chamberlain,** Joseph. English Radical statesman; President of the Board of Trade.............................. 1836 ——

**Chamisso,** Adelbert von. German poet, traveler, and novelist. *Peter Schlemihl*............................. 1781—1838

**Champollion,** Jean F. French Egyptologist and antiquary. *Hieroglyphic Dictionary*........................... 1790—1832

**Channing,** William Ellery. American Unitarian theologian and reformer; opponent of slavery. *Remarks on the Life and Character of Napoleon Bonaparte; Self Culture; The Elevation of the Laboring Classes; Evidences of Christianity*............................................. 1780—1841

**Chantrey,** Sir Francis. English sculptor. *The Sleeping Children*.................................................. 1782—1841

**Charlemagne.** King of France. Emperor of the West. Son of Pepin the Short; became master of the whole territory of the Franks in 771; began a war against the Saxons, 772, which lasted thirty years; conquered Desiderius, King of the Lombards; received the crown of Lombardy, 774; he was defeated by the Saracens at Roncesvalles, 778; was crowned Emperor of the West, with the title of Cæsar Augustus, by Pope Leo. III., 800 His empire extended from the Elbe to the Ebro, and from Calabria to Hungary. He was the founder of the Carlovingian line of kings.............................. 742— 814

**Charles II.** (I. of France). "The Bald." Emperor of Germany. Invaded Italy, and was crowned Emperor ..... 823— 877

**Charles V.** (I. of Spain). Emperor of Germany; son of Philip, archduke of Austria, and Joanna, daughter and heiress of Ferdinand and Isabella; inherited the Low Countries from his father; succeeded to the Spanish throne in 1516, and became Emperor of Germany in 1519; summoned the Diet of Worms to put down Luther in 1521. Warring against Francis I. of France, and Pope Clement VII. in 1527, his army captured and sacked Rome; opposed the Protestants, but made concession to them by the treaty of Passau 1552; abdicated 1552, and withdrew to the monastery of St. Yuste, Spain. 1500—1538

**Charles VI.** ("The Well-Beloved"). King of France. Became deranged, 1392; his reign memorable for troubles between Armagnacs and Burgundians.................. 1368—1422

**Charles VII.** ("The Victorious"). King of France. Expeller of the English........................................ 1403—1461

**Charles XII.** King of Sweden, 1697-1718. Soldier and conqueror. Came to the throne in 1697. Peter the Great of Russia, Frederick IV. of Denmark, and Augustus of Poland made a league against him in 1700. He besieged Copenhagen, and forced Denmark to make peace; beat the Russians, and in the next campaign invaded Poland, where he compelled Augustus to resign; invaded Russia, and was defeated (1709) at Pultowa, losing 9,000 killed, and 6,000 prisoners; found refuge in Turkey, from which he soon returned; invading Norway, he was killed at the siege of Fredrickshalle ..................... 1682—1718

**Charles I.** King of England. Beheaded after vainly attempting to subdue his rebellious subjects............ 1600—1649

**Charles II.** King of England. (1660-1685.) Careless, witty, and licentious ..................................... 1630—1685

**Charles the Bold.** Duke of Burgundy. Warred with Louis XI. of France, and René of Lorraine; killed fighting the Swiss allies of the latter. ................... 1433—1477

**Charron,** Pierre. French moralist. *De la Sagesse*...... 1531—1603

**Chartier,** Alain. French poet. *Book of the four Ladies*.. 1385—1455

BORN. DIED.

**Chase, Salmon P.** American statesman and jurist. Sec'y of the Treasury. Chief Justice of the U. S. ........... 1808—1873

**Chateaubriand**, Francis A., Viscount of. French poet and prose writer. *Genie du Christianisme. Atala* .... 1768—1848

**Chatham**, William Pitt, First Earl of. English statesman and orator. "The Great Commoner;" entered Parliament, 1735; opposed Walpole's ministry; Premier, 1757; formed coalition ministry with Newcastle; resigned, 1761; opposed taxation of the American Colonies........................... 1708—1778

**Chatterton**, Thomas. English poet and literary impostor; fabricated works which he attributed to Rowley, a monk of the 15th century. *The Battle of Hastings. The Tournament; Ode to Ella*........................ 1752—1770

**Chaucer**, Geoffrey. English poet. *The Canterbury Tales;* in the household of Edward III.; ambassador to Genoa, 1373; comptroller of customs at London; knight of the shire for Kent, 1386; among his works are *The Court of Love; Legend of Good Women; Troilus and Cresseide*.. 1328—1400

**Chénier**, André M. de. French lyric poet. *The Young Captive*......................... 1764—1794

**Cherbuliez**, Victor. French novelist. *Prosper Randoce; L'Idée de Jean Teterol* ........................ 1832 ——

**Cherubini**, Maria L. C. Z. S. Italian musical composer. Produced at London in 1784 his operas *The Pretended Princess*, and *Giulio Sabino;* after 1786 he lived in Paris, where his opera *Lodoiska* appeared in 1791. Among his other works are *Medée, Elisa, Ali Baba*, and, in sacred music, the *Requiem* ........................ 1760—1842

**Chesterfield**, Philip D. Stanhope, Earl of. English wit and man of fashion. *Letters*. ..................... 1694—1773

**Chevalier**, Michael. French political economist. *On the Material Interests of France* ...................... 1806—1879

**Chillingworth**, William. English theologian. *The Religion of Protestants; a Safe Way to Salvation*......... 1602—1644

**Choate**, Rufus. American lawyer, orator, and statesman. Most eloquent advocate of his time; U. S. Senator from Mass.............................. 1799—1859

**Chopin**, Frederick. Polish composer and pianist. Went to Paris in 1832, where he was most admired; was himself an accomplished and successful performer. Among his works are many mazurkas, waltzes and concertos. His works are perhaps the best of piano music. His life has been written by Liszt .................... 1810—1849

**Christina**, Queen of Sweden. Eccentric and learned; daughter of Gustavus Adolphus; abdicated in 1654..... 1626—1689

**Chrysostom**, John. "The Golden-mouthed." Greek preacher and theologian; Archbishop of Constantinople. 347— 407

**Churchill**, Charles. English poet; schoolmate of Cowper; entered Church against his will; became dissipated; assisted Wilkes on *North Briton; The Rosciad; The Bard; The Prophecy of Famine; The Conference*.. 1731—1764

**Cibber**, Colley. English actor and dramatist. Poet Laureate. *Richard III. altered*...................... 1671—1757

**Cicero**, Marcus Tullius. Roman orator, statesman, and author. Received a thorough education, becoming familiar with Greek literature. After travelling, he began (at 25) his successful career as an advocate; was quaestor 76 B.C.; aedile 70 B.C.; and consul 63 B.C. In his consulship suppressed the conspiracy of Catiline; went in exile in 58 B.C. but was recalled; was a Pompeian, but enjoyed the favor of Cæsar; was slain by the soldiers of Antony. Among his orations are his great speeches against Catiline, and against Verres, in defence of Milo, and of Archas. Among his philosophical works are *De Natura Deorum* and *Tusculan Disputations*. His work *On Old Age* is perhaps the best known of his writings........................B.C. 103— 46

**Cimabue**, John. Early Italian painter. Restorer of painting in Italy .............................. 1240—1300

**Cincinnatus,** Lucius Quintus. Roman general and statesman. Taken from the plow and made Dictator; conquered the Æquians................................B.C. 516— 438

**Cinna**, Lucius Cornelius. Roman demagogue. Partisan of Marius, with whom he captured Rome and massacred the adherents of Sulla............................B.C. —— 84

**Cinq-Mars**, Henri C. de Ruze, Marquis of. Favorite of Louis XIII. of France; Grand-equerry; executed on a charge of treason.............................. 1620—1642

**Clarendon**, Edward Hyde, 1st Earl of. Lord Chancellor of England; chief adviser of Charles II. in his exile, and his Prime Minister, 1660-7. Historian. *History of the Rebellion*.................................. 1608—1674

**Clarke**, Adam. Irish Methodist Biblical commentator. *Commentary on the Holy Bible*......................... 1762—1832

**Claude Lorraine** (Claude Gelée). French painter. *Esther and Ahasuerus*.............................. 1600—1682

**Cimarosa**, Domenico. Italian composer. *The Secret Marriage*................................ 1755—1801

**Claudian**, Claudius. Latin poet. *The Rape of Proserpine* 365— 410

**Claudius**. Fourth Roman Emperor. (41-54.) Made a successful invasion of Britain......................B.C. 10—A.D. 54

**Clay**, Henry. American orator and statesman; born in Virginia; removed to Kentucky in 1797, and practiced law; Speaker of U. S. Congress, 1811; signed treaty of Ghent, 1815; elected Speaker, 1815, and thrice re-elected; advocated U. S. Bank and Missouri Compromise; Sec'y of State, 1825; U. S. Senator, 1832-42; Whig candidate for President, 1844; re-elected to Senate, 1848. 1777—1852

**Clemens**, Samuel L. American humorist. "Mark Twain." *The Innocents Abroad*......................... 1835 ——

**Cleon**. Athenian demagogue; for a time a successful general; defeated and slain at Amphipolis..........B.C. —— 422

**Cleopatra.** Queen of Egypt. Mistress of Cæsar and Antony. Daughter of Ptolemy Auletes, upon whose death, 51 B.C., she became joint sovereign of Egypt with her brother Ptolemy; was beautiful and accomplished, but voluptuous; was expelled from the throne by Ptolemy but reinstated by Julius Cæsar (48); lived with Cæsar at Rome (46-44); in 41, became the favorite of Mark Antony; at the battle of Actium she fled; she escaped Augustus by killing herself with an asp.....B.C. 69— 30

**Clinton**, De Witt. American statesman. Governor of New York; U. S. Senator; Federal candidate for President; promoter of the Erie Canal........................ 1769—1828

**Clive**, Robert, 1st Lord. British general, founder of the British empire in India......................... 1725—1774

**Clodius**, Publius. Roman tribune and demagogue. Opponent of Milo, who finally killed him ..............B.C. —— 52

**Clootz**, John Baptist, Baron. German traveller and French Revolutionist. Guillotined................ 1753—1794

**Clough**, Arthur Hugh. English poet. *Dypsychus; Amours de Voyage; Long-Vacation Pastoral; Ambarvalia*..... 1819—1861

**Clovis I.** King of the Franks. Conquerer of the Gauls... 465— 511

**Cobbett**, William. English radical, reformer, and writer. *Cottage Economy*.............................. 1762—1835

**Cobden**, Richard. English statesman and economist, leader of the Anti-Corn Law League .... .............. 1804—1865

**Coke**, Sir Edward. English Lord Chief Justice. *Reports*.. 1552—1633

**Colbert**, Jean Baptiste. French statesman and financier. Controller-general of the finances; principal minister of Louis XIV.............................. 1619—1683

**Colenso**, John W. English theologian. Bishop of Natal. *The Pentateuch and Book of Joshua critically considered.* 1814 ——

**Coleridge**, Samuel Taylor. English poet and philosopher. *The Ancient Mariner;* educated at Cambridge; with Southey, came near emigrating to America to found democratic community in 1794; with Wordsworth wrote *Lyrical Ballads;* studied German literature in Göttingen; 1816-25, published *Christabel; A Lay Sermon; Zapoyla; Biographia Literaria; Aids to Reflection;* was a slave to opium............................. 1772—1834

BORN. DIED.

**Coligny**, Gaspard de. French admiral. Huguenot leader; killed in the massacre of St. Bartholomew. . . .. ....... 1517—1572

**Collingwood**, Cuthbert. Lord High Admiral of England; second in command at the battle of Trafalgar.......... 1750—1810

**Collins**, William. English poet; educated at Oxford; friend of Dr. Johnson; published *Odes* 1747; insane latter part of his life. *The Passions*....... ......... 1720—1756

**Colman**, George (The Younger). English dramatist. *John Bull*........................................ 1762—1836

**Colt**, Samuel. American inventor; Colt's revolver........ 1814—1862

**Columbus**, Christopher. Discoverer of America; born in Genoa; studied at University of Padua; a sailor at 14; removed to Lisbon 1470; went with Portuguese navigators to Western Africa; expected by sailing westward to find India; left Palos (Aug. 3, 1492) with 3 vessels; discovered San Salvador Oct. 12; visited Cuba and Hayti; 1493 discovered Porto Rico and Jamaica: 1498 continent at mouth of Orinoco; 1502 Honduras; died in poverty and neglect.......................... .. 1436—1506

**Combe**, George. English phrenologist and educator. *Constitution of Man*........................................ 1788—1858

**Comines**, Philippe de. French statesman and historian. *Memoirs*........................................ 1445—1509

**Commodus**. Emperor of Rome (180-192). Cruel and vicious. Poisoned... .................................. 161— 192

**Comte**, Auguste. French philosopher. Founder of positivism. *Course of Positive Philosophy*............ 1798—1857

**Condé**, Louis II, Prince de. "The Great Condé." French general; defeated Spaniards at Rocroi, 1643; and the Germans at Nordlingen, 1645; returned to France, 1659; entered the Spanish service, 1653; defeated William of Orange, 1674........................................ 1621—1686

**Condillac**, Stephen B. de. French philosopher. *Treatise on Sensations*........................................ 1715—1780

**Condorcet**, Marie J. A. N., Caritat, Marquis of. French metaphysician. *Historical Sketch of the Progress of the Human Mind*........................................ 1743—1794

**Confucius**, (Kung-futse). Chinese philosopher and theologian. Came forward as a religious teacher at 22; was for a time minister of crime; subsequently he traveled extensively. His influence in the East has been enormous. His philosophy related to the present life only; had nothing to do with physics or metaphysics; his sole object was to promote human happiness......B. C. 551— 479

**Congreve**, William. English dramatist, man of fashion and wit. *The Old Bachelor*, 1693; *The Double Dealer*, 1694; *Love for Love*, 1695; *The Mourning Bride*, 1697; *The Way of the World*, 1700. Was appointed Secretary of Jamaica, 1714. Pope dedicated his translation of the *Iliad* to him.... ...................................... 1670—1729

**Conkling**, Roscoe. American Republican, lawyer and statesman. U. S. Senator from N. Y........................... 1828 —

**Constantine I.**, ("The Great"). Roman Emperor (306-337). Removed the Capital of the Empire to Byzantium........................................ 272— 337

**Cook**, Captain James. English circumnavigator of the globe, and discoverer. Killed by Hawaians. *Journal*.. 1728—1779

**Cooke**, George Frederick. English actor. Great as *Richard III.* and *Iago* ........................................ 1755—1812

**Cooper**, Sir Astley P. English surgeon. *Anatomy and Diseases of the Breast*........................................ 1768—1841

**Cooper**, Peter. American philanthropist; founder of Cooper Union ........................................ 1791 —

**Cooper**, James Fennimore. American novelist. Studied for a time at Yale College, and was a midshipman for a few years; published his first novel, *Precaution*, in 1809. The sea stories are his best. Among his works are *The Spy*, *The Pioneers*, *The Pilot*, *Lionel Lincoln*, *The Prairie*, *The Bravo*, *The Red Rover*, *The Pathfinder*, *The Deerslayer*, *Wing and Wing*, *Afloat and Ashore*, *Oak Openings* ........................................ 1789—1851

BORN. DIED.

**Copernicus**, Nicholas. German astronomer. Demolished the Ptolemaic theory of the universe and demonstrated that the sun is the center of the universe in his great work *The Revolution of the Celestial Orbs*. Its publication was delayed (for fear of persecution, it is said) so that a copy of it did not reach him till the day of his death........................................ 1473—1543

**Copley**, John Singleton. English (American born) painter. *The Death of Lord Chatham*........................................ 1737—1815

**Corday**, Charlotte de. Slayer of Marat.............. 1768—1793

**Coriolanus**. Roman patrician and general. Conqueror of the Volscians, to whom he afterwards deserted...B. C. 5th Cent'y.

**Corneille**, Pierre. French dramatist. The *Cid*; founder of the classical French drama; produced the *Cid* in 1636; among his other works are *Les Horaces*, *Cinna*, and *Polyeucte*........................................ 1606—1684

**Cornell**, Ezra. American philanthropist. Founder of Cornell University........................................ 1807—1874

**Correggio**, Antonio Allegri da. Italian painter. *The Assumption of the Virgin*. Was extremely skillful in the use of *chiaroscuro*, and foreshortening. Among his works are a *Penitent Magdalen* (at Dresden); *St. Jerome*; *Notte* (a picture of the Nativity); *Ecce Homo*; and a Holy Family called *La Vierge au Panier*................ 1474—1534

**Cortez**, Hernando. Spanish Conqueror of Mexico...... .. 1485—1547

**Corvinus**, Matthias. King of Hungary; conqueror of Austria........................................ 1443—1490

**Cousin**, Victor. French eclectic philosopher and writer. *Course of Moral Philosophy* ........................................ 1792—1867

**Couture**, Thomas. French painter. *Romans of the Decadence* 1815—1867

**Cowley**, Abraham. English poet. *Pindaric Odes*........ 1618—1667

**Cowper**, William. English poet; came of good family; studied at Westminster school; was called to the bar but never practiced; suffered mental derangement for several years. Published his great work, *The Task*, in 1785. His letters are among the best in the language. His translation of Homer is a most faithful rendering...... 1731—1800

**Crabbe**, George. English poet; at first a surgeon; went to London where he was befriended by Edmund Burke; published *The Library* in 1781; soon after he was ordained a priest in the Church of England; published *The Village*, his best work, in 1783; *The Parish Register*, 1807; *The Borough*, 1810; *Tales in Verse*, 1812. 1754—1832

**Cranach**, Lucius. German painter. *Crucifixion*......... 1472—1553

**Cranmer**, Thomas. Archbishop of Canterbury. Reformer. Burnt ........................................ 1489—1556

**Crassus**, Marcus Licinius. Roman plutocrat. Triumvir with Cæsar and Pompey. Defeated and slain by the Parthians........................................B.C. 115— 53

**Crœsus**. King of Lydia. Famous for his wealth......B.C. 590— 546

**Cromwell**, Oliver. Lord Protector of England. M.P. in 1628 and 1640; entered army as Captain of Cavalry, 1642; led left wing at Marston Moor, 1644; as Fairfax's lieut. gen. led right wing at Naseby, 1645; won at Preston, 1648; signed death warrant of Charles I., 1649; made Commander-in-Chief, 1650; routed the Scotch at Dunbar, beat Charles at Worcester, 1651; dissolved Parliament, 1653; was created Protector, 1654.......................... 1599—1658

**Cromwell**, Thomas. Earl of Essex. English statesman. Minister of Henry VIII. Prominent in the suppression of monasteries........................................ 1490—1540

**Cruikshank**, George. English caricaturist. *Comic Almanack*........................................ 1792—1878

**Cudworth**, Ralph. English metaphysician. *The True Intellectual System*........................................ 1617—1688

**Cumberland**, William Augustus, Duke of. Son of George II. Conqueror at Culloden.................... 1721—1765

**Curran**, John Philpot. Irish barrister and orator. *Speech in Defence of Rowan*........................................ 1750—1817

**Curtis**, Benjamin Robbins. American Jurist. Justice of the United States Supreme Court........................ 1809—1874

BORN. DIED.

**Curtis,** George William. American orator, author and journalist. *Nile Notes ; Potiphar Papers*.............. 1824 —

**Curtius** Ernest. German scholar and author. *History of Greece*.............. 1814 —

**Curtius,** Rufus Quintus. Roman Historian. *Alexander the Great*.............. 1st Cent'y.

**Cushing,** Caleb. American lawyer, diplomatist and statesman. Attorney-General of the United States ; Minister to China. *The Treaty of Geneva*.............. 1800—1879

**Cushman,** Charlotte S. American actress. Great as *Meg Merrilies*.............. 1816—1876

**Cuvier,** George C. L. D., Baron de. French naturalist. *Animal Kingdom.* Assistant professor of comparative anatomy at Paris Museum of Natural History, 1795; published, 1817, his *Animal Kingdom*, in which he divided animals into four classes; began in 1823 his *Natural History of Fishes ;* was founder of the science of comparative anatomy.............. 1769—1832

**Cyprian,** Saint. Bishop of Carthage. Martyr. *On the Unity of God*.............. 200— 258

**Cyrus** (The Elder). King of Persia. Conqueror of Babylon.............. B. C. — 529

**Cyrus** (The Younger). Hero of Xenophon's *Anabasis.* Defeated and slain at Cunaxa.............. B. C. — 401

**Dacier,** André. French scholar and critic. *Commentary on Horace*.............. 1651—1722

**Dacier,** Anne Lefèvre. Wife of the above. Classical scholar and translator of Homer.............. 1654—1720

**Daguerre,** Louis J. M. French photographer. Daguerreotypes.............. 1789—1851

**Daguesseau,** Henri F. French chancellor, orator and lawyer; defended Gallican Church; instituted legislative reforms.............. 1668—1751

**D'Albret,** Jeanne. Queen of Navarre. Supporter of French Protestantism. Mother of Henry IV.............. 1528—1572

**D'Alembert,** Jean le Rond. French mathematician and philosopher. *Elements of Philosophy*.............. 1717—1783

**Dallas,** George M. American Democratic politician. Vice-President, 1845-49.............. 1792—1864

**Dalton,** John. English natural philosopher. Propounder of the atomic theory. *New System of Chemical Philosophy*.............. 1766—1844

**D'Amboise,** George. Cardinal. Minister of Louis XII. of France.............. 1460—1510

**Damiani,** Peter. Italian ecclesiastic and author. Cardinal Bishop of Ostia. Attempted to check simony.... 990—1072

**Damiens,** Robert F. French fanatic. Attempted to murder Louis XV. of France.............. 1714—1757

**Dampier,** William. English explorer and navigator. *Voyage Round the World*.............. 1652—1712

**Dana,** Charles A. American journalist. Editor of the New York *Sun*.............. 1819 —

**Dana,** Richard Henry. American poet and man of letters. *The Buccaneer ; The Dying Rover ; The Idle Man*....... 1787—1879

**Dana,** Richard Henry. Son of the above. American lawyer and author. *Two Years Before the Mast.* Editor of *Wheaton's International Law*.............. 1815—1882

**Dancer,** Daniel. English miser.............. 1716—1794

**Dandolo,** Enrico. The Blind Doge of Venice. Took Byzantium by storm.............. 1108—1205

**Dane,** Nathan. American lawyer and statesman. Author of the *Ordinance of 1787. Digest*.............. 1752—1835

**Daniel,** Jewish prophet of the 6th Cent. B. C. Reputed author of the book bearing his name.

**Daniel,** Arnaud. Greatest of the Provincial troubadours. — 1198

**Daniel,** Samuel. English poet and antiquarian. *Musophilus ; The Tragedy of Cleopatra ; The Civil Wars of York and Lancaster ; History of England*.............. 1562—1619

**Dante degli Alighieri.** Greatest Italian Poet. *The Divine Comedy.* Passed much of his time in exile from Florence for political causes. Wrote *The New Life* (*Vita Nuova*), the *Convito*, treatise on the Italian language *De Vulgari Eloquio*, and *De Monarchia*.......... 1265—1321

**Danton,** George J. French Revolutionist. Head of the "Dantonists." Minister of Justice.............. 1759—1794

**D'Arblay,** Mme. Frances (Miss Burney). English novelist. *Evelina ; Cecilia, Camilla*.............. 1752—1840

**Dare,** Virginia. First American-born child of English parents.............. 1587 —

**D'Argensola,** Lupercio L. Spanish poet and dramatist. *Filis*.............. 1565—1613

**Darius I.** (Hytaspes). King of Persia B. C. 521-485. Began the wars with the Greeks. His Satraps Datis and Artaphernes were defeated at Marathon.......... B. C. — 485

**Darius III.** (Codomannus). King of Persia B. C. 336-330. Defeated and dethroned by Alexander the Great... B. C. 380— 330

**Darling,** Grace. English heroine and lighthouse keeper. 1815—1842

**Darnley,** Henry, Earl of. Married Mary Queen of Scots. Murdered (it is supposed) by the Earl of Bothwell...... 1541—1567

**Darwin,** Charles. English naturalist. Originator of the theory of evolution ; held that all the various forms of animal and vegetable life have been produced by a series of gradual changes in natural descent. *Origin of Species ; The Descent of Man; The Fertilization of Orchids*.............. 1809—1882

**Darwin,** Erasmus. English poet. *The Loves of the Plants*.............. 1731—1802

**D'Aubigné,** Theodore. French soldier, historian and poet. *Les Tragiques*.............. 1550—1630

**Daudet,** Alphonse. French novelist. *Jack*.............. 1840 —

**Daunou,** Pierre C. F. French author and statesman. *Course of Historical Studies*.............. 1761—1840

**Davenant,** Sir William. English dramatist and poet. (The unfinished) epic poem, *Gorborduc*.............. 1605—1668

**David.** King of Israel. Author of many of the psalms. B. C. 1090—1015

**David,** Jacques Louis. French historical painter. *Rape of the Sabines*.............. 1748—1825

**David,** Pierre J. French sculptor. *Bust of Washington*.. 1789—1856

**Da Vinci,** Leonardo. Italian painter, sculptor, engineer and universal genius. *The Lord's Supper.* Among his works are *Madonna, Lisa del Giocondo* and *The Virgin on the Knees of St. Anne.* In the last part of his life he was in the service of Francis I. of France.............. 1452—1519

**Davis,** Jefferson. American statesman. Graduated at West Point ; served in Black Hawk war; colonel in Mexican war; elected to U. S. Senate, 1847; Secretary of War, 1853-57; re-elected to Senate, 1857; President Southern Confederacy, 1861-65.............. 1808 —

**Davoust,** Louis N. Duke of Auerstadt. One of Napoleon's marshals. Defeated the Prussians at Auerstadt. 1770—1823

**Davy,** Sir Humphrey. English physicist. Discovered that the fixed alkalies are metallic oxides. Published *Researches, Chemical and Philosophical*.............. 1778—1829

**Decatur,** Stephen. American naval commander. Captured the British frigate Macedonian; defeated Algerines.............. 1779—1820

**De Foe,** Daniel. English novelist ; son of a Dissenting London butcher ; took part in Monmouth's rebellion. 1701, published *The True-Born Englishman ;* 1702, *The Shortest Way with Dissenters*, for which he was imprisoned and pilloried ; was subsequently committed to Newgate ; produced his great work, *Robinson Crusoe*, in 1719 ; *Moll Flanders*, 1721 ; *Colonel Jack*, 1721.......... 1661—1731

**Dekker,** Thomas. English dramatist ; wrote plays in conjunction with Rowley and Ford. *The Gulls Hornbook ; Fortunatus, or the Wishing Cap*.............. — 1641

**Delacroix,** Ferdinand V. E. French painter. *The Women of Algiers*.............. 1799—1863

**Delane,** W. F. A. Chief editor of the London *Times*..... 1793—1857

**Delaroche,** Paul. French painter. *The Girondist in Prison*.............. 1797—1856

| | BORN. DIED. |
|---|---|
| **Delavigne,** Jean F. C. French poet and dramatist. *The Sicilian Vespers* | 1793—1843 |
| **Delorme,** Marion. French prostitute and beauty. Friend of Richelieu and St. Evremond | 1612—1650 |
| **Del Sarto,** Andrea Vannuchi. Italian painter. *Madonna di S. Francesco* | 1488—1530 |
| **Demetrius Poliorcetes.** King of Macedonia. One of Alexander the Great's generals; famed for the number of cities he had captured B.C. | 37— 283 |
| **Democritus** (of Abdera). "The Laughing Philosopher." B.C. | 460— 357 |
| **Demosthenes.** Greatest Greek orator; had an impediment in his speech which he conquered with persistent effort; was an opponent of Philip of Macedon, against whom, between 352 and 340 B.C., he delivered his 11 *Philippics.* It being proposed to give him a crown, Æschines opposed; this was the cause of the noblest speech of Demosthenes, that *On the Crown;* finally committed suicide; left 60 speeches B.C. | 385— 322 |
| **Denham,** Sir John. English poet. *Cooper's Hill* | 1615—1668 |
| **Denman,** Thomas, Lord. Chief Justice of England | 1779—1854 |
| **Denys,** Saint. Apostle of France. *First Bishop of Paris. Martyr* | — 272 |
| **De Quincey,** Thomas. English author; son of wealthy Manchester merchant; educated at Oxford, where he contracted opium habit; was a brilliant magazine writer. *Confessions of an Opium Eater* | 1785—1859 |
| **Derby,** Geoffrey Smith Stanley, Earl of. English Tory statesman. Translator of Homer. Prime Minister | 1799—1868 |
| **Desaugiers,** Marc A. M. French lyric poet. Famous writer of drinking songs | 1772—1827 |
| **Descartes,** René. French philosopher and metaphysician. *Discourse on the Method of Reasoning Well;* published, 1641, *Meditationes de Prima Philosophia;* in 1644, *Principles of Philosophy;* made many discoveries in algebra and geometry. "I think, therefore I am." | 1596—1650 |
| **Desmoulins,** B. Camille. French Revolutionist. Editor of the *Vieux Cordelier;* guillotined | 1762—1794 |
| **De Soto,** Ferdinand. Spanish adventurer. Discoverer of the Mississippi | 1500—1542 |
| **Desportes,** Philippe. French lyric poet; author of many erotic and anacreontic songs | 1545—1606 |
| **D'Estrées,** Gabrielle. Mistress of Henry IV. of France. | 1570—1599 |
| **De Vigny,** Alfred, Count. French poet and novelist. *Cinq Mars* | 1799—1863 |
| **Devonshire,** Georgiana Cavendish, Duchess of. English beauty and woman of fashion | 1757—1806 |
| **De Witt,** John. Grand Pensionary of Holland. Leader of the Anti-Orange party | 1625—1672 |
| **Dibdin,** Charles. English song writer. *Tom Bowling* | 1745—1814 |
| **Dickens,** Charles. English novelist; parliamentary reporter and journalist; published *Sketches by Boz,* 1836; next appeared *Pickwick Papers, Oliver Twist, Nicholas Nickleby, The Old Curiosity Shop, Barnaby Rudge, American Notes, Martin Chuzzlewit, Dombey and Son, David Copperfield, Bleak House, Hard Times, Little Dorrit, The Tale of Two Cities, Great Expectations, Our Mutual Friend, Edwin Drood* | 1812—1870 |
| **Diderot,** Denis. French philosopher and novelist. *Encyclopédie* | 1713—1784 |
| **Digby,** Sir Kenelm. English author. *Chemical Secrets* | 1603—1663 |
| **Diocletian.** Roman Emperor, 284—305. Divided the Empire for administrative purposes. Persecuted the Christians | 245— 313 |
| **Diodorus Siculus.** Greek historian. *Historical Library* B.C. | 1st Cent'y |
| **Diogenes.** Greek cynic philosopher. Surly and independent inhabitant of a tub B.C. | — 323 |
| **Diogenes Laertius.** Greek historian. *Lives of the Philosophers* | 2d Cent'y |
| **Dion Cassius.** Greek historian. *History of Rome* | 155— 230 |
| **Dion Chrysoston.** Greek rhetorician. 80 of his orations are extant | 2d Cent'y |
| **Dionysius** (the Elder) of Syracuse. Greek general who made himself tyrant B.C. | 430— 367 |
| **Dionysius** of Syracuse (the Younger). Tyrant. Deposed by Conuth. Afterward taught school B.C. | 398— 340 |
| **Dionysius of Halicarnassus.** Greek historian. *Roman Antiquities* | 1st Cent'y |
| **Disraeli,** Benjamin, Earl of Beaconsfield. English statesman and novelist. Premier (1874-1880). English repsentative at the Congress of Berlin. *Coningsby, Vivian Grey, The Young Duke, Contarini Fleming, Henrietta Temple, Endymion, Lothair* | 1805—1881 |
| **Disraeli,** Isaac. English author. *Curiosities of Literature* | 1767—1848 |
| **Dix,** John A. American statesman and general; senator. Minister to France | 1798—1879 |
| **Doddridge,** Philip. English dissenting minister. *The Rise and Progress of Religion in the Soul* | 1702—1751 |
| **Dodington,** George Bubb, Lord Melcombe. English politian and writer. *Diary.* Ambassador to Spain. Patron of Thomson and Young | 1691—1762 |
| **Dolce,** Carlo. Italian painter. *Christ on Mount Olivet* | 1616—1686 |
| **Domenichino** (Dominic Zampieri). Italian painter. *The Martyrdom of St. Agnes* | 1581—1641 |
| **Dominic de Guzman,** Saint. Spanish inquisitor; founder of the Dominican monks | 1170—1221 |
| **Domitian.** Roman Emperor. Rapacious and cruel; assassinated | 52— 96 |
| **Donatello** (Donato di Belto di Bardi). Italian sculptor. *Judith holding the head of Holofernes* | 1383—1486 |
| **Donizetti,** Gaetano. Italian composer. *Lucia di Lammermoor; Lucrezia Borgia; Anna Bolena; Linda di Chamouni* | 1798—1848 |
| **Donne,** John. English poet and divine; Works consist of elegies, satires, epigrams, religious poems; first of the "metaphysical poets." *Pseudo-Martyrs* | 1573—1631 |
| **Doria,** Andrew. Genoese naval commander. Defeated the Turks | 1468—1560 |
| **D'Orsay,** Alfred G. G., Count. French artist, and man of fashion in England | 1798—1852 |
| **Dorset,** Charles Sackville, Earl of. English poet and patron of letters. Rescued Dryden from poverty | 1637—1706 |
| **Douglas,** Gawayn. Scotch poet. *Palace of Honor; King Hart;* and a translation of the *Æneid* into Scottish verse | 1475—1522 |
| **Douglas,** Stephen A. American democratic politician. Senator from Illinois. *The Kansas-Nebraska Bill* | 1813—1861 |
| **Draco.** Athenian legislator; noted for the severity of his laws B.C. | 7th Cent'y |
| **Drake,** Sir Francis. English navigator and admiral; preyed upon Spanish commerce; burned 100 Spanish vessels in Cadiz | 1545—1596 |
| **Drake,** Joseph Rodman. American poet. *The Culprit Fay; The American Flag* | 1795—1820 |
| **Drayton,** Michael. English poet. *Polyolbion; The Shepherd's Garland; The Baron's Wars* | 1563—1631 |
| **Drummond,** William (of Hawthornden.) Scotch poet. *Praise of a Solitary Life; Tears on the Death of Mœliades; Poems; Forth Feasting; Polemo; Middinia;* friend of Drayton and Ben Jonson | 1585-1649 |
| **Dryden,** John. English poet and dramatist; educated at Cambridge; appointed poet-laureate, 1670; produced *Absalom and Achitophel,* 1681; also, *The Medal;* 1682 the second part of *Absalom and Achitophel* and *Mac Flecknoe;* became Roman Catholic and produced *The Hind and the Panther;* 1694-6, translated Virgil; 1696 appeared *Ode on Alexander's Feast;* 1698-1700, *Fables.* Of his dramatic works, *All for Love* is the best | 1631—1700 |
| **Dubarry,** Marie Jeanne, Countess. Mistress of Louis XV. of France | 1746—1793 |

BORN. DIED.

**Dubellay,** Joachim. French poet; one of the "Pleiad." 1523—1560

**Dubois,** William, Cardinal. French Prime Minister. Teacher of the Regent Duke of Orleans; Archbishop of Cambray ........ 1656—1723

**Duguesclin,** Bertrand. Constable of France. Expelled the English from France........ 1315—1380

**Dumas,** Alexandre. French novelist. *The Three Musketeers*........ 1803—1870

**Dumas,** Alexandre (Jr.). French novelist and dramatist. *La Dame aux Camélias*........ 1824—

**Dundas,** Henry, Viscount Melville. English statesman. Secretary of War, friend and supporter of Pitt........ 1740—1811

**Duns Scotus,** John. Scotch schoolman. Founder of the Scotists who opposed the Thomists, *i.e.*, followers of Thomas Aquinas........ 1265—1308

**Dunstan,** Saint. Saxon Archbishop of Canterbury, and statesman. Increased the power of the monks as against the secular clergy........ 925— 988

**Dupanloup,** Félix, A. P., Bishop of Orleans. *Treatise on Education*........ 1802—1878

**Dupin,** Andre M. J. J. Eloquent French advocate and statesman. *Principia Juris Civilis*........ 1783—1865

**Dürer,** Albert. German painter and engraver. *The Crucifixion.* Born at Nurenberg, where he painted *Orpheus;* at Venice (1505), painted *The Martyrdom of St. Bartholomew*, and became the friend of Raphael; was court painter to Maximilian and Charles V. Among his works are *Adam and Eve*, *Adoration of the Magi*, and portraits of Erasmus and Raphael; among his best engravings are *The Revelation of St. John.* and *Adam and Eve.* 1471—1528

**Duroc,** Gerard C. W., Duke of Friuli. French Marshal. Aide-de-camp and confidential friend of Napoleon I... 1772—1813

**Duval,** Claude. French highwayman........ —— 1670

**Dwight,** Timothy. American clergyman and author. President of Yale College. *Travels in New England and New York*........ 1752—1817

**Edgeworth,** Maria, Miss. English novelist. *Belinda; Castle Rackrent; Popular Tales; Senoria; The Absentee; Ennui; Essay on Irish Bulls*........ 1767—1849

**Edgeworth,** Richard Lovell. Father of the above. English writer. *Professional Education*........ 1744—1817

**Edmund, Saint.** Saxon king of East Anglia; defeated and put to death by Danes........ 841— 870

**Edward I.** King of England; conqueror of Wales and Scotland........ 1239—1307

**Edward III.** King of England; carried on war (Hundred Years' War) with France; won battle of Crecy........ 1312—1377

**Edward the Black Prince.** Son of Edward III.; hero of the French-English wars (Hundred Years' War); won battle of Poitiers........ 1330—1376

**Edward the Confessor.** King of England; under Norman influence; virtuous and weak........ 1004—1066

**Edwards,** Jonathan. American metaphysician; ablest Defender of Calvinism. *On the Freedom of the Will*... 1703—1758

**Eginhard.** Secretary to Charlemagne; supposed author of a life of Charlemagne........ 775— 840

**Egmont,** Lamoral, Count of. Dutch statesman and general; hero of Goethe's *Egmont;* won battle of Gravelines. Executed........ 1522—1568

**Eldon,** John Scott, Earl of. English jurist; Lord Chancellor of England........ 1751—1838

**Elijah.** Jewish prophet; translated to heaven........ B.C. 910— 896

**Eliot,** John. Apostle of the Indians *The Indian Bible*.. 1604—1690

**Eliot,** Sir John. English Parliamentary leader; head of the popular party........ 1590—1632

**Elisha.** Prophet of the Jews succeeding Elijah. Flourished........ B.C. 9th Cent'y.

**Elizabeth.** The great queen of England; daughter of Henry VIII. Educated by Roger Ascham. Among the great events of her reign were the repulse of the Spanish Armada, and the execution of Mary Queen of Scots. Among her favorites were Essex, Leicester, and Raleigh 1533—1603

**Elizabeth Petrovna.** Empress of Russia; daughter of Peter the Great; opponent of Frederick the Great in Seven Years' War; licentious........ 1709—1761

**Elizabeth Woodville.** Queen of Edward IV. of England —— 1488

**Elizabeth of York.** Queen of Henry VII. of England; daughter of Edward IV.; mother of Henry VIII........ 1466—1502

**Ellenborough,** Edward Law, Earl of. English jurist; Lord Chief Justice of England........ 1748—1818

**Elliott,** Ebenezer. English poet. "The Corn Law Rhymer." *Corn Law Rhymes; The Ranter; The Village Patriarch;* painted social condition of the poor........ 1781—1849

**Ellsworth,** Oliver. American jurist; Chief Justice of the United States........ 1745—1807

**Elyot,** Sir Thomas. English author. *The Governor*........ 1495—1546

**Elzevirs.** A celebrated family of printers at Leyden in the 16th and 17th Cent........

**Emerson,** Ralph Waldo. American transcendental philosopher and poet; graduated at Harvard; was for a time a Unitarian minister in Boston; settled in Concord in 1835; published *Essays on Representative Men*, 1850; *English Traits*, 1856; *The Conduct of Life*, 1860; *Poems*, 1840 and 1867; *Society and Solitude*, 1870, and several volumes of *Essays*........ 1803—1882

**Emmett,** Robert. Irish patriot; executed for treason.... 1780—1803

**Emmett,** Thomas Addis. Brother of the above Irish patriot, and leading member of the American Bar........ 1763—1827

**Empedocles.** Greek (Sicilian) natural philosopher; held that Nature is composed of four elements; flourished B.C. 5th Cent'y.

**Endicott,** John. Governor of the colony of Massachusetts Bay; emigrated to Salem from England in 1628........ 1589—1665

**Enghien,** Louis A. H. de Bourbon, Duke of. Executed by Napoleon I........ 1772—1804

**Ennius,** Quintus. Early Roman poet. *Annals*......B.C. 239— 169

**Enzio.** Bastard son of Frederick II. of Germany; nominal king of Sardinia; won naval victory over Genoese..... 1225—1272

**Epaminondas.** Theban general; defeated Spartans at Leuctra; slain at Mantinea........ B.C. —— 362

**Epictetus.** Greek Stoic philosopher and moralist. *Enchiridion.* Flourished in........ 2d Cent'y.

**Epicurus.** Greek philosopher. Founder of the Epicureans........ B.C. 342— 270

**Epimenides** (Legendary) Hero and sage of Crete; famed for his long sleep. Flourished........ B.C. 6th Cent'y.

**Erasmus,** Desiderius. Dutch scholar, restorer of learning, and author. *Enconium Moriae, Colloquia; Adagia* 1467—1536

**Eratosthenes.** Greek geographer and scientist; measured the obliquity of the ecliptic........ B.C. 275— 196

**Erigena,** John Scotus. Irish schoolman and theologian. *On the Division of Nature.* Flourished in........ 9th Cent'y.

**Ernesti,** John A. German philologist and classical scholar; edited Cicero, Homer, Tacitus........ 1707—1781

**Erostratus.** Greek incendiary; burner of the temple of Diana at Ephesus........ B.C. 4th Cent'y.

**Erskine,** Henry. Scotch advocate and orator........ 1746—1817

**Erskine,** Thomas, Lord. Scotch advocate and orator. Entered the Bar 1778; was instantaneously successful, and was soon recognized as the first advocate of his time; made a noble defense of Lord G. Gordon in 1781; defended the liberty of the press in the Stockdale trial, in 1789, and in the state trials of 1794 secured the acquittal of Hardy and Horne Tooke; was made Lord Chancellor and raised to the peerage in 1806........ 1750—1823

**Eschenbach,** Wolfram von. German minnesinger. *Titurel.* Flourished in........ 13th Cent.

**Escobar y Mendoza,** Antonio. Spanish Jesuit theologian and casuist. *Cases of Conscience*........ 1589—1669

**Espartero,** Joaquin B. Spanish general and politician. Regent during the minority of Isabella; defeated the Carlists........ 1792—1879

BORN. DIED.

**Esquirol,** Jean S. D. French physician and alienist. *Des Maladies Mentales* .... 1772—1840

**Essex,** Robert Devereux, 2d Earl of. Favorite of Elizabeth, and by her beheaded .... 1567—1601

**Essex,** Robert Devereux, 3d Earl of. English parliamentary general in the early part of the English Rebellion. 1592—1647

**Ethelred the Unready.** King of Wessex during the Danish invasion; ordered general massacre of all Danes in England in 1002 .... 968—1016

**Etherege,** Sir George. English comedy writer and wit. *Sir Fopling Flutter; She Would If She Could* .... 1635—1689

**Euclid.** Alexandrian mathematician. *Elements of Geometry*. B.C. 4th Cent.

**Eudoxia.** Wife of the Roman Emperor Arcadius (395–408); secured the exile of Chrysostom .... —— 404

**Eudoxus,** of Cnidus. Greek astronomer; determined the length of the year .... B.C. 4th Cent'y.

**Eugene,** Francis, Prince of Savoy. One of the greatest generals of his time; coöperated with Marlborough at Blenheim, Oudenarde, and Malplaquet .... 1663—1736

**Eupolis.** Greek comedy writer; next to Aristophanes in merit; only fragments of his work are extant .... B.C. 446— 410

**Euripides.** Third in merit of the great Greek tragedy writers. *Alcestis* .... B.C. 480— 406

**Eusebius.** Bishop of Cæsarea, and historian. *Ecclesiastical History* .... 265— 337

**Eutropius,** Flavius. Roman historian. *Epitome of Roman History* .... 4th Cent'y.

**Evans,** Marian (George Eliot). English novelist; daughter of a clergyman; was educated by Herbert Spencer; lived with G. H. Lewes, and afterwards married J. W. Cross; published *Scenes of Clerical Life*, 1857; *Adam Bede*, 1858; *The Mill on the Floss*, 1859; *Romola*, 1863; *Felix Holt*, 1866; *Middlemarch*, 1871; *Daniel Deronda*, 1876; *Theophrastus Such*, 1879; *The Spanish Gypsy* (a poem), 1868 .... 1820—1880

**Evarts,** William M. American lawyer and statesman; Attorney-General of the United States; Secretary of State 1816 ——

**Evelyn,** John. English author. *Diary; Sylva* .... 1620—1706

**Everett,** Edward. American orator, statesman and diplomatist; U. S. Senator; Minister to Great Britain. *Orations and Speeches* .... 1794—1865

**Ewald,** George H. A. von. German Orientalist and Biblical critic. *History of the People of Israel* .... 1803—1875

**Ewing,** Thomas. American statesman. Sec'y of Treasury under Taylor .... 1789—1871

**Eyck,** John van. Flemish painter. *Adoration of the Magi*. 1370—1441

**Ezekiel.** Hebrew prophet: *Book of Ezekiel* .... B.C. 7th Cent'y.

**Ezra.** Hebrew lawmaker; led Jews back to Jerusalem B.C. 5th Cent'y.

**Fabius Maximus,** Quintus. Roman consul and general; opponent of Hannibal; famous for his cautious "Fabian" policy .... B.C. —— 203

**Fahrenheit,** Gabriel D. German natural philosopher. Fahrenheit's thermometer .... 1686—1736

**Fairfax,** Thomas, Lord. Roundhead general in the English Rebellion; commander-in-chief before Cromwell; won battle of Naseby .... 1611—1671

**Falconer,** William. Scottish poet. *The Shipwreck* .... 1735—1769

**Faliero,** Marino. Doge of Venice. Immortalized by Byron; attempted to overthrow nobles by conspiracy of plebeians .... 1278—1350

**Faneuil,** Peter. American merchant. Founder of Faneuil Hall, Boston .... 1700—1743

**Fanshawe,** Sir Richard. English poet and politician. Translator of Guarini's *Pastor Fido* .... 1608—1666

**Faraday,** Michael. English man of science. Founder of the science of magneto-electricity. *Experimental Researches in Electricity* .... 1791—1867

**Farquhar,** George. English dramatist. *The Beaux' Stratagem; The Constant Couple* .... 1678—1707

**Farragut,** David Glascoe. American Admiral. Entered navy, 1812; commander, 1841; passed New Orleans forts and took New Orleans, 1862; made Rear Admiral same year; attacked defenses at Mobile, 1864; Admiral, 1866. 1801—1870

**Fauriel,** Claude. French author. *History of Provençal Literature* .... 1772—1844

**Faustina,** Annia. Daughter of Antoninus Pius; wife of M. Aurelius; of infamous character .... —— 175

**Fawkes,** Guy. Chief conspirator in "Gunpowder Plot." .. —— 1606

**Fearne,** Charles. English lawyer. *Contingent Remainders*. 1749—1794

**Fechter,** Charles Albert. English actor; famous in England and America. Best in *Hamlet* .... 1824—1879

**Felton,** Cornelius Conway. American scholar; president Harvard University; editor of Greek classics .... 1807—1862

**Fénelon,** Francis de Salignac de la Mothe. Archbishop of Cambray. French prelate and author. *Télémaque* .... 1765—1818

**Ferdinand Maximilian Joseph** (Maximilian I.). Emperor of Mexico. Executed. Brother of Francis Joseph. 1832—1867

**Ferdusi** (Firdousee). Persian poet. *The Shah-Nameh* (*Book of Kings*) .... 940—1020

**Fesch,** Joseph, Cardinal. French prelate. Half-brother of Napoleon's mother .... 1763—1839

**Fessenden,** William Pitt. American Republican Senator, and Secretary of the Treasury; ablest debater of his time in the Senate .... 1806—1869

**Feuillet,** Octave. French novelist and dramatist; *The Sphinx* .... 1812 ——

**Fichte,** John Gottlieb. German metaphysician. *Principles of Science* .... 1762—1814

**Ficinus,** Marselius. Italian scholar and Platonist. *Life of Plato* .... 1433—1499

**Field,** Cyrus W. American capitalist. Laid the first Atlantic cable .... 1819 ——

**Fielding,** Henry. English novelist; educated at Eton and University of Leyden; wrote much for stage; was called to the bar; published *Tom Jones; Joseph Andrews; Jonathan Wild; Amelia* .... 1707—1754

**Filelfo,** Francis. Italian scholar and philologist. *Epistles*. 1398—1481

**Fillmore,** Millard. American statesman. President of the United States, 1850–53; born in N. Y.; learned fuller's trade; studied law; M.C., 1832–42; elected Vice-President, 1848; became President on death of Taylor. 1800—1874

**Finlay,** George. British historian. *Greece Under the Romans* .... 1800—1875

**Firenzuola,** Angelo. Italian author. *Novelle* .... 1493—1545

**Fitzherbert,** Maria Anna, Mrs. Wife of George IV... 1756—1837

**Flaccus,** Caius Valerius. Roman poet. *Argonautica* .... —— 90

**Flaminius,** Titus Quinctius. Roman consul and general. Conqueror at Cynoscephalæ (197 B.C.) .... B.C. 230— 174

**Flaxman,** John. English sculptor and artist. *Illustrations of Homer* .... 1755—1826

**Fleetwood,** Charles. English Puritan and general in the Civil War. Lord Deputy of Ireland; lieut.-gen. at Dunbar and Worcester .... —— 1692

**Fletcher,** John. English dramatist. Associate of Beaumont. *The Maid's Tragedy; The Faithful Shepherdess*. 1576—1620

**Fleury,** Andrew Hercules de, Cardinal. French statesman and historian. *Ecclesiastical History* .... 1640—1723

**Flodoard.** French chronicler and priest. *Events in France, 919–966* .... 894— 966

**Flood,** Henry. Irish orator and statesman; leader of opposition in Irish Parliament; rival of Grattan .... 1732—1791

**Florence of Worcester.** English chronicler (in Latin). *Events in England* .... —— 1118

**Florus,** Lucius Annæus. Roman historian. *Epitome de Gestis Romanorum* .... 2d Cent'y.

**Foix,** Gaston de. French General and hero. Conqueror at Ravenna .... 1489—1512

**Fontanelle,** Bernard Le Bovier de. French author. *Discourse on the Plurality of Worlds* .... 1657—1757

**Foote,** Samuel. Comedian and wit. *The Englishman in Paris* .... 1720—1777

BORN. DIED.

**Ford**, John. English dramatist. *The Broken Heart; The Lover's Melancholy; Love's Sacrifice; Perkin Warbeck*.. 1586—1639

**Forrest**, Edwin. American tragedian; eminent as *Metamora; the Gladiator; Virginius*.......... 1806—1872

**Forster**, John. English biographer. *Life of Charles Dickens; Life and Times of Oliver Goldsmith*.......... 1812—1876

**Forster**, William E. English Liberal statesman; Chief Secretary for Ireland (1880-2).. ....... .......... 1818 —

**Fortescue**, Sir John. English Lord Chief Justice. *De Laudibus Legum Angliæ*.. ........ 1395—1485

**Foscari**, Francesco. Doge of Venice. Fought the Milanese........ 1373—1457

**Foscolo**, Nicolo Ugo. Italian scholar, poet, and patriot. *The Monuments*........ 1777—1827

**Foster**, John. English essayist. *On Decision of Character; Essay on the Evils of Popular Ignorance*........ 1770—1843

**Fouché**, Joseph. Duke of Otranto. French Minister of Police........ 1763—1820

**Fourier**, Francis C. M. French socialist and reformer. *Theory of Universal Unity*........ 1772—1837

**Fox**, Charles James. English orator and statesman; entered Parliament, 1768, as a Tory; joined opposition, 1773; became leader of the Whigs; Foreign Secretary, 1783 and 1806; opposed policy of Pitt ........ 1749—1806

**Fox**, George. English religionist. Founder of the Quakers........ 1624—1690

**Fox**, John. English author. *Book of Martyrs*........ 1517—1587

**Foy**, Maximilian Sebastian. French general; led a division at Waterloo........ 1775—1825

**Fra Bartolomeo di S. Marco** (Baccio della Porta). Italian painter. *The Last Judgment*........ 1469—1517

**Fra Diavolo** (Michael Rozzo). Neapolitan brigand...... 1769—1806

**Francia**, Joseph G. R. Dictator of Paraguay; adopted policy of non-intercourse with foreign nations........ 1757—1840

**Francis I.** King of France. Patron of literature and art. Opponent of Charles V.; defeated at Pavia....... 1494—1547

**Francis**, Sir Philip. English statesman. Prominent opponent of Warren Hastings. Alleged author of the *Letters of Junius*........ 1740—1818

**Francis, Saint** (of Assisi). Founder of the Franciscans 1182—1226

**Francis, Saint** (de Sales). French missionary and author. *Treatise on the Love of God*........ 1567—1622

**Franklin**, Benjamin. American statesman and philosopher. Born in Boston; learned printer's trade; removed to Pennsylvania; published *Poor Richard's Almanac*; discovered identity of lightning and electric fluid, 1752; deputy postmaster-general of the colony; agent of Penn in England; delegate to Continental Congress; Minister to France, 1776-85; President of Pennsylvania, 1785-87; member Convention of 1787.. 1706—1790

**Franklin**, Sir John. English Arctic explorer; lost in Arctic regions........ 1786—1847

**Frédégonde.** Queen of Chilperic of France. Famous for her crimes........ 545— 596

**Frederick I.** ("Barbarossa"). Holy Roman Emperor; at war with Pope and Lombard cities; died in Holy Land. 1121—1190

**Frederick II.** (grandson of the above). Emperor, 1210-50. Excommunicated by Gregory IX.; warred with Guelphs; led expedition to Palestine. Poet, and patron of literature and art........ 1194—1250

**Frederick II.** ("The Great"). King of Prussia; came to the throne in 1740, and invaded Silesia, which Maria Theresa ceded to him in 1742. Russia, France, and Austria began Seven Years' War against him and England (1756). He won a great victory at Prague (1757), but was defeated by Daun soon afterward; the same year defeated the French at Rossbach, and the Austrians at Leuthen. Peace was made in 1763. At the partition of Poland (1772) he got Prussian Poland...... 1712—1786

**Freeman**, Edward A. English historian. *The Norman Conquest; History of Federal Government*........ 1823 —

**Freiligrath**, Ferdinand. German lyric poet and patriot. 1810—1876

**Fremont**, John Charles. American explorer, politician, and general. Republican candidate for President in 1856........ 1813 —

**Frere**, John Hookham. English diplomatist, poet, and wit. *Prospectus and Specimen of an Intended National Work*........ 1769—1846

**Freytag**, Gustav. German novelist. *Debt and Credit*.... 1816 —

**Frœbel**, Frederick. German educator. Introducer of the "Kindergarten" system........ 1782—1852

**Froissart**, Jean. French chronicler. *Les Chroniques*.... 1337—1410

**Frontinus**, Sextus Julius. Roman architect and general. *Stratagematica*........ — 106

**Froude**, James A. English historian. *History of Henry VIII; Short Studies on Great Subjects*........ 1818 —

**Fuller**, Thomas. English divine and author. *Worthies of England; Holy and Profane States*........ 1608—1661

**Fulton**, Robert. American inventor of the steamboat. In 1793 tried to improve inland navigation, and in 1796 published a treatise on *Canal Navigation*. Lived in Paris for several years, and while there invented the submarine torpedo. Returning to New York in 1806, with Robert Livingston, he discovered steam navigation; built (1807) the steamer *Clermont*, which made regular trips between New York and Albany........ 1765—1815

**Fuseli**, John H. Swiss historical painter. *Shakespeare Gallery*........ 1742—1825

**Fust**, John. A German inventor of printing........ — 1460

**Gaddi**, Taddeo. Italian painter. *Virgin and Christ Between Four Prophets*........ 1300—1350

**Gainsborough**, Thomas. English landscape painter. *The Shepherd Boy*........ 1727—1788

**Galen**, Claudius. Greek physician. *De Locis Affectis*.... 130— 200

**Galilei**, Galileo. Italian astronomer. Professor of mathematics at Padua and Pisa. Discovered isochronism of the vibrations of the pendulum, and law by which the velocity of falling bodies is accelerated. Constructed a telescope in 1619. Discovered satellites of Jupiter, and adopted the Copernican system. Meanwhile he had removed to Florence, where he was compelled to recant his views on the Copernican system; published *Dialogues on the Ptolemaic and Copernican Systems*........ 1564—1642

**Gallatin**, Albert. American statesman. Secretary of the Treasury........ 1761—1849

**Gallaudet**, Thomas H. American clergyman. Instructor of the deaf and dumb........ 1787—1851

**Galt**, John. Scottish novelist. *Lawrie Todd*........ 1779—1839

**Galvani**, Louis. Italian physicist. Discoverer of galvanism........ 1737—1798

**Gambetta**, Leon. French radical orator and statesman. President of the Chamber of Deputies........ 1838 1882

**Garfield**, James A. American statesman; born in Ohio; educated at Williams College; teacher and lawyer; brigadier-gen., 1862; chief of staff to Rosecrans, 1862; major-gen. for services at Chickamauga; M.C., 1862-1881; elected to Senate, 1880; elected President, 1881; shot by Charles J. Guiteau, July 2, 1881; died Sept. 19. 1831—1881

**Garibaldi**, Giuseppe. Italian patriot and general; liberator of Italy........ 1807—1882

**Garrick**, David. English actor. Made his debut as *Richard III.* in 1741. Among his great parts were *Lear, Macbeth, Romeo, Hamlet, Abel Drugger*; made his last appearance in 1776; buried in Westminster Abbey........ 1716—1779

**Garrison**, William Lloyd. American Abolitionist...... 1804—1879

**Gascoigne**, George. English poet. *The Comedy of Supposes; Posie; The Princely Pleasures*........ 1536—1577

**Gaskell**, Mrs. Mary E. C. English novelist. *Mary Barton*........ 1820—1865

BORN. DIED.

**Gassendi,** Peter. French mathematician and philosopher. *System of Epicurean Philosophy* .......... 1592—1655

**Gates,** Horatio. American Revolutionary general; captured Burgoyne's army at Saratoga.......... 1728—1806

**Gauss,** Charles Friedrich. German mathematician. *Theory of the Motion of the Celestial Bodies*.......... 1777—1855

**Gautier,** Théophile French poet and novelist. *Mlle. de Maupan*.......... 1811—1872

**Gaveston,** Piers. Favorite and chief minister of Edward of England. Executed by the nobles.......... — 1312

**Gay** John. English poet. *The Beggar's Opera; Trivia; The Fan; Fables; The Captives* .. 1688—1732

**Gay-Lussac,** Joseph L. French physicist. Discoverer of cyanogen.......... 1778—1850

**Gaza,** Theodore Greek scholar and humanist.......... 1398—1478

**Gellert,** Christian F. German theologian and poet. *Tales; Sacred Songs* .......... 1715—1769

**Gellius,** Aulus. Latin author. *Noctes Atticæ*.......... 115— 180

**Genghis,** Khan. Mogul warrior and conqueror; subjugated China and Persia.......... 1163—1227

**Geoffrey of Monmouth.** English Latin historian. *History of the Britons* .......... 1112—1154

**Geoffroy,** Julian S. French critic and scholar; dramatic critic of the *Journal des Débats*.......... 1743—1814

**George I.** King of England. Favored the Whigs....... 1660—1727

**George II.** King of England. The Jacobites were beaten at Culloden, the French in Canada and India, during his reign .......... 1683—1760

**George III.** King of England. Arbitrary ruler; lost American colonies; insane latter part of his life.... 1738—1820

**George IV.** King of England. "The First Gentleman" in Europe; took no interest in public affairs.......... 1762—1830

**George,** Prince of Denmark. Husband of Queen Anne.. 1653—1708

**Gerard,** Balthazar. French fanatic. Assassin of William of Orange.......... 1558—1584

**Gerry,** Elbridge. American Revolutionary statesman. Vice-President; Governor of Massachusetts... ....... 1744—1814

**Gerson,** John Charles de. French theologian. "The Most Christian Doctor." Prominent at Council of Constance. *Consolation*.......... 1363—1429

**Gesenius,** Frederick H. N. German Orientalist. *Hebrew Lexicon*.......... 1786—1842

**Gesner,** Conrad von. Swiss botanist and naturalist. *History of Animals*.......... 1516—1565

**Ghiberti,** Lorenzo. Florentine sculptor. *Gate of the Baptistery of S. Giovanni at Florence*.......... 1378—1455

**Ghirlandajo,** Il. (Dominic Currodo). Italian painter. *Massacre of the Innocents* .......... 1449—1498

**Gibbon,** Edward. English historian; educated at Oxford and on the Continent; passed most of his life at Lausanne; *Memoirs. Decline and Fall of the Roman Empire*.......... 1737—1794

**Gibson,** John. English sculptor. *Venus*.......... 1790—1865

**Giddings,** Joshua R. American Abolitionist.......... 1795—1864

**Gifford,** William. English satirist. *The Baviad*.......... 1757—1826

**Gilray,** James. English caricaturist. *House of Hanover*. 1785—1815

**Ginguené,** Pierre L. French historian. *Literary History of Italy* .......... 1748—1816

**Giorgione,** Giorgio Barbarelli. Venetian painter. *Christ Allaying the Storm* .......... 1477—1511

**Giotto.** Florentine sculptor and architect. *Navicello*.. 1276—1336

**Giovanni da Fiesole** (Fra Angelico). Italian painter. *Coronation of Mary* .......... 1387—1455

**Giovio,** Paolo. Italian scholar and historian. *Lives of Illustrious Men* .......... 1483—1552

**Giraldus Cambrensis.** English Latin historian *Descriptio Cambriæ*.......... 1147—1220

**Girardin,** Mme. Emile de. French author. *Lettres Parisiennes* .......... 1804—1855

**Giulio,** Romano. Italian painter. *Giants Struck by the Thunderbolts of Jupiter*.......... 1492—1546

BORN. DIED.

**Gleim,** Johann W. L. German poet. *War Songs*.......... 1719—1803

**Glendower,** Owen. Welsh warrior; fought Henry IV... 1350—1415

**Glück,** Christopher W. von. German composer. *Iphigenia in Tauris*.......... 1714—1787

**Godfrey of Bouillon.** King of Jerusalem. Hero of the first Crusade.......... 1058—1100

**Godolphin,** Sidney, Earl of. English statesman. Lord High Treasurer under Anne.......... 1630—1712

**Godoy,** Manuel de. Spanish statesman. "The Prince of the Peace," from his unpopular peace with France in 1795; favorite of Charles IV.......... 1767—1851

**Godwin,** Mary Wollstonecraft. English writer. *Vindication of the Rights of Woman*.......... 1759—1797

**Godwin,** William. English philosopher and novelist. *Caleb Williams; St. Leon; Fleetwood*.......... 1756—1836

**Goethe,** John Wolfgang von. German poet, dramatist, critic, novelist, man of science, statesman. *Faust; Iphigenia in Tauris; Wilhelm Meister; Egmont; West-Eastern Divan; The Sorrows of Werther*, and many noble lyrical poems. In almost every department of literature, first among the Germans.......... 1749—1832

**Goldoni,** Charles. Venetian dramatist. *La Donna di Garbo* .......... 1707—1793

**Goldsmith,** Oliver. Irish poet, novelist and historian. *Vicar of Wakefield; The Traveller; The Deserted Village;* studied at Trinity College, Dublin, and at Edinburgh; led wandering life on Continent; published *The Good-Natured Man*, 1767; *She Stoops to Conquer*, 1773; *Retaliation*, 1777; was a gambler, and always in debt.......... 1728—1774

**Goodrich,** Samuel G., "Peter Parley." American writer. *Peter Parley's Own Story* .......... 1793—1860

**Gordon,** Lord George. English anti-Catholic agitator; fomenter of the Gordon riots in 1780 .......... 1750—1793

**Gortschakoff,** Alexander M., Prince. Russian statesman; Chancellor and Minister of Foreign Affairs.. .......... 1798 —

**Gottsched,** John C. German poet and author. *German Theatre According to the Rules and Examples of the Ancients*.......... 1700—1766

**Gough,** John B. American temperance orator.......... 1817 —

**Gower,** John. English poet. *Confessio Amantis*.......... 1320—1402

**Gozzi,** Charles, Count. Italian dramatist. *The Loves of the Three Oranges* .......... 1772—1806

**Gracchus,** Caius. Roman tribune and demagogue. Proposed extension of franchise to the Latins; murdered by patricians.......... B C. 154— 121

**Gracchus,** Tiberius. Roman tribune and demagogue. Passed agrarian law; murdered by patricians .... B C. 163— 133

**Grammont,** Antoine, Duke de. French marshal. *Memoirs*. 1604—1678

**Grant,** Ulysses S. American general. Born in Ohio; graduated at West Point, 1839; served in Mexican War; afterwards engaged in the leather business; brigadier-general, 1861; took Fort Donelson, 1862; Vicksburg, 1863; lieutenant-general, 1864; President, 1869-77 ..... 1822 —

**Granvelle,** Anthony Perrenot, Cardinal. French statesman; chief counselor of Margaret of Austria in the Netherlands .......... 1516—1586

**Granville,** Granville G. S. Gower, Earl of. English Liberal statesman; Secretary for Foreign Affairs.. 1815 —

**Grattan,** Henry. Irish orator and statesman. Advocate of Catholic emancipation; member of Irish and Imperial Parliament .......... 1750—1820

**Gray,** Thomas. English poet. Son of a London money-scrivener; educated at Eton and Oxford; friend of Horace Walpole, with whom he traveled on the Continent; professor of modern history at Cambridge. *Pindaric Odes; Elegy Written in a Country Churchyard* ........ 1716—1771

**Greeley,** Horace. American journalist. Founder of the N. Y. *Tribune*.......... 1811—1872

**Greene,** Nathaniel. General in the American Revolution; commander in the South.......... 1742—1786

BORN. DIED.

**Greene,** Robert. English poet and pamphleteer. *Comical History of Alphonsus, King of Aragon*.................. 1560—1592

**Greenough,** Horatio. American sculptor. *The Angel and Child*.................................................. 1805—1852

**Gregory,** Saint. Bishop of Tours. French Latin historian. *Historia Francorum*.................................... 544— 595

**Gregory I.,** "The Great." Pope. Converter of Britain. 545— 604

**Gregory VII.** (Hildebrand.) Greatest of the Popes. Elected Pope in 1073, and at once began to reform the Church and correct the abuses of simony; determined to take from secular rulers the power of disposition of sees; convened a council in 1074 which anathematized persons guilty of simony, and debased from holy orders persons not vowed to celibacy. His council of 1075 forbade kings, under penalty of excommunication, to invest with benefices. The Emperor, Henry IV., of Germany, deposed him, and was excommunicated. After a humiliating penance at Canossa, Henry was pardoned, but the reconciliation was only temporary... 1015—1085

**Grenville,** George. English statesman. Prime Minister; Chancellor of the Exchequer (1762-5).................. 1712—1770

**Gresset,** Jean B. L. French poet. *Vert Vert*.......... 1709—1777

**Grétry,** André E. M. French composer. *Richard Cœur de Lion*.................................................. 1741—1813

**Greuze,** Jean Baptiste. French painter. *St. Mary in Egypt*.................................................. 1726—1805

**Grey,** Lady Jane. Beheaded. Pretendant to English throne 1537—1554

**Grimm,** Jacob L. C. German philologist and mythologist. Discoverer of Grimm's Law.............................. 1785—1863

**Grimm,** Wilhelm C. German philologist and mythologist. *Deutsch Mythologie*.................................... 1786—1859

**Grote,** George. English historian. *History of Greece*.... 1794—1871

**Grotius,** Hugo. Dutch publicist and theologian. *De Jure Belli et Pacis*........................................ 1583—1645

**Grouchy,** Emanuel, Marquis of. French marshal. Conspicuous at Eylau; failed to move at Waterloo........ 1766—1847

**Guarini,** Giovanni B. Italian poet. *Pastor Fido*....... 1537—1612

**Guericke,** Otto von. German natural philosopher. Inventor of the air-pump................................... 1602—1686

**Guicciardini,** Francis. Florentine historian. *History of Florence*............................................. 1482—1540

**Guillotine,** Joseph G. French inventor of the guillotine. 1738—1814

**Guise,** Charles de, Cardinal of Lorraine. French statesman; Minister of Finance; opponent of the Protestants.............................................. 1525—1574

**Guise,** Francis of Lorraine, Duc de. French general; won battle of Guines; captured Calais from the English.... 1519—1563

**Guizot,** François P. G. French statesman and historian. Minister of Foreign Affairs. *History of France*........ 1787—1874

**Gustavus I.** (Vasa.) King of Sweden. Won back crown of Sweden from the King of Denmark..................... 1490—1560

**Gustavus II.** (Adolphus.) King of Sweden. General. Began to reign in his 17th year; soon afterward defeated the Czar and the King of Poland; invited to become the head of the Protestant party in Germany, he entered Pomerania with 8,000 men, and took town after town; defeated (1631) Marshal Tilly at Leipzig, and the next year on the banks of the Lech, where Tilly was slain. The Emperor now called in the great Wallenstein to oppose Gustavus; the two generals met at Lützen; Gustavus was mortally wounded, but the imperial army under Wallenstein was repulsed........... 1594—1632

**Gutenberg,** John. German inventor of printing......... 1400—1468

**Guyon,** Mme. Jeanne M. B. de la Mothe. French mystic. *The Song of Songs of Solomon*........................ 1648—1717

**Gwynn,** Eleanor (Nell). Actress. Mistress of Charles II. —— 1687

**Habakkuk.** One of the minor Jewish prophets. Flourished 600 B.C.

**Hackländer,** Friedrich M. German novelist. *Nameless Histories*............................................. 1816—1877

BORN. DIED.

**Hadrian.** Emperor of Rome (117-138); built wall across Britain; patron of art and letters..................... 76— 138

**Hafiz,** Mohammed. Persian poet. *Divan*............... 1300—1389

**Hahnemann,** Samuel C. F. German founder of homœopathy; proposed homœopathy, 1796; every affection to be cured by medicine having power to produce similar affection in healthy patients; published *Organum of Rational Medicine*, 1810.............................. 1755—1843

**Hakluyt,** Richard. English writer. Collector of *Voyages*. 1554—1616

**Hale,** Sir Matthew. English judge and law writer. *Pleas of the Crown*........................................... 1609—1676

**Hale,** Nathan. American Revolutionary soldier. Shot as a spy.................................................... 1755—1776

**Haliburton,** Thomas C. ("Sam Slick.") Nova Scotian judge and humorist. *Clockmaker; or, the Sayings and Doings of Sam Slick, of Slickville*...................... 1796—1865

**Halifax,** Charles Montague, Earl of. English statesman and scholar; leader of the Whigs; Chancellor of the Exchequer; patron of art and letters..................... 1661—1715

**Hall,** Joseph, Bishop of Norwich. English writer and satirist. *Poetical Satires*................................. 1574—1656

**Hall,** Robert. English Baptist divine and eloquent preacher. *Apology for the Freedom of the Press*.............. 1764—1831

**Hallam,** Arthur Henry. Hero of Tennyson's *In Memoriam*............................................... 1811—1833

**Hallam,** Henry. English historian. *Constitutional History of England; Middle Ages*.......................... 1778—1859

**Halleck,** Fitz-Greene. American poet. *Marco Bozzaris*. 1790—1867

**Haller,** Albert von. German philosopher and physician. *Elements of the Physiology of the Human Body*.......... 1708—1777

**Halley,** Edmund. English astronomer; first to calculate return of a comet.................................... 1656—1742

**Hamilcar.** Carthaginian general. Father of Hannibal. Made conquests in Spain; leader of popular party..B.C. —— 229

**Hamilton,** Alexander. American statesman and financier; born in Island of Nevis, West Indies. Aide-de-camp and secretary to Washington in Revolutionary War; began practice of law in New York, 1783; leading member of the Convention of 1787; principal author of the *Federalist;* Secretary of the Treasury, 1789-95; killed in a duel by Aaron Burr.................. 1757—1804

**Hamilton,** Anthony, Count. Irish courtier and writer. *Memoirs of Grammont*................................... 1646—1726

**Hamilton,** James, Duke of. Scotch Royalist general; defeated by Cromwell at Preston; executed for treason 1606—1649

**Hamilton,** Sir William. Scotch metaphysician.......... 1788—1856

**Hamilton,** Sir William R. Irish mathematician. *Elements of Quaternions*.................................. 1805—1865

**Hampden,** John. English statesman and patriot. Refused to pay ship money, 1636; one of the leaders of the opposition in the Long Parliament; slain in a skirmish with Prince Rupert's forces........................ 1594—1643

**Hancock,** John. American Revolutionary statesman; President of the Continental Congress.................. 1737—1793

**Hancock,** Winfield S. American general; commanded corps at Gettysburg; Democratic candidate for President in 1880.......................................... 1824 ——

**Handel,** George F. German composer; composed sonatas at 10; produced *Almeric*, 1706; *Roderigo*, 1708; *Rinaldo*, 1710; became chapel-master to George I., 1714, and spent the rest of his life in England. His oratorio of *Saul* was produced, 1740; his masterpiece, the *Messiah*, 1741. Among his other works are *Moses in Egypt, Samson,* and *Jephthah*............................ 1684—1759

**Hannibal.** Carthaginian general against Rome. Son of Hamilcar, who swore him to eternal enmity with the Romans. He became commander of the Carthaginian army, 221 B.C.; captured Saguntum, 219; crossed the Alps, 218; defeated the Romans at the Ticino and the Trebia; routed Flaminius at Lake Thrasybulus, 217; destroyed Roman army at Cannæ; took Tarentum, 213;

BORN. DIED.

was called back to Carthage, 203; defeated by Scipio at Zama, 202; finally poisoned himself to escape falling into the hands of the Romans ..... B.C. 247— 183

**Hardenberg,** Frederick von. "Novalis." German author. *Heinrich von Ofterdingen* ..... 1772—1801

**Hardinge,** Henry, Viscount. British statesman and general in India; conquered the Sikhs; commander-in-chief of English army ..... 1785—1856

**Hardwicke,** Philip York, first Earl of. English jurist. Lord Chancellor of England ..... 1690—1764

**Hardy,** Thomas. English novelist. *Far from the Madding Crowd* ..... 1840 —

**Hardy,** Sir Thomas M. English admiral; one of the officers of Nelson's flag-ship at Trafalgar ..... 1769—1839

**Hare,** Augustus W. English divine and author. *Guesses at Truth* ..... 1792—1834

**Hare,** Julius C. English divine and author. *Guesses at Truth* ..... 1795—1850

**Harley,** Robert. First Earl of Oxford. English statesman; Chancellor of the Exchequer; secured Treaty of Utrecht ..... 1661—1724

**Harrington,** James. English speculative writer. *Oceana* 1611—1677

**Harrison,** William Henry. American general and statesman; signer of Declaration of Independence; Governor of Virginia; born in Va.; entered army in 1791; aide-de-camp to Gen. Wayne; Gov. of Indiana, 1801-13; defeated Indians at Tippecanoe; made major-gen., 1813; elected to Congress, 1817; to the Senate, 1824; Minister to Columbia, 1828; Whig candidate for President, 1836; elected President, 1840 ..... 1773—1841

**Harte,** Francis Bret. American novelist and poet. *The Heathen Chinee; Gabriel Conroy; Luck of Roaring Camp; Flip* ..... 1839 —

**Hartington,** Spencer C. Cavendish, Marquis of. English Liberal statesman; leader of the Liberals ..... 1833 —

**Hartley,** David. English philosophical writer. *Observations on Man* ..... 1705—1777

**Harvard,** John. Colonial divine. Benefactor of Harvard College ..... 1608—1688

**Harvey,** William. English physician. Discoverer of the circulation of the blood ..... 1578—1657

**Hasdrubal.** Punic general. Brother of Hannibal; defeated the Scipios in Spain; defeated and slain at the river Metaurus ..... B.C. — 207

**Hastings,** Warren. British statesman and general; President of the Council of Bengal; conqueror of Hyder Aly; impeached, but acquitted ..... 1733—1818

**Havelock,** Sir Henry. British general in Sepoy rebellion; defeated Sepoys at Cawnpore; relieved Lucknow ..... 1795—1857

**Hawkins,** Sir John. British naval commander; served against Armada. First Englishman to engage in slave trade ..... 1521—1595

**Hawthorne,** Nathaniel. American romance writer. *Marble Fawn; The Scarlet Letter; The House of Seven Gables; The Blithedale Romance; Mosses from an Old Manse; Septimius; Twice-told Tales; English Note-Books* ..... 1804—1864

**Haydn,** Francis Joseph. German composer. When a boy he became a chorister at Vienna; learned Italian from Metastasio; between the ages of 19 and 26, composed many sonatas, concertos, and symphonies; from 1760 to 1790 was chapel-master to Prince Esterhazy at Eisenstadt; produced (1791) six noble symphonies at London; 1798, his masterpiece, *The Creation* ..... 1732—1809

**Hayes,** Rutherford B. American politician; born in Ohio; admitted to bar, 1845; brigadier-gen. in Civil War; entered Congress at its close; re-elected, 1866; Gov. of Ohio, 1868-76: President, 1877-81 ..... 1822 —

**Hayne,** Robert H. American lawyer and senator. Nullifier; Governor of S. C.; opponent of Webster in discussing Constitution ..... 1791—1839

BORN. DIED.

**Hazlitt,** William. English critic and author. *Characters of Shakespeare's Plays* ..... 1778—1830

**Heathfield,** George Augustus Eliot, Lord. English governor of Gibraltar, which he successfully defended against France and Spain for three years ..... 1718—1790

**Heber,** Reginald. Bishop of Calcutta. English author. *Hymns Adapted to the Weekly Church Service* ..... 1783—1826

**Hegel,** George W. F. German philosopher; professor of philosophy at Heidelberg and Berlin. He develops his system of philosophy (claimed by his disciples to be the most logical of systems) in the *Encyclopædia of the Philosophical Sciences.* Logics and metaphysics are identical in his system. He continues and completes Kant, Fichte, Schelling ..... 1770—1831

**Heine,** Heinrich. German lyric poet and satirist. *Reisebilde; Lieder* ..... 1799—1856

**Heliogabalus.** Roman emperor and gourmand. Infamous, cruel, extravagant; slain by his soldiers ..... 205— 222

**Heloise.** French nun, beloved by Abelard ..... 1101—1164

**Helps,** Sir Arthur. English author. *History of the Spanish Conquest of America* ..... 1817—1875

**Helvetius,** Claude A. French philosopher and writer. *On the Mind* ..... 1715—1771

**Hemans,** Felicia D., Mrs. English poetess. *Restoration of the Works of Art to Italy* ..... 1794—1835

**Hennepin,** Louis. French explorer of the Mississippi ..... 1640—1699

**Henrietta Maria.** French queen of Charles I. of England; daughter of Henry IV. and Marie de Medici ..... 1609—1669

**Henry I.** "The Fowler." Emperor of Germany. Defeated the Hungarians at Merseburg ..... 876— 936

**Henry IV.** Emperor of Germany. Opponent of Hildebrand ..... 1050—1106

**Henry IV.** "The Great." (Henry of Navarre.) King of France. Won battle of Ivry; issued Edict of Nantes ..... 1553—1610

**Henry I.** King of England. "Beauclerc." Defeated his brother Robert, from whom he usurped the throne ..... 1068—1135

**Henry II.** King of England; conqueror of Ireland. Issued *Constitutions of Clarendon* ..... 1133—1189

**Henry V.** King of England. Conqueror at Agincourt ..... 1388—1422

**Henry VIII.** King of England. "Defender of the Faith." Suppressed the monasteries; much-married ..... 1491—1547

**Henry,** Patrick. American orator and Revolutionary patriot. "Give me Liberty, or give me Death." ..... 1736—1799

**Herbert,** Rev. George. English Christian lyric poet. *Poems; Our Country Parson* ..... 1593—1633

**Herder,** Johann E. von. German scholar and author. *Ideas on the Philosophy of the History of Mankind* ..... 1744—1803

**Herod.** "The Great." King of the Jews. Ordered assassination of infants at birth of Christ ..... B.C. 73— 4

**Herodotus.** Greek historian. *History* ..... B.C. 484— 408

**Herrick,** Robert. English clergyman and poet. *Hesperides: or, Poems Human and Divine* ..... 1591—1674

**Herschel,** Sir Frederick N. English astronomer; discoverer of Uranus ..... 1738—1822

**Herschel,** Sir John F. N. English astronomer. *Preliminary Discourse on the Study of Natural Philosophy* ..... 1792—1871

**Hesiod.** Greek poet. *Works and Days.* Flourished 800 B.C.

**Heyne,** Christian G. German classical scholar. Editor of *Virgil* ..... 1729—1812

**Hezekiah.** King of Judah. Defeated the Assyrian king, Sennacherib ..... B.C. 750— 698

**Hildreth,** Richard. American historian. *History of the United States* ..... 1807—1863

**Hill,** Rowland. English Calvinistic Methodist preacher. *Village Dialogues* ..... 1744—1833

**Hill,** Sir Rowland. English originator of cheap postage ..... 1795—1876

**Hillard,** George S. American lawyer and scholar. *Six Months in Italy* ..... 1808—1879

**Hippocrates.** Greek physician and writer. *On Air, Water, and Locality* ..... B.C. 460— 357

BORN. DIED.

**Hobbes,** Thomas. English philosopher. *Human Nature; Leviathan* ........ 1588—1679

**Hoffman,** Ernest T. W. German romantic novelist. *Serapion's Brüder* ........ 1776—1822

**Hogarth,** William. English painter. *The Rake's Progress* ........ 1697—1764

**Hogg,** James. Scottish poet. "The Ettrick Shepherd." *The Queen's Wake* ........ 1772—1835

**Holbein,** Hans. German painter. *The Dance of Death.* Pensioned by Henry VIII., and during his residence in England painted portraits of the principal persons in Henry's court. Among his most admired works are a *Last Supper*, an *Adoration of the Shepherds and Kings*, and portraits of Erasmus and Sir Thomas More ........ 1498—1543

**Holmes,** Oliver Wendell. American poet, physician, and novelist. *Elsie Venner; The Autocrat of the Breakfast Table; The Guardian Angel; Poems; The Iron Gate; The Poet at the Breakfast Table.* Professor at Harvard Medical School ........ 1809 —

**Holt,** Sir John. English jurist. Lord Chief Justice of England ........ 1642—1709

**Homer.** Greek epic poet. *Iliad* and *Odyssey.* Seven cities claimed the honor of his birth, but his actual birthplace is unknown; probably it was in Asia Minor. According to tradition, he was blind and poor—a sort of wandering minstrel. The times of his birth and death are likewise uncertain, and his existence is doubted by some, who maintain that the *Iliad* and *Odyssey* are collections of songs by different authors ........ B.C. 10th cent'y.

**Hood,** Thomas. English poet and humorist. *Song of the Shirt; Whims and Oddities; Eugene Aram's Dream* ........ 1798—1845

**Hook,** Theodore E. English novelist and wit. *Sayings and Doings* ........ 1788—1841

**Hooker,** Richard. English theologian. *Ecclesiastical Polity* ........ 1553—1600

**Hooker,** Joseph. American general; commander of the Army of the Potomac, 1863; defeated at Chancellorsville ........ 1815—1879

**Horace** (Q. Horatius Flaccus). Latin poet and satirist. *Odes, Epistles, Satires* ........ B.C. 65— 8

**Hortensius,** Quintus. Roman lawyer and orator; consul: rival of Cicero in eloquence ........ B.C. 114— 50

**Houston,** Samuel. American general and statesman; commander-in-chief of the Texan army; captured Santa Anna; Governor of Texas ........ 1793—1863

**Howard,** John. English philanthropist and prison reformer. *The State of the Prisons in England* ........ 1726—1790

**Howe,** Samuel G. American philanthropist. Teacher of the blind ........ 1801—1876

**Hugo,** Victor. French poet, dramatist, and novelist. *Les Miserables; Nôtre Dame* ........ 1809 —

**Humboldt,** C. Wilhelm von. German philologist. *Memoir on Comparative Linguistics* ........ 1767—1835

**Humboldt,** F. H. Alexander von. German naturalist. Traveled in South America, Mexico, and the United States, 1799-1804; lived in Paris for next twenty years, and published scientific results of his travels; traveled in Asiatic Russia in 1829; published *Cosmos, an Essay of a Physical Description of the Universe*, 1845-58 ........ 1769—1859

**Hume,** David. Scottish philosopher and historian. *History of England; Enquiry into the Principles of Human Nature* ........ 1711—1776

**Hunt,** J. H. Leigh. English author. *The Seer* ........ 1784—1859

**Hunt,** William H. English painter. *The Light of the World* ........ 1827 —

**Hunter,** John. British surgeon and anatomist ........ 1728—1793

**Huss,** John. Bohemian reformer. *On the Church.* At Council of Constance, given up by Emperor Sigismund, and burned ........ 1376—1415

BORN. DIED.

**Hutten,** Ulrich von. German soldier and author. *Epistolæ Obscurorum Virorum* ........ 1488—1523

**Huxley,** Thomas H. English physicist. *Physiology* ........ 1825 —

**Ingres,** Jean D. A. French painter. *The Apotheosis of Homer* ........ 1781—1867

**Innocent III.** One of the greatest of the popes. Elected Pope in 1198; put France under the ban, 1199, because Philip Augustus repudiated his queen; Innocent compelled him to take her back. He organized the fourth Crusade, which resulted in the capture of Constantinople; excommunicated and deposed Otho, Emperor of Germany, 1212, and crowned Frederick II. in his place. In a dispute with King John, he put England under the ban, till John (1213) agreed to hold England and Ireland as fiefs of the Holy See, and to pay an annual tribute of 1,000 marks. In 1214 he crushed the Albigensians ........ 1161—1216

**Irving,** Edward. Scotch Presbyterian clergyman; celebrated preacher; claimed "gift of tongues." *For the Oracles of God* ........ 1792—1834

**Irving,** J. Henry B. English actor. Great in Shakespearian parts ........ 1838 —

**Irving,** Washington. American author. *Bracebridge Hall; The Sketch Book.* Born in New York; studied law; lived much abroad; was Minister to Spain, 1842; *History of New York; The Conquest of Granada; Life of Washington; Columbus; Tales of a Traveller; Wolfert's Roost* ........ 1783—1859

**Isabella.** "The Catholic" Queen of Castile. Patroness of Christopher Columbus ........ 1451—1504

**Isaiah.** Hebrew prophet. Flourished ........ B.C. 740

**Isocrates.** Athenian orator; said to have died of grief at hearing of battle of Chæronea. Twenty-one of his *Orations* are extant ........ B.C. 436— 338

**Ivan II.** "The Terrible." Czar of Russia. Fought Sweden and Poland. Established first printing-press in Russia, 1582 ........ 1529—1584

**Jackson,** Andrew. American general and statesman; born in N. C.; began to practice law at Nashville, Tenn., 1788; M.C., 1796; Senator, 1797; resigned, 1798; Judge Tenn. Supreme Court, 1798-1804; defeated Creek Indians, 1814; won battle of New Orleans, 1815; in Seminole War, 1817-18; Senator, 1823; President, 1829-37 ........ 1767—1845

**Jackson,** Thomas J. ("Stonewall.") American Confederate general. Captured Harper's Ferry with 11,000 prisoners; defeated Banks ........ 1826—1863

**James I.** King of Scotland (1406-37). Assassinated by his nobles. *The King's Quhair* ........ 1394—1431

**James IV.** King of Scotland. Defeated and killed at Flodden ........ 1473—1513

**James I.** King of England. Pedantic and narrow-minded; truckled to Spain; failed to support Elector Palatine; executed Raleigh. *A Counterblast to Tobacco* ........ 1566—1625

**James II.** King of England. Lost his throne by revolution ........ 1633—1701

**James,** George P. R. English novelist. *Adra; or, The Peruvian* ........ 1801—1860

**James,** Henry, Jr. American novelist. *Portrait of a Lady* ........ 1843 —

**Jameson,** Mrs. Anna. English art writer. *Legends of the Madonna* ........ 1797—1869

**Jansenius,** Cornelius. Bishop of Ypres. Flemish theologian; founder of the Jansenists ........ 1585—1638

**Jasmin,** Jacques. French (Provençal) poet. "The Barber Poet." *The Blind Girl of Castel Cuillé* ........ 1798—1864

**Jay,** John. American jurist, diplomatist and statesman; negotiated treaty with England; one of the authors of *Federalist* ........ 1754—1829

**Jeanne D'Arc** (The Maid of Orleans). A peasant girl in

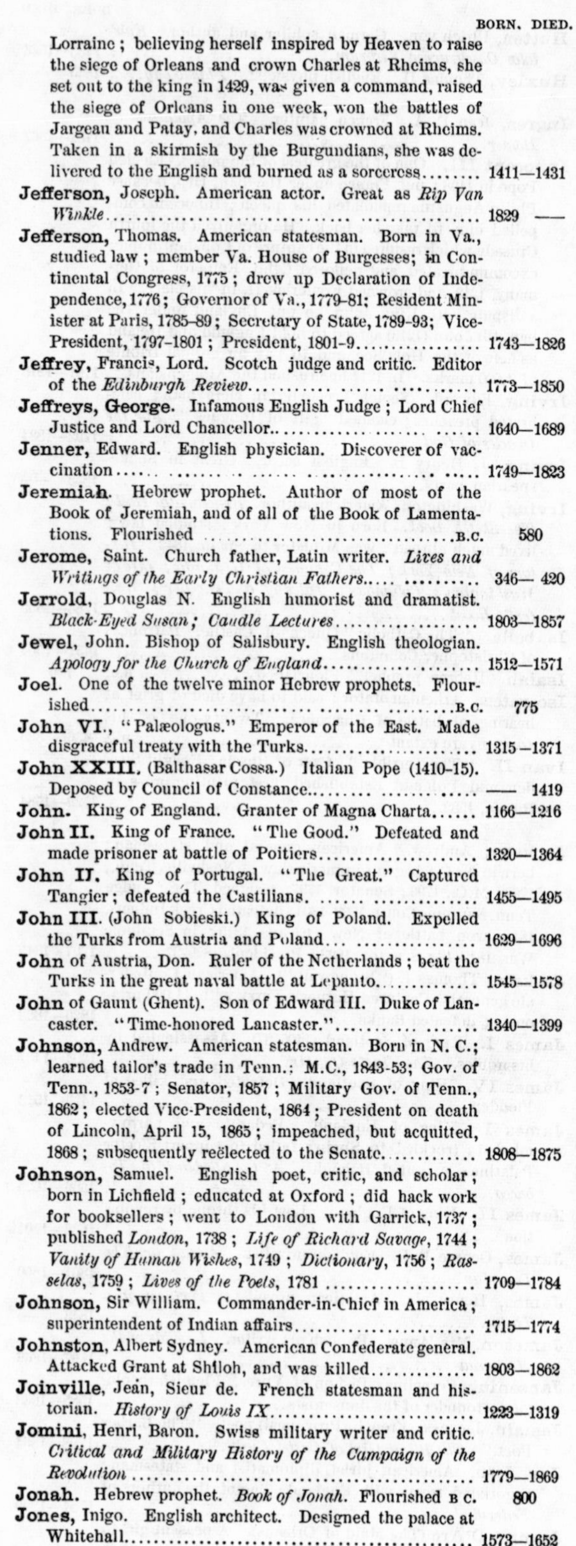

BORN. DIED.

Lorraine; believing herself inspired by Heaven to raise the siege of Orleans and crown Charles at Rheims, she set out to the king in 1429, was given a command, raised the siege of Orleans in one week, won the battles of Jargeau and Patay, and Charles was crowned at Rheims. Taken in a skirmish by the Burgundians, she was delivered to the English and burned as a sorceress........ 1411–1431

**Jefferson**, Joseph. American actor. Great as *Rip Van Winkle*........................................ 1829 —

**Jefferson**, Thomas. American statesman. Born in Va., studied law; member Va. House of Burgesses; in Continental Congress, 1775; drew up Declaration of Independence, 1776; Governor of Va., 1779-81; Resident Minister at Paris, 1785-89; Secretary of State, 1789-93; Vice-President, 1797-1801; President, 1801-9............ 1743–1826

**Jeffrey**, Francis, Lord. Scotch judge and critic. Editor of the *Edinburgh Review*.......... ........... 1773–1850

**Jeffreys, George**. Infamous English Judge; Lord Chief Justice and Lord Chancellor.................. 1640–1689

**Jenner**, Edward. English physician. Discoverer of vaccination........................................ 1749–1823

**Jeremiah**. Hebrew prophet. Author of most of the Book of Jeremiah, and of all of the Book of Lamentations. Flourished ..................................B.C. 580

**Jerome**, Saint. Church father, Latin writer. *Lives and Writings of the Early Christian Fathers*..... .......... 346– 420

**Jerrold**, Douglas N. English humorist and dramatist. *Black-Eyed Susan; Caudle Lectures*.............. 1803–1857

**Jewel**, John. Bishop of Salisbury. English theologian. *Apology for the Church of England*.................. 1512–1571

**Joel**. One of the twelve minor Hebrew prophets. Flourished..........................................B.C. 775

**John VI.**, "Palæologus." Emperor of the East. Made disgraceful treaty with the Turks.................. 1315–1371

**John XXIII.** (Balthasar Cossa.) Italian Pope (1410-15). Deposed by Council of Constance........................ — 1419

**John.** King of England. Granter of Magna Charta...... 1166–1216

**John II.** King of France. "The Good." Defeated and made prisoner at battle of Poitiers.................. 1320–1364

**John II.** King of Portugal. "The Great." Captured Tangier; defeated the Castilians. ................ 1455–1495

**John III.** (John Sobieski.) King of Poland. Expelled the Turks from Austria and Poland.................. 1629–1696

**John of Austria**, Don. Ruler of the Netherlands; beat the Turks in the great naval battle at Lepanto........ 1545–1578

**John** of Gaunt (Ghent). Son of Edward III. Duke of Lancaster. "Time-honored Lancaster."............ ...... 1340–1399

**Johnson**, Andrew. American statesman. Born in N. C.; learned tailor's trade in Tenn.: M.C., 1843-53; Gov. of Tenn., 1853-7; Senator, 1857; Military Gov. of Tenn., 1862; elected Vice-President, 1864; President on death of Lincoln, April 15, 1865; impeached, but acquitted, 1868; subsequently reëlected to the Senate............ 1808–1875

**Johnson**, Samuel. English poet, critic, and scholar; born in Lichfield; educated at Oxford; did hack work for booksellers; went to London with Garrick, 1737; published *London*, 1738; *Life of Richard Savage*, 1744; *Vanity of Human Wishes*, 1749; *Dictionary*, 1756; *Rasselas*, 1759; *Lives of the Poets*, 1781 .................. 1709–1784

**Johnson**, Sir William. Commander-in-Chief in America; superintendent of Indian affairs........................ 1715–1774

**Johnston**, Albert Sydney. American Confederate general. Attacked Grant at Shiloh, and was killed.............. 1803–1862

**Joinville**, Jean, Sieur de. French statesman and historian. *History of Louis IX*........................ 1223–1319

**Jomini**, Henri, Baron. Swiss military writer and critic. *Critical and Military History of the Campaign of the Revolution*............................................. 1779–1869

**Jonah.** Hebrew prophet. *Book of Jonah*. Flourished B C. 800

**Jones**, Inigo. English architect. Designed the palace at Whitehall........................................ 1573–1652

BORN. DIED

**Jones**, John Paul. American Revolutionary naval officer; naval victories over British........................ 1747–1792

**Jones**, Sir William. English scholar and Orientalist. *Persian Grammar*........................................ 1746–1794

**Jonson**, Ben. English poet and dramatist, bricklayer and soldier. *Every Man in his Humor; Volpone; The Alchemist; The Silent Woman; Sejanus; Masques*....... 1574–1637

**Joseph II.** Emperor of Germany. Abolished feudal serfdom; mitigated condition of the Jews.............. 1741–1790

**Josephine.** Wife of Napoleon I.; Empress of France; divorced; widow of Alexander de Beauharnais........ 1763–1814

**Josephus**, Flavius. Jewish historian. *History of the Jews.* 35– 100

**Joshua.** Hebrew general and statesman. Commander of the Israelites after Moses........................B.C. 1537–1427

**Judas Maccabeus.** Hebrew patriot and general. Conquered several Syrian armies; finally defeated and slain..............................................B.C. 160

**Judson**, Adoniram. American missionary to Burmah.... 1788–1850

**Julian.** "The Apostate." Roman emperor. Restored Pagan worship........................................ 331– 363

**Jung Stilling** (John H. Jung). German mystic and author. *Scenes from the Spirit Land*.................. 1740–1817

**Junot**, Andoche, Duc d'Abrantés. French marshal. Commanded army which took Lisbon ...................... 1771–1813

**Justin Martyr.** Greek Christian author. *Apology for the Christian Religion* ............................ 103– 165

**Justinian I.** "The Great." Emperor of the East. Had revised and published the *Code, Pandects Institutes* ... 483– 565

**Juvenal** (Decimus Junius Juvenalis). Latin satirist. *Satires*........... ......................................... 40– 125

**Kames**, Henry Home, Lord. Scotch judge and philosopher. *Elements of Criticism* ........................ 1696–1782

**Kane**, Elisha K. American Arctic explorer. *Arctic Explorations*........................................ 1820–1857

**Kant**, Immanuel. German philosopher. *Critique of Pure Reason.* In his *Universal Natural History and Theory of the Universe* he anticipated the discovery of Uranus. Another of his important works is the *Critique of Practical Reason.* It was his aim to determine the laws and limits of human reason and of the human intellect in relation to the objects of human knowledge........... 1724–1804

**Kean**, Edward. English actor. Among his greatest parts were *Shylock, Richard III., Othello, Iago, King Lear*, and *Sir Giles Overreach* in Massinger's *A New Way to Pay Old Debts*........................................ 1787–1833

**Keats**, John. English poet; born in London; apprenticed to a surgeon; died at Rome. *Endymion; Hyperion; The Eve of St. Agnes*.................................. 1795–1821

**Kemble**, John. English divine and poet. *The Christian Year*............................................. 1792–1866

**Kemble**, John Philip. English actor. Great in Shakesperian parts; *Coriolanus* was his most famous role..... 1757–1823

**Kempis**, Thomas à. German Ascetic writer. *Imitatio Christi*.......................................... 1380–1471

**Kent**, James. American lawyer and judge. Chief Justice of New York. *Commentaries*........................ 1763–1847

**Kenyon**, Lloyd, Lord. English jurist. Lord Chief Justice. 1733–1802

**Kepler**, John. German astronomer. Published, in 1609, *Astronomia Nova, Seu Physica celestis tradita de Motibus Stellae Martis.* His celebrated *Laws* are: 1. The orbits of the planets are elliptical. 2. The radius vector, or line passing from a planet to the sun, passes over equal spaces in equal times. 3. The squares of the periodic times of the planets are proportional to the cubes of their mean distances from the sun. He was mathematician to the Emperor Rudolph.......................... 1571–1630

**Key**, Francis Scott. American song writer. *Star Spangled Banner*........................................... 1779–1843

**Kidd**, William. American pirate in the East Indies. Executed ........................................... — 1701

BORN. DIED.

**King,** Rufus. American Federalist statesman. U. S. Senator; Minister to Great Britain........ 1755—1827
**King,** Thomas Starr. American Unitarian clergyman. *The White Hills*........ 1824—1864
**King,** William R. American Democratic statesman. Vice-President; U. S. Senator; Minister to France........ 1786—1853
**Kingsley,** Charles. English divine and novelist. *Hypatia.* 1819—1875
**Kirkland,** John T. American divine. President of Harvard College........ 1770—1840
**Kitto,** John. English Biblical scholar and divine. *History of the Bible*........ 1804—1854
**Kleber,** Jean B. French general. Drove the Turks from Cairo in Egyptian campaign; assassinated........ 1755—1800
**Klopstock,** Friedrich T. German poet. *Messiah*........ 1724—1803
**Kneller,** Sir Godfrey. English painter of portraits. Court painter from the time of Charles I. to that of George II. 1650—1723
**Knowles,** James Sheridan. English dramatist. *Virginius; The Hunchback*........ 1784—1862
**Knox,** Henry. American general. Directed artillery at Brandywine; Secretary of War........ 1750—1806
**Knox,** John. Scotch reformer. Fierce anti-Catholic. *The First Blast of the Trumpet*........ 1505—1572
**Kock,** C. Paul de. French novelist. Many immoral novels. 1794—1871
**Körner,** Charles T. German soldier and lyric poet. Author of many stirring war songs........ 1791—1813
**Kosciuszko,** Thaddeus. Polish patriot and general. Commander of the Polish insurgent army; defeated at Warsaw, which he bravely defended........ 1745—1817
**Kotzebue,** Augustus F. F. von. German author. *The Stranger; Pizarro*........ 1761—1819
**Krummacher,** Frederick A. German theologian and author. *Parables*........ 1768—1845
**Kyd,** Thomas. English dramatist. *The Spanish Tragedy.* Flourished about 1580.

**Lablache,** Louis. Italian vocalist. His voice embraced two full octaves........ 1794—1858
**Lacordaire,** Jean B. H. French preacher and author. *Life of St. Dominic*........ 1802—1861
**Lactantius,** Lucius C. F. Christian Latin writer. *Institutiones Divinæ*........ —— 325
**La Fayette,** Louise Motier, Mlle. de. French beauty. Exerted great influence over Louis XIII. and his policy........ 1615—1665
**La Fayette,** Marie J. P. R. P. Gilbert Motier, Marquis de. French patriot general in the American Revolution. Joined American army major-general, 1775; commanded advance guard of Washington at Yorktown: commander of French national guard, 1789; revisited America, 1824; took part in revolution of 1830........ 1757—1834
**Lafontaine,** Jean. French poet and fabulist. *Fables*... 1621—1695
**Lagrange,** Joseph L. French mathematician. Discovered equalities of the planets. *Mécanique Analytique*........ 1736—1813
**Lamartine,** Alphonse M. L. de. French poet and statesman. *Jocelyn*........ 1790—1869
**Lamb,** Charles. English essayist, "Elia." *Essays of Elia.* 1775—1834
**Lamballe,** Marie T. L. de Savoie Carignon, Princess de. Friend of Marie Antoinette. Guillotined........ 1747—1792
**Lambert,** Daniel. English fat man........ 1767—1809
**Lambert,** John. English parliamentary general. Led the van at Dunbar........ 1621—1694
**La Mothe le Vayer,** Francis de. French skeptic and writer. *On the Virtue of the Pagans*........ 1588—1672
**La Motte Fouqué,** Frederick, Baron. German novelist *Undine*........ 1777—1843
**Landon,** Letitia E. English authoress. "L. E. L." *Romance and Reality*........ 1802—1838
**Landor,** Walter Savage. English poet and prosist. *Imaginary Conversations*........ 1775—1864
**Landseer,** Sir Edwin. English painter. *The Old Shepherd's Chief Mourner*........ 1802—1873

BORN. DIED.

**Langland,** or **Longland,** Robert. English poet. *Piers Plowman* (1369).
**Langton,** Stephen, Cardinal. English ecclesiastic. Archbishop of Canterbury; statesman. Coöperated with the barons against King John........ —— 1228
**Lannes,** Jean, Duke of Montebello. French marshal. Commander-in-chief at Saragossa........ 1769—1809
**Lansdowne,** William Petty, 1st Marquis of. English statesman. Secretary of State; opposed coercion of American colonies........ 1737—1805
**Laplace,** Pierre Simon, Marquis of. French mathematician. Discovered the theory of Jupiter's satellites and the causes of the acceleration of the moon's mean motion, and of the inequality of Jupiter and Saturn. His *Exposition of the System of the Universe* is a popular form of his great work *La Mécanique Celeste.* He was one of the greatest mathematicians and astronomers... 1749—1827
**La Rochefoucauld,** François, Duke de. French statesman and author. *Maxims*........ 1613—1680
**Latimer,** Hugh, Bishop of Worcester. English reformer. Burned........ 1480—1555
**Latini,** Brunetto. Florentine scholar and poet. Dante's master. *Il Tesoro*........ 1230—1294
**Lauderdale,** John Maitland, Duke of. English statesman. Favorite of Charles II.; member of "Cabal" ministry........ 1616—1682
**Laura** (de Sade) of Vaucluse. Beloved by Petrarch, who celebrates her in his sonnets........ 1310—1348
**Laurens,** Henry. American Revolutionary patriot. President of Congress; ambassador to The Hague........ 1724—1792
**Lauzun,** Antoine N de Caumont, Duke de. Favorite of Louis XIV.; commander of the French troops at the battle of the Boyne........ 1633—1723
**La Vallière,** Françoise Louise, Duchess de. Mistress of Louis XIV........ 1644—1710
**Lavater,** John G. C. Swiss scientist and physiognomist. 1741—1801
**Lavoisier,** Antoine L. French chemist. Inventor of the gasometer. *Physical and Chemical Essays*........ 1743—1794
**Law,** John. Scottish financier in France. Promoter of the "South Sea Bubble." [*See Dictionary of Allusions.*] 1671—1729
**Lawrence,** Amos. American merchant. Philanthropist. 1786—1852
**Lawrence,** James American naval commander. Commander of the Chesapeake; killed fighting the British *Shannon.* "Don't give up the ship."........ 1781—1813
**Lawrence,** Sir Thomas. English painter. *Portrait of Mrs. Siddons*........ 1769—1830
**Lebrun,** Charles. French painter. *The Family of Darius.* 1619—1690
**Lebrun,** Charles François, Duke of Placentia. French politician. Third consul; Governor General of Holland. 1739—1824
**Lee,** Arthur. American statesman and diplomatist. Member of Congress; Minister to France........ 1740—1792
**Lee,** Charles. American Revolutionary general. Dismissed for disobedience of orders at Monmouth........ 1730—1782
**Lee,** Francis Lightfoot. American Revolutionary patriot. Member Congress; signed Declaration of Independence 1734—1797
**Lee,** Henry. American Revolutionary soldier. "Light Horse Harry." Served under Greene; Governor of Virginia........ 1756—1818
**Lee,** Nathaniel. English dramatist. "The Mad Poet."... 1655—1692
**Lee,** Richard Henry. American Revolutionary statesman. Signed Declaration of Independence; President of Congress; U. S. Senator........ 1732—1794
**Lee,** Robert Edward. American Confederate general. Commander-in-chief of Confederate army........ 1807—1876
**Leech,** John. English humorous artist and caricaturist. Drawings in *Punch*........ 1817—1864
**Lefebvre,** François J., Duke of Dantzic. French marshal. Conspicuous at battle of Wagram........ 1755—1820
**Legaré,** Hugh S. American lawyer and statesman. Attorney-General of the United States. *Essay on Roman Literature*........ 1797—1843

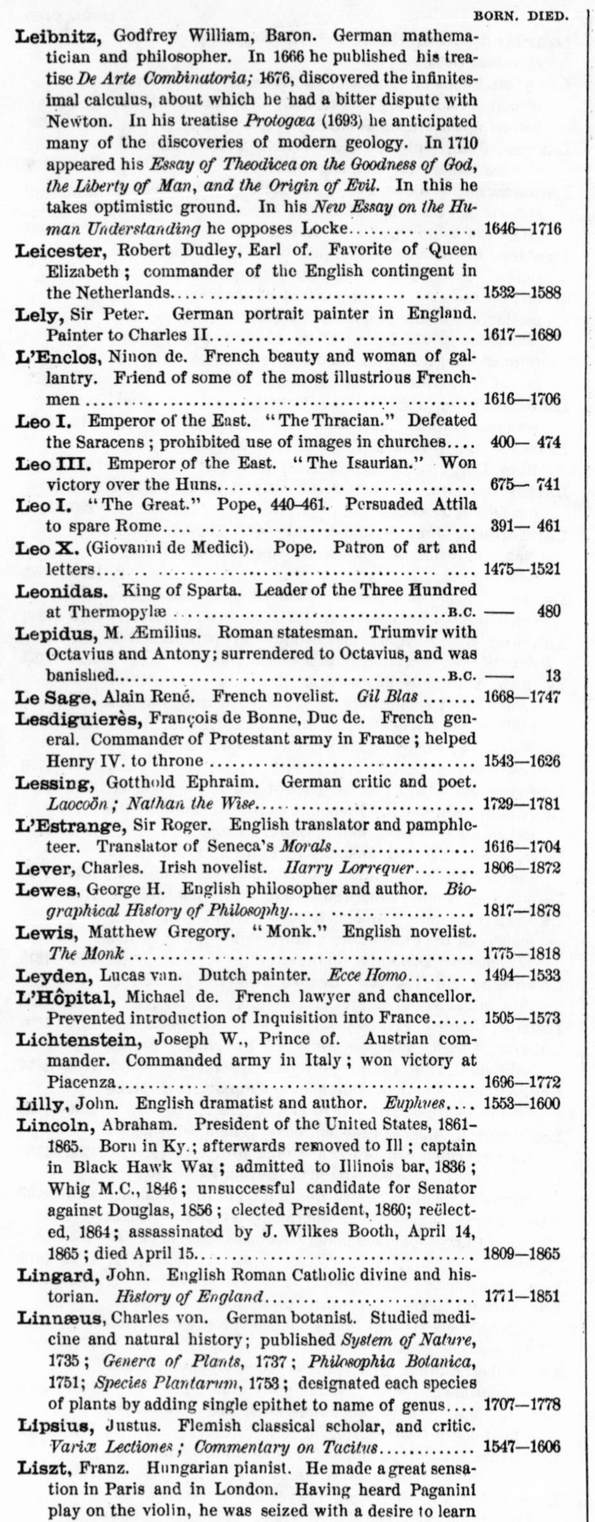

BORN. DIED.

**Leibnitz,** Godfrey William, Baron. German mathematician and philosopher. In 1666 he published his treatise *De Arte Combinatoria;* 1676, discovered the infinitesimal calculus, about which he had a bitter dispute with Newton. In his treatise *Protogæa* (1693) he anticipated many of the discoveries of modern geology. In 1710 appeared his *Essay of Theodicea on the Goodness of God, the Liberty of Man, and the Origin of Evil.* In this he takes optimistic ground. In his *New Essay on the Human Understanding* he opposes Locke.......... 1646—1716

**Leicester,** Robert Dudley, Earl of. Favorite of Queen Elizabeth; commander of the English contingent in the Netherlands.......... 1532—1588

**Lely,** Sir Peter. German portrait painter in England. Painter to Charles II.......... 1617—1680

**L'Enclos,** Ninon de. French beauty and woman of gallantry. Friend of some of the most illustrious Frenchmen.......... 1616—1706

**Leo I.** Emperor of the East. "The Thracian." Defeated the Saracens; prohibited use of images in churches.... 400— 474

**Leo III.** Emperor of the East. "The Isaurian." Won victory over the Huns.......... 675— 741

**Leo I.** "The Great." Pope, 440-461. Persuaded Attila to spare Rome.......... 391— 461

**Leo X.** (Giovanni de Medici). Pope. Patron of art and letters.......... 1475—1521

**Leonidas.** King of Sparta. Leader of the Three Hundred at Thermopylæ..........B.C. — 480

**Lepidus,** M. Æmilius. Roman statesman. Triumvir with Octavius and Antony; surrendered to Octavius, and was banished..........B.C. — 13

**Le Sage,** Alain René. French novelist. *Gil Blas*....... 1668—1747

**Lesdiguierès,** François de Bonne, Duc de. French general. Commander of Protestant army in France; helped Henry IV. to throne.......... 1543—1626

**Lessing,** Gotthold Ephraim. German critic and poet. *Laocoön; Nathan the Wise*.......... 1729—1781

**L'Estrange,** Sir Roger. English translator and pamphleteer. Translator of Seneca's *Morals*.......... 1616—1704

**Lever,** Charles. Irish novelist. *Harry Lorrequer*........ 1806—1872

**Lewes,** George H. English philosopher and author. *Biographical History of Philosophy*.......... 1817—1878

**Lewis,** Matthew Gregory. "Monk." English novelist. *The Monk*.......... 1775—1818

**Leyden,** Lucas van. Dutch painter. *Ecce Homo*......... 1494—1533

**L'Hôpital,** Michael de. French lawyer and chancellor. Prevented introduction of Inquisition into France...... 1505—1573

**Lichtenstein,** Joseph W., Prince of. Austrian commander. Commanded army in Italy; won victory at Piacenza.......... 1696—1772

**Lilly,** John. English dramatist and author. *Euphues*.... 1553—1600

**Lincoln,** Abraham. President of the United States, 1861-1865. Born in Ky.; afterwards removed to Ill; captain in Black Hawk War; admitted to Illinois bar, 1836; Whig M.C., 1846; unsuccessful candidate for Senator against Douglas, 1856; elected President, 1860; reëlected, 1864; assassinated by J. Wilkes Booth, April 14, 1865; died April 15.......... 1809—1865

**Lingard,** John. English Roman Catholic divine and historian. *History of England*.......... 1771—1851

**Linnæus,** Charles von. German botanist. Studied medicine and natural history; published *System of Nature*, 1735; *Genera of Plants*, 1737; *Philosophia Botanica*, 1751; *Species Plantarum*, 1753; designated each species of plants by adding single epithet to name of genus.... 1707—1778

**Lipsius,** Justus. Flemish classical scholar, and critic. *Variæ Lectiones; Commentary on Tacitus*.......... 1547—1606

**Liszt,** Franz. Hungarian pianist. He made a great sensation in Paris and in London. Having heard Paganini play on the violin, he was seized with a desire to learn that instrument, on which he soon became a skilled performer; is hardly less noted for his love affairs than for his musical proficiency; now (1882) lives in Italy....... 1811 —

BORN. DIED

**Liverpool,** Charles Jenkinson, 1st Earl of. English statesman. Secretary of War under Lord North.......... 1727—1808

**Liverpool,** Robert B. Jenkinson, 2d Earl of. English Whig statesman. Prime Minister, 1812-27.......... 1770—1828

**Livingston,** David. African explorer. *Narrative of an Expedition to the Zambesi*.......... 1817—1873

**Livingston,** Edward. American lawyer and statesman. Secretary of State; Minister to France. *System of Penal Law*.......... 1764—1836

**Livingston,** Philip. American Revolutionary statesman. Signer of Declaration of Independence.......... 1716—1778

**Livingston,** Robert R. American statesman and diplomatist. Member of Congress; Minister to France..... 1746—1813

**Lobeira,** Vasco de. Portuguese author. *Amadis de Gaul*. 1360—1403

**Locke,** John. English philosopher. *Human Understanding*. In *Essay on the Human Understanding* (1690) maintains human mind has no innate ideas, but latter are result of sensation and reflection. *Letters on Toleration; Treatise on Education; The Reasonableness of Christianity*.......... 1632—1704

**Lockhart,** John Gibson. Scottish scholar and author. *Life of Scott*.......... 1794—1854

**Longfellow,** Henry Wadsworth. American poet; born in Portland, Maine; educated at Bowdoin College, where he was professor of modern languages; held a similar chair at Harvard, 1835-54; published *Hyperion*, 1839; *Ballads and other Poems*, 1841; *Poems on Slavery*, 1842; *The Spanish Student*, 1843; *Poets and Poetry of Europe*, 1845; *The Belfry of Bruges*, 1846; *Evangeline*, 1847; *The Golden Legend*, 1851; *Hiawatha*, 1855; *Miles Standish, Tales of a Wayside Inn, Translation of Dante, Aftermath, Keramos, Ultima Thule*.......... 1807—1882

**Longinus,** Dionysius C. Greek philosopher and critic. *The Sublime*.......... 212— 273

**Lorris,** William de. French poet. *Roman de la Rose*.... — 1240

**Louis I.** Emperor of the West. "Le Débonnaire." Divided the empire among his sons.......... 778— 840

**Louis IX.** "Saint." King of France. Crusader. Captured by the Saracens; famous for his virtue.......... 1215—1270

**Louis XI.** King of France. Builder up of the monarchy; opponent of Charles of Burgundy.......... 1423—1483

**Louis XIV.** King of France. Son of Louis XIII. and Anne of Austria; ascended throne under regency of his mother, 1643; after the death of Mazarin, acted as his own minister, Colbert being his Minister of Finance; annexed large part of Flanders and Franche Comté (1667); revoked Edict of Nantes, 1685; fought England, Austria, Spain, and Prince of Orange, and engaged in the war of the Spanish Succession, his grandson having been appointed heir to the Spanish throne; was a patron of literature and the arts.......... 1638—1715

**Louis XV.** King of France. Defeated the English at Fontenoy; sensual and careless.......... 1710—1774

**Louis XVI.** King of France. Guillotined by his people. 1754—1793

**Louis Philippe.** King of France. "The citizen king." Abdicated in 1848.......... 1773—1850

**Louvois,** François M. Le Tellier, Marquis of. French statesman. Minister of Louis XIV.; caused revocation of Edict of Nantes.......... 1641—1691

**Lovejoy,** Elijah P. American Abolitionist. Murdered by a mob at Alton, Illinois.......... 1802—1837

**Lover,** Samuel. Irish novelist. *Handy Andy*.......... 1797—1868

**Lowell,** James Russell. American poet, critic and diplomatist. *The Bigelow Papers; The Vision of Sir Launfal; The Commemoration Ode; Fable for Critics; The Cathedral; Among my Books; My Study Windows.* Minister to Spain and England.......... 1819 —

**Lowell,** John. American statesman and lawyer. Promoted abolition of slavery in Massachusetts.......... 1743—1802

BORN. DIED.

**Loyola,** Ignatius. Spanish founder of the Jesuits. Was at first a soldier, then became a monk and preacher; (1523) made a pigrimage to Jerusalem; 1534, in association with St. Francis Xavier and Laïnez, he founded the Society of Jesus, with the object of renovating the Church and converting the infidels; became its superior in 1540; left a devotional work called *Spiritual Exercise* 1491—1536

**Lubbock,** Sir John. English banker and naturalist. M.P. *The Origin of Civilization* ... 1834 —

**Lucan** (Lucanus), M. Annæus. Roman poet. *Pharsalia.* 39— 65

**Lucian.** Greek satirist. *Dialogues of the Dead* ... 125— 200

**Lucretius.** Roman philosophical poet. *De Rerum Natura.* Committed suicide; his work *On the Nature of Things* expounds the physical and ethical doctrines of Epicurus ... B.C. 95— 55

**Lucullus,** L. Licinius. Roman general. Conqueror of Mithridates; celebrated for wealth and good dinners. B.C. 110— 57

**Lully,** Raymond. French philosopher. *Ars Magna* ... 1234—1315

**Luther,** Martin. German reformer. Became a priest in 1507; published (1517) 95 propositions against indulgences, which Tetzel was then selling in Germany. A great controversy arose, and Luther's works were condemned by Leo X. Luther burnt the Pope's Bull at Wittenburg; attended the Diet of Worms, and was protected; left monasticism (1524), and married Catherine de Bora, an ex-nun (1525). Justification by faith was the central point of his theology ... 1483—1546

**Lycurgus.** Spartan legislator. Instituted community of property and double executive at Sparta in the 9th. Cent ... B.C.

**Lyell,** Sir Charles. English geologist. *Geological Evidence of the Antiquity of Man* 1797—1875

**Lyndhurst,** John S. Copley, Lord. English Lord Chancellor ... 1772—1863

**Lyon,** Nathaniel. American general. Commander of the Department of Missouri; killed at battle of Wilson's Creek ... 1819—1861

**Lysias.** Athenian orator. *Thirty-five orations* ... B.C. 458— 378

**Lyttelton,** Sir Thomas. English lawyer and judge. *Tenures* 1420—1481

**Lytton,** Sir Edward G. E. Lytton Bulwer, Baron. English novelist and dramatist. *The Caxtons; Richelieu* ... 1805—1873

**Lytton,** Lord Edward Robert Bulwer. ("Owen Meredith.") English statesman and novelist. *Lucille* ... 1831 —

**Macaulay,** Thomas Babington, Lord. English historian and essayist. *History of England. Essays; Lays of Ancient Rome* ... 1809—1859

**Maccabæus,** Judas. [See Judas Maccabæus.]

**Macchiavelli,** Nicolo. Italian statesman (Secretary of the Republic) and author. *The Prince; History of Florence* ... 1419—1527

**McClellan,** George B. American general. Won battle of Antietam in the late civil war ... 1826 —

**McClosky,** John, Cardinal. American Catholic divine ... 1810 —

**Mackenzie,** Henry. English novelist. *Man of Feeling* .. 1745—1831

**Mackintosh,** Sir James. Scotch historian. *History of the Revolution in England* ... 1765—1832

**Macpherson,** James. Scotch scholar and poet. *Ossian.* 1738—1796

**MacPherson,** James P. American general. Commanded army of Tennessee; made Jackson retreat to Atlanta. 1828—1864

**Macready,** William C. English actor. Great in Shakespearian parts Made his *début* (1816) as *Orestes*; played Richard III., and other Shakespearian parts; visited U. S., 1848-9; retired from the stage in 1861 ... 1793—1873

**Madison,** James. American statesman. Member of the Virginia Legislature, of the convention of 1787, and a strenuous advocate of the Constitution; joint author with Hamilton and Jay of the *Federalist;* M. C., 1789-97; Secretary of State, 1801-9; President, 1809-17 ... 1751—1836

**Magellan,** Ferdinand de. Portuguese navigator. Magellan's Straits is named after him ... 1470—1521

BORN. DIED.

**Mahomet.** Arabian prophet. Founder of Mohammedanism. Lived in the practice of the regular religion till he was 40 years of age. Receiving a pretended revelation from Allah, he devoted himself henceforth to the propagation of his new religion. His faith was rejected at Mecca, but taken up at Medina. He fled from Mecca 622 (The Hegira); was originally a monogamist, and at first asserted liberty of conscience ... 570— 632

**Mahomet II.** "The Great." Sultan of Turkey. Captor of Constantinople ... 1430—1481

**Mai,** Angelo, Cardinal. Italian antiquarian and scholar. Discovered and published six books of Cicero's lost *Republic* ... 1782—1854

**Maintenon,** Françoise d'Aubigné, Mme. de. Mistress of Louis XIV.; married the comic poet Scarron, 1652; (he died, 1660); made governess of the Duc du Maine, 1670; given estate of Maintenon, 1674; secretly married Louis XIV., 1685; exerted great religious influence over him. 1635—1719

**Maistre,** Joseph de. French author. *Soirées de St.-Petersburg* ... 1753—1821

**Maistre,** Xavier de. French author. *Walk Around My Room* ... 1763—1852

**Malthus,** Thomas Robert, Rev. English political economist. *Essay on the Principle of Population* ... 1766—1834

**Mandeville,** Sir John. English traveler in the East. Often called the first English prose writer ... 1300—1372

**Manfred.** Son of the Emperor Frederick II. King of Naples and Sicily. Defeated by Charles of Aragon ... 1233—1266

**Manning,** Henry Edward, Cardinal. English Catholic prelate and author ... 1808 —

**Mansfield,** William Murray, Earl of. English Lord Chief Justice. Born in Scotland, educated at Oxford, and called to the bar in 1731; became Solicitor-General in 1743, having previously acquired a large practice. In Parliament he distinguished himself by his oratory; was made Attorney-General in 1754, and Chief Justice of the King's Bench in 1756, being at the same time created Baron Mansfield ... 1705—1793

**Mantegna,** Andrea. Italian painter. *The Triumph of Julius Cæsar* ... 1431—1506

**Manutius,** Aldus. Venetian printer and scholar. Inventor of Italic type. The Aldine Editions ... 1449—1515

**Manutius,** Aldus. Venetian printer and author. *On the Roman Senate* ... 1547—1597

**Manzoni,** Alessandro, Count. Italian author. *I Promessi Sposi* ... 1784—1873

**Marat,** Jean P. French Revolutionist. Assassinated ... 1744—1793

**Marcellus,** Marcus Claudius. Roman general and statesman. Conqueror of Syracuse ... B.C. 270— 208

**Margaret,** "Semiramis of the North." Queen of Norway, Sweden and Denmark ... 1353—1412

**Margaret** of Austria. Regent of the Netherlands. Took part in the league of Cambray ... 1480—1530

**Margaret** of Parma. Regent of the Netherlands. Mother of Alexander Farnese ... 1522—1586

**Margaret** of Valois. Sister of Francis I. of France. Authoress. *Heptameron.* Queen of Navarre ... 1492—1549

**Maria Louisa.** Empress of Napoleon I.; daughter of Francis I. of Austria ... 1791—1847

**Maria Theresa.** Empress of Austria and Queen of Hungary. Daughter of Charles VI., Emperor of Germany, and wife of Francis, Duke of Lorraine. Prussia, Spain, Sardinia, Bavaria and Saxony disputed her title to her father's estate. She drove out the French and Bavarians, and made peace with Prussia. Francis was chosen Emperor in 1745, but she was the real power; took part in the Seven Years' War; abolished feudal service ... 1717—1780

**Marius,** Caius. Roman general and statesman. Consul. Defeated Cimbri and Teutones; leader of the popular faction; rival of Sulla ... B.C. 157— 86

**Marlborough,** John Churchill, Duke of. English com-

BORN. DIED.

mander. Married Sarah Jennings, 1678; favorite of the Duke of York; made Earl of Marlborough, 1689; commanded English forces in Low Countries, 1689; deposed for his Jacobite intrigue, 1692; restored, 1696; commander of allied armies in Holland, 1702; won battle of Blenheim, 1704; Ramillies, 1706; Malplaquet, 1709. His wife was the confidante of Queen Anne. In disgrace from 1711 till accession of George I........ 1650—1722

**Marlborough,** Sarah Jennings, Duchess of. Wife of the above; had great influence with Queen Anne.......... 1660—1744

**Marlowe,** Christopher. English poet and dramatist. *Doctor Faustus; Hero and Leander; The Jew of Malta; Dido, Queen of Carthage*........ 1564—1593

**Marmont,** Augustus F. L. V. de, Duke of Ragusa. French general. Fought Austrian, Prussian and Russian troops near Paris, 1814........ 1774—1852

**Marmontel,** Jean F. French author and philosopher. *Moral Tales*........ 1723—1799

**Marryat,** Frederick. English naval officer and novelist. *Peter Simple; Midshipman Easy; Jacob Faithful; Japhet in Search of a Father*........ 1792—1848

**Mars,** Anne F. H. B. French actress. Famous in genteel comedy........ 1778—1847

**Marsh,** George P. American philologist. *History of the English Language*........ 1801—1882

**Marshal,** John. Chief Justice of the United States. Captain in the Revolutionary War, at the close of which he began to practice law in Virginia; a member of the Virginia Convention (1788); in 1797, with Pinckney and Gerry, he went on a diplomatic mission to France; elected to congress in 1799; appointed Secretary of State 1800, and resigned that office to become Chief Justice. Was the greatest judge that ever held the latter office... 1755—1835

**Martel,** [*i. e.*, "The Hammer"] Charles, Mayor of the Palace. Austrasian Duke and general. Conquered Saracens in a great battle at Poitiers........ 694— 741

**Martial** (M. Valerius Martialis). Roman epigrammatic poet. *Epigrams*........ 43— 105

**Martin,** Bon Henri. French historian. *History of France*. 1810 ——

**Martineau,** Harriet. English writer. *Society in America*. 1804—1876

**Martyn,** Justin. Christian writer. *Apology for the Christian Religion*........ 103— 165

**Mary.** Queen of England. Married Philip II. of Spain. Persecutor of the Protestants........ 1516—1558

**Mary de' Medici.** Queen of Henry IV. of France. Regent after his death; deposed........ 1573—1642

**Mary Stuart** Queen of Scots. Daughter of James V. and Mary of Guise; married (1558) the French Dauphin, (who came to the throne in 1559 as Francis II., and died childless, 1560); was invited to the throne of Scotland (1560); married her cousin, Lord Darnley (1565). Her secretary and favorite, Rizzio, was murdered (1566); her husband was blown up (1567), and she married the Earl of Bothwell the same year. Compelled to take refuge in England, she was finally beheaded by Elizabeth on a charge of conspiracy........ 1542—1587

**Masaniello** (Tommasso Anniello). Neapolitan patriot. Led popular revolt against Viceroy of Naples........ 1623—1643

**Mason,** James M. American statesman. Author of Fugitive Slave Law of 1850........ 1797—1871

**Massinger,** Philip. English dramatist. *New Way to Pay Old Debts; The Virgin Martyr; The City Madam*..... 1584—1640

**Mather,** Cotton. American theologian and writer. *Magnalia Christi*........ 1663—1728

**Mather,** Increase. American theologian and author. *Essay on Remarkable Providences*........ 1639—1723

**Mathew,** Theobald. "Father Mathew." Irish temperance reformer........ 1790—1856

**Mathews,** Charles. English comedian. *A Trip to America*........ 1776—1833

**Maurice.** Protestant Elector of Saxony. German general and statesman. Secured Treaty of Passau, guaranteeing religious liberty to Protestants........ 1521—1553

**Maurice** of Nassau. Prince of Orange. Son of William the Silent. Stadtholder. Defeated Spaniards at Turnhout, Austrians at Nieuwport........ 1567—1625

**Maximilian I.** Emperor of Germany. With Henry VIII. defeated the French at battle of the Spurs; created standing army........ 1459—1519

**Mazarin,** Julius, Cardinal. French statesman. Negotiated treaty of Westphalia; adviser of Anne of Austria and Louis XIV........ 1602—1661

**Mazzini,** Guiseppe. Italian patriot. Coöperated with Garibaldi; founder of Young Italy........ 1808—1872

**Meade,** George G. American general. Won battle of Gettysburg........ 1815—1872

**Medici,** Catherine de'. Queen of Henry II. of France. Instigated massacre of St. Bartholomew........ 1519—1589

**Medici,** Cosmo de'. Florentine statesman. "Father of his country." Patron of art and learning; collected MSS.. 1389—1464

**Medici,** Cosmo de'. Grand Duke of Tuscany. "The Great." Defeated Florentines and French. First Grand Duke........ 1519—1574

**Medici,** Lorenzo de'. Grand Duke of Florence. "The Magnificent." Patron of art and literature; adorned Florence........ 1448—1492

**Mehemet Ali.** Pasha of Egypt. General. Destroyed the monuments; conquered Syria; conquests stopped by European powers........ 1769—1849

**Melanchthon,** Philip (Schwarzerdt). German Reformer and scholar. Succeeded Luther as leader of the Reformers. *The Augsburg Confession*........ 1497—1560

**Melbourne,** William Lamb, Viscount. English statesman. Moderate Whig Minister, 1835-41........ 1779—1848

**Melchthal,** Arnold von. Swiss patriot. One of the founders of Swiss independence........ — 1317

**Melville,** Andrew. Scotch reformer and scholar. Abolished Episcopacy in Scotland........ 1545—1622

**Mendelssohn-Bartholdy,** Felix. German composer. In 1827 he produced *The Midsummer Night's Dream* and the opera *The Wedding of Camache*. In 1836 appeared his *St. Paul*, and in 1846 the oratorio of *Elijah*. Among his most famous works are his *Songs Without Words*. He produced many instrumental pieces and sonatas.... 1809—1847

**Mengs,** Anthony Raphael. German painter. *Apollo and the Muses*........ 1728—1779

**Merimée,** Prosper. French novelist and dramatist. *Colomba*........ 1803—1870

**Mesmer,** Frederick B. Suabian physician. Founder of Mesmerism........ 1734—1815

**Metellus,** Quintus Cæcilius. Roman commander. Victor over Jugurtha. Flourished 100 B.C.

**Metternich,** Clement W. N. L., Prince de. Austrian statesman and diplomatist. Chancellor; Minister of Foreign Affairs; represented Austria at Congress of Vienna........ 1773—1859

**Meyerbeer,** James. German composer. *Robert Le Diable. Romilda e Costanza*, 1818; *Semiramide Riconosciuta*, 1819; *Crociato in Egypto*, 1824; *Robert le Diable*, 1831; *Huguenots*, 1836; *L'Étoile du Nord*, 1854........ 1791—1864

**Mezzofanti,** Guiseppe G., Cardinal. Italian linguist..... 1774—1849

**Michael Angelo** (Buonarotti). Italian painter, sculptor, and architect. Painted the fresco of the *Last Judgment*, and prophets, sibyls, etc., at the Sistine Chapel. Among his great sculptures are the gigantic marble *David* at Florence, a *Pietà* and *Moses*; was appointed architect of St. Peter's, and formed a model for the dome; wrote sonnets and poems........ 1474—1564

**Mickiewicz,** Adam. Polish patriot and poet. *The Ancestors*........ 1798—1855

**Middleton,** Thomas. English dramatist. *The Roaring Girl; A Mad World, My Masters*........ 1570—1625

BORN. DIED.

**Mifflin,** Thomas. American statesman. President of the Continental Congress.................................. 1744—1800

**Mill,** James. English metaphysician and historian. *History of British India*............................ ...... 1773—1836

**Mill,** John Stuart. English political economist and philosopher. *Examination of Sir W. Hamilton's Philosophy*... 1806—1873

**Millais,** John E. English painter. *Return of the Dove to the Ark*.................................................... 1829 —

**Miller,** Hugh. Scotch geologist. *Old Red Sandstone*.... 1802—1856

**Milman,** Henry H. English divine and historian. *History of Latin Christianity*.................................. 1791—1868

**Miltiades.** Athenian general. Commander at Marathon. Flourished 500 B.C.

**Milton,** John. English poet. *Paradise Lost.* Educated at Cambridge, and passed some years in study and travel; was a Republican, and Latin Secretary of the English Commonwealth; wrote many prose political and controversial works. His sonnets are among the best in the language. His other works are *Comus, L'Allegro, Il Penseroso, Samson Agonistes, Paradise Regained, Lycidas*.. 1608—1674

**Minto,** Sir Gilbert Elliott, 1st Earl of. English Administrator in India; Governor General...................... 1751—1814

**Mirabeau,** Gabriel H. de Riquetti, Count of. French orator and revolutionist. Entered army, 1767; imprisoned by his father at various times for intrigues and debts; wandered in England, France, and Germany, 1783-8; represented Aix in States General, 1789; president of National Convention, 1791.............................. 1749—1791

**Mirandola,** John Picus, Count della. Italian scholar and reviver of learning.................................... 1463—1494

**Mitchell,** Donald G. ("Ik. Marvel.") American author. *My Farm at Edgewood; Reveries of a Bachelor*........ 1822 —

**Mitchell,** Ormsby M. American astronomer and general. Director of Dudley Observatory at Albany; surprised Huntsville ........ .................................. ........ 1810—1862

**Mitford,** Mary Russell. English author. *Our Village*.... 1786—1855

**Mithridates.** "The Great." King of Pontus. With Tigranes of Armenia fought the Romans for many years.............................. ..............B. C. 130— 63

**Molière,** Jean Baptiste Poquelin de. French dramatist. Became *valet du chambre* to Louis XIII. in 1640; four years later he took the name of Molière, and became a comic actor. After playing in the provinces for some time he opened a theatre at Paris, in 1658. His *Précieuses Ridicules* appeared in 1659; *École des Maris* in 1661; *Misanthrope* in 1666; and *Tartuffe*, his masterpiece, in 1667. Among his other works are *Le Malade Imaginaire* and *Les Femmes Savantes*.................. 1622—1673

**Moltke,** Hillmuth, Count von. German general. Conqueror in the Franco-Prussian war .................... 1800 —

**Mommsen,** Theodore. German historian. *History of Rome*.................................................... 1817 —

**Monk,** George, Duke of Albemarle. Restorer of the English monarchy .............................................. 1608—1670

**Monmouth,** James Scott, Duke of. Natural son of Charles II. Rebelled and was executed........................ 1649—1685

**Monroe,** James. American statesman. Captain in Revolutionary War; studied law with Jefferson; delegate to Congress, 1783; opponent of Constitution; Senator, 1790; Minister to France, 1794-6; Governor of Virginia, 1799-1802; Envoy-Extraordinary to France, 1802; Minister to England, 1803; Governor of Virginia, 1811; Secretary of State, 1811-17; President, 1817-25.......... 1758—1831

**Montagu,** Lady Mary Wortley. English author. *Letters*. 1690—1762

**Montaigne,** Michael de. French author. *Essais.* Studied law; judge at Bordeaux, 1554; Mayor of Bordeaux, 1581-5; published the *Essays*, 1580.......................... 1533—1592

**Montalembert,** Charles Forbes, Comte de. French publicist. Leader of Liberal Catholic party. *The Free Church in the Free State*.............................. 1810—1870

**Montcalm,** Louis J. de St. Véran, Marquis of. French commander in Canada. Killed on Abraham's Heights, in the battle with Wolfe.................................... 1712—1759

**Montemayor,** George de. Spanish poet. *Diana*........ 1520—1562

**Montespan,** Françoise A. de R. de Montemart, Marchioness de. Mistress of Louis XIV.......................... 1641—1707

**Montesquieu,** Charles de Secondat, Baron de. French author. *Spirit of the Laws*.............................. 1689—1755

**Montez,** Lola, Countess of Landsfeld. Spanish adventuress. Mistress of King Louis of Bavaria. *The Art of Beauty*. 1824—1861

**Montezuma II.** Last Emperor of Mexico. Mortally wounded while attempting to quell insurrection of his subjects against Cortez.................................. 1470—1520

**Montfort,** Simon de. Norman soldier and Crusader. Conspicuous in the war against the Albigenses........ .... 1150—1218

**Montfort,** Simon de, Earl of Leicester. English soldier and statesman. Called first House of Commons; led barons against Henry III.; killed at battle of Leicester.. 1205—1265

**Montgolfier,** Jacques S. French inventor of balloons.... 1745—1799

**Montgomery,** James. English poet. *The World Before the Flood; The Wanderer of Switzerland*.............. 1771—1854

**Montgomery,** Richard. American Revolutionary soldier. Killed at Quebec.................................... 1736—1775

**Montmorency,** Anne de. Constable of France. Chief Minister of Francis I.; beat Huguenots at Greux........ 1493—1567

**Montmorency,** Henri de. Constable of France. Took up arms against Louis XIII.; beheaded................ 1534—1614

**Montmorency,** Matthew de. Constable of France. "The Great." General at the victory of Bouvines............ 1175—1230

**Montpensier,** Anne M. L. d'Orleans, Duchess of. French writer. Adherent of Condé in the Wars of the Fronde. *Memoirs* ................................................ 1627—1693

**Montrose,** James Graham, Marquis of. Scotch Royalist general. Executed for treason.......................... 1612—1650

**Moore,** Sir John. British commander. Killed at Corunna 1761—1809

**Moore,** Thomas. Irish poet. *Lalla Rookh; Irish Melodies; The Twopenny Postbag; The Fudge Family; The Loves of the Angels; The Epicurean; Life of Sheridan; Life of Lord Byron*.......................... 1779—1852

**Morales,** Luis. Spanish painter. "The Divine." *Via Dolorosa*.................................................. 1509—1586

**More,** Hannah. English authoress. *Cœlebs in Search of a Wife*.................................................... 1745—1833

**More,** Sir Thomas. English statesman and author. Lord Chancellor. Educated at Oxford, where he knew Erasmus; entered Parliament, 1504; published *History of Richard III.*, 1513; became favorite of Henry VIII.; published *Utopia*, 1516; speaker of House of Commons, 1523; Lord Chancellor, 1532; refused to acknowledge the validity of Henry's marriage to Anne Boleyn ............. 1480—1530

**Moreau,** Jean Victor. French commander. Won battles of Hochstadt and Hohenlinden; killed at Dresden...... 1763—1818

**Morgan,** Sir Henry J. Welsh buccaneer. Captured Panama and Porto Bello .......................................... 1636—1696

**Mornay,** Philippe de, Sieur du Plessis-Morlay. French Protestant statesman. *Treatise on the Institution of the Eucharist*.................................................. 1549—1623

**Morny,** Charles A. L. J. de, Count of. French statesman. Reputed son of Hortense de Beauharnais; prominent in *coup d' état*................................................ 1811—1865

**Morris,** George P. American journalist and poet. *Woodman, Spare that Tree*.......................... .............. 1802—1864

**Morris,** Gouverneur. American Revolutionary statesman and orator. Minister to France; U. S. Senator; promoter of Erie Canal.................................. .......... 1754—1816

**Morris,** Robert. American financier and statesman. Superintendent of Finances, 1781-4.......................... 1734—1806

**Morris,** William. English poet. *The Earthly Paradise*.. 1834 —

**Morse,** Samuel Finley Breese. American inventor of telegraph. Studied painting at first; suggested electric telegraph in 1832, while returning from Europe; constructed small recording electric telegraph in 1835; ap-

BORN. DIED.

plied vainly for Congressional aid in 1837; got it in 1843; constructed telegraph line from Washington to Baltimore, and brought telegraph into successful operation in 1846 ... 1794—1872

**Morton,** James Douglas, Earl of. Regent of Scotland; Lord Chancellor. Beheaded as accessory to murder of Darnley ... 1530—1581

**Morton** (or **Moreton**), John, Cardinal. Archbishop of Canterbury. English statesman. Lord Chancellor; proposed marriage of Henry VII. to daughter of Edward IV ... 1410—1500

**Moses.** Hebrew legislator and statesman. Led the Israelites out of Egypt. Mosaic *Code* of Laws ... B.C. 1570—1450

**Motley,** John Lothrop. American historian and diplomatist. Minister to England and Austria. *The Rise of the Dutch Republic* ... 1814—1877

**Mott,** Valentine. American surgeon. First to exsert entire right clavicle ... 1785—1865

**Moultrie,** William. American Revolutionary soldier. Defended fort on Sullivan's Island (1776), afterward called Fort Moultrie ... 1731—1805

**Mozart,** Johann C. N. A. German composer. Composed short pieces when 6 years old; gave concerts in Paris and London, 1763-4; in 1781, composed *Idomeneo;* 1783, *The Abduction from the Seraglio;* 1785, *Davidde Penitente;* 1786, the comic opera of *The Marriage of Figaro;* 1787, his masterpiece of *Don Giovanni;* 1791, *The Magic Flute;* his latest work, the *Requiem,* is his most sublime 1756—1791

**Müller,** F. Max. German philologist in England. *Chips from a German Workshop* ... 1823 —

**Müller,** Wilhelm. German lyric poet. *Lyrical Promenades* ... 1794—1827

**Münchausen,** Jerome C. F. von. German traveller and liar ... 1720—1797

**Münzer,** Thomas. German Anabaptist and insurgent. Led 40,000 fanatics; committed great excesses; executed — 1525

**Murat,** Joachim. French Marshal and King of Naples. Dashing cavalry leader ... 1770—1815

**Murger,** Henri. French author. *Vie de Bohême* ... 1822—1860

**Murillo,** Bartholomew Stephen. Spanish painter. Enjoyed the advice and friendship of Velasquez at Madrid. Many of his works were painted for churches there, and at Cadiz and Seville. His virgin saints and his beggar boys are famous. Among his great works are *St. Elizabeth of Hungary, The Prodigal Son, The Young Beggar, Moses Striking the Rock, St. Anthony of Padua,* and the *Marriage of St. Catherine* ... 1618—1682

**Murner,** Thomas. German satirist and poet. *The World of Fools* ... 1475—1535

**Murray,** James Stuart, Earl of. Regent of Scotland. Leader of Protestant faction; opponent of Mary Stuart. 1531—1570

**Murray,** Lindley. American grammarian. *Grammar of the English Language* ... 1745—1826

**Musset,** Louis C. Alfred de. French poet and novelist. *Les Marrons du Feu; Namouna* ... 1810—1857

**Nadir Shah.** King of Persia. Expelled Afghans; dethroned Shah and usurped crown; conquered part of India ... 1687—1747

**Napier,** Sir Charles J. English general in India. Conqueror of the Scinde ... 1782—1853

**Napier,** John, Lord. Scotch mathematician. Inventor of logarithms ... 1550—1617

**Napier,** Sir William F. P. English general and historian. *History of the War in the Peninsula* ... 1785—1860

**Nash,** Thomas. English satirist and dramatist. *The Supplication of Pierre Penniless to the Devil* ... 1567—1600

**Neander,** Johann A. N. German historian. *Universal History of the Christian Religion* ... 1789—1850

**Nebuchadnezzar.** King of Babylon. Conqueror of Jerusalem, Tyre, Egypt ... B.C. — 562

BORN. DIED.

**Necker,** James. French financier and statesman. Controller-General of the Finances. *On the Administration of the Finances.* Father of Mme. de Staël ... 1732—1804

**Nelson,** Horatio, Viscount. English naval commander. Went to sea at 13; post captain, 1779; rear admiral, 1797; distinguished himself at battle of Mount Vincent; won battle of the Nile, 1798; second in command at Copenhagen, 1801 (but really won the fight); in 1805, with 27 sail of the line and four frigates, defeated combined French and Spanish fleets at Trafalgar, where he was mortally wounded ... 1758—1805

**Nepos,** Cornelius. Roman biographer. *Lives of the Emperors.* Flourished 5 B.C.

**Nero.** Roman Emperor (54-68). Put his mother to death; persecuted Christians; said to have burned Rome ... 37— 68

**Nerva.** Roman Emperor (76-98). Humane ruler; recalled exiles banished by his predecessors ... 32— 98

**Nesselrode,** Charles R., Count of. Russian diplomatist. Minister of Foreign Affairs under three Emperors ... 1780—1862

**Newman,** John Henry, Cardinal. English Catholic theologian. *A Grammar of Assent* ... 1801 —

**Newton,** Sir Isaac. English mathematician and philosopher. *Principia.* In 1665 discovered the method of fluxions; in 1668, that light is not homogeneous, but consists of rays of different refrangibility; in 1675, published his *Theory of Light and Color.* His great work, the *Principia,* appeared in 1687. (He had really discovered the extent of the force of gravity in 1666.) In this he shows that every particle of matter is attracted by every other particle with a force inversely proportional to the squares of the distances ... 1642—1727

**Ney,** Michael. "The Bravest of the Brave." One of Napoleon's marshals. Led Guard at Waterloo; shot ... 1769—1815

**Nicholas I.** Czar of Russia. Warred with Turkey and Persia; put down Polish insurrection; engaged in Crimean War ... 1796—1855

**Nicias.** Athenian commander. Leader of the disastrous expedition into Sicily ... B.C. — 413

**Nicole,** Pierre. French Jansenist. *Essais de Morale* ... 1625—1695

**Niebuhr,** Barthold G. German historian. *History of Rome* ... 1776—1831

**Nightingale,** Florence. English philanthropist. *Notes on Nursing* ... 1820 —

**Noailles,** Adrian M., Duke of. French general and statesman; commanded in war with Germany, 1734 ... 1678—1766

**Nillson,** Christine. Swedish singer ... 1843 —

**Nodier,** Charles. French novelist. *Thérèse Aubert* ... 1783—1844

**Nollekens,** Joseph. Dutch sculptor. *Timoleon and Alexander* ... 1737—1823

**Norfolk,** Thomas Howard, 3d Duke of. English general; defeated the Scotch at Flodden Field ... 1473—1554

**Normanby,** Constantine A. Phipps, Marquis of. English statesman; home Secretary; advocate of Catholic Emancipation ... 1797—1863

**North,** Frederick, Lord. English statesman; leader of Commons; Prime Minister during the American War ... 1732—1792

**North,** Sir Thomas. English translator. *Plutarch's Lives.* 1535—1580

**Northcote,** Sir Stafford H. English Conservative statesman; Chancellor of the Exchequer (1874-'80) ... 1818 —

**Nostradamus,** Michael de. French astrologer. *Centuries* (a collection of prophesies) ... 1503—1566

**Nottingham,** Daniel Finch, Earl of. English statesman; Secretary of State; one of the Counsellors of William III ... 1647—1730

**Nottingham,** Heneage Finch, Earl of. English jurist; Attorney General, and Lord Chancellor ... 1621—1682

**"Novalis,"** (Friedrich von Hardenberg). German author. *Heinrich von Ofterdingen* ... 1772—1801

**Noyes,** George R. American theologian and biblical scholar. Translation of the *Psalms* ... 1798—1860

BORN. DIED.

**Oates,** Titus. English informer; inventor of the "Popish Plot." .......... 1620—1705
**Oberlin,** Jean F. French philanthropist .......... 1740—1826
**O'Brien,** William Smith. Irish politician; leader of "Young Ireland;" banished for "treason" .......... 1803—1864
**Occam,** William, English theologian. *On the Power of the Sovereign Pontiff* .......... —— 1347
**Occleve,** Thomas. English poet. *The Story of Jonathan.* 1370—1450
**O'Connell,** Daniel. Irish orator and agitator; advocate of Catholic Emancipation, and the repeal of the union.. 1775—1847
**O'Connor,** Charles. American lawyer .......... 1804 ——
**Odoacer.** Gothic King of Italy. Executed by Theodoric, who besieged him in Ravenna .......... —— 493
**Oecolampadius,** John. German reformer; adherent of Zwingle. *On the Passover* .......... 1482—1531
**Oehlenschläger,** Adam G.. Danish dramatist. *Axel and Valborg* .......... 1779—1850
**Oersted,** Hans C. Danish scientist; founder of the science of electro-magnetism .......... 1775—1851
**Oglethorpe,** James. British general; colonizer of Georgia .......... 1688—1785
**Olaus,** Magnus. Danish historian. *On the Peoples of the North* .......... 1500—1568
**Oldcastle,** Sir John, Lord Cobham. English reformer. Head of the insurgent Lollards. Executed .......... 1360—1407
**Oldfield,** Anne. English actress; equally famous in tragedy and comedy .......... 1683—1730
**Oldham,** John. English poet. *Pindaric Odes* .......... 1653—1683
**Oldmixon,** John. English historian and antiquarian. *History of the Stuarts* .......... 1673—1742
**Olivarez,** Gaspard Engman, Duke of. Spanish statesman and general. First Minister of State; opponent of Richelieu; fought France and the Netherlands .......... 1587—1645
**Omar I.** Arabian Caliph. Conqueror of Jerusalem .......... 581— 644
**Opie,** Mrs. Amelia. English novelist. *The Orphan* .......... 1761—1807
**Opitz,** Martin. German poet. *Poem of Consolation* .......... 1597—1639
**Orcagna,** Andrea di Cioni. Italian painter and sculptor. *The Triumph of Death,* at Pisa .......... 1329—1389
**Orelli,** John G. German philologist and classical scholar. *Inscriptions* .......... 1787—1849
**Origen.** Greek Father of the Church. *Hexapla.* Held universal restoration of the dead .......... 185— 253
**Orléans,** Charles d'. French poet; captured at Agincourt 1391—1465
**Orléans,** Louis Philippe Joseph, Duke of. "Egalité" (Equality). French revolutionist .......... 1747—1793
**Orléans,** Phillippe, Duke of. Regent of France. Profligate in morals and politics .......... 1674—1723
**Orloff,** Gregory Gregorievitch, Count. Favorite of Catherine of Russia, whom he helped to the throne .......... 1734—1783
**Ormond,** James Butler, Duke of. Irish statesman; put down Irish Rebellion .......... 1610—1688
**Orosius,** Paulus. Spanish ecclesiastic and historian. *Historiarum Libri VII. Adversus Paganos.* Flourished... 5th Cent'y.
**Orsini,** Felix. Italian conspirator and revolutionist; attempted to assassinate Napoleon III.; executed .......... 1819—1858
**Osceola.** Seminole Indian chief; fought whites 2 years.. 1803—1838
**Osman I.** Turkish Sultan. (1299-1326.) Founder of the Ottoman Empire .......... 1259—1326
**Ostade,** Adrian von. Dutch painter. *A Smoker Lighting his Pipe* .......... 1610—1685
**Otho I.** ("The Great.") Emperor of Germany. Defeated and Christianized Danes; deposed Pope John XI .......... 912— 973
**Otis,** Harrison Gray. American statesman and orator; a Federalist leader in Congress .......... 1765—1848
**Otis,** James. American Revolutionary statesman and orator; argued against writs of assistance; led popular party .......... 1726—1783
**Otway,** Thomas. English dramatist. *Venice Preserved*.. 1651—1680
**Outram,** Sir James. English general in India; led expedition against Persia, 1836 .......... 1802—1863
**Overbury,** Sir Thomas, English poet. *The Wife* .......... 1581—1613

BORN. DIED.

**Ovid,** (Publius Ovidius Naso). Roman poet. *Metamorphoses* .......... B.C. 43 18 A.D.
**Owen,** Richard. English anatomist and palæontologist. *History of British Fossil Mammals* .......... 1804 ——
**Owen,** Robert. English Socialist in America; founded colony of New Harmony. *New View of Society* .......... 1771—1858
**Oxenstiern,** Axel, Count. Swedish statesman .......... 1583—1634

**Paganini,** Niccolo. Italian violinist; celebrated for his performances on a single string .......... 1784—1840
**Paine,** Robert Treat. American lawyer and statesman; signed Declaration of Independence .......... 1731—1814
**Paine,** Thomas. American (English born) deist and political writer. *The Age of Reason; Common Sense* .......... 1737—1809
**Paley,** William. English divine and theologian. *Evidences* .......... 1743—1805
**Palgrave,** Sir Francis. English historian. *History of Normandy* .......... 1788—1861
**Palissy,** Bernard. French potter and enameller. *Treatise on the Origin of Fountains* .......... 1510—1596
**Palladio,** Jacopo. Italian architect. *Church of S. Ridentore,* at Venice. Founder of "Palladian" architecture. 1518—1580
**Palmerston,** Henry John Temple, 3d Viscount. English statesman; Minister of Foreign Affairs; long Prime Minister .......... 1784—1865
**Paoli,** Pascal de. Corsican patriot and General-in-Chief in Corsican revolt against the Genoese .......... 1726—1807
**Papin,** Denys. French natural philosopher; inventor of Papin's Digester; one of the inventors of the steam engine .......... 1647—1716
**Pappenheim,** Godfrey H., Count von. German General; won Imperialist victory at Magdeburg .......... 1594—1632
**Paracelsus,** Philippus A. T. von Hohenheim. Swiss physician and philosopher; introduced mercury and opium into medical use .......... 1493—1541
**Pardoe,** Julia. English writer. *Louis XIV* .......... 1806—1862
**Park,** Mungo. Scotch traveler in Africa. *Travels in the Interior of Africa* .......... 1771—1805
**Parker,** Isaac. American jurist; Chief Justice of Massachusetts .......... 1768—1830
**Parker,** Matthew. Archbishop of Canterbury. Published the *Bishops' Bible* .......... 1504—1575
**Parker,** Theodore. American theologian and reformer. *Transient and Permanent in Christianity* .......... 1810—1860
**Parkman,** Francis. American historian. *Conspiracy of Pontiac* .......... 1823 ——
**Parma,** Alexander Farnese, Duke of. Italian General; Regent of the Netherlands; commanded the Spanish Armada; fought Maurice and William of Orange .......... 1541—1592
**Parmigiano,** Il. (F. Mazzuoli). Italian painter. *Madonna della Rosa* .......... 1503—1540
**Parnell,** Charles Stewart. Irish politician and agitator; M. P.; head of the Land League movement .......... 1847 ——
**Parnell,** Thomas. English poet. *The Hermit* .......... 1679—1717
**Parny,** Evariste D.E. French lyric poet. Author of many amatory poems .......... 1753—1814
**Parr,** Catherine. Queen of Henry VIII. of England, whom she succeeded in surviving .......... 1509—1548
**Parr,** Samuel. English divine, scholar and author. *Character of Charles James Fox* .......... 1747—1825
**Parr,** Thomas ("Old Parr"). English centenarian .......... 1483—1635
**Parry,** Sir William E. English arctic explorer; sought for northwest passage; discovered Barrow's Strait .......... 1790—1855
**Parsons,** Theophilus. American jurist and Chief Justice of Massachusetts .......... 1750—1813
**Parsons,** Thomas William. American poet. Translator of Dante's *Divina Commedia* .......... 1819 ——
**Pascal,** Blaise. French philosopher and writer. (*Pensées*). He wrote a treatise on conic sections at 16; invented a calculating machine at 18; established the theory of atmospheric pressure 1648; entered the cloister of Port

BORN. DIED.

Royal, where, in 1656, he produced the famous *Provincial Letters* against the Jesuits. His *Pensées* is really the fragments of a great work on the fundamental truths of religion. He was one of the greatest of French thinkers 1623—1662

**Patrick**, Saint. Apostle of Ireland. Born in Scotland. One of the first to preach Christianity in Ireland ........ 372— 463

**Paul**, Saint, of Tarsus. Apostle of the Gentiles .......... — 65

**Paul III.** (Alexander Farnese). Pope of Rome. Called Council of Trent; excommunicated Henry VIII ........ 1468—1549

**Paulding**, James K. American author. *Bulls and Jonathans* ........ 1779—1860

**Payne**, John Howard. American dramatist and poet. *Home, Sweet Home* ........ 1792—1852

**Peabody**, George. American banker in London, philanthropist. Founder of homes for workingmen in London, of museums, etc ........ 1795—1869

**Peel**, Sir Robert. English statesman and Prime Minister. Repealed the Corn Laws ........ 1788—1850

**Peirce**, Benjamin. American mathematician, author of many works on mathematics and mechanics ........ 1809—1880

**Pellico**, Silvio. Italian patriot and author. *My Prisons* .. 1789—1854

**Pendleton**, Edmund. American lawyer and statesman; an able debater; Member of Congress; President of Virginia Convention of 1789 ........ 1721—1803

**Penn**, Sir William. English admiral. Commander-in-chief of fleet which defeated Dutch, 1665, father of William below ........ 1621—1770

**Penn**, William. English Quaker. Proprietor of Pennsylvania, courtier, statesman, philanthropist, author ........ 1644—1718

**Pepin**, ("The Short"). Mayor of the Palace. King of France. Usurped throne; defeated Saxons and Lombards ........ 714— 768

**Pepperell**, Sir William. American colonial general, commanded at siege of Louisville, 1755 ........ 1697—1759

**Pepys**, Samuel. English author. *Diary* ........ 1632—1703

**Perceval**, Spencer. English Prime Minister. Opposed reform; assassinated ........ 1762—1812

**Pereira**, Nunez Alvarez. "The Portuguese Cid." Portuguese commander; won many victories over the Spaniards ........ 1360—1431

**Pergolesi**, John Baptist. Italian composer. *Stabat Mater*. 1710—1736

**Periander**. Tyrant of Corinth. One of the Seven Sages of Greece ........ B. C. 665— 585

**Pericles.** Athenian orator and statesman; came forward as a leader of the democracy 470 B. C. He secured the ostracism of Cimon, and after that event, and the ostracism of Thucydides, was the first man in Athens. He was commander in the Samian war, and conquered Samos; founded many colonies, made new alliances, and greatly increased the influence of Athens, which he adorned with noble public works; his funeral oration on the victims of the first Peloponnesian war was sublimely eloquent ........ B. C. — 429

**Perrault**, Charles. French scholar and author. *Parallel between the Ancients and the Moderns* ........ 1628—1703

**Perry**. Matthew C. American commodore. Chief of expedition to Japan ........ 1795—1858

**Perry**, Oliver H. American naval commander. Won battle of Lake Erie ........ 1785—1820

**Persius**, (Aulus Persius Flaccus). Roman satirist. *Satires* 34— 62

**Pestalozzi**, Giovanni H. Swiss educator. *Leinhard und Gertrude* ........ 1746—1827

**Peter**, Saint. Apostle ........ — 66

**Peter the Hermit.** Preacher of the First Crusade ...... 1050—1115

**Peter.** (The Cruel). King of Castile. Put his wife to death; driven out; restored by Edward the Black Prince 1319—1369

**Peter I.** ("The Great.") Czar of Russia. Visited Western Europe in 1697; was for a time a shipcarpenter in Holland, and spent 8 months in England: on his return to Russia, he reorganized the army and navy, founded schools, and took measures to increase Russian commerce; he made an alliance with Poland and Denmark, (1701) against Charles XII., whom he defeated at Pultowa (1709); founded St. Petersburg (1703); his son Alexis was poisoned by him ........ 1672—1725

**Peterborough**, Charles Mordaunt. Third Earl of. English general. Captured Barcelona and Valencia. Of splendid talents but eccentric ........ 1658—1735

**Petrarch**, Francis. (Francesco Petrarca). Italian poet and scholar. *Sonnets* ........ 1304—1374

**Phalaris.** Tyrant of Agrigentum. Famed for cruelty B.C. — 554

**Phidias.** Greatest of Greek sculptors. Pericles made him superintendent of public buildings at Athens, and he made the sculptured ornaments of the Parthenon; his masterpieces were the colossal ivory-and-gold statues (40 feet high) of Minerva at the Parthenon, and of Zeus at Olympia in Elis; the latter being counted one of the wonders of the world ........ B. C. 490— 432

**Philip II.** King of Macedonia. Father of Alexander the Great. Came to throne 359 B. C.; married Olympia, daughter of the King of Epirus; he was an ally of Thebes against Athens; took Olynthos 347; defeated Athenians and Thebans at Chaeronæa; assassinated B.C. 382— 336

**Philip II.** ("Augustus.") King of France. Annexed Normandy, Anjou, Lorraine; won battle of Bouvines 1165—1223

**Philip IV.** ("The Fair.") King of France. Suppressed the Templars; imprisoned Pope Boniface III ........ 1268—1314

**Philip II.** King of Spain. Son of Charles V. Caused revolt in Netherlands; despatched Armada against England ........ 1527—1598

**Philips**, Ambrose. English poet. *The Distressed Mother* 1671—1749

**Phillips**, Charles. Irish lawyer and orator. *Recollections of Curran* ........ 1789—1859

**Phillips**, Wendell. American orator, abolitionist. *Speech in Faneuil Hall*, 1836 ........ 1811 —

**Phips**, Sir William. Colonial governor of Massachusetts. Captured Port Royal, 1690 ........ 1651—1695

**Phocion.** Athenian statesman and general. Leader of aristocratic party; opponent of Demosthenes ...... B.C. 402— 317

**Piccolomini**, Octavius. Austrian general. Conspirator against Wallenstein; led Spanish army in Flanders .... 1599—1656

**Pickering**, Timothy. American statesman. Postmaster-General, Secretary of War and State under Washington 1746—1829

**Pierce**, Franklin. American statesman; born in N. H.; studied law; Democratic M.C., 1832-7; U. S. Senator, 1837-42; brigadier general in Mexican war; President, 1853-57; opposed coercion of seceding States ........ 1804—1869

**Pilate**, Pontius. Roman governor of Palestine. Acquiesced in condemnation of Christ ........ — 38

**Pinckney**, Charles C. American soldier and statesman. Leader of Federalists; Minister to France ........ 1740—1825

**Pindar.** Lyric poet of Thebes. *Odes* ........ B.C. 518— 442

**Piranese**, Giovanni B. Italian architect and engraver. *The Magnificence of the Romans* ........ 1720—1728

**Piron**, Alexander. French dramatic poet. *The Mania for Writing Verse* ........ 1689—1773

**Pisano**, Andrea. Italian architect and sculptor. His greatest work is the bronze gate of the Baptistry at Florence ........ 1270—1345

**Pisano**, Il. (Nicolo di Pisa). Italian sculptor and architect. Architect of the Campo Santo, at Pisa ........ 1200—1273

**Pisistratus.** Tyrant of Athens. Patron of learning. Had *Iliad and Odyssey* reduced to writing for the first time ........ B.C. 612— 527

**Pitt**, William. English statesman and orator. He was the second son of Lord Chatham; received a careful education, and entered parliament in 1781; he was made Chancellor of the Exchequer (1782); became First Lord of the Treasury, and Prime Minister 1783; resigned in 1801, but took office again in 1804; was the head and front of the great coalition against Bonaparte; an eloquent orator and a quick debater ........ 1759—1806

BORN. DIED.

**Pius IX.** (Giovanni Maria Mastai Ferretti.) Pope. Dogmas of Immaculate Conception and Papal Infallibility promulgated during his incumbency; temporal power lost 1870 .......... 1792—1878

**Pizarro,** Francis. Spanish conqueror of Peru .......... 1475—1541

**Plato.** Greek philosopher and writer; held that the human soul has always existed; an idea is an eternal thought of the divine mind; among his works are *The Republic, Phaedo, Gorgias, Crito,* and *Apology for Socrates* .. B.C. 428— 347

**Pliny,** The Elder. Roman savant and writer *Natural History* .......... 23— 79

**Pliny,** The Younger. Roman writer and statesman. *Panegyric on Trajan* .......... 61— 106

**Plotinus.** Greek Neo-Platonic philosopher. Author of many metaphysical works .......... 205— 270

**Plutarch,** Greek biographer. *Lives* .......... 45— 120

**Poe,** Edgar Allen. American poet. *The Raven* .......... 1811—1849

**Poitiers,** Diana de. Duchess de Valentinois. Mistress of Henry II. of France .......... 1500—1556

**Pole,** Reginald. Cardinal. English catholic prelate. Papal legate to England in the reign of Queen Mary. *For the Unity of the Church* .......... 1500—1556

**Polk,** James K. American statesman. Born North Carolina; removed to Tennessee, 1806; studied law; member of Congress, 1825; elected speaker, 1835 and 1837; governor of Tennessee, 1839-41; Democratic President, 1845-49; prosecuted Mexican war .......... 1795—1849

**Polk,** Leonidas, Bishop. American Confederate general and Episcopal prelate. Conspicuous at Shiloh and Stone River .......... 1806—1864

**Pollok,** Robert. Scotch poet. *Course of Time* .......... 1798—1827

**Polo,** Marco. Venetian traveler in the East. *The Book of Marco Polo* .......... 1256—1333

**Polybius.** Greek historian of Rome. *Universal History* .......... B.C. 204— 122

**Polycarp.** Bishop of Smyrna; Christian martyr .......... 80— 160

**Pompadour,** Jeanne A. P., Marchioness of. Mistress of Louis XIV.; married, 1741, M. de Etioles; attracted notice of Louis XV., 1744: made Marquise de Pompadour, 1745; controlled him and the policy of France; caused the coalition of France and Austria against Frederick the Great .......... 1722—1764

**Pompey** (Cnæus Pompeius). Roman general and statesman; conqueror of Suetonius and Mithridates; leader of aristocracy; rival of Cæsar; defeated at Pharsalia B.C. 106— 48

**Ponce de Leon,** Juan. Spanish discoverer of Florida .... 1460—1521

**Poniatowski,** John. Polish commander; led Poles against Prussia and Russia in service of France .......... 1762—1813

**Pontiac.** American Indian chief; formed coalition of Western tribes against the whites .......... 1742—1769

**Pope,** Alexander. English poet; son of a London linen draper; educated by a priest named Tavernier. *Pastorals; Essay on Criticism; Essay on Man; Windsor Forest; The Dunciad; Rape of the Lock;*. Translation of *The Iliad* and *The Odyssey; Satires; Epistles* .......... 1688—1744

**Porter,** David. American naval officer; commander of the *Essex* .......... 1780—1843

**Porter,** David D. American naval officer; admiral; bombarded Fort Fisher .......... 1813 ——

**Portsmouth,** Louisa de Querouaille, Duchess of. French *Cattle* .......... 1652—1734

**Poussin,** Nicholas. French painter. *The Last Supper* ... 1594—1665

**Praed,** Winthrop M. English poet and wit. Writer of vers de societé. *Athens* .......... 1802—1839

**Prentiss,** Seargent S. American orator and lawyer; member of Congress; leading lawyer of the Southwest ...... 1808—1850

**Prescott,** William. American Revolutionary officer; commanded (probably) at Bunker Hill .......... 1725—1795

**Prescott,** William Hickling. American historian. *Ferdinand and Isabella* .......... 1796—1859

**Priestley,** Joseph. English natural philosopher. *History of the Corruptions of Christianity* .......... 1733—1804

**Prior,** Matthew. English poet and diplomatist. *Carmen Seculare* .......... 1664—1721

**Probus,** M. Aurelius. Roman Emperor. Defeated the Germans in Gaul .......... 232— 282

**Procter,** Bryan W. English poet. *The Sea* .......... 1787—1874

**Proudhon,** Pierre J. French Socialist. *What is Property* 1809—1860

**Ptolemy I.** ("Soter.") King of Egypt. Founder of the dynasty of Greek sovereigns in Egypt; patron of literature .......... B.C. 367— 282

**Ptolemy II.** (Philadelphus.) King of Egypt. Founder of Alexandrian Library; Theocritus, Euclid, Aratus lived at his court .......... B.C. 309— 247

**Ptolemy,** Claudius. Greek mathematician and geographer. *Almagest*. Flourished .......... 2nd Cent'y.

**Pugin,** Augustus W. N. English architect; designed many churches. *True Principles of Pointed Architecture* .......... 1811—1852

**Pulaski,** Count. Polish general in the American Revolution; leader of "Pulaski's Legion;" killed at siege of Savannah .......... 1747—1779

**Pushkin,** Alexander S. Russian poet and author. *Boris Godoonof* .......... 1799—1837

**Putnam,** Israel. General in the American Revolution; conspicuous at Bunker Hill .......... 1718—1790

**Pym,** John. English Republican statesman; leader of the popular party in Parliament .......... 1584—1643

**Pyrrho.** Greek skeptic and philosopher; founder of "Pyrrhonism:" recommended suspension of judgment in religious matters .......... B.C. 375— 290

**Pyrrhus.** King of Epirus. Defeated the Romans; conquered Macedonia; one of greatest generals of antiquity .......... B.C. 318— 272

**Pythagoras.** Greek philosopher and writer; taught doctrine of transmigration of souls .......... B.C. 570— 510

**Quarles,** Francis. English poet. *Emblems* .......... 1592—1644

**Quatremère de Quincy,** Antonio C. French antiquarian. *Dictionary of Architecture* .......... 1755—1849

**Queensberry,** William Douglas, 4th Duke of. Scotch profligate .......... 1724—1810

**Quin,** James. English actor; famous as *Falstaff* .......... 1693—1766

**Quincy,** Josiah. American statesman and author; Federalist member of Congress. *History of Harvard University* .......... 1772—1864

**Quincy,** Josiah, Jr. American Revolutionary patriot and orator. *Observations on the Boston Port Bill* .......... 1744—1775

**Quintilian.** (M. Fabius Quintilianus.) Roman author. *Rhetoric* .......... 42— 118

**Rabelais,** François. French satirist and scholar. *Gargantua.* Joined Franciscans, but left the order; was absolved of his neglect of his vows by the Pope in 1536; studied medicine; gained an extensive erudition. The full title of his great work is *The Pleasant Story of the Giant Gargantua and his Son Pantagruel* .......... 1495—1553

**Rachel,** (Eliza Rachel Félix). French actress at the Comedie Français; was famous in classic and modern plays; as *Marie Stuart; Joan of Arc* .......... 1820—1858

**Racine,** Louis. French dramatist. Among his best works the comedy *Les Plaideurs* (The Litigants); and the tragedies *Britannicus; Iphigenie; Phèdre;* and *Athalie.* 1639—1699

**Radcliffe,** Ann M. English novelist. *Mysteries of Udolpho* .......... 1764—1823

**Raglan,** Fitzroy Somerset, Lord. English general; commander of British army in the Crimean War .......... 1788—1855

**Raleigh,** Sir Walter. English courtier, statesman, and author. *History of the World.* A favorite of Queen Elizabeth; executed by James I .......... 1552—1618

**Ramsay,** Allan. Scotch poet. *Gentle Shepherd* .......... 1685—1758

BORN. DIED.

**Randolph**, John, of Roanoke. American politician; member of Congress; Minister to Russia; opposed Missouri compromise; caustic wit .......... 1773—1833

**Raphael**, (Raffaele Sanzio) of Urbino. Italian painter. *Sistine Madonna.* Among his other works are the frescoes called *The School of Athens; The Transfiguration; The Marriage of the Virgin; Galatea;* and the cartoons (designs for tapestry of the Pope's Chapel).... 1483—1520

**Ravaillac**, François. Assassin of Henry IV. of France.. 1579—1610

**Read**, Thomas Buchanan. American poet and artist. *The Wagoner of the Alleghanies* .......... 1822—1872

**Réaumur**, René A. F. de. French physicist; inventor of Reaumur thermometer. *Memoirs Illustrating the History of Insects* .......... 1683—1757

**Récamier**, Jeanne F. J. A. French woman of fashion and letters. Friend of Chateaubriand, Lamartine, etc.. 1777—1849

**Red Jacket.** American Seneca Indian chief. Famous for his eloquence .......... 1760—1830

**Regnier**, Mathurin. French satirical poet. *Satires*...... 1573—1613

**Regulus**, Marcus Aurelius. Roman statesman and general. Captured by Carthaginians; sent to Rome to secure peace; advised Romans against it; tortured by Carthaginians ..........B.C. — 250

**Reid**, Thomas. Scotch metaphysician. *Essay on the Intellectual Powers of Man* .......... 1710—1796

**Rembrandt van Ryn**, Paul Gerritz. Dutch painter. *The Woman Taken in Adultery* .......... 1606—1669

**Renan**, J. Ernest. French Orientalist and author. *Life of Jesus* .......... 1823 —

**Rémusat**, François M. C., Count de. French statesman and writer. *Essays on Philosophy* .......... 1797—1875

**Retz**, Jean F. P. de Gondi, Cardinal. French statesman and writer. *Memoirs.* Head of the Frondeurs .......... 1614—1679

**Reuchlin**, Johann. German scholar and reviver of learning; defender of Hebrew studies. *Speculum Oculare*... 1455—1522

**Revere**, Paul. American Revolutionary patriot. Carried to Concord news of impending attack of Gage.......... 1735—1818

**Reynolds**, Sir Joshua. English painter. *Mrs. Siddons as the Tragic Muse* .......... 1723—1792

**Ricardo**, David. English political economist. *Principles of Political Economy* .......... 1772—1823

**Richard I.** (Coeur de Lion.) King of England. Conquered Acre; defeated Saladin .......... 1157—1199

**Richard II.** King of England. Put down Wat Tyler's Rebellion; deposed .......... 1366—1400

**Richard III.** King of England. Put Edward V. to death and usurped his crown; killed at Bosworth.......... 1452—1485

**Richardson**, Samuel. English novelist. *Clarissa Harlowe; Sir Charles Grandison; Pamela.* .......... 1689—1761

**Richelieu**, Armand Jean Duplessis, Cardinal. French statesman. Made Cardinal, 1622; Prime Minister, 1624; secured exile of his foe, Marie de Medicis, 1630; reduced the Huguenots and captured Rochelle; supported German Protestants against Austria; founded French Academy (1635); added Alsace, Lorraine, and Roussillon to France .......... 1585—1642

**Richter**, John Paul Friederich (Jean Paul). German novelist. *Thorn, Fruit, and Flower Pieces* .......... 1763—1825

**Rienzi**, Nicolo Gabrini. Italian patriot and enthusiast. Tribune; for a short time ruler of Rome: "the friend of Petrarch, hope of Italy" .......... 1313—1354

**Ripley**, George. American divine, journalist, and critic. Founder of the Brook Farm Community; editor of *Appleton's Cyclopædia* .......... 1802—1880

**Ristori**, Adelaide. Italian actress .......... 1822 —

**Ritter**, Charles. German geographer. *Geography in Relation to the Nature and History of Man* .......... 1779—1859

**Rizzio**, David. Italian favorite and secretary of Mary Queen of Scots. Murdered .......... 1540—1566

**Robert** ("The Devil"). Duke of Normandy. Famed for "devilish" courage. Father of William the Conqueror. — 1035

BORN. DIED.

**Robert I.** (Bruce.) King of Scotland. See Bruce, R... 1276—1329

**Robertson**, Frederick W. English divine. *Sermons*..... 1816—1853

**Robespierre**, François J. M. French Revolutionist. Guillotined; leader of the extreme radicals; ruler during the Reign of Terror .......... 1759—1794

**Rochefoucauld**, Francis, Duke de la. French wit and author. *Maxims* .......... 1613—1680

**Rochester**, John Wilmot, 2d Earl of. English courtier, wit, and poet. Author of many songs and satires...... 1647—1680

**Rockingham**, Charles N. Wentworth, Marquis of. English statesman. Prime Minister; repealed the Stamp Act.. 1730—1782

**Rodgers**, John. American naval officer; captured 7 British merchantmen in War of 1812... 1771—1838

**Rodolph**, of Hapsburg. Emperor of Germany. Reduced power of the feudal barons .......... 1218—1291

**Rogers**, John. English Protestant. (Apostate Catholic.) Burned .......... 1500—1555

**Rohan**, Henry, Prince of. French Huguenot commander. Defeated Imperialists in Italy. *The Perfect Captain* .......... 1579—1638

**Roland**, Madame Manon J. P. French Republican and writer. *Memoirs.* Guillotined .......... 1754—1793

**Rollin**, Charles. French historian. *Ancient History*..... 1661—1741

**Rollo**, or Rou, Northman. Pirate who made Frank King grant him Normandy. First Duke of Normandy....... — 931

**Romilly**, Sir Samuel. English lawyer. Opposed slave trade; reformed Penal Code; great Chancery lawyer.. 1757—1818

**Romney**, George. English painter. *Milton and his Daughter* .......... 1734—1802

**Ronsard**, Pierre de. French poet. Head and founder of the "Pleiad." Many odes, etc .......... 1524-1585

**Rosamond.** ("Fair Rosamond.") Daughter of Lord Clifford. Mistress of Henry II. of England. Poisoned by Queen Eleanor .......... — 1177

**Roscius**, Quintus. Greatest of Roman actors.........B.C. — 62

**Roscoe**, William. English banker and author. *Life of Leo X.* .......... 1753—1831

**Roscommon**, Wentworth Dillon, Earl of. English poet. *Poems* (odes, prologues, etc.) .......... 1633—1684

**Rossetti**, Gabriel. Italian commentator on Dante.... ... 1783—1854

**Rossetti**, Dante Gabriel. English poet and painter. *House of Life* .......... 1828—1882

**Rossini**, Gioacchno Antonio. Italian composer. *William Tell* .......... 1792—1868

**Rothschild**, Meyer A. German banker .......... 1743—1812

**Rousseau**, Jean Baptiste. French lyric poet. *Odes*...... 1670—1741

**Rousseau**, Jean Jacques. French philosopher and author. *Confessions.* Born at Geneva; apprenticed to an engraver, but wandered about in a wretched manner, and was successively a servant, a clerk, and a music teacher; went to Paris (1745), where he met Diderot and Grimme, and formed a connection with Thérèse le Vasseur, an ignorant woman, whom he afterward married. In 1760 appeared his *Julie; or, The New Heloïse;* and in 1762 *The Social Contract.* His *Emile, or Education,* was burned at Geneva, and he would have been arrested had he not taken refuge in England with Hume.......... 1712—1778

**Rowley**, William. English dramatist. *Watch at Midnight.* 17th Cent.

**Rubens**, Peter Paul. Dutch painter. *Descent from the Cross; Last Judgment; Battle of the Amazons; Judgment of Paris; Rape of the Sabines* .......... 1577—1640

**Rumford**, Benjamin Thompson, Count. American natural philosopher in France .......... 1753—1814

**Rupert**, Prince, of Bavaria. Nephew and general of Charles II. of England. Brilliant cavalry leader .......... 1619—1682

**Ruskin**, John. English art critic. *Modern Painters*..... 1819 —

**Russel**, John, Earl. English statesman. Principal author of the Reform Bill .......... 1792—1878

**Russell**, Lord William. English statesman. Beheaded on a charge of complicity in Rye House Plot .......... 1639—1683

**Ruysdaal**, Jacob. Dutch painter. *The Stag Hunt* .......... 1636—1681

BORN. DIED.

**Sacheverell,** Henry. Tory English divine. Convicted of libelling Parliament and Ministry .... 1672—1724

**Sachs,** Hans. Nurnberg shoemaker and poet. A Meister Singer .... 1494—1578

**Sadi,** or **Saadi.** Persian poet. *Gulistán* .... 1175—1291

**Sage,** Alain René le. French novelist. *Gil Blas* .... 1668—1747

**Saint Clair,** Arthur. American Revolutionary general. Brigadier-General at Trenton and Princeton; defeated by Miami Indians 1791 .... 1735—1818

**Saint-Evremond,** Charles de M. de St. Denis. French wit and courtier .... 1613—1703

**Saint-Pierre,** Jacques H. Bernadin de. French author. *Paul et Virginia* .... 1737—1814

**Saint-Simon,** Claudius H., Comte de. French philosopher. *The New Christianity* .... 1760—1825

**Saint-Simon,** Louis Rouvroy, Duc de. French author. *Memoirs* .... 1675—1755

**Sainte-Beuve,** Charles A. French poet and critic. *Causeries de Lundi* .... 1804—1869

**Saladin** [Salah-ed-Deen]. Sultan of Egypt. Opponent of the Crusaders; defeated the Christians at Tiberias; a chivalrous prince .... 1137—1193

**Salisbury,** Robert A. T. G. Cavendish, Marquis of. English Tory statesman .... 1830 —

**Sallust** (C. Sallustius Crispus). Roman historian. *Catiline* .... B.C. 86— 34

**Salvini,** Tommaso. Italian actor. Great as *Othello* .... 1833 —

**Samuel.** Last of the Israelite judges. Anointed Saul and David .... B.C. 1170—1060

**Sand,** George. (Amoutine L. A. Dupin-Dudevant.) French novelist. *Consuelo; Indiana; Valentine; André* .... 1804—1876

**Sandwich,** Edward Montague, 1st Earl of. English naval commander. Led squadron against De Ruyter; lost in the wreck of the *Royal James* .... 1625—1672

**Santillana,** Iñigo L. de Mendoza, Marquis of. Spanish poet and politician. *Elegy on the Marquis of Villena* .. 1398—1458

**Sappho.** Greek lyric poetess. Wrote elegies, hymns, and erotic poems. Only a fragment of her works is preserved. Flourished 600 B.C.

**Sardanapalus.** King of Nineveh. Famed for luxury. B.C. — 875

**Saul.** First King of Israel (1095-1055 B.C.). Fought the Ammonites and Philistines .... B.C. — 1055

**Savage,** Richard. English poet. Famed for his misfortunes. *The Wanderer* .... 1698—1743

**Savonarola,** Girolamo. Italian reformer. A Dominican monk and preacher; denounced the corruptions of the Church; prior of the convent of St. Mark, at Florence, 1491; became a leader of the liberals; was excommunicated by Pope Alexander VI., in 1497; deserted by his followers; strangled .... 1452—1498

**Saxe,** Hermann Maurice, Count of. French marshal. Born in Saxony; son of Augustus II. of Poland; lover of Anna Ivanovna, afterwards Empress of Russia; fought the Austrians, 1742; took Prague, 1744; was made Marshal of France; won battles of Fontenoy, Rancon, and Laufeldt .... 1696—1750

**Scanderbeg,** George Castriota, Prince of. Albanian general. Defeated the Turks .... 1404—1467

**Scarron,** Paul. French humorist. *Le Roman Comique* ... 1610—1660

**Scheffer,** Ary. French historical painter. *Christ the Comforter* .... 1795—1858

**Schelling,** Frederick W. J. German metaphysician. *First Sketch of System of Philosophy of Nature* .... 1775—1854

**Schiller,** John C. F. von. German dramatist and poet. Studied law and medicine, but finally followed his own inclination to literature. In 1777 appeared his drama of *The Robbers*; in 1791, his *Thirty Years' War*; and in 1799, his *Wallenstein*, upon which he had been long engaged. The same year he removed to Weimar, where he enjoyed the friendship and advice of Goethe. Among his other works are *The Maid of Orleans, Mary Stuart,* and *William Tell.* Of his minor poems, *The Song of the Bell* is perhaps the best .... 1759—1805

**Schlegel,** Augustus W. von. German scholar and critic. *Lectures on Dramatic Literature* .... 1767—1845

**Schlegel,** Friedrich W. von. German scholar and philosopher. *Lectures on the Philosophy of History* .... 1772—1829

**Schleiermacher,** Friederich D. E. German divine and author. *Critical Essay on the Writings of Luke* .... 1768—1834

**Schoeffer,** Peter. One of the German inventors of printing .... 1430—1500

**Schomberg,** Henry. Count of. French general; Marshal of France. One of the greatest generals of his time ... 1583—1632

**Schopenhauer,** Arthur. German pessimistic philosopher. *The World as Will* .... 1788—1860

**Schubert,** Francis. German composer. *Lieder.* While still very young was made one of the singers in the court chapel at Vienna; received an excellent musical education; his Songs (*Lieder*) and Ballads are his best work; musical, tender, and expressive in the rarest degree.... 1797—1828

**Schumann,** Robert. German composer. *Paradise and the Peri* .... 1815—1856

**Schuyler,** Philip. American revolutionary general; afterwards member of Congress and Senator .... 1733—1804

**Schurz,** Carl. American journalist and politician. Secretary of the Interior, 1877-1881 .... 1829 —

**Schwarz,** Berthold. German monk. Alleged inventor of gunpowder .... 14th cent'y.

**Scipio,** Africanus (The Elder). Roman General and statesman. Defeated Hannibal at Zama .... B.C. 234— 183

**Scipio,** Africanus (The Younger). Roman general. Conqueror of Carthage .... B.C. 185— 129

**Scott,** Sir Walter. Scotch novelist, poet and historian. *Waverley* novels; *Marmion; Lay of the Last Minstrel; The Lady of the Lake; Rokeby; The Vision of Don Roderick.* Son of an Edinburgh writer to the signet; educated at University of Edinburgh; sheriff depute of Selkirkshire; lived at Abbotsford: ruined by commercial speculation .... 1771—1852

**Scribe,** Augustine E. French dramatist. *The Glass of Water* .... 1791—1861

**Scroggs,** Sir William. Infamous Lord Chief Justice of England. Removed .... 1623—1683

**Scudéry,** Mlle., Magdalen de. French romancist. *Le Grand Cyrus* .... 1607—1701

**Sebastian.** King of Portugal. General. Invaded Morocco and was defeated and killed .... 1554—1578

**Secundus,** Johannes. (Everard.) Dutch statesman. Latin poet. *Basia.* Latin Secretary to Charles II .... 1511—1536

**Sedgwick,** Theodore. American lawyer and statesman. U. S. Senator; Speaker House of Representatives; opposed slavery .... 1746—1813

**Sedley,** Sir Charles. English poet, profligate and wit.... 1639—1701

**Selden,** John. English statesman and jurist. *Mare Clausum; Table Talk* .... 1584—1654

**Selkirk,** Alexander. Scotch sailor. His adventures suggested *Robinson Crusoe.* Lived alone on Juan Fernandez, 1704-09 .... 1675—1723

**Selwyn,** George Augustus. English wit and man of fashion 1719—1791

**Semiramis.** Queen of Assyria. Wife of Omnes, an Assyrian general, but attracted the notice of Ninus, King of Assyria, who married her; she came to the throne at his death, built Babylon and other cities, and annexed to her dominion large portions of Persia and Ethiopia; invaded India but was defeated; is said to have been murdered by her son, Ninyas. Flourished 1250 B.C.

**Seneca,** Lucius Annaeus. Roman philosopher. *Morals.* 5— 65

**Servetus,** Michael. Spanish scientist and theologian. Opposed the doctrine of the Trinity. *On the Errors of the Trinity* Burned at Geneva .... 1509—1553

**Severus,** Alexander. Roman Emperor. Defeated the Persians; a mild and humane ruler .... 205— 235

BORN. DIED.

**Sévigné,** Marie de Rabutin-Chantal, Marchioness of. French authoress. Educated by her uncle, the Abbe de Coulanges; familiar with Latin, Italian, and Spanish; married (1644) the Marquis de Sevigné, a profligate nobleman who was killed in a duel in 1651, leaving a son and a daughter; Turenne, the Prince of Conti, and others, in vain, solicited her to a second marriage; she was one of the most distinguished ornaments of the Hôtel de Rambouillet; her *Letters* are models .......... 1626—1696

**Seward,** William H. American republican statesman, Secretary of State, 1861-69 .......... 1801—1872

**Seymour,** Horatio. American statesman. Democratic candidate for President in 1868 .......... 1811 ——

**Sforza,** Francis A. Duke of. Milan general and statesman. Built canal between Milan and the Adda .......... 1401—1466

**Sforza,** Ludovico (Il Moro). Italian general and statesman. Drove French from Italy .......... 1453—1510

**Shadwell,** Thomas. English dramatist, poet laureate. *The Sullen Lovers* .......... 1640—1692

**Shaftesbury,** Anthony Ashley Cooper, first Earl of. English statesman. Lord Chancellor. "Achitophel." Author of Habeas Corpus Act .......... 1621—1683

**Shaftesbury,** Anthony Ashley Cooper, third Earl of. English author. *Characteristics* .......... 1671—1713

**Shakespeare,** William. Greatest English poet and dramatist. *Lear; Hamlet; Macbeth; Othello; The Tempest; Midsummer Night's Dream;* born at Stratford-on-Avon; went to London about 1586 and became an actor and playwright; after amassing a competence returned to his native town, where he spent the rest of his life. Was son of a glover, and farmer; educated at Stratford grammar school; married Anne Hathaway 1582; became dramatist and shareholder at Blackfriars theater, and subsequently part proprietor of the Globe; left London about 1608; produced *Venus and Adonis*, and the *Rape of Lucrece*, 1593-94, the only works published under his own hand. The first collected edition of his works appeared in 1623 .......... 1564—1616

**Sheil,** Richard Lalor. Irish orator and politician; member of Parliament. *Sketches of the Irish Bar* .......... 1794—1851

**Shelley,** Percy Bysshe. English poet. *Cenci, Adonais, Prometheus; Revolt of Islam; Alastor; The Witch of Atlas.* Came of an old Sussex family; was expelled from Oxford for circulating a *Defence of Atheism*; married against his father's will the daughter of an innkeeper; separated from her in 1813; afterwards married Mary Godwin; was drowned off coast of Italy .......... 1792—1822

**Sheppard,** Jack. English burglar. Hanged .......... —— 1724

**Sheridan,** Philip H. American general. Won battle of Winchester, Cedar Creek, Five Forks .......... 1831 ——

**Sheridan,** Richard Brinsley. Irish orator, wit, and dramatist. *The School for Scandal; The Rivals; The Critic;* friend of Fox; member of Parliament; made great speech at impeachment of Warren Hastings .......... 1751—1816

**Sherman,** John. American politician and financier. Secretary of the Treasury, 1877-81; resumed specie payments 1823 ——

**Sherman,** Roger. American Revolutionary patriot and statesman. Signed Declaration of Independence; U. S. Senator .......... 1721—1793

**Sherman,** William Tecumseh. American general. Made the "March to the Sea"; commander American army .. 1820 ——

**Shrewsbury,** Charles Talbot, Duke of. English statesman. Secretary of State and Lord Treasurer. "The King of Hearts" .......... 1660—1717

**Shrewsbury,** John Talbot, 1st Earl of. English warrior in France. Conquered French; repulsed by Joan of Arc 1373—1453

**Siddons,** Mrs. Sarah Kemble. English tragic actress. sister of J. P. Kemble, married Henry Siddons in 1773; made her London debut in 1775. Among her great parts were *Belvidere, Isabella, Lady Macbeth.* She retired from the stage in 1812 .......... 1755—1831

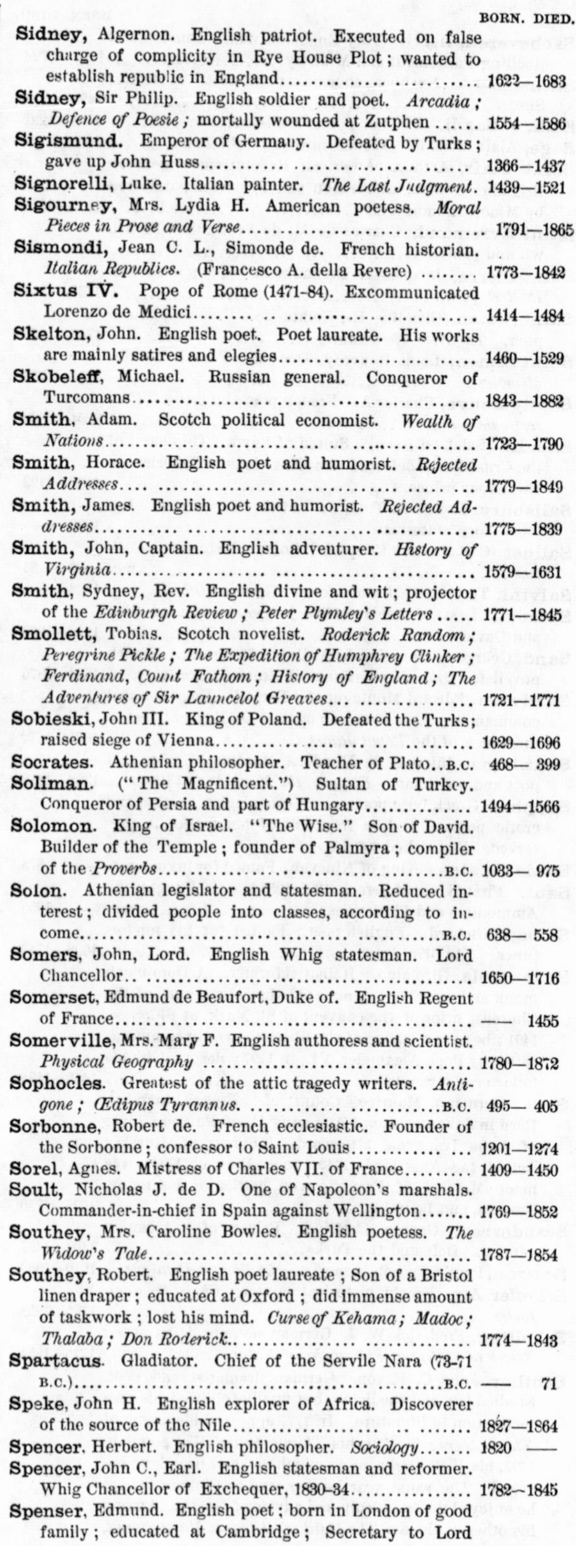

BORN. DIED.

**Sidney,** Algernon. English patriot. Executed on false charge of complicity in Rye House Plot; wanted to establish republic in England .......... 1622—1683

**Sidney,** Sir Philip. English soldier and poet. *Arcadia; Defence of Poesie;* mortally wounded at Zutphen .......... 1554—1586

**Sigismund.** Emperor of Germany. Defeated by Turks; gave up John Huss .......... 1366—1437

**Signorelli,** Luke. Italian painter. *The Last Judgment.* 1439—1521

**Sigourney,** Mrs. Lydia H. American poetess. *Moral Pieces in Prose and Verse* .......... 1791—1865

**Sismondi,** Jean C. L., Simonde de. French historian. *Italian Republics.* (Francesco A. della Revere) .......... 1773—1842

**Sixtus IV.** Pope of Rome (1471-84). Excommunicated Lorenzo de Medici .......... 1414—1484

**Skelton,** John. English poet. Poet laureate. His works are mainly satires and elegies .......... 1460—1529

**Skobeleff,** Michael. Russian general. Conqueror of Turcomans .......... 1843—1882

**Smith,** Adam. Scotch political economist. *Wealth of Nations* .......... 1723—1790

**Smith,** Horace. English poet and humorist. *Rejected Addresses* .......... 1779—1849

**Smith,** James. English poet and humorist. *Rejected Addresses* .......... 1775—1839

**Smith,** John, Captain. English adventurer. *History of Virginia* .......... 1579—1631

**Smith,** Sydney, Rev. English divine and wit; projector of the *Edinburgh Review; Peter Plymley's Letters* .......... 1771—1845

**Smollett,** Tobias. Scotch novelist. *Roderick Random; Peregrine Pickle; The Expedition of Humphrey Clinker; Ferdinand, Count Fathom; History of England; The Adventures of Sir Launcelot Greaves* .......... 1721—1771

**Sobieski,** John III. King of Poland. Defeated the Turks; raised siege of Vienna .......... 1629—1696

**Socrates.** Athenian philosopher. Teacher of Plato .. B.C. 468— 399

**Soliman.** ("The Magnificent.") Sultan of Turkey. Conqueror of Persia and part of Hungary .......... 1494—1566

**Solomon.** King of Israel. "The Wise." Son of David. Builder of the Temple; founder of Palmyra; compiler of the *Proverbs* .......... B.C. 1033— 975

**Solon.** Athenian legislator and statesman. Reduced interest; divided people into classes, according to income .......... B.C. 638— 558

**Somers,** John, Lord. English Whig statesman. Lord Chancellor .......... 1650—1716

**Somerset,** Edmund de Beaufort, Duke of. English Regent of France .......... —— 1455

**Somerville,** Mrs. Mary F. English authoress and scientist. *Physical Geography* .......... 1780—1872

**Sophocles.** Greatest of the attic tragedy writers. *Antigone; Œdipus Tyrannus.* .......... B.C. 495— 405

**Sorbonne,** Robert de. French ecclesiastic. Founder of the Sorbonne; confessor to Saint Louis .......... 1201—1274

**Sorel,** Agnes. Mistress of Charles VII. of France .......... 1409—1450

**Soult,** Nicholas J. de D. One of Napoleon's marshals. Commander-in-chief in Spain against Wellington .......... 1769—1852

**Southey,** Mrs. Caroline Bowles. English poetess. *The Widow's Tale* .......... 1787—1854

**Southey,** Robert. English poet laureate; Son of a Bristol linen draper; educated at Oxford; did immense amount of taskwork; lost his mind. *Curse of Kehama; Madoc; Thalaba; Don Roderick* .......... 1774—1843

**Spartacus.** Gladiator. Chief of the Servile Nara (73-71 B.C.) .......... B.C. —— 71

**Speke,** John H. English explorer of Africa. Discoverer of the source of the Nile .......... 1827—1864

**Spencer.** Herbert. English philosopher. *Sociology* .......... 1820 ——

**Spencer,** John C., Earl. English statesman and reformer. Whig Chancellor of Exchequer, 1830-34 .......... 1782—1845

**Spenser,** Edmund. English poet; born in London of good family; educated at Cambridge; Secretary to Lord

BORN. DIED.

Grey; the Queen's deputy in Ireland; Sheriff of Cork in 1598, there his house was sacked and burned, and his youngest child perished in the flames. *Faerie Queene; The Shepherds' Calendar; View of Ireland*.......... 1553—1599

**Spinoza**, Benedict. Dutch philosopher. His parents were Spanish Jews at Amsterdam; he supported himself by making lenses for telescopes and microscopes; his great work is his *Ethics Demonstrated by a Geometric Method;* a pantheist, who conceived that the infinity of God requires the exclusion of all other substances. He was abused as an atheist in his own time.................. 1632—1677

**Spontini**, Gaspar. Italian composer. *La Vestale*....... 1778—1851

**Spurzheim**, John G. German phrenologist........... 1776—1832

**Staël**, Anna M. L. G., Baroness de. French authoress. *Corinne*................................ 1766—1817

**Standish**, Miles. Captain. Plymouth colonist and soldier. 1584—1656

**Stanhope**, Philip Henry, Earl of. English historian. *History of England*..... 1805—1875

**Stanley**, Arthur Penryhn. English divine and historian. *Lectures on the History of the Jewish Church*.......... 1813—1881

**Stedman**, Edmund Clarence. American poet and critic. *Victorian Poets*........ 1833 —

**Steele**, Sir Richard. English essayist. Essays in *The Tattler, The Spectator*, and *The Guardian*............... 1671—1729

**Steen**, Jan. Dutch painter. His specialty was tavern scenes................ 1636—1689

**Stein**, Heinrich F. C., Baron von. Russian statesman. Opponent of Napoleon.............................. 1757—1831

**Stephen**. King of England. Carried on war against partisans of Matilda, daughter of Henry I.............. 1105—1154

**Stephens**, Alexander H. American statesman. Vice-President of the Southern Confederacy.............. 1812 —

**Stephenson**, George. English inventor of the railroad and locomotive. In 1814 constructed a locomotive which drew 8 cars; made great improvements on this the next year; invented the steam blast pipe, and greatly improved the construction of the railroad; finally built an engine running 30 miles an hour; did for the locomotive what Watt did for the condensing steam engine........ 1781—1848

**Stephenson**, Robert. English inventor of the tubular bridge........................................ 1803—1859

**Sterling**, John. Scotch essayist. *Arthur Coningsby*..... 1806—1844

**Sterne**, Lawrence, Rev. Irish novelist. *Tristram Shandy; The Sentimental Journey*.............................. 1713—1768

**Steuben**, Friedrich N. A., Baron von. German officer in the American Revolution............................ 1730—1794

**Stewart**, Alexander T. American millionaire merchant.. 1803—1876

**Stewart**, Dugald. Scotch metaphysician. *Elements of the Philosophy of the Human Mind*.......................... 1753—1828

**Stilicho**, Flavius. Roman general. Drove Alaric out of Italy and the Goths out of Thrace...................... — 408

**Story**, Joseph. American jurist. Justice of the Supreme Court. *Commentaries on the Constitution*............. 1779—1845

**Story**, William W. American sculptor and poet. *Cleopatra; Roba di Roma*......... 1819 —

**Stowe**, Harriet E. Beecher. American novelist. *Uncle Tom's Cabin*........ 1812 —

**Strabo**. Greek geographer. *Geography*..........B.C. 54 A.D. 24

**Strafford**, Thomas Wentworth. Earl of. "Thorough." Minister of Charles I. Beheaded..................... 1593—1641

**Strauss**, Johann. German composer of waltzes.......... 1804—1849

**Strongbow**, Richard de Clare. Conqueror of Ireland..... — 1176

**Strozzi**, Philippo. Florentine Republican. Led an army of French and Italian mercenaries against the Medici.. 1488—1538

**Stuart**, Charles Edward. "The Young Pretender."...... 1720—1788

**Stuart**, Gilbert C. American portrait painter. *Portrait of George Washington*............................. 1756—1828

**Stuart**, James F. E. Son of James II. "The Elder Pretender.".......................................... 1688—1765

**Stuyvesant**, Peter. Dutch Governor of the colony of New Netherlands (New York).......................... 1602—1682

BORN. DIED.

**Suckling**, Sir John. English poet. *Poems* (amatory or witty)............................................. 1609—1642

**Sue**, Eugene. French novelist. *Le Juif Errant*.......... 1804—1857

**Suetonius**, Caius (Tranquillus). Biographer of the Roman Emperors. *Lives of the Twelve Cæsars*.......... 70 —

**Suffolk**, Michael de la Pole, 1st Earl of. English statesman. Lord Chancellor of England................ — 1389

**Sulla**, Lucius Cornelius. Roman general and statesman. Prominent in Social War; led aristocratic party; opponent of Marius; introduced proscription; dictator; abdicated voluntarily..........B.C. 138— 78

**Sully**, Maximilian de Bethune, Duke of. French general and statesman. Superintendent-General of Finances; Minister of Henry IV. *Memoirs*...................... 1539—1641

**Sumner**, Charles. American Republican statesman, orator, and Senator. *True Grandeur of Nations*............... 1811—1874

**Sunderland**, Charles Spencer, 3d Earl of. English statesman. Minister of James II., and (after several changes of religion) Counsellor of William III.............. 1674—1722

**Surrey**, Henry Howard, Earl of. English poet. First to use English blank verse.............................. 1515—1547

**Suwarrof**, Alexander T., Count. Russian general. Defeated Turks; revolted Poles and French............. 1729—1800

**Swedenborg**, Emanuel. Swedish religionist and naturalist. Up to 57 he devoted himself to mathematics and the natural sciences. Among his works on those subjects are *Principia; The Animal Kingdom;* and *Miscellaneous Observations Connected with the Physical Sciences.* After 57 he engaged in religious speculations. Among his religious works are *The True Christian Religion;* and *The Mysteries of Heaven*. The central point of his theosophy is the correspondence of the natural and the supernatural.............................................. 1689—1722

**Swift**, Jonathan. Irish divine and satirist; educated at Trinity College, Dublin; admitted into the house of Sir W. Temple; entered church; became Dean of St. Patrick's; at first a Whig, afterwards a strenuous Tory. *Tale of a Tub; Gulliver's Travels*.................... 1667—1745

**Swinburne**, Algernon C. English poet. *Atalanta in Calydon*................................................ 1837 —

**Tacitus**, Caius Cornelius. Roman historian. *Germania*. 50— 118

**Talfourd**, Sir Thomas Noon. English author. *Ion*...... 1795—1854

**Talleyrand-Périgord**, Charles Maurice, Prince of. French diplomatist and wit. Minister of Foreign Affairs 1754—1836

**Tallien**, Jean Lambert. French Revolutionist. Leader of the party which overthrew the Robespierres........... 1769—1820

**Talma**, François J. French actor. Son of a dentist, and practiced dentistry for some time; lived several years in London when young; made his début at the Française, in 1787, as *Seide* in *Mahomet*. Among his great roles were *Orestes, Hamlet, Sulla, Othello,* and *Leonidas.* 1763—1826

**Tamerlane** (Tamour-leng, *i. e.*, "Tamour the Lame"). Tartar general and conqueror. Subjugated Armenia, Georgia, Persia, India................................. 1335—1405

**Tancred**. Last Norman King of Sicily (1189-1194)........ — 1194

**Taney**, Roger B. American jurist and Democratic statesman. Chief Justice of the United States............ 1777—1864

**Tarquinius Superbus**. Last King of Rome. Expelled by the Romans under the elder Brutus.............B.C. — 495

**Tasso**, Bernardo. Italian poet. *Amadis*. Father of Torquato................................................ 1493—1569

**Tasso**, Torquato. Italian poet. *Jerusalem Delivered.* Lived at the Court, and under the patronage of Alphonso, Duke of Este; produced (1593) *Aminta*, a pastoral drama; completed his great work, the *Gerusalemme Liberata*, in 1575. For falling in love with Leonora, sister of the Duke of Este, he was shut up seven years as a madman. Among his works is the romantic poem *Rinaldo*................................................ 1544—1595

**Taylor**, Bayard. American traveler, novelist, poet; printer

BORN. DIED.

and journalist; Minister to Germany. Translator of Goethe's *Faust; Prince Deucalion; Masque of the Gods; John Godfrey's Fortunes* .......... 1825—1878

**Taylor,** Jeremy, Bishop. English author. *Holy Living*.. 1613—1667

**Taylor,** Zachary. American general; 12th President of the U. S. Born in Va.; entered army in 1808; served in Black Hawk and Seminole wars, and was commander in Florida; major-gen. in Mexican War; won battles of Resaca de la Palma and Buena Vista; elected President by the Whigs in 1848.......... 1784—1850

**Tecumseh.** American Indian chief. Formed alliance of the Western Indians; defeated by Harrison at Tippecanoe.......... 1770—1813

**Tell,** William. Swiss patriot and legendary hero.......... —— 1354

**Temple,** Sir William. English statesman and author. Negotiated the Triple Alliance of 1668. *Account of the United Provinces*.......... 1628—1699

**Teniers,** David. (The Elder.) Flemish painter. His specialty was tavern scenes.......... 1582—1649

**Teniers,** David. (The Younger.) Flemish marine and landscape painter.......... 1610—1694

**Tennyson,** Alfred. English poet; educated at Cambridge; made poet-laureate in 1850. *In Memoriam; Enoch Arden; The Princess; Maud; The Idylls of the King; Locksley Hall; The Lotus Eaters; Ulysses; Ode on the Death of the Duke of Wellington; The Holy Grail; Queen Mary; Harold*.......... 1809 ——

**Terence** (P. Terentius Afer). Roman comedy writer..B.C. 195— 159

**Tertullian,** Quintus Septimius Florens. Church father. *On the Resurrection of the Body*.......... 160— 240

**Tetzel,** John. German seller of indulgences.......... 1450—1519

**Thackeray,** William Makepeace. English novelist; born in Calcutta; educated at Cambridge; tried to be an artist. *Henry Esmond; Vanity Fair; The Newcomes; Pendennis; The Adventures of Philip; The Virginians; The Book of Snobs; The Four Georges; English Humorists*. 1811—1863

**Thais.** Celebrated courtesan of Athens. Mistress of Alexander the Great; afterward married Ptolemy of Egypt.B.C. 4th Cent.

**Thales** of Miletus. Greek natural philosopher. Fixed length of year at 365 days; believed water the origin of things..........B.C. 635— 550

**Themistocles.** Athenian statesman and general. Commander-in-chief against Xerxes; won battle of Salamis; rebuilt walls to Peraeus..........B.C. 515— 449

**Theocritus.** Greek bucolic poet. He has left 30 *Idyls*. Flourished 270 B.C.

**Theodora.** Wife of Justinian I. Empress of the East. A reformed courtesan.......... —— 548

**Theodoric** ("The Great"). King of Ostro-Goths. Conquered Odoacer; a wise, humane prince.......... 445— 526

**Theodosius** ("The Great"). Roman Emperor. Defeated the Goths; persecuted Christians.......... 345— 395

**Theophrastus.** Greek philosopher and moralist. *Characters*..........B.C. 360— 285

**Thierry,** Jacques U. Augustin. French historian. *Norman Conquests*.......... 1795—1836

**Thiers,** Louis Adolphe. French statesman and historian. *History of the Consulate and Empire*.......... 1797—1877

**Thomas,** George H. American Federal general. Won battles Chickamaugua and Nashville.......... 1816—1870

**Thomson,** James. Scotch poet; son of a minister; educated at Cambridge; lived at London; secretary of the briefs. *The Seasons; The Castle of Indolence; Tancred and Sigismunda*.......... 1700—1748

**Thoreau,** Henry D. American author. *The Concord and Merrimac Rivers; The Maine Woods*.......... 1817—1862

**Thorwaldsen,** Albert D. Danish sculptor. *Triumphal March of Alexander*.......... 1770—1844

**Thucydides.** Greek historian. *Sicilian Expedition*..B.C. 470— 400

**Tiberius.** Roman Emperor (14-37). Gave control of affairs to infamous Sejanni; retired to Capri, 26.....B.C. 42A.D.37

BORN. DIED.

**Ticknor,** George. American scholar. *History of Spanish Literature*.......... 1791—1871

**Tieck,** Louis. German writer. *Puss in Boots*.......... 1773—1853

**Tilden,** Samuel J. American Democratic statesman. Candidate for President in 1876.......... 1814 ——

**Timoleon.** Corinthian general. Liberator of Syracuse.B.C. 395— 337

**Tintoretto,** Il. (Jacopo Robusti.) Italian painter. *The Worship of the Golden Calf*.......... 1512—1594

**Titian.** (Tiziano Vecelli.) Italian painter. Greatest of the Venetian colonists; a fellow pupil with Giorgione. Among his masterpieces are the *Assumption of the Virgin, Presentation of the Virgin, Peter Martyr, The Last Supper, Sleeping Venus, Bacchus and Ariadne, Pharisee Showing the Tribute Money to Christ, Homage of Frederick Barbarossa to the Pope*.......... 1477—1566

**Tocqueville,** Alexis C. H. C. de. French author. *American Democracy*.......... 1805—1859

**Tone,** Theobald Wolfe. Irish patriot. Founder of the "United Irishmen;" condemned to death for treason.. 1763—1798

**Tooke,** John Horne. English philologist and radical. *The Diversions of Purley*.......... 1736—1812

**Töpfer,** Rudolph. Swiss novelist. *Nouvelles Genevoises*.. 1779—1846

**Torquemada,** Thomas de. Spanish grand inquisitor. Said to have burned 8,000 people in 16 years.......... 1420—1498

**Torricelli,** Evangelista. Italian physicist. Inventor of the barometer.......... 1608—1647

**Toussaint l'Ouverture,** François. Negro chief of the Haytien Rebellion.......... 1743—1803

**Trajan.** (Marcus Ulpius Nerva Trajanus.) Roman Emperor, 98-117. Defeated Dacians and Parthians.......... 52— 117

**Trollope,** Anthony. English novelist. *Barchester Towers*. 1815 ——

**Tromp,** Marten H. van. Dutch admiral. Defeated Spanish and Portuguese, 1639; English under Blake, 1652... 1597—1653

**Trumbull,** Jonathan. American Revolutionary statesman. Governor of Connecticut; friend of Washington. 1710—1783

**Trumbull,** Jonathan. American revolutionary patriot; Speaker House of Representatives; U. S. Senator, and Governor of Connecticut.......... 1740—1809

**Turenne,** Henri de la Tour d'Auvergne, Vicomte de. French commander. Defeated Condé and the Spanish at Dunes; invaded Holland.......... 1611—1675

**Turgeneff,** Ivan S. Russian novelist. *Virgin Soil; Fathers and Sons*.......... 1818

**Turner,** Joseph M. W. English painter. *The Slave Ship*. 1775—1851

**Turpin,** (Dick) Richard. English highwayman.......... 1711—1739

**Tyler,** John. American statesman. President of the U. S.; born in Va.; practiced law; M. C. 1816-21; Governor of Virginia 1825; elected U. S. Senator 1827; sympathised with the nullifiers and opposed Jackson; resigned 1836; elected Vice-President on Whig ticket 1840; succeeded Harrison on his death in 1841.......... 1790—1862

**Tyler,** Wat. English rebel. Led revolt in southeast England against capitation tax.......... —— 1381

**Tyndall,** John. Irish physicist. Heat considered as a mode of motion.......... 1820 ——

**Ub rti,** Fazio. Italian poet. *Il Dittamondo*.......... —— 1370

**Udal,** Nicholas. English author. *Ralph Roister Doister*, the earliest English comedy.......... 1506—1574

**Uhland,** John L. German lyric poet and scholar. *Ballads* 1787—1862

**Ulfilas.** Gothic bishop. Translator of the Scriptures into Gothic.......... 311— 381

**Ulpian,** Domitius. Roman jurist. *Ad Edictum*.......... 170—228

**Unger,** John F. F. German engraver. Inventor of "Ungerian" type.......... 1750—1804

**Urban II.** Pope. 1088-1099. Organizer of the first crusade.......... —— 1099

**Usher,** James. Archbishop. Chronologist and theologian. *Annals of the Old and New Testaments*.......... 1580—1656

**Valens,** Flavius. Emperor of the East (364-378). An

BORN. DIED.

Arian. Persecuted the Orthodox; defeated and killed by Goths........ 327— 378

**Valentinian I.** Emperor of Rome (364-375). Fought the Picts, Scots and Germans........ 321— 375

**Valerian.** Emperor of Rome (253-260). Captured by the Persians at Edessa........ — 260

**Vallière,** Françoise L. Duchesse de la. Mistress of Louis XIV. of France........ 1644—1710

**Van Buren,** Martin. American politician. Entered bar 1803; served in N. Y. Senate; Attorney-General of N. Y. 1815; leading man of the "Albany Regency"; elected U. S. Senator by the Democrats 1821; Governor of N. Y. 1828; Secretary of State 1829-31; Vice-President 1833-37; President 1837-41........ 1782—1862

**Vanbrugh,** Sir John. English architect and dramatist. *The Relapse; The Provoked Wife*........ 1666—1726

**Vandyke,** Sir Anthony. Flemish painter in England. Pupil of Rubens; traveled and studied in Italy; settled in England in 1632, and painted several portraits of Charles I.; among his best works are *The Erection of the Cross; Portrait of the Earl of Strafford;* and a *Crucifixion*; is considered the greatest of modern portrait painters........ 1599—1641

**Van Ostade,** Adrian. Dutch painter. *A Smoker Lighting his Pipe*........ 1610—1685

**Van Renselaer,** Stephen. American landholder. "The Patroon."........ 1764—1839

**Van der Weyde,** Roger (Roger of Bruges). Flemish painter. *The Descent from the Cross*........ 1455—1529

**Vancouver,** George. English navigator. Discoverer of Vancouver's Island........ 1758—1798

**Vanderbilt,** Cornelius. American capitalist........ 1794—1877

**Vandervelde,** Adrian. Flemish painter. His specialty was landscapes with cattle........ 1639—1672

**Vane,** Sir Henry. English statesman. Ambassador to Denmark and Sweden; Secretary of State; convicted of treason........ 1589—1634

**Vane,** Sir Henry. English painter. Statesman; beheaded; leader of independents; head of navy........ 1612—1662

**Vanloo,** Charles A. French historical painter. *Apotheosis of S. Isidore*........ 1705—1765

**Varnhagen von Ense,** Charles A. S. P. German writer. *Biographic Memorials*........ 1785—1808

**Varro,** Marcus Terentius. Roman scholar. *De Re Rustica*........B.C. 116— 28

**Vasari,** George. Italian painter and biographer. *Lives of the Painters*........ 1512—1574

**Vattel,** Emmerich de. Swiss jurist. *International Law.* 1714—1767

**Vauban,** Sebastian Leprestre Seigneur de. French military engineer. Captured fortress of Norma. *Practice on the Attack of Places*........ 1633—1707

**Vega,** Garcilasso de la. Spanish historian. *History of Peru*........ 1530—1568

**Vega,** Lope de. Spanish dramatist and poet. Educated at the University of Alcala; enjoyed the patronage of the Duke of Alva; was in the Invincible Armada, but left the army in 1590; became a priest in 1609; wrote some 2,000 dramas, besides several epics; among his best works are *Estella de Sevilla; The Prude;* and *The Beautiful Deformed*........ 1562—1635

**Velasquez,** James R. de Silva Y. Spanish painter. Court painter to Philip II.; greatest Spanish painter in history, landscape and portraits; among his works are *The Crucifixion; The Spinners;* and a portrait of Innocent X........ 1599—1660

**Vendôme,** Louis Joseph, Duke de. French commander. Captured Barcelona; defeated at Oudenarde........ 1634—1712

**Vergennes,** Charles Gravier. Comte de. French statesman. Louis XVI.'s Minister of Foreign Affairs; negotiated treaty of alliance with the United States 1778........ 1717—1787

**Vernet,** Antoine C. H. French painter. *The Battle of Wagram*........ 1758—1836

BORN. DIED.

**Vernon,** Edward. English admiral. Captured Porto Bello, 1739........ 1684—1757

**Veronese,** Paul (Cagliari). Worked in Rome and Venice; among his greatest works are *The Marriage at Cana; The Pilgrims of Emmaus;* and *The Rape of Europa*........ 1530—15[illegible]

**Vespasian,** Titus Flavius. Emperor of Rome (70-79). Captured Jerusalem........ 9— 79

**Vespucius,** Americus. Italian navigator. America was named after him........ 1451—15[illegible]

**Vestris,** Gaetano A. B. Italian dancer. Master of the ballet at Grand Opera, Paris. "The God of Dancers."........ 1729—1808

**Vicente,** Gil. Portuguese. Dramatist and poet. *The Judge of Beyra*........ 1485—1557

**Victor,** Emmanuel. King of Sardinia; first King of Italy; restorer of Italian unity........ 1820—1878

**Vidocq,** Eugéne F. French thief, gambler, soldier, and detective. *Memoirs*........ 1775—1850

**Vigny,** Alfred Victor. Comte de. French poet and novelist. *Poems; Cinq-Mars*........ 1799—1863

**Villars,** Charles L. H., Duc de. French general. Subdued the Camisards........ 1653—1734

**Villèle,** Joseph de. Count. French politician. Prime Minister (1822-28)........ 1773—1854

**Villena,** Enrique d'Aragon, Marquis de. Spanish poet. *Gaya Sciencia*........1384—1434

**Villiers,** George. First Duke of Buckingham. Favorite of Charles I. Assassinated........ 1592—1628

**Villiers,** George. Second Duke of Buckingham. Profligate. *The Rehearsal*........ 1627—1688

**Vincent de Paul,** Saint. Founder of the Sisters of Charity 1576—1660

**Virgil** or **Vergil** (Publius Virgilius Maro). Roman poet. *Æneid.* Enjoyed the friendship and patronage of Augustus and Maecaenas; previous to the production of the *Æneid,* wrote the *Eclogues* and the *Georgics*....B. C. 70— 19

**Visconti,** Matteo. "The Great." Duke of Milan. A leader of the Ghibellines........ 1250—1322

**Voiture,** Vincent. French poet, wit, and courtier. His letters to ladies were imitated by Pope........ 1598—1648

**Volney,** Constantine F. C. Comte de. French traveler and skeptic. *Ruins*........ 1757—1820

**Voltaire,** François M. Arouet de. French philosopher, poet, historian, wit, skeptic. Voltaire is an anagram of Arouet; the son of a notary; produced *Œdipe;* and wrote part of the *Henriade* while quite young: was in England 1726-29, passing much time in the society of Bolingbroke; his drama of *Zaïre* appeared in 1730, and about the same time he finished his *History of Charles XII.;* produced *Alzire* in 1736; *Mahomet* in 1741; and *Merope* in 1743; passed the years 1750-53 with Frederick the Great; took up his residence (1755) at Ferney; among his abler works are *The Age of Louis XIV; Essay on the Manners of Nations;* and *Candide*........ 1694—1778

**Vossius,** Gerard J. German. Scholar and critic. *Aristarchus*; or, *Seven Books on the Dramatic Art*........ 1577—1649

**Vulpius,** Christian A. German author. *Rinaldo Rinaldini*........ 1762—1827

**Wace,** Robert. Anglo-Norman poet. *Roman de Rou*.... 1112—1184

**Wade,** Benjamin F. American politician. Republican Senator from Ohio. Abolitionist........ 1800—1878

**Wagner,** Richard. German composer. *Lohengrin; Götterdämmerung; Tannhaüser; Rheingold; Nibelungenlied:* held great musical festival at Bayreuth 1876; produced *Parsifal* at Bayreuth, 1882........ 1813 1883

**Waldemar I.** "The Great." King of Denmark. Subjugated the Wends and Southern Norway........ 1131—1181

**Waldis,** Burchard. German fabulist. "The German Æsop Fables."........ — 1554

**Walker,** John. English lexicographer. *Dictionary*........ 1732—1807

**Wallace,** Sir William. Scotch patriot and general. Fought Edward I. of England; executed........ 1270—1305

BORN. DIED.

**Wallack**, James W. English actor in America. Founder of Wallack's Theater, New York........ 1795—1864

**Wallack**, John Lester. American actor. A finished comedian; manager of Wallack's Theater, New York........ 1819 ——

**Wallenstein**, Albert N. E. von. Count. German general. Opponent of Gustavus Adolphus. Quartermaster-General of the Imperial army 1619; raised a mercenary army of his own in 1625; defeated Count Mansfield and invaded Denmark 1626; was defeated by Gustavus Adolphus at Lützen, 1632; the Emperor was turned against him, and in 1634 he was deprived of his command and assassinated........ 1583—1634

**Walpole**, Horace. Fourth Earl of Oxford. English wit and writer. *Catalogue of Noble Authors*........ 1717—1797

**Walpole**, Sir Robert. English Whig statesman. Prime Minister (1721-42)........ 1676—1745

**Walsingham**, Sir Francis. English statesman. Elizabeth's Minister of Foreign Affairs........ 1536—1590

**Walter**, John. English printer. Founder of the London *Times*........ 1739—1812

**Walther von der Vogelweide.** German minnessinger. *Tristram*........ 1170—1228

**Walton**, Izaak. English writer. *The Complete Angler*... 1593—1683

**Warbeck**, Perkin. Pretender to the English crown. Pretended to be younger son of Edward IV.; raised revolt —— 1499

**Warner**, Charles Dudley. American humorist. *My Summer in a Garden*........1829 ——

**Warren**, Joseph. American Revolutionary patriot and orator. Killed at Bunker Hill........ 1741—1775

**Warren**, Samuel. English barrister and novelist. *Ten Thousand a Year*........ 1807—1877

**Warwick**, Richard Neville. Earl of, "The King Maker." English statesman. Set up and deposed Henry IV..... 1420—1471

**Washington**, George. Commander-in-chief in the American revolution. First President of the United States; aide-de-camp to Braddock in the Indian campaign of 1755; married Martha Custis, 1759; chosen to Congress, 1774; appointed Commander-in-chief, 1775; President, 1789-97........ 1732—1799

**Watt**, James. Scotch inventor. Improver of the steam engine; discovered (1764) that water converted into steam expands to 1,800 times its bulk; learned (1765) to condense steam; a cool separate vessel exhausted of air; used the expansive force of steam to depress a piston; discovered the composition of water (though the honor of this discovery is disputed); and improved engines for pumping water........ 1736—1819

**Watteau**, Antoine. French painter. His favorite subjects are small landscapes, festivals, etc........ 1684—1721

**Watts**, Isaac. English divine and hymn writer. *Divine Songs Attempted in Easy Language*........ 1674—1748

**Wayne**, Anthony, "Mad Anthony." American revolutionary general. Captured Stony Point........ 1745—1796

**Weber**, Charles M. F. E. Baron von. German composer. *Freischütz*; produced *Das Waldmädchen*, 1800; was director of opera at Prague, 1813; manager of German opera at Dresden, 1817; produced *Der Freischütz*, 1822; *Oberon*, 1826........ 1786—1826

**Webster**, Daniel. American lawyer, orator, and statesman. Member of Congress, 1812-16, and 1822-28; entered the Senate (1828), where he remained till 1841, when he became Secretary of State; reëntered the Senate in 1844; again became Secretary of State in 1850; his greatest legal effort was in the Dartmouth College case; his greatest Congressional speech was his reply to Hayne .. 1782—1852

**Webster**, Noah. American lexicographer. *Dictionary of the English Language*........ 1758—1843

**Wedgewood**, Josiah. English potter. "Wedgewood" ware........ 1730—1795

**Wellington**, Arthur Wellesley. Duke of. British general and statesman. Conqueror at Waterloo; beat the Mahrattas at Assaye, India, 1803; was made commander-in-chief in Spain and Portugal; fought against Soult, whom he defeated at Oporto; crossed the Douro; fought the battles of Talavera, Sabagal, and Albuera; captured Badajos, 1812; won at Waterloo, 1815; was afterwards Prime Minister and Minister of Foreign Affairs........ 1769—1852

**Wenceslaus**, King of Bohemia. Emperor of Germany. Supported Anti-Pope against Boniface IX.; deposed... 1361—1419

**Wesley**, Charles, Rev. English poet and divine. *Hymns.* 1708—1788

**Wesley**, John, Rev. Founder of the Methodist Wesleyans 1703—1791

**West**, Benjamin. American painter in England. *The Death of Wolfe*........ 1738—1820

**Weyde**, Roger van der (Roger of Bruges). Flemish painter. *Descent from the Cross*........ 1455—1529

**Whately**, Richard. Archbishop of Dublin. British divine and logician. *Logic*........ 1787—1863

**Wharton**, Henry. American diplomatist and law writer. *International Law*........ 1785—1848

**Wheelock**, Eleazar. American clergyman. Founder of Dartmouth College........ 1711—1779

**Whewell**, William. English philosopher and educator. *Philosophy of the Inductive Sciences*........ 1794—1866

**White**, Henry Kirke. English poet. *Poems* (largely religious and devotional)........ 1785—1806

**White**, Joseph Blanco. Spanish ex-priest. English poet. His sonnet, *Night*, is thought by some the finest in the English language........ 1775—1841

**Whitefield**, George, Rev. English Methodist preacher and revivalist........ 1714—1770

**Whitney**, Eli. American inventor. The cotton-gin...... 1765—1825

**Whittier**, John Greenleaf. American poet; born at Haverhill, Mass.; farmer, shoemaker, journalist, anti-slavery agitator. *Snow Bound; Voices of Freedom; Songs of Labor; Home Ballads; In War Time; National Lyrics; The Tent on the Beach; Ballads of New England; Hazel Blossoms*........ 1808 ——

**Wieland**, Christopher M. German poet. *Oberon*........ 1733—1813

**Whitman**, Walt. American poet; born at West Hills, Long Island; educated in public schools; editor, carpenter, nurse, government clerk. *Leaves of Grass; The Two Rivulets; Drum Taps; Democratic Vistas*........ 1819 ——

**Wilberforce**, William. English philanthropist, statesman, and reformer. Secured abolition of slave trade... 1759—1833

**Wilkie**, Sir David. Scotch painter. *The Village Festival* 1785—1841

**William I.** ("The Conqueror.") Duke of Normandy. Conqueror and King of England (1066-87)........ 1027—1087

**William I.** ("The Silent.") Prince of Orange. Stadtholder of Holland; son of William, Count of Nassau; when young, page to Charles V.; head of the insurrection which broke out, in 1566, on the attempt to introduce the Inquisition in the Netherlands; led army against Duke of Alva; made Republic of 7 Protestant provinces; assassinated by Balthasar Gerard........ 1533—1584

**William II.** (Rufus.) Son of William the Conqueror. King of England (1087-1100). Put down Anglo-Norman Barons........ 1056—1100

**William III.** Stadtholder of Holland. King of England (1688-1702). Won battle of the Boyne........ 1650—1702

**Williams**, Roger. Founder of Rhode Island Colony. *The Hireling Ministry None of Christ's*........ 1606—1683

**Willis**, Nathaniel P. American author. *Pencillings by the Way*........ 1807—1867

**Wilson**, Henry. American Republican politician. Senator; Vice-President........ 1812—1875

**Wilson**, John. ("Christopher North.") Scotch poet and essayist. *Noctes Ambrosianæ*........ 1785—1854

**Winckelmann**, John J. German archæologist. *History of Greek Art*........ 1717—1768

**Winkelried**, Arnold S. von. Swiss patriot and hero. Broke Austrian phalanx at Sempach by grasping numbers of their spears into his body........ —— 1386

BORN. DIED.

**Winthrop,** John. Governor and founder of the Massachusetts Bay Colony ........ 1588—1649

**Winthrop,** Robert C. American orator and statesman. Speaker of the U. S. House of Representatives ........ 1808 ——

**Winthrop,** Theodore. American novelist and soldier. *Cecil Dreeme* ........ 1828—1861

**Wirt,** William. American lawyer and statesman. Attorney-General of the U. S. *Life of Patrick Henry* ........ 1772—1834

**Wiseman,** Nicholas P. S., Cardinal. English Catholic prelate ........ 1802—1865

**Woffington,** Margaret. ("Peg.") Irish actress. Famous as *Sir Harry Wildair* in the *Constant Couple* ........ 1719—1766

**Wolcott,** John. ("Peter Pindar.") English satirist, *Peter Pindar's Odes* ........ 1738—1819

**Wolf,** Frederick A. German classical scholar. *Prolegomena.* Advancer of the theory that the *Iliad* and the *Odyssey* are collections of ballads and not the work of a single author. ........ 1759—1824

**Wolfe,** Charles. Irish poet. *The Burial of Sir John Moore.* 1791—1823

**Wolseley,** Sir Garnet Joseph. English General. Reduced Ashantees to submission, 1873; Administrator of Cyprus, 1878; ended Zulu war, 1879; commanded English army in Egypt against Arabi Bey, 1882 ........ 1833 ——

**Wolsey,** Thomas, Cardinal. English statesman. Chancellor of Henry VIII.; secured Henry's divorce from Catherine ........ 1471—1530

**Woodworth,** Samuel. American journalist and author. *The Old Oaken Bucket* ........ 1785—1842

**Worcester,** Edward Somerset, Marquis of. English inventor. (Steam engine, etc,) ........ 1601—1667

**Worcester,** J. E. American lexicographer. *Dictionary*.. 1734—1866

**Wordsworth,** William. English poet; educated at Cambridge; with Coleridge produced *Lyrical Ballads*, 1798; settled at Rydal Mount, 1803; published *Poems*, 1807; *The Excursion*, 1814; *The White Doe of Rylstone*, 1815; *Peter Bell*, 1816. Among his other works are *Ecclesiastical Sonnets*; *The Wagoner*; *Yarrow Revisited*; *The Prelude* ........ 1770—1850

**Wotton,** Sir Henry, English diplomatist and poet. *The State of Christendom* ........ 1568—1639

**Wrangel,** Charles G. von, Count. Swedish general. Prominent at Lützen; defeated Danes and Dutch ........ 1613—1675

**Wren,** Sir Christopher. English architect. *St. Paul's Cathedral* ........ 1632—1723

**Wright,** Silas. American Democratic statesman. United States Senator; opposed U. S. Bank ........ 1795—1847

**Wycherly,** William. English comedy writer. *Country Wife; Love in a Wood; The Plain Dealer* ........ 1640—1715

**Wycliffe,** John de. English reformer. Translator of the Scriptures ........ 1324—1384

**Wyckham,** William of. English statesman and architect. Lord Chancellor; founder of New College, Oxford... 1324—1404

**Wythe,** George. American lawyer and statesman. Chancellor of Virginia; signer of Declaration of Independence. 1726—1806

**Xavier,** Saint, Francis. "Apostle of the Indies." Jesuit missionary to India and Japan ........ 1506—1552

**Xenocrates.** Greek philosopher. Held that unity and duality are 2 deities ........ B.C. 396— 314

**Xenophanes.** Greek philosopher. Greek originator of the doctrine of the unity of God ........ B.C. 546— 500

**Xenophon.** Greek historian. *Anabasis; Cyropædia.* B.C. 444— 350

**Xerxes I.** King of Persia. Invader of Greece; beaten at Salamis ........ B.C. —— 465

**Ximenes de Cisneros,** Cardinal. Spanish ecclesiastic and statesman. Published *Polyglot Bible;* founded University of Alcala; regent ........ 1436—1517

**Yakoob Ibn Lais.** ("Suffar.") First of the Persian dynasty of the Suffaride. Conquered Seistan and Faristan ........ —— 879

**Yale,** Elihu. Founder of Yale College ........ 1648—1721

**Yancey,** William L. American politician. Member of Congress; extreme "State Sovereignty" advocate ........ 1815—1863

**Yates,** Mrs. Anne M. English actress. Great in tragic parts ........ —— 1787

**York and Albany,** Frederick, Duke of. Son of George III. of England. Defeated at Bergen, 1799 ........ 1763—1827

**Yorke,** Charles. English lawyer. Lord Chancellor (as Lord Morden) ........ 1722—1770

**Young,** Arthur. English agricultural writer. *Annals of Agriculture* ........ 1741—1820

**Young,** Brigham. American religionist. Head of the Mormons ........ 1801—1877

**Young,** Charles. English actor. Eminent in Shakespearean parts ........ 1777—1856

**Young,** Edward. English poet; educated at Oxford; a persistent toady; rector of Welwyn in Hertfordshire. *Night Thoughts; The Revenge; The Love of Fame* ........ 1684—1756

**Yriarte,** Thomas de. Spanish poet. *Literary Fables* ........ 1750—1791

**Zacharia,** Justus F. N. German humorist. *The Brawler* 1723—1777

**Zaleucus.** Legislator and reformer at Locris. First of the Greeks to make a written code of laws ........ B.C. 7th Cent'y.

**Zamoyski,** John S. Polish statesman. Grand Chancellor; defeated Maximilian of Austria ........ 1541—1605

**Zechariah.** One of the 12 Minor Hebrew prophets. B.C. 6th Century ........

**Zeno,** of Elea. Greek philosopher. Inventor of dialectic. B.C. 5th Century ........

**Zeno.** Greek philosopher. Founder of the Stoics. "*Pain is no Evil.*" ........ B.C. 362— 264

**Zenobia,** Septimia. Queen of Palmyra (266–73). Daughter of an Arab chief; beautiful; familiar with Latin, Greek, Syriac, and Egyptian; and of a warlike and masculine temper. Her husband, Odenathus, died in 266, leaving two minor sons. She then took the title of Queen of the East. Her dominions extended from the Mediterranean to the Euphrates, and included a large part of Asia Minor. She refused allegiance to Aurelian, who defeated her and captured Palmyra; passed the rest of her life at Tibur, in Italy ........ —— 275

**Zephaniah.** One of 12 minor Hebrew prophets. Foretold destruction of Jerusalem. Flourished in the reign of Josiah.

**Zeuxis.** Greek painter. *The Infant Hercules Strangling a Serpent.* Flourished B.C. 5th Century ........

**Zimmermann,** Johann G. v. Swiss philosopher. *On Solitude* ........ 1728—1795

**Zinzendorf,** Nicholas Louis, Count of. Founder of the Moravians. *The Journey of Atticus Through the World* ........ 1700—1760

**Ziska,** John. Hussite chief. Beat Imperial armies 13 times ........ 1360—1424

**Zoilus.** Greek critic. Severe on Homer. Flourished B.C. 4th Century ........

**Zollicoffer,** Felix K. American Confederate general. Defeated and killed at Mill Spring ........ 1812—1862

**Zosimus.** Greek historian. *History of the Roman Empire.* 5th Century ........

**Zumpt,** Charles G. German classical scholar. *Latin Grammar* ........ 1792—1858

**Zurbaran,** Francis. Spanish painter. *Virgin and St. John returning from the Sepulcher* ........ 1598—1662

**Zurlauben,** Béat F. A. J. D. Swiss general. *Military History of the Swiss* ........ 1720—1795

**Zwingli,** Ulric. Swiss reformer. *Exposition of the Christian Faith.* Killed in battle ........ 1484—1531

## HEADS OF THE PRINCIPAL NATIONS OF THE WORLD.

| Governments. | Ruler. | Title. | Year of Birth. | Date of Accession. |
|---|---|---|---|---|
| Argentine Republic | Julio A. Roca | President | | Oct. 12, 1880 |
| Austria-Hungary | Franz Joseph I. | Emperor | 1830 | Dec. 2, 1848 |
| Belgium | Leopold II | King | 1835 | Dec. 10, 1865 |
| Bolivia | Nicolas Campero | President | | June 1, 1880 |
| Brazil | Pedro II. Alcántara | Emperor | 1825 | April 7, 1831 |
| Chili | Domingo Santa Maria | President | | Sept. 18, 1881 |
| China | Kwong Shu | Emperor | 1871 | Jan. 12, 1875 |
| Colombia | R. Nuñez | President | | April 1, 1880 |
| Costa Rica | Tomas Guardia | President | | Provisional. |
| Denmark | Christian IX | King | 1818 | Nov. 15, 1863 |
| Ecuador | José de Vintimilla | President | | Sept. 8, 1876 |
| France | François P. Jules Grévy | President | 1813 | Jan. 30, 1879 |
| Germany | Wilhelm I. | Emperor | 1797 | Jan. 18, 1871 |
| Alsace-Lorraine | F. M. Baron Manteuffel | Oberpräsident | | ——, 1880 |
| Anhalt | Friedrich | Duke | 1831 | May 22, 1871 |
| Baden | Friedrich I. | Grand Duke | 1826 | April 24, 1852 |
| Bavaria | Ludwig II. | King | 1845 | March 10, 1864 |
| Bremen | | Burgomasters | | |
| Brunswick | Wilhelm I. | Duke | 1806 | April 20, 1831 |
| Hamburg | | Burgomasters | | |
| Hesse | Ludwig IV. | Grand Duke | 1837 | June 13, 1877 |
| Lippe | G. F. Waldemar | Prince | 1824 | Dec. 8, 1875 |
| Lubeck | | Burgomasters | | |
| Mecklenburg-Schwerin | Friedrich Franz II | Grand Duke | 1823 | March 7, 1842 |
| Mecklenburg-Strelitz | Friedrich Wilhelm | Grand Duke | 1819 | Sept. 6, 1860 |
| Oldenburg | Peter | Grand Duke | 1827 | Feb. 27, 1853 |
| Prussia | Wilhelm I. | King | 1797 | Jan. 2, 1861 |
| Reuss-Greiz | Henrich XXII | Prince | 1846 | Nov. 8, 1859 |
| Reuss-Schleiz | Heinrich XIV | Prince | 1832 | July 10, 1867 |
| Saxe-Altenburg | Ernst | Duke | 1826 | Aug. 3, 1853 |
| Saxe Coburg and Gotha | Ernst II | Duke | 1818 | Jan. 29, 1844 |
| Saxe-Meiningen | Georg II. | Duke | 1826 | Sept. 20, 1866 |
| Saxe-Weimar Eisenach | Karl Alexander | Grand Duke | 1818 | July 8, 1853 |
| Saxony | Albert | King | 1828 | Oct. 29, 1873 |
| Schaumburg-Lippe | Adolf | Prince | 1817 | Nov. 21, 1860 |
| Schwarzburg-Rudolstadt | Georg | Prince | 1838 | Nov. 26, 1869 |
| Schwarzburg-Sondershausen | Günther III | Prince | 1830 | July 17, 1880 |
| Waldeck | Georg Victor | Prince | 1831 | May 14, 1845 |
| Würtemberg | Karl I | King | 1823 | June 25, 1864 |
| Great Britain and Ireland | Victoria I | Queen, and Empress of India | 1819 | June 20, 1837 |
| Greece | Georgios I. | King | 1845 | June 6, 1863 |
| Guatemala | J. Rufino Barrios | President | | May 7, 1873 |
| Hayti | Gen. Salomon | President | | Nov. 25, 1879 |
| Hawaiian Islands | Kalakaua I. | King | 1836 | Feb. 12, 1874 |
| Honduras | M. A. Soto | President | | May 29, 1877 |
| Italy | Humbert I. | King | 1844 | Jan. 9, 1878 |
| Japan | Mutsu Hito | Mikado | 1852 | Feb. 13, 1867 |
| Mexico | Manuel Gonzalez | President | | Dec. 1, 1880 |
| Morocco | Muley-Hassan | Sultan | 1831 | Sept. 25, 1873 |
| Netherlands | Willem III | King | 1817 | March 17, 1849 |
| Nicaragua | Joaquin Zavala | President | | March 1, 1879 |
| Paraguay | Gen. B. Caballero | President | | Oct. —, 1880 |
| Persia | Nassr-ed-deen | Shah | 1829 | Sept. 10, 1848 |
| Peru | Montero | President, acting | | Dec. —, 1881 |
| Portugal | Luis I. | King | 1838 | Nov. 11, 1861 |
| Roumania | Karl I. | King | 1839 | March 26, 1881 |
| Russia | Alexander III | Emperor | 1845 | March 10, 1881 |
| Salvador | Rafael Zaldivar | President | | April 30, 1876 |
| Santo Domingo | F. A. de Moreño | President | | July 23, 1880 |
| Servia | Milan IV., Obrenovic | Prince | 1855 | July 2, 1868 |
| Spain | Alfonso XII | King | 1857 | Dec. 30, 1874 |
| Sweden and Norway | Oscar II | King | 1829 | Sept. 18, 1872 |
| Switzerland | Numa Droz | President | | Jan. 1, 1881 |
| Turkey | Abdul-Hamid Khan | Sultan | 1842 | Aug. 31, 1876 |
| Egypt | Tewfik Pasha | Khedive | 1852 | Aug. 8, 1879 |
| United States | Chester A. Arthur | President | 1830 | Sept. 20, 1881 |
| Uruguay | F. A. Vidal | President | | March 17, 1880 |
| Venezuela | Guzman Blanco | President | | Feb. 26, 1879 |

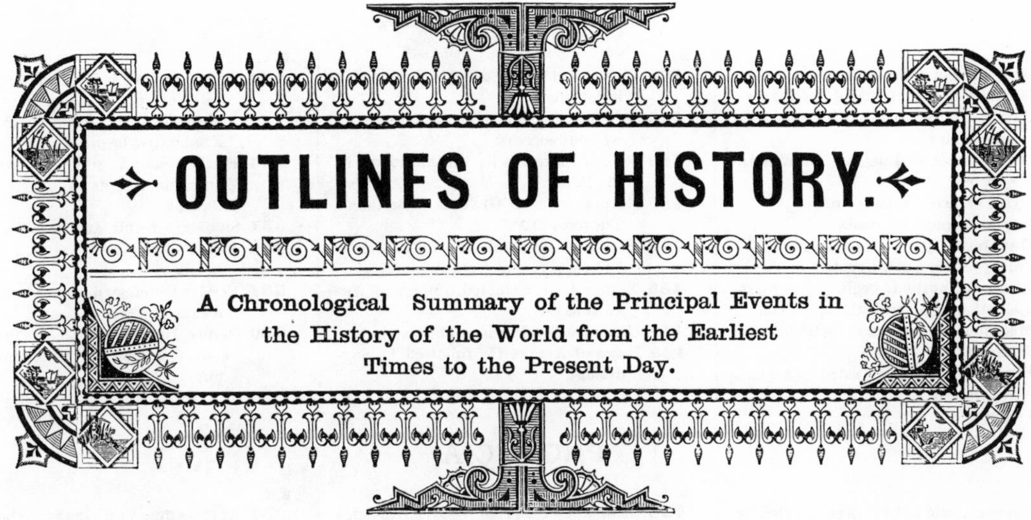


[For convenience of arrangement the following arbitrary division as to periods has been adopted:—1. **Ancient History,** from the earliest times to the fall of the Western Roman Empire, 476 A.D.—2. **Mediæval History,** from the fall of the Western Roman Empire to the close of the fifteenth century. 3. **The History of Modern Nations**]

# Ancient History.

## EGYPT.

B. C.

**2717** Reign of Menes, founder of the Thinite dynasty.
**2122** HIEROGLYPHICS invented.
**2120** **Pyramids built,** north of Memphis.
**1822** Memnon invents EGYPTIAN ALPHABET.
**1706** Jacob and his family settle in Egypt.
**1618** Accession of Sesostris.
**1491** **Exodus of the Hebrews,** after the ten plagues.
**1308** Reign of Sethos, who builds Temple of Vulcan at Memphis and other works.
**781** Saite dynasty begins.
**711** Assyrian invasion of Sennacherib.
**686** Egypt divided between **12** kings.
**610** Attempt to cut a canal across the ISTHMUS OF SUEZ. Failure after the loss of **120,000** men.
**581** Babylon invaded by Nebuchadnezzar.
**535** Egypt becomes subject to CYRUS THE GREAT.

B. C.

**418** Visit of HERODOTUS to Thebes.
**332** Egypt conquered by ALEXANDER THE GREAT. ALEXANDRIA founded.
**322** Ptolemy I. makes Egypt independent.
**320** Revolt of Phœnicia. Immigration of 100,000 Jews.
**301** Battle of Ipsus, between Ptolemy Soter and Antigonus.
**217** Battle of Raphia. Ptolemy IV. defeats Antiochus III. of Syria.
**198** SYRIA becomes independent.
**145** Reign of Ptolemy VII., who marries Cleopatra.
**130** Ptolemy VII. flees to Cyprus; returns in B. C. 128; dies, B. C. 117.
**117** Reign of Ptolemy VIII. and CLEOPATRA, his mother.
**82** THEBES destroyed.
**47** ALEXANDRIAN LIBRARY burned in siege by CÆSAR.

B. C.

**43** Cleopatra poisons her brother and reigns alone.
**41** MARC ANTONY follows Cleopatra to Egypt.
**31** **Battle of Actium.** Antony and Cleopatra defeated by OCTAVIUS.
**30** Suicide of Antony and Cleopatra. Egypt becomes a ROMAN province.

A. D.

**122** Hadrian visits Egypt.
**171** Revolt against ROME.
**273** Aurelian regains possession.
**288** Rebellion of Achilleus in upper Egypt.
**297** DIOCLETIAN captures Alexandria and puts down rebellion.
**379** Pagan worship prohibited by THEODOSIUS. Many famous temples destroyed.

## CHALDÆA, ASSYRIA, AND BABYLONIA.

B. C.

**2458** Chaldæa said to have been conquered by Medes or Armenians.
**2234** First authentic date. Beginning of Chaldæan astronomical tablets.
**2093** Reign of Uruch, the architect.
**1850** Reign of Ismi-dagon, who conquers ASSYRIA.
**1500** Arabians subdue Chaldæa and establish a new dynasty.
**1250** ASSYRIA absorbs CHALDÆA or Early Babylonia about this time.
**1150** Nebuchadnezzar I. of Babylon invades Assyria.
**1130** Tiglath-Pileser I. invades Babylonia.

B. C.

**1110** Tiglath-Pileser I. seizes Babylon, but is soon driven out.
**880** The Assyrians again invade Babylonia.
**820** Babylon becomes subject to Assyria.
**750** Independence regained by Babylon.
**747** Reign of Nabonassur.
**709** Sargon of Assyria conquers Babylon.
**625** Naborpolassar establishes independence of Babylon. SARDANAPALUS burns himself in his palace.
**598** **Nebuchadnezzar conquers the Jews,** and carries away King Jehoiakim.

B. C.

**588** Siege of Jerusalem.
**587** JERUSALEM SURRENDERS.
**581** Nebuchadnezzar invades Egypt, and makes Amasis king.
**570** Second invasion of Egypt.
**561** Nebuchadnezzar dies.
**539** CYRUS THE GREAT, of Persia, drives out Nabonadius, whose son BELSHAZZAR becomes king of Babylon.
**538** Cyrus turns the EUPHRATES from its course and enters BABYLON, which becomes subject to Persia.

## PERSIAN EMPIRE.

B. C.

**2160** First Persian dynasty founded.
**642** Kaianite dynasty founded by Cyaxares.
**640** Invasion of Scythians, who subjugate the country.
**559** CYRUS becomes king, and defeats Assyrians.
**543** Cyrus annexes ASIA MINOR.
**538** Cyrus conquers BABYLON.
**529** **Death of Cyrus the Great.**
**525** Cambyses conquers Egypt.
**531** Reign of DARIUS I. begins, after assassination of Smerdis the Magician.
**508** Macedon and Thrace subdued by Darius.
**495** Revolt of the IONIANS, aided by Athens, suppressed.

B. C.

**492** Invasion of GREECE by Mardonius. He is defeated.
**490** Artaphernes and Datis invade Greece without success.
**485** Reign of XERXES I., the Ahasuerus of the Bible.
**480** Xerxes invades GREECE. Battle of THERMOPYLÆ.
**479** Persians, defeated at MYCALE and PLATÆA, retreat from Greece.
**465** Xerxes I. assassinated. Reign of ARTAXERXES.
**449** Greeks defeat Persians at Salamis.
**425** Reign of Xerxes II., followed by Sogdianus.

B. C.

**401** CYRUS rebels; is defeated and slain at battle of Cunaxa, where the "Retreat of the Ten Thousand" Greeks, under XENOPHON, begins.
**394** Persians assist Athenians and defeat Spartans at naval battle of the CNIDUS.
**351** Sidonians revolt, and burn their city.
**334** ALEXANDER THE GREAT invades Persia.
**331** Persians defeated by Alexander at ARBELA.
**330** Darius III. assassinated. Persia becomes part of the Macedonian Empire.

## PHŒNICIA.

B. C.

**2800** Phœnicia said to have been peopled by the "sons of Anak."
**1497** Reign of Agenor, the first historical king of Phœnicia.
**1050** Tyre becomes the leading city.
**870** The Assyrians conquer the country.
**850** A colony led by Elissa, or Dido, founds Carthage.

B. C.

**723** Shalmaneser IV. of Assyria, invades Phœnicia.
**587** Invasion by Nebuchadnezzar of Babylon.
**536** CYRUS THE GREAT subdues the country.
**466** BATTLE OF EURYMEDON; Phœnicians, aiding Persia, are defeated by the Greeks under Cimon.
**352** Revolt from the Persian monarchy.

B. C.

**331** ALEXANDER THE GREAT subdues the land.
**323** Phœnicia annexed to EGYPT by Ptolemy Soter I.
**315** Conquest of Antigonus of Phrygia.
**83** Tigranes I. of Armenia, annexes Phrygia.
**63** Absorbed in the province of Syria.

## SYRIA.

B. C.

**1920** ABRAHAM arrives in Syria.
**1047** Reign of HIRAM, King of Tyre, who assists David.
**1040** KING DAVID of Israel subdues the Syrians.
**975** Independence recovered after the death of Solomon.
**901** War with the Israelites; Syrians defeated.
**892** Samaria besieged by the Syrians.
**740** Alliance with ISRAEL against JUDAH. Syria subject to ASSYRIA.
**604** Nebuchadnezzar subdues the land.

B. C.

**596** **Invasion of Persians**; Syria subject to Persia for three centuries.
**333** **Battle of Issus.** Alexander the Great conquers Syria.
**323** Seleucus I. founds a dynasty.
**300** **Antioch** becomes the capital of the country.
**246** The Egyptians conquer Syria.
**198** Independence regained.
**170** ANTIOCHUS EPIPHANES besieges and captures Jerusalem.
**65** **Syria subject to Rome.** Pompey defeats Antiochus XII.

B. C.

**57** The pro-consul, Gabinius, restores many devastated cities.
**47** JULIUS CÆSAR confirms the liberties of the cities.

A. D.

**6** JUDAH and SAMARIA added to the province.
**120** Eastern boundary fixed at the Euphrates, by HADRIAN.
**258** War with Persia; Syria successful after six years.

## THE HEBREWS.

B. C.

**1996** Birth of ABRAHAM.
**1882** Death of Abraham.
**1729** Joseph sold into Egypt.
**1571** Birth of MOSES. Male infants destroyed.
**1491** **Exodus from Egypt.** Passover instituted. **Crossing of the Red Sea.** Giving of the law from Mount Sinai.
**1490** TABERNACLE established in the wilderness.
**1451** JOSHUA leads the nation into CANAAN.
**1413** From this date to B. C. 1136 the Hebrews are subject to six periods of bondage; to Mesopotamia, Moab, Canaan, the Midianites, the Ammonites, and the Philistines.

B. C.

**1136** Samson defeats Philistines.
**1123** Samuel becomes Judge of Israel.
**1095** SAUL is made king.
**1093** Saul defeats Philistines.
**1081** Birth of **David.**
**1055** Death of Saul and accession of David.
**1040** David defeats Philistines and recovers the ark.
**1023** Death of ABSALOM after his rebellion.
**1015** Death of David. SOLOMON becomes king.
**1011** Solomon begins to build the TEMPLE.
**1004** **Temple Completed.**
**990** Visit of QUEEN OF SHEBA to Solomon.
**975** Death of Solomon; revolt of the ten tribes; division into kingdoms of JUDAH and ISRAEL.

### Kingdom of Israel.

B. C.

**975** Reign of JEROBOAM.
**906** Great famine, predicted by Elijah.
**901** Syrians besiege Samaria.
**771** Assyrian invasion under Phul.
**721** The Assyrians invest Samaria; ten tribes carried into captivity; the kingdom is destroyed.

### Kingdom of Judah.

**971** Jerusalem pillaged by Egyptians.
**896** JEHOSHAPHAT defeats Ammonites.
**741** Pekah, King of Israel, besieges Jerusalem.
**726** HEZEKIAH abolishes idolatry.
**710** Sennacherib the Assyrian invades JUDÆA. The destroying angel slays 185,000 Assyrians in the night.

B. C.
605 Nebuchadnezzar invades Judæa.
588 Jerusalem captured, after a long siege.
587 **Jerusalem razed to the ground. Temple burnt.**

**Babylonish Captivity.**

603 Daniel prophesies at Babylon.
587 Golden image set up; Shadrach, Meshach and Abednego thrown into a furnace. Prophecies of Obadiah.

B. C.
538 Daniel interprets handwriting on the wall. Belshazzar slain.
536 Cyrus allows the Jews to return to Jerusalem.
515 **Temple rebuilt.**
458 Ezra reforms abuses.
445 Walls of Jerusalem rebuilt.
415 Malachi prophesies.
332 Alexander the Great visits Jerusalem and worships at the temple.
320 Ptolemy Soter takes Jerusalem.

B. C.
170 Antiochus takes the city; temple pillaged, 40,000 Jews slain.
161 Treaty with Rome, the first on record.
40 Herod becomes king.
37 Jerusalem taken by Herod and the Romans.
18 Temple rebuilt by Herod.
A. D.
4 Birth of Jesus Christ.
33 **Crucifixion and Resurrection of Christ.**

## GREECE.

B. C.
2042 Uranus arrives in Greece, according to legend.
1856 Kingdom of Argos founded by Inachus.
1710 Arcadians emigrate to Italy, and found a colony.
1503 Mythical deluge of Deucalion.
1493 Cadmus founds Thebes.
1459 Reign of Hellen.
1453 First Olympic games founded.
1384 Corinth built.
1326 Eleusinian mysteries instituted.
1313 Kingdom of Mycenæ created.
1283 Pelops settles in South Greece.
1263 Argonautic expedition.
1198 Helen carried off by Paris.
1193 Trojan war begins.
1184 **Troy Destroyed** by Greeks.
1103 Return of the Heraclidæ. Æolians settle in Asia Minor.
1044 Ionians settle in Asia Minor.
916 Rhodians found navigation laws.
846 Lycurgus flourishes. Olympian games revived at Elis.
776 **First Olympiad.**
752 Athens establishes decennial instead of perpetual *archons*.
743 Messenian wars; Sparta victorious.
683 Creon becomes first annual archon of Athens.
657 Byzantium built by Bysas, from Argos.
621 Draconian laws published.
594 Code of Solon published.
590 The Seven Wise Men of Greece flourish; Solon, Periander, Pittacus, Chilon, Thales, Cleobulus and Bias.
560 Pisistratus becomes tyrant of Athens.
522 Greeks colonize the Thracian Chersonese. Sestos founded.
510 Banishment of Hippias and the Pisistratidæ.
504 Sardis burnt by the Greeks.
499 Ionian war; the rebellion put down.
492 Mardonius with a Persian fleet is wrecked near Mount Athos.
490 Second Persian invasion under Datis and Artaphernes. **Battle of Marathon**, in which the Persians are defeated by the Greeks under Miltiades.
483 Aristides banished from Greece.
480 Third and greatest invasion of Persians, under Xerxes. Battles of **Artemisium, Thermopylæ and Salamis.**
479 Battles of **Mycale and Platæa**; Greeks victorious in both; Persians retreat home.
477 Athens becomes the chief Greek state.
471 Themistocles banished from Athens.
469 Cimon overruns all Thrace. Pericles begins to take part in public affairs.
464 Third Messenian war; Sparta defeats Messenia.
445 Thirty years' truce between Athens and Lacedæmonia.
443 Herodotus flourishes.
440 Samian war. Pericles defeats the Samians.
433 Treaty between Athens and Corcyra.
431 Beginning of Peloponnesian war, between Athens and a confederacy with Sparta at the head. This war lasted 27 years, and ended in the defeat of Athens.
418 Battle of Mantinea; Spartans defeated.
415 Invasion of Sicily by the Athenians.
413 Athenian fleet destroyed by Gelippus.
400 **Death of Socrates.** Retreat of the Ten Thousand.
395 Corinthian war begins; Corinth, Athens, Argos, Thebes and Thessaly unite against Sparta.
388 Plato founds Athenian academy.
387 Peace of Antalcidas closes Corinthian war, and establishes independence of all Greek cities except Lemnos, Imbros and Scyros, which become subject to Athens.
382 Olynthian war begins; after three years Sparta subdues the Olynthians.
378 Thebes and Athens unite against Sparta.
376 Lacedæmonian fleet defeated at Naxos.
371 Treaty of Callias, between Athens, Sparta and the allies; all Greek cities made independent, but acknowledge Sparta as supreme on land, and Athens as queen of the sea.
368 Epaminondas leads Thebans into the Peloponnesus.
362 Death of Epaminondas at battle of Mantinea.
357 Social war. Chios, Rhodes and Byzantium revolt from Athens.
356 Third Sacred war, the Phocians having seized the temple of Delphi.
346 Athens makes peace with Macedon.
339 Fourth Sacred war, between Philip of Macedon and the Athenians.
338 Battle of Chæronea; Philip defeats Athenians and Bœotians.
336 Accession of Alexander the Great.
335 Athens submits to Alexander.
323 Samian war. Antipater, a Macedonian general, defeats Athens and allies.
300 Athenian Democracy restored.
280 Achæan League, between twelve cities of Achæa.
277 League between Athens, Sparta, and Egypt.
268 Antigonus of Macedon takes Athens.
229 Athens joins Achæan league.
211 Treaty concluded with the Romans against Philip V. of Macedon.
200 The allies attack Macedon and defeat Philip.
196 Greece declared free from Macedon.
167 Romans ravage Epirus and Achæa.
146 Greece becomes a Roman province.
88 Mithridates of Pontus seizes Athens.
86 Sylla besieges and reduces Athens.
21 Augustus Cæsar founds Confederacy of Laconian cities.
A. D.
52 The apostle Paul visits Athens.
54 Nero visits Greece and takes part in the games.
122 Hadrian visits Greece.
262 Greece invaded by the Goths.
395 Alaric I. invades Greece.
442 Attila ravages Thrace and Macedon.
475 Theodoric, the Ostrogoth, devastates Thessaly and Thrace.

# ROME.

B. C.

**753** **Rome founded** by Romulus on the Palatine hill (legendary).

**750** Sabine war follows the abduction of the Sabine women.

**747** League between Romans and Sabines.

**716** Assassination of Romulus.

**715** NUMA POMPILIUS becomes king.

**670** Alban invasion and battle of the HORATII and CURIATII.

**665** King TULLUS HOSTILIUS defeats the Albans and destroys Alba Longa.

**640** Reign of Ancus Marcius.

**616** TARQUINIUS PRISCUS begins to reign.

**615** The CAPITOL is begun, in honor of Jupiter, Juno and Minerva.

**605** The Circus Maximus is erected.

**600** The Cloacæ Maximæ (great sewers) are built ; still in use.

**578** Accession of SERVIUS TULLIUS. First coinage.

**566** The first census makes the number of inhabitants 84,700.

**534** Servius assassinated by Tullia, his daughter. Her husband, TARQUINIUS SUPERBUS, reigns.

**520** Sibylline books brought from Cumæ.

**510** Rape of Lucretia. **The Tarquins are banished.** Foundation of the REPUBLIC; L. Junius Brutus and L. Tarquinius Collatinus consuls.

**509** Commercial treaty with Carthage.

**507** Capitol completed and dedicated.

**501** Titus Lartius made DICTATOR.

**498** or **496** Battle of Lake Regillus. Tarquin and his Latin allies defeated by Romans.

**494** Patricians secede. Tribunes of the people appointed.

**493** Independence of the Latins recognized. Corioli taken by Caius Martius (CORIOLANUS.)

**491** Coriolanus banished; he is received by the Volscians.

**489** The Volscians and Coriolanus besiege Rome.

**488** Coriolanus withdraws at his mother's entreaty ; is slain by the Volscians.

**484** First Agrarian Law proposed.

**477** The Fabii perish in a battle with the Veientes.

**471** Election of plebeian magistrates given to the Comitia Tributa.

**458** CINCINNATUS made DICTATOR; defeats the Æqui.

**451** DECEMVIRI, or counsel of ten, govern. They institute the ten tables or code of laws.

**449** VIRGINIUS kills his daughter VIRGINIA to save her from Appius Claudius; decemvirate abolished.

**440** Terrible famine in Rome.

**434** War with the Etruscans declared.

**431** Battle of Mount Algidus; the Æqui and Volsci defeated.

B. C.

**423** The Samnites capture Vulternium.

**409** Three plebeian quæstors elected.

**407** The Volscians defeat the Romans.

**405** Siege of Veii.

**396** The dictator Camillus captures Veii.

**391** Camillus impeached and exiled.

**390** Battle of Allia. The Romans defeated by Brennus and the Gauls. **Rome burnt.** Siege of the Capitol.

**389** Gauls expelled and city rebuilt.

**387** Capitoline games are established.

**384** Manlius hurled from Tarpeian rock for having aimed at sovereignty.

**376** CIVIL WAR between patricians and plebeians. Law passed that one consul shall be a plebeian.

**362** CURTIUS leaps into a gulf to save Rome.

**350** The Gauls are defeated by Popilius.

**343** War with Samnites; this war lasts more than fifty years.

**340** War with Latins; after two years the Romans are victorious.

**332** Treaty made with Alexander the Great.

**321** **Battle of the Caudine Forks.** Romans terribly defeated by Pontius.

**312** The Via Appia, a great military road, completed.

**295** Quintus Fabius defeats the Samnites, Etruscans, and Gauls.

**290** The third Samnite war ends in subjection to Rome.

**281** War with PYRRHUS, KING OF EPIRUS.

**280** Battle of Pandosia; Romans defeated.

**279** Second Victory of Pyrrhus at Asculum.

**275** Battle of BENEVENTUM; Pyrrhus defeated.

**266** All Italy now subject to Rome.

**264** **First Punic War;** Carthage disputes Rome's empire.

**256** Naval victory over the Carthaginians by REGULUS.

**250** Regulus slain at Carthage.

**241** End of First Punic War. Sicily made a Roman province.

**235** No war existing, the TEMPLE OF JANUS is closed for the first time in nearly 500 years.

**225** Invasion of Gauls; BATTLE OF CLUSIUM; defeat of Gauls.

**218** **Second Punic War.** HANNIBAL defeats SCIPIO.

**217** Battle of Lake Thrasymene. Flaminius defeated by Hannibal.

**216** **Battle of Cannæ.** Romans defeated with loss of 80,000 men.

**202** SCIPIO AFRICANUS defeats Hannibal at ZAMA in Africa.

**201** End of Second Punic War.

**197** War with Philip of Macedon ended by his defeat.

**192** War with Antiochus of Syria; peace concluded in B. C. 188.

B. C.

**172** Second war with Macedon begun.

**168** BATTLE OF PYDNA; Perseus killed and Macedon subject to Rome.

**149** **Third Punic War.** Scipio invades Africa.

**146** **Carthage destroyed** by order of the Senate.

**134** SERVILE WAR; Sicilian slaves rebel; in B. C. 132 are conquered and slain.

**121** Civil war arising from agrarian troubles; Caius Gracchus killed.

**111** JUGURTHINE WAR; peace concluded, but war renewed two years later; in B. C. 106 Jugurtha defeated and Numidia subjected.

**102** Another SERVILE WAR breaks out in Sicily.

**101** Battle of Campus Raudius. Marius and Catullus defeat the Cimbri.

**91** SOCIAL WAR. The Marsians, at first successful, are, B. C. 89, defeated.

**88** **Mithridatic War.** The King of Pontus sues for peace in B. C. 83.

**87** Civil war between SYLLA and MARIUS; Marius is slain.

**82** Proscriptions of Sylla, who becomes dictator.

**79** Abdication of Sylla.

**74** SPARTACUS leads revolt of the slaves; is defeated and killed in B. C. 71.

**65** Pompey subdues Syria.

**63** **Conspiracy of Catiline** suppressed by CICERO.

**60** FIRST TRIUMVIRATE; Julius Cæsar, Pompey, and Crassus.

**58** Banishment of Cicero. Cæsar invades Gaul.

**55** Cæsar invades Britain.

**51** Gaul made a Roman province.

**48** **Battle of Pharsalia;** Cæsar defeats Pompey.

**46** Cæsar becomes dictator. Suicide of Cato.

**44** **Assassination of Julius Cæsar** by Brutus, Cassius, and others.

**43** SECOND TRIUMVIRATE; Octavius, Antony and Lepidus. Cicero put to death.

**42** **Battle of Philippi;** defeat and death of Brutus and Cassius.

**41** War between Antony and Octavius, ended by the marriage of Antony and Octavia.

**32** Civil war of Antony and Octavius.

**31** **Battle of Actium;** defeat and death of Antony.

**30** Temple of Janus closed; first time in 200 years.

**27** Octavius becomes emperor under the title of AUGUSTUS CÆSAR.

**25** The Pantheon is erected.

# Mediaeval History.

## 476 A.D. TO 500 A.D.

A.D.
476 Odoacer captures and sacks Rome. **Fall of the Western Empire.**
477 Second Saxon invasion of Britain.
481 Clovis I. reigns in Belgic Gaul.

A.D.
486 Battle of Soissons. Clovis I. defeats the Romans.
489 Ostrogoths invade Italy.
491 Ella founds the kingdom of Sussex.

A.D.
493 Theodoric establishes the Ostrogothic Kingdom of Italy, South Germany, and Hungary.
495 Third Saxon invasion of Britain.
496 Clovis of France becomes a Christian.

## THE SIXTH CENTURY.

A.D.
501 Laws of Burgundy published.
502 Charbades the Persian ravages the Greek Empire.
503 Fergus lands in Scotland from Ireland.
507 Clovis founds the Kingdom of the Franks; total overthrow of the Visigoths.
510 Paris becomes the capital of the Franks.
511 Salic Law established in France.
514 Vitalianus, the Goth, besieges Constantinople.
519 Cerdic founds the Kingdom of Wessex in Britain.

A.D.
527 Fourth Saxon invasion of Britain. Essex founded.
529 Justinian Code published.
534 Belisarius conquers Africa.
538 The Franks appear in Italy.
539 Italy made subject to Belisarius. Goths ravage Milan.
545 The Turks enter Asia.
547 Northumbria founded in Britain.
552 Totila, the Ostrogoth, defeated in Italy.
554 Narses overthrows Gothic power in Italy.
562 St. Colombo lands in Scotland.
563 Constantinople destroyed by fire.

A.D.
565 Æthelbert becomes King of Kent.
568 Italy invaded by the Longobardi, who found the Kingdom of Lombardy.
569 **Birth of Mohammed.**
577 Battle of Durham; West-Saxons defeat the Britons.
581 Paris mostly destroyed by fire. Slavonians ravage Thrace.
584 Franks invade Italy and are repelled.
586 Kingdom of Mercia founded in Britain.
587 Franks expelled from Spain.
590 **Gregory the Great becomes Pope.**
595 The Lombards besiege Rome.
597 St. Augustine lands in England.

## THE SEVENTH CENTURY.

A.D.
600 Italy ravaged by Sclavonians.
603 Scots invade Bernicia; are driven back.
611 The Persians make conquests in Syria, Egypt, and Asia Minor, and besiege Rome.
612 Jews persecuted in Spain.
614 Jerusalem captured by Persians.
622 Mohammed enters Medina. **The Hegira.**
630 Mohammed reënters Mecca; installed as prince and prophet.

A.D.
632 **Death of Mohammed.** His religion spreads through Persia.
638 Syria occupied by Saracens.
640 Alexandrian Library burnt.
642 In Britain the Mercians defeat the Bernicians.
653 Rhodes taken by the Saracens.
656 Clovis II. becomes King of France.
662 In Italy, Constans II., Emperor of the East, is defeated by the Lombards.
668 Constantinople besieged by Saracens.
672 Saracens driven from Spain.

A.D.
678 Bulgarians occupy Bulgaria, in Northern Greece.
681 Mebrouin, last of the Merovingians, assassinated.
685 Saxons drive Britons into Wales and Cornwall.
687 Sussex united to Wessex. In France, Pepin defeats Thierry.
694 Kent devastated by West Saxons.
697 Anafesto becomes the first Doge of Venice.

## THE EIGHTH CENTURY.

A.D.
711 The Arabs cross from Africa to Spain. The Bulgarians ravage the Eastern Empire.
712 The Gothic kingdom of Spain overthrown by the Arabs.
714 **Charles Martel** becomes Duke of France.
716 Independent Gothic monarchy founded in the Asturias.
720 The Saracens are defeated at Constantinople.
730 Pope Gregory excommunicates the Emperor Leo.
732 **Battle of Tours**, or Poitiers; Saracens defeated by the Franks.

A.D.
739 Charles Martel conquers Provence.
746 Slavic settlements in Grecian Peloponnesus.
747 Carloman of France abdicates.
752 Pepin le Bref becomes King of France.
755 Insurrection in Mercia, Britain. Abderahman I. becomes King of Cordova.
756 Pepin annexes Ravenna to the See of Rome.
760 Insurrection of Toledo.
768 Charlemagne and Carloman rule in France and Germany.

A.D.
771 Charlemagne rules alone.
774 Charlemagne annexes Italy, after conquering the Lombards.
778 Battle of Roncesvalles. Beginning of the age of chivalry. Charlemagne invades Spain.
785 Saxons, subdued by Charlemagne, become Christians.
787 **The Danes land in England.**
791 Reign of Alphonso the Chaste in Spain; independence of Christians established.
799 The Avars subdued by Charlemagne.

## THE NINTH CENTURY.

A.D.

**800** **Charlemagne crowned at Rome;** becomes Emperor of the West.

**807** War between Slaves and Peloponnesian Greeks.

**820** Michael II. of the Byzantine Empire founds the Amorian dynasty.

**823** In England, Essex (and, two years later, Kent and Northumbria) are annexed to Wessex.

**825** The Servians occupy Dalmatia.

**827** EGBERT becomes king of all England.

**830** Louis the Debonair imprisoned in France.

A.D.

**843** TREATY OF VERDUN; the sons of Louis divide the empire. Spain ravaged by the Northmen.

**846** The Saracens sack Rome.

**848** Brittany becomes independent.

**850** Russian monarchy established by Rusic.

**851** **Northmen pillage France.**

**858** Kingdom of Navarre founded.

**865** Russians attack Constantinople.

**867** Basilian Dynasty founded at Constantinople.

**869** Œcumenical Council of Constantinople. (*Latin Church.*)

A.D.

**871** The DANES defeat Alfred at Battle of MERTON.

**875** Charles the Bald becomes Emperor.

**878** ALFRED THE GREAT driven from England.

**879** Œcumenical Council of Constantinople. (*Greek Church.*)

**881** Danes ravage Scotland.

**888** Paris attacked by Northmen.

**890** Italy subjected to the Eastern Empire. ALFRED of England founds Oxford, and establishes a code of laws.

**896** The Germans under Arnold seize Rome.

## THE TENTH CENTURY.

A.D.

**901** Death of Alfred the Great.

**907** The Russians receive tribute from Constantinople.

**911** Death of Louis the Child, last of the German CAROLINGIANS.

**912** Rollo the Northman becomes Robert, Duke of Normandy.

**921** Italy invaded by Burgundians.

**928** Five emperors rule the Byzantine Empire.

A.D.

**933** Athelstan ravages Scotland.

**934** Henry I. of Germany defeats the Danes.

**937** ATHELSTAN becomes first king of England.

**939** Louis IV. of France subdues Hugh Capet, Count of Paris.

**951** **Otho invades Italy.**

**962** OTHO THE GREAT becomes Emperor of the West; Italy and Germany united.

**978** Otho II. invades France.

A.D.

**979** Assassination of EDWARD THE MARTYR of England.

**982** BATTLE OF BASIENTELLO; Otho III. of Germany defeated by Greeks and Saracens.

**987** **Hugh Capet made King of France.**

**988** Vladimir I. of Russia embraces Christianity.

**996** Otho III. makes the German Emperor elective.

## THE ELEVENTH CENTURY.

A.D.

**1002** **Massacre of Danes in England.** Reign of Robert II. in Burgundy.

**1013** Sveyn conquers England.

**1014** Battle of Zetunium; Basil II. of Constantinople defeats the Bulgarians.

**1015** Vladimir I. dies; Russia is divided.

**1016** Ethelred dies; Edmund Ironsides and Canute divide England. Italy invaded by Northmen.

**1017** CANUTE becomes king of all England.

**1019** The Moors enter Spain.

**1026** Sancho founds kingdom of Castile.

**1035** Aragon becomes a kingdom.

**1037** Union of Leon and Castile.

A.D.

**1039** Duncan I. of Scotland murdered by Macbeth.

**1040** Sicily restored and Servia lost to the Eastern Empire.

**1041** Danes driven from Scotland.

**1042** Reign of Edward the Confessor in England.

**1043** Russians defeated before Constantinople.

**1051** Rebellion of Godfrey in Kent.

**1052** War of Roderigo the Cid with the Moors.

**1058** Moors expelled from Italy.

**1065** Jerusalem captured by the Turks.

**1066** **Battle of Hastings.** WILLIAM OF NORMANDY conquers England.

A.D.

**1073** Hildebrand made Pope; Henry IV. of Germany disputes his title.

**1077** Henry IV. submits and does penance.

**1081** Italy invaded by the Germans.

**1084** Henry IV. takes Rome and makes Clement III. Pope.

**1086** DOMESDAY BOOK completed in England.

**1090** Mantua taken by Henry IV.

**1095** Portugal becomes a separate principality.

**1096** **First Crusade.**

**1098** War between France and England.

**1099** Death of THE CID. Jerusalem captured by GODFREY DE BOUILLON.

## THE TWELFTH CENTURY.

A.D.

**1100** HENRY I. crowned in England.

**1104** Crusaders capture Acre.

**1106** Milan becomes a free republic.

**1110** Henry V. of Germany invades Italy.

**1114** Henry V. marries Matilda of England.

**1122** TREATY OF WORMS, between the Emperor and Pope.

**1135** STEPHEN becomes King of England.

**1139** Portugal becomes a kingdom. Maud crowned in England.

**1143** Moors rebel in Spain.

**1146** **Second Crusade;** Louis VII. of France and Conrad of Germany are defeated, A.D. 1148. Greece plundered by Roger of Sicily.

A.D.

**1152** FREDERICK BARBAROSSA made Emperor of Germany.

**1154** Frederick Barbarossa invades Italy. Henry II., King of England, the first Plantagenet.

**1159** War of Guelphs and Ghibellines.

**1162** Barbarossa destroys MILAN.

**1167** Frederick Barbarossa takes Rome. Italian League formed.

**1170** Thomas à Becket murdered in England.

**1172** The Sultan Saladin makes great conquests in Asia. Conquest of Ireland.

**1176** BATTLE OF LEGNANO. Barbarossa defeated by the Lombard League.

A.D.

**1183** Peace of Constance establishes the free cities of Italy.

**1185** Provinces of Amiens and Valois annexed to France.

**1187** Saladin seizes Jerusalem.

**1189** **Third Crusade,** by England, France and Germany. SIEGE OF ACRE begun. Richard I. crowned in England.

**1190** Barbarossa drowned. Henry V. invades Italy.

**1191** Acre captured. Jerusalem opened to pilgrims. Kingdom of Cyprus founded. Artois annexed to France.

**1192** Richard Cœur de Lion imprisoned in Germany; ransomed (1194) for £300,000.

**1199** JOHN becomes King of England.

## THE THIRTEENTH CENTURY.

A.D.

1202 **Fourth Crusade**; capture of Zora.
1203 Constantinople besieged and captured by the Crusaders.
1204 Normandy lost to England. Latins possess and divide GREECE.
1208 OTHO crowned Emperor of Germany at Rome.
1209 French crusade against the Albegeoise. INQUISITION established.
1210 War between Venice and Genoa.
1213 Battle of Muret; defeat of Albigenses.
1214 French defeat Germans at Bouvines.
1215 **Magna Charta signed at Runnymede.**
1216 Henry III. becomes King of England.
1217 **Fifth Crusade**, by Germans and Hungarians.
1220 Frederick II. becomes Emperor of Italy.
1228 **Sixth Crusade**; Frederick II. at Acre.
1229 Ten years' truce with the Sultan. Jerusalem restored to the Christians. Albigenses defeated in France.
1235 The Mongolians invade Russia.
1236 War between the Emperor and the Lombard League.
1238 Moorish kingdom of Grenada founded by Mohammed I.
1239 **Seventh Crusade**, by Thibaud, Count of Champagne.
1244 Jerusalem seized by the Carismians.
1248 **Eighth Crusade**, under Louis IX. of France.
1250 Louis captured by the Saracens; truce for ten years. Mamelukes rule Egypt.
1251 Rise of MEDICI family in Italy.
1252 Reign of Alexander I. of Russia.
1259 Kubla Khan builds Pekin.
1262 Barons' War in England.
1268 **Ninth Crusade**, by Louis IX. and Edward, Prince of Wales.
1270 Louis IX. dies at Carthage.
1271 The English quit Palestine.
1272 Reign of EDWARD I. of England.
1273 Rudolph of Hapsburg, Emperor of Germany.
1275 Wars of Robert Bruce and John Baliot for the crown of Scotland.
1276 House of Hapsburg of Austria founded.
1282 **Sicilian Vespers**; massacre of Sicilians by the French. Crusade against Aragon.
1283 Wales subjected to England.
1287 Jews banished from England.
1289 Second invasion of the Mongols.
1291 MAMELUKES take Acre. Christian power in Syria destroyed.
1297 Sir William Wallace fights for the independence of Scotland.
1299 **Battle of Falkirk**; Bruce and Douglas defeated by Edward I. Osman I. establishes the Turkish Empire.

## THE FOURTEENTH CENTURY.

A.D.

1300 Moscow becomes capital of Russia.
1302 First convocation of STATES-GENERAL in France.
1303 Edward I. invades Scotland.
1305 WILLIAM WALLACE executed.
1306 ROBERT BRUCE crowned as King of Scotland
1307 Edward II. King of England.
1308 Revolt of Swiss in Austria; WILLIAM TELL.(?)
1310 Henry VII. subdues the Lombards.
1313 Louis V. and Frederick of Austria contend for the German Empire.
1314 **Battle of Bannockburn**; the Scots defeat the English.
1315 Insurrection of English Barons. The Swiss defeat the Austrians at MORGARTEN.
1321 Death of DANTE.
1322 Battle of Mühldorf; Louis V. defeats Frederick.
1326 Germany invaded by Turks.
1327 Reign of Edward III.; INDEPENDENCE OF SCOTLAND.
1328 Charles the Fair of France dies; House of Valois reigns. Ivan I. rules Russia.
1334 First Doge of Genoa.
1337 War between France and Flanders.
1339 The COLONNA rise to power in Italy.
1340 Battle of Tarifa in Spain; the Moors defeated.
1346 **Battle of Crecy**; French routed by the English under Edward III. and the Black Prince. In Scotland, battle of Durban.
1347 The English take Calais. RIENZI, last of the Tribunes, establishes a democracy in Rome.
1349 Order of the Garter instituted.
1353 Turks enter Greece.
1354 Rienzi slain at Rome.
1356 **Battle of Poitiers**; 8,000 English defeat 60,000 French; the Black Prince takes John II. captive. Charles IV. of Germany signs the GOLDEN BULL, the basis of the German Constitution until 1806.
1358 Insurrection of the JACQUERIE in France.
1360 **Peace of Bretigny**, between English and French.
1361 Italy overrun by the Free Lances. Turks enter Greece.
1363 Austria acquires the Tyrol.
1364 Charles V. King of France; Philip the Bold Duke of Burgundy. Treaty between Austria and Bohemia.
1367 The Mamelukes conquer Armenia.
1369 Empire of TAMERLANE founded.
1370 Pope Gregory XI. goes to AVIGNON.
1371 STUART line begins with Robert II. of Scotland.
1374 Death of PETRARCH. Rebellion against the Pope.
1375 Death of BOCCACCIO.
1377 Reign of Richard II. of England. Papacy restored to Rome.
1380 BATTLE OF THE DON; Dimitri II. of Russia defeats the Tartars. WICKLIFFE's translation of the Bible published.
1381 **Wat Tyler's insurrection** in London suppressed.
1382 Tartars burn Moscow.
1387 German Empire divided.
1388 BATTLE OF CHEVY CHASE, or Otterburn, between Scots and English.
1390 The Eastern Empire loses power in Asia.
1392 Portuguese discover the Cape of Good Hope.
1395 Timour the Tartar invades Russia.
1396 BATTLE OF NICOPOLIS; the Turks under Bajazet I. defeat the Hungarian Christians.
1397 Persecution of the Wycklifites or Lollards.
1399 Reign of Henry IV. in England; Order of the Bath founded.

## THE FIFTEENTH CENTURY.

A.D.

1400 Death of CHAUCER and FROISSART.
1401 Rebellion in Wales; Glendower and the Percies defeated.
1402 BATTLE OF ANGORA; Timour the Tartar defeats the Turks and captures Bajazet I.
1409 Alexander V. made Pope by Council of Pisa.
1410 Sigismund of Hungary becomes Emperor of Germany.
1411 Battle of Harlaw; the Lowland defeat the Highland Scots.
1413 HENRY V. King of England.
1414 COUNCIL OF CONSTANCE; Pope John XXIII. deposed.
1415 **Battle of Agincourt**; 10,000 English defeat 50,000 French. JOHN HUSS burned at the stake.
1420 Paris captured by the English; Treaty of Troyes.
1422 Henry VI. proclaimed King of France and England. Ottoman Empire reunited by Amurath II.
1425 War between Milan and Venice.
1429 JOAN OF ARC raises siege of Orleans; Charles VII. King of France.
1430 Henry VI. crowned at Paris. Amurath II. conquers Macedonia.
1431 **Joan of Arc burned** at Rouen.
1433 Lisbon the capital of Portugal.

A.D.

**1435** TREATY OF ARRAS, between France and Burgundy. Sicily and Naples united. End of Hussite wars. War of Turks with Venice.

**1436** **Invention of Printing** by Guttenberg.

**1437** James I. of Scotland murdered.

**1438** THE PRAGMATIC SANCTION; Albert V. of Austria becomes Emperor of Germany.

**1439** Title of Emperor limited to the Austrian Hapsburgs.

**1442** Battle of Vasag; Turks routed by Hungarians.

**1443** Battle of Nissa; Turks again defeated.

**1445** Birth of LEONARDO DA VINCI.

**1452** Earl Douglas murdered by James II.

**1453** **Constantinople captured by Mohammed II.**; end of the Eastern Empire. End of the French and English wars.

**1455** **War of the Roses**; between Henry VI. and the Duke of York, afterwards Edward IV.

**1456** Battle of Belgrade; Turks repulsed by Hungarians.

**1460** The Turks conquer Greece.

**1461** Edward IV. deposes Henry VI.

**1462** Ivan the Great of Russia founds the modern Russian Empire.

**1463** Turkish war with Venice.

**1471** League of Italian cities against the Turks. WILLIAM CAXTON establishes first English printing-press.

**1473** Birth of Copernicus.

**1474** **Ferdinand and Isabella** rule in Castile. Birth of Michael Angelo.

**1475** Edward IV. invades France.

**1477** Russian war with Tartars. Artois and Burgundy united to France.

**1479** Union of Aragon and Castile under Ferdinand and Isabella.

**1480** Mongolian power in Russia destroyed. Mohammed II. takes Otranto.

**1483** Edward V. of England murdered in the Tower; RICHARD III. usurps the throne.

**1484** Spain invaded by Turks; first *auto da fé* at Seville.

**1485** **Bosworth Field**; death of Richard III.; Henry VII. crowned.

**1487** Star Chamber instituted in England.

**1488** War between Russia and Sweden.

**1492** **COLUMBUS DISCOVERS AMERICA.** Conquest of Grenada. CÆSAR BORGIA poisons Pope Alexander VII.

**1493** Treaty of Barcelona, between France and Spain. League between Russia and Denmark.

**1494** Charles VIII. invades Italy. Lollards persecuted in England.

**1499** The French seize Milan. BATTLE OF LEPANTO; victory of the Turks. Moors expelled from Spain.

# History of Modern Nations.

## 1500 A.D. TO THE PRESENT TIME.

### CHINA.

A.D.

**1517** Europeans first obtain a footing in China.

**1536** Macao granted to PORTUGUESE.

**1616** Mantchou Tartars establish the Tsing dynasty (still reigning).

**1662** Terrible earthquake; 300,000 killed at Pekin.

**1680** Trading with India Company begins.

**1724** JESUITS expelled.

**1793** English embassy received at Pekin.

**1812** Edict against Christianity.

**1816** Lord Amherst's embassy fails.

**1834** **Opium trade prohibited.**

**1839** Opium seized; trouble with British; outrages in Canton; Hong Kong captured; naval battles.

**1840** Trade with England forbidden by the emperor; Canton and coast blockaded; war ends in a truce, but—

**1841** Chinese break faith; war renewed; Chinese defeated; treaty giving England Hong Kong and $6,000,000 repudiated by emperor; Canton ransomed; English victorious.

**1842** **Treaty of peace**; Hong Kong ceded to England; Canton, Amoy, Foochoofoo, Ningpo and Shang-hae opened to British; China pays $21,000,000.

**1843** Treaty ratified by Queen Victoria and the Emperor Taou-Kwang.

**1850** REBELLION in Quang-Si gains head.

**1853** Rebels take Nankin and Shang-hae.

**1856** Outrages on Europeans; war renewed; Commodore Elliott, U.S.N., destroys Chinese fleet.

**1857** CANTON blockaded.

**1858** Canton captured by English and French; treaty of Lord Elgin; pirates destroyed.

**1859** Commercial treaty with UNITED STATES; English envoy attacked.

**1860** **War with England and France**; Europeans victorious; Pekin surrenders, Oct. 12; treaty signed, Oct. 24; Chinese apologize, pay indemnity, and ratify former treaty. Treaty with Russia.

**1861** Canton restored to Chinese. Rebels defeated by French and English aid.

**1864** Tien-wang, the rebel Emperor, commits suicide.

**1865** Prince Kung becomes regent.

**1868** **Burlingame Embassy** visit United States and sign treaty.

**1869** Chinese Embassy visits PARIS.

**1870** **Tien-tsin massacres**; French consul and many priests killed.

**1871** Chinese Government apologizes and gives indemnities. Marriage of emperor.

**1873** Ki-Tsiang of age; becomes Emperor as TOUNG-CHI.

**1875** Emperor dies; accession of TSAI-TIEN. First Chinese railway, from Shanghae to Woosung.

**1877** Terrible famine; opium smoking forbidden.

**1880** Troubles with RUSSIA.

**1881** Peace concluded with Russia.

### EGYPT.

A.D.

**1517** SELIM I. defeats Mamelukes and adds Egypt to the OTTOMAN EMPIRE.

**1770** Rebellion of Ali Bey suppressed.

**1798** NAPOLEON invades Egypt.

**1799** **Battle of Aboukir**; Turks defeated by the French.

**1801** The English aid Turks; Napoleon forced to leave the country.

**1806** Mehemet Ali becomes Pasha.

**1811** **Massacre of the Mamelukes**; Mehemet becomes supreme.

**1815** Discoveries of Belzoni.

**1831** Revolt of MEHEMET ALI; Syria invaded.

**1832** Defeat of Turks at Konieh.

**1833** Treaty of Kutayah; rebellion suppressed.

**1839** Second revolt of Mehemet; battle of

A.D.

Nezib; IBRAHIM, Ali's son, defeats the Turks.

**1840** England, Russia, Austria, and Prussia aid Turkey; Battle of BEYROUT; Egyptians defeated.

**1841** Treaty with Turkey; Mehemet made Viceroy, but deprived of Syria.

**1858** **Suez Canal begun.**

**1863** Death of Said Pasha; ISMAIL PASHA becomes Viceroy.

**1864** Arabian rebellion suppressed.

**1865** Suez Canal opened in part.

**1867** The Khedive (Viceroy) visits France and England.

**1869** **Suez Canal inaugurated.**

**1870** Sir Samuel Baker sent to suppress slave trade.

**1872** Baker returns after considerable success.

**1873** By the Sultan's firman the Khedive becomes independent in most points.

**1875** Abyssinian expedition; unsuccessful. Suez Canal stock sold to British Government.

**1876** War with Abyssinia. Debt consolidated.

**1877** Treaty of peace with Abyssinia made by Col. Gordon.

**1879** Nubar Pasha resigns. The Khedive deposed by the Sultan, June 26. His son Tewfik succeeds him.

**1881** **Decree of abolition of slavery.**

**1882** **Arabi Pasha**, Minister of War, heads opposition to the Khedive. Alleged conspiracy against Arabi Pasha, minister of war, leads to international complications. English and French fleets appear at Alexandria (May). On June 11, a riot breaks out in Alexandria, the natives killing 340 Europeans. The powers called upon to aid the Khedive. Arabi erects fortifications, and threatens to blow up the Suez Canal. Admiral Seymour takes command of English forces, and orders Arabi to cease fortifying; he refuses. **Bombardment of Alexandrian Forts** (July 12); they are destroyed by the English fleets. Arabi Pasha retreats into the country under cover of a flag of truce. The Khedive declares him a rebel. **Gen. Sir Garnet Wolseley** arrives at Alexandria (Aug. 15). Ramleh fortified; skirmish between Egyptians and the English. Arrival of more English troops. The fleet sails to Aboukir under sealed orders; proceeds to Port Said; reaches Ismailia; the English occupy the Suez Canal. Arabs attack the British at KASSASSIN, and are repulsed with heavy loss. Battle of **Tel-el-Kebir** in which the whole Egyptian army is routed (Sept. 13). Zagazig occupied. Kafr-el-Dwar surrenders. CAIRO opens its gates; ARABI PASHA and 10,000 troops surrender unconditionally; end of the war (Sept. 15).

## MEXICO.

A.D.

**1503** Reign of MONTEZUMA.

**1519** **Landing of Cortez.**

**1522** Charles V. makes Cortez Governor of Mexico or New Spain.

**1653** Negro insurrection suppressed.

**1659** *Auto da fé* of the Inquisition.

**1692** Insurrection in City of Mexico.

**1767** Jesuits expelled.

**1815** Insurrection of MORELOS.

**1821** **Mexico becomes independent.**

**1822** Iturbide declared Emperor.

**1823** Iturbide abdicates; federal constitution.

**1829** Spaniards expelled; Spanish expedition surrenders to SANTA ANNA. Slavery abolished.

**1832** Revolt of the Texans.

**1833** Santa Anna elected President; Mexicans defeated by Texans under Houston.

**1838** War with France; concluded next year.

**1844** **Treaty of annexation** between Texans and the United States.

**1845** War declared with the United States.

**1846** Mexicans defeated at Palo Alto and Matamoras (May 8), Santa Fe (Aug. 18), and Monterey (Sept. 24).

**1847** Battles of BUENA VISTA, CERRO GORDA, and CONTRERAS; victories of TAYLOR and SCOTT. **City of Mexico taken** (Sept. 15).

**1848** Peace ratified with the United States.

**1853** Santa Anna becomes Dictator.

**1855** Abdication of Santa Anna and Alvarez.

**1858** JUAREZ declared President; civil war with Miramon.

**1860** BATTLE OF SILOA; defeat of Miramon.

**1861** Juarez President and Dictator. England, France, and Spain intervene.

**1862** Truce with the Allies; England and Spain withdraw; France declares war against Juarez.

**1863** **War with France**; Gen. Forey enters the capital; provisional government established; the Assembly adopts imperial form of government. **Archduke Maximilian of Austria invited to become Emperor.** Contest with Republicans; French occupy Tampico, Morelia and Queretaro.

**1864** War continues; Juarez occupies Monterey. MAXIMILIAN accepts the crown and arrives at the capital. Successes of the Imperialists and French.

**1865** The Imperialists generally successful, but defeated at Tacambuso.

**1866** Juarists seize Toluca, Alarmos, Chihuahua, and Matamoras.

**1867** **Surrender and execution of Maximilian**, the French having left Mexico. Juarez re-elected President.

**1872** Death of Juarez; LERDA DE TEJADA made President.

**1873** Insurrection of Lozada suppressed.

**1875** Religious riots; Protestants murdered.

**1876** **Revolt of Gen. Diaz**, who occupies Matamoras; flight of Lerda de Tejada.

**1877** Gen. Diaz installed as President of the republic.

**1880** Manuel Gonzales elected President.

**1881** San Morelos railway accident; 200 lives lost.

**1882** Extensive grants of land to American railroad construction companies.

## SWITZERLAND.

A.D.

**1501** Basle and Schaffhausen join the Swiss Confederacy.

**1530** Reformation makes progress.

**1544** Grison League joins the Confederacy.

**1599** Appenzel joins the cantons.

**1602** **Siege of Geneva**; Charles of Savoy defeated.

**1648** **Treaty of Westphalia**; independence of Switzerland acknowledged.

**1712** Peace of AARGAU; end of religious war.

**1777** Alliance with France.

**1781** Civil strife; France interferes.

**1798** Helvetian Confederation dissolved; REPUBLIC founded.

**1800** Internal dissensions; 19 cantons.

**1811** Switzerland aids France.

**1814** Allies enter Switzerland.

**1815** **Treaty of Vienna** secures Swiss independence; 22 cantons.

**1842** Dissensions between Protestants and Catholics.

**1847** Jesuits expelled; civil war.

**1857** NEUFCHATEL DISPUTE; the Swiss retain the canton.

**1859** Neutrality in Italian war declared.

**1861** French violate Swiss territory; treaty of mutual cession.

**1864** Election riots at GENEVA.

**1865** International Social Science Congress at Berne.

**1868** Neutrality in Franco-Prussian war declared.

**1872** St. Gothard Tunnel commenced.

**1874** International Postal Congress at Berne.

**1877** J. Philippin elected President of National Congress.

**1880** Suicide of Herr Anderwert, President-elect.

## HOLLAND.

A.D.

**1477** Holland annexed to Austria.
**1506** Rule of Charles V. of Spain, Emperor of Germany.
**1555** Reign of PHILIP II.
**1565** Philip establishes the Inquisition.
**1566** CONFEDERACY OF "GUEUX" (beggars) against Philip's cruelty.
**1572** **Rebellion of William of Orange.**
**1575** Sovereignty offered to Elizabeth of England; she refuses.
**1576** PACIFICATION OF GHENT; provinces in North and South unite against Spain.
**1579** **League of Utrecht**; northern provinces declare their independence.
**1584** **Assassination of William of Orange.**
**1585** Southern provinces subdued by the Prince of Parma. Treaty with England.
**1586** BATTLE OF ZUTPHEN; Sir Philip Sydney killed.
**1587** Prince Maurice becomes Stadtholder.
**1598** Death of Philip II. Netherlands ceded to Austria.
**1600** Prince Maurice invades Flanders.
**1609** **Truce of Antwerp**; independence of United Provinces.
**1619** Execution of BARNEVELDT.
**1621** War with Spain. Dutch West India Company formed.
**1625** Rule of Prince Frederick Henry.
**1635** The "tulip mania" prevails.

A.D.

**1639** VAN TROMP captures two Spanish fleets.
**1648** PEACE OF WESTPHALIA; republic recognized by Europe.
**1652** **War with England**; Van Tromp "sweeps the channel;" De Ruyter defeated by Blake.
**1653** Peace with England; death of Van Tromp.
**1665** Second war with England; Monk defeats De Ruyter (1666).
**1667** Perpetual edict abolishes office of Stadtholder.
**1668** **Triple Alliance**: England, Holland and Sweden against France.
**1670** France and Sweden break alliance, and declare war against Holland.
**1672** Condé and Turenne overrun Holland; PERPETUAL EDICT revoked; William of Orange Stadtholder; the De Witts assassinated. **The dikes opened** and French driven out.
**1677** WILLIAM OF ORANGE marries MARY.
**1689** William and Mary ascend the English throne. War with France.
**1697** **Treaty of Ryswick,** between England, France, Spain and Holland.
**1707** Holland, Germany and England war against France.
**1713** **Treaty of Utrecht**, between the great powers.
**1747** French invade Flanders; Stadtholdership revived.

A.D.

**1748** **Peace of Aix-la-Chapelle**: France takes part of Flanders.
**1780** Another war with England; lasts three years.
**1793** French army invades the Netherlands.
**1806** Napoleon I. makes his brother LOUIS KING OF HOLLAND.
**1810** Louis abdicates in favor of his son; Holland annexed to France.
**1813** Revolt from France; Prince of Orange proclaimed sovereign.
**1814** Free constitution adopted. Belgium annexed to the Netherlands.
**1815** Most of Belgium ceded to Austria.
**1830** Revolt of Belgium, which becomes independent.
**1840** William I. abdicates; reign of William II.
**1849** Accession of William III.
**1856** Treaty with Japan.
**1861** Terrible inundations.
**1863** Slavery abolished in the colonies.
**1871** Dutch Guinea colonies ceded to Great Britain.
**1873** War with the Sultan of Atschin.
**1875** Rupture with Venezuela.
**1876** Victories over Sultan of Atschin. North Sea Canal opened.
**1877** General Vander Heyden ends the war in Atschin.
**1881** New tumults break out in Atschin.

## GREECE.

A.D.

**1540** Greece subjected to the OTTOMAN power.
**1684** Invasion by VENETIANS.
**1687** Athens captured by the Venetians.
**1699** PEACE OF CARLOWITZ; the Morea ceded to Venice.
**1718** **Turkish supremacy re-established.**
**1770** Russia assists insurgent Greeks; defeated by the Turks.
**1788** SULIOT rebellion suppressed.
**1803** Turks put down second Suliot rebellion (incited by the French.)
**1821** **Revolt of Ipsylanti**; the Greeks gain the Peloponnesus.
**1822** Independence of Greece; massacre at Scio.
**1823** National Congress at Argos. Death of MARCO BOZZARIS.
**1824** Death of LORD BYRON at Missolonghi. Turks destroy Ipsara.
**1826** **Siege of Missolonghi**; taken by Turks.

A.D.

**1827** Turks take ATHENS. Interference of foreign powers rejected by Turkey. **Battle of Navarino**; British, French, and Russian fleets defeat Turks and Egyptians. Independence of Greece established.
**1828** The Turks quit the Morea.
**1829** Turks surrender Missolonghi; treaty of Hadrianople.
**1831** President D'Istria assassinated.
**1833** Accession of OTHO I.
**1843** Insurrection in Athens; National Assembly; new constitution.
**1850** British fleet blockades the Piræus; indemnity for injury to British subjects demanded; French intervention; Greece yields.
**1854** Revolt of Albanians; English and French occupy Greece. Neutrality in Russo-Turkish war declared.
**1857** French and English evacuate Greece.

A.D.

**1862** Many insurrections; Otho I. leaves Greece. Prince Alfred declared King. Austria declares for Otho I.
**1863** National Assembly declares Alfred elected King; England prevents his accession; Prince William of Denmark becomes King as GEORGE I.; new constitution.
**1867** King George marries Princess Olga of Russia.
**1870** Trouble with brigands, who kill several English prisoners.
**1875** Greece observes neutrality in HERZEGOVINIAN insurrection.
**1876** Neutrality in SERVIAN war.
**1878** Greeks aid Thessalians against the Turks.
**1880** Berlin Conference considers question of Greek and Turkish frontiers.
**1881** **Convention with Turkey** (July 2); Thessaly ceded to Greece.

## TURKEY.

A.D.

**1512** SELIM I. made king by Janissaries; murders his male relatives.
**1516** Turks gain Egypt.
**1526** Selim defeats Hungarians.
**1571** **Battle of Lepanto**; Turkish power crippled.
**1606** Great fire in Constantinople.

A.D.

**1638** Turks defeat Persians and take BAGDAD.
**1683** Mahomet I. besieges Vienna, but fails.
**1715** Occupation of the Morea.
**1717** Turks abandon BELGRADE.
**1784** Crimea ceded to Russia.

D.A.

**1787** War with Russia and Austria; defeat of the Turks.
**1798** War with the French, who invade Egypt.
**1803** Insurrection of MAMELUKES at Cairo.
**1807** War with England and Russia; British fleet passes the DARDANELLES.

A. D.

**1812 Treaty of Bucharest**; Pruth made frontier of Turkey and Russia.

**1821** Insurrection in Moldavia and Wallachia. Independence of Greece (q v.).

**1824** Turks defeated at Mitylene.

**1827 Battle of Navarino**; Turkish fleet destroyed.

**1828** War with Russia; surrender of Anapa (June 23); Bajazet taken (Sept. 9); Varna yields to Russians (Oct. 11).

**1829** BATTLE OF SHUMLA; Russians victorious; they take Erzeroum and enter Adrianople; treaty of peace (Sept. 14).

**1831 Battle of Konieh**; Egyptians defeat Turks.

**1833** Russians enter Constantinople; offensive and defensive treaty with Russia.

**1849** Turkey refuses to surrender Polish refugees; sustained by England.

**1851** Rebellion in CROATIA.

**1852** Treaty with France regarding the HOLY PLACES.

**1853** Russian army crosses the Pruth. **War declared by Turkey**; approved by the "four powers," England, France, Austria and Prussia.

**1854 Crimean War.** Allied fleets enter Black Sea (Jan. 4); Russia refuses intervention (March 19). Treaty with England and France. Four powers guarantee Turkish integrity. Allied fleets bombard ODESSA and blockade the Danube; siege of Silistria; allies defeat Russians at Giurgero; Turks worsted at Bayazid; Russians evacuate principalities; **Battle of the Alma**, great victory of allies (Sept. 20); **siege of Sebastopol** begins.

**1855** Russians evacuate Anapa (June 5); attack on the Malakhoff tower (June 18); destruction of Kertch; death of Lord Raglan; MALAKHOFF taken by assault (Sept. 8); **Sebastopol evacuated**; Russian fleet sunk; battle at Kars, Russian defeat; Turks under Omar Pasha win victory at the Ingour (Nov. 6); allies take Kars (Nov. 26).

**1856** Negotiations for peace. Suspension of hostilities (Feb. 29). **Treaty of Peace** signed at Paris (April 29). CRIMEA evacuated (July 9). Independence of Turkey guaranteed.

**1858** Conflict with Montenegrins. Massacre of Christians at Jedda. Montenegrin boundaries determined.

**1859** Great fire at Constantinople. Conspiracy against the Sultan.

**1860** Druse and Maronite war. Christians massacred at Damascus. Convention of Great Powers.

**1861** Insurrection in HERZEGOVINA and MONTENEGRO.

**1862** Omar Pasha invades Montenegro. Trouble with SERVIA.

**1866** Revolt in CANDIA. Cretan Greeks rise against Turks.

**1874** Circular letter to the Powers protesting against treaties with Turkish tributaries.

**1875 Insurrection in Herzegovina and Bosnia.** Battle of Gatschko; Bosnians victorious.

**1876** BATTLE OF TREBINGE, indecisive. Germany, Austria and Russia demand reforms. BULGARIA revolts. Death of Sultan ABDUL-AZIZ (suicide or murder?). **Montenegro and Servia declare war** against Turkey. Deposition of MURAD V.; accession of ABDUL HAMID II.; defeat of Servians at Alexinatz. Conference of Great Powers about Turkish affairs.

**1877** Turkey rejects proposals of the Powers. MIDHAT PASHA banished. **War with Russia** declared. Hostilities with Montenegro. Russians cross the Danube (June 23); Nicopolis lost; Turkish success in Armenia; Plevna abandoned (July 6); recaptured (July 28); terrible battles in the SHIPKA PASS (Aug. 21-28); Russians repulsed at Plevna (Sept. 7-11), great loss on both sides; **relief of Plevna** (Sept. 22) by Chefket Pasha; retreat of Turks (Sept. 24); dismissal of Mehemet Ali as commander-in-chief; appointment of Suleiman Pasha; Mukhtar Pasha gains victories in Armenia. Total defeat of Mukhtar Pasha at Battle of Aladja-Dagh (Oct. 15); **Kars taken by storm** (Nov. 18). **Surrender of Plevna** (Dec. 10). Continued Russian successes.

**1878** ERZEROUM evacuated (Sept. 17). End of Russo-Turkish war; complete defeat of Turkey; treaty of peace signed (March 3). CONFERENCE of the Powers at BERLIN to settle Turkish question. TREATY OF BERLIN ratified (Aug. 3). Cyprus ceded to Great Britain (July 3).

**1879** Final treaty with Russia signed (Feb. 8); Russians leave the country. England demands reforms.

**1880** Protest of the Powers regarding delay in executing provisions of Berlin Treaty. Naval demonstration. Cession of Dulcigno (Nov. 26).

**1881** Conference of the Powers at Constantinople. Trial of MIDHAT PASHA and others for murder of Abdul-Aziz; Midhat and alleged accomplices condemned to death; sentence commuted to exile.

**1882** The Porte declines to enter conference of Powers regarding Egypt, but subsequently yields. Remonstrates with England for intended bombardment of Alexandria. Dervish Pasha sent as envoy to Egypt. Turkey declines to send troops to Egypt, but after the bombardment consents. The Sultan refuses to proclaim ARABI PASHA a rebel until Turkish troops shall have landed.

## SPAIN.

A.D.

**1500** Moorish rebellion suppressed.

**1502** Spanish Moors compelled to adopt Christianity.

**1503** Louis XII. of France invades Spain.

**1504** Death of ISABELLA.

**1506** Death of COLUMBUS.

**1512** NAVARRE annexed to Spain.

**1516** Death of Ferdinand. Rule of Cardinal Ximenes.

**1527** Insurrection of MORISCOES suppressed.

**1554** PHILIP of Spain marries Queen MARY of England.

**1556** CHARLES V. abdicates in favor of PHILIP.

**1557 War with France**; Battle of St. Quentin; Alva takes Rome.

**1563** The ESCORIAL Palace founded.

**1567 Alva enters the Netherlands.** (*See* HOLLAND.)

**1570** Rebellion of Moriscoes put down.

**1571** Alliance with Venice and the Pope against the Turks. BATTLE OF LEPANTO; Turks routed.

**1580** Alva conquers Portugal. United Provinces renounce their allegiance.

**1588 Destruction of Spanish Armada** off the English coast.

**1598** Death of Philip II.

**1609** Moriscoes expelled by Philip III. Peace with the Dutch.

**1616** Death of CERVANTES, author of "Don Quixote."

**1621** War renewed with HOLLAND (q. v.).

**1634** War with France, which is invaded.

**1640** John of Bragança drives Spaniards from Portugal.

**1648 Peace of Westphalia**; Spain gives up Holland.

**1655** War with England, lasting five years.

**1665** Death of Philip II.; regency of Anne.

**1668 Treaty of Lisbon**; independence of Portugal recognized.

**1690** Spain joins the "Grand Alliance" against France.

**1691** Invasion of the French; Aragon and Catalonia ravaged.

**1697 Treaty of Ryswick**; peace with France.

**1698** First PARTITION TREATY; regulates Spanish succession and cedes territory to France.

**1700** Second PARTITION TREATY; declares the Archduke Charles next in succession. Charles II. succeeded by Philip V.

**1701** Alliance with France and Mantua concluded.

**1702** War of the SPANISH SUCCESSION; Holland, Austria and England declare war with France and Spain.

A.D.

**1703** Portugal joins alliance against Spain.

**1704** GIBRALTAR taken by the British.

**1705** Charles acknowledged king at Barcelona.

**1710** BATTLE OF ALMENARA; Spaniards under Philip V. routed.

**1713** **Treaty of Utrecht**; Naples ceded to Austria.

**1715** Rule of CARDINAL ALBERONI.

**1724** Philip V. abdicates, but resumes power at death of Louis, his son.

**1729** Seville Alliance with England and France.

**1735** Don Carlos crowned King of the Two Sicilies.

**1736** War breaks out with Portugal.

**1739** England again declares war with Spain.

**1748** Treaty of Aix-la-Chapelle restores peace.

**1750** Treaty of Madrid with England.

**1753** Charles III. mounts the Spanish throne.

**1762** Spain again declares war with Portugal and England; Portugal invaded.

**1763** Treaty of Madrid restores peace.

**1767** Expulsion of the Jesuits.

**1771** Falkland Islands ceded to England.

**1775** War resumed with Portugal.

**1779** War renewed with England; siege of Gibraltar by French and Spanish.

**1783** TREATY OF VERSAILLES; England cedes Balearic Isles to Spain.

**1794** Spain invaded by the French.

**1796** War again begins with England.

**1797** **Battle of St. Vincent**; Spanish fleet defeated.

**1800** Parma ceded to the French.

**1801** Peace of Badajos ends war with Portugal. Treaty of Madrid, with France.

**1802** PEACE OF AMIENS ends English war.

**1804** War again declared with England.

**1805** **Battle of Trafalgar**; the English fleet under NELSON defeats French and Spanish fleets.

**1807** France signs treaty with Spain for partition of Portugal.

**1808** French demand territory and seize fortresses; Charles IV. abdicates; MURAT enters Madrid; massacre of 200 French at Madrid; French retaliate; Ferdinand VII. abdicates. NAPOLEON I. gives crown to his brother Joseph, who is driven from Madrid; Battle of Vimeira; English defeat French; Battle of Logrono; patriots defeated; French victory at Durange; NAPOLEON takes command (Nov. 3); enters Madrid (Dec. 4).

**1809** BATTLE OF CORUNNA (Jan. 16), death of Moore; Joseph returns to Madrid; surrender of Saragossa; Sir Arthur Wellesley enters Spain by crossing the Douro; BATTLE OF TALAVERA (July 28); defeat of French; Spanish defeated at Ocana (Nov. 12); Battle of MOLINOS DL REY (Dec. 21).

**1810** French seize Granada (Jan. 27), Seville (Jan. 31), Astorga (April 21); Ciudad-Roderigo surrenders to Massena (July 10).

**1811** Battle of Fuentes de Onoro; English victory; Suchet takes Tarragova; Joseph returns to Madrid; Soult defeats Spanish army at Lorca.

**1812** **Ciudad-Roderigo taken by Wellesley** (Jan. 19); STORMING OF BADAJOS (April 6); BATTLE OF SALAMANCA (July 22); defeat of the French; English enter Madrid.

**1813** Battle of Castella (April 13), Vittoria (June 21); the Pyrenees (July 28); Wellesley takes St. Sebastian, crosses the Bidasoa and enters France.

**1814** **Ferdinand VII. restored.**

**1820** Revolution of Raphael y Nunez del Riego. Ferdinand accepts constitution of the Cortes.

**1823** French enter Spain and invest Cadiz; Battle of the Trocadero; rebels defeated; Riego executed.

**1828** French evacuate Cadiz, which is proclaimed a free port.

**1829** Salique Law abolished in Spain.

**1833** Death of Ferdinand VII.; Don Carlos claims the throne; Queen Christina acts as regent for Isabella II.

**1834** The quadruple alliance of France, England, Spain, and Portugal, guarantee the throne to Isabella; Don Carlos expelled.

**1836** Battle of Bilbao; defeat of Carlists.

**1837** Dissolution of the monasteries.

**1839** Don Carlos retreats to France.

**1840** ESPARTERO subdues Carlists and heads the ministry; the Queen-Regent abdicates.

**1841** Espartero declared Regent by the Cortes. Insurrection in favor of Christina quelled.

**1842** Insurrection at Barcelona; the city bombarded (Dec. 3); surrenders to Espartero (Dec. 4).

**1843** Continued revolutionary movements in Barcelona, Corunna, Seville, Burgos and Santiago; Seville bombarded (July 21); siege raised (July 27). **Espartero defeated and deprived of power.** Isabella II. (13 years old) declared to be of age by the Cortes.

**1845** Carlos assigns his claims to his son.

**1846** Marriage of ISABELLA to Francisco, Duke of Cadiz, and of the Infanta to the Duc de Montpensier. England protests against these marriages.

**1847** Espartero restored. Attempt on the Queen's life.

**1848** British envoy ordered to leave Spain.

**1851** Lopez expedition against Cuba defeated. Birth of a princess.

**1853** Narvaez exiled to Vienna.

**1854** Disturbances at Saragossa; ESPARTERO heads the insurrection, which is successful; Espartero forms a ministry.

**1855** Death of Don Carlos.

**1856** Insurrection of Valencia; Espartero resigns; O'Donnel becomes Dictator, but is forced to resign; NARVAEZ becomes Minister.

**1857** Birth of a prince royal.

**1859** War with Morocco.

**1860** Moors defeated at Tetuan and Guad-el-ras. Ortega proclaims the Comte de Montemolin king as Charles VI.; Ortega shot (April 19).

**1861** Ratification of annexation of St. Domingo to Spain.

**1863** Juan de Bourbon renounces his right to the throne. Insurrection in St. Domingo.

**1864** General Prim exiled; Christina returns to Spain.

**1865** Peru pays indemnity to Spain. Student riots at Madrid. Insurrection and riots in Barcelona, Aragon and New Castile.

**1866** General Prim lays down his arms. Revolt in favor of Prim quelled at Madrid; O'Donnel resigns and Narvaez succeeds as Minister. The Queen dismisses the Cortes.

**1867** Insurrection in Catalonia and Aragon suppressed.

**1868** General amnesty; death of Narvaez; ministry of Murillo. Marshal Serrano exiled. Insurrection begins at Cadiz, headed by Prim; spreads rapidly; the ministers resign; **Isabella flees to France and is deposed** (Sept. 29); Prim, Serrano and Olozaga form provisional government (Oct. 5); universal suffrage, free press and education declared for (Oct. 26); various reactionary revolts suppressed.

**1869** Insurrection in Cuba; Serrano elected regent (June 15); Prim forms a ministry; Carlist risings suppressed; Republicans defeated at Taragona, Reuss and Saragossa.

**1870** Espartero declines the crown; ISABELLA abdicates in favor of her son ALFONSO; Prince Leopold accepted as king, but resigns; AMADEUS elected king by the Cortes (Nov. 16); Prim assassinated.

**1871** Serrano forms ministry (Jan. 5); Cortes dissolved (Nov. 25.)

**1872** Sagasta's ministry resigns; **Carlist War**; Serrano enters Navarre with 600,000 men; BATTLE OF OROQUITA; Carlists routed; attempted assassination of king and queen; Republican and Carlist risings suppressed.

**1873** **King Amadeus abdicates**; Republic proclaimed; Carlists defeated at various points; Don Carlos enters Spain (July 13); Cadiz yields to him (July 31); Castelar President of the Cortes; Carlist War continues.

**1874** Serrano forms new ministry; Carlists besiege Bilbao; Serrano takes command of army. **Battle of Irun**; Carlists routed. Prince Alfonso declared king by troops as Alfonso XII.

**1875** Alfonso enters Madrid; takes command of the army; VITTORIA taken from Carlists (July 9).

**1876** Bilbao taken (Feb. 5); Battle of Durango; Carlists defeated; surrender of Carlists at Pamplona (Feb. 26); flight of Don Carlos into France; Alfonso enters Madrid in triumph.

A.D.

**1877** General amnesty to Carlists. Isabella visits Spain.

**1878** Marriage of Alfonso to MERCEDES, daughter of the Duc de Montpensier (Jan. 23); death of Mercedes (June 26). Attempt to kill the King (Oct. 25.)

**1879** Great inundations in Granada, Seville and elsewhere. Alfonso XII. marries the Archduchess Maria Christina of Austria (Nov. 29); attempted assassination of King and Queen (Dec. 30).

**1880** Law for gradual abolition of slavery in Cuba (Feb. 18). Execution of the assassin Otero (April 14).

**1881** Calderon Centenary (May 23). Don Carlos expelled from France (July 17).

**1882** The Chamber of Deputies approves the Franco-Spanish Commercial Treaty (April 23). Bill introduced to abolish slavery in Cuba (June 10).

## ITALY.

A.D.

**1508** LEAGUE OF CAMBRAY against Venice.

**1515** Francis I. invades Italy; BATTLE OF MARIGNANO — Italians, Swiss and Germans defeated.

**1523** Italian league against Francis I.

**1525** **Battle of Pavia**; Francis I. defeated.

**1527** Death of MACHIAVELLI.

**1530** Charles V. conquers Italy.

**1627** War of the Mantuan Succession.

**1631** Treaty of Cherasco, between Louis XIII. of France and Victor Amadeus I. of Savoy.

**1642** Death of Galileo.

**1701** War with France about the Spanish succession.

**1706** The French raise the siege of Turin and surrender Naples and Lombardy.

**1713** Treaty between Spain and Savoy.

**1720** SARDINIA is made a kingdom.

**1748** Italian States assent to Treaty of Aix-la-Chapelle.

**1793** Naples declares war against France.

**1796** **Napoleon I. invades Italy.**

**1797** TREATY OF CAMPO FORMIO divides Venetian States between France and Austria. Cis-alpine Republic formed.

**1798** Second invasion by the French; Napoleon deposes Pius VI.

**1799** French in Italy defeated by Russians under Suwarrow.

**1800** Napoleon crosses the Alps; **Battle of Marengo** (June 24); Austrians totally defeated.

**1802** Cis-alpine Republic remodeled as the Italian Republic (Napoleon president).

**1805** Napoleon crowned King of Italy (May 26); Eugéne Beauharnois made viceroy.

**1806** TREATY OF PRESBURG; Austria loses Italian possessions.

**1814** Dissolution of the Kingdom of Italy; Lombardo-Venetian Kingdom established for Austria.

**1831** MAZZINI forms the "Young Italy Party;" insurrections inCentral Italy.

**1848** LOMBARDY and VENICE revolt against the Austrians. The Pope and the King of Sardinia support the revolution; Lombardy annexed to Sardinia (June 29).

**1849** BATTLE OF NOVARA; Austria defeats the Sardinians and regains Lombardy.

**1853** Revolt in Milan subdued.

**1856** Unsuccessful insurrection in Sicily.

**1859** Sardinia refuses to disarm; Austrians cross the Ticino; VICTOR EMANUEL declares war against Austria; revolutions at Florence and Parma. Napoleon III. assists Sardinia; **Battles of Montebello** (May 20), **Palestro** (May 30), **Magenta** (June 4), **Malegnano** (June 8), and **Solferino** (June 24); total defeat of Austria. Victor Emanuel proclaims annexation of Lombardy to Sardinia; Treaty of Villafranca (July 11); Tuscany protests, and declares for a united kingdom; GARIBALDI incites the people to arms; Tuscany, Modena, Parma and the Romagna enter into alliance (Oct. 10); Treaty of Zurich, by which the Pope was made head of an Italian confederation.

**1860** CAVOUR forms a ministry (Jan. 16); Parma, Modena, the Romagna and Tuscany vote for annexation to Sardinia: Savoy and Nice ceded to France; **Garibaldi lands in Sicily** (May 11); declares himself Dictator and defeats Neapolitans at Calatifimi and Melazzo (July 20); Sicily evacuated by Neapolitans; Garibaldi enters Naples (Sep. 7); insurrection in Papal States; Sardinians defeat Papal troops (Sept. 18); capture Ancano (Sept. 29); Garibaldi defeats Neapolitans at the VOLTURNO (Oct. 1); Sicily and Naples vote for annexation to Sardinia (Oct. 21); Victor Emanuel enters Naples as king (Nov. 7); GARIBALDI resigns DICTATORSHIP and retires to Caprera.

**1861** **Victor Emanuel declar d king of Italy** by the first Italian parliament (March 14); Cavour forms a ministry; death of Cavour (June 6). Rising of José Borges for Francis II. in Calabria; he is shot.

**1862** Ratazzi forms a ministry. Naples declared in a state of siege. Ratazzi resigns and Farina forms a ministry.

**1864** Elections favorable to "Moderates." Treaty with France for the evacuation of Rome; capital transferred from Turin to Florence.

**1865** Insurrection at Turin suppressed. Much trouble with brigands. New parliament meets at Florence.

**1866** Alliance with Prussia (May 12). **War declared against Austria** (June 18). Italians cross the Mincio (June 23); BATTLE OF CUSTOZZA (June 24); Italians defeated; Austria cedes Venetia to France (July 3); Italians defeated at Versa (July 26); Treaty of Vienna cedes Venetia to the Italian kingdom (Nov. 3); Victor Emanuel enters Venice (Nov. 7).

**1867** Ministry of Ratazzi. Insurrection in Papal States; Garibaldi arrested; French enter Rome; Garibaldi defeated at MENTANA; French leave Rome (Dec. 3).

**1868** Marriage of Crown Prince Humbert to Princess Margherita.

**1869** **Œcumenical Council at Rome.** Earthquake at Florence.

**1870** Dogma of Papal infallibility decreed by the Council. Mazzini arrested at Palermo. Italian army enters the Papal States and occupies Rome (Sept. 20); Papal States proclaimed part of the kingdom of Italy (Oct. 9); Pius IX. excommunicates the government (Nov. 1).

**1871** Capital transferred from Florence to Rome. Mont Cenis tunnel opened.

**1872** Death of MAZZINI. Great inundations. Eruption of Vesuvius.

**1873** Death of Manzoni and Ratazzi. Jesuits expelled by law.

**1874** Trouble with brigands and *Camorra* (secret societies for extortion).

**1875** GARIBALDI takes oath of allegiance to the king and enters chamber of deputies. Treaty of commerce with England. Six new cardinals created.

**1876** Launch of the iron-clad *Duilio*; elections give great majority for the Depretis ministry.

**1877** The celebrated "Antonelli case," brought by the Countess Lambertini, dismissed. Ministry resigns and is re-formed by Depretis.

**1878** **Death of Victor Emanuel** (Jan. 8). POPE PIUS IX. DIES (Feb. 7); Leo XIII. elected Pope (Feb. 20). Attempted assassination of King Humbert (Nov. 17).

**1880** Ministry of Cairoli. Elections give majority for Cairoli ministry. Launch of *Italia*, monster iron-clad. Garibaldi resigns his seat as deputy and goes to Genoa.

**1881** Cairoli ministry again resigns and Depretis forms a new ministry. Senate passes Reform Bill (Dec. 21).

**1882** Death of Garibaldi (June 2).

# RUSSIA.

A.D.

**1510** Tartars invade Russia.
**1521** Battle of Razan; Poland defeated.
**1530** Peace concluded with the Tartars.
**1541** Great invasion of Tartars repelled.
**1543** IVAN IV. (the Terrible) assumes the government at the age of fourteen.
**1545** Ivan IV. crowned by the patriarch.
**1552** Massacre of Cazan.
**1562** Russia and Sweden unite against Poland.
**1570** Ivan the Terrible massacres 25,000 people at Novgorod.
**1571** Moscow burned by the Tartars.
**1606** MATINS OF MOSCOW: Demetrius, a pretended son of Ivan, and many Poles are massacred.
**1613** **Accession of Romanoff Dynasty.**
**1618** LADISLAUS of Poland marches on Moscow.
**1656** Truce of Niemetz, or Wilma, with Poland.
**1668** Russian ambassadors sent to France and Spain.
**1678** War begins with the Turks.
**1686** Alliance between Russia and Poland against the Turks.
**1689** **Accession of Peter the Great.**
**1697** Peter I. visits Holland and England.
**1698** Revolt of the Strelitzes; they are slain by Peter.
**1700** Sweden defeats Russia. Peter builds the first Russian frigate.
**1703** Foundation of St. Petersburg.
**1706** Kamtschatka is subdued by Russia.
**1708** Revolt of MAZEPPA and the Cossacks.
**1709** Battle of POLTAVA; Peter defeats Charles XII. of Sweden.
**1710** War again begins with Turkey.
**1721** Peace of Nystadt with Sweden.
**1725** Death of PETER THE GREAT.
**1730** Death of Peter II.; extinction of the Romanoff dynasty. Anne becomes empress.
**1733** The Russians invade Poland.
**1739** **Treaty of Belgrade** between Russia, Austria and Turkey. Russia renounces her rights on the Black Sea.
**1741** War with Sweden. Ivan VI. deposed.
**1742** Elizabeth, daughter of Peter I., becomes empress.
**1757** Russia takes part in the Seven Years' War; invasion of PRUSSIA.
**1760** Russians and Austrians take BERLIN.
**1762** Treaty with Russia. Revolution at St. Petersburg; Peter III. deposed. Reign of CATHERINE THE GREAT.
**1764** Ivan VI. put to death in prison.
**1768** War declared against Russia by Turkey.
**1772** **First partition of Poland.**
**1778** Prince Potemkin becomes prime minister.
**1780** ARMED NEUTRALITY. Russia, Sweden and Denmark declare that "free ships make free goods."
**1787** War with Turkey renewed.
**1788** War with Sweden. Treaty of Werelow.
**1793** **Second Partition of Poland.** Alliance with England.
**1795** **Final Partition of Poland** between Russia, Prussia and Austria.
**1798** Russia, England and Austria coalesce against France.
**1799** SUWARROW assists Austrians in Italy. Russia forms an alliance with France.
**1801** **Assassination of Paul I.** Convention with England. Accession of Alexander I.
**1805** Russia joins the coalition against France. BATTLE OF AUSTERLITZ; allies defeated.
**1809** Battle of Silistria; victory of the Turks.
**1812** Invasion of Napoleon I.; BATTLES OF SMOLENSKO and BORODINO (Aug. 17); Russians defeated; **Moscow burned by the Russians** (Sept. 14); retreat of the French.
**1814** Alexander enters Paris with the Allies.
**1815** HOLY ALLIANCE between Russia, Austria and Prussia. Alexander proclaimed king of Poland.
**1822** Succession renounced by the Grand Duke Constantine.
**1825** Death of Alexander; accession of Nicholas I.; insurrection of troops at Moscow.
**1828** War with Persia and Turkey.
**1829** Peace of Adrianople with Turkey.
**1830** Insurrection in POLAND suppressed.
**1840** Expedition against Khiva fails. Treaty of London signed by Russia.
**1841** War with Circassians.
**1848** Russia aids Austria against the Hungarians.
**1849** Russia demands that Polish and Hungarian exiles be expelled from Turkey.
**1850** Exiles sent to Konish, Asia Minor.
**1853** Army sent to Turkish frontier; dispute about the Holy Places; origin of CRIMEAN WAR (*see also* TURKEY); conference of the Powers. War declared by Turkey (Oct. 5); English and French fleets enter the Bosphorus (Nov. 2).
**1854** Allies enter the Black Sea. Battle of Citate (Jan. 6). Russians defeated; ultimatum of England and France unanswered; treaty between France, England and Turkey (Mar. 12); bombardment of Odessa (Apr. 22); siege of Silistria (May 17); siege raised (June 26); Russia evacuates the principalities (Sept.); **Battle of the Alma** (Sept. 20); victory of the allies; **Siege of Sebastopol** begins (Oct. 17); BATTLE OF BALAKLAVA (Oct. 25); attack at INKERMAN (Nov. 5).
**1855** Death of NICHOLAS; accession of Alexander II. Sortie of Malakhoff tower (Mar. 22); Kars invested (July 15); Malakhoff taken by French; **Evacuation of Sebastopol**; Russian assault on Kars fails; Russians defeated by Turks at the Ingour (Nov. 6); Kars surrendered to Russians (Nov. 26).
**1856** Council of war at Paris (Jan. 11); armistice agreed upon (Feb. 25); **Treaty of Peace** (Mar. 30); CRIMEA evacuated (July 9). Amnesty to Poles.
**1857** Meeting of the emperors at Stutgardt and Weimar.
**1858** Partial emancipation of royal serfs.
**1859** Treaty with Great Britain.
**1860** Commercial treaty with China.
**1861** **Emancipation Decree**; 23,000,000 serfs to be freed within two years. Revolts in Poland. Student riots.
**1863** Insurrection in Poland suppressed. Serfdom ended.
**1864** War with Asiatic nations.
**1865** Death of the Czarowitch Nicholas. Province of Turkestan created.
**1866** Attempt to assassinate the Czar (Sept. 15); marriage of Prince Alexander.
**1867** Sale of ALASKA to UNITED STATES for $7,000,000; attempt to assassinate the Czar in Paris by a Pole.
**1868** Amnesty for political offenses.
**1869** SOCIALIST conspiracy among students.
**1870** Neutrality in Franco-Prussian war declared. Gortschakoff repudiates treaty of 1856 as regards the Black Sea.
**1871** Conference of the powers at London abrogates the Black Sea clauses. Many socialists imprisoned.
**1873** Expedition against KHIVA, which surrenders (June 10).
**1875** War with Khokand. Baltic provinces incorporated into the empire.
**1876** Sympathy and aid given to Servia and Bulgaria in their struggles with Turkey.
**1877** **Second Russo-Turkish War** (*see also* TURKEY). War declared (Apr. 24); Melikoff enters Armenia and seizes Bayazid (Apr. 30); Russians defeated at Batoum (May 4); Melikoff storms Ardahan (May 17); Kars invested (June 3); **Grand Duke Nicholas crosses the Danube** (June 27); Plevna occupied (July 6); **Plevna retaken by Turks** (July 30); great defeat of Russians by Mukhtar Pasha; terrible fighting at Schipka Pass (Aug. 20–27); assaults on Plevna, partly successful (Sept. 7–11); BATTLE OF ALADJA DAGH, great victory of Russians; **Kars taken by storm** (Nov. 18); with great slaughter; **Surrender of Plevna** (Dec. 10); ERZEROUM invested (Dec. 24); Gourko crosses the Balkans (Dec. 31).
**1878** Servians defeated (Jan. 7); Skobeleff and Radetzky capture Turkish army in Asia Minor; Russians attack Batoum without success; advance of Russians on Constantinople; ERZE-

A.D.

ROUM evacuated by Turks (Feb. 21); **Treaty of Peace signed at San Stefano** (Mar. 3). Conference of powers at Berlin (June 13); BERLIN TREATY signed (July 13).

**1879** Final treaty with Turkey signed (Feb. 8). Attempt to assassinate the Czar by Solovieff (Apr. 14); conviction of many Nihilists at Kieff and Odessa. Another attempt on the Czar's life by mining railway (Dec. 1); plot to blow up the Winter Palace discovered (Dec. 12).

**1880** Explosion under dining-room of Winter Palace, 11 soldiers killed, 47 wounded (Feb. 17); arrest of Hartmann at Paris (Feb. 20); Melikoff made virtual dictator (Feb. 24); extradition of Hartmann refused by France; many Nihilists convicted at St. Petersburg and Kieff.

**1881** **Assassination of Alexander II.** by bombs thrown at his carriage (Mar. 13); one assassin killed by explosion, another seized. **Accession of Alexander III.** (who has not been crowned up to present time (August, 1882), on account of fear of assassination). Trial of Nihilists (Apr. 8); Russakoff, Sophie Picoffsky, Jelaboff and others condemned to death. Treaty of peace with China. Resignation of Melikoff (May 13); manifesto of Ignatieff (May 23); counter - manifesto of Nihilists. New plots discovered (Nov.).

**1882** Retirement of Prince Gortschakoff; anti-Jewish riots; Pan-Slavist speech of Gen. Skobeleff at Paris; postponement of coronation of the Czar. Death of Gen. Skobeleff (July 6).

# AUSTRO-HUNGARIAN EMPIRE.

A.D.

**1453** Archduchy of Austria created by Emperor Frederick III.

**1515** Maximilian I. secures the Hungarian succession.

**1526** Ferdinand I. unites Bohemia and Hungary to Austria.

**1529** Austria overrun for many years by Turks.

**1556** Charles V. rules Austria, Bohemia and Hungary.

**1570** Hungary definitely annexed to Austria.

**1606** Treaty of Vienna gives liberty of worship to Protestants.

**1618** **Thirty Years' War** begins in Bohemia; Matthias II. of Hungary abdicates; accession of Ferdinand II.

**1620** BATTLE OF PRAGUE; Hungarian Protestants defeated.

**1625** Accession of Ferdinand III. of Hungary.

**1648** End of the Thirty Years' War between Catholics and Protestants.

**1658** Leopold I. is made king of Hungary.

**1683** SOBIESKI defeats the Turks before Vienna.

**1687** Hungarian crown declared to be in the Austrian male line. Accession of JOSEPH I.

**1695** Turks again invade Hungary.

**1699** TREATY OF CARLOWITZ, between Turkey and the Allies.

**1701** Austria enters war of Spanish Succession, which lasts thirteen years.

**1708** Mantua ceded to Joseph I.

**1712** Accession of CHARLES, as emperor.

**1713** TREATY OF UTRECHT gives the emperor Milan; the Netherlands and Naples added in 1714, 1715.

**1718** PEACE OF PASSAROWITZ increases Austrian dominions.

**1735** Naples and Sicily ceded to Spain.

**1737** Hungary again wars with the Turks.

**1740** Death of CHARLES VI. and accession of MARIA THERESA as empress of Germany and queen of Hungary.

**1741** SILESIAN WARS; Austria attacked by Prussia, France, Bavaria and Saxony, aided by England.

**1745** FRANCIS I., consort of Maria Theresa, elected emperor.

**1748** PEACE OF AIX-LA-CHAPELLE; Austria cedes Parma and Milan to Spain.

**1756** **Seven Years' War** begins. Frederick the Great invades Saxony and captures Saxon army.

**1757** Austria concludes treaty with France for division of Prussia. **Battle of Breslau** (Nov. 22); defeat of Prussians.

**1758** BATTLE OF HOCHKIRKEN; Frederick defeated.

**1759** Battles of Minden, Cunersdorf and Maxen; Prussians defeated.

**1760** The Austrians and allies enter BERLIN. Battle of TORGAU; Austrians defeated.

**1762** Battles of Freiberg and Burkersdorf; Frederick defeats the Austrians in Silesia.

**1763** **End of Seven Years' War.** Treaty of Hubertsburg. Silesia ceded to Prussia.

**1772** Galicia and other provinces acquired from Poland.

**1785** Vassalage abolished in Hungary.

**1792** **War with France** begins.

**1793** Battles of Neerwinden and Quesnoy; Austrians victorious.

**1794** French war continues with varying result.

**1795** Battle of Loano; Austrians defeated.

**1796** Severe defeats by Napoleon at Montenotte, LODI, Radstadt, Roreredo and elsewhere.

**1797** TREATY OF CAMPO FORMIO. Napoleon gives up Lombardy and receives VENICE.

**1799** Austria renews the war with some success, but is defeated at Zurich and Bergen.

**1800** BATTLES OF ENGEN (May 3), MONTEBELLO (June 9), MARENGO (June 14), HOCHSTADT (June 19), HOHENLINDEN (Dec. 3), and MINCIO; Napoleon defeats the Austrians in all.

**1801** TREATY OF LUNEVILLE; Austria loses more territory.

**1804** Francis II. of Germany becomes FRANCIS I. of Austria.

**1805** War against France declared by Francis. Ney defeats Austrians at Elchingen and Ulm. **Battle of Austerlitz**: complete defeat of Russians and Austrians.

**1806** **Treaty of Presburg**; Venice and the Tyrol ceded by Austria. Dissolution of the Germanic confederation; Francis abdicates.

**1809** Battle of Abensberg; French enter Vienna; Vienna restored (Oct. 24).

**1810** Marriage of MARIA LOUISA, daughter of Francis II. to Napoleon I.

**1814** Congress of sovereigns at Vienna.

**1815** **Treaty of Vienna**; Austria regains her Italian territory; Lombardo-Venetian empire established.

**1825** Hungarian Diet assembles.

**1835** Death of Francis I.; accession of FERDINAND I.

**1848** Insurrections at Vienna and in Italy; the emperor flees to Inspruck. **Revolution in Hungary**; imperial troops capture Raab and defeat Hungarians at Szikiszo and Mohr. Ferdinand abdicates in favor of FRANCIS JOSEPH.

**1849** War between Austria and Hungary; Hungarian independence declared (Apr. 14); KOSSUTH proclaimed governor; Hungarians defeated at SZEGEDIN; the revolution is suppressed. Execution of Count Bathyany.

**1853** Attempted assassination of the emperor.

**1854** Austria enters Danubian provinces.

**1856** Amnesty to Hungarian revolutionists.

**1857** The Danubian provinces are evacuated; trouble with Sardinia.

**1859** Diplomatic differences with France regarding Sardinia. Austrians cross the Ticino and enter Piedmont; **Napoleon III. declares war with Austria** (May 31); BATTLES OF MONTEBELLO (May 20); PALESTRO (May 30); **Magenta** (June 4); and MARIGNANO (June 8); Austrians defeated in all. **Battle of Solferino** (June 24); French victory. TREATY OF ZURICH (Nov. 10) gives Lombardy to Sardinia. (*See also* FRANCE AND ITALY.)

**1860** Reichsrath (imperial council) meets at Vienna; unsettled state of Hungary.

**1861** New constitution of the empire published; civil rights granted to Prot-

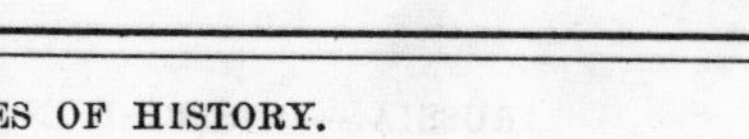

A.D.

estants, except in Hungary and Venice; Hungary protests and sends no deputies to Reichsrath.

1862 Great inundations. Amnesty to Hungarian revolutionists.

1863 Meeting of German sovereigns at Frankfort; federal constitution reformed.

1864 Austria assists Prussia against Denmark. Maximilian becomes emperor of MEXICO.

1865 Union of Hungary and Transylvania affirmed; the emperor visits Pesth; autonomy of Hungary asserted.

1866 **War with Prussia**, on the Holstein question; Austrians enter Silesia, and Prussians enter Bohemia: **Battle of Sadowa or Koniggrätz**; total defeat of Austrians under Count Benedek (July 3); Venetia ceded to France (July 4) and intervention asked for. TREATY OF PRAGUE (Aug. 23); Austria cedes Hanover, Hesse Cassel, Nassau and Frankfort to Prussia.

1867 Hungarian autonomy established; constitution of 1848 restored; ANDRASSY president of Hungarian Diet; emperor and empress of Austria crowned king and queen of Hungary at Buda.

1869 Insurrection in Dalmatia against conscription.

1870 Neutrality declared in Franco-Prussian war. Contest between national and federal parties.

1871 New German empire recognized by Austria. "Old Catholic" movement at Vienna. Struggle between German constitutionalists and Slavonian conservatives; resignation of Count Beust; Count Andrassy becomes minister of foreign affairs.

1872 New law in regard to elections passed.

A.D.

Meeting of the emperors at Berlin.

1873 **International Exhibition opened at Vienna** (May 1). Constitutionalists defeat the federalists in elections.

1874 Emperor visits Russia. The Pope condemns Austrian ecclesiastical laws. Death of Ferdinand, ex-emperor.

1876 Neutrality declared in Servian war.

1877 Neutrality declared in Russo-Turkish war.

1878 Austrian ministry resigns and withdraws resignation twice. Andrassy takes part in the Berlin conference, which permits Austria to occupy Bosnia and Herzegovina. War with BOSNIA ensues.

1879 Count Andrassy resigns; success of liberals in elections.

1881 Marriage of Archduke Rudolph and Princess Stephanie of Belgium.

## GERMANY.

A. D.

1517 **Era of the Reformation.**

1519 CHARLES V. of Spain elected emperor.

1521 MARTIN LUTHER excommunicated at the Diet of Worms.

1527 Germans storm Rome; Papal war.

1530 Confession of Augsburg published.

1536 John of Leyden slain at Munster.

1546 **Death of Martin Luther.**

1552 "Peace of Religion" at Passau.

1556 Charles V. abdicates and is succeeded by FERDINAND, his brother.

1564 Accession of Maximilian II.

1576 Accession of RUDOLPH II.

1612 MATTHIAS becomes emperor.

1618 **Thirty Years' War**, between the Protestants under the elector palatine and the Catholic Bavarian league. The elector of Brandenburg assumes the title of Duke of Prussia.

1619 Accession of Ferdinand II., king of Hungary.

1620 BATTLE OF PRAGUE (*see* AUSTRO-HUNGARIAN EMPIRE).

1630 GUSTAVUS-ADOLPHUS of Sweden invades Germany.

1632 Death of Gustavus at the batttle of LUTZEN, which he won.

1634 Assassination of WALLENSTEIN.

1648 **Treaty of Westphalia**, establishing religious tolerance. Pomerania and other territory annexed to Prussia.

1637 Accession of Frederick III.

1656 PRUSSIA declared independent of Poland.

1658 Accession of Leopold I.

1683 SOBIESKI of Poland raises the siege of Vienna.

1697 PEACE OF RYSWICK ends war with France.

1699 Peace of Carlowitz, between Turks and the emperor.

A.D.

1700 Leopold recognizes the Elector Frederick as King of Prussia.

1702 War with France.

1704 **Battle of Blenheim**; victory of Marlborough and his allies.

1705 JOSEPH I. becomes Emperor.

1711 Accession of CHARLES VI.

1713 PEACE OF UTRECHT signed by foreign powers.

1715 War between Prussia and Sweden.

1722 The PRAGMATIC SANCTION settles the succession.

1726 Prussia concludes a league with the empire.

1740 Accession of FREDERICK WILLIAM II. (the Great) of Prussia. Death of Charles VI.; accession of MARIA THERESA of Austria; Prussians enter Silesia.

1741 BATTLE OF MOLWITZ; Prussian victory.

1742 France supports the claim of the Elector of Bavari aas CHARLES VII. Glatz and Silesia ceded to Prussia.

1744 Friesland annexed to Prussia.

1745 FRANCIS I. elected Emperor.

1756 **Seven Years War** begins (*see* AUSTRIA *for details*).

1765 Joseph II. becomes Emperor.

1766 Lorraine ceded to France.

1769 Convention between Frederick of Prussia and Austria.

1772 Germany shares in the partition of Poland.

1788 War with Turkey.

1790 Accession of Leopold II.

1791 CONFERENCE OF PELNIZ between the Emperor and Frederick.

1792 Accession of FRANCIS II. of Austria.

1793 Rhenish provinces revolt. Prussians seize Dantzic and acquire Posen.

1795 Prussia obtains Warsaw in the partition of Poland.

A.D.

1795-1803 **War with France**; Germany loses the Netherlands, the Italian States, and territory west of the Rhine. TREATY OF LUNEVILLE (1801).

1797 Accession of FREDERICK WILLIAM III. of Prussia.

1801 Prussians seize Hanover.

1805 TREATY OF VIENNA; Napoleon establishes the kingdoms of WESTPHALIA, BAVARIA and WURTEMBURG; **Downfall of the German Empire.**

1806 **Confederation of the Rhine formed.** The Prussians seize Hanover; declare war with Napoleon (Sept. 24); **Battles of Auerstadt and Jena** (Oct. 14); French enter Berlin (Oct. 21).

1807 TREATY OF TILSIT between France and Prussia.

1808 Serfdom abolished in Prussia.

1810 North Germany annexed to France.

1812 Prussia concludes an alliance with France and Austria.

1813 The French evacuate Berlin (March 4). War declared against France (March 16); Napoleon invades Silesia (May 31); BATTLE OF KATZBACH (Aug. 16); Blücher defeats Ney; **Battle of Leipsic** (Oct. 16); the allies completely defeat Napoleon.

1814 The allies invade France; Battles of Brienne, Creon, and Laon.

1815 CONGRESS OF VIENNA. **Germanic Confederation formed**, including Prussia, Austria, Bavaria, Saxony, Hanover, Würtemberg, Baden, Hesse, Holstein, Luxemburg, and smaller powers. Prussia enters the HOLY ALLIANCE with Russia and Austria.

1817 Insurrection in Breslau suppressed.

1818 Formation of the Prussian Zollverein (commercial union).

A.D.

**1819** Congress of Carlsbad (anti-revolutionary).

**1830** Revolution at Brunswick; flight of the Duke. Abdication of the King of Saxony.

**1832 Death of the poet Goethe.**

**1833** Other states join the Zollverein.

**1834** Thuringia and Saxony join the Zollverein.

**1840** Accession of FREDERICK WILLIAM IV. of Prussia.

**1844** Disputes about the "Holy Coat" of Treves. Attempt to assassinate the King of Prussia.

**1848** Insurrection in Berlin; revolts in Schleswig, Holstein, and throughout Germany. German National Assembly meets at Frankfort.

**1849** King of Prussia elected Emperor by the Assembly (March 28); he declines (April 3); Frankfort Assembly moves to Stuttgart; Austria protests against alliance of Prussia and smaller states.

**1850** TREATY OF MUNICH, between Bavaria, Saxony and Würtemberg (Feb. 27); Parliament at Erfurt; the German Confederation assembles at Frankfort (Sept. 2). Forces of Austria, Bavaria and Prussia enter Hesse-Cassel (Nov. 12); attempt to assassinate the King of Prussia (May 22).

**1851** Diet of Germanic Confederation at Frankfort.

**1853** Revolutionary plot discovered in Berlin.

**1854** Prussia enters into treaty with Austria.

**1856** Prussia takes part in Paris Conference (*see* RUSSIA). Crown-Prince becomes Regent in Prussia.

**1858** Marriage of Prince Frederick William (son of Crown-Prince) to the Princess Royal of England.

**1859** Prussia invited to take the initiative in a national movement; declines.

**1860** Federal Diet maintains Hesse-Cassel Constitution against Prussia. Holstein-Schleswig dispute with Denmark.

**1861** Death of Frederick William IV.; accession of Crown-Prince as WILLIAM I.; National Association meets at Heidelberg; attempt to assassinate the King of Prussia.

**1862** The National Assembly at Berlin declares in favor of unification. **Bismarck** becomes Minister.

**1863** William I. closes the Lower House for the second time. German States (outside of Prussia) meet at Frankfort, and approve a plan of federal reform. Prussian decree against the freedom of the press. The Crown Prince protests; decree recalled; The Schleswig-Holstein rights maintained by Germany.

**1864** Prussia invades Holstein; Prussian ports blockaded by Denmark; peace restored (Oct. 30).

**1865** The Diet calls on Prussia and Austria to give up Holstein; they refuse. Prussian treaty with Belgium. Bismarck visits Napoleon III. at Paris.

**1866** The Diet calls on Prussia and Austria to disarm; they refuse. Attempt on Bismarck's life (May 7); Prussians invade Holstein (June 7) and Saxony (June 15); **War with Austria**, supported by the Diet. (*For particulars see* AUSTRIA.) Peace with Würtemberg (Aug. 13), with Bavaria (Aug. 22), with Austria (Aug. 23); treaty of Prussia and Hesse-Darmstadt (Sept. 15); Frankfort, Hanover, Hesse-Cassel, and Nassau annexed to Prussia (Sept. 20). **North German Confederation formed** (Aug. 18). Schleswig-Holstein incorporated with Prussia (Dec. 24).

**1867** North German Constitution settled Feb. 9). Extraordinary session of Prussian Diet (April 29). Deputies from Bavaria, Würtemberg, Baden, and Hesse-Darmstadt declare union with North Germany necessary. First meeting of new North German Parliament.

**1868** South German Military Commission appointed. Prussia passes the Rhine Navigation Treaty.

**1870 France declares war against Prussia** (July 15). (*For details of* FRANCO-PRUSSIAN WAR *see* FRANCE). Bavaria, Würtemberg, Hesse-Darmstadt, and Baden support Prussia in the war. Munich, Stuttgart, and other cities declare for union with North Germany. Baden and Hesse-Darmstadt join the North German Confederation (Nov. 15), Würtemberg (Nov. 25), Bavaria (Nov. 23). North German Parliament opens at Berlin (Nov. 24). By a vote of 188 to 6 the Parliament asks the King of Prussia to become Emperor of Germany (Dec. 10).

**1871 German Empire re-established** (Jan. 1); William I. of Prussia declared Emperor at VERSAILLES (Jan. 18). Preliminaries of peace with France signed at Versailles (Feb. 26). First Reichstag opened (March 21). PRINCE BISMARCK becomes Chancellor (May 12). **Treaty of Peace ratified** (May 16). Triumphal entry of victorious troops into Berlin (June 16). German Parliament opened by the Emperor (Oct. 16).

**1872** Bill for expulsion of Jesuits passed (July 5). Meeting of the Emperors of Germany, Russia, and Austria at Berlin (Sept. 6). Bismarck resigns the premiership of Prussia.

**1873** TREATY WITH FRANCE for payment of indemnity and evacuation of territory (March 15). Last payment of indemnity (Sept. 5). Monetary Reform Law passed (June 23).

**1874** National Liberals successful in elections (Jan. 10). Attempt to assassinate Bismarck (July 13). Arrest of Count Arnim (Oct. 4); released (Oct. 28). Bismarck resigns chancellorship (Dec. 16); withdraws resignation on receiving vote of confidence. Count Arnim convicted of tampering with official papers.

**1875** Civil Marriage Bill passed (Jan. 25). Religious agitation in Prussia; Government aid withdrawn from Catholic clergy.

**1876** Inundations in Prussia. The Czar visits Berlin.

**1877** Code of laws enacted (March 21). Bismarck resigns as Chancellor (April 3); withdraws resignation (April 8).

**1878** Attempted assassination of the Emperor by Hödel, a Socialist (May 11) Bill to repress Socialism rejected (May 24). Attempt to assassinate the Emperor by Dr. Karl Nobiling (June 2); the Emperor wounded; the Crown Prince takes charge of the empire. Death of King George of Hanover (June 12). BERLIN CONFERENCE (June-July); (*see* RUSSIA and TURKEY). Hödel executed (Aug. 16). Nobiling commits suicide (Sept. 10). Conservatives gain in the elections; Liberal majority. Many newspapers and clubs suppressed.

**1879** Bismarck's Protectionist Bill adopted (May 9). Falk and other ministers resign (June 30). Meeting of Bismarck and Andrassy at Vienna (Sept.). Code of 1877 goes into operation (Nov.).

**1880** Small states outvote Prussia, Saxony, and Bavaria on stamp duties; Bismarck resigns and the states yield. "New Liberal" Party formed (Aug.).

**1881** German Reichstag opened (Feb. 16). October elections for Reichstag favorable to the Liberals.

**1882** Imperial rescript of Jan. 4 asserts extreme rights of the Emperor, and slight constitutional restraints. Rescript modified by explanation.

## FRANCE.

A.D.

**1508** LEAGUE OF CAMBRAY, between Louis XII. and Maximilian against Venice.

**1511** Pope Julius II. forms the HOLY LEAGUE with Venice and Ferdinand.

**1513** English invasion; battle of Guinegate or Spurs.

**1520** "Field of the Cloth of Gold:" meeting of Francis I. with HENRY VIII. of England.

**1525 Battle of Pavia**; defeat and capture of Francis I.

**1529** Peace of Cambria, between Francis I. and Charles V.

**1532** France annexes Brittany.

A.D.

**1544** Invasion of English under Henry VIII.
**1546** Peace concluded with England.
**1558** CALAIS taken by the Duke of Guise.
**1560** Accession of CHARLES IX.; regency of CATHERINE DE MEDICI.
**1562** Vassy massacre of Protestants; defeat of Huguenots at Dreux by Guise.
**1563** Siege of Orléans; Guise killed; temporary peace.
**1567** Battle of St. Denis; Huguenots defeated.
**1572** **Massacre of St. Bartholomew.**
**1574** Accession of HENRY III., last of the Valois.
**1585** Henry III. killed by the friar Jacques Clement; accession of HENRY IV., of NAVARRE, first of Bourbon line.
**1588** Assassination of the Duke of Guise and his brother.
**1590** **Battle of Ivry**; Henry IV. defeats the League.
**1593** Henry adopts the Catholic religion.
**1598** EDICT OF NANTES in favor of Protestants.
**1610** Henry IV. assassinated by Ravaillac; accession of LOUIS XIII.; regency of Marie de Medici.
**1620** France annexes Navarre.
**1624** **Administration of Richelieu.**
**1628** SIEGE OF ROCHELLE; Richelieu reduces the place.
**1642** Death of Richelieu.
**1643** Accession of LOUIS XIV., THE GREAT; regency of Anne of Austria; ascendancy of MAZARIN.
**1648** Civil wars of the FRONDE.
**1661** Death of Mazarin; Colbert Minister of Finance.
**1664** War begins with HOLLAND (*which see*).
**1678** Peace of Nimeguen.
**1685** **Revocation of Edict of Nantes.**
**1697** Peace of Ryswick, with England and Holland.
**1701** War of the Spanish Succession (*see* SPAIN *and* AUSTRIA).
**1704** BATTLE OF BLENHEIM; French defeated by Marlborough.
**1706** Battle of Ramillies; defeat of French.
**1713** TREATY OF UTRECHT, between France, England, and the other powers.
**1715** Death of LOUIS THE GREAT; accession of LOUIS XV., his grandson.
**1720** Law's Mississippi scheme collapses.
**1743** BATTLE OF DETTINGEN; English drive back French.
**1748** Peace of Aix-la-Chapelle, between the great powers.
**1756** Beginning of Seven Years War (*see* AUSTRIA).
**1757** Damiens attempts to kill Louis IV.
**1763** Peace of Paris cedes Canada to England.
**1769** Power of Madame du Barry begins.
**1770** Marriage of the Dauphine to MARIE ANTOINETTE of Austria.
**1774** Death of Louis XV.; accession of LOUIS XVI.
**1776** Turgot dismissed from office.
**1777** NECKER becomes Minister of Finance.
**1778** France declares war against England in aid of the American colonies.

A.D.

**1781** Resignation of Necker.
**1783** TREATY OF VERSAILLES; peace with England and Spain.
**1785** "Diamond necklace affair" creates great excitement.
**1787** Assembly of Notables. Dispute about taxes.
**1788** Second Assembly; Necker recalled.
**1789** **The French Revolution.** States-General meet and declare themselves the National Assembly. **Overthrow of the Bastile** (July 14); mob at Versailles compel King and Queen to go to Paris (Oct. 6); Assembly meets at Paris (Oct. 9); confiscation of clerical property (Nov. 2); France divided into 83 departments (Dec. 22).
**1790** Louis accepts the revolution (Feb. 4); *lettres de cachet*, titles of honor, and hereditary nobility abolished; *fête* in the Champ de Mars (July 14); flight of Necker.
**1791** Death of MIRABEAU (April 2). Escape of the royal family from Paris (June 20); arrest at Varrennes (June 21). Imprisonment of Louis and the Queen in the Tuileries. Louis assents to the National Constitution (Sept. 15). National Assembly dissolves, (Sept. 29), and Legislative Assembly meets (Oct. 1).
**1792** War with Austria declared (April 20); Tuileries mobbed (June 20); **Tuileries captured by mob.** Swiss guards murdered; royal family imprisoned in the Temple (Aug. 10); massacre of prisoners (Sept. 2-5); royalty abolished by National Convention (Sept. 21) and FRENCH REPUBLIC declared. Debate on trial of the King (Nov. 12—Dec. 3).
**1793** **Execution of Louis XVI.** (Jan. 21). War declared with Spain, Holland, and England (Feb. 1). Insurrection in the Vendée. Robespierre becomes Dictator (March 25). **Reign of Terror begins** (May). MARAT assassinated by CHARLOTTE CORDAY (July 13). Siege of Toulon; first victory of Napoleon Bonaparte. **Execution of Marie Antoinette** (Oct. 16). Execution of the DUKE OF ORLEANS (Philip Egalité); of MADAME ROLAND (Nov. 8). Vendée revolt suppressed (Dec. 12).
**1794** DANTON guillotined (April 5); Madame Elizabeth, sister of Louis, executed. Robespierre becomes President (June); festival of "God of Nature" (June 7). **Fall of Robespierre** (July 27); execution of Robespierre, St. Just, and 70 others; end of Reign of Terror.
**1795** Death of Louis XVII. in prison; Bonaparte suppresses royalist rebellion (Oct. 5); establishment of the DIRECTORY (Oct. 28).
**1796** Campaign of Napoleon in ITALY. Battles of Montenotte (April 12), Mondovi (April 22), LODI (May 10), Attenkirchen (June 1), Radstadt (July 5), Roveredo (Sept. 4), ARCOLA (Nov. 14-17) and others; French victorious everywhere.

A.D.

**1797** Babœuf's conspiracy fails. Napoleon returns to Paris.
**1798** Napoleon embarks in the Egyptian expedition (*see* EGYPT). BATTLE OF THE PYRAMIDS (July 13-21); defeat at the NILE by NELSON (Aug. 1).
**1799** Coalition between England, Germany, Russia, Turkey, Portugal, and Naples against Napoleon (June 22); Directory dissolved (Nov. 10); Napoleon elected First Consul (Dec. 13).
**1800** **Battle of Marengo** (June 14); total defeat of Austrians. Attempt to assassinate Napoleon by infernal machine (Dec. 24).
**1801** Treaty of Luneville, with Germany; the Rhine made French boundary. Peace with Russia (Oct. 8), with Turkey (Oct. 9) Defeat at ABOUKIR (March 8).
**1802** TREATY OF AMIENS, with England, Spain and Holland (May 27). Napoleon made Consul for life (Aug. 2).
**1803** War with England declared (May 22).
**1804** George's conspiracy against Napoleon fails. Execution of the DUC D'ENGHIEN March 21). **Napoleon proclaimed Emperor** (May 18); crowned by the Pope (Dec. 2).
**1805** Napoleon crowned King of Italy (May 26). Annexation of Genoa (June 4). Coalition of Russia, England, Prussia and Saxony against Napoleon. Germany invaded (Sept. 26). BATTLE OF TRAFALGAR; great victory of NELSON (Oct. 21). **Battle of Austerlitz** (Dec. 2); total defeat of Austrians and Russians. TREATY OF PRESBURG (Dec. 26.)
**1806** Confederation of the Rhine ratified at Paris (July 12). Fourth coalition against France (same powers as before); Prussia declares war (Oct. 8); **Battle of Jena**; defeat of the Prussian army (Oct. 14); capture of Erfurt (Oct. 15).
**1807** **Battle of Eylau**; Russians defeated (Feb. 8); Napoleon meets Alexander at Tilsit (June 26); peace signed (July 7); publication of MILAN DECREE (Dec. 17).
**1808** Abdication of Charles IV. of Spain; Peninsular War begins (*see* SPAIN).
**1809** Coalition of England and Austria against France. Napoleon enters Vienna (May). TREATY OF VIENNA (Oct. 14). Divorce of JOSEPHINE (Dec. 15).
**1810** Napoleon marries Maria Louise of Austria (April 1). Holland annexed to France.
**1811** Birth of the King of Rome, afterwards Napoleon II.
**1812** **War declared with Russia** (*see also* RUSSIA); battle of BORODINO (Sept. 7); retreat from Moscow (Oct.).
**1813** The Concordat (treaty with the Pope).

A.D.

Alliance of Austria, Russia and Prussia against France (March 16); Wellington enters France (Oct. 7).

**1814** Surrender of Paris to the Allies (March 30). **Abdication of Napoleon I.** in favor of his son. Bourbon dynasty restored; LOUIS XVIII. arrives in Paris. Napoleon I. at Elba (May 4). Constitutional Charter decreed (June).

**1815** **Return of Napoleon from Elba;** he lands at Cannes (March 1); alliance of England, Austria, Prussia and Russia (March 15); Louis XVIII. leaves Paris; restoration of the Empire. Napoleon invades Belgium (June 15); **Battle of Waterloo** (June 18); final defeat of Napoleon by English under WELLINGTON and Prussians under BLUCHER; Louis XVIII. returns (July 6); Napoleon sent to ST. HELENA (Aug. 8); execution of Marshal Ney (Dec. 7).

**1816** Decree of Amnesty excludes the Bonapartes from the throne forever.

**1820** Assassination of the Duc de Berri.

**1821** Death of Napoleon at St. Helena.

**1824** Death of Louis XVIII.; accession of CHARLES X.

**1830** Chamber of Deputies dissolved (May 16). Algiers taken (July 5). Ordinances passed regarding the election of deputies and the press (July 26); very unpopular. Revolution of 1830 begins with street barricades (July 27); **Charles X. abdicates** (July 31); the DUKE OF ORLEANS becomes LOUIS PHILLIPE I.

**1831** Riots in Paris (Feb. 14 and 15).

**1832** Death of Napoleon's son, the Duke of Reichstadt (July 22). Attempt on the King's life (Dec. 27).

**1835** Fieschi's infernal machine plot.

**1836** Failure of LOUIS NAPOLEON'S Strasburg insurrection.

**1838** Death of TALLEYRAND. War with Mexico (q. v.).

**1839** Insurrections in Paris.

**1840** Louis Napoleon makes another attempt at Boulogne (Aug. 6); fails and is imprisoned. Attempt on the King's life by Darmés. Reinterment of Napoleon I. in the Hôtel des Invalides (Dec. 15).

**1842** Death of the Duke of Orleans.

**1846** Lecompte's attempt on the King's life (April 16). **Louis Napoleon escapes from Ham** (May 25). Henri attempts to kill the King (July 29).

**1847** Surrender of Abd-el-Kader to the French.

**1848** "Reform banquet" prohibited; dissatisfaction culminates in revolution; barricades thrown up (Feb. 22); **abdication of Louis XVIII.** (Feb. 24); Republic proclaimed (Feb. 26); Louis Napoleon elected to National Assembly (June 13); insurrection of extreme Republicans in Paris (June 23); Paris in a state of siege (June 25); surrender of insurgents (June 26). Napoleon proclaimed President-elect of the French Republic (Dec. 20).

**1850** Death of Louis Phillippe at Claremont.

**1851** (The) ***Coup d'état*** (Dec. 2); Napoleon dissolves the Assembly, proclaims universal suffrage, calls for election of president for ten years, and declares Paris in a state of siege; THIERS and others arrested; 180 members of Assembly arrested; resistance in streets put down with great loss of life (Dec. 3–4); elections for president (Dec. 21–22); affirmative votes, 7,473,431; negative, 644,351.

**1852** Napoleon installed as Prince-President (Jan. 1); banishment of 83 members of Assembly and transportation of 575 persons for resisting *coup d'état*; the Senate asks Napoleon to assume the title of Emperor (Nov. 7); vote on the subject (Nov. 21–22); ayes, 7,864,189; noes, 253,145. **Louis proclaimed as Napoleon III.** (Dec. 2).

**1853** Marriage of Louis Napoleon to EUGÉNIE DE MONTIGO; pardon of 8,000 political offenders; plot to assassinate the Emperor.

**1854** TREATY OF CONSTANTINOPLE (March 12). **War declared with Russia** (March 27). (*For details of* CRIMEAN WAR *see* RUSSIA, TURKEY, *and* GREAT BRITAIN).

**1855** Opening of Paris Exposition. Two attempts on the Emperor's life.

**1856** Birth of the Prince Imperial (March 16). Peace with Russia (March 30).

**1857** Archbishop of Paris assassinated (Jan. 3). Conference on Neuchatel difficulty (March 15).

**1858** ORSINI'S attempt to assassinate the Emperor (Jan. 4); trial of the Count de Montalembert.

**1859** **France declares war with Austria** (*see* AUSTRIA *and* ITALY); MAGENTA (June 4); SOLFERINO (June 24); treaty of ZURICH (Nov. 10).

**1860** France demands the cession of Savoy and Nice.

**1861** Sardinian boundary treaty (March 7). Intervention in Mexico (*which see*).

**1863** Election of Thiers, Favre, Ollivier, and others in opposition to the Government.

**1864** Death of Marshal Pelissier, Duke of Malakoff. France agrees to evacuate Rome (Sept. 15).

**1865** Death of Proudhon, Morny, and Magnan.

**1866** Congress at Paris on Roumanian affairs.

**1867** **International Exhibition opened** (April 1); visit of many crowned heads; attempt to assassinate the Emperor of Russia (June 6).

**1868** Treaties with Italy, Prussia, and Mecklenburg.

**1869** Death of Lamartine (Feb. 28). Election riots at Paris (June 11); new constitution promulgated (Sept. 10); resignation of ministers (Dec. 27).

**1870** Prince Pierre Bonaparte shoots Victor Noir (Jan. 10); tried and acquitted (March 26); riots in Paris (Feb. 8–9); plots against the Emperor's life discovered; plebiscite on change of constitution (May 8); vote affirmative; nomination of Leopold for the Spanish throne creates warlike feeling; Leopold withdraws. France requires guarantees from Prussia; refused; **war declared by France against Prussia** (July 15); English mediation refused (July 20); Prussians blow up bridge of Kehl; engagements at SAARBRUCK (Aug. 2–4); alternate success; **Battle of Woerth** (Aug. 6); defeat of the French; Forbach taken by Germans (Aug. 6); STRASBURG invested (Aug. 10); battle of Courcelles (Aug. 14); Prussians take NANCY; **Battle of Gravelotte** (Aug. 18); defeat of French; METZ invested (Aug. 24); Battle of VERDUN, Germans repulsed (Aug. 25); **Battle of Sedan**, great victory of the Prussians (Sept. 1); surrender of Napoleon and the army (Sept. 2); Paris invested (Sept. 19); Strasburg surrenders (Sept. 27); Metz capitulates (Oct. 27); general success of the Germans; defeat of the Army of the North (Dec. 23).

**1871** Rocroy taken (Jan. 6); Alençon (Jan. 17); King of Prussia proclaimed Emperor of Germany at Versailles (Jan. 18); last sortie from Paris (Jan. 19); **peace signed** (Feb. 27); France agrees to give up Alsace (except Belfort), a fifth of Lorraine, with Metz and Thionville, and to pay five milliards of francs. Prussians enter Paris (March 1). National Assembly deposes the Bonapartes; Versailles evacuated (March 12). **Outbreak of the Commune** (March 18); Paris taken by storm (May 28). THIERS elected President of the FRENCH REPUBLIC (Aug. 31).

**1872** Death of the Duke de Persigny (Jan. 12). Commercial treaty with Belgium and England abrogated (Feb. 2).

**1873** **Death of Napoleon III.** at Chiselhurst (Jan. 9). New treaty of evacuation signed with Germany (March 15). Thiers resigns (May 24); MCMAHON becomes President (May 25); war indemnity paid in full (Sept. 5); Germans leave Verdun (Sept. 13); presidential term fixed at seven years (Nov. 19): BAZAINE condemned to death for having surrendered Metz (Dec. 10); sentence commuted to twenty years imprisonment (Dec. 12).

**1874** Execution of Communists. Escape of Bazaine (Aug. 11).

**1875** Ministry resigns (Jan. 6). New constitution adopted (Jan. 29). M. Buffet forms a ministry (March 12). Pilgrimage of Paray-le-Monial. Great inundations. Amended constitution adopted (July 16).

A.D.

**1876** Elections for Senate and Deputies; Buffet replaced by Dufaure; Amnesty for Communists (June 28); Dufaure resigns; Jules Simon forms a ministry.

**1877** Resignation of the Jules Simon ministry (May 17); the Duc de Broglie forms new ministry; President McMahon dissolves the Chamber of Deputies (June 25); prosecution of Gambetta (Aug. 25); DEATH OF THIERS (Sept. 8); General elections (Oct. 14); great Republican majorities; Dufaure forms a ministry (Dec. 13).

**1878** International Exhibition opened at Paris (May 1); The COMTE DE CHAMBORD (Henry V.) writes a letter asserting his "divine right."

**1879** **McMahon resigns** (Jan. 28); Jules Grevy elected President by the Senate (Jan. 30); Gambetta becomes President of the Chamber; new ministry formed by Waddington (Feb. 1); Communist amnesty bill passed (Feb. 21); M. Ferry introduces education bills to abolish Jesuit colleges; **Prince Louis Napoleon killed** in Zululand (June 1); Waddington ministry resigns (Dec. 21); M. De Freycinet forms new ministry.

**1880** Death of Duc de Gramont and Jules Favre; Ferry's education bills rejected (March 9); decree dissolves Jesuit and other orders in France; many protest; expulsion carried out (June 30); general amnesty bill passed (July 3); Jules Ferry forms new ministry (Sept. 20).

**1881** Municipal elections favor the Government; loan of 40,000,000*l*. taken up three times over; discussion on *scrutin de liste* (March 21); **invasion of Tunis** (April); treaty signed with the Bey (May 12) gives France virtual suzerainty; excitement in Italy; treaty ratified by the Senate (May 23); reception of Gambetta at Cahors (May 25); *scrutin de liste* rejected (May 9); elections give large Republican gains (Sept.); French troops enter Tunis (Oct. 10); Ferry cabinet resigns (Nov. 10); Gambetta becomes Premier.

**1882** In Senate the Republicans gain 22 seats (Jan. 8); *scrutin de liste* rejected (Jan. 26); Gambetta's ministry resign (Jan. 30); Freycinet forms a ministry: resigns (July 29), on rejection of vote of credit to protect Suez Canal; Duclerc forms a ministry (Aug. 7).

## GREAT BRITAIN AND IRELAND.

A.D.

**1509** Accession of HENRY VIII.; he marries Catherine of Aragon.

**1510** Execution of Dudley and Empson.

**1513** JAMES IV. of Scotland invades England; **Battle of Flodden Field**; Scots defeated.

**1520** "Field of the Cloth of Gold" (*see* FRANCE).

**1529** Fall of CARDINAL WOLSEY.

**1533** Henry VIII. marries ANNE BOLEYN; Cranmer declares former marriage void.

**1534** Rebellion of Fitzgerald in Ireland. Papal supremacy denied in England.

**1535** Execution of Sir Thomas More.

**1536** Anne Boleyn executed (May 19); Henry marries LADY JANE SEYMOUR (May 20).

**1537** Death of Lady Jane Seymour.

**1538** Henry suppresses the monasteries.

**1540** Henry marries ANNE of Cleves (Jan. 6); divorced (July 9); marries CATHERINE HOWARD (Aug. 8); Execution of CROMWELL; James V. of Scotland dies; MARY proclaimed Queen of Scots; regency of Cardinal Beaton.

**1542** Catherine Howard executed; Henry VIII. takes the title of King of Ireland.

**1543** Henry marries CATHERINE PARR.

**1546** Assassination of Cardinal Beaton, Regent of Scotland.

**1547** Execution of the Earl of Surrey (Jan. 19); Death of Henry VIII.; accession of EDWARD VI., under protectorship of the Duke of Somerset.

**1549** Execution of Lord Seymour; arrest of his brother, the Duke of Somerset.

**1552** Execution of the Duke of Somerset.

**1553** Death of Edward VI.; LADY JANE GREY proclaimed Queen (July 10); she relinquishes the title; MARY (daughter of Catherine of Aragon) proclaimed.

**1554** Wyatt's insurrection suppressed; Execution of Lady Jane Grey and Lord Guilford Dudley (Feb. 12); Queen Mary marries Philip II. of Spain.

**1555** John Rodgers burnt at the stake (Feb. 4); RIDLEY and LATIMER burnt (Oct. 16).

**1556** Continued persecution of Protestants; burning of CRANMER (Oct. 16).

**1558** CALAIS lost to England; Mary of Scotland marries the Dauphine; **accession of Elizabeth** (Nov. 17). Knox's Scotch reformation (1550-1560).

**1559** Act of Uniformity restores Protestant religion.

**1565** Mary, Queen of Scots, marries Lord Darnley.

**1566** MURDER OF RIZZIO by Darnley (March 9).

**1567** Assassination of Darnley (Feb. 10); Mary accused of connivance; Mary marries Bothwell (May 15); abdicates in favor of her son, JAMES VI.; Earl of Murray regent.

**1568** Mary escapes from prison; defeated by Murray at Langside (May 13); seeks shelter in England.

**1570** Regent Murray murdered; Lennox becomes regent.

**1571** Lennox murdered; Mar becomes regent.

**1579** Fitzgerald's Irish rebellion suppressed.

**1580** Lord Grey and Admiral Winter take fortress of Smerwick in Ireland from Italians, and butcher 700 prisoners.

**1581** Campian's Jesuit conspiracy suppressed.

**1587** **Execution of Mary, Queen of Scots**, at Fotheringay Castle.

**1588** **Spanish Armada repulsed** see SPAIN).

**1598** Irish rebellion of O'Neil or Tyrone; English defeated at Blackwater.

**1601** Execution of the Earl of Essex (Feb. 25).

**1603** Death of QUEEN ELIZABETH; accession of James VI. of Scotland as JAMES I. of Great Britain; **union of Scotland and England.**

**1605** Discovery of the Gunpowder Plot (Nov. 6) of Guy Fawkes, Catesby, Digby, and others to blow up king, lords, and commons.

**1609** James drives Irish from Ulster and divides the land among English and Scotch.

**1611** Title of baronet created by James I.

**1616** **Death of William Shakespeare.**

**1618** Sir Walter Raleigh executed.

**1621** Impeachment of LORD BACON.

**1625** Accession of CHARLES I.; he marries Princess Henrietta Maria of France.

**1628** Duke of Buckingham assassinated by John Felton.

**1637** Trial of JOHN HAMPDEN for resisting ship money levy.

**1638** SOLEMN LEAGUE AND COVENANT subscribed in Scotland.

**1639** Pacification of Dunse; Charles I. withdraws army from Scotland.

**1641** **Earl of Stafford beheaded**; Judgment against Hampden annulled; Ulster rebellion in Ireland.

**1642** Charles attempts to seize members in the House; **outbreak of the Civil War**; Battle of Edgehill (Oct. 23).

**1643** Battles of Chalgrove (June 18) and Newbury (Sept. 20); covenant approved by Parliament.

**1644** **Battle of Marston Moor**; victory of CROMWELL; second battle of Newbury (Oct. 27).

**1645** Archbishop Laud beheaded (Jan. 10); **Battle of Naseby** (June 14); decisive defeat of Royalists; Battle of Philiphaugh; Montrose defeated by the Covenanters.

**1646** Charles I. seeks refuge in Scotland; is given up to the Parliament.

**1649** Trial of the king; sentenced (Jan 27); **execution of Charles I.** (Jan. 30); massacre and capture of Drog-

A.D.

HEDA (Ireland) by Cromwell (Sept. 11).

**1650** Marquis of Montrose beheaded in Scotland.

**1651** CHARLES II. crowned at Scone, Scotland (Jan. 1); **Battle of Worcester** (Sept. 3); defeat of Royalists; Charles escapes to France.

**1653** LONG PARLIAMENT dissolved by Cromwell (April 20); he becomes Lord Protector (Dec. 16).

**1657** Convention gives Cromwell power to appoint his successor; Death of Admiral Blake.

**1658** **Death of Oliver Cromwell** (Sept. 13); Richard Cromwell succeeds him.

**1659** Richard resigns title of Lord Protector.

**1660** **The Restoration**; CHARLES II. returns to England.

**1661** Execution of Marquis of Argyle in Scotland.

**1662** Act of Uniformity (May 19); Charles marries Catherine of Bragança (May 20).

**1665** The Great Plague in London.

**1666** The Great London Fire.

**1674** Death of the poet JOHN MILTON.

**1678** Titus Oates alarms the country by stories of a false "popish plot." Sir Edmond Berry Godfrey found murdered.

**1679** HABEAS CORPUS ACT passed (31 Charles II., C. 2); Archbishop Sharpe murdered by Covenanters, who defeat Claverhouse at London Hill, but are routed at BOTHWELL BRIDGE.

**1680** Execution of Lord Stafford (Dec. 29).

**1683** Discovery of Rye-house Plot (to secure succession for Duke of Monmouth); execution of Lord Russell (July 21); of Algernon Sydney (Dec. 7).

**1685** Accession of JAMES II. (Feb. 6); ARGYLE's rebellion suppressed; he is executed (June 30): DUKE OF MONMOUTH (natural son of Charles II.) lands at Lyme (June 11); proclaimed king at Taunton (June 20); **Battle of Sedgemoor** (July 6); defeat of the rebels; Monmouth executed (July 15).

**1688** Acquittal of the seven bishops (June 30); **Abdication of James II.** (Dec. 23).

**1689** WILLIAM and MARY proclaimed King and Queen (Feb. 13): James II. lands in Ireland; Claverhouse's rebellion in Scotland suppressed.

**1690** William III. lands in Ireland (June 14); **Battle of the Boyne** (July 1); James defeated.

**1691** TREATY OF LIMERICK deprives James of power in Ireland, and grants amnesty to rebels.

**1692** Massacre of Glencoe.

**1694** Death of Queen Mary.

**1701** Death of James II. at St. Germain (Sept 16).

**1702** Death of William III.; accession of QUEEN ANNE.

**1704** Irish "Popery Act" passed; Battle of Donauwerth.

A.D.

**1706** BATTLE OF RAMILIES; MARLBOROUGH victorious.

**1707** Union of England and Scotland as GREAT BRITAIN.

**1708** French squadron routed by Admiral Byng.

**1709** **Battle of Malplaquet**; defeat of French by Marlborough.

**1710** Sacheverell's riots; dissenting meeting-houses destroyed.

**1713** TREATY OF UTRECHT terminates the wars of Queen Anne.

**1714** Death of Queen Anne (Aug. 1); accession of GEORGE I.; Hanoverian succession begins.

**1715** Insurrection of the Earl of Mar in Scotland in favor of the Pretender. **Battles of Preston and Sheriffmuir**; defeat of the rebels; Landing of the Chevalier at Peterhead (Dec. 22).

**1719** Battle of Glensheil.

**1720** "South Sea Bubble" collapses.

**1722** Death of the Duke of Marlborough.

**1724** "Wood's half-pence" excitement in Ireland.

**1727** Death of George I.; accession of GEORGE II.

**1737** Death of Queen Caroline.

**1743** BATTLE OF DETTINGEN (June 16); English and Hessians defeat the French.

**1745** The Young Pretender lands at Moidart, Scotland; **Battle of Preston Pans** (Jan. 17); defeat of Royalists; the rebels enter England.

**1746** BATTLE OF FALKIRK (Jan. 17); Royalists defeated; **Battle of Culloden** (April 16); total route of the Pretender.

**1747** Execution of Lord Lovat.

**1752** "New Style" chronology adopted; Sept. 3 counted as Sept. 14.

**1756** Commencement of Seven Years War.

**1757** Conquest of India begun (*see* INDIA); Admiral Byng executed (March 14).

**1760** Death of George II.; accession of GEORGE III; conquest of CANADA (*which see*); Thurot's invasion of Ireland.

**1761** George III. marries Charlotte Sophia of Mecklenburg-Strelitz.

**1762** War declared with Spain (*see* SPAIN).

**1763** PEACE OF PARIS ends Seven Years War; arrest of John Wilkes for sedition.

**1765** **American Stamp Act passed** (March 22); death of the Pretender, at Rome.

**1772** Royal Marriage Act passed.

**1773** Revolt in American Colonies (*see* UNITED STATES).

**1778** Death of LORD CHATHAM; Relief Bill for Irish Catholics passed.

**1780** Lord George Gordon's anti-popery riots in London.

**1781** Trial and acquittal of Gordon.

**1782** **Independence of United States** acknowledged by provisional treaty at Paris (Nov. 30).

**1786** Attempt on the king's life by Margaret Nicholson (insane).

A.D.

**1788** **Impeachment of Warren Hastings** opened by Edmund Burke (Feb. 13); death of Young Pretender at Rome (March 3); insanity of the king made known (Nov. 19).

**1789** Regency Bill withdrawn on account of the king's recovery; public thanksgiving (April 23).

**1792** First Coalition against France.

**1793** War declared against France.

**1794** *Habeas Corpus* suspended; Battle of Brest (June 1); LORD HOWE defeats the French fleet.

**1795** The Prince of Wales marries Caroline of Brunswick (April 8); Warren Hastings acquitted (April 23); Orange clubs formed in Ireland.

**1796** Birth of PRINCESS CHARLOTTE; death of ROBERT BURNS.

**1797** Bank of England stops payment (Feb. 27); death of EDMUND BURKE (July 29).

**1798** *Habeas Corpus* Act suspended; rebellion in Ireland; Battle of Kilcullen (May 23); rebels successful; Battle of ANTRIM (June 7); rebels defeated; **Battle of the Nile** (Aug. 1); great victory of Nelson over the French.

**1799** Irish rebellion completely suppressed.

**1800** Attempt on the king's life by Hatfield.

**1801** **Legislative Union of Great Britain and Ireland**; BATTLE OF COPENHAGEN (April 2); Nelson victorious; *Habeas Corpus* suspended (April 19); Peace of Amiens (Oct. 1).

**1803** War again declared against France (*which see*); Emmett's rebellion in Ireland suppressed; he is executed (Sept. 20).

**1805** **Battle of Trafalgar** (Oct. 21); victory and death of HORATIO NELSON.

**1806** Death of WILLIAM PITT; "Delicate Investigation" into conduct of Princess Caroline (May); death of CHARLES JAMES FOX (Sept. 13).

**1807** "Orders in Council" (Jan. 7); slave trade abolished (March 25); death of Cardinal Henry Stuart, claimant of the English throne.

**1808** **Peninsular War begins** (*see* SPAIN).

**1809** BATTLE OF CORUNNA (Jan. 16); death of SIR JOHN MOORE; impeachment of the Duke of York; Walcheren Expedition (Aug.).

**1810** Irish agitation for repeal of the Union; the king's insanity returns (Nov. 2); commercial depression.

**1811** The PRINCE OF WALES becomes REGENT (Feb. 5); Luddite riots (Nov.); DANIEL O'CONNELL forms the Roman Catholic Board (Dec. 26).

**1812** Mr. Perceval, the Premier, assassinated by Bellingham in the House; the United States declare war against Great Britain (June 18) (*see* UNITED STATES).

**1814** Peace with France (*which see*); TREATY OF GHENT closes war with the United States (Dec. 24).

**1815** **Battle of Waterloo** (June 18); final

A.D.

defeat of Napoleon I. by the DUKE OF WELLINGTON and BLUCHER in Belgium; insurrection in Tipperary, Ireland; marriage of Princess Charlotte to Prince Leopold of Saxe-Coburg.

**1817** *Habeas Corpus* Act suspended; death of Princess Charlotte (Nov. 6).

**1819** Birth of QUEEN VICTORIA (May 24).

**1820** Death of George III.; accession of GEORGE IV. (Jan. 29); Cato Street conspiracy discovered (Feb. 23); trial of Queen Caroline (Aug.-Nov.).

**1821** Coronation of George IV. (July 19); death of Queen Caroline (Aug. 7); outrages in Ireland.

**1822** George IV. visits Scotland; "Whiteboy" outrages in Ireland.

**1824** Death of LORD BYRON.

**1826** Commercial panic.

**1827** BATTLE OF NAVARINO: the allies defeat Turkish and Egyptian fleets.

**1829** Roman Catholic Relief Bill passed (April 13); riots in London.

**1830** Death of George IV.; accession of WILLIAM IV. (June 26); ministry of the Duke of Wellington.

**1831** REFORM BILL rejected by the Lords (Oct. 7); riots in Bristol (Oct. 29).

**1832** **English Reform Bill passed** (June 7); death of SIR WALTER SCOTT (Sept. 21); Irish Reform Bill passed (Aug. 7).

**1834** Slavery ceases in the colonies.

**1835** Corporation Reform Bill passed (Sept. 9); Peel ministry.

**1837** Death of William IV.: **accession of Queen Victoria** (June 20); Hanover separated from Great Britain.

**1838** Coronation of Victoria (June 28); Irish Poor Law Bill passed (July 31); ministry of Viscount Melbourne.

**1839** War with CHINA (*which see*); murder of Lord Norbury in Ireland.

**1840** MARRIAGE OF VICTORIA with PRINCE ALBERT of Saxe Coburg (Feb. 10); assault of Oxford on the Queen (June 10).

**1841** Birth of ALBERT EDWARD, Prince of Wales; Peel ministry formed.

**1842** Attacks on the Queen by Francis (May 30), by Bean (June 3); Income Tax passed (Aug); peace with China (Dec.).

**1844** Trial of DANIEL O'CONNELL at Dublin for sedition (Feb. 12): convicted, fined, and imprisoned; released from prison (Sept. 5).

**1845** Great famine in Ireland; Puseyite or Tractarian controversy; railway mania; anti-corn-law agitation.

**1846** Commercial panic; **repeal of the Corn Laws** (June 26); food riots in Tipperary; Russell ministry formed.

**1847** Death of O'Connell (May 15); Government expends £10,000,000 for relief of Irish sufferers.

**1848** Chartist demonstration in London; Irish rebellion, headed by Smith O'Brien, Meagher, and others, suppressed; the leaders condemned to death (Oct. 9).

**1849** Sentence of Irish insurgents commuted to transportation; Encumbered Estates Act (Irish) passed; cholera reappears in England.

**1850** Death of the poet WORDSWORTH, SIR ROBERT PEEL, and the Duke of Cambridge; Pate assaults the Queen.

**1851** The GREAT EXHIBITION OPENED (May 1).

**1852** Death of the poet Thomas Moore; riots in Belfast; death of the Duke of Wellington (Sept. 14); Aberdeen ministry.

**1853** English and French fleets enter the Bosphorus (Oct. 22); protocol between England, France, Austria, and Prussia signed (Dec. 5).

**1854** Alliance between England, France, and Turkey (March 12); **war declared against Russia** (March 28). (*For events of Russo-Turkish or Crimean War see* RUSSIA *and* TURKEY.) Crystal Palace opened June 10); Washington Treaty with United States, regarding fishery claims.

**1855** Aberdeen Ministry resigns (Jan. 29). Palmerston forms a ministry (Feb.).

**1856** Peace with Russia proclaimed (April 19); war with CHINA (*which see*); war with Persia (Nov.); Persians take Herat (Oct. 25); Bushire taken by English (Dec. 10).

**1857** **Indian Mutiny begins** (*see* INDIA); Persian War concluded by Peace of Teheran; Herat restored; commercial panic (Nov.).

**1858** Marriage of the Princess-Royal to Prince Frederick William of Prussia (Jan. 25); Derby-Disraeli Ministry formed (Feb. 26); Jewish Disabilities Bill passed (July 23); India Bill passed (Aug. 2).

**1859** Neutrality in Italian war declared; Derby Ministry defeated on the REFORM BILL; resigns (June 11); Palmerston-Russell Ministry formed (June 18); death of LORD MACAULAY (Dec. 28).

**1860** Commercial treaty with France(March); peace with China (Oct. 24).

**1861** Complications with United States in regard to the TRENT AFFAIR: Slidell and Mason taken from a British mail steamer (Nov. 8); **Death of Albert, the Prince-Consort** (Dec. 14); Slidell and Mason released (Dec. 28).

**1862** Second International Exhibition (May 1); Princess Alice marries Louis of Hesse (July 1); Prince Alfred declines the throne of Greece (Oct 23); distress in cotton manufacturing districts; riots in Ireland.

**1863** Marriage of the PRINCE OF WALES to PRINCESS ALEXANDRA of Denmark (March 10); death of the novelist THACKERAY (Dec. 24).

**1864** Birth of a son to the Prince of Wales (Jan. 8); Ionian Islands given to Greece; powers as to Confederate privateers discussed; Schleswig-Holstein conference.

**1865** Death of Richard Cobden (April 2); of Lord Palmerston (Oct. 18); cattle plague in England and Ireland; Fenian movement in Ireland; James Stephens, "Head-Center," arrested (Nov. 11); escapes (Nov. 24); Earl Russell, Premier; commercial treaty with Austria (Dec. 16).

**1866** GLADSTONE introduces Reform Bill (March 12); defeated (June 18); ministers resign (June 26); third Derby cabinet formed (July 6); marriage of Princess Helena to Prince Christian of Schleswig-Holstein (July 5); Atlantic cable a success; *Habeas Corpus* suspended in Ireland; Fenians in CANADA (*which see*).

**1867** New Reform Act passed (Aug. 15); Fenian outbreaks; **war with Abyssinia**, on account of imprisonment of British subjects; Sir Robert Napier made chief of expedition.

**1868** Earl of Derby resigns (Feb. 25); Disraeli Ministry formed (Feb. 29); Theodore of Abyssinia defeated (April 10); commits suicide (April 13); Gladstone's resolution for Disestablishment of Irish Church passes Commons (April 30); death of Lord Brougham (May 7); Scotch and Irish reform acts passed (July 13); Parliament dissolved (Nov. 11); new Parliament meets (Dec. 10); Disraeli resigns; Gladstone forms a ministry (Dec. 9).

**1869** Convention on "Alabama Claims" signed; rejected by the United States. Earl Spencer made Lord-Lieutenant of Ireland: IRISH CHURCH BILL receives the royal assent (July 26); death of the Earl of Derby (Oct. 23).

**1870** Death of CHARLES DICKENS (June 9); **Irish Land Bill** brought in (Feb. 15); receives royal assent (July 8); neutrality in Franco-Prussian war proclaimed (July 19); Treaty with Prussia and France for neutrality of Belgium (Aug. 11); Mr. John Bright resigns (Dec. 20).

**1871** Princess Louise marries the Marquis of Lorne (March 20); death of Sir John F. Herschel (May 11); of GROTE the historian (June 18); Black Sea Conference (March 13) (*see* RUSSIA); serious illness of Prince of Wales (Dec.); SCOTT Centenary at Edinburgh; riots in Dublin; Washington Treaty with United States, regarding *Alabama* Claims May 8).

**1872** National thanksgiving for recovery of the Prince of Wales (Feb. 27); O'Connor threatens the Queen (Feb. 29); supplemental treaty about *Alabama* Claims (Feb. 3; award of *Alabama* arbitrators (Sept. 14); commercial treaty with France (Nov. 5); riots in Belfast.

A.D.

**1873** Death of Lord Lytton (Edward Bulwer) (Jan. 18); Mr. Gladstone resigns after defeat on Dublin University Bill (March 13); resumes office (March 17); visit of the Shah of Persia; Judicature Bill passed (Aug. 5). **War with Ashantee**; Sir Garnet Wolseley in command.

**1874** Marriage of the Duke of Edinburgh to the Grand Duchess Marie Alexandrovna of Russia (Jan. 23); general elections; Conservative gains; Gladstone resigns (Feb. 17); Mr. Disraeli forms a ministry. End of "Tichborne" trial (Feb. 28); Ashantees defeated (Jan. 31); treaty signed (Feb. 13).

**1875** Moody and Sankey "revival;" Prince of Wales visits England; Suez Canal stock bought by England (Nov. 1). O'Connell Centenary in Ireland.

**1876** The Queen proclaimed "Empress of India" (May 1); Excitement about Bulgarian atrocities; "Home Rule" for Ireland defeated, 291 against 61 votes; DISRAELI raised to the peerage as the EARL OF BEACONSFIELD.

**1877** Neutrality in Russo-Turkish war proclaimed (April 30); Duke of Marlborough made Lord-Lieutenant of Ireland; Gladstone's resolutions in regard to Turkey defeated.

**1878** Excitement in regard to Russian advance on Constantinople; resignation of Lord Carnavon (Jan. 24); of the Earl of Derby (March 28); Earl of Salisbury's circular (April 2); death of Earl Russell (May 28); Earl of Leitrim shot in Ireland; Beaconsfield and Salisbury attend the Berlin Conference in behalf of England; TREATY OF BERLIN signed (July 13); **War in Afghanistan**; Gen. Roberts victorious at PEIWAR PASS (Dec. 2); British occupy Jellalabad (Dec. 20).

**1879** Yakoob Khan recognized as Ameer (May 9); British troops retire; treaty of peace (May 30); massacre of British residents of Cabul (Sept. 3); Gen. Roberts reaches Cabul (Sept. 28); abdication of Yakoob Khan (Oct. 19); Afghans defeated at Sherpur (Dec. 23). **Zulu War**; British troops enter Zululand (Jan. 12); massacre of ISANDULA, 837 killed (Jan. 22); victory at Kambula (March 29); PRINCE LOUIS NAPOLEON killed by Zulus (June 1); Sir Garnet Wolseley takes command (June 23); **Battle of Ulundi**; total defeat of CETEWAYO (July 4); he is captured (Aug. 28). Marriage of the Duke of Connaught to Princess Louise Margaret of Prussia (Mar. 13). Great distress and famine in Ireland; Mr. Parnell visits the United States in behalf of the Land League; anti-rent agitation.

**1880** Fighting continues in Afghanistan; Shere Ali made Governor of Candahar; Ayoob Khan attacks Candahar and repulses Gen. Burrows (July 27); sortie from Candahar fails (Aug. 16); Gen. Roberts relieves Candahar (Aug. 31); defeats Ayoob (Sept. 1). General election, great Liberal gains; Beaconsfield Ministry resigns (April 22); Gladstone forms a ministry (April 29); Bradlaugh refuses to take the oath. In Ireland, resistance to evictions; great contributions to relieve distress from United States, Canada, and elsewhere; Compensation for Disturbance Bill rejected; speech of Dillon at Kildare (Aug. 15); Lord Mountmorris shot (Sept. 25); "Boycotting" practiced; arrest of Parnell, Healy, and others on charge of conspiracy to prevent payment of rent; trial of Parnell begins (Dec. 28).

**1881** Duke of Argyle resigns from cabinet (April 8). **Death of Lord Beaconsfield**; Lord Salisbury becomes the Conservative leader. Jury in Parnell case disagree; Bradlaugh excluded from House of Commons; Coercion Act for Ireland passed (March 21); many arrests; Irish Land Bill passed by vote of 220 to 14; Lords agree to it (Aug. 16). Ayoob Khan routs the Ameer and enters Candahar. Parnell arrested under Coercion Act (Oct. 13); Land League declared illegal (Oct. 20). Ayoob defeated by the Ameer (Sept. 22). Agrarian outrages in Ireland.

**1882** Parliament opens (Feb. 7); Bradlaugh prevented from taking the oath. Attempt on the Queen's life by McLean (March 2). House again refuses to allow Bradlaugh to take the oath (March 6). State trial of McLean; he is adjudged insane. Prince Leopold married to Princess Helena of Waldeck (April 27). Earl Cowper resigns (April 28); Earl Spencer appointed Lord Lieutenant of Ireland. W. G. Foster resigns (May 2); Lord Frederick Cavendish appointed Chief Secretary of Ireland; Lord Cavendish and Mr. Burke (Under Secretary) assassinated in Dublin (May 6); Otto Trevelyan succeeds Lord Cavendish; the Repression of Crime Bill passed (July 11). John Bright resigns (July 15) as a member of Gladstone's Cabinet, owing to Egyptian policy. The "Clôture" bill passed, permitting closing of debate by majority vote. Irish constabulary demand increased pay; 234 of the Dublin police force dismissed; 208 reinstated. Arrest of E. Dwyer Grey. Arrears of Rent Bill passed. Anglo-Turkish Military Convention informally signed (Sept. 6). *See* EGYPT for particulars of the **war in Egypt** to coerce ARABI BEY.

# AUSTRALIA.

A.D.

**1601** Alleged discovery by Portuguese.

**1606** The Dutch observe Australia.

**1618** Coast surveyed by Zeachen and others.

**1642** TASMAN coasts S. Australia and Van Diemen's Land.

**1665** Western Australia named New Holland by Dutch.

**1686** WILLIAM DAMPIER lands in Australia.

**1763** Explorations of WILLIS and CARTERET.

**1770** CAPT. COOK and others land at Botany Bay, and name the country NEW SOUTH WALES.

**1773** Explorations of Furneaux.

**1774** Capt. Cook explores Australia and NEW ZEALAND.

**1777** Third voyage of Capt. Cook.

**1788** First landing of English convicts at Port Jackson; Phillips, first governor, founds Sydney.

**1789** Voyages of Bligh.

**1798** Bass and Flinders discover Bass's Straits.

**1800–1805** Explorations and surveys of Grant and Flinders.

**1803** VAN DIEMEN'S LAND (now Tasmania) discovered; settlement at Port Phillip.

**1804** Insurrection of convicts repressed.

**1808** Gov. Bligh deposed for tyranny; succeeded by McQuarrie.

**1829** WEST AUSTRALIA made a province.

**1830** Stuart's explorations in South Australia.

**1835** Port Phillip (now VICTORIA) colonized.

**1836** SOUTH AUSTRALIA made a province.

**1837** Founding of MELBOURNE.

**1838** Explorations of Grey in North-West Australia.

**1839** New South Wales and Tasmania explored by Stizelecki; alleged discovery of gold in Bathurst kept secret by Gov. Gipps.

**1840** Eyre explores West Australia.

**1842** SYDNEY incorporated.

**1814–48** Explorations of Leichhardt Stuart, Mitchell, Gregory, and Kennedy.

**1846** Fitzroy made Governor-General.

**1848** Leichhardt starts on second exploration; party never heard of again; Kennedy killed by natives.

**1850** Province of VICTORIA established.

**1851** **Gold discovered near Bathurst** by Edward Hargreaves; intense excitement in Victoria, New South Wales, and elsewhere; rush to the mines. Between May, 1851, and May, 1861, gold to the value of £96,000,000 was sent to England from Victoria and New South Wales.

A.D.

**1854** Sir William Dennison becomes Governor-General.

**1855** GREGORY'S expeditions into interior begin.

**1858-62** Stuart's expeditions.

**1859** Province of QUEENSLAND established.

**1860** BURKE and WILLIS cross the continent, but perish on the return next year; Sir John Young, governor of New South Wales.

**1861** Stuart and M'Kinlay cross from shore to shore.

**1865** Death of Morgan, desperate Bushranger chief; boundary disputes between New South Wales and Victoria settled.

**1866** Population of Australia (natives excluded), 1,298,667.

**1867** Capt. Cadell explores South Australia.

**1872** Telegraphic communication with England.

**1876** Willshire explores Daly and Victoria rivers.

**1879** International Exhibition at Sydney opened (Sept. 17.)

**1880** Melbourne Exhibition opened (Oct. 1); Tahiti annexed to France; the Queensland Government authorize construction of the Trans-continental Railway, to bring the colonies within thirty days of England.

**1881** Railroad completed from Sydney to Murray River, connecting with Melbourne; inter-colonial conference at Sydney to consider federal action; majority vote in favor of a tariff commission and the establishment of an Australian Court of Appeal.

## CANADA.

A.D.

**1497** Canada discovered by JOHN and SEBASTIAN CABOT.

**1524** Settlement of New France.

**1535** JACQUES CARTIER ascends the St. Lawrence to the site of Montreal.

**1598** Henry IV. of France commissions the Marquis de la Roche to conquer Canada; he fails.

**1608** QUEBEC founded by CHAMPLAIN.

**1629** English seize French posessions in Canada.

**1632** Canada restored to French by Treaty of St. Germain.

**1642** MONTREAL founded.

**1663** Canada becomes a royal government under Louis XIV.

**1665** Canada granted to French West India Company.

**1690** Fruitless expedition of Sir William Phipps.

**1711** Wreck of fleet from American colonies in the St. Lawrence.

**1746** Invasion of Shirley in Nova Scotia.

**1759** **Battle of Quebec**, on the "Heights of Abraham;" great English victory (Sept. 13); death of GEN. WOLFE and the MARQUIS DE MONTCALM; Quebec surrenders.

**1763** Treaty of Paris cedes Canada to Great Britain.

**1765** Canada accepts the Stamp Act.

**1775** **Invasion of Canada** by American forces under Montgomery and Arnold; Montgomery takes Fort St. John (Nov. 3); Montreal (Nov. 12); Arnold's attack on Quebec repulsed (Nov. 14); joint attack on Quebec (Dec. 31); Americans defeated; MONTGOMERY killed.

**1776** Canada evacuated by the Americans.

**1791** The "Quebec Bill" divides Canada into Upper and Lower Provinces.

**1812** United States troops under Gen. Hull surrender (Aug. 15); Gen. Wordsworth surrenders (Oct. 14); Gen. Van Rensselear surrenders (Nov.27).

**1813** Capture of York by United States troops (April 27); Fort George (May 27); they defeat British at Sackett's Harbor (May 29); defeated at Stony Creek (June 6); Battle of Williamsburg (Nov. 11), indecisive; **Battle of Lake Erie** (Sept. 10); COMMODORE PERRY (U. S.) captures English squadron.

**1814** Battle of Longwood; success of United States troops (March 4); they take Fort Erie (July 3); win Battle of Chippewa (July 25); of Bridgewater (Dec. 24); Treaty of Ghent puts an end to hostilities.

**1828** Petition against misuse of revenues.

**1836** Supplies refused by the House of Assembly.

**1837** PAPINEAU'S rebellion; "Sons of Liberty" rise in Montreal; attempt to take Toronto (Dec. 4); defeated at St. Eustace (Dec. 14).

**1838** Resignation of Sir Francis Head; Lord Durham succeeds him.

**1841** Consolidation of Upper and Lower Canada.

**1844** Seat of government transferred from Kingston to Montreal.

**1846** Earl Cathcart, Governor; Earl of Elgin becomes Governor-General (Oct.).

**1850** Riots in Montreal; Parliament House burned (April 26).

**1853** Clergy "reserves" abolished by British Parliament.

**1854** Treaty with the United States.

**1856** Quebec made the seat of government.

**1858** OTTAWA made the capital by Queen Victoria.

**1860** Visit of the PRINCE OF WALES.

**1861** Lord Monck made Governor-General; troops sent to Canada on account of Trent affair.

**1862** Ministry resigns; McDonald forms a cabinet.

**1864** Meeting of delegates at Quebec to discuss confederation of American colonies; raid of Confederates upon St. Albans, Vt., from Canada; they return and are arrested; discharged (Dec. 14); Gen. Dix proclaims reprisals; proclamation rescinded by Pres. Lincoln.

**1865** Canadian Parliament agrees to Confederation.

**1866** First DOMINION Parliament meets at Ottawa. **Fenian invasion threatened**; *Habeas Corpus* suspended; Fenians under O'Neill cross Niagara river; are driven back and dispersed by volunteers.

**1867** **Union of Canada, Nova Scotia, and New Brunswick** as Dominion of Canada; act passed (March 29); LORD MONCK becomes Viceroy (July 2).

**1868** SIR JOHN YOUNG becomes Governor-General (Nov. 27).

**1869** Hudson's Bay territories bought for £300,000.

**1870** Fenian raid repelled by militia; O'Neill captured by United States troops. Province of MANITOBA formed.

**1871** Discussion on the fishery question; British Columbia united to the Dominion.

**1872** Earl of Dufferin becomes Governor-General.

**1873** Prince Edward's Isle added to Dominion; charges of corruption against the McDonald Ministry; he resigns; McKensie forms a ministry.

**1875** Reciprocity Treaty rejected by the United States.

**1877** Canadian and United States Fishery Commission at Halifax; award of $5,500,000 to Canada.

**1878** Fortune Bay outrages; MARQUIS OF LORNE appointed Governor-General (Oct. 14); Halifax award paid (Nov. 21); arrival of PRINCESS LOUISE and MARQUIS OF LORNE (Nov. 25).

**1879** Industrial Exhibition at Ottawa (Sept.).

**1880** Compensation for Fortune Bay affair refused by the Earl of Salisbury; granted by Lord Granville.

**1881** Award of £15,000 for Fortune Bay outrages. Bill to construct a railroad from Halifax to Buzzard inlet passed (Jan. 31); and letters patent issued to the Canadian Pacific Railway Company (Feb. 16).

# INDIA.

A.D.

**1497** VASCO DA GAMA discovers the passage to India.
**1503** Portuguese in Cochin.
**1526** Mongol dynasty founded in India.
**1579** SIR FRANCIS DRAKE lands in the Moluccas.
**1600** First charter of EAST INDIA COMPANY.
**1612** English factories established.
**1614** English defeat Portuguese in BOMBAY.
**1641** Fort St. George built at MADRAS.
**1672** The French acquire PONDICHERRY.
**1719** Ostend East India Company founded.
**1739** **Persian invasion**; NADIR SHAH sacks DELHI.
**1746** **War between French and English**: French take MADRAS.
**1751** CLIVE takes Arcot.
**1754** Peace between French and English.
**1756** Dowlah, Viceroy of Bengal, captures CALCUTTA, after heroic defense by Holwell; "**Black Hole**" **tragedy** (June 20).
**1757** Clive retakes Calcutta (Jan. 2); Chandernagore (March 23); **Battle of Plassey** (June 23) establishes English power in India.
**1758** The French seize Fort St. David and Arcot.
**1759** French driven back; much territory ceded to the British by the Subadhar of Deccan.
**1760** ARCOT retaken by Coote.
**1761** PONDICHERRY surrendered by the French.
**1763** Treaty of Paris restores Pondicherry to France. Battle of Buxar (Oct. 23); great defeat of native princes.
**1765** Nabob of Oudh becomes tributary to British; Company made receiver of Bengal, Bahar, and Orissa.
**1766** Treaty with Nizam of the Deccan.
**1767** Alliance of the Nizam and Hyder Ali; they attack the English and are defeated at Vellore.
**1769** Hyder Ali marches on Madras and compels English to form alliance.
**1770** Terrible famine in Bengal.
**1771** The Mahrattas enter Delhi.
**1772** WARREN HASTINGS becomes Governor of Bengal.
**1774** Rohilla army defeated.
**1775** Benares ceded to the company; charges of bribery against Hastings.
**1778** Pondicherry surrenders to the English.
**1780** Hyder Ali takes Arcot.
**1781** BATTLE OF NOVO PORTO (July 1); Treaty of Chunar, between Hastings and the Subadhar of Oudh.
**1782** French assist TIPPOO SAIB against the English; they take Trincomlee; Tippoo Saib succeeds Hyder Ali.
**1783** Arrival of Bussy with French troops; Tippoo takes Bedmore.
**1784** Treaty concluded with Tippoo Saib.
**1785** Warren Hastings returns to England; Sir John Macpherson succeeds him.
**1786** Cornwallis becomes Governor-General of India.
**1788** **Trial of Warren Hastings** begins in Westminster Hall; Burke opens (Feb. 15-19); Sheridan presents charges in relation to the Begums (June 3-13).
**1789** Tippoo attacks Travancore (Dec. 24); defeated.
**1790** Tippoo plunders Travancore; concludes treaty with Mahrattas.
**1791** Lord Cornwallis takes Bengalore; **Battle of Arikera** (May 14); Tippoo routed; Hastings begins his defense.
**1792** Peace concluded with Tippoo Saib.
**1793** Pondicherry taken by the English.
**1795** **Acquittal of Warren Hastings**.
**1798** Marquis of Wellesley becomes Governor-General.
**1799** SERINGAPATAM taken by English; Tippoo killed (May 4); partition of Mysore; Rajah of Tanjore surrenders his power to English.
**1800** Surrender of SURAT; Nizam cedes Mysore to English.
**1802** Treaty of Amiens gives Pondicherry to France; further cessions to English; Treaty of Bassein, between the Company and the Peishwa.
**1803** Mahratta War; BATTLE OF DELHI; Gen. Lake defeats French and Mahrattas (Sept. 11); **Battle of Assaye**; Wellesley with 4,500 men defeats 50,000 natives (Sept. 23); Lake takes Agra (Oct. 17); peace with Scindia (Dec. 30).
**1804** Siege of Delhi by Holkar; BATTLE OF DEEG; Gen. Frazer defeats Holkar (Nov. 13).
**1805** Peace with Holkar, who cedes Bundelcund, etc.
**1806** Mutiny among Sepoys.
**1808** War with Travancore.
**1809** Travancore subdued; mutiny at Seringapatam.
**1813** India trade thrown open to any British subject.
**1817** Mahratta confederacy dissolved; Ahmednuggur ceded to English; defeat of Holkar at Mehudpore; Pindarrie War.
**1818** End of Pindarrie War; peace with Holkar; the Peishwa surrenders and cedes the Deccan.
**1819** Oudh becomes independent.
**1824** **Burmese War** begins; Rangoon taken (May 11).
**1825** Capture of ASSAM (Feb. 1); Battle of Prome; Burmese defeated.
**1826** Battle of Pagham Mew ends Burmese War; English take Bhurtpore.
**1838** Slavery abolished in the East. **Afghan War**; Cabul captured (Aug. 7).
**1843** SIR CHARLES NAPIER defeats Ameers of Scinde (Feb. 17).
**1845** England purchases Danish possessions in India; war with Sikhs; Battle of Moodkee (Sept. 6).
**1846** Defeat of Sikhs at Sobraon (Feb.); Treaty of Lasore.
**1848** Gen. Gough takes Ramnuggur; Sikhs defeated at Vyseerabad; second Sikh War continues.
**1849** BATTLE OF GOOJERAT (Feb. 21) ends Sikh War; Napier becomes Commander-in-chief; **Annexation of the Punjaub**.
**1850** Mutiny in Bengal native infantry.
**1851** Second Burmese War begins.
**1853** End of the Burmese War.
**1856** Annexation of Oudh.
**1857** **Great Indian Mutiny**; native regiments mutiny at Barrackpore, Burhampore, and Lucknow (May 6); they seize Delhi and proclaim the king emperor; mutinies at Cawnpore and Allahabad; British at Cawnpore surrender to Nana Sahib (June 25); **Siege of Lucknow** begins (July 1); Havelock enters Cawnpore (July 17); defeats Nana Sahib at Bithoor (July 19); **Capture of Delhi** (Sept. 20); Havelock relieves Lucknow (Sept. 25); **Battle of Cawnpore** (Dec. 6); rebels routed.
**1858** Battle of Futteghur (Jan. 2); SIR COLIN CAMPBELL captures Lucknow (March 21); rebels defeated at Kotara (July 14); other defeats subdue the country. Government takes control of India from the East India Company; Lord Canning made first Viceroy.
**1859** The Punjaub is made a presidency. Pacification of Oudh announced (Jan. 25).
**1862** Lord Elgin becomes Viceroy of India.
**1863** Death of Elgin; Sir John Lawrence made Viceroy.
**1866** Severe famine in Bengal.
**1868** Earl of Mayo becomes Viceroy.
**1870** Railway between Calcutta and Bombay.
**1872** Lord Northbrook appointed Viceroy.
**1874** Terrible famine throughout Bengal.
**1875** Tour of the PRINCE OF WALES through India.
**1876** Appointment of Lord Lytton as Governor-General; cyclone causes loss of 220,000 lives.
**1877** Queen Victoria proclaimed Empress of India at Delhi (Jan. 1).
**1879** Massacres at Cabul (*see* GREAT BRITAIN); attempt on Lord Lytton's life.
**1880** Marquis of Ripon made Governor-General.
**1882** Riot between Hindoos and Mohammedans in the presidency of Madras.

# UNITED STATES OF AMERICA.

A.D.

**1492 America discovered by Christopher Columbus.**
**1497** Coast of Newfoundland discovered by JOHN CABOT.
**1498** The Cabots discover the Atlantic coast.
**1499** Voyage of AMERIGO VESPUCII to America.
**1512** Coast of FLORIDA discovered by PONCE DE LEON.
**1517** MEXICO discovered by CORDOVA.
**1521** CORTEZ conquers Mexico.
**1524** Verazzani's discoveries in North America.
**1526** PIZARRO discovers Quito.
**1528** Narvaez's expedition to Florida coast.
**1532** Conquest of Peru begins.
**1534** Cartier discovers the St. Lawrence.
**1541** DE SOTO discovers the Mississippi River.
**1562** Port Royal founded by Huguenots.
**1564** FLORIDA colonized by Huguenots.
**1565** St. Augustine founded by Melendez.
**1576** Frobisher enters San Francisco Bay.
**1582** Santa Fé founded by Espego.
**1584** Expedition of Amidas and Barlow.
**1585** RALEIGH'S Roanoke settlements fail.
**1604** Settlements in Novia Scotia.
**1607 First English settlement, at Jamestown, Va.**
**1608** Quebec settled by Champlain.
**1609** Henry Hudson discovers the Hudson River. Champlain's discoveries. Virginia obtains a new charter.
**1612** Virginia receives a third charter.
**1614** New Amsterdam (now New York) built by the Dutch. Smith explores New England coast.
**1620 Puritans arrive at Plymouth.** "Great Patent" to Virginia Company.
**1623** NEW HAMPSHIRE first settled.
**1627** DELAWARE settled by Swedes and Dutch.
**1629** Charter granted to Massachusetts Bay Colony.
**1630** City of Boston founded.
**1632** LORD BALTIMORE receives grant of MARYLAND.
**1635** CONNECTICUT settlements at Hartford, Windsor, and Wethersfield under grant to Lords Say and Brooke. ROGER WILLIAMS, driven from Massachusetts, settles in RHODE ISLAND.
**1637** Pequod Indian War in Connecticut.
**1638** New Haven Colony founded.
**1644** Charter granted to Rhode Island. Indian massacre in Virginia.
**1664** New Jersey sold to Lord Berkeley; settled at Elizabethtown. The English take New Amsterdam. NORTH CAROLINA settled.
**1670** SOUTH CAROLINA settled by the English.
**1673** Virginia granted to Arlington and Culpepper. Discoveries of Marquette and Joliet.
**1675** King Philip's War in New England.
**1680** Mississippi River explored by Hennepin. Charleston founded.
**1682** WILLIAM PENN settles in PENNSYLVANIA. Delaware granted to Penn. LA SALLE sails down the Mississippi and names LOUISIANA.
**1685** TEXAS colonized.
**1689** King William's War. French and Indians ravage New England frontier. Canadian expedition fails.
**1692** Salem witchcraft delusion.
**1697** End of King William's War.
**1699** Further exploration of the Mississippi.
**1701** The French found Detroit.
**1702** Queen Anne's War begins; treaty of French with the Five Nations; Massachusetts frontier ravaged.
**1707** First expedition against Port Royal fails.
**1710** Port Royal taken and named Annapolis.
**1711** Expedition against Quebec wrecked in the St. Lawrence.
**1713** Treaty of Utrecht ends Queen Anne's War.
**1717** New Orleans settled.
**1732** Birth of GEORGE WASHINGTON (Feb. 22).
**1733** GEORGIA settled at Savannah by Oglethorpe.
**1744** King George's War begun (third intercolonial war).
**1745** Capture of Louisburg by Pepperell.
**1748** War ended by Treaty of Aix-la-Chapelle.
**1753** French seize Hudson Bay Company's trading posts. Washington sent to St. Pierre.
**1754 French and Indian War** begins; Fort Necessity built at Great Meadows; Washington surrenders it to De Villiers with honors of war. KENTUCKY settled by Daniel Boone.
**1755** Gen. Braddock takes command of English forces. French Acadians taken from homes. Expedition against Fort Du Quesne; defeat of Braddock; Niagara expedition fails; Battle of Crown Point; Dieskau defeated.
**1756** Failure of expeditions against Fort Du Quesne, Niagara, and Crown Point; Montcalm takes Oswego forts.
**1757** Expedition against Louisburg fails; Montcalm captures and destroys Fort William Henry.
**1758** Abercrombie takes command; English take Louisburg, Cape Breton Island, and Prince Edward's Island; repulse at Ticonderoga, Fort George built; Fort Du Quesne taken by Washington.
**1759** Fort Niagara surrenders (July 23); Ticonderoga and Crown Point abandoned; Wolfe's expedition against Quebec: **Battle of the Heights of Abraham** (Sep. 13); English victory; death of Wolfe and Montcalm; QUEBEC surrenders (Sept. 18).
**1760** French fail to retake Quebec; Montreal surrenders (Sept. 8); end of French and Indian War.
**1763** Treaty of peace with France. PONTIAC'S WAR; Indians capture English forts and massacre garrisons.
**1764** Indians sue for peace. End of Pontiac's War. Heavy duties on imports decreed by British Parliament.
**1765 The Stamp Act passed in England** (March 22). Colonial Congress at New York (Oct. 7). Massachusetts, Rhode Island, Pennsylvania, Delaware, and Maryland unite. Stamp Act resisted (Nov.).
**1766** Repeal of the Stamp Act (March 18).
**1767** Tax imposed on tea, paper, glass, etc.
**1768** Petition against tax from Massachusetts. Gen. Gates sent to Boston.
**1770** Affray between soldiers and citizens in Boston (March 5).
**1771** Gov. Tyrone defeats insurgents in North Carolina.
**1773** The "Boston Tea Party" (Dec. 16).
**1774** Boston Port Bill deprives Boston of its port rights. "Continental" or second Colonial Congress at Philadelphia (Sept. 5); Declaration of Rights (Nov. 4).
**1775 Battle of Lexington** (April 18); British retreat. Ethan Allen seizes TICONDEROGA (May 10); union of the States (May 20); Howe, Burgoyne, and Clinton arrive from England; GEORGE WASHINGTON appointed Commander-in-Chief (June 15). **Battle of Bunker Hill** (June 17); Americans retreat after stubborn resistance, only when ammunition is exhausted. Gens. Montgomery and Arnold invade Canada; capture of St. John (Nov. 3); of MONTREAL (Nov. 12); repulse of Arnold at Quebec (Nov. 14); second and joint assault; MONTGOMERY killed (Dec. 31); Americans defeated.
**1776** Evacuation of Boston by British (March 17). **Declaration of Independence** adopted by the thirteen States (July 4) (New Hampshire, Massachusetts, Rhode Island, Connecticut, Delaware, Maryland, Virginia, North Carolina, South Carolina, New York, Pennsylvania, and Georgia). BATTLE OF LONG ISLAND (Aug. 27); defeat of Americans by Gen. Howe; he occupies New York (Sept. 15); BATTLE OF WHITE PLAINS (Oct. 28); Gen. Howe defeats American forces; Battle of Lake Champlain (Oct. 11-13); American fleet captured; Fort Washington taken by English (Nov. 16); they occupy Rhode Island; **Battle of Trenton** (Dec. 26); surrender of Hessians to Washington.
**1777 Battle of Princeton** (Jan. 3); British forces defeated by Washington. Arrival of LA FAYETTE; he is made a major-general. BATTLE OF BRANDYWINE (Sept. 11); Lord Cornwallis de-

A.D.

feats Americans; he takes Philadelphia (Sept. 26); BATTLE OF GERMANTOWN (Oct. 3-4); Burgoyne defeats Americans; his army is surrounded by Washington; **Burgoyne surrenders at Saratoga** (Oct. 17); ARTICLES OF CONFEDERATION adopted by Congress (Nov. 15). France recognizes American independence (Dec. 16).

**1778** Alliance with France concluded at Paris (Feb. 6). English evacuate Philadelphia (June 18). BATTLE OF MONMOUTH (June 28); MASSACRE OF WYOMING (July 3). Savannah seized by British forces (Dec. 29).

**1779** Battle of Briar Creek (March 3); Americans repulsed.

**1780** Surrender of Charlestown to the English. BATTLE OF CAMDEN (Aug. 16); Cornwallis defeats Gates. BENEDICT ARNOLD betrays his country; capture of Major André (Sept. 23); he is hung as a spy (Oct. 2).

**1781** Congress assembles (March 2), Articles of Confederation having been accepted by all the States. BATTLE OF COWPENS; British defeated by Americans. Cornwallis defeats Green at Guildford; Battle of Eutaw; Americans defeated. **Surrender of Cornwallis at Yorktown** (Oct. 19).

**1782** Holland acknowledges the independence of the United States.

**1783** Armistice with Great Britain (Jan. 20). **Peace with England concluded** by Treaty of Paris (Sept. 3). New York evacuated (Nov. 25). Washington resigns (Dec. 23).

**1784** Treaty of Paris ratified by Congress (Jan. 4).

**1785** John Adams of Massachusetts received as Minister to England.

**1786** Shay's Rebellion in Massachusetts and New Hampshire. Delegates meet at Annapolis and recommend a convention to *revise* Articles of Confederation (Sept.).

**1787** Convention meets at Philadelphia (May); George Washington presides; **United States Constitution agreed upon** (Sept. 17).

**1788** Constitution ratified by eleven States.

**1789** First Congress meets at New York; WASHINGTON becomes first PRESIDENT. North Carolina ratifies Constitution.

**1790** Alexander Hamilton's financial scheme proposed. Rhode Island ratifies the Constitution.

**1791** VERMONT admitted as a State. St. Clair defeated by Indians. United States Bank at Philadelphia.

**1792** KENTUCKY admitted into the Union. Capt. Grey discovers the Columbia River.

**1793** Trouble with Genet, French Ambassador. Washington's second term begins.

**1794** "Whisky Rebellion" in Pennsylvania. Genet recalled. Jay's Treaty with Great Britain.

**1795** Jay's Treaty ratified by Congress.

**1796** TENNESSEE admitted into the Union. Washington resigns.

**1797** JOHN ADAMS inaugurated. Treaty with France annulled.

**1798** War with France imminent. Naval conflicts.

**1799** **Death of Washington at Mount Vernon.**

**1800** Capital removed from Philadelphia to Washington. Treaty signed with France.

**1801** THOMAS JEFFERSON inaugurated. War with Tripoli.

**1802** OHIO admitted into the Union.

**1803** LOUISIANA purchased from the French.

**1804** ALEXANDER HAMILTON killed in a duel with Aaron Burr.

**1805** Treaty of peace with Tripoli.

**1806** Blockade of French and English coasts ("*paper* blockades") affects American commerce.

**1807** Aaron Burr tried for conspiracy; acquitted. *Chesapeake* fired upon by the *Leopard;* British "Orders in Council" prohibit trade with France. Embargo on American ships declared (Dec. 22).

**1809** Embargo repealed (March 1); Congress prohibits trade with Great Britain and France. JAMES MADISON inaugurated.

**1810** Napoleon prohibits trade with United States.

**1811** United States frigate *President* defeats English cruiser *Little Bell*. BATTLE OF TIPPECANOE; Harrison defeats Indians under Tecumseh.

**1812** LOUISIANA admitted as a State. **War declared with Great Britain** (June 18); Gen. Hull invades Canada; surrender of Mackinaw (June 17); *Constitution* captures the *Guerriere* (Aug. 19); Battle of Queenstown (Oct. 13); British victory; United States frigate *Wasp* takes the *Frolic* (Oct. 18); *United States* (frigate) takes *Macedonia* (Oct. 25); *Constitution* takes the *Java*.

**1813** Battle of Frenchtown (Jan. 24); American defeat; *Hornet* takes the *Peacock* (Feb. 25); capture of York (Toronto) by Americans (April 27); *Chesapeake* (United States frigate) captured by the *Shannon* (June 1); Battles of Stony Creek and Burlington Heights (June 6); American defeat; **Battle of Lake Erie** (Sept. 10); COMMODORE PERRY captures English fleet; Battle of the Thames (Oct. 5); English burn Buffalo (Dec. 13). Madison's second term begins.

**1814** English defeated at Longwood (March 4); Creek Indians subdued; English seize Oswego (May 6); Americans take Fort Erie (July 3); Battle of Chippewa (July 5); **Battle of Lundy's Lane** (July 25); American victory; British victory at Bladensburg; **Public Buildings of Washington burnt** (Aug. 24); Battle of Lake Champlain; English fleet taken; United States army defeated at Baltimore (Sept. 12); Hartford Convention (Dec. 14). **Treaty of peace signed at Ghent** (Dec. 24).

**1815** **Battle of New Orleans** (Jan. 8); JACKSON repels British under **Packenham**. Treaty of Ghent ratified (Feb. 17). War with Algiers.

**1816** INDIANA admitted into the Union.

**1817** JAMES MONROE inaugurated; MISSISSIPPI admitted.

**1818** Florida War; Jackson takes Pensacola. ILLINOIS admitted.

**1819** ALABAMA admitted; Arkansas made separate territory.

**1820** Florida ceded by Spain; "Missouri Compromise" Act passed; MAINE admitted.

**1821** MISSOURI accepts Compromise Act and is admitted. Monroe's second term begins.

**1822** "Monroe Doctrine" declared; independence of South American republics acknowledged.

**1824** La Fayette visits the United States.

**1825** JOHN QUINCY ADAMS inaugurated.

**1828** A "protective" tariff is adopted.

**1829** ANDREW JACKSON inaugurated.

**1832** New tariff law. Commercial crisis. Black Hawk War. Excitement about United States Bank and South Carolina "nullification."

**1833** Jackson's second term.

**1835** Seminole War in Florida. Great fire in New York.

**1836** ARKANSAS made a State.

**1837** MARTIN VAN BUREN inaugurated; Michigan admitted.

**1839** United States Bank suspends payment.

**1841** WILLIAM H. HARRISON inaugurated; dies (April 4); JOHN TYLER inaugurated (April 6). M'Leod difficulty.

**1842** Ashburton or first Washington Treaty signed with England.

**1843** Dorr Rebellion in Rhode Island.

**1844** Texas asks for annexation. First telegraph line. Joseph Smith, Mormon prophet, shot by the mob.

**1845** TEXAS annexed by Act of Congress; FLORIDA and IOWA admitted. JAMES K. POLK inaugurated. **War declared by Mexico** (June 4).

**1846** Northwestern boundary fixed at 49°. Hostilities begin in Mexico; BATTLE OF PALO ALTO (May 8); victory of Gen. Taylor; Matamoras taken (May 18); Monterey taken (Sept. 24). IOWA admitted as a State.

**1847** **Battle of Buena Vista** (Feb. 23); Taylor defeats Santa Anna; BATTLE OF CERRO GORDO (April 18); Scott defeats Mexicans; also at Contreras (Aug. 20); Molino del Rey taken (Sept. 8); Gen. Scott enters the city of Mexico (Sept. 15).

**1848** Treaty signed with Mexico (Feb. 2); Upper California ceded to United

A.D.

States; gold discovered there. WISCONSIN admitted.

**1849** ZACHARY TAYLOR inaugurated. California "gold fever." Territory of Minnesota established. Astor Place riot in New York.

**1850** Death of Pres. Taylor (July 9); MILLARD FILLMORE inaugurated (July 10). CALIFORNIA admitted; New Mexico and Utah made Territories. Fugitive Slave Bill passed.

**1851** Lopez's expedition to Cuba. Visit of Louis Kossuth. Fire in Capitol at Washington.

**1853** FRANKLIN PIERCE inaugurated. Martin Kossta complications; he is surrendered. New York International Exhibition. Washington made a Territory.

**1854** Commodore Perry's treaty with Japan. Anti-Slavery riots at Boston. Nebraska and Kansas made Territories. Free-Soil and Pro-Slavery struggle in Kansas.

**1855** Treaty with Denmark annulled.

**1856** Slavery question much agitated. Attack on Sumner by Preston Brooks in the Senate. Walker's Nicaragua Expedition. Freemont, candidate of new Republican Party, defeated by James Buchanan in Presidential election.

**1857** JAMES BUCHANAN inaugurated. Riots in New York. Commercial panic.

**1858** Trouble with Mormons. MINNESOTA admitted as a State. Atlantic telegraph completed (Aug. 5).

**1859** OREGON made a State. San Juan occupied. Death of the historian Prescott. Treaty with China. Walker's filibusters seized by United States troops. Harper's Ferry Insurrection; JOHN BROWN hanged (Dec. 2). Death of Washington Irving.

**1860** Stephen Douglass nominated by Charleston Convention (April 23); John Bell by Baltimore Convention; Abraham Lincoln by Chicago (Republican) Convention; second Democratic convention at Baltimore splits, Southern delegates nominating John Breckenridge. Walker shot at Honduras (Sept. 12). Prince of Wales visits the country. Presidential election in favor of ABRAHAM LINCOLN. **South Carolina secedes from the Union** (Dec. 20); Floyd, Cobb, and Cass resign from Cabinet. *Star of the West* fired on at Charleston.

**1861** KANSAS admitted into the Union (Jan. 29). Pres. Bucha an refuses to withdraw forces from Fort Sumter. Mississippi secedes (Jan. 9); Florida (Jan. 10); Alabama (Jan. 11); Georgia (Jan. 19); Louisiana (Jan. 26); Texas (Feb. 1). **Confederated States of America** formed (Feb. 4); JEFFERSON DAVIS declared President (Feb. 8); inaugurated (Feb. 18). **Abraham Lincoln inaugurated** (March 4). **Attack on Fort Sumter** (April 12-13). Morrill Tariff Bill goes into operation (April 11). Pres. Lincoln calls for 75,000 volunteers; Northern States respond. Virginia secedes (April 17). Mob attacks Massachusetts' troops in Baltimore (April 19); Norfolk Navy-yard abandoned (April 21); Lincoln calls for three years' volunteers (May 4). Arkansas secedes (May 6); North Carolina (May 20); Tennessee (June 8). Skirmish at Philippi (June 3). BATTLE OF BIG BETHEL (June 10); Federal defeat. *Missouri:*— Gen. Lyon defeats Confederates; Fremont takes command in the State; BATTLE OF WILSON'S CREEK, Lyon killed (Aug. 10); Fremont proclaims martial law and freedom to slaves (Aug. 31); Lexington surrenders (Sept. 20); Fremont blamed and retired (Nov. 2). *Virginia:*—Federals take Harper's Ferry (June 16); Rich Mountain (July 11); **Battle of Bull Run** or Manasses, Federals routed (July 21); McClellan takes command of Army of the Potomac (Aug.). Fort Hatteras taken by Gen. Butler (Aug. 29). BATTLE OF BALL'S BLUFF (Oct. 21); Federals defeated. Port Royal (S. C) taken (Nov. 8); **Trent affair**: Capt. Wilkes of United States steamer *San Jacinto* takes Mason and Slidell (Confederate commissioners) from British mail packet *Trent* (Nov. 8). Missouri and Kentucky secede (Nov.).

**1862** Mason and Slidell surrendered (Jan. 1). Battle of Big Sandy River (Jan. 9); Mill Spring (Jan. 19); Federal victory; capture of FORT HENRY (Feb. 6); of FORT DONELSON (Feb. 16); of Roanoke Island, N. C. (Feb. 8); of Nashville (Feb. 23); BATTLE OF PEA RIDGE, Confederate defeat (March 7). The *Merrimac* sinks *Cumberland* and *Congress* at Hampton Roads (March 8); defeated by *Monitor* (March 9). Newbern, N. C., taken by Federals; Battle of Winchester, Confederate defeat (March 23). Charleston blockaded; Shiloh (April 6); Island No. 10 (April 7); Fort Pulaski (April 11); Yorktown evacuated by Confederates (May 3); Battle of Williamsburg (May 5). FARRAGUT passes forts at mouth of Mississippi (April 24); New Orleans taken (April 25). Federals take Corinth (May 30). Battle of Fair Oaks (May 31–June 1); Memphis taken (June 6). Fort Pillow taken. Pope placed over Fremont, Banks, and McDowell (June 27); Lee drives McClellan back; seven days battles from the Chickahominy to the James (June 25–July 1). Pres. Lincoln calls for 300,000 volunteers. BATTLE OF CEDAR MOUNTAIN; Banks defeated by "Stonewall" Jackson (Aug. 9); second Battle of Bull Run (Sept. 1); Pope defeated by Jackson; Pope sent to the Northwest; McDowell superseded; McCLELLAN made Commander-in-Chief (Sept. 5); Confederates defeated at South Mountain (Sept. 15); at ANTIETAM (Sept. 17); Harper's Ferry taken by Jackson (Sept. 15); he joins Lee; Federals lose Lexington and Mumfordsville; Pres. Lincoln declares slaves free after Jan. 1, if States do not return; Battle of Corinth (Oct. 4); indecisive; Gen. Stuart (Confederate) enters Pennsylvania; Morgan's raid in Kentucky; *Alabama*, Confederate cruiser, does much damage to commerce. **Battle of Fredericksburg** (Dec. 13); Burnside repelled; BATTLE OF MURFREESBORO' (Dec. 31–Jan. 1); Gen. Bragg (Confederate) defeated.

**1863** **Emancipation Proclamation by Pres. Lincoln** (Jan. 1). Gen. Hooker given command of Army of the Potomac. Federal attack on Charleston repelled (April 7). Battles of Grand Gulf and Port Gibson in Mississippi. **Battle of Chancellorsville** (May 2-3); Hooker defeated; Jackson mortally wounded; dies (May 10). Defeat of Confede rates at Jackson, Miss. (May 14); Grant invests Vicksburg (May 18); assault repelled (May 22); Gen. Lee invades Maryland and Pennsylvania (June). WEST VIRGINIA admitted as a State (June 20). Hooker superseded by Mead (June 27); **Battle of Gettysburg** (July 1-3); Confederates retreat. **Surrender of Vicksburgh** (July 4); of Port Hudson (July 8). Draft riots in New York (July 13-16). Siege of Charleston (Aug. 21); Fort Sumter destroyed. Quantrell burns Lawrence, Kan. (Aug. 21). BATTLE OF CHICKAMAUGA (Sept. 19-20); Bragg defeats Rosencrans, who is superseded by Grant, Thomas, and Sherman. BATTLE OF LOOKOUT MOUNTAIN; Thomas defeats Bragg (Nov. 25); MISSIONARY RIDGE (Nov. 26); Longstreet driven back (Nov. 29).

**1864** Attack on Richmond fails (Feb.-March). GRANT succeeds Halleck as Commander-in-Chief. Sherman driven back by Kirby Smith (April 5). Fort Pillow Massacre. (April 12). Army of the Potomac crosses the Rapidan (May 4). Forrest's raids. **Battles of the Wilderness** (May 5–7); Spottsylvania Court House (May 7-12); Federal success. Gen. Sherman marches on Atlanta (May 7). Lee driven back on Richmond; Grant invests PETERSBURG (June 15); assault repulsed (June 18). *Alabama* sunk by *Kearsage* off Cherbourg. EARLY invades Maryland (July 5). Battles before Atlanta (July 20, 22, 28). Explosion of Petersburg mine; assault repulsed (July 30). FARRA-

A.D.

GUT's fleet enters MOBILE BAY (Aug. 5); Fort Gaines taken (Aug. 8). McClellan nominated for President by Democrats. Capture of Atlanta (Sept. 1). Gen. Sheridan defeats Early at WINCHESTER; Battle of Cedar Creek (Oct. 19); St. Alban's raid (*see* CANADA). NEVADA admitted as a State. Re-election of Lincoln (Nov. 8). Sherman begins his "march to the sea" (Nov. 14). Thomas defeats Hood (Confederate) in Tennessee (Dec. 14-16). Sherman takes Savannah (Dec. 21). First assault on Fort Fisher (Dec. 24).

**1865** FORT FISHER taken (Jan. 15). Columbia, S. C., captured (Feb. 17). Charleston evacuated (Feb. 17). Wilmington taken (Feb. 22). Sheridan in Shenandoah Valley; defeats Early (March 2). Lincoln's second term begins; Andrew Johnson, Vice-President (March 4). Battle of Goldsborough, N. C. (March 21); **Battle of Five Forks** (Mar. 31); Sheridan defeats Lee, who retreats; Petersburg and Richmond captured (April 2-3). **Surrender of Gen. Lee to Grant** (April 9). Sherman enters Raleigh, N. C. (April 13). **Abraham Lincoln assassinated by Wilkes Booth** at Ford's Theater (April 14); Mr. Seward and his son wounded. ANDREW JOHNSON takes oath as President (April 15). Surrender of Gen. Johnston (April 26). Jefferson Davis captured (May 10). Surrender of Kirby Smith (May 26); **end of the Civil War.** Pres. Johnson issues an amnesty (May 30). Execution of Mrs. Surratt and others for complicity in Lincoln's assassination (July 7). *Shenandoah* surrenders to England. *Habeas Corpus* restored.

**1866** Johnson vetoes Freedmen's Bureau Bill (Feb. 19); also Civil Rights Bill; veto overruled; bill to admit COLORADO vetoed (May); overruled. Fenian raids on Canada (May-June) (*see* CANADA). Fourteenth Amendment passes the Senate. State elections sustain Congress as against the President. Pres. Johnson makes a speech-making tour.

**1867** Further vetoes overruled by two-thirds vote. NEBRASKA admitted as a State. Reconstruction Bill passed (March 20). ALASKA purchased from Russia for $7,000,000. General amnesty proclaimed (Sept. 9). Republicans gain supremacy in the South through negro votes.

**1868** **Articles of Impeachment against Pres. Johnson** agreed upon by House, 127—47 (March 22); trial begins (March 23); acquittal (May 26). Wyoming Territory organized. Southern States re-admitted over Johnson's veto. Presidential election; Grant defeats Seymour; Indian troubles (Nov.).

A.D.

**1869** Convention on *Alabama Claims* signed with Great Britain (Jan. 14). Fifteenth Amendment passed. Prosecution of Jefferson Davis dropped. ULYSSES S. GRANT inaugurated (March 4).

**1870** Virginia and Mississippi re-admitted to Congress (Feb. 3); also Texas and Georgia (April 20). Grant recalls Motley, Minister to Great Britain. New tariff bill passed. Death of GEN. ROBERT E. LEE (Oct. 12). St. Domingo project fails.

**1871** "Ku Klux Klan" outrages in North and South Carolina. Treaty of Washington (on *Alabama* Claims) signed, agreeing to Geneva arbitration (May). Corean forts destroyed (June). **Great Fire in Chicago** (Oct. 8-11). Visit of Grand Duke Alexis. Geneva Commission meets.

**1872** General Amnesty Bill passed. HORACE GREELEY nominated for President by "Liberal Republicans" (May 4); by Democrats (July 10). "Straight-out" Democrats nominate O'Connor. Award of Geneva Arbitration, over £3,000,000. Death of W. H. SEWARD. San Juan difficulty settled. Grant defeats Greeley in elections (Nov. 5); death of HORACE GREELEY (Nov. 29).

**1873** Defeat of troops by Modoc Indians in Oregon. Grant's second term begins. Credit Mobilier scandal. Death of CHIEF-JUSTICE CHASE. Murder of Gen. Canby and others by Modocs (June 1). *Virginius* troubles with Spain (Nov.).

**1874** Death of CHARLES SUMNER (March 11). Grant vetoes Currency Bill (April 22). Beecher-Tilton scandal in Brooklyn. Race conflicts in the South. Democratic gains in Congressional elections. RESUMPTION BILL passed (Dec.). Troops eject members of Legislature at New Orleans.

**1875** COLORADO made a State (Feb.). Civil Rights Bill passed. Death of Andrew Johnson (July 31). Centenary celebrations of Lexington and Bunker's Hill.

**1876** Whisky frauds exposed. Belknap, Secretary of War, accused of corruption; resigns (March). Emma Mine frauds in England; Minister Schenck resigns; John Walsh succeeds him. Hayes and Wheeler nominated by Cincinnati (Republican) Convention (June 16). Massacre of CUSTER and his army by the Sioux. Tilden nominated by St. Louis (Democratic) Convention. Centenary of the founding of the Republic (July 4). **International Exhibition at Philadelphia** (May-Nov.). Presidential election (Nov. 7); doubtful result; South Carolina, Florida, and Louisiana claimed by both parties; Louisiana "Returning Board" throw out many votes on charges of intimidation. Electoral College casts 185 votes for Hayes, 184 for Tilden.

A.D.

**1877** Electoral Commission (to settle presidential dispute) agreed upon in Congress (Jan. 30). It confirms the election of Hayes and Wheeler; inauguration of RUTHERFORD B. HAYES (March 4). Great railway strikes and riots in Pennsylvania and West Virginia (July). Much property destroyed at Pittsburg (July 22); loss of life; Chicago mob suppressed (July 26). Death of BRIGHAM YOUNG (Aug. 7).

**1878** Bland's Silver Bill passed; vetoed by Pres. Hayes. Kearney agitation in California. Yellow fever spreads through the South. Congressional elections leave Congress 149 Democrats, 130 Republicans, 10 Greenbackers. **Gold reaches par.**

**1879** **Specie resumption.** Caleb Cushing dies at Madrid. "Exodus" of negroes from South to West. LOWELL made Minister to England. Fall elections favor Republicans.

**1880** Garfield and Arthur nominated by Chicago (Republican) Convention (June 9); Hancock and English by Cincinnati (Democratic) Convention. "Morey letter" forgery. Presidential election; Republicans receive 213 out of 369 electoral votes.

**1881** JAMES A. GARFIELD inaugurated (March 4). Contest between Garfield and Senator Conkling (N. Y.) about New York Collectorship. Commercial treaty with China signed (May 5). Senators Conkling and Platt resign (May 16). Great Britain pays $15,000 award for Fortune Bay affair. **Assassination of Pres. Garfield by Charles J. Guiteau** at railway depot in Washington (July 2). "Dead lock" in New York broken by election of Miller and Lapham to the United States Senate. **Death of Pres. Garfield** at Elberon, N. J. (Sept. 19); burial at Cleveland (Sept. 26). Special session of the Senate (Oct. 10). Trial of GUITEAU begins (Nov. 14). News of destruction of *Jeannette*, Arctic exploring vessel (Dec. 30).

**1882** Guiteau convicted (Jan. 25); sentenced (Feb. 4); hanged (June 30). Great overflow of Mississippi River (March). ANTI CHINESE bill (twenty years) passed (March 23); vetoed (April 4). Second Anti-Chinese bill (ten years) passed; signed by the President. RIVER AND HARBOR bill passed over the President's veto. Return of survivors of North Pole expedition. STAR ROUTE trial ended by verdict of jury (Sept. 11) acquitting Turner, convicting Miner and Rerdell, and disagreeing as to Brady, the Dorsey brothers, and Vail. Democrats carry elections in Arkansas (Sept. 4); Republicans successful in Vermont (Sept. 4), and Maine (Sept. 11).

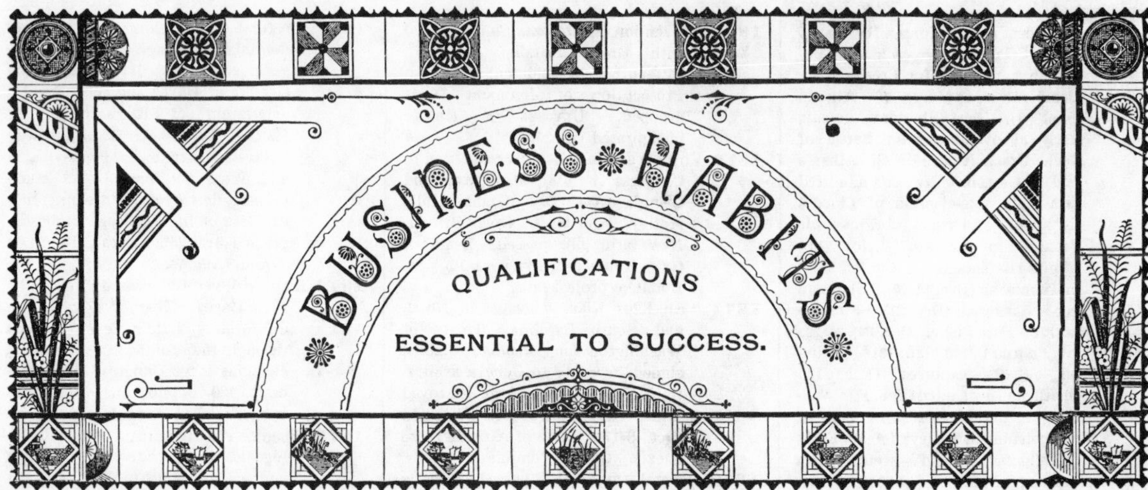


WHILE Sydney Smith was of the opinion that "every man should be occupied in the highest employment of which his nature is capable, and die with the consciousness that he has done his best," Longfellow maintained that "the talent of success is nothing more than doing what you can do well without a thought of fame." It would be a comparatively easy task to quote suitable proverbs, maxims, and epigrams on this subject; but no one but a charlatan would deem himself qualified to lay down infallible rules, or pretend to furnish the multitude with an "*open sesame*" to the secrets of success. There is no royal road to learning, and the path to fortune leads generally up-hill. It cannot be ignored that *Luck* and *Opportunity* often win the race, while *Merit* and *Ability* lag behind, but those who have "greatness thrust upon them" are few and far between. The great prizes of life are seldom won by those who do not possess the necessary qualifications for the attainment of permanent success.

**Health.**—A vigorous constitution is invaluable for those who desire to succeed in a mercantile career, for health is essentially the requirement of our time. Machinery has been carried to such perfection, that a large proportion of mankind, who formerly gained ascendency by superiority of bodily strength, are now compelled to submit to long hours of intense brainwork. This strain upon the mental powers of the modern business man can only be endured for any length of time by those who resort to the antidote of proportional physical action and outdoor exercise. Firmness of purpose and ability to perform great deeds are rarely found in a puny and effeminate body. It has been truly said that health is a large ingredient in what the world calls talent, and that the first requisite of success is to be a good animal.

**Education** is almost indispensable at the present time, although there are numerous instances of ignorant men rising to wealth and position by native ability and unusual force of character. The average man, however, will not be able to make up his deficiency in rudimentary knowledge by inherent talent and common-sense qualities. The reason why so many self-made men of inferior education have attained success in business is owing to the fact that it is not so much what a man knows, as the use he is able to make of his knowledge for practical purposes that tells in mercantile pursuits. It stands to reason that the great merchant, who gathers and distributes the products of every clime, would be an impossibility without the aids of educational knowledge. Books of instruction are so numerous, that there is no excuse for ignorance of the elementary branches of education, and the lack of early training can be overcome by continuous application in leisure hours.

**Industry.**—Rely above all on Industry in your fight to win in the battle of life. Do not take things easily, with no thought of the future, nor trust to favorable turns of the tide. "What men want," says Bulwer, "is, not talent, it is purpose; in other words, not the power to achieve, but the will to labor." "Know what thou canst work at," says Carlyle, "and work at it like a Hercules;" and the same author has defined genius as merely "a great capacity for taking pains." It matters not what branch of trade you are engaged in, it is impossible for you to succeed without the habit of industry. "It is the philosopher's stone," says Clarendon, "that turns all metals, and even stones into gold; it conquers all enemies, and makes fortune itself pay contributions." You must give your whole mind, heart, and soul to your work. To do this, you must love your work, for it is not talents nor acquirements, but enthusiasm and energy that win the great prizes of life. Whatever your business, master all its bearings and details, all its principles, instruments, and applications. Let nothing about it escape your notice; sound it "from the lowest note to the top of the compass."

**Method.**—There is no business which does not demand system. The meanest trade exacts it, and will go to ruin without it, but in a complicated business it is indispensable. It is method that binds all its parts together, and gives unity to all its details. Commissioners of insolvency say that the books of nine bankrupts out of ten are found to be in a muddle, kept without plan or method. Arrangement digests the matter that industry collects. It apportions time to duties, and keeps an exact register of its transactions; it has a post for every man, a place for every tool, a pigeon-hole for every paper, and a time for every settlement. A perfectly methodical man leaves his books, accounts, etc., in so complete a shape on going to bed, that if he were to be taken sick for a year, everything could be perfectly understood. On the first of every month a tradesman should know what he owed, what he bought and sold, and what his expenses were for the same month the preceding year; and you cannot be too methodical in knowing what you have to pay as soon as possible each month, and calculating and arranging how to pay it. "Successful men," says Carlyle, "possess the great gift of a methodical, well-balanced, arranging mind; they are men who cannot work in disorder, but will have things straight, and know all the details, which enables them so to arrange the machinery of their affairs, that they are fully cognizant alike of its strength, weakness, and capability, and they judiciously and discreetly exercise all its power to the uttermost."

**Accuracy.**—The necessity of accuracy to success in any calling is so obvious, as to hardly call for comment. "Whatever is worth doing is worth doing well," has, no doubt, become a hackneyed truism, but how many reputations have been ruined owing to the non-observance of this fact. It is better do a few things carefully than to do ten times as many in a loose and slovenly manner. Careful observation of facts, exactness in stating them, and accuracy in whatever work you undertake to perform, rank among the highest qualifications for a successful career.

**Punctuality** is a virtue that all men reverence in theory, but comparatively few carry into practice. Nothing inspires confidence in a business man sooner than this quality, nor is there any habit which is more disadvantageous than that of always being behind time. If that which is first at hand be not despatched at the proper time, other things accumulate, and the opportunity to attend to it may not arrive again. Punctuality has reference to time, money, and engagements for work. A want of system, defective calculation, and imprudence in making promises, when the probabilities of fulfilling are very uncertain, are among the most frequent causes of persons lacking punctuality. The successful men in every calling have had a keen sense of the value of time.

**Dispatch** is the knack of doing one's work quickly, which, of course, should always be secondary to accuracy. It is the result of skill, system, and experience, and can be employed to advantage by those only who are thoroughly familiar with the work they are about to undertake.

**Readiness** is the ability to use all one's resources instantly, and at the right moment; it is a gift of great value in commercial transactions.

**Decision** is of vital importance to those who have to deal with the practical affairs of life. A vacillating man, no matter what his abilities, is invariably pushed aside by the man of determined will. It has been wisely remarked, that it is probable every man possesses a germ of this quality, which can be cultivated by favorable circumstances; and by method and order in the prosecution of his duties and tasks, he may by habit greatly augment his will-power, or beget a frame of mind so nearly resembling decision, that it would be difficult to decide between the two. "In order to do anything in this world that is worth doing," says Sydney Smith, "we must not stand shivering on the bank, and thinking of the cold and the danger, but jump in and scramble through as well as we can."

**Perseverance** means the steady pursuit of a plan that has been determined upon. There is hardly an employment in life so trifling that it will not afford a subsistence, if constantly and faithfully followed; and it is by indefatigable diligence alone that a fortune can be acquired in any business whatever.

**Calculation**, as a business habit, means more than arithmetical computation. It is synonymous with prudence, and implies the ability to weigh probabilities, measure risks, and distinguish between the true and the false. In its comprehensive sense, it also demonstrates to a man that honesty is the best policy, and that to be a rogue is to be a fool.

To sum up, it should not be overlooked that practical talent, common sense, and a thorough knowledge of human nature, are at the foundation of all prosperity in commercial pursuits. How to act in an emergency, how to say the right thing in the right place, and how to deal with customers cannot be taught in books. The Rothschilds, Astors, and Stewarts of the mercantile world are generally shrewd men, of great enterprise and wonderful executive ability, but it will be found, on close examination of their characters, that they also possess, in greater or less degree, all the business qualities mentioned above. In order to become a successful merchant, it is necessary to acquire the habit of watching the markets, and studying the laws of demand and supply. He must be able to devise shrewd and ingenious methods of attracting trade; should know how to calculate to a nicety at what price he can sell his goods with a fair and reasonable profit; and never drive customers away by affixing a high price to an inferior quality of goods. He should regard the interests of the buyer, and sell him goods that are adapted to his market, or such as he can resell quickly and advantageously. He should use good judgment in extending credit, and not allow himself to be swindled by false representations. He should use discretion in selecting a location for his business, and use all proper means for advertising his trade. The man of business must think for himself, for the days when a man could get rich by plodding on without enterprise have passed. Industry and economy will not suffice; the modern business man requires intelligence and original thought, whether he be a *shipping*, *importing*, or *commission* merchant—a *wholesale* or a *retail* dealer. Every calling is filled with bold, keen, subtle-witted men, fertile in devices and expedients, who are perpetually inventing new ways of buying cheaply, in order to attract customers by selling at lower prices than their competitors in the same branch of trade. The man, therefore, who runs in a perpetual groove will fall behind, instead of advancing his interests. "Commerce," says Dr. Mathews, "is no longer a mere dollar-and-cent traffic, requiring no apprenticeship, but a matter tasking the mind to the utmost, to be mastered by the highest sagacity, and after the profoundest study of facts, circumstances and prospects. The times demand men of large and energetic soul, and the man who insists on doing business in the old-fashioned, jog-trot, humdrum way is as much out of place as he who insists on traveling with an ox-team instead of by railway, or upon getting news by the old stage-coach instead of by the lightning telegraph."

In conclusion, it should be remembered that circumstances alter cases, and that every individual must find out by practical experience the proper methods of conducting his business. Natural ability and enthusiasm are more likely to lead a man to the goal of his ambition than all the rules and wise sayings that have been written on the subject of success since the world began. Find out what you are best fitted for, choose a congenial occupation, acquire as much information as possible relating to the profession or business you propose to follow, work with all your heart and soul to get on in the world, and the chances are that sooner or later—you will succeed.

## HABITS OF A BUSINESS MAN.

He is strict in keeping his engagements.

Does nothing carelessly or in a hurry.

Employs nobody to do what he can easily do himself.

Keeps everything in its proper place.

Leaves nothing undone that ought to be done, and which circumstances permit him to do.

Keeps his designs and business from the view of others.

Is prompt and decisive with his customers, and does not overtrade his capital.

Prefers short credits to long ones ; and cash to credit at all times, either in buying or selling ; and small profits, in credit cases, with little risk, to the chance of better gains with more hazard.

He is clear and explicit in all his bargains.

Leaves nothing of consequence to memory which he can and ought to commit to writing.

Keeps copies of all his important letters which he sends away, and has every letter, invoice, &c., relating to his business, titled, classed, and put away.

Never suffers his desk to be confused by many papers lying upon it.

Is always at the head of his business, well knowing that if he leaves it, it will leave him.

Holds it as a maxim that he whose credit is suspected is not one to be trusted.

Is constantly examining his books, and sees through all his affairs as far as care and attention will enable him.

Balances regularly at stated times, and then makes out and transmits all his accounts current to his customers both at home and abroad.

Avoids as much as possible all sorts of accommodation in money matters and lawsuits where there is the least hazard.

He is economical in his expenditure, always living within his income.

Keeps a memorandum book in his pocket in which he notes every particular relative to appointments, addresses, and petty cash matters.

Is cautious how he becomes security for any person, and is generous when urged by motives of humanity.

## BUSINESS MAXIMS.

God helps them that help themselves. Diligence is the mother of good luck.

Time is money. What we call time enough, always proves little enough.

God gives all things to industry ; then plough deep while sluggards sleep, and you will have corn to sell and to keep.

The sleeping fox catches no poultry, and there will be sleeping enough in the grave.

He that rises late must trot all day, and shall scarce overtake his business at night.

Drive thy business, let not that drive thee.

Early to bed, and early to rise, makes a man healthy, wealthy and wise.

He that hath a trade hath an estate.

One to-day is worth two to-morrows. Have you somewhat to do to-morrow, do it to-day.

Handle your tools without mittens. A cat in gloves catches no mice.

Three removes are as bad as a fire. A rolling stone gathers no moss.

If you would have your business done, go; if not, send.

If you would be wealthy, think of saving as well as getting. A fat kitchen makes a lean will.

Beware of little expenses. A small leak will sink a great ship.

Buy what thou hast need of, and ere long thou shalt sell thy necessaries. Silks and satins, scarlet and velvet, put out the kitchen fire.

If you would know the value of money, go and try to borrow some. A child and a fool imagine twenty shillings and twenty years can never be spent.

Pride is as loud a beggar as want, and a great deal more saucy.

Rather go to bed supperless than rise in debt. The borrower is a slave to the lender, and the debtor to the creditor.

They that will not be counseled cannot be helped. If you will not hear reason, she will surely rap your knuckles.

THERE is probably no attainment more desirable than the art of LETTER WRITING, and no lady or gentleman should neglect the opportunity of becoming proficient in this accomplishment. An elegant and well written letter is generally considered a mark of refinement and education, while a letter bearing the stamp of slovenliness and ignorance gives the person to whom it is sent a very poor opinion of the writer's character and ability.

In this progressive age, the increased facilities for writing and transmitting letters are fully proportionate to the advance in other matters, the opportunities and necessities for correspondence are equally increased; and the individual is sadly behind the times who does not appreciate the value of a knowledge that enables us to properly communicate ideas through the medium of "written language."

There is no condition of life, humble or elevated, in which the "art of letter writing" will not at times be found of much importance. It is a comfort and blessing to the poor; with the middle and upper classes an indispensable acquirement—a boundless means of pleasure and gratification.

The way to prosperity has been opened for many persons by means of well-written letters; and happy marriages, lasting friendships, and important services have been promoted in the same manner; for letters, in a certain sense, are the reflections or photographs of the writers, and their perusal may inspire affection or hatred, esteem or aversion, just as a portrait often creates our opinion of the person it represents. It may, therefore, be conceded that proficiency in the epistolary art is one of the paths to success in all the affairs of life.

## METHOD AND STYLE.

A proper study of the rules of penmanship, orthography, punctuation, grammar, and com position, as treated under their respective headings, is of primary importance to the accomplishment of the art of letter writing. After these subjects have been thoroughly mastered, it should be remembered that letter writing is simply "speaking with the pen." The pervading idea of the writer should, therefore, be to express his ideas as easily and naturally as in conversation, but with more brevity and method. Carefully consider the purport of any letter you are about to write; think of the circumstances you wish to state before beginning it. You will find this practice of great assistance in obtaining clearness of expression, which is the essential feature to be acquired. You will also be enabled to bring out the principal points of your subject more effectively, while the less important ones may be more lightly touched upon.

A certain amount of tact, however, is necessary to avoid a formal or studied effect, frequently caused by this pre-arrangement of ideas. The use of short sentences by the inexperienced will greatly aid in promoting the lucidity of their letters. Long sentences, even when their composition is perfect, often obscure the meaning of the writer, and are less forcible than short ones. The parenthesis tends to a similar effect, and should be used as seldom as possible. Care should be taken to avoid an unnecessary repetition of the same words. Avoid also tautology, which is always a fault, being a repetition of the same meaning in different words, and adding nothing either to the sense or sound; consult our dictionary of synonyms frequently, as it will cause a familiarity with the exact meaning of words, and in what cases they should be applied.

### A PROPERLY ARRANGED LETTER.

(Heading.)
*17 Barclay St., New York,*
*May 25th, 1882.*

(Address.)
*Mr. E. A. Chastenay,*
*Paris, France.*

(Salutation.)
*My dear Sir,*

(Body of the Letter.)
*As you will perceive from the heading of my letter, I have safely arrived home, and settled down to business once more. The ocean trip was a pleasant one, the weather being favorable and the passengers congenial.*

*Permit me to renew my thanks for the many courtesies extended to me while visiting your city, and to assure you that it will give me great pleasure to reciprocate whenever the opportunity may occur.*

*Present my regards to your estimable wife, and believe me,*

(Complimentary Closing.)
*Very sincerely yours,*

(Subscription.)
*George A. Ferris.*

The ***Style*** of a letter should be governed, in a measure, by the nature of the subject, but the comparative social position, age, sex, and the degree of intimacy between the writer and the person addressed, should influence it to a greater degree. In writing to superiors or seniors, a certain deference of expression should be exercised; to inferiors be courteous, without familiarity, and say nothing to remind them of the difference in station; to relatives and intimate friends be as affectionate and familiar as your own judgment may dictate. There can be no better general rule to follow, with regard to style, than to adopt the same tone and manner of expression in your correspondence that you would use in speaking personally to the person addressed.

## *ARRANGEMENT OF THE PARTS OF A LETTER.*

Every complete letter has six distinct parts:—

1. The ***Date*** or ***Heading,*** which embraces the place of writing as well as the day of the month and year.

2. The ***Address,*** which con-

sists of the name and residence of the person to whom it is written.

3. The ***Salutation,*** or complimentary opening, such as *Dear Sir,* or *Dear Madam.*

4. The ***Body of the Letter,*** which contains the subjects or circumstances you wish to state.

5. The ***Complimentary Closing,*** as, *I remain, Yours truly,* or, *believe me, Yours sincerely,* etc.

6. The ***Subscription,*** which is simply the signature of the writer.

### THE HEADING.

If the letter be written from a country town or small city, the name of the place, county, and state should occupy the first line, commencing about the middle, and the date the next line below, beginning a little to the right, *viz.* :—

*Eureka, Woodford Co., Ill.,*
*June* 15*th*, 1882.

If you are writing from a large city, and it is necessary to specify the street and number of your address, it should be written thus :—

22 *Park Place, New York,*
*August* 5*th*, 1882

or,

22 *Park Place,*
*New York, August* 5*th*, 1882.

In writing from large, well-known cities like New York, Philadelphia, Chicago, etc., it is unnecessary to indicate the State. In the case of smaller cities it is better to include the State, as,

*Providence, R. I., May* 10*th*, 1882.

When writing from a Hotel or Institution, its name should be included, thus :—

***St. Nicholas Hotel,***
*New York, August* 5*th*, 1882.

***Yale College,***
*New Haven, Conn.,*
*May* 5*th*, 1882.

The heading should invariably indicate with accuracy the place from which the letter is written and to which a reply may be sent, unless otherwise specified in the body of the letter.

### COMPLIMENTARY ADDRESS AND SALUTATION.

The NAME and ADDRESS are often written at the conclusion of the letter on the left hand side, but as frequently, especially in business letters, they occupy one or two lines immediately below the date, on the left side of the page, and may include the name and address, or the name alone, *viz.* :—

***17 Barclay Street, New York,***
*July* 10*th*, 1882.

*Mr. John Masters,*
*New Haven, Conn.*

The SALUTATION is written on the line below the address, commencing a little to the right of the left hand margin. The wording depends entirely on the mutual relations of the parties concerned. In business letters the words *Sir, Dear Sir,* or *Gentlemen* are all correct. In very formal letters to ladies, married or single, the word *Madam* should be used; a more friendly form would be *Dear Madam,* or *My dear Madam.* A lady should never be addressed by her Christian name in a letter, unless you would use it in her presence.

### BODY OF THE LETTER.

The BODY OF THE LETTER should commence about the middle of the page on the line below the salutation. Each topic or subject should form a new paragraph commencing on the next line, a little to the right of the left hand margin ; uniformity in this respect tending greatly to improve the general appearance of the letter.

### COMPLIMENTARY CLOSING.

The terms used in *closing a letter* precede the signature of the writer, and admit of great variety ; as a rule, the formality or friendliness of the closing should correspond with the mode of salutation. A very formal letter beginning with *Sir* or *Madam* may be closed as follows :—

*I have the honor to be, Sir* (or *Madam*),
*Your obedient Servant,*
EDWARD CHESTERFIELD.

A more friendly form, commencing with *My dear Sir,* or *My dear Madam,* would be :—

*I beg to remain,*
*Yours very respectfully,*
HENRY B. SANDERSON.

In letters between friends and intimate acquaintances, there is more latitude of expression allowable. *Yours very truly, Sincerely your friend, Affectionately yours,* or any other forms of respect or endearment compatible with the state of intimacy or relationship.

### SUBSCRIPTION OR SIGNATURE.

The name of the writer should be plainly written immediately below the closing phrase, so that it will end near the right margin of the page; and to important communications the full signature is requisite.

In writing to strangers a lady should make her signature indicate her sex and condition; the latter designation being inclosed in parenthesis, as (*Mrs.*) EDITH HASTINGS, or (*Miss*) ELLEN JOHNSON, otherwise her correspondent, in answering, might be unable to properly address her.

## THE SUPERSCRIPTION.

Last but not least in importance is the SUPERSCRIPTION or ADDRESS to be written on the envelope. Legibility is of primary consequence, and every item necessary to insure safe delivery should be included in proper arrangement: first, the name of the person to whom the letter is sent, written a trifle below the middle of the envelope; next, the name of the post-office; then the county, and lastly the state.

If the address requires a street number, it should follow the name, then the city and state as before.

If necessary to direct the letter in care of another person the additional name occupies the second line.

In writing to a person in a large city, where there is no street or special address, it is well to add the words "*General Delivery*" in the lower left-hand corner. The post-office clerk will then understand that it is to be called for.

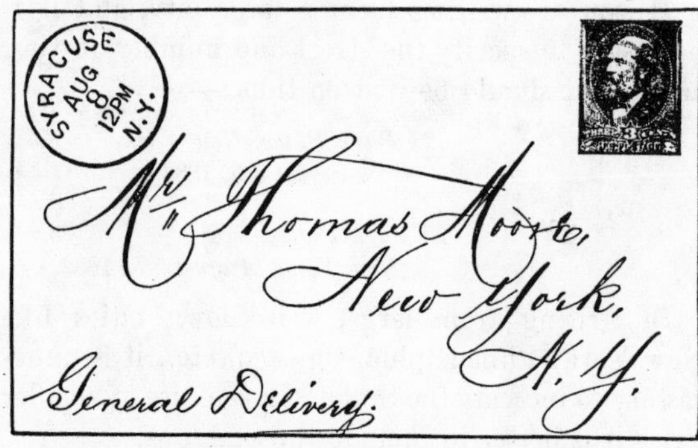


## HONORARY TITLES.

In the United States the use of titles is determined by the social, professional, or official position of the person addressed, and their proper application is an additional evidence of the courtesy and refinement of the writer. Every person, whether of high or low degree is entitled respectively to the appelation of *Mr.* (mister), *Master*, *Mrs.* (contraction of mistress), or *Miss*.

In addressing gentlemen of high social standing or members of the legal profession the prefix *Mr.* may be omitted and the complimentary title of *Esq.* (esquire) added. This latter term is, however, a distinction more strictly English, and should seldom be used unless really appropriate. One title or the other should always be used, but never both together. Members of any profession should be addressed by their professional title, which takes the place of other forms. Neither *Mr.* nor *Esq.* can be used for *Professor, Doctor,* etc.

## PROFESSIONAL TITLES USED IN THE UNITED STATES.

*Rt. Rev.* Charles Smith—A Bishop.
*Rev.* Charles Smith, *D. D.*—Doctor of Divinity.
*Rev.* Charles Smith—Minister or Priest of any persuasion.
**Rev.* (or *Prof.*) Charles Smith, *L.L. D.*—Doctor of Laws.
*Dr.* Charles Smith, or Charles Smith, *M. D.* }—Doctor of Medicine.
*Prof.* Charles Smith—Professor of Art or Science.
*Hon.* Charles Smith—Judge of Law Courts.
Charles Smith, *Esq.*—Attorney at Law.

In addition to the above, the following titles are used in addressing the Roman Catholic clergy :—

*His Holiness*—The Pope.
*His Eminence*—A Cardinal.
*His Grace*—An Archbishop.

Persons occupying prominent public positions acquire the right to be addressed by the titles prescribed by custom and courtesy as distinctive of their offices.

## OFFICIAL TITLES USED IN THE UNITED STATES.

**His Excellency.**† { The President of the United States, Governors of States, and Ministers to foreign countries.

**Honorable.** { The Vice-President of the United States, Heads of the Executive Department of the United States Government, Members of Congress, Lieutenant-Governors of States, State Senators and Representatives, Judges, Mayors.

*A person may be a Doctor of Laws and also a Professor of some Art or Science instead of a Minister of the Gospel. See the list of abbreviations in another part of this book.

† The use of this title is considered objectionable by some critics. In Massachusetts and South Carolina the title is conferred upon the Governor by the State Constitution.

All officers of the army or navy should be addressed according to their rank.

We give a few examples of superscriptions where professional and official titles are required :

Stamp.

Hon. Jasper M. Gilbert,
Supreme Court,
Brooklyn,
N. Y.

Maj-Gen. Winfield S. Hancock,
Headquarters, Dep't of the Atlantic,
Governor's Island,
New York,
N. Y.

One title only may be *prefixed* to any name, such as *Hon., Prof., Dr.;* but it is correct to *affix* several if they exist, and in the order in which they were conferred ; for instance, *A.M., M.D., LL.D ;* or *D.D., LL.D.,* etc.

In addressing men in the plural, or a firm of several members, the proper title to use is *Messrs.*, a contraction of the French word *Messieurs*, signifying gentlemen ; to unmarried ladies it would be *Misses*, and to married ladies *Mesdames.*

## ENGLISH TITLES.

Appended are the forms for addressing persons of different ranks in England, and the proper superscriptions :

***The Queen***—Madam—To the Queen's Most Excellent Majesty.

***Members of the Royal Family***—Sir—Madam—To His or Her Royal Highness.

***Archbishops***—My Lord Archbishop—His Grace the Archbishop of—
***Duke***—My Lord Duke—His Grace the Duke of——
***Marquis***—My Lord Marquis—the Most Hon. the Marquis of——
***Earl***—My Lord—The Right Hon. the Earl of——
***Viscount***—My Lord—The Right Hon. the Viscount——
***Baron***—My Lord—the Right Hon. the Lord F——
***Bishops***—My Lord Bishop—The Right Rev. the Bishop of——

Honorary titles, as "K.G.," "K.C.B.," "M.P.," etc., may be added to the name. All members of the Privy Council are addressed as "Right Hon.," and the title of "Esq." is dropped, as "The Right Hon. W. E. Gladstone, M.P."

Peeresses of all the five orders are addressed as:

***Duchess***—My Lady—Her Grace the Duchess of——
***Marchioness***—My Lady—The Most Hon. the Marchioness of——
***Countess***—My Lady—The Right Hon. the Countess of——
***Viscountess***—My Lady—The Right Hon. the Viscountess of——
***Baroness***—My Lady—the Right Hon. the Lady F——

Widows of peers, if the successors to the title are married :—

Her Grace the Duchess Dowager of——
The Most Noble the Marchioness Dowager of——

The younger sons and daughters of dukes and marquises, and the daughters of dukes, marquises, and earls, are styled *lords* and *ladies*.

Younger sons of earls and younger sons and daughters of viscounts and barons are styled "The Hon." Baronets, in order to distinguish them from Knights, are addressed thus, "Sir H. Grey, Bart."

## GENERAL ADVICE.

Always answer a letter as soon after its receipt as possible. If it contains commissions that require time to execute, acknowledge its receipt at once, and state the cause of delay in complying with its requests.

Write invariably with ink. Pencil writing denotes carelessness. If compelled to use a pencil, apologize for it.

Black ink is preferable to all others. A violet ink for ladies' use is fashionable at present. Red ink should never be used in correspondence.

When writing about your own affairs, necessitating a reply, inclose a stamp for return postage, unless a relationship or intimacy exists between yourself and correspondent.

Never cross your letters (a practice prevalent among some young ladies) ; use an extra half sheet if necessary.

If you are in doubt about the spelling of a word, always consult the dictionary ; the search will impress the orthography on the mind.

No respectable person will write an anonymous letter ; it is cowardly.

Avoid the use of slang words or phrases, even harmless ones.

If you are in a state of dejection or ill temper, do not manifest it in your letters.

A half sheet of paper is not permissible, except for business purposes.

Mourning paper should not be used in a letter of congratulation.

In order to make our letters pleasant to our friends, we should write as we speak, just what we have to say, and exactly in the words we should use if our correspondent were sitting by us ; and then all that stiff formality, those long strings of questions, those meaningless sentences with which the mass of letters are burdened, would die a natural death.

The handwriting should be clear, and yet not too large and bold ; it should possess some character and style, but not be adorned or ornamented with fine flourishes and dashes. The minute Italian handwriting—in which the words and letters appeared to possess no individuality of their own—has now passed out of date, and a freer, nobler style has taken its place. There is a fashion in letter paper and envelopes which is ever-varying as to size and shape—sometimes small, at other times large ; now oblong, now square ; but one thing never alters, and that is the desirability of using good thick paper and envelopes, whatever the shape may be. Nothing looks more mean and untidy than thin sheets and envelopes of the same quality, through which the writing exhibits itself.

The latest styles and devices, as well as their special application, can always be ascertained by consulting the stationer who provides your writing materials.

BUSINESS LETTERS, in this great trading and money-making century, are necessarily of great importance, and since the time of both sender and receiver is valuable, brevity becomes an essential characteristic. As Ben Jonson has so well written, "Brevity is attained in matter by avoiding idle compliments, prefaces, protestations, parentheses, superfluous circuits of figures, and digressions; in the composition, by omitting conjunctions, and such like idle particles that have no great business in a serious letter except the breaking of sentences, as oftentimes a journey is made long by unnecessary halts."

The letter must not, however, be so curt that its clearness is interfered with; every statement should be perfectly free from obscurity, so that the dullest person may not be liable to mistake its meaning, nor be compelled to read it twice in order to understand it. This necessary clearness implies correctness without excluding elegance of style.

In business letters an elegant simplicity combined with the usual terms of politeness and good breeding are essential features. Misunderstanding arising out of a carelessly worded letter has often created much mischief and been the cause of costly proceedings in the law courts. Brevity and perspicuity must, then, go hand in hand in a good business letter, and with them should be linked vigor of style and tact. By tact is meant that knowledge of men and manners, which enables the writer to compose his letter in a style befitting the person addressed.

The handwriting itself should be free, neat, and legible, but it is well to avoid pretensions to excessive elegance. A free hand, which is neither crabbed nor formal, nor abounding in flourishes, is the most desirable. Legibility cannot be too strongly advocated; it is exceedingly selfish in a writer to occupy the time of his correspondent by providing him with a mass of hieroglyphics to decipher.

The inexperienced will find it of great assistance, before commencing a letter of any extent, to note down the different subjects they desire to embrace, so that they may be taken up in proper order. This practice is especially valuable when instructions concerning the topics of the letter are communicated verbally to a clerk.

In reading business correspondence it is a good plan to underline the important points that require consideration in the answer, with a colored lead pencil; this will save time by enabling the correspondent to avoid reading the second time matter that is not pertinent, and also promote the method of replying to the various subjects in the same order in which they occur.

# FORMS OF BUSINESS LETTERS.

## NOTICE OF COPARTNERSHIP.

New York, June 1st, 1882.

M________________________

______________________

We beg to inform you that we have this day formed a copartnership under the firm name of *Rice & Farrington*, for the purpose of carrying on the importing and jobbing of photograph albums and leather fancy goods, at No. 22 Park Place, New York.

The possession of ample capital, combined with a long and varied experience in this line, enables us to assure our friends and the trade generally that they will consult their best interests by favoring us with their patronage.

Very respectfully,
Edward M. Rice.
Charles Farrington.

## DISSOLUTION OF COPARTNERSHIP.

Sidney, Sept. 15, 1882.

M________________________

______________________

You are hereby respectfully advised that the copartnership hitherto existing under the firm name of Gregg, Brown & Co., is this day dissolved by mutual consent. Mr. Henry Brown will sign in liquidation, and is empowered to receive and pay all debts of the late copartnership.

Very respectfully,
Jonathan Gregg,
Henry Brown,
Robert W. Sanders.

## REQUEST FOR CATALOGUE AND TERMS.

Cincinnati, Aug. 25, 1882.

American Publishing Co.,
New York.

*Gentlemen:* —

Please favor me with your catalogue, and quote your best prices and terms on your publications generally. I beg to refer you, concerning my standing, to Mr. Thomas Kelly, 17 Barclay St., New York, with whom I have had considerable dealing; and, awaiting the pleasure of an early reply, I remain,

Very respectfully,
Lucien H. Barkdull.

## ORDER TO A PUBLISHER.

New Orleans, Sept. 5, 1882.

Mr. Thomas Kelly,
New York.

*Dear Sir:* —

Please ship us by first Mallory line steamer, the following goods:
100 copies History of U. S., half mor.
250 " Universal Self-Instructor, cloth.
25 " Brown's Bible, No. 65.

Please effect insurance for full amount of invoice, and send certificate of same together with B/L., and oblige,

Yours truly,
N. D. McDonald & Co.

## NOTICE OF DRAFT.

Boston, Oct. 10, 1882.

Messrs. W. Chambers & Co.,
Philadelphia.

*Gentlemen:* —

We have this day drawn on you at five days' sight for three hundred dollars ($300), which please honor and oblige,

Yours respectfully,
Brown, Smith & Co.

## REQUESTING AN EXTENSION OF NOTE.

Buffalo, N. Y., Oct. 9, 1882.

Messrs. J. J. Little & Co.,
New York.

*Gentlemen:* —

We are reluctantly compelled to advise you that we shall be unable to meet our note for seven hundred dollars, maturing 14th inst., without your assistance to the extent of three hundred dollars ($300). If you will kindly forward us draft for that amount, we will return you our note for same at thirty days, interest added; and assure you that there is scarcely a doubt of our being able to pay it when due. Our lack of funds in the present instance is entirely owing to the depression of trade, caused by the lateness of the season, and the consequent dullness of collections. Hoping you may find it convenient to oblige us, we remain,

Very truly yours,
Jones, Robinson & Co.

## ASKING A SETTLEMENT OF ACCOUNT.

New Haven, Conn., Aug. 15, 1883.

Messrs. Wade & Clark,
Worcester, Mass.

*Gentlemen:* —

We are under the necessity of reminding you that your account for May is considerably past due, and as we have especial need of all our available funds this month, we trust you will make us a remittance without further delay.

Respectfully,
Carter & Phillips.

## REPLY TO FOREGOING.

Worcester, Mass., Aug. 17, 1882.

Messrs Carter & Phillips,
New Haven, Conn.

*Gentlemen:* —

Yours of the 15th inst. is duly received. We inclose you herewith a draft on New York payable to your order, for $112.46, the amount due you upon our books. We greatly regret having put you to any inconvenience by delay in payment, but have been temporarily embarrassed by the tardiness of our own debtors. Henceforth, as in the past, we hope to remit promptly at the close of each month.

Yours respectfully,
Wade & Clark,
*per W.*

## UNFAVORABLE ANSWER.

Worcester, Mass., Aug. 17, 1882.

Messrs. Carter & Phillips,
New Haven, Conn.

*Gentlemen:* —

Yours of the 15th inst. received and contents noted. We find ourselves obliged to defer payment of your account for a few days longer, but will surely send it before the end of next week. We hope that this will put you to no serious inconvenience, and assure you that our delay arises from circumstances beyond our power to control, and is not likely to occur again.

Yours truly,
Wade & Clark,
*per W.*

## OFFERING PROMISSORY NOTE.

Cleveland, O., Nov. 8, 1881.

Messrs. Wilcox, Field & Black,
Chicago, Ill.

*Gentlemen:* —

Yours of the 6th inst. is received, requesting immediate payment. I am sorry to say that the failure of the Tradesmen's Bank of this city, with which I had an account, has thrown me into great embarrassment. I am confident that ultimately I shall be able to meet all my liabilities in full. At present the best I can do is to offer you my note at three months for the amount due, $285.50, with legal interest, payable at the First National Bank of Chicago. I have little doubt but that by the time it is due, I shall be able to take it up. Hoping that this proposal will meet with acceptance on your part and that you will recognize the fact that I am not personally to blame in the matter, I remain,

Yours respectfully,
William Hatch.

## THREATENING LAW PROCEEDINGS.

412 Seventh Ave., NEW YORK,
May 17, 1882.

JAMES BOLLMAN, ESQ.,
322 W. 18th St.

*Sir :—*

I have waited patiently for three months to receive payment of your bill for groceries and provisions purchased of me. The last item was bought Feb. 10, and it is now the middle of May. The bill has been sent to you several times, but has met with no response. I am obliged to inform you that if payment is not made before the first of next month, I shall put the account into the hands of an attorney for collection.

STEPHEN DUNSCOMBE.

## ATTORNEY'S DEMAND FOR PAYMENT.

Room 12, No. 523 Sixth Ave.
June 3, 1882.

JAMES BOLLMAN,
322 W. 18th St.

*Sir :—*

A bill against you to the amount of $196.85 for groceries and provisions has been put in my hands for collection by Mr. Stephen Dunscombe. I inclose a copy of the bill. You will find it to your advantage to call at my office *at once* and settle the account, as otherwise legal proceedings will be instituted and the amount considerably increased by the charges.

Yours truly,
SIMON STRAUSS, *Attorney at Law.*

## OFFER TO OPEN AN ACCOUNT.

PEORIA, ILL., Dec. 18, 1879.

MESSRS. HART & SYLVESTER,
Chicago, Ill.

*Gentlemen :—*

I have lately opened a millinery and fancy goods store in this place, and as I am not yet fully stocked, I propose opening an account with your house, if agreeable to you. I can refer you to Disbrow & Sellers, of your city, with whom I have had dealings in the past, and also to Edward Wilcox & Co., of this city, who are well acquainted with my financial standing, and with whom I believe you correspond. Should the information you may receive from them prove satisfactory, please inform me to that effect, and I will at once forward an order for what goods I require at present.

Very respectfully,
MARY J. RAWLINGS.

## LETTER OF CREDIT.

NEW ORLEANS, Sept. 25, 1881.

MESSRS. VERMILYEA & Co.,
New York City.

*Gentlemen :—*

Please give the bearer, George Ashdown, a cash credit to the extent of $12,000, taking his receipt for the amount required and drawing on us at short sight for your advances. We inclose Mr. Ashdown's signature.

Yours truly,
COX & LATHROP.

(*Mr. Ashdown's signature.*)
GEORGE ASHDOWN.

## INTRODUCTION AND CREDIT.

ST. LOUIS, MO., Jan. 8, 1876.

MESSRS. LORD & TAYLOR,

*Gentlemen :—*

We beg leave to introduce to you the bearer, Frederick S. Bush, of this city, of the firm of Colt, Sanders & Bush, dry goods merchants. Mr. Bush is visiting New York to purchase an extensive line of goods, and we have recommended him to your house as a favorable one to deal with. We will become responsible to you for the payment of the price of goods and merchandise purchased, to the value of six thousand dollars ($6,000), holding ourselves accountable in case Mr. Bush should make default, of which default you are to give us reasonable notice.

Yours very truly,
J. T. & L. F. WILLIAMS.

## ANNOUNCING INSOLVENCY.

INDIANAPOLIS, IND., May 12, 1883.

J. C. WATSON & Co.,
Chicago, Ill.

*Gentlemen : —*

It becomes our painful duty to announce to you, in common with our other creditors, that upon a careful examination of our books and assets, we find that we are no longer able to meet our outstanding engagements, and have therefore this day suspended payment.

Our insolvency arises from two causes, the general depression of trade which has been so extensively felt in this section of the country, and our losses by the fire of last November, from which, though partly insured, we have never fully recovered. We propose to call a meeting of our creditors, at the earliest possible date, to lay before them a full and unreserved statement of our assets and liabilities. Of this meeting we will give you due notice, and hope your firm will be there represented. It is impossible at this time to state what percentage of our indebtedness we may be able to pay, but we have hopes it will be a large one and that the matter will be arranged in a friendly manner. We earnestly hope that you will believe us when we say that we have done all in our power to avert this misfortune, and propose to deal with our creditors in the most frank and open manner.

Yours with regret,
STEPHEN BISHOP & SON.

## RECOMMENDATION OF SUCCESSORS.

NEW YORK CITY, Aug. 12, 1880.

JARED HOFFMEIER, ESQ.
Atlanta, Ga.

*Sir :—*

As an old and esteemed customer of this firm, we desire to inform you that on and after the first of next month, we shall retire entirely from the business we have hitherto conducted. On that date our lease of premises and stock on hand will be transferred to Maurice Gordon and Joseph Heller, who will carry on the business under the firm name of Gordon & Co. We beg leave to recommend the new firm to your notice. We are well acquainted with the business integrity and capacity of both members, and feel sure that if you honor them with your custom the result will be in every way to your satisfaction. Thanking you for the favors of the past, we remain,

Your obliged servants,
HOLLIS & JENNINGHAM.

## ASKING FOR PRICE LIST.

PITTSBURG, PA., April 4, 1882.

MESSRS. GOELET & KIRSCHNER,
New York City.

*Gentlemen :—*

I am assured by Mr. William Allen, an old customer of yours, that by dealing with you I can obtain an excellent assortment of wines and liquors, and at a moderate price. I should be glad to obtain your price list. If your rates are satisfactory I may give you a very considerable order upon my next visit to your city. I understand from Mr. Allen that your usual terms of sale are three months' notes or a discount of two per cent. for cash. If I desire credit I will, of course, furnish you with satisfactory references before ordering.

Yours truly,
ELMER G. HOWD.

## INQUIRY ABOUT OVERDUE SHIPMENT.

PHILADELPHIA, July 8, 1883.

S. S. HOLTON & Co.,
San Francisco, Cal.

*Sir :—*

We are informed by yours of the 12th ult. that upon that day you shipped to us fifty cases California wine per Union Pacific Railroad, marked with our firm name as above, and charges prepaid. The goods should have arrived before this, but have not ; and inquiry at this end of the line fails to elicit any information as to their whereabouts. Will you do us the favor to make inquiry at the office where you shipped the goods and, if possible, expedite their transportation ?

Yours to command,
BETTS & HOWLAND.

## RELATING TO PAYMENT OF MORTGAGE.

12 Scranton St., ALBANY, N. Y.
Oct. 19, 1882.

JAMES WINTHROP, ESQ.

*Dear Sir :—*

The note for $2,500, for the security of which you hold a mortgage deed on my house and lot, No. 12 Scranton St., is payable on the first of next month. After that date I understand that you can, if you choose, at once bring suit for foreclosure. It is not in my power to raise the sum necessary to discharge the debt, and I should be greatly obliged for information as to your intentions on the subject. As you know, I have always paid the interest regularly, and I inclose herewith a check for the last quarter ($37.50) payable to your order. You are probably aware that I have a small but regular income and am certain to keep up the interest. Under these circumstances I have great hopes that you will allow matters to stand as they are at the present.

Yours respectfully,
JANET C. SUTTON.

## ANSWER TO FOREGOING.

56 Grafton St., ALBANY,
Oct. 21, 1882.

MRS. JANET C. SUTTON.

*Dear Madam :—*

Your letter of the 19th inst., inclosing check for $37.50 in payment of a quarter's interest on mortgage note, has just been received. Inclosed find receipt for the amount. As to foreclosure, feel assured that I have no intention of taking such a step. You have been most prompt in the payment of interest, and I regard the mortgage as a very satisfactory investment. In case it should be necessary at any furture time for me to realize the cash, I will give you ample notice, so that you may, if you desire, obtain the transfer of the mortgage to some other party, which no doubt could easily be done. I am, madam,

Your obedient servant,
JAMES WINTHROP.

## APPLICATION FOR PERSONAL LOAN.

BUCKINGHAM HOTEL, BOSTON,
March 15, 1882.

*Dear Friend :—*

I find myself obliged to do what I never before attempted, *viz.*, to borrow money. I was foolish enough last month to indorse a note for a college friend, "just as a mere matter of form, you know," and it seems to be included in the "matter of form" that I must cash up or be sued. As you know, my income is payable quarterly, and I shall be in funds about the first of next month. If you can lend me $150 until that time, you will confer a great favor. I should hesitate to ask for the accommodation, if it were not that I feel assured you know me well enough to believe that I am both honest and good for the amount. If the loan would inconvenience you at all, do not hesitate to say so, and I shall still be

Yours with sincere regard,

MR. DANIEL S. FULLER.
Cambridge, Mass.

ALEXANDER MCPHERSON.

## FAVORABLE REPLY.

CAMBRIDGE, March 16, 1882.

*Dear Alec :—*

I am very glad to be able to do you the little favor you mention. Inclosed please find my check for the amount ($150). I also inclose a blank note form, which please return after filling it out. I do not ask this because I have the least doubt of your word being as good as your bond, but "business is business," as you will probably remember the next time some one asks for the "loan of your name." Pay me whenever convenient, and do not consider yourself at all under obligations to

Your old friend,

MR. ALEX. MCPHERSON.
Boston.

DAN FULLER.

## COMMISSION SALES.

RUTLAND, VT., June 12, 1878.

MESSRS. SPRAGUE & CO.,
Boston, Mass.

*Gentlemen :—*

I have to-day consigned to you eight hundred bushels of prime Early Rose potatoes in good condition, and packed in barrels, *via* the Rutland and Burlington Railroad, time freight, due in Boston on the 14th inst.

Please take charge of the goods upon their arrival, dispose of them at the best market prices, and hold proceeds subject to my order. Make the sale within a week after receipt.

Yours, etc.,
SELAH THORNTON.

## REPORT OF SALES.

148 Parker Street, BOSTON,
June 15, 1878.

MR. SELAH THORNTON,
Rutland, Vt.

*Dear Sir :—*

Your shipment of potatoes came safely to hand yesterday, by railroad. As we think we see signs of a falling in the market, we sold at once, and herewith forward our Account Sales. The proceeds are subject to your draft or order. We hope you will be satisfied with the price obtained, and shall be glad to do further business for you.

Respectfully,
SPRAGUE & CO.
*per K.*

## INCLOSED ACCOUNT SALES.

Boston, June 15, 1878.

*Sold by* SPRAGUE & CO., COMMISSION MERCHANTS,
*for Account* SELAH THORNTON, Rutland, Vt.

| | | |
|---|---|---|
| 800 bush. Early Rose Potatoes @ 89c....... | | $712 00 |
| PAID. | | |
| Freight R. & B. R. R.......................... | $73 25 | |
| Cartage and labor............................. | 13 00 | |
| Commission (5 per cent.)...................... | 35 60 | |
| | | 121 85 |
| Net Proceeds to your Credit........ | | $590 15 |

## OFFER TO SELL GOODS ON COMMISSION.

PORTSMOUTH, OHIO, Oct. 14, 1882.

MESSRS. BACON & HOLT,
Chicago.

*Gentlemen :—*

The orders which I have hitherto sent you from this place have probably made you aware that I have been doing a good business in your line for some time. I now see an opportunity for a large increase of sales, and, as my capital is not large, would be glad to sell for you on commission. The business relations already existing between us will, I presume, be sufficient guarantee of my dealing fairly with you, but if necessary, I can give you full security against loss.

If my proposition meets with your approval, please let me know your most favorable terms at once.

Respectfully,
EDWARD NORRIS.

## COMPLAINING OF AN ERROR IN BILL.

RALEIGH, N. C., Feb. 12, 1881.

MESSRS. RIPLEY & CO.,
Richmond, Va.

*Gentlemen :—*

I find, on examining the bill sent by you with the last consignment of goods, that I am charged with 100 yards of merino cloth, which I neither ordered nor received. I inclose bill and copy of invoice that the error may be corrected.

Yours respectfully,
CHARLES P. TURNER.

A MOST important step in procuring employment of any kind is to furnish assurance that the past character and services of the applicant have been satisfactory and valuable. Such a guarantee may be presented in the form of letters of recommendation from previous employers, or persons well acquainted with one's character and capacity. No hesitation or false modesty should be felt in asking for such testimonial. To assist a faithful employee or acquaintance in this manner is to all well-disposed persons not only a duty but a pleasure. On the other hand, it must be remembered that to ask such a favor of a slight acquaintance, or one who has no means of judging of your fitness, is a gratuitous impertinence. The value and force of the recommendation depend on the position and influence of the person giving it, and the relation he has held to the applicant.

The more precise and explicit the testimonial, the greater will be its effect. A general statement of trust and confidence in the bearer may seem to have been given out of mere compliment. Much better is a detailed statement of the opportunities the writer has had to judge of the applicant and the results of his observation. In speaking of an employee, it is well to give the reasons for the severance of the relation, or to state in general terms that it was through no fault of the applicant. Silence upon points which it would seem natural to speak of is very apt to be construed in an unfavorable manner.

To refuse a letter of recommendation is a most unpleasant duty, but it sometimes *is* a duty, and should not be shirked. Remember that in vouching for another your own credit is to some extent involved; and that to place an unworthy person in another's service is an act of dishonesty toward the new employer and the public at large.

A general form of recommendation addressed to all concerned is not likely to be as advantageous as one to a special person from one whom he knows and trusts. Yet, when the writer is well known or occupies a prominent position, a testimonial not restricted as to person or time may be of value.

### FORM OF GENERAL RECOMMENDATION.

CHESTER, PA., Aug. 12, 1880.

TO WHOM IT MAY CONCERN:—

I take great pleasure in certifying to the worth and character of the bearer, Mr. Edwin Ralston of Wilkesbarre. Mr. Ralston has for two years been a member of the Collegiate Institute of which I am Principal. His attention to his studies and rapid progress in them have been marked. To the branches of bookkeeping and accounts he has paid special attention, and is, I believe, well fitted to enter upon mercantile pursuits. From constant observation while under my care I feel justified in asserting that his character and habits are in all respects steady, and his deportment gentlemanly. I feel sure that in whatever employment he may engage, he will be found a valuable and reliable assistant

JAMES K. SHARPE, *Principal.*

### RECOMMENDING A COACHMAN.

NEW YORK.

The bearer, Terence O'Brien, has served me as coachman for five years. He thoroughly understands driving and the care of horses, and is a steady, sober, honest man. I part with him only through necessity, as I am closing my establishment previous to a European trip.

*462 Fifth Ave.* V. P. GILMORE.

## RECOMMENDING A HOUSEMAID.

82 Beacon St., Boston.

Mary Sullivan has been in my employ as housemaid for six months, and has proved a faithful and competent servant. I have no hesitation in recommending her to any lady looking for a servant. She leaves me of her own accord and through no fault of hers.

Respectfully,

Mrs. Margaret Grey.

## RECOMMENDING A SALESMAN.

Galveston, Texas, May 13, 1883.

Edward L. Hurd, Esq.,
Austin, Texas.

*Dear Sir:—*

We beg to recommend to your notice the bearer, Orville Dixon, for the past two years a salesman in our house. Mr. Dixon, for personal reasons, is desirous of settling in Austin, and, to our great regret, has decided to leave us. If you have a vacancy in your store, you cannot do better than to employ him. He is a clever and expert salesman, and is well acquainted with the dry goods business. He has given our house satisfaction in every respect.

Wade & Grinnell.

## REFUSAL TO RECOMMEND SALESMAN.

Worcester, Mass., Dec. 28, 1882.

Edward G. Lawrence, Esq.

*Dear Sir:—*

Yours of the 24th inst. is duly received. I am sorry to say that I cannot honestly speak in very laudatory terms of Mr. John Saunders, in regard to whose qualifications you ask my opinion.

Mr. Saunders was for some months in my employment as a salesman, but did not seem suited for that situation. His manner was brusque and at times rude, and I have learned that he displeased some of my best customers. It was for this reason that I parted with him. He is a good penman, and, I am told, well qualified to act as bookkeeper, but of that I cannot speak from personal knowledge. In the counting house he might prove a very useful man, but as a salesman I cannot recommend him.

Very respectfully,

James T. Howland.

## RECOMMENDING FARM LABORER.

Mr. Jonas Stebbins.

*Dear Sir:—*

In reply to your inquiries, I would state that the bearer, Simon Wilson, is fully competent to discharge any and all the duties of a farm laborer. He has been in my employ for two years, and has a thorough knowledge of farm work in all its branches. He is accustomed to the care of cattle and horses, and is a good and careful driver. I should not hesitate to give him entire charge of a farm.

Yours truly,

R. E. Clarke.

## RECOMMENDING A MUSIC TEACHER.

Annapolis, Md., July 14.

It gives me much pleasure to testify to the ability of Miss Delia Ellesly as a teacher of instrumental music. Miss Ellesly has taught my four daughters for the past five years. Her system of instruction is admirable and thorough, and the proficiency of my daughters has greatly increased under her tuition.

Wyatt Sinclair.

## RECOMMENDATION OF A BOOK-KEEPER.

Toledo, O., July 12, 1871.

We take pleasure in certifying that Mr. Willis Lowell has filled the position of chief book-keeper for many years, having, in fact, been in our employ in various capacities since he was a boy. Mr. Lowell is a thorough accountant, a neat penman, and implicit confidence may be placed both in his capacity and personal integrity. His personal character and practical knowledge of business are such that he would prove a valuable acquisition to any establishment. In whatever sphere he may hereafter be placed, we wish him every success, and feel sure that he will attain it.

Elmore & Roxden.

## SCHOOL TEACHER'S TESTIMONIAL.

Knoxville, Tenn., July 15, 1882.

Miss Prudence Thorpe,
*Oakland School,*
Columbus, S. C.

I have received your letter requesting information as to the character and capacity of Miss Gertrude Miller, lately employed as a teacher in the Young Ladies' Institute of this place, of which I am one of the trustees. Miss Miller, during the year in which she was connected with our school, gave great satisfaction, and we esteem her highly. She leaves us only because we are unable to offer her the remuneration which she undoubtedly deserves. She has taught French, music, and some English branches, and her pupils have made notable progress in all classes. We have no hesitation in recommending her to you or any others desiring to find a competent and successful instructress.

Yours respectfully,

Gideon Wylie, *Trustee.*

## REFUSAL TO RECOMMEND.

Bay City, Mich., Oct. 28, 1871.

Henry Statmeyer, Esq.

*Sir:—*

I have received your letter requesting me to recommend you to Howard, Gager & Smith as book-keeper. This, I regret to say, I am unable to do, and must confess that I am surprised at your request. You are well aware that it was only after repeated offenses on your part that the position you held with me was forfeited. Those offenses were so serious in their nature, and the repetition of the fault such convincing proof of a hardened character, that however earnestly I may hope that your reform is, as you now assure me, sincere and lasting, yet I cannot conscientiously aid you to obtain a position where you would be exposed to the same temptation.

I would not willingly stand in the way of your advancement, but cannot honestly assist in it.

Yours,

Henry G. Blackman.

## RECOMMENDING A WAITER.

Elliot House, Brooklyn, May 21, 1883.

The bearer, George Somers, who is now leaving my employ, has been a waiter in this hotel for the last six months, and has given full satisfaction to myself and the guests of the house. He knows the duties of a dining-room waiter thoroughly, and is neat, honest, obliging, and sober. I cheerfully recommend him to any one wishing to obtain a first-class and thoroughly competent waiter.

Henry Keator,
*Proprietor Elliot House.*

In answering newspaper advertisements for "Help Wanted," be prompt, explicit and frank. Other things being equal, the answers first received will be most likely to obtain careful notice. An advertisement in any of our large city papers is almost sure to meet with scores of answers, and only the best written and worded will stand a chance of being considered. Elegant penmanship is the gift of a few only, but all can attain neatness in writing, accuracy in spelling, and clearness in stating what is needful. Much may be inferred in regard to an applicant's character from the outward appearance of his application. Use in preference square letter paper or commercial note, with plain business envelope.

Observe with care the directions already given in regard to method of address, signature and date. It is well to inclose the advertisement referred to, or to paste it neatly at the head of the letter, but this is by no means essential. State in what paper the notice was seen. Use no unnecessary words in stating your case. Be brief and business-like. Avoid, on the one hand, discursive talk about yourself, and, on the other, mock-modesty in describing your qualifications. To apply for a position, the duties of which you are entirely unfamiliar with, is a sheer waste of time.

Letters of recommendation and testimonials of character should be inclosed either in the original or by copies. Do not state, in a general way, that you can refer to past employers, but give name and address in full. State age, condition of life (married or single), employment in the past, and any special experience which may seem to fit you for the peculiar requirements of the position sought. Say nothing in regard to your integrity and good character. Let your testimonials speak for themselves. To plead for employment as a favor, and represent oneself as greatly in need of it, destitute, or in great trouble, is not advisable. Take rather a business tone—the style of a capable man who respects himself, and is ready to render service for equivalent.

## APPLICATION FOR SITUATION AS LADY'S MAID.

212 Bleecker St., N. Y. City.

Mrs. M. T. Shaw,
220 Irving Place.

*Madam:—*

I am informed that you wish to employ a lady's maid and light seamstress, and should be glad to obtain the situation. I have held positions of the kind with three ladies, and have a testimonial of character from each. I inclose that from the lady with whom I last lived, Mrs. Lambert, who now lives at No. 49 Park Avenue. Before engaging as lady's maid, I was for some time employed in a hair-dressing establishment, and am considered proficient in that direction. I am able to do plain and fancy sewing, and would be willing, when necessary, to assist in dressmaking. If you will honor me with a line to the above address, I will call upon you at any hour you may indicate.

Yours very respectfully,
Elise Maderot.

## APPLICATION FOR POSITION AS PORTER.

Wanted.—In bonded warehouse, strictly temperate, extra strong, experienced porter; steady employment if found capable. Address Box 1426, Brooklyn.

114 Greene St., Hoboken, N. J., Oct. 14, 1883.

Box 1426, Brooklyn.

In answer to the above advertisement, I respectfully offer my services. I am thirty-two years of age, unmarried, six feet in height, and am considered unusually strong. I have been porter for four years in the house of Armstrong & Wilson, and by their failure have recently been thrown out of employment. I believe that I thoroughly understand the shipping and unloading of goods, and am competent to act as tally man if desired. I inclose a letter of recommendation from Mr. Wm. S. Armstrong, late of Armstrong & Wilson. I should be glad to go at once to Brooklyn for a personal interview, if you think it likely I would suit you, and will drop me a card to that effect.

Your obedient servant,

FREDERICK BAUER.

### APPLICATION FOR OFFICE BOY'S POSITION.

BURLINGTON, IA., Feb. 19, 1877.

T. J. C.
Box 241, P. O.

*Sir:—*

I respectfully apply for the position advertised in the *Hawkeye* of this morning. I am thirteen years old, and reside with my parents at No. 46 William Street. Until this time I have attended the public school, and I send you a certificate of character from my late teacher. I am very willing to accept small wages if there is good opportunity to acquire business knowledge and a chance of gradual advancement.

Very respectfully,

GIDEON S. HALL.

### FOR SCHOOL TEACHER'S SITUATION.

GREENVILLE, May 16, 1880.

TO THE SCHOOL COMMITTEE OF THE
FOURTH DISTRICT, HUDSON CO.

*Gentlemen:—*

Having been informed that a vacancy exists in School No. 3 of your district, I beg leave to offer myself as a candidate for the position. I inclose testimonials and my certificate of examination from the State Board of Education. Among others will be found one from the school committee of this district, where I taught last winter, and a commendatory set of resolutions passed at a meeting of the parents of my pupils. Should you see fit to choose me, I assure you that I will endeavor to discharge the duties of the position to the best of my ability, and, I hope, to your entire satisfaction.

Yours with respect,

MARION C. TAY.

### APPLICATION FOR POSITION OF HOTEL CLERK.

WANTED—An experienced hotel clerk for a seaside resort. State age, previous positions, salary required, and inclose testimonials. Address J. C., Glen Cove, L. I.

NEW LONDON, CONN., May 20.

"J. C.," GLEN COVE, L. I.

*Sir:—*

In answer to your advertisement in to-day's *Herald* I would state that I am thirty-six years of age, unmarried, and have had considerable experience in the hotel business. I am now engaged at the Pequot House, near this town, and inclose a testimonial from the proprietor. I wish to leave because, owing to the dullness of the season, the proprietor cannot pay me what I think I should receive. As you ask that the salary desired should be stated, I will say that my terms are $75 per month, with board, of course. I send you recommendations from other places where I have been engaged, and would specially refer you to Mr. Wilkins Smith, of Glen Cove, who is well acquainted with me, and can give you any further information you may desire.

Yours very truly,

DANIEL M. CALHOUN.

### BOOKKEEPER'S APPLICATION.

212 Walnut St., PHILADELPHIA,
November 21, 1883.

MESSRS. GOLDING & WELCH,
571 Market Street,

*Gentlemen:—*

In reply to your advertisement in the *Ledger* of this date for a competent bookkeeper, I beg to offer my services for the position.

I am 24 years of age, single, and until last spring was assistant bookkeeper in the large establishment of Griggs, Potter & Dunscombe. This position I was obliged to relinquish on account of a severe attack of typhoid fever, from which I have now entirely recovered. I am thoroughly conversant with the system of double entry, and familiar with general mercantile correspondence.

I refer, by permission, to my last employers, Messrs. Griggs, Potter & Dunscombe, and to George Atkins, Esq., President of the Fourth National Bank of this city.

I shall be happy to furnish you with any further information you may desire, or to wait upon you for a personal interview.

Your obedient servant,

WALLACE D. HOLT.

### APPLICATION IN BEHALF OF ANOTHER.

HOWARD GROVE, Jan. 30.

*Dear Friend:—*

You mentioned in conversation last night that you were looking for a gardener. To-day I met Alexander McClure, who formerly served me in that capacity, and find that he is looking for a place. I have advised him to call upon you, and believe you could not do better than to engage him. He thoroughly understands his business, which he learned, he tells me, on the estate of the Duke of Cumberland, in Shropshire, England. He is inclined to be a little arbitrary in his gardening plans, but that seems to be a fault common to all of his trade. Otherwise I can heartily recommend him. He does not drink, and is very quiet and steady. In the management of green-houses and hot-houses he is greatly skilled. Yours sincerely,

WM. P. GRAFTON.

### APPLICATION BY APPRENTICE.

*(Advertisement pasted in.)*

MERIDEN, CONN., October 12, 1880.

GEORGE S. GORDON, Esq.:

*Sir:—*

I beg to apply for the situation mentioned in the above advertisement, clipped from to-day's *Morning Post.* I have been employed for the last four months in the foundry of Wheeler & Co., where I was bound apprentice. The recent failure of that concern and closing of the foundry has caused the canceling of my articles, and I am now anxious to obtain work elsewhere. I am permitted to refer to Mr. Charles Wheeler and Mr. Edwin Hoyt.

Hoping that you will be willing to take me on trial, I remain,

Very respectfully,

SAMUEL HENDERSON,
220 Main Street.

### ANSWERING ADVERTISEMENT FOR GOVERNESS.

218 Elm Street, BOSTON,
November 6, 1883.

MRS. ELLEN COOPER:

*Dear Madam:—*

In answer to your advertisement for a governess in to-day's *Post*, I would state that I wish to obtain such a position as you mention. I have been engaged as governess for the last two years in the family of Mr. Clarence Seward, residing at 115 Marks Place in this city, and would refer to him and Mrs. Seward as to my capacity and character. Mr. Seward is on the point of leaving for Europe with his family, and for that reason will not desire my services longer. I have been teaching music, drawing and French, as well as the common English branches.

I should be happy to call upon you at any hour you may name for a personal interview. Very respectfully,

MARGARET PRESTON.

WHEN it is desired to bring one friend into acquaintance with another at a distance, a note or card will answer the purpose as well as a personal introduction. Though the card is often used, it is not, in our opinion, in as good taste as a letter. The former may seem to indicate a lack of interest and a desire to avoid the trifling labor of preparing a note.

Letters of introduction may be of a social or business character. Those of the first class should be brief, free from general compliments, and to the point. In social introductions grace in style and polite compliments are to be aimed at. In both the note should be left unsealed, but inclosed in an open envelope. When formality is desired, the letter may be written in the third person.

Business letters of introduction may very properly be delivered in person, but in the case of social introductions, etiquette requires that the note should be left at the door with the card of the person introduced, and the recipient should acknowledge the formation of acquaintance by calling within a short time upon the person introduced. When the card is used, the introducing lady or gentleman should write distinctly the name of the person to be introduced in the upper left-hand corner of his or her own visiting card. This card with that of the person desiring the presentation should be inclosed in an envelope and sent by post or messenger. The recipient of the two cards should call in person or send a polite message or invitation within three days.

> *Mr. Howard Tyler,*
>
> *Savannah, Ga.*
>
> *Introducing*
> *James A. Hoye, Esq.,*
> *of Boston.*

If a letter is used, then the person desiring the introduction must inclose his or her own card and send both by post or messenger. The messenger is always to be preferred. The envelope inclosing both cards (or letter and card) should be addressed as if to be sent by mail with the word "Introducing," and the name of the person to be introduced written in the lower left-hand corner. When delivered by post the whole should be inclosed in a second envelope. The card formula will be found in the chapter on card etiquette.

Introductions are often far too freely given, and especially is this true of social introductions. When one business man brings a casual acquaintance to the notice of another business man he does not necessarily vouch for the personal character or standing of the bearer. His letter can be construed to mean no more than it explicitly expresses. But in social introduction it is implied that the person introduced is one who can safely and with propriety be admitted to friendship and hospitality. If he fail to answer this description a reflection is thrown back upon the character or standing in society of his introducer. If he prove to be a boor or an ignoramus the inference is natural that the writer of the letter must be accustomed to such society. Too great care cannot be taken, therefore, in offering such favors, and, when granting them, in abstaining from extravagant praise.

*New York, January 10, 1883.*

*Dear Sir:*

*I have the pleasure of introducing to your acquaintance, my friend, Mr. James A. Hoye, whom I commend to your kind attention.*

*Very truly yours,*

*Edwin Morris.*

*Mr. Howard Tyler,*
*Savannah, Ga.*

### INTRODUCING A YOUNG GENTLEMAN.

FIFTH AVENUE HOTEL, NEW YORK, Feb. 11, 1880.

*Dear Madam :—*

Allow me to present to you my friend, Mr. Hamilton Froude, a gentleman whose pleasant manners and irreproachable character have emboldened me to request for him your particular favor. Will you kindly do me the honor to give my best wishes to Miss Halls, and accept for yourself my most respectful compliments.

Most sincerely,

CLAYTON ABBOT.

MRS. H. P. HALLS,
Charleston, S. C.

### FORM IN THE THIRD PERSON.

Mr. Bolton presents his compliments to Mrs. Lancaster, and begs to be allowed to introduce to her acquaintance Mr. Arthur Vere, of Boston. Mr. Vere is a stranger in this city, but has the pleasure of being acquainted with many of Mrs. Lancaster's Boston friends. Any social attention shown to him will be regarded as a personal favor by Mr. Bolton.

148 Madison Avenue,
New York.

### BUSINESS INTRODUCTION.

TOPEKA, KAN., July 20, 1883.

MESSRS. HOLDEN & CUTLER,
Chicago.

*Gentlemen :—*

I beg to introduce to you the bearer of this letter, Mr. Charles E. Goldthwaite, of this place. Mr. Goldthwaite is about to take up his residence in your city, and I have mentioned the name of your firm to him as one which he will find valuable and prompt in all dealings in grain. I think you will find that Mr. Goldthwaite can give you much valuable information in regard to the state of the crops in this section. Any services you may render him will be regarded as a favor to myself.

Respectfully,

WM. G. HOFFMAN.

*Melbourne, May 14, 1883.*

*My dear Mrs. Morton:*

*I take the liberty of introducing to you an old and valued friend, Miss Sarah Hart, who is visiting your city for a short time, and whose acquaintance I am sure you will value.*

*Most sincerely yours,*

*Madeline Graham.*

### INTRODUCING AN OFFICE-SEEKER.

INDIANAPOLIS, Dec. 14, 1880.

HON. BARDWELL SLOCUMB,
*Member of Congress for the 4th District, Indiana.*
Washington, D. C.

*Dear Sir :—*

I take pleasure in introducing to you Mr. Wilson McGuire of this city, with whose name you are doubtless acquainted through the public press. The friends of Mr. McGuire are desirous that he should obtain a public appointment. He would accept an important consulship or a first-class bureau appointment in one of the departments. I have no hesitation in saying that he possesses ample capacity to fill any such position, and his knowledge of French and German would make a foreign consulship specially suitable. As a supporter of our party during the last election, Mr. McGuire rendered most valuable service. He took the stump throughout the southern part of the State, and was also most useful in organizing the local committees. You will find that Senator Balston is well acquainted with his claims to recognition. Hoping that your influence may bring about the success of Mr McGuire's wishes, I remain,

Yours with respect,

ROBERT K. BILLUP.

NEVER delay the writing of a letter of apology or excuse. The sincerity of the writer is very likely to be judged of by his promptness in offering his explanation. If delay is unavoidable, then a very thorough explanation of circumstances should be made, and the reason for delay stated.

In all cases the paper, penmanship, construction, and the delivery of the letter must be carefully attended to. A gentleman who receives a note of apology from a lady, if it consist only of a dozen words beautifully written, on thick creamy or tinted paper, and delicately perfumed, will prize it far more than a whole page of excuses badly written and penned upon coarse paper. In the latter case he will be very careful not to give the lady another opportunity to apologize. The same rule holds good with a lady, for if she receives a note of apology from a gentleman, written in a clear distinct hand upon his private (not business) paper, and it is accompanied with a bunch of cut flowers, she cannot easily refuse to accept it; but if delayed, and then written upon office paper and sent through the post, the lady will not soon forget the slight.

Do not treat the matter in question as a trifle. If it is worth while to give an excuse at all, it is worth while to do it seriously. When the offense or neglect for which excuse is made is slight, waste few words on the topic, and introduce at once some other subject. When there is reason to fear that the person to whom the excuse is offered has been seriously offended or wounded in feeling, earnestly disclaim any intention to offend, and express your desire to replace yourself in his or her good opinion. There is no occasion to invent ingenious excuses for such faults as neglect of correspondence. The best way is simply to admit your fault, ask indulgence, and promise greater attention in the future.

If the excuse is in relation to a business matter, explain the circumstances briefly but very clearly, and state exactly what steps you propose to take to remedy the delay or failure to act.

### AN APOLOGY FOR A BROKEN ENGAGEMENT.

322 Bay Street, Aug. 1, 1883.

*My Dear Bella:—*

I feel sure you will accept an apology for my failure to be present at your birthday party last evening. Very unexpected circumstances prevented me from enjoying that pleasure. If I am thoroughly forgiven, you will call and take tea with me to-morrow evening, when I will explain the reasons of my absence more fully.

Wishing you all the joys that you so well deserve in the coming years, I am,

Affectionately yours,
Ella Clarke.

Miss Bella Adams.

### EXCUSE ON ACCOUNT OF BEREAVEMENT.

Glen Cove, L. I., Aug. 12, 1882.

*My Dear Friend:—*

Your kind invitation to spend a week with you at your beautiful country house has just arrived. You will, I doubt not, sympathize with me, when you learn that my dear sister Julia calmly and hopefully passed away from this world of suffering (as for many years it had been to her) on Wednesday morning last. Under these circumstances, it is, of course, impossible that I should accept your invitation, but I sincerely thank you for it, and remain now and ever,

Yours faithfully,
Maude Seymour.

Mrs. Willard Shaw.

### PUPIL'S EXCUSE.

THURSDAY MORNING,
April 6, 1881.

MRS. MORTON :—

Will you please excuse John for absence from school yesterday afternoon. I was compelled to keep him at home on account of the severe illness of his father. Respectfully.

MRS. SARAH MOORE.

### FAILURE TO KEEP APPOINTMENT.

WESTPORT, N. Y., Jan. 12, 1881.

WM. PATTERSON, ESQ.,
19 Wall St., N. Y. City.
*Dear Sir :—*

I owe you an apology for not meeting you according to agreement at the Astor House yesterday noon. My failure to do so was owing to a telegram which reached me from this town calling for my immediate presence. As the matter in question was of considerable importance, I felt it to be necessary to start at once. I shall again be in the city in the early part of next week, and will at once call upon you, and hope we can settle our business in a manner satisfactory to both of us. Yours, etc.,

ALMET F. JENKINSON.

### EXCUSE FOR NON-PAYMENT OF MONEY.

UNION CLUB, Feb. 12, 1876.

*Dear Salters:—*

I find, to my great annoyance and regret, that I am unable to repay the sum which you loaned me yesterday, and which I promised to refund before the end of the week. Pray excuse me for my failure. Next week you shall surely have the money. If this delay really causes you inconvenience, my dear fellow, tell me so, and I will borrow the money, while waiting for remittances.

Your obliged friend,
WILKINS MICAWBER.

JOHN P. SALTERS.

### APOLOGY TO YOUNG LADY FRIEND.

TERRE HAUTE, Ind., June 18.

*Dear Miss Talcott:—*

In parting from you at the party last night, I was greatly pained to feel that your manner towards myself was much cooler than I have hitherto found it. It may be very presumptuous in me to allude to this, and even more so to speak of what I think was the cause, but I cannot bear that the pleasant terms of intimacy with which you have honored me in the past should be broken by an unfortunate misunderstanding. It is true that I paid considerable attention to Miss Mamie Woodhouse last evening, but it was because she was comparatively a stranger and had been specially recommended to my politeness by my old schoolfellow, Ned Collins, to whom she is to be *married* next month. If I seemed to neglect you, be sure it was not for "greater attractions," for such there cannot be to me.

I hope to see you to-morrow at the Jardines' ball, and trust to find that you have forgiven,

Yours most sincerely,
JOSEPH E. DART.

MISS JESSIE TALCOTT.

### NEGLECT IN EXECUTING A COMMISSION.

HARTFORD, Sept. 11, 1882.

MRS. WM. S. GRANT.
*Dear Madam :—*

I am really ashamed of myself for having so long neglected to fulfill the promise I gave you to buy the books you wanted. To be sure, I have been unusually busy since my return, but that is not sufficient excuse for leaving your little commission unattended to. So I can only ask your pardon, and promise to do better next time. I have at last bought the books you want, and forward them by express. Please let me know when they reach you.

Yours truly,
ROSCOE HUDSON.

### DELAY IN RETURNING BOOKS.

SEAVIEW, June 10, 1883.

*My dear Maud :—*

I send you by the messenger the books which you so kindly loaned me, and which I found very interesting. I hope you will excuse me for having kept them so long. I have had so many visitors that I have found little time for reading. One, "The Last of the Mohicans," was unfortunately lost from the yacht by my boy Freddie, but upon returning to town I will not fail to send you another copy.

Yours affectionately,
EMMA GLEASON.

### RUDENESS OF A SERVANT.

46 GEORGE ST., October 14, 1882.

*My dear Mrs. Stapler :—*

I cannot tell you how mortified and annoyed I was to-day, upon returning to the house, to learn from my sister of the rudeness with which you were treated by the servant. I knew very well that she was stupid and sullen, but did not think her capable of such insolence. I at once discharged her and hope you will accept my apologies for her rude behavior.

Hoping that you will soon call again, I am, with sincere regret,

Your friend,
ELLA MARTIN.

### DELAY IN ACKNOWLEDGING RECEIPT OF PRESENT.

BALTIMORE, August 4, 1883.

*Dear Mr. Sturgis :—*

You must think me both ungrateful and ill-mannered in neglecting so long to thank you for your most beautiful present. You will, I am sure, accept my excuses when I tell you that I have but this morning returned from the seashore, whither your parcel should have been, but, through some stupidity of the servants, was not forwarded.

Though tardy, my thanks are none the less hearty, and I hope you will not delay calling to receive them in person.

Your sincere friend,
MAMIE LAMBERT.

### DELAY IN ANSWERING LETTERS.

BATH, 1797.

If I *do* write, quoth I to myself, in the humor I am in, I shall convince my most honored friend that I have no wit ; and if I do not write I shall prove to a demonstration that I have no gratitude. Thus the matter stood for a long time in exact equipoise ; but at last recollecting that wit was only a *talent*, and gratitude a *virtue*, I was resolved to secure to myself the reputation and comfort of the one, though at the risk, nay the certainty, of forfeiting all pretensions to the other. * * * *

Alas ! my dear Madam, your letter has just arrived which announces the affecting tidings of Lord Oxford's death—affecting in no small degree ; though I have been in daily expectation of such an event taking place, my feelings are quite overcome when I call to remembrance that kindness which knew no interruption during twenty years.

I am, dear Madam,
Affectionately yours,
H. MORE.

DELICATE as is the task of offering advice to others, it sometimes becomes a most important duty. Unless justified by relationship or intimacy, advice should rarely be volunteered. Letters of this kind are often thoughtlessly written, but not thoughtlessly read, and, therefore, the writers should thoroughly understand the responsibilities they incur. Letters of advice should be kind, strong, and always written by those who really take an interest in the person addressed. Rules and forms are of little service to the writer of such a letter, for if he cannot trust his own judgment, he had better leave the matter to some one better qualified to undertake it. A safe rule to follow is rarely to proffer advice unasked, but never to refuse it when asked.

To offer *advice* when *assistance* is desired is not only disappointing, but often positively offensive. What can be more dispiriting than to receive in answer to a request for pecuniary aid a homily on the virtues of prudence and foresight, and the evil results of borrowing? If you can give, give generously; if you must refuse, refuse politely.

Even in replying to a request for advice it is desirable to use the greatest caution not to offend the self-esteem of the applicant. Men are often more willing to censure themselves than to allow others that privilege; and a request for advice as to a line of conduct to be pursued is not infrequently intended only to elicit approval for that determined upon.

## ADVICE AS TO SPECULATION.

N. Y. CITY, Nov. 24, 1883.

MR. SOLOMON HERCHFELDT,

*Dear Sir:—*

I have received your note asking if, in my judgment, there is a good prospect of a rise in "Union Pacific," and if I would advise you to "go long" on that stock. In reply I will say that though many years a broker, I make it a rule never to express an opinion as to future movements of the market, so uncertain and irregular are its fluctuations. Experience seems to show that one man's opinion is about as good as another's.

I hope you will excuse the liberty of an old friend of your father, if I go further and earnestly advise you to leave speculation alone altogether. This may seem strange as coming from a broker, but I have seen so many small fortunes engulfed in "the street," and so many young men rendered miserable by trying a short cut to wealth, that I cannot refrain from letting you know my opinion. You have a good business, and by close attention to it will in all likelihood become a successful merchant. That is the true road to fortune. Pray excuse my freedom, and believe me,

Most truly yours,

BERTRAND KOPSTEIN.

## CONCERNING A SON'S DISSIPATION.

NEW YORK, June 11, 1880.

*My Dear Friend:—*

I have learned with much pain your distress concerning your son's dissipation; but knowing what a good father he possesses, and the excellent bringing up he has had, I cannot despair. My advice is to continue his allowance as usual. Nor would I for a moment allow him to suppose that you intend to disinherit him, for he will in that case be very apt to "not care" what he does. It is my belief that should his mother continue her loving letters, and you your kind, firm advice, treating him as a friend, he will return to you a penitent prodigal. Patience and kindness are great helps in such cases.

Hoping to hear more favorable news soon,

I remain your friend,

MR. J. C. SAMUELS, Richmond, Va. JOHN W. TIMS.

## ADVICE AS TO LETTER-WRITING.

Here is a genuine letter of advice as to style and tone to be observed in correspondence, written to his son by the noted Lord Chesterfield, whose name has become proverbial for grace and elegance of manners:—

*Dear Boy:—*

Your letters, except when upon a given subject, are exceedingly laconic, and neither answer my desires nor the purpose of letters, which should be familiar conversation between absent friends. As I desire to live with you upon the footing of an intimate friend, and not of a parent, I could wish that your letters gave me more particular accounts of yourself and of your lesser transactions. When you write to me, suppose yourself conversing freely with me by the fireside. In that case, you would naturally mention the incidents of the day, as where you had been, whom you had seen, what you thought of them, etc. Do this in your letters; acquaint me sometimes with your studies, sometimes with your diversions; tell me of any new persons and characters that you meet with in company, and add your own observations upon them; in short, let me see more of you in your letters. How do you get on with Lord Pulteney, and how does he go on at Leipzig? Has he learning, has he parts, has he application? Is he good or ill-natured? In short, what is he? You may tell me without reserve, for I promise secrecy. You are now of an age that I am desirous of beginning a confidential correspondence with you; and, as I shall on my part write you very freely my opinions upon men and things, which I should often be very unwilling that anybody but you and Mr. Harte should see, so, on your part, if you write to me without reserve, you may depend upon my inviolable secrecy.

If you have ever looked into the correspondence of Madame Sévigné to her daughter, Madame de Grignan, you must have observed the ease, freedom, and friendship of that correspondence; and yet I hope and believe that they did not love one another better than we do. * *

## ADVICE CONCERNING A SUITOR.

WORCESTER, MASS., April 3, 1882.

*My Dear Niece:—*

You ask my opinion and advice concerning Mr. Hopkins, a young gentleman of whom I know very little. I have made inquiries about him, and find that he is held in high esteem among all who know him. He has the highest possible reputation for honesty and truthfulness, and does not owe a penny to any one. I am assured that by industry and economy he has acquired some property, and, although he is at present only a clerk in Hoyte & Co.'s employ, it is not at all impossible that the firm may one day be Hoyte, Hopkins & Co.

Besides all this, my dear, he is a good son to his mother, and "a good son makes a good husband." If it is possible, I shall be very proud and happy to call him my nephew.

Affectionately,

MISS MARY SMITH. AUNT ANN.

## CHOICE OF EMPLOYMENT.

BOSTON, Sept. 11, 1882.

*Dear Madam:—*

The request you make for my advice concerning your son's future employment is a very flattering one, and I wish I were more capable of answering it.

As no man can do a business well that he does not do with all his heart, let me ask, has your son business or professional tastes? If he wishes to be a clergyman, lawyer, or physician, do not try to make a merchant of him. From your letter I take it that he has a taste for trade; if so, give him the opportunity he desires, and he will be, I trust, a credit to you.

If not too old, he should begin as office boy, no matter what business he chooses. In this way he will learn all the details of business life, and by close observation and attention discover many things that will be of great advantage to him later in his career. If too old for this, let him take a clerkship for a year or more, even if you have mo ey to start him in business, as it is well for a man to serve a good house until he has made himself thoroughly acquainted with all the details of the business; he makes many friends in this way, and becomes acquainted with the best systems and the most advantageous localities, and learns in his own clerkship the qualities necessary to a succes-ful merchant.

In selecting a business in which to place your son, you must be guided by the opportunities at hand. In general, a wholesale house is to be preferred to a retail establishment, and one dealing in staple commodities to one dependent on the whims or fashions of the day. Locality, capital, and prospect of advancement must also be carefully considered. To you immediate salary should be a matter of indifference.

When started in business for himself, let your son observe these principles:—

Politeness to customers.
Prompt delivery of goods.
Goods sold for what they are.
Fixed prices.
Cash dealings when practicable.
Short credit, both in buying and selling.
Politeness, but firmness, in collecting accounts.

Following these rules of action, and bearing in mind that truthfulness, promptness, and politeness are three of the most necessary qualities required for any business, your son may in time attain the highest mercantile success.

Hoping most heartily that such will prove the case,

I remain,

Respectfully yours,

MRS. C. E. BROWN, Hartford, Conn. DAVID D. PONNER.

## ADVICE TO YOUNG MAN ENTERING COLLEGE.

FARMINGTON, CONN., June 10, 1876.

*My Dear Leslie:—*

You are about to pass from my care as your tutor, and to enter one of our best and largest colleges. Will you allow me to say a few words to you about your prospects and conduct there? I well know that advice is not particularly palatable to young men, flushed as they are with new-gained independence and self-confidence, but I will try to be neither verbose nor puritanical.

I need say little about your studies. You have always proved an apt and intelligent scholar, and no doubt will continue to be so. Do not fall into the mistake of thinking that your only object should be to obtain high marks in the class-room. I have seen more than one high-rank scholar, who, in general company, has exhibited the most lamentable ignorance about everything not included in the *curriculum*. Keep abreast with the times. Read the best papers and reviews, and have an opinion of your own on the topics discussed. Remember that you will probably never again have the same opportunities of gleaning in the golden fields of history, literature, and science. "Reading," says Lord Bacon, "maketh the full man."

Do not be in haste to form intimacies. Distrust those who at the outset pose as "popular men." If your experience is like mine, you will see great changes before the close of a single year in this matter of popularity. On the other hand, sedulously avoid making a recluse of yourself. If you do so, you will miss a great part, not only of the pleasure, but of the profit, of college life. It is the constant intercourse and study of character which give a foretaste of actual business and social life.

It is a mistake to allow motives of economy to have extreme influence in such matters as dress, furnishing of rooms, and general manner of living. Of course, a man may be shabby and yet be a gentleman; but we unconsciously judge, in great measure, by outward appearances.

Bodily exercise is a most excellent and needful thing for a student. Excess is of course to be avoided, but, with the exception of the few who train for intercollegiate contests, I think the danger lies in the other direction. You will find it of advantage to have some means of exercising in your own room, as with clubs or dumb-bells, to break the monotony and tedium of long continued study.

In regard to your moral conduct, be governed by your own self-respect. Do not ask whether a given thing is sanctioned by practice or general opinion, but whether it meets with your own honest approval; whether it is an act which you are at all times willing to acknowledge and uphold. That is the true test, and if you observe it you cannot go very far out of the path of virtue.

I shall always be pleased to hear from my old friend and pupil, and hope to have an opportunity of greeting you personally in your new surroundings.

Yours with regard,

MR. LESLIE HOLBROOK. JONATHAN STURGIS.

# LETTERS OF CONGRATULATION.

CONGRATULATORY messages are always pleasant to receive, both as proving that any honor or distinction obtained is known and appreciated, and as evidence of the writer's kindly feeling and regard. When good fortune or prosperity falls to our lot the pleasure is doubled by learning that our friends join in our elation. Better, however, say nothing, than send a cold, formal, and curt letter of congratulation. The expression of feeling must be cordial, hearty and full of life and spirit. If written to an intimate friend, a tone of playfulness may often be taken with pleasing results.

It is not often desirable to express one's congratulations at length or in labored phrase. A brief note is to be preferred, provided the wording is such as to preserve it from the appearance of curtness or carelessness. Remember that the sooner your congratulation is sent after the event the more welcome it will be. Delay indicates indifference, and renders absurd the air of eager interest which should be exhibited.

Write as though you were clasping the hand of the friend you congratulate.

Cards are seldom used except on occasions of great ceremony, and then should be of plain white with envelopes to match. The post is the most convenient and fashionable way of delivery.

*Oct. 11, 1881.*

*Please accept my most hearty congratulations for the good fortune that has fallen to you.*

*Sincerely Yours,*

*John Thurston.*

*J. K. King,*
*N. Y. City.*

*May 14, 1882.*

*Mr. and Mrs. Welton offer their sincere congratulations upon your recent success.*

*S. L. Clarke,*
*Washington, D. C.*

### CONVALESCENCE OF AN INVALID.

Mr. and Mrs. Burns beg leave to offer Mr. and Mrs. Brown their most sincere congratulations on the convalescence of Miss Rebecca Brown, and to express the hope that she will soon regain her usual good health.

100 Madison Ave. May 3, 1869.

### UPON THE BIRTH OF A CHILD.

Mr. and Mrs. Kay desire to offer to Mr. and Mrs. Munroe their hearty congratulations upon the fulfillment of their wish for a son and heir.

Clark Street. Nov. 12, 1874.

### BIRTHDAY CONGRATULATIONS.

BAY CITY, MICH., Dec. 14, 1883.

*My Dear Niece:—*

I am reminded as I look at my morning paper that the birthday of my little relative Madeline has again arrived. But I suppose I must no longer call you my "little" friend, as this is actually your seventeenth anniversary, and you now stand, blushing, yet confident, on the threshold of womanhood. How short a time it seems since you were playing, a wee thing by my side, and now you are already looking forward, I suppose, to social triumphs, and counting the future victims of your beauty. Well, my dear, accept an old man's congratulations for the present and best wishes for the future. I send a little memento of my regard in the shape of a bracelet, and hope it will please you. Among the faces you will see at your reception to-night, will be many younger and more attractive, but none more abounding in affection and regard than that of

Your loving uncle,
BENJAMIN ELLIOTT.

MISS MADELINE GREY.

### UPON BUSINESS ADVANCEMENT.

MARIETTA, OHIO, Feb. 26, 1883.

MR. CARLOS TALCOTT,
Springfield, Ill.

*My Dear Carlos:—*

I have just learned through our mutual friend, Booth, that you have recently been appointed to a lucrative and responsible position as Assistant Superintendent of the West Illinois and Chicago Railroad, and hasten to offer you my sincere and earnest congratulations. To those who do not know you, it may seem remarkable that so important a post should be intrusted to one so young as yourself, but for those who, like myself, have had opportunities of appreciating your business capacity, clear-headed style of action, and steady habits, it is easy to see that a better man could not have been selected for the place. I hope some day to see you at the head of your line.

Believe me, my dear Talcott, to be,

Truly your friend,
JACOBUS T. WALRADT.

### TO A LADY UPON HER MARRIAGE.

NEW ORLEANS, Sept. 6, 1876.

*My Dear Marion:—*

I have just received your letter from San Francisco announcing your intended marriage to Mr. Julien De Lamar, on the first of this month, and hasten to offer my warmest congratulations. You are before this, doubtless, the happy bride of your chosen husband, and I have doubts as to when or how this note will reach you. But wherever you may be, you have my sincerest wishes for your happiness; and if my congratulation is late in reaching you, be assured it is none the less heartfelt and earnest.

As I have not the pleasure of a personal acquaintance with Mr. De Lamar, I cannot say so many pleasant things about him as I am certain he deserves, but I know you well enough to unhesitatingly assert that the man of *your* choice *must be* a gentleman of honor, refinement and courage.

Your old friend,
CECILIA PASTEAU.

MRS. JULIEN DE LAMAR,
San Francisco, Cal.

### MARRIAGE OF A FRIEND.

SPRINGFIELD, MASS., July 12, 1877.

*My Dear Cook:—*

The invitation to your wedding on the 20th has just reached me, and as I shall be unavoidably absent from the city on that day, and therefore, to my great regret, unable to witness the ceremony, I send you my congratulations by letter.

You are surely to be envied! What could one desire which fortune has not given you, or your own merit and industry attained? Successful in business, influential in politics, popular in society, you now crown your happiness by taking as a helpmeet one of the loveliest, brightest, most intellectual young ladies in the city. That you have a brilliant future and a delightful home life before you seems beyond question. Such at all events is my ardent wish. So, as Rip Van Winkle says, "Here's to you and your family, may you live long and prosper!"

Yours very truly,
S. WOOLSEY BARNETT.

PETER D. COOK, ESQ.

### ELECTION OF A CANDIDATE.

DOVER, N. H., Oct. 12, 1882.

HON. JAMES T. WATKINS.

*Dear Sir:—*

I hope to be among the first to offer my congratulations upon your glorious triumph at the polls yesterday. The first thing I looked at in the newspaper this morning was the vote for State Senator of this district, and while I have been confident of success throughout, I must admit that I was not a little surprised at the large majority you obtained. It can be ascribed only to your wide personal popularity and undoubted superiority over your opponent in the qualities of statesmanship.

Though I always take a great interest in the success of the party, you may be sure that the presence of the name of an old and valued friend on the ticket redoubled my efforts. I say this the more freely as I want office and political advancement neither for myself nor my friends. Hoping some day to have the pleasure of voting for you for some still higher office, I am,

Your obedient servant,
EPHRAIM D. SPERRY.

### UPON LITERARY SUCCESS.

WHEELING, W. Va., Aug. 16, 1880.

MISS EDITH WYLIE,
Richmond, Va.

*Dear Miss Wylie:—*

I have received the copy of your beautiful book of poems which you were good enough to send me. The greater part of the verses I have already perused with interest and pleasure, and I wish to express to you my appreciation of your literary ability, and congratulate you on the success which "The Southern Wreath" has obtained. I hear it spoken of with enthusiasm on all sides. The favorable criticism of our local press, and even of the great metropolitan reviews, must have assured you that you have touched the popular heart and gained a worthy place among the sons and daughters of song. The pathos of many of the poems is genuine, honest, and deep. It is the hope of all your friends that before long we shall have the pleasure of reading some new product of your pen.

Yours sincerely,
MARTHA TAYLOR.

RESPECT for the sorrow of others and sympathy in their grief may often be more effectively evinced by correspondence than by personal interviews. Perhaps there is no class of letters more difficult to write with taste and judgment. To really *console* a friend for loss by death is not within the power of man. But to give proof of our own affection and sympathy, to let our bereaved friends know that we feel and suffer with them, is prompted by all the instincts of love. The expression of such sympathy is always grateful to those addressed, and will knit the bond of friendship closer in the future. Letters of condolence should be written from the heart, and the simplest language is always the best. Never strive after effect nor indulge in fine writing, but think carefully of the trouble your friend is in, and try to write what you would say if you were speaking to him. Never make light of any trouble. Such a course tends only to vex the sufferer, and leaves a bad impression of the reality of the writer's sympathy and appreciation. In most cases brevity is desirable. Intimate friendship or relationship only can justify prolonged attempts at consolation. If strict etiquette is to be followed, letters of condolence for a death should be written upon black-edged paper, and sealed with black wax, if wax is used.

### ON THE DEATH OF A WIFE.

BUFFALO, N. Y., Sept. 12, 1883.

*My Dear Friend Edward:—*

I cannot tell you how deeply I feel for you in the loss of your lovely wife, whose sudden death I heard of this morning. If sympathy could comfort you, then the many expressions of regret and sorrow for your terrible affliction would heal your heart; but we all feel how impossible that can be; only time can soften your grief and diminish the bitterness of your sorrow. Please accept my sincere sympathy and kindest regards.

Yours sincerely,

FRANK LOW.

MR. E. J. BENSON,
Ridgefield, Conn.

### TO A FRIEND ON THE DEATH OF A SISTER.

NEW YORK, Aug. 20, 1883.

*My Dear Friend:—*

It is impossible for me to tell you how troubled I am for you, in this, your great trial. Words cannot comfort, but there is a comforter—he who bears all our burdens—and unto him we may carry all our troubles without fear. Your sweet sister, and my friend, was a lovely Christian, and it is a comfort to us to know that death had no terror for her, and that never again will she be weary or troubled.

"Now by the bright water her lot is cast."

Yet, dear friend, we have still her sweet memory and many tokens of her love to continue with us. With kind love,

LULU MOORE.

MISS K. OTIS,
Brooklyn, L. I.

### ANNOUNCING THE DEATH OF A RELATIVE.

DENVER, COL., Dec. 18, 1883.

MR. WILLIAM MONTROSE,
Princeton, N. J.

*Dear Sir:—*

It becomes my painful duty to announce to you the death of your brother James, at this place, last evening. You have doubtless long been aware that there was but slight probability of permanent improvement, but I fear the news of his death will come upon you as a sudden shock. Up to last week he had seemed to hold his own, but then began to fail rapidly, and at ten last evening breathed his last

It will be a comfort to you to know that he suffered but little, if any, bodily pain. He had borne his weakness and confinement with true fortitude and retained his faculties to the last moment. His devoted wife was with him to the end, and received his dying words of love. She is in such a state of prostration that she finds herself unequal to the task of writing, and has desired me, as the most intimate friend of her late husband, to communicate to you these sad tidings.

It would be impertinent for a comparative stranger to attempt to offer words of consolation. I can only say that even in your sorrow it must be pleasant to remember how beloved your brother was by all who knew him. Upright, earnest, charitable, and sweet-tempered, I believe he never made an enemy or lost a friend. Truly he was a man "without fear and without reproach." Accept, dear sir, my sincere sympathy in your loss, and believe me to be, Sincerely yours,

WILLARD BARTON.

## ON THE DEATH OF A CHILD.

RIVERSIDE, June 2, 1883.

*My Dear Eliza:—*

How can I attempt to comfort you in the bitter affliction which has befallen you! Words are but empty things at best, and I can feel far more than I can say. Your boy was to you the highest treasure and greatest joy of life. He has left you; but you may yet hope to see him again where sorrow and parting are no more. Trust in God, dear Lizzie, and, hard though it may seem, remember that "He doeth all things well."

Your darling Frankie has gone to Him who said, "Suffer little children to come unto me, for of such is the kingdom of heaven." Your memory of him will be as of an innocent, unspotted soul. He has escaped the weariness, the toils, the struggles, and temptations of this chequered life, and who shall say, sorrow-laden though we be, that it is not better so? That a higher than human power may console and support you under this heavy stroke is the earnest prayer of,

Your loving friend,
LOUISA STROBAL.

MRS. ELIZA STANTON,
Jersey City, N. J.

## DEATH OF AN AGED MAN.

CLEVELAND, O., Oct. 14, 1883.

MR. HERMANN LENHART,
Chicago.

*Dear Sir:—*

Your letter announcing the death of your father, and my old friend, has just reached me. Truly it may be said that he was "full of years and honors." Though ten years his junior, I was for a long time honored with his confidence and friendship, and few, I think, better knew the sterling integrity of his character and the keen but liberal sweep of his thought. His circle of friends was large and yet select. Though neither a politician nor a writer on public topics, his influence on public questions was by no means inconsiderable. In short, he was one of those men who make a distinct impression on the history of the day. Could his personal experiences and letters be collected they would make a most interesting volume.

I am pleased to hear that his old age was spent in quiet retirement, free from the cares and anxieties of life; that a useful career was crowned by a happy and contented end. At the extreme age which he had attained, his death could not have been unexpected. I sympathize sincerely with you in your loss. Would there were more like him.

Yours very truly,
HIRAM P. LANGDON.

## LOSS BY FIRE.

518 MARKET STREET,
ALBANY, N. Y., March 14, 1883.

JULIUS CALTER, ESQ.,
City.

*Dear Sir:—*

I am sincerely sorry to hear of your loss by fire. I understand that you were only partially insured, but hope your loss is not great enough to seriously embarass you. It is by the way in which misfortunes like yours are met and overcome that we judge of the spirit, courage, and endurance possessed by the sufferer. With your active mind and business shrewdness I have no doubt you will soon be in even a better position than before. In the meantime, if I can be of assistance to you in any way, pray let me know at once, and rely upon my sympathy and aid. Yours respectfully,

RUFUS G. HALL.

## BUSINESS LOSS.

112 BROADWAY,
NEW YORK, Oct. 1, 1883.

MR. THEODORE MOORE.

*Dear Sir:—*

I am inexpressibly sorry to hear of your embarrassments and despondency over your misfortune, and write to offer my services in any way you may require them. Hoping to hear better news of you soon, I remain,

Sincerely yours,
JOHN H. BROWN.

MR. THEODORE MOORE,
Boston, Mass.

## COMMERCIAL FAILURE.

PITTSBURG, PA., May 3, 1882.

WM. S. GRIGGS, Esq.,
Reading, Pa.

*Dear Sir:—*

I was deeply pained when I learned by your letter that you had been compelled to suspend payment. The trifle due me is of little consequence, and you need not fear that its non-payment will interrupt our old friendship. I sympathize with you deeply, knowing by personal experience how hard it is to meet with disappointment and adverse fortune after straining every nerve in the effort to meet one's obligations. But do not be despondent. You are young, the world is still before you, and many of our merchant princes can look back to failures more disastrous than this of yours. Courage, my friend; all is not lost while health and hope remain. I know that your embarrassment is due to causes which only most extraordinary foresight could have provided for, and in the business world your integrity and capacity still remain beyond doubt.

If my services can in any way assist you, do not hesitate to ask for them.

Yours as ever,
BERTRAM HOLDEN.

## TO AN INVALID LADY.

12 Williams St., CHESTER, PA.,
August 22, 1880.

*Dear Emma:—*

I cannot tell you how sad I was to hear of your continued indisposition, but hope that before long you may return to your wonted health and energy. I was not surprised to learn from your cousin of your patience and quiet endurance of pain, for I know your sweet, uncomplaining spirit. I should rejoice if I could be with you to nurse and comfort you, but I can only send you my sympathy and best wishes for your speedy and complete recovery.

Your loving friend,
MISS EMMA LAMBERT. KATE COWLES.

## FROM HON. WILLIAM WIRT TO HIS WIFE.

"BALTIMORE, December 27, 1822.

* * * * * * * *

"The image of your pensive face is on my heart, and continually before my eyes. May the Father of Mercies support you, and pour into your bosom the rich consolations of his grace, and preserve and strengthen you for your family! What can we do, if you suffer yourself to sink under the sorrow that afflicts you? Let us bear up, and endeavor to fulfill our duty to our surviving children. Let us not overcast the morning of their lives with unavailing gloom by exhibiting to them continually the picture of despair. Trouble comes soon enough, whatever we do to avert it; and the sombre side of life will early enough show itself to them without any haste on our part to draw aside the curtain. Let them be unusually gay and happy as long as they can; and let us rather promote than dissipate the pleasing illusions of hope and fancy. Let us endeavor to show religion to them in a cheering light: the hopes and promises it sets before us; the patience and resignation which it inspires under affliction; the peace and serenity which it spreads around us; the joyful assurance with which it gilds even the night of death.

* * * * * * * *

"May God bless you, and breathe into your bosom peace and cheerful resignation.

"W. W."

# Letters to Friends and Relatives.

LETTERS of friendship and affection are valuable in proportion to the naturalness of the writer. The day has long gone by when elaborate and polished compliments were indispensable; when a son was expected to address his father as "Honored Sir," and his mother as "Respected Madam." Write to your friends as you talk to them, in easy, familiar, unstudied language. Give the details of your life; excursions made, books read, amusing incidents met with. Relate the news in regard to friends known to your correspondent, and ask about others. If you have been blessed with wit, do not fear to display it. A light and playful tone is the very best to take in a friendly letter. The subjects spoken of should be such as your correspondent is known to be interested in.

A long, pleasant letter to or from home is always a work of love, but how few ever take the pains to write such a letter. We are too apt in the hurry of life to say: "I am well and doing well; hope all are the same at home; will not be back till next week. Love to all," or something similar, forgetting that the home folk would be glad to know where we have been, where we are going, who we have seen, and even little trifles that when together pass by unnoticed. Such trifles, says Madame de Sévigné, "are as dear to us from those we love, as they are tedious and disagreeable from others."

Never put off writing till you have more time. It is better to send only a message of love than to disappoint those who will be expecting a letter.

Many men and women have a delightful way of dropping little notes of love and cheerfulness at all times. It is one of those pleasant little courtesies of life that bind us very close, and that make the old young, and the sorrowful happy. Lovers have indulged in the custom from the time that lovers have existed, and were separated; and why should not the rest of mankind?

It is a common saying with young friends, as an excuse for remissness in correspondence, that they have nothing to write about; but surely between friends there must be a similarity of taste on some subjects, and a discussion of their sentiments and opinions on any one of them, in a course of correspondence, would be acceptable and also valuable, as tending to mutual improvement.

It would not be an easy task to give models for the class of letters under discussion, as they should be prompted by the individual taste, thought and feelings of the writer, and adapted to the circumstances of each particular case. We have thought it better, therefore, to give selections from the letters of some of the most noted authors and letter writers in the English tongue. These may be perused with much profit, both as models of style and for the subject matter they contain. We may mention the following as among the most delightful letter-writers: —William Cowper, Thomas Gray, Lady Mary Wortley Montague, Madame Sévigné, Charles Lamb, Madame Récamier, Horace Walpole, Thomas Moore, Washington Irving, Charles Dickens, Henry Crabb Robinson, Mary Russell Mitford, Mendelssohn, Beethoven, Goethe, Sir Walter Scott, John Adams, John Quincy

Adams, Thomas Jefferson, John Randolph, and William Wirt.

## LETTER OF FAREWELL FROM WILLIAM PENN TO HIS FAMILY.

*My dear Wife and Children:*

*My love, which neither sea, nor land, nor death itself can extinguish or lessen toward you, most endearedly visits you with eternal embraces, and will abide with you forever.* * * * * * *

*So farewell to my thrice dearly beloved wife and children.*

*Yours, as God pleaseth, in that which no waters can quench, no time forget, nor distance wear away, but remains forever.*

*William Penn.*

*Worminghurst, 4th of 6th mo., 1683.*

## FROM WILLIAM WIRT TO HIS DAUGHTER.

BALTIMORE, April 18, 1822.

*My Dear Child:—*

You wrote me a dutiful letter, equally honorable to your head and heart, for which I thank you; and when I grow to be a light-hearted, light-headed, happy, thoughtless young girl, I will give you a *quid pro quo*. As it is, you must take such a letter as a man of sense can write, although it has been remarked, that the more sensible the man, the more dull his letter. Don't ask me by whom remarked, or I shall refer you, with Jenkinson, in the Vicar of Wakefield, to Sanconiathon, Manetho, and Berosus.

This puts me in mind of the card of impressions from the pencil seals, which I intended to inclose last mail, for you, to your mother, but forgot. Lo! here they are: these are the best I can find in Baltimore. I have marked them according to my taste; but exercise your own *exclusively*, and choose for yourself, if either of them please you.

Shall I bring you a Spanish guitar of Giles' choosing? Can you be certain that you will stick to it? And some music for the Spanish guitar? What say you?

There are three necklaces that tempt me—a beautiful mock emerald, a still *more* beautiful mock ruby with pearl, and a still *most* beautiful real topaz—what say you?

Will you have either of the scarfs described to your mother, and which—the blue or black? They are very fashionable and beautiful. Any of those wreaths and flowers? Consult your dear mother; always consult her, always respect her. This is the only way to make yourself respectable and lovely. God bless you, and make you happy.

Your affectionate father,

WILLIAM WIRT.

## FROM EMILY CHUBBUCK (FANNY FORRESTER) TO MRS. DR. NOTT.

UTICA FEMALE SEMINARY, October, 1842.

*My Dear M——:—*

There it is again! I cannot write "Miss Sheldon," and I am sure such a bashful body as I could not be expected to address so dignified a personage as Mrs. Nott. So what shall I do? I am very lonely just now, and feel inclined to be somewhat sentimental; for I have been up the hall and found a certain corner room, looking not desolate—oh, no; it is wondrous cozy and comfortable—but as though it *ought* to be desolate. Yet I will spare you all the things I could say, and turn to some other subject. * * * * * *

T. sits studying close by; somebody is thumping Miss F.'s piano over our head tremendously; M. B. is passing the door. There! the bell rings—study-hour is over; there is a general increase of sound in the house, and I know by the voices in the hall that many a door has been flung open within the last half minute. How I wish—but no, there is no use in wishing! I will go to bed, and dream (I have few day-dreams now) of pleasant things, and wake in the morning and see everything pleasant; for this *is* a happy world, in spite of its perplexities. Fine dreams to you, too, both waking and sleeping; yet now and then intermingling may there come a little (though it were the least in the world) thought of

Your truly affectionate

EMILY.

The following, selected from Jefferson's letters to his children, is an excellent example of the clear and serious style of the great statesman, and combines the noblest precepts with the most touching affection.

## THOMAS JEFFERSON TO HIS DAUGHTER MARTHA.

TOULON, April 7, 1787.

*My Dear Patsy:—*

I received yesterday, at Marseilles, your letter of March 25th, and I received it with pleasure, because it announced to me that you were well. Experience teaches us to be always anxious about the health of those whom we love. * * * * * * *

I have received letters which inform me that our dear Polly will certainly come to us this summer. When she arrives she will become a precious charge on your hands. The difference of your age and your common loss of a mother, will put that office upon you. Teach her above all things to be good; because without that we can neither be valued by others, nor set any value on ourselves. Teach her to be always true; no vice is so mean as the want of truth, and at the same time so useless. Teach her never to be angry; anger only serves to torment ourselves, to divert others, and to alienate their esteem. And teach her industry and application to useful pursuits. I will venture to assure you that, if you inculcate this in her mind, you will make her a happy being in herself, a most estimable friend to you and precious to all the world. In teaching her these dispositions of mind, you will be more fixed in them yourself, and render yourself dear to all your acquaintances. Practice them, my dear, without ceasing. If ever you find yourself in difficulty and doubt how to extricate yourself, *do what is right*, and you will find it the easiest way of getting out of the difficulty. Do it for the additional incitement of increasing the happiness of him who loves you infinitely, and who is, my dear Patsy,

Yours affectionately,

THOMAS JEFFERSON.

The quaint humor of Lamb is nowhere better seen than in the following letter, where he treats a friend's desire for travel and adventure as a disease demanding speedy treatment.

## CHARLES LAMB TO A FRIEND.

*My Dear Manning:—*

The general scope of your letter afforded no indications of insanity, but some particular points raised a scruple. For God's sake, don't think any more of Independent Tartary. What are you to do among such Ethiopians? Is there no *lineal descendant* of Prester John? Is the chair empty? Is the sword unswayed? Depend upon it, they'll never make you their king as long as any branch of that great stock is remaining. I tremble for your Christianity. Read Sir John Mandeville's travels to cure you, or come over to England. There is a Tartar man now exhibiting at Exeter Change. Come and talk with him, and hear what he says first. Indeed, he is no very favorable specimen of his countrymen! But perhaps the best thing you can do is to *try* to get the idea out of your head. For this purpose, repeat to yourself every night, after you have said your prayers, the words "Independent Tartary, Independent Tartary," two or three times, and associate with them the *idea* of *oblivion* ('tis Hartley's method with obstinate memories); or say, Independent, independent—have I not already got *an independence?* That was a clever way of the old Puritans, *pun-divinity.* My dear friend, think what a sad pity it would be to bury such parts in heathen countries, among nasty, unconversible, Tartar people. Some say they are cannibals; and then conceive a Tartar fellow *eating* my friend and adding the *cool malignity* of mustard and vinegar! I am afraid 'tis the reading of Chaucer has misled you; his foolish stories about Cambuscan, and the ring, and the horse of brass. Believe me, there are no such things, 'tis all the poet's *invention;* but if there were such darling things as old Chaucer sings, I would *up* behind you on the horse of brass and frisk off to Prester John's country. But these are all tales; a horse of brass never flew, and a king's daughter never talked with birds! The Tartars really are a cold, insipid, smouchey set. You'll be sadly moped (if you are not eaten) among them. Pray *try* and cure yourself. Take hellebore (the counsel is Horace's, 'twas none of my thought *originally*). Shave yourself oftener. Eat no saffron, for saffron-eaters contract a terrible Tartar-like yellow. Pray to avoid the fiend. Eat nothing that gives the heart-burn. Shave the *upper lip.* Go about like a European. Read no books of voyages (they are nothing but lies), only now and then a romance to keep the fancy under. Above all, don't go to any sights of wild beasts. *That has been your ruin.* Accustom yourself to write familiar letters on common subjects to your friends in England, such as are of a moderate understanding. And think about common things more. I supped last night with Rickman, and met a merry, *natural* captain, who pleases himself vastly with having once made a pun at Otaheite in the O. language. 'Tis the same man who said Shakespeare he liked because he was *so much of the gentleman.* Rickman is a man "absolute in all numbers." I think I may one day bring you acquainted, if you do not go to Tartary first; for you'll never come back. Have a care, my dear friend, of Anthropophagi! their stomachs are always craving. 'Tis terrible to be weighed out at five-pence a pound. To sit at a table (the reverse of fishes in Holland), not as a guest, but as a meat.

God bless you; do come to England. Air and exercise may do great things. Talk with some minister. Why not your father? God dispose all for the best. I have discharged my duty.

Your sincere friend,

19th February, 1803, London. CHARLES LAMB.

Wm. Cowper, the poet, was a thorough master of the art of letter writing. His "Life and Works" by Southey will well repay the reader. His unaffected, easy, playful letters have been called "the finest specimens of epistolary style in the language." We give two examples:—

## WILLIAM COWPER TO MR. UNWIN.

*My Dear Friend:—*

You like to hear from me; this is a very good reason why I should write. But I have nothing to say; this seems equally a good reason why I should not. Yet if you had alighted from your horse at our door this morning, and at this present writing, being 5 o'clock in the afternoon, had found occasion to say to me: "Mr. Cowper, you have not spoke since I came in; have you resolved never to speak again?" it would be but a poor reply if, in answer to the summons, I should plead inability as my best and only excuse. And this, by the way, suggests to me a seasonable piece of instruction, and reminds me of what I am very apt to forget when I have any epistolary business in hand, that a letter may be written upon anything or nothing, just as that anything or nothing happens to occur. A man that has a journey before him twenty miles in length, which he is to perform on foot, will not hesitate and doubt whether he shall set out or not, because he does not readily conceive how he shall ever reach the end of it; for he knows that by the simple operation of moving one foot forward first and then the other, he shall be sure to accomplish it. So it is in the present case, and so it is in every similar case. A letter is written as a conversation is maintained, or a journey performed, not by preconcerted or premeditated means, a new contrivance, or an invention never heard of before, but merely by maintaining a progress and resolving, as a postilion does, having once set out, never to stop till we reach the appointed end. If a man may talk without thinking, why may he not write upon the same terms? A grave gentleman of the last century, a tie-wig, square-toe, Steinkirk figure, would say, "My good sir, a man has no right to do either." But it is to be hoped that the present century has nothing to do with the mouldy opinions of the last, and so good Sir Launcelot, or Sir Paul, or whatever be your name, step into your picture-frame again and look as if you thought for another century, and leave us moderns in the mean-time to think when we can and to write whether we can or not, else we might as well be as dead as you are.

When we look at our forefathers we seem to look back upon the people of another nation, almost upon creatures of another species. Their vast rambling mansions, spacious halls and painted casements, the gothic porch smothered with honeysuckles, their little gardens and high walls, the box-edgings, balls of holly and yew-tree statues, are become so entirely unfashionable now that we can hardly believe it possible that a people who resemble us so little in their taste should resemble us in anything else. But in everything else I suppose they were our counterparts exactly; and time, that has sewed up the slashed sleeve and reduced the large trunk hose to a neat pair of silk stockings, has left human nature just where he found it. The inside of the man at least has undergone no change. His passions, appetites, and aims are just what they ever were. They wear perhaps a handsomer disguise than they did in days of yore, for philosophy and literature will have their effect upon the exterior, but in every other respect a modern is only an ancient in a different dress.

Yours,

WILLIAM COWPER.

## COWPER'S RHYMING LETTER.

*My Very Dear Friend:—*

I am going to send. what when you have read, you will scratch your head, and say, I suppose, there's nobody knows whether what I have got be verse or not—by the tune and the time, it ought to be rhyme; but if it be, did you ever see, of late or yore, such a ditty before?

I have writ *Charity*, not for popularity, but as well as I could, in hopes to do good; and if the reviewer should say: "To be sure, the gentleman's muse wears Methodist shoes; you may know by her face, and talk about grace, that she and her bard have but little regard for the taste and fashions, and ruling passions, and hoydening play, of the modern day; and though she assume a borrowed plume, and now and then wear a tittering air, 'tis only her plan to catch, if she can, the giddy and gay, as they go that way, by a production on a strict construction; she has baited her trap in hopes to snap all that may come, with a sugar plum." His opinion in this will not be amiss; 'tis what I intend, my principal end; and if I succeed, and folks should read, till a few are brought to a serious thought, I shall think I am paid for all I have said and all I have done, though I have run many a time after a rhyme, as far as from hence to the end of my sense, and by hook or crook, write another book, if I live and am here, another year.

I have heard before, of a room with a floor laid upon springs and such like things, with so much art, in every part, that when you went in you were forced to begin in a minuet pace, with an air and a grace, swimming about, now in and now out, with a deal of state, in a figure of eight, without pipe or string or any such thing; and now I have writ, in a rhyming fit, what will make you dance, and as you advance, will keep you still, against your will, dancing away alert and gay, till you come to an end of what I have penned; which that you may do ere madam and you are quite worn out with jigging about, I take my leave, and here you receive, a bow profound, down to the ground, from your humble me,

W. C.

## LORD TO LADY COLLINGWOOD.

OCEAN, June 16, 1806.

This day, my love, is the anniversary of our marriage, and I wish you many happy returns of it. If ever we have peace, I hope to spend my latter days amid my family, which is the only sort of happiness I can enjoy. After this life of labor to retire to peace and quietness is all I look for in the world. Should we decide to change the place of our dwelling, our route would, of course, be to the southward of Morpeth; but then I should be forever regretting those beautiful views which are nowhere to be exceeded; and even the rattling of that old wagon that used to pass our door at six o'clock on a winter's morning had its charms. The fact is, whenever I think how I am to be happy again, my thoughts carry me back to Morpeth, where, out of the fuss and parade of the whole world, surrounded by those I loved most dearly, I enjoyed as much happiness as my nature is capable of. Many things that I see in the world give me a distaste to the finery of it. The great knaves are not like those poor unfortunates who, driven perhaps to distress from accidents which they could not prevent, or at least not educated in principles of honor and honesty, are hanged for some little thievery, while a knave of education and high-breeding, who brandishes his honor in the eyes of the world, would rob a state to its ruin. For the first I feel pity and compassion; for the latter, abhorrence and contempt; they are the ten-fold vicious.

Have you read—but what I am more interested about, is your sister with you, and is she well and happy? Tell her—God bless her!—I wish I were with you, that we might have a good laugh. God bless me! I have scarcely laughed these three years.

* * * * * * *

How do the dear girls go on? I would have them taught geometry, which is, of all sciences in the world, the most entertaining; it expands the mind more to the knowledge of all things in nature, and better teaches to distinguish between truths and such things as have the appearance of being truths, yet are not, than any other. Their education, and the proper cultivation of the sense which God has given them, are the objects on which my happiness most depends. To inspire them with a love of everything that is honorable and virtuous though in rags, and with contempt for vanity in embroidery, is the way to make them the darlings of my heart. They should not only read, but it requires a careful selection of books; nor should they ever have access to two at the same time; but when a subject is begun, it should be finished before anything else is undertaken. How it would enlarge their minds if they could acquire a sufficient knowledge of mathematics and astronomy to give them an idea of the beauty and wonders of the creation. I am persuaded that the generality of people, and particularly fine ladies, only adore God because they are told it is proper, and the fashion to go to church; but I would have my girls gain such knowledge of the works of the creation that they may have a fixed idea of the nature of that Being who could be the author of such a world. Whenever they have that, nothing on this side the moon will give them much uneasiness of mind. I do not mean that they should be stoics, or want the common feelings for the suffering that flesh is heir to, but they would then have a source of consolation for the worst that could happen. * * *

Here is a delightfully witty letter from the grand-daughter of Sheridan, the dramatist. It is an excellent illustration of the amusement which may be excited by treating a common-place topic in a vivacious, sprightly manner.

## LADY DUFFERIN TO MISS BERRY.

HAMPTON HALL, Dorchester, 1846.

Your kind little note followed me here, dear Miss Berry, which must account for my not having answered it sooner. As you guessed, I was obliged to follow my "things" (as the maids always call their raiment) into the very jaws of the law. I think the Old Bailey is a charming place. We were introduced to a live lord mayor, and I sat between two sheriffs. The common sergeant talked to me familiarly, and I am not sure that the governor of Newgate did not call me "Nelly." As for the Rev. Mr. Carver (the ordinary), if the inherent vanity of my sex does not mislead me, I *think* I have made a deep impression there. Altogether, my Old Bailey recollections are of the most pleasing and gratifying nature. It is true that I have only got back three pairs and a half of stockings, one gown, and two shawls; but that is but a trifling consideration in studying the glorious institutions of our country. We were treated with the greatest respect and—ham sandwiches; and two magistrates handed us down to the carriage. For my part I do not think we were in a *criminal* court, as the law was so uncommonly *civil*.

* * * * * * * *

I find that the idea of *personal property* is a fascinating illusion, for our goods belong, in fact, to our country, and not to us; and that the petticoats and stockings I have fondly imagined *mine*, are really the petticoats of Great Britain and Ireland. I am now and then indulged with a distant glimpse of my most necessary garments in the hands of different policemen; but "in this stage of the proceedings" may do no more than wistfully recognize them. Even on such occasions the words of Justice are: "Policeman B, 25, produce *your* gowns." "Letter A, 36, identify *your* laces." "Letter C, tie up *your* stockings." All this is harrowing to the feelings, but one cannot have everything in this life. We have obtained *justice*, and can easily wait for a change of linen.

Hopes are held out to us that at some vague period in the lapse of time we may be allowed to *wear* our raiment—at least, so much of it as may have resisted the wear and tear of justice; and my poor mother looks confidently forward to being restored to the bosom of her silver teapot. But I don't know! etc., etc. * * * * * *

## SIR WALTER SCOTT TO HIS SON.

ABBOTSFORD, 22d October, 1824.

*My Dear Charles:—*

I am glad to hear you are safely settled at college, I trust, with the intention of making your residence there subservient to the purposes of steady study, without which it will be only a waste of expense and of leisure. I believe the matter depends very much on a youth himself, and, therefore, hope to hear that you are strenuously exerting yourself to hold an honorable situation among the students of your celebrated university. Your course will not be unmarked, as something is expected from the son of any literary person: and in this case I sincerely hope those expectations will be amply gratified.

I am obliged to Mr. Hughes for his kind intentions in your favor, as I dare say that any one to whom he introduces you will be acquaintance worth cultivating. I shall be glad to hear that you have taken up your ground at college, and who are like to compose your set. I hope you will make your way to the clever fellows and not put up with Doldrums. Every man soon falls behind that does not aspire to keep with the foremost in the race.

I have little domestic news to tell you. Old Maida died quietly in his straw last week after a good supper, which, considering his weak state, was rather a deliverance. He is buried below his monument, on which the following epitaph is engraved—though it is great audacity to send Teviotdale Latin to Brazenose:—

> "Maidæ marmoreæ dormis sub imagine Maida,
> Ad januam domini; sit tibi terra levis."

Thus Englished by an eminent hand:—

> "Beneath the sculptured form which late you wore,
> Sleep soundly, Maida, at your master's door."

Yesterday we had our solemn hunt, and killed fourteen hares, but a dog of Sir Adam's broke her leg, and was obliged to be put to death in the field. Little Johnnie talks the strangest gibberish I ever heard, by way of repeating his little poems. I wish the child may ever speak plain. Mamma, Sophia, Anne, and I send love.

Always your affectionate father,

WALTER SCOTT.

# LETTERS OF NARRATIVE AND DESCRIPTION.

WE add a few letters of a descriptive and narrative kind. Nothing is pleasanter to the friends of a traveler or distant relative than to receive a well-written account of the places he has visited, the scenery which has pleased him, and the adventures he has encountered. The great sights of foreign lands, familiar as they may be in reading, are brought more closely before us when pictured in the well-known language of a friend.

## LADY MARY WORTLEY MONTAGUE TO HER SISTER.

ROTTERDAM, Aug. 3 (O. S.), 1716.

I flatter myself, dear sister, that I shall give you some pleasure in letting you know that I have safely passed the sea, though we had the ill-fortune of a storm. We were persuaded by the captain of the yacht to set out in a calm, and he pretended there was nothing so easy as to tide it over; but after two days slowly moving, the wind blew so hard that none of the sailors could keep their feet, and we were all Sunday night tossed very handsomely. I never saw a man more frightened than the captain. For my part, I have been so lucky, neither to suffer from fear or seasickness, though, I confess, I was so impatient to see myself once more upon dry land that I would not stay till the yacht could get to Rotterdam, but went in the long-boat to Helvoetsluys, where we had *voitures* to carry us to the Briel. I was charmed with the neatness of that little town; but my arrival at Rotterdam presented me with a new scene of pleasure. All the streets are paved with broad stones, and before many of the meanest artificers' doors are placed seats of various colored marbles, so neatly kept that I assure you I walked almost all over the town yesterday, *incognito*, in my slippers without receiving one spot of dirt; and you may see the Dutch maids washing the pavement of the street with more application than ours do our bed-chambers. The town seems so full of people, with such busy faces, all in motion, that I can hardly fancy it is not some celebrated fair, but I see it is every day the same. 'Tis certain no town can be more advantageously situated for commerce. Here are seven large canals, on which the merchant ships come up to the very doors of their houses. The shops and warehouses are of a surprising neatness and magnificence, filled with an incredible quantity of merchandise, and so much cheaper than what we see in England, that I have much ado to persuade myself that I am so near it. Here is neither dirt nor beggary to be seen. One is not shocked with those loathsome cripples so common in London, nor teased with the importunity of idle fellows and wenches that choose to be nasty and lazy. The common servants and little shop-women here are more nicely clean than most of our ladies; and the great variety of neat dresses (every woman dressing her head after her own fashion) is an additional pleasure in seeing the town. You see, hitherto, I make no complaint, dear sister, and if I continue to like traveling as well as I do at present, I shall not repent my project. It will go a great way in making me satisfied with it, if it affords me an opportunity of entertaining you. But it is not from Holland that you must expect a disinterested offer. I can write enough in the style of Rotterdam to tell you plainly in one word that I expect returns of all the London news. You see I have already learnt to make a good bargain, and that it is not for nothing I will so much as tell you I am your affectionate sister.

## THOMAS GRAY TO HIS MOTHER.

LYONS, Oct. 13 (N. S.), 1739.

It is now almost five weeks since I left Dijon, one of the gayest and most agreeable little cities of France, for Lyons, its reverse in all these particulars. It is the second in the kingdom in bigness and rank; the streets are excessively narrow and nasty; the houses immensely high and large (that, for instance, where we are lodged has twenty-five rooms on a floor, and that for five stories); it swarms with inhabitants like Paris itself, but chiefly a mercantile people, too much given up to commerce to think of their own, much less of a stranger's diversions. We have no acquaintance in the town, but such English as happen to be passing through here on their way to Italy and the South, which at present happen to be nearly thirty in number. It is a fortnight since we set out from hence upon a little excursion to Geneva. We took the longest road, which lies through Savoy, on purpose to see a famous monastery called the Grand Chartreuse, and had no reason to think our time lost. After having traveled seven days very slow (for we did not change horses, it being impossible for a chaise to go post in these roads) we arrived at a little village, among the mountains of Savoy, called Echelles, from thence we proceeded on horses, who are used to the way, to the mountain of the Chartreuse. It is six miles to the top; the road runs winding up it, commonly not six feet broad; on one hand is the rock with woods of pine trees hanging overhead, on the other, a monstrous precipice, almost perpendicular, at the bottom of which rolls a torrent, that sometimes tumbling among the fragments of stone that have fallen from on high, and sometimes precipitating itself down vast descents with a noise like thunder, which is still made greater by the echo from the mountains on each side, concurs to form one of the most solemn, most romantic, and the most astonishing scenes I have ever beheld. Add to this the strange views made by the crags and cliffs on the other hand; the cascades that in many places throw themselves from the very summit down into the vale and the river below, and many other particulars impossible to describe; you will conclude we had no occasion to repent our pains.

* * * * * * * * *

## CHARLES LAMB TO WORDSWORTH

(*Description of London Life.*)

I ought before this to have replied to your very kind invitation into Cumberland. With you and your sister I could gang anywhere, but I am afraid whether I shall ever be able to afford so desperate a journey. Separate from the pleasures of your company I don't now care if I never see a mountain in my life. I have passed all my life in London, until I have formed as many and intense local attachments as any of your mountaineers can have done with dead nature. The lighted shops of the Strand and Fleet street, the innumerable trades, tradesmen and customers, coaches, wagons, playhouses; all the bustle and wickedness about Covent Garden, the watchmen, drunken scenes, rattles; life awake, if you awake, at all hours of the night; the impossibility of being dull in Fleet street; the crowds, the very dirt and mud, the sun shining upon houses and pavements, the printshops, the old bookstalls, parsons cheapening books, coffee houses, steam of soups from kitchens, the pantomime—London itself a pantomime and masquerade—all these things work themselves into my mind and feed me without a power of satiating me. The wonder of these sights impels me into night-walks about her crowded streets, and I often shed tears in the motley Strand from fullness of joy at so much life. All these emotions must be strange to you; as are your rural emotions to me. But consider, what must I have been doing all my life not to have lent great portions of my heart with usury to such scenes?

My attachments are all local, purely local; I have no passions (or have had none since I was in love, and then it was the spurious engendering of poetry and books) to groves and valleys. The room where I was born, the furniture which has been before my eyes all my life, a bookcase which has followed me about like a faithful dog, only exceeding him in knowledge, wherever I have moved; old chairs, old tables, streets, squares, where I have sunned myself, my old school—these are my mistresses—have I not enough without your mountains? I do not envy you. I should pity you, did I not know that the mind will make friends of anything. Your sun and moon and skies and hills and lakes affect me no more, or scarcely come to me in more venerable characters, than as a gilded room with tapestry and tapers, where I might live with handsome visible objects. I consider the clouds above me but as a roof beautifully painted, but unable to satify the mind; and at last, like the pictures of the apartment of a connoisseur, unable to afford him any longer a pleasure. So fading upon me, from disuse, have been the beauties of Nature, as they have been confinedly called; so ever fresh, and green, and warm are all the inventions of men and assemblies of men in this great city. * * * * * * * *

CHARLES LAMB.

**LOVE LETTERS** form part of the choicest machinery of the poet and the novelist, and one of our most popular lady novelists discusses with much force the *great value* of these letters, showing how men who are unable by word of mouth to do themselves justice can thoroughly reveal their whole nature in their love letters.

Yet we regard as correct the popular sentiment which considers the lover who would propose marriage by letter as a moral coward. Instances there may be where such a course is *necessary*, and others where it is not open to serious objection; but, with few exceptions, an offer couched in the language suggested by the inspiration of passion, hurried and almost incoherent though it be, will find more ready acceptance than pages of eloquently turned sentences composed in the study and sent by post. It is *after* the proposal and acceptance that the love letter becomes the sweet messenger of absent lovers, to be written with confidence and passion, read with tears and smiles, and preserved till death as the relic of the brightest, most joyous period of man and woman's life.

Some of the most beautiful examples have come from the heart and pen of the greatest men and women representing Literature, Science, and Art. The old poet, Thomson, the author of The Four Seasons, in his advice to a sister about to be married, is worth reading; he says:—

"I must chiefly recommend to you to cultivate by every method that union of hearts, that agreement and sympathy of tempers, in which consists the true happiness of the marriage state. The economy and gentle management of a family is a woman's natural province, and from that arises her best praise." The famous Rousseau says: "To write a good love letter you ought to begin without knowing what you mean to say, and finish without knowing what you have written."

Love letters are in the strictest sense confidential; and, therefore, one is apt to unfold the heart and lay bare the feelings on many subjects in a way that would not be thought of under other circumstances. It often happens that a man of genius with a gift of utterance causes decided wonderment to his *fiancée* in an intellectual effusion that relieves his mind of some burden, but only mystifies his correspondent. Then there are those who in a few short sentences give worlds of love, and make life inexpressibly glorious. A famous reviewer was once detected in writing a love letter. "I'll not detain you long," he observed, "I never give the young woman more than a short notice." Women are for the most part the writers of love letters, because they generally have more time and are less afraid to express their feelings.

Letter-writing is a very convenient way of making love, for an answer may be thought of that could not be spoken right on the spot; and it is most subtle and entangling for the heart, for spoken words may be forgotten or misunderstood, but when written, words are apt to inspire belief. If, as Pope declares, "*love letters* lie at the foundation of all literature, and are the language of souls that without them would be speechless," we can believe as he does that—

"In Maiden Meditation Fancy Free."

"Heaven first taught letters for some wretch's aid,
Some banished lover, or some captive maid;
They live, they speak, they breathe what love inspires,
Warm from the soul and faithful to its fires,
The virgin's wish, without her fears, impart,
Excuse the blush, and pour out all the heart."

Few of us have not read Tennyson's poem called "The Letters," and have not felt all the delicious associations of the young lover who refuses to receive or give back the letters that had passed between them.

"She told me all her friends had said,
I raged against the public liar:
She spoke as if her love were dead,
But in my words were seeds of fire.
I spoke with heat and strength and force,
I shook her breast with vague alarms.
Like torrents from a mountain source
We rushed into each other's arms."

From time immemorial love has found its richest expression in poetry. If one has the slightest spark of the divine afflatus, it will surely manifest itself in the days of love. Those who dare not soar on the wings of original poesy will find many choice citations relating to the tender passion in the select extracts and quotations given elsewhere in this book. For the benefit of young ladies whose sweethearts are absent, we quote the following Finland love song, which, with very little alteration, makes a beautiful love letter:—

"Oh that my beloved were now here! Alas! why have not the winds understanding? and why is the breeze bereft of speech? The winds might exchange thoughts between my beloved and me; the breezes might every instant carry my words to him, and bring back his to me.

"Then how would the delicacies of my table be neglected, how inattentive should I be to my dress. I should leave everything to attend to my beloved, who is the dear object of my summer thought and winter cares."

A clever girl who had not heard from her lover for two days, sent the following: "?," and received this answer, "!!!" This is probably the briefest love correspondence on record. It is not seldom that lovers' quarrels can be traced to a neglected letter, and on the principle of like cures like, a letter carefully worded will smooth all uneven places. Seldom, very seldom, can a woman resist the delight of opening a letter, no matter how angry she may be; and, having done so, she is *sure* to read. Of all letters, love letters are the hardest and the easiest to write, and our advice to those who read this chapter is to write even more freely than they would speak, and to follow as far as possible the promptings of the heart.

Among published love letters those of Cowper and Lady Scott are elegant specimens. We give one of each. Cowper begins and ends in a stately way, characteristic of the manners of the times. He addresses his sweetheart as:—

*Dearest Madam:*—

I wish my thoughts that are so often with you, when I am not, were not invisible; then you might save yourself the trouble of reading such notes, and see in one view how discontented and vexed they are when I cannot wait on you. You would see how forward and impatient they are, under any other business, and I'm sure without further apology, would excuse me and forgive my absence for their very looks.

Your very Humble and
Affectionate Servant.

## LETTER TO WALTER SCOTT.

If I could but really believe that my letter gave you only half the pleasure you express I should almost think, my dearest Scott, that I should get very fond of writing, merely for the pleasure to indulge you —that is saying a great deal. I hope you are sensible of the compliment I pay you; I don't expect I shall *always* be so pretty behaved. You may depend on me, my dearest friend, for fixing as *early* a day as I possibly can; and if it happens to be not quite so soon as you wish, you must not be angry with me. It is very unlucky you are such a bad housekeeper, as I am no better. I shall try. I hope to have very soon the pleasure of seeing you, and to tell you how much I love you; but I wish the first fortnight was over.

With all my love and those sort of pretty things, adieu!

CHARLOTTE.

## LOVE LETTER OF RICHARD STEELE.

(*Published in the "Spectator."*)

September 1, 1807.

***Madam:***—

It is the hardest thing in the world to be in love, and yet attend business. As for me, all that speak to me find me out, and I must lock myself up, or other people will do it for me. A gentleman asked me this morning, "What news from Holland?" and I answered: "She is exquisitely handsome!" Another desired to know when I had been at Windsor. I replied: "She designs to go with me." Prithee allow me at least to kiss your hand before the appointed day, that my mind may be in some composure. Methinks I could write a volume to you, but all the language on earth would fail in saying how much and with what disinterested passion

I am ever yours,
RICH. STEELE.

The following is taken from "The H—— Family," a novel by Miss Fredrika Bremer:—

TROMSOE, May 28, 184-.

If you were but here, my Alette! I miss you every moment, while I am preparing my dwelling to receive you. I am continually wishing to ask you: "How will you have this, Alette?" Ah, my ever beloved, that you were here at this moment! You would be enraptured with this "land of ice and bears," at the thought of which I know you inwardly shudder.

* * * * * * * * *

"But the winter!" I hear you say, "the summer may pass well enough, but the long, dark winter!" Well, the winter, too, my Alette, passes happily away with people who love each other, when it is warm at home. Do you remember, last summer, how we read together at Christiansand, in the morning paper, this extract from the *Tromsoe Gazette*:—

"We have had snow-storms for several days together, and at this moment the snow-plow is at work opening a path to the churches. The death-like stillness of night and winter extends over meadow and valley, only a few cows wander about, like ghosts, over the snowy tracts, to pluck a scanty meal from the twigs of the trees that are not yet buried in the snow."

This little winter sketch pleased me, but you shuddered involuntarily at that expression, "The death-like stillness of the night and winter," and bowed your sweet dear face, with closed eyes, upon my breast.

Oh! my Alette, thus it will be when, in future, the terror of the cold and darkness seizes thee, and, upon my breast, listening to the beatings of my heart, the words of my love, wilt thou forget these dark images of storm and gloom?

* * * * * * * * *

Close thine eyes, slumber, my beloved one, while I watch over thee. Thou sha't one day look upon night and winter and own that their power is not so fearful. Love, that geyser of the soul, can melt the ice and snow of the most frozen regions; wherever its warm springs well up there glows a southern climate.

## LORD BYRON TO THE MARCHESA GUICCIOLI.

BOLOGNA, August 25, 1819.

*My dearest Teresa :—*

I have read this book in your garden ;—my love, you were absent, or else I could not have read it. It is a favorite book of yours, and the writer was a friend of mine. You will not understand these English words, and others will not understand them—which is the reason I have not scrawled them in Italian. But you will recognize the handwriting of him who passionately loved you, and you will divine that, over a book which was yours, he could only think of love. In that word, beautiful in all languages, but most so in yours—*Amor mio.* * * *

But all this is too late. I love you, and you love me,—at least, you say so, and act as if you did so, which last is a great consolation in all events. But I more than love you, and cannot cease to love you.

Think of me sometimes, when the Alps and the ocean divide us,—but they never will, unless you wish it.

BYRON.

## WELLINGTON TO MADAME DE STAËL.

PARIS, June 13.

I confess, madame, that I am not very sorry that business matters will prevent my calling upon you after dinner: since every time I see you, I leave you more deeply impressed with your charms, and less disposed to give my attention to politics ! I shall call upon you to-morrow, provided you are at home, upon my return from the Abbé Sicard's, and in spite of the effect such dangerous visits have upon me.

Your very faithful servant,

WELLINGTON.

## THOMAS OTWAY TO MADAM BARRY.

[1682.]

Could I see you without passion, or be absent from you without pain, I need not beg your pardon for thus renewing my vows that I love you more than health, or any happiness here or hereafter. Everything you do is a new charm to me, and though I have languished for seven long tedious years of desire, jealously despairing, yet every minute I see you, I still discover something new and more bewitching. Consider how I love you ; what would I not renounce, or enterprise for you? * * * * * This minute my heart aches for you ; and, if I cannot have a right in yours, I wish it would ache till I could complain to you no longer.

REMEMBER POOR OTWAY.

## CHARLES I. TO QUEEN HENRIETTA MARIA.

OXFORD, 1646.

*Dear Heart :—*

Whatsoever may make thee mistake my actions, yet nothing can make me doubt of thy love, nor alter my way of kindness and freedom to thee. * * * * * * * *

Whereas, now, men have more reason to trust to my promises, find [ing] me constant to my grounds, and thou that I am eternally thine,

CHARLES R.

## THOMAS HOOD TO MARY ELLIOT.

MONDAY, April, 1844.

*My dear May :—*

I promised you a letter, and here it is. I was sure to remember it ; for you are as hard to forget, as you are soft to roll down a hill with. What fun it was ! only so prickly, I thought I had a porcupine in one pocket, and a hedgehog in the other. The next time, before we kiss the earth we will have its face well shaved. * * * * * *

However, I hope we shall all have a merry Christmas ; I mean to come in my ticklesome waistcoat, and to laugh till I grow fat, or at least streaky. Fanny is to be allowed a glass of wine, Tom's mouth is to have a *hole* holiday, and Mrs. Hood is to sit up to supper ! There will be doings ! And then such good things to eat ; but pray, pray, pray, mind they don't boil the baby by mistake for the plump pudding, instead of a plum one.

Give my love to everybody, from yourself down to Willy, with which and a kiss, I remain, up hill and down dale,

Your affectionate lover,

THOMAS HOOD.

## ROBERT BURNS TO MISS ELLISON BEGBIE.

LOCHLEA, 1783.

I verily believe, my dear E., that the pure genuine feelings of love are as rare in the world as the pure genuine principles of virtue and piety. This I hope will account for the uncommon style of all my letters to you. * * * *

I don't know how it is, my dear, for though, except your company, there is nothing on earth gives me so much pleasure as writing to you, yet it never gives me those giddy raptures so much talked of among lovers. * * * *

The sordid earth-worm may profess love to a woman's person, whilst in reality his affection is centered in her pocket ; and the slavish drudge may go a-wooing as he goes to the horse-market to choose one who is stout and firm, and as we may say of an old horse, one who will be a good drudge and draw kindly. I disdain their dirty puny ideas. I would be heartily out of humor with myself, if I thought I were capable of having so poor a notion of the sex, which were designed to crown the pleasures of society.

R. B.

## JAMES HOWELL TO THE RIGHT HON. LADY E. D—.

April 8, 1649.

*Madam :—*

There is a French saying that courtesies and favors are like flowers, which are sweet only while they are fresh, but afterward they quickly fade and wither. * * *

But, Madam, I honor you not so much for favors, as for that precious brood of virtues which shine in you with that brightness, but specially for those high motions whereby your soul soars up so often toward heaven ; insomuch, Madam, that if it were safe to call any mortal a saint, you should have that title from me, and I would be one of your chiefest votaries ; howsoever, I may without any superstition subscribe myself

Your truly devoted servant,

J. H.

## BONAPARTE TO JOSEPHINE.

MARMIROLO, July, 17, 1796.

I have received your letter, my adorable friend. It has filled my heart with joy. * * Ah ! I entreat you to permit me to see some of your faults. Be less beautiful, less gracious, less affectionate, less good. Especially be not over anxious, and never weep. Your tears rob me of reason, and inflame my blood. Believe me it is not in my power to have a single thought which is not of thee, or a wish which I could not reveal to thee. * * * *

A thousand kisses,

BONAPARTE.

## JOSEPHINE TO BONAPARTE.

April, 1810.

A thousand, thousand, tender thanks that you have not forgotten me. My son has just brought me your letter. With what eagerness have I read it, and yet it required much time, for there was not one word in it which did not make me weep. But these tears were very sweet. I have recovered my heart all entire, and such it will ever remain. There are sentiments which are even life, and which can only pass away with life. * * * Adieu, my love, I thank you as tenderly as I always love you.

JOSEPHINE.

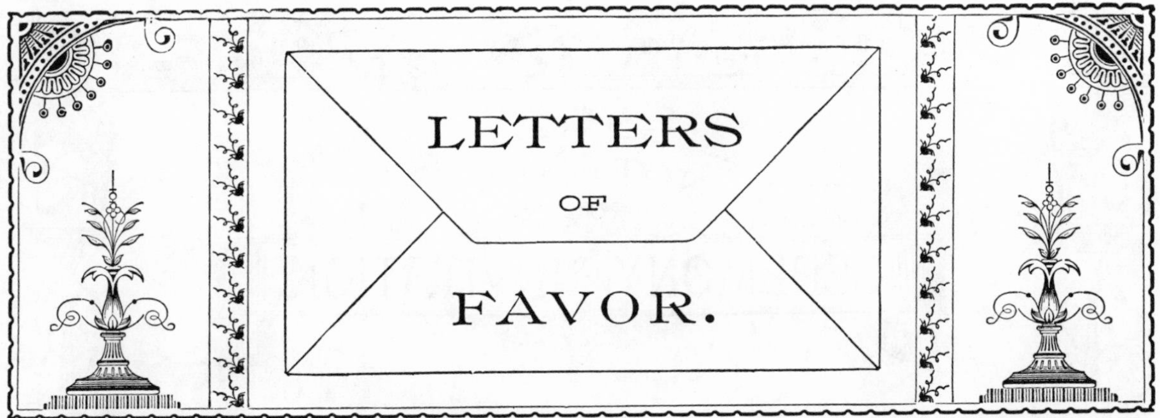

ALL persons, at some time, have occasion to ask for favors, and to be able to do so with tact and self-respect is a very delicate matter.

Such a letter should be worded as simply and plainly as possible. A request should not be urged too strongly, although it should be so stated as to be plainly understood, and should show that the writer would fully appreciate compliance with his request. In conferring a favor one should be very careful to avoid any expression that may tend to wound the feelings. To give grudgingly is as bad as to refuse outright.

Letters declining to grant favors require tact and kindness; the reasons for refusing should be expressed in as sincere and kind a manner as possible. Answers to requests of any kind should be sent with the least possible delay, whether favorable or otherwise.

### REQUESTING THE LOAN OF A BOOK.

111 W. 59TH ST.,
NEW YORK CITY, April 13, 1879.

*Dear Mattie:—*

Will you kindly loan me your copy of Rossetti's "Ballads and Sonnets?" I will take great care of it, and return by Friday evening.

Lovingly,
ALICE.

MISS MATTIE DAY.

### A REQUEST FOR MONEY.

BOSTON, Sept. 2, 1874.

MR. JOHN BROWN,
Worcester, Mass.

*Dear Sir:—*

Through unforeseen circumstances I find myself in a temporary embarrassment. If you can accommodate me with a loan of $150 until the 15th of this month, I will esteem it as a great favor.

Respectfully,
S. S. TELFORD.

### FAVORABLE ANSWER TO FOREGOING.

WORCESTER, MASS., Sept. 3, 1874.

MR. S. S. TELFORD,
Boston.

*Dear Sir:—*

Your note requesting a loan of $150 has just been received, and I take great pleasure in complying with your request. Inclosed find my check for the amount mentioned, and a note of hand for $150, which please sign and return.

Yours truly,
JOHN BROWN.

### UNFAVORABLE ANSWER.

WORCESTER, MASS., Sept. 3, 1874.

MR. S. S. TELFORD,
Boston.

*Dear Sir:—*

I have just received your note asking the loan of $150 until the 15th inst. I regret to say that my funds are so placed in permanent investments that I cannot spare the sum from my business. I am truly sorry not to be able to oblige you, and trust you will have no difficulty in obtaining the amount elsewhere.

Yours sincerely,
JOHN BROWN.

### ASKING A FRIEND TO EXECUTE A COMMISSION.

WILKESBARRE, PA., May 8, 1876.

*My Dear Marion:—*

Will you be so very good as to do a little shopping for me at Wannemaker's. I wish to obtain the following articles (*here give list of purchases to be made*). If you will give my address to the salesman he will see that the goods are properly packed and sent to me "C. O. D."

I hope you will soon find time to make me a little visit. Pray write and tell me when you can come, and thus give me an opportunity to thank you personally for your kindness.

Yours faithfully,
GRACE HOWARD

TO MRS. MARION BURR,
No. 14 Elm street, Philadelphia.

BRIEF messages of ceremony or compliment, expressed in a formal manner, are called notes, though the term note may properly be used of any short letter. Notes differ from ordinary letters in being more formal, in being expressed in the third person, and, usually, in being without signature. A very awkward blunder frequently made is the expression of a note partly in the third person and partly in the first. This should be most carefully avoided.

Both in the style of writing and in the materials, notes of ceremony should be at the same time *simple* and *elegant.* Paper and envelope should be plain, but of the finest and heaviest quality. As to color, it should be either white or a very delicate tint. For weddings white only is allowable. A very delicate cream-white is the fashionable color at present. The size of paper and envelope depends upon individual taste. For most purposes a long sheet folding once into a square envelope, or a square sheet folding into an oblong envelope, are to be chosen.

CARDS may be substituted for notes in most cases; in the present style of printing and engraving it would be hard to distinguish the note from the card. The finest English cardboard, *unglazed,* should be used. A delicate tint is allowable for other occasions than weddings, but white is to be preferred. Visiting cards for ladies should be a trifle larger than for gentlemen, and the address, if given at all, should be in the lower left hand corner. Cards of ceremony are usually 3 by 5, or 4 by 6 inches in size. Both cards and notes should be inclosed in envelopes bearing only the name and title of the person addressed. If it is necessary to mail the note or card, the whole should be inclosed in a second envelope. It is no longer considered necessary to add the word *Present* in the right hand corner of the envelope. Delivery by private messenger is preferable to the use of the post, if practicable. The etiquette to be observed with visiting and other ceremonial cards is explained under the head of "Social Etiquette."

The French words and phrases given below are often used in notes and cards :—

*R.S.V.P. Répondez, s'il vous plait,* answer, if you please.
*E.V.*, or *en ville,* in the town or city.
*P.P.C. Pour prendre congé,* to take leave.
*Costume de rigueur,* full dress ; in character.
*Soirée dansante,* a dancing party.
*Bal masqué,* masquerade ball.
*Fête champêtre,* a rural or out-doors party.

## INVITATIONS.

The note form is generally used for invitations, but they may be printed or engraved, as well as written. In all cases they should be concise, polite, and *definite.*

An invitation to dine "*to-morrow*" would be a violation of this rule. Formality should be adhered to, except in cases of great intimacy. Great taste may be exercised in selecting the size of paper, style of engraving, etc. The envelope only should have the monogram or coat of arms of the sender. We give first examples of invitations to various social entertainments :—

DINNER INVITATION.

Mr. and Mrs. John W. Howard
request the pleasure of
Mr. and Mrs. William H. Griffen's company,
At Dinner,
on Monday, February ninth, 1883,
at seven o'clock.

R.S.V.P. — Fifth Avenue.

PARTY INVITATION.

Mr. and Mrs. John W. Howard
request the pleasure of your company
on Friday Evening, October First,
at half past eight o'clock.

Dancing at eleven.

—— Fifth Avenue.

MASQUERADE BALL.

Mr. and Mrs. Henry M. Frost
request the pleasure of your company, in fancy dress, on Monday Evg., February Fifth,
at nine o'clock.

52 Lafayette Avenue.

R. S. V. P.

INVITATION TO "THE GERMAN."

Mr. and Mrs. Charles H. Armstrong
request the pleasure of
Miss Daisy Miller's
company on Monday Evening,
December twenty-third,
at eight o'clock.

72 Fingerboard Row.

"The German."

SOCIABLE INVITATION.

**The Home Circle**

*requests the pleasure of your company*

..............................................*at the residence of*

*M*..............................................

*Secretary.*

*R. S. V. P.*

"KETTLE DRUM" RECEPTION.

**Mrs. R. G. Howard,**
**Misses Howard.**

*Kettle Drum,*
*Thursday, Three o'clock,*
*January Tenth.*

48 CLINTON AVENUE.

EVENING RECEPTION.

*Miss Bunker*

*requests the pleasure of your company*

*April third, at eight o'clock.*

*117 Second Place.*

CHILDREN'S PARTIES.

**Master Harry H. Peck**

*requests the pleasure of your company*
*at his*

**Birthday Celebration,**

*on Monday Evening, September 23d,*
*from six until ten o'clock.*

*— Lexington Avenue.*

*R.S.V.P.*

*Miss Agnes, Mamie and Master Frank Armstrong*

*request the pleasure of your company*

*Wednesday, March second, from five until ten o'clock.*

*Punch and Judy,*
*half past five.*

*12 Fingerboard Row.*

R. S. V. P.

Mr. and Mrs. C. H. Armstrong

request the pleasure of your presence

at a

**Social Gathering,**

Thursday Evg., December Second,

at half past eight o'clock.

12 Fingerboard Row.

---

Mr. and Mrs. Vanderbilt

request the pleasure of

..............................................................

company, on Tuesday Evening,

May 20th,

at half past nine o'clock precisely,

to meet

PRESIDENT ARTHUR.

........ Fifth Avenue.

*The favor of an answer is requested.*

## WEDDING ANNIVERSARIES.

THE celebration of the recurrence of the marriage day is a most pleasing custom which has rapidly grown into favor. We give a list of the names usually given to these anniversaries. Sometimes the first is called the paper instead of the cotton wedding. The first three are rarely celebrated under the names given:—

The first anniversary is called the cotton wedding.
The second, the paper wedding.
The third, the leather wedding.
The fifth, the wooden wedding.
The seventh, the woolen wedding.
The tenth, the tin wedding.
The twelfth, the silk and fine linen wedding.
The fifteenth, the crystal (glass) wedding.
The twentieth, the china wedding.
The twenty-fifth, the silver wedding.
The fiftieth, the golden wedding.
The seventy-fifth, the diamond wedding.

The twentieth is sometimes celebrated as the *Floral Wedding*, the thirtieth as the *Pearl Wedding*, the thirty-fifth as the *China Wedding*, the fortieth as the *Coral Wedding*, and the forty-fifth as the *Bronze Wedding*. The list given above is that adopted by most fashionable people. The notice "No Gifts Received" is sometimes added to these forms, when many persons are invited with whom the parties issuing the invitations are not on intimate terms.

### WOODEN WEDDING.

(The invitations may be engraved on wood or imitation.)

1813. 1818.

Mr. and Mrs. Alexander S. Hamilton,

At Home.

*Wednesday Evening, June Eleventh,*
*at eight o'clock.*

*10 Bowling Green.*

### CRYSTAL WEDDING.

(The invitations can be engraved on crystallized cards.)

*1813. 1828.*

*Mr. and Mrs. Alexander S. Hamilton*
*request the pleasure of your company at their*

Fifteenth Wedding Anniversary,

*Wednesday Evening, June Eleventh, at eight o'clock*
*503 Broadway.*

### TIN WEDDING.

(Can be engraved on paper in imitation of tin.)

1813. 1823.

*Mr. and Mrs. Alexander S. Hamilton,*

At Home,

*Tuesday Evening, June Eleventh,*
*at eight o'clock,*

*53 Beekman Street.*

### DIAMOND WEDDING.

(Engraved on cream-white paper of fine quality.)

*1813. 1888.*

*Alexander S. Hamilton,*
*Sarah Ogden,*

*Married June eleventh, 1813,*

SEVENTY-FIFTH ANNIVERSARY,

*Saturday Evening, June Eleventh, 1888,*
*at eight o'clock.*

*The pleasure of your company is requested,*
*314 Madison Avenue.*

*NO GIFTS RECEIVED.*

→1858.←  →1883.←

**Mr. & Mrs. Chas. H. Desbrosses**

*request the pleasure of your company at the celebration of their*

**SILVER WEDDING,**

*Monday Evening June Eleventh, 1883, at eight o'clock.*

1845 UNIVERSITY PLACE.

NO GIFTS RECEIVED.

THE INVITATIONS CAN BE ENGRAVED ON SILVER-BORDERED PAPER OR CARDS.

1834.  1884.

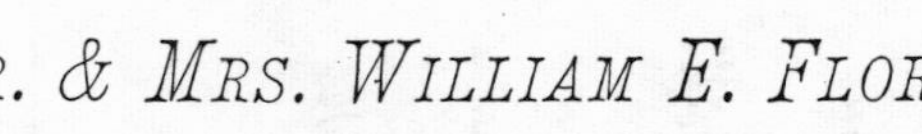

MR. & MRS. WILLIAM E. FLORENCE

*request the pleasure of your company at the celebration of their*

**GOLDEN WEDDING,**

*Wednesday Evening May Tenth, 1884.*

2314 MADISON AVENUE.

THE INVITATIONS CAN BE ENGRAVED ON GOLD-BORDERED PAPER OR CARDS.

DINNER invitations should always be promptly accepted or declined.

Wedding and reception invitations do not require an answer, unless they bear the letters R. S. V. P., when a prompt acceptance or note of regret should be sent.

It is always well to state the reason why an invitation is not accepted. Three days is the limit that courtesy allows for an answer. An acceptance or regret should always be written on handsome paper, and should correspond in style to the invitation.

### INVITATION TO THE OPERA.

Mr. Raymond's compliments, and requests the pleasure of Miss Lawton's company at the opera, *La Favorita*, Wednesday evening.

No. — W. 59th street. January 4th.

### FORM OF ACCEPTANCE.

*Mr. and Mrs. William H. Griffen*

*accept with pleasure*

*Mr. and Mrs. John W. Howard's*

*invitation for Monday Evening,*
*February ninth.*

### INVITATION TO DRIVE.

Mr. Carlton's compliments, and may he have the honor of Miss Burgoyne's company for a drive in Central Park to-morrow afternoon; if so, will Miss Burgoyne kindly state what time will be convenient to have him call?

Hotel St. Nicholas. March 28th.

### ACCEPTANCE.

Miss Burgoyne's compliments, and will be delighted to accept Mr. Carlton's kind invitation to drive, at half-past four.

No. — Lexington avenue. March 28th.

### INVITATION DECLINED.

Miss Burgoyne's compliments to Mr. Carlton, and regrets that a previous engagement prevents her from accepting Mr. Carlton's kind invitation to drive to-morrow afternoon.

No. — Lexington avenue. March 28th.

### REVOKING ACCEPTANCE.

Mr. and Mrs. Williams regret that on account of the sudden illness of Mrs. Williams they are obliged to revoke their acceptance of Mrs. Wetmore's kind invitation for to-morrow evening.

413 Broad street. Friday, Jan. 20th.

### FORM OF DECLINING.

*Mr. and Mrs. Wm. H. Griffen*

*regret that a previous engagement*
*prevents the acceptance of*

*Mr. and Mrs. John W. Howard's*

*invitation for Monday Evening,*
*February ninth.*

WHEN a gift is sent to a friend it may be accompanied by either note or card. For ordinary occasions a card is to be preferred. When some message is to be added the note may be adopted. It should be brief and rather more formal in style than general letters of friendship. If it is desired to be ceremonious, the third person may be used; between relations and intimate friends it is better to avoid this formality.

## CARD FORMS.

*With Compliments*

*Mr. E. M. Dudley*

---

*Miss Langdon sends her Christmas greeting to Mr. Sanders, and begs his acceptance of the accompanying trifle as a token of her esteem.*

*Christmas, 1883.*

### ACCOMPANYING A BOUQUET.

BELLEVUE, May 12, 1881.

Will Miss Bella Haines accept this little token of regard from a sincere admirer?

FRANK BISHOP.

### TICKETS TO A MATINEE.

BOSTON, May 20, 1883.

*My Dear Mrs. Sayres:—*

May I request your acceptance of the inclosed tickets for the afternoon performance at the Athenæum to-day? I am sure you and the young ladies would enjoy the play (Hazel Kirke). I am just leaving town, or would call in person.

Yours most truly,

JULIUS FELTON.

MRS. E. P. SAYRES,
618 Beacon street.

### ACCOMPANYING A PHOTOGRAPH.

OAK HILL, May 10, 1882.

MR. EDWARD LANSING,
Washington, Conn.

*Dear Friend:—*

I send you what you have so often asked for—a photograph of myself. I think it a good one, and hope it will please you, and that when you see it you may be reminded of the many pleasant hours we have spent together. Write and tell me what you think of it.

Yours sincerely,

ELLA WHEELER.

### REPLY TO THE ABOVE.

WASHINGTON, June 1, 1882.

*Dear Miss Wheeler:—*

Thanks for the capital likeness of your well-remembered face, which has just reached me. The expression is perfect. Hamlet tells Horatio that he can see his father with his "mind's eye," but though the memory is tenacious of the images of those who are dear to us, a good portrait of a friend seems to bring the face more palpably before us than any exercise of the mental vision. I shall keep the picture where I can pay my respects to it daily, and hope soon to see the fascinating original of which it is the shadow.

Yours faithfully,

EDWARD LANSING.

Agnes, Georgia and Willie May's

COMPLIMENTS FOR

MONDAY EVE'G, OCT. 31, 1882.

1680 MADISON AVENUE.

---

MOONLIGHT EXCURSION

OF THE

**NEW YORK PRESS CLUB,**

TO NEWBURGH, N. Y.,

**Monday Evening, June 17th, 1883.**

MUSIC BY GILMORE.

BOAT LEAVES PIER 35, N. R., AT 7 O'CLOCK.

---

CANDY PULL.

You are cordially invited to attend a Candy Pull, at the residence of

*MR. & MRS. JOHN FULTON,*

THURSDAY EVENING, FEB. 2, 1883.

2163 MADISON AVENUE.

---

PRIVATE THEATRICALS

AND

MUSICAL ENTERTAINMENT,

TO BE GIVEN ON

**Monday Evening, January 9, 1883,**

AT 8 O'CLOCK.

4173 LEXINGTON AVE.

---

THIRD ANNUAL HOP

OF THE

AT ACADEMY OF MUSIC,

**Monday, May 28, 1883.**

COMMITTEE OF ARRANGEMENTS:

| | | |
|---|---|---|
| WM. ARMITAGE. | G. F. SULLIVAN. | THOS. RUSSELL. |
| C. F. BRIGHT. | JOS. CARTER. | JNO. S. ALLEN. |

MUSIC BY WERNIG.

---

TRIENNIAL SOCIAL

OF THE

HOLOYKE LIGHT INFANTRY,

FRIDAY EVENING, DEC. 16, 1882.

MUSIC BY ORCHESTRAL CLUB,

DANCING AT 10 O'CLOCK.

---

SECOND ANNUAL

CALICO RECEPTION

OF THE

*WINDSOR CLUB,*

IRVING HALL JANUARY 10, 1882

---

PROMENADE CONCERT

AND

FAIR

AT

AMERICAN INSTITUTE,

WEDNESDAY, DECEMBER 20, 1883.

TICKETS, 50 CENTS. OPEN FROM 10 A. M. UNTIL 11 P. M

---

TENTH ANNUAL BALL

OF THE

**CALEDONIAN SOCIETY,**

Thursday Evening, Jan. 14, 1883,

AT ACADEMY OF MUSIC.

TICKETS, ADMITTING GENTLEMAN AND 2 LADIES, $1.

---

PICNIC

OF THE

YOUNG PEOPLE'S UNION,

SPRING HILL GROVE,

**Tuesday, September 12th, 1883.**

TICKETS, 50 CENTS.

---

MASQUERADE SURPRISE.

M____________

YOU ARE INVITED TO ATTEND THE MASQUERADE SURPRISE OF THE

**Violet Social Club,**

AT THE RESIDENCE OF

JOHN LOVELL, BROOKLYN HEIGHTS,

Monday Eve'g, June 3, 1883.

FROM the beginning of the world, and even among the most savage races, there has generally been found existing some conception of a deity, and certain ideas, which might be termed religion. Beginning with Fetishism—the worship of animals, trees, insects, etc.—these ideas ran into personification and symbolism, and produced idolatry, which was the next form. The savage tribes of Africa and America were, and, to some extent, are still, fetish-worshippers. Idolatry, or Paganism, marked an advance step of intelligence, and was an element of early civilization. From these points diverged, in different lands, and among different races of men, notions of religion and theology, which eventually became systems, nearly all of which were based upon a personality, or individual god-head, or mediator. The existing great systems of religion are those held by the following named sects: Jews, Christians, Mohammedans, Hindus (Brahmanism), Buddhists, Guebers (Fire-worshippers). The relative proportions in numbers of these sects are as follows:

| | | | |
|---|---|---|---|
| Jews | | | 7,931,080 |
| Christians | Roman Catholics | 186,860,076 | |
| | Greek Church | 82,926,049 | |
| | Protestants | 101,091,941 | 370,878,066 |
| Mohammedans | | | 103,453,594 |
| Hindus | | | 139,248,568 |
| Magian Religion (Guebers) and Parsees | | | 1,007,190 |
| Buddhism and Religions of China and Japan | | | 483,015,475 |
| | | | 1,105,533,973 |

To this total must be added the number of aborigines in Africa, America, etc., still practicing Fetishism, say 189,000,000, and the grand total of inhabitants of the world (as given by accepted authorities), divided here according to religious belief, is 1,294,533,973.

***Jews.***—This remarkable people emigrated from Mesopotamia about 2000 B. C., and sojourned in Palestine. They were the descendants of the patriarch, Abraham, who accompanied them, and differed from other nations, and particularly from the Egyptians, in their religious belief, as well as in peculiarities of dress, customs, etc. This belief was, and is, Monotheism, the recognition of one God; they practiced circumcision, and they confidently expected to one day possess the land in which they then sojourned. They were afterwards enslaved by the Egyptians, and were delivered by Moses, who conducted the exodus out of Egypt 1600 B. C. From that period, for more than thirty centuries, the Jews have led a wandering life, being found in all countries, but in nearly all, at one time or another, proscribed, rejected, and persecuted. Meanwhile, they have held closely to the tenets of their faith, and have generally prospered in affairs wherever they have been permitted to remain

***Buddhism.***—This religion was founded about 2500 years ago, in Hindostan, where now, however, it has but little hold. It is the religion of China, Japan, the Malay Peninsula, and the Polynesian Islands, and governs the largest number of souls of any existing faith. Buddhism originated in northern Hindostan, in the sixth century B. C., and was founded by a Prince Siddhartha, Gautama, or Sakya (see Arnold's "Light of Asia"). To this prince, after the period of his ascetic and mendicant life, was given the name "Buddha," meaning, "he to whom truth is known," and from which is derived the name of the sect. The Buddhist faith is based upon belief in the doctrine of the transmigration of souls, by which every individual changes the nature of his existence at death, for better or for worse, in accordance with his behaviour during that existence, being thus exalted or degraded, through all imaginable forms, from a clod to a divinity. This faith accepts no ultimate creator, and only finds final rest and happiness in "nirvana," annihilation.

***Brahmanism, or Hinduism.***—This religion antedated Buddhism by an unknown period. It recognizes a trinity of deities, to each of which is ascribed all power, in such wise that no one of the three is complete without the other two. Briefly, the gods, Brahma, Vischnu, and Siva, would seem to indicate the powers of Creation, Existence, and Destruction Transmigration of souls exists in this belief, as in Buddhism, with the qualification that those who arrive at a perfect conception of Brahma, as the potential creator and infusing spirit of the universe, are enabled to avoid the varied curse of perpetual and multiform existence, and to gain eternal rest, and the knowledge of the TRUTH in the bosom of the triune Deity

***Christianity.***—The Christian religion, predicted by the prophets, and anticipated in the teachings of John the Baptist, is based on the preaching of Jesus Christ and of His disciples, and the epistles of certain of the latter. Like Brahmanism, it assumes the existence of a triune Deity—"God the Father, God the Son, and God the Holy Ghost." As is the case with all previous religions, that of Christ is subdivided into sects, each of which is different from the others, in minor forms of doctrine or ritual. Following is a list of these sects among Protestant races, with the number of those accepting the peculiar doctrines or forms of each of them:

| | | |
|---|---|---|
| Roman Catholics | | 186,860,076 |
| Greek Church | | 82,926,049 |
| Protestants: | | |
| Lutherans | 33,767,924 | |
| Anglican Church | 14,459,000 | |
| Calvinists | 13,716,958 | |
| Presbyterians | 3,866,000 | |
| Baptists | 2,439,436 | |
| Methodists | 4,406,422 | |
| Congregationalists | 1,445,683 | |
| Universalists | 656,000 | |
| Quakers | 203,091 | |
| Unitarians | 183,000 | |
| Moravians | 157,925 | |
| Brethren | 108,422 | |
| Mormons | 100,902 | |
| Swedenborgians | 12,000 | |
| Evangelical Union | 10,319 | |
| Irvingites | 6,000 | |
| Shakers | 3,000 | |
| Christian Disciples | 2,471 | |
| Sandemanians | 1,700 | |
| Campbellites | 710 | |
| Free Christian Brethren | 340 | |
| Christian Chartists | 220 | |
| | 75,547,523 | |
| Add in Asia, Africa, etc. | 25,544,418 | 101,091,941 |
| Total Christians | | 370,878,066 |

***Mohammedanism.***—The Mohammedan doctrine was founded by Mohammed, of the tribe of Koreish, who was born in Mecca, in 570 A. D., though it was not until he had reached his fortieth year that he first discovered the gift of prophecy, and began to see visions. He thereafter preached the doctrines which he claimed to have received by direct inspiration, and which are contained in the Koran, of which, translations in French, English, and German can be found in the public libraries. Mohammedanism is made up of parts of Judaism and Christianity, the theory of its founder being that he was one (but the greatest) of a series of prophets, including both Abraham and Christ. It comprises belief in one God—"there is no God but God, and Mohammed is God's apostle" It also peoples the unknown universe with angels—good and evil, and accepts the resurrection and the final judgment. It establishes a Paradise and seven Hells, the lowest and deepest of which is for the "Hypocrites: those, who, outwardly professing a religion, in reality had none." The Mohammedan belief further recognizes the inutility of "works" in influencing the final condition of man, assuming that it is not by these, but by God's mercy, that he is saved, and not damned. Predestination is a part of the creed, man's whole life and destiny being prefigured by Fate (Kismet). The efficacy of prayer is, however, established, and this form of worship enjoined upon "the Faithful;" this, with the sensual nature and characteristics of the Mohammedan Paradise, completes a superficial view of the peculiarities of this religion, as presented in the Koran.

***Fire-Worshippers.***—The Parsees are at present the only devotees of Zoroaster, who is supposed to have founded the religion of the Fire-Worshippers about one thousand years before Christ. Its doctrines are set forth in the Zend Avesta, the sacred books of the Parsees, who are supposed to have been the "Magi" of the scriptures. Like the Koran of Mohammed, the Zend Avesta is made up of the so-called inspired visions of the prophet Zoroaster, who preached Monotheism (one God), added to which were the principles of Good and Evil, having power over Men, the Good being recognized in the blazing flame, the Evil in the burned-out wood or charcoal: Night and Day, Sleeping and Waking, Death and Life. The Fire-Worshippers believed in the resurrection of the body, and held the idea of a Messiah, who was to be the awakener and mediator; they also recognized the doctrine of future rewards and punishments, and the efficacy of the prayers of the Good, who would become immortal, while for the wicked, the end was annihilation.

***Mormonism.***—Although the Mormons are counted as a sect among Protestants, their faith is sufficiently individual to deserve special mention. This faith is mainly contained in the volume known as the "Book of Mormon," which is claimed to have been the inspired revelations made to Joseph Smith, the founder and first prophet of this sect. Smith was born in Vermont in 1805, and received the revelations of the Book of Mormon in 1827, after which date the church was founded, and grew to its present significance. Twenty years later the "Latter-day Saints," as they called themselves, settled about Salt Lake, in Utah, establishing the city of that name as the centre of their church. The Mormons enjoin and practice polygamy, and their doctrine is a modification of Buddhism. They, however, believe that any man may, by devotion and the practice of good works, achieve the spirit of prophecy and the right to rule; in this, following somewhat after the doctrine of Mohammed. They recognize a rather materialized conception of the trinity, believe that men will be punished only for their own sins, that inspiration and miraculous gifts are still possible, and in the resurrection of the body.

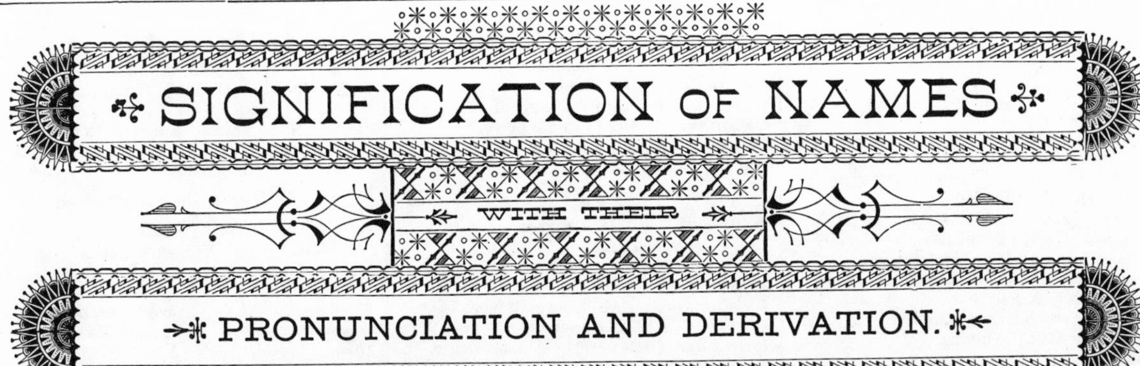


The following Abbreviations of Languages are used in this list to designate the Derivation of Names: A.-S., for Anglo-Saxon; Brit., for British; Celt., for Celtic; Fr., for French; O. Ger., for Old German; Gr., for Greek; Heb., for Hebrew; It., for Italian; Lat., for Latin.

## NAMES OF MEN.

### A.

***Aaron.*** [Heb.] A mountain.
***A'bel.*** [Heb.] Breath; vanity.
***Ab'ner.*** [Heb.] Father of light.
***A'bra-ham.*** [Heb.] Father of a multitude.
***A'bram.*** [Heb.] Father of loftiness.
***Ab'sa-lom.*** [Heb.] Father of peace.
***Ad'am.*** [Heb.] Man; red earth.
***A-dolph'.*** [O. Ger.] Noble warrior.
***Al'bert.*** [O. Ger.] Noble; bright; distinguished.
***Al'ex-an'der.*** [Gr.] A defender of men.
***Al'fred.*** [O. Ger.] Wise counselor.
***Al'mon.*** [Heb.] Hidden.
***A-lon'zo.*** [O. Ger.] See ALPHONSO.
***Al-phon'so.*** [O. Ger.] All-ready; willing.
***Am'brose.*** [Gr.] Immortal; godlike.
***An'drew.*** [Gr.] Strong; manly.
***An'tho-ny.*** [Lat.] Priceless; praiseworthy.
***Ar'thur.*** [Celt.] High; noble.
***Au-gus'tus.*** [Lat.] Majestic; imperial.

### B.

***Bald'win.*** [O. Ger.] Bold; brave friend.
***Bar'na-bas.*** [Heb.] Son of consolation.
***Bar-thol'o-mew.*** [Heb.] A warlike son.
***Bas'il.*** [Gr.] Kingly; royal.
***Ben'e-dict.*** [Lat.] Blessed.
***Ben'ja-min.*** [Heb.] Son of the right hand.
***Ber'nard.*** [O. Ger.] Bold as a bear.
***Ber'tram.*** [O. Ger.] Bright raven.
***Bon'i-face*** [Lat.] A benefactor.
***Bri'an.*** [Celt.] Strong.
***Bru'no.*** [O. Ger.] Brown.

### C.

***Cæ'sar.*** [Lat.] Hairy; blue-eyed.
***Ca'leb.*** [Heb.] A dog.
***Cal'vin.*** [Lat.] Bald.
***Cecil.*** [Lat.] Dim-sighted.
***Charles.*** [O. Ger.] Strong; manly.
***Christ'ian.*** [Lat.] Belonging to Christ.
***Chris'to-pher.*** [Gr.] Bearing Christ.
***Clar'ence.*** [Lat.] Illustrious.
***Clau'di-us, Claude.*** [Lat.] Lame.
***Clem'ent.*** [Lat.] Merciful.
***Con'rad.*** [O. Ger.] Bold in council.
***Con'stant.*** [Lat.] Firm; faithful.
***Con'stan-tine.*** [Lat.] Resolute; firm.
***Cuth'bert.*** [A.-S.] Splendid.
***Cyr'il.*** [Gr.] Lordly.
***Cy'rus.*** [Persian.] The sun.

### D.

***Dan.*** [Heb.] A judge.
***Dan'i-el.*** [Heb.] A divine judge.
***Da-ri'us.*** [Persian.] Preserver.
***Da'vid.*** [Heb.] Beloved.
***De-me'tri-us.*** [Gr.] Belonging to Demeter.
***Den'is, Den'nis.*** [Gr.] Belonging to Dionysos or Bacchus, the god of wine.
***Don'ald.*** [Celt.] Proud chief.
***Dun'can.*** [Celt.] Brown chief.

### E.

***Eb'en.*** [Heb.] A stone.
***Eb'en-e'zer.*** [Heb.] The stone of help.
***Ed'gar.*** [A.-S.] A javelin or protector of property.
***Ed'mund.*** [A.-S.] Defender of property.
***Ed'ward.*** [A.-S.] Guardian of property.
***Ed'win.*** [A.-S.] Gainer of property.
***Eg'bert.*** [O. Ger.] The sword's brightness.
***E'li.*** [Heb.] A foster son.
***E-li'jah.*** [Heb.] Jehovah is my God.
***El'mer.*** [A.-S.] Noble; excellent.
***Em-man'u-el.*** [Heb.] God with us.
***E'no-ch.*** [Heb.] Consecrated.
***E'phra-im.*** [Heb.] Very fruitful.
***Er'nest.*** [Gr.] Earnest.
***E'than.*** [Heb.] Firmness; strength.
***Eu'gene,*** or ***Eu-gene'.*** [Gr.] Well-born.
***Ev'er-ard.*** [O. Ger.] Strong as a wild boar.
***E-ze'ki-el.*** [Heb.] Strength of God.
***Ez'ra.*** [Heb.] Help.

### F.

***Fe'lix.*** [Lat.] Happy; prosperous.
***Fer'di-nand.*** [O. Ger.] Brave.
***Fes'tus.*** [Lat.] Joyful.
***Fran'cis.*** [Fr.] Free.
***Fred'er-ic, Fred'er-ick.*** [O. Ger.] Abounding in peace; *or* peaceful ruler.

### G.

***Ga'bri-el.*** [Heb.] Man of God.
***Ga-ma'li-el.*** [Heb.] Reward of God.
***Geof'frey.*** [O. Ger.] See GODFREY.
***George.*** [Gr.] A landholder; husbandman.
***Ger'ald.*** [O. Ger.] Strong with the spear.
***Gid'e-on.*** [Heb.] A destroyer.
***Gil'bert.*** [O. Ger.] Bright as gold.
***Giles.*** [Gr.] A kid.
***God'frey.*** [O. Ger.] At peace with God.
***God'win.*** [A.-S.] Good in war.
***Greg'o-ry.*** [Gr.] Watchful.
***Grif'fith.*** [Brit.] With faith.
***Gus-ta'vus.*** [Swedish.] A warrior; hero.
***Guy.*** [Fr.] A leader.

### H.

***Han'ni-bal.*** [Punic.] A gracious lord.
***Har'old.*** [A.-S.] A champion; general.
***He'man.*** [Heb.] Faithful.
***Hen'ry.*** [O. Ger.] The head of a house.
***Her'bert.*** [A.-S.] Glory of the army.
***Her'cu-les.*** [Gr.] Lordly fame.
***Her'man.*** [O. Ger.] A warrior.
***Hez'e-ki'ah.*** [Heb.] Strength of God.
***Hi'ram.*** [Heb.] Most noble.
***Ho-se'a.*** [Heb.] Salvation.
***Hu'bert.*** [O. Ger.] Bright in spirit.
***Hugh, Hu'go.*** [Dutch.] High; lofty.
***Humph'rey.*** [A.-S.] Protector of the home.

### I.

***Ig-na'ti-us*** [Gr.] Fiery.
***I'ra.*** [Heb.] Watchful.
***I saac.*** [Heb.] Laughter.
***I-sa'iah.*** [Heb.] Salvation of God.
***Is'ra-el.*** [Heb.] A soldier of God.

### J.

***Ja'cob.*** [Heb.] A supplanter.
***James.*** [Heb.] See JACOB.
***Jes'se.*** [Heb.] Wealth.
***John.*** [Heb.] The gift of God.
***Jo'nah.*** [Heb.] A dove.
***Jon'a-than.*** [Heb.] Gift of Jehovah.
***Jo'seph.*** [Heb.] He shall add.
***Josh'u-a.*** [Heb.] A Saviour.
***Ju'li-us.*** [Gr.] Soft-haired.
***Jus'tin.*** [Lat.] Just.

K.

***Ken'elm.*** [A.-S.] A defender of his kindred.

L.

***Law'rence,*** ***Law'rence.*** } [Lat.] Crowned with laurel.
***Lem'u-el.*** [Heb.] Created by God.
***Leon'ard.*** [Ger.] Lion-hearted.
***Le'o-pold.*** [O. Ger.] Defending the people.
***Le'vi.*** [Heb.] Adhesion.
***Lew'is.*** [O. Ger.] Bold warrior.
***Li'o-nel.*** [Lat.] Young lion.
***Llew-el'lyn.*** [Celt.] Lightning.
***Lo-ren'zo.*** [Lat.] See LAURENCE.
***Lot.*** [Heb.] A veil.
***Lou'is.*** French form of LEWIS.
***Lu'ci-us.*** [Lat.] Shining.
***Luke.*** [Lat.] A wood or grave.
***Lu'ther.*** [Ger.] Illustrious warrior.
***Ly-cur'gus.*** [Gr.] Wolf-driver.

M.

***Mal'a-chi.*** [Heb.] Messenger of the Lord.
***Mark.*** [Lat.] A hammer.
***Mar'tin.*** [Lat.] Of Mars; warlike; martial.
***Mat'thew.*** [Heb. A gift.
***Mau'rice.*** [Lat.] Moorish; dark-colored.
***Mi'cha-el.*** [Heb.] Who is like God.
***Miles.*** [Lat.] A soldier.
***Mor'gan.*** [Brit.] A mariner.
***Mo'ses.*** [Egyptian.] Drawn out of the water.

N.

***Na-po'le-on.*** [Gr.] Lion of the forest-dell.
***Na'than.*** [Heb.] A gift.
***Na-than'i-el.*** [Heb.] The gift of God.
***Neal.*** [Celt.] Chief.
***Nich'o-las.*** [Gr.] Victorious over the people.
***No'ah.*** [Heb.] Rest; comfort.
***No'el.*** [Lat.] Christmas.
***Nor'man.*** [Ger.] A Northman; born in Normandy.

O.

***O-ba-di'ah.*** [Heb.] Servant of God.
***Oc-ta'vi-us.*** [Lat.] The eighth-born.
***Ol'i-ver.*** [Lat.] An olive.
***O-res'tes.*** [Gr.] A mountaineer.
***Or-lan'do.*** [It.] Counsel for the land.
***Os'car.*** [Celt.] Leaping warrior.
***Os'mund.*** [O. Ger.] House peace.
***Os'wald.*** [O. Ger.] Ruler of a house.
***Ow'en.*** [Celt.] Lamb, *or*, young warrior.

P.

***Pat'rick.*** [Lat.] A nobleman.
***Paul.*** [Lat.] Little.
***Per'e-grine.*** [Lat.] A traveler.
***Pe'ter.*** [Gr.] A rock or stone.
***Phi-lan'der.*** [Gr.] A lover of men.
***Phil'ip.*** [Gr.] A lover of horses.
***Phin'e-as.*** [Heb.] Of bold countenance.
***Pi'us.*** [Lat.] Pious.

Q.

***Quin'tin.*** [Lat.] The fifth.

R.

***Ralph.*** [O. Ger.] Contraction of Rodolph.
***Ray'mond,*** ***Ray'mund.*** } [O. Ger.] Wise protection.
***Reg'i-nald.*** [O. Ger.] Strong ruler.
***Reu'ben.*** [Heb.] Behold, a son.
***Rich'ard.*** [O. Ger.] Rich-hearted; powerful.
***Rob'ert.*** [O. Ger.] Bright in fame.
***Rod'er-ic,*** ***Rod'er-ick.*** } [O. Ger.] Rich in glory.
***Ro'dolph,*** ***Ro-dol'phus.*** } [O. Ger.] Famous wolf, *or* hero.
***Rog'er.*** [O. Ger.] Strong counsel.
***Ro'land,*** ***Row'land.*** } [O. Ger.] Counsel of the land.
***Ru'dolph.*** See RODOLPH.
***Ru'fus.*** [Lat.] Red; reddish.
***Ru'pert.*** [O. Ger.] See ROBERT.

S.

***Sam'son.*** [Heb.] Sun-like.
***Sam'u-el.*** [Heb.] Heard of God.
***Saul.*** [Heb.] Desired.
***Se-bas'tian.*** [Gr.] Venerable.
***Seth.*** [Heb.] Appointed.
***Sig'is-mund.*** [O. Ger.] Victorious protection.
***Si'las.*** [Lat.] A contraction of SILVANUS.
***Sil-va'nus.*** [Lat.] Dwelling in the woods.
***Sil-ves'ter.*** [Lat.] Rustic.
***Sim'e-on,*** ***Si'mon.*** } [Heb.] Hearing graciously.
***Sol'o-mon.*** [Heb.] Peaceable.
***Ste'phen.*** [Gr.] A crown or garland.

T.

***The'o-bald.*** [O. Ger.] Bold over the people.
***The'o-dore.*** [Gr.] The gift of God
***The-oph'i-lus.*** [Gr.] A lover of God.
***The'ron.*** [Gr.] A hunter.
***Thom'as.*** [Heb.] A twin.
***Tim'o-thy.*** [Gr.] Fearing God.
***Tris'tam.*** [Lat.] Grave.

U.

***U-lys'ses.*** [Gr.] A hater.
***Ur'ban.*** [Lat.] Of the town; polite.
***U-ri'ah.*** [Heb.] Light of the Lord.

V.

***Val'en-tine.*** [Lat.] Strong; powerful.
***Vic'tor.*** [Lat.] A conqueror.
***Vin'cent.*** [Lat.] Triumphant.
***Viv'i-an.*** [Lat.] Lively.

W.

***Wal'ter.*** [O. Ger.] Ruling the army.
***Will'iam.*** [O. Ger.] Resolute helmet; protector.
***Win'fred.*** [A.-S.] Winning peace.

Z.

***Zach'a-ri'ah.*** [Heb.] Remembered of God.
***Za'dok.*** [Heb.] Just.
***Zed'e-ki'ah.*** [Heb.] Justice of God.
***Ze'nas.*** [Gr.] Gift of Zeus.

## NAMES OF WOMEN.

A.

***Ab'i-gail.*** [Heb.] Father's joy.
***A'da.*** [O. Ger.] See EDITH.
***Ad'e-la,*** ***Ad'e-laide.*** } [O. Ger.] See ADELINE.
***A-de'li-a.*** [O. Ger.] See ADELA.
***Ad'e-li'na,*** ***Ad'e-line.*** } [O. Ger.] Of noble birth; a princess.
***Ag'a-tha.*** [Gr.] Good.
***Ag'nes.*** [Gr.] Chaste.
***Al-ber'ta.*** [O. Ger.] Feminine of ALBERT.
***Al'e-the'a.*** [Gr.] Truth.
***Al'ex-an'dra.*** [Gr.] Feminine of ALEXANDER.
***Al'ice.*** [O. Ger.] See ADELINE.
***Al-mi'ra.*** [Arabic.] Lofty; a princess.
***A-man'da.*** [Lat.] Worthy of love.
***A-me'li-a.*** [O. Ger.] Energetic; beloved.
***An-gel'i-ca,*** ***An-ge-li'na.*** } [Gr.] Angelic.
***An'na.*** [Heb.] Gracious.
***An-to'ni-a.*** [Lat.] Feminine of ANTHONY.
***Ar'a-bel'la.*** [Lat.] A fair altar.
***Au-gus'ta.*** [Lat.] Feminine of AUGUSTUS.
***Au-re'li-a.*** [Lat.] Golden.
***Au-ro'ra.*** [Lat.] Morning redness; dawn.

B.

***Bar'ba-ra.*** [Gr.] Foreign.
***Be'a-trice.*** [Lat.] Making happy.
***Ber'tha.*** [O. Ger.] Bright.
***Blanche.*** [Fr.] White.
***Bridg'et.*** [Celt.] Strength; bright.

C.

***Car'o-line.*** [O. Ger.] Feminine of CHARLES.
***Cath'a-ri'na,*** ***Cath'a-rine,*** ***Cath'er-ine.*** } [Gr.] Pure.
***Ce-cil'i-a.*** [Lat.] Feminine of CECIL.
***Ce-les'tine.*** [Lat.] Heavenly.
***Char'lotte.*** [O. Ger.] Feminine of CHARLES.
***Chris'ti-na.*** [Gr.] Feminine of CHRISTIAN.
***Clar'a.*** [Lat.] Bright.
***Clem'en-ti'na,*** ***Clem'en-tine.*** } [Lat.] Mild.
***Con'stance.*** [Lat.] Constant.
***Co'ra.*** [Gr.] Maiden.
***Cor-de'li-a.*** [Lat.] Warm-hearted.
***Co-rin'na.*** [Gr.] Maiden.
***Cor-ne'li-a.*** [Lat.] Feminine of CORNELIUS.

D.

***Deb'o-rah.*** [Heb.] A bee.
***De'li-a.*** [Gr.] Belonging to Delos.
***Di-an'a.*** [Lat.] Goddess of Hunting.
***Di'nah.*** [Heb.] Judged.
***Do'ra.*** [Gr.] Contraction of DOROTHEA.
***Dor'cas.*** [Gr.] A gazelle.
***Do-rin'da.*** [Gr.] See DOROTHEA.
***Dor'o-the'a,*** ***Dor'o-thy.*** } [Gr.] The gift of God.

E.

***E'dith.*** [O. Ger.] Happiness.
***Ed'na.*** [Heb.] Pleasure.
***El'e-a-nor.*** [Gr.] Light.
***E-lis'a-beth,*** ***E-liz'a-beth,*** ***E-li'za.*** } [Heb.] Worshiper of God.

*El'la.* [Gr.] Contraction of ELEANOR.
*El-vi'ra.* [Lat.] White.
*Em'e-line,* *Em'me-line.* [O. Ger.] Industrious.
*Em'i-ly,* *Em'ma.* [O. Ger.] See EMELINE.
*Es'ther.* [Persian.] A star; good luck.
*Eth'el.* [O. Ger.] Of noble birth.
*Eth'e-lind,* *Eth'e-lin'da.* [O. Ger.] Noble snake.
*Eu-ge'ni-a.* [Gr.] Feminine of EUGENE.
*Eu'nice.* [Gr.] Happy victory.
*E'va.* [Heb.] Life.
*E-van'ge-line.* [Gr.] Bringing glad news.
*Eve.* [Heb.] See EVA.
*Ev'e-li'na,* *Ev'e-line.* [Heb.] Diminutive of EVA.

F.

*Fan'ny.* [Gr.] Diminutive of FRANCES.
*Fe-lic'ia.* [Lat.] Happy.
*Fi-de'l-ia.* [Lat.] Faithful.
*Flo'ra.* [Lat.] Flowers.
*Flor'ence.* [Lat.] Flourishing.
*Fran'ces.* [Ger.] Feminine of FRANCIS.
*Fred-er-i'ca.* [O. Ger.] Feminine of FREDERICK.

G.

*Geor-gi-an'a,* *Geor-gi'na.* [Gr.] Feminine of GEORGE.
*Ger'al-dine.* [O. Ger.] Feminine of GERALD.
*Ger'trude.* [O Ger.] Spear-maiden.
*Grace.* [Lat.] Grace.

H

*Han'nah.* [Heb.] See ANNA.
*Har'ri-et.* [O. Ger.] Feminine of HENRY.
*Hel'en,* *Hel'e-na.* [Gr.] Light. Diminutive: Nell, Nelly.
*Hen'ri-et'ta.* [O. Ger.] Feminine of HENRY. Diminutive: Etta, Hetty.
*Hes'ter.* [Per.] See ESTHER.
*Hon-o'ra,* *Hon-o'ri-a.* [Lat.] Honorable.
*Hor-ten'si-a.* [Lat.] A female gardener.
*Hul'dah.* [Heb.] A weasel.

I.

*I'da.* [O. Ger.] Godlike.
*I-re'ne.* [Gr.] Peace.
*Is'a-bel,* *Is-a-bel'la.* [Heb.] See ELIZABETH.

J.

*Jane.* [Heb.] Feminine of JOHN.
*Ja-net'.* [Heb.] Diminutive of JANE.
*Jean,* *Jeanne,* *Jean-nette'.* French forms of JANE.
*Je-mi'ma.* [Heb.] A dove.
*Je-ru'sha.* [Heb.] Married.
*Joan'.* *Joan'na.* [Heb.] Feminine of JOHN.
*Jo'sephine.* [Heb.] Feminine of JOSEPH.
*Ju'lia.* [Lat.] Feminine of JULIUS.
*Ju'liet.* [Lat.] Diminutive of JULIA.

K.

*Kath'ar-ine.* [Gr.] See CATHARINE.
*Ke-zi'ah.* [Heb.] Cassia.

L.

*Lau'ra.* [Lat.] Laurel.
*La-vin'i-a.* [Lat.] Belonging to Lavinium.
*Leti't-ia.* [Lat.] Joy.
*Lil'i-an.* [Lat.] A lily.
*Lou-i'sa,* *Lou-ise'.* [O. Ger.] Feminine of LOUIS.
*Lu-cin'da.* [Lat.] See LUCY.
*Lu-cre'tia.* [Lat.] Light.
*Lu'cy.* [Lat.] Feminine of LUCIUS.
*Lyd'i-a.* [Gr.] A Lydian.

M.

*Ma'bel.* [Lat.] Lovable.
*Mad'e-line,* *Mag'da-lene.* [Heb.] Of MAGDALA.
*Mar'ga-ret.* [Gr.] A pearl.
*Ma-ri'a,* *Mar'i-on.* [Heb.] See MARY.
*Mar'tha.* [Heb.] Sorrowful.
*Ma'ry.* [Heb.] Star of the sea.
*Ma-til'da.* [O. Ger.] A woman warrior.
*Maud.* See MAGDALENE.
*Me-lis'sa.* [Gr.] A bee.
*Mi-ran'da.* [Lat.] Wonderful; admirable.
*Mir'i-am.* [Heb.] See MARY.

N.

*Nan'cy.* See ANNE.
*No'ra.* See HONORA.

O.

*Ol'ive,* *O-liv'i-a.* [Lat.] The olive.
*O-phe'li-a.* [Gr.] Belonging to a serpent.

P.

*Pau-li'na,* *Pau-line'.* [Lat.] Feminine of PAUL.
*Pe-nel'o-pe.* [Gr.] A weaver.
*Per'sis.* [Gr.] A Persian woman.
*Phœ'be.* [Gr.] Shining.
*Pol'ly.* [Eng.] See MARY.
*Pris-cil'la.* [Lat.] A little old.

R.

*Ra'chel.* [Heb.] An ear.
*Re-bec'ca.* [Heb.] Beautiful.
*Rho'da.* [Gr.] A rose.
*Ro'sa.* [Lat.] A rose.
*Ros'a-lind.* [Lat.] Fair as roses.
*Ro'sa-mond.* [Lat.] The rose of the world.
*Ruth.* [Heb.] Beauty.

S.

*Sa'ra,* *Sa'rah.* [Heb.] A princess.
*Sib'yl,* *Si-byl'la.* [Gr.] Prophetess.
*So-phi'a.* [Gr.] Wisdom.
*So-phro'ni-a.* [Gr.] Wise minded.
*Stel'la.* [Lat.] A star.
*Su'san,* *Su-san'na,* *Su-san'nah.* [Heb.] A lily.

T.

*Tab'i-tha.* [Syrian.] A gazelle.
*The-o-do'ra.* [Gr.] Feminine of THEODORE.
*The-re'sa.* [Gr.] Bearing corn-ears.

U.

*U-ra'ni-a.* [Gr.] Heavenly.
*Ur'su-la.* [Lat.] She-bear.

V.

*Vic-to'ri-a.* [Lat.] Feminine of VICTOR.
*Vi'o-la.* [Lat.] A violet.
*Vir-gin'i-a.* [Lat.] Virginal.
*Viv'i-an.* [Lat.] Vivacious.

W.

*Wil-hel-mi'na.* [O. Ger.] Feminine of WILLIAM.
*Win'i-fred.* [A.-S.] Feminine of WINFRED.

Z.

*Ze-no'bi-a.* [Gr.] Deriving life from Zeus.

## TYPOGRAPHICAL MARKS EXEMPLIFIED.

1 a/ THOUGH severel differing opinions exist as to
the individual by wyom the art of printing was 2 ∂
first discovered; yet all authorities concur in
admitting Peter Schoeffer to be the person 3 *Caps.*
who invented *cast metal types*, having learned
4 ∂ the art ~~of~~ of *cutting* the letters from the Gu-
5 :/ tenbergs/ he is also supposed to have been
6 # the first whoengraved on copper plates. The 7 /-/
following testimony is preseved in the family, 8 r/
9 ✓ by ✓Jo. ✓Fred. ✓Faustus, ✓of ✓Ascheffenburg:
10 □ ∧ 'Peter Schoeffer, of Gernsheim, perceiving 3 *S. Caps*
11 ∨ his master Fausts design, and being himself
12 *tr.* desirous ardently to improve the art, found
out (by the good providence of God) the
method of cutting (~~*incidendi*~~) the characters 13 *stet.*
in a *matrix*, that the letters might easily be
5 ,/ singly *cast*/ instead of bieng *cut*. He pri- 12 *tr.*
14 ▮ vately *cut matrices*▮ for the whole alphabet: 15
Faust was so pleased with the contrivance,
that he promised Peter to give him his only 17 *w.f.*
16 daughter Christina in marriage, a promise 3 *Ital.*
which he soon after performed.
19 *as*/ But there were many difficulties at first 18 *no* ¶
with these *letters*, as there had been before 3 *Rom.*
20 + with wooden ones, the metal being too soft 3 *Ital.*
to support the force of the im pression: but 21 ⁀
this defect was soon remedied, by mixing
a substance with the metal which sufficiently 12 *tr.*
5 ⊙ hardened it/

*and when he showed his master the letters cast from these matrices,*

THOUGH several differing opinions exist as to the individual by whom the art of printing was first discovered; yet all authorities concur in admitting PETER SCHOEFFER to be the person who invented *cast metal types*, having learned the art of *cutting* the letters from the Gutenbergs: he is also supposed to have been the first who engraved on copper-plates. The following testimony is preserved in the family, by Jo. Fred. Faustus of Ascheffenburg:

"PETER SCHOEFFER, of Gernsheim, perceiving his master Faust's design, and being himself ardently desirous to improve the art, found out (by the good providence of God) the method of cutting (*incidendi*) the characters in a *matrix*, that the letters might easily be singly *cast*, instead of being *cut*. He privately *cut matrices* for the whole alphabet; and when he showed his master the letters cast from these matrices, Faust was so pleased with the contrivance, that he promised Peter to give him his only daughter *Christina* in marriage, a promise which he soon after performed. But there were as many difficulties at first with these letters, as there had been before with *wooden ones*, the metal being too soft to support the force of the impression: but this defect was soon remedied, by mixing the metal with a substance which sufficiently hardened it."

# HOW TO CORRECT PROOF.

The following rules for correcting proof are given in *MacKellar's American Printer*. Professional proof-readers and all persons who may have occasion to revise proofs of their articles will find these rules very convenient for reference.

A wrong letter in a word is noted by drawing a short perpendicular line through it, and making another short line in the margin, behind which the right letter is placed. (See No. 1.) In this manner whole words are corrected, by drawing a line across the wrong word and making the right one in the margin opposite.

A turned letter is noted by drawing a line through it, and writing the mark No. 2 in the margin.

If letters or words require to be altered from one character to another, a parallel line or lines must be made underneath the word or letter,—viz., for capitals, three lines; small capitals, two lines; Italics, one line; and, in the margin opposite the line where the alteration occurs, *Caps*, *Small Caps*, or *Ital.* must be written. (See No. 3.)

When letters or words are set double, or are required to be taken out, a line is drawn through the superfluous word or letter, and the mark No. 4 placed opposite in the margin.

Where the punctuation requires to be altered, the correct point, marked in the margin, should be encircled.

When a space is omitted between two words or letters which should be separated, a caret must be made where the separation ought to be, and the sign No. 6 placed opposite in the margin.

No. 7 describes the manner in which the hyphen and ellipsis line are marked.

When a letter has been omitted, a caret is put at the place of omission, and the letter marked as No. 8.

Where letters that should be joined are separated, or where a line is too widely spaced, the mark No. 9 must be placed under them, and the correction denoted by the marks in the margin.

Where a new paragraph is required, a quadrangle is drawn in the margin, and a caret placed at the beginning of the sentence. (See No. 10.)

No. 11 shows the way in which the apostrophe, inverted commas, the star and other references, and superior letters and figures, are marked.

Where two words are transposed, a line is drawn over one word and below the other, and the mark No. 12 placed in the margin; but where several words require to be transposed, their right order is signified by a figure placed over each word, and the mark No. 12 in the margin.

Where words have been struck out, that have afterward been approved of, dots should be marked under them, and *Stet.* written in the margin. (See No. 13.)

Where a space sticks up between two words, a horizontal line is drawn under it, and the mark No. 14 placed opposite, in the margin.

Where several words have been left out, they are transcribed at the bottom of the page, and a line drawn from the place of omission to the written words (see No. 15); but if the omitted matter is too extensive to be copied at the foot of the page, *Out, see copy*, is written in the margin, and the missing lines are enclosed between brackets, and the word *Out*, is inserted in the margin of the copy.

Where letters stand crooked, they are noted by a line (see No. 16); but, where a page hangs, lines are drawn across the entire part affected.

When a smaller or larger letter, of a different font, is improperly introduced into the page, it is noted by the mark No. 17, which signifies wrong font.

If a paragraph is improperly made, a line is drawn from the broken-off matter to the next paragraph, and *No* ¶ written in the margin. (See No. 18.)

Where a word has been left out or is to be added, a caret must be made in the place where it should come in, and the word written in the margin. (See No. 19.)

Where a faulty letter appears, it is marked by making a cross under it, and placing a similar one in the margin (see No. 20); though some prefer to draw a perpendicular line through it, as in the case of a wrong letter.

# MARKS USED IN CORRECTING PROOF-SHEETS.

|  |  |
|---|---|
| ℘ | Turn reversed letter. |
| □ | Indent line one em quadrat. |
| ℘ | (*dele.*) Take out; expunge. |
| ∧ | The caret shows that something omitted in the line is interlined above, or written in the margin, and should be inserted in that place. |
| # | Insert space between words, letters, or lines. |
| ⌒ | Less space. |
| ⁀‿ | Close up. |
| ℘ # | Take out type, and insert a space, in place of what is taken out. |
| ℘ ⁀‿ | Take out type, and close up. |
| × | Calls attention to bad type. |
| ⊥ | Push down space. |
| ⊥ | Plane down a letter. |
| ⁓ | No paragraph. |
| ...... | Placed under erased words in order to have them remain. |
| *Stet.* | Written in the margin to restore words (with dots placed under them) that have been struck out by mistake. |
| ¶ | New paragraph. |
| / | Letters stand crooked. |
| /-/ | Hypnen omitted. |
| ⌊ | Carry further to the left. |
| ⌋ | Carry further to the right. |
| ⌐¬ | Carry higher up on page. |
| ⌴ | Carry down. |
| ≡ | Three lines, beneath writing, call for capitals. |
| = | Two lines, beneath writing, call for small capitals. |
| — | One line, beneath writing, calls for italics. |
| *w. f.* | Wrong font type. |
| *tr.* | Transpose letters, words, or sentences. |
| *l. c.* | Lower case, or small letters. |
| *s. c.* | Small capitals. |
| ⊙ | Period. |
| ? | Query as to some doubtful word, sentence, or statement. |

# THE CALENDAR.

OUR English term "*Calendar*" means a method of reckoning time. The name is from *Calendæ*, the first division of the Roman month, when the pontiffs called the people together and informed them what days were to be observed during the month.

Man's first conception of time or duration would naturally have come from observing the regular recurrence of light and darkness. He would next notice the changing appearance and position of the moon. Hence, whatever he might have called them, he would have a tolerable idea of the day and the month. In the temperate zone he would observe the changes of heat and cold and the recurrence of what we call seasons, and so get a notion of the year. These only are natural divisions of time. Weeks, hours, minutes and seconds are purely artificial and arbitrary. Before the appearance of clocks or watches, men would measure time by the movements of the sun, moon, and stars; the first artificial measures were made by sun-dials, water-clocks or clepsydra, (on the principle of the modern hour-glass,) by sand-glasses, or by the burning of candles.

## THE DAY.

This would naturally have been at first only the time of the duration of light, or from sunrise to sunset. Modern observation makes the solar or common day the period between the passage of the sun over a given meridian and its return to that meridian. This period is so nearly uniform that its variations are of no account in ordinary reckoning. This solar day is the unit of time.

The ancient Egyptians, and most early people of Europe, began the day as we do now, at midnight, and divided it into two periods of twelve hours each. Astronomers, however, count the hours from one to twenty-four, and begin their day at noon. Thus where we would write Jan. 1, 1882, 10½ A. M., they say Dec. 31, 1881, 22h. 30m. The Chaldeans and Greeks began the day at sunrise; the Italians and Bohemians at sunset. [Not many years ago there was a custom in the New England States of "keeping Saturday night," as if Sunday began at sunset. This especial night was devoted by the young people to love-making, and was sometimes called "courting night."]

In early Rome, down to about the year 200 B. C., the only divisions of the day were morning or sunrise, mid-day, and sunset. Mid-day was known when the sun shone straight along between the Forum and the Graciostasis, a place where foreign ambassadors came to deliver their messages. This must have been the original noon-mark, traces of which may still be seen on the floor under a southward-looking window in many a farm house in New York and other States.

The division of the day into hours must have been of extreme antiquity. Evening and morning, days and weeks, seasons and years are spoken of in the Hebrew scriptures; but the first mention of the hour is in the book of Daniel, who lived about 550 B. C. It reads: "Then Daniel, whose name was Belteshazzar, was astonished for one hour, and his thoughts troubled him." The division into hours, minutes and seconds may have been made before the invention of the decimal system; at any rate it is on the duodecimal system, increasing and diminishing by twelves; $12 \times 5 = 60$ seconds make a minute; $12 \times 5 = 60$ minutes make an hour; $2 \times 12 = 24$ hours make a day. The Chinese, who are nothing if not contrary, divide the day into twelve parts of two hours each.

If one desires to know the length of day and night, add 12 hours to the time of sunset and from the sum subtract the time of sunrise—the remainder gives the length of the day. To find the length of the night, subtract 12 hours from the time of sunset, and to the remainder add the time of sunrise for the next morning; the product shows the length of the night.

## THE WEEK.

The week is a purely arbitrary division of time and of very great antiquity. It is peculiar in being uniform and unbroken. Whatever has been done in rectifying the length of years or months, the days of the week have gone on in regular succession, entirely undisturbed. In England and her Colonies the change from old to new style was made in 1752, by ordering the day following the 2d of September to be numbered the 14th. Here were eleven days stifled before their birth—all between the 2d and 14th; but the 2d was Wednesday and the 14th was Thursday, the days of the week going on without interruption.

Most Eastern nations used the week, though the Greeks did not, nor did the Romans until about 400 A. D. Probably the week was suggested by the changes of the moon, as the return of these changes in regular order suggested the month. There are seven days in a week, and the fourth part of a lunar month is seven days and three eights of a day—seven days and nine hours, nearly.

The names of the days are variously accounted for. Assuming that the week was of Egyption origin, and the days named after the heavenly bodies. the theory is that the seven planets (or what were called planets) presided over the hours. Beginning with the most remote, Saturn presided over the first hour of the day, Jupiter the second, Mars the third, the Sun the fourth, Venus fifth, Mercury sixth, and the Moon seventh; then Saturn eighth, and so on. By this rule, the planet presiding over the first hour gave its name to the day; and so came Saturn's, Sun's, Moon's, Mars's, Mercury's, Jupiter's, and Venus's days. The Egyptian week began with Saturday; but the Jews, in taking the weeks along with them, out of hatred to their oppressors, made Saturday the last day of the week in their calendar.

The English names of the days are a mixture of astronomical and Old Norse or Scandinavian mythological names. Sunday and Monday are clear enough; Tuesday is variously derived; but it comes from the Norse divinity Tyr, the god of valor, or bravery, who put his hand in the mouth of the Fenris wolf while the other gods chained the monster, and had the hand bitten off when the wolf found himself a captive. Tuesday was Tyr's day. Wednesday is named from Odin, the principal deity of the Norsemen. The Saxons called him Woden, and the day Woden's day. Thursday is called after Thor, the god of thunder, the Norse Mars. Friday is Freya's day. She was the wife of Ottar, and goddess of love and fruitfulness, and nearly answers to the Roman Venus. whose name was given to the same day. Saturday is undoubtedly from Saturn. The Northmen called it "Thvatt-dag," washing or bathing day.

## THE MONTH.

This division must have been made with reference to the moon. The Egyptians had twelve months of thirty days each, and put five extra days to the last month to make up the year. The Greeks divided the month into three decades of ten days each. This was imitated in the short-lived calendar of the French Revolution. The Romans had a remarkable division, not easy to understand. Instead of naming the days, first, second, third, and so on, they counted backward from three fixed points in each month—the calends, the nones, and the ides. What we call the 14th of January, they would call the 19th day before the calends of February.

The names of months used by most nations are those given by the Romans. January from Janus, who had two faces, could look out before and behind, and presided over doors and entrances (hence our *janitor*). February, from *februare*, to purify or offer expiation. March, from Mars (this was originally the beginning of the Roman year, when it had but ten months). April, from Aphrilis (probably) a name of Venus. May, probably from the Majores, the first senators of Rome. June, probably from Junores, or next class of law-givers—some think from Juno. July, after Julius Cæsar; August, after Augustus Cæsar, and the others by numerals—Septem, Octo, Novem, Decem, or, seventh, eighth, ninth and tenth. Among the northern nations some of the names indicated the character of the season or things to be done. The Norsemen had a gore month, when cattle were slaughtered for winter food a freezing month, breeding month, sacrifice month, reaping month, the sun's month, and Thor's month. The Saxons called January wolf month, because of the roaming of wolves for prey; February was sprout month, or sun month; March, the lengthening month, the days growing longer; April, the last wind month; May, the milking month; July, the hay month; September, barley month; October, wine month; November, wind month; December, winter month. In Holland the months are still designated in a similar way, such as snowy, rainy, and chilly, grass, hay, harvest, etc.

## THE SEASONS.

In the extreme north of Europe there were but two seasons—winter and summer, and it is so now in Iceland. Summer had six months of 30 days each, with four *ekke*, or eke-out, nights interpolated near the close of July. Winter began Oct. 26, and had six months of 30 days each. In Iceland it is still the custom to reckon one's age by winters, and not by years.

In southern Europe spring and autumn were clearly defined, and were the most delightful portions of the year. The seasons are natural divisions: Spring begins when the sun is over the equator; Summer when the sun reaches its highest northern declination; Autumn when it is again over the equator, and Winter when at the remotest southern declination. Our months ought to conform to these natural divisions, and the year should begin at the vernal equinox, about March 21 or 22. Then should come, for common years, seven months of 30 and five of 31 days, and for leap years, six months of each number, which would be as nearly as possible equalized months. Julius Cæsar tried to equalize the months by so arranging that no two of 31 days should come together, but his nephew, Augustus, was vain enough to disturb the arrangement, not only ordering Sextilis (sixth) month to be named August, after himself, but insisting that his month should be as long as his uncle's; so a day was stolen from February to give August as many days as there were in July.

## THE YEAR.

The most important division of time is the year, and no effort has been spared to determine its exact length. The civil year, employed in chronology, consists of 365 days 5 hours 48 minutes and 49 and 7-10 seconds, or 36,556,930 seconds, nearly, or a trifle over 11 minutes less than 365¼ days. The year, as we now reckon it, consists of 365.2425 days. The ancient astronomers made pretty near guesses at the length of the year, but the nations had various methods of computation, and no approach to correct time was made until Julius Cæsar took the business in hand. With the help of Sosigenes, the astronomer, he concocted the Julian Calender, which we call Old Style, making three years of 365 days, and giving the fourth year 366 days, which was pretty near the truth. But the year at that time was so confused that, to get a fair start, Cæsar added 67 days to the year 47 B. C., making it 445 days long. This is known as "the last year of confusion." He began his calendar Jan. 1, 46 B. C. Carrying back the old style reckoning, it appears that the Julian era would have begun on Thursday, if any such day of the week had been known. He also made a common-sense division into months, giving 30 and 31 days alternately as nearly as possible. This was disarranged by Augustus Cæsar, as we have said, and when he tried to separate months of 30 and 31 days he failed, as the almanac still shows by July and September, and December and January, each having 31 days, falling together. Augustus gave the leap-year day to February, not, as we do, by putting it last, but as the Roman Calendar called the 25th of February the sixth before the calends of March, he put it in there as a second sixth, or *bis-sextilis*. Hence the name bis-sextile for leap year. Some church calendars still follow this method.

Cæsar's calendar was carelessly kept. For a considerable period the pontiffs gave a leap day to every third instead of fourth year. This was rectified by omitting all leap days from 48 to 37 B. C. Thence downward the Julian Calendar went on correctly. But its year was too long, and in about three-and-a-half centuries (at the Council of Nice, A. D. 325), it was found that the vernal equinox, fixed by Cæsar on the 25th of March, had gone back to the 21st. If this were to go on the seasons would in time be reversed, and summer come when the calendar called for mid-winter. Furthermore, it was reckoning days that never existed.

In 1582 the Julian Calendar, as compared with the actual time, was ten days too far ahead. Then Pope Gregory XIII., aided by the best-learned men of the age, promulgated the Reformed Calendar, for a long period known as the Gregorian or New Style—the Julian Calendar being called Old Style. He directed that the 5th of October of 1582 should be reckoned as the 15th, and, to avoid errors of the kind in the future, that three of the one hundred leap days coming in 400 years by the Julian Calendar should be dropped. It was ordered that if the first two figures of the year ending a century were divisible by 4 without remainder, it should be a leap year; those not so divisible were to be common years. Thus, the year 1600, then near at hand, was a leap year; 1700 and 1800 are not, nor 1900; but 2000 will be. This regulation makes cycles of 400 years, and, though not exact, is so near to precise time that it will take 3,323 years to accumulate a superfluous day. Even this may be provided for by calling the year 4000 a common, instead of a leap, year, as it would be under the Calendar. A still nearer approach to exactness might be made by omitting one leap day in 128 years, or allowing 31 only instead of 32 leap days in such a period. This would come so near that it would take 100,000 years to accumulate a superfluous day.

Gregory's Calendar was immediately adopted in most of the Catholic countries of Europe; in Scotland in 1600; by Protestant Germany in 1700; and, finally, in England in 1752. An Act of Parliament, adopted in 1751, directed that the year 1752 should be reckoned from the 1st of January, and not from the 25th of March; and that the day following the 2d of September should be reckoned the 14th of September. So the year 1751 lost 83 days, and 1752 lost 11—the two years having only 637, instead of 731, days.

The beginning of the year varied with various nations. The Norsemen began at the winter solstice, rejoicing at the return of the sun; Eastern nations generally with the autumnal equinox, and so did the early Germans; the Jewish civil year began at the same time, but their ecclesiastical year six months earlier; Greeks at the summer, and then at the winter solstice; the early Romans at the winter solstice; in France, March 1, Dec. 25, and Easter; in England, March 25; Russia, until Peter the Great, Sept. 1; ancient Mexicans at the vernal equinox [they had 18 months of 20 days each, and a leap year]; in the East Indies, with the first quarter of the moon harvest, the beginning of December. But all these have been superseded by a purely arbitrary point that has not the slightest reference to seasons or planetary motions. Why was Jan. 1 fixed upon? Thus it was: In the year 353 B. C. there was a revolt against Roman rule in Spain. It was deemed necessary to send a consul there, and, to hasten his departure, it was ordered that the consuls just selected should take office two-and-a-half months before the regular time. The regular time was at the beginning of the year in March, but on this occasion they took their seats at the time now known as the 1st of January. That began the consular year for them, and, it seems, the common year for all mankind. With all his overhauling of the calendar, Cæsar did not disturb this point for commencing the year.

## LEGAL HOLIDAYS.

The law of most states provides that the 1st of January, Washington's Birthday (Feb. 22), Decoration Day (May 30), the 4th of July, Christmas, any day of a general election, Thanksgiving Day, and any days of fasting and prayer, or other religious observance, appointed by the Governor of the State, or the President, shall, for all purposes whatsoever, as regards the presenting for payment or acceptance, and of the protesting and giving notice of the dishonor of bills of exchange, bank checks, and promissory notes, be treated and considered as the first day of the week, commonly called Sunday, and as public holidays. And the days aforesaid shall be considered the same as Sunday and public holidays for the transaction of business in public offices. When such days fall on a Sunday, the Monday next following is deemed a public holiday for all purposes.

## ALMANACS.

Fifty years ago no family was well served that did not have a nail somewhere in the wall on which to hang the almanac. The oldest almanac known is in the British Museum, found in Egypt, and dating back almost 3,000 years. The days are written in red ink, and certain characters follow each day, prophesying the probable nature of the morning, the day, and the evening. Then come various directions and predictions relating to religious ceremonies, events that happened on the day, cautions against doing certain things on the day, fates of children born on the day, and so on, much like almanacs made in Europe a few centuries ago, and still made by Zadkiel and other so-called astrologists.

The oldest Roman church almanac is one composed in the fourth century by Pope Julius, giving both Pagan and Christian festivals. Another was made in 448 A. D., and one at Carthage in 483, still preserved in Paris. There is also one in existence made in 826. Nearly all these were devoted to feast and fast days, saints' days, and other church matters. There are Saxon almanacs of the ninth and tenth centuries; one of 940 A. D. giving an obituary of Alfred the Great.

The earliest almanacs of the northern nations of Europe were made by cutting notches in a wooden stick, on an axe helve, or some domestic article of furniture. Weeks, months, and notable days were known by their large or small or duplicate notches. Many of these are preserved in England, and are known as Clog Almanacs. There were symbols for certain points of time, such as, an axe for St. Paul's Day, a harp for St. David's, a gridiron for St. Lawrence's, and a true-lover's knot for St. Valentine's. When almanacs came to be written, and long before printing was known, weather predictions appeared. There is one which is yet remembered and often repeated in England, the United States, and other countries, viz:

> The evening red, the morning gray,
> Are certain signs of a fair day;
> The evening gray, the morning red,
> Makes the shepherd hang his head.

But this is precisely what the Saviour said in rebuking the Pharisees: "When it is evening ye say, 'it will be fair, for the sky is red,'" etc. These weather prophecies are almost innumerable.

One of the earliest almanacs coming from a seat of learning was made at Oxford in 1386, and its contents embraced: "1—The Houses of the Planets and their Properties. 2—The Exposition of the Signs. 3—Chronicle of Events from the Birth of Cain. 4—How to find the Prime Numbers. 5—Short Notes on Medicine. 6—On Blood-letting. 7—A Description of the Table of Signs and Movable Feasts. 8—Artificial Quantities." The style of our language at that period is shown in this extract: "Aquarius is a syne in the whitk, the son es in Jan'y, and in that moneth are seven pylos days, the 1, 2, 4, 5, 6, 15, 19, and if thonar is heard in that moneth it betokens great wynde, mykel fruite, and batel." [Pylos = perilous.]

The first printed almanac was the "Kalendarium Novum" (or New Calendar), by Regiomontanus, calculated for 1475, 1494, and 1573. It was the first to give eclipses to come, and the places of the planets, and sold for ten crowns in gold. The first almanac printed in England was the "Sheapherd's Kalendar," a translation from the French, brought out in 1497. Thenceforward almanacs multiplied rapidly, and were common enough at the end of the fifteenth century. Here are the peculiar titles of two of them:

"Prognossiacion and an Almanac fastened together, declaring the dyspocission of the People and also of the Weather, with certain Electyons and Tymes chosen both for Physicke and Surgerye, and for the Husbandman."

"A Newe Almanache and Prognostication collected for the yere of our Lord MDLVIII, wherein is expressed the Change and Full of the Moone with the Quarters. The varieties of the Ayre and also of the Windes throughout the yere, with unfortunate times to by and sell, and take Medicine, Sowe, Plant, and Journey."

One of the most popular in England was "Poor Robin's Almanack," issued in 1664, under the title:

"An Almanack after a new fashion, wherein the reader may find remarkable things if he be not blinde. Written by Poor Robin, Knight of the Burnt Island, a well-wisher of mathematics. Calculated for the Meridian of Saffron Walden, where the pole is 5° and 6′ above the Horizon."

It was full of wit and sarcasm of a low order, and was published annually until 1828. Almanac publishing in England was, from about 1600 to about 1750, monopolized by the Stationers' Company. There were almanacs in great variety, and nearly all were crowded with predictions, astrological and meteorological. Among the compilers were, Lily, Dr. Dee, and Partridge the Shoemaker. Finally, true science came up, and the Nautical and British Almanacs began to do credit to the nation.

In America, the first almanac worth notice was made by Benjamin Franklin, under the name of Richard Saunders, and was known as "Poor Richard's Almanac." It was issued in 1733, and for twenty-five years supervised by Franklin. The next widely popular American almanac was that of Isaiah Thomas, the editor of the *Massachusetts Spy*. Other notable works were the "American Nautical Almanac," begun in 1849; the "American Almanac and Repository of Useful Knowledge," 1828 to 1861. In these days calendar tables and almanacs are without number, and millions of them are given away for the sake of advertising a warehouse, a patent medicine, an invention, a railroad, or almost any imaginable enterprise. The most important statistical publications are, "The Tribune Almanac," begun in 1838; and the "American Almanac," edited by A. R. Spofford, Librarian of Congress. Many newspapers also publish, or have published, almanacs, such as the *New York Herald*, the *Albany Evening Journal*, the *New York World*, the *Philadelphia Ledger*, and many more almanacs are also published by bible societies, tract societies, and by every considerable denomination in the country. Comic almanacs are issued, but have little popularity.

The familiar features of the almanac of the fathers have disappeared. The well-known figure of a partially-disemboweled man, with head, hands, and feet pointing to the signs of the zodiac, is rarely seen. The dominical letter, to point out Sundays, is also gone. The once invaluable weather predictions have been cast aside, and in most publications the record of events, births, deaths, etc., has fallen into disuse. Aside from its statistics of elections, laws passed, names of Congressmen, Legislators, Governors, and days of election, a political almanac is of little account. All that remains of the almanac of old times is, eclipses, positions of planets, church days and cycles, mean time, rising and setting of sun and moon, changes of the moon, and time of high water. The reports of weather bureaus have superseded the guess-work of other days, and even the rising and setting of the sun and moon, and high water, are printed in all important newspapers. Almanacs and card calendars, given away by millions, cease to have any practical value, and so the traditional nail in the farmhouse is no longer driven, or, if remaining, is unoccupied

## PAST AND FUTURE TIME.

If one were to ask, "On what day of the week was grandfather born?" or, "On what day will come the American Millennial—the 4th of July, 2776?" how should we set about answering? There are many ways, and it is not difficult to find calendars for the century, or, perpetual calendars. Some use the dominical letters; some have more or less intricate tables of common and leap years, and centuries; some have numbers for the various months, and work out answers by addition and division. Putting these aside, I will give here a calendar of my own construction, by which any person may find any day of the week, from the first day of the year *one*, of the Christian era (according to the Gregorian, or New Style, now in use), to the 28th day of February of the year 4000. There is small gain every year over the present reckoning, so that it will be necessary to omit the 29th of February, in the year 4000, to regulate the computation, and then the whole calendar will go back one day; that is, if 4000 were a leap year, 4001 would begin on Monday; but, as it will not be a leap year, 4001 will begin on Sunday. By the present reckoning, every 400 years make a cycle, and then the days of the week, month, and year, return in precisely the same order. Therefore, if you find the order for the first 400 years, you have it for the second 400, and so on to the change in the year 4000.

All we need to learn is the day of the week on which the first century began. This we learn by calculation, and find that, under the reckoning of New Style, the first day of January, of the Christian era, was Monday. We then give the day on which each successive year began, up to 400. Then the order returns at periods of 400 years. Along with the beginning of the years, we give two calendars—one for common years, and one for leap years. The leap years in the first table are marked with a star (*), and the blank following shows that the next year begins two days later, instead of one day later, as in common years.

## GREGORIAN, OR NEW STYLE.

*Calendar of Days of the Week, from the Year* 1 *to the 28th of February, of the Year* 4000.

### YEARS BEGINNING ON

| SUN. | MON. | TUES. | WED. | THURS. | FRI. | SAT. |
|---|---|---|---|---|---|---|
| —.... | 1.... | 2.... | 3.... | *4.... | —.... | 5 |
| 6.... | 7.... | *8.... | —.... | 9.... | 10.... | 11 |
| *12.... | —.... | 13.... | 14.... | 15.... | *16.... | — |
| 17.... | 18.... | 19.... | *20.... | —.... | 21.... | 22 |
| 23.... | *24.... | —.... | 25.... | 26.... | 27.... | *28 |
| —.... | 29.... | 30.... | 31.... | *32.... | —.... | 33 |
| 34.... | 35.... | *36.... | —.... | 37.... | 38.... | 39 |
| *40.... | —.... | 41.. | 42.... | 43.... | *44.... | — |
| 45.... | 46.... | 47.... | *48.... | —.... | 49.... | 50 |
| 51.... | *52.... | —.... | 53.... | 54.... | 55.... | *56 |
| —.... | 57.... | 58.... | 59.... | *60.. | —.... | 61 |
| 62.... | 63.... | *64.... | —.... | 65.... | 66.... | 67 |
| *68.... | —.... | 69.... | 70.... | 71.... | *72.... | — |
| 73.... | 74.... | 75.... | *76.... | —.... | 77.... | 78 |
| 79.... | *80.... | —.... | 81.... | 82.... | 83.... | *84 |
| —.... | 85.... | 86.... | 87.... | *88.... | —.... | 89 |
| 90.... | 91.... | *92.... | —.... | 93.... | 94.... | 95 |
| *96 ... | —.... | 97.... | 98.... | 99.... | 100.... | 101 |
| 102.... | 103.... | *104.... | —.... | 105.... | 106.... | 107 |
| *108.... | —.... | 109.... | 110.... | 111.... | *112.... | — |
| 113.... | 114.... | 115.... | *116.... | —.... | 117.... | 118 |
| 119.... | *120.... | —.... | 121.... | 122.... | 123.... | *124 |
| —.... | 125.... | 126.... | 127.... | *128.... | —.... | 129 |
| 130.... | 131.... | *132.... | —.... | 133.... | 134.... | 135 |
| *136.... | —.... | 137.... | 138.... | 139.... | *140.... | — |
| 141.... | 142.... | 143.... | *144.... | —.... | 145.... | 146 |
| 147.... | *148.... | —.... | 149.... | 150.... | 151.... | *152 |
| —.... | 153.... | 154... | 155.... | *156.... | —.... | 157 |
| 158.... | 159.... | *160.... | —.... | 161.... | 162.... | 163 |
| *164.... | —.... | 165.... | 166.... | 167.... | *168.... | — |
| 169.... | 170.... | 171.... | *172.... | —.... | 173.... | 174 |
| 175.... | *176.... | —.... | 177.... | 178.... | 179.... | *180 |
| —.... | 181.... | 182.... | 183.... | *184.... | —.... | 185 |
| 186.... | 187.... | *188.... | —.... | 189.... | 190 ... | 191 |
| *192.... | —.... | 193.... | 194.... | 195.... | *196.... | — |
| 197... | 198.... | 199.... | 200.... | 201.... | 202.... | 203 |

| SUN. | MON. | TUES. | WED. | THURS. | FRI. | SAT. |
|---|---|---|---|---|---|---|
| *204 | — | 205 | 206 | 207 | *208 | — |
| 209 | 210 | 211 | *212 | — | 213 | 214 |
| 215 | *216 | — | 217 | 218 | 219 | *220 |
| — | 221 | 222 | 223 | *224 | — | 225 |
| 226 | 227 | *228 | — | 229 | 230 | 231 |
| *232 | — | 233 | 234 | 235 | *236 | — |
| 237 | 238 | 239 | *240 | — | 241 | 242 |
| 243 | *244 | — | 245 | 246 | 247 | *248 |
| — | 249 | 250 | 251 | *252 | — | 253 |
| 254 | 255 | *256 | — | 257 | 258 | 259 |
| *260 | — | 261 | 262 | 263 | *264 | — |
| 265 | 266 | 267 | *268 | — | 269 | 270 |
| 271 | *272 | — | 273 | 274 | 275 | *276 |
| — | 277 | 278 | 279 | *280 | — | 281 |
| 282 | 283 | *284 | — | 285 | 286 | 287 |
| *288 | — | 289 | 290 | 291 | *292 | — |
| 293 | 294 | 295 | *296 | — | 297 | 298 |
| 299 | 300 | 301 | 302 | 303 | *304 | — |
| 305 | 306 | 307 | *308 | — | 309 | 310 |
| 311 | *312 | — | 313 | 314 | 315 | *316 |
| — | 317 | 318 | 319 | *320 | — | 321 |
| 322 | 323 | *324 | — | 325 | 326 | 327 |
| *328 | — | 329 | 330 | 331 | *332 | — |
| 333 | 334 | 335 | *336 | — | 337 | 338 |
| 339 | *340 | — | 341 | 342 | 343 | *344 |
| — | 345 | 346 | 347 | *348 | — | 349 |
| 350 | 351 | *352 | — | 353 | 354 | 355 |
| *356 | — | 357 | 358 | 359 | *360 | — |
| 361 | 362 | 363 | *364 | — | 365 | 366 |
| 367 | *368 | — | 369 | 370 | 371 | *372 |
| — | 373 | 374 | 375 | *376 | — | 377 |
| 378 | 379 | *380 | — | 381 | 382 | 383 |
| *384 | — | 385 | 386 | 387 | *388 | — |
| 389 | 390 | 391 | *392 | — | 393 | 394 |
| 395 | *396 | — | 397 | 398 | 399 | *400 |

## COMMON YEAR ALMANAC.

| JANUARY. | | | | | FEBRUARY. | | | | MARCH. | | | |
|---|---|---|---|---|---|---|---|---|---|---|---|---|
| 1 | 8 | 15 | 22 | 29..— | 5 | 12 | 19 | 26..— | 5 | 12 | 19 | 26 |
| 2 | 9 | 16 | 23 | 30..— | 6 | 13 | 20 | 27..— | 6 | 13 | 20 | 27 |
| 3 | 10 | 17 | 24 | 31..— | 7 | 14 | 21 | 28..— | 7 | 14 | 21 | 28 |
| 4 | 11 | 18 | 25 | —.. 1 | 8 | 15 | 22 | —.. 1 | 8 | 15 | 22 | 29 |
| 5 | 12 | 19 | 26 | —.. 2 | 9 | 16 | 23 | —.. 2 | 9 | 16 | 23 | 30 |
| 6 | 13 | 20 | 27 | —.. 3 | 10 | 17 | 24 | —.. 3 | 10 | 17 | 24 | 31 |
| 7 | 14 | 21 | 28 | —.. 4 | 11 | 18 | 25 | —.. 4 | 11 | 18 | 25 | — |

| APRIL. | | | | | | MAY. | | | | JUNE. | | | |
|---|---|---|---|---|---|---|---|---|---|---|---|---|---|
| — | 2 | 9 | 16 | 23 | 30..— | 7 | 14 | 21 | 28..— | 4 | 11 | 18 | 25 |
| — | 3 | 10 | 17 | 24 | —.. 1 | 8 | 15 | 22 | 29..— | 5 | 12 | 19 | 26 |
| — | 4 | 11 | 18 | 25 | —.. 2 | 9 | 16 | 23 | 30..— | 6 | 13 | 20 | 27 |
| — | 5 | 12 | 19 | 26 | —.. 3 | 10 | 17 | 24 | 31..— | 7 | 14 | 21 | 28 |
| — | 6 | 13 | 20 | 27 | —.. 4 | 11 | 18 | 25 | —.. 1 | 8 | 15 | 22 | 29 |
| — | 7 | 14 | 21 | 28 | —.. 5 | 12 | 19 | 26 | —.. 2 | 9 | 16 | 23 | 30 |
| 1 | 8 | 15 | 22 | 29 | —.. 6 | 13 | 20 | 27 | —.. 3 | 10 | 17 | 24 | — |

| JULY. | | | | | | AUGUST. | | | | SEPTEMBER. | | | |
|---|---|---|---|---|---|---|---|---|---|---|---|---|---|
| — | 2 | 9 | 16 | 23 | 30..— | 6 | 13 | 20 | 27..— | 3 | 10 | 17 | 24 |
| — | 3 | 10 | 17 | 24 | 31..— | 7 | 14 | 21 | 28..— | 4 | 11 | 18 | 25 |
| — | 4 | 11 | 18 | 25 | —.. 1 | 8 | 15 | 22 | 29..— | 5 | 12 | 19 | 26 |
| — | 5 | 12 | 19 | 26 | —.. 2 | 9 | 16 | 23 | 30..— | 6 | 13 | 20 | 27 |
| — | 6 | 13 | 20 | 27 | —.. 3 | 10 | 17 | 24 | 31..— | 7 | 14 | 21 | 28 |
| — | 7 | 14 | 21 | 28 | —.. 4 | 11 | 18 | 25 | —.. 1 | 8 | 15 | 22 | 29 |
| 1 | 8 | 15 | 22 | 29 | —.. 5 | 12 | 19 | 26 | —.. 2 | 9 | 16 | 23 | 30 |

| OCTOBER. | | | | | NOVEMBER. | | | | DECEMBER. | | | | |
|---|---|---|---|---|---|---|---|---|---|---|---|---|---|
| 1 | 8 | 15 | 22 | 29..— | 5 | 12 | 19 | 26..— | 3 | 10 | 17 | 24 | 31 |
| 2 | 9 | 16 | 23 | 30..— | 6 | 13 | 20 | 27..— | 4 | 11 | 18 | 25 | — |
| 3 | 10 | 17 | 24 | 31..— | 7 | 14 | 21 | 28..— | 5 | 12 | 19 | 26 | — |
| 4 | 11 | 18 | 25 | —.. 1 | 8 | 15 | 22 | 29..— | 6 | 13 | 20 | 27 | — |
| 5 | 12 | 19 | 26 | —.. 2 | 9 | 16 | 23 | 30..— | 7 | 14 | 21 | 28 | — |
| 6 | 13 | 20 | 27 | —.. 3 | 10 | 17 | 24 | —.. 1 | 8 | 15 | 22 | 29 | — |
| 7 | 14 | 21 | 28 | —.. 4 | 11 | 18 | 25 | —.. 2 | 9 | 16 | 23 | 30 | — |

## LEAP YEAR ALMANAC.

| JANUARY. | | | | | FEBRUARY. | | | | MARCH. | | | |
|---|---|---|---|---|---|---|---|---|---|---|---|---|
| 1 | 8 | 15 | 22 | 29..— | 5 | 12 | 19 | 26..— | 4 | 11 | 18 | 25 |
| 2 | 9 | 16 | 23 | 30..— | 6 | 13 | 20 | 27..— | 5 | 12 | 19 | 26 |
| 3 | 10 | 17 | 24 | 31..— | 7 | 14 | 21 | 28..— | 6 | 13 | 20 | 27 |
| 4 | 11 | 18 | 25 | —.. 1 | 8 | 15 | 22 | 29..— | 7 | 14 | 21 | 28 |
| 5 | 12 | 19 | 26 | —.. 2 | 9 | 16 | 23 | —.. 1 | 8 | 15 | 22 | 29 |
| 6 | 13 | 20 | 27 | —.. 3 | 10 | 17 | 24 | —.. 2 | 9 | 16 | 23 | 30 |
| 7 | 14 | 21 | 28 | —.. 4 | 11 | 18 | 25 | —.. 3 | 10 | 17 | 24 | 31 |

| APRIL. | | | | | MAY. | | | | JUNE. | | | |
|---|---|---|---|---|---|---|---|---|---|---|---|---|
| 1 | 8 | 15 | 22 | 29..— | 6 | 13 | 20 | 27..— | 3 | 10 | 17 | 24 |
| 2 | 9 | 16 | 23 | 30..— | 7 | 14 | 21 | 28..— | 4 | 11 | 18 | 25 |
| 3 | 10 | 17 | 24 | —.. 1 | 8 | 15 | 22 | 29..— | 5 | 12 | 19 | 26 |
| 4 | 11 | 18 | 25 | —.. 2 | 9 | 16 | 23 | 30..— | 6 | 13 | 20 | 27 |
| 5 | 12 | 19 | 26 | —.. 3 | 10 | 17 | 24 | 31..— | 7 | 14 | 21 | 28 |
| 6 | 13 | 20 | 27 | —.. 4 | 11 | 18 | 25 | —.. 1 | 8 | 15 | 22 | 29 |
| 7 | 14 | 21 | 28 | —.. 5 | 12 | 19 | 26 | —.. 2 | 9 | 16 | 23 | 30 |

| JULY. | | | | | AUGUST. | | | | SEPTEMBER. | | | | |
|---|---|---|---|---|---|---|---|---|---|---|---|---|---|
| 1 | 8 | 15 | 22 | 29..— | 5 | 12 | 19 | 26..— | 2 | 9 | 16 | 23 | 30 |
| 2 | 9 | 16 | 23 | 30..— | 6 | 13 | 20 | 27..— | 3 | 10 | 17 | 24 | — |
| 3 | 10 | 17 | 24 | 31..— | 7 | 14 | 21 | 28..— | 4 | 11 | 18 | 25 | — |
| 4 | 11 | 18 | 25 | —.. 1 | 8 | 15 | 22 | 29..— | 5 | 12 | 19 | 26 | — |
| 5 | 12 | 19 | 26 | —.. 2 | 9 | 16 | 23 | 30..— | 6 | 13 | 20 | 27 | — |
| 6 | 13 | 20 | 27 | —.. 3 | 10 | 17 | 24 | 31..— | 7 | 14 | 21 | 28 | — |
| 7 | 14 | 21 | 28 | —.. 4 | 11 | 18 | 25 | —.. 1 | 8 | 15 | 22 | 29 | — |

| OCTOBER. | | | | | NOVEMBER. | | | | DECEMBER. | | | | |
|---|---|---|---|---|---|---|---|---|---|---|---|---|---|
| — | 7 | 14 | 21 | 28..— | 4 | 11 | 18 | 25..— | 2 | 9 | 16 | 23 | 30 |
| 1 | 8 | 15 | 22 | 29..— | 5 | 12 | 19 | 26..— | 3 | 10 | 17 | 24 | 31 |
| 2 | 9 | 16 | 23 | 30..— | 6 | 13 | 20 | 27..— | 4 | 11 | 18 | 25 | — |
| 3 | 10 | 17 | 24 | 31..— | 7 | 14 | 21 | 28..— | 5 | 12 | 19 | 26 | — |
| 4 | 11 | 18 | 25 | —.. 1 | 8 | 15 | 22 | 29..— | 6 | 13 | 20 | 27 | — |
| 5 | 12 | 19 | 26 | —.. 2 | 9 | 16 | 23 | 30..— | 7 | 14 | 21 | 28 | — |
| 6 | 13 | 20 | 27 | —.. 3 | 10 | 17 | 24 | —.. 1 | 8 | 15 | 22 | 29 | — |

### Rule for Finding any Day of the Week.

Set off the two right-hand figures, and divide the left-hand figures by 4. Put the remainder at the left of the figures set off, and the sum will be found in the table under the day that begins the year. *Ex.*—1882; divide 18 by 4: remainder, 2, which, before the figures set off, makes 282, which, in the table, is under Sunday. Take 1907; set off, as before, and divide; the answer will be 307, which year, as also 1907, begins on Tuesday. Take the Millennial of American Independence, or the year 2776; set off the 76, divide the 27 by 4, and 3 remains, which shows 376—a leap year, under Thursday.

For any day in any year, you find in the Calendar table the first day of the year to be, say Sunday. Then all the dates in the first line of the almanac table, from left to right, are Sundays; the next, Mondays, and the last, Saturdays. For leap years, which appear only under a star (*), consult the leap year almanac. *Ex.*—On what day of the week was the Declaration of Independence made? The date was July 4, 1776; 17 divided by 4 leaves 1, which, prefixed to the right-hand figures, makes 176, which, in the table, is under Monday, and a leap year. The first day of July, in the leap year almanac, is Monday, and the fourth is Thursday. In the same way, we find that the one thousandth anniversary, July 4, 2776, will come on a Sunday.

HUMAN nature is the highest subject of human study. Man looks at his fellow man who is a stranger to him, and wonders who and what he is. For many ages men have been seeking for a rule by which to judge strangers, and learn, without the necessity of a long experience, the disposition, capacity and tendency of men. The face has been studied, the hand has been studied, the stars have been invoked to tell us what men may expect in the way of fate and fortune.

In 1796, an eminent physician of Vienna commenced giving lectures on human character as exhibited through peculiar developments of the brain. From that day to this, Phrenology, as Dr. GALL'S system of character-reading is called, has been widely disseminated and much discussed. A brief description of this subject, in connection with some illustration, may be interesting to our readers.

The symbolical head here presented shows the location of the Phrenological organs, and in the field of each organ a picture is made designed to illustrate the character of the organ in question. ***Firmness,*** on the top of the head, is indicated by the stability of the pyramid, and the obstinacy of the mule, or the man who is contending with him. ***Veneration*** is shown by the attitude of prayer and the courtesy which the boy extends to the venerable man. ***Benevolence*** is shown by the picture of the Good Samaritan; ***Constructiveness*** by the cog-wheel, as a part of machinery; ***Cautiousness,*** by the frightened hen, who fears detriment to her chicks; ***Secretiveness,*** by the fox; ***Acquisitiveness,*** by the miser counting his gain. These illustrations, of course, are simply to help the memory and make vivid the impression.

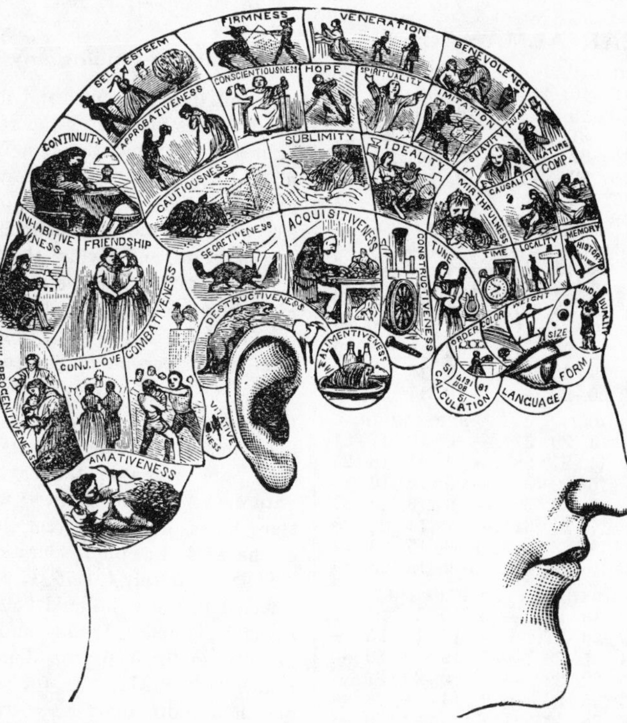


SYMBOLICAL HEAD.—ILLUSTRATING THE NATURE OF EACH ORGAN OF THE BRAIN.

## THE PRINCIPLES OF PHRENOLOGY.

The term Phrenology signifies *discourse on the mind*, and advocates of this science claim that it is based on certain definite principles, which are as easily understood as the science of chemistry or the laws of natural philosophy.

Phrenology claims to explain the powers and faculties of the mind by studying the organization of the brain during life. Its doctrines, briefly stated, are:

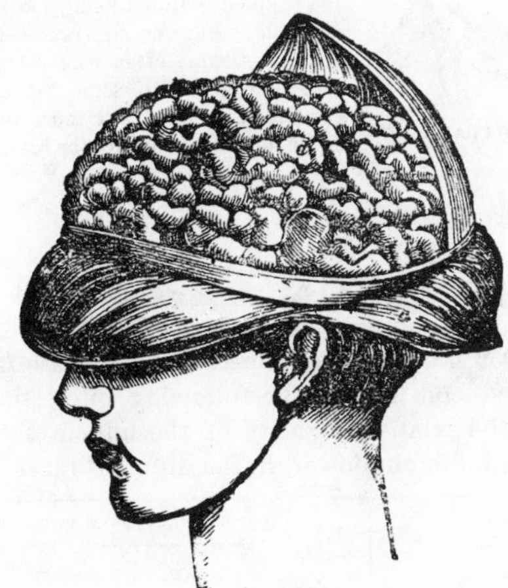

BRAIN IN THE SKULL.

1.—The brain is the organ or instrument of the mind.

2.—The mind has many faculties, some of which may be stronger or weaker than the rest in the same person.

3.—Each faculty, or propensity of the mind, has its special organ.

4.—Size of brain, if the quality be good, is the true measure of its power. The brain, when deficient in size, or low in quality, is always connected with a low degree of mental power. Among the lower animals, the brain is found to be large and complicated in proportion to the variety and strength of the faculties.

THE OBSERVER.

THE PHILOSOPHER.

5.—Organs related to each other in function are grouped together in the brain. For example, the organs of intellect are located in the forehead; those of the social nature in the back-head; those of passion, appetite, and self-preservation in the side-head; those of aspiration, pride, and ambition, in the crown; and those of sentiment, morality, sympathy, and religion, in the top-head.

6.—As each function of the body has its specific organ, so each faculty of the mind, each sentiment and propensity has its own organ. If this were not so, each person would exhibit the same amount of talent or power on all subjects, such as arithmetic, language, music, mechanism, memory, reasoning, love of property, courage, prudence, pride, etc. Everybody knows that persons rarely show equal talent on all topics. A man may be a genius at one thing, and find it impossible, by long training, to become even respectable in other things. This would not be the case if the mind were a single power and the brain a single organ. As the senses of seeing, hearing, tasting, smelling, etc., are not always possessed by each person in an equal degree of perfection, these several powers being dependent on different organs, so the mental faculties and dispositions are sometimes very unequal in a given person, owing to the greater strength or weakness of their respective organs in the brain. Partial genius, partial idiocy, and partial insanity sustain the phrenological theory of the mind.

7.—The quality or temperament of the organization determines the degree of vigor, activity, and endurance of the mental powers. These temperaments are indicated by external signs, including the build, complexion, and texture.

There are three Temperaments, known as the Motive, Vital, and Mental.

The MOTIVE temperament, corresponding to the *bilious*, has a strong, bony system, an abundance of muscle, dark, wiry hair, dark eyes, rough, prominent features, dark complexion, and a great disposition to locomotive effort.

MOTIVE TEMPERAMENT.

VERAZZANO.

The motive temperament, in its influence on mental manifestation, is favorable to dignity, sternness, determination, power of will, and desire to govern and control others. It gives slowness of passion, desire for heavy labor or large business, and a liability to miasmatic diseases.

VITAL TEMPERAMENT.

WHITEFIELD.

The VITAL temperament is evinced by large lungs, a powerful circulatory system, and large digestive and assimilating organs, abundance of blood, and animal spirits. The form is plump, the limbs rounded and tapering, the complexion light or florid, with an inclination to take on flesh as age advances. This temperament is a combination of the *sanguine* and the *lymphatic* as set forth by Mr. COMBE and other writers; but as the digestive and assimilating organs, which constitute the lymphatic temperament, together with the respiratory and circulatory systems, which constitute the sanguine temperament, are really vital organs, we regard their combination into one, under the name of vital temperament, as both convenient and philosophical.

MENTAL TEMPERAMENT.

MELANCTHON.

The MENTAL temperament (formerly called *nervous*) depends on the development of the brain and nervous system, and is indicated by mental activity, light frame, thin skin, fine hair, delicate features, and large brain as compared with the body. It imparts sensitiveness and vivacity to the mind, a disposition to think, study, or follow some light and delicate business.

The structures which, in excess of great predominance, determine these temperaments, exist in each individual. In one person one temperament may predominate—in the next, another. They can be modified by proper training. When combined, they give harmony of character and excellent health.

The strong, black hair, rough, prominent features, and bony development of Verazzano indicate toughness and endurance; the power and hardihood of the Motive temperament. The deep chest, rounded face, and glowing countenance of Whitefield indicate the Vital temperament; and he was known for ardor, strong affection, and impassioned eloquence.

The large top-head of Melancthon indicates a predominance of the mental temperament, which gives a tendency to thought, philosophy, moral sentiment, and an appreciation of the beautiful and æsthetical.

TEMPERAMENTS COMBINED.

SIR JOHN FRANKLIN.

In Sir John Franklin we find the strength of the Motive temperament, the plumpness and ardor of the Vital temperament, and sufficient amplitude of the brain to indicate a full degree of the Mental temperament; thus, all being combined, he was harmonious; strong without being rough; ardent without impulsiveness; thoughtful and studious, without being too abstract or excitable. Persons so organized are fortunate. Genius often comes from unbalanced development, some faculties being greatly in excess; but more often, vice, crime, or misfortune are the result.

## COMPOSITION OF THE BRAIN.

The brain is a large, organized mass which, with its enveloping membranes, completely fills the cavity of the skull. It is a soft, jelly-like substance, very much like the marrow in our bones. The interior portion, which is of a whitish color, is composed of exceedingly small tubes, which are the beginnings of the nerves. There are two sets of nerves—those of feeling, and those of motion; both are, as far as can be discovered, the same in structure and composition, but as the offices which they perform are entirely different, there is something about them that the keenest physiologist cannot understand. Nor can we understand how the brain receives impressions through one set, and sends out messages and causes motion through another set, for this would be to understand how mind acts upon matter, and how the spiritual is connected with the material. The nerves are telegraph wires; and, to illustrate their uses, suppose you place your finger upon a pin point, which piercing the nerves of feeling, they instantly convey the intelligence to the brain, and, quick as a lightning flash, a command is sent down over the nerves of motion to remove the finger. The nerves of feeling and motion spread all over and throughout the body, but in the head are found the still more wonderful nerves of hearing, seeing, smelling, and tasting, each different in its functions from all the others, and capable of performing no other.

PROPORTION OF SUBSTANCES IN BRAIN.

| | | |
|---|---|---|
| Water | about | 75½ |
| Fat | " | 9½ |
| Albumen | " | 7 |
| Phosphorous | " | 2½ |
| Salts, Acids, etc. | " | 5½ |
| | | 100 |

Out of 256 skulls carefully measured by himself, the late Dr. Morton constructed the following interesting table, showing the relative capacity of the human skull, and, indirectly, the brain-power, in the different races:

| RACE. | NO. OF SKULLS. | CAPACITY IN CUBIC INCHES. | | |
|---|---|---|---|---|
| | | MEAN. | LARGEST. | SMALLEST. |
| Caucasian | 52 | 87 | 109 | 75 |
| Mongolian | 10 | 83 | 93 | 69 |
| Malay | 18 | 81 | 89 | 64 |
| American | 147 | 82 | 109 | 60 |
| Ethiopian | 29 | 78 | 94 | 65 |

WEIGHT OF SKULLS

(*Of very nearly the same size*).

| | |
|---|---|
| A Greek | 27½ ounces. |
| " Mulatto | 26 " |
| " Negro | 32 " |
| Another Negro | 28½ " |
| " " | 21¼ " |
| A Congo " | 27¾ " |
| " New Zealander | 26¾ " |
| " Chinese | 23½ " |
| " Gipsy | 32 " |

AVERAGE WEIGHT OF THE BRAIN.

| | |
|---|---|
| Anglo-Saxons (English and American) | 45.70 ounces. |
| French | 44.58 " |
| Germans | 44.10 " |
| Italians | 44.00 " |
| Americans (aboriginal race) | 44.37 " |
| Hindoos | 42.11 " |
| Kaffirs (Africans) | 45.00 " |
| Negroes " | 40.50 " |
| Bushmen " | 38.00 " |
| Malays and Oceanic race, from 39.56 to | 48.70 " |

## THE TELEGRAPH.

NO application of electricity has contributed more towards advancing the convenience and comfort of man than the invention of the Electric Telegraph. The telephone enables us to converse by word of mouth with persons within circumscribed distances; the electric signal calls the engine to subdue the flames that threaten to destroy our homes; but the telegraph alone has power to convey our thoughts with immeasurable rapidity over land and under sea, enabling us to communicate with friends and places in distant lands. The merchant, sitting at his desk, quotes to his customer the prices of the hour in cities thousand of miles away; the statesman, pondering over some knotty question of political economy, turns for reference and assistance to speeches and opinions delivered perhaps but a few hours previous by diplomats in another part of the globe. To circumscribe the power of electricity and the value of the telegraph were to attempt the impossible; it vanquishes thought in speed, annihilates distance, and almost outspeeds time itself. Millions of dollars are invested in lines of telegraph, and thousands of persons are employed in their construction and operation. Lawyer and client, doctor and patient, manufacturer and merchant consult together, and the business men of the world effect transactions for millions every day.

### ANCIENT METHODS OF COMMUNICATION.

Before the application of electricity to methods of conveying news from place to place there were many crude inventions for that purpose, which, while they answered the requirements demanded of them, performed their work so imperfectly that they were constantly liable to error. Important news, in France, a century or two ago, was shouted from the top of a high hill; a person at a distance hearing it answered the sender, and shouted it to a third party, who in turn cried the message, and news traveled in this manner long distances quickly. This method was employed in the time of Cæsar in calling the people to arms. Fires lighted upon elevations gave signs in their arrangement which could be readily understood. A signal fire upon Hero's tower lighted Leander across the Hellespont. In the Middle Ages a fiery cross shone along the British coast, announcing the approach of the Normans. Signal posts were organized systematically in France by Louis XI., and for a long time this method was sufficient for all purposes of transmission.

The aerial telegraph came next, consisting of great towers erected on rising ground in the country. These towers were surmounted by movable turrets which could be turned to any point to which it was desired to send a message. Above the tower were two long black arms connected by an immovable bar. The arms, moving in vari us ways, made signs which represented words and even complete phrases. This worked well enough in clear weather, but in rainy or foggy atmospheres its operation was ineffectual.

### INVENTION OF THE ELECTRIC TELEGRAPH.

For a time the electric telegraph was considered a mere curiosity. The system invented by Professor Morse in 1831 was looked upon as chimerical, and he was obliged to wait eight years before he succeeded in getting his invention before the public, although its machinery was almost as perfect as it is at the present day. Many savants in ancient times astonished the world with experiments, the chief motor of which was electricity. Among these may be mentioned the Abbé Noblet, Dafay, Mesmer, and Cagliostro. In 1790, Galvani discovered a singular fact which has been followed by the most splendid results, and later Volta brought to light the voltaic pile. Many persons claim that the true inventor of the electric telegraph was Wheatstone, who set up the first telegraph line in England and afterwards one in France ; but the Morse system is the simplest, and has been generally adopted in nearly all countries. There are now in all about fifty systems.

### THE DIGNEY SYSTEM.

The DIGNEY prepares the dispatch by means of a special machine called a perforator. A band of paper passes under two keys, one of which being depressed the paper passes under without indentation ; when the other is depressed a steel punch cuts into the paper, making a single point. Two consecutive pressures upon the second key give two points run together, or a dash. The dot and dash used by Morse as an alphabet are employed in this method. The band of paper unrolls from the perforator with a message written upon it in these characters, and it can be revised, if it is desired, before sending. The band of paper is placed in a manipulator.

This instrument is composed of an elbowed lever easily movable, one arm of which rests constantly upon the perforated paper. The battery communicates with the lever and the line instrument with the metallic plate over which the paper rolls ; when the lever drops on the paper no current passes ; when it falls on a perforation it touches the metallic plate, and the current passes into the line, thus repeating the message as it is cut into the band. In this manner the receiver will register a dispatch exactly similar to the one placed in the manipulator. A skillful operator will send by this system 175 letters a minute ; the ordinary, or Morse method, will send about one hundred and fifty.

### OTHER SYSTEMS.

The HUGHES TELEGRAPH is beginning to be employed on great lines ; it is very ingenious, but very complicated. CASSELLI'S PANTELEGRAPH transmits even the autograph of the operator, and works perfectly during a thunder-shower.

### THE MORSE SYSTEM.

The MORSE SYSTEM operates entirely by sound, and it is said that *sound reading* was discovered by the operators noticing the action of the *armature* in writing the message on the paper band made peculiar sounds. In time they became so familiar with these sounds that they read without recourse to the written message. The operators became so proficient that the register or receiver was entirely done away with, which proved to be a great saving to the companies. In this system the armature is furnished with a steel point or style, which makes marks in the form of dots and dashes on a strip of paper where the receiver is used ; these arranged in combinations form an alphabet. Without the receiver the letters are formed in the same manner, and are read by the duration of the sound of the armature striking on the upper and lower binding screws. Shadow-reading by means of a point of light reflected upon a scale from a mirror inclosed in a magnetized frame suspended by a human hair, is used in long distances, where it is impossible to locate intermediate stations, as in submarine cables.

### TELEGRAPH LINES.

Construction of telegraph lines is a work of no ordinary undertaking. The country through which it is to pass has to be explored, and the services of experienced engineers must be engaged. The shortest route is generally chosen, running along a highway or railway if possible ; forests must be avoided ; sudden turns should not occur ; where curves are necessary, they should be designed as long as possible, so that the solidity of the supports are not endangered. The posts should be 150 to 200 feet apart ; new supports may be added if the weight of the wires is too great. Posts are sometimes charred to avoid decay. Across them arms are placed, on which porcelain or glass cups are fixed in a reversed position, to avoid accumulation of moisture. The wire passes around these cups, and is thus insulated from the earth. The wire is galvanized, size from 9 to 12, a mile of wire weighing about 375 pounds. When wire is being run, the ends are twisted firmly together by means of a tackle and vise. When wire runs through damp places like tunnels, it should be covered with gutta percha.

## HOW TO TELEGRAPH.

Those who desire to instruct themselves in telegraphy will find below the MORSE ALPHABET, FIGURES, PUNCTUATION POINTS, and a correct form of a telegram. Diagrams showing a constructed line, illustrations of a way station, and cuts of the INSTRUMENTS used in transmitting messages, will also be found in the following pages.

### TELEGRAPH ALPHABET.

| A | B | C | D | E | F | G | H | I |
|---|---|---|---|---|---|---|---|---|
| -— | —--- | -- - | —-- | - | -—- | ——- | ---- | -- |

| J | K | L | M | N | O | P | Q |
|---|---|---|---|---|---|---|---|
| —-—- | —-— | —— | — — | —- | - - | ----- | --—- |

| R | S | T | U | V | W | X | Y | Z |
|---|---|---|---|---|---|---|---|---|
| - -- | --- | — | --— | ---— | -—— | -—-- | -- -- | --- - |

&

- ---

### FIGURES.

| 1 | 2 | 3 | 4 | 5 | 6 |
|---|---|---|---|---|---|
| -——- | --—-- | ---—- | ----— | ——— | ------ |

| 7 | 8 | 9 | 0 |
|---|---|---|---|
| ——-- | —---- | —--— | —— |

| Period | Comma | Interrogation | Exclamation |
|---|---|---|---|
| --——-- | -—-— | —--—- | —-—- |

| Semicolon | Italics | Quotation | Paragraph |
|---|---|---|---|
| -—-—- | —---— | -—-—-—-— | ———— |

Fraction ⅛

-——- - —----

## CORRECT FORM OF TELEGRAM.

6 Pd 25. TRENTON, N. J., May 24th, 1882.

To Thompson's Telegraph Institute,
New York.

Send me circular of your institution.

J. L. DAVIS.

The foregoing message should be thus written on the line:

```
------ ----- —-- --—-- ——— -—- - -- —
- -- - —- — -- —- --—-- ----— — -- - —
--- - -- —— ----- --- -- —- --- — - -—
- ——- - -- -— ----- ---- -- —- --- — --
— --— — - —- - -—— ----- - - - -- —-—
--——-- --- - —- —-- —— - -- - -- - --
-- - --— —— -— - -- - - -—- -- -- -- --—
- -- -- —- --- — -- — --— — -- - - —-
--- -- ——- —-—- —— —-- -— ---— --
---
```

The check (CK) 6 Pd 25 signifies that there are six words in the message, and that the price of transmission is 25 cents; the abbreviation "Pd." shows that the dispatch is prepaid. When "Col." accompanies the check, it indicates that the charges are to be collected. The month and year of the date are never sent over the line. The abbreviations "Fr." (from) "Sig." (signature) are never copied by the receiver.

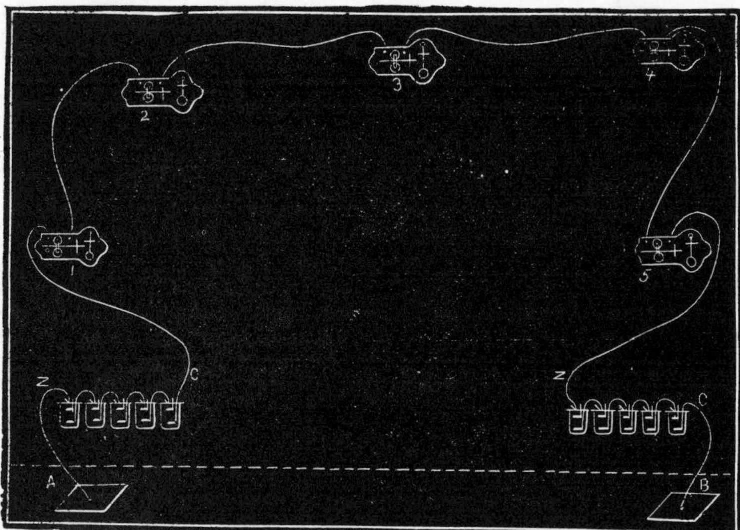


The above diagram illustrates the manner of connecting wires, instruments, and batteries on such a line, batteries being placed at each end of the wire. Battery A has its zinc pole connected to the earth and its copper to the line; and the other battery at B presents its zinc pole to the line and its copper to the earth. If both batteries were connected with the same pole to the line, they would neutralize each other, and no current whatever would be produced. The line is connected, as shown, from the battery to the first instrument, and on to the next, in such a way that the current is made to pass through each and every instrument on the route.

Each office has a call or signal for itself. Any one or two letters of the alphabet will suit, and serves in working over the line as the name of whatever office it is applied to. One office desiring to communicate with another writes on the line the call of that office three or four times, followed by his own call, and repeats this operation indefinitely, or until he is answered by the office called. The office answering the call makes the letter "I" three or four times, and signs his own call. The receipt of a communication is answered by the signal "O. K." followed by the signal or call of the office receiving it. If the receiver, from any cause, fails to read or understand any portion of the communication, he calls for a repetition by "breaking in" and saying "G. A." (go ahead), and giving the last word understood by him. If he wishes it repeated entirely he says "R. R" (Repeat).

With wires of many miles in length, main batteries, containing a large number of cells are placed at the end stations. The return circuit is made through the entire distance of the earth, and each office connected with the line in the manner here described. The means employed to "tap" a telegraph line (which is sometimes done in case of railway accidents and for other purposes) are very simple. The wire is cut, and its two ends connected to a portable instrument in the hands of a "sound" operator, who may then easily read all that passes over the wire.

As lightning is frequently attracted to out-door lines, and thereby enters the offices, sometimes damaging the instruments or even setting fire to curtains or other inflammable material about the instrument table, a simple instrument called "Lightning Arrester and Cut-out" is used for the purpose of intercepting and carrying to the earth such discharges of lightning as would be liable to cause damage. This apparatus is entirely effective, and is a complete safeguard against lightning.

## RELAY.

The Relay is used only on main lines, and is made with greater or less resistance, according to the length of the wire. It is connected in the main line, and is operated by the key. The Armature of the relay closes the local circuit by striking the screw above the magnet, and is simply the key to work the local sounder.

In the previous description it is assumed that the instrument is worked directly by the current sent along the line. In long circuits, however, direct working could only be accomplished by great battery power, as, owing to inevitable loss by leakage, a current loses greatly before it reaches its destination. It is found to be a much better arrangement to have the instrument worked by a "local current" derived from a local battery at the receiving station.

When two stations far apart are to be connected by telegraph, it is usual to transmit the signal to a half-way station, and thence to re-transmit it. This is done by making the intermediate instrument act as a

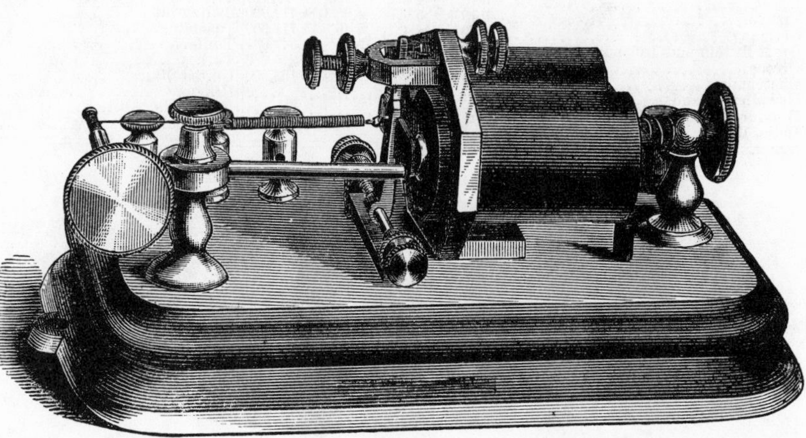

THE RELAY.

relay. The mechanical contrivance for this purpose is too complicated to be described here.

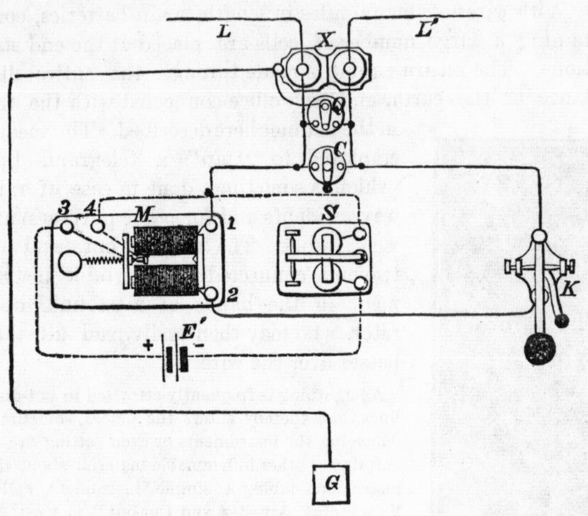


## ARRANGEMENT OF A WAY STATION.

The annexed plan shows the instruments and connections of a way station. The line enters at L, passes through the lightning arrester, X, and thence through the relay, M, key, K, and back to the lightning arrester, and thence to the next station by the line L′. The button C, arranged as shown in the figure, is called a "Cut-out." When turned so as to connect the two wires leading into the office, it allows the line current to pass across from one to the other without going through the instruments. The instruments should always be cut out, by means of this apparatus, when leaving the office temporarily or for the night, and also during a thunder-storm, to avoid damage to the apparatus. The local circuit commences at the X pole of the local battery, E′, and through the platinum points of the relay by the binding screws 3, 4, thence through the sounder coils, S, and back to the other pole of the battery.

Other essential parts are the Pony Sounder (used in offices to receive from), the Key, with circuit-breaker, and the Battery, by means of which action is produced. If the battery is a gravity battery, it has the copper in the bottom of a glass jar, and the zinc suspended in the top. The circuit is formed by connecting with wire the copper (or positive pole) to the binding screw of the key, and the zinc (or negative pole) to the binding screw of the sounder. A small quantity of blue vitriol is placed in the bottom of the jar, and the jar filled with water to cover the zinc; the instrument is then in condition for operation.

## THE TELEGRAPHS OF THE WORLD.

| | Date. | Length of Lines, Miles. | Number of offices. | Number of Messages sent | | Date. | Length of Lines, Miles. | Number of offices. | Number of Messages sent |
|---|---|---|---|---|---|---|---|---|---|
| Algeria, French | 1876 | 3,470 | 106 | | Indies, Dutch | 1878 | 3,513 | 82 | 334,006 |
| Argentine Republic | 1877 | 4,819 | 485 | 214,000 | Italy | 1879 | 15,864 | 1,462 | 5,502,000 |
| Australia | 1879 | 26,842 | 675 | | Japan | 1879 | 5,000 | 125 | 410,000 |
| Austria-Hungary | 1879 | 30,403 | 3,444 | 8,371,000 | Luxemburg | 1877 | 192 | 21 | 58,000 |
| Belgium | 1879 | 3,361 | 708 | 3,242,000 | Mexico | 1879 | 10,140 | 237 | |
| Bolivia | | 475 | 15 | | Montenegro | | 275 | 11 | |
| Brazil | 1879 | 4,313 | 123 | 232,000 | Netherlands | 1879 | 2,336 | 185 | 2,705,000 |
| British Columbia | | 642 | | | Norway | 1879 | 4,663 | 127 | 677,000 |
| Bulgaria | 1879 | 1.278 | | 65,000 | New Zealand, | 1879 | 4,538 | 206 | 1,448,943 |
| Canada | | 10,994 | 830 | 52,000 | Orange Free State | | 1,274 | | |
| Ceylon | | 812 | | | Paraguay | 1878 | 44 | | |
| Cape Colony | | 2,712 | | | Persia | 1878 | 3,375 | 71 | 500,000 |
| Chili | 1878 | 4,450 | 73 | 138,000 | Peru | | 608 | 25 | |
| China | | 24 | | | Philippines | 1880 | 713 | 37 | |
| Cochin China, French | 1878 | 1,249 | | 32,000 | Porto Rico | | 466 | | |
| Colombia | 1879 | 1,839 | 36 | 124,000 | Portugal | 1878 | 2,305 | 191 | 662,000 |
| Costa Rica | | 389 | 16 | | Roumania | 1879 | 3,254 | 98 | 879,000 |
| Cuba | 1880 | 2,796 | 187 | | Russia | 1879 | 56,170 | 2,561 | 4,710,120 |
| Denmark | 1878 | 2,097 | 127 | 939,000 | Servia | 1874 | 907 | 37 | 165,000 |
| Ecuador | | 210 | 10 | | Spain | 1877 | 9,624 | 324 | 2,023,000 |
| Egypt | 1878 | 4.872 | 168 | | Sweden | 1879 | 5,145 | 177 | 859,000 |
| France | 1879 | 36,970 | 4,965 | 14,414,000 | Switzerland | 1879 | 4,071 | 995 | 2,614,000 |
| Germany | 1879 | 41,431 | 6,467 | 15,711,000 | Tasmania | | 754 | | |
| Great Britain and Ireland | 1879 | 23,156 | 5,331 | 26,547,037 | Tunis | | 599 | 10 | |
| Greece | 1878 | 1,906 | 82 | 315,000 | Turkey | 1878 | 17,085 | 417 | 1,344,000 |
| Guatemala | 1879 | 1,160 | 52 | 185,000 | United States | 1880 | 107,103 | 11,317 | 33,155,991 |
| Hawaiian Islands | | 39 | | | Uruguay | 1878 | 654 | 20 | 38,000 |
| Honduras | | 649 | | | Venezuela | | 334 | | |
| India, British | 1878 | 18,209 | 239 | 1,431,000 | Total, miles | | 492,573 | | |

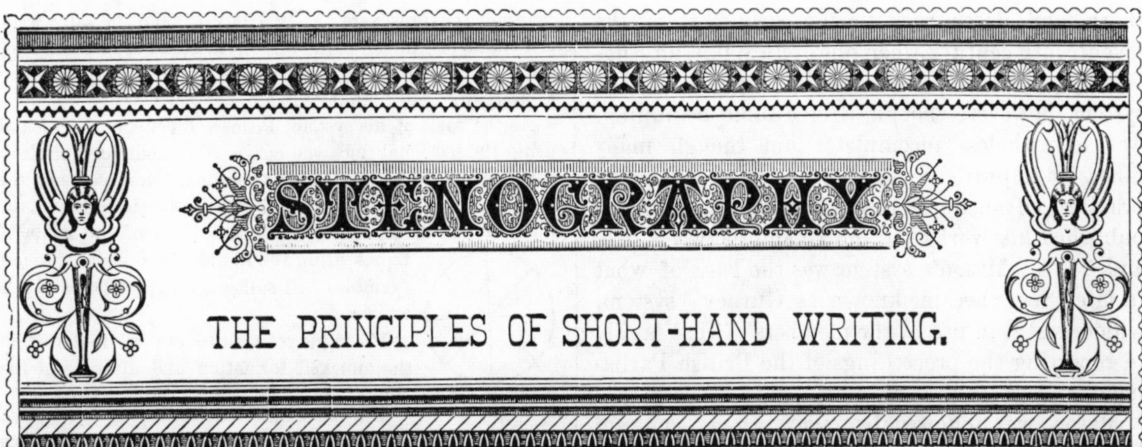


THE art of writing by signs, other than those in ordinary use as the written signs of speech, and so brief and simple of formation that the writer may record the utterances of a speaker as fast, or nearly as fast, as they proceed from his lips, is commonly known as "Short-hand Writing." The best known of the modern systems of writing in this style is called phonography, or more generally, perhaps, stenography—the former word signifying *writing by sound*, and the latter *short*, or *brief writing*. There are numerous other methods or systems of writing in short-hand, such as brachygraphy and tachygraphy, but none of these are in such popular repute or use as stenography.

Short-hand writing in some form has been in use to a greater or less extent for nearly two thousand years, and it is said that the first short-hand writer who has left us any remnants of his work was Marcus Tullius Tiro, a freedman of Cicero, whose records of the oratory of his time are preserved and known in the form of the "Tironian Notes." The system by which he wrote the orations of the great Roman orators must have been something of the most arbitrary and complex character, for Seneca, the philosopher, who lived about the beginning of the Christian era, is said to have added about five thousand characters or signs. And, as if the system were still incomplete, Cyprian, a Carthaginian bishop, added to it many notes.

The "Tironian Notes" flourished and were popular with the learned for about five hundred years, and then the Emperor Justinian practically suppressed them by forbidding the chroniclers to write the text of his codex by the "catches and short-cut riddles of signs." This would seem to indicate that the characters were used not merely for the purpose of catching the extemporaneous language of orators and speakers, but also as the means of recording matters of history, the inscription of laws, decrees, and statutes in the empire. It is the opinion of scholars, who have made close research into the antiquity of short-hand writing, that the Tironian system required the labors, at one time, of several writers to take the words of a single orator, each one taking all the words he could, and that then the notes of all the writers were united and matched or dove-tailed together, so as to furnish the complete transcription. It is claimed also that Xenophon used a system of short-hand in writing the record of his "Memorabilia" of Socrates, but there is no existing evidence of it, and many scholars are at variance on the point.

The origin of any thing approaching a system, or alphabetical method of writing English by short-hand, dates back to the early part of the seventeenth century, when one John Willis, an Englishman, devised a stenographic alphabet. His system, however, though a creditable beginning, was nevertheless incomplete, and though many others "improved" on it, no very important practical advance was made until William Mason published his works on short-hand between 1672 and 1707. Mason's system was the basis of what in later years became known as Gurney's system, which is still in use by the members of that family in reporting the proceedings of the British Parliament.

Mason was followed by many others, some of whom developed great improvements in the art up to the close of the eighteenth century, among the best known being Byron, Taylor, Odell, and Mavor.

It was in the years 1837–40, however, that short-hand writing was reduced to philosophical exactitude, and was made comparatively easy of acquirement by Isaac Pitman. His manual has run through thirteen or fourteen editions, and in each there are "improvements" of real practical value. Besides this it has been improved on by his relative Benn Pitman, of Cincinnati, James E. Munson and Andrew J. Graham, of New York, and other practical phonographers, until it is now equal, in the hands of an accomplished writer, to the task of recording verbatim the most fluent and scholarly orators and lecturers of our time.

Next to the English and American authors, the Germans have been most industrious in the improvement of short-hand, and the French are third. There are, however, systems for writing in short-hand the Russian, Swedish, Danish, Spanish, Italian, and other languages. Types have been invented for the printing of books in short-hand, and the literature of the art, printed both in the ordinary alphabets and the short-hand characters of these languages, would make a library of many hundred volumes.

## THE PRINCIPLE OF MODERN SHORTHAND.

The principle of the modern system of phonetic short-hand writing is exceedingly simple, while singularly complete; and the credit for the invention or discovery of a plan of systematizing the signs in short-hand writing so as to philosophically represent the sounds in our language is due to Isaac Pitman. In every one of the methods of writing by short-hand which preceded his there was a lack of system. Many of the signs were purely arbitrary, and the same written character, in comparatively slight changes of position or relation to other written characters, frequently represented entirely different sounds.

As the basis of his system, Pitman hit upon the idea of using the sectional lines and curves of a subdivided circle as the signs to represent all of the consonant and some of the occasional vowel sounds. To illustrate the simplicity of the plan, and at the same time give some idea of the mode of representing the sounds by the signs, a few examples will suffice for the purposes of this article.

The signs referred to are all included in the annexed formation and division of the parts of a circle.

### THE CONSONANT SOUNDS.

The primary or elementary consonant sound signs obtained from this configuration, are the following:—

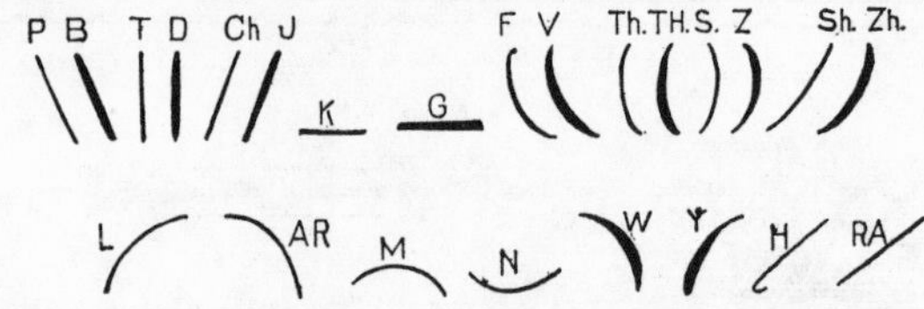


### THE VOWEL SOUNDS.

The vowel sounds are represented by minute signs, in the form of dots and dashes, placed before and after, and in certain relations to these consonant signs. To briefly illustrate this idea, it is only necessary to give a single example. A dot, a trifle larger than the usual sign for a period (thus .) in one position is used as the sign of the vowel E; in another as the sign of A. Place that dot before the stroke representing T, and we have the signs of the two sounds which belong to and form the spoken word, "*Eat*," while the superfluous center letter a, with its unuttered sound, is omitted, and it gives the full sound thus, ·| of the word ET. Take the same dot vowel sign, and place it after the "t" sign, thus |·, and it gives the sign for the sounds in the word "tea," but again omitting the superfluous letter A, as though the word were spelled TE. Put the same dot in this position ·| and it gives us the sound of the word "ate," as though it were spelled AT. Place the vowel dot behind or after the "t" stroke and it produces the sound of the word "Tay," thus, |·.

All of these consonant signs are capable of being united to each other at their initial or terminal points, forming words, thus, |·—*take*—as if it was spelled TAK, the final e being in any case a superfluity.

Examples of other junctions of the consonants are these:

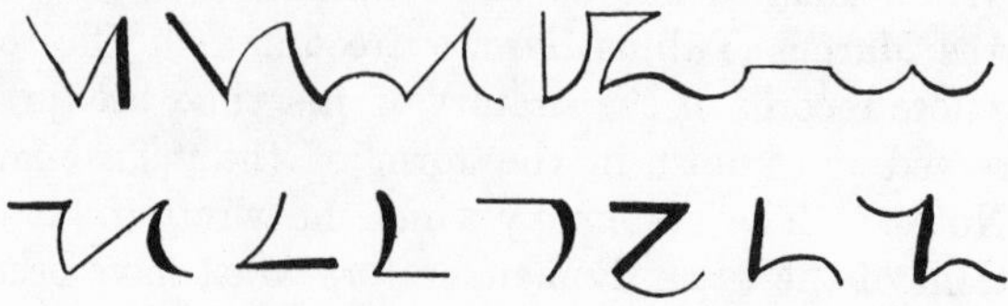

In this way words are formed, and the simplicity of the method of forming them, as compared with the ordinary forms required in English spelling and writing, cannot be better or more forcibly illustrated than in the word "take," given above, a vertical and a horizontal sign joined, with a dot between them. It is this easy form of expressing the sounds of spoken words that makes it practicable by the use of short-hand writers to record the extemporaneous words and speeches of orators, actors, and preachers.

## TIME REQUIRED TO MASTER THE ART.

The art of writing short-hand is altogether a relative art—one of degree. For example, it is quite possible to learn the art, so as to be able to write a letter in phonographic characters, in two or three weeks of vigorous study. But between that degree of the mastery of the art and the expert accomplishment of reporting a sermon or address as the words issue from the lips of a fluent speaker, there is a gulf as wide as that which separates a sign-painter from a Bierstadt, or a brewer's truck-horse from a racer or trotter. But to learn short-hand so as to write 160 words a minute, generally requires two years of study and practice.

The acquirement of the art so as to be truly expert, requires a vast amount of practice and persistence added to natural capacity and aptitude for the work. Out of every one hundred young persons who undertake to learn short-hand writing, not over five per cent. become first-class, expert writers ; ten per cent. become fairly good ; twenty per cent. will be good dabblers merely, and the other sixty-five per cent., after losing months of time in study and practice, will give it up in disgust.

## THE BEST AGE TO BEGIN THE STUDY.

To become a good short-hand writer one needs to begin the study and practice of the art between the ages of 14 and 18 years. Of course much depends, in short-hand as in every-thing else, upon the natural aptitude and tact of the individual, and there may be some expert phonographers who began to study the art as early as 12 years or as late as 24 years. But the chances of success between these extreme ranges are largely in favor of the 12 year-old. Being more or less intimately acquainted with nearly all of the most rapid and accomplished stenographic writers in the United States—and American short-hand writers are the equals, perhaps the superiors, of any in the world—the writer has taken pains to inquire as to this question of age, and the result of such inquiries is that 14 years to 17 years may be considered the best time at which a lad or girl should begin their studies.

## WHAT IS REQUIRED OF SHORT-HAND WRITERS.

To become successful as a short-hand writer, the beginner must set out with an abundant stock of energy and considerable patience. Behind these qualities there must be: first, a good liberal education, a quick, clear intelligence, rapid faculties of perception and distinction, excellent hearing, and a quick, nimble hand and wrist for the use of pen or pencil. The necessity of all these qualities will be understood and appreciated when it is remembered how rapidly the syllables, the words, the sentences of speech flow from the mouths of speakers, and that the phonographer must keep pace with them, and not only hear them correctly, but record them legibly in the short-hand characters.

The logic, or reason, or coherence of the ideas conveyed by the speaker is not necessarily a matter for which the reporter is accountable, nor is the style, or felicity, or elegance of the form of expression an affair which need concern him—but the phonographer should be able to correct all errors or misconceptions in grammatical rule or style of construction, if required to do so.

The process of transferring instantly to a written record the extemporaneous, perhaps unstudied, utterances of a speaker calls for a most singular, prompt, and clear exercise of both mental and physical powers. The ear must be alert to carry to the brain the chain of word-sounds ; the brain is required to interpret the meaning of these sounds, and at the same instant mentally call up the phonetic sign which in writing records the words. Next it telegraphs through the nerves to the hand the recollection or original suggestion of the forms of the characters or signs which will express the words, and finally, it is required to guide the muscular action of the fingers, hand, and arm, in making these signs.

To think merely of the lightning-like rapidity with which these mental and physical operations, acting in concert, must be carried out, and that every syllable calls for their exercise, while these minute syllabic operations follow each other at the rate of five hundred to one thousand per minute, and are sometimes required to be maintained for hours without any intermission, save the almost unappreciable rest of the ordinary rhetorical pauses, one may be led to suspect that the art is at once delicate and its practice straining to the last degree. It is no idle remark to say that a day's sharp work at short-hand writing involves a greater amount of fatigue and exhaustion than does an equal number of hours spent at brick-making or at lumbering in the back-woods. The writer of this article has had actual experience in all three of the occupations, and submits the statement as one of actual fact.

## SPEED IN WRITING.

The speed attained in short-hand writing is a matter about which there is no little diversity of opinion among short-hand writers themselves, and there is probably about as much imagination indulged in respecting it as there is among turfmen concerning the "time" made by their own private trotters.

The New York Stenographers' Association adopted a rule providing for a test examination of candidates as a condition upon which their election depended, and the rate required to be reached was an average of one hundred and fifty words per minute, in a trial of six minutes' duration. But such a test of itself proves very little as to the actual merit or ability of the writer. He may be put to great disadvantage, or he may be favored by the examining committee.

It does not necessarily follow that the most rapid speaker is the most difficult to report verbatim. Henry Ward Beecher, for example, rates as a speaker who utters about two hundred words per minute, but most short-hand writers will admit that they prefer to report him instead of many other clergymen who do not exceed one hundred and sixty or one hundred and seventy words per minute. This is due to the fact that Mr. Beecher's style and method is so clear, even, fluent, and distinct. He has bursts of rapid and fervid eloquence, but even these are even and well-balanced, not jerky, confused, or indistinct, as is the case with many speakers.

Many years ago the writer sat beside an accomplished short-hand writer, and saw him write, while "the watch was held on him," as the horse jockeys say, for two minutes and a half at the rate of three hundred and two words a minute. But he was not writing from dictation. He wrote, from memory, a selection from the tragedy of Julius Cæsar, and it is doubtful whether any man, or woman even, could have clearly and distinctly uttered the words at that rate of speed. The aspirant for phonographic honors, however, need not surrender because he fails to attain such speed as that. If he gets to the point where he can write one hundred and fifty words per minute, and read or transcribe the notes readily either an hour or a month afterward, he may consider himself an efficient writer. Of course a higher rate of speed without any diminution in legibility makes him still more proficient.

The beginner should carefully avoid sacrificing legibility to rapidity. Charles Dickens, himself an expert stenographer, gives an amusing account in "David Copperfield," of a learner who has attained the power of writing, but who cannot decipher his own notes.

It is almost superfluous to state that persons taking down a speech in short-hand should have about half a dozen pencils sharpened, so that no time need be lost, if the point of one of them should happen to break.

## REMUNERATION OF STENOGRAPHERS.

A stenographer who can write from one hundred and sixty to two hundred words a minute can earn anywhere from $2,000 to $10,000 a year, according to the patronage he can command, and if it could be "picked up" in three or six months, there would soon be thousands of stenographers, instead of the few score, perhaps fifty, really *accomplished* writers to be found in the whole State of New York to-day.

There are five hundred phonographers in New York City who are fairly fast and legible writers, but as they are only of mediocre ability, they are employed mainly as amanuenses and stenographic secretaries, and earn from $600 to $2,000 a year.

## SYSTEMS OF STENOGRAPHY.

According to the claims of stenographic authors there are some five or six "systems" of phonetic short-hand, for each of which text-books and manuals have been published, but coming to the consideration of phonographic short-hand only, we may say that there is *only one system* in fact, and that is the original Isaac Pitman system.

The systems of Benn Pitman, Andrew J. Graham, James E. Munson, and D. L. Scott-Browne, are nothing more than modifications and elaborations of Isaac Pitman's system or principle of writing. They are, however, very careful and conscientious efforts, and there is not one of them that is not an improvement on the original work. But the Isaac Pitman manual of to-day, the thirteenth edition, is a long way in advance of his manual of thirty years ago. Isaac Pitman holds the same relation to these other authors that Watt, the inventor of the steam engine, does to modern engine builders; granting, of course, that if Watt were alive to-day and building engines, he would not be still building the old style engines, but would be putting them together with "improvements" and "modifications," as the other builders are doing.

Riding
Introduction
Kettle-Drum
W P Snyder
This Train for N.Y.
Party
Traveling

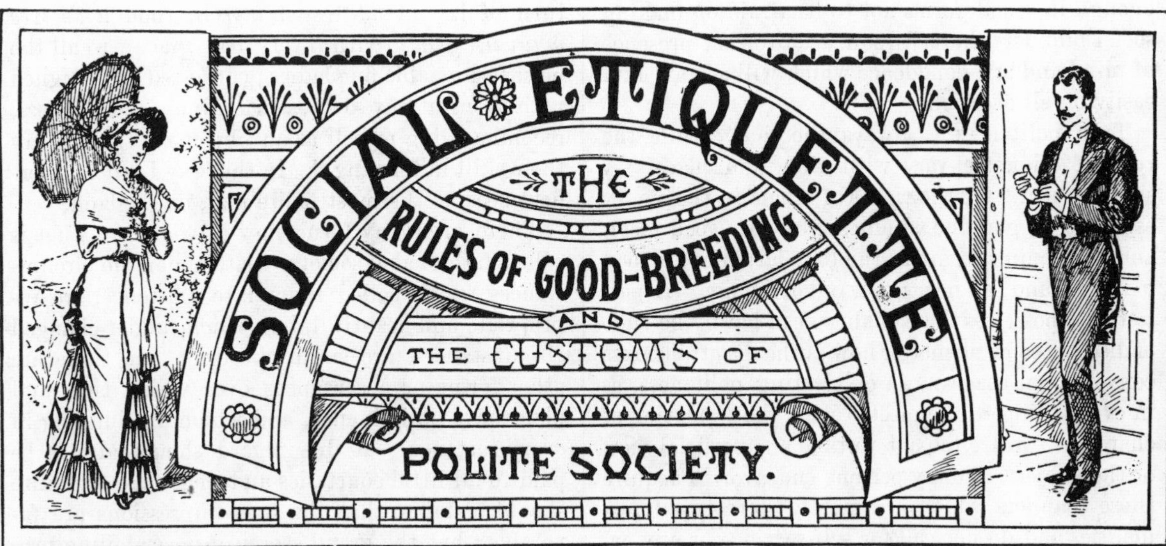


CHESTERFIELD defined *Politeness* as the art of pleasing. It denotes that ease and gracefulness of manners which first sprung up in cities, connected with a desire to please others by anticipating their wants and wishes, and studiously avoiding whatever might give them pain.

*Courtesy* displays itself in the address and manners; it is shown more especially in receiving and entertaining others, and is a union of dignified complaisance and kindness. The word *Etiquette* is of Anglo-Norman origin, and formerly conveyed to those who used it a far different signification from what it does to-day. Etiquette originally specified the ticket tied to the neck of bags, or affixed to bundles to denote their contents, and a bag or bundle thus ticketed passed unchallenged. The present meaning of the word was developed from the fact that our ancestors had their codes of manners written or printed upon cards or tickets, and hence the modern slang phrase "the ticket" is not so meaningless as one might suppose.

Etiquette is the code of politeness enforced in well-bred society. It relates entirely to the observance of certain exterior forms in the social intercourse of men and women; so that a person may be polite with that innate and unstudied courtesy, which the French call the politeness of the heart, and yet be entirely ignorant of etiquette.

But there is no reason why one who is naturally polite should not master that acquired and artificial politeness which is called etiquette, for etiquette can be taught; politeness must be born in a man. He may understand the minutest details of formal etiquette, he may pass with ease and distinction all the tests of social life, and yet remain a boor at heart. On the other hand, a man may be rude in his manners, may transgress etiquette continually, and yet be a gentleman at heart, because deference to women, and kindness to and consideration for all are natural to him.

A man or woman possessing already this genuine substance of politeness can easily master the established rules of etiquette, that pass-word by which polished society defends itself from vulgar intrusion.

When a man is fully conversant with etiquette, he may still fear to move in society for some time before he obtains that self-unconscious ease which is the highest distinction of the well-bred man. "True politeness," says Pope, "consists in being easy one's self, and in making everybody about one as easy as one can." But when one has practice enough in social forms not to be afraid of making social blunders, he will soon acquire that presence of mind and self-confidence which will sustain him easily on all occasions.

True politeness is always the same, while the rules of etiquette vary with time and place. A sincere regard for the rights of others in the smallest matters, genuine kindness of heart, good taste, and self-command are at the foundation of all good manners, and can never grow out of fashion. A person who possesses these qualities can hardly be rude or discourteous, no matter how far he may transgress conventional usages. In cultivating politeness, as in every-thing else connected with the formation of character, we are too apt to take a superficial view of the subject. Many persons endeavor to acquire those manners which are merely stereotyped formalities and do not call for self-sacrifice or any action prompted by a good heart. They forget that the golden rule, do unto others as you would they should do unto you, contains the very soul and life of genuine politeness. Unless children and young people are taught by precept and example to abhor what is selfish and to prefer another's pleasure and comfort to their own, their politeness will be entirely artificial, and exercised only when dictated by self-interest and policy. The essence of the worldly code of ethics is selfishness; that of the Christian is disinterestedness.

Some persons have the "instinct of courtesy" so largely developed that they hardly need to cultivate politeness, but the great majority of us must be content to acquire the rules of good breeding by study and practice. Lord Chesterfield, who was naturally deficient in that grace which afterward distinguished him as the most polished gentleman in England, said, "I had a strong desire to please, and was sensible that I had nothing but the desire. I therefore resolved, if possible, to acquire the means too. I studied attentively and minutely the dress, the air, the manner, the address, and the turn of conversation of all those whom I found to be the people in position, and most generally allowed to please. I imitated them as well as I could; if I heard that one man was reckoned remarkably genteel, I carefully watched his dress, motions, and attitudes, and formed my own upon them. When I heard of another whose conversation was agreeable and engaging, I listened and attended to the turn of it. I addressed myself, though *de très mauvaise grâce* (with a very bad grace), to all the most fashionable fine ladies; confessed and laughed with them at my own awkwardness and rawness, recommending myself as an object for them to try their skill in forming." In this way Lord Chesterfield became the most polite man in England.

There are many forms now in vogue, in what is called fashionable society, that, under the circumstances which called them into existence, are appropriate and beautiful, but which, under changed circumstances, are simply absurd; and there are other forms or observances over which time and place have no influence, and which are binding in every instance. A due regard should always be paid to all little courtesies and elegances, and care should be taken that the first impressions are favorable; but the grand secret of never-failing propriety of deportment, says Madame Celnart, "*is to have an intention of always doing right.*"

"Manners makyth man" has the same force as ever. Goodness of heart, however boundless; learning, however profound; and accomplishments, the most brilliant and varied, are not in themselves sufficient to make us pleasant and agreeable members of society—a knowledge and practice of the laws of good-breeding must be added, to make a perfect whole. Your character may be inestimable; but if you speak loudly, or with a vulgar twang, if you are boisterous in your behavior and eschew the requirements of society, your best friends will—behind your back—lament that you are so little endowed with manners, although "an excellent creature." "Manners recommend, prepare, and draw people together; manners make the fortune of the ambitious youth—for the most part, his manners marry him, and he marries manners." The principle and groundwork of these laws is, that they tend to add materially to the happiness and comfort of those around us, smooth and soften the contact of the individual atoms which are incessantly coming against each other in the restless intercourse of the busy world, and add a charm to the quiet monotony of every-day life. Acts of attention and thoughtfulness shown to those around not only make their days pass more easily and happily, but at the same time ennoble the doer, and provoke a sweet return of kindly feeling and good-will.

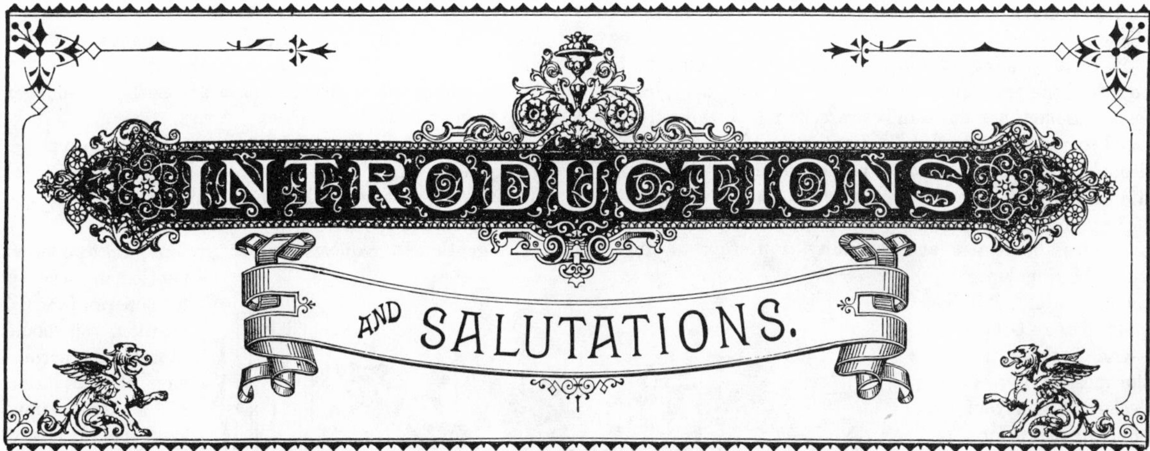

## SALUTATIONS.

ALTHOUGH there are many every-day forms of salutation, good sense will teach that they should vary in style with persons, time, place, and circumstances.

Never present a passive hand, or one or two fingers, but grasp the right hand of a friend for a moment only.

Gentlemen introduced to an unmarried lady do not extend their hands, unless she offers hers.

A gentleman takes off or touches the hat on meeting an acquaintance. He rises when visitors enter or leave the room, bows to strangers, and extends his right hand to friends. On entering a drawing-room where there is a party, he salutes the lady of the house before speaking to any one else.

Gentlemen when saluted by gentlemen need not uncover the head. When saluting a lady a gentleman raises his hat.

Unless the right hand is disabled, a gentleman does not use the left ; he should apologize if compelled to extend his left hand.

In meeting in the street, the lady generally first bows to the gentleman, in America, unless the gentleman be much older or a very intimate acquaintance. If he wishes to address the lady, he will turn round and accompany her for a little, or even a long distance.

Many persons maintain, however, that a gentleman should always bow first to a lady, no matter whether she returns it or not. If he sees by her face that she does not wish to return it, he can refrain from bowing the next time.

A gentleman takes off his hat to a lady who is with a gentleman whom he knows, the latter being the first to salute.

If a gentleman meets a lady on a stairway, he lifts his hat respectfully. If both are about to ascend the stairs, the lady stands aside for a moment and allows the gentleman, who will bow, to go first; should they be descending the stairs, the gentleman bows and allows the lady to go down first.

A gentleman carries his hat, cane, and gloves in his left hand on entering a room, as the right hand must be free to salute his friends. He need not, and at present does not, remove the glove from his right hand. The hands should not be gloved while receiving friends.

Should a gentleman on the street see a lady at a window, he may salute her, if she has recognized him first; but a lady cannot, while on the street, recognize a gentleman at a window.

In bowing to a lady a gentleman lifts his hat with the hand farthest from the lady.

If a lady with whom a gentleman is walking is saluted by another gentleman, the former acknowledges the salutation by removing his hat.

In meeting a friend with whom he is likely to shake hands, a gentleman removes his hat with the left hand, in order to leave the right hand free; and he does not put out his hand until he is quite near the person whom he is about to salute.

He always returns a salutation, no matter how humble the person who gives it may be.

"A bow," La Fontaine says, "is a note drawn at sight. If you acknowledge it, you must pay full amount."

As grace should attend all the movements, whether of man or woman, the manner of bowing, shaking the hand, walking, and speaking should be at once refined and elegant.

The bow should be a graceful bend, or inclination of the head ; not a hasty movement, nor a stiff jerk. A gentleman should raise his hat, indeed take it off his head, but not with a flourish, nor seize it with a sudden dash, as is now so often seen. There is great art in making a bow, dignified and stately, but at the same time neither stiff nor awkward ;

and how much more difficult is it than people suppose to shake hands well!

In what a variety of ways are our hands shaken in the course of the year, and how few of those ways are pleasant ones! Sometimes our hands are seized and violently agitated to and fro; at others, a limp, nerveless something is dropped into our outstretched palm, which shows no sign of life while in our possession. There are people, who from no feeling of affection, but simply from a vicious habit intended to express heartiness and cordiality, squeeze your fingers until the rings upon them enter into your flesh. Others—and I think this the most trying ordeal—retain your hand in theirs for a length of time, and ever and anon give it a little shake by way of adding *empressement* to their inquiries about your welfare. This latter custom is a very old-fashioned one, but now and then one is rendered uncomfortable by encountering it. Each one of these forms of hand-shaking is most irritating and objectionable. Take the hand offered you firmly; be careful to grasp the *hand*, not the fingers merely, which has a ridiculous effect; give it a gentle pressure, and then relinquish it; do not lift it up to shake, neither let it drop—heartiness and cordiality should be expressed.

THE SALUTATION.

## INTRODUCTIONS.

T is neither necessary nor desirable to introduce everybody to everybody. Before introducing persons to each other, endeavor to discover if such is the wish of both. When people are thrown together accidentally or unavoidably, it is much better not to hesitate, but to make them known to one another. The rules of introductions are substantially the same for both sexes.

### GENTLEMEN.

In making introductions be careful to present the inferior to the superior, as Mr. B. to the Rev. Dr. C.

When neither difference of rank or sex exists, the younger person is introduced to the elder.

Friends may present friends at the house of a mutual acquaintance.

When two gentlemen call upon a stranger on business, each should present the other.

If a gentleman requests you to present him to another gentleman, who is his superior in social position, you should first obtain permission of the latter, and a lady's permission should always be asked before one gentleman presents another to her.

Gentlemen are always introduced to ladies, not ladies to gentlemen.

The form required for introductions is very simple, viz.: "Mr. Ross, permit me to introduce to you my friend, Captain Lockwood," then (turning to the Captain), "Captain Lockwood, Mr. Ross." The two gentlemen may then shake hands and exchange courteous remarks, or merely bow.

The members of your own family are always introduced by mentioning their relations, in this way: "My father, Mr. Ross," "My daughter, Miss Ross," or "Miss Mary, Mr. Ross." A gentleman's wife is simply "Mrs. Ross," and if there be another Mrs. Ross in the family she is spoken of as "My sister-in-law, etc." It is not considered good form for a gentleman to speak of his wife as his "lady," nor to enter his name on a hotel register as "Mr. Ross and lady."

When introducing persons, be very careful to speak their names plainly, and on being introduced to another, if you do not catch his name, say without hesitation or embarrassment, "I beg your pardon, I did not hear the name."

If a gentleman meets an agreeable person at the house of a friend, he may converse with him without the ceremony of an introduction. Their presence in a friend's house is a sufficient guaranty of their respectability.

When many persons are to be presented to one person, as at a reception, it is necessary only to name the honored guest once, as "Allow me to present Mr. Johnson, Mr. Gray, Mr. Morton," and so on, a bow emphasizing each name.

When introducing persons of rank, never forget their titles.

Persons that are known to have achieved fame in any way are always given the credit due them. If a foreigner, who is not otherwise noteworthy, is to be introduced, it is as "Monsieur Vincent, from Paris," or "Lord Killoway, from Dublin," and so on. If a painter or author is presented, the introduction should be "Mr. Lossing, the author," or "the well-known painter, Mr. Brown," &c.

If a gentleman should meet in a friend's house a person with whom he is not on friendly terms, etiquette requires that he should be courteous towards him for the time.

A gentleman should never let the lack of an introduction prevent him from promptly offering his services to any unattended lady who may require them; he should lift his hat and politely ask permission to assist her, and, when the service has been accomplished, bow and retire.

The act of "cutting" can only be justified by some strong instance of bad conduct in the person to be cut, but a cold bow, which discourages familiarity without offering insult, is the best mode to adopt towards those with whom an acquaintance is not deemed desirable.

Introductions, given at a party to a stranger visiting in a city, must be followed by recognition as long as the visit continues.

To introduce to a friend a person who is in any way objectionable, is an insult which fully justifies a withdrawal of friendship.

## RULES FOR LADIES.

Unmarried ladies are presented to married ladies, the younger to the elder.

When two ladies are introduced they shake hands.

Young ladies simply bow when introduced to unmarried men.

A lady may present another lady at the house of a friend, but it is always better to allow the hostess to perform the ceremony.

Ladies should not dance with gentlemen to whom they have not been formally introduced, although an introduction by the master of ceremonies is perfectly in order; even then the lady's permission should be asked, if the entertainment be a public one. At a private ball, the lady of the house may introduce a gentleman to a lady without the permission of the latter, in order that he may ask her guest to dance; but the lady is not obliged to consider her partner as an acquaintance afterwards unless she please.

The manner in which an introduction is made is very simple:

"Miss Morton, permit me to introduce you to my friend, Mrs. Howard," or "My sister, Mrs. Howard," or "My mother, Mrs. Howard," or "My sister-in-law, Mrs. Howard," as the case may be, and then (turning to Mrs. Howard), "Mrs. Howard, Miss Morton."

It is often better to have one's relatives introduced to friends by other friends instead of directly. Of course there are many exceptions to this rule.

The relatives of one's friends, when introduced by the latter, become acquaintances, but may be dropped if they seem objectionable.

Ladies may pass or "cut" a gentleman on the street, but it should be very carefully done, and never without good cause; it is better to bow coldly.

## FOR LADIES.

LADIES' visiting cards should be of fine material, and a little larger than those of gentlemen. They should be engraved in plain script with letters of a medium size. "Mrs." or "Miss" should be prefixed, unless there is a title of some kind. No *lady* will allude to her husband's political, religious, military, naval, or professional position or titles on her card. Her husband's rank or honoring designation may be alluded to by others, but she should never herself parade them.

Old English characters are often used, but are not "good form." Cards should be engraved in simple Italian characters and without flourish, embossed surface, or even ostentatiously large letters. When the address is given, it should be engraved in the lower left-hand corner.

Persons in mourning use a card with a black border with the inscription in heavy shaded script.

In England, if a person thinks a stranger who has left a card a desirable acquaintance, he sends him an invitation to call. In America, however, it is the prevailing custom to require an introduction, which may take place by card; indeed, the card has, to a certain extent, taken the place of formal letters of introduction, unless there is some special reason for the latter. The introducing lady writes upon the upper left-hand corner of her visiting card,

*Introducing*

*Mrs. John S. Smith.*

This card is put in a fine envelope with that of the lady wishing to be introduced. The envelope may be sent by either post or messenger. The lady to whom the two cards are forwarded, or some of her family, must call in person, or send special message by private messenger to explain. If the call is made, the introduction should take place within three days. This visit must be promptly returned unless an "At Home" day is noted upon the visiting card, or mentioned during the conversation. If the lady introduced lives at a distance, and there have been no special courtesies, she must leave a card with P. P. C. (*pour prendre congé*, to take leave) written upon it, to show that she has left town. If only one visit has taken place on each side she need not call again, and her P. P. C. card is the final courtesy required. If she lives in town she may put her acquaintance in her visiting-list, but the first hospitalities are the privilege of the person whose acquaintance was sought.

After a personal introduction, the lady residing in town may leave a card, which must be responded to by a return card within a week. But if a reception day is mentioned upon the card, that particular time cannot be passed over without a card or an apology. No further visits need be paid.

When a lady changes her residence she must leave her card, with her new address, with those who have paid her visits. She may send the card by post to those who owe her a call. On leaving town for the summer, or to go on a journey, a lady must send her friends by post her own and her family's card marked P. P. C., with her temporary address. When she returns she sends out her cards, which may have an "At Home" day upon them.

Three weeks before a young lady's marriage she leaves her card in *person*, but she does not visit; her mother's or *chaperon's* card is left with her own; and, although the young lady's name may have been engraved together with theirs before, at this time she has her own card and address.

On the death, birth, private wedding, the entering of a new house, etc., of a friend, a card with some appropriate recognition of the event may be sent. A bouquet of cut flowers and a card are sent directly in case of a death among one's friends. Written expressions of sympathy are confined to friends. The card must be *left in person*, or sent by special messenger. On such occasion no acknowledgment is necessary or expected.

On entering a reception, cards are left in the hall. If an invitation has to be declined after it has been accepted, cards are left (by messenger) in the evening, and an explanation sent the next day. Invitations, cards, and replies may be sent by mail, but a card of sympathy or of congratulation must be left in person or by special messenger.

Upon all formal occasions the husband's card goes with his wife's, but their names are not usually engraved upon the same card except immediately after marriage. The mother's and the eldest daughter's names are engraved upon the same card, during the first season of the latter.

*Mrs. Max Moore,*

*Miss Moore,*

*25 Ocean Row.*

If there is more than one daughter, the form is, "Misses Moore."

If a *chaperon* introduces the young lady or ladies, then her visiting card is left with theirs, so that their connection is understood.

When a son enters society his mother leaves his card with his father's and her own. Within a week the cards of all persons invited to an entertainment must be left by a member of the family upon the host and hostess, and also upon the person, if any, in whose honor it was given. This is strict etiquette, whether the invitation was accepted or declined. This duty must be performed by the ladies of the family, or some one of them, and cannot be shared by gentlemen. In the case of death at a friend's house, however, a gentleman may leave a lady's card.

### FOR GENTLEMEN.

A gentleman's card is smaller than a lady's, engraved in plain *fac-simile* or script, and has his address in the lower right hand corner. If it be engraved, *Mr.* should be prefixed to the name, otherwise not. Visiting cards must never bear a business address.

All merely honorary or official designations must be omitted, except in cards intended for official visits only. Officers of the army or navy may use their title if they choose. It is also customary for judges and physicians to use their titles, but it should be omitted by other professional men.

A gentleman who has been introduced to a lady, and wishes to be put on her list of acquaintances, leaves his card at her house. If her mother or *chaperon* does not desire to enlarge her acquaintance, she pays no attention to his card. If she wishes his acquaintance, she invites him to visit, or to an entertainment, and he must then call.

If introduced by card or letter, he calls, asks after the ladies, and sends his own card and that of his introducer.

An indefinite invitation given to a new acquaintance, without mentioning any particular time for calling, amounts to nothing, and he should not call upon the strength of such a vague courtesy.

When a gentleman makes a call and acts for all the ladies of the family, he sends in a card for each person. If he calls upon a young lady who is staying with friends with whom he is not acquainted, he sends in his card to the lady of the house, and asks to see her also ; it is customary for her to come into the room before he goes away, and tell him that the friends of her guest are always welcome.

If he calls upon a young lady, she may (if she has been "in society" for one season) receive him without her mother or *chaperon*, or they may be present during the call. The absence and not the presence of the mother or *chaperon* is more common in America, less common in England.

A purely formal call should not exceed a quarter of an hour. On leaving, "good bye" should be said, in preference to "good morning," or "good evening."

A gentleman who has asked an introduction to a married or elderly lady has no right to expect that she will care to continue the acquaintance, or will invite him to call, though she may do so. At their next meeting he should wait for her to recognize him.

A gentleman who is at leisure in the day-time should call between two and five P. M. If engaged during the day, he should call between half past eight and nine in the evening, *and not earlier*.

Within a week after a gentleman has received an invitation to an entertainment, whether he accepted or not, he should call or leave a card upon the senders of the invitation.

Every invitation, no matter what its nature, should be answered at once, and either accepted or declined.

If a gentleman receives a card introducing another gentleman, whose card he incloses, he must call within three days, or if unable to do so, send a messenger with explanations and courteous offers.

### MORNING AND AFTERNOON CALLS.

IT is not the practice of good society to make calls before noon. From two until five in the afternoon is the proper time. Such calls are, however, often called morning calls. All ladies who are in society have their reception days, and if these are known, it is very impolite, except in a case of necessity, to intrude at other times. Often ladies choose the evening for their reception time, but, whether it is the morning or evening, their hours should be regarded. The only exception to this rule is when visitors to the city or town, who could not otherwise pay their respects, are permitted to make calls when they can. Formal calls are always made in the morning, and should not exceed twenty minutes. A gentleman making a morning call should go alone, unless he has gained permission to bring a friend with him.

Gentlemen retain their hats in their hands, and do not remove their gloves.

Ladies do not remove their gloves, and retain their parasol in their hands.

The hostess will ring the bell for a servant to open the door for her callers when they take their leave.

Callers should always send up their cards first, and ladies who call in carriages do this by the footman before they alight from their equipage.

### EVENING CALLS

Are less formal, and more pleasant than those made in the morning, and intimate friends may prolong an evening call beyond the usual hour.

Calls made by strangers should be returned within one week.

New comers to any neighborhood are called on by the former residents first.

On ceremonial occasions married ladies leave their husband's cards with their own.

Never keep a visitor waiting ; it is better to receive him just as you are than to delay.

Visitors from a distance may call earlier or later, and stay longer than neighbors.

When your friends are entertaining visitors from a distance, you should call upon both, and they should return your call within a week.

It is not customary to offer refreshments to callers unless they come from a long distance.

Cards should be left within a week after any social festival. When one has been prevented from accepting an invitation, it is polite to call as soon as possible, and express regrets.

When a lady receives a gentleman, she rises from her seat to meet him, but resumes it at once.

The hostess advances to meet a lady guest.

A gentleman calling on a gentleman is received at the door, and relieved by him of hat, overcoat, and cane.

Never, while waiting the appearance of the hostess, be guilty of handling anything, or walking about the room, or interfering with the furniture in any way. Be careful not to turn your back on visitors, or to take out your watch, or in any way to manifest tedious anxiety to be going.

When one has said "good bye," or "good day," it is awkward to linger.

If your friend is dressed ready to go out, do not make any remark about it, but take your departure at the earliest moment without remark

DR. JOHNSON says that in order to converse well, "there must, in the first place, be knowledge—there must be materials; in the second place, there must be a command of words; in the third place, there must be imagination to place things in such views as they are not commonly seen in; and in the fourth place, there must be a presence of mind, and a resolution that is not to be overcome by failure—this last is an essential requisite; for want of it many people do not excel in conversation."

The art of expressing one's thoughts in clear, simple English, is one of the utmost importance to those who mix in good society. A half-opened mouth, a perpetual smile, a vacant stare, and a wandering eye are all evidences of ill-breeding. One should try to suppress all excessive emotion of whatever kind. As conversation is the principal business in company, we cannot pay too much attention to it.

Wit in conversation consists more in finding it in others than in showing a great deal one's self; for if a man goes from our company pleased with himself and his own wit, he is perfectly well pleased with us.

A gentleman will never permit himself to lose his temper in society, and he will never talk *at* people, or "show off" in strange company.

Women, clergymen, and men of learning or years should always be addressed with respect and attention.

It is bad taste to talk of fevers to a physician, or stocks to a broker, or in fact to talk "shop" of any kind.

Conversation ought not to relate to domestic matters. Yet, as people take more interest in their own affairs than in any thing else, it is a mark of tact to lead a mother to speak of her children, a young lady to talk of her summer at a watering place, or, in winter, of her last ball. Ask the author about his forthcoming book, or the artist about his exhibition picture, and after having furnished the topic, you need only listen.

Some persons spoil every party they join by making it their only object to prove that every one present is in the wrong but themselves; such ill-bred and ill-timed argumentativeness should be strictly avoided.

Advice is never to be given unasked, and information should be asked for and given with caution.

A gentleman will not make a statement, unless he is absolutely convinced of its truth.

He is attentive to any person who may be speaking to him, and is equally ready to speak or to listen as the case may require.

He never descends to flattery, although he will not withhold a deserved compliment.

If he has traveled he does not introduce that information into his conversation at every opportunity.

He does not help out, or forestall, the slow speaker, but in conversing with foreigners, who do not not understand our language perfectly, and at times are unable to find the right word, politely assists them by suggesting it.

He converses with a foreigner in his own language; if not competent to do so, he apologizes and begs permission to speak English.

He does not try to use fine language, long words, or high-sounding phrases.

He does not boast of birth, money, or friends.

The initial of a person's name as, "Mr. H.," should never be used to designate him.

Long stories should be avoided.

One's country or customs should be defended without hesitation, but also without anger or undue warmth.

Scandal is the least excusable of all conversational vulgarities.

When a grammatical or verbal error is committed by

persons with whom one is conversing, it is not to be corrected.

Words and phrases that have a double meaning are to be avoided.

Politics, religion, and all topics specially interesting to gentlemen, such as the turf, the exchange, or the farm, should be excluded from general conversation when ladies are present.

Gentlemen should not make use of classical quotations in the presence of ladies, without apologizing for, or translating them, although there are many women now, whose education has made them quite able to understand and appreciate almost any subject, and a gentleman who is a good conversationist, will always adapt his conversation as skillfully as may be to his company.

Polite vulgarisms, or slang, should be scrupulously guarded against, *e. g.*, "awfully nice," "just so."

Long arguments in general company, no matter how entertaining to the disputants, are to the last degree tiresome.

Anecdotes should be very sparsely introduced, unless they are short, witty, and appropriate.

Proverbs should be as carefully used as puns ; and a pun should never be perpetrated unless it rises to the rank of witticism. There is no greater nuisance in society than a dull and persevering punster.

It is always silly to try to be witty.

It is bad breeding to interrupt a person when conversing.

Refrain from the use of satire, even if you are master of the art. It is permissible only as a guard against impertinence, or for the purpose of checking personalities, or troublesome intrusions. Under no circumstances whatever should it be used merely for amusement's sake, to produce an effect, or in order to show off one's own wit. It must never be employed by a gentleman against a lady, though ladies are prone to indulge in the use of this wordy weapon. Their acknowledged position should, in the eyes of a true gentleman, shield them from all shafts of satire. If they, on the other hand, choose to indulge in satire, it is the part of a gentleman to remonstrate gently, and if the invective be continued, to withdraw.

THE TETE-A-TETE.

It is extremely ill-bred to whisper in company, but a "gentle and low voice" is always an "excellent thing" in men as well as in women.

A gentleman looks, but never stares at those with whom he converses.

Loud laughter is objectionable, although often it is excusable.

The name of any person, present or absent, to whom reference is made, should be given if possible.

Place should always be given to one's elders.

Death is not a proper subject for conversation with a delicate person, or shipwreck with a sea-captain's wife, or deformities before a deformed person, or failures in the presence of a bankrupt. For, as Heine says, "God has given us speech in order that we may say pleasant things to our friends." We should let it be the object of our conversation to please, and in order to do this, we should not converse on subjects that might prove distasteful to any person present.

## SHOPPING.

IT should be remembered that a shop is a public place, where one is seen and heard by strangers.

A genuine lady marks her goodness and wisdom by using polite forms of speech. She will not say "I want such a thing," but "show me, if you please, that article." A woman of good sense ought to have a very clear idea of what she requires before going shopping, and she will do well to fix in her own mind just what she wants to buy, and how much she is able to pay for it. Clerks have been heard to say: "It is a pleasure to wait upon that lady, for she always knows what she wants, and she is so polite." A lady will always find that those little phrases "if you please," and "thank you" will assist her very much in her shopping. If some other lady should be examining goods that you wish to look at, wait until she is through. Never draw comparisons with goods of another store. When you leave the counter a slight bow is never out of place. On the other hand, familiarity on the part of the clerk should not be allowed, and if he is asked for advice it should be done in such a way that he will give it respectfully.

SHOPPING.

## STREET ETIQUETTE.

Nowhere has a man or a woman greater occasion to exercise the virtue of courtesy than on the street, and in no place is the distinction between the polite and the vulgar more clearly marked.

In England and America it is not customary, as a general rule, for a gentleman to salute a lady with whom he is not intimate, unless he has received a slight bow of recognition, in order to give her an opportunity of discontinuing his acquaintance. But many gentlemen adopt the rule of the (European) continent, where the gentleman always bows *first*, leaving it optional with the lady to return his bow or not. The hat is raised with the hand farthest from the person saluted.

When gentlemen are escorting ladies it is their duty to insist on carrying any article the latter may have in their hands, except the parasol.

Ladies and persons of rank or age are always entitled to the inner path, and a gentleman walking with any person should accommodate his speed to that of his companion.

Never leave a friend suddenly on the street without a brief apology.

If a gentleman wishes to speak to a lady whom he meets on the street, he must turn and walk with her.

Never, except in a case of necessity, stop a business man; if you must speak with him, walk in his direction, or if compelled to detain him, state your errand briefly, and apologize for the detention.

A gentleman always throws away his cigar when he turns to walk with ladies.

In stopping to speak to an acquaintance on the street, always step aside. If you are compelled to detain a friend when he is walking with a stranger, apologize to the stranger, who will then withdraw a step or two in order not to hear the conversation.

It is rude to stare at ladies in the street.

Information asked by a lady or stranger should always be promptly and courteously given.

A gentleman should offer his arm to a lady or elderly person on long walks at night, or in ascending the stairs of a public building.

A gentleman cannot under any circumstances "cut" a lady who has bowed to him.

A gentleman who renders any service to a lady whom he does not know will take his leave as soon as his good deed has been accomplished. She may recognize him the next time they meet or not, as she pleases; it is not considered amiss to do so.

Do not look back after persons, or eat in the street, or walk too rapidly, or talk or laugh so as to attract attention.

To talk of domestic affairs in a public vehicle or on the street, is very rude.

FANCY FAIR.

Never nod to a lady in the street, but take off your hat; it is a courtesy her sex demands.

A lady should never leave a friend on the street suddenly without an apology.

If a lady with whom you are walking recognizes the salute of a person who is a stranger to you, you should return it.

When a lady whom you accompany wishes to enter a store, you should hold the door open and allow her to enter first, if practicable; and you must never pass before a lady anywhere without apology.

Ladies should avoid walking too rapidly. Loud talking on the street or in public conveyances is a sure sign of bad training.

No gentleman will stand in the doors of hotels to stare at ladies as they pass.

Do not eat in the street, or attempt to force your way through a crowd.

Ladies should never bow to gentlemen unless they are sure of their identity.

When a lady is crossing a muddy street, she should gather her dress in her right hand, and draw it to the right side. It is very vulgar to use both hands for that purpose.

Ladies do not often take a gentleman's arm during the day, unless he is a near relative or *fiancé*, and in ascending the steps of a public building, or on long walks, and in the country.

## FANCY FAIRS.

A gentleman should wear an opera or dress hat to these entertainments. He should not "chaff" about the price appended to any article, nor demand change; should he overpay for any thing, the lady should hand the change without delay, leaving him the opportunity of offering the excess as a contribution.

It is always well for gentlemen to provide themselves with such sums as they are willing to spend on such occasions, and ladies should remember that even the smallest purchase deserves a "thank you."

## LIBRARY ETIQUETTE.

Libraries are generally visited by persons who know the

value of books and quiet too well to disturb others. Visitors to a library should remember to be careful not to turn the leaves of a volume noisily, or to laugh or converse with acquaintances so as to annoy other readers. It is but miserable vandalism to make pencil marks, turn down a leaf, or bend back a book. Readers should be careful not to tear or soil a volume; and visitors who go through the library building merely as sight-seers should move quietly, and if asked to write their names in the visitors' book, do so at once.

## AT CHURCH.

Church goers should always be in season, so as not to interrupt the congregation. A gentleman removes his hat on entering a church. If he is accompanied by ladies, he opens the door of the pew and allows them to enter first.

It should be remembered that a pew is generally private property, and it is well for a stranger not to enter one uninvited, but to wait quietly for the usher to show him to a seat.

Laughing or loud talking is inexcusable in church, and if children are present, they should be taught to keep still.

Social greetings should be exchanged before or after the service, but never in the body of the church during the hours of worship. Whatever act of civility is offered or received should be acknowledged quietly, and every-thing arranged to prevent a noise. Hat, cane, and umbrella must be carried into the pew, and care taken that they do not fall.

Due respect should always be paid to the observances of the church which one attends.

It is not a mark of good breeding to crowd about the church door when the congregation is entering or leaving.

On ceremonial occasions, the guests should always remain in the pew until the persons immediately interested have passed; they may then fall into position, and move with them to the exit.

## ETIQUETTE AT PLACES OF AMUSEMENT.

When a gentleman takes a lady to the theater, he should endeavor to secure seats in advance.

No gentleman will leave his lady companion unattended between acts, unless requested to do so by her, or to obtain something for her.

Never whisper during the performance of a play, nor hum the melody that is being sung on the stage.

If a gentleman is in full dress he can visit any part of the house to speak with a friend, and it is permissible at the present time for gentlemen to appear without gloves.

The rule of English theaters forbids ladies wearing bonnets to occupy boxes. In the United States bonnets are often worn in the boxes of a theater, and even at the opera.

When an invitation is given to the opera or theater it is proper to inquire if a box is preferred; if it is accepted, a carriage should always be ordered, if the ladies propose to wear full dress or to go unbonneted. Light opera cloaks may be worn. A light evening bonnet and gloves are sufficient evening dress for a concert or theater, unless one occupies a box. Gentlemen of course need not wear full dress unless ladies do, and a gentleman may escort a lady in such a costume to the opera in any of the public conveyances. The fashion of wearing large hats has made it quite permissible for young ladies to remove their hats after taking their seats. Both at matinées and evening performances if she be in demi-toilet she may visit with her escort the *foyer* to chat with promenaders between acts.

AT THE THEATER.

## ETIQUETTE OF TRAVELING.

Whether one travels for pleasure or business, it is always well to know the times for the departure and arrival of trains, and the hotel accommodations along the way, and to secure the tickets the day before. In this way a crowd and much discomfort may be avoided.

The lower berth both of steamers and cars is always desirable. It should be as near the middle of a train as possible, as the middle car is less likely to meet with an accident.

It is always easy to obtain guide-books, and it is well to do so.

When a gentleman is escorting a lady, he will, of course,

secure before starting all that can be obtained for her comfort. He should attend to tickets and checks for baggage, study the railway time-table, and secure a carriage to take her to the train or steamer. If they are going by train, he should learn where they are to stop for refreshments or rest, and what hotel accommodations he can secure.

No gentleman will address a lady while traveling, unless he can be of some service to her.

If a gentleman is requested by a lady to close a window that he may have thoughtlessly opened, he will do so at once, for he can go to the platform for fresh air, while the lady must necessarily keep her seat.

Friendships made while traveling usually end with a courteous bow at the termination of the journey.

Ladies can travel without an escort, and may accept the aid of any gentleman whose services are courteously offered; but the officers and employés of railroads or steamers are always willing to assist a lady when asked, and she will do well to accept their aid rather than that of a stranger.

Ladies should carry as few parcels as possible, and be careful not to inconvenience other people with them.

STUDIO ETIQUETTE.

If a lady is traveling by train and without escort, she should not leave the train for exercise unless accompanied by another lady, and then they should not leave the walk beside which the train stands. The porter will always bring refreshments to the cars for ladies who do not wish to go out for them.

## STUDIO ETIQUETTE.

It is not right to enter a studio without being asked by the artist; nor, if invited, to go late.

Children should never be taken to a studio merely to see things. It is contrary to etiquette to touch the artist's portfolio, or disturb any article that may be of interest, without first asking permission.

If a person is to have a sitting, he should attend at the exact time. If the artist be at work, any notice of his operations may annoy and disturb him, and the sitter has no right to look about the studio unasked.

All artists have reception days, and ladies who count artists among their social friends, will pay their respects to them on such days. "Studio days" have become very fashionable in all large cities the last few years, and many ladies go in parties of four and six: but etiquette allows a lady to go alone, if she chooses. Loud talking, laughing, or pushing before others who are examining a picture is very rude. Gentlemen always remove their hats in studios and picture galleries, and ladies should be very careful not to pass remarks or exchange opinions about pictures with their friends in a loud or offensive manner.

It is not proper to ask the artist whether a picture has been executed upon an order, nor even to ask whether it is for sale, unless entertaining seriously the thought of purchase.

In art galleries the rules given for studio etiquette should be observed. Canes, umbrellas, and parasols should be left with the custodian. Conversation should be carried on in a low tone. Do not stand too long before one picture, as others may wish to view it from your position. Disparaging comments should not be too freely or too loudly made, as they may reach the ear of the artist or of his friends. To decline buying a catalogue, and afterward seek for information from those who have, is a confession of either poverty or meanness.

REMEMBER that politeness is an article for every-day wear. If we only use it on special and rare occasions it will be sure to set awkwardly upon us; and if we are not well-behaved in our own family circle we are not likely to be so elsewhere. A man who acts rudely to the members of his own family and forgets to exercise the common courtesies of life at the table or around the fireside of his own home, will be a boor in the houses of others. For the same rights exist in a man's own house as on the street or in public life, and the natural respect and affectionate courtesy that should be shown by each member of the family to other members add infinitely to the sacredness of the home.

Parents who desire that their children should grow up beloved and respected must teach them good manners in their childhood, and brothers and sisters should be taught to be as respectful to each other as they would be to strangers. To say "thank you," "if you please," "yes, sir," or "no, madam," to open the door or hand a chair to one's elders, are but trifling words and acts of politeness; but it is the constant practice of courtesy in even the smallest matters that distinguishes the well-bred and perfectly-trained gentleman and gentlewoman.

## HUSBAND AND WIFE.

A husband should never cease to be a *lover*, or fail in any of those delicate attentions which are due a wife, and which are doubly due her as wife and as woman.

An unkind word should never be said to the wife, or of her.

It is wrong to jest with one's wife upon subjects in which there is danger of wounding her feelings.

It is foolish to praise some virtue in another man's wife before one's own.

A husband ought not to reproach his wife with personal defects, physical or mental, or upbraid her in the presence of servants or strangers, or treat her with inattention in company. He should always speak of her to strangers as Mrs. ——, and to servants as "your mistress," or Mrs. (giving her surname).

A lady will always speak of her husband as Mr. (with surname), except to very intimate friends.

To wait for her husband at meals, to ask his advice upon subjects about which she is not certain, to dress for him, and to pay him all the respect that she did during their engagement, are among the many courtesies that a lady practices toward her husband.

When once a man has established a home, his most important duties have fairly begun. The errors of youth may be overlooked ; want of purpose, and even of honor, in his earlier days, may be forgotten. But from the moment of his marriage he begins to write his indelible history ; not by pen and ink, but by actions—by which he must ever afterward be reported and judged. His conduct at home ; his solicitude for his family ; the training of his children ; his devotion to his wife—these are the tests by which his worth will ever afterward be estimated by all who think or care about him.

## COURTESY TO THE AGED.

Never allow yourself to retain a seat while old persons, no matter who they are, are standing. The door should always be opened for them, and every possible assistance rendered them.

It should not be forgotten in making inquiries at a friend's house to ask after the older members of the family. They should always be remembered in invitations.

In conversation, no matter how tiresome people may be, those to whom they are talking should show good breeding by listening politely and attentively.

One's elders should never be contradicted. They are to be given the preference in everything. If they have peculiarities, we have them too; nor are the peculiarities of old folks a proper subject for criticism or mirth. Only an ill-natured and heartless boor will under any circumstances make fun of the old in any way. An old person should be always spoken of, or to, by his or her full name.

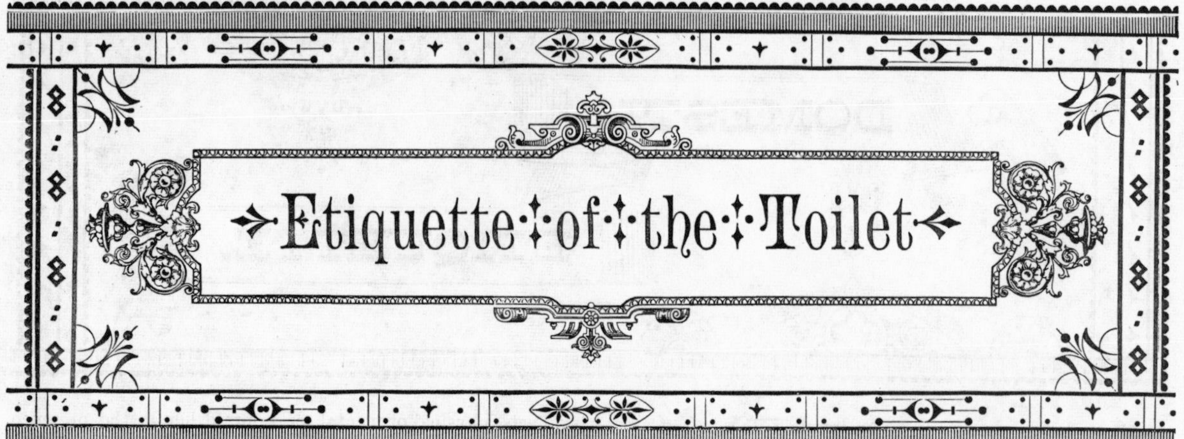

IN no way do genuine ladies and gentlemen show their superiority over vulgar pretenders to those honorable distinctions than in their dress, which is always neat and suitable to the particular occasion where it is worn. Vulgar people may order the most costly garments in the latest fashion, but there will always be something "loud" and inappropriate in their dress, something tawdry in their finery.

"Dress makes the man, the want of it the fellow." For the "fellow" is often *over*-dressed, but never *well*-dressed.

A person may be well-dressed without being fashionably dressed, and nothing is more common than to see persons fashionably dressed who are not well-dressed.

The only test is suitability. A costume may be perfectly becoming at one time and place, and perfectly ridiculous at another. A costume which is charming when worn by a young girl, may move to inextinguishable laughter when decorating the ruins of a would-be juvenile of seventy.

In this place it is, of course, impossible to say anything in regard to the ever-changing *fashions* of dress, but it may not be amiss to give a few practical hints as to what is appropriate to the various social occasions.

A mother at the christening of her child should wear a plain but handsome silk dress; muslin would be out of place.

When paying calls on foot the costume should be plainer than when calling in a carriage. It may be light or dark, as the season demands, but it should not be gay enough to attract attention.

Carriage dress is much more elaborate. The fine silks, the heavily-trimmed skirts, the gay bonnets, and the lace parasols, which would be in bad taste when walking, are quite in place when driving. At present long, many-buttoned, black kid gloves are fashionable with every style of dress.

## OUT-DOOR DRESSES.

For lawn parties, flower shows, fancy fairs, etc., the dress is much gayer. Young ladies wear beautiful, soft, fine materials in delicate tints, and make their costumes as gay and coquettish as morning attire is allowed to be. They wear a bonnet or hat—in cities usually the former. Older ladies wear silk, or some rich and handsome material, elegantly trimmed with lace, a lace mantle or imported shawl, and bonnets, not hats.

For the seaside or for excursions and picnics, use is the chief thing to be considered in choosing a costume. Some strong material that will stand hard wear is best. A shabby silk is out of the question, and any sort of flimsy material, liable to tear every moment, is not to be thought of. Serge and tweed are the usual materials for yachting dresses, as those fabrics, besides being warm and durable, are not injured by the sea air or by water.

Lawn-tennis dresses are made of some thick and strong fabric, in white, cream-color, or some other pale shade. They have a short, plain skirt, with no frills or flounces, ornamented with embroidery in colored crewels. The full bodice is inserted in a band stitched to the neck. Another favorite lawn-tennis costume consists of a dark blue or black jersey, with a skirt of the same color. This costume fits tightly to the figure without fastening.

## IN-DOOR DRESSES.

A lady's morning dress should be fresh, clean, simple, and suitable to the time of day. Lace, unless it be very thick, is not worn with morning dress. Very little jewelry is worn, and must be plain gold or silver. Precious stones are worn only in rings. When on a visit, the style of morning dress may be a little increased; thus, a silk dress may be worn where a woolen or cotton one would be worn at home. Morning dress, however, should not be too smart.

Although both ball dress and dinner dress are "full dress," they are not alike. For a dinner costume, brocades, silks, satins, and velvets, trimmed with lace, are worn. The neck and arms are usually covered ; the bodice is high, but open in front ; the sleeves come to the elbow, or slightly below.

Caps of soft silk lace and flowers are sometimes worn by young ladies at dinner parties ; and sometimes they put natural flowers in their hair. Elderly ladies wear larger caps, with flowers and feathers.

In the ball-room, "full dress" is indispensable. For young ladies, dresses of some light gossamer fabric are chosen—net, tulle, grenadine, or gauze, trimmed with ribbon or flowers, made low and with short sleeves. The wreaths of flowers worn in the hair are generally artificial, because natural ones so soon fall to pieces from the heat of the room and the movements of the dancers.

The dress of the chaperons should be similar in character to that worn at a dinner. Jewelry is generally worn in sets; ornaments never look so well if pieces of different sets are displayed together ; that is to say, if diamonds are in the brooch, a necklet of pearls and ear-rings set with emeralds would not look well if worn on the same occasion. All the ornaments should match in character as much as possible, but variety is allowed in the matter of bracelets.

## WEDDING DRESS.

The bride's costume now demands attention. Brides of the present day are dressed entirely in white, unless for a second marriage, when it is usual to choose some delicate color for the dress, such as silver-gray, pearl-white, or dove-color, and also to wear a bonnet instead of a virginal veil. The dress of a young bride is made of silk or satin, trimmed with rich white lace – Honiton or Brussels—and a large veil of the same description of lace as that on the dress. This is placed on the head so as to fall on to the skirt of the dress, equally behind and in front. If the bride has been married before, the veil is dispensed with.

Some twenty or thirty years ago it was *à la mode* to wear "full dress" at a wedding : that is, the bride's dress was made low, with short sleeves, and the bridegroom wore an evening suit. Now, morning attire is proper for gentlemen, and the bride's costume is also much more simple. A wreath of white flowers is worn under the veil, gloves and boots are white, and the bouquet is composed of white flowers only. Any great display of jewelry is in bad taste, and the little that may be allowed should not be florid or elaborate. A set of pearls, or something of the same plain or simple character, looks well.

There is more variety in bridesmaids' dresses than in that of a bride. A picturesque costume is often chosen which combines two colors, or is made entirely of one pale shade of color. The hats or bonnets are composed of the same material as the dress, or else of that which trims it. The flowers worn are generally those kinds which would be naturally blooming at that season. Sometimes veils of plain tulle are worn, and wreaths take the place of bonnets. When this is the case the veil does not fall over the face like that of the bride, but entirely down the back. All the bridesmaids are dressed alike, and their bouquets are composed of colored flowers. Neither the bride nor her maids wear any-thing over their shoulders except their dresses and veils.

The young ladies who do not hold the office of bridesmaids should choose some dainty material.

If children are present at a wedding, girls look the best in costumes of white or pale colors, and little boys in some fancy costume, or black velvet suits with gold buttons.

The older guests at a wedding should choose some handsome, rich material—of course avoiding black—and have it trimmed with either white or black lace. Over the shoulders should be worn a lace mantle or a foreign shawl, and their bonnets trimmed with feathers and flowers.

## MOURNING DRESS.

Formerly mourning was worn both for a longer period and of a much deeper character than is usual at the present time. Two years was not considered too long a time for a near relative, such as father or mother. Now, one year for relations of that degree, and six months for uncles, aunts, or cousins is the general time. In these days it is considered better taste to wear plainer and less heavy, expensive, and ostentatious habiliments than heretofore. Widows wear their weeds, which consist of crape dress, large black silk cloak, crape bonnet and veil, plain muslin collar, and broad cuffs or "weepers," as they are termed, and "widow's cap," usually for a year, and then discontinue the particular signs which distinguish a widow, such as cap, weepers, and veil, and wear ordinary mourning for as long a time as they may wish. Deep mourning is considered to be stuff and crape. What is called "second mourning" is black silk trimmed with crape.

## GENTLEMAN'S DRESS.

Of course it will be thought that there cannot be much to say about the toilet of gentlemen, since they are supposed never to think about dress, nor talk about it, and rarely to change their fashions. At garden parties they wear black or dark blue frock coats, white waistcoats, gray trousers, and hats. At the seaside and in the country, dark blue serge or gray tweed is common. Their evening dress is a black "swallow-tail" coat, waistcoat, and trousers, and white tie. It is best to wear a cloth or "fob" watch-chain with a dress suit.

A gentleman wears very little jewelry. A plain ring, small shirt studs, cuff buttons, and an unostentatious watch chain are sufficient.

Gentlemen were formerly supposed to wear gloves everywhere, except at dinner and in the country; but at present (1882) it is the fashion to wear gloves as little as possible.

A gentleman should take care to have his dress suitable to the occasion.

Morning and evening dress are not to be combined. Light and not black trousers should go with a black frock coat.

## THE ENGAGEMENT.

THE engagement is made known in some pleasant manner that is entirely left to the will of the intended bride. Sometimes a small dinner-party is given by the family of the future bride, the host announcing the engagement just before rising from the table; of course good wishes and congratulations follow.

Notes of congratulation should be sent the lady soon afterward, and flowers very frequently accompany them.

Sometimes the engagement is announced through the daily papers, and yet another way is for the mother of the bride or the bride herself to send notes to her most intimate friends. The groom does the same.

These notes should be immediately answered.

If the lady has many friends, it is a very pretty and pleasant custom for them to give parties of all kinds to the engaged couple.

As soon as the engagement is known, the friends of the bride should call upon her or leave their cards.

If the wedding is to follow soon after the engagement is announced, the bride does not pay any ceremonious calls, but leaves her visiting card in person at the houses of her friends just before the wedding invitations are issued. This call, which is the last she will make in her family name, is of the strictest etiquette. The wedding invitations are forwarded at least ten days before the marriage ceremony.

They are issued in the name of the parents or parent, if she has both or one living. If the bride is a ward, niece, cousin, granddaughter, or friend, that relationship appears on the invitation instead of the word daughter. With the invitation is a card to the wedding breakfast or reception. Often tickets of admission to the church ceremony are sent. This is sometimes necessary at large weddings in the city. As many of the "church cards" as the bride chooses may be sent with the invitations.

One sheet of paper is now used for wedding invitations. The engraving is in plain script, and the paper should be fine and thick, made to fold once only. If the monogram of the bride's family is on the paper, it should be printed without color or tint, on the middle of the top of the page. At present (1882) it is more fashionable to place the monogram upon the envelope instead of the note.

To the personal friends of the family, cards of invitation are sent for the reception at the house of the bride's father and mother.

A bride can thus select her company early on this all-important occasion; for invitation to the wedding may not include the "At Home" cards, and yet the receiver will not feel slighted if it should be omitted. The "admission card" is generally inclosed to friends, to be used by their friends, and the bride thus shows a confidence which no lady or gentleman will use thoughtlessly. Of course in country towns the "admission card" is generally unnecessary.

## THE WEDDING.

The groom selects a personal friend to act as "best man," and arrange the business and social formalities of the wedding. Some one of the ushers is made master of ceremonies. He should be at the church early to see that the awning and carpet have been properly arranged. He must know how

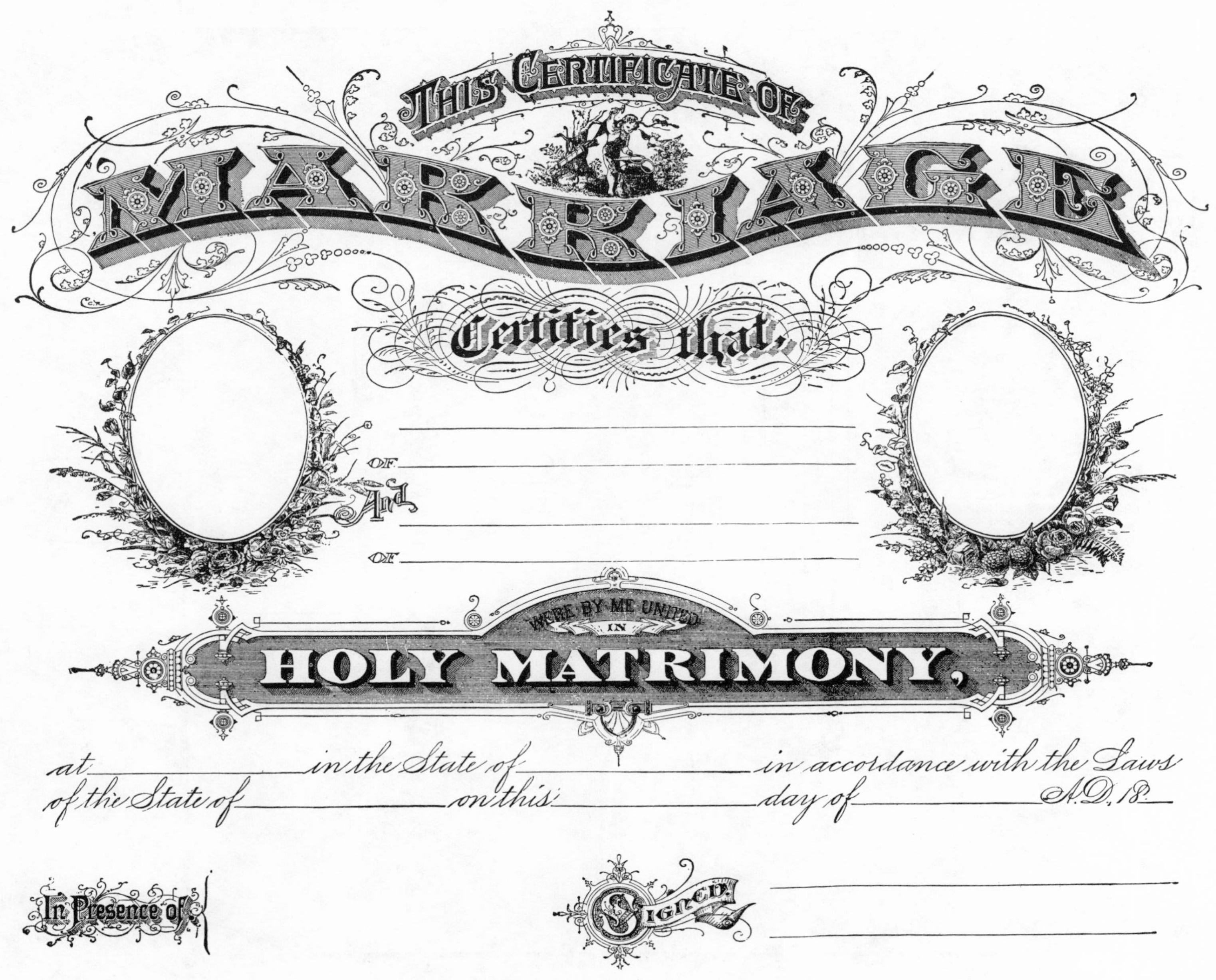
This Certificate of

MARRIAGE

Certifies that,

____________________

of ____________________

And ____________________

of ____________________

WERE BY ME UNITED IN

HOLY MATRIMONY,

at __________ in the State of __________ in accordance with the Laws of the State of __________ on this __________ day of __________ A.D. 18__

In Presence of

Signed ____________________

____________________

Family Record
Of
BORN
AT
MARRIED
DIED
And
BORN
AT
DIED
THY CHILDREN SHALL BE LIKE OLIVE PLANTS ROUND ABOUT THY TABLE
BIRTHS.
Name. Place. Date. Name. Place. Date.
WHAT GOD HATH JOINED TOGETHER LET NOT MAN PUT ASUNDER.
MARRIAGES.
Name. Place. Date. Name. Place. Date.
DEATHS.
Name. Place. Date. Name. Place. Date.
BLESSED ARE THE DEAD THAT DIE IN THE LORD.
COPYRIGHTED 1882

many guests are expected and estimate the space needed for their accommodation. He puts a ribbon across the aisle far enough from the altar to afford sufficient room. Often an arch of flowers is used instead of a ribbon. He must see that the organist is present, that the kneeling-stool is in the proper place, that all the ushers are at hand and ready to show the ladies their seats. The usher must offer the lady his right arm, and if he does not know her must ask if she is a friend of the bride or of the groom. If a friend of the bride he gives her a seat upon the left, if of the groom, upon the right of the main aisle. If the lady is accompanied by a gentleman, he follows her to her seat.

THE WEDDING.

When the bride with her companions has arrived, and taken her place in the vestibule, the groom and "best man" come from the vestry and wait at the altar with their faces turned toward the bride, the organ meanwhile playing some air selected by the bride. The ushers generally walk in pairs before the ladies, and take their stand on the right of the groom and the "best man." Sometimes the bridesmaids go before the bride, and sometimes they follow her; they always stand at her left. All this is according to the wishes of the pair. The younger sisters and brothers are very frequently in attendance to carry flowers, and are usually dressed in some fancy costume.

The bride always wears white with natural flowers, unless she is married in traveling costume. She is veiled, and enters the church on the arm of the person who is to give her away. The bridesmaids wear simple costumes in delicate colors and without trains, and usually all dress alike, their bouquets or flowers only varying.

If the wedding is by day, the gentleman wears a morning dress, *i.e.*, dark coat and vest, and light trousers, white necktie, and no gloves (if he chooses to take advantage of the present extreme fashion). If the ceremony is in the evening, gentlemen wear full dress.

The ring has, of late, been the one used to bind the engagement, a jeweled ring being given afterward.

It is not considered "good form," at present, for the clergyman or any friend to kiss the bride, and, indeed, kissing in public has passed out of fashion. Two of the ushers should hurry from the church to the home of the bride, so as to be ready to receive the newly-married pair.

When receiving congratulations the bridal party stand in the center of the room, half the bridesmaids on the right of the bride, and the other half on the left of the groom. The parents of the bride stand at a short distance to her right, that of the groom at his left.

At the breakfast the host sits at one end of the table with the bride at his right side. The hostess occupies the other end with the groom at her right side. The oldest man at table proposes the toast. After breakfast the pair may retire to their drawing-room, and only a few friends may see them leave the house. The bride's favorite sister or friend must throw the slipper after the carriage.

It is not polite to ask them where they are going, and generally no one except the "best man" is informed. He must go to the steamer or train after breakfast, and see that their luggage is properly checked, and that everything possible has been done, to make their leave-taking perfect.

The bride must acknowledge by note, with her own hand, every gift she receives, and this should be done before she returns from her wedding trip. The groom generally presents *souvenirs* to the bridesmaids and ushers—they should not be chosen for cost, but as novelties.

There is generally a reception when the young people return, and the cards for this are small and very simple.

Weddings at home differ but little from those in the church, and every-thing connected with them should be conducted on very nearly the same principles.

After-calls or card leaving within ten days after the wedding are strict etiquette.

The marriage of a widow is very little different from a young girl, except that neither veil nor orange blossoms are used. She may dress in white if she chooses, and she may also have bridesmaids. On her wedding cards her maiden name is used as part of her proper name.

**WEDDING INVITATION.**

*Mr. and Mrs. Louis Howe*
*request your presence*
*at the marriage of their daughter,*
*Alice,*
*to*
*Mr. Alexander Hamilton,*
*on Tuesday Morning,*
*June eleventh, 1884,*
*at eleven o'clock,*
*Grace Church,*
*Broadway and Tenth St.,*
*New York.*

**ADMISSION CARD.**

*Grace Church,*
*Ceremony at eleven o'clock.*

**RECEPTION AFTER THE WEDDING JOURNEY.**

*Mr & Mrs. Alexander Hamilton,*
*At Home,*
*Thursday Evening, September 6th,*
*from eight to eleven o'clock.*
*22 E.————Street.*

**CARD ANNOUNCING A MARRIAGE.**

*Mr. and Mrs. Louis Howe*
*announce the marriage of their daughter*
*Alice*
*to*
*Mr. Alexander Hamilton,*
*Tuesday, June eleventh, 1884.*
*48 W.————Street.*

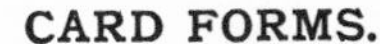


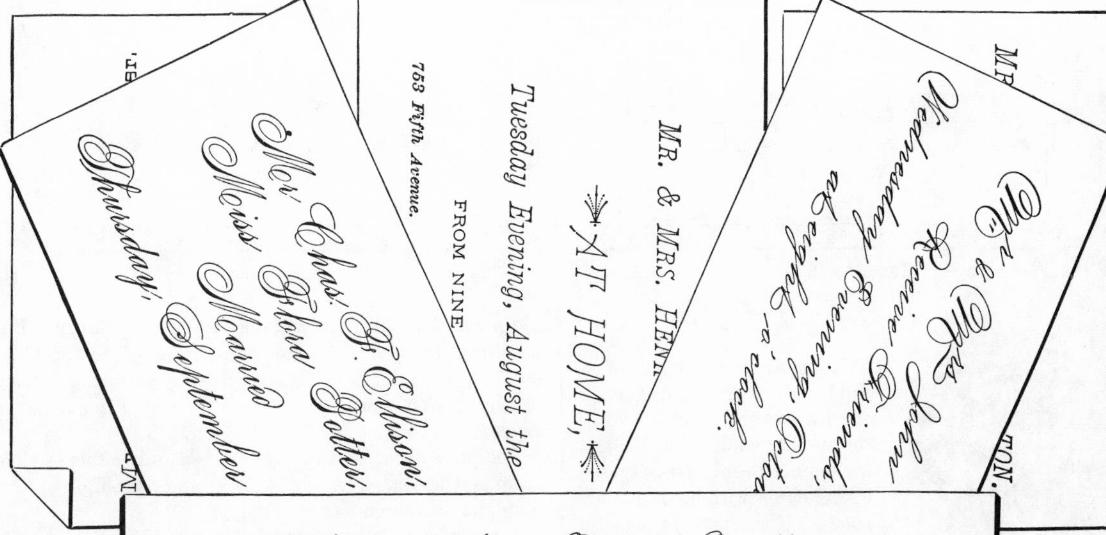


GEORGIA S. WILLIAMS.

*Mr. & Mrs. B. A. Williams,*
*request your presence at the marriage of their daughter,*
MISS GEORGIA,
TO
MR. HERBERT R. HORTON,
*Wednesday Afternoon, August the tenth,*
*at two o'clock.*
*123 Fifth Avenue, New York.*
1882.

HERBERT R. HORTON.

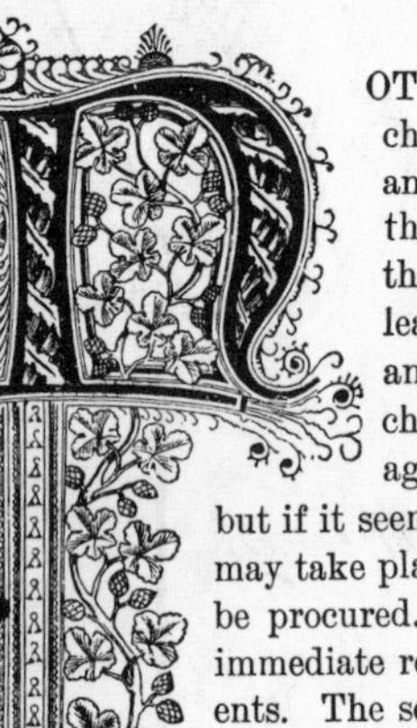

NOT long after the birth of a child, friends of its parents call and leave cards, inquiring after the mother and child. When the mother re-enters society, she leaves cards with her acquaintances. The child is usually christened when it reaches the age of one month or thereabouts; but if it seems likely to die, the ceremony may take place as soon as a clergyman can be procured. The godparents are usually immediate relatives or friends of the parents. The selection of godparents is often a matter of considerable delicacy and difficulty; for many people are reluctant to accept the office, while others again, who think they have a strong claim to the honor, are offended if they are overlooked.

Formerly there were two godfathers and two godmothers. Now, if the infant be a boy, he has two godfathers and one godmother; and if a girl, then the order is reversed. The godparents are chosen from the relatives and friends of the parents. For the first-born the sponsors should be near relatives, preference being given to the father's family. It is not advisable to choose elderly people for this office; for, although its duties are supposed to cease with confirmation, yet the association often lasts a lifetime, and kindly help and counsel may be given in later days by the godparent to the godchild, should the battle of life prove hard, should parents die, or friends depart. At a baptism which took place in 1744, the sponsors must have been very aged relatives, judging from their kinship to the infant. Its godmothers were three in number—its great-great-grandmother, great-grandmother, and great-great-great-aunt. Its great-great-great-great-uncle and two of its great-great-uncles were the godfathers.

That it was the general custom for the baptism to take place very soon after the birth, may be gathered from Mr. Pepys, who writes in his voluminous Diary, "We went to Mrs. Brown's, where Sir W. Pen and I were godfathers, and Mrs. Jordan and Slopman were godmothers. I did give the nurse five shillings, and the maid two shillings. But, inasmuch as I expected to give the name to the child, but did not, I forebore then to give my plate which I had in my pocket, namely, six spoons and a porringer of silver."

The presents at christenings are generally either a silver basin and spoon, or a knife, fork, and spoon, or a silver mug and a Bible in elegant binding.

The christening ceremony in England and her colonies takes place in a church or chapel, and varies according to the customs of the religious denomination to which the parents of the infant belong. After it is completed the guests are entertained at luncheon, or invited to a dinner in the evening, in honor of the child. The officiating clergyman is asked to these entertainments, where the infant and the christening presents are usually exhibited.

In many parts of America the christening ceremony takes place at the house of the parents, who send out the following engraved or written invitation:—

*Mr. and Mrs. James Otis request the honor of your presence at the Christening Ceremony of their Son (or Daughter), at five o'clock Wednesday, February first.*

*Reception from three to six o'clock.*

*No. 14 Blank Street.*

The guests wear reception costumes. The house is often decorated, and musicians are in attendance. In the room selected for the ceremony a font is placed, to which, at the appointed hour, the child is carried. The parents and sponsors surround the font, and a clergyman performs the rite. After music and the benediction the parents are congratulated. Refreshments are served as at other receptions.

WHEN a death occurs, some sign of bereavement should be shown, black crape on the bell-handle or door-knob if the person was advanced in years or married, white ribbon and white crape if young and unmarried.

Printed or engraved cards or notes, bordered with black, are sometimes used to announce a death. These should bear the date of birth and death, and are sent to acquaintances after the interment.

After the funeral the friends and acquaintances leave their cards at the door, writing beneath their names the words: "With kind inquiries."

Before the funeral, friends may call and leave cards, but the ladies of the family are rarely visible, save to their most intimate relatives and friends. It is but common decency on the part of acquaintances to avoid any intrusive curiosity or loud-spoken sympathy.

Notice of the death and funeral should be inserted in the newspapers, and relatives and intimate friends should be immediately informed by letter.

The remains should be arranged as naturally as possible, and clad in tasteful manner. The coffin should be plain elm or oak, lined with white, and having simple metal handles. On the lid should be a white metal or brass plate, engraved with the name, age, and time of death.

The funeral arrangements are in the hands of the undertaker, who follows the directions of the head of the family.

Six or eight persons are selected as pall-bearers if the burial is immediately after the funeral.

The funeral may be at the house or at a church; if in the latter, private services are generally held in the house before the public ceremony. Flowers are now used only sparingly at funerals, and frequently the family request their friends through the newspapers to "kindly omit flowers." Whatever flowers are used should be simple and appropriate. The family and intimate friends take their final leave of the deceased privately.

The immediate family ought to be out of sight during the progress of the religious rites, but not beyond the hearing of the service. Those who are in deep mourning are excused from paying visits of condolence or from attending the funerals of friends. If the deceased was carried off by a contagious disease, the fact should be mentioned in the funeral notice.

Guests will not salute the mourners, but will stand with uncovered heads as the coffin passes them, and also as the bereaved move on their way. The carriage next the hearse always contains the nearest of kin. The clergyman generally precedes the hearse.

**In Memoriam.**

**Maud S. Hamilton,**

Born May 12th, 1866,

Died October 2d, 1883.

"He giveth His beloved sleep."

A widow wears a perfectly plain bombazine costume trimmed with crape and a small cap border of tarletan. For father or mother or children mourning is worn for a year. For sister and brother it is worn for six months, and quiet colors are worn for grandparents, aunts, uncles, and distant relatives for the period of three months. Widowers should wear deep mourning for one year at least. This includes black clothes, gloves, neckties, and a weed on the hat.

Every one who goes to a funeral shonld dress in black or quiet colored garments.

# Etiquette of the Drive.

THE seats facing the horses are always reserved for ladies, the guests, or older persons.

When a coachman holds the reins, the seat on the right facing the horses is the lady's privilege.

Do not turn after you have entered the carriage, and be careful when ladies are present that their wraps are out of danger of being crushed or trodden on.

Gentlemen enter the carriage after the ladies, and leave it first, so as to assist them in alighting. They should also guard the ladies' apparel from being soiled by the dust, or from the mud on the wheels of the carriage.

Attendants, when present, will open the carriage door, but the lady's escort should hand her out.

The gentleman should consult the lady or ladies as to the course to be taken during the drive. Orders to the coachman are given by the gentleman in attendance.

When a gentleman drives, he should take the right hand seat, so that he may have a clear view of the road, and that his right arm may be untrammeled. He will drive close to the sidewalk and then turn the horses toward the middle of the road. This will leave room between the wheels for ladies to be handed in conveniently. When they have taken their seats, their dresses should be covered with a lap robe, after being carefully tucked in. When about to dismount where there is no groom to hold the horses' heads, the horses should be tied up to avoid a possible runaway, before assisting the ladies to alight.

Ladies should never grasp the reins, nor interfere with the driver in any way. In driving or riding the right side of the way is always taken. If there is no post to which the horses may be hitched while the ladies are alighting, the driver should grasp the reins tightly with one hand, while with the other he helps the lady down. A gentleman driving with a lady should never put his arm along the back of the seat which she occupies. A gentleman should drive in the pace acceptable to the lady. If a lady and gentleman are in a carriage with a coachman, but with no other occupants than themselves in the body of the vehicle, the gentleman sits opposite to the lady unless she asks him to take a seat by her side.

In America the rule of the road is to always turn to the right. In England, drivers turn to the left..

HELPING A LADY TO ALIGHT.

No exercisé is more conducive to health and grace. A gentleman who asks a lady to ride should be sure that the horse which he offers her, if not his own, is accustomed to the side-saddle. He should also examine carefully the curb, bridle, girths, headstall, reins, and stirrup leathers, and all the buckles and straps on her horse, to see that they are sound. Both the lady and gentleman should be exactly punctual, for waiting is not only tedious but it is liable to make the horses difficult to manage.

A lady's horse should be up to her weight, trained, and docile.

She should never strike the horse on the head or neck.

Neither gentlemen nor ladies should wear flashy dress; the hat should sit tightly to the head, for the hands are needed for the reins and whip.

RIDING.

In mounting, a lady should stand close to and on the near side of the horse, with the right hand on the pommel of the saddle, her skirt gathered in the left hand. The gentleman faces her, and standing by the horse's shoulder bends down so that she may put her left foot on his left hand. As she springs into the saddle, he easily but firmly guides her foot, which, when the lady is in the saddle, he fixes in the stirrup. He should also adjust her skirts. The lady should sit well down, leaning rather back than forward, and holding the reins a little above the level of the knee.

A rider never touches the horse of his companion, unless she needs aid, when riding. The pace must be determined by the lady.

Should a gentleman while on horseback receive an intimation from a lady that she wishes to speak to him, he is bound to dismount and give the lady his attention.

If a gentleman is saluted when riding, etiquette permits him to touch the rim of his hat with his whip, or to bow, for his hands may be too closely occupied to lift his hat.

A gentleman always rides on the lady's right, unless the wind or other circumstances make it advantageous for the lady that he should take the left.

No gentleman will display any power as a horseman, however accomplished he is, when with a lady. When the ride is finished, the lady should prepare to dismount in a correct way, and not tumble off her horse, nor fall into the gentleman's arms, as a bad rider is apt to do. She puts her left hand in the gentleman's or groom's right, putting her foot in his left hand, which he lowers easily as she rises from the saddle before springing.

## DEBUT IN SOCIETY.

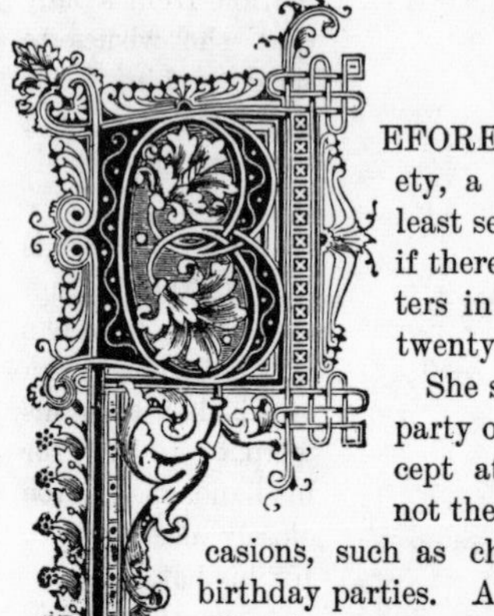

BEFORE making her *début* in society, a young lady should be at least seventeen years of age, and if there are older unmarried sisters in the family she may be twenty.

She should not be present at a party of "grown-up" people except at her father's house, and not there save on anniversary occasions, such as christenings, marriages, or birthday parties. About two weeks before her *début*, her mother and elder unmarried sisters—if there be any—call or leave their cards and those of their father and brothers, upon all whom they expect to invite to the *début*. To these persons engraved invitations are sent some ten days before the *début*. They may be sent by post or messenger.

The envelope bears the direction "To Mr. and Mrs. Blank." If there is more than one daughter, the direction is "Misses Blank," or "The Misses Blank." Each son receives a separate invitation. Replies bear the names addressed on the envelope.

The ordinary form of party invitation is used, and the card of the young *débutante* is inclosed in the same envelope with the invitation. The reply should be written and sent immediately, and should correspond in form to the invitation.

Young ladies use the same form, only they begin their note with "The Misses Hope." Young men adopt a similar custom.

The young lady stands at her mother's left during the reception. She is welcomed, and congratulations are offered to her as she is presented to the guests. When supper is announced, in the absence of a brother her father escorts her to the table. The mother and the most honored gentleman present come last. If there be a brother, the father goes first with the eldest or most distinguished lady guest, and the brother escorts the *débutante*, and seats her at her father's left hand at the table.

Her partner in the first dance is selected by the mother, and is usually a kinsman or near friend of the family. No gentleman should dance with her more than once. All visits of ceremony paid her mother after the *début* include the *débutante*, but in her first season she has no card, and does not pay formal visits alone. If she is the eldest unmarried daughter, her name is engraved as *Miss Blank* beneath her mother's. If she has elder sisters, her name is engraved in full. She cannot receive gentlemen without a *chaperon* under any circumstances in her first season. After it she may leave her own card either alone or with her family's. Of course all these customs may not be observed in the country, where people are more familiar with each other, but in all large cities they are rigidly carried out.

## THE KETTLE-DRUM,

Or "social matinée," as some call it, which has become so popular, is given between the hours of three and seven, and is largely attended by ladies, gentlemen dropping in after four o'clock. Bonnets and wraps may be laid aside, but not necessarily so, unless it is a full dress reception. For a "kettle-drum," the invitations are issued in the name of the hostess, with the addition beneath it, if she chooses, of a daughter or friend.

The "at home" should not be engraved upon a reception card, except after a wedding. A servant in dress suit and white thread gloves should await the arrival of guests, and open the door without waiting for the bell to be rung.

In full dress receptions a little girl prettily dressed is often in waiting to show ladies to the dressing-room, but at "four o'clock teas" the ladies seldom remove their wraps, and the gentlemen may carry their hats into the drawing room with them.

A lady enters the drawing-room on the gentleman's right; if she be a *chaperon* unattended by a gentleman, she enters with her charge at her right.

Salutations should be very brief, and half an hour is long enough to stay.

Both ladies and gentlemen may partake of some slight refreshment. A ceremonious leave-taking of the hostess is not expected or desired.

After-calls are not considered necessary if the reception was informal or a kettledrum. Gloves for gentlemen are not worn at all now, and white gloves for ladies are not seen at kettle-drums or small day parties.

## DINNER ETIQUETTE.

Forms of dinner invitations for ordinary and special occasions are given under "Letter Writing," where forms for accepting and declining will also be found.

Every diner out should be strictly punctual. From five to fifteen minutes before the dinner hour is correct. The host tells each gentleman the name of the lady whom he is to take in to dinner; and, if they are strangers, introduces him to the lady.

THE DINNER PARTY.

When dinner is announced by the butler or chief waiter, the host offers his arm to the oldest lady, or the lady of greatest rank, or the greatest stranger present, or to a bride if there is one. The guests follow arm-in-arm, the hostess bringing up the rear with the gentleman entitled to the greatest distinction. A gentleman offers his left arm to the lady whom he is to take in to dinner. When they come to the table he fixes her chair with his right hand, seating her on his right side; but the gentleman who escorts the hostess is seated on her right. The host sits at the bottom of the table, and his wife at the top, unless (as happens when the table is very long) they sit opposite to each other in the middle of each side. Each couple of guests find their places by means of cards laid at each plate. At formal dinners the *menu*, or bill of fare, is placed under these cards.

Soup is first served, of which every guest eats, or pretends to. After soup he can take or refuse as he chooses. If a silver knife is furnished, the fish is cut with that; if not, with the fork in the right hand, a piece of bread being held in the left. It is best to take out the fish-bones before putting the fish in the mouth.

The knife is used to cut, not to convey food to the mouth. Cheese is taken up with a knife, but the knife should never be put in the mouth.

The napkin should be partially unfolded, and laid across the knees, not tucked into one's collar or waistcoat like a bib.

Soup is to be sipped *noiselessly* from the *side* of the spoon.

Bread is to be broken into small pieces, not cut.

The man who picks his teeth at table, talks with his mouth full, breathes hard as he eats or drinks, smacks his lips, uses his own knife instead of the butter knife, or eats too rapidly, should be kept on bread and water till he learns better.

When one is through with his plate, he should lay his knife and fork across it with the handles turned to the right.

When dinner is through, the hostess, looking at the lady on her husband's right, rises; the rest of the ladies and the gentlemen do the same. The gentleman nearest the door opens it, and the ladies return to the drawing-room. After their withdrawal the gentlemen linger over their cigars and wine. They soon rejoin the ladies, and the tea-tray is brought in. Sometimes coffee, instead of being served at table after dessert, is served in the drawing-room a little later. By half past ten the guests begin to take their departure. A servant announces to its owner the arrival of each carriage.

Ladies and gentlemen wear full evening dress to a dinner party. The ladies take off their gloves as soon as they are seated.

Each guest should, if possible, call upon his hostess within a week; and if she has a regular receiving day the call should be made then. If for any reason it is inconvenient to call on that day, a card, with the upper right hand corner turned down, should be left (in person) for each adult member of the family.

Gentlemen without female relatives to leave their cards may, when unable to call in person, send their cards by mail.

## BREAKFASTS AND SUPPERS.

The hour for a formal breakfast is twelve, but an ordinary social breakfast begins at ten or half-past ten. Invitations to breakfast are usually written and sent out five days beforehand. The invitation may be an informal note, or the lady's visiting card with the following words below the name:—

*Breakfast at ten o'clock,*

*December 16th.*

Ladies and gentlemen wear walking dress, including gloves, which are taken off at the table. The meeting between the hostess and her guests does not differ from that at a dinner.

If there are many guests, cards are put beside the plates, to show each guest his or her seat. If there are more ladies than gentlemen, the hostess assigns ladies to take ladies in to breakfast.

The host takes in the lady to whom the greatest respect is due, either on account of her age, because she is a stranger, or a bride, or from any other reason. In the absence of the host, the hostess goes first to the breakfast room, taking with her the gentleman or lady to whom the greatest consideration is due.

The gentlemen find out what ladies they are to escort, by cards left in the dressing-room, or brought in by a servant. If a gentleman is a stranger to the lady whom he is to escort, he should ask the hostess for an introduction. On the announcement of breakfast, the gentleman offers to the lady his left arm. He finds their seats by means of the cards, assists the lady to her seat, and sits down himself when all the ladies are seated.

The breakfast is served in courses on the table, or from the sideboard. The hostess attends to the dispensing of the coffee, chocolate, and tea. At a signal given by the hostess to the lady opposite, all the guests rise, and repair to the drawing-room, where they remain for not more than half an hour.

A call must be made after a breakfast party. The proper time is either upon the first "at home" day of the hostess, or at least within ten days after the breakfast.

### SUPPERS.

As a general rule only gentlemen are invited to "suppers"; the viands and the wines are, in consequence, if it be not ungallant to say so, generally better than at feasts where flirting usurps the place of eating and drinking.

Suppers are usually informal, and so are the invitations, which may be made verbally or by note, or by sending out the visiting card of the host with the following words written upon it:—

*Supper at ten o'clock,*

*Thursday, December 1st.*

Suppers are variously named, according to the nature of the *menu.* A game supper consists mostly of game, witn dessert, coffee, and wines. A champagne or wine supper consists of cold meats, etc., with wines and a rich dessert. A fish supper is mostly made up of fish, oysters, lobsters, etc., with fruit, salads, coffee, and wines.

Suppers usually end by two o'clock at the latest.

A supper at an evening party or ball is almost as elaborate as a wedding breakfast. Fruits and flowers run along the whole length of the table in the middle. Every-thing is cold except the soup. Vegetables and cheese are conspicuous by their absence. There is a vast amount of creams, jellies, bonbons, decorated cakes, and crackers. Game pie, boiled and roasted fowls and turkey, cold salmon, salads, ham, tongues, game, etc., are the substantials. Ices are always served. The beverages are sherry, claret, and sparkling wines.

## LUNCHEONS AND TEAS.

Some dyspeptic, angry because his physician would not allow him to eat four meals a day, has called luncheon "an insult to one's breakfast, and an outrage to one's dinner." However that may be, luncheon has sandwiched itself between breakfast and dinner in many houses.

It has this great merit, that there is nothing stiff and formal about it. Gentlemen do not take in the ladies. The hostess goes first, the ladies follow in her wake, and the gentlemen bring up the rear. The hostess wears indoor morning dress, but her lady guests invited to lunch keep on their hats.

Every-thing is put on the table at the start, and guests help one another and themselves. It is quite correct to push to one side a plate on which one has had jelly or tart, and take a fresh plate with fruit or cheese. While luncheon is usually what was left from yesterday's dinner, nothing should be brought on in exactly the same shape in which it was the day before.

### TEAS.

"Tea" is supposed to be essentially the ladies' meal; but there are countless numbers of the opposite sex who, while they swallow "just an odd cup because it is made," experience as much enjoyment as those for whose delectation it was said to have been brewed. There are two classes of teas—"great teas" and "little teas;" the "high" or "meat" teas which come under the first denomination, and "handed tea," or "afternoon tea," which place themselves under the latter. The first of these is quite a country institution, and scarcely known to dwellers in towns. But a tea, of whatever kind, may be made one of the most agreeable of meals, for tea always seems to produce sociability, cheerfulness, and vivacity.

A white cloth is always laid on the table for "high tea," and on it, down the center, are placed flowers, and, in summer, fruits. Nothing looks more tempting than bowls of old china filled with ripe red strawberries, and jugs of rich cream by their side. Glass dishes containing preserved fruits of different colors, such as apricots, strawberries, marmalade, etc. take their stands at short intervals. Cakes of various kinds—plum, rice, and sponge; and then within easy reach of the "tea drinkers" are hot muffins, crumpets, toast, tea cakes, and so forth. At one end of the table the tea tray stands, with its adjuncts; at the other the coffee is placed, also on a tray. The sideboard is the receptacle of the weightier matters, such as cold salmon, pigeon and veal and ham pies, boiled and roast fowls, tongues, ham, veal, cake; and should it be a very "hungry tea," roast beef and lamb may be there for the gentlemen of the party.

THE QUADRILLE.

The servants should be expert and handy, as there is a good deal of waiting to be done. One should hand the cups of tea on a tray, together with sugar and cream; another should do the same with coffee, and both should take notice of the empty cups, and take them to be refilled. Then there should be one to carve and help at the sideboard, and another to change the plates, hand bread and butter, etc. Very often the gentlemen wait to a great extent upon the ladies and themselves on these occasions. After the fruit has been handed, the servants leave the room. It is usual for the party to remain a short time at the table after the conclusion of the meal.

Sometimes a dance on the lawn or on the drawing-room carpet, music, talk, or charades end an entertainment of this kind; but if dancing is not introduced, the success of a tea depends much upon the attractiveness of the reception rooms.

"Little teas" take place in the afternoon. Now that dinners are so late, and that "teas proper" are postponed in consequence to such an unnatural hour as ten P.M., the want is felt of the old-fashioned meal at five, and so it has been reinstated, though not in quite the same form as before. The modern afternoon tea takes place about five, and the invitation is by card, intimating that Mrs. —— will be "At home" on such an afternoon. No answer is necessary. When the day arrives, if you are disengaged, and so disposed, you call upon your friend, are ushered into her drawing-room, and there you find her and others who have come on the same errand as yourself. The tea equipage is placed on a table near to the lady of the house, who pours out the tea herself. Usually this equipage is one specially designed for these occasions. The cups and saucers are smaller than those in use at other meals, and are of a more dainty and refined character. The other accompaniments also are on a smaller scale—the spoons, sugar-basin, and cream-jug, are distinctively small. No plates are brought into the room except those which hold cake or rolled bread and butter. Gentlemen, of course, will tender their services; but they should not be too officious or over anxious to do their duty. There are men who will perpetually be handing cake, and offering to do this, that, and the other about the tea-tray. People do not assemble at these five o'clock teas to eat and drink, but merely to see and talk to each other, and take a cup of tea merely as a refreshment. Small tables should be placed about the room, so that people can group round them and use them.

## ETIQUETTE OF BALLS AND EVENING PARTIES.

Good music is indispensable, otherwise the entertainment is very apt to be a failure.

A ball is exclusively for dancing; a party includes dancing.

When a lady concludes to give such an entertainment she should call first in person or by card upon all persons whom she intends to invite.

The hours mentioned on the invitations for a ball are usually nine to eleven ; for a party, eight to half-past ten o'clock.

Invitations for a ball are issued about three weeks in advance ; for a party ten days or a week. Both the post and private messengers can be used to distribute them.

Unless the affair is to be very formal, one envelope is sufficient.

Party invitations mention in the lower left corner the hour at which dancing begins.

All invitations must be promptly accepted or declined.

That the supper-room should be provided with choice refreshments is of course necessary, and if the hostess does not understand their arrangement she should employ an expert caterer.

Iced or cool drinks should be obtainable in the supper-room until the close of the ball.

The hostess should see that each lady guest is provided with a partner.

Seats will not be provided at the supper, unless at small parties, when the gentleman in attendance stands behind the chair of his lady partner.

At a party or private ball a lady may accept the attentions of any gentleman in the supper-room if her escort is absent. The gentlemen should see that the ladies are fully supplied before they help themselves.

It is customary for the young lady's *chaperon* to visit the supper room with the gentleman who has been dancing with her charge.

Ladies should not remain long in the supper-room, but they may visit it more than once if they choose.

The ball-room should be without carpet, but if there is one on the floor it can be covered with a crash cloth. Most of the furniture should be removed, and the room made as handsome as possible with plants and flowers, and small trees should be placed where they will not limit dancing room, as a screen for the musicians.

The comforts of the dressing-room should be thoroughly considered, and an abundance of water, soap, towels, several washstands, with toilet necessaries for the ladies, and for large balls a hair-dresser and modiste in the ladies' room to assist the ladies with their toilet, should be provided.

In the gentlemen's dressing-rooms brushes, combs, towels, etc., should be furnished.

In another room near the entrance door is an attendant to receive the cloaks, overcoats, hats, and wraps of the guests, giving a duplicate check for each.

The number of guests that can be invited is of course to be decided by the giver of the entertainment. If the room is large enough to accommodate one hundred guests, more than that number may be invited, but care should be taken not to overcrowd.

The number of dances must not exceed twenty-four, and should not be less than eighteen at a ball.

At a party dancing does not generally begin until after supper, conversation, music, and so on, taking up the earlier part of the evening. The dancing may cease at this entertainment as early as one o'clock. Balls are prolonged till two or three o'clock.

The programmes for dancing will of course be arranged so that the card will have space for the names of partners. Great taste and skill can be displayed in these cards ; often they are hand painted, and when filled with pleasant names become pretty *souvenirs*.

The host and hostess stand near the door to receive guests, and greet each person by name, saying a few pleasant words. Other members of the family may present guests,

THE ESCORT.

and do their best to acquaint themselves with the wants of all present.

Gentlemen not in attendance on ladies are at the disposal of the hostess.

Married gentlemen will escort their wives to balls and attend upon them, but it is not etiquette for them to dance together all the evening.

A lady may wish to sit down before a square dance is at an end ; in that case the gentleman will offer her his arm and conduct her to a seat without questions, merely expressing regret.

The lady's waist should be but lightly touched when the dance begins, and the gentleman's arm should be dropped as soon as the dance ends.

When a gentleman is not familiar with a dance he should not invite a lady to try it with him.

Introduction by the hostess or some friend is necessary, before a gentleman can ask a lady to dance.

The arm, not the hand, should be offered to a lady when conducting her to or from the dance.

### ESCORTS.

A gentleman who is accepted as an escort by a lady for such an occasion, should attend the lady during the evening, when she is not dancing with some one else. A bouquet may be sent her during the afternoon. The escort must be in time at her residence with a carriage to convey her to the house of the entertainer, and the carriage should be in attendance to take her home after the ball.

Having arrived at the house where the ball is given, the gentleman should first conduct the lady to the cloak-room, where her wraps are to be left. He should then take her to the door of the ladies' dressing-room, go on to the gentlemen's dressing-room, and having arranged his toilet, return to the door of the ladies' dressing-room, and wait the lady's coming. He should then conduct her to the hostess, and continue in attendance during the rest of the evening. The first dance belongs to him, and he should attend her to supper, as well as escort her home after the ball.

A lady may refuse to dance with any gentleman if she chooses, but she should do so courteously, and he must not take offense. She may also dance with another gentleman immediately, but the gentleman who has been refused should not take notice of the fact, and be very careful not to offer to dance with another lady who may have heard the declination. If, on the other hand, the lady pleads fatigue, he should remain by her side, unless dismissed, until the end of the dance. When the lady has no escort the gentleman who dances the last dance preceding supper escorts her to the supper-room, and attends her until she returns to the ball-room. When there is an escort, he should surrender the lady to the gentleman who has the first right to her hand and company for the time.

### DRESS.

The proper dress at balls for both ladies and gentlemen is always full evening costume. Ladies wear gloves, but according to the latest London fashion, gentlemen do not, even on the grandest occasions. Fashions change so frequently that it is impossible to say what should or should not be worn, but the modiste and tailor can always give information about what is both correct and becoming.

Full-dress is not absolutely required at parties, but every lady and gentleman should present a neat appearance, and endeavor to appear in evening dress.

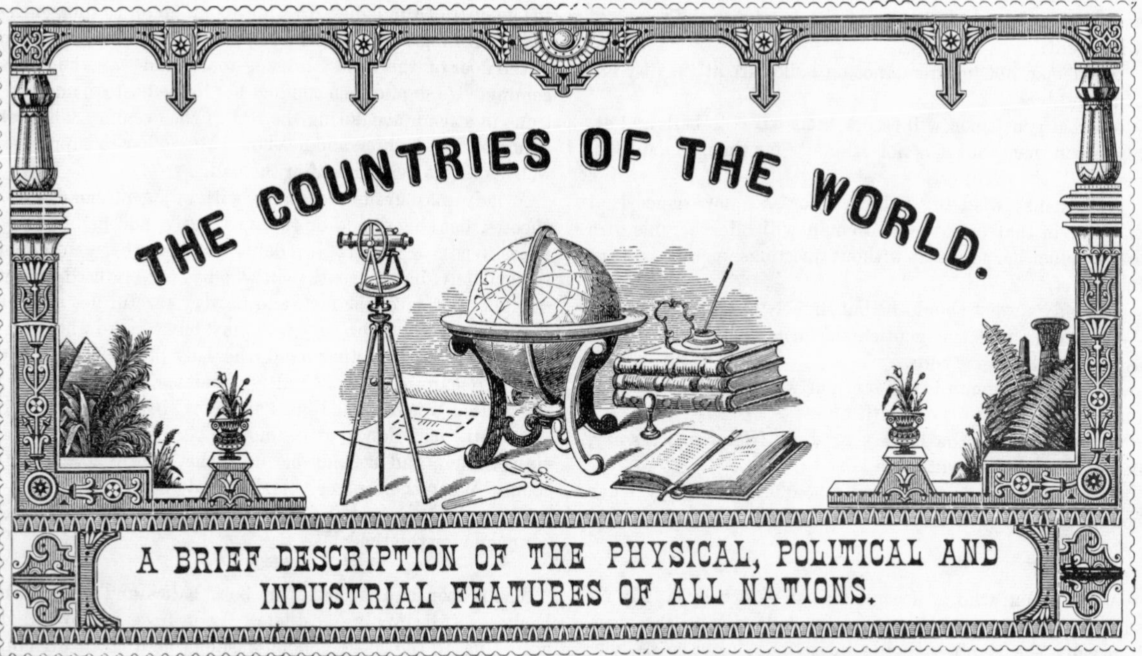


BEFORE proceeding to describe the countries of the world separately and in alphabetical order, it may be useful and interesting to speak of the Geography of the Earth in general, and enter into an explanation of the most important geographical terms. Geography deals principally with the surface of the earth. It treats also of the earth as a whole and of its relations to the sun; of the atmosphere by which it is surrounded; of the various plants, minerals, and animals distributed throughout the globe; and of the divisions made by man with regard to its industries, institutions and government. The whole subject is accordingly divided into three branches—Mathematical Geography, Physical Geography, and Political Geography.

**Mathematical Geography** is a description of the form, size, position, motions, circles, and zones of the earth, and of the relative positions of places on its surface.

**Physical Geography** is a description of the natural divisions of the surface of the earth.

**Political Geography** is a description of the nations and peoples of the earth, their social condition, and the countries they inhabit. It includes an account of towns, cities, states, industrial productions, and commerce.

## I. MATHEMATICAL GEOGRAPHY.

The **shape** of the earth is nearly that of a sphere or round ball. This fact was long ago suspected by the philosophers, because, in watching a ship departing from the shore, they observed that it sinks gradually below the horizon, until the tips of the masts are all that can be seen. Early navigators thought the earth must be round, because whenever they came in sight of land, they first saw the tops of trees, or the summits of the mountains, while the land beneath lay concealed from view. In 1519 Ferdinand Magellan, a bold sailor of Portugal, proved these conjectures to be correct by actually sailing round the world. The exact figure of the earth is that of an *oblate spheroid*, a globe flattened at the poles.

The **diameter** of the earth, or distance through its center in a straight line, is 8,000 miles.

The **circumference** of the earth, or greatest distance round it, is nearly 25,000 miles.

The **surface** of the earth contains about 197,000,000 square miles.

The **daily motion** of the earth is its rotation on one of its diameters in the direction from west to east. One rotation is completed in a period which we call a *day*, and divide into twenty-four hours.

**Axis.**—The earth turns on its shortest diameter, which is called its Axis.

The **Poles** of the earth are the extremities of the axis. The pole toward the north star is known as the North Pole; the opposite one is called the South Pole.

The **Equator** is a great circle equally distant from the Poles.

**Cardinal Points.** To tell which way one place is from another, certain names of directions are necessary—NORTH, SOUTH, EAST, and WEST. **North** is the direction along the earth's surface toward the North Pole: **South** is the opposite direction. **East** is the direction in which the earth turns on its axis: **West** is the opposite direction of East.

**Latitude and Longitude.** Distance north and south from the equator is called *Latitude*, and is measured by degrees. The longest degree is $69\frac{3}{5}$ miles; the shortest, $68\frac{7}{10}$. *Longitude* is distance east and west from a given meridian, measured in degrees, which at the equator include $69\frac{1}{6}$ miles, and decrease as we go toward the poles. The meridian usually taken is that passing through Greenwich, near London. In the United States the meridian of Washington is sometimes taken.

**Zones.** As regards temperature the surface of the earth is divided into five belts or *Zones:* the *North Frigid*, extending from the North Pole $23\frac{1}{2}°$ to an imaginary line called the *Arctic Circle;* the *North Temperate*, extending 43° from the Arctic Circle to an imaginary line called the *Tropic of Cancer;* the *Torrid*, extending 47° from the Tropic of Cancer to an imaginary line called the *Tropic of Capricorn;* the *South Temperate*, extending 43° from the Tropic of Capricorn to the *Antarctic Circle;* and the *South Frigid*, extending thence $23\frac{1}{2}°$ to the South Pole.

## II. PHYSICAL GEOGRAPHY.

**Land and Water.** The surface of the earth contains three times as much water as land. Nearly three-fourths of the land lies north of the equator.

**Divisions of Land.** The two largest divisions of land are called the Eastern and Western *Continents*. By some the island of Australia is also called a continent. *Grand Divisions* (by some geographers called continents) are: Europe, Asia, Africa, Australia, North America and South America. An *Island* is a body of land surrounded by water. A group of islands is an *Archipelago*. A *Peninsula* is a body of land nearly surrounded by water. A *Cape* is a point of land extending into the water. An *Isthmus* is a neck of land connecting two larger bodies. As regards elevation, the land of islands and continents consists of *lowland plains, table-lands* or *plateaus* (broad extents of high land), *hills, valleys, mountains, mountain ranges* and *systems*, and *volcanoes*.

**Divisions of Water.** The vast body of salt water surrounding the land is called the *Ocean*. Its principal divisions are the Atlantic, Pacific, Indian, Arctic, and Antarctic Oceans. *Seas, Bays*, and *Gulfs* are arms of the ocean partly inclosed by land. Small bays are known as *Bights, Estuaries*, and *Firths*. *Straits* and *Channels* are passages connecting larger bodies of water. Inland waters are either *rivers, lakes*, or *ponds*. Salt lakes have no outlet. A *river-basin* is a tract drained by a river and its branches. A *delta* is the space included between several mouths of a river.

**Races of Mankind.** The population of the globe is about fourteen hundred and fifty millions. It may be divided into five races, distinguished by physical characteristics, viz.: 1. *Caucasian*, about six hundred millions, the main body inhabiting Europe, South-western Asia, and North America, but scattered over the world by emigration; fair complexion, full forehead, soft hair, heavy beard. 2. *Mongolian*, about five hundred and ninety millions, found throughout Asia, Arctic America, and North-eastern Europe; complexion yellowish, black straight hair, flat forehead, narrow oblique eyes. 3. *Malay*, about fifty-five millions, found in Oceanica and the Malay Peninsula in Asia; brown complexion, narrow head, low broad forehead, black and curly hair and beard. 4. *Negro*, about one hundred and eighty-five millions, found throughout Africa; black or very dark complexion, receding forehead, black woolly hair, flat nose, thick lips, thin beard. 5. *American* (Indian) about eleven millions, including all American aborigines, except the Mongols of the Arctic coasts and perhaps the Aztec races; copper-colored, broad strong face, low forehead, high cheek-bones, straight, coarse, black hair.

## III. POLITICAL GEOGRAPHY.

**Government.** The lowest savages, as Australian blacks, have no form of government whatever. More intelligent savages are ruled by a chief chosen for his physical courage. The next highest form is that found among pastoral and nomadic tribes, and is essentially of a *family* type. Among highly advanced peoples there are two forms of government, *Republican* and *Monarchical*. In the first, the laws are made and executed by persons elected by the people. The chief executive is called the President. The United States and France are the two greatest Republics of the world. In a *Monarchy* the ruler obtains the throne by inheritance and holds it for life. A monarchy may be *limited* by a *constitution*, as in England, or *unlimited*, when the sovereign has supreme power, as in Russia. An *Empire* is a monarchy of great extent. Titles of monarchs are: kings, queens, emperors, empresses, sultans, shahs, czars, and mikados.

The *Capital* of a country is its seat of government. The *Metropolis* is the largest city. States, Provinces, Colonies, Departments, Shires, Counties, and Districts, are subdivisions or dependencies of a country. A Town is a collection of houses and people. A City is an incorporated town.

**Religions.** The most extensive religious systems of the world are the CHRISTIAN, the JEWISH, the MOHAMMEDAN, and the HINDOO. In the first three the existence of one God and one only is acknowledged. *Christianity* rests on the belief that Jesus Christ is the Son of God, and the Bible God's inspired word. There are about three hundred and seventy-five million Christians, occupying the most civilized countries of the earth. Of these one hundred and eighty-seven millions are Catholics, one hundred and one millions

Protestants, and eighty-two millions members of the Greek Church. The *Jewish Religion* recognizes the Old Testament as the word of God, but rejects Christ as the Messiah. There are about eight million Jews scattered over the globe. The *Mohammedan* creed recognizes Christ as a prophet, but believes in Mohammed as the last and greatest. Its religious book is the Koran. The faith was founded by Mohammed in Arabia about A.D. 625, and now has one hundred and three million followers in Asia, Africa, and Turkey in Europe. The *Hindoo* religion exists in India, and is founded on idolatry and polytheism. It has about one hundred and forty million followers. Many other forms of pagan worship are found, and it is estimated that more than half of the world's population is pagan.

**Social Condition.** In regard to intelligence, civilization, and culture, four grades are sometimes recognized: the *Civilized, Half-civilized, Barbarous,* and *Savage.* It is impossible, however, to classify the nations strictly under such a division.

[In addition to the facts given below about the various countries, much interesting information will be found in the articles on Commerce and Transportation, Agriculture, Manufactures, Mining, and Outlines of History.]

## ABYSSINIA.

This country lies in North Africa, southwest of the Red Sea, and has an area of one hundred and fifty-eight thousand square miles. The population is about three millions. The natives are mainly Coptic Christians, but there are many Jews and Mohammedans. The sources of the Blue Nile lie in Abyssinia. The surface consists of a series of plateaus, from which rise lofty mountain ranges. The climate is temperate and the soil fertile. The chief exports are coffee, ivory, gold dust, and musk. Since the death of King Theodore in the war of 1868, the government has been divided among petty states. The present king, Johannes II., was crowned in 1872.

## AFGHANISTAN.

A country of Asia, northwest of Hindostan and east of Persia. Area, two hundred and twelve thousand square miles, mostly table land or mountainous. The Hindoo-Coosh range forms the north boundary, and the Suliman range on the east is penetrated by only three passes. The population is about ten millions, a third being Afghans. The large towns are inhabited by Persians and Hindoos. The Afghans are a hardy and warlike race, as shown by their frequent contests with the English. CABUL, Candahar, Herat, and Jellalabad, are the chief towns. Principal exports are woolen stuff, silk, carpets, shawls, chemicals, and fruits.

## ALGERIA.

The chief colonial possession of France lies in North Africa, bounded north by the Mediterranean, east by Tunis, south by the Great Desert, and west by Morocco. The area is about one hundred and sixty-five thousand five hundred square miles, a little larger than France. A rugged coast rises to inclose an extensive and fertile table-land, varied by beautiful hills and rich valleys, producing all kinds of fruit and timber. In 1877, the population was two millions eight hundred and sixty-seven thousand six hundred and twenty-six. Before 1871 the government was entirely military. At that time three civil and three military departments were instituted. Besides Europeans there are eight distinct races: Arabs, Moors, Turks, Kooloolis, Jews, Berbers, Negroes, and Mozabites. Algiers, Constantine, and Oran, are the capitals of the three provinces bearing the same names. Manufactures are slight. Principal exports are cotton, sugar, dates, fruit, barley, rice, iron, zinc, and coal. Total exports (1879), £7,081,000; imports, £8,560,020.

Algeria embraces ancient Numidia, and has been successively conquered by Romans, Vandals, Greeks, Arabs, and finally, in 1842, by the French, after a gallant struggle by Abd-el-Kader.

## ARGENTINE REPUBLIC.

The Argentine Republic is a confederation of South American States, formerly known by the name of Provincias Unidas del Rio de la Plata. It is bounded on the west by the Andes, which separate it from Chili and the desert of Atacama; on the north by Bolivia; by Paraguay, Brazil, Uruguay, and the Atlantic on the east; and on the south by Patagonia.

**Area and Population.** This country has an area as great as all Central and Western Europe combined—about 1,619,500 square miles. Its average length is about 1,200 miles, and its breadth about 650. According to the census of 1869, the population was 1,768,681, but is now estimated at 2,400,000, consisting of the various types common in South America. Among the Creoles are the Gauchos, who claim to be descended from the best blood of Castile.

**Mountains.** The Andes descend on the Argentine side by gentle slopes towards the sea-coast. The Balchitta chain is in the southwest, and extends into Patagonia. The Vulcan Mountains are in the south.

**Rivers.** The Parana River, which rises in Brazil, unites with the Uruguay, and forms the Rio de la Plata. The Vermego flows into the Paraguay, while the Salado, the Colorado, and the Rio Negro flow into the Atlantic Ocean.

**Chief Towns.** The capital, BUENOS AYRES (population 248,110), is the second city in South America, and thirteen lines of steamers connect it with foreign ports. The other important cities are Rosario, Mendoza, Cordova, Tucuman, and Corientes, with from 10,000 to 28,000 inhabitants.

**Products and Industry.** It is eminently a pastoral country, with about eighteen million horned cattle, and 100 million sheep. In proportion to the population, it contains more of these than any other country in the world. In the State of Buenos Ayres alone, four millions of cattle graze upon the pampas; they are caught by the mounted herdsmen, called Gauchos, who throw the lasso with great skill. The commerce consists chiefly in the exportation of wool, hides, tallow, sheep-skins, and live cattle, and the importation of woven fabrics, iron-ware, and other manufactures. The Republic has nearly 1,500 miles of railway, and 10,000 miles of telegraph, besides an Atlantic cable communicating with London.

**Government.** The goverment is a Federal Republic, modeled on the Constitution of the United States, except that the ministry is responsible to Congress, an adverse vote in the Senate and House leading to the formation of a new Cabinet.

## AUSTRALIAN COLONIES.

Under this head are included the five colonies of the Australian continent—New South Wales, Victoria, Queensland, South Australia, and West Australia, and the Islands Tasmania and New Zealand. All belong to Great Britain, and each has its distinct government and legislature.

**Area and Population.** The mainland is washed by the Indian Ocean on the west and the Pacific on the east; its nearest point to Asia is 1,600 miles southeast of Singapore. It covers an area of 2,983,386 square miles. Tasmania has 26,215 square miles. New Zealand, 106,260 square miles. The population of Australia in 1881 was estimated at 2,850,000; of Tasmania, 115,705; of New Zealand, 534,008. The natives on the mainland are rapidly decreasing in numbers. They are among the most degraded tribes in the world. The Maoris of New Zealand are of a different race, being very warlike; they are admitted to a small share in the government.

MELBOURNE.

**Physical Features.** It is only near the coast that Australia is favorable for settlement. The high ranges on the east absorb the moisture of the trade winds, and render the interior and west coast in main part a sterile desert, covered with spinifex and salt marshes. The principal rivers are the Murray, Murrumbidgee, and Darling in the south; the Swan and Murchison in the west; and in the north, the Victoria, Mitchell, and Flinders. New Zealand comprises three large islands, North, Middle, and Stewart's, and numerous small islands. The plant and animal life of Australia comprise many interesting and remarkable species.

**Government.** Each colony is ruled by a governor appointed by the crown, and a legislature of two houses, in whole or in part elective. In New Zealand, four native members are elected to the legislature by the Maoris.

**Principal Cities.** The chief cities are SYDNEY (population, 1881, 220,427) the capital of New South Wales, and first settlement on the continent; MELBOURNE, capital of Victoria (population, 1881, 280,836); ADELAIDE, capital of South Australia (population, 1881, 37,892 exclusive of suburbs); BRISBANE, capital of Queensland (population, 33,000); PERTH, capital of Western Australia (population, 7,000); HOBART, capital of Tasmania (population, 21,000); and WELLINGTON, capital of New Zealand (population, 21,582).

**Commerce and Industry.** Sheep-farming is the preeminent industry, and the export of wool is enormous. Full statistics as to the exports of wool and gold will be found under the head Commerce of Various Countries (page 128). Besides gold, mercury, copper, silver, tin, zinc, and antimony, are found in large quantities. Already 4,500 miles of railway, and 30,000 miles of telegraph wire have been constructed. Total imports (1879), £43,378,783; exports, £41,229,957. This is exclusive of Tasmania and New Zealand, which exported in 1880 to the amount of £7,864,623, and imported to the amount of £7,531,234.

## AUSTRIA-HUNGARY.

The Empire of Austria, or Austro-Hungarian Monarchy, is a country in the interior of Europe, bordering on Italy, Switzerland, Bavaria, Saxony, Prussia, Russia, Roumania, Servia, Turkey, and Montenegro It has 500 miles of sea-coast on the Adriatic, and a circumference of about 5,350 miles. The Austrian Empire, exclusive of the Turkish provinces annexed in 1878, has an area of 240,942 English square miles, with a population, at the last census, December 31, 1880, of 37,754,972, or 159 inhabitants to the square mile.

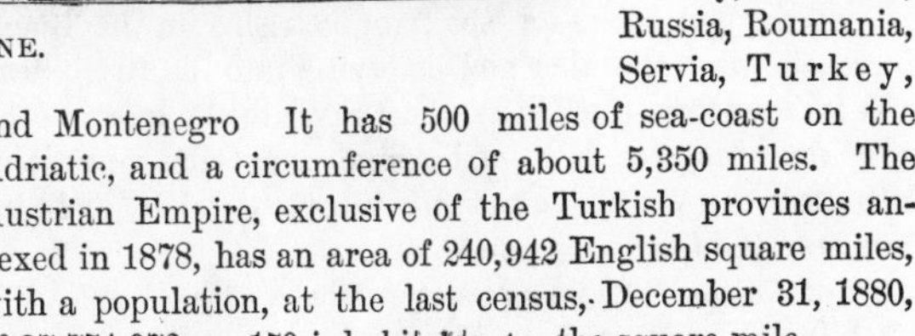

It was decided in 1878 by the Congress of Berlin that the provinces of Bosnia and Herzegovina should be occupied and administered by Austria-Hungary. In 1879, these new provinces had the following area and population:

| PROVINCES. | AREA. | POPULATION. |
|---|---|---|
| Bosnia | 16,417 | 862,202 |
| Herzegovina | 4,308 | 207,970 |
| Novi-Bazar | 3,522 | 142,000 |
| Total | 24,247 | 1,212,172 |

The following table gives the area, and total number of inhabitants, of the various provinces of the empire in 1880, and after the previous census of 1869.

| PROVINCES OF THE EMPIRE. | AREA. SQ. M. | POPULATION. | |
|---|---|---|---|
| | | 1869. | 1880. |
| *German Monarchy.* | | | |
| Lower Austria | 7,654 | 1,990,708 | 2,330,621 |
| Upper Austria | 4,631 | 736,557 | 759,620 |
| Salzburg | 2,767 | 153,159 | 163,570 |
| Styria | 8,670 | 1,137,990 | 1,213,597 |
| Corinthia | 4,005 | 337,694 | 348,730 |
| Carniola | 3,856 | 446,334 | 481,243 |
| Coast-land | 3,084 | 600,525 | 647,834 |
| Tyrol and Vorarlberg | 11,324 | 885,789 | 912,549 |
| Bohemia | 20,060 | 5,140,544 | 5,560,819 |
| Moravia | 8,583 | 2,017,274 | 2,153,406 |
| Silesia | 1,987 | 513,352 | 565,475 |
| Galicia | 30,307 | 544,683 | 5,958,907 |
| Bukowina | 4,035 | 513,404 | 571,671 |
| Dalmatia | 4,940 | 456,961 | 476,101 |
| Total, German Monarchy. | 115,908 | 20,374,974 | 22,144,243 |
| *Kingdom of Hungary.* | | | |
| Hungary Proper | 87,043 | 11,530,397 | 11,744,471 |
| Croatia and Slavonica | 16,773 | 1,846,150 | 1,732,261 |
| Transylvania | 21,215 | 2,115,024 | 2,116,132 |
| Town of Fiume | 8 | 17,844 | 17,865 |
| Total, Hungary | 125,039 | 15.509,415 | 15,610,729 |
| Total, Austria-Hungary | 240,942 | 35,884,389 | 37,754,972 |

**Physical Features.** Three-fourths of Austria is mountainous or hilly, being traversed by three great mountain chains--the Alps, Carpathians, and Sudetes.

The chief lakes are the Platten See (400 square miles), and the Neusiedler See (100 square miles), both in Hungary.

The principal rivers are the Danube, rising in the Black Forest, flowing 849 miles and emptying into the Black Sea, with its branches, the Theiss, the Drave, the Save, and others ; the Dneister, Po, and Adige, emptying into the Adriatic ; the Vistula, emptying into the Baltic, and the Elbe, into the German ocean.

**Chief Cities.** There are eleven towns with over 50,000 inhabitants ; the capital, Vienna, has 726,105 ; Prague, 162,318 ; Trieste, 144,437 ; Lemberg, 110,250 ; Gratz, 97,-727 ; Brünn, 82,665 ; and Cracow, 66,095.

VIENNA is situated on the Danube, and is one of the finest cities in Europe. Trieste, on the Adriatic, is the principal seaport. Jaspruch is the chief city of the Tyrol ; Prague, of Bosnia ; Brünn, of Moravia. Buda and Pesth, situated opposite each other on the Danube, and connected by a fine suspension bridge, are considered as one city and regarded as the capital of Hungary. Tokay, on the Theiss, is famous for its rare wines. Lintz and Salzburg are seats of important manufactures. Carlsbad, Töplitz, and Seidlitz, are celebrated for their baths and mineral springs.

**Religion.** About two-thirds of the people profess the Roman Catholic religion, while of the remainder, 11 per cent. are Greek Catholics, 10 per cent. Evangelical Protestants, 9 per cent. Byzantine Greeks, and 3 per cent. Jews.

**Education,** since 1849, is under the care of a minister of public worship and instruction. The law enforces compulsory attendance at the "Volks-schulen, or national schools, of all between the ages of 6 and 12 ; and 76 per cent. actually attend. The eight universities are at Vienna, Prague, Grätz, Insbruck, Pesth, Cracow, Lemberg, and Czernowitz.

**Races.** The Slavs are the most numerous race, amounting to 16,500,000, or 46 per cent., including Poles, Croats, Serbians, Czechs, Moravians, etc. The Magyars, or Hungarians, number 5,500,000, or 16 per cent.; the Wallachians, nearly 3,000,000 ; the Jews, 1,100,000 ; the Italians, 515,000 ; and Gypsies, 140,000.

**Trade and Industry.** Austria, being an inland country, is not favorably situated for commerce. The majority of the people pursue agriculture, and about 39 per cent. are engaged in trade and manufactures. The great crop is grain, yielding over 400,000,000 bushels annually. The total imports average $303,000,000, and exports $330,000,000. The principal seaport is Trieste.

**Finances.** Austria pays 70 per cent. and Hungary 30 per cent. of the expenses of the empire. The receipts are at present $58,000,000 ; expenditures about the same. The public debt is $1,589,600,000.

The Army on a peace footing consists of 289,190 men and 16,635 officers. Military service is compulsory for ten years.

The Navy consists of 68 vessels, 11 of which are ironclads, and 30 steam vessels, with 320 guns.

**Government.** Since the year 1867, the Austro-Hungarian Monarchy forms a bipartite state, consisting of a German, or Cisleithan Monarchy, and a Magyar, or Transleithan Kingdom, the former officially designated as Austria, and the latter as Hungary. Each of the two countries has its own parliament, ministers, and government, while the connecting ties between them consist in the person of the hereditary sovereign, in a common army, navy, and diplomacy, and in a controlling body known as the Delegations, forming a parliament of 120 members, one half of whom are chosen by and represent the legislature of Austria, and the other half that of Hungary, the Upper House of each returning 20, and the Lower House 40 delegates.

## BELGIUM.

The Kingdom of Belgium is one of the smaller European States, and consists of the southern portion of the former Kingdom of the Netherlands. It is bounded on the north by Holland ; on the east by Dutch Limbourg and Rhenish Prussia ; on the southwest by France ; and on the northwest by the North Sea.

**Area and Population.** Its length is about 120 miles ; breadth about 94 miles, and the whole area 11,373 square miles. It is the most densely peopled country in Europe, the population at the end of 1879 being 5,536,664, or 487 per square mile.

The inhabitants are mainly French, Walloons, Frisians, and Germans; they combine the qualities of the French and the Dutch character, and are generally well educated. Most of the people are Roman Catholics, there being about 15,000 Protestants and 3,000 Jews.

The principal rivers are the Meuse and Scheldt. The celebrated watering place of Spa is near the frontier of Rhenish Prussia.

**Chief Towns.** BRUSSELS (population 399,936 with suburbs) the capital, on the Senne, is particularly famous for its lace. Antwerp (population 163,011) is a great commercial center. Ghent (population 132,839) is largely engaged in the manufacture of cotton goods. Liege (population 121,787) is the seat of extensive iron works, and the seaport, Ostend, is the headquarters of the Belgian cod and herring fisheries. Bruges (population 44,833) noted for its linens, firearms and cutlery, derives its name from the 54 bridges in the place.

CITY SQUARE, BRUSSELS.

**Products and Industry.** Belgium is rich in soil, forests, and minerals. Its manufactures have a world-wide reputation, and it is one of the best cultivated countries in Europe. The coal mines produce an average of 14,000,000 tons of coal per annum, and the timber and iron exist in great quantities. There are also extensive quarries of black marble, slate, and stones for building and paving.

**Government.** Belgium is a limited constitutional monarchy, established in its present form by the revolution of 1830. The legislative body consists of two chambers—that of the Senate, and that of the Representatives. A responsible ministry, with the king as president, is at the head of public affairs, and its measures are carried into effect by the governors of the several provinces.

**Historical Events.** Belgium has been for many centuries one of the principal battlefields in European warfare. The great battle of Waterloo, between the Duke of Wellington and General Blücher commanding the allied troops of England and Germany on one side, and Napoleon at the head of a French army on the other, was fought near Brussels in 1815, resulting in the downfall of Napoleon I.

## BOLIVIA.

Bolivia, or Upper Peru, is a Republican State on the west side of South America; deriving the name from its "Liberator," General Bolivar. It is bounded on the south-west by the Pacific; on the west and north by Peru; by Brazil on the north and east; and on the south by the Plate Provinces and Chili.

**Area and Population.** As a result of the war with Chili, 1879–80, Bolivia has ceded to that country all her coast territory, but the exact area ceded is not ascertained. The whole area is about 536,000 square miles, and the total population, 2,080,000. The aboriginal, or Indian population of Bolivia is variously estimated at from 24,000 to 700,000 souls. A small number of them have been converted to Christianity.

**Mountains, Lakes, and Rivers.** The Andes Mountains range through Bolivia, extending eastward about 300 miles. Lake Titicaca, on the boundary line of Peru, is about 180 miles long and 40 miles wide. The principal rivers are the Madeira, the Pilcomayo, and the Paraguay.

**Chief Towns.** The largest town, La Paz (pop. 76,000), is the chief center of the home and foreign trade of Bolivia, exporting great quantities of cinchona. The capital, SUCRE, (pop. 24,000), has a good university. Potosi (pop. 23,000), at the foot of the famous mountain, Cerro de Potosi, was formerly the seat of extensive mining operations.

**Products and Industry.** Bolivia abounds in high plateaus, constituting granaries of wheat production, has much valuable timber, and the lowlands are the seat of tropical forests and swamps, with every variety of climate, and two or more zones of production. It produces coffee, cotton, sugar-canes, garden vegetables, and fruits in surprising luxuriance and abundance. The famous silver mines of Potosi have yielded over $1,600,000,000 since 1545. Gold, copper, lead, tin, sulphur, nitre, and salt are also obtained in considerable quantities.

**Government and History.** The government is popular in form, three legislative chambers being elected for four years, eight, and for life. The executive power is vested in a President elected for four years. Bolivia, under the name of Upper Peru, was formerly comprised in the Spanish viceroyalty of Buenos Ayres, but on gaining its independence in 1825 it assumed its present name. In 1879 a war broke out between Chili and Bolivia, allied with Peru, which proved very disastrous to Bolivia.

## BORNEO.

Borneo, with the exception of Australia, the largest island in the world, is situated in the Pacific, south-east of Indo-China, and is about 800 miles in length and 600 in breadth; area, 290,000 square miles; population, about 1,750,000, consisting of Dyaks, Malays, Kyans, Negritos, and Chinese. About two-thirds of the island belong to the Dutch, the rest being ruled by three native sultans. The chief exports are sago, camphor, hides, rattans, tortoise-shell, coal, diamonds, and gold.

## BRAZIL.

Brazil is an immense empire of South America, occupying nearly one half of the continent. It is bordered on the east by the Atlantic ocean; on the north by French, Dutch, and English Guiana and Venezuela; and west and south-west by Ecuador, Peru, Bolivia, Paraguay, the Argentine Republic, and Uruguay.

**Area and Population.** The area of the empire is estimated at 3,287,964 square miles. It extends from the north to the south 2,500 miles, the breadth is about the same, and the coast-line is above 3,700 miles in length. The last census was taken in 1872, when the population was 10,108,291, giving on the average about three inhabitants to the square mile. The inhabitants are of different races, Whites, Indians, and Negroes.

**Education and Religion.** Free public schools supported by the state exist throughout the empire, and in some of the provinces instruction is compulsory. There are about 200 newspapers, of which six are dailies, published at Rio de Janeiro. The Roman Catholic religion is established, other forms being tolerated, though they must only be practiced privately. The language spoken by the majority of the people is Portuguese.

**Mountains, Lakes, and Rivers.** The principal mountain ranges are the Brazilian Coast Range, the Organ mountains, and the Geral mountains. In the interior are dense forests of great extent. The Amazon flows across the northern part, and with its numerous tributaries drains the largest river-basin in the world. The Madeira is the largest affluent of the Amazon, and the other principal tributaries are the Tapajos, Xinga, Negro, and Purus. The other streams are the San Francisco, Parana, and Paraguay. There are few lakes of great extent. The Lagoa dos Platos is the largest, being 150 miles long, and 35 miles in its broadest part.

**Chief Towns.** Rio Janeiro (pop. 420,000), the capital of the empire, has an excellent harbor, and is the greatest commercial metropolis of South America. It has a large diamond trade, and is the greatest coffee market in the world. Bahia (pop. 120,000) exports large quantities of sugar, cotton, tobacco, rum, and hides. The other towns of importance are Pernambuco (pop. 90,000), Maranhao (pop. 40,000), Para (pop. 35,000), Porto Alegre (pop. 24,000), and San Paulo (pop. 20,000) distinguished by its superior educational institutions and fine public library.

**Products, Industry, and Commerce.** The mines of Brazil are among the richest in the world, abounding in diamonds, emeralds, rubies, gold, quicksilver, copper, and iron. Three-fourths of the world's supply of coffee is produced in Brazil, and in the production of sugar this country ranks next to Cuba. The forests furnish our chief supplies of India-rubber, and yield large quantities of timber, spices, nuts, and drugs. The soil is extremely fertile, and yields, besides coffee and sugar, tobacco, rice, maize, etc., in great abundance. The immense pastures are covered with cattle and horses, and the forests abound with birds of the most beautiful plumage. Commerce is flourishing, and there are eighteen lines of steam vessels, receiving annual subsidies from the State. In 1874, a submarine telegraph cable was completed from Europe. Over twenty railway lines have been constructed, and are being rapidly extended by the State.

**Government and History.** The legislative power is vested in a Senate of 58 members elected for life, and a Chamber of Deputies, 122 members, chosen for four years by indirect suffrage, involving a property qualification. The executive power is vested in the emperor, ministers, and secretaries of State. Brazil, originally a Portuguese colony, became a kingdom in 1808. In 1841 Dom Pedro II. ascended the throne, his father having abdicated. From 1865 till 1870 Brazil was engaged in an exhausting war with Paraguay, which terminated in the defeat of the Paraguayans.

## BULGARIA.

The principality of Bulgaria was created by the Berlin Treaty of 1878, and is under the suzerainty of Turkey. It is bounded on the east by the Black Sea, west by Servia, separated on the north from Roumania by the Danube, and from Eastern Roumania on the south by the Balkan Mountains; area, 24,659 square miles; population, 1,959,000. It is governed by a Prince (present monarch, Prince Alexander of Hesse), chosen by the National Assembly, and has a popular legislature and constitutional government. The exports are grain, timber, wool, and skins. Capital, Sofia (population about 20,000). Bulgaria contains the five famous fortresses of Varna, Schumla, Widdin, Rustchuck and Silistria.

## CANADA.

The Dominion of Canada includes all the British territory in North America, except Newfoundland. It comprises a vast territory, stretching from Atlantic to Pacific, about as large as Europe. The following table will show the extent and population of the several provinces.

| PROVINCE. | AREA. sq. m. | POPULATION 1881. | CAPITAL. |
|---|---|---|---|
| Ontario | 300,290 | 1,913,460 | Toronto. |
| Quebec | 193,355 | 1,358,469 | Quebec. |
| Nova Scotia | 21,731 | 440,585 | Halifax. |
| New Brunswick | 27,322 | 331,129 | St. John. |
| Manitoba | 120,000 | 49,509 | Winnipeg. |
| British Columbia | 213,000 | 60,000 | Victoria. |
| Prince Edward Island | 2,713 | 107,781 | Charlottetown. |
| North West Territory | 1,900,000 | 100,000 | Battleford. |
| Total | 2,778,411 | 4,360,933 | |

**Rivers and Lakes.** The great chain of fresh water lakes, far the largest in the world, includes Lakes Superior, Michigan, Huron, Erie, and Ontario, and forms in part the southern boundary. There are many other inland lakes, of which the Winnipeg, Great Slave, and Great Bear, are the largest. The chief rivers are the St. Lawrence and its tributaries, draining more than 560,000 square miles, the Ottawa, 450 miles long, Saguenay, St. Maurice or Three Rivers, Richelieu, Chaudière, and St. Francis.

**Surface and Climate.** The provinces differ widely in climate and surface. Ontario is generally even, while Quebec has three principal mountain ranges, the Green, Mealy, and Wotchish. The greater part of the country is still covered by forests of great variety and value.

**Historical Note.** The first discovery was by the Cabots, 1497. First settlement was by the French at Quebec in 1608. In 1759 the French succumbed to the English forces under General Wolfe, at the famous battle of the Heights of Abraham, and in 1763 the whole territory was ceded to Great Britain. The Dominion was established by an Act of 1867, uniting Upper and Lower Canada (Quebec and Ontario). Manitoba was formed and admitted in 1870, British Columbia and Vancouver's Island in 1871, and lastly, in 1873, Prince Edward Island.

**Government.** The Queen's authority is exercised by a Governor-General (at present the Most Hon. the Marquis of Lorne), aided by a Privy Council. The Parliament consists of an Upper House or Senate, and a House of Commons. In the Senate, Ontario and Quebec have twenty-four members each; Nova Scotia, New Brunswick, and Prince Edward Island twenty-four in all; British Columbia, three; Manitoba, two. In the lower house, Ontario has eighty-eight members; Quebec, sixty-five; Nova Scotia, twenty-one; New Brunswick, sixteen; Manitoba, four; British Columbia, six; Prince Edward Island, six. Each province has also a separate legislature and administration, with a Lieutenant-Governor appointed by the Governor-General at the head of the administration. The Dominion capital is Ottawa.

**Chief Cities.** In addition to the provincial capitals already mentioned, other cities of note are Montreal, on the St. Lawrence, an old town of great historic interest, Kingston, Richmond, Hamilton, London, Three Rivers, and Frederickston (N. B.)

**Finances.** The total public revenue (1881) was £6,105,210; public expenditure, £5,255,072; total public debt (1880), £32,248,408; value of imports (1880), £17,734,454; value of exports (1880), £18,063,973.

**Trade and Products.** The principal articles of export are timber, fish, and bread-stuffs. An immense capital is invested in saw-mills and log-ponds. Many minerals are found; copper, lead, and iron in large quantities. The agricultural products are varied, including wheat, rye, oats, peas, maize, buckwheat, and potatoes. Fur, lumber, and wool are important subjects of trade. About 6,000 miles of railways are now open to traffic. There are seven canals, the largest being the Rideau, from Kingston to Ottawa, 132 miles; the Welland, from Erie to Ontario, 41 miles; and the Grenville, from Rideau to Montreal. Over £6,500,000 has been expended on these canals, and £6,000,000 is being laid out in canalizing the St. Lawrence from Lake Erie to Montreal. The Dominion has 5,378 post offices. The Canadian fisheries yielded in 1880 £2,899,996.

## CAPE COLONY.

The Cape of Good Hope or Cape Colony is an extensive possession of Great Britain in South Africa, washed by the Atlantic and Indian Oceans on the west and south, and extending north to 28° south latitude. The area, including Basutoland, Transkei, and Griqualand West is 240,110 square miles; estimated population in 1881, 1,249,824, of which about 250,000 were Europeans, 337,000 Kafirs, and the rest Hottentots, Malays, Fingos, and mixed races. The territory was nominally taken possession of by the English in 1620, and colonized by the Dutch East India Company in 1652. In 1795 the English took possession, but yielded at the Peace of Amiens. It was again taken by the English in 1806, and their possession confirmed by the peace of 1815. The government is by a Governor and Commander-in-chief named by the Crown (at present Sir Hercules G. R. Robinson), a Council of twenty-two, and House of Assembly of seventy-two members, both elected. Among the chief articles of export are wool, copper, ivory, hides, fish, and ostrich feathers. Ostrich farming is extensively carried on. But the most interesting industry of the colony centers at the great diamond mines, of which the most famous are the Kimberley and Old de Beer's. The gross weight of diamonds passing through the Kimberley post office in 1880 was 1,440 lbs. 12 oz., valued at £3,367,897. About 900 miles of railway and 4,000 miles of telegraph are in operation. The capital of the colony is Capetown (population, with suburbs, 45,240); other important towns are Kimberley (population 13,590), Port Elizabeth (population 13,049), and Grahamstown (population 6,903).

## CEYLON.

This island is a British possession in the Indian Ocean, southeast of Hindostan, having an area of about 24,702 square miles and a population of 2,758,166, the great part being Siamese, descendants of colonists from the Ganges valley who settled here B. C. 543. Settlements were made by the Portuguese in 1505, but they were driven out by the Dutch in the next century. The English took possession in 1795, and in 1801 Ceylon was made a separate colony. The

Governor is aided by an Executive Council of five, and a Legislative Council of fifteen. The capital is Colombo (population 1881, 111,942). There are 137 miles of railway and 813 miles of telegraph in operation ; post offices number 122. Chief articles of export are cinnamon, coir-stuff, cinchona, coffee, cocoanut oil, plumbago, and tea.

## CHILI.

Chili is a republic of South America, and the most southerly State on the west side of that continent. It is bounded west and south by the Pacific Ocean ; north by Bolivia, and east by La Plata, or the Argentine confederation, and Patagonia. The country is generally hilly, with many fertile valleys. Owing, however, to the great quantity of nitrous and sulphurous substances with which the country abounds, it is subject to volcanic eruptions. The climate is considered healthy.

**Area and Population.** Chili is divided into sixteen provinces, of which the aggregate area is officially stated at nearly 130,000 square miles ; the extreme length is about 1,240 miles ; and the average breadth fully 120 miles. In 1878 the population numbered 2,400,396 souls, and comprises the usual South American races. The Araucanian Indians, a brave and warlike tribe, though often assailed, maintain their independence in the Andes, not 400 miles from the capital ; their number is estimated to be 50,000. As contrasted with Spanish America in general, Chili contains an unusually large proportion of Europeans. The language spoken by the people is Spanish.

**Education and Religion.** Roman Catholicism is the prevailing religion, but other religions are protected by a law of 1875. There are about 10,000 monks and nuns in the country. Education is largely aided by the government, which supports 810 schools through the country, besides lyceums and the University of Chili, a well conducted government institution with 700 students, 37 professors, and free instruction.

**Mountains, Lakes, and Rivers.** The great chain of the Andes runs along the eastern boundary of Chili, at an average height of from 13,000 to 14,000 feet above the level of the sea. The loftiest peak is Aconcagua, 22,296 feet in height. There are eleven mountain passes ; only two, however, are now passable by wagons. There are eight active volcances, varying in height from 7,500 to upwards of 20,000 feet. The rivers are all short, as they have their sources in the Andes. The largest are the Maule, the Brobio (200 miles long), the Copiapo, the Huasco, and the Chuapa. There are no lakes properly so called, although collections of water, both salt and fresh, are common.

**Chief Towns.** SANTIAGO (population 129,807), the capital, is situated on an elevated plateau, 90 miles from the sea. Valparaiso (population 97,737) is the chief sea-port. Talcahuana has a fine harbor, and the other towns are Huasco, Carizal, Tougoy, Coquimbo, Concepcion, Valdivia, San Carlos, Castro, and Caldera.

**Products and Industry.** Chili is rich in gold, silver, and especially in copper. Agriculture flourishes, although about 82 per cent. of the entire surface is desert. Wheat is the most important product. the crops averaging ten million bushels, two-thirds of which is exported.

**Government and History.** By the constitution of 1833, the legislative power is in a National Congress, composed of 37 members, elected for six years, and a Chamber of Deputies, 109 members, for three years. Suffrage is universal to citizens able to read and write, and paying a small annual tax. The executive power resides in a President elected for five years, a Council of State, and five cabinet ministers.

Chili, originally a Spanish settlement, became independent in 1810-17. In 1859 a dangerous revolution was suppressed at the battle of Coquimbo. In the recent war (1879-81) against Peru and Bolivia, Chili came off victorious, and demanded a large war indemnity, in land and money.

## CHINA.

With the exception of Egypt the Chinese Empire is historically the oldest nation on the face of the globe. Only of late years has it condescended to open commercial and diplomatic relations with other countries.

**Area and Population.** China occupies the south-east part of Asia, forming the eastern slope of the great tableland of the continent. China Proper includes eighteen provinces, is 1,860 miles in length by 1,520 miles in breadth, and contains about 1,554,000 square miles ; on the north lie Mongolia and Manchuria ; on the west Mongolia, Thibet, and Burma ; on the south Burma, Anam, and the China Sea, and on the east the Pacific, the Yellow Sea, and Corea. Beyond these limits, China possesses as tributaries Mongolia, Manchuria, Turkestan (in part), Kouldja, Thibet, and Corea. No census has ever been taken, but the best computations place the population at from 350 to 400 millions.

**Rivers and Mountains.** There are four great mountain ranges, whence proceed some of the greatest rivers in the world—the Yangtzé (3,200 miles long) draining 950,000 square miles; the Houng-Ho or Yellow River (3,000 miles long); the Amur (2,400 miles long), and the Brahmaputra, which flows 1,000 miles within the empire. In the northern part of the empire lies the great desert of Gobi. The Chinese Wall, one of the wonders of the world, divides China Proper from Mantchooria, and is 1,250 miles in length.

**Chief Cities.** PEKIN, the capital, lies on a gulf of the Yellow Sea. Its population is variously estimated at from 500,000 to 1,500,000. CANTON, on the south-east coast, has a population of a million and a half, and is the most important trading place. Other cities of importance are Amoy, Foochoofoo, Ningpo, Shanghai, Siangtan, Singanfu, Tientsin, and Woochung.

HONG KONG, one of the Ladrone (thieves) Islands, lies at the mouth of the Canton River, on the south-east coast of China. It was ceded to Great Britain in 1841. The area is 29 square miles, and the population (1876) was 139,144, of which 7,525 were whites. The harbor is one of the finest in the world, and the port is a military and naval station for the protection of English commerce. It is a free port, and possesses excellent docks. The main articles of trade are opium, sugar, flour, oil, ivory, sandalwood, betel, rice, tea, and silk. The governor is aided by a legislative council of eight, and an executive council of four members.

**Government.** The Emperor (at present Kuang Sü or Tsai-tien) is absolute, but is bound to observe a code of laws. The Administration is carried on by a cabinet of Manchus and Chinese. There are also a Board of Works, Board of War, Board of Law or Punishment, a Colonial Office, and a Foreign Office. The Present or Tsin dynasty dates from 247 B. C. For a history of the wars with England and the opening of the country to commerce, see article on "Outlines of History."

**Religion and Education.** The educated classes profess the Confucian religion or philosophy. The mass of the people are Buddhists, and there are many thousand Buddhist monks or professional beggars. Mingled with these beliefs is a superstitious compound of astrology and belief in demons and spells, which is a degenerated Taonism. There are many temples dedicated to Confucius and Buddha, but any settled form of public worship is unknown. Proficiency in poetical and philosophical literature, as shown in the annual examinations, is the passport to official rank. Printing from blocks was known long before discovered in Europe.

HONG KONG.

**Trade and Commerce.** The exports amount to about $110,000,000 a year, about half of which is tea, and about $35,000,000 silk. Great skill is shown in the manufacture of porcelain, in carving ivory and tortoise-shell, and making lacquered cabinets and fans. The imports are chiefly cotton, woolens, metals, and opium, the latter to the amount of $40,000,000 per annum. Coal exists in immense quantities, but is little worked. The internal commerce is immense. A railway from Shanghai to Kangwang was opened in 1876, but excited superstitious fear, and in 1877 was purchased and closed by the government. A telegraph line from Shanghai to Pekin was completed in 1881.

## COLOMBIA.

Colombia, formerly New Granada, now officially known as the United States of Colombia, is a republic of South and Central America, including the north-western part of the continent and the Isthmus of Panama. It is bounded on the west by the Pacific Ocean ; on the north-west by the Caribbean Sea; on the east by Venezuela; and on the south and south-west by Ecuador and Brazil. The soil is very fertile. There is perpetual spring on the table-lands, but on the coast and lowlands it is very unhealthy at certain seasons of the year.

**Area and Population.** The area of the republic is estimated to embrace 504,773 square miles. The population numbers 3,000,000, composed of Spaniards, Creoles, Mulattos, Mestizoes, and other mixed races; also Indians, and a few negroes. The educated Creoles rank first in South America for scientific and literary culture. The Llaneros are expert horsemen, and use the lasso in catching cattle. The Roman Catholic religion is established by law, and other creeds are tolerated.

**Mountains and Rivers.** The Andes, extending from the Ecuador, branch off into three ranges, the Eastern, Central, and Western Andes, forming two beautiful valleys. The highest point in Colombia is the peak of Tolima, 18,020 feet above the sea. The principal rivers in the west are the Magdalena and Cauca, which empty into the Caribbean Sea. The rivers in the eastern and southern parts are tributaries of the Amazon or the Orinoco.

**Chief Towns.** BOGOTÁ (population 50,000), the capital, is situated 8,700 feet above the sea-level. It is distinguished for its fine climate and superior educational institutions. Popayan (population 33,000) was the first city built by European settlers in the western part of South America. The principal seaports are Carthagena, Santa Martha, and Porto Bello. In the Isthmus of Panama, Chagres and Aspinwall are ports on the Caribbean Sea, while Buenaventura and Panama are on the Pacific Ocean, the latter port being the Southern terminus of the Panama railroad across the Isthmus, and connected by a line of steamers with San Francisco.

**Products and Industry.** The chief products are coffee, tobacco, sugar, cotton, rice, wheat, and Indian corn, and tropical fruits abound in great variety. Immense herds of cattle and horses are pastured upon the pampas. The native products resemble those of Brazil. Silver, gold, platinum, and precious stones are found, and the emeralds are the purest in the world. Peruvian bark, dyewoods, and hides are largely exported.

**Government and History.** The legislative power resides in a Senate of 27 members, and a Representative Chamber of 61, elected by general suffrage. The executive power is exercised by a president chosen for two years by the people of the different States, and by four ministers. The republic of New Granada was formed in 1831. The present constitution was promulgated in 1861. The present republic consists, in addition to six territories, of nine States: Antioquia, Bolivar, Boyaca, Cauca, Cundinamarca, Magdalena, Panama, Santander, and Tolima.

## COSTA RICA.

Costa Rica is the most southern republic of Central America. It is bounded on the north-east by the Gulf of Mexico; south-west by the Pacific Ocean; north-west by Nicaragua; and south-east by Veragua. It is mountainous and volcanic, with extensive forests. Along the Pacific coast the country is fertile, and the climate is mild and temperate.

**Area and Population.** The area of the republic is calculated to embrace 26,040 square miles, including some disputed territories on the northern frontier. There exist only vague estimates as regards the population, calculated to number 180,000 to 190,000 souls, but stated at twice the amount in government returns. Nearly one-third of the inhabitants are Aborigines or Indians. The population of European descent, many of them of pure Spanish blood, dwell mostly in a small district on the Rio Grande, around the city of San José. The State religion is Roman Catholic, but full religious liberty is guaranteed by the Constitution.

**Chief Towns.** SAN JOSÉ, the capital, has a population of 25,000, and the other towns are Cartago, Heredia, Estralla, Esparza, and Ujanas.

**Products and Industry.** The country produces mahogany, ebony, Brazil-wood, and India-rubber trees.

**Government and History.** The government is vested in a President elected for four years, two Vice-Presidents, and four ministers. The legislative power is in a Congress of Deputies chosen for four years. Costa Rica has been an independent State, since 1821, and from 1824–39 formed part of the confederation of Central America. The present constitution dates from 1871.

## CUBA.

Cuba, the largest of the West Indian islands, "the pearl of the Antilles," and the most important colonial possession of Spain, is situated at the entrance of the Gulf of Mexico. It is about 130 miles south of Florida, from which it is separated by the Bahama channel; 48 miles from Hayti on the east; 95 miles from Jamaica on the south; and separated by the Yucatan channel, 130 miles wide, from the north-eastern point of the peninsula of Yucatan, in Central America. The healthfulness of the climate is affirmed by some and denied by others. Yellow fever often prevails in the towns on the coasts, but is unknown in the interior.

**Area and Population.** The area of Cuba is 43,220 miles, and it is about 650 miles long and 60 miles in breadth. The population at the census of 1877 was 1,394,516, distributed as follows: whites, 764,164; free negroes, 344,050; negro slaves, 227,902, and Chinese, 58,400. The established religion is Roman Catholic.

**Mountains and Rivers.** A mountain-range, part of which is called Sierra del Cobre, runs through the island from east to west. The longest river is the Cauto, which empties into the Bay of Buena Esperanza, and is navigable (for schooners) for 60 miles from its mouth.

**Chief Towns.** HAVANA (population 230,000), the capital, is the principal city, and is the center of a large commerce. Its harbor is one of the finest in the world, and is strongly fortified by Moro Castle. The remains of Columbus are deposited in the Cathedral of Havana. The other towns are Matanzas, Cienfuegos, Santiago de Cuba, and Puerto Principe.

**Products.** Coffee is extensively cultivated, and two crops of corn are obtained in a year. Mahogany and ebony are among the valuable woods. Sugar and tobacco are the leading productions, and are largely exported. Molasses, rum, honey, oranges, and pineapples are also exported.

**Government and History.** Cuba is now entitled to representation in the Spanish Cortes, or Parliament, and is governed by a Captain-General appointed by the Spanish crown. The island was discovered by Columbus in 1794. In recent years, efforts have been made by the Cubans, in several revolutions, to release themselves from the dominion of Spain, with great loss of life on both sides.

## DENMARK.

Denmark is a kingdom of Europe, occupying an almost insular position between the North Sea and the Baltic, and bounded on the south by the States of the German Empire. It comprises the peninsula of Jutland, a part of Sleswick, and several low islands, the largest of which is Zealand. The colonial possessions of Denmark are Iceland, Greenland, several of the West Indies, and the Faroe Islands.

**Area and Population.** The whole area is about 14,784 square miles; the length from north to south is about 200 miles, and the breadth about 160 miles. The population in 1880 was 1,969,454. The majority are of Scandinavian origin. The prevailing religion is Protestant. Education is compulsory.

**Rivers and Lakes.** The most important river is the Guden, and the smaller streams are the Holm, the Lunborg, and the Stor Aa. There are also numerous small lakes, mostly in Zealand.

**Chief Towns.** Copenhagen (population, with suburbs 273,727), on the island of Zealand, is the capital, and the only large town in the kingdom. Elsinore, on the Danish Sound, is an important naval station.

**Products and Industry.** The inhabitants are chiefly devoted to agriculture, stock-raising, and fisheries, and the principal exports are grain, cheese, and cattle.

**Government.** The constitutional charter of 1849 vests the legislative power in the Rigsdag, consisting of a Folkething, 102 members, and a Landsthing, 66 members. The Folkething is elected for three years by universal suffrage, and the Landsthing for eight years by electoral districts, except twelve members who are named for life by the king.

**Historical Note.** Until 1864 Denmark embraced the entire peninsula of Jutland and a narrow belt of the adjacent coast, but a war with Austria and Prussia in that year reduced it to its present dimensions.

## ECUADOR.

Ecuador is a republic on the west side of South America, constituted in 1830 after the civil war which separated the members of the Central American Free-state, founded by Bolivar. It takes its name from the equator, by which it is traversed. The area is 248,312 square miles, and the population in 1878 was 1,146,000, besides about 200,000 Indians. The country is traversed by two great ranges of the Cordilleras, with the snow-clad peaks of Chimborazo and Cotopaxi. The capital, Quito, is 9,500 feet above the sea level, and has 80,000 inhabitants ; Guayaquil (population 26,000), is the chief sea-port. The government consists of a President, chosen by 900 electors selected by popular vote, a Vice-President, who is also Minister of the interior, three other cabinet officers, a Senate of sixteen, and a House of thirty-two members, elected by popular suffrage. The Roman Catholic is the sole religion. Ecuador is deeply in debt, and the imports exceed the exports. Cocoa is the chief export.

## EGYPT.

Egypt, the oldest historical country of the world, abounds in interest to the archæologist and historian. (" See Outlines of History.") On the north lies the Mediterranean; on the east, the Red Sea and Isthmus of Suez; on the south, Nubia; and on the west, the desert. Nominally a dependency of the Turkish Empire, Egypt has been practically independent since 1811, when Mehemet Ali made himself master of the country. Sovereign power was given to the Khedive by a firman of 1873. He is assisted by a council of four military and four civil dignitaries. A representative body, called the Chamber of Delegates, was created in 1867.

**Area and Population.** Egypt Proper includes only the valley and delta of the Nile ; politically, Nubia and other sterile country is included. The total area is 1,152,948 square miles, and the population in 1877 was 17,419,980, of which about 75,000 are Europeans, and the rest Arabs, Syrians, Copts, Abyssinians, Armenians, and negroes.

**Cities.** Alexandria (population 165,752), the scene of the bombardment of July, 1882, is one of the most ancient cities of the world. Cairo, the capital, is the largest city of Africa (population in 1877, 327,462).

**Trade, Commerce, and Products.** The commerce of the world has derived great advantages from the Suez Canal, connecting the Red Sea with the Mediterranean, opened for navigation in 1869. In 1879, 1,477 vessels of 3,236,942 tonnage passed through. The country is irrigated by canals cut from the Nile, there being almost no rainfall. Cotton, grain, and sugar are the chief exports; total exports in 1880, £13,307,783, or $66,538,915.

**Finances.** The debt of Egypt is not far from £100,000,000. In 1879, a decree of the Khedive invested the French and British governments, as represented each by a " Controller-General," with great powers in administering the finances. It is altogether probable that in consequence of the recent war great changes will be made in the political and financial administration. In 1879, there were 1,500 miles of railway and 5,260 miles of telegraph.

## FIJI ISLANDS.

The Fiji archipelago in the South Pacific has been a colony of Great Britain since 1874. There are about 255 islands ; 80 being inhabited. The largest are Viti-levu (4,112 square miles) and Vanua-levu (2,432 square miles). There are 140,000 inhabitants, of which 3,000 are whites and the rest natives, nominally Christians, but retaining many savage characteristics. Cannibalism prevailed until 1860. Tropical fruits abound, and the cultivation of cotton, coffee, sugar, and tobacco has been introduced. The group was discovered by Tasman in 1646, and visited by Captain Cook.

## FRANCE.

The Republic of France is the most westerly state of Central Europe, and is bounded on the north-west by the English Channel, separating it from Great Britain ; north-east by Belgium; east by Germany, Switzerland, and Italy; south by the Mediterranean and Spain; and west by the Bay of Biscay and the Atlantic. Area, 204,030 square miles ; population (1876), 36,905,788.

**Constitution and Government.** The present constitution dates from the fall of the Empire in 1870. The executive is vested in a President, elected for seven years by the joint legislature. He is aided by a ministry of nine members responsible to the Chamber of Deputies, and a Council of State presided over by the Minister of Justice. The *Corps Legislatif* consists of a Senate of 300 members—of whom 75 are elected for life by the Assembly, and the others chosen for 9 years by the departments and colonies—and a Chamber of Deputies elected by universal suffrage, one to every 100,000 of the population. The country is divided into 87 Departments, subdivided into 362 " arrondissements " and about 36,000 communes. The government is represented in each department by an officer of administrative duties called a prefect. The State aids three religious denominations, Protestant, Jewish, and Roman Catholic, the last by far the most numerous, receiving about 40,000,000 francs yearly. Systematic provision is made for public instruction, though education is neither gratuitous nor compulsory.

**Physical Features.** The coast line measures about 1,500 miles. That of the Atlantic side is irregular, jutting out in two peninsulas ; the Mediterranean coast is generally low, with lagoons, but east of Toulon becomes bolder. The

Pyrenees form the southern boundary, having several peaks over 10,000 feet in height. The Jura and Vosges ranges form the eastern boundary, and meet the Alps, which extend from Switzerland into Savoy and Nice. A little further west, between the Rhone and the Loire, extends the Cevennes range. The principal rivers are the Seine, flowing into the English Channel; the Loire and Garonne, emptying into the Atlantic; the Rhone into the Mediterranean; and the Meuse, Sombre, and Scheldt into the North Sea. The surface is for the most part level. Vast tracts in Brittany, Anjou, and Gascony are sandy heaths unfit for culture, and a striking feature is the extent of marsh and desert, called the Landes, between the Adour and the Gironde. The climate in four-fifths of the country is healthy and delightful.

**Colonial Possessions.** These embrace 463,827 square miles, exclusive of Algeria, and are: AFRICA—Algeria, Senegal, Islands of Reumon, St. Marie, Nossi Bé, and Mayotte; ASIA—Cochin China, and East Indian Possessions; POLYNESIA—New Caledonia, Marquesas, and Royalty Islands; AMERICA—Guiana, Guadaloupe, Martinique, St. Pierre, and Miquelon.

TUILERIES AND LOUVRE, FROM THE PONT NEUF, PARIS.

**Chief Cities.** The capital, PARIS, is, after London, the largest and most populous city of Europe. It lies on both banks of the Seine, 111 miles from its mouth, and near its juncture with the Marne. In the center are two islands, Ile St. Louis and Ile de la Cité, the latter the oldest part and original nucleus of Paris. The census of 1881 fixes the population at 2,225,900. The entire city is inclosed by a belt of fortifications. Extensive thoroughfares and broad avenues were opened by the last emperor. Among the churches, palaces, museums, public gardens, and other places of interest, we can only mention the Louvre, the Tuileries, the Luxembourg Palace, the Cathedral of Notre Dame, the new Hôtel de Ville (City Hall), the superb Opera house, completed in 1875, the public offices, the Hôtel des Invalides, the Bois de Boulogne, the Champs Elysées, with the Arc de Triomphe at its entrance, and, in the suburbs, Versailles and Vincennes. Twenty-three other cities have a population of more than 50,000, the largest being LYONS (342,815) on the Rhone; MARSEILLES (318,688) a Mediterranean port, and BORDEAUX (215,140) on the Garonne—all important commercial cities.

**Products, Manufactures, and Finances.** Chief agricultural products are wheat, barley, maize, rye, oats, potatoes, hops, and beet root (for sugar). The vine flourishes, as the wines of Bordeaux, Burgundy, Champagne, etc., testify. The mineral resources include iron, coal, copper, lead, silver, and antimony. The manufactures are very varied, including woolen, linen, carpets, paper, glass, porcelain, silk, lace, watches, jewelry, cabinet-work, chemicals, etc., etc. Total exports (1880) about 3,075,200,000 francs; total imports about 4,076,250,000 francs; public debt (1881) 23,500,000,000 francs; revenue 2,862,475,000 francs; expenditure 2,837,485,000 francs; standing army, 502,866 men; navy, 258 vessels; railway, 15,265 miles; telegraph, 40,954. The revenue is mainly raised from excise income and stamp duties, only ten per cent. being derived from custom duties.

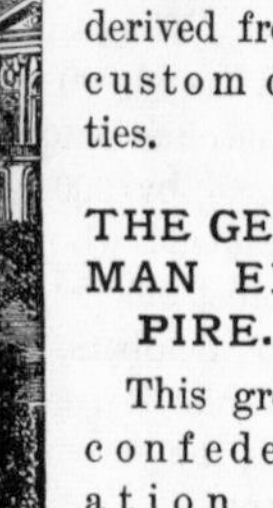

## THE GERMAN EMPIRE.

This great confederation of States of Central Europe is bounded north by the Baltic, Denmark and the North Sea; east by Russia and Austria; west by Belgium, France, and the Netherlands; south by Switzerland, Austria, and the Alps; lying between latitude 47°18′-55°52′ North, and longitude 5°20′—22°50′ East. Total area, 208,744 square miles; population (1880), 45,194,177.

**Government and Constitution.** The Empire was founded in 1871 by the confederation of 25 distinct States and the newly acquired territory of Alsace-Lorraine. Each State retains a separate legislature and king, prince, or duke. The head of the empire is the King of Prussia, bearing the hereditary title of the German Emperor (the present Emperor, William I., ascended the throne of Prussia in 1861), and representing the empire in declaring war, making peace and treaties, and for all purposes of international law. He is commander-in-chief of the entire army and navy, except the powers of Würtemberg and Bavaria, which in time of peace form separate corps. His edicts must be countersigned by the Chancellor (at present Prince Bismarck). The *Bundes-*

*rath*, or federal council, has 59 members appointed by the several States. The *Reichstag*, or legislative parliament, has 397 members, elected for three years by universal suffrage. The matters properly pertaining to the control of the empire, and in which the State governments are subordinate, are: Military, naval, and telegraphic business, civil laws, passports, emigration and colonization, political laws, coinage, banking, commerce, navigation, and railways. Alsace-Lorraine belongs to the whole empire, and is governed by an officer appointed by the Emperor. The following are the names of the separate States, area, population, capitals, and representation in the Bundesrath and Reichstag:—

| | | ENGLISH SQ. MILES. | POPULATION 1880. | CAPITALS | BUNDESRATH. | REICHSTAG |
|---|---|---|---|---|---|---|
| 1. | Prussia | 134,499 | 27,251,067 | Berlin | 17 | 236 |
| 2. | Bavaria | 29,292 | 5,271,516 | Munich | 6 | 48 |
| 3. | Saxony | 5,788 | 2,973,220 | Dresden | 4 | 23 |
| 4. | Würtemberg | 7,531 | 1,970,132 | Stuttgardt | 4 | 17 |
| 5. | Baden | 5,821 | 1,570,189 | Carlsruhe | 3 | 14 |
| 6. | Hesse | 2,965 | 936,944 | Darmstadt | 3 | 9 |
| 7. | Mechlenburg-Schwerin | 5,138 | 576,827 | Schwerin | 2 | 6 |
| 8. | Saxe-Weimar | 1,404 | 309,503 | Weimar | 1 | 3 |
| 9. | Mecklenburg-Strelitz | 1,131 | 100,269 | Strelitz | 1 | 1 |
| 10. | Oldenburg | 2,470 | 337,454 | Oldenburg | 1 | 3 |
| 11. | Brunswick | 1,425 | 349,429 | Brunswick | 2 | 3 |
| 12. | Saxe-Meiningen | 952 | 207,147 | Meiningen | 1 | 2 |
| 13 | Saxe-Altenberg | 510 | 155 062 | Altenberg | 1 | 1 |
| 14. | Saxe-Coburg and Gotha | 760 | 194,479 | Coburg and Gotha | 1 | 2 |
| 15 | Anhalt | 907 | 232,747 | Dessau | 1 | 2 |
| 16. | Schwarzburg Rudolstadt | 364 | 80,149 | Rudolstadt | 1 | 1 |
| 17. | Schwarz Sondershausen | 332 | 71,083 | Sonderhausen | 1 | 1 |
| 18. | Waldeck | 438 | 56,548 | Korbach | 1 | 1 |
| 19. | Reuss (elder line) | 122 | 50,782 | Greiz | 1 | 1 |
| 20. | Reuss (younger line) | 320 | 101,265 | Schleiz | 1 | 1 |
| 21. | Schaumburg Lippe | 171 | 35,332 | Bückeburg | 1 | 1 |
| 22. | Lippe | 438 | 120,214 | Detmold | 1 | 1 |
| 23. | Lubeck | 109 | 63,571 | | 1 | 1 |
| 24. | Bremen | 97 | 156,229 | | 1 | 1 |
| 25. | Hamburg | 157 | 454,041 | | 1 | 3 |
| 26. | Alsace-Lorraine | 5,603 | 1,571,971 | Strasburg | 1 | 15 |
| | Total of all Germany | 208,744 | 45,194,177 | | 59 | 397 |

**Physical Features.** Germany is naturally divided into two parts, North and South Germany, by the great line of mountains ending on the frontiers of Poland and Hungary in the Carpathians, and including the Hartz, the Erzegebirge, the Riesenbirge, the Thuringerwald, and other ranges. North of this line the country is flat. South Germany is more diversified, being traversed by the Schwarzwald (Black Forest) and the Bavarian Alps. On all the elevated lands are valuable timber forests. The coast line is about 950 miles in extent. There are about 50 navigable rivers, draining three great river-basins into the North, Baltic, and Black Seas. The Rhine, famous for its castles and vineyards; the Danube, the Main, the Weser, the Elbe, the Ems, and the Oder, rank among the noblest and largest rivers of Europe. The lakes, though numerous, are small and unimportant. The climate is remarkably uniform and is especially mild in the valleys of the Rhine and Main.

**Principal Cities.** The capitals of the various States have already been mentioned. BERLIN, the capital of the empire as well as of Prussia, had in 1880 a population of 1,122,385. It lies on a small stream called the Spree, a tributary of the Elbe. It is the seat of a great university and of important industrial establishments. Among the finest public buildings are the royal palaces, the Prussian and Imperial houses of legislature, the Museum, Exchange, University, National Gallery, and Opera House. *Unter der Linden* is a magnificent promenade, three-quarters of a mile long and 160 feet wide, with a double avenue of lime trees. HAMBURG and BREMEN are free cities and of great commercial importance. The former (population, 290,055) lies on the Elbe about 70 miles from the sea, and is the leading commercial city of Europe. BREMEN (population, 112,158) is situated on the Weser. BRESLAU (population, 272,390) is the greatest wool market of the continent. MUNICH (population, 229,343), the capital of Bavaria, is renowned for its library, university, and art gallery. FRANKFORT-ON-THE-MAIN (population, 137,600) is a great financial and banking center. DRESDEN (population, 220,216) is noted for its porcelain and china.

**Religion and Education.** Of the entire population, about 27 millions are Protestants, 15 millions Roman Catholics, and 500,000 Jews. Education is compulsory. There are 21 universities, those at Berlin, Heidelberg, Munich, Leipsic, Göttingen, and Freiburg being unrivaled. There are also 16 polytechnic institutes, 500 high schools, and many schools of agriculture, commerce, and other technical subjects. Primary education is supported from the local rates.

**Products, Manufactures, and Finance.** The principal agricultural products are wheat, barley, buckwheat, oats, flax, hemp, potatoes, madder, chicory, rape-seed, tobacco, and hops. The vine is extensively cultivated in the valleys of the Middle Rhine, the Danube, Main, Moselle, and Neckar. Among the chief manufactures are linen (in Silesia, Saxony, and Westphalia), cotton and woolen goods (in Prussia, Silesia, Saxony, and Brandenburg), silk (in the Rhine provinces), hardware, glass, musical instruments, leather, clocks, and toys. Total exports (1880), $705,375,000; imports, $973,200,000; revenue (1881), $148,239,138, half derived from customs; total expenditure, $147,695,846, of which $90,600,000 was for the army; public debt about $88,000,000. The army on a peace footing is 445,402 men; navy 86 vessels, 15,800 men. Military service is compulsory on every German capable of bearing arms. Railways, 21,367 miles, about 10,000 owned by the government; telegraph lines, 33,660 miles; number of post-offices, 7,540; the telegraph and postal service is worked by the government; emigration (1880), 106,180, the greater part to the United States.

BERLIN.

## GREAT BRITAIN AND IRELAND.

Great Britain, the largest of the British isles, is bounded north by the North Sea; east by the German Ocean; south by the English Channel; and west by St. George's Channel and the Atlantic. It constitutes the larger portion of the United Kingdom of Great Britain and Ireland, and includes England, Wales, Scotland, the Channel Islands, and the Isle of Man. Its length from north to south is 587 miles, and its greatest breadth from east to west about 360; area, 89,539 square miles; population (1881), including army, navy, and seamen abroad, 30,086,723. To the west lies Ireland, separated from Scotland on the north-east by the North Channel, from England by the Irish Sea and St. George's Channel, and surrounded by the Atlantic; area, 31,784 square miles; population (1881), 5,159,839. The colonial possessions of the British Empire, on which "the sun never sets," are described under their respective names, but to give a comprehensive view of the whole, we annex the following table :—

| NAME OF COUNTRY. | Area in Sq. Mls. | Populat'n | Revenue. | Public Debt |
|---|---|---|---|---|
| | | | £ | £ |
| Great Britain and Ireland... | 121,115 | 35,250,000 | 84,045,000 | 769,000,000 |
| Indian Possessions, etc.... | 1,558,254 | 253,000,000 | 68,500,000 | 152,000,000 |
| Other Eastern Possessions.. | 30,000 | 3,700,000 | 2,500,000 | 2,000,000 |
| Australasia.... ............ | 3,173,310 | 2,850,000 | 16,000,000 | 80,000,000 |
| North America............ | 3,620,500 | 4,350,000 | 6,105,000 | 32,500,000 |
| Guiana, etc................ | 100,000 | 200,000 | 400,000 | 500,000 |
| Africa ..................... | 270,000 | 2,250,000 | 3,500,000 | 12,500,000 |
| West Indies, etc........... | 12,707 | 1,250,000 | 1,500,000 | 1,400,000 |
| European Possessions...... | 120 | 160,000 | 250,000 | 350,000 |
| Various Settlements........ | 96,171 | 200,000 | 550,000 | 650,000 |
| Totals................ | 8,982,177 | 303,210,000 | 183,750,000 | 1,050,900,000 |

**Government and Constitution.** The British Empire is under a limited or constitutional monarchy. The present, or Hanoverian, family have occupied the throne since the peaceful Revolution of 1714. Queen Victoria succeeded to the Crown in 1837. There is no written constitution, but by the term British Constitution is meant the system of fundamental principles and rules of government established by long usage and ancient precedent. By this constitution the supreme legislative function is vested in Parliament, which has exclusive power over taxation. As the Mutiny Act and the Supplies are granted for a year only, the Crown is obliged to assemble Parliament at least annually. The Upper House, or House of Lords, consisted in 1880 of 537 members; there were 5 peers of the Queen's family, two archbishops and 24 bishops, 201 dukes, marquises, earls, and viscounts, 261 barons, 16 Scottish and 18 Irish representative peers. The Lower House, or House of Commons, had 658 members, elected by limited suffrage. Though the executive power is theoretically in the Crown, it is practically exercised by a Cabinet of 13 members, headed by the First Lord of the Treasury, known as the Premier (at present the Right Hon. Wm. Ewart Gladstone). The tenure of office of the Premier and his Ministry depends upon their receiving the support of a majority in the House. If the Premier fails to do this on a test measure, a custom, as strong as law, though not a law, compels him to resign. A summary of English history will be found elsewhere. For purposes of administration, England is divided into 40 counties, Wales into 12, Scotland into 33, and Ireland into 32. In each are found a lord-lieutenant, sheriff, and justices of the peace.

**Religion and Education.** The Church of England is established as the state religion in England and Wales, though full freedom is granted to all sects. In Ireland the Church has been dis-established by an act taking effect in 1871. In Scotland the Presbyterian is the established Church. The members of the Episcopal Church in the kingdom are estimated at about 13 millions; of the Roman Catholic, about 6,200,000. Education is widely extended, about £4,000,000 being spent annually for elementary schools. The great universities of Oxford and Cambridge are seconded by the University of London, King's College, and the Victoria University of Manchester, in England; by St. Andrews, Aberdeen, Edinburgh and Glasgow Universities, in Scotland; and the Dublin University, in Ireland.

HOUSES OF PARLIAMENT.

**Physical Features.** The form of ENGLAND somewhat resembles a triangle, the base being the south coast. The entire coast line, with its bold sweeps, capacious bays, and wide estuaries, is at least 2,000 miles in length. In the north the Cheviot Hills and Solway Frith mark the Scottish boundary. Extending south lie the Northern, Cumbrian, and Devonian mountain ranges, and in the smaller counties are many chalk cliffs; but the greater part of the country is level or rolling plains, presenting a beautiful variety of scenery and fertile fields. The richest parts are in general the midland and southern counties. The principal river systems are those of the Thames in the south, the affluents of the Wash, the Humber (all flowing eastward), and the Mersey and Severn, emptying into the Irish Sea and Bristol Channel. The lakes of Windermere, Ulleswater, Derwentwater, and others in Cumberland and Westmoreland, are famous for their beauty and poetical associations. WALES has a coast line of 360 miles, inclosing the Cardigan Bay in a great curve. It approaches in form a peninsula. The surface is generally mountainous, the Snowdonian, Cambrian, and Plinlimmon ranges having many projecting spurs. Mt. Snowdon rises to a height of 3,590 feet. The chief rivers are the Dee, Severn, Wye, and Usk. SCOTLAND is very irregular in shape, with a continually indented coast. Its surface is almost covered with rugged mountain chains, moors, and forests. The Grampian Mountains are the highest in Great Britain, the loftiest summit being that of Ben Nevis, 4,406 feet in height. In the south the river Tweed and the Forth discharge into the North Sea, and the Clyde into the Firth of Clyde. Further north are the Tay, the Esk, the Dee, and the Spey. The inland lakes, or *lochs*, are numerous; among the largest and most famous are Lochs Lomond, Ness, Tay, and Katrine. The principal groups of islands are the Orkneys and Shetlands to the north-east, and the Hebrides on the west coast. IRELAND has also a deeply indented coast on the west, that on the east being comparatively regular; the total coast line is about 2,200 miles in length. The mountain chains are few and of little importance. Chief among the rivers are the Shannon (215 miles long), the Lee, the Blackwater, the Liffey, the Boyne, and the Bann. Of the lakes or *loughs*, Lough Neagh is noted for its size (150 square miles), and the three Lakes of Killarney for their wonderful beauty.

**Chief Cities.** LONDON, the capital of the kingdom, is the largest and richest city in the world (population, 1881, with suburbs, 4,764,312). It lies on both side of the Thames, and has an area of 118 square miles. Among the chief public buildings and places of interest we can merely mention the Tower, the Houses of Parliament, St. Paul's Cathedral, Westminster Abbey, the Guild Hall, the Post-Office, the Royal Exchange, the Monument, the Tunnel, London Bridge, Buckingham and St. James Places, Hyde and Regent Parks, the British Museum, South Kensington Museum, the National Gallery, and the Albert Memorial. London engrosses a large share of the trade of the kingdom, and carries on a variety of manufactures. Next in size is the city of LIVERPOOL (population, 1881, 552,425), situated at the mouth of the Mersey, on the west coast. It is famous for its splendid system of docks, and is of great commercial importance. Here is the landing-place of the great steamship lines to America and Australia. Among the great manufacturing cities are Manchester (population 341,508), famous for its cotton mills; Leeds (population 309,126), for its woolens; Birmingham (population 400,757), for its hardware, and Sheffield (population 284,410), for its cutlery. There are in England eighteen cities with over 100,000 inhabitants. EDINBURGH, the ancient capital of Scotland (population, 1881, 228,190), stands near the Firth of Forth, Leith being its sea-port. It is picturesquely situated on high ground, guarded by the ancient castle on a precipitous rock to the west. It is specially noted as a literary center, and for its excellent university. The chief commercial city, GLASGOW (population 571,532), owes its rapid growth to both commerce and manufactures. The greatest iron ship-building establishments of the world are at Glasgow on the Clyde. Other important towns are Dundee (population 140,465), Aberdeen (105,818), Greenock, Leith, and Perth. In Ireland the chief cities are DUBLIN, the metropolis (population Dublin, 1881, 249,486), situated at the mouth of the Liffey, and the residence of the lord-lieutenant; Cork, the chief seaport; Belfast, Galway, and Queenstown.

LONDON.

Dublin is built in rectangular form, and surrounded by a road, 9 miles long, called the Circular. The business part is chiefly on the west side of the Liffey. The poorer portion is called "the Liberties." The finest street is Sackville Street, half a mile long and 120 ft. wide. At the west end of the city lies Phœnix Park, a royal demesne. Among the finest buildings are the Royal Exchange, Post Office, Bank (formerly the Parliament House), Trinity College, and St. Patrick's Cathedral.

**Agriculture, Manufactures, and Finances.** The land is in the hands of comparatively few proprietors, and is very closely cultivated. The usual cereals are produced in large quantities, but breadstuffs and all kinds of provisions are imported to an enormous extent, chiefly from the United States. There are few indigenous fruits, but most temperate fruit is cultivated. The growing of hops constitutes a large industry in Kent. Timber of excellent quality is abundant. The minerals are valuable and varied. Coal abounds in the northern counties; iron in Lancashire, Shropshire, and elsewhere; tin in Cornwall and Devonshire; copper in several counties. There are also mines of freestone, marble, rock salt, and clay. But it is to her manufactures that England owes her commercial greatness. The six principal articles of export and the amount of each sent out in 1880, were: 1. Cotton manufactures, £75,564,056; 2. Woolen and worsted manufactures, £20,609,917; 3. Iron and steel, £28,390,316; 4. Coal and fuel, £8,372,933; 5. Linen manufactures, £7,047,361; 6. Machinery, £9,263,516. Total imports (1880), £411,229,565; total exports (including exports of colonial and foreign produce), £286,405,466; net revenue (1880–81), £84,041,288; gross expenditure, £83,107,294; total public debt (March 31, 1881), £709,708,527. The revenue is derived principally from excise, customs, stamp, land, and income duties, in relative importance as given. The army embraces 113,190 men and 7,221 officers; the volunteer militia system is unexcelled; navy, 243 vessels, 58,800 officers and men; 68 ironclads carry 438 guns. The mercantile shipping statistics show, as employed in foreign trade, 4,518 sailing vessels of 2,924,407 tonnage, and 2,293 steam vessels of 2,289,179 tonnage. The railway system includes 17,696 miles of line, with receipts of nearly £62,000,000. The telegraph is consolidated with the postal system; miles of line, 5,735; miles of wire, 117,100; number of post-offices, 13,982, of which 5,269 were open for telegraph business; number of letters carried, about 1,176 millions; cards, 126 millions; newspapers, etc., 381 millions.

## GREECE.

Modern Greece is a maritime country, in south-east Europe, having an area of 20,018 square miles, and a population of 1,679,775. After the Turko-Russian war Greece acquired from Turkey a portion of Thessaly and Epirus, an area of about 5,000 square miles, with 388,000 inhabitants.

The continental part of Greece is nearly divided by the gulfs of Lepanto and Patras on the west, and Ægina on the east. Greece includes the Ionian Isles and the Ægean archipelago. The surface is very mountainous, the coasts elevated and irregular. The Constitution of 1864 established a Legislative Chamber of 187 deputies, elected for four years by universal suffrage. King George I. was elected in 1863. The principal exports are fruit, olive oil, and raw products. Public debt, $86,264,800 ; exports, about $15,000,000 per annum. Capital, ATHENS, population (1879), 84,992, including the Piræus. There are only seven and a half miles of railway, from Athens to the Piræus ; telegraph, 1,540 miles. The inhabitants mostly belong to the Orthodox Greek Church.

## GUIANA.

Guiana lies on the northern coast of South America, east of Venezuela, bounded by the Atlantic, the Amazon, and the Orinoco. The western part belongs to England, the eastern to France, and the center to Holland. The soil is very fertile, and the climate is hot and unhealthy. There are two wet and two dry seasons, and thunder-storms are frequent and violent. The total area is about 178,370 square miles, being 560 miles long from east to west, and about 200 miles broad. The entire population is estimated at 286,000. Of these, 193,000 are in the British, 69,000 in the Dutch, and 24,000 in the French colonies. The population is of a diversified character, consisting of the aboriginal Indians, the creole negro, the mixed race, the immigrants from Madeira, from the East Indies, and from China, with a sprinkling of Europeans, chiefly British, French, and Dutch. The prevailing religion of these colonies is the same as the countries they belong to. The Acaray Mountains form the southern boundary, and have an average height of 4,000 feet. The Essequibo is the principal river. There are many picturesque cataracts. Georgetown, on the Demerara River, is the capital of British Guiana ; Paramaribo, that of Dutch Guiana ; and Cayenne, on an island near the coast, that of French Guiana. New Amsterdam is a flourishing settlement in the Dutch colony. The principal products are coffee, sugar, tobacco, timber, dye-stuffs, rum, cloves, and nutmegs. The *Victoria regia* of Guiana is the most beautiful specimen of the flora of the Western Hemisphere. British Guiana has a governor, appointed by the British Crown, while French and Dutch Guiana have no special form of local government. The first settlement in Guiana was formed by the Dutch in 1580 ; the greater part since 1803, has belonged to Great Britain. The present limits of Dutch Guiana were settled by the Congress of Vienna. The first French settlement was made in 1604. In 1809 the colony was captured by the English and Portuguese, but restored to France at the peace of 1815.

EDINBURGH.

## GUATEMALA.

Guatemala is a republic of Central America, bounded on the north by Yucatan and British Honduras; on the south by the Pacific Ocean; by Honduras and San Salvador on the east; and by Mexico on the west. The country is subject to earthquakes, and abounds in active volcanoes. The surface presents great variety, mountains and valleys, plains and table lands; and the separate levels have different climate and temperature. Guatemala has an area of 44,800 square miles. The population in 1872 was 1,197,054, of which 360,608 were whites, and 830,146 Indians. Public instruction is cared for by the government. The Roman Catholic is the established religion, but others are tolerated. The country is traversed by the Andes near the Pacific shores, sending off ranges toward the Atlantic with numerous peaks, some of which are more than 13,000 feet in elevation. The Lacantum, forming a part of the Mexican boundary, and the Montagua and the Polochic, flowing into the Bay of Honduras, are the chief rivers, but there are numerous short streams which discharge into the Pacific. The most important lakes are Dulce, Amatitlan, Atitlan, and Peten. The capital, NEW GUATEMALA (population, 40,000), is the chief town, being an inland city on a plateau 5,000 feet above the sea. The houses are low, and the walls very thick, as a precaution against earthquakes. Old Guatemala, the former capital, twelve miles from New Guatemala, was destroyed by an earthquake in 1773. The soil is very fertile, but ill-cultivated. Large flocks of sheep are reared in the northern parts of the State. The chief products are cochineal, indigo, sugar, hides, sarsaparilla, and mahogany. The republic was established in 1839, having previously, for eighteen years, formed a part of the confederation of Central America. The President is elected for four years, and there are two Chambers, known as the Council of State and the House of Representatives.

## HAYTI.

Hayti is a republic of the West Indies, occupying the west end of the island of which Santo Domingo forms the eastern or Spanish part. In climate and products it is similar to Cuba, from which it is separated on the west by the Windward Passage (50 miles broad). The soil is very fertile and well-watered. The area of the whole island is 28,000 square miles, being about 300 miles long from east to west, and about 140 broad. The population is about 550,000, nine-tenths of whom are negroes, the rest chiefly mulattos. The language in use is French, and the state religion Catholic. The island is mountainous in the center, where Mount Cibao attains a height of 7,200 feet. The salt lake Enriquillo is 20 miles long by 8 wide, and abounds in caymans. The Artibonite is the principal river, besides which the Yuma, the Yacki, the Nisao, and the Ozama deserve mention. PORT AU PRINCE is the capital and chief sea-port of the republic of Hayti. Aux Cayes is a sea-port in the south-western part of the island. St. Domingo (population, 15,000), on the southern coast, is the capital of the Dominican republic. It is fortified, and was founded in 1504. The productions are coffee, logwood, mahogany, tobacco, cotton, cocoa, wax, ginger, and sugar; and mines of gold, silver, copper, tin, and iron, though not worked now, are found in many places. Hayti was originally a Spanish possession, but it was afterward divided between France and Spain. Until recently the State of Hayti was an empire under a black Emperor. According to the constitution of 1867, the legislative power vests in a National Assembly, divided into two chambers, respectively called the Senate and House of Commons. The executive power is in the hands of a President, whose nominal term of office is four years, but it is generally cut short by insurrections. The eastern portion of the island, the *republica Dominica*, formerly belonging to Spain, is now a separate republic.

DUBLIN, GRAFTON STREET.

## HONDURAS.

Honduras is one of the five Central American republics, extending from the Caribbean Sea to the Pacific Ocean, having Guatemala on the north-west, and Nicaragua on the south-east. It is generally mountainous, being traversed by the Cordilleras, and contains extensive forests. The soil is fertile, and the climate, though very hot, is not unhealthy. The area is about 47,068 square miles, including a portion of the Mosquito territory. The inhabitants number 351,700, most of them wholly or partly of aboriginal blood. The white inhabitants are chiefly of Spanish origin. The principal rivers are the Chamelicon, Ulna, Aguan, and Choluteca; the last flowing into the Pacific, the others into the

Caribbean Sea. Comayagua, in the interior, is the capital, and Omoa and Truxillo are the chief sea-ports. The products are mahogany, maize, cotton, sugar, coffee, indigo, tobacco, and other tropical products. Honduras also abounds in mineral wealth. The country is governed by a President, a single Minister, and thirty-seven Representatives. The republic was established in 1839, on the dissolution of the Confederation of Central America.

## INDIA.

India, Hindostan, or the East Indies, as the country is variously called, is an extensive region, consisting of the central of the three great peninsulas of Southern Asia. It is bounded north-east by the Chinese empire; east by Indo-China and the Bay of Bengal; south and west by the Indian Ocean and Arabian Sea; north-west by Beloochistan and Afghanistan; area, about 1,477,763 square miles; population, 252,833,683, including the feudatory or native States. About 65,000 are of English birth. As to religion, 139,248,568 are Hindoos, 40,882,537 Mahomedans, 2,832,851 Buddhists; 1,174,436 Sikhs, and 897,216 Christians.

BOMBAY, STREET SCENE.

**Government.** The government of the territory formerly under the rule of the East India Company was vested in the British sovereign by an Act of 1858. Queen Victoria assumed the title of Empress of India in 1877. The chief executive is a Viceroy or Governor-General, appointed by the Crown, and acting under the Secretary of State for India. Present Viceroy, Right Hon. George F. S. Robinson, Earl De Grey and Ripon, appointed in 1880. He is assisted by a council of five "ordinary," and one "extraordinary," members, the latter usually the commander-in-chief of the forces. The Secretary for India is aided by a Council of State of fifteen members. A summary of the Indian wars will be found under "Outlines of History."

**Physical Features.** On the north lies the great range of the Himalaya Mountains; immediately below is a wide strip of lowland plain, while the rest of the peninsula is a plateau, bordered on the coasts by the East and West Ghauts—high hills. The Ganges flows from west to east, and the Brahmapootra from north to south, through the lowland plain, both emptying at the head of the Bay of Bengal. Other important streams are the Indus and Nerbudda in the west; and in the east, the Godavery, Krishna, and Hoogly.

**Chief Cities.** The three great commercial emporiums are CALCUTTA (population, 1881, 683,329), at the mouth of the Hoogly; BOMBAY (population, 753,000), on the west coast, and MADRAS, on the south-east, or Coromandel coast (population, 405,948). There are 41 other towns with a population of over 50,000, the largest being Lucknow, Benares, and Allahabad.

**Products, Trade, and Finances.** The principal articles of export are raw cotton, jute, rice, indigo, tea, hides, and opium. The opium trade is a government monopoly, the export being almost wholly to China, and amounting to nearly £7,000,000 yearly. The chief article of import is cotton goods. Total exports (1880–81), £71,962,240; total imports, £50,278,995 (this is exclusive of the opium trade); public debt (1880), £151,563,802; railroads, 9,325 miles; telegraph, 20,468 miles; army, about 195,000 officers and men, 125,000 being natives; there is also a native force of 190,000 men for police and frontier duty.

## ITALY.

A kingdom of Southern Europe, consisting of a large peninsula, bounded north by Austria and Switzerland; west by France and the Mediterranean; south by the Mediterranean, and east by the Ionian and Adriatic seas; and including also the islands of Sicily, Sardinia, and Elba, and many smaller; area, 114,408 square miles; population (1878), 28,209,620.

**Constitution and Government.** The present constitution is an expansion of that of 1848. The government is a constitutional monarchy, with a senate of 270 members, appointed for life, and a chamber of deputies of 508 members, elected by universal suffrage. King Humbert ascended the throne in 1878. The Roman Catholic is nominally the

State religion, but legislative acts have subordinated the power of the church to civil authority, and secured perfect religious freedom. Education is free and compulsory. The kingdom is divided into 69 provinces. The struggle which resulted in the unification of Italy (in 1870) is outlined elsewhere. San Marino alone retains an independent form of government.

**Physical Features.** The coast line of the mainland is 1,999 miles, of the islands 1,946 miles, having several large bays and gulfs, as the Gulf of Genoa in the north, and of Taranto in the "instep of the foot," the whole peninsula bearing a resemblance to a human leg or boot. The Alps on the north form a natural barrier between Italy and France, while the Appennines traverse the length of the peninsula. There are three volcanic mountains, Vesuvius, (near Naples), Ætna (Sicily), and Stromboli (Lipari Islands). At the foot of Vesuvius lie the buried cities of Herculaneum and Pompeii. The chief rivers are the Po, about 300 miles long, with its numerous tributaries, the historical Tiber, the Adige, and the Arno. Nestled in the Alps lie the beautiful lakes of Como, Maggiore, Iseo, and Garda.

**Principal Cities.** The capital, Rome (population, 303,-383), the most famous of ancient cities, for nearly eighteen centuries the residence of the bishops and popes of the Roman Church, is situated on both sides of the Tiber, fifteen miles from the mouth, on its seven-storied hills. It is replete with objects of interest to the antiquarian, the archæologist, the classicist, and the artist. St. Peter's, the largest cathedral in the world, is 600 feet in length, and 458 feet from the pavement to the cross on the dome. Adjoining it on the north, stands the great Vatican palace, the residence of the pontiffs since the return from Avignon in 1377. Space forbids us to enumerate the magnificent palaces, libraries, and museums, the glorious churches and cathedrals, the renowned monuments of antiquity, with which the "eternal city" is thronged.

**Naples** (population, 450,804), is the largest city of Italy, and is beautifully situated on the Bay of Naples, usually called the finest bay of the world. Other important cities are Florence, with its splendid cathedral; Venice, the city of canals; Milan, Turin, Leghorn, Genoa, Parma, Padua, Bologna, Ravenna, and Palermo, in Sicily.

**Products and Finances.** Agriculture is the principal Italian interest, though the manufactures of silk, cotton, straw, and woolen goods are important. Fruits abound, and are of exquisite flavor. The supply of sea and fresh-water fish is large; sardines and anchovies are exported in large quantities. The chief exports are olive oil, wine, fruit, raw and thrown silk, hemp, straw hats, cattle, marble, zinc, iron and copper ores, and sulphur. Total exports (1880), £45,291,567; total imports, £49,025,776; public revenue (1881), £54,-107,543; expenditure, £53,403,601; public debt, £508,500,000; standing army, 736,-502; navy, 66 vessels, 339 guns; railway, 5,191 miles; telegraph, 14,391 miles.

VESUVIUS AND THE BAY OF NAPLES.

## JAMAICA.

Jamaica is the largest and most valuable of the British West India Islands, having an area of 4,256 square miles, and a population of 560,000. It was discovered by Columbus in 1494, and named St. Jago. In 1670 it was formally ceded to Great Britain by the treaty of Madrid. Excellent harbors exist, and more than seventy streams flow from the central mountains. Sugar, rum, tobacco, and fruit are the exports, amounting in 1879 to £1,357,571. The capital, chief port, and largest town is Kingston (population about 35,000). The governor is assisted by a privy council of eight, and a legislative council of sixteen members.

## JAPAN.

Japan is an extensive empire, consisting of several large and about 3,800 small islands, situated at the eastern extremity of Asia in the North Pacific Ocean. It is bounded on the north by the Sea of Okhotsk, on the east and south by the Pacific Ocean, and on the north-west by the Strait of

Corea, the Sea of Japan, and the Gulf of Tartary. The principal of the islands are Hondo, Shikoku, and Kiushiu. The large island of Jesso or Yesso is immediately north of Hondo. The most important of the smaller islands are Sado, Tsoussima, Amadsi, Yki, Yaksima, Oosima, Tanegasima, with the groups of Okisima, Gohissima, and Kosikisima. The general aspect of these islands is rugged and irregular. Volcanoes and earthquakes occur frequently. The climate is intensely cold in the north, and very genial in the south. The total area of Japan is 146,568 square miles. The population in 1876 was 34,338,404. The people are a mixed race, sprung from Chinese, Malay, and the aboriginal Aino stock. They are divided into three classes—nobles, gentry, and common people. The state religion is Buddhism, and education is very general. The capital, YEDDO or TOKIO, is situated on the island of Hondo; has a population of 594,283, and covers about 100 square miles of ground. The buildings are chiefly of wood in Japan, and only one or two stories high. Kioto and Ozaka are important towns on the same island. Yokohama, Matsumea and Hakodati are the chief towns of Yesso, and Nagasaki that of Kiushiu. Yeddo is the capital. The soil is productive, teeming with every variety of agricultural produce. Gold and silver mining is prosecuted on a small scale, and there is a fair supply of coal. Forest trees, flowers, and fruits abound. In manufactures the Japanese are very skillful, and silk, cotton, porcelain, paper, and lacquered ware are largely exported. The empire is ruled by a mikado, aided by a great council, and without a legislative body. The first account of Japan was given by Marco Polo in the thirteenth century. The Portuguese about 1542 began to trade with Japan, and in 1600 were succeeded by the Dutch, and later by the English. In the reign of James I. all ports were closed against Europeans, but in 1854 a treaty was concluded by which they were reopened.

SHOPS IN YEDDO.

## JAVA.

Java, an island of the Indian Archipelago, and the chief seat of the Dutch power in the East, is separated from Sumatra by the Straits of Sunda. Area (including Madura), 51,336 square miles; population in 1878, 19,067,829, of which 27,000 are Europeans, 190,000 Chinese, 27,000 Arabs, and the rest natives. The professed religion is Mohammedanism. The island was conquered by the Dutch in 1596. In 1811 it was seized by England, but surrendered in 1814. The soil is of wonderful richness. Chief exports are rice, sugar, coffee, indigo, tobacco, teak timber, and spices, and they amount to about $45,000,000 yearly. Slavery was abolished in 1860, by a law passed in 1856. Two lines of railroad exist of about 240 miles, owned by the government. The governor-general has almost absolute power, a council of five members acting as a court of advice.

## LIBERIA.

An independent negro republic of west Africa, occupying that part of North Guinea between the San Pedro and the Yong, 500 miles on the coast and 100 miles inland. This tract has been purchased, improved, and colonized by the American Colonization Society. The population is about 1,000,000, of which about 20,000 are American immigrants or their descendants, the rest aborigines. Capital, MONROVIA (population about 14,000). The climate is dangerous to Europeans. Chief exports, coffee, cotton, ivory, hides, gold dust, and indigo. The government is modeled after that of the United States.

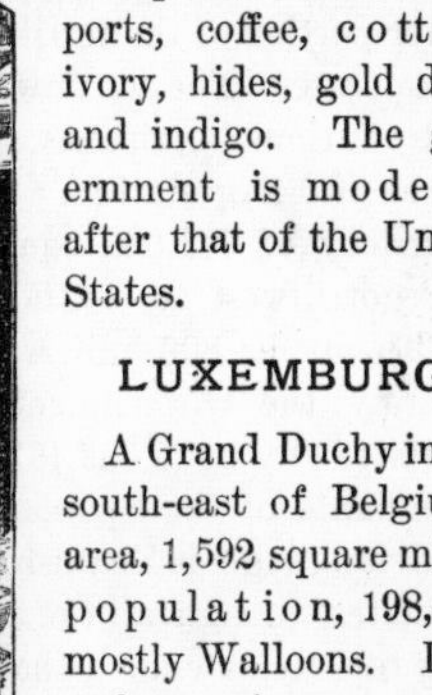

## LUXEMBURG.

A Grand Duchy in the south-east of Belgium; area, 1,592 square miles; population, 198,000, mostly Walloons. Luxemburg is connected with the Netherlands, as regards the sovereign, but has a constitution and administration of its own, and is, by the treaty of London, of May, 1867, a neutral country, under the protection of the great European powers. The surface is generally level, and the chief products are corn, hemp, flax, hops, and wine. Capital, LUXEMBURG.

## MADAGASCAR.

This, the largest African island, is separated from the east coast by the Mozambique Channel. Its area is 228,570 square miles, twice that of the British Isles, and its population is about 3,000,000. The natives were formerly cruel and hostile, but some progress has been made under the present Christian queen, Ranaralona. The government is an absolute monarchy. Tropical products and fruits are exported to a small extent. Capital, Antananarino (population 80,000).

## MAURITIUS.

An island in the Indian Ocean, 600 miles east of Madagascar, and a colony of Great Britain; area, 700 square miles; population, 320,000, two-thirds Indian coolies. The surface is mostly rugged. The main products are coffee, cotton, indigo, sugar, and cloves. The chief towns are St. Louis, the capital, and Grande Porte. The island was discovered by the Portuguese in 1505, colonized by the Dutch in 1598, but soon abandoned. The French formed an establishment in 1644, and the English came into possession in 1810.

## MEXICO.

Mexico is a republic of North America on the southern boundary of the United States, and is chiefly included between the Gulf of Mexico and the Pacific Ocean. It comprises 27 States, one territory, and the federal district, making in all 29 political divisions. It includes three different regions ; on the coast, the hot lands; upon the upper terraces, the temperate lands, from 4,000 to 8,000 feet above the sea ; and in the mountain regions, the cold lands. The soil of Mexico is fertile, but in some portions there is great want of water. There are two seasons—the dry, from June to November, and the rainy, from November to June. The greater portion of the territory is so elevated that the climate is temperate. The south western shores are frequently visited by furious hurricanes.

**Area and Population.** The area is estimated to embrace a territory of 741,598 square miles. Its extreme length from north-west to south-east is 2,000 miles, its extreme breadth about 800 miles. According to an enumeration made by the Government in 1877 the population was calculated to be 9,389,461. It is composed of Indians, descendants of the Spaniards, and mixed races. The national language is Spanish, and the Catholic religion predominates, though all are equally protected. Education is being rapidly extended, there being 4,000 public schools.

**Mountains, Lakes, and Rivers.** The principal chain is the Sierra Madre, which divides into three main branches. Among the loftiest peaks are Istarchihuatl (white lady), 15,700 feet, the Pico del Trayle, 15,250 feet ; and the Coffre de Perote, 13,400 feet. Earthquakes occur on the coasts of the Pacific and in the environs of the capital. The great volcano of Popocatapetl (smoking mountain) is 17,880 ft. high. Orizara, another volcano, is 17,374 ft. high. The principal rivers are the Rio Grande, separating Mexico from Texas ; the Colorado ; and the Rio Grande de Santiago.

**Chief Towns.** Mexico, the capital, has a population of 236,500 souls. It is situated in a valley 7,450 feet above the sea, and surrounded by lofty mountains. It was founded in 1325, and is the oldest city in America of which we have any account. The other cities of Mexico containing from 50,000 to 100,000 inhabitants are Guadalajara, Puebla, Guanajuato, Merida, Xacatecas, and Queretaro. Vera Cruz lies on the gulf coast, and is a walled town.

**Products and Industry.** The country is rich in agriculture and mineral wealth, vast table-lands producing almost every variety of grain and vegetables, while in the warmer regions oranges and other tropical fruits grow profusely. Coffee and cotton are largely cultivated, and the northern states are full of vast herds of cattle and sheep. The formerly valuable silver mines of Mexico, neglected for a long time, were partly reopened in 1864. There are about 7,000 miles of telegraph, and 1,070 miles of railway.

**Government and History.** By the terms of the present constitution, dating from 1857, Mexico is a federative republic. A President is elected for four years, a Senate of 56 members chosen for six years, and a House of Deputies of 331 members for two years. The Chief Justice of the Supreme Court, elected for six years, is ex-officio vice-president of the republic. Each state has its local constitution, with elective governors and legislatures. The earliest inhabitants were the Toltecs, superseded by the Aztecs, who in 1519 were conquered by the Spaniards. After a long struggle with Spain, Mexico was declared independent in 1822. In 1847 it was obliged to yield a large part of valuable territory to the United States, after an unsuccessful war. Maximilian, an Austrian prince, became Emperor in 1864, but was shot by Juarez in 1867.

## MONTENEGRO.

The small principality of Montenegro is situated on the west frontier of European Turkey, south of Herzegovina, having an area of 1710 square miles, and a population of 245,380, the great majority orthodox Slavs. Independence has been claimed from time immemorial and has recently been admitted by Turkey. The surface is very rugged, and agriculture is the chief occupation. Capital, Cetigne (population 1,400). Prince Nicholas was proclaimed King in 1860.

## MOROCCO.

The largest of the Barbary States lies in north-west Africa, and is bounded north by the Mediterranean, west by the Atlantic, and east and south by the Great Desert. The area is about 260,000 square miles, and the population is estimated at from five to seven millions, two thirds being Moors, and the rest Bedouin Arabs, Jews, and Negroes. The emperor or sultan has absolute power. Agriculture is neglected, though the soil is fertile. Wool, hides, almonds, carpets, oil, and ostrich feathers are the chief exports. There are three capitals, Fez (population 80,000), Morocco (population 50,000), and Mequinez (population 56,000).

## NATAL.

The British possession of Natal lies on the south-east coast of Africa about 800 miles from the Cape of Good Hope. The Drankensberg Mountains separate it from the Cape Colony and Orange Free State. It has a sea coast of 200 miles, an area of 18,750 square miles, and a population (1879) of 361,537, about 25,000 whites included. The name Natal was given because of its discovery by Vasco de Gama on Christmas Day. The governor is assisted by a legislative and executive council. Natal became a separate colony in 1856. The fertile coast region produces all tropical vegetation, the midland is suited to European cereals, and the uplands form a fine grazing country. Chief exports are wool, sugar, coffee, ivory, hides, and ostrich feathers. Capital, Pietermaritzburg (population 10,144).

## NETHERLANDS.

This maritime kingdom of west central Europe, situate on the North Sea, consists of eleven provinces, and has an area of 12,680 square miles, and a population (1880) of 4,060,578. Of these the majority belong to the Dutch Reformed Church. The king (Willem III. succeeded in 1849 to the throne) is also sovereign of the Grand-Duchy of Luxemburg, with 999 square miles and 299,520 inhabitants. The surface is flat and low, intersected by numerous canals and streams. The Rhine, Maas, Yssel, and Scheldt are the principal rivers. THE HAGUE is the political, and AMSTERDAM the commercial, capital ; the former has 117,856 and the latter 326,196 inhabitants. Diamond cutting employs about 1,000 hands in Amsterdam. The chief exports are refined sugar, flax, cheese, butter, cattle, sheep, madder, and gin; total exports (1881) £48,500,000; public debt (1881) £83,072,418. There is an army of 65,000 men and a navy of 122 vessels. There are 1,390 miles of railway, partly managed by the state, and 2,196 miles of telegraph. The present constitution was adopted in 1848 and vests the legislative power in a States-General, with 39 members in the upper and 86 in the lower house. Property qualifications exist.

## NEWFOUNDLAND.

This island is the only British possession in North America not included in the Dominion of Canada. It lies on the north-east side of the Gulf of Lawrence, has an area of 40,200 square miles, and a population of about 165,000. Labrador, on the mainland, is a dependency. The chief industry is fishing. The government is at present by a responsible Executive Council, a Legislative Council, named by the Crown, and an Assembly of 31 members. Capital, ST. JOHN'S (population, 22,533), a fine sea-port town.

## NICARAGUA.

Nicaragua, one of the five republics of Central America, has Honduras on the north and Costa Rica on the south, with an area of 58,000 square miles, and a population of about 300,000, half of whom are Indians. It is in large part covered with great forests furnishing the finest mahogany, rosewood, and dyewoods. The republic was founded in 1858. There is a President, responsible Ministers, a Senate of ten, and a House of eleven members. Internal dissensions are common. Besides valuable woods the principal exports are coffee, gum, and gold and silver bullion. The commerce is small. The capital, MANAGUA, on the lake of the same name, has about 8,000 inhabitants.

## ORANGE FREE STATE.

A South African Republic of Dutch Boers, on the head streams of the Orange River, surrounded by Natal and the Transvaal. Area, 42,470 square miles ; population, about 50,000, of whom half are white. Diamonds, garnets, and other precious stones are found. Capital, BLOEMFONTEIN (population, 1,250).

## PARAGUAY.

A small inland country of South America, bounded north by Bolivia and Brazil, and separated from Brazil and the Argentine Confederation on the east, west, and south by the forks of the Parana and Paraguay Rivers ; area, 91,980 square miles ; population, 293,844. Paraguay is a republic in form, but is practically under the control of Brazil. Sugar, rum, tobacco, indigo, "maté" or Paraguay tea, coffee, etc., are raised. There is scarcely any export trade. The country is hopelessly insolvent and subject to constant political quarrels. Capital, ASCUNCION (population, about 15,000). A new Constitution was adopted in 1870, modeled closely after that of the Argentine Confederation.

## PATAGONIA.

Patagonia is the most southern country of South America, having the Atlantic and Pacific on the east and west, and lying south of the Argentine Confederation and Chili ; area, about 350,000 square miles ; population, estimated at 4,000, mostly Indians, who are steadily decreasing. The surface has been little explored, but is mostly sterile and uninviting. There is a station at the mouth of the Rio Negro with about 2,000 inhabitants, including many Spaniards and other Europeans.

## PERSIA.

Persia, called by the natives Iran, is the most important country of Asia west of India. It is bounded by Asiatic Turkey on the west, the Caspian Sea and Turkestan on the north, Afghanistan and Beloochistan on the east, and southwest by the Persian Gulf. The area is about 636,000 square miles, and the population is variously estimated at from five to eight millions, including nomadic tribes. In the north and west are the great mountain chains of the Caucasus, and further south those of Armenia and Kurdistan. The provinces on the Caspian Sea are of great fertility, but the central and eastern regions form a vast and irreclaimable salt desert. There are many rivers, but none navigable. The country produces most valuable vegetable productions, including wheat and other cereals, rice, sugar, tobacco, cotton, and opium. The wines are celebrated. The most important manufacture is of silk. Carpets, shawls, brocade, and embroidery are also exported. There is no public debt, the revenue being greater than the expenditure. The Shah is an absolute monarch and may appoint his successor. The vast majority of the inhabitants are Mohammedans, but there are many Armenians, Parsees, Nestorians, and Jews. Capital, TEHERAN (population, 85,000).

## PERU.

Peru, one of the oldest Spanish colonies in America, whose conquest is vividly described by Prescott, the American historian, is a republic of South America, having on the north, Ecuador ; on the east, Brazil ; south, Bolivia ; and west, the Pacific ; area, 503,360 square miles ; population (1876), 3,050,000, of which 57 per cent. are aboriginal Indians, 23 per cent. "Cholos and Zambos," and 20 per cent. Europeans and descendants of Spaniards, negroes, and Chinese. The country is traversed from north to south by the Andes, and the table-lands of the Sierra are the highest in the world (22,000 feet). Lake Titicaca is 115 miles long and 30 broad. The chief rivers are the Maranon, Hualga (700 miles long), the Ucayali, the Purus, and the Rio Negro.

**History and Government.** Peru was invaded by Pizarro in 1513, and he found the subjects of the Incas far advanced beyond other American natives in architecture, government, and general civilization. Peruvian independence was achieved in 1821. The present Constitution dates from 1867, and is modeled on that of the United States. The state religion is the Roman Catholic. In 1879 broke out the disastrous war with Chili, in which Peru sustained a crushing defeat.

**Products and Finances.** The chief exports are guano, nitrate of soda, sheep, sugar, silver, and cinchona (quinine). The ancient silver mines are still worked with profit. The public debt in 1876 was about $215,000. To-day the amount is enormous but unestimated. There are 1,020 miles of railway and 1,374 miles of telegraph.

**Chief Towns.** Capital, LIMA (population, about 100,000). Other important places are Callao, the chief sea-port, Arequipa, Cuzco, and Huamanga. Lima has been wholly or partly destroyed by earthquakes half a dozen times, the most dreadful being that of 1697.

## PORTUGAL.

This, the most westerly kingdom of Europe, forms the western part of the Spanish peninsula, bounded north and east by Spain, south and west by the Atlantic. The coast line is 500 miles long and the average breadth about 100 miles. The area is 34,595 square miles, and the population (1878), 4,348,551. There are six provinces, and the kingdom also owns the Azores Islands (area, 966 square miles; population, 264,352), and Madeira and Porto Santo (area, 317 square miles; population, 123,222). The government is a constitutional monarchy, hereditary in both the male and female lines. The Peers, 100 in number, are named for life by the sovereign. The Second Chamber, of 149 members, is elected under a property qualification. The Roman Catholic is the state religion, but other creeds are tolerated.

The interior of the country is mountainous, the loftiest chain being the Serra de Estrella. Between the many mountain ranges lie beautiful and fertile valleys. The largest rivers are the Minho, the Douro, part of the north boundary, and the Tagus, all rising in Spain. Every species of European and many semi-tropical vegetables and fruits grow abundantly. The chief exports are wine, oil, fruit, and salt; total exports (1880), $20,520,000; imports, $34,046,000; public debt, $387,659,575; railways, 750 miles; telegraph, 2,300 miles; post-offices, 616.

The capital, LISBON, at the mouth of the Tagus, has a population of 203,681; Oporto, famous for the shipment of port wine, lies at the mouth of the Douro (population, 108,346). Other important places are Braga, Coimbra, and Elvas.

## ROUMANIA.

The kingdom of Roumania consists of the Moldo-Wallachian provinces formerly belonging to Turkey, but recognized as independent, with the Dobrudscha territory annexed, by the Berlin Treaty of 1878, and recognized as a Kingdom in 1881. Area, 49,262 square miles; population, 5,376,000, mostly members of the Greek Church. Wallachia, the largest province, has a fine soil, but is subject to fearful droughts. Stock-raising is the most important industry. Moldavia produces large quantities of grains, fruit and wine. The chief exports are wheat, barley, cattle and wine. Capital, BUCHAREST (population, 221,805).

## ROUMELIA, EASTERN.

This is another creation of the Berlin Congress. It is bounded by the Black Sea on the east, and extends south and west from Cape Leityn to the Rhodope mountains, and thence north to the Rilo Dagh. Area, 13,663 square miles; population, 815,951. The general character of the country is similar to Roumania. Capital, PHILIPPOPOLIS (population, in 1880, 24,053).

## RUSSIA.

The Russian empire comprises an immense territory, including a considerable portion of the north and the whole of the north-eastern and eastern part of Europe, and the whole of northern and a part of central Asia, extending from the Baltic on the west to the Pacific on the east; area, 8,138,541 square miles; population, 82,230,264, of which 56,000,000 are Russians and the rest Poles, Lithuanians, Fins, Tartars, Baschkires, Jews, Germans, and Turks.

**Government.** This is an absolute hereditary monarchy. The executive power centers in the "Private Council of the Emperor," aided by four great boards, or councils:—the Council of the Empire, the Directing Senate, the Holy Synod, and the Council of Ministers. Alexander III. ascended the throne March, 1881, but has not yet (September, 1882) been crowned. The established religion is the Russo-Greek church, to which 60,000,000 of the people belong. There are 98 governments, or provinces, 81 in Europe and 17 in Asia, and 14 military general governors. Russia in Asia consists of Central Asia and Siberia; Russia in Europe comprises Poland, Finland, Cis-Caucasia, Trans-Caucasia, and Russia Proper, which is subdivided into Great Russia, Little Russia, East, South, and West Russia, and the Baltic provinces.

**Physical Features.** Russia in Europe consists of an immense plain, without a single mountain. The principal rivers are, the Volga, Ural, Dneiper, Dniester, Don, Dwina, Duna, and Neva. The Volga is the largest river in Europe, empties into the Caspian, and is navigable almost to its source. In Siberia the surface is mountainous, rising in many places far above the level of perpetual snow. Of the rivers, the Ob, Yeniseï, Lena, and Amur, are all larger than the Volga, and have many important branches. A great part of Russian territory is totally unfit for cultivation, consisting of frozen wastes, sandy deserts, and dense forests. The woodland occupies about 500,000,000 acres. The Ural Mountains divide Europe from Asia, and contain great mineral wealth. The Gulf of Finland, the White Sea, and the Sea of Azof lie entirely within Russian territory, and the coast of Russia in Europe skirts the Arctic Ocean, the Gulf of Bothnia, and the Baltic, Black, and Caspian Seas.

**Chief Cities.** The capital, ST. PETERSBURG (population, 670,000), lies on the Neva river, where it enters the Gulf of Finland. About 150 bridges span the Neva. The Winter Palace, built in 1837, is probably the most magnificent palace in the world. The city contains nearly 200 churches; the church of the Metropolitan, or cathedral, is richly adorned, and surmounted by a dome and cross reaching to the height of 345 feet. Among the finest buildings are the Academy of Sciences, the University, the Imperial Library, and the National Museum. Moscow (population, 620,000) is almost exactly at the center of the country, and from it converges the whole railway system. It derives its name from the river Moskwa, on which it lies, 400 miles south-east of St. Petersburg. From the ruins of Moscow, burned by the citizens, the French set out upon their disastrous retreat of 1812. Within the walls of the Kremlin are many fine public buildings, including the University (having 1,500 students), and the Public Museum and Library (150,000 volumes). There are 15 other cities of over 50,000 inhabitants, the largest being Warsaw, Odessa, Kicheneff, Riga, Kieff, Tiflis, and Kharkoff, all having over 100,000 population.

**Products, Trade, and Finances.** The most fertile region is that between the Baltic and Black Seas. The chief exports are grain, timber, hides, flax, tallow, wool, linseed, and hempseed. Wheat, barley, oats, buckwheat, millet, and rye, are cultivated, the last being the staple food. Potatoes and tobacco are grown on a small scale. Silver, gold, iron, of fine quality, platinum, copper, salt, and marble, are found in the Ural and Altai mountains. The principal manufactures are in tanning, fur-dressing, weaving, etc. Total exports (1880), £83,693,000 ; imports, £79,090,000 ; expenditure, £93,820,500 ; income, £87,109,000 ; public debt, £416,283,500; army, 974,771 men ; navy, 389 vessels, 561 guns ; railways, 16,715 miles ; telegraph, 42,595 miles; post offices, 3,678. The issue of irredeemable paper money is about £170,000,000, and it is depreciated about 30 per cent.

## SANDWICH ISLANDS.

This group of the North Pacific consists of thirteen islands (five uninhabited), lying in latitude 19°-22° N., and longitude 154°-160° W.; population about 58,000. The largest islands are Hawaii, Papu, and Kauai. They are all mountainous and of volcanic origin. In 1810 they were placed under British protection, but are now independent. The islands were discovered in 1778 by Capt. Cook, who lost his life at Hawaii. Considerable trade is carried on with whaling and other vessels.

## SAN SALVADOR,

The smallest of the Central American republics, is bounded north and north-east by Honduras, north-west by Guatemala, east by Nicaragua, and south by the Pacific ; area, 9,594 square miles ; population 434,500, mostly aborigines and of mixed race. The government consists of a president, five ministers, and a Congress of twelve senators and twenty-four deputies. The Roman Catholic religion is recognized, but others protected. The surface is covered with lofty mountains of volcanic origin. Indigo, maize, sugar, coffee, tobacco, and cotton are successfully cultivated. The capital, San Salvador (population about 16,000), has twice been destroyed by earthquakes.

## SANTO DOMINGO.

This West Indian republic forms the largest part of the island of Hayti (which see), but is politically distinct from the republic of that name. Area, 20,591 square miles ; population about 250,000. The capital, Santo Domingo, has 15,000 inhabitants. The government consists of a president, council of four ministers, senate of nine members, and lower house of fifteen members. The Roman Catholic is the established religion. Exports, chiefly tobacco and sugar, amount to $1,500,000 a year. The physical features of the country are described under Hayti.

## SERVIA.

Servia is a kingdom of eastern Europe, separated from Hungary by the Danube. It received large accessions of territory after the Turko-Russian war of 1878, and now has an area of 18,787 square miles, and a population of 1,670,000, nearly all orthodox Greeks. It is governed by a hereditary prince, and an elected parliament or "Skuptschina." Independence from Turkey was solemnly declared by Prince Milan II., in 1878. In March, 1882, Prince Milan accepted the royal title of King Milan I.

The country is mountainous, and the inhabitants warlike and brave. The valleys are fertile, but not thoroughly cultivated. Lumber, cattle (especially hogs), and grain are the chief exports ; public debt (1881) about £4,000,000. The capital, BELGRADE, has a population of 27,675.

## SIAM.

The kingdom of Siam lies in the heart of the peninsula, between India and China, in south-eastern Asia. The limits have varied greatly and cannot be exactly defined. The area is between 250,000 and 300,000 square miles, and the population has been roughly estimated at about 16,000,000, of which nearly half are Siamese, and a majority of the rest Chinese, Malays, and Laotians. Siam is divided into forty-one provinces, each with a chief. The monarchy is partly hereditary, but the king may name his successor from among his own family. There are really two kings ; one civil, the other military. The natives are practically serfs. The foreign commerce centers at the capital, BANGKOK (population 255,000) ; rice is the staple export ; sugar, gum, hides, dye-woods, and timber are also exported. There are several ports of little importance on the Gulf of Siam.

## SPAIN.

A kingdom of south-western Europe, bounded by the Atlantic, the Mediterranean, Portugal, and France. Area, 193,171 square miles ; population (1877), 333,293, the vast majority being natives.

**Government and Constitution.** The present constitution was proclaimed in 1876. The government is a constitutional monarchy, the legislative power vesting in a Cortes, of which the Senate includes members of the royal family, grandees, and certain officials, 100 life members named by the crown, and 132 elected members ; and the Congress is composed of elected members, one to every 50,000 of the population. Alfonso XII. ascended the throne in 1874.

There are forty-nine provinces, subdivisions of the fourteen ancient provinces: New Castile, Old Castile, La Mancha, Leon, Asturias, Galicia, Andalusia, Estremadura, Murcia, Valencia, Aragon, Catalonia, Basque Provinces, and the Canary and Balearic Isles. The Roman Catholic is the state religion.

**Physical Features.** The coast line is 1,370 miles in length. No country in Europe, except Switzerland, has such an extent of mountainous surface. On the north the Pyrenees divide Spain from France, and four other ranges traverse the peninsula from east to west: the Sierra Gaudarama, the mountains of Toledo, the Sierra Morena, and the Sierra Nevada. The interior consists of lofty table-lands. In the valleys flow the Douro, the Tagus, the Guadalquivir, the Guadianha, the Minho, the Ebro, and other streams. There are altogether 230 rivers.

**Chief Towns.** The capital, MADRID (population 397,960), a walled city, noted for the beauty of its architecture, stands on a high table-land, 300 miles from the sea, lying on a small affluent of the Tagus. Other important towns are Seville (population 133,938) on the Guadalquivir, Cadiz (population 72,000), a southern sea-port; Barcelona, Granada, Malaga, Murcia, Valencia, Valladolid, and Saragossa.

**Trade and Finances.** The country is generally fertile, and, besides the cereals, produces olives, oranges, dates, lemons, pomegranates, and other tropical fruit. The vine is everywhere cultivated. In Xeres and the south-west fine sherry is made; in the south-east, Malaga and Alicante. The chief exports are wine, silk, iron, quicksilver, fruit, olive oil, wool, cork, and salt. Iron, copper, and lead abound. Manufactures are neglected. Total exports (1880), $100,980,000; imports, $88,660,000; revenue, $163,347,097; expenditure, $156,529,840; standing army, 90,000; navy, 139 ships, 552 guns; miles of railway, 4,023; of telegraphs, 8,190; post-offices, 2,358.

## SUMATRA.

This large island of the Indian Archipelago lies immediately under the equator, south-west of the Malay peninsula, being 1,500 miles long and 250 miles broad; area, 160,000 square miles; population, 3,500,000, mostly Malay Mohammedans. There are four Dutch colonial establishments, the first settlement dating from 1649. The British held the island from 1795 to 1815, restored all but Bencoolen in 1815, and gave that up in 1824. The climate is warm and moist, and the soil yields large crops of rice, coffee, pepper, tobacco, and cotton. Tigers, elephants, rhinoceroses, apes, crocodiles, and pythons abound. The chief towns are Acheen, Bencoolen, Padang, and Palembang.

## SWEDEN AND NORWAY.

The kingdoms of Norway and Sweden, now united under one sovereign, form an extensive peninsula, bounded by Russia on the north-east, and surrounded on the other sides by the Atlantic on the west, the Skager Rack and Categat on the south, and on the west the Baltic sea and the gulf of Bothnia. Area of Sweden (1878), 170,297 square miles; population, 4,531,863. Area of Norway, 122,823 square miles; population, 1,806,900. The union of the two took place in 1814, each maintaining a separate code of laws, constitution, and legislative assembly. The present king, Oscar II., ascended the throne in 1872.

**Sweden** comprises the eastern half of the peninsula, and is divided into twenty-four governments or "Vor Län." The country is for the most part flat, rising in the north-west into the Kiolen range, which forms the boundary of Norway. Agriculture is the principal occupation, but valuable iron, copper, and other mines exist. Timber, cattle, iron, copper, and butter are the chief exports; total exports (1880), £12,500,000; imports, £16,000,000; public debt, £12,792,537; miles of railway, 3,528, of which 1,203 belong to the state; miles of telegraph lines, 6,787; standing army, 41,280 men; navy, 42 vessels. Capital, STOCKHOLM, a port on an inlet of the Baltic (population, 169,249). The Lutheran is the established church, but all sects are tolerated.

**Norway,** occupying the west side of the peninsula, is divided into twenty provinces or *amts.* It has a deeply indented coast line, and a mountainous surface, of which one-fourth is forest land, and not more than a thirtieth cultivated. Fishing is the chief industry; cod, herring, salmon, fur, and timber being the principal exports. Agriculture is somewhat neglected. Total exports, about £5,000,000; total imports about £9,000,000; public debt (1881), £5,834,000; miles of railway, 828; miles of telegraph lines, 5,315, mostly belonging to the state; army (including reserves), 40,000 men; navy, thirty steamers, ninety sailing vessels, mostly small. Capital, CHRISTIANIA, on an inlet of the Skager Rack (population, 119,407).

## SWITZERLAND.

Switzerland, the oldest of existing republics, lies in central Europe, bounded west by France, south by Italy and France, east by Austria, and north by Germany; area, 15,908 square miles; population (1880), 2,831,887, of whom 2,030,792 speak German, 608,007 French, and 161,293 Italian; about three-fifths are Protestants and two-fifths Catholics.

**Government.** There are twenty-two cantons, each of which sends two members to the Ständerath or Upper House; the Nationalrath, or Lower House, has 135 members elected by the people, one for every 20,000. The two houses elect the "Federal Council" of seven members to serve three years, two being designated to act as President and Vice-President for one year. Manhood suffrage prevails. The present constitution was approved in 1874.

**Physical Features.** This is the most mountainous country of Europe. The Alps lie not only along the southern and eastern frontiers, but throughout the chief part of the interior. Among the highest and most famous peaks are Mt. Blanc (15,781 feet high), Monte Rosa and the Matterhorn, nearly as high, and the Jungfrau (13,671 feet). From the Alps the most wonderful glaciers of the world roll down to fill some of the finest rivers, among others, the Rhone, the Rhine, the Ticino, the Aar, and the Reuss. The lakes are numerous and beautiful. The principal are those of

Geneva, Constance, Zurich, Lucerne, and Neufchatel. The scenery embracing these remarkable lakes, rivers, waterfalls, and mountains, draws yearly a throng of sight-seers from distant lands.

**Cities.** BERNE, the political capital, lies near the Aar, and is a beautiful fortified town of 36,000 inhabitants. Geneva, on the lake of that name (pop. 75,000) is even more attractive. It is the center of a trade in watches, musical boxes, and jewelry. Other important places are Fribourg, Lausanne, Neufchatel (noted for its cheese), and Zurich.

**Finances and Commerce.** Switzerland is in the main an agricultural country, but with highly developed manufactures. There is an excess of food imports over exports. The chief manufactures are of watches (500,000 a year), jewelry, embroidery, silk, cotton goods, and hand carvings. The aggregate debt of the cantons is about £8,000,000; federal revenue (1881), £1,629,660; expenditure, £1,638,200; army, on a war footing, 215,000 men; miles of railway, 1,478 (the great Mt. Cenis tunnel was opened in 1872); miles of telegraph lines, 4,924, over nine-tenths owned by the state.

CONSTANTINOPLE.

## TRANSVAAL.

A South African republic, lying between the Vaal and Limpopo or Crocodile rivers; area, 114,360 square miles; population about 300,000, of whom 25,000 are white. The colony was founded by Dutch Boers, dissatisfied with the Cape Colony and Natal government. The Cape government recognized the independence of the Boers, but in 1877 attempted to annex it. The Boers resisted manfully, and drove back the British troops. The English poured more troops into the Transvaal, but before further fighting took place acknowledged the political independence of the Boers under a merely formal admission of the sovereignty of Great Britain over the soil. Cattle raising is the great occupation. Gold, copper, lead, iron, and coal are found. The chief towns are Potchefstroom and Pretoria.

## TRIPOLI.

This is the most easterly of the Barbary States in Africa, and is a province or *vilayet* of the Turkish empire; area, 344,400 square miles; population about 1,200,000, including Fezzan and Barca. There are no rivers, and rain seldom falls. Principal articles of export are cattle, iron, oil, ostrich feathers, wool, and esparto grass. Capital, TRIPOLI (pop. 25,000); Bengazi, the second city, has about 22,000 inhabitants.

## TUNIS.

This country lies in North Africa, on the Mediterranean, east of Algeria; area, 45,716 square miles; population about 1,500,000. Tunis is theoretically a dependency of the Ottoman Empire, but since the action of the French in 1881 is practically subject to the power of France, embodied in a Resident. The capital, TUNIS, is a large, prosperous city (population, 125,000), with considerable manufactures of silk and woolen stuffs, shawls, fez caps, carpets, and perfumes. North of Tunis is the site of Carthage.

## TURKISH EMPIRE.

The Ottoman Empire embraces, besides the dependencies of Egypt, Tripoli and Tunis, already described, and the island of Crete, the two great divisions of Turkey in Europe and Turkey in Asia.

**Government and Constitution.** Until 1876 the Sultan was an absolute though not an hereditary monarch, the sovereignty devolving on the senior male descendant of Othman, the founder of the empire. A new constitution was granted in 1876, providing two legislative bodies, a Senate nominated by the Sultan, and a Chamber of Deputies elected by ballot every four years, one for every 100,000 inhabitants. Mohammedanism is the state religion. Abdul-Hamid II. ascended the throne in 1876.

**Finances.** Turkey is practically bankrupt. The debt (1880) was $1,289,565,000; the expenditures were over $125,000,000, and the receipts about $63,000,000. The exports are about $100,000,000, and the imports $110,000,000 yearly, thus leaving an adverse balance every way. An army of 350,000 men is maintained in time of peace; navy, 156 vessels, 1600 guns; railways, 900 miles; telegraph, 17,950 miles. The whole empire is divided into *vilayets* or provinces, for collection of taxes and government.

### TURKEY IN EUROPE.

**Area and Population.** As limited by the concessions consequent on the disastrous war with Russia, of 1878, Turkey in Europe is bounded north by Bulgaria, Servia, and Montenegro ; east by the Black Sea ; south by Greece and the Archipelago ; west by the Adriatic, and the Straits of Otranto; area (exclusive of Bulgaria, Eastern Roumelia, and Bosnia), about 80,000 square miles; population, 5,275,000.

**Physical Features.** A great part of the surface is covered with mountains of moderate elevation, the Carpathians forming part of the northern limits. Rivers are numerous, but of little importance, unless we include the Danube, forming the northern boundary of Bulgaria. The soil is for the most part fertile, but is not thoroughly cultivated.

**Products.** Maize, rice, cotton, barley, and millet are cultivated; in Albania are found the orange, citron, vine, peach, and plum; and in the valley of the Maritza roses are grown in abundance, from which ottar of roses is distilled. Cotton and silk are manufactured. Iron in large quantities, copper, galena, sulphur, alum, and salt are found.

COTTON PICKING.

**Chief Cities.** CONSTANTINOPLE, the capital of the empire, is beautifully situated on the west side of the Bosphorus. Its harbor, the Golden Horn, is an inlet five miles long, on the north side of the city. Within its limits are included Stamboul, Galata, and on the east side of the Bosphorus, Scutari. The population is about 1,075,000, including suburbs and floating population. Constantinople has been four times devastated by fire, and many times besieged, but only twice captured—in 1204, A. D., by the Crusaders, and in 1453 by the Turks, who then overthrew the Eastern Roman Empire. It occupies the site of ancient Byzantium. Other important towns are Adrianople on the Fundja (population, 150,000), formerly the seat of empire, and Salonica (population, 75,000), the chief commercial town, situated on the gulf of the same name on the Ægean, 270 miles from Constantinople.

### TURKEY IN ASIA.

The larger division of the Turkish Empire, is bounded north by the Black Sea and the Sea of Marmora; east by Persia and Trans-Caucasia ; south by Arabia and the Gulf of Aden, and west by the Archipelago, the Mediterranean, the Isthmus of Suez, and the Red Sea. It includes Asia Minor, Syria, Palestine, part of Armenia, Kurdistan, Mesopotamia, and that part of Arabia bordering on the Red Sea; area, 729,981 square miles; population, about 15,000,000, of which at least 13,000,000 are Mohammedans. The Ægean islands of Rhodes, Samos, Lemnos, Mitylene, Scio, and others are included in the kingdom. A range of mountains skirts the entire coast, and the Taurus chain stretches from west to east; the Tigris and Euphrates are the largest rivers. In such an extent of territory the productions are varied, including nearly all temperate and semi-tropical grains and fruits. There are few manufactures. The most famous cities are Smyrna (population, 170,000), a great trading port on the Ægean, famous for its raisins and wine, ALEPPO (population, 12,000), another commercial center, DAMASCUS (population, 150,000), probably the oldest city in the world, MECCA, the birthplace of Mahomet, and place of pilgrimage for the faithful, and JERUSALEM (population, 18,000), with its precious historical and Biblical associations.

## UNITED STATES OF AMERICA.

The great Republic of the western world comprises the central portion of the continent of North America, lying between latitude 24° 30′ and 49° north; and longitude 66° 50′ and 124° 45′ west; and also the territory of Alaska, purchased from Russia in 1867, separated from the main country by British Columbia. The United States are bounded north by the Dominion of Canada ; east by New Brunswick and the Atlantic ; south by the Gulf and Republic of Mexico; and west by the Pacific. The greatest length from the Atlantic to the Pacific is 2,800 miles; the greatest breadth from north to south about 1,200 miles; total area, 3,602,990 square miles; population, 1880, 50,155,783. The colored population amounted to 6,577,151 ; the Indians to 255,938 ;

and the Chinese to 105,717, of which 75,122 were in California. There are thirty-eight States and ten territories, which may be grouped as follows: 1. North Atlantic, or New England States—Maine, New Hampshire, Vermont, Mass. Conn., Rhode Island. 2. Middle Atlantic States—New York, New Jersey, Pennsylvania, Delaware, Maryland, and District of Columbia. 3. South Atlantic States—Virginia, North and South Carolina, Georgia, and Florida. 4. North Central States—Ohio, Indiana, Illinois, Wisconsin, and Michigan. 5. South Central States—West Virginia, Kentucky, Tennessee, Alabama, and Mississippi. 6. West Central States—Minnesota, Iowa, Missouri, Arkansas, and Louisiana.

7. Western or Highland States and Territories, including;—1. States of the Plain—Dakota Territory, Nebraska, Kansas, Indian Territory and Texas. 2. Rocky Mountain States—Montana Territory, Wyoming Territory, Colorado and New Mexico Territory. 3. Basin States—Idaho Territory, Nevada, Utah Territory, and Arizona Territory. 5. Pacific States—Alaska Territory, Washington Territory, Oregon, and California.

**Constitution and Government.** The text of the constitution and full information as to the various departments of government will be found elsewhere. A detailed and carefully prepared summary of noteworthy historical events is given in "Outlines of History."

**Physical Features.** The coast line of the Atlantic measures 2,350 miles; that of the Gulf of Mexico 1,556 miles: of the Pacific 1,810 miles, and of the Great Lakes 3,450 miles. The surface may be divided into two nearly equal parts the *low eastern half* and the *high western half.* The first is fertile and well watered. The Appalachian mountain system, of which the Alleghany, Cumberland, Blue, and White ranges are the largest branches, stretches in a north-east to south-west direction from Maine to Alabama. Mount Washington in the White Mountains attains the height of 6,428 feet. Mount Guyot in North Carolina is a little higher. East of the range many rivers flow to the indented Atlantic

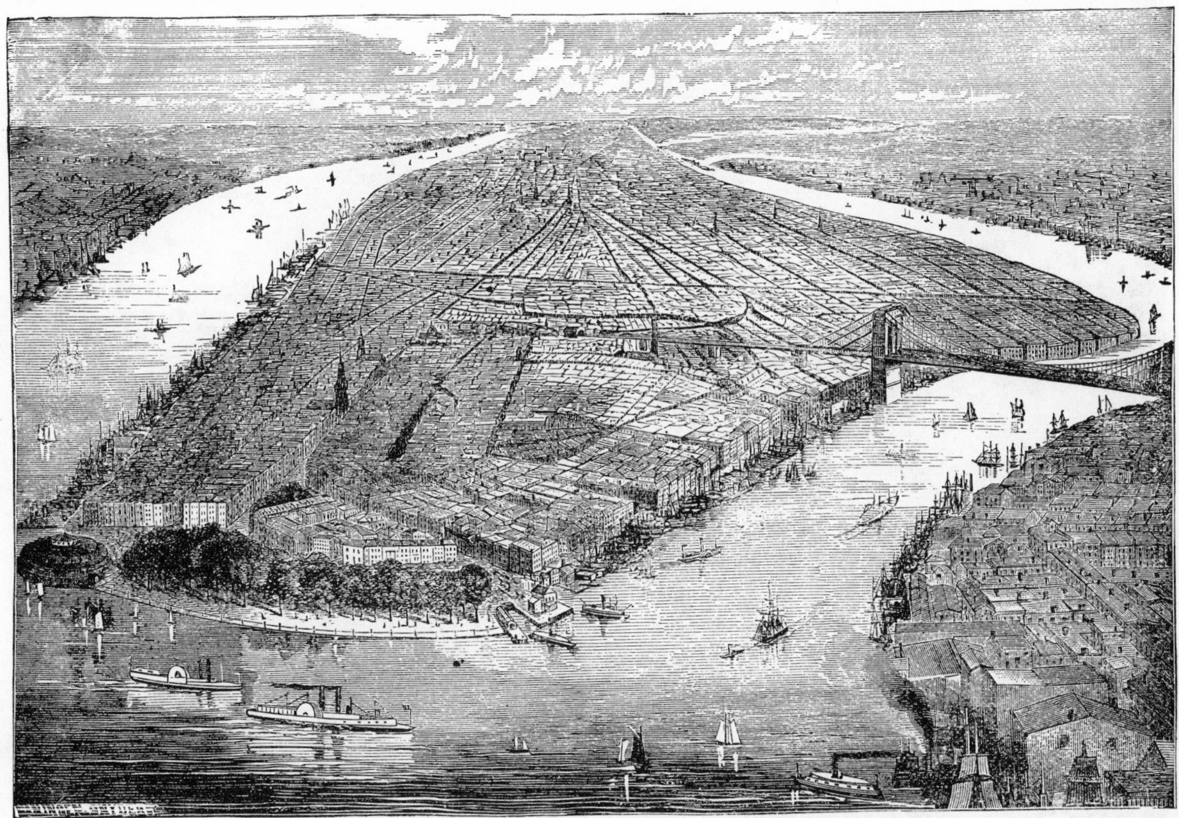

NEW YORK CITY.

coast, as the Penobscot, the Kennebec, the Connecticut, the Hudson, the Delaware, the Susquehanna, the Potomac, and the James. The southern portion of this section is drained into the Gulf by the Chattahoochee, the Appalachicola, the Tombigbee, and other streams. To the north lie the Great Lakes, covering 114,000 square miles, and between Ontario and Erie lie the Niagara Falls, one of the world's wonders. West of the Alleghanies stretches out the great central plain drained by the Mississippi and its tributaries, the most extensive system of navigated rivers in the world, having a drainage basin of 1,350,000 square miles. The Missouri, miscalled a branch of the Mississippi, is in reality the main stream, and from its source to the Gulf is 4,300 miles, navigable for nearly 3,000 miles; the chief branches on the east are the Ohio, and its great tributaries the Tennessee, Kentucky, Cumberland, and Wabash; on the west the Red, Arkansas, Kansas, and Platte. The great wheat, cotton, and tobacco plains of this region extend into the great prairies of the far West.

Turning now to the western and highland half, we find the vast, gently undulating plain of Dakota, Nebraska, Indian Territory, and Texas sloping slowly toward the Gulf of Mexico, drained in the north by the Missouri and its branches, and in the south by the Trinity, Brazos, Colorado, and Rio Grande, the last forming the Mexican boundary. These great plains are walled in on the west by the Rocky Mountains, extending from north-east to south-west across the whole country, culminating in Colorado in Mount Lincoln, 14,300 feet high. West of the Rockies is found another great plain or table-land, varied by small ranges, and containing what is known as the Great Basin, in the center of which is Great Salt Lake, and others having no outlets. In this section rise the Snake, Columbia, Grand, and Colorado, the great rivers of the far West. Between this extensive plateau, which is in great part unfit for cultivation, and the Pacific lie the Cascade and Sierra Nevada ranges, the highest peak being Mount Whitney, 14,900 feet. The small rich lowland of the California Basin lies at the foot of the Nevadas, drained by the Sacramento and Joaquin Rivers.

**Chief Cities.** The capitals and principal cities of the several States are given elsewhere. Twenty cities have a population of over 100,000 and thirty-five have more than 50,000. New York, the metropolis (population, 1880, 1,206,577) is admirably situated for purposes of commerce, standing at the head of a deep, safe, and beautiful bay, and having the Hudson and East Rivers on either side. Within a radius of twenty miles from the City Hall the population exceeds 2,500,000. Manhattan Island proper has an area of 22 square miles. Twenty-seven steam ferries, twenty converging railways, and numerous steam-boat lines connect the metropolis with its suburbs. The most important of the public parks are the Battery, commanding a fine view of the Bay; the City Hall Park, containing the city and county offices, and the immense granite Post-office; and the Central Park, a beautiful public pleasure ground, two and a half miles long and half a mile broad. Among the principal buildings we may note the Post-office, the City Hall, the County Court-House, Trinity Church, the Western Union Telegraph building, the Equity Insurance building, the *Tribune* office, Astor Library, Lennox Library, Art Gallery, and the Metropolitan Museum in Central Park, near which stands the obelisk

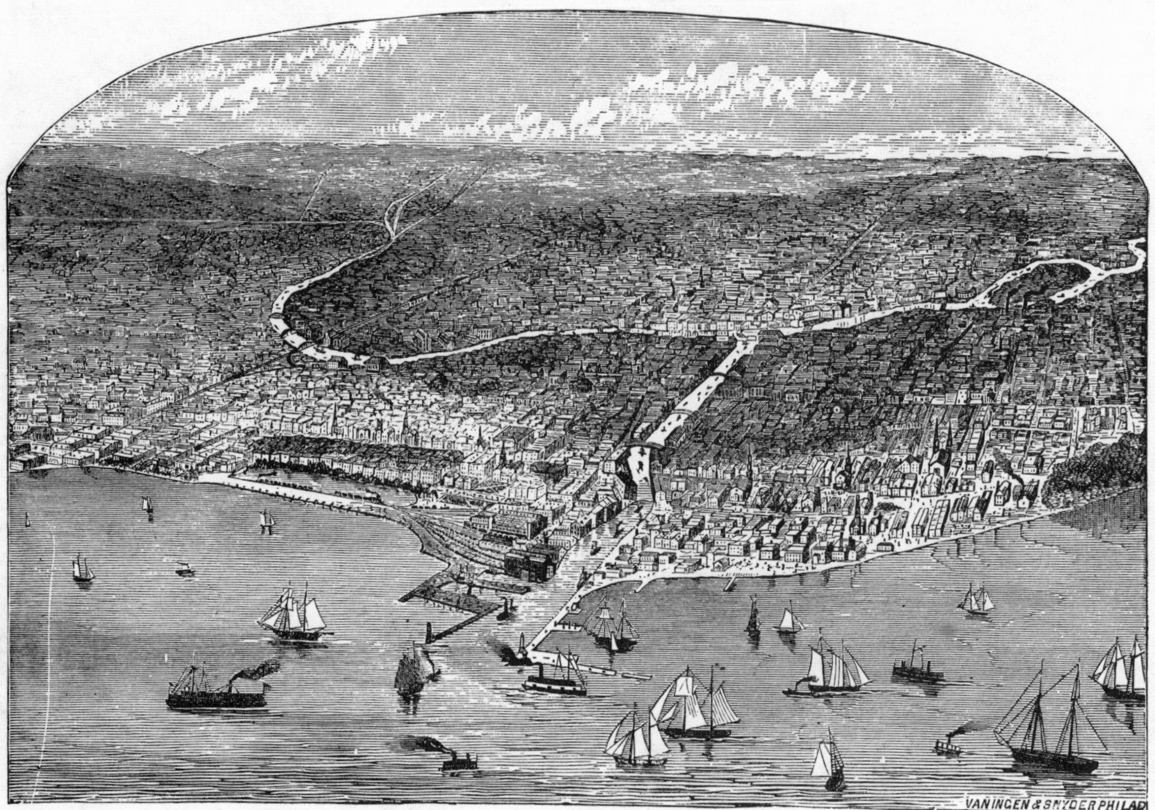

CHICAGO

brought from Egypt. Though preëminently a commercial city, New York surpasses every other in the total value of its manufactures.

Across the East River, and connected by the Brooklyn bridge, lies BROOKLYN, the third city of the United States (population, 1880, 566,689). The gigantic suspension bridge, now (1882) nearly completed, is the largest in the world. The central span is 1595 feet in length, and the total length is about 6,000 feet. The two massive piers by which it is supported are 268 feet in height. The total cost of the bridge will be nearly $15,000,000. Prospect Park is the great pleasure ground of the city, and near by is Greenwood Cemetery, noted for its natural and artificial beauties. From its numerous church edifices, Brooklyn is sometimes called the "City of Churches." Not far behind in population is CHICAGO, the commercial center of the West (population 503,304). The marvelous growth of this city is unparalleled in history; and the wonderful energy with which the ravages of the great fire of 1871 were repaired illustrates the vigor and business energy of the people. PHILADELPHIA (population, 1880, 847,170), the second city in population, is the first in manufactures and the greatest coal-depot in the country. Its historic associations made it a most fitting place for the great Centennial exhibition of 1876. BOSTON, the capital of Massachusetts (population, 369,832), may be called the literary center of the country, and is the third commercial city. ST. LOUIS (population 350,522) stands fifth in point of population, and is the center of the immense river traffic of the Mississippi.

SAN FRANCISCO, the only great city of the Pacific coast, has a population of 233,959. It lies on a narrow strip of land between the ocean and San Francisco bay. From the inlet which unites the two it gains its name of "The City of the Golden Gate." In 1848, the site was occupied by a struggling village called Serba Buena, of less than 500 inhabitants. Among the finest buildings are the United States branch mint, the Custom House, and the Palace Hotel, said to be the finest in the world. The Chinese quarter is built with narrow crooked streets and contains a Chinese theater, opium dens, gambling houses, and joss-houses or temples. NEW ORLEANS (population 216,090), the metropolis of the southwest, is second only in commercial importance to New York. It is situated below the sea level and in a swampy soil, the climate being very dangerous to strangers in the hot months. New Orleans was originally a French city, and retains to this day many of the characteristic features of European towns. Among the other cities, the most important are WASHINGTON, the seat of general government (population 147,293), with its expensive public buildings and regular network of avenues and streets converging at the capitol; BALTIMORE (population 332,330), sometimes called the "Monumental City," from the fine public monuments which adorn it, the most noticeable being that of Washington, 200 feet high; PITTSBURG (population 156,389), the center of

SAN FRANCISCO.

the great iron and coal interests of Pennsylvania and CINCINNATI (population 255,809), the great pork market of the United States.

**Religion and Education.** The Constitution guarantees perfect equality to all creeds and religions. About twenty-five different sects exist, the largest being the Methodist, the Baptist, the Presbyterian, the Roman Catholic, the Congregational, and the Protestant Episcopal. Education is general. The proportion of illiterate persons is very small as compared with that of other countries. Education is compulsory and free. The largest and best universities are not supported by the States. Harvard, at Cambridge ; Yale, at New Haven; Columbia, in New York City, and the University of Michigan may be named as among the best.

**Products, Commerce, and Finances.** The natural and artificial productions of the United States have been so extensively discussed under the various articles on agriculture, mining, manufactures, and commerce and transportation, that further mention here is unnecessary. The total exports in 1881 amounted to $902,377,346; imports, $642,664,628; revenue, mainly derived from imports and internal revenue duties (1880), $333,526,610; total expenditure, $267,642,957; net public debt (1881), $1,778,285,340; the separate debts of the States amount to about $600,000,000; standing army, 25,000; navy, 113 ships (many in process of repair or construction), 11,115 men, 900 officers; miles of railway, 86,497; telegraph lines, 107,103 miles; miles of wire, 309,279; number of post-offices, 44,512; letters carried (1880), 1,053,252,876; postal cards, 324,556,440.

## URUGUAY.

A small republic of South America, bounded north and east by Brazil, south by the mouth of the Plata, and south and southwest by the Argentine Confederation; area, 72,151 square miles; population, 455,000, more than half foreigners. Formerly a Brazilian province, Uruguay declared its independence in 1828 and adopted a constitution modeled on that of the United States. It is divided into East and West Uruguay by the river of the same name, of which the Rio Negro is the chief branch. The most striking feature is the vast extent of pampas or grassy plains, supporting great herds of cattle, horses, and sheep. Gold is found in paying quantities. The capital is MONTE VIDEO (population, 91,167).

## VENEZUELA.

A South American republic, bounded north by the Caribbean, east by the Atlantic and British Guiana, south by Brazil, and west by Colombia; area, 439,119 square miles; population, 1,784,197. The coast line is nearly 2,000 miles long, and the interior is mountainous ; the coast is intensely hot and unhealthy, while the elevated regions are temperate. There are about 1,000 streams, the Orinoco (1,800 miles long, draining 400,000 square miles, and having 50 mouths), and the Rio Negro being the largest. All kinds of tropical produce is abundant. Earthquakes are frequent. Capital, CARACAS (population, 48,897). The Confederation consists of twenty States, besides the federal district, each having an Executive and Legislature and sending delegates to a general Congress. The prevailing religion is the Roman Catholic, but all are tolerated. Education is gratuitous and compulsory. From 1819 to 1830 Venezuela formed part of Colombia. The chief exports are coffee and cocoa; total exports about $11,500,000; total imports, $15,000,000; miles of railway, seventy.

## ZANZIBAR.

This kingdom, off the eastern coast of Africa, includes the islands of Zanzibar and Pemba and several small isles. The main island contains about 400,000 acres, and the population is about 150,000, composed of Arab proprietors, negro slaves, free blacks, and about 6,000 Indians. Independence was obtained in 1862. The chief ruler is called a Sultan. The soil is wonderfully fertile, and produces rice, sugar-cane, cocoa-nuts, oranges, and other tropical fruits. The chief exports are ivory, gum-copal, india rubber, and cocoa-oil; they amount to about £500,000. The export of slaves has never wholly ceased. Capital, ZANZIBAR (population, 80,000). There are other important towns on the coast, from which caravans are sent into the interior to collect ivory.

# POLITICAL AND STATISTICAL RECORD OF STATES AND TERRITORIES.

| States and Territories. | Capitals. | Area in sq. miles. | Mean Annual Temperature. | Date of Settlement. | Date of Admission to the Union. | Electoral Vote. | Representatives. | Governor's Salary. | Governor's Term. | Miles of Railroad in 1880. | ¶Number of persons 10 years of age and upward who cannot read. |
|---|---|---|---|---|---|---|---|---|---|---|---|
| Alabama | Montgomery | 52,250 | 66° | 1711 | 1819 | 10 | 8 | $3,000 | 2 years. | 2,086 | 349,771 |
| Arkansas | Little Rock | 53,850 | 63 | 1685 | 1836 | 6 | 4 | 3,500 | 2 " | 591 | 111,799 |
| California | Sacramento | 158,360 | 55 | 1769 | 1850 | 6 | 4 | 6,000 | 3 " | 2,828 | 24,877 |
| Colorado | Denver | 103,925 | 48 | .... | 1876 | 3 | 1 | 3,000 | 2 " | 684 | 6,297 |
| *Connecticut | Hartford | 4,990 | 50 | 1633 | 1788† | 6 | 4 | 2,000 | 2 " | 906 | 19,680 |
| *Delaware | Dover | 2,050 | 53 | 1627 | 1787† | 3 | 1 | 2,000 | 4 " | 222 | 19,356 |
| Florida | Tallahassee | 58,680 | 69 | 1565 | 1845 | 4 | 2 | 3,500 | 4 " | 454 | 66,238 |
| *Georgia | Atlanta | 59,475 | 58 | 1733 | 1788† | 11 | 9 | 3,000 | 2 " | 2,616 | 418,553 |
| Illinois | Springfield | 56,650 | 50 | 1720 | 1818 | 21 | 19 | 6,000 | 4 " | 9,383 | 86,368 |
| Indiana | Indianapolis | 36,350 | 51 | 1690 | 1816 | 15 | 13 | 5,000 | 4 " | 5,069 | 76,634 |
| Iowa | Des Moines | 56,025 | 49 | 1833 | 1846 | 11 | 9 | 4,000 | 2 " | 2,852 | 24,115 |
| Kansas | Topeka | 82,080 | 51 | 1850 | 1861 | 5 | 3 | 3,000 | 2 " | 1,844 | 16,369. |
| Kentucky | Frankfort | 40,400 | 56 | 1775 | 1792 | 12 | 10 | 5,000 | 4 " | 1,906 | 249,567 |
| Louisiana | Baton Rouge | 48,720 | 69 | 1699 | 1812 | 8 | 6 | 4,000 | 4 " | 1,231 | 257,184 |
| Maine | Augusta | 33,040 | 45 | 1625 | 1820 | 7 | 5 | 2,000 | 2 " | 1,059 | 13,486 |
| *Maryland | Annapolis | 12,210 | 54 | 1634 | 1788† | 8 | 6 | 4,500 | 4 " | 1,072 | 114,100 |
| *Massachusetts | Boston | 8,315 | 48 | 1620 | 1788† | 13 | 11 | 4,000 | 1 " | 2,128 | 74,935 |
| Michigan | Lansing | 58,915 | 47 | 1670 | 1837 | 11 | 9 | 1,000 | 2 " | 3,607 | 34,613 |
| Minnesota | St. Paul | 83,365 | 42 | 1846 | 1858 | 5 | 3 | 3,800 | 2 " | 4,025 | 12,747 |
| Mississippi | Jackson | 46,810 | 64 | 1716 | 1817 | 8 | 6 | 4,000 | 4 " | 1,420 | 291,718 |
| Missouri | Jefferson City | 69,415 | 55 | 1764 | 1821 | 15 | 13 | 5,000 | 4 " | 3,875 | 146,771 |
| Nebraska | Lincoln | 76,855 | 49 | 1854 | 1867 | 3 | 1 | 2,500 | 2 " | 2,782 | 2,365 |
| Nevada | Carson City | 110,700 | 50 | 1861 | 1864 | 3 | 1 | 6,000 | 4 " | 322 | 727 |
| *New Hampshire | Concord | 9,305 | 46 | 1623 | 1788† | 5 | 3 | 1,000 | 2 " | 876 | 7,618 |
| *New Jersey | Trenton | 7,815 | 53 | 1624 | 1787† | 9 | 7 | 5,000 | 3 " | 1,687 | 37,057 |
| *New York | Albany | 49,170 | 48 | 1614 | 1788† | 35 | 33 | 10,000 | 3 " | 5,975 | 163,501 |
| *North Carolina | Raleigh | 52,250 | 59 | 1663 | 1789† | 10 | 8 | 3,000 | 4 " | 1,469 | 339,789 |
| Ohio | Columbus | 41,060 | 53 | 1788 | 1802 | 22 | 20 | 4,000 | 2 " | 7,046 | 92,720 |
| Oregon | Salem | 96,030 | 53 | 1811 | 1859 | 3 | 1 | 1,500 | 4 " | 588 | 2,609 |
| *Pennsylvania | Harrisburg | 45,215 | 54 | 1682 | 1787† | 29 | 27 | 10,000 | 3 " | 6,081 | 131,728 |
| *Rhode Island | Providence & Newport | 1,250 | 48 | 1636 | 1790† | 4 | 2 | 1,000 | 1 " | 153 | 15,416 |
| *South Carolina | Columbia | 30,570 | 62 | 1670 | 1788† | 7 | 5 | 3,500 | 2 " | 1,221 | 265,892 |
| Tennessee | Nashville | 42,050 | 58 | 1757 | 1796 | 12 | 10 | 4,000 | 2 " | 1,476 | 290,549 |
| Texas | Austin | 265,780 | 67 | 1690 | 1845 | 8 | 6 | 4,000 | 2 " | 3,219 | 189,423 |
| Vermont | Montpelier | 9,565 | 43 | 1725 | 1791 | 5 | 3 | 1,000 | 2 " | 836 | 15,185 |
| *Virginia | Richmond | 42,450 | 57 | 1607 | 1788† | 11 | 9 | 5,000 | 4 " | 2,028 | 390,913 |
| West Virginia | Wheeling | 24,780 | 52 | .... | 1862 | 5 | 3 | 2,700 | 4 " | 295 | 48,802 |
| Wisconsin | Madison | 56,040 | 45 | 1669 | 1848 | 10 | 8 | 5,000 | 2 " | 5,034 | 35,031 |
| Alaska | Sitka | 577,390 | 46 | .... | .... | .. | .. | .... | ........ | .... | ... |
| Arizona | Prescott | 113,020 | 69 | 1590 | .... | .. | ‡ | 2,600 | 4 " | 384 | 2,690 |
| Dakota | Yankton | 149,100 | 47 | 1859 | .... | .. | .. | 2,600 | 4 " | 209 | 1,249 |
| District of Columbia | ........ | 70 | 55 | .... | .... | .. | .. | .... | ........ | .... | 22,845 |
| Idaho | Boise City | 84,800 | 52 | 1842 | .... | .. | .. | 2,600 | 4 " | .... | 3,293 |
| Indian Territory | Tahlaquah | 64,690 | 60 | .... | .... | .. | .. | .... | ........ | .... | .... |
| Montana | Helena | 146,080 | 43 | 1852 | .... | .. | .. | 2,600 | 4 " | .... | 667 |
| New Mexico | Santa Fé | 122,580 | 51 | 1537 | .... | .. | .. | 2,600 | 4 " | 664 | 48,836 |
| Utah | Salt Lake City | 84,970 | 52 | 1847 | .... | .. | .. | 2,600 | 4 " | 815 | 2,515 |
| Washington | Olympia | 69,180 | 51 | 1845 | .... | .. | .. | 2,600 | 4 " | 274 | 1,018 |
| Wyoming | Cheyenne | 97,890 | 41 | 1867 | .... | .. | .. | 2,600 | 4 " | .... | 468 |
| United States | Washington, D. C. | 3,696,530 | | | | 369 | 293 | | | §93,669 | 4,528,084 |

* The thirteen original States. † Date of adoption of the Constitution. ‡ The Territories of Arizona, Dakota, Idaho, Montana, New Mexico, Utah, Washington, and Wyoming have each one Delegate. ¶ Census of 1870. § Fractions of a mile are not given for each State, but are included in the total.

# AGGREGATE POPULATION OF THE UNITED STATES

## AT EACH CENSUS.

*NOTE.—The narrow column under each census year shows the order of the States and Territories when arranged according to magnitude of Population.*

| States and Territories. | | 1880. | | 1870. | | 1860. | | 1850. | | 1840. | | 1830. | | 1820. | | 1810. | | 1800. | | 1790. |
|---|---|---|---|---|---|---|---|---|---|---|---|---|---|---|---|---|---|---|---|---|
| Total | | 50,155,783 | | 38,558,371 | | 31,443,321 | | 23,191,876 | | *17,069,453 | | †12,866,020 | | 9,633,822 | | 7,239,881 | | 5,308,483 | | 3,929,214 |
| Alabama | 17 | 1,262,505 | 16 | 996,992 | 13 | 964,201 | 12 | 771,623 | 12 | 590,756 | 15 | 309,527 | 19 | 127,901 | | | | | | |
| Arizona | 44 | 40,440 | 46 | 9,658 | | | | | | | | | | | | | | | | |
| Arkansas | 25 | 802,525 | 26 | 484,471 | 25 | 435,450 | 26 | 209,897 | 25 | 97,574 | 28 | 30,388 | 26 | 14,255 | | | | | | |
| California | 24 | 864,694 | 24 | 560,247 | 26 | 379,994 | 29 | 92,597 | | | | | | | | | | | | |
| Colorado | 35 | 194,327 | 41 | 39,864 | 38 | 34,277 | | | | | | | | | | | | | | |
| Connecticut | 28 | 622,700 | 25 | 537,454 | 24 | 460,147 | 21 | 370,792 | 20 | 309,978 | 16 | 297,675 | 14 | 275,148 | 9 | 261,942 | 8 | 251,002 | 8 | 237,946 |
| Dakota | 40 | 135,177 | 45 | 14,181 | 42 | 4,837 | | | | | | | | | | | | | | |
| Delaware | 38 | 146,608 | 35 | 125,015 | 32 | 112,216 | 30 | 91,532 | 26 | 78,085 | 24 | 76,748 | 22 | 72,749 | 19 | 72,647 | 17 | 64,273 | 16 | 59,096 |
| Dist. of Columbia | 36 | 177,624 | 34 | 131,700 | 35 | 75,080 | 33 | 51,687 | 28 | 43,712 | 25 | 39,834 | 25 | 33,039 | 22 | 24,023 | 19 | 14,093 | | |
| Florida | 34 | 269,493 | 33 | 187,748 | 31 | 140,424 | 31 | 87,445 | 27 | 54,477 | 26 | 34,730 | | | | | | | | |
| Georgia | 13 | 1,542,180 | 12 | 1,184,109 | 11 | 1,057,286 | 9 | 906,185 | 9 | 691,392 | 10 | 516,823 | 11 | 340,985 | 11 | 252,433 | 12 | 162,686 | 13 | 82,548 |
| Idaho | 46 | 32,610 | 44 | 14,999 | | | | | | | | | | | | | | | | |
| Illinois | 4 | 3,077,871 | 4 | 2,539,891 | 4 | 1,711,951 | 11 | 851,470 | 14 | 476,183 | 20 | 157,445 | 24 | 55,162 | 24 | 12,282 | | | | |
| Indiana | 6 | 1,978,301 | 6 | 1,680,637 | 6 | 1,350,428 | 7 | 988,416 | 10 | 685,866 | 13 | 343,031 | 18 | 147,178 | 21 | 24,520 | 21 | 5,641 | | |
| Iowa | 10 | 1,624,615 | 11 | 1,194,020 | 20 | 674,913 | 27 | 192,214 | 29 | 43,112 | | | | | | | | | | |
| Kansas | 20 | 996,096 | 29 | 264,399 | 33 | 107,206 | | | | | | | | | | | | | | |
| Kentucky | 8 | 1,648,690 | 8 | 1,321,011 | 9 | 1,155,684 | 8 | 982,405 | 6 | 779,828 | 6 | 687,917 | 6 | 564,135 | 7 | 406,511 | 9 | 220,955 | 14 | 73,677 |
| Louisiana | 22 | 939,946 | 21 | 726,915 | 17 | 708,002 | 18 | 517,762 | 19 | 552,411 | 19 | 215,739 | 17 | 152,923 | 18 | 76,556 | | | | |
| Maine | 27 | 648,936 | 23 | 626,915 | 22 | 628,279 | 16 | 583,169 | 13 | 501,793 | 12 | 399,455 | 12 | 298,269 | 14 | 228,705 | 14 | 151,719 | 11 | 96,540 |
| Maryland | 23 | 934,943 | 20 | 780,894 | 19 | 687,049 | 17 | 583,034 | 15 | 470,019 | 11 | 447,040 | 10 | 407,350 | 8 | 380,546 | 7 | 341,548 | 6 | 319,728 |
| Massachusetts | 7 | 1,783,085 | 7 | 1,457,351 | 7 | 1,231,066 | 6 | 994,514 | 8 | 737,699 | 8 | 610,408 | 7 | 523,159 | 5 | 472,040 | 5 | 422,845 | 4 | 378,787 |
| Michigan | 9 | 1,636,937 | 13 | 1,184,059 | 16 | 749,113 | 20 | 097,654 | 23 | 212,267 | 27 | 31.639 | 27 | 8,765 | 25 | 4,762 | | | | |
| Minnesota | 26 | 780,773 | 28 | 439,706 | 30 | 172,023 | 36 | 6,077 | | | | | | | | | | | | |
| Mississippi | 18 | 1,131,597 | 18 | 827,922 | 14 | 791,305 | 15 | 606,526 | 17 | 375,651 | 22 | 136,621 | 21 | 75,448 | 20 | 40,352 | 20 | 8,850 | | |
| Missouri | 5 | 2,168,380 | 5 | 1,721,295 | 8 | 1,182,012 | 13 | 682,044 | 16 | 383,702 | 21 | 140,455 | 23 | 66,557 | 23 | 20,845 | | | | |
| Montana | 45 | 39,159 | 43 | 20,595 | | | | | | | | | | | | | | | | |
| Nebraska | 30 | 452,402 | 36 | 122,993 | 39 | 28,841 | | | | | | | | | | | | | | |
| Nevada | 43 | 62,266 | 40 | 42,491 | 41 | 6.857 | | | | | | | | | | | | | | |
| New Hampshire | 31 | 346,991 | 31 | 318,300 | 27 | 326,073 | 22 | 317,976 | 22 | 284,574 | 18 | 269,328 | 15 | 244,022 | 16 | 214,460 | 11 | 183,858 | 10 | 141,885 |
| New Jersey | 19 | 1,131,116 | 17 | 906,096 | 21 | 672,035 | 19 | 489,555 | 18 | 373,306 | 14 | 320,823 | 13 | 277,426 | 12 | 245,562 | 10 | 211,149 | 9 | 184,139 |
| New Mexico | 41 | 119,565 | 37 | 91,874 | 34 | 93,516 | 32 | 61,547 | | | | | | | | | | | | |
| New York | 1 | 5,082,871 | 1 | 4,382,759 | 1 | 3,880,735 | 1 | 3,097,394 | 1 | 2,428,921 | 1 | 1,918,608 | 1 | 1,372,111 | 2 | 959,049 | 3 | 589,051 | 5 | 340,120 |
| North Carolina | 15 | 1,399,750 | 14 | 1,071,361 | 12 | 992,622 | 10 | 869,039 | 7 | 753,419 | 5 | 737,987 | 4 | 638,829 | 4 | 555,500 | 4 | 478,103 | 3 | 393,751 |
| Ohio | 3 | 3,198,062 | 3 | 2,665,260 | 3 | 2,339,511 | 3 | 1,980,329 | 3 | 1,519,467 | 4 | 937,903 | 5 | 581,295 | 13 | 230,760 | 18 | 45,365 | | |
| Oregon | 37 | 174,768 | 38 | 90,923 | 36 | 52,465 | 34 | 13,294 | | | | | | | | | | | | |
| Pennsylvania | 2 | 4,282,891 | 2 | 3,521,951 | 2 | 2,906,215 | 2 | 2,311,786 | 2 | 1,724,033 | 2 | 1,348,233 | 3 | 1,047,507 | 3 | 810,091 | 2 | 602,365 | 2 | 434,373 |
| Rhode Island | 33 | 276,531 | 32 | 217,353 | 29 | 174,620 | 28 | 147,545 | 24 | 108,830 | 23 | 97,199 | 20 | 83,015 | 17 | 76,931 | 16 | 69,122 | 15 | 68,825 |
| South Carolina | 21 | 995,577 | 22 | 705,606 | 18 | 703,708 | 14 | 668,507 | 11 | 594,398 | 9 | 581,185 | 8 | 502,741 | 6 | 415,115 | 6 | 345,591 | 7 | 249,073 |
| Tennessee | 12 | 1,542,359 | 9 | 1,258,520 | 10 | 1,109,801 | 5 | 1,002,717 | 5 | 829,210 | 7 | 681,904 | 9 | 422,771 | 10 | 261,727 | 15 | 105,602 | 17 | 35,691 |
| Texas | 11 | 1,591,749 | 19 | 818,579 | 23 | 604,215 | 25 | 212,592 | | | | | | | | | | | | |
| Utah | 39 | 143,963 | 39 | 86,786 | 37 | 40,273 | 35 | 11,380 | | | | | | | | | | | | |
| Vermont | 32 | 332,286 | 30 | 330,551 | 28 | 315,098 | 23 | 314,120 | 21 | 291,948 | 17 | 280,652 | 16 | 235,966 | 15 | 217,895 | 13 | 154,465 | 12 | 85,425 |
| Virginia | 14 | 1,512,565 | 10 | 1,225,163 | 5 | 1,596,318 | 4 | 1,421,661 | 4 | 1,239,797 | 3 | 1,211,405 | 2 | 1,065,116 | 1 | 974,600 | 1 | 880,200 | 1 | 747,610 |
| Washington | 42 | 75,116 | 42 | 23,955 | 40 | 11,594 | | | | | | | | | | | | | | |
| West Virginia | 29 | 618,457 | 27 | 442,014 | | | | | | | | | | | | | | | | |
| Wisconsin | 16 | 1,315,497 | 15 | 1,054,670 | 15 | 775,881 | 24 | 305,391 | 30 | 30,945 | | | | | | | | | | |
| Wyoming | 47 | 20,789 | 47 | 9,118 | | | | | | | | | | | | | | | | |

* Including 6,100 persons on public ships in the service of the United States.

† Including 5,318 persons on public ships in the service of the United States.

# POPULATION OF THE UNITED STATES

## BY STATES AND TERRITORIES, IN 1880.

## IN THE AGGREGATE, AND BY SEX, NATIVITY AND RACE.

| States and Territories. | Total. | Male. | Female. | Native. | Foreign. | White. | Colored. | Chinese. | Japanese. | Indians. |
|---|---|---|---|---|---|---|---|---|---|---|
| The United States | 50,155,784 | 25,518,820 | 24,636,963 | 43,475,840 | 6,679,943 | 43,402,970 | 6,580,793 | 105,465 | 148 | 66,407 |
| The States | 49,371,340 | 25,075,619 | 24,295,721 | 42,871,556 | 6,499,784 | 42,714,479 | 6,513,372 | 93,782 | 141 | 44,566 |
| Alabama | 1,262,505 | 622,629 | 639,876 | 1,252,771 | 9,734 | 662,185 | 600,103 | 4 | ....... | 213 |
| Arkansas | 802,525 | 416,279 | 386,246 | 792,175 | 10,350 | 591,531 | 210,666 | 133 | ....... | 195 |
| California | 864,694 | 518,176 | 346,518 | 571,820 | 292,874 | 767,181 | 6,018 | 75,132 | 86 | 16,277 |
| Colorado | 194,327 | 129,131 | 65,196 | 154,537 | 39,790 | 191,126 | 2,435 | 612 | ....... | 154 |
| Connecticut | 622,700 | 305,782 | 316,918 | 492,708 | 129,992 | 610,769 | 11,547 | 123 | 6 | 255 |
| Delaware | 146,608 | 74,108 | 72,500 | 137,140 | 9,468 | 120,160 | 26,442 | 1 | ....... | 5 |
| Florida | 269,493 | 136,444 | 133,049 | 259,584 | 9,909 | 142,605 | 126,690 | 18 | ....... | 180 |
| Georgia | 1,542,180 | 762,981 | 779,199 | 1,531,616 | 10,564 | 816,906 | 725,133 | 17 | ....... | 124 |
| Illinois | 3,077,871 | 1,586,523 | 1,491,348 | 2,494,295 | 583,576 | 3,031,151 | 46,368 | 209 | 3 | 140 |
| Indiana | 1,978,301 | 1,010,361 | 967,940 | 1,834,123 | 144,178 | 1,938,798 | 39,228 | 29 | ....... | 246 |
| Iowa | 1,624,615 | 848,136 | 776,479 | 1,362,965 | 261,650 | 1,614,600 | 9,516 | 33 | ....... | 466 |
| Kansas | 996,096 | 536,667 | 459,429 | 886,010 | 110,086 | 952,155 | 43,107 | 19 | ....... | 815 |
| Kentucky | 1,648,690 | 832,590 | 816,100 | 1,589,173 | 59,517 | 1,377,179 | 271,451 | 10 | ....... | 50 |
| Louisiana | 939,946 | 468,754 | 471,192 | 885,800 | 54,146 | 454,954 | 483,655 | 489 | ....... | 848 |
| Maine | 648,936 | 324,058 | 324,878 | 590,053 | 58,883 | 646,852 | 1,451 | 8 | ....... | 625 |
| Maryland | 934,943 | 462,187 | 472,756 | 852,137 | 82,806 | 724,693 | 210,230 | 5 | ....... | 15 |
| Massachusetts | 1,783,085 | 858,440 | 924,645 | 1,339,594 | 443,491 | 1,763,782 | 18,697 | 229 | 8 | 369 |
| Michigan | 1,636,937 | 862,355 | 774,582 | 1,248,429 | 388,508 | 1,614,560 | 15,100 | 27 | 1 | 7,249 |
| Minnesota | 780,773 | 419,149 | 361,624 | 513,097 | 267,676 | 776,884 | 1,564 | 24 | 1 | 2,300 |
| Mississippi | 1,131,597 | 567,177 | 564,420 | 1,122,388 | 9,209 | 479,398 | 650,291 | 51 | ....... | 1,857 |
| Missouri | 2,168,380 | 1,127,187 | 1,041,193 | 1,956,802 | 211,578 | 2,022,826 | 145,350 | 91 | ....... | 113 |
| Nebraska | 452,402 | 249,241 | 203,161 | 354,988 | 97,414 | 449,764 | 2,385 | 18 | ....... | 235 |
| Nevada | 62,266 | 42,019 | 20,247 | 36,613 | 25,653 | 53,556 | 488 | 5,416 | 3 | 2,803 |
| New Hampshire | 346,991 | 170,526 | 176,465 | 300,697 | 46,294 | 346,229 | 685 | 14 | ....... | 63 |
| New Jersey | 1,131,116 | 559,922 | 571,194 | 909,416 | 221,700 | 1,092,017 | 38,853 | 170 | 2 | 74 |
| New York | 5,082,871 | 2,505,322 | 2,577,549 | 3.871,492 | 1,211,379 | 5,016,022 | 65,104 | 909 | 17 | 819 |
| North Carolina | 1,399,750 | 687,908 | 711,842 | 1,396,008 | 3,742 | 867,242 | 531,277 | ....... | 1 | 1,230 |
| Ohio | 3,198,062 | 1,613,936 | 1,584,126 | 2,803,119 | 394,943 | 3,117,920 | 79,900 | 109 | 3 | 130 |
| Oregon | 174,768 | 103,381 | 71,387 | 144,265 | 30,503 | 163,075 | 487 | 9,510 | 2 | 1,694 |
| Pennsylvania | 4,282,891 | 2,136,655 | 2,146,236 | 3,695,062 | 587,829 | 4,197,016 | 85,535 | 148 | 8 | 184 |
| Rhode Island | 276,531 | 133,030 | 143,501 | 202,538 | 73,993 | 269,939 | 6,488 | 27 | ....... | 77 |
| South Carolina | 995,577 | 490,408 | 505,169 | 987,891 | 7,686 | 391,105 | 604,332 | 9 | ....... | 131 |
| Tennessee | 1,542,359 | 769,277 | 773,082 | 1,525,657 | 16,702 | 1,138,831 | 403,151 | 25 | ....... | 352 |
| Texas | 1,591,749 | 837,840 | 753,909 | 1,477,133 | 114,616 | 1,197,237 | 393,384 | 136 | ....... | 992 |
| Vermont | 332,286 | 166,887 | 165,399 | 291,327 | 40,959 | 331,218 | 1,057 | ....... | ....... | 11 |
| Virginia | 1,512,565 | 745,589 | 766,976 | 1,497,869 | 14,696 | 880,858 | 631,616 | 6 | ....... | 85 |
| West Virginia | 618,457 | 314,495 | 303,962 | 600,192 | 18,265 | 592,537 | 25,886 | 5 | ....... | 29 |
| Wisconsin | 1,315,497 | 680,069 | 635,428 | 910,072 | 405,425 | 1,309,618 | 2,702 | 16 | ....... | 3,161 |
| The Territories | 784,443 | 443,201 | 341,242 | 604,284 | 180,159 | 688,491 | 62,421 | 11,683 | 7 | 21,841 |
| Arizona | 40,440 | 28,202 | 12,238 | 24,391 | 16,049 | 35,160 | 155 | 1,630 | 2 | 3,493 |
| Dakota | 135,177 | 82,296 | 52,881 | 83,382 | 51,795 | 133,147 | 401 | 238 | ....... | 1,391 |
| District of Columbia | 177,624 | 83,578 | 94,046 | 160,502 | 17,122 | 118,006 | 59,596 | 13 | 4 | 5 |
| Idaho | 32,610 | 21,818 | 10,792 | 22,636 | 9,974 | 29,013 | 53 | 3,379 | ....... | 165 |
| Montana | 39,159 | 28,177 | 10,982 | 27,638 | 11,521 | 35,385 | 346 | 1,765 | ....... | 1,663 |
| New Mexico | 119,565 | 64,496 | 55,069 | 111,514 | 8,051 | 108,721 | 1,015 | 57 | ....... | 9,772 |
| Utah | 143,963 | 74,509 | 69,454 | 99,969 | 43,994 | 142,423 | 232 | 501 | ....... | 807 |
| Washington | 75,116 | 45,973 | 29,143 | 59,313 | 15,803 | 67,199 | 325 | 3,186 | 1 | 4,405 |
| Wyoming | 20,789 | 14,152 | 6,637 | 14,939 | 5,850 | 19,437 | 298 | 914 | ....... | 140 |

# POLITICAL HISTORY OF THE UNITED STATES.

| President. | Inaugurated. | Vice-President. | Inaugurated. | Secretary of State. | Appointed. | Secretary of Treasury. | Appointed. |
|---|---|---|---|---|---|---|---|
| George Washington | 1789 | John Adams | 1789 | Thomas Jefferson | 1789 | Alex. Hamilton | 1789 |
| George Washington | 1793 | John Adams | 1793 | Edm. Randolph | 1794 | Oliver Wolcott | 1795 |
| | | | | Tim. Pickering | 1795 | | |
| John Adams | 1797 | Thomas Jefferson | 1797 | Tim. Pickering | 1797 | Oliver Wolcott | 1797 |
| | | | | John Marshall | 1800 | S. Dexter | 1800 |
| Thomas Jefferson | 1801 | Aaron Burr | 1801 | James Madison | 1801 | S. Dexter | 1801 |
| Thomas Jefferson | 1805 | George Clinton | 1805 | | | Albert Gallatin | 1802 |
| James Madison | 1809 | George Clinton | 1809 | Robert Smith | 1809 | Albert Gallatin | 1809 |
| James Madison | 1813 | Elbridge Gerry | 1813 | James Monroe | 1811 | G. W. Campbell | 1814 |
| | | | | | | Alex. J. Dallas | 1814 |
| James Monroe | 1817 | Dan. D. Tompkins | 1817 | John Q. Adams | 1817 | W. H. Crawford | 1817 |
| James Monroe | 1821 | | | | | | |
| John Q. Adams | 1825 | John C. Calhoun | 1825 | Henry Clay | 1825 | Richard Rush | 1825 |
| Andrew Jackson | 1829 | John C. Calhoun | 1829 | Martin Van Buren | 1829 | Samuel D. Ingham | 1829 |
| Andrew Jackson | 1833 | Martin Van Buren | 1833 | Ed. Livingston | 1831 | Louis McLane | 1831 |
| | | | | Louis McLane | 1833 | William J. Duane | 1833 |
| | | | | John Forsyth | 1834 | Roger B. Taney | 1833 |
| | | | | | | Levi Woodbury | 1834 |
| Martin Van Buren | 1837 | Richard M. Johnson | 1837 | John Forsyth | 1837 | Levi Woodbury | 1837 |
| Wm. H. Harrison | 1841 | John Tyler | 1841 | Daniel Webster | 1841 | Thomas Ewing | 1841 |
| John Tyler | 1841 | | | Hugh S. Legare | 1843 | Walter Forward | 1841 |
| | | | | Abel P. Upshur | 1843 | John C. Spencer | 1843 |
| | | | | John Nelson | 1844 | George M. Bibb | 1844 |
| | | | | John C. Calhoun | 1844 | | |
| James Knox Polk | 1845 | George M. Dallas | 1845 | James Buchanan | 1845 | Robt. J. Walker | 1845 |
| Zachary Taylor | 1849 | Millard Fillmore | 1849 | John M. Clayton | 1849 | W. M. Meredith | 1849 |
| Millard Fillmore | 1850 | | | Daniel Webster | 1850 | Thomas Corwin | 1850 |
| | | | | Edward Everett | 1852 | | |
| Franklin Pierce | 1853 | Wm. R. King | 1853 | William L. Marcy | 1853 | James Guthrie | 1853 |
| James Buchanan | 1857 | J. C. Breckenridge | 1857 | Lewis Cass | 1857 | Howell Cobb | 1857 |
| | | | | Jeremiah S. Black | 1860 | Philip F. Thomas | 1860 |
| | | | | | | John A. Dix | 1861 |
| Abraham Lincoln | 1861 | Hannibal Hamblin | 1861 | William H. Seward | 1861 | Salmon P. Chase | 1861 |
| | | | | | | W. P. Fessenden | 1864 |
| Abraham Lincoln | 1865 | Andrew Johnson | 1865 | | | Hugh McCulloch | 1865 |
| Andrew Johnson | 1865 | | | | | | |
| Ulysses S. Grant | 1869 | Schuyler Colfax | 1869 | E. B. Washburne | 1869 | Alex. T. Stewart | 1869 |
| Ulysses S. Grant | 1873 | Henry Wilson | 1873 | Hamilton Fish | 1869 | Geo. S. Boutwell | 1869 |
| | | | | | | W. A. Richardson | 1873 |
| | | | | | | Benj. H. Bristow | 1874 |
| | | | | | | L. M. Morrill | 1876 |
| Rutherford B. Hayes | 1877 | Wm. A. Wheeler | 1877 | Wm. M. Evarts | 1877 | John Sherman | 1877 |
| James A. Garfield | 1881 | Chester A. Arthur | 1881 | James G. Blaine | 1881 | William Windom | 1881 |
| Chester A. Arthur | 1881 | | | F. T. Frelinghuysen | 1881 | Charles J. Folger | 1881 |

# POLITICAL HISTORY OF THE UNITED STATES.—Continued.

| Secretary of War. | Appointed. | Secretary of Navy. | Appointed. | Sec'y of Interior. | Appointed. | Postmaster General. | Appointed. | Attorney General. | Appointed. |
|---|---|---|---|---|---|---|---|---|---|
| Henry Knox | 1789 | Henry Knox | 1789 | Interior Department created 1849. | | Samuel Osgood | 1789 | E. Randolph | 1789 |
| T. Pickering | 1794 | T. Pickering | 1794 | | | T. Pickering | 1791 | Wm. Bradford | 1794 |
| J. McHenry | 1796 | J. McHenry | 1796 | | | Jos. Habersham | 1795 | Charles Lee | 1795 |
| J. McHenry | 1797 | George Cabot | 1798 | | | Jos. Habersham | 1797 | Charles Lee | 1797 |
| S. Dexter | 1800 | B. Stoddert | 1798 | | | | | | |
| John Marshall | 1800 | | | | | | | | |
| Rog. Griswold | 1801 | | | | | | | | |
| H. Dearborn | 1801 | B. Stoddert | 1801 | | | Jos. Habersham | 1801 | Th. Parsons | 1801 |
| | | Robert Smith | 1802 | | | Gideon Granger | 1802 | Levi Lincoln | 1801 |
| | | J. Crowinshield | 1805 | | | | | Robert Smith | 1805 |
| | | | | | | | | J. Breckenridge | 1805 |
| | | | | | | | | C. A. Rodney | 1807 |
| William Eustis | 1809 | Paul Hamilton | 1809 | | | Gideon Granger | 1809 | C. A. Rodney | 1809 |
| J. Armstrong | 1813 | William Jones | 1813 | | | R. J. Meigs | 1814 | W. Pinckney | 1811 |
| James Monroe | 1814 | B. W. Crowinshield | 1814 | | | | | Richard Rush | 1814 |
| W. H. Crawford | 1815 | | | | | | | | |
| Isaac Shelby | 1817 | B. W. Crowinshield | 1817 | | | R. J. Meigs | 1817 | William Wirt | 1817 |
| J. C. Calhoun | 1817 | S. Thompson | 1818 | | | John McLean | 1823 | | |
| | | John Rodgers | 1823 | | | | | | |
| | | S. L. Southard | 1823 | | | | | | |
| James Barbour | 1825 | S. L. Southard | 1825 | | | John McLean | 1825 | William Wirt | 1825 |
| P. B. Porter | 1828 | | | | | | | | |
| John H. Eaton | 1829 | John Branch | 1829 | | | W. T. Barry | 1829 | J. M. Berrien | 1829 |
| Lewis Cass | 1831 | L. Woodbury | 1831 | | | Amos Kendall | 1835 | R. B. Taney | 1831 |
| | | M. Dickerson | 1834 | | | | | B. F. Butler | 1834 |
| J. R. Poinsett | 1837 | M. Dickerson | 1837 | | | Amos Kendall | 1837 | B. F. Butler | 1837 |
| | | J. K. Paulding | 1838 | | | John M. Niles | 1840 | Felix Grundy | 1838 |
| | | | | | | | | H. D. Gilpin | 1840 |
| John Bell | 1841 | Geo. E. Badger | 1841 | | | Francis Granger | 1841 | J. J. Crittenden | 1841 |
| John C. Spencer | 1841 | Abel P. Upshur | 1841 | | | C. A. Wickliffe | 1841 | H. S. Legare | 1841 |
| James M. Porter | 1843 | David Henshaw, | 1843 | | | | | John Nelson | 1844 |
| Wm. Wilkins | 1844 | T. W. Gilmer | 1844 | | | | | | |
| | | John Y. Mason | 1844 | | | | | | |
| W. L. Marcy | 1845 | Geo. Bancroft | 1845 | | | Cave Johnson | 1845 | J. Y. Mason | 1845 |
| | | John Y. Mason | 1846 | | | | | N. Clifford | 1846 |
| | | | | | | | | Isaac Toucey | 1848 |
| G. W. Crawford | 1849 | Wm. B. Preston | 1849 | Thomas Ewing | 1849 | Jacob Collamer | 1849 | R. Johnson | 1849 |
| Winfield Scott | 1850 | Wm. A. Graham | 1850 | A. H. H. Stuart | 1850 | Nathan K. Hall | 1850 | J. J. Crittenden | 1850 |
| Chas. M. Conrad | 1850 | J. P. Kennedy | 1852 | | | S. D. Hubbard | 1852 | | |
| Jefferson Davis | 1853 | James C. Dobbin | 1853 | R. McClelland | 1853 | James Campbell | 1853 | Caleb Cushing | 1853 |
| John B. Floyd | 1857 | Isaac Toucey | 1857 | J. Thompson | 1857 | Aaron V. Brown | 1857 | J. S. Black | 1857 |
| Joseph Holt | 1860 | | | | | Joseph Holt | 1859 | E. M. Stanton | 1860 |
| | | | | | | Horatio King | 1861 | | |
| S. Cameron | 1861 | Gideon Welles | 1861 | Caleb B. Smith | 1861 | Montg. Blair | 1861 | Edw. Bates | 1861 |
| E. M. Stanton | 1861 | | | John P. Usher | 1863 | Wm. Dennison | 1864 | James Speed | 1864 |
| | | | | James Harlan | 1865 | | | | |
| Ulysses S. Grant | 1867 | | | O. H. Browning | 1866 | A. W. Randall | 1866 | H. F. Stanberry | 1866 |
| Lorenzo Thomas | 1868 | | | | | | | O. H. Browning | 1868 |
| J. M. Schofield | 1868 | | | | | | | W. M. Evarts | 1868 |
| J. M. Schofield | 1869 | Adolph E. Borie | 1869 | J. D. Cox | 1869 | J. A. J. Cresswell | 1869 | E. R. Hoar | 1869 |
| J. A. Rawlins | 1869 | G. W. Robeson | 1869 | C. Delano | 1870 | Jas. W. Marshall | 1874 | A. T. Ackerman | 1870 |
| W. W. Belknap | 1869 | | | Zach. Chandler | 1875 | Marshall Jewell | 1874 | E. S. Pierrepont | 1875 |
| Jas. D. Cameron | 1876 | | | | | Jas. N. Tyner | 1876 | G. H. Williams | 1876 |
| | | | | | | | | A. Taft | 1876 |
| G. W. McCrary | 1877 | R. W. Thompson | 1877 | Carl Schurz | 1877 | D. M. Keys | 1877 | H. Devens | 1877 |
| | | Nathan Goff, Jr. | 1881 | | | | | | |
| Robt. T. Lincoln | 1881 | Wm. H. Hunt | 1881 | Sam'l J. Kirkwood | 1881 | Thomas L. James | 1881 | Wayne MacVeagh | 1881 |
| | | William E. Chandler | | Henry M. Teller | | Timothy O. Howe | 1881 | B. H. Brewster | 1881 |

# THE ARMIES AND NAVIES OF THE WORLD.

## ARMY.

| COUNTRIES. | Population. | Regular Army. | War Footing. | Annual Cost of Army. | Cost per Head. | *Per cent of total expenditure. |
|---|---|---|---|---|---|---|
| Argentine Republic | 2,400,000 | 8,227 | 304,000 | $3,374,518 | $1.46 | 19.53 |
| Austria-Hungary | 37,739,407 | 289,190 | 1,125,833 | 53,386,915 | 1.41 | 87.38 |
| Belgium | 5,476,668 | 46,383 | 165,877 | 8,776,429 | 1.60 | 15.73 |
| Bolivia | 2,080,000 | 3,021 | ........ | 1,126,916 | .54 | 25.01 |
| Brazil | 11,108,291 | 15,304 | 32,000 | 8,690,000 | .78 | 14.54 |
| Canada | 4,352,080 | 2,000 | 700,152 | 777,399 | .17 | 3.11 |
| Chili | 2,400,396 | 3,573 | 50,000 | ........ | .... | .... |
| China | 434,626,000 | 300,000 | 1,000,000 | ........ | .... | .... |
| Colombia | 2,774,000 | 3,000 | 30,740 | 982,432 | .35 | 11.37 |
| Denmark | 1,969,454 | 35,727 | 49,054 | 2,359,027 | 1.19 | 20.96 |
| Egypt | 17,419,980 | 15,000 | 43,000 | ‡2,198,216 | .12 | 5.31 |
| France | 36,905,788 | 502,764 | 3,753,164 | 114,279,761 | 3.09 | 20.88 |
| Germany | 45,194,172 | 445,402 | 1,492,104 | 98,330,429 | 2.17 | 66.57 |
| Great Britain | 35,246,562 | 131,636 | 577,906 | 74,901,500 | 2.12 | 18.02 |
| Greece | 1,679,775 | 12,118 | 35,000 | 2,264,716 | 1.34 | 12.06 |
| India, British | 252,541,210 | 189,597 | 380,000 | 84,481,195 | .33 | 26.74 |
| Italy | 28,209,620 | 736,502 | 1,718,933 | 42,947,263 | 1.52 | 15.15 |
| Japan | 34,338,404 | 36,777 | 51,721 | 8,151,000 | .23 | 13.76 |
| Luxembourg | 209,673 | 377 | ........ | 90,980 | .43 | 5.64 |
| Mexico | 9,389,461 | 24,830 | ........ | 9,786,964 | 1.04 | 42.31 |
| Netherlands | 3,981,887 | 65,113 | 163,198 | 8,397,000 | 2.10 | 16.86 |
| Norway | 1,806,900 | 18,750 | 241,600 | 1,626,750 | .90 | 13.62 |
| Persia | 7,000,000 | 57,600 | ........ | 3,392,000 | .48 | 41.71 |
| Peru | 3,050,000 | 4,670 | 40,000 | ........ | .... | .... |
| Portugal | 4,348,551 | 34,874 | 78,024 | 4,373,833 | 1.00 | 12.68 |
| Roumania | 5,376,000 | 19,812 | 200,000 | 5,222,227 | .97 | 21.61 |
| Russia | 72,520,000 | 974,771 | 2,733,305 | 137,812,202 | 1.90 | 29.37 |
| Servia | 1,589,650 | 50.000 | 265,000 | 1,765,021 | 1.11 | 34.42 |
| Spain | 16,333,293 | 90,000 | 450,000 | 24,802,930 | 1.51 | 15.84 |
| Sweden | 4,531,863 | 41,280 | 202,783 | 4,649,940 | 1.02 | 23.13 |
| Switzerland | 2,831.787 | 117,500 | 210,495 | 2,352,160 | .83 | 29.32 |
| Turkey | 8,866,532 | 350,000 | 610,200 | 19,642,090 | 2.21 | 34.19 |
| United States | 50,155,783 | 25,745 | †3,165,000 | 40,466,460 | .80 | 15.52 |
| Uruguay | 447,000 | 2,357 | 22,357 | ‡1,870,686 | 4.18 | 40.53 |
| Venezuela | 1,784,197 | 2,240 | 185,000 | ........ | .... | .... |

## NAVY.

| COUNTRIES. | No. of Vessels. | No. of Men. | Cost of Navy. |
|---|---|---|---|
| Argentine Republic | 27 | 991 | $550,439 |
| Austria-Hungary | 68 | 6,369 | 4,633,669 |
| Belgium | 10 | 172 | ........ |
| Brazil | 41 | 4,984 | 5,898,132 |
| Canada, Dominion of | 7 | .... | ........ |
| Chili | 23 | 1,468 | ....... |
| China | 56 | .... | ........ |
| Colombia | .. | .... | 1,000,000 |
| Denmark | 33 | 1,125 | 1,383,940 |
| Egypt | 14 | .... | ........ |
| France | 258 | 48,283 | 32,267,498 |
| Germany | 86 | 15,815 | 9,722,721 |
| Great Britain & Ireland | 238 | 58,800 | 51,607,175 |
| Greece | 18 | 652 | 1,056,536 |
| Italy | 67 | 16,140 | 9,227,132 |
| Japan | 27 | 5,551 | 3,015,000 |
| Mexico | 4 | .... | ........ |
| Netherlands | 122 | 5,914 | 4,849,776 |
| Norway | 123 | 4,342 | 448,632 |
| Peru | 18 | .... | ........ |
| Portugal | 44 | 3,569 | 1,607,411 |
| Roumania | 10 | 530 | ........ |
| Russia | 389 | 30,194 | 19,268,755 |
| Spain | 139 | 15,179 | 6,429,163 |
| Sweden | 131 | 5,925 | 1,424,250 |
| Turkey | 78 | 23,000 | 2,816,000 |
| United States | 139 | 11,115 | 15,686,671 |
| Venezuela | 4 | 200 | ....... |

* This column shows the ratio which the military expenditure bears to the total annual expenditure of each nation. † Militia force *plus* the regular army. ‡ This includes the army and navy.

# RATE OF MORTALITY IN AMERICAN CITIES.

| CITIES. | Population. | | Deaths in every 1,000 of Population. | | | | | |
|---|---|---|---|---|---|---|---|---|
| | 1880. | 1870. | 1875. | 1876. | 1877. | 1878. | 1879. | 1880. |
| Atlanta, Ga | 37,409 | 21,789 | ..... | ..... | ..... | ..... | 17.20 | 19.3 |
| Baltimore | 332,313 | 267,354 | 21.23 | 21.26 | 21.25 | 17.26 | 19.34 | 24.7 |
| Boston | 369,832 | 250,526 | 25.00 | 23.58 | 21.43 | 21.66 | 19.80 | 23.5 |
| Brooklyn | 566,663 | 396,099 | 25.91 | 24.92 | 21.61 | 19.72 | 20.40 | 24.0 |
| Charleston, S. C | 49,999 | 48,956 | 34.60 | 30.72 | 24.34 | 27.18 | 28.40 | 31.9 |
| Chicago | 503,185 | 298,977 | 20.29 | 20.42 | 18.24 | 15.70 | 17.20 | 20.8 |
| Cincinnati | 255,139 | 216,239 | 20.39 | 23.10 | 17.81 | 18.33 | 18.89 | 20.9 |
| Cleveland, Ohio | 160,146 | 92,829 | ..... | ..... | ..... | ..... | 17.50 | 20.4 |
| Dayton, Ohio | 38,678 | 30,473 | 14.22 | 14.04 | 12.29 | 15.00 | 13.80 | 15.3 |
| Erie, Pa | 27,737 | 19,646 | 18.74 | 13.40 | 13.71 | 13.88 | ..... | 17.1 |
| Jacksonville, Fla | 7,650 | 6,912 | ..... | ..... | ..... | ..... | 18.10 | 28.4 |
| Louisville, Ky | 123,758 | 100,753 | ..... | ..... | ..... | . ... | 13.90 | 21.2 |
| Lowell, Mass | 59,475 | 40,928 | ..... | ..... | ..... | ..... | 19.60 | 22.4 |
| Memphis, Tenn | 33,593 | 40,226 | 29.79 | 24.78 | 26.06 | ..... | ..... | 31.0 |
| Mobile, Ala | 29,132 | 32,034 | 22.00 | 24.34 | 24.14 | 15.93 | 21.00 | 24.4 |
| Milwaukee, Wis | 115,712 | 71,440 | 14.64 | 18.78 | 16.84 | 13.37 | 15.85 | 21.5 |
| Nashville, Tenn | 43,377 | 25,865 | 43.17 | 31.82 | 29.57 | 20.00 | 25.00 | 23.3 |
| Newark, N. J | 136,508 | 105,059 | 20.29 | 27.15 | 23.17 | ..... | 22.40 | 21.4 |
| New Haven, Conn | 62,882 | 50,840 | 20.79 | 17.89 | 19.66 | 17.90 | 15.40 | 18.5 |
| New Orleans | 216,090 | 191,418 | 27.80 | 26.89 | 34.83 | 30.10 | 21.60 | 24.2 |
| New York | 1,206,299 | 942,292 | 29.79 | 27.23 | 24.36 | 25.24 | 25.82 | 26.7 |
| Paterson, N. J | 51,031 | 33,579 | 30.94 | 26.72 | 24.28 | 19.29 | 24.85 | .... |
| Philadelphia | 847,170 | 674,022 | 24.35 | 24.51 | 19.02 | 18.03 | 17.20 | 20.9 |
| Pittsburgh, Pa | 156,389 | 86,076 | 21.69 | 21.90 | 23.87 | 19.49 | 19.40 | 22.1 |
| Providence, R I | 104,857 | 68,904 | 18.94 | 18.30 | 18.81 | 19.75 | 19.60 | 20.0 |
| Reading, Pa | 43,280 | 33,930 | 19.55 | 27.95 | 22.50 | ..... | ..... | 18.8 |
| Richmond, Va | 64,670 | 51,038 | 24.97 | 22.18 | 21.93 | 17.37 | 20.10 | 27.6 |
| Rochester, N. Y | 89,366 | 62,386 | 24.39 | 21.27 | 18.41 | 15.65 | 16.90 | .... |
| Salt Lake City, Utah | 20,768 | 12,854 | ..... | ..... | ..... | ..... | 24.60 | 20.4 |
| San Francisco | 233,959 | 149,473 | 19.28 | 18.89 | 19.86 | 15.86 | 14.40 | 19.3 |
| Savannah, Ga | 30,709 | 28,235 | ..... | ..... | : | ..... | 29.80 | 32.6 |
| Selma, Ala | 7,529 | 6,484 | 22.53 | 16.87 | 19.62 | 30.81 | 28.99 | 26.8 |
| St. Louis | 350,518 | 310,864 | 23.88 | 19.89 | 17.24 | 21.66 | 18.19 | 19.2 |
| Syracuse, N. Y | 51,792 | 43,051 | ..... | 10.26 | 13.20 | 13.79 | 13.09 | .... |
| Toledo, Ohio | 50,137 | 31,584 | 24.90 | 14.80 | 13.54 | 12.32 | ..... | .... |
| Washington, D. C | 147,293 | 109,199 | 29.03 | 25.81 | 24.39 | 24.20 | 25.20 | 22.9 |
| Yonkers, N. Y | 18,892 | 12,733 | 19.29 | 23.37 | 17.81 | 12.60 | ..... | 14.3 |

## FINANCIAL HISTORY OF THE WORLD.

| Countries. | Fiscal Year. | Public Debt. | Revenue. | Expenditures. | Imports.[1] | Exports.[1] |
|---|---|---|---|---|---|---|
| Argentine Republic | 1880 | $57,068,979 | $19,594,305 | $17,270,516 | $44,660,204 | $66,497,423 |
| Australia[2] | 1879 | 462,760,515 | 79,637,540 | 93,225,515 | 236,893,913 | 206,149,785 |
| Austria-Hungary | 1881 | 1,582,222,008 | 57,922,954 | 61,092,009 | 302,900,000 | 329,995,000 |
| Austria proper | 1881 | 204,308,213 | 204,827,997 | 231,556,152 | (In Austria- | Hungary.) |
| Hungary proper | 1881 | 500,665,178 | 132,207,358 | 143,590,048 | (In Austria- | Hungary.) |
| Belgium | 1880 | 351,967,293 | 54,501,284 | 55,763,710 | 452,265,000 | 428,149,065 |
| Bolivia | 1879 | 30,000,000 | 2,929,574 | 4,500,504 | 5,000,000 | 5,647,000 |
| Brazil | 1880 | 407,716,027 | 57,423,412 | 59,762,289 | 81,752,900 | 102,029,250 |
| Canada | 1880 | 199,125,323 | 23,307,406 | 24,850,634 | 86,489,747 | 87,911,458 |
| Ceylon | 1880 | 6,650,000 | 7,374,335 | 7,343,915 | 25,197,175 | 24,804,690 |
| Chili | 1879 | 77,654,238 | 27,693,087 | 24,777,360 | 22,740,000 | 36,620,226 |
| China | 1878 | 64,500,000 | 121,482,000 | 121,475,000 | 70,804,027 | 67,172,179 |
| Colombia | 1879 | 19,971,219 | 4,910,000 | 8,634,571 | 10,787,634 | 13,711,511 |
| Denmark | 1880 | 46,798,190 | 12,756,571 | 11,251,561 | 53,744,310 | 42,576,810 |
| Ecuador | 1879 | 18,350,400 | 1,853,600 | 2,688,000 | 7,596,264 | 8,634,331 |
| Egypt | 1879 | 411,820,700 | 42,097,105 | 41,544,350 | 32,749,664 | 64,916,017 |
| France | 1881 | 4,700,860,700 | 552,496,163 | 547,241,755 | 981,509,400 | 680,129,800 |
| Germany | 1881 | 88,385,022 | 148,239,138 | 147,695,846 | 973,200,000 | 705,375,000 |
| Prussia | 1881 | 477,210,581 | 125,439,802 | 228,267,605 | (In German | Empire.) |
| Other German States | 1880 | 792,858,492 | 121,396,304 | 116,032,115 | (In German | Empire.) |
| Great Britain | 1881 | 3,843,518,460 | 420,207,440 | 415,509,620 | 2,056,147,825 | 1,432,072,330 |
| Greece | 1880 | 58,572,730 | 8,759,000 | 18,765,000 | 29,101,400 | 17,992,000 |
| Hawaii | 1880 | 388,900 | 1,780,080 | 2,196,006 | 3,673,000 | 4,968,000 |
| India, British | 1879 | 754,979,810 | 325,998,010 | 315,826,780 | 224,286,715 | 324,598,705 |
| Italy | 1880 | 2,042,000,000 | 286,904,471 | 283,340,500 | 244,548,042 | 225,128,904 |
| Japan | 1880 | 363,721,776 | 59,933,507 | 59,204,609 | 32,631,000 | 28,364,000 |
| Luxembourg | 1880 | 2,400,000 | 1,347,000 | 1,612,400 | ........... | ........... |
| Mexico | 1880 | 144,953,785 | 17,811,125 | 23,128,218 | 29,962,407 | 31,659,151 |
| Netherlands | 1881 | 376,908,500 | 42,044,240 | 49,786,774 | 338,680,000 | 232,680,000 |
| Norway | 1881 | 24,705,000 | 13,454,670 | 11,937,340 | 40,715,976 | 29,359,530 |
| Paraguay | 1879 | 12,098,417 | 216,599 | 270,031 | 956,000 | 1,046,700 |
| Persia | 1876 | No debt. | 8,216,000 | 8,131,000 | 7,500,000 | 4,500,000 |
| Peru | 1879 | 254,000,000 | 38,900,000 | 54,600,000 | 27,000,000 | 45,000,000 |
| Portugal | 1880 | 387,659,575 | 30,794,012 | 34,478,143 | 34,046,000 | 20,502,000 |
| Roumania | 1881 | 114,210,075 | 24,152,940 | 24,164,876 | 51,057,200 | 43,782,000 |
| Russia | 1880 | 2,081,417,932 | 435,548,352 | 469.121,794 | 395,466,667 | 418.466,667 |
| Servia | 1880 | 20,248,090 | 5,125,216 | 5,127,108 | 5,244,100 | 7,002,975 |
| Siam | 1879 | ........... | 4,000,000 | 4,000,000 | 5,200,000 | 10,200,000 |
| Spain | 1880 | 2,504,571,684 | 163,347,097 | 156,529,840 | 88,660,000 | 100,980,000 |
| Sweden | 1881 | 62,196,184 | 20,503,260 | 20,098,260 | 62,139,340 | 50,264,280 |
| Switzerland | 1880 | 6,120,780 | 8,502,901 | 8,020,764 | Not given. | Not given. |
| Turkey | 1880 | 1,289,565,000 | 62,681,608 | 57,390,803 | 107,500,000 | 99,250.000 |
| United States | 1881 | 2,018,869,698 | 360,782,292 | 260,712.887 | 753,240,125 | 921,784,193 |
| Uruguay | 1879 | 47,861,042 | 8,936.714 | 10,090,260 | 18,328,225 | 19,752,201 |
| Venezuela | 1880 | 67,309,990 | 4,680,000 | 4,448,000 | 14,800,000 | 11,300,000 |
| Total debts | | $26,979,170,506 | | | | |

[1] Including merchandise, specie, and bullion.
[2] Including New South Wales, New Zealand, Queensland, South Australia, Tasmania, Victoria, and Western Australia.

## AMERICAN TROTTING RECORD.

Horses that have trotted a mile in less than 2 minutes and 20¾ seconds.

| Name. | Time. | Year. | Name. | Time. | Year. | Name. | Time. | Year. |
|---|---|---|---|---|---|---|---|---|
| Maud S | 2.10¼ | 1881 | Midnight | 2.18¼ | 1878 | Deck Wright | 2.19¾ | 1880 |
| St. Julien | 2.11¼ | 1880 | Slow Go | 2.18½ | 1877 | Daisydale | 2.19¾ | 1880 |
| Rarus | 2.13¼ | 1878 | Col. Lewis | 2.18½ | 1878 | Mambrino Gift | 2.20 | 1874 |
| Goldsmith Maid | 2.14 | 1874 | Nutwood | 2.18½ | 1880 | Fleety Golddust | 2.20 | 1874 |
| Hopeful | 2.14¾ | 1878 | Patchen | 2.18¾ | 1880 | May Queen | 2.20 | 1875 |
| Lula | 2.15 | 1875 | Cozette | 2.19 | 1876 | Little Fred | 2.20 | 1877 |
| Smuggler | 2.15¼ | 1876 | Albermarle | 2.19 | 1878 | Prospero | 2.20 | 1877 |
| Hattie Woodward | 2.15½ | 1880 | Edward | 2.19 | 1878 | Frank | 2.20 | 1877 |
| Lucille Golddust | 2.16¼ | 1877 | Alley | 2.19 | 1879 | Nancy Hackett | 2.20 | 1878 |
| American Girl | 2.16½ | 1874 | Bonesetter | 2.19 | 1879 | John H | 2.20 | 1878 |
| Darby | 2.16½ | 1879 | George Palmer | 2.19¼ | 1869 | Belle Brassfield | 2.20 | 1879 |
| Charlie Ford | 2.16¾ | 1880 | Bodine | 2.19¼ | 1875 | Etta Jones | 2.20 | 1879 |
| Occident | 2.16¾ | 1873 | Comee | 2.19¼ | 1877 | Graves | 2.20 | 1879 |
| Gloster | 2.17 | 1874 | Hannis | 2.19¼ | 1877 | Elaine | 2.20 | 1880 |
| Dexter | 2.17¼ | 1867 | Croxie | 2.19¼ | 1878 | Captain Emmons | 2.20 | 1880 |
| Red Cloud | 2.18 | 1874 | Trinket | 2.19¼ | 1880 | Orange Girl | 2.20 | 1880 |
| Nettie | 2 18 | 1874 | Parana | 2.19¼ | 1880 | Henry | 2.20¼ | 1871 |
| Judge Fullerton | 2.18 | 1875 | Jim Keene | 2.19¼ | 1880 | Martha Washington | 2.20¼ | 1877 |
| Great Eastern | 2.18 | 1878 | T. L. Young | 2.19½ | 1875 | Mazo-Manie | 2.20¼ | 1877 |
| Edwin Forrest | 2.18 | 1878 | Moose | 2.19½ | 1880 | Amy | 2.20¼ | 1879 |
| Protine | 2.18 | 1878 | Will Cody | 2.19½ | 1880 | Fannie Robinson | 2.20¼ | 1879 |
| Dick Swiveller | 2.18 | 1879 | Driver | 2.19½ | 1880 | Sam Purdy | 2.20½ | 1876 |
| Santa Claus | 2.18 | 1879 | Flora Temple | 2.19¾ | 1859 | Governor Sprague | 2.20½ | 1876 |
| Lady Thorn | 2.18¼ | 1869 | Camorse | 2.19¾ | 1874 | Lida Bassett | 2.20½ | 1879 |
| Lucy | 2.18¼ | 1882 | Adelaide | 2.19¾ | 1878 | Chance | 2.20½ | 1879 |
| Lady Maud | 2.18¼ | 1875 | | | | | | |

# POPULATION OF THE CHIEF CITIES OF THE GLOBE.

| City | Date | Population |
|---|---|---|
| **AMERICA.** | | |
| **United States.** | | |
| Albany, N. Y. | 1880 | 87,584 |
| Allegheny, Pa. | " | 78,682 |
| Baltimore, Md. | " | 332,313 |
| Boston, Mass. | " | 369,832 |
| Brooklyn, N. Y. | " | 566,689 |
| Buffalo, N. Y. | " | 149,500 |
| Chicago, Ill. | " | 503,185 |
| Cincinnati, O. | " | 255,809 |
| Cleveland, O. | " | 155,946 |
| Columbus, O. | " | 51,337 |
| Detroit, Mich. | " | 116,340 |
| Indianapolis, Ind. | " | 75,056 |
| Jersey City, N. J. | " | 120,722 |
| Kansas City, Mo. | " | 55,785 |
| Louisville, Ky. | " | 123,758 |
| Lowell, Mass. | " | 59,475 |
| Milwaukee, Wis. | " | 115,587 |
| Newark, N. J. | " | 136,508 |
| New Haven, Conn. | " | 62,882 |
| New Orleans, La. | " | 216,090 |
| New York, N. Y. | " | 1,206,577 |
| Paterson, N. J. | " | 50,887 |
| Philadelphia, Pa. | " | 847,170 |
| Pittsburg, Pa. | " | 156,389 |
| Providence, R. I. | " | 104,857 |
| Richmond, Va. | " | 63,600 |
| Rochester, N. Y. | " | 87,057 |
| St. Louis, Mo. | " | 350,518 |
| San Francisco, Cal. | " | 233,959 |
| Syracuse, N. Y. | " | 51,791 |
| Toledo, O. | " | 50,143 |
| Troy, N. Y. | " | 56,747 |
| Washington, D. C. | " | 147,293 |
| Worcester, Mass. | " | 58,291 |
| **British North Am.** | | |
| Montreal | 1871 | 107,225 |
| Quebec | " | 59,699 |
| Toronto | 1878 | 70,865 |
| **Mexico.** | | |
| Guadalajara | Est. | 93,875 |
| Guanajuato | " | 63,000 |
| Mexico | 1879 | 236,500 |
| Puebla | Est. | 70,000 |
| Xacatecas | " | 62,000 |
| **South America.** | | |
| Bahia | 1872 | 128,929 |
| Buenos Ayres | 1869 | 177,787 |
| Caracas | 1873 | 48,897 |
| La Paz | 1878 | 76,372 |
| Lima | 1876 | 101,488 |
| Montevideo | 1878 | 92,260 |
| Pernambuco | 1872 | 116,671 |
| Quito | Est. | 80,000 |
| Rio de Janeiro | 1872 | 274,972 |
| Santa Fé de Bogota | | 50,000 |
| Santiago | 1875 | 129,807 |
| Valparaiso | " | 97,737 |
| **AFRICA.** | | |
| Abeokuta | Est. | 130,000 |
| Alexandria | 1878 | 165,752 |
| Antananarivo | Est. | 75,000 |
| Bida | " | 80,000 |
| Cairo | 1877 | 327,462 |
| Fez | Est. | 100,000 |
| Kumasi | " | 70,000 |
| Ojo | " | 70,000 |
| Porto Novo | " | 100,000 |
| Tunis | " | 125,000 |
| Zanzibar | " | 80,000 |
| **ASIA.** | | |
| **Afghanistan.** | | |
| Cabul | Est. | 60,000 |
| Chulum | " | 60,000 |
| Herat | " | 50,000 |
| Maimene | " | 60,000 |
| **Arabia.** | | |
| Sana | Est. | 50,000 |
| **China.** | | |
| Amoy | Est. | 88,000 |
| Canton | " | 1,500,000 |
| Fatschan | " | 400,000 |
| **China.—*Continued.*** | | |
| Foochow | Est | 600,000 |
| Hangtscheu-fu | " | 400,000 |
| Hankow | " | 600,000 |
| Hutcheu | " | 200,000 |
| Jangtschau | " | 360,000 |
| Jongping | " | 200,000 |
| Kirin | " | 120,000 |
| Leinkong | " | 250,000 |
| Nangkin | " | 450,900 |
| Ningpo | " | 120,000 |
| Pauting-fu | " | 120,000 |
| Peking | " | 500,000 |
| Schaohing | " | 500,000 |
| Shanghai | " | 278,000 |
| Siangtan | " | 1,000,000 |
| Singan-fu | " | 1,000,000 |
| Sutschau | " | 500,000 |
| Taijuen-fu | " | 250,000 |
| Taiwan-fu | " | 235,000 |
| Tengtschau-fu | " | 230,000 |
| Tientsin | " | 950,000 |
| Tschangtjiakheu | " | 200,000 |
| Tschantschau-fu | " | 1,000,000 |
| Tschaujang | " | 200,000 |
| Tschingtu-fu, | " | 800,000 |
| Tschungking-fu | " | 600,000 |
| Tsinan-fu | " | 200,000 |
| Weihein | " | 250,000 |
| Wutschang | " | 200,000 |
| **Corea.** | | |
| Saoul | Est. | 100,000 |
| **India.** | | |
| Agra | 1871 | 149,008 |
| Ahmedabad | " | 116,873 |
| Allahabad | " | 143,693 |
| Amritsur | 1876 | 142,381 |
| Bangalore | 1871 | 142,513 |
| Bangkok | Est. | 600,000 |
| Bareilly | 1871 | 102,982 |
| Baroda | " | 112,057 |
| Benares | " | 175,188 |
| Bombay | 1872 | 644,405 |
| Calcutta | 1881 | 683,329 |
| Cawnpore | 1871 | 122,770 |
| Colombo (Ceylon) | 1881 | 111,942 |
| Delhi | 1876 | 160,553 |
| Dhar | Est. | 100,000 |
| Gwalior | " | 200,000 |
| Hyderabad | " | 200,000 |
| Jondpore | " | 150,000 |
| Kescho | " | 150,000 |
| Lahore | 1876 | 128,441 |
| Lucknow | 1871 | 284,779 |
| Madras | " | 397,552 |
| Mandalah | Est. | 100,000 |
| Patna | 1871 | 158,900 |
| Puna | " | 118,886 |
| Rangoon | 1881 | 132,004 |
| Singapore | 1871 | 97,111 |
| Surat | " | 107,149 |
| **Indian Archipelago** | | |
| Batavia | 1875 | 99,109 |
| Manila | Est. | 160,000 |
| Surabaja | " | 90,000 |
| **Japan.** | | |
| Hakodate | 1877 | 112,494 |
| Kagoshima | " | 200,000 |
| Kanagawa | " | 108,263 |
| Kioto | " | 229,810 |
| Nagoya | " | 135,715 |
| Osaka | " | 284,105 |
| Tokio | " | 594,283 |
| Yokohama | " | 64,313 |
| **Persia.** | | |
| Ispahan | Est. | 60,000 |
| Meschhed | " | 60,000 |
| Rescht | " | 60,000 |
| Täbris | " | 120,000 |
| Teheran | " | 200,000 |
| **Russia in Asia.** | | |
| Khokand | Est. | 50,000 |
| Taschkent | " | 86,233 |
| Tiflis | 1876 | 104,024 |
| **Turkey in Asia.** | | |
| Aleppo | Est. | 75,000 |
| Bagdad | " | 67,000 |
| Beirut | " | 80,000 |
| Brusa | " | 70,000 |
| Damascus | " | 150,000 |
| Erzerum | " | 55,000 |
| Mossul | " | 75,000 |
| Smyrna | " | 150,000 |
| **Turkistan.** | | |
| Buchara | Est. | 70,000 |
| Jarkand | " | 80,000 |
| Kaschgar | " | 70,000 |
| **Australia.** | | |
| Adelaide | 1881 | 31,573 |
| Auckland | " | 24,712 |
| Ballarat | " | 34,219 |
| Brisbane | " | 32,012 |
| Dunedin | " | 22,525 |
| Hobart Town | " | 19,092 |
| Melbourne | " | 252,000 |
| Sydney | 1879 | 187,381 |
| Wellington | 1881 | 18,953 |
| **EUROPE.** | | |
| **Austria-Hungary.** | | |
| Brunn | 1880 | 82,655 |
| Budapesth | " | 347,536 |
| Lemberg | " | 110,250 |
| Prague | " | 162,318 |
| Trieste | " | 144,437 |
| Wien (Vienna) | " | 726,105 |
| **Belgium.** | | |
| Antwerp | 1878 | 159,579 |
| Brussels | " | 391,393 |
| Ghent | " | 130,671 |
| Liége | " | 119,942 |
| **Denmark.** | | |
| Copenhagen | 1880 | 273,727 |
| **France.** | | |
| Bordeaux | 1876 | 215,140 |
| Brest | " | 66,828 |
| Havre | " | 92,068 |
| Lille | " | 162,775 |
| Lyons | " | 342,815 |
| Marseilles | " | 318,868 |
| Nantes | " | 122,247 |
| Paris | " | 1,988,806 |
| Reims | " | 81,328 |
| Rouen | " | 104,902 |
| Saint-Etienne | " | 126,019 |
| Toulon | " | 70,509 |
| Toulouse | " | 131,642 |
| Versailles | " | 49,847 |
| **Germany.** | | |
| Aachen | 1880 | 85,432 |
| Berlin | " | 1,122,385 |
| Bremen | " | 112,158 |
| Breslau | " | 272,390 |
| Danzig | " | 108,549 |
| Dresden | " | 220,216 |
| Düsseldorf | " | 95,459 |
| Frankfort | " | 137,600 |
| Hamburg | " | 290,055 |
| Hanover | " | 122,860 |
| Köln (Cologne) | " | 144,751 |
| Königsberg | " | 150,396 |
| Leipzig | " | 148,760 |
| Magdeburg | " | 97,529 |
| Mainz (Mayence) | " | 61,322 |
| München (Munich) | " | 229,343 |
| Nürnberg (Nuremb'g) | " | 99,889 |
| Stettin | " | 91,745 |
| Strasburg | " | 104,501 |
| Stuttgart | " | 117,021 |
| **Great Britain.** | | |
| Aberdeen | 1881 | 105,818 |
| Belfast | " | 207,671 |
| Birmingham | " | 400,757 |
| Bolton | " | 105,422 |
| Bradford | " | 183,032 |
| Bristol | " | 206,503 |
| Cork | " | 78,361 |
| Derby | " | 80,410 |
| Dublin | " | 249,486 |
| Dundee | " | 140,466 |
| **Gt. Britain.—*Cont.*** | | |
| Edinburgh | 1881 | 228,075 |
| Glasgow | " | 555,289 |
| Halifax | " | 73,633 |
| Huddersfield | " | 81,825 |
| Kingston-upon-Hull | " | 154,250 |
| Leeds | " | 309,126 |
| Leicester | " | 122,351 |
| Liverpool | " | 552,425 |
| London | " | 3,832,441 |
| Manchester | " | 341,508 |
| Newcastle-on-Tyne | " | 145,228 |
| Nottingham | " | 186,656 |
| Oldham | " | 111,343 |
| Plymouth | " | 75,096 |
| Portsmouth | " | 127,953 |
| Preston | " | 96,532 |
| Salford | " | 176,233 |
| Sheffield | " | 284,410 |
| Southampton | " | 60,235 |
| Sunderland | " | 116,262 |
| West Ham | " | 128,692 |
| York | " | 54,198 |
| **Italy.** | | |
| Alessandria | 1878 | 59,241 |
| Bari | " | 55,166 |
| Bologna | " | 111,969 |
| Catania | " | 90,886 |
| Ferrara | " | 75,494 |
| Firenze (Florence) | " | 168,423 |
| Genoa | " | 163,234 |
| Livorno | " | 97,908 |
| Messina | " | 120,917 |
| Milan | " | 262,283 |
| Naples | " | 450,804 |
| Palermo | " | 231,836 |
| Perugia | " | 49,389 |
| Rome | 1880 | 303,383 |
| Turin | 1878 | 214,200 |
| Venice | " | 125,276 |
| **Netherlands.** | | |
| Amsterdam | 1878 | 308,948 |
| s'Gravenhage (Hague) | " | 111,016 |
| Rotterdam | " | 147,082 |
| Utrecht | " | 68,280 |
| **Portugal.** | | |
| Lisbon | 1878 | 203,681 |
| Porto | " | 108,346 |
| **Roumania.** | | |
| Bucharest | 1878 | 177,646 |
| Galacz | " | 80,000 |
| Jassy | " | 90,000 |
| **Russia.** | | |
| Charkow | 1879 | 101,175 |
| Kijew | 1874 | 127,251 |
| Kischenew | | 102,427 |
| Moscow | 1871 | 601,969 |
| Odessa | 1873 | 184,819 |
| Riga | | 103,000 |
| St. Petersburg | 1869 | 667,963 |
| Warsaw | 1877 | 308,548 |
| **Spain.** | | |
| Barcelona | 1877 | 249,106 |
| Cadiz | " | 65,028 |
| Carthagena | " | 75,908 |
| Cordova | " | 49,855 |
| Granada | " | 76,108 |
| Jeres de la Frontera | " | 64,533 |
| Madrid | " | 397,690 |
| Malaga | " | 115,882 |
| Murcia | " | 91,805 |
| Saragossa | " | 84,575 |
| Seville | " | 133,938 |
| Valencia | " | 143,856 |
| **Sweden & Norway.** | | |
| Christiania | 1880 | 119,407 |
| Göteborg | 1878 | 74,418 |
| Stockholm | 1880 | 169,429 |
| **Switzerland.** | | |
| Geneva | 1870 | 68,165 |
| Zurich | " | 56,695 |
| **Turkey.** | | |
| Adrianople | Est. | 62,000 |
| Constantinople | " | 600,000 |
| Saloniki | " | 80,000 |

# PRINCIPAL NATIONS OF THE WORLD.

## Population, Capitals, Area, Religion, and Government.

| Countries. | Capitals. | Last Census. | Population. | Area Square Miles. | Inhabitants to the Square Mile. | Prevailing Religion. | Government. |
|---|---|---|---|---|---|---|---|
| Argentine Republic | Buenos Ayres | 1875 | 2,400,000 | 827,177 | 2 90 | Catholic. | Republic. |
| Austria-Hungary | Vienna | 1880 | 37,741,413 | 240,415 | 156.98 | Catholic. | Monarchy. |
| Belgium | Brussels | 1878 | 5,476,668 | 11,369 | 481.71 | Catholic. | Monarchy. |
| Bolivia | La Paz | 1878 | 2,080,000 | 500,740 | 4.15 | Catholic. | Republic. |
| Brazil | Rio de Janeiro | 1872 | 10,108,291 | 3,218,166 | 3 14 | Catholic. | Monarchy. |
| Canada, Dominion of | Ottawa | 1881 | 4,352,080 | 3,204,381 | 1.35 | Protestant. | Colony. |
| Ceylon | Colombo | 1881 | 2,758,166 | 24,702 | 111.65 | Buddhist. | Colony. |
| Chili | Santiago | 1878 | 2,400,396 | 124,084 | 19.34 | Catholic. | Republic. |
| Chinese Empire | Pekin | Est. | 400,000,000 | 4,560,107 | 95.31 | Buddhist. | Empire. |
| Colombia, United States of | Bogota | 1870 | 2,951,323 | 320,638 | 9 20 | Catholic. | Republic. |
| Denmark | Copenhagen | 1878 | 1,969,454 | 14,784 | 133.21 | Protestant. | Monarchy. |
| Ecuador | Quito | 1878 | 1,146,000 | 248,312 | 4.61 | Catholic. | Republic. |
| Egypt (Turkish Dependency) | Cairo | 1877 | 17,419,980 | 1,152,948 | 15.19 | Mohammedan. | Province. |
| France | Paris | 1876 | 36,905,788 | 204,030 | 180.88 | Catholic. | Republic. |
| Germany | Berlin | 1880 | 45,194,172 | 208,624 | 216.62 | Protestant. | Empire. |
| Great Britain and Ireland | London | 1881 | 35,246,633 | 121,571 | 289.92 | Protestant. | Monarchy. |
| Greece | Athens | 1879 | 1,679,775 | 20,018 | 83.91 | Greek Church. | Monarchy. |
| India, British | Calcutta | 1881 | 252,541,210 | 810,542 | 311.57 | Hindoo. | Monarchy. |
| Italy | Rome | 1878 | 28,209,620 | 114,380 | 246.63 | Catholic. | Monarchy. |
| Japan | Yeddo | 1876 | 34,338,404 | 146,568 | 234 28 | Buddhist. | Monarchy. |
| Mexico | Mexico | 1877 | 9,389,461 | 741,598 | 12.66 | Catholic. | Republic. |
| Morocco | Morocco | Est. | 6,370.000 | 313,560 | 20.31 | Mohammedan. | Sultanate. |
| Netherlands | The Hague | 1878 | 3,981,887 | 12,727 | 312 86 | Protestant. | Monarchy. |
| Norway | Christiania | 1876 | 1,806,900 | 122,823 | 14.71 | Protestant. | Monarchy. |
| Paraguay | Asuncion | 1876 | 293.844 | 91,980 | 3.19 | Catholic. | Republic. |
| Persia | Teheran | Est. | 7,000.000 | 636,203 | 11.00 | Mohammedan. | Monarchy. |
| Peru | Lima | 1876 | 3,050,000 | 72,413 | 42.11 | Catholic. | Republic. |
| Portugal | Lisbon | 1878 | 4,348,551 | 34,595 | 125.69 | Catholic. | Monarchy. |
| Russian Empire | St. Petersburg | 18 7 | 82,330,864 | 8,138,541 | 10.11 | Greek Church. | Empire. |
| Roumania | Bucharest | Est. | 5,376,000 | 50,159 | 107.17 | Greek Church | Monarchy. |
| Servia | Belgrade | 1876 | 1,589,650 | 18,781 | 84 64 | Greek Church. | Monarchy. |
| Siam | Bangkok | Est. | 5,750,000 | 280,564 | 20.49 | Buddhist. | Monarchy. |
| Spain | Madrid | 1877 | 16,333,293 | 193,171 | 84.55 | Catholic. | Monarchy. |
| Sweden | Stockholm | 1878 | 4,531,863 | 170,927 | 26.51 | Protestant. | Monarchy. |
| Switzerland | Berne. | 1880 | 2.831,787 | 15,908 | 177.10 | Protestant. | Republic. |
| Turkey | Constantinople | Est. | 25,036,480 | 860,322 | 29.10 | Mohammedan. | Monarchy. |
| Uruguay | Montevideo | 1877 | 447,000 | 72.151 | 6.19 | Catholic. | Republic. |
| United States | Washington | 1880 | 50.155,783 | 3,602,990 | 13.92 | Protestant. | Republic. |
| Venezuela | Caracas | 1873 | 1,784,197 | 439 119 | 4.06 | Catholic. | Republic. |

## HEIGHTS OF PRINCIPAL MOUNTAINS.

| | | Feet. |
|---|---|---|
| **NORTH AMERICA.** | | |
| Mount St. Elias | Coast Mountains | 17,900 |
| Popocatepetl (volcano) | Mexico | 17,784 |
| Orizaba | " | 17,380 |
| Mount Whitney | Sierra Nevada | 14,887 |
| Mount Rainier | Cascade Range | 14,444 |
| Mount Shasta | Sierra Nevada | 14,440 |
| Mount Tyndall | " | 14,386 |
| Mount Dana | " | 13,277 |
| Mount Hood | Cascade Range | 11,225 |
| Long's Peak | Rocky Mountains | 14,271 |
| Pike's Peak | " | 14,147 |
| **SOUTH AMERICA.** | | |
| Illampu | Andes | 24,812 |
| Illimani | " | 24,155 |
| Aconcagua | " | 23,421 |
| Chimborazo (volcano) | " | 21,244 |
| Nevada de Sorata | " | 21,290 |
| Arequipa | " | 20,320 |
| Antisana (volcano) | " | 19,137 |
| Cotopaxi " | " | 18,875 |
| **EUROPE.** | | |
| Elbruz (highest of Caucasus Mountains) | | 18,526 |
| Mont Blanc | Alps | 15,784 |
| Monte Rosa | " | 15,223 |
| Matterhorn | " | 14,835 |
| Finsteraar-horn | " | 14,039 |
| Jungfrau | " | 13,718 |
| Highest of Pyrenees | | 11.200 |
| Mount Ætna (volcano) | Sicily | 10,874 |
| Mount Olympus | Greece | 9,745 |
| Mount Vesuvius (volcano) | Italy | 3,948 |
| **AFRICA.** | | |
| Killima-Ndjaro | Central Africa | 20,000 |
| Teneriffe | Canary Islands | 12,182 |
| Atlas Mountains (highest) | | 11.400 |
| Kenia | Central Africa | 18,000 |

### HEIGHTS OF PRINCIPAL MOUNTAINS.—*Continued.*

| | | Feet. |
|---|---|---|
| **ASIA.** | | |
| Everest | Himalaya Mountains. | 29,100 |
| Kanchinginga | " " | 28,156 |
| Dhawalagiri | " " | 28,000 |
| Hindoo Koosh Mountains | | 20,000 |
| Ararat | Armenia | 17,260 |
| Fusiyama | Japan | 14,000 |
| **AUSTRALASIA.** | | |
| Mount Kosciusko | Australian Alps | 7,176 |
| Mount Hotham | " " | 6,414 |
| Mount Cook | New Zealand Alps | 13,200 |

### THE OCEANS, SEAS, BAYS, AND LAKES OF THE WORLD.

| Oceans. | Sq. Miles. |
|---|---|
| Pacific, about | 80,000,000 |
| Atlantic, " | 40,000,000 |
| Indian, " | 20,000,000 |
| Southern, " | 10,000,000 |
| Arctic, " | 5,000,000 |

Note.—The seas, bays, gulfs, etc., connected with each ocean, are included in the list given above. Most geographers concede, however, that the exact superficial extent of the several oceans is not known with certainty, nor the exact proportion of land and water.

| Seas. | Length in Miles. |
|---|---|
| Mediterranean, about | 2,000 |
| Caribbean, about | 1,800 |
| China, " | 1,700 |
| Red, " | 1,400 |
| Japan, " | 1,000 |
| Black, " | 932 |
| Caspian, " | 640 |
| Baltic " | 600 |
| Okhotsk, " | 600 |
| White, " | 450 |
| Aral, " | 250 |

| Bays. | Length in Miles. |
|---|---|
| Hudson's, about | 1,200 |
| Baffin's, " | 600 |
| Chesapeake, " | 250 |

| Lakes. | Length. Miles. | Width. Miles. |
|---|---|---|
| Superior | 380 | 120 |
| Baikal | 360 | 35 |
| Michigan | 350 | 60 |
| Great Slave | 300 | 45 |
| Huron | 250 | 90 |
| Winnipeg | 240 | 40 |
| Erie | 270 | 50 |
| Athabasca | 200 | 20 |
| Ontario | 180 | 40 |
| Maracaybo | 150 | 60 |
| Great Bear | 150 | 40 |
| Ladoga | 125 | 75 |
| Champlain | 123 | 12 |
| Nicaragua | 120 | 40 |
| Lake of the Woods, | 70 | 25 |
| Geneva | 50 | 10 |
| Constance | 45 | 10 |
| Cayuga | 36 | 4 |
| George | 36 | 3 |

## CAPACITY OF PUBLIC BUILDINGS.

| Building. | City. | Capacity. |
|---|---|---|
| Coliseum | Rome | 87,000 |
| St. Peter's | Rome | 54,000 |
| Theatre of Pompey | Rome | 40,000 |
| Cathedral | Milan | 37,000 |
| St. Paul's | Rome | 32,000 |
| St. Paul's | London | 31,000 |
| St. Petronia | Bologna | 26,000 |
| Cathedral | Florence | 24,300 |
| Cathedral | Antwerp | 24,000 |
| St. John's Lateran | Rome | 23,000 |
| St. Sophia's | Constantinople | 23,000 |
| Notre Dame | Paris | 21,500 |
| Theatre of Marcellus | Rome | 20,000 |
| Cathedral | Pisa | 13,000 |
| St. Stephen's | Vienna | 12,400 |
| St. Dominic's | Bologna | 12,000 |
| St. Peter's | Bologna | 11,400 |
| Cathedral | Vienna | 11,000 |
| Gilmore's Garden | New York | 8,443 |
| Mormon Temple | Salt Lake City | 8,000 |
| St. Mark's | Venice | 7,500 |
| Spurgeon's Tabernacle | London | 6,000 |
| Bolshoi Theatre | St. Petersburg | 5,000 |
| Tabernacle, (Talmage's) | Brooklyn | 5,000 |
| Music Hall | Cincinnati | 4,824 |
| La Scala | Milan | 3,600 |
| University Hall | Ann Arbor | 3,500 |
| Exeter Hall | London | 3,500 |
| Washington Hall | Paterson, N. J | 3,000 |
| St. James' Methodist Church | Montreal | 3,000 |
| Plymouth Church | Brooklyn | 3,000 |
| City Hall | Columbus, O | 3,000 |
| Boston Theatre | Boston | 2,972 |
| Academy of Music | Philadelphia | 2,865 |
| Covent Garden | London | 2,684 |
| Music Hall | Boston | 2,585 |
| Carlo Felice | Genoa | 2,560 |
| Academy of Music | New York | 2,526 |
| Cooper Union | New York | 2,500 |
| Opera House | New Haven | 2,500 |
| Mobile Theatre | Mobile, Ala | 2,500 |
| Opera House | Birmingham, Pa | 2,500 |
| Chestnut Street Theatre | Philadelphia | 2,380 |
| Alexander | St. Petersburg | 2,332 |
| Opera House | Munich | 2,307 |
| Grand Opera House | Paris | 2,300 |
| Grand Opera House | Cincinnati | 2,250 |
| Collingwood Opera House | Poughkeepsie | 2,250 |
| San Carlos | Naples | 2,240 |
| Haverly's Theatre | Chicago | 2,238 |
| Globe Theatre | Boston | 2,200 |
| St. Charles Theatre | New Orleans | 2,178 |
| Imperial | St. Petersburg | 2,160 |
| Academy of Music | Paris | 2,092 |
| Grand Opera Hall | New Orleans | 2,052 |
| Lafayette Ave. Presbyterian Church | Brooklyn | 2,000 |
| Opera House | Terre Haute | 2,000 |
| Academy of Music | Peoria, Ill | 2,000 |
| Burtis' Opera House | Davenport, Ia | 2,000 |
| Opera House | Columbus, O | 2,000 |
| Academy of Music | Charleston | 2,000 |
| Opera House | Canton, O | 2,000 |
| Opera House | Atlanta, Ga | 2,000 |
| Opera House | Battle Creek | 2,000 |
| Niblo's Garden | New York | 1,978 |
| Tremont Temple | Boston | 1,942 |
| Ambigu Comique | Paris | 1,900 |
| Grand Opera House | New York | 1,883 |
| Booth's Theatre | New York | 1,807 |
| Porte St. Martin | Paris | 1,800 |
| Academy of Music | Indianapolis | 1,800 |
| Opera House | Pittsburgh | 1,800 |
| Opera House | Detroit | 1,790 |
| M'Vicker's Theatre | Chicago | 1,786 |
| New Music Hall | Chicago | 1,786 |
| Ford's Opera House | Baltimore | 1,720 |
| Walnut Street Theatre | Philadelphia | 1,720 |
| National Theatre | Washington | 1,709 |
| Théâtre Italien | Paris | 1,700 |
| Théâtre Lyrique | Paris | 1,700 |
| De Bar's Opera House | St. Louis | 1,696 |
| Academy of Music | New Orleans | 1,674 |
| California Theatre | San Francisco | 1,651 |
| Euclid Avenue Opera House | Cleveland | 1,650 |
| Odeon | Paris | 1,650 |
| Opera House | Berlin | 1,636 |
| Arch Street Theatre | Philadelphia | 1,614 |
| Wallack's Theatre | New York | 1,605 |
| Grand Opera House | Toronto | 1,600 |
| Fifth Avenue Presbyterian Church | New York | 1,600 |
| Front Street Theatre | Baltimore | 1,561 |
| Greenlaw Opera House | Memphis | 1,507 |
| Academy | Des Moines | 1,500 |
| Opera House | Adrian, Mich | 1,500 |
| Opera House | Allentown, Pa | 1,500 |
| Opera House | Altoona, Pa | 1,500 |
| Hill's Opera House | Ann Arbor, Pa | 1,500 |
| Beethoven Hall | Boston | 1,500 |
| Howard Athenæum | Boston | 1,500 |
| St. John's Methodist Church | Brooklyn | 1,500 |
| Martin's Opera House | Albany | 1,400 |
| St. Paul's Methodist Church | New York | 1,400 |
| Theatre Royal | Montreal | 1,368 |
| Museum | Boston | 1,275 |
| Union Square Theatre | New York | 1,210 |
| Durley Hall | Bloomington, Ill | 1,200 |

## THE LONGEST RIVERS OF THE WORLD.

| Rivers. | Locality. | Rise. | Discharge. | Miles. |
|---|---|---|---|---|
| Missouri | North America | Rocky Mountains | Gulf of Mexico | 4,194 |
| Mississippi | North America | Lake Itaska | Gulf of Mexico | 3,200 |
| Amazon | Brazil | Andes | Atlantic Ocean | 3,800 |
| Hoang-Ho | China | Koulkoun Mountains | Yellow Sea | 3,000 |
| Murray | Australia | Australian Alps | Encounter Bay | 3,000 |
| Obi | Siberia | Altaian Mountains | Arctic Ocean | 2,800 |
| Nile | Egypt, Nubia | Blue Nile, Aby sinia | Mediterranean | 2,750 |
| Yang-tse-Kiang | China | Thibet | China Sea | 3,200 |
| Lena | Siberia | Heights of Irkutsk | Arctic Ocean | 2,500 |
| Niger | Soudan | Base of Mt. Loma | Gulf of Guinea | 2,300 |
| St. Lawrence | Canada | River St. Louis | Gulf of St. Lawrence | 1,900 |
| Volga | Russia | Lake in Volhonsky | Caspian Sea | 1,900 |
| Maykiang | Siam | Thibet | Chinese Gulf | 1,700 |
| Indus | Hindostan | Little Thibet | Arabian Sea | 1,700 |
| Danube | Germany | Black Forest | Black Sea | 1,630 |
| Mackenzie | North America | River Athabasca | Arctic Ocean | 2,500 |
| Brahmapootra | Thibet | Himalaya | Bay of Bengal | 1,500 |
| Columbia | North America | Rocky Mountains | Pacific Ocean | 1,090 |
| Colorado | North America | San Iaba | Gulf of California | 1,000 |
| Susquehanna | North America | Lake Otsego | Chesapeake Bay | 400 |
| James | North America | Allegheny Mountains | Chesapeake Bay | 500 |
| Potomac | North America | Great Black Bone Mountain | Chesapeake Bay | 400 |
| Hudson | North America | Adirondacks, Mt. Marcy | Bay of New York | 325 |

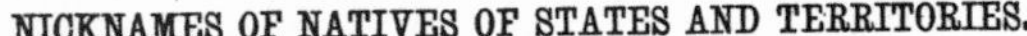

## NICKNAMES OF NATIVES OF STATES AND TERRITORIES.

| States. | Nicknames. |
|---|---|
| Alabama | Lizards. |
| Arkansas | Toothpicks. |
| California | Gold-Hunters. |
| Colorado | Rovers. |
| Connecticut | Wooden Nutmegs. |
| Dakota | Squatters. |
| Delaware | Muskrats. |
| Florida | Fly-up-the-creeks. |
| Georgia | Buzzards. |
| Idaho | Fortune Seekers. |
| Illinois | Suckers. |
| Indiana | Hoosiers. |
| Iowa | Hawkeyes. |
| Kansas | Jayhawkers. |
| Kentucky | Corn Crackers. |
| Louisiana | Creoles. |
| Maine | Foxes. |
| Maryland | Clam-Humpers. |
| Massachusettts | Yankees. |
| Michigan | Wolverines. |
| Minnesota | Gophers. |
| Mississippi | Tadpoles. |
| Missouri | Pukes. |
| Nebraska | Bug-Eaters. |
| Nevada | Sage Hens. |
| New Hampshire | Granite Boys. |
| New Jersey | Blues, or Clam-Catchers. |
| New Mexico | Spanish Indians. |
| New York | Knickerbockers. |
| North Carolina | Tarheels. |
| Ohio | Buckeyes. |
| Oregon | Hard Cases. |
| Pennsylvania | Pennamites, or Leather-Heads. |
| Rhode Island | Gunflints. |
| South Carolina | Weazles. |
| Tennessee | Whelps. |
| Texas | Beefheads. |
| Utah | Polygamists. |
| Vermont | Green Mountain Boys. |
| Virginia | Beagles. |
| Wisconsin | Badgers. |

## HEIGHT OF NOTED CATHEDRALS, PYRAMIDS, TOWERS, ETC.

| | | |
|---|---|---|
| Pyramid of Cheops | Egypt | 543 ft. |
| Cologne Cathedral | Germany | 501 " |
| Antwerp Cathedral | Belgium | 476 " |
| Strasburg Cathedral | Germany | 474 " |
| Tower of Utrecht | Holland | 464 " |
| Steeple of St. Stephen's, Vienna | Austria | 460 " |
| Pyramid of Cephenes | Egypt | 456 " |
| St. Martin's Church | Bavaria | 456 " |
| St. Peter's, Rome | Italy | 448 " |
| Notre Dame, Amiens | France | 422 " |
| Salisbury Spire | England | 410 " |
| St. Paul's, London | England | 404 " |
| Cathedral at Florence | Italy | 384 " |
| Cremona Cathedral | Italy | 372 " |
| Freiberg Cathedral | Germany | 367 " |
| Seville Cathedral | Spain | 360 " |
| Milan Cathedral | Italy | 355 " |
| Notre Dame, Munich | Bavaria | 348 " |
| Dome des Invalides, Paris | France | 347 " |
| Magdeburg Cathedral | Germany | 337 " |
| St. Patrick's, New York | United States | 328 " |
| St. Mark's Church, Venice | Italy | 328 " |
| Norwich Cathedral | England | 309 " |
| Chichester Cathedral | England | 300 " |
| Trinity Church, New York | United States | 283 " |
| Canterbury Tower | England | 235 " |
| Notre Dame Cathedral, Paris | France | 232 " |
| St. Patrick's, Dublin | Ireland | 226 " |
| Glasgow Cathedral | Scotland | 225 " |
| Bunker Hill, Monument | Massachusetts | 220 " |
| Notre Dame, Montreal | Canada | 220 " |
| Lima Cathedral | Peru | 220 " |
| Garden City Cathedral, Long Island | United States | 219 " |
| St. Peter and St. Paul's, Philadelphia | United States | 210 " |

## LENGTH AND COST OF AMERICAN WARS.

| Wars. | Length. | Cost. |
|---|---|---|
| 1. War of the Revolution | 7 years—1775–1782 | $135,193,703 |
| 2. Indian War in Ohio Territory | 1790 | .......... |
| 3. War with the Barbary States | 1803–1804 | .......... |
| 4. Tecumseh Indian War | 1811 | .......... |
| 5. War with Great Britain | 3 years—1812–1815 | 107,159,003 |
| 6. Algerine War | 1815 | .......... |
| 7. First Seminole War | 1817 | .......... |
| 8. Black Hawk War | 1832 | .......... |
| 9. Second Seminole War | 1845 | .......... |
| 10. Mexican War | 2 years—1846–1848 | 66,000,000 |
| 11. Mormon War | 1856 | .......... |
| 12. Civil War | 4 years—1861–1865 | 6,500,000,000 |

## QUOTA OF TROOPS FURNISHED BY THE STATES AND TERRITORIES DURING THE CIVIL WAR.

| States and Territories. | Troops furnished 1861-65. | Colored Troops furnished 1861-65 | Number of men drafted. | Per cent. of Troops to Population. |
|---|---|---|---|---|
| New England States | 375,131 | 7,916 | 103,807 | 12.0 |
| Middle States | 914,164 | 13,922 | 362,686 | 12.2 |
| Western States and Territories | 1,098,088 | 12,711 | 203,924 | 13.6 |
| Pacific States | 19,579 | | ...... | 4.3 |
| Border States | 301,062 | 45,184 | 106,412 | 8.3 |
| Southern States | 54,137 | 63,571 | ... .. | .6 |
| Indian Nation | 3,530 | ...... | ...... | .... |
| Colored Troops* | 93,441 | ...... | ...... | .... |
| Grand Total | †2,859,132 | 143,304 | 776,829 | 9.1 |
| At large | .. ... | 733 | | |
| Not accounted for | ...... | 5,083 | | |
| Officers | ...... | 7,122 | | |
| | | 156,242 | | |

* This gives colored troops enlisted in the States in rebellion; besides this, there were 92,576 colored troops, included (with the white soldiers) in the quotas of the several States; the second column gives the aggregate of colored, but many enlisted South were credited to the Northern States.

† This is the aggregate of troops furnished for all periods of service—from three months to three years time. Reduced to a uniform three years standard, the whole number of troops enlisted amounted to 2,320,272.

## NUMBER OF OFFICERS AND MEN IN THE WAR OF 1812.

| Date. | Officers | Men. | Total. | Date. | Officers | Men. | Total. |
|---|---|---|---|---|---|---|---|
| July, 1812.. | 301 | 6,385 | 6,686 | Sept., 1814.. | 2,395 | 35,791 | 38,186 |
| Feb., 1813.. | 1,476 | 17,560 | 19,036 | Feb., 1815.. | 2,396 | 31,028 | 33,424 |

The whole militia force raised during the war was 31,210 officers, and 440,412 men; total, 471,622.

## COMPARATIVE RATES OF WEEKLY WAGES PAID IN EUROPE AND IN THE UNITED STATES.

| | France. | Germany. | Italy. | Great Britain. | United States. | |
|---|---|---|---|---|---|---|
| | | | | | New York. | Chicago. |
| Bakers | $5.55 | $3.50 | $3.90 | $6.50- 6.60 | $5- 8 | $8- 12 |
| Blacksmiths | 5 45 | 3.55 | 3.94 | 7.04- 8.12 | 10-14 | 9- 12 |
| Bookbinders | 4.85 | 3.82 | 3.90 | 6.50- 7.83 | 12-18 | 9- 20 |
| Bricklayers | 4.00 | 3.60 | 3.45 | 7.58- 9.63 | 12-15 | 6- 10½ |
| Cabinetmakers | 6 00 | 3.97 | 4.95 | 7.70- 8.48 | 9-13 | 7- 15 |
| Carpenters & Joiners | 5.42 | 4 00 | 4.18 | 7 33- 8.25 | 9-12 | 7½-12 |
| Farm Laborers | 3.15 | 2 87 | 3 50 | 3.40- 4.25 | .... | ...... |
| Laborers, Porters, etc. | .... | 2.92 | 2.60 | 4.50- 5.00 | 6- 9 | 5½- 9 |
| Painters | 4.90 | 3.92 | 4 60 | 7.25- 8 16 | 10-16 | 6- 12 |
| Plasterers | .... | 3.80 | 4.35 | 7.68-10.13 | 10-15 | 9- 15 |
| Plumbers | 5.50 | 3.60 | 3.90 | 7.13- 8.46 | 12-18 | 12- 20 |
| Printers | 4.70 | 4.80 | 3.90 | 7.52- 7 75 | 8-18 | 12- 18 |
| Shoemakers | 4 75 | 3 12 | 4.32 | 7.35 | 12-18 | 9- 18 |
| Tailors | 5.10 | 3.58 | 4.30 | 5.00- 7 30 | 10-18 | 6- 18 |
| Tinsmiths | 4.40 | 3.65 | 3.60 | 6.00- 7.30 | 10-14 | 9- 12 |

# WAGES TABLE.

Ten hours as the basis of one day's labor.

| WEEK. | HOURS. | | | | | | | | | | DAYS. | | | | | |
|---|---|---|---|---|---|---|---|---|---|---|---|---|---|---|---|---|
| | Half. | One. | Two. | Three. | Four. | Five. | Six. | Seven. | Eight. | Nine. | One. | Two. | Three. | Four. | Five. | Six. |
| **$1** | 5-6 | 1⅔ | 3⅓ | 5 | 6⅔ | 8⅓ | 10 | 11⅔ | 13⅓ | 15 | 16⅔ | 33⅓ | 50 | 66⅔ | 83⅓ | $1.00 |
| **$2** | 1⅔ | 3⅓ | 6⅔ | 10 | 13⅓ | 16⅔ | 20 | 23⅓ | 26⅔ | 30 | 33⅓ | 66⅔ | $1.00 | $1.33⅓ | $1.66⅔ | 2.00 |
| **$3** | 2½ | 5 | 10 | 15 | 20 | 25 | 30 | 35 | 40 | 45 | 50 | $1.00 | 1.50 | 2.00 | 2.50 | 3.00 |
| **$4** | 3⅓ | 6⅔ | 13⅓ | 20 | 26⅔ | 33⅓ | 40 | 46⅔ | 53⅓ | 60 | 66⅔ | 1.33⅓ | 2.00 | 2.66⅔ | 3.33⅓ | 4.00 |
| **$5** | 4⅓ | 8⅓ | 16⅔ | 25 | 33⅓ | 41⅔ | 50 | 58⅓ | 66⅔ | 75 | 83⅓ | 1.66⅔ | 2.50 | 3.33⅓ | 4.16⅔ | 5.00 |
| **$6** | 5 | 10 | 20 | 30 | 40 | 50 | 60 | 70 | 80 | 90 | $1.00 | 2.00 | 3.00 | 4.00 | 5.00 | 6.00 |
| **$7** | 5 | 11⅔ | 23⅓ | 35 | 46⅔ | 58⅓ | 70 | 81⅔ | 93⅓ | $1.05 | 1.16⅔ | 2.33⅓ | 3.50 | 4.66⅔ | 5.83⅓ | 7.00 |
| **$8** | 6⅔ | 13⅓ | 26⅔ | 40 | 53⅓ | 66⅔ | 80 | 93⅓ | $1.06⅔ | 1.20 | 1.33⅓ | 2.66⅔ | 4.00 | 5.33⅓ | 6.66⅔ | 8.00 |
| **$9** | 7½ | 15 | 30 | 45 | 60 | 75 | 90 | $1.05 | 1.20 | 1.35 | 1.80 | 3.00 | 4.50 | 6.00 | 7.50 | 9.00 |
| **$10** | 8⅓ | 16⅔ | 33⅓ | 50 | 66⅔ | 83⅓ | $1.00 | 1.16⅔ | 1.33⅓ | 1.50 | 1.66⅔ | 3.33⅓ | 5.00 | 6.66⅔ | 8.33⅓ | 10.00 |
| **$11** | 9⅓ | 18⅓ | 36⅔ | 55 | 73⅓ | 91⅔ | 1.10 | 1.28⅓ | 1.46⅔ | 1.65 | 1.83⅓ | 3.66⅔ | 5.50 | 7.33⅓ | 9.16⅔ | 11.00 |
| **$12** | 10 | 20 | 40 | 60 | 80 | $1.00 | 1.20 | 1.40 | 1.60 | 1.80 | 2.00 | 4.00 | 6.00 | 8.00 | 10.00 | 12.00 |
| **$13** | 10¾ | 21⅔ | 43⅓ | 65 | 86⅔ | 1.08⅓ | 1.30 | 1,51⅔ | 1.73⅓ | 1.95 | 2.16⅔ | 4.33⅓ | 6.50 | 8.66⅔ | 10.83⅓ | 13.00 |
| **$14** | 11⅔ | 23⅓ | 46⅔ | 70 | 93⅓ | 1.16⅔ | 1.40 | 1.63⅓ | 1.86⅔ | 2.10 | 2.33⅓ | 4.66⅔ | 7.00 | 9.33⅓ | 11.66⅔ | 14.00 |
| **$15** | 12½ | 25 | 50 | 75 | $1.00 | 1.25 | 1.50 | 1.75 | 2.00 | 2.25 | 2.50 | 5.00 | 7.50 | 10.00 | 12.50 | 15.00 |
| **$16** | 13⅓ | 26⅔ | 53⅓ | 80 | 1.06⅔ | 1.33⅓ | 1.60 | 1.86⅔ | 2.13⅓ | 2.40 | 2.66⅔ | 5.33⅓ | 8.00 | 10.66⅔ | 13.33⅓ | 16.00 |
| **$17** | 14⅓ | 28⅓ | 56⅔ | 85 | 1.13⅓ | 1.41⅔ | 1.70 | 1.98⅓ | 2.26⅔ | 2.55 | 2.83⅓ | 5.66⅔ | 8.50 | 11.33⅓ | 14.16⅔ | 17.00 |
| **$18** | 15 | 30 | 60 | 90 | 1.20 | 1.50 | 1.80 | 2.10 | 2.40 | 2.70 | 3.00 | 6.00 | 9.00 | 12.00 | 15.00 | 18.00 |

EXPLANATION.—The full-face figures at the side of the columns show the rate of wages per week, the other figures the rate per hour or per day. For instance, in order to find the rate per hour at $10 per week, trace your finger along the column headed one hour till you reach the column crossing it at right angles and headed $10, where 16⅔ cents is found—the rate of pay for one hour's labor at $10 per week. In similar manner the rate for several hours or days may be found.

## DIFFERENCE IN TIME BETWEEN WASHINGTON AND OTHER CITIES OF THE WORLD.

12.00 noon.........Washington.
12.01 P. M.........Harrisburg.
12.02 " .........Annapolis.
12.06 " .........Wilmington.
12.09 " .........Trenton.
12.12 " .........New York.
12.14 " .........Montreal.
12.17 " .........Hartford.
12.22 " .........Providence.
12.23 " .........Quebec.
12.24 " .........Boston.
12.29 " .........Augusta.
1.37 " .........St. John.
2.15 " .........Rio Janeiro.
3.19 " .........Angra.
4.31 " .........Lisbon.
4.43 " .........Dublin.
4.55 " .........Edinburgh.
5.07 " .........London.
5.17 " .........Paris.
5.25 " .........Brussels.
5.28 " .........Amsterdam.
5.58 " .........Rome.
6.02 " .........Berlin.
6.14 " .........Vienna.
6.22 " .........Cape Town.
6.43 " .........Athens.
7.04 " .........Constantinople.
7.13 " .........Cairo.
7.38 " .........Moscow.
10.00 P. M.........Bombay.
11 01 ,, .........Calcutta.
12.41 A. M.........Canton.
2.48 " .........Melbourne.
4.51 " .........Auckland.
8.56 " .........Portland.
8.58 " .........San Francisco.
9.40 " .........Salt Lake City.
10.04 " .........Santa Fé.
10.08 " .........Denver.
10.44 " .........Omaha.
10.49 " .........Leavenworth.
10.53 " .........Des Moines.
10.56 " .........St. Paul.
10.59 " .........Little Rock.
11.07 " .........Jackson.
11.07 " .........St. Louis.
11.08 " .........New Orleans.
11.18 " .........Chicago.
11.21 " .........Nashville.
11.23 " .........Montgomery.
11.24 " .........Indianapolis.
11.29 " .........Frankfort.
11.35 " .........Milledgeville.
11.36 " .........Detroit.
11.41 " .........Key West.
11.44 " .........Columbia.
11.45 " .........Wheeling.
11.50 " .........Raleigh.
11.58 " .........Richmond.

## VELOCITY AND PRESSURE OF WIND.

The relation between the velocity of the wind and the pressure it exerts upon any surface opposed to it, varies according as the opposing surface is at right angles or inclined more or less to the wind, or as the surface may be curved or flat. The rule generally followed for surfaces at right angles to the direction of the wind, is to consider the pressure in pounds per square foot of exposed surface to be equal to the square of the velocity in miles, divided by 200. By this rule the following table has been prepared.

| Velocity in miles per hour. | Velocity in feet per second. | Pressure in pounds per square foot | Remarks. |
|---|---|---|---|
| 1 | 1.467 | .005 | Hardly perceptible. |
| 2 | 2.933 | .020 | " " |
| 3 | 4.400 | .045 | Pleasant. |
| 4 | 5.867 | .080 | " |
| 5 | 7.330 | .125 | " |
| 10 | 14.670 | .500 | Cooling. |
| 12½ | 18.330 | .781 | Fresh breeze. |
| 15 | 22.000 | 1.125 | " |
| 20 | 29.330 | 2.000 | Brisk wind. |
| 25 | 36.670 | 3.125 | " " |
| 30 | 44.000 | 4.500 | Strong wind. |
| 40 | 58.670 | 8.000 | High wind. |
| 50 | 73.330 | 12.500 | Storm. |
| 60 | 88.000 | 18.000 | Violent storm. |
| 80 | 117.300 | 32.000 | Hurricane. |
| 100 | 146.700 | *50.000 | Tornado. |

* This force will uproot the largest trees.

## Table showing Variations of Time, Distances from New York City, Hours by Railway, and Passenger Fares from New York to the Principal Places in the United States.

| NAMES OF CITIES. | Time when it is 12 noon at N. Y. | Miles by rail from N. Y. | Mail time from N. Y. | R. R. fares from N. Y. | NAMES OF CITIES. | Time when it is 12 noon at N. Y. | Miles by rail from N. Y. | Mail time from N. Y. | R. R. fares from N. Y. |
|---|---|---|---|---|---|---|---|---|---|
| Albany, N. Y. | 12.01 P. M. | 145 | 4.15 | $ 3.10 | Montgomery, Ala. | 11.10 A. M. | 1056 | 45. | $32.90 |
| Atlanta, Ga. | 11.18 A. M. | 881 | 52.15 | 25.50 | Nashville, Tenn. | 11.09 A. M. | 1053 | 43. | 29.45 |
| Auburn, N. Y. | 11.50 A. M. | 319 | 9.30 | 6.58 | Newark, N. J. | 11.59 A. M. | 10 | .30 | .20 |
| Baltimore, Md. | 11.50 A. M. | 188 | 6. | 6.20 | Newburgh, N. Y. | 12.00 M. | 63 | 2.35 | 1.45 |
| Bangor, Me. | 12.21 P. M. | 478 | 19.40 | 12.00 | Newburyport, Mass. | 12.12 P. M. | 270 | 9.20 | 7.00 |
| Boston, Mass. | 12.12 P. M. | 233 | 8. | 6.00 | New Haven, Conn. | 12.04 P. M. | 77 | 2.45 | 1.75 |
| Bridgeport, Conn. | 12.03 P. M. | 59 | 2. | 1.30 | New Orleans, La. | 10.56 A. M. | 1377 | 58. | 42.75 |
| Brooklyn, N. Y. | 12.00 M. | 2 | .30 | .02 | Newport, R. I. | 12.11 P. M. | 185 | 10. | 2.00 |
| Buffalo, N. Y. | 11.40 A. M. | 424 | 14. | 9.25 | Norfolk, Va. | 11.51 A. M. | 372 | 18. | 8.50 |
| Burlington, Iowa | 10.51 A. M. | 1120 | 47. | 27.25 | Northampton, Mass. | 12.05 P. M. | 156 | 6. | 3.65 |
| Burlington, Vt. | 12.03 P. M. | 302 | 11. | 8.00 | Norwich, Conn. | 12.07 P. M. | 140 | 5.15 | 2.00 |
| Charleston, S. C. | 11.36 A. M. | 804 | 33. | 24.00 | Ogdensburg, N. Y. | 11.54 A. M. | 374 | 14.30 | 9.60 |
| Chicago, Ill. | 11.05 A. M. | 913 | 35. | 20.00 | Omaha, Neb. | 10.32 A. M. | 1406 | 56.20 | 36.00 |
| Cincinnati, O. | 11.18 A. M. | 758 | 28. | 18.00 | Philadelphia, Pa. | 11.55 A. M. | 89 | 2. | 2.50 |
| Cleveland, O. | 11 29 A. M. | 585 | 20. | 13.00 | Pittsburgh, Pa. | 11.36 A. M. | 445 | 15. | 12.50 |
| Columbus, O. | 11.24 A. M. | 639 | 22. | 16.25 | Pittsfield, Mass. | 12 02 P. M. | 161 | 6. | 3.50 |
| Concord, N. H. | 12.10 P. M. | 274 | 10.30 | 7.15 | Portland, Me. | 12.15 P. M. | 341 | 14. | 9.00 |
| Council Bluffs, Iowa | 10.34 A. M. | 1389 | 56. | 35.50 | Poughkeepsie, N. Y. | 12.00 M. | 76 | 3. | 1.46 |
| Davenport, Iowa | 10.53 A. M. | 1096 | 41.40 | 26.00 | Providence, R. I. | 12.10 P. M. | 189 | 6.30 | 5.00 |
| Dayton, O. | 11.19 A. M. | 709 | 25. | 17.50 | Richmond, Va. | 11.46 A. M. | 343 | 13. | 12.85 |
| Denver, Col. | 9.57 A. M. | 1982 | 92. | 59.75 | Rochester, N. Y. | 11.43 A. M. | 374 | 10. | 7.70 |
| Des Moines, Iowa | 10.42 A. M. | 1270 | 51.10 | 31.20 | Sacramento, Cal. | 8.50 A. M. | 3183 | 146.15 | 136.00 |
| Detroit, Mich. | 11.24 A. M. | 776 | 24. | 15.00 | St. Louis, Mo. | 10 55 A. M. | 1066 | 38. | 24.25 |
| Dubuque, Iowa | 10.54 A. M. | 1103 | 43. | 26.60 | St. Paul, Minn. | 10.44 A. M. | 1322 | 54. | 31.35 |
| Easton, Pa. | 11.55 A. M. | 76 | 2.30 | 2.25 | Salt Lake City, Utah | 9.28 A. M. | 2476 | 120. | 115.50 |
| Elmira, N. Y. | 11.49 A. M. | 275 | 22.30 | 7.25 | San Antonio, Tex. | 10.23 A. M. | 1952 | 104. | 67.05 |
| Evansville, Ind. | 11.07 A. M. | 995 | 36.25 | 25.00 | San Francisco, Cal. | 8.46 A. M. | 3273 | 151. | 136.00 |
| Fort Wayne, Ind. | 11.15 A. M. | 765 | 29. | 16.75 | Savannah, Ga. | 11.32 A. M. | 919 | 39. | 25.00 |
| Galveston, Tex. | 10.37 A. M. | 1789 | 97.30 | 49.25 | Springfield, Ill. | 10.58 A. M. | 1032 | 42.30 | 24 00 |
| Harrisburg, Pa. | 11.49 A. M. | 183 | 5.10 | 5.50 | Springfield, Mass. | 12.05 P. M. | 139 | 4.30 | 3.30 |
| Hartford, Conn. | 12.05 P. M. | 113 | 3.45 | 2.65 | Syracuse, N. Y. | 11 51 A. M. | 293 | 8.30 | 6.06 |
| Indianapolis, Ind. | 11.12 A. M. | 826 | 30. | 19.00 | Terre Haute, Ind. | 11.07 A. M. | 899 | 32. | 21.25 |
| Kansas City, Mo. | 10.37 A. M. | 1343 | 60. | 32.75 | Toledo, O. | 11.22 A. M. | 706 | 24. | 16.25 |
| Keokuk, Iowa | 10.50 A. M. | 1128 | 48. | 26.25 | Trenton, N. J. | 11.54 A. M. | 58 | 1.30 | 1.75 |
| Leavenworth, Kan. | 10.37 A. M. | 1369 | 62. | 32.75 | Troy, N. Y. | 11.58 A. M. | 151 | 4.20 | 3.15 |
| Little Rock, Ark. | 10.47 A. M. | 1411 | 54.20 | 42.85 | Utica, N. Y. | 11.56 A. M. | 240 | 7.30 | 5.00 |
| Louisville, Ky. | 11.14 A. M. | 868 | 35. | 22.00 | Vicksburg, Miss. | 10.53 A. M. | 1287 | 63.30 | 39.25 |
| Lowell, Mass. | 12.10 P. M. | 245 | 9. | 7.00 | Washington, D. C. | 11.48 A. M. | 228 | 8. | 7.50 |
| Memphis, Tenn. | 10.55 A. M. | 1245 | 50. | 32.00 | Wheeling, W. Va. | 11 33 A. M. | 511 | 21. | 14.25 |
| Milwaukee, Wis. | 11.05 A. M. | 998 | 40. | 23.00 | Wilmington, Del. | 11.54 A. M. | 118 | 3. | 3.10 |
| Mobile, Ala. | 11.04 A. M. | 1236 | 52. | 40.75 | Worcester, Mass. | 12.10 P. M. | 193 | 7.15 | 4.65 |

NOTE.—As the fares by railway are constantly varying, and time tables vary widely by different trains, the mail time and passenger fares above given are to be taken as approximately correct.

### ANNUAL SALARIES OF THE PRINCIPAL CIVIL OFFICERS OF THE UNITED STATES.

| LEGISLATIVE. | |
|---|---|
| President | $50,000 |
| Vice-President | 8,000 |
| Secretary of State | 8,000 |
| Secretary of the Treasury | 8,000 |
| Secretary of the Interior | 8,000 |
| Secretary of the Navy | 8,000 |
| Secretary of War | 8,000 |
| Postmaster-General | 8,000 |
| Attorney-General | 8,000 |
| Speaker House of Representatives | 8,000 |
| United States Senators | 5,000 |
| Representatives in Congress | 5,000 |

| HEADS OF DEPARTMENTS. | |
|---|---|
| Director Geological Surveys | $6,000 |
| Auditor Railroad Accounts | 5,000 |
| Superintendent of Census | 5,000 |
| Superin't Naval Observatory | 5,000 |
| Commissioner of Patents | 4,500 |
| Director of the Mint | 4,500 |
| Commis'r Gen'l Land Office | 4,000 |
| Superintend't Signal Service | 4,000 |
| Commissioner of Pensions | 3,600 |
| Superin't Nautical Almanac | 3,500 |
| Commander of Marine Corps | 3,500 |
| Commis'r of Agriculture | 3,000 |
| Commis'r of Indian Affairs | 3,000 |
| Commissioner of Education | 3,000 |

| UNITED STATES' MINISTER TO | |
|---|---|
| England | $17,500 |
| France | 17,500 |
| Germany | 17,500 |
| Russia | 17,500 |
| Spain | 12,000 |
| China | 12,000 |
| Japan | 12,000 |
| Mexico | 12,000 |
| Brazil | 12,000 |
| Chili | 10,000 |
| Peru | 10,000 |
| Central America | 10,000 |
| Venezuela | 7,500 |
| Turkey | 7,500 |
| Sweden and Norway | 7,500 |
| Netherlands | 7,500 |
| Denmark | 5,000 |
| Greece | 5,000 |
| Uruguay | 5,000 |
| Portugal | 5,000 |
| Switzerland | 5,000 |
| Liberia | 4,000 |

| JUDGES. | |
|---|---|
| Chief Justice of the United States Supreme Court | $10,500 |
| Associate Judges | 10,000 |
| U. S. Circuit Judges | 6,000 |
| U. S. Distr. Judges, $3,500 to | 5,000 |
| Judge of the U. S. Court of Claims | 4,500 |

### PAY TABLE OF THE ARMY AND NAVY OF THE UNITED STATES.

**ARMY.**

| GRADE OR RANK. | Yearly pay first five years. |
|---|---|
| General | $13,500 |
| Lieutenant-General | 11,000 |
| Major-General | 7,500 |
| Brigadier-General | 5,500 |
| *Colonel | †3,500 |
| *Lieutenant-Colonel | †3,000 |
| *Major | 2,500 |
| *Captain, mounted | 2,000 |
| *Captain, not mounted | 1,800 |
| *Regimental Adjutant | 1,800 |
| *Regimental Quarterm'st'r | 1,800 |
| *1st Lieutenant, mounted | 1,600 |
| *1st Lieutenant, not m't'd | 1,500 |
| *2d Lieutenant, mounted | 1,500 |
| *2d Lieutenant, not m't'd | 1,400 |
| *Chaplain | 1,500 |

† The maximum pay of colonels is limited to $4,500, and of lieutenant-colonels to $4,000.

**NAVY.**

| GRADE OR RANK. | At Sea. |
|---|---|
| Admiral | $13,000 |
| Vice-Admiral | 9,000 |
| Rear-Admiral | 6,000 |
| Commodore | 5,000 |
| Captain | 4,500 |
| Commander | 3,500 |
| ‡Lieutenant-Commander | 2,800 |
| *Lieutenant | 2,400 |
| *Master | 1,800 |
| *Ensign | 1,200 |
| Midshipman | 1,000 |
| Cadet Midshipman | 500 |
| Mate | 900 |
| Medical and Pay Director, Medical and Pay Inspector and Chief Engineer | 4,400 |
| *Fleet* Surgeon, Paymaster and Engineer | 4,400 |
| *Surgeon, Paymaster and Chief Engineer | 2,800 |
| **Passed Assist't* Surgeon, Paymaster and Engineer | 2,000 |
| **Assistant* Surgeon, Paymaster and Engineer | 1,700 |

*The pay of these officers is increased after the first five years service.
‡ Increased to $3,000 after four years from date of commission.

# WEIGHTS AND MEASURES.

## AVOIRDUPOIS WEIGHT.

16 Drachms.........1 Ounce (oz.)=28.35 gr'm's
16 Ounces .........1 Pound (lb.)=453.6 "
14 Pounds ..........1 Stone.
2 Stone ...........1 Quarter (qr.), 28 pounds.
4 Quarters..........1 Hundred-w't, 112 pounds
20 Hundred-weight..1 Ton, 2,240 pounds.

The standard avoirdupois pound of the United States, copied from the British standard, is 0.00734 grain too heavy. The gramme is legal at 15.432 grains, and the kilogramme at 2.2046 pounds. In some States the ton rates at 2,240 pounds, and in others at only 2,000—the latter value being the more usual.

## TROY WEIGHT.

24 Grains..........1 Pennyweight. (dwt.)
20 Pennyweights..... 1 Ounce,=480 grains.
12 Ounces .......... 1 Pound,=5,760 grains.

Gold, silver, platinum, and some gems are weighed by this scale. Pearls and diamonds are weighed by the carat of 4 grains, 5 diamond grains being equal to 4 grains troy.

## APOTHECARIES' WEIGHT.

20 Grains.............................1 Scruple.
3 Scruple ............................1 Drachm.
*8 Drachms............................1 Ounce.
*12 Ounces............................1 Pound.

* Same as in troy weight, as is also the grain.

## LINEAR MEASURE.

3 Barleycorns..........1 Inch.
12 Inches..............1 Foot=0.3047 metre.
3 Feet.................1 Yard=0.91438 metre.
5½ Yards...............1 Rod, Perch, or Pole.
4 Poles, or 100 Links...1 Chain.
10 Chains..............1 Furlong.
8 Furlongs ............1 Mile=1.6093 kilom'rs

1 Line.............................$\frac{1}{12}$ Inch.
1 Nail (cloth measure).............2¼ Inches.
1 Palm.............................3 "
1 Hand (used for height of horses)4 "
1 Span.............................9 "
1 Cubit............................18 "
1 Scotch Ell........................37.06 "
1 English Ell.......................45 "
1 Fathom............................6 Feet.
1 Cable's Length....................120 Fathoms.
1 League............................3 Miles.
1 Degree of the Equator.............69.1613 Miles.
1 Degree of Meridian................69.046 "

## SQUARE, OR SURFACE MEASURE.

144 Square Inches...1 Sq. Foot, = 9.29 square decimetres.
9 " Feet......1 Sq. Yard,=0.836 square metre.
30¼ " Yards.....1 Square Rod.
16 " Rods.....1 Chain.
40 " " .....1 Rood.
4 Roods............1 Acre, or 43.560 sq. fect.
640 Acres..........1 Sq. Mile,=259 hectares.
The acre, = 0.405 hectare.

## CUBIC, OR SOLID MEASURE.

1728 Cubic Inches ..............1 Cubic Foot.
27 Cubic Feet ..................1 Cubic Yard.
40 Cubic Feet of rough, or... } 1 Ton or Load.
50 Cubic Feet of hewn timber }
42 Cubic Feet of timber .......1 British Shipping Ton.
40 Cubic Feet....................1 American Ship'g Ton.
108 Cubic Feet....................1 Stack wood.
128 Cubic Feet....................1 Cord wood.

## APOTHECARIES' MEASURE.

60 Minims...................1 Fluid Drachm.
8 Drachms ..................1 " Ounce.
20 Ounces...................1 Pint.
8 Pints ....................1 Imperial Gallon.

## LIQUID MEASURE.

4 Gills.....................1 Pint. (pt.)
2 Pints.....................1 Quart. (qt.)
4 Quarts....................1 Gallon. (gal.)
42 Gallons..................1 Tierce.
63 " .....................1 Hogshead. (hhd.)
84 " .....................1 Puncheon.
126 " .....................1 Pipe.
252 " .....................1 Ton.
10 " .....................1 Anker.
18 " .....................1 Runlet.
*31½ " .....................1 Barrel. (bbl.)

* In some of the States 32 gallons make a barrel.

## DRY MEASURE.

The Bushel is 2150.42 cubic inches, that of England being 2218.192 cubic inches. The imperial bushel is, therefore, 1.0315 United States bushels. In dry measure the litre is legal at 0.908 quart. The following table is generally used:

2 Pints.....1 Quart.
4 Quarts.....1 Gallon of 268.8 cubic inches.
2 Gallons.....1 Peck. (pk.)
4 Pecks.......1 Bushel. (bush.)
36 Bushels.....1 Chaldron. (For coke and coal.)

## MEASURES OF TIME.

60 Seconds...................1 Minute.
60 Minutes...................1 Hour.
24 Hours.....................1 Day.
7 Days.......................1 Week.
28 Days......................1 Lunar Month.
28, 29, 30, or 31 Days ......1 Calendar Month.
12 Calendar Months...........1 Year.
365 Days.....................1 Common Year.
366 Days.....................1 Leap Year.

## ANGULAR MEASURE.

60 Seconds....................1 Minute.
60 Minutes....................1 Degree.
30 Degrees....................1 Sign.
90 Degrees....................1 Quadrant.
4 Quadrants, or 360°..........1 Circumference, or great circle.

## MEASURES FOR HOUSE-KEEPERS.

Wheat flour..................1 pound = 1 quart.
Indian meal...........1 pound 2 oz. = 1 "
Butter, when soft............1 pound = 1 "
Loaf sugar, broken...........1 pound = 1 "
White sugar, pow'd....1 pound 1 oz. = 1 "
Brown sugar...........1 pound 2 oz. = 1 "
Eggs.........................10 eggs = 1 pound
Flour........................8 quarts = 1 peck.
Flour........................4 pecks = 1 bushel

### LIQUIDS.

16 Large tablespoonfuls..............½ Pint.
8 Large tablespoonfuls...............1 Gill.
4 Large tablespoonfuls...............½ Gill.
2 Gills..............................½ Pint.
2 Pints .............................1 Quart.
4 Quarts.............................1 Gallon.
1 Common sized tumbler holds ....½ a Pint.
1 Common sized wine glass holds...½ a Gill.
25 Drops are equal to........... 1 Teaspoonful.

## AMERICAN MONEY.

10 Mills.............................1 Cent.
10 Cents.............................1 Dime.
10 Dimes.............................1 Dollar.
10 Dollars...........................1 Eagle.

In the West and South, 12½ cents make a *bit*; in New York the same sum is called a *shilling*. The New England States call 16⅔ cents a shilling, but all of these values are not legal.

## ENGLISH MONEY.

4 Farthings....1 Penny.
12 Pence.......1 Shilling.
20 Shillings...*1 Pound or Sovereign—$4.8666.

*In United States custom houses it rates at $4.84.

## FOREIGN WEIGHTS AND MEASURES.

With their value given in the standard of the United States.

### FRANCE.

Metre.............................. 3.28 Feet.
Decimetre (1-10th metre)........... 3.94 Inches.
Velt............................... 2.00 Gallons.
Hectolitre ........................ 26.42 Gallons.
Decalitre.......................... 2.64 Gallons.
Litre.............................. 2.11 Pints.
Kilolitre.......................... 35.32 Feet.
Hectolitre ........................ 2.84 Bushels.
Decalitre.......................... 9.08 Quarts.
Millier............................ 22.05 Pounds.
Quintal............................220.54 Pounds.
Kilogramme......................... 2.21 Pounds.

### PRUSSIA.

100 Pounds of 2 Cologne marks each...........................103.11 Pounds.
Quintal, 110 pounds................113.42 Pounds.
Sheffel of grain................... 1.56 Bushels.
Eimer of wine...................... 18 14 Gallons.
Ell of cloth....................... 2.19 Feet.
Foot............................... 1.03 Feet.

### RUSSIA.

100 Pounds of 32 laths each ....... 90.26 Pounds.
Chertwert of grain................. 5.95 Bushels.
Vedro of wine ..................... 3.25 Gallons.
Petersburgh foot................... 1.18 Feet.
Moscow foot........................ 1.10 Feet.
Pood............................... 36.00 Pounds.

### *SPAIN.

Quintal, or 4 arrobas..............101.44 Pounds.
Arroba............................. 25.36 Pounds.
Arroba of wine..................... 4.43 Gallons.
Fanega of grain.................... 1.60 Bushels.

### NETHERLANDS.

Ell................................ 3.28 Feet.
Mudde of Zak....................... 2.84 Bushels.
Vat hectolitre..................... 26.42 Gallons.
Kan litre.......................... 2.11 Pints.
Pond kilogramme.................... 2.21 Pounds.

### DENMARK.

100 Pounds, 1 centner..............110.28 Pounds.
Barrel or toende of corn........... 3.95 Bushels.
Viertel of wine.................... 2.04 Gallons.
Copenhagen or Rhineland foot....... 1.03 Feet.

### SWEDEN.

100 Pounds, or 5 lispunds ......... 73.76 Pounds.
Kan of corn........................ 7.42 Bushels.
Last............................... 75.00 Bushels.
Cann of wine....................... 69.09 Gallons.
Ell of cloth....................... 1.95 Feet.

### *PORTUGAL.

100 Pounds ........................101.19 Pounds.
22 Pounds (1 arroba)............... 22.26 Pounds.
Alquiere........................... 4.75 Bushels.
Almude of wine .................... 4.37 Gallons.

### CHINA.

Tail............................... 1.33 Ounces.
16 Tails 1 catty .................. 1.33 Pounds.
100 Catties 1 picul ...............133.25 Pounds.

In the following countries the French metric system has been either introduced or legalized: Argentine Confederation, Austria, Belgium, Bolivia, Brazil, Chili, Colombia, Ecuador, Egypt, German Empire, Greece, Italy, Mexico, *Portugal, *Spain.

In the United States the metric system was legalized by an act of Congress, passed in 1866, but it has not yet come into use.

The present uniform system of Switzerland is upon a semi-metric basis.

In Turkey the weights and measures vary in the different provinces, and with the nature of the substances to be measured.

# THE RAILROADS OF THE WORLD IN 1880.

| Countries. | | Miles. |
|---|---|---|
| 1. North America. | United States | 93,671 |
| | Canada | 6,891 |
| | Mexico | 678 |
| Total | | 101,240 |
| 2. Middle America. | Honduras | 56 |
| | Costa Rica | 74 |
| | Cuba (Spanish) | 858 |
| | Jamaica (British) | 24 |
| | Panama (Colombia) | 48 |
| Total | | 1,060 |
| 3. South America. | Bolivia | 31 |
| | Ecuador | 76 |
| | Venezuela | 70 |
| | Guiana (British) | 21 |
| | Brazil | 1,711 |
| | Peru | 1,750 |
| | Chili | 1,049 |
| | Argentine Republic | 1,439 |
| | Paraguay | 44 |
| | Uruguay | 233 |
| Total | | 6,424 |
| 4. Europe | Great Britain and Ireland | 17,696 |
| | France | 15,287 |
| | Spain | 4,264 |
| | Portugal | 795 |
| | Belgium | 2,324 |
| | Netherlands | 1,199 |
| | Denmark | 849 |
| | Sweden | 3,260 |
| | Norway | 658 |
| | Russia | 13,571 |
| | Germany | 21,037 |
| | Austria-Hungary | 11,471 |
| 4. Europe, continued | Switzerland | 1,609 |
| | Italy | 4,999 |
| | Turkey | 1,032 |
| | Roumania | 862 |
| | Greece | 7 |
| Total | | 100,920 |
| 5. Asia | Turkey in Asia | 250 |
| | India (British) | 8,615 |
| | Ceylon (British) | 108 |
| | Java (Dutch) | 499 |
| | Philippines (Spanish) | 279 |
| | China | |
| | Japan | 67 |
| Total | | 9,818 |
| 6. Africa | Egypt | 928 |
| | Tunis | 115 |
| | Algeria (French) | 708 |
| | Cape Colony (British) | 662 |
| | Namaqualand | 95 |
| | Natal (British) | 5 |
| | Mauritius | 65 |
| Total | | 2,578 |
| 7. Australia | New South Wales | 736 |
| | Queensland | 503 |
| | Victoria | 1,125 |
| | South Australia | 559 |
| | Western Australia | 72 |
| | Tasmania | 172 |
| | New Zealand | 1,171 |
| Total | | 4,338 |
| Grand Total | | 226,378 |

## QUICK PASSAGES OF OCEAN STEAMERS.

| | Miles. | Steamer. | Date. | D. | H. | M. |
|---|---|---|---|---|---|---|
| New York to Queenstown | 2,950 | Arizona | June, 1879 | 7 | 9 | 23 |
| New York to Queenstown | 2,950 | Britannic | Dec., 1876 | 7 | 12 | 46 |
| New York to Queenstown | 2,950 | City of Berlin | Oct., 1875 | 7 | 15 | 48 |
| Queenstown to New York | 2,950 | City of Berlin | Sept., 1875 | 7 | 18 | 02 |
| New York to Queenstown | 2,950 | Russia | July, 1869 | 8 | 6 | 30 |
| Queenstown to New York | 2,950 | Russia | June, 1869 | 8 | 2 | 58 |
| Liverpool to New York | 3,050 | Russia | 1869 | 9 | 8 | 12 |
| Philadelphia to Queenstown | 3,010 | Illinois | Dec., 1876 | 8 | 18 | 13 |
| New York to Havana | 1,225 | City of Vera Cruz | Aug., 1876 | 4 | 0 | 43 |
| Havana to New York | 1,225 | City of New York | May, 1875 | 3 | 10 | 7 |
| New York to Aspinwall | 2,300 | Henry Chauncey | 1875 | 6 | 14 | .. |
| Aspinwall to New York | 2,300 | Henry Chauncey | 1875 | 6 | 5 | 30 |
| San Francisco to Yokohama | 4,764 | City of Peeking | ——, | 15 | 9 | .. |
| Yokohama to San Francisco | 4,764 | Oceanic | 1876 | 14 | 13 | .. |

### Velocity of Various Bodies.

| | Per Hour. | Per Second. |
|---|---|---|
| A man walks | 3 miles. | 4 feet |
| A horse trots | 7 " | 10 " |
| A horse runs | 20 " | 29 " |
| Steamboat runs | 18 " | 26 " |
| Sailing vessel runs | 10 " | 14 " |
| Slow rivers flow | 3 " | 4 " |
| Rapid rivers flow | 7 " | 10 " |
| A rifle ball moves | 1,000 " | 1466 " |
| Sound " | 743 " | 1142 " |
| Light " | 192,000 miles per second. | |
| Electricity " | 288,000 " " " | |

**SIZES OF TYPE.**—It requires 205 lines of *Diamond* type to make 12 inches; of *Pearl*, 178; of *Ruby*, 166; of *Nonpareil*, 143; of *Minion*, 128; of *Brevier*, 112½; of *Bourgeois*, 102½; of *Long Primer*, 89; of *Small Pica*, 83; of *Pica*, 71½; of *English*, 64.

**Strength of Ice.**—Solid ice 2 inches thick will bear men on foot; 4 inches thick will bear men on horseback; 6 inches thick will bear cattle and teams with light loads; 8 inches thick will bear teams with heavy loads; 10 inches thick will bear a pressure of 1,000 pounds per square foot.

**Counted in Groups**—12 things make 1 *dozen*, 12 doz. (144) 1 *gross*, 12 gross, (1,728) 1 *great gross*, 2 things 1 *pair*, 6 things 1 *set*, 20 things 1 *score*.

**In Counting Paper**—24 sheets make 1 *quire*, 20 quires (480 sheets), 1 *ream*, 2 reams (960 sheets), 1 *bundle*, 5 bundles (4,800 sheets), 1 *bale*.

**Classification of Books.**—The terms *folio*, *quarto*, *octavo*, etc., point out the *number of leaves* into which a sheet of paper is folded in making a book, the number of pages in each sheet being termed *a signature*; A *folio* book or paper is made of sheets folded in 2 leaves; a *quarto* (4to) of sheets folded into 4 leaves; an *octavo* (8vo), 8 leaves; *duodecimo* (12mo), 12 leaves; 18*mo*, in 18 leaves; a 24*mo*, in 24 leaves; a 32*mo*, in 32 leaves, etc.

**In Copying**—72 words make one folio, or sheet of common law; 9 words one folio in chancery.

# MODERN ABBREVIATIONS.

*A.A.S.* (*Academiæ Americanæ Socius.*) Member of the American Academy.
*A.B.* (*Artium Baccalaureus.*) Bachelor of Arts.
*A.B.C.F.M.* American Board of Commissioners for Foreign Missions.
*A.C.* (*Ante Christum.*) Before Christ.
*Æt.* (*Ætatis.*) Of age; aged.
*Al.* Alabama.
*A.M.* (*Artium Magister.*) Master of Arts.
*A.M.* (*Ante Meridiem.*) Before noon.
*A.M.* (*Anno Mundi.*) In the year of the world.
*An.* (*Anno.*) In the year.
*Apr.* April.
*A.R.* (*Anno Regni.*) In the year of the reign.
*Ark.* Arkansas.
*A.U.C.* (*Anno Urbis Conditæ.*) In the year from the foundation of the city.
*Aug.* August.
*Avoir.* Avoirdupois.
*b.* Born.
*B.* Book.
*B.A.* Bachelor of Arts.
*Bal.* Balance.
*Bart.* Baronet.
*B.C.* Before Christ.
*B.C.L.* Bachelor of Civil Law.
*B.D.* Bachelor of Divinity.
*Bd.* Bound.
*Bds.* Bound in boards.
*Benj.* Benjamin.
*Bk.* Book.
*B.L.* Bachelor of Laws.
*Bp.* Bishop.
*Brig. Gen.* Brigadier-General.
*C.*, or *Cap.* (*Caput.*) Chapter.
*Cal.* California.
*Cam.*, or *Camb.* Cambridge.
*Caps.* Capitals.
*Capt.* Captain.
*C.B.* Companion of the Bath.
*C.C.P.* Court of Common Pleas.
*C.E.* Civil Engineer.
*C.J.* Chief Justice.
*Co.* Company.
*Col.* Colonel; Colorado.
*Com.* Commodore.
*Conn.*, or *Ct.* Connecticut.
*Cor.* Corinthians.
*Cor. Sec.* Corresponding Secretary.
*Crim. Con.* Criminal Conversation; Adultery.
*Ct.* Cent; *Cts.* Cents.
*Cwt.* Hundredweight.
*D.*, or *d.* Penny, *or* pence.
*Dan.* Daniel.
*D.C.* District of Columbia.
*D.C.L.* Doctor of Civil Law.
*D.D.* (*Divinitatis Doctor.*) Doctor of Divinity.
*Dea.* Deacon.
*Dec.* December.
*Del.* Delaware.
*Dept.* Department.
*Deut.* Deuteronomy.
*Deft.*, or *dft.* Defendant.
*Dist.* District.
*Dist. Atty.* District Attorney.
*D.M.* Doctor of Music.
*Do.* (*Ditto.*) The same.
*Dols.* ($) Dollars.
*Doz.* Dozen.
*Dr.* Doctor; Debtor; Dram.
*D.V.* (*Deo Volente.*) God willing.
*Dwt.* Pennyweight.
*E.* East.
*Ed.* Edition; Editor.
*Edw.* Edward.
*E.G.*, or *e.g.* (*exempli gratia.*) For example.
*Eliz.* Elizabeth.
*E.N.E.* East-north-east.
*Eph.* Ephesians.
*Esq.* Esquire.
*Et. al.* (*et alii.*) And others.
*Etc.*, or *&c.* (*et cætera.*) And so forth.
*Et. seq.* (*et sequentia.*) And what follows.
*Exod.* Exodus.
*Ez.* Ezra.
*Ezek.* Ezekiel.
*Fahr.* Fahrenheit.
*Feb.* February.
*Fl.*, or *Flor.* Florida.
*Fred.* Frederic.
*F.R.S.* Fellow of the Royal Society.
*Ft.* Foot, *or* feet.
*Fur.* Furlong.
*Ga.* Georgia.
*G.B.* Great Britain.
*G.C.B.* Grand Cross of the Bath.
*Gen.* General; Genesis.
*Geo.* George; Georgia.
*Gov.* Governor.
*Gov. Gen.* Governor-General.
*H.*, or *h.* Hour.
*Hab.* Habakkuk.
*H.B.M.* His, *or* Her, Britannic Majesty.
*H.C.* House of Commons.
*Heb.* Hebrews.
*Hhd.* Hogshead.
*H.L.* House of Lords.
*H.M.* His, *or* Her, Majesty.
*H.M.S.* His, *or* Her, Majesty's Ship, *or* Service.
*Hon.* Honorable.
*Hos.* Hosea.
*H.R.* House of Representatives.
*H.R.H.* His, *or* Her, Royal Highness.
*Hund.* Hundred.
*I.*, or *Isl.* Island.
*Ib.*, *Ibid.* (*Ibidem.*) In the same place.
*Id.* (*Idem.*) The same.
*i.e.* (*id est.*) That is.
*I.H.S.* (*Iesus Hominum Salvator.*) Jesus the Saviour of Men.
*Ill.* Illinois.
*In.* Inches.
*Incog.* (*Incognito.*) Unknown.
*Ind.* Indiana.
*I.N.R.I.* (*Iesus Nazarenus, Rex Iudæorum.*) Jesus of Nazareth, King of the Jews.
*Inst.* Instant (the current month).
*Io.* Iowa.
*i.q.* (*idem quod.*) The same as.
*Is.* Isaiah.
*It.* Italics.
*J.* Justice; Judge.
*Jan.* January.
*Jas.* James.
*Jer.* Jeremiah.
*Jno.* John.
*Jona.* Jonathan.
*Jos.* Joseph.
*Josh.* Joshua.
*J.P.* Justice of the Peace.
*Jr.* Junior.
*Judg.* Judges.
*Jul.* July.
*Jun.* Junior.
*Kan.* Kansas.
*K.B.* Knight of the Bath; King's Bench.
*K.C.B.* Knight Commander of the Bath.
*Ken.*, or *Ky.* Kentucky.
*K.G.* Knight of the Garter.
*K.G.C.* Knight of the Grand Cross.
*Ki.* Kings.
*Knt.*, or *Kt.* Knight.
*L.*, or *lb.* Pound (weight).
*L.*, *l.*, or *£.* Pound Sterling.
*La.* Louisiana.
*Lat.* Latitude.
*L. I.* Long Island.
*Lieut.* Lieutenant.
*LL.B.* Bachelor of Laws.
*LL.D.* Doctor of Laws.
*M.*, or *m.* Masculine.
*M.A.* Master of Arts; Military Academy.
*Maj.* Major.
*Mar.* March.
*Mass.* Massachusetts.

*Matt.* Matthew.
*M.C.* Member of Congress.
*M.D.* Doctor of Medicine.
*Md.* Maryland.
*Mdlle.* Mademoiselle.
*M.E.* Mechanical Engineer; Methodist Episcopal; Most Excellent.
*Me.* Maine.
*Mem.* Memorandum.
*Messrs.* Gentlemen.
*Meth.* Methodist.
*Mich.* Michigan.
*Min.*, or *min.* Minute; minutes.
*Minn.* Minnesota.
*Miss.* Mississippi.
*Mlle.* Mademoiselle.
*MM.* (*Messieurs.*) Gentlemen; Their Majesties.
*Mme.* Madame.
*Mo.* Missouri.
*Mo.*, or *mo.* Month.
*Mons.* Monsieur; Sir.
*Mos.*, or *mos.* Months.
*M.P.* Member of Parliament; Member of Police.
*M.P.P.* Member of the Provincial Parliament.
*Mr.* Master, *or* Mister.
*Mrs.* Mistress, *or* Missis.
*MS.* Manuscript.
*MSS.* Manuscripts.
*Mt.* Mount, *or* Mountain.
*Mus. D.*, *Mus. Doc.*, or *Mus. Doct.* Doctor of Music.
*N.* North.
*N.*, or *n.* Noun; Neuter.
*N. A.* North America.
*Nath.* Nathaniel.
*N. B.* New Brunswick.
*Nota Bene.* Note well, *or* take notice.
*N. C.* North Carolina.
*N.E.* North-East; New England.
*Neb.* Nebraska.
*N. F.* Newfoundland.
*N. H.* New Hampshire.
*N. J.* New Jersey.
*N.L.* or *N. Lat.* North Latitude.
*N.N.E.* North-North-East.
*N.N.W.* North-North-West.
*No.*, or *no.* (*Numero.*) Number.
*Non. seq.*, or *non. seq.* (*Non sequitur.*) It does not follow.
*Nos.*, or *nos.* Numbers.
*Nov.* November.
*N. S.* Nova Scotia; New Style (since 1752).
*N. T.* New Testament.
*N.W.* North-West.
*N. Y.* New York.
*O.* Ohio.
*Ob.*, or *ob.* (*Obiit.*) Died.
*Ob.*, or *Obdt.* Obedient.
*Oct.* October.
*Or.* Oregon.
*O. S.* Old Style.
*O.T.* Old Testament.
*Oxf.*, or *Oxon.* (*Oxonia.*) Oxford.
*Oz.*, or *oz.* Ounce, *or* ounces.
*P.*, or *p.* Page.
*Pa.* Pennsylvania.
*Parl.* Parliament.
*Pd.* Paid.
*P. E. I.* Prince Edward Island.
*Penn.* Pennsylvania.
*Per cent.*, or *per ct.* (*Per centum.*) By the hundred.
*Ph.D.* (*Philosophiæ Doctor.*) Doctor of Philosophy.
*Phil.* Philippians.
*Phila.* Philadelphia.
*Pinx.*, or *pxt.* (*Pinxit.*) He, *or* she, painted it.
*Pk.*, or *pk.* Peck.
*Pl.*, or *pl.* Plural.
*Plff.* Plaintiff.
*P.M.* Post-Master; Past Master. (*Post Meridiem.*) Afternoon.
*P.M.G.* Post-Master-General.
*P. O.* Post-Office.
*pp.* Pages.
*P.P.C.* (*Pour Prende Congé.*) To take leave.
*Pr.*, *pr.*, or ℘. (*Per.*) By the.
*Pres.* President.
*Prof.* Professor.
*Pro tem.*, or *pro tem.* (*Pro tempore.*) For the time being.
*Prov.* Proverbs; Province.
*Prox.* (*Proximo.*) Next (the next month).
*P.S.* (*Post Scriptum.*) Postscript.
*Ps.* Psalm, *or* Psalms.
*Pt.* Pint.
*Pub. Doc.* Public Documents.
*Pwt.*, or *pwt.* Pennyweight.
*Pxt.*, or *pxt.* (*Pinxit.*) He, *or* she, painted it.
*Q.* Question.
*Q.*, or *Qu.* Query; Question; Queen.
*Q.B.* Queen's Bench.
*Q.C.* Queen's Council.
*Q.E.D.* (*Quod Erat Demonstrandum.*) Which was to be demonstrated.
*Q.M.* Quartermaster.
*Q.M.G.* Quartermaster-General.
*Qr.*, or *qr.* Quarter. (28 pounds); Farthing; Quire.
*Qt.*, or *qt.* Quart; Quantity.
*Q.v.*, or *q.v.* (*Quod vide.*) Which see.
*R.* (*Rex.*) King. (*Regina.*) Queen.
*R.A.* Royal Academy, *or* Academician; Rear Admiral; Right Ascension.
*Rec. Sec.* Recording Secretary.
*Rev.* Revelation; Reverend.
*R. I.* Rhode Island.
*R.N.* Royal Navy.
*Rom.* Roman; Romans.
*Rom. Cath.* Roman Catholic.
*R.R.* Railroad.
*Rt. Hon.* Right Honorable.
*Rt. Rev.* Right Reverend.
*S.* South; Signor; Shilling.
*S. A.* South America; South Africa.
*Sam.* Samuel.
*Sat.* Saturday.
*S. C.* South Carolina.
*Sc.*, or *Sculp.* (*Sculpsit.*) He, *or* she, engraved it.
*Sch.*, or *Schr.* Schooner.
*Scil.*, or *Sc.* (*Scilicet.*) To wit; namely.
*Script.* Scripture.
*Sculp.*, or *sculp.* (*Sculpsit.*) He, *or* she, engraved it.
*S E.* South-East.
*Sec.* Secretary; Section.
*Sen.* Senate; Senator; Senior.
*Sep.*, or *Sept.* September.
*Serg.* Sergeant.
*Serv.*, or *Servt.* Servant.
*S.J.* Society of Jesus.
*S.J.C.* Supreme Judicial Court.
*S. Lat.* South Latitude.
*Sld.*, or *sld.* Sailed.
*S.M.I.* (*Sa Majesté Imperiale.*) His, *or* Her, Imperial Majesty.
*Soc.* Society.
*Sq.*, or *sq.* Square.
*Sq. ft.*, or *sq. ft.* Square feet.
*Sq. in.*, or *sq. in.* Square inches.
*Sq. m.*, or *sq. m.* Square miles.
*Sr.* Sir, *or* Senior.
*SS.*, or *ss.* (*Scilicet.*) Namely.
*S.S.* Sunday-school.
*S.S.E.* South-South-East.
*S.S.W.* South-South-West.
*St.* Saint; Street.
*Stat.* Statute.
*S.T.D.* (*Sacræ Theologiæ Doctor.*) Doctor of Divinity.
*Sun.*, or *Sund.* Sunday.
*Supt.* Superintendent.
*S.W.* South-West.
*Ten.*, or *Tenn.* Tennessee.
*Tex.* Texas.
*Th.* Thursday.
*Theo.* Theodore.
*Thurs.* Thursday.
*Tier.*, or *tier.* Tierce.
*Tr.* Translation; Transpose; Treasurer; Trustee.
*Tu.*, or *Tues.* Tuesday.
*Ult.*, or *ult.* (*Ultimo.*) Last month.
*U. S.* United States.
*U. S. A.* United States of America; United States Army.
*U. S. M.* United States Mail; United States Marine.
*U. S. M. A.* United States Military Academy.
*U. S. N.* United States Navy.
*U. S. V.* United States Volunteers.
*U. T.* Utah Territory.
*Va.* Virginia.
*Vice Pres.* Vice President.
*Vid.*, or *vid.* (*Vide.*) See.
*Vis.*, or *Visc.* Viscount.
*Viz.*, or *viz.* (*Videlicet.*) Namely; To wit.
*V. n.*, or *v. n.* Verb neuter.
*Voc.*, or *voc.* Vocative.
*Vol.*, or *vol.* Volume.
*V.P.* Vice President.
*V.R.* (*Victoria Regina.*) Queen Victoria.
*Vs.*, or *vs.* (*Versus.*) Against.
*Vt.* Vermont.
*W.* West.
*W.*, or *w.* Week.
*Wed.* Wednesday.
*W. I.* West India; West Indies.
*W. Lon.* West Longitude.
*Wm.* William.
*W.M.* Worshipful Master.
*W.N.W.* West-North-West.
*Wp.* Worship.
*W.S.W.* West-South-West.
*Wt.*, or *wt.* Weight.
*Xm.*, or *Xmas.* Christmas.
*Y.*, or *Yr.* Year.
*Yd.*, or *yd.* Yard.
*Yr.* Your.
*Zach.* Zachary.
*Zech.* Zechariah.
*Zeph.* Zephaniah.

*Ab ante.* (L.) Before; previously.
*A bas.* (Fr.) Down.
*Ab extra.* (L.) From the outside.
*Ab initio.* (L.) From the beginning.
*Ab origine.* (L.) From the origin.
*Ab ovo usque ad mala.* (L.) From the egg to the apples; from first to last. Roman banquets began with eggs, and ended with apples.
*Ab urbe conditâ.* (L.) From the foundation of the city.
*A compte.* (Fr.) On account.
*Ad infinitum.* (L.) To infinity.
*Ad interim.* (L.) In the meanwhile.
*Ad libitum.* (L.) At one's pleasure.
*Ad nauseam.* (L.) To disgust; till disgust is excited.
*Ad patres.* (L.) To his fathers, *i. e.*, dead.
*Ad referendum.* (L.) Till further consideration.
*Ad valorem.* (L.) According to; upon the value.
*Affaire d'amour.* (Fr.) An intrigue; a love affair.
*Affaire d'honneur.* (Fr.) An affair of honor, *i.e.*, a duel.
*A fortiori.* (L.) With stronger reason.
*A gusto.* (Ital.) To one's heart's content.
*A la bonne heure.* (Fr.) In happy time; at a good hour.
*A la mode.* (Fr.) In fashion; fashionable.
*Al fresco.* (Ital.) In the open air.
*Alias.* (L.) Otherwise, *e.g.*, Jones, *alias* the Count Johannes.
*Alibi.* (L.) Elsewhere. A legal defense by which the defendant attempts to show that he was absent at the time and from the place of the commission of the crime.
*A la Française.* (Fr.) In the French manner.
*A l'Anglaise.* (Fr.) In the English manner.
*Allons.* (Fr.) Come on; let us go.
*Alma mater.* (L.) A nourishing mother. A name frequently applied by students to their college.
*A l'outrance.* (Fr.) To the uttermost; the last extremity.
*Alter ego.* (L.) A second self.
*Alumnus.* (L.) A foster child; a pupil. The graduates of American colleges are often called *alumni.*
*Amende honorable.* (Fr.) To make the *amende honorable* is to make a suitable apology for and confession of one's offense.
*Amor patriæ.* (L.) Love of country; patriotism.
*Amour propre.* (Fr.) Self-esteem.
*Ancien régime.* (Fr.) The old government; the French monarchy before the Revolution.
*Anno Domini.* (L.) In the year of our Lord.
*Anno mundi.* (L.) In the year of the world.
*Annus mirabilis.* (L.) The wonderful year.
*Ante bellum.* (L.) Before the war.
*Ante meridiem.* (L.) Before noon.
*A posteriori.* (L.) From the latter; the cause from the effect.
*A priori.* (L.) From the former; the effect from the cause.
*A propos.* (Fr.) Appositely; seasonably; in regard to.
*Argumentum ad hominem.* (L.) An argument to the man, *i. e.*, personal.
*Audi alteram partem.* (L.) Hear the other part; both sides.
*Au fait.* (Fr.) Skilled; accomplished; competent.
*Au fond.* (Fr.) To the bottom; thoroughly.
*Au revoir.* (Fr.) Good-by, till we meet again.
*Auto da fè.* (Sp.) An act of faith, *i.e.*,burning heretics.
*Aux armes.* (Fr.) To arms.
*A votre santé.* (Fr.) To your health.

*Bas bleu.* (Fr.) A blue stocking; a literary woman.
*Beau ideal.* (Fr.) Ideal beauty. The absolute beauty which exists only in the mind.
*Beau monde.* (Fr.) The gay world; the world of fashion.
*Bel esprit.* (Fr.) A fine mind; wit.
*Ben trovato.* (Ital.) Well found; "a happy thought."
*Bête noir.* (Fr.) A scarecrow; a bugbear.
*Billet doux.* (Fr.) A love letter; a "sweet" note.
*Bizarre.* (Fr.) Strange; eccentric; fanciful.
*Blasé.* (Fr.) One who has seen and enjoyed everything, and upon whom pleasure falls, is called *blasé.*
*Bonâ fide.* (L.) In good faith; genuine; actual.
*Bon gré, mal gré.* (Fr.) With a good or ill grace; willy-nilly.
*Bonhomie.* (Fr.) Simple, unaffected goodnature.
*Bon jour.* (Fr.) Good-day; good-morning.
*Bon mot.* (Fr.) A good word, *i.e.*, a witty saying.

*Cœteris paribus.* (L.) Other things being equal.
*Canaille.* (Fr.) The rabble; the common multitude.
*Carte blanche.* (Fr.) Blank sheet of paper. To give a person *carte blanche* is to give him an unconditional discretion.
*Casus belli.* (L.) A case of war; an act which justifies war.
*Cedant arma togæ.* (L.) Let arms yield to the gown; *i. e.*, military to civil power.
*Cela va sans dire.* (Fr.) That goes without saying; follows as a matter of course and necessarily.
*Chacun à son gout.* (Fr.) Every man to his taste.
*Cha sarà, sarà.* What is to be, will be.
*Châteaux en Espagne.* (Fr.) Castles in Spain; air-castles.
*Chef d'œuvre.* (Fr.) A masterpiece; an unequaled work.
*Chevalier d'industrie.* (Fr.) An adventurer; one who lives by his wits.
*Chronique scandaleuse.* (Fr.) A record of scandals.
*Cicerone.* (Ital.) A person who acts as guide to sight-seers.
*Comme il faut.* (Fr.) Neatly; properly; rightly; in "good form."
*Compagnon de voyage.* (Fr.) Companion of one's travels.
*Compos mentis.* (L.) Sane; of sound mind.
*Con amore.* (It.) Earnestly; zealously.
*Con spirito.* (It.) In a spirited manner.
*Corps diplomatique.* (Fr.) The foreign ambassadors.
*Corpus delicti.* (L.) The body of the offense.
*Coup d'état.* (Fr.) A bold stroke in politics.
*Coup de grâce.* (Fr.) A stroke of mercy; a final blow.
*Coup de main.* (Fr.) A bold, swift undertaking.
*Coup d'œil.* (Fr.) A swift glance of the eye.
*Coute qu'il coute.* (Fr.) Let it cost what it may.
*Cui bono.* (L.) To what (for whose) good.
*Cum grano salis.* (L.) With a grain of salt; not unqualifiedly.
*Currente calamo.* (L.) Rapidly and fluently.

*Da capo.* (It.) From the beginning.
*De bonne grace.* (Fr.) Readily; with good will.
*Début.* (Fr.) One's first appearance in society, on the stage.
*De facto.* (L.) Actual; in fact.
*De jure.* (L.) Rightfully; lawfully; lawful.
*De gustibus non est disputandum.* (L.) There is no disputing about tastes.
*De mortuis nil nisi bonum.* (L.) Say nothing but good of the dead.
*De novo.* (L.) Anew; over again; afresh.
*Denouement.* (Fr.) The catastrophe of a plot.
*Deo volente.* (L.) If it please God.
*Dernier ressort.* (Fr.) The last resource.
*De trop.* (Fr.) In the way; too much.

*Dieu et mon droit.* (Fr.) God and my right.
*Distingué.* (Fr.) Distinguished in manner.
*Distrait.* (Fr.) Preoccupied; absent-minded.
*Divide et impera.* (L.) Divide and govern.
*Dolce far niente.* (It.) Lazy; luxurious idleness.
*Double entente.* (Fr.) Double meaning; obscenity in disguise. (Often erroneously written *double entendre.*)
*Douceur.* (Fr.) Sweetness; compensation; a gratuity.
*Dramatis personæ.* (L.) The characters of a drama.
*Dulce domum.* (L.) Sweet Home.
*Dum vivimus, vivamus.* (L.) While we live, let us live; enjoy life to the full.

*Eclat.* (Fr.) Splendor; distinction; brilliancy.
*Elan.* (Fr.) A spring; fire; dash; impetuosity.
*Embarras de richesses.* (Fr.) Embarrassment of riches; excess of any thing.
*Embonpoint.* (Fr.) Plumpness of figure.
*Empressement.* (Fr.) Enthusiasm; eagerness.
*En famille.* (Fr.) In family; by themselves.
*Enfant gâté.* (Fr.) A spoiled child.
*Enfant terrible.* (Fr.) A terrible child; making ill timed remarks.
*En grande toilette.* (Fr.) In full dress; toilet.
*En masse.* (Fr.) In a body.
*En rapport.* (Fr.) In communication.
*En règle.* (Fr.) As it should be; in rule.
*En revanche.* (Fr.) To make up for it.
*En route.* (Fr.) On one's way.
*En suite.* (Fr.) In company together.
*Entente cordiale.* (Fr.) A cordial understanding.
*Entourage.* (Fr.) Surroundings; adjuncts.
*Entre nous.* (Fr.) Between ourselves.
*E pluribus unum.* (L.) One of many. Motto of the United States.
*Ergo.* (L.) Therefore.
*Esprit de corps.* (Fr.) The spirit of the body; a feeling for the honor and interest of an organization.
*Esprit fort.* (Fr.) A skeptic; a free thinker.
*Et cætera.* (L.). And the rest; etc.
*Ex cathedra.* (L.) From the chair; with authority.
*Excelsior.* (L.) Higher.
*Exeunt omnes.* (L.) They all go out.
*Ex nihilo nihil fit.* (L.) From nothing, nothing comes.
*Ex officio.* (L) By virtue of his office.
*Ex parte.* (L.) From a part; one-sided.
*Ex post facto.* (L.) After the deed is done.
*Ex tempore.* (L.) Off-hand.

*Facile princeps.* (L.) Easily the chief.
*Facilis est descensus Averni.* (L.) The descent into hell is easy.
*Fait accompli.* (Fr.) An accomplished fact.
*Faux pas.* (Fr.) A false step; a mistake.
*Fecit.* (L.) He (or she) made. This word is put after an artist's name on a picture.
*Felo de se.* (L.) A felon of himself; a suicide.
*Femme de chambre.* (Fr.) A chambermaid.
*Femme sole.* (Fr.) An unmarried woman.
*Festina lentè.* (L.) Make haste slowly.
*Fête champêtre.* (Fr.) A rural party; a party in the open air.
*Feuilleton.* (Fr.) The bottoms of the pages in French newspapers are so called, being given up to light literature.

*Fiat justitia, ruat cœlum.* (L.) Let justice be done, though the heavens fall.
*Finis coronat opus.* (L.) The end crowns the work.
*Flagrante delicto.* (L.) "In the act."
*Fugit irreparable tempus.* (L.) Irrevocably time flies.

*Gamin.* (Fr.) A street urchin.
*Garçon.* (Fr.) A waiter.
*Garde du corps.* (Fr.) A body guard.
*Garde mobile.* (Fr.) Troops liable for general service.
*Gasconnade.* (Fr.) Boasting; bragging.
*Gaucherie.* (Fr.) Awkwardness; clumsiness.
*Gendarme.* (Fr.) An armed policeman.
*Genius loci.* (L.) The genius of the place.
*Gentilhomme.* (Fr.) A gentleman; nobleman.
*Genus homo.* (L.) The human race.
*Gloria in excelsis.* (L.) Glory to God in the highest.
*Gloria Patri.* (L.) Glory to the Father.
*Grand Siècle.* (Fr.) A great century.
*Grossièreté.* (Fr.) Grossness; rudeness.

*Habeas corpus.* (L.) You may have the body.
*Hauteur.* (Fr.) Haughtiness; loftiness.
*Hic et ubique.* (L.) Here and everywhere.
*Hic jacet.* (L.) Here lies.
*Homme d'Etat.* (Fr.) A statesman.
*Honi soit qui mal y pense.* (Fr.) Shame to him who evil thinks.
*Horribile dictu.* (L.) Horrible to say.
*Hors de combat.* (Fr.) Out of condition to fight.
*Hotel de ville.* (Fr.) A town hall.

*Ibidem.* (L.) In the same place.
*Ich dien.* (Ger.) I serve. (Motto of the Prince of Wales.)
*Ici on parle Français.* (Fr.) French spoken here.
*Idem sonans.* (L.) Sounding the same.
*Id est.* (L.) That is; i. e.
*Ignis fatuus.* (L.) A foolish fire; a delusion.
*Ignobile vulgus.* (L.) The ignoble crowd.
*Ignotum per ignotius.* (L.) The unknown by something more unknown.
*Imprimis.* (L.) In the first place.
*In articulo mortis.* (L) At the point of death.
*Index expurgatorius.* (L.) A purging index; a list of works prohibited to be read.
*In embryo.* (L.) In the rudiments.
*In esse.* (L.) Actual; in existence.
*In extremis.* (L.) At the point of death.
*In flagrante delicto.* L.) In the very act.
*Infra dignitatem.* (L.) Beneath one's dignity.
*In futuro.* (L.) In the future.
*In hoc signo vinces.* (L.) In this sign thou shalt conquer.
*In loco.* (L.) In place; on the spot.
*In medias res.* (L.) In the middle of a subject.
*In pace.* (L.) In peace.
*In perpetuum.* (L.) Forever.
*In propriâ personâ.* (L.) In one's own person.
*In re.* (L.) In the thing; in the matter of.
*In rem.* (L.) Against the thing.
*In sæcula sæculorum.* (L.) For ages of ages.
*Instanter.* (L.) Instantly.
*In statu quo.* (L.) In the state in which it was.

*Inter alia.* (L.) Among other things.
*Inter nos.* (L.) Between ourselves.
*Inter se.* (L.) Among themselves.
*In toto.* (L.) Entirely; wholly.
*In transitu.* (L.) In the passage; on the way.
*In vino veritas.* (L.) In wine there is truth.
*Ipse dixit.* (L.) He said it himself.
*Ipso facto.* (L.) By the fact itself.

*Je ne sais quoi.* (Fr.) I know not what.
*Jeu de mots.* (Fr.) A play upon words.
*Jour de fête.* (Fr.) A saints' day; a festival.
*Jubilate Deo.* (L.) Be joyful to God.
*Jupiter tonans.* (L.) Jupiter the thunderer.
*Jure divino.* (L.) By divine law.
*Jure humano.* (L.) By human law.
*Jus civile.* (L.) The civil law.
*Jus gentium.* (L.) The law of nations.
*Juste milieu.* (Fr.) The golden mean.

*Labor omnia vincit.* (L.) Labor conquers all things.
*Laissez faire.* (Fr.) Let things alone.
*Lapsus linguæ.* (L.) A slip of the tongue.
*Lares et penates.* (L.) The household gods.
*Laus Deo.* (L.) Praise be to God.
*L'avenir.* (Fr.) The future.
*Le beau monde.* (Fr.) The world of fashion.
*Lèse majesté.* (Fr.) High treason.
*Lex loci.* (L.) The law of the place.
*Lex scripta.* (L.) The written law.
*Lex talionis.* (L.) The law of retaliation.
*Literatim.* (L.) Letter for letter.
*Litterateur.* (Fr.) A literary man.
*Locus Sigilli.* (L.) The place of the seal.

*Ma chère.* (Fr.) My dear.
*Ma foi.* (Fr.) My faith; upon my faith.
*Magnum bonum.* (L.) A great good.
*Maison de ville.* (Fr.) The town-house.
*Maitre d'hôtel.* (Fr.) A house-steward.
*Major domo.* (It.) A chief steward.
*Maladie du pays.* (Fr.) Home sickness.
*Materfamilias.* (L.) The mother of a family.
*Mauvaise honte.* (Fr.) Bashfulness.
*Maximum.* (L.) The greatest possible.
*Me judice.* (L.) In my judgment.
*Memento mori.* (L.) Remember death.
*Memorabilia.* (L.) Things deserving to be remembered.
*Mens sana in corpore sano.* (L.) A sound mind in a sound body.
*Meum et tuum.* (L.) Mine and thine.
*Mirabile dictu.* (L.) Wonderful to tell.
*Mise en scène.* (Fr.) Putting on the stage.
*Modus operandi.* (L.) The method of operating.
*Mon ami.* (Fr.) My friend.
*Mot d'ordre.* (Fr.) The password; countersign.
*Multum in parvo.* (L.) Much in little.

*Nemine contradicente.* (L.) No one contradicting.
*Ne plus ultra.* (L.) Nothing more beyond; the utmost.
*Nil admirari.* (L.) To wonder at nothing.
*Nil desperandum.* (L.) We must not despair.
*Ni l'un ni l'autre.* (Fr.) Neither the one, nor the other.
*N'importe.* (Fr.) It does not matter.
*Nisi prius.* (L.) Unless before.

*Noblesse oblige.* (Fr.) Nobility obliges; noble must act nobly.
*Nolens volens.* (L.) Willy-nilly.
*Noli me tangere.* (L.) Don't touch me; hands off.
*Nolle prosequi.* (L.) To abandon prosecution.
*Nom de guerre.* (Fr.) A war name; an assumed name.
*Nom de plume.* (Fr.) Pen-name; name assumed by an author.
*Non compos mentis.* (L.) Not in one's right mind.
*Non est inventus.* (L.) He has not been found.
*Non multa, sed multum.* (L.) Not many things, but much.
*Nota bene.* (L.) Mark well.
*Nous avons changé tout cela.* (Fr.) We have changed all that.
*Nous verrons.* (Fr.) We shall see.

*Odium theologicum.* (L.) Theological hatred.
*Olla podrida.* (Sp.) A mixture.
*Omnia vincit amor.* (L.) Love conquers all things.
*On dit.* (Fr.) They say; people say.
*Onus probandi.* (L.) The burden of proof.
*Ora pro nobis.* (L.) Pray for us.
*O tempora! O mores!* (L.) Oh, the times! Oh, the manners.
*Otium cum dignitate.* (L.) Ease with dignity.
*Outré.* (Fr.) Extravagant; extreme.

*Par excellence.* (Fr.) By way of eminence; in the highest degree.
*Par hasard.* (Fr.) By chance.
*Pari passu.* (L.) With equal step.
*Parvenu.* (Fr.) An upstart; a rich "snob."
*Pater familias.* (L.) The father of a family.
*Pater patriæ.* (L.) The father of his country.
*Pax vobiscum.* (L.) Peace be with you.
*Peccavi.* (L.) I have sinned.
*Pendente lite.* (L.) While the suit is pending.
*Per annum.* (L.) By the year.
*Per capita.* (L.) By the head; on each person.
*Per contra.* (L.) On the other hand.
*Per diem.* (L.) By the day; every day.
*Per se.* (L.) By itself.
*Personnel.* (Fr.) The staff; persons in any service.
*Petitio principii.* (L.) Begging the question.
*Petite.* (Fr.) Small; little.
*Pièce de resistance.* (Fr.) A joint of meat.
*Pinxit.* (L.) He (or she) painted it.
*Pis aller.* (Fr.) A last expedient.
*Plebs.* (L.) The common people.
*Poeta nascitur, non fit.* (L.) A poet is born, not made.
*Point d'appui.* (Fr.) Point of support.
*Posse comitatus.* (L.) The power of the country; the force that may be summoned by the sheriff.
*Poste restante.* (Fr.) To be left till called for.
*Post meridiem.* (L.) Afternoon.
*Post mortem.* (L.) After death.
*Post obitum.* (L.) After death.
*Pour parler.* (Fr.) A consultation.
*Pour prendre congé.* (Fr.) To take leave.
*Precieuse.* (Fr.) A blue stocking; a conceited woman.
*Preux chevalier.* (Fr.) A gallant gentleman.
*Prima donna.* (It.) The first lady; the principal female singer in Italian opera.
*Primâ facie.* (L.) On the first face; at first sight.
*Primus inter pares.* (L.) First among his peers.
*Pro bono publico.* (L.) For the public good.
*Procès verbal.* (Fr.) Verbal process; the taking of testimony in writing.
*Pro et con.* (L.) For and against.
*Pro formâ.* (L.) For the sake of form.
*Pro patriâ.* (L.) For one's country.
*Pro tempore.* (L.) For the time.
*Punica fides.* (L.) Punic faith, *i. e.*, treachery.

*Quantum sufficit.* (L.) As much as is sufficient.
*Quelque chose.* (Fr.) As if.
*Quid nunc.* (L.) What now; a gossip.
*Quid pro quo.* (L.) An equivalent.
*Qui vive.* (Fr.) Who goes there?
*Quod erat demonstrandum.* (L.) Which was to be demonstrated.
*Quondam.* (L.) At one time; once.

*Rara avis.* (L.) A rare bird.
*Rechauffé.* (Fr.) Warmed over; stale.
*Recherchè.* (Fr.) Choice; elegant.
*Redacteur.* (Fr.) An editor.
*Redivivus.* (L.) Restored to life.
*Reductio ad absurdum.* (L.) Reduction to an absurdity.
*Rentes.* (Fr.) Public funds; national securities.
*Requiescat in pace.* (L.) May he (or she) rest in peace.
*Res gestæ.* (L.) Things done.
*Resurgam.* (L.) I shall rise again.
*Revenons à nos moutons.* (Fr.) Let us return to our sheep; come back to the subject.
*Robe de chambre.* (Fr.) A dressing-gown.
*Roué.* (Fr.) A rake.
*Rouge et noir.* (Fr.) Red and black; a game.

*Sanctum sanctorum.* (L.) The holy of holies.
*Sang froid.* (Fr.) Cold blood; self-possession.
*Sans culottes.* (Fr.) Without breeches; red republicans.
*Sartor resartus.* (L.) The tailor patched.
*Sauve qui peut.* (Fr.) Save himself who can.
*Savoir faire.* (Fr.) Knowing how to do things.
*Savoir vivre.* (Fr.) Knowledge of the world.
*Semper idem.* (L.) Always the same.
*Semper paratus.* (L.) Always prepared.
*Sequitur.* (L.) It follows.
*Seriatim.* (L.) In order.
*Sic itur ad astra.* (L.) Thus men go to the stars.
*Sic semper tyrannis.* (L.) Thus always with tyrants.
*Sic transit gloria mundi.* (L.) So passes the glory of the world.
*Similia similibus curantur.* (L.) Like is cured by like.
*Sine die.* (L.) Without a day.
*Sine qua non.* (L.) Without which, not; an indispensable condition.
*Soi disant.* (Fr.) Self-styled.
*Spirituel.* (Fr.) Witty.
*Status quo.* (L.) The state in which; the former state.
*Stet.* (L.) Let it stand.
*Suaviter in modo, fortiter in re.* (L.) Gently in manner, bravely in action.
*Sub rosâ.* (L.) Under the rose; secretly.
*Sui generis.* L.) Of its own kind.
*Summum bonum.* (L.) The supreme good.

*Tableau vivante.* (Fr.) A living picture.
*Table d'hôte.* (Fr.) A public ordinary; dinner at a fixed price.
*Tabula rasa.* (L.) A smoothed tablet; a blank.
*Tant mieux.* (Fr.) So much the better.
*Tant pis.* (Fr.) So much the worse.
*Te Deum laudamus.* (L.) Thee, God, we praise.
*Tempora mutantur, et nos mutamur in illis.* (L.) Times change and we change with them.
*Tempus fugit.* (L.) Time flies.
*Terra firma.* (L.) Solid earth.
*Terra incognita.* (L.) An unknown country.
*Tête-à-tête.* (Fr.) Head to head; in private conversation.
*Tiers état.* (Fr.) The third estate; *i. e.*, the commons.
*Totidem verbis.* (L.) In just so many words.
*Tour de force.* (Fr.) A turn of strength; a feat of skill.
*Tout ensemble.* (Fr.) The whole taken together.
*Tout le monde.* (Fr.) Everybody.
*Trottoir.* (Fr.) The pavement.
*Tu quoque, Brute.* (L.) Thou, too, Brutus.

*Ubi libertas, ibi patria.* (L.) Where liberty is there is my country.
*Ubi supra.* (L.) As mentioned above.
*Ultima Thule.* (L.) Uttermost Thule; the end of the earth.
*Usque ad nauseam.* (L.) Till it was (or is) absolutely sickening.
*Ut infra.* (L.) As below.
*Ut supra.* (L.) As above.
*Utile dulci.* (L.) The useful with the sweet.

*Vade mecum.* (L.) Go with me; a companion.
*Væ victis.* (L.) Woe to the vanquished.
*Vale.* (L.) Farewell.
*Valet de chambre.* (F.) A servant.
*Veni, vidi, vici.* (L.) I came, I saw, I conquered.
*Verbatim et literatim.* (L.) Word for word; letter for letter.
*Verbum sat sapienti.* (L.) A word to the wise is sufficient.
*Viâ.* (L.) By way of.
*Vide.* (L.) See.
*Videlicet.* (L.) Namely.
*Vinculum matrimonii.* (L.) The bond of matrimony.
*Vis à vis.* (Fr.) Face to face.
*Vis inertiæ.* (L.) The force of inactivity
*Vivâ voce.* (L.) By the living voice.
*Vive la bagatelle.* (Fr.) Success to trifles.
*Vive l'empereur.* (Fr.) Long live the emperor.
*Vive la reine.* (Fr.) Long live the queen.
*Vive le roi.* (Fr.) Long live the king.
*Voilà.* (Fr.) See there: behold.
*Vox et præterea nihil.* (L.) A voice, and nothing more.
*Vox populi, vox Dei.* (L.) The voice of the people is the voice of God.

# English Versification.

ETTERS are the elements of verse; from them are formed syllables, from syllables, feet; and from feet, verses.

QUANTITY is the time necessary to pronounce a syllable. Syllables are long or short, according as the time is greater or less.

## SHORT SYLLABLES.

1. A short vowel, if alone or not followed by a consonant, is a short syllable, as *a, the.*

2. A short vowel, followed by a single consonant, or by the same consonant doubled, is short, as, *man, manner.*

3. In some instances a short vowel before two consonants makes a short syllable, as *reprove.*

## LONG SYLLABLES.

1. A long vowel or diphthong makes its syllable long, as *flee, toy.*

2. A syllable consisting of short vowels before two different consonants (other than a mute and a liquid) is long by position, as *number, into.*

ACCENT is the force of the voice used in uttering a syllable; it may be placed either on long or short syllables. Syllables, accordingly, are long, accented or unaccented, or short, accented or unaccented. To *scan* verse is to divide it metrically.

A certain number of syllables combined make a foot.

### FEET OF TWO SYLLABLES.

These are four in number :—

The *Iambic,* which has one accented syllable, viz., the last as *Be'gin, declare'.*

The *Trochaic,* which has one accented syllable, viz., the first, *pi'ous, lof'ty.*

The *Spondee,* which has two accented syllables, as *hárk, hárk.*

The *Pyrrhic,* which has no accented syllable, as [*va*]*nity.*

### FEET OF THREE SYLLABLES.

There are eight of these, but only three are found in English verse :—

The *Dactyl,* which has an accent on the first syllable only. *Rev'erence.*

The *Anapest,* which has an accent on the last syllable only. *Incomplete'.*

The *Amphibrachys,* which has an accent on the middle syllable only. *Delight'ed.*

English verse is iambic, trochaic, anapestic, or dactylic, according to the feet of which it is composed.

### IAMBIC VERSE.

Iambic verse may consist of one foot only, or of any greater number, up to six or seven.

> Trŭst nót | ĭn wórld | lў̆ prín | cĕs thén,
> Thŏŭgh théy | ăboúnd | ĭn weálth;
> Nŏr ín | thĕ sóns | ŏf mór | tăl mén,
> In whóm | thĕre ís | nŏ heálth.

Iambic lines of two, three, four, and five feet, are the commonest. Iambic verse of one foot only is rare. The following, from Donne, is an example:—

> As mén | dŏ whén | thĕ súm | mĕr sún
> *Grŏws gr'eat.*

Iambic verse of six feet (called the Alexandrine) is not at present in use.

### TROCHAIC VERSE.

Three syllables is the shortest line in the measure; thus in Pope's *Ode on St. Cecilia's Day :—*

> Hóllŏw | gróans,
> Súllĕn | móans.

Trochaic lines of seven or eight syllables are common. The following, from Gray, is an example of the first :—

> | Rúĭn | séize thĕe, | rúthlĕss | ki'ng. |

The following line consists of four complete feet :

> | Héncе, ă | wáy, thŏu | si'rĕn, | leáve mĕ. |

### ANAPESTIC VERSE.

This may be in two feet, as in the following, from Dryden:

> | Sĕe thĕ fú | ríes-ăríse, |

or in three, as in Shenstone's :—

> I hăve nó | thĭng tŏ dó | bŭt tŏ we'ep,

or in four, as in Beattie's :—

> At thĕ clóse | ŏf thĕ dáy, | whĕn thĕ hám | lĕt ĭs stíll.

### DACTYLIC VERSE.

This form of verse is generally used in songs and pieces.

It is of three kinds. Dactylic verse of two feet is the measure of the English national air, *God Save the King.*

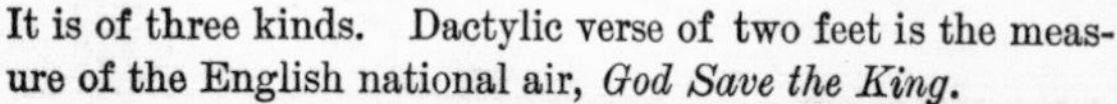

Sénd hĭm vïc | to'rĭoŭs,
Háppy̆ ănd | glo'rĭoŭs,
Lóng tŏ rĕign—o'vĕr ŭs.

## RHYMES.

Rhymes are syllables corresponding in sound, but not identical. They are of one syllable or more. The latter are called double rhymes.

Rhymes are good (1) which have an exact consonance in the vowel and the consonants (if any) which follow it, as:

Dear Harley, generous youth, admit
What friendship dictates more than wit.—SWIFT.

(2) Which have a decided dissimilarity between the consonants before the vowel.

(3) Which are made by long, full sounding syllables.

Terminations in a long vowel, or a liquid consonant preceded by a long vowel, are the most harmonious. Terminations in a liquid consonant, preceded by a short vowel, though inferior to the former, are still euphonious, and so are mutes preceded by a long vowel.

## DIVISIONS OF POETICAL COMPOSITIONS.

A *Verse* is a line in meter, its length and rhyme depending upon certain fixed rules.

A *Hemistich* is a half verse.

A *Couplet*, or Distich, is composed of two rhymed verses, as:

Willing to wound, and yet afraid to strike,
Just hint a fault, and hesitate dislike.—POPE.

A *Triplet* is composed of three rhymed verses, as:—

Be to her faults a little blind,
Be to her virtues not unkind,
And clap the padlock on the mind.—PRIOR.

A *Stanza* is a uniform division of a poetical composition into parts, composed of at least two lines. There is no fixed rule for the nature of a stanza, except that within the same work the stanzas should be alike in structure.

## VARIETIES OF METER.

Meter, or measure, is the plan in accordance with which verses are made, and it varies with the kind and number of feet used. By the nature of the feet of which they are composed, meters are divided intc iambic, dactylic, trochaic, and anapestic.

## BLANK VERSE.

Verse devoid of rhyme is called blank verse. This is of frequent occurrence in tragedy. Milton, in his "Paradise Lost" and "Paradise Regained," has employed blank verse with wonderful success. Excellent specimens of blank verse will also be found in the works of Shakespeare.

## NUMBER OF RHYMES.

There is no arbitrary rule as to how many lines in a stanza may rhyme; but there is a fixed principle that the lines which rhyme should occur at regular intervals. Two rhymes in a stanza constitute the most common rhyme, but three, four, and sometimes five are found; four are always used in the Spenserian stanza and the sonnet. Of course, the more rhymes in a stanza the greater the difficulty in the construction.

## SPECIES OF POETRY.

The chief divisions of poetry are into Epic, Dramatic, Lyric, Didactic, Elegiac, Pastoral, and Satirical poems. Of course several of these species may be found in the same work.

Epic poetry narrates the exploits of heroes. It is chiefly narrative in character. The greatest example of this form of poetry is the "Iliad" of Homer. Other epics are Virgil's "Æneid," Tasso's "Jerusalem Delivered," and Milton's "Paradise Lost." The epic is written in an elevated style.

A Drama is a composition in which the action is not narrated, but represented upon the stage.

## LESSER DIVISIONS OF POETRY.

A Parody is a composition in which an author's words are imitated so as to be made ridiculous or turned to a new purpose.

A Prologue is a piece in verse recited before the representation of a play.

An Epilogue is a piece in verse recited to the spectators at the end of a play.

Lyric poetry was originally poetry sung to the lyre, or composed for musical recitation, but in its broader signification it denotes poetry which depicts only the feelings and thoughts of the author.

Among the chief divisions of lyric poetry is the Ode, which among the ancients was a short lyric composition intended to be sung, but which in its modern sense is a long, various-metered poem of high imagination and sentiment. Among the well-known compositions in this species may be mentioned Gray's "Ode on the Progress of Poesy," Collins' "Odes to the Passions," and Lowell's "Commemoration Ode."

A Ballad is a tale of love or adventure, in iambic hexameter verse.

An Epigram is a pointed stanza or a short poem ending "with some unexpected and some biting thought."

A Madrigal is a short pastoral or love poem containing some ingenious or gallant thought.

A Hymn is a song of praise; in the modern sense, a short poem to be sung in religious services.

A Psalm is a sacred lyric song.

Elegiac poetry is a poetical composition of a mournful character. Gray's "Elegy Written in a Country Churchyard" is the finest English specimen.

An Epitaph is a short composition to be placed on the tomb or monument of a deceased person.

Pastoral poetry describes rural life—the life and pursuits of a shepherd.

An Idyl is a short, highly-wrought poem on pastoral subjects.

An Eclogue, or Bucolic, is a pastoral poem.

Didactic poetry seeks to communicate instruction. Young's "Night Thoughts" is an example.

Satirical poetry holds vice and folly up to contempt. Pope's "Dunciad" is the most famous English satire.

A Lampoon, or Pasquinade, is a personal attack.

# Album Verses.

LBUMS," said Leigh Hunt, "are records kept by gentle dames, to show us that their friends can write their names." In writing for albums, the contributor should be original, if possible; the verses should be short, and the sentiment complimentary, but not extravagant. Acrostics, *i. e.*, verses in which the initial letters of the lines, in their order, form a Christian name, are considered very appropriate. But if one cannot venture upon original composition, an apt quotation from some eminent poet may be fittingly used. We give below a few selections, and many more will be found among "Poetical Quotations" in another part of the book.

My heart is ever at your service.

SHAKESPEARE.

Absence makes the heart grow fonder.

BAYLEY.

Love me little, love me long
Is the burden of my song.

Thou'rt fairer than the poets can express,
Or happy painters fancy when they love.

Otway.

Love reckons hours for months, and days for years;
And every little absence is an age.

DRYDEN.

If grief thy steps attend,
If want, if sickness be thy lot,
And thou require a soothing friend,
Forget me not! forget me not!

OPIE.

Doubt thou the stars are fire;
Doubt thou the sun doth move;
Doubt Truth to be a liar;
But never doubt I love!

SHAKESPEARE.

I hold it true, whate'er befall—
I feel it when I sorrow most—
'Tis better to have loved and lost,
Than never to have loved at all.

TENNYSON.

Forget thee? Bid the forest-birds
Forget their sweetest tune;
Forget thee? Bid the sea forget
To swell beneath the moon.

MOULTRIE.

Albums are, after all, pleasant inventions,
Make friends more friendly, grace one's good intentions,
Brighten dull names, give great ones kinder looks,
Nay, now and then produce right curious books,
And make the scoffer (now the case with me)
Blush to look round on deathless company.

LEIGH HUNT.

As half in shade, and half in sun,
This world along its path advances,
Oh! may that side the sun shines on
Be all that ever meets thy glances;
May Time, who casts his blight on all,
And daily dooms some joy to death,
On thee let years so gently fall
They shall not crush one flower beneath.

MOORE.

I have seen the wild flowers springing,
In wood, and field, and glen,
Where a thousand birds were singing,
And my thoughts were of thee then;
For there's nothing gladsome round me,
Or beautiful to see,
Since thy beauty's spell has bound me,
But is eloquent of thee.

RICHARD HOWITT.

The changeful sand doth only know
The shallow tide and latest;
The rocks have marked its highest flow,
The deepest and the greatest:
And deeper still the flood-marks grow;—
So, since the hour I met thee,
The more the tide of time doth flow,
The less can I forget thee!

SAMUEL LOVER.

As o'er the cold sepulchral stone
Some name arrests the passer-by,
Thus, when thou view'st this page alone,
May mine attract thy pensive eye!

And when by thee that name is read,
Perchance in some succeeding year,
Reflect on me as on the dead,
And think my heart is buried here.

BYRON.

Here is one leaf reserved for me,
From all thy sweet memorials free;
And here my simple song might tell
The feelings thou must guess so well.
But could I thus within thy mind
One little vacant corner find,
Where no impression yet is seen,
Where no memorial yet has been;
Oh, it should be my sweetest care
To write my name forever there!

MOORE.

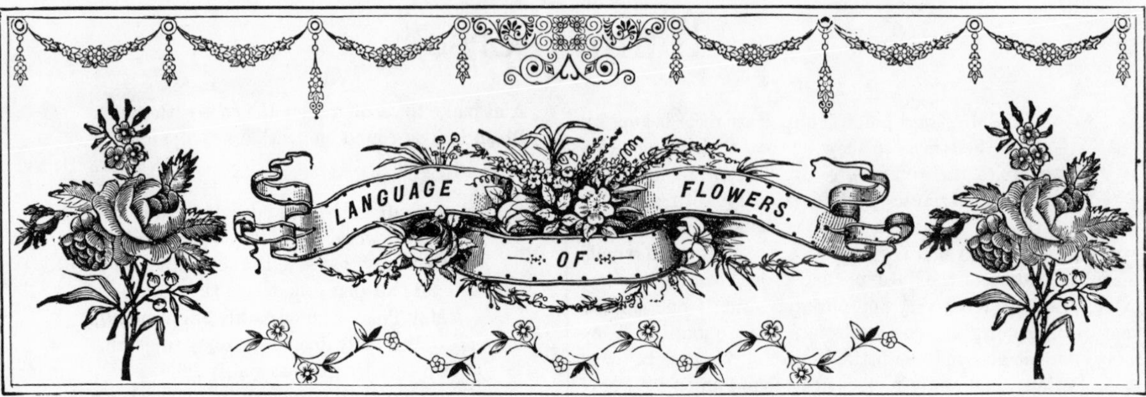


FROM time immemorial sentiments of various kinds have been associated with particular flowers, and flowers have been held to denote certain human attributes, or expressions of feeling.

The first principle to be observed in the construction of the floral love-letter is that the pronoun *I* or *me* is expressed by inclining the flower to the left, and the pronoun *thou* or *thee* by sloping it to the right; but when represented by drawings on paper, those positions should be reversed, as the flower should lean to the heart of the person whom it is to signify. The articles *a*, *an*, and *the* may be expressed by tendrils—the first by a single tendril, the second by a double tendril, and the third by one with three branches.

The second rule is that, if a flower presented upright expresses a particular sentiment, when reversed it has a contrary meaning. Thus, for example, a rose-bud upright, with its thorns and its leaves, means, "I fear, but I hope." If the same bud is returned, held downward, it signifies, "You must neither hope nor fear." But, if the thorns be stripped off, it expresses, "There is everything to hope." Deprived of its leaves it signifies, there is everything to fear." Thus the expression may be varied of almost all the flowers by changing their position. The flower of the marigold, for example, placed on the head, signifies, "Trouble of spirits;" on the heart, "Trouble of love;" on the bosom, "Weariness." The pansy, held upright, denotes "Heart's-ease;" reversed, it speaks the contrary; when presented upright it is understood to say, "Think of me;" but when offered pendant, it means, "Forget me." And thus the amaryllis, which is the emblem of pride, may be made to express, "My pride is humbled," or "Your pride is checked," by holding it downward, either to the left or the right, as the sense requires. In the same manner, the wallflower, which is made the emblem of fidelity in misfortune, if presented with the stalk upward, would insinuate that the person was considered no friend to the unfortunate.

## Vocabulary of Floral Sentiments.

| | |
|---|---|
| Acacia, Rose, | Platonic affection. |
| " White or Pink, | Elegance. |
| " Yellow, | Secret affection. |
| Acanthus, | Artifice. |
| Amaranth, Globe, | Unchangeable. |
| Amaryllis, | Pride. |
| Anemone, Field, | Sickness. |
| Apple Blossom, | Temptation. |
| Arbor Vitæ, | Unchanging friendship |
| Arune (Wake Robin), | Ardor in pursuit. |
| Auricula, | Painting. |
| " Scarlet, | Avarice. |
| Bachelors' Buttons, | Single blessedness. |
| Balm, | Sympathy. |
| Basil, Sweet, | Hatred. |
| Bay Leaf, | I change but in dying. |
| Bay Tree, | Glory. |
| Bay Wreath, | Reward of merit. |
| Bee Orchis, | Industry. |
| Belladonna, | Silence. |
| Betony, | Surprise. |
| Bindweed, | Humility. |
| Birch, | Gracefulness. |
| Birdsfoot, Trefoil, | Revenge. |
| Bitter Sweet, Nightshade, | Truth. |
| Blackthorne, | Difficulty. |
| Blue Bell, | Constancy. |
| Blue Bottle (Centaury), | Delicacy. |
| Box, | Stoicism. |
| Bramble, | Envy, Remorse. |
| Broom, | Neatness. |
| Bryony, | Prosperity. |
| Bulrush, | Docility. |
| Bur, | Importunity. |
| Buttercup, | Childishness, Riches. |
| Butterfly Orchis, | Gayety. |
| Cactus, | Horror. |
| Camelia, | Unpretending excellence. |

| | |
|---|---|
| Candy Tuft, | Indifference. |
| Canterbury Bell, | Acknowledgment. |
| Cardamine, | Paternal error. |
| Carnation, | Woman's love. |
| " Striped, | Refusal. |
| " Yellow, | Disdain. |
| Centaury, | Felicity. |
| Chamomile, | Energy in adversity. |
| Cherry Tree, | Education. |
| Cherry, White, | Deception. |
| Chestnut, | Luxury. |
| Chickweed, | Rendezvous. |
| Chrysanthemum, Red, | I love. |
| " White, | Truth. |
| " Yellow, | Slighted love. |
| Cinquefoil, | Beloved daughter. |
| Cistus, or Red Rose, | Popular favor. |
| Clematis, | Mental beauty. |
| " Evergreen, | Poverty. |
| Clover, Red, | Industry. |
| Cloves, | Dignity. |
| Cockscomb, | Singularity. |
| Columbine, | Folly. |
| " Purple, | Resolute. |
| " Red, | Anxious and trembling |
| Coriander, | Concealed merit. |
| Cowslip, | Pensiveness. |
| Cranberry, | Cure for heart-ache. |
| Cresses, Water, | Stability. |
| Crocus, | Abuse not. |
| Crow Foot, | Ingratitude. |
| Currants, Bunch of, | You please all. |
| Cypress, | Mourning, Despair, Death. |
| Dahlia, | Dignity. |
| Daisy, | Beauty, Innocence. |
| " Double, | Participation. |
| " White, | Innocent. |
| " Red, | Beauty. |
| Dandelion, | Oracle, Coquetry. |
| Dittany, | Birth. |
| Dock, | Patience. |
| Dog's Bane, | Deceit. |
| Dragon Plants, | Snare. |
| Ebony, | Darkness. |
| Eglantine(Sweet Briar), | Poetry. |
| Elder, | Zealousness. |
| Elm, | Dignity. |
| Endive, | Frugality. |
| Everlasting Pea, | Lasting pleasure. |
| Everlasting Thorn, | Solace in adversity. |
| Fennel, | Force. |
| Fern, | Sincerity. |
| " Flowering, | Fascination. |
| Flax, | Domestic Industry. |
| Forget-me-not, | Forget-me-not, True love. |
| Foxglove, | Insincerity, a wish. |
| Gentian, | Virgin pride. |
| Hawkweed, | Quicksightedness. |
| Hawthorn, | Hope. |
| Heart's-ease, Purple, | You occupy my thoughts. |
| " " Wild, | Love in idleness. |
| Heath, | Solitude. |
| Heliotrope, | Devoted to you. |
| Hellebore, | Calumny. |
| Hemlock, | You will cause my death. |
| Hemp, | Fate. |
| Holly, | Foresight. |
| Honeysuckle, | Bond of love. |

| | |
|---|---|
| Hop Blossom, | Injustice. |
| Hyacinth, | Sport, Amusement. |
| Indian Cress, | Resignation. |
| Iris, Yellow, | Passion, Fire. |
| Ivy, | Fidelity. |
| Jasmine, or Jessamine, | Amiability. |
| Jonquil, | Affection, Return. |
| King Cup, | Wish to be rich. |
| Laburnum, | Forsaken. |
| Larch, | Audacity. |
| Larkspur, Double, | Haughtiness. |
| " Pink, | Fickleness. |
| Laurel, Mountain, | Ambition, Glory. |
| Lavender, | Distrust, Assiduity. |
| Lemon Blossom, | Fidelity in love. |
| Lilac, Purple, | First emotions of love. |
| " White, | Modesty. |
| Lily, White, | Purity and sweetness. |
| Lily of the Valley, | Return of happiness. |
| Lime, or Linden Tree, | Conjugal fidelity. |
| Lobelia, | Arrogance. |
| London Pride, | Frivolity. |
| Lotus Flower, | Estranged love, Silence |
| Love in a Mist, | Perplexity. |
| Love Lies Bleeding, | Hopeless,not heartless. |
| Lucerne, | Life. |
| Lupine, | Voraciousness. |
| Madder, | Calumny. |
| Magnolia, | Love of nature. |
| Maiden Hair (Fern), | Discretion. |
| Mallow, | Mild disposition. |
| Mandrake, | Rarity. |
| Maple, | Reserve. |
| Marigold, | Chagrin, Pain. |
| " African, | Vulgar-minded. |
| " Garden, | Jealousy; Uneasiness. |
| Marjoram, | Blushes. |
| Marsh Mallow, | Humanity. |
| Mignonette, | Your qualities surpass your beauty. |
| Mint, | Virtue. |
| Mistletoe, | Obstacles to be overcome. |
| Moss, | Maternal love. |
| Mountain Ash, | Prudence. |
| Myrtle, | Love. |
| Narcissus, | Self-esteem. |
| Nasturtium, | Patriotism. |
| Nettle, | Cruelty, Slander. |
| Nightshade, | Sorcery, Witchcraft. |
| Oak Leaf, | Bravery. |
| Oats, | Music. |
| Olive, | Peace. |
| Orange Tree, | Generosity. |
| Orange Blossom, | Your purity equals your loveliness. |
| Osier, | Frankness. |
| Ox Eye, | Patience. |
| Pansy (Heart's Ease), | Thoughts. |
| Parsley, | Feasting. |
| Passion Flower, | Belief. |
| Pea, Sweet, | Respect. |
| Peach Blossom, | I am your captive. |
| Peony, | Bashfulness. |
| Periwinkle, Blue, | Pleasure of memory. |
| Pimpernel, | Change. |
| Pink, | Boldness. |
| " Carnation, | Woman's love. |
| " Indian Double, | Always lovely. |
| " Variegated, | Refusal. |
| Plane Tree, | Serious. |
| Plum Tree, | Perform your promises |
| Polyanthus, | Pride of riches. |

| | |
|---|---|
| Polyanthus, Lilac, | Confidence. |
| Pomegranate, Flower, | Mature elegance. |
| Poppy, Red, | Consolation. |
| " Scarlet, | Fantastic extravagance |
| " White, | Sleep. |
| Primrose, | Early youth. |
| " Evening, | Inconstancy. |
| " Red, | Unpatronized merit. |
| Queen's Rocket, | Fashionable. |
| Ragged Robin, | Wit. |
| Ranunculus, Garden, | Rich in attraction. |
| Rhododendron, | Danger. |
| Rocket, | Rivalry. |
| Rose, Cabbage, | Love's ambassador. |
| " Champion, | Deserve my love. |
| " Christmas, | Relieve my anxiety. |
| " Damask, | Youthful love. |
| " Deep Red, | Bashful, Love. |
| " Guelder, | Touch of life. |
| " Moss, | Confession of love. |
| " Musk, | Capricious beauty. |
| " Cluster of, | You charm me. |
| " Red (bud), | Youth and beauty. |
| " Red (full), | Beauty. |
| " Thornless, | Ingratitude. |
| " Wild, | Romance. |
| " White, | Heedless of love. |
| " " withered, | Forgetfulness. |
| " York, | War. |
| " Lancaster, | Union of sentiment. |
| Rue, | Disdain. |
| Saffron, | Marriage. |
| Sage, | Esteem. |
| Scabious, Sweet, | Widowhood. |
| Shamrock, | Light-heartedness. |
| Snap Dragon, | Presumption. |
| Snowdrop, | Hope. |
| Sorrel, Wild, | Wit ill-timed. |
| Spearmint, | Warmth of sentiment. |
| Speedwell, | Fidelity. |
| Star of Bethlehem, | Guidance. |
| Starwort, | Welcome. |
| Stock (Gilly Flower), | Lasting beauty. |
| Straw (Broken), | Rupture. |
| " (Whole), | Union. |
| Sunflower, | Haughtiness. |
| Sweet Basil, | Good wishes. |
| Sweet Sultan(Centaury) | Felicity. |
| Sweet William, | Gallantry. |
| Sycamore, | Curiosity. |
| Tansy, | Resistance. |
| Thistle, Common, | Austerity. |
| " Scotch, | Retaliation. |
| Thorn, Branch of, | Severity. |
| Thyme, | Activity. |
| Traveler's Joy, | Safety. |
| Tulip, Red, | Declaration of love. |
| " Variegated, | Beautiful eyes. |
| " Yellow, | Hopeless love. |
| Venus's Looking-glass, | Flattery. |
| Vine Leaf, | Intoxication. |
| Violet, Blue, | Faithfulness. |
| " Sweet, | Modesty. |
| Wallflower, | Fidelity in misfortune. |
| Wheat, | Prosperity. |
| Willow, Weeping, | Forsaken. |
| Woodbine, | Fraternal affection. |
| Woodsorrel, | Joy in absence. |
| Wormwood, | Sorrow in absence. |
| Xanthium, | Rudeness. |
| Yew, | Sadness. |
| Zinnia, | Absence. |

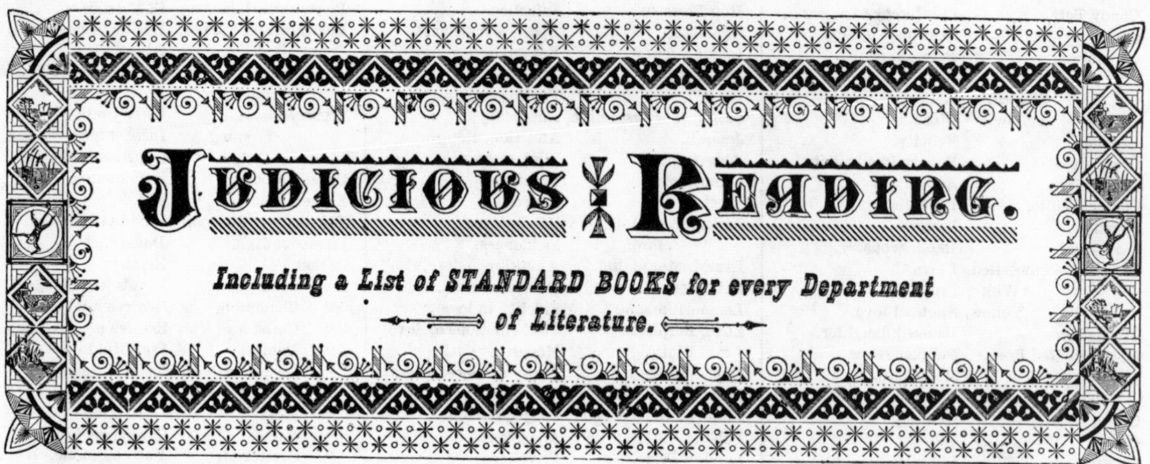


THE number of books worth reading is so great that no person, however great his leisure and his industry, can hope to read more than a small part of them. If all the printing presses in the world were stopped today, it would still be impossible for any man in one lifetime to read all the noteworthy books in literature, or indeed to exhaust the literature of many subjects. But new books of great interest and value are constantly appearing, and between the old and indispensable works, and the newer works about which everybody is talking, even the most universal reader must feel the necessity of exercising some principle of choice. Besides, there are so many good books that it is foolish to waste one's time in reading bad ones. We, therefore, append a list of standard works for the various departments of literature, which will enable readers to make a judicious selection of books on subjects in which they take an interest :—

**Architecture.**—FERGUSSON'S *History of Architecture* is expensive, but invaluable. RUSKIN'S *Stones of Venice*, and *Lectures on Architecture* are, perhaps, more distinguished for style than for judgment. MIRSAY'S *Cathedral Hand Books* are useful for gothic. EASTLAKE'S *History of the Gothic Revival* is good authority. C. J. RICHARDSON'S *Housebuilding*, and CALVER and VAUX'S *Villas and Cottages* are practical works. So is HATFIELD'S *American House Carpenter*.

**Astronomy.**—LOCKE'S *Astronomy*, MITCHELL'S *Popular Astronomy*, and *Planetary and Stellar Worlds*, are good general works. SIMON NEWCOMB'S *Astronomy*, is the most scientific popular treatise. J. F. CLARKE'S *How to find the Stars*, is useful in connection with an orrery. R. A. PROCTOR'S works are interesting, but to be followed with great caution. DENISON'S *Astronomy Without Mathematics* is clear and simple.

**Atlases.**—BLACK'S *Atlas of the World*, COLTON'S *General Atlas*, and JOHNSON'S *Atlas of the World* are quite expensive, but full. JOHNSON'S *Royal Atlas of Modern Geography* is still more expensive, but nobody will regret money spent in buying a good atlas. Among the smaller works, MACMILLAN'S *Globe Atlas of the World* is the best. Of the numerous school geographies, CORNELL'S are as good as any. Of the historical atlases, FREEMAN'S is the best; then SPRUNER BRYCE'S *Student's Atlas* is good for physical geography.

**Bible.**—GLEIG'S *History of the Bible* is well written, and trustworthy. WILLIAM SMITH'S *History of the Old Testament* and *History of the New Testament* are more elaborate. BROWN'S *Self-interpreting Bible* (Protestant) and HAYDOCK'S *Catholic Family Bible* are among the best editions.

**Biography.**—THOMAS'S *Cyclopædia of Biography* is the standard. BEETON'S *Dictionary of Universal Biography*, and GODWIN'S *Cyclopædia of Biography* are cheap, and contain a great deal of condensed information. *Men of the Time* has a full list of English and Continental celebrities; on Americans, it is of small value. To choose among the countless separate biographies a short satisfactory list, is a matter of no small difficulty. Read all the biography you can get. The following list may be useful :—**American Biography.**—WELLS'S *Life of Samuel Adams* gives a circumstantial account of the life and times of one of the fathers of the American Revolution. J. T. MORSE'S *Life of John Quincy Adams* is the best, and latest. CHAS. BEECHER'S *Autobiography of Lyman Beecher*, WEISS'S *Life of Theodore Parker*, and SPRAGUE'S *Annals of the American Pulpit* represent a good deal of American (Protestant) ecclesiastical history. SPARK'S *American Biography* is invaluable for the early history. SHEA'S *Life and Epoch of Alexander Hamilton*, RANDALL'S *Life of Jefferson*, J. Q. and C. F. ADAMS'S *Life of John Adams*, BIGELOW'S and PARTON'S *Lives of Franklin*, G. W. GREENE'S *Nathaniel Greene*, PARTON'S *Life of Aaron Burr*, PARTON'S *Life of Andrew Jackson*, H. C. LODGE'S *Life of George Cabot*, H. ADAMS'S *Life of Albert Gallatin*, ARNOLD'S *Life of Abraham Lincoln*, RIVES'S *Life of Madison*, J. E. COOKE'S *Life of General Lee*, *The Memoirs of W. H. Seward*, G. T. CURTIS'S *Life of D. Webster*, BROWN'S *Life of Rufus Choate*, COLTON'S *Henry Clay*, *The Life and Writings of J. C. Calhoun*, include what is most essential for American political biography. The *Journals and Letters of George Ticknor* is the most interesting literary biography ever written by an American.—**General Biography.**—BOSWELL'S *Johnson* is the best biography ever written. The *English Men of Letters* series, now in course of publication, is useful, especially for biographies of the English poets. TREVELYAN'S *Macaulay* is interesting. CARLYLE'S *Reminiscences*, *The Life of Benvenuto Cellini*, GIBBON'S *Autobiography*, and GREELEY'S *Recollections of a Busy Life* are autobiographies of value in widely differing lines. The *Greville Memoirs* are highly seasoned. CARLYLE'S *Cromwell*, and *Frederick the Great*, are famous. PARTON'S *Voltaire* is good. MASSON'S *Milton* is full, but tedious. SPEDDING'S *Life and Letters of Lord Bacon* is the definite work on that important subject. LOCKHART'S *Life of Scott* is one of the best biographies in the language. MOORE'S *Byron*, SWINBURNE'S *Critical Memoir of W. Blake*, FOSTER'S *Life of Swift*, and *Life of Dickens*, IRVING'S *Michael Angelo*, and PROCTOR'S *Edmund Kean*, are good specimens of artistic and literary biography. THACKERAY'S *Four Georges*, and BROUGHAM'S *Statesmen of the Time of George III.*, are valuable. MRS. OLIPHANT'S *Frances of Assissi*, VENN'S *S. Francis Xavier*, and SOUTHEY'S *Wesley*, are good ecclesiastical biographies. DE QUINCEY'S *Autobiographical Sketches*, and COLERIDGE'S *Biographia Literaria* are valuable, especially the latter. LUBY'S *Lives of Illustrious Irishmen* is very complete.

**Botany.**—Prof. ASA GRAY'S text books are the best for this subject.

**Chemistry.**—COOKE'S *First Principles of Chemical Philosophy*, Ros-

COE'S *Elementary Chemistry*, and YOUMAN'S *Class Book of Chemistry*, are the best elementary works.

**Constitution of the United States.**—CURTIS'S *History of the Constitution*, ELLIOT'S *Debates*, and the *Federalist*, are best authorities on its history. VAN HOLZ, in his *Constitutional History*, comes down to Polk's administration. STORY'S *Commentaries on the Constitution* is a standard. ALDEN'S *Science of Government* is a useful little work.

**English Constitution.**—STUBBS'S *Constitutional History* is the standard. Next in value, though better known, is HALLAM'S. MAY'S *Constitutional History of England* begins at 1760.

**Correspondence.**—HORACE WALPOLE'S *Letters* are full of gossip. GRAY'S *Letters* are perhaps the best in the language. MME. DE SEVIGNE'S *Letters*, and LADY MARY WORTLEY MONTAGUE'S *Letters* are classics.

**Criticism, Art.**—HAMERTON'S *Thoughts About Art*, and *Contemporary French Painters*. ROSETTI'S *Fine Art*, and RUSKIN'S works in general.

**Criticism, Literary.**—MATTHEW ARNOLD'S *Essays in Criticism*. LOWELL'S *Among My Books*, and *My Study Windows* (2 series). Arnold is easily the first of living critics.

**Decorative Art.**—EASTLAKE'S *Hint on Household Taste* is the standard work.

**Demonology.**—CONWAY'S *Demonology* is the latest. UPHAM'S *History of the Salem Witchcraft* is a well-written account of a famous delusion.

**Devotion.**—BUNYAN'S *Pilgrim's Progress* is an English classic. THOMAS A KEMPIS'S *Imitation of Christ* is a world classic. KEBLE'S *Christian Year* is likely to become a classic.

**Dictionaries—English.**—WEBSTER'S *Unabridged Dictionary*, and WORCESTER'S *Dictionary* (new edition) are the standards. **French**—SPIER and SURENNE'S dictionary is full. The best, so far as it goes, is MASSON'S little *French-English Dictionary*. **German**—ADLER'S. **Greek**—LIDDELL and SCOTT'S (latest edition, revised). **Italian**—MILLHOUSE. GRAGLIA'S small work is useful. **Latin**—ANDREWS'S, revised by DRISLER and SHORT.

**Drama.**—COLLIER'S *History of the English Drama* gives a good account of the beginning of the drama in England. DORAN'S *Annals of the English Stage*, and *His Majesty's Servants*, are learned and entertaining in regard to the dramatic profession. ABBOTT'S *Shakespearean Grammar* is useful not only for Shakespeare but for all the Elizabethan dramatists. CLARKE'S *Concordance to Shakespeare* is handy. The so-called *Leopold Shakespeare* is as convenient an edition as any. Of the larger editions, DYCE'S is as good as any. FUNESS'S *Variorum* edition is the richest in notes. The following dramatists are too well known to be more than mentioned. The works of most of them can generally be picked up at second-hand book-stores, at low prices. BEAUMONT and FLETCHER, MRS. CENTLIVRE, CONGREVE, DEKKER, DRYDEN, FARQUHAR, FIELDING, FORD, GOLDSMITH, BEN JONSON, SHERIDAN KNOWLES, C. MARLOW, MARSTON, MASSINGER, OTWAY, PEELE, ROWE, SHERIDAN, TALFOURD, HENRY TAYLOR, VANBURGH, VILLIERS, WEBSTER, and WYCHERLY. LAMB'S *Specimens of the Dramatic Poets* is valuable, and easily to be found.

**Education.**—LOCKE, *On Study and Reading*; MILTON, *On Education*; SPENCER, *On Education*; HART'S *German Universities*; JEX-BLAKE'S *American Schools and Colleges*; STAUNTON'S, *The Great Schools of England*; BRISTED'S *Five Years in an English University*, *Four Years at Yale*: PORTER'S *American Colleges*. The last six books will give a practical idea of the systems of education prevalent in England, Germany, and America. They may be agreeably supplemented by SEVERANCE'S *Hammersmith*, and WASHBURNE'S *Fair Harvard*.

**Elocution.**—DAY'S book is useful. BACON'S *Manual of Gesture* is good for action. MONROE'S *Physical and Vocal Training* is full of practical exercises.

**Encyclopædias.**—The *Britannica* has the best scientific and literary articles. ZELL'S is short, and cheap. CHAMBERS'S *Encyclopedia* with American Additions is the most complete edition of that work. APPLETON'S and JOHNSON'S are good. The latter is very full on American subjects.

**English Language.**—MARSH'S *Lectures on the English Language*, and *Origin and History of the English Language* are standard works. MORRISS'S *Historical Outlines of English Accidence* is a useful text book.

**Fiction.**—Among the standard works are the novels of FIELDING, SMOLLETT, SCOTT, COOPER, HAWTHORNE, THACKERAY, DICKENS, and GEORGE ELIOT. After these authors, read at least one of the works of the novelists mentioned below. We have indicated the book which seems to us best. This is, of course, a matter of personal taste, and many of our readers may prefer some other work of the same author. But any work by the authors we mention is worth reading. We have not space to indicate the characteristics of the different authors:—LOUISA M. ALCOTT, *Little Women*; MRS. ALEXANDER, *Her Dearest Foe*; H. C. ANDERSEN, *The Improvisatore*; *The Arabian Night's Entertainments*; B. AURRBACH, *On the Heights*; JANE AUSTIN, *Sense and Sensibility*; BALZAC, *Father Goriot*; W. BECKFORD, *Vathek*; W. BLACK, *A Princess of Thule*; W. BLACKMORE, *Lorna Doone*; CHARLOTTE BRONTE, *Jane Eyre*; MRS. BURNETT, *Lass o' Lowrie*; MISS BURNEY, *Evelina*; G. W. CABLE, *The Grandissimes*; CERVANTES, *Don Quixote*; A. VON CHAMISSO, *Peter Schlemihl*; WILKIE COLLINS, *The Woman in White*; MRS. CRAIK (Miss Mulock), *John Halifax, Gentleman*; DANIEL DE FOE, *Robinson Crusoe*: JAS. DE MILLE, *The Dodge Club*; Mme. DE STAEL, *Corinne*; B. DISRAELI, *Vivian Grey*; G. EBERS, *Uarda*; MRS. EDWARDS, *Archie Lovell*; G. FREYTAG, *Debt and Credit*; J. W. VON GOETHE, *Wilhelm Meister*; O. GOLDSMITH, *The Vicar of Wakefield*; THOMAS HARDY, *Far from the Madding Crowd*; BRET HARTE, *Gabriel Conroy*; O. W. HOLMES, *Elsie Venner*; W. D. HOWELLS, *A Foregone Conclusion*; T. HUGHES, *Tom Brown at Oxford*; VICTOR HUGO, *Les Miserables*; W. IRVING, *Bracebridge Hall*; H. JAMES, JUN., *The Portrait of a Lady*; J. P. KENNEDY, *Horse-Shoe Robinson*; CHARLES KINGSLEY, *Hypatia*; HENRY KINGSLEY, *The Hillyars and the Burtons*; LE SAGE, *Gil Blas*; C. LEVER, *Harry Lorrequer*; H. W. LONGFELLOW, *Hyperion*; Lord LYTTON (E. BULWER), *The Caxtons*; GEORGE MACDONALD, *David Elginbrood*; "E. MARLITT," *Gold Elsie*; Captain MARRYATT, *Midshipman Easy*; G. MEREDITH, *The Tragic Comedians*; MRS. OLIPHANT, *Carlingford*; E. A. POE, *Tales*; JANE PORTER, *The Scottish Chiefs*; MRS. RADCLIFFE, *The Mysteries of Udalpho*; C. READE, *Cloister and Hearth*; S. RICHARDSON, *Clarissa Harlowe*; G. SAND, *Consuelo*; F. SPIELHAGEN, *Problematical Characters*; L. STERNE, *Tristram Shandy*; MRS. STOWE, *Uncle Tom's Cabin*; J. SWIFT, *Gulliver's Travels*; A. TROLLOPE, *Barchester Towers*; TURGENEFF, *Virgin Soil*; S. WARREN, *Ten Thousand a Year*; MISS YONGE, *The Heir of Redcliffe*.

**Fine Arts.**—CLEMENT'S *Legendary Art*, and MRS. JAMIESON'S books are useful for the legends so much used by painters and sculptors. LUBKE'S *History of Art* and *History of Sculpture*. KUGLER'S *Handbooks* give a general idea of the subject. WINCKELMANN'S *History of Ancient Art*, exhausts that part of art. CLEMENT'S *Handbook of Painters and Sculptors* contains much information.

**Gazeteers.**—LIPPINCOTT'S *Pronouncing Gazeteer* is the best.

**Geography.**—RITTER'S *Comparative Geography* is the standard.

**Geology.**—DANA'S *Manual of Geology* and *Text Book of Geology*. LYELL'S *Elements of Geology*, and HITCHCOCK'S *Elementary Geology* give a fair knowledge of this subject.

**Government.**—DE TOCQUEVILLE'S *Democracy in America* is indispensable to the student of American institutions. MULFORD'S *The Nation* is a thoughtful study of the same subject. Other good books are LAMPHERE'S *U. S. Government*, NORDHOFF'S *Politics for Young Americans*, and YOUNG'S *Government Class-book*. Among recent books on the English Government are GLADSTONE'S *The Country and the Government*, PALGRAVE'S *House of Commons*, and SYME'S *Representative Government in England*.

**Gymnastics.**—BLAIKIE'S *How to Get Strong* is concise, clear, and practical.

**History—Ancient.**—RAWLINSON'S *Manual of Ancient History* and *Five Great Monarchies*, give a good idea of ancient history. SMITH'S *Ancient History of the World* may be read in connection with them.

**History—American.**—HILDRETH'S *History of the United States* is the best. BRYANT'S (really GAY'S) comes down to the present time. LOSSING'S *Pictorial History*, is a useful, popular work. LODGE'S *Short History of the English Colonies in America* gives a graphic account of society, manners, etc., in the colonies. SCHOULER'S *History of the United States*, etc., is the newest work on the subject. BANCROFT'S *History* goes into full detail. There are good small histories by HIGGINSON and SWINTON. SPARK'S *Life and Times of Washington* is a valuable work. A good history of the civil war remains to be written. DRAPER'S *History of the American Civil War* aims at a scientific treatment. POLLARD'S *Southern History of the War* considers the subject from a Southern standpoint; so does JEFFERSON DAVIS's recent *Memoirs*. HEADLEY'S and ABBOTT'S books are interesting rather than trustworthy. WATSON and PATTON'S *History of the United States* is a popular illustrated work. PARKMAN'S different histories, such as *The Conspiracy of Pontiac* are models of style, and to be depended upon.

**History—English.**—LINGARD'S *History of England* is the most impartial general history. GREEN'S *Short History of the English People* gives the most graphic account of English history every written, in a popular form and in a small compass. FREEMAN'S *Old English History for Children* is indispensable for the time preceding the conquest. His *History of the Norman Conquest* has superseded all other works upon the subject. MACAULAY and FROUDE have treated brief periods brilliantly, but their works are full of prejudice and misstatement. Lord MAHON'S *England under Anne* is trustworthy. MCCARTHY S *History of Our Own Times* is a useful work. The diaries of EVELYN and of PEPYS throw much light upon the reigns of Charles II., and James II., and are full of entertaining gossip.

**History—German.**—MENZEL'S *History of Germany*. KOLRANCH'S *History of Germany*; BRYCE'S *Holy Roman Empire*, and COXE'S *History of the House of Austria* will give a good idea of German history.

**History—Grecian.**—Whoever is unable to find time to read the great histories by GROTE, THIRLWALL, and CURTIUS will find much condensed information in SMITH'S *Student's History of Greece*. FINLAY'S *History of Greece* has the later history. MAHAFFY'S *Social Life in Greece* is useful in connection with the political histories.

**History—French.**—KITCHIN'S *History of France* is the best account in a small compass. *The Student's History of France* is condensed and fair. MICHELET'S is brilliant, but often misleading.

**History—Roman.**—MOMMIER'S is the standard for the earlier history; GIBBON'S for the last days of the empire. LIDDELL'S *Student's History of Rome* and SMITH'S *Smaller History of Rome* are useful, short histories.

**History—Irish.**—MCGEE'S *History of Ireland*, and MOORE'S *History of Ireland* are useful. HAVERTY'S *National History of Ireland* is considered impartial and reliable.

**History—Italian.**—MACHIAVELLI'S *History of Florence*; RANKE'S *History of the Popes*, and SISMONDI'S *Italian Republics* will give a general idea of Italian history.

**History—Spanish.**—MRS. CALCOTT'S *History of Spain and Portugal*, and DUNHAM'S *History of Spain and Portugal* are the best general works in English on Peninsular history. They are not especially good, however. PRESCOTT'S histories should of course, be read, for the special periods which they cover.

**Literature—American.**—TYLER'S *History of American Literature* has superseded all other works upon that subject. RICHARDSON'S *Primer of American Literature* gives a good deal of information in a very condensed form.

**Literature—English.**—TAINE'S *History of English Literature* gives a brilliant sketch. CRAIK'S *History of English Literature and Language* is a standard work. CHAMBERS'S *Cyclopædia of English Literature* is excellent for reference.

**Logic.**—JEVON'S *Logic*, and BAIN'S *System of Logic* are enough for the general reader. Sir W. HAMILTON and MILL may be read by those who wish to go deeper into the subject.

**Metaphysics.**—LEWES'S *History of Philosophy* and RITTER'S *History of Philosophy* give a general view of the subject. BAIN'S *Mental Science*, HAVEN'S *Mental Philosophy* and *Moral Philosophy*, and BOWEN'S edition of Sir W. HAMILTON'S *Metaphysics* are useful, especially the last. SPENCER'S *Psychology* is rather difficult. BACON, LOCKE, FICHTE, KANT, and COMTE require more study than most persons have time for.

**Moral Science.**—HOPKINS'S *Moral Science* and WAYLAND'S *Moral Science* are sufficient.

**Physiology.**—HUXLEY'S *Physiology* is the best elementary work upon the subject ever written.

**Poetry.**—WARD'S *English Poets* is the best work for persons of moderate means. It does not contain every-thing, to be sure; but it contains the best. The biographical and critical sketches in it, too, are of high value. BRYANT'S *Library of Poetry and Song*, and LONGFELLOW'S *Poems of Places*, and *Poets and Poetry of Europe* are useful collections. PERCY'S *Reliques*, containing the old ballads, can be picked up cheaply. CHILD'S *English Ballads* is a much better work than PERCY'S, but expensive. As it is useless to read any other than good poetry, only poets of universally acknowledged merit are included in our list. Read (and own if you can afford it) the whole or greater part of the works of MATTHEW ARNOLD, EDWIN ARNOLD, ROBERT BROWNING, MRS. BROWNING, BRYANT, BURNS, SAMUEL BUTLER, BYRON, CAMPBELL, CHAUCER (GILMAN'S edition), CLOUGH, COLERIDGE, COLLINS, COWLEY, COWPER, CRABBE, DONNE, DRYDEN, EMERSON, GOLDSMITH, GRAY, GEORGE HERBERT, HERRICK, HOLMES, HOMER (CHAPMAN'S translation), HOOD, KEATS, LONGFELLOW, LOWELL, MARVELL, MILTON, MOORE, MORRIS, POE, POPE, PRIOR, ROGERS, ROSETTI, SCOTT, SHAKESPEARE, SHELLEY, SPENSER, SWINBURNE, BAYARD TAYLOR, TENNYSON, THOMPSON, VIRGIL (DRYDEN'S translation), WALLER, WHITMAN, WHITTIER, and WORDSWORTH.

**Political Economy.**—BOWEN'S *Political Economy*, PERRY'S *Elements of Political Economy*, MRS. FAWCETT'S *Political Economy for Beginners*, and FAWCETT'S *Manual of Political Economy* are useful to the beginner. ADAM SMITH'S *Wealth of Nations* is a standard authority. MILL'S *Principles of Political Economy*, and *System of Political Economy* are clearly and cogently written, and may be read after the above.

**Science, Natural.**—The *International Scientific Series*, containing books by such men as HUXLEY and TYNDALL, is a good and cheap scientific library in itself. WELLS'S *Science of Common Things* is packed with useful information. GANOT'S *Physics*, and BALFOUR STEWART'S *Physics* are valuable elementary works. (The first requires considerable study.) TYNDALL'S, *On Sound* is all the ordinary reader will want on the subject of acoustics. TYNDALL *On Radiation*, and AIRY'S *Undulation Theory of Optics* are enough on optics. HUXLEY'S *Lay Sermons and Addresses*, SPENCER'S *Principles of Biology*, TYNDALL'S *Fragments of Science*, and YOUMAN'S *Correlation and Conservation of Forces* are more generally interesting.

**Science, Social.**—SPENCER'S *Social Statics* is thoughtful, however much we may dissent from his conclusions. The same may be said of H. C. CAREY'S *Principles of Social Science*, and FAWCETT'S *Essays on Political and Social Subjects*.

**Travels and Voyages.**—The number of these is so vast that it is impossible to mention many discriminatingly. Besides, hardly any traveler is so stupid as not to be able to give some information about the country which he visits. BAYARD TAYLOR'S works of travel are entertaining; so are C. D. WARNER'S. S. L. CLEMENS'S (MARK TWAIN) *Innocents Abroad* is vastly amusing. KINGLAKE'S *Eothen* is perhaps the best book of Eastern travels ever written. The works of the early travelers, MAUNDEVILLE and MARCO POLO deserve especial mention. EMERSON'S *English Traits*, and HAWTHORNE'S *Our Old Home* and *English Note-Books* are the most valuable American accounts of English society. MACKENZIE'S *Russia* is a standard work. SIR FRANCIS HEAD'S *Faggot of French Sticks* is very entertaining. HILLARD'S *Six Months in Italy*, and HOWELL'S *Italian Journeys*, and *Venetian Life* are of the best works of Italian travel. Sir F. HEAD'S *Bubbles from the Brunnen* is a vivacious bit of German travel. SAVAGE'S *Picturesque Ireland* is an attractive work, and contains much valuable information. MACKENZIE'S *A Year in Spain*, HAYS'S *Castilian Days*, and HARE'S *Wanderings in Spain* are to be commended. G. W. CURTIS'S *Nile Notes*, and *The Howadji in Syria* are delightful reading.

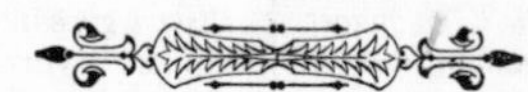

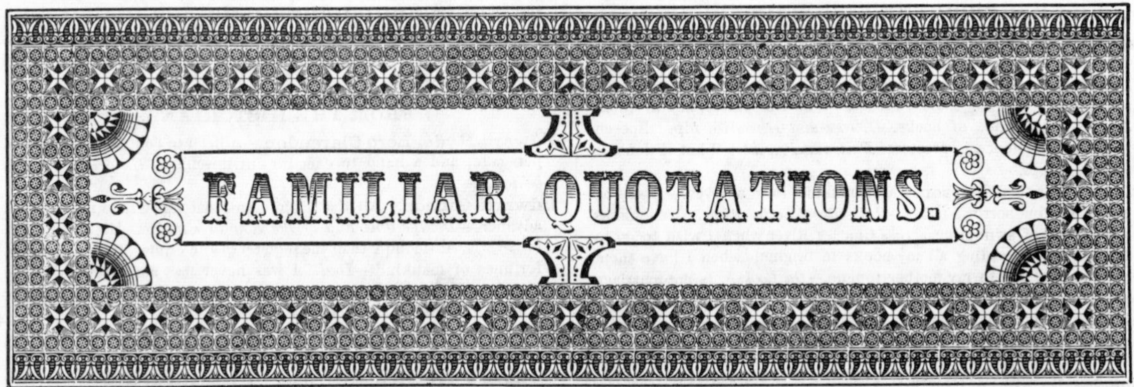


## FROM AMERICAN STATESMEN.

**John Adams.**—It [The 2nd day of July, 1776, when the Declaration of Independence was reported] ought to be commemorated as the day of deliverance, by solemn acts of devotion to God Almighty. It ought to be solemnized with pomp and parade, with shows, games, sports, guns, bells, bonfires, and illuminations, from one end of this continent to the other, from this time forward forevermore.—*Letter to Mrs. Adams.*

**John Quincy Adams.**—This is the last of earth. I am content. [Said when stricken with paralysis in the Capitol, 1848.]

**John A. Dix.**—If any man attempts to haul down the American flag, shoot him down. [1861.]

**Rufus Choate.**—Glittering generalities.—*Letter to Maine Whig Committee.* We join ourselves to no party that does not carry the flag, and keep step to the music of the Union.—*Letter to the Whig Convention.*

**Benjamin Franklin.**—There never was a good war or a bad peace.—*Letter to J. Quincy*, 1773. They that can give up essential liberty to obtain a little temporary safety deserve neither liberty nor safety.—*Historical Review of Pennsylvania.*

**Ulysses S. Grant.**—I propose to fight it out on this line if it takes all summer.—*Dispatch.* Let us have peace.—*Inaugural Address.*

**Horace Greeley.**—The way to resume [specie payments] is to resume. —Young man, go West'!

**Patrick Henry.**—I know not what course others may take, but, as for me, give me liberty or give me death !—*Speech in the Virginia House of Burgesses*, 1775.

**Andrew Jackson.**—Our Federal Union; it must be preserved.—*Speech*, 1830.

**Thomas Jefferson.**—Error of opinion may be tolerated where reason is left free to combat it.—*Inaugural Address.* If a due participtation of office is a matter of right, how are vacancies to be obtained ? Those by death are few ; those by resignation none.—*Letter to a Committee of the Merchants of New Haven*, 1801. We hold these truths to be self-evident : that all men are created equal. . . . . .—*Declaration of Independence.* We mutually pledge to each other our lives, our fortunes, and our sacred honor.—*Ibid.*

**Henry Lee.**—To the memory of the man, first in war, first in peace, first in the hearts of his countrymen.—*Eulogy on Washington*, 1799.

**Abraham Lincoln.**—That government of the people, by the people, for the people, shall not perish from the earth.—*Gettysburg Speech*, 1863. With malice towards none, with charity for all, with firmness in the right, as God gives us to see the right.—*Inaugural Address*, 1865.

**William L. Marcy.**—To the victors belong the spoils of the enemy.—*Speech in the Senate*, 1832.

**Charles C. Pinckney.**—Millions for defense, but not one cent for tribute. [In answer to the French Directory, 1796.]

**Josiah Quincy.**—Under God we are determined that, wheresoever, whensoever, or howsoever, we shall be called upon to make our exit, we will die freemen.—*Observations on the Boston Port Bill*, 1774.

**William H. Seward.**—There is a higher law than the Constitution. —*Speech*, 1850. An irrepressible conflict [between slavery and freedom].—*Speech*, 1858.

**George Washington.**—To be prepared for war is one of the most effectual means of preserving peace.—*Speech to both Houses of Congress*, 1790.

**Daniel Webster.**—He smote the rock of the national resources and abundant streams of revenue gushed forth. He touched the dead corpse of public credit, and it sprung upon its feet.—*Speech on Hamilton.* I was born an American, I live an American, I shall die an American.—*Speech*, July 17, 1850. Independence now and Independence forever.—*Eulogy on Adams and Jefferson.* Liberty and Union, now and forever, one and inseparable.—*Second Speech on Foote's Resolution.* One country, one constitution, one destiny.—*Speech*, March 15th, 1837. Sea of upturned faces.—*Speech*, September 30th, 1842. Sink or swim, live or die, survive or perish, I give my hand and my heart to this vote. [Sentiment attributed to John Adams.]—*Eulogy on Adams and Jefferson.*—Whose morning drum-beat following the sun, and keeping company with the hours, circles the earth with one continuous and unbroken strain of the martial airs of England.—*Speech*, May 7th, 1834.

**Robert C. Winthrop.**—A star for every State, and a State for every star.—*Address at Boston*, 1862.

## FROM ENGLISH STATESMEN.

**Edmund Burke.**—All government, indeed every human benefit and enjoyment, every virtue and every prudent act, is founded on compromise and barter.—*Speech on Conciliation with America.*

And having looked to government for bread, on the very first scarcity they will turn and bite the hand that fed them.—*Thoughts and Details on Scarcity.*

Early and provident fear is the mother of safety.—*Speech on the Petition of the Unitarians.* I would rather sleep in the southern corner of a little country churchyard than in the tomb of the Capulets.—*Letter to Matthew Smith.*

That chastity of honor which felt a stain like a wound.—*Reflections on the Revolution in France.* The age of chivalry is gone. That of sophisters, economists, and calculators has succeeded.—*Ibid.* The unbought grace of life, the cheap defense of nations, the nurse of manly sentiment and heroic enterprise is gone.—*Ibid.* They made and recorded a sort of institute and digest of anarchy called the Rights of Man.—*On the Army Estimates.* Kings will be tyrants from policy, when subjects are rebels from principle.—*Reflections on the Revolution in France.* Vice itself lost half its evil, by losing all its grossness.—*Ibid.* What shadows we are, and what shadows we pursue.—*Speech at Bristol on Declining the Poll.*

**George Canning.**—I called the New world into existence to redress the balance of the Old.—*King's Message*, 1826.

**William Pitt, Earl of Chatham.**—Confidence is a plant of slow growth.—*Speech*, 1766. If I were an American, as I am an Englishman, while a foreign troop was landed in my country, I would never lay down my arms, never, never, never.—*Speech*, 1777. Where law ends, tyranny begins.—*Speech*, 1770.

**William Pitt [1759-1806].**—Necessity is the argument of tyrants, it is the creed of slaves.—*Speech on the India Bill*, 1783.

### FROM THE ESSAYISTS.

**Joseph Addison.**—Much may be said on both sides.—*Spectator.* There is no living with thee, nor without thee.—*Ibid.*

**Thomas Carlyle.**—All true work is sacred.—*Work.* Literature is the thought of thinking souls.—*Essays.* The true university of these days is a collection of books.—*Heroes and Hero Worship.* Speech is great, but silence is greater.—*Past and Present.* What is done, is done.—*Essays.*

**Ralph Waldo Emerson.**—All mankind love a lover.—*Essay on Love.* Genius borrows nobly.—*Letters and Social Aims.* I should as soon think of swimming across Charles River when I wish to go to Boston, as of reading all my books in originals when I have them rendered for me in my mother tongue.—*On Books.* Is not marriage an open question, when it is alleged . . . . that such as are in the institution wish to get out, and such as are out wish to get in?—*Essay on Montaigne.* Thought is the property of him who can entertain it.—*Essay on Shakespeare.*

**Charles Lamb.**—A clear fire, a clean hearth, and the rigor of the game.—*Mrs. Battle's Opinions on Whist.* Books which are not books.—*Detached Thoughts on Books.* If dirt was trumps, what hands you would hold.—*Lamb's Suppers.* Neat, not gaudy.—*Letter to Wordsworth.* Not if I know myself at all.—*The Old and New Schoolmaster.* Sentimentally I am disposed to harmony, but organically I am incapable of a tune.—*A Chapter on Ears.*

**Thomas Babington Macaulay.**—In that temple of silence and reconciliation. [Westminster Abbey.]—*Essay on Warren Hastings.* Nobles by the right of an earlier creation, and priests by the interposition of a mightier hand.—*Milton.* She [the Roman Catholic Church] may still exist in undiminished vigor when some traveler from New Zealand shall, in the midst of a vast solitude, take his stand on a broken arch of London Bridge to sketch the ruins of St. Paul's.—*Review of Ranke's History of the Popes.*

**Sir Richard Steele.**—To love her [Lady Elizabeth Hastings] was a liberal education.—*The Tattler.*

### FROM LAWYERS AND JUDGES.

**Lord Avonmore.**—He [Sir William Blackstone] it was that first gave to the law the air of a science. · He found it a skeleton, and clothed it with life, color and complexion ; he embraced the cold statue, and by his touch it grew into youth, health, and beauty.—*On Blackstone.*

**Sir William Blackstone.**—It [the English navy] is . . . the floating bulwark of our island.—*Commentaries.* Time whereof the memory of man runneth not to the contrary.—*Ibid.*

**Henry, Lord Brougham.**—The schoolmaster is abroad.—*Speech,* Jan. 29, 1828. The whole machinery of the State, all the apparatus of the system, and its varied workings, end in bringing simply twelve good men into the box.—*Present State of the Law.*

**Sir Edward Coke.**—A man's house is his castle.—*Third Institute.* Reason is the life of the law : nay, the common law itself is nothing else but reason.—*First Institute.* The gladsome light of jurisprudence.—*Ibid.* They [corporations] cannot commit treason . . for they have no souls.—*Reports, vol.* 10.

**Thomas, Lord Denham.**—A delusion, a mockery, and a snare.—*Case of O'Connell against the Queen.*

**Sir John Holt.**—The better day the better deed.—*Sir William Moore's Case. Raymond's Reports.*

**Lord Stowell.**—A dinner lubricates business.—Boswell's *Johnson.* The elegant simplicity of the three per cents.—Campbell's *Lives of the Lord Chancellors.*

**Lord Thurlow.**—The accident of an accident.—*Speech in Reply to the Duke of Grafton.* When I forget my sovereign may my God forget me.—Brougham's *Statesmen of the Time of George III.*

### FROM MEN OF SCIENCE.

**Louis Agassiz.**—I cannot afford to make money.

**John Kepler.**—It [his book] may well wait a century for a reader, as God has waited six thousand years for an observer.—Quoted in Brewster's *Martyrs of Science.*

**Sir Isaac Newton.**—To myself I seem to have been only a boy playing on the sea-shore, and diverting myself now and then in finding a smoother pebble or a prettier shell than ordinary, whilst the great ocean of truth lay all undiscovered before me.—Quoted in Brewster's *Memoirs of Newton.*

### FROM THE HISTORIANS.

**Edward Hyde, Lord Clarendon.**—A head to contrive, a tongue to persuade, and a hand to execute any mischief.—*History of the Rebellion.*

**Edward Gibbon.**—All that is human must retrograde if it do not advance.—*Decline and Fall of the Roman Empire.* History . . . is . . . little more than the register of the crimes, follies, and misfortunes of mankind.—*Ibid.* I was never less alone than when by myself.—*Memoirs.* Revenge is profitable ; gratitude is expensive.—*Decline and Fall of the Roman Empire.*

**David Hume.**—The sport of it [bear-baiting], not the inhumanity, gave offense.—*History of England.*

**Thomas Babington Macaulay.**—There were gentlemen and there were seamen in the navy of Charles II. But the seamen were not gentlemen, and the gentlemen were not seamen.—*History of England.*

### FROM THE NOVELISTS.

**Miguel de Cervantes.**—Blessings on him who invented sleep.—*Don Quixote.* Every one is as God has made him, and oftentimes a great deal worse.—*Ibid.* He had a face like a benediction.—*Ibid.* Let me sit where I will, that is the upper end.—*Ibid.* Patience, and shuffle the cards.—*Ibid.* Sancho Panza I am, unless I was changed in the cradle.—*Ibid.*

**Charles Dickens.**—A demd, damp, moist, unpleasant body. [Remark of Mantalini.*]—*Nicholas Nickleby.* Barkis is willin'.—*David Copperfield.* Ha'penny be demd.—*Nicholas Nickleby.* In a Pickwickian sense.—*Pickwick Papers.* Literary man with a wooden leg.—*Our Mutual Friend.* May the wing of friendship never moult a feather.—*Old Curiosity Shop.* My life is one demd horrid grind.—*Nicholas Nickleby.* Samivel, Samivel, bevare of the vidders. [See Weller.*]—*Pickwick Papers.* Tough is J. B.—Tough and de-vil-ish sly. [See Bagstock.*]—*Dombey and Son.* Whatever was required to be done, the Circumlocution Office was beforehand with all the public departments in the art of perceiving How Not To Do It.—*Little Dorrit.* When found, make a note of. [See Cuttle.*]—*Dombey and Son.*

**Maria Edgeworth.**—The bore is usually considered as harmless, or of that class of irrational bipeds who hurt only themselves.—*Thoughts on Bores.*

**George Eliot.**—I could not live in peace if I put the shadow of a willful sin between myself and God.—*The Mill on the Floss.* More helpful than all human wisdom is one draught of simple human pity that will not forsake us.—*Ibid.* The beauty of a lovely woman is like music.—*Adam Bede.* Thoughts are so great—ar'n't they, sir? They seem to lie upon us like a flood.—*Ibid.* Vanity is ill at ease under indifference, as tenderness is under the love which it cannot return.—*Daniel Deronda.* What furniture can give such finish to a room as a tender woman's face ?—*Ibid.*

**Henry Fielding.**—An author ought to consider himself, not as a gentleman who gives a private eleemosynary treat, but rather as one who keeps a public ordinary, at which all persons are welcome for their money.—*Tom Jones.* "He [Garrick in 'Hamlet'] the best player !" cries Partridge, contemptuously sneering. "Why I could act as well as he myself. I am sure, if I had seen a ghost, I should have looked in the very same manner, and done just as he did. . . . Why, Lord help me ! any man, that is any good man, that had such a mother, would have done exactly the same."—*Ibid.* Rhymes are difficult things.—*Amelia.*

**Oliver Wendell Holmes.**—The Brahmin caste [*i. e.*, the New England aristocracy].—*Elsie Venner.*

**Henry James, Jr.**—Not much talk—a great, sweet silence.—*A Bundle of Letters.* Rotten before it is ripe [American civilization.]—*Ibid.*

**Samuel Johnson.**—The endearing elegance of female friendship.—

* See "Celebrated Characters of Fiction" in another part of the book.

*Rasselas.* Who listen with credulity to the whispers of fancy, and pursue with eagerness the phantoms of hope.—*Ibid.*

**Henry Wadsworth Longfellow.**—Music is the universal language of mankind.—*Outre-Mer.*

**Samuel Lover.**—For drames always go by *conthraries*, my dear.—*Rory O'More.* Reproof on her lips, but a smile in her eye.—*Ibid.*

**Sir Edward Bulwer-Lytton.**—I do loves poetry, sir, specially the sacred.—*Eugene Aram.* Laws die, books never.—*Richelieu.*

**Sir Walter Scott.**—My foot is on my native heath, and my name is MacGregor.—*Rob Roy.* Sca ed out of his seven senses.—*Ibid.* Sea of upturned faces.—*Ibid.* [Often attributed to Daniel Webster.] The longest kingly line in Europe . . . runs back to a successful soldier.—*Woodstock.* Rouse the lion from his lair.—*The Talisman.* There's a good time coming.—*Rob Roy.*

**Sir Philip Sidney.**—High erected thoughts seated in the heart of courtesy.—*Arcadia.* My dear, my better half.—*Ibid.* The many-headed multitude.—*Ibid.* They are never alone that are accompanied with noble thoughts.—*Ibid.*

**Tobias Smollett.**—One wit, like a knuckle of ham in soup, gives a zest and flavor to the dish, but more than one serves only to spoil the pottage.—*Humphrey Clinker.*

**Laurence Sterne.**—Go, poor devil [a fly], get thee gone; why should I hurt thee? This world is surely wide enough to hold both thee and me.—*Tristram Shandy.* God tempers the wind to the shorn lamb. [A translation of the French proverb: *A brebis tondue Dieu mesure le vent.*]—*Sentimental Journey.* "Our armies swore terribly in Flanders," cried Uncle Toby, "but nothing to this."—*Tristram Shandy.* The recording angel, as he wrote it [an oath] down, dropped a tear upon the word and blotted it out forever.—*Ibid.* "They order," said I, "this matter better in France."—*Sentimental Journey.*

**Harriet Beecher Stowe.**—Cause I's wicked, I is. I's mighty wicked, anyhow. I can't help it.—Topsy in *Uncle Tom's Cabin.*

**William Makepeace Thackeray.**—It is best to love wisely, no doubt: but to love foolishly is better than not to be able to love at all.—*Pendennis.* Not a hero, but a man and a brother.—*Ibid.* Novel without a hero.—*Vanity Fair.* Pretty voice, but no cultivation.—*Newcomes.* "Why *Pall Mall Gazette*?" asked Wagg. "Because the editor was born at Dublin, the sub-editor at Cork; because the proprietor lives in Paternoster Row, and the paper is published in Catharine Street, Strand.—*Pendennis.*

## FROM THE PHILOSOPHERS AND MORALISTS.

**Lord Bacon.**—A little philosophy inclineth a man's mind to atheism, but depth in philosophy bringeth men's minds about to religion.—*Essay XVI.* Books must follow sciences, and not sciences books.—*Proposition touching Amendment of the Law.* Cleanness of body was ever esteemed to proceed from a due reverence to God.—*Advancement of Learning.* Come home to men's business and bosoms.—*Dedication to the Essays.* For the glory of the Creator and the relief of man's estate.—*A. of Learning.* God Almighty first planted a garden.—*Essay XLVI.* He that hath wife and children hath given hostages to fortune; for they are impediments to great enterprises, either of virtue or mischief.—*Essay VIII.* Histories make men wise; poets, witty; the mathematics, sublime; natural philosophy, deep, moral, grave; logic and rhetoric, able to contend.—*Essay I.* Reading maketh a full man, conference a ready man, and writing an exact man.—*Ibid.* Some books are to be tasted, others swallowed, and some few to be chewed and digested.—*Ibid.* Virtue is like precious odors, most fragrant when they are incensed [burned] or crushed.—*Essay V.*

**Jeremy Bentham.**—The greatest happiness of the greatest number [the phrase is taken from Beccaria] is the foundation of morals and legislation.—*Works, Vol. X., p.* 142.

**Henry St. John. Viscount Bolingbroke.**—I have read . . . . that history is philosophy teaching by example.—*On the Study and Use of History.*

**Sir Thomas Browne.**—Man is a noble animal, splendid in ashes and pompous [magnificent] in the grave.—*Urn Burial.* Rich with the spoils of nature.—*Religio-Medici.*

**Thomas Fuller.**—Learning hath gained most by those books which the printers have lost.—*The Holy and the Profane State.* Often the cockloft is empty in those whom Nature hath built many stories high.—*Ibid.* The image of God . . . cut in ivory.—*Ibid.* The pyramids themselves, doting with age, have forgotten the names of their founders.—*Ibid.* They that marry ancient people, merely in expectation to bury them, hang themselves, in hope that one will come and cut the halter.—*Ibid.* To smell of fresh earth is wholesome for the body; no less are thoughts of mortality cordial to the soul.—*Ibid.*

**Bishop Joseph Hall.**—Death borders upon our birth, and our cradle stands in the grave.—*Christian Moderation.*

**Thomas Hobbes.**—The life of man solitary, poor, nasty, brutish, and short.—*The Leviathan.*

**Samuel Johnson.**—His [David Garrick's] death eclipsed the gayety of nations, and impoverished the public stock of harmless pleasure.—*Life of Edmund Smith.*

**Sir James Mackintosh.**—Disciplined inaction.—*Causes of the Revolution of* 1688. The frivolous work of polished idleness.—*Dissertation on Ethical Philosophy.* Wise and masterly inactivity.—*Vindiciæ Gallicæ.*

**William Paley.**—Who can refute a sneer?—*Moral Philosophy.*

## FROM POLITICAL WRITERS.

**"Junius."**—I do not give you to posterity as a pattern to imitate, but as an example to deter.—*Letter XII. To the Duke of Grafton.* Private credit is wealth, public honor is security.—*Letter XLII. The Affair of the Falkland Islands.*

**John Milton.**—A good book is the precious life-blood of a master spirit embalmed and treasured up on purpose to a life beyond a life.—*Areopagitica.* As good almost kill a man as kill a good book.—*Ibid.* I cannot praise a fugitive and cloistered virtue, unexercised and unbreathed, that never sallies out and sees her adversary, but slinks out of the race where that immortal garland is to be run for not without dust and heat.—*Ibid.* Methinks I see in my mind a noble and puissant nation rousing herself like a strong man after sleep, and shaking her invincible locks; methinks I see her as an eagle rousing her mighty youth, and kindling her undazzled eye at the full mid-day beam.—*Ibid.* Who ever knew truth put to the worse in a free and open encounter?—*Ibid.*

**Thomas Paine.**—As he [Edmund Burke] rose like a rocket, he fell like a stick.—*Letter to the Addressers.* Times that try men's souls.—*The American Crisis.*

## FROM THEOLOGICAL WRITERS.

**Henry Ward Beecher.**—We sleep, but the loom of life never stops—*Life Thoughts.*

**Robert Hall.**—Glass of brandy and water. That is the current, but not the appropriate name; ask for a glass of liquid fire and distilled damnation. [From his *Life* by Gregory.]. He laid so many books upon his head that his brain could not move.—*Ibid.* His [Edmund Burke's] imperial fancy had laid all nature under tribute.—*Apology for the Freedom of the Press.*

**Matthew Henry.**—Bread which strengthens man's heart.—*Commentaries.* Rolled under the tongue as a sweet morsel.—*Ibid.* Their own second and sober thoughts.—*Exposition. Job VI.*, 29. [Compare Fisher Ames' *Speech on Biennial Elections.* "The sober, second thought of the people."]

**Richard Hooker.**—Of Law there can be no less acknowledged than that her seat is the bosom of God, her voice the harmony of the world; all things in heaven and earth do her homage; the very least as feeling her care, and the very greatest as not exempted from her homage.—*Ecclesiastical Polity.* To live by one man's will became the cause of all men's misery.—*Ibid.*

**John Milton.**—Beholding the bright countenance of truth in the quiet and still air of delightful studies.—*The Reason of Church Government.* I might, perhaps leave something so written to aftertimes, as they should not willingly let die.—*Ibid.* Poet soaring in the high reason of his fancies, with his garland and singing robes about him.—*Ibid.* Truth is as impossible to be soiled by any outward touch as the sunbeam.—*The Doctrine and Discipline of Divorce.*

**Theodore Parker.**—All men desire to be immortal.—*A Sermon of Immortal Life.* A government of all the people, by all the people, for all the people.—Speech at the *Anti-Slavery Convention at Boston*, May 29, 1850. [Compare Lincoln's *Gettysburg Speech.*]

**Jeremy Taylor.**—The sun reflecting upon the mud of strands and shores is unpolluted in his beam.—*Holy Living.* You have often been

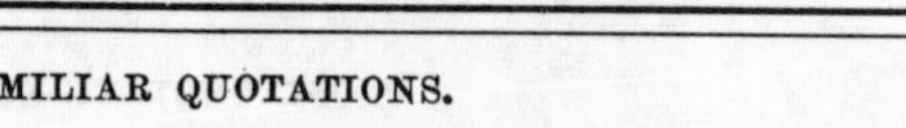

told . . . . . that ignorance is the mother of devotion.—*Letter to a Person Newly Converted.* [Compare Dryden's "Your ignorance is the mother of your devotion to me."—*The Maiden Queen. Act I., sc.,* 2.]

**John Tillotson.**—If God were not a necessary Being of himself, He might almost seem to be made for the use and benefit of men.—*Sermon* 93.

**John Wesley.**—A duty not a sin. Cleanliness is indeed next to godliness.—*Sermon on Dress.* That execrable sum of all villainies commonly called a slave trade.—*Journal.*

## FROM THE WITS AND SATIRISTS.

**Lord Chesterfield.**—A chapter of accidents.—*Letters.* Dispatch is the soul of business.—*Ibid.* He [Pulteney] shrank into insignificancy and an earldom.—*Character of Pulteney.* I assisted at the birth of that most significant word "flirtation."—*The World.* Manners must adorn knowledge.—*Letters.* Style is the dress of thoughts.—*Ibid.*

**Thomas C. Haliburton.**—They are all upper-crust here.—*Sam Slick in England.*

**Oliver Wendell Holmes.**—Boston State House is the hub of the solar system.—*The Autocrat of the Breakfast Table.*

**Alexander Pope.**—I never knew any man in my life who could not bear another's misfortunes perfectly like a Christian.—*Thoughts on Various Subjects.* Party is the madness of many for the gain of a few. *Ibid.*

**Sydney Smith.**—Heat, ma'am! it was so dreadful here that I found nothing left for it but to take off my flesh and sit in my bones.—Lady Holland's *Memoir.* In the four quarters of the globe, who reads an American book?—*Edinburgh Review,* 1820. It is not more than a month ago that I heard him [Jeffrey] speak disrespectfully of the equator.—*Memoir.* It requires a surgical operation to get a joke well into a Scotch understanding.—*Ibid.* Macaulay is like a book in breeches. . . . He has occasional flashes of silence.—*Ibid.* Webster struck me much like a steam engine in trowsers.—*Ibid.*

**Jonathan Swift.**—A nice man is a man of nasty ideas.—*Thoughts on Various Subjects.* Bread is the staff of life.—*Tale of a Tub.* Censure is the tax a man pays to the public for being eminent.—*Thoughts on Various Subjects.* The two noblest things, which are sweetness and light.—*Battle of the Books.*

**Horace Walpole.**—A careless song, with a little nonsense in it, now and then, does not misbecome a monarch.—*Letters.* Pulteney's toad-eater.—*Ibid.* The world is a comedy to those that think; a tragedy to those who feel.—*Ibid.*

## FROM THE DRAMATISTS.

### WILLIAM CONGREVE.

"Ferdinand Mendez Pinto was but a type of thee, thou liar of the first magnitude."—*Love for Love.* "Hannibal was a very pretty fellow in those days."—*Ibid.* "I came up stairs into the world, for I was born in a cellar."—*Ibid.*

### GEORGE COLMAN.

"I had a soul above buttons."—*Sylvester Daggerwood.* "Thank you, good sir, I owe you one."—*The Poor Gentleman.*

### GEORGE FARQUHAR.

"I believe they talked of me, for they laughed consumedly."—*The Beaux' Stratagem.*

### THOMAS MORTON.

"Approbation from Sir Hubert Stanley is praise, indeed."—*A Cure for the Heartache.* "What will Mrs. Grundy say?"—*Speed the Plough.*

### WILLIAM SHAKESPEARE.

***All 's Well That Ends Well.***—"The web of our life is of a mingled yarn, good and ill together."—*Act IV., sc.* 3.

***Antony and Cleopatra.***—"A woman is a dish for the gods."—*Act V., sc.* 2. "There is never a fair woman has a true face."—*Act II., sc.* 6.

***As You Like It.***—"An ill-favored thing, sir, but my own."—*Act V., sc.* 4. "For ever and a day."—*Act IV., sc.* 1. "How full of briars is this working-day world."—*Act I., sc.* 3. "I had rather have a fool to make me merry, than experience to make me sad."—*Act IV., sc.* 1. "Men have died from time to time, and worms have eaten them, but not for love."—*Act IV., sc.* 1. "The Retort Courteous."—*Act V., sc.* 4. "Too much of a good thing."—*Act IV., sc.* 1.

***Comedy of Errors.***—"Many a man hath more hair than wit."—*Act II., sc.* 2. "There 's a time for all things."—*Ibid.*

***Coriolanus.***—"The many-headed multitude."—*Act II., sc.* 2. "The wounds become him."—*Act II., sc.* 1.

***Cymbeline.***—"Winning will put any man into courage."—*Act II., sc.* 3.

***Hamlet.***—"Alas, poor Yorick! I knew him, Horatio; a fellow of infinite wit, of most excellent fancy."—*Act V., sc.* 1. "Be thou as chaste as ice, as pure as snow, thou shalt not escape calumny. Get thee to a nunnery; go."—*Act III., sc.* 1. "Cudgel thy brains no more about it."—*Ibid.* "Here's metal more attractive."—*Act III., sc.* 2. "How absolute the knave is."—*Act V., sc.* 1. "In the very torrent, tempest, and (as I may say) the whirlwind of passion, you must acquire and beget a temperance that may give it smoothness."—*Act III., sc.* 2. "It out-Herods Herod."—*Ibid.* "Not to speak it profanely."—*Ibid.* "There's rosemary, that's for remembrance."—*Act IV., sc.* 5. "'Tis as easy as lying."—*Act III., sc.* 2. "To what base uses may we return, Horatio."—*Act V., sc.* 1. "'Twas caviare to the general."—*Act II., sc.* 2. "Very like a whale."—*Ibid.* "What a piece of work is man!"—*Act II., sc.* 2.

***Julius Cæsar.***—"As proper men as ever trod upon neat's leather." *Act I., sc.* 1. "Not that I loved Cæsar less, but that I loved Rome more."—*Act III., sc.* 2. "Who is here so base, that would be a bondman? If any, speak; for him have I offended. I pause for a reply."—*Ibid.*

***King Henry IV., First Part.***—"A good mouth-filling oath."—*Act III., sc.* 1. "A plague of all cowards."—*Act II., sc.* 4. "Call you that backing of your friends?"—*Ibid.* "I am a Jew, else."—*Ibid.* "Food for powder."—*Act IV., sc.* 2. "I know a trick worth two of that."—*Act II., sc.* 1. "No more of that, Hal, an' if thou lovest me."—*Act II., sc.* 4. "O, monstrous! but one-half pennyworth of bread to this intolerable deal of sack."—*Ibid.* "Out of this nettle danger we pluck the flower safety."—*Act II., sc.* 3. "Shall I not take mine ease in mine inn?"—*Ibid.* The better part of valor is discretion."—*Act V., sc.* 4. "Thou hast damnable iteration."—*Act I., sc.* 2.

***King Henry IV., Part Second.***—"A man can die but once."—*Act III., sc.* 2. "I am not only witty myself, but the cause that wit is in other men."—*Act I., sc.* 2. "He hath eaten me out of house and home."—*Act II., sc.* 1. "Most forcible feeble."—*Act III., sc.* 2. "Under which king, Bezonian? Speak, or die."—*Act V., sc.* 3. "We have heard the chimes at midnight."—*Act III., sc.* 2.

***King Henry V.***—"'A [he] babbled of green fields."—*Act II., sc.* 1.

***King Henry VI., Second Part.***—"There shall be, in England, seven half-penny loaves sold for a penny, * * * and I will make it a felony to drink small beer."—*Act IV., sc.* 2.

***Love's Labor Lost.***—"The world was very guilty of such a ballad some three ages since."—*Act I., sc* 2. Priscian [a famous Latin grammarian] a little scratch'd."—*Act V., sc.* 1.

***Merchant of Venice.***—"God made him, and therefore let him pass for a man."—*Act I., sc.* 2. "Gratiano speaks an infinite deal of nothing."—*Act I., sc.* 1. "Hath not a Jew eyes, hath not a Jew hands, organs, dimensions, senses, affections, passions?"—*Act III., sc.* 1.

***Merry Wives of Windsor.***—"A man of my kidney."—*Act III., sc.* 5. "As good luck would have it."—*Ibid.* "All his successors, gone before him, have done 't, and all his ancestors that come after him may."—*Act I., sc.* 1. "Mine host of the Garter."—*Ibid.*

***Midsummer Night's Dream.***—"A proper man as one shall see in a summer's day."—*Act I., sc.* 2. "Bless thee, Bottom! * * * thou art translated."—*Act III., sc.* 1. "I will roar you as gently as any sucking dove."—*Act I., sc.* 2. "This is Ercles' vein."—*Ibid.*

***Much Ado About Nothing.***—"Are you good men and true?"—*Act III., sc.* 3. "As merry as the day is long."—*Act II., sc.* 1. "Benedick, the married man."—*Act I., sc.* 1. "Comparisons are odorous."—*Act III., sc.* 5. "Flat burglary as was ever committed."—*Act IV., sc.* 2. "O, that he were here to write me down an ass! *Act IV., sc.* 2. "Sits the wind in that corner?"—*Act II., sc.* 3.

***Othello.***—"For I am nothing if not critical."—*Act II., sc.* 1. "O, that a man should put an enemy into his mouth to steal away his brains." *Act II., sc.* 3.
***Romeo and Juliet.***—"'Tis not so deep as a well, nor so wide as a church door; but 'tis enough."—*Act III., sc.* 1.
***Taming of the Shrew.***—"Let the world slide."—*Induction.*
***Tempest.***—"Misery acquaints a man with strange bedfellows."—*Act II., sc.* 2.
***Twelfth Night.***—"Dost thou think, because thou art virtuous, there shall be no more cakes and ale?"—*Act II., sc.* 3. "Midsummer madness."—*Act III., sc.* 4. "Some are born great, some achieve greatness, and some have greatness thrust upon them."—*Act II., sc.* 5.
***The Winter's Tale.***—"A snapper-up of unconsidered trifles" [*i. e.*, a thief].—*Act IV., sc.* 2.

[See also "Quotations from Shakespeare."]

### RICHARD BRINSLEY SHERIDAN.

"A progeny of learning."—[Remark of Mrs. Malaprop.]—*The Rivals.* "As headstrong as an allegory on the banks of the Nile."—*Ibid.* "I feel it [my valor] oozing out, as it were, at the palms of my hands."—*Ibid.* "I own the soft impeachment."—*Ibid.* "The quarrel is a very pretty quarrel as it stands."—*Ibid.* "The Right Honorable gentleman [Dundas] is indebted to his memory for his jests, and to his imagination for his facts."—*Sheridiana.* "Too civil by half."—*The Rivals.* "You are not like Cerberus, three gentlemen at once, are you?"—*Ibid.*

## APHORISMS AND EPIGRAMS.

A good hater.—*Samuel Johnson.* A man who could make so vile a pun would not scruple to pick a pocket.—*John Dennis* [1657–1734]. A man will turn over half a library to make one book.—*Samuel Johnson.* A very unclubable man.—*Samuel Johnson.* Actions of the last age are like almanacs of the last year.—*Sir John Denham.* All is lost save honor.—*Francis I.* of France. [*Letter to his Mother* after the battle of Pavia. He really said: "Out of everything nothing is left me save honor and my life which is safe."] All men have their price.—*Sir Robert Walpole.* Ambition has no rest.—*Sir E. Bulwer Lytton.* Angling is somewhat like poetry; men are to be born to it.—*Izaak Walton.* Attack is the reaction; I never think I have hit hard unless it rebounds.—*Samuel Johnson.*

Do well and right, and let the world sink.—*George Herbert.*

For words are wise men's counters, but they are the money of fools.—*Thomas Hobbes.*

He had only one idea, and that was wrong.—*Benjamin Disraeli.* He that is down need fear no fall.—*John Bunyan.* History must be false.—*Sir Robert Walpole.* Honest labor bears a lovely face.—*Thomas Dekker.*

If a man were permitted to make all the ballads, he need not care who should make the laws of a nation.—*Andrew Fletcher.* [1653–1716]. Imagination rules the world.—*Napoleon Bonaparte.* It is more than a crime, it is a political fault.—*Joseph Fouché.* [Generally ascribed to Talleyrand, "It is worse than a crime, it is a blunder."] It is the cause and not the death that makes the martyr.—*Napoleon Bonaparte.*

Love begets love.—*Jean de la Bruyère.*

Much may be made of a Scotchman if he be caught young.—*Samuel Johnson.* Much may be said on both sides.—*Joseph Addison.*

Nature is the art of God.—*Sir Thomas Browne.* No man can lose what he never had.—*Izaak Walton.* No man is the wiser for his learning.—*John Seldon.* No man was ever written out of reputation save by himself.—*Richard Bentley.* No pleasure is comparable to the standing on the vantage ground of truth.—*Francis Bacon.* Nothing except a battle lost can be half so melancholy as a battle won.—*Duke of Wellington.*

O liberty, what crimes are committed in thy name!—*Madame Roland.* Of two evils the less is always to be chosen.—*Thomas à Kempis.* Old friends are best.—*John Selden.*

Patriotism is the last refuge of a scoundrel.—*Samuel Johnson.* Poverty is want of much, but avarice of everything.—*Publius Synes.*

Rich soils are often to be weeded.—*Francis Bacon.*

Syllables govern the world.—*John Selden.*

The gratitude of place-hunters is a lively sense of future favors.—*Sir Robert Walpole.* [Compare Rochefoucault.]—The tree of liberty only grows when watered by the blood of tyrants.—*Bertrand Barrère.* The true use of speech is not so much to express our thoughts as to conceal them.—*Oliver Goldsmith.* [Compare Voltaire's similar saying.] They are never alone that are accompanied with noble thoughts.—*Sir Philip Sydney.* Time tries the truth in everything.—*Thomas Tusser.*

Virtue is not left to stand alone.—*Confucius.*

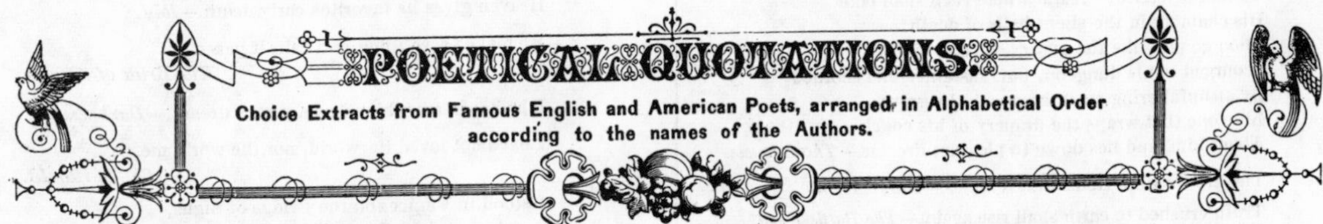


**Joseph Addison.**

A day, an hour of virtuous liberty
Is worth a whole eternity of bondage—*Cato, Act II., sc.* 1.

Eternity, thou pleasing, dreadful thought.—*Cato, Act V., sc.* 1.

Forever singing as they shine,
The hand that made us is divine.—*Ode.*

It must be so—Plato, thou reasonest well!
Else whence this pleasing hope, this fond desire,
This longing after immortality?—*Cato, Act V., sc.* 1.

Rides on the whirlwind, and directs the storm.—*The Campaign.*

The dawn is overcast, the morning lowers,
And heavily in clouds brings on the day.—*Cato, Act I., sc.* 1.

The soul, secure in her existence, smiles
At the drawn dagger, and defies its point.—*Cato, Act V., sc.* 1.
The spacious firmament on high,
With all the blue ethereal sky.—*Ode.*

When vice prevails and impious men bear sway,
The post of honor is the private station.—*Cato, Act IV., sc.* 4.

**Mark Akenside.**

Seeks painted trifles and fantastic toys,
And eagerly pursues imaginary joys.—*The Virtuoso.*

**James Aldrich.**

She passed through Glory's morning gate
And walked in Paradise.—*A Death Bed.*

**Richard Allison.**

There is a garden in her face,
Where roses and white lilies grow;
A heavenly paradise is that place,
Wherein all pleasant fruits do grow.
—From *An Houres Recreation in Musike.*

**Matthew Arnold.**

Calm's not life's crown, though calm is well.—*Youth and Calm.*

Change doth unknit the tranquil strength of men.—*A Question.*

Who saw life steadily, and saw it whole.—*To a Friend.*

**Philip J. Bailey.**

We live in deeds, not years; in thoughts, not breaths;
In feelings, not in figures on a dial.—*Festus.*

**Anne Letitia Aikin Barbauld.**

Life ! we've been long together,
Through pleasant and through cloudy weather ;
'Tis hard to part when friends are dear,
Perhaps 'twill cost a sigh, a tear ;
Then steal away, give little warning,
Choose thine own time ;
Say not "Good night," but in some better clime,
Bid me "Good morning."—*Life.*

**George Barrington.**

True patriots all ; for be it understood
We left our country for our country's good.—*Prologue*, 1796.

Mine be the breezy hill that skirts the downs.—*The Minstrel.*

Patient of toil, serene amidst alarms ;
Inflexible in faith, invincible in arms.—*Ibid.*

**Beaumont and Fletcher.**

A soul as white as heaven.—*The Maid's Tragedy.*

Calamity is man's true touchstone.—*Four Plays in One.*

Nothing can cover his high fame but heaven.—*The False One.*

**Francis Beaumont.**

What things have we seen
Done at the Mermaid ; heard words that have been
So nimble and so full of subtile flame.
*Letter to Ben Jonson.*

**Bishop Berkeley.**

Westward the course of empire takes its way ;
The four first acts already past :
A fifth shall close the drama with the day ;
Time's noblest offspring is the last.
*On the Prospect of Planting Arts and Learning in America.*

**Lord Brooke.**

O wearisome condition of humanity.—*Mustapha.*

**William Cullen Bryant.**

Old Ocean's gray and melancholy waste.—*Thanatopsis.*

So live that when thy summons comes to join
The innumerable caravan which moves
To that mysterious realm where each shall take
His chamber in the silent halls of death,
Thou go not, like the quarry-slave at night,
Scourged to his dungeon, but, sustained and soothed
By an unfaltering trust, approach thy grave,
Like one that wraps the drapery of his couch
About him, and lies down to pleasant dreams.—*Thanatopsis.*

The groves were God's first temples.—*Forest Hymn.*

Truth crushed to earth shall rise again.—*The Battle Field.*

**Robert Burns.**

Had we never loved sae kindly,
Had we never loved sae blindly,
Never met or never parted,
We had ne'er been broken hearted.
*Song, Ae Fond Kiss.*

If there's a hole in a' your coats,
I rede [advise] ye tent [take care of] it,
A chiel [young fellow] 's amang ye taking notes,
And faith he'll prent [print] it.
*On Captain Grose's Peregrinations through Scotland.*

Man's inhumanity to man
Mak's countless thousands mourn.
*Man was Made to Mourn.*

O wad some power the giftie gie [give] us
To see ourselves as others see us.—*To a Louse.*

Should auld acquaintance be forgot,
And never brought to min',
Should auld acquaintance be forgot,
And days o' lang syne.—*Auld Lang Syne.*

The best laid schemes o' mice and men
Gang [go] aft [often] a-gley [wrong].—*To a Mouse.*

The mirth and fun grew fast and furious.—*Tam O'Shanter.*

The rank is but the guinea's stamp,
The man's the gowd [gold] for a' that.
*Is there for Honest Poverty.*

**Samuel Butler.**

And pulpit, drum ecclesiastic,
Was beat with fist instead of a stick.—*Hudibras.*

Compound for sins they are inclined to,
By damning those they have no mind to.—*Ibid.*

He that complies against his will
Is of the same opinion still.—*Ibid.*

To swallow gudgeons ere they're catched,
And count their chickens ere they're hatched.—*Ibid.*

'T was Presbyterian true blue.—*Ibid.*

**Lord Byron.**

A change came o'er the spirit of my dream.—*The Dream.*

Ada ! sole daughter of my house and heart.
*Childe Harold.*

Adieu, adieu, my native shore
Fades o'er the waters blue.—*Childe Harold.*

Better to sink beneath the shock
Than moulder piecemeal on the rock !—*The Giaour.*

Fare thee well ! and if forever,
Still forever fare thee well.—*Fare thee Well.*

For freedom's battle, once begun,
Bequeathed from bleeding sire to son,
Though baffled oft is ever won.—*The Giaour.*

Had sighed to many, though he loved but one.
*Childe Harold.*

Heaven gives its favorites early death.—*Ibid.*

He makes a solitude and calls it peace.
*The Bride of Abydos.*

I had a dream which was not all a dream.—*Darkness.*

I have not loved the world, nor the world me.
*Childe Harold.*

I stood in Venice, on the Bridge of Sighs,
A palace and a prison on each hand.—*Ibid.*

Land of lost gods, and godlike men.—*Ibid.*

Maid of Athens, ere we part,
Give, oh give, me back my heart.—*Maid of Athens.*

My boat is on the shore,
And my bark is on the sea.—*To Thomas Moore.*

My days are in the yellow leaf,
The flowers and fruits of love are gone,
The worm, the canker, and the grief
Are mine alone.—*On my Thirty-sixth Year.*

My native land, good night !—*Childe Harold.*

Oh, mirth and innocence ! Oh, milk and water !
Ye happy mixtures of more happy days !—*Beppo.*

Oh ! that the desert were my dwelling-place,
With one fair spirit for my minister.—*Childe Harold.*

On with the dance ! let joy be unconfined.—*Ibid.*

Roll on, thou deep and dark blue Ocean, roll !
Ten thousand fleets sweep over thee in vain.—*Ibid.*

Seek roses in December, ice in June,
Hope constancy in mind, or corn in chaff,
Believe a woman, or an epitaph.
*English Bards and Scotch Reviewers.*

She walks the waters like a thing of life.—*The Corsair.*

The Assyrian came down like the wolf on the fold,
And his cohorts were gleaming in purple and gold.
*The Destruction of Sennacherib.*

The dome of Thought, the palace of the Soul.—*Childe Harold.*

There was a sound of revelry by night.—*Ibid.*

And all went merry as a marriage bell.—*Ibid.*

There's naught, no doubt, so much the spirit calms
As rum and true religion.—*Don Juan.*

Time writes no wrinkles on thine azure brow.—*Ibid.*

'Tis pleasant, sure, to see one's name in print;
A book's a book, although there's nothing in 't.
*English Bards and Scotch Reviewers.*

With just enough of learning to misquote.
*English Bards and Scotch Reviewers.*

**Thomas Campbell.**

And freedom shrieked as Kosciusko fell.—*Pleasures of Hope.*

Britannia needs no bulwarks,
No towers along the steep ;
Her march is o'er the mountain waves,
Her home is on the deep.—*Ye Mariners of England.*

Few, few shall part where many meet !
The snow shall be their winding-sheet.—*Hohenlinden.*

Like angel-visits, few and far between.—*Pleasures of Hope.*

O, Star-eyed Science, hast thou wandered there.—*Ibid.*

The sentinel stars set their watch in the sky.
*The Soldier's Dream.*

There came to the beach a poor exile of Erin.
*The Exile of Erin.*

'Tis distance lends enchantment to the view.
*Pleasures of Hope.*

'Tis the sunset of life gives me mystical lore,
And coming events cast their shadows before.
*Lochiel's Warning.*

**Samuel Taylor Coleridge.**

O sleep ! it is a gentle thing,
Beloved from pole to pole.—*The Ancient Mariner.*

Red as a rose is she.—*Ibid.*

The river Rhine, it is well known,
Doth wash your city of Cologne;
But tell me, nymphs ! what power divine
Shall henceforth wash the river Rhine.—*Cologne.*

Water, water, everywhere,
Nor any drop to drink.—*The Ancient Mariner.*

**George Colman.**

When taken,
To be well shaken.—*The Newcastle Apothecary.*

**William Congreve.**

Heaven has no rage like love to hatred turned,
Nor hell a fury like a woman scorned.—*The Mourning Bride.*

Music hath charms to soothe the savage breast.—*Ibid.*

**William Cowper.**

A hat not much the worse for wear.—*History of John Gilpin.*

God made the country, and man made the town.—*The Task.*

God moves in a mysterious way
His wonders to perform.—*Light Shining out of Darkness.*

I am monarch of all I survey.—*Alexander Selkirk.*

I would not enter on my list of friends
(Though graced with polished manners and fine sense,
Yet wanting sensibility) the man
Who needlessly sets foot upon a worm.—*The Task.*

O for a lodge in some vast wilderness,
Some boundless contiguity of shade.—*Ibid.*

O that those lips had language.
*On the Receipt of My Mother's Picture.*

The cups
That cheer but not inebriate.—*The Task.*

Though on pleasure she was bent,
She had a frugal mind.—*History of John Gilpin.*

Variety's the very spice of life.—*The Task.*

**Daniel Defoe.**

Wherever God erects a house of prayer,
The devil always builds a chapel there ;
And 'twill be found upon examination,
The latter has the larger congregation.
*The True Born Englishman.*

**Charles Dibdin.**

For though his body's under hatches,
His soul has gone aloft.—*Tom Bowling.*

He was all for love and a little for the bottle.
*Captain Wattle and Miss Roe.*

There's a sweet little cherub that sits up aloft,
To keep watch for the life of poor Jack.—*Poor Jack.*

**Joseph Rodman Drake.**

Flag of the free heart's hope and home !
By angel hands to valor given.—*The American Flag.*

Forever float that standard sheet.—*Ibid.*

**John Dryden.**

And whistled as he went for want of thought.
*Cymon and Iphigeneia*

Great wits are sure to madness near allied,
And thin partitions do their bounds divide.
*Absalom and Achitophel.*

Men are but children of a larger growth.—*All for Love.*

None but the brave deserve the fair.—*Alexander's Feast.*

**Timothy Dwight.**

Columbia, Columbia, to glory arise,
The queen of the world, and child of the skies.—*Columbia.*

**Ralph Waldo Emerson.**

Earth proudly wears the Parthenon
As the best gem upon her zone.—*The Problem.*

Good bye, proud world, I'm going home.—*Good-Bye.*

He builded better than he knew.—*The Problem.*

Here once the embattled farmer stood,
And fired the shot heard round the world.—
*Hymn at the completion of the Concord Monument.*

**David Garrick.**

Let others hail the rising sun ;
I bow to that whose course is run.
*On the Death of Mrs. Pelham.*

Their cause I plead ; plead it in heart and mind ;
A fellow feeling makes one wondrous kind.
*Prologue on Quitting the Stage.*

**John Gay.**

How happy I could be with either,
Were t' other dear charmer away.

*The Beggar's Opera.*

Over the hills and far away.—*Ibid.*

**Oliver Goldsmith.**

And drags at each remove a lengthening chain.—*The Traveller.*

And learn the luxury of doing good.—*The Traveller.*

And still they gazed, and still the wonder grew,
That one small head could carry all he knew.

*The Deserted Village.*

Creation's heir, the world, the world is mine.—*The Traveller.*

Ill fares the land, to hastening ills a prey,
Where wealth accumulates, and men decay.

*The Deserted Village.*

Man wants but little here below,
Nor wants that little long.—*The Hermit.*

Remote, unfriended, melancholy, slow.—*The Traveller.*

The man recover'd of the bite,
The dog it was that died.

*Elegy on the Death of a Mad Dog.*

The watch dog's voice that bay'd the whispering wind,
And the loud laugh that spoke the vacant mind.

*The Deserted Village.*

Truth from his lips prevailed with double sway,
And fools who came to scoff, remain'd to pray.—*Ibid.*

When lovely woman stoops to folly,
And finds too late that men betray,
What charm can soothe her melancholy?
What art can wash her guilt away?

*Vicar of Wakefield.*

**Thomas Gray.**

Full many a flower is born to blush unseen,
And waste its sweetness on the desert air.

*Elegy written in a Country Churchyard.*

He passed the flaming bounds of space and time.

*Progress of Poesy.*

Ruin seize thee, ruthless king!
Confusion on thy banners wait.—*The Bard.*

**Fitz-Green Halleck.**

Green be the turf above thee
Friend of my better days;
None knew thee but to love thee,
Nor named thee but to praise.

*On the death of Joseph Rodman Drake.*

One of the few, the immortal names,
That were not born to die.—*Marco Bozzaris.*

**Bret Harte.**

And the subsequent proceedings interested him no more.

*The Society upon the Stanislaus.*

For ways that are dark,
And for tricks that are vain,
The Heathen Chinee is peculiar,
Which the same I am free to maintain.

*Plain Language from Truthful James.*

With the smile that was childlike and bland.—*Ibid.*

**Reginald Heber.**

By cool Siloam's shady rill.—*First Sunday after Epiphany.*

From Greenland's icy mountains,
From India's coral strand.—*Missionary Hymn.*

Though every prospect pleases
And only man is vile.—*Missionary Hymn.*

**George Herbert.**

Sweet day, so cool, so calm, so bright,
The bridal of the earth and sky.—*Virtue.*

Who sweeps a room as for thy laws,
Makes that and th' action fine.

**Robert Herrick.**

Gather ye rosebuds while ye may,
Old Time is still a-flying;
And this same flower that smiles to-day,
To-morrow will be dying.

*To the Virgins to make much of Time.*

**Oliver Wendell Holmes.**

And since, I never dare to write,
As funny as I can.—*The Height of the Ridiculous.*

Ay, tear her tattered ensign down!
Long has it waved on high,
And many an eye has danced to see
That banner in the sky.—*Old Ironsides.*

**Thomas Hood.**

Alas for the rarity
Of Christian charity
Under the sun!—*The Bridge of Sighs.*

One more unfortunate
Weary of breath,
Rashly importunate,
Gone to her death.—*Ibid.*

Take her up tenderly,
Lift her with care.—*Ibid.*

**Joseph Hopkinson.**

Hail, Columbia! happy land!
Hail, ye heroes! heaven-born band!

*Hail Columbia.*

**Samuel Howard.**

Gentle Shepherd, tell me where?—*Song.*

**Leigh Hunt.**

And lo! Ben Adhem's name led all the rest.

*Abou Ben Adhem.*

**Samuel Johnson.**

Fears of the brave! and follies of the wise!

*Vanity of Human Wishes.*

How small, of all that human hearts endure.
That part which laws or kings can cause or cure!

*Lines added to Goldsmith's Traveller.*

Slow rises worth by poverty depress'd.

*Vanity of Human Wishes.*

Superfluous lags the veteran on the stage.—*Ibid.*

To point a moral, or adorn a tale.—*Ibid.*

**Sir William Jones.**

Men who their duties know,
But know their rights, and knowing, dare maintain.

*Ode in imitation of Alcaeus.*

**Ben Jonson.**

Drink to me only with thine eyes,
And I will pledge with mine;
Or leave a kiss within the cup,
And I'll not look for wine.—*To Celia.*

He was not for an age, but for all time.

*To the memory of Shakespeare.*

**John Keats.**

A thing of beauty is a joy forever.—*Endymion.*

Heard melodies are sweet, but those unheard are sweeter.

*Ode on a Grecian Urn.*

That large utterance of the early gods.—*Hyperion.*

**J. P. Kemble.**

Perhaps it was right to dissemble your love,
But why did you kick me down stairs?—*The Panel.*

**Thomas Ken.**

Praise God, from whom all blessings flow,
Praise Him all creatures here below!
*Morning and Evening Hymn.*

**Francis S. Key.**

And the star-spangled banner, O long may it wave
O'er the land of the free and the home of the brave!
*The Star-spangled Banner.*

**Nathaniel Lee.**

Then he will talk—good gods! how he will talk!
*Alexander the Great.*

When Greeks joined Greeks, then was the tug of war.—*Ibid.*

**Henry W. Longfellow.**

And the night shall be filled with music,
And the cares that infest the day
Shall fold their tents like the Arabs,
And as silently steal away.—*The Day is Done.*

Art is long, and Time is fleeting.—*A Psalm of Life.*

Know how sublime a thing it is
To suffer and be strong.—*The Light of Stars.*

Lives of great men all remind us
We can make our lives sublime;
And, departing, leave behind us,
Footprints on the sands of time.—*A Psalm of Life.*

Sail on, O ship of state!
Sail on, O Union, strong and great!—*Building of the Ship.*

There is a Reaper whose name is Death.
*The Reaper and the Flowers.*

There is no flock, however watched and tended,
But one dead lamb is there!
There is no fireside, howsoe'er defended,
But has one vacant chair.—*Resignation.*

**Richard Lovelace.**

I could not love thee, dear, so much
Loved I not honor more.
*To Lucasta, on going to the Wars.*

Stone walls do not a prison make,
Nor iron bars a cage.—*To Althea, from Prison.*

**James Russell Lowell.**

And what is so rare as a day in June.
Then, if ever, come perfect days.
*The Vision of Sir Launfal.*

An' you'v gut to git up airly,
Ef you want to take in God.—*The Biglow Papers.*

Don't never prophesy onless ye know.—*Ibid.*

But John P.
Robinson, he
Sez they didn't know everythin' down in Judee.—*Ibid.*

Truth forever on the scaffold, Wrong forever on the throne.
*The Present Crisis.*

We kind o'thought Christ went agin war an' pillage.
*The Biglow Papers.*

**Edward Bulwer Lytton.**

Beneath the rule of men entirely great,
The pen is mightier than the sword.—*Richelieu.*

In the lexicon of youth, which fate reserves
For a bright manhood, there is no such word
As—*fail.*—*Ibid.*

Frank, haughty, rash.—the Rupert of debate.
*The New Timon.*

**Christopher Marlow.**

And I will make thee beds of roses,
And a thousand fragrant posies.
*The Passionate Shepherd to his Love.*

Infinite riches in a little room.—*The Jew of Malta.*

Who ever loved that loved not at first sight?
*Hero and Leander.*

**John Milton.**

All hell broke loose.—*Paradise Lost.*

And storied windows richly dight
Casting a dim, religious light.—*Il Penseroso.*

At whose sight all the stars,
Hide their diminish'd heads.—*Paradise Lost.*

Better to reign in hell than serve in heaven.—*Ibid.*

Come, and trip it as you go
On the light fantastic toe.—*L'Allegro.*

Confusion worse confounded.—*Paradise Lost.*

To noon he fell, from noon to dewy eve.—*Ibid.*

Gorgons and Hydras, and Chimæras dire.—*Ibid.*

Grace was in all her steps, heaven in her eye,
In every gesture dignity and love.—*Ibid.*

Grinned horrible a ghastly smile.—*Ibid.*

Hail, holy light! offspring of heaven first born.—*Ibid.*

I was all ear,
And took in strains that might create a soul,
Under the ribs of death.—*Momus.*

In notes with many a winding bout,
Of linked sweetness long drawn out.—*L'Allegro.*

Married to immortal verse.—*L'Allegro.*

O'er many a frozen, many a fiery Alp.—*Paradise Lost.*

Peace hath her victories
No less renowned than war.
*To the Lord General Cromwell.*

That old man eloquent.—*To the Lady Margaret Ley.*

The mind is its own place, and in itself
Can make a heaven of hell, a hell of heaven.
*Paradise Lost.*

The world was all before them, where to choose
Their place of rest, and Providence their guide.—*Ibid.*

They also serve who only stand and wait.
*On his blindness.*

Things unattempted yet in prose or rhyme.—*Paradise Lost.*

To-morrow to fresh woods and pastures new.—*Lycidas.*

To sport with Amaryllis in the shade,
Or with the tangles of Neæra's hair.—*Ibid.*

Where perhaps some beauty lies,
The cynosure of neighboring eyes.—*L'Allegro.*

Without the meed of some melodious tear.—*Lycidas.*

**James Montgomery.**

Friend after friend departs,—
Who hath not lost a friend?
There is no union here of hearts,
That finds not here an end.—*Friends.*

Prayer is the soul's sincere desire,
Uttered or unexpressed.—*What is Prayer?*

'Tis not the whole of life to live,
Nor all of death to die.—*The Issues of Life and Death.*

**The Marquis of Montrose.**

He either fears his fate too much,
Or his deserts are small,
That dares not put it to the touch
To gain or lose it all.—*My Dear and only Love.*

**Thomas Moore.**

But the trail of the serpent is over them all.
*Paradise and the Peri.*

But there's nothing half so sweet in life
As love's young dream.—*Love's Young Dream.*

Earth has no sorrow that Heaven cannot heal.
*Sacred Songs.*

Go where glory waits thee;
But while fame elates thee,
O, still remember me.—*Irish Melodies.*

O, ever thus, from childhood's hour,
I've seen my fondest hopes decay.—*The Fire Worshipers.*

My only books
Were woman's looks.—*The Time I've lost.*

Oft in the stilly night
Ere slumber's chain has bound me,
Fond memory brings the light
Of other days around me.—*Oft in the Stilly Night.*

The harp that once through Tara's halls
The soul of music shed.—*The Harp that once.*

Those evening bells! those evening bells!
How many a tale their music tells.—*Those Evening Bells.*

'Tis the last rose of summer,
Left blooming alone.—*The Last Rose of Summer.*

You may break, you may shatter the vase if you will,
But the scent of the rose will hang round it still.
*Farewell! But whenever you welcome the hour.*

**George P. Morris.**

The union of hearts—the union of hands,—
And the Flag of our Union forever!—*The Flag of our Union.*

**William Morris.**

The idle singer of an empty day.—*The Earthly Paradise.*

**Thomas Moss.**

Pity the sorrows of a poor old man.—*The Beggar.*

**Thomas Otway.**

Angels are painted fair to look like you;
There's in you all that we believe of heaven;
Amazing brightness, purity, and truth,
Eternal joy and everlasting love.—*Venice Preserved.*

**Robert T. Paine.**

And ne'er shall the sons of Columbia be slaves,
While the earth bears a plant, or the sea rolls its waves.
*Adams and Liberty.*

**John Howard Payne.**

'Mid pleasures and palaces though we may roam,
Be it ever so humble, there's no place like home.
*Home, Sweet Home.*

**George Peele.**

His golden locks time hath to silver turned.
*Polyhymnia.*

**Edgar A. Poe.**

Take thy beak from out my heart, and take thy form from off my door!
Quoth the raven, "Nevermore."—*The Raven.*

**Alexander Pope.**

Damn with faint praise, assent with civil leer,
And without sneering, teach the rest to sneer.
*Epistle to Dr. Arbuthnot.*

I lisped in numbers, for the numbers came.—*Ibid.*

A little learning is a dangerous thing;
Drink deep, or taste not the Pierian spring.
*Essay on Criticism.*

For fools rush in where angels fear to tread.—*Ibid.*

To err is human, to forgive divine.—*Ibid.*

True wit is nature to advantage dress'd,
What oft was thought, but ne'er so well express'd.—*Ibid.*

All are but parts of one stupendous whole.—*Essay on Man.*

An honest man's the noblest work of God.—*Ibid.*

From grave to gay, from lively to severe.—*Ibid.*

Honor and shame from no conditions rise,
Act well your part, there all the honor lies.—*Ibid.*

Lo, the poor Indian! whose untutored mind
Sees God in clouds, or hears Him in the wind.—*Ibid.*

The proper study of mankind is man.—*Ibid.*

The wisest, brightest, meanest of mankind. [Bacon.]—*Ibid.*

Vice is a monster of so frightful mien,
As, to be hated, needs but to be seen;
Yet seen too oft, familiar with her face,
We first endure, then pity, then embrace.—*Ibid.*

Whatever is, is right.—*Ibid.*

Worth makes the man, the want of it, the fellow.—*Ibid.*

Just as the twig is bent, the tree's inclined.—*Ibid.*

Who shall decide, when doctors disagree?—*Ibid.*

**Matthew Prior.**

Be to her virtues very kind!
Be to her faults a little blind.—*An English Padlock.*

Fine by degrees, and beautifully less.—*Henry and Emma.*

**Sir Walter Raleigh.**

Fear not to touch the best,
The truth shall be thy warrant;
Go, since I needs must die,
And give the world the lie.—*The Lie.*

The shallows murmur, but the deeps are dumb.
*The Silent Lover.*

**The Earl of Rochester.**

Here lies our sovereign lord the king,
Whose word no man relies on;
He never says a foolish thing,
Nor ever does a wise one.
*Epigram on Charles II.*

**Samuel Rogers.**

Not dead, but gone before.—*Human Life.*

To know her was to love her.—*Jacqueline.*

**Nicholas Rowe.**

Is this, that haughty, gallant, gay Lothario?—*The fair Penitent.*

**Sir Walter Scott.**

And dar'st thou then
To beard the lion in his den,
The Douglas in his hall?—*Marmion.*

Breathes there a man, with soul so dead,
Who never to himself hath said,
This is my own, my native land!
*Lay of the Last Minstrel.*

"Charge, Chester, charge! on, Stanley, on!"
Were the last words of Marmion.—*Marmion.*

O woman! in our hours of ease,
Uncertain, coy, and hard to please,
. . . . . .
When pain and anguish wring the brow,
A ministering angel thou.—*Marmion.*

Unwept, unhonored, and unsung.—*Lay of the Last Minstrel.*

**William Shakespeare.**

A collection of the most familiar Shakespearean quotations will be found on the following page.

**Percy Bysshe Shelley.**

The pilgrim of eternity. [Lord Byron.]—*Adonais.*

We look before and after,
And pine for what is not;
Our sincerest laughter
With some pain is fraught!
Our sweetest songs are those that tell of saddest thought.
*To a Skylark.*

**Robert Southey.**

"But what good came of it at last?"
Quoth little Peterkin.
"Why, that I cannot tell," said he,
"But 'twas a famous victory.
*The Battle of Blenheim.*

They sin who tells us Love can die.—*The Curse of Kehama.*

**Edmund Spenser.**

A bold bad man.—*Faerie Queene.*

Be bold, be bold; and everywhere be bold.—*Ibid.*

Dan [*Lord, master*] Chaucer, well of English undefiled.—*Ibid.*

**Sir John Suckling.**

Her feet beneath her petticoat
Like little mice stole in and out.—*Ballad upon a Wedding.*

Why so pale and wan, fond love?
Prithee, why so pale?—*Song.*

**Algernon C. Swinburne.**

The lilies and languors of virtue,
For the roses and raptures of vice.—*Dolores.*

**Alfred Tennyson.**

And thus he bore without abuse
The grand old name of gentleman.—*In Memoriam.*

Better fifty years of Europe than a cycle of Cathay.
*Locksley Hall.*

Blow, bugle, blow; set the wild echoes flying,
Blow, bugle; answer echoes, dying, dying, dying.
*The Princess.*

But O! for the touch of a vanish'd hand,
And the sound of a voice that is still!—*Break, break, break.*

But the tender grace of a day that is dead
Will never come back to me.—*Ibid.*

I am a part of all that I have met.—*Ulysses.*

I hold it truth, with him who sings
To one clear harp in divers tones,
That men may rise on stepping stones
Of their dead selves to higher things.—*In Memoriam.*

In the spring a young man's fancy lightly turns to thoughts of love.—*Locksley Hall.*

Kind hearts are more than coronets,
And simple faith than Norman blood.
*Lady Clara Vere de Vere.*

Ring out, wild bells to the wild sky.—*In Memoriam.*

Tears, idle tears, I know not what they mean.
*The Princess.*

'Tis better to have loved and lost,
Than never to have loved at all.—*In Memoriam.*

You must wake and call me early, call me early, mother dear.
*The May-Queen.*

**James Thomson.**

Come gentle Spring! ethereal Mildness! come.—*The Seasons.*

Delightful task! to rear the tender thought,
To teach the young idea how to shoot.—*The Seasons.*

Rule Britannia! Britannia rules the waves!
Britons never shall be slaves.—*Alfred.*

Sigh'd, and looked unutterable things.—*The Seasons.*

**John Tobin.**

The man that lays his hand upon a woman,
Save in the way of kindness, is a wretch,
Whom 'twere gross flattery to name a coward.
*The Honey-moon.*

**John Trumbull.**

No man e'er felt the halter draw,
With good opinion of the law.—*M'Fingal.*

**John G. Whittier.**

For of all sad words of tongue or pen,
The saddest are these: "It might have been."
*Maud Muller.*

The hope of all who suffer,
The dread of all who wrong.
*The Mantle of St. John de Matha.*

**Charles Wolfe.**

Not a drum was heard, not a funeral note,
As his corse to the ramparts we hurried.
*The Burial of Sir John Moore.*

We carved not a line, and we raised not a stone,
But we left him alone in his glory.—*Ibid.*

**William Wordsworth.**

A perfect woman, nobly planned,
To warn, to comfort, and command.
*She was a Phantom of Delight.*

Elysian beauty, melancholy grace.—*Laodamia.*

Plain living and high thinking are no more.
*Written in London*, 1802.

The Child is father of the Man.—*My Heart Leaps Up.*

The good die first!
And they whose hearts are dry as summer dust,
Burn to the socket.—*The Excursion.*

The light that never was on sea or land.
*Suggested by a picture of Peele Castle in a storm.*

The monumental pomp of age.
Was in their goodly personage.
*The White Doe of Rylstone.*

Heaven lies about us in our infancy.
*Imitation of Immortality.*

The vision and the faculty divine.—*The Excursion.*

**Edward Young.**

An undevout astronomer is mad.—*Night Thoughts.*

Death loves a shining mark, a signal blow.—*Ibid.*

How blessings brighten as they take their flight!—*Ibid.*

Insatiate archer! could not one suffice?—*Ibid.*

Tired Nature's sweet restorer, balmy sleep!—*Ibid.*

A BRIGHT particular star.—My friends were poor but honest.—The inaudible and noiseless foot of time.—***All's Well that Ends Well.***

Age cannot wither her, nor custom stale her infinite variety.—It beggared all description.—Let's do it after the high Roman fashion.—My salad days, when I was green in judgment.—***Antony and Cleopatra.***

All the world's a stage, and all the men and women merely players.—And thereby hangs a tale.—Finds tongues in trees, books in the running brooks, sermons in stones, and good in everything.—Full of strange oaths, and bearded like the pard.—Full of wise saws and modern instances.—Sweet are the uses of adversity.—***As You Like It.***

Angels and ministers of grace defend us.—And then it started like a guilty thing, upon a fearful summons.—Brevity is the soul of wit.—But soft! methink I scent the morning air.—Cut off even in the blossom of my sin.—Dead, for a ducat, dead.—Diseases desperate grown, by desperate appliances are relieved.—False as dicers oaths.—Frailty, thy name is woman!—Give thy thoughts no tongue.—He was a man, take him for all in all, I shall not look upon his like again.—Hyperion to a Satyr.—Hyperion's curls; the front of Jove himself; An eye like Mars to threaten and command.—I could a tale unfold.—Imperial Cæsar dead, and turned to clay, Might stop a hole to keep the wind away.—In my mind's eye, Horatio.—Lay her i' the earth; And from her fair and unpolluted flesh, may violets spring.—Lay not that fluttering unction to your soul.—Like Niobe, all tears.—Making night hideous.—Meat it is, I set it down, that one may smile, and smile, and be a villain.—More honor'd in the breach than the observance.—More in sorrow than in anger.—Like sweet bells jangled out of tune and harsh.—Nymph in thy orisons, be all my sins remembered.—O, my offense is rank, it smells to heaven!—O, that this too, too solid flesh would melt.—Rest, rest, perturbed spirit.—Something is rotten in the state of Denmark.—Sweets to the sweet.—The time is out of joint; O, cursed spite! That ever I was born to set it right.—The undiscovered country, from whose bourne no traveler returns.—There's a divinity that shapes our ends, rough hew them how we will.—Thrift, thrift, Horatio!—To be, or not to be; that is the question.—To the manner born.—What's Hecuba to him, or he to Hecuba?—When we have shuffled off this mortal coil.—***Hamlet.***

Ambition should be made of sterner stuff.—Cry havoc and let slip the dogs of war.—For Brutus is an honorable man; So are they all, all honorable men.—His life was gentle, and the elements so mixed in him, that Nature might stand up and say to all the world, "This was a man!"—I had rather be a dog and bay the moon, than such a Roman.—If you have tears, prepare to shed them now.—The evil that men do lives after them; The good is oft interred with their bones.—This was the most unkindest cut of all.—This was the noblest Roman of them all.—Though last, not least in love.—***Julius Cæsar.***

But if it be a sin to covet honor, I am the most offending soul alive.—Once more unto the breach, dear friends, once more, or close the wall up with our English dead.—Familiar in their mouths as household words.—***King Henry V.***

A poor, infirm, weak, and despised old man.—Ay, every inch a king. | Blow, winds, and crack your cheeks!—Her voice was ever soft, gentle, and low—an excellent thing in woman.—How sharper than a serpent's tooth it is, to have a thankless child.—More sinn'd against than sinning.—***King Lear.***

A horse! a horse! my kingdom for a horse!—Give me another horse!—bind up my wounds!—Now is the winter of our discontent made glorious summer by this sun of York.—O, coward conscience, how dost thou afflict me!—Off with his head!—***King Richard III.***

A deed without a name.—After life's fitful fever, he sleeps well,—Blow wind! come, wrack! At least we'll die with harness on our back.—Can'st thou not minister to a mind diseas'd?—Come what come may, Time and the hour runs through the roughest day.—Curses, not loud, but deep.—Double, double toil and trouble.—Dwindle, peak, and pine.—Fair is foul, and foul is fair.—Golden opinions from all sorts of people.—Hear it not, Duncan; for it is a knell, That summons thee to Heaven or to Hell.—Hence horrible shadow! Unreal mockery, hence!—I dare do all that may become a man; who dares do more is none.—I 'gin to be a-weary of the sun—I'll make assurance doubly sure.—Is this a dagger which I see before me?—Lay on, Macduff, and damn'd be him that first cries, "Hold, enough!"—Letting "I dare not," wait upon "I would."—It is a tale told by an idiot, full of sound and fury, signifying nothing.—My hand will rather the multitudinous seas incarnadine.—My way of life is fall'n into the sear, the yellow leaf.—Nothing in his life became him like the leaving it.—Now, good digestion wait on appetite.—Screw your courage to the sticking-place.—The deep damnation of his taking-off.—Thou can'st not say I did it; never shake thy gory locks at me.—Throw physic to the dogs.—***Macbeth.***

A looker on here in Vienna.—Drest in a little brief authority.—Plays such fantastic tricks before high Heaven, as make the angels weep.—***Measure for Measure.***

A Daniel come to judgment.—How sweet the moonlight sleeps upon this bank.—I am Sir Oracle, and, when I ope my lips, let no dog bark!—Now, infidel, I have thee on the hip.—The devil can cite Scripture for his purpose.—The man that hath no music in himself, nor is not mov'd with concord of sweet sounds, is fit for treason's stratagems and spoils.—The quality of mercy is not strain'd.—***Merchant of Venice.***

I'll put a girdle round about the earth.—In maiden meditation, fancy-free.—The course of true love never did run smooth.—The poet's eye, in a fine frenzy rolling.—***Midsummer Night's Dream.***

A round, unvarnished tale.—And smooth as monumental alabaster.—But I will wear my heart upon my sleeve, for daws to peck at.—Farewell! Othello's occupation's gone.—Good name in man or woman, dear my lord, is the immediate jewel of their souls.—Of one that loved, not wisely, but too well.—On horror's head horrors accumulate.—She swore,—in faith, 'twas strange, 'twas passing strange; 'twas pitiful, 'twas wondrous pitiful.—The very head and front of my offending.—Trifles, light as air.—***Othello.***

He jests at scars, that never felt a wound.—How silver-sweet sound lovers' tongues at night.—It is the East, and Juliet is the sun.—O, that I were a glove upon that hand; That I might touch that cheek.—O, Romeo, Romeo! wherefore art thou Romeo?—Parting is such sweet sorrow.—What's in a name? that which we call a rose, by any other name would smell as sweet.—***Romeo and Juliet.***

Deeper than did ever plummet sound.—From the still-vex'd Bermoothes.—In the dark backward and abysm of time.—The cloud-capp'd towers, the gorgeous palaces, the solemn temples, the great globe itself, yea, all which it inherit, shall dissolve, and like this insubstantial pageant faded, leave not a rack behind.—We are such stuff as dreams are made on; and our little life is rounded with a sleep.—***The Tempest.***

O, it came o'er my ear like the sweet south, that breathes upon a bank of violets, stealing and giving odour.—She never told her love; but let concealment, like a worm i' the bud, feed on her damask cheek.—She sat, like Patience on a monument, smiling at grief.—***Twelfth Night.***

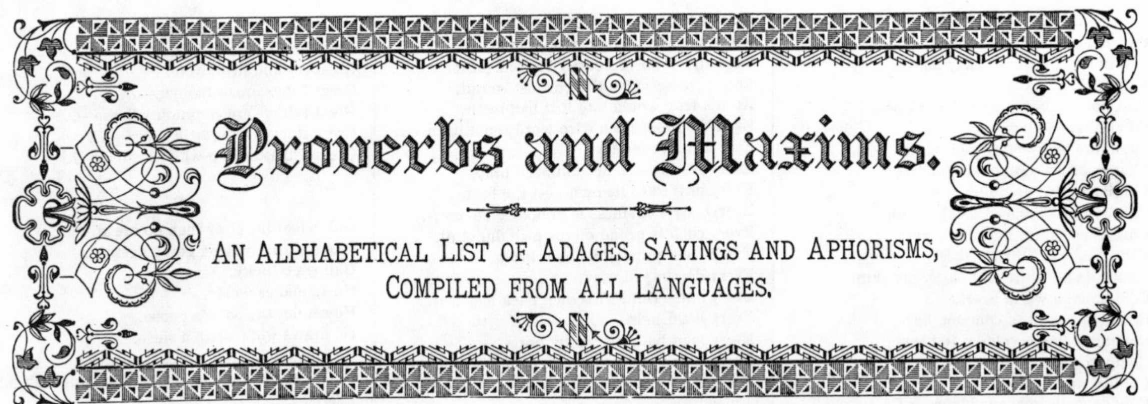

# Proverbs and Maxims.

## An Alphabetical List of Adages, Sayings and Aphorisms, Compiled from All Languages.

"Jewels five words long,
That on the stretched forefinger of all time
Sparkle forever."—TENNYSON.

PROVERBS are wise or witty sayings of unknown authorship and universal currency. Some well-known proverbs are often attributed to Shakespeare, or Rabelais, or other famous writers in whose works they occur; but these authors merely quote them. They are, as all genuine proverbs are, the offspring of a wisdom and a wit infinitely greater than that of Shakespeare or Rabelais, the homely wisdom, the sly wit of the people. They are the collective experience of many laborious generations. Side by side with famous sayings of the most illustrious authors, we place the works of these thousand nameless philosophers and wits; nor will the comparison be entirely to the disadvantage of the latter.

The present collection includes the principal English proverbs, and the most interesting ones (not found in English) from the French, Italian, German, Spanish, Portuguese, Dutch, and Danish languages. It should be said that most of the proverbs here given as English, occur in one form or another in many of the Continental languages; but none are here specially credited to another language if they are found in the English collections.

*F.* stands for French; *D.* for Dutch; *Dan.* for Danish; *G.* for German; *I.* for Italian: *P.* for Portuguese, and *S,* for Spanish.

### A.

A bad penny always comes back.
A bald head is soon shaved.
A bargain is a bargain.
A bird in the hand is worth two in the bush.
A bow long bent at last waxeth weak.
A braying ass eats little hay.—*I.*
A burnt child dreads the fire.
A cat has nine lives, and a woman has nine cats' lives.
A cat may look at a king.
A chip of the old block.
A clear conscience is a good pillow.—*F.*
A contented mind is a continual feast.
A dog in the manger, that neither eats nor lets others eat.—*P.*
A drowning man will catch at a straw.
A fair exchange is no robbery.
A fool and his money are soon parted.
A fool may ask more questions in an hour than a wise man can answer in seven years.
A fool's bolt is soon shot.
A friend in need is a friend indeed.
A good name is better than riches.
A green winter makes a fat churchyard.
A liar must have a good memory.
A living dog is better than a dead lion.
A man may lead his horse to water but cannot make him drink.
A man's house is his castle.
A penny saved is a penny gained.
A pitcher that goes oft to the well is broken at last.
A rolling stone gathers no moss.
A short horse is soon curried.
A stitch in time saves nine.
A word to the wise is sufficient.
All cats are gray in the night.—*F.*
All is not gold that glitters.
All's well that ends well.
All roads lead to Rome.—*I.*
All work and no play make Jack a dull boy.
All your geese are swans.
Always in love, never married.—*F.*
An honest miller has a golden thumb.
An inch in a man's nose is much.
As a cat loves mustard.
As busy as a bee.
As clear as a bell.
As cross as a bear with a sore head.
As dark as pitch.
As drunk as a lord.
As good out of the world as out of fashion.
As like as two peas.
As merry as a cricket.
As plain as a pike-staff.
As poor as a church-mouse.
As you make your bed, so you must lie in it.
As you sow, you shall reap.
At Rome, do as the Romans do.

### B.

Bachelors' wives and maids' children are well taught.
Bad news travels fast.
Barking dogs seldom bite.
Beauty is but skin deep.
Beggars must not be choosers.
Better alone than in bad company.
Better bend than break.
Better fall from the window than the roof.
Better late than never.
Better lose a jest than a friend.
Birds of a feather flock together.
Blind men should not judge of colors.
Blood is thicker than water.
Borrowed garments never set well.
Brag's a good dog, but Holdfast's a better.
Brave actions never want a trumpet.
Bring up a raven and he will peck out your eyes.—*G.*
Broken sacks will hold no corn.
Burning the candle at both ends.
Buy and sell, and live by the loss.
Buying is cheaper than asking.—*G.*
By candle-light a goat looks like a lady.—*F.*
By hook or by crook.
By Tre, Pol, and Pen, you shall know the Cornish men.
By and by is easily said.

C.

Can you make a pipe of a pig's tail ?
Cap in hand never did any harm.—*I.*
Care will kill a cat.
Cast not the helve after the hatchet.
Catch that catch can.
Catch the bear before you sell his skin.
Change of pasture makes fat calves.
Charity begins at home.
Children and fools speak the truth.
Christmas comes but once a year.
Claw me, and I'll claw thee.
Close sits my shirt, but closer my skin.
Cold hand, a warm heart.
Common fame is a common liar.
Common fame is seldom to blame.
Comparisons are odious.
Confess and be hanged.
Confidence begets confidence.—*G.*
Conscience is as good as a thousand witnesses. —*I.*
Constant dropping wears the stone.
Cooks are not to be taught in their own kitchen.
Counsel is no command.
Counsel over cups is crazy.
Count not your chickens before they're hatched.
Cover yourself with honey, and the flies will have at you.
Cowards are cruel.
Cowards have no luck.—*G.*
Creaking carts last the longest.—*D.*
Credit is dead ; bad pay killed it.—*I.*
Creditors have better memories than debtors.
Crooked by nature is never made straight by education.
Crooked logs make straight fires.
Crows are never the whiter for washing themselves.
Crows bewail the dead sheep and then eat them.
Crows do not peck out crows' eyes.—*P.*
Custom is a second nature.
Cut your coat according to your cloth.

D.

Danger past, God is forgotten.
Daughter-in-law hates mother-in-law.—*G.*
Daughters and dead fish are no keeping wares.
Dead dogs don't bite.—*D.*
Death defies the doctor.
Death is the grand leveler.
Deep swimmers and high climbers seldom die in their beds.—*D.*
Delays are dangerous.
Desperate ills require desperate remedies.
Diamond cut diamond.
Do not halloo till you are out of the wood.
Do not hang all on one nail.—*G.*
Don't buy a pig in a poke.
Don't reckon without your host.
Don't teach fishes to swim.—*F.*
Drink little that ye may drink lang.
Drop by drop fills the tub.—*F.*
Drunken folks seldom take harm.

E.

Each bird loves to hear himself sing.
Eagles catch no fleas.
Early ripe, early rotten.
Early to bed, early to rise, makes a man healthy, wealthy, and wise.
East or west, home is best.
Eat at pleasure, drink by measure.
Eggs and oaths are easily broken.—*Dan.*
Empty vessels give the greatest sound.
Even a frog would bite if it had teeth.
Even the fool says a wise word sometimes.—*I.*
Ever drunk, ever dry.
Every ass loves to hear himself bray.
Every bird likes its own nest the best.
Everybody's business is nobody's business.
Every cock is proud on his own dunghill.
Every cook praises his own broth.
Every dog has his day.
Every horse thinks his own pack heaviest.
Every little helps.
Every man hath his hobby horse.
Every man is the son of his own works.
Every man must eat a peck of dirt before he dies.
Every one can keep house better than her mother till she trieth.
Every one hath a penny for a new ale-house.
Every rose has its thorn.—*I.*
Everything has a beginning.—*F.*
Every tide has its ebb.
Every tub must stand on its own bottom.
Every why has its wherefore.
Evil communications corrupt good manners.
Example is better than precept.
Experience is the mistress of fools.
Extremes meet.—*F.*

F.

Faint heart ne'er won fair lady.
Fair and softly goes far.—*P.* and *F.*
Fair words and rotten apples.—*I.*
Fair words butter no parsnips.
Far from the eyes, far from the heart.
Fast bind, fast find.
Few have luck, all have death.
Few words are best.
Fire and water are good servants, but bad masters.
First come, first served.
Fools build houses, and wise men buy them.
Forbidden fruit is sweet.
Forewarned, forearmed.
Fortune favors the brave.
Fortune favors fools.
Foul linen should be washed at home.—*F.*
Froth is not beer.
Funeral sermon, lying sermon.—*G.*

G.

Give a dog an ill name and hang him.
Give a rogue an inch and he will take an ell.—*D.*
Give a thief rope enough and he'll hang himself.
Give even the devil his due.
Give to him that has.—*I.*
Go farther and fare worse.
God alone understands fools.—*F.*
God deliver me from a man of one book.
God gives a cursed cow short horns.—*I.*
God helps those who help themselves.
God send you more wit and me more money.
God tempers the wind to the shorn lamb.—*F.*
Gold is proved in the fire, friendship in need.—*Dan.*
Good ale is meat, drink, and cloth.
Good tree, good fruit.—*D.*
Good wine needs no bush.
Good words fill not a sack.
Great boast, small roast.
Great cry and little wool.
Great fishes break the net.—*D.*
Great talkers are commonly liars.—*G.*
Great thieves hang little ones.—*F.*
Green Christmas, a white Easter.—*G.*

H.

Half a loaf is better than no bread.
Hanging and wiving go by destiny.
Happy go lucky.
Haste makes waste.
He cannot say *bo* to a goose.
He draws water with a sieve.
He gives twice that gives in a trice.
He has need of a long spoon that sups with the devil.
He has a bee in his bonnet.
He has given leg bail.
He has two strings to his bow.
He is nothing but skin and bones.
He is teaching iron to swim.
He is up to snuff.
He knows which side of his bread is buttered.
He lies as fast as a horse can trot.
He must needs go where the devil drives.
He takes the bull by the horns.
He that is born to be hanged shall never be drowned.
He that waits for dead men's shoes may go long enough barefoot.
He will never set the Thames on fire.
He would bite a cent in two.—*D.*
He would flay a flint.
He would slaughter a bug to drink its blood.—*I.*
He'd skin a louse and send the hide to market.
He'll swear the devil out of hell.
Hell and chancery are always open.
Hell is paved with good intentions.
His bark is worse than his bite.
His bread is buttered on both sides.
His room's better than his company.
Hit the nail on the head.
Home is home, be it ever so homely.
Honesty is the best policy.
Hunger is the best sauce.

I.

I can see as far into a millstone as another man.
I have a crow to pluck with you.
I have other fish to fry.
I smell a rat.
I would not touch him with a pair of tongs.
If the mountain will not go to Mahomet, Mahomet must go to the mountain.
If the sky falls, we shall catch larks.
If the young man knew, if the old man could, there is nothing but would be done.—*F.*
If today will not, to-morrow may.
If wishes were horses, beggars would ride.
If you can kiss the mistress, never kiss the maid.
If you can't get it in bushels, take it in spoonfulls.—*G.*
If you swear, you'll catch no fish.
Ill got, ill spent.
Ill gotten goods seldom prosper.
Ill weeds grow apace.

In at one ear and out at the other.
In for a penny, in for a pound.
It is a long lane that has no turning.
It is a silly fish that is caught twice with the same bait.
It is an ill-wind that blows nobody good.
It is better to be a beggar than a fool.
It is good to have two strings to one's bow.
It is good to sleep in a whole skin.
It is hard to teach an old dog tricks.—*Dan.*
It is never too late to learn.
It is never too late to mend.
It is not the big oxen that do the best day's work.—*F.*
It is past joking when the head's off.
It is too late to lock the stable door when the steed is stolen.—*F.*
It never rains but it pours.
It is neither rhyme nor reason.
It's not good to wake a sleeping lion.
It's ill jesting with edged tools.—*D.*

J.

Jack of all trades and master of none.
Jacob's voice, Esau's hands.—*G.*
Jest with your equals.—*Dan.*

K.

Ka me, and I'll ka thee.
Keep no more cats than will catch mice.
Keep the wolf from the door.
Keep your nose out of another's mess.—*Dan.*
Keep your breath to cool your porridge.
Kill two birds with one stone.
Kings have long ears.
Kings have long hands.—*F.*
Knowledge is power.

L.

Laws were made for rogues.—*I.*
Lazy folks take the most pains.
Learn to creep before you run.
Let the dead rest.—*G.*
Let the cobbler stick to his last.
Let them laugh that win.
Like blood, like good, and like age, make the happiest marriage.
Like master like man.
Like the tailor who sewed for nothing, and found thread himself.
Little pitchers have great ears,
Little pots soon boil over.—*G.*
Little strokes fell great oaks.
Live and let live.
Lock the stable door before the steed is stolen.
Look not a gift horse in the mouth.
Look to the main chance.
Losers are always in the wrong.—*S.*
Love is blind.
Love me little, love me long
Love me, love my dog.
Lying pays no tax.—*P.*

M.

Maidens say no and mean yes.—*G.*
Make a virtue of necessity.
Make hay while the sun shines.
Make the best of a bad bargain.
Man proposes, God disposes.
Many a slip 'twixt the cup and the lip.
Many a truth is spoken in jest.
Many go out for wool and come home shorn.—*S.*
Many littles make a mickle.
Many talk of Robin Hood that never shot his bow.
Marriages are made in heaven.
Marry in haste, repent at leisure.
Misfortunes never come singly.
Money begets money.
Money makes the mare go.
Much memory and little judgment.—*F.*
Murder will out.
My teeth are nearer than my kindred.—*S.*

N.

Naught is never in danger.
Necessity hath no law.
Necessity is the mother of invention.
Neck or nothing; for the king loves no cripples.
Needs must when the devil drives.
Neither fish nor flesh, nor good red herring.
Never limp before the lame.—*F.*
Never ride a free horse to death.
Never too old to learn.
New brooms sweep clean.
Nine tailors make a man.
No great loss but some small gain.
No man cries stinking fish.
No news is good news.
No sooner said than done.
None so blind as those that won't see.
None so deaf as those that won't hear.
Nothing dries sooner than tears.—*G.*
Nothing is had for nothing.—*F.*
Nothing venture, nothing have.

O.

Of all birds, give me mutton.
Of oil, wine, and friends, the oldest.—*P.*
Of two evils choose the less.
Old birds are not caught with chaff.
Old foxes are hard to catch.—*D.*
One fool makes many.
One good turn deserves another.
One man's meat is another man's poison.
One nail drives out another.
One swallow doesn't make a summer.
One tale is good till another is told.
Opportunity makes the thief.
Our neighbors' children are always the worst. —*G.*
Out of debt out of danger.
Out of sight out of mind.
Out of the frying-pan into the fire.
Oysters are not good in a month that has not an R in it.

P.

Penny wise, pound foolish.
Physician, heal thyself.—*I.* and *G.*
Play with an ass, and he will whisk his tail in your face.—*S.*
Plenty makes dainty.
Poor and proud.
Poor men have no souls.
Poor men's tables are soon spread.
Possession is nine points of the law.
Poverty is no sin.—*F.*
Practice makes perfect.
Praise the sea, but keep on land.
Pride feels no cold.
Pride will have a fall.
Procrastination is the thief of time
Proffered service stinks.
Promises don't fill the belly.
Put not all your eggs into one basket.—*E.*
Put the light out, and all women are alike.

Q.

Quick at meat, quick at work.
Quick come, quick go.
Quoth the young cock, "I'll neither meddle nor make."

R.

Ragged colts may make fine horses.
Raining cats and dogs.
Rather lose the wool than the sheep.—*P.*
Raw leather will stretch.
Ready money is ready medicine.
Report hangs a man.
Revenge is sweet.
Rich men have no faults.
Riches have wings.
Riches rule the roost.
Rolling stones gather no moss.
Rome was not built in a day.

S.

Safe bind, safe find.
Salt spilled is never all gathered.—*P.*
Saving is getting.
Saying and doing are two things.
See Naples and then die.—*I.*
Seldom seen, soon forgotten.
Set a beggar on horseback, he'll ride to the devil.
Set a thief to catch a thief.
Sharp stomachs make short devotion.
Short and sweet.
Silence gives consent.
Singed cats live long.—*G.*
Six feet of earth makes all men equal.
Small rains lay great dust.
Smoke, raining into the house, and a scolding wife, will make a man run out of doors.
Soon got, soon spent.
Sooner said than done.
Sour grapes, as the fox said when he could not reach them.
Speak the truth and shame the devil.
Speak well of the dead.
Still waters run deep.
Strike while the iron is hot.
Sweat makes good mortar.—*G.*

T.

Take a hair of the same dog that bit you.
Take a man by his word, and a cow by her horns.
Take care of the pence, and the pounds will take care of themselves.
Take the will for the deed.
Take time by the forelock.
Talk of the devil and his imp appears.
Teach your grandame to suck eggs.
Tell me the company you keep, and I'll tell you what you are.
Tell me the moon is made of green cheese.
Tell no tales out of school.
Ten noes are better than one lie.—*Dan.*
That must be true which all men say.
That was laid on with a trowel.
That's the cream of the jest.
The accomplice is as bad as the thief.
The better the day, the better the deed.
The cat is fain the fish to eat, but hath no will to wet her feet.

The course of true love never did run smooth.
The devil was sick, the devil a monk would be; the devil was well, the devil a monk was he.
The early bird catches the worm.
The first cut, and all the loaf besides.
The fox may grow gray, but never good.
The full cask makes no noise.—*I.*
The gray mare is the better horse.
The kettle calls the pot black.
The last drop makes the cup run over.
The lion's not half so fierce as he's painted.
The longest day must have an end.
The longest way round is the shortest way home.—*I.*
The more haste the less speed.
The nearer the church, the farther from God.
The poor man pays for all.
The pot that goes often to the well, comes home broken at last.
The proof of the pudding is in the eating.
The receiver is as bad as the thief.
The remedy is worse than the disease.
The sleeping fox catches no poultry.
The smiles of a pretty woman are the tears of the purse.—*I.*
The sow prefers the mire.—*Dan.*
The sun is never the worse for shining on a dunghill.
The sweeetest grapes hang highest.—*G.*
The thirteenth man brings death.—*D.*
The thunderbolt hath but its clap.
The voice of the people is the voice of God.—*Lat.*
The weakest goes to the wall.
The weeds o'ergrow the corn.
The white coat does not make the miller.—*I.*
The wind keeps not always in one quarter.
The wise drunkard is a sober fool.—*G.*
The wise make jests, and fools repeat them.
The wolf loseth his teeth, but not his inclinations.—*S.*
The worst pig often gets the best pear.
The worth of a thing is what it will bring.
The young cock crows as he heard the old one.
The young may die, the old must die
There are more threatened than struck.
There is a remedy for everything but death.—*F.*
There is a time for all things.
There is no day without the night.—*T.*
There is no disputing of tastes.
There is no fire without some smoke.
There is no love without jealousy.—*F.*
There is no medicine against death.—*I.*
There is no worse joke than a true one.—*I.*
There was never a looking-glass that told a woman she was ugly.—*F. 2.*
There's a salve for every sore.
There's many a slip 'twixt the cup and the lip.
There's no fool like an old fool.
There's nothing new under the sun.—*G.*
They agree like cats and dogs.
They say so is half a lie.
They that hide can find.
They who live in glass houses should not throw stones.
Think much, speak little, and work less.
Thorns make the greatest cracking.
Those who climb high, often have a fall.
Threatened folks live long.
Time and tide wait for no man.
'Tis a wise child that knows its own father.
'Tis better to be happy than wise.
To a good spender God is a treasure.
To a rogue, a rogue and a half.
To add fuel to the fire.
To be hail fellow well met with every one.
To blow hot and cold with the same breath.
To build castles in the air.
To call a spade a spade.
To carry coals to Newcastle.
To catch a Tartar.
To curse with bell, book, and candle.
To give a Roland for an Oliver.
To go the whole hog.
To hold one's nose to the grindstone.
To lead one by the nose.
To make both ends meet.
To-morrow will be another day.—*S.*
To pay one in his own coin.
To piece the lion's skin with that of the fox.—*D.*
To pick a hole in a man's coat.
To put one's nose out of joint.
To rob Peter to pay Paul.
To send one away with a flea in his ear.
To set all at sixes and sevens.
To sow one's wild oats.
To spare at the spigot, and let run through the bung hole.
To strain at a gnat, and swallow a camel.
To strut like a crow in a gutter.
To turn over a new leaf.
To wash a blackamoor white.
Too many cooks spoil the broth.
Too much is stark naught.
Too much wisdom is folly.—*G.*
Touch pitch and you'll be defiled.
Train up a child in the way he should go.
Tread on a worm and it will turn.
Trust, but not too much.
Two eyes see more than one.
Two fools in a house are too many by a couple.
Two heads are better than one.
Two of a trade never agree.

U.

Unkindness has no remedy at law.
Under a good cloak may be a bad man.—*S.*
Union is strength.—*D.*
Unknown, unkissed.
Unlooked for, often comes.—*G.*
Unwilling service earns no thanks.—*Dan.*
Use soft words and hard arguments.

V.

Vain glory blossoms, but never bears.
Varnishing hides a crack.
Venture a small fish to catch a great.
Venture not all in one bottom.
Very good corn grows in little fields.—*F.*
Vipers breed vipers.—*Dan.*
Virtue is its own reward.
Virtue never dies.—*G.*
Vows made in storms are forgotten in calms.

W.

Wait is a hard word to the hungry.—*G.*
Wake not a sleeping lion.
Walls have ears.
Want is the mother of industry.
Waste makes want.
Waste not, want not.
We cannot all be Pope of Rome.—*G.*
We shall see, as the blind man said.—*F.*
Wedlock's a padlock.
Weeds want no sowing.
Well begun is half done.
Well lathered is half shaven.
Were it not for "if," and "but," we should all be rich for ever.—*F.*
What a dust have I raised, quoth the fly upon the coach.
What belongs to the public belongs to nobody.
What cannot be cured must be endured.
What is one man's meat is another man's poison.
What is sauce for the goose is sauce for the gander.
What three know, everybody knows.—*S.*
What you do yourself is well done.—*Dan.*
When a dog is drowning, every one offers him water.
When Adam delved and Eve span, where was then the gentleman?
When drink enters, wisdom departs.—*S.*
When God pleases, it rains with every wind.
When it thunders, the thief becomes honest.
When rogues fall out, honest men come by their own.
When the cat's away, the mice will play.
When the devil grows old, he turns hermit.—*F.*
When the fool has made up his mind, the market is over.—*S.*
When the fox preaches, beware of your geese.
When the measure is full, it runs over.—*G.*
When the wine is in, the wit is out.
When the hostess is handsome, the wine is good.—*F.*
Where there's a will, there's a way.
While there's life, there's hope.
Who cannot sing, may whistle.—*G.*
Who has nothing, fears nothing.—*I.*
Who loves not women, wine, and song, he is a fool his whole life long.—*G.*
Who so blind as he that will not see.
Wise men change their minds; fools, never.
Wit may be bought too dear.
With foxes we must play the fox.
Women rouge that they may not blush.—*I.*
Words won't feed cats.—*I.*
Would you live long, be healthy and fat, drink like a dog, and eat like a cat.
Wounds heal, but not ill words.—*S.*

Y.

You are a sweet nut, if you were well cracked.
You are always best when asleep.
You cannot catch old birds with chaff.
You cannot make a silk purse of a sow's ear.
You cannot take a cow from a man who has none.—*Dan.*
You can't eat your cake and have it too.
You come a day after the fair.
You cry out before you are hurt.
You have brought your pigs to a fine market.
You have got the wrong sow by the ear.
You know good manners, but use but few.
You may know the lion by his claw.—*F.*
You must shift your sail with the wind.—*I.*
You must take the fat with the lean.
You pour water into a sieve.
Young dogs have sharp teeth.—*Dan.*
Young gambler, old beggar.—*S.*
Your belly will never let your back be warm.
Your cake is dough.
Your tongue runs before your wit.
Your wits are gone a wool-gathering.
Youth will have its swing.

## THE CROWDED STREET.

WILLIAM CULLEN BRYANT.

LET me move slowly through the street,
Filled with an ever-shifting train,
Amid the sound of steps that beat
The murmuring walks like autumn rain.

How fast the flitting figures come!
The mild, the fierce, the stony face:
Some bright with thoughtless smiles, and some
Where secret tears have left their trace!

They pass—to toil, to strife, to rest:
To halls in which the feast is spread,
To chambers where the funeral guest
In silence sits beside the dead.

And some to happy homes repair,
Where children, pressing cheek to cheek
With mute caresses, shall declare
The tenderness they cannot speak.

And some, who walk in calmness here,
Shall shudder as they reach the door
Where one who made their dwelling dear,
Its flower, its light, is seen no more.

Youth, with pale cheek and slender frame,
And dreams of greatness in thine eye,
Go'st thou to build an early name,
Or early in the task to die?

Keen son of trade, with eager brow,
Who is now fluttering in thy snare?
Thy golden fortunes, tower they now?
Or melt the glittering spires in air?

Who of this crowd to-night shall tread
The dance, till daylight gleams again?
Who sorrow o'er the untimely dead?
Who writhe in throes of mortal pain?

* * * * * * * * *

Each where his tasks or pleasures call,
They pass, and heed each other not;
There is who heeds, who holds them all,
In His large love and boundless thought.

These struggling tides of life, that seem
In wayward, aimless course to tend,
Are eddies of the mighty stream
That rolls to its appointed end.

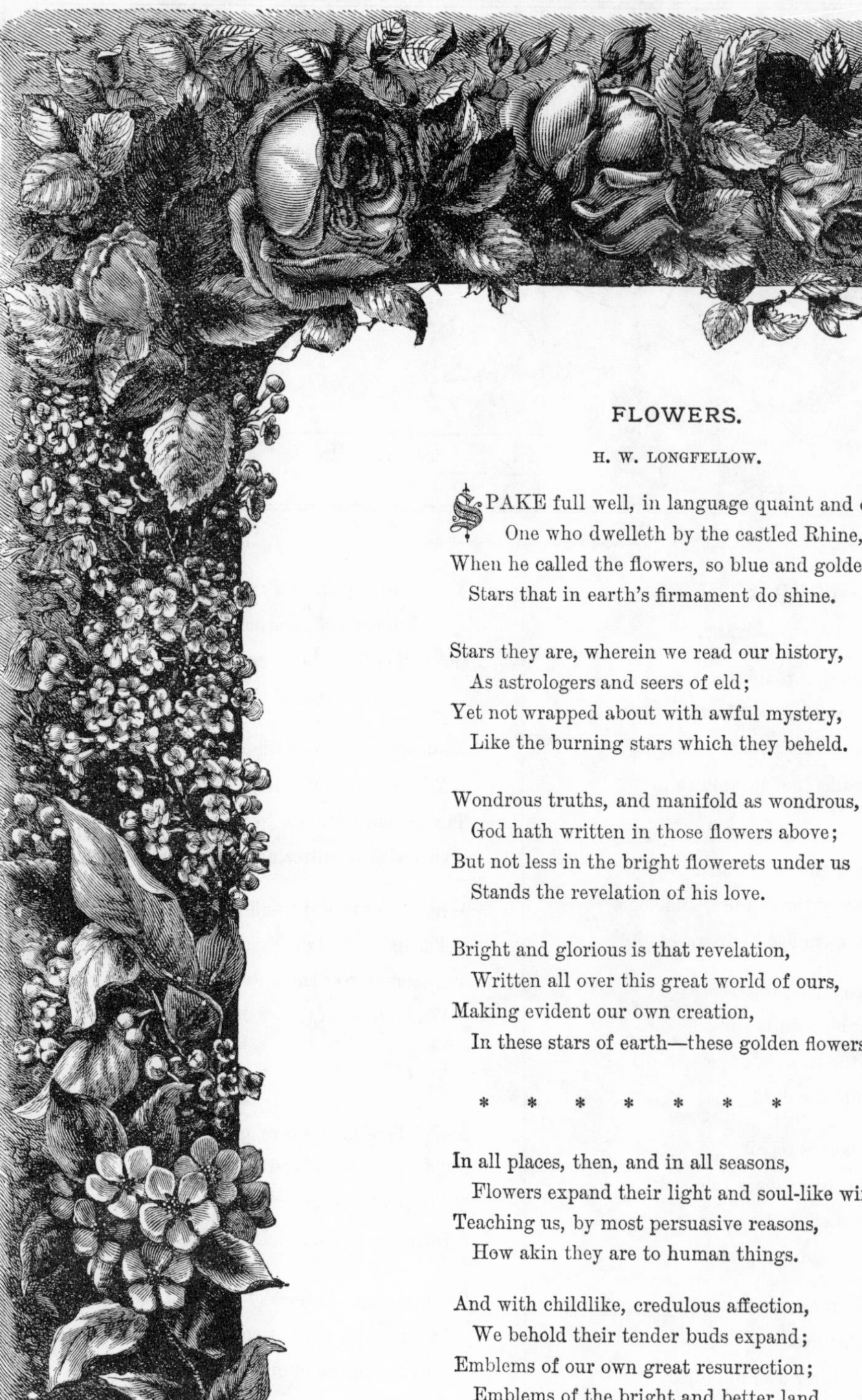

## FLOWERS.

H. W. LONGFELLOW.

SPAKE full well, in language quaint and olden,
One who dwelleth by the castled Rhine,
When he called the flowers, so blue and golden,
Stars that in earth's firmament do shine.

Stars they are, wherein we read our history,
As astrologers and seers of eld;
Yet not wrapped about with awful mystery,
Like the burning stars which they beheld.

Wondrous truths, and manifold as wondrous,
God hath written in those flowers above;
But not less in the bright flowerets under us
Stands the revelation of his love.

Bright and glorious is that revelation,
Written all over this great world of ours,
Making evident our own creation,
In these stars of earth—these golden flowers.

* * * * * * *

In all places, then, and in all seasons,
Flowers expand their light and soul-like wings,
Teaching us, by most persuasive reasons,
How akin they are to human things.

And with childlike, credulous affection,
We behold their tender buds expand;
Emblems of our own great resurrection;
Emblems of the bright and better land.

## THE DEATH OF THE FLOWERS.

WILLIAM CULLEN BRYANT.

THE melancholy days are come, the saddest of the year,
Of wailing winds, and naked woods, and meadows brown and sear.
Heaped in the hollows of the grove, the autumn leaves lie dead;
They rustle to the eddying gust, and to the rabbit's tread.
The robin and the wren are flown, and from the shrubs the jay,
And from the wood-top calls the crow through all the gloomy day.

Where are the flowers, the fair young flowers, that lately sprang and stood
In brighter light and softer airs, a beauteous sisterhood?
Alas! they all are in their graves; the gentle race of flowers
Are lying in their lowly beds with the fair and good of ours.
The rain is falling where they lie; but the cold November rain
Calls not from out the gloomy earth the lovely ones again.

The wind-flower and the violet, they perished long ago,
And the brier-rose and the orchis died amid the summer glow;
But on the hill the golden-rod, and the aster in the wood,
And the yellow sunflower by the brook in autumn beauty stood,
Till fell the frost from the clear cold heaven, as falls the plague on men,
And the brightness of their smile was gone from upland, glade, and glen.

And now, when comes the calm mild day, as still such days will come,
To call the squirrel and the bee from out their winter home;
When the sound of dropping nuts is heard, though all the trees are still,
And twinkle in the smoky light the waters of the rill,
The south-wind searches for the flowers whose fragrance late he bore,
And sighs to find them in the wood and by the stream no more.

And then I think of one who in her youthful beauty died,
The fair meek blossom that grew up and faded by my side.
In the cold moist earth we laid her, when the forest cast the leaf,
And we wept that one so lovely should have a life so brief;
Yet not unmeet it was that one, like that young friend of ours,
So gentle and so beautiful, should perish with the flowers.

## MAUD MULLER.

JOHN GREENLEAF WHITTIER.

MAUD MULLER, on a summer's day
Raked the meadow sweet with hay.

Beneath her torn hat glowed the wealth
Of simple beauty and rustic health.

Singing, she wrought, and her merry glee
The mock-bird echoed from his tree.

But, when she glanced to the far-off town,
White from its hill-slope looking down,

The sweet song died, and a vague unrest
And a nameless longing filled her breast,—

A wish, that she hardly dared to own,
For something better than she had known.

The Judge rode slowly down the lane,
Smoothing his horse's chestnut mane.

He drew his bridle in the shade
Of the apple-trees, to greet the maid,

And ask a draft from the spring that flowed
Through the meadow, across the road.

She stopped where the cool spring bubbled up,
And filled for him her small tin cup,

And blushed as she gave it, looking down
On her feet so bare, and her tattered gown.

"Thanks!" said the Judge, "a sweeter draught
From a fairer hand was never quaffed."

He spoke of the grass and flowers and trees,
Of the singing birds and the humming bees;

Then talked of the haying, and wondered whether
The cloud in the west would bring foul weather.

And Maud forgot her brier-torn gown,
And her graceful ankles, bare and brown,

And listened, while a pleased surprise
Looked from her long-lashed hazel eyes.

At last, like one who for delay
Seeks a vain excuse, he rode away.

Maud Muller looked and sighed: "Ah me!
That I the Judge's bride might be!

"He would dress me up in silks so fine,
And praise and toast me at his wine.

"My father should wear a broadcloth coat,
My brother should sail a painted boat.

"I'd dress my mother so grand and gay,
And the baby should have a new toy each day.

"And I'd feed the hungry and clothe the poor
And all should bless me who left our door."

The Judge looked back as he climbed the hill,
And saw Maud Muller standing still:

"A form more fair, a face more sweet,
Ne'er hath it been my lot to meet.

"And her modest answer and graceful air
Show her wise and good as she is fair.

"Would she were mine, and I to-day,
Like her, a harvester of hay.

"No doubtful balance of rights and wrongs,
Nor weary lawyers with endless tongues,

"But low of cattle, and song of birds,
And health, and quiet, and loving words."

But he thought of his sister, proud and cold,
And his mother, vain of her rank and gold.

So, closing his heart, the Judge rode on,
And Maud was left in the field alone.

But the lawyers smiled that afternoon,
When he hummed in court an old love tune;

And the young girl mused beside the well,
Till the rain on the unraked clover fell.

He wedded a wife of richest dower,
Who lived for fashion as he for power.

Yet oft, in his marble hearth's bright glow,
He watched a picture come and go;

And sweet Maud Muller's hazel eyes
Looked out in their innocent surprise.

Oft, when the wine in his glass was red,
He longed for the wayside well instead,

And closed his eyes on his garnished rooms,
To dream of meadows and clover blooms;

And the proud man sighed with a secret pain,
"Ah, that I were free again!

"Free as when I rode that day
Where the barefoot maiden raked the hay."

She wedded a man unlearned and poor,
And many children played round her door.

But care and sorrow and child-birth pain,
Left their traces on heart and brain.

And oft, when the summer sun shone hot
On the new-mown hay in the meadow lot,

And she heard the little spring brook fall
Over the roadside, through the wall,

In the shade of the apple-tree again
She saw a rider draw his rein,

And, gazing down with a timid grace,
She felt his pleased eyes read her face.

Sometimes her narrow kitchen walls
Stretched away into stately halls;

The weary wheel to a spinnet turned,
The tallow-candle an astral burned;

And for him who sat by the chimney lug,
Dozing and grumbling o'er pipe and mug,

A manly form at her side she saw,
And joy was duty and love was law.

Then she took up her burden of life again,
Saying only, "It might have been."

Alas for maiden, alas for judge,
For rich repiner and household drudge!

God pity them both! and pity us all,
Who vainly the dreams of youth recall;

For of all sad words of tongue or pen,
The saddest are these: "It might have been!"

Ah, well! for us all some sweet hope lies
Deeply buried from human eyes;

And, in the hereafter, angels may
Roll the stone from its grave away!

## THE DEATH OF THE OLD YEAR.

ALFRED TENNYSON.

FULL knee-deep lies the winter snow,
And the winter winds are wearily sighing:
Toll ye the church-bell sad and slow,
And tread softly and speak low,
For the old year lies a-dying.
Old year, you must not die;
You came to us so readily,
You lived with us so steadily,
Old year, you shall not die.

He lieth still: he doth not move:
He will not see the dawn of day.
He hath no other life above.
He gave me a friend and a true true-love,
And the New-year will take 'em away.
Old year, you must not go;
So long as you have been with us,
Such joy as you have seen with us,
Old year, you shall not go.

He froth'd his bumpers to the brim;
A jollier year we shall not see.
But though his eyes are waxing dim,
And though his foes speak ill of him,
He was a friend to me.
Old year, you shall not die;
We did so laugh and cry with you,
I've half a mind to die with you,
Old year, if you must die.

He was full of joke and jest,
But all his merry quips are o'er.
To see him die, across the waste
His son and heir doth ride post-haste,
But he'll be dead before.
Every one for his own.
The night is starry and cold, my friend,
And the New-year blithe and bold, my friend,
Comes up to take his own.

How hard he breathes! over the snow
I heard just now the crowing cock.
The shadows flicker to and fro:
The cricket chirps: the light burns low:
'T is nearly twelve o'clock.
Shake hands, before you die.
Old year, we'll dearly rue for you:
What is it that we can do for you?
Speak out before you die.

His face is growing sharp and thin.
Alack! our friend is gone.
Close up his eyes: tie up his chin:
Step from the corpse, and let him in
That standeth there alone,
And waiteth at the door.
There's a new foot on the floor, my friend,
And a new face at the door, my friend,
A new face at the door.

## TIME.

SHAKESPEARE.

TIME'S glory is to calm contending kings,
To unmask falsehood and bring truth to light,
To stamp the seal of time in aged things,
To wake the morn and sentinel the night,
To wrong the wronger till he render right,
To ruinate proud buildings with thy hours,
And smear with dust their glittering golden towers;

To fill with worm-holes stately monuments,
To feed oblivion with decay of things,
To blot old books and alter their contents,
To pluck the quills from ancient ravens' wings,
To dry the old oak's sap and cherish springs,
To spoil antiquities of hammer'd steel,
And turn the giddy round of Fortune's wheel;

To show the beldam daughters of her daughter,
To make the child a man, the man a child,
To slay the tiger that doth live by slaughter,
To tame the unicorn and lion wild,
To mock the subtle in themselves beguiled,
To cheer the ploughman with increaseful crops,
And waste huge stones with little water-drops.

## LITTLE BREECHES.

JOHN HAY.

I DON'T go much on religion,
 I never ain't had no show;
But I've got a middlin' tight grip, sir,
 On the handful o' things I know.
I don't pan out on the prophets,
 And free-will, and that sort of thing;
But I b'lieve in God and the angels,
 Ever sence one night last spring.

I come into town with some turnips,
 And my little Gabe come along—
No four-year old in the county
 Could beat him for pretty and strong.
Peart and chipper and sassy,
 Always ready to swear and fight;
And I'd larnt him to chaw terbacker,
 Jest to keep his milk-teeth white.

The snow come down like a blanket
 As I passed by Taggart's store;
I went in for a jug of molasses,
 And left the team at the door.
They skeered at something and started—
 I heerd one little squall,
And hell-to-split over the prairie
 Went team, Little Breeches, and all.

Hell-to-split over the prairie!
 I was almost froze with skeer;
But we rousted up some torches,
 And sarched for 'em far and near.
At last we struck hosses and wagon,
 Snowed under a soft white mound,
Upsot, dead beat—but of little Gabe
 No hide nor hair was found.

And here all hope soured on me,
 Of my fellow-critters' aid—
I jest flopped down on my marrow-bones,
 Crotch-deep in the snow, and prayed.

* * * * * * *

By this the torches was played out,
 And me and Isrul Parr
Went off for some wood to a sheep-fold
 That he said was somewhar thar.

We found it at last, and a little shed
 Whar they shut up the lambs at night,
We looked in, and seen them huddled thar,
 So warm and sleepy and white.
And *thar* sot Little Breeches, and chirped
 As peart as ever you see,
"I want a chaw of terbacker,
 And that's what's the matter of me."

How did he git thar? Angels.
 He could never have walked in that storm,
They jest scooped down and toted him
 To whar it was safe and warm.
And I think that saving a little child
 And bringing him to his own,
Is a derned sight better business
 Than loafing around the Throne.

---

## ROCK ME TO SLEEP.

ELIZABETH AKERS ALLEN.

BACKWARD, turn backward, Oh, Time, in your flight,
 Make me a child again just for to-night!
Mother, come back from the echoless shore,
Take me again to your heart as of yore;
Kiss from my forehead the furrows of care,
Smooth the few silver threads out of my hair;
Over my slumbers your loving watch keep;—
Rock me to sleep, mother,—rock me to sleep!

Backward, flow backward, O tide of the years!
I am so weary of toil and of tears,—
Toil without recompense, tears all in vain,—
Take them, and give me my childhood again!
I have grown weary of dust and decay,—
Weary of flinging my soul-wealth away;
Weary of sowing for others to reap;—
Rock me to sleep, mother,—rock me to sleep!

Tired of the hollow, the base, the untrue,
Mother, O mother, my heart calls for you!
Many a summer the grass has grown green,
Blossomed, and faded our faces between;
Yet with strong yearning and passionate pain
Long I to-night for your presence again.
Come from the silence so long and so deep;—
Rock me to sleep, mother,—rock me to sleep!

Over my heart, in the days that are flown,
No love like mother-love ever has shone;
No other worship abides and endures,—
Faithful, unselfish and patient like yours:
None like a mother can charm away pain
From the sick soul and the world-weary brain.
Slumber's soft calms o'er my heavy lids creep;—
Rock me to sleep, mother,—rock me to sleep!

Come, let your brown hair, just lighted with gold,
Fall on your shoulders again as of old;
Let it drop over my forehead to-night,
Shading my faint eyes away from the light;
For with its sunny-edged shadows once more
Haply will throng the sweet visions of yore;
Lovingly, softly, its bright billows sweep;—
Rock me to sleep, mother,—rock me to sleep!

Mother, dear mother, the years have oeen long
Since I last listened your lullaby song:
Sing, then, and unto my soul it shall seem
Womanhood's years have been only a dream.
Clasped to your heart in a loving embrace,
With your light lashes just sweeping my face,
Never hereafter to wake or to weep;—
Rock me to sleep, mother,—rock me to sleep!

## THE VILLAGE BLACKSMITH.

H. W. LONGFELLOW.

UNDER a spreading chestnut-tree
The village smithy stands;
The smith, a mighty man is he,
With large and sinewy hands;
And the muscles of his brawny arms
Are strong as iron bands.

His hair is crisp and black and long;
His face is like the tan;
His brow is wet with honest sweat,—
He earns whate'er he can;
And looks the whole world in the face,
For he owes not any man.

Week in, week out, from morn till night,
You can hear his bellows blow;
You can hear him swing his heavy sledge,
With measured beat and slow,
Like sexton ringing the village bell,
When the evening sun is low.

And children, coming home from school,
Look in at the open door;
They love to see the flaming forge,
And hear the bellows roar,
And catch the burning sparks that fly
Like chaff from a threshing-floor.

He goes on Sunday to the church,
And sits among his boys;
He hears the parson pray and preach,
He hears his daughter's voice,
Singing in the village choir,
And it makes his heart rejoice.

It sounds to him like her mother's voice,
Singing in Paradise!
He needs must think of her once more,
How in the grave she lies;
And with his hard, rough hand he wipes
A tear out of his eyes.

Toiling, rejoicing, sorrowing,
Onward through life he goes;
Each morning sees some task begin,
Each evening sees it close;
Something attempted, something done,
Has earned a night's repose.

Thanks, thanks to thee, my worthy friend,
For the lesson thou hast taught!
Thus at the flaming forge of life
Our fortunes must be wrought;
Thus on its sounding anvil shaped
Each burning deed and thought!

## ALADDIN.

JAMES RUSSELL LOWELL.

WHEN I was a beggarly boy,
And lived in a cellar damp,
I had not a friend nor a toy,
But I had Aladdin's lamp;
When I could not sleep for cold,
I had fire enough in my brain,
And builded, with roofs of gold,
My beautiful castles in Spain!

Since then I have toiled day and night,
I have money and power good store,
But I'd give all my lamps of silver bright,
For the one that is mine no more;
Take, Fortune, whatever you choose,
You gave, and may snatch again;
I have nothing 'twould pain me to lose,
For I own no more castles in Spain!

## MEMORY.

OLIVER GOLDSMITH.

O MEMORY! thou fond deceiver,
Still importunate and vain,
To former joys recurring ever,
And turning all the past to pain;

Thou, like the world, oppress oppressing,
Thy smiles increase the wretch's woe!
And he who wants each other blessing,
In thee must ever find a foe.

## LETTERS.

AARON HILL.

LETTERS from absent friends extinguish fear,
Unite division and draw distance near
Their magic force each silent wish conveys,
And wafts embodied thought a thousand ways.
Could souls to bodies write, death's power were mean,
For minds could then meet minds with heav'n between.

## LOVE'S PHILOSOPHY.

PERCY BYSSHE SHELLEY.

THE fountains mingle with the river,
And the rivers with the ocean;
The winds of heaven mix forever,
With a sweet emotion;
Nothing in the world is single;
All things by a law divine
In one another's being mingle:—
Why not I with thine?

See! the mountains kiss high heaven,
And the waves clasp one other;
No sister flower would be forgiven
If it disdained its brother;
And the sunlight clasps the earth,
And the moonbeams kiss the sea;—
What are all these kissings worth,
If thou kiss not me?

## "JIM."

BRET HARTE.

SAY, there! P'r'aps
Some on you chaps
Might know Jim Wild?
Well—no offence;
Thar ain't no sense
In gettin' riled!
Jim was my chum
Up on the Bar;
That's why I come
Down from up yar,
Looking for Jim.

Thank ye, sir! *You*
Ain't of that crew—
Blest if you are!
Money!—Not much;
That ain't my kind;
I ain't no such,
Rum?—I don't mind,
Seein' it's you.

Well, this yer Jim,
Did you know him?—
Jess about your size;
Same kind of eyes—
Well, that is strange;
Why, it's two year
Since he came here,
Sick, for a change.

Well, here's to us;
Eh?
The h—— you say!
Dead?—
That little cuss?
What makes you star—
You over thar?
Can't a man drop
'S glass in yer shop
But you must r'ar?
It wouldn't take
D—— much to break
You and your bar.

Dead!
Poor—little—Jim!
Why, thar was me,
Jones, and Bob Lee,
Harry and Ben—
No-account men;
Then to take *him!*
Well, thar— Good-bye—
No more, sir—I—

Eh?
What's that you say?
Why, dern it!—sho!—
No? Yes? By Jo!
Sold!
Sold! Why, you limb,
You ornery,
Derned old
Long-legged Jim!

## MINGUILLO.

J. G. LOCKHART.

"SINCE for kissing thee, Minguillo,
My mother scolds me all the day,
Let me have it quickly, darling!
Give me back the kiss, I pray.

"If we have done aught amiss,
Let's undo it while we may.
Quickly give me back the kiss,
That she may have nought to say.

"Do—she keeps so great a pother,
Chides so sharply, looks so grave;
Do, my love, to please my mother,
Give me back the kiss I gave."

"Out upon you, false Minguillo!
One you give, but two you take;
Give me back the two, my darling!
Give them, for my mother's sake."—

—*From the Spanish.*

## IN EARLY SPRING.

ANONYMOUS.

PALE yellow sunlight tints the wave,
The glowing skies are blue and clear;
How languidly the waters lave
The sands that glimmer near!

The shady nooks along the hill
Are dappled yet with wasting snow;
I hear the earliest blue-birds trill;
Soft winds are breathing low.

Beyond the shining harbor bar
A dim sail lingers like a pearl,
While busy sea gulls near and far
Hover and swoop and whirl.

Oh! heart and day in sweet accord,
Oh! waves ye seem as fair to me
As if the feet of Christ, the Lord,
Had walked the morning sea.

## THE OLD OAKEN BUCKET.

SAMUEL WOODWORTH.

HOW dear to this heart are the scenes of my childhood
When fond recollection presents them to view!
The orchard, the meadow, the deep-tangled wild-wood,
And every loved spot which my infancy knew;—
The wide-spreading pond and the mill which stood by it,
The bridge, and the rock where the cataract fell;
The cot of my father, the dairy-house nigh it,
And e'en the rude bucket which hung in the well.
The old oaken bucket, the iron-bound bucket,
The moss-covered bucket which hung in the well.

That moss-covered vessel I hail as a treasure,
For often at noon when returned from the field,
I found it the source of an exquisite pleasure,
The purest and sweetest that nature can yield.
How ardent I seized it, with hands that were glowing!
And quick to the white-pebbled bottom it fell;
Then soon, with the emblem of truth overflowing,
And dripping with coolness, it rose from the well;
The old oaken bucket, the iron-bound bucket,
The moss-covered bucket, arose from the well.

How sweet from the green mossy brim to receive it,
As, poised on the curb it inclined to my lips!
Not a full blushing goblet could tempt me to leave it
Though filled with the nectar that Jupiter sips.
And, now, far removed from the loved situation,
The tear of regret will intrusively swell,
As fancy reverts to my father's plantation,
And sighs for the bucket which hangs in the well;
The old oaken bucket, the iron-bound bucket,
The moss-covered bucket which hangs in the well.

## SOMEBODY'S DARLING.

MARIE R. LACOSTE.

INTO a ward of the whitewashed walls,
Where the dead and dying lay,
Wounded by bayonets, shells and balls,
Somebody's darling was borne one day.

Somebody's darling, so young and so brave,
Wearing yet on his pale, sweet face,
Soon to be hid by the dust of the grave,
The lingering light of his boyhood grace.

Matted and damp are the curls of gold
Kissing the snow of that fair young brow,
Pale are the lips, of delicate mold—
Somebody's darling is dying now.

Back from his beautiful blue-veined brow,
Brush all the wandering waves of gold;
Cross his hands on his bosom now,
Somebody's darling is stiff and cold.

Kiss him once for somebody's sake,
Murmur a prayer soft and low,
One bright curl from its fair mates take—
They were somebody's pride, you know.

Somebody's hand had rested there;
Was it a mother's, soft and white?
And have the lips of a sister fair
Been baptized in the waves of light?

God knows best! He was somebody's love,
Somebody's heart enshrined him there;
Somebody wafted his name above,
Night and noon, on the wings of prayer.

Somebody wept when he marched away,
Looking so handsome, brave and grand,
Somebody's kiss on his forehead lay,
Somebody clung to his parting hand.

Somebody's waiting and watching for him,
Yearning to hold him again to their heart,
And there he lies, with his blue eyes dim,
And the smiling, child-like lips apart.

Tenderly bury the fair young dead,
Pausing to drop on his grave a tear;
Carve on the wooden slab at his head,
"Somebody's darling slumbers here."

## MODESTY.

COVENTRY PATMORE.

NOT to unvail before the gaze
Of an imperfect sympathy
In aught we are, is the sweet praise
And the main sum of modesty.

## HOHENLINDEN.

THOMAS CAMPBELL.

On Linden, when the sun was low,
All bloodless lay the untrodden snow,
And dark as winter was the flow
Of Iser, rolling rapidly.

But Linden saw another sight,
When the drum beat at dead of night,
Commanding fires of death to light
The darkness of her scenery.

By torch and trumpet fast arrayed,
Each horseman drew his battle-blade,
And furious every charger neighed,
To join the dreadful revelry.

Then shook the hills with thunder riven,
Then rushed the steed to battle driven,
And louder than the bolts of heaven,
Far flashed the red artillery.

But redder yet that light shall glow
On Linden's hills of stainéd snow,
And bloodier yet the torrent flow
Of Iser, rolling rapidly.

'Tis morn, but scarce yon level sun
Can pierce the war-clouds, rolling dun,
Where furious Frank, and fiery Hun,
Shout in their sulphurous canopy.

The combat deepens. On, ye brave,
Who rush to glory, or the grave!
Wave, Munich! all thy banners wave!
And charge with all thy chivalry!

Few, few shall part when many meet!
The snow shall be their winding-sheet,
And every turf beneath their feet
Shall be a soldier's sepulchre.

## THOSE EVENING BELLS.

THOMAS MOORE.

Those evening bells! those evening bells!
How many a tale their music tells,
Of youth, and home, and that sweet time
When last I heard their soothing chime.

Those joyous hours are passed away;
And many a heart that then was gay
Within the tomb now darkly dwells,
And hears no more those evening bells.

And so 'twill be when I am gone;
That tuneful peal will still ring on,
While other bards shall walk these dells,
And sing your praise, sweet evening bells!

## OFT, IN THE STILLY NIGHT.

THOMAS MOORE.

Oft, in the stilly night,
Ere Slumber's chain has bound me,
Fond Memory brings the light
Of other days around me:
The smiles, the tears,
Of boyhood's years,
The words of love then spoken;
The eyes that shone,
Now dimmed and gone,
The cheerful hearts now broken!
Thus in the stilly night,
Ere Slumber's chain has bound me,
Sad Memory brings the light
Of other days around me.

When I remember all
The friends, so linked together,
I've seen around me fall,
Like leaves in wintry weather,
I feel like one
Who treads alone
Some banquet-hall deserted,
Whose lights are fled,
Whose garlands dead,
And all but he departed!
Thus in the stilly night,
Ere Slumber's chain has bound me,
Sad Memory brings the light
Of other days around me.

## VIRTUE.

OLIVER GOLDSMITH.

The triumphs that on vice attend
Shall ever in confusion end;
The good man suffers but to gain,
And every virtue springs from pain:

As aromatic plants bestow
No spicy fragrance while they grow,
But crushed, or trodden to the ground,
Diffuse their balmy sweets around.

## HOPE.

OLIVER GOLDSMITH.

The wretch, condemned with life to part,
Still, still on hope relies;
And every pang that rends the heart
Bids expectation rise.

Hope, like the gleaming taper's light,
Adorns and cheers the way;
And still, as darker grows the night,
Emits a brighter ray.

## TIRED MOTHERS.

MAY RILEY SMITH.

A LITTLE elbow leans upon your knee,
  Your tired knee that has so much to bear;
A child's dear eyes are looking lovingly
  From underneath a thatch of tangled hair.
Perhaps you do not heed the velvet touch
  Of warm, moist fingers holding yours so tight;
You do not prize this blessing overmuch;
  You almost are too tired to pray, to-night.

But it is blessedness! A year ago
  I did not see it as I do to-day—
We are so dull and thankless, and so slow
  To catch the sunshine till it slips away.
And now it seems surpassing strange to me
  That, while I wore the badge of motherhood,
I did not kiss more oft and tenderly
  The little child that brought me only good.

* * * * * * *

I wonder so that mothers ever fret
  At little children clinging to their gown;
Or that the foot-prints, when the days are wet,
  Are ever black enough to make them frown.
If I could find a little muddy boot,
  Or cap or jacket, on my chamber floor;
If I could kiss a rosy, restless foot,
  And hear it patter in my home once more:

If I could mend a broken cart to-day,
  To-morrow make a kite to reach the sky—
There is no woman in God's world could say
  She was more blissfully content than I.
But, ah! the dainty pillow next my own
  Is never rumpled by a shining head;
My singing birdling from its nest has flown;
  The little boy I used to kiss is dead!

## SHE WALKS IN BEAUTY.

LORD BYRON.

SHE walks in beauty, like the night
  Of cloudless climes and starry skies;
And all that's best of dark and bright
  Meet in her aspect and her eyes:
Thus mellowed to that tender light
  Which heaven to gaudy day denies.

One shade the more, one ray the less,
  Had half-impaired the nameless grace
Which waves in every raven tress,
  Or softly lightens o'er her face;
Where thoughts serenely sweet express
  How pure, how dear their dwelling-place.

And on that cheek, and o'er that brow,
  So soft, so calm, yet eloquent,
The smiles that win, the tints that glow,
  But tell of days in goodness spent,
A mind at peace with all below,
  A heart whose love is innocent!

## A RED, RED ROSE.

ROBERT BURNS.

O MY luve's like a red, red rose,
  That's newly sprung in June;
O my luve's like the melodie
  That's sweetly played in tune.
As fair art thou, my bonnie lass,
  So deep in luve am I;
And I will luve thee still, my dear,
  Till a' the seas gang dry.

Till a' the seas gang dry, my dear,
  And the rocks melt wi' the sun:
I will luve thee still, my dear,
  While the sands o' life shall run.
And fare thee weel, my only luve!
  And fare thee weel awhile!
And I will come again, my luve,
  Though it were ten thousand mile.

## OUR OWN.

MARGARET E. SANGSTER.

IF I had known in the morning
  How wearily all the day
The words unkind would trouble my mind
  That I said when you went away,
I had been more careful, darling,
  Nor given you needless pain;
But we vex our own with look and tone
  We may never take back again.

For though in the quiet evening
  You may give me the kiss of peace,
Yet it well might be that never for me
  The pain of the heart should cease!
How many go forth at morning
  Who never come home at night!
And hearts have broken for harsh words spoken,
  That sorrow can ne'er set right.

We have careful thought for the stranger,
  And smiles for the sometime guest;
But oft for our own the bitter tone,
  Though we love our own the best.
Ah! lips with the curve impatient,
  Ah! brow with the shade of scorn,
'T were a cruel fate, were the night too late
  To undo the work of the morn!

## THE BLUE AND THE GRAY.

F. M. FINCH.

By the flow of the inland river,
Whence the fleets of iron have fled,
Where the blades of the grave-grass quiver,
Asleep are the ranks of the dead:—
Under the sod and the dew,
Waiting the judgment day;
Under the one, the Blue,
Under the other, the Gray.

These in the robings of glory,
Those in the gloom of defeat,
All with the battle-blood gory,
In the dusk of eternity meet:—
Under the sod and the dew,
Waiting the judgment day;
Under the laurel, the Blue,
Under the willow, the Gray.

From the silence of sorrowful hours
The desolate mourners go,
Lovingly laden with flowers,
Alike for the friend and the foe:—
Under the sod and the dew,
Waiting the judgment day;
Under the roses, the Blue,
Under the lilies, the Gray.

So, with an equal splendor,
The morning sun-rays fall,
With a touch impartially tender,
On the blossoms blooming for all:—
Under the sod and the dew,
Waiting the judgment day;
Broidered with gold, the Blue,
Mellowed with gold, the Gray.

So, when the summer calleth
On forest and field of grain,
With an equal murmur falleth
The cooling drip of the rain:—
Under the sod and the dew,
Waiting the judgment day;
Wet with the rain, the Blue,
Wet with the rain, the Gray.

Sadly, but not with upbraiding,
The generous deed was done;
In the storm of the years that are fading
No braver battle was won:—
Under the sod and the dew,
Waiting the judgment day;
Under the blossoms, the Blue,
Under the garlands, the Gray.

No more shall the war-cry sever,
Or the winding rivers be red;
They banish our anger forever,
When they laurel the graves of our dead,—
Under the sod and the dew,
Waiting the judgment day;
Love and tears for the Blue,
Tears and love for the Gray.

## WHAT MAIDENS PRIZE.

ANONYMOUS.

There's many a thing that the maidens wish
As they travel the road of life,
While taking their part in this busy world,
And sharing its cares and strife.
Perhaps they may long for a cosy home
With its furniture "spick and span,"
But to crown the whole, they care the most
For the love of an honest man.

Oh! sweet little maiden, wherever you are,
In palace or humble cot;
And whether your life be fair and bright,
Or toil and trouble your lot;
And whether your name be Flora May,
Or homely Mary Ann,
You will be in luck if you win that love:
The love of an honest man.

A maiden may prize her diamond set,
Or dresses of latest style,
And live in a home of costly build
With carpets of velvet pile;
But the noblest thing in a woman's life—
Let her gain it while she can—
From her golden curls to her silvery hair,
Is the love of an honest man.

## HOME, SWEET HOME.

JOHN HOWARD PAYNE.

Mid pleasures and palaces though we may roam,
Be it ever so humble, there's no place like home!
A charm from the skies seems to hallow us here,
Which, seek through the world, is ne'er met with elsewhere.
Home! home! sweet, sweet home!
There's no place like home!

An exile from home, splendor dazzles in vain!
Oh, give me my lowly thatched cottage again!
The birds singing gayly that came at my call;—
Give me them,—and the peace of mind dearer than all!
Home! home, etc.

PLATE III.

HONI SOIT QUI MAL Y PENSE

What does little birdie say
In her nest at peep of day?
Let me fly says little birdie
Mother let me fly away.

Birdie rest a little longer.
Till the little wings are stronger.
So she rests a little longer.
Then she flies away.

Tennyson.

PLATE IV.

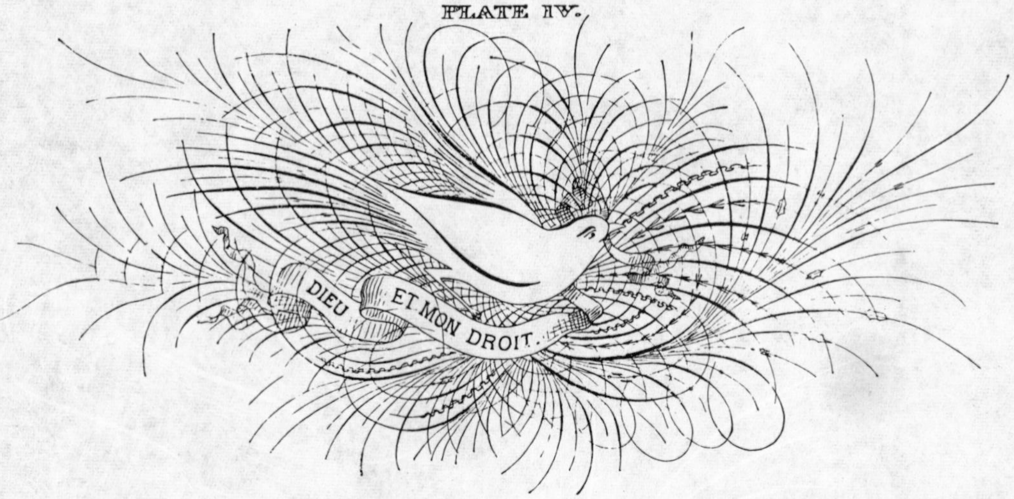

DIEU ET MON DROIT.

Brooklyn, July 23, 1883.

Dear Sir:-

My daughter Florence requests the pleasure of your company at a small garden party next Wednesday afternoon at two o'clock.

The programme includes a game of Lawn Tennis, in which we shall be delighted to have you take part, as we are aware what an authority you are on out-door sports.

Yours very truly,

Alice C. Parker.

To Benj. Hardwick, Esq.
135 Broadway, N.Y.

New York, July 24, 1883.

Mrs. Alice Parker,

Dear Madam,

I regret exceedingly that my journalistic duties make it impossible for me to accept your daughter's kind invitation.

Please present my compliments to the young lady, and tell her that I hope to have the pleasure of initiating her into the mysteries of Lawn Tennis on some future occasion.

Yours Sincerely,

Benjamin Hardwick.

"KILLING TIME" is not a very worthy object to have in view, but even the busiest of grown-up mortals find it necessary on some occasions to resort to home occupations when "time hangs heavily on their hands." Young people, however, who have not lived long enough to appreciate the value of time, are too apt to spend their leisure hours in frivolous pastimes. It is true that "all work and no play make Jack a dull boy," but Jack's play might just as well partake of the *utile cum dulce* (the useful along with the sweet), instead of consisting altogether of base-ball, cards, billiards, and even harmful amusements. Your sixteen-year-old daughter might certainly indulge in more profitable occupations than gossiping, reading novels, and flirting at her window with the young gentleman over the way. There are many useful and beautiful arts which may be practiced at home, greatly increasing the sum of home enjoyment, and adding also to the elegance of the familiar rooms where the better part of our lives is spent.

It is a one-sided and incomplete education which neglects the training of the eye and hand. Every girl should acquire some technical skill, which she might apply to the decoration of her own parlor, and if need were, to the earning of money for herself and her private uses. Every boy, however deeply he may plunge into the classics, should know how to use tools, to drive a nail, to wield a hammer, to mend a hinge, or to make some pretty article for his mother and sisters. Head and hands should help each other.

There has been a revival of taste in common things, and we care much more than our grandparents did about surrounding ourselves with beauty. The struggle of life was harder for them, and they had not time, as we have, for adorning tables and chairs, arranging corners so that they are artistic and not hideous, and making windows and walls rich with color and fair with softly falling drapery.

## EMBROIDERY.

Among the most popular home occupations for ladies at the present day, we may name embroidery. The loom and the spinning-wheel, in one simple form or another, are as old as history, and our devotion to the embroidery frame is only a return to the work which mediæval ladies found delightful. True, few of them could read and write, and so the needle was their only form of expression, while all doors are open to us. But, though not shut up to embroidery, it is pleasant work for a group of merry girls or thoughtful women.

To speak of materials, the most expensive are silk, velvet, tissue, gold and silver cloth, velveteen, and plush. Among cheaper materials which are available in household art, are linens of various degrees of fineness, crash, sateen, Bolton, sheeting, scrym, serge, and canton flannel.

Imagine the old funereal parlor with ghostly windows, hung with white shades, a marble mantel deathly white, a marble-topped table with a few ambrotypes and animals in red and gilt on its chilly surface, and then think how even such a room may bloom in brightness when a fair magician has touched it with her needle. Behold! Creamy curtains drape the windows, a lambrequin covers the frozen mantel, the tables are hidden under cloths which make each a warm and glowing spot to attract the eye, and

Why is a son who objects to his mother's second marriage like an exhausted pedestrian?
Because he can't go a step farther.

Why is lip-salve like a duenna?
Because it's meant to keep the chaps off!

When is a door not a door?
When it is a jar (a-jar).

Why are good resolutions like fainting ladies?
Because they want carrying out.

What is the "sweetest thing in bonnets?"
A lady's two-lips.

What sort of music should a girl sing whose voice is cracked and broken?
Pieces!

What animal took most luggage into the Ark, and which the least?
The elephant who had his trunk; while the fox and the cock had only a brush and a comb between them!

In what place did the cock crow so loud that all the world heard him?
In the Ark.

Why is the root of the tongue like a dejected man?
Because it's down in the mouth.

Why is a dog biting his own tail like a good manager?
Because he makes both ends meet!

When does the House of Representatives present one of the most ludicrous spectacles?
When its ayes (eyes) are on one side, and its noes (nose) on the other!

What is the difference between an accepted and a rejected lover?
One kisses his miss, the other misses his kiss!

When is a schoolmaster like a man with one eye?
When he has a vacancy for a pupil!

Which are the lightest men—Scotchmen, Irishmen, or Englishmen?
In Ireland there are men of Cork; in Scotland men of Ayr; but in England, on the Thames, they have lighter-men!

Which would you rather, look a greater fool than you are, or be a greater fool than you look?
After somebody has chosen you will create a laugh by saying, "that is impossible!"

Why is a young man engaged to a young lady like a person sailing for France?
Because he's going to Havre (have her).

Why is a man who never lays a wager as bad as a regular gambler?
Because he's no better.

What should be a soldier's definition of a kiss?
A report at head-quarters!

Why are two young ladies kissing each other an emblem of Christianity?
Because they are doing unto each other as they would men should do unto them!

When is a baby most like a cherub?
When it continually doth cry!

What is the difference between an old maid and a girl fond of a red-haired Irishman?
One loves a cat and parrots, the other—a Pat and carrots!

Why is an author the most wonderful man in the world?
Because his tail (tale) comes out of his head!

What is the difference between the manner of the death of a barber and a sculptor?
One curls up and dies, and the other makes faces and busts!

When did Moses sleep five in a bed?
When he slept with his forefathers.

What part of speech is kissing?
A conjunction!

Why are married men like steamboats?
Because they are subject to get blown up occasionally.

Why is a very demure young lady like a steampacket?
Because she pays no attention to the swells that follow her.

When are kisses sweetest?
When sirup-titiously obtained.

Why is a kiss like a sermon?
Because it requires two heads and an application!

How do you spell "blind pig" in two letters?
P G—pig without an I!

Why is I the luckiest of all the vowels?
Because it is in the center of bliss, while e is in hell, and all the others in *purgatory*!

What one letter in the alphabet will spell the word potato?
The letter O; put them down one at a time until you have *put eight o's*.

What do lawyers do when they die?
Lie still!

Why do girls kiss each other while men do not?
Because girls have nothing better to kiss and men have.

Why are hogs more intelligent than human beings?
Because they nose (knows) everything!

What is the difference between a mother with a large family and a barber?
One shaves with his razors, and the other raises her shavers.

What shape is a kiss?
A-lip-tickle (elliptical).

In what key should a declaration of love be made?
Be mine ah! (B minor)

Why are there more marriages in winter than in summer?
Because then men seek comforters, and ladies seek muffs!

Why are country girls' cheeks like well-printed cottons?
Because they are warranted to wash and—keep color!

What game do the waves play at?
At pitch and toss!

What is a button?
A small event that is always coming off!

When is a girl like a mirror?
When she's a good-looking (g)lass!

Why is love like a potato?
Because it shoots from the eyes, and gets less by pairing (paring).

Why is a youth encouraging a mustache like a cow's tail?
Because he grows down.

Why is a judge's nose like the middle of the earth?
Because it's the center of gravity.

Why is it almost certain that Shakespeare was a broker?
Because no man has furnished so many stock quotations.

Why is a dirty man like flannel?
Because he shrinks from washing?

Why is twice ten like twice eleven?
Because twice ten are twenty, and twice eleven are twenty-two (too).

What is the most dangerous time of the year to go into the country?
When the trees are shooting and the bull-rushes out!

Why was "Uncle Tom's Cabin" not written by a female hand?
Because it was written by Mrs. Beecher's toe (Stowe).

Which one of the Seven Wonders of the World are locomotive engines like?
The coal-horses of roads (Colossus of Rhodes).

What did Queen Elizabeth take her pills in?
In cider (inside her).

Why was Blackstone like an Irish vegetable?
Because he was a common tatur.

Why was Eve made?
For Adam's Express Company.

Why is a dead doctor like a dead duck?
Because the both have done quacking!

## HOW TO ROW.

In rowing, throw the hands well forward with the back straight, and eyes fixed on the back of the man in front. The chest should be well out, with the arms forward, and the knees separated about twelve inches, until the hands are over the toes. In making the stroke, immerse the oar so that the blade is just covered, no deeper. Then pull the oar well back, straightening the back and drawing in the arms, till the oar is well home at the chest. The forward movement for the next stroke involves feathering. Bend the wrists well down which will bring the plane of the oar parallel with the water, and again thrust out the arms, until the hands reach a point over the toes, and so pull again.

The movement of the body has been much facilitated by the sliding American seat. It enables the crew to slide all together into position with less muscular effect.

FOUR-OARED SHELL.

The three great points in rowing are: 1st, perfect time; 2d, to get the oar in square; 3d, to row the stroke right out and use the legs well. If the oarsman keeps his eyes firmly fixed on the man in front, corresponding motion for motion with him, then it will not be his fault if the time is bad. Let there be no hurry. Bring the hands well up to the chest, or "home," as it is termed, but let them not rest there. A quick recovery and the free use of the legs will lift the boat with every stroke. Nothing is a better sign of a well coached crew than to see the boat lift with every stroke, and for this it is the part of the stroke in front of the rowlocks which is most important. When the oar is brought home to the chest, the hands should be dropped, which will lift the oar out of the water, then by turning the wrists down the oar is feathered, and the arms should be shot out to their full stretch, the body following them without pause but as part of a continuous motion. A quick recovery is produced by keeping the back straight. The knees should not cease to be slightly bent, the contraction of the knees and the abdominal muscles must come into play, and the body be slung evenly forward (not jerked) as if working by machinery. It is all important to get the oar in square. If it gets in obliquely, it will go too deep and pull the boat down. Avoid beginning the feathering motion with the wrists before the oar is well out of the water, or you will splash. Holding water is required in a stream before starting or *bringing to* after a race. Reverse the blade of the oar, and press gently against the water. Backing is the opposite motion to rowing. The blade is pushed through the water, feathered, brought back, and then pushed again. It should be done very gently, as it has a great tendency to strain a boat. Paddling is simply the art of rowing at half power, about twenty or thirty strokes a minute so as to enable the coach to detect faults more easily.

A spurt is a simultaneous effort of all the crew, a pull all together at their greatest strength. Easing, stopping or starting must be effected by the whole crew together.

With regard to the length of the stroke, it must be borne in mind that the measure of the shortest oarsman in the boat must govern all. "The stroke" must not overreach his crew or any one of them.

## COACHING.

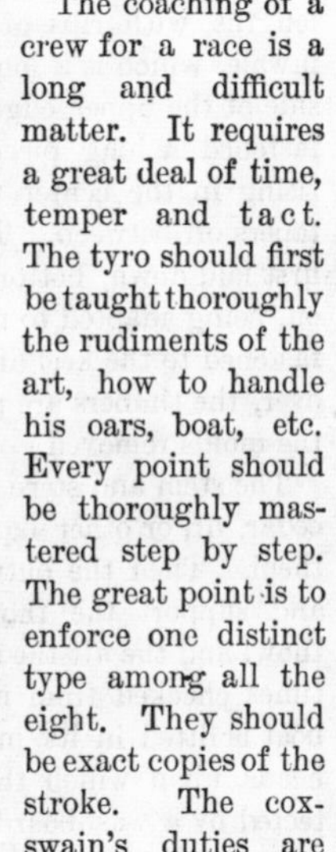

The coaching of a crew for a race is a long and difficult matter. It requires a great deal of time, temper and tact. The tyro should first be taught thoroughly the rudiments of the art, how to handle his oars, boat, etc. Every point should be thoroughly mastered step by step. The great point is to enforce one distinct type among all the eight. They should be exact copies of the stroke. The coxswain's duties are many and important, and many a race is lost or won by his skill or the want of it. He should know the currents, and be careful not to expose the side of the boat more than absolutely necessary to the full force of the current. It is also his duty to give the word of command what to do, when to stop, start or ease. He should keep his yoke lines taut, and not allow the rudder to be swayed by the current. The pull at the lines should be very gentle, and the movement very slight. A hard pull seriously interferes with the speed of the boat. In turning corners the outside oars should be pulled harder and the inner slackened, according to the orders "pull bow side," "pull stroke side."

## ROW BOATS.

The rowing boats consist mostly of eight-oared boats, four-oared and two-oared. The last have to be built somewhat stiffer as the strain of one oar on each side is more unequal, and has a tendency to make the boat twist and tremble and slightly veer from side to side.

# ROWING.

NTO the various modes of boat-building now in vogue it is not proposed to enter, nor into the arguments used in favor of this or that particular build.

The body of an ordinary sculling-boat is built of cedar, in lengths, with ribs of ash, chestnut, or beech, fixed to the inwale, which is a long strip of deal running along the inside of the upper edge of the boat. Upon the inner keel is fastened a long piece of wood, generally of deal, which, rising in the center under the seats supports them, and tapers off between. The inner keel, kelson, and inwale, are first laid down, bottom upwards. To these the skin is laid on, being adapted to the molds by hot water or steam, and fastened to the keel and inwale. The boat is then turned over, the timbers are put in, the thwarts or seats added, and the molds removed.

The stem and stern are of solid pieces, either mahogany, cedar, fir, or other hard wood, and the skin worked up to them. Then the outriggers are added, which are of iron, and support the thowls, of which the fore is called the thowl and the aft the stopper; within these the oar is sometimes checked from unshipping by a twisted string. The boat is fitted in its interior with three divisions or bulkheads, upon which the deck rests. The fore part is protected by a washboard, and in front of that and behind the coxswain the whole is covered with canvas.

The skulls and oars are made of white deal and their three divisions are known as the handle, loom, and blade. The loom and handle are the part inside the row-locks. The rest is called the blade. The handles of the oars are rounded and smoothed. From the handle to the row-lock the oar is square, with a button nailed on to the back of the oar, so as to catch the thowls, and keep the oar from sliding out. Outboard the oar is rounded at the back, so that it can turn easily in the thowls; where it begins to slope into the blade it is thinned off, and the blade as it approaches the end is slightly curved.

## HOW TO SIT.

In rowing, you should sit about two-thirds of the seat away from the row-lock. The mat and pad should be firmly tied on to the seat. The feet should be straight in front, heels together. If they are nearer the side the rower swings towards the middle, or, as it is called, "rows into the boat," but if they are too near the middle, he "rows out of it." Both are bad faults and destroy the equilibrium, making the boat roll. The stretcher should be adjusted so that the oar just clears the knees as it is thrust forward, and the strap buckled tight over the left foot. The thwart on which the rower sits should be so tight that he can easily command his oar, and low enough to enable him to get the oar well over his knees. The lower the oarsman sits, the more he has a tendency to pull the boat under water; and higher, the more he lifts the boat with his stroke.

ROWING—THE REACH.

ROWING—THE RECOVER.

is the general term, and includes the others. We are *deluded* by false hopes, *imposed upon* by others for gain. We may be *deceived* without any fault of our own; but not *deluded*.

***Decide,*** *v.* Determine, conclude upon. We *decide* more quickly than we *determine*. We *conclude upon* a thing when we arrive at a final *determination* in regard to it.

***Declare,*** *v.* Publish, proclaim. We *publish* or *proclaim* publicly only; we *declare* privately or publicly. Facts and opinions are *declared;* events *published;* public measures proclaimed.

***Deed,*** *n.* Act, action, exploit, feat, achievement.

***Defeat,*** *v.* Conquer, repulse, overthrow, frustrate, foil. CONQUER.

***Defend,*** *v.* Protect, vindicate. *Defend* is the general term. *Vindication* is a moral *defense; protection* a permanant defense. ATTACK.

***Delay,*** *v.* Defer, postpone, procrastinate, prolong, protract, retard. We *delay* a thing by not beginning it; *defer* and *postpone* by fixing the beginning at a later period. The continuance of a thing is *prolonged* or *protracted;* the end *retarded*. *Procrastination* is a blameworthy *delay*.

***Delightful,*** *a.* Charming. *Charming* is a stronger term than *delightful;* and mostly applied to pleasures of the senses. DISAGREEABLE.

***Demand,*** *v.* We *demand* what is due us; *require* what we expect to have done.

***Demolish,*** *v.* Destroy, dismantle, raze, ruin, overthrow.

***Deny,*** *v.* Refuse, disavow, contradict. We *deny* facts; *contradict* erroneous statements; *refuse* requests; *disavow* what is wrongly attributed to us. AFFIRM. (See VOUCH.)

***Deplore,*** *v.* Lament, bewail; mourn, bemoan.

***Deposit,*** *n.* Pawn, pledge, security.

***Deride,*** *v.* Banter, rally, mock, ridicule. *Banter* and *rally* are slight ridicule; *mockery* is a direct personal attack; *derision* is stronger than *ridicule*, but weaker than *mockery*.

***Design,*** *n.* Plan, project, purpose, scheme, intention. CHANCE.

***Desire,*** *v.* Wish, hanker after, long for, covet.

***Destiny,*** *n.* Fate, doom, lot.

***Determined,*** *a.* Resolute, decided, firm. UNDETERMINED.

***Deviate,*** *v.* Err, stray, wander, swerve.

***Diction,*** *n.* Phraseology, style.

***Dictionary,*** *n.* Glossary, lexicon, vocabulary. A *lexicon* is a *dictionary* of dead languages. A *vocabulary* is a list of words; a *glossary* is a *vocabulary* with explanations.

***Differ,*** *v.* Disagree, dissent, vary. AGREE. (See SUIT.)

***Different,*** *a.* Distinct, separate. *Different* refers to internal qualities; *distinct* to things as seen by the eye or mind; *separate* is what is apart to be seen by itself. LIKE. (See LIKENESS.)

***Difficulty,*** *n.* Impediment, obstacle, obstruction, perplexity. EASE.

***Disadvantage,*** *n.* Detriment, hurt, injury, prejudice. ADVANTAGE. (See BENEFIT.)

***Disagreeable,*** *a.* Unpleasant, offensive. DELIGHTFUL.

***Discernment,*** *n.* Discrimination, judgment, penetration. *Discernment* estimates rightly persons or things; *penetration* pierces through what has been hidden by cunning; *discrimination* finds the difference between two objects; *judgment* is a practical power, the result of inward deduction.

***Discredit,*** *n.* Disgrace. scandal, reproach, dishonor. CREDIT. (See NAME)

***Dishonesty,*** *n.* Fraud, knavery. HONESTY.

***Dislike,*** *n.* Disgust, displeasure, distaste, dissatisfaction.

***Displease,*** *v.* Offend, vex. *Displease* relates rather to the inward feeling; *offend* and *vex* to the exterior cause. *Vex* is stronger than *offend* and *displease;* but temporary. CEASE.

***Disposition,*** *n.* Inclination, temper. *Disposition* is permanent; *inclination* and *temper* transitory; *disposition* is stronger and more positive than *inclination*.

***Dissimilarity,*** *n.* Unlikeness. LIKENESS.

***Dissolute,*** *a.* Lax, loose, licentious. AUSTERE.

***Distinguished,*** *a.* Famous, eminent, illustrious, conspicuous, noted. UNDISTINGUISHED. (See OBSCURE.)

***Distress,*** *n.* Agony, anguish, anxiety. *Distress* is the result of present evil; *agony* of immediate evil; *anguish* of reflection on past evil; *anxiety* of the fear of future evil.

***Distribute,*** *v.* Allot, apportion, assign.

***Distrust,*** *n.* Suspicion. CONFIDENCE. (See HOPE.)

***Divide,*** *v.* Separate, part, disunite, distribute.

***Doctrine,*** *n.* Dogma, tenet. A *doctrine* rests on individual authority; a *dogma* on the authority of a body; a *tenet* on its merits.

***Doubt,*** *n.* Disbelief, suspense. BELIEF.

***Doubtful,*** *a.* Dubious, uncertain, precarious. CERTAIN.

***Dregs,*** *n.* Dross, scum, refuse, sediment.

***Dull,*** *a.* Dismal, gloomy, sad. A thing is *dull* and *gloomy* when it wants light and life; *dismal*, when it has what is also offensive to the sense. *Sad* is generally used in regard to moral objects. BRIGHT.

***Durable,*** *a.* Lasting, permanent. *Durable* applies more properly to things material, a *durable* structure; *lasting* to non-material things, a *lasting* feud. *Permanent* is weaker than durable; a *permanent* situation. TEMPORARY.

***Duty,*** *n.* Obligation. *Duty* relates to the whole conduct of men; *obligation* to particular circumstances.

## E.

***Eager,*** *a.* Earnest, serious. *Earnest* is exclusively moral; *eager*, either physical or moral. *Eagerness* is usually a fault; *earnestness* a virtue. A person or thing is *serious;* only a person *earnest*. INDIFFERENT. (See INDIFFERENCE.)

***Eagerness,*** *n.* Avidity, greediness. INDIFFERENCE.

***Earn,*** *v.* Win, obtain, acquire, get, attain, gain. SPEND.

***Ease,*** *n.* Quiet, rest, repose. *Rest* is cessation of motion; *ease* is freedom from anything painful; *quiet*, freedom from disturbance caused by others; *repose* is the necessary rest after labor.

***Ease,*** *n.* Easiness, facility. DIFFICULTY.

***Ebullition,*** *n.* Effervescence, fermentation, ferment.

***Ecclesiastic,*** *n.* Divine, theologian. An *ecclesiastic* has a station in the church a *theologian* writes on theology; a *divine* teaches, besides having a station in the church.

***Eclipse,*** *v.* Obscure, darken, cloud, veil.

***Ecstasy,*** *n.* Rapture, transport. *Ecstasy* and *rapture* are pleasurable; *transport* pleasurable or painful.

***Edifice,*** *n.* Fabric, structure.

***Education,*** *n.* Breeding, instruction, nurture, tuition. *Education* includes *instruction* and *breeding; breeding* relates to the manners; *instruction* to imparting knowledge; *tuition* is the act of teaching; *nurture* the bringing up of children.

***Effect,*** *v.* Perform, produce. *Effect* includes *perform* and *produce*. Only a rational agent can *effect*.

***Effective,*** *a.* Effectual, efficient, efficacious. INEFFECTUAL.

***Elderly,*** *a.* Aged, old. *Aged* denotes greater age than elderly; *old* than *aged*. *Elderly* and *aged* are more respectful than *old*. YOUTHFUL.

***Elocution,*** *n.* Eloquence, oratory, rhetoric. *Elocution* is the manner of delivery; *eloquence* the matter. *Oratory* is an acquired art; *eloquence* a natural gift; *rhetoric* is the theory of oratory (in common use as a display of *oratory*).

***Embarrass,*** *v.* Entangle, perplex.

***Embellish,*** *v.* Adorn, decorate, beautify.

***Embrace,*** *v.* Clasp, hug.

***Empire,*** *n.* Reign, kingdom, dominion. An *empire* is a great country composed of different people; a *kingdom* is smaller. As implying the exercise of power, *empire* relates to the country governed; *reign* to the ruler; a vast *empire;* a long *reign*. *Dominion* denotes either the act or power of ruling.

***Employ,*** *v.* Act. What is *employed* acts; what is *used* is acted upon.

***Empty,*** *a.* Devoid, vacant, void. An *empty* building; a *vacant* chair; *void* of reason; *devoid* of sense. FULL.

***Encomium,*** *n.* Eulogy, eulogium, panegyric.

***Encourage,*** *v.* Animate, embolden, impel, incite, stimulate, urge. ABASH.

***Encourage,*** *v.* Advance, forward, prefer, promote.

***Encroach,*** *v.* Infringe, intrude, invade.

***Endeavor,*** *v.* Aim, strive, struggle.

***Endeavor,*** *n.* Effort, exertion, attempt, aim.

***Enemy,*** *n.* Adversary, antagonist, foe, opponent. *Foe* is stronger than *enemy*. An *opponent* opposes one's opinions, etc. An *adversary*, from personal reasons, opposes one's claims; an *antagonist* is a kind of *opponent*. *Enemy* and *foe* convey the idea of personal hostility. FRIEND.

***Energy,*** *n.* Force, vigor, strength, power, spirit.

***Enormous,*** *a.* Huge, immense, vast. *Enor-*

***Care,*** *n.* Heed, attention. NEGLIGENCE.

***Carnage,*** *n.* Butchery, massacre, slaughter.

***Cause,*** *n.* Motive, reason. *Cause* relates to the connection of things; *motive*, mental and physical operation; *reason*, mental operations. EFFECT. (See CONSEQUENCE.)

***Cease,*** *v.* Discontinue, leave off, end. CONTINUE.

***Censure,*** *v.* Animadvert, criticise. *Censure* finds fault, assertively; *criticism*, argumentatively; *animadversion*, states the reasons for its objections. PRAISE.

***Certain,*** *a.* Secure, sure. DOUBTFUL.

***Cessation,*** *n.* Intermission, rest, stop. CONTINUANCE.

***Chance,*** *n.* Fate, fortune. *Chance* relates to all things; *fate* and *fortune* (generally) to things personal. *Chance* is variable without plan; *fortune* plans blindly; *fate* plans with knowledge and attains the result intended. DESIGN.

***Change,*** *v.* Barter, exchange, substitute.

***Changeable,*** *a.* Fickle, inconstant, mutable, variable. UNCHANGEABLE.

***Changeableness,*** *n.* Fickleness, inconstancy. CONSTANCY.

***Charm,*** *v.* Captivate, enchant, enrapture, fascinate.

***Cheerful,*** *a.* Gay, merry, sprightly. *Cheerfulness* is an habitual state; *mirth*, a temporary exhilaration; *gayety* the result of circumstances; *sprightfulness*, the buoyancy of health and temperament. MOURNFUL.

***Chief,*** *n.* Chieftain, head, leader. SUBORDINATE. (See SUBJECT.)

***Circumstance,*** *n.* Fact, incident. A *fact* is something done; an *incident*, something that happens; a *circumstance* denotes everything connected with a thing.

***Class,*** *n.* Degree, order, rank. Persons hold a *rank;* belong to a *class* or *order;* are of high or low *degree.*

***Clear,*** *a.* Bright, lucid, vivid. OPAKE. (See DARK.)

***Clever,*** *a.* Adroit, dexterous, expert, skillful. *Cleverness* is mental; *skill*, mental and physical; *expertness* and *dexterousness*, chiefly physical; *adroitness*, wholly physical. STUPID.

***Clothed,*** *n.* Clad, dressed. NAKED.

***Coarse,*** *a.* Rude, rough. All denote things unpolished. *Coarse* relates to material; *rough*, to surface; *rude*, to construction. *Coarse* is the opposite of fine; *rough* of smooth; *rude* of polished. FINE.

***Coax,*** *v.* Cajole, fawn, wheedle.

***Color,*** *v.* Dye, stain, tinge. *Color* is generic; *dye*, a term of art (but also used figuratively); *tinge* is poetical; *stain* is used either with its proper meaning or figuratively.

***Colorable,*** *a.* Ostensible, plausible, specious.

***Combination,*** *n.* Cabal, conspiracy, plot. A *cabal* is a party intrigue; a *combination*, the union of many for mutual protection; a *plot* is a secret union of two or more persons, for bad purposes; a *conspiracy* is a secret concert among a number of persons to bring about a change.

***Command,*** *n.* Injunction, order, precept.

***Commodity,*** *n.* Goods, merchandise, ware.

***Common,*** *a.* Mean, ordinary, vulgar. *Common* is the opposite of refined; *mean* of noble; *ordinary* of distinguished; *vulgar* of cultivated. UNCOMMON. (See EXCEPTIONAL.)

***Compel,*** *v.* Force, oblige, necessitate.

***Compensation,*** *n.* Amends, recompense, remuneration, requital, reward. *Amends* is the return for a fault; *recompense*, voluntary payment for voluntary service; *compensation* is a payment for service; *requital* pays kindness with kindness; *remuneration* is as indefinite as but less voluntary than *recompense; reward* is a voluntary return for service or conduct.

***Complain,*** *v.* Lament, murmur, regret, repine.

***Comply,*** *v.* Accede, conform, submit, yield. REFUSE.

***Compound,*** *a.* Complex. SIMPLE.

***Comprise,*** *v.* Comprehend, contain, embrace, include.

***Conceal,*** *v.* Hide, secrete. UNCOVER.

***Conceive,*** *v.* Comprehend, understand. We *conceive* a thing when we form an idea of it; we *understand* or *comprehend* it only when we possess all the ideas which the thing presents. *Understanding* relates to familiar things; *comprehension* to principles.

***Conclusion,*** *n.* Inference, deduction. A *conclusion* is *decisive;* an *inference*, incomplete; a *deduction* is drawn from arguments; a *conclusion* from facts.

***Conduct,*** *v.* Direct, guide, lead, govern, regulate, manage.

***Confirm,*** *v.* Corroborate. CONTRADICT.

***Conflict,*** *n.* Combat, contest, contention, struggle.

***Confute,*** *v.* Disprove, refute, oppugn. An argument is *confuted;* a charge *refuted;* a statement disputed; an erroneous doctrine *oppugned.*

***Conquer,*** *v.* Overcome, subdue, surmount, vanquish. DEFEAT.

***Consequence,*** *n.* Effect, event, issue, result. There may be several *consequences;* there can be but one *result. Issue* and *event* are final; *consequences* may be intermediate. *Effect* relates to things physical or moral; *consequences* to moral things only. CAUSE.

***Consider,*** *v.* Reflect. *Consider* is practical; *flect*, speculative, or moral.

***Consistent,*** *a.* Constant, compatible. INCONSISTENT.

***Console,*** *v.* Comfort, solace. *Comfort* gives pleasure; *console* and *solace* alleviate pain. *Consolation* is of a higher kind than *solace.*

***Constancy,*** *n.* Firmness, stability, steadiness. *Constancy* relates to the affections; *firmness* to the will; *stability* to the opinions; steadiness to conduct and action. INCONSTANCY. (See CHANGEABLENESS.)

***Contaminate,*** *v.* Corrupt, defile, pollute, taint.

***Contemn,*** *v.* Despise, disdain, scorn. ESTEEM.

***Contemplate,*** *v.* Meditate, muse. We *contemplate* what is before our eyes; *meditate* on actions or qualities; *muse* on recent events.

***Contemptible,*** *a.* Despicable, paltry, pitiful, vile, mean. NOBLE.

***Contend,*** *v.* Contest, dispute, strive, struggle, combat.

***Continual,*** *a.* Constant, continuous, perpetual, incessant. INTERMITTENT. (See ALTERNATING.)

***Continuance,*** *n.* Continuation, duration. CESSATION.

***Continue,*** *v.* Persist, persevere, pursue, prosecute. CEASE.

***Contradict,*** *v.* Deny, gainsay, oppose. CONFIRM.

***Cool,*** *a.* Cold, frigid. *Cool* implies the opposite of warmth; *cold* and *frigid* are the opposite of warm. Figuratively, *cool* is opposed to friendly; *cold* to warm-hearted; *frigid* to animated. HOT.

***Correct,*** *v.* Rectify, reform. We *rectify* mistakes; *correct* substantial faults; *reform* the public service.

***Cost,*** *n.* Charge, expense, price. *Cost* or *expense* is what is paid for a thing; *price* or *charge* what is asked for it.

***Covetousness,*** *n.* Avarice, cupidity. *Cupidity* is an acquired disposition to mass and to keep. An *avaricious* man seeks to keep what he has; a *covetous* man to get more. BENEFICENCE.

***Cowardice,*** *n.* Fear, timidity, pusillanimity. COURAGE.

***Crime,*** *n.* Sin, vice, misdemeanor. *Crime* is a violation of human law; *vice*, of moral law; *sin*, of the law of God. *Sin* includes *crime* and *vice; misdemeanor* is a minor offence.

***Criminal,*** *n.* Convict, culprit, felon, malefactor. *Criminal* is a general term for violator of law; *culprit* is brought before a court; *malefactor*, any evil-doer; *felon*, person guilty of felony; *convict*, sentenced criminal.

***Crooked,*** *a.* Bent, curved, oblique. STRAIGHT.

***Cruel,*** *a.* Barbarous, brutal, inhuman, savage. KIND. (See AFFECTIONATE.)

***Cultivation,*** *n.* Culture, refinement.

***Cursory,*** *a.* Desultory, hasty, slight. EXHAUSTIVE.

***Custom,*** *n.* Fashion, manner, practice. *Custom* is relative; *practice*, absolute; *manner* or *manners* is the way in which we behave in social intercourse; *fashion* is a temporary, arbitrary mode of doing or making things.

## D.

***Danger,*** *n.* Hazard, peril. *Hazard* may be a good; danger and *peril* are evils. A *peril* is a (far-off), extraordinary *danger.* SAFETY. (See SAFE.)

***Dark,*** *a.* Dismal, opaque, obscure, dim. LIGHT.

***Deadly,*** *a.* Fatal, destructive, mortal. Whatever produces death is *deadly;* whatever ends in death, *mortal. Fatal* and *destructive* apply also to things which produce great harm.

***Death,*** *n.* Departure, decease, demise. *Death* is the general term. *Departure, decease,* and *demise* relate to human beings only. *Decease* is the legal term; *demise* is used of the death of great personages. LIFE.

***Decay,*** *n.* Decline, consumption. *Decay* is a gradual loss of health; *decline*, of vigor; *consumption*, of existence.

***Deceive,*** *v.* Delude, impose upon. *Deceive*